by Thomas Rowlandson

Founded in 1744 to auction fine books, Sotheby's is now the leading firm of art auctioneers and appraisers in the world.

Sotheby's, 1334 York Avenue, New York, New York 10021.
Telephone: (212) 606-7385

Sotheby's, 34-35 Bond Street, London W1A 2AA.
Telephone: 44 (71) 493-8080.

THE WORLD'S LEADING AUCTION HOUSE

SOTHEBY'S
FOUNDED 1744

# The Book Collector

In its forty and more years of publication THE BOOK COLLECTOR
has firmly established itself as the most interesting and lively
current journal for collectors, bibliographers,
antiquarian booksellers and custodians of rare books.
Leading authorities contribute regularly on all aspects of
bibliophily, from medieval manuscripts to modern first editions
and each issue offers new and original insight into
the world of books
THE BOOK COLLECTOR is generously illustrated
It remains remarkably inexpensive
THE BOOK COLLECTOR is published quarterly
in March, June, September, December

*Subscription rates on request from*
THE BOOK COLLECTOR
20 Maple Grove, London NW9 8QY
*Tel/Fax 0181 200 5004*

# METROPOLITAN
## BOOK AUCTION

*New York City's*
*Rare Book Source*

#867203

123 WEST 18TH ST. 4TH FL., NEW YORK, N.Y. 10011
TEL 212.929.4488 | FAX 212.463.7099

## METROPOLITAN BOOK AUCTION

### Regularly Scheduled
# FINE BOOK AUCTIONS

Colorplate Books
Science & Technology
Voyages & Travels
Americana
Children's & Illustrated Books
Art & Architecture
Fine Art & Prints
Photography
Autographs
Maps & Atlases
Fine Bindings
First Editions
Ephemera

We Offer Consignors:
Established International Clientelé
Fast Turnover • Prompt Payment
Outright Purchase • Free Appraisals

*Catalog Subscriptions Available*

#867203

123 W. 18TH ST., 4TH FLOOR, NEW YORK, N.Y. 10011
TEL **212.929.4488** | FAX 212.463.7099

# BLOOMSBURY BOOK AUCTIONS

## hold 24 Sales a year

There are usually about 400 lots in a catalogue

*The catalogues are arranged broadly by categories of interest, such as*

- Travel & Topography
  Science & Natural History
- Bibliography & Art Reference
  English Literature & History
- Continental Literature & History
  Modern First Editions & Private Press Books
- Illustrated Books & Limited Editions
  Hebraica & Judaica
- Sport, Fishing, Mountaineering, Railways
  Genealogy & Heraldry
- Economics & Social History
  Manuscript Material of all kinds
- Maps, Atlases, Prints & Drawings
  and, of course,
- Horology, Music & Photography

You can, of course, subscribe to our catalogues but, if you have specific areas of interest, we can advise you in plenty of time when items in your field come up for sale, through a simple and inexpensive **WANTS SERVICE.**

*Phone us for details at:* 3 & 4 Hardwick St, London EC1R 4RY England
*Tel:* 011 44 171 833 2636/7 or 011 44 171 636 1945  *Fax:* 011 44 171 833 3954

Anna Atkins, 'Photographs of British Algae, 3 Vols., 1843-1853
Sold for £134,000. From the Library of the Eton College Natural History Museum

**The Book & Manuscript Department**

David Park
44 (171) 393 3986

Montpelier Street, London SW7 1HH England. Tel: 00 44 171 393 3900
Fax: 00 44 171 393 3905 Internet Address: http://www.Bonhams.com/

# BONHAMS

AUCTIONEERS & VALUERS SINCE 1793

# Harvey W. Brewer, Bookseller

BOX 322, CLOSTER, NEW JERSEY 07624
Telephone 768-4414. Area Code 201
BY APPOINTMENT

We are interested in the following subjects

**FINE ARTS
COLOR PLATE BOOKS
TOPOGRAPHY - VIEW BOOKS
ATLASES
FINE ILLUSTRATED BOOKS
COSTUME & FASHION
ART NOUVEAU
ART DECO**

# CHRISTIE'S

## FOR AUCTIONS OF PRINTED BOOKS, MANUSCRIPTS AND AUTOGRAPH LETTERS

### NEW YORK
Christie, Manson & Woods International, Inc.
502 Park Avenue, New York, NY 10022
Telephone: (212) 546 1197 Telex: 672-0315 Fax: (212) 980 2043

Christie's East, 219 East 67th Street, New York, NY 10022
Tel: (212) 606 0520 Fax: (212) 717 4725

### LONDON
Christie, Manson & Woods, Ltd.
8 King Street, St. James, London SW1Y 6QT
Telephone: (44171) 389 2151 Fax: (44171) 389 2263

Christie's South Kensington
85 Old Brompton Road, London SW7 3LD
Telephone: (44171) 321 3205 Fax: (44171) 321 3321

### PARIS
Christie's France S.A. 6 rue Paul Baudry, 75008 Paris
Telephone: (331) 40 76 85 93 Fax: (331) 42 89 87 78

### ROME
Christie's International S.A. 114 Piazza Navona, 00186 Rome
Telephone: (389) 687 2787 Fax: (396) 686 9902

### MELBOURNE
Christie's Australia Pty. Ltd
1 Darling Street, South Yarra, Melbourne, Victoria 3141
Telephone: (613) 9820 4311 Fax: (613) 9820 4876

# Jahrbuch der Auktionspreise für Bücher, Handschriften und Autographen
## Vol. 46

Auction prices for books, manuscripts and autographs
in Germany, the Netherlands, Austria
and Switzerland

The "Jahrbuch der Auktionspreise" has since 1950 reported annually and through Index sets (issued every five years) on auction sales prices achieved by books, manuscripts, and autographs. Vol 46/1995 describes 32,000 sales prices at 65 auctions for books, manuscripts and autographs. Among the appendices of the book is to be found a list of antiquarian booksellers according to their specialties and an English\German index of the keywords used in the list.

**Volume 46/1995.** *Describes 32,000 sales prices.*
*1996. Royal Octavo. 800 pages. Cloth. Approx. 380 DM.*
*ISBN 3-7762-0409-5*

Catalog sent on request

Dr. Ernst Hauswedell & Co. • Postfach 14 01 55
D-70071 Stuttgart Germany

# Book Auction On Your Mind?

**Discover our reputation for fair dealing, prompt payment, and results!**

Let our professional, courteous staff of experienced auctioneers, appraisers, and cataloguers sell for you. Check our results in <u>American Book Prices Current</u> (since 1990) for atlases, scarce Americana, early printed books, bibles, plate books, and more. We are New England's market place for books, maps, autographs, historical prints, letters, ephemera, and photographs.

## QUALITY CONSIGNMENTS INVITED FOR THE 1997 SEASON

Catalogue subscription w/prices realized
$15 Domestic; $22 Foreign

Richard & Mary Sykes, Frank Sykes
Robinson Murray III

*Beginning Our 13th Year*

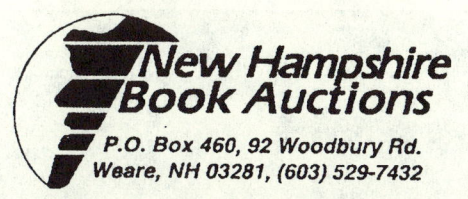

**New Hampshire Book Auctions**
P.O. Box 460, 92 Woodbury Rd.
Weare, NH 03281, (603) 529-7432

# PBA
## Pacific Book Auction Galleries

PBA invites your consignments for our sales of
Autographs & Manuscripts, Fine & Rare Books, Cartography,
Travel & Exploration, Western Americana, Photography,
and Modern Literature

Please contact Marjorie Shaw or Douglas C. Johns

---

Pacific Currents, the Galleries' newsletter and schedule of auctions, is available upon request. Auction catalogues and prices realized are available on-line at http://www.nbn.com/pba, by subscription, or individually. Bids are welcome by mail, fax, phone, or E-mail.

---

Pacific Book Auction Galleries takes particular pride in the personalized service we offer to each of our consignors and bidders.

---

Pacific Book Auction Galleries
133 Kearny Street, 4th Floor
San Francisco, CA 94108
Phone 415 989-2665   Fax 415 989-1664
E-Mail pba@slip.net   Web http://www.nbn.com/pba

# Rare Books

## Autograph Letters
## Historical Documents
## Atlases & Maps

For information on buying or selling at auction, details of our forthcoming sales programme or our catalogue subscription services please contact Elizabeth Merry at Phillips in London.

Direct line : (00 44) 171 468 8351
Fax : (00 44) 171 465 0224

http://www.phillips-auctions.com

LONDON   NEW YORK   HOUSTON

**Phillips**
INTERNATIONAL
AUCTIONEERS & VALUERS

Phillips London, 101 New Bond Street, London W1Y 0AS. Tel : (44) 171 629 6602
Phillips New York, 406 East 79th Street, New York, 10021. Tel : (212) 570 4830

# - POLYGRAPHICUM -

Books • Paintings • Prints • Drawings

## PETER A. HELM

Backgasse1  Tel. 06271 • 1387
D-69412 EBERBACH AM NECKAR
EURO-BOOK AUCTION SERVICE

We wish to buy Fine Prints & Books i.e. single titles and collections of Old Master & Decorative Prints, European Travel, Art, Natural History, Literature, etc.
(Colour) Plate Books

Fine Topographical Paintings & Works of Art relating Mannheim, Heidelberg, Heilbronn (River Neckar Valley)
– **Fine Paintings by R. EPP (1834-1910)** –

We are always interested in acquisition and would be pleased to discuss outright purchase or other possible arrangements with collectors interested in disposal. Consultations with bankers and attorneys representing estates are welcome.

# When you can't find it in ABPC... you should try us

***BOOK COLLECTING:*** *A Comprehensive Guide*  New York: G.P. Putnam, 1995. The 1995 edition with over 5,000 first books by collected authors with estimated prices. Over 100 pages on book collecting; and lists of Literary Prize Winners (including the Booker, Caldecott, Edgar, Hugo, Newbery, Pulitzer) and High Spot lists (including Burgess, Connolly, Haycraft-Queen, Merle Johnson and Blanck). 480 pages in hardcover. ISBN: 0-399-14049-2.
*\*$35.00 plus postage*

***COLLECTED BOOKS:*** *The Guide to Values*  New York: G.P. Putnam (new/enlarged edition scheduled for July 1997). 20,000 collected books with bibliographical first edition identification and price estimates. Over 17,000 copies of the last edition (1991) edition were sold. The one book you'll see in practically all the out of print book stores in the country. Approximately 800 pages in hardcover.
*\*$75.00 plus postage* **(Advance orders now being taken)**

***AUTHOR PRICE GUIDES***  Individual author guides with first edition identification and estimated prices for each American and English edition of each of the author's titles. Faulkner, Fitzgerald, Hemingway, Steinbeck and 165 others (approximately 25 additional guides will be added in 1997). Available individually in three-ring binder format; or, standing order in 2 cloth volumes and notebook. Priced individually from $1.00 to $30.00 plus postage. (No discounts unless the whole series is purchased.) Send for complete list.

Patricia & Allen Ahearn
## Quill & Brush
Box 5365
Rockville, MD 20848
(301) 460-3700
FAX: (301) 871-5425 E-Mail: orders@qb.com
HOME PAGE: http://www.qb.com/pub/q-and-b

**\*Dealer discounts:** *10% on one copy, 20% on 2 or 3, 30% on 4 or 5, and 40% on 6 or more copies*

# AUCTIONS AT SWANN

SWANN GALLERIES is the oldest and largest U.S. auctioneer specializing in

## RARE & ANTIQUARIAN BOOKS

## AUTOGRAPHS & MANUSCRIPTS

## MAPS & ATLASES

## 19TH & 20TH CENTURY PHOTOGRAPHS

## WORKS OF ART ON PAPER

We conduct some 35 sales a year. For our Newsletter and Catalogues, and to discuss consignments to future sales, please call Swann at (212) 254-4710.

IAA *Member International Association of Auctioneers*

# SWANN GALLERIES
104 East 25 Street, New York, N.Y. 10010 ▪ (212) 254-4710

# Titles, Inc.

FLORENCE SHAY
1931 Sheridan Road
Highland Park, IL 60035

847-432-3690
FAX: 847-432-3699

DEALERS IN
RARE & FINE BOOKS
IN ALL CATEGORIES

SEARCH SERVICE

Do you have books to
sell us?

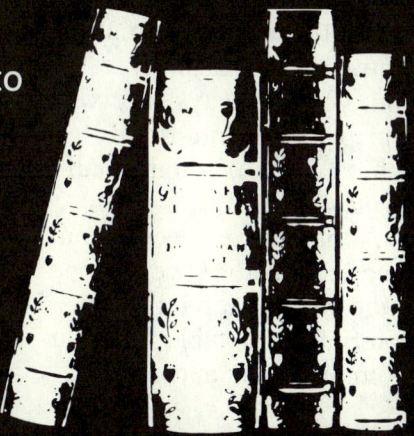

# We're Prepared To Do Battle For Your Autographs.

In the battle for autographs, University Archives has at its disposal an arsenal of superior client services.

With our virtually unlimited funds to purchase, you can be assured of receiving top dollar for your merchandise. Our toll free number makes contacting us hassle-free. And, you'll always receive your payment in a timely fashion -- by overnight mail if you so desire.

Although we specialize in American history, we are one of the world's top buyers of materials by notable individuals in all fields; autographed documents, manuscripts, letters, family correspondence, and more.

We are actively seeking items ranging in value from one hundred dollars to one million dollars.

You can reach us by calling (800) 237-5692, by faxing (203) 348-3560, or by writing us at 600 Summer Street, Stamford, CT 06901.

University Archives. If there's one signature collectors recognize, it's ours.

**University Archives**
A division of UNIVERSITY STAMP CO., INC.
Serving collectors since 1979

Member: ASDA, APS, Antiquarian Booksellers Assoc. of America, Manuscript Society, UACC, Ephemera Society of America, PADA

# 20 YEARS

We celebrate our 20th Anniversary on March 4, 1997. We have earned the right to describe ourselves, immodestly but accurately, as the premier fine and rare book auction house of the middle Atlantic states, and our role in auctioning prints, maps, atlases, manuscripts, and autographs is growing rapidly. We hold eight to twelve auctions annually, and mail our catalog to an international audience. We accept consignments (at competitive rates) from dealers, institutions and individuals.

Subscriptions to our catalog are available for $35*us*, or $7 for a single issue. Subscriptions include domestic postage and prices realized.

Please contact Dr. Dale Sorenson for consignment information.

**Waverly Auctions**

4931 CORDELL AVENUE   BETHESDA MD 20814          VOICE : (301) 951-8883   FAX : (301) 718-8375

## Wilsey Rare Books

23 MILL ROAD, OLIVEBRIDGE, NY 12461, USA

## WE SPECIALIZE IN

## THE ARTS OF THE BOOK

*Printing History*  *Art Nouveau & Deco*
*Paper-making*  *Illustrated Books*
*Bookbinding*  *Fine Bindings*
*Typography*  *Private Press*
*Calligraphy*  *Incunabula*
*Type Specimens*  *Manuscripts*
*Color Plate Books*  *Livres D'Artistes*
*Early Lithography*  *Rare and Unusual*

## FREQUENT CATALOGUES ISSUED

## FINE BOOKS AND COLLECTIONS PURCHASED

PH: (914) 657–7057    MEMBER ABAA & ILAB    FAX: (914) 657–2366

## The PHILADELPHIA RARE BOOKS & MANUSCRIPTS COMPANY

☞ *ALWAYS SEEKING* ☞ English and European Imprints to 1700
English Illustrated Books to 1750
U.S. Imprints to 1820
Mexican Imprints to 1850

Bibles in English, Pre-1750 or Fine Press
American Bibles in Any Language, Pre-1840
Bibles in Exotic Languages, Pre-1875

Broadsides, Any Language, Pre-1850
*PMM* Books, in First and Early Editions of the Pre-1800 Texts
American Publishers' Cloth Bindings, Illustrated and Embossed, Pre-1880
(Bindings *in Excellent Condition Only* — Please Send Photocopies)

Post Office Box 9536  Philadelphia, Pennsylvania 19124
Phone (215) 744-6734   e-mail rarebks@prbm.com   FAX (215) 744-6137
Members: ABAA, ILAB, ALA   ☞ *We Appreciate All Offers!* ☜

---

# TITLES
## OF
# OXFORD
### FOR
### ANTIQUARIAN
SECONDHAND
AND
FINE MODERN BOOKS

15 Turl St., Oxford
OXI 3DQ England

Tel: (0865) 727928
Fax: (0865) 727928

Open
9:30 to 5:30 • Monday to Saturday

# AMERICAN
# BOOK PRICES
# CURRENT
# VOLUME 102

## 1995-1996

# AMERICAN BOOK PRICES CURRENT 1996

**VOLUME 102**
The Auction Season September 1995-August 1996

BANCROFT-PARKMAN, INC.

1996

EDITORS

KATHARINE KYES LEAB
DANIEL J. LEAB
MARIE-LUISE FRINGS
ABIGAIL LEAB
KATHLEEN THORP

Please send all inquiries and suggestions to:

American Book Prices Current
P.O. Box 1236
Washington, CT 06793
TEL: (212) RE 7-2715
TEL: (860) 868-7408
FAX: (860) 868-0080

Copyright © 1996 Bancroft-Parkman, Inc. All rights reserved.
ISBN: 0-914022-32-6
ISSN: 0091-9357
Library of Congress Card No. 3-14557
Printed in the United States of America

# CONTENTS

**Page**

Abbreviations .............................................. vi

Introduction ............................................... vii

Auction Houses ............................................ ix

Named Consignors ........................................ xii

Season's Sales ............................................ xvi

Exchange Rates .......................................... xxiii

Part I: Autographs & Manuscripts ....................... 1

Part II: Books, Broadsides, Maps & Charts .............. 233

# ABBREVIATIONS

**ad, ads**  Advertising
**ACs**  Autograph Card, signed
**ADs**  Autograph Document, signed
**ALs**  Autograph Letter. signed
**A Ls s**  Autograph Letters, signed
**Amst.**  Amsterdam
**anr**  Another
**Anon**  Anonymous
**ANs**  Autograph Note, signed
**armorial bdg**  Binding with coat of arms on cover
**Balt.**  Baltimore
**bdg**  Binding
**bds**  Boards
**Birm.**  Birmingham
**Bost.**  Boston
**c.**  Circa
**Cambr.**  Cambridge
**cat**  catalogue
**cent**  Century
**contemp**  Contemporary
**def**  Defective
**Ds**  Document, signed
**d/j**  Dust jacket
**Ed**  Edition; Edited; Editor
**Edin.**  Edinburgh
**extra bdg**  Elaborate binding
**f, ff**  Folio(s)
**frontis**  Frontispiece
**H of R**  House of Representatives
**illus, illusts**  Illustrate(d);  Illustrations
**imperf**  Imperfect
**inscr**  Inscribed; Inscription
**intro**  Introduction

**L**  London
**Lea**  Leather
**lev**  Levant
**litho**  Lithograph
**L.p.**  Large paper
**Ls**  Letter, signed
**Ls s**  Letters, signed
**Ltd**  Limited
**Mor**  Morocco
**Ms, Mss**  Manuscript; Manuscripts
**mtd**  Mounted
**n.d.**  No date
**n.p.**  No place
**n.y.**  No year
**NY**  New York
**no, nos**  Number; Numbers
**orig**  Original
**pbd, pbr**  Published; Publisher
**Phila.**  Philadelphia
**port**  Portrait
**pp**  Pages
**prelim**  Preliminary
**pseud.**  Pseudonym
**ptd, ptg, ptr**  Printed; Printing; Printer
**pvtly**  Privately
**Sen.**  Senate
**sgd**  Signed
**syn**  Synthetic
**tp**  Title page
**trans**  Translated; Translation; Translator
**vol, vols**  Volume; Volumes
**w.a.f.**  With all faults
**Wash.**  Washington
**wrap, wraps**  Wrapper; Wrappers

Books are listed as:
 folio    12 mo
 4to     16 mo
 8vo     etc.

# INTRODUCTION

Volume 102 of *American Book Prices Current* has been prepared by a team of editors highly experienced in the field of rare books and manuscripts. As its users know, ABPC is not just a transcribed record of titles and prices, copied unquestioningly from the season's auction catalogues. It is, on the contrary, the only work in English in which every listing of printed material has been checked as to title, format, date of publication, edition, and limitation. Bindings are described, with condition when relevant, and whenever possible maps and plates in books are verified. Moreover, sales of autographs and manuscripts are reported. Because of this, ABPC is an essential tool for buying, selling and evaluating books, serials, autographs, manuscripts, broadsides, and maps, based on actual figures realized at auction. In the words of a reviewer in *The Times Literary Supplement,* it is "an accurate, indispensable tool for the antiquarian bookseller and collector." And, in addition to meeting the need for a dependable guide in determining the value of old and out-of-print books, ABPC serves as a reference work and as an aid to scholars in locating printed works and manuscripts of all centuries, from the earliest years to the present.

*American Book Prices Current* is composed of two parts. Part I, Autographs & Manuscripts, includes original illustrations for printed books, documents, letters, typescripts, corrected proofs, signed photographs, and signatures, as well as manuscripts. Part II, Books, includes broadsides, single-sheet printings, maps, and charts and uncorrected proof copies of books.

Entries are listed alphabetically by author whenever possible, by title when the author's name is unknown, or by Private Press and Club, printer, or publisher headings if such are the associations which attract the collector. In general, illustrated books are listed under the author of the text. Subject headings such as England, Maps & Charts, Hebrew Books and Miniature Books or those for individual U.S. states or cities have also been used. Individual works are in turn listed alphabetically under each heading and include: Title; place & date of publication; edition designation; number of volumes when more than one; size; binding; condition of binding; descriptive material; limitation notes, and the sale record—auction houses (in code), date or number of sale, lot number, price and purchaser (buyers' names are given when and as listed in price lists.) There are cross-references to Club or Press books, to books bound together, and to books by more than one author.

Volume 102 lists only those books and manuscripts which sold for at least $50 or its equivalent in another currency. In keeping with previous editorial policy, auction lots consisting of groupings of miscellaneous volumes are not listed, for the prices realized by such lots can give no accurate indication of the value of individual items. Similarly, listings of badly broken runs or seriously incomplete sets of printed books do not appear. Listings of books in non-Western languages realizing less than $100 have been selectively excluded, as have peripheral works as printings of musical scores, collections of plates, and panoramas. We are selective in approaching German and Dutch sales, for our aim here is to include some items of particular interest to our readers.

Listings of 20th century books frequently appear without format or binding information. In such instances it may be assumed that these books are octavo or doudecimo and bound in cloth or boards. Items which are sold by auction house as "a collection of plates" or which are deemed to be bound prints rather than books, are excluded from these pages. Considerable effort has been made to secure price lists for all of the relevant sales held by the auction houses listed herein. We make great efforts to be comprehensive, but not all auction houses are equally diligent in sending us price lists, or equally responsive to our inquiries.

## Buyer's Surcharges

All prices listed in this book are hammer prices, that is, the price actually called out in the sale room when the lot is knocked down to a buyer. What the buyer actually pays for the lot has become complicated. Taxes vary from country, and may depend on who buys the lot — dealer, institution or private buyer — and where the buyer lives. The buyer's premium charged by auction houses also varies. Most houses in England charged 15% on the first £30,000 and 10% thereafter. The exceptions are as follows: Bloomsbury made the change at £20,000; Christie's South Kensington charged 12.5% and then 10% until mid-February of 1996, when they joined the majority at 15%; Lawrence, Woolley & Wallis and Dominic Winter charged 10%. In Germany, the surcharge was 15%. Christie's Australia charged 15% on the first AU$50,000, and then 10%. In the United States the majority of houses charged 15% on the first $50,000 and then 10%. Exceptions were: Baltimore, Darvick, Freeman, New Hampshire, Oinonen, Eldred, Waverly, and Zubal — all charging 10%; Dorothy Sloan and Pacific 15%.

# AUCTION HOUSES

The sales recorded in this volume are from the auction houses listed below and are designated by code letters. On the following pages are a list of the season's sales from each house and a record of the named consignors of merchandise.

| | |
|---|---|
| b | W & FC Bonham & Sons Ltd.<br>Montpelier Street, London SW7 1HH England |
| bba | Bloomsbury Book Auctions<br>3 & 4 Hardwick Street, London EC1 England |
| bbc | Baltimore Book Company<br>2114 N. Charles Street, Baltimore, MD 21218 |
| C | Christie, Manson & Woods<br>8 King Street, St. James's, London SW1Y 6QT England |
| CA | Christie, Manson & Woods (Australia) Ltd<br>298 New South Head Rd., Double Bay, NSW 2028, Austraila |
| cb | California Book Auction Galleries<br>965 Mission St., Ste. #730, San Francisco, CA 94103 |
| CE | Christie's East<br>219 East 67th Street, New York, NY 10021 |
| Cg | Christie's Scotland<br>164-166 Bath St., Glasgow, Scotland G24 TG |
| Ck | Christie's South Kensington<br>85 Old Brompton Road, London SW7 3JS England |
| CNY | Christie, Manson & Woods International, Inc.<br>502 Park Avenue, New York, NY 10022 |
| Dar | Herman Darvick Autograph Auctions<br>P. O. Box 467, Rockville Centre, NY 11571-0467 |
| ds | Dorothy Sloan<br>Box 49670, Austin, TX 78765-9670 |
| dw | Dominic Winter<br>The Old School, Maxwell Street,<br>Swindon, Wiltshire SW1 5DR England |
| F | Freeman/Fine Arts<br>1808 Chestnut Street, Philadelphia, PA 19103 |

ix

## AUCTION HOUSES

FD      F. Doerling
Neuer Wall 40-42, 2000 Hamburg 36 Germany

HH      Hartung und Hartung
Karolinenplatz 5a, D 8000 Munich 2 Germany

HN      Hauswedell und Nolte
Poseldorfer Weg 1, D 2000 Hamburg 13 Germany

JG      Jochen Granier
4800 Bielefeld 1 Welle 9 Germany

K      Kane Antiquarian Auction
1525 Shenkel Road, Pottstown PA 19464

L      Lawrence Fine Art
South Street, Crewkerne, Somerset TA18 8AB England

Met      Metropolitan Book Auction
123 W. 18th St., 4th floor, New York, NY 10011

NH      New Hampshire Book Auction
Woodcurry Road, Weare, NH 03281

O      Richard E. Oinonen Book Auctions
Box 470, Sunderland, MA 01375

P      Sotheby Parke Bernet, Inc.
1334 York Avenue, New York NY 10021

pba      Pacific Book Auction Galleries
133 Kearny St., 4th floor, San Francisco CA 94108

pn      Phillips, Son & Neale
101 New Bond Street, London W1Y OAS England

pnE      Phillips in Scotland
65 George Street, Edinburgh EH2 2JL Scotland

rce      Robert C. Eldred Co., Inc.
1483 Rte. 6A, P.O. Box 796, East Dennis, MA 02641-0796

Rms      R.M. Smythe & Co., Inc.
26 Broadway, Suite #271, New York, Ny 10004-1701

rs      Skinner, Inc.
357 Main Street, Bolton, MA 01740

S      Sotheby Parke Bernet & Co.
34-35 New Bond Street, London W1A 2AA England

sg      Swann Galleries
104 East 25th Street, New York, NY 10010

## AUCTION HOUSES

Si
Sotheby's Italia
Via Broggi, 19-20129 Milano, Italy

star
J. A. Stargardt
Rade-Strasse 10, D-3550 Marburg, Germany

W
Woolley & Wallis
Castle Street, Salisbury, Wiltshire, England

wa
Waverly Auctions
4931 Cordell Avenue, Suite AA, Bethesda, MD 10814

wad
Waddington's
189 Queen Street East, Toronto, Ontario M5A 152 Canada

wd
William Doyle Galleries
175 East 87th Street, New York, NY 10128

Z
Zubal Auction Company
2969 W. 25th St., Cleveland, Oh 44113

# NAMED CONSIGNORS

| | | | |
|---|---|---|---|
| Afanasenko, Galina I. | P Mar 16 | Colonial Williamsburg Foundation | CE June 12 |
| Aksenov, Vladimir V. | P Mar 16 | Conefry, Hal | pba Apr 18 |
| Akulinichev, I. T. | P Mar 16 | Conger, Jay | CNY May 17 |
| Amis, Kingsley | S July 11 | Cushing, Peter | pn July 11 |
| Arthur, Robert P. | O June 4 | Daniels, Mr. D. & Mrs. K. E. | S Oct 26, 27 |
| Avoca Museum | CNY May 17 | Davies, Mansel | S Mar 28, 29 |
| Baginsky, Yuri M. | P Mar 16 | De Mille, Cecil B. | CE Sept 27 |
| Ball, Abraham | dw May 16 | Dennis, Frank & Kitty | CE Nov 8 |
| Beregovoy, Georgy T. | P Mar 16 | Douwma, Robert | bba Oct 5 |
| Berezovoy, Anatoly N. | P Mar 16 | Dukov, Vyacheslav | P Mar 16 |
| Bersudsky, Sidney | wad Oct 18 | Engelhard, Mrs. Charles W. | CNY Oct 27 / CNY Jan 26 |
| BMI Foundation, Inc. | CNY May 17 / CE June 12 | Ernst, Kate | rms Oct 11 / rms Nov 30 |
| Boehler, Julius | S Oct 26, 27 | Fearon, H. B. | b Dec 5 |
| Booth, Robert | pn June 13 | Feoktistov, Konstantin | P Mar 16 |
| Borthwick of that Ilk, The Rt. Hon. Lord | pnE May 15 / Cg May 25 / pn E Aug 14 | Filipchenko, Anatoly V. | P Mar 16 |
| | | Fisher, Kurt | sg Mar 28 |
| Breslin, George M., Jr. | pba Jan 18 | Fleming, George | dw Dec 12 |
| British Rail Pension Fund | S Apr 23 | Forbes Magazine Collection | CNY Dec 15 / CNY May 17 |
| Bunker, Isabel Leighton | P Dec 12 | Fort Myers Historical Museum | CNY May 17 |
| Carey, Macdonald | pba Jan 25 | Frank, Maud | wd May 8 |
| Catalfimo, Donald F. | O June 25 | Fuerstenberg, Hans | S Dec 7, 8 |
| Chertok, Boris E. | P Mar 16 | Gargarin, Yuri | P March 16 |
| Colin, Mr. & Mrs. Ralph F. | CE Sept 27 | | |

# NAMED CONSIGNORS

| | | | |
|---|---|---|---|
| Garver, Virginia R. | wd May 8 | Jones, Frances Hunter | CE Sept 27 |
| Geiger, George L. | pba July 25 | Kanner, Ken | O Dec 5 |
| Gerasimenko-Kartenko, Oleg F. | P Mar 16 | Karpov, E. A. | P Mar 16 |
| Gilberg, Lev | P Mar 16 | Kaufmann, William | pba July 11 |
| Goalby, Margaret M. | S Dec 18 | Kerimov, Kerim A. | P Mar 16 |
| Goldschmidt, Lucien | sg Nov 2 | Khokhlov, Vladimir A. | P Mar 16 |
| Goldstein, David | bba Apr 25 | Kubasov, Valery | P Mar 16 |
| Goodspeed's Bookshop Inc. | CE Sept 27 | Larson, Roger K. | pba Sept 28 pba Feb 12 |
| Gordon, Phyliss W. G. | wd Nov 15 | Law Society of England & Wales | |
| Goshorn, Robert | CE June 12 | | bba Sept 21 bba Nov 1, 2 |
| Grechko, Georgy M. | P Mar 16 | | bba Dec 14 |
| Gridgman, Norman | wad Oct 18 | Lawson-Tancred, Andrew | b Sept 20 |
| Grosse Pointe Public Library | sg Apr 18 | Lazarus, Allan | S May 15 |
| Gubarev, Alexei A. | P Mar 16 | Lentz, William M., Jr. | sg June 6 |
| Haas, Marc | CE Sept 27 | Leonov, Alexei A. | P Mar 16 |
| Hammond Museum | CE Sept 27 | Levchenko, Anatoly | P Mar 16 |
| Hefner, Robert A., III | CNY May 17 | Ligne, Le Prince | de S June 18 |
| Hidy, Vernon S. | O Feb 6 | Lyakhov, Vladimir | P Mar 16 |
| Hilson, Mildred S. | CE Sept 27 | Mc Cabe, George E. | O Feb 6 |
| Hobson, Anthony | S June 28 | Madsen, Soren | S Mar 14 |
| Hotchner, A. E. | P June 5 | Makarov, Oleg | P Mar 16 |
| Howell, Alfred | sg Oct 19 | Maksimov, Greb Y. | P Mar 16 |
| Hunt, Derrick | bba Jan 11 | Malyshev, Yuri M. | P Mar 16 |
| Investment Economic Association | P Mar 16 | Mamleyev, Dmitry | P Mar 16 |
| Ivanchenkov, Aleksandr S. | P Mar 16 | Manakov, Gennady | P Mar 16 |
| Ivanovsky, Oleg | P Mar 16 | Manarov, Musa K. | P Mar 16 |
| | | Marans, Wesley M. | CE Apr 17 |

# NAMED CONSIGNORS

| | | | |
|---|---|---|---|
| Marsh, Anthony | bba Nov 1, 2 | Prins, Warner | CE Dec 6 |
| Martin, Dick | sg Oct 19 | Purchase College Foundation | CNY May 17 |
| Mashinsky, Aleksandr | P Mar 16 | Pym, Horace N. | S Apr 23 |
| Mellon, Paul | CE June 12 | Robb-Smith, A. H. T. | bba June 20 |
| Mikhailov, Boris | P Mar 16 | Robbins, Irving W., Jr. | pba Oct 5 |
| | | | pba Mar 21 |
| Morris, David | W Nov 8 | | pba Apr 25 |
| Mosimann Collection | S Oct 12 | Roberts, W. S. | rms Oct 11 |
| | | | rms Nov 30 |
| Moody Medical Library | CE Nov 8 | | |
| | | Robertson-Glasgow, Robert Foxcroft | |
| Morrison, Stuart | bba May 9 | | Ck Feb 9 |
| Neufeld, Philip M. | CE Sept 27 | Roche, Emeline Clark | wd May 8 |
| Nevill, Lady Dorothy | CK Apr 12 | Rockefeller, Blanchette H. | CE Sept 27 |
| Newberry Library | sg Sept 21 | Rohner, Ernst | wd May 8 |
| New-York Historical Society | sg Mar 7 | Romanenko, Yuri V. | P Mar 16 |
| | sg Apr 18 | Romanov, Aleksandr P. | P Mar 16 |
| Nicholls, John V. V. | wad Oct 18 | | |
| | wad Mar 19, 20 | Rothman, Algernon | C Oct 5 |
| Nikolayev, Andrian G. | P Mar 16 | Royal Institute of Chartered Surveyors | |
| | | | bba Dec 14 |
| Nikolayev, Yuri V. | P Mar 16 | | |
| | | Rozhdestvensky, Valery I. | P Mar 16 |
| Nissen, Harlan | CE June 12 | Russell, John & Vera | dw May 16 |
| Novello, Vincent | S May 15 | Ryan, Tomas L. | CE Dec 6 |
| Parham Park Trust | C May 13, 14 | Savinykh, Viktor P. | P Mar 16 |
| Phoenix Arts Museum | CE Sept 27 | Schaefer, Otto | S Dec 7, 8 |
| Poleshchuk, Aleksandr | P Mar 16 | Scott, Edgar & Helen Hope Montgomery | |
| Popovich, John A. | pba June 25 | | CNY May 17 |
| | | | CE June 12 |
| Portsmouth Athenaeum | CNY May 17 | Serebrov, Aleksandr A. | P Mar 16 |
| Power, Robert H. | CNY May 17 | | |
| | CE June 12 | Sergeev, Aleksandr N. | P Mar 16 |
| Prins, Carol | CE Dec 6 | Shatalov, Vladimir A. | P Mar 16 |

# NAMED CONSIGNORS

| | | | |
|---|---|---|---|
| Shonin, Georgy S. | P Mar 16 | Vanasse, Sally & Louis | O May 7 |
| Shrub, Derek | bba Dec 14 | Vasyutin, Vladimir V. | P Mar 16 |
| Simon Family | CE Feb 21 | Volkov, Alexsandr A. | P Mar 16 |
| Sloan, Frances S. | CE Sept 27 | Wales, Cyril Arthur | S Mar 28, 29 |
| Solovyev, Anatoly | P Mar 16 | Walters, Angela & Stephen | b Mar 20 |
| Soudek, Josef | P Dec 12 | Ward, Carrie Duffy | CE Sept 27 |
| Southworth-Anthoensen Press | O Dec 5 | Webb, J. Watson | O Jan 9 |
| | | Weiner, Alan L. | CNY May 17 |
| Steinbrugge, Karl V. | pba Feb 13 | | CE May 22 |
| | | | CE June 12 |
| Strekalov, Gennady | P Mar 16 | Weller, Eleanor | wa Dec 14 |
| Stewart, Sir Michael | b Sept 20 | Witt, Mario Max | bba Oct 5 |
| Tarasova, Ilya | P Mar 16 | Wittkower, Rudolf & Margot | CE Nov 8 |
| Taubenheim, Siegfried | dw Mar 13 | Wood, Charles B., III | O Feb 6 |
| Thieriot, Barbara T. | CE Sept 27 | Worcester Public Library | P Dec 12 |
| Thomson, Chilton | CNY May 17 | Yazinsky, Stanislav | P Mar 16 |
| Titov, Vladimir | P Mar 16 | Yefimov, Viktor P. | P Mar 16 |
| Tully, Alice | CE Sept 27 | Yudkin, John | Ck Mar 22 |
| Turner, Lana | CE June 20, 25 | Zaytsev, Sergei | P Mar 16 |
| Tyulin, Georgy A. | P Mar 16 | Zvezda | P Mar 16 |
| Universal Autograph Collectors' Club | wa Oct 28 | | |

xv

# SEASON'S SALES
(arranged alphabetically by code letters)

Please note that September-December are 1995, January-August are 1996

### W. & F. C. BONHAM

| | |
|---|---|
| b Sept 20 | Printed Books |
| b Dec 5 | Printed Books |
| b Dec 5-6 | Provincial Poetry 1789-1839 |
| b Jan 31 | Printed Books |
| b Mar 20 | William Bligh & the Bounty Mutineers |
| b May 30 | Printed Books |
| b June 28 | Printed Books |

### BLOOMSBURY BOOK AUCTIONS

| | |
|---|---|
| bba Sept 7 | Printed Books |
| bba Sept 21 | Printed Books |
| bba Oct 5 | Printed Books |
| bba Oct 19 | Printed Books |
| bba Nov 1-2 | Printed Books |
| bba Nov 16 | Printed Books |
| bba Nov 30 | Decorative & Topographical Prints |
| bba Dec 14 | Printed Books |
| bba Jan 11 | Printed Books |
| bba Jan 25 | Printed Books |
| bba Feb 8 | Printed Books |
| bba Feb 22 | Printed Books |
| bba Mar 7 | Printed Books |
| bba Mar 21 | Printed Books |
| bba Apr 11 | Printed Books |
| bba Apr 25 | Printed Books |
| bba May 9 | Printed Books |
| bba May 30 | Printed Books |
| bba June 6 | Illustrated Books, Maps |
| bba June 20 | Printed Books |
| bba July 4 | Printed Books |
| bba July 18 | Printed Books |
| bba Aug 15 | Printed Books |

### BALTIMORE BOOK COMPANY

| | |
|---|---|
| bbc Sept 18 | Books, Autographs, Maps |
| bbc Dec 18 | Books, Autographs |
| bbc Feb 26 | Books, Autographs |
| bbc Apr 22 | U.S. Civil War, Photography |
| bbc June 24 | Books, Autographs, Maps |

# SEASON'S SALES

## CHRISTIE, MANSON & WOODS

| | |
|---|---|
| C Oct 5 | Algernon Rothman Collection |
| C Oct 25 | Valuable Natural History & Travel Books |
| C Nov 29 | Valuable Printed Books & Manuscripts |
| C Apr 3 | Valuable Continental Books & Fine Bindings |
| C May 1 | Fine Historical & Modern Decorated Bookbindings |
| C May 13-14 | Parham Park |
| C May 31 | Valuable Atlases, Natural History & Travel Books |
| C June 26 | Valuable Printed Books, Music & Manuscripts |
| C July 1 | Ashwell Lodge |

## CHRISTIE'S AUSTRALIA

| | |
|---|---|
| CA Mar 26 | Printed Books, Autograph Letters |

## CALIFORNIA BOOK AUCTION

| | |
|---|---|
| cb Oct 17 | Fine & Rare Books |
| cb Feb 14 | Fine & Rare Books |
| cb June 25 | Fine & Rare Books |

## CHRISTIE'S EAST

| | |
|---|---|
| CE Sept 27 | Books & Autographs |
| CE Nov 8 | Books & Autographs |
| CE Dec 6 | Warner Prins Collection |
| CE Feb 21 | Printed Books & Autographs |
| CE Apr 17 | M. Wesley Marans Collection |
| CE May 22 | Alan L. Weiner Collection |
| CE June 12 | Autographs, Maps |

## CHRISTIE'S SCOTLAND

| | |
|---|---|
| Cg May 15 | Scottish Books |
| Cg June 12 | The Jacobites & their Adversaries |

## CHRISTIE'S SOUTH KENSINGTON

| | |
|---|---|
| Ck Sept 8 | Printed Books |
| Ck Oct 20 | Printed Books |
| Ck Nov 17 | Autograph Letters & Modern First Editions |
| Ck Dec 8 | Antiquarian Books |
| Ck Dec 14 | Film & Entertainment |
| Ck Jan 24 | Frank Williams Collection |
| Ck Feb 9 | Printed Books |
| Ck Feb 14 | Bonsack Collection |
| Ck Mar 22 | John Yudkin Collection |
| Ck Apr 12 | Autograph Letters, Modern First Editions |
| Ck May 3 | Trade, Politics & Finance |
| Ck May 31 | Illustrated & Private Press Books |
| Ck June 14 | Printed Books |

# SEASON'S SALES

### CHRISTIE'S NEW YORK

| | |
|---|---|
| CNY Oct 27 | Mrs. Charles W. Engelhard Collection |
| CNY Dec 15 | Manuscripts & Printed Books; Forbes Magazine Collection |
| CNY Jan 26 | Americana |
| CNY May 17 | Hefner Collection; Forbes Magazine Collection |

### HERMAN DARVICK AUTOGRAPH AUCTIONS

| | |
|---|---|
| Dar Oct 19 | Autographs |

### DOROTHY SLOAN

| | |
|---|---|
| ds July 27 | Printed Books |

### FREEMAN / FINE ARTS

| | |
|---|---|
| F Sept 21 | Printed Books |
| F Mar 28 | Books, Autographs |
| F June 20 | Books |

### F. DOERLING

| | |
|---|---|
| FD May 14 | Autographen |

### HARTUNG & HARTUNG

| | |
|---|---|
| HH Nov 14 | Autographen |
| HH Nov 17 | Autographen |
| HH May 7 | Autographen |

### HAUSWEDELL & NOLTE

| | |
|---|---|
| HN Nov 24 | Autographen |
| HN May 15 | Autographen |

### JOCHEN GRANIER

| | |
|---|---|
| JG Sept 29 | Autographen |
| JG Mar 29 | Autographen |

### KANE ANTIQUARIAN AUCTION

| | |
|---|---|
| K Oct 1 | Printed Books |
| K Feb 11 | Printed Books |
| K June 23 | Printed Books |

### LAWRENCE FINE ART

| | |
|---|---|
| L Nov 16 | Printed Books & Documents |
| L May 30 | Books |

# SEASON'S SALES

## METROPOLITAN ART & ANTIQUES PAVILION

| | |
|---|---|
| Met Sept 27 | Fine Books |
| Met Dec 5 | Children's Book |
| Met Dec 14 | Textile Swatchbooks |
| Met Feb 24 | Fine Books |
| Met May 22 | Fine Books |
| Met June 6 | Swatchbook Auction |

## NEW HAMPSHIRE BOOK AUCTIONS

| | |
|---|---|
| NH Sept 16 | Printed Books |
| NH June 1 | Printed Books |
| NH July 21 | Printed Books |

## RICHARD E. OINONEN BOOK AUCTIONS

| | |
|---|---|
| O Sept 12 | Children's Books |
| O Oct 10 | Big Game Hunting |
| O Nov 14 | Americana |
| O Dec 5 | Printed Books |
| O Jan 9 | Webb Sporting Library |
| O Feb 6 | Angling Books |
| O Mar 5 | Rare Books & Manuscripts |
| O Mar 26 | Printed Books |
| O May 7 | Vanasse Library |
| O June 4 | Arthur Sporting Library, Part Ii |
| O June 25 | Catalfimo Sporting Library |
| O July 9 | Ephemera |

## SOTHEBY'S NEW YORK

| | |
|---|---|
| P Oct 5 | Photographs |
| P Nov 1 | Otto Schaefer Collection, Part III - Illustrated Books & Historical Bindings |
| P Dec 12 | Fine Books & Manuscripts |
| P Dec 13 | Fine Manuscript & Printed Americana |
| P Mar 16 | Einstein's Theory of Relativity |
| P Mar 16 | Russian Space History |
| P Apr 18 | Photographs |
| P Apr 23-25 | Jacqueline Kennedy Onassis |
| P June 5 | Fine Books & Manuscripts |

## PACIFIC BOOK AUCTION GALLERIES

| | |
|---|---|
| pba Sept 14 | Fine & Rare Books |
| pba Sept 28 | Larson Library, Part Ii |
| pba Oct 5 | Irving W. Robbins, Jr. Collection |
| pba Oct 9 | Cartography |
| pba Oct 26 | Autographs & Manuscripts |
| pba Nov 9 | Golf Books |
| pba Nov 16 | Western Americana |
| pba Nov 30 | Fine & Rare Books |

# SEASON'S SALES

| | |
|---|---|
| pba Dec 7 | Science Fiction |
| pba Dec 14 | 19th Century Literature |
| pba Jan 4 | January Miscellany |
| pba Jan 18 | L. Frank Baum |
| pba Jan 25 | Modern Literature |
| pba Feb 12 | Larson Library, Part III |
| pba Feb 13 | Steinbrugge Library |
| pba Feb 22 | Autographs & Manuscripts |
| pba Mar 7 | Fine & Rare Books |
| pba Mar 21 | Irving W. Robbins, Jr. Collection |
| pba Apr 4 | April Miscellany |
| pba Apr 18 | Hal Conefry Collection |
| pba Apr 25 | Cartography |
| pba May 4 | Science Fiction |
| pba May 23 | Modern Literature |
| pba June 13 | Autographs & Manuscripts |
| pba June 20 | Fine & Rare Books |
| pba June 25 | John A. Popovich Collection |
| pba July 11 | William Kaufmann Collection |
| pba July 25 | Printed Books |
| pba Aug 8 | August Miscellany Part I |
| pba Aug 22 | August Miscellany Part Ii |

### PHILLIPS, SON & NEALE

| | |
|---|---|
| pn Sept 7 | Books & Maps |
| pn Oct 12 | Sporting Books |
| pn Nov 9 | Books, Autograph Letters, Manuscripts |
| pn Dec 7 | Printed Books, Atlases & Maps |
| pn Feb 15 | Printed Books, Atlases & Maps |
| pn Mar 14 | Books, Autograph Letters, Manuscripts |
| pn May 16 | Printed Books, Atlases, Maps |
| pn June 13 | Books, Autograph Letters, Manuscripts, Part I |
| pn June 13 | Booth Collection, Part Ii |
| pn July 11 | Printed Books & Maps |

### PHILLIPS IN SCOTLAND

| | |
|---|---|
| pnE Sept 20 | Printed Books |
| pnE Nov 29 | Printed Books, Maps, Documents |
| pnE Mar 20 | Printed Books, Maps |
| pnE May 15 | Scottish Books |
| pnE Aug 14 | Printed Books |

### R.C. ELDRED

| | |
|---|---|
| rce Nov 16 | Printed Books |
| rce Nov 17-18 | Americana |
| rce July 25 | Marine Art |

# SEASON'S SALES

### R.M. SMYTHE & CO., INC.

| | |
|---|---|
| rms Oct 11 | Autographs |
| rms Nov 30 | Autographs |
| rms Mar 21 | Autographs |
| rms June 6 | Autographs |

### ROBERT SKINNER

| | |
|---|---|
| rs Nov 11 | Books & Manuscripts |

### SOTHEBY'S

| | |
|---|---|
| S Oct 12 | Food & Drink |
| S Oct 18 | Oriental Manuscripts & Miniatures |
| S Oct 26-27 | Printed Books & Maps |
| S Nov 2 | Illustrated Books, Children's Books |
| S Nov 21 | The Book as Art |
| S Nov 30 | Valuable Printed Books |
| S Dec 1 | Important Printed & Manuscript Music & Continental Manuscripts |
| S Dec 5 | Western Manuscripts & Miniatures |
| S Dec 7-8 | Otto Schaefer Collection, Part IV: 18th Century French Books |
| S Dec 18 | English Literature & History |
| S Mar 14 | Madsen Scientific Library |
| S Mar 28-29 | Printed Books & Maps |
| S Apr 23 | Horace N. Pym Library |
| S Apr 23 | Persian & Indian Manuscripts & Miniatures |
| S May 15 | Novello Collection |
| S May 15 | Fine Continental Manuscripts, Printed & Manuscript Music |
| S May 16 | Illustrated Books & Drawings |
| S June 12-13 | Printed Books & Maps |
| S June 18 | Western Manuscripts & Miniatures |
| S June 27 | Valuable Printed Books |
| S June 28 | Anthony Hobson Collection |
| S July 11 | English Literature & History |

### SWANN GALLERIES

| | |
|---|---|
| sg Sept 7 | Art & Architecture |
| sg Sept 14 | Modern Press & Illustrated Books |
| sg Sept 21 | Sets & Bindings |
| sg Sept 28 | Autographs |
| sg Oct 7 | Photographs |
| sg Oct 19 | Rare Books |
| sg Oct 26 | Americana |
| sg Nov 2 | Early Printed Books |
| sg Nov 9 | Limited Editions Club |
| sg Dec 7 | Maps & Atlases |
| sg Dec 14 | Modern Literature, Detective Fiction |
| sg Jan 11 | Art & Architecture |
| sg Feb 1 | Autographs |
| sg Feb 8 | Sets & Bindings, Literature |
| sg Feb 15 | Modern Press & Illustrated Books |
| sg Feb 29 | Photographic Literature |

# SEASON'S SALES

| | |
|---|---|
| sg Mar 7 | Travel & Sporting Books |
| sg Mar 21 | Early Printed Books |
| sg Mar 28 | African-Americana |
| sg Apr 11 | Bibliography |
| sg Apr 18 | Rare Books |
| sg Apr 24 | Photographs |
| sg May 9 | Maps & Atlases |
| sg May 16 | Science & Technology |
| sg May 23 | Works of Art on Paper |
| sg June 6 | Autographs |
| sg June 13 | Art & Architecture |
| sg June 20 | Fantasy & Detective Fiction |
| sg June 27 | Limited Editions Club |

## J. A. STARGARDT

| | |
|---|---|
| star Mar 21-22 | Autographen |

## WOOLLEY & WALLIS

| | |
|---|---|
| W Nov 8 | Printed Books |
| W Nov 8 | David Morris Collection |
| W Nov 8 | Antiquarian & Modern Books, Maps |
| W Mar 6 | Antiquarian & Modern Books, Maps |
| W June 19 | Antiquarian & Modern Books, Maps |

## WAVERLY AUCTION

| | |
|---|---|
| wa Oct 28 | Autographs & Manuscripts |
| wa Nov 16 | Fine Books |
| wa Dec 14 | Fine Books |
| wa Feb 1 | Fine Books |
| wa Feb 29 | Fine Books, Maps & Atlases, Autographs |
| wa June 20 | Fine Books |

## WADDINGTONS

| | |
|---|---|
| wad Oct 18 | Fine Books, Autographs |

## WILLIAM DOYLE GALLERIES

| | |
|---|---|
| wd Nov 15 | Books, Maps & Autographs |
| wd May 18 | Books, Maps & Autographs |

## ZUBAL AUCTION COMPANY

| | |
|---|---|
| Z Oct 27 | Antiquarian & Rare Books |
| Z Jan 30 | Antiquarian & Rare Books |
| Z Apr 19 | Art History & Reference |

# EXCHANGE RATES IN TERMS OF DOLLARS

The following is set forth as an aid in dealing with prices in foreign currencies. It is not meant to be precise (for that you need to go day by day to 8 or 9 places) but as a useful approximation. In each instance the following represent the number of US cents required to buy 1 dollar, pound, mark, or franc, as the case may be, in the foreign currency. For some currencies, we have included only those months in which sales covered herein occurred.

### AUSTRALIAN DOLLAR

Mar 1996  77.13

### CANADIAN DOLLAR

Oct 1995  74.31

### GERMAN MARK

Sept 1995  68.51
Nov 1995  70.56
Mar 1996  67.67
May 1996  65.23

### ITALIAN LIRA

Nov 1995  0.06

### BRITISH POUND

Sept 1995  156.67
Oct 1995  157.79
Nov 1995  156.24
Dec 1995  154.05
Jan 1996  152.90
Feb 1996  153.59
Mar 1996  152.70
Apr 1996  151.60
May 1996  151.46
June 1996  154.15
July 1996  155.30
Aug 1996  154.98

# PART I

# Autographs & Manuscripts

## A

**Abbott, Bud, 1894-1974 —&**
**Costello, Lou, 1906-59**
Photograph, sgd & inscr, [n.d.]. 4to. Inscr to Lena & Bill, Illus in cat rms Oct 11 (130) $800

**Abeille, Ludwig, 1761-1838**
ALs, 18 Dec 1804. 1 p, folio. To unnamed officials. Responding to an inquiry about some scores. star Mar 22 (730) DM400

**Abelard & Heloise**
Ms, Historia Calamitatum, & Epistolae. [Central or Eastern France, c.1350]. 74 leaves (some lacking), vellum, 231mm by 155mm. Modern blindstamped off-white lea. In a very neat compressed gothic bookhand, with some decorative descenders into lower margins. With 2-line initials in red or blue with penwork infilling & marginal flourishing in purple or red, & many medieval notes & readers' marks. S Dec 5 (33) £30,000 [Quaritch]

**Aberdeen, George Hamilton Gordon, 4th Earl**
Series of 61 A Ls s, 22 June 1828 to 12 Aug 1852. About 160 pp, various sizes. To Sec. to the Admiralty John Wilson Croker. Written as Foreign Secretary. With copies of 9 of Crokers replies. Bound in mor extra by Riviere. P June 5 (148) $1,700

**Abt, Franz, 1819-85**
ALs, 24 Apr 1865. 1 p, 4to. Recipient unnamed. Sending a photograph. HN May 15 (2482) DM220

**Adams, Abigail Smith, 1744-1818**
AL, [Feb 1788]. 1 p, 121mm by 187mm, cut from larger sheet. To Sir Clement Cotterell. About the Adams's official farewells to George III & Queen Charlotte. P June 5 (1) $4,200

**Adams, Abigail Smith, 1744-1818 —&**
**Adams, John, 1735-1826**
ALs, 14 Jan 1799. 1 p, 8vo. Recipient unnamed. Withdrawing his nomination of H. P. Schuyler as Captain of Infantry. CE June 12 (1) $3,750

**Adams, Jane, 1860-1935**
Ls, 12 Nov 1931. 1 p, 8vo. To Eugene Prussing. Sending thanks for books. sg June 6 (6) $80

**Adams, John, 1735-1826**
ALs, 2 Dec 1788. 3 pp, 4to. To Benjamin Rush. Thanking for Rush's praise of his Defence of the Constitutions of the United States, & discussing the possibility of his election to office. CNY May 17 (202) $26,000

— 30 Mar 1798. 2 pp, 4to. To Tristam Dalton. Thanking for some letters, responding to rumors about an unnamed politician, & discussing historical memory. Illus in cat. rms Mar 21 (8) $14,000

— 17 Sept 1798. 1 p, 4to. To James McHenry. Asking the Secretary of War for a commission for the grandson of General Palmer,a veteran of the Revolution. Mtd & framed with a bronze port medallion. CNY Dec 15 (134) $8,000

— 30 Nov 1798. 1 p, 4to. To Gov. Tichenor. Thanking for a laudatory address by the Vermont legislature. Illus in cat. P Dec 13 (7) $5,000

— 13 Apr 1799. 2 pp, 4to. To James McHenry. Deploring the recent rebellion against the property tax & proposing a new regimental organization for the army. Forbes Magazine collection. CNY May 17 (112) $26,000

— 1 Sept 1807. 3 pp, 4to. To Dr. Benjamin Rush. Speaking against the Jefferson government: "Our Monarchical, Anti-republican administration conceal from us, the People, all information which I a zealous Republican was always prompt to communicate..." With holograph free frank from Adams to Dr. Rush. Docketed by Rush. CNY Dec 15 (45) $26,000

— 8 Sept 1808. 3 pp, 4to. To Dr. Benjamin Rush. Discussing European politics & lamenting "the narrow selfish spirit" of American political parties. P Dec 13 (9) $27,000

— 8 Nov 1811. 1 p, 4 by 5.5 inches. To Hon W. Plummer [sic] Esq. About a Boston Newspaper: "...like you as mentioned in your last he has the Patriot bound in volumes. I hope however that the Correspondence will not be continued much loner. I am weary of it, and my dim Eyes and palsied Fingers admonish me to desist..."Free franked. Illus in cat pba Oct 26 (194) $2,500

— [26] June 1812. 3 pp, 4to. To Dr. Benjamin Rush. Criticizing the Madison Administration for undoing his work as President and bringing on War: "The Prudence of the 18 Century is called now in the 19th 'The Profligate Administration of John Adams'! ...Is

1

this the Reasoning, the Veracity, the Justice, the Gravity, the Dignity, the deliberation of a Legislative Assembly? Or the Raving of your Patients in your tranquilizing Chairs?...War! War! War! Sure enough. Whose 'Profligacy' is this?..." Illus in cat CNY Dec 15 (135) $40,000

— 6 Aug 1812. 2 pp, 4to. To Samuel B. Malcolm. Discussing the necessity of political parties & referring to Aaron Burr & other political acquaintances. Forbes Magazine collection. CNY May 17 (113) $24,000

— 14 Mar 1813. 1 p, 4to. To James Madison. Recommending Henry Coleman's brother for a commission in the army, & referring to the war. Repaired. Illus in cat. P Dec 13 (10) $10,000

— 3 May 1818. 1 p, 4to. To Justin Griswold. Responding to an inquiry about his & his son's birthdates. Silked. rms Mar 21 (10) $3,500

— 21 June 1821. 2 pp, 4to. To W. S. Shaw. Writing his nephew about Alexander McGillivray and attempts to learn about Native American religion. Worn & spotted. CNY Dec 15 (46) $5,000

— 25 Oct 1802. 1 p, 4to. To General Benjamin Lincoln. Recommending his friend Lemuel Clark for a position in Customs in Boston. CNY Dec 15 (44) $4,200

**Ls**, 20 Oct 1781. 2 pp, 4to. To James Searle. About problems obtaining a loan for Pensylvania from France & Holland & his illness. Signature restored. Detail in cat rms Oct 11 (1) $1,700

— 9 May 1823. 1 p, 4to. Recipient unnamed. Reflecting on his Presidency. Forbes Magazine collection. CNY May 17 (114) $6,500

**ADs**, 28 Nov 1780. 1 p, 111mm by 187mm. Order draft to Horneca, Fizeaux & Co. to pay Francis data on account of Mr. F. Grand at Paris. Endorsed by Dana. P June 5 (2) $3,750

— 23 June 1792. 1 p, 4to. Order to attach goods or estate of Elisha Wilder & James Wilder. With 18 lines in his hand, 8 of them covered by a paper repair. Sgd twice. sg Feb 1 (3) $375

**Ds**, 19 Feb 1774. 1 p, oblong 4to. Legal writ of attachment & summons against James Bryant of Cambridge MA. With c.8 lines in Adams's hand on verso, sgd. sg Feb 1 (2) $1,200

— 29 Mar 1798. 1 p, 17 by 21 inches. Ship's papers for the schooner Industry. Countersgd by Secretary of State Timothy Pickering. sg June 6 (1) $2,000

— 7 June 1799. 1 p, folio. Four-language ship's papers for the brig Lavinia. Countersgd by Secretary of State Timothy Pickering. Browned. Mtd & framed under glass. rms Oct 11 (2) $3,000

— 29 Oct 1799. 1 p, 17 by 21 inches. Ship's papers for the schooner Industry. Countersgd by Secretary of State Timothy Pickering. sg June 6 (2) $1,800

— 18 Apr 1800. 1 p, 15.2 by 13 inches, on vellum. Land grant. Countersgd by Timothy Pickering. rs Nov 11 (2) $1,400

— 14 May 1800. 1 p, folio. Land grant to Hugh Stephenson. P Dec 13 (8) $2,500

**Address leaf**, 21 Apr [n.y.]. Addressed to John Quincy Adams & with John Adams's Free Frank. wd Nov 15 (1) $750

**Cut signature**, 7 Dec 1797. On 5.5 by 8.5 inch slip of paper. Fragment of ship's paper. Countersgd by Secretary of State Timothy Pickering. Browned and with tape repairs. pba Feb 22 (209) $1,000

— Anr, [n.d.]. 1 by 6 inches; mtd. Including subscription. rms Mar 21 (9) $950

See also: Adams, Abigail Smith & Adams

**Adams, John Quincy, 1767-1848**

A Ls s (2), 25 March 1800 & 14 Oct 1801. 2 pp, 4to. To Joseph Pitcairn. About mutual acquaintances, financial dealings with the Spanish Minister, and his return to the US from Prussia. Stained. With tears in the margins. CNY Dec 15 (140) $900

— A Ls s (2), 18 April 1801 & 16 Dec 1815. 2 pp, 4to. To Joseph Pitcairn. About both political and personal matters. With worn edges. CNY Dec 15 (139) $2,200

**ALs**, 29 Aug 1792. 1 p, 8vo. To his mother. Forwarding letters & discussing a delivery of oats. Illus in cat. P Dec 13 (2) $4,000

— 12 Mar 1799. 2 pp, 4to. To Joseph Pitcairn. Asking the US Consul for intelligence to be sent to his father, the President: "Your situation at Hamburg indeed puts you often in possession of interesting intelligence, which you have opportunities of communicating earlier than any other of the public officers in Europe, and it is perhaps a desirable object to the Government to have the different views of several persons upon the same circumstances..." Docketed on verso. Illus in cat CNY Dec 15 (136) $2,100

— 27 Dec 1800. 1 p, 4to. To Joseph Pitcairn. Asking the Consul about the status of the Prussian-American Treaty: "My special concern at present is however for the Treaty- I have no acknowledgement of its being received at the department of State..." CNY Dec 15 (137) $900

— 17 July 1804. 4 pp, 4to. To Uriah Tracy. Insisting that "Love of retirement ... forms no item in [his] Catalogue of Virtues," & hoping for a constitutional amendment counting freemen only for the purposes of representation. Silked. Illus in cat. P Dec 13 (3) $16,000

— 17 Jan 1817. 4 pp, 4to. To Gov. William Plumer. Praising Plumer's speech & analyzing European attitudes towards America. Illus in cat. Pratt collection. P Dec 13 (4) $19,000

— 7 May 1818. 1 p, 4to. To Dr. George Bates. Reporting on letters of recommendation sent to the Secretary of Treasury. Illus in cat rms Nov 30 (51) $900

— 28 Oct 1818. 1 p, 4to, framed with port. To Kias Pimpton. About property captured by the British Government. CE June 12 (2) $1,300

— 4 Nov 1819. 1 p, 4to. To Gov. [Isaac H. Williamson]. Sending Congressional documents for the New Jersey legislature. Framed with a port. Illus in cat. rms Mar 21 (25) $1,400

— 22 Aug 1828. 2 pp, 4to. To Richard Rush. Accepting the resignation of his Secretary of the Treasury: "You will leave a place never easy to be filled, and never less easy when vacated by you..." Docketed on verso. Adams has written "Private"at top. With tear at fold. CNY Dec 15 (138) $5,500

— 25 Oct 1832. 3 pp, 4to. To John M. Patton. Reflecting on the history of weights & measures & explaining that the French metre would be well suited as a general standard. P Dec 13 (6) $7,000

**Ls,** 6 Apr 1819. 1 p, 4to. To Henry Hill. Sending Hill his commission as Counsel of the United States at Rio de Janeiro. With faulty edges. Framed with a color port. pba Oct 26 (196) $600

— 1 May 1822. 1 p, 4to. To Benjamin C. Wilcocks. Introducing Philip Ammidon who is claiming indemnities after his ship was wrecked & robbed on a Chinese island. Illus in cat. rms June 6 (302) $1,450

— 11 June 1822. 1 p, 4to. To Benjamin Robertson. Notifying him of his appointment as Marshal for West Florida. Illus in cat. rms Mar 21 (26) $850

**ANs,** 5 Sept 1842. 1 p, 8vo. To Mr. Seaton. Saying that the reports must be folded to be of use to him. wa Oct 28 (170) $500

**Collection** of 8 account statements, receipts & Ls s, 2 autograph receitps sgd & autograph address leaf with franking signature, 1806-19. Mostly 1 page. All to Thomas Hill Hubbard. P June 5 (4) $6,000

**Series of Ds s,** 4 Ds s, 1 Aug & 1 Sept 1827. 4 pp, on vellum, oblong folio. Land grants to William Wirt for land in Tallahassee. Countersgd by George Graham. bbc June 24 (29) $1,125

**Ds,** 3 Dec 1821. 1 p, folio. Detailing an agreement between the U.S. Dept of State & Darius Clark: "Sir, Your Newspaper has been selected as one among the numbers designated for publishing the Orders, Resolutions and Laws...which may be approved and ratified during the First Session of the Seventeenth Congress..." Clark was editor of the Vermont Gazette. Illus in cat pba Oct 26 (198) $800

— 1 Apr 1825. 1 p, oblong folio. Land grant in Missouri. sg June 6 (4) $325

— 1 Sept 1825. 1 p, folio, vellum. Land grant to Justus & Ebenezer Gage of New York for 160 acres in "the North East quarter of Section Twenty nine in Township One North of Range Ten East in the District of Detroit and Territory of Michigan..." With related material. pba Oct 26 (199) $400

— 15 Mar 1826. 9.8 by 15.8 inches. Land grant. rs Nov 11 (3) $250

— 15 June 1826. 1 p, folio. Grant of land in Alabama to Robert Jamison. Framed with a port. Illus in cat. rms Mar 21 (24) $560

— 29 July 1826. 1 p, folio. Land grant to Isaac Bell. P Dec 13 (5) $300

— 30 Oct 1827. 1 p, 4to, vellum. Appointing Thomas W. Brent as Midshipman in the U. S. Navy. Countersgd by Secretary of the Navy S. L. Southard. With 4 related documents concerning Brent. Detail in cat rms Oct 11 (3) $800

— 1 Nov 1827. 1 p, oblong folio. Land grant in Tallahassee. sg June 6 (5) $325

**Autograph endorsement,** 13 Dec 1831. On verso for check for $13.25 payable to his order. In full: " Pay the contents to Sidney Brooks or order J. Q. Adams". With repaired chipped edges. Also with a port. Illus in cat. rms Oct 11 (74) $300

**Envelope,** [n.d.]. 1 p, 2.2 by 5 inches. Address portion of an envelope. To Mrs. Adams. With franking signature. Illus in cat sg Sept 28 (5) $300

**Franking signature,** [27 June n.y.]. 3.25 by 5 inches. Sgd as " J. Q. Adams". Addressed to James F. Babcock. pba Oct 26 (200) $325

— DEARBORN, N. - Engraving, port of Adams; [c.1825]. 96mm by 83mm. Sgd by Adams. Illus in cat. Marans collection. CE Apr 17 (104) $2,600

See also: Monroe, James & Adams

**Adams, John Quincy, 1767-1848 —& Clay, Henry, 1777-1852**

**Ds,** 24 May 1827. 1 p, 4to. Appointing Martin Mantin as Vice Consul to " His Majesty The King of the Two Sicilies for the Port of New York". With ports of Clay & Adams. Framed. Over-all sized 25. by 20 inches. Illus in cat rms Oct 11 (304) $750

— 17 Jan 1828. 1 p, 4to, vellum. Portion only. A Ship's passport. Framed with ports of both men, a Lafayette commemorative ribbon & related material. Over-all size 27 by 39 inches. Illus in cat rms Oct 11 (5) $800

**Adams, Samuel, Signer from Massachusetts**

**ALs,** 11 Aug 1777. 1 p, folio. To Roger Sherman. Blaming Gen. Schuyler for the recent defeat at Ticonderoga. Silked. Illus in cat. P Dec 13 (11) $12,000

**Adenauer, Konrad, 1876-1967 —& Johnson, Lyndon B., 1908-73**

**Group photograph,** Jan 1961. 197mm by 247mm. Sgd by both. With letter of transferral by Max Adenauer. star Mar 22 (1200) DM1,600

**Adler, Alfred, 1870-1937**

**Collection** of 2 A Ls s, 1 Ls & 1 Ns, 11 Apr to 1 Aug 1933. 4 pp. To Dr. Knauer. CE June 12 (4) $850

**Adolf Frederick, King of Sweden, 1710-71**

**Endorsement,** sgd, 20 Nov 1741, on a sentence by a military court, 6 pp, folio; confirming sentence. star Mar 22 (1651) DM300

**Adolf Friedrich, Herzog von Mecklenburg-Schwerin, 1873-1969**

**Ls,** 26 Apr 1916. 3 pp, 4to. To Count Bernstorff. Reporting about the war in Mesopotamia. HN May 15 (2485) DM850

**Adorno, Theodor Wiesengrund, 1903-69**

**Collection** of ALs, 44 Ls s, & 2 autograph postcards, sgd, 27 July 1957 to 7 May 1969. 50 pp, mostly folio. To Carla Henius. Important correspondence concerning performances of his compositions, literary & academic matters. With c.70 letters from Henius to Adorno. star Mar 21 (388) DM13,000

**Akhmatova, Anna, 1889-1966**

**Typescript,** early version of her Poem without a Hero [here subtitled Triptych 1940-1955], sgd; 18 Aug 1942 to 1955. 46 pp, 8vo, in limp green wraps. Including autograph revisions. Containing notable differences from ptd text. With related material. S May 15 (152) £7,500

**Akihito, Emperor of Japan**
**Photograph, sgd,** [n.d.]. 4to. Full length; as crown prince. Illus in cat. rms Mar 21 (307) $570

**Alastair.** See: Voight, Hans Henning

**Albany, Louise Stuart, Countess of, 1753-1824**
**AL,** 12 Apr [n.d.]. 3 pp, 4to. To Karl Viktor von Bonstetten. Discussing Vittorio Alfieri, Johannes von Mueller, F. R. de Chateaubriand, & others. star Mar 22 (1344) DM1,900

**Albert, Prince Consort of Victoria of England, 1819-61.** See: Victoria & Albert

**Albrecht, Johann Lorenz, 1732-73.** See: Silbermann, Gottfried

**Alchemical Manuscripts**
— NICOLLIS, LORENZO VIRGILIO. - Autograph Ms, Thesaurus M[iraculi] M[undi?] Descriptus, [Vienna, 1723]. 2 parts in 1 vol, 288 pp (some blank), 198mm by 155mm. Contemp vellum bdg. Including 7 mostly full-page drawings. HH Nov 14 (3) DM3,000

**Alcock, Sir John William, 1892-1919 —& Brown, Arthur Whitten, Sir, 1886-1948**
**Group photograph,** [c.1919]. 152mm by 202mm. Seated; by International Newsreel, NY. Sgd by both. Marans collection. CE Apr 17 (1) $650

**Aldiss, Brian**
**Ms,** working draft of Burnell's Travels [pbd as Somewhere East of Life]. Several hundred pages, folio, typed or photocopied pages with holograph revisions & corrections throughout. Sgd & dated on tp, 1994. S Dec 18 (364) £200 [Fenelon]

**Aldrin, Edwin E.**
**Photograph, sgd & inscr,** [n.d.]. 16 by 20 inch color photo of Aldrin stepping onto the moon. Inscr to Ken Sharp. pba June 13 (128) $150

**Aldringen, Johann, Graf von, 1588-1634**
**Ls,** 31 Aug 1626. 1 p, folio. Recipient unnamed. Giving instructions concerning the building of a bridge across the Elbe at Dessau. With engraved port. star Mar 22 (1224) DM860

**Aleichem, Sholem, 1859-1916.** See: Sholem Aleichem

**Alexander I, Emperor of Russia, 1777-1825**
**ALs,** 1 Oct 1806. 2 pp, 4to. To Queen Luise of Prussia. Thanking for a letter delivered by the Duchess of Kurland & promising to respond by courier. Illus in cat. HN Nov 24 (2739) DM3,000
— 1 Sept 1814. 1 p, 4to. To an unnamed Prince of Oldenburg. Expressing thanks. star Mar 22 (1617) DM700
**Ds,** 27 Jan 1797. 1 p, folio. Order to provide horses for a traveller. star Mar 22 (1616) DM300

— 19 Dec 1823. 1 p, folio. Awarding Order of St. Anne to an officer. With related material. sg June 6 (8) $550
— 9 June 1825. 1 p, folio. Awarding the Order of St. Vladimir to the 1st Naval Complement for saving a boy from drowning. Detail in cat rms Oct 11 (4) $475

**Alexander III, Emperor of Russia, 1845-94**
**ALs,** 23 Sept 1879. 4 pp, 8vo. To Nikolai Alekseevich. Discussing a present for the King of Denmark, referring to a text about Tsar Alexander I, & hoping to see him in Paris. star Mar 22 (1625) DM900

**Alexander III, Pope, c.1105-81**
**Ds,** [10 Mar] 1181. 1 p, vellum, 68cm by 59cm. Papal Bull confirming the reform & the property of the cloister at Flotin. Also sgd by others, including the future Popes Lucius III & Celestine III. Nibbled by rodents. Illus in cat. star Mar 22 (1496) DM13,500

**Alexander VIII, Pope, 1610-91**
**Ls,** 22 Feb 1686. 1 p, 4to. To Francesco Alberti di Poja. Thanking for a favor accorded to Paolo Cariboni. star Mar 22 (1499) DM750

**Alexandra, Queen of Edward VII of England, 1844-1925**
**Photograph, sgd,** 1901. 360mm by 260mm. b May 30 (359) £140
— Anr, 1901. 200mm by 150mm. In ceremonial robes with Edward VII. Sgd by her "Edward VII. Alexandra 1901" on mount. b May 30 (363) £90
— Anr, [c.1903]. 285mm by 175mm. Sgd on image. b May 30 (361) £65
— Anr, 1910. 200mm by 150mm. In ceremonial robes with Edward VII. Sgd by her "Edward VII. Alexandra 1910" on mount. b May 30 (362) £75
— Anr, [n.d.]. 205mm by 140mm. Showing her embracing Prince Olav. Sgd on image. b May 30 (358) £50
**Photograph, sgd & inscr,** in Coronation robes, sgd Alexandra Coronation day, 1902. 200mm by 150mm. b May 30 (357) £95

**Alexis, Willibald, 1798-1871**
**Autograph Ms,** novel, Der Roland von Berlin, vol 1, parts of chapter 8, & vol 3, chapters 1 - 14; [1840]. 258 pp, 4to. Ptr's copy; including numerous revisions. star Mar 21 (1) DM3,200

**Alfonso, Prince of Fez, fl.1500-10**
**Ds,** 16 Dec 1507. 1 p, 8vo. Receipt for 10 florins from Denis Bruin. HN May 15 (2490) DM200
— 30 Apr 1508. 1 p, 8vo. Receipt for travel expenses in the Emperor's service. HN Nov 24 (2864) DM480

**Alfonso VII, King of Castile & Leon, 1104?-57**
**Ds,** [23 Aug 1149]. 1 p, vellum, 225mm by 437mm. Confirmation of the inheritance of Fernando Gutteriz of lands in the Val de Salze. Sgd with a cross. Illus in cat. S Dec 5 (21) £1,700 [Fonseca]

**Allenby, Edmund Henry Hynman, 1st Viscount Allenby of Megiddo, 1861-1936**

Group photograph, [11 Dec 1917]. 116mm by 163mm. Entering Jerusalem at the Jaffa Gate; sgd by Allenby. Illus in cat. Marans collection. CE Apr 17 (105) $3,000

**Alma-Tadema, Sir Lawrence, 1836-1912**

ALs, 6 Aug [n.d.]. 3 pp, 4to. To an unnamed lady. Criticizing her trans of one of his works. Illus in cat. star Mar 21 (646) DM230

**Altenberg, Peter, 1859-1919**

ALs, [1905]. 3 pp, 4to. To the pbr Samuel Fischer. Describing his financial misery & asking for recipient's help. star Mar 21 (3) DM900

— [7 Dec 1917]. 2 pp, 4to. To the Ed of the journal Berliner Boersen-Courier. Sending a hymn on Alfred Kerr (included) as a contribution to the magazine. star Mar 21 (2) DM460

Autograph postcard, sgd, [2 Aug 1901]. To Karl Kraus. Asking for picture postcards. HH Nov 17 (3187) DM240

**Ambrosiaster**

Ms, commentary on St. Paul's Epistle to Timothy. [Northern or northeastern France, 2d half of 8th cent]. Bifolium, vellum, 300mm by 245mm. In dark brown ink in a very fine pre-Caroline minuscule. With headings & some biblical lemmata in large red majuscules, 21 initials in pale red, & running titles in a 12th cent hand. Trimmed, worn; recovered from a bdg. Illus in cat. S Dec 5 (7) £12,500 [Quaritch]

**American Revolution**

Ms, Orderly Book, kept at the headquarters of British Major John Dyke Acland at Crown Point, Ticonderoga, & camps in Canada, 8 Oct 1776 to 4 Mar 1777. 93 leaves, 8vo, in modern half brown mor. With typed transcript. P Dec 13 (321) $14,000

— BOSTON PORT ACT. - Letter sgd by John Rowe, John Hancock & Samuel Adams as members of a Boston merchants' committee, 12 July 1774. 1 p, 254mm by 181mm. In a clerical hand. Probably to Richard Derby of Salem. About assistance from neighboring townspeople to Boston merchants. P June 5 (19) $9,750

— BRITISH SECRET SERVICE. - Ms, notebook recording military expenditures at Montreal & Cambridge, including expenses for espionage activities, 1777 & 1778. 44 leaves, 8vo, in limp sheep wraps. P Dec 13 (33) $3,250

— BURGOYNE'S ARMY. - Ms, muster roll of a regiment of American troops guarding Burgoyne's army after the surrender, 3 Mar 1778. 1 p, folio. Illus in cat. P Dec 13 (53) $1,500

— CLIFT, SAMUEL. - ALs, 8 Oct 1781. 2 pp, folio. To his wife Sally. Reporting from the Yorktown campaign. CNY May 17 (296) $5,500

— GAY, MARTIN. - ALs, 8 & 27 July 1775. 4 pp, 4to. To his brother Jotham. Sending an eyewitness account of the Battle of Bunker Hill. P Dec 13 (35) $15,000

— MERRICK, SAMUEL J. - ALs, 1 June 1835. 5 pp, 4to. To John Trumbull. Reminiscing about the invasion of Canada in 1776 & the Saratoga campaign. P Dec 13 (15) $1,000

— STAMP ACT CONGRESS. - Document headed The Names of the Gentn. of the Congress, listing the 27 delegates to the Stamp Act Congress. [c.Oct 1765]. 1 p, 314mm by 200mm. Addressed to Samuel Gray in Windham CT by the offices of Mr. Bricknell. P June 5 (101) $1,600

**Amherst, Jeffrey Amherst, Baron, 1717-97**

ALs, 26 Apr 1788. 1 p, 4to. To Sir George Yonge. About Lt. Henry Graydon's death & the need for a replacement. rms Nov 30 (62) $700

— 17 May 1794. 2 pp, 4to. To Henry, Lord Dundas. Reporting to the King that "when the Colours taken at Louisbourg were sent to St. Pauls Cathedrall [sic] the Tower and Park Guns were fired at their arrival..." With ptd map of Louisbourg. Illus in cat sg Sept 28 (105) $650

— [n.d.]. 2 pp, 4to. To Lord Dover. Expressing uneasiness about problems between army members. rms June 6 (308) $525

**Ampere, Andre Marie, 1775-1836**

Autograph Ms, notes about multidimensional bodies, [n.d.]. 1 p, folio. Imperf. Illus in cat. HH May 9 (2420) DM650

**Amundsen, Roald, 1872-1928**

ALs, 28 Jan 1907. 4 pp, 8vo. To Mrs. G. Wiik. About her husband's death during his recent expedition, & promising to visit her. star Mar 21 (390) DM840

**Andersen, Hans Christian, 1805-75**

Photograph, sgd & inscr, 20 May 1870. 107mm by 64mm, mtd. By Thora Hallager; inscr to Miss Rye on verso. Illus in cat. Marans collection. CE Apr 17 (59) $1,800

**Anderson, Marian**

Concert program, sgd, 21 Nov 1947. For appearance at Ryman Auditoriu, in Nashville, 21 Nov 1947. Also sgd by accompanist Franz Rupp. sg Feb 1 (11) $100

**Anderson, Robert, 1805-71**

ALs, 11 Feb 1861. 2 pp, 8vo. To Mr. Mickles. About his command at Fort Sumter: "The Gov't has...given me every assurance that I shall have re-enforcements as soon as I need them. I have some slight hope that the present difficulties may be cleared up without bloodshed..." Folds. sg Sept 28 (15) $15,000

**Andre, Julius, 1808-80.** See: Mozart, Wolfgang Amadeus

**Andreae, Volkmar, 1879-1962**

Autograph quotation, 3 bars from his opera Ratcliff, 7 June 1938. 1 p, 8vo. Sgd. star Mar 22 (737) DM240

**Andreas-Salome, Lou, 1861-1937**

Collection of 4 A Ls s, autograph postcard, sgd, & AN, 3 Mar 1925 to 18 Apr 1935 & [n.d.]. 9 pp, various

sizes. To Charlotte Goetz. About personal matters. star Mar 21 (8) DM2,100
**Series** of 6 A Ls s, 1909. 10 pp, 4to & 8vo. To Sophie Hoechstetter. Concerning recipient's projected biography of Frieda von Buelow. With related material. star Mar 21 (7) DM2,200

### Angely, Louis, 1787-1835
**ALs,** 29 Oct 1827. 2 pp, 4to. To the bookseller Trautwein. Discussing a publication of his plays. star Mar 22 (1143) DM350

### Anna Ivanovna, Empress of Russia, 1693-1740
**Ds,** 31 Jan 1738. 1 p, 14 by 19 inches. Confirming Andrei Brunts as captain commander. sg June 6 (10) $600

### Anne, Queen of England, 1665-1714
**Ds,** 27 Oct 1712. 1 p, folio. Warrant for court regalia to be made up for Henry, Duke of Kent. Ck Apr 12 (20) £380
— [n.d.]. 1 p, folio. Appointment for an Ensign in a Regiment of Foot; unaccomplished. Illus in cat. rms June 6 (309) $525

### Anstey, F.
**Autograph Ms,** novel, The Giant's Robe. [1884] About 360 pp, 4to, interleaved, in contemp mor by Tout. With many revisions; with 80 india-proof illusts by W. Ralston. Inscr to Horace Pym. S Apr 23 (66) £2,500
— Autograph Ms, novel, The Tinted Venus. Sgd & dated 14 Jan 1885 Revised 18 Mar 1885. 166 pp, 4to, in contemp mor by Tout. With tipped-in ALs sending Horace Pym the above & a copy of the novel on 13 June 1885. S Apr 23 (70) £1,900

### Anthony, Susan B., 1820-1906
**Ls,** 28 Nov [19]02. 1 p, 4to. To Mrs. Arthur Sutherland. Sending an inquiry about the history of Woman Suffrage (present). With autograph postscript on verso. Illus in cat. rms June 6 (310) $675
**Photograph, sgd,** 15 Feb 1896. 279mm by 214mm, mtd. 3-quarter length; by Marceau. Illus in cat. Marans collection. CE Apr 17 (180) $1,700

### Antiphoner
— Antiphoner for the feast of Corpus Christi & other offices between Easter & Pentecost. [Spain, Toledo?, c.1600]. 95 leaves & 2 flyleaves, vellum, 618mm by 430mm. Extra contemp bdg of blindstamped dark brown goatskin gilt over massive wooden bds with brass fittings. With 4 lines each of text in a large rounded liturgical hand & of music on a 5-line red stave. With some words written in gold ink, c.60 large painted initials up to half-page in height usually on grounds of colored penwork, & 2 very large historiated initials. S Dec 5 (42) £5,500 [Damms]
**Ms,** [Bologna, c.1320]. Single leaf, vellum, 530mm by 338mm. With 7 lines each of text in a gothic rotunda & of music on a 4-line red stave. With large historiated initial & 3-quarter border in gold & colors. Illus in cat. HH May 7 (26) DM10,500

— Ms, [Italy, c.1400]. 10 leaves only, vellum, 450mm by 350mm. With 6 lines each of text in a textura hand & of music on a 5-line stave. With numerous large & small penwork initials in red & blue. Trimmed. HH May 7 (28) DM1,000
— Ms, [Italy, c.1400]. Single leaf, vellum, 515mm by 370mm. With 6 lines each of text in a gothic textura & of music on a 4-line red stave. With large historiated initial with marginal extension in colors. Imperf. HH May 7 (29) DM1,700
— Ms, [Lombardy, Milan?, c.1450]. Single leaf, vellum, 450mm by 310mm. With 7 lines each of text in a rounded gothic hand & of music on a 4-line brown stave with 1 line re-ruled in red. With small initials in red & blue with penwork in purple & red, & large historiated initial in colors & burnished gold with long marginal extensions. Framed. S June 18 (23) £2,600
— Ms, [Northwest Italy, c.1490]. Single leaf, vellum, 525mm by 375mm. With 7 lines of text & music. With very large illuminated initial in leafy design in colors & burnished gold with full-length illuminated border. Worn. S June 18 (25) £500
— Ms, [Siena, c.1350]]. Single leaf, vellum, 550mm by 380mm. With 7 lines each of text in a gothic rotunda & of music on a 4-line red stave. With large historiated initial attributable to the circles of Niccolo di Ser Sozzo or Lippo Vanni. Illus in cat. HH Nov 14 (30) DM7,500
— Ms, [Spain, 15th cent]. 10 leaves only, vellum, 460mm by 360mm. With 6 lines each of text in a gothic textura & of music on a 5-line stave. Including 56 initials in red & blue penwork. HH Nov 14 (31) DM900

### Apafi, Michael I, Prince of Transylvania, 1632-90
**Ms,** Ad Sacr. Roman. Imperium ex Cives Pannonia Rescriptum sive Declaratio, Cur Hungari ad Portam Ottomanicam Confugerint, [c.1683]. 15 leaves, 186mm by 146mm, in half lea. Contemp copy of his declaration of war against Austria. HH May 7 (21) DM900

### Apostel, Hans Erich, 1901-72
**Collection** of A Ls s & Ls s, [mostly 1966-1969]. 13 pp, mostly folio. To Egon Wellesz. Discussing music life in Vienna & various composers. S May 15 (539) £400

### Arabic & Persian Manuscripts
— JAMAL AL-DIN HUSAIN AL-KASHIFI. - Tafsir al-Qur'an. [Persia, c.1550]. 572 ff, 370mm by 244mm. Later black mor gilt. In naskhi script. With sura headings in white on illuminated panels, illuminated headpiece, & double page of illumination. S Oct 18 (45) £1,500

### Arabic Manuscripts
**Ms,** compendium of religious poetry. [North West Africa, A.H. 669/ A.D. 1270]. 185 ff, 212mm by 154mm. Medieval tooled brown mor bdg. In a cursive hand on thick pink paper. S Oct 18 (36) £5,500

— Ms, grammatical treatise. [Ottoman, 18th cent]. 86 leaves, 164mm by 107mm. Contemp blindstamped lea. In naskhi script. With 3 half-page illuminated headpieces & marginal commentary throughout. HH May 7 (83) DM1,000

— Ms, prayers & pious phrases. [North India, A.H. 1285/ A.D. 1868]. Scroll, 180cm by 6.1cm. In fine script in the form of birds, animals, & other designs. With floral sprays in gold on gold-sprinkled paper. S Oct 18 (48) £2,800

— ABDALLLAH BEN YUSUF BEN HISAM AL-ANSARI AL-HANBALI. - Mugni al-labib 'an kutub al-a'arib. [Ottoman, 1st half of 19th cent]. 243 leaves, 215mm by 135mm. Contemp lea. In naskhi script. With full page of illuminiation. HH Nov 14 (89) DM200

— ABU'L QASIM MAHMUD BIN UMAR AL-ZAMAKHSHARI. - Kitab al-Kasshaf an Haqa'iq al-Tanzil al-Qur'an. [Mesopotamia or Western Iran, A.H. 681/ A.D. 1282]. 277 ff, 326mm by 242mm. Rebacked later stamped brown mor. In cursive script on cream-colored paper with headings in thuluth or muhaqqaq scripts. With illuminated tp & opening page of text in superb eastern kufic script on a ground of scrolling gold arabesques. S Oct 18 (42) £10,000

— ABU'L QASIM MAHMUD BIN UMAR AL-ZAMAKHSHARI. - Kitab al-Mufassal. [Samarkand, A.H. 730/ A.D. 1329]. 251 ff, 175mm by 141mm. Worn rebacked brown paper bds. In cursive script on thick buff paper by Muhammad bin Ali bin Abu Shahid. With numerous marginal glosses. S Oct 18 (44) £6,000

— AHMAD BEN MUHAMMAD BEN IBRAHIM AL-UMAWI, KNOWN AS MAIBUDI. - Risalat rasm al-'utman ... bi-maurid az-zam'an. [Cairo, A.H. 1149/ A.D. 1737]. 278 leaves, 212mm by 158mm. Contemp blindstamped lea. In naskhi script by 'Abd al-Latif. HH Nov 14 (90) DM400

— AL-JAZULI. - Dala'il al Khayrat. [Ottoman?, early 19th cent]. 89 leaves, 172mm by 113mm. Contemp brown lea gilt. In naskhi script with headings in red thuluth. With double page of illumination & 2 full-page miniatures of Mecca & Medina in gold & colors. HH Nov 14 (92) DM2,600

— AL-JAZULI. - Dala'il al-Khayrat. [Persia?, A.H. 1184/ A.D. 1770]. 99 leaves, 165mm by 95mm. Contemp? lacquer bdg. In naskhi script by Abdullah bin Abdulrahman. With 8 double pages of illumination & 2 full-page drawings of Mecca & Medina. HH May 7 (73) DM6,500

— AL-JAZULI. - Dala'il al-Khayrat. [ A.H. 1247/ A.D. 1831]. 99 leaves, 165mm by 100mm. Contemp dark brown lea gilt. In naskhi script. With 2 illuminated headpieces & 2 full-page drawings of Mecca & Medina. HH May 7 (74) DM1,600

— IBN YAZID AL-'ATTAR. - Kitab at-tidkar aban Ibn-Yazid, & other texts. [Ottoman, 2d half of 19th cent]. 494 pp, 202mm by 140mm. Contemp blindstamped lea. In naskhi script in several hands. HH Nov 14 (95) DM250

— ISMA'IL BEN MUSTAFA KALANBAWI. - Hada kitab Kalanbawi 'ala 'l-mir. [Ottoman, 1st half of 19th cent]. 166 pp, 217mm by 154mm. Contemp blindstamped lea. In naskhi script. Ownership inscr of el-Hafiz Mahmud Prilepevi. HH Nov 14 (97) DM260

— MALIK IBN ANAS. - Kitab al-Muwatta, parts 18 & 19. [Southern Spain or North Africa, A.H. 391/ A.D. 1001]. 78 ff, vellum, 280mm by 221mm, disbound. In small maghribi script, with headings in larger script & numerous minute marginal glosses. Ownership inscr of Abu Muhammad Abdallah. Imperf. S Oct 18 (35) £6,000

— MUHAMMAD BIN MUHAMMAD AL-AQSARA'I. - Sharh Mujaz Ibn an-Nafis. [Levant, A.H. 968/ A.D. 1560]. 196 ff, 227mm by 126mm. Modern red mor. In a cursive hand verging on naskhi. With marginal glosses throughout. S Oct 18 (46) £800

— MUSA BIN MUHAMMAD QADIZADEH AL-RUMI. - Tuhfat al-Ra'is fi Askal al-Ta'sis. [Mesopotamia or Western Persia, A.H. 879/ A.D. 1474]. 44 ff, 214mm by 130mm. Red & brown mor. In a cursive hand. With numerous diagrams in text & glosses in margins. S Oct 18 (37) £800

— NIZAMUDDIN AL-HASSAN BIN MUHAMMAD AL-NISHAPURI. - Sharh Tadkira al-Nasiriya; with Mir Sayyid Sharif, Sharh Tadkira. [Persia, A.H. 844-845/ A.D. 1441-1442]. 314 ff, 247mm by 151mm. Contemp brown mor. In nasta'liq script by Amir Muhammad bin Amir Mahmud al-Qantari. With numerous red & black diagrams throughout. S Oct 18 (54) £5,000

— QUTB AL-DIN MAHMUD BIN MA'SUD AL-SHIRAZI. - Al-Tuhfa al-Shahiya fi 'l-Hai'a. [Mesopotamia or Western Persia, A.H. 734/ A.D. 1334]. 200 ff, 185mm by 119mm. Modern brown mor. In a neat cursive hand. With numerous diagrams in text & glosses in margins. Repaired. S Oct 18 (38) £2,400

— SHIHAB AL-DIN AHMAD IBN MUHAMMAD IBN AL-HA'IM. - Kitab al-Wasila fi 'ilm al-hisab al-jabr. [Jerusalem, A.H. 792/ A.D. 1390]. 56 ff, 182mm by 129mm. Modern brown mor. In a cursive hand on thick cream paper by Muhammad ibn Ali Nuhad [?] al-Maqdisi. With occasional glosses in margins. Opening leaf replaced. S Oct 18 (41) £3,800

— SIRAJ AL-DIN MAHMUD BIN ABU BAKR AL-URMAWI. - Matali' al-Anwar fi 'l-Mantiq. [Northern Mesopotamia, A.H. 670/ A.D. 1271]. 49 ff, 164mm by 123mm, in marbled paper bds. In a spidery cursive hand on thick cream paper, with headings in larger thuluth script & numerous marginal glosses. S Oct 18 (40) £3,000

### Arbuthnot, Marriot, 1711-94

Ls, 21 Apr 1781. 1 p, folio. To George Washington. Protesting the treatment of British prisoners of war. P Dec 13 (19) $5,500

### Ariosti, Alexander de, 1484?

Ms, Tractatus contractuum editus a fratre Alexandro de Ariostis de feraria ordis minorum. [Italy, 3d quarter of 15th cent] 100 leaves, on vellum, 138mm by 96mm, in 18th-cent sheep with mor back. In brown ink in a small & rather archaic Bolognese gothic bookhand. C Apr 3 (3) £3,800

# ARISTOTLE

### Aristotle, 384-322 B.C.

**Ms,** Libellus de admirandis in natura auditis per Antonium Beccaria veronense traductus. [Italy, 2d half of 16th cent]. 40 leaves, 186mm by 128mm. 19th-cent bds. Containing excerpts of works by Sotion Peripateticus & Athenaeus Naucratita, all attributed to Aristotle. HH Nov 14 (5) DM1,400

— Ms, Physica. [Paris, 1639]. 468 leaves (32 blank), 220mm by 165mm. Contemp brown calf gilt. In the hand of St. Germain de Posse. HH May 7 (1) DM750

### Armenian Manuscripts

**Ms,** Gospel of St. Mark. [Armenia, c.1655]. 143 leaves & 3 flyleaves, vellum, 90mm by 62mm. Worn contemp Armenian blindstamped lea over bds. In dark brown ink in a small bolorgir hand. With decorated initials throughout in elaborate designs of animals & plants with marginal extensions, tp with half-page headpiece, 2-sided border & historiated initial, & 10 large or full-page miniatures in full colors. S June 18 (55) £2,600

— Ms, Gospels, with prefaces & Canon Tables. [Ostan, Lake Van, 1411]. 249 leaves (1 blank) & 4 earlier vellum flyleaves, 248m by 182mm. Worn blindstamped medieval bdg of tanned lea over thin wooden bds by the priest Atom. In black ink in a sloping bolorgir hand by the artist Tserun for the monk Yohannes. With c.200 large chapter openings with large initials of colored birds or other devices, 4 full-page openings of books with elaborate half-page interlaced headpieces & symbols of the Evangelists, 10 full-page canon pages in elaborate architectural designs, & 14 full-page miniatures in full colors. With endleaves from an earlier liturgical Ms in Georgian. S June 18 (54) £28,000

— Ms, Missal. [Georgia, Tiflis?, 1721]. 30 leaves, 240mm by 180mm, in 19th cent marbled bds. In black & red ink in a handsome bolorgir hand. With 21 large illuminated initials formed of animals, angels & people in colors & gold, 22 illuminated borders, 10 column-width miniatures, half-page & full-page miniature, & illuminated tp. Fragile. S Dec 5 (25) £4,000 [Sam Fogg]

### Armstrong, Louis, d.1971

**Concert program,** 1963. For a New Zealand tour by "Louis Armstrong and His All Stars with Jewel Brown and Eddie Cano". Sgd by Armstrong & also by the members of the group, the promoter, the publicist, etc. sg Feb 1 (119) $150

**Photograph, sgd & inscr,** [1920s]. 9.5 by 13 inch pubicity photo. Of Armstrong and his band. Inscr to Ernie. Tipped to a backing board. Inscr faint. Illus in cat sg Sept 28 (16) $375

— Anr, [c.1940]. 205mm by 253mm. Seated, blowing his trumpet; inscr to Andy. Illus in cat. Marans collection. CE Apr 17 (236) $450

**Signature,** 1949. On Program of the Zulu Social Club in New Orleans. Also sgd by Leonard Feather. F Mar 28 (702) $260

### Armstrong, Louis, d.1971 —& Others

**Concert program,** [1950s]. Program of Louis Armstrong And His Concert Group, 16 pp. Sgd on his port. Also sgd by 6 other members of the company. Illus in cat. rms June 6 (198) $200

### Arndt, Ernst Moritz, 1769-1860

**Autograph Ms,** poem, Des Teutschen Vaterland, [n.d.]. 2 pp, 4to. 10 stanzas; differing from ptd version. Illus in cat. star Mar 21 (9) DM26,000

**ALs,** 13 July 1855. 2 pp, 4to. To [Wilhelm Schoepff]. Praising his work, but requesting him not to use his name in the publication. star Mar 21 (10) DM650

### Arnim, Bettina von, 1785-1859

**ALs,** [n.d.]. 1 p, 8vo. To the ptr Buexenstein. Giving instructions to wait with the bdg of the new Ed of Des Knaben Wunderhorn until she has seen the proofs. star Mar 21 (11) DM1,300

### Arnim, Ludwig Achim von, 1781-1831

**ALs,** 26 Sept 1808. 2 pp, 4to. To Johann Gustav Buesching. Concerning the failure of his journal Zeitung fuer Einsiedler. Illus in cat. star Mar 21 (13a) DM4,200

— 30 Aug 1824. 2 pp, 4to. To Friedrich Karl von Savigny. Discussing family matters. star Mar 21 (13b) DM2,000

### Arnold, Benedict, 1741-1801

**ALs,** 10 Jan 1766. 1 p folio. Recipient unnamed. Concerning the payment of a debt. Repaired. CNY May 17 (204) $1,800

— 8 May 1769. 1 p, folio. To his first wife. Giving a brief account of his travels in the West Indies. cb June 25 (2301) $3,750

— 8 June 1777. 1 p, 8vo. To Thomas Mumford. Letter of recommendation for Samuel Griffin. Illus in cat. P Dec 13 (20) $6,000

— 6 June 1783. 2 pp, 8vo. To Lord Sheffield. Forwarding a letter from Henry Clinton (not included) & asking for assistance in his request for monetary rewards from the British government. Illus in cat. P Dec 13 (21) $4,000

— 28 Oct 1794. 3 pp on 2 sheets. To Col. Fisher. About deliveries of foodstuffs for the troops. cb June 25 (2302) $3,000

**ADs,** 8 May 1776. 1 p, 3.6 by 7.25 inches. Permit allowing Josiah Blakely to travel from Montreal to Albany with a "Battteau loaded with Bale Goods." Aged but professionally restored. Illus in cat sg Sept 28 (17) $3,200

— OFFICER IN ARNOLD'S COMMAND. - ALs, 5 June 1776. 4 pp, 4to. To "My dear Love." Describing engagements with the enemies & the burning of an Indian town. Sgd "Philander". cb June 25 (2303) $2,000

### Arnold, Hannah

**ALs,** June 1775. 1 p, 4to. To her brother Benedict Arnold. Congratulating him on his success at Ticonderoga. Sang collection. P Dec 13 (22) $2,500

## Arouet, Francois, 1650-1722
Ds, 7 Aug 1705. 1 p, 8vo. Chambre de Comptes receipt. Repaired. rms June 6 (495) $700

## Arp, Jean (or Hans), 1887-1966
ALs, 24 Nov 1954. 1 p, folio. Recipient unnamed. Thanking for an article. HN May 15 (2492) DM260

## Arrhenius, Svante, 1859-1927
ALs, 15 Mar 1904. 4 pp, 4to. To Gustav Adolf Hagemann. Promising to attend a conference in St. Louis. star Mar 21 (392) DM420

## Arthur, Chester A., 1830-86
ALs, 19 Nov 1864. 1 p, 8vo. To D. F. Tyler. Regarding his possible appointment to Quarter Master General. CE June 12 (5) $450
— 24 Dec 1882. 1 p, 8vo. To Judge Edwards Pierrepont. Concerning his being unable to leave Washington over the holidays. CNY Dec 15 (141) $2,000
Ls, 24 May 1884. 2 pp, 8vo. To Edwards Pierrepont. Thanking for his endorsement for renomination by a Cooper Union meeting. Forbes Magazine collection. CNY May 17 (117) $750
Ds, 22 Oct 1881. 1 p, folio. Appointing Haile C. T. Nye as a Lieutenant of the Navy. Countersgd by Secretary of the Navy William H. Hunt. With folds. Illus in cat rms Oct 11 (274) $700
— 4 May 1882. 1 p, 4to. Order to affix the U.S. Seal to be affixed to an envelope containing a letter of recall of James O. Putnam addressed to King Leopold II of the Belgians. Framed. wa Oct 28 (172) $425
— 11 Apr 1883. 1 p, oblong folio. Appointment of Allen B. Croasman as Postmaster at Salem, Ohio. CE June 12 (6) $350
— 21 Jan 1884. 1 p, folio. Appointing Samuel J. Logan a First Lieutenant in the Marine Corps. Countersgd by Secretary of the Navy W. E. Chandler. Signature light. Illus in cat rms Oct 11 (38) $700
— 3 Mar 1885. 1 p, 17 by 13.5 inches, framed. Appointment of Henry L. Howison as Captain in the Navy. rs Nov 11 (9) $400
Check, 29 Aug 1881. 1 p, 4to. $25 payable to his son Chester A. Arthur, Jr. Endorsed by Jr on verso & intialed by him. With pinholes & folds. Illus in cat rms Oct 11 (75) $625
Executive Mansion card, sgd, 14 Jan 1885. Inscr to Master Bayard Marston Smith. Framed with port. wa Oct 28 (173) $325
— Anr, [n.d.]. No size given. On an Executive Mansion card. pba Feb 22 (212) $325
Signature, 12 Apr 1881. On a card. sg June 6 (11) $225
— Anr, [n.d.]. No size given. On a card. Sgd as "C. A. Arthur". Soiled. Illus in cat pba Oct 26 (201) $250
— Anr, [n.d.]. No size given. On Executive Mansion card. With oval port & stereo card of the Brooklyn Bridge by Underwood & Underwood. Framed. Over-all size 15.5 by 23.5 inches. Illus in cat rms Oct 11 (305) $600
White House card, [n.d.]. Sgd in full. pba June 13 (47) $275

See also: Garfield, James A. & Arthur

## Astor, John Jacob, 1763-1848
Ds, 6 Nov 1816. 1 p, folio. Columbian Insurance Company financial report, 13 Oct 1814 to 6 Nov 1816. Also sgd by others. Illus in cat. rms June 6 (364) $900

## Astrid, Queen of Leopold III, King of the Belgians, 1905-35
ALs, 22 Mar 1926. 4 pp, 4to. To Miss Atterling. Sending family news. star Mar 22 (1177) DM1,300

## Astrological Manuscripts
— GEUSS, WOLFGANG. - Ms, [Nativitet Buch], astrological treatise, [Nuernberg, 1580]. 268 pp (2 lacking, 4 blank), 194mm by 162mm. Contemp blindstamped lea gilt over wooden bds. Lacking tp. HH May 7 (13) DM3,200

## Astronauts
— APOLLO 11. - Signatures of Neil Armstrong, Buzz Aldrin & Michael Collins. [n. d.]. On 1 p, no size given. pba June 13 (129) $325
— APOLLO 12 . - Signatures of Frank Borman, William Anders & James Lovell. [n. d.]. On Chicago Police calling card. No size given. pba June 13 (130) $150
— APOLLO XI. - Group photograph, [c.1969]. 206mm by 201mm. Posed before an image of the moon; sgd by all 3. Illus in cat. Marans collection. CE Apr 17 (3) $1,200
— LOVELL, JAMES. - Photo sgd. [n.d.]. No size given. pba June 13 (133) $50
— MERCURY. - Group photograph, [c.1962]. 202mm by 255mm. In front of a flight training jet; sgd by 6 of the 7 flight members. Illus in cat. Marans collection. CE Apr 17 (2) $950

## Atchison, David Rice, 1807-86
ALs, 18 June 1858. 1 p, 8vo. Recipient unnamed. Promising to provide a copy of his address to the people of Missouri. rms Mar 21 (40) $800

## Atwood, Margaret
Collection of Collection of 5 ALs s, 17 Ls s & 2 Letters, 1970-76, No size or length given. Concerning her works, chicken-rearing, the birth of her daughter & her stance on America: "I'm not anti-Americans (singular); in fact I'm married to one. Just anti-U. S. imperialism, which I suppose we all are. Canadians do tend to be overly touchy, but then its their country they see being sucked down the drain..." Illus in cat pba Jan 25 (11) $2,000

## Auber, Daniel Francois, 1782-1871
Ds, 16 Dec 1850. 2 pp, folio. Contract ceding the German & Austrian rights to his opera L'enfant prodigue to Heinrich Schlesinger. Also sgd by Schlesinger & Eugene Scribe. star Mar 22 (738) DM200

## Auden, Wystan Hugh, 1907-73
Autograph Ms, 2 stanzas of the poem "Our hunting fathers told the story". 1934. 1 p, folio. In half mor. Hinged in a volume. Illus in cat S June 28 (9) £1,900
— Autograph Ms, A Review of T. E. Lawrence by B. H. Liddell Hart. 1934. 2 pp, folio. With many deletions & corrections. S June 28 (2) £600

## AUDEN

— Autograph Ms, draft of an unidentified 25-line verse beginning "Of these the false Achitophel was". 1 p., 4to. wa Oct 28 (4) $210
— Autograph Ms, Introductory Essay from Robert Frost's Selected Poems. 1936. 7 pp, 4to. With deletions & corrections. S June 28 (3) £1,000
Collection of 3 A Ls s & 1 autograph postcard, sgd, [c.1931-35, the postcard after World War II]. 6 pp, 8vo. To Olive Mangeot. Discussing poems & other matters, including A Bride of the Thirties, which he had dedicated to Mangeot. S Dec 18 (287) £700 [Bertram]
ALs, 22 May [n. y.]. 1 p, folio. To Marshall Bean. Sending a poem to an ill person: "I am very sorry to hear you are ill. Now and again I have been ill myself and the worst thing, next to the pain, was feeling lonely, because those who are well can't know what it is like. It's quite true they can't, but they can think of you with love as I shall, often, even though we've never met." With a 1 p poem, " On Reading a Child's Guide to Modern Physiics: If all a top physicist knows..." Sgd with initials. S June 28 (22) £600

**Audubon, John James, 1785-1851**
ALs, 7 June 1835. 2 pp, folio. To James Clarke Ross. Asking for recipient's observations of arctic birds & including a list of 54 species of birds. Illus in cat. CNY May 17 (205) $4,200

**Auersperg, Anton Alexander von, 1806-76.** See: Gruen, Anastasius

**Augereau, Pierre Francois Charles, Duc de Castiglione, 1757-1816**
Ls, 27 May 1805. 1 p, 4to. To M Perregard. Arranging credit for Madame Augerau. Illus in cat P Dec 12 (303) $140
— 30 July 1813. 1 p, folio. To Comte Cessac. Recommending Andre Julien Fossey. star Mar 22 (1435) DM280

**August, Herzog von Braunschweig-Wolfenbuettel, 1579-1666.** See: August & August

**August, Herzog von Sachsen-Weissenfels, 1614-80 — &**
**August, Herzog von Braunschweig-Wolfenbuettel, 1579-1666**
Ls s (2), 10 Mar 1652. 4 pp, folio. To the magistrates of an unnamed town. Protesting against the Imperial order that Protestants in Duderstadt must convert to Catholicism. star Mar 22 (1225) DM530

**August, Kurfuerst von Sachsen, 1526-86**
Ls, [1 Apr] 1545. 2 pp, folio. To the chapter of the cathedral at Merseburg. Instructing them to accept Prince Georg of Anhalt as new bishop of Merseburg. star Mar 22 (1627) DM650
See also: William I & August

**August II, King of Poland, 1670-1733**
Ls, 16 Apr 1729. 3 pp, folio. To Duke Georg Albert of Saxony. Concerning a recent rebellion in Augsburg. star Mar 22 (1632) DM900

**August III, King of Poland, 1696-1763**
ALs, 15 Feb 1740. 1 p, folio. To Count Wackerbarth. Thanking for news about his daughter & son-in-law, & asking for some relics from Italy. star Mar 22 (1633) DM550

**Augusta, Empress of Wilhelm I of Germany, 1811-90**
Ls, 12 Sept 1856. 2 pp, 4to. To an unnamed manufacturer. About a contribution to a charity. star Mar 22 (1555) DM250

**Auster, Paul**
ALs, 25 May 1984. 1 p, no size given. To Stephen Vincent. Writing the editor about the lack of women mentioned in his The Invention of Solitude & also discussing the New York Trilogy on which he was working. With original envelope & letter from Vincent to which this was a response. Illus in cat pba Jan 25 (13) $250

**Austin, Stephen F., 1793-1836**
Ds, 11 Jan 1836. 1 p, 4to. A Texas Loan Certificate. Countersgd by Branch Arthur Tanner & William Harris Wharton as Commissioners of Consultation. CNY Dec 15 (51) $1,800
— 11 Jan 1836. 1 p, 4to. Texian Loan Certificate. Countersgd by Archer & Wharton. wa Oct 28 (392) $900

**Austria**
Ms, Urbar zu Gmuend [Cadastral register of rate payers]. [Gmuend, c.1500] 36 leaves, folio. Bound in contemp austrian wallet bdg of blind-tooled mor with 2 decorated brass buckles & lea clasps with brass finials. C May 1 (6) £7,000

**Ayers, James J.**
Autograph Ms, Pioneer Times: The First and the Last Gold-hunters. A Lecture Delivered at Good Templar Hall, March 15, 1878. Los Angeles, 1878. 24 pp, 12.75 inches by 7.5 inches. Larson collection pba Sept 24 (302) $1,100

# B

**Bach, Carl Philipp Emanuel, 1714-88**
Ms, cantata, Gottes Groesse in der Natur, in full score; sgd & dated by the scribe Johann Georg Walther, 1792. 21 pp, size not stated, in wraps. Comprising an opening movement for orchestra & chorus, & an aria for soprano & tenor. Possibly unrecorded. S May 15 (271) £800

**Bach, Johann Christian, 1743-1814**
ALs, 29 May 1762. 1 p, 4to. To Maria Testagrossa. Informing her that he is unable to write an opera for the carnival in Naples because he has sgd a contract to write operas for London. Illus in cat. S Dec 1 (69) £10,000
Ds, 22 Feb 1762. 1 p, 8vo. Receipt for payment for the composition of a cantata written for the birthday of King Charles III of Spain. Illus in cat. S May 15 (272) £13,000

### Bach, Johann Sebastian, 1685-1750
**Autograph music,** cantata, Ach Gott vom Himmel sieh darein, BWV 2; June 1724. 12 pp, folio, in contemp wraps inscr by Johann Anton Kuhnau. Working Ms of the full score; including autograph title at head. S May 15 (278) £450,000

### Bachmeir von Regenbrun, Huldrich
**Ms,** Introduction Hominis, das ist, Was der Mensch inn disem Leben fuernemblich Studiern und lernnen soll, 1607. 69 leaves, 198mm by 164mm. Red-brown lea gilt over contemp wooden bds. HH May 7 (2) DM3,600

### Bacon, Henry, 1866-1924
**Original drawings,** (18) architectural sketches & plans for the Lincoln Memorial in Washington DC, 24 Feb 1912 to 21 Nov 1917. With related blueprints. rs Nov 11 (29) $25,000

### Baden-Powell of Gilwell, Robert S. S. Baden-Powell, 1st Baron, 1857-1941
**ALs,** 25 Jan 1884. 4 pp. To Henry Blaghorne. Asking for Corporal Jackson's papers. With related material. Ck Apr 12 (21) £260

— 17 May 1895. 4 pp. To Capt. Anstruther-Thomson. About the necessity for Car Machine Guns. Ck Apr 12 (22) £180

— 29 Aug [n.y.]. 3 pp, on single sheet, 8vo. Recipient unnamed. praising his work in the movement. wa Oct 28 (90) $300

### Baden-Powell of Gilwell, Robert S. S. Baden-Powell, 1st Baron, 1857-1941 —&
### Beard, Daniel C., 1850-1941
**Group photograph,** [c.1925]. 180mm by 230mm. Seated on a stage; sgd by both & inscr by Beard. Marans collection. CE Apr 17 (116) $320

### Baggesen, Jens Immanuel, 1764-1826
**ALs,** 15 Oct 1816. 2 pp, 4to. To "Liebster Courlaender". Discussing the refusal of the theater at Kopenhagen to play A. G. Oehlenschlaeger's comedy Freyas Altar. star Mar 21 (15) DM850

— 8 to 14 Sept 1817. 3 pp, folio. To "Liebster Courlaender". About his travels in northern Germany. star Mar 21 (16) DM1,700

### Baillie, Joanna, 1762-1851
**ALs,** 28 Aug [1836?]. 3 pp, no size given. To Mrs. Lawrence. Concerning Mrs. Lawrence's verses about the death of Felicia Dorothea Hermans. With related material. Ck Nov 17 (1) £70

### Baker, Josephine, 1906-75
**ALs,** 2 Feb [n.y.]. 2 pp, 8vo. Recipient unnamed. About her recovery from an operation. cb June 25 (2489) $150

**Photograph,** sgd & inscr, 16 Oct 1927. 253mm by 194mm. Inscr to Hope & Edgar. CE June 12 (8) $750

— Anr, 1929. 79mm by 129mm. Shoulder-length port, by G. L. Manuel Freres. Inscr to Louis Consiglieri. Repaired. Illus in cat. Marans collection. CE Apr 17 (221) $750

### Baker, Newton D. See: Wilson, Woodrow & Baker

### Balakirev, Mily Alekseyevich, 1837-1910
**ALs,** 17 Aug 1886. 4 pp, 8vo. To an unnamed conductor. Sending some compositions, & asking him to forward some of Glinka's works. star Mar 22 (740) DM1,200

### Balbi, Adriano, 1782-1848
**ALs,** 24 June [c.1825]. 2 pp, 4to. To Auguste de St.-Hilaire. Praising recipient's work. star Mar 21 (395) DM270

### Baldner, Leonhard, 1612-94
**Ms,** Rechts natuerliche Beschreibung und Abmahlung der Wasservoegel, Fischen, Vierfuessigen Thier, Insekten und Gewirm.... Strasbourg, 1666-87. 299 leaves (including 4 blanks) & 129 full-page watercolor drawings, oblong folio, in contemp bds covered with vellum from a legal document. One of 5 known copies. Baldner - Spielmann - Fattorini copy C Oct 25 (56) £48,000

### Baldwin, James —&
### Haley, Alex, 1921-92
[A collection of correspondence between the two on literary and film matters, 1967, sold at Swann on 28 Mar 1996, lot 10, for $1,600]

### Balfe, Michael William, 1808-70
**Autograph quotation,** Andantino, Cara Evelina sei bella, Sept 1849. 1 p, 8vo. 4 bars, sgd. star Mar 22 (741) DM280

### Baner, Johan, 1596-1641
**Ls,** 28 July 1632. 1 p, size not stated. To the magistrate of Dinkelsbuehl in Franconia. Urging them to procure information about the enemy's troops, & offering his help. HH May 9 (2440) DM600

— 25 Nov 1639. 1 p, folio. To the magistrates of Loebau. Instructing them to raze their fortifications and to prevent enemy troops from entering their town. star Mar 22 (1226) DM700

### Bankhead, Tallulah, 1902-68
**Photograph,** sgd, [n.d.]. 13.25 by 9.75 inches. Head-&-shoulders port, by G. Maillard Kesslere. Illus in cat. rms June 6 (103) $250

### Banks, Sir Joseph, 1743-1820
**ALs,** 1 May 1818. 2 pp, 8vo. To Dr. Adams. Asking him to cooperate with a committee investigating contagious diseases. rms June 6 (320) $450

### Banks, Nathaniel P., 1816-94
**ALs,** 5 June 1884. 1 p. To H. F. Lamb. Saying that he is unable to comply with a request in regard to a letter of Judge Gray. Framed with port & engraving from Harper's Weekly showing his forces landing at Baton Rouge. rms Nov 30 (11) $370

**Ds,** 13 Aug 1863. 1 p, 4to. Appointing Otis R. Colby as 2d Lieutenant of the 2d Regiment of the 'Corps d'Afrique". pba Oct 26 (151) $375

**Banting, Frederick Grant, 1891-1941**
Photograph, sgd, [c.1930]. 151m by 100mm, mtd. Shoulder-length port. Illus in cat. Marans collection. CE Apr 17 (33) $850

**Bantock, Granville, 1868-1946**
Autograph music, Prometheus Unbound, [1934]. 41 pp, 4to. Notated on one system per page, each of 18 staves. Including autograph title. S May 15 (281) £900

**Baraka, Amiri**
Ls, [1960s]. 1 p, 4to. To a black writer in Europe. Sgd as Le Roi Jones. sg Mar 28 (179) $80

**Barbe-Marbois, Francois, Marquis de, 1745-1837.**
See: United States of America

**Barclay, Robert, 1648-90**
ALs, 9 Oct 1685. 2 pp, folio (large fragment torn from 2d leaf with loss of address panel). To William Penn. On matters concerning the governance of East Jersey, New York & Pennsylvania & whether the charters of the private colonies would be vacated. C June 26 (300) £2,800
— 12 Sept 1685. 1 p, folio. To William Penn. On such matters as meetings & the relationship between East Jersey, the King & New York. C June 26 (299) £2,800

**Barkley, Alban William.** See: Truman, Harry S. & Barkley

**Barlach, Ernst, 1870-1938**
ALs, 6 Feb 1931. 1 p, folio. To Karl Paetow. Responding to a request (carbon copy included) to make a sculpture for a war memorial. star Mar 21 (648) DM2,400

**Barnum, Phineas Taylor, 1810-91**
ALs, 3 Feb 1865. 1 p, 8vo. To one of his clerks. Requesting that he locate James Keathram. CE Sept 27 (6) $550
— 2 Sept 1866. 1 p, size not stated. To Mr. Hodge. Discussing dates for lectures. Illus in cat. rms Mar 21 (233) $300
Photograph, sgd, 1866. No size given. Sepia carte bust photo. By Black & Case. Sgd & dated. Illus in cat sg Sept 28 (32) $600
— Anr, 1867. 100mm by 61mm. Shoulder-length vignette port, by Black & Case. Marans collection. CE Apr 17 (5) $800
— Anr, 1874. Cabinet size; oval. Bust pose, by Landy. Illus in cat. rms June 6 (105) $1,100
Signature, 24 Dec 1868. Inscr to E. Beauman. Tipped to a larger sheet. cb June 25 (2307) $110
— Anr, 5 April 1890. No size given. On a white card. pba Feb 22 (6) $85

**Barrie, Sir James Matthew, 1860-1937**
ALs, 8 May 1892. 1 p, 12mo. Recipient unnamed. Commenting on his correspondent's play. Mtd with photos of Barrie & 4 early Pan players. wa Oct 28 (5) $200

**Barrow, Clyde, 1909-34**
Group photograph, [c.1933]. 114mm by 62mm. With Bonnie Parker & her brother Jim; sgd & inscr by Barrow on verso. Illus in cat. Marans collection. CE Apr 17 (7) $19,000

**Barrow, Edward G., 1868-1953 —&**
**Ruppert, Jacob, 1867-1939**
Group photograph, [c.1925]. 273mm by 357mm. Shoulder-length port, seated; sgd by both. Marans collection. CE Apr 17 (267) $650

**Barrymore, John, 1882-1942**
ALs, [c.1919]. 1 p, 8vo. To [David] Belasco. Sending 2 acts of an Italian drama in a literal trans. Illus in cat. rms June 6 (104) $235

**Bartholdi, Frederic A., 1834-1904**
ALs, [1899]. 1 p, 12mo. To Mme Lumley. Explaining that he is not able to see her the next day. rms Mar 21 (234) $450

**Bartlett, Josiah, Signer from New Hampshire**
ALs, 18 Aug 1776. 2 pp, 4to. To William Whipple. Reporting on the work of Congress. Imperf. Illus in cat. P Dec 13 (24) $4,750
— 25 Nov 1776. 2 pp, 4to. To William Whipple. Reporting about military matters. Illus in cat. P Dec 13 (25) $7,000
ADs, [July 1767]. 2 pp, 12mo. Accounting record concerning money from Lt. Peter Morse. With list of his perscriptions on verso. Trimmed. Dated in anr hand. rms Oct 11 (123) $400

**Bartok, Bela, 1881-1945**
ALs, 2 Feb 1922. 2 pp, c.34cm by 21cm. To Jelly d'Aranyi. About the difficulties of his Violin Sonata [no 1]. S Dec 1 (71) £1,000
— 28 Nov 1922. 1 p, 4to. To Herr Windisch. In German, about concert arrangements & his Eight Hungarian Folksongs. C June 26 (247) £600
Autograph quotation, 7 bars of the 1st movement of his 4th String Quartet, [n.d.]. 1 p, c.16cm by 12.5cm. Notated on 2 systems of 4 staves each; sgd. Illus in cat. S Dec 1 (72) £3,000
Photograph, sgd & inscr, 21 Jan 1928. 237mm by 190mm. Bust port, inscr to Sue Prosser. Marans collection. CE Apr 17 (222) $1,500

**Barton, Clara, 1821-1912**
Autograph Ms, 23-line poem entitled "It's the Fourth of July, My dear sister". [n. d.]. On verso 6 by 9 inch photo of Barton with 2 Russian men. Poem begins "Does she remember the sad same day..." Inscr to "Princess Agnees of Salm Salm..." With unsgd carte-de-visite photo of Princess Agness. Some minor damage. Dar Oct 19 (24) $750
ALs, 10 Mar 1905. 4 pp, 4to. Recipient unnamed. About the Red Cross & her declining to take positions in other organizations. rms Nov 30 (96) $500
— 1 Sept 1905. 1 p, no size given. On a US Government Postcard. To Mary J. Kenrel. About the National

First Aid Society of America. Sgd as ⁓' ⁓' C B. ". pba Feb 22 (152) $275

— 15 May 1906. 4 pp, 8vo. To Roscoe & Harriette [Reed]. Discussing problems with the Red Cross organization. rms Mar 21 (236) $350

— 28 July 1906. 5 pp, 8vo. To her secretary. About The National First Aid Society of America. pba Feb 22 (151) $650

— 7 Feb 1910. 4 pp, 8vo. To "Dear 'children'" [Roscoe & Mary]. Discussing the Red Cross after her resignation from it: "The longer I wait, and the more I think and observe, the less I know what to say. If it were not decidedly unsafe...I should go to you and try by counsel...what is wise or possible to do." Illus in cat rms Oct 11 (44) $800

— 31 May 1910. 1 p, 8vo. To " my dear children". About travel plans. Browned. pba June 13 (3) $225

— 11 June 1910. 1 p, 4to. To Roscoe G. Wells. Trying to clear The National First Aid association of America of debt by sending a check: "which I hope will serve to lighten the hearts of both the payees and the prayers..." Illus in cat pba June 13 (2) $250

— 22 Apr 1911. 6 pp, 8vo. To a colleague at the National First Aid Association of America. About her health & letters. Sgd as "Sister Clara". pba June 13 (1) $275

— 22 Aug 1911. 2 pp, 8vo. To Mr. Stebbins. Hoping that Mrs. Stebbins will visit her. Illus in cat. rms June 6 (321) $500

Ls, 28 June 1900. 1 p, 4to. To Harriette Reed. Making plans for a business meeting. rms Mar 21 (235) $400

— 25 Apr 1910. 1 p, no size given. About her brisk & busy schedule. pba Oct 26 (152) $170

ADs, 7 Apr 1885. 1 p, 4to. Resolutions of a Red Cross meeting acknowledging the labors of a group of ladies in New Orleans. P Dec 13 (26) $1,700

Ds, 25 Dec 1910. 4 pp, 4to. Program from "Tribute of Clara Barton to Julia Ward Howe." Tribute from 12 Nov 1910 but sgd Christmas 1910. With holograph note "Dearest sister Harriette I am rending out 1000 of these little ⁓'Tributes' this Xmas for my rememberance to almost that number who are remembering me...Love you C. B." Illus in cat pba Oct 26 (153) $350

Photograph, sgd & inscr, July-Aug 1865. 10 by 6.5 inches. Inscr "very truly yours". rms Nov 30 (97) $380

— Anr, [c.1875]. 100mm by 60mm, mtd. Bust port, inscr on recto & verso. Illus in cat. Marans collection. CE Apr 17 (115) $1,000

**Baruch, Bernard M., 1870-1965**

Ls, 10 Jan 1917. 1 p, 4to. To Norman de Mauriac. Thanking him for a letter. pba June 13 (48) $50

— 7 June 1921. 1 p, 4to. To Mr. Millington. About Clarence Barron's writings. pba Oct 26 (88) $160

Photograph, sgd, [n.d.]. 4to size. Framed with old photo of Broad Street. rms Nov 30 (1) $650

**Baryshnikov, Mikhail —& Makarova, Natalia**

Group photograph, [n.d.]. 10 by 8 inches. Full-length pose, in Giselle. Sgd by both & inscr by Makarova. Illus in cat. rms June 6 (213) $375

**Baseball**

Signature, [c.1934]. 1 p, 3.5 by 5 inches. Including Adolfo Luque, Roy Parmelee, George Watkins & Walter Johnson. Illus in cat bbc Sept 18 (62) $460

**Baskin, Leonard**

Original drawings, for the dust jacket of Crow, by Ted Hughes. [c.1969-70] 11 by 7.75 inches, in crayon & ink, sgd, framed. S Dec 18 (316) £1,200 [Jaffe]

**Bassermann, Albert, 1869-1952**

ALs, 19 Feb 1925. 2 pp, 8vo. To Alice Stein-Landesmann. Commenting on recipient's play Daemon. HN May 15 (2496) DM220

**Batista Y Zaldivar, Fulgencio, 1901-73**

Ds, 25 Nov 1958. 1 p, folio. Letter of state congratulating Rodrigues Thomaz as his election of President of Portugal. With orig envelope. pba Oct 26 (182) $350

**Battle of Waterloo**

— JOHNSTON, SERJEANT ARCHIBALD. - Ms journal of this member of the 2d Regiment of Dragoons, 14 Apr to 3 Dec 1815. About 150 pp, 4to, becoming detached from bds. S July 11 (370) £1,050

**Baudelaire, Charles, 1821-67**

Autograph Ms, poem, Sisina [Les Fleurs du Mal, no 59]; [c.1858-59]. 1 p, 8vo. Including autograph revisions. With autograph list of poems on verso. Illus in cat. S May 15 (153) £10,000

ALs, 11 Aug 1854. 1 p, 4to. To Louis Ulbach. Requesting him to return a Ms for revisions. Illus in cat. star Mar 21 (17) DM1,800

— [c.20 Oct 1859]. 1 p, 4to. To Paul Meurice. Reminding him of a promised favor. CNY Oct 27 (5) $900

**Baxter, Alexander.** See: Napoleon I

**Baxter, Anne**

[An archive of material concerning Anne Baxter & her relationship with Russell Birdwell. Sold at Pacific on Oct 26, 1995 as lot 1 for $2,000.]

**Bean, Roy, 1825?-1904**

Ds, 9 Aug 1853. 2 pp, folio. As defendant in a case of assault & murder, confirming that he will apppear in court to answer the charges. Also sgd by others. CNY May 17 (206) $3,500

**Beard, Daniel C., 1850-1941.** See: Baden-Powell of Gilwell, Robert S. S. Baden-Powell & Beard

**Beardsley, Aubrey, 1872-98**

Series of 7 A Ls s, 8 Oct 1892 & [n.d.]. 17 pp, 8vo. To J. M. Dent. About drawings & terms for Morte d'Arthur. With related material. S Nov 21 (34) £7,000

ALs, [c.July 1891]. 4 pp, folio. To [G. F. Scotson-] Clark. Reporting about a letter from Burne-Jones concerning London art schools & his own plans. Including a drawing; man climbing up a mountain to reach the valley of art. S Nov 21 (32) £2,000

**Photograph,** sgd & inscr, [c.1896]. 303mm by 250mm. Shoulder-length port, inscr to Mrs. Beerbohm. Illus in cat. Marans collection. CE Apr 17 (198) $2,000

## Beatles, The

**Signature,** [1964]. On postcard of the Southern Cross Hotel. Sgd by all 4. CA Mar 26 (107A) A$1,100

## Beaton, Cecil, 1904-80

**ALs,** [c.1932-33]. 4 pp, 8vo. To Anita Loos. Chatting about his holiday in Southern France, friends & Hollywood celebrities. rms June 6 (107) $500

**Photograph,** sgd & inscr, [c.1965]. 244mm by 190mm. Self-port, inscr to Anita [Loos]. Marans collection. CE Apr 17 (199) $450

## Beauharnais, Hortense de, 1783-1837

**ALs,** 15 June 1837. 1 p, 8vo. To the lawyer Lehon. Sending some presents for his sister-in-law. star Mar 22 (1429) DM650

## Beauharnais, Stephanie, Grossherzogin von Baden, 1789-1860. See: Stephanie, 1789-1860

## Beaumarchais, Pierre Augustin Caron de, 1732-99

**ALs,** 5 Dec 1767. 3 pp, 4to. To his lawyer. About some business matters. star Mar 21 (18) DM2,000

— 11 Apr 1769. 3 pp, 8vo. To M. Sonnet. Concerning a joint business venture. HN Nov 24 (2744) DM2,500

## Beauregard, Pierre G. T., 1818-93

**Ls,** 14 Jan 1862. 2 pp, 4to. To an unnamed general. Advising that " circumstances may favor a sudden blow at your immediate adversary opposite some clear night when the passage of the river on the ice may be practicable and safe..." In the hand of Adjutant General Thomas Jordan. With annotation by Beauregard "The above properly revised will do..." Sgd twice with initials. With newspaper clipping affixed to the second page. Also with marginal defects. Illus in cat rms Oct 11 (88) $800

**Check,** sgd, 14 May 1879. Payable to N.O. Gaslight Co for $24. cb June 25 (2426) $350

**Signature,** 1874. On 2 by 4 inch slip of paper. Sgd as " " G. T. Beauregard". pba Feb 22 (153) $225

## Beauvoir, Simone de, 1908-86

**Autograph Ms,** novel, Les Mandarins. 956 leaves, 270mm by 232mm. With revisions; a few typed pages scattered through, these with extensive holograph emendations. With 4-page holograph dedicatory preface sgd, 9 July 1957 & with Ls of L. Arega providing further information, 3 Feb 1956. All bound in mor extra by P. L. Martin. P June 5 (168) $18,000

## Beaverbrook, William Maxwell Aitken, Ist Baron

**Ls s** (2), 13 Jan 1942 & 11 Jul 1946. 2 pp, 4to. To Leon Henderson. sg June 6 (19) $1,000

## Bechstein, Ludwig, 1801-60

**Collection** of 12 A Ls s & 3 autograph Mss, 14 Oct 1841 to 3 Dec 1843. 31 pp, various sizes. To Ernst von Bibra. About his own & recipient's work, & lists of his publications. star Mar 21 (19) DM2,600

**Becker, Heinrich, 1764-1822.** See: Schiller, Friedrich von

## Becker, Juergen

**Collection** of ALs & 4 Ls s, 5 May to 21 Dec 1957. 12 pp, folio. Recipient unnamed. Offering his poems for print, & commenting on his own & other authors' works. star Mar 21 (20) DM420

## Becker, Rudolf Zacharias, 1752-1822

**ALs,** 25 Mar 1786. 4 pp, 8vo. To Dr. Stein. Planning a farmer's manual. star Mar 21 (21) DM280

## Beckett, Samuel, 1906-89

**Original drawing,** Three-quarter view of the author in pencil by Yale Saffro. [n.d.]. 1 p, 16mo. Sgd by Beckett & the artist. Illus in cat rms Oct 11 (47) $280

**Collection** of 2 A Ls s, 1 Ls & 20 autograph postcards, sgd, 13 Jan 1965 to 5 Aug 1980. To Sean O'Casey's daughter Shivaun. On various matters, including advising her on how to dramatize From an Abandoned Work. S July 11 (255) £4,400

**ALs,** 24 July 1931. 1 p, 4to. To Mr. Prentice of Chatto & Windus. Arranging a meeting. S Dec 18 (369) £360 [Pearson]

## Beckmann, Max, 1884-1950

**ALs,** 5 Feb 1930. 1 p, 4to. To Simon. Hoping to see him in Frankfurt. star Mar 21 (649) DM550

## Becquerel, Antoine Cesar, 1788-1878

**ALs,** [17 July 1849]. 2 pp, 8vo. To his uncle [Ferriere]. Expressing condolences on the death of recipient's child. star Mar 21 (398) DM260

## Beecher, Henry Ward, 1813-87

**Autograph Ms,** Notes for a sermon based on Luke 13:24. 6 June 1886. 3 pp, 8vo. Unsgd. pba June 13 (240) $250

**Photograph,** sgd, [c.1875). 165mm by 105mm, mtd. 3-quarter-length port, by Sarony. Marans collection. CE Apr 17 (117) $550

## Beerbohm, Max, 1872-1956

**Original drawing,** caricature of Sir Herbert Vansittart, sgd Max & dated 1873. 320mm by 200mm, pencil & wash, mtd on card. On verso is parody verse beginning Ah, did you once see "Penny" plain.... S Dec 18 (289) £450 [Levine]

**Autograph transcript,** Triolets - To be inscribed in any book by A. C. B. [A. C. Benson]. 1 p, folio. Inscr to Egan, 1919. S July 11 (261) £1,450

— Autograph transcript, verse, Drinking Song. 1 p, folio. Inscr to Egan, Feb 1919. S July 11 (259) £850

**ALs,** 2 Apr 1913. 3 pp, 8vo. To Miss Norton. Declining her proposal for a published selection of his writings. S July 11 (256) £380

— [n.d.]. 4 pp, 8vo. To Egan Mew. Asking about his recovery from flu. S July 11 (258) £260

**Beery, Wallace**

**Photograph, sgd,** [1934]. 8 by 10 inch still from the film Viva Villa! Sgd as "Wally Beery/ VILLA". With anr signature from an unnamed cast member. rms Oct 11 (48) $375

**Beethoven, Ludwig van, 1770-1827**

[An autograph address leaf to Rovantini in Wuerzburg..., [n.d.], 80mm by 190mm, framed, sold at Christie's on 29 Nov 1995, lot 198, for £1,100.]

**Autograph music,** sketches for his 5th Piano Concerto in E flat major, Op.73; [1809]. 2 pp, 308mm by 238mm. Illus in cat. star Mar 22 (745) DM55,000

**ALs,** [Mar 1808]. 3 pp, 4to. To Count von Oppersdorf. Announcing the completion of his 5th Symphony, describing its last movement, & discussing financial arrangements. S May 15 (285) £50,000

— [c.1826]. 1 p, 4to. To [Karl Holz?]. Apologizing for mistaking the day of a meeting. Illus in cat. S Dec 1 (80) £13,500

— FURTWAENGLER, WILHELM. - Overture no 2 zur Oper Leonore, from the complete Ed by Breitkopf & Haertel, 1920. 4to. Furtwaengler's performing copy, sgd; with autograph annotations throughout. S May 15 (287) £2,400

— RAZUMOVSKII, ANDREI KIRILLOVICH. - Ls, 29 Feb 1804. 2 pp, 4to. To Ivan M. Muraviev Apostol. As Russian minister in Vienna, informing him of his return to his post. HN Nov 24 (2745) DM1,600

**Begas, Oskar, 1828-83**

**Series** of 3 A Ls s, 14 Aug [1837], 4 Jan 1847, & [n.d.]. 6 pp, 4to. To his mother Wilhelmine (1 to his parents). Reporting from visits. Including half-page watercolor. star Mar 21 (650) DM760

**Begin, Menachem, 1913-92**

**Ls,** 11 Aug 1977. 1 p, 8vo. To the President of the Jerusalem Chamber of Commerce. Concerning Jerusalem: " ...I have myself become a resident of Jerusalem, and it is superfluous to say that I will do all I can to strengthen and fortify the standing of our capital, both in foreign and internal relations." With orig envelope & translation. Illus in cat rms Oct 11 (49) $325

**Photograph, sgd,** [n.d.]. 8vo. With typewritten quotation in English sgd by Anwar Sadat, a photo of Sadat & the Mar 27 1979 front page of the Daily News. With transmittal letter from Sadat's secretary on verso. Framed. Over-all size 25 by 31 inches. Illus in cat . rms Oct 11 (407) $525

**Behmer, Marcus, 1879-1958**

**Autograph Ms,** description of a meeting with Klabund in a bar in Berlin, 1950. 3 pp, 4to. In pencil. With typescript version with autograph revisions, 3 pp, folio. star Mar 21 (652) DM450

**Belafonte, Harry.** See: Robinson, Jackie & Belafonte

**Belcher, Jonathan, 1682-1757**

**ALs,** 18 Sept 1738. 2 pp, 4to. To Mr Waldron. Discussing business with his secretary and also praying for his recovery. Foxed. rms Oct 11 (124) $350

**Ds,** 6 Aug 1739. 1 p, double folio. Appointment of Ebenezer Alden as a lieutenant in Militia. Countersgd by J. Willard. Featuring a woodcut. With related material. s'g Sept 28 (7) $200

**Belknap, Jeremy**

**ALs,** 23 Nov 1792. 1 p, 4to. To Judge Increase Sumner. About his duties as an Elector for the Commonwealth. pba June 13 (241) $225

**Bell, Alexander Graham, 1847-1922**

**Ls,** 4 Aug 1919. 1 p, 4to. To Rev. Frank Tucker. Thanking Tucker for "interesting information regarding large families and longevity among the New England Tuckers....the active work of our office has been somewhat interrupted owing to war conditions...for the present we could not undertake any investigation for the genealogical data concerning the Bermuda or Virginia branches of the Tucker family..." With small envelope. Illus in cat sg Sept 28 (35) $900

**Photograph, sgd,** [c.1905]. 166mm by 108mm, mtd. Half length, by NY Photographic Co. Illus in cat. Marans collection. CE Apr 17 (34) $3,200

**Bellini, Vincenzo, 1801-35**

**Autograph music,** bass part of the aria Dolente immagine, [c.1824]. 1 p, c.13cm by 29cm, cut from larger sheet. Notated on 4 staves; sgd. S Dec 1 (85) £1,400

**Ms,** full score of Norma. [c.1830-50]. About 480 pp in 2 vols, Oblong 4to, in modern half mor. Notated mainly in 3 separate hands. S June 13 (677) £900

**Bendemann, Eduard, 1811-89**

**ALs,** 23 Jan 1846. 2 pp, 8vo. Recipient unnamed. Responding to an inquiry about crayons. star Mar 21 (653) DM240

**Benedict, Sir Julius, 1804-85**

**Autograph Ms,** working Ms of the Symphony in C. About 200 pp, oblong 4to, in wraps. Sgd & dated 6 Apr 1874-Sept 1875-1877. Notated in black, brown & red ink, with some phrasing & markings in blue & red crayon. With extensive revisions. S May 15 (10) £1,100

**Benedict XIII, Pope, 1649-1730**

**Document,** 15 Aug 1726. 12 vellum leaves (last blank) plus prelim leaf on paper, 237mm by 175mm, in contemp mor gilt bdg by the Vatican Bindery, with Gambiano arms on lower cover & Braschi arms on upper cover. Papal diploma appointing Giovanni Antonio Gambinio as Protonotary Apostolic. With engraved, hand-colored ports of Benedict XIII & of Bishop Braschius; with port of Gambinio in body color & wash & his arms on facing leaf C Apr 3 (9) £900

**Benedict XIV, Pope, 1675-1758**

**Document,** 22 May 1749. 1 p, folio. Brief granting permission for the ordination of J. B. Carosi as priest. star Mar 22 (1500) DM350

## Ben-Gurion, David, 1886-1973

**Collection** of 7 A Ls s & 2 Ls s, 1949 to 1959. 10 pp, various sizes. To Moshe Sharett. Discussing political matters. rms June 6 (322) $4,000

**ALs,** 23 Feb 1955. 1 p, 8o. To Prime Minister Moshe Sharett. Concerning his perceptions of the U. N. policies towards Israel: " We have recently witnessed a tendency in the administration of the UN to act towards Israel as if it were an unclaimed area or an international mandate. The Government of Israel cannot accept this harmful tendency, which is detrimental to our sovereignity and contradicts the UN Charter..." With translation. Illus in cat rms Oct 11 (210) $1,300

— 30 July 1967. 1 p, 8vo. To an unnamed recipient. Concerning the removal of Arabs from occupied territories by force: "we cannot, in my opinion, replace them by force. I am aware of the ugly things that the Arabs did to us - but we cannot act like them. If it is possible to arrange...by agreement, this can be done. This should not be done in my opinion with violence..." With some show-through in margins. With translation from Hebrew. Illus in cat rms Oct 11 (51) $1,000

— 10 Apr 1970. 2 pp, 8vo. To an unnamed recipient. Concerning his attempts to convince Israel's government to wage war against Jordan: "In the Six Day War we conquered all the western part of our land, the Sinai, Golan - and Old Jerusalem. Till the Six Day War I considered it all an irreparable disaster... The second ceasefire was arranged on condition Jordan would not damage the Jerusalem pipeline which was in its territory...They did not honor the decision and destroyed the pipe...since Jordan violated the conditions...I proposed starting a war with Jordan for the purpose of conquering...the entire Jerusalem District and Hebron District..." Mtd. Toned. rms Oct 11 (52) $1,000

**Ls,** 5 July 1938. 1 p, 4to. To Abraham Shlonsky. About his suggestion that the Histradut should support the weekly Turim. Framed with composite photo. rms Nov 30 (43) $950

— 4 Nov 1954. 1 p, 4to. To Moshe Rohn. Regretting misinformation about the Israeli army spread by the media. star Mar 22 (1178) DM320

— 5715 Tamuz 19 (9 July 1955). 1 p, 6 by 8 inches. To Moshe Sharett. About an upcoming visit by Burma's Prime Minister: "The importance...is twofold. To establish cultural relationships with peace loving nations in the Far East. For Israel to maintain its international contacts during difficult times..." Dar Oct 19 (114) $500

— 13 Aug 1956. 1 p, 4to. To M. Hockshtein. Appointing him as a member of the Council of the Principal Archives. rms Nov 30 (99) $360

**Photograph, sgd,** [c.1956]. 130mm by 90mm. Shoulder-length port. Marans collection. CE Apr 17 (118) $400

## Benjamin, Judah P., 1811-84

**Ls,** 7 Jan 1864. 1 p, 4to. To Messrs. Fraser & Trenholm. Informing them of the appointment of William Preston as Confederate envoy to Mexico. P Dec 13 (29) $2,250

## Benn, Gottfried, 1886-1956

**Autograph Ms** (2), list of receipts & list of telephone nos, 1952 & [1955]. 2 pp, 8vo & 4to. star Mar 21 (23) DM500

**Autograph Ms,** draft of a 12-line poem, & further notes, [1953]. 2 pp, 8vo. Illus in cat. star Mar 21 (24) DM2,800

**Collection** of 2 A Ls s & 5 Ls s, 4 Feb 1952 to 1 Oct 1955. 15 pp, 4to & 8vo. To Edgar Lohner. Interesting literary correspondence. With related material. star Mar 21 (22) DM8,500

## Bennett, James Gordon, 1841-1918

**ALs,** 24 Jan 1889. 1 p, 8vo. Recipient unnamed. Requesting him to send some reports about baseball in Florida. Illus in cat. rms June 6 (323) $250

## Bentham , Jeremy, 1748-1832

**Signature,** [n.d.]. 4 by 3 inch address leaf sgd. Dar Oct 19 (42) $75

## Berenson, Bernard, 1865-1959

**Series** of 67 A Ls s & 3 Ls s, 10 Dec 1949 to 10 Dec 1957. About 156 pp, 8vo & 4to. To Mally Dienemann. With photocopies of her replies & 3 cards by Nicky Mariano. C June 26 (304) £850

## Berg, Alban, 1885-1935

**ALs,** 23 Oct 1931. 2 pp, 8vo. To [Robert Kolisko?]. Referring to performances of his Wozzeck in Zurich. star Mar 22 (747b) DM3,200

— 8 Oct 1932. 2 pp, 8vo. To Egon Wellesz. Discussing a matter of musical politics in Vienna. S May 15 (540) £650

**Autograph postcard, sgd,** [5 Feb 1930]. To Egon Wellesz. Thanking for his good wishes for a performance [of Wozzek]. S May 15 (541) £750

**ANs,** 25 June 1931. 1 p, 12mo, on ptd visiting card. Authorizing Julius Schloss to enter his apartment. With a photograph. star Mar 22 (747a) DM950

**Autograph quotation,** 2 bars from Der Wein, in piano score; 29 Nov [19]31. 1 p, 8vo. Sgd & inscr to Torsten Carlander. Illus in cat. S Dec 1 (84) £1,800

— BERG, HELENE. - 6 A Ls s, [mostly 1946]. 10 pp, folio & 8vo. To Egon Wellesz. Discussing life after the war, performances of her husband's music, etc. S May 15 (542) £250

## Bergengruen, Werner, 1892-1964

**Collection** of ALs & Ls, 4 & 18 May 1933. 6 pp, 4to & 8vo. To Karl Paetow. Discussing contributions to an anthology. star Mar 21 (25) DM250

## Berger, Gottlob, 1896-1975

**Ls,** 7 Dec 1943. 1 p, 8vo. To Philipp Bouhler. Sending a book as a Christmas present & referring to the hardships of the war. Illus in cat. rms June 6 (611) $235

**Berger, Ludwig, 1777-1839**
**Autograph music,** song, Katzenpastete v. Goethe, Nov 1819. 1 p, 8vo. Scored for voice & piano; sgd at head. Trimmed. star Mar 22 (748) DM520

**Berkeley, Busby, 1895-1976**
**Ds,** 16 Nov 1932. 1 p, 4to. Agreement with Warner Bros. specifying the beginning of his new contract. Carbon copy. rms June 6 (133) $285

**Berlichingen, Goetz von, 1480-1562**
**ALs,** 8 Oct 1542. 1 p, 8vo. To Schultes. Insisting on his legal rights. HH May 9 (2422) DM6,000

**Berlin, Irving, 1888-1989**
**Photograph, sgd & inscr,** [c.1915]. 232mm by 189mm. Shoulder-length port, by Tycko. Illus in cat. Marans collection. CE Apr 17 (223) $1,900
— **Anr,** [n.d.]. 4to portrait photo. Inscr to Al Goodhart. With surface crack & ink blots. Illus in cat pba Feb 22 (9) $475
**Signature,** [n.d.]. On cover of sheet music of Oh! How I Hate To Get Up In The Morning. rms Nov 30 (101) $600

**Berlioz, Hector, 1803-69**
**ALs,** [May 1834]. 3 pp, 4to. To Liszt. Inviting him to visit, contrasting the beauties of nature with his sad state of mind, & including a long musical quotation from Spontini's La Vestale. S May 15 (291) £3,800
— 9 Dec 1849. 1 p, 8vo. To [the Societe des Concerts de l'Union Musicale]. Asking for admission to their concerts so that he can review them. S Dec 1 (90) £460
— 4 June 1859. 2 pp, 16mo. To Biedermann. Reporting about a performance of scenes from Romeo et Juliette at Bordeaux, the cancellation of the festival at Baden-Baden, etc. S May 15 (290) £460
— 23 Oct 1867. 3 pp, 8vo. To Ferdinand Christian Wilhelm Praeger. Expressing frustration about music & theaters in Paris. Mtd. Illus in cat. HN Nov 24 (2746) DM1,400
— 24 Aug [n.y.]. 1 p, 8vo. To Madam. Declining a dinner invitation. cb June 25 (2493) $350
— [n.d.]. 2 pp, 8vo. To Pauline Viardot-Garcia. Expressing satisfaction to find everything as he left it, & hoping to see her the next day. star Mar 22 (750) DM1,300
**Autograph quotation,** opening 20 bars from his cantata L'Imperiale, in A flat major; 5 Dec 1853. 1 p, c.20.5cm by 26.5cm. Sgd. Illus in cat. S Dec 1 (89) £3,000

**Bernadotte, Jean Baptiste, 1763-1844.** See: Charles XIV John, 1763-1844

**Bernhard, Herzog von Sachsen-Weimar, 1604-39**
**Ds,** 8 July 1637. 1 p, folio. Pay order. star Mar 22 (1227) DM600

**Bernhardt, Sarah, d.1923**
**ANs,** [n.d.]. 2 pp, oblong 16mo. To Germain. Asking her to post 3 letters for New York. CE June 12 (9) $100

**Photograph, sgd,** [c.1878]. No size given. Sepia cabinet photo by Navar. Illus in cat pba June 13 (179) $180
**Photograph, sgd & inscr,** 1909. 14 by 10.5 inches. Swooning, as Adrienne Lecouvreur; by W. & D. Downey. Illus in cat. rms June 6 (108) $2,100
— **Anr,** 1916. 19.5 by 15 inches. sg June 6 (20) $950
— **Anr,** Carte size. sg June 6 (21) $250

**Bernis, Francois Joachim de Pierres de, Cardinal, 1715-94**
**ALs,** 3 June 1778. 2 pp, 4to. To the Vicomte de Monteil. Congratulating him on his marriage. star Mar 22 (1297) DM240

**Bernoulli, Johann, 1744-1807**
**ALs,** 15 Jan 1776. 1 p, 8vo. To Friedrich Nicolai. Inquiring about reviews of his works. star Mar 21 (400) DM400

**Bernsen, Corbin.** See: Smits; Bernsen & Others

**Bernstein, Leonard, 1918-90**
**Autograph music,** The Victory Jive. [n.d.]. 8 pp, folio. A wartime anti-Nazi tune. On 12-stave sheets. Inscr "My apologies to Sam for being so free with his words, Love L." Second page featuring a letter to Donna suggesting she ask Harold Shapero to arrange the piece. Sgd as Lenny. Soiled & torn. With waterstains on second and third pages. sg Sept 28 (37) $2,200

**Bertram, Ernst, 1884-1957.** See: George, Stefan

**Bertuch, Friedrich Justin, 1747-1822**
**ALs,** 26 June 1814. 1 p, 4to. To the bookseller Hartknoch. Discussing action against unauthorized reprints. star Mar 21 (127) DM650

**Berzelius, Jons Jacob von, 1779-1848**
**ALs,** 16 May 1845. 3 pp, 4to. To Ernst von Bibra. Expressing satisfaction that his own research results have been confirmed by recipient's findings. star Mar 21 (403) DM800

**Besant, Annie, 1847-1933**
**ALs,** 2 May 1907. 2 pp, 8vo. Recipient unnamed. Explaining her beliefs as a theosophist. star Mar 21 (404) DM600

**Bethmann-Unzelmann, Friederike, 1760-1815**
**ALs,** 6 Feb 1793. 2 pp, 4to. To an unnamed royal highness. Hoping for the King's permission to give a performance for the support of her family. star Mar 22 (1159) DM900

**Beurnonville, Pierre Riel, Marquis de, 1752-1821**
**ALs,** [6 July 1798]. 2 pp, folio. To the departmental administration at Epinal. Requesting papers about the recent war & mentioning Josephine Bonaparte & the conquest of Malta. star Mar 22 (1440) DM340

**Beuys, Joseph, 1921-86**
**Autograph sentiment,** sgd, [n.d.]. On art postcard. star Mar 21 (655) DM200

## Beyle, Marie Henri ("Stendhal"), 1783-1842

ALs, 6 May 1815. 2 pp, 4to. To his sister Pauline Perier-Lagrange. Asking her to send him some books from his library & to subscribe to a Swiss journal. Sgd Lauzanne. star Mar 21 (353) DM4,500

## Bialas, Guenter

**Autograph music,** score of the music for a film about the sculptor Loercher, 1959. 4 pp, 4to. Sgd & inscr at foot, 16 Mar 1981. star Mar 22 (752) DM470

— Autograph music, sketches for a song, Apollo 8, sgd; June 1984. 2 pp, 4to. With ANs, 27 July 1984, 1 p, 8vo. HN May 15 (2501) DM240

## Bible Manuscripts, Latin

— Paris, c.1250]. 552 (of 576) leaves, on vellum, 290mm by 188mm, later paper bds covered with leaf from a 15th-cent vellum Ms, with old calf back. With the Prologues ascribed to St. Jerome & the Interpretation of Hebrew Names. In a small gothic liturgical hand in blank ink. With 61 illuminated initials & 39 historiated initials. 22 other initials cut out & partly replaced by illuminated initials or by squares of text. Illus in cat C June 26 (14) £40,000

— [Padua or Bologna?, c.1250]. 350 leaves (2 lacking), vellum, 200mm by 138mm. Late 19th-cent blind-stamped brown mor. With Prologues, but without Psalms. In a very small rounded gothic bookhand. With very large decorated initials at the beginning of every book & Prologue in divided blue & red with extensive penwork infilling & surround with full-length marginal decoration including a drawing of an eagle. S Dec 5 (30) £9,500 [Brake]

— [England, c.1250 & 15th cent]. 398 leaves (some missing), vellum, 156mm by 105mm. Residue of medieval bdg of white tawed lea, in old wraps from a vellum bifolium of a 14th-cent Breviary. By several scribes in dark brown ink in small early gothic bookhands, with 13 leaves in a later English gothic ('anglicana') hand. With decoration throughout inserted in the 15th cent with large blue initials with extensive penwork in red often enclosing faces, & chapter initials throughout in bright red & pink gesso. Worn. S June 18 (56) £5,000

— [Paris, c.1250]. 405 leaves, vellum, 187mm by 130mm. Early 19th-cent English dark blue mor gilt. With Prologues & Interpretation of Hebrew Names. In dark brown ink in a very small early gothic bookhand. With large decorated initials at the start of every book & prologue in divided red & blue with elaborate penwork extending into margins, & many medieval sidenotes in several hands. S June 18 (57) £7,500

— [Paris?, c.1265]. 8 leaves only, vellum, 161mm by 116mm. In an extremely small gothic bookhand. With 5 large painted initials in leafy designs in colors on panelled ground & 8 large historiated initials with marginal extensions. S Dec 5 (6) £3,500 [Pirages]

— [Northern France, Paris?, 2d half of 13th cent]. 550 leaves (c.35 lacking), vellum, 147mm by 98mm. Early 19th-cent red mor gilt. With Prologues & Interpretation of Hebrew Names. In an extremely small gothic bookhand. With large decorated initials at the beginning of every book in divided red & blue with extensive penwork decoration & some contemp sidenotes. S Dec 5 (31) £7,000 [Santo]

— [Paris, c.1275]. 579 leaves (some lacking) & 2 flyleaves, vellum, 152mm by 102mm. Old red velvet over pastebds. With Prologues. In dark brown ink in a very small well-formed gothic hand. With c.90 large painted & illuminated initials in a wide variety of designs often including animals & grotesques, some marginal vignettes, & 3 large historiated initials. Worn. S June 18 (58) £14,000

— [France, c.1280]. Single leaf, vellum, 200mm by 140mm. In a light brown rotunda hand. With large decorated initial, large historiated initial in silver & colors, & 3 penwork initials with full-length baguette borders in red & blue. HH May 7 (35) DM1,100

— [Northern France, c.1300]. Single leaf, vellum, 240mm by 155mm. In a small rounded gothic hand. With historiated initial with 2-sided bar borders. Illus in cat. HH Nov 14 (33) DM2,400

— [Northern France, c.1300]. Single leaf, vellum, 240mm by 156mm. In a black rotunda hand. With small & 2 large initials in gold & colors. HH May 7 (36) DM2,000

— [Central Spain, c.1300]. 68 (non-consecutive) leaves, vellum, 365mm by 260mm. Modern vellum over pastebds. In dark brown ink in a large angular gothic hand. With illuminated chapter initials throughout in soft colors & highly burnished gold, very large illuminated initial, & 5 very large historiated initials in eleborate plant designs with long marginal extensions. Recovered from use as wraps. S June 18 (59) £15,000

— The St. Albans Bible. [Paris, 2d quarter of 14th cent]. Bifolium, vellum, 270mm by 190mm. Interpretation of Hebrew Names (Aegla - Atrocite), attributed to Stephen Langton. In fine gothic script, with cadels including a bird & a face. With 3 large illuminated initials with full-length bar borders. Stained. S June 18 (9) £300

## Biddle, Clement, 1740-1814

ALs, 15 Mar 1786. 3 pp, 4to. To John Groves of Richmond. Asking him to make inquiries about a large interest that belongs to his estate in Virginia Military Warrants. Seal cut out partially affecting last 3 letters of Biddle's signature. rms Nov 30 (102) $470

## Biddle, Nicholas, 1786-1844

ALs, 9 June 1841. 1 p, 4to. To William Racole. About a financial matter. With 19th-Century steel engraving of Biddle. pba Oct 26 (202) $150

Ls, 23 Dec 1806. 1 p, 4to. To Mon. Joseph Mattia Ferrari. Requesting that his mail in Naples be forwarded to him in Paris. Illus in cat pba June 13 (137) $100

**Bidwell, John, 1819-1900**

**A Ls s** (2), [c.1860]. 2 pp, 9.75 inches by 7.75 inches, laid in cloth folder with 2 photo ports. About construction of a bridge on his Chico property. pba Feb 18 (319) $325

**Ds,** 18 Oct 1867. Certificate No 25 for 10 shares in the Chico Gold and Silver Mining Co. 4.75 by 9 inches. Sgd as president. Larson collection pba Sept 24 (320) $350

**Bierce, Ambrose, 1842-1914?**

**ALs,** 26 Feb 1904. 2 pp, 8vo. To "dear Reagles". Referring to a recent meeting in Washington & hoping to meet him again. rms Mar 21 (238) $470

**Signature,** [n.d.]. On 8vo page. In pencil. pba Feb 22 (11) $80

**Bilibin, Ivan Iakovlevich, 1876-1942**

**Autograph Ms,** poem, ode on the year 1942, 1 Jan 1942. 3 pp, folio. 9-line & 6 ten-line stanzas, sgd & inscr to V. I. Zvetkov. HH Nov 17 (3190) DM380

**Billings, John Shaw, 1838-1913**

**ALs,** 7 Mar 1876. 2 pp, 8vo. To I. M. Hays. Discussing the program of a medical conference. rms Mar 21 (319) $225

**Birdman of Alcatraz.** See: Stroud, Robert

**Birney, Earle**

[A collection of correspondence from 1966 to the 1980s & poems by Birney. Sold at Pacific on 25 Jan 1996 as lot 19 for $450.]

**Bishop, Sir Henry R., 1786-1855**

**Series** of 14 A Ls s, mostly 1835. 22 pp, various sizes. To Vincent & Alfred Novello. About the publishing of his works. S May 15 (12) £120

**Bismarck, Otto von, 1815-98**

**ALs,** 18 May 1846. To Herr von Muenchhausen. Discussing plans for an excursion. HN Nov 24 (2749) DM800

— 7 June 1856. 1 p, 8vo. Recipient unnamed. Discussing a financial matter. star Mar 22 (1179) DM1,200

— 6 May 1867. 4 pp, 8vo. To Helmuth von Moltke. Discussing the occupation of Luxembourg, French & Prussian rights & the possibility of war. star Mar 22 (1180) DM18,000

— 5 Nov 1871. 1 p, folio. To Herr von Boehn. Thanking for condolences & informing him of the date of a funeral. HN May 15 (2505) DM520

— 17 July 1873. 3 pp, 8vo. To [Bernhard von Buelow]. Discussing an appointment. star Mar 22 (1181) DM1,300

**Ls,** 28 Nov 1874. 2 pp, folio. To Herr von Krieger. Draft, regarding the sale of the manor of Sachsenwaldau. Including extensive autograph additions & corrections. star Mar 22 (1182) DM320

— 16 Mar 1882. 1 p, 4to. To Moritz Busch. Sending condolences. HN May 15 (2507) DM240

**Ns,** 4 Apr 1879. 1 p, 4to. To Major von Stobbe. Thanking for congratulations on his birthday. HN May 15 (2506) DM260

**Photograph, sgd,** [c.1870]. 105mm by 65mm, mtd. Seated. Illus in cat. Marans collection. CE Apr 17 (119) $800

**Bissett, Bill**

**A Ls s** (2), 1983. No size or length given. To John Gill. Concerning Gill's publications of his works. pba Jan 25 (22) $70

**Bissier, Julius, 1893-1965**

**ALs,** 23 Nov 1961. 1 p, 4to. To Otto W. Brodnitz. About the sale of his works in NY. HN Nov 24 (2751) DM220

— 17 Dec 1963. 1 p, folio. To Felix H. Man. Expressing dissatisfaction with some proofs of lithographs. star Mar 21 (657) DM360

**Blaine, James G., 1830-93.** See: Cleveland, Grover & Blaine

**Blatty, William Peter**

**Autograph Ms,** Closing text from The Exorcist. [n.d.]. 1 p, 8 by 10 inches. Inscr for Mrs. Bessie Holmes "with a hug and a Happy Birthday from William Peter Blatty." Dar Oct 19 (48) $100

**Blei, Franz, 1871-1942**

**Series** of 4 A Ls s, 25 Oct 1908 & [n.d.]. 4 pp, 4to & 8vo. To Max Mell. About various publishing matters. HH Nov 17 (3191) DM420

**Bleriot, Louis, 1872-1936**

**Photograph, sgd,** [c.1912]. 139mm by 88mm. Shoulder-length port; sgd in lower margin. Illus in cat. Marans collection. CE Apr 17 (6) $200

**Signature,** 23 Oct 1909. On a postcard of his airplane. star Mar 22 (1391) DM340

**Bligh, William, 1754-1817**

**Ms,** fragment, "H.M.S. Bounty 1789. Hand with me on the launch. John Fryer. Master. Thomas Ledward. Surgeon.... W[illiam Bli]gh. Commander." [1789] 100mm by 250mm, ink on paper, laid down on wood, fire damage, framed. With a copy of Uffa Fox's Second Book, sgd by Fox, in which the fragment is reproduced. With a history of White's of Cowes. b Mar 20 (62) £650

**Ds,** 29 Dec 1787. 1 p. Lower portion of an order addressed to John Fry, William Cole & 2 master's mates of the Bounty. b Mar 20 (14) £6,200

— 14 May 1798. 1 p, folio. Order for provisions to be supplied to H.M.S. Director by William Dearl, countersgd by Bligh. b Mar 20 (32) £550

**Autograph endorsement,** sgd, 9 Mar 1790. On a letter from William Dearl requesting provisions for the ship Director. Giving his approval. Framed with port & biographical plaque. cb June 25 (2494) $6,000

**Blind, Karl, 1826-1907**

**ALs,** 3 Dec 1868. 3 pp, 8vo. To his future sister-in-law. Thanking for photographs & hoping she will visit him in London. HN Nov 24 (2752) DM240

### Blitzstein, Marc

**Autograph Ms,** piano & vocal score of Regina. NY, 1946-48. 132 leaves. Inscr to Jane Pickens & sgd by her on tp. With related material. wd May 8 (5) $2,400

**Autograph quotation,** 31 Jan 1955. 1 p, 8vo. 5 bars of music with words from Act I, Scene I of his opera Reuben, Reuben. rms Oct 11 (53) $250

### Bluecher von Wahlstatt, Gebhard Leberecht, Fuerst, 1742-1819

**ALs,** 2 Nov 1816. 3 pp, 4to. To Count von der Asseburg. Family letter. star Mar 22 (1186) DM1,700

**Ls,** 18 May 1798. 2 pp, 4to. To Lieut. Preuss. Thanking for some maps. Including autograph postscript. star Mar 22 (1184) DM500

### Blum, Robert, 1807-48

**ALs,** 16 Jan 1844. 1 p, 4to. To K. G. Th. Winkler. Recommending a stage manager. With engraved port. star Mar 22 (1187) DM460

— [n.d.]. 1 p, 4to. To an unnamed Ed. Insisting that at least 3 copies of the liturgy for services in Chemnitz & Annaberg be furnished immediately. star Mar 22 (1188) DM220

### Blumenbach, Johann Friedrich, 1752-1840

**ALs,** 7 Dec 1823. 2 pp, 4to. Recipient unnamed. Thanking for some historical illusts. star Mar 21 (406) DM320

### Blunden, Edmund Charles, 1896-1974

**Autograph Ms,** poem, The Prologue. 6 stanzas. With ptd version of the poem annotated & corrected by Blunden. With 3 related A Ls s. Ck Apr 12 (26) £180

### Bly, Robert

**Collection** of A Collection of 10 ALs s & 3 APs s, 1968-70, No size or length given. To John & Elaine Gill. pba Jan 25 (25) $250

### Boccherini, Luigi, 1743-1805

**Autograph music,** String Quartet in E flat, Op.31 no 1, [c.1780]. 33 pp, 4to; sewn. Complete parts for 2 violins, viola & 2 cellos, with tp for each part; 1 sgd. Notated on up to 10 staves per page; including some alterations. S Dec 1 (95) £17,000

### Bode, Johann Joachim Christoph, 1730-93

**A Ls s** (2), 8 July & 15 Nov 1777. 2 pp, 4to. To Philipp Erasmus Reich. Sending a Ms & thanking for a payment. star Mar 21 (128) DM650

### Bodenstedt, Friedrich von, 1819-92

**Autograph Ms,** poem, beginning "Wenn das Glueck sich wenig um mich kuemmert...", 14 Apr 1855. 1 p, 4to. 2 stanzas, sgd. HN May 15 (2510) DM200

### Bodman, Emanuel von, 1874-1946

**Autograph Ms,** poem, Das verstossene Glueck, [n.d.]. 1 p, 4to. 2 four-line stanzas, sgd. star Mar 21 (26) DM300

### Bodoni, Giovanni Battista, 1740-1813

**ALs,** 3 May 1803. 1 p, 8vo. To Giusti, Ferrario & Co. Confirming receipt of a payment. star Mar 21 (658) DM1,600

### Boell, Heinrich, 1917-85

**ALs,** 12 Nov 1964. 2 pp, 8vo. To an unnamed actress. Giving advice. star Mar 21 (28) DM580

### Boerne, Ludwig, 1786-1837

**ALs,** 10 June 1836. 1 p, 8vo. To Konrad Ott. Praising recipient's work. HH Nov 17 (3192) DM850

**Boetticher, Hans, 1883-1934.** See: Ringelnatz, Joachim

### Bogart, Humphrey, 1899-1957

**Ds,** 13 Aug 1947. 2 pp, 4to. Contract with Warner Bros. concerning his appearance in the film Always Together. Carbon copy. Illus in cat. rms June 6 (134) $1,300

**Photograph, sgd,** [1954?] 7 by 9 inch b&w publicity photo from "The Barefoot Contessa". Worn & creased. bbc Sept 18 (65) $325

— Anr, [1954?] 7 by 9 inch b&w publicity photo from "The Barefoot Contessa". Worn & creased. Sgd on middle tones of the image. wa Oct 28 (415) $300

### Bohr, Niels, 1885-1962

**Photograph, sgd,** [c.1950]. 126mm by 82mm. Shoulder-length port. Marans collection. CE Apr 17 (35) $1,500

— Anr, Dec 1957. 6 by 5 inches on larger mount. Sgd & dated on mount. sg Feb 1 (31) $700

### Boie, Heinrich Christian, 1744-1806

**ALs,** 26 Feb 1777. 1 p, 4to. To Philipp Erasmus Reich. Complaining about the pbr C. F. Weygand. star Mar 21 (27) DM900

**Boito, Arrigo, 1842-1918.** See: Verdi, Giuseppe

### Bonaparte, Jerome, 1784-1860

**ALs,** 20 Aug 1807. 1 p, 4to. To Eugene Beauharnais. Announcing his forthcoming wedding. HH May 9 (2524) DM420

— 5 Oct 1830. 1 p, 8vo. To Prince Felice Bacciocchi. Informing him that he will not travel to Germany this year. star Mar 22 (1431) DM480

### Bonaparte, Joseph, 1768-1844

**ALs,** [13 Dec 1799]. 1 p, 4to. To an unnamed minister. Interceding in favor of his brother-in-law Clary. star Mar 22 (1425) DM280

— 8 Aug 1811. 1 p, 4to. To an uncle. Introducing M. d'Almenara who will bring his news. star Mar 22 (1426) DM230

**AL,** 15 Mar 1822. 1 p, 4to. To Mr. Nancrede. Approving design for engraving. In 3d person. sg June 6 (22) $175

**Bonaparte, Joseph Charles Paul Napoleon, 1822-91.**
See: Bonaparte, Napoleon Jerome ("Plon-Plon")

**Bonaparte, Louis, King of Holland, 1778-1846**
ALs, 9 Jan 1810. 1 p, 4to. To his brother Joseph Bonaparte. About his difficulties with his brother Napoleon. HH May 9 (2527) DM900
Ls, 2 Feb 1809. 1 p, 4to. To Jan Hendrik van Swinden. Regretting recipient's illness but hoping to convene a committee soon. star Mar 22 (1428) DM460

**Bonaparte, Maria Anna Elisa, 1777-1820**
Ls, 11 Mar 1809. 1 p, 4to. To M. Ruville. Promising to recommend him to the Emperor. star Mar 22 (1427) DM280

**Bonaparte, Napoleon Jerome ("Plon-Plon"), 1822-91**
ALs, 26 Dec 1848. 2 pp, 8vo. To the Duchesse de Decres. Commenting on his cousin's election as President of the French Republic. star Mar 22 (1432) DM550

**Bonheur, Rosa, 1822-99**
ALs, 24 Dec 1866. 3 pp, 8vo. To an unnamed lady. Regretting she did not see her in Paris & sending a port. HN Nov 24 (2755) DM360

**Bonpland, Aime J. A., 1773-1858**
ALs, [c.Oct 1799]. 2 pp, 4to. Recipient unnamed. Reporting about their travels & findings in South America. star Mar 21 (515a) DM5,200

**Boone, Daniel, 1734-1820**
ADs, 31 Aug 1806. 1 p, 4to. Statement of costs incurred in conducting the trial of James Davis. Framed with a port. Illus in cat. CNY May 17 (207) $11,000
Ds, 12 Mar 1783. 1 p, 8 by 2.25 inches. Attestation to the value of a horse lost in battle. Also sgd by David Mitchell & David Vance. cb June 25 (2311) $5,500

**Booth, Edwin, 1833-93**
ALs, 27 Feb 1878. 4 pp, 4to. To "My dear Stedman". About Othello: "I am pleased beyond measure that you like my conception of the Moor. My execution of it is frequently awry, for it depends so much upon the pliability & view of my Ancient..." With engraving of Booth in costume. pba Oct 26 (2) $325
Photograph, sgd & inscr, 1891. 21 by 16.5 inches. Inscr to St. Clair Smith. sg June 6 (23) $1,100

**Borchardt, Rudolf, 1877-1945**
Autograph Ms, poem, An Hugo von Hofmannsthal, [c.1903?]. 2 pp, folio. 52 lines; differing from ptd version. Illus in cat. star Mar 21 (29) DM9,500

**Borglum, Gutzon de la Mothe, 1867-1941**
Ls, 19 July 1938. 1 p, 4to. To Congressman J. A. Martin of Colorado. Concerning the Mount Rushmore head of Theodore Roosevelt. With file holes and pencil dockets. sg Sept 28 (39) $2,100
Photograph, sgd & inscr, [c.1930]. 252mm by 210mm. Seated, by O. A. Vik. Illus in cat. Marans collection. CE Apr 17 (200) $650

**Bormann, Martin, 1900-45?**
Ls, 23 Dec 1935. 1 p, 4to. To Philipp Bouhler. Thanking for a book & sending New Year's wishes. Illus in cat. rms Mar 21 (359) $445
— 23 Oct 1944. 1 p, folio. To Heinrich Lohse. About Lohses party duties. " I have presented to the Fuehrer this evening the contents of your letter of the 18th of October. The Fuehrer agrees that you should resume your occupation as area commander. However, the Fuerher wishes you to be careful with your health and that you therefore refrain from taking up again your duties of Reich Commissioner until further notice..." Age-stained & with file holes in the margin. With translation. rms Oct 11 (277) $650

**Born, Max, 1882-1970**
Ls, 2 Apr 1968. 1 p, folio. To Kenneth Heuer at Scribner's. Planning an American Ed of his correspondence with Einstein. star Mar 21 (407) DM320

**Borodin, Aleksandr Porfirevich, 1833-87**
ALs, 8 Feb 1887. 4 pp, 8vo. To an unnamed lady musician. Expressing pleasure at her success in Paris & sending personal news. S Dec 1 (97) £1,600

**Boswell, James, 1740-95**
ALs, 10 May 1791. 3 pp, 4to. To Thomas Percy. About the proof of the "altered leaf concerning Grainger" & inserting Percy's praisful comments. With Boswell's seal. S Dec 18 (122) £5,200 [Maggs]
AN, [n.d.], In 3d person, to Lady Diana Beauclerk. Asking when he may call on her. wd May 8 (6) $1,200

**Botanic Manuscripts**
Original drawings, (398 on 233 leaves) of flowers in watercolor & bodycolor arranged by genus. Germany, c.1660-70. 384mm by 250mm, in contemp mor gilt. 1st leaf headed "De Place" & final leaf initialed P.A. in a contemp hand. Fattorini Ms C Oct 25 (63) £170,000

**Bottesini, Giovanni, 1821-89**
Autograph music, song, Romanza; [n.d.]. 3 pp, 4to. 54 bars, scored for voice & piano. Sgd & inscr to Madonnina Malaspina. star Mar 22 (758) DM520

**Boulanger, Nadia, 1887-1979**
Photograph, sgd & inscr, [n.d.]. 3 by 5 inch photo. Inscr to Reginald Steward. Affixed to matting with masking tape. Also with vertical surface crack. pba June 13 (191) $160

**Bourke-White, Margaret, 1904-71**
Photograph, sgd, [c.1955]. 252mm by 203mm. Shoulder-length port. Marans collection. CE Apr 17 (201) $750

**Boxer Rebellion**
— HYNDE, R. R. - ALs of this employee of the Hongkong & Shanghai Banking Corporation, stationed in Tientsin, 28 June 1900. 8 pp, 8vo. To his parents. Describing the week's fighting. pn Nov 9 (375) £180

## Brachmann, Luise, 1777-1822
**ALs**, 5 Oct 1821. 1 p, 8vo. To the bookseller Heinrichshofen. Offering a vol of poems for print. Margin trimmed. star Mar 21 (31) DM350

## Brahms, Johannes, 1833-97
**Autograph music**, song, Gold ueberwiegt die Liebe, Op.48, no 4, [1868]. 1 p, 8vo. Stichvorlage, notated on 3 systems, each of 3 staves. Illus in cat. S May 15 (299) £7,500

— Autograph music, song, Salamander, Op.107, no 2, to a text by Carl Lemcke; [July 1888]. 2 pp, 250mm by 325mm. Illus in cat. star Mar 22 (759) DM30,000

**ALs**, [24 Oct 1876]. 3 pp, 8vo. To Fritz Simrock. Humorous comments regarding fees & the ptg of his 3rd String Quartet. star Mar 22 (760) DM7,000

— Jan 1879. 2 pp, 8vo. To the widow of Adolf Jensen. Offering his condolences. S May 15 (304) £1,300

— Apr 1879. 2 pp, 8vo. Recipient unnamed. Explaining that he will not be able to act as a judge for a foundation in Vienna. star Mar 22 (761) DM3,000

— 16 Dec 1883. 3 pp, 8vo. To Fritz Simrock. Inquiring about works of Scarlatti & folksong collections. S Dec 1 (103) £2,100

— 2 Nov 1886. 1 p, 8vo. To Fritz Simrock. Requesting him to send the collected works of Schuetz. S May 15 (307) £1,000

— [25 May 1891]. 4 pp, 8vo. To his sister Elise Grund. Discussing her last will. star Mar 22 (765) DM7,000

— [28 Aug 1894]. 4 pp, 8vo. To Fritz Simrock. Expressing thanks, discussing acquaintances, & chatting about his songs. star Mar 22 (767) DM3,300

— [n.d.]. 1 p, 8vo. Recipient unnamed. Discussing his travel plans. Framed with a port. S Dec 1 (100) £700

**Autograph postcard, sgd**, [4 Jan 1882]. To Carl Reinthaler. Planning a meeting the next day. star Mar 22 (762) DM1,100

— [3 Feb 1886]. To Adolf Brodsky. Declining an invitation. Illus in cat. star Mar 22 (763) DM3,000

— 28 May 1886. To Fritz Simrock. About his stay on Lake Thun & asking whether he will be in Cologne. S May 15 (309) £650

— 19 Dec 1886. To Fritz Simrock. Complaining about mistakes in an arrangement of his 4th Symphony. S May 15 (305) £650

— 18 Mar 1888. To Fritz Simrock. Referring to some recent mishaps. S May 15 (308) £550

— 1 Aug 1888. To Fritz Simrock. Offering to meet him in Bern. S May 15 (311) £450

— [7 Oct 1888]. To Wilhelm Kupfer. Inquiring whether he is able to accept a copying job. star Mar 22 (764) DM850

— 6 Nov 1889. To Fritz Simrock. Asking if he has recovered from a waltz evening. S May 15 (302) £550

— 11 Nov 1889. To Fritz Simrock. About his 3 Motets Op.110. S May 15 (306) £580

— [17 Feb 1893]. To Philipp Spitta. Returning a publication & thanking for an evening spent together. star Mar 22 (766) DM2,400

— 23 Oct 1893. To Fritz Simrock. Concerning the publication of his German Folksongs & the piano pieces Op.116 & 117. Illus in cat. S May 15 (310) £680

— 22 Nov 1893. To Fritz Simrock. About the publication of the German Folksongs. S May 15 (303) £440

— 5 Jan 1894. To Fritz Simrock. Asking for Max Klinger's address. S May 15 (301) £490

**Ds**, 13 Feb 1872. 1 p, folio. Publication agreement for Brahms's piano transcription of a Gavotte by Gluck. Sgd by Brahms & dated by him 20 Feb. S May 15 (15) £1,700

**Autograph quotation**, 4 bars from the Magelone Romanzen, Op.33 no 3, Sept 1865. 1 p, 11cm by 22.8cm, cut from larger sheet. Sgd. Illus in cat. S Dec 1 (102) £4,600

**Photograph, sgd**, May [18]96. 99mm by 63mm, mtd. Bust port, by C. Brasch. Imperf. Illus in cat. Marans collection. CE Apr 17 (225) $1,300

## Brancusi, Constantin, 1876-1957
**Collection** of 15 A Ls s & photographs, sgd & inscr, 17 July 1933 to 27 Dec 1947. 32 pp, 8vo & folio. To Florence Meyer Homolka. About his work, her photographs, parcels sent during the war, health concerns, etc. With related photographs by Homolka. S Dec 1 (5) £8,500

## Brandeis, Louis D., 1856-1941
**ALs**, 24 Apr 1930. 1 p, 8vo. To David Freiberger. With orig holograph envelope. sg June 6 (24) $300

— 30 Jul 1930. 1 p, 8vo. To David Freiberger. Asking for a copy of a report concerning the American Zionist Commonwealth. sg June 6 (25) $450

— 19 May 1934. 1 p, 4to. To Dr. Knapp. Responding to some financial questions. Illus in cat. rms Mar 21 (338) $495

— 29 Sept 1939. 1 p, 8vo. To Charles Schwager. Saying that what is asked is an opinion in this matter. rms Nov 30 (104) $260

**Photograph, sgd & inscr**, 1934. 270mm by 184mm. Shoulder-length port, by Harris & Ewing. Illus in cat. Marans collection. CE Apr 17 (120) $1,000

**Signature**, [n.d.]. On letter requesting an autograph. No size given. With port. Framed. Over-all size 15.75 by 19.75 inches. Illus in cat rms Oct 11 (6) $450

## Brandes, Heinrich Wilhelm, 1777-1834
**Autograph Ms**, essay, Beitraege zur Geschichte und Theorie der Cometen-Schweife, [n.d.]. 7 pp, 4to. Including astronomical drawing. star Mar 21 (410) DM320

## Braun, Eva, 1912-45
**ALs**, [n.d.]. 1 p, 8vo (card). To [Helli] Bouhler. Thanking for a Christmas package & sending Christmas & New Year's wishes. Illus in cat. rms Mar 21 (358) $2,800

**ANs**, 16 Dec [19]42. 2 pp, 8vo (card). To Helli Bouhler. Thanking for some books & sending Christmas wishes. Illus in cat. rms June 6 (602) $1,700

**Braun, Johann, 1753-1811**

ALs, 12 Nov 1794. 1 p, 4to. To a royal chamberlain. Sending the program of some concerts. star Mar 22 (768) DM600

**Braune, Helene**

[Her guest book mainly kept at Dresden, [c.1900-1930], 81 pp, 8vo, in brown lea gilt, containing c.110 entries by authors, painters, musicians, actors, & others, including Thomas Mann, Richard Strauss, Enrico Caruso, Orville Wright & Adolf Hitler, sold at Stargardt on 21 Mar 1996, lot 78, for DM8,500.]

**Braxton, Carter, Signer from Virginia**

ALs, 15 Mar 1781. 1 p, folio. To [Landon Carter?]. Requesting a quantity of tobacco & discussing a bill. P Dec 13 (32) $1,100

**Brecht, Bertolt, 1898-1956**

Autograph Ms, poem, beginning "Seine Musse zu geniessen", [c.1920-23]. 1 p, folio. 7 four-line stanzas, differing from ptd version. star Mar 21 (32) DM7,500

Ls, 8 June 1955. 1 p, folio. To Alberto Cavalcanti. Referring to recipient's film version of Herr Puntila und sein Knecht Matti. star Mar 21 (33) DM1,200

— NEHER, CASPAR. - ALs, 25 Sept 1946. 1 p, folio. To the pbr Reiss. Draft, concerning illusts for Brecht's works. star Mar 21 (34) DM300

**Breckinridge, John Cabell, 1821-75**

ALs, 15 May 1858. 1 p, 8vo. To H. N. Otterson. Sending his autograph. rms Nov 30 (105) $280

**Breidbach-Buerresheim, Emmerich Joseph von, Kurfuerst von Mainz, 1707-74**

ALs, [n.d.]. 1 p, 4to. To Herr Carove. Returning New Year's wishes. star Mar 22 (1330) DM520

**Breviarium -- Latin Manuscripts**

— [Southwestern France, Toulouse?, c.1310). 2 leaves only, vellum, 495mm by 370mm. In fine angular gothic script, with music on a 4-line red stave. With red & blue initial with contrasting penwork, large illuminated initial with long marginal extensions, & 2 large historiated initials. S June 18 (13) £4,800

— [Northern France, c.1415]. 218 leaves, vellum, 135mm by 90mm. Late 17th-cent lea gilt. In a slightly sloping gothic textura. With numerous small initials in gold & colors & 28 large illuminated initals extending into full or 3-quarter borders sometimes including animals or grotesques. HH Nov 14 (7) DM16,000

— [Southern France, c.1450]. 28 lines, double column, on 17 leaves. With 2-line initials in red or blue. bba Apr 11 (213) £260 [Jordan]

— The Llangattock Breviary. [Ferrara, c.1456-69]. 3 leaves only, vellum, 273mm by 202mm; framed. In 2 sizes of a rounded gothic script. With 17 two-line initials in highly burnished gold on blue or pink grounds, & 12 full-length illuminated borders in several styles. Probably illuminated for Borso d'Este, Duke of Ferrara. S June 18 (12) £2,400

— [Florence, c.1460]. 334 leaves (3 blank, 1 lacking), vellum, 132mm by 95mm. Faded yellow-green velvet over pastebds of c.1860. In a very small rounded gothic hand. With 19 large illuminated initials in leafy designs in colors & burnished gold & 3 large historiated initials with 3-quarter or full historiated borders in the style of Francesco d'Antonio del Chierico. S Dec 5 (40) £4,000 [Smith]

— [Beuerberg, Germany, 1594). Of Augustinian Use. 42 leaves, vellum, 187mm by 160mm. Contemp blindstamped lea over wooden bds. With numerous small & 12 large decorated initials, mostly with red penwork. In the hand of F. Conr. Widman. HH Nov 14 (8) DM3,200

— [El Burgo de Osma, Castile, late 17th cent]. 143 leaves, vellum (1 lacking, 2 paper), 223mm by 185mm. Worn contemp blindstamped lea over thick wooden bds. In brown & red ink in a neat round roman hand in imitation of ptd type. With initials in red. S Dec 5 (41) £300 [Santo]

**Briez, Philippe Constant Joseph, 1759-95**

ALs, [17 Dec 1794]. 4 pp, 4to. To Nicolas Haussmann. About the situation in Belgium, & insisting that the Rhine is the natural border of France. star Mar 22 (1317) DM200

**Brillat-Savarin, Anthelme, 1755-1826**

ALs, [20 Aug 1799]. 1 p, 4to. To a division of the criminal court at Versailles. Concerning the suit against Citoyen Demasis. star Mar 22 (1309) DM240

**Brinckmann, John, 1814-70**

Autograph Ms, poem, Twaeschens, [n.d.]. 2 pp, 4to. 3 eight-line stanzas, differing considerably from ptd version. star Mar 21 (36) DM1,200

**Britten, Benjamin, 1913-76**

Collection of ALs & photograph, sgd, 20 Aug 1946 & [n.d.]. 1 p, 8vo, & size not stated. Recipient unnamed. Sending his autograph. Including musical quotation. star Mar 22 (769) DM800

— Collection of 10 A Ls s & 4 Ls s, 1948-73. To James Lawrie, Deputy Chairman of the English Opera Group. Ck Apr 12 (27) £950

Photograph, sgd & inscr, 1971. 4to. Close-up outdoor pose. Illus in cat. rms June 6 (179) $220

**Brod, Max, 1884-1968**

ALs, 28 Nov 1950. 2 pp, 8vo. To Lena Gedin. Thanking for a book, requesting review copies of others, & mentioning his current literary work. HH Nov 17 (3193) DM1,700

**Broglie, Louis Victor, Prince de, 1892-1987**

Autograph Ms, Apercu sur l'oeuvre de Pierre Curie, 19 Apr 1956. 4 pp, 4to. Sgd. With photograph, sgd. star Mar 21 (411) DM2,200

ALs, 30 Dec 1937. 2 pp, 8vo. Recipient unnamed. Regarding the Polish trans of his work Matiere et lumiere. HN May 15 (2516) DM500

— 20 Dec 1938. 2 pp, 8vo. To his pbr. Forwarding two requests regarding his works. star Mar 21 (412) DM320

**Bronsart von Schellendorf, Hans, 1830-1913**
ALs, 12 Feb 1862. 3 pp, 4to. To Bernhard Friedel. Discussing a projected concert in Dresden. HN May 15 (2517) DM420

**Bronstein, Lev Davydovich, 1879-1940.** See: Trotsky, Leon

**Brooke, Rupert, 1887-1915**
Photograph, sgd, [n.d.]. 12 by 10 inches, framed. Unsgd but with clipped signature mtd below. Ck Apr 12 (28) £160

**Brown, Arthur Whitten, Sir, 1886-1948.** See: Alcock, John William & Brown

**Brown, Ford Madox, 1821-93**
[A collection of his papers, including holograph lecture notes, drafts of outgoing correspondence & a very large collection of letters to him, sold at Sotheby's on 18 Dec 1995, lot 537, for £26,000 to Quaritch]

**Brown, John, of Osawatomie, 1800-59**
Autograph Ms, notes for a speech delivered several times in New England, 1857. 2 pp on 1 leaf, 4to. About his experiences, the wounding of his son & the burning of Osowatamie. sg Mar 28 (275) $11,000
ALs, 26 Oct 1833. 1 p, 4to. To "Dear Brother"[Frederick Brown]. Concerning the death of their brother: "I had received Newspaper respecting the death of our brother. I believe I was to write Father as soon as I returned, but I have nothing further to write, & you can shew [sic] him this..." Franked. Restored. Illus in cat pba Oct 26 (155) $3,000
— 3 June 1839. 1 p, 4to. To O. O. Brown & William H. Munroe. About a land purchase. Browned. CNY Dec 15 (53) $2,000
Cut signature, [n.d.]. 1 by 4 inches. With a closing sentiment. Cut from a letter to his son John Brown, Jr. With ALs by John Brown, Jr. to Eleanor Sherman sending her the signature. Illus in cat pba Oct 26 (156) $800
Photograph, [c.1859]. Oval, 252mm by 205mm, mtd. 3-quarter-length sepia port; with clipped inscr & signature mtd below. Illus in cat. Marans collection. CE Apr 17 (121) $2,200

**Browning, Elizabeth Barrett, 1806-61**
Autograph transcript, poem, Fortune-telling. 1 p, 16 lines, 137mm by 162mm. [c.4 Mar 1825]. Illus in cat P June 5 (181) $2,000

**Browning, Robert, 1812-89**
ALs, 3 Nov 1845. 2 pp, 8vo. To Eliot Warburton. Responding to praise of Bells and Pomegranates. pn Nov 9 (438) £550
— 28 Nov [1845]. 2 pp, 16mo. To Eliot Warburton. Commenting on the verses written by Landor in his honor. pn Nov 9 (439) £520
— 6 Jan 1846. 2 pp, 8vo. To Eliot Warburton. Offering sympathy after hearing of a bereavement. pn Nov 9 (440) £380
— 23 Mar 1867. 2 pp, 8vo. To J.B.F.E. de Chatelain. Responding graciously to his praise for Browning's work. pn June 13 (227) £500
— 17 Mar [18]77. 1 p, 8vo. To Mr. Nevelyan. Concerning an election: " I had appended my name to your nomination card at the Club...I voted for you yesterday..." Wrinkled. Illus in cat rms Oct 11 (55) $450
— 12 May [18]79. 1 p, 8vo. To Helen Zimmerman. Arranging an appointment for the next Saturday. rms Oct 11 (56) $500
Photograph, sgd, [c.1867]. 104mm by 62mm, mtd. Shoulder-length profile port, by Elliott & Fry. Illus in cat. Marans collection. CE Apr 17 (60) $1,000

**Bruce, Blanche K., 1841-98**
Ds, Aug 1890. 3 pp, folio. Indenture & land deed release for a parcel of land in the city of Washington DC. cb June 25 (2314) $130
— 9 Sept 1890. 1 p, folio. As Recorder of Deeds in the District of Columbia, confirmation of a land deed. rms Mar 21 (242) $350

**Bruch, Max, 1838-1920**
ALs, 11 Feb 1881. 4 pp, 8vo. To Siegfried Ochs. Expressing satisfaction that Ochs has returned to Berlin. star Mar 22 (771) DM340
Autograph quotation, sgd, 23 Dec 1906. 7cm by 12cm. From Das Lied von der Glocke. S May 15 (314) £200

**Bruckner, Anton, 1824-96**
Autograph music, sketches for the Adagio of his 9th Symphony, 1 May 1894. 2 pp, 4to. Repaired. Illus in cat. star Mar 22 (773a) DM32,000
ALs, 11 May 1885. 1 p, 8vo. To Johannes Peregrin Hupfauf. Concerning the publication of his Te Deum. Illus in cat. star Mar 22 (773b) DM9,000

**Bruening, Heinrich, 1885-1970**
ALs, 14 July 1941. 2 pp, folio. Recipient unnamed. Concerning the publication of recipient's work on Feuerbach & Marx. star Mar 22 (1197) DM270

**Bruhn, Erik Belton Evers, 1928-86**
Photograph, sgd & inscr, [n.d.]. 10 by 8 inches (image). Inscr to Lucia. Framed. Illus in cat. rms June 6 (215) $210

**Bryan, William Jennings, 1860-1925**
ALs, 13 July [n.y.]. 1 p, 4to. To Howard Thompson. A letter of introduction for D. L. Baumgarten for St. Petersburg. Toning. pba Oct 26 (204) $110
Ls, 4 Dec 1902. 3 pp, 4to. To Erving Winslow. Discussing the Democratic Party, President Cleveland's political positions, the Philippines & imperialism. Illus in cat. rms June 6 (328) $850
— 19 June 1912. 1 p, 4to. To W. P. Carmichael. Announcing that he will take on the presidency of the Board of Directors of the Winona Assembly and Bible Conference "when the debt is cleared and the

reorganization is effected". Folds. sg Sept 28 (40) $120
— 18 June 1923. 1 p, 8vo. To Mr. D. Lloyd Claycomb. Explaining that he will be travelling less due to his wife's ill health. pba Feb 22 (118) $80

**Bryant, William Cullen, 1794-1878**
Photograph, sgd, [n.d.]. 2.5 by 4 inch sepia portrait. By J. Gurney & son. With elegant gold border. Illus in cat pba Oct 26 (5) $225

**Buber, Martin, 1878-1965**
Series of 3 A Ls s, 3 Dec 1922 to 4 Dec 1928. 3 pp, 4to & 8vo. To Dr. Danzel. About recipient's & his own work. S May 15 (155) £420
Ls, 12 July 1962. 1 p, 8vo. To Mr. Cohen. Sending copies of letters for his information. rms Mar 21 (243) $340

**Buchanan, James, 1791-1868**
ALs, 13 Apr 1852. 4 pp. About holding the Union together & the slavery question. rs Nov 11 (8) $14,000
— 10 Apr 1836. 2 pp, 4to. To Thomas Elder. About an agreement: "I was and still am under the impression that there was a positive agreement to continue these causes until after the adjournment of the present session of Congress..." With copy of his return letter to Buchanan on bottom of page 2 & copy of anr letter to Buchanan from Elder on page 3. pba Oct 26 (205) $700
— 7 Jan 1837. 1 p, 4to. To James Caldwell. About his poor health, business and Martin Van Buren: " Speculation has nearly ceased here as to who shall compose the new Cabinet. On this subject M. Van Buren keeps his own counsel..." With fold break in margins. Illus in cat rms Oct 11 (57) $850
— 16 May 1840. 2 pp, 4to. To Dr. Francis Barclay. About the Whig party & its policies & the upcoming elections: "They have no common principle of action but hostility to the present administration; and they think so meanly, as they always have done, of the intelligence of the people as to expect their support, by raising the senseless cry of 'Hard Cider and Log Cabins'. This will be 'no go' before the month of November..." CNY Dec 15 (144) $2,200
— 9 Jan 1842. 2 pp, 4to. To General Isaac Winters. About the resignation of President Tyler's Cabinet over his opposition to the restoration of the National Bank. Browned. With pinholes. CNY Dec 15 (145) $1,300
— 10 Dec 1847. 1 p, 4to. To John Wadman. Assessing his chances for the presidential nomination. Forbes Magazine collection. CNY May 17 (118) $950
— 18 Jan 1849. 1 p, 4to. To Robert J. Walker. Mentioning two gentlemen to the Secretary of the Treasury: "Permit me again to call your attention to the cases of William M. Weles & David Pool...you would do me an especial favor personally by deciding the cases finally...." rms Oct 11 (58) $475
— 16 July 1851. 2 pp, 4to. To Isaac G. McKinley. About the importance of "the maintenance of the Fugitive Slave law, without modification; and the repeal of our State laws denying the use of our jails for the detention of fugitive slaves..." CNY Dec 15 (146) $4,500
— 13 June 1853. 2 pp, 4to. To Isaac McKinley. Explaining that he would have preferred McKinley for a post office appointment. Forbes Magazine collection. CNY May 17 (119) $900
— 19 Dec 1853. 1 p, 4to. To Lady Stafford. Expressing condolences on the death of her sister. rms Mar 21 (46) $570
— 7 Jan 1859. 1 p, 4to. To Messrs. Riggs & Co. About the payment of dividends due him from the Planters Bank of Tennessee. Illus in cat. rms June 6 (325) $1,600
— 13 Mar 1859. 1 p, 4to. To James William Denver. Accepting Denver's resignation as Commissioner of Indian Affairs: " I cannot consent to sever our official connection, without expressing my lasting obligation to you for the able, discreet, firm & successful, manner in which you performed you duties..." With orig holograph envelope. Spotted. CNY Dec 15 (147) $3,000
— 17 Feb 1860. 1 p, 8vo. To Mrs. John R. Thompson. Asking her to act as hostess at a White House Dinner. Illus in cat pba Oct 26 (206) $1,300
— 5 Sept 1860. 1 p, 8vo. To Dr. Hall. Politely calling the Doctor to the White House. CNY Dec 15 (148) $800
— 29 Feb 1868. 1 p, 8vo. To E. M. Walton. Thanking Walton for a calendar & a kind note. pba Oct 26 (207) $400
— 26 Apr [n. y.]. 1 p, 8vo. To H. D. Gelpin. An invitation to dine. Illus in cat pba Feb 22 (213) $160
Ds, 27 July 1847. 1 p, folio. Passport issued to George Endicott. rms June 6 (326) $600
— 8 Sept 1853. 1 p, folio. American passport (in French) for Thomas & Mary F. White. Fold line through B of signature. wa Feb 29 (237) $220
— 23 Sept 1858. 1 p, oblong folio. Appointment of John P. Brown as Secretary & Dragoman of the U.S. legation at Constantinople. Countersgd by Sec. of State Lewis Cass. wa Oct 28 (174) $450
— 25 Jan 1861. 1 p, folio. Appointment of a 1st lieutenant in the militia of DC. Countersgd by Sec of War Joseph Holt. Framed with port. sg Feb 1 (32) $550
Cut signature, [n.d.]. No size given. A free frank cut from an envelope. With sepia-toned reprints of his inauguration and a port of Buchanan as President. Framed. Over-all size 15.5 by 23.75 inches. Illus in cat rms Oct 11 (306) $280
Signature, [n.d.]. No size given. With others. Trimmed. Mtd. pba Feb 22 (214) $90

**Buck, Pearl S., 1892-1973**
[2 typescript carbon copies of essays, Space and Sky, & Elements of Democracy in the Chinese Traditional Culture, [n.d.], 17 pp, 4to, with a few autograph corrections, sold at Hartung & Hartung on 17 Nov 1995, lot 3195, for DM340.]
Typescript carbon copy, Short story entitled Faithfully Yours. 1936. 43 pp, 4to. pba Feb 22 (17) $130

## BUELOW

**Buelow, Hans von, 1830-94**
ALs, [c.1860]. 2 pp, 4to. To Bernhard Friedel. Sending a corrected version of a French announcement of a concert in Dresden. HN May 15 (2518) DM500
— 8 Nov 1868. 1 p, 8vo. To Ferdinand David. Introducing Wilhelm Schwendemann. star Mar 22 (775) DM400
— 31 Dec 1868. 1 p, 8vo. To [Georg Vierling]. Reporting about a performance of recipient's overture to Schiller's Maria Stuart. star Mar 22 (776) DM280
— 6 Apr 1878. 2 pp, 8vo. To Franz Ries. Concerning concerts in Dresden & Liege, & including a quote about Chopin. star Mar 22 (777) DM420

**Buerckel, Josef, 1895-1944**
Ls, 23 Dec 1935. 1 p, 8vo. To [Philipp] Bouhler. Sending some wine as a Christmas present. Illus in cat. rms June 6 (609) $200

**Buffalo Bill.** See: Cody, William F. ("Buffalo Bill")

**Buffon, Georges Louis Marie Leclerc, Comte de, 1707-88 —&**
**Seve, Jacques de, 1742-88**
Original drawings, for Buffon's Histoire naturelle. [1770s-80] 233 wash drawings, sheet size 245mm by 160mm, all within a black line frame, some sgd & dated, all mtd on blue paper & bound in contemp red half mor. Fuerstenberg - Schaefer copy S Dec 7 (87) £20,000

**Bull, Ole**
Autograph quotation, 4 bars in B flat major, 15 Nov 1876. 1 p, 8vo. Sgd. star Mar 22 (774) DM580

**Bunsen, Robert Wilhelm, 1811-99**
Photograph, sgd, [c.1865]. 102mm by 62mm. Full length, standing. Illus in cat. Marans collection. CE Apr 17 (36) $1,200

**Buntline, Ned.** See: Judson, Edward Zane Carroll

**Burbank, Luther, 1849-1926**
Ls, 14 Sept 1917. 1 p, 4to. To Mrs. E. B. Power. Concerning the quality of French marigolds. pba Feb 22 (119) $225

**Burckhardt, Carl Jacob, 1891-1974**
ALs, 17 Apr 1946. 4 pp, 8vo. To Wilhelm Furtwaengler. Praising Grillparzer as a political mind. star Mar 21 (414) DM700

**Burgoyne, John, 1722-92**
ALs, 9 June 1769. 5 pp, 4to. To George Townshend. Hoping for an appointment. Repaired. P Dec 13 (40) $1,500
— 15 Apr 1772. 2 pp, 4to. Recipient unnamed. Recommending Lieut. Williams for promotion. P Dec 13 (41) $2,500
— 11 Sept 1777. 2 pp, 4to. To Major Gen. Riedesel. Discussing troop movements. P Dec 13 (42) $13,000
— 22 Mar 1778. 2 pp, 4to. To Major Gen. William Heath. Referring to matters pertaining to his army. P Dec 13 (44) $5,000

## AMERICAN BOOK PRICES CURRENT

— 30 Aug 1778. 2 pp, 4to. To Robert Kingston. About the threat to send him back to America because of his status as prisoner of war. Illus in cat. P Dec 13 (46) $4,750
— 20 Jan 1781. 2 pp, 4to. To Lord McCartney. Introducing Mr. Shaw. P Dec 13 (47) $1,500
— 26 May 1789. 3 pp, 4to. To John Dick & William Mollerton. Providing information regarding Mr. Atherton's pay. P Dec 13 (48) $1,500
— KINGSTON, ROBERT. - A collection of his papers, comprising 82 letters, documents & reports relating to the Saratoga Campaign, Dec 1776 to Mar 1779, 128 pp, various sizes. P Dec 13 (52) $34,000

**Burke, Edmund, 1729-97**
ALs, [c.7 Aug 1770]. 4 pp, 4to. To Richard Shakleton. Discussing his wife's illness, recipient's approval of his recent book, & current affairs. P Dec 13 (56) $1,500
— 17 Oct 1792. 2 pp, 4to. To the Earl of Sheffield. Thanking him for helping French refugees. P Dec 13 (57) $800

**Burne-Jones, Sir Edward Coley, 1833-98**
ALs, 14 July 1887. 4 pp, 8vo. To Ellen Terry. Sending her his drawing Now Walk the Angels on the Walls of Heaven (not present). S Nov 21 (57) £500

**Burney, Charles, 1726-1814**
Transcript, letter to William Crotch, 3 Nov 1790. 2 pp, 4to. Congratulating him on his appointment as organist, invoking Handel & Haydn, & giving advice on a rounded education in music & literature. Transcript in Crotch's hand. S May 15 (317) £500
— BENINCASA, SIGNOR. - ALs, 4 Feb 1786. 4 pp, size not stated. To Charles Burney. Acknowledging receipt of Burney's publication about the Handel commemoration & discussing the music scene in Italy. S May 15 (318) £2,900

**Burney, Frances, 1752-1840**
Autograph Ms, T. Tembaron. [c.1913] About 600 leaves bound in 3 vols, 4to, in mor. Covers & edges singed O Mar 5 (36) $4,100

**Burns, Robert, 1759-96**
AL, [n.d.]. About 35mm by 185mm. Fragment of 28 words. On verso is sgd inscr of Robert Ainsle, saying that this is part of a letter addressed to Ainsle. CE June 12 (12) $350

**Burnside, Ambrose E., 1824-81**
Signature, [n.d.]. On a 2 by 5 inch slip of paper. pba Feb 22 (155) $60

**Burr, Aaron, 1756-1836**
ALs, 4 Dec 1800. 1 p, 4to. To James Binny. Apologizing for taking so long to return a book. F June 20 (768) $750
— 21 Apr 1801. 2 pp, 4to. To Thomas Jefferson. Writing the President about political rivals & adding a nasty comment about Alexander Hamilton: "Hamilton seems to be literally mad with spleen and envy and disappointment...his efforts are practically impo-

tent..." Docketed by Jefferson. With a portion cut from the letter deleting an individual's name. Illus in cat CNY Dec 15 (54) $11,000

— 3 Dec 1803. 1 p, 4to. To Rob. G. Harper. Introducing Mr. Astor but urging that Mrs. Harper give "particular protection" to Miss Astor. With related material. wa Oct 28 (321) $1,200

**ADs,** 1 Oct 1812. 1 p, 8vo. Certification that "John Greenwood has commenced a Clerkship with me as an attorney at Law." Docketed by Burr on integral leaf. rms Mar 21 (14) $500

**Burr, Theodosia, 1783-1813**

**ALs,** 9 Mar 1811. 2 pp on 1 leaf, 4to. "Apparently addressed to Secretary of the Treasury Albert Gallatin". Concerning the possible return of her father from exile. Sgd "Theo Burr Aston". wa Oct 28 (322) $375

**Burroughs, Edgar Rice, 1875-1950**

**Ls,** 6 Mar 1939. 1 p, 4to. To John Roth. Concerning a Tarzan club: " In the matter of the national Tarzan club which you mentioned, I may say that we have been working on this for a number of years. Just when we shall launch such an organization I don't know..." rms Oct 11 (59) $280

— 4 Dec 1946. 1 p. To A. Atlas Leve. Sending his autograph pba May 4 (89) $225

**Signature,** [n.d.]. On a 2 by 3.5 inch piece of paper pba May 4 (90) $120

**Burroughs, John, 1837-1921**

**Photograph, sgd,** [c.1909]. 340mm by 235mm. Shoulder-length port. Marans collection. CE Apr 17 (37) $500

**Burton, Sir Richard Francis, 1821-90**

**ALs,** 21 Feb 1855. 1 p, folio. To the British assistant political resident at Aden. Telling him about problems encountered by Speke in Somaliland. CNY May 17 (53) $2,800

— [1876]. 1 p, 8vo, mtd. To Henry Schuetz Wilson. Thanking him for a list. pn June 13 (228) £320 [Maggs]

— Jan 1880. 4 pp, 8vo. To Mr. Arvafield. Writing from Trieste about the Italians: " I will tell the truth...about Italy and the Italians. There is not an honest man in this country; and Knife is King. The upper clans are such cowards that they do not dare support an anti-Cruelty Society; and Englishmen...who do dare are threatened with and must expect assasination. There! I won't trouble you anymore..." Illus in cat rms Oct 11 (60) $800

**Busch, Wilhelm, 1832-1908**

**ALs,** 2 Dec 1875. 1 p, 8vo. Recipient unnamed. Admitting that he loves smoking a pipe. star Mar 21 (40) DM1,300

**Autograph postcard, sgd,** Dec 1903. To Baroness S. Nadherny-Borntin. Sending his photograph (on verso; also sgd). Illus in cat. HH Nov 17 (3196) DM3,000

**Photograph, sgd & inscr,** 1903. 8vo. Inscr with 2-line verse. star Mar 21 (41) DM2,600

**Bush, George Herbert Walker**

**Ds,** 10 Oct 1990. 1 p, folio. Ptd proclamation naming Oct 14, 1990 Dwight D. Eisenhower Day. Illus in cat. rms Mar 21 (173) $850

**Bushnell, David, c.1742-1824**

**Ds,** 15 June 1782. 1 p, 8vo. Receipt for a pay order; sgd on behalf of Jonathan Russ. rms Mar 21 (244) $1,750

**Busoni, Ferruccio B., 1866-1924**

**Series** of 3 A Ls s, 1921. 6 pp, 4to & 8vo. To Egon Wellesz. About the works of Schoenberg & of Wellesz. S May 15 (543) £700

**ALs,** 16 Oct 1907. 2 pp, 8vo. To Arthur Dandelot. Informing him that he has instructed Breitkopf & Haertel to send him the score of a concert. star Mar 22 (778) DM600

**Autograph quotation,** 4 bars from his Variazioni per Violoncello, Oct 1910. 1 p, folio. Sgd & inscr to [Enrico Mainardi]. Illus in cat. star Mar 22 (779) DM2,200

**Butler, Benjamin F., 1795-1858**

**Ds,** 19 July 1864. Provisional commission for Richard F. Andrews as Lieutenant in the U.S. Colored Troops. Ptd oath sgd by Andrews on verso. rms Mar 21 (261) $750

**Signature,** [n.d.]. No size given. With a 3 pp 1862 soldier's letter & patriotic envelope about occupying Hatteras. Also with port of Butler in uniform & a vintage map. Over-all size 29 by 33 inches. Detail in cat rms Oct 11 (102) $390

See also: Morrissey, John & Others

**Butler, Benjamin F., 1818-93**

[A collection of material sold at R. M. Smythe on 11 Oct 1995 as lot 89 for $5,000.] Illus in cat

**Ls,** 2 Aug 1861. 2 pp, 4to. To Edwin D. Morgan. Concerning problems with the 20th Regiment N.Y. Volunteers & Col. Weber. With response from Morgan dated 6 Aug on 2d page. Illus in cat pba Oct 26 (157) $1,000

— 24 Aug 1868. 2 pp, 8vo. To Anson Burlingame. Presenting Captain Meigs in order that he introduce the rapid-fire gun to China. pba Oct 26 (158) $450

**Butler, Frank S., 1850-1926**

**ALs,** 9 Sept [n.y.]. 1 p, 4to. To the sales manager of the Colt Arms Company. Ordering a custom made pistol for his wife Annie Oakley. CNY May 17 (278) $2,400

**Byrd, Richard E., 1888-1957**

**Ls,** 23 Sept 1933. 1 p, 4to. To Struys, Jones & Co. About forthcoming South Polar expedition and seeking support in form of necessary supplies. sg June 6 (27) $425

— 10 Oct 1935. 2 pp, 4to. Sending news "about what has happened since the expedition broke up." With related material. CA Mar 26 (111A) A$600

**Check,** 2 Aug 1928. Payable to Byrd Antarctic Expedition for $34,000. Mtd with 2 photos & copy of a document. wa Oct 28 (334) $200

**Signature**, [n.d.]. No size given. On a fly-leaf from his book Little America, Aerial Exploration in the Antartic. With a 1935 photo of Byrd & his plane & related material. Framed. Over-all size 16 by 20 inches. Illus in cat rms Oct 11 (7) $325

### Byron, George Gordon Noel, Lord, 1788-1824

**ALs**, 21 Nov 1815. 1 p, 8vo. To "Sir James"[Bland Burges]. Trying to arrange a meeting. Illus in cat pba Oct 26 (6) $2,250

**AL**, [29 May 1823]. Postscript cut from letter to Stendhal. 1 p, 1.25 by 4.75 inches, attached to a 4to leaf. "I do not apologize for addressing you in English -- as you understand the language I am told -- which is less difficult than my handwriting." S July 11 (143) £520

**ANs**, 22 July [n. y.]. Requesting the filling of a perscription: " ld. Byron presents his comp[limen]ts to Mr. Hudson & requests him to send immediately to this place 6 boxes of the pills to the perscription of Sir W. Thrighton. Ld. B. hopes to receive them immediately." Foxed & with repaired tear. Inlaid. Illus in cat rms Oct 11 (61) $1,000

# C

### Caesar, Caius Julius, 100-44 B.C.

**Ms**, Commentaires de Cesar avec des notes historiques, critiques et militaires par M. le comte Turpin de Crisse.... 4 parts in 2 vols, 4to, in contemp red mor gilt. Fuerstenberg - Schaefer copy S Dec 7 (92) £2,400

### Cage, John

**Autograph Ms** (2), working notebooks containing literary & compositional writings later collected in "M", [c.1970-71]. About 117 pp, 8vo, in 2 spiral-bound notebooks. 1 notebook sgd & inscr to Bob Moran. S May 15 (320) £13,500

**Autograph music**, sketches of pieces from Etudes Australes. 6 pp, 314mm by 240mm & 352mm by 278mm, 1 sheet framed, the others mtd loose on card within perspex frames. In pencil & blue crayon on ptd Ms sheets & 1 sheet of lined paper. C June 26 (250) £3,200

### Cagney, James, 1899-1986

**Ls s** (2), 27 Jul 1974 & 29 Oct 1975. 3 pp, 8vo & 4to. To Joseph Shipley, Jr. sg June 6 (29) $225

### Calder, Alexander, 1898-1976

**ALs**, 30 Sept 1944. 1 p, 4to. To Agnes Rindge Claflin. Suggesting dates for a meeting. star Mar 21 (660) DM370

— [1957]. 1 p. To George Staempfli. About works in progress. With a sgd sketch of a mobile design for the Brussels Theatre. wa Oct 28 (74) $900

— [n.d.]. 2 pp, 4to. To George Staempfli. About an alteration to a mobile. Sgd "Sandy". wa Oct 28 (73) $220

### California

— GOLD RUSH. - 2 A Ls s of W. H. Stoakes, written from San Francisco, 12 Sept 1850 & 13 June 1853. 8 pp, 4to. To Allen. The first about is inability to make a living at the mines; the second about his life as a farmer. cb June 25 (2404) $250

— GOLD RUSH. - 2 account ledgers of John Ball, dentist in California, 1851-62. Length not given, 8vo size, in calf gilt. pba Nov 16 (111) $550

— GOLD RUSH. - A Ls s (5) of J. H. Gamble, 12 Feb 1852 to 25 Dec 1859. 9 pp. To Joseph Kelly. From a later participant in the California gold rush over a span of 7 years. Larson collection pba Sept 24 (489) $950

— GOLD RUSH. - ALs of Alonzo W. Merrill, 9 July 1854. 3 pp, 9.75 by 7.75 inches. To his sister. Describing his life at Angel's Camp, Calaveras County CA. Larson collection pba Sept 24 (482) $475

— GOLD RUSH. - ALs of Charles Tyler of Pawtucket RI, 29 Jan 1849. 3 pp, 10 by 8 inches. Recipient unnamed. About his preparations to sail to California on the barque Velasco. Larson collection pba Sept 24 (478) $225

— GOLD RUSH. - ALs of Chauncey Taylor, 29 Sept 1850. 4 pp, 9.75 by 7.5 inches. About his life in San Francisco. Larson collection pba Sept 24 (480) $550

— GOLD RUSH. - ALs of D. Perkins, from Marysville, 29 June [1851]. 1 p, folio. To Master Perkins Nutte. About stabbings & hangings in San Francisco. cb June 25 (2413) $160

— GOLD RUSH. - ALs of G. W. Harris in San Francisco, 21 Apr 1855. 1 p, 4to. To Dr. Harry. Asking for money to buy dental instruments. cb June 25 (2407) $350

— GOLD RUSH. - ALs of H. L. Simpson, 16 June 1850. 5 pp, 10.75 by 8.5 inches. To Noah Simpson. About his overland trip in '49 and his experiences mining. Larson collection pba Sept 24 (476) $800

— GOLD RUSH. - ALs of James Nelson, 22 Jan 1859. 4 pp, 9.75 by 7.75 inches. Written from Weavervlle, to his sister, Mary Leavitt, in Wisconsin. About his own status as a gold seeker & giving his opinion of CA. Larson collection pba Sept 24 (488) $375

— GOLD RUSH. - ALs of Jason Whitmore, from Marysville, 19 Mar 1855. 4 pp, 4to. To Ann Griggs. Giving an account of his daily life. cb June 25 (2405) $220

— GOLD RUSH. - ALs of Jim H. Hardy from Sacramento, 19 May 1856. To a General. Deploring the plans of the vigilance committee of San Francisco to hang Jim Casey & Charley Cora. cb June 25 (2403) $550

— GOLD RUSH. - ALs of John D. Thomas, 21 Apr 1850, to Jacob Jones in Philadelphia. 4 pp, 4to. About his life in California & the town of Linda. cb June 25 (2398) $375

— GOLD RUSH. - ALs of John H. McKing, 28 July 1855. 4 pp, 975 by 7.75 inches. To Mrs. Harriet, his wife. Written from Sacramento, hoping that she will join him in CA as he is not going back to Illinois. Larson collection pba Sept 24 (485) $550

— GOLD RUSH. - ALs of John Nelsen, Jr., 21 Sept 1858. 2 pp, 9.75 by 7.75 inches. To his nephew, James. Written from San Francisco. About hunting for gold, which has become a way of life to him. Larson collection pba Sept 24 (487) $130

- GOLD RUSH. - ALs of Joseph Howard in Downieville to his brother in Philadelphia, 14 Aug 1852. 3 pp, 10 by 8 inch paper folded to 3 by 5. Sending his brother gold dust (not present) & describing his life. Larson collection pba Feb 12 (507) $325

- GOLD RUSH. - ALs of Mark Wooster, 11 Sept 1852. Written from Marysville CA to Burton N. Smith in CT. 6 pp, 10 by 7.5 pp. About his mining activities & giving advice about coming to California. Larson collection pba Sept 24 (479) $500

- GOLD RUSH. - ALs of Patrick Doyle, 6 Oct 1854. 3 pp, 9.75 by 7.75 inches, on single folded sheet. Written from Whiskey Bar CA to a friend. Asking for a loan & relating his experiences in the gold fields. Larson collection pba Sept 24 (483) $190

- GOLD RUSH. - ALs of R. C. Newton, 17 Nov 1855. 4 pp, 9.75 by 7.75 inches. To his aunt & uncle in VT. Written from San Francisco, expressing his enthusiasm for CA: "My plan would be for evey man woman and child in Vt. to pack up their dudds and start for Cal." Larson collection pba Sept 24 (484) $325

- GOLD RUSH. - ALs of Sanford O. Pease, 25 Feb 1855. 2 pp, 9.75 by 8 inches. To an uncle. Written from Orleans Flat, asking about a legacy; sends gloomy news about the status of gold mining in CA. Larson collection pba Sept 24 (486) $225

- GOLD RUSH. - ALs of Sullivan G. Morris, 1 Jan 1849. 3 pp, folio. To Ruben Button. Written aboard the U.S. Ship Yarmouth at San Francisco, about his trip to California in 1849. cb June 25 (2407) $350

- GOLD RUSH. - ALs of William T. Reynolds, 31 Aug 1851. 32 pp in a Gregory Express Pocket Letter Book, with transmittal envelope. Detailing his time in San Francisco and his joining of the Vigilance Committee. cb June 25 (2414) $1,300

- GOLD RUSH. - ALs of Wm. & Chas. E. Hense of San Francisco to Francis Fisher of Boston, 26 Apr 1850. 2 pp on 4-page lettersheet folded to form self-envelope. pba Nov 16 (112) $200

- GOLD RUSH. - Autograph Ms reminiscences of the California Gold Rush by a returned Australian. Australia, [n.d.]. 18 pp, 10 by 8 inches. Larson collection pba Sept 24 (493) $1,300

- GOLD RUSH. - Certificate for 1 share in the Stanislaus Central Bridge Company. Sonora, 4 Mar 1853. Filled out in ink to Benj. F. Moulton & sgd by Lewis F. Gunn & W. O. Byrne. pba Nov 16 (113) $325

- GOLD RUSH. - Certificate for 1 share in the South Fork Canal Company, Placerville, Eldorado County. Placerville, 1852. Filled out in ink & sgd by A. L. Taylor & B. F. Keene. pba Nov 16 (114) $200

- GOLD RUSH. - Document, 27 Mar 1854. 1 p, 12 by 7.75 inches. Bill of sale for mining claims of Peter Suthy in Sierra County to William R. Morgan along with a cabin, utensils & tools. Larson collection pba Sept 24 (490) $425

- GOLD RUSH. - Ds. 11 Dec 1863. 1 p, 8vo. Stock Certificate for the Tiunfo Gold & Silver Mining Co. Sgd by Edward P. Flint as president. pba Oct 26 (94) $190

- GOLD RUSH. - Ms overland diary of Jonathon Wykoff, 1 Apr to 25 July 1852. 132 pp, 5.75 by 3.75 inches, in diary vol. Detailing his journey from Cincinnati as far as Salt Lake City. Larson collection pba Sept 24 (620) $6,500

- GOLD RUSH. - Ms overland diary, 1 Apr 1849 at Pontotoc MS to 31 July 1851 in the California gold fields. About 156 pp. With related material. Larson collection pba Sept 24 (619) $9,000

- GOLD RUSH. - Ms, Record of Persons buried by C. H. Townswnd, Sexton and Undertaker - Placerville, Call. Placerville, 1858-65. 38 pp, in 11.75 by 7.25 lea-backed ledger. Giving name, place of origin, date of death, age at death, cause of death, grave site & remarks. At end are financial records. Larson collection pba Feb 12 (508) $2,500

- GOLD RUSH. - Partially ptd deed granting a town lot in Sonoma to Manuel Espinola, 20 Apr 1849. Has ptd Territory of California legend at top. pba Aug 8 (62) $400

- GOLD RUSH. - Series of 20 A Ls s of Leander Cummings, a schoolmaster in Occidental, 1878-1886. 40 pp, folio & 4to. To Edgar Cummings of Montpelier VT. cb June 25 (2406) $1,700

- GOLD RUSH. - Series of 4 A Ls s of W. H. Gardner, from Marysville, 10 July 1850 to 6 Sept 1853 & [n.d.], to his mother & sister. About life in California. cb June 25 (2399) $600

- GOLD RUSH. - Series of 47 A Ls s of S. S. Huey, 1852-71. 156 pp. mostly 4to. Recipient unnamed. Giving a running journal of places & events in Nevada City, Santa Clara, Stockton & Fort Reno. cb June 25 (2417) $8,000

- GOLD RUSH. - Typescript of Ms journal of Nathan W. Blanchard, 1853-1863. Maine & California, 1853-63. 45 pp, 10.75 by 7.5 inches, bound in cloth. About his experiences in California. Larson collection pba Sept 24 (475) $2,750

- GREAT SEAL. - Document sgd by Jno. McDougal, Governor, 26 Feb 1851. 1 p. Certification that the annexed (present) is a correct impression of the Great Seal of the State of California. Larson collection pba Sept 24 (347) $250

- SAN FRANCISCO FIRE. - ALs of Charles King to his mother in Maine, 29 June 1851. 3 pp, 9.75 by 7.5 inches. About restarting his life as a merchant after the May 1851 fire. Larson collection pba Sept 24 (477) $225

## Callas, Maria, 1923-77

ALs, 1 Sept 1973. 3 pp, 4to. To Leonidas Lantzounis. Apologizing that she did not help his friend; gives her schedule. sg Feb 1 (36) $750

- 26 June 1975. 3 pp, 4to. To Leonidas Lantzounis. About her love life. sg Feb 1 (37) $1,100

- 22 Aug 1975. 5 pp. To Leonidas Lantzounis. Reporting on her life. Ck Apr 12 (29) £1,400

- 22 Aug 1976. 2 pp. To Leonidas Lantzounis. Asking him for news; says she did not buy the house in Palm Beach. Ck Apr 12 (30) £380

# CALLAS

— 2 Oct 1976. 2 pp, 4to. To Leonidas Lantzounis. Commenting on her recently finished love affair. sg Feb 1 (38) $1,400

**Photograph, sgd,** [n.d.]. 8vo. As Tosca. Illus in cat. rms June 6 (180) $550

— Anr, [n.d.]. 14.5cm by 9cm. By Vivienne. S Dec 1 (108) £360

**Photograph, sgd & inscr,** 1971. 252mm by 204mm. Shoulder-length port, by Capital Records. Inscr to "my dearest children". Illus in cat. Marans collection. CE Apr 17 (226) $1,600

## Calligraphy

**Ms,** calligraphic arithmetical exercise book belonging to George Bishopp of Martocke, 1634. About 70 leaves written on 1 side only, 4to, in contemp vellum. Incorporates decorative borders, strapwork, emblematic flowers & beasts, most colored. pn Mar 14 (345) £3,200

— **Ms,** calligraphic arithmetical exercise book belonging to Cornelius Jesson, 30 July 1699. Some leaves lacking, 4to, in vellum. Sold w.a.f. pn Mar 14 (346) £220

— **Ms,** Formulary of sample letters. [Flanders, c.1525] 21 (of 22 leaves; lacking 1st leaf), 297mm by 220mm, sewn, loose in vellum portfolio. Each recto bears sample letter in alphabetical succession, each dated on a successive Saturday. Schaefer copy P Nov 1 (54) $6,000

— ADAM, JOSEPH. - Autograph Ms, Collection de Pieces d'Ecriture Anglaise Avec differentes Manieres de faire des Encres; Collection de Pieces d'Ecriture; Collection de Pieces D'Ecriture Latine; & Anleitung zur Schoenschreibkunst. [Wertheim, Germany, 1813]. 67 leaves, 405mm by 250mm. Contemp white silk. With numerous illusts in pen-&-ink & wash. HH Nov 14 (1) DM2,300

— ADAM, JOSEPH. - Autograph Ms, Principes et tous Genres d'ecriture. [Wertheim, Germany, 1811]. 36 leaves (3 blank), 350mm by 510mm. With numerous illus in pen-&-ink & wash. HH Nov 14 (2) DM2,500

— BARLOW, A. E. - Ms, The Raven by Edgar Allan Poe. [c.1915] 37 pp & colophon, on vellum, 35mm by 27mm, in mor gilt by Sangorski & Sutcliffe. S Nov 2 (332) £800 [Marlborough]

— CAMERON, SISTER MARY GERTRUDE, FOR RIVIERE. - The Rubaiyat of Omar Khayyam. [L, c.1920] 21 leaves plus 2 blank flyleaves, on vellum, in mor extra tree of life (upper cover) peacock (lower cover) bdg by Riviere, upper cover detached. With 6 historiated initials with watercolor landscape scenes & 8 vignettes of similar watercolor landscape scenes incorporating gilt & colored borders. With 44 four- to six-line opening initials heightened in gold & incorporating intricate floral borders. CE Feb 21 (14) $6,000

— DOBE, FRIEDRICH. - Roemische Elegien, by Johann Wolfgang von Goethe, [Berlin, 1922-23]. 20 leaves, vellum, 226mm by 175mm, in vellum bdg. In an uncial script imitating a 15th-cent humanistic hand. With 17 illuminated initials (1 large) & floral border. HH May 7 (14) DM220

— HEWITT, GRAILY. - Carmina quaedam by Catullus. [mid-20th cent] 9 leaves, 180mm by 125mm, in half

# AMERICAN BOOK PRICES CURRENT

mor by A. V. Hughes. Written in a humanistic hand in black ink with capitals in blue, red & burnished gold. sg Oct 19 (116) $950

— HORAE B. M. V. - Ms, miniature Book of Hours. [England, late 19th cent]. 92 leaves, vellum, 60mm by 41mm. In repousse silver bdg over red mor by Zaehnsdorf. In a fine gothic script. With 2- & 3-line illuminated initials in colors on gold ground, & 3 full-page miniatures. C Nov 29 (12) £2,100

— HUBERT OF SPROXTON, HENRY. - Autograph Ms, The Writing Schoolemaster... January the 11 1661. About 45 pp, oblong 4to, in cover formed from a vellum indenture. With ink & watercolor vignettes & decorations, including self-port of the scribe holding a pen, a port of Gen. George Monck, a bagpiper, a cellists & others. S Dec 18 (115) £5,500 [Quaritch]

— JARRY, NICHOLAS. - Prieres devotes. Paris, 1649. 90 leaves, including 3 blanks, on vellum, 123mm by 80mm, in contemp olive mor gilt by Florimond Badier to a fanfare design. With 4 full-page & 5 half-page miniatures. On final leaf a full-page monogram of interlacing capital letters BEEIIRRY in gold within a wreath of palm leaves. Each page within frame of burnished gold; Latin text in roman hand in sepia ink; French text & headings in italic hand in red or gold ink; main headings in gold & blue; versal initials in red; larger initials in blue, red & gold; 8 three-line initials in gold with floral decoration; 5 floral headpieces. Lignerolles - Hoe - Rahir - Rosset - l'Oncle copy C May 1 (84) £45,000

— MISSAL. - Ms, Missal, in English. [England, c.1892]. 268 leaves, vellum, 177mm by 142mm. White pigskin over wooden bds tooled in blind, by Johanna Birkenruth. In a gothic bookhand, written & illuminated in the manner of an early 15th-cent Ms. With 3-line initials in colors on gold ground, 5 small & 6 large miniatures, & 13 pp with full or partial borders of ivy leaves. C Nov 29 (11) £650

— POMFRET, LADY. - Ms, The Flower and the Leaf, by John Dryden. Illuminated Ms on vellum, title & 26 leaves, 229mm by 185mm, in orig velvet. Made by Lady Pomfret for presentation to Anne, Princess Royal, 1733. pn Nov 9 (432) £2,300

— SANGORSKI & SUTCLIFFE. - Ms on vellum, A Deserted Village, by Oliver Goldsmith. [N.d.]. 23 pp plus 8 vellum blanks, 9.25 by 6.75 inches, in mor extra. Title & 1st page of text with large initials in gold, blue & red with decorative surround of acanthus leaves, title with large miniature of man seated outside a village. S Dec 18 (540) £1,400 [Parker]

— ZSCHAU, ELSE. - Ms, Die Weise von Liebe und Tod des Christoph Rilke von Rainer Maria Rilke, [c.1928]. 52 pp, 26cm by 23.5cm, in vellum bdg. Including 29 illuminated initials. JG Sept 29 (336) DM200

## Cameron, Simon, 1799-1889

**ALs,** 14 Nov 1864. 1 p, 8vo. To Major General Hough. Concerning the arrangement of a furlough for private David Krouse. Illus in cat pba June 13 (8) $500

**Ds,** 6 Apr 1861. 1 p, 4to. Order that Amos Stickney is to be received as Cadet at West Point. Illus in cat. rms June 6 (7) $100

## Campbell, John W., 1910-71 —& Smith, Edward E., 1890-1965
**Typescript,** Piracy Preferred by Campbell. [1950s] 84 leaves, 279mm by 218mm, loose sheets. Heavily corrected & rewritten throughout by Smith. cb Oct 17 (523) $1,500

## Campe, Johann Heinrich, 1746-1818
**ALs,** [6 Mar 1773]. 2 pp, 4to. To [Prorektor Ferber]. Hoping to see his friends from his time at Helmstaedt again & giving his new address. Postscript to ALs from J.B. Ballenstedt to Ferber. star Mar 21 (417) DM700

## Campendonk, Heinrich, 1889-1957
**ALs,** 18 May 1922. 2 pp, folio. To Alfred Kubin. Thanking for some of Kubin's lithographs & talking about his new house. HH Nov 17 (3280) DM350

## Canetti, Elias, 1905-94
**ALs,** 20 Sept 1973. 1 p, 8vo. To Viktor Suchy. Thanking for a publication, & declining an invitation to a conference. HN May 15 (2519) DM1,200

— 12 July 1978. 1 p, 8vo. Recipient unnamed. Sending his autograph. star Mar 21 (42) DM620

## Canova, Antonio, 1757-1822
**AL,** 2 Sept 1815. 3 pp, 4to. To Mme Tambroni. Informing her that he has talked to the Emperor & to Prince Metternich about her husband. star Mar 21 (661) DM430

## Capek, Karel, 1890-1938
**ALs,** 22 Nov 1930. 1 p, 4to. Recipient unnamed. Saying he has never had to make a major decision in his life. star Mar 21 (43) DM550

## Capote, Truman, 1924-84
**Ms,** Excerpt from In Cold Blood. [n.d.] 1 p, 4to. Sgd. Detail in cat rms Oct 11 (63) $350

**Autograph postcard, sgd,** 24 June 1973. 1 p, no size given. To Mrs Ellis. Sending compliments. On card showing Claude Monet's painting The Poppy Field. pba June 13 (192) $100

## Cardozo, Benjamin Nathan, 1841-1935
**Ls,** 4 March 1930. 1 p, 8vo. To Carl Weinstein. Declining an invitation to speak for the Politics Club of CCNY. 2 letters of signature waterstained. sg Sept 28 (44) $275

## Cardozo, Benjamin Nathan, 1870-1938
**ALs,** 24 Jan 1916. 1 p, 8vo. To Joseph L. Gitterman. Expressing condolences on the death of his father. rms Mar 21 (339) $400

— BARMORE, CHARLES. - Engraving, bust port of Cardozo, [n.d.]. Framed, overall size 23.75 by 17.75 inches. Sgd by Cardozo & Barmore. Illus in cat. rms Mar 21 (340) $700

## Carlota, Empress of Mexico, 1840-1927
**AL,** [n.d.]. 1 p, 8vo. Recipient unnamed. Sending a dried flower for the Countess Schoenborn's collection. HN May 15 (2557) DM1,900

## Carlyle, Thomas, 1795-1881
**ALs,** 10 May 1850. 2 pp, 8vo. To Espinasse. Informing him that "the sublime veiled prophet" gives no hope of any employment; hopes to see him soon. pn June 13 (229) £300

**Photograph, sgd,** sgd, [July 1854]. Carte size. pn June 13 (230) £260

## Carmichael, Hoagy, 1899-1981
**Autograph quotation,** 3 bars from Stardust. [n.d.]. 1 p, 8.5 by 5.5 inches. Sgd. Illus in cat sg Sept 28 (45) $350

## Carnegie, Andrew, 1835-1919
**ALs,** 22 May 1903. 1 p, 8vo. To E. Bruce Low. Responding to a request for some words of advice to young men. rms Mar 21 (287) $510

**Cut signature,** 25 June 1899. No size given. Cut from an ALs. With a Brown Brother's print & 3 Keystone stereographs. Framed. Over-all size 18 by 22 inches. Illus in cat rms Oct 11 (9) $550

**Photograph, sgd,** [c.1905]. 139mm by 85mm. Bust port, by Pach Bros. Illus in cat. Marans collection. CE Apr 17 (122) $550

— Anr, [n.d.]. Postcard. Bust pose, by J. Beagles. Addressed to Winnie Robinson on verso. Illus in cat. rms Mar 21 (288) $450

**Photograph, sgd & inscr,** [n.d.]. 6.25 by 8.25 inch photo. Inscr to A. G. Foster. Mtd. Over-all size 10 by 12 inches. pba Oct 26 (95) $450

## Carol I, King of Romania, 1839-1914
**ALs,** 24 July 1867. 4 pp, 8vo. To [the future Emperor] Friedrich III. Insisting that efforts to contain the Jews in Moldavia are not antisemitic religious persecution but necessary police actions. star Mar 22 (1610) DM1,100

## Carol II, King of Romania, 1893-1953
**Ls,** 25 Aug 1938. 2 pp, 4to. To King Farouk of Egypt. Notifying him of the death of his mother. star Mar 22 (1611) DM250

## Caroline Matilda, Queen of Christian VII of Denmark, 1751-75
**ALs,** 9 July 1774. 2 pp, 4to. To Frau von Ompteda. Reporting about her situation in Celle. star Mar 22 (1210) DM850

## Carossa, Hans, 1878-1956
**Autograph Ms,** poem, beginning "Der Acker der Zeit...", 27 Feb 1939. 1 p, folio. Sgd & inscr to Johannes & Kaete Linke. star Mar 21 (44) DM750

**ALs,** 1 Sept 1943. 1 p, 4to. To Max Stebich. Accepting an invitation to lecture in Vienna. star Mar 21 (45) DM300

— 10 Feb 1951. 2 pp, 4to. To Herr Sturz. Thanking for a letter, referring to a new book, & praising Martin Buber. HN May 15 (2520) DM280

## Carrel, Alexis, 1873-1944
**Ls,** 22 Sept 1933. 1 p, 4to. To Dr. Frank H. Vizetelly. Discussing the way he pronounces his name: "It is

difficult to indicate the prounciation of my name. The first syllable is stressed, and the pronounciation is very similar to the American "Carroll"..." rms Oct 11 (64) $250

**Carroll, Charles, Signer from Maryland, 1737-1832**
ALs, 4 Nov 1800. 7 pp, 4to. To James McHenry. Discussing the "present critical situation of this country" & criticizing John Adams. P Dec 13 (59) $7,000
— 28-29 Mar 1822. 3 pp, 4to. To William Gibbons. About wheat rents & the growing of wheat. sg Feb 1 (40) $450
— 27 Nov 1827. 1 p, oblong 8vo. To William Gibbons. Giving instructions on farm work. sg Feb 1 (41) $425
**Check**, sgd, 20 Jan 1830. Payable to Prime, Ward, King & Co for $1,950. sg Feb 1 (42) $225

**Carroll, Lewis.** See: Dodgson, Charles Lutwidge

**Carter, James Earl ("Jimmy")**
Ls, 25 Feb 1991. 1 p, 4to. Recipient unnamed. Stating that he will not run for President in 1992 but will continue his work at the Carter Center. rms Mar 21 (167) $520
**Photograph**, sgd & inscr, [n.d.]. 8 by 10 inch photo. Color port photo. Inscr to Olen Jones. pba Feb 22 (216) $90

**Carter, James Earl ("Jimmy") —& Thatcher, Margaret**
**Photograph**, sgd, sgd by both, [n.d.]. 4to size, in color. rms Nov 30 (108) $350

**Carteret, Sir George, 1599?-1680**
Ds, 17 July 1663. 1 p, folio. Allocating money to the maintenance of over 4,000 men at sea for six months. Soiled & waterstained. rms Oct 11 (67) $950

**Cartlidge, Daniel**
**Autograph Ms**, Icones Plantarum aliquot primo Exoticarum tum Indigenarum, or the Figures of Several Plants...Drawn for Dr. Thos. Shortt.... L, 1734. Ms title, 4 pp of index & 202 leaves of watercolor drawings, 360cm by 225cm, in contemp calf, worn & rebacked. bba June 6 (76) £3,000 [Kafka]

**Cartwright, Alexander Joy, 1820-92**
ADs, 30 Aug 1862. 1 p, 4to. To George Richard. About money that he owes him. cb June 25 (2310) $700

**Carus, Carl Gustav, 1789-1869**
ALs, 10 Dec 1856. 1 p, 4to. To an unnamed pbr. Requesting copies of one of his works. star Mar 21 (131) DM320

**Caruso, Enrico, 1873-1921**
**Original drawing**, double caricature of himself & Umberto Giordano, sgd twice, 15 May 1905. 1 p, c.18.5cm by 27cm; framed. Sgd by Giordano & inscr with 2 bars from the aria Amor ti vieta from the opera Fedora. Illus in cat. S Dec 1 (122) £2,000
ALs, 28 Oct 1904. 4 pp on single sheet, 8vo. To a lady. Seeking help in geting specific types of stamped envelopes or postcards. With small sketch of a stamp. wa Oct 28 (129) $260
— 20 Nov 1913. 2 pp, 8vo. To [Rosa Scognamillo]. Sending theater tickets. rms June 6 (181) $425
— 16 Aug 1916. 4 pp on both sides, 4to. To Enrico Scognamillo. About his holiday in Italy & matters concerning the Metropolitan Opera. cb June 25 (2500) $950
— 3 Sept 1916. 4 pp, 4to. To Errico Scognamillo. Reporting that he has just returned from Southern Italy. rms June 6 (182) $500
— 26 May 1919. 2 pp, 8vo. To Enricao & Rosa Scognamillo. Thanking them for a gift & reminding them that they will be his guests the following Saturday. cb June 25 (2506) $220
— [n.d.]. 1 p, 4to, on a Western Union Cablegram. To Mrs. Rosa Scognamillo. Sending his regrets because he feels ill & sending New Year's greetings. With a self-caricature of himself, unshaven & unkempt. cb June 25 (2507) $1,300
**Autograph postcard**, sgd, 14 July 1914. To Enrico Scognamillo. Sending regards. Postcard has photo of Caruso in white suit, shoes & top hat. cb June 25 (2516) $275
— [n.d.]. To E. M. Scognamillo. Saying that he is busy & sending greetings. cb June 25 (2512) $350
— [n.d.]. To Gabriel Scognamillo. In a mixture of Italian & English, thanking him for a letter & says that he will soon be back in NY. cb June 25 (2513) $300
— [n.d.]. To Rosa Scognamillo. Sending greetings. On port postcard, sgd on recto. Illus in cat. rms June 6 (189) $325
ANs, 14 Nov 1916. 1 p, 8vo. To Gabriel Scognamillo. Sending thanks. On verso of a correspondence card with ptd self-caricature of Caruso as Canio. cb June 25 (2511) $150
— [n.d.]. 1 p, 8vo. Sending regards & thanks for the portrait of Peppinella. cb June 25 (2504) $160
**Caricature**, sgd, [n.d.]. 1 p, 4to. Of H. H. Higgins, General Manager of Covent Garden. cb June 25 (2509) $275
**Concert program**, 3 Sept 1909. 4to. For a concert given in Glasgow. Sgd on cover photo. Spotted. Ck Nov 17 (5) £95
**Group photograph**, [1914]. Postcard. Alighting from an open touring car. Sgd & inscr by Caruso. Addressed to Rosa Scognamillo on verso. Illus in cat. rms June 6 (190) $325
**Photograph**, sgd, [11 Oct 1911]. Postcard. Half length, by Hofmann. star Mar 22 (781) DM420
— Anr, [n.d.]. 5.75 by 4.25 inches; trimmed. 3-quarter length, by A. Dupont. Illus in cat. rms Mar 21 (247) $400
**Photograph**, sgd & inscr, 1907. 6.25 by 4.05 inches. As Don Jose in Carmen, by Aime Dupont. Inscr to Errico Scognamillo. Illus in cat. rms June 6 (188) $900
— Anr, [c.1910]. 195mm by 129mm. Half length, by C. Mishkin. Inscr to Margherita Cirindelli. Illus in cat. Marans collection. CE Apr 17 (227) $550
— Anr, 1 Jan 1911. 5 by 7.5 inches. Inscr to Rosa Scognamillo. cb June 25 (2503) $425

— Anr, 1914. 5.25 by 9.75 inches. Inscr diagonally in ink. cb June 25 (2502) $600
— Anr, [n.d.]. 5.5 by 10 inches. Inscr to Rosa. cb June 25 (2505) $275
— Anr, [n.d.]. 5.5 by 10 inches. In costume as Rodolfo. Inscr "Juliena Scognone!". cb June 25 (2515) $300
**Self-caricature,** sgd, 1905. 8vo. Mtd. Illus in cat. S May 15 (325) £580
— Anr, 1910. 39cm by 28.5cm. Playing golf; sgd. Illus in cat. S Dec 1 (116) £1,200
— Anr, [n.d.]. 7 by 4 inches (card). In ink & wash, sgd & inscr My Brother. Illus in cat. rms June 6 (186) $400
**Signature,** on a dinner invitation for Caruso at the Lotos Club, 5 Feb 1916. 300mm by 440mm. Sgd in lower right corner. wad Oct 18 (147) C$460

### Carver, George Washington, 1864-1943
**ALs,** 24 Jan 1927. 1 p, 4to. To Miss Ovington. Sending her an article & thanking her for a letter. Illus in cat sg Sept 28 (46) $500
— 24 Jan 1927. 1 p, 4to. To Mary White Ovington. Expressing pleasure that the information he had sent was of help to her. sg Mar 28 (28) $500
— 21 Apr 1927. 1 p, 4to. To Mary White Ovington. Praising her articles. sg Mar 28 (29) $600
— 24 Nov 1931. 2 pp, 4to. To Ralph Douberly. About spiritual inspiration: "...I write to my dear boys as I do not write to other people...Just as Paul's dear little Timothy was to him, and indeed for the same reason." With original holograph envelope. pba Oct 26 (96) $425

### Casals, Pablo, 1876-1973
**ALs,** 20 May [1910]. 1 p, 8vo. To A. Daudelot. About the music he will perform at a concert on the 28th. Addressed Casals on verso. pba June 13 (193) $100
**Photograph, sgd & inscr,** 1906. 164mm by 106mm. Shoulder-length port, by M. Buettinghausen. Inscr to Mme Ladenburg. Marans collection. CE Apr 17 (228) $550

### Castro, Fidel
**Ptd photograph,** 12 Feb [19]59. 278mm by 198mm, mtd. Stylized shoulder-length port, sgd & inscr to Hans Faxdal. Marans collection. CE Apr 17 (123) $900
**Signature,** [n.d.]. On Cuban 5-peso bill. rms Nov 30 (111) $600

### Castro, Manuel
**AL,** 23 May 1846. 1 page only, 11.75 by 8.25 inches. Recipient unidentified. Inquiring about a rumor of a civilian movement to preserve peace & order in the district. Larson collection pba Sept 24 (56) $500

### Cather, Willa, 1873-1947
**Ls,** 4 Dec 1943. 1 p, 4to. To Miss Pruette. About Death Comes for the Archbishop. wa Oct 28 (11) $850

### Catherine de Medicis, Queen of France, 1519-89
**ALs,** [c.13 June 1562]. 2 pp, folio. To her daughter Elizabeth, Queen of Spain. About the political situation in France. Illus in cat. star Mar 22 (1283) DM6,500

### Catherine I, Empress of Russia, 1684-1727
**Ds,** 10 Nov 1726. 1 p, folio. Grant of the proceeds from the sale of the Martem'yanov lands to Peter Chicherin. Forbes Magazine collection. CNY May 17 (212) $700

### Catherine II, Empress of Russia, 1729-96
**ALs,** 22 Jun 1775. 1 p, 4to. To Count Munnich. Ordering books and artwork. sg June 6 (30) $1,100
**AL,** [n.d.]. 1 p, 4to. To Count Munich. Inviting him to see her since she needs to talk to him. In French. Illus in cat. S May 15 (156) £600
**Ds,** 11 Jan 1763. 1 p, folio. Appointment of Katerina Maslova as chambermaid. Illus in cat. rms June 6 (330) $850
— 8 Nov 1768. 1 p, folio. Order to collect 2 rubles per year from all government peasants. Illus in cat. rms Mar 21 (248) $1,200
— 20 July 1771. 1 p, folio. Military discharge for Ludwig von Fock. star Mar 22 (1613) DM800

### Celan, Paul, 1920-70
**Ls,** 16 Aug 1957. 1 p, folio. Recipient unnamed. Reporting about his current work & recommending Klaus Demus's poems. star Mar 21 (47) DM2,000

### Celine, Louis Ferdinand Destouches, 1894-1961
**Autograph Ms,** chapter 3 of novel, D'un Chateau l'Autre [pbd 1957]. 18 pp, 4to. With revisions. With 3 pp from a later chapter. CE May 22 (78) $1,300
**Collection** of 5 A Ls s & 1 postcard photograph sgd, [1926-34]. 9 pp, various sizes. To Elizabeth Craig. In English. Laminated. CE May 22 (79) $2,200

### Certificates
— GARDENER'S CERTIFICATE. - Document, 28 Mar 1677. 1 leaf, 320mm by 583mm. Certificate that Melchart Hiesinger completed a year as journeyman in the service of Count Wolfgang zu Oettingen-Wallerstein; sgd by Michael Thier. HH Nov 14 (74) DM360
— GARDENER'S CERTIFICATE. - Document, 1 Apr 1678. 1 leaf, 314mm by 428mm. Certificate that Melchart Hiesinger completed a year as journeyman in the service of Prince Johann Adolff von Schwarzenberg; sgd by Georg Kubata. HH Nov 14 (75) DM360
— GARDENER'S CERTIFICATE. - Document, 23 Jan 1764. 1 p, folio. Journeyman's certificate for Johannes Oberleutner, sgd by Johann Valentin Schultz. In a calligraphic hand; including ornamental border & the arms of Prince Victor I Amadeus Adolph von Anhalt-Bernburg-Schaumburg-Hoym. star Mar 22 (1351) DM1,250

### Cervino, Marcello, 1501-55. See: Marcellus II, 1501-55

### Cezanne, Paul, 1839-1906
**ALs,** 30 Nov 1896. 2 pp, 8vo. To [Emile] Solari. Trying to set up a meeting. With minor fold breaks and a small piece missing from the margin. Illus in cat rms Oct 11 (72) $8,000

## Chadwick, James, 1891-1974

**Collection** of ALs & ANs, 7 June 1972. 2 pp, 4to & 8vo. Recipient unnamed. Referring to "the formal relations between the proton and the neutron". star Mar 21 (419) DM750

## Chagall, Marc, 1887-1985

**Ls,** 20 Oct 1965. 1 p, 4to. To Varian Fry. Saying he cannot be present for the Jewish Theological Seminary award ceremony. sg June 6 (31) $375

— 15 Nov 1965. 1 p, 4to. To Varian Fry. Concerning the lithograph format for the Emergency Rescue Committee. sg June 6 (32) $275

— 29 Nov 1967. 1 p, 4to. To Mrs. Kermit Roosevelt. Saying he has long since sent the lithograph for the International Rescue Committee. sg June 6 (33) $325

**Ns,** 29 Dec 1961. 1 p, 8vo. Recipient unnamed. Accepting the invitation "de faire partie de votre Comite encyclopedique". HN May 15 (2521) DM400

— 7 July 1973. 8vo. Ptd invitation to the opening of an exhibition in Paris; including colored lithograph. HH May 9 (2427) DM700

**Ptd photograph,** 1934. 166mm by 109mm, mtd. Shoulder-length port. Illus in cat. Marans collection. CE Apr 17 (203) $600

## Chailly, Luciano

**Autograph music,** sketches for his Improvvisazione N. 7 per flauto (Dialogo), [n.d.]. 2 pp, 4to. In pencil. With a photograph. star Mar 22 (782) DM220

## Chamberlain, Houston Stewart, 1855-1927

**ALs,** 19 Aug 1896. 3 pp, 8vo. To George Davidsohn. Offering information about the Bayreuth festival. HN May 15 (2522) DM310

## Chamberlain, Joshua Lawrence, 1828-1914

**Check,** 23 Sept 1867. 1 p, 3 by 7.25 inches. $70.60 payable to J E Kingsley & Co. or order. Sgd as "J. L. Chamberlain". Illus in cat pba Oct 26 (160) $750

## Chamberlain, Neville, 1869-1940

**Ls,** 25 Apr 1940. 1 p, 4to. To Sir Walter Halsey. Thanking for some tickets. With a photograph. Illus in cat. rms June 6 (624) $275

## Chamisso, Adelbert von, 1781-1838

**ANs,** [n.d.]. 1 pp, 12mo. To Franz von Gaudy. Referring to a Ms by G. Schwab. star Mar 21 (48) DM320

## Chandrasekhar, Subrahmanyan

**Autograph Ms,** essay, Of Some Famous Men, [pbd 1976]. 8 pp, 4to. Fragment; sgd at head. With Ls, 1978; letter of transmittal. star Mar 21 (420) DM440

## Channing, William Ellery, 1780-1842

**ALs,** 14 Jan 1825. 1 p, 4to. To unnamed recipient. Concerning probabting a will. pba June 13 (242) $80

## Chaplin, Charles, 1889-1977

**Ms,** comedy sketch, Twelve Just Men. 22 pp, part typescript & part hand-written in an unknown hand. With anr version in Ms. Ck Dec 14 (244) $2,600

**Group photograph,** sgd, 11 Jan 1917. Showing him on a fishing trip. Also sgd by Cecil E. Reynolds & Capt. Edmunon. Ck Dec 14 (246) £420

**Photograph, sgd & inscr,** 1928. 13.5 by 10.5 inches. "Yours Faithfully Charlie Chaplin, 1928". Ck Apr 12 (31) £300

— Anr, 1941. 4to. Waist-length pose. Illus in cat. rms Mar 21 (249) $650

— Anr, [n.d.]. Postcard size. Showing Chaplin & Edna Purviance. Inscr by Chaplin later. Ck Dec 14 (243) £150

**Signature,** 5 Oct 1921. On program cover for his movie The Kid. CE June 12 (14) $600

## Charcot, Jean Martin, 1825-93

**ALs,** [n.d.]. 1 p, 8vo. Recipient & content not indicated. Framed with port. CE June 12 (15) $160

## Charles I, King of England, 1600-49

**Ls,** 4 June 1628. 2 pp, folio. To Viscount Falkland, Deputy General of Ireland. Confirming a land grant to Sir William Talbot. S Dec 18 (448) £700 [De Burca]

**Ds,** 29 May 1627. 1 p, on vellum, 9.25 by 13 inches. Authorizing payments to be made to the Gardener at Theobalds, seat of the Earl of Salisbury. S Dec 18 (447) £700 [Maggs]

— 21 Apr 1643. 1 p, 406mm by 305mm. Ordering an annual pension for William Earl of Landwirk. Countersgd by 14 nobles. Spotted. With frayed margins and a repaired fold. Docketed on verso. P Dec 12 (52) $1,200

— Pictures & Furniture. - Ms, 1649. 29 leaves only, folio, later wraps. Inventory of his pictures & furniture drawn up by the Commonwealth Committee of Trustees for the Sale of the Late King's Goods. Sgd by 4 Commissioners, including George Wither. Illus in cat S July 11 (379) £10,000

## Charles II, King of England, 1630-85

**ALs,** 27 Sept [1650]. 1 p, 4to. To Middleton. About mutual understanding: "I shall be in redines to meete you, and keep time and, be you sure to sease upon disafected persons, and to prevent the troups dispersed in Angus and Mairnes...." S Dec 18 (450) £950 [Maggs]

**Ls s** (2), 27 Apr & 28 May 1650. 2 pp, 4to. To Sir Edward Walker. Authorizing payments. S Dec 18 (451) £1,100 [Browning]

**Ds,** 29 Oct 1660. 1 p, folio. Righting the fact that Captain Abraham Davis has mistakenly been deprived of a land grant: " forthwith put into the same condicon [sic] with others in actuall service that he may partake of Our gracious favour intended to such Our officers & souldiers [sic] as have served faithfully..." Foxed. Signature light. rms Oct 11 (73) $950

— Jan 1663. 1 p. Warrant for the Privy Council to pay Henrietta & Elizabeth Killigrew. With related material. Ck Apr 12 (32) £180

— 23 Aug 1672. 1 p, folio. Order to appoint Charles Cotterell assistant to his father, Sir Charles Cotterell. Countersgd by Arlington. pn Nov 9 (381) £550

— 6 Sept 1672. 1 p, folio. Appointment of John Knight as an Under- or Sub-Searcher of the Port of London. Countersgd by Lord Arlington. pn Nov 9 (382) £460

— 16 Sept 1672. 1 p, folio. Pardon of Susanna Mansell & Tabitha Stone for forging or defacing coin of the realm. Countersgd by Sec. of State Henry Coventry. pn Nov 9 (383) £800

**Charles III, Prince de Monaco, 1818-89**

ALs, 16 July 1856. 1 p, folio. To King Ferdinand II of the Two Sicilies. Notifying him of the death of his father. star Mar 22 (1409) DM340

**Charles V, Emperor, 1500-58**

Ls, 28 Apr 1520. 1 p, folio. To Markgraf Ernst I von Baden. Requesting him not to acquire any further property in Austrian territories. Silked. star Mar 22 (1574) DM2,000

— 23 July 1523. 1 p, folio. To the Duke of Arcos. Concerning the purchase of bread in Andalucia for the use of troops. C Nov 29 (144) £550

— 21 June 1540. 1 p, 4to. To Francisco Vasquez De Coronado. Written by President of the Council of the Indies, Francisco Garcia de Loyasa, on behalf of Charles. Officially authorizing Coronado's North American expedition & discussing the Niza expedition report. Verso initialed by Diego Beltran, Licenciado Juan Suarez de Carvajal, Bishop of Lugo & Licenciado Guttierez Velazquez de Lugo. Docketed. with old folds & a marginal stain. Illus in cat CNY Dec 15 (58) $80,000

— 27 May 1543. 1 p, folio. To the Abbess of Herford. Inviting her to a diet at Speyer. star Mar 22 (1576) DM1,200

— 20 Feb 1548. 45cm by 62cm. To the magistrate of the town of Lueneburg. Giving instructions concering a prebend. HH May 9 (2490) DM1,100

Document, 6 June 1546. Grant of Nobility to Juan de Soto & Andres de Soto. 42 leaves, vellum, 320mm by 220mm, orig lea extra with 2 red velvet panels embroidered with the arms of the father & the mother. With 2 full-page miniatures added in 1547, 3 illuminated borders, 1 large illuminated initials, 34 words or phrases & 53 initials in gold on red grounds. Illuminated border on vellum cut out & pasted over border painted on last page. CE Sept 27 (17) $4,200

— 3 July 1553. 1 p, folio. Order addressed to the Governor of Tournai concerning improvements in the cavalry. star Mar 22 (1577) DM300

**Charles VI, Emperor, 1685-1740**

ALs, 27 May 1711. 1 p, folio. To an unnamed prince. Referring to his brother's death & promising his friendship. Illus in cat. HH May 9 (2491) DM1,300

Ls, 10 May 1718. 3 pp, folio. To the mayor & council of the city of Ulm. Inquiring about Swiss merchants. star Mar 22 (1593) DM350

Ds, 15 Dec 1719. 21 pp, 4to, in red velvet. Patent of nobility for Johann Jacob Matheser. Including full-page achievement of the arms in gold, silver & colors. star Mar 22 (1594) DM1,300

**Charles VII, Emperor, 1697-1745**

Ls, 7 Jan 1734. 1 p, folio. To Herzog Friedrich III of Sachsen-Gotha. As Elector of Bavaria, returning New Year's wishes. star Mar 22 (1166) DM440

— 23 Apr 1742. 1 p, folio. To an unnamed Elector. Announcing an envoy. HH May 9 (2492) DM450

**Charles X, King of France, 1757-1836**

Ds, 1 July 1827. 2 pp, folio. Naming four men as "Conseiller de Prefecture" and replacing others to serve in other functions. sg June 6 (34) $200

**Charles XI, King of Sweden, 1655-97**

Ds, 30 May 1687. 3 pp, folio. Order addressed to Johan Egegreens concerning a financial matter. HH May 9 (2494) DM600

— 4 June 1695. 4 pp, folio. Appointment for Hindrich Schefer as master of mines. star Mar 22 (1648) DM320

**Charles XII, King of Sweden, 1682-1718**

ALs, 17 Feb [1716]. 1 p, 4to. To [the future King] Frederik I of Sweden. Informing him that he has instructed Major Delvich to put monies in his possession at recipient's disposal. star Mar 22 (1649) DM2,800

**Charles XIII, King of Sweden, 1748-1818**

Ls, 29 Jan 1810. 2 pp, folio. To Jerome Bonaparte, King of Westfalia. Notifying him of the arrival of his appointed successor Christian von Holstein at the Swedish court. star Mar 22 (1652) DM500

**Charles XIV John, King of Sweden, 1763-1844**

Ls, [16 Fructidor 13]. 1 p, no size given. About payment for reparations concerning the camp at Lunebourg. Sgd as " J. Bernadotte". P Dec 12 (304) $150

Ds, [6 Sept 1800]. 1 p, folio. Military promotion for Lieut. Alexandre Villatte. HH May 9 (2523) DM500

**Chase, Samuel, Signer from Maryland**

ALs, 31 May 1803. 2 pp, folio. To James Winchester. Discussing "the amount of the salvage to be allowed on the french Ship Blaireau". P Dec 13 (63) $3,250

Ds, 27 Mar 1858. 1 p, oblong folio. Appointment of Solomon Hoover as a Notary Public. Countersgd by A. P. Russell. Framed with Brady photo. rms Nov 30 (13) $400

**Chekhov, Anton, 1860-1904**

Collection of ALs & photograph, sgd & inscr, 29 Feb 1899 & 16 Oct 1900. 1 p, 8vo, & 14cm by 10cm (image). To Dora V. Zhook. Expressing pleasure at her request to trans his short stories into English. With related material. S May 15 (157) £3,000

ALs, 13 May 1902. 1 p, 8vo. Recipient unnamed. Recommending a sanatorium & giving details of the treatment. Illus in cat. S May 15 (158) £2,600

— 13 Apr 1904. 3 pp, 8vo. To Alexander Amfiteatrov. Commenting on recipient's reviews & various works he has been reading. Illus in cat. star Mar 21 (363) DM9,500

**Chelard, Hippolyte Andre, 1789-1861**
**Autograph quotation,** trio of the witches, from his opera Macbeth, 4 June 1859. 1 p, 8vo. Sgd. star Mar 22 (785) DM300

**Chennault, Claire Lee, 1893-1958**
**Ls,** 12 Sept 1947. 1 p, 4to. To J. H. Leib. Sending a resume of an address (not present). rms Mar 21 (221) $320

**Chertok, Boris E.**
[A group of 5 documents relating to Chertok's activities at Pennemuende at the end of World War II sold at Sotheby's New York on 16 Mar 1996, lot 8, for $2,400]

**Cherubini, Luigi, 1760-1842**
**Autograph music,** draft of a song, [n.d.]. 1 p, 4to. 14 bars, scored for voice. Including musical Ms in a scribe's hand on verso. star Mar 22 (786) DM1,250
**Collection** of 8 ALs s & 2 Ls s, 1806-42, no size given. To various French government officials concerning finances for his company & his music. With engraved port. Illus in cat pba Feb 22 (30) $950
**ALs,** 9 Oct 1813. 1 p, 4to. To Joachim Lebreton. Declining to compete against Pierre Alexandre Monsigny as a candidate for election to an academy. star Mar 22 (787) DM650

**Chiang Kai-shek, 1887-1975**
**Photograph, sgd,** [c.1950]. 145mm by 94mm. By Hu Chung Hsien. Marans collection. CE Apr 17 (124) $950

**Chiang Kai-shek, 1887-1975 —&**
**Soong Mei-ling (Mme. Chiang Kai-shek)**
**Photograph, sgd & inscr,** [1927]. 9.5 by 7 inches. Wedding picture inscr to Captain & Mrs. Steele. sg June 6 (35) $2,000

**China**
— OPIUM WAR. - Ms, 2 journals kept by an army officer stationed in India, 1838-44. 70 pp & c.40 pp, foio & 4to, calf & wraps. One describing his voyage as part of the British expeditionary force dispatched to the Yangtze; the other kept during a recruiting tour in the Carnatic. S July 11 (389) £700

**Chodowiecki, Daniel, 1726-1801**
**Proof copy,** 12 etchings to illus Salomon Gessner's Idyllen, 9 Jan 1771. On a single sheet, 22cm by 36.5cm. Including autograph draft of captions & note of approval sgd by 4 members of the Berlin Academy of Science. star Mar 21 (662) DM5,000

**Chopin, Frederic, 1810-49**
**Autograph music,** Nocturne in C minor, Op.48 no 1, & Nocturne in F sharp minor, Op.48 no 2, [1841]. 20 pp, folio. Working Ms, notated on 4 systems per page of 2 & 3 staves. Including 3 tpp; sgd & inscr to Emilie Duperre. S Dec 1 (123) £170,400
**ALs,** [n.d.], "Thursday". 1 p, 4to. To Fromental Halevy. Asking for opera tickets. Illus in cat. star Mar 22 (788) DM17,000
See also: Sand, George

**Christian, Herzog von Braunschweig-Lueneburg, 1566-1633**
**Ds,** 17 Mar 1618. 1 p, folio. Order regarding houses belonging to the Duke at Celle. FD May 14 (1098) DM480

**Christian I, Fuerst von Anhalt-Bernburg, 1568-1630**
**Ls,** 20 June 1629. 1 p, folio. To [his brother Ludwig?]. Informing him about the peace treaty between Denmark & the Emperor, & discussing troop movements. star Mar 22 (1228) DM950

**Christian IV, King of Denmark, 1577-1648**
**Ls,** 10 Mar 1619. 2 pp, folio. To Lady Ruthven. Asking her to support his sister Queen Anne of England in her depressed state of mind. star Mar 22 (1229) DM950

**Christie, Agatha, 1891-1976**
**Ls s** (2), 2 May 1969 & 24 Nov 1970. To Mr. & Mrs. Holden. With a paperback Ed of Death Comes as the End, sgd by Christie on half-title. Ck Apr 12 (33) £540
**Signature,** [n.d.]. On a 12mo card. Mtd & framed. rms Oct 11 (82) $325

**Christina, Queen of Sweden, 1626-89**
**Ds,** 13 Jan 1645. 1 p, folio. Safeguard for Franciscus Marree. star Mar 22 (1230) DM700

**Christy, Howard Chandler, 1873-1952**
**Original drawing,** Pen & ink sketch of a woman's profile. 26 May 1912. 1 p, 4to. Inscr to Mr. McCarthy. Toned. pba Oct 26 (8) $150
**Photograph, sgd & inscr,** [n.d.]. Sepia 8vo bust photo. A close view of Christy with pipe in mouth. Inscr & sgd. sg Sept 28 (50) $110

**Chrysler, Walter P., 1875-1940**
**Ls,** 1 May 1926. 2 pp, 4to. To Walter Chrysler, Jr. About colors of cars: " One of the new color schemes is Pheasant Green, which is a very beautiful shade of light green, with beads painted black and Partridge Cream striping. I would not suggest silver because it tarnishes and looks very bad in time." rms Oct 11 (83) $1,700
— 29 Nov 1926. 1 p, 4to. To his son, Walter. Sending family news; comments on the special report he has received from Hotchkiss & suggests ways for Walter to improve his grades. rms Nov 30 (121) $1,400
— 29 Oct 1930. 1 p, 4to. To his son, Walter, at Dartmouth. Sending family news. rms Nov 30 (122) $900
— 31 Mar 1937. 1 p, 4to. To Edna Harvey. About his nieces' recovery: "Your mother has told me that you are out at Poettenger Sanatorium and that you have been put on a strict routine by the doctors there. I am quite sure that with the fine care and attention you are having and the wonderful climate that you will be able to get yourself back into shape..." Illus in cat rms Oct 11 (84) $2,200
**Photograph, sgd,** 22 Aug [19]33. 252mm by 202mm. Shoulder-length port, by Blank & Stoller. Illus in cat. Marans collection. CE Apr 17 (108) $750

## Churchill, Sir Winston L. S., 1874-1965

**Typescript,** memorandum to Sir Robert Chambers written while preparing the People's Budget of 1909. 1 p, 4to, sgd & dated 19 July 1909. pn Nov 9 (386) £500

— Typescript, message commemorating the Battle of Britain broadcast on 16 Sept 1961. 1 p, 4to, sgd. pn Mar 14 (367) £1,500

**ALs,** 7 Nov 1913. 1 p, 8vo. To Admiral Mundy. Offering him the appointment of Admiral Superintendent of HM Dockyard, Devonport. sg June 6 (36) $2,000

— 6 Jan 1931. 1 p, no size given. To Mr. Wethersall. Thanks his old school friend for a supportive letter. Creased. With tape repair. Ck Nov 17 (35) £450

— 5 Feb 1939. 1 p, 8vo. To Lord Beaverbrook. Expressing surprise at what appeared in the Sunday Express about Epping. S Dec 18 (487) £1,300 [Levine]

— 10 Sept 1944. 2 pp, 4to. To Lorna Wingate. Letter of condolence, paying tribute to Gen. Wingate. S July 11 (377) £10,500

**Ls,** 15 Mar 1901. 1 p, 8vo. To Sir John Puleston. About the Colville debate. Lower half discolored, affecting signature. wd Nov 15 (6) $225

— 12 Jan 1905. 1 p, 8vo. To A. D. Armour. Thanking him for a letter. cb June 25 (2518) $1,800

— 29 July 1909. 1 p, 4to. To Sir Robert Chalmers. Asking about the possible outcome should Lloyd George's People's Budget of 1909 be defeated in the House of Lords. pn Mar 14 (364) £880

— 11 Jan 1919. 1 p, 4to. To Mr. Stevenson. Informing him of his appointment as Surveyor General of Supply at the War Office. Framed with a port. Illus in cat. rms Mar 21 (257) $1,200

— 21 June 1923. 1 p, no size given. To Mr. Tilden. About a bore hole for a water supply. Creased. With holes. With ALs from Clementine Churchill to Mr. Tilden about Chartwell. Ck Nov 17 (34) £360

— 22 Apr 1938. 1 p, 4to. To Philip Guedalla. Commenting that "I feel sure that what has happened has done no end of harm in the United States." With retained copy of Guedalla's letter to Churchill of 20 Apr 1938 on public opinion in America going against the British following the government decision to "fraternize" with the Nazis. S Dec 18 (499) £800 [Bennett]

— 8 Dec 1939. 1 p, 4to. To Minister of Shipping Sir John Gilmour. Written as first Lord of the Admiralty, pressing for an agreement of figures & methods of calculation. S Dec 18 (497) £1,400 [Fairfax]

— 1 Jan 1940. 3 pp, 4to. To Minister of Shipping Sir John Gilmour. Written as first Lord of the Admiralty, discussing shipping losses. S Dec 18 (498) £3,000 [Wilson]

— 15 Mar 1941. 1 p, 4to. To Philip Guedalla. About his proposed biography of Churchill. S Dec 18 (500) £700 [Wilson]

— 8 Oct 1941. 1 p, 4to. To Doris Harrison. Thanking her for a poster from Cuba. With holograph salutation & subscription. With retained draft of Miss Harrison's letter. S Dec 18 (493) £600 [Stodolski]

— 26 Nov 1941. 1 p, 4to. To Philip Guedalla. Thanking him for a copy of his biography of Churchill. With autograph salutation & subscription. S Dec 18 (501) £850 [Levine]

— 23 Mar 1943. 1 p, no size given. To Sir Adrian Pollock. Thanking "the Court Common Council of the City of London an expression of my deep appreciation of the honor they have done me in proposing to confer upon me the Freedom of the City". With orig envelope. Illus in cat Ck Nov 17 (39) £650

— 10 July 1944. 1 p, 4to. To Sir Alexander Walker. Denying a report that a visit by the President to Scotland had been arranged. S July 11 (395) £1,000

— 10 Jan 1945. 1 p, 4to. To Mrs. Guedalla. Sending her condolences on her husband's death. S Dec 18 (502) £850 [Stodolski]

— 14 Mar 1945. 1 p, 4to. To Lorna Wingate. Supporting her plan for a memorial to her husband in Jerusalem. S July 11 (378) £6,000

— 9 Aug 1946. 1 p, no size given. To Mr. Dalkmann. Thanking him for a box of cigars "made especially for Goring, which you have kindly sent me...I shall keep these cigars as an interesting curiosity." Mtd. Signature faded. Ck Nov 17 (43) £550

— 4 Apr 1950. 1 p, 8vo. To H. D. Wiggins. Thanking him for help in the General Election. pn Nov 9 (391) £320

— 14 Aug 1951. 1 p, no size given. To Mr. Gray. Thanking him for making " the film of the robin. It is a great success and gives much amusement to the family." With sgd 6 by 4 inch port photo & orig envelope. Ck Nov 17 (46) £1,200

— 20 Nov 1951. 1 p, 4to. To Mrs. Gravener of Woodford Green. Thanking her for valuable service in the election campaign. With related material. S Dec 18 (496) £600 [Bennett]

— 19 Apr 1954. 1 p, 8vo. To Wolfgang von Tirpitz. Thanking for a letter. HH May 9 (2428) DM1,050

— 22 Nov 1954. 1 p, 8vo. To Fieldfare [Henry Fearon]. Acknowledging receipt of his book on Poy [cartoonist Percy Hutton Fearon]. With holograph addition. Sold with a copy of Poy's Churchill, by Fieldfare. b Dec 5 (238) £550

— 18 June 1955. 1 p, 4to. To Mr. K. Lilley. Thanking him for help with the General Election. Illus in cat pba Oct 26 (347) $1,300

— June 1955. 1 p. To Miss D. M. Bayes. Thanking her for help in the election. Ck Apr 12 (45) £420

— 10 Dec 1955. 1 p, 8vo. To Kenneth Lilley. Thanking Lilley for his letter. pba Feb 22 (296) $850

— 3 May 1961. 1 p, 4to. To the Marquess of Angelsey. Thanking him for a book on his ancestor & for the inscr in it. S Dec 18 (380) £340 [Levine]

**Ds,** 28 March 1910. 1 p, no size given. Certificate of naturalization for Samuel Shevloff. Sgd as Home Secretary. Browned & soiled and creased. With related material. Ck Nov 17 (31) £320

— 28 Mar 1910. 2 pp, folio. Certificate of Naturalization for Samuel Sherloff. rms June 6 (338) $550

— 1 Feb 1911. 2 pp, folio. Certificate of Naturalisation, sgd as Home Secretary. bba Apr 11 (245) £340 [Linehan]

# CHURCHILL

— [1951]. 2 pp, no size given. Press release about government: "The Socialist Government have drifted from crisis to crisis with shifting and vacillating policies. In this grave hour the return of a united and stable government with the widest national support, is essential to our continued national existence as a world power. The Socialist government is deeply divided and could not form such a Government..." Sgd. Signature faded. Overall size is 16.5 by 18.5 inches. Framed. Ck Nov 17 (48) £320

**Check,** sgd, 21 July 1956. Payable for 8 shillings to the Hon Mrs. Henley. Framed. S July 11 (393) £680

**Lithographed port,** 1911. 15.5 by 10.5 inch chromolithograph by Nibs. Mtd. Soiled. With abrasions. Ck Nov 17 (32) £70

**Photograph, sgd,** 1905. 136mm by 85mm. Half length, by Thomson. Newspaper clipping attached to verso. Illus in cat. Marans collection. CE Apr 17 (125) $3,000

— Anr, [c.9 May 1908]. Postcard size. With holograph addressed envelope to Grace Rattray. S Dec 18 (491) £800 [Levine]

— Anr, 1908. 5.5 by 3.5 inch copy photo. Sgd as "Winston S. Churchill". Creased. Ck Nov 17 (30) £300

— Anr, Dec 1941. 9 by 7.5 inches, port by Cecil Beaton. With Ls of Clementine Churchill, 16 Dec 1941, returning the photograph, which her husband has sgd, to Mrs. Bigsworth. S Dec 18 (490) £1,100 [Bennett]

— Anr, 1941. 4to size. Sgd on bottom margin. rms Nov 30 (123) £1,300

— Anr, 26 July 1945. 7 by 5 inch port photo. Sgd as "W. S. Churchill". With related material. Ck Nov 17 (40) £650

— Anr, 1948. 9 by 7.25 inch photo. Of Churchill riding. Sgd. Spotted. Framed. Ck Nov 17 (45) £900

— Anr, [c.1955]. 5.5 by 4 inch photo. Of Churchill smoking a cigar and painting a landscape. Mtd. Ck Nov 17 (50) £750

— Anr, [n.d.]. 9 by 6 inch port photo. Sgd as " W. S. Churchill". Ck Nov 17 (37) £350

— Anr, [n.d.]. 13 by 10.5 inch port photo. Scratched & stained with some fading of signature. Framed. Illus in cat Ck Nov 17 (41) £700

**Ptd photograph,** 1943. Port medallion, 121mm by 96mm. Sgd & dated below. CE June 12 (16) $750
See also: Roosevelt, Franklin D. & Churchill

## Cicero, Marcus Tullius, 106-43 B.C.

**Ms,** De Senectute, De Amicitia, Paradoxica Stoicorum & 2 other texts in Latin. [Northeast Italy, 3d quarter of 15th cent] 60 leaves plus 2 orig flyleaves (torn), on vellum, 204mm by 135mm, in contemp panelled sheep over wooden bds. In brown ink in a humanistic minuscule bookhand. With 2 3-line illuminated initials in gold on blue, green & red ground & 3 larger white-vine initials in burnished gold on blue grounds, the intertwined vinestems infilled in red & green. C Apr 3 (4) £15,000

## Cimarosa, Domenico, 1749-1801

**Autograph music,** fragment from the duet Carolina - Paolino from the 2d act of his opera Il matrimonio segreto, [n.d.]. 2 pp, 4to. 6 bars, in full score. Illus in cat. star Mar 22 (789) DM2,600

— Autograph music, recitativo accompagnato for soprano & orchestra from an unidentified opera, [n.d.]. 6 pp, 4to, on 16- & 12-stave papers, in vellum-backed bds. Beginning "D'un incostante, e perfido amatore..."; in full score. S May 15 (329) £500

## Citroen, Andre, 1878-1935

**Photograph, sgd & inscr,** [c.1915]. 190mm by 105mm, mtd. 3-quarter-length port, in uniform; by Cautin & Berger. Marans collection. CE Apr 17 (109) $350

## Civil War, American

**Ms,** Roster of Company J of the 100th U.S. Colored Infantry, Oct 1864 1 p, folio. cb June 25 (2427) $420

**Signature,** [28 Jan to 8 Mar 1869]. 1 p, 4to. Signatures of 8 important Union generals including Grant, Sherman & Farragut gathered for a court of inquiry. Detail in cat sg Sept 28 (65) $3,200

— BATCHELDER, FRANK A. - ALs, 14 Apr 1862. 4 pp, 4to. To an unnamed cousin. Giving an eyewitness account of the Battle of the Monitor & Merrimac. P Dec 13 (65) $1,500

— BENEDICT, WILLIS. - Collection of c.140 letters, 31 Aug 1861 to 18 June 1865. Length not stated. To his brother Edward. Reporting about his life as a member of the 15th Connecticut Volunteers. P Dec 13 (64) $7,000

— BRATTON, JOHN. - Ls. 20 Sept 1861. 3 pp, 8vo. To Major Manigault. Releasing arms from the express office in Richmond. Sgd as Lieutenant, Company C, 6th Regiment. Confederate. sg Sept 28 (54) $550

— DAVIS, JAMES M. M. - Journal. 1864-5. 56 pp, 24mo. In black oilcloth binding. Concerning his battery's activities. CNY Dec 15 (56) $3,500

— GREENHOW, ROSE O'NEAL. - ALs. 15 Dec [c.1850]. 4 pp, 8vo. To "My dear Judge" [John Y. Mason]. About her life in California. CNY Dec 15 (55) $2,800

— HAMMOND, J. H. - ALs. 15 Dec 1863. 8 pp, 4to. To General McClellan. Analysis of the Battle of Chickamauga compiled as Assistant Adjutant-General, 15th Army Corps: "Rosecrans has been badly beaten at Chickamauga, and with a loss of 23,000 men killed, wounded & prisoners, had retreated in confusion to Chattanooga & then lay at the mercy of the enemy..." Featuring a map of the attack on Missionary Ridge. Inlaid to larger sheets. Illus in cat sg Sept 28 (53) $3,800

— LASIMES, J. W. - ALs.9 July 1865. 4 pp, no size given. To unnamed recipient. Concerning volunteers leaving home to fight in Sherman's army. pba June 13 (6) $375

— LITTLEJOHN, DEWITT CLINTON. - ALs. 13 Mar 1865. 1 p, 8vo. To unnamed recipient. About his support for the war. With port & sepia-toned reprint of a scene depicting the burial of soldiers. By A. J. Riddle. Illus in cat rms Oct 11 (108) $260

— LONGSTREET, JAMES. - ANs. [n.d.]. 1 p, 4.5 by 7 inches. "James Longstreet/Lieut. General C. S. A./Who used to try to catch Dr./Talmadge, but was finally/captured by him." Aged. With related material. sg Sept 28 (55) $550

— McGraw, Capt. John S. - Diary of the Colonel of the 57th Indiana Volunteers, 1863-14 Dec 1865. 82 pp, 3.5 by 6.5 inches, in lea gilt, some leaves loose. cb June 25 (2443) $2,250

— Mercer, Hugh W. - Ls. 5 Dec 1867. 2 pp, 8vo. To Col. C. C. Jones. Seeking help to apply for a pardon: "I write to ask you the best way to proceed in the matter. I would not ask for a pardon nor would I give a fig for it, except as it may aid in getting my money." sg Sept 28 (56) $350

— Pickett's Charge. - ALs of Knowles Croskey, once a private in Company G of the 1st Virginia Volunteers, 18 Mar 1937. 1 p, 276mm by 216mm, in pencil. To Virginia Dryer. Giving an first-hand account of Pickett's Charge. P June 5 (93) $2,000

— Powers, John. - ALs. 31 May 1865. 4 pp, 8vo. To Miss Annie Baker. Concerning the media's criticism of Sherman for Jefferson Davis' escape to Mexico. Browned. With orig envelope. pba June 13 (11) $50

— Preble, George Henry. - Photo sgd 1869. 3.7 by 5.75 inches. Sepia photo. Of Preble in uniform. Mtd. Dated in anr hand. sg Sept 28 (70) $150

— Samuel, Harry S.- ALs. 24 Feb 1865. 2 pp, 4to. To his cousin Matilda. Concerning R. J. Moses, a Jewish prisoner of war in a Union jail. pba June 13 (20) $2,500

— Stacey, Manly. - Ms diary & 9 A Ls s sgd by this member of Company D of the 111th Regiment of NY State Volunteers, 1853. About 365 pp, 12mo, in wallet-style mor. A Ls s, 27 pp, 8vo & 4to. sg Oct 26 (66) $2,600

— Tees, Lewis. - Ds. 2 June 1863. 4 pp, folio. Letters Patent for "Improved Iron-clad Vessels". Issued to Tees. Sgd by Acting Secretary of the Interior W. T. Otto & Commissioner of Patents D. P. Holloway & Tees. With related material. pba Oct 26 (162) $650

— Titus, Jerome. - Ms diary of this musician in Company H, 2d CT Volunteer Artillery, 2d Brigade, 1st Division, 6th Corps, for 1864 & 1865. About 775 pp, in 2 12mo wallet-style mor bdgs. sg Oct 26 (67) $1,600

— Tuttle, Dennis. - over 166 ALs s, 640 pp, 4to & 12mo, Jan 1862 to December 1865. To his wife.. Concerning his service in the 20th Regiment Indiana Volunteer Infantry including battles, politics, conditions and family matters. Illus in cat rms Oct 11 (97) $9,000

— Washington, D.C. - Letter, 27 Apr 1861. 4 pp, 8vo. Soldier's report about the current crisis, rumors of an attack, & Lincoln's administration. Sgd George. P Dec 13 (66) $1,000

— Weeks, Andrew. - Collection of c.34 A Ls s from Weeks to his sister & 2 military documents, 9 Mar 1861 to 23 Jan 1868. About his life on board various warships & at various camps & forts. Weeks was with Company D of the 10th Regiments of New York Infantry Volunteers. P June 5 (29) $2,500

— Wright, Brigadier General George. - ALs. 8 Mar 1865. 1 p, 4to. To Col. Franklin Haven. Concerning the arrest & sending to Alcatraz of a Laurence Mur-phy for " enticing and carrying away a Soldier in the Service of the United States..." pba June 13 (9) $150

**Clanton, Newman Haynes**
Signature, 16 July 1878. 1 p, 4to. Endorsement on verso of a sight draft of George Cottreal. CNY May 17 (224) $9,000

**Clark, Galen**
Photograph, sgd, 1904. 7.75 by 5.25 inches, on 10 by 7.5 inch mtd bd. Sgd on verso "Galen Clark, Yosemite Valley." Larson collection pba Feb 12 (25) $500

**Clark, William, 1770-1838**
ALs, 10 Oct 1810. 2 pp, 4to. To his nephew John O'Fallon. Giving advice about the importance of making profitable use of his time & encouraging him to write often. CNY May 17 (225) $4,500

**Clarke, Joseph Clayton ("Kyd")**. See: Dickens, Charles & Clarke

**Claudel, Paul, 1868-1955**
ALs, 14 Aug 1946. 1 p, 8vo. To the pbr Egloff. Sending a poem (not present). star Mar 21 (51) DM200

**Clay, Henry, 1777-1852**
ALs, 5 Apr 1803. 1 p, 4to. To William Taylor. Explaining why he cannot settle an account. sg Feb 1 (48) $400

— 24 Mar 1806. 1 p, 4to. Recipient unnamed. Concerning a legal suit. rms Mar 21 (272) $250

— 8 Aug 1818. 1 p, 4to. To Henry Franklin. About land interests: "Since my return from Washington to Kentucky I have redeemed the 10,000 Acres of land in the name of Samuel Franklin, and paid the taxes to the present year." Repaired at central fold & with other defects. pba Oct 26 (209) $350

— 10 June 1820. 1 p, 4to. To Caesar Augustus Rodney. Expressing satisfaction about the vote of the House of Representatives "in favor of recognizing the Patriot Governments of South America." Forbes Magazine collection. CNY May 17 (121) $1,700

— 21 Oct 1821. 1 p, 4to. To Hon. Benj. Mills. Legal letter about a case in which Clay offers assistance. sg June 6 (41) $375

— 5 Mar 1837. 1 p, 8vo. To [Daniel] Webster. Thanking for pine nuts which he will grow on his plantation. Illus in cat. rms Mar 21 (273) $540

— 30 Dec 1842. 1 p, 4to. To F. T. Brooke. Pondering his chances in the next presidential election. Forbes Magazine collection. CNY May 17 (122) $1,000

— 24 Jan 1844. 1 p, 8vo. To Nicholas Williams. Confirming the day of his arrival in Raleigh. P Dec 13 (68) $400

— 12 Feb 1848. 1 p, 4to. To George Getz. Thanking Getz for a friendly letter. Illus in cat pba Oct 26 (210) $1,100

— Apr 1850. 1 p, 4to. A letter of introduction for Jonathan Edwards, esq. Framed with engraved port. pba Feb 22 (217) $300

ANs, 7 Feb 1851. 1 p, 8vo. To Mr. J. Williams. Thanking him for tickets sent but regretting that he cannot attend. With original enevlope & frank. pba Oct 26 (212) $275

**ADs,** June 1804. 2 pp, 4to. Legal pleading in case of Beard vs. Cullin. 2 holes in text (affecting 4 words). sg June 6 (40) $110

— 1804. 1 p, 4to. Copy of a suit he has filed on behalf of Richard Fox for nonpayment of debt. Toned & with breaks in folds & a ragged bottom edge. rms Oct 11 (115) $280

**Cut signature,** [n.d.]. No size given. Clipped. Sgd as " H. Clay". pba Feb 22 (218) $60
See also: Adams, John Quincy & Clay

### Clay, Lucius D., 1897-1978

**Ls,** [n.d.]. 1 p, folio. Excerpt from Decision in Germany in which he describes his final days of in Moscow during the war. With 2 photos of the Russians occupying Berlin. Framed. Over-all size 25.5 by 35 inches. Illus in cat rms Oct 11 (8) $320

### Clem, John Lincoln, 1851-1937

**Photograph, sgd & inscr,** [c.1863]. 102mm by 61mmm, mtd. In uniform. Illus in cat. Marans collection. CE Apr 17 (126) $2,400

### Clemenceau, Georges, 1841-1929

**ALs,** 19 Oct 1926. 1 p, 4to. To [W. G. McAlexander]. Declining an offer to come to America for medical treatment. Including ANs by McAlexander at foot. With a port. Illus in cat. rms Mar 21 (274) $380

### Clemens, Samuel Langhorne, 1835-1910

**Collection** of 2 A Ls s & 1 Ls (typed), 5 to 7 June 1909. 7 pp. 8vo. To Mrs. Hookway. About her children's theater project. With photograph of Twain. CE Sept 27 (8) $2,800

**ALs,** [31 Oct 1870]. 4 pp, 181mm by 114mm. To Frank Bliss. Requesting help in finding a position for his brother, Orion Clemens. P June 5 (124) $1,800

— 21 Aug [1879]. 4 pp, 200mm by 127mm. To Dr. John Brown. Regretting that he has not seen Brown during his 15-month stay in England. P June 5 (127) $1,800

— 14 Aug 1880. 7 pp, 178mm by 114mm. To Dr. John Brown. Sending personal & professional news. P June 5 (128) $3,500

— 1 June 1881. 2 pp, 12mo (card). To J. S. Wood. Complying with a request & regretting the delay. Sgd as Twain. rms Mar 21 (275) $900

— 6 July 1885. 4 pp, 8vo. To Robert U. Johnson. Concerning his business sense, & expressing irritation about an error involving the publication of a chapter of Huckleberry Finn. CNY May 17 (60) $3,500

— 6 Aug 1886. 2 pp, 225mm by 140mm. To Mrs. William Laffan. Sending thanks for a stay with the Laffans. P June 5 (130) $1,600

— 17 Mar 1887. 1 p, 8vo. To Annie Adams Field. Accepting an invitation. CE May 22 (104) $1,100

— 17 Mar 1887. 2 pp, 8vo. To Richard W. Gilder. Requesting proofs of English as She is Taught for a reading for the benefit of the Longfellow Memorial. CNY May 17 (61) $1,600

— 26 Jan 1889. 2 pp, 225mm by 140mm. Recipient unnamed. Acknowledging praise for The Prince and the Pauper; explains attempts to dramatize the book for the stage. P June 5 (131) $3,000

— 22 Feb 1892. 1 p, 8vo. To E. A. Reynolds Ball. Acknowledging receipt of a book. CE Sept 27 (7) $900

— 1 Sept 1894. 5 pp, 178mm by 114mm. To Morse. Humorously explaining a recommendation for a friend of his daughter, Clara. P June 5 (132) $2,250

— 14 Aug [1896]. 3 pp, 12mo. To Anna Goodenough. Sending family news & mentioning his daughter's illness. CE May 22 (105) $1,300

— 21 Oct 1896. 1 p, 8vo. To Frank Bliss. Attempting to find out if it is yet necessary to renew the copyright of The Innocents Abroad & how to go about it. CNY May 17 (62) $1,700

— 28 Oct 1897. 2 pp, 8vo. To Bettina Wirth. About sitting for her. CE May 22 (106) $1,300

— 2 June 1899. 1 p, 203mm by 130mm. To Y. M. MacAlister. About arrangements for the Savage supper. P June 5 (134) $900

— 21 Jan [1901]. 2 pp, 8vo. To Robert Reid. Sending regrets for not having been able to join him on Sunday. Sold with letter of explanation by Robert H. Hirst. cb June 25 (2519) $1,500

— 3 Feb 1901. 1 p, 175mm by 114mm. To Kate Douglas Wiggin Riggs. About unreturned foul weather gear. Illus in cat P June 5 (136) $1,200

— 21 Nov [n.y.]. 1 p, 4to. To W. A. Willard. Politely declining some request. pba Feb 22 (31) $1,400

**ANs,** 31 Oct 1908. 1 p, 8vo. To Miss Davies. "Admonition: We ought always to behave, when people are looking." S July 11 (148) £1,500

**Ds,** 7 Aug 1862. 3 pp, folio. Sale of his shares in 15 different mining claims to George Turner. Partly autograph. CNY May 17 (59) $9,500

**Autograph quotation,** [Aug 1894]. 2 pp, 10 by 7.5 inches. From a Guest Book. Provides Name, Residence, Arrived & Left. Also: "GOING TO: take a drink.....EVENTS, ADVENTURES, REMARKS: It is human beings that make climate. - Pudd'nhead Wilson's Calendar." Illus in cat pba Oct 26 (79) $2,000

**Check,** sgd, 24 May 1875. Payable to Patrick McAleer for $100. P June 5 (126) $700

**Cut signature,** as Twain [n.d.]. Framed with port. cb June 25 (2520) $500

**Menu,** 23 May 1888. Sgd on verso of menu to the First Annual Dinner of the American Watercolor Society. Also sgd by 38 other members of the Society. cb June 25 (2522) $425

**Photograph, sgd,** [c.1900]. 138mm by 87mm. Shoulder-length port, sgd as Twain. Illus in cat. Marans collection. CE Apr 17 (61) $2,800

**Photograph, sgd & inscr,** 3 Aug 1907. Port mtd on card inscr to lady Campbell Clarke, adding the quotation"Let us save the tomorrows for work." The whole about 7 by 10.5 inches. Sgd as Twain. Illus in cat S Dec 18 (171) £2,200 [Bennett]

**Signature,** on a steamer ticket, 9/12 Nov 1903. For Miss Margharita Sherry of the Villa di Quarto, Florence. pn Mar 14 (403) £460

— Anr, 20 Sept 1907. Sgd as Clemens, with his grasshopped signature vertically down the center of the page. Inscr to Mrs. Cutting. sg Feb 1 (233) $2,600

— Anr, [n.d.]. Sgd as Clemens & as Twain. With port. cb June 25 (2521) $650

— Anr, [n.d.]. On card. Framed with photograph. CE Feb 21 (39) $300

— Anr, [n.d.]. "Yrs. Truly Saml. L. Clemens Mark Twain". Mtd with port & framed under glass. Over-all size 13.25 by 8.75 inches. rms Oct 11 (116) $475

— Anr, [n.d.]. On 1 p, 8vo album leaf. Sgd as " S. L. Clemens/ Mark Twain". Also sgd by "Th Nast". With a 19th century photo of a river boat and a silevr print postcard photo of Twain. Framed. Over-all size 15.5 by 12.5 inches. Illus in cat rms Oct 11 (235) $1,200

**Clemens, Samuel Langhorne, 1835-1910 —& Kipling, Rudyard, 1865-1936**

**Commencement program,** for the ceremony at Oxford University, 26 June 1907. 4 pp. Sgd by both. S July 11 (264) £460

**Clemens, Samuel Langhorne, 1835-1910 —& Warner, Charles Dudley, 1829-1900**

[2 autograph Ms leaves by Warner & 1 leaf by Clemens, leaves from The Gilded Age, 8vo, on rectos only, [c.1872], paginated 1410, 33 & 1444, sold at Sotheby's New York on 5 June 1996, lot 125, for $1,500.]

**Clement XIII, Pope, 1693-1769**

**Document,** 4 Sept 1766. 1 p, folio. Papal Bull; contents not stated. HN May 15 (2528) DM360

**Clementina, Princess of Salerno, 1798-1881**

**ALs,** 7 June [1812]. 3 pp, 8vo. To her brother [the future Emperor] Ferdinand. Reporting about a family meeting. HN May 15 (2656) DM560

**Cleveland, Frances Folsom, 1864-1947**

**Photograph, sgd,** 2 June 1886. No size given. Sepia cabinet photo. Sgd as "Frances F. Cleveland". On verso imprint states "This photograph...is the first one of Mrs. Cleveland...since her marriage". Illus in cat pba Feb 22 (220) $160

**Cleveland, Grover, 1837-1908**

**ALs,** 13 July 1884. 2 pp, 8vo. To Shepard F. Knapp. Declining an invitation to visit a fishing club. rms Nov 30 (126) $210

— 30 Apr 1887. 2 pp, 8vo. To E. O. Graves. Asking the Chief of the Bureau of Engraving and Printing in Washington for help: " The bearer Mr. Morse of Boston claims to see the photograph from which the steel engraving of me was made in your Department. Will you please afford him any facilities possible, in his efforts to gain an idea of my features?" Aged & with reapired fold breaks. With orig holograph envelope. rms Oct 11 (117) $400

— 12 Apr 1892. 3 pp, 8vo. To Frederic A. Tupper. Declining to attend a dinner for the alumni of the Principal Arms Academy. rms Nov 30 (127) $350

— 28 Aug 1894. 3 pp, 8vo. To Judge D. Cady Herrick. Explaining his decision to decline an appointment: "I have turned the Mastman (?) appointment over and over again in my mind, but I feel that if it were made it would become a source of embarrassment to all of us including the appointee...." With holograph envelope. CNY Dec 15 (151) $500

— 2 Mar 1900. 2 pp, 8vo. To Richard Underwood Johnson. About the editor's request for an article for "The Century Magazine". Also concerning his cancer: "Perhaps faith cure is the best thing; and it may well be that we had better pray that the crisis may be reached and safely past..." With original holograph enevelope. sg Sept 28 (72) $425

— 29 Dec 1902. 1 p, 8vo. To Elliot H. Goodwin. Accepting his re-election as Vice President of the National Civil Service Reform League. Illus in cat pba Oct 26 (213) $200

— 14 Jan 1903. 2 pp, 8vo. To Dr. C. J. Cigrand. Commenting on recipient's plan to write a story of the Great Seal of the United States. P Dec 13 (71) $500

— 17 Dec 1905. 1 p, 8vo. To J. W. Baer. Sending a cut signature of Joseph Jefferson (present). rms Mar 21 (87) $400

**ADs,** 23 Jan 1872. 2 pp, folio. Summons for jurors to appear at the Superior Court in Buffalo. pba Feb 22 (219) $110

**Ds,** 28 July 1885. 1 p, folio. Designating William Jewell to continue his duties as Postmaster in Danville, Illinois. With archival tape repair of center fold break. pba June 13 (53) $160

**Photograph, sgd,** [n.d.]. Size not given but oval. Sgd on lower mount. sg Feb 1 (60) $250

**Signature,** 26 Mar 1888. On 4.75 by 7.5 inch card. pba Oct 26 (215) $170

**White House card,** [n.d.]. 2.75 by 4.5 inch card. Illus in cat pba Oct 26 (214) $180

**Cleveland, Grover, 1837-1908 —& Blaine, James G., 1830-93**

**Signature,** [n.d.]. No size given. A signature and a cabinet-sized port from each individual. Also with ballots from the 1884 election. Framed. Over-all size 19.5 by 26.5 inches. Illus in cat rms Oct 11 (308) $500

**Clift, Montgomery, 1920-66**

**Signature,** [n.d.]. No size given. On album page. To Carmela. pba Feb 22 (32) $100

**Clinton, George, 1739-1812**

**Ls,** 5 May 1789. 1 p, 4to. To the Governor of Connecticut. Sending a resolution of the NY legislature regarding a Bill of Rights. Illus in cat. P Dec 13 (72) $5,000

**Ds,** 24 Apr 1787. 1 p, folio. Military commission appointing John Johnson "Lieutenant of Captain Hen-

drick Van Cleef's Company..." pba Oct 26 (133) $160
— 12 Feb 1803. 1 p, oblong 8vo, framed. Approval of 3 Council resolutions. sg Feb 1 (61) $175

**Clodius, Johannes, 1645-1733**
Ls, 5 May 1702. 3 pp, folio. To Gottfried Hermann von Beichling. Discussing the building of a church at Lenz near Dresden. With related material. HH Nov 17 (3197) DM220

**Clough, Arthur Hugh, 1819-61**
Autograph Ms, 2 vols of his holograph notes on parts of the scriptures, 1835-37. About 200 pp & about 50 pp, 4to, in mor. pn June 13 (262) £8,500
— Autograph Ms, notebook for Ethics II, kept when an undergraduate at Balliol. [c.1841] About 15 pp, 4to, in mor-backed card wraps. pn June 13 (268) £400
— Autograph Ms, notes of conversations with Florence Nightingale, Mar to May 1859 & [n.d.]. About 30 pp, 8vo. pn June 13 (282) £3,600
— Autograph Ms, Salsette and Elephanta, his Newdigate Prize Poem for 1839. 264 lines, 15 leaves (including wraps). With notes on the setting. Upper wrap initialled by 5 examiners. pn June 13 (265) £2,700
ALs, 5 Oct [1837]. 4 pp, 4to. To his mother. Sending news of Rugby a week before going up to Balliol. pn June 13 (263) £1,300
— [postmarked 12 July 1838]. 4 pp, 4to. To his sister, Anne. About the illness of his Rugby friend Burgidge. Sends news of Balliol. pn June 13 (264) £1,300
— 2 Jan 1854. 5 pp, 8vo. To his wife's cousin Beatrice. Telling her of Froude's praise of Matthew Arnold's poems; discusses educational matters. pn June 13 (280) £550 [Sawyer]

**Clum, John, 1851-1932**
Ds, 18 Aug 1881. 1 p, 39 by 22.5 inches. Oath of office of Tombstone City Attorney V. A. Gregg, in Gregg's hand. Sgd as mayor of Tombstone. Framed. cb June 25 (2316) $2,250

**Clymer, George, Signer from Pennsylvania**
ALs, [1789]. 3 pp, 4to. To Dr. Benjamin Rush. Discussing Capt. French's petition & political matters. P Dec 13 (75) $3,750
Autograph check, sgd, 27 May 1796. 1 p, 12mo. Order to pay Capt. Arthur Simkins $14. rms Nov 30 (128) $190

**Cobb, Howell, 1815-68**
Ls, 24 Mar 1860. 1 p, 8vo. To John Glancy Jones. Introducing Hudson E. Bridge. rms Mar 21 (262) $230

**Cobb, Tyrus Raymond ("Ty"), 1886-1961**
ALs, 13 Oct 1949. 2 pp, no size given. To Ken. Concerning his 1949 trip to New York for the World Series: " Enjoyed series, my league won. Frances and I had a great time in N. Y...' Also Concerning obtaining a Nevada driver's license for his wife. Illus in cat pba June 13 (181) $1,300
— 26 Oct 1952. 2 pp, 4to. To an unnamed restaurant owner. Reacting to having been stood up for dinner: "I feel I should write and express to you my disappointment in your apparent attitue in taking our proffer so lightly." With original holograph enevelope. Illus in cat pba Feb 22 (33) $850
Check, 12 Oct 1946. 1 p, 3 by 8 inches. $174.34 payable to Southern Pacific R. R. pba Oct 26 (12) $375
Photograph, sgd, 17 Aug 1949. 8.5 by 11 inch ptd photo. Of Cobb rounding third base. With torn margin. Illus in cat pba Feb 22 (34) $700
Photograph, sgd & inscr, [n.d.]. 8 by 10 inch b & w photo in uniform. Inscr to Ken Johnson. Scuffed in lower left. Illus in cat pba June 13 (182) $1,300
Ptd photograph, 5 Aug [19]50. 242mm by 194mm. Action photograph of Cobb of c.1915; sgd & inscr. Illus in cat. Marans collection. CE Apr 17 (270) $1,500

**Cobbe, Francis Power**
Collection of 8 A Ls s, [c.1901], No size or length given. To Dr. Authur Walker. About vivisection. Ck Nov 17 (54) £90

**Cocceji, Samuel, Freiherr von, 1679-1755**
ALs, 16 June 1727. 1 p, 4to. Recipients unnamed. Thanking for congratulations on his appointment as Minister of War. star Mar 22 (1535) DM800

**Cocchi, Gioacchino, c.1720-1804?**
ALs, [n.d.]. 1 p, 4to. To Michele Fontana. Discussing a singer. Illus in cat. S Dec 1 (130) £600

**Cochin, Charles Nicolas, 1715-90**
Original drawings, (4) in sanguine, with tablette & quotations added in ink, for the 1771 Terence. 216mm by 130mm. With 5 plates. Fuerstenberg - Schaefer collection S Dec 8 (605) £2,000
— Original drawings, (6) in pencil, for an almanac. [Paris, c.1745] Each 96mm by 58mm, mtd within gold frame & blue wash border. Fuerstenberg - Schaefer copy S Dec 7 (126) £900

**Cochlaeus, Johannes, 1479-1552**
ALs, 6 June 1547. 2 pp, folio. To Julius von Pflug, Prince Bishop of Naumburg. About reinstating him to his diocese, the Council of Trent, literary matters, etc. star Mar 22 (1565) DM650

**Cocteau, Jean, 1889-1963**
Autograph Ms, draft of his tribute to Jean Giraudoux, [n.d.]. 1 p, folio. On verso of cardboard backing of a photograph of Cocteau by Harcourt, sgd & inscr to Abelardo Arias, 1961. S May 15 (159) £300
ALs, [18 Apr 1932]. 1 p, 4to. To Manuel Gasser. Saying he needs time after a recent illness. star Mar 21 (52) DM420
— 29 July 1955. 1 p, 4to. To John Arcesi Darcy. Commenting on their lack of a common language. Sgd twice with a pencil sketch of a woman's profile. sg June 6 (42) $600
Photograph, sgd & inscr, [c.1960]. 252mm by 202mm. In uniform as a member of the Academie Francaise;

inscr to Cornelius Greenway. Marans collection. CE Apr 17 (62) $550

**Cody, William F. ("Buffalo Bill"), 1846-1917**
**ALs,** 1 Aug 1894. 1 p, 4to. To Major M. C. Harrington. Requesting extra time to pay a loan. sg June 6 (199) $1,300
— 21 Sept [1903]. 2 pp, 8vo. To Julia. Reporting that his health is improved. Sgd "Brother". sg June 6 (201) $375
— 7 July 1904. 1 p, 4to. To Mike [Stockton]. About a new mining venture. Yellowed. CNY Dec 15 (57) $1,300
— 16 July [1905?]. 1 p. To Julia. Offering to help her pay for her new hope but speaking of hard financial times. Sgd "Brother". sg June 6 (203) $425
— 10 Oct [1905?]. 1 p. To Julia. Complaining of his sister Nellie's treatment of him; mentions his financial troubles. Sgd "Brother". sg June 6 (204) $800
— "Thursday morning" [probably 1905]. 1 p, 4to. To Joseph T. McCaddon. Declining a request for "my shooting in the Garden" because there are too many big glass lights. sg June 6 (206) $1,400
— 22 June 1907. 1 p, 4to. To Joseph T. McCaddon. Referring to corporate litigation over the Wild West Corp. stock. sg June 6 (208) $1,300
— 24 Aug [1907?]. 1 p, 4to. To several gentlement. Accepting their invitation. sg June 6 (210) $1,000
— 26 Sept 1907. 1 p, 4to. To Deedo. Thanking him for an album of photos. sg June 6 (211) $1,400
— 14 June 1908. 1 p, 4to. To Julia. Sending news of his circumstances. Sgd "Brother". sg June 6 (212) $900
— 14 Dec 1913. 1 p, 4to. To Julia. Sending 10 shares of his mining stock. Sgd "Brother". sg June 6 (217) $550
— 31 Mar [1915?]. 1 p, 8vo. To Frank & Nellie. Saying it will a month before they will know whether the mines are sold. Sgd "Will". sg June 6 (218) $700
— 25 Apr [1915?]. 2 pp, 8vo. To Frank. About problems associated with his Arizona mine. Sgd "Will". sg June 6 (220) $900
— 13 May 1915. 1 p, 4to. To Frank & Nellie. Telling of hard times in California for his show. Sgd "Cousin Will". sg June 6 (221) $850
— 3 Aug [1915]. 1 p, 4to. To his cousins. About his Arizona mining claims & the raining out of a Chicago engagement. Sgd "Will". sg June 6 (222) $750
— 22 Aug [1915]. 2 pp, 4to. To his sister, Julia Cody Goodman. About his show being sold at a sheriff sale & his continuing indebtedness. Sgd "Brother". sg June 6 (223) $2,000
— 23 Nov 1915. 2 pp, 8vo. To Henry Hersey. About how he hopes to break with Tammen. sg June 6 (224) $1,400
— 25 Nov 1915. To Henry Hersey. About his immediate plans & difficulties. sg June 6 (225) $1,200
— 11 Dec 1915. 2 pp, 8vo. To Henry Hersey. Hoping to arrange funding for his show. sg June 6 (226) $2,600
— 1915. 1 p, 4to. To Frank & Nellie. Complaining of financial bad luck, partly caused by Tammen. Sgd "Cousin Will". sg June 6 (227) $850

— 13 July [1916]. 1 p, 4to. To Henry Hersey. Sending funds as requested & explaining how a violent storm "came near putting us out of business". sg June 6 (228) $1,900
— 18 Sept 1916. 2 pp, 4to. To Henry Hersey. Giving detailed information on his financial situation. sg June 6 (229) $3,200
— 21 Dec 1916. 1 p, 8vo. To Frank & Nellie. About his health & finances. Sgd "Cousin Will". sg June 6 (231) $750
— 20 May [n.y.]. 1 p, 4to. To Cousin Frank. Complaining of medical problems after a storm during which "I overtaxed myself rescuing women and children". Sgd "Will". sg June 6 (236) $1,900
— 2 June [n.y.]. 1 p, 4to. To Frank. Expressing concern about the mines & money. Sgd "Cousin Will". sg June 6 (235) $1,200
— 18 June [n.y.]. 1 p, 4to. To Frank. Saying that he had to have an operation in Knoxville. Sgd "Cousin Will". sg June 6 (234) $1,300
— [n.d.]. 1 p, 4to. To his cousins. Regretting that he can't visit because of his financial problems. sg June 6 (237) $1,200
**Ls,** 28 Jan 1907. 3 pp, 4to. To Joseph T. McCaddon. Writing to of his Wild West Show executives: " I am now corresponding with six or seven Union Pacific bandit hunters, one or two ex-sheriffs, who actually participated in the great train robbery. I will get them for the same salary that we pay to cowboys, and will have in their contracts that they are not only to assist in the great train robbery, but also in...other battle scenes." With 3-line holograph postscript "I presume the horses will be shipped direct to Bridgeport when the Circus moves out?" With file holes and paper clip stains. Illus in cat sg Sept 28 (73) $2,400
— 29 Apr 1909. 1 p, 4to. To Loie Fuller. Inviting her to a show. With holograph addition. b Dec 5 (52) £360
— 18 May 1911. 1 p, folio. To Edwin T. Pollock. Apologizing for an accident. CNY May 17 (226) $950
— 5 Dec 1913. 1 p, 4to. To Cousin Frank. About travel plans & business negotiations. sg June 6 (216) $650
**Autograph postcard, sgd,** 18 Oct 1916. To Henry Hersey. Predicting that Wilson would beat Hughes. On verso is a rendering of Buffalo Bill welcoming guests to Yellowstone Park. Sgd & dated as both Cody & Buffalo Bill. sg June 6 (230) $1,900
**ANs,** 21 Sept 1911. 1 p, oblong 8vo. To Julia. About books he was supposed to sign. Sgd "Brother". sg June 6 (215) $325
— 18 Apr [1915?]. 1 p, 4to. To Frank & Nellie. Invites them to Detroit. Sgd "Cousin Will". sg June 6 (219) $375
**Ds,** 8 Jan 1876. 1 p, 2.5 by 8 inches. Receipt acknowledging payment to him of $1,638.93 by DeBar's opera House in St. Louis. sg June 6 (198) $750
— 24 Mar 1913. 1 p, size not stated. Stock certificate in the Cody-Dyer Arizona Mining & Milling Company for 1,000 shares made out to himself. Illus in cat. sg June 6 (364) $3,400
**Autograph sentiment,** sgd both ways, 1887. "True to friend & foe." On a card. Ck Dec 14 (1) £300

## CODY

— Anr, sgd both ways, [n.d.] "True to friend & foe." 1 p, 12mo. sg June 6 (238) $1,000

**Photograph, sgd,** [c.1900]. 165mm by 108mm. Shoulder-length vignette port by Stacy; sgd as Cody & as Buffalo Bill. Illus in cat. Marans collection. CE Apr 17 (9) $1,600

— Anr, 1890. Cabinet size. Sgd as Cody & as Buffalo Bill. sg June 6 (241) $3,200

**Signature,** 1896. Size not stated. Sgd as Cody & as Buffalo Bill. Framed with a photograph. Illus in cat. rms Mar 21 (214) $1,100

— Anr, [n.d.]. On a card. Sgd both ways. Framed with port. cb June 25 (2317) $350

— CODY, MARY G. - Ds. 17 June 1905. 1 p, 8vo. Receipt for $125 as a settlement "of claim of Mary G. Cody against Henrietta Shaw upon a promissory note..." rms Oct 11 (120) $325

### Colbert, Claudette

A Ls s (2), Sept [n.y.] & Nov [n.y.]. 4 pp, 4to. To Arnold Weissberger. About a book of photographs that he sent her & about a contract. rms Nov 30 (129) $275

### Cole, Sir Henry, 1808-82

**Proof copy,** of the 1st Christmas card, designed for Cole by J. C. Horsley in 1843, sgd & inscr by Cole to Mr. & Lady Dorothy Nevill, 1865. With a later facsimile, also inscr. Ck Apr 12 (6) £2,600

### Coleridge, Samuel Taylor, 1772-1834

**ALs,** 21 june 1822. 2 pp, 4to. To John Anster. Humorous letter about the confusion surrounding an invitation. S Dec 18 (172) £850 [Mandl]

### Colette, Sidonie Gabrielle, 1873-1954

**Autograph postcard, sgd,** 8 Sept 1941. 1 p, 6 by 4 inches. To Mme Margauerite Moreno. About itineraries. In French. Not translated. Dar Oct 19 (68) $75

**Photograph, sgd,** [c.1905]. 138mm by 88mm. 3-quarter-length port; by Henri Manuel. Sgd Colette Willy. Illus in cat. Marans collection. CE Apr 17 (63) $700

### Colfax, Schuyler, 1823-85

**ALs,** 7 July 1869. 1 p, 8vo. To E. B. Fairfield. About his honorary degree from Hillsdale College. pba Feb 22 (221) $75

**Photograph, sgd,** [n.d.]. Carte size. Bust pose, by M. J. Powers. Illus in cat. rms Mar 21 (70) $320

**Signature,** [n.d.]. On 3.5 by 5.5 inch slip of paper. Sgd as "Schuyler Colfax Speaker H. Rep." pba Oct 26 (216) $50

**Colfax, Schyler, 1823-85.** See: Grant, Ulysses S. & Colfax

### Colgate, James B., 1818-1904

**ALs,** 5 Oct 1882. 2 pp, 8vo. To Benson J. Lossing. About a sketch of his life. rms Oct 11 (121) $375

### Colgate, Samuel, 1822-92

**ALs,** 1 Mar 1869. 2 pp, 8vo. To the Rev. Leonard Bacon. About ministerial education. Detail in cat rms Oct 11 (122) $575

### Collalto, Ramboldo, Graf von, 1579-1630

**Ls,** 22 June 1629. 1 p, folio. To Capt. von Bellinghausen. About the recruiting of a cavalry regiment under the command of Count Montecuccoli. star Mar 22 (1232) DM860

### Collings, William Knibbs

**Autograph Ms,** diary in the Cameroons, Cuba & Paraguay, 1860s-80s. About 230 pp including blanks, 4to, in 19th-cent lea gilt. S Mar 28 (359) £850

### Collins, Wilkie, 1824-89

**ALs,** 9 Feb 1877. 2 pp, 8vo. To "Madam". Regretting that the French translation rights to a story have already been purchased. pn Mar 14 (405) £340

— 25 Apr 1887. 2 pp, 8vo. To Felix Moscheles. Declining an invitation. rms Nov 30 (131) $250

— 5 Dec 1887. 4 pp, 8vo. To Horace Pym. Thanking him for his abstract of the insurance fraud case; comments on Pym's having Dickens's copy of Collins's book about his (Collins's) father. S Apr 23 (32) £950

**Photograph, sgd,** [c.1870]. 100mm by 64mm, mtd. Seated; by Cundall, Downes & Co. Illus in cat. Marans collection. CE Apr 17 (64) $1,200

— PYM, HORACE. - Autograph ms notes by Pym about the Insurance Fraud Case used by Wilkie Collins for his last novel, Blind Love. 7 pp, folio. With related material, including a copy of the New Ed of Blind Love. S Apr 23 (42) £1,200

### Colloredo-Waldsee, Rudolf, Graf von, 1585-1657

**Endorsement,** sgd, 16 Dec 1621. 1 p, folio. Note regarding the summons addressed to Adam von Herberstein to appear before the estates of Lower Austria. star Mar 22 (1233) DM380

### Colt, Samuel, 1814-62

**ALs,** 26 Feb 1839. 2 pp, 4to. To D[udley] Seldin. Explaining that he is not able to ship the requested arms because of an exhibition of his guns in Washington. CNY May 17 (227) $4,500

— 17 Feb 1852. 1 p, 4to. To Messrs. Pearson & Taylors. Ordering clothes. cb June 25 (2318) $2,250

### Colton, Walter

**Ds,** 25 Sept 1847. 1 p, 13 by 8 inches, folded to make 4 pp. Transfer of ownership of a building lot in Monterey to Charles Wooster. Sgd by Colton as Alcade of Monterey. Larson collection pba Sept 24 (388) $150

### Conde, Louis II, Prince de, 1621-86

**ALs,** 17 Mar 1665. 1 p, 4to. Recipient unnamed. Inquiring about "Iaffaire de ce secretaire de vandes". star Mar 22 (1293) DM400

### Conrad, Joseph, 1857-1924

**Typescript,** short story, Falk. [late May-early June 1901] 59 pp, 4to. Incomplete. With holograph revisions. CNY Oct 27 (22) $30,000

**Ls,** 27 Mar 1918. 2 pp, 4to. To Edward Garnett. About his distressed mental state. With orig envelope, which is pasted into Vol I only of Conrad's Works, 1920. CE Sept 27 (10) $1,100

— 11 Dec 1918. 1 p, 4to. To Chatto & Windus. Upbraiding the firm for treating him as a writing-machine. S Dec 18 (381) £620 [Maggs]

— 14 Oct 1922. 2 pp, 4to. To the producer J. harry Benrimo. About a dramatization of The Secret Agent. S July 11 (266) £3,000

**Constant de Rebecque, Benjamin Henri, 1767-1830**
ALs, 26 July 1827. 1 p, 4to. Recipient unnamed. Inquiring whether he is listed with the "Electeurs du Departement de la Seine". star Mar 21 (352) DM420

**Constant, Samuel Victor**
Typescript, Calls, Sounds and Merchandise of the Peking Street Peddlers. [Peking, c.1920s] 103 leaves, on rectos only. With c.64 blueprint reproductions of line drawings; 13 orig orig photographs laid on leaves. pba Apr 25 (166) $140

**Constitution of the United States**
[A collection of 20 A Ls s, 4 Ls s, 6 A Ds s, & 10 Ds s of the 39 signers of the Constitution at Philadelphia on 17 Sept 1787 & the Secretary of the Convention, sold at Sotheby's New York on 13 Dec 1995, lot 342, for $75,000.]

Ms, list of amendments to the Constitution proposed by Massachusetts, New Hampshire, Virginia & South Carolina, [after late June 1788]. 3 pp, folio. Illus in cat. P Dec 13 (79) $29,000

**Continental Congress**
Ms, account book, 1 Apr 1778 to 10 June 1779. 101 pp, folio, in orig marbled wraps. Documenting moneys appropiated by & directed to the Congress by Joseph Nourse, Pay Master to the Board of War & Ordnance. In 2 different hands. Sang collection. P Dec 13 (83) $5,500

**Cooke, Jay, 1821-1905**
ALs, 30 Dec 1870. 2 pp, 8vo. To George F. Anderson. About his gift to Cook's mother. rms Nov 30 (134) $700

— 6 Oct 1888. 1 p, 4to. To "Gentlemen of the Committee". Thanking them for an invitation to Honor Thos. F. Oakes: "Your telegram of 3d only reached me this evening. I thank you sincerely for your kind invitation to attend a dinner to be given the new President of the Northern Pacific RRd...I should have been glad to have assisted in doing honor to Mr. Oakes whom I regard most sincerely personally & estimate him as one of the best Railroad Managers..." Smudged. Illus in cat rms Oct 11 (132) $950

**Cookery Manuscripts**
Ms, Allerley Zuggerwerch zu machen..., [Southern Germany or Austria, c.1780]. 190 leaves, 200mm by 155mm. Contemp bds. In several hands. Ownership inscr of Rossina Marie Baronesse d'Aycholt. HH Nov 14 (17) DM900

— GUERTLER, JOHANN. - Beschriebene so woll Berecht= alss wahrhaffte Koch= und Artzney Recepten..., [Bohemia?, 1743]. About 370 pp, 203mm by 165mm. Contemp vellum over wooden bds. Culinary & medical recipes, in German & Czech. HH Nov 14 (18) DM800

— HARINGTON, KATHERINA E. - Booke of Recipts. 1672 [& later]. About 180 pp, folio, in contemp vellum. Sgd & inscr. S Oct 12 (105) £1,300

**Coolidge, Calvin, 1872-1933**
Autograph Ms, notes for a speech about the war, [c.1918]. 6 pp, 4to. In pencil; sgd. P Dec 13 (86) $2,250

ALs, 21 Sept 1931. 1 p, 4to. To R. H. Waldo. Expressing non-interventionist sentiments. Illus in cat CNY Dec 15 (156) $1,800

— [n.d.]. 1 p, 4to. To Mr. L. L. Seely. Thanking Seely for a note: "We are having a good rest and perfect service in your house. I hope to see you and express my appreciation in person." Illus in cat pba Oct 26 (221) $550

Ls s (2), 11 Dec 1931 & 19 Jan 1932. 2 pp, 4to. To Thomas Buckner. About problems resulting from his radio address warning listeners about unscrupulous insurance agents. rms Nov 30 (136) $550

Ls, 26 Sept 1921. 1 p, 4to. To Rev. William E. Barton. About an upcoming address: "I have your very kind favor relative to your coming address at Washington. It is possible that we may be able to be present..." pba Oct 26 (217) $130

— 26 July 1923. 1 p, 4to. To Wellington Hodgkins. Declining an invitation to speak. Dampstained. With Ptd declaration of Warren G. Harding's death sgd in type as President. Also with ptd photo sgd. CNY Dec 15 (158) $750

— 11 Nov 1924. 1 p, 4to. To Senator Elmer J. Burkett. Thanking him for a note of congratulations. pba Oct 26 (219) $200

— 16 Dec 1924. 1 p, 4to. To Martin B. Madden. Protesting against a Congressional proviso restricting his appointment power. rms June 6 (345) $375

— 2 Mar 1929. 1 p, 4to. To Henry J. Ryan. Thanking him for kind words. Soiled. pba Oct 26 (220) $250

Ds, 27 May 1924. 1 p, oblong folio. Appointment of Harry W. Burgess as Postmarked at Rose Hill, Iowa. Countersgd by Postmaster General Harry S. New. CE June 12 (21) $180

— 5 June 1924. 1 p, folio. Conferring powers & authority on William W. Russell Envoy Extraordinary and Minister Plenipotentiary to the Dominican Republic. Also sgd by Secretary of State Charles E. Hughes. Illus in cat pba Oct 26 (218) $700

— 29 May 1926. 1 p, folio. Appointment of Edgar Jadwin to an advisory committee. Illus in cat. rms Mar 21 (126) $600

— 22 Dec 1926. 1 p, folio. Appointment of Sam C. Loomis as a Captain in the Navy. Countersgd by Sec of the Navy Curtis D. Wilbur. With embossed Presidential Seal. Signature smeared. With 3 staple holes. sg Sept 28 (79) $300

— 7 Jan 1927. 4 pp, folio. Requesting an appropriation from Congress for the "expenses of American participation in the work of the Preparatory Commission for the Disarmament Conference..." CNY Dec 15 (155) $3,000

— 20 Feb 1928. 1 p, folio. Reducing the sentence of Joseph Propper. pba Feb 22 (224) $225

**Check,** accomplished & sgd, 9 Dec 1911. Drawn on the Hampshire County National Bank for $1.40 payable to George S. Buckner. Illus in cat. rms June 6 (331) $150

**Coolidge, Calvin, 1872-1933 —& Others**
**Group photograph,** [c.1925]. 245mm by 345mm photo port of the Coolidge Cabinet. Also sgd by Herbert Hoover, Dwight F. Davis, Frank B. Kellogg and the rest of the Cabinet. Mtd. CNY Dec 15 (154) $2,000

**Coolidge, Calvin, 1872-1933 —&**
**Coolidge, Grace Goodhue**
**Signature,** 20 July 1953. Each on a card 3 by 5 inches. With orig envelope with Grace Goodhue Coolidge's free frank. pba Oct 26 (222) $140

**Coolidge, Grace Goodhue.** See: Coolidge, Calvin & Coolidge

**Cooper, Dennis**
**Series** of 13 Ls s, 1980s, no size or length given. To John Gill. Concerning the publication of The Tenderness of Wolves. Also with photcopies & notes of original poems for the work. pba Jan 25 (55) $300

**Cooper, Gary, 1901-61**
**Ls,** (carbon copy), 21 Nov 1945. 1 p, 4to. To Warner Brothers Pictures. Approval of the distribution policy of Saratoga Trunk. sg Feb 1 (65) $100

**Ds,** 9 Feb 1944. 1 p, 4to. Contractual letter to Jacob Karp concerning his billing in the film The Story of Dr. Wassell. rms June 6 (137) $300

**Photograph,** sgd & inscr, [n.d.]. 4to. Close-up port. Illus in cat. rms June 6 (138) $500

**Cooper, James Fenimore, 1789-1851**
**Autograph Ms,** fragment from his novel The Heidenmauer, [c.1832]. 2 pp, 4to, cut from larger sheet. Paginated 9 & 10. Including authentication by his grandson J. F. Cooper. star Mar 21 (53) DM850

**ALs,** 19 Apr 1820. 2 pp, 4to. To Brigadier General Peter Gansevoort. About the political climate in Westchester, NY. CNY May 17 (63) $1,600

— 23 Mar 1850. 1 p, 8vo. To his publisher. About the printing of The Ways of the Hour. CE Sept 27 (11) $380

**Cope, Sir John**
**Ls,** 16 Aug 1745. 4 pp, folio. To Col. Halkett. Giving instructions for a detachment of 300 men in preparation for a long march to Fort William. S July 11 (364) £800

**Copland, Aaron, 1900-90**
**Ds,** 25 Aug 1952. 2 pp, 4to. Official ASCAP-ACA Survey form, giving publishing details on his "Piano Sonata". sg June 6 (46) $275

**Copley, John Singleton, 1737-1815**
**ANs,** May 1796. 1 p. Requesting that 6 proofs of Major Picsons Death be delivered to the bearer. With a sgd receipt, 2 Apr 1787 for a print of the Siege & Relief of Gibraltar & the subscription prospectus for same, 1791. rs Nov 11 (13) $1,800

**Coptic Manuscripts.** See: Psalms & Psalters

**Corbusier, Le.** See: Le Corbusier

**Corcoran, William Wilson, 1798-1888**
**Ls,** 28 Jan 1884. 1 p, 8vo. To James F. Rodgers. Sending an "order of exercises on the re-internment of Mr. (John Howard) Payne's remains; a card of invitation & one with two photographs, and a copy of the song Home, Sweet Home..." pba June 13 (141) $50

**Cornell, Ezra**
**ALs,** 30 Sept 1867. 1 p, 8vo. To Messrs. Kenyon. Saying they can have the job for making "Sash for Casadilla Place as you proposed". rms Nov 30 (138) $550

**Cornforth, John Warcup**
**ALs,** 27 Feb 1984. 2 pp, 4to. To a colleague ("Bill"). Draft, discussing recipient's "results and those of Brown". star Mar 21 (421) DM260

**Cornwallis, Charles Cornwallis, 1st Marquis, 1738-1805**
**Ls,** 18 July 1781. 2 pp, 4to. To the Marquis de Lafayette. Discussing an exchange of prisoners of war. P Dec 13 (87) $9,500

**Cortot, Alfred, 1877-1962**
**Series** of 31 A Ls s, 1 Mar [1909] to 2 Apr 1962. 63 pp, 4to & 8vo. To Gustave Samazeuilh. Interesting correspondence about musical matters. star Mar 22 (791) DM1,700

**Costello, Lou, 1906-59.** See: Abbott, Bud & Costello

**Coward, Noel, 1899-1973**
**ALs,** 24 July 1941. 2 pp, 8vo. To "C. V.". Insisting that he "did not steal a song from [him]." rms June 6 (109) $350

**Photograph,** sgd & inscr, [c.1925]. 138mm by 85mm. Seated, by Maurice Beck & McGregor. Illus in cat. Marans collection. CE Apr 17 (65) $300

**Crane, Hart, 1899-1932**
**Autograph postcard,** sgd, 5 March 1929. 1 p, 3.5 by 5.5 inches. To Sam Loveman. Concerning a visit to Paris: "Still waiting for some word from you! Jack Taylor, freshly arrived, is staying at my hotel. Also met Forrest Anderson, who manages to live here somehow and who haunts the cafes. Yes, I'm more than enthusiastic. Never want to leave. Such grace, such intelligence, such courtesy! Whoever thinks the French to be decadent just doesn't know..." 2 blank corners broken off & anr creased. Illus in cat sg Sept 28 (81) $800

**Crane, Stephen, 1871-1900**
**ALs,** 6 Mar 1895. 3 pp, 8vo. To James H. Mosher. About corrections made to The Red Badge of Courage before its publication & his trip to Galveston. CNY May 17 (64) $5,500

### Crane, Walter, 1845-1915
ALs, 5 Apr 1890. 4 pp, 8vo. To Mrs. Morell. Thanking her for woodcuts sent: "Few things are more interesting & suggestive than early woodcuts from the middle of the 15th to the middle of the 16th Century." The line "Walter Crane, Eng Painter" in anr hand. Foxed. pba Oct 26 (14) $225

### Crawford, William H., 1772-1834
Ls, 12 Sept 1816. 2 pp, 4to. To Andrew Jackson, David Merriwether & Jesse Franklin. Giving instructions concerning their negotiations with the Cherokee Indians. rms Mar 21 (31) $4,250

### Crimean War
— JAMES, CORPORAL. - Series of 7 A Ls s by a member of the 1st Battalion, Rifle Brigade, describing the siege of Sebastopol & other events, May 1855 to June 1856. 26 pp, 4to & 8vo. pn Mar 14 (355) £420
— WARD, MAJOR FRANCIS BECKFORD. - Series of c.70 A Ls s, Dec 1854 to June 1856 & later. About 500 pp, 8vo. To his parents. With related material. pn Mar 14 (354) £5,200

### Crockett, David, 1786-1836
ALs, 31 May 1830. 1 p, 4to. To Maj. Wm. B. Lewis. Introducing Thomas Graham. cb June 25 (2319) $14,000
ADs, 2 Sept 1829. 1 p, 90mm by 200mm. Receipt for compensation for testifying in a court suit. Framed with a port. Illus in cat. CNY May 17 (228) $9,500

### Cromwell, Oliver, 1599-1658
Ds, 25 June 1649. 1 p, vellum, 8.25 by 12.5 inches. Commission of Thomas Stone as Lieutenant in the Troop of Horse. Sgd as Lieutenant-General of Horse. S Dec 18 (469) £1,000 [Webb]

### Crosby, Harry Lillis ("Bing"), 1904-77
Photograph, sgd & inscr, [n.d.]. 11 by 14 inch sepia photo. Inscr to Maria. Framed. pba Oct 26 (15) $250
Ptd photograph, [n.d.]. 4to. Youthful bust-length pose; sgd & inscr to Mary. Illus in cat. rms June 6 (203) $160

### Cruciger, Caspar, 1504-48
ALs, 8 July 1544. 3 pp, folio. To Veit Dietrich. Discussing personal matters, health problems, Baumgaertner's imprisonment, Melanchthon, Osiander,& Luther. Kuenzel collection. star Mar 22 (1566) DM2,600

### Cruikshank, George, 1792-1878
[A Collection of 11 ink, watercolor & pencil drawings, bound together in an album & mainly on theatrical subjects, sold at Sotheby's on 21 Nov 1996 for £2,250.]
Original drawings, (14), in bdg lettered Original Drawings 1846. Folio, ink & watercolor, in mor. Most sgd. Sold w.a.f CE May 22 (116) $1,100
Original drawing, Sketch of figures for a book illustration in pencil. [n.d.]. 1 p, 8vo. Sgd in ink. pba June 13 (195) $190

### Crumb, George
A Ls s (2), 15 May & 1 Aug 1975. 2 pp, 4to & 8vo. To Oscar White. Discussing his photographic port. star Mar 22 (793) DM260

### Cui, Cesar, 1835-1918
Series of 3 A Ls s, 13 June 1891 & [n.d.]. 3 pp, 8vo. To Frederic Due & Olga Due (2). Thanking for an intercession in Paris, mentioning the Countess Mercy-Argenteau, etc. star Mar 22 (794) DM320

### Cumberland, William Augustus, Duke of
Ls, 8 Feb 1746. 1 p, folio. To Granville. Thanking him for a letter of congratulations. CG June 12 (46) £1,300

### Cummings, Edward Estlin, 1894-1962
Photograph, sgd & inscr, [c.1935]. 252mm by 202mm. Half length, by Wide World Photos; inscr to Cornelius Greenway. Marans collection. CE Apr 17 (66) $600

### Cunard, Edward
Document, 1876. 1 p, folio, on vellum. Indenture releasing executors William Cunnard & Charles Gilbert Francklyn from any indemnity concerning Edward Cunard's estate. Sgd by all parties. rce July 25 (15) $100

### Cunningham, Allan, 1784-1842
Autograph Ms, poem, Mariners Song. 3 stanzas, 1 p, sgd. [1826] Addressed to Miss Hemrey. Ck Apr 12 (48) £65

### Curie, Marie, 1867-1934
ALs, 12 Oct 1908. 1 p, 8vo. Recipient unnamed. Declining an invitation to a conference in Switzerland. Illus in cat. star Mar 21 (422) DM5,000
— 1 Nov 1920. 1 p, 8vo. Recipient unnamed. Thanks for helping her acquire a tube of mesothorium. sg June 6 (48) $2,400
Group photograph, [c.1921]. 275mm by 355mm, mtd. With President Harding & others, by Harris & Ewing; sgd by Curie. Illus in cat. Marans collection. CE Apr 17 (38) $4,200
— CURIE, EVE. - ALs, 17 Dec 1924. 6 pp, 4to & 12mo. To Mr. Johnson. Reporting about her mother's work in the laboratory & her need to take a vacation. star Mar 21 (423) DM360

### Curtius, Ernst, 1814-96
Series of 3 A Ls s, 28 Aug 1870 to 15 Aug 1887. 4 pp, 8vo. To an unnamed colleague. About the war & family matters. star Mar 21 (424) DM320

### Curtius, Ernst Robert, 1886-1956
Collection of 6 A Ls s, 2 Ls s & autograph postcard, 3 Feb 1952 to 27 Nov 1953. 12 pp, various sizes. To Edgar Lohner. About Gottfried Benn & other literary matters. star Mar 21 (54) DM520

### Custer, George Armstrong, 1839-76
Ls, 11 Aug 1875. 1 p, 4to. To John Bunker. Instructing him to supply rations to the families of some Indian

scouts. Framed with a port. Illus in cat. CNY May 17 (229) $8,500

**Photograph, sgd & inscr,** 27 Feb [18]65. 93mm by 61mm, mtd. Seated, in uniform; by Brady. Illus in cat. Marans collection. CE Apr 17 (128) $7,500

### Cyprianus, Saint

**Ms,** Epistolae. [North-east Italy, 2d quarter of 15th cent]. 90 leaves (incomplete), vellum, 243mm by 174mm. Worn 18th-cent Italian sheep. In a small neat rounded gothic bookhand with punctus flexus. With c.33 three-line initials in red or blue with penwork in purple or red, & large illuminated initial in colors & burnished gold with 2-sided border. S Dec 5 (35) £2,800 [Maggs]

### Czerny, Carl, 1791-1857

**Autograph music,** Romanzina, 9 June 1846. 1 p, 8vo. 32 bars, scored for piano; sgd. S May 15 (334) £1,100

**ALs,** 19 Jan 1855. 1 p, 8vo. To Herr von Schubert. Asking him to forward some music to Gustav Nottebohm. star Mar 22 (795) DM900

# D

### Dalberg, Johann Friedrich Hugo, Freiherr von, 1760-1812

**ALs,** 12 Dec 1803. 1 p, 4to. To an unnamed bookseller. Thanking for an art journal & ordering Gessner's letters to his son. star Mar 22 (796) DM240

### Dalberg, Karl, Reichsfreiherr von, Kurfuerst von Mainz, 1744-1817

**ALs,** 27 June 1811. 1 p, 4to. To Miss Cochelet. Inviting her & her brother to dine with him. Illus in cat. star Mar 22 (1331) DM850

### Dali, Salvador, 1904-89

**ALs,** [postmarked 24 Dec 1942]. 1 p, 8vo. To Allene Talmey. Wishing her "bon Noel et Nouvel An..." Sgd twice. Dali has drawn three figures on perspective lines with stars above. With original holograph envelope. sg June 6 (50) $750

— 1951. 1 p, 8vo. To an unnamed recipient. In a mix of French and English. Requesting money and concerninng his desire to improve his English. Sgd as "Dali". sg Sept 28 (83) $350

— 1952. 1 p, 8vo. To an unnamed recipient at Vogue. Concerning money matters. In a mix of French & English. Illus in cat sg Sept 28 (84) $500

— 1955. 2 pp, 8vo. To "Tres cher ami" at Vogue Magazine. Concerning his works & his planned projects. In a mix of French and English. sg Sept 28 (85) $900

**Ls,** 18 July 1966. 1 p, 4to. To Manheim Fox. Asking that all business be conducted through his attorney, Arnold Grant. sg Feb 1 (67) $350

— 8 Dec 1966. 1 p, 8vo. To his lawyer, Arnold Grant. About contract conditions for prints being done for the United Nations. sg Feb 1 (68) $275

**Photograph, sgd,** of a painting in the Dali style. On verso Dali has sgd a statement in anr hand certifying that the painting is a copy & not painted by him. Dated 19 Feb 1975. sg Feb 1 (73) $130

**Photograph, sgd & inscr,** 1936. 256mm by 202mm. Shoulder-length port. Illus in cat. Marans collection. CE Apr 17 (204) $700

— Anr, 1970. About 7.25 by 9.35 inches. Inscr in French to Arnold Grant & sgd in blue ink. sg Feb 1 (71) $375

— Anr, 1970. About 6.25 by 9 inches, depicting him at work on a sculpture. Has sketch of warrior with lance on horseback with signature Dali as part of design. Inscr to Arnold Grant. sg Feb 1 (72) $1,900

### Dallapiccola, Luigi, 1904-75

**ALs,** 18 May 1964. 1 p, 4to. To Rolf Liebermann. Regarding changes in his opera Il Prigioniero. With carbon copy of Liebermann's answer. star Mar 22 (797) DM550

### Dalton, Emmett, 1871-1937

**Ls,** 26 Feb 1935. 1 p, 4to. To C. W. Mowre. Praising Chuck Martin's fiction. Illus in cat. CNY May 17 (231) $7,500

**Photograph, sgd & inscr,** [c.1912]. 88mm by 138mm. On horseback. Illus in cat. Marans collection. CE Apr 17 (11) $4,000

### Dalton, Gratton, 1861-92

**Ds,** 4 Jan 1890. 1 p, 8vo. Oath of Office as Deputy Marshal. Illus in cat. rms Mar 21 (215) $12,000

### Dampierre, Guy de, Count of Flanders, 1225-1305

**Document,** [12 Dec] 1274. 1 p, vellum, 230mm by 280mm. Charter granting & confirming the privileges of the butchers of the city of Namur. Together with a transcript of 1581 of a related charter of 1388 in a folder covered with 2 vellum leaves from an early 16th-cent breviary. S June 18 (34) £1,900

### Dana, Richard Henry, Jr., 1815-82

**ALs,** 26 Feb 1856. 3 pp on 1 folded sheet, 8vo. To Francis Henry Underwood. Celebrating Nathan Prentiss Banks's election as Speaker of the House as a blow against slavery. CE Sept 27 (12) $200

— 26 Jan 1857. 2 pp, 8vo. To a friend in England. Accepting an invitation for another year. bbc June 24 (38) $100

— 24 March 1859. 1 p, no size given. To unnamed recipient. Letter of introduction for Mr. K. King. pba Feb 22 (38) $110

— 11 Feb 1878. 1 p, 8vo. To Mrs F. D. Perkins. Declining a dinner invitation. pba June 13 (197) $120

### D'Annunzio, Gabriele, 1863-1938

**Photograph, sgd & inscr,** Apr 1928. 223mm by 165mm (image). 3-quarter length; inscr to Edith Gardner. Marans collection. CE Apr 17 (12) $500

### Danton, Georges Jacques, 1759-94 —& Others

**Ds,** 5 Sept 1792. 1 p, folio. Appointment of Jacques Vialla as commissary. Also sgd by 5 other members of the Executive Council. star Mar 22 (1312) DM950

## Darrow, Clarence, 1857-1938

**ALs,** 14 Mar 1932. 1 p, 8vo. To "My Dear Prussing". Commenting about his book The Story of My Life. Tipped into a copy of the book in question. sg June 6 (52) $2,200

**Ptd photograph,** 31 Jan 1935. 263mm by 210mm. Shoulder-length port, sgd & inscr to Herbert Clinton Branch. Illus in cat. Marans collection. CE Apr 17 (129) $2,200

## Darwin, Charles, 1809-82

**ALs,** [postmarked 1847]. 3 pp, 8vo. To Richard Owen. Sending him a box of important fossils. S Dec 18 (530) £2,200 [Quaritch]

— 30 Mar 1877. 1 p, 8vo. To O. Schimmler. Sending his autograph. HH Nov 17 (3199) DM860

— [n.d.]. 1 p, 8o. To "My dear [Sir Joseph] Hooker". A request for a friend: "Will you please read the enclosed memorial & as I hope [you will] sign it, & then put it in enclosed envelope for Huxley...." With marginal defects & mounting traces. Illus in cat rms Oct 11 (135) $1,500

**Ls,** 16 Dec 1876. 1 p, no size given. To unnamed recipient. Thanking them for a present. Ck Nov 17 (56) £550

**Photograph, sgd,** Jan 1864. 4 by 2.5 inch cabinet photo. With orig envelope. Envelope inscr " With compliments and thanks. C. D.". With related material. Illus in cat Ck Nov 17 (55) £1,300

— Anr, [c.1872]. 99mm by 64mm, mtd. Seated, by Julia Margaret Cameron. Illus in cat. Marans collection. CE Apr 17 (39) $8,500

## Daumer, Georg Friedrich, 1800-75

**ALs,** 18 Jan 1869. 2 pp, 8vo. To an unnamed pbr. Reminding him of the fee for an article pbd in recipient's journal. star Mar 21 (426) DM380

## Daun, Leopold, Graf von, 1705-66

**Ls,** 24 Dec 1764. 2 pp, folio. To Count Ferdinand Philipp von Harsch. Explaining a new tax levied by the Emperor. HN May 15 (2531) DM420

## Dauthendey, Max, 1867-1918

**ALs,** 30 Nov 1912. 4 pp, 4to. To Alexander von Gleichen-Russwurm. Asking him to support his application for financial help from the Schiller Foundation. star Mar 21 (55) DM950

## David, Johann Nepomuk, 1895-1977

**Collection** of ALs & Ls, 11 Oct 1943 & 28 Oct 1949. 2 pp, folio & 8vo. To Alfred Morgenroth. Sending a score, & declining to succeed Paul Hoeffer as the head of the musical academy in Berlin. star Mar 22 (798) DM320

## Davis, Bette, 1908-89

**Photograph, sgd & inscr,** [1969]. 4to. Head-&-shoulders port; inscr to Barrie Davis. Illus in cat. rms June 6 (140) $400

## Davis, Jefferson, 1808-89

**Series** of 3 A Ls s, 17 Aug 1867 to 5 Oct 1876. 11 pp. To his biographer, Frank H. Alfriend. With a cut signature, an ANs & related material. In part giving a point-by-point justification for "the exercise of the sovereign right of state revocation of its grants and withdrawal from the Union." Illus in cat P June 5 (33) $42,500

**ALs,** 29 Sept 1849. 1 p, 4to. To Navy Sec. W. B. Preston. Nominating Samuel Dabney for a midshipman's warrant. sg Feb 1 (74) $1,100

— 21 June 1862. 1 p, 4to. To Gen. L. T. Wigfall. Inviting him for dinner. Illus in cat. rms June 6 (19) $4,250

— 21 Sept 1863. 4 pp, 4to. Recipient unnamed. Explaining why he was not able to satisfy the wish of Robert A. Toombs for military promotion. Silked. CNY May 17 (216) $6,500

— 16 Mar 1865. 2 pp, 8vo. To his son, Jefferson. Telling him how much he is missed & how anxious the family is to have him return. With a related letter by Margaret Howell Davis. CE June 12 (22) $2,600

— 1 Sept 1870. 3 pp, 8vo. To Dr. Charles Mackay. Reminiscing about a tour of Scotland the previous summer. P Dec 13 (90) $2,500

— 4 Apr 1877. 1 p, 8vo. To P. Van Doren. About mistaken identity: "I was never a student in the Virginia University, and neither as such, or otherwise, have been connected with a change in the Regulations of that Institution, in regard to the employment of a Chaplain..." Trimmed & dustsoiled. With port. Illus in cat rms Oct 11 (91) $1,300

— 29 Jan 1883. 1 p, 8vo. To Mrs. Crawford. About the South: "Though you are far away from our beloved Mississippi, the land of your nativity, I am sure you are not unmindful of her and rejoice with us that she is emerging from the pall of disaster which so heavily enshrouded her...." Illus in cat sg Sept 28 (88) $2,400

— 20 Oct 1884. 1 p, 8vo. To Ed Richardson. Recommending Col. F. G. Skinner for employment. Signature faded. wa Oct 28 (330) $900

— 3 Sept 1885. 2 pp, 8vo. To Mr. Clegg. Sending an autograph & discussing Confederate principles: " In the fullness of time the restoration shall come that they may enjoy the blessings of the liberty and community independence which the Constitution of the Union was designed to secure..." Soiled. CNY Dec 15 (59) $3,000

**Ls,** 16 Mar 1863. 1 p, 4to. To Gov. John Letcher. Forwarding a letter regarding slaves called for to work on fortifications. Illus in cat. rms Mar 21 (57) $6,250

— 9 Nov 1863. 4 pp. To Gen. H. A. Wise. About the misunderstanding of a gift of a wooden spoon. rs Nov 11 (14) $2,500

**Letter,** 29 Nov 1887. 1 p, 200mm by 127mm. To R. M. Orme. Defending the Southern cause against the pbd criticisms of Gen. James V. Longstreet. P June 5 (34) $4,000

— 21 July 1888. 1 p, 8vo. To C. F. Lee. Responding to a request for a letter of R. E. Lee. Written & sgd Jefferson Davis in his wife Varina Howell Davis's hand. With related material. Illus in cat. rms Mar 21 (58) $600

**Autograph endorsement,** sgd, on verso of a letter addressed to him by H. K. Craig, 2 Nov 1855, 3 pp, 4to, refuting claims of the Whitney Arms Company; concurring with the report. Illus in cat. rms June 6 (18) $1,800

**Autograph quotation,** [n.d.]. 1 p, 3.25 by 4.25 inches. "The rightful powers of government are derived/from the consent of the/governed." Stained in blank bottom margin. sg Sept 28 (89) $3,000

**Check,** sgd, 16 May 1873. Payable to Oliver Finnie & Co. for $125.62. rms Nov 30 (115) $1,000

**Signature,** [n.d.]. On 2 by 3.5 inch card. Stained at lower edge. Illus in cat pba Oct 26 (164) $550

— Anr, [n.d.]. On 2 by 3.5 inch card. pba Feb 22 (161) $325

— Anr, [n.d.]. 16mo. Including subscription. Framed with a port. Illus in cat. rms June 6 (21) $425

**Davis, Varina Howell, 1826-1906**
**ALs,** 14 May 1902. 1 p, 8vo. To Susie. Asking her to see her on Friday. rms Mar 21 (59) $160

**Davis, Varina Howelll, 1826-1906.** See: Davis, Jefferson

**Davout, Louis Nicolas, Marshal of France, 1770-1823**
**Ls,** 24 Jan 1812. 3 pp, folio. To M. Lefebvre. Sending some estimates concerning a salt mine. star Mar 22 (1446) DM250

**Dayan, Moshe, 1915-81**
**ALs,** 7 June 1959. 1 p, no size given. To unnamed recipient. Concerning his activities. With a photo of Dayan with Israeli troops. Framed. Over-all size 15.5 by 19.5 inches. Illus in cat rms Oct 11 (399) $350

**De Forest, Lee, 1873-1961**
**ALs,** 14 Mar 1934. 1 p, 4to, To Theodore Vandervelden. Returning a sgd cartoon (not present). rms June 6 (348) $300

— [n.d.]. 1 p, 4to. To Carl Haverlin. Cancelling a luncheon. Also sgd by his wife, Marie. pba Oct 26 (91) $325

**Ls,** 26 Jan 1954. 1 p, 4to. To Eugene Blode. About amatuer radio. rms Oct 11 (136) $280

**De Gaulle, Charles, 1890-1970**
**Group photograph,** [1944]. 200mm by 250mm. Entering Paris, surrounded by men & children. Sgd by De Gaulle. Illus in cat. Marans collection. CE Apr 17 (130) $2,200

**Photograph, sgd,** 1943. 5 by 7 inches. sg June 6 (53) $1,000

**De Seversky, Alexander Procofieff, 1894-1974**
**Ls,** 19 Jan 1971. 1 p, 4to. To Lawrence E. Spivak. About his ecological activities: "Working in this field for eighteen years, I am encountering the same human inertia, indifference, misapprehension and downright stupidity that I encountered in my fight for air power. (Incidentally, even greater stupidity in connection with air power is now being demonstrated in Vietnam.)" pba Oct 26 (92) $140

**De Valera, Eamon**
**Signature,** 1919. With photos of De Valera & the 1916 Easter Rebellion. Framed. Over-all size 15 by 25.5 inches. Illus in cat rms Oct 11 (400) $350

**Dearborn, Henry, 1751-1829**
**Ls,** 16 July 1801. 1 p, 4to. To Thomas Mounger. Advising him of the need to prepare rations for the holding of a treaty with Indians at Fort Wilkinson. Including franking signature. rms Mar 21 (278) $400

**Debussy, Claude, 1862-1918**
**ALs,** [n.d.], "Wednesday". 1 p, 4to. To Rene Peter. About the time for a meeting the next day. star Mar 22 (799) DM1,300

**ANs,** [n.d.]. 1 p, 8vo. To Andre Caplet. Informing him that "le No 9 est devenue le No 15". star Mar 22 (800) DM520

**Decatur, Stephen, 1779-1820.** See: McHenry; Decatur & Others

**Degas, Edgar, 1834-1917**
**Autograph telegram,** sgd, [16 Oct 1896]. 1 p, size not stated. To Dr. Goubert. Asking to see him. HH May 9 (2431) DM700

**Dehmel, Richard, 1863-1920**
**Autograph Ms,** essay, Tippel und Tappel, [n.d.]. 2 pp, 4to. Ptr's copy; sgd at head. star Mar 21 (56) DM280

**Delandine de St. Esprit, Jean Louis Catherine Jerome, 1787-1855**
**Ms,** Tableau historique du chateau de Rambouillet... pour servir a l'histoire des maisons royales de France.... N.p., c.1813. 2 vols. 190mm by 135mm, in orig half mor gilt. Folding table slightly torn. Fuerstenberg - Schaefer copy S Dec 7 (150) £360

**Delbrueck, Johann Friedrich Gottlieb, 1768-1830**
**A Ls s** (2), 30 Dec 1797 & 6 Jan 1798. 6 pp, 4to. Recipient unnamed. Discussing a recent order by the Prussian king. star Mar 21 (427) DM540

**Delius, Frederick, 1862-1934**
**ALs,** 20 July 1908. 4 pp, 8vo. To Mr. Lam. Explaining that he will not be able to meet his friends because he is just beginning work on "the Suite of Dowson's songs". S May 15 (336) £550

**Dempsey, Jack, 1895-1983**
**Menu,** sgd, [c.1950]. On the Drink List for Jack Dempsey's Restaurant. sg Feb 1 (75) $200

**Photograph, sgd & inscr,** [c.1915]. 255mm by 202mm. Full length, by Apeda; inscr to Edward Quimby. Illus in cat. Marans collection. CE Apr 17 (271) $400

**Derain, Andre, 1880-1954**
**ALs,** [n.d.], "Wednesday". 2 pp, 8vo. To "cher Gabout". Discussing some joint projects. star Mar 21 (663) DM350

## 1995 - 1996 · AUTOGRAPHS & MANUSCRIPTS        DICKENS

**Desaix de Veygoux, Louis Charles Antoine, 1768-1800**
ALs, 12 Oct 1795. 1 p, folio. To Gen. Jean Jacques Ambert. Requesting soldiers & arms for a reconnoitering mission. Illus in cat. star Mar 22 (1447) DM530

**Dessalines, Jean Jacques, Emperor of Haiti, c.1758-1806**
Ls, 11 Feb 1804. 2 pp, 4to. To George Dundas. Thanking for the care Lord Duckworth is taking of Haitians in Jamaica, & referring to Haitians taken prisoner by the French & to foreign troops in Haiti. S May 15 (167) £850

**Dessau, Paul, 1894-1979**
[2 autograph Mss (1 sgd) & typescript with autograph additions, [n.d.], 4 pp, 4to, dealing with fascism & other political matters, sold at Stargardt on 22 Mar 1996, lot 805, for DM470.]
Autograph music, 3 songs to Shakespeare's Sonnets nos 32, 88 & 8, scored for voice; [n.d.]. 6 pp, folio. star Mar 22 (803) DM2,700
— Autograph music, the cook's song, from his music to Brecht's Mutter Courage und ihre Kinder, [n.d.]. 1 p, folio. Scored for voice & piano. With 4 unrelated bars of music on verso. star Mar 22 (804) DM1,500
Ls, 6 Aug 1938. 1 p, 4to. To an unnamed lady. Explaining that she has insulted him. star Mar 22 (806) DM240

**Dewey, George, 1837-1917**
Photograph, sgd, [c.early 1900s]. 4 by 5.5 inch photo. Of Dewey in full dress uniform as Admiral of the Navy. Mtd. Over-all size 4.6 by 6.75 inches. Trimmed. sg Sept 28 (90) $225
— Anr, [n.d.]. 5 by 8.75 inch photo. Mtd. Over-all size 11 by 14 inches. Foxed & soiled. Illus in cat pba Oct 26 (183) $180
Signature, 1 May 1898. No size given. With soiled lower left corner. pba Feb 22 (201) $60

**Dickens, Charles, 1812-70**
Series of 5 A Ls s, 13 Dec 1841 to 10 Mar [1850]. 10 pp, mostly 8vo. To Alfred, Count D'Orsay. About his port, & other matters. CNY May 17 (71) $4,500
— Series of 8 A Ls s, 14 Nov 1850 to 17 Jan 1869. 17 pp, 8vo. To The Rev. Gilbert Eliot, Dean of Bristol (1 to Eliot's daughter Maggie). Sending news to his old friend & minister. S Dec 18 (175) £4,000 [Stodolski]
A Ls s (2), 1 Mar 1867 to 5 Jan 1869. 4 pp, 8vo. To Lord Chief Justice James Whiteside. Declining invitations. With a Cs. S July 11 (176) £1,300
ALs, 8 Feb 1836. 3 pp, 4to. To Lord Stanley. Presenting him with a copy of his 1st book. CNY May 17 (69) $4,000
— [1838?]. 2 pp, 184mm by 114mm. To John Pritt Harley. Politely declining a dinner invitation but inquiring whether Sunday would be possible. Soiled. With frayed margins. P Dec 12 (57) $1,600
— [July 1839]. 1 p, 8vo. To J. H. Daly. Asking him to address his letters to Dickens's summer residence in Surrey. S July 11 (173) £480
— 3 June 1841. 1 p, 8vo. To Dr. Thomas Southwood Smith. Declining to attend a committee meeting. With photo. CE May 22 (177) $800
— 2 Mar 1846. 3 pp, 8vo. To William Locke. Requesting information on the Ragged Schools. CE May 22 (178) $750
— 14 July 1847. 1 p, 8vo. To "Indan". Telling his correspondant to "tell Andersen not to let the Nimrods of London kill him, but to live and write more books". Framed with port. wd Nov 15 (7) $3,200
— 14 Apr 1848. 3 pp, 8vo. To Ann Romer. About fund raising performances to be played at the request of the Shakespeare House Committee. CE May 22 (179) $1,100
— [1848]. 2 pp, 8vo. To F. Crewe. An invitation to a private dinner. sg June 6 (54) $1,100
— 23 Nov 1849. 2 pp, 8vo. Recipient unnamed. Commenting on the bad influence of public executions. CE May 22 (180) $1,200
— 12 Apr 1852. 2 pp, 8vo. To G. L. Chesterton. About the troublesome charity girl, Mary Anne Church. S Dec 18 (176) £750 [Finch]
— 6 July 1853. 1 p, 8vo. To H. K. Browne ("Phiz"). Returning sketches & looking forward to seeing him at Boulogne. In "Franglais". CE May 22 (182) $850
— 17 Mar 1854. 2 pp, 8vo. To Lady Talfourd. Sending condolences on the death of her husband. Framed with port. CE May 22 (183) $950
— 9 Dec 1855. 1 p, 8vo. To Mrs. Brown. About the improved health of Angela Burdette-Coutts. CE May 22 (184) $650
— 7 Jan 1856. 1 p, 8vo. To Edmund Wardley. Regretting that he is unable to see the girl in whom he is interested as he has no occasion to visit London. Written from Paris. pn Nov 9 (441) $440
— 24 Apr 1857. 3 pp, 8vo. To Thomas Oldham Barlow. Promising to forward engravings by Daniel Maclise. CE May 22 (185) $900
— 8 Oct 1859. 2 pp, 8vo. To Arthur Hill. Sending thanks for a book. sg Feb 1 (78) $950
— 1 Mar 1862. 1 p, 8vo. To A. W. Arnold. Setting a date for a meeting. Framed with a port. Illus in cat. rms June 6 (349) $850
— 27 Mar 1862. 1 p, 8vo. To Mr. Finlay. Saying that what Finlay has written about him is wildly untrue. CE May 22 (186) $700
— 1 Apr 1862. 1 p, 8vo. To F. W. Devey. Stating that he cannot advise him on his proposed pamphlet. CE May 22 (187) $700
— 12 Oct 1864. 1 p, 8vo. To Charles Manly. Apologizing for not responding: " Seeing you at the Theater the other night has brought it to my mind that I fear you have never had an answer from me to your note...Pray excuse it, on the ground that I have been working very hard..." Illus in cat rms Oct 11 (138) $1,400
— 21 Oct 1864. 1 p, 8vo. To Frederick Mills. Declining the offer of a position. S July 11 (172) £360
— 13 June 1865. 1 p, 7.25 by 4.3 inches. To Charles Kent. Inviting him to come along to Gravesend. Sgd

## DICKENS

as " C. D. ". With holograph envelope. Mtd & framed. P Dec 12 (58) $600
— 13 June 1866. 1 p, 8vo. To Mary. Inviting her & Cavendish to see him. Framed with an engraving & with a plate from a Dickens novel. Sgd with initials. cb June 25 (2525) $800
— 24 Sept 1866. 2 pp, 8vo. To the Board of Commissioners or Trustees of Roads. Requesting permission to plant lime trees along the wall at Gad's Hill. S July 11 (155) £1,000
— 20 Nov 1866. 1 p, 8vo. To the photographer Mason. Approving all the photographs sent. With a carte-de-visite photo of Dickens by Mason. S Dec 18 (174) £680 [Bennett]
— 19 Dec 1866. 2 pp, 8vo. To Miss Horner. Thanking her for offering her novel to him. CE May 22 (188) $550
— 19 Apr 1867. 1 p, 8vo. To E. M. Ward. About seeing Mr. Schulze. S July 11 (157) £360
— 28 July 1868. 2 pp, 180mm by 114mm. To H. D. Palmer. About a business meeting. With holograph envelope. Soiled. CE May 22 (190) $750
— 17 May 1870. 1 p, 8vo. To Florence Marryat Church. About neuralgia in his foot. CE Sept 27 (13) $1,200
— "Monday morning". 1 p, 8vo. To the Rev. Whittington Landon. Apologizing for having forgotten his note. CE May 22 (191) $850
AL, 29 Sept 1847. 1 p. To the Proprietor of the Bull Inn at Rochester. In 3d person, making arrangements for the Dickens's arrival the following day. Ck Apr 12 (49) £380
— 7 Sept 1852. In 3d person. To John Gilson. Acknowledging receipt of a note; declines his proposal. sg Feb 1 (77) $550
— 10 Dec 1858. 1 p, 8vo. In 3d person, to Constable James Steed. Arranging to meet him in Whitechapel. With related material. pn Nov 9 (442) £340 [Maggs]
Ls, 31 Aug 1858. 1 p, no size given. To Captain Chads. Declining an invitation. Creased. Ck Nov 17 (59) £280
Check, 1 Aug 1859. 1 p, 3 by 7 inches. Five pounds payable to House. Illus in cat pba Oct 26 (18) $600
— Anr, sgd, 9 Aug 1859. Payable to self for £5. rms Nov 30 (141) $550
— Anr, sgd, 3 July 1860. Payable to N. V. Cremer for £4 5s. rms Nov 30 (116) $420
— Anr, sgd, 26 Apr 1864. Payable to House for £8. Framed. b Jan 31 (4) £170
— Anr, sgd, 11 Dec 1863. Payable to Jackson & Graham for £4 15s. Framed. CE Feb 21 (89) $300
— Anr, sgd, 22 Jan 1866. Payable to Wages & House for £23. b Jan 31 (3) £220
— Anr, 14 Jan 1867. 1 p, 8vo. For 11 pounds and 1 shilling. To Mess. Coutts & Co. Illus in cat pba Feb 22 (39) $450
— Anr, 7 Apr 1870. 1 p, 4to. 25 Pounds payable to Charles Dickens, Jr. Aged & with ink blots. Also with a portrait. Illus in cat rms Oct 11 (76) $600
Cut signature, [n.d.]. 1 p, 2 by 4 inches. Cut from an autograph letter. Mounted. pba Feb 22 (40) $375

## AMERICAN BOOK PRICES CURRENT

— Anr, sgd, [n.d.]. Cut from an ALs. With closing. To W. Bridge Adams. Framed with illust from a Dickens novel. sg Feb 1 (79) $350
Envelope, [n.d.]. 6 by 8 inch sheet folded into 2.5 by 4 inch envelope. Addressed to W. J. Ward. Franked. Tipped to a backing sheet. Ink faded, paper worn, soiled & torn. sg Sept 28 (91) $175
Photograph, sgd, [c.1868]. 97mm by 64mm, mtd. Standing beside a table, by Watkins; sgd in margin & on verso. Illus in cat. Marans collection. CE Apr 17 (67) $5,500
Signature, [1847]. No size given. On holograph enevelope. Stamped & postmarked 1847. rms Oct 11 (139) $325
— Anr, [n.d.]. 4to, on autograph envelope addressed to John Henry Chamberlain. Framed with a port. Illus in cat. rms June 6 (350) $400

**Dickens, Charles, 1812-70 —& Clarke, Joseph Clayton ("Kyd")**
ALs, 16 June 1863. 1 p, no size given. To Augustus Frederick Gore. Thanking him for some chapters but "I do not find enough of novelty of manner or incident in them to instigate a new interest". With 3 orig pen, ink & watercolor drawings by Clarke and other related material. In 2 mts. Framed. Overall size 27.5 by 15 inches and 17.5 by 14.5 inches. Illus in cat Ck Nov 17 (61) £1,200

**Dickinson, Emily, 1830-86**
Autograph Ms, Poem. [c.1858]. 1 p, 4to. Beginning "Morns like these--we parted"Mtd. In mor gilt case. Illus in cat CNY Dec 15 (14) $10,000
ALs, [n.d.]. 3 pp, 8vo. To Mrs. Samuel E. Mack. Expressing pleasure at her visit. Sgd as "Emily". Stained. With related material. CNY Dec 15 (16) $16,000
— [n.d.]. 2 pp, 8vo. To Jennie Bates. Extending sympathy on the illness of her father. With envelope, addressed in her hand. sg June 6 (55) $7,500

**Dickinson, John, 1732-1808**
Ds, 11 Oct 1787. 1 p, folio. Confirmation of the marriage of John James & Rachel Woodcock. Also sgd by 45 other members of the Quaker community. rms June 6 (454) $350

**Dietrich, Marlene, 1901-92**
Collection of A collection of 4 ALs s, 2 ANs s & 7 Ls s, July 1955 to Dec 1977, 26 pp, various sizes. To Arnold Weissberger. Concerning business matters & show business. rms Oct 11 (140) $1,700

**Dingelstedt, Franz von, 1814-81**
Autograph Ms, poem, beginning "In das Album Rudolf's von Habsburg," 15 May 1857. 1 p, 4to. 2 four-line stanzas, sgd. HN Nov 24 (2763) DM200

**Disney Studios, Walt**
Original drawing, Original production drawing for Little Golden Books of Mickey Mouse in blue pencil. [c. 1970]. By Joe Morrison. Mtd. Over-all size 14.75 by 16.75 inches. Illus in cat rms Oct 11 (251) $500

— MORRISON, JOE. - Orig drawing, 2 depictions of Mickey Mouse, [c.1987]. Matted, overall size 17 by 15 inches. Sgd. Illus in cat. rms June 6 (163) $650

**Disney, Walter Elias, 1901-66**

Ls, 3 Jan 195[2]. 1 p, 4to. To Joseph Kleinberg. Responding to an inquiry about a locomotive that Disney had built. Illus in cat. rms June 6 (142) $6,500

ANs, [c.1932]. 1 p, 12mo. To Carl Sollmann. Reporting that he is feeling better. On verso of ptd Mickey Mouse greeting card by Hall Brothers. Illus in cat. rms Mar 21 (280) $4,000

Photograph, sgd & inscr, [c.1931]. 10 by 8 inches. With Mickey Mouse; by Clarence Sinclair Bull. Inscr to Carl Sollmann. Illus in cat. rms Mar 21 (279) $4,750

Signature, [n.d.]. 1 p, 4 by 5.5 inches. On paper with ptd name & small caricature of Mickey Mouse. Wrinkled & stained. Illus in cat bbc Sept 18 (71) $700

— Anr, [n.d.]. On 8 by 10 inch page. Inscr "to Mary Marg". Detail in cat Dar Oct 19 (71) $900

— Anr, [n.d.]. 12mo, on hotel card. Matted with a photograph. Illus in cat. rms June 6 (143) $1,800

**Disraeli, Benjamin, 1st Earl of Beaconsfield, 1804-81**

ALs, [1825?]. 4 pp, 200mm by 130mm. To J. G. Lockhart. About a meeting. Browned & spotted. With some holes. P Dec 12 (66) $400

Ls, 20 Jan 1876. 8 p, no size given. To the Lord Mayor. Asking for a postponement of a public meeting on slavery: " there should be as little agitation as possible on the Slavery Question before the meeting of Parliament...otherwise men get committed to views, which, if attempted to be put into practice only aggrivate the evils..." Split & creased. With portion of orig envelope. Ck Nov 17 (62) £650

**Divine, M. J. ("Father")**

Ls, 11 Oct 1945. 1 p, 4to. To Mrs. R. L. Guttman. Responding to her acknowledgment of the service of Miss Angel Love during her recent illness. wa Oct 28 (152) $250

**Dix, John A., 1798-1879**

AL, 26 June 1852. 5 pp, 4to. To George E. Shepley & others. Giving his views on the upcoming election. With secretarial signature. rms June 6 (23) $440

**Dix, Otto, 1891-1969**

ALs, [n.d.]. 1 p, folio. Recipient unnamed. Making plans for his visit & informing him about an exhibition in Freiburg. star Mar 21 (665) DM300

**Dizengoff, Meir, 1861-1937**

ALs, 25 Aug 1910. 1 p, 4to. To The Anglo Palestine Company Ltd. Concerning a line of credit: " Upon receipt of my memorandum of today,will you kindly pay to M. S. Levitzky during my absence the sums he may need, debiting my account up to 4,000 francs." With translation. rms Oct 11 (211) $260

**Doderer, Heimito von, 1896-1966**

Collection of ALs & 2 A Ns s, 5 Jan to 27 Dec 1960. 3 pp, 8vo. To Fanny Thoma. Sending New Year's wishes, expressing condolences, & referring to a death in his family. HN May 15 (2537) DM600

**Dodgson, Charles Lutwidge, 1832-98**

Series of 7 A Ls s, 9 Jan 1884 to 21 May 1890. Length not given, 8vo. To Lucy Walters. Signature cut out from 5 letters. With 6 accompanying holograph envelopes. S Nov 2 (293) £4,600 [Fogg]

ALs, 24 Feb 1856. 2 pp, 8vo. To Mrs. Kitchin. Containing an 8-line poem. With a copy of Morton N. Cohen's Lewis Carroll and the Kithins, 1980. CE May 22 (201) $3,800

— 14 Apr 1867. 2 pp, 8vo. To James Leathart. Enclosing (present) 3 photographs by Dodgson of the Ward sisters & Christina Rossetti. Photos illus in cat S Dec 18 (185) £3,600 [Lindseth]

— 12 Nov 1872. 3 pp, 8vo. To [Percy Fitzgerald]. Thanking and discussing with Fitzgerald his suggestions for turning one of his Alice books into a play. Offset & with abraisons. CNY Dec 15 (18) $6,500

— 19 Apr 1877. 3 pp, 8vo. To Mr. Draper. Thanking him for photographs; writers of Draper's daughter Dolly & The hunting of the Snark. With a postcard photograph of Dolly by Dodgson, inscr by Dodgson on back, 24 Jan 1877. Illus in cat S Dec 18 (186) £2,200 [Lindseth]

— 29 Mar 1878. 2 pp, 8vo. To Amy Walters. Apologizing for forgetting about her request for a copy of An Easter Greeting...; sends several copies (not present). With a Dodgson photo of Walters inscr to her, 30 June 1875. S July 11 (180) £2,000

— 26 Dec 1878. 1 p, 16mo. To a young lady. Sending birthday greetings. sg Feb 1 (43) $1,600

— 4 Marc 1887. 3 pp, 12mo. To Mrs Cooke. Concerning lectures he had given at her school. CNY Dec 15 (19) $3,800

— 7 Oct 1890. 2, pp, on both sides of a 4.5 by 7 inch sheet. To his niece Edith. Congratulating her on passing the entrance examination to Lady Margaret Hall at Oxford. Sgd with initials. sg Feb 8 (193) $1,300

— 11 July 1894. 3 pp, 8vo. To Ethel Hatch. About her work & mutual friends. sg Feb 8 (194) $2,600

— 16 Apr 1895. 2 pp, 8vo. To Amy Walters. About no giving away his present to her unless she really does not want it. S July 11 (181) £1,100

— "Friday". 1 p, 12mo. To Mrs. Chambers. Returning books. sg Feb 1 (44) $800

ANs, "Saturday". 1 p, 8vo. Recipient's name cut away. Asking whether the person can come to a tasting luncheon on Monday. pn June 13 (231) £140

Photograph, sgd, [n.d.]. About 6.5 by 4.25 inches. Showing him seated at his desk. Sgd in pencil on verso. With an In Memorian card for Dodgson, 1898, in which head & shoulders of this port are reproduced. S July 11 (182) £1,900

**Doeblin, Alfred, 1878-1957**

[A copy of the 1st Ed of his book Buerger und Soldaten 1918, Stockholm & Amsterdam 1939, 435 pp, 8vo, in orig cloth, with extensive autograph revisions throughout for a projected new Ed (but differing from the version pbd 1948), [c.1947?], sold at Stargardt on 21 Mar 1996, lot 80, for DM4,700.]

**ALs,** [c.July 1933]. 4 pp, 8vo. To Arthur & Elvira Rosin. Reporting about their situation in Switzerland & their plans to move to Paris. HH May 9 (2433) DM1,000

— 14 Feb 1936. 1 p, 4to. To Arthur & Elvira Rosin. Complaining that an outline for a film which he submitted has not been acknowledged. On ALs by his wife Erna. HH May 9 (2435) DM1,300

— [c.1936]. 2 pp, 8vo. To Arthur & Elvira Rosin. Referring to health problems & a film project. On ALs by his wife Erna. HH May 9 (2434) DM600

— 12 June 1938. 1 p, 4to. To Elvira Rosin. About his new project & news from America. On ALs by his wife Erna. HH May 9 (2436) DM550

— 21 July 1938. 3 pp, 4to & 8vo. To Elvira Rosin. Sending family news, mentioning a trans project, & promising to send books for her husband. On ALs by his son Peter. HH May 9 (2437) DM550

— 28 Mar 1941. 3 pp, 8vo. To Arthur & Elvira Rosin. About their residence in America & his efforts to write for the American market. On Ls by his wife Erna. With related family letters. HH May 9 (2438) DM700

— 8 Oct 1947. 6 pp, 8vo. To Arthur & Elvira Rosin. Sending personal news. HH Nov 17 (3200) DM850

— 23 Feb 1948. 4 pp, 8vo. To Arthur & Elvira Rosin. Reporting about lectures in Goettingen & Berlin. HH Nov 17 (3202) DM950

— 30 Sept 1948. 4 pp, 8vo. To Arthur & Elvira Rosin. About his recent birthday, a visit with his sons, the situation in Germany, etc. HH Nov 17 (3203) DM1,100

**Series** of 7 Ls s, 2 Jan 1948 to 24 Nov 1950. 7 pp, 8vo & 4to. To Herr Niedermeyer at the Limes Press. About various publications. HH Nov 17 (3201) DM650

**Ls,** 22 Jan 1950. 2 pp, 4to. To Arthur & Elvira Rosin. About his health problems, his literary work, his book Schicksalsreise, etc. HH Nov 17 (3204) DM750

— 20 Aug 1951. 2 pp, 4to. To Arthur & Elvira Rosin. Hoping to meet them in Paris, & expressing disillusionment with the situation in Germany. HH Nov 17 (3205) DM450

**Letter,** 7 May 1957. 3 pp, 8vo. To Arthur & Elvira Rosin. Pessimistic letter about his failing health & the situation in Germany & the world. In the hand of a nurse. With related material. HH Nov 17 (3206) DM650

**Doell, Friedrich Wilhelm, 1750-1816**

**Autograph Ms,** Pro Memoria, commenting on his statue of Basedow; [n.d.]. 2 pp, folio. Sgd. star Mar 21 (666) DM350

**Dolgorukaya, Yekaterina Mikhailovna, Princess Iurievskaya, 1847-1922**

**AL,** 21 & 22 June 1869. 12 pp, 8vo. To Emperor Alexander II of Russia. Love letter, reporting about her day. In French. HN May 15 (2489) DM320

**Donaueschingen**

**Ms,** catalogue of the medical theses in the library at Donaueschingen. [c.1826-57] About 160 leaves, folio, loose in modern half mor case. O Mar 26 (106) $325

**Donizetti, Gaetano, 1797-1848**

**Autograph music,** 2do finale del primo atto di [Maria] Padilla, [c.1842]. 1 p, 4to. 7 systems of 2 staves each; sgd. S May 15 (339) £900

— Autograph music, arias Quanno n'ommo sta senza maglia, Ecco cca se pitta a guazzo, & other Arie Napolitane, including revisions; in Donizetti's or a scribe's hand; [c.1820s or 1830s]. 42 pp, 4to (18 in Donizetti's hand). In a Ms collection of arias by Donizetti, Mercadante, Pacini, & others, c.320 pp, in half vellum bdg. S Dec 1 (142) £2,200

— Autograph music, draft of an aria, beginning "'Se un dio", [c.1830s]. 1 p, 4to. 6 systems of 2 staves each; sgd. Illus in cat. S May 15 (337) £1,000

— Autograph music, recitativo for a Salve Regina, [n.d.]. 4 pp, folio. Scored for voice & piano. HH May 9 (2439) DM2,800

— Autograph music, sketches for his opera Alahor in Granata, [n.d.]. 2 pp, folio. Illus in cat. star Mar 22 (809) DM2,400

— Autograph music, waltz in C major, 1841. 1 p, 4to. 24 bars, notated on 3 systems of 2 staves each. Sgd & inscr to Buchot. Apparently unrecorded. Illus in cat. S Dec 1 (145) £1,050

**Autograph quotation,** 8 bars from Act 1 of his opera Roberto Devereux, sgd; 13/14 June 1838. 1 p, c.12.5cm by 19.5cm. Including unidentified quotation at foot. S Dec 1 (143) £1,200

**Doolittle, Hilda, 1886-1961**

**Ls,** 13 May [1925]. 2 pp, 8vo. Recipient unnamed. Giving and requesting personal information. sg June 6 (56) $150

**Dorothea, Herzogin von Kurland, 1761-1821**

**ALs,** 29 Sept 1785. 3 pp, 8vo. To Wilhelm Gottlieb Becker. About a visit with her sister in Berlin after her father's death. star Mar 22 (1385) DM850

**Dos Passos, John, 1896-1970**

**Collection** of 2 Ls s & typescript, sgd, 22 May to 20 July 1962. 11 pp, 4to. To Antonio Aita. Thanking for an invitation to a PEN meeting & sending a copy of his speech (included). In Spanish. star Mar 21 (81) DM440

**Douglass, Frederick, 1817-95**

**Ds,** 19 Apr 1884. 1 p, 4to. Lan.d.cument. Sgd on the docket. With a port of Douglass & a reprint of a 19th-cent photo of Battery A, 2d U. S. Colored Artillery, Dept. of the Cumberland. Framed. Over-all size 16 by 26 inches. Illus in cat rms Oct 11 (10) $475

— 23 Apr 1884. 5 pp, folio. As Recorder of Deeds for the District of Columbia, sale of land to William T. Collins. rms June 6 (26) $225

— 19 Apr 1886. 2 pp, 4to. Land-related document sgd as Recorder of Deeds.. Framed with photo & 2 19th-cent sterographs of African-American laborers picking cotton. rms Nov 30 (9) $550

**Autograph sentiment,** sgd, 26 Apr 1872. 1 p, 3.75 by 2.25 inches. "Though Slavery is dead the negro will remain a slave until all of the rights common to man shall be secured." cb June 25 (2321) $4,000

**Photograph, sgd & inscr,** [c.1885]. 162mm by 166mm. Shoulder-length port, by C. M. Bell. Sgd on recto & verso. Illus in cat. Marans collection. CE Apr 17 (131) $5,500

**Doyle, Sir Arthur Conan, 1859-1930**

**Autograph Ms,** Poem entitled "A Forgotten Tale". 27 Nov 1893. 3 pp, 8vo. "Say, what saw you on the hill, Garcia the herdsman? I saw my bridled heifer there, a trail of bowmen, spent and bare, a little man on a roan mare and a tattered flag before them..." Soiled. Illus in cat pba Oct 26 (19) $2,500

— Autograph Ms, story, Tales of the High Seas. The Governor of St. Kitts, [1896]. 23 pp, 8vo & 4to. Including some revisions; sgd. CNY May 17 (74) $11,000

**ALs,** 27 Mar 1890. 1 p, 8vo. To a member of a publishing firm. About royalties. pn Mar 14 (407) £260

— 2 June [n.y.]. 1 p, 8vo. Recipient unnamed. About experiences in World War I. S Dec 18 (179) £360 [Maggs]

— 6 June [n.y.]. 1 p, 4to. To Dr. Ernest. About a story: "No, the name in the story was June Chance. I fear the other matter is quite beyond me." With 2 file holes. pba Oct 26 (20) $600

— [n.d.]. 1 p, 8vo. To Dr. Bogart. A Thank you letter. Sgd as " A. Conan Doyle ". Tipped to anr page. Illus in cat pba Feb 22 (42) $500

**ANs,** [n.d.]. No size given. On correspondence card. To unnamed recipient. " If you compare these two bits, and if you add the extra names...we shall really have it complete." With fold crease at center. pba June 13 (202) $200

**Photograph, sgd,** [c.1900]. 139mm by 89mm. Bust port, by Elliott & Fry. Marans collection. CE Apr 17 (69) $1,300

**Signature,** 21 Oct 1907. On 8vo sheet. With port. Mtd & framed. Over-all size 15.75 by 12 inches. Illus in cat rms Oct 11 (141) $400

**Doyle, Richard, 1824-83**

**ALs,** 1 Aug 1960. 1 p, 8vo, mtd. To John Leech. Soliciting work for the then little known artist Edward Burne-Jones. S Nov 21 (118) £750

**Dragonetti, Domenico, 1763-1846**

**ALs,** 18 Dec 1842. 1 p, 8vo. To Archibald Billing. In 3d person, inviting him to visit. star Mar 22 (810) DM560

**Draper, John William, 1811-82**

**Ds,** c.1850. 1 p, 12mo. Medical school pass issued to J. Alex Klein for admission to the Surgical and Medical Clinque at the School of Medicine at the University. Toned & with chipped margins. rms Oct 11 (142) $260

**Drayton, Stephen**

**ALs,** 1 Oct 1772. 2 pp, 4to. To John Houston. About Button Gwinett's unauthorized use of one of Drayton's bonds. P Dec 13 (99) $1,500

**Ls,** 8 Dec 1773. 2 pp, folio. To John Houstoun. About Button Gwinnett and a failed real estate transaction "Gwin[net]t...by whom I have been basely abused, as also that sickness...rendered me incapable of seeing me to my affairs..." With repairs in the margins and a small piece torn away. rms Oct 11 (178) $375

**Drechsler, Joseph, 1782-1852.** See: Schubert, Ferdinand

**Dreiser, Theodore, 1871-1945**

**Series** of 3 A Ls s, 2 Jan 1901 to 30 Mar 1902. 8 pp, 8vo. To Richard I. Duffy. About family matters, a review of Sister Carrie, financial matters, etc. CNY May 17 (75) $750

**ALs,** 19 June 1945. 1 p, 4to. To Senora Baff. Concerning film scripts: " If you are work free...I would like to work out a movie script with you for I fell that you have realistic as well as romantic points of view..." With port and 2 early 20th Century silver print photographs. Framed. Over-all size 17.5 by 27.5 inches. Illus in cat rms Oct 11 (236) $550

**Photograph, sgd,** [n.d.]. 11 by 14 inch portrait photo. With age discoloration. pba Feb 22 (44) $160

**Dreyfus, Alfred, 1859-1935**

**ANs,** 5 Dec [1894?]. 1 p, 8vo (card). Recipient unnamed. Requesting the bill for some photographs. HN Nov 24 (2764) DM380

**Photograph, sgd,** [c.1905). 138mm by 88mm, mtd. In uniform, by Coquelin. Illus in cat. Marans collection. CE Apr 17 (132) $1,700

— Anr, [n.d.]. 5.5 by 3.5 inches. Bust pose, by C. Coquelin. Illus in cat. rms Mar 21 (282) $950

— ESTERHAZY, FERDINAND WALSIN. - ALs & autograph Ms, 5 Aug 1899. 5 pp, 8vo & folio. Recipient unnamed. Outlining his part in the Dreyfus Affair. S May 15 (164) £5,800

**Du Barry, Jeanne Becu, Comtesse, 1743-93**

**ADs,** 7 Nov 1784. 1 p, 8vo. Pay order in favor of M. Fremineau. star Mar 22 (1298) DM950

**Du Bois, William Edward Burghardt, 1868-1963**

**Ls,** 12 June 1913. 1 p, 8vo. To Butler Davenport. Accepting an invitation to his home. Framed with photo. sg Mar 28 (51) $550

**Du Bois-Reymond, Emil, 1818-96**

**ALs,** [n.d.]. 2 pp, 8vo. To Theodor Mommsen. Sending a draft of a letter concerning O. Finsch for his approval. star Mar 21 (430) DM340

**Du Maurier, Daphne, 1907-89**

**Ls s** (2), 15 & 28 July 1965. 6 pp, 8vo. To Mr. Sullivan. About her background. CE June 12 (23) $400

# DUCHAMP

**Duchamp, Marcel, 1887-1968**
ALs, 23 Mar 1958. 1 p, 4to. To George Staempfli. Mainly about the American artist John Ferren. In French, with close in English. wa Oct 28 (77) $350
Photograph, sgd & inscr, 1963. 253mm by 205mm. Playing chess, by NY Times. Inscr to McPherson. Illus in cat. Marans collection. CE Apr 17 (205) $900

**Dudevant, Amandine Aurore Lucie Dupin, Baronne, 1804-76.** See: Sand, George

**Dudley, Joseph, 1647-1720**
Ds, 1 Apr 1710. 1 p, 8vo. Order addressed to the Marshal of the Admiralty that the sloop Swallow & her passengers must be kept in quarantine. Framed. rms June 6 (352) $1,100

**Duerrenmatt, Friedrich, 1921-90**
Photograph, sgd, [n.d.]. 19cm by 12.5cm. HH Nov 17 (3209) DM220

**Dufy, Raoul, 1877-1953**
ALs, 17 Dec 1914. 1 p, 8vo. To Miss B. Weill. Hoping to hear from her. star Mar 21 (667) DM520
Ls, 4 June 1949. 2 pp, 4to. To George Jackowski. About his health & work: " I am distraught at all the details you gave me of the hardship of your life. Happily for me today, despite the problems occasioned by my illness, I have pulled out of them...I continue to look after myself and that keeps up my hope. Don't give up hope either..." With translation. rms Oct 11 (145) $950

**Duisberg, Friedrich Carl, 1861-1935**
Photograph, sgd, 1933. 21cm by 15.5cm. Mtd. JG Sept 29 (255) DM200

**Dumas, Alexandre, 1802-70, pere**
ALs, [postmarked 10 Sept 1852]. 2 pp, 8vo. To Henry Vizetelly. In French, on publishing matters. sg Feb 1 (81) $200
— [n.d.]. 1 p, 8vo. To an unnamed lady. Referring to "l'adorable Moment que vous m'avez faite". star Mar 21 (83) DM340
ANs, [n.d.]. Recipient unnamed. Complaining about translation errors. Sgd with initials. sg Feb 1 (82) $300

**Dumas, Alexandre, 1824-95, fils**
ALs, [n.d.]. 1 p, 8vo. Recipient unnamed. Exchanging a photograph. star Mar 21 (84) DM260

**Dumas, Charles Guillaume Frederic, 1721-96**
ALs, 7 Oct 1777. 4 pp, 4to. To Arthur Lee. Sending diplomatic information from the Netherlands. Silked. P Dec 13 (100) $400

**Dunbar, Sir William, 1749-1810**
Ms, Account of the Commencement and Progress of the First 18 Miles of the Line of Demarcation... between the Territories of Spain and the United States of America...." [New Orleans, 1798] 71 pp, including 6 blanks, 230mm by 200mm, in contemp wraps. With-

# AMERICAN BOOK PRICES CURRENT

out the annexed map noted on page 1. Illus in cat CNY Jan 26 (167) $28,000

**Duncan, Isadora, 1878-1927**
ALs, 12 Nov 1906. 2 pp, 4to. To Herr Kretzschmar. Asking for a loan & offering a security. star Mar 22 (1147) DM800
Photograph, sgd & inscr, [c.1914]. 139mm by 88mm. Bust profile pose. Illus in cat. Marans collection. CE Apr 17 (229) $900

**Dunlap, John, 1747-1812**
Ds, 15 Mar 1784. 2 pp, folio. Power of attorney by Hannah Harris authorizing John Hunter to survey her lands in Kentucky. Sgd as witness. rms June 6 (455) $550

**Dunster, Henry, 1609?-59**
ADs, [1648]. 1 p, 8vo. Concerning a suit in which " Henry Dunster as Guardian to John Glover will pay all damages justly cleared by hand falling since ye 11th of 7 [July] 1648..." Also sgd by Stedman. With transcription. In lea presentation folder. Detail in cat rms Oct 11 (126) $800

**Dupin, Amandine Aurore Lucie, Baronne Dudevant, 1804-76.** See: Sand, George

**Dupont, Gabriel, 1878-1914**
Autograph postcards (2), sgd, 4 July 1904 & 31 Oct 1906. To Miss Kohl. Sending his new address & reporting from his holidays. star Mar 22 (811) DM280

**Duryea, Charles Edgar, 1861-1938**
Photograph, sgd & inscr, [c.1895]. 166mm by 109mm, mtd. Shoulder-length port, by Lasswell. Illus in cat. Marans collection. CE Apr 17 (110) $1,500

**Duse, Eleonora, 1858-1924**
Photograph, sgd, [c.1896]. 165mm by 107mm, mtd. 3-quarter length, by Aime Dupont. Illus in cat. Marans collection. CE Apr 17 (230) $500

**Dutilleux, Henri**
Collection of ALs & photograph, sgd, 3 Oct 1970. 2 pp, 8vo & 178mm by 240mm. Recipient unnamed. Sending his autograph. star Mar 22 (812) DM250

**Duvalier, Francois ("Papa Doc")**
Ls, 12 Feb 1959. 2 pp, folio. To President Americo Rodrigues Thomaz of Portugal. Sending congratulations on his Presidency & confirming the desire for friendly relations between Haiti & Portugal. sg Mar 28 (104) $225
ANs, [31 Dec 1957]. On verso correspondence card. No size given. With official holograph envelope. To unnamed recipient. With tape remnants. pba June 13 (106) $75

**Dvorak, Antonin, 1841-1904**

ALs, 26 Feb 1892. 2 pp, 8vo. To Alfred Littleton. About the Eighth Symphony & Requiem Mass. S May 15 (33) £1,300

— 25 Aug 1892. 1 p, 8vo. To Alfred Littleton. About the Mass in D major. In English. S May 15 (26) £1,300

— 29 Mar 1896. 4 pp, 8vo. To Leo Stern. Urging him to come to Prague to rehearse his cello concerto for a projected performance. C Nov 29 (209) £2,000

**Autograph postcard, sgd,** 28 Aug 1891. To Novello's. Stating that he wishes no dedication on the title of the Requiem Mass. With corrected proof of the title with pbr's question about whether there is to be a dedication to Cardinal Newman. S May 15 (31) £950

— 21 July 1892. 1 p, 8vo. To Alfred Littleton at Novello's. Saying that the full score of the Mass in D major is on its way to him. S May 15 (29) £1,400

**ANs,** 21 July 1892. 1 p, 8vo. To Novello's. Urging them to be careful to include the Bohemian title on the tp of the Requiem Mass, Op. 89. With related material. S May 15 (30) £750

# E

**Eakins, Thomas**

**Photograph,** of The Gross Clinic (Portrait of Professor Gross), sgd & inscr to Dr. John H. Brinton. [1876]. 18.25 by 13.75 inches, dampstained, 10-inch horizontal tear in center of image. F Mar 28 (678A) $2,100

**Earhart, Amelia, 1897-1937**

**Ds,** 23 Apr 1927. 4 pp, folio. Insurance application sgd by her as Aviation Editor of Cosmopolitan Magazine. sg Feb 1 (22) $1,100

— 12 Jan 1929. 1 p, 4 inches square. New York Bureau of Motor Vehicles registration for her 1922 "Kissel Speedster". With 4to glossy print of her "1922 Kissel Goldbug". Worn but retsored. Embossed with Motor Vehicles Seal. Illus in cat sg Sept 28 (94) $1,100

**Cut signature,** [n.d.]. Framed with photo. rms Nov 30 (2) $550

**Photograph, sgd,** [c.1932]. 166mm by 121mm. Full length. Illus in cat. Marans collection. CE Apr 17 (13) $2,600

**Signature,** [n.d.]. On 1.75 by 3.5 inch piece of paper. Mtd. Detail in cat rms Oct 11 (147) $225

**Early, Jubal Anderson, 1816-94**

**ALs,** 26 Sept 1861. 1 p, 4to. To Col. Thomas Jordan. Informing him of his arrival at Sangster's Cross Roads. Illus in cat. rms Mar 21 (264) $2,600

**Signature,** [n.d.]. 1 p, on sheet of lined notepaper. Framed with ports. rms Nov 30 (14) $440

**Eberhard IV Ludwig, Herzog von Wuerttemberg, 1676-1733**

**Ls,** 28 Nov 1707. 2 pp, folio. To Count Albrecht Ernst von Oettingen. Recommending Capt. von Hahnstein for a promotion. Kuenzel collection. star Mar 22 (1687) DM450

**Eberhard, Johann August, 1739-1809**

**A Ls s** (2), 19 May 1781 & 15 Aug 1785. 2 pp, 4to. To Moses Mendelssohn. Reporting about a visit with J. C. Adelung & inquiring about the cabala. star Mar 21 (556) DM1,100

**Eckermann, Johann Peter, 1792-1854**

**ALs,** 1 Oct 1849. 1 p, 8vo. To an unnamed lady. Informing her that he has sent their friend's prologue to a newspaper. star Mar 21 (132) DM650

**Eddy, Mary Baker Glover, 1821-1910**

**ALs,** 27 Nov 1888. 1 p, 8vo. To "dear child". Expressing good wishes for recipient's marriage. Illus in cat. rms June 6 (353) $3,000

**Edgeworth, Maria, 1767-1849**

**Collection** of 3 Ls s & 2 letters, 19 July 1831 to 18 July 1835, Over 7 p, no size given. To the Reverend C. W. or Mrs. Lawrence. About accounts, political disturbances, and railway shares. With adhesive marks and some text loss. Detail in cat Ck Nov 17 (66) £280

**Edison, Thomas A., 1847-1931**

**Autograph Ms,** Speech from the Telegraph Operators Dinner in his honor. 19 Oct 1915. No size given. On inside front cover of program. "I am delighted to meet the old pioneers of the telegraphic profession as well as the younger generation...My capacity for slinging conversation to an audience is zero, so my lifelong friend Samuel Insull will keep me out and do the act..." Sgd. pba Oct 26 (100) $1,600

**Collection** of 2 A Ls s, Ls, & 2 letters, 9 June 1888 to 30 Sept 1890. 6 pp, 4to. To John Birkinbine. Concerning business matters. 2 letters with secretarial signature. P Dec 13 (101) $3,000

**ALs,** 29 June 1923. 1 p, 4to. To an unnamed recipient. Concerning the Standard Essence Company. On a letter to Edison from Dr. Herman Reinbold. Sgd as " E ". pba Feb 22 (127) $325

— [30 June 1923]. 6 pp, no size given. To Henry Lanahan. Writing his general counsel about a mining claim. Sgd as "E". Toned. pba Feb 22 (128) $700

— [14 Nov 1923]. 1 p, 8vo. To Henry Lanahan. Concerning the Bull Con mining claim. Sgd as "E". Browned & with file holes in margin. Illus in cat pba June 13 (148) $400

— [3 July 1925]. 1 p, 8vo. To Henry Lanahan. Concerning a final patent on " the Lithia property". Browned & with file holes at top. pba June 13 (146) $325

— 2 Apr [n.y.]. 1 p, 4to. To his wife, concerning progress at his brick manufacturing plant. sg June 6 (57) $500

— [n.d.]. 2 pp, 4to. To his wife. Reassuring her. Sgd with initials. CE May 22 (207) $800

— [n.d.]. 4 pp, 8vo. To his wife. About a trip to the city & Eliot's Chemical Solubilities. Sgd with initials. CE May 22 (208) $1,900

**Ls,** 16 Jan 1905. 1 p, 4to. To Herman E. Dick. Concerning batteries & royalties: "...it occurs to me that in Japan, Australia and possibly other countries, it might be found desirable to supply the demand for storage batteries by manufacture in the United States..." Illus in cat pba Oct 26 (99) $1,000

— 9 June 1926. 1 p, 4to. Declining to join the Woodrow Wilson Young Men's and Young Ladies' Club of NYC. Port mtd in upper right margin. rms Nov 30 (145) $800

**ANs,** 24 Nov 1923. 1 p, 4to. To Henry Lanahan. Advising Lanahan to proceed on a patent application. Written on a letter from Lanahan. Illus in cat pba Feb 22 (129) $550

— 4 Feb 1924. 1 p, 8vo. To Henry Lanahan. About a mining claim. Written on a letter to Edison from Lanahan. Illus in cat pba Feb 22 (130) $350

— [n.d.]. On bottom of 1 p, 8vo letter to him from Henry Lanahan dated 14 Nov 1923. Concerning the Bull Con mining claim: " Of course I would like to patent the claim to get rid of the develpment work..." With 2 file holes at top. pba June 13 (145) $350

— [n.d.]. On 1p, 4to Ls from Henry Lanahan dated 10 Sept 1923. Concerning whether or not to purchase the Bull Con mining claim from Dr. Herman Reinbold for $3,000. In full: " OK - go ahead & clean up matters, we can arrange to have assessment work done by Mr. Swanzy from whom we got the other mine." Sgd as "E". With 2 file holes in margin. pba June 13 (149) $400

**Ns,** 19 Apr 1930. 1 p, 6 by 3 inches. Sending his autograph. With a letter of transmittal from Edison's secretary, Helen Dixon, to Helen Burket of Boswell, Pennsylvania. cb June 25 (2530) $325

**Ds,** 28 July 1890. 2 pp, folio. Deed for real estate in Harrison Township, Hudson County, NJ. Sold by Edison Lamp company to Edison General Electric Company. Docketed. With color port. Illus in cat rms Oct 11 (148) $1,000

— 9 Mar 1919. 1 p, 4to. Edison Storage Battery Company Stock Certificate. Framed with port. Sgd twice by Edison. pba Oct 26 (101) $1,500

— 30 June 1926. 4 pp, 4to. Minutes from a Meeting of the Edison Storage Battery Co.'s Board of Directors. Also sgd by Charles Edison as Chairman and others. Detail in cat rms Oct 11 (149) $700

**Autograph endorsement,** [n.d.]. On 1 p, 4to Ls to him from Henry Lanahan dated 14 July 1925. Concerning the Bull Con mining claim: " Noted TAE". pba June 13 (147) $300

**Check,** sgd, 9 Feb 1928. Drawn on the Savings Investment & Trust Company for $70.36 payable to U.S. Industrial Alcohol Co. Illus in cat. rms Mar 21 (252) $550

— Anr, sgd, 9 Feb 1928. Drawn on the Savings & Trust Co. for $4.46 payable to Western Union Telegraph Co. Illus in cat. rms June 6 (332) $425

— Anr, 8 Dec 1928. 1 p, no size given. $107.70 payable to H. Nehrberg. pba June 13 (144) $300

— Anr, [n.d.], 3 by 8 inch check. From the Edison Botanic Reserach Corporation. Framed with port of Edison. pba Oct 26 (102) $340

**Photograph, sgd,** [c.1906] 9.9 by 7.7 inches. Sgd on mount. CE May 22 (209) $1,400

— Anr, [c.1912]. 312mm by 219mm; matted. Half-length, seated; by Walter Scott Sherin. Illus in cat. Marans collection. CE Apr 17 (42) $3,200

— Anr, [n.d.]. 8,5 by 6.5 inch b&w silver print photo portrait. Mtd. Over-all size 12 by 10 inches. bbc Sept 18 (72) $650

— Anr, [n.d.]. 4to sepia photo. By Scott Shinn. Backed. With corner crease. Illus in cat rms Oct 11 (201) $1,200

**Signature,** [n.d.]. No size given. On a white card. pba Feb 22 (131) $225

### Edward VII, King of England, 1841-1910

**Series** of 22 A Ls s & cards, 22 Oct 1913 to 1 Sept 1915. To Bertram Pawle. Ck Apr 12 (52) £3,600

**ALs,** 16 Jan 1879. 1 p, 8vo. To a nobleman. Requesting that he sent the enclosed [not present] to the Crown Princess by tomorrow's messenger. Framed with photo. rms Nov 30 (44) $400

— 15 Jan [n. y.]. 2 pp, 4.75 by 3.25 inches. To Mrs. James. About a London engagement. Dar Oct 19 (74) $75

— [n.d.]. 2 pp, 8vo. To Mrs. Walker. Accepting an invitation. star Mar 22 (1348) DM480

**Photograph, sgd,** 3 Feb 1873. 7 by 5.5 inches, sgd as Prince of Wales. In orig folding velvet case with his feathers & initials. Ck Apr 12 (50) £260

### Edward VIII, King of England, 1894-1972. See: Windsor, Edward

See also: Windsor, Edward & Windsor

### Edwards, Edward

**Autograph Ms,** rough notes detailing the most important aspects of the voyage of H.M.S. Pandora, including information about the Bounty mutineers. [c.1792] 4 pp, 4to. b Mar 20 (87) £2,800

### Effingham, Charles Howard, 2d Baron, 1536-1624.
See: Howard, Charles

### Egmont, Lamoraal, Count of, 1522-68

**Ls,** 18 Sept 1552. 1 p, folio. To M. De Ham. Requesting him to observe Albrecht Alcibiades of Brandenburg & referring to the Emperor's march on Metz. Including long autograph postscript. Illus in cat. star Mar 22 (1480) DM7,500

### Egyptian Manuscripts

**Ms,** Book of the Dead. [Egypt, c.300-150 B.C.]. 9 rectangular fragments from 142mm by 80mm to 59mm by 65mm. Inset into card pages, in late 19th-cent red mor gilt. In black & red ink in hieratic script. Illus throughout with skilful drawings outlined in black & infilled with black, red-brown, yellow & purple. S June 18 (60) £4,000

### Ehlers, Martin, 1732-1800

**ALs,** 14 July 1772. 4 pp, 4to. To Elias Kaspar Reichard. Referring to Johann Heinrich Rolle's visit in Hamburg & Bernhard Basedow's move to Dessau. star Mar 21 (431) DM320

## Ehrenburg, Ilya Grigoryevich, 1891-1967
**ALs,** 28 Sept [n.y.]. 1 p, 4to. To Mr. Goldschmidt. Expressing thanks for help extended to his daughter. In French. star Mar 21 (85) DM300

## Ehrlich, Paul, 1854-1915
**Ls,** [n.d.]. 1 p, 8vo. Recipient & content not indicated. Framed with port. CE June 12 (26) $300

**Photograph, sgd,** [c.1911]. 160mm by 106mm. Bust-length profile port. Marans collection. CE Apr 17 (43) $1,200

## Eich, Guenter, 1907-72
**Autograph Ms,** poem, Ende eines Sommers, [n.d.]. 1 p, folio. 12 lines, sgd. Illus in cat. star Mar 21 (86) DM1,200

## Eichstaedt, Heinrich Karl Abraham, 1772-1848
**Series** of 9 A Ls s, 24 Aug 1838 to 29 July 1847. 30 pp, 4to.To an unnamed official at Weimar. Discussing various academic & literary matters. star Mar 21 (133) DM650

## Eiffel, Gustave, 1832-1923
**Photograph, sgd,** [c.1885]. 163mm by 108mm, mtd. Half length, by Nadar. Illus in cat. Marans collection. CE Apr 17 (206) $1,400

## Eigen, Manfred
**Autograph Ms,** essay about chemical prerequisites of cellular development, [17 Feb 1981]. 10 pp, folio. In English. Possibly incomplete; sgd later, at head. star Mar 21 (434) DM500

— Autograph Ms, lecture, Evolutionsexperimente, [15 Sept 1979]. 30 pp, folio. Sgd later, at head. star Mar 21 (433) DM1,400

## Einem, Gottfried von
**Collection** of 3 A Ls s & 6 autograph postcards, sgd, 25 July 1944 to 17 June 1954. 8 pp, folio & 8vo, & cards. To Alfred Morgenroth. About political & musical matters. star Mar 22 (814) DM600

## Einstein, Albert, 1879-1955
**Autograph Ms,** differential equations, including explanations & 2 diagrams, [n.d.]. 4 pp, folio. star Mar 21 (437) DM7,500

— Autograph Ms, Elektron und allgemeine Relativitaetstheorie, [1925]. 1 p, folio. Introduction of an article for the periodical Physica; including a few autograph corrections. Illus in cat. S May 15 (170) £3,200

— Autograph Ms, equations & discussions relating to his unified field theory, [n.d.]. 2 leaves, 8vo. With ALs requesting help for Max Wertheimer's children on versos; draft. star Mar 21 (436) DM3,900

— Autograph Ms, Inwiefern laesst sich die moderne Gravitationstheorie ohne die Relativitaet begrunden? [Nov 1920] 3 pp, 289mm by 225mm. Printer's copy for the article. Presented on 1 Dec 1920 to Dr. Hans Muehsam as a contribution to Jewish philanthropy. P June 5 (216) $20,000

— Autograph Ms, resume of the thinking which lead him to the Special & General Theories of Relativity, sgd; [Feb 1924]. 2 pp, folio. With related material. Illus in cat. S Dec 1 (11) £18,000

— Autograph Ms, statement, in German about Nature. 1 p, 8vo, sgd. rms Nov 30 (147) $4,500

— Autograph Ms, thoughts about schools in America, [c.1934]. 1 p, folio. Sgd. Trimmed. On verso of letter addressed to him. star Mar 21 (442) DM3,200

**Collection** of 6 A Ls s, 4 Ls s, & autograph Ms, [c.Aug 1935] to 2 Jan 1955. 20 pp, mostly 4to. To Janos Plesch. Important correspondence covering biographical matters, personal relations & political opinions. star Mar 21 (443) DM40,000

**ALs,** 25 Apr [1911?]. 2 pp, 8vo. To Emil Warburg. Discussing recipient's photochemical research. star Mar 21 (438) DM3,800

— 2 March 1913. 3 pp, no size given. To uknown recipient. Sending a copy of one of his lectures on relativity & explaining that he is entirely sick of the subject. Illus in cat P Dec 12 (70) $4,000

— 16 Dec [1921]. 1 p, 4to. To Anatole France. Inviting him to dinner after winnining the Nobel Prize. pba Oct 26 (106) $4,250

— 13 July 1925. 1 p, 8vo. To John F. Kendrick. Covering letter, returning a ptd inquiry about his father with autograph additions (on verso). star Mar 21 (439) DM1,900

— 23 Mar 1930. 1 p, folio. Recipient unnamed. Testimonial for the pianist Iso Elinson. S May 15 (169) £800

— 10 Jan 1938. 1 p, 159mm by 187mm. To Felix Frankfurter. Congratulating him on being appointed Associate Justice of the United States. P Dec 12 (74) $2,250

**Series** of 3 Ls s, 20 Jan to 16 Feb 1943. 3 pp. 276mm by 216mm. To Helen Lorz. One with holograph postscript. P June 5 (218) $6,500

**Ls,** 27 June 1931. 1 p, no size given. To the "Secretariat of the 'Kulturbund'"in Vienna. Declining an invitation due to "my generally heavy burdens as well as the special atmosphere I sense among the Viennese academics..." With translation. Illus in cat rms Oct 11 (212) $1,400

— 9 Dec 1935. 2 pp, 4to. To Anton Lampa. Responding to a request to support efforts to preserve the scientific papers of Ernst Mach. star Mar 21 (441) DM3,400

— 4 Feb 1941. 1 p, 4to. In German, to Dr. Ludwig Reiss. Saying that he cannot help him to obtain a position but that he has written to the Council of Jewish Women & asked them to help Reiss. sg Feb 1 (84) $950

— 26 Apr 1944. 1 p, 4to. To Erwin F. Freundlich. Discussing stellar motion. star Mar 21 (445) DM5,500

— 26 Sept 1946. 1 p, 4to. To Alice K. Orlan. Sending condolences on the death of her mother. rms Mar 21 (286) $950

— 26 Aug 1949. 1 p, 4to. To Mrs. J. E. van den Bergh v. Dantzig. In German, discussing his reading of her paper on metaphysical concepts. CE May 22 (210) $1,400

— 19 Apr 1950. 1 p, 4to. To Murray Siegel. Inviting him to the first dinner & conference for the American Committee for the Hebrew University, the Weizmann Institute of Science & Technion. CE June 12 (28) $1,200

— 23 Feb 1952. 4 pp, 279mm by 216mm. To Dr. Martin Rosenthal. About the Special Theory of Relativity applied to the collission of two masses. In German. Illus in cat P June 5 (219) $60,000

— 6 Nov 1953. 1 p, folio. To Zoya Frahy. Commenting on a port of himself. S Dec 1 (12) £650

— Jan [n. y]. 1 p, 8.5 by 11 inches. To unknown recipient. Concerning the Emergency Committee of Atomic Scientists: " Dear Friend: I thank you sincerely for the interest you have shown in our work, and for your generous support. We need all possible help in carrying to our fellow citizens the facts of atomic energy and in explaining their vast implications in the fields of international relations and world peace..." Illus in cat Dar Oct 19 (75) $3,000

ANs, [1930?]. 1 p, no size given. Mathematical notes on recto & quotation on verso translates as " Nature hides her secret through the loftiness of her character, not through slyness". In morocco box by Renaud Vernier. Sgd & dated by Vernier, 1994. Illus in cat P Dec 12 (71) $11,000

Ds, 15 Dec 1950. 1 p, 4to. Preliminary draft of a public statement for the United Nations to settle the conflict in Korea. With related material. sg June 6 (58) $2,000

Photograph, sgd, 1925. Mtd on postcard, showing Einstein standing with 2 women. Sgd & dated below photo. CE June 12 (27) $800

— Anr, 1930. On a photo of Professor & Mrs. Einstein on the deck of an ocean liner. 251mm by 203mm. P June 5 (217) $2,500

— Anr, [1954]. 241mm by 200mm photo. Sgd as " A. Einstein". Mtd & framed. Creased. With related material. P Dec 12 (76) $2,500

Photograph, sgd & inscr, 1945. 348mm by 250mm, matted. By Furman(?); inscr to David Paul Jaffa. Illus in cat. Marans collection. CE Apr 17 (44) $4,200

Signature, 1921. On engraved half-length port, 21cm by 26cm. Framed. S May 15 (168) £750

— Anr, 1949. On a card. rms Nov 30 (206) $500

— Anr, 1950. On a 2 by 4 inch slip of paper. Sgd as " A. Einstein ". pba Feb 22 (132) $500

— Anr, [n.d.]. No size given. With port. Mtd & framed. Over-all size 14.25 by 9.75 inches. Illus in cat rms Oct 11 (150) $900

**Einstein, Albert, 1879-1955 —& Einstein, Elsa, 1876-1936**

Photograph, sgd, [c.1931]. 108mm by 82mm, sgd on image. With unsgd photo of Einstein in Indian regalia. CE May 22 (211) $2,300

— Anr, [c.1932]. 8 by 10 inches. Sgd by both on lower portion of image. CE June 12 (29) $1,600

**Einstein, Elsa, 1876-1936**

ALs, 12 Mar [n.y.]. 2 pp, 4to. To Dr. Strecker. Commenting on her husband's forgetfulness. star Mar 21 (446) DM1,200

See also: Einstein, Albert & Einstein

**Eisenhower, Dwight D., 1890-1969**

Ms, Typescript of his Oath of Office as President of the US. 20 Jan 1953. 1 p, 4to. Sgd. With port. Illus in cat rms Oct 11 (151) $1,300

ALs, 20 Jan [1945]. 2 pp, 4to. To Mamie Doud Eisenhower. About a new post for their son John: "Yesterday I received Johnny's letter, telling me he'd be willing to take a job where I could see him...The problem is to find a job where John KNOWS he is doing USEFUL work & I don't want to do anything to hurt his self-respect of his reputation..." Browned. Illus in cat CNY Dec 15 (159) $1,800

— 12 Oct [1945]. 2 pp, 4to. To his wife. Reflecting about his future & expressing the desire "to be a one-mule farmer". Forbes Magazine collection. CNY May 17 (124) $2,200

Ls, 1 Aug 1945. 1 p, 8vo. To Serena Tucker. Thanking her for a copy of her poem. CE June 12 (31) $180

— 10 Jan 1949. 1 p, 4to. To Merle Thorpe. Thanking for a journal. star Mar 22 (1673) DM320

— 29 June 1949. 1 p, 8vo. Recipient unnamed. Acknowledging a nice letter about W. T. Cheswell. sg Feb 1 (85) $110

— 16 Mar 1955. 1 p, 4to. To Mr. Ludwick. Thanking him for a dinner. Framed with port. rms Nov 30 (149) $200

— 19 Oct 1955. 1 p, 4to. To Congressman John Kluczynski. Sending thanks for birthday greetings. sg Feb 1 (86) $225

— 13 Sept 1957. 1 p, 4to. To Mrs. Olive D. Ellis. Thanking her for " the cordial welcome you have extended to us on behalf of the Alexander K. McLellan Chapter No.40 of the Telephone Pioneers of America..." With original envelope & a vintage International Soundphoto from 11 July 1952 of Eisenhower with news clipping on verso. rms Oct 11 (307) $400

— 16 Oct 1958. 1 p, 4to. To Major General Henry Clay Hodges. Thanking him for birthday wishes. Worn at folds. rms Oct 11 (152) $270

— 6 Apr 1965. 1 p, 4to. To General Julius Klein. Thanking him for having sent him Bob Considine's column of March 29th. With file holes in margin. pba June 13 (56) $250

— 4 Apr 1967. 1 p, 4to. To Robert M. Smith. Praising Ronald Reagan & Richard Nixon but insisting that he will support "whoever may be the Republican nominee in 1968". Illus in cat. rms June 6 (357) $3,250

— 1 Feb 1968. 1 p. To Virgil M. Pinkley. About the press and the misconceptions about him it breeds. Sgd with initials. rms Nov 30 (151) $500

Ns, 24 Oct 1949. 1 p, 8vo. To Mr. Koza. Thanking him for his letter. sg June 6 (60) $110

Ds, 7 May 1945. 1 p, 4to. Copy No 13 of Special Cable 355, reading "The mission of this Allied Force was fulfilled at 0241 local time, May 7th, 1945." Sgd later. P Dec 13 (103) $13,000

— 12 Oct 1948. 1 p, 5.5 by 3.5 inch card. Excerpt from Eisenhower's Inaugural Address as President of Columbia University: "...the principal purpose of education itself- to prepare the student for effective personal and social life in a free society..." With newspaper article relating to the circumstances of the signing. Dar Oct 19 (76) $375

— 21 Jan 1957. 1 p, 7 by 10 inches. Engraved invitation to Inaugural Ball. Mtd. Toned at edges. Dar Oct 19 (77) $90

— 29 Jan 1957. 1 p, folio. Appointing Raymond A. Hare U.S. Ambassador Extraordinary to Egypt. Countersgd by Sec of State John Foster Dulles. With a minor smudge. rms Nov 30 (150) $750

**Photograph, sgd,** [n.d.]. 8 by 10 inch photo. With original letter of transmittal. Illus in cat pba Oct 26 (226) $450

— Anr, [n.d.]. 7.5 by 9.25 inch photo. Mtd. Over-all size 9.75 by 12.7 inches. sg Sept 28 (98) $275

**Eisenhower, Dwight D., 1890-1969 —& Nixon, Richard M., 1913-94**
[A ptd pamphlet from the Los Angeles Chamber of Commerce Seventy-First Annual Banquet on 31 Jan 1962, sgd by both, sold at California on 25 June 1996, lot 2368, for $300]

**Eisenhower, Mamie Doud, 1896-1975**
**White House card,** [n.d.]. 2.75 by 4.25 inches. pba Oct 26 (227) $150

**Elgar, Sir Edward, 1857-1934**
**Autograph music,** corrections for the full score of Falstaff, Op. 68. 1 p, oblong 8vo, cut from larger sheet. [1913] Providing an alteration to the cello & bassoon parts. S May 15 (59) £700

**Collection** of 30 A Ls s & Ls s, 1896-1928. Length not given. To Novello's. On publishing matters. S May 15 (39) £1,500

— Collection of c.90 mostly A Ls s, 1903-6. Over 200 pp. To Alfred Littleton & A. J. Jaeger at Novello's. About The Apostles & The Kingdom & other works. Includes a corrected proof page & holograph musical examples. S May 15 (45) £6,500

— Collection of 2 A Ls s & 2 Ls s, 1928. 6 pp, 4to & 8vo. To H. W. Gray & Co. Discussing the renewal of the American copyright of The Dream of Gerontius. S May 15 (64) £420

— Collection of 4 A Ls s & 1 Ls, 1932. 6 pp. To Novello's. About the performance of his music in South Africa. With related material. S May 15 (66) £550

**Series** of 14 A Ls s, 13 Jan 1890 to 17 Nov 1892. 28 pp, 8vo. To Novello & Co. Drafts of the replies on the letters & on separate sheets. S May 15 (34) £1,100

— Series of 20 A Ls s, 1892-94. About 40 pp, 8vo. To Novello & Co. About the cantata, The Black Knight. S May 15 (35) £1,500

— Series of 30 A Ls s, 1900-2. About 80 pp, various sizes. To A J. Jaeger & Alfred Littleton at Novello's. About publication of his works, with musical examples. S May 15 (41) £5,500

— Series of c.40 A Ls s, 1900-32. Length not given. To A. J. Jaeger of Novello's. S May 15 (61) £3,200

— Series of 26 A Ls s, 1909. About 70 pp, 4to & 8vo. To Alfred Littleton & Henry Clayton of Novello's. About performances of his music. With copies of their replies. S May 15 (54) £2,700

**A Ls s** (2), 27 & 30 June 1911. 7 pp, 4to. To Novello's. Formally terminating his contract with Novello's. With a draft of the firm's reply in the hand of Henry Clayton. S May 15 (55) £1,150

**ALs,** 11 Apr 1901. 1 p, 8vo. To Novello's. Agreeing to the publication of the piano arrangement of the Intermezzo from the Enigma Variations. S May 15 (44) £350

— 23 May 1902. 2 pp, 8vo. To Alfred Littleton. Reporting on the triumphant German premiere of Gerontius & the approbal of Richard Strauss. S May 15 (42) £1,600

— 22 Nov 1904. 3 pp, 8vo. To Alfred Littleton. About The Apostles, describing his over-all scheme. S May 15 (46) £1,150

— 18 Dec 1908. 1 p, 4to. To Mrs. E. M. Underwood. Thanking for a present. C Nov 29 (211) £300

— 24 Aug 1910. 3 pp, 4to. To Henry Clayton of Novello's. About Fritz Kreisler & the Violin Concerto. S May 15 (56) £700

— 13 Apr 1911. 6 pp, 4to. To Alfred Littleton of Novello's. Containing the long description of the Second Symphony used in the program notes for the 1st performance. Sgd 3 times. S May 15 (57) £2,200

— 17 Nov 1932. 1 p, 4to. To Mrs. Hobday. Sending a photograph (not present). star Mar 22 (816) DM380

**ANs,** [postmarked 28 Aug 1899]. 1 p, 4to. To A. J. Jaeger at Novello's. About the Enigma Variations. Sgd with initials. Signature smudged. S May 15 (40) £420

**Photograph, sgd & inscr,** 12 Dec 1933. 15cm by 21cm. In bed, inspecting one of his records. Inscr to Landon Streeton. Illus in cat. S May 15 (342) £3,500

**Eliot, George, 1819-80**
**ALs,** [5 June 1862]. 4 pp, 8vo. To Frederick Leighton. Praising his illusts for her novel. rms June 6 (358) $2,200

— 21 Dec 1863. 2 pp, 8vo. To Joseph Langford of Blackwood's. Asking for a copy of Silas Marner. Sgd "MELewes". pn June 13 (234) £620 [Sawyer]

— 17 May 1873. 1 p, 8vo. To Joseph Langford of Blackwood's. Thanking him for a copy of her poems in presentation bdg. Sgd "MELewes". pn June 13 (235) £420 [Wilson]

— 4 May 1874. 1 p, 8vo. To Joseph Langford of Blackwood's. Asking that 4 copies of the thick-paper Jubal be sent to the binder; thanks him for the offer of the Birket Foster proof. Sgd "MELewes". pn June 13 (237) £480 [Sawyer]

— 7 May 1874. 1 p, 8vo. To Joseph Langford of Blackwood's. Giving qualified approval to a Birket Foster illust for Middlemarch. Sgd "MELewes". pn June 13 (238) £720

— 22 June [1877]. 1 p, 8vo. To Joseph Langford of Blackwood's. Giving permission for extracts from

# ELIOT

Silas Marner to be ptd in the 6th National Reading Book. pn June 13 (240) £550 [Wilson]
— 22 Dec 1877. 1 p, 8vo. To Joseph Langford of Blackwood's. Asking for help in tracing the daughter of the Rev John Gwyther; approves of the new Ed of Romola. With Langford's answer. pn June 13 (239) £550 [Sawyer]
— 19 Oct 1879. 1 p, 8vo. To Joseph Langford of Blackwood's. Saying that she will manage her correspondence. pn June 13 (241) £780 [Sawyer]
— 17 Dec 1879. 1 p, 8vo. To Joseph Langford of Blackwood's. Giving permission, but with many strings attached, for publication of a series of drawings based on Impressions of Theophrastus Such. pn June 13 (242) £680

**Eliot, Thomas Stearns, 1888-1965**

ALs, 4 Sept 1918. 2 pp, 8vo. To Robert Ross. Thanking him for an introduction to [Arnold] Bennett. S June 28 (43) £550
**Collection** of 64 Ls s, 1 autograph postcard, sgd & a 1-page typescript, 13 Feb 1934 to 9 Feb 1951. To Desmond Hawkins. S July 11 (288) £13,500
**Series** of 3 Ls s, 8 Mar to 30 May 1934. 3 pp, 4to. To Thomas Earp. About the possible publication of Erp's book. S July 11 (281) £380
**Photograph, sgd,** [c.1950]. 208mm by 160mm. Half length, by B.B.C. Publications. Illus in cat. Marans collection. CE Apr 17 (70) $650

**Elisabeth, Princess of Braunschweig-Wolfenbuettel, 1746-1840**

ALs, 26 Dec 1795. 1 p, 4to. To Herr Roemer. Concerning an inheritance. star Mar 22 (1543) DM320

**Elisabeth, Empress of Franz Joseph I of Austria, 1837-98**

AN, [n.d.]. 1 p, 8vo. To her husband. Brief note in Hungarian. HN May 15 (2541) DM1,800

**Elisabeth Charlotte, Duchesse d'Orleans, 1652-1722**

ALs, 2 Mar 1710. 4 pp, 4to. To her sister Louise. Reporting about her activities. HN May 15 (2547) DM8,400

**Elizabeth, Queen of George VI of England**

Ds, 3 March 1960. 1 p, folio. Appointing Sir Alexander Francis Morley "Commander of Our Most Excelelnt Order of the British Empire". pba Feb 22 (298) $375
See also: George VI & Elizabeth

**Elizabeth, Queen of Frederick V of Bohemia, 1596-1662**

ALs, 6 Apr [n.y.]. 1 p, 4to. To Sir Benjamin Rudyerd. Asking help to find £500 support for his sister & her servant, Lady Harrington. S Dec 18 (445) £1,200 [Mandl]

**Elizabeth I, Queen of England, 1533-1603**

Ds, 27 June [1559]. 1 p, 4to, parchment. Ordering money to be paid to Isabell Wright to settle an account dating from the reign of her sister Mary. Foxed. Illus in cat CNY Dec 15 (21) $15,000

— 26 May 1564. 1 p, 4to. Grant of privileges as a merchant trader in London to Paul Harwarde. Countersgd by 5 members of her Privy Council on verso. CNY May 17 (232) $7,000
— 26 Sept 1586. 1 p, on vellum. Warrant to the Treasurer of her Chamber, Sir Thomas Hennage for an allowance to Richard Mondaye. C June 26 (309) £9,000
**Document,** 19 Mar 1593. 1 p, on vellum, 310mm by 175mm, framed. Land grant to Richard Lewknor & John Lampton. Sgd by Sir John Fortescue. 2d Great Seal appended. bba Apr 11 (221) £450 [Krown & Spellman]
— PRIVY COUNCIL. - Letter, 5 May 1561. 2 pp, folio, in red half mor. To Sir Nicholas Throckmorton. Explaining the denial of the Spanish Ambassador's request that the Papal Nuncio be permitted to visit England to persuade the Queen to allow English representatives to attend the Council of Trent. In Latin, sgd by 15 members of the Privy Council. C Nov 29 (146) £2,000

**Elizabeth II, Queen of England —& Philip, Prince, Duke of Edinburgh**

**Christmas card,** sgd & dated 1961. 4 pp, folder, c.8.5 by 8.75 inches. sg Feb 1 (88) $450
**Group photograph,** 1957. 225mm by 175mm. With Prince Charles & Princess Anne; sgd by both. Marans collection. CE Apr 17 (134) $750

**Ellery, William, Signer from Rhode Island**

ALs, May 1778. 9 pp, 4to. To William Whipple. Sending news about recent military & political developments. P Dec 13 (106) $8,000
— 1 Nov 1792. 4 pp, 4to. To his daughter Nancy. About her smallpox inoculation. P Dec 13 (107) $2,750
— 1 Aug 1807. 2 pp, 4to. To Benj. Bourne. About the administration of an estate. sg Feb 1 (89) $275
ADs, 8 Oct 1805. 1 p, 8vo. Receipt to Benjamin Bowers for $22.65, proceeds from the auction of the effects of John Wood. wa Oct 28 (373) $260

**Ellis, Havelock, 1859-1939**

**Photograph, sgd,** Dec 1935. 126mm by 106mm. Shoulder-length profile port, by Cheltenham. Marans collection. CE Apr 17 (45) $240

**Ellison, Ralph**

Ms, Opening paragraph from Invisible Man. [n.d.]. 1 p, 8vo. In full: " I am an invisible man. No, I am not a spook like those who haunted Edgar Allen Poe; nor am I one of your Hollywood-movie ectoplasms. I am a man of substance, of flesh and bone, fiber and liquids - and I might even be said to possess a mind. I am invisible, simply because people refuse to see me." With port. Framed. Over-all size 16.5 by 20 inches. Illus in cat rms Oct 11 (237) $700

**Ellsworth, Oliver, 1745-1807**

Ds, 12 Aug 1775. 1 p, 8vo. Requesting that the Treasurer of Connecticut pay Mr. Moses Butler for "Victualing Capt. James Chambers's Company of Rifle Men on their March thro. this Colony..."Countersgd by Thos.

Seymour. Seymour's signature light. Docket sgd by Butler. rms Oct 11 (21) $290

— 12 Mar 1776. Order of payment of "three pound ten shillings and seven pence for boarding and tending...a sick soldier of the Connecticut troops" go to Nathaniel Hibberd. Illus in cat pba Oct 26 (135) $200

**Emerson, Ralph Waldo, 1803-82**
ALs, 19 Oct 1845. 2 pp, 4to. To H. G. O. Blake, Esq. Concerning payment for lectures. With holograph address leaf. With tape repair. Illus in cat pba Feb 22 (46) $325

— 14 July 1859. 4 pp, 8vo. To Mrs. Houghton. Reporting that a sprained ankle has forced cancellation of his trip to Waterford. CE May 22 (214) $480

— August [n. y.]. 2 pp, 8vo. To Rev. J. H. Hedge. Concerning his desire for counsel at the club on Sunday. Foxed. With related material. pba Feb 22 (47) $300

— [n.d.]. 3 pp, 8vo. To a minister. Declining an invitation. With a sepia portrait. Framed with plexiglass on both sides. Over-all size 16 by 24 inches. Illus in cat rms Oct 11 (238) $400

**Photograph, sgd**, [c.1860]. 105mm by 63mm. Profile port, by Whipple. Marans collection. CE Apr 17 (71) $2,200

**Englaender, Richard, 1859-1919.** See: Altenberg, Peter

**England**
Ms, Register of Writs and Formulary, from 1390 to 1407. [L, 1st quarter of 15th cent] 234 leaves, on vellum, 263mm by 180mm, in later 15th-cent blindstamped calf over wooden bds. Phillipps Ms 10349. C June 26 (16) £5,500

— Ms, Royal chronicle & Genealogy of the Kings of England from Bladuth, father of King Lear, to Edward IV; in Latin. [London, c.1461-64]. Scroll of 6 membranes of vellum, 5024mm by 295mm. In a small neat professional English bookhand. With c.125 paragraphs each opening with large initial in blue or burnished gold, elaborately interconnected family tree with names of c.250 kings in colored cartouches beneath highly burnished gold crowns, & names of wives & children in red cartouches. S Dec 5 (36) £5,000 [Abraham]

**Document,** 19 Sept 1598. 1 p, folio. Privy Council warrant, sgd by Sir Thomas Egerton, Essex, North, Buckhurst, Sir Robert Cecil, & Sir John Fortescue for payment of the account of the Mayor of Chester for shipping & food for soldiers. Addressed to Buckhurst & Sir John Fortescue as Chancellor & Under Treasurer of the Exchequer. C June 26 (308) £800

— HERTFORDSHIRE. - Ms, The Court of Survey of all those Lands... belonging to the Mannour of Great Hormead. [c.1593]. 259 leaves plus blanks, folio, in orig vellum. bba Apr 11 (234) £460 [Hertfordshire Record Office]

— REIGN OF CHARLES II. - Journall for the King's Maiestie's Silver, 3 Feb [1 June] 1662. Chronological accounts by weight of silver & allow received, molten, cast & deliverd by Edward Backwell. 94 pp, folio. In vellum wraps. S July 11 (416) £800

**Entrecasteaux, Joseph Antoine Bruni d', 1737-93**
ALs, 16 Aug 1792. 1 p, 4to. Recipient unnamed. Aboard ship near New Guinea, acknowledging receipt of a message. HN Nov 24 (2750) DM2,800

**Epp, Franz, Ritter von, 1868-1946**
Ds, 20 Aug 1934. 1 p, 4to. Appointment of Philipp Bouhler as President of the Police Department in Munich. Illus in cat. rms Mar 21 (360) $420

**Equestrianism**
Ms, Abrege de l'art de monter a cheval... [France?, c.1700]. About 110 pp, 230mm by 170mm, in wraps. HH Nov 14 (21) DM700

**Ericsson, John, 1803-89**
ALs, 17 July 1862. 1 p, 8vo. Recipient unnamed. Promising to provide material on the new iron-clad vessels & predicting "the inevitable downfall of England as a great naval power". CNY May 17 (217) $10,000

**Erni, Hans**
Ls, 3 June 1958. 1 p, 4to. To Jean-Robert Delahaut. Thanking him for a letter & arranging a meeting in Paris. Featuring the drawing of a ram as part of the signature. With translation. Illus in cat rms Oct 11 (154) $180

**Ernst, Erzherzog von Oesterreich, 1553-95**
Ls, 10 Jan 1591. 2 pp, folio. To Emperor Rudolf II. Referring to potential problems between noblemen & other members of the army. HN Nov 24 (2765) DM1,400

**Ernst August II, King of Hannover, 1771-1851**
Ds, 11 Dec 1837. 5 pp, folio. Dismissal of Wilhelm Albrecht as professor at Goettingen. HN Nov 24 (2785) DM5,800

— 11 Dec 1837. 5 pp, folio. Dismissal of G. H. A. Ewald as professor at Goettingen. Trimmed. HN Nov 24 (2786) DM3,400

**Ernst I, Herzog von Sachsen-Gotha, 1601-75**
Ls, 26 Jan 1652. 3 pp, folio. To the preacher Jakob Weller. Worrying about the increasing number of conversions to catholicism among members of aristocratic families. star Mar 22 (1637) DM300

**Ernst, Max, 1891-1976**
ALs, 25 June [c.1950]. 1 p, 4to. To "Bekky". Enjoying his stay in Arizona. star Mar 21 (668) DM650

— 19 Aug 1966. 1 p, 4to. To Varian Fry. Regarding newspaper articles and the case of Mr. Straus. sg June 6 (65) $225

— 6 Oct 1966. 1 p, 4to. To Varian Fry. Sending thanks for the obtaining of refugee documents for friends. He wishes improved health for Fry. sg June 6 (66) $450

— May [n. y.]. To unnamed artist. About sculpture & exhibitions. With postscript featuring his first initial. With translation. Detail in cat rms Oct 11 (155) $400

Ls, 29 Oct 1966. 1 p, 4to. To Varian Fry. Thanking him for sending all the documents concerning that "dirty business in the newspapers of my country". With 2 holograph additions and envelope with last name penned on flap. sg June 6 (67) $275

**Erzberger, Matthias, 1875-1921**
Ds, 4 June 1919. 1 p, 4to. Passport for Paul Diedrichs to travel from Berlin to Cologne. star Mar 22 (1273) DM420

**Esswein, Hermann**
ALs, 8 July 1922. 4 pp, 8vo. To Alfred Kubin. Thanking for a letter & a port. HH Nov 17 (3281) DM420

**Este, Leonora d', 1537-81**
Ls, 20 Aug 1575. 1 p, folio. To an unnamed Marchesa. Sending condolences. star Mar 22 (1372) DM650

**Esterhazy, Ferdinand Walsin, 1847-1923.** See: Dreyfus, Alfred

**Ethiopic Manuscripts**
Ms, lectionary. [Ethiopia, c.1800]. 121 leaves, vellum, 215mm by 165mm. Contemp blindstamped brown lea over wooden bds. Imperf. HH May 7 (101) DM1,000
— Ms, Mas'hafa Gebra Letit [Book of Offices for the Night], with S Lams [Hymns of Praise to the Twelve Apostles]. [Ethiopia, c.1800] 29 leaves only including 2 blanks, 200mm by 142mm, in contemp goat-backed wooden bds. With 17 full-page miniatures. C June 26 (25) £1,200
See also: Psalms & Psalters

**Eucken, Rudolf, 1846-1926**
Collection of ALs, 2 autograph Mss, & 3 typescripts (1 with autograph corrections), 19 Dec 1921. 8 pp, 8vo & 4to. To Professor Doegen. Sending excerpts from several of his works (included). JG Sept 29 (256) DM400

**Eugene of Savoy, Prince, 1663-1736**
ALs, 21 June 1723. 4 p, folio. To an unnamed prince. Sending condolences. HH May 9 (2452) DM4,600
Ls, 30 June 1708. 2 pp, folio. To an unnamed prince. Informing him that he is proceeding to the Netherlands with his army to join forces with the Duke of Marlborough. star Mar 22 (1275) DM1,700
— 23 Feb 1732. 2 pp, folio. To Count Virmond. Responding to a request for his intercession with the Emperor. HN May 15 (2549) DM500

**Eugenie, Empress of the French, 1826-1920**
ALs, 26 Dec 1891. 2 pp, 8vo. To Mrs. Corman. Regarding the marriage of her godson and inquiring where to send a gift. sg June 6 (68) $400

**Eugenius IV, Pope, 1383-1447**
Document, [13 Mar] 1444. 1 p, vellum, folio. Brief addressed to Francesco Foscari, Doge of Venice, confirming the arrival of recipient's envoy. star Mar 22 (1497) DM1,250
— COUNCIL OF BASEL. - Letter, 9 Nov 1434. 1 p, folio. To Pope Eugenius IV. Asking him to mediate between the Count of Hoya & Baldwin, Abbot of St. Michael in Lueneburg, in their differences over the nomination of an archbishop for Bremen. S May 15 (163) £700

**Eulenburg-Hertefeld, Philipp, Fuerst zu, 1847-1921**
A Ls s (2), 30 Mar 1899 & 20 Feb 1904. 7 pp, 8vo & 4to. To an unnamed lady. Planning meetings & sending personal news. star Mar 22 (1276) DM300

**Everett, Edward, 1794-1865**
Autograph quotation, 2 Aug 1861. 1 p, 2.5 by 4 inches. Concerning Washington: " Washington was the greatest of good men and the best of great men." With mounting traces on verso. pba June 13 (59) $50

**Ewers, Hanns Heinz, 1871-1943**
Collection of 3 postcards, sgd (2 autograph), 2 Oct 1941 to 17 Apr 1943. To Karl Rosner. About a variety of business matters. HN Nov 24 (2766) DM220

**Eybler, Joseph Leopold von, 1765-1846**
ADs, Feb 1841. 1 p, folio. Receipt for 220 guilders. star Mar 22 (820) DM400

# F

**Fabricius, Georg, 1516-71**
ALs, [10 Aug 1554]. 1 p, 4to. To Wolfgang Meurer. Concerning affairs at the new school at Leipzig, & requesting the return of one of his works. In Latin. star Mar 21 (447) DM450

**Faella, Giovanni, Count**
Ms, Instrumenta feudorum castri sone cum privilegio comitatus in personam D. Ioannis et fratrum ac descendentium de Faelis. [Verona, c.1505] 27 leaves, vellum, 307mm by 186mm, in contemp lea over wooden bds. Comprising copies of documents from 1332 to 1504 concerning the possession by the Faella of the castle of Sona. Abbey 7387. C Apr 3 (8) £12,000

**Fairfax, Edward, d.1635**
Ms, A Discourse of Witchcraft as it was acted in the Family of Mr Edward Fairfax of Fuystone in the County of Yorke in the Year 1621, [c.1650]. 128 pp, folio, disbound. S July 11 (119) £2,200

**Fairfax, Thomas, 6th Baron, 1692-1782**
Ds, 1 Mar 1754. 1 p, on vellum, oblong folio. Land grant to William Kernes. Framed with port. CE June 12 (32) $600

**Fall, Leo, 1873-1925**
ALs, [n.d.]. 3 pp, 4to. To an unnamed Ed. Saying that he does not feel like a foreigner in Berlin. Including 2 musical quotations. star Mar 22 (822) DM550

**Falla, Manuel de, 1876-1946**
Ls, 8 Oct 1933. 1 p, 4to. To an unnamed composer. Thanking for news & medicine. In Spanish & French. star Mar 22 (823) DM370

**Faraday, Michael, 1791-1867**
ALs, 20 Aug 1831. 1 p, 4to. To the Rev. Buckland. About the properties of a stone his correspondent has given him. Framed with port. CE June 12 (33) $500
— 25 Apr [1834]. 1 p, 4to. To Richard Phillips. Making plans for a meeting. star Mar 21 (448) DM480
— 28 Oct 1862. 1 p, 8vo. To Henri Victor Regnault. Thanking for his work on the steam engine. star Mar 21 (449) DM470

**Fargo, William George, 1818-81**
Ds, 10 Sept 1877. 1 p, 4to. Stock certificate of the American Express Company issued to William Lacy. Illus in cat. rms June 6 (360) $275
See also: Wells, Henry & Fargo

**Farragut, David G., 1801-70**
Photograph, sgd, [c.1865]. 100mm by 60mm. 3-quarter-length port, by C. D. Fredericks & Co. Sgd on verso. Illus in cat. Marans collection. CE Apr 17 (135) $750
— Anr, [n.d.]. Carte size. Seated, by J. Gurney & Son. Sgd on recto & on verso. Framed. Illus in cat. rms June 6 (28) $850

**Farrell, James T., 1904-79**
Series of 3 A Ls s, 6 Oct 1970 to 5 Dec 1973. 4 pp, 4to & 8vo. To Catherine Peters of Jonathan Cape. About his novel, Troubles. S Dec 18 (383) £350 [Strauss]

**Faulkner, William, 1897-1962**
Ls, [c.11 Sept 1945]. 1 p, 4to. To Richard Wright. About Black Boy and Native Son. CNY Oct 27 (39) $7,000
Photograph, sgd & inscr, 3 Apr [19]37. 252mm by 203mm; matted. Shoulder-length port, holding his pipe; sgd Bill & inscr to Meta. Illus in cat. Marans collection. CE Apr 17 (72) $3,200

**Faure, Gabriel, 1845-1924**
Autograph music, Le pas espagnol, from his "Dolly" Suite, Op.56, 17 Nov 1896. 11 pp, folio. Working Ms, notated on 6 or 7 systems per page, 2 staves each. Including autograph title; sgd. S May 15 (350) £8,500
ALs, [c.1878]. 2.5 pp, 8vo, on folded sheet. Recipient unnamed. Discussing the choice of a soloist for a performance of his violin concerto. sg Feb 1 (92) £350

**Feininger, Lyonel, 1871-1956**
ALs, 13 June 1952. 2 pp, 4to. To his daughter. Discussing personal matters. HN Nov 24 (2769) DM480

**Ferdinand, Prince of Prussia, 1730-1813**
A Ls s (2), 12 Sept 1760 & 1789. 3 pp, 4to. To Luigi d'Angelelli de Malvezzi. About his military service, & thanking for New Year's wishes. star Mar 22 (1534) DM380

**Ferdinand, Erzherzog, 1529-95**
Ds, 1551. 1 p, folio. Ptd orders addressed to Bishop Jan Dubrowsky concerning the production of alum at Olmuetz. HH Nov 17 (3211a) DM200
— 5 Dec 1587. 1 p, 495mm by 685mm. Grant of arms for Georg Klingler. Including large painting of the arms in gold & colors. Framed. FD May 14 (1140) DM1,350

**Ferdinand I, Emperor, 1503-64**
Ls, 20 Jan 1529. 2 pp, folio. To his treasury for Bohemia. Discussing payments to Hans von Pflugk & others. star Mar 22 (1579) DM580
— 26 July 1536. 1 p, folio. To the mayor & magistrates at Goerlitz. Requesting them to support his officials in Bohemia. HN Nov 24 (2771) DM600
— 3 May 1549. 1 p, folio. To Count Wilhelm von Nassau. Letter of recommendation for Jacob Jonas. HH May 9 (2453) DM500
— 3 May 1552. 2 pp, folio. To Georg von Pappenheim, Prince Bishop of Regensburg. Reminding him of contributions for the defense of the city. star Mar 22 (1581) DM750

**Ferdinand II, Emperor, 1578-1637**
Ls, 9 Apr 1625. 3 pp, folio. To Prince Karl of Liechtenstein. Concerning a decoration for 3 of his Bohemian councillors. star Mar 22 (1234) DM780
— 24 July 1626. 2 pp, size not stated. To the magistrate of Ulm. Requesting them to support movements of newly recruited troops. HH May 9 (2441) DM1,000
Ds, 14 Apr 1625. 1 leaf, vellum, 550mm by 705mm. Grant of an hereditary title to the manor of Lamperssdorff. HH Nov 14 (69) DM500
— 3 Nov 1626. 1 p, folio. Appointment for Landgraf Georg II of Hessen-Darmstadt to settle claims to an inheritance in the House of Hanau. star Mar 22 (1588) DM500
— 27 May 1632. 1 p, folio. Ptd order not to help deserted soldiers. star Mar 22 (1235) DM350

**Ferdinand III, Emperor, 1608-57**
Ls, 1 Mar 1650. 2 pp, folio. To the magistrate of Nuernberg. Requesting a contribution of 20,000 guilders for the war chest. HH May 9 (2442) DM450
— 7 May 1654. 2 pp, folio. Recipient unnamed. Appointing him as guardian of Maximilian Ferdinand zu Oettingen. star Mar 22 (1589b) DM400

**Ferdinand IV, Grand Duke of Tuscany, 1835-1908**
ALs, 9 Nov 1859. 3 pp, 8vo. To Luigi Bargagli. Reporting about a visit with his sister, & discussing the situation in Italy. HN Nov 24 (2873) DM420

**Ferdinand V, King of Spain, 1452-1516**
Ds s (2), 20 Nov 1504 & 5 Feb 1515. 2 pp, folio. Instructions addressed to the Conde de Tendilla concerning payments for troops. CNY May 17 (234) $1,800

**Ferdinand V, King of Spain, 1452-1516 —& Isabella I, Queen of Spain, 1451-1504**
Ls, 28 Dec [c.1480]. 1 p, 4to. To Rodrigo de Verdesoto. Appointing him Produrador of the Royal Court & summoning him to take the oath. b Dec 5 (165) £2,100
— 13 Apr 1491. To Alonso de Arevalo. Ordering him to give money to the Conde de Salinas & those who accompanied him, on their arrival from Brittany. b June 28 (20) £2,500

## FERDINAND

— 13 Nov 1483. 1 p, oblong 4to. To Inigo de Artieta, Captain-General of the Armada of Biscay. Telling him to sail for Cadiz when he returns from escorting King Muly Boabdil (Abu Abdullah Muhammad) into exile. Illus in cat CNY Jan 26 (151) $13,400

Ds, 28 Mar 1494. 3 pp, folio. Order confirming privileges of the Santa Hermandad of Toledo in penal matters. Illus in cat. star Mar 22 (1661) DM8,000

Document, 2 Dec 1497. 26 leaves, vellum, 313mm by 213mm. Carta executoria de hidalguia in favor of Francisco de Caceres. With 2 four-sided illuminated borders including half-length port of Ferdinand V & 2 full-page coats-of-arms probably added in the 17th cent. S June 18 (38) £1,100

### Fernow, Ludwig, 1763-1808

Autograph Ms, extensive comments on 33 pp of an interleaved copy of Immanuel Kant's Anthropologie in pragmatischer Hinsicht. Koenigsberg, 1798; in contemmp bds. FD May 14 (1103) DM7,200

### Ferrari, Enzo, 1898-1988

Photograph, sgd, [c.1955]. 232mm by 166mm. Shoulder-length port. Marans collection. CE Apr 17 (111) $700

### Fesca, Alexander Ernst, 1820-49

Autograph quotation, initial bars of the 4 movements of an unnamed composition, 14 Sept 1838. 1 p, 4to. Sgd. star Mar 22 (824) DM320

### Fesch, Joseph, Cardinal, 1763-1839

Ls, 23 Nov 1805. 1 p, folio. To Eugene Beauharnais. Asking him to forward dispatches for Talleyrand & others. star Mar 22 (1433) DM320

### Ficker, Ludwig von, 1880-1967

Series of 16 A Ls s, 1913 to 1952. 51 pp, 8vo & 4to. To Martina Wied. Literary correspondence. HN May 15 (2551) DM1,300

### Field, Cyrus W., 1819-92

Ls, 15 Nov 1851. 1 p, 8vo. To Mr. Rieves. Arranging a meeting. pba June 13 (150) $100

### Field, Eugene, 1850-95

Autograph Ms, poem, Rare Roast Beef. 19 Aug 1889. 3 pp, with separate calligraphic title page. 6 8-line stanzas in Field's hand. sg June 6 (74) $650

A Ls s (2), 2 Dec 1892 & 21 Oct 1893. Each 1 p, 8vo. To Professor Child. The first arranging a meeting, the other literary. With a holograph envelope. sg June 6 (73) $150

ALs, 21 Aug 1891. 4 pp, 8vo. To Professor Child. Literary letter about his book Echoes from the Sabine Farm. sg June 6 (69) $600

— 27 May 1892. 2 pp, 4to. To Professor Child. Effusive letter on literary matters and works of Whitman, Lowell and Whittier. Initial letter hand-illuminated by Field. sg June 6 (70) $550

— 1 Dec 1892. 1 p, 8vo. To Professor Child. Trying to arrange a meeting. sg June 6 (71) $100

— 22 Dec 1892. 4 pp, 8vo. To Professor Child. Sending thanks for a pamphlet. Also discussing mortality. sg June 6 (72) $150

### Fields, W. C., 1880-1946

Ls, 2 Aug 1939. 1 p, 4to. To Carlotta Douglas. Concerning books he will be sending. Sgd as "W". With original enevelope. pba Feb 22 (49) $650

— 23 Sept 1940. 1 p, 4to. To Carlotta Douglas. Regarding a mix-up on her 1935 California tax return. Sgd "Great Man". sg June 6 (75) $350

Photograph, sgd & inscr, [1936]. 4to. Depicting the actor in costume on the set & being shaved by a barber. Inscr "To Harry Shirley/ cut my throat/ I've heard everything..." Upper half of image toned. With surface defects. Illus in cat rms Oct 11 (156) $420

### Figueroa, Jose, 1792-1835

Ds, 20 June 1835. 3 pp on 4-page lettersheet, 8.5 by 6 inches. To David Sopence, Alcade of Monterey. Demand for a delinquent report. Larson collection pba Sept 24 (101) $400

### Fillmore, Millard, 1800-74

Autograph Ms, His "Copperhead" speech. 22 Feb 1864. 16 pp, 8vo. Speech in which Fillmore revealed his displeasure with the way the Lincoln government handled the war. Bound with 1 p, 8vo letter of 9 Mar 1864 to H. P. McIntosh sending the manuscript. Bound in contemp half mor gilt. Edges rubbed. Illus in cat CNY Dec 15 (60) $18,000

ALs, 30 Jan 1841. 2 pp, 4to. To Solomon G. Haven. Writing one of his law partners about " the merit of Canadian PATRIOTISM. I know not why Doct. Stagg published my letter to him; but no matter. It was written in too much haste for the public eye..." CNY Dec 15 (163) $650

— 6 Mar 1844. 2 pp, 4to. To Truman Smith. Declaring that Connecticut could be carried as a Whig state and that it must be. CNY Dec 15 (164) $850

— 8 May 1851. 2 pp, 4to. To John Bell. Regretting that he was not able to see him before his departure. Forbes Magazine collection. CNY May 17 (125) $1,300

— 7 June 1864. 1 p, 8vo. To Miss A. J. Edsall. Forwarding autographs in order to aid Union wounded: "Our brave soldiers will need all the relief that it is possible to give, and the sympathetic heart of woman must be their best hope..." With related material. CNY Dec 15 (61) $1,800.

— 26 Nov 1866. 2 pp, 8vo. To John R. Bartlett. About the Historical Society in Buffalo & requesting, as its President, a copy of the list of publications of the Historical Society of Rhode Island. pba Oct 26 (229) $550

Ds, 12 Oct 1850. 1 p, folio. Appointment of Robert Townsend as Lieutenant in the Navy. Countersgd by William A. Graham. Framed with related material. Illus in cat. rms Mar 21 (42) $850

— 14 Aug 1852. 1 p, folio. Four-language ship's papers for the Golden Fleece. Countersgd by Sec of State Daniel Webster. CE June 12 (34) $1,000

— 2 Sept 1852. 1 p, vellum, 17 by 13.25 inches, framed. Appointment of Stephen V. Benet as 2d Lieutenant in the Ordnance Department. rs Nov 11 (16) $550

**Autograph sentiment,** 30 Mar 1863. 1 p. "Respectfully yours". Framed with photo. rms Nov 30 (34) $470

**Cut signature,** 11 Apr 1865. No size given. Cut from a letter. pba Feb 22 (229) $150

**Signature,** [n.d.]. No size given. Mtd on a card. With a captioned port of Washington and a vintage American Republican party silk. Framed. Over-all size 15.5 by 19.5 inches. Illus in cat rms Oct 11 (309) $375

**Finck von Finckenstein, Karl Wilhelm, Graf, 1714-1800**

ALs, [n.d.]. 4 pp, 4to. Recipient unnamed. Reporting about events at the court of Frederick the Great. star Mar 22 (1536) DM920

**Firestone, Harvey Samuel, 1868-1938**

**Group photograph,** [c.1915]. 260mm by 155mm. Seated with Henry Ford; sgd by Firestone. Marans collection. CE Apr 17 (112) $750

**First Ladies of the United States.** See: Presidents of the United States & First Ladies of the United States

**Fish, Hamilton, 1808-93**

Ds, 2 June 1869. 1 p, folio. Requesting safe passage for James Gary Jewell, United States Counsel & his family in "Singapore, India". With Department of State frank. pba Oct 26 (230) $50

**Fitsimons, Thomas**

**Series** of 4 ALs s, 30 Mar 1784 to 25 July 1786, 5 pp, 4to. To Nicholas Low. Concerning business matters & requesting payment: "I must beg to know of you whether I may be allowed to draw on you for the amt. & at what time..." Toned. rms Oct 11 (157) $1,300

ALs, 30 May 1797. 1 p, 4to. To John Nicholson. Concerning financial matter: "The Securitie promised to me is so Long delayed as to Create anxiety in my Mind least the pressure of your other officers should put it out of your power to fullfill your intention if either the Population or Aslym shares should be put in a situation to Operate as Eventual Securitie to me I will be satisfied..." With mounting remnant on verso. Illus in cat rms Oct 11 (158) $6,500

**Fitzgerald, F. Scott, 1896-1940**

**Autograph Ms,** unpublished poem to Anita Loos. [1930s]. 1 p, 8vo. Beginning " This book tells that Anita Loos/ Is a friend of Caesar, a friend of Zeus..." Sgd. Darkening at bottom margin. CNY Dec 15 (22) $4,000

ALs, [Autumn 1922]. 3 pp, 4to. To Arthur W. Brown. About the illustrations for Winter Dreams. With a sketch by Fitzgerald of a golf scene in the text. CNY Oct 27 (46) $4,000

— [c.1923]. 1 p, 4to. To Thomas R. Smith at Boni & Liveright. Saying that the Waldo Frank novel is rubbish; wishes that they would republish Gertrude Stein's Three Lives. CNY Oct 27 (47) $2,100

— [n.d., received 12 Feb 1926]. 1 p, 4to. To Chatto & Windus. About The Great Gatsby. S Dec 18 (384) £2,400 [Dupre]

**Photograph, sgd & inscr,** [c.1920]. 190mm by 114mm; matted. Bust port, inscr to Charles T. Scott. Illus in cat. Marans collection. CE Apr 17 (73) $3,000

**Flagg, James Montgomery, 1877-1960**

**Original drawing,** pen-&-ink profile sketch of a young woman, [n.d.]. 4to. Sgd & inscr to William W. Seward. rms June 6 (312) $235

**Self-caricature,** [n.d.]. On 6 by 4.5 inch slip of paper . With note " You say --- ~'If you have time perhaps you would write your title' -- certainly -- just ~'Crown Prince' ...' Detail in cat Dar Oct 19 (80) $110

**Flammarion, Camille, 1842-1925**

Ms, essay, Sur la planete Mars, [c.Feb 1918]. 4 pp, 8vo. Including some autograph corrections; sgd. With ALs, letter of transmittal, 16 Feb 1918. star Mar 21 (450) DM250

**Fleetwood, Charles, d.1692**

ALs, 10 Sept 1650. 2 pp, 4to. To Sir Peter Wentworth. About the battle of Dunbar. S July 11 (363) £1,100

**Fleury, Andre Hercule de, Cardinal, 1653-1743**

ALs, 10 Aug [1707]. 3 pp, 4to. Recipient unnamed. As Bishop of Frejus, referring to the devastation of his diocese by the enemy. star Mar 22 (1294) DM350

**Flotow, Friedrich von, 1812-83**

ALs, 17 Feb 1860. 2 pp, 8vo. To M. Brandus. Discussing the price of some scores. star Mar 22 (825) DM550

**Floyd, John Buchanan, 1806-63**

Ls, 30 Jan 1860. 4 pp, 4to. Recipient unnamed. Informing him of his appointment as a cadet at West Point. rms June 6 (29) $100

**Foch, Ferdinand, 1851-1929**

Ds, 7 Nov 1913. Proceedings of the Army Correctional Court ordering 10 days of detention for Private Lejune. Signature light. With rear in the margins. Also with translation. rms Oct 11 (160) $160

**Photograph, sgd,** 25 Jan 1927. No size given. By Harris & Ewing. With flaw in background. Also with 2 World War I photos of the trenches & tanks. Framed. Over-all size 18 by 22 inches. Illus in cat rms Oct 11 (401) $300

**Foerster-Nietzsche, Elisabeth, 1846-1935**

Ls, 3 Mar 1927. 3 pp, 4to. To [Ulrich von Hassell]. Referring to the death of Georg Brandes & his appreciation of her brother. HH May 9 (2458) DM320

**Fontane, Theodor, 1819-98**

ALs, 24 Aug 1869. 4 pp, 8vo. To Herr Prediger. Informing him that he is leaving for Silesia & discussing various spellings of a woman's name. S May 15 (174) £1,200

— 28 Nov 1887. 2 pp, 8vo. Recipient unnamed. Declining an election to a jury. HN May 15 (2552) DM3,800
— 3 Oct 1889. 1 p, 8vo. To [Carl Robert Lessing]. Accepting an invitation to a meeting in honor of Ludwig Pietsch. star Mar 21 (90) DM4,200
— 12 Sept 1898. 1 p, 8vo. To Paul Warncke. Thanking for some friendly comments. star Mar 21 (91) DM3,200

**Fonteyn, Dame Margot, 1919-91**
Photograph, sgd & inscr, [n.d.]. 8 by 10 inches. Next to a mirror, where her image is reflected. Inscr to Lucia. Illus in cat. rms June 6 (216) $225
— Anr, [n.d.]. 4to. With an armful of flowers; inscr to Lucia Wayne. Framed. Illus in cat. rms June 6 (217) $215

**Football**
— FOUR HORSEMEN OF NOTRE DAME. - Ptd photograph, [c.1924]. 89mm by 120mm, mtd. Full length; inscr by Don Miller & sgd by Miller, Harry Stuhldreher, Jim Crowley & Elmer Layden. Illus in cat. Marans collection. CE Apr 17 (273) $1,300

**Ford, Gerald R.**
Ls, 13 Jan 1954. 1 p, 4to. To Mrs. Eleanor Gilleo. Concerning legal immigration proceedings. pba Oct 26 (231) $120
— 20 Mar 1963. 1 p, 4to. To Theresa Sherman. About the addition of Great Britain to the Common Market: "I thought France will let Great Britain's Entry into the Common Market...President DeGaulle has said 'No." This means there will not be an immediate entrance..."With minor defects. rms Oct 11 (161) $250

**Ford, Henry, 1863-1947**
Ls, 3 Feb 1937. 1 p, 4to. To James C. Colgate. About a coach: "...I have been advised of the safe arrival in Dearborn of the old coach which belonged to your grandfather...I am much pleased you have passed this conveyance and the account of its history on to us..." pba Oct 26 (109) $2,250
Group photograph, [c.1930]. 201mm by 251mm. Showing him with a group of men, including his son Edsel. Sgd by both Henry & Edsel Ford. CE May 22 (237) $1,300
Photograph, sgd, [c.1921]. 240mm by 175mm. Half length. Illus in cat. Marans collection. CE Apr 17 (113) $2,000
— Anr, [n.d.]. 4to. Bust-length pose. Illus in cat. rms June 6 (374) $1,300

**Ford, John Thomson, 1829-94**
ALs, 23 Aug 1866. 1 p, 8vo. To Mr. Boyd. Responding to an inquiry: "Dear Sir The only bills I have of the eventful night you name ar[e] in scrap books at home. Should I find more I will save one for you with pleasure. Very truly Yours J. T. Ford." pba Oct 26 (272) $8,000

**Formey, Johann Heinrich Samuel, 1711-97**
Autograph Ms, excerpts from the Mercure de France of 12 June 1718 concerning J. P. Gundling's election as President of the Berlin Academy of Sciences; 21 Mar 1779. 2 pp, 4to. Sgd. star Mar 21 (451) DM420

**Forrest, Edwin, 1806-72**
ALs, 13 Jan 1847. 3 pp, 8vo. To James Lawson. Giving instructions for financial investments. rms June 6 (111) $200

**Forrest, Nathan B., 1821-77**
Ds, 1 Sept 1869. 2 pp, folio. $1,000 bond of the Selma, Marion & Memphis Railroad Company; sgd twice. rms June 6 (30) $1,200

**Forster, Edward Morgan, 1879-1970**
Collection of 1 ALs & 1 Ls, 29 Mar 1949 & 11 Oct 1946. To John Gawsworth. The first agreeing to a reprint of "Entrance to an Unwritten Novel", the second saying that due to his schedule he cannot review a book. sg June 6 (76) $250
— Collection of 1 ALs, 4 Ls s & 2 autograph postcards, sgd, 1965-67. All to James Lawrie. With a large quantity of related material, all relating to the play version of Howards End. Ck Apr 12 (54) £500
ALs, 4 Aug 1959. 1 p, 8vo. To Dr. Anthony Storr. Granting him permission to quote passages from his work. S Dec 18 (386) £120 [Osborn]

**Forster, Georg, 1754-94**
— SANDER, JOHANN DANIEL. - ALs, 18 Feb 1794. 3 pp, 8vo. To [Friedrich Koepken]. Reminiscing about Georg Forster's life & work. star Mar 21 (455) DM850

**Forster, Johann Reinhold, 1729-98**
ANs, [c.1785]. 1 p, 8vo. To Johann Christian Christoph Ruediger. Asking for the cat of Robert Hoblyn's library. star Mar 21 (454) DM420

**Foscolo, Ugo, 1778-1827**
Series of 5 A L s s, [n.d.]. 8 pp, 4to & 8vo. To Xavier Labensky. Concerning his Ed of Dante's works. S May 15 (175) £5,000

**Fouche, Joseph, Duc d'Otrante, 1759-1820**
Ls, [11 Feb 1800]. 1 p, 4to. To Comte Berthier. Recommending Gen. D'Auvergne. star Mar 22 (1450) DM280

**Fouque, Friedrich de la Motte, 1777-1843**
A Ls s (2), 4 May 1823 & 5 Oct 1824. 2 pp, 4to. To the Weygand Press. Concerning the publication of Luise Brachmann's poems. star Mar 21 (92) DM800
ALs, 7 Feb 1829. 2 pp, 4to. To Friedrich Kind. Asking for contributions to his journal Berlinische Blaetter fuer Deutsche Frauen. On ptd advertisement for the journal. star Mar 21 (93) DM550

**France**
— DE LEUSE, GOSSES & BIETRIS. - Document, Apr 1264. 1 p, vellum, 305mm by 392mm. Last will & testament,

bequeathing money from rents at Tournai to various churches. Framed. S June 18 (33) £400

— REVOLUTION. - Letter, 30 Sept 1793. 1 p, folio. From the Comite de Salut Public to the Comite de Surveillance de Seine inferieure. Responding to their letter "sur la situation de nos villes maritimes." Sgd by Collot d'Herbois & Carnot. star Mar 22 (1310) DM280

**Francis I, Emperor, 1708-65**

**Ls,** 27 Nov 1754. 1 p, folio. To Count Ludwig zu Hohenlohe-Langenburg. Regarding an inheritance in the Loewenstein-Wertheim family. star Mar 22 (1595) DM300

**Autograph endorsement,** sgd, on a report addressed to him by Johann Adam von Posch, 19 May 1765, 1 p, 4to, concerning a suit pending before the Imperial appellate court at Wetzlar; hoping for an end of the matter. HN May 15 (2554) DM360

**Francis II, Emperor, 1768-1835.** See: Franz I, 1768-1835

**Franck, Cesar, 1822-90**

**ALs,** [c.1876]. 4 pp, 8vo. To an unnamed musician. Sending a list of his works. star Mar 22 (826) DM1,000

— [3 May 1884]. 3 pp, 8vo. To M. Brandus. Requesting him to send scores of his Beatitudes to M. Gamboti & M. Danbe. star Mar 22 (827) DM480

**Francke, August Hermann, 1663-1727**

**ALs,** 19 Apr 1723. 1 p, 4to. To [a son of Julius Elers?]. Describing a thunderstorm. star Mar 21 (456) DM620

**Franco, Francisco, 1892-1975**

**Photograph, sgd,** 2 Apr [n.y.]. 5.25 by 3.5 inches. Showing him in uniform. Matted. sg June 6 (77) $500

**Photograph, sgd & inscr,** 1956. 271mm by 213mm, including mount. Inscr on lower portion of the mount to "Coronel de U.S. Army Don Roberto F. Carter". CE June 12 (35) $600

**Francoeur, Francois, 1698-1787**

**Ds,** 1747. 1 p, 8vo. Receipt for 365 livres as his salary. Trimmed. star Mar 22 (829) DM520

**Francois I, King of France, 1494-1547**

**Ds,** [early 1525]. 1 p, c.11 by 10.5 inches. Pay warrant. sg Feb 1 (93) £400

**Frank, Hans, 1900-46**

**Ls,** 29 Dec 1934. 1 p, 4to. To Philipp Bouhler. Sending New Year's wishes. Illus in cat. rms June 6 (618) $400

**Frank, Leonhard, 1882-1961**

**Collection** of Ls & autograph postcard, sgd, 22 Mar 1951 & 2 Feb 1953. 2 pp, 4to, & card. To Nymphenburg Press. About fees, etc. HH Nov 17 (3213) DM340

**Frankfurter, Felix, 1882-1965**

**Ms,** Quotation. 30 Nov 1959. 1 p, 12mo. In full: "It is important not to give the appearance of a predisposed mind. And it is important not to let the mind become predisposed." With port & 1st page of the 23 Aug 1927 Dallas Morning News concerning the Sacco & Vanzetti electrocution. Framed 23.5 by 23.5 inches. Illus in cat rms Oct 11 (11) $525

**Ls,** 17 Oct 1924. 1 p, 4to. To Mr. Hornbeck. Comparing Robert La Follette & James MacDonald. Illus in cat. rms Mar 21 (341) $440

— 18 Nov 1937. 1 p, 4to. To Donald MacCampbell. About an interview & his feelings about public opinion. wa Oct 28 (389) $550

**Autograph sentiment,** sgd, [n.d.]. On ptd waist-length port, framed; overall size 18.75 by 18.75 inches. Illus in cat. rms Mar 21 (342) $340

**Franklin, Benjamin, 1706-90**

**ALs,** 16 Mar 1755. 1 p, folio. To his brother John Franklin. Complaining about a blacksmith. Illus in cat. Forbes Magazine collection. CNY May 17 (126) $19,000

**ADs,** 7 May 1770. 1 p, folio. Agreement concerning the purchase of lands on the Ohio River. Sgd twice; also sgd by 4 others. With related material. Illus in cat. P Dec 13 (110) $13,000

**Ds,** 5 Nov 1785. 1 p, oblong 4to. Order to pay Private James Allen a year's interest on his depreciation certificate. Illus in cat pn June 13 (222) £3,400

— 2 May 1786. 1 p, folio. Receipt for payment for a tract of land by Peter Louason. Countersgd by James Trimble. Framed with a port. P Dec 13 (111) $5,000

— 25 Oct 1786. 1 p, on vellum 254mm by 686mm. Declaration of bankruptcy against John Meng, William Goodwin Jr, James Smith & Robert Cumming. Sgd as President of the Supreme Executive Council of Pennsylvania. Also sgd by the bankruptcy commissioners. Framed. P June 5 (37) $5,500

— 13 June 1787. 1 p, folio. Grant of land "on the North West Side of the River Ohio" to Francis Johnston. CNY May 17 (238) $6,000

— 14 June 1787. 1 p, folio. On vellum. Land grant to Joseph Lewis Finley. rms Nov 30 (157) $5,750

— 14 Mar 1788. 1 p, folio. As President of the Supreme Executive Council of Pennsylvania, sale of land in Bethel Township to Henry Dubes. Illus in cat. P Dec 13 (113) $7,000

— 12 July 1788. Size not stated. Land grant to Joseph Till. rms Mar 21 (204) $4,000

**Franklin, William, 1731-1813**

**Ds,** 26 Sept 1772. 3 pp, folio. Legislation concerning meadow & swamp maintenance in Salem County. On page 3 he has noted "I assent to this Bill enacting the same and order it to be Enrolled." With signatures of other unnamed statesmen. Sgd as "Wm. Franklin". Folds & margins defective & with tape repairs. Detail in cat rms Oct 11 (22) $1,350

— 11 Mar 1774. 1 p, folio. Defraying charges and reimbursing himself for costs as Colonial Royal Governor. Also sgd on verso by Charles Pettit. Paper brit-

# FRANKLIN

tle. Margins chipped & with tape strengthening on verso. sg Sept 28 (8) $450

**Franklin, William Buel, 1823-1903**
ALs, 17 May 1861. 1 p, 8vo. To L. J. Cist Discussing when he was appointed a Brigadier General & when he was made a Major General. pba June 13 (15) $225

**Franz Albrecht, Herzog von Sachsen-Lauenburg, 1598-1642**
Ls, 4 Mar 1642. 1 p, folio. To an unnamed count. Humorous letter referring to a recent death. star Mar 22 (1237) DM900

**Franz Ferdinand, Erzherzog, 1863-1914**
Autograph postcard, sgd, [27 Mar 1902]. To Countess Aja Pueckler. Sending good wishes for Easter & hoping for a meeting. star Mar 22 (1494) DM650
Photograph, sgd, [c.1885]. 175mm by 118mm. Shoulder-length port. Illus in cat. Marans collection. CE Apr 17 (136) $1,200
Signature, 2 June 1908. On 1 p, 4to sheet. With unrelated material. sg Sept 28 (102A) $130

**Franz I, Emperor of Austria, 1768-1835**
ALs, 12 Dec 1791. 1 p, 4to. To Queen Caroline of Naples & Sicily. Announcing the birth of his daughter Marie Louise [the future Empress of the French]. Illus in cat. star Mar 22 (1606) DM1,900
Ls, 15 July 1792. 2 pp, folio. To [Archduke Maximilian Franz, Elector of Cologne?]. Notifying him of the appointment of Joseph Heinrich von Schlick as envoy to the estates on the Upper Rhine. HH May 9 (2460) DM200
— 24 Jan 1798. 3 pp, 4to. To King Ferdinand I of Naples & Sicily. As Holy Roman Emperor, regarding the conferral of a decoration on the Marchese di Gallo. star Mar 22 (1607) DM500
— 23 Aug 1832. 1 p, folio. To Pope Gregory XVI. Agreeing to the conferral of the cardinalate on Pietro Spinola. star Mar 22 (1485) DM370
Ds, 12 June 1801. 16 pp, 4to, in red velvet. Patent of nobility for Ignaz Stuermer. Including full-page painting of the arms in gold, silver & colors. star Mar 22 (1608) DM1,300

**Franz Joseph I, Emperor of Austria, 1830-1916**
Autograph Ms, draft of telegrams to 2 of his daughters, [1910]. 1 p, 4to. Sgd with paraph. star Mar 22 (1489) DM450
Ls, 4 July 1895. 1 p, 4to. To Archduke Leopold Salvator. Informing him of a change in his attendants. star Mar 22 (1488) DM450
Ds, 30 Nov 1892. 13 pp, folio. Patent of nobility for Ferencz Nadasdy. Illuminated throughout, & with painting of the arms. S Dec 1 (14) £460
— 25 Jan 1911. 4 leaves, 375mm by 285mm, in red velvet. Patent of nobility & grant of arms for Josef Koudela. Including achievement of the arms in gold, silver & colors. HH Nov 14 (71) DM1,300
Autograph telegram, sgd, 9 July 1888. 1 p, 4to. To his wife. Thanking for her news. star Mar 22 (1487) DM860

# AMERICAN BOOK PRICES CURRENT

**Franz Karl, Erzherzog von Oesterreich, 1802-78**
ALs, 13 June 1809. 3 pp, 4to. To his brother Ferdinand. Family news. HN May 15 (2556) DM650

**Franz, Robert, 1815-92**
ALs, 29 Mar 1852. 1 p, 4to. To Hans von Buelow. Hoping to meet him in his hotel in Weimar. star Mar 22 (830) DM240

**Frederick, Prince of the Netherlands, 1797-1881**
Series of 3 A Ls s, 3 Dec 1823 to 13 June 1825. 11 pp, 4to. To Empress Alexandra of Russia. Sending family news. HN May 15 (2563) DM750
— Series of 5 A Ls s, 1824 to 1834. 10 pp, 4to. To King Friedrich Wilhelm II of Prussia. Mostly about family matters. HN May 15 (2564) DM900

**Freeman, Douglas Southall, 1886-1953**
Series of 11 Ls s, 1927-45. 11 pp, 4to. To Charles Lee Lewis. bbc June 24 (43) $350
Ls, 17 Aug 1943. 2 pp, 4to. To Charles Lee Lewis. Mainly concerning portraits of Robert E. Lee. bbc June 24 (42) $200

**Freiligrath, Ferdinand, 1810-76**
A Ls s (2), 30 Aug & 17 Sept 1859. 4 pp, 8vo. To the booksellers Williams & Norgate. About a book order & a recommendation. star Mar 21 (96) DM850

**Fremont, John Charles, 1813-90**
ALs, 2 Sept [n. y.]. 1 p, 8vo. To Rev. Edmond B. Fairfield. Arranging a visit. Right edge soiled. pba Feb 22 (133) $275
Ds, 2 Mar 1868. 1 p, 8vo. Transfer of 50 acres of land from Freemont to the Trans-Continental Railroad, Texas Division for $1000. Also sgd by 3 railroad officials. sg Sept 28 (104) $325

**French & Indian War**
— HOLDEN, DAVID - Autograph Ms, A Jurnal of what was Transacted in the Expedition for the Total Reduction of Canada from the French, 20 Feb to 28 Nov 1760. In the margins of ptd book, Jesus Christ God-man: or, the Constitution of Christ's person..., L, 1719, in rebacked contemp calf. Ptd as Samuel A. Green, Ed.: French & Indian War..., Cambridge, 1889. P Dec 13 (117) $3,250

**French, Daniel Chester**
A Ls s (2), 14 Sept 1879 & 24 Nov 1913. 2 pp, 4to. To unnamed recipient. About a dinner & providing personal news. pba Feb 22 (52) $200

**French, John Denton Pinkstone, 1st Earl of Ypres, 1852-1925**
ALs, 11 May 1901. 3 pp, 4to. To "dear old Pashe". Congratulating him on an appointment & referring to a bout with malaria & the Boer War. rms June 6 (324) $325

**French Revolution**
— COMMUNE OF LONGPONT. - Ms Register. Dec 1792-Sept 1802. 100 pp, 4to. Record of marriages, births &

other communal matters. Half lea over bds. Worn. pba June 13 (105) $225

**Freuchen, Lorentz Peter Elfred**
**Typescript**, Min gronlandske Ungdom. [Copenhagen, 1936] 421 leaves, 4to. WIth corrections & editorial markings in ink. S Mar 14 (130) £700

**Freud, Sigmund, 1856-1939**
[A collection of essays written for Freud's 75th birthday, comprising an autograph Ms by Erich Schilf & typescripts (partly with autograph corrections) by Max Dessoir, Herbert Frenzel, Dr. Heimsoth, Marie Kalau vom Hofe, Viktor Mueller-Hess, Theodor Reik & Robert Saudek sold at Stargardt on 21 Mar 1996, lot 460, for DM1,900.]
**Series** of 1899-1911. About 34 pp, various sizes, some on card. To Alfred Adler. With related material. C June 26 (310) £24,000
**ALs**, 9 Mar 1909. 2 pp, 8vo. Recipient unnamed. Looking forward to reading his book. S May 15 (179) £1,600
— 11 May 1933. 2 pp, 8vo. Recipient unnamed. Asking him to help a young lady who wants to get married. star Mar 21 (457) DM4,600
— 7 Aug 1938. 1 p, 8vo. To an unnamed lady. Responding to a request for help after recipient's emigration. star Mar 21 (459) DM3,600
**Autograph postcard, sgd**, 18 June 1910. To Dr. Wilhelm Stekel. Asking him to send an announcement to the Ed of a scholarly journal in Leipzig. C June 26 (314) £800
**ADs**, 26 July 1905. 1 p, folio. Testimonial (Zeugniss) for Alfred Adler. C June 26 (312) £3,000
— Sept 1905. 1 p, folio. Testimonial (Zeugniss) for Alfred Adler. C June 26 (313) £3,000
**Photograph, sgd & inscr**, 1921. 225mm by 167mm (image). Holding a cigar, by Max Halberstadt. Illus in cat. Marans collection. CE Apr 17 (46) $13,000

**Frey, Alexander Moritz, 1881-1957**
**Collection** of 3 A Ls s & 2 Ls s, 24 Feb to 19 Mar 1956. 7 pp, 8vo & 4to. To Herr Niedermeyer at Limes Press. About publishing matters. HH Nov 17 (3216) DM340

**Freytag, Gustav, 1816-95**
**ALs** 28 Jan 1864. 2 pp, 4to. To [a carnival society in Cologne]. Responding to a carnival decoration awarded to him. HN Nov 24 (2775) DM220
— 26 June 1878. 3 pp, 8vo. Recipient unnamed. About recipient's plan to apply for a position at Molinari's in Breslau. HH Nov 17 (3217) DM380

**Frick, Wilhelm, 1877-1946**
**Ls**, 21 Dec 1935. 1 p, 4to. To Philipp Bouhler. Returning Christmas & New Year's wishes. Illus in cat. rms Mar 21 (361) $250

**Friedeburg, Hans Georg von, 1895-1945**
**ALs**, 11 to 14 May 1945. 10 pp, 4to. To his wife. Reporting about his negotiations with the allied powers for a surrender of the German forces. HN May 15 (2748) DM13,000

**Friedell, Egon, 1878-1938**
**ALs**, [c.1930]. 2 pp, 8vo. Recipient unnamed. Thanking for favorable comments on his work. star Mar 21 (98) DM700

**Friederike, Queen of Ernst August II of Hannover, 1778-1841**
**Series** of 4 A Ls s, 1825 to 1838. 12 pp, 8vo. To Princess Luise of the Netherlands. Family letters. HN May 15 (2561) DM900

**Friedrich August I, King of Saxony, 1750-1827**
**Ds**, 12 June 1809. 21 pp, folio. Ratification of a convention with King Jerome of Westfalia regarding deserted soldiers. star Mar 22 (1634) DM320

**Friedrich I, King of Prussia, 1657-1713**
**Ls**, 2 Dec 1680. 2 pp, folio. To the magistrate of Magdeburg. Discussing an ordinance to regulate the work of carpenters. star Mar 22 (1191) DM800
— 15 Apr 1696. 3 pp, folio. To an organization of French merchants in Berlin. Announcing restrictions on the importation of luxuries. star Mar 22 (1192) DM1,000
— 15 Sept 1710. 2 pp, folio. To the magistrate at Halberstadt. Instructing them to respond to a complaint by the Markgraf of Kulmbach. star Mar 22 (1515) DM460

**Friedrich I, King of Wuerttemberg, 1754-1816**
**Ds**, 14 Jan 1808. 1 p, folio. Commission for Lieut. Jakob von Molsberg. star Mar 22 (1689) DM560

**Friedrich I, Grossherzog von Baden, 1826-1907**
**Photograph, sgd**, [c.1890]. Folio. Knee-length. HH May 9 (2463) DM240

**Friedrich II, Landgraf von Hessen-Homburg, 1633-1708**
**Ls**, 2 Jan 1663. 1 p, folio. To Heinrich Bennen. About fees due to the cloister at Marienthal from the Manor of Hoetensleben. Including autograph postscript. star Mar 22 (1362) DM1,200

**Friedrich II, Landgraf von Hessen-Kassel, 1720-85**
**Ls**, 7 Jan 1759. 3 pp, 4to. To [Luigi d'Angelelli de Malvezzi]. About finances & the recruiting of soldiers. star Mar 22 (1363) DM320

**Friedrich II, King of Prussia, 1712-86**
**ALs**, 4 Nov 1736. 2 pp, 4to. To his father. Thanking for a letter & reporting about his wife's health. star Mar 22 (1522) DM6,000
— 11 [May 1757]. 1 p, 4to. To his sisters Philippine Charlotte, Duchess of Braunschweig-Wolfenbuettel, & Amalie, Abbess of Quedlinburg. Reporting about the siege of Prague & recent military actions. Illus in cat. star Mar 22 (1527) DM14,000
— 6 Dec 1784. 1 p, 4to. To [his brother Heinrich?]. Assuring him of his attachment. Thorek collection. HN Nov 24 (2776) DM5,200

# FRIEDRICH

**Series** of 11 Ls s, 30 Oct 1754 to 19 Oct 1769. 11 pp, 4to. To Major Binius (3) & his son-in-law Ricaud de Tiregale. About various requests & military orders, granting leave, etc. star Mar 22 (1525) DM7,500

— Series of 23 Ls s, 12 Dec 1756 to 5 Apr 1774. 23 pp, 4to. To Luigi d'Angelelli de Malvezzi. Giving various instructions regarding recipient's regiment. star Mar 22 (1526) DM13,000

**Ls,** 8 May 1735. 1 p, 4to. To Samuel von Marschall. As Crown Prince, requesting his help in finding a tall soldier in time for the inspection of his regiment by the King. Including autograph postscript. star Mar 22 (1521) DM2,200

— 8 Oct 1740. 1 p, folio. To his administration in Stettin. Giving orders to procure grain for a regiment. star Mar 22 (1523) DM1,100

— 2 Apr 1752. 1 p, 4to. To the Prussian secretary in Hamburg, Ludewig. Instructing him to ignore an unfriendly act by Hannoverian authorities. star Mar 22 (1524) DM650

— 7 May 1778. 1 p, 4to. To Georg Ernst von Holtzendorff. Informing him about instructions to replace horses in his regiment. star Mar 22 (1528) DM950

— 7 Feb 1783. 1 p, 4to. To a literary society in Mannheim. Declining to subscribe to a projected work. star Mar 22 (1529) DM1,600

— 26 Sept 1784. 1 p, 4to. To his treasury for Pommerania. Giving instructions to audit expenses for works in the port of Swinemuende. star Mar 22 (1530) DM950

— 9 Aug 1785. 1 p, 4to. To Col. Fox. Inviting him to a parade of troops in Silesia. star Mar 22 (1531) DM950

**Friedrich III, Landgraf von Hessen-Kassel, 1771-1845**

A Ls s (2), 2 Apr & 18 Aug 1816. 6 pp, 4to. To Prince Frederick of the Netherlands. About some military matters. HN May 15 (2562) DM260

**Friedrich III, Kurfuerst von der Pfalz, 1515-76**

Ls, 18 Sept 1550. 1 p, folio. To Emperor Charles V. Introducing two envoys. HH May 9 (2464) DM800

**Friedrich III, Deutscher Kaiser, 1831-88**

ALs, 22 July 1880. 1 p, 8vo. Recipient unnamed. Returning some information about his grandfather. star Mar 22 (1217) DM200

— 29 Dec 1887. 4 pp, 8vo. To Gen. Hugo von Winterfeld. Giving instructions for messages to some ministers, discussing Russian military matters, & referring to a visit by Sir Morell Mackenzie. star Mar 22 (1218) DM3,600

**Friedrich IV, Kurfuerst von der Pfalz, 1574-1610**

Ls, 1 Mar 1597. 2 pp, folio. To Queen Elizabeth I of England. Asking for her help in effecting the release of Wilhelm von Trcka from Turkish captivity. star Mar 22 (1510) DM2,200

— 8 June 1603. 1 p, folio. To [Prince Christian I von Anhalt-Bernburg?]. Requesting permission to drive cattle bought in Poland or Silesia through recipient's territory. HH Nov 17 (3218a) DM650

# AMERICAN BOOK PRICES CURRENT

— 15 June 1607. 1 p, folio. To Prince Christian I von Anhalt-Bernburg. Concerning the hunting of deer in the district of Amberg. HH Nov 17 (3218b) DM650

**Friedrich Karl, Herzog von Wuerttemberg, 1652-98**

Ls, 26 Apr 1678. 1 p, folio. To Count Albrecht Ernst von Oettingen. Recommending his former servant Joseph Melchior Hofmann. star Mar 22 (1686) DM360

**Friedrich V, Kurfuerst von der Pfalz, 1596-1632**

Ls, 8 Aug 1629. 1 p, size not stated. To M. Voillot. About a reconciliation with the Emperor. HH May 9 (2443) DM1,500

**Friedrich Wilhelm, Herzog von Braunschweig-Wolfenbuettel, 1771-1815**

ALs, 20 Feb 1814. 3 pp, 4to. Recipient unnamed. About arms for his troops & the military situation in France. star Mar 22 (1196) DM750

**Friedrich Wilhelm, Kurfuerst von Brandenburg, 1620-88**

Ls, 27 Apr 1641. 2 pp, folio. To Duchess Anna Sophie of Braunschweig-Lueneburg. Informing her that he released the Swedish envoy & assuring her that he ordered his army not to attack Swedish towns. star Mar 22 (1240) DM3,800

**Friedrich Wilhelm I, King of Prussia, 1688-1740**

Ls, 6 Sept 1727. 1 p, 4to. To Graf von Schlieben. Approving of recipient's return to his regiment. Including autograph postscript. star Mar 22 (1516) DM1,500

— 7 Jan 1734. 1 p, 4to. To the merchants Saturgus. Thanking for New Year's wishes & presents. star Mar 22 (1517) DM350

— 15 Apr 1735. 13 pp, folio. To his treasury for Pommerania. Giving instructions for a fair distribution of expenses for troops. star Mar 22 (1518) DM370

**Autograph endorsement,** sgd, on a report addressed to him by an administrative department, 17 Feb 1740, 1 p, folio, concerning payment for a mill builder; declining the builder's demands. Illus in cat. star Mar 22 (1520) DM1,300

**Friedrich Wilhelm II, King of Prussia, 1744-97**

Ls s (2), 9 Jan 1789 & 3 Jan 1790. 2 pp, 4to. To Luigi d'Angelelli de Malvezzi. Thanking for New Year's wishes. star Mar 22 (1540) DM340

Ds, 3 Mar 1790. 3 pp, folio. Military promotion for Major von Weyrach. star Mar 22 (1541) DM380

**Friedrich Wilhelm III, King of Prussia, 1770-1840**

Ls s (2), 20 Mar 1822 & 3 July 1832. 2 pp, 4to. To August Wilhelm Francke, Mayor of Magdeburg. About a convention of the estates & the award of a decoration. star Mar 22 (1548) DM380

Ls, 19 Mar 1813. 1 pp, 4to. To Count Yorck von Wartenburg. Informing him that Prince Biron of Curland has been assigned to his regiment. star Mar 22 (1547) DM450

**Friedrich Wilhelm IV, King of Prussia, 1795-1861**
**Ls,** 13 Mar 1848. 2 pp, 4to. To his brother Carl. About a military appointment for recipient's son. star Mar 22 (1550) DM420

**Friesen, Karl Friedrich, 1784-1814**
**ALs,** 2 May 1813. 3 pp, 4to. To an unnamed aunt. Reporting from the war. HN May 15 (2567) DM500

**Frommann, Friedrich, 1765-1837**
**ALs,** 28 May 1787. 3 pp, 4to. To Johann Gottlieb Schummel. Discussing a work by G. S. Roetger. Including ALs from Schummel on verso. star Mar 21 (134) DM600

**Frommann, Johanna, 1765-1830**
**Series** of 8 A Ls s, 22 June 1824 to 2 May 1826. 35 pp, 8vo. To Friedrich Adolph Karl Meyer. Interesting letters mostly about literary matters, mentioning Goethe, Jean Paul, Kleist, & others. star Mar 21 (135) DM2,200

**Frost, Robert, 1874-1963**
**Signature,** [n.d.]. On card. Framed with port. CE Feb 21 (105) $450

**Fry, Elizabeth Gurney, 1780-1845**
**ALs,** 28 Jan 1837. 3 pp, no size given. To Catherine Gurney about Joseph Gurney's illness. With related material such as her Texts for Every Day in the Year & ANs about the book. Ck Nov 17 (90) £100

**Fuchs, Guenter Bruno, 1928-77**
**Collection** of 5 A Ls s, 2 Ls s, 4 postcards, sgd (2 autograph), ANs, & woodcut, sgd, 11 July 1956 to 9 June 1958. 15 pp, various sizes. Recipient unnamed. Discussing his literary work. star Mar 21 (99) DM1,300

**Fuessli, Johann Heinrich, 1745-1832**
**AL,** 22 Aug 1802. 4 pp, 8vo. To Karl Viktor von Bonstetten. Fragment, discussing political developments in Switzerland. star Mar 21 (461) DM1,100

**Fuller, Loie, 1862-1928**
**Photograph, sgd & inscr,** [c.1880s]. 1 p, 4 by 5.5 inches. Sepia cabinet photo of the dancer in costume. By Langfier. Sgd & Inscr. sg Sept 28 (86) $175

**Fuller, Roy**
**Autograph Ms,** Notebook containin.d.afts & versions of poems such as Versions of Love, Monologue in Autumn & Brother Serene. [1960-63]. 57 pp, 8vo. In bds. Illus in cat S June 28 (62) £900

**Fulton, Robert, 1765-1815**
**ALs,** 25 Feb 1813. 2 pp, 4to. To John D. Delacy. Inquiring about the failure of Oliver Evans's steam engine. Illus in cat. P Dec 13 (118) $5,500
— 14 Oct 1814. 1 p, 4to. To David Cooke. Sending $500 for " ...the account of the New Orleans hull..." Illus in cat rms Oct 11 (164) $3,000
**Ds,** 1 Aug 1814. 1 p, 4to. Promissory note for $600 from Joseph C. Yates for steamboats to be built by Fulton.

Also sgd by Yates & Thomas Morris. Illus in cat. rms June 6 (376) $13,000

**Furtwaengler, Wilhelm, 1886-1954**
**ALs,** 5 Sept [n.y.]. 1 p, 4to. To Firtz Hirt. Saying that he cannot include the Landischer Symphony in his upcoming concert. wa Oct 28 (130) $300
**Ls,** 4 Mar 1930. 1 p, 4to. To [Ulrich von Hassell]. Declining an invitation. HH May 9 (2468) DM450
See also: Beethoven, Ludwig van

# G

**Gable, Clark, 1901-60**
**Check,** 10 Jan 1950. 1 p, 8vo. Payable for $9.32 to E. Des Baillets. pba Feb 22 (53) $250
— Anr, 10 Jan 1950. 1 p, no size given. $80.33 payable to Chubby's. pba June 13 (183) $200
— Anr, 10 Jan 1950. $3.79 payable to Book-of-the-Month-Club,Inc. Cancellation perforation just affecting signature. sg June 6 (80) $300
— Anr, 20 Apr 1950. 1 p, 3 by 8.5 inches. $23.09 payable to Pacific Telephone and Telegraph Company. Ink cancellation stamp affecting the first 2 letters in Clark. pba Oct 26 (24) $325
**Ptd photograph,** [n.d.]. 11.37 by 7.75 inches. Bust-length magazine port with caption; sgd & inscr. Illus in cat. rms June 6 (168) $280

**Gabor, Dennis, 1900-79**
**Series** of 3 Ls s, 21 June to 9 Aug 1972. 3 pp, 8vo. Recipient unnamed. Discussing the German Ed of his work The Mature Society. star Mar 21 (462) DM360

**Gade, Niels Wilhelm, 1817-90**
**ALs,** [n.d.]. 1 p, 8vo. To Ferdinand David. Discussing the program of a concert with Clara Schumann. star Mar 22 (836) DM720

**Gagarin, Yuri, 1934-68**
[The records file on the flight of Gagarin on 12 Aopr 1961 on the Vostok I, prepared for submission to the International Aeronautics Federation & sgd by Gagarin, sold at Sotheby New York on 16 Mar 1996, lot 39, for $28,000]
**Typescript,** orig draft of 1st article written by Gagarin for the newspaper Ivestiya. 6 pp, 298mm by 210mm, sgd & dated 27 Apr 1961 & countersgd by the commander of the Cosmonauts' Center, Nikolai Kamanin. With some emendations in an unidentified hand. P Mar 16 (40) $3,750
**Photograph, sgd,** of Vostok I, sgd [c.Apr 1961]. 90mm by 140mm. P Mar 16 (36) $1,800
— Anr, 4 July 1961. 171mm by 241mm. Showing him with fellow cosmonaut Gherman Titov. Sgd & dated by Gagarin. Yuri M. Baginsky collection P Mar 16 (56) $1,700
**Photograph, sgd & inscr,** 21 May 1961. 276mm by 197mm. Inscr at lower margin. Taken by Aleksandr N. Sergeev & with related material. P Mar 16 (43) $1,800

**Gagarin, Yuri, 1934-68 —& Korolev, Sergei G.**
Photograph, sgd, May 1961. 128mm by 238mm. Sgd on recto by Gagarin & on verso by many in the Russian Space Program. Yuri M. Baginsky collection P Mar 16 (50) $2,750
— Anr, May 1961. 133mm by 229mm. Sgd on verso by many in Russian Space Program. Yuri M. Baginsky collection P Mar 16 (51) $2,000

**Gagarin, Yuri, 1934-68 —& Titov, Gherman S.**
Photograph, sgd, [n.d.]. 197mm by 273mm, sgd by both. Yuri M. Baginsky collection P Mar 16 (67) $1,200

**Gagnebin, Henri, 1886-1977**
ALs, 6 July 1938. 2 pp, 8vo. Recipients unnamed. Supporting "l'initiative de la Lincoln Memorial University". star Mar 22 (837) DM220

**Gal, Hans, 1890-1987**
Autograph music, Divertimento fuer Fagott & Violoncello, Op.90, no 1, 1st movement; 1968. 2 pp, folio. Sgd. star Mar 22 (838) DM300

**Galenus, Claudius, 129-c.199**
Ms, Liber Tegni, Book of Medicine, Ktav Yad Refuah al Kalph, in Hebrew, with other medical texts in Hebrew. [Spain, 14th cent]. 49 leaves, vellum, 192mm by 134mm. Modern dark red blindstamped mor. In a small elegant Spanish rabbinic cursive hand, with headings in larger square script, by several scribes. S June 18 (45) £6,000

**Gall, Franz Joseph, 1758-1828**
Autograph Ms, medical report about a baby girl, sgd; 28 May 1828. 3 pp, 4to. In French. HN Nov 24 (2779) DM420

**Gallas, Matthias, Duke of Lucera, 1584-1647**
Ls, 20 Sept 1644. 2 pp, folio. To Duke August of Sachsen-Weissenfels, Archbishop of Magdeburg. Responding to complaints about requisitions in Halle. star Mar 22 (1241) DM950

**Gallatin, Albert, 1761-1849**
Ls, 14 Jan 1809. 3 pp, 4to. To William Ellery. Treasury circular concerning the enforcement of the embargo acts. Including franking signature on integral address leaf. rms June 6 (368) $350
— 27 June 1810. 2 pp, folio. To Isaac Van Horne. Authorizing William Wells to inspect the books of Zanesville concerning public lands disposal. Toned. With defects. pba Oct 26 (235) $250

**Gallaudet, Thomas Hopkins, 1787-1851**
ALs, 21 Aug [n.y.]. 1 p, 12mo. To [John] Trumbull. Asking permission for his students to see Trumbull's "very interesting national painting." rms June 6 (377) $450

**Galvani, Luigi, 1737-98**
Autograph Ms (2), scientific memoranda about "animal electricity" & experiments he has performed on muscles, [n.d.]. 5 pp, 4to. S May 15 (182) £6,000

**Gandhi, Mohandas K., 1869-1948**
ALs, 10 Jan 1930. 1 p, 4to. To Syed Mahmud. Regretting the death of a Muslim prince. star Mar 22 (1326) DM4,000
— 10 Apr 1931. 2 pp, 8vo. To Mr. Garrett. Requesting an interview "regarding Gujarat affairs arising out of the settlement." With marginal defects and pinholes. sg Sept 28 (107) $800
Photograph, sgd, 9 Oct [19]31. 179mm by 130mm. Seated. Illus in cat. Marans collection. CE Apr 17 (137) $3,800

**Garbo, Greta, 1905-90**
ALs, [n.d.]. 1 p, 4to. To Cecil Beaton. Thanking for an invitation & sending the address where she can be reached in Stockholm. Sgd "Harry, for short". With a port. Illus in cat. rms June 6 (144) $850
Autograph sentiment, sgd, [c.1970]. 4 lines, on Zarah Leander record cover (imperf). "To my angel, Get well soon." HH Nov 17 (3221) DM1,050
Signature, [n.d.]. 1 p, 12mo. With Photo port of Garbo and 3 others from movie star book. bbc Sept 18 (75) $110

**Gardner, Alan, 1st Baron Gardner, 1742-1809.** See: Nelson, Horatio Nelson & Gardner

**Gardner, John, 1933-82**
Original drawing, of the character Ork from his 1971 novel Grendel. Folio size. In color crayon. Sgd & titled in crayon. Framed. wa Oct 28 (23) $280

**Garfield, James A., 1831-81**
ALs, 16 March 1864. 1 p, 8vo. To A. T. Goodman. Explaining that he cannot send a copy of a speech because it "was Entirely extemporaneous..." CNY Dec 15 (62) $1,500
— 5 Dec 1867. 2 pp, 4to. To an unnamed general. Discussing a nomination for the consulate in Havana & Andrew Johnson's impeachment. P Dec 13 (122) $1,900
— 10 Nov 1869. 1 p, 8vo. To John Gourlie. Replying to Gourlie's autograph request. pba June 13 (66) $350
— 5 June 1871. 1 p, 8vo. To A. Morgan. About the Southington Post Office in Hiram, Ohio. CE June 12 (37) $300
— 26 Mar 1880. 1 p, 8vo. To [John?] Sherman. Returning a letter. rms Mar 21 (78) $220
— 23 Dec 1880. 2 pp, 4to, on 1 leaf. To Senator George F. Edmunds. Thanking him for his suggestions in reference to his declination of the Senatorship. CE June 12 (38) $4,000
— 30 June 1881. 1 p, 8vo. To Charles W Clark. Offering him the appointment as Marshal for Mississippi. Illus in cat. Forbes Magazine collection. CNY May 17 (128) $18,000
Ls, 8 Feb 1876. 1 p, 8vo. To Henry Hubbard. Concerning a petition to stop the bridging of the Detroit River: "I will present the petition tomorrow and do all I can to

prevent any obstruction of our lake navigation." rms Oct 11 (165) $230

— 6 July 1877. 1 p, 4to. To H. E. Parsons. Explaining that there is no change in Deputy Collector of Customs at Ashtabula Ohio:"I should be exceedingly glad to aid Major Hubbard in any way in my power; but the rules of the Civil Service, it seems, allow me no chance under present circumstances..." rms Oct 11 (166) $230

— 9 July 1878. 3 pp, 8vo. To Henry Hubbard. "My experience with the present administration makes it clear that I can accomplish nothing in the direction of your desire...." rms Nov 30 (161) $300

— 25 Dec 1879. 2 pp, 8vo. To President R. B. Hayes. Supporting John J. Williams' bid for a territorial judgeship. pba Feb 22 (235) $300

— 30 June 1880. 1 p, 8vo. To C. J. Hill. Sending thanks. Sgd as "J. A. Garfield". sg Sept 28 (109) $225

— 28 Oct [18]80. 1 p, 8vo. To B. H. Stinemetz. Thanking for a hat. rms Mar 21 (80) $360

**ANs,** 15 Sept 1880. 1 p, 8vo. [To Chester A. Arthur]. Merely asking "What do you think of this ?"Browned. CNY Dec 15 (167) $400

— 11 Apr 1881. 1 p, 16mo. Recipient unnamed. Stating that he will see Mr. Bullitt the next day. Illus in cat. rms June 6 (380) $5,000

**Ds,** 10 June 1881. 1 p, 4to. Authorizing the sending of a letter of state to the King of the Belgians on the marriage of Princess Stephanie to the Austrian Prince Rudolphe. Illus in cat CNY Dec 15 (168) $8,500

**Autograph quotation,** Latin phrase. 8 June 1872. 1 p, 8vo. "Per angusta, ad augusta". (Through the tight places, on to the august.) In purple ink. Sgd as "J. A. Garfield/Hiram/Ohio". sg Sept 28 (108) $475

**Photograph, sgd,** [9 Feb 1881]. Cabinet size. Bust port, by Harroun & Bierstadt. Inscr in anr hand on verso. Illus in cat. rms Mar 21 (79) $1,500

— Anr, [n.d.]. Carte size. By Brady. Illus in cat. P Dec 13 (123) $1,800

**Signature,** [n.d.]. No size given. On a card. With a sepia-toned port & a reproduced photo of his coffin lying in state. Also with a broadside describing his final hours. Framed. Over-all size 24.5 by 30.5 inches. Illus in cat rms Oct 11 (311) $550

— ROCKWELLL, ALMON FERDINAND. - ALs, 17 Sept 1881. 3 pp, 8vo. To John Sherman. Conveying President Garfield's condition for a letter & reporting about his condition. rms Mar 21 (84) $400

— WOODWARD, JOSEPH JANVIER. - ALs, 26 Sept 1881. 2 pp, 8vo. To Dr. I. Minis Hays. Enclosing (not present) a copy of "the proceedings of a meeting of the late President's physicians held last night" & a copy of the post-mortem. rms Nov 30 (162) $440

**Garfield, James A., 1831-81 —&**
**Arthur, Chester A., 1830-86**

**Signature,** [n.d.]. No size given. Signatures & vintage cabinet photos of each individual. Also with a vintage silk from the 1880 campaign. Framed. Over-all size 13.5 by 18 inches. Illus in cat rms Oct 11 (310) $600

**Garfield, Lucretia R., 1832-1918**

**ALs,** 27 Feb 1882. 4 pp, 8vo. To Ezra Boot Taylor. Protesting the decision of the Committee to audit the expenses of Gen. Garfield's illness to pay Dr. Reyburn $10,000 but to pay Miss Dr. Edson $5,000. With port. rms Nov 30 (163) $1,100

**Garibaldi, Giuseppe, 1807-82**

**ALs,** 17 May 1877. 1 p, 4to, framed. To Mrs. Chamber. Thanking for "l'eccelente bacon". pn June 13 (202) £140 [Wilson]

**ANs,** 4 Apr 1875. 1 p, no size given. Sending his autograph to a collector. pba Feb 22 (299) $110

— [n.d.]. 1 p, 8vo. Recipient unnamed. Expressing regrets. HN Nov 24 (2780) DM280

**Garrett, Patrick Floyd, 1850-1908**

**Ds,** 12 Dec 1899. 1 p, 4to. Stock certificate of the Alabama Gold and Copper Mining Company for D. M. Goodrich. CNY May 17 (242) $2,400

**Garrick, David, 1717-79**

**Collection** of 1 ALs & 1 autograph card, sgd, 16 Apr & 2 July [n.y.]. 1 p, oblong 8vo & card. To Thomas Percy. About theatrical performances. S Dec 18 (439) £600 [Levine]

**Garrison, William Lloyd, 1805-79**

**Autograph Ms,** Poem entitled Equal Rights. 26 Apr 1875. 1 p, 8vo. Poem supporting women's suffrage. Beginning " Though woman never can be man..."With fold strengthened by tape on verso. Trimmed & age stained. rms Oct 11 (167) $230

**ALs,** 15 Sept 1870. 1 p, size not stated. To T. B. Pugh. Declining an invitation to lecture & referring to his health & age. rms Mar 21 (297) $340

**Garvey, Marcus Moziah, 1887-1940**

**Ls,** 27 Sept 1928. 1 p, 4to. To Uriah Gittens. Sending thanks for a contribution. sg Mar 28 (90) $850

**Gastoldi, Giovanni Giacomo, 1550s-1622?**

**Ms,** balletto, A lieta vita. [Germany, early 17th cent]. 2 pp, folio. Notated in open score in German organ tablature, with letter names for the notes. Illus in cat. S Dec 1 (158) £1,700

— Ms, balletto, Tutti venite Armanti. [Germany, early 17th cent]. 2 pp, folio. Notated in score in German organ tablature. Illus in cat. S Dec 1 (157) £800

**Gates, Horatio, 1728-1806**

**ALs,** 1 Aug 1775. 1 p, 4to, mtd. To Artemas Ward. Requesting surgeons to attend wounded British marines. P Dec 13 (124) $9,000

— [c.20 Sept 1777]. 1 p, 4to. To Mathew Vischer. Expressing his conviction that "Albany ... is undoubtedly General Burgoyne's object". P Dec 13 (125) $3,000

— 19 Sept 1780. 2 pp, 4to. To Brigadier General Jethro Sumner. About the defense of Charlotte, N. C. With address leaf featuring Gates's free frank. With a second signature. Soiled. CNY Dec 15 (64) $2,800

— 23 Nov 1797. 2 pp, 4to. To Dr. Benjamin Rush. Concerning Rush's move to New York & introducing a friend of his : "Your Friends here say you are coming to live in New York...I am quiet Satisfied; but I never will believe, until I see it that the Philadelphians will permit you to leave their City...Mr Garnet...This Gentleman, my Relation and particular Friend, I take the Liberty to Introduce to Your Notice. He is lately with his Family from England, intending to make this Country of Freedom Theirs..." With postscript about Benedict Arnold. Toned. Detail in cat rms Oct 11 (168) $2,600

Document, [17 Oct 1777]. 3 pp, 4to. Articles of Convention between Lt. Gen. Burgoyne & Maj. Gen. Gates; retained copy in a secretarial hand. Repaired. Sang collection. P Dec 13 (126) $9,000

**Gatling, Richard Jordan, 1818-1903**
ALs, 7 June 1884. 1 p, 4to. To the Colt Fire Arms Company. Forwarding an order for guns for the U. S. Navy Department. Illus in cat. CNY May 17 (243) $5,000

Ls, 11 July 1885. 1 p, 4to. To [Samuel] Colt's Patent Fire Arms Manufacturing Co. Ordering a gun. Typed in purple ink. CNY Dec 15 (63) $4,800

Signature, 3 Mar 1891. On card. Framed with photograph. CE June 12 (39) $260

**Gatty, Harold, 1903-57.** See: Post, Wiley & Gatty

**Gauguin, Paul, 1848-1903**
ALs, Jeudi, 28th, 1886. 1 p, 8vo. To Felix Bracquemond. Making an appointment to see him on Saturday. wad Oct 18 (149) C$4,200

— [n.d.]. 1 p, 8vo. To unnamed recipient. Sending a La Meuse article: " I am sending you this small article hoping that you will give it the same welcome as you did for the first one. I think that it has its usefulness at this time. If you find things you would like to change, go ahead. If you run it, be kind enough to send me a copy." tipped to a mat. With a copy of La Meuse & translation. Illus in cat rms Oct 11 (169) $7,250

**Gauss, Karl Friedrich, 1777-1855 —& Others**
Ds, 7 Nov 1843. 2 pp, folio. Statement concerning students arriving at Goettingen University after the regular registration period; sgd by 53 professors. In the hand of F. Ch. Bergmann. star Mar 21 (463) DM720

**Gay, Martin, c.1727-1809.** See: American Revolution

**Geary, John White, 1819-73**
Ds, 4 Jan 1862. 1 p, 4to. Requisition for plank & scantling for a government telegraph office in Maryland. pba June 13 (16) $225

— 15 June 1868. 1 p, folio. Appointing Andrew Hero, Jr. a Commissioner. Folds reinforced. pba Oct 26 (166) $70

**Gehrig, Henry Louis ("Lou"), 1903-41**
Photograph, sgd & inscr, [c.1935]. 232mm by 172m. Shoulder-length port, by Morgan; inscr to Perry. Illus in cat. Marans collection. CE Apr 17 (274) $3,000

**Geibel, Emanuel, 1815-84**
Autograph Ms, 5 poems, Jugendlieder; [n.d.]. 4 pp, 8vo. star Mar 21 (100) DM460

**Gellhorn, Martha**
Collection of 8 A Ls s & 15 Ls s, 8 May 1939 to 23 Feb 1942. 26 pp, 4to. To Jane Armstrong. With related material, including a ptd announcement of her marriage to Ernest Hemingway. CE Feb 21 (141) $2,400

**Genlis, Stephanie de, 1746-1830**
AL, [n.d.]. 1 p, 4to. To [G. J. L.] Lambert. Announcing that Mr. Fitzgerald is planning to attend recipient's concert & giving instructions for the singer. Including authentication by K. A. Varnhagen von Ense at foot. star Mar 21 (103) DM340

**Genzmer, Harald**
Autograph music, Mistral, Kantate ... Adagio molto, [n.d.]. 2 pp, folio. Draft; sgd & inscr on verso. star Mar 22 (841) DM240

**Geoffroy Saint-Hilaire, Etienne, 1772-1844**
Autograph Ms, philosophical reflections about natural history, [n.d.]. 4 pp, 4to. Possibly incomplete. star Mar 21 (466) DM300

**Georg, Herzog von Braunschweig-Lueneburg, 1583-1641**
Ds, 25 Dec 1626. 1 p, folio. Order to arrest marauding soldiers. star Mar 22 (1242) DM660

**Georg Wilhelm, Herzog von Braunschweig-Lueneburg, 1624-1705**
Ls, 28 Dec 1648. 2 pp, folio. To an unnamed prince. Informing him about the succession after the death of his brother Friedrich. star Mar 22 (1243) DM380

**Georg Wilhelm, Kurfuerst von Brandenburg,1595-1640**
ALs, 15 May 1618. 1 p, folio. To his father Kurfuerst Johann Sigismund. Reporting his arrival at Neuenhof on his journey to East Prussia. Illus in cat. star Mar 22 (1189) DM3,200

**George I, King of England, 1660-1727**
Ds, 16 Feb 1718/9. 1 p, folio. Ratification of a Convention for Establishing a free and regulated Trade for Herrings and other Fish. Countersgd by Lord Stanhope. Ck Apr 12 (57) £600

Document, [early 18th-cent]. 1 p, oblong folio. In Latin, content not given. Contains initial port; with Great Seal suspended from vellum ribbon. wa Oct 28 (155) $325

**George I, King of Greece, 1845-1913**
ALs, 31 May 1887. 4 pp, 8vo. To Mr. Tuckermann. Planning to travel to England to attend Queen Victoria's jubilee. star Mar 22 (1339) DM480

**George II, King of England, 1683-1760**
Ds, 22 July 1738. 1 p, folio. Commission of Thomas Eaton as Captain in the Horse Guards. star Mar 22 (1342) DM200

— 29 July 1757. 2 pp, 292mm by 190mm. Pardon for William York. Framed with engraving. P June 5 (233) $600

— 26 June 1758. 1 p, folio. Appointing John Kelsey a Captain in the 32nd Regiment of Foot. Countersgd by [Robert D'Arcy, Fourth Earl of ] Holderness & other officials. Soiled at edges. rms Oct 11 (170) $275

— 17 Sept 1759. 1 p, folio. Warrant to pay Mathew Woodford for supplying food to the Garrison of Annapolis Royal Officers. Ck Apr 12 (58) £260

### George III, King of England, 1738-1820

**ALs,** 22 Aug 1787. 1 p, 4to. Sgd " The King". To unnamed recipient. Rearranging an audience with Joseph Banks. rms Oct 11 (172) $400

**Ds,** 27 Oct 1760. 1 p, folio, vellum. Appointing Hugh McKenzie as captain in 77th Regiment of Foot. Countersgd by [the 4th Earl of] Holderness. Edges soiled. rms Oct 11 (171) $350

— 27 Oct 1760. 1 p, folio. Appointment of Hugh McKenzie as Captain in the 77th Regiment of Foot. rms Mar 21 (298) $360

— 14 Sept 1761. 1 p, folio. To William Lord King. Summoning him to " Our and the Queen's coronation."With defects. Illus in cat rms Oct 11 (173) $1,100

— 9 Oct 1801. 5 pp, folio. Order to the Lord Chancellor to affix the Great seal to the ratification of the Secret Article in the Treaty of Amiens regulating the borders of Spain & Portugal. pn Nov 9 (397) £550 [Wilson]

— 10 Sept 1802. Order to affix the Great Seal to the commission of James Talbot as Secretary of the "Extraordinary Embassy to the First Consul of the French Republic". pn Nov 9 (398) £170 [Maggs]

— 11 Jan 1805. 2 pp, folio. Order to affix the Great Seal to a warrant empowering British ships to seize any Spanish vessel. Countersgd by Lord Hawkesbury. pn Mar 14 (371) £320

— 15 Aug 1807. 2 pp, folio. Warrant requiring the Lord Chancellor to draw up Full Powers enabling Lord Granville Leveson Gower full powers to treat with the Russian Minister or Ministers. Sewn with text of the full powers. pn Mar 14 (372) £300

— 24 Apr 1808. 6 pp, folio. Order to affix the Great Seal to the appointment of Edward Thornton as Envoy to Sweden. Countersgd by George Canning. Illus in cat. rms June 6 (382) $625

— 19 May 1808. 1 p, folio. Licence for Greffulhe Brothers to import goods to England with 4 ships. star Mar 22 (1343) DM230

— 31 Jan 1809. 5 pp, folio. Order to affix the Great Seal to the commission of Andrew Snape Douglas. Includes text. Countersgd by Canning. rms Nov 30 (164) $400

— 28 Oct 1809. 2 pp, folio. Warrant requiring the Lord Chancellor to draw up an instrument ratifying the convention between the King & the Prince Regent of Portugal. Sewn with the text. pn Mar 14 (373) £160

### George IV, King of England, 1762-1830

**ANs,** 12 June 1825. 1 p, oblong 8vo. In 3d person. To Lt. Jervens. Commanding him to appear at Carlton House at noon the following day. CE June 12 (40) $200

**Ds,** 13 Mar 1813. 2 pp, folio. Warrant to affix the Great Seal to the instrument granting Major General Sir Charles Steward full powers to negotiate with Prussia. Sewn with the text. pn Mar 14 (374) £160

— 3 May 1813. 2 pp, folio. Warrant to affix the Great Seal to instrument granting Major General Alexander Hope full powers to negotiate with Denmark. Sewn with text. Countersgd by Castlereagh. pn Mar 14 (375) £95

— 27 Dec 1813. 2 pp, folio. Warrant to affix the Great Seal to a warrant granting Castlereagh full powers to treat with the Northern Powers. 2 pp, folio. Sewn with the text. Countersgd by Castlereagh. pn Mar 14 (376) £380

— 3 Mar 1814. 1 p, size not stated. Appointment of Alexander Campbell as lieutenant. rms June 6 (383) $300

— 31 Mar 1814. 17 pp, folio. As Prince Regent, warrant to affix the Great Seal to the ratification of the treaty with Austria sgd at Chaumont; countersgd by Bathurst. pn Nov 9 (400) £780

— 17 May 1815. 2 pp, folio. Order to affix the Great Seal to an instrument authorizing payment of a subsudy to enable Prussia to take the field against Napoleon before Waterloo. 2 pp, folio. Sewn with text. Countersgd by Castlereagh. pn Mar 14 (377) £1,300

— 19 May 1815. 2 pp, folio. Order to affix the Great Seal to an instrument regulating the Russian Loan contracted by the King of the Netherlands in "the final Reunion of the Belgic Provinces with Holland". Sewn with text. Countersgd by Castlereagh. pn Mar 14 (379) £300

— 12 June 1815. 2 pp, folio. Order to affix the Great Seal to a ratification of the alliance between Britain & Switzerland during the Napoleonic Wars. Sewn with text. Countersgd by Castlereagh. pn Mar 14 (378) £340

— 7 Feb 1816. 2 pp, folio. Order to affix the Great Seal to Commission of John Innes, Commander of the Ship Fort William. Countersgd by Lord Sidmouth. pn Mar 14 (380) £220

— 9 Mar 1816. 2 pp, folio. Authorization for the marriage of Princess Charlotte to Prince Leopold of Saxe-Coburg.. Countersgd by the Lord Chetwynd; with the text of the commission. pn Nov 9 (402) £180

— 28 June 1816. 2 pp, folio. Order to affix the Great Seal to the commission appointing Lord Fitzroy Somerset Secretary at the Paris Embassy. Sewn with the text of the commission. pn Nov 9 (403) £95

— 28 July 1816. 4 pp, folio. Appointment of Lord Fitzroy Somerset as Secretary to the embassy in France. Countersgd by Castlereagh. rms June 6 (384) $300

— 16 Nov 1818. 6 pp, folio. Order to affix the Great Seal to the ratification "of an Act of Acceptance of the

Accession of His Majesty The King of Bavaria" to a convention sgd in Paris. rms June 6 (385) $525

— 14 Feb 1822. 2 pp, folio. Order to affix the Great Seal to commission of Henry Andrews Drummond of the Castle Huntley. pn Mar 14 (384) £300

— 15 Apr 1823. 2 pp, folio. Order to affix the Great Seal to a commission appointing George Jackson & John McTavish as Commissioner & Arbitrator to treat with the President of the United States on the King's behalf with reference to claims outstanding after the Treaty of Ghent. pn Nov 9 (405) £4,400

— 29 Nov 1823. 2 pp, folio. Order to affix the Great Seal to an instrument (present) granting full powers to William Huskisson & Stratford Canning to deal with the United States of America. Sewn with the text. pn Nov 9 (406) £2,600

— 2 Sept 1824. 2 pp, folio. Order to affix the Great Seal to an instrument granting full powers to Henry Unwin Addington to negotiate with america "a Treaty for the more effectual suppression of the Slave Trade". pn Nov 9 (407) £4,000

— 7 Mar 1825. 2 pp, folio. Order to affix the Great Seal to an instrument granting Sir Charles Stuart full power to mediate on his behalf between the King of Portugal & his son, Don Pedro, newly proclaimed Emperor of Brazil. Sewn with the text. pn Nov 9 (408) £850

**George, Stefan, 1868-1933**

ALs, June 1917. 1 p, 4to. To Ernst Gloeckner. Promising to explain why he did not come to Brueckenau. Mtd in a Ms in Ernst Bertram's hand, Ernst Gloeckner ueber Stefan George..., I, Wiederherstellung; [n.d.], 150 pg, 4to, in vellum bdg; containing excerpts from Gloeckner's diaries & letters relating to George, 1906 to 1918. Illus in cat. star Mar 21 (104) DM8,500

— 3 Jan 1919. 1 p, 4to. To Ernst Gloeckner. Asking him to come to Munich for a while. Mtd in a Ms in Ernst Bertram's hand, Briefe Stefan Georges an Ernst Gloeckner, [n.d.], c.150 pp, 4to, in red lea gilt, containing transcripts of 51 letters by George, 1913 to 1928, & copies of numerous letters written by members of George's circle, with related material. star Mar 21 (105) DM8,000

**George V, King of England, 1865-1936**

ALs, 13 Nov 1901. 3 pp, 8vo. To Mrs. (Lillie) Langtry. Thanking his father's mistress for a letter of congratulations: "I must call you by the name which I have known you by for so many years. I send you my best thanks for your kind letter of congratulations on my being created 'Prince of Wales'..." With orig envelope. Torn. Illus in cat sg Sept 28 (111) $1,000

Ds, 3 June 1916. 1 p, folio. Appointment of Reginalf Chalmers Hammond as Major in the Royal Engineers. Countersgd by David Lloyd George. rms Nov 30 (165) $400

— 1 Jan 1918. 2 pp, folio. Award of the Order of the British Empire to Baroness Wolverton. Countersgd by Edward, Prince of Wales (later the Duke of Windsor) as Grand Master. CE June 12 (25) $240

— 21 Apr 1928. 1 p, folio. Official document concerning the appoinment of Harvey J. Goodier as US Consul at Vancouver. pba Oct 26 (351) $180

Group photograph, 31 Dec 1918. Showing him with Queen Mary, Princess Mary, President & Mrs. Woodrow Wilson. 13 by 15.25 inches, framed. Sgd by all. Ck Apr 12 (63) £920

Photograph, sgd, 1932. 8vo. Matching ports, his by Vandyke & hers by Hay Wrightson. Sgd as " George R. I." & " Mary R.". Mary's port silvered. Framed. Over-all size 14 by 18 inches. Illus in cat rms Oct 11 (402) $650

— Anr, Dec 1934. 10.25 by 7.5 inches, framed. Showing him giving his Christmas speech. Sgd & dated Christmas, 1934. Ck Apr 12 (67) £100

— Anr, 1934. 6 by 8 inches, framed. Equestrian port. Sgd & dated by him. Ck Apr 12 (66) £160

**George V, King of England, 1865-1936 —& Mary, Queen of George V of England, 1867-1953**

Photograph, sgd, 12 Dec 1911. 19.5 by 14.5 inches, framed. Showing them in Coronation robes. Sgd at Delhi. Ck Apr 12 (61) £280

— Anr, 1911. 12.5 by 12 inches, in elaborate frame. Showing them in Coronation robes. Sgd by both. Ck Apr 12 (60) £950

**George V, King of England, 1865-1936 —& Wilson, Woodrow, 1856-1924**

Photograph, sgd, 31 Dec 1918. 10.5 by 8.25 inches, framed. Sgd by both. Ck Apr 12 (62) £550

**George VI, King of England, 1895-1952**

ALs, 5 Sept 1915. 1 p. To Capt. Brown. Sending a sgd photograph of himself (present). b May 30 (356) £180

Ls, 18 Nov 1917. 2 pp, 8vo. To "Victoria". Letter of condolence. Also sgd by Mary, Princess Royal. sg Feb 1 (95) $200

Ds, 21 May 1940. 1 p, oblong folio. Appointment of Douglas Young as Consul General for the Portuguese possessions in West Africa. Countersgd by Halifax. rms Nov 30 (166) $350

Group photograph, sgd, 1937. 11.25 by 8.25 inches, framed. Showing him with Queen Mary & Princesses Elizabeth & Margaret in Coronation dress. Ck Apr 12 (69) £380

— Anr, sgd, 1939. 8 by 5.5 inches, framed. Showing him with his family. Ck Apr 12 (70) £1,200

Photograph, sgd, 1942. 503mm by 405mm. Sgd on mount. CE June 12 (41) $550

**George VI, King of England, 1895-1952 —& Elizabeth, Queen of George VI of England**

Group photograph, [Dec 1946]. 150mm by 170mm. Group photo of the family; sgd by both beneath engraved Christmas wishes. Marans collection. CE Apr 17 (139) $700

**Georgia**

— JONES, GEORGE. - Ds. 7 May 1806. 4 pp, folio. Legal document concerning a petition by Joseph Hour which Jones attests to a presiding judge of the Superior Courts of the state of Georgia. Browned. pba June 13 (36) $140

**Germain, George Sackville, 1st Viscount Sackville, 1716-85**

**ALs,** 7 Oct 1775. 5 pp, 4to. Recipient unnamed. About the draft of a speech concerning the "disturbances in America." Repaired. Sang collection. P Dec 13 (128) $2,500

**Germany**

**Ms,** Consignation Derer jenigen Victualien ...Welche Ihro May. der Koenigin Kuechelmeister ... in die Koenigl. Kuechel zu verschaffen verlangen thut, & Lista deren bey der Koenigl. Hoffstadt befundenen Personen..., [c.1700]. 5 leaves, 317mm by 205mm; stitched. HH Nov 14 (9) DM360

— BAVARIA. - Ms, Origo ducatus Bavariae... Duces Francorum... Duces Australes... Duces Karinthie... Duces Bohemie. [Southern Germany, c.1500]. 24 leaves (5 blank), 209mm by 147mm, in wraps. HH May 7 (15) DM500

— FUHRMANN, THEOPHILUS CHRISTOPHERUS. - Ms, Haus-Buch, 1724 to [c.1835]. 180 leaves, 20.5cm by 16cm. Contemp vellum bdg. Memoranda concerning bonds & other financial matters, & funerals, mostly from the area of Bielefeld. In several hands. JG Mar 29 (256) DM1,100

— MOSEL RIVER. - Ms, list of feudal property of the House of Pyrmont situated in the districts of Elz, Cochem & Ehrenburg on the Mosel River, 1444. 40 leaves, 215mm by 150mm. HH May 7 (17) DM1,500

— WUERTTEMBERG. - Ms, Ordnung fuer die Communen, auch deren Vorstehere u. Bediente in dem Herzogthum Wuerttemberg..., [c.1750]. 304 pp, 340mm by 220mm. Contemp half lea. HH Nov 14 (28) DM650

— WUERZBURG. - Ms, Kurze Geschichte der Fuersten und Bischofen zu Wirzburg..., 1792. 168 pp, 210mm by 170mm. Contemp half lea. HH Nov 14 (29) DM420

**Gerning, Johann Isaak von, 1767-1837**

**ALs,** 20 Nov 1807. 4 pp, 4to. To Karl Ludwig von Knebel. Announcing Zacharias Werner's visit. Sgd G. star Mar 21 (136) DM220

**Gerry, Elbridge, Signer from Massachusetts**

**ALs,** 30 Dec 1776. 1 p, 213mm by 162mm. Recipient unnamed, but inlaid to larger sheet with notation "Patrick Henry". Reporting Washington's crossing of the Delaware. P June 5 (42) $21,000

— 28 Dec 1796. 2 pp, 4to. To Abigail Adams. On the 1796 election. Sang collection. P Dec 13 (129) $4,500

**AL,** 2 Jan 1812. 1 p, 4to. To James Monroe. Asking for information on the Office of Counsel at London for an interested friend. pba Oct 26 (236) $250

**Gersdorff, Rudolf Christoph von, 1905-80**

**Ls,** 26 Aug 1978. 1 p, 4to.. To Randall Sutherland. Discussing his wartime activities & the part he played in a plan to kill Hitler in 1943. rms June 6 (627) $425

**Gershwin, George, 1898-1937**

**Ls,** 15 Apr 1931. 1 p, 4to. To Albert Sirmay. Returning a list of recordings of Gershwin's compositions (not present). wd May 8 (15) $1,300

— 8 Sept 1936. 2 pp, 4to. To Albert Sirmay. About getting started on new songs for Shall We Dance. wd May 8 (11) $3,000

— 6 Oct 1936. 1 p, 4to. To Tessie. About his work in Hollywood & his house in Beverly Hills. wd May 8 (13) $3,000

— 15 Feb 1937. 2 pp, 4to. To Albert Sirmay. Sending him a copy of They Can't Take That Away From Me (not present). With 3-line holograph postscript. wd May 8 (12) $6,250

— 18 Feb 1937. 2 pp, 4to. To his secretary, Miss Hannenfeldt. Sending news of concerts he has played in Los Angeles. wd May 8 (14) $3,000

— 4 March 1937. 1 p, 4to. To "Bob". Concerning a business proposition: "my picture contracts will take up so much of my time that I couldn't do it and...if I could I would ask for more money for myself than you could offer for the whole show...." sg Sept 28 (113) $2,800

**Ds,** 10 Apr 1935. 1 p. Filled out order form for the Hammond Organ Company, ordering an organ. With holograph annotation "It is understood the first organ to be sold in New York sometime in May 1935 is to be mine. G.G." With related material. wd May 8 (16) $2,500

**Caricature,** [n.d.]. 1 p, 6 by 4 inches. On a hotel telephone message sheet. With signature from a cancelled check, Over-all size 8 by 6 inches. With a letter from the Ira and Leonore Gershwin Trusts authenticating & offering the origin of the drawing. Framed. Illus in cat sg Sept 28 (114) $1,200

**Check,** accomplished & sgd, 1 Nov 1935. Drawn on the National City Bank of NY for $199.11 payable to Rabsons. Illus in cat. star Mar 22 (842) DM1,700

**Concert program,** sgd, 16 Jan 1934. From a Concert at the Worcest Auditorium with James Melton & the Reisman Symphonic Orchestra. Also sgd by Melton. sg Feb 1 (96) $950

**Photograph, sgd & inscr,** July 1929. 202mm by 252mm. Playing the piano; inscr to Edgar A. Moss. Illus in cat. Marans collection. CE Apr 17 (231) $7,500

— Anr, [n.d.]. 15 by 11.25 inches (image 6.5 by 9.75 inches). Inscr & with 1st bar of Rhapsody in Blue, sgd. Part of inscr erased. Framed. wd May 8 (10) $2,700

**Signature,** Aug 1929. 35 pp, folio. On the score for An American in Paris. With chipping at edges & age stains. Toned. Inscr " For C. S. Evans - from an appreciative American in New York." Illus in cat rms Oct 11 (174) $2,250

**Gershwin, George, 1898-1937 —& Gershwin, Ira, 1896-1983**

**Photograph, sgd & inscr,** [n.d. - c.1837]. 9.75 by 8 inches. Of the brothers seated at worktable. Inscr by Ira to Albert Sirmay. Framed. wd May 8 (17) $1,500

## GERSHWIN

**Gershwin, Ira, 1896-1983.** See: Gershwin, George & Gershwin

**Gerstaecker, Friedrich, 1816-72**
Series of 14 A Ls s, 25 Oct 1852 to 27 July 1864. 28 pp, 4to & 8vo. To Ernst von Bibra. About products from foreign countries, literary & personal matters. star Mar 21 (106) DM3,400

**Gerster, Ottmar, 1897-1969**
Autograph music, song, Nur nicht denken (Helga Hoeffken), [n.d.]. 8 pp, 4to. Scored for voice & piano; sgd on tp. star Mar 22 (843) DM250

**Gert, Valeska**
Collection of 3 A Ls s & autograph postcard, sgd, 20 Sept 1970 to 9 Apr 1972 & [n.d.]. 6 pp, 4to & 8vo, & card. Recipient unnamed. Discussing the publication of her memoirs. star Mar 22 (1148) DM210

**Gertler, Mark**
Autograph Ms, First Memories. About 51 pp, 4to. Dated 18 Oct 1934. pn Nov 9 (423) £2,000

**Gervinus, Georg, 1805-71**
ALs, 13 Dec 1841. 1 p, 8vo. To Joachim Meyer. Thanking for recipient's work on Schiller's Wilhelm Tell. star Mar 21 (468) DM280

**Gesner, Johann Matthias, 1691-1761**
ALs, 25 Mar 1742. 2 pp, 4to. To Tobias Roenicke. Asking him to send his Latin poems to Mr. Uhl for publication. star Mar 21 (469) DM450

**Getty, J. Paul, 1892-1976**
Ds, 15 May 1936. His United States Passport. cb June 25 (2329) $1,500
Check, sgd, 21 Nov 1945. Drawn on the 1st National Bank of Los Angeles for $55.25 payable to Quandt Hardware. star Mar 22 (1674) DM260
— Anr, sgd, 3 Feb 1947. Drawn on the Security First National Bank of Los Angeles for $8350 payable to Claude I. Parker. rms Mar 21 (253) $230
Photograph, sgd, [c.1960]. 88mm by 88mm. Seated. Marans collection. CE Apr 17 (140) $380

**Geuss, Wolfgang, fl.16th cent.** See: Astrological Manuscripts

**Giannini, Amadeo Peter**
Ls, 9 Feb 1932. 2 pp, 8vo. To Cecil B. De Mille. About the campaign for proxies for the annual meeting of stockholders of Transamerica Corporation. pba Oct 26 (112) $700

**Giardini, Felice, 1716-96**
Autograph music, Trio in F major [for violin, viola & cello], 1792. 11 pp; 4to; stitched. Notated on 3 systems per page, 3 staves each; including revisions. Sgd & inscr to Lord Aylesford. Probably unpbd. S Dec 1 (162) £2,200
— Autograph music, Trio in G major [for violin, viola & cello], 1792. 11 pp, 4to; stitched. Notated on 3 systems per page, 3 staves each; including revisions.

## AMERICAN BOOK PRICES CURRENT

Sgd & inscr to Lord Aylesford. Probably unpbd. S Dec 1 (161) £1,900

**Gide, Andre, 1869-1951**
ALs, 20 Feb 1929. 1 p, 4to. To M. Challage. Looking forward to seeing him. rms Mar 21 (300) $260
— 27 June 1929. 1 p, 4to. To Monsiuer Samson DeBrier. Regretting the distance between them. With orig mailing envelope. pba Oct 26 (27) $170
Ls, 30 Jan 1929. 1 p, 4to. To Monsiuer Samson DeBrier. Asking him if he will come to Paris & urging him to visit. With orig envelope. pba Oct 26 (26) $190
Autograph postcard, 14 Nov 1926. To Gene Espesset. Postponing a meeting. Sgd in full. Illus in cat sg Feb 1 (97) $200

**Gilbert, Jack**
Ls, 1966. 2 pp, no size given. To Steve Vincent. About his travel plans & comparing Nigerian & American women. Sgd as "Jack". With holograph collections. pba Jan 25 (110) $50

**Gilbert, Sir William Schwenck, 1836-1911**
Photograph, sgd & inscr, 9 Nov 1900. 184mm by 118mm, mtd. 3-quarter length; by Langfierz. Inscr to Brandon Thomas. Illus in cat. Marans collection. CE Apr 17 (232) $600

**Gilly, David, 1748-1808**
ALs, 12 June 1803. 4 pp, 8vo. To Herr Morgenlaender. Discussing purchases for the Berlin Academy of Architecture & reporting about his stay in France. star Mar 21 (670) DM900

**Giordani, Tommaso, c.1733-1806**
Autograph music, aria, My Morn of Life was Wounderous fair, for voice, obligato accompaniment & continuo, [1790s]. 4 pp, 4to. Notated on 4 systems per page, 3 staves each; sgd. Upper margin trimmed. S Dec 1 (163) £450

**Giordano, Umberto, 1867-1948.** See: Caruso, Enrico

**Gissing, George, 1857-1903**
ALs, 7 Dec 1886. 3 pp, 8vo. To the pbr Walter Scott. About establishing a new review. pn Mar 14 (409) £950

**Gladstone, William E., 1809-98**
Ls, 26 Mar 1870. 3 pp, 8vo. To J.B.F.E. de Chatelain. Justifying his government's denial of an amnesty towards Fenian agents. pn June 13 (204) £160
Photograph, sgd, [n.d.]. No size given. Sepia cabinet photo bust pose. By Russell & Sons. Sgd on mount. sg Sept 28 (115) $175

**Glazunov, Aleksandr Konstantinovich, 1865-1936**
Autograph music, opening 32 bars of the Adagio from his ballet Raymonda, scored for piano, with details or orchestration added; [n.d.]. 3 pp, folio. Notated on 5 or 6 systems per page, each of 2 or 3 staves. Including revisions; sgd. S Dec 1 (164) £700
Autograph postcard, sgd, 21 Jan 1935. To Nikolai de Kouroff. Informing him that his concert for saxo-

phone will be performed on the radio. star Mar 22 (846) DM320

**Autograph quotation,** 3 bars of music, 26 Jan 1929. 1 p, 8vo. Sgd & inscr to Mme Dulce Capper Alves de Souza. rms June 6 (222) $400

### Gleim, Johann Wilhelm Ludwig, 1719-1803

**Series** of 160 A Ls s, 6 letters, & ANs, 24 July 1768 to 7 Feb 1803. Over 500 pp, mostly 8vo. To Lorenz Benzler. Important correspondence touching personal & literary matters. star Mar 21 (107b) DM32,000

— Series of 3 A Ls s, 9 Aug 1788 to 3 Aug 1790. 5 pp, 8vo. Recipient unnamed. About a variety of matters. star Mar 21 (107a) DM4,000

### Glier, Reyngol'd Moritsevich, 1875-1956

**ALs,** 9 May 1933. 2 pp, 8vo. To Ivan Grigorievich. Informing him that the score of his Po procheny psalma may not be sent abroad & inviting him to come to Moscow. star Mar 22 (847) DM580

### Gloeckner, Ernst, 1885-1934. See: George, Stefan

### Gluck, Christoph Willibald, 1714-87

**ALs,** 31 Mar 1780. 1 p, 4to. To Franz Kruthoffer. Announcing that he has received the score of Echo et Narcisse & expressing his exasperation with the Gluck-Piccinni controversies. Illus in cat. S Dec 1 (165) £6,200

### Gmelin, Wilhelm Friedrich, 1760-1820

**ALs,** 28 Nov 1818. 1 p, 4to. To [Ludwig Daniel] Jacoby. Concerning the shipping of some etchings. star Mar 21 (671) DM210

### Gneisenau, August, Graf Neithardt von, 1760-1831

**ALs,** 20 Dec 1816. 1 p, 4to. To Georg Baersch. Hoping that he has no material problems. With a port. star Mar 22 (1335) DM800

— 25 June 1823. 1 p, 4to. To [Major von Fehrentheil]. Referring to recipient's promotion. star Mar 22 (1336) DM600

**Ls,** [n.d.]. 1 p, 8vo. Recipient unnamed. Giving instructions to illus a map. HN May 15 (2573) DM350

### Goddard, Robert H., 1882-1945

**Photograph,** sgd & inscr, [c.1930]. 304mm by 202mm, mtd. Half length. Illus in cat. Marans collection. CE Apr 17 (47) $2,600

### Godowsky, Leopold, 1870-1938

**Autograph quotation,** 3 bars of music, 9 July 1926. 1 p, 8vo. Sgd & inscr to Helen Beck. star Mar 22 (848) DM210

### Goebbels, Joseph, 1897-1945

**Ls,** 16 Oct 1935. 1 p, 4to. To [Philipp] Bouhler. Thanking for congratulations on the birth of his son. Illus in cat. rms June 6 (614) $700

— [25 Dec 1935]. 1 p, 4to. To Philipp & Helli Bouhler. Sending Christmas greetings & including a family photograph & a book (not present). Illus in cat. rms Mar 21 (362) $1,100

### Goeckingk, Leopold Friedrich Guenther von, 1748-1828

**ALs,** 23 Sept 1783. 2 pp, 4to. To the Rev. Dannenberg. Regarding subscriptions to a projected literary journal. star Mar 21 (108) DM340

### Goercke, Johann, 1750-1822

**ALs,** 4 July 1817. 2 pp, 4to. To Dr. Haase. About Otto von Guericke's seal & coat-of-arms sent to him by Mrs. von Kalkstein & his collection of portraits. star Mar 21 (470) DM420

### Goering, Emmy, 1899-1973

**Group photograph,** with husband Hermann & baby daughter Edda, [n.d.]. 5.25 by 3.25 inches. Sgd by Emmy & inscr with a lengthy note to [Helli] Bouhler. Illus in cat. rms Mar 21 (363) $450

— Anr, [n.d.]. 9 by 6.5 inches. With daughter Edda, in formal pose; by Rosemarie Clausen. Sgd & inscr to [Helli] Bouhler. Illus in cat. rms June 6 (608) $260

### Goering, Hermann, 1893-1946

**Ls,** 30 Nov 1939. 2 pp, 4to. To [Philipp] Bouhler. Instructing him to report on complaints and suggestions brought forward by the people. rms Mar 21 (364) $900

**Ds,** 19 May 1933. 1 p, folio. Appointing Heinrich Lohse President of the Province of Schleswig Holstein. With translation. rms Oct 11 (278) $450

— 5 Apr 1940. 1 p, folio. Appointment for Regierungsrat Helmuth Rautenkranz. Including Hitler's stamped signature. HH May 9 (2470) DM240

### Goes, Albrecht

**Autograph Ms,** poem, beginning "Nicht den Fels zu erschuettern vermag ich...", [n.d.]. 1 p, 4to. 4 lines, sgd. HN Nov 24 (2781) DM280

### Goethals, George W., 1858-1928

**Signature,** 30 Sept 1919. On a card. Framed with photo & related document. rms Nov 30 (3) $450

### Goethe, August von, 1789-1830

**Ls,** 30 May 1816. 1 p, 4to. To Herr Ramann. Sending a payment & ordering wine. star Mar 21 (121) DM850

### Goethe, Johann Wolfgang von, 1749-1832

**Autograph Ms,** 1st verse of his poem Was es gilt, [25 May] 1817. 1 p, 4to. Inscr in the hand of Friedrich T. Kraeuter at foot, 1843. CNY May 17 (80) $2,300

— Autograph Ms, two lines from his Faust, part 2, act 5; [c.May 1831]. 2.2cm by 20.5cm, cut from larger sheet. Illus in cat. star Mar 21 (109) DM13,000

**ALs,** 10 Feb 1810. 1 p, 8vo. To Prof. Reimer. Asking that "you, my dear professor, come to me...so that we can go together to Madame Schopenhauer..." The 0 in 1810 looks like 4. With contemporary transcript. Detail in cat sg Sept 28 (116) $1,500

— 16 June 1813. 4 pp, 4to. To Constanze von Fritsch. Interesting letter explaining why he is unable to visit Prague, referring to "Docktor Faust", various friends, etc. Illus in cat. star Mar 21 (113) DM24,000

## GOETHE

— [n.d.]. 1 p, 4to. Recipient unnamed. Referring to Herr Woechner's report. star Mar 21 (117) DM3,500

Ls, 2 June 1783. 1 p, 4to. Recipient unnamed. Concerning Professor Buettner's departure from Weimar. S Dec 1 (17) £1,300

— 13 Dec 1783. 1 p, folio. To [Johann Jakob Griesbach]. Referring to a payment. star Mar 21 (111) DM3,200

— 14 June 1796. 2 pp, 4to. To Christian Gottlob von Voigt. Sending several documents. Sgd with paraph. Illus in cat. HN Nov 24 (2782) DM4,200

— 16 Mar 1798. 1 p, folio. To Johannes Daniel Falk. Commenting on recipient's comedy. star Mar 21 (112) DM3,600

— 29 Dec 1822. 1 p, 4to. To Ludwig Wilhelm Cramer. Sending a mineral specimen for recipient's collection. HN Nov 24 (2783) DM5,400

— 1 Sept 1826. 3 pp, 4to. To Clementine Cuvier. Thanking for her father's works. Including autograph subscription. star Mar 21 (115) DM8,000

ANs, 3 May 1808. 1 p, 8vo. Recipient unnamed. Acknowledging receipt of writing materials. C Nov 29 (149) £950

— [11 Nov 1831]. 1 p, 8vo, on fragment of address leaf. Recipient unnamed. Book order (title). star Mar 21 (116) DM1,400

— [n.d.]. 1 p, 8vo. To [Johann Peter Eckermann]. Saying that some headings need to be discussed. star Mar 21 (119) DM750

Ns, 26 Jan 1819. 1 p, 4to. Recipient unnamed. Providing information about a work by J. B. Graser. star Mar 21 (114) DM1,500

Cut signature, 26 Apr 1779. 1 p, 8vo. Also sgd by K. A. von Volgstedt. star Mar 21 (110) DM850

Single sheet ptg, poem, Am acht und zwanzigsten August 1826. 8vo. Sgd & dated 23 June 1829. HN Nov 24 (2784) DM5,000

— RIEMER, FRIEDRICH WILHELM. - ALs, 16 Mar 1811. 4 pp, 8vo. To [Karl Ludwig von Knebel]. Conveying some messages from Goethe who has not been well. star Mar 21 (148) DM500

### Goethe, Ottilie von, 1796-1872

ALs, [May 1849]. 3 pp, 4to. To her mother Henriette von Pogwisch. Sending family news. On a letter by her uncle Wilhelm Henckel von Donnersmark to Henriette von Pogwisch, 6 May 1849. star Mar 21 (122) DM950

### Goethe, Walther von, 1818-85

Collection of ALs & signature, 31 Jan 1885 & [n.d.]. 2 pp, 8vo, & visiting card. To his gardener. Concerning business matters. star Mar 21 (123) DM250

### Goethe, Wolfgang von, 1820-83

ALs, 17 Feb 1871. 2 pp, 8vo. Recipient unnamed. Expressing thanks. star Mar 21 (124) DM440

### Goldsmith, Oliver, 1728-74

AL, [c.27 July 1770]. 1 p, oblong 4to. To Sir Joshua Reynolds. Giving an account of his journey to France. Unfinished & unsgd. Docketed in the hand of James Boswell "Original Letter of Dr. Goldsmith to Sir Joshua Reynolds who gave it to me James Boswell". Illus in cat S Dec 18 (129) £7,500 [Mandl] See also: Calligraphy

### Goll, Claire, 1890-1977

Autograph transcript, Das Geheimnis, excerpt from her story Der gestohlene Himmel; [c.1962]. 1 p, folio. Sgd. HN May 15 (2574) DM200

### Gomes, Antonio Carlos, 1836-96

Collection of ALs & ANs, 26 June 1875 & [n.d.]. 3 pp, 8vo, & visiting card. To Gabbi Centurio. Responding to a request for help. star Mar 22 (849) DM450

### Gompers, Samuel, 1850-1924

Ls, 9 Oct 1903. 1 p, 4to. To H. L. Sayles. Regretting that he will be unable to furnish him with the extract of his remarks in advance. sg June 6 (83) $70

### Goodman, Julia Cody

A Ls s (2), 10 & 16 Oct 1928. 8 pp, 4to. To her daughter, Josie Thurston. Personal news. sg June 6 (286) $750

### Gorbachev, Mikhail Sergeyevich

Group photograph, [12 June 1989]. 177mm by 239mm. With Helmut Kohl; sgd by Gorbachev. Illus in cat. HH Nov 17 (3223) DM320

Photograph, sgd, [n.d.]. No size given. Color photo of him with his wife. Sgd in Russian. rms Oct 11 (175) $400

### Gordimer, Nadine

Typescript, article, Mandela: What He Means to Us. [1993] 5 pp, folio, stapled. With holograph corrections, sgd & with holograph note about its genesis. S Dec 18 (391) £3,600 [Gekoski]

### Gordon, Charles George, 1833-85

Autograph Ms, 2 maps of the Nile, with comments, & Observations on the Lower Nile, [Aug 1875] to 2 Nov 1875. 7 pp, 8vo. Probably extracts from correspondence with Major Wilson & Mrs. Freese, sent to his brother during his visit to the Sudan. C Nov 29 (150) £1,500

Collection of 6 A Ls s & 3 A Ls, 4 Dec 1874 to 2 Nov 1883. 38 pp, various sizes. To his brother Enderby & his wife Margaret (3). Recounting his activities in Egypt & the Sudan, & discussing family matters. C Nov 29 (151) £3,000

ALs, 18 Apr 1883. 3 pp, 8vo. To Mr. Campbell. Writing to help the grandson of a friend [LeMesurier] a position in Chinese customs. pba Oct 26 (352) £350

— 18 Apr 1883. 3 pp, 8vo. To Mr. Campbell Gordon. Trying to get the grandson of the Director of Egyptian Railways a position in Chinese Customs. With some show-through on verso. pba June 13 (109) $250

Gordon, John, d.1649. See: Thirty Years' War

Gorenko, Anna Andreyevna, 1889-1966. See: Akhmatova, Anna

**Gorki, Maxim, 1868-1936**

**Photograph, sgd,** [15 Mar 1906]. 138mm by 87mm. Seated at his desk. Addressed to Oskar Popper on verso in anr hand. Illus in cat. Marans collection. CE Apr 17 (74) $1,100

**Gospel Manuscripts.** See: Armenian Manuscripts

**Gosse, Sir Edmund W., 1849-1928**

[A collection of material in an album, including autograph Ms s of 12 poems, letters, galley proofs, etc, c.1876-1915, sold at Sotheby's on 18 Dec 1995, lot 190, for £1,400 to Quaritch]

**Gottschalk, Louis Moreau, 1829-69**

**Photograph, sgd & inscr,** 6 May 1862. 98mm by 61mm, mtd. 3-quarter length, by Charles D. Fredricks. Inscr to his "ami Appi". Marans collection. CE Apr 17 (233) $2,200

**Gould, Elizabeth Coxen.** See: Lear, Edward & Gould

**Gould, Jay, 1836-92**

**ALs,** 30 Sept 1861. 1 p, 8vo. To Thomas A. Brooks. About financial dealings. pba Oct 26 (113) $1,500

— 28 Oct 1867. 2 pp, 8vo. To D. G. Morgan. Introducing his broker D. L. Miller. CNY May 17 (245) $2,000

**Gould, John, 1804-81**

**ALs,** 14 Jan 1880. 2 p, no size given. To Mr. Peckover. About the publication of Birds of Asia. Creased & soiled. Ck Nov 17 (91) £330

**Gounod, Charles, 1818-93**

**Autograph Ms,** commentary on his oratorio The Redemption. 12 pp, 4to. [c.1882] S May 15 (73) £1,100

**Autograph music,** 1er Hosannah du Sanctus (en Style fugue), [n.d.]. 10 pp, folio. Full score, notated on up to 24 staves per page, with chorus parts for 2 sopranos, 2 tenors & Bass; including revisions & autograph title. S Dec 1 (167) £600

— Autograph music, recitative of Marguerite in his Faust, Act 3, [n.d.]. 1 p, 4to. 7-bar working draft, notated on 3 systems of 3 staves each. Sgd & inscr to Marquis Bouisson. S May 15 (359) £450

**ALs,** 8 May 1883. 2 pp, 8vo. To an unnamed lady. Declining a dinner invitation. star Mar 22 (851) DM320

**Gourgaud, Gaspard, 1783-1853**

**Autograph Ms,** account "du 18 brumaire", [c.1815-18]. 9 pp, folio. Draft, recounting events leading up to Napoleon's coup d'etat of 9 Nov 1799. S May 15 (206) £1,200

**Grace, William Gilbert, 1848-1915**

**ALs,** 10 Dec 1876. 2 pp, 8vo. Recipient's name cut away. Arranging a cricket match. pn June 13 (205) £130

**Gradual**

— [Southern Germany, 13th cent]. Single leaf, vellum, 229mm by 160mm. With 10 lines each of text in a liturgical hand & of music in hufnagelschrift neumes. With 6 decorated initals & historated initial in red & brown ink colored with red & blue. Recovered from a bdg. S June 18 (14) £400

— [Tuscany, Siena?, c.1450]. Single leaf, vellum, 519mm by 371mm. With 7 lines each of text in a rounded gothic hand & of music on a 4-line brown stave, with 2 lines re-ruled in yellow & red. With initials in red or blue with contrasting penwork, & very large historiated initial in colors & highly burnished gold with illuminated border of scrolling leaves & gold bezants along 2 margins. Illuminated by a follower of Giovanni di Paolo. S June 18 (24) £5,500

— [Toledo?, 17th cent]. About 100 leaves only, with lacunae & some leaves misbound, folio, in contemp sheep over wooden bds, bronze bosses & clasps. On vellum. Madsen Ms S Mar 14 (341) £1,300

**Graedener, Hermann, 1844-1929**

**Autograph quotation,** 8 bars from his opera Die heilige Zita, 12 Oct 1919. 1 p, 4to. Sgd & inscr. star Mar 22 (852) DM260

**Grahame, Kenneth, 1859-1932**

**Ls,** 5 June 1927. 1 p, 4to. Recipient unnamed. Giving permission to use A Harvesting in an anthology. rms Nov 30 (170) $550

**Granados, Enrique, 1867-1916**

**Autograph quotation,** 7 bars from his Goyescas, 1911. 1 p, folio. Notated on 3 systems of 3 staves each; sgd. S Dec 1 (168) £850

**Grant, Cary, 1904-86**

**Ds,** 15 Sept 1954. 2 pp, 4to. Contract with Paramount Pictures concerning his salary for the film To Catch a Thief. rms June 6 (146) $325

**Grant, Ulysses S., Jr. ("Buck")**

**Ls,** 7 Jan 1877. 1 p, 8vo. To The Postmaster General. Concerning a meeting with President Grant. With original envelope. pba Oct 26 (238) $190

— 7 Jan 1877. 1 p, 8vo. To the Postmaster General. Arranging an appointment with his father. pba Oct 26 (238) $190

**Grant, Ulysses S., 1822-85**

**ALs,** 26 Nov 1862. 3 pp, 4to. To Gen. Charles Hamilton. Instructing him to move his troops southward. Silked. Forbes Magazine collection. CNY May 17 (129) $4,800

— 17 Dec 1862. 2 pp, 4to. To Senator Elihu B. Washburn. Requesting a promotion for a Captain G. A. Williams. Detail in cat CNY Dec 15 (170) $6,000

— 11 July 1864. 1 p, 8vo. To Major Gen. Burnside. Instructing him to send an ambulance to take [John Mitchell] Ashley to his headquarters. Illus in cat. rms Mar 21 (65) $2,700

— 30 Dec 1864. 1 p, 4to. To Major Gen. [Benjamin] Butler. Asking him to forward a letter to Jefferson Davis. Illus in cat. rms June 6 (33) $7,500

# GRANT

— 2 Apr 1865. 1 p, 8vo. To Major General George Meade. Directing Meade in preparations to break Petersburg siege lines. Top third of letter is separated. Mtd. With related material. Illus in cat CNY Dec 15 (171) $7,500

— 18 Dec 1865. 2 pp, 8vo. To William D. Lewis. Thanking him for sending "The Tribute Book". CNY Dec 15 (67) $1,100

— 16 Jan 1871. 3 pp, 8vo. To Franz Sigel. Offering him the appointment as Secretary of the commission going to Santo Domingo. Forbes Magazine collection. CNY May 17 (131) $2,400

— 21 Feb 1871. 1 p, 4to. To Senator Hannibal Hamlin. Complying with a request. CE June 12 (46) $650

— 13 Sept 1872. 4 pp, 8vo. Recipient unnamed. Discussing his wife, children & campaign stops. rms Nov 30 (171) $3,500

— 19 Oct 1873. 2 pp, 8vo. To John E. Williams. Discussing the banking crisis. P Dec 13 (133) $2,250

— 7 Aug [18]75. 3 pp, 8vo. To Dr. Silas Reed. Accepting his resignation as Surveyor General. rms Nov 30 (172) $1,000

— 30 Sept 1878. 1 p, 8vo. To Edward Steel & William Justice. In 3rd person in his & his wife's name; accepting a dinner invitation. rms Mar 21 (66) $850

— 25 Nov 1879. 1 p, 8vo. To J.W. Thymes. Declining dinner invitation of Caledonia Club. With related material. sg June 6 (86) $550

— 2 Oct 1880. 1 p, 8vo. To H. C. Tuttle. Commenting on a letter received from Tuttle. Framed with port. wa Oct 28 (192) $800

— 12 Dec 1880. 2 pp, 8vo. To General William Rowley. About relations with Mexico: "I hope however my efforts may have something to do with the development of the railroad, commercial & friendly relations with our sister Republic, Mexico." CNY Dec 15 (172) $1,400

— 21 Feb 1881. 2 pp, 8vo. To "My Dear Ex P M G". Mentioning that he will not be attending Garfield's inauguration. CNY Dec 15 (68) $1,200

— 27 July 1882. 2 pp, 197mm by 121mm. To Adam Badeau. Declining to participate in the promotion of a recreational festival being planned by Badeau. P June 5 (43) $900

**Ls,** 2 June 1863. 2 pp, 4to. To Col. James B. Fry. Sending a list of deserters. Sgd as "U. S. Grant Major General Commd'g." pba Oct 26 (168) $2,500

— 15 June 1865. 1 p, 8vo. To unnamed recipient. A receipt for a donation to a sanitary fair to benefit Union Soldiers. With mat burn in lower margin. CNY Dec 15 (66) $800

**Series** of 25 A Ns, 1869 to 1877. 25 notecards, various sizes. To his secretary C. C. Striffen. Giving various instructions. Forbes Magazine collection. CNY May 17 (132) $2,600

**Ds,** 25 Dec 1868. 1 p, size not stated. Certificate that Hiram Ruggles has contributed $150.00 "to the Building Fund of the Metropolitan Memorial M. E. Church, in the City of Washington". Also sgd by S. P. Chase. Illus in cat. rms June 6 (386) $2,100

— 9 Apr 1869. 1 p, folio. Appointment of John Ely as US Marshal in Pennsylvania. Countersgd by Hamilton Fish. Illus in cat. rms June 6 (34) $1,100

— 7 July 1870. 1 p, 4to. Order to affix the US Seal to a warrant for the remission of a fine. rms June 6 (387) $700

— 30 Jan 1871. 1 p, 4to. Order to affix the U.S. seal to a pardon warrant for E. Bloomfield. CE June 12 (45) $550

— 5 Oct 1872. 2 pp, folio. Pardon of Henry Smith, convicted of "passing counterfeit money". Countersgd by Secretary of State Hamilton Fish. With fold breaks. sg Sept 28 (117) $1,000

— 22 Oct 1874. 1 p, 4to. Pardon warrant for H. A. Berry. cb June 25 (2330) $750

— 15 Dec 1875. 1 p, folio. Appointing Samuel J. Logan as a Second Lieutenant in the Marine Corps. Countersgd by Secretary of the Navy George M. Robeson. Signature light. rms Oct 11 (275) $800

— 25 Apr 1876. 1 p, 4to. Directing Sec of State to affix U.S. Seal to pardon warrant. sg June 6 (85) $650

— 13 Feb 1877. 11.5 by 15.25 inches, framed. Appointment of a postmaster in Auburne ME. rs Nov 11 (18) $500

— [n.d.]. 1 p, folio. Unaccomplished ship's passport. Countersgd by Sec. of State Hamilton Fish. CE June 12 (47) $1,300

**Autograph sentiment,** 30 March 1864. 1 p, 4to. "Liberal patronage for the benefit of the sick and wounded soldiers is respectfully solicited..." Browned. CNY Dec 15 (65) $3,800

**Autograph telegram,** sgd, 31 Jan 1865. 1 p, 8vo. To Major Gen. George G. Meade. Asking him to return immediately. With ALs by John G. Stevenson, 14 May 1865, forwarding Grant's telegram to Mary E. Carson. Illus in cat. Forbes Magazine collection. CNY May 17 (130) $4,000

**Check,** accomplished & sgd, 1 Dec 1873. Drawn on the National Metropolitan Bank for $700 payable to John F. Long. Endorsed by Long on verso. Illus in cat. rms Mar 21 (67) $1,500

— Anr, sgd, 21 mar 1876. Payable to L. Johnson & Co for $750. Repaired. rms Nov 30 (118) $900

**Photograph, sgd,** [c.1862]. 105mm by 60mm. Half length, by E. & H. T. Anthony. Illus in cat. Marans collection. CE Apr 17 (141) $2,400

— Anr, [n.d.]. Carte size. Mtd. Illus in cat. P Dec 13 (130) $3,250

— Anr, [n.d.]. Carte size. sg June 6 (84) $2,600

**Signature,** 29 Sept 1868. 1 p, 5 by 2.75 inches. With engraving cb June 25 (2331) $600

— Anr, 29 Jan 1876. No size given. With a port & a double page from Harper's Weekly with engravings of the Surrender of Vicksburg. Framed. Over-all size 22.5 by 38.5 inches. Detail in cat rms Oct 11 (100) $900

— Anr, [n.d.]. No size given. On a card. pba Feb 22 (236) $400

— Anr, [n.d.]. Size not stated. Framed with engraved port. rms Mar 21 (69) $420

— Anr, [n.d.]. On a card, matted with a photograph. sg June 6 (87) $350

**Grant, Ulysses S., 1822-85 —&**
**Colfax, Schyler, 1823-85**
**Signature,** [n.d.]. On 1 p, 8vo album page. With an 1868 election ticket from California & an 1868 campaign silk. Framed. Over-all size 15.5 by 19.5 inches. Illus in cat rms Oct 11 (312) $800

**Grass, Guenter**
**Typescript,** part of Ms (p 108) of his Das Treffen in Telgte, [c.1978]. 1 p, folio. Including autograph corrections. Sgd later. star Mar 21 (155) DM340
**Ls,** 26 Nov 1968. 1 p, 4to. To Edgar Lohner. Explaining some passages in one of his works. star Mar 21 (156) DM390

**Grassi, Joseph, 1757-1838**
**Ds,** 8 Sept 1804. 1 p, folio. Receipt for 300 ducats from the Duke of Sachsen-Gotha-Altenburg. star Mar 21 (672) DM400

**Gratz, Hyman**
**ADs,** 1808. 2 pp, folio. Bond for $60,000 filled out by Gratz as court-appointed treasurer of a lottery organized under an Act of the General Assembly of Pennsylvania from February 8, 1806. Toned & with marginal repair. rms Oct 11 (213) $280

**Gratz, Rebecca, 1781-1869**
**ALs,** 18 July 1804. 7 pp, 4to. To her sister Rachel. Sending news from NY & reporting about Alexander Hamilton's death. P Dec 13 (14) $10,000

**Graves, Robert, 1895-1985**
[Collection of correspondence from 1915-16 relating to Robert Graves's service in World War I. Sold at Sotheby's on 28 June 1996 as lot 66 for £24,000. Hinged in a 4to volume of half mor with typed list of contents.] Detail in cat
**Autograph Ms,** 6 stanzas of Whipperginny. [1922]. 2 pp, 8vo. Sgd. Marked up for printing. S June 28 (71) £350
**Series** of 17 ALs s, 16 Sept 1916 to 19 July 1917 & [n.d.]. , 34 pp, 8vo & 4to. To Robert Ross. About Graves's writings. S June 28 (67) £17,000
— Series of 36 A Ls s, 24 Mar 1917 to 5 Mar 1961. 93 pp, 4to & 8vo. To W. K. T. Barrett. About his life, works & loves, including the here-identified Marjorie Machin. S Dec 18 (305) £4,200 [Maggs]
**A Ls s** (2), 1 Oct 1965 & 13 Apr 1970. 3 pp, 4to & 8vo. To Dr. Louis Rodriguez. About writing poetry; gives his publication history. S Dec 18 (389) £250 [Fenelon]
**ALs,** [1922]. 5 pp, 8vo. To W. K. T. Barrett. About T. E. Lawrence & his capture by the Turks. S Dec 18 (306) £1,500 [Maggs]

**Greece**
— CYCLADES. - Archive of diplomatic correspondence relating to the Austrian & Sardinian missions in the island of Siros in the Cyclades, 1827 to 1899. Several hundred pages, mostly folio. S May 15 (184) £3,600

**Greeley, Horace, 1811-72**
**ALs,** 12 Sept 1858. 2 pp, 8vo. To George S. Phillips. About a request for work at the New York Tribune: "I am not now and hope never to be the manager of the Tribune. Mr. Dana has relieved me of that woe to my great satisfaction. I don't see how any place could be made for you unless you can take mine (which I would very cheerfully resign to the right person) of chief political writer and Director of the paper. pba Oct 26 (114) $250
— 26 Feb 1865. 1 p, 8vo. To General Irvine. Recommending his cousin William O'Connell for promotion. pba Oct 26 (171) $150
— 6 Oct 1872. No size given. No length given. To V. R. Vrooman. Concerning his wife's health. pba Oct 26 (239) $250

**Greely, Adolphus Washington, 1844-1935**
**ALs,** 23 Oct 1862. 2 pp, 4to. To unnamed recipient. About a wound to his face, which is healing. Worn. pba June 13 (18) $225

**Greenaway, Kate, 1846-1901**
**Original drawings,** (2) to illus Bluebeard. [c.1870] 226mm by 165mm & 227mm by 167mm, in watercolor. Depicting Bluebeard handing the key to his wife & the wife on bended knee pleading for her life. S Nov 21 (344) £4,100
— Original drawings, complete set of 16 watercolor illusts for Mary Annette Russell's The April Baby's Book of Tunes, 1900; each initialled. With calligraphic tp, Ms music & verses of nursery rhymes. Blue mor gilt bdg; large 4to. S Nov 21 (390) £40,000
**Series** of (12) A Ls s, 20 Feb 1889 to 27 Apr 1894. To Mary Anderson. Sgd with initials, 2 with ink or ink & watercolor sketches. S May 16 (164) £1,900

**Greene, Graham, 1904-91**
**Autograph Ms,** Short story entitled "The Blessing". 1964. 6 pp, 4to. Stained. With 1st top typescript, carbon typescript of revised text & carbons of the 2 achieved versions. S June 28 (126) £2,200
— Autograph Ms, The Quiet American. 1932. 147 pp, folio, with inserts on smaller sheets. Heavily revised. CNY Oct 27 (61) $60,000
**A Ls s** (2), 17 June 1986 & 7 Apr [n.y.]. 2 pp, 4to. To John Mortimer. Thanking him for the latest Rumpole; listing 7 errors made in a profile of him. S Dec 18 (390) £600 [Mandl]

**Gregoire, Henri Baptiste, 1750-1831**
**ALs,** 1 Feb 1804. 1 p, 8vo. To M. de Vos. Thanking for his hospitality. HH May 9 (2531) DM260

**Gregory IX, Pope, d.1241**
**Ms,** Decretales, with the gloss of Bernardo Bottoni of Parma. [Bologna?, c.1265]. 252 leaves (some lacking), vellum, 380mm by 230mm. Brown lea over contemp bevelled wooden bds, with 15th-cent pastedown in a French notarial hand. In a neat rounded gothic bookhand surrounded by gloss in smaller script. With 2-line initials throughout in blue & red, 4 very large decorated book openings formed of the

name Gregorius in tall combined capitals, & extensive medieval notes added throughout. S Dec 5 (32) £14,000 [Sam Fogg]

**Gregory of Nazianzus, Saint, 329-389**
Ms, Homilies. [Constantinople?, c.1075]. With Johannes Chrysostomus. in sanctum Pascha Concio. Fragment of 14 leaves, on vellum, 325mm by 257mm, disbound. In brown ink in a small Greek miniscule, headpieces & headings in red, first large decorative initials to each work & other initials in red. C June 26 (11) £5,000

**Gregory XVI, Pope, 1765-1846**
Ls, 1 Dec 1829. 1 p, folio. To Cardinal Remigio Crescini. Sending Christmas wishes. star Mar 22 (1504) DM250
Autograph sentiment, 2 Apr 1845. 1 p, 4to. Benediction, under a request for his Apostolic Blessing. Was mtd. HH May 9 (2472) DM340

**Grenville, George, 1712-70**
ALs, 24 Sept 1763. 2 pp, 4to. To Lord Cowper. About recommending Cowper's son. rms Nov 30 (174) $400

**Gretry, Andre Ernest Modeste, 1741-1813**
ALs, [9 May 1797]. 1 p, folio. To the French Directoire. Referring to his "essais sur la musique". With a port. star Mar 22 (853) DM400

**Grey, Zane, 1875-1939**
ALs, 1 Oct 1901. 2 pp, 8vo. To Lina E. Roth. A love letter: " I am your captive; your slave if you will..." With holograph envelope. pba Feb 22 (58) $190
ANs, 23 Nov 1932. 1 p, no size given. On a card. To Wildemere. Wishing the recipient a Merry Christmas. Illus in cat pba Feb 22 (57) $180
Check, 8 Jan 1928. 1 p, no size given. $5,000 payable to Mrs. Zane Grey. pba June 13 (207) $75

**Grieg, Edvard, 1843-1907**
Autograph transcript, 4 double-bars of music, captioned Berceuse. Sgd & dated 28 Aug 1896. rms Nov 30 (175) $1,500
Collection of 3 A Ls s & 2 Ns s, 20 Dec 1899 to 20 Apr 1901. Length not stated (2 visiting cards). To Borresen. Thanking for flowers & invitations, sending New Year's greetings, etc. S May 15 (362) £750
ALs, 29 June 1892. 2 pp on bifolium, 181mm by 114mm. Recipient unnamed. Saying that he cannot answer his foolish questions; includes 4 bars, sgd, from the violin sonata no 2 in G. C June 26 (257) £750
— 10 Oct 1894. 3 pp, 8vo. To the singer Hansen. Concerning recipient's application for a position in Christiania. S May 15 (363) £500
Autograph postcard, sgd, [12 Feb 1907]. To J. H. Smither-Jackson. Inscr with 3 bars from his Peer Gynt. Illus in cat. S May 15 (369) £1,000
Autograph quotation, 9 bars from the prelude of his Foran Sydens Kloster, Op.20, sgd & inscr; [28 Mar] 1875. 1 p, 8vo. Framed with a photograph. S May 15 (368) £950

— Anr, 8 bars from his Ballade, Op.24; 29 Apr [19]03. 1 p, 4to. Notated on 2 systems of 2 staves each; sgd & inscr to M. D. Calvocoressi. Illus in cat. S May 15 (366) £1,300
Photograph, sgd, [1882]. 163mm by 106mm, mtd. Bust-length vignette port, by Georg Brokesch. Marans collection. CE Apr 17 (234) $950
— Anr, [n.d.]. 16.5cm by 10.5cm. By Elliott & Fry. Illus in cat. S May 15 (360) £950

**Griffith, David Wark, 1875-1948**
Group photograph, 1927. Showing him on a set with Douglas Fairbanks & 12 others. Inscr by both Griffith & Fairbanks. Fairbanks's surname a little light. wa Oct 28 (437) $500

**Grillparzer, Franz, 1791-1872**
ALs, [n.d.]. 1 p, folio. Recipient unnamed. Letter of recommendation for Mansvetus Riedt. Illus in cat. star Mar 21 (158) DM1,700
Ds, 6 May 1870. 1 p, 8vo. Receipt for books from a library. star Mar 21 (157) DM700

**Grimm, Hermann, 1828-1901**
ALs, 20 Apr 1870. 2 pp, 8vo. To an unnamed Ed. Sending a cat for review. star Mar 21 (473) DM250

**Grimm, Jacob, 1785-1863**
ALs, 12 Feb 1859. 3 pp, 8vo. To Werthester Freund. About news from Raszmann of a manuscript of the complete Hildebrands Lied. C June 26 (316) £5,200
ANs, 3 Dec 1853. 1 p, 8vo. Recipient unnamed. Sending a contract [not present] & asking the recipient to recommend him to Mr. Lillewen. Framed with port & plaque. Vertical crease affecting the J in the signature. cb June 25 (2537) $650

**Grimm, Jacob, 1785-1863 —& Others**
Signature, 7 Feb 1836. 1 p, folio. Academic circular in the hand of F. Ch. Bergmann, sgd by 53 professors at Goettingen University. star Mar 21 (472) DM800

**Grimm, Wilhelm, 1786-1859**
ALs, 8 Sept 1838. 1 p, 8vo. Recipient unnamed. Informing him that he has forwarded 3 prize essays to his brother in Kassel. S Dec 1 (21) £420

**Groener, Wilhelm, 1867-1939**
Autograph Ms, speech analyzing actions of military leaders at the end of the war, 17 May 1922. 3 pp, 4to. Sgd. With typescript of the same text. JG Sept 29 (267) DM240

**Gropius, Walter, 1883-1969**
Photograph, sgd, 1969. 179mm by 125mm. Shoulder-length port. Marans collection. CE Apr 17 (209) $380

**Grosse, Karl Friedrich August, 1768-1847**
ALs, 7 Jan 1791. 4 pp, 8vo. To Herr [Stegemann]. Colorful report about his recent experiences. star Mar 21 (159) DM1,100

### Grossmann, Rudolf, 1882-1941
ALs, 12 Nov 1925. 2 pp, 4to. Recipient unnamed. Sending portraits of some actors & authors. star Mar 21 (673) DM340

### Grotefend, Georg Friedrich, 1775-1853
ALs, 1 & 2 Dec 1822. 3 pp, 4to. To an unnamed colleague. Discussing a project concerning cuneiform writing & other scholarly matters. star Mar 21 (474) DM1,600

### Groth, Klaus, 1819-99
ALs, 13 Apr 1899. Length not stated. To Ferdinand Braune. Agreeing to sit for his port. HN May 15 (2578) DM230

### Gruen, Anastasius
A Ls s (2), 10 Nov 1842 & 4 June 1847. 2 pp, 8vo. To the booksellers Weidmann. Mostly regarding his work Der letzte Ritter. star Mar 21 (160) DM320

### Gruithuisen, Franz Paula von, 1774-1852
Ls, 3 Apr 1841. 4 pp, 4to. To an unnamed Italian astronomer. Reporting about the optical institute in Munich. star Mar 21 (475) DM650

### Guardini, Romano, 1885-1968
Typescript, theological work, Der Mensch. Umriss einer christlichen Anthropologie; [c.1948]. Over 120 pp, 4to. Including extensive autograph revisions. Sgd on tp. star Mar 21 (476) DM2,600

### Guericke, Otto von, 1602-86
Ds, 25 Oct 1676. 1 p, 8vo. Receipt for 50 talers. star Mar 21 (477) DM780

### Guetersloh, Albert Paris
Autograph Ms, fragment from his novel Sonne und Mond, [c.1961]. 1 p, 8vo; sgd later. Including ALs, letter of transmittal, 1963. Illus in cat. star Mar 21 (161) DM750

### Guilbert, Yvette, 1867-1944
ALs, [n.d.]. 2 pp, 4to. To Mr. de Bonneford. Asking his help in gaining financial support from important clerics in Paris. rms Nov 30 (176) $210

### Guillotin, Joseph Ignace, 1738-1814
Cut signature, 26 Feb 1807. 114mm by 128mm, framed with port. CE June 12 (49) $350

### Guiteau, Charles, 1840?-82
Autograph Ms, entitled Facts touching Miss Early's Case. 187? 1 p, 4to. "I was present on the trial. Two of the best lawyers in Chicago defended the Times..." Illus in cat sg Sept 28 (119) $600

Signature, 10 Feb 1882. Card, 2.1 by 4.5 inches. Sgd on recto & verso. With a photograph. Illus in cat. rms June 6 (381) $425

### Gundry, Stephen G.
Autograph Ms, private log onboard H.M.S. Pelican describing a voyage on the Pacific Station, including Tahiti & Pitcairn. [c.1886] About 200 pp, folio, in half calf. Includes autographs of several Pitcairners & with photographs of H.M.S. Pelican inserted b Mar 20 (167) £350

### Gunn, Thom
Proof copy, 1967. 1 p, 8vo. Proofs of Touch. Corrected & revised. With ALs returning them to the publisher. S June 28 (136) £190

### Gurckhaus, Carl, 1821-84
[A collection of c.180 autograph musical quotations dedicated to him by composers & musicians, 1853 to 1883, 4to, sold at Stargardt on 22 Mar 1996, lot 980, for DM9,000.]

### Gustav II Adolf, King of Sweden, 1594-1632
Ds, 5 Apr 1625. 1 p, folio. Order to furnish corn to Niels Bielke. Including Bielke's receipt at foot. star Mar 22 (1245) DM1,000

### Gustav V, King of Sweden, 1858-1950
ALs, 17 Nov 1890. 4 pp, 8vo. To his foster mother. Chatting about his stay in Egypt. HN May 15 (2579) DM480

### Gustav VI Adolf, King of Sweden, 1882-1973 —& Louise, Queen of Gustav Adolf VI of Sweden, 1889-1965
Ls, 1 Dec 1923. 1 p, 8vo. To a sports society. Thanking for congratulations on their wedding. star Mar 22 (1655) DM400

### Guthrie, Thomas Anstey, 1856-1934. See: Anstey, F.

### Gutzkow, Karl Ferdinand, 1811-78
Series of 8 A Ls s, 7 Apr 1853 to 5 June 1868. 27 pp, various sizes. To [Feodor Loewe]. Discussing a variety of theatrical matters. HH Nov 17 (3225) DM2,200

A Ls s (2), 5 June 1872 & 5 May 1874. 3 pp, 8vo. Recipient unnamed. About his financial problems. HH Nov 17 (3226) DM260

# H

### Haalilio, Timoteo
ALs, [c.1842]. Recipient unnamed. In Hawaiian, Asking for a meeting "before the army will start a war". rms Nov 30 (185) $3,200

### Haber, Fritz, 1868-1934
Ls, 1 July 1932. 5 pp, 4to. To Prince Andronikov. Expressing condolences on the death of recipient's wife Margarethe von Wrangell. star Mar 21 (478) DM1,000

### Haeckel, Ernst, 1834-1919
Collection of 5 A Ls s & 5 autograph postcards, sgd, 3 Sept 1906 to 24 Nov 1910. 11 pp, 4to & 8vo. To Hermine & Alfred Heimendahl. About a variety of matters. HN Nov 24 (2791) DM1,400

ALs, 13 Dec 1864. 3 pp, 8vo. Recipient unnamed. Ordering plaster casts of some zoological specimens. star Mar 21 (479) DM360

**Haering, Wilhelm, 1798-1871.** See: Alexis, Willibald

**Haertling, Peter**
Autograph Ms, poem, Zwischen den Altern, 16 Apr 1985. 1 p, folio. 4 lines, sgd. star Mar 21 (166) DM320

**Haggard, Sir Henry Rider, 1856-1925**
Ls, 1 Jan 1898. 1 p, 4to. To B. Knowles. About the origins of Umslopogaas the Zulu in She. pn Nov 9 (443) £110

**Hahn, Otto, 1879-1968**
Autograph Ms, 4 additions to a paper on the practical use of nuclear energy, [n.d.]. 2 pp, folio. Illus in cat. star Mar 21 (481) DM2,400

Ls, 15 Dec 1962. 1 p, folio. To Max Flesch-Thebesius. Thanking for information on an old obstetrical hospital in Goettingen. star Mar 21 (482) DM320

**Hahnemann, Samuel, 1755-1843**
ALs, 3 Apr 1825. 1 p, 12mo. Recipient unnamed. Giving medical advice. star Mar 21 (484) DM5,500

**Hahn-Hahn, Ida, Graefin von, 1805-80**
ALs, 9 June 1849. 4 pp, 8vo. To an unnamed countess. Mourning for Adolf von Bistramb. star Mar 21 (162) DM580

**Haile Selassie, Emperor of Ethiopia, 1892-1975**
Ls, 23 Sept 1958. 1 p, folio. To Hector Trujillo Molina, President of the Dominican Republic. Expressing congratulations on his election. Illus in cat. rms June 6 (390) $1,500

Photograph, sgd, 1942. 9.25 by 6.75 inches. Sgd on image. Ck Apr 12 (113) £380

**Hales, Stephen, 1677-1761**
ALs, 25 Dec 1750. 1 p, 4to. To Mr. Joyns. Sending condolences on the death of his brother & discussing a financial matter. Illus in cat. star Mar 21 (485) DM1,300

**Haley, Alex, 1921-92**
[An archive of typed drafts for his article Search For Roots, with holograph revisions & related material, sold at Swann on 28 Mar 1996, lot 142, for $3,000]

Typescript, article on Roots for the London Observer. San Francisco, 24 Jan 1973. 32 pp. Heavily corrected by Haley in green ink. With related material. sg Mar 28 (143) $2,200

Collection of 6 Ls s, ANS, & AN, 3 Mar to 30 Nov 1973. 10 pp, 4to. To an Ed of Reader's Digest. Referring to the writing of his novel Roots. CE May 22 (249) $1,300

See also: Baldwin, James & Haley

**Haley, Alex, 1921-92 —&**
**Malcolm X, 1925-65**
Typescript, draft of Playboy Magazine interview with Malcolm X. [c.Jan-Feb 1963] 40 pp, 4to. Extensively annotated by Haley & with 38 corrections in ink by Malcolm X, sgd & intialled. sg Mar 28 (196) $9,500

Typescript carbon copy, p. 29 of the Playboy interview with Malcolm X. With 4 holograph revisions & sgd by Malcolm X. cb June 25 (2361) $1,500

**Hall, Basil, 1788-1844**
ALs, 27 June 1835. 1 p, 4to. To Karl K. Kraukling. Returning books & thanking for introducing him to Ludwig Tieck. FD May 14 (1109) DM200

**Hall, Lyman, Signer from Georgia**
ALs, 11 May 1784. 2 pp, folio. To " my D[ea]r Sister Susa". About family news including: " I am glad I knew nothing of my Hon[ore]d Mother's Illness till it was past, it was not my Happiness, to Rock the Cradle of the Declining Age of my ever Revered parents, but I am Thankfull to You & Others who did it..." Foxed. rms Oct 11 (179) $5,250

**Hallam, Lewis, c.1740-1808**
Ds, [late 1780s]. 1 p, folio. Petition addressed to the Pennsylvania Assembly asking that he be granted the management of the theater to be licensed by the Assembly. Illus in cat. rms June 6 (101) $1,000

**Halleck, Henry W., 1815-72**
ALs, 11 May 1865. 1 p, 8vo. To Brig. Gen. [Marsena] Patrick. Inquiring about the alleged mining of Libby Prison. Framed with a port. Illus in cat. rms June 6 (35) $1,300

Cut signature, [n.d.]. Framed with photo & related material. rms Nov 30 (16) $500

**Haller, Albrecht von, 1708-77**
ALs, 26 May 1751. 1 p, 4to. To Tobias Roenicke. Promising to print a review of recipient's work. star Mar 21 (163) DM800

**Hamilton, Alexander, 1739-1802**
Ls, 22 July 1792. 3 pp, 4to. To collectors of customs. Explaining in great detail they way he feels their duties, such as taxation of cargoes & issuance of permits, should be carried out. Foxed & worn. rms Oct 11 (180) $4,000

**Hamilton, Alexander, 1757-1804**
ALs, 10 Sept 1779. 1 p, 8vo. To John Fitch. As aide-de camp of George Washington, giving orders concerning an account of stores at 2 army camps. Illus in cat. P Dec 13 (136) $5,000

— 16 Aug 1791. 3 pp, 4to. To William Seton. Confidential letter discussing the national debt & giving instructions for purchases on behalf of the government. P Dec 13 (138) $27,000

— 8 July 1793. 1 p, 4to. To Benjamin Bourne. About financial matters: "The papers you mention after a diligent search cannot be found. Did you not take them back? I am not well informed of the office of the Settlement of account, but from some circumstances which have fallen under my view I am led to conclude that your State will have a ballance [sic] in its favour of somewhere about 30,000 Dollars. The pardons have gone forward..." Maked "Personal and Confidential". Sgd as " A. Hamilton". With integral overleaf, franked. Illus in cat pba Oct 26 (240) $4,000

**Ls,** 21 May 1792. 1 p, 4to. To John Kean, Cashier of the Bank of the U.S. Transmitting (not present) a warrant to be applied towards the interest of the registered debt. Signature & title of recipient in Hamilton's hand. rms Nov 30 (177) $6,500

— 6 Apr 1793. 1 p, 222mm by 184mm. To John Brooks, U.S. Marshall for the District of Massachusetts. Apologizing for the delay in reimbursing one of Brooks's expense reports. P June 5 (44) $2,500

— 26 Mar 1794. 1 p, 238mm by 194mm. To Samuel Hodgdon. Forwarding a warrant (not present) to suply the Philadelphia Army comissary. Framed with port. P June 5 (45) $2,500

— 5 Dec 1794. 1 p, 4to. To John Quincy Adams. Asking Minister Adams to open a bank for Special Commissioner to Spain William Pinckney. Right margin trimmed. Browned. With small piece neatly pasted at top corner. Illus in cat CNY Dec 15 (69) $3,500

— 22 Jan 1795. 1 p, 4to. To Sharp Delany. Giving instructions for the commissioning of a new revenue cutter. CNY May 17 (246) $2,800

**Hammerstein, Oscar, 1895-1960.** See: Rodgers, Richard & Hammerstein

**Hammett, Dashiell, 1894-1961 —& Huston, John**

**Typescript,** The Maltese Falcon. From the Novel by Dashiell Hammett. Screen Play by John Huston. Final. 26 May 1941. Length not given, 285mm by 223mm, in wraps with metal brad fasteners. cb Oct 17 (371) $800

**Hampton, Wade, 1818-1902**

**Signature,** [n.d.]. On small slip. Framed with photo & map. rms Nov 30 (17) $480

— Anr, [n.d.]. On small slip. Framed with port. rms Nov 30 (179) $225

**Hamsun, Knut, 1859-1952**

**ALs,** 7 Mar 1918. 1 p, 8vo. To Albert Langen. Informing him that he does not need copies of his collected works. star Mar 21 (164) DM370

— [n.d.]. 1 p, 8vo. To unnamed friends. Wondering whether he can call Gladstone "a bigoted cow" in his book. star Mar 21 (165) DM450

**Hancock, John, 1737-93**

**ALs,** 29 Oct 1760. 2 pp, 4to. To the Reverend Daniel Perkins. About political happenings in England: "I am very busy getting my self mourning upon the Occasion of the melancholy event of the Death of his late Majesty King George the 2nd...His death was very sudden last Saturday morning....On Sunday last the Prince of Wales was proclaim'd King..." With tape repairs. Illus in cat CNY Dec 15 (174) $21,000

— 16 Aug 1775. 1 p removed from larger sheet, 162mm by 168mm. To Richard Derby. Calling in a debt. Illus in cat. P June 5 (46) $4,250

— 8 Aug 1782. 1 p, 4to. To Levi Lincoln. Asking him to accept a bill from Mr. Leggatt. Illus in cat. P Dec 13 (141) $6,000

**Ls,** 10 Aug 1776. 1 p, folio. To William Palfrey. Informing him that Samuel Adams will bring things for Capt. Palms on his return to Massachusetts. Including autograph postscript. Illus in cat. Forbes Magazine collection. CNY May 17 (133) $8,000

**Ds,** 16 Jan 1771. 1 p, 8vo. Certifying accuracy of the expenses turned in for " the Province Hospital at Ransford Island". Also sgd by 4 others. Toned. With repairs in margins. Also with a port of Hancock. Illus in cat rms Oct 11 (182) $2,000

— 22 June 1775. Appointment of Daniel Morgan as Captain of a Company of Riflemen. Accomplished in George Washington's hand; countersgd by Charles Thomson. Illus in cat. P Dec 13 (282) $11,000

— 27 Feb 1777. 1 p, 190mm by 184mm. Appointment of 3 men to appraise woolens brought into the port of Baltimore by a Privateer from the State of NY. Framed Illus in cat P June 5 (47) $6,000

— 14 by 9 inches. Appointment of Isaac Adams as coroner of Essex MA. Countersgd by John Avery rs Nov 11 (19) $2,200

— 11 May 1784. 1 p, folio. Ship's registry for the sloop Ranger. Framed with a port. Illus in cat. rms Mar 21 (205) $2,800

— 7 June 1784. 1 p, 4to. Assignment to Godfrey Malbone of the outstanding balance of a bond (on verso) made by Hancock to Andrew Johonnot. Framed. P Dec 13 (143) $2,500

— 10 Apr 1787. 2 pp, 4to. Sale of land in Pittston, Lincoln County, to Jonathan Bowman. Also sgd by Dorothy Hancock & 2 others. Illus in cat. P Dec 13 (140) $3,000

— 23 Feb 1788. 1 p, 298mm by 181mm. Certification that Christopher Gore is a justice of the peace for Suffolk County. Countersgd by John Avery. P June 5 (48) $2,500

— 18 Nov 1788. 1 p, folio. Appointment of Nathan Alden as Captain, 3rd Regiment, 1st Brigade of Militia. Countersgd by John Avery, Jr. Folds worn & reinforced on verso. Browning. sg Sept 28 (121) $2,400

— 30 May 1791. 1 p. Appointment of William Hood as an Ensign in a Massachusetts regiment. Framed with port. cb June 25 (2332) $2,250

— [n.d.]. 1 p, 45mm by 94mm. Ticket no 581 for the lottery to rebuild Faneuil Hall. CNY May 17 (247) $2,400

**Autograph endorsement,** 23 Mar 1762. 1 p, 3.75 by 8.9 inches. On verso of promissory note payable to him. sg Feb 1 (98) $1,500

**Autograph sentiment,** [n.d.]. 1 p, 3.5 by 7 inches. Cut from an ALs. "I wish you happy, and am/Your most obed Serv./John Hancock." Addressed to Benjamin Lincoln Esq. Mtd. Detail in cat sg Sept 28 (122) $1,600

**Lottery ticket,** sgd, June 1765. For Faneuil-Hall Lottery No. 5, number 4190. sg Feb 1 (99) $2,800

## Hancock, Winfield Scott, 1824-86

**Ls,** 1 Sept 1879. 2 pp, 8vo. To General T. T. Locke. Declining an invitation to join an excursion. pba Feb 22 (166) $110

— 14 Aug 1884. 2 pp, 8vo. To Committee Chairman Frank R. Lawrence. Declining an invitation to meet members of the "Greeley Relief" Expedition due to his wife's poor health. rms Oct 11 (37) $230

**ANs,** 5 Oct 1864. 1 p, 12mo. Recipient unnamed. Sending his autograph. Framed. wd Nov 15 (11) $175

**Signature,** 20 Mar 1878. On album leaf. Framed with related ports & views. rms Nov 30 (18) $460

— Anr, [n.d.]. No size given. On a card. With port of Scott in uniform, a three-ring Minie ball & 2 original stereos of the painted battle cyclorama in Gettysburg. Over-all size 16 by 24 inches. Detail in cat rms Oct 11 (101) $450

## Hand, Edward, 1744-1802

**Ds,** 7 Apr 1792. 1 p, 4to. Appointing Jasper Yeats as his attorney to receive all interests due on " Six per Cent and three per Cent Stock standing in my Name in the Books of the Commissioner of Loans for the State of Pennsylvania..." Also sgd by 2 witnesses. Mtd & framed. Top margin trimmed. Over-all size 10.3 by 10.11 inches. rms Oct 11 (183) $1,300

## Handy, William Christopher, 1873-1958

**Ls,** 12 Apr 1946. 2 pp, 4to. To Mary E. Clarke. About his recent tour through the South. sg Mar 28 (166) $275

## Hanley, James

**Autograph Ms,** story, A Breath of Air. 7 pp, 4to. Sgd & dated 1937. pn Nov 9 (444) £140

## Hanson, Howard Harold

**Autograph quotation,** [n.d.]. 1 p, 12mo. 2 bars from Symphony No 2, Romantic. Illus in cat rms Oct 11 (184) $200

## Hardee, William Joseph, 1815-73

**Signature,** 4 June 1869. No size given. On a card. With 2 sepia-toned reprints of Hardee & ruins of Columbia. With related material. Framed. Over-all size 15.5 by 26 inches. Detail in cat rms Oct 11 (103) $400

## Harden, Maximilian, 1861-1927

**Collection** of 40 A Ls s & postcards, sgd, 1899 to 1900. About 46 pp, 8vo. To Karl Kraus. About matters pertaining to Kraus's journal Die Fackel. S Dec 1 (22) £3,600

## Hardenberg, Karl August, Fuerst von, 1750-1822

**ALs,** 23 June 1810. 2 pp, 4to. To an unnamed Prussian princess. Hoping that he will be able to justify the King's confidence. star Mar 22 (1354) DM1,100

**Ls,** 27 Dec 1815. 1 p, 4to. To the Prince'of Salm-Krautheim. Responding to a request for an appointment. star Mar 22 (1355) DM220

## Harding, Warren G., 1865-1923

[An archive of material concerning the correspondence of Warren G. Harding sold at Pacific on Oct 26, 1995 as lot 242 for $9,000.] Illus in cat

**Autograph Ms,** Draft of a speech to the Benevolent and Protective Order of Elks. [n.d.]. 27 pp, 4to. On the theme of greatness. With chipped & brittle edges. With a typed transcription. CNY Dec 15 (176) $1,400

**ALs,** 5 Mar 1903. 1 p, 8vo. To Fred B. Crow. Thanking him for kind wishes. Sgd as "W G Harding". Illus in cat pba Oct 26 (241) $850

**Ls,** 31 Jan 1921. 2 pp, 4to. To Henry A. Wise Wood. Discussing potential alignments of nations in the future. With a small paperclip stain. rms Oct 11 (185) $700

— 15 Nov 1921. 1 p, 4to. To Caroline Cox. Responding to an invitation to the opening of a theater. Framed with a port. Illus in cat. rms Mar 21 (122) $540

— 8 May 1922. 3 pp, 4to. To Congressman Madden. Concerning reducing the cost of government. sg Sept 28 (123) $1,100

— 28 Nov 1928. 1 p, 4to. To Henry A. Wallace. Thanking his Secretary of Agriculture for the proof sheets of his annual report: " I am very sure it is an excellent, forward looking, and comprehensive report..." CNY Dec 15 (175) $1,100

**Ds,** 27 Dec 1895. 1 p, 12mo. Receipt for $14.00 in payment of a dividend. Illus in cat. rms Mar 21 (121) $175

— 1 Feb 1909. 1 p, folio. Stock certificate no 19 for 10 shares in The Harding Publishing Company. Illus in cat. rms Mar 21 (120) $800

— 12 Aug 1921. 1 p, 18 by 14 inches. Appointing Charles C. Malosh as Postmaster for Lake, Michigan. Countersgd by Postmaster General Will H. Hays. Stained with waterstain on signature. Dar Oct 19 (94) $75

**Signature,** [n.d.]. No size given. On a White House Card. With ticket stubs from the 1920 Republican Collection & a news archive photo of Harding. Framed. Over-all size 13.5 by 17.5 inches. Illus in cat rms Oct 11 (313) $500

## Hardy, Josiah

**Ds,** 10 Mar 1762. 1 p, oblong 8vo. Colonial pay warrant No 36. Also sgd by Charles Read. rms Nov 30 (181) $200

## Hardy, Oliver, 1892-1957. See: Laurel, Stan & Hardy

## Harris, Sir Arthur Travers

**Photograph,** sgd, [n.d.]. 8 by 10 inches. Photo of Harris in RAF uniform. Sgd as "Arthur T. Harris/MRAF". sg Sept 28 (30) $200

## Harris, Frank, 1856-1931

**Collection** of 12 Ls s, 1926 c. 27 pp, 4to. To Lincoln Torrey. About writings. Also with 6 Ls s to Torrey by Harris' secretary B. D. Kentner concerning Harris's financial problems. Bound in half calf. Withrealted material. pba June 13 (208) $1,500

## Harrison, Benjamin, 1833-1901

**ALs,** 17 Jan 1893. 1 p, 8vo. To his brother John Scott Harrison. Worrying about recipient's health. Forbes Magazine collection. CNY May 17 (134) $700

Ls, 21 Aug 1884. 2 pp, 8vo. To Dr. J. B. Green. Declining to deliver an oration at a soldier's reunion. rms June 6 (37) $400

— 12 Mar 1888. 1 p, 4to. To Capt. A. H. Mattox. Hoping to be able to attend a soldier's reunion. rms June 6 (38) $375

— 21 Mar 1888. 1 p, 4to. To A. H. Mattox. Explaining that he will not be able to attend a banquet. Illus in cat. rms June 6 (391) $285

— 28 Jan 1884. 1 p, oblong 12mo. Receipt for a registered letter. wa Oct 28 (196) $200

— 6 May 1897. 2 pp, 8vo. To Maysie E. Shelley. Concerning the volume of requests for his autograph & thanking her for a gift for his daughter Elizabeth. Sgd as "Benj Harrison". Mended & stained. pba Oct 26 (244) $950

Series of Letters, 12 Oct 1896, 27 Oct 1897 & 2 Nov 1898, 1 p each, 4to. To unnamed recipient. Declining invitation to speak. sg Sept 28 (125) $425

Ds, 7 Nov 1863. 1 p, folio. Report on the strength of his regiment. rms June 6 (36) $2,100

— 23 Apr 1889. 1 p, folio. Appointment of postmaster at Winnebago City. Countersgd by Postmaster-General John Wanamaker. 1 p, folio. Many folds. sg Sept 28 (124) $325

— 17 Jan 1890. 1 p, oblong folio. Appointment of Daniel C. Pearson as a Captain in the 2d Regiment of Cavalry. Countersgd by Sec. of War Redfield Proctor. CE June 12 (52) $450

Check, accomplished & sgd, 26 Oct 1886. Drawn on Fletcher's Bank for $250 payable to himself. rms Mar 21 (90) $200

Group photograph, of the 4 Division & Brigade Commanders of his Division, 1865. 203mm by 165mm. Sgd at foot of mount; also sgd by the other 3 flag officers. P June 5 (51) $4,250

Signature, [n.d.]. On 8vo album page. pba Feb 22 (240) $150

See also: Roosevelt, Theodore

### Harrison, John Scott

Ls, 23 Oct 1841. 1 p, 4to. Letter of recommendation for an engineer of the White Water Canal Co. pba Feb 22 (242) $90

### Harrison, Mary Lord, 1858-1948

Franking signature, [n.d.]. 5 free franks. Various sizes. All sgd & dated but dates not given. All sgd in full. pba Oct 26 (245) $85

Photograph, sgd & inscr, 20 May 1937. 8 by 10 inch sepia photo. Inscr to Harriet Sprague. pba Feb 22 (243) $200

### Harrison, Robert Hanson

ALs, 12 Mar 1788. 2 pp, 4to. To Mr. Walton Stone. Making arrangements for his salary as Chief Justice of Maryland. pba June 13 (37) $250

### Harrison, William Henry, 1773-1841

ALs, 22 Nov 1820. 2 pp, 4to. To Secretary of the Navy Irving Thomson. Recommending Joseph G. Blake for appointment as Midshipman in the Navy. With mat burn. CNY Dec 15 (71) $1,200

— 17 Feb 1834. 15 pp, folio. To Thomas Chilton. Recounting the wars in the Northwest Territory to justify the veterans' claims to military pensions. CNY May 17 (250) $18,000

ADs, 6 Aug 1795. 1 p, 16mo. Order to issue beef & flour to the Chippawas. rms Nov 30 (183) $900

— 24 Aug 1805. 1 p, 8vo. Telling the Cashier of the Bank of the United States to pay his father-in-law John Cleve Symmes from his next salary payment. Endorsed by Symmes on verso. With repaired fold break. Illus in cat rms Oct 11 (186) $1,700

Ds, 27 Nov 1796. 1 p, 4to. A survey of the U.S. and (Spanish) Florida border for 1796. Also sgd by the surveyor, Andrew Ellicott. Docketed on verso. Illus in cat CNY Dec 15 (178) $2,600

— 13 Feb 1799. 1 p, 4to. Land grant to George Atchison in St. Clair County. Also sgd by Arthur St. Clair. sg June 6 (90) $1,400

— 19 Mar 1841. 1 p, 4to. Asking his Secretary of State Daniel Webster to the pardon of James P. Smith. Docketed on verso. Yellowing along fold. Illus in cat CNY Dec 15 (179) $70,000

— 29 Mar 1841. 1 p, folio. Ship's passport for the brigantine Virginia Trader. Illus in cat. Forbes Magazine collection. CNY May 17 (136) $75,000

Document, 25 Mar 1841. 1 p, oblong folio. Land grant to Hohn Hustis in the District of Sands. Secretarial signature. CE June 12 (53) $700

### Hart, John, Signer from New Jersey

Ds, 27 Apr 1768. 1 p, folio. As member of the Committee on Public Accounts, statement of the account of Hendrick Fisher. Also sgd by others. Illus in cat. rms June 6 (456) $750

— 1776. 1 p, 57mm by 102mm. 18 pence New Jersey colonial currency note. Also sgd by Robert Smith & John Stevens, Jr. Framed. P Dec 13 (150) $250

### Hartmann, Karl Amadeus, 1905-63

Ls, 1 Feb 1948. 1 p, folio. To Egon Wellesz. Bemoaning the attitude of the German public towards modern music, criticizing Orff, & offering to give the German premiere of Wellesz's 5th String Quartet. S May 15 (544) £280

— 10 Aug 1961. 1 p, folio. To Pavel Eckstein. Arranging a meeting to discuss Janacek's opera. star Mar 22 (860) DM250

### Hassler, Hans Leo, 1562-1612

Ms, song, Mein Lieb will mit mir kriegen, for 8 instrumental parts; [c.1600?]. 2 pp, folio. In German organ tablature. Illus in cat. S Dec 1 (177) £1,800

### Hauer, Josef Matthias, 1883-1959

Autograph music, diagrammatical representation of the opening of his opera Die schwarze Spinne, 26 Dec 1931. 1 p, 8vo. In ink & colored crayon; sgd & inscr. Illus in cat. S Dec 1 (179) £400

## Haug, Friedrich, 1761-1829
**Autograph Ms,** poem, Das Vater unser, [n.d.]. 1 p, 8vo. Sgd. star Mar 21 (168) DM280

## Hauptmann, Gerhart, 1862-1946
**ALs,** 13 Mar [18]99. 2 pp, 8vo. Recipient unnamed. Regretting he was not able to see a play & thanking for a poem. HH May 9 (2477) DM320

— [17 Apr 1903]. 2 pp, 4to. To Paul Jonas. Concerning a judicial matter. star Mar 21 (169) DM320

— [c.Apr 1905]. 1 p, 8vo. To Herr Block. Declining to write an essay about Schiller. star Mar 21 (171) DM320

**Ls,** 28 Apr 1905. 3 pp, 8vo. To Lily Braun. Explaining that he will continue to influence people only with his art. star Mar 21 (170) DM850

— ORLIK, EMIL. - Engraving, port of Hauptmann, [c.1924]. 21cm by 16cm (image). Sgd by Orlik & Hauptmann. Framed. FD May 14 (1110) DM380

## Hauser, Kaspar, c.1812-33
**Autograph Ms,** report about a dream, [n.d.]. 1 p, 4to. Including authentication by Georg Friedrich Daumer at head. Illus in cat. star Mar 22 (1356) DM7,500

**ALs,** 3 Nov 1832. 2 pp, 4to. To [J. G. Meyer]. Sending congratulations. star Mar 22 (1357) DM7,000

## Hausmann, Manfred, 1898-1986
**Autograph transcript,** Die Nienburger Revolution. Szene aus dem 2. Akt, [1975]. 4 pp, 8vo. With ALs, 30 Sept 1975, letter of transmittal. star Mar 21 (172) DM320

**Collection** of 4 A Ls s, 2 Ls s, & 7 autograph postcards, sgd, 24 July 1953 to 30 Apr 1966. 10 pp, 8vo, & cards. To Karl Paetow. About various literary matters. With related material. star Mar 21 (173) DM620

## Hausmann, Raoul, 1886-1971
**Ls,** 9 Apr 1968. 2 pp, 4to. To Herr Niedermayer at Limes Press. Concerning contributions for a publication about Hans Arp. HH Nov 17 (3231) DM250

## Hawks, Frank Monroe, 1897-1938
**Ls,** 22 Nov 1929. 2 pp, 4to. To the Contest Committee, National Aeronautical Assn. Giving details of his transcontinental flights. rms Mar 21 (226) $1,000

## Hawthorne, Nathaniel, 1804-64
**Autograph Ms,** Brief notation on Eclipses. [n.d.]. 1 p, 4to. In full: " In 1851, there will be four Eclipses - two of the sun, and two of the moon."With mounting remnant on verso. Illus in cat rms Oct 11 (190) $2,000

**Ds,** 20 Dec 1855. 1 p, 4to. Passport for John S. Williston.. Also sgd by Williston. With visa issued by French Consulate on verso. With break in blank area. Illus in cat rms Oct 11 (189) $900

**Cut signature,** 8 Mar 1856. On verso of fragment from a document. Framed with port. wa Oct 28 (27) $220

## Hay, John Milton, 1838-1905
**ALs,** 21 Dec 1864. 1 p, 4to. Recipient unnamed. Concerning President Lincoln's order for the release of a Confederate officer. Illus in cat. rms June 6 (9) $450

**Ds,** 16 June 1905. 1 p, folio. U. S. Passport of Eliza B. Bacon. Signature light. Waterstained in margin. rms Oct 11 (293) $300

## Haydon, Benjamin Robert, 1786-1846
**Series** of 17 May 1833 to 19 Feb 1839. 7 pp, 4to to 8vo. To his landlord, Newton. pn Nov 9 (445) £550 [Quaritch]

## Hayes, Isaac Israel, 1832-81
**ALs,** 3 Dec 1861. 1 p, 4to. To a Committee of the American Philosophical Society. Accepting an invitation to speak about the scientific results of his expedition. Illus in cat. rms Mar 21 (266) $250

## Hayes, Rutherford B., 1822-93
**ALs,** 29 Aug 1870. 1 p, 4to. To the Honorable J. A. Bingham. Concerning arrangements for a visit. With a tape repair on verso & a minor fold split. rms Oct 11 (191) $400

— 11 Mar 1881. 1 p, 8vo. To D. A. James. Thanking for a letter praising his administration. Illus in cat. rms Mar 21 (71) $420

— 4 Jan 1883. 1 p, 8vo. To J. D. Cox. Declining an invitation to attend a banquet. rms Mar 21 (72) $460

— 14 Sept 1884. 2 pp, 8vo. To Major F. B. James. Discussing an unspecified offense. rms June 6 (39) $450

— 24 Jan 1885. 1 p, 8vo. To [A. H.] M[attox?]. Thanking for an "account of the coming feast." Illus in cat. rms June 6 (40) $150

— 13 July 1889. 1 p, 8vo. To Wm. H. Reisling. Declining an invitation. Illus in cat pba Oct 26 (247) $350

— 26 July 1889. 1 p, 8vo. To Capt. [Hunter]. Thanking for some circulars. rms Mar 21 (74) $400

— 20 Dec 1889. 1 p, 8vo. To Major [Hosea] & Companion. Declining to speak at a soldiers' gathering. rms Mar 21 (75) $420

— 29 Dec 1889. 1 p, 8vo. Recipient unnamed. Agreeing to attend a banquet. Illus in cat. rms June 6 (394) $270

**ANs,** 6 Feb 1878. 1 p, 12mo. To Senator George F. Edmunds. Saying that the honorary Commissioner for KY was a gallant Union soldier under Hayes's command. cb June 25 (2335) $250

**Ds,** 16 Mar 1877. 1 p, folio. Appointing Francis W. Seely as Postmaster at Lake City, Minnesota. Toned. Folds separated & reinforced. pba Oct 26 (246) $170

— 23 Oct 1877. 1 p, folio. Four-language ship's papers for the whaler Union. Countersgd by Sec. of State William M. Evarts. CE June 12 (55) $950

**Signature,** 29 Apr 1881. No size given. With a port & 3 Civil war era musket precussion caps. Also with a stereo card of "Army Blacksmith and Forge, Antietam, Sept., 1862"from 1885. Framed. Over-all size 15.5 by 19.5 inches. Detail in cat rms Oct 11 (104) $450

— Anr, 2 Aug 1892. On 8.75 by 1.5 inch portion cut from a portrait of First Lady Lucy Webb Hayes.

Inscr to Judge & Mrs. L. B. Otis. Dar Oct 19 (95) $90
— Anr, [n.d.]. No size given. With a reprint photo of Hayes, an 1878 L'Exposition Universelle de Paris & a receipt from the same year for the National Yellow Fever Relief Commission. Framed. Over-all size 15.5 by 19.5 inches. Illus in cat rms Oct 11 (314) $500

**Hays, Moses Michael**
ALs, 4 June 1765. 1 p, 4to. To Michael Gratz. Requesting him to forward a letter. P Dec 13 (201) $600

**Hazen, William Babcock, 1830-87**
Ds, 19 June 1886. 1 p, 4to. $20 bank check, With a port & an artist's rendering of the Battle of Chickamauga. Framed. Illus in cat rms Oct 11 (105) $280

**Hearst, William Randolph, 1863-1951**
Ls, 2 May 1942. 1 p, 4to. To Cobina Wright. Thanking her for birthday wishes. Detail in cat rms Oct 11 (192) $285
— 16 Apr 1944. 1 p, 4to. To Miss Linda Ryan. Thanking her for a letter. With orig enevelope. Sgd as " W. R. Hearst". pba Feb 22 (135) $225

**Heath, William, 1737-1814**
Ms, Pay warrant. 5 Oct 1778. 1 p, 4to. $50 to be paid to Lieutenant Benjamin Netherland by "Ebenezer Hancock, Deputy Pay Master General to the Forces of the United States of America."Toned & with breaks in the folds. rms Oct 11 (23) $650
Collection of ALs & letter, 9 June & 1 Aug 1778. 4 pp, 4to. To William Phillips. Discussing matters pertaining to Burgoyne's army. Letter retained copy. P Dec 13 (154) $3,500
ALs, 16 Dec 1777. 1 p 4to. To John Burgoyne. Retained draft, informing him that his troops must embark from Boston for their return to England. Illus in cat. P Dec 13 (152) $5,000
Ls, 11 Feb 1778. 2 pp, 4to. To William R. Lee. Giving orders to investigate frauds by members of Burgoyne's army. P Dec 13 (153) $2,750
Ds, 3 Apr 1778. 1 p, 4to. Pay order for $309. With holograph certification on verso by Gen. Henry Knox. Needs restoration. sg Feb 1 (7) $225

**Hebbel, Friedrich, 1813-63**
ALs, 31 Jan 1851. 1 p, 8vo. To [Heinrich Laube]. Sending his play Genoveva. star Mar 21 (174) DM3,200
— 8 Aug 1856. 3 pp, 8vo. To [Herr Grailich]. Looking back on his earliest theatrical works Judith & Genoveva. S May 15 (185) £600

**Hebrew Manuscripts**
Ms, Bible fragments, comprising parts of I & II Kings, Zechariah, Joshua, Micah, Jeremiah, Isaiah & Samuel. [Near East, c.1100]. 14 leaves, vellum, 168mm by 130mm. In dark brown ink in a square Hebrew hand with nikud, with headings in larger script & 7 marginal headings with decorative brackets resembling a flower growing on a hill. S June 18 (41) £11,500

— Ms, Ketubim. 10 July 1831. 18 lines, 1 p, on vellum, 285mm by 215mm. For the earliest recorded Jewish marriage in Australia, between John Moses & Mary Connolly. CA Mar 26 (120) A$13,000
— Ms, Megillah Esther, [c.17th Century]. 11 by 64 inches over-all. On 4 connected membrane vellum sheets. In Hebrew. Ms text of this book of the Old Testament. Unbound & rolled. Worn at beginning & end. Smudged & soiled. Edges of last panel stained & ragged but still complete. Notation in upper left corner that this was "brought from Jerusalem by Gen. S. W. Crawford." bbc Sept 18 (77) $450
— Ms, Megillah Esther. [Italy, 2d half of 18th cent]. Scroll of 3 membranes of vellum, 170mm by 1560mm. In a small square Sephardic script within 10 compartments with arabesque borders. With endpieces of colored flowers & leaves, & 20 miniatures in upper & lower borders. C Nov 29 (14) £6,500
— Ms, Seder Selichot, penitential prayers. [Italy, 15th cent]. 51 leaves, vellum, 110mm by 75mm. Modern blindstamped black mor. In dark brown ink in a small near semi-cursive Hebrew hand with nikud, with headings in square script. S June 18 (50) £6,000
— TANCHUM BEN JOSEPH YERUSHALMI. - Al-Murshid al-Kafi. [Egypt or New East, 13th cent]. 38 leaves (some missing), 200mm by 130mm. Early 20th cent dark red mor gilt. In Oriental rabbinic cursive script with headings in square script. Sassoon Ms 410. S June 18 (42) £5,500
See also: Galenus, Claudius

**Hedin, Sven, 1865-1952**
ALs, 30 June 1918. 4 pp, 8vo. To Admiral von Tirpitz. Sending a text for publication in a calendar, hoping that Germany will win the war. HH May 9 (2479) DM440

**Hedio, Caspar, 1494-1552**
ALs, [25 July 1523]. 1 p, folio. To Wolfgang Fabricius Capito. Sending news about the Reformation, protestant martyrs, & matters in Mainz. Illus in cat. star Mar 22 (1567) DM3,500

**Hedouville, Gabriel Marie Joseph Theodore, Comte d', 1755-1825**
ALs, 30 Sept 1813. 1 p, 4to. To the Baron de Latour-Maubourg. Reporting about Jerome Bonaparte's retreat to Wetzlar. star Mar 22 (1452) DM420

**Hegel, Georg Wilhelm Friedrich, 1770-1831**
ALs, 12 Oct 1802. 1 p, 4to. To the winesellers Ramann. Ordering wine. Illus in cat. star Mar 21 (489) DM4,200

**Heidegger, Martin, 1889-1976**
ALs, [n.d.]. 3 pp on 2 leaves, 8vo. Content not given. wa Oct 28 (143) $240
Autograph postcard, sgd, 12 Apr 1954. To an unnamed student. Thanking for congratulations on his birthday. star Mar 21 (491) DM440

### Heifetz, Jascha, 1901-87
**Ptd photograph,** sgd, 1946. 4to. Waist-length pose, on Carnegie Hall program cover. Framed. rms Mar 21 (302) $320

### Heine, Heinrich, 1797-1856
**Autograph Ms,** draft of an article for the Augsburg Allgemeine Zeitung concerning problems in the Dardanelles & the copyright question, [ptd 31 Mar 1841]. 1 p, 4to. Differing from ptd version. star Mar 21 (175) DM16,000

**ALs,** [late 1829?]. 2 pp, 4to. To Immanuel Wohlwill. Interesting letter referring to his Jewish heritage & several Jewish authors. star Mar 21 (176) DM27,000

— [31 Oct 1843]. 3 pp, 4to. To his wife Mathilde. Reporting about a family reunion. Including a note by his nephew Louis. star Mar 21 (177) DM14,000

— 7 Feb [1847]. 2 pp, 4to. To Gustav Kolb. Asking him to print an article about Jenny Lind immediately. star Mar 21 (178) DM13,000

**Ls,** 31 Jan 1852. 2 pp, 8vo. To Heinrich Wilhelm Ernst. Thanking for concert tickets. Illus in cat. HN Nov 24 (2794) DM7,200

— 9 May 1854. 2 pp, folio. To Prince Pueckler-Muskau. Thanking for his intervention with the pbr Campe. S May 15 (186) £3,200

### Heine, Mathilde, 1815-83
**Letter,** [18 Feb 1856]. 1 p, 8vo. To an unnamed Ed. Letter in her name, asking him to print a note announcing Heinrich Heine's funeral. star Mar 21 (180) DM850

### Heinrich, Prinz von Preussen, 1726-1802
**ALs,** 20 Dec 1796. 2 pp, 4to. To [Stanislas Jean de Boufflers]. Discussing the military situation in Europe & stressing that his communications are confidential. star Mar 22 (1533a) DM680

**Ls,** [n.d.]. 1 p, 4to. Recipient unnamed. Sending a medal to thank for recipient's work. star Mar 22 (1533b) DM200

### Heinrich, Prinz von Preussen, 1862-1929
**ALs,** 20 Sept 1896. 4 pp, 4vo. To Admiral von Tirpitz. Discussing a variety of naval matters & military strategy. HH May 9 (2480) DM200

### Heiszmeyer, August
**Ls,** 21 Dec 1935. 1 p, 4to. To Philipp Bouhler. Returning Christmas wishes. Illus in cat. rms June 6 (612) $200

### Hemingway, Ernest, 1899-1961
**Typescript,** article on crime in Chicago. [1921] 3 pp, 4to. With 6-word holograph revision. Goodwin Ms. CNY Oct 27 (75) $2,000

— Typescript, Introduction for Illustrated Ed of A Farewell to Arms. 1948. 7 pp, 4to. With 43 words of holograph revision. Goodwin Collection. Illus in cat CNY Oct 27 (78) $8,000

**Typescript carbon copy,** Green Hills of Africa. [c.1935]. 323 pp, 4to. With 2 Ls s about the work to Richard & Jane Armstrong, 7 Jan & 8 Dec 1935 & other related material. CE Feb 21 (135) $9,400

**Collection** of 1 A Ls & 3 Ls s & 1 Letter, 20 Nov 1935 to 6 Sept 1943. 6 pp, 4to. To Prudencio de Pereda. In folder with 2 unrelated checks endorsed by Hemingway. CNY Oct 27 (77) $7,500

— Collection of 1 ALs & 1 ANs, [1930s]. 3 pp, 12mo. To Richard & Jane Armstrong. One sgd "Hemingstein". CE Feb 21 (138) $3,100

— Collection of 1 ALs & 3 Ls s, [1939-40]. 5 pp, 8vo & 4to. To Jane Armstrong. ALs in pencil. With 9 related items, primarily regarding the mailing of the typescript of For Whom the Bell Tolls. CE Feb 21 (139) $6,000

**A Ls s** (2), 12 & 17 Apr 1931. 3 pp, folio. To Dr. Carlos Guffey. Goodwin Collection. CNY Oct 27 (76) $4,200

**ALs,** [c.1916). 5 pp, 12mo. To "Emily." About John Masefield & about how he received a bloody nose. Goodwin Ms. CNY Oct 27 (73) $3,500

— 18 Sept 1919. 4 pp, 12mo. To Coles Van Brunt Seeley, Jr. About the war & his return; "Have cursed every day that I've been back in this god damned dry arid, friendless country..." Goodwin Ms. CNY Oct 27 (74) $1,800

— 16 Aug [1920s]. 3 pp, 4to. To "Weeley" [Smith]. Describing whiskey & women on a stopover in Quebec. CNY May 17 (87) $1,500

— 17 May 1934. 1 p, 4to. Recipient unnamed. Explaining the meaning of "C. & M." in his Winner Take All. With related material. sg June 6 (91) $2,000

— 25 July 1936. 1 p, 4to. To Richard Armstrong. About Cuba & his work on To Have and Have Not. With related material. With 13-word holograph closing. CE Feb 21 (137) $3,200

— 22 Feb [19]59. 1 p, 4to. To Wendell Palmer. Ordering books. CE May 22 (266) $1,600

— 17 [June 1959]. 1 p, 279mm by 216mm. To A. E. Hotchner. Arranging to meet in Alicante; writes of bullfights and boxing. Illus in cat P June 5 (254) $1,500

**Collection** of 6 Ls s, ANs, & 4 telegrams, 10 May 1939 to 7 Nov 1941. 16 pp, 4to & 8vo. To Gustavo Duran. Expressing feelings of friendship, referring to the work on his For Whom the Bell Tolls, & thanking for help with the book. C Nov 29 (155) £7,500

**Series** of [n.d.], 15 Aug & 9 Apr? 1940, 4 pp, 4to. To Lester J. Bowman. About writing, women, drinking & the war in Spain. Each featuring holograph closings. Holes. With orig envelopes. Illus in cat CNY Dec 15 (25) $8,500

**Ls,** 16 Feb 1920. 2 pp, 4to. To "Dear Roy". To a journalist friend about Toronto: "This is a pretty good town. About half a million inmates, one good paper, on whose stationery I'm writing." pba Oct 26 (31) $3,500

— 29 July [1932]. 4 pp, legal folio. To Charles [P. Thompson). About Michael Henry [Strater]'s inability to visit. Dated "July 29 or 30th - can't tell anymore" Sgd as "Ernest", With minor separations at fold corners. pba Oct 26 (32) $3,200

— 8 Jan 1942. 1 p, 4to. To Miss Margaret Hyman. About a book for her brother-in-law: "sorry that it is too late to get the book off for your brother-in-law. Would it do any good to have it for his birthday, or to save it for next Christmas? I remember Viola with much affection and would do anything for either her or her husband...." Illus in cat pba Oct 26 (33) $1,300

— 13 Oct 1950. 1 p, 279mm by 216mm. To A. E. Hotchner. With 6 words added in holograph. About the critical reception of Across the River and Into the Trees. Sgd "Papa". P June 5 (243) $2,000

— 13 Apr 1951. 2 pp, 279mm by 216mm. To A. E. Hotchner. Sgd "Papa". About his writing, fishing and why he doesn't like From Here to Eternity. P June 5 (245) $2,000

— 5 Jan 1951. 2 p, 279mm by 216mm. To A. E. Hotchner. Sending news about his writing & gossip as the new year begins. P June 5 (246) $2,000

**ANs,** 7 Mar 1958. On a letter to him soliciting him to sit for a portrait bust. Refusing on the grounds of work & travel. cb Oct 17 (403) $850

**Ds,** [c.1950s]. 1 p, 8vo. Permission for N. M. & Anna B. Davis to drive his car anywhere in Europe. rms Mar 21 (303) $1,100

— [c.1959]. Authorizing the transfer of 10 shares of AT&T stock. sg June 6 (92) $1,100

**Christmas card,** [n.d.]. To Harris. With holograph greetings by both Ernest & Mary Hemingway, sgd "Ernest" & "M". Mtd with photo in green-doored display case with bas-relief Christmas tree on outside & plaques inside each door. cb June 25 (2540) $800

**Cut signature,** [n.d.]. 22mm by 101mm. With closing. Sgd with initials. Framed with port. CE Feb 21 (140) $400

**Photograph, sgd & inscr,** [c.1941]. 10.25 by 13.5 sepia profile port. Of Hemingway & Martha Gellhorn. Inscr "To that great tennis player, George Tilden Brown, with love from Marty and Ernest." Illus in cat pba Oct 26 (34) $3,500

— Anr, [c.1960]. 252mm by 202mm. Shoulder-length, by Wide World Photos; inscr to Cornelius Greenway. Illus in cat. Marans collection. CE Apr 17 (76) $2,200

**Signature,** [4 Feb 1940?]. On 3 by 5 inch card. Inscr to Mildred Davis. featuring Habana, Cuba postmark dated 4 Feb 1940. Illus in cat pba June 13 (209) $600

### Henckell, Karl, 1864-1929

**Autograph Ms,** poem, Sommermittag, 17 Nov 1910. 1 p, 4to. 4 four-line stanzas, sgd. star Mar 21 (181) DM280

### Henicke, F. W.

**Ms,** Sammlung verschiedener Raetsel, Charaden und Logogryphs. Erster Band, von No. 1 bis 384, [c.1835]. 142 leaves, 20cm by 17cm. Contemp half lea. Riddles by various authors. JG Mar 29 (261) DM350

### Henri III, King of France, 1551-89

**Ls,** 17 Nov 1586. 1 p, folio. To Capt. de Poyanne. About an exchange of prisoners. star Mar 22 (1285) DM1,050

### Henry, Patrick, 1736-99

**ADs,** 22 Dec 1776. 1 p, 4to. Discharge by John Keeling from "all Bargains & Contracts heretofore made Between us". Sgd by Henry in text; also sgd by Keeling & 3 others. Illus in cat. P Dec 13 (155) $1,500

**Ds,** 27 July 1786. 1 p, folio, vellum Land grant for 1,500 acres of land in Fayette County to Henry Watkins. Stained. With an engraved port. Illus in cat rms Oct 11 (193) $1,300

— 2 Oct 1786. 1 p, oblong folio. Land grant to Stephen West. cb June 25 (2336) $2,750

**Henschke, Alfred, 1890-1928.** See: Klabund

### Hensel, Fanny Mendelssohn-Bartholdy, 1805-47

**ALs,** 24 May 1837. 2 pp, 8vo. To Ferdinand David. Asking for some scores of her brother's oratorio Paulus & mentioning her brother's return to Frankfurt. star Mar 22 (943) DM2,400

### Hepburn, Katharine

**Photograph, sgd,** [n.d.]. 4 by 5 inch photo. Mtd. Dar Oct 19 (96) $200

### Hepburn, Katharine —& Tracy, Spencer, 1900-67

**Photograph, sgd,** [n.d.]. 4.5 by 6 inch sepia bust photo of Tracy. With unsgd photo of Hepburn & 2 June 1992 TNs thanking John Andrews. Mtd. Over-all size 20 by 16 inches. Dar Oct 19 (97) $140

### Heraldic Manuscripts

**Ms,** armorial of the nobility of England from William the Conqueror to Elizabeth I. [late 16th cent] 96 leaves, vellum, 4to, 19th-cent mor gilt. Containing 8 full-page & 525 smaller coats-of-arms, in gold & colors. C June 26 (21) £2,200

— Ms, Armorial roll for the Hastings Family, 16 Dec 1552. 2,340mm by 510mm, on 3 vellum membranes, framed. With 65 fully emblazoned shields of arms; at foot the larger coat of Hastings. Sgd by William Hervey, Norroy King of Arms. C June 26 (20) £2,000

— Ms, The Names and Armes of All the Nobilitie Which Were in England at the Tyme of K. Wm. the Conqueror and which have been Created or Called since untill this 14 April 1597. 85 leaves, 285mm by 190mm. About half the arms emblazoned in colors. C June 26 (22A) £800

— BAHAMONDE FAMILY OF GALICIA. - Ms, Carta executoria de hidalguia, [Granada?, c.1620-30]. 2 leaves only, vellum, 280mm by 188mm; framed. With text in a rounded hand including 2 panels in gold on purple ground, full-page miniature, & large achievement of the arms within full border including elaborate military trophies & several vignettes. S Dec 5 (18) £2,600 [Petrus]

— HERBERTZ, J. M. - Ms, Annotationes privatae, 7 July 1768 [& later]. 86 pp, size not stated, in 19th-cent half lea. Including c.300 small coats-of-arms in pen-&-ink, mostly in colors. JG Mar 29 (262) DM240

# HERBERT

### Herbert, Sir Henry, 1595-1673
**Ls,** 13 Oct 1660. 1 p, folio. To the actors of the Cockpit Theatre. Official demand for a lowering of the rates & for the right to censor plays. With address, last 4 lines of text & endorsement in Herbert's hand. S Dec 18 (441) £3,600 [Folger]

### Herbert, Victor, 1859-1924
**Autograph music,** 28 compositions form various musical shows. 124 pp, folio. With related material. wd May 8 (18) $7,000

**Autograph transcript,** 4 bars captioned Kiss Me Again, sgd & dated Apr 1919. Inscr. Mtd. rms Nov 30 (186) $220

— Autograph transcript, 6 bars from The Singing Girl. Dec 1900. 1 p, c.3.25 by 6.5 inches. Sgd & dated. sg Feb 1 (101) $120

**Autograph quotation,** 4 Sept 1897. 1 p, 8o. Four bars of music called "Bandinage". With related material. rms Oct 11 (194) $260

**Photograph, sgd & inscr,** May 1912. 7.25 by 9.25 inch sepia cabinet bust photo. Inscr with 3 bars of music from "Natoma". Over-all size 8 by 10.75 inches. Illus in cat sg Sept 28 (126) $175

— Anr, Feb 1914. 136mm by 84mm. 3-quarter length; inscr with 2 bars of music. Marans collection. CE Apr 17 (235) $240

— Anr, [n.d.]. 1 p, no size given. Cabinet photo. Inscr to Mr. Frank Paul. Featuring unnamed AMQ. Mtd. Illus in cat pba Feb 22 (62) $100

### Herder, Johann Gottfried von, 1744-1803
**ALs,** [c.1780]. 1 p, folio. To church authorities at Weimar. Discussing some bills. star Mar 21 (182) DM1,100

**Ls,** 24 Dec 1793. 1 p, folio. To church authorities at Gotha. About the validity of a marriage. star Mar 21 (183) DM550

### Herndon, William H., 1818-91
**ALs,** 7 Dec 1883. 4 pp, 4to. To "Friend Macdonald". Discussion concerning Lincoln's religion: "This letter reads badly, but it is facts--facts & I can't make it ring better." With corrections. sg Sept 28 (164) $1,200

### Herriot, James
**Typescript,** A Vet Goes to War. 253 pp, 4to. Setting copy with holograph revisions. CE Feb 21 (145) $520

### Herschel, Sir John Frederick William, 1792-1871
**Photograph, sgd,** May 1864. 102mm by 64mm, mtd. Seated at a desk, by Maull & Polyblank. Marans collection. CE Apr 17 (48) $1,100

### Herzberg, Gerhard
**Autograph Ms,** scientific paper, Absorption Spectrum of SiH in the Vacuum Ultraviolet; [n.d.]. 12 pp, folio. In pencil; sgd at head. With Ls, 1973; note of transmittal. star Mar 21 (493) DM620

# AMERICAN BOOK PRICES CURRENT

### Herzl, Theodor, 1860-1904
**ALs,** 6 Mar 1899. 2 pp, 8vo. To Ulla Wolff. About her Ms sent to the journal Die Welt for publication, an ungrateful person who has become an enemy, & other matters. Illus in cat. star Mar 22 (1360) DM5,500

### Hess, Rudolf, 1894-1987
**Ls,** 8 Sept 1933. 1 p, 4to. To [Philipp] Bouhler. Conveying Hitler's wishes for his speedy recovery & suggesting that he see some specialists. Illus in cat. rms June 6 (617) $650

**Photograph, sgd & inscr,** 13 May 1938. Folio. Inscr to Heinrich Lohse " In War association and companionship..." Torn in margin and slightly affecting image. Illus in cat rms Oct 11 (279) $600

### Hess, Victor Franz, 1883-1964
**Autograph Ms,** scientific paper, B. E. & Temp. effect; [c.1939?]. 4 pp, 8vo. star Mar 21 (494) DM800

### Hesse, Hermann, 1877-1962
**Autograph Ms,** 12 poems, sgd & inscr to Hugo Frey 1938. 16 pp, 4to, in green mor gilt. Including 15 watercolored pen-&-ink sketches. star Mar 21 (185) DM21,000

— Autograph Ms, poem, Beim Schlafengehen, [n.d.]. 2 pp, 4to. 3 four-line stanzas. Including watercolored pen-&-ink sketch. star Mar 21 (187) DM3,600

— Autograph Ms, poem, Schicksal, [n.d.]. 2 pp, 4to. 2 four-line stanzas, sgd later. Including watercolored pen-&-ink sketch. star Mar 21 (186) DM3,200

**Autograph transcript,** 12 poems, sgd; [1959]. 13 bifolia, 8vo. Including 12 watercolors. HN May 15 (2591) DM26,000

— Autograph transcript, poem, Blauer Schmetterling, [n.d.]. 1 p, 8vo. 2 quatrains, sgd. Including small watercolored sketch at head. S May 15 (187) £1,600

**Typescript,** poem, Ein Traum, Sept 1958. 1 p, 8vo. Sgd, & with autograph addition. Addressed to K. Pfeiffer on verso. HN May 15 (2592) DM250

**Typescript carbon copy,** poem, Skizzenblatt, sgd & inscr; 5 Dec 1946. 1 p, 8vo. Addressed to Lise Isenberg in Hesse's hand, on verso. star Mar 21 (188) DM580

**ALs,** 20 Sept 1904. 2 pp, 8vo. To Frau Lichtenhahn. Describing his situation in Gaienhofen after his marriage. star Mar 21 (190) DM1,600

**Ls s** (2), [1942 & 1945]. 3 pp, 8vo. To an unnamed friend. About the publication of his works, & worrying about the times. star Mar 21 (193) DM2,000

**Ls,** 24 Sept 1960. 1 p, 8vo. To Kurt Pfeiffer. Announcing a transcript of a poem. HN May 15 (2595) DM220

**Autograph postcard, sgd,** [4 Apr 1961]. To Kurt Pfeiffer. Inviting him to see his garden. HN May 15 (2596) DM320

### Heuss, Theodor, 1884-1963
**Ds,** 21 May 1955. 1 p, folio. Conferral of a decoration on Ferdinando Baldelli. star Mar 22 (1204) DM440

## Hevesy, George Charles de, 1885-1966
**Collection** of Ls & Ds, 2 Jan 1956 & [n.d.]. 2 pp, folio. To Rolf Hosemann. Discussing some scientific experiments. Confirmation that R. Hosemann completed his doctoral dissertation under his guidance. star Mar 21 (495) DM1,100

## Hewes, Joseph, Signer from North Carolina
**ALs,** 4 June 1775. 3 pp, 4to. To Samuel Johnston. Discussing business before the Continental Congress & wondering about the ability of the colonies to pay for an army. P Dec 13 (156) $8,000

## Hewitt, Graily, 1864-1952
[The publisher's file for his book, Lettering for Students and Craftsmen, including calligraphic Ms s & 90 A Ls s or cards, sold at Phillips on 9 Nov 1995, lot 434, for £2,200.]
See also: Calligraphy

## Heyne, Christian Gottlob, 1729-1812
**ALs,** 11 Feb 1811. 1 p, 8vo. To Heinrich von Struve. Confirming receipt of a piece of art. star Mar 21 (497) DM260

**AL,** 12 Jan 1808. 4 pp, 4to. To [Matthisson?]. Draft, discussing Vergil's Aeneid. star Mar 21 (496) DM1,300

## Heyse, Paul, 1830-1914
**Autograph Ms,** poem, beginning "O heil'ges Wunder!...", Apr 1857. 1 p, 4to. Sgd. HN May 15 (2599) DM300

**ALs,** 26 May 1867. 3 pp, 8vo. Recipient unnamed. Requesting his help in organizing a charity concert. star Mar 21 (198) DM270

## Heyward, Thomas, Signer from South Carolina
**Ds,** 18 Mar 1788. 1 p, folio. A Summons for the State of South Carolina. Sgd by Heyward as Associate Justice. pba Oct 26 (141) $500

## Heywood, Peter
**Ms,** album with transcriptions of poems and letters in the possession of Heywood's sister Nessy. [c.1793]. About 284 pp plus blanks & index, 4to size. Contains source material for his court-martial. b Mar 20 (99) £6,500

**Transcript,** relating to the court-martial & defense of Heywood. [1792] 30 pp, sewn. b Mar 20 (102) £1,700

**Ds,** 28 Dec 1801. 1 p. Order to the purser to purchase a quantity of tobacco. Bound into a copy of Nathan Heywood's Captain Peter Heywood, 1889. b Mar 20 (101) £480

## Higginson, Thomas Wentworth
**ALs,** 1 July 1910. 1 p, 4.5 by 7 inches. To Mr. Jones. About Francis Higginson's work & sending off some volumes of it. Dar Oct 19 (46) $75

**Ls,** 9 Dec 1904. 1 p, 5.5 by 8.5 inches. To Mrs. Davenport. Thanking her for a volume of her sister's poetry. Dar Oct 19 (98) $75

## Hildesheimer, Wolfgang, 1916-91
**Autograph Ms,** sketches for a lecture about Mozart, sgd & inscr; [24 Nov 1973]. 1 p, 8vo. star Mar 21 (199) DM850

## Hiller, Ferdinand, 1811-85
**ALs,** 18 June 1864. 1 p, 4to. To [Bernhard Friedel]. Responding to a request for a composition. HN May 15 (2600) DM200

— [n.d.]. 3 pp, 8vo. To [Ferdinand David?]. Chatting about personal matters, & praising recipient's book. star Mar 22 (862) DM450

## Hiller, Johann Adam, 1728-1804
**ALs,** 20 July 1785. 1 p, 4to. To Moses Levin. Discussing the price of a grand piano. Kuenzel collection. star Mar 22 (863) DM3,400

## Hillerman, Tony
**Ls,** 28 Apr 1984. 4 pp, 4to. To his pbr, Dennis McMillan. The final 28 corrections & revisions for The Ghostway. CE Feb 21 (146A) $160

## Hilpert, Heinz, 1890-1967
**Collection** of ALs, 5 Ls s, & autograph sentiment, sgd, 30 Apr 1955 to 10 May 1957. 8 pp, various sizes. To Claus Leininger. About performances of Schiller's Kabale und Liebe & recipient's changes in a trans of Macbeth. Inscr in a textbook of Kabale und Liebe. star Mar 22 (1149) DM900

## Himmel, Friedrich Heinrich, 1765-1814
**Autograph music,** Polonaise in C major, [n.d.]. 4 pp, 4to. 57 bars, scored for piano. Sgd on tp. star Mar 22 (864) DM1,200

**ADs,** 1 Apr 1803. 1 p, 4to. Receipt for 300 talers for Pierre Rode. star Mar 22 (865) DM340

## Himmler, Heinrich, 1900-45
**ALs,** 20 Apr 1940. 1 p, 8vo. To [Helli] Bouhler. Sending congratulations on her birthday. Illus in cat. rms June 6 (610) $600

**Ls,** 14 Oct 1937. 1 p, 4to. To [Philipp] Bouhler. Thanking for a birthday present. Illus in cat. rms Mar 21 (365) $800

**Ds,** 10 Mar 1932. 1 p, 4to. To Hitler. Concerning the naming of a military unit. With translation & a vintage photo of Himmler by Friedrich Franz Bauer with a newsclip on verso. Illus in cat rms Oct 11 (280) $500

## Hindemith, Paul, 1895-1963
**Autograph music,** several additions to the cello part of the 1st Ed of his Konzert fuer Violoncello und Orchester, Feb 1962. Parts for cello & piano only, 4to. Sgd & inscr to Pierre Fournier. Annotated throughout by Fournier. S May 15 (383) £1,600

**Autograph postcard, sgd,** 1 Sept 1922. To Paul Aron. Discussing the program for a concert in Dresden. star Mar 22 (866) DM800

## Hindenburg, Paul von, 1847-1934
**Ds,** 13 July 1893. 2 pp, 4to. Approving orders for the 37th Infantry Brigade. With sgd endorsements on

both pages by other officers including Field Marshal von Bock. sg Sept 28 (126A) $200
— 21 June 1927. 2 pp, folio. Military appointments & discharges. star Mar 22 (1364) DM200
**Photograph, sgd,** [c.1925]. 428mm by 334mm. Shoulder-length port. Illus in cat. Marans collection. CE Apr 17 (142) $500

### Hirohito, Emperor of Japan, 1901-89
**Photograph, sgd,** [1921]. 8 by 5 inches, tipped to a 13 by 8.5 inch mount. sg June 6 (94) $6,500

### Hitchcock, Alfred, 1899-1980
**Photograph, sgd,** [c.1950s]. 11 by 14 inch bust pose with 2 french poodles. Mtd. Over-all size 15 by 20 inches. sg Sept 28 (127) $300

### Hitler, Adolf, 1889-1945
**Ls,** 1 Apr 1941. 2 pp, folio. To Paty member Lutze. Presenting a War Service Cross to Viktor Lutze. Illus in cat pba June 13 (111) $1,300
**Ds,** 29 Sept 1928. 1 p, folio. Appointing Heinrich Lohse "area commander of the German National Socialist Workers Party in Schleswig-Holstein." Margins frayed. With translation. Illus in cat rms Oct 11 (281) $1,300
— 25 June 1935. 1 p, 4to. Discharge of Leopold Wenger from a judicial appointment in Bavaria. With related material. HH Nov 17 (3314) DM950
— 30 Jan 1936. 1 p, 4to. Promotion for Philipp Bouhler to Obergruppenfuehrer in the SS. Illus in cat. rms June 6 (601) $1,700

### Hobbes, Thomas, 1588-1679
**ALs,** 8 Aug 1645. 1 p, 4to. To Edmund Waller. About how he spends his time in Rouen; mentions the possibility of Waller's translating De Cive. Illus in cat S Dec 18 (106) £13,500 [Schram]

### Hofer, Andreas, 1767-1810
**Ds,** 12 Oct 1809. 1 p, folio. To the authorities in the village of Igls. Order to support Philip Marquard during his recovery. star Mar 22 (1367) DM3,600

### Hoffa, James R., 1913-75?
**Photograph, sgd & inscr,** [n.d.]. 11 by 14 inch color port photo. Inscr to Bob Wolf. Creased & torn. pba Feb 22 (136) $325

### Hoffmann, Heinrich, 1809-94
**ALs,** [n.d.]. 2 pp, 8vo. Recipient unnamed. Requesting him to visit a patient. star Mar 21 (201) DM480

### Hoffmann, Heinrich, 1885-1957
**Ls,** 13 Apr 1942. 1 p, 4to. To Philipp Bouhler. Praising recipient's book about Napoleon. Illus in cat. rms June 6 (603) $300

### Hoffmann, Karl Christoph von, 1735-1801
**ALs,** 22 Dec 1795. 3 pp, 4to. Recipient unnamed. Sending a sketch (included) to illus a projected monument for J. B. Basedow. star Mar 21 (502) DM320

### Hoffmann von Fallersleben, August Heinrich, 1798-1874
**Autograph Ms,** Wismar. Meklenburgischer Butterkrawall, [c.1848]. 2 pp, 8vo; trimmed. Notes about a stay in Mecklenburg. star Mar 21 (202) DM850

### Hofmann, Albert
**Autograph quotation,** chemical formulas for LSD & Psilocybin, sgd [n.d.]. 1 p, 8vo (card). HH Nov 17 (3235) DM240

### Hofmann von Hofmannswaldau, Christian, 1616-79
**Autograph Ms,** poem, An M... als sie die schoenen Haende der M... gelobet; [n.d.]. 2 pp, folio. 6 four-line stanzas. Illus in cat. HH May 9 (2483) DM2,200
— **Autograph Ms,** poem, Auf die gewoehnliche Maertinsganss, [n.d.]. 2 pp, folio. 7 six-line stanzas. Illus in cat. HH May 9 (2484) DM2,200

### Hofmannsthal, Hugo von, 1874-1929
**ALs,** 20 Mar [1903?]. 4 pp, 8vo. To Otto Brahm. Reminiscing about their meeting in Italy, chatting about his way of writing poetry, etc. HN Nov 24 (2798) DM2,600

### Hohenlohe, Georg Friedrich, Graf von, 1569-1645
**Ds,** 8 Aug 1613. 1 p, folio. Power of attorney in a feudal matter, sgd as guardian of Count Philipp Moritz of Hanau-Muenzenberg. star Mar 22 (1246) DM400

### Hohenlohe-Schillingsfuerst, Chlodwig, Fuerst zu, 1819-1901
**ALs,** 29 Oct 1900. 2 pp, 4to. To K. H. von Boetticher. Inviting him for breakfast & expressing thanks for his support. star Mar 22 (1368) DM220

### Holiday, Billie, 1915-59
**Photograph, sgd & inscr,** [c.1950]. 252mm by 205mm. Shoulder-length profile port, inscr "For My Namesake". Illus in cat. Marans collection. CE Apr 17 (237) $1,200

### Holladay, Ben, 1819-87
**Check,** 28 June 1870. 1 p, 4to. $313 payble to George W. Weidler. Illus in cat rms Oct 11 (78) $125

### Holly, Buddy, 1936-59
**Signature,** [n.d.]. 1 p, 8vo. Sgd as " Buddy Holly & The Crickets". Also with other pages sgd by the Crickets. detail in cat rms Oct 11 (195) $850

### Holmes, Oliver Wendell, 1809-94
**Autograph transcript,** last stanza of The Last Leaf. 1 p, 8vo. Sgd & dated 15 Mar 1887. rms Nov 30 (188) $450
**Photograph, sgd,** 17 Oct 1882. No size given. Sepia carte bust pose photo. By Pach. Sgd & dated on verso. sg Sept 28 (128) $110

### Holmes, Oliver Wendell, 1841-1935
**Photograph, sgd,** 12 Nov 1923. 350mm by 246mm. Seated; by Harris & Ewing. Marans collection. CE Apr 17 (143) $850

**Holst, Gustav, 1874-1934**
ALs, 7 Sept 1930. 2 pp, 8vo. To Edmond Kapp. Thanking for a book with caricatures of musicians. star Mar 22 (868) DM600

**Holstein, Friedrich von, 1837-1909**
ALs, [17 Mar 1892]. 7 pp, 4to. To Graf Philip zu Eulenburg. Discussing political strategy. star Mar 22 (1369) DM700

**Honegger, Arthur, 1892-1955**
Autograph music, calme et doux, compositon for piano, July 1922. 2 pp, 4to. In ink over pencil; sgd. Illus in cat. star Mar 22 (869) DM3,000
Autograph postcard, sgd, [6 May 1923]. To Paul Pelissier. Hoping to see him at the station in Toulouse. star Mar 22 (870) DM210

**Hooker, Joseph, 1814-79**
Signature, [n.d.]. On 2 by 5 inch page. Sgd as " Joseph Hooker/ Brig. Gen". pba Feb 22 (167) $110

**Hooper, William, Signer from North Carolina**
ALs, [c.July - Aug 1779]. 3 pp, 4to. To Joseph Hewes. Asking a favor concerning a hat. Illus in cat. P Dec 13 (157) $5,000
Ds, 22 May 1790. 1 p, folio. Bond for 100 pounds. Sgd by Hooper as a witness. Toned & with defects. With port. Illus in cat rms Oct 11 (196) $2,500

**Hoover, Herbert, 1874-1964**
ALs, 5 Nov 1934. 2 pp, 4to. To Rufus C. Dawes. Congratulations on the Century of Progress Exposition. CNY Dec 15 (182) $2,600
Ls, 5 Sept 1917. No size given. Worrying about the potential waste of food during the war. pba Feb 22 (247) $150
— 6 Jan 1930. 1 p, 4to. To the Baron de Cartier de Marchienne. Thanking for New Year's wishes. star Mar 22 (1675) DM280
— 12 Feb 1932. 1 p, 4to. To Eugene E. Prussing. About the possible appointment of Mr. Chandler. With orig White House envelope. sg June 6 (96) $175
— 27 Feb 1934. 1 p, 4to. To John Watkin. Sending him an autograph. pba Feb 22 (250) $85
— 6 Apr 1943. 2 pp, 4to. To James J. Rick. About peace policies & Problems of Lasting Peace. rms Nov 30 (190) $500
— 3 Dec 1954. 1 p, 8vo. To Lawrence E. Spivak. Declining to appear on the TV program Meet the Press. rms June 6 (396) $110
— 29 Mar 1962. 1 p, 4to. To A. C. Harlander. About economics: "As our governments grow and grow, they always become more expensive. A periodic search for economics is imperative." pba Oct 26 (249) $190
— [n.d.]. No size given. To Mr. Thomas Dawson. Soiled. pba Feb 22 (252) $650
Letter, 21 May 1932. 6 pp, 4to. To the President of the American Society of Civil Engineers. About means to break the back of the Depression. Sgd by a secretary & incorrectly addressed to Richard S. Parker rather than Herbert S. Crocker, with Ls rectifying the error. sg Feb 1 (105) $1,700

ADs, [n.d.]. 2 pp, 4to. Inventory of his autograph collection. Illus in cat pba Feb 22 (248) $400
Ds, [2 Nov 1939]. Quotation on 5 by 3.25 inch card. About youth from a speech at the Centennial Committee Dinner of the YMCA: "And it is the frustrated and disappointed youth who cannot get a chance who has the greatest right to complain of our civilization..."Stained on verso. Dar Oct 19 (99) $160
Photograph, sgd & inscr, [c.1925]. 252mm by 203mm. Inscr on lower margin to Col. Robert F. Carter. CE June 12 (58) $240
— Anr, [n.d.]. 12 by 9 inch b&w photo. Inscr to the Hayward Review. pba Oct 26 (250) $160
Signature, [n.d.]. On a 3.3 by 5.3 inch Waldorf Astoria card. pba Oct 26 (253) $55
— Anr, [n.d.]. No size given. With 1932 photo of Hoover & a 1931 photo of a soup kitchen line. Also with 3 mercury dimes minted in 1929, 1930 & 1931. Illus in cat rms Oct 11 (315) $400

**Hoover, J. Edgar, 1895-1972**
Ls, 1 May 1951. 1 p, 8 by 10 inches. To Joseph Lieb. Responding to an earlier letter from Lieb: "I am led to conclude that you feel the FBI was basically at fault in creating a situation which you said caused you great personal harm and humiliation...the FBI would have absolutely no right to intervene and attempt to control the use of a record..." With carbon of Lieb's letter to Hoover & other related items. Dar Oct 19 (100) $80

**Hopkins, Johns, 1795-1873**
ALs, 5 Nov 1830. 2 pp, 4to. To John Lisle. Concerning " the sale of the mill & other property pledged by John Allensworth to you..." With age stains & a minor fold break. Detail in cat rms Oct 11 (197) $1,300

**Hopkins, Stephen, Signer from Rhode Island**
ALs, 5 June 1755. 2 pp, 4to. To Gov. William Shirley. Mobilizing for the ill-fated assaults on Niagara & Crown Point. P Dec 13 (158) $4,000
Ds, 13 Aug 1744. 1 p, folio. Sgd as witness to a bond for $4,700 from the Grand Committee & Trustees of Providence. Also sgd by 4 colony trustees. rms Nov 30 (191) $550

**Hopkinson, Francis, Signer from New Jersey**
ALs, 17 July 1789. 2 pp, 4to. To Messers Samuel Clark and Thomas Penrose. Writing the "Sitting Managers at the Pennsylvania Hospital" to recommend the reception and support of a patient into the hospital: "" This Girl was once before in the hospital as a Lunatic...she has however relapsed again...Mrs. Lewis is by no means able to pay weekly for her Support...I hope you will have no difficulty in admitting this Unfortunate Person..." Tipped to a larger sheet with an engraving of Hopkinson's house. Detail in cat rms Oct 11 (198) $1,600
— [n.d.], "Tuesday 20th". 2 pp, 4to. To Thomas McKean. Asking for a loan & sending family news. P Dec 13 (159) $1,000
Ds s (2), [before 12 Feb 1779]. 1 p, 4to. As Continental Treasurer of Loans, 3d & 4th bills of a 30-day sight

draft payable to Ebenezer Plummer. P Dec 13 (160) $800

**Ds,** 20 Sept 1779. Sight note for $24 payable to Samuel Ridgway. Countersgd by Nathaniel Appleton. rms Nov 30 (192) $400

— 29 Sept 1779. 1 p, 8vo. Sight bill payable to Calvin Scott. rms Mar 21 (208) $350

**Horae B. M. V.**

— [Bologna, c.1400]. Single leaf, vellum, 237mm by 168mm. In a rounded gothic hand. With 2-line initials in burnished gold with blue penwork, large historiated initial in rich jewel-like colors on burnished gold ground, & 3-quarter illuminated border of colored flowers & burnished gold bezants. Text roughly erased & smudged. S June 18 (20) £3,600

— [Paris, c.1410]. 2 leaves only, vellum, 211mm by 153mm. In a gothic textura. With numerous small initials & linefillers in gold & colors & 4 three-quarter foliate & floral borders. Illus in cat. HH May 7 (37) DM1,200

— [Normandy, c.1420]. Single leaf, vellum, 170mm by 113mm. In a slightly sloping textura. With 11 small initials, 4 linefillers & 2 three-sided borders in gold & colors. HH Nov 14 (38) DM1,400

— [Normandy, c.1420]. Single leaf, vellum, 170mm by 113mm. In a slightly sloping textura. With very large miniature above 3-line illuminated initial & within 3-sided foliate border. Illus in cat. HH Nov 14 (40) DM3,600

— [Normandy, c.1420]. Single leaf, vellum, 167mm by 115mm. In a slightly sloping textura. With 11 initials & 2 three-quarter foliate borders, including a monk & an animal. HH May 7 (39) DM1,300

— [Paris, c.1420]. Use of Rome. 64 leaves only, vellum, 211mm by 154mm. Late 18th-cent French red mor gilt. In 2 sizes of an extremely fine gothic liturgical hand. With 2-line initials throughout in colors on highly burnished gold grounds, 4-line illuminated initial, 3-quarter illuminated borders throughout of broad panels of burnished gold leaves with colored flowers, acanthus sprays or fruit, & 11 large or full-page miniatures from 16th-cent choirbooks pasted in. S Dec 5 (43) £8,800 [Neumann-Walter]

— [Besancon, c.1440]. Use of Paris. In Latin, with prayers in French. 103 leaves (1 lacking) & 2 orig flyleaves, 203mm by 147mm. Modern red mor gilt over wooden bds. In a gothic textura. With 8 four-line initials in red or blue on gold ground with foliate branchwork decoration, with full foliate borders containing grotesques & birds, surrounding 3-quarter baguette frames, & 5 large miniatures with similar borders & armorial shields in each corner. Ownership inscr of Etienne Cauquohin & the Rougier family of Dijon. C Nov 29 (9) £24,000

— [Southern Netherlands, Bruges?, c.1430-50]. 5 leaves only, vellum, 141mm by 103mm; framed. In a semi-round gothic liturgical hand. With 2-line initials in burnished gold on red & blue grounds, & 5 large miniatures above 3-line illuminated initials in crisp colors on burnished gold grounds with 3-sided baguettes & full borders of gold leaves & colored flowers. S Dec 5 (14) £6,500 [Maggs]

— [Utrecht, c.1440]. Use of Utrecht. In Dutch. 149 leaves (2 blank) & 2 pastedowns, vellum, 137mm by 97mm. 16th-cent calf gilt over partially bevelled wooden bds, with sewing guards from pieces of a 13th-cent Ms. In a neat gothic liturgical hand. With 25 large illuminated initials in heavily raised burnished gold with partial or full borders, & 5 full-page miniatures on burnished & tooled gold grounds within full borders. Illuminated in the style of the Masters of Zweder van Culembourg. S Dec 5 (53) £12,000 [Sam Fogg]

— [France, c.1450]. Single leaf, vellum, 135mm by 92mm. In 2 sizes of a lettre batarde. With illuminated initial & 2 large historiated initials in camaieu d'or. HH May 7 (41) DM1,000

— [West central France, Angers?, c.1450]. Use of Angers. In Latin & French. 136 leaves (c.14 lacking), vellum, 169mm by 122mm. Worn 16th-cent French calf gilt. In 2 sizes of a compressed gothic liturgical hand. With 2-line initials throughout in leafy designs in colors & white tracery on burnished gold panels with c.150 illuminated panel borders of flowers & burnished gold leaves, & 13 full illuminated borders including birds, animals & people. S June 18 (72) £6,500

— [Chartres, c.1450]. Use of Chartres. In Latin, with Calendar & Prayers in French. 145 leaves (1 lacking) & flyleaf, vellum, 174mm by 120mm. Repaired contemp blindstamped bdg of tanned calf over wooden bds. In 2 sizes of a gothic liturgical hand by more than one scribe. With 11 large illuminated initials in divided blue & burnished gold with extensive penwork in red & dark blue. S June 18 (73) £2,800

— The Milburn Hours. [Bruges, c.1450]. Use of Sarum. 129 leaves & 3 flyleaves, vellum, 192mm by 132mm. Bdg of vellum over pastebds by Roger Powell, 1947. In a compact gothic liturgical hand. With 2-line initials throughout in burnished gold, 25 small miniatures with 3-quarter illuminated borders, 13 large miniatures with full borders, & full-page miniature in full border with large initial & full border on facing page. Some erasures. S June 18 (74) £16,000

— [Flanders, c.1460]. Single leaf, vellum, 153mm by 109mm. In a lettre batarde. With full-page miniature within full foliate borders in gold & colors. Illus in cat. HH Nov 14 (43) DM2,200

— [Flanders, c.1460]. Single leaf, vellum, 154mm by 110mm. In a slightly sloping lettre batarde. With small illuminated initial & full-page miniature. Illus in cat. HH May 7 (45) DM3,000

— [Rouen, c.1460]. Use of Rouen. In Latin, with Calendar & prayers in French. 138 leaves (4 blank), vellum, 202mm by 135mm. Late 16th-cent blind-stamped armorial calf over wooden bds. In a compressed gothic liturgical hand. With 13 large illuminated initials with 3-quarter borders of flowers & acanthus leaves, & 4 large miniatures within 2-sided illuminated baguettes & full borders. S Dec 5 (46) £15,000 [Abraham]

— [Florence, c.1460-75]. Use of Rome. 282 leaves (10 blank), vellum, 126mm by 85mm. Early 19th-cent English dark blue mor gilt. In 2 sizes of a rounded gothic hand. With 2-line initials throughout in blue or red with fine penwork extending the full height of the page, 14 large historiated initials in full colors on highly burnished gold grounds with partial or full-length illuminated borders, & 5 very large historiated initials with full historiated borders. Illumination attributable to Francesco d'Antonio Chierico. S June 18 (70) £30,000

— [France, c.15th cent]. Unknown use. 95 leaves, 185mm by 124mm, in 16th-cent vellum wraps, lacking spine. With 4 large miniatures with three-quarter borders & 13 small miniatures with quarter borders; miniatures overpainted with flaking. Lacking some leaves & miniatures; stained. Sold w.a.f CE June 12 (218) $2,400

— [Burges, c.1465]. 20 leaves only (1 blank), vellum, 173mm by 115mm. In a slightly sloping lettre batarde. With numerous initials & 13 borders of leaves, flowers & fruit in gold & colors. HH May 7 (46) DM1,000

— [Burges, c.1465]. Single leaf, vellum, 173mm by 115mm. In a slightly sloping lettre batarde. With very large miniature above 3-line illuminated initial & 4 lines of text, all within full border of leaves, flowers & fruit in gold & colors. Illus in cat. HH May 7 (47) DM1,800

— [France, 3d quarter of 15th cent]. Use of Rome. 97 leaves only, including 2 blanks & 4 vellum flyleaves, 168mm by 122mm, in 19th-cent russia. Written in brown ink in a gothic textura, with rubrics in red, versals & 2-line initials in gold on blue & red grounds with white tracery & line fillers. With 24 calendar miniatures within three-quarter borders enclosing panels with floral decoration on gold grounds & 1 other small miniature; 11 large miniatures in arched compartments, 3 of them just shaved into lower ruled border at fore-edge. pn Mar 14 (337) £11,000

— [Chartres?, c.1470]. Of uncertain use. 157 leaves & flyleaf, vellum, 121mm by 90mm. 18th-cent red mor gilt. With 2-line illuminated initials in gold on blue & red ground with white tracery, 12 three- & four-line initials in blue on gold ground with branchwork decoration & outer panel border, & 4 large miniatures with full borders of leaves & flowers. Herzogliche Sachsen-Meiningische Bibliothek Ms 61. C Nov 29 (10) £5,000

— [Tours, c.1470] Use of Paris. in Latin, with calendar in French. 104 (of 106) leaves, on vellum, 140mm by 95mm, in 18th-cent calf. In brown ink in a small batarde. With 24 ten- to eleven-line miniatures, each within three-quarter border, some parti-colored on gold ground with colored flowers, fruit & acorn leaves. With 6 large miniatures within arched compartments & full borders. C June 26 (18) £12,000

— [Northern France or Flanders, c.1470]. Single leaf, vellum, 176mm by 110mm. In a gothic textura. With large illuminated initial & 2 full-length borders, 1 including miniature. Illus in cat. HH Nov 14 (46) DM2,000

— [Flanders, 3d quarter of 15th cent]. Of English use. 25 leaves, 105mm by 70mm. With gold & blue initials, decorated in red & blue. bba Apr 11 (211) £520 [Sol-mi]

— [Southern Netherlands, Bruges or Antwerp?, c.1475]. Use of Rome. 100 leaves, vellum, 182mm by 123mm. 18th-cent mottled calf gilt. In a neat gothic liturgical hand. With 2-line initials throughout in burnished gold on red & blue grounds, 28 small miniatures with 3-quarter iluminated borders, & 7 full-page miniatures in full borders all facing pages with 6-line initials & full matching borders. S Dec 5 (54) £11,500 [Holland]

— [Southwestern France, 1479]. Use of Rome. In Latin, with a rubric in Languedoc. 140 leaves (1 lacking), vellum, 99mm by 74mm. Repaired partly contemp blindstamped bdg of calf over wooden bds. In 2 sizes of a gothic hand. With large & small initials throughout in red with purple penwork. S June 18 (75) £6,500

— [Northern Italy, last quarter of 15th cent] In Latin. 157 leaves, on vellum, 89mm by 70mm, cut down from 124mm by 85mm, in late 16th-cent mor gilt. In brown ink in an upright humanist bookhand. With 5 large but folded decorated pages within interlacing white vine-stam border on colored & gold ground surrounding a 4-line gold initial (5 historiated) on blue & red ground, heading in gold on a purple or red plaque. These leaves mostly very rubbed & worn. Illus in cat C June 26 (15) £2,000

— [Northern France, c.1480]. Single leaf, vellum, 175mm by 111mm. In a lettre batarde. With small illuminated initials & 2 full-length foliate & floral borders. HH Nov 14 (48) DM700

— [Rome, c.1480-85]. Use of Rome. 216 leaves (2 blank), vellum, 123mm by 80mm. Old red velvet over pastebds. In a rounded gothic hand, with rubrics in burnished gold. With 2-line initials throughout in burnished gold or dark blue with extensive penwork & full-length marginal decoration, 13 large illuminated or historiated initials with 3-quarter historiated borders of flowers & acanthus leaves with putti, people & animals, & 5 large historiated initials with full historiated borders. Illuminated by the Master of the della Rovere Missals. S June 18 (71) £27,000

101

# HORAE

— [Rouen, c.1485]. Single leaf, vellum, 166mm by 112mm. In a slightly sloping lettre batarde. With 4 illumined initials (2 large), full-length border, & large miniature within full border including a bird & an animal. Illus in cat. HH May 7 (50) DM3,200

— [France, late 15th cent]. Use of Angers. 27 leaves, 150mm by 115mm. Initials & line-fillers in red & blue. bba Apr 11 (212) £500 [Solmi]

— [Rouen, late 15th cent]. Use of Rouen. In Latin, with Calendar in French. 94 leaves (9 lacking, 1 replacement), vellum, 197mm by 124mm. Blindstamped calf of c.1900. In 2 sizes of a neat lettre batarde. With panel borders throughout in outer margins, 16 small calendar miniatures at top & bottom of panel borders, & 9 large miniatures with elaborate borders. Illuminated in the style of the Master of the Geneva Latini. S Dec 5 (45) £7,000 [H. P. Kraus]

— [Troyes, c.1490]. Use of Troyes. In Latin, with Calendar in French. 115 leaves (2 lacking), vellum, 169mm by 115mm. 18th-cent olive mor gilt. In a small gothic liturgical hand. With 2-line initials throughout in highly burnished gold on red & blue grounds, 8 small miniatures with 3-quarter illuminated borders, & 3 large miniatures with full borders including birds & grotesques. S Dec 5 (47) £6,000 [Sam Fogg]

— [Northeast? France, c.1490]. Use of Rome. In Latin, with Calendar in French. 133 leaves (2 lacking), vellum, 171mm by 107mm. 19th-cent blindstamped brown mor. In a gothic liturgical hand. With small initials throughout in burnished gold on red & blue grounds, 8 large illuminated initials with 3-quarter illuminated borders of colored flowers & acanthus leaves, & 5 large miniatures with full borders. Imperf. S Dec 5 (50) £2,800 [Schwing]

— [Angers, c.1490]. Use of Angers. In Latin, with prayers in French. 192 leaves (2 blank, 3 lacking), vellum, 151mm by 103mm. 16th-cent French red mor gilt. In 2 sizes of a gothic liturgical hand. With small initials throughout in liquid gold on blue & red grounds, & 18 large or full-page miniatures within full borders of leaves & flowers on liquid gold grounds. Worn. S Dec 5 (52) £6,500 [Holland]

— [Netherlands, c.1500] In dutch. 212 leaves, on vellum, 137mm by 94mm, in early vellum gilt with crowns at corners & initialled clasp with letters A.G.K. With 5 full-page miniatures & 37 illuminated initials with elaborate floral borders. cb Feb 14 (2500) [US24,000]

— [Bourges, c.1500]. Use of Rome. In Latin, with Calendar in French. 249 leaves (1 blank), vellum, 177mm by 110mm. 17th-cent pale brown mor gilt. In 2 sizes of a widely-spaced lettre batarde. With 2-line initials throughout in colors on liquid gold grounds, 12 double Calendar miniatures with panel borders, 22 small miniatures with panel borders of naturalistic flowers in trompe l'oeil designs, & 13 large miniatures within full borders on parti-colored grounds. Attributable to the Master of the Lallement Boethius. Ownership inscr of Agnes le Dieu, 1607. S Dec 5 (51) £29,000 [Sam Fogg]

# AMERICAN BOOK PRICES CURRENT

— [Bruges or Ghent, c.1500]. Use of Rome. 191 leaves (3 blank), vellum, 83mm by 61mm. 18th-cent French olive-brown mor gilt. In a very small gothic liturgical hand. With small initials throughout in delicate designs in liquid gold on blue or red grounds, 8 half-page miniatures with 3-quarter illuminated borders in designs of naturalistic flowers with trompe l'oeil insects, & 8 full-page miniatures in full borders with large initials & full borders on facing pages. Possibly illuminated in the workshop of Alexander Bening. S June 18 (76) £11,000

— [Bruges, c.1500-1510]. Use of Rome. 173 leaves (4 blank), 108mm by 80mm. Late 19th-cent French dark brown mor gilt. In a skilful rounded gothic hand. With large historiated initial with 3-quarter border, & 15 large illuminated initials & full borders of flowers, fruit, insects & grotesques in full colors on liquid gold grounds. S June 18 (77) £6,500

— [Central France, Orleans?, early 16th cent]. Use of Orleans. 108 leaves & 3 flyleaves, vellum, 185mm by 130mm. French red mor gilt of c.1770. In a compressed gothic liturgical hand. With 2-line initials throughout usually in pink heightened in white & infilled in colors & liquid gold, panel borders throughout in designs of colored flowers & acanthus leaves, 28 small or half-page miniatures within elaborate liquid gold architectural borders, & 14 full-page miniatures within full architectural borders often including angels, lion masks, etc. S Dec 5 (49) £16,000 [Damm]

— [Southern Netherlands, Bruges, c.1510]. Use of Rome. 235 leaves (a few lacking), vellum, 116mm by 87mm. 18th-cent red mor gilt. In a well-formed lettre batarde. With small initials throughout in grey with delicate leafy designs, 23 small miniatures or historiated initials, 15 with 3-quarter illuminated borders of naturalistic flowers & fruit in trompe l'oeil designs & including birds & insects, & 7 full-page miniatures within full borders. S Dec 5 (55) £32,000 [Sam Fogg]

— [France, Bourges?, c.1510]. Use of Rome. 14 separate leaves only, vellum, 190mm by 130mm, mtd in an album. In a large lettre batarde. With versal initials in liquid silver or gold on blue or red grounds, 2- to 4-line initials in leafy designs enclosing colored flowers on liquid gold panels, large historiated initial, & 2 small, 8 very large, & 3 half-page miniatures. S June 18 (28) £13,000

— [N.p.], 1654. 139 leaves, on vellum, 744mm by 525mm, in vellum-covered wooden bds. Text & music with 5 or 6 staves. With initials in colors, some with floral designs. cb Feb 14 (2501) [US3,750]

See also: Calligraphy

**Horner, Francis**

ALs, 28 Nov [1810] 3 pp, 8vo. To Thomas R. Malthus. Written as Chairman of the Bullion Committee, commissioning an article from him on Reicardo's Theory of Depreciation for The Edinburgh Review. pn June 13 (209) £2,100 [Wilson]

**Horton, George Moses, c.1797-1883**
**Autograph Ms**, poem, Departing Love. [Chapel Hill NC, 1 Aug 1856] 1 p, 4to. 23 lines. With contemp transcript made by the recipient of the poem, Martha Suggs Dixon. sg Mar 28 (292) $8,500

**Hossack, David, 1769-1835**
**Signature**, [n.d.]. On 1814 ptd pamphlet paying tribute to Dr. Benjamin Rush. Toned & with binding remnants. rms Oct 11 (199) $300

**Houdini, Harry, 1874-1926**
**ALs**, 8 Feb 1920. 1 p. To Mr. Pesty. About his movements; gives his address in London. Sgd with initials. bbc Dec 18 (79) $450

— 3 Jan 1923. 1 p, 8vo. To Olive R. Barrett. Concerning an upcoming visit to Chicago. Sgd as "Houdini". pba Feb 22 (63) $850

**Photograph, sgd & inscr**, 27 Sept [19]24. 176mm by 127mm. Shoulder-length port; inscr to F. L. Pleadwell. Illus in cat. Marans collection. CE Apr 17 (15) $2,400

— Anr, [n.d.]. 6.5 by 9 inch sepia glossy photo. Inscr to a lady. Over-all size 8 by 10 inches. Illus in cat sg Sept 28 (133) $1,500

**Houston, Samuel, 1793-1863**
**ALs**, 10 Dec 1836. 1 p, folio. To "the Hon. the Senate (of Texas)". Recommending F. Catlett Esq as an envoy of the Republic of Texas to the United States. Docketed. With a tiny hole near the signature. CNY Dec 15 (183) $2,600

— 10 July 1838. 3 pp, folio. To Ashbel Smith. Asking him to come to the aid of a young patient. CNY May 17 (252) $4,500

**Ls**, 27 Dec 1845. 2 pp, 4to. To Francis P. Blair. Praising Andrew Jackson & discussing contributions to a fund for a monument to him. CNY May 17 (253) $6,500

— 12 Jan 1857. 3 pp, 4to. To Capt. John G. Tod. About a contract to build the Custom House. With 3 line postscript. Restored. Detail in cat sg Sept 28 (135) $1,300

**Ds**, 1 Dec 1827. 1 p, folio. Commission for Henry W. Coffin as Colonel in the Tennessee militia. CNY May 17 (251) $1,000

— 14 Sept 1860. 1 p, oblong folio. Land grant to Robert M. Rowland. Also sgd by Francis M. White. cb June 25 (2337) $1,400

**Cut signature**, [n.d.]. 16mo. rms June 6 (397) $550

**Howard, Charles, 1st Earl of Nottingham, 1536-1624**
**Ds**, July 1595. 2 leaves, 4to. Detailed orders for the victualling of the Vangard. b Jan 31 (13) £260

— 31 May 1594. 1 p, 4to. Order for victualling the Victory, the Dreadnought & other ships. Also sgd by Sir John Hawkins & William Borough & subscribed by Lord Burghley. pn Nov 9 (378) £1,050 [Maggs]

**Howard, John Eager, 1752-1827**
**ALs**, 12 Dec 1785. 2 pp, 4to. To Charles Carroll of Carrollton. Recommending Dr. Reuben Gilder for Port Physician for Baltimore. With repairs to address leaf. rms Oct 11 (24) $400

**Howard, Leslie, 1893-1943**
**ALs**, [n.d.]. 1 p, 4to. To M.G.M. Studios, Culver City. Introducing some actors. Framed. Illus in cat. rms June 6 (170) $800

**Photograph, sgd & inscr**, [n.d.]. 4.75 by 7 inches. As Hamlet, by Vandaman. Inscr to Lucia. Illus in cat. rms June 6 (171) $575

— Anr, [n.d.]. 7.25 by 10.5 inches. As Scarlet Pimpernel, by Tunbridge. Inscr to Lucia. Illus in cat. rms June 6 (173) $550

**Howard, Leslie, 1893-1943 —& Others**
**Playbill**, program for Howard's production of Hamlet, [1936]. 16 pp, size not stated. Sgd & inscr by Howard; also sgd by 10 cast members. rms June 6 (172) $350

**Howe, Julia Ward, 1819-1910**
**ALs**, 4 Sept 1903. 2 pp, 8vo. To an old friend. About her health & plans. bbc June 24 (47) $100

— 9 Mar [n. y.]. 1 p, 5 by 8 inches. To Mrs. Classin. Inviting Mrs. Classin & her husband for "some recitations by a lady in whom we are much interested..." Dar Oct 19 (101) $100

**Howe, Richard Howe, Earl, 1726-99**
**Ds**, 25 July 1790. 16 pp, folio, stitched. Ptd Instructions and Standing Orders for the General Government and Discipline of the Ships of War. Countersgd by Admiral Joseph Davies. P Dec 13 (162) $400

**Howe, Sir William, 1729-1814**
**Franking signature**, [n.d.]. On autograph address leaf to Mark Huish. P Dec 13 (163) $350

**Hubbard, L. Ron, 1911-86**
**Ls**, 3 Apr 1975. 1 p, 4to. To the manager of the Baldwin Piano & Organ Company. Discussing the shipping of an organ. With related material. rms Mar 21 (306) $370

**Huch, Ricarda, 1864-1947**
**ALs**, 8 Dec 1908. 7 pp, 4to. To [Richard Moritz Meyer & his wife?]. Discussing her works about Garibaldi & the Risorgimento. star Mar 21 (206) DM950

**Autograph postcard, sgd**, 22 Oct 1897. To Marie Herzfeld. Concerning a meeting. JG Mar 29 (234) DM200

**Huehnlein, Adolf**
**Ls**, 22 Dec 1935. 1 p, 4to. To [Philipp] Bouhler. Thanking for his book & sending greetings for Christmas & the New Year. Illus in cat. rms June 6 (613) $200

**Huerta, Victoriano**
**Photograph, sgd & inscr**, 18 Aug 1913. Approx 5 by 6.75 inches. Inscr to A. Nelson O'Shaughnessy. sg June 6 (98) $130

**Hufeland, Christoph Wilhelm, 1762-1836**
**Series** of 9 A Ls s, 27 Nov 1823 to 6 Apr 1836 & [n.d.]. 30 pp, 8vo. To his daughter Hulda. Discussing financial & family matters. star Mar 21 (137) DM2,400

**ALs,** 14 May 1825. 8 pp, 4to. Recipient unnamed. Explaining why he cannot allow his daughter to marry a Catholic. star Mar 21 (138) DM1,300

### Hughes, Howard, 1905-76
[An archive of material relating to Hughes's 1938 round-the-world flight sold at California on 25 June 1996, lot 2338, for $1,300]

**Cut signature,** [n.d.]. In blue ink on green paper. Mtd with ptd photo & brass plate. wa Oct 28 (325) $450

**Group photograph,** [c.1938]. 253mm by 202mm. Driving in a parade. Sgd by Hughes. Illus in cat. Marans collection. CE Apr 17 (16) $2,600

— Anr, of the crew of his 1938 glob-circling flight, sgd by Hughs. 8 by 10 inches. With related material. sg Feb 1 (23) $1,600

**Hughes, Judge Sarah T.** See: Johnson, Lyndon B. & Hughes

### Hughes, Langston, 1902-67
**Ls,** 7 June 1961. 1 p, 8vo. To unnamed recipient. About traveling, and his pleasure that 2 of his works has been performed. Illus in cat pba Oct 26 (39) $600

**Autograph quotation,** [n.d.]. 1 p, 12mo. In full "I wish the rent/ Was heaven-sent". With the indication that it was written for Ashley Cole. With port & 2 vintage 1940s photos of Harlem. Framed. Over-all size 15.5 by 23.5 inches. Illus in cat rms Oct 11 (239) $800

### Hughes, Ted
**Autograph Ms,** verse, The Zeet Saga, or Pale Tale. [c.1846] 3 pp, 88 lines, on 2 leaves from school exercise book. CA Mar 26 (78) A$750

### Hugo, Victor, 1802-85
**ALs,** 19 Aug [n.y.]. 2 pp, 8vo. To Comte Rambuteau. Concerning rumors that the roof of the Hotel de Ville in Paris may be altered. S May 15 (189) £260

— [n.d.]. 1 p, 8vo. Recipient unnamed. Invitation to dinner. Sgd with initials. sg Feb 1 (113) $300

**Photograph, sgd & inscr,** [c.1870]. 97mm by 59mm, mtd. Full length, by Ghemar Freres; inscr to Duncumb Pike(?). Marans collection. CE Apr 17 (77) $1,300

### Humann, Karl, 1839-96
**ALs,** 21 Mar 1892. 3 pp, 8vo. To Joseph Hallbauer. Giving advice for recipient's travels to the Near East. star Mar 21 (504) DM300

### Humboldt, Alexander von, 1769-1859
**Autograph Ms,** sur l'Hygrometre par Mr Tralles, June 1807. 1 p, 4to, on final sheet of a paper by Johann Georg Tralles discussing the barometer, 7 pp, 4to (included). Illus in cat. star Mar 21 (505) DM1,500

**Series** of 4 A Ls s, 17 Mar 1856 & [n.d.]. 4 pp, 8vo. To Oskar Begas. Concerning various portraits. star Mar 21 (513) DM1,200

**ALs,** [c.Dec 1804]. 6 pp, 4to. To Jean Baptiste Nompere de Champagny. Asking that a pension be granted to his travel companion Aime Bonpland. star Mar 21 (506) DM3,600

— [c.1827-1831]. 1 p, 8vo. To [August Leopold Crelle]. About the plan to found a polytechnical school in Berlin. star Mar 21 (507) DM420

— [c.1831?]. 1 p, 8vo. To Pierre Berthier. Sending two books. star Mar 21 (508) DM360

— [23 Apr 1832]. 1 p, 8vo. To [Edme Francois Jomard]. Making plans to see him the next day. star Mar 21 (509) DM400

— [c.30 Sept 1834]. 1 p, 8vo. Recipient unnamed. Referring to Elisa Radziwill's death, & inviting him for breakfast. With engraved port. star Mar 21 (510) DM460

— 22 Apr 1855. 2 pp, 8vo. Recipients unnamed. Concerning the nomination of Marie Jean Pierre Flourens as member of a scientific academy. HN Nov 24 (2800) DM1,200

— [n.d.], "Saturday". 2 pp, 8vo. To [Benjamin A. Gould?]. Discussing optical manufactures. star Mar 21 (511) DM1,100

— [n.d.], "Tuesday". 1 p, 8vo. To an unnamed minister. Inviting him for dinner. star Mar 21 (514) DM300

— [n.d.], "Saturday". 1 p, 8vo. To E. P. E. de Rossel. Asking for a recent map to compare with one of his own maps of South America. Illus in cat. HN Nov 24 (2799) DM1,400

— [n.d.]. 1 p, 8vo. Recipient unnamed. Concerning a decoration. HN May 15 (2601) DM380

**ANs,** [n.d.]. 1 p, 8vo. To Herr Loeffler. Notifying him that the King will receive him the next day. Mtd. HN Nov 24 (2801) DM260

### Humboldt, Wilhelm von, 1767-1835
**ALs,** 29 July 1828. 2 pp, 4to. To Heinrich von Buelow. Sending family news, & reporting about meetings with diplomats in Paris. Illus in cat. star Mar 21 (515b) DM3,200

### Hummel, Johann Nepomuk, 1778-1837
**Autograph music,** Ex abrupto, for piano. 5 pp, oblong 8vo, in modern bds. Sgd & inscr, 21 July 1835. In brown ink on up to 3 systems per page, each of 2 staves. Repairs at central fold; lower corner of 1st leaf lacking, affecting text. S July 13 (714) £2,050

### Humperdinck, Engelbert, 1854-1921
**ALs,** 15 Feb 1896. 2 pp, 8vo. To [Emil Claar). Asking for opera tickets. star Mar 22 (871) DM500

**Autograph postcard, sgd,** 24 Mar 1899. To Fritz Schaum. Looking forward to seeing him in Rome. star Mar 22 (872) DM210

**Autograph quotation,** 3 bars from Haensel und Gretel, sgd; 1921. 1 p, 8vo. Including lengthy inscr. HH Nov 17 (3239) DM550

### Humphrey, Hubert Horatio
**Ls,** 7 Feb 1955. 1 p, 8 by 10.5 inches. To Simon Epstein. About Formosa & the Pacific. Dar Oct 19 (103) $150

— 26 Oct 1968. 2 pp, 8 by 10.5 inches. To "the Students of Ohio State University". Discussing the positive development of America's youth. Dar Oct 19 (104) $225

**Hunter, David, 1802-86**

**ALs,** 17 June 1865. 1 p, 8vo. Recipient unnamed. Complying with a request. rms June 6 (11) $210

**Ds,** 12 May 1865. 1 p, 16mo. Pass for Dr. Robert K. Stone to attend the proceedings of the Military Commission for the trial of Lincoln's assassins. Illus in cat. rms June 6 (10) $1,700

**Hunter, John, 1728-93**

**ALs,** 1793. 1 p, 4to. To unnamed recipient. Explaining that he will be unable " to attend the meeting of the Gentlemen of the Veterinary College to day." Docket on veros dated 1832 in anr hand. Torn in margins & aged. rms Oct 11 (200) $600

**Huntington, Henry Edwards, 1850-1927**

**Series** of 4 Ls, 1922-25. Each 1 p, 4to. To Eugene Prussing, rejecting a painting, making appointments, and thanking him. sg June 6 (99) $175

**Huntington, Jedediah, 1743-1818**

**ALs,** 31 Oct 1777. 2 pp, 4to. To Col. [William?] Williams. Rejoicing about Burgoyne's surrender & speculating about Gen. Howe's plans. P Dec 13 (164) $9,000

**Ds,** 24 Feb 1809. 1 p, 4to. Manifest for the sloop Rising Sun transporting 20 cords of wood to New York. Sgd as Collector of the Port of New London. pba June 13 (38) $70

**Huntington, Samuel, Signer from Connecticut**

**ALs,** 4 Apr 1774. 1 p, folio. To Mayor Jedidiah Edderkin. Sending "my amount in the Case of Mr. Cogswell..." With holograph address & docket on verso. Silked. rms Oct 11 (25) $290

**Ds,** 30 May 1780. 1 p, 6.5 by 11 inches, vellum. Comissioning Alexander Benstead as Lieutenant in the 10th Pennsylvania Regiment. Sgd as President of the Continental Congress. Countersgd by Ben Stoddert as Secretary of the Board of War. With folds & a narrow border of cellotape. Browned & stained. Ink faded. sg Sept 28 (137) $225

— 2 June 1790. 1 p, 8 by 12.75 inches, laid down. Commission. rs Nov 11 (23) $175

— 20 July 1790. 1 p, 4to. Notice to be attached to Daniel Edwards's estate. Browned & offset. Also with 2 tears in top margin. pba June 13 (39) $225

— 18 May 1791. 1 p, oblong folio. Commission of Samuel Bliss as an ensign of the 2d Company of Militia in the 12th Regiment. rms Nov 30 (193) $320

**Endorsement,** 5 June 1795. 1 p, 2.9 by 7.8 inches. Sgd as witness on promissory note of Stephen Stemson to Joshua Lathrop. sg Feb 1 (114) $150

**Huston, John.** See: Hammett, Dashiell & Huston

**Hutchinson, Capt. Edward**

**ADs,** 6 Dec 1670. 1 p, folio. Legal indenture about payments as trustee. With related material. pba June 13 (40) $1,600

**Hutton, E. F.**

**Ls,** 17 June 1930. 1 p, 4to. To George Worthington. Sending on a carbon copy of a letter to the Mayor [not present]. With coffee stain in right margin. pba June 13 (151) $180

**Hutton, Edward**

**Autograph Ms,** Ravenna. [c.1913] About 150pp, 4to, in half mor with E. H. in gilt. With many corrections. b May 30 (404) £60

**Huxley, Aldous, 1894-1963**

**ALs,** 5 Dec 1959. 1 p, 4to. To Werner H. Guttmann. Responding to a suggestion that he write a play. rms June 6 (398) $260

**Huxley, Andrew F.**

**Autograph Ms,** fragment of a draft of a scientific paper, [ptd 1977]. 4 pp, 4to. With Ls, note of transmittal, 11 Jan 1978. HN May 15 (2602) DM200

# I

**Ibert, Jacques, 1890-1962**

**Autograph quotation,** Rondo (Hommage a Mozart), 1956. 1 p, 8vo. 4 bars, sgd. star Mar 22 (874) DM550

**Ibsen, Henrik, 1828-1906**

**Series** of 3 A L s s, 13 Jan to 21 Apr 1870. 4 pp, 8vo. To Watt. About his works, plans for a meeting, etc. S May 15 (191) £1,650

**ALs,** 7 Oct 1890. 1 p. To an unidentified woman. Thanking her for flowers & a ticket. Ck Apr 12 (72) £450

**Photograph, sgd,** 10 Nov [18]96. 168mm by 109mm. Bust port, by J. C. Schaarwaechter. Illus in cat. Marans collection. CE Apr 17 (78) $1,000

**Ickes, Harold L.**

**Series** of 4 Ls s, Mar 1940 to July 1941, 5 pp, 8 by 10.5 inches. To Joseph Lieb. About Lieb's political writings. Dar Oct 19 (105) $170

**Iffland, August Wilhelm, 1759-1814**

**ALs,** 12 Nov 1790. 3 pp, 4to. To [Georg Forster]. Explaining that he declined an offer to work in Vienna because he prefers to stay among his friends in Mannheim. star Mar 22 (1150) DM1,900

— 21 Sept [n.y.]. 1 p, 8vo. Recipient unnamed. Discussing the possibility of an Ed of his collected works. HN May 15 (2603) DM240

**Illiger, Johann Karl Wilhelm, 1775-1813**

**ALs,** 27 June 1798. 3 pp, 4to. To the bookseller Keil. Promising to review a botanical work. star Mar 21 (516) DM210

**Illo, Christian, Freiherr von, c.1585-1634.** See: Ilow, Christian

**Ilow, Christian, Freiherr von, c.1585-1634**

**Ls,** 7 Feb 1634. 1 p, folio. To Princess Polyxena Lobkovitz. Assuring her that he is not persecuting her deliberately. star Mar 22 (1247) DM2,600

## INDIANS

**Indians, North American**

— FITCH, JOHN G. - ADs, Dec 1837 to Feb 1838. 7 pp, folio. Ledger recording purchases, rents & other expenses charged to members of the Mohican tribe in Norwich, Connecticut. CNY May 17 (273) $2,600

— SENECA TRIBE. - Document, 28 Oct 1841. 3 pp, folio. Petition addressed to Gov. William H. Seward complaining of land transactions with the Ogden Land Company. Sgd by 58 chiefs of the tribe. Framed. CNY May 17 (274) $6,500

— SIWANOY TRIBE. - Document, 12 Nov 1661. 1 p, 4to. Sale of land on Long Island to John Budd. Sgd by Chief Shenorock & 5 other chiefs of the tribe, each with their totem marks. Framed. CNY May 17 (275) $7,500

— WAMPANOAG TRIBE. - Document, 16 Nov 1671. 1 p, 4to. Sale of land on Cape Cod to Richard Bourne. Sgd by Sachem Quechatoset & 2 other members of his tribe. Framed. CNY May 17 (276) $7,500

**Ingelheim, Anselm Franz von, Kurfuerst & Erzbischof von Mainz, 1634-95**

Ls, 24 Apr 1687. 2 pp, folio. To Quirin Kunkel & Christoph Balthasar Heppe. Instructing them to investigate the complaints of Wilhelm Gottfried Philipp against the parson at Kiedrich. star Mar 22 (1329) DM550

**Ingemann, Bernhard Severin, 1789-1862**

ALs, [25 Dec] 1835. 3 pp, 4to. To Hans Christian Andersen. Praising his fairy tales, looking forward to his forthcoming novel, & expecting his visit. star Mar 21 (5) DM700

**Ireland, John, 1879-1962**

Autograph quotation, 4 bars from his Sonatina for piano, 24 Feb 1928. 1 p, folio. Sgd. star Mar 22 (875) DM300

**Irving, Washington, 1783-1859**

Autograph Ms, fragment from the draft of his History of the Life and Voyages of Christopher Columbus, [ptd 1828]. 1 p, 8vo. About 26 lines, corresponding to pages 454 & 455 of the 1st Ed. Illus in cat. rms June 6 (400) $500

**Irwin, James**

Photograph, sgd & inscr, [n.d.]. 6 by 4 inch postcard photo. Of Irwin saluting the American Flag on the moon. Inscr to Fran. Dar Oct 19 (106) $95

**Isabella Clara Eugenia of Austria, Regent of the Netherlands, 1566-1633**

Ls, 2 Nov 1625. 1 p, folio. To the Sieur de Guernouval. Ordering troop movements. star Mar 22 (1483) DM350

**Isabella I, Queen of Spain, 1451-1504**

Ls, 23 July 1499. 1 p, 4to. To Pedro Gomez de Setubal. Ordering him to take up the post of Oidor in Vallodolid. b June 28 (21) £1,500
See also: Ferdinand V & Isabella I

**Isherwood, Christopher, 1904-86**

Collection of Collection of 3 APS s & 1 PS, 22 April 1958 to 21 Jan 1968, 4 pp, no size given. to Arnold Weissberger. Thanking Weissberger for kodachromes, a drawing, a review & discussing a personal memo. rms Oct 11 (203) $200

**Isolani, Johann Ludwig, Graf von, 1586-1640**

Ls, 23 Jan 1635. 1 p, folio. To Ottavio Piccolomini. Informing him about Swedish troop movements & discussing a newly recruited company of dragoons. star Mar 22 (1249) DM1,200

**Italy**

Ms, Liber statutorum comunis vogoniae et ordinacionum anno domini millesimo trecentesimo septuagesimo quarto. [Northwestern Italy, 1374] 20 leaves, 203mm by 152mm, in contemp lea-backed wooden bds. In a gothic bookhand. C Apr 3 (1) £2,800

— Ms, Statuti della Corporazione dei fabbri di Genova. [Genoa, c.1440 to 1539] 42 leaves, on vellum, 235mm by 167mm, in 18th-cent calf. In brown ink in a gothic bookhand, with additions in various gothic 7 humanist cursive hands. C Apr 3 (2) £2,600

— BOLOGNA. - Document, medical doctorate for Petrus Franciscus Peratinus, 11 Feb 1640. 8 leaves, vellum, 218mm by 162mm. Contemp lea gilt. In an elegant cursive script. With 2 illuminated initials, fully illuminated page with large miniature & coat-of-arms, & half-page border in gold & colors. HH May 7 (58) DM1,200

— PADUA. - Document, 1631. 6 leaves, vellum, & paper endleaves, 201mm by 140mm, in contemp dark brown goatskin gilt. Doctorate in law granted to Taddeo Pechata. With full borders throughout & illuminated floral border & coat-of-arms on 1st page. With seal of the Chapter of Padua. S June 18 (40) £800

— PADUA. - Document, 7 June 1714. 4 leaves (2 blank), vellum, 235mm by 165mm. Contemp lea gilt. Doctorate in law for Josephus Victorius. HH May 7 (69) DM320

— ROME. - Document, June 1604. 9 leaves, vellum, 213mm by 148mm. Contemp red-brown mor gilt. Doctorate in medicine awarded to Francesco Jarubeo; in Latin. In a sloping italic script with names throughout in liquid gold capitals. With 3 full-page miniatures. S Dec 5 (20) £850 [Nadell]

**Iturbide, Agustin de, 1783-1824**

Ls, 9 Dec 1821. 1 p, 8vo. Recipient unnamed. Informing him that his letter has been forwarded to the Ministers of the Treasury. Illus in cat. rms June 6 (419) $425

## J

**Jackson, Andrew, 1767-1845**

ALs, 27 Jan 1818. 2 pp, 4to. To his wife Rachel. Reporting about his progress during the Seminole Campaign. Illus in cat. Sang collection. P Dec 13 (168) $7,000

## 1995 - 1996 · AUTOGRAPHS & MANUSCRIPTS — JACKSON

— 28 Aug 1822. 3 pp, 4to. To Richard Coll. Giving advice concerning new settlements & referring to his own political career. Illus in cat. P Dec 13 (170) $8,500

— 6 Nov 1829. 1 p, size not stated. To the Sec. of the Navy. Recommending Samuel P. Walker. P Dec 13 (171) $1,000

— 12 Aug 1831. 1 p, 4to. To Martin Van Buren. Sending an undisclosed something on to his Minister to Great Britain. Mtd with an engraved port. CNY Dec 15 (73) $1,400

— 31 July 1835. 1 p, 4to. To Postmaster General Amos Kendall. Sending on a letter [not present] and personal news: "I am much afflicted here, as I was at the City with headache - my general health is improved - the children all well, & as fat as little pugs - we are comfortably fixed & would be glad to see you here..." Illus in cat CNY Dec 15 (185) $2,800

— 14 Feb 1837. 1 p, 8vo. To Benjamin F. Butler. Directing a variety of matters to the attention of his Secretary of War. CNY Dec 15 (186) $1,800

— [c.1838]. 1 p, 4to. To Frederick W. Porter. Concerning a charitable gesture: " I feel greatly indebted to this unknown friend who has without my knowledge contributed to make me a member [of the American Sunday School Union]...an institution that its intended for the best and noblest purpose...But charity begins at home, and I have never yet had that I could spare without neglecting more charitable objects - the poor & the needy with the widows & orphans - therefore I cannot consent..." With small burnhole affecting text. CNY Dec 15 (187) $1,600

— 11 Mar 1839. 1 p, 4to. To James Kirke Paulding. Sending on letters from Tennessee merchants [not present] to the Secretary of the Navy "...with their great anxiety to serve their friend Mr. Ewing in the appointment solicited for his son..." Docketed by Paulding & others. Illus in cat pba Oct 26 (255) $2,800

— 5 June 1843. 2 pp, 4to. To Alexander Mouton. Writing the Governor of Louisiana about the resolution of an old quarrel relative to the refund of a $1,000 fine to Jackson: "...My grateful acknowledgements for this act of Justice in wiping from my memory the past imputations cast upon it by this unjust, illegal, and unconstitutional decree of a vindictive...Judge..." CNY Dec 15 (188) $5,000

— 22 Sept 1843. 1 p, 4to. To John C. Rives. About problems with his gift of a horse to F. P. Blair, & commenting on current politics. Illus in cat. Forbes Magazine collection. CNY May 17 (141) $2,500

— 22 Feb 1844. 3 pp, 4to. To Benjamin F. Butler. Concerning his actions during the defense of New Orleans. Including franking signature. Illus in cat. Forbes Magazine collection. CNY May 17 (142) $8,500

— 29 Apr 1844. 2 pp, 4to. To Benjamin F. Butler. About the upcoming annexation of Texas: "From what I learn of the Texan Treaty from a friend, it is such a one as you suggested, a field left open for a friendly adjustment with Mexico by Treaty...We will get Texas & have a lasting peace & friendship with Mexico, & put the entrigues of Great Britain at a distance..." Also wrongly predicting Van Buren's political success. Dampstained. With autograph free frank. Illus in cat CNY Dec 15 (189) $20,000

— 6 May 1844. 2 pp, 4to. To Benjamin F. Butler. Referring to the forthcoming Democratic Convention & his failing health. Forbes Magazine collection. CNY May 17 (143) $2,000

**AL,** 13 May 1835. 1 p, 4to. To Sec of War Lewis Cass. In 3d person, sending a report about the Battle of New Orleans (not present). Forbes Magazine collection. CNY May 17 (139) $2,000

**Ls,** 9 Oct 1836. 2 pp, 4to. To Major E. B. Penrose. Declining an invitation to a militia encampment in Pennsylvania. Forbes Magazine collection. CNY May 17 (140) $4,500

**Ds,** 2 May 1826. 1 p, on vellum, foliio. Ship's passport for the Meilwood. Countersgd by Sec. of State Edward Livingstone. CE June 12 (61) $1,600

— 1 Nov 1830. 1 p, folio, vellum. Land grant for 79 acres in Tuscaloosa, Alabama. Countersgd by Commissioner of the General Land Office Elijah Hayward. Signature light. With a port of Jacksonin military gear. Also with a reprint of the Battle of New Orleans. Over-all size 24 by 34 inches. Illus in cat rms Oct 11 (316) $750

— 2 Dec 1830. 1 p, folio, vellum. Land grant for 80 acres at Crawfordsville, Indiana to Perrine Kent. Countersgd by Elijah Hayward as Commissioner of the General Land Office. sg Sept 28 (138) $700

— 1 July 1831. 1 p, folio. Granting 79 acres of land to Adam Taylor. Mtd. With color port & statistical data. Soiled in margins. Over-all size 21.75 by 31.5 inches. rms Oct 11 (204) $800

— 13 Apr 1834. 1 p, folio. Patent for Elijah Skinner for an improvement in locks for furniture. Countersgd by Van Buren & J. M. Berrien. Framed. P Dec 13 (172) $1,200

— 25 Oct 1834. 2 pp, folio. Land deed by which Creek Indian "Ful lote Ho gan" conveys to Benjamin Mattison her claim. Sgd with her mark. Also sgd with 2 witnesses & Certifying Agent Leonard Tarrant. Deed & Cerification dated 9 May 1834. Browned & restored. sg Sept 28 (139) $1,400

— 26 Dec 1834. 1 p, vellum, laid down. Signature light. Ship's passport. rs Nov 11 (24) $700

— 21 July 1835. 1 p, folio. Patent for Jordan L. Mott for an "improvement in the Stove". Countersgd by John Forsyth & B. F. Butler. Framed. P Dec 13 (175) $1,200

— 20 Feb 1836. 3 pp, on vellum folio. Patent awarded to James cooper for an improvement in the threshing machine. Countersgd by Sec of State John Forsyth & Attorney General B. F. Butler. With related material. cb June 25 (2339) $2,750

**Autograph endorsement,** 2 March 1817. 2 pp, folio. Requisition for expenses of Thomas Fearn, Acting Hospital Surgeon, " The Quartermaster Gen[eral]...will pay the within account..." Browned & silked. CNY Dec 15 (72) $800

**Franking signature,** [1 May n.y.]. On envelope addressed to Mrs. Lucius J. Polk in anr hand. Illus in cat. rms Mar 21 (30) $850

### Jackson, Andrew, 1767-1845 — & Van Buren, Martin, 1782-1862
Ds, 11 June 1830. 1 p, folio, parchment. A ship's passport for the maiden voyage of the whaler Brandt. Illus in cat CNY Dec 15 (184) $2,600

### Jackson, Michael
Signature, Boxed album with promotional copy of stories from E. T. [1982?] On color ptd booklet. Inscr to Alexandrea. Also inscr & sgd by Quincy Jones. pba June 13 (184) $130

### Jackson, Thomas J. ("Stonewall"), 1824-63
ALs, 13 July 1861. 2 pp, 4to. To an unnamed Colonel. Hoping to be able to assign him to his staff. Illus in cat. P Dec 13 (179) $15,000

Ds, 6 Sept 1849. 1 p, folio. Requisition for pay for the month of August as a Lt. Mtd with engraved port. Framed. Illus in cat CNY Dec 15 (74) $6,000

### Jacobi, Johann Georg, 1740-1814
ALs, [n.d.]. 1 p, 4to. To Jettchen. In his sister Lotte's name (& sgd Lotte). Making plans for a visit. star Mar 21 (210) DM1,000

### Jagemann, Caroline, 1777-1848
ALs, 15 Jan 1842. 1 p, 8vo. To Herr von Spiegel. Asking for a comedy which she wants to read. star Mar 21 (139) DM470

### Jahnn, Hans Henny, 1894-1959
Collection of 7 A Ls s, 27 Ls s, postcard, sgd, 2 Ns s, & autograph Ms, 1931 to 1956. 57 p, 4to & 8vo. To Ludwig Voss & his family. Personal correspondence discussing private matters & his work. HN May 15 (2605) DM8,000

Corrected proof, poem, beginning "Den Greis liebt die Schoepfung nicht", [c.1951]. Postcard. Including autograph corrections & addition; sgd. File holes. star Mar 21 (211) DM550

### James, Frank, 1843-1915
ALs, 10 - 12 July 1883. 10 pp, 8vo. To his wife. Worrying about his forthcoming trial. Sgd Ben. CNY May 17 (255) $6,000

### James, Henry, 1843-1916
Collection of 2 A Ls s & 1 Ls, 1 June 1904 to 25 Oct 1914. 15 pp, 4to. To Mr. Phillips. CNY Oct 27 (96) $1,600

Series of 9 A Ls s, [1888-92]. 23 pp, mainly 8vo. To Mrs. Alma-Tadema. On social matters. S Dec 18 (196) £1,500 [Stodelski]

— Series of 5 A Ls s, 6 Feb to 17 Aug 1915. 9 pp, 4to. To Marie Belloc Lowndes. About the loss of Rupert Brooke; reports that he himself has become a British citizen. CNY Oct 27 (98) $4,800

— Series of 9 A Ls s, 9 June 1917 & [n.d.]. 27 pp, 8vo. To Douglas Ainslie. With an inscr photo of James. CNY Oct 27 (99) $3,800

ALs, 17 Nov 1891. 18 pp, 8vo. To Mme Helena Modjeska. Describing his dramatic work. With related material. CNY Oct 27 (94) $3,000

— 3 Oct 1899. 6 pp, 4to. To Edmund Gosse. About Gosse's health, guests & writing. CNY Oct 27 (95) $900

— 10 Mar 1912. 9 pp, 8vo. To Dr. Percy Wells. Recommending H. G. Wells's election to the Royal Society of Literature. CNY Oct 27 (97) $1,400

### James, P. D.
Autograph Ms, draft & working notes for her novel Original Sin. About 250 pp, folio, on 3 ruled notepads. 1 pad dated 18 Dec 1993, each titled & sgd. S Dec 18 (398) £1,400 [Fenelon]

### James V, King of Scotland, 1513-42
Ls, 6 Mar [1538]. 1 p, 200mm by 210mm. To the Constable of France. About sending the Cardinal of St. Andrews to the King [concerning the marriage to Mary of Guise]. C June 26 (320) £500

### James, William, 1842-1910
ALs, 21 June 1877. Recommending his student, W. S. Gooding, for a position teaching philosophy. wa Oct 28 (144) $240

### Janacek, Leos, 1854-1928
Autograph music, leaf of score for voice & full orchestra from the opera Vec makropulos. 1 p, 313mm by 236mm. [c.1926] Sold with 5 photos of Czech musicians, including Janacek. C June 26 (265) £4,100

### Jarry, Nicholas, c.1615-70. See: Calligraphy

### Jaspers, Karl, 1883-1969
ALs, 26 Mar 1949. 2 pp, folio. To Frau Victorius. Thanking for sending a work by Heidegger, & criticizing Heidegger's approach to philosophy. S Dec 1 (24) £1,400

### Jay, John, 1745-1829
ALs, 6 Sept 1787. 1 p, 4to. To George Washington. Expressing the wish of NY for "an occasion of giving you fresh Proofs of Esteem" for consenting to serve in the Constitutional Convention. Inlaid. Illus in cat. Doheny collection. P Dec 13 (180) $15,000

Ds, [1778-79]. 1 p, folio. Ptd Instructions to the Commanders of Private Ships or Vessels of War, dated 3 Apr 1776. Sgd as President of Congress. P Dec 13 (182) $2,500

— [1778-79]. 1 p, folio. Ptd Instructions to the Commanders of Private Ships or Vessels of War, dated 3 Apr 1776. Sgd as President of Congress. Illus in cat. P Dec 13 (183) $4,250

— 29 June 1779. 1 p, folio, vellum. Appointing Philip Dubois Bevoir as a Captain in "the fifth New York Regiment". Signature irregular. Aged & with holes & folds. rms Oct 11 (26) $900

### Jean Paul, 1763-1825. See: Richter, Jean Paul

### Jeanneret, Charles Eduard, 1887-1965. See: Le Corbusier

**Jeffers, Robinson, 1887-1962 —&**
**Weston, Edward**
**Photograph, sgd & inscr,** by Edward Weston, 1931. 3.75 by 2.75 inches, mtd on sheet & sgd by Weston 1931. Inscr by Jeffers to Libby Reynold, 1937. pba June 20 (360) $2,000

**Jefferson, Joseph, 1829-1905.** See: Cleveland, Grover

**Jefferson, Thomas, 1743-1826**
**Autograph Ms,** "Extract of a letter from J. Blair to Th: Jefferson dated W[illia]msburg June 13, 1795"; [n.d.]. 1 p, 4to. Recording a stock transaction. Illus in cat. Forbes Magazine collection. CNY May 17 (145) $12,000

**ALs,** 8 Nov 1779. 1 p, 238mm by 187mm. To the Speaker of Virginia's House of Delegates (Benjamin Harrison). Letter of enclosure. P June 5 (55) $5,000

— 23 Nov 1780. 1 p, folio. To Brigadier Gen. Robert Lawson. Asking him to visit to discuss the defense of Virginia with Baron von Steuben. Forbes Magazine collection. CNY May 17 (144) $17,000

— 12 Aug 1790. 2 pp, 4to. To Gouverneur Morris. About diplomatic relations with Britain: "they talk of a minister, a treaty of commerce and alliance. If the object of the latter be honorable, it is useless; if dishonorable, inadmissable." Separated at center fold. Silked. Laid into a larger sheet. CNY Dec 15 (76) $35,000

— 2 Aug 1791. 4 pp, 4to. To Philip Mazzei. About his settlement of Mazzei's affairs with news of political activities & family events. Illus in cat CNY Jan 26 (157) $65,000

— 26 Aug 1793. 1 p, 4to. To Messrs. Thayer Bartlett & Co. About a shipment of china that has arrived after 4 years, which is too late. cb June 25 (2344) $9,000

— 11 Nov 1793. 2 pp, 4to. To Herman Le Roy. Discussing payment of a mortage on land in Henrico County belonging to his son-in-law. Illus in cat. P Dec 13 (185) $16,000

— 17 Dec 1795. 1 p, 4to. To Henry Remsen. Discussing the planting of peas, thanking for newspapers, & commenting on Jay's Treaty. Illus in cat. P Dec 13 (186) $29,000

— 21 May 1803. 2 pp, 4to. To Jared Mansfield. Asking Mansfield to replace an incompetent surveyor of the Northwest Territory: "the present Surveyor General in the Northern quarter is totally incompetent to the office he holds. The errors he has committed...have fixed an indelible blot on the map of the U. S....I am happy in possessing proof of your being entirely master of this subject, and therefore in proposing to you to undertake the office..." Illus in cat CNY Dec 15 (191) $28,000

— 1 Dec 1803. 1 p, 8vo. To [William] Eustis. Sending him greetings and thanking Eustis for a fish he had sent Jefferson. In 3d person. Illus in cat rms Oct 11 (205) $5,500

— 25 Feb 1804. 1 p, 4to. To Craven Payton. Discussing the purchase of an old mill. Illus in cat. P Dec 13 (193) $12,000

— 30 Mar 1804. 2 pp, 4to. To the Marquis De Lafayette. Concerning Lafayette's thousands of acres of land in America that had be voted to him by Congress as a reward for his service in the Revolutionary War. Also concerning Jefferson's hope that Lafayette's presence in America might aid the trasnaition of French citizens to the US after the Louisana Purchase. Illus in cat CNY Dec 15 (192) $55,000

— 26 Mar 1807. 1 p, 4to. About tree planting in his orchards. With a spray of leaves & 3 pecans supposedly collected from trees grown from seeds enclosed in the letter. CNY Dec 15 (79) $18,000

— 13 Sept 1808. 1 p, 4to. To Edgar Patterson. About a letter to be forwarded. Stained & browned. With separations & losses of folds. CNY Dec 15 (80) $6,500

— 17 Jan 1810. 2 pp, 4to. To John Eppes. Proposing a solution to the problem of long speeches in the House of Representatives. Repaired. Illus in cat. P Dec 13 (194) $7,500

— 30 Apr 1812. 1 p, 4to. To John Williams. About a parcel of coffee. cb June 25 (2341) $10,500

— 31 May 1826. 1 p, 232mm by 190mm. To William Hilliard. About the shipping of books to the library at the University of Virginia. Illus in cat P June 5 (61) $27,000

**AL,** 17 Mar 1801. 2 pp, 4to. To Philip Mazzei. Congratulating him on his marriage, thanking for seeds, & sending news about the new administration. Illus in cat. P Dec 13 (190) $18,000

**Ls,** 19 July 1790. 1 p, 4to. To the President of New Hampshire. Circular letter establishing the District of Columbia as the seat of the U. S. Government. Edges browned, paper brittle & some ink has bled. Illus in cat CNY Dec 15 (75) $8,000

— 11 Jan 1791. 1 p, 4to. To Gov. Thomas Mifflin. Forwarding some acts of Congress. Framed. P Dec 13 (189) $7,000

— [1808]. 1 p, 4to. Recipient unnamed. Ptd circular letter defending the Embargo Act. Illus in cat. Forbes Magazine collection. CNY May 17 (146) $8,500

**ANs,** 14 Nov 1811. 1 p, 4to. To [David] Gelston. Thanking Gelston for information about steamboats & expressing his belief that a steamboat "will materially improve the condition of our country..." CNY Dec 15 (193) $13,000

**ADs,** 14 Aug 1783. 1 p, folio. Land indenture between Jefferson, James & Hanah Hickman, & Thomas & Ann Garth; sgd 10 times in text. Also sgd by others. Illus in cat. P Dec 13 (184) $15,000

— Sept 1798. 1 p, 8vo. Promissory note to John Barnes. P Dec 13 (187) $4,000

— 12 July 1802. 1 p, 8vo. Ordering John Barnes to pay Mr. Lemaire for "value received on account..." Also sgd by Lemaire. CNY Dec 15 (77) $4,200

**Ds,** 4 June 1790. 1 p, folio. Ptd Act for finally adjusting and satisfying the claims of Frederick William De Steuben; sgd as Sec of State. With related material. Illus in cat. P Dec 13 (188) $16,000

— 1791. 1 p, folio. An act approving a loan from the Netherlands to the US. Countersgd in type by George Washington as President and John Adams as Vice-President. Illus in cat CNY Dec 15 (190) $23,000

## JEFFERSON

— 16 Feb 1792. 3 pp, 4to. Act "Concerning Certain Fisheries of the United States, and the Regulation and Government of the Fishermen Employed Therein." Sgd as Secretary of State. sg Sept 28 (142) $4,600

— 2 Mar 1793. 2 pp, folio. Providing for collection of duties on ships. cb June 25 (2342) $5,000

— 14 Apr 1801. 1 p, folio. Ship's passport for the schooner Saratoga. Countersgd by James Madison & Joseph Wilson. Framed. P June 5 (58) $3,000

— Aug 1801. 1 p, folio. Ship's passport for the Defiance of New York. Countersgd by James Madison & David Gelston. Framed P June 5 (57) $3,500

— 4 Nov 1801. 1 p, folio. Land grant to William Triplett. Countersgd by James Madison. P Dec 13 (191) $2,750

— 19 Jan 1802. 17 by 21 inches, oblong folio. Four-language ship's papers for the schooner Industry. Countersgd by Sec of State James Madison. sg June 6 (101) $3,000

— 18 Apr 1803. Notification to Napoleon that R. R. Livingston has been authorized to "take his leave of you" as Minister Plenipotentiary. Duplicate copy. Also sgd by Madison. Sang - Engelhard collections. CNY Jan 26 (171) $26,000

— 23 May 1803. 1 p, on vellum, folio. Ship's passport for the Eagle of Nantucket. Countersgd by Sec. of State James Madison. CE June 12 (62) $3,200

— 18 Nov 1803. 1 p, 257mm by 346mm, on vellum. Appointment of Levett Harris as Consul for the port of St. Petersburg. Countersgd by James Madison. P June 5 (60) $3,250

— 15 Aug 1805. 1 p, folio. Land grant. Countersgd by Madison. sg Feb 1 (120) $3,000

— 19 Dec 1805. 1 p, folio. Four-language ship's papers for the brig Danube. Countersgd by Port Collector David Gelston. cb June 25 (2345A) $2,500

— 6 Mar 1806. 1 p, folio, parchment. Granting land to Benjamin Ruffner of Virginia. Countersgd by James Madison. Soiled. CNY Dec 15 (78) $2,800

— 27 May 1806. 1 p, folio. Ship's passport for the brig Jane. Countersgd by James Madison. Illus in cat. rms Mar 21 (13) $7,000

— 9 Dec 1806. 1 p, 8vo. Fragment only. Sgd by Jefferson & countersgd by James Madison. cb June 25 (2345) $2,000

— 14 Dec 1807. 1 p, folio. Land grant. Countersgd by Sec of State James Madison. Jefferson's signature poor. sg Feb 1 (121) $1,000

— 20 Jan 1809. 1 p, oblong folio, on vellum. Land grant to James Douglass in Kings County, New York. Countersgd by James Madison as Sec. of State. CE June 12 (63) $1,900

— 20 Feb 1809. 1 p, folio. Grant of land in the Northwest Territory to William Alman. Countersgd by James Madison. rms Mar 21 (12) $4,000

— [n.d.]. 1 p, folio. Four-language ship's paper. Also sgd by Secretary of State James Madison. With folds reinforced and margins restored. pba Oct 26 (258) $2,500

## AMERICAN BOOK PRICES CURRENT

Cut signature, 31 Dec 1802. From a Ds. Countersgd by James Madison. Framed with ports of both. P June 5 (59) $3,000

— Anr, [n.d.]. 6.5 by 1.5 inches. With closing. Framed with port. cb June 25 (2343) $5,000

— Anr, [n.d.]. Sold w.a.f F Mar 28 (697) $150

Franking signature, [n.d.]. 4.25 by 5 inches. To Edgar Patterson. Front panel only. Worn & soiled. CNY Dec 15 (81) $2,000

**Jefferson, Thomas, 1743-1826 — & Madison, James, 1751-1836**

Ds, 24 Oct 1804. 1 p, 10.5 by 15 inches, vellum. Ship's papers for "Hero of New York". Dar Oct 19 (109) $5,500

— 6 Sept 1805. 1 p, 10.5 by 15 inches, vellum. Ship's Papers for the "Independence of New York". Fold through Madison's signature. Dar Oct 19 (108) $5,000

— 27 Jan 1808. 1 p, folio, vellum. Granting 23 acres of land to John Garrett. Signatures light. Foxed & with damaged seal. Mtd with ports of both Madison & Jefferson. Framed under glass. Over-all size 35 by 29 inches. rms Oct 11 (206) $2,500

— [n.d.]. 1 p, 4to. Four-language ship's paper. Unaccomplished. Margins restored & folds reinforced. pba Oct 26 (258) $2,500

**Jelinek, Elfriede**

Autograph Ms, poem, der Kuss; [n.d.]. 1 p, folio. 4 four-line stanzas, sgd. star Mar 21 (212) DM550

**Jenifer, Daniel, 1723-90**

— Brice, James. - ADs, 31 Aug 1779. 1 p, 8vo. Certification that Daniel Jenifer took the trade-restriction oath prescribed by the Maryland legislature. P Dec 13 (197) $800

**Jenkinson, Charles, 1st Earl of Liverpool, 1727-1808**

Ls, 3 Nov 1779. 4 pp, folio. To Major Gen. William Phillips. Duplicate, reassuring him that army promotions will not affect the careers of officers of Burgoyne's army. P Dec 13 (198) $800

**Jensen, Hans Daniel, 1907-73**

Ls, 22 Feb 1969. 6 pp, 4to. To the journal Die Zeit. Draft, responding to a recent article. star Mar 21 (517) DM1,500

**Jerusalem, Johann Friedrich Wilhelm, 1709-89**

ALs, 9 May 1782. 3 pp, 4to. Recipient unnamed. Recommending a young author. star Mar 21 (140) DM320

**Johann Albrecht, Herzog von Mecklenburg-Schwerin, 1857-1920**

Ls, 10 Jan 1899. 1 p, folio. To Paul Warncke. Thanking for his biography of Fritz Reuter. star Mar 22 (1399) DM580

**Johann Georg I, Kurfuerst von Sachsen, 1585-1656**

Ls, 4 Jan 1623. 4 pp, folio. To a forest official. Giving instructions regarding a white hart. star Mar 22 (1628) DM320

— 24 May 1639. 1 p, folio. To the magistrates of the town of Loebau. Expressing sympathy for the plight of the occupied town. star Mar 22 (1250) DM250

### Johann Georg II, Kurfuerst von Sachsen, 1613-80
Ls, 21 Mar 1676. 1 p, folio. To Johann Caspar Knoche. Instructing him to furnish wood to some manors belonging to his son. star Mar 22 (1629) DM220

### John, Don, of Austria, 1547-78
Ls, 3 June 1570. 1 p, folio. To Martin de Caruajal. Giving instructions concerning the war against the Moriscos in Andalusia. S Dec 1 (10) £1,000

— 29 Nov 1573. 1 p, folio. To King Philipp II of Spain. Interceding in favor of Juan Enriquez. Including long autograph addition. star Mar 22 (1578) DM4,000

### John, Augustus, 1878-1961
ALs, 21 June 1901. 1 p, 8vo. To Charles Conder. About seeing his work at the Carfax gallery. pn Nov 9 (425) £180

### John III, King of Portugal, 1502-57
Ls, 30 Mar 1553. 1 p, oblong folio. To Pope Julius III. Concerning the administration of his affairs in Portugal. sg June 6 (102) $700

### John Paul II, Pope
Group photograph, [14 June 1980]. 4to. With Josef Stimpfle, Bishop of Augsburg. Sgd by both. HH May 9 (2487) DM440

### Johnson, Andrew, 1767-1875
Autograph endorsement, 5 May 1865. 1 p, 8vo. To Surgeon General William Hammond. On verso of letter from Adele Douglas to President. Supporting Mrs. Douglas' request that the Government not terminate its lease on a property she owns. CNY Dec 15 (82) $1,500

### Johnson, Andrew, 1808-75
[A Congressional document stating the resolution of the House of Representatives to impeach Johnson, 24 Feb 1868, 1 p, folio, sgd by Speaker Schuyler Colfax & 126 Congressmen who voted in favor of the resolution, with a Matthew Brady photograph of the managers of the impeachment in the House of Representatives, sold on 17 May 1996, lot 147, for $55,000 at Christie's New York.]

ALs, 15 May 1853. 2 pp, 8vo. Recipient unnamed. Discussing his political prospects, Tennessee politics, & internal improvements. Illus in cat. rms June 6 (404) $3,200

Ls, 11 Dec 1865. 3 pp, folio. To the President of the Republic of Chile. A Letter of Credence introducing Judson Kilpatrick as the American Minister to his country. Countersgd by Secretary of War William Seward. In caligraphic style in gold and colors. Flaking. With some separations. Illus in cat CNY Dec 15 (194) $2,000

— 8 July 1868. 1 p, 8vo. To The Sentae of the United States. Nominating J. Rowan Boone as United States Marshal for the District of Kentucky. Stained. Illus in cat pba Oct 26 (261) $650

Ds, 20 Mar 1854. 1 p, 4to. Appointment of 23 Justices of the Peace. Illus in cat. rms Mar 21 (60) $850

— 10 Oct 1856. 1 p, folio. As Governor of Tennessee, land grant to William Nash. P Dec 13 (199A) $800

— 10 Apr 1866, 1 p, folio. Appointment of Alfred Russell as District Attorney. Framed with related material. Countersgd by Wm. H. Seward. P Dec 13 (199) $900

— 13 June 1866. 2 pp, folio. Pardon for Thomas McNaney. Countersgd by William H. Seward. rms Mar 21 (63) $1,300

— 3 Jan 1867. 1 p, folio. Directing Secretary of State to affix the U. S. seal for "commutation of the sentence of death imposed upon James Brown." Browned in upper left quarter. Illus in cat sg Sept 28 (143) $750

— 2 Mar 1867. 11.25 by 17.5 inches. Commission of Sherlock Andrews as U.S. Attorney for the Northern District of Ohio. rs Nov 11 (25) $400

— 3 June 1868. 1 p, 4to. Order to affix the U.S. Seal to an instrument authorizing George P. Marsh to negotiate with the government of Italy on the subject of naturalization. rms Nov 30 (198) $800

— 22 June 1868. 1 p, 4to. Directing the Secretary of State to affix the Seal to " the ratification of a Convention between the United States and His Majesty the King of Italy..." Discolored at folds & edges. sg Sept 28 (144) $800

— 25 Aug 1868. 1 p, 4to. Order to affix the U.S. Seal to a pardon warrant for Charles Floyd Hopkins. CE June 12 (64) $700

Autograph endorsement, 4 Jan 1868. On 1 p, 8vo ALs from James W. Bradbury dated 25 Dec 1867. Concerning a request in aiding Daniel F. Baker an appointment to Naval School: "Let the application be entered for special consideration." pba Oct 26 (260) $1,500

Endorsement, sgd, 18 May 1865, 1 p, 4to, on ALs by John S. Carlile concerning claims by Mr. Harder; asking the Quartermaster General to examine the case. Also endorsed by M. C. Meigs. Illus in cat. rms Mar 21 (61) $800

Envelope, [n.d.]. Front panel only. Addressed to John H. Gourlie. pba Feb 22 (253) $300

Signature, 27 June 1867. Framed with photo & composite photo of impeachment committee & Michigan 1864 ballot. rms Nov 30 (36) $600

### Johnson, John A. ("Jack"), 1878-1946
Photograph, sgd & inscr, [c.1910]. 138mm by 87mm, mtd. 3-quarter length; by Birmingham Smallwares. Illus in cat. Marans collection. CE Apr 17 (275) $3,000

### Johnson, Lyndon B., 1908-73
Collection of 9 Dec 1959. 1 p, 8 by 10.5 inches. To unnamed recipient. Sending along a quotation. With Quotation sgd. 1 p, 5.5 by 3.5 inches: " It's my job in the Senate to keep the thing moving. You might say it's my job to prove that democracy can work. You have a lot of work to do with a lot of different people - Republicans as well as Democrats. But it gives you a sense of achievement, like almost nothing else,

when the system is working the way it ought to work." Dar Oct 19 (111) $425

**Ls,** 26 March 1953. 1 p, 4to. To Tim Carroll. Thanking Carroll for mentioning in his Dallas Morning News column. pba Feb 22 (255) $130

— 23 Nov 1957. 1 p, 6 by 7 inches. To Lawrence E. Spivak. Declining an invitation to appear on Meet The Press. Dar Oct 19 (112) $160

— 22 Sept 1962. 1 p, 4to. To Lawrence Spivak. Praising Meet the Press. Sgd "Lyndon". rms Nov 30 (199) $285

— 21 Sept 1966. 1 p, 4to. To Under Secretary of State George W. Ball. Accepting his resignation. rms Nov 30 (201) $1,300

**Group photograph,** [n.d.]. Framed, overall size 14.75 by 17.75 inches. In his rocking chair, with George Ball. Sgd by Johnson & inscr to Ball in anr hand. rms June 6 (407) $500

**Photograph, sgd,** [n.d.]. 4.25 by 6.25 inches, mtd on card. rs Nov 11 (26) $150

**Photograph, sgd & inscr,** 11 Apr 1968. 8 by 7.25 inches. Photo of Johnson shaking Walter F. Mondale's hand. Inscr to Fritz Mondale. Over-all size 114 by 11 inches. Dar Oct 19 (110) $425

— **Anr,** [n.d.]. 4to. Inscr to George Ball "a patriot". Framed under glass. Over-all size c. 11.11 by 14.5 inches. Illus in cat rms Oct 11 (207) $325

— **Anr,** [n.d.]. 4to. Inscribed to George Ball "May we always be this relaxed". Framed under glass. Over-all size 12 by 14.7 inches. rms Oct 11 (208) $425

— **Anr,** [n.d.]. 4to. Inscr to George Ball. Mtd to folio. Framed under glass. Over-all size 16.1 by 12 inches. rms Oct 11 (209) $350

See also: Adenauer, Konrad & Johnson

**Johnson, Lyndon B., 1908-73 —& Hughes, Judge Sarah T.**

**Photograph, sgd,** [n.d.]. 4to. Photo of Johnson being sworn in as President on Air Force One. Hughes has noted: " I administered the presidential oath to Lyndon B. Johnson on November 22, 1960 at 2:38 P. M. " With ptd reproduction of the photo from Time. Illus in cat rms Oct 11 (223) $2,000

**Johnson, Pamela Hansford**

[A collection of material including the Autograph Ms of Important to Me, 11 A Ls s & 10 Ls s to her doctor, David Sofaer, sold at Sotheby's on 18 Dec 1995, lot 319, to Fenelon for £750]

**Johnson, Richard Mentor, 1780-1850**

**ANs,** 3 Aug 1848. 1 p, 8vo. Recipient unnamed. Sending his autograph. rms Mar 21 (33) $200

**Johnson, Samuel, 1709-84**

**ALs,** 10 Nov 1769. 1 p, 4to. To Thomas Percy. About an arrangement with some ladies for Percy to preach at a charity school. S Dec 18 (132) £3,200 [Edwards]

— 17 Oct 1778. 1 p, 4to. To Thomas Cadell. On the progress of The Works of the English Poets. C June 26 (319) £4,800

— 25 Feb 1780. 2 pp, 4to. Recipient unnamed but possibly George Colman. Asking for the return of Mr. Walpole's tragedy. S July 11 (127) £4,400

**Johnson, Uwe, 1934-84**

**Autograph Ms,** quotation from Christian Morgenstern (possibly imitated by Johnson); [c.1954/55]. 1 p, folio. star Mar 21 (217) DM680

— Autograph Ms, story, It comes then and now but fades again, [Oct 1954]. 4 pp, 4to. Probably unpbd. star Mar 21 (214) DM7,000

— Autograph Ms, story, Jedenfalls am 2. Januar LV, [Oct 1954]. 2 pp, 4to. Sgd with paraph. Probably unpbd. star Mar 21 (215) DM4,500

**Corrected galley proof,** essay, Gespraeche ueber Jerichow, [ptd 1972]. 1 p, folio. Including extensive autograph revisions. Sgd & inscr at head. star Mar 21 (218) DM550

**Johnson, Walter Perry, 1887-1946 —& Vance, Dazzy, 1891-1961**

**Ptd photograph,** [c.1924]. 228mm by 180mm, mtd. Full length; sgd by both. Illus in cat. Marans collection. CE Apr 17 (276) $650

**Johnston, Albert Sidney, 1803-62**

**ALs,** 15 Sept 1846. 1 p, 4to. To his wife. Reporting from the Mexican War. Illus in cat. CNY May 17 (218) $5,000

**Ds,** 8 Jan 1840. 1 p, 4to. Discharge certificate from the Army of Texas for D. Cooper. Including autograph addition. Illus in cat. rms June 6 (42) $1,800

**Johnston, Joseph E., 1807-91**

**ANs,** 14 Mar 1865. On bottom of letter from C. B. Harrison. Concerning whether or not public funds should be moved. Sgd as "J. E. Johnston". pba Oct 26 (172) $2,750

**Cut signature,** [n.d.] No size given. With port and excerpt from the 2 June 1862 New York Tribune concerning "The Battle Before Richmond". Also with 2 stereos by Taylor & Huntington. Framed. Over-all size 24.1 by 34.1 inches. Illus in cat rms Oct 11 (106) $450

**Johnston, Samuel, 1733-1816**

**Ds,** 2 Aug 1788. 1 p, 4to. Resolution of the North Carolina Constitutional Convention concerning the collection of impost on goods exported from & imported to North Carolina; sgd as President of the Convention. Illus in cat. P Dec 13 (333) $4,750

**Jolson, Al, 1886-1950**

**Signature,** [c.1928]. 4to. On front cover of Warner Brothers Theatre In Hollywood program for the play Glorious Betsy. Illus in cat. rms June 6 (150) $235

**Jones, Jennifer**

**Collection** of 1967. 8 pp, 4to & 8vo. To Arnold Weissberger. Thank you notes and friendly letters. rms Oct 11 (350) $550

**Jones, John Paul, 1747-92**
ALs, 13 Nov 1778. 4 pp, 4to. To Robert Morris. Describing his frustrations in trying to obtain a warship in France. P Dec 13 (200) $36,000

**Jones, Le Roi.** See: Baraka, Amiri

**Jonnart, J.**
Autograph Ms, Petit recueil de prieres. 1896. 60 pp, 174mm by 144mm, in ink & watercolor heightened with gold, in mor extra by Gruel to a design by J. Chadel. With ornamental tp, 3 pictorial subtitles, 43 pictorial or ornamental borders & 9 smaller decorations. Henri Vever's copy, with 2 bdg designs by Chadel & an ALs from her to Vever about her work S Nov 21 (345) £2,100

**Jordan, Pascual, 1902-80**
Autograph Ms, scientific paper about a question of abstract algebra, [n.d.]. 19 pp, folio. Fragment, including numerous mathematical formulae. star Mar 21 (518) DM650

**Jorden, Thomas, 1819-95**
Ds, 13 July 1861. 2 pp, 4to. Special Orders No. 111. Assigment of artilery batteries to battalion officers. pba Feb 22 (169) $800

**Joseph I, Emperor, 1678-1711**
ALs, May 1691. 1 p, folio. To Princess Hedwig Elisabeth of Poland. Responding to her report about her arrival in Warsaw. Illus in cat. star Mar 22 (1592) DM2,500
— [n.d.]. 1 p, folio. To Friedrich Karl von Schoenborn. Giving instructions regarding a loan. Illus in cat. HH May 9 (2488) DM2,000

**Joseph II, Emperor, 1741-90**
Ls, 26 May 1776. 1 p, 4to. To some Freemasons in Berlin. Responding to a request for protection. star Mar 22 (1604) DM1,200
— 6 Jan 1788. 1 p, folio. To an unnamed prince. Announcing his nephew's marriage. HH May 9 (2489) DM300
Ds, 29 Aug 1786. 15 pp, 4to, in new velvet. Patent of nobility & grant of arms for Friedrich Creutz von Ehrenkampf. Including full-page painting of the arms in gold, silver & colors. star Mar 22 (1603) DM650

**Josephine, Empress of the French, 1763-1814**
Ls, 2 Nov 1807. 1 p, oblong 4to. Recipient unnamed. Recommending a retired soldier, Diebecker, for a post as a guard. Cut from a longer letter. rms Nov 30 (246) $1,100
See also: Napoleon I; Josephine & Others

**Joyce, James, 1882-1941**
ALs, 11 Aug 1920. 1 p, 4to. To Henry Davray. About his life in Paris & Ludmila Savitsky's translation of A Portrait of the Artist as a Young Man. CNY Oct 27 (102) $3,200
— 9 Feb 1927. 1 p, 4to. To Arthur Laubenstein. Sending thanks for birthday greetings; Reports that his son Giorgio, Laubenstein's former singing pupil, has taken up singing again. Illus in cat CNY Oct 27 (103) $2,800
Photograph, sgd, 31 July 1925. 212mm by 141mm. Seated, by C. Rap. Illus in cat. Marans collection. CE Apr 17 (79) $5,500

**Judson, Edward Zane Carroll, 1823-86**
Photograph, sgd & inscr, [c.1870]. 165mm by 107mm. Seated; by Sarony's. Illus in cat. Marans collection. CE Apr 17 (8) $1,400

**Juenger, Ernst**
Ls, 21 Sept 1969. 1 p, folio. Recipient unnamed. Responding to an inquiry about authors and political groups. star Mar 21 (220) DM600
Autograph quotation, beginning "Die Schwalben kreisen immer noch...", [n.d.]. 1 p, 8vo. Excerpt from a novel, sgd. HH Nov 17 (3241) DM260

**Juin, Alphonse, 1888-1967.** See: Montgomery, Bernard Law & Juin

**Julius III, Pope**
Ls, 8 Feb 1543?. 1 p, 4to. Recipient unnamed. Sgd as Cardinal del Monte. Regarding the Cavalieri Pellegrini. Lightly dampstained in lower margin, slightly affecting the signature. sg June 6 (103) $325

**Jung, Carl Gustav, 1875-1961**
Collection of 2 A Ls s & 1 autograph postcard, sgd, 3 June 1909 to 10 July 1911. 4 pp. To Alfred Adler. C June 26 (315) £1,800
Series of 3 Ls s, 9 Jan 1939 to 25 July 1946. 3 pp, folio. To Alfred Wuerfel. About India, the western world after the war, Indian thought & Christian philosophy, etc. With related material. S Dec 1 (25) £2,600
Ls, 23 July 1957. 1 p, 8vo. To Dr. Anthony Storr. In English, informing him of the spread of psychoanalytical jargon. S Dec 18 (400) £500 [Gadney]

**Junot, Andoche, Duc d'Abrantes, 1771-1813**
ALs, 27 Aug 1811. 1 p, 4to. Recipient unnamed. Accepting an invitation to a hunt. star Mar 22 (1454) DM230

# K

**Kabalevsky, Dimitri Borisovich**
ALs, 7 Sept 1957. 2 pp, 8vo. To Eva. Thanking for photographs & promising to send his new compositions for piano. star Mar 22 (885) DM300

**Kaestner, Abraham Gotthelf, 1719-1800**
Autograph Ms, poem, Das Marienbild an den Herzog, [n.d.]. 1 p, 4to. 4 lines, inscr to Duke Friedrich August of Braunschweig-Lueneburg. star Mar 21 (223) DM320

**Kafka, Franz, 1883-1924**
AL, [late June 1922]. 4 pp, 8vo. To Max Brod. About personal & political news. Sgd Dein. star Mar 21 (222) DM44,000

## KAFKA

**Corrected galley proof,** collection of stories, Ein Landarzt, Feb to Sept 1919. 13 long galleys (3 lacking), size not stated. Including autograph corrections & revisions in ink & pencil. star Mar 21 (221) DM42,000

**Signature,** [n.d.]. No size given. On verso of a holograph envelope addressed to Felice Bauer. rms Oct 11 (216) $850

**Kalakaua, King of the Hawaiian Islands, 1836-91**
ALs, 25 Aug 1883. 1 p, 8vo. To G. W. MacFarlane & Co. Requesting delivery of small bottles. sg June 6 (104) $700

**Photograph, sgd,** [c.1891]. 165mm by 108mm, mtd. Full length, in uniform; by J. Williams & Co. Illus in cat. Marans collection. CE Apr 17 (106) $1,400

**Kalakaua, King of the Hawaiian Islands, 1836-91 —& Phillips, Wendell, 1811-84**
**Signature,** [n.d.]. 4to autograph sheet, sgd by both. rms Mar 21 (301) $440

**Kalb, Johann, 1721-80**
Ds, 13 Apr 1778. 1 p, folio. Oath of Allegiance administered to Balser Geehr. P Dec 13 (92) $3,000

**Kalman, Emmerich, 1882-1953**
**Autograph quotation,** themes from 3 of his operettas, 28 June 1937. 1 p, 8vo. Sgd. star Mar 22 (886) DM520

**Kane, Elisha Kent, 1820-57**
ALs, 7 Sept 1849. 1 p, 4to. To Dr. Francis Tuckerman. Concerning a need to take a leave. rms Oct 11 (217) $250

**Kant, Immanuel, 1724-1804**
Ds, 17 Oct 1792. 1 p, folio. List of students attending his lectures in anthropology. Introductory statement & confirmations of payment in Kant's hand; c.50 names of students in their own hands. star Mar 21 (522) DM4,200

**Kapiolani, Queen of Kalakaua of the Hawaiian Islands, 1835-99**
**Photograph, sgd,** [c.1891]. 165mm by 108mm, mtd. Seated, holding a fan; by J. Williams & Co. Illus in cat. Marans collection. CE Apr 17 (107) $1,100

**Karl, Erzherzog von Oesterreich, 1771-1847**
Ls, 3 Nov 1793. 2 pp, folio. To the administration of Brabant. Concerning supplies of hay & oats. star Mar 22 (1486) DM250

**Karl August, Grossherzog von Sachsen-Weimar, 1757-1828**
Ls, 26 Mar 1814. 1 p, folio. To Baron von der Horst. Forwarding some information by Count von Hogenberg concerning the occupation of Apell & Kulst. star Mar 21 (129) DM280

— 3 Nov 1821. 2 pp, 4to. To Herr von Donop. Promising more funds for excavations. star Mar 21 (130) DM470

## AMERICAN BOOK PRICES CURRENT

**Karl I Ludwig, Kurfuerst von Pfalz-Neuburg, 1617-80.** See: Leyen, Damian Hartard von der & Karl I Ludwig

**Karl II Eugen, Herzog von Wuerttemberg, 1728-93**
Ls, 20 Dec 1756. 2 pp, folio. To Duchess Luise Dorothea von Sachsen-Gotha. Sending New Year's wishes. star Mar 22 (1688) DM550

**Karl Joseph, Herzog von Lothringen, Kurfuerst von Trier, 1680-1715**
Ls, 24 Mar 1713. 1 p, folio. To Alessandro Borgia. Promising to support the 4th article of the Treaty of Rijswijk in the negotiations at Utrecht. star Mar 22 (1334) DM450

**Karl Theodor, Kurfuerst von Bayern, 1724-99**
**Document,** 7 July 1792. 9 leaves, 341mm by 275mm. Light blue velvet. Patent of nobility for Anton Fuchs. With achievement of the arms in gold, silver & colors. HH May 7 (67) DM2,300

**Karl Wilhelm Ferdinand, Herzog von Braunschweig-Wolfenbuettel, 1735-1806**
ALs, 8 Aug 1804. 2 pp, 4to. To Markgraefin Amalie von Baden. Inviting her to come to Braunschweig for the confinement of her daughter, the wife of his son. star Mar 22 (1195) DM400

**Karloff, Boris, 1887-1969**
**Photograph, sgd & inscr,** c.1934. 10 by 8 inch photo of a scene from "The Black Cat". Inscr & sgd. With marginal creases. sg Sept 28 (146) $400

**Signature,** [n.d.]. No size given. On small sheet. trimmed. Mtd. bbc Sept 18 (79) $110

**Karoline Auguste, Empress of Franz I of Austria, 1792-1873**
ALs, 12 Nov 1846. 4 pp, 8vo. To Elisabeth Berthier. Sending family news. In French. HN May 15 (2615) DM600

**Kastler, Alfred, 1902-84**
**Autograph Ms,** biographical essay about Marguerite Perey, May 1975. 9 pp, folio. Sgd later, at beginning & end. star Mar 21 (524) DM360

— Autograph Ms, lecture, Optical Methods of Radiofrequency Spectroscopy, [1968]. 22 pp, folio. Sgd later, at end. With ALs, 19 May 1969; letter of transmittal. star Mar 21 (523) DM1,700

**Katz, Sir Bernard**
**Autograph Ms,** Results. Effect of curare on end-plate membrane potentials..., [1977]. 2 pp, folio. Sgd B. K., at head. With ALs, 23 Mar 1977. star Mar 21 (525) DM300

**Keats, John, 1795-1821**
ALs, [30 Jan 1818]. 3 pp, 4to. To his brothers Thomas & George Keats. Discussing the publication of Endymion & including an unpbd version of his Lines on the Mermaid Tavern. Repaired. CNY May 17 (92) $70,000

**Keene, Laura, 1826-73**
**Autograph sentiment,** "A severe Snow Storm ushers in December 1872"; sgd. 1 p, 8vo. Illus in cat. rms June 6 (12) $950

**Kellar, Harry, 1849-1922**
**ALs,** 8 Mar 1915. 2 pp, 4to. To Powers. Concerning the itinerary for the magician Ching Ling Foo's visit to Southern California. pba Feb 22 (71) $250

**Keller, Gottfried, 1819-90**
**ALs,** 6 Oct 1883. 3 pp, 8vo. To Wilhelm Hertz. Discussing a 2d Ed of his collected poems & sending 2 corrections. Fold tear. star Mar 21 (224) DM8,500

**Keller, Helen, 1880-1968**
**Photograph, sgd,** [c.1950]. 251mm by 200mm. Sgd on lower margin. CE June 12 (66) $650
**Photograph, sgd & inscr,** May 1924. 242mm by 192mm (image). With her dog; by Muray. Inscr to Helen Thompson. Illus in cat. Marans collection. CE Apr 17 (145) $1,900
— Anr, [c.1950]. 242mm by 189mm. Inscr on lower portion of image to Arthur H. Ailey CE June 12 (65) $600

**Kellermann, Francois Christophe, Duc de Valmy, 1735-1820**
**Ls,** 6 Nov 1813. 3 pp, folio. To Baron Desbureaux. Conveying the Emperor's defense instructions. star Mar 22 (1455) DM230

**Kennedy, Jacqueline Bouvier.** See: Onassis, Jacqueline Bouvier Kennedy

**Kennedy, John F., 1917-63**
**Autograph Ms,** Concerning an appoitnment for Mr. Lee. [n.d.]. 2 pp, 8vo. rms Oct 11 (220) $2,500
— Autograph Ms, draft of a Memorial Day speech. [c.1952-60] 4 pp, 4to. rms Nov 30 (207) $5,000
**Transcript,** Statement on what it takes for a democratic society to remain strong. 1 p, 4to, sgd. CE June 12 (67) $1,100
**Typescript,** Remarks of Senator John F. Kennedy (Dem.-Mass.) Jefferson-Jackson Day Dinner -- Bristol, Virginia, Friday Evening, March 7, 1958. 11 pp, 4to. With holograph revisions. CNY Jan 26 (161) $6,500
— Typescript, text of a speech made on New England. 11 pp only, 4to. With corrections in ink & pencil throughout in his & anr hand. rms Nov 30 (208) $700
**Typescript carbon copy,** Carbon typescript of a speech entitled "Address...at Executive Committee Meeting American Legion". 16 Oct 1953. 5 pp, 4to. With emendations both holograph and in the hand of Jacqueline Kennedy. With 2-inch strip of corrected text taped to page 3. CNY Dec 15 (198) $950
— Typescript carbon copy, Courage in the Senate, comprising the 1st 10 chapters of Profiles in Courage. 176 pp, 4to (lacking 1st 2 pages of the sequence). With holograph notes of material for the chapter Courage & Politics, 3 pp, 4to. Sang - Engelhard collections CNY Jan 26 (160) $8,000

**ALs,** [c.1943]. 4 pp, folio. To Mrs. Mead. About his stay in the naval hospital: "We live a very rugged life here. Conditions are somewhat similar to a 15th century Dominican monastery..."Browned. CNY Dec 15 (83) $2,800
— [n.d.]. 1 p, folio. To Anne-Marie Ostinger. Thanking her for a letter & saying that he will be in touch after the election. cb June 25 (2347) $3,000
**Ls,** 6 Feb 1953. 1 p, 4to. Recipient unnamed. About his delay in taking up a matter concerning claims against Yugoslavia. rms Nov 30 (209) $1,100
— 14 July 1955. 1 p, 4to. To Lawrence Spivak. Agreeing to go on Meet the Press. wa Oct 28 (207) $600
— 22 Oct 1953. 1 p, 8 by 10 inches. To Private S. F. Curran. Thanking the Private for his good wishes on his marriage. Detail in cat Dar Oct 19 (117) $1,100
— 22 Oct 1953. 1 p, 4to. To Lawrence Spivak. Recommending Charles Bartlett if there ever is a vacancy for Meet the Press. wa Oct 28 (206) $650
— 24 May 1956. 1 p, 4to. To Ann V. Penderrgast. Thanking a campaign worker. Illus in cat pba Feb 22 (258) $950
— 6 June 1956. 1 p, 4to. To Ann V. Pendergast. Hoping to arrange a meeting with a devoted campaign worker at the Democratic Convention. Illus in cat pba Oct 26 (266) $850
— 30 Nov 1956. 1 p, 4to. To Doris M. Racicot. Thanking for her help in the recent election. rms Mar 21 (157) $650
— 27 Mar 1957. 1 p, 4to. To Hyman Fisch. Thanking him for kind remarks. With holograph postscript. Mtd with a port. Framed. Over-all size 11. 1 by 17.5 inches. Illus in cat rms Oct 11 (219) $1,000
— 29 Apr 1957. 1 p, 4to. To William Kelly. Forwarding a copy of a telegram (present) sent to Commissioner Callahan in recipient's behalf. Including autograph postscript. Illus in cat. rms Mar 21 (156) $1,100
— 19 June 1957. 1 p, 4to. To Judge Wendell Green. Sending thanks for hospitality in Chicago. sg Feb 1 (123) $1,500
— 27 Apr 1961. 1 p, 4to. To Hanns Hubmann. Sending thanks for a book. sg Feb 1 (124) $2,000
— 30 June 1961. 1 p, 4to. To George Copping. About the relationship between the U. S. and Canada; declines an invitation. CNY Dec 15 (199) $2,100
— 10 Mar 1962. 1 p, 4to. To Congressman William K. Van Pelt. Sending birthday wishes. With original envelope. rms Oct 11 (221) $1,500
— [n.d.]. 1 p, 4to. To Ann V. Pendergast. Thanking her for aiding in his campaign for Senate. pba Oct 26 (265) $850
**Ds,** 29 Nov 1961. 1 p, folio. Appointment of George W. Ball as Under Secretary of State. Countersgd by Dean Rusk. Illus in cat. rms Mar 21 (155) $5,000
**Autograph sentiment,** sgd, "with thanks & best wishes," 1963. On memo sheet. With photograph with secretarial inscr. sg Feb 1 (125) $1,500
**Group photograph,** [c.1958]. 205mm by 254mm. Seated at a table during a campaign tour; sgd & inscr by Kennedy. Illus in cat. Marans collection. CE Apr 17 (146) $1,900

### Kennedy, Joseph, 1888-1969
**ALs,** 31 July 1916. 2 pp, 8vo. To "Arthur". Returning a gift: "Rose made up her mind that market conditions did not warrant any expensive gift, hence the return of them all..." rms Oct 11 (224) $375

### Kennedy, Robert F., 1925-68
**Ls,** 5 Dec 1964. 1 p, 8.5 by 11 inches. To Louis G. Fields, Jr. Thanking him for congratulations sent. With holograph postscript concerning Burr Harrison's introduction of Kennedy at a Law Day celebration. With reproduction of that introduction & carbon of Fields's letter. Detail in cat Dar Oct 19 (120) $450

**Photograph,** sgd & inscr, [n.d.]. 8 by 10 inches. Inscr to Jeff Mitchell. wa Oct 28 (338) $350

### Kenner, Albert W., 1880-1959
[An archive of material mainly dealing with his service as the Allies' chief medical officer in Europe sold at California on 25 June 1996, lot 2391, for $950]

### Kent, Rockwell, 1882-1971
**Ls,** 30 Sept 1927. 1 p, 4to. To Frank Crowninshield. Agreeing to make his Christmas card design. F Mar 28 (875) $130

### Kerensky, Aleksandr Fyodorovich, 1881-1970
**Telegram,** sgd, 29 Sept [c.1917]. 1 p, 4to, framed with port. To the Commander in Chief of the Northern Front. CE June 12 (68) $450

### Kern, Jerome, 1885-1945
**Ms,** vocal score of the musical play Show Boat [c.1927]. About 290 pp, various sizes, in 2 contemp carf folders. In the hand of 2 copyists, with holograph additions & 2 sections of holograph music, including a draft of Ol' Man River. P June 5 (283) $80,000

**Ls,** 4 June 1936. 1 p, 8vo. To Peggy Wood. Complaining about his collaboration with the Spewacks. Matted with photogravure. sg June 6 (106) $400

**Ds,** 5 Apr 1934. Assigning Canadian copyright for Smoke Gets in Your Eyes. pba June 13 (214) $400

— 26 Dec 1944. 1 p, 4to. Assignment of copyright of Sweetest Sight That I Have Seen. Attached is the LC copyright document. sg June 6 (107) $175

### Kerouac, Jack, 1922-69
**Ms,** New School Term Paper about Sinclair Lewis & Theodore Dreiser. 21 Dec 1948. 6 pp, 279mm by 216mm. "Dreiser is calm and his people are cautious and the whole is overlaid with the mild grace of Classical tragedy; but the Lewis tragedy is a Dionysian, crazy Faustian tragedy." With Kerouac's registration card from the course and the Professor's note attesting to the authenticity of the paper. P Dec 12 (100) $2,250

— Ms, Term paper on Thomas Wolfe. [1949]. 9 pp, 279mm by 216mm. With chipped & browned edges & tape repairs. With Kerouac's registration card, his examination book and Lenrow's note authenticating the material. P Dec 12 (106) $2,250

**ALs,** 26 Apr 1949. 1 p, 216mm by 152mm. To Elbert Lenrow. About Allen Ginsberg "...an important, perhaps great, young poet...". Browned. P Dec 12 (103) $2,000

**Ls s** (2), 28 Dec 1957 & 13 Jan 1958. 3 pp, 279mm by 216mm & 216mm by 140mm. To Elbert Lenrow. About Visions of Neal and On the Road. First letter is fragile and has a chipped right margin. P Dec 12 (108) $1,800

**Ls,** 28 June 1949. 3 pp, 356mm by 216mm. To Elbert Lenrow. About his work including On the Road. With some passages underlined in red ink. P Dec 12 (104) $2,500

— 28 Sept 1949. 1 p, 225mm by 149mm. To Elbert Lenrow. Concerning how Ginsberg has been confined to Columbia University Hospital for pyschiatric observation. Stained in margins. With some underlining in red ink. P Dec 12 (105) $1,300

**Autograph postcard, sgd,** 7 Feb 1949. 1 p, 83mm by 140mm. To Elbert Lenrow. About a trip west. Sgd as "John Kerouac". P Dec 12 (101) $900

### Kerr, Alfred, 1867-1948
**Typescript,** reflections on visiting an ocean steamer, [n.d.]. 1 p, 4to. Sgd. star Mar 21 (226) DM300

### Key, Francis Scott, 1779-1843
**Autograph Ms,** Receipt to Mr. Bevesky. 21 Oct 1817. 1 p, 4to. With show through tape repairs. Also with port. mtd & framed under glass in oval frame. Over-all size 20 by 24 inches. rms Oct 11 (225) $500

**ALs,** 20 Apr 1807. 6 pp, 4to. To Roger B. Taney. Discussing his professional prospects. P Dec 13 (204) $3,500

— 9 Apr 1840. 1 p, 7.5 by 12 inches. To Franklin Bache. Enclosing documents. Dar Oct 19 (121) $400

— 26 June 1840. 3 pp, 8.75 by 11 inches. To his son Charles. About his education. rs Nov 11 (27) $650

**ADs,** [n.d.]. 1 p, 1 by 8 inches. Ground in Georgetown assigned to Key & his heirs. Cut from larger document. Framed with sepia photo of a portrait. pba Feb 22 (196) $325

### Keynes family
**Autograph Ms,** Gem magazine, written & drawn by the children of the Keynes family, 1898. About 220 pp, 4to & 8vo, in 11 vols. With c.65 pp in whole or part by John Maynard Keynes. Contributors include Geoffrey & Margaret Keynes, their mother & children of neighboring families. With related material. pn Nov 9 (411) £2,800 [Quaritch]

### Keynes, John Maynard, 1st Baron, 1883-1946
**Ls,** 13 Jan 1927. 1 p, 4to. To A. R. Blanco. Discussing Board of Trade estimates for foreign profits. rms Mar 21 (289) $800

### Khrushchev, Nikita Sergeyevich, 1894-1971
**Ptd photograph,** sgd, [c.1960]. 185mm by 175mm; mtd. Bust port, by Sovfoto. Illus in cat. Marans collection. CE Apr 17 (147) $1,100

### Kiehtreiber, Albert Konrad, 1887-1973. See: Guetersloh, Albert Paris

**Kienzl, Wilhelm, 1857-1941**
**Autograph quotation,** 8 bars from his opera Der Evangelimann, scored for voice & piano, 28 Apr 1920. 1 p, 8vo. Sgd. star Mar 22 (888) DM450

**King, Martin Luther, 1929-68**
**Ls,** 2 Nov 1961. 1 p, 4to. To Robert Thomas of Northwestern University. Declining an offer to appear on the television program Your Right to Say It. sg Feb 1 (126) $2,400
**Autograph quotation,** [n.d.]. 1 p, 12mo. To Dr. Bernard Weinstein. With 2 photos, including a 1950s photo of a burning KKK cross. Over-all size 16 by 20 inches. Illus in cat rms Oct 11 (13) $1,350

**Kingdom Come**
[A publishing archive of the magazine Kingdom Come, 1939-43, sold at Phillips on 14 Mar 1996, lot 417, for £7,800] pn Mar 14 (417) £7,800

**Kinkel, Gottfried, 1815-82**
**Autograph Ms,** poem, Neujahrsgruss, [n.d.]. 7 pp, 8vo. Sgd at head. star Mar 22 (1378) DM480
**ALs,** 17 Apr 1873. 1 p, 8vo. To an unnamed Ed. Thanking for reviews & discussing a projected lecture in Moenchengladbach. star Mar 22 (1379) DM290

**Kipling, Rudyard, 1865-1936**
**ALs,** 20 Jan 1902. 2 pp, 8vo. To "Dear Stiassny". Regretting that recipient was unable to find the way to his house. star Mar 21 (228) DM300
— 4 July 1907. 2 pp, 8vo. To Mrs. Schofield. Sending condolences on the death of her husband, the original of Foxy in Stalky & Co. With related material. pn Mar 14 (410) £260
— 8 Dec 1916. 2 pp, 7 by 5 inches. To Mr. Bush. About military matters. Framed. Ck Nov 17 (97) £320
— 8 Jan 1923. 1 p, 12mo. To Mrs. Trevelyan. Agreeing to have a letter of his to her mother (Mrs. Humphry Ward) included in the biography she was writing. rms Oct 11 (226) $230
**Photograph, sgd,** [c.1925]. 198m by 152mm, mtd. Seated at a table, by Elliott & Fry. Illus in cat. Marans collection. CE Apr 17 (80) $1,200
**Signature,** [n.d.]. 12mo (card). Including subscription. Framed with a port. Illus in cat. rms June 6 (409) $250
See also: Clemens, Samuel Langhorne & Kipling

**Kirkpatrick, William**
**Collection** of 3 A Ls s & 1 Ls, Jan-Aug 1804. 11 pp, 4to. To Tobias Lear. Written from Malaga, Spain, during the reign of the Barbary Pirates. rms Nov 30 (94) $3,300

**Kirsch, Sarah**
**Autograph Ms,** story, Galoschen, 5 poems, & sketches for a short film, 1982 & 1983. 24 pp, 8vo, in stitched school notebook. Sgd on cover. star Mar 21 (229) DM1,700
**Autograph transcript,** poem, Maerz, [22 Apr 1986]. 1 p, 4to. 5 lines, sgd. HN May 15 (2617) DM240

**Klabund**
[A group of 6 A Ls s & 13 autograph postcards, sgd, 1912 to 1921, addressed to Klabund by various authors, sold at Hartung & Hartung on 17 Nov 1995, lot 3248, for DM850.]

**Kleber, Jean Baptiste, 1753-1800**
**Autograph endorsement,** sgd, [8 Jan 1797]. On a petition addressed to him, 3 pp, 4to; 11 lines granting a request for leave. star Mar 22 (1456) DM440

**Kleist von Nollendorf, Friedrich, Graf, 1762-1823**
**Ls,** 11 Feb 1806. 2 pp, 4to. Recipient unnamed. About the necessity of reforms in the army. star Mar 22 (1380) DM1,400

**Klemperer, Otto, 1885-1973.** See: Mahler, Gustav

**Kletke, Hermann, 1813-85**
**ALs,** 24 Jan 1844. 2 pp, 4to. To Hans Christian Andersen. Praising Andersen's works, & announcing a book of his own. star Mar 21 (6) DM340

**Klinger, Max, 1857-1920**
**ALs,** 20 Mar 1906. 2 pp, 8vo. Recipient unnamed. Inviting him & his wife to a concert at his house. star Mar 21 (675) DM500

**Knebel, Karl Ludwig von, 1744-1834**
**ALs,** 29 Dec 1797. 4 pp, folio. To Karl August Boettiger. Asking him to edit his notes to his trans of Propertius. star Mar 21 (141) DM650
— 4 Jan 1825. 1 p, 8vo. To Friedrich Theodor Kraeuter. Thanking for New Year's wishes. star Mar 21 (142) DM320

**Kneipp, Sebastian, 1821-97**
**Autograph Ms,** instructions for a patient taking a cure at Woerishofen, [c.Oct 1889]. 1 p, 16mo. star Mar 21 (526) DM1,100

**Knoderer, Hans, fl.1508**
**Ds,** 22 Feb 1508. 1 p, 8vo. Receipt for 2 guilders. star Mar 21 (676) DM1,200

**Knox, Henry, 1750-1806**
**Ms,** 28 Apr 1791. 1 p, folio. To Governor Ames Clinton of New York. About Native American Affairs. Illus in cat pba Feb 22 (197) $400

**Koch, Robert, 1843-1910**
**Autograph postcard, sgd,** 24 Jan 1883. To Dr. Krieger. Responding to a request for a remedy for book lice. star Mar 21 (527) DM2,200
**Photograph, sgd,** [c.1905]. 290mm by 224mm. Seated; by H. Fechner. Illus in cat. Marans collection. CE Apr 17 (49) $2,000

**Koenigsmarck, Hans Christoph, Graf von, 1600-63**
**Ls,** 20 Jan 1649. 1 p, folio. To the magistrate of an unnamed town. Ordering the payment of a contribution of 8,800 talers. Including receipt by his servant O. W. Lueders at bottom. star Mar 22 (1252) DM860

### Koerner, Anna Maria Jakobine, 1762-1843
ALs, 8 Jan 1837. 4 pp, 8vo. To Karoline Pichler. Introducing Carl Kuenzel, & reminiscing about old friends. star Mar 21 (236) DM800

### Koerner, Theodor, 1791-1813
Autograph Ms, poem, Ballade, & draft of a love poem, [n.d.]. 4 pp, 4to. 11 four-line stanzas, & 20 lines. star Mar 21 (234) DM2,000

### Koestler, Arthur, 1905-83
Series of 5 Ls s, 15 Jan 1972 to 19 Mar 1980. 5 pp, 4to. Recipient unnamed. Concering the German Ed of his novel The Call-Girls & other publication matters. star Mar 21 (237) DM260

### Kokoschka, Oskar, 1886-1980
ALs, 10 June 1966. 2 pp, 8vo. To Dr. Ludwig Goldschneider. Interpreting his port of Konrad Adenauer. star Mar 21 (677) DM8,000

Signature, [n.d.]. No size given. Mtd. With color print of his portrait of Tilla Durieux. pba Feb 22 (73) $130

### Kolb, Alois, 1875-1942. See: Strauss, Richard

### Kolb, Annette, 1870-1967
ALs, 20 Mar 1933. 2 pp, 4to. To Carl Jacob Burckhardt. Referring to the sale of her house & deploring the situation in Germany. star Mar 21 (232) DM750

### Kollmann, Albert, 1837-1915
Collection of 24 A Ls s & 2 autograph postcards, sgd, 1898 to 1913. 108 pp, 8vo & 4to. To Dr. Max Linde. Reporting about artists & the art scene in Berlin. HN May 15 (2622) DM2,700

### Kollwitz, Kaethe, 1867-1945
Collection of 5 A Ls s, 2 autograph postcards, sgd, & 2 A Ns s, 26 Feb 1934 to 2 Sept 1942. 12 pp, 4to & 8vo, & cards. To Dorothea Eskuchen. Concerning the care for a sick young lady, & news about family & friends. 1 ANs postscript on a letter from her husband. star Mar 21 (679) DM4,800

ALs, 18 Mar 1943. 2 pp, 8vo. To Mr. & Mrs. Diepolder. Referring to efforts to save her works after an air raid, & thanking for some eggs. star Mar 21 (680) DM1,200

Autograph postcard, sgd, 27 Aug 1928. To editors in Paris. Promising to send a woodcut. star Mar 21 (678) DM450

### Kopisch, August, 1799-1853
Autograph Ms, poem, Prolog zum 1 Maerz 1850; 1850. 1 p, folio. 26 lines, sgd. star Mar 21 (233) DM280

### Koran
— [Near East, late 8th cent]. Sura XXIX, vv.33 - 41. Single leaf, vellum, 302mm by 367mm. In elegant mashq script with diacritics in red & green. With diagonal dashes between verses. Def. Illus in cat. S Oct 18 (5) £6,000

— [Near East, Arabia?, 9th cent]. Sura XI, vv.10 - 21. Single leaf, vellum, 315mm by 414mm. In kufic script, with diacritics in red. With diagonal dashes & colored star or rectangle between verses. Frayed. Illus in cat. S Oct 18 (3) £5,500

— [Qairawan, 10th cent]. Sura XVIII, vv.85 - 87. Single leaf, vellum, 147mm by 204mm; framed. In gold kufic script. With gold florets with blue surround between verses. Illus in cat. S Oct 18 (16) £9,500

— [Cairo or Qairawan?, 11th cent]. Suras CXIII - CXIV. Single leaf, 340mm by 240mm. In eastern kufic script on buff paper. With colored circular devices between verses, sura heading in white on a panel of bold illumination extending into marginal palmette, & fully illuminated page on verso. Illus in cat. S Oct 18 (17) £15,000

— [Cairo or Qairawan?, 11th cent]. 52 leaves (composite section), 359mm by 234mm. Modern brown mor gilt. In eastern kufic script on thick brown paper. With illuminated roundels between verses, twenty verses marked with marginal illuminated roundel with verse count in gold kufic, sura headings in gold kufic on illuminated panels with stylised palmettes extending into margins, & fully illuminated page of bold foliate & geometric illumination. S Oct 18 (21) £65,000

— [Southern Spain or North Africa, c.1200]. 4 leaves only, vellum, 185mm by 195mm. In maghribi script, with diacritics in colors. With gold roundels between verses, & 10 verses marked with a gold pear-shaped device in margin. S Oct 18 (4) £500

— [North Africa or Southern Spain, c.1200]. Sura XVI, vv.1 - 11. 9 leaves only, vellum, 183mm by 155mm. In maghribi script, with diacritics in red, orange & blue. With gold florets between verses, 10 verses marked with gold roundel, & sura heading in gold kufic script with illuminated palmette extending into margin. S Oct 18 (7) £1,500

— [Southern Spain or North Africa, c.1200]. 17 leaves only, vellum, 168mm by 145mm, in later brown mor. In maghribi script, with diacritics in colors. With gold trefoil devices between verses. Worn. S Oct 18 (9) £1,000

— [North Africa or Southern Spain, c.13th cent]. Juz XVII only. 43 leaves, vellum, 165mm by 150mm, in modern red mor. In maghribi script, with diacritics in red, green & orange. With large illuminated roundels in margins, sura headings in gold kufic with illuminated palmette extending into margin, & opening page with large square panel of geometric illumination. S Oct 18 (8) £1,900

— [Spain, c.1300]. 69 leaves only, 180mm by 163mm. Blindstamped brown lea of c.1500. In maghribi script. With gold markers between verses, 2 sura headings in western kufic script, illuminated medallions in margins, & full-page & half-page of illumination. HH May 7 (99) DM38,000

# 1995 - 1996 · AUTOGRAPHS & MANUSCRIPTS — KORAN

— [Southern Spain or North Africa, c.1300]. Sura XCVI, v.15 - Sura XCVIII, v.5. Bifolium, vellum, 271mm by 263mm. In maghribi script, with diacritics in yellow, green & blue. With gold trefoil devices between verses & sura headings in large gold kufic script with extending palmette of intricate illumination. Illus in cat. S Oct 18 (1) £1,500

— [Southern Spain or North Africa, c.1300]. Sura LXXX, v.38 - Sura LXXXI, v.9. Single leaf, vellum, 269mm by 261mm. In maghribi script, with diacritics in yellow, green & blue. With gold trefoil devices between verses & sura heading in large gold kufic script with extending palmette of intricate illumination. Illus in cat. S Oct 18 (2) £1,600

— [Egypt, c.1300-50]. Sura XXIX, v.46 - Sura XXXI, v.23. 28 leaves, 306mm by 215mm. Def stamped contemp brown mor covers, rebacked. In gold muhaqqaq script on thick cream paper. With illuminated roundels between verses, large illuminated roundels in margins, sura headings in white ornamental kufic script on illuminated rectangular panels with a marginal palmette, finely illuminated shamsa, & double page of fine illumination. S Oct 18 (25) £24,000

— [Mamluk, c.1350]. 268 leaves, 364mm by 276mm. Modern stamped brown mor. In muhaqqaq script on thick cream paper. With gold rosettes between verses & sura headings in gold with blue diacritics. Opening double page of illumination damaged & repaired. S Oct 18 (14) £3,500

— [Egypt or Syria, c.1400]. 30 leaves only, 292mm by 202mm. Blindstamped contemp lea gilt. In muhaqqaq script on pink paper. With significant words in gold, headings in white thuluth, gold rosettes between verses, marginal medallions in gold & colors, & full-page & double page of fine illumination. HH May 7 (100) DM15,000

— [Persia, c.1420-30]. 487 leaves, 212mm by 141mm. Later brown mor gilt. In fine muhaqqaq script on buff paper. With gold roundels between verses, further textual divisions in margins & sura headings in gold thuluth. Opening double page remargined with 19th cent Ottoman illumination. S Oct 18 (18) £2,400

— [Persia, A.H. 890/ A.D. 1485]. 363 leaves (1 missing), 185mm by 117mm. Contemp blindstamped red-brown lea. In naskhi script, with commentary by Sidi Mohammad bin Abdullah. With gold dots between verses, sura headings in white or gold thuluth, illuminated borders throughout & full page of illumination. HH May 7 (86) DM5,000

— [Ottoman, late 15th cent]. Sura VI. 29 leaves (1 blank), 240mm by 158mm, in red mor with stamped central medallions. In naskhi script on cream paper. With gold discs between verses, illuminated headpiece, & marginal inscr attributing calligraphy to Hamdullah. S Oct 18 (23) £1,300

— [Turkey or Persia, c.1500]. 212 leaves (incomplete), 292mm by 183mm, in lea bdg. In naskhi script, with sura headings in red thuluth. Repaired. HH May 7 (87) DM750

— [Persia, early 16th cent]. Suras I, VI, XVIII, XXXIV & XXXV. 50 leaves, 250mm by 160mm. Modern brown mor gilt. In black & gold muhaqqaq & naskhi scripts. With sura headings in white thuluth on illuminated panels of foliate motifs, illuminated circular devices in margins, double page of fine illumination, & fictitious colophon of Yaqut al-Musta'simi dated A.H.690/A.D.1291. S Oct 18 (20) £3,000

— [Ottoman, 1st half of 16th cent]. 28 leaves only, 357mm by 240mm. Contemp lea richly gilt with colored lea onlay. In elegant muhaqqaq script with diacritics in black & 2 sura headings in gold thuluth. With double page of fine illumination in colors & gold. HH Nov 14 (98) DM13,000

— [Persia, 16th cent]. 306 leaves, 227mm by 140mm. 19th cent floral lacquer bdg. In naskhi script by Abdallah ibn Sultan Muhammad Harawi. With gold florets between verses, illuminated devices in margins, sura headings in gold thuluth, & double page of fine illumination. S Oct 18 (19) £2,800

— [Ottoman, A.H. 1131/ A.D. 1718]. 388 leaves, 162mm by 1055mm. Contemp brown mor gilt. In naskhi script on cream paper by Ibrahim Kamali. With gold roundels between verses, sura headings in white on finely illuminated panels, & double page of illumination. S Oct 18 (28) £2,400

— [Mughal, A.H. 1146/ A.D. 1733]. 547 leaves (12 blank), 280mm by 170mm. Contemp brown mor covered with finely stamped foliate motifs in gold & colors. In naskhi script on gold-sprinkled paper. With interlinear gold decoration throughout, gold roundels between verses, marginal bands of scrolling leaves in red & gold, sura headings in white on finely illuminated panels, & 7 double pages of fine illumination. S Oct 18 (26) £17,000

— [Afghanistan, 18th cent]. 598 leaves, 125mm by 75mm. Contemp lea gilt. In naskhi script on gold panels. With sura headings in white thuluth, gold, red & black dots between verses, numerous illuminated roundels in margins, & 8 double pages of illumination. Worn; repaired. HH May 7 (94) DM1,200

— [China, 18th cent]. Juz IV. 47 leaves, 220mm by 173mm. Brown mor with stamped Chinese motifs. In sini script on thick buff paper. With sura heading in red & opening & closing double pages with panels of foliate decoration. S Oct 18 (13) £1,800

— [Ottoman, A.H. 1172/ A.D. 1758]. 256 leaves, 36mm by 36mm, octagonal. Unbound, in silver casket. In ghubari script on thin paper. With gold dots between verses, sura headings in red on gold ground, & double page of illumination. S Oct 18 (31) £1,900

— [South East Asia, Malaysia?, A.H. 1200/ A.D. 1785]. 433 leaves, 350mm by 219mm. Brown mor with stamped paper onlay. In naskhi script by Salih al-Hafiz al-Malawi. With gold roundels between verses, sura headings in red, double page of foliate illumination, & numerous ownership inscriptions on flyleaves. S Oct 18 (22) £2,500

# KORAN

— [Kashmir, A.H. 1213/ A.D. 1798]. 416 leaves, 160mm by 98mm. Contemp floral lacquer bdg. In naskhi script, with interlinear Persian trans in red nasta'liq. With gold dots between verses, sura headings in white thuluth on gold grounds, & double page of illumination. HH May 7 (93) DM4,000

— [Ottoman, c.1800]. 256 leaves (1 blank), 161mm by 110mm. Contemp red-brown lea gilt. In naskhi script. With gold dots between verses, sura headings on gold panels, numerous illuminated roundels in margins, 2 illuminated vignettes & double page of illumination. HH May 7 (95) DM2,200

— [Indonesia or Borneo?, c.1800]. About 180 leaves, 407mm by 300mm. Wooden covers. In Brunawi script on coarse paper. With red roundels between verses, sura headings in red, & 3 double pages of elaborate border decoration. Many leaves bound upside down. S Oct 18 (24) £4,500

— [Persia, c.1800]. Scroll, 336cm by 6cm, in fitted ivory box. In ghubari script in panels & letterforms making up larger thuluth script of pious phrases. With gold rules between panels, 2 sura headings in larger script in red & black, & illuminated headpiece. S Oct 18 (30) £2,600

— [Ottoman, A.H. 1222/ A.D. 1808/09]. 294 leaves, 14.5cm by 10cm, in new cloth bdg. In naskhi script on polished paper by Mehmed Emin bin 'Osman. With marginal decorations in gold & colors & double page of illumination. JG Sept 29 (328) DM950

— [Ottoman, A.H. 1245/ A.D. 1829]. 152 leaves, 173mm by 109mm. Contemp brown mor gilt. In naskhi script by Yusuf Rifa'at. With illuminated florets between verses, sura headings in white on illuminated panels, & double page of illumination. Illuminated by Muhammad ibn Muhammad ibn Ahmad. S Oct 18 (27) £2,800

— [Qajar, A.H. 1249/ A.D. 1833]. 389 leaves, 321mm by 202mm. Contemp floral lacquer bdg. In naskhi script on burnished paper by Bint Shah Umm Salma, with interlinear Persian trans in red. With gold florets between verses, marginal glosses in nasta'liq, illuminated devices in margins, & double page of fine illumination. S Oct 18 (33) £7,000

— [Qajar, 19th cent]. Scroll, 506cm by 8cm. In 3 columns of ghubari script, with further pious phrases in thuluth & nasta'liq scripts. With sura headings in red, illuminated headpiece & lea endpiece. S Oct 18 (29) £1,900

— [Kandahar, A.H. 1269/ A.D. 1853]. 1110 pp, 240mm by 150mm. Contemp red lea gilt. In black naskhi script, with commentary throughout in red. With sura headings in blue or green thuluth on gold panels, numerous illuminated medallions in margins, & double page of illumination. HH May 7 (98) DM7,000

— [Qajar, A.H. 1310/ A.D. 1892]. 334 leaves, 243mm by 161mm. Contemp floral lacquer bdg. In naskhi script on polished paper by Muhammad Ali Al-Khurasani, at the instance of Prince Muhammad Taqi Mirza Rukn al-Daulah. With decorated gold rosettes between verses, sura headings in red on illuminated panels, marginal commentary in black nasta'liq, illuminated marginal devices throughout, & 2 double pages of fine illumination. S Oct 18 (34) £6,000

— [Turkey or Levant, c.1900]. 6 leaves only, 368mm by 251mm. Modern brown mor. In fine gold diwani jali script. With elaborate illuminated floral devices at beginning & end. S Oct 18 (32) £4,800

### Korngold, Erich Wolfgang, 1897-1957
Collection of ALs & autograph quotation, 10 Jan 1928. 2 pp, 4to & 8vo. To Hans Zesewitz. Referring to a performance of his new opera, & sending a musical quotation (included, sgd). star Mar 22 (889) DM540

Korolev, Sergei G. See: Gagarin, Yuri & Korolev

### Kosciuszko, Tadeusz, 1746-1817
ALs, 14 Mar 1815. 2 pp, 4to. To Henry Brougham. Expressing his wish for the independence of Poland. In French. P Dec 13 (207) $3,750

### Kossuth, Lajos, 1802-94
ALs, 23 Oct 1852. 1 p, 8vo. To Alexander Ireland. Introducing a Hungarian artist. With a photograph. rms Mar 21 (308) $250

Ls, 12 Jan 1852. 4 pp, 4to. To President Millard Fillmore. Letter of departure from the United States. With a photo. rms Nov 30 (212) $550

Cut signature, 27 Feb 1850. On 8.25 by 3.5 inch piece of paper. Sgd as "Louis Kossuth/Gouverneur de la Hongrie". Dar Oct 19 (123) $75

### Kotzebue, August von, 1761-1819
ALs, 8 Mar 1803. 1 p, 4to. To Friederike Lohmann. Concerning a review of her novel in his journal Der Freimuethige. star Mar 21 (238a) DM660

— 14 Apr 1804. 1 p, 4to. To [Johann Wilhelm von Archenholz]. Requesting him to print a statement correcting some "silly rumours" in his journal Minerva. star Mar 21 (238b) DM1,000

### Kreisler, Fritz, 1875-1962
Photograph, sgd, [n.d.]. 5 by 7.75 inch bust pose sepia photo. sg Sept 28 (148) $100

### Krenek, Ernst, 1900-91
ALs, 14 May 1933. 1 p, 4to. To Paul Aron. Discussing possibilities for emigration. star Mar 22 (890a) DM750

### Kreutzer, Konradin, 1780-1849
ALs, 11 July 1815. 2 pp, 4to. To [Count Dillen?]. Reminding him of fees due to him. star Mar 22 (891) DM1,700

— 4 - 16 May 1826. 1 p, 4to. To Friedrich Kind. Doubting that an opera about Das Kaethchen von Heilbronn will be a success in Vienna at this time. Illus in cat. star Mar 22 (892) DM1,700

— 17 May 1838. 3 pp, 4to. To Martin Blessing. About the closing of his theater because of financial problems, & discussing the adaptation of compositions for barrel organs. star Mar 22 (893) DM1,700

— 15 Dec 1844. 6 pp, 8vo & 16mo. To Giacomo Meyerbeer. Inquiring about a position in Berlin. star Mar 22 (894) DM1,200

— 2 June [1846]. 3 pp, 4to. To the conductor Ott. About concerts in Graz & his daughter, who is an opera singer. HN Nov 24 (2809) DM920

**Krolow, Karl**
**Autograph Ms,** poem, Erwachen, 14 Jan 1988. 1 p, 8vo. 12 lines, sgd. star Mar 21 (240) DM220

**Kropotkin, Petr Alekseevich, Prince, 1842-1921**
**ALs,** 1 Dec 1910. 1 p, 8vo. Recipient unnamed. Sending a receipt. star Mar 22 (1381) DM280

**Kruenitz, Johann Georg, 1728-96**
**ALs,** 11 Dec 1750. 2 pp, 4to. To [J. J. Wippel]. Praising the program of recipient's school. star Mar 21 (528) DM550

**Kruger, Stephanus Johannes Paulus ("Oom Paul"), 1825-1904**
**Ds,** 30 Aug 1898. 1 p, folio. Confirmation of property at Christiana issued to Marthinus Christoffel van Niekerk. star Mar 22 (1382) DM320

**Photograph,** sgd, [c.1900]. 225mm by 160mm, mtd. Seated, by Ebner. Illus in cat. Marans collection. CE Apr 17 (148) $400

**Krupp, Friedrich Alfred, 1854-1902**
**Ls,** 4 Apr 1879. 1 p, 8vo. To a society of artists at Duesseldorf. Concerning the renewal of his ticket of admission. HN Nov 24 (2813) DM200

**Krusenstern, Adam Johann von, 1770-1846**
**ALs,** 15 Sept 1817. 1 p, 4to. To [Friedrich Theodor von Schubert]. Informing him that he has received Otto von Kotzebue's papers, & referring to a discovery in Alaska. star Mar 21 (529) DM1,300

**Kubin, Alfred, 1877-1959**
[A group of 5 A Ls s, Ls & 6 autograph postcards, sgd, addressed to Kubin by various artists & authors, 1921 to 1924, sold at Hartung & Hartung on 24 Nov 1995, lot 3284, for DM500.]

**Collection** of ALs & 4 autograph postcards, sgd, 1918. 1 p, 4to, & cards. To Max & Irene Heberle. About various matters. HH Nov 17 (3251) DM420

— Collection of ALs & 6 autograph postcards, sgd, 1919. Length not stated. To Max & Irene Heberle. About meetings, the political situation, an exhibition, etc. HH Nov 17 (3253) DM750

— Collection of ALs & 2 autograph postcards, sgd, 1924. Length not stated. To Max & Irene Heberle. Suggesting a meeting, etc. HH Nov 17 (3259) DM320

— Collection of 2 A Ls s & 2 autograph postcards, sgd, 1927. Length not stated. To Max & Irene Heberle. About a visit to his parental home, birthday celebrations, etc. With related material. HH Nov 17 (3265) DM400

**ALs,** 15 May 1919. 1 p, 4to. To Max Heberle. Sending Oswald Spengler's Der Untergang des Abendlandes. HH Nov 17 (3254) DM340

— 2 Dec 1921. 2 pp, folio. To Max & Irene Heberle. Reporting from Berlin. HH Nov 17 (3257) DM420

— [1921]. 2 pp, 8vo. To Max & Irene Heberle. Describing his holiday resort. HH Nov 17 (3256) DM320

— [June 1924]. 2 pp, 8vo. To Max & Irene Heberle. Postponing a visit because of fish poisoning. Including pen-&-ink sketch. Illus in cat. HH Nov 17 (3260) DM850

— [30 Nov 1924]. 1 p, 4to. To an unnamed professor. Thanking for a pen. HH Nov 17 (3277) DM200

— 14 Jan 1926. 2 pp, 8vo. To Max & Irene Heberle. Asking for a special Ed of a journal. HH Nov 17 (3264) DM350

— 10 Oct 1926. 2 pp, folio. Recipient unnamed. Describing his work Daemone und Nachtgesichte, & making plans for anr publication. Including small sketch. HH Nov 17 (3278) DM600

— 5 Mar 1927. 2 pp, 4to. To Irene Heberle. Referring to a forthcoming exhibition in Munich & asking her to forward some sketches. star Mar 21 (681) DM360

— 5 Apr 1927. 2 pp, folio. To Max & Irene Heberle. About his birthday celebrations. Including pen-&-ink sketch. Illus in cat. HH Nov 17 (3266) DM1,000

— 10 July 1927. 1 p, folio. To Max & Irene Heberle. Discussing Georg Brandes's work Voltaire. HH Nov 17 (3267) DM260

— 21 May 1928. 2 pp, folio. To Irene Heberle. Thanking for congratulations & referrring to her husband's death. HH Nov 17 (3268) DM600

— [18 Apr 1929]. 3 pp, folio & 8vo. To Irene Heberle. Sending news about his family, some friends, & his work. HH Nov 17 (3269) DM500

— 17 Jan 1933. 2 pp, 4to. To Irene Heberle. About his work, personal matters, & the future. HH Nov 17 (3271) DM750

— 10 Oct 1934. 2 pp, 8vo. To Irene Heberle. About his current work. HH Nov 17 (3272) DM400

— 24 Feb 1942. 1 p, size not stated. To Herr Hessel. Thanking for reviews & information. Illus in cat. JG Sept 29 (277) DM400

**Series** of 4 autograph postcards, sgd, 1920 & 1921. To Max & Irene Heberle. Reporting from his travels. HH Nov 17 (3255) DM370

— Series of 7 autograph postcards, sgd, 1922 & 1923. To Max & Irene Heberle. About a variety of matters. HH Nov 17 (3258) DM700

— Series of 8 autograph postcards, sgd, 1925. To Max & Irene Heberle. About a variety of matters. HH Nov 17 (3261) DM650

— Series of 10 autograph postcards, sgd, & 3 A Ns s, 1926. Length not stated. To Max & Irene Heberle. About various matters. Including pen-&-ink sketch. HH Nov 17 (3263) DM1,100

**Autograph postcards (2),** sgd, 1930 & 1932. To Irene Heberle. About various matters. With related material. HH Nov 17 (3270) DM800

**Autograph postcard, sgd,** 22 Dec 1918. To Irene Heberle. Making plans for a visit. Including pen-&-ink sketch. Illus in cat. HH Nov 17 (3252) DM900

— 4 July 1919. To Horst Stobbe. Inquiring about some works that recipient sent to him. Including pen-&-ink sketch. Illus in cat. HH Nov 17 (3274) DM800

— 27 Dec 1920. To Herr Schranzhofer. Thanking for recipient's work. HH Nov 17 (3275) DM200

— [20 Apr 1925]. To Max & Irene Heberle. Complaining about the rain. Including pen-&-ink sketch. Illus in cat. HH Nov 17 (3262) DM1,400

**Kuenneke, Eduard, 1885-1953**
**Autograph quotation,** opening bars of his song Ich bin nur ein armer Wandergesell, 10 Mar 1934. 1 p, 8vo. Sgd. star Mar 22 (896) DM600

**Kuernberger, Ferdinand, 1821-79**
**Series** of 4 A Ls s, 15 May to 18 Nov 1863. 12 pp, 8vo. To Heinrich Laube. About a performance of his play Catilina in Vienna. star Mar 21 (242) DM900

**Kunert, Guenter**
**Autograph Ms,** poem, Fensterblicke II, [21 Nov 1990]. 1 p, 4to. Draft; sgd. HN May 15 (2624) DM300

# L

**La Roche, Georg Michael Frank von, 1720-88**
**ALs,** 4 Nov 1782. 3 pp, folio. To Johann Heinrich Merck. Referring to family matters, old age, his scientific interests, etc. star Mar 21 (12) DM3,000

**La Valette, Louis de Norgaret de, Cardinal, 1593-1639**
**ALs,** 26 Apr 1635. 3 pp, folio. To Cardinal Richelieu. Concerning the fortification of Metz. star Mar 22 (1289) DM420

**Lachenmann, Helmut**
**Autograph music,** fragment of Les Consolations, in full score, 15 Oct 1977. 3 pp, folio. Sgd & inscr at head. star Mar 22 (898) DM520

**Lachner, Franz, 1803-90**
**ALs,** 12 Dec 1852. 2 pp, 4to. To [Ferdinand David]. Discussing a performance of his new symphony in Leipzig. star Mar 22 (899) DM240

**Laemmle, Carl, 1867-1939**
**Ls,** 14 June 1932. 1 p, 4to. To Forest J. Ackerman. About the film The Doomed Battalion. Illus in cat pba Feb 22 (74) $375

**Lafayette, Gilbert du Motier, Marquis de, 1757-1834**
[A collection of letters & documents relating to the administration & sale of Lafayette's lands in Louisiana, sold at Sotheby's New York on 3 June 1980, lot 957, for $2,100 and at Christie's New York on 26 Jan 1996, lot 185, for $11,000.]

**Autograph Ms,** expression of gratitude to members of both houses of the Pennsylvania Legislature. [1824] 1 p, 8vo. sg Feb 1 (127) $1,400

**ALs,** [6 Mar 1779]. 1 p, 8vo. To Benjamin Franklin. Forwarding a letter concerning Mr. Blodget's wish to visit Paris. P Dec 13 (208) $5,500

— [8 July 1781]. 2 pp, 8vo. To George Washington. Announcing that Cornwallis seems to have given up the conquest of Virginia; reports on his troops. Docketed by Jared Sparks. Illus in cat pn June 13 (223) £12,000

— 9 July 1803. 2 pp, 4to. To Charles James Fox. About the purchase of the Louisiana Territory, & introducing James Monroe. Repaired. Sang collection. P Dec 13 (210) $3,750

— 10 Mar 1811. 1 p, 8vo. In English. To "Monsieur Charge d'affair des etats unis." Forwarding a package (not present). CE Sept 27 (14) $450

— 18 Nov 1828. 4 pp, 4to. To Jeremy Bentham. Discussing his retirement, a general system of national guards & state militia, & the issue of impeachment. P Dec 13 (211) $2,500

— 27 Sept 1830. 1 p, 4to. Recipient unnamed. Answering inquiries about the the slave trade. Sang collection. P Dec 13 (212) $2,750

— [n.d.]. 2 pp, 4to. To General Henry Dearborn. Expressing his gratitutude for a land grant in Louisiana made to him by Congress. Foxed. Sang - Engelhard collections. Illus in cat CNY Jan 26 (180) $12,000

**ANs,** 6 Sept 1825. 1 p, 92mm by 148mm. To Elizabeth Coombs Adams. Sending thanks for birthday greetings. CE June 12 (69) $500

**ADs,** 30 Aug 1781. 2 pp, folio. In the hand of James McHenry. To Col. William Davie. About the plans to trap Cornwallis. CNY Jan 26 (154) $4,500

**Ds,** Jan 1805. 4 pp, folio. Power of attorney to James Madison & James Monroe to dispose of the lands granted to him by Congress. With document in a secretarial hand listing Lafayette's assets & expenses before 1792. Illus in cat. rms June 6 (408) $4,500

**Lagerkvist, Par Fabian, 1891-1974**
**ALs,** 24 June 1951. On 3.5 by 5 inch card. To Professor Gustafson. About his work: "...it is impossible to procure for you some of my earliest books, because they are costly and hard to find. Some of them I don't own myself..." With transcription in Swedish, English translation, a history of the letter & typed notes. sg Sept 28 (149) $300

**Lagerlof, Selma, 1858-1940**
**Autograph Ms,** autobiographical essay, [c.1910]. 2 pp, 4to & folio. Sgd at head & in text. star Mar 21 (244a) DM950

— Autograph Ms, poem entitled Pa Fred[e]riksborg. [n.d.]. 4 pp, 8vo. With holograph corrections. Separated at folds. Paper discolored. sg Sept 28 (151) $225

**ALs,** 22 July 1935. 1 p, on a 3.5 by 5 inch card. To Professor Gustafson. Thanking him for kind words: "...your letter came as a great encouragment. It pleased me that you have paid special attention to my little confession of faith in the story..." Soiled, worn & creased. With typed transcription in Swedish,

English translation & history of the letter. sg Sept 28 (150) $200

**Lam, Wilfredo**
**Ls,** 15 Nov 1966. 1 p, 4to. To Varian Fry. About a lithograph he is making for the Rescue Committee. sg June 6 (108) $300

**Lamarck, Jean Baptiste de, 1744-1829**
**ALs,** [10 Oct 1800]. 1 p, 4to. Recipient unnamed. Inviting him to a meeting. star Mar 21 (532) DM360

**Lamb, Charles, 1775-1834**
**ALs,** 10 Aug 1822. 1 p, 4to. Recipient unnamed. Asking that John Skelton be given a licence to drive a Hackney Coach. pn Nov 9 (448) £420

**Lamb, William, 2d Viscount Melbourne, 1779-1848**
**Series** of 4 A Ls s, 28 Apr to 9 Nov 1831. 7 pp, 4to. To the Lord Mayor of London. About unrest in London, the King's visit, etc. rms June 6 (389) $350

**Langen, Albert, 1869-1909**
**ALs,** 13 May 1896. 2 pp, 4to. To Hermann Bahr. Enlisting his help in protesting against the Austrian confiscation of the 1st Ed of the journal Simplicissimus. HH Nov 17 (3318) DM240

**Langhans, Carl Gotthard, 1733-1808**
**Ds,** 17 July 1793. 1 p, folio. Pass for the transportation of materials for some royal buildings in Berlin. Also sgd by others. star Mar 21 (682) DM1,600

**Langtry, Lillie, 1852-1929**
**Series** of c.50 A Ls s, [n.d.]. About 270 pp, 8vo. To Arthur Henry Jones. Love letters. S July 11 (301) £6,200

**Lanza, Mario, 1921-59**
**Photograph, sgd & inscr,** [n.d.]. Folio. Bust-length pose, inscr to Andy Roy. rms June 6 (152) $550

**Laplace, Pierre Simon de, Marquis, 1749-1827**
**ALs,** 20 Oct [1815]. 2 pp, 8vo. To an unnamed colleague. Concerning the use of probability calculus. star Mar 21 (533) DM570

**Larkin, Philip, 1922-85**
**Autograph Ms,** listing 4 words & their definitions for the Dictionary Game, initialled. 1 p, 4to. With a photograph of Larkin by Ann Thwaite & a related note by Ann & Anthony Thwaite. S Dec 18 (407) £320 [Mandl]
**Collection** of 4 A Ls s, 13 Ls s, 1 Letter & 1 autograph postcard, sgd, 27 Mar 1963 to 21 Mar 1985. To Patrick Garland. Mainly about the making of a BBC Television Monitor documentary. With carbon copies of 2 of Garland's letters to Larkin. "Nearly all unpublished." S July 11 (303) £3,600

**Larkin, Rachel.** See: Larkin, Thomas Oliver & Larkin

**Larkin, Thomas Oliver**
**Ds,** 28 Apr 1848. 2 pp, on 15 by 20 inch leaf folded to 15 by 10. Sale of a parcel of land in San Francisco by Larkin's half-brother John B. R. Cooper & his wife Encarnacion Vallejo Cooper to Andrew Jackson McDuffee. Sgd by the Coopers, Larkin, Walter Colton & Moses Schallenberger. Larson collection pba Feb 12 (376) $800

**Larkin, Thomas Oliver —&**
**Larkin, Rachel**
**Ds,** 9 Feb 1849. 4 pp, 12.5 by 7.5 inches. Sale by the Larkins of land in Benecia to C. V. Gillespie. Sgd by both Larkins, P. K. Woodside, Moses Schallenberger & Milton Sittler & by Monterey Alcalde Florncio Serrano. pba July 25 (309) $750

**Larned, Simon, 1753?-1817**
**ALs,** 22 Oct 1781. 4 pp, 8vo. To his brother. Describing the Battle of Eutaw Springs. P Dec 13 (16) $3,250

**Lasker-Schueler, Else, 1869-1945**
**Autograph Ms,** poem, Charlotte Bara [ptd as Die Taenzerin Wally]; [n.d.]. 2 pp, 4to. 11 lines, sgd & inscr to [Carl] Ruetters. Illus in cat. star Mar 21 (245a) DM5,500
**ALs,** 3 Apr 1926. 1 p, 4to. To Mechtilde Lichnowski. About her husband's illness, & inquiring about a loan. C Nov 29 (156) £950

**Lassalle, Ferdinand, 1825-64**
**ALs,** 16 July 1859. 8 pp, 8vo. To his brother-in-law Ferdinand Friedlaender. Discussing recipient's marital problems & financial matters. star Mar 22 (1386) DM1,600
— 24 May 1861. 1 p, 8vo. To [his niece Elise Friedlaender]. Reprimanding her for failing to keep a secret. star Mar 22 (1387) DM450
— [n.d.]. 3 pp, 4to. To his parents. About his need to feel loved. star Mar 22 (1388) DM800

**Laue, Max von, 1879-1960**
**Collection** of 3 Ls s & Ns, 1953 to 19 July 1954. 5 pp, mostly folio. To Rolf Hosemann. Commenting on recipient's work, expressing thanks, etc. With related Ls, draft. star Mar 21 (534) DM6,500

**Laurel, Stan, 1890-1965**
**ALs,** 24 Nov 1956. 1 p, 6 by 3.5 inches. To unnamed recipient. Concerning a reporter: "I really don't know how this reporter figured that Mr. Hardy made that statement, due to the fact that Mr. Hardy's speech was affected & he is unable to talk yet..." On his personal note card. Dar Oct 19 (127) $170
**Ls,** 14 June 1957. 1 p, 6 by 9 inches. To unnamed recipient. About his films being run on television: "The way they cut the films now to make room for the commercial ads sure ruins them & makes them uninteresting..." Dar Oct 19 (126) $350
— 8 July 1959. 1 p, 8 by 10 inches. To unnamed recipient. About the 3 Stooges & Ted Healey: "I met the original boys many times - two of them have since passed on. I was a very good friend of the late Ted Healey who discovered them & gave them their start in the business..." Dar Oct 19 (128) $300

## LAUREL

**Autograph postcard, sgd,** 24 Sept 1956. 1 p, 5.5 by 3.25 inches. To unnamed recipient. Thanking the recipient for a letter: "your kind thoughts & wishes for Mr. Hardy were deeply appreciated. Pleased to tell you he is slowly improving..." Spotted. Dar Oct 19 (125) $130

### Laurel, Stan, 1890-1965 —& Hardy, Oliver, 1892-1957

**Photograph, sgd,** 25 Aug 1947 & 6 Sept 1947. Showing them arriving at Coventry railway station accompanied by their wives. Sgd by both in ink. Ck Dec 14 (235) £280

— Anr, [n.d.]. Postcard sgd. Sgd in ink. Ck Dec 14 (231) £130

— Anr, [n.d.]. 5 by 7 inches. Sgd in margin in blue ink. Ck Dec 14 (233) £160

**Photograph, sgd & inscr,** [n.d.]. Inscr by Laurel to Odette & sgd by both in blue ink. Ck Dec 14 (234) £120

— Anr, [n.d.]. Oblong 12mo. Both sgd in blue ink in bottom margin. with "Hello Daphne!" at top, probably in Laurel's hand. wa Oct 28 (454) $600

### Laurens, Henry, 1724-92

**Collection** of ALs & Ls, 17 Feb & 13 July 1792. 2 pp, 4to. To Samuel Johnston. Discussing a financial settlement. P Dec 13 (216) $1,600

**ALs,** 11 May 1778. 1 p, folio. To Caesar Rodney. Sending a ptd proclamation of Congress concerning the conduct of armed vessels (included). P Dec 13 (214) $4,000

— 13 Sept 1778. 1 p, 4to. To Brigadier General William Maxwell. Asking for information about 6'6'the Number & strength of the whole naval power of Great Britain on this Continent from New York to Hallifax..." Dampstained. With worn edges. CNY Dec 15 (84) $2,400

**ADs,** 16 Oct 1778. 1 p, 4to. Fair copy of a congressional resolution concerning the use of flags of truce by British Commissioners. P Dec 13 (215) $2,750

### Lavater, Johann Kaspar, 1741-1801

**Autograph Ms,** Vermischte physiognomische Regeln, 1789. 102 leaves, 8vo, in lea box. Including illusts. HN May 15 (2628) DM8,000

**ALs,** 18 Feb 1767. 2 pp, 4to. To Johann Georg Zimmermann. Inquiring about a position for Pestalozzi, & discussing his family & other authors. Illus in cat. star Mar 21 (245b) DM5,500

— 18 Aug 1790. 2 pp, 8vo. To M. de Pougens. Giving some brief physiognomical judgments. S May 15 (194) £400

### Law, John, 1671-1729

**Ls,** 14 Jan 1720. 1 p, folio. Recipient unnamed. Thanking for congratulations on his recent appointment. star Mar 21 (535) DM2,200

### Lawrence, David Herbert, 1885-1930

**Collection** of 29 A Ls s & 11 autograph postcards sgd, 10 Feb 1913 to 30 Jan 1930. 80 pp plus postcards. To his sister-in-law, Dr. Else Jaffe-Richthofen. Partly in German. Illus in cat P June 5 (287) $17,000

**Series** of 9 A Ls s. [1928] to 23 Dec 1929. 20 pp, 4to & 8vo. To Rhys Davies. pba Mar 7 (161) $9,500

### Lawrence, Frieda, 1879-1956

**ALs,** "Friday"[c.1932]. 3 pp, 4to. To Desmond Hawkins. Recalling her anger towards D. H. Lawrence for loving humanity more than her. Sgd with initials. S July 11 (289) £500

### Lawrence, Sir Thomas, 1769-1830

**ALs,** 25 Nov 1824. 1 p, 4to. To his sister. Informing her of his nephew's arrival at Madeira & stating that he cannot eat the goodies she sent. rms June 6 (313) $100

### Lawrence, Thomas Edward, 1888-1935

**ALs,** 9 Jan 1919. 2 pp. To B. E. Leeson. Announcing his departure for the Paris Peace Conference. Sgd "TELawrence". pn Mar 14 (392) £3,400 [Irani]

— 9 Jan 1919. 2 pp, 4to. To B. E. Leeson. About the "Arab Adventure," his resulting self-disgust, early drafts of The Seven Pillars of Wisdom, the press & his reasons for changing his name. Sgd "J. H. Ross". pn Mar 14 (393) £5,800 [Irani]

— 16 Feb 1923. 1 p, 4to. To B. E. Leeson. Refusing to write an account of the "Arab Show"; eulogises his motor bicycle. Sgd "JR". pn Mar 14 (394) £3,800 [Irani]

— 28 Sept 1923. 2 pp, 8vo. To B. E. Leeson. Congratulating him on his engagement but not on his choice of transport. Sgd "R". pn Mar 14 (395) £3,600 [Irani]

— 30 Dec 1925. 1 p, 4to. To B. E. Leeson. Promising him a copy of The Seven Pillars of Wisdom & informing him of his new persona as Shaw. Sgd "TES". pn Mar 14 (396) £2,300 [Irani]

— 23 June 1927. 2 pp, 4to. To B. E. Leeson. About Seven Pillars of Wisdom & his being stationed in India. pn Mar 14 (397) £3,400 [Irani]

— 1 Apr 1929. 2 pp, 4to. To B. E. Leeson. Saying that he should have sold is copy of The Seven Pillars of Wisdom "in the boom years"; dreads the prospect of a film on his life. Sgd "TEShaw". pn Mar 14 (398) £4,600 [Irani]

— 18 Apr 1929. 1 p, 4to. To B. E. Leeson. Discounting newspaper rumors about him; defends his attitude towards women. Sgd "TES". pn Mar 14 (398A) £3,800 [Irani]

— 11 Oct 1929. 1 p, folio. To B. E. Leeson. Describing his recent life. Sgd "T.E.S." pn Mar 14 (399) £3,400 [Irani]

— 8 Jan 1930. 2 pp, 4to. To B. E. Leeson. Anticipating the manner of his death. Sgd "TEShaw". pn Mar 14 (400) £4,600 [Irani]

— 15 Jan 1932. 2 pp, 4to. To Flight Lieutenant Beauforte-Greenwood. Discussing his progress on motor boat engines. S Dec 18 (340) £1,500 [Marriott]

— 21 Dec 1933. 2 pp, folio. To B. E. Leeson. Fretting about the publicity he still generates. Sgd "T.E.S." pn Mar 14 (401) £3,600 [Irani]

— 13 Apr 1934. 2 pp, 4to. To B. E. Leeson. Pouring scorn on bogus reminiscences of the Arabian campaign. Sgd "T.E.S." pn Mar 14 (402) £2,700 [Irani]

— [postmarked 11 May 1934]. 2 pp, 4to. To K. W. Marshall. About work going on at Clouds Hill. Sgd T. E. S. pn Nov 9 (449) £1,250 [Wilson]

**Photograph,** sgd & inscr, [c.1934]. 207mm by 158mm (image). Shoulder-length vignette port, inscr to J. E. Illus in cat. Marans collection. CE Apr 17 (17) $2,600

### Lawson, Henry Hertzberg, 1867-1922

**Autograph Ms,** 4-line verse ending "and mine was a light that failed". [c.1910] CA Mar 26 (121) A$800

### Layton, Irving

**Collection** of A collection of 2 ALs s, 2 Ls s, 1 ANs & a 2 pp typed poem with a holograph note, 1970-3, no size or length given. To John Gill. Concerning poems. pba Jan 25 (194) $225

### Lazarus, Julius Samuel

[A collection of material including his field notes at Gallipoli & ink & pencil sketches of views at Gallipoli sold at Christie's Australia on 26 Mar 1996, lot 124, for Australian $1,900]

### Lazarus, Samuel

**Autograph Ms,** diary kept on the Ballarat Goldfields, 24 Sept 1853 to 21 Jan 1855. 168pp, 8vo, in vellum. Includes an eyewitness account of the Eureka Stockade events of Nov-Dec 1854. CA Mar 26 (123) A$32,000

### Le Corbusier, 1887-1965

**Ls,** 2 Feb 1963. 2 pp, 4to. To Hilary Harris. Declining to get involved in an architectural project in New York. sg Feb 1 (129) $325

— 3 Dec 1963. 1 p, 4to. To Henri Perruchot. Congratulating him on some works of art. star Mar 21 (684) DM260

**Photograph,** sgd & inscr, Aug 1931. 163mm by 106mm, mtd. With a bull. Illus in cat. Marans collection. CE Apr 17 (210) $500

### Le Sueur, Jean Francois, 1760-1837

**Autograph music,** 2 fragments of 5 bars each from the score of an unnamed opera, [n.d.]. 2 pp, 8vo, cut from larger sheet. Including authentication in his wife's hand. Illus in cat. star Mar 22 (908) DM620

### Lear, Edward, 1812-88 —& Gould, Elizabeth Coxen

**Autograph sketchbook,** Trogon Gigas, watercolor over graphite sketching, [c.1835-36] 547mm by 368mm, hinged to early mat. P Dec 12 (218) $5,000

### Leclerc, Charles Victor Emmanuel, 1772-1802

**ALs,** [17 Aug 1802]. 1 p, 4to. To Gen. Rochambeau. About payments for his troops. Illus in cat. star Mar 22 (1458) DM600

### Lectionary

— [North-central Italy, Citta di Castello?, 15th cent]. 93 leaves & flyleaf, vellum, 209mm by 210mm. Contemp blindstamped bdg of brown goatskin over wooden bds, with spurious coat-of-arms added in 19th cent. Epistle & Gospel Lectionary. In a large skilful rounded gothic liturgical hand. With large & small decorated initials throughout in red or blue with penwork in blue or purple, & some illumination added in the 19th cent. S June 18 (67) £2,300
See also: Ethiopic Manuscripts

### Lee, Arthur, 1740-92

**ALs,** 8 Aug 1785. 2 pp, 4to. To John Fitzgerald. Instructing him to purchase land in Alexandria. P Dec 13 (217) $550

### Lee, Bruce, 1940-73

**Ds,** 16 Apr 1968. 1 p, Orig top copy of Carte Blanche credit card receipt for $23.10 charged to his account. Computer punch affecting final stroke of signature. wa Oct 28 (455) $400

### Lee, Charles, 1731-82

**ALs,** 10 Jan 1780. 4 pp, 4to. To Dr. Benjamin Rush. Discussing his disenchament with the U. S.: " I am...most heartily sick of this Country, and have thoughts of quitting it soon...." rms Oct 11 (27) $4,600

### Lee, Fitzhugh, 1835-1905

**Signature,** [n.d.]. With photo of Lee in uniform & a reproduction of Alexander Gardner's "The Dead at Chancellorsville". Also with 30th reunion silk for the 123rd Regiment N. Y. S. V. Framed. Over-all size 15.5 by 25.5 inches. Detail in cat rms Oct 11 (107) $400

— Anr, [n.d.]. On card. Framed with port & wartime ALs of Confederate Dr. Hollingsworth, 4 July 1862. rms Nov 30 (20) $550

### Lee, Francis Lightfoot, Signer from Virginia

**AL,** 30 Jan 1776. 3 pp, 4to. To John Page. Giving an account of the failure of the Olive Branch Petition & discussing some military appointments. Silked. Sang collection. P Dec 13 (219) $9,000

**Ls,** 23 Mar 1778. 2 pp, folio. To Patrick Henry. About troops & the shortness of supplies. Also sgd by John Banister, & with Banister's franking signature. Thorek collection. P Dec 13 (220) $8,000

### Lee, Gypsy Rose, 1914-70

**Photograph,** sgd & inscr, [c.1940]. 233mm by 183mm, possibly trimmed. Full length, seated; by Maurice Seymour. Inscr to Eddie. Illus in cat. Marans collection. CE Apr 17 (240) $700

### Lee, Henry ("Light-Horse Harry"), 1756-1818

**ALs,** 19 June 1794. 1 p, folio, vellum. Land grant for 290 acres of land in Greenbrier County. With some small holes. Soiled. sg Sept 28 (152) $500

— 11 Feb 1796. 1 p, oblong 8vo. To Aaron Burr. Requesting that he give John Hopkins "the pattent for 300,000 acres of land left with you". At top is Burr's autograph endorsement, sgd, to Timothy Green requesting that this be done. On verso are sgd endorsements by Hopkins & anr person. Folds split & fragile. wa Oct 28 (344) $110

— 12 Sept 1796. 2 pp, 4to. To unnamed recipient. About recipient's financial problems. sg Sept 28 (153) $550

**Lee, Mary Custis, 1806-73**

**Photograph, sgd & inscr,** [n.d.]. No size given. By Boude & Miley of Lexington. Hand-tinted. With dedication on verso: "For my dear little Julie Davidson from her friend..." Writing light. Waterstained & scuffed. rms Oct 11 (92) $650

**Lee, Richard Henry, Signer from Virginia**

[Four sgd true copies of letters exchanged between Lee & Ulysses S. Grant detailing the terms of the Confederate surrender at Appomattox, 9-10 Apr 1865, sold at Skinner on 11 Nov 1995, lot 28, for $130,000]

**ALs,** 28 May 1776. 2 pp, folio. To his brother [Thomas Ludwell Lee]. Sending war news. Silked. P Dec 13 (222) $9,000

— 24 Nov 1777. 4 pp, 4to. To [Roger Sherman]. Discussing military developments & diplomatic news, & supporting the Articles of Confederation. P Dec 13 (221) $10,000

— 18 Apr 1864. 1 p, 248mm by 197mm. To Col. Edward Willis. Thanking him for a gift of foodstuffs from the 12th Georgia Infantry. P June 5 (66) $4,500

— 14 June 1865. 2 pp, 8vo. To Mrs. E. H. Stevens. Sending a copy of a paper (not present) & sends greetings to a child. cb June 25 (2454) $9,500

— 17 Nov 1866. 1 p, 4to. Recipient unnamed. Recommendation of William Poindexter. Framed with port & C.S.A. belt buckle. rms Nov 30 (19) $5,500

**Lee, Robert E., 1807-70**

**A Ls s** (2), 23 Aug 1865. 1 p, 4to. To D. Barnes. Replying to a father searching for his Yankee son missing in action: "I regret I can give you no information on the subject, nor have I the means of pursuing any...I hope he is safe & may speedily be restored to you...."With 4 pp, 4to letter from the son to his father. CNY Dec 15 (85) $8,500

**ALs,** 30 Aug 1853. 2 pp, 4to. To Sophia Bursley. Expressing his favorable opinion of her son. With a photograph. Illus in cat. CNY May 17 (219) $5,500

— 20 Nov 1854. 1 p, 4to. To Capt. Favrot. Asking him to forward some boxes for his son. Illus in cat. rms June 6 (43) $4,250

— 11 Oct 1867. 4 pp, 4to. To Gen. E. G. W. Butler. Reflecting on the execution of Emperor Maximilian of Mexico, the sufferings of people in the South, & expressing his conviction that the Federal government rules by force of arms rather than by the consent of the people. Illus in cat. Forbes Magazine collection. CNY May 17 (149) $14,000

**Ls,** 29 Apr 1835. 1 p, 8vo. To John Campbell. Asking him to deliver a warrant for the salaries to be paid at the Department of Engineers. Illus in cat. rms June 6 (45) $3,500

— 6 May 1836. 1 p, 4to. To Brig. Gen. Jones. Enclosing a muster roll of musicians attached to the Military Academy. cb June 25 (2455) $4,000

**Ds,** 1838. 2 pp, 8vo. Certifiying the necessity of mentioned expenditures for the St. Louis Harbor. Sgd by " Captain R. E. Lee, Corps of Engrs." Margin torn. pba Feb 22 (171) $4,500

— June 1851 to 1855. 30 pp, 8vo, in contemp calf. Account book of West Point cadet William Babcock Hazen, sgd R. E. L. 32 times as Superintendent of Cadets. rms June 6 (44) $10,000

**Check,** 29 Sept 1838. $179.16 payable to William Beaumont. Endorsed by Beaumont on verso. Illus in cat rms Oct 11 (93) $4,250

**Cut signature,** [n.d.]. 1 by 2.5 inch signature, Light. sg Sept 28 (154) $1,700

**Photograph, sgd,** [c.1862). 105mm by 63mm. Shoulder-length vignette port, by John W. Davies. Illus in cat. Marans collection. CE Apr 17 (150) $7,000

— Anr, [n.d.]. 92mm by 57mm. By Vannerson & Jones. Illus in cat. P Dec 13 (224) $6,000

**Signature,** [n.d.]. No size given. With a print photo of Matthew Brady's picture of Lee at Appomatox. pba Oct 26 (173) $2,000

**Lee, Thomas Sim, 1745-1819**

**ALs,** 7 Sept 1778. 2 pp. To Daniel Carroll. About defences around Annapolis. bbc Feb 26 (117) $280

**Legrand, Jacques.** See: Magni, Jacobus

**Legrenzi, Giovanni, 1626-90**

**ALs,** 15 Feb 1659. 1 p, folio. To [Conte Hippolito Bentivoglio?]. Paying his respects, & mentioning the singer Rascarini. Illus in cat. star Mar 22 (901) DM3,400

**Lehar, Franz, 1870-1948**

**Collection** of ALs, 2 postcards, sgd, & photograph, sgd & inscr, 4 Jan 1941 to 31 May 1942. 1 p, 8vo, & postcards. To Maria Likar. Referring to performances of his works. star Mar 22 (904) DM650

**Ls,** 12 May 1932. 1 p, 4to. Recipient unnamed. Concerning "Es war einmal ein Walzer..." pba Oct 26 (42) $180

**Photograph, sgd & inscr,** 9 July 1907. Postcard. Inscr with 8 bars from his operetta Die Lustige Witwe. star Mar 22 (902) DM780

**Leibl, Wilhelm, 1844-1900**

**Autograph Ms,** curriculum vitae, [c.1890]. 2 pp, 8vo. Repaired. HN Nov 24 (2817) DM850

**ALs,** 15 Sept 1879. 2 pp, 8vo. To [Friedrich Pecht?]. Explaining why he is not able to send a promised drawing right away. star Mar 21 (686) DM2,300

**Leibniz, Gottfried Wilhelm von, 1646-1716**

**ALs,** 30 Oct 1710. 2 pp, 8vo. To Jean Paul Bignon. Discussing several scholarly problems, announcing a collection of his essays, & hoping for better times. Illus in cat. star Mar 21 (537) DM11,000

## Leigh, Vivien, 1913-67
**ALs,** 7 Nov [1966]. 2 pp, 12mo. To Stanley Hall. Thanking for congratulations on her birthday. Illus in cat. rms June 6 (177) $300

**Photograph, sgd,** [n.d.]. 8.75 by 6.25 inches (image). Bust-length pose. Framed. Illus in cat. rms June 6 (178) $225

**Ptd photograph,** [n.d.]. 5 by 6.5 inch bust port of Leigh as Scarlett O'Hara. Inscr. pba Oct 26 (43) $425

## Leigh, Vivien, 1913-67 —& Olivier, Laurence, Sir, 1907-89
**Playbill, sgd by both,** 1955. For Twelfth Night at the Shakespeare Memorial Theatre in Stratford-Upon-Avon. Ck Dec 14 (29) £100

## Leigh, Vivien, 1913-67 —& Olivier, Laurence, Sir, 1905-89 —& Others
**Signature,** [n.d.]. On 60 pp, folio program of "The Old Vic Theatre Company - A Tour of Australia and New Zealand". Sgd by c. 37 members of the company. Worn. rms Oct 11 (372) $425

## Leiva, Antonio, Prince of Ascoli, 1480-1536
**Ls,** [7 Oct n.y.]. 2 pp, 4to. Recipient unnamed. Concerning payments & provisions for 5 companies of soldiers. FD May 14 (1114) DM290

## Lekeu, Guillaume, 1870-94
**Autograph music,** fragments of an Adagio pour Violon, Alto et Violoncello & 3 other works, [n.d.]. 2 pp, folio. Sgd at head. Including authentication by P. Cornuau. star Mar 22 (905) DM1,100

## Lenau, Nikolaus, 1802-50
**Autograph Ms,** poem, An einen Jugendfreund, [1831]. 3 pp, 8vo. 8 six-line stanzas. star Mar 21 (246) DM4,200

## Lenbach, Franz von, 1836-1904
**ALs,** 24 Sept 1890. 3 pp, 8vo. Recipient unnamed. Promising to paint Moltke's port for the art gallery in Hamburg. star Mar 21 (687) DM400

— 2 Dec 1897. 1 p, 8vo. Recipient unnamed. Responding to an inquiry about the lease of a house. HN May 15 (2633) DM200

## L'Enfant, Pierre Charles, 1754-1825
**ALs,** 13 Feb 1787. 4 pp, 4to. To his parents in France. Complaining of money owed him by the Society of the Cincinnati. Forbes Magazine collection. CNY May 17 (150) $3,800

## Lenne, Peter Joseph, 1789-1866
**ALs,** 12 July 1829. 1 p, 4to. To [August Wilhelm Francke]. Asking him to procure fresh figs for the Prussian king's visit in Magdeburg. star Mar 21 (538) DM1,800

## Leo XII, Pope, 1760-1829
**Document,** 29 July 1825. 1 p, folio. Brief addressed to a vicar of the Bishop of Citta di Castello granting permission for the marriage of Philipp Gallinella & Theodora Beltroni. star Mar 22 (1503) DM220

## Leoncavallo, Ruggiero, 1858-1919
**Autograph music,** sketch of Dufresne's waltz-song E il riso gentil, including introductory passage, from his opera Zaza; [c.1900]. 8 pp, 4to. Notated in short score on 2 or 3 systems per page & including revisions; sgd twice. Differing from final version. S Dec 1 (201) £900

**ALs,** 7 Sept 1894. 3 pp, 8vo. To Ernst von Possart. Concerning a performance of his opera I Medici. star Mar 22 (906) DM800

## Leonov, Alexei
**Autograph Ms,** draft for the book Soyuz-Apollo. 51 pp, 298mm by 213mm, with extensive deletions & corrections. With sgd holograph statement describing the material. P June 16 (195) $4,000

— Autograph Ms, statement about his space walk. [c.1994] 3 pp, 298mm by 210mm, sgd. With accompanying typescript, sgd. P June 16 (100) $1,000

— Autograph Ms, [A Walk in Space, in Russian]. 26 pp, 295mm by 210mm. With orig typescript with ink & pencil emendations & autograph statement describing the above. With a copy of the pbd book, 1980, sgd by Leonov, presented to him & inscr by a group of Russian school children. P June 16 (98) $8,000
See also: Space Program, Soviet

## Leopold I, King of the Belgians, 1790-1865
**ALs,** 2 Aug 1865. 1 p, 8vo. Recipient unnamed. About some business matters. star Mar 22 (1176) DM290

## Leopold I, Emperor, 1640-1705
**ALs,** 15 Nov 1681. 2 pp, folio. To [Prince Johann Wilhelm von der Pfalz?]. About political & family matters. Illus in cat. HN May 15 (2635) DM2,400

— 12 Aug 1693. 1 p, folio. To Princess Hedwig Elisabeth of Poland. Concerning a godparenthood. star Mar 22 (1590) DM1,200

**Ls,** 28 Aug 1668. 1 p, folio. To an unnamed Elector. Thanking for support promised to him. HH May 9 (2500) DM250

**Ds,** 15 Nov 1667. 1 p, folio. Ptd order concerning the devaluation of Polish coins. In German & Polish. HH Nov 17 (3285) DM220

## Leopold II, Emperor, 1747-92
**Ls,** 19 Sept 1790. 1 p, folio. To an unnamed Elector. Announcing the marriages of three of his children. HH May 9 (2501) DM260

## Leopold III Friedrich Franz, Herzog von Anhalt-Dessau, 1740-1817
**Collection** of 8 A Ls s & Ls, 1 Nov 1768 to 12 Apr 1778. 16 pp, folio & 4to. To Oberamtmann Pfeiffer. About agricultural improvements & the administration of his manor in Norkitten. star Mar 22 (1162) DM500

## Leopold V, Erzherzog von Oesterreich, Regent of Tirol, 1586-1632
**Ls,** 10 Oct 1627. 1 p, folio. To his mother-in-law Grand Duchess Christina of Tuscany. Announcing an envoy. star Mar 22 (1253) DM240

— STARHEMBERG, GOTTHARD VON. - Letter, 20 May 1611. 1 p, folio. To his cousin Erasmus von Starhemberg. Referring to the occupation of Bohemia by Archduke Leopold's troops from Passau. star Mar 22 (1254) DM850

**Leopold Wilhelm, Erzherzog von Oesterreich, 1614-62**
ALs, 16 Jan 1640. 1 p, folio. Recipient unnamed. Contents not stated. HN May 15 (2638) DM1,200
Ls, 22 Sept 1634. 1 p, folio. To an unnamed prince. Sending condolences on the death of recipient's brother who died in the Emperor's service. With engraved port. star Mar 22 (1255) DM280

**Leopoldine, Empress of Pedro I of Brasil, 1797-1826**
ALs, 1 Dec 1817. 2 pp, 8vo. To her brother Ferdinand. Detailed report about her first impressions of Brasil. HN May 15 (2513) DM3,200

**Leslie, Walter, Graf von, 1607-67**
ALs, 9 Mar 1655. 1 p, folio. Recipient unnamed. Sending news from Paris. In Italian. HH May 9 (2444) DM440
Ls, 4 Sept 1641. 2 pp, folio. To Francesco Useppi. Referring to money promised him by the Emperor. With engraved port. star Mar 22 (1256) DM1,600

**Lesseps, Ferdinand, Vicomte de, 1805-94 —&**
**Lesseps, Heloise, Vicomtesse de**
[A pair of photographs, sgd, of De Lesseps & his wife, [c.1870], each 105mm by 63mm, sold at Christie's East on 17 Apr 1996, lot 40, for $600.]

**Lesseps, Heloise, Vicomtesse de.** See: Lesseps, Ferdinand & Lesseps

**Leverett, John, 1616-79**
ADs, 2 Dec 1665. 1 p, folio. As notary, certifying a deed by Henry Way (on verso). With a port. rms Mar 21 (310) $245

**Levetzow, Ulrike von, 1804-99**
ALs, 13 Mar 1889. 1 p, 8vo. To Franz von Rauch. Sending congratulations. star Mar 21 (143) DM500

**Lewes, Mary Anne Evans, 1819-80.** See: Eliot, George

**Lewis, Cecil Day, 1904-72**
Collection of Collection of 13 ALs s, 1 APs & 6 Ls s, 1945-46, 28 pp, 8vo. To Denys Kilham Roberts. Concerning difficulties with publishers and other business matters as well as works by Stevie Smith, A. S. J. Tessimond & others. S June 28 (35) £600

**Lewis, Clive Staples, 1898-1963 —&**
**Lewis, Joy, d.1960**
Collection of 8 A Ls s by Lewis & 10 A Ls s & 1 Ls by Joy Lewis, 13 Sept 1957 to 21 Mar 1961. All to Jane Gaskell. Ck Apr 12 (75) £3,500

**Lewis, Francis, Signer from New York**
ADs, 20 June 1777. 2 pp, folio. Balance sheet of loans by, & payments to, the Board of Admiralty by the owners of the sloop Montgomery & the NY Convention. P Dec 13 (226) $1,400

**Lewis, Jerry.** See: Martin, Dean & Lewis

**Lewis, Joy, d.1960.** See: Lewis, Clive Staples & Lewis

**Lewis, Meriwether, 1774-1809**
ADs, 24 Aug 1809. 1 p, 78mm by 132mm. Promissory note to Falconer & Carmegyes. CNY May 17 (259) $14,000

**Lewis, Sinclair, 1885-1951**
Ls, 22 Jan 1920. 1 p, 4to. To Ms. Curtis. About how one judges short stories rms Oct 11 (230) $800

**Leyen, Damian Hartard von der, Kurfuerst von Mainz, 1624-78 —&**
**Karl I Ludwig, Kurfuerst von Pfalz-Neuburg, 1617-80**
Ls, 20 Apr 1676. 1 p, folio. To Count Johann August von Solms-Muenzenberg. Sending an Imperial order. star Mar 22 (1328) DM1,100

**Leyva, Antonio, Prince of Ascoli, 1480-1536.** See: Leiva, Antonio

**Library Catalogues**
Ms, list of 16th-cent books shelved by subject & size, including 26 Mss. [Paderborn, Germany, 1612]. 38 pp, 312mm by 88mm. Part of an inventory of lands & possessions, 81 leaves, vellum, bound in a vellum leaf of a 12th-cent geographical Ms. S June 18 (39) £500
— HUEFFE, WESTFALIA. - Ms, Verzeichnis der in der Bibliothek zu Hueffe befindlichen Werke ueber Westfaelische Provinzial-Geschichte, 1876 & 1877. About 550 pp in 2 vols. Contemp cloth, & wraps. JG Mar 29 (274) DM420

**Lie, Trygve, 1896-1968**
Ls, 31 Dec 1935. 1 p, 8 by 11.5 inches. To unnamed recipient. About civilian aid for mobilization should it prove necessary. With full English translation. Dar Oct 19 (129) $75

**Liebermann, Max, 1847-1935**
Series of 20 A Ls s, 25 Feb 1897 to 17 Apr 1907 & [n.d.]. 59 pp, 8vo. To Dr. Max Linde. Reporting about his paintings, exhibitions & sales, visitors, travels, etc. 1 ALs fragment. HN May 15 (2640) DM7,800
ALs, 2 Dec 1909. 4 pp, 8vo. To an unnamed official. Asking him to support his request for a special building permission. star Mar 21 (688) DM880
— 16 Mar 1911. 2 pp, 8vo. Recipient unnamed. Expressing satisfaction about recipient's praise of a port. star Mar 21 (689) DM950

**Liebig, Justus, Freiherr von, 1803-73**
Autograph Ms, essay, Der Ernaehrungsprocess der Pflanzen und Thiere, [n.d.]. Single leaf, folio. Fragment of introduction; including corrections. Repaired. star Mar 21 (541) DM1,100

**Series** of 21 A Ls s, 6 May 1844 to 3 Mar 1861. 26 pp, 4to & 8vo. To Ernst von Bibra. Discussing personal & scientific questions. star Mar 21 (543) DM6,000

**ALs,** 3 Nov 1840. 2 pp, 4to. To an unnamed colleague in England. Thanking for a decoration, & reporting that he has been offered a position in Vienna. star Mar 21 (542) DM1,400

— 6 Dec 1847. 4 pp, 8vo. To [Th. J. Pelouze?]. Discussing scientific matters. star Mar 21 (544) DM1,100

— Sept 1860. 1 p, 8vo. To an unnamed Marquise. Informing her about his itinerary & announcing his visit. HN May 15 (2641) DM680

— 26 Oct 1864. 2 pp, 8vo. To an unnamed colleague. Referring to a suit pending against Dr. Volhard. star Mar 21 (545) DM1,400

### Liliencron, Detlev von, 1844-1909

**ALs,** 20 Nov 1897. 4 pp, 8vo. To an unnamed baroness. Requesting her help in placing his poems in literary journals. Repaired. star Mar 21 (249) DM360

— 30 Dec 1903. 2 pp, 8vo. To Karl Kraus. Reporting about a visit to a cemetary. HN May 15 (2642) DM620

### Lilienthal, Otto, 1848-96

**ALs,** 5 Apr 1895. 1 p, 4to. To H. Moedebeck. About the importance of recipient's book for aviation. Illus in cat. star Mar 22 (1392) DM8,000

### Lillie, Gordon William, 1860-1942

**Photograph, sgd & inscr,** [c.1905]. Cabinet size, framed. Showing him sitting with Buffalo Bill. Inscr to V. W. Marshall & sgd both ways. sg June 6 (266) $1,200

### Lincke, Paul, 1866-1946

**Photograph, sgd & inscr,** 25 Mar 1909. 4to. Inscr with 7 bars from his Luna Waltz. star Mar 22 (909) DM470

— Anr, 19 May 1944. 4.5 by 6.5 inch bust photo. Sgd & Inscr. With 6-line holograph letter concerning a poem on verso. sg Sept 28 (157) $140

### Lincoln, Abraham, 1809-65

[An Archive of documents related to Lincoln and his Generals. Sold at auction at Swann on Sept 28 as lot 162 for $9,000.] Illus in cat

**Autograph Ms,** concluding portion of a speech prepared during the Lincoln-Douglas debates, [c.July 1858]. 2 pp, folio, in mor case. Predicting the abolition of slavery. Professionally repaired. Illus in cat. CNY May 17 (261) $450,000

**Ms,** Legal fragment. 1843. 1 p, 1 by 8 inches. " This day came the Petitioner and it appearing to the court that due notice..." With photocopy of the entire document. Illus in cat pba Feb 22 (261) $1,300

**ALs,** 25 May 1849. 1 p, 4to. To Elisha Embree. Reacting indignantly to rumors that Justin Butterfield will be named to head the General Land Office. Illus in cat. Forbes Magazine collection. CNY May 17 (151) $55,000

— 21 Dec 1857. 1 p, 8vo. To Jesse K. Dubois. Attempting to settle a tax case for the Illinois Central Railroad. Forbes Magazine collection. CNY May 17 (152) $24,000

— 29 Apr 1859. 1 p, 4to. To Norman Judd. Proposing the purchase of a printing press to promote the Republican cause among German-American voters. Illus in cat. Forbes Magazine collection. CNY May 17 (153) $13,000

— 29 Aug 1860. 1 p, 8vo. To Harriet W. Chase. Responding to a recommendation of [Cassius M.] Clay for a post in his administration. Illus in cat. rms Mar 21 (50) $19,000

— 6 Aug 1861. 1 p, 8vo. To Secretary of War. Appointments of various officers such as Capt. Samuel Sammons as Commissary in the new Regular Army & Joseph S. York as captain. Blank left margin worn. Mtd. Illus in cat sg Sept 28 (158) $12,000

— 18 Feb 1862. 1 p, 8vo. To William A. Newell. Concerning the question as to whether or not Governor Newell of New Jersey had used his influence for a Colonel Hatfield: "Your advocacy of ...Hatfield for Brigadier-General has been earnest, without reservation..." Darkened. With stained right margin. Mtd with colored engraved port of Lincoln. Illus in cat CNY Dec 15 (203) $15,000

— 29 Aug 1863. 1 p, 8vo. To Edwin M. Stanton. About a request by Dr. Brown, who would later embalm Lincoln. Dust-soiled and stained. Leaves separated. With 1 p, 24mo Ds from the War Dept inviting Dr. Brown to accompany the remains of the President from D. C. to Illinois. Mtd. Illus in cat CNY Dec 15 (205) $14,000

**Ls,** 17 Sept 1860. 1 p, 8vo. To H. H. Marvin. Sending an autograph upon request. CNY Dec 15 (201) $5,000

— 26 Nov 1860. 1 p, 8vo. To J. D. Mansfield. Sending his autograph. Text in the hand of Mary Todd Lincoln. CNY May 17 (262) $5,000

— 28 Jan 1861. 1 p, size not stated. To Henry C. Meyer. Sending his autograph. Text in the hand of Mary Todd Lincoln. Framed. CNY May 17 (263) $4,800

— 23 July 1861. 1 p. 238mm by 190mm. To the Superintendent of the U.S. Mint at Philadelphia, James Pollock. About an appointment for Charles Stewart, son of Hon. Andrew Stewart. Illus in cat P June 5 (71) $5,500

— 24 Aug 1863. 2 pp, 4to. To Gov. Horatio Seymour. About differences of opinion concerning the enlistment of soldiers under the recent draft calls. Forbes Magazine collection. CNY May 17 (155) $10,000

— 9 Nov 1863. 1 p, 4to. To 21 "important" New Yorkers including Robert B. Roosevelt, John J. Astor, Jr., and Nathaniel Sands. Declining to endorse General Dix for Mayor of New York. With loss in left-hand margin. Torn at bottom. Mtd with transcription of petition with signatures. Detail in cat CNY Dec 15 (206) $14,000

**ANs,** [c.1845-47]. 1 p, 51mm by 197mm, removed from a larger sheet. To Gibson William Harris. About staying at his home that evening. Sgd "Lincoln". P June 5 (70) $2,000

— 4 Aug 1862. 1 p, 8vo. Recommending Edward Hall as a "competent, faithful & genteel man". cb June 25 (2353) $5,000

# LINCOLN

— 30 Oct 1862. 1 p, no size given. On bottom left-hand corner of a letter from Colonel George C. Buling. Revoking an order by General Mc Clellan: " I know nothing of this recruiting for the regulars, from the volunteer regiments. How is this?..." CNY Dec 15 (204) $6,500

— 31 Jan 1863. On card, 54mm by 86mm. To William Gallaer. Saying he cannot do what Gallaer desires. Framed. P June 5 (74) $3,750

— 14 Sept 1863. 1 p, 8vo. To Sec of State [Seward]. Asking him to convene the Cabinet. Illus in cat. P Dec 13 (238) $10,000

— 30 Apr 1864. On a card, 51mm by 83mm. To Brig. Gen. Edward R .S. Canby. Asking him to give the bearer a hearing. Framed with port. P June 5 (76) $3,750

— 20 June 1864. On a card, 51mm by 83mm. To a State Dept. administrator. Emphatically requestion a consular appointment for Capt. Bailey. P June 5 (77) $3,750

— 20 June 1864. On a card, 52mm by 85mm. To Sec. of State Seward. Explaining that the bearer, Mr. Ingersoll, is the successor of Lovejoy & asking Seward to see & hear him. Mtd. Sold with an ALs of Seward, 5 Mar 1866, to Mrs. Adams, forwarding the card. pn June 13 (224) £2,400

— 4 Aug 1864. 1 p, 45mm by 75mm. Asking for the record in the case of A. J. Smith. Framed. CE June 12 (73) $4,200

— 16 Aug 1864. 1 p, 12mo. To [Ethan Allen] Hitchcock. Asking him to see Mr. Christophe. Illus in cat. P Dec 13 (241) $4,500

— 21 Sept 1864. Recipient unnamed. Giving permission for W. W. Glenn to return to Baltimore. Illus in cat. rms June 6 (2) $7,000

— 1 Feb 1865. 7 lines, size not stated; inlaid in larger sheet. Recipient unnamed. Giving instructions for a deserter "to enter any regiment having as much as two years to serve". With related note by Gen. John A. Dix on verso. Illus in cat. Forbes Magazine collection. CNY May 17 (158) $6,000

— 13 Feb 1865. 1 p, 53mm by 78mm, cut from larger document. Recipient unnamed. Giving instructions for a young soldier to be discharged. Forbes Magazine collection. CNY May 17 (159) $3,600

— 18 Mar 1865. 1 p, size not stated, on verso of ALs addressed to him by J. R. Dorsett. Giving instructions to discharge Mr. Dorsett's son from the army. Illus in cat. Forbes Magazine collection. CNY May 17 (160) $9,500

**Ds,** 29 Nov 1852. 1 p, folio. Ptd mortgage indenture taken by Lincoln on land owned by Thomas & Elizabeth Cantrall; sgd twice & accomplished in Lincoln's hand. Also sgd by others. Endorsed by Lincoln on verso. Illus in cat. P Dec 13 (228) $13,000

— 27 Mar 1861. 1 p, 4to. Order to affix the US Seal to a the envelope of letter to Queen Victoria regarding the recall of G. M. Dallas. Illus in cat. rms June 6 (1) $8,500

— 29 Mar 1861. 1 p, folio. Appointment of James E. Harrison as Lieutenant in the 2d Regiment of Cavalry. Framed with a port. P Dec 13 (230) $3,500

— 6 June 1861. 1 p, oblong 4to. Appointment of Thomas E. Lloyd as Captain of the National Guard Battalion, Militia of the District of Columbia. CE Sept 27 (15) $3,100

— 26 July 1861. 1 p, 368mm by 464mm. Appointment of Nathan Sargent as Commissioner of Customs. Countersgd by Sec. of State William H. Seward. P June 5 (72) $3,250

— 10 Aug 1861. 1 p, 19 by 15 inches, vellum. Commission of James B. McPherson as Captain, Corps of Engineers. Countersgd by Simon Cameron as Secretary of War. sg Sept 28 (160) $10,000

— 14 Aug 1861. 1 p, on vellum, folio. Appointment of Charles C. McConnell as 2d Lieut. in the 5th Regiment of Artillery. Countersgd by Sec. of War Simon Cameron (his signature faded). wa Oct 28 (209) $3,200

— 19 Aug 1861. 1 p, folio, parchment. Appointment of Aaron Smith as First Lieutenant of an infantry regiment. Countersgd by Secretary of War Simon Cameron. Mtd with port. Framed. Illus in cat CNY Dec 15 (88) $3,200

— 17 Sept 1861. 1 p, folio. Appointment of George L. Willard as Captain of Infantry. Framed. P Dec 13 (233) $2,750

— 3 Oct 1861. 1 p, folio. Appointing John W. Dawson as Governor of the Territory of Utah. Countersgd by Secretary of War William H. Seward. broken along vertical center fold & with weakness of folds. Also with holograph statement by Justice James M. Wayne certifying that Wayne has been sworn in. On verso is anr statment by Frank Fuller as Secretary of the Territory of Utah noting that "John W. Dawson...presented to me this commission...." Framed under glass to reveal both sides of the document. Illus in cat pba June 13 (74) $8,000

— 5 Feb 1862. 1 p, folio, parchment. Appointing D. B. Sacket an "Inspector General with the Rank of Colonel". Pale. CNY Dec 15 (89) $3,200

— 12 Feb 1862. 1 p, folio. Appointment of Robert H. Insley as Assistant Quartermaster of Volunteers with rank of Captain. Countersgd by Sec. of War Edwin M. Stanton. Framed with port. cb June 25 (2360) $3,250

— 20 Feb 1862. 1 p, on vellum, folio. Appointment of Cornelius L. King as Captain in the 12th Regiment of Infantry. Countersgd by Sec. of War Edwin M. Stanton. CE June 12 (71) $4,000

— 21 Feb 1862. 1 p, on vellum, 17.5 by 13.5 inches, framed. Commission of Daniel W. Benham as 2d Lieut. in the 18th Regiment of Infantry. Countersgd by Sec. of War Edwin Stanton. rs Nov 11 (30) $3,750

— 11 Mar 1862. 1 p, 4to. Order to affix the U.S. Seal to a pardon warrant for Nathaniel W. Watkins. CE June 12 (72) $4,000

— 3 July 1862. 1 p, folio, parchment. Appointing U. L. M. Burger as Assistant Adjutant General of Volunteers with the rank of Captain. Countersgd by Scretary of War Edwin M. Stanton. Pale. CNY Dec 15 (90) $5,000

— 8 Nov 1862. 1 p, 4to. Order to affix the U.S. Seal to the envelope of a duplicate of the letter addressed to the President of Salvador. Fold through signature. wa Oct 28 (210) $3,000

— 10 Jan 1863. 1 p, folio. Appointment of Noah Gaylord as Hospital Chaplain. Countersgd by E. M. Stanton. Framed. CNY May 17 (264) $3,600

— 21 Feb 1863. 1 p, folio, parchment. Appointing William C. Nicholson as "...a Commodore in the Navy, on the Retired List..." Countersgd by Secretary of the Navy Gideon Welles. CNY Dec 15 (93) $4,800

— 26 Feb 1863. 1 p, folio. Appointment of Jacob R. Ludlow as Surgeon of Volunteers. Countersgd by E. M. Stanton. Framed. CNY May 17 (265) $3,600

— 26 Feb 1863. 1 p, folio, vellum. Appointing Francis Bacon a Surgeon of Volunteers. Illus in cat rms Oct 11 (231) $5,500

— 26 Feb 1863. 1 p, folio. Appointment of Francis Bacon as Surgeon of Volunteers. Countersgd by E. Stanton. Illus in cat. rms June 6 (3) $6,500

— 16 Mar 1863. 1 p, on vellum. Countersgd by Edwin M. Stanton. Appointment of Franklin S. Nickerson as Brigadier General of Volunteers. Countersgd by Edwin M. Stanton. Framed with ports & scenes. rms Nov 30 (21) $4,300

— 1 July 1863. 1 p, 4to. Draft order for troops to be furnished by Connecticut. Illus in cat. P Dec 13 (237) $9,000

— [c.1863]. 1 p, folio. Ship's papers in 4 languages for the whaling ship Arnolda of New Bedford. Illus in cat. P Dec 13 (239) $6,000

— 25 Jan 1864. 1 p, 16 by 21 inches. Appointment of John C. Underwood as District Court Judge for the Eastern District of Virginia. Countersgd by Sec. of State William H. Seward. sg June 6 (109) $3,200

— 1 Mar 1864. 1 p, on vellum, folio. Commission of H. P. Whitsel as Assistant Quartermaster of Volunteers with rank of Captain. Framed. Countersgd by Sec. of War Edwin Stanton. wd May 8 (19) $2,750

— 8 June 1864. 1 p, folio. Appointment of Henry G. Nims as Additional Pay Master. Countersgd by Sec. of War E. M. Stanton. Framed with port. sg Feb 1 (131) $3,800

— 21 June 1864. 1 p, folio. Four-language ship's papers for the whaler Stephania. Countersgd by Secretary of State William H. Seward. Mtd & framed with engraving of Lincoln & pencil drawing of a sperm whale fishery. Illus in cat CNY Dec 15 (208) $9,500

— 1 Aug 1864. 1 p, folio. Appointment of Rowland M. Jones as a 1st Lieutenant in the Veteran Reserve Corp. Countersgd by Sec of War Stanton. Fold crease across Lincoln's signature. rms Nov 30 (213) $6,500

— 21 Sept 1864. 1 p, 12mo. Pass for W. W. Glenn to return to Baltimore. P Dec 13 (242) $5,000

— 26 Sept 1864. 1 p, folio Recognizing Carl Schmidt of Cincinnati as Consul of the Duchy of Brunswick & Lunenburg for Ohio, Indiana, Kentucky & Illinois. Countersgd by Secretary of State William H. Seward. Wrinkled. sg Sept 28 (161) $4,000

— 15 Nov 1864. 1 p, 254mm by 391mm. Appointment of Oscar T. Crandall as Deputy Postmaster at Sedalia MO. Countersgd by Sec. of State William H. Seward. P June 5 (78) $3,250

— 7 Mar 1865. 1 p, folio. Commission for Abram Wakeman as Surveyor of Customs for New York. CE June 12 (74) $3,500

— 23 Mar 1865. 1 p, folio. Appointment of James C. Duane as Lieut. Colonel. Countersgd by E. Stanton. rms June 6 (4) $5,750

— 1 May 1865. 1 p, folio. Ship's papers in four languages for the whaleship Osprey. Countersgd by William H. Seward. Forbes Magazine collection. CNY May 17 (161) $8,000

**Autograph endorsement,** sgd, 5 Aug 1861. At bottom of ANs by Sen. O. H. Browning requesting that John Gillson be appointed a Captain. Agreeing with the recommendation. Tipped into a copy of Alonzo Rothschild's Honest Abe, 1917, bound in calf gilt by Zaehnsdorf & extra-illus with plates. wa Feb 29 (243) $4,100

— Anr, sgd, 17 Aug 1861. 1 p, 8vo. On fragment of a letter addressed to him by Gen. William B. Franklin regarding the rejection of A. J. Dallas's appointment by the Senate; suggesting that Dallas be reappointed. Also endorsed by Adjutant Gen. L. Thomas. Illus in cat. P Dec 13 (232) $5,500

— Anr, sgd, 12 Dec 1861. On verso of a letter addressed to him by the Maryland delegation in Congress, 10 Dec 1861, 3 pp, 8vo, recommending the appointment of Robert H. Thompson als Lieutenant of Marines; suggesting that Thompson be appointed. With related material. Illus in cat. P Dec 13 (234) $3,250

— Anr, sgd, on integral blank of a letter addressed to him by P. D. Gurley, 10 Jan 1862, 1 p, 8vo, recommending R. H. Thompson for an appointment; stating that Thompson is expected to be appointed to the Marine Corps. P Dec 13 (234A) $4,000

— Anr, sgd, 15 Jan 1862, size not stated, on a letter addressed to Sec of War Simon Cameron by James Oakes, recommending Thomas E. Maley for an appointment; agreeing to the appointment if a vacancy exists. Also endorsed by others. Illus in cat. rms Mar 21 (51) $8,000

— Anr, 10 Jan 1863. On U. S. Sanitary Commission envelope addressed to Lincoln. Requesting Surgeon General Hammond's input on a appointment for Mr. Bushnell. Hammond has replied in the affirmative. CNY Dec 15 (92) $4,000

— Anr, sgd, 2 Nov 1863. 8 lines on ALs by J. B. Stonehouse to Col. Tompkins, 22 Oct 1863, concerning the raising of troops in NY State; suggesting that 1,000 soldiers be raised. Also endorsed by Gov. Horatio Seymour. Forbes Magazine collection. CNY May 17 (156) $5,500

— Anr, 2 Mar 1864. On ALs from Mrs. A. H. Hoge. Passing on her request that her son appointed Brigadier. Browned. Torn at folds. CNY Dec 15 (94) $4,800

— Anr, sgd, 4 Mar 1864; on a petition addressed to him by the 2d Presbyterian Church of Memphis, 7 pp, size not stated, requesting the return of their church

# LINCOLN

now under control of Union troops to the local Presbytery; 20 lines insisting that the "Government must not undertake to run the churches." With related material. Illus in cat. P Dec 13 (240) $75,000

— Anr, sgd, 28 Apr 1864. On slip cut from larger paper. Releasing an unidentified boy from military service on return of the volunteer bounty. P June 5 (75) $3,750

**Autograph telegram,** 27 Aug 1862. 1 p, 8vo. To Major General George McClellan. Asking "What news from the front?". Sgd as " A. Lincoln." With transmission marking and ink blot. Illus in cat sg Sept 28 (159) $34,000

**Check,** 7 July 1862. 1 p, 66mm by 195mm. $20 payable to John Hay, his personal secretary. Framed with Confederate bond for $100 and a $10 Confederate bill. Sold w. a. f Illus in cat CNY Dec 15 (91) $7,000

**Endorsement,** 2 Nov 1861. 1 p, 4to. To Secretary of War Simon Cameron. On verso of letter from 1st. Lieutenant George T. Balch. Responding favorably to a request from Capt. John McNab that he be able to testify for himself in a court of inquiry. Dockted. Browned. CNY Dec 15 (202) $8,500

— Anr, 20 Feb 1864. 1 p, 24mo. Noting "I forget what it is that I am to do in this case. Will not the same trouble...arise, about the oath in Col Edwards' case?..." Bottom margin cropped. Clipped. Detail in cat CNY Dec 15 (207) $5,500

**Franking signature,** [7 Nov 1864]. 1 p, 2.7 by 5.25 inches. On envelope in Lincoln's hand to A. Chester. CNY Dec 15 (96) $3,500

**Photograph, sgd,** [Feb 1861]. 94mm by 62mm, mtd. Seated at a table, facing to the left. By Alexander Gardner for Mathew Brady, pbd by E. Anthony. Including authentication by John Hay on verso. Illus in cat. Marans collection. CE Apr 17 (151) $34,000

**Signature,** 1864. 1 p, 8vo; on ptd card "Autographs of the President and Cabinet". Also sgd by 7 cabinet members. Illus in cat. Forbes Magazine collection. CNY May 17 (157) $11,500

— ASSASSINATION. - ALs, 30 July 1866, 4 pp, 4to, of an unnamed Union soldier to his sister. Giving an account of the hanging of the Lincoln conspirators. CNY May 17 (267) $9,000

— DEGEN, JOHN ALDEN. - ALs. 18 Apr 1908. 3 pp, 8vo. To the Editor of the Bookman. Concerning the existence of a public memorial to John Wilkes Booth: "Erected by Pink Perkins in honor of John Wilkes Booth for killling old Abe Lincoln. I prefer not to name the town or even the state as the people there are ashamed of the monument and are at some pains to make clear that, so far as known, not a single person in town is in sympathy with Mr. Perkins..." pba Oct 26 (276) $225

— DEGEN, JOHN ALDEN. - ALs. 18 Apr 1908. 3 pp, 8vo. To The Editor of The Bookman. Concerning the monument "...Erected by Pink Perkins in honor of John Wilkes Booth for killing Old Abe Lincoln." pba Oct 26 (276) $225

— ROBBINS, Z. C. - ALs, 25 June 1862. 1 p, 8vo. To Abraham Lincoln. Reminding him of a promised appointment. rms Mar 21 (52) $650

# AMERICAN BOOK PRICES CURRENT

— TAFT, CHARLES S. - AMS. Entitled "Abraham Lincoln's Last Hours - The Note Book of an Army Surgeon present ". [n. d.]. 10 pp, 4to. Detailing the assassination, death & autopsy of President Lincoln: " He was totally inconsious...breathing regularly but heavily, an occaasional sigh escaping with breath...the saddest and most pathetic death scene I have ever witnessed..." Illus in cat rms Oct 11 (234) $47,500

**Lincoln, Abraham, 1809-65 —&**
**Seward, William Henry, 1801-72**

Ds, 4 May 1861. 1 p, folio. Appointing Edgar H. Bates as Justie of the Peace in the county of Washington. Toned. With repaired folds. pba Oct 26 (270) $4,250

**Lincoln, Benjamin, 1733-1810**

Ds, 11 Sept 1797. 1 p, 8vo. Importation certificate issued to James Scobie. Framed with a port. P Dec 13 (245) $150

— 23 June 1806. 1 p, 4to. Certifying that rum has been imported by R. D. Finken from Grenada. Sgd as Collector of the Port of Boston. Countersgd by Thomas Melville. Browned. pba Feb 22 (198) $200

**Lincoln, Mary Todd, 1818-82**

ALs, 27 Mar 1866. 3 pp, 8vo. To Mary Ann Dana Foot[e]. Consoling a Senator's wife over her husband's illness: "I pray that our Heavenly Father, may be merciful to you, and restore the Senator to health & spare you the cup of affliction which I have been called upon, so freely to drink." Fold separations strengthed with archival tape. Illus in cat CNY Dec 15 (209) $17,000

— 15 Dec [n.y.]. 2 pp, 12mo. To General Sykes. Letter recommending Peter Vermin. Framed. wd Nov 15 (12) $3,250

**Lind, Jenny, 1820-87**

Series of 5 A Ls s, [c.1841] to 6 Aug 1849. 10 pp, 4to & 8vo. To George Blumm. Personal letters to her "Parisian Father", thanking for help & reporting about her travels. star Mar 22 (910) DM1,100

ALs, 1 July 1856. 3 pp, no size given. To unnamed recipient. Apologizing for being slow to write as "if life and time was not so short one could do much more..." Browned. With related material. Ck Nov 17 (100) £50

— 14 May 1858. 4 pp, 8vo. To an unnamed lady. Thanking for some sewing gear, & reporting about her children. star Mar 22 (911) DM320

**Photograph, sgd & inscr,** 19 May 1872. 106mm by 64mm, mtd. Shoulder-length vignette port, by Schemboche. Inscr to Mme Stals. Marans collection. CE Apr 17 (241) $1,100

**Signature,** July 1862. No size given. Mtd & framed. pba Feb 22 (75) $80

**Lindbergh, Anne Morrow.** See: Lindbergh, Charles A. & Lindbergh

**Lindbergh, Charles A., 1902-74**
**ALs,** 12 March 1971. 1 p, 4to. To Edna Swedback. Commiseration on the loss of her uncle, Martin Engstrom. With original enevelope. pba Feb 22 (138) $750
**Ls,** 2 June 1930. 1 p, 4to. To Commander P. V. H. Weems. About sextant readings & a system of navigation. rms Nov 30 (73) $1,600
**Check,** 8 Apr 1919. 1 p, 7.5 by 3 inches. $250 payable to Charles A. Lindbergh, Jr. Lindbergh Jr. himself has filled in the "Pay to the Order of" space. Endorsed on verso by Lindbergh, Jr. With metal plaque & front page photo of the New York Times concerning Lindbergh's transatlantic flight. Mtd. Over-all size 14 by 18 inches. Illus in cat Dar Oct 19 (131) $950
**Photograph, sgd,** sgd, 9 Dec 1927. 9 by 7 inches. With The Spirit of St. Louis. wa Oct 28 (261) $1,700
— Anr, [c.1927]. 200mm by 253mm. Beside his airplane; by Underwood. Illus in cat. Marans collection. CE Apr 17 (18) $3,500
— Anr, [c.1927]. 358mm by 256mm. Shoulder-length port. Marans collection. CE Apr 17 (19) $1,000
— Anr, [n.d.]. 8 by 10 inch port photo. Creased. pba Oct 26 (116) $850
**Signature,** 1 Aug 1934. No size given. On an Airmail envelope. Also sgd by Boris Sergievsky and Edwin Musick. Illus in cat pba Feb 22 (140) $375
— Anr, 12 June 1949. On British one pound note. Also sgd by a variety of other famous people. Worn. pba Feb 22 (139) $400

**Lindbergh, Charles A., 1902-74 —&**
**Lindbergh, Anne Morrow**
**Photograph, sgd,** 2 Feb 1938. Showing them by a small personal plane. Sgd by both in black ink. With letter of transmittal by AML's sister Elisabeth & other related material. rms Nov 30 (76) $1,500

**Lindpaintner, Peter Joseph von, 1791-1856**
**ALs,** 18 Mar 1855. 1 p, 4to. Recipient unnamed. Reporting about some new songs. star Mar 22 (912) DM260

**Lindsay, Vachel, 1879-1931**
**Collection** of 8 A Ls s & 1 Ls, 11 Jan 1916 - 23 July 1929. 47 pp, various sizes. To either or both Mr. & Mrs. Carl and Julia Vrooman. Discussing his concern over the progress of his career as a poet. With further related material. CE May 22 (313) $350

**Lips, Johann Heinrich, 1758-1817**
**Series** of 4 A Ls s, 7 Nov 1801 to 29 June 1802. 8 pp, size not stated. To Johann Heinrich von Dannecker. Concerning a bust of Lavater. HN May 15 (2643) DM2,000

**Lipton, Sir Thomas Johnstone, 1850-1931**
**Photograph, sgd & inscr,** 1 Jan 1926. 299mm by 248mm, mtd. Full length. Marans collection. CE Apr 17 (152) $400

**Lister, Joseph Lister, Baron, 1827-1912**
**Ds,** 6 Nov 1868. 1 p, 16mo. Surgery class admission ticket for Thomas B. Henderson for the 1868-69 session at the University of Glasgow. rms Nov 30 (216) $700

**Liszt, Franz, 1811-86**
**Autograph music,** Aufruf zum Kampf, 4 bars in D major from his Phantasiestueck on themes from Wagner's Rienzi, scored for piano, [n.d.]. 1 p, 8vo. Including autograph instructions for insertion. S Dec 1 (208) £800
— Autograph music, concluding part of his cantata Sainte Cecile, Legende; 21 Aug 1874. 4 pp, folio. Full score, for orchestra, voice, chorus & organ, notated on 1 or 2 systems per page of up to 24 staves each. Working Ms. S Dec 1 (204) £2,200
— Autograph music, Petrarch Sonnet no 47, for voice & piano, 12 Dec 1851. 8 pp, folio. Unpbd version in F-sharp major, notated on 3 systems per page of 3 staves each. Sgd & inscr to Salvatore Marchesi. S May 15 (403) £5,000
**Ms,** Ungarischer Koenigs-Hymnus, in short score; [c.1883]. 4 pp, folio, in Liszt's lea portfolio. In a scribal hand, with the autograph Ms by Liszt of an 8-bar introduction laid down at head, 11.5cm by 23.5cm. S Dec 1 (216) £1,400
**ALs,** 21 May [1846]. 2 pp, 8vo. To Jules Janin. Discussing his literary activity & announcing that he will travel to Hungary. S Dec 1 (206) £1,100
— 18 Sept 1848. 5 pp, 4to. To the pbr Kistner. Discussing the publication of several of his works. S Dec 1 (210) £1,400
— 25 Dec 1851. 4 pp, 8vo. To Mme Karlowa. About her son's promising debut as an actor. star Mar 22 (913) DM1,300
— 9 July 1853. 2 pp, 8vo. Recipient unnamed. Discussing the date for a performance of Tannhaeuser, & mentioning Wagner. S Dec 1 (215) £600
— 29 Aug 1871. 1 p, 8vo. To Gottlieb Hemleb. Asking him to forward a letter. star Mar 22 (914) DM550
— [Oct 1871]. 3 pp, 4to. Draft, agreeing to a request by Breitkopf & Haertel (on verso) to help decide a question of disputed authorship. Illus in cat. S Dec 1 (214) £800
— 19 Aug 1873. 4 pp, 8vo. To Eduard Liszt. Reporting on a visit to Bayreuth, festivities in Weimar, his travel plans, etc. S May 15 (394) £2,200
— 11 Mar 1882. 3 pp, 8vo. Recipient unnamed. Discussing recipient's 2 sacred works & sending a Mass of his own. S Dec 1 (205) £680
— 8 May 1885. 2 pp, 8vo. To Carl Riedel. Advising him on a recital program. S May 15 (396) £500
**ANs,** 10 Nov [n.y.]. 1 p, on engraved visiting card. To [Josef] Tichatschek. Hoping to see him in Ballenstedt. star Mar 22 (917) DM280
**Autograph quotation,** 8 bars from the Fantasia on Themes from Berlioz's Lelio, May 183[5?]. 1 p, 20cm by 25.5cm. Sgd. S May 15 (399) £700
— Anr, Preludio, 5 bars notated on 2 systems of 2 staves each, 30 Aug 1841. 1 p, 18cm by 21.5cm, cut from larger sheet. Sgd. With a photograph. Illus in cat. S Dec 1 (207) £1,400
— Anr, 27 bars from his symphonic poem Orpheus, scored for piano; [n.d.]. 1 p, c.20cm by 27cm. Sgd. Illus in cat. S Dec 1 (211) £1,800

**Autograph sentiment,** inscr to Alban Stolz, sgd, 21 Sept 1879. 1 p, 4to. Mtd. star Mar 22 (915) DM380

**Photograph,** sgd, [c.1875]. 104mm by 60mm, mtd. Half-length vignette port, by Fratelli d'Alessandri. Illus in cat. Marans collection. CE Apr 17 (242) $1,100

— Anr, [1870s]. 28cm by 23cm. By Luckhardt. Illus in cat. S Dec 1 (213) £1,700

— Orsay, Alfred Guillaume Gabriel, Comte d'. - Orig drawing, port of Liszt, 27 May 1840. Framed, overall size 43cm by 33cm. In pencil; sgd by d'Orsay & Liszt. Illus in cat. S May 15 (402) £2,600

**Little, Malcolm.** See: Malcolm X

**Litvinov Maxim.** See: Vishinsky, Andrei & Litvinov Maxim

**Liverpool, Charles Jenkinson, 1st Earl of, 1727-1808.** See: Jenkinson, Charles

**Livingston, Robert R., 1746-1813**
**Ls,** 23 June 1782. 4 pp, folio. To John Jay. Discussing relations with Spain, the recognition of American independence, & a proposal for the cessation of hostilities. P Dec 13 (247) $8,500
See also: United States of America

**Livingstone, David, 1813-73**
**ALs,** 20 July 1858. 4 pp, 8vo. To Lady Franklin. Sending news of his children. S Dec 18 (508) £400 [Stodolski]
— 6 May 1861. 8 pp, no size given. To Thomas Berry Horsfall. Concerning his attempts to find a way into Africa that does not involve travelling through Portuguese territories & describing the Rovuma. Creased & folds faded. With a second letter sgd about a vessel to survey the Zambesi. Creased. Illus in cat Ck Nov 17 (101) £5,000

**Lockwood, Belva Ann Bennett, 1830-1917**
**ALs,** 4 Aug 1906. 1 p, 4to. To Julia Babbitt. Suggesting that they travel to a women's conference together. rms Mar 21 (353) $650
**Signature,** [n.d.]. Size not stated (card). Including address. With a port. Illus in cat. rms Mar 21 (313) $420

**Loewe, Carl, 1796-1869**
**ALs,** 24 Feb 1850. 1 p, 4to. To H. L. E. Dorn. Congratulating him on an appointment & praising his Te Deum. star Mar 22 (920) DM1,000

**Loewenstein, Carlo Frederico de**
**Ms,** III Quartetti concertanti..., & III Quintetti ... al Signor Federico Witt, [c.1820]. 6 vols, 355mm by 250mm. Contemp bds. Including numerous corrections & additions. HH Nov 14 (20) DM360

**Log Books**
— "Cyclamen." - Ms, private log of an anonymous crew member of the armed sloop H.M.S. Cyclamen, 4 Apr 1916 to 17 Mar 1919. About 250 pp, folio, in leabacked ledger. b May 30 (281) £250

— "Discovery." - Ms, meteorological log from the expedition ship Discovery, Feb 1930 to 31 Mar 1930. 106 pp, 4to, in orig cloth. CA Mar 26 (111) A$500

— "Gorch Fock". - Ms, log kept by the sailor Karl Kreuzer on S.S. Gorch Fock, April to June 1938. 98 pp (6 blank), 275mm by 225mm, in half cloth. Including 8 drawings & 23 maps & photographs pasted in. JG Sept 29 (320) DM360

— "Imperieuse" & "Coromandel". - Ms log book kept by Lt. G. A. Doublas R.N. on the flagships of Adm. Sir James Hope, the commander in chief in China, 1861-65. About 100 pp. Wraps. With coastal profiles, sketches & contemp newspaper cuttings pasted in or loosely inserted. S July 11 (390) £800

**Logan, John Alexander, 1826-86**
**ALs,** 25 Feb 1868. 1 p, 4to. To Francis De Grass. Promising to recommend recipient's friend if possible. Illus in cat. rms June 6 (46) $170

**Lombard, Carole, 1908-42**
**Photograph,** sgd & inscr, [25 Nov 1938]. Folio. A studio pose in a glamourous gown. Inscr to Joan. Dated on verso. With chipped edges. Illus in cat rms Oct 11 (244) $900

**Lombardi, Vincent Thomas, 1913-70**
**Photograph,** sgd, [c.1965]. 250mm by 205mm. Shoulder-length port. Illus in cat. Marans collection. CE Apr 17 (277) $450

**Lombroso, Cesare, 1835-1909**
**ALs,** 29 Oct 1890. 1 p, 8vo. Recipient unnamed. Stating that socialism is not possible at this time but remains a theoretical concept. star Mar 21 (547) DM240

**London, Charmian K.**
**Series** of 4 Ls s, 26 July 1929 to 31 Jan 1931. 9 pp, 8vo. To Jack Harries. cb June 25 (2548) $400

**London, Jack, 1876-1916**
**ALs,** 31 July 1910. 1 p, no size given. To Charmian London. About Charmian's aunt's wedding plans. Sgd as "Your man" Creased. Illus in cat pba Oct 5 (205) $1,200
— 17 Aug 1912. 4 pp, no size given. To his wife Charmian. About visits he has made in London. Sgd as "Mate-man". pba Oct 5 (207) $2,250
— 19 Aug 1912. 5 pp, no size given. To his Wife Charmian ("White Woman, alias Mate, alias Miss Legs"). Concerning his travel plans & his irritation at her for not writing to him. pba Oct 5 (208) $3,250
— 14 Oct 1912. 3 pp, no size given. To his wife Charmian. About her miscarriage: " But everything is all right for you and me and ours that is to be. We have been patient and we will leave our heart's desire. I never loved you more than I love you now." Sgd as "Your Own Man". pba Oct 5 (206) $3,000
**Ls,** [n.d.] 1 p, 4to. To unnamed recipient. Second page only. Recommending resources related to his work "The War of the Classes". Folds separated & some archival repairs. pba Oct 26 (44) $500

**Check,** sgd, 23 Dec 1909. Payable to cash for $150. Perforations affecting 1st 2 letters. wa Oct 28 (34) $260

**Photograph,** sgd, [c.1915]. 180mm by 233mm. Half length, by Arnold Genthe. Illus in cat. Marans collection. CE Apr 17 (81) $1,700

### Long, Huey Pierce, 1893-1935

**Ds,** Dec 1930. 1 p, double 4to. $1,000 State of Louisiana Gold Bond bearing 4% interest. Countersgd by 3 other unnamed Louisiana Officials. With cancelation holes. Bond due 1957. sg Sept 28 (171) $250

### Longfellow, Henry Wadsworth, 1807-82

**Autograph Ms,** quatrain beginning "Lives of great men all remind us...." 1 p, 4.25 by 6.25 inches, tipped to bd. rs Nov 11 (31) $750

**ALs,** 14 Jan 1842. 4 pp, 248mm by 200mm. To Samuel Ward. About his work & other literary matters. With repaired seal tear. P Dec 12 (114) $1,800

— 21 Jan 1851. 4 pp, 8vo. Recipient unnamed. Declining an invitation because he will not be able to visit England that year. CE May 22 (319) $260

— 12 Nov 1860. 4 pp, 8vo. To F. O. C. Darley. About a portrait : "...the main business has not for a moment [been] neglected. I have been twice to Whipple; and should have been again, but for the rainy week we have had. The report thus far is; body and looks successful; face not satisfactory to Gods or men. Hawthorne and Emerson have already sat for you, but not with entire success..." With Signature excised & a blank sheet containing his signature affixed. Mtd with ports of Longfellow & Darley. Framed under glass so it is visible on both sides. Over-all size c. 23.2 by 18.5 inches. rms Oct 11 (245) $350

— 29 Mar 1867. 1 p, 8vo. Recipient unnamed. Accepting an invitation. Framed with port. sg Feb 1 (135) $225

**Photograph,** sgd, [c.1874]. 164mm by 107mm, mtd. Seated; by Warren. Illus in cat. Marans collection. CE Apr 17 (82) $950

**Signature,** 1875. On 2 by 4 inch slip of paper. pba Feb 22 (76) $120 ·

### Longueville, Henri II d'Orléans, Duc de, 1595-1663

**Ls,** 18 Dec 1640. 1 p, 4to. To Landgraf Georg II von Hessen-Darmstadt. Assuming that his envoy has arrived with his messages by now. Including engraved port. Kuenzel collection. star Mar 22 (1257) DM340

### Lopez, Aaron, 1731-82

**Ds,** Oct 1775. 2 pp, 4to. Bankruptcy petition of Nathaniel Tibbits to the General Assembly of the Colony of Rhode Island, sgd by Lopez as a Subscriber Creditor. Also sgd by 11 others. sg June 6 (111) $450

### Lortzing, Albert, 1801-51

**ALs,** 2 Nov 1844. 1 p, 4to. To Ferdinand David. Declining an invitation because of a previous engagement. star Mar 22 (919) DM900

### Lossing, Benson John, 1813-91

**Autograph Ms,** article, account of the Battle of Bunker Hill, sgd; [1875]. Length not stated. Ptd in the Poughkeepsie Eagle on the centennial anniversary of the battle. P Dec 13 (34) $550

### Louis Napoleon, Crown Prince of France, 1856-79

**Ms,** text of the words found on his body. Illuminated Ms in the hand of Minna Parkes Smith, 1880. Mtd in a triptych in imperial velvet with engraved ormulu fittings in gothic style, height 370mm. Illus in cat b Sept 20 (19) £2,800

**Photograph,** sgd, 28 July 1877. 164mm by 109mm, mtd. Leaning against a cabinet, by Alexander Bassano. Illus in cat. Marans collection. CE Apr 17 (160) $500

### Louis Philippe, King of France, 1773-1850

**ALs,** 21 June 1826. 2 pp, 4to. To an unnamed count. Discussing a legal matter. star Mar 22 (1303) DM500

### Louis XIII, King of France, 1601-43

**Ds,** 8 May 1628. 1 p, folio. Order to procure wood for the fortification of the town of Brouage. star Mar 22 (1286) DM440

### Louis XIV, King of France, 1638-1715

**AL,** 22 Apr 1709. 2 pp, 4to. To Maria Anna of Pfalz-Neuburg, Queen of Spain. About the payment of her debts & her future residence in Toulouse. Illus in cat. HN May 15 (2646) DM10,500

**Ds,** 1676. 1 p, folio. Military appointment. Toned. With 19th century engraving of the King. Framed. Over-all size 18 by 22 inches. Illus in cat rms Oct 11 (404) $950

— 15 Apr 1687. 12 by 18.5 inches, on vellum. rs Nov 11 (32) $300

— Nov 1704. 6 pp, on vellum, folio. Edict making clear his intention to set proper standards for wine, cider & spirits. Also sgd by Colbert. This copy addressed to the Parlement of Rennes. S Oct 12 (77) £800

— 11 July 1790. 1 p, folio, framed with port. Authorization for a pension payment. Countersgd by Jacques Necker. CE June 12 (81) $650

**Document,** 12 Apr 1702. 1 p, folio. Appointment of Bonnaventure Testu as kitchen boy. Including secretarial signature. star Mar 22 (1290) DM240

— 13 Dec 1714. 1 p, folio. Approval of the nomination of a prior for the Cistercian monastery at Mouchy-le-Chatel. Including secretarial signature. star Mar 22 (1291) DM200

### Louis XV, King of France, 1710-74

**Ds,** 1 June 1757. 1 p. Commission of Ch. d'Omonville into an infantry regiment destined for Santo Domingo. b Dec 5 (173) £85

— 1 Oct 1766. 1 p, folio. Pay order in favor of the daughter of the drummer Bressier. star Mar 22 (1295) DM580

### Louis XVI, King of France, 1754-93

**Ds,** 3 Oct 1776. 2 pp, folio. Appointment of Henri Jacques de Millau as Commissioner to Louisiana. CNY Jan 26 (164) $6,000

— 5 Apr 1789. 1 p, folio. Pay order in favor of Sieur Dufeu. HH May 9 (2507) DM600

## LOUIS

— 3 Jan 1790. 1 p, folio. Pay order addressed to the treasurer of the Invalides. With ALs by Thomas Charles Naudet on verso. S May 15 (195) £500

— 19 Apr 1791. 1 p, folio. Pay order in favor of M. de la Garde. star Mar 22 (1299) DM900

**Louis XVIII, King of France, 1755-1824**

Ds, 9 Nov 1776. 1 p, 10.25 by 15 inches. Ordering payment for laundry & purchases at Brunoy. Sgd as "Louis Stanislas Xavier". With a separating fold. Dar Oct 19 (132) $130

— 21 Jan 1818. 1 p, oblong folio. Appointment of Baron Hubert Callier de St. Apollin to honorary rank of lieutenant general. Countersgd by Gouvion de St. Cyr. sg June 6 (114) $325

**Louise, Queen of Gustav Adolf VI of Sweden, 1889-1965.** See: Gustav VI Adolf & Louise

**Louvois, Francois Michel le Tellier, Marquis de, 1639-91**

Ms, inventory of his property for his will. 1 July 1726. 78 pp, folio, sewn. C June 26 (321) £300

**Louys, Pierre, 1870-1925**

ALs, 22 Mar 1894. 7 pp, 8vo. To Mme de St. Marceaux. Defending Claude Debussy whose honor has been attacked. star Mar 21 (251) DM750

**Lovecraft, Howard Phillips, 1890-1937**

ALs, 26 Feb 1932. 2 pp. To Clark Ashton Smith. About the supernatural & his & Smith's writings. pba May 23 (226) $950

— [1935]. 2 pp, 8vo. To Clark Ashton Smith. Answering questions about politics & current events. Addressed to Klarkash-Ton & sgd as Ech-Pi-El. sg Dec 14 (204) $1,600

**Lovejoy, Owen**

ALs, 3 Jan 1860. 1 p, 8vo. To " Friend Grimes". Accepting the offer of a loan. pba June 13 (247) $50

**Lowe, Sir Hudson, 1769-1844**

Ls, 12 July 1817. 25 pp, 4to, stitched. To Sir Pulteney Malcolm. Listing Malcolm's various visits to Napoleon & complaining of his conduct. Lazarus collection. S May 15 (240) £800

— 12 July 1818. 4 pp, 4to. To Count Montholon. Discussing medical care for Napoleon on St. Helena. rms June 6 (431) $3,750

**Lowe, Thaddeus Sobieski Coulincourt, 1832-1913**

Ds, 7 Feb 1868. 1 p, 4to. Promissory note to James T. Ames for $100. Illus in cat. rms Mar 21 (254) $325

— 25 July 1868. 1 p, 4to. To James T. Ames, the manufacturer of his mechanical works. About an experiment. rms Nov 30 (78) $1,000

Autograph endorsement, sgd, on ALs addressed to him by James T. Ames, 18 Apr 1868, 1 p, 4to, concerning the cost of experiments with his machinery; accepting Ames's conditions. Illus in cat. rms Mar 21 (228) $900

**Lowell, James Russell, 1819-91**

Autograph Ms, poem, Invita Minerva. 30 lines in 5 stanzas, 2 pp. Bound with port in mor gilt by Walters. Neufeld copy CE Sept 27 (16) $380

Autograph quotation, sgd, 7 July 1859. 8 lines beginning "Sincere & genuine autographs". rms Nov 30 (220) $340

**Lowry, Malcolm, 1909-57**

Autograph Ms, diary, 10 Apr to 2 Sept 1945. 18 pp, 4to, in a binder. About his private life, his drinking, reading & writing. CNY May 17 (93) $2,200

**Luckner, Felix, Graf von, 1881-1966**

Series of 4 A Ns s, 17 Sept 1963. 4 pp, 8vo. To an unnamed lady. Sending greetings. HN May 15 (2644) DM200

**Ludwig I, King of Bavaria, 1786-1868**

ALs, 4 July 1809. 2 pp, 4to. To [Heinrich Luden]. Expressing interest in German historiography. star Mar 22 (1169) DM1,100

— 29 Oct 1819. 2 pp, 4to. To an unnamed Cardinal. Thanking for sending him a sculpture. In Italian. star Mar 22 (1170) DM1,100

Ls, 18 Apr 1841. 1 p, 4to. To Ferdinand, King of the Two Sicilies. Sending congratulations on the birth of a son. rms June 6 (411) $260

ANs, 8 Mar [18]28. 1 p, 8vo. To Cornelius. Concering etchings to be made of some frescoes. HH May 9 (2504) DM260

**Ludwig II, King of Bavaria, 1845-86**

ALs, [n.d.]. 2 pp, 8vo. To Karl [Hesselschwert]. Inquiring about an actor & a painter in Bologna. Illus in cat. star Mar 22 (1175) DM3,000

Ls, 20 Apr 1868. 1 p, 4to. To Cardinal Innocenzo Ferrieri. Sending congratulations on his elevation to the cardinalate. star Mar 22 (1173) DM750

— 3 June 1877. 1 p, folio. To Prince Chlodwig von Hohenlohe-Schillingsfuerst. Inviting him to a meeting of a diet. star Mar 22 (1174) DM950

Ds, 30 Jan 1871. 1 p, folio. Presentation of a medal [not present]. sg Feb 1 (137) $175

— 23 Aug 1879. 1 p, 4to. Judicial appointment for Hermann von Sonnenberg. JG Sept 29 (321) DM450

— 6 Apr 1884. 1 p, folio. Administrative appointment for Herr von Kissingen. HH May 9 (2505) DM600

**Ludwig III, King of Bavaria, 1845-1921**

ALs, 19 June 1908. 6 pp, 8vo. To Admiral von Tirpitz. Reporting about his visits in several German ports. HH May 9 (2506) DM800

**Ludwig IX, Herzog von Bayern-Landshut, 1417-79**

Ds, [Aug] 1471. 1 p, vellum, 188mm by 343mm. Confirmation of rights & benefits. Illus in cat. JG Mar 29 (267) DM1,500

**Luettwitz, Hinko von, 1855-1928**

Ls, 4 Aug 1919. 2 pp, 4to. To Herr Hoffmann. Responding to an inquiry concerning relations between Goethe & his daughter-in-law & some of his ancestors. HN May 15 (2647) DM260

**Luise, Queen of Friedrich Wilhelm III of Prussia, 1776-1810**
**ALs,** 7 Oct 1803. 3 pp, 4to. To her sisters Therese & Friederike. About several deaths in the family & other family matters. HN Nov 24 (2820) DM2,800

**Luise, Grossherzogin von Baden, 1838-1923**
**ALs,** 5 Apr 1871. 3 pp, 8vo. To Prince Frederick of the Netherlands. Sending condolences on the death of his daughter, the Queen of Sweden. HN May 15 (2648) DM260

**Lully, Jean Baptiste, 1632-87**
**Ds,** 12 Oct 1675. 1 p, folio. Receipt for 105 livres as his salary. Illus in cat. star Mar 22 (921) DM5,500

**Lutoslawski, Witold**
**Autograph music,** sketches for a piano concerto, [n.d.]. 1 p, 4to, cut from larger sheet. In pencil; sgd & inscr later. star Mar 22 (922) DM650

**Lutyens, Sir Edwin**
**Series** of 7 A Ls s, 1906-14. 23 pp, 8vo. To the Princess Alexis Dolgorouki. About the house he is building for her. pn Nov 9 (427) £650

**Lyell, Sir Charles, 1797-1875**
**Ls,** 21 Nov 1833. 1 p, folio. To Dr. Isaac Hays. Official expression of thanks on behalf of the Geological Society of London for the donation of Hays's Descriptions of the Inferior Maxillary bones of Mastodons in the Cabinet of the American Philosophical Society. rms Nov 30 (221) $500

**Lynch, Thomas, Signer from South Carolina**
**Ds,** 22 Aug 1775. 1 p, 4to. Receipt for legal compensation for an executed slave belonging to his father. Illus in cat. Doheny collection. P Dec 13 (248) $36,000
**Cut signature,** [n.d.]. Clipped from an endorsement, with portions in his hand. 16mm by 48mm, mtd. P June 5 (80) $9,000

**Lytton, Edward Robert Bulwer, 1st Earl, 1831-91**
**A Ls s (2),** 22 May & 29 Dec 1878. 28 pp, 4to. To Sir WIlliam Henry Haggard. About the british invasion of Afghanistan. S July 11 (360) £400

# M

**Maas, Joachim, 1901-72**
**Autograph Ms,** 5 poems & 3 additional verses, [c.1949]. 4 pp, 8vo, in a copy of his book Des Nachts und am Tage. Hamburg, 1948. Additions & corrections for the 2d Ed. HN Nov 24 (2821) DM800

**MacArthur, Douglas, 1880-1964**
**Ls,** 15 Feb 1956. 1 p, 4to. To Philip L. Dickinson. Thanking him for birthday wishes. pba Oct 26 (186) $150
**ANs,** [31 Dec 1947.] In lower blank margin of a letter from Jack M. Small in lower margin requesting MacArthur to sign 3 blocks of stamps: "Glad to-". pba June 13 (93) $80
**Ds,** 1918. Size not stated. American Expeditionary Forces Identity Card including shoulder-length photograph pasted on, 38mm by 27mm. Illus in cat. Marans collection. CE Apr 17 (153) $7,500
**Photograph, sgd & inscr,** [c.1930-35]. 7 by 9.75 inch sepia photo in uniform as a 4-star general. Inscr to General Gibbins. Over-all size 9.25 by 13.1 inches. sg Sept 28 (172) $650
— **Anr,** [n.d.]. About 11 by 14 inches. Inscr to Sams. Signature uneven from poor ink flow. sg June 6 (116) $325

**McCarthy, Joseph R., 1908-57**
**Ds,** 20 May 1952. 1 p, folio. Certificate for 100 shares of capital stock of Four Wheel Drive Auto Company issued to McCarthy. With transfer endorsement on verso. Sgd as "Joe McCarthy". sg Sept 28 (176) $200

**McClellan, George B., 1826-85**
**Photograph, sgd,** [c.1863]. Carte size; framed, overall size 12.25 by 11 inches. Bust pose, in uniform; by F. Gutekunst. Illus in cat. rms June 6 (47) $1,500
**Signature,** [n.d.]. On 2 by 4 inch slip. Sgd as "Geo. B. McClellan". Mtd. Stained. pba Feb 22 (172) $65

**Macdonald, Etienne Jacques Joseph Alexandre, Duc de Tarente, 1765-1840**
**Ds,** 13 May 1818. 1 p, 4to. Certificate honoring Le Comte Muraire for serving in the Midi Canal campaign. Sgd as "Macdonald". Illus in cat pba Feb 22 (305) $130

**McDougall, Alexander**
**Ds,** 1 July 1760. 1 p, 4to. Tax levy stating that " We John Robertson, Mariner and Alexander McDougall of New York, Merchant are held firmly bound unto our Sovereign Lord George..." pba Oct 26 (145) $325

**Macer, Aemilius.** See: Odo de Meung

**McHenry, James, 1753-1816**
**ALs,** 28 Oct 1778. 4 pp, folio. To Dr. Hugh Williamson. About his service as senior Surgeon at Valley Forge: "We are still much perplexed as to the enemy. A confusion of intelligence from New-York, and the season of the year, renders the total evacuation of that place or the State in general rather a matter of doubt and uncertainty...we have lately adopted in wounds of the breast - Harsh dressings...The success...has been very remarkable..." Browned at folds. Illus in cat rms Oct 11 (28) $3,400
— 26 July 1783. 1 p, folio. To Thomas Stone. Referring to the appointment of a minister for foreign affairs. Illus in cat. rms Mar 21 (209) $1,800

**McHenry, James, 1753-1816 —& Decatur, Stephen, 1779-1820 —& Others**
**Ls,** 7 June 1798. 1 p, 8vo. To the War Dept. Ordering a set of Signal flags. Also sgd by Samuel Hodgson. With defects. sg Sept 28 (9) $700

**McIntosh, Lachlan, 1725-1806**
ALs, 25 Aug 1778. 1 p, folio. To the Lieutenant of Berkeley County, Virginia. Requesting troops for a western expedition. Including franking signature. P Dec 13 (267) $3,500

Ds, 5 May 1791. 1 p, 4to. Sailing permit for the sloop "Anna" to proceed to New York. Countersgd by port collector John Habersham. Lacking upper left blank corner. Detail in cat sg Sept 28 (177) $600

**McKean, Thomas, Signer from Delaware**
ALs, 3 Aug 1791. 2 pp, 4to. To Thomas Rodney. Defending recipient's brother Caesar Rodney against political attacks. Illus in cat. P Dec 13 (268) $4,750

Ds, 30 July 1803. 1 p, oblong folio, on vellum. Land grant in Luzerne County called Mount Holly. Countersgd on verso by T. Matlock. Framed. rms Nov 30 (226) $200

**Mackenzie, Sir Alexander C., 1847-1935**
Series of 65 A Ls s, 1880-1924. About 230 pp, 8vo. To Alfred & Jack Littleton of Novello's. About his compositions. S May 15 (89) £1,700

**Mackenzie, Sir Compton, 1883-1972**
Ms, entitled "Recollection of Henry James". [14 Jan 1955]. 8 pp, no size given. A recollection of the author: "I first remember him with a beard, which suited him. Although it concealed its sensitive mouth...." Ck Nov 17 (103) £120

**MacKenzie, William Lyon, 1795-1861**
ALs, 30 Jan 1836. 3 pp, 4to. To the Cashier of the U.S. Branch Bank in Buffalo. Inquiring about a financial transaction. rms Mar 21 (245) $275

**McKinley, William, 1843-1901**
Ls, 23 May 1888. 1 p, 8vo. To M. M. Garrett. Thanking for congratulations & promising to send his speech. Illus in cat. rms Mar 21 (96) $250

— 11 Aug 1896 1 p, 8vo. To Gen. Wm. M. Osborn. Introducing Charles H. Gray, a newspaperman. Framed with McKinley campaign pin & ribbon & pass for 1896 Republican convention. rms Nov 30 (37) $500

— 12 Nov 1896. 1 p, 8vo. To Henry C. Potter. Thanking for congratulations on his election. rms June 6 (416) $195

— 21 Nov 1896. 1 p, no size given. To W. G. Raines. Thanking Raines for his letter. With an annotation in Raines's hand: " May 31st 1900 I had a long, confidential interview with him alone in the Cabinet Room at the White House - He allowed me to give him some advice as well as information - He neither desires, nor expects reelection because as he said to me, the responsibilities are too great for mortal men. W. G. R." With holograph footnotes as well dated 1 June 1900. Also with a mourning ribbon & McKinley's port. Also with souvenir ticket to the Pan American Exposition. Over-all size 13.5 by 17.5 inches. Illus in cat rms Oct 11 (317) $500

ANs, 6 June 1898. On 2.75 by 4.3 inch card. To Genl. Corbin: "If eligible appoint Frank Hain Martin of Iowa a 2d Lieutenant in the 2nd U.S. Vol Eng, to be detailed on the staff of Gnl Lincoln...." pba Oct 26 (289) $325

Ds, 19 Feb 1898. 1 p, 17 by 22 inches. Appointment of Richard F. Lawson as postmaster at Effingham, Illinois. Margins stained. With related material. sg Sept 28 (178) $275

— 24 June 1898. 1 p, oblong folio. Appointment of Isaac R. Huggins as Postmaster at Palmyra, Missouri. Countersgd by Charles Emory Smith as Postmaster General. CE June 12 (82) $210

— 12 Aug 1899. 2 pp, 10 by 6 inches. A Pardon for Charles Anderson who was charged with "selling liquor to Indians". Countersgd by Acting Attorney General James E. Boyd. With folds. Dar Oct 19 (139) $950

— 18 Dec 1899. 1 p, 4to. Disapproval of an act in the Legislature of the Chickasaw Nation passed in Nov 1899. Framed with photo. wa Oct 28 (211) $350

— 26 Dec 1899. 1 p, 18.5 by 14.5 inches, framed. Appointment of Harry D. Humphrey as Captain of Infantry. rs Nov 11 (34) $275

— 8 Feb 1900. 1 p, folio, on vellum. Appointing Edgar Gadwin as a Captain in the Corps of Engineers. Countersgd by Secretary of War Elihu Root. First name in McKinley's signature is light. pba Oct 26 (288) $275

Autograph telegram, sgd, 30 May 1897. 1 p, on imprinted Executive Mansion telegram form. To Dr. J. N. Bishop in New work. Requesting a bottle of medicine to be sent immediately to Mrs. McKinley. rms Nov 30 (227) $700

Group photograph, sgd, 1898. Of McKinley with his Cabinet. Also sgd by John W. Griggs, James Wilson, William R. Day, C. N. Bliss & others. F Mar 28 (828) $1,900

Photograph, sgd, [c.1890s]. 4 by 5.5 inch bust photo. By Courtney, McKinley & Block. Mtd Over-all size 5.25 by 7.25 inches. Illus in cat sg Sept 28 (179) $450

Signature, 3 Feb 1882. No size given. On Album page. Sgd as " Wm. McKinley". pba Feb 22 (265) $130

**McManus, George, 1884-1954 —& Others**
Group photograph, [c.1945]. 181mm by 238mm. Sgd by Alex Raymond & George McManus; sgd & inscr by Otto Sorglow, Harry Foster Welch, Arthur "Bugs" Baer, & Ross Westover. Illus in cat. Marans collection. CE Apr 17 (202) $420

**McQueen, Steve, 1930-80**
Ls, 18 Aug 1972. 1 p, 4to. To Kenneth Ziffren. concerning their relationship: " I'm going to try very hard not to have any kind of detached relationship with you..." pba June 13 (185) $130

**Madariaga y Rojo, Salvador de, 1886-1978**
Collection of 4 A Ls s & 9 Ls s, 17 Aug 1933 to 19 Dec 1963. 14 pp, 4to & 8vo. To Antonio Aita. About various literary matters. star Mar 21 (253) DM650

**Madison, Dorothy Payne Todd ("Dolley"), 1768-1849**

**ALs,** [c.1785]. 3 pp, 4to. To Eliza Brooke. Chatting about friends & their marriages. rms Mar 21 (18) $4,500

**Ls,** 9 Oct 1835. 1 p, 4to. To Ann Maury. Describing her eye problems at length to her cousin: " the pain from the inflamed eyes and lids calls for continual bathing with milk & water-sassafras teas & thereby I derive the only ease that I can experience..." Illus in cat rms Oct 11 (247) $1,700

**Madison, James, 1751-1836**

**Autograph Ms,** draft of 2 resolutions addressed to the Senate & House of Representatives, [21 Dec 1816 & 3 Feb 1817]. 2 pp, 4to. Concerning tariff questions. Forbes Magazine collection. CNY May 17 (163) $3,000

**ALs,** 28 Aug 1799. 1 p, 238mm by 187mm. To Thomas Jefferson. Recommending a plasterer for work at Jefferson's home. Docketed in Jefferson's hand. P June 5 (81) $2,500

— 15 Apr 1803. 1 p, 4to. To Robert Purviance. Writing the Baltimore Collector of the Customs about a Captain Lewis. Illus in cat pba Oct 26 (282) $2,500

— 24 June 1805. 2 pp, 4to. To Theodorus Bailey. Concerning the problem of obtaining overseas newspapers for United States's envoys. Mtd. Spotted. With Madison's free frank. With related material. CNY Dec 15 (97) $2,200

— 21 Feb 1806. 2 pp, 4to. To the Marquis de Lafayette. Regretting that the United States will not be able to assist him with a loan. Illus in cat. P Dec 13 (249) $13,000

— 30 Oct 1807. 2 pp, 4to. To William Jarvis. Sending information about the attack on USS Chesapeake, & referring to the crops. rms Mar 21 (15) $5,500

— 30 Aug 1815. 2 pp, 4to. To George Graham. Referring to the commercial treaty with Great Britain & discussing various matters pertaining to the Department of War. Illus in cat. P Dec 13 (252) $6,000

— 18 Apr 1821. 1 p, 4to. To [Anthony Charles Cazenove]. Ordering sugar, coffee and "Lisbon Wine". Margins trimmed. CNY Dec 15 (211) $1,700

**Ls,** 23 July 1802. 3 pp, 4to. To Rufus King. About monetary problems & political matters including the "Cession of Louisiana & the Floridas to France..." Sang - Engelhard collections. CNY Jan 26 (169) $6,500

— 31 Jan 1804. 18 pp, 4to. To Robert R. Livingston, U. S. minister in Paris. Informing him of the progress of the transfer of the rule of the Louisiana territory from France to the U. S. Partly written in numerical cipher. Sang - Engelhard collections. Illus in cat CNY Jan 26 (178) $26,000

— 23 Apr 1807. 1 p, 244mm by 197mm. To Gov. John T. Gilman of New Hampshire. Circular letter accompanying a printed collection of laws passed by the 9th Congress [not present]. Illus in cat P June 5 (82) $2,200

**Ds,** 23 July 1804. 1 p, 4to. Laisser-passer for Daniel Nicholas Morice. sg Feb 1 (139) $550

— 16 Aug 1807. 1 p, 15.5 by 10.25 inches. Ship's passport for the Citizen of NY. Countersgd by Robert Smith. rs Nov 11 (33) $375

— 6 Aug 1810. 1 p, folio. Ship's passport for the ship Hunter. Countersgd by R. Smith. Illus in cat. rms June 6 (412) $800

— 1 Dec 1810. 1 p, folio. A Four-language Ship's Papers to the Schooner the Ann. Countersgd by Secretary of State Robert Smith. Illus in cat pba Oct 26 (283) $1,100

— 1 Dec 1810. 1 p, folio. Four-language Ships' Papers for William Doliber of the schooner The Ann. Countersgd by Secretary of State Robert Smith. Illus in cat pba Oct 26 (283) $1,100

— 20 Feb 1811. 1 p, folio. Ship's Papers in 4 languages for the brig Ida. Countersgd by R. Smith. rms Mar 21 (16) $1,200

— 14 June 1811. 1 p, 15 by 11 inches. 1 p, 17 by 21 inches. Four-language ship's papers for the sloop Laura. sg Feb 1 (141) $1,100

— 30 Sept 1811. 2 pp, 244mm by 197mm. To Richard Cutts. Predicting that Congress will seek a declaration of war unless British maritime policy changes. Mtd. P June 5 (84) $3,750

— 23 Dec 1811. 1 p, folio. Land grant to Philip Kuhn. Countersgd by Monroe. P Dec 13 (250) $750

— 15 Feb 1812. 1 p, folio. Ship's papers. Countersgd by James Monroe. F Mar 28 (694A) $1,050

— 11 Apr 1812. 17 by 21 inches. Four-language ship's papers for the ship Gossypium. Countersgd by Sec. of State James Monroe. sg Feb 1 (142) $1,400

— 21 Mar 1815. 1 p, folio. Appointing Roger Skinner Attorney of the United States "in and for the Northern District of the State of New York..." Countersgd by Secretary of State James Monroe. Mtd & framed with engraved ports of Madison & Monroe. Overall size 9.5 by 15.5 inches. Edges worn. CNY Dec 15 (98) $900

— 12 Sept 1815. 1 p, folio. Patent for Bracket Greenough for a "machine for facilitating the making of Carriage Wheels". Framed. P Dec 13 (253) $1,500

— [n.d.]. 1 p, on vellum, folio. Unaccomplished ship's passport. CE June 12 (83) $1,000

**Check,** sgd, 8 Mar 1813. Payable to A.B. or Bearer for $300. Perforations affecting signature in 2 places. rms Nov 30 (119) $875

**Anr,** 8 May 1817. 1 p, 4to. $600 payble to Richard Cutts, Congressman. Enorsed by Cutts on verso. Toned. With repaired margins. With port. Illus in cat rms Oct 11 (79) $850

**Cut signature,** [n.d.]. No size given. pba Feb 22 (263) $200

See also: Jefferson, Thomas & Madison

**Madison, James, 1751-1836 —&**
**Monroe, James, 1758-1831**

**Ds,** 23 Dec 1811. 1 p, folio. Land grant for Josiah Robe for "...the North East Quarter of Section...of the unappropriated Lands in the Military District of the Lands directed to be sold at Lanesville..." Stained. pba Oct 26 (284) $750

— [n.d.]. 1 p, folio. Military Commission which has not been filled in. Stained & restored. With defects. pba Oct 26 (285) $1,500

### Maeterlinck, Maurice, 1862-1949

Collection of ALs & Ls, 7 Oct 1900 & 16 Oct 1913. 4 pp, 8vo & 4to. To the actress Rejane. About performances of his plays. HH Nov 17 (3287) DM300

— Collection of 25 A Ls s & Ls s, 10 Nov 1921 to 21 Oct 1925. About 30 pp, 8vo, tipped into brown mor album. To Mr. Colles of the Authors' Syndicate in London. Discussing contracts & financial matters concerning many of his works. S Dec 1 (28) £700

ALs, 11 June 1917. 2 pp, 8vo. To an unnamed lady. Discussing film rights to his play The Bluebird. rms June 6 (155) £200

### Magni, Jacobus

Ms, Livre de Bonnes Moeurs, in the French trans prepared by the author for the Duc de Berry. [Northern France (Burgundy?), c.1465]. 57 leaves, 307mm by 220mm, disbound. In brown ink in a lettre batarde by the scribe Lambert. With large painted initials throughout in red. S June 18 (66) £2,000

### Magnus, Gustav, 1802-70

ALs, 13 June 1837. 2 pp, 4to. To Theophile Jules Pelouze. Referring to his research about blood. star Mar 21 (548) DM350

### Mahler, Gustav, 1860-1911

Autograph music, sketches for the choral section of the final movement of his 2d Symphony, [c.1893]. 2 pp, folio. Drafts of 2 passages of 76 & 70 bars, respectively, in short score. Including revisions; differing from final version. S Dec 1 (228) £13,000

ALs, [c.1908]. 2 pp, 8vo. To Egon Wellesz. Referring to his "2 new symphonies" & his travel plans. With related material. S May 15 (546) £1,800

Autograph postcard, sgd, 22 Apr 1893. To Emil Freund. Asking for a statement about his finances. Illus in cat. star Mar 22 (924) DM2,400

Photograph, sgd & inscr, Mar 1909. 337mm by 274mm, mtd. Profile port, by A. Dupont. Inscr to Lionel S. Mapleson. Illus in cat. Marans collection. CE Apr 17 (243) $22,000

— Klemperer, Otto. - Ls, 4 July 1970. 2 pp, 8vo. To Egon Wellesz. Reminiscing about performances of Wagner's Die Walkuere & Gluck's Iphigenie in Aulis by Mahler, & disapproving of Deryck Cooke's version of Mahler's 10th Symphony. S May 15 (547) £200

### Mahone, William, 1826-95

Signature, 1886. No size given. On a card. With port & Anthony stereograph of a soldier killed at Petersburg. Also with a Taylor & Huntington stereograph of a large gun. Framed. Over-all size 15.75 by 23.75 inches. Illus in cat rms Oct 11 (109) $280

### Makarova, Natalia. See: Baryshnikov, Mikhail & Makarova

### Malcolm X, 1925-65

ALs, 9 Nov 1964. 2 pp, 4to. To Alex Haley. Reporting about his meetings with African leaders & announcing his return to the US. Illus in cat. P Dec 13 (255) $9,500

See also: Haley, Alex & Malcolm X

### Mallarme, Stephane, 1842-98

ALs, 12 Jan 1888. 2 pp, 8vo. To M. Rey. Thanking him for an effort on behalf of a sick friend. sg Feb 1 (145) $200

### Mann, Golo, 1909-94

Series of 7 Ls s, 21 Nov 1963 to 11 Jan 1968. 8 pp, folio & 8vo. Recipient unnamed. Discussing publishing matters. star Mar 21 (267) DM800

### Mann, Klaus, 1906-49

Collection of ALs & autograph postcard, sgd, 11 May & 25 July 1931. 4 pp, 8vo. To Franz Goldstein. Thanking for a review & discussing Martin Buber. HH Nov 17 (3288) DM800

### Mann, Thomas, 1875-1955

Autograph Ms, notes for a speech at Amsterdam upon receipt of the Oranje-Nassau Order, [1 July 1955]. 1 p, 8vo. With explanatory Ls by his daughter Erika, 22 Aug 1955. HH Nov 17 (3289) DM3,000

Typescript, 3 leaves (numbered 9, 23 & 98) from the final vol of his novel Joseph der Ernaehrer, [c.1943]. 4to. Including a few autograph corrections. HN Nov 24 (2831) DM1,000

— Typescript, draft of a speech supporting Churchill's idea of a union between Great Britain & America, [c.1941]. 6 pp, 4to. In German & English; including a few autograph corrections. HN Nov 24 (2824) DM2,000

ALs, 15 Apr 1911. 2 pp, 8vo. To an unnamed lady. Declining to have some photographs pbd. star Mar 21 (255) DM1,150

— 4 Dec 1924. 3 pp, 8vo. To Arthur Eloesser. Praising recipient's review of Der Zauberberg. star Mar 21 (257) DM2,600

— 4 Feb 1933. 2 pp, folio. To Mr. Schlesinger. About the political situation in Germany. S Dec 1 (27) £1,050

— 4 Oct 1939. 2 pp, 8vo. To an unnamed lady. Concerning the publication of a poetical work & the continuation of the journal Mass und Wert after the outbreak of the war. star Mar 21 (261) DM1,400

— [1941]. 1 p, 8vo. To the widow of Max Herrmann. Draft, sending condolences on the death of her husband. HN Nov 24 (2823) DM1,100

— [1943]. 6 pp, 4to. To Alexei Tolstoy. Draft, discussing democracy & socialism, American help for Russia, Russian culture, etc. Lacking 1st leaf. HN Nov 24 (2830) DM5,200

— 15 Dec 1948. 1 p, 8vo. To Marga Bauer. Responding to the news of Samuel Singer's death. star Mar 21 (263) DM2,200

— 18 Apr 1950. 2 pp, 8vo. To Walter H. Perl. Informing him about his travel plans. HN Nov 24 (2832) DM1,100

AL, [1942]. 3 pp, 4to. To John T. Frederick. Draft, sending comments for a radio program reviewing his political works, & discussing the war. In German & English. HN Nov 24 (2826) DM4,600

**Ls,** 19 Dec 1925. 1 p, 4to. Recipient unnamed. Thanking for an invitation. Torn. star Mar 21 (258) DM540
— 19 July 1926. 1 p, 4to. To Alfred Morgenroth. Carbon copy, thanking for comments on a lecture. star Mar 21 (259) DM560
— 4 Aug 1931. 2 pp, 4to. Recipient unnamed. Expressing satisfaction that young people in America are reading his works. star Mar 21 (260) DM1,100
— 31 May 1946. 1 p. In English. Letter of recommendation for Hugo Simon. With covering Ls to Hugo Simon, sgd by Katia Mann. Ck Apr 12 (76) £260
— 24 Aug 1948. 2 pp, folio. To Walter A. Weiss. Discussing suggestions to adapt "the Joseph stories" for the stage or for a film. star Mar 21 (264) DM1,100
**Autograph postcard, sgd,** 24 Feb 1914. To Hulda Eggart. Thanking for a poem. On port postcard. star Mar 21 (256) DM720
**Autograph endorsement,** on a letter addressed to him by Charles B. Sherman of the Jewish Labor Committee, 3 Sept 1942, 1 p, 4to, asking him to set a date for a meeting; explaining why Sherman's visit will not be necessary. HN Nov 24 (2827) DM270
**Photograph, sgd,** 21 Mar 1938. 252mm by 199mm. Seated. Marans collection. CE Apr 17 (83) $400

### Mansfeld, Ernst, Graf von, 1580-1626

**Ls,** 29 Aug 1623. Length not stated. To Prince Thomas of Savoy. Offering his services. star Mar 22 (1258) DM660

### Mansfield, Katherine, 1888-1923

**ALs,** [c. Feb-Apr 1920]. 2 pp, no size given. To Anne [Estelle Drey]. About Bliss and Other Stories : "Constable has accepted my book and that you may perhaps do some drawings for it. This last fact simply fills me with joy..." With related material. Illus in cat Ck Nov 17 (113) £1,400

### Maps & Charts

**Ms,** Johnson's Map of the Vicinity of Richmond and Peninsular Campaign in Virginia. [c.1862] 27 by 20 inches, hand-painted. cb June 25 (2462) $300
— Ms, Johnson's New Military Map of the United States Showing the Forts, Military Posts &c. with Enlarged Plans of Southern Harbors. 1861. 24 by 17 inches, hand-painted. cb June 25 (2463) $250
— Ms, map of Malta. Valletta, 2 Apr 1822. 500mm by 690mm, on vellum in ink & wash, areas ceded to the Ryal Navy colored in blue wash. With later Ms documentations. Sgd by Sir Thomas Maitland, Vice Admiral G. Moore & H. Wolsey. Later annotations sgd by others, including Sir Pulteney Malcolm. C Oct 25 (134) £1,050
— Ms, map of Timor. Amst or Java, [c.1760] 900mm by 585mm. Coastlines in green, black & yellow. Mountains in green & brown washes. C Oct 25 (150) £3,000
— Ms, plan, Plano Geometrico de la Cuidad de Santa Fe de Bogota... 1791 por D. Domingo Esquiaqui. 4 sheets joined, 990mm by 880mm, in ink & colors. S Nov 30 (149) £5,500
— Ms, [Map of the route from the Missouri River at Council Bluffs westward to the Idaho & Utah border, as it appeared in 1850. 325mm by 800mm, backed; some loss along folds; soiled. sg May 9 (200) $1,100
— ADAMS, JOHN. - A Map of Churchelans Farm Woodchurch Kent the Estate of Mr. W. Kingschurch. 1808. 358mm by 468mm, on vellum, with added decoration in watercolor, framed. b Sept 20 (278) £160
— BRAILES, WARWICKSHIRE. - Ms, estate survey, The Description of the Maners, Ouer Brayles, Nether Brayles, and Chemscote.... [c.1585]. 4 sheets joined, 685mm by 838mm, in ink & wash colors. Attributed to Christopher Saxton. S Nov 30 (49) £7,500
— CIVIL WAR, AMERICAN. - Spy map sketched on verso of a prd form, Quarterly Return and Inventory of Negro Slaves belonging to the State of Louisiana. [1863]. Showing the headquarters of Gens. Banks & Andrews. cb June 25 (2464) $2,000
— ECKART, ANSELM. - Mappa V - Provinciae Maragonii Societatis Jesu cum adjacentibus quibusdam terris Hispanorum, Gallorum & Batavorum. [N.p.], 1755. 380mm by 465mm, in sepia ink. Showing the Amazon river. C Oct 25 (100) £2,500
— MILLO, ANTONIO. - [World map]. Venice, c.1580. 4 (of 6) sheets (lacking North America & Africa), ink & colors on vellum, each sheet c.600mm by c.830mm. Some features heightened with gold. C Oct 25 (135) £16,500

### Marcellus II, Pope, 1501-55

**Ls,** 14 Jan 1539. 1 p, 4to. Recipient unnamed. Requesting the return of his horse. Sgd as Marcello Cervino. sg Feb 1 (146) $500

### Marciano, Rocky, 1923-69

**Photograph, sgd & inscr,** [c.1952]. 253mm by 204mm. Full length, by Bob Gaffney. Inscr to Roy Pitts. Illus in cat. Marans collection. CE Apr 17 (278) $700

### Marconi, Guglielmo, 1874-1937

**Photograph, sgd,** [c.1905]. 136mm by 89mm. Shoulder-length port, by Rotary Photo Co. Marans collection. CE Apr 17 (50) $850

**Marcy, William Learned, 1786-1857.** See: Pierce, Franklin & Marcy

### Margaret, Duchess of Parma, Regent of the Netherlands, 1522-86

**Ls,** 18 Sept 1565. 5 pp, folio. To Emperor Maximilian II. Interceding in favor of the Countess of Rittberg in a controversy with the estates of the Netherlands & Westfalia. HH May 9 (2509) DM450

**Maria, Empress of Maximilian II, 1528-1603.** See: Maximilian II & Maria

### Maria Anna, Queen of Charles II of Spain, 1667-1740

**Ls,** 10 Dec 1697. 2 pp, folio. To Count Georg Adam von Martinitz. Asking him to find a benefice in Rome for Prince Friedrich of Hessen. star Mar 22 (1666) DM200

## MARIA

**Maria Anna, Erzherzogin von Oesterreich, 1738-89**
ALs, [n.d.]. 1 p, 8vo. To Count Franz Dietrichstein. Recommending the "pauvre Princesse Trautson". HN May 15 (2650) DM2,400

**Maria Fyodorovna, Empress of Paul I of Russia, 1759-1828**
ALs, 25 Aug 1819. 1 p, 8vo. To an unnamed count. Congratulating him on his marriage. star Mar 22 (1615) DM380

**Maria Paulowna, Grossherzogin von Sachsen-Weimar, 1786-1859**
AL, [n.d.]. 2 pp, 8vo. To Henriette von Fritsch. Discussing an appointment. star Mar 21 (144) DM340

**Maria Theresa, Empress, 1717-80**
Ls, 19 Aug 1755. 5 pp, folio. To the administration at Temesvar. Giving instructions to modify a court sentence. star Mar 22 (1597) DM480
— 6 Aug 1765. 1 p, folio. To an unnamed Elector. Announcing the marriage of her son Leopold. HH May 9 (2512) DM800
— 13 Nov 1766. 2 pp, 4to. To Count Ludwig von Zinzendorf. Instructing him to audit Prince Kaunitz's accounts of the recent war. star Mar 22 (1598) DM1,400
— 12 Jan 1778. 1 p, 4to. To Count Auersperg. Confirming receipt of 17,820 guilders from Galicia. star Mar 22 (1600) DM340
**Autograph endorsement,** sgd, on verso of a fragment of a petition concerning differences between the Serbian bishop & priests in Hungary, 16 Nov 1753, 1 p, folio; 29 lines giving orders to settle the matter. HN May 15 (2652) DM1,000
**Autograph sentiment,** sgd, admonition inscr to her daughter Marie Amalie on the occasion of her marriage, 1769. On verso of gouache painting sgd by Wilhelm Kleinhart, 1743, 161mm by 107mm, depicting the Holy Family. star Mar 22 (1599) DM1,500

**Marie Antoinette, Queen of Louis XVI of France, 1755-93**
Ls, 19 May 1782. 1 p, 4to. To the Ferdinand IV, King of Naples & Sicily. Expressing pleasure about the birth of a daughter to his wife, her sister. C Nov 29 (158) £2,200
— 30 July 1783. 1 p, folio. To the Royal Tailor. Guaranteeing 200 francs for his services in aiding the upkeep of seceral officers. Framed. pba Oct 26 (346) $5,500
Ds, 1 Oct 1785. 1 p, folio. Pay order addressed to her Treasurer Randon de la Tour. C Nov 29 (157) £2,000

**Marie Louise, Empress of the French, 1791-1847**
Ms, list of ladies at her court, sgd by the Duchesse de Montebello, 31 Jan 1813. 1 p, folio. HH May 9 (2522) DM260
ALs, 24 Apr 1810. 2 pp, 8vo. To Victoire de Poutet, Countess Colloredo. Expressing satisfaction with her husband & her new life. Illus in cat. S May 15 (198) £2,400

## AMERICAN BOOK PRICES CURRENT

Ds, 2 Oct 1813. 1 p, folio. Permission for Pierre Joseph d'Houdetot to enter the King of Westfalia's services. star Mar 22 (1421) DM650
— 22 Jan 1824. 1 p, folio. As Duchess of Parma, pay order in favor of 8 servants. star Mar 22 (1422) DM400

**Marlborough, Consuelo, Duchess of, 1878-1964**
Photograph, sgd, 1902. 340mm by 250mm. Full-length formal port. Illus in cat. Marans collection. CE Apr 17 (127) $800

**Marot, Samuel, 1770-1865**
[His album kept at Frankfurt on the Oder, Magdeburg, Berlin, & other places, containing 135 entries mostly by fellow students including Heinrich Zschokke & Johann Friedrich Gottlieb Delbrueck, 1788 & later, in contemp lea gilt, sold at Stargardt on 22 Mar 1996, lot 1280, for DM2,800.]

**Marschner, Heinrich, 1795-1861**
— KASKEL, SOPHIE. - ALs, 21 Aug [n.y.]. 5 pp, 8vo. To Lily Bernhard. Reporting Marschner's gossip about [Franz Xaver Wolfgang] Mozart & Chopin. star Mar 22 (1050b) DM1,100

**Marsh, George Perkins, 1801-82**
ALs, 10 June 1848. 2 pp, 8vo. To The House of Representatives. About a package containing Congressional documents & foreign newspapers which he has already sent to the House. pba Oct 26 (287) $250
— 10 June 1848. 2 pp, 8vo. To unnamed recipient. Sending things & on making arrangements for things to be sent on before leaving to be Minister to Turkey. pba Oct 26 (287) $250

**Marshall, George Catlett, 1880-1959**
Ls, 16 Oct 1945. 1 p, 4to. To Leland Stowe. Discussing measures to shield American soldiers from German propaganda. Illus in cat. rms Mar 21 (356) $850
— 16 Sept 1950. 1 p, 4to. To Morris Luxenberg. Thanking him for congratulations on Marshall's appointment as Secretary of Defense. pba Feb 22 (205) $160
Photograph, sgd, [1948]. Oblong 4to. Signature slightly light. Also sgd by Ambassador to Great Britain Lewis Douglas. With calligraphic lettering on inner mat stating "Sectetary of State George C. Marahall presenting The Marshall Plan to the Senate in early 1948...." rms Nov 30 (223) $650
— WOODRING, H. HARRY. - Ls. 1 Sept 1939. 1 p, 8.5 by 11 inches. To Joseph Lieb. On Lieb's letter to him requesting information about Marshall: " Yes, I appointed General Marshall, Chief of Staff...I passed over some 34 senior (many of them West Point) to name him. I had quite a battle with President Roosevelt..." Seperated at folds. Dar Oct 19 (136) $250

**Marshall, John, 1755-1835**
ALs, 2 July 1789. 2 pp, 4to. To unnamed recipient. Offering legal advice about inherited debts. With edges worn. With loss at left margin. CNY Dec 15 (99) $1,400

— 27 Sept 1821. 2 pp, 4to. To Walter L. Fontaine. Discussing a payment which is overdue. Illus in cat. P Dec 13 (262) $2,750

**Ds**, 25 July 1820. 1 p, 4to. Concerning a financial matter involving Isham Scruggs. Illus in cat pba Oct 26 (340) $950

### Marshall, Thurgood, 1908-93
**Ls**, 19 Sept 1953. 1 p, 8.5 by 11 inches. To Joseph Lieb. About his lack of availability: "I do not expect to be in Washington any time within the next three weeks or a month..." With notes in Lieb's hand on letter. Dar Oct 19 (137) $275

### Martin, Archer John Porter
**Autograph Ms**, calculations relating to electrophoresis; [n.d.]. 3 pp, folio. Sgd at end. With secretarial covering letter. star Mar 21 (550) DM400

### Martin, Dean —& Lewis, Jerry
**Signature**, [1994?] On 10.5 by 14 inch lobby card from the film The Caddy. Lewis' signature dated 94. Framed. Over-all size 14 by 11 inches. Dar Oct 19 (138) $160

### Martin, Frank, 1890-1974
**Autograph quotation**, 3 bars from his 6th Prelude pour le piano, June 1960. 1 p, 8vo. Sgd. star Mar 22 (929) DM320

### Martius, Carl Friedrich Philipp von, 1794-1868
**ALs**, 9 Oct 1851. 1 p, 4to. To the booksellers Perthes, Besser & Mauke. Discussing terms for the sale of a complete copy of his work about Brasil. star Mar 21 (551) DM460

### Marx, Adolph Bernhard, 1795-1866
**ALs**, 5 Dec 1825. 3 pp, 4to. To Ferdinand von Biedenfeld. Calling for a new opera to fit the times & the North German character. star Mar 22 (930) DM700

### Marx, Karl, 1818-83
**Autograph Ms**, essay, Das philosophische Manifest der historischen Rechtsschule, [ptd 9 Aug 1842]. 8 pp, 4to, in wraps. Commenting on Gustav Hugo's work. Fair copy, with a few corrections. star Mar 22 (1395) DM100,000

**Photograph, sgd & inscr**, 11 Jan 1883. 164mm by 109mm. Seated, by Mayall; inscr to Mme James M. Williamson on verso. Illus in cat. Marans collection. CE Apr 17 (51) $11,000

### Mary, Queen of George V of England, 1867-1953
**Photograph, sgd**, 1916. 195mm by 150mm. Sgd Mary R. 1916 on mount. b May 30 (372) £60

— Anr, 1925. 5.3 by 6.9 inches (image). 3-quarter length; by W. & D. Downey. Framed. Illus in cat. rms June 6 (414) $675

See also: George V & Mary

### Masaryk, Thomas Garrigue, 1850-1937
**ALs**, 26 Apr 1918. 1 p, 8vo. To Mr. Pleschner. Concerning a payment. star Mar 22 (1396) DM260

— 16 July 1932. 3 pp, 4to. To Emil Ludwig. About Ludwig's study of Mussolini. pn Nov 9 (393) £140

### Mascagni, Pietro, 1863-1945
**Autograph music**, song, beginning "Per l'Italia e giunta l'ora!", 1915. 9 pp, 4to. Short score, notated on 4 systems per page of up to 3 staves each. Working Ms; sgd. Probably composed for insertion in a play by Antonio Traversa. S Dec 1 (231) £1,800

### Massachusetts
**Ms**, preliminary draft of resolution by the Governor & Council for a "day of humiliation." 7 Sept 1689. 1 p, folio. Mostly in the hand of & sgd by Ebenezer Prout. sg Feb 1 (5) $850

— WITCHCRAFT. - ADs. 24 June 1737. 1 p , 8vo. Sgd by "Tho. Barton" acknowledging receipt of 45 pounds from Miels Ward. Noted in anr hand that Barton "Examined the Witches in 1692 to see if they had anything unnatural about their bodies." Illus in cat rms Oct 11 (127) $400

### Massena, Andre, 1758-1817
**Ls**, [7 Apr 1801]. 1 p, 4to. To Gautier. Thanking for information about some rumours. star Mar 22 (1463) DM230

### Massenet, Jules, 1842-1912
[An archive of c.150 A Ls s, 1864 to 1908, c.300 pp, 8vo, mostly to Emma Borch & various members of her family, & several other correspondents, about personal matters & the composition & performance of almost all his operas, sold at Sotheby's on 15 May 1996, lot 408, for £7,500.]

**ALs**, 6 Mar 1889. 1 p, 8vo. Recipient unnamed. Arranging a luncheon for the following Sunday. sg June 6 (118) $50

**Autograph quotation**, [n.d.]. No size given. On his calling card. With port. Mtd & framed under glass. Over-all size c.13.11 by 9.3 icnhes. rms Oct 11 (249) $210

### Mata Hari
**Ptd photograph**, sgd, [c.1907]. 51mm by 109mm (image). Full-length profile pose, lying nearly naked on her stomach. Illus in cat. Marans collection. CE Apr 17 (20) $3,800

### Matisse, Henri, 1869-1954
**ALs**, 20 July 1941. 1 p, 4to. To Varian Fry. About paintings available for sale, with photo (present) of a painting he will sell Fry for F50,000. sg June 6 (119) $1,200

— 4 Sept 1941. 1 p, 4to. To Varian Fry. Asking him to sent the photos Fry took of him at work to his son Pierre in NY. sg June 6 (120) $850

— 11 Apr 1942. 3 pp, folio & 8vo. To Harold Tooby. Making arrangements for a meeting & explaining how to mix oil colors. Including explanatory sketch. S May 15 (199) £1,700

— 2 Nov 1948. 3 pp, 4to. To Professor Leriche. Concerning health problems and a gift. Detail in cat rms Oct 11 (250) $1,000

**Autograph postcard, sgd,** 20 Dec 1950. To Mrs. Alexandra Prober. Sending thanks for a holiday gift. cb June 25 (2552) $550

— [n.d.]. On verso of postcard of the Chapel at Vence. Recipient unnamed. Thanking for a Christmas parcel & for a contribution to the chapel. cb June 25 (2553) $400

**Photograph, sgd & inscr,** [c.1910]. 139mm by 84mm. On horseback, inscr to M. Torrey. Illus in cat. Marans collection. CE Apr 17 (211) $2,800

### Matthias, Emperor, 1557-1619

**ALs,** 20 Oct 1592. 1 p, folio. To Pope Clement VIII. Sending an envoy & repeating his request for a cardinalate for Archbishop Albani. Illus in cat. star Mar 22 (1585) DM3,800

**Ls,** 12 Dec 1615. 2 pp, folio. To Hans von Wiedebach. Concerning instructions for the territory of Niederlausitz. star Mar 22 (1586) DM650

### Matthisson, Friedrich von, 1761-1831

**ALs,** 2 May 1830. 1 p, 4to. To Ch. A. G. Eberhard. Hoping to see him before his journey to the Alps. star Mar 21 (270) DM560

### Maugham, William Somerset, 1874-1965

**ALs,** 21 Jan [n.y.]. 1 p, 8vo. To Patrick. Inviting him to visit Villa Mauresque. wd Nov 15 (15) $100

**Ls,** 24 January [1924]. 1 p, 8vo. To Mr. Bernheimer. Agreeing to autograph some books. With original envelope and a port of Maugham. Also with a photo of Malaya. Framed. Over-all size 15.75 by 23.75 inches. Illus in cat rms Oct 11 (241) $270

### Maupassant, Guy de, 1850-93

**ALs,** [27 July 1891]. 2 pp, 12mo. To M. Maynard of Le Figaro. Requesting that he counter in print a wrongful charge of plagiarism against Maupassant. sg Feb 1 (149) $275

— [n.d.]. 2 pp, 12mo. Recipient unnamed but with pencil note in anr hand identifying Octave Mirbeau as the recipient. Thanking him for a letter; refers to a suit against Le Figaro. sg Feb 1 (150) $275

— [n.d.]. 2 pp, 12mo. Recipient unnamed but with pencil note in anr hand identifying Octave Mirbeau as the recipient. Inviting him to dine. sg Feb 1 (151) $300

— [n.d.]. 2 pp, 12mo. To Octave Mirbaur. About some forged bills. sg Feb 1 (152) $475

### Maurice, Prince of Orange, 1567-1625

**Ls,** 30 Apr 1591. 1 p, 4to. Recipient unnamed. Credentials for some envoys. star Mar 22 (1482) DM600

### Maury, Dabney H., 1822-1900

**Signature,** [c.1865]. Framed with photo & newspaper front page. rms Nov 30 (22) $460

### Maximilian I, Kurfuerst von Bayern, 1573-1651

**Ls,** 30 Aug 1627. 2 pp, folio. To Georg Friedrich von Greiffenklau, Kurfuerst von Mainz. Discussing a complaint by the city of Erfurt concerning an unauthorized request for a contribution. star Mar 22 (1261) DM580

### Maximilian I Joseph, King of Bavaria, 1756-1825

**Ds,** 1 Aug 1808. 1 p, folio. To Jerome Bonaparte, King of Westfalia. Discharge for recipient's envoy Baron von Moltke. Countersgd by Count Montgelas. star Mar 22 (1168) DM330

### Maximilian II, King of Bavaria, 1811-64

**ALs,** 22 Dec 1842. 1 p, 8vo. To Philipp von Lichtenthaler. Thanking for congratulations on his forthcoming marriage. star Mar 22 (1171) DM1,000

### Maximilian II, Emperor, 1527-76

**ALs,** [n.d.]. 1 p, 8vo. To Richard Strein. Concerning a payment due in Hungary. Illus in cat. HN Nov 24 (2836) DM2,500

**Ls,** 27 Feb 1566. 2 pp, 4to. To his brother Archduke Ferdinand of Tirol. Informing him about the purchase of 2 houses in Prague. HH Nov 17 (3292) DM650

— IMPERIAL COURT OF CHANCERY. - Letter, 6 Sept 1575. 1 p, folio. Interim report in the case concerning the last will of Count Friedrich von Diepholz; sgd by Johannes Syfridus. HH Nov 14 (79) DM320

### Maximilian II, Emperor, 1527-76 —& Maria, Empress of Maximilian II, 1528-1603

**Ds,** 13 Jan 1550. 1 p, folio. As Regents in Spain, order addressed to the members of the "audiencia Real de la nueva espana" regarding a report to the Council of the Indies by Juan Cano. star Mar 22 (1582) DM750

### Maximilian II Emanuel, Kurfuerst von Bayern, 1662-1726

**Ls,** 1 Sept 1702. 2 pp, folio. To the magistrate of the city of Frankfurt. Requesting help for his agent Hans Peter von Borrnhofer who is going to Frankfurt to redeem some pawned pearls. star Mar 22 (1165) DM260

**Ds,** 29 May 1705. 1 p, folio. Ptd safeguard for the ship La belle Catherine. HH May 9 (2514) DM200

### Maximilian of Mexico, Emperor, 1832-67

**ALs,** 24 Mar 1855. 2 pp, 8vo. To an unamed baroness. Praising a play by Ernst Ritter. star Mar 22 (1404) DM560

**Ls,** 19 July 1864. 1 p, 4to. To Under-Secretary of Gobernacion. Authorizing in reply to Prefect of Tula that if Jinoco is serving with rebels, then the prefect of Ixmiquilpan not to issue safe conduct requested by Military Court of Queretato. sg Sept 28 (181) $600

### Maximilian zu Wied-Neuwied, Prince, 1782-1867

**Series** of 6 A Ls s, 8 Jan 1854 to 15 Mar 1864. 16 pp, 4to & 8vo. To Ernst von Bibra. Mostly concerning anthropological & zoological specimens. star Mar 21 (638) DM2,800

### May, Karl, 1842-1912

**ALs,** 27 Mar 1906. 1 p, size not stated. Recipient unnamed. Thanking for a letter. JG Sept 29 (286) DM1,100

— 22 Jan 1907. 1 p, size not stated. To Leopold Gheri. Regretting that the January Ed of the journal Der Kunstfreund has not been published yet, & announcing a contribution. JG Sept 29 (288) DM1,300

— 1 Mar 1907. 4 pp, size not stated. To Leopold Gheri. Concerning contributions to the journal Der Kunstfreund. JG Sept 29 (289) DM2,000

— 21 Apr 1907. 2 pp, size not stated. To Leopold Gheri. Responding to recipient's wish to print two of May's articles pbd in America. JG Sept 29 (293) DM1,500

— 30 Apr 1907. 1 p, size not stated. To Leopold Gheri. Asking him to return a Ms & to send some copies of a ptd letter. Illus in cat. JG Sept 29 (294) DM2,400

— 4 Aug 1907. 3 pp, size not stated. To Leopold Gheri. Discussing a response by Herr Cardanus to an article in the journal Sonntagsglocken. JG Sept 29 (291) DM1,800

— 3 May 1908. 2 pp, size not stated. To Philipp Rauer. Requesting information about Rudolf Lebius who has pbd a pamphlet attacking May. JG Sept 29 (298) DM1,800

**Autograph postcard, sgd,** [24 Apr 1899]. To Price Adelbert of Bavaria. Sending greetings from Egypt. JG Sept 29 (281) DM1,200

— 25 Apr 1899. To Richard Ploehn. Asking him to write. Illus in cat. JG Sept 29 (282) DM1,400

— 10 June 1900. To Dr. Eser. 2-line poem, referring to his travels in Syria. star Mar 21 (272) DM1,400

— 30 July 1902. Recipient unnamed. Sending greetings. JG Mar 29 (237) DM500

— [1 Dec 1908]. Recipient unnamed. Sending greetings from England. Addressed in the hand of Klara May. JG Sept 29 (300) DM600

**Photograph, sgd,** 28 Dec 1904. Postcard. Addressed by Klara May. JG Mar 29 (238) DM340

— Anr, 13 Mar 1908. Postcard. Addressed by Klara May. JG Mar 29 (240) DM380

— Anr, [14 Mar 1908]. Postcard. Addressed in the hand of Klara May. JG Sept 29 (297) DM460

**Photograph, sgd & inscr,** 10 Jan 1906. Postcard. Addressed by Klara May. JG Mar 29 (239) DM300

— Anr, [c.1906]. Postcard. JG Sept 29 (303) DM500

— Anr, [17 Jan 1907]. Postcard. Addressed in the hand of Klara May. JG Sept 29 (287) DM400

— Anr, [3 Mar 1907]. Postcard. Addressed in the hand of Klara May. JG Sept 29 (290) DM450

— Anr, [31 Mar 1909]. Postcard. Addressed in the hand of Klara May. JG Sept 29 (301) DM550

**Signature,** [n.d.]. On photograph postcard of his residence in Canada. Also sgd by Klara May. JG Sept 29 (302) DM500

### Mayer, Louis B., 1885-1957

**Ls,** 30 Jan 1933. 2 pp, 4to. To Joseph R. Knowland. About Herbert Hoover's presidency. pba Feb 22 (79) $225

### Mazarin, Jules, Cardinal, 1602-61

**ALs,** 23 Aug 1647. 1 p, 331mm by 227mm. To Giovanni Battista in Florence. In Italian, assuring him of his esteem & offering support. C June 26 (270) £700

### Mazzei, Philip, 1730-1816

**ALs,** 2 Nov 1791. 4 pp, 4to. To the Marquis de Lafayette. Regretting the departure of many friends. Sgd Ph. M. Sang collection. P Dec 13 (265) $1,800

### Mazzini, Giuseppe, 1805-72

**ALs,** [14 Oct 1852]. 2 pp, 12mo. To Dr. Epps. Asking him to convey his thanks to Mr. Stuart for a "liberal contribution". rms June 6 (415) $280

— [c.1860]. 1 p, 12mo. To [Jacob Feis]. Changing a date for an appointment. star Mar 22 (1397) DM330

**AL,** 21 Apr [1859]. 1 p, 8vo. In 3d person, to Arthur hugh Clough. Arranging a meeting. Sold with the museum pass that Mazzini halped Clough get. pn June 13 (293) £250

### McLeod, Geertruida Zelle, 1876-1917. See: Mata Hari

### Medical Manuscripts

— TADDEO DA BOLOGNA. - Autograph Ms, articles describing medical conditions & remedies. [Italy, c.1500]. About 200 pp, 4to, in vellum wraps. With annotations in other hands. S Dec 1 (31) £1,600

### Medici, Cosimo I de, 1519-74

**Ls,** 21 Apr 1560. 1 p, 4to. To the Marchese di Foschinuovo. Concerning orders given to his agent Domenico Bonsi. star Mar 22 (1374) DM480

**Ns,** 29 Sept 1542. 1 p, oblong 8vo. About a delay in making an appointment to an office. sg Feb 1 (155) $325

### Medina, Daniel de

**Ms,** Noticias del Comercio Maritimo y trafico entre Espana y fu America, 1740. 35 pp, size not stated. Contemp lea gilt. JG Mar 29 (257) DM300

### Meigs, Montgomery C., 1816-92

**ALs,** 21 Oct 1864. 2 pp, 8vo. To E. L. Baker. Praising the St. Louis Depot and its supervision during the war. pba June 13 (22) $225

### Meir, Golda, 1898-1978

**Signature,** [n.d.]. No size given. In English & Hebrew. With 1973 wirephoto of her as Foreign Minister. Framed. Over-all size 13.5 by 17.5 inches. Illus in cat rms Oct 11 (405) $210

### Melanchthon, Philipp, 1497-1560

**ALs,** [8 Sept] 1551. 3 pp, folio. To Count Wilhelm IV of Henneberg-Schleusingen & his son Georg Ernst. Advising them not to allow individual priests to excommunicate offenders but to institute proper proceedings in a consistory. star Mar 22 (1571) DM22,000

**Signature,** 1544. 1 p, 8vo. Ownership inscr on detached flyleaf of a book. HN May 15 (2661) DM600

### Melba, Dame Nellie, 1861-1913

**Photograph, sgd & inscr,** 1907. 310mm by 245mm. Standing beside a table; inscr to Mr. Rogers(?). Marans collection. CE Apr 17 (244) $750

### Mellon, Andrew William, 1855-1937

**Ls,** 4 Dec 1923. 1 p, 4to. To Hon. Ernest R. Ackerman. Thanking him for support of Mellon's recommendations for tax revision. rms Nov 30 (230) $440

— 4 Feb 1928. 2 pp, 4to. To Earle B. Mayfield. Responding to an inquiry about the supervision of banks created by the Federal Farm Loan Act. rms Mar 21 (290) $325

**Signature,** May 1935. On a card. "Autograph of A. W. Mellon Pittsburgh Pa. May 1935". Framed with photo, showing him with Coolidge & Hoover. rms Nov 30 (5) $320

### Melville, Herman, 1819-91

**ALs,** 31 Mar 1847. 3 pp, 4to. To John Romeyn Brodhead. Concerning the sale of his work Omoo in England. CNY May 17 (98) $11,000

— 22 Jan 1885. 3 pp, 8vo. To James Billson. Commenting on James Thomson's poems & sending a copy of his own work Clarel. CNY May 17 (99) $11,000

— 20 Dec 1885. 4 pp, 8vo. To James Billson. Discussing works by James Thomson. CNY May 17 (100) $13,000

— 10 Aug 1890. 2 pp, 8vo. To T. Fisher Unwin. Concerning his first book: "My disinclination to recast an old book--tho' as you suggest, some excisions & would undoubtedly improve 'Redburn', as I remember it..." Unpublished. Illus in cat pba Oct 26 (48) $18,000

### Memminger, Christopher Gustavus, 1803-88

**Ds,** 28 Oct 1863. 1 p, 4to. Certifying that J. S. Jackson is an employee of the Treasury Note Division. Right margin nicked. pba June 13 (23) $425

### Mencken, Henry Louis, 1880-1956

**Ls,** 8 July 1941. 1 p, 8vo. To Mr. Allen. About the word Goon and its age. pba Feb 22 (81) $80

— 27 Jan 1944. 1 p, 8o. To Mr. Miller. About a "dictionary of trade argots" compiled by the Federal Writer's Project. pba June 13 (217) $110

— 21 Aug [n.y.]. 1 p, 8vo. To [Arthur G.] Sedgwick. Concerning articles on Neitzsche: "The Nietzsche articles are both very interesting. Old Frau Foerster-Nietzsche is a remarkable woman...at least eighty and yet is constantly printing articles on her brother..." sg Sept 28 (182) $110

### Mendelssohn, Moses, 1729-86

**ALs,** 24 Apr 1761. 2 pp, 4to. To [Friedrich Nicolai]. Chatting about his stay in Hamburg & about literary matters. Illus in cat. star Mar 21 (555) DM6,500

### Mendelssohn-Bartholdy, Cecile, 1817-53

**Series** of 5 A Ls s, [n.d.]. 13 pp, 8vo. To Ferdinand David & his wife Sophie (1). About the publication of her husband's works & personal matters. star Mar 22 (941) DM2,800

**ALs,** [19 Oct 1843]. 2 pp, 8vo. To her husband Felix. Chatting about her activities, concerts, visitors, etc. star Mar 22 (940) DM4,400

— [1848]. 3 pp, 8vo. To Ferdinand David. Chatting about activities in Frankfurt. star Mar 22 (942) DM900

### Mendelssohn-Bartholdy, Fanny, 1805-47. See: Hensel, Fanny Mendelssohn-Bartholdy

### Mendelssohn-Bartholdy, Felix, 1809-47

**Collection** of 10 A Ls s & 1 LS, 27 Sept 1836 to 21 Jan 1840. 24 pp, folio. To Alfred Novello. On musical matters. S May 15 (96) £4,350

**Series** of 8 A Ls s, 18 Nov 1830 to 16 Nov 1844. 22 pp, 4to & 8vo. To Julius Schubring. Letters to a personal friend about a variety of private & musical matters. 3 letters def. star Mar 22 (933) DM26,000

**ALs,** 30 July 1829. 3 pp, 4to. Expressing thanks for a song & for his hospitality. With numerous corrections; possibly draft. Framed. Illus in cat. C Nov 29 (226) £1,900

— 17 June 1833. 1 p, 8vo. To John Murray. Declining a dinner invitation. Illus in cat. S Dec 1 (235) £1,300

— 3 Nov 1836. 1 p, 8vo. To the singer Hering. Asking him to sing the tenor solos in [Handel's] Israel [in Egypt]. Illus in cat. S May 15 (412) £2,900

— 27 Jan 1840. 1 p, 8vo. To the pbr Kistner. Sending his Maennerchorlieder, Op.50, & discussing the ptg. S May 15 (411) £1,900

— 29 June 1842. 1 p, 4to. To Johannes Bernardus van Bree. Regretting that he will not be able to come to Amsterdam. star Mar 22 (937) DM3,800

— 19 Jan 1843. 4 pp, 8vo. Recipient unnamed. Giving a detailed critique of recipient's compositions & offering help in his misfortune. C Nov 29 (229) £3,500

— 18 Feb 1843. 2 pp, 8vo. Recipient unnamed. Sending money to help him during his illness. C Nov 29 (228) £950

— 8 Apr 1846. 1 p, 8vo. To Franz Bernus. Explaining that he is not able to accompany him to Hanau as promised. S May 15 (413) £2,200

— 5 Feb 1847. 1 p, 8vo. To Elise Vogel. Hoping she will sing in his next concert. star Mar 22 (939) DM3,400

**AL,** 4 Apr 1845. 1 p, 8vo. To [Wilhelm Taubert]. Introducing Ernst & Josephine Reiter. Sgd with a musical quotation. star Mar 22 (938) DM3,300

**ANs,** 18 July 1840. 1 p, 8vo. To publisher F. Hofmeister. Concerning the visit of "the son of the famous Weimar composer. He wants some words of recommendation from me for his songs..." Sgd as "FMB". With impression of Mendelssohn's small red wax monogram seal. Illus in cat sg Sept 28 (183) $750

**ADs,** 28 May 1839. 1 p, 8vo, tipped to larger sheet. Acknowledgment of receipt of 5 guineas from J. A. Novello for the English copyright to his Prayer for Chorus and Orchestra in E flat. With related material. S May 15 (92) £1,100

**Ds,** 7 Jan 1834. 1 p, folio. Receipt for 100 talers as an advance on his salary at Duesseldorf. star Mar 22 (934) DM1,100

— 15 Oct 1836. 1 p, folio. Assignment of copyright in the oratiorio Saint Paul, Op. 36 to Joseph Alfred Novello. S May 15 (98) £1,600

— 5 Oct 1837. 1 p, folio. Assignment of copyright in his Second Piano Concerto in D to Joseph Alfred Novello. S May 15 (93) £1,200

— 15 June 1838. 1 p, folio. Assignment to Joseph Alfred Novello of copyright in the 42nd Psalm. S May 15 (94) £1,200

— 29 Sept 1840. 1 p, folio. Assignment of the copyright in When Israel Out of Egypt Came to Joseph Alfred Novello. S May 15 (91) £1,150

**Autograph endorsement,** sgd, on a bill by C. Simnowski for scores copied for the Verein fuer Tonkunst at Duesseldorf, 19 Dec 1834; accepting statement. star Mar 22 (935) DM800
— Anr, sgd, on a bill by J. G. Schauseil for scores copied for the Verein fuer Tonkunst at Duesseldorf, 13 Feb 1835; accepting statement. Also sgd by Schauseil in receipt. star Mar 22 (936) DM1,200

### Menuhin, Yehudi
**Photograph,** sgd & inscr, 11 Jan 1940. 8 by 10 inches. Inscr to Thankfull Everett. sg June 6 (123) $110

### Menzel, Adolph von, 1815-1905
A Ls s (2), 9 Nov 1875 & 20 Apr 1876. 5 pp, 12mo. To Oskar Begas. Concerning meetings. star Mar 21 (697) DM1,400
**ALs,** 16 Aug 1854. 2 pp, 8vo. Recipient unnamed. About the examination of recipient's son. HN May 15 (2662) DM400
— [n.d.]. 1 p, 4to. To an unnamed lady. Declining a request. star Mar 21 (698) DM600

### Mercadante, Saverio, 1795-1870
**ALs,** 23 Sept 1837. 2 pp, folio. To the pbr Pacini. Asking for some recent plays because he must write an opera for the opening of the Teatro Fenice in Venice. star Mar 22 (944) DM480

### Meredith, William Morris, 1799-1873
**Series** of 10 Ls s, 18 Jan to 3 July 1850. 10 pp, 4to. To Hugh Maxwell. Relating to shipments through the Port of NY. rms Mar 21 (41) $285

### Merian, Matthaeus, 1621-87
**Autograph quotation,** 2 quotes from the Bible, sgd & inscr to Johann Achilles Greuff, 28 July 1640. 1 p, 8vo. Illus in cat. star Mar 21 (699) DM2,200

### Merimee, Prosper, 1803-70
**ALs,** [c.25 Sept 1854]. 1 p, 8vo. Recipient unnamed. Conveying a dinner invitation. star Mar 21 (274) DM220

### Metcalf, Theophilus
**Ms,** Short Writing. L, 1717. 8vo, calf. In the hand of William Sweet. F June 20 (765) $275

### Methfessel, Albert, 1785-1869
**ALs,** 2 Oct 1850. 1 p, 8vo. To Eduard Maria Oettinger. Discussing a new Ed of his Commersbuch. star Mar 22 (945) DM420

### Metternich, Klemens Wenzel Nepomuk Lothar von, 1773-1859
**ALs,** 1 Aug 1824. 4 pp, 4to. To an unnamed English diplomat. Suggesting a meeting to discuss the Greek question. star Mar 22 (1401) DM500
— 13 Dec 1848. 3 pp, 8vo. To Sir Travers Twiss. Sending corrections for recipient's article Austria and Germany [ptd 1849]. HN May 15 (2663a) DM1,600
— 2 Apr 1854. 3 pp, 4to. To Countess Colloredo. Acknowledging condolences on the death of his wife. star Mar 22 (1403) DM360

— 14 Mar [n.y.]. 2 pp, 8vo. To an unnamed ambassador. Referring to a report by Prince Esterhazy. HN May 15 (2665) DM380
**Ls,** 14 June 1842. 3 pp, folio. To Salomon von Rothschild. Discussing the transfer of funds for the inhabitants of Hamburg after the conflagration of their city. star Mar 22 (1402) DM1,200

### Meusel, Johann Georg, 1743-1820
**ALs,** 2 Apr 1775. 4 pp, 4to. Recipient unnamed. Thanking for supporting his journal & requesting news from Magdeburg. star Mar 21 (558) DM340

### Mexico
[A group of 3 illus Aztec Ms s & a map, [c.17th cent], written in a European alphabet in the Nahuatl language on amatl (fig tree bark) paper, comprising c.40 leaves of Techialoyan Mss recording landholding claims in San Cristobal Texcalucan, Santa Maria Iztacapan & San Juan Tolcayuca, also including a ptd broadside Bull of Paul V, sold at Sotheby's on 5 Dec 1995, lot 24, for £195,000 to Summers.]

### Meyer, Hannes, 1889-1954
**Ls,** 5 Sept 1930. 1 p, 4to. To V. Polacek. Thanking for support & announcing his visit in Prague. JG Mar 29 (220) DM450

### Meyerbeer, Giacomo, 1791-1864
**ALs,** 20 June 1856. 1 p, 8vo. To Pietro Romani. Recommending a singer. star Mar 22 (946) DM320
— 12 May 1863. 2 pp, 4to. To the architect [Hennicke?]. Discussing works in a new apartment. star Mar 22 (947) DM600
— 20 Dec [n.y.]. 1 p, 8vo. To Mme Millaud. Announcing his visit. star Mar 22 (948) DM210
— [n.d.], "Thursday". 1 p, 8vo. To Karl Helmuth Dammas. Concerning the renewal of a ticket. star Mar 22 (949) DM260

### Meyr, Melchior, 1810-71
**Autograph Ms,** poem, beginning "Schoen ist das Leben, reich und schoen", May 1854. 1 p, 4to. 6 stanzas, sgd & inscr. HN Nov 24 (2840) DM220

### Miaskovskii, Nikolai Iakovlevich, 1881-1950
**ALs,** 28 Nov 1929. 3 pp, 8vo. To Nikolai Andreevich. Discussing corrections in the proofs of his 9th Symphony. Including 3 musical quotations. Illus in cat. star Mar 22 (954) DM2,200

### Michelin, Edouard, 1859-1940
**Ds,** 14 Mar 1907. 1 p, folio. Invitation to & agenda of the 1st meeting of the directors of the Michelin Tire Company. rms June 6 (370) $550

### Middleton, Arthur, Signer from South Carolina
**ALs,** 15 Sept 1775. 2 pp, folio. To William Henry Drayton. About the Revolution in South Carolina & the fate of local loyalists. Illus in cat. Sang collection. P Dec 13 (272) $8,000
— 1 Mar 1783. 3 pp, 4to. To Gov. Lyman Hall. About a slave seized by the enemy during the British occupa-

tion of South Carolina. Illus in cat. P Dec 13 (273) $13,000

**Miegel, Agnes, 1879-1964**
**Collection** of ALs, Ls, & autograph postcard, sgd, 16 Jan 1933 to 22 Sept 1960. 3 pp, various sizes. To Karl Paetow. Concerning a reprint & mutual visits. star Mar 21 (275) DM480

**Mifflin, Thomas, 1744-1800**
**Series of Ds s,** 3 Ds s, all dated 6 Mar 1795. 3 pp, on vellum, folio folded to 5.75 by 7.25 inches. Land grants to Samuel Wallis. 2 Mifflin signatures faded. sg Feb 1 (158) $250

**Ds,** 16 June 1794. 1 p, folio, vellum. Land grant for 439 acres in Northampton County, PA to John Nicholson. Countersgd by A. J. Dallas. Detail in cat rms Oct 11 (253) $240

— 27 Feb 1795. 1 p, oblong folio. Land grant to James Wilson. Countersgd by A. J. Dallas. sg Feb 1 (157) $140

— 16 May 1796. 1 p, 11 by 21 inches. Land grant to William Bingham of "Amhurst" in Lycoming County. sg June 6 (124) $90

— 20 May 1796. 1 p, 11 by 21 inches, on vellum. Grant of land called "Middleton" in Lycoming County fo William Bingham. sg June 6 (125) $90

— 14 Oct 1796. 1 p, oblong folio. Land grant to Joseph Demett of land called "Othello" in Luzerne county. rms Nov 30 (235) $150

**Milchmeyer, Peter Johann, 1750-1813.** See: Milchmeyer, Philipp Jakob

**Milchmeyer, Philipp Jakob, 1750-1813**
**ALs,** 5 Dec 1797. 2 pp, 4to. To the bookseller Keil. Sending the 1st installment of his Piano-Forte-Schule & explaining its advantages. star Mar 22 (951) DM300

**Milhaud, Darius, 1892-1974**
**ALs,** [1946?]. 3 pp, 4to. To Nikolai Malko. Suggesting that he perform his Suite Francaise instead of his ballet The Bells. star Mar 22 (952) DM450

**Military Manuscripts**
— PETERSEN, HANS. - Ms, Kurtzer Tractat vom Anfang dess Kriegs Kunstes zu Fuess Zum Unter Richt der Jungen Soldaten..., [Genua, 1639]. Over 450 pp, 145mm by 70mm. Contemp black lea. Treatise on military training & fortifications, in German & Italian. With painted coat-of-arms & hundreds of small drawings & diagrams. HH May 7 (16) DM1,100

**Mill, John Stuart, 1806-73**
**Series** of 3 A Ls s, 18 Apr 1866 to 17 Aug 1867. 8 pp, 12mo. To Charles J. Grece. Concerning discussions about the electoral franchise. C Nov 29 (159) £1,400

**Miller, Arthur**
**Autograph postcard, sgd,** 23 Dec 1964. To John Hunt. Declining to write a contribution for The Saturday Evening Post. sg June 6 (126) $90

**Miller, Glenn, 1904-44**
**ALs,** [postmarked 30 Sept 1936]. 2 pp, 4to. To Jerry Braden. About shirts sent to him; says he has remembered Braden to his mother. sg Feb 1 (159) $325

**Photograph, sgd,** [c. early 1940s]. 5 by 7 inch sepia informal bust photo. Of the bandleader with his trombone. sg Sept 28 (141) $175

— Anr, [n.d.]. 8vo. Holding a trombone. Illus in cat. rms June 6 (200) $375

**Miller, Henry, 1891-1980**
[An archive of Miller material, most of it correspondence with Irving Stettner, editor of Stroke, 1978-80, sold at Christie's East on 22 May 1996, lot 345, for $3,500]

**Typescript,** draft of Peace! It's Wonderful! 8 pp. Loose sheets. Accompanied by photocopy of much-different ptd essay. Sgd & titled by Miller pba Aug 22 (356) $170

**Typescript carbon copy,** Peace! It's Wonderful! [Paris, 1930s] 8 pp, 4to. Inscr & sgd Henry "Divine" Miller. CE Feb 21 (187) $600

**Collection** of 1 ALs & 1 Ls, 1938-39. To Derek Savage. Rejecting some of Savage's poetry; stating Miller's objectives for his literary magazine, Phoenix. pba Nov 30 (328) $325

**Series** of 7 A Ls s, 1967-68. To Michiyo Watanabe. With related material by Watanabe with Miller's holograph corrections. Total of c.17 pp, 8vo & 4to. CE Feb 21 (188) $1,300

**ALs,** 27 May 1940. 2 pp, 4to. To M. Everitt. Concerning the publication of his book about Greece. star Mar 21 (276) DM800

— 23 May 1978. 1 p, 4to. To Irving Stettner. Admitting that "poetry is one of [his] weak points." star Mar 21 (277) DM620

— 1979. 2 pp. To Jeff Carpenter. Recommending John Chescko for a job. pba Aug 22 (358) $85

**Miller, Joaquin, 1839-1913**
**Series** of 5 A Ls s, 17 Aug 1867 to 19 July 1869. 17 pp, 8vo. To Richard D. Webb. About The Subjection of Women. S July 11 (196) £4,600

**ALs,** 25 Sept 1904. 1 p, 4to. To Mr. Alden. Sending a picture of a man & woman sitting beneath a tree. pba Oct 26 (52) $120

— [n.d.]. 1 p, 8vo. To unnamed recipient. About a note sent. pba Feb 22 (86) $110

**Milloecker, Carl, 1842-99**
**Autograph quotation,** opening bars of a song from his operetta Gasparone, 28 Jan 1885. 1 p, 12mo. Sgd. star Mar 22 (953) DM530

**Mills, Clark, 1810-83**
**Check,** accomplished & sgd, 15 Oct 1869. Drawn on the Treasurer of the Lincoln Monument Association for $300 payable to himself. Illus in cat. rms June 6 (13) $500

## Milne, Alan Alexander, 1882-1956

**Autograph Ms,** comic dialogue between 2 characters, Weekes & Wrench, as they perform unsuccessfully as a conjurer & his assistant. 1917. 18 pp, 4to. wd May 8 (21) $1,500

**Autograph transcript,** poem, Vespers. 1 p on stiff card, 8vo. Sgd & dated 6.3.35. b Jan 31 (12) £750

## Minckwitz, Erasmus von, fl.1550

**A Ds s** (2), [Apr] 1537 & 4 May 1539. 2 pp, 4to & 8vo. Receipts to Hans von Taubenheim for his salary as a member of a judicial court. star Mar 22 (1573a) DM300

## Miro, Joan, 1893-1983

**Signature,** [n.d.]. On postcard with reproduction of his work, Siesta. cb June 25 (2557) $225

## Missal

— [Bari or Apulia, 2d half of 11th cent] Beneventan Missal. Fragment of 12 leaves on vellum, 207mm by 93mm, in modern vellum bdg. Includes 1st leaf of melodies with neumes. In brown ink, with rubrics in red; small initials with yellow, red or blue wash; 106 3-line capitals. C June 26 (12) £22,000

— [N.p., c.1585]. 108 leaves, on vellum 840mm by 580mm, in contemp calf over wooden bds. With 3 large illuminated intials in colors & gold, with peacocks, human faces, butterflies, snails, flowers & grotesques, with borders having embellishments of flying dragons & other winged creatures; some other initials with fantastical images of birds & reptiles. Various initials dated 1585, one also bearing the name "F. Hier de C". cb Feb 14 (2505) $19,000

— [Northeastern France, Diocese of Soissons, c.1265]. 199 leaves, vellum, 334mm by 220mm. Mottled calf of c.1800 with the arms of the Prince de Ligne. Use of Soissons. In dark brown ink in a very fine formal gothic liturgical hand (littera gothica textualis formata sine pedibus), with music on many pages on a 4-line red stave. With decorated initials throughout with very fine penwork, 19 very large decorated initials in divided blue & red with elaborate infilling & full-length penwork in both colors, 22 large historiated initials in elaborate gothic designs in colors & burnished gold mostly with full-length branching borders including dragons, faces, & birds, & full-page miniature. S June 18 (61) £330,000

— [Alsace, Neubourg Abbey?, c.1450]. 4 leaves only, vellum, 311mm by 224mm; framed. In 2 sizes of a compressed gothic liturgical hand. With 17 two-line illuminated initials usually with marginal sprays of burnished gold leaves, large historiated initial with full-length bar border with panels of illumination in upper & lower margins, & 4 column-width miniatures with similar borders. S Dec 5 (8) £8,500 [Maggs]

— [Lyons, c.1450]. 40 leaves (2 lacking), vellum, 187mm by 137mm. Rebacked 17th-cent French calf over pastebds. Including Order of Baptism & Litany. In a gothic liturgical hand, with music on 26 pages on a 4-line red stave. With full-page miniature. Worn. S June 18 (64) £2,000

— [Paris or Rouen, c.1490-1510]. 2 leaves only, vellum, 238mm by 154mm; mtd together. In a very fine gothic liturgical hand. With 8 small illuminated initials & linefillers, large illuminated initial, & 2 full-page miniatures within architectural borders, probably by Jos Coene. S June 18 (27) £3,000

— [Spain, 17th cent]. 118 leaves plus vellum pastedowns, 392mm by 266mm, in contemp calf over wooden bds. With 7 staves & lines of text per page. With 3 3-line & 1 2-line initials in pink on glue ground with white pen flourishes & floral designs in gold; smaller lombard initials in red or blue throughout, many with red pen flourishes. With ecclesiastical coat-of-arms on 1st leaf. Some large initials smeared; 1 small initial nearly obliterated; some ink burns. cb Feb 14 (2504) [US3,250]

See also: Armenian Manuscripts
See also: Calligraphy

## Mitchell, Margaret, 1900-49

**Ls,** 17 Nov 1936. 1 p. To Frances Hjort. About the ending of Gone With the Wind. cb Oct 17 (441) $1,100

— 11 July 1940. 2 pp, 4to. To Miss Ruth Williamson. Thanking her for her interest in Tara: "I felt embarrassed at having to write you that all of them are fictional...I went to an enormous amount of trouble, during the ten years I worked upon my book, to make sure the houses and people I described would not accidentally coincide with actual houses and people..." With pamphlet. Illus in cat pba Oct 26 (53) $4,500

## Mitchell, William ("Billy"), 1879-1936

**Photograph, sgd,** [c.1924]. 292mm by 220mm. Half length, in uniform. Illus in cat. Marans collection. CE Apr 17 (155) $1,300

## Mitscherlich, Alexander, 1908-82

**ALs,** 12 Feb 1973. 2 pp, 8vo. To Edgar Lohner. Concerning the trans of his & his wife's works into English. star Mar 21 (560) DM380

## Mitscherlich, Eilhard, 1794-1863

**ALs,** 20 Mar 1862. 3 pp, 8vo. Recipient unnamed. Discussing his research of isomorphism. star Mar 21 (561) DM550

## Mitterer, Erika

**Autograph Ms,** poem, Trost, 4 Dec 1937. 2 pp, 4to. 4 four-line stanzas, sgd. star Mar 21 (278) DM250

## Moehsen, Johann Karl Wilhelm, 1722-95

**ALs,** 1 Mar 1777. 1 p, folio. To Christian Ludwig von Rebeur. Sending his works & commenting on the dangers of arsenic in medicines. star Mar 22 (1539) DM340

## Moellendorff, Wichard Joachim Heinrich von, 1724-1816

**Ls,** 11 June 1785. 1 p, 4to. To Gen. von Zieten. Discussing the appointment of a parson at Stuedenitz. star Mar 22 (1405) DM200

**Moerike, Eduard, 1804-75**
Autograph Ms, poem, Frankfurter Brennten, sgd; [c.1852]. 2 pp, 4to, in the album of Bernhard von Gugler, cloth gilt, containing c.50 entries by Gugler's friends. Illus in cat. star Mar 21 (282) DM8,000
ALs, [n.d.]. 1 p, 8vo. Recipient unnamed. Trying to postpone a meeting because of a headache. star Mar 21 (285) DM1,300
Photograph, sgd, [1864]. 9cm by 5.5cm (image). By Brandseph. Illus in cat. star Mar 21 (283) DM3,500

**Mohn, Johann Friedrich**
Ms, Abschieds-Lied, an Herrn Johann Friedrich Mohn, bisheriger Praeses der loeblichen Hamburger Bank, von Seinen Collegen und Freuenden... 31 December, 1804. Length not given, 4to. In 4 different calligraphic hands. Bound in contemp mor extra neoclassical bdg. C May 1 (107) £1,300

**Moholy-Nagy, Laszlo, 1895-1936**
Ls, 22 Sept 1927. 1 p, 4to. To Herr Ralfs. Planning a meeting in Braunschweig. JG Mar 29 (242) DM460

**Molitor, Gabriel Jean Joseph, Comte, 1770-1849**
Ls, 19 June 1813. 1 p, folio. To Gen. Clarke. Sending information about troops. star Mar 22 (1464) DM220

**Molo, Walter von, 1880-1958**
Collection of ALs, 8 Ls s, & autograph postcard, sgd, 17 Dec 1923 to 15 July 1950. 17 pp, various sizes. To Alfred Morgenroth. About personal & political matters. star Mar 21 (279) DM420
— Collection of ALs, 5 Ls s, & postcard, sgd, 1934 to 1955. 8 pp, various sizes. To Ellen von Biedermann & her husband (1). Concerning affairs of the Goethe Society. star Mar 21 (280) DM320

**Moltke, Helmuth, Graf von, 1800-91**
ALs, 27 Oct 1876. 1 p, 8vo. To the mayor of Schweidnitz. Thanking for congratulations on his birthday. star Mar 22 (1407) DM400

**Mommsen, Theodor, 1817-1903**
ALs, 24 Nov 1866. 2 pp, 8vo. Recipient unnamed. Thanking for a newspaper report about relics in Trier. star Mar 21 (565) DM270
— 13 Dec 1899. 4 pp, 8vo. To an unnamed English journalist. Commenting on British politics in South Africa. star Mar 21 (566) DM500

**Mondrian, Piet, 1872-1944**
Autograph postcard, sgd, [14 Jan 1915]. To Dr. van Assendelft. Changing the date for a meeting. S May 15 (203) £800

**Monet, Claude, 1840-1926**
A Ls s (2), 28 June [1897] & 28 June 1917. 4 pp, 12mo & 8vo. To G. Geffroy. rms Nov 30 (238) $1,700
ALs, 9 Feb 1890. 2 pp. To a friend. Asking him to send a ticket through his childhood friend Billecoaq. With related ALs of Billecoaq. Ck Apr 12 (77) £600
— 26 Apr 1899. 2 pp, 8vo. To Gustave Geffroy. About the advertising of Sisley's sale. S May 15 (204) £1,700
— 30 Dec 1899. 2 pp, 8vo. To G. Geffroy. About sending a painting to Clemenceau & his coming to Giverny when Clemenceau is there. rms Nov 30 (237) $1,800
— 13 Nov 1916. 3 pp, 8vo. To " Monsieur G. Geffroy". Thanking him for advice on his work: " Clemenceau has just left full of enthusiasm for what I do. I told him how happy I was to have your advice about this tremendous work which to be honest is madness." rms Oct 11 (255) $1,100
— 25 Jan 1917. 3 pp, 8vo. To Gustave Geffroy. Discouraged letter about the war & his personal situation. star Mar 21 (700) DM2,000
— 1 May [n.y.]. 1 p, 8vo. To G. Geffroy. Detailing his plans for a return to Paris. Illus in cat pba Oct 26 (55) $1,500
ANs, 6 Oct 1907. 1 p, 12mo. To Ambrose Vollard. Authorizing him to have photographs taken of his works for an exposition. Framed with photo. wd Nov 15 (16) $1,200
Ptd photograph, sgd, [c.1920]. 240mm by 198mm. Half length. Illus in cat. Marans collection. CE Apr 17 (212) $1,600

**Monfreid, Georges Daniel de**
Series of 18 A Ls s, [1895-1905]. 48 pp, 4to & smaller. To Ambrose Vollard. In a spiral-bound album. Mostly concerning Paul Gauguin's affairs. wad Oct 18 (151) C$8,400

**Monroe, James, 1758-1831**
ALs, 9 May 1794. 2 pp, 4to. To Robert R. Livingston. Urging him to accept the nomination as US Minister to France. Including franking signature. P Dec 13 (274) $5,500
— 17 Jan 1795. 2 pp, 4to. To John Jay. About France's unease over Jay's Treaty. Wrinkled. CNY Dec 15 (213) $3,200
— 27 Jan 1803. 1 p, 219mm by 184mm. To William C. Claiborne. Letter of introduction for Robert Hanard. P June 5 (86) $2,750
— 21 Aug 1803. 4 pp, 4to. To Joel Barlow. About the negotiations following the treaty for the Louisiana Purchase & Monroe's disagreements with Robert Livingston. Illus in cat CNY Jan 26 (173) $17,000
— 3 May 1805. 1 p, 4to. Recipient unnamed. Enclosing letters for the Sec of State & others. Illus in cat. rms Mar 21 (20) $1,200
— 31 Jan 1815. 2 pp, 4to. To unnamed recipient. Concerning the purchase of a great deal of gun powder. Browned. Upper third of leaf separated. Docketed. CNY Dec 15 (101) $1,500
— 14 Sept 1815. 2 pp, folio. Recipient unnamed. Referring to Napoleon's downfall, the return of Albert Gallatin & Henry Clay from Europe, & the treaty with Algiers. Forbes Magazine collection. CNY May 17 (165) $3,200
— 27 Apr 1821. 2 pp, 4to. To William Benton. About commodities: " In consequence of the prospect of war with Naples, I understand that flour has risen...it will be well for you to keep back the sale of the flour..." With autograph free frank. CNY Dec 15 (216) $4,200

— 9 July 1821. 2 pp, 4to. To a banker. About his checking account with the Bank of Columbia; asks for increase in a loan. sg Feb 1 (161) $800

— 28 Feb 1823. 2 pp, 4to. Recipient unnamed. Discussing the settlement of a debt. CNY May 17 (270) $1,300

— 1 Oct 1823. 1 p, 4to. To unnamed recipient. About a dispute over a pea patch. Edge separations at folds repaired. Illus in cat pba Oct 26 (293) $2,250

— 6 Nov 1824. 1 p, 4to. To Lord Holland. Introducing Mr. Lynch. Illus in cat. P Dec 13 (278) $2,500

**Ls**, 11 Jan 1815. 2 pp, 4to. Recipient unnamed. Discussing a standing militia & the protection of the Springfield arsenal. Forbes Magazine collection. CNY May 17 (164) $1,500

— 14 July 1815. 1 p, 4to. To Joel R. Poinsett. About a warrant: "I have this day requested the Secretary of the Treasury to issue a Warrant in your favor for one thousand dollars..." A .75 inch restoration in the lower left margin. pba Oct 26 (292) $475

**Ds**, 6 May 1801. 1 p, folio, vellum. Land grant for 130 acres in Greenbrier County. With holes & worming. Soiled. With related material. sg Sept 28 (184) $420

— 26 June 1812. 3 pp, folio. "An ACT concerning Letters of Marque, Prizes and Prize Goods" pba Oct 26 (291) $2,250

— 28 Aug 1812. 1 p, 4to. "Additional Instruction to the public and private armed vessels of the United States"; ptd. Sgd as Sec of State. P Dec 13 (275) $800

— 28 Aug 1812. 1 p, 4to. Order that the public & private armed vessels of the United States not interrupt American vessels coming from British ports to the United States carrying British merchandise. rms Nov 30 (239) $1,300

— 7 Nov 1812. 1 p, 8vo. Ordering that " The public and private armed vessels of the United States are not to interrupt any British unamred vessels bound to Sable Island, and laden with supplies for the humane establishment of that place." Mtd & framed under glass. Over-all size c.12.5 by 12.5 inches. Illus in cat rms Oct 11 (384) $1,500

— 1 p, 4to. Passport for the safe passage of Stephen Jumel. sg Feb 1 (160) $800

— 7 Mar 1818. 1 p, folio, vellum. land grant for 160 acres in Illinois to Anthony Daly. Soiled & worn. sg Sept 28 (185) $225

— 26 Nov 1818. 1 p, folio. Patent for Jacob Bromwell for an "improvement in the Wheat Fan of Winnowing Machine." Countersgd by J. Q. Adams & William Wirt. Framed. P Dec 13 (276) $1,500

— 27 Nov 1820. 1 p, folio. Land grant. Foxed & soiled. CE June 12 (87) $250

— 11 Apr 1821. 1 p, , on vellum, folio. Ship's passport for the Residens of Fairhaven. Countersgd by Sec. of State J. Q. Adams. CE June 12 (88) $1,400

— 20 June 1821. 1 p, 14.25 by 10.25 inches, on vellum. Mediterranean passport. Countersgd by John Quincy Adams. rs Nov 11 (35) $800

— 30 July 1821. 1 p, oblong folio. Land grant to Elizabeth Weldon in Arkansas. Countersgd by Josiah Meigs. Framed with port. sg Feb 1 (162) $325

— 13 Dec 1822. 1 p, folio. Ship's papers for the brig Venus. Countersgd by J. Q. Adams. Trimmed; framed. rms Nov 30 (38) $1,500

— 14 Jan 1823. 1 p, folio. Land grant. Countersgd by John McLean. rms Mar 21 (22) $400

— 1 May 1824. 1 p, folio. Land grant to William Donelson. Framed with a port. P Dec 13 (277) $350

**Cut signature**, [n.d.]. 1 p, no size given, vellum. pba Feb 22 (266) $180

— YATES, JOSEPH C. - Ls. 21 July 1823. 2 pp, 4to. To James Monroe. Concerning "the restrictions contained in the Act of Parliament of Great Britain passed the 5th day of August 1822 alledged to be unjust and unwarrantable in their operation on a great portion of our western citizens who...be virtually prevented access to the Atlantic Ocean..." Endorsed by Monroe & his Secreatry of State J. Q. Adams. Docketed. sg Sept 28 (206) $1,000

See also: Madison, James & Monroe

**Monroe, James, 1758-1831 —&
Adams, John Quincy, 1767-1848**

**Ds**, 5 Jan 1818. 1 p, folio, parchment. Whaler passport for the "Brig Active". Framed. Stained. CNY Dec 15 (215) $1,000

**Monroe, James, 1758-1831.** See: United States of America

**Monroe, Marilyn, 1926-62**

**Ds**, 11 May 1950. 1 p, 4to. Contract with 20th Century-Fox. Carbon copy. Illus in cat. rms June 6 (156) $4,000

**Check**, sgd, 15 Aug 1960. Drawn on Colonial Trust Co. for $146.88 payable to the Pacific Telephone Co. Illus in cat. rms June 6 (157) $1,550

**Montesquieu, Charles de Secondat, 1689-1755**

**ALs**, 25 Aug 1726. 2 pp, 4to. To an unnamed priest. Concerning a funeral oration. S May 15 (205) £700

**Montgomery, Bernard Law, 1st Viscount
Montgomery of Alamein, 1887-1976**

**Photograph, sgd**, [n.d.]. 10 by 8 inches. Showing him with Churchill. Sgd by Montgomery through the brim of Churchill's hat. sg June 6 (128) $450

**Montgomery, Bernard Law, 1st Viscount
Montgomery of Alamein, 1887-1976 —&
Juin, Alphonse, 1888-1967**

**Group photograph**, [c.1958]. 250mm by 200mm. Montgomery receiving a decoration from Juin; inscr & sgd by both. Marans collection. CE Apr 17 (156) $320

**Montmorency, Anne, Duc de, 1493-1567**

**Ls**, 16 Sept 1550. 1 p, 4to. To the Seneschal of Agenois. Sending 20 archers & asking him to report about the health of the Queen & the Dauphin. star Mar 22 (1284) DM750

**Moore, Henry, 1898-1986**
Photograph, sgd, [n.d.]. 4 by 6 inches. Sgd in black ink. Framed with photo of one of his sculptures, also sgd. cb June 25 (2558) $200

**Moore, Thomas, 1779-1852**
ALs, [docketed 16 Feb 1825]. 1 p, 16mo. Recipient unnamed. Transmitting (not present) poems for engraving. sg Feb 1 (164) $90

**Moreau, Jean Michel, 1741-1814**
Autograph Ms, [Carnet de voyage. Italy, 1785] 81 leaves, 130mm by 110mm, in contemp calf lettered Mr Moreal le Jne. 1785. Colored drawing pasted on p.[1], pencil drawing of man with plough on p.[iii], 2 small drawings of St. Peter's on p.[iv] & architectural sketches on pp. 28 & 33. sgd Fuerstenberg - Schaefer copy S Dec 7 (443) £9,500

**Moreau, Jean Victor, 1763-1813**
ALs, 16 Mar 1812. 3 pp, 4to. To his lawyer St. Paul. Asking him to find replacements for his books, referring to his wife's bad health, etc. star Mar 22 (1465) DM450

**Morgan, Daniel, 1736-1802**
ALs, 16 July 1799. 3 pp, 4to. To William Cobbett. Explaining why he did not pay his subscription fee for recipient's journal. P Dec 13 (283) $1,300
See also: Hancock, John

**Morgan, Edwin Denison, 1811-83**
Collection of ALs & ADs, 26 July 1856. 1 p, 4to. Recipient unnamed. Sending a power of attorney (included, at head) for recipient to accomplish. Illus in cat. rms June 6 (421) $225

**Morgan, John Pierpont, 1837-1913**
Ls, 14 Jan 1896. 2 pp, 8vo. To George H. Earle, president of the Finance Co. of Pennsylvania. About a possible adjustment with the Poughkeepsie Bridge interest. sg Feb 1 (165) $400

— 7 Dec 1910. 1 p. To his physician, C. R. Holmes. Saying that his bill is inadequate & paying him more. rms Nov 30 (240) $1,300

Ds, 13 June 1886. 2 pp, folio. Bond no 2510 of the New Jersey Junction Railroad Company. CNY May 17 (271) $550

— 30 June 1886. 1 p, folio. Trustee's Certificate of the New Jersey Junction Railroad Company. Also sgd by Harris C. Fahnestock. Framed with port. rms Nov 30 (6) $600

— 30 June 1886. 1 p, folio. Trustee's Certificate of the New Jersey Junction Railroad Company; including 32 orig bond coupons. rms June 6 (422) $300

— [1886]. 6 leaves, oblong 4to. Mortgage bond certificate, sgd as Trustee of the New Jersey Junction Railroad Co. CE June 12 (89) $550

**Morgenroth, Alfred, 1900-54**
[A collection of c.170 letters & cards addressed to him by numerous composers, singers & musicians, 1921 to 1951, sold at Stargardt on 22 Mar 1996, lot 955, for DM1,700.]

**Morgenstern, Christian, 1871-1914**
ALs, 10 May 1904. 1 p, 4to. To Albert Langen. Inquiring about the publication of his trans of a work by Knut Hamsun. star Mar 21 (281) DM800

**Moritz, Kurfuerst von Sachsen, 1521-53**
Ls, 4 Mar 1552. 2 pp, folio. To the chapter of the archbishopric of Magdeburg in Halle. Introducing two envoys. star Mar 22 (1626) DM500

**Morlacchi, Francesco, 1784-1841**
ALs, 6 Mar 1835. 1 p, 8vo. To [Johann Peter] Pixis. Offering an engagement for his adopted daughter Francilla Pixis-Goehringer at the Dresden opera. star Mar 22 (956) DM260

**Morley, Christopher, 1890-1957**
Autograph Ms, essay, The Fight. 6 pp, 4to. With revisions. sg Feb 1 (166) $225

**Morris, Gouverneur, 1752-1816**
ALs, 18 Nov 1811. 1 p, 4to. To Jonathan Dayton. Informing him that he is unable to invest in a financial scheme. P Dec 13 (284) $750

**Morris, James or Jan**
Typescript, drafts of Morris's Venice [pbd 1960]. About 400 leaves, folio, with extensive holograph revisions in ink. S Dec 18 (409) £900 [Gekoski]

**Morris, Lewis, Signer from New York**
Ds, 9 Nov 1750. 1 p, folio. Bond of Richard & Lewis Morris to Peter Van Pelt. Some staining. rms Nov 30 (241) $550

**Morris, Robert, Signer from Pennsylvania**
ALs, 25 June - 22 July 1780. 11 pp, 4to. To Elbridge Gerry. On Continental finances. Sang collection. P Dec 13 (285) $27,000

— 31 May 1795. 2 pp, 4to. To Sylvanus Bourne. Reporting on the progress of his North American Land Company; asks for money. sg Feb 1 (177) $1,700

— 10 Feb 1797. 2 pp, 4to. To James Greenleaf. About payments & possible problems with Mr. Duncanson. sg June 6 (131) $650

— 2 May 1798. 1 p, folio. To John Nicholson. About financial and legal matters: "...I agree...when you say our wants teach us economy, and I add that our Catch Creditors are daily trying to teach us the practice of care & caution..." Docketed by Nicholson on verso. rms Oct 11 (258) $1,100

Ls, 29 Oct 1783. 1 p, 4to. To Gov. [George Clinton]. Sending the copy of a letter from Henry Sherburne. Illus in cat. rms Mar 21 (210) $900

— 3 Oct 1792. 1 p, 4to. Recipient unnamed. Inquiring about a missing certificate issued by the Comptroller of the Treasury. rms June 6 (424) $350

— 14 Oct 1797. 1 p, 4to. To the Trustees of the Aggregate Fund. Hoping that the Fund witll pay the balance of a fee to Mr. Martin. Body in the hand of & also sgd by John Nicholson. sg June 6 (133) $600

**ADs,** 8 May 1795. 1 p, 4to. To James Greenleaf. About a list of Greenleaf's bills. Illus in cat rms Oct 11 (256) $850

**Ds,** 22 Oct 1782. 1 p, 4to. Sixth bill of exchange for 656 Livres Tournois issued to Haym Salomon. Endorsed by Salomon on verso. Both signatures with ink corrosion cracks. rms Nov 30 (294) $4,200

— 13 June 1794. 3 pp on 2 sheets, 4to. Articles of agreement between Morris & John Nicholson and Thomas Stokeley & John Hodge to purchasewarrants for surveying 120,000 acres between the Ohio & Allegheny Rivers. Sgd by all 4 parties & witnesses. Worn & torn at folds. Sold w.a.f sg June 6 (129) $650

— 8 Jan 1795. 1 p, 7 by 4 inches. Promissory note for ten thousand dollars payable to Morris. Sgd on verso. pba Oct 26 (146) $325

— Feb 1795. 1 p, 4to. North American Land Co. Certificate. F Mar 28 (827) $310

— 17 Apr 1795. 1 p, folio. Certificate of entitlement to 5 shares in the North American Land Co. sg June 6 (130) $650

— 25 Aug 1797. 1 p, 4to. Power of attorney from Morris & John Nicolson to the Trustees of the Aggregate funds to negotiates for land sales or purchases. Sgd by both & by witnesses. Some ink erosion to Morris's signature. sg June 6 (132) $900

### Morrissey, John, 1831-78 —& Others

**Signature,** [n.d.]. On 4to autograph sheet, also sgd by Benjamin F. Butler & Thaddeus Stevens. Illus in cat. rms Mar 21 (239) $460

### Morse, Samuel F. B., 1791-1872

**Autograph Ms,** introductory address to the American Society for the Promotion of National Unity, a pro-slavery society. [1860-61] 2 pp, 203mm by 127mm. P June 5 (88) $4,250

**ALs,** 3 Dec 1841. 2 pp, 4to. To "Isaac N. Coffin, Esq." Seeking financial backing from Congress for his new invention, the telegraph. Illus in cat rms Oct 11 (260) $3,000

— 25 Jan 1870. 1 p, 8vo. To Charles Bretler. Declining an invitation. With a rust stain. Illus in cat rms Oct 11 (202) $750

**ADs,** 10 Apr 1843. 3 pp, folio. Statement of expenditures for constructing the first telegraph line. CNY Dec 15 (104) $4,800

**Cut signature,** [n.d.]. No size given. Cut from letter. pba Feb 22 (141) $190

**Engraving,** sgd & inscr, Sept 1851. 212mm by 166mm. Shoulder-length port, inscr to E. Willis. Illus in cat. Marans collection. CE Apr 17 (52) $7,000

### Morton, John, Signer from Pennsylvania

**ADs,** 23 June 1770. 1 p, 4to. As Justice of the Peace, deposition of Mary Crozer in a breach of contract suit. P Dec 13 (288) $700

### Mosby, John Singleton, 1833-1916

**Photograph,** sgd, [c.1865]. 95mm by 62mm. In uniform; by Vannerson. Illus in cat. CNY May 17 (221) $13,000

**Signature,** [n.d.]. No size given. On a card. Toned & with shadowing. rms Oct 11 (94) $410

### Moscheles, Ignaz, 1794-1870

**ALs,** 8 Jan 1833. 3 pp, 4to. To Johann Peter Pixis. Discussing the difficulties in recipient's composition Clochette Rondo. star Mar 22 (957) DM800

**Autograph quotation,** Thema aus der "belle Union", 22 June 1860. 1 p, 4to. 9 bars on 4 systems, sgd. Inscr [in his wife's hand?] at foot. star Mar 22 (959) DM400

### Moses, Anna Mary Robertson ("Grandma"), 1860-1961

**Photograph,** sgd, [c.1950]. 215mm by 165mm. Painting at a table. Marans collection. CE Apr 17 (213) $500

### Mott, Sir Nevill Francis

**Ls,** 30 Mar 1979. 1 p, 4to. Recipient unnamed. Responding to an inquiry about the most important discovery of the 20th cent. star Mar 21 (568) DM380

### Mott, Valentine, 1785-1865

**Ds,** c.1847-48. 1 p, 12mo. Pass to his lectures on "Operative Surgery with Surgical and Pathological Anatomy" at the University of City of New York. Filled out to J. P. Webster by Mott. rms Oct 11 (261) $210

### Motzfeld, Heinrich, d.1697

**Ls,** 4 Dec 1686. 1 p, folio. To Friedrich van der Capellen. Informing him of a meeting in Xanten. With draft of reply. HN Nov 24 (2806) DM300

### Mountbatten, Louis, 1st Earl Montbatten of Burma, 1900-79

**Ls,** 5 Jan 1957. 2 pp, 4to. To an unnamed lady. Sending condolences on the death of her husband. star Mar 22 (1411) DM230

### Mozart, Constanze, 1762-1842

**ALs,** 16 Mar 1830. 2 pp, 4to. To Marie Celeste Spontini. Referring to the Spontinis' friendship, & thanking for a letter & various favors. star Mar 22 (964) DM10,000

### Mozart, Wolfgang Amadeus, 1756-91

**Autograph music,** leaf from unrecorded part of a soprano aria [c.1778-80]. 219mm by 302mm. Scored for strings, horn & soprano on 2 systems of 6 staves per page. Sgd at head of page. C June 26 (275) £78,000

— Autograph music, sketches for a Sanctus, KV 296c for a Mass in E flat major, [c.1779?]. 1 p, 16cm by 21cm. 18 bars, notated for 4 voices & instruments. Illus in cat. star Mar 22 (962) DM72,000

**ALs,** 26 May 1784. 3 pp, 4to. To his father Leopold Mozart. Discussing his Piano Concertos K.449, 450, 451 & 453, & recounting problems with a maid. Sgd W et C: Mozart. S Dec 1 (243) £60,000

— [c.June 1788). 2 pp, 4to. To Michael Puchberg. Explaining his financial situation & his projected move to a suburb, & asking for a substantial loan. Illus in cat. star Mar 22 (963) DM120,000

## MOZART

— ANDRE, JULIUS. - ALs, [26 Jan 1852]. 3 pp, 8vo. To Karl August Krebs. Responding to an inquiry about the orig score of Mozart's Die Zauberfloete. HH May 9 (2518) DM420

**Mueller, Johannes Peter, 1801-58**
ALs, 20 Jan 1845. 2 pp, 4to. To Ernst von Bibra. Thanking for recipient's work & discussing bone & tooth diseases. star Mar 21 (570) DM380

**Mueller, Johannes von, 1752-1809**
ALs, 13 Mar 1802. 3 pp, 4to. To [John Spencer Smith?]. Asking him to intercede in favor of a young man whose employer has died. star Mar 21 (569) DM700

**Mueller, Max, 1823-1900**
ALs, 13 Feb 1876. 3 pp, 8vo. Recipient unnamed. Wondering whether he would still want to return to Germany at this time. star Mar 21 (572) DM340

**Mueller, Wilhelm, 1794-1827**
ANs, 27 July 1826. 1 p, 8vo, cut from larger sheet. To his wife Adelheid. Postscript to anr letter, sending news about Simolin who has fallen in love with the countess Wolkenstein. star Mar 21 (286) DM900

**Muenchhausen, Boerries, Freiherr von, 1874-1945**
ALs, 6 July 1908. 3 pp, 4to. To [Leo] Berg. Giving permission to reprint some of his poems. star Mar 21 (287) DM320

**Muhammad, Elijah, 1897-1975**
Check, sgd, 16 Aug 1971. Payable to Willie Warren for $125. sg Mar 28 (214) $110

**Munch, Edvard, 1863-1944**
Collection of 4 A Ls s & 4 A Ns s, 1902 to 1936. 17 pp, 8vo & 4to. To Dr. Max Linde. About his work, his travels, exhibitions, & personal matters. HN May 15 (2673) DM6,200

**Murat, Joachim, 1767?-1815**
Ls, 15 July 1802. 1 p, folio. To Minister of War (Marshal Berthier). Requesting "you take definite measures for disarming the places of the Italian Republic...The artillery officers urgently request this...prod the government to make a decision..." Dated "26 Messidor, year 10". With ANs at left head sgd B (Berthier) noting that an attempt had been made to fulfill his request. With bust engraving of Murat. Illus in cat sg Sept 28 (197) $250

**Mursinna, Christian Ludwig, 1744-1823**
ALs, 24 May 1803. 2 pp, 4to. To Herr Wildegans. Commenting on a medical case history. star Mar 21 (573) DM300

**Musical Manuscripts**
Ms, bass part of an unrecorded motet beginning "Te reformator". [England, 2d quarter of 16th cent]. 1 p, vellum, 18cm by 18cm; front pastedown of an early 17th-cent Ms survey for the manor of Wetton in Staffordshire, 21 pp, in old roll-tooled calf over wooden bds. Notated in dark brown ink on 5 staves ruled with a dry-point pen. Illus in cat. S May 15 (348) £2,800

— Ms, collection of over 20 songs, motets & dances by Josquin des Pres, Heinrich Isaac, Ludwig Senfl, Paul Hofhaimer & others, notated in German lute tablature; [c.1525]. 24 pp, folio; stitched, in vellum wraps. By 2 or more hands on up to 11 systems per page. S Dec 1 (220) £27,000

— Ms, collection of over 60 pieces for Lyra-viol. [England or Low Countries, c.1670s?]. 38 pp, folio, in contemp vellum bds. Including 9 or 10 pieces by John Jenkins & others by Dietrich Steffkens, William Lawes, Thomas Mace, etc. S Dec 1 (186) £8,500

— Ms, motet, Suspiret corde quia deo placens nequit homo. [Germany, c.1600]. 4 leaves, folio. 4 parts for Discantus, Altus, Tenor & Bassus, notated on 7 staves per page. Illus in cat. S Dec 1 (241) £1,700

— Ms, song, beginning "Last unss Frisch"; [Germany, c.1610]. 2 pp, folio. Notated in German organ tablature on 3 systems, with 3 stanzas of the words on 2d page. Including 2 presentation inscriptions by the author of the Ms. S Dec 1 (160) £1,150

**Musorgsky, Modest Petrovich, 1839-81**
Autograph music, song, Trepak, no 3 of his 4 Songs & Dances of Death, 17 Feb 1875. 3 pp, 262mm by 377mm. Fragment comprising the final 29 bars, scored for voice & piano. Sgd on tp & at foot; inscr to Ossip Petrov. Illus in cat. star Mar 22 (984) DM60,000

**Musset, Alfred de, 1810-57**
Ms, Les Nuits. [c.1900] 55 pp, each with watercolor drawing by G. Fraipont, comprising pictorial tp to each of the 4 nights & 51 pp of text with large pictorial border, last page of each poem sgd in full, the rest with initials. In mor extra by Marius Michel. S Nov 21 (329) £700

**Mussolini, Benito, 1883-1945**
Autograph Ms, address to Italian fascists, praising the achievements of the movement, Mar 1923. 3 pp, folio. Sgd at end. Illus in cat. star Mar 22 (1413) DM4,400

— Autograph Ms, speech about the Demanio Agricolo Communale. 1 Sept 1942. 12 pp, 4to. Illus in cat rms Nov 30 (244) $1,600

ALs, 2 Apr 1921. 1 p, 4to. To an unnamed recipient. "I am sending this letter to you for your review and for appropriate assessment and action. I repeat that which I have published--Fascist violence, when necessary, must be intelligent and timely." Sgd as Editor of Il Popolo d'Italia. Creased, folded, and foxed. With pinholes, tears & repairs. sg Sept 28 (202) $800

— 10 Apr 1925. 1 p. To Paolo Orano. Telling him they will talk at length as soon as Orano gets well. sg June 6 (139) $800

Ls, 28 Feb 1923. 1 p, 4to. To General Alberto De Marinis Stendaro. Thanking him & all members of the Italian Mixed Commission for their work in Geneva. sg Sept 28 (203) $375

## 1995 - 1996 · AUTOGRAPHS & MANUSCRIPTS                    NAPOLEON

— 28 Sept 1942. 1 p, folio. To King Vittorio Emanuele III. Suggesting a candidate for an appointment. star Mar 22 (1414) DM600

**Ds,** 22 Sept 1927. No size or length given. Authorizing a proposal to change the name of a captain in Corps of Engineers. Countersgd by King Vittorio Emanuele and issued in his name. With translation. rms Oct 11 (267) $350

— 2 Dec 1928. 1 p, folio. Appointment of Carlo Scorza as Commissioner Extraordinaire. Framed with photo. rms Nov 30 (45) $650

**Photograph, sgd,** 7 Sept 1928. 350mm by 175mm. Full length, in uniform. Imperf. Illus in cat. Marans collection. CE Apr 17 (157) $1,200

— Anr, May 1931. 12.5 by 7.5 inches. Bust-length port, by Victor Laviosa. Illus in cat. rms June 6 (629) $375
See also: Vittorio Emanuele III, 1869-1947

**Mussolini, Benito, 1883-1945 —&**
**Vittorio Emanuele III, King of Italy, 1869-1947**

**Ds,** 28 Nov 1938. 1 p, folio. Authorization of the retirement of Brigade General Baseggio Ottoniello. sg June 6 (138) $600

## N

**Nabokov, Vladimir, 1899-1977**

**ALs,** [n.d.]. 1 p, 4to. To Gleb Petrovich Struve. In Russian, praising a poem; discusses possible readings to be undertake in Brussels or Paris. CE May 22 (363) $650

**Photograph, sgd,** 1961. 105mm by 150mm (image). Half-length profile port. Illus in cat. Marans collection. CE Apr 17 (86) $950

**Nadar**

**ALs,** 1 Oct 1869. To a respected person. Recommending Mlle Perrot to him. rms Nov 30 (79) $375

— 7 Sept [1890]. 1 p, 8vo. To his son Paul. Urging him to keep a diary. star Mar 21 (702) DM420

**Naegeli, Hans Georg, 1773-1836**

**ALs,** 27 Nov 1828. 3 pp, 4to. To the printers Wegelin & Stuetzer. Stating conditions for a commission. Kuenzel collection. star Mar 22 (985) DM700

**Nagaoka, Gaishi, 1858-1933**

**Photograph, sgd,** 1932. 225mm by 150mm. 3-quarter length, in uniform. Illus in cat. Marans collection. CE Apr 17 (158) $850

**Napoleon I, 1769-1821**

[2 Ls s by Robert Lambert to John Wilson Crocker, 2 & 6 May 1821, duplicates, reporting about Napoleon's illness & death, with a copy of the report on the autopsy performed on Napoleon, 6 May 1821, sgd by Lambert, 6 pp, folio, sold at Smythe on 6 June 1996, lot 430, for $6,000.]

**Autograph Ms,** fragment from his memoirs, [1816]. 1 p, 8vo. 5 lines, dealing with 1795. Including authentication by Las Cases at foot, 1 June 1824. Framed with a port. Lazarus collection. S May 15 (235) £950

**ALs,** [17?] Aug [1819]. 2 pp, 8vo. To Count Bertrand. Sending the codicil of his will & giving instructions for the disposal of his belongings on St. Helena. Illus in cat. C Nov 29 (161A) £8,000

**Series** of 3 Ls s, [6 May 1802 to 10 Aug 1803]. 4 pp, 4to. To the Minister of War. Concerning the recent duel between Generals Reynier & D'Estaing, & giving instructions for the deployment of cavalry. S Dec 1 (37) £1,500

**Ls,** [5 Nov 1793]. 1 p, 8vo. To Citoyen Constantin. Requesting wood from La Ciotat for the siege of Toulon. star Mar 22 (1415) DM3,000

— [15 Aug 1796]. 1 p, folio. To the paymaster in chief. Ordering him to pay the soldiers of the 8th division immediately. S Dec 1 (34) £340

— [15 Nov 1797]. 1 p, 324mm by 232mm. To Citizen Hallen. Arranging to buy some minerals in Corsica. Featuring engraved vignette. Spotted & soiled. Mtd & framed with an image of Napoleon. P Dec 12 (126) $800

— [12 Aug 1799]. 1 p, folio. To Pou Vielgue(?). Giving orders concerning the payment of taxes by hostages from Jaffa & Gaza. Illus in cat. rms June 6 (427) $2,300

— [22 Jan 1800]. 2 pp, 4to. To Gen. Lefebvre. Giving orders for military action in Normandy. S Dec 1 (35) £400

— 12 May 1802 [An 10 de La Republique]. 3 pp, 4to. To the Minister of War. Giving orders for the subjugation of Haiti. Sgd Bonaparte. sg Mar 28 (122) $3,000

— 8 Germinal an XIII [29 Mar 1805]. 4 pp, folio. To M. Kellermann. Ordering him to obtain information for the government secretly, reporting on officials & clerics & identifying men of influence. Sgd Napoleon. C June 26 (324) £1,400

— 2 Sept 1808. 2 pp, 4to. To Gen. Clarke. Giving orders for troops to move to Paris. star Mar 22 (1416) DM1,100

— 24 Oct 1808. 2 pp, 4to. To Gen. Clarke. Giving orders to find soldiers for his guard & to find quarters for troops at Hanau. star Mar 22 (1417) DM2,600

— 12 Oct 1811. 1 p, 229mm by 184mm. To his son. Admonishing him: "I am surprised that you have not taken possession of this regiment , as I have commanded you to do. Do it without delay...." Spotted. P Dec 12 (127) $700

— 22 May 1812. 1 p, 4to. To Comte Mollien. Concerning funds for his Russian campaign. star Mar 22 (1419) DM1,800

— 9 Apr 1813. 1 p, 4to. To Marshal Marmont. Giving instructions for troop movements preceding the battles of Luetzen & Bautzen. cb June 25 (2561) $2,250

— 28 Apr 1813. 2 pp, 4to. To Comte Bertrand. Giving detailed instructions for troop movements in anticipation of the Battle of Luetzen. star Mar 22 (1420) DM2,200

**Ns,** [1796-97]. 1 p, folio. Recipient unnamed. Reassigning an officer. CE Sept 27 (21) $1,100

**Ds,** [15 Sept 1798]. (fructidor, Year 6). 2 pp, folio. Givin.d.tailed orders to the Paymaster of the Army with regards to reimbursement of payments made by

# NAPOLEON

some merchants. He is to "give receipts to the merchants of Catte for the 200,000 thalaris which they have paid. Each receipt will represent a payment of 3,000 francs on the Nation's assets and will be issued by the Paymaster, countersgd by the Administrator of Finance..." With translation & an engraved port. Illus in cat rms Oct 11 (269) $1,500

— [after 1799]. 1 p, folio, on vellum. Brevet of honor issued to Corporal Beguca. Also sgd by Berthier & Maret. Writing faded. sg June 6 (140) $200

— 19 July 1802. 1 p. Orders for the embarkation of a battalion for Marginique. Sgd "Bonaparte". Ck Apr 12 (78) £500

— 1803. 1 p. About the disposition of his troops in Italy. Sgd "Bonaparte". Framed with port & view. rms Nov 30 (46) $1,350

— Feb 1805. 1 p, folio. Denonciation for M. de Bouillon. Sgd "Napoleon". Ck Apr 12 (79) £480

— 25 Mar 1810. 35 pp on 10 vellum bifolia, 450mm by 290mm. Letters Patent for Francois Charles Marie de Mercy Argenteau conferring lands & the title of Count. With Imperial seal. Sgd Napoleon. C June 26 (326) £2,000

— 3 Jan 1813. 1 p, folio. Permission for Lieut. Jean Nicholas Thomas to remain in the Spanish service. Lazarus collection. S May 15 (236) £360

— 4 Mar 1813. 1 p, folio, ptd on parchment. grant of freedom to 13 political prisoners. Sgd "Napoleon." CE Sept 27 (23) $1,600

**Autograph endorsement,** sgd, 10 Feb 1809. Note of approval on a report addressed to him by Gen. Clarke, 8 Feb 1809, 1 p, folio, concerning the future employment of several generals. star Mar 22 (1418) DM650

— Anr, on letter to him of Gen Bertrand, the Duc de Feltre, Minister of War, 28 June 1811, asking if he wishes to retain 2 companies of elite troops from the heavy infantry. Saying that they should be kept. Sgd "Np". rms Nov 30 (245) $900

**Endorsement,** sgd, 1 Mar 1802, on a letter addressed to him by D. J. Larrey, 5 Feb 1802, 1 p, folio, forwarding a petition by Citizen Guirard requesting that he be taken off the list of emigrants; requesting a police report on the matter. Illus in cat. rms Mar 21 (323) $2,000

— Anr, 5 Apr 1804 [15 Germinal An XII]. On an ALs of Senator Tronchet, 2 Apr 1804, asking that his relative, Citizen Durieux, be given a post. Referring request to the Minister of Finance. Sgd "Buon't". sg Feb 1 (181) $950

— Anr, sgd, on a memorandum addressed to him by the Minister of the Treasury Mollien, reporting a complaint about the quality of coins in Piedmont, 30 Mar 1812. 3 pp, folio. C Nov 29 (160A) £350

— Anr, 24 Jan 1815. On 1 p, 4to letter from Henri Bertran dated 22 Jan 1815. Approving Bertrand's request for expenditures necessary to repair damage from a chimney fire. Illus in cat pba June 13 (118) $950

**Signature,** 4 Mar 1810. 1 p, folio. 1 p, folio. On a 28 Feb 1810 report by the Minsiter of War about the retirement of General Hanicque & the nomination of General Pernetty to fill his position. Marked approved

# AMERICAN BOOK PRICES CURRENT

and dated 4 Mar 1810 in anr hand. Signature smudged. Illus in cat rms Oct 11 (270) $1,000

— BAXTER, ALEXANDER. - ALs, 11 June 1819. 1 p, 8vo. To Dr. Verling. Discussing an accident which happened to the apothecary Simpson on St. Helena. Illus in cat. rms June 6 (434) $400

— PEARCE, LIEUT. ROBERT. - ALs, [c.1816]. 4 pp, 4to. To his sister Eliza. Giving a description of Napoleon's captivity. Including watercolor sketch of Longwood. In acrylic mount. Illus in cat. Lazarus collection. S May 15 (241) £2,500

— ST. HELENA. - A group of 3 A Ls s by Capt. George Nicholls & ALs by Capt. Engelbert Lutyens, 3 Sept 1819 to 18 Nov 1820, 7 pp, 8vo & folio, to Major Gideon Gorrequer, concerning the surveillance of Napoleon. Lazarus collection. S May 15 (242) £380

— ST. HELENA. - Collection of 7 letters by various Englishmen concerning Napoleon's exile, 1816 to 1819, 16 pp, various sizes. Lazarus collection. S May 15 (239) £500

**Napoleon I, 1769-1821 —&**
**Josephine, Empress of the French, 1763-1814 —&**
**Others**

**Collection** of Collection of 9 ALs s, 3 Ds s & 1 ADs by Josephine, Napoleon, Josephine's daughter Hortense & Eugene Beauharnais. 1795-1900. c. 28 pp, 4to & 8vo. A variety of personal and political matters. Including a minature of Josephine sgd by J. Isabey & a letter of authentication by Noel Charavay. Illus in cat rms Oct 11 (268) $15,000

**Napoleon III, 1808-73**

**ALs,** 27 Dec 1819. 1 p, 4to. To his aunt Julie. Sending good wishes for her recovery. star Mar 22 (1476) DM1,200

— 26 Apr 1868. 1 p, 8vo. Recipient unnamed. Agreeing to see him on Monday. With a photograph. rms June 6 (435) $350

**Ls,** 19 Feb 1860. 1 p, 4to. To an unnamed Church official. Thanking for Christmas greetings. rms Mar 21 (325) $250

**ANs,** 10 Apr 1842. 1 p, 8vo. Recipient unnamed. Wondering why the military people have so little influence. HH May 9 (2541) DM260

**Ds,** 10 Aug 1860. 1 p, folio. Conferral of a decoration. star Mar 22 (1478) DM200

— 23 Oct 1867. 1 p, about 18 by 23.5 inches, on vellum. Commutation of a death sentence of a woman who killed her children to life imprisonment. Sgd "Napoleon". With port. sg June 6 (142) $600

**Photograph,** sgd, [c.1870]. 110mm by 60mm, mtd. Bust port, by Le Jeune. Marans collection. CE Apr 17 (159) $750

**Nash, Ogden, 1902-71**

**Autograph quotation,** "The cow is of the bovine ilk...", sgd. 1 p, 4to. rms Nov 30 (247) $550

**Nation, Carry A., 1846-1911**

**Photograph,** sgd, [c.1900]. 181mm by 130mm, mtd. 3-quarter length, holding a hatchet; by Hall's Studio.

Illus in cat. Marans collection. CE Apr 17 (161) $1,900

**Nay, Ernst Wilhelm, 1902-68**
**Series** of 4 A Ls s, 24 Sept 1946 to 17 Jan 1948. 6 pp, 8vo. To the art dealer Herrmann. Regarding exhibitions & sales of his works. star Mar 21 (704) DM1,000

**Necker, Jacques, 1732-1804**
**Ls,** 9 Jan 1778. 1 p, 4to. Recipient unnamed. Thanking for New Year's wishes. star Mar 22 (1300) DM320

**Neher, Caspar, 1897-1962**
[An archive of 70 letters addressed to him by various correspondents, 1946 & 1947, mostly concerning theatrical matters, sold at Stargardt on 21 Mar 1996, lot 35, for DM1,700.]
See also: Brecht, Bertolt

**Neilsen, Kay**
**Original drawing,** to illus East of the Sun, West of the Moon, 1914. "And there lay the Lad, so lovely, and white and red, just as the Princess had seen him in the morning sun." Sgd & dated 1914. 35cm by 25.5cm, in pencil & watercolor heightened with gold; framed. Ck May 31 (258) £19,000
— Original drawing, "The Prince sets off for the Castle which stands east of the Sun and west of the Moon." Sgd & dated 1913. 28.5cm by 22cm, in pencil & watercolor heightened with gold; framed. To illus East of the Sun, West of the Moon, 1914. Ck May 31 (257) £22,000

**Nelson, Eric Hilliard ("Rick"), 1940-85**
**Photograph,** sgd & inscr, [n.d.]. 4to. Waist-length pose; inscr to Barry. Illus in cat. rms June 6 (204) $175

**Nelson, Horatio Nelson, Viscount, 1758-1805**
**Autograph Ms,** Extract from the Admiralty Orders to Earl St. Vincent dated May 2nd 1798. 1 p. Ck Apr 12 (83) £550
**Collection** of 1 A Ls & 1 Ls, Feb 1799 & 31 May 1799. 8 pp. To Perkins Magra, British Consul at Tunis. About his efforts at Tunis. Ck Apr 12 (84) £750
**A Ls s** (2), 5 & 13 Aug 1794. 4 pp. To Lieutenant St. Hill. Instructions for naval operations. Ck Apr 12 (82) £1,800
**ALs,** 7 Aug 1794. 1 p, 8vo. To Lieut. St. Hill. Giving orders to move transports near Calvi. C Nov 29 (164) £600
— 14 Aug 1794. 2 pp, 4to. To Lieut. St. Hill. Giving instructions to expedite powder on board HMS Scarborough. C Nov 29 (167) £750
— 24 Aug [1794]. 1 p. To Lieut. St. Hill. Summoning him to Calvi to transport some soldiers to Bastia. Illus in cat. C Nov 29 (166) £700
— 7 Jan 1799. 3 pp, 4to. To Lieut. Gen. Sir Charles Stuart. Expressing shock at the capitulation of the Neapolitan army to the French. C June 26 (327) £1,400

— 1 Feb 1799. 2 pp, 4to. To Lady Parker. Writing to an old friend about his depression. C June 26 (329) £1,600
— 30 Mar 1799. 1 p. To Sir Charles Stuart. About the campaign to restore the King of Naples. Ck Apr 12 (81) £700
— 12 Apr 1799. 2 pp, 4to. To Admiral Duckworth. Discussing naval actions in the Bay of Naples. C Nov 29 (172) £1,000
— 7 Dec 1799. 2 pp, 4to. To Captain [Alexander] Ball. Praising the Governor of the Island of Malta for his accomplishments. Sgd as "Bronte Nelson". Foxed. Illus in cat rms Oct 11 (284) $2,200
— 4 Oct 1801. 1 p, 4to. To Lieut. Langford. Saying that he is trying to get him a commission. S Dec 18 (517) £450 [Mandl]
— 17 Oct 1801. 3 pp, 4to. To Sir Thomas Rich. About their long-standing friendship & why Rich's protege, Lieut. Owen, has been paid off rather than promoted. Sgd Nelson & Bronte. S July 11 (367) £700
— 8 Nov 1802. 3 pp, 4to. To the Lord Mayor Elect of London. In 3d person, declining a dinner invitation because the City of London has not paid due approbation to the men under his command at Copenhagen. Illus in cat. C Nov 29 (174) £1,700
— 25 May - 4 June 1803. 3 pp, 4to. To Lady Hamilton. Reporting from his voyage to the Mediterranean. C Nov 29 (175) £2,600
— 14 Oct 1803. 2 pp, 4to. To Sir Peter Parker. Reporting the arrival of recipient's grandson on his ship. C Nov 29 (176) £900
— 1 May 1804. 5 pp, 4to. To Sir Edward Pellew. About his infirmities & his hope to fight 1 more battle. S July 11 (365) £4,400
— 24 May 1804. 3 pp, 4to. To William Haslewood. Concerning prize money arrangements. S Dec 18 (523) £800 [Browning]
— 4 Aug 1804. 1 p, 4to. To J. S. Blankley. Responding to a request for a favor. C Nov 29 (178) £800
— 8 Oct 1804. 1 p. To Capt Richard Thomas. In 3d person, requesting him to receive a parcel from Mr. Falconet & to check on a case sent from Mr. Fagan. Ck Apr 12 (93) £500
— 22 Dec 1804. 2 pp. To the Captains of "any of His Majesty's Ships or Vessels arriving from the Westward in search of the Squadron." Announcing that he is proceeding of Toulon & will be at the Madalena islands about the 7th of Jan. Sgd as Nelson & Bronte. Ck Apr 12 (97) £600
— 19 Jan 1805. 2 pp. To Capt. Richard Thomas. Giving urgent news on the movements of the French fleet. Sgd as Nelson & Bronte. Ck Apr 12 (99) £700
— 28 Mar 1805. 3 pp. To Dr. Sewell. Commenting on the regulations for the distribution of prize money. Sgd as Nelson & Bronte. Ck Apr 12 (101) £1,100
— 4 Apr 1805. 1 p, 4to. To Capt. Richard Thomas. Announcing that the French fleet is at sea. C Nov 29 (182) £1,100
— 16 Apr 1805. 3 pp. To Capt. Richard Thomas. About a sighting of the French Fleet. Sgd as Nelson & Bronte. Ck Apr 12 (103) £950

# NELSON

— 30 Aug 1805. 2 pp, 4to, framed. To the Rev. J. Glasse. Attacking his old servant, Tom Allen; sends greeting to his Burnham friends. pn Nov 9 (380) £7,200

**Ls s (2)**, 9 & 11 Apr 1805. 3 pp. To Richard Thomas. About his movements. Ck Apr 12 (102) £1,200

**Ls,** 30 May 1801. 1 p, folio. To Rear Admiral Thomas Graves. Ordering him & 6 ships to Kjoge Bay. S Dec 18 (515) £420 [Stodolski]

— 19 May 1804. 3 pp. To Capt. Richard Thomas. Ordering him to deliver the relevant Act to the officer of Artillery on the Aetna so that in future he may not plead ignorance. Sgd as Nelson & Bronte. Ck Apr 12 (87) £600

— 16 Aug 1804. 1 p, folio. To Capt. Jonathan Chambers White. Ordering an exchange of guns. CNY May 17 (272) $3,200

**Ds s (2)**, 20 June & 20 July 1794. 2 pp, 8vo. Orders addressed to Lieut. Richard Sainthill to land military stores. C Nov 29 (162) £550

— Ds s (2),4 & 6 July 1799. 3 pp. To Adm. Duckworth. Giving instructions for a court martial to try John Jolly. Ck Apr 12 (85) £650

— Ds s (2),29 Sept & 8 Oct 1804. To Capt. Thomas. Instructions about wine & dispatches. Sgd as Nelson & Bronte. Ck Apr 12 (91) £1,100

— Ds s (2),3 Jan & 30 Mar 1805. 3 pp, folio. Memoranda to Capt. Thomas about supplies & requiring that he join him on the Fleet's return from Pula. Ck Apr 12 (98) £1,000

— Ds s (2),14 Mar & 9 Apr 1805. 5 pp, folio. To Capt. Thomas. Instructions concerning ordnance stores & intelligence. Sgd as Nelson & Bronte. Ck Apr 12 (100) £1,000

**Ds,** 22 Sept 1799. 1 p, 4to. Appointment of Lieut. Robert Cameron as Commander of the gunboat Urchin. CE June 12 (90) $1,100

— 8 Aug 1804. 2 pp, folio. To the Masters of the Donegal, Leviathan & Ambuscade. Ordering a report on unfit food, as reported by Captain Stuart. Sgd as Nelson & Bronte Ck Apr 12 (88) £350

— 14 Aug 1804. 2 pp, folio. Appointment of Alfred Smyth as Master of H.M. Sloop Medusa. Countersgd by John Scott. pn Mar 14 (360) £350

— 20 Aug 1804. 2 pp, folio. To the Masters of the Victory, Royal Sovereign & Seahorse. Order to report on the condition of a suspect cask of pork. Sgd as Nelson & Bronte. Ck Apr 12 (89) £480

— 5 Sept 1804. 3 pp, folio. About water supplies & purchasing bullocks. Sgd as Nelson & Bronte. Ck Apr 12 (90) £550

— 9 Nov 1804. 1 p, 4to. To Joseph King. About King's recovery & sending him money. Framed. S July 11 (366) £400

— 15 Nov 1804. 2 pp, folio. To Capt. Thomas. Instructions to proceed off Toulon with a letter for the Phoebe & Hydra. Sgd as Nelson & Bronte. Ck Apr 12 (94) £420

— 22 Dec 1804. 1 p, folio. To Capt. Thomas. Instructions to Thomas to join him off the Madalena islands if the Aetna needs supplies. With added holograph note. Sgd Nelson & Bronte in margin & at foot. Ck Apr 12 (96) £1,100

— 26 Sept 1805. 1 p. Formally placing Richard Thomas under his orders. With related memoranda of orders, with 6-line note by Nelson extending the order for 10 days, after which Thomas is to join him off Cadiz. Illus in cat Ck Apr 12 (105) £1,800

— 10 Oct 1805. 1 p, folio. Memorandum to Capt. Thomas. Ordering him to proceed to Gibraltar & then to rejoin Nelson. Ck Apr 12 (106) £1,100

**Endorsement,** sgd, on secretarial copy of a letter from Admiral Hood to Nelson, 24 July 1794, 2 pp, 4to, regarding supplies & personnel; certifying as true copy. sg Feb 1 (184) $1,100

— SCOTT, JOHN. - Ms, letterbook including 54 letters to various correspondents on Nelson's business, 30 July 1803 to 27 Sept 1805, 44 pp, folio, in contemp calf. C Nov 29 (184) £1,300

**Nelson, Horatio Nelson, Viscount, 1758-1805 —& Gardner, Alan, 1st Baron Gardner, 1742-1809**

**Ms,** Letterbook containing transcriptions of 13 letters of Nelson & c.180 letters of Gardner, 7 July 1800 to 7 Sept 1801. 13 pp of Nelson letters in the hand of John Scott & 117 pp of Gardner letters, folio, in calf. C June 26 (330) £1,400

**Nelson, Samuel, 1792-1873**

**Ds,** 17 May 1839. 1 p, folio. License for John W. Mitchell allowing him to practice as an attorney in New York State Supreme Court. rms Oct 11 (285) $325

**Nelson, Thomas, Signer from Virginia**

**ALs,** 15 June 1781. 1 p, 4to. To Benjamin Harrison. Accepting his appointment as Governor of Virginia. Illus in cat. P Dec 13 (290) $5,500

**ANs,** 2 Sept 1781. 1 p, folio. To the Lieutenant of Berkeley County. Postscript to ptd circular letter asking for troops & horses for the battle against Cornwallis's army; stating that large supplies are needed. Illus in cat. P Dec 13 (291) $14,000

**Nernst, Walter, 1864-1941**

**ALs,** 4 Mar 1922. 2 pp, 4to. To Ernesto Quesada. Discussing recipient's projected visit in Berlin. star Mar 21 (577) DM750

**Ls,** 26 June 1905. 2 pp, 4to. To [the physicist Merriam]. Disussing experiments with ammonia. star Mar 21 (576) DM420

**Nesbit, Evelyn Florence, 1884-1967**

**Photograph, sgd & inscr,** [1902]. 165mm by 108mm, mtd. Shoulder-length port, by Sarony. Inscr on verso. Illus in cat. Marans collection. CE Apr 17 (245) $1,100

**Nevada**

— BLASDEL, HENRY G. - Ds. 1 Mar 1867. 1 p, folio. $1000 bond of the State of Nevada. Sgd as Governor. pba June 13 (158) $190

— BRADLEY, LEWIS R. - Ds. 1 Mar 1872. 1 p, folio. $1000 Bond of the State of Nevada. Sgd as Governor. pba June 13 (159) $110

## New Jersey

**Ms,** Minute Book of the Lords Proprietors of East Jersey, 1664-83. Containing minutes, transcripts of letters & documents, extracts from Robert Barclay's journal, maps & other material. About 316 pp, folio, in 19th-cent mor. C June 26 (298) £45,000

**Document,** 2 Feb 1681/2. 2 sheets (of 3), vellum, 615mm by 815mm, with 4 wax seals & vellum tags. Deed of conveyance form Elizabeth Cartered, widow of Sir George Carteret, & his trustees to William Penn & 11 others of the province of East New Jersey. Sgd by Elizabeth Cartered & the 7 trustees. With a single vellum sheet from an indenture referring to the same subject. C June 26 (296) £13,000

— [1683]. 4 sheets only (1, 3, 4 & 5), various sizes. The Fundamental Constitutions for the Province of East New Jersey in America. Sgd by 17 proprietors, including Robert Barclay as Governor. Fragments cut away from head of 1st sheet, affecting 1 word of title & preamble; some other losses. C June 26 (297) £17,500

## New York (Colony & State)

**Document,** sgd by Horatio Seymour as governor, proclaiming Thursday, 26 Nov 1863, a day of Thanksgiving & Prayer & a legal holiday. 1 p, 4to. Sgd 10 Nov 1863. sg Feb 1 (225) $650

## Newton, John, 1725-1807

**ALs,** [n.d.]. 3 pp, 4to. Recipient & content unknown. F Mar 28 (686) $600

## Ney, Elly, 1882-1968

**ALs,** 15 Oct 1931. 4 pp, 4to. To Herr Kuehn. About her mother's death. star Mar 22 (986b) DM360

## Ney, Michel, Prince de la Moskowa, 1769-1815

**Ls,** [29 Mar 1804]. 3 pp, 4to. To Gen. Dutaillis. Giving instructions to house troops in tents along the coast. star Mar 22 (1467) DM550

— MEYRONNET, MAJOR. - Ls, 12 Aug 1815. 1 p, 4to. Recipient unnamed. Discussing Ney's arrest & requesting orders. star Mar 22 (1469) DM500

## Nicholas, Crown Prince of Russia, 1843-65

**A Ls s** (2), 18 July 1856 & 12 Sept 1857. 3 pp, 4to & 8vo. To his mother. From his holidays, sending congratulations on her name day, & sending a drawing. star Mar 22 (1623) DM800

## Nicholas I, Emperor of Russia, 1796-1855

**Ls,** 25 June 1831. 2 pp, 4to. To Count Michael Semyonevich. Telling him to keep under strict supervision Admiral Greg, who has been sent to serve as Military Governor of Sevastopol, accompanied by Count General Witte. rms Nov 30 (254) $160

## Nicholas I, King of Montenegro, 1841-1921

**Ds,** 4 Feb 1911. 2 pp, folio. Treaty of commerce between Montenegro & Switzerland. star Mar 22 (1410) DM460

## Nicholas II, Emperor of Russia, 1868-1918

**ALs,** 5 Mar 1903. 3 pp, 4to. To Alexandra Paulovna. Thanking for her letter about his manifesto, & referring to her husband's diary. S May 15 (207) £1,500

**Ds,** 5 Oct 1904. 1 p, folio. Decoration for Mikhail Usov. Illus in cat. rms June 6 (439) $1,250

— 10 Feb 1914. 1 p, no size given. Honoring Count Vladimir Sapozhnikov & Collegiate Councillor Innokenitiy Tolmachev. Sgd as "Nikolai". Browned. With related material. Ck Nov 17 (151) £550

— 6 June 1914. 2 pp, folio. Directing the head of the Dept of Russiam Imperial and Royal Orders to grant the appropriate isignia to various nobles. Countersgd by Chancellor Count Frederick. With stamp of Imperial Court in lower margin dated 6 June 1914. sg Sept 28 (207) $700

— 24 Dec 1914. 1 p, folio. Awarding the Order of St. Anna to a military officer and the Order of St. Stanislav to 2 other officers. With translation. Detail in cat rms Oct 11 (287) $950

**Photograph,** sgd, 1901. 4to. In uniform. Ownership inscr by Margot von Tirpitz on mount. HH May 9 (2542) DM2,800

## Nichols Family

[An archive of letters & ptd ephemera relating to John Nichols, John Bowyer Nichols, John Gough Nichols, their family & circle, 1816-54, bound in 8 vols, sold at Bonham's on 5 Dec 1995, lot 186 for £5,200]

## Nichols Ruth R.

**Ls,** 11 Jan 1929. 1 p, 4to. To the Contest Committee of the National Aeronautic Association. Quoting from Amelia Erhart & urging that separate air records be established for women. rms Nov 30 (80) $800

— 23 June 1934. 1 p, 4to. To the National Aeronautic Association. Asking for information about speed records. rms Nov 30 (81) $600

## Nicolai, Otto, 1810-49

**ALs,** 14 Mar 1840. 1 p, 4to. To Francesco Lucca. Concerning changes in his opera Il templario. star Mar 22 (987) DM500

**Nicolaus de Byard, d.1261.** See: Pierre de St. Benedict

**Nicollis, Lorenzo Virgilio, fl.1720-40.** See: Alchemical Manuscripts

## Nicolovius, Alfred, 1806-90

**ALs,** 22 May 1827. 2 pp, 8vo. Recipient unnamed. Sending silhouettes of Goethe's parents (his own great grandparents). star Mar 21 (145) DM900

**Niembsch, Nikolaus, Edler von Strehlenau, 1802-50.** See: Lenau, Nikolaus

## Nietzsche, Friedrich, 1844-1900

**ALs,** 16 Dec 1876. 4 pp, 8vo. To Reinhart von Seydlitz. Reporting about his stay in Sorrent & meetings with M. von Meysenbug & Richard Wagner. star Mar 21 (578) DM20,000

# NIETZSCHE

**Autograph postcard, sgd,** [28 Aug 1877]. To Reinhart von Seydlitz. Commenting on recipient's novella. star Mar 21 (579) DM6,450

## Nightingale, Florence, 1820-1910

**Series** of 11 A Ls s, 1887-88 & [n.d.]. About 50 pp, 8vo, most written pencil, some possibly incomplete. To Mary Shore Smith ("Aunt Mai"). Containing a retrospective of her life's achievements. pn June 13 (310) £3,000

**A Ls s** (2), 1 Apr & 12 May 1881. 3 pp, no size given. To Miss Isabel Johnston. About appointments & about her work in Sarajevo. Also with 5 ANs s & other material. Illus in cat Ck Nov 17 (152) £900

**ALs,** 24 Feb 1828. 3 pp, 8vo. To her cousin, Hilary Bonham Carter. Thanking her for a gift; sending nursery news. Partly in French. pn June 13 (296) £1,700

— [Docketed Nov 1855]. 2 pp, 8vo, incomplete & partly scratched out. To a relative in the Crimea. Reporting the death of Sister Winifred. pn June 13 (304) £400

— 24 Apr 1863. 8 pp, 8vo. To "Dear Lord Nelson". Concerning the nursing profession: "Indeed there is a great lack of suitable persons...Not a week of my life passes but that I am asked to recommend a Lady Sup[erintendent] for some Training...[Hospital]...."Browned. CNY Dec 15 (33) $1,300

— 15 June 1865. 4 pp, 16mo. To Dr. R. Angus Smith. congratulating him on his work. With 2 incomplete letters to Smith & a photograph. pn Nov 9 (412) £440

— 7 Nov 1893. 3 pp, 8vo. To her cousin Blanche. On the death of Jowett & Jowett's last thoughts of Clough. pn June 13 (312) £440

— 21 Oct 1895. 11 pp, 203mm by 127mm. To the Rev. Thomas P. Clarke. Writing at length for the anniversary of the Balaclava charge. P June 5 (306) $4,400

— 11 Dec [18]96. 3 pp, 8vo. Concerning articles regarding the improvement of sanitary conditions. Including autograph postscript, sgd F.N. rms Mar 21 (326) $650

— 3 June 1900. 1 p, 16mo. To T. DeWitt Talmage. Agreeing to see him. Trimmed. Pencil smudging. sg Sept 28 (208) $350

**AN,** [c.1861]. Postscript to a letter to her cousin Blanche Clough. 5 pp, 8vo. Giving her views on right sainthood & nursing; says that she has asked Cardinal Manning to burn her letters. pn June 13 (307) £340

## Nijinsky, Waslav, 1890-1950

**Ptd photograph,** [c.1915]. 130mm by 94mm, in folding mount. Shoulder-length port, sgd & inscr to Andre. Illus in cat. Marans collection. CE Apr 17 (246) $1,400

## Nimitz, Chester W., 1885-1966

**Photograph, sgd,** [n.d.]. 8vo photo in uniform. Sgd as "C. W. Nimitz". With photo of Marines fighting on Marshall Island. With related material. Framed. Over-all size 15.5 by 19.75 inches. Illus in cat rms Oct 11 (14) $450

## Nin, Anais, 1903-77

**ALs,** 16 Aug 1973. 1 p, 4to. To Lawrence Lopez. Discussing a Spanish trans of her story Under a Glass Bell. star Mar 21 (289) DM320

## Nixon, Richard M., 1913-94

**Transcript,** later souvenir copy of his letter of resignation, [9 Aug 1974]. 1 p, 8vo. Sgd. Illus in cat. rms Mar 21 (165) $5,250

**Ls,** 26 July 1950. 1 p, 4to. To Mrs. A. T. Spring. Thanking for congratulations & informing her that he has forwarded her information about a former colleague to the Un-American Activities Committee. Illus in cat. rms Mar 21 (162) $1,500

— 1 Nov 1968. 1 p, 4to. To Col. Robert F. Carter. Asking him to help get the vote out. CE June 12 (91) $300

— 22 Feb 1985. 1 p, 4to. To George Romney. Concerning "...the tenth anniversary of the fall of Saigon [and] we shall probably be indundated in the weeks ahead with scores of book columns, and television documentaries criticizing and lamenting the American role in Vietnam...There can be an honest difference of opinion whether we should have become involved in Vietnam...Whatever our mistakes, the United States tried and failed in a just cause in Vietnam..." Illus in cat pba June 13 (76) $3,000

**Ds,** 15 May 1969. 1 p, 18 by 22 inches, framed. Appointment of John E. Nidecker as Deputy Special Assistant to the President. Countersgd by H. R. Haldeman. rs Nov 11 (36) $800

**Menu, sgd,** [n.d.]. From a TWA flight. Inscr to Mark Clark II & Michael Clark. Framed with photo of Nixon in Peking. rms Nov 30 (39) $210

**Signature,** [n.d.]. No size given. On a title page taken from his book No More Vietnams. With a photo of Nixon welcoming home a woundeed veteran. Framed. Over-all size 18 by 14 inches. Illus in cat rms Oct 11 (318) $280

— Anr, [n.d.]. On souvenir typescript of his letter of resignation. rms Nov 30 (255) $800

See also: Eisenhower, Dwight D. & Nixon

## Noah, Mordecai Manuel, 1785-1851

**ALs,** 27 Aug 1830. 6 pp, 4to. To Mr. Nyham. Complaining of the Treasury Department's interference with his authority as Surveyor of the Port of NY. P Dec 13 (202) $3,750

— 6 Apr 1832. 1 p, 4to. To E. Hayward. Interceding in favor of Wm. A Barton who is trying to sell parchment to the government. P Dec 13 (203) $1,600

## Nolde, Emil, 1867-1956

**ALs,** 24 Apr 1948. 2 pp, 8vo. To Professor Federmann. Announcing his 2d marriage. JG Mar 29 (242a) DM800

## Nordau, Max, 1849-1923

**ALs,** [Feb 1882?]. 2 pp, 8vo. To Sarah Hutzler. Love letter; fragment. HN Nov 24 (2844) DM420

**AL,** [14 Oct 1884?]. 4 pp, 8vo. To Sarah Hutzler. Fragment, discussing their relationship. HN May 15 (2676) DM500

**Nordenskjold, Nils Adolf Erik, 1832-1901**

**Collection** of ALs & Ls, 14 May 1895 & 1896. 4 pp, 8vo. To Frederik & Olga Due. Introducing his nephew & his niece. star Mar 21 (581) DM400

**North, Frederick, 2d Earl of Guilford, 1732-92**

**Ds,** 11 July 1777. 2 pp, folio. Noting receipt of 400 pounds due to him for services as Chancellor of the Exchequer. Also sgd by William Lyttleton as "Wescote". With tape repair of a fold break. pba June 13 (41) $225

**North, William, 1755-1836**

**ALs,** 25 Jan 1781. 4 pp, folio. To Lewis Morris. Discussing the military situation. P Dec 13 (292) $900

**Norton, Charles Eliot**

**Series** of 5 A Ls s, 31 Dec 1861 to 21 Jan 1867. About 35 pp, 8vo. To Blanche Clough. About her husband's poetry & its publication. pn June 13 (316) £1,500

**ALs,** 11 May 1856. 4 pp. To Arthur Hugh Clough. Giving an account of his tour of Sicily with Lowell & Fields. pn June 13 (314) £90 [Sawyer]

— 31 Oct 1859. 4 pp, 8vo. To Arthur Hugh Clough. Informing him of the good sale of his Plutarch in America & of the purchase of the Atlantic by Ticknor & Fields; writes of John Brown. pn June 13 (315) £180 [Sawyer]

**Nossack, Hans Erich, 1901-77**

**Ls,** 10 Apr 1950. 2 pp, folio. Recipient unnamed. Responding to questions about his poems. star Mar 21 (290) DM380

**Novarro, Ramon**

**Photograph, sgd & inscr,** [n.d.]. 10 by 13 inch portrait photo. Inscr to Ferdinand and Charlotte. Photo by Henry Waxman. Also sgd by Waxman. Browned with age & with break in right margin. pba Feb 22 (89) $110

**Nuremberg**

— CHURCH OF ST. WALPURGIS. - Illuminated calligraphic Ms, Stuelbuch ober die Kirchen zu Sanct Walburgen gehoerig vom Herrn Georg Volckhamer damals verordneter Kirchenpfleger offgerichtet worden den 1 August Anno 1615. 149 leaves, folio, in orig calf gilt with Nuremberg arms, 1615. Coats of arms of Volckhamer on title & 334 illuminated armorials of holders of pews. C May 1 (113) £2,500

**Nureyev, Rudolf, 1938-93**

**Ds,** French travel document, [c.1972]. 15cm by 10cm. Including 3 photographs. Illus in cat. S May 15 (437) £850

**Photograph, sgd,** [n.d.]. 8 by 10 inches. Head-&-shoulders port, in casual clothes. Illus in cat. rms June 6 (219) $300

**Signature,** [c.1974]. On his photograph within a program of The National Ballet of Canada, folio. Illus in cat. rms June 6 (220) $250

**Nussbaum, Johann Nepomuk von, 1829-90**

**ALs,** 24 June 1890. 1 p, 8vo. Recipient unnamed. Explaining that his university duties do not allow him to move to the country. HH Nov 17 (3299) DM320

# O

**Oakley, Annie, 1860-1926**

**ALs,** 17 Nov 1923. 3 pp, 8vo. To an unnamed young girl. Describing her recent show appearances & hoping to see her & her family before they go to California. Illus in cat. CNY May 17 (277) $11,000

**Photograph, sgd & inscr,** 19 Feb 1906. 226mm by 150mm, mtd. Full length, taking aim; by Duryer. Illus in cat. Marans collection. CE Apr 17 (21) $10,000

**Occom, Samson**

**ALs,** 7 Nov 1752. 1 p, 4to. To the Rev Solomon Williams. About his financial difficulties. rms Nov 30 (54) $440

**O'Connor, Sandra Day**

**Cut signature,** [n.d.]. No szie given. On Supreme Court Card. With port. Framed. Over-all size 13.75 by 17.5 inches. Illus in cat rms Oct 11 (15) $260

**Odo de Meung, fl.11th cent**

**Ms,** De Virtutibus Herbarum. [Germany, c.1185]. Fragment of 22 leaves, vellum, page height 175mm. Antique-style bdg of wooden bds with calf back & endpapers from a 15th-cent Ms. 1245 of 2269 lines only, in a late Caroline minuscule in 2 different hands, partly with 14th-cent marginal annotations. With 2- & 3-line decorated initials introducing each verse & 6-line initial of strapwork design in red & blue. Partly palimpsest of an earlier medical text. C Nov 29 (6) £7,000

**O'Faolain, Sean**

**Typescript,** 3 drafts of his short story, Marmalade. About 70 leaves, 4to. With extensive holograph revisions. S Dec 18 (411) £850 [Quaritch]

**Offenbach, Jacques, 1819-80**

**Autograph music,** part of Edwige's waltz-song in Act 2 of his Robinson Crusoe, [c.1867]. 2 pp, folio. Working Ms of the full score, comprising 25 bars of music, notated on up to 13 staves per page. S May 15 (439) £600

— Autograph music, sketches for various unidentified works, [n.d.]. 9 pp, folio. About 100 bars, mostly scored for a single instrumental voice. C Nov 29 (235) £850

**ALs,** [10 Dec 1860]. 1 p, 8vo. Recipient unnamed. About plans to visit Berlin & performances of his works. HN Nov 24 (2845) DM950

— 4 May [n.y.]. 1 p, 8vo. To the pbr Brandus, Dufour & Cie. Concerning theater tickets & a shipment of Mss. star Mar 22 (989) DM550

— Saturday. 1 p, 8vo. To Mr. Henry of the New York Herald. Inviting him to dinner. cb June 25 (2563) $375

## Officium

**Ms**, Office de la Pentecote. 1768. 83 leaves, 197mm by 122mm, in contemp red mor gilt with arms of Jourdan de Launay. Fuerstenberg - Schaefer copy S Dec 8 (464) £950

## Oglethorpe, James Edward, 1696-1785

**Ds**, 7 Feb 1743. 1 p, 8vo. Colony of Georgia sight bill. Illus in cat. rms June 6 (440) $3,750

## O'Higgins, Ambrosio, 1720?-1801

**Ls**, 26 Mar 1789. 1 p, folio. Recipient unnamed. Requesting a statement of income & expenses of the Royal Treasury. rms June 6 (441) $600

## Ohm, Martin, 1792-1872

**ALs**, 15 Dec 1821. 1 p, 4to. To his pbr. Urging him not to delay the publication of his algebraic handbook. star Mar 21 (583) DM470

## O'Keeffe, Georgia, 1887-1986

**ALs**, 30 Oct 1957. 1 p, 4to. To George Staempfli. Saying that she does not like to loan from the Stieglitz collections. wa Oct 28 (80) $700

## Oken, Lorenz, 1779-1851

**ALs**, 11 Sept 1812. 2 pp, 4to. Recipient unnamed. Sending the 1st part of his Naturgeschichte & requesting some books to continue the work. star Mar 21 (584) DM650

## Olga Konstantinovna, Queen of George I of Greece, 1851-1926

**ALs**, 20 Nov 1900. 2 pp, 8vo. To the Red Cross Society. Wishing them well for their work. Also sgd by her husband King George I. star Mar 22 (1340) DM380

## Olivier, Laurence, Sir, 1905-89. See: Leigh; Olivier & Others

## Olivier, Laurence, Sir, 1907-89. See: Leigh, Vivien & Olivier

## O'Meara, Barry Edward, 1786-1836

**ALs**, 23 June 1817. 2 pp, 4to. To Sir Pulteney Malcolm. Reporting Napoleon's account of his last conversation with Malcolm. Lazarus collection. S May 15 (243) £380

— 22 May 1821. 4 pp, 8vo. Recipient unnamed. About Napoleon's illness & the return of Napoleon's chaplain Abbe Buonavista to Europe due to ill health. Illus in cat. rms June 6 (433) $1,550

## Onassis, Jacqueline Bouvier Kennedy, 1929-94

**ALs**, 23 May [1962]. 2 pp, 12mo. To Betty Beale. Referring to a meeting the night before. Illus in cat. rms Mar 21 (159) $950

## Ondaatje, Michael

**Collection** of A Collection of an ALs & 2 TLs s, 1970-73, no size or length given. To John Gill. Concerning the worth of his poems. Bottom of ALs torn & with notes in Gill's hand. pba Jan 25 (281) $275

## O'Neill, Eugene, 1888-1953

**ALs**, 15 Aug 1921. 1 p, 4to. To his wife. Reporting on a storm. Mtd with envelope & framed. wa Oct 28 (47) $1,300

**Photograph, sgd & inscr**, [1923]. 237mm by 180mm. Seated on a handrailing, by Muray. Illus in cat. Marans collection. CE Apr 17 (87) $1,900

## Oppenheimer, Joseph Suess, 1698-1738

**Ls**, 27 June 1736. 3 pp, folio. To Duke Karl Alexander of Wuerttemberg. Reporting about negotiations with the Elector Palatine's ministers. HH May 9 (2544) DM3,800

## Oppenheimer, Julius Robert, 1904-67

**ANs**, [n.d.]. 1 p, 8vo. To I. I. Rabi. "Wednesdays it is". bbc Dec 18 (82) $120

## Ord, Edward Otho Cresap, 1818-83

**Ds**, 31 May 1879. 1 p, 16mo. An approval endorsement cut from anr document. With a stereo card of A dead Southern soldier. Framed. Over-all size 19.5 by 15.5 inches. Detail in cat rms Oct 11 (110) $200

## Orleans, Charles, Duc d', 1394-1465

— RENIER, PIERRE. - Ds, 19 Nov 1421. 1 p, vellum, 320mm by 238mm. Receipt for items of silver, gold, jewels & coinage received from Jehan le Mercier, Charles's valet de chambre. S June 18 (35) £600

## Orleans, Gaston Jean Baptiste, Duc d', 1608-60

**Endorsement**, sgd, 29 Oct 1650, on a list of interest payments, 28 Oct 1650, 3 pp, folio; instructing his treasurer to retain money for current expenses. star Mar 22 (1287) DM220

## Orlik, Emil, 1870-1932. See: Hauptmann, Gerhart

## Ormerod, George Wareing, 1810-91

**Autograph Ms**, diaries, 1829-38. 2 vols, c.200 pp, calf & half calf, worn. With related materials. S July 11 (413) £500

## Orsay, Alfred Guillaume Gabriel, Comte d', 1801-52. See: Liszt, Franz

## Orsbeck, Johann Hugo von, Kurfuerst von Trier, 1634-1711

**Ls**, 26 Nov 1703. 2 pp, folio. To Johann Friedrich Ignaz Karg von Bebenburg. Asking him to recommend Bertram Scheben for a prebend at Lohe. star Mar 22 (1333) DM900

## Orwell, George, 1903-50

**Ls s** (2), 22 Mar 1941 & 17 Nov 1942. 2 pp, 4to. To Desmond Hawkins. Discussing a proposed BBC series; gives permission for Hawkins to republish a previous broadcast. S July 11 (290) £2,300

## Osgood, Samuel, 1748-1813

**Ls**, 25 Feb 1788. 1 p, 4to. To Thomas Smith Esq., "Commissioner of the L. Office" for Pennsylvania. Asking for an estimate of debts incurred by the state in the Revolutionary War. Illus in cat pba Oct 26 (147) $650

**Osler, Sir William, 1849-1919**
**Photograph, sgd & inscr,** [c.1900]. By Meany of Baltimore. 136mm by 96mm, on mount measuring 256mm by 206mm. Inscr on mount. sg May 16 (464) $1,900
— BRADLEY, ALFRED E. - Ls. 12 June 1917. 1 p, 4to. To Osler. Thanking him for any suggestions on " ...the venereal situation...one of the most serious of the many problems which are confronting us..." Margins chipped & with file & pin holes. rms Oct 11 (290) $175

**Ottheinrich, Kurfuerst von der Pfalz, 1502-59**
**Ls,** 9 Feb 1548. 3 pp, folio. To Mary Queen of Hungary. Asking her to intercede in his favor with the Emperor. HH May 9 (2546) DM2,800

**Otto, King of Greece, 1815-67**
**Ls,** 5 July 1850. 1 p, 4to. To Ferdinand II, King of the Two Sicilies. Congratulating him on the marriage of his brother. rms June 6 (442) $250

**Overbeck, Franz, 1837-1905**
**A Ls s** (2), 9 Dec 1869 & 14 Feb 1870. 12 pp, 8vo. Recipient unnamed. Discussing recipient's dissertation. star Mar 21 (585) DM750

**Overbeck, Johann Friedrich, 1789-1869**
**Autograph Ms,** statement of the artistic & religious creed of the Nazarene School. 1 p, 4to. Sgd & dated at Rome, 14 May 1835. pn Nov 9 (428) £110

**Ovington, Mary White**
[An Archive of personal diaries, photographs & family ephemera sold at Swann on 28 Mar 1996, lot 225, for $2,400]

**Owen, Robert, 1771-1858**
**ALs,** 17 Nov 1860. 4 pp, 8vo. To "My dear Neighbour". Declining an invitation because of the pressures of work. Detail in cat rms Nov 30 (261) $300
**Autograph sentiment,** sgd, 27 May 1830. 1 p, 8vo. Referring to practical truths, the character of man, & the necessity "to relieve mankind from moral error". star Mar 22 (1495) DM250

**Oxenstierna, Axel, Count, 1583-1654**
**Ls,** 31 Aug 1633. 1 p, folio. To Count Albert zu Hanau-Muenzenberg. Informing him that he is not able to visit him but must go to Frankfurt. star Mar 22 (1262) DM500

**Oxenstierna, Johan, Count, 1611-57**
**Ls,** 22 Sept 1642. 3 pp, folio. To Landgraefin Amalie Elisabeth von Hessen-Kassel. Informing her about diplomatic negotiations & actions of the Swedish troops. star Mar 22 (1263) DM350

# P

**Paca, William, Signer from Maryland**
**ALs,** 3 Dec 1782. 2 pp, folio. To Jacques Rene de La Villebrune. Draft, requesting assistance in expelling British barges from the Chesapeake Bay. P Dec 13 (294) $1,800

**Paderewski, Ignace Jan, 1860-1941**
**Photograph, sgd,** [n.d.]. 4to. By Hartsook Photo, S.F. Mount margins trimmed. rms Oct 11 (291) $350
— Anr, [n.d.]. 9.5 by 7.5 inches (image). Waist-length pose; by Hartsook. Illus in cat. rms June 6 (443) $325
**Photograph, sgd & inscr,** [c.1890s]. 4.5 by 6 inch sepia bust photo. Inscr & sgd in French. sg Sept 28 (212) $175

**Paer, Ferdinando, 1771-1839**
**ALs,** 27 Oct 1828. 1 p, 4to. To an unnamed baron. Apologizing for an indiscretion. star Mar 22 (990) DM220

**Paganini, Nicolo, 1782-1840**
**ALs,** 9 Mar 1834. 1 p, 4to. Recipient unnamed. Introducing the lawyer Tabacchi. C Nov 29 (241) £950

**Paget, Thomas Guy Frederick, 1886-1952**
**Series** of hundreds of A Ls s, 1914-18. Pinned together in sheaves. To his wife. Covering his experiences with the 7th Northants Regiments. S Dec 18 (527) £400 [Imperial War Museum]

**Paine, Robert Treat, Signer from Massachusetts**
**Ds,** 2 May 1767. 1 p, oblong 16mo. Witnessing signature of Jonathan Hill on promissory note to John King. sg Feb 1 (188) $225
— 2 July 1780. 1 p, folio. Order to confiscate the property of Margaret Draper. Sgd twice. P Dec 13 (296) $1,000

**Paine, Thomas, 1737-1809**
**ALs,** [c.1805]. 3 pp on both sides, 4to. To Citizen Director. About the case of Captain Hayley & a prize cargo. cb June 25 (2370) $11,000

**Palmerston, Henry John Temple, 3d Viscount, 1784-1865**
**Series** of 90 A Ls s, 9 Nov 1810 to 16 Oct 1856. About 200 pp, various sizes. To Sec. to the Admiralty John Wilson Croker. On political & military matters. With related material. Bound in mor extra by Riviere. P June 5 (308) $3,000

**Pankhurst, Christabel, 1880-1958**
**ALs,** 3 Mar 1913. 2 pp. To the Editor of The Daily Mail. Enclosing a telegram (present) stating that an explosion at Devonport was not the work of Suffragettes. Ck Apr 12 (108) £250

**Pankhurst, Emmeline, 1858-1928**
**Photograph, sgd,** [c.1910). 165mm by 218mm, mtd. Seated at her desk. Illus in cat. Marans collection. CE Apr 17 (181) $400

**Pankhurst, Sylvia, 1882-1960**
**Photograph, sgd & inscr,** [c.1920). 288mm by 230mm, mtd. Shoulder-length port. Marans collection. CE Apr 17 (182) $400

**Pannwitz, Rudolf, 1881-1969**
Typescript, Aiaia. Hyperboraeisches Epos. Zweiter Gesang, [n.d.]. 9 pp, 4to. 12 stanzas, sgd & inscr to Karl [Carlo] Schmid. HH Nov 17 (3302) DM260

**Papen, Franz von, 1879-1969**
Ds, 1 Sept 1945. 1 p, 5 by 8 inches. Form certifying that "the following is my proper signature." Mtd with photo. sg June 6 (144) $200

**Pappenheim, Gottfried Heinrich, Graf von, 1594-1632**
Ls, 13 Oct 1630. 2 pp, folio. To [the magistrate of Braunschweig?]. Warning them not to allow the Swedish to recruit soldiers in their city. star Mar 22 (1264) DM1,650

**Parker, Charlie, 1920-55**
Photograph, sgd & inscr, [c.1950]. 246mm by 197mm. Shoulder-length port, holding his saxophone, by James J. Kriegsmann. Inscr to Kayo. Illus in cat. Marans collection. CE Apr 17 (238) $3,000

**Parrish, Maxfield, 1870-1966**
ALs, 20 Mar 1942. 2 pp, 280mm by 215mm. To a female correspondent. About commercial art, family & watercolor painting. cb Oct 17 (664) $550
Photograph, sgd & inscr, [c.1935]. 185mm by 125mm, including folding mount. Half length, by Levesque Studio. Inscr to Edgar A. Moss. Marans collection. CE Apr 17 (214) $350

**Parsons, Samuel Holden, 1737-89**
ALs, 19 Nov 1780. 2 pp, 4to. To [Jeremiah?] Wadsworth. Urging improvements in the treatment of army officers by Congress & provisions for discharging the interest on Continental securities. P Dec 13 (297) $900

**Pasternak, Boris, 1890-1960**
Collection of ALs & autograph sentiment, sgd, 12 July 1959. 1 p, folio, with dust jacket of English Ed of Dr. Zhivago. To Miss De Cruz. Discussing the possibility of a trans of The Last Summer. Inscr to Miss De Cruz, sgd twice. S May 15 (209) £350
ALs, 5 Apr 1953. 2 pp, folio. To Boris & Evgenia Livanov. Giving his assessment of King Lear. S Dec 1 (38) £440
— 30 May 1959. 2 pp, folio. To Miss De Cruz. Commenting on Dr. Zhivago & The Last Summer. S Dec 1 (40) £800

**Pasteur, Louis, 1822-95**
Autograph Ms, Commentary on the proper way of treating rabies. 3 Sept 1886. 1 p, 8vo. In part: " Even the most serious cases at the very beginning, I am confident that one could cure them all, that is to say that one could prevent rabies from breaking out..." Unsgd. With transcription & translation. Illus in cat rms Oct 11 (294) $3,250
— Autograph Ms, notebook of experiments entitled Fermentation Alcoolique. 1868. 9 pp, 4to, in modern half cloth. Illus in cat C June 23 (331) £8,000
ALs, 9 June 1882. 1 p, 8vo. To an unnamed recipient. Letting the recipient know that " I have received the beautiful work...and I beg you to accept with all my thanks to the family..." With a sepia reprint of a 19th century photo of Pasteur in the lab. Framed. Over-all size 14 by 18 inches. Illus in cat rms Oct 11 (406) $1,350
— 9 June 1883. 1 p, 8vo. To the Vice Chancellor of Cambridge University. Regretting that he cannot return to Cambridge for an event. Framed with photo & in lacquer display cabinet with brass plaques. cb June 25 (2565) $650
— 20 July 1884. 1 p, 4to. To Professor Rodriguez Mendez. Thanking for an honor bestowed upon him. Illus in cat. rms June 6 (444) $2,200
— June 1886. 1 p, 32mo. To Emile Corra of L'Evenement. About his dog, evidently cured by Pasteur of rabies. sg June 6 (146) $1,500
ANs, 25 May 1888. 1 p, 8vo. To an unnamed lady. Thanking for good wishes for his recovery. HH May 9 (2547) DM750
Photograph, sgd, [c.1886]. 162mm by 107mm, mtd. Seated; by A. Gerschel. Illus in cat. Marans collection. CE Apr 17 (53) $2,600
Ptd photograph, [n.d.]. 17cm by 11cm. In his laboratory, sgd & inscr to the Mayor of Le Havre. S May 15 (210) £750

**Paterson, Andrew Barton ("Banjo"), 1864-1941**
ALs, 16 June 1939. 1 p. To Laurie Copping. About his composition of Walzing Matilda. "The only known record by Banjo Paterson to confirm his authorship of Australia's national song...." CA Mar 26 (130) A$30,000

**Patkul, Johann Reinhold von, 1660-1707**
ALs, [18 Apr] 1694. 1 p, folio. To Johann Fischer. Making plans to leave for Stockholm, since the King has now granted him safe conduct. In Latin. star Mar 22 (1650) DM480

**Patrick, Marsena Rudolph**
ALs, 16 Apr 1879. 1 p, 8vo. To Col. D. C. Robinson. About a police order that will be issued the following day. Framed with port & 30th reunion silk of the I Corps survivors. rms Nov 30 (23) $320

**Patti, Adelina, 1843-1919**
Photograph, sgd & inscr, 1890. 11.25 by 7.12 (image). Standing, in elaborate gown; by Barraud. Illus in cat. rms June 6 (194) $650

**Patton, George S., Jr., 1885-1945**
ALs, 19 Nov 1912. 2 pp, 4to. To Beatrice Ayer. Telling his wife about his 27th birthday and barracks gossip. With orig envelope. CNY Dec 15 (105) $4,200
— 19 Oct 1917. 2 pp, 4to. To his mother. Chatting about his stay in the hospital after being wounded in the Meuse-Argonne offensive. CNY May 17 (280) $4,500
— 14 June 1918. 2 pp, 4to. To Ruth Wilson Patton. Concerning tanks: " ...rain in moderation is good for tanks...A tank in spite of its ferocious appearance is in reality a delicate animal and subject to more ills than horses..." Yellowed. With holograph envelope.

Sgd again as commader under "Passed as Censored" stamp. CNY Dec 15 (106) $5,500
— 14 July 1918. 2 pp, folio. To his mother. About a party with French officers & his lectures about the necessity of tanks. CNY May 17 (281) $5,500
— 18 Nov 1918. 2 pp, folio. To his mother. About family matters, his own health, acquaintances, etc. CNY May 17 (282) $2,600
**Ls,** 27 Apr 1935. 2 pp, 8vo. To Col. Kenyon A. Joyce. Thanking him for his "kindness and consideration evinced almost daily during the time I had the pleasure of serving under you." rms Nov 30 (264) $3,500
— 4 Sept 1935. 1 p, folio. To "Jerry". Concerning his plan to invest in munitions firms. CNY May 17 (283) $5,000
— 20 July 1943. 1 p, 4to. To Mrs. Suzanne Miner. Thanking her for a letter & looking forward to a post-war visit: "You will have to excuse this brief note as we are having a battle at the moment. G S Patton Jr. Lieut. General, U. S. Army, Commanding." Illus in cat pba Oct 26 (190) $2,500
— 30 Sept 1943. 1 p, 267mm by 203mm. To Brig. Gen. Albert Kenner, the Army Surgeon General. Speculating about who will be put in charge of the continental invasion; refers to his enforced ideleness after having been relieved of command for hitting a soldier. With Kenner's personal file on Patton's final medical history & other related material. P June 5 (90) $9,500
— 30 Sept 1944. 1 p, 4to. To Dr. W. C. Loft. Thanking him for a letter & a cartoon. With holograph correction. Illus in cat rms Oct 11 (409) $1,600
— 4 Dec 1944. 1 p, 4to. To Howell E. Dodd. Thanking him for his coverage of combat activities. sg June 6 (147) $3,000
**Menu,** 7 June 1945. 6 by 9 inch engraved program of official dinner given by Commonwealth of Massachusetts in his honor. Sgd on cover in pencil. Includes listing of "General Patton's Party from Overseas". With cords & tassels. Cover browned. sg Sept 28 (213) $750
**Photograph, sgd & inscr,** [c.1945]. 246mm by 199mm. Half length, in uniform. Inscr referring to the church where he was baptized & confirmed. Illus in cat. Marans collection. CE Apr 17 (163) $7,000

### Paul, Bruno, 1874-1968
**ALs,** 15 Apr 1915. 1 p, 4to. To the Lord Mayor of Berlin. About a council for the arts & the journal Wieland. HN May 15 (2681) DM200

### Paul I, Emperor of Russia, 1754-1801
**Ls,** 14 Aug 1789. 1 p, 8vo. To Friedrich Nicolai. Thanking for "le second cahier des anecdotes du feu Roi de Prusse". HN Nov 24 (2846) DM550

### Paul, Jean, 1763-1825. See: Richter, Jean Paul

### Paul VI, Pope, 1897-1978
**ALs,** 7 July 1937. 2 pp, 4to. To an unnamed marchese. Responding to a request for help in a difficult matter. star Mar 22 (1508) DM950

**Photograph, sgd,** 28 July 1964. 253mm by 188mm, mtd. Shoulder-length port. Marans collection. CE Apr 17 (164) $750

### Paulin, Tom
**Autograph Ms,** poem, The Rooks. 6 pp, 4to, sgd. With an earlier autograph draft & revised typescript. S Dec 18 (412) £150 [Quaritch]

### Pauling, Linus Carl, 1901-95
**Autograph Ms,** conclusion of a larger work, referring to war & militarism; [n.d.]. 3 pp, folio. Sgd; inscr at head. star Mar 21 (586) DM480
— Autograph Ms, Examples of Energy-rich Molecules; [n.d.]. 5 pp, 4to, paginated 8-26 & 8-30. Part of a larger work; sgd at head. star Mar 21 (587) DM380
— Autograph Ms, fragment of a scientific paper about Vitamin C, [4 Mar 1977]. 4 pp, 4to, paginated 3 - 6. Sgd at head. HN May 15 (2682) DM420

### Pavlov, Ivan Petrovich, 1849-1936
**Ptd photograph,** [c.1925]. 213mm by 121mm, mtd. Shoulder-length port, inscr to Seymour Halpern. Illus in cat. Marans collection. CE Apr 17 (54) $6,500

### Pavlova, Anna, 1881-1931
**Photograph, sgd,** [c.1920]. 146mm by 102mm, mtd. 3-quarter length, in a white dress, by Alfred Ellis & Walery. Illus in cat. Marans collection. CE Apr 17 (248) $500
— Anr, [n.d.]. Postcard. Full length, in costume; by Schneider. Illus in cat. rms June 6 (224) $350
**Photograph, sgd & inscr,** 1 Jan 1917. About 172mm by 120mm, apparently cut from larger photo. Inscr across lower portion of image to Mrs. Reins. CE June 12 (93) $220
— Anr, 1925. 1 p, 7 by 8 inches. By Abbe. Sgd & Inscr. Ink Splattered. Trimmed. Illus in cat sg Sept 28 (87) $325
— Anr, [n.d.]. Showing her as the dying swan. Inscr to Mr. Smalley in white ink. Framed. Illus in cat rms Nov 30 (265) $750

### Pawnee Bill. See: Lillie, Gordon William

### Payn, James, 1830-98
**Autograph Ms,** novel, A Confidential Agent. About 560 pp, 4to, in contemp mor by Tout. With extensive revisions. Inscr to Horace Pym, 11 Aug 1883. S Apr 23 (126) £2,300

### Peabody, George Foster, 1852-1938
**Photograph, sgd & inscr,** [n.d.]. Folio. Sepia-toned. Inscr to Louis Wiley. Inscr shadowed & mount trimmed. Also with edge chip. Illus in cat rms Oct 11 (295) $210

### Peale, Rembrandt, 1778-1860
**Autograph sentiment,** [n.d.]. "I remain with great respect Yours, Rem. Peale". On 3.5 by 2-inch card. cb June 25 (2566) $275

**Peary, Robert Edwin, 1856-1920**
**Collection** of 1 May & 6 July 1903. 3 pp & 1 p, 4to. To William Porter Allen. About Aluminum transit. Also with 2 Ls s by H. C. Bridgman about the purchase of the transit. With orig postmarked envelope. rms Oct 11 (296) $280
**ALs,** 6 Sept 1916. 1 p, 4to. To Mr. Cole. Referring to a bill before Congress & promising to send some publications. Illus in cat. rms Mar 21 (230) $380
**Ls,** 12 July 1905. 1 p, 4to. To Robert Underwood Johnson. Thanking Johnson for his encouragement in attempting to reach the North Pole. Sgd as "' "' R. E. Peary". pba Feb 22 (144) $140
**Photograph, sgd,** 9 [Oct?] 1910. 121mm by 80mm. 3-quarter-length. Marans collection. CE Apr 17 (22) $500

**Penn, John, Signer from North Carolina**
**ALs,** 22 Sept 1780. 1 p, folio. To [Gen. Butler or Gen. Sumner]. Advising him to expect the arrival of Gen. Smallwood to command the state's militia & discussing military strategy. Including franking signature. Illus in cat. P Dec 13 (300) $8,000
**ADs,** [after 10 June 1783]. 1 p, 4to. Indictment of Pomfritt Herndon for assault on Susannah Lankford. P Dec 13 (301) $2,750

**Penn, William, 1644-1718**
**Ds,** 7 Sept 1681. 1 p, folio. Grant of land in Pennsylvania to Francis Smith. rms June 6 (445) $1,650
— 17 Oct 1681. 1 p, folio. Appointment of an assistant surveyor for his colony. CNY May 17 (284) $1,900
— CLAYTON, JOSHUA. - Ds. Indenture. Feb 1750. 2 pp, folio. Indenture concerns a dispute over land boundaries for Clayton's land obtained from Penn. pba June 13 (42) $85

**Penn, Sir William, 1621-70 —&**
**Pepys, Samuel, 1633-1703**
**Ds,** 26 Oct 1661. 1 p, folio. As Captain of the Fleet & Secretary General of the Victualling Office respectively, naval requisition addressed to the Chancellor of the Exchequer. Countersgd by Sir George Carteret. CNY May 17 (285) $2,200

**Penney, James Cash**
**Photograph, sgd & inscr,** 25 Jan 1949. 4to. Inscr to Henry Kendall. Mtd. Illus in cat rms Oct 11 (297) $600

**Pennsylvania**
— MATHER, RICHARD. - Ds. 25 Oct 1746. Land indenture for Richard Mather & his wife Sarah of "Cheltenham in the County of Philadelphia". Soiled & discolored. pba Oct 26 (134) $150
— PHILADELPHIA ACADEMY. - Ds. 17 Nov 1767. 1 p, folio. Master of Arts diploma of John Andrews. Sgd by "Gul: Smith" as President of the College & others. rms Oct 11 (129) $275
— UNIVERSITY OF PENNSYLVANIA. - Diploma conferring a Medical Arts degree upon Charles B. Martin, 2 May 1887. 1 p, folio. Sgd by David Hayes Agnew, William William Pepper & others. rms Nov 30 (260) $1,500

**Penzias, Arno Allan**
**Typescript,** lecture, Globecom Talk, Nov 1984. 19 pp, 4to. With lengthy autograph revisions; sgd & inscr. HH Nov 17 (3303) DM200

**Pepperell, Sir William, 1696-1759**
**ALs,** 20 Dec 1725. 1 p, 4to. To John Stafford. Ordering fishing gear. sg Feb 1 (191) $400

**Pepys, Samuel, 1633-1703.** See: Penn, William & Pepys

**Pergolesi, Giovanni Battista, 1710-36**
**Ms,** contemp score of Intermezzo Prima & Intermezzo Seconda from Livietta e Tracollo. 120pp, oblong 4to, disbound. Scored for voice with occasional instrumental accompaniment. C June 26 (276) £280

**Peron, Juan Domingo, 1895-1974**
**Ls,** Apr 1948. 1 p, 4to. To D. Pedro Radio. Announcing a shipment of wine for Francisco Franco. star Mar 22 (1509) DM600
**Photograph, sgd,** sgd, 27 Nov 1950. 11 by 8.5 inches. Sgd beneath calligraphic inscr. sg Feb 1 (193) $225
**Photograph, sgd & inscr,** [c.1965]. 255mm by 200mm. On horseback; inscr to Cornelius Greenway. Illus in cat. Marans collection. CE Apr 17 (165) $400

**Peron, Maria Eva Duarte ("Evita"), 1919-52**
**Photograph, sgd,** sgd, 27 Nov 1950. 9 by 6.5 inches. Sgd under calligraphic inscr. sg Feb 1 (192) $600

**Perry, Matthew Calbraith, 1794-1858**
**ALs,** 20 May 1849. 2 pp, 4to. To J. Ws. M. Rodgers. "I do not apprehend much risk from the unhealthfulness of the climate as I shall be careful myself and enquire upon others Do request precautions to guard against sickness..." pba Oct 26 (191) $950
**Ds,** 27 Dec 1847. 1 p, folio. General Orders No 14 addressed to Lieut. Commander H. J. Hartstine instructing commanders of his squadron to collect information for the improvement of charts of the coast. Illus in cat. rms Mar 21 (328) $750

**Perry, Oliver H., 1785-1819**
**Ds,** 31 Mar 1819. 1 p, oblong 12mo. Receipt for his pay & subsistence in the amount of $295. With port. Illus in cat rms Nov 30 (266) $650

**Pershing, John J., 1860-1948**
**Photograph, sgd,** [n.d.]. 4to. In uniform, on horseback. Illus in cat. rms June 6 (446) $400
**Photograph, sgd & inscr,** [n.d.]. 14 by 11 inches. Inscr "with cordial good wishes". sg Feb 1 (196) $325
**Signature,** [n.d.]. No size given. With a port of him in a 1919 parade & related material. Framed. Over-all size 15.5 by 19.5 inches. Illus in cat rms Oct 11 (17) $350

**Persian Manuscripts**
**Ms,** album of calligraphy. [Mughal, c.1590-1600]. 73 ff, 372mm by 239mm. Qajar lacquer bdg. In nasta'liq

script on gold sprinkled colored & marbled paper by Muhammad Husain al-Kashmiri Zarin Qalam & others. With borders of decorated colored paper & double page of illumination. S Oct 18 (68) £50,000

— Ms, album page of calligraphy (Hafiz). [Mughal, c.1619]. Single leaf, 388mm by 263mm. In fine nasta'liq on gold ground, by Mir 'Ali al-Husayni al-Katib. With outer margins decorated with flowers on gold on pink-tinted background. Including full-page miniature by Bishan Das on verso depicting Shah 'Abbas I of Persia receiving the Mughal ambassador Khan 'Alam. Illus in cat. British Rail Pension Fund collection. S Apr 23 (6) £48,000

— Ms, album page of poetic calligraphy. [Mughal, c.1635]. Single leaf, 388mm by 260mm. In fine nasta'liq on blue paper, by Mir 'Ali al-Husayni al-Katib. With outer margins decorated with flowers in colors & gold & 2 small corner miniatures of a goose & a cheetah. Including full-page miniature by Murad on verso depicting Christ enthroned holding an orb. Illus in cat. British Rail Pension Fund collection. S Apr 23 (7) £26,000

— Ms, album page of poetic calligraphy. [Mughal, c.1635]. Single leaf, 385mm by 263mm. In black & gold nasta'liq, by Mir 'Ali al-Husayni al-Katib. With surround decorated with flowers on gold grounds & outer margins with a variety of flowers in colors & gold. Including full-page miniature by Manohar on verso depicting King David playing a harp. Illus in cat. British Rail Pension Fund collection. S Apr 23 (8) £28,000

— Ms, album page of poetic calligraphy. [Mughal, c.1635]. Single leaf, 388mm by 265mm. In black nasta'liq within a border of smaller calligraphy, by Mir 'Ali al-Husayni al-Katib. With interstices decorated with flowers on gold ground by Daulat, outer margin of blue paper decorated with flowering plants in gold, & full-page miniature by Bichitr depicting Prince Aurangzeb on verso. Illus in cat. British Rail Pension Fund collection. S Apr 23 (9) £42,000

— Ms, astronomical treatise. [Persia?, A.H. 1250/ A.D. 1834]. 152 leaves, 273mm by 158mm. Contemp blindstamped half lea gilt. In nasta'liq script, with some additions in a later hand. HH May 7 (75) DM1,500

— Ms, calligraphy. [Herat?, c.1510]. Single page, 408mm by 347mm. In nasta'liq script by Ali al-Katib. With scrolling floral designs on gold ground & 4 panels of fine illumination. Illus in cat. S Oct 18 (73) £2,400

— Ms, calligraphy. [Mughal, c.1600]. Single page, 393mm by 265mm. In nasta'liq script on gold-sprinkled paper by Muhammad Husain al-Katib al-Kashmiri. Mtd. S Oct 18 (71) £2,600

— Ms, grammatical treatise; [17th cent]. 243 pp, 139mm by 72mm. Contemp dark brown lea gilt. In nasta'liq script. With 5 illuminated headpieces & marginal commentary throughout. HH May 7 (82) DM1,500

— Ms, Kitab-i Mihr wa mustari. [Persia, A.H. 954/ A.D. 1547]. 213 leaves, 215mm by 128mm. Contemp lea gilt. In nasta'liq script by Husain al-Hwarizmi. With headings in gold, double page of illumination, & endpiece in gold & colors. HH May 7 (85) DM4,000

— FIRDAUSI. - Shahnama. [Persia, Tabriz, c.1525]. Single leaf, 47cm by 31.8cm. With illumination between columns, broad gold-sprinkled margin, triangular cornerpieces in colors & gold, & full-page miniature attributed to Sultam Muhammad. F.36 from Shah Tahmasp's Shahnama [the Houghton Shahnama]. Illus in cat. British Rail Pension Fund collection. S Apr 23 (11) £380,000

— FIRDAUSI. - Shahnama. [Persia, Tabriz, c.1525]. Single leaf, 47cm by 31.3cm. With triangular cornerpieces in colors & gold, broad gold-sprinkled margin, & full-page miniature attributed to Aqa Mirak. F.110 from Shah Tahmasp's Shahnama [the Houghton Shahnama]. Illus in cat. British Rail Pension Fund collection. S Apr 23 (12) £720,000

— FIRDAUSI. - Shahnama. [Persia, Tabriz, c.1525]. Single leaf of gold-sprinkled paper, 47cm by 31.4cm. With 2 illuminated headings, broad gold-sprinkled margin, & full-page miniature by Mir Musavir. F.60 from Shah Tahmasp's Shahnama [the Houghton Shahnama]. Illus in cat. British Rail Pension Fund collection. S Apr 23 (13) £320,000

— FIRDAUSI. - Shahnama. [Persia, Tabriz, c.1530]. Single leaf, 47.2cm by 32.1cm. With broad gold-sprinkled margin, illuminated heading, & very large miniature in colors & gold attributed to Aqa Mirak. F.451 from Shah Tahmasp's Shahnama [the Houghton Shahnama]. Illus in cat. British Rail Pension Fund collection. S Apr 23 (14) £360,000

— FIRDAUSI. - Shahnama. [Shiraz, c.1570]. Single leaf, 43.5cm by 31.2cm. In nasta'liq script. With 2 illuminated panels, intercolumnar decoration in colors, & full-page miniature extending into margins. Illus in cat. British Rail Pension Fund collection. S Apr 23 (15) £6,500

— HAFIZ. - Diwan. [Shiraz, A.H. 938/ A.D. 1532]. 194 ff, 196mm by 114mm. Brown mor bdg with red velvet panels. In nasta'liq script written horizontally & diagonally, with headings in blue thuluth. With double page of illumination & 5 miniatures. S Oct 18 (59) £5,000

— HAQANI. - Diwan. [Persia, A.H. 1059/ A.D. 1649]. 225 ff, 281mm by 160mm. Later red mor gilt. In nasta'liq script on cream paper by Muhammad Shafi'. With 3 illuminated headpieces. S Oct 18 (56) £650

— HATIFI. - Timurnama. [Persia, Mashhad?, c.1550]. 97 ff, 230mm by 151mm. Qajar floral lacquer bdg. In small nasta'liq script on gold-sprinkled paper by Shah Mahmud al-Nishapuri. With pink paper borders throughout, illuminated headpiece, & 7 miniatures. S Oct 18 (66) £2,600

— JALAL AL-DIN RUMI. - Mathnawi, parts 5 & 6. [Konya, A.H. 743/ A.D. 1342]. 102 ff, 229mm by 157mm. Tooled brown mor. In cursive script on thick cream paper by Abu Hamid ibn Muhammad ibn al-Naqib al-Mevlevi. With marginal glosses in various hands. S Oct 18 (62) £5,000

— JAMI. - Diwan. [Herat, A.H. 901/ A.D. 1495]. 313 ff (c.10 lacking), 289mm by 196mm. Later Indian lacquer bdg. In nasta'liq script on thick burnished paper by Sultan Ali al-Mashhadi. With headings in fine nasta'liq & thuluth scripts in gold & colors on illuminated panels, & double page of superb intricate illumination. S Oct 18 (61) £42,000

— JAMI. - Nafahat al-Uns. [Herat?, A.H. 883/ A.D. 1478]. 265 ff, 242mm by 181mm. Later brown mor with gilt lea onlay. In nasta'liq script on cream paper. With illuminated headpiece & a lengthy note in the author's own hand. S Oct 18 (52) £10,500

— JAMI. - Poetry. [Herat?, c.1490]. Single leaf, 241mm by 166mm. In fine nasta'liq calligraphy in colored ink on green paper. With borders of gold-sprinkled cream paper. S Oct 18 (72) £1,200

— JAMI. - Subhat al-Abrar. [Persia, A.H. 950/ A.D. 1543]. 71 ff, 228mm by 120mm. Later brown mor gilt. In 2 columns of nasta'liq script. With illuminated headpiece. S Oct 18 (50) £700

— JAMI. - Tuhfat al-Ahrar. [Khurasan, c.1575]. 81 ff, 231mm by 162mm. Contemp painted lacquer covers. In 2 columns of nasta'liq script on thick cream paper. With illuminated headpiece, six miniatures, & borders of colored paper stencilled with floral motifs & scenes of animals among trees. S Oct 18 (57) £5,500

— JAMI. - Yusuf va Zuleykha. [Bukhara, A.H. 972/ A.D. 1564]. 138 ff, 248mm by 170mm. Rebacked red mor with painted floral designs. In 2 columns of nasta'liq script on thick cream paper by Abd al-Rahman al Bukhari. With illuminated headpiece & 8 miniatures. S Oct 18 (58) £8,500

— MANSUR IBN MUHAMMAD IBN AHMAD AL-KASHMIRI AL-BALKHI. - Tashrih Mansuri. [A.H. 813/ A.D. 1411]. 30 ff, 243mm by 174mm. Later red mor. In cursive script by the author himself. With 5 full-page anatomical diagrams. S Oct 18 (51) £13,000

— NIZAMI. - Khamsa. [Mughal, c.1625]. 354 leaves, 29.2cm by 18cm. 18th-cent Indian black lea gilt. In nasta'liq script on gold-sprinkled paper by the scribe Mustafa. With gold decoration in margins & 17 miniatures. Illus in cat. British Rail Pension Fund collection; Phillipps MS.3665. S Apr 23 (10) £17,000

— NIZAMI. - Khamsa. [Qazwin, c.1570]. 343 ff (3 later replacements), 229mm by 144mm. Modern red mor gilt. In four columns of nasta'liq script on cream paper. With 5 illuminated headpieces & 10 miniatures. S Oct 18 (64) £15,000

— SA'DI. - Bustan. [Ottoman?, c.1675]. 134 pp, 215mm by 125mm. Def 19th-cent half lea. In calligraphic nasta'liq on polished paper, with some interlinear or marginal glosses. With double page of illumination. JG Sept 29 (330) DM650

— SA'DI. - Gulistan. [Qajar, c.1850]. 113 ff, 212mm by 140mm. Contemp painted lacquer bdg. In nasta'liq script on thick burnished paper. With illuminated headpiece & double page with interlinear gold decoration. S Oct 18 (70) £3,200

— SA'DI. - Gulistan. [Tabriz, A.H. 952/ A.D. 1546]. 128 ff, 255mm by 146mm. Brown mor gilt. In nasta'liq script on cream paper written horizontally & diagonally. With double page of illumination & 2 miniatures. S Oct 18 (60) £6,500

— SA'DI. - Kulliyat. [Persia?, c.1800]. 295 leaves, 286mm by 168mm. Contemp floral lacquer bdg. In nasta'liq script, with commentary throughout in margin. With 5 illuminated headpieces & 7 double pages of illumination. HH May 7 (107) DM1,800

— SHARAF AD-DIN 'ALI YAZDI. - Zafarnama. [Shiraz, 1436). 393 leaves, 35.2cm by 24.5cm, in modern black mor; with earlier Qajar lacquer panels preserved separately. In elegant naskhi script by Ya'qub ibn Hasan probably for Ibrahim Sultan. With headings in gold, 3 finely illuminated headpieces in colors & gold & 9 miniatures (some imperf). With introduction added by the scribe Muhammad ibn 'Ali at Herat, 1480. British Rail Pension Fund collection. S Apr 23 (16) £55,000

— SHEIKH ABU'L-FAZL IBN MUBARAK. - Ayar-i-Danish. [A.H. 1137/ A.D. 1725]. 138 ff, 251mm by 170mm. Marbled paper bds. In nasta'liq script on cream paper by Abu Muhammad of Kura for Bhagwant Rai. With 32 brightly colored miniatures. S Oct 18 (53) £2,600

— VAHSHI. - Diwan. [Persia, late 16th cent]. 232 ff, 208mm by 125mm. Def Qajar floral lacquer bdg. In 2 columns of nasta'liq script on pink paper. With borders of colored & sprinkled paper, 3 illuminated headpieces, & 10 miniatures. S Oct 18 (55) £1,600

**Perutz, Max Ferdinand**
Autograph Ms, 2d chapter of a scientific paper about biotechnology, [1994]. 8 pp, 4to, on rectos only. Sgd at head. HH Nov 17 (3304) DM220

**Pestalozzi, Johann Heinrich, 1746-1827**
ALs, 6 Aug 1781. 2 pp, 4to. To Professor La Croix de Sauvage at University of Montpellier. Saying that the Ms he sent was incorrect because the copyist didn't know Greek & left out certain passages; asks whether changes should be made. sg Feb 1 (197) $850

**Peter I, Emperor of Russia, 1672-1725**
Ls, 18 Oct 1710. 1 p, folio. To Louis XIV of France. Offering his fellow monarch congratulations on the birth of his son. Illus in cat pba Feb 22 (307) $2,500

**Peters, Richard, 1744-1828**
ALs, 12 Sept 1785. 3 pp, 4to. To Baron von Steuben. About the future employment of von Steuben. P Dec 13 (302) $450

— 19 Aug 1811. 1 p, 8vo. To G[eorge] Vaux. Asking him to leave "the Draft Book of [his] lands" at his son's office. Illus in cat. rms June 6 (457) $350

**Petrarca, Francesco, 1304-74**
Ms, Trionfi. [Florence, 3d quarter of 15th cent] 53 leaves & medieval flyleaf, on vellum, 200mm by 130mm, in contemp goatskin over wooden bds, panelled 7 tooled in blind. In brown ink in a humanistic cursive bookhand. With 13 three-line illuminated initials & large historiated initial containing the figure of a blindfolded Cupid within a full border of interlaced white vine stems on blue & rose ground historiated with 5 small framed vignettes depicting a hound, a hare, the figure of Laura, the face of a cherub; at bottom 4 putti supporting an armorial shield. C Apr 3 (5) £24,000

**Petrus Damianus, Saint, 1007-72.** See: Suso, Heinrich

**Petrus de Alliaco, 1350-c.1422**

**Ms,** Meditationes super Psalmos Penitentiales, & texts by Lotario de'Conti di Segni, Jacob de Gruytrode, & others. [Northern France, Paris?, c.1500]. 103 leaves, vellum, 200mm by 138mm. 19th-cent dark blue-green velvet. In a small regular lettre batarde. With 1- to 5-line initials throughout in liquid gold on red or blue grounds & large miniature with full border. S Dec 5 (34) £3,800 [Sam Fogg]

**Pettenkofer, Max von, 1818-1901**

**ALs,** 29 Sept 1864. 2 pp, 8vo. To Bernhard Tollens. Discussing a joint project. star Mar 21 (590) DM550

**Pfitzner, Hans, 1869-1949**

**Series** of 4 A Ls s, 2 autograph postcards, sgd, & autograph music, 21 Oct 1944 to 30 Aug 1947. 5 pp, various sizes, & cards. To Alfred Morgenroth. Discussing the times & his personal situation. Fragment of 2 bars from his cantata, Op.57. With related material. star Mar 22 (995) DM3,500

**ALs,** 12 Oct 1947. 2 pp, 8vo. To Vera von Falkenhayn. Thanking for a testimony to help his denazification procedures. Including musical quotation. star Mar 22 (996) DM1,200

**Autograph quotation,** some bars from his Die Heinzelmaennchen, 2 Dec 1905. 1 p, 4to. Sgd. star Mar 22 (994) DM480

**Pharmacology**

**Ms,** compilation of medical recipes, kept in a pharmacy. [Germany, Hesse?, c.1730]. 172 pp, 8vo; stitched. Including c.130 recipes & a list of alchemical terms. star Mar 21 (591) DM750

**Philby, Harry St. John Bridger, 1885-1960**

**Autograph Ms,** leaf of his Heart of Arabia, describing the 1st sighting of Wadi Dawasir. Folio size, corresponding to text of Vol II, pp 183-86. [c.1922]. b Sept 20 (370) £500

**Philip, Prince, Duke of Edinburgh.** See: Elizabeth II & Philip

**Philip II, King of Spain, 1527-98**

**ALs,** [n.d.]. 1 p, folio. To Catherine de Medicis, Queen of France. Introducing his envoy Diego de Zuniga. Illus in cat. star Mar 22 (1664) DM6,800

**Ls,** 4 Dec 1555. 4 pp, folio. To the council of an unnamed German city. Informing them that his father has ceded the government of the Netherlands to him. star Mar 22 (1662) DM4,000

— 17 Oct 1558. 1 p, folio. To the Duchess of Parma. About his father's death. HH May 9 (2548) DM600

— 16 July 1559. 2 pp & docket leaf, folio. To the Duque de Arcos. Giving him instructions on how to conduct himself when congratulating Francois II on his accession to the throne. b June 28 (55) £900

— 7 June 1562. 2 pp, folio. To Ottavio Farnese. Discussing the political situation in France. HH May 9 (2549) DM650

— 27 July 1568. 1 p, folio. Recipients unnamed. Informing them of the death of Don Carlos. b Dec 5 (174) £520

— 5 Mar 1570. 1 p, folio. To Martin de Caruajal. Inquiring about supplies in Granada. S Dec 1 (42) £600

**Document,** 1570. 24 leaves (1 blank), folio, in later brown lea gilt. Carta executoria de hidalguia in favor of Diego Devera. Including historiated initial, 18 illuminated initials, & painting of the arms in gold & colors. HN May 15 (2479) DM3,400

**Philip III, King of Spain, 1578-1621**

**Document,** 1608. 101 leaves, 307mm by 210mm. Worn contemp lea gilt. Carta executoria de hidalguia in favor of Don Juan de Lara y Fernan Mexia. With 30 large illuminated initials & 2 full-page miniatures. S Dec 5 (19) £1,800 [Petrus]

**Philip V, King of Spain, 1683-1746**

**Ds,** 1 Mar 1712. 2 pp, folio. Authorizing the transfer of land in Guadalajara. Sgd as "Yo el Rey". pba Oct 26 (357) $300

**Philipp Ludwig, Pfalzgraf zu Neuburg, 1547-1614**

**Ls,** 27 Dec 1602. 2 pp, folio. To Gottfried von Oettingen. Sending New Year's wishes. star Mar 22 (1511) DM230

**Phillipps, Sir Thomas, 1792-1872**

**Autograph Ms,** "Catalogue of the 4 Vedas (Vaids) with the Openshuds on them. Also a Large number of Sanscrit MSS... Collected by Sir Robt Chambers...." [c.1830] 37 pp, 4to, formerly sewn. S July 11 (199) £750

**Phillips, Wendell, 1811-84.** See: Kalakaua & Phillips

**Physick, Philip Syng, 1768-1837**

**ALs,** 19 Nov 1827. 2 pp, 8vo. To John Vaughan. About Mrs. Vaughan's health. Detail in cat rms Oct 11 (298) $850

See also: Rush; Physick & Others

**Picasso, Pablo, 1881-1973**

**Group photograph,** [c.1945]. 175mm by 117mmm. With unnamed friend, lighting a cigarette. Inscr to Pierre Bertrand. Illus in cat. Marans collection. CE Apr 17 (215) $900

**Photograph, sgd,** [c.1956]. 18cm by 13cm. Posing as bullfighter. S May 15 (211) £700

— Anr, 1957. 235mm by 175mm. Showing him in front of a sculpture & a painting. Sgd in 3 colors "Picasso Cannes A.M. (France) 12.6.57". CE June 12 (94) $1,300

**Signature,** 25 June 1967. On Time Magazine cover for 26 June 1950. Sgd 3 places & dated 25.6.67. CE June 12 (95) $550

**Piccinni, Niccolo, 1728-1800**

**Autograph music,** psalm, Da te solo, 27 Mar 1794. 69 pp, folio, in 19th-cent bds. Working Ms of the full score, notated on up to 10 staves per page. Partly written in anr hand & revised by Piccinni. Sgd in several places. S Dec 1 (269) £950

**ADs,** 20 June 1778. 1 p, 8vo. Receipt for 2,400 livres. Illus in cat. star Mar 22 (998) DM650

### Piccolomini, Ottavio, 1599-1656

**Ls,** 17 Nov 1637. 3 pp, folio. To an unnamed count. Informing him about the Emperor's orders to establish winter quarters. star Mar 22 (1265) DM860

### Pickering, Timothy, 1745-1829

**ALs,** 30 Aug 1798. 2 pp, 4to. To Rufus King. Forwarding a letter for James Cramond, & discussing the XYZ-Affair. Illus in cat. rms Mar 21 (11) $2,800

— 6 Jan 1816. 1 p, 4to. To John McHenry. Sending "Dr. Price's little volume of sermons" & explaining his Christian beliefs. P Dec 13 (304) $1,300

**Ls,** 15 Dec 1798. 1 p, 4to. To Nathaniel Cutting. Revoking a commission as a result of the X. Y. Z. Affair: "I am directed by the President of the United States hereby to declare to you his revocation of your commission of Consul for the Port of Havre de Grace in France..." pba Oct 26 (296) $650

**Ds,** 10 Nov 1782. 1 p, 8vo. Issuing a certificate to an aide de camp, Winthrop Sargeant, for "Rations of Forage". Sgd as Quartermaster General. Countersgd by David Wolfe. With related material. Illus in cat rms Oct 11 (29) $975

### Pierce, Franklin, 1804-69

**ALs,** 23 Dec 1850. 2 pp, 248mm by 194mm, on a bifolium. To Edmund Burke at Newport. About supporting John Atwood for Governor & regaining editorial control of several New Hampshire newspapers for the Democrats. P June 5 (94) $2,500

— 27 June 1852. 4 pp, 4to. To Mary Aiken. Thanking his sister-in-law for her congratulations after winning the Democratic presidential nomination. Yellowed at folds. CNY Dec 15 (217) $1,500

— [c.1853-57]. 1 p, 8vo. To Sec. of War Jefferson Davis. Introducing C. L. Richter. CE June 12 (96) $600

— 16 Sept 1856. 2 pp, 4to. To Dr. Boardman. Discussing his wife's health Illus in cat CNY Dec 15 (218) $1,400

— 18 June 1860. 2 pp, 8vo. To George M. Dallas. A letter of Introduction to the Minister of Great Britain for Sidney Webster. Fold separations repaired. Illus in cat pba Oct 26 (299) $425

— 4 June 1869. 3 pp, 8vo. To Sidney Webster. Expressing opposition to African-American government appointments during the Grant adminsitration: "Can he afford to lend his well earned reputation and honorable character to confer respectablity upon the men who are associated with him?..." CNY Dec 15 (109) $5,500

**Ds,** 6 Jan 1854. 1 p, 8vo. Order to affix the US Seal. Framed with a port. P Dec 13 (306) $450

— 9 Feb 1854. 1 p, on vellum, 17.5 by 13 inches. Commission of Patrick Calhoun as Captain of the 2d Regiment. Countersgd by Jefferson Davis. In poor condition. rs Nov 11 (38) $175

— 19 July 1854. 1 p, 4to. Authorizing Secretary of State to affix the seal of the United States to a pardon for Noah C. Hansen. Illus in cat pba Oct 26 (297) $650

— 13 Oct 1854. 1 p, folio. Four-language ship's papers for the whaler Atlantic. Countersgd by Sec. of State William L. Marcy. CE June 12 (97) $900

— 18 Apr 1856. 1 p, folio. Commission of Philip S. Wales as Assistant Surgeon in the Navy. Countersgd by J. G. Dobbin. cb June 25 (2369) $450

**Envelope,** [n.d.]. No size given. To Mrs. Comm'd Paulding. Franked. pba Feb 22 (270) $250

### Pierce, Franklin, 1804-69 —& Marcy, William Learned, 1786-1857

**Cut signature,** [n.d.]. 8vo. With double-page engraved sheet taken from Gleason's Pictorial Drawing Room Companion depicting his Cabinet & " Presidents from Washington to Pierce". Illus in cat rms Oct 11 (319) $350

### Piercy, Marge

**Collection** of A collection of 41 Ls s & a carbon typesccript of Laying the Tower III. 1968-83. Letters to John & Elaine Gill. Typescript featuring holograph collections. pba Jan 25 (291) $550

### Pierre de St. Benedict, fl.1280

**Ms,** Sermones, in Latin & French, with Nicolaus de Byard, Summa Abstinentia. [Paris?, c.1290]. 255 leaves & 2 flyleaves, vellum, 121mm by 85mm. Modern brown mor incorporating part of medieval bdg of blindstamped calf. In dark brown ink in a neat gothic bookhand. With painted initials throughout. S June 18 (63) £6,500

### Pillney, Karl Hermann, 1896-1980

**Autograph music,** J. S. Bach BWV947 (Orgelfuge) Instrumentiert fuer Kammerorchester; [n.d.]. 5 pp, folio. Fair copy of his arrangement of Bach's fugue for chamber orchestra; sgd at head. star Mar 22 (999) DM210

### Pillow, Gideon Johnson, 1806-78

**Signature,** [n.d.]. No size given. With port & a 15 Mar 1862 front page of Harper's Weekly. Also with 2 engravings. Framed. Over-all size 21.5 by 25.5 inches. Illus in cat rms Oct 11 (111) $400

### Pinchot, Gifford, 1865-1946

**Photograph, sgd & inscr,** 1931. 9.5 by 7.5 inches. Silver print photo port. By Marceau. Inscr. bbc Sept 18 (89) $50

— Anr, 1931. 9.5 by 7.5 inch b&w silver print photo port. Inscr. bbc Sept 18 (89) $50

### Pinkerton, Allan, 1819-84

**Ds,** 2 Sept 1856. 1 p, 4to. Deposition in a case of theft from a railroad. CNY May 17 (288) $2,500

**Photograph, sgd,** [c.1866]. 253mm by 205m. Salt print shoulder-length port. Illus in cat. Marans collection. CE Apr 17 (166) $1,000

### Pinkerton, William Allan

**Ls,** 29 Apr 1897. 1 p, 8vo. To Alf Hayman. About pictures of the Secret Service division during the war. Stained. pba Oct 26 (118) $400

## Pirandello, Luigi, 1867-1936

**Autograph postcard, sgd,** 5 Mar 1904. To Nini Knoblich. Announcing a new vol of stories. star Mar 21 (293) DM280

## Piscator, Erwin, 1893-1966

**Collection** of 7 A Ls s, 6 Ls s, autograph postcard, sgd, Ns, & autograph Ms, 20 Sept 1954 to 27 Nov 1959 & [n.d.]. 24 pp, various sizes. To Claus Leininger. About various theatrical matters. star Mar 22 (1154) DM1,100

## Pissarro, Camille, 1830-1903

**ALs,** 23 Oct [18]96. 1 p, 8vo. To an unnamed doctor. About a syringe. With a sketch of the syringe on the opposite page. Illus in cat rms Oct 11 (299) $4,225

## Pius IX, Pope, 1792-1878

**Ls,** 28 Apr 1873. 1 p, folio. To the Bishop of Rieti. Acknowledging Christmas wishes. star Mar 22 (1505) DM380

## Pius VI, Pope, 1717-99

**Document,** 13 Mar 1775. 1 p, folio. Brief granting permission for the ordination of Vincenzo Valerio Curti as priest. star Mar 22 (1501) DM450

## Pius VII, Pope, 1742-1823

**Document,** 18 Aug 1818. 1 p, folio. Brief addressed to the Bishop of Alessandria permitting Francesco de Salomone to read mass at his own house. star Mar 22 (1502) DM350

## Pius VIII, Pope, 1761-1830

**Ds,** [n.d.]. 1 p, 4to. Granting a year's permission "to bear in the countryside and district of Rome, the long arquebus for hunting with the customary ammunition for the same, provided that in Rome in the walled areas it be carried unloaded and without powder in it, subject to the usual punishments..." Sgd as Bishop of Palestrina. Illus in cat sg Sept 28 (215) $275

## Pius XI, Pope, 1857-1939

**Ls,** 22 Apr 1922. 1 p, folio. To the Archbishop of Montevideo. Thanking for congratulations on his election as Pope. star Mar 22 (1506) DM850

**Photograph, sgd,** [n.d.]. 6.5 inch-diameter circular port. Framed. Sgd in lower margin of mat. wa Oct 28 (147) $400

## Pius XII, Pope, 1876-1958

**Ds,** [n.d.]. 1 p, 15 by 11 inches. Apostolic benediction for Joseph Kinsley & family. Mtd with oval photograph. sg Feb 1 (198) $550

**Photograph, sgd,** 28 Nov 1939. Framed, overall size 27 by 20 inches. Sgd under a request for his Apostolic Blessing. Illus in cat. rms Mar 21 (330) $520

## Planck, Max, 1858-1947

**ALs,** 3 Apr 1942. 2 pp, 8vo. To Oberkirchenrat Neuberg. Thanking for a lecture sent to him. Illus in cat. star Mar 21 (594) DM2,200

## Platen, August, Graf von, 1796-1835

**ANs,** [n.d.]. 1 p, 8vo, cut from larger sheet. To [Emilie Linder?]. Inquiring where he can find her. Sgd at head. star Mar 21 (294) DM460

## Platt, Thomas Collier, 1833-1910

**Ds,** 1 Aug 1887. 1 p, folio. $500 six per cent Income Bond . Designed & ptd by the American Bank Note CO. With anr Bond. pba June 13 (80) $110

## Podbielski, Viktor von, 1844-1916

**ALs,** 18 Apr 1914. 2 pp, 8vo. Recipient unnamed. Concerning a recommendation of recipient's son for a position with the justice department. HN Nov 24 (2848) DM360

## Poe, Edgar Allan, 1809-49

**ALs,** 16 Nov 1843. 1 p, 4to. To Joseph H. Hedge. Responding to a request for autographs by his father & grandfather: "I regret to say, however, that, owing to peculiar circumstances, I have in my possession no autograph of either...." With repaired hole in seal. CNY Dec 15 (34) $12,000

See also: Calligraphy

## Poelzig, Hans, 1869-1936

**ALs,** 25 Sept 1915. 4 pp, 8vo. To [Gerhard] Haenisch. Discussing affairs of the art academy at Wroclaw. star Mar 21 (707) DM280

## Pogwisch, Henriette von, 1776-1851

**ALs,** [c.Oct 1842]. 2 pp, 8vo. To her daughter Ottilie von Goethe. Complaining about recipient's sons. star Mar 21 (147) DM1,400

## Polk, James K., 1795-1849

**ALs,** 22 Mar 1826. 2 pp, 4to. To his cousin William Polk. Sending his 1st speech in Congress (not present) & predicting the downfall of John Quincy Adams. Including franking signature. Forbes Magazine collection. CNY May 17 (169) $3,500

— 24 Apr 1838. 1 p, 4to. to Hon. Levi P. Woodbury. Agreeing to appoint R. J. Powell "for a clerkship in some of the Departments at Washington...." Illus in cat sg Sept 28 (217) $2,200

— 13 June 1845. 1 p, 251mm by 200mm. To Postmaster General Cave Johnson. About potential openings in the Post Office Department. P June 5 (95) $1,400

— 31 Oct 1846. 2 pp, 4to. To George M. Dallas. Discussing appointments with his Vice-President and asking for research assistance concerning the Madison Papers. Illus in cat CNY Dec 15 (220) $1,800

**Ls,** 2 Jan 1849. 1 p, 4to. Circular letter to US Senators convening the Senate on March 5. Illus in cat. rms Mar 21 (38) $4,000

**Ds,** 31 Dec 1839. 1 p, 4to. As Governor of Tennessee, land grant to Matthew Wynn. Framed with a port. P Dec 13 (308) $550

— 17 Aug 1848. 1 p, folio, on vellum. Promotion of David R. Jones to 1st Lieut. Countersgd by Sec. of War W. L. Marcy. Polk's signature light. Framed with port. wa Oct 28 (221) $600

— 24 Aug 1848. 1 p, folio. A Mexican War commission for Shuyler Hamilton as First Lieutenant of Infantry. Countersgd by Secretary of War W. L. Marcy. rms Oct 11 (300) $1,300
— 22 Dec 1848. 1 p, folio. Appointment of O. C. Pratt as Associate Justice of the Oregon Territory Supreme Court. CNY May 17 (290) $1,000
— [n.d.]. 1 p, folio. Unaccomplished four-language ship's papers. Countersgd by Sec. of State James Buchanan. CE June 12 (98) $1,000
**Endorsement,** 17 July 1846. 1 p, folio. About spectacles: "Mr. Siga has finished me with a pair of spectacles which I think superior to any I have ever used..." With anr testimonial by Thomas J. Rusk & others. Browned & silked on verso. With one hole from acidic ink. CNY Dec 15 (219) $1,800

### Ponchielli, Amilcare, 1834-86
**Autograph music,** Improvviso for piano, 13 Sept 1880. 1 p, folio. 27 bars, notated on 7 systems of 2 staves each. Including revisions; sgd & inscr. S Dec 1 (274) £800
**ALs,** 14 Feb 1871. 3 pp, 8vo. To Mascardi. Discussing changes in Bellini's opera Norma. Including 2 musical quotations. S Dec 1 (275) £850

### Poniatowski, Jozef Antoni, Prince, 1763-1813
**Ls,** 21 June 1802. 2 pp, 4to. To the Prussian state bank, the Seehandlungs-Societaet. Sending a receipt for payments made to him. star Mar 22 (1471) DM1,900

### Pontifical
**Ms,** [Central Italy, Gubbio?, c.1473-82]. 356 leaves (2 blank), vellum, 308mm by 236mm. Contemp black lea over wooden bds with elaborate bookmark. In black & red ink in a rather compressed prickly rounded gothic liturgical hand, with many contemp textual corrections in a fine sloping humanistic cursive minuscule. Spaces left blank for illumination throughout. S Dec 5 (38) £5,200 [Sam Fogg]

### Pope, Alexander, 1688-1744
**Cut signature,** [n.d.]. Cut from an ADs. Framed with port. wa Oct 28 (49) $350

### Porsche, Ferdinand Anton Ernst
**Photograph,** sgd & inscr, [c.1970]. 173mm by 120mm. Shoulder-length port, by Werkphoto Porsche; inscr to Bill Wood. Marans collection. CE Apr 17 (114) $700

### Porter, Cole, 1893-1964
**Photograph,** sgd, [c.1930]. 98mm by 70mm. Bust port. Illus in cat. Marans collection. CE Apr 17 (249) $700
**Photograph,** sgd & inscr, [n.d.]. 8vo. Bust port, by Hal Phyfe. Inscr to Ralph Botsford. Illus in cat. rms June 6 (115) $550

### Porter, David Dixon, 1813-91
**Ls,** 26 July 1812. 1 p, 4to. To Midshipman George Pearce. Giving him instructions on how to proceed with "the prize under your command". sg Feb 1 (199) $300
— 19 May 1869. 1 p, 4to. To Commodore John G. Walker. Complying with Walker's request to have seamen shipped to Boston. Framed with port. rms Nov 30 (24) $300

### Porter, Fitz-John, 1822-1901
**Series** of 4 A Ls s, 1892 to 1894. Length not stated. To William B. Franklin. Mentioning other Civil War generals. rms Mar 21 (270) $280

### Porter, Horace, 1837-1921
**Ls,** 14 Nov [18]87. 2 pp, 8vo. To John M. Burt.. Discussing the illness of his former employer: " General Grant...had no symptons whatever of his last illness while in the war, nor until the summer of '84...."With a strengthed corner. rms Oct 11 (177) $325
**Signature,** [n.d.]. On a card. Framed with photo & Civil War canteen cover. rms Nov 30 (25) $320

### Porter, William Sydney ("O. Henry"), 1862-1910
**ALs,** 17 Feb 1907. 2 pp, 8vo. To Alexander Black of the NY Sunday World. Saying that he wll write an Easter piece for the paper. rms Nov 30 (267) $950

### Post, Wiley, 1900-35
**Ls,** 20 Feb 1931. 1 p, 4to. To the contest committee of the National Aeronautical Association. About his plan for a solo flight around the world. With typed Proposed Route of Wiley Post - Around-the-world Flight. rms Nov 30 (82) $1,700
**Ds,** [26 July 1933]. 1 p, 4to. Official Observer's Report on World Flight, documenting Post's record-breaking solo flight around the world. Sgd by J. Wilson Kelly, the observer. Endorsed by post. rms Nov 30 (83) $1,900

### Post, Wiley, 1900-35 —& Gatty, Harold, 1903-57
**Group photograph,** [c.1931]. 273mm by 217mm, mtd. Full length, sgd by both & inscr to Bill Deegan in Gatty's hand. Marans collection. CE Apr 17 (23) $700

### Potter, Beatrix, 1866-1943
**Original drawings,** (2) for The Tale of Benjamin Bunny: "One morning a little rabbit sat on a bank..." and "Benjamin pricked his ears and listened.... 11.5cm by 11.5cm, in ink & watercolor heightened in white. Captions in anr hand. 1904. Ck May 31 (245) £9,000
— Original drawings, (2) for The Tale of Benjamin Bunny: "Benjamin Bunny slid down into the road..." and "Old Mrs. Rabbit was a widow...." 1904. 11.5cm by 11.5cm, in ink & watercolor heightened in white, on silk. With captions in anr hand Ck May 31 (246) £7,000
— Original drawings, (2) for The Tale of Benjamin Bunny: "Little Benjamin did not very much want to see his Aunt..." & "They took Peter's clothes off the scare-crow...." 1904. 11.5cm by 11.5cm, in ink & watercolor heightened in white, on silk. With captions in anr hand Ck May 31 (247) £7,500
— Original drawings, (2) for The Tale of Benjamin Bunny: "Peter looked poorly and was dressed in a red cotton pocket-handkerchief" & "Peter replied -- The Scare-crow in Mr. McGregor's garden...." 1904. 11.5cm by 11.5cm, in ink & watercolor heightened in

white, on silk. With captions in anr hand Ck May 31 (248) £11,000

— Original drawings, (2) for The Tale of Benjamin Bunny: "Mrs. Rabbit's voice was heard inside the rabbit hole..." & "Peter's coat and shoes were plainly to be seen upon the scarecrow...." 1904. 11.5cm by 11.5cm, in ink & watercolor heightened in white, on silk. With captions in anr hand Ck May 31 (249) £9,500

— Original drawings, (2) for The Tale of Benjamin Bunny: "Little Benjamin said It spoils people's clothes to squeeze under a gate..." & It had been sown with lettuces...." 1904. 11.5cm by 11.5cm, in ink & watercolor heightened in white, on silk. With captions in anr hand Ck May 31 (250) £8,000

**Collection** of 1 ALs & 1 autograph postcard, sgd, 22 Dec 1934 & 22 Oct 1943. To or about Anthony "Tant" Benson. With related material. Ck May 31 (80) £700

### Poulenc, Francis, 1899-1963

**Autograph postcard, sgd,** 10 Apr 1956. To an unnamed lady. Thanking for congratulations on his birthday & mentioning his travels. star Mar 22 (1001) DM400

### Pound, Ezra, 1885-1972

[A collection of material, 1957-58 of material from the files of Congressman Usher Burdick leading to Pound's release from St. Elizabeth's Hospital sold at Pacific on 7 Mar 1996 for $8,000.]

**Collection** of 10 A Ls s & Ls s, 3 autograph postcards, sgd & ANs listing the neglected writers of an earlier generation, [1937-40]. 23 pp, 4to. To Desmond Hawkins. S July 11 (291) £2,500

**Series** of 3 A Ls s, 14 Aug to 31 Oct 1953. 3 pp, 4to. To Samuel Hynes. About his life at St. Elizabeth's Hospital. S Dec 18 (415) £340 [Mandl]

**ALs,** 27 Dec [1909]. 4 pp, folio, on 2 sheets. Recipient's name unclear, possibly Antrobus. On literary matters. CNY Oct 27 (117) $1,500

### Pousseur, Henri

**Autograph music,** detailed sketches for a work for "Marimba/Orgue/Synthi/Piano & Clarin. CB"; [n.d.]. 4 pp, folio. Including numerous corrections & annotations. star Mar 22 (1002) DM460

### Powell, Adam Clayton, Jr., 1908-72

**Photograph, sgd,** [n.d.]. 5 by 7.25 inches. Sgd, but ink skipped on a few letters sg Mar 28 (243) $130

### Powys, John Cowper, 1872-1963

**Photograph, sgd & inscr,** 1 May 1929. 9 by 12 inch profile port photo. On a 14 by 14.5 inch photographer's matte. Inscr to Puck Durant. Creased. pba Oct 26 (60) $375

### Prayer Books

**Ms,** Andachts Uebungen Auss unterschiedlichen Gebettern zusammengetragen, [c.1750]. 105 pp, 168mm by 119mm. Contemp lea gilt. Including 17 pen-&-ink drawings. Ownership(?) inscr of Hieronymus a S. Antonio. HH May 7 (5) DM850

— Ms, Ein Kussliches Betbuech warinnen Schone Hertzerquickende Gebete auss Gottes Wort. [Arnstadt, 1574]. 246 leaves (6 blank), vellum, 180mm by 150mm. Old calf over wooden bds. In a very fine calligraphic compressed gothic hand by Caspar Leo Schueller. With illuminated initials throughout in gold in elaborate calligraphic designs, 4 full-page miniatures in gold & colors, & 18 pp at end in bizarre calligraphic hands, 10 pp with pictures & designs formed entirely of micrographic writing (sometimes in mirror writing), & 8 full-page calligraphic or illuminated pages with elaborate designs & penwork fantasies. S Dec 5 (37) £22,000 [Abraham]

— Ms, in Low German, Prayer Book. [Lower Rhine or Netherlands, late 15th cent]. 330 leaves & 36 blanks, 15cm by 10cm. Def blindstamped 16th-cent calf over wooden bds. In red & black ink in a lettre batarde. With 13 illuminated initials & very large miniature on vellum leaf. Ownership inscr of Sibilla Schaupin. HN Nov 24 (2737) DM4,800

— ADRIAN, FR. - Geistliches Tag buch auff alle Tage des gantzen Jahres, parts 5 & 6; [c.1750]. 282 leaves, 100mm by 147mm. Contemp lea gilt. Including 135 full-page engravings by Goez & Klauber. HH May 7 (4) DM700

### Presidents of the United States

[An album of 39 letters, documents & signatures of Presidents from Washington to Truman, each bound with a port, folio, in mor gilt, sold at Christie's East on 27 Sept 1995, lot 25, for $32,000]

**Group photograph,** Presidents Reagan, Ford, Carter & Nixon in the White House, 8 Oct 1981. 4to. Sgd by all 4. Illus in cat. rms Mar 21 (177) $1,000

— Anr, Presidents Reagan, Carter, Ford & Nixon in the White House, Oct 1981. 8 by 10 inches. Sgd by all 4. rms Nov 30 (268) $1,000

— Anr, [n.d.]. 4to. Color photo of Presidents Reagan, Ford, Carter & Nixon. Illus in cat rms Oct 11 (301) $1,400

— Anr, Presidents Bush, Ford, & Carter, [n.d.]. Oblong 4to. Sgd by all 3. rms Nov 30 (269) $550

### Presidents of the United States —& First Ladies of the United States

**Group photograph,** [n.d.]. Folio. Color photo of Ronald and Nancy Reagan & George and Barbara Bush at a formal affair. Inscr to Terri Anderson by Nancy Reagan & Barbara Bush. Illus in cat rms Oct 11 (302) $700

### Presley, Elvis, 1935-77

**Ds,** 22 Apr 194. 1 p, 4to. Authorization for reports to be furnished to his attorney regarding an accident at Sunset Blvd. & Delfern Drive. Fold line through initial P in signature. wa Oct 28 (478) $650

**Photograph, sgd,** [n.d.]. 8 by 10 inch glossy photo. Of Presley clad only in black shorts. Illus in cat sg Sept 28 (222) $500

# PRICE

**Price, Sir Uvedale**
**ALs,** 10 Oct 1769. 3 pp, 4to. To Sir William Hamilton. About books, Mount Aetna, Raphael & the delights of macaroni. pn Nov 9 (450) £880

**Prinzhorn, Hans, 1866-1933**
**Series** of 3 autograph postcards, sgd, 10 June 1922 to [11 June 1923]. To Alfred Kubin. Thanking for a work by Kubin, referring to experiments with drugs, etc. HH Nov 17 (3282) DM280

**Processional**
**Ms,** [Vallombrosa near Florence, c.1600]. Use of Vallombrosa. 112 leaves, 203mm by 135mm. Contemp calf over pastebds. With 5 lines each of music on a 4-line red stave & of text in a rounded gothic hand with calligraphic flourishes. With large colored initial; other initials lightly marked or left blank. S June 18 (69) £2,200

**Prochnow-Kohlguth, J. D.**
**Autograph Ms,** Journal from Septr 11 1848 to June 12 1851 including 2 trips in the Himalayas. [Northern India, 1848-51] About 90 leaves, folio, in contemp calf. S Mar 28 (376) £250

**Prokofiev, Sergei Sergeevich, 1891-1953**
**Autograph quotation,** 2 bars from his String Quartet, Op.50, sgd; 1932. 1 p, 8vo. On hotel letterhead. S May 15 (447) £750
— Anr, one bar of music, sgd; 1934. 9.5cm by 16cm (card). Inscr by others on verso. Illus in cat. S Dec 1 (278) £850
**Photograph,** sgd & inscr, 1920. 226mm by 177mm. Shoulder-length port; inscr to E. F. Gottlieb. Illus in cat. Marans collection. CE Apr 17 (250) $1,300

**Proust, Marcel, 1871-1922**
**Original drawing,** caricature [of Reynaldo Hahn?], [c.1900?]. 1 p, 8vo; framed. In pen-&-ink, showing him with 3 other men. Illus in cat. S Dec 1 (44) £1,600
**ALs,** 23 Mar [1908]. 6 pp, 8vo. To Princess Marthe Bibesco. About her writing. C June 26 (334) £1,500
— "Mercredi" [24 Apr 1912]. 12 pp, 8vo. To Princess Marthe Bibesco. Thanking her for & commenting on her book, Alexandre Asiatique. C June 26 (332) £2,400
— [Sept 1917]. 11 pp, 8vo. To Princess Marthe Bibesco. About writing to Antoine Bibesco at the time of the death of his brother Emmanuel. Illus in cat C June 26 (335) £1,600
— [Feb 1921]. 1 p, 8vo. To Princes Marthe Bibesco. Hoping to see her soon. C June 26 (336) £850
— [n.d.]. 1 p, 4to. Recipient unnamed. Apologizing for his delay in writing & explaining that he is not able to promise collaborating on a project. S May 15 (212) £700

**Psalms & Psalters**
**Ms,** Ethiopic Psalter, with Canticles. [Ethiopia, 1918]. 243mm by 178mm, vellum, 243mm by 178mm. Blind-tooled goatskin over wooden bds. With 17 headpieces in full colors & 2 full-page miniatures. Written by the scribe Gabra Egziabeger for Habta Maryam. C Nov 29 (16) £1,100
— **Ms,** in Coptic, Psalter. [Upper Egypt, White Monastery near Sohag?, 4th or 5th cent]. Fragment of 1 leaf, vellum, 195mm by 160mm. In dark brown ink in a fine large clear round uncial script, in the Sahidic dialect. Def. S Dec 5 (28) £7,500 [Quaritch]
— **Ms,** in Ge'ez, Psalter, with Weddase Maryam. [Ethiopia, late 18th cent]. 139 leaves, vellum, 176mm by 124mm. Contemp blindstamped lea over wooden bds. With 6 ornamental headpieces in red, black & yellow, & 2 full-page miniatures. HH Nov 14 (102) DM2,600
— **Ms,** in Ge'ez, Psalter, with Weddase Maryam. [Ethiopia, 19th cent]. 171 leaves, vellum, 213mm by 161mm. Contemp blindstamped lea over wooden bds. With 16 ornamental headpieces & 7 miniatures (6 full-page). HH Nov 14 (103) DM2,000
— **Ms,** in Latin, content not given. [N.p., 1479] 208 leaves, on vellum, 179mm by 129mm. In black ink with some words in red; single column of 21 lines. First leaf with full illuminated floral border & coat-of-arms with initials O.M. & 10-line historiated initial in colors with gold highlights on a gold ground. Formerly J. William Smith Collection, Syracuse Public Library. cb Feb 14 (2507) $8,000
— **Ms,** in Latin, Ferial Psalter, with Calendar, Canticles & Litany. [Auxerre, c.1350]. 128 leaves, vellum, 205mm by 138mm. Def late 15th-cent blindtooled calf over wooden bds. In a gothic liturgical bookhand, with musical notation throughout on a 4-line red stave. With calligraphic initials & 8 large historiated initials with full-page baguette & ivy-leaf border extensions containing grotesques. C Nov 29 (8) £22,000
— **Ms,** in Latin, Ferial Psalter, with Hymnal, Canticles & Calendar. Of Carthusian Use. [Paular Abbey near Segovia, Castile, c.1500]. 211 leaves, vellum, 385mm by 272mm. Old massive wooden bds covered with blindstamped brown lea. By several scribes in various forms of gothic liturgical hands, partly with 6 lines of text & of music on a 5-line red stave. With large & small initials throughout in red or purple, some with extensive penwork. Including some 16th-cent insertions. S June 18 (68) £4,000
— **Ms,** in Latin, Psalter with Hours of the Cross, the Seven Joys of the Virgin, the Passion of the Virgin & other texts. [England, 2d half of 15th cent] 230 leaves (lacking c.23 leaves throughout & imperf at end), on vellum 220mm by 150mm, in contemp doeskin over wooden bds. In brown ink in a gothic textura, with rubrics & leaf numbers in red; large initials in gold on blue, brown & white grounds, occasionally forming short borders. pn June 13 (189) £2,700
— **Ms,** in Latin, Psalter, with Canticles. [Northern France or Flanders, c.1285]. 196 leaves, vellum, 164mm by 112mm. Early 19th-cent roan. In a gothic textura. With 178 two-line illuminated initials in red & blue on burnished gold & contrasting ground, & 8 large historiated initials. C Nov 29 (7) £8,500

— Ms, in Latin, Psalter. [Brabant, Brussels?, c.1275]. Single leaf, vellum, 123mm by 91mm; mtd. In a gothic hand. With large historiated initial in colors & burnished gold with long extension formed of a leafy dragon scrolling the height of the page & along upper margin. S Dec 5 (10) £1,500 [Sam Fogg]

— Ms, in Latin, with Canticles & Litany. [Cologne or Munster, c.1440] 229 (of 230) leaves, on vellum, 123mm by 88mm, in 15th-cent Westphalian blind-tooled calf over wooden bds. In brown ink in a gothic liturgical hand. With 8 six-line initials in burnished gold, blue & red, with thre-quarter of full-page border extensions; intials in gold or blue. C June 26 (13) £7,200

**Puccini, Giacomo, 1858-1924**

**Autograph Ms,** pencil notes for the text of La Canzone di Dorette in Act I of La Rondine. 2 pp, 4to. sg June 6 (153) $250

**Autograph transcript,** 2 bars of music on card, sgd 14 Dec 1910. Mtd. sg Feb 1 (202) $1,200

— Autograph transcript, Flauto, opening 38 bars of Boccherini's Minuet from his String Quintet Op.11 no 5, scored for flute; [n.d.]. 1 p, folio. star Mar 22 (1004) DM2,000

**Collection** of ALs & AL, 8 & 11 June 1884. 2 pp, 8cm by 13.7cm (cards). To his brother Michele Puccini. About Mascagni & other friends, the port of himself & Fontana, etc. S May 15 (452) £450

— Collection of ALs & 2 autograph postcards, sgd, 1905 to 1908. 4 pp, 8vo. To his sister Ramelde. About his opera Edgar, his travels & health, family news, etc. S May 15 (463) £650

**A Ls s** (2), 23 Apr & 2 May 1895. 2 pp, 9cm by 14cm (cards). To his brother-in-law Raffaello. About Manon Lescaut & La Boheme, his return to Lucca, etc. S May 15 (464) £550

— A Ls s (2), 28 Apr 1912 & [6 Oct 1917]. 4 pp, 8vo. To his niece Albina del Panta. About the forthcoming premiere of La rondine, a financial matter, & family news. S May 15 (462) £500

**ALs,** 10 Apr 1896. 2 pp, 12mo. To Giuseppe Razzi. About the premieres of 2 of his operas in Palermo. S Dec 1 (282) £500

— 6 Aug 1897. 4 pp, 8vo. To his sister Ramelde. About a production of La Boheme, the composition of Tosca, travels, etc. S May 15 (448) £620

— 14 Oct 1906. 1 p, 8vo. To Sybil Seligman. Postponing a visit & mentioning the projected opera Conchita. S May 15 (458) £700

— 31 Oct [1909]. 4 pp, 8vo. To his sister Ramelde. In verse, describing his journey home from Basel to Milan with his relatives. S May 15 (457) £620

— 30 Oct 1915. 1 p, 8vo. To his niece Albina del Panta. Family news; including musical quotation. S May 15 (453) £450

— 28 Apr 1919. 1 p, 4to. To " Distinguished Mr. Carminati". Thanking him for a letter and wishing " to express to her Highness The Princess my deepest respects. So many distinguished greetings to you and your very kind wife..." With port. Mtd & framed.

Over-all size 16.75 by 19.5 inches. Illus in cat rms Oct 11 (328) $650

— 15 Dec 1920. 1 p, 4to. To "Dear Otto". About Franz Lehar & his work. sg Sept 28 (224) $550

**AL,** 4 Feb 1884. 1 p, 8cm by 14cm (card). To his mother. Reporting that Ponchielli has promised to talk to Ricordi about his work. Illus in cat. S May 15 (450) £700

— 10 Feb 1884. 1 p, 8cm by 13.8cm (card). To his mother. Explaining that he has not been able to meet the pbr Lucca. S May 15 (451) £520

**Ls,** [c.Mar 1905]. 12 pp, 8vo. To his sister Ramelde. Describing the production of Manon Lescaut at Leghorn. S May 15 (455) £1,150

**Autograph postcard,** [c.1906]. To his brother-in-law Raffaello. In verse, teasing him about the postcard which is showing a naked girl. S May 15 (449) £500

**Autograph quotation,** 2 bars from La Boheme (Mi chiamano Mimi), 1 Mar 1908. 1 p, 8vo. Sgd. On hotel letterhead. Illus in cat. S May 15 (461) £1,400

— Anr, 3 bars from Madama Butterfly, 1923. 1 p, 107mm by 162mm. Sgd. Illus in cat. S May 15 (456) £1,100

**Photograph, sgd & inscr,** 22 Oct 1904. 25cm by 20cm. By Vandyk; inscr to Rina Giachetti. Illus in cat. S Dec 1 (280) £1,000

— Anr, [c.1907]. 138mm by 88mm. Half length, seated; inscr to Violet Leverson. Illus in cat. Marans collection. CE Apr 17 (251) $700

— Anr, 1916. 36cm by 26cm; mtd. By Valdemaro; inscr to Lucio d'Ambra. Illus in cat. S Dec 1 (283) £1,000

— Anr, 20 Apr 1921. 5.75 by 8.5 inches. Inscr to Maya Ader. cb June 25 (2569) $900

**Ptd photograph,** 1912. 3.5 by 5.5 inch photo. By A. Dupuis. Sgd in upper left. Inscr to Constance L. PRag (?) on verso. 2 corners worn. Illus in cat sg Sept 28 (223) $950

**Pueckler-Muskau, Hermann, Fuerst von, 1785-1871**

**ALs,** [n.d.]. 2 pp, 8vo. To Klara Mundt. About a date for a meeting. star Mar 21 (295) DM500

**Pugno, Raoul, 1852-1914**

**Autograph quotation,** opening 2 bars of his Serenade a la lune, 22 May 1905. 1 p, 8vo. Sgd & inscr to Comtesse Agnel de Bourbon. star Mar 22 (1005) DM300

**Putnam, Israel, 1718-90**

**ADs,** 6 Jan 1781. 2 by 7.5 inches. Receipt for the full discharge of an obligation by Jonathan Taylor. sg June 6 (154) $550

**Pyle, Howard, 1853-1911**

**ALs,** 9 Dec 1881. 1 p, 8vo. To Miss Sartain. Transmitting an illustration (not present) for Under Green Apple Boughs; with invoice for $60 on integral leaf. sg June 6 (155) $425

## Q

**Quantrill, William Clark, 1837-65**
— BALDWIN, MARY COLAMER. - Autograph Ms, Historical Account and Experience of a Survivor of Quantrell's Massacre at Lawrence, Kansas, During the Civil War, August 21, 1863. 31 pp, folio. [c.1893]. cb June 25 (2376) $4,500

## R

**Raabe, Wilhelm, 1831-1910**
ALs, 24 Mar 1869. 2 pp, 8vo. To [Eduard Hallberger]. Offering his novel Der Schuedderump for publication. star Mar 21 (296) DM1,000
— 2 June 1870. 2 pp, 8vo. To his friend Adolf. Introducing Arnold Wellmer. HN May 15 (2685) DM800
ADs, 20 Nov 1909. 1 p, 8vo. Receipt for 650 marks in fees from Otto Janke. star Mar 21 (297) DM330

**Rabinowitz, Shalom, 1859-1916.** See: Sholem Aleichem

**Rachmaninoff, Sergei, 1873-1943**
Autograph quotation, 6 bars from the last movement of his 2d Piano Concerto, 28 Feb 1911. 1 p, 23cm by 18cm. Sgd. Illus in cat. S Dec 1 (287) £1,600
Photograph, sgd, [n.d.]. 1.5 by 3 inches. Sgd on upper center. cb June 25 (2570) $550
Photograph, sgd & inscr, 28 May 1908. 5.25 by 3.25 inches. Inscr with 2-bar musical quotation from the Prelude for Piano, Op. 3. Ck Apr 12 (109) £1,000
— Anr, 1924. Postcard. Inscr to John Kite. Affixed to flyleaf of an early miniature score of The Isle of the Dead. S May 15 (466) £600
— Anr, 1942. 25cm by 20cm. Lighting a cigarette; inscr to Irma Schenuit. Illus in cat. S May 15 (467) £1,600

**Rackham, Arthur, 1867-1939**
ALs, 24 Aug 1920. 4 pp, 8vo. To N. M. Penzer. Giving reasons why he doesn't think he will ever illustrate the Arabian Nights. bba Apr 11 (254) £170 [Browning]
Autograph sentiment, sgd, 6 Feb 1911 & with drawing of a devil's head. "With kind regards". sg Feb 1 (203) $475

**Raff, Joseph Joachim, 1822-82**
Autograph music, fragment of his String Quartet in D flat Op.77, [n.d.]. 35 pp, 4to. Comprising the 1st movement & parts of the 3d movement. star Mar 22 (1006) DM1,300
ALs, 17 Nov 1870. 2 pp, 8vo. To [Robert] Seitz. Returning some documents & discussing projected publications. star Mar 22 (1007) DM300

**Rain-in-the-Face, Chief of the Sioux Indians, c.1835-1905**
Photograph, sgd, [c.1893]. 165mm by 108mm, mtd. Half length, by George E. Spencer, U.S. Army Photo. Sgd on verso. Illus in cat. Marans collection. CE Apr 17 (167) $4,800

**Ramuz, Charles Ferdinand, 1878-1947**
ALs, [n.d.]. 1 p, 8vo. To an unnamed lady. Thanking for flowers, & reporting that he must return to the hospital for anr operation. HH May 9 (2551) DM220
See also: Stravinsky, Igor

**Randall, James R., 1839-1908**
Autograph transcript, 7th stanza of his poem Maryland, My Maryland; [n.d.]. 1 p, 8vo. Sgd. Illus in cat. rms June 6 (49) $950
— Autograph transcript, poem, Maryland, My Maryland; [13 June 1893]. 5 pp, 4to. 9 eight-line stanzas, sgd. With ALs to Isaac Roland, letter of transmittal. CNY May 17 (223) $4,200

**Randolph, Edmund, 1753-1813**
Ls, 6 Dec 1786. 1 p, 4to. To [Gov. Samuel Huntington]. Sending a duplicate of a resolution of the Virginia Legislature (not present) & naming the Virginia delegates to the proposed convention in Philadelphia. P Dec 13 (314) $12,000
— 29 May 1794. 1 p, 4to. To Sylvanus Bourne. Sending on the commission for Randolph to serve as "Vice-Consul of the United States of America for the Court of Amsterdam in the United Netherlands..." Illus in cat pba Oct 26 (148) $225
Ds, 5 Jan 1787. 1 p, folio. Land grant to Burgess Ball. P Dec 13 (315) $350

**Randolph, Edward, c.1632-1703**
Ls, 22 Mar 1699. 3 pp, folio. To Mr. Blaythwayt. Regarding mines in South Carolina, & forwarding letter on the subject by James Moore (present). CNY May 17 (305) $6,000

**Rasputin, Grigory Efimovich, 1872?-1916**
[A copy of the report of the committee of enquiry set up by Kerensky's provisional government to investigate Rasputin's role in the collapse of the Imperial monarchy, comprising testimony by members of the Imperial household & others, Apr to Aug 1917, more than 500 pp, mostly folio, in bds, in Ms & typescript, sold on 1 Dec 1995, lot 45, for £4,200 at Sotheby's.]
AN, [envelope postmarked 17 Apr 1914]. 1 p, 8vo. To the Countess Witte. Saying that he is visiting with his reverence & they remember her & talk with her. sg Feb 1 (204) $3,200

**Rauch, Christian Daniel, 1777-1857**
ALs, 16 Nov 1828. 2 pp, 4to. To Peter von Cornelius. Refuting an accusation that he has made disparaging remarks about recipient. Illus in cat. star Mar 21 (708) DM400
— 30 July 1846. 2 pp, 8vo. To [Gabriele von Buelow]. Informing her that he has found Thorvaldsen's bust of her mother. star Mar 21 (709) DM500

**Ravel, Maurice, 1875-1937**
ALs, 29 Mar 1911. 3 pp, 8vo. To [Natasha Trouhanova]. Discussing compositions suited for ballet. star Mar 22 (1008) DM2,600

**Autograph quotation,** 3 bars from his Bolero, [24 Mar 1932]. 1 p, 11.5cm by 12cm. Sgd. Illus in cat. S Dec 1 (290) £1,700

**Photograph, sgd & inscr,** [c.1928]. 163mm by 111mm. Bust profile port, by Henri Manuel; inscr to Mme Paul Prosser. Illus in cat. Marans collection. CE Apr 17 (252) $1,300

### Ray, James Earl

**ALs,** [n.d.]. 1 p, 8 by 4 inches. To Rev. Jackson. About the fact he is no longer to sign photos. Dar Oct 19 (122) $75

**Razumovskii, Andrei Kirillovich, 1752-1836.** See: Beethoven, Ludwig van

### Read, George, Signer from Delaware

**ALs,** 29 Feb 1796. 3 pp, 4to. To Samuel Meredith. About the impending marriage of their children & his son's "means to provide for a family." With related material. P Dec 13 (317) $3,000

**AL,** 27 July 1779. 2 pp, 4to. To John Dunlap. Sending a public notice for insertion in recipient's newspaper refuting charges of misappropriation of 2 barrels of flour. P Dec 13 (316) $1,600

### Reagan, Ronald

**ALs,** 14 Apr 1967. 3 pp, 8vo. To Jack Warner. Draft, defending the decision to cut health care for the mentally ill. Forbes Magazine collection. CNY May 17 (175) $950

— 2 June 1967. 1 p, folio. To George Putnam. Thanking a reporter: " Thanks for using the letter about the man whose life was saved by mentioning the gas chamber..."Sgd as "Ron". Illus in cat CNY Dec 15 (223) $750

— 19 July 1967. 2 pp, 8vo. To Mr. deBrettville. Writing the Chairman of the Board and President of the Bank of California about A. B. 1362. With note "Copy to Wm. French Smith" in left margin . Lacking piece of right corner. Illus in cat pba June 13 (81) $1,500

— 15 Aug 1967. 1 p, 4to. To Glenn Dumke. About freedom of expression in academia: "How far do we go in tolerating these people & this trash under the excuse of academic freedom & freedom of expression?..." Sgd as "Ron". CNY Dec 15 (224) $1,200

**Ds,** 15 Aug 1968. 1 p, folio. Extradition of Johnny C. Novello from Nevada to San Francisco. With 30 pp of case history & police photos. Illus in cat pba Oct 26 (303) $350

**Signature,** [n.d.]. On 3 by 5 inch card. pba June 13 (82) $100

— Anr, [n.d.]. No size given. On a small sheet of paper. With tape stains. Also with a campaign button from the 1980 Presidential race. Framed. Over-all size 14 by 10.5 inches. Illus in cat rms Oct 11 (320) $200

### Reagan, Ronald —& Others

**Group photograph,** taking the Presidential oath of office, 1981. 8 by 10 inches. Sgd by Reagan, Nancy Reagan, Warren E. Burger & Elvera S. Burger. Illus in cat. rms Mar 21 (172) $950

### Reagan, Ronald —& Wyman, Jane

**Signature,** [c.late 1930s]. On 2 by 3.5 inch card. Mtd. bbc Sept 18 (90) $125

### Recke, Elisa von der, 1756-1833

**ALs,** 11 July 1826. 2 pp, 4to. To Gerhard Fleischer. Concerning the publication of an earlier play & her new literary projects. star Mar 21 (298) DM280
See also: Tiedge, Christoph August

### Reed, John, 1887-1920

**Ls,** 29 July [c.1917]. 1 p, 4to. To Art Young. Asking him to create a cartoon for the cover of the 1st number of a new labor magazine. CE May 22 (402) $700

### Reed, Joseph, 1741-85

**Ls,** 12 July 1781. 1 p, 4to. To "Auditors of the Publick Accounts". Requesting that they make an official demand to procure an account from Col. Matthew Smith. pba Oct 26 (149) $375

### Reed, Walter, 1851-1902

**Ds,** 30 Aug 1901. 2 pp, folio. Mortgage on a six acre property in Maryland. Sgd by Reed & his wife Emily. Detail in cat rms Oct 11 (330) $700

### Reger, Max, 1873-1916

**Autograph music,** Chorale Prelude for Organ, Komm' suesser Tod!, [c.1893-1901]. 4 pp, folio. In red & black inks on up to 3 systems per page, each of 3 staves, & including autograph notes to the ptr. Sgd twice. S May 15 (470) £4,000

**ALs,** [Oct 1912]. 4 pp, 8vo. To Hans von Ohlendorff. Complaining about the unauthorized premiere of his Konzert im alten Stil, Op.123 in Frankfurt. star Mar 22 (1011) DM1,800

— 29 Dec 1913. 2 pp, folio. To R. Bignell. Recommending piano teachers. S May 15 (472) £180

**Autograph postcard, sgd,** [25 Jan 1908]. To Gustav Herrmann. Asking him to visit. star Mar 22 (1010) DM310

**Reich, Jacques, 1852-1923.** See: Roosevelt, Theodore

### Rellstab, Johann Carl Friedrich, 1759-1813

**ALs,** 6 Oct 1795. 1 p, 4to. To the Rev. Sievers. Explaining that he is not able to send the desired scores because they were misplaced in his move. star Mar 22 (1013) DM200

### Remarque, Erich Maria, 1898-1970

**Autograph Ms,** novel, Im Westen nichts Neues, [c.1927-28]. About 120 pp, folio, in 11 gatherings. Working Ms of the complete text in an early version, differing in important respects from the ptd version. In pencil. S Dec 1 (46) £250,000

**Typescript (duplicated),** Geborgtes Leben. [before 1960] 349 pp, cyclostyled, sgd & inscr to Alvise. C June 26 (338) £1,000

### Remington, Frederic, 1861-1909

## REMINGTON

ALs, 1 Apr 1894. 1 p, 16mo. To Mr. Johnson. "I am not in the market for Froissart, so please don't bother about the matter." cb June 25 (2378) $900

**Renoir, Pierre Auguste, 1841-1919**
ALs, 28 Dec 1902. 2 pp, 8vo. To [Paul Gallimard]. Remembering a previous engagement. star Mar 21 (710) DM1,300

**Requesens y Zuniga, Luis de, 1528-76**
Ls, 11 Aug 1574. 2 pp, folio. To the enyoys of a regiment. Explaining his financial difficulties but promising to pay them soon. star Mar 22 (1481) DM320

**Respighi, Ottorino, 1879-1936**
ALs, 29 May 1914. 2 pp, 4to. To an unnamed Ed at Ricordi's. Providing biographical information. star Mar 22 (1014) DM350

**Reuter, Fritz, 1810-74**
Collection of 5 A Ls s, Ls, & 2 autograph postcards, sgd, 11 Oct 1870 to 26 Nov 1871. 7 pp, 8vo, & cards. To Franz Lipperheide. Concerning poems for recipient's anthology Lieder zu Schutz und Trutz. star Mar 21 (300) DM13,000

ALs, 4 Sept 1866. 2 pp, 8vo. Recipient unnamed. Responding to a request for an autograph & discussing a charity. star Mar 21 (299) DM900

**Revere, Paul, 1735-1818**
ALs, 29 Oct 1795. 1 p, 4to. To Capt. James Byers. Discussing a shipment of copper & work on some cannons. With a related letter of Revere's son Joseph Warren Revere, 26 Mar 1808. CE June 12 (102) $12,000

ADs, [c.24 Apr 1779]. 1 p, 50mm by 190mm. Certificate "that John Vaughan ... is not Endebted to the Regiment". Silked. CNY May 17 (294) $7,000

— 19 Aug 1793. 1 p, 12mo, cut from larger sheet. Receipt to David Greenough for payment for iron materials. Framed with a port. Illus in cat. P Dec 13 (320) $8,500

**Rhodes, Cecil John, 1853-1902**
ALs, 15 Mar 1893. 2 pp, 8vo. To [James Rennell] Rodd. Introducing a man travelling to Zanzibar. star Mar 22 (1573b) DM850

— [c.1895]. 1 p, 8vo. To George Elliot. Makin.d.nner arrangements. pba June 13 (165) $225

**Rhys, Jean**
Autograph Ms, leaf from her unfinished autobiography, Smile Please. [1977] 1 p, folio, written in pencil on both sides. With holograph note by David Plante about Rhys's effort in writing it. S Dec 18 (416) £460 [Davids]

**Ribbentrop, Joachim von, 1893-1946**
Ls, 23 Dec 1935. 1 p, 4to. To Philipp Bouhler. Returning Christmas wishes. Illus in cat. rms Mar 21 (366) $1,100

## AMERICAN BOOK PRICES CURRENT

**Richard, 3d Duke of York, 1411-60**
— GREFILLE, JEHAN. - Ds, 13 July 1437. 1 p, vellum, 90mm by 263mm. Receipt for wages for a herald carrying secret letters from the Duke of York to cities in Normandy. S June 18 (36) £800

**Richelieu, Armand Jean du Plessis, Duc de, Cardinal, 1585-1642**
Ds, 8 Sept 1634. 2 pp, folio. Power of attorney for Nicolas Le Camus to audit some accounts & to purchase a manor. star Mar 22 (1288) DM1,400

**Richet, Charles, 1850-1935**
Autograph Ms, De l'Anaphylaxie. 33 leaves. With holograph revisions & ptr's pencil markings. bba Nov 16 (116) £550 [Rota]

**Richter, Adrian Ludwig, 1803-84**
ALs, 23 June 1861. 1 p, 4to. Recipient unnamed. Sending 2 drawings. HN May 15 (2691) DM640

**Richter, Jean Paul, 1763-1825**
Autograph Ms, deliberations about jokes and puns, Feb 1814. 2 pp, 8vo. star Mar 21 (302) DM2,600

— Autograph Ms, diagnostic description of his eye problems, [summer 1824]. 2 pp, 4to. Illus in cat. star Mar 21 (301) DM4,200

AL, 31 Jan 1803. 2 pp, 8vo. To his wife Karoline. Chatting about his stay in Weimar. star Mar 21 (304) DM4,200

AN, [3 Dec 1796]. 1 p, 8vo. To [Christian Otto]. Sending his latest publications. star Mar 21 (303) DM650

— RICHTER, MAX. - ALs, 21 Mar 1815. 1 p, 8vo. To his father J. P. Richter. Congratulating him on his birthday. star Mar 21 (308) DM320

**Richter, Max, 1803-21.** See: Richter, Jean Paul

**Richthofen, Manfred, Freiherr von, 1892-1918**
Photograph, sgd, [c.1918]. 135mm by 84mm. Shoulder-length port, by C. J. von Duehren. Illus in cat. Marans collection. CE Apr 17 (24) $10,000

**Rickard, Tex**
Photograph, sgd & inscr, [n.d.]. 13 by 10 inches. Inscr to R. R. Barrett. Framed. wa Oct 28 (313) $220

**Rickenbacker, Edward Vernon, 1890-1973**
Ls, 10 June 1940. 1 p, 4to. To the General Manager of The National Aeronautic Association. Agreeing to serve on the 1940 Collier Trophy Committee. rms Nov 30 (84) $700

— 26 Apr 1944. No size given. To John W. Snyder. A thank you letter. pba Feb 22 (146) $75

— 15 July 1959. 1 p, 4to. To Luis St. Bernard. Apologizing for the discourtesy of one of the Eastern Airlines staff. rms Mar 21 (232) $500

— 4 Feb 1964. 1 p, 4to. To W. D. Nice. Concerning pictures. pba June 13 (167) $75

— 1 Aug 1968. 2 pp, 4to. To Col. A. C. Harlander. Thanking him for praise & sending a sgd photo. With 8 by 10 inch mtd, inscr & sgd photo. Illus in cat pba Oct 26 (192) $500

### Rickover, Hyman G., 1900-86
**Ls,** 29 July 1964. 2 pp, 4to. To Congressman William H. Natcher. Concerning sea trials for the 26th Polaris nuclear submarine & offering a biography of John Caldwell Calhoun, the ship's namesake. With original enevelope. rms Oct 11 (331) $200

— 9 June 1969. 1 p, 4to. To Congressman William Natcher. Discussing details of the first sea trials of the nuclear submarine Spadefish. wa Feb 29 (255) $95

— 16 June 1969. 1 p, 4to. To Congressman William Natcher. Discussing details of the first sea trials of the nuclear submarine Seahorse. wa Feb 29 (254) $95

— 27 May 1969. 1 p, 4to. To Congressman William Natcher. Discussing details of the 1st sea trials of the nuclear submarine Puffer. wa Feb 29 (256) $95

— 11 Aug 1969. 1 p, 4to. To Congressman William Natcher. Discussing details of the 1st sea trials of the nuclear submarine Grayling. wa Feb 29 (253) $95

— 3 June 1974. 1 p, 4to. To Congressman William Natcher concerning sea trials of the USS Parche. pba June 13 (95) $300

— 9 Feb 1981. 1 p, 4to. To William H. Natcher. Concerning the first sea trial of the USS San Francisco. pba Oct 26 (193) $150

### Riding, Laura
**Series** of 4 A Ls s, 1933-34. 23 pp, 4to to 8vo. To W. K. T. Barrett. On sex and the differences between men & women & other matters. With an offprint of her pamphlet The First Leaf, which she sent him. S Dec 18 (344) £780 [Maggs]

### Riel, Louis, 1844-85
**Ls,** 19 Feb 1880. 1 p. To the Rev. George Young. Giving permission to see Shutts & Scott before their execution. wad Oct 18 (154) C$1,600

### Riemer, Friedrich Wilhelm, 1774-1845
**Autograph Ms,** 15 aphorisms, 26 Dec 1829, 3 Feb 1842 & [n.d.]. 15 p, 8vo. 2 to 8 lines each; 3 sgd R. star Mar 21 (149) DM950
See also: Goethe, Johann Wolfgang von

### Ries, Ferdinand, 1784-1838
**ALs,** 11 Feb 1835. 2 pp, 4to. To Francois Antoine Habeneck. Explaining that he does not have a copy of his 4th Symphony. star Mar 22 (1018) DM290

### Rietz, Julius, 1812-77
**ALs,** 6 Feb 1865. 1 p, 4to. To Bernhard Friedel. Sending the piano reduction of his Te Deum. HN May 15 (2692) DM300

### Righini, Vincenzo, 1756-1812
**Ds,** 27 Aug 1810. 1 p, folio. Minutes of court proceedings in his suit against the brothers von Kahle. star Mar 22 (1019) DM400

### Riley, James Whitcomb, 1849-1916
**Photograph, sgd & inscr,** 4 July 1908. 7.1 by 8.75 inch sepia photo. A reproduction of a painting by H. Lieber. Inscr to Howard Chandler Christy: "With best greetings and esteem of your old Hoosier friend...." Tipped to mount. Over-all size 11 by 14 inches. sg Sept 28 (227) $375

### Rilke, Rainer Maria, 1875-1926
**ALs,** 14 Jan 1902. 4 pp, 8vo. To Arthur Schnitzler. Describing his financial problems & asking for his help in finding a position in Vienna. star Mar 21 (310) DM4,600

— 6 Mar 1903. 4 pp, 8vo. To [Ignacio Zuloaga]. Praising recipient's works, promising to send his book about Rodin, & hoping to spend some time in the Mediterranean. HN Nov 24 (2850) DM3,800

— 4 Feb 1907. 2 pp, 8vo. To Fraulein Franziska Bruck. A letter of thanks. pba Oct 26 (62) $3,000

— 20 Aug 1908. 4 pp, 8vo, in red mor folder. To the pbr S. Fischer. Thanking for some money & reporting about his mood, his current work, & his situation in Paris. FD May 14 (1123) DM4,300

— 6 Sept 1908. 4 pp, 8vo. To Hedwig Fischer. Chatting about travels in Belgium, her children, other authors, etc. HN Nov 24 (2851) DM5,200

— 10 June 1912. 2 pp, 8vo. Recipient unnamed. Responding to an inquiry about his trans of E. Barrett Browning's Sonnets. star Mar 21 (311) DM1,400

— 8 Sept 1916. 4 pp, 8vo. To [Hedwig Jaenichen-Woermann]. Poetical letter about Dresden, Toledo, his work & his mood. star Mar 21 (312) DM5,600

— [c.1920]. 1 p, 8vo. To the bookseller Jaffe. Apologizing for a delay. HH Nov 17 (3306) DM1,400

— 31 Mar 1921. 1 p, 8vo, on verso of picture postcard. To Hedwig Fischer. Forwarding a letter. star Mar 21 (313) DM1,400

— 11 Apr 1921. 4 pp, 8vo. To the bookseller Jaffe. Ordering books for his wife who is ill. HH Nov 17 (3307) DM2,600

— 24 Feb 1922. 2 pp, 8vo. To Thury-Baumgartner & Co.in Geneva. Ordering books. HN Nov 24 (2852) DM650

### Rimbault, Edward Francis
[Rimbault's letter books for 1840-1855, including letters from Vincent Novello, John Payne Collier & others, sold at Sotheby's on 15 May 1996, lot 123, for £7,500]

### Rimsky-Korsakov, Nikolai Andreevich, 1844-1908
**Autograph quotation,** 7 bars from the 1st movement of his work Scheherezade, [Apr 1889]. 1 p, 4to. Sgd. Illus in cat. S Dec 1 (295) £3,000

**Photograph, sgd & inscr,** 30 May 1907. Framed, overall size 41cm by 31cm. By Boissonas & Eggler. Inscr to M. D. Calvocoressi with a 5-bar musical quotation from Tsar Saltan. Illus in cat. S May 15 (474) £2,500

### Ringelnatz, Joachim, 1883-1934
**Autograph Ms,** poem, Kind, spiele!; [n.d.]. 1 p, 4to. 21 lines, sgd. Stanzas differing from ptd version. Illus in cat. star Mar 21 (314) DM2,500

**ALs,** 13 Nov 1918. 2 pp, 8vo. To his fiancee Annemarie Ruland. From the army, worrying about the times. star Mar 21 (315) DM420

**Riotte, Philipp Jakob, 1776-1856**
**ALs,** 3 June 1805. 2 pp, 4to. To the pbr Anton Andre. About his situation in Erfurt & the publication of some compositions. star Mar 22 (1020) DM350

**Ritter, Karl, 1779-1859**
**Autograph sketchbooks,** (2), kept during his travels in Greece, July 1837 to Jan 1838. 112 sketches in 2 vols, 8vo & folio, in contemp half lea. Landscapes, buildings, geological strata, etc.; mostly in pen-&-ink & pencil. star Mar 21 (601) DM55,000

**Robeson, Paul, 1898-1976**
**Transcript,** radio interview, 25 July 1933. 11 mimeographed pp, 4to. With 12 additions & corrections in Robeson's hand. With 7 family photographs by Eslanda Goode Robeson. sg Mar 28 (257) $2,000
**Photograph, sgd & inscr,** [c.1928]. 140mm by 89mm. Bust port, by Sasha. Illus in cat. Marans collection. CE Apr 17 (253) $500

**Robinson, Jackie, 1919-72**
**Check,** accomplished & sgd, 11 Feb 1966. Drawn on the Freedom National Bank of NY for $22.00 payable to Topaz. Illus in cat. rms Mar 21 (255) $360

**Robinson, Jackie, 1919-72 —&**
**Belafonte, Harry**
**Group photograph,** 1964. Framed, overall size 12.75 by 10.75 inches. With anr man in a law office. Sgd & inscr by both to John Ball. Illus in cat. rms June 6 (458) $325

**Rochambeau, Jean Baptiste Donatien de Vimeur, Comte de, 1725-1807**
**ALs,** 20 Feb 1794 (2 Ventose, Vn II). 1 p, folio. To Vice Admiral LaTouche Treville. Ordering that M. Lapeyrere be placed aboard the first ship possible destined for France & imprisoned upon arrival. sg June 6 (156) $200
**Ls,** 28 Mar 1782. 1 p, 4to. To [Gov. Patrick Henry]. Sending a copy of a letter concerning a confusion in differentiating between slaves & freedmen serving with the French army. P Dec 13 (322) $1,400

**Rochester, John Wilmot, Earl of, 1647-80**
**Ms,** Poems by the Right Honourable John Earle of Rochester. [c.1680s] 216 pp plus c.100 blanks, 4to, in early 19th-cent half russia. The Hartwell Ms, comprising 25 poems, the full text of his play Lucinas Rape or the Tragedy of Vallentinian & Sir Francis Fane's Masque in this play, together with an address To the Reader by William Lovesey. With port. Illus in cat S Dec 18 (114) £48,000 [Quaritch]

**Rochow, Friedrich Eberhard von, 1734-1805**
**ALs,** 6 May 1773. 1 p, 4to. To Herr Luetcke. Asking him to recommend a teacher. star Mar 21 (602) DM330

**Rockefeller, John D., 1839-1937**
**Ls,** 6 July 1905. 1 p, 4to. To the Rev. Henry A. Stimson. About a recent donation to Yale University. bbc Dec 18 (84) $550
**Ds,** 22 Dec 1883. 1 p, folio. Standard Oil Trust Certificate issued to Fannie Freeman. Illus in cat. CNY May 17 (298) $2,500
— 1 July 1891. 1 p, 7.25 by 11.5 inches. Stock certificate for 100 shares of common capital stock of Missouri, Kansas and Texas Railway Company issued to Rockefeller. With sgd transfer endorsement on verso. With cancellation holes. sg Sept 28 (228) $850
— 1 July 1894. 1 p, 4to. Certificate for 100 shares of the Missouri, Kansas & Texas Railway Co., issued to Rockefeller. Sgd in transfer endorsement on verso. rms Mar 21 (292) $600
**Photograph, sgd,** [c.1900]. 350mm by 230mm. Seated; by Edward Tou. Illus in cat. Marans collection. CE Apr 17 (168) $1,300
**Signature,** [n.d.]. On verso of 4to Certificate for 100 shares of Common Capital Stock of Missouri, Kansas and Texas Railway Company issued to Rockefeller. Endorsing a transfer of the stock. With glue-stains & cancellation holes. rms Oct 11 (332) $1,300

**Rockwell, Norman, 1894-1978**
**Ls,** 20 June 1950. 1 p, 4to. To Mabel Saloomey. Praising & making suggestions about her drawing of 2 boys with a baseball bat. rms Nov 30 (279) $850

**Rodgers, Richard, 1902-79 —&**
**Hammerstein, Oscar, 1895-1960**
**Ms,** Vocal selections from Oklahoma, arranged by Dr. Albert Sirmay. Piano & vocal score in pencil. 50 pp, 4to. wd May 8 (25) $450
**Concert program,** 27 Mar 1960. 4 pp, 5.5 by 8.5 inch program for "A Special Dinner to pay Tribute to Richard Rodgers and Oscar Hammerstein II." Inscr for Stephanie. Dar Feb 23 (217) $200

**Rodin, Auguste, 1840-1917**
**Photograph, sgd,** [c.1890]. 135mm by 86mm. Sitting in front of a sculpture, by Manuel. Illus in cat. Marans collection. CE Apr 17 (216) $1,000

**Rodney, Caesar, Signer from Delaware**
**ALs,** 8 May 1775. 1 p, 4to. To his brother Thomas. Reporting about delegates travelling to Philadelphia & taxes being paid in Newcastle County. Illus in cat. P Dec 13 (323) $8,000
**ADs,** 4 Jan 1771. 3 pp, folio. Leasing a plantation and some slaves to a William Sneap. Also sgd by Sneap. With full transcription. Toned & with repaired margins. rms Oct 11 (30) $3,250

**Roebling, Washington Augustus, 1837-1926**
**ALs,** 6 Dec 1898. 2 pp, 4to. To C. C. Marlin. Discussing cables: " Your report and letter of the 3d came duly to hand - owing to the fact that the 4 cables are not loaded alike I scarcely think it proper to dvide the total strain evenly among the 4 cables...Neither do I consider that we are warranted in assuming the total

strength of a cable to be equal to the combined maximum strength of all the individual wires..." Toned & waterstained in the fold of the second page. rms Oct 11 (333) $450

**Roehm, Ernst, 1887-1934**
**Ns,** Dec 1933. 1 p, 4to. To [Philipp Bouhler]. Ptd note of thanks for congratulations on his birthday. Illus in cat. rms Mar 21 (367) $700

**Roentgen, Wilhelm Conrad, 1845-1923**
**ALs,** 30 Mar 1909. 1 p, 8vo. To the secretary of Prince Alfons of Bavaria. Sending his rent & requesting a receipt. star Mar 21 (603) DM1,500
**AN,** 5 Jan 1906. On 2.25 by 4.1 inch card. Content not given. pba Oct 26 (121) $600

**Rogendas, G. P.**
**Ms,** Der Harnisch von seinem Entstehn bis zu seinem Wiedervergehen in Bildern dargestellt und gezeichnet v. G. P. Rugendas, 1714. [19th cent] 17 pp text, interleaved with English trans & 14 full-page watercolor drawings. Bound with: I Gradi della Cavalleria inv. e delin. per Mat. Argenteocorno, 1688. With watercolor title & 17 full-page watercolor drawings plus an additional watercolor drawing loosely inserted at end. Possibly in the hand of Matthaeus Silberhorn. b June 28 (61) £6,000

**Rogers, Will, 1879-1935**
**Signature,** [n.d.]. On 1.7 by 3.3 inch card. With related material. pba Oct 26 (65) $160

**Roget, Peter Mark, 1779-1869**
**ALs,** 13 Dec 1834. 4 pp, 4to. To Mr. Wood, an M.P. On political matters. rms Nov 30 (229) $210

**Rohlfs, Christian, 1849-1938**
**ALs,** 11 Feb 1925. 1 p, 4to. To Wilhelm Koehler. Thanking for congratulations on his birthday. JG Mar 29 (247) DM420
— 31 Dec 1928. 2 pp, folio. To Herr Kirchhoff. Referring to the building of an art gallery in Ascona & an exhibition in Berlin. Including sketch, at foot. star Mar 21 (711) DM900

**Roland de la Platiere, Jeanne Manon Philipon, 1754-93**
**ALs,** [c.Dec 1792]. 4 pp, 8vo. To her friend Lanthenas. Predicting that she & her husband will lose their lives in the revolution. With the warrant for her arrest & further related material. S Dec 1 (47) £1,200

**Rolland, Romain, 1866-1944**
**Series** of 3 A Ls s, 16 to 21 Sept 1931. 9 pp, 8vo. To Gustav Goldstein. Giving advice in a personal crisis. star Mar 21 (316) DM850

**Rommel, Erwin, 1891-1944**
**Ds,** certificate for Johannes Mayer, issued by the military academy at Potsdam; 21 Aug 1937. 2 pp, folio, on ptd form. HH Nov 17 (3308) DM1,300

**Photograph, sgd,** [c.1943]. 140mm by 91mm. In uniform, by Valtingojer. Illus in cat. Marans collection. CE Apr 17 (169) $4,500

**Roosevelt, Edith K.** See: Roosevelt, Theodore & Roosevelt

**Roosevelt, Eleanor, 1884-1962**
[An archive of correspondence to Elizabeth von Hesse & her daughter Maxeda from 1938 to 1961 sold at Swann on Sept 28, 1995, lot 229 for $1,700.]
**Series** of 3 L s s, 5 Jan to 2 June 1959. 3 pp, 8vo. To Frederick R. Lachman. Concerning a chair at Hebrew University. HN May 15 (2694) DM200
**Ls,** 15 Apr 1939. 1 p, 4to. To Eddie Rickenbacker. Hoping the current strike will soon come to an end by a fair agreement. Illus in cat. rms Mar 21 (141) $1,200
**Photograph, sgd,** [c.1940]. 250mm by 200mm. At her desk; by Bachrach. Marans collection. CE Apr 17 (170) $700

**Roosevelt, Franklin D., 1882-1945**
**Autograph Ms,** memorandum concerning an "[a]greement offered D. Hart in August" regarding shares in the Fidelity & Deposit Company of Maryland, 23 Sept [n.y.]. 2 pp, 4to. rms Mar 21 (139) $300
— Autograph Ms, outline map of the Roosevelt family's property at Hyde Park, 27 Sept 1939. 1 p, 4to. Initialled four times. With authentication by Basil O'Connor. P Dec 13 (326) $550
**Typescript (duplicated),** mimeographed Address of the President, at Chautauqua, 14 Aug 1936. 4 pp, 4to. Discussing America & developments in Europe; sgd. P Dec 13 (324) $2,750
— Typescript (duplicated) mimeographed copy of his Address to the Congress declaring a state of war between Japan & the USA, 8 Dec 1941. 2 pp, 4to. Including 3 autograph emendations; sgd FDR. Illus in cat. P Dec 13 (327) $90,000
**ALs,** [31 May 1937]. 2 pp, 4to. To Harold Ickes. About recipient's illness. Illus in cat. rms Mar 21 (134) $25,000
— [1941]. 1 p, 4to. To Norman Davis. Thanking him for aiding in the vocational training of Barbara Rotherford: "...she & I are very grateful. If this war does break out she will be working at it somewhere..." With orig holograph envelope. Illus in cat CNY Dec 15 (116) $15,000
**Ls s** (2), 6 & 17 May 1921. 1 p each, no size given. To the British Consulate-General, Commissioner of Immigration & Collector of the Port of New York City. Trying to assist the safe passage of a servant to England & back. With her baptism certificate. Ck Nov 17 (155) £480
— Ls s (2), 24 Mar & 31 Oct 1938. 2 pp, 4to. To Symon Gould. About a Stephen Foster memorial postage stamp. CE June 12 (105) $600
**Ls,** 23 Dec 1926. 1 p, 4to. To Miss Conklin. Wishing her a Merry Christmas and noting that he is " much pleased that my letters have brought you some relief from the business of scrub woman...The office is going to beat last year's total volume...Missy was on

## ROOSEVELT

week before last for a few days and will be here again in January I hope." With port. Mtd & framed uner glass. Over-all size 12.25 by 18.25 inches. rms Oct 11 (334) $350
— 19 Nov 1928. 1 p, 4to. To Major Oliver P. Newman. About a letter sent: "I wrote you the other day I believe, but since then my late opponent has since conceded my election, so I send a line to say that the second letter is appreciated also." pba Oct 26 (307) $225
— 27 May 1932. 1 p, 4to. To James E. Beverly. Concerning Beverly's suggestion for a parade of ex-servicemen. Illus in cat pba Oct 26 (308) $250
— 20 June 1932. 1p, 4to. To James E. Beverly. Thanking him for information from Chicago just before the Democratic National Convention: "I am glad that you feel that public sentiment is growing more and more friendly toward me. However, as you say, we cannot tell until the convention actually takes place what will be the final outcome..." pba Oct 26 (309) $300
— 6 July 1933. 2 pp, 4to. To Gov. Fred Balzar of Nevada. Asking him to meet with state bankers to discuss "necessary legislative changes or Constitutional amendments to bring about the desired effect" of the Banking Act of 1933. rms Nov 30 (281) $900
— 26 July 1933. 2 pp, 4to. To William George Bruce. Discussing recipient's appointment to the advisory committee of the Public Works Administration. rms Mar 21 (135) $950
— 9 Nov 1933. 1 p, 4to. To Ruth Bryan Owen, Minister to Denmark. Extending holiday greetings to Foreign Service staff in Denmark. Framed with FDR telegram, 30 Aug [n.y.] accepting her resignation. wd Nov 15 (17) $250
— 24 Aug 1936. 1 p, 8vo. To Felix M. Cornell. Thanking for an old book. rms June 6 (460) $325
— 20 May 1937. 1 p, 4to. To G. F. Neuhaeuser, Editor of the Texas Free Press at San Antonio. Sending congratulations on the 73rd anniversary. sg Feb 1 (206) $275
— 10 Mar 1939. 1 p, 4to. To Col. Frank K. Hyatt. Concerning an appointment for Hyatt's nephew: " It is quite interesting to know that three generations of Hyatts have directed a military college...The Presidential appointments given me by law have been, over a period of forty years, reserved for the sons of Army, Navy and Marine Corps officers and enlisted men....Unfortunately, there is no way that I could bestow one of these appointments on your nephew unless he actually comes under the above policy..." With tape stain in corner. Illus in cat rms Oct 11 (335) $425
— 20 Apr 1939. 1 p, 4to. To Frederic W. Lord. Sending thanks for his letter about Roosevelt's message. wa Oct 28 (228) $350
— 25 Sept 1939. 1 p, 4to. To Gov. Clyde R. Hoey. Thanking "for that fine telegram about the Address to the Congress." Illus in cat. rms June 6 (620) $1,300
— 21 Nov 1939. 1 p, 4to. To the Administrator of the Federal Works Agency, John M. Carmody. Concerning funds for the radio station in the Department of the Interior. rms June 6 (621) $475

— 26 Dec 1939. 1 p, 4to. To Charles Schwager. Congratulating him on the 40th anniversary of First Solotwiner Sick & Benevolent Society of N.Y.: "I trust that for long years to come the Society will continue its good work in the relief of human suffering..." sg Sept 28 (231) $375
— 18 Apr 1940. 1 p, 4to. To Hon. Charles C. Burlingham. Thanking him for a letter about George Martin for a court post. Framed with photo, campaign buttons & delegate floor pass to 1940 Democratic convention. rms Nov 30 (40) $675
— 18 Apr 1940. 2 pp, 4to. To Frederic W. Lord. Responding to a booklet by Lord on the subject of contracting for construction. wa Oct 28 (229) $600
— 8 Nov 1940. 1 p, 4to. To Frederic W. Lord. Thanking him for a congratulatory letter on Roosevelt's reelection. With related material. wa Oct 28 (230) $300
— 30 Nov 1944. 2 pp, folio. To the Senate of the US. Sending a convention with France (not present) for their approval. Illus in cat. rms June 6 (622) $2,500
**Ns,** 14 Oct 1942. 1 p, 4to. Recipient unnamed. Sending thanks for a message. Framed with port. Sgd with initials. sg June 6 (157) $375
**Ds,** 11 Sept 1917. 1 p, 4to. Carbon of document promoting John D. Hall as clerk, sgd with initials. CE June 12 (103) $90
— 26 Jan 1931. 1 p, 15 by 18 inches. Appointment of Lida Waldorf Waterhouse as a Member of the Board of Visitors of the New York School for the Blind. Wrinkled. sg Sept 28 (230) $150
— 3 Dec 1933. 1 p, oblong 8vo. NY passenger vehicle registration form for a 1933 De Soto sedan convertible. rms Nov 30 (282) $2,900
— 12 Sept 1939. Size not given. Appointment of Cornelius Eldert as State Delegate. Framed with port. rs Nov 11 (42) $425
— 26 Mar 1943. 1 p, 4to. Memorandum of the Secretary of Labor concerning attempts to settle a coal operators & mine workers' union dispute. Offset. With paperclip stain in the margin. rms Nov 30 (283) $1,100
— 2 Oct 1943. 1 p, 11.25 by 15 inches, framed. Appointment of Leslie E. Given as U.S. Attorney for the Southern District of West Virginia. rs Nov 11 (39) $425
**Check,** sgd, 18 Mar 1930. Payable to John Wilson for $10.92 as "Pay Refund, Spanish War." Repair affecting 2 letters of signature. wa Oct 28 (226) $220
— **Anr,** 31 Mar 1934. 1 p, 8vo. $937.50 payable to "Franklin D. Roosevelt President of the United States". Sgd twice. CNY Dec 15 (226) $6,000
**Endorsement,** 31 July 1936. On the back of his monthly salary check for $937.50. CE June 12 (104) $2,900
**Photograph, sgd,** [c.1933]. 350mm by 265mm. Seated; by Underwood. Illus in cat. Marans collection. CE Apr 17 (171) $1,200
**Photograph, sgd & inscr,** [c.1934]. About 8.25 by 11.5 inches. Inscr to Charles Edward Addams. sg Feb 1 (205) $325
— **Anr,** [n.d.]. 8 by 10 inches, on bd. Inscr to James F. J. Archibald. sg June 6 (159) $375

— Anr, [n.d.]. 4to size. Inscr to Samuel Eliot Morison. Framed. wa Oct 28 (227) $550

**Signature,** [n.d.]. No size given. On State of New York card. pba Feb 22 (275) $95

— Anr, [n.d.]. No size given. On a White House card. Rust-stained in margin. Also with a photo of the President with Churchill & Stalin at Yalta & the front page of the 13 Feb 1945 Daily News covering development at Yalta. Framed. Over-all size 20.5 by 26.5 inches. Illus in cat rms Oct 11 (321) $475

**Roosevelt, Franklin D., 1882-1945 —&**
**Churchill, Winston L. S., Sir, 1874-1965**

**Photograph,** of a painting of Churchill by George W. Fisher, sgd by Churchill. [N.d.] 8 by 6 inches plus borders. pn Mar 14 (365) £580

**Roosevelt, Theodore, 1858-1919**

[A group of 3 working typescripts of his article Advertising and Concealing Coloration in Birds and Mammals, [c.1910], 550 pp, 4to, including c.2,000 autograph revisions, sold on 17 May 1996, lot 179, for $5,500 at Christie's New York.]

**Autograph Ms,** Guildhall lecture on the British in Egypt, [c.1911]. 7 pp, 8vo. Including numerous corrections. With typescript of the speech, [c.1911], 5 pp, 4to. P Dec 13 (329) $5,000

**Typescript,** speech for the Progressive Party, 19 Oct 1914. 25 pp, 4to. Including c.150 words of autograph emendations. With carbon copy of revised speech. Forbes Magazine collection. CNY May 17 (180) $2,600

**ALs,** 11 Nov 1893. 3 pp, 8vo. To Joseph E. Brown. About speaking before the Civil Service Commission. CNY Dec 15 (228) $900

— 31 May 1901. 2 pp, 8vo. To Mrs. New. Wishing her luck. CNY Dec 15 (229) $1,300

**AL,** 3 Ls s & 6 letters, 15 Dec 1898 to 2 May 1900. 9 pp, 4to & 8vo. To William Cary Sanger. Commenting on international & domestic politics. Partly with stamped or secretarial signatures. Forbes Magazine collection. CNY May 17 (178) $1,600

**Ls,** 6 May 1890. 1 p, folio. As a member of the U.S. Civil Service Commission, recommending 2 promotions. Also sgd by others. Including autograph endorsement, sgd, by President Benjamin Harrison at bottom, 8 May 1890. Illus in cat. Forbes Magazine collection. CNY May 17 (177) $1,400

— 7 Apr 1892. 1 p, 4to. To Bernard D. Rowe. Referring to a recent hunting trip in Texas. CNY May 17 (299) $1,100

— 13 May 1902. 1 p, 4to. To Hugh S. Thompson. Sending some letters (not present) showing "how difficult it is to get at the facts concerning any public man." Illus in cat. rms June 6 (461) $525

— 3 June 1902. 1p, 8vo. To General James H. Wilson. Replying to criticism that had been levelled at him: "It is above all to the interests of the men of great wealth that the people at large should understand that they also have to obey the law." With a correction in his hand. sg Sept 28 (235) $2,200

— 12 Sept 1903. 1 p, 4to. To Judge Theodore Brentano. About the Miller case. rms Nov 30 (284) $800

— 14 Oct 1906. 1 p, 4to. To Dr. C. F. Stokes. Approving of recipient's actions. Illus in cat. rms Mar 21 (100) $540

— 27 Aug 1908. 3 pp, 4to. To Congressman Herbert Parsons. Denying that he is trying to use influence to aid Charles Evans Hughes in his gubernatorial race. With holograph postscript. Illus in cat CNY Dec 15 (230) $4,000

— 26 May 1911. 1 p, 4to. To Elmer J. Burkett. Declining an invitation from the Nebraska Senator. Illus in cat pba Oct 26 (312) $450

— 25 Sept 1911. 34 pp, 4to. To Gray. Giving an account of his trip to Great Britain for the funeral of Edward VII. P Dec 13 (328) $8,000

— 24 May 1912. 1 p, 4to. To Hon. John Allison. Thanking him for assistance at the Republican State Convention of Tennessee. Detail in cat rms Oct 11 (337) $550

— 19 Feb 1913. 1 p, 4to. To L. F. Packer. Informing him that he is referring his letter to a legislative committee of the Progressive Party. rms June 6 (462) $300

— 1 Nov 1915. 1 p, 4to. To Reverend Paul R. Hickock. About Abraham Lincoln's drinking habits: "Hay mentioned to me on two or three occasions the fact that President Lincoln occasionally drank alcoholic liquor as a beverage but said that he never drank it in the least to excess....I shall ask you to treat this as purely confidential and not for general use..." Signature pale. Mtd in wooden case. Unexamined out of case. CNY Dec 15 (117) $3,800

— 27 May 1916. 2 pp, 4to. To Mrs. A. W. Nicholson. About his volume of mail and appointments. With holograph corrections & additions. Pale. CNY Dec 15 (231) $550

— 23 Dec 1916. 2 pp, 4to. To Henry Fairfield Osborn. About his plans for a scientific expedition to the Pacific. With holograph corrections. sg June 6 (161) $1,300

— 23 Jan 1918. 1 p, 4to. To Willis C. Cook. About his policies: "There is not one word of truth in that statement. It has never entered my head to make any such offer..." With holograph insertion. Marked PRIVATE. CNY Dec 15 (232) $800

**ANs,** 25 Oct 1895. On calling card with mourning border. About Professor Donovan's sparring & wrestling exhibition. wd Nov 15 (18) $275

**Ns,** 23 Nov 1898. 1 p, 4to. To his cousin, Marcia Roosevelt Scovel. "Hearty thanks!" pn Mar 14 (389) £110

**Ds,** 5 Apr 1902. 1 p, 17 by 22 inches. Appointment of Richard F. Lawson as Postmaster at Effingham, Illinois. Browned, mostly in margins. sg Sept 28 (234) $300

— 22 July 1902. 1 p, folio. Appointing William P. Leete as Postmaster at North Haven, Connecticut. Mtd. Illus in cat pba Oct 26 (311) $375

— 3 Dec 1903. 1 p, folio. Appointment of Elvid Hunt to rank of 2d Lieut. of Infantry. Countersgd by Sec. of War Elihu Root. sg Feb 1 (208) $450

## ROOSEVELT

— 2 Mar 1906. 1 p, 17 by 22 inches. Reappointment of Richard F. Lawson as Postmaster at Effingham, Illinois. Countersgd by George B. Cortelyou. Browned, stained & with tears at the lower left edge. sg Sept 28 (236) $275

— 23 July 1906. 1 p, folio. Postmaster's appointment for F. H. Hitchcock. Illus in cat. rms June 6 (465) $325

— 10 Aug 1906. 1 p, folio. Appointment of Cyrus Sears as Honorary Consul of Cuba at Baltimore. Countersgd by Acting Sec. of State Robert Bacon. rms Nov 30 (285) $340

— 4 Dec 1906. 1 p, folio. Appointing Lionello Scelsi as Consul of Italy at New Orleans for the States of Louisiana, Texas, Mississippi, Alabama, Florida Tennessee and Arkansas. pba June 13 (83) $500

— [1912]. 1 p, folio. Statement trying to regain the Republican nomination from Wm. Howard Taft: "I do not regard the handing back to us, obviously as a mere sop to us and with the hope of confusing the issue, of a few of the delegates stolen from us as of any use unless it is immediately followed by a real and substantial purging of the role of the fraudulent delegates generally." Sgd & annotated in pencil. With 2 burns in right blank margin. sg Sept 28 (239) $1,200

**Cut signature,** [1898]. Framed with depiction of the Rough Riders charge up San Juan Hill. cb June 25 (2380) $500

— Anr, [n.d.]. F Mar 28 (696) $100

**Group photograph,** sgd, [c.1898]. 208mm by 307mm. At the head of his Rough Riders; sepia print. Illus in cat. Marans collection. CE Apr 17 (173) $7,000

**Photograph, sgd & inscr,** 20 Nov 1903. 10 by 7 inches. Inscr to Francis Fitzgerald. Ck Apr 12 (111) £480

— Anr, 22 May 1905. 304mm by 200mm. 3-quarter length, by G. Rockwood. Inscr to William Deacon Murphy. Marans collection. CE Apr 17 (172) $1,500

— Anr, 25 May 1905. 5.75 by 7.75 inches. Inscr on lower border of mat sg June 6 (160) $750

— Anr, 3 Apr 1907. 9 by 6.25 inches, framed but glass lacking. Inscr but name of recipient scratched out. pn Nov 9 (415) £340

— Anr, 21 Nov 1912. 16.5 by 12.5 inch portrait bust photo. Inscr for Mrs. L. R. Carpenter. Creased but repaired. Mtd. Illus in cat sg Sept 28 (238) $1,100

— Anr, [n.d.]. 6 by 8 inches (image). Inscr to E. H. Lawrence. Mtd on card. Showing him outside the National Bank of India in Nairbi, wearing a pith helmet. With 2 unsgd photos. pn Mar 14 (390) £580

**Ptd photograph,** sgd, 14 May 1910. 4to. HH May 9 (2552) DM260

**Signature,** [n.d.]. No size given. On a White House card. Toned. With a sepia-toned reprint photo of Roosevelt in Panama & an original photo of a troopship in the Panama canal. Also with a public debt subscription to finance the Canal dated 1899. Framed. Over-all size 23 by 29 inches. Illus in cat rms Oct 11 (322) $550

— Anr, [n.d.]. No size given. On White House card. Toned. rms Oct 11 (338) $295

— Anr, [n.d.]. On card. sg Feb 1 (209) $200

— HAMNER, GEORGE P. - A Collection of 2 Ms sgd & 2 Ls s. [1950] 7 pp, no size given. Recollecting his experiences as a Rough Rider with Theodore Roosevelt. pba Oct 26 (313) $500

— HAMNER, GEORGE P., DR. - Ms. [1950s]. 3 pp, no size given. About his service with the Rough Riders. With related material. pba Oct 26 (313) $500

— REICH, JACQUES. - Engraving, bust pose of Roosevelt, 1900. 18 by 14 inches. Sgd by Reich & by Roosevelt. Illus in cat. rms Mar 21 (106) $850

**Roosevelt, Theodore, 1858-1919 —&**
**Roosevelt, Edith K.**

**Check,** 13 Sept 1910. 1 p, 4to. $369.97 to Theodore Roosevelt. Filled out in the hand of Mrs. Roosevelt. With beginnings of Mrs. Roosevelt's signature crossed out. Sgd by Mr. Roosevelt & endorsed by him on verso & indication that the check had been cashed on 1 Oct 1910. Illus in cat rms Oct 11 (80) $700

**Root, George F., 1820-95**

**Autograph quotation,** 9 Jan 1884. 1 p, 8vo. Two bars of music from The Battle Cry of Freedom. With the words "Yes, we'll rally 'round the flag, boys!" rms Oct 11 (96) $400

**Rosas, Juan Manuel de, 1793-1877**

**ALs,** 6 Nov 1862. 2 pp, 4to. To Dr. Fraser. Concerning a consultation & the doctor's fee. In Spanish & English. rms June 6 (466) $500

**Rosecrans, William Starke, 1819-98**

**Signature,** [n.d.]. No size given. With a carte-de-visite portrait & a bayonette scabard tip from Stones River. Framed. Over-all size 10.5 by 14 inches. Detail in cat rms Oct 11 (112) $350

**Rossetti, Dante Gabriel, 1828-82**

**Series** of 9 A Ls s, 4 Apr 1876 to 11 Dec 1879 & [n.d.]. 17 pp, 8vo, sgd with initials. To Theodore Watts-Dunton. With a 3-page holograph memorandum on a sonnet & on the appropriate viewing for certain paintings. S Dec 18 (202) £700 [Yablon]

**ALs,** 30 Nov 1875. 4 pp, 8vo. To Philip Bourke Marston. Suggesting that Marston make "a series of poems derived from the most subtle & exquisite impressions of nature". CE May 22 (409) $400

— [n.d.]. 4 pp, 8vo. To Mrs. Sumner. Referring to her kindness to the painter, F. J. Shields. bba Apr 11 (255) £220 [Silverman]

**Rossini, Gioacchino, 1792-1868**

**Autograph music,** 8 bars in C major, scored for piano, 5 Feb 1851. 1 p, 8vo. Sgd. Illus in cat. S May 15 (479) £2,300

— Autograph music, fragment of an unknown opera, [c.1820?]. 2 pp, 4to; trimmed. 12 bars, scored for voice & orchestra. Some later corrections. star Mar 22 (1022) DM3,200

**Ms,** 35 piano pieces, each sgd & corrected by Rossini throughout, [c.1866-68]. Over 200 pp, folio. Notated on 5 two-stave systems per page. Stichvorlage for the Oeuvres Posthumes de Rossini, 1880. With material concerning the publication. S Dec 1 (299) £5,000

— Ms, Requiem eternam for contralto & piano. [1859] 5 pp, oblong folio & oblong 8vo. Sgd & dated, 18 Aug 1859. With separate vocal part marked by the printer. S May 15 (131) £550

— Ms, song, La Lontananza. [Paris, 1860s] 16 pp, oblong folio. In a scribal hand but extensively annotated by Rossini throughout & sgd by him. S May 15 (130) £1,200

ALs, 8 June 1839. 1 p, 4to. To an unnamed countess. Recommending a musician. star Mar 22 (1023) DM700

— 19 June 1839. 1 p, 8vo. To Signor Fabbri. Informing him of his arrival to discuss a confidential matter. S May 15 (481) £460

— 14 Sept 1849. 1 p, 4to. To Countess Antonietta Orsini. About a Ms of Semiramide & other Mss, & promising to visit her. S May 15 (480) £480

— 12 Mar 1851. 1 p, 4to. To Signor della Ripa. Discussing financial matters. S May 15 (478) £500

— Feb 1858. 3 pp, 8vo. To Leopoldo Pini. About emptying a house in Florence. sg June 6 (162) $375

— 24 May 1862. 1 p, 4to. To Salvatore Marchesi. Praising his hymn dedicated to the King of Italy. S May 15 (477) £500

— [n.d.]. 1 p, 8vo. To Felice Schiassi. Content not given b Sept 20 (25) £190

Autograph quotation, 3 bars in A minor, 13 Sept 1860. 1 p, 16mo. Sgd & inscr to Ferdinand Falk. With a photograph. Illus in cat. star Mar 22 (1024) DM1,300

Photograph, sgd, 26 Jan 1866. 105mm by 62mm, mtd. Full length, standing, by Erwin Freier. Sgd on recto; sgd & inscr to Alfred de Rothschild on verso. Illus in cat. Marans collection. CE Apr 17 (256) $1,600

**Rostand, Edmond, 1868-1918**

Photograph, sgd, 1906. 162mm by 106mm; mtd. 3-quarter length; by Paul Boyer. Marans collection. CE Apr 17 (88) $750

**Roth, Eugen, 1895-1976**

Autograph Ms, story, Eis; [n.d.]. 13 pp, 4to. Some corrections. HH May 9 (2553) DM750

ALs, 29 June 1959. 2 pp, 8vo. To Otto Henning. 22 lines of verse, expressing congratulations. star Mar 21 (319) DM450

**Rother, Christian von, 1778-1849**

Ls, 22 Oct 1826. 2 pp, 4to. To P. W. D. Tonnies. Responding to his suggestions to assure the freedom of navigation in the Mediterranean. star Mar 22 (1609) DM350

**Rouget de Lisle, Claude Joseph, 1760-1836**

ALs, [n.d.]. 1 p, 8vo. Recipient unnamed. Referring to some music & to an earlier discussion. star Mar 22 (1319) DM900

**Rousseau, Jean Jacques, 1712-78**

ALs, 2 June 1763. 2 pp, 4to. To Marianne Francoise de Luze. Regretting he could not continue his travels and see her, & requesting her help in a financial matter. Illus in cat. star Mar 21 (320) DM7,200

**Rowe, Susan**

Original drawings, (29) to illus Tales for a Winter's Night [1983]. 13 for full-page designs, the remainder for illusts in the text, the majority sgd with initials. The full-page illusts measure c.200mm by 145mm. S Nov 2 (559) £3,200 [George]

— Original drawings, (35) to illus Charles Kingsley's The Water-Babies. [c.1980] Most c.185mm by 140mm, all but 3 in color, 3 double-page. S Nov 2 (558) £4,400 [Vallejo]

**Rubbra, Edmund**

Autograph music, Symphony No 4, Op.53, 30 Aug 1940 to 2 Mar 1942. 75 pp, folio, in bds. Full score, notated on up to 20 staves per page, with revisions. Sgd later & inscr to Maurice, 15 Sept [19]65. S Dec 1 (300) £1,150

**Rubinstein, Anton, 1829-94**

Autograph music, Barcarolle no 5 for Piano, [c.1873]. 4 pp, folio. Sgd on tp & inscr to Comtesse Marie Doehnhof. Silked. rms June 6 (467) $725

Autograph quotation, 39 bars of a piano piece in A minor, notated on 6 two-stave systems, 21 Nov 1854. 1 p, 4to. Sgd. Illus in cat. S Dec 1 (302) £650

— Anr, 8 bars with tempo marking. 1 June 1890. 1 p, 8vo. With sepia cabinet photo of Rubenstein by J. Ganz. Sgd on mount. Illus in cat sg Sept 28 (241) $300

**Rudolf, Erzherzog, 1858-89**

ALs, 1 Mar 1882. 2 pp, 8vo. Recipient unnamed. Forwarding a letter from Egypt & promising some zoological specimens. star Mar 22 (1491) DM680

— 1 Nov 1885. 3 pp, 8vo. To an unnamed count. Hoping that a forthcoming "patriotic work" about Austria & Hungary will be read in the schools. star Mar 22 (1492) DM1,700

**Rudolf II, Emperor, 1552-1612**

ALs, 18 Jan 1593. 1 p, folio. To Pope Clement VIII. Discussing differences between the Archbishop of Salzburg & the Duke of Bavaria about the abbey at Berchtesgaden. Illus in cat. star Mar 22 (1583) DM6,000

Ls, 7 May 1603. 3 pp, folio. Recipients unnamed. Requesting that Georg Rueber & his brothers be granted an exemption from duties. star Mar 22 (1584) DM400

Ds, 7 Feb 1603. 1 p, 412mm by 572mm. Order concerning a suit of the chapter of the cathedral in Brussels against innkeepers at Odenheim & Rohrbach. Illus in cat. HH May 9 (2555) DM650

**Rueckert, Friedrich, 1788-1866**

Ms, Gedichte..., zusammengestellt fuer die erste Jugend...; [n.d.]. About 600 pp, 4to, in cardboard

folder. Including poems from 10 of his collections, in a scribal hand. S May 15 (219) £1,500
— Ms, Life of Saint Hadumod, trans from the Latin; [pbd 1845]. 52 pp, 4to. In an elegant scribal hand. S May 15 (218) £500
Series of 3 A Ls s, 14 June 1838 & [n.d.]. 3 pp, 4to & 8vo. To Ferdinand Scheler. Discussing the purchase of a house, planning a meeting, etc. S May 15 (216) £1,150
ALs, 9 Feb 1864. 1 p, 8vo. To [Wilhelm Schoepfl]. Commenting on recipient's anthology of German verse. star Mar 21 (321) DM1,300
— RUECKERT, HEINRICH. - 7 A Ls s, 2 Oct 1858 to 29 Apr 1867. 16 pp, 8vo. To Ferdinand & Lisette Scheler. About the publishing of his father's Mss. With related family letters. S May 15 (220) £650

Rueckert, Heinrich, 1823-75. See: Rueckert, Friedrich

**Ruggles, Daniel, 1810-97**
ALs, 28 Feb [1865]. 1 p, 8vo. To Major General Polk. Asking for "1000 lbs. of common powder..." Illus in cat pba Feb 22 (177) $350

**Runge, Friedlieb Ferdinand, 1795-1867**
ALs, 10 July 1863. 2 pp, 8vo. To Ernst von Bibra. Sending copies of his book for recipient & the King. star Mar 21 (605) DM1,400

**Rungenhagen, Karl Friedrich, 1778-1851**
ALs, 16 Feb 1849. 1 p, 4to. To [K. T. von Kuestner]. Asking for 3 singers for a performance of Mendelssohn's oratorio Paulus. star Mar 22 (1025) DM340

Ruppert, Jacob, 1867-1939. See: Barrow, Edward G. & Ruppert

**Rush, Benjamin, Signer from Pennsylvania**
Autograph Ms (2), A List of Mrs. Rush's excellent qualities ... for the benefit & imitation of her children, & A List of my husband's Dr. Rush's faults kept by me Julia Rush..., [n.d.]. 11 pp, 8vo; stitched. Sgd in text. rms June 6 (468) $8,000
ALs, 1 Oct 1787. 4 pp, 4to. To [David Ramsay]. Discussing some of his publications, praising the new Constitution, & predicting its ratification by Pennsylvania. P Dec 13 (330) $14,000
— 20 Nov 1801. 1 p, 4to. To Dr. James Currie. Concerning the US & written in the third person: " Dr. Rush is happy being able to inform his friend Dr. Currie, that liberty, peace, order and plenty continue to pervade every part of the United States...." Repaired, silked, toned & foxed. rms Oct 11 (339) $2,800
— 21 Sept 1811. 1 p, 4to. Recipient unnamed. Asking that a letter thanking the Russian emperor for a diamond ring be forwarded to John Quincy Adams at St. Petersburg. P Dec 13 (331) $1,800
Collection of 1 ADs & 1 Document unsgd but filled out, 17 Feb 1797 & Nov 1796. Certification that Samuel Taylor has "attended the medical Lectures on Anatomy, Chemistry, & on the Institutes & clinical cases in the Pennsylvania hospital; pass for admission of Taylor to Rush's "Lectures on the Institutes of Medicine, and Clinical Cases". rms Nov 30 (288) $1,500
ADs, Mar 1794. Receipt for 5.5 pounds issued by the Estate of Major General Anthony Wayne to Rush for "Medicines and advice for his Son". Soiled in margin. Illus in cat rms Oct 11 (389) $1,300
— [Oct 1805]. 1 p, 8vo. Statement to the estate of Manuel Eyre for medicines & medical services. With related material. P Dec 13 (332) $1,400
Ds, 17 Nov 1791. 1 p, vellum, 15.5 by 16.75 inches. Deed of Rush & his wife to Thomas Ketland. Sgd & sealed by both Rushes & by William Bradford. With port. O Mar 5 (195) $1,200
— 20 Nov 1791. 1 p, folio, vellum. Deed of sale for a property in Philadelphia. Also sgd by William Bradford. pba June 13 (44) $900
— 20 Feb 1806. 1 p, 13 by 9 inches, vellum. Medical Diploma. In Latin. Sgd as President of the Medical Society of Philadelphia. License granted to Peter Wendell. Browned with age. sg Sept 28 (242) $2,300

**Rush, Benjamin, Signer from Pennsylvania —& Physick, Philip Syng, 1768-1837 —& Others**
Ds, Apr 1810. 1 p, folio, vellum. In Latin. Medical arts degree diploma of Joseph B. Stuart. Featuring University of Pennsylvania seal. Soiled. Illus in cat rms Oct 11 (340) $3,250

**Rusk, Thomas Jefferson, 1803-57**
Ds, 8 July 1845. 1 p, 4to. Resolution expressing gratitude to former President Tyler that "restore[d] Texas to the bosom of the Republican Family..." Sgd as Rusk. With Ls transmitting the document to Tyler. CNY Dec 15 (123) $6,000

**Ruskin, John, 1819-1900**
ALs, 30 Aug 1882. 2 pp, 8vo. To unnamed recipient. Concerning Pre-Raphaelite artists. CNY Dec 15 (36) $650

**Russwurm, John Brown**
Ms, Essay entitled "Toussaint L'Overture, the Principal Chief in the Revolution of St. Domingo". c.1828. 22 pp, 4to. Unsgd. Dampstained & faded. With ragged edges. bbc Sept 18 (91) $800

**Rust, Wilhelm, 1822-92**
A Ls s (2), 18 Dec 1886 & 4 Mar 1887. 8 pp, 8vo. To [Wilhelm Tappert]. Discussing works for lute, & sending some of his grandfather's compositions. Including some musical quotations. star Mar 22 (1026) DM750

**Ruth, George Herman ("Babe"), 1895-1948**
Ls, 7 Nov 1947. 1 p, 4to. To a father of a fan. Concerning his son: " Thank you very much for the photos of your little son Nicholas in his baseball togs. They are very amusing and he must be a bright little fellow. I would like very much to meet him sometime although for the present I am doing a great deal of travelling...In the mean time I am sending the little fellow an autographed picture [not present]..."Worn at folds & soiled. Illus in cat rms Oct 11 (360) $2,700

**Check,** 15 Dec 1937. 1 p, 3.25 by 8.5 inches. $50 payable to cash. Sgd as "G. H. Ruth". Illus in cat pba Oct 26 (66) $1,300

— **Anr,** 29 Mar 1946. 1 p, 4to. $100 payable to Claire Ruth. Illus in cat rms Oct 11 (81) $1,300

**Christmas card,** sgd & inscr, [n.d.]. Framed within 2-door red lacquer display case with bas-relief Christmas tree hung with baseball equipment & with biographical plaque. cb June 25 (2308) $1,100

**Photograph, sgd & inscr,** [c.1930]. 86mm by 136mm. During a baseball game; inscr to Frederick Smith. Illus in cat. Marans collection. CE Apr 17 (281) $3,500

**Signature,** [n.d.]. No size given. Inscr to "To My Pal Joe". With 7 by 8 inch photo of Ruth in his New York Yankee uniform. Mtd. Overall size 11 by 14 inches. Dar Oct 19 (38) $350

— **Anr,** [n.d.]. No size given. On notebook sheet. Smudged. Detail in cat rms Oct 11 (45) $500

— **Anr,** [n.d.]. On a prelim leaf of the remains of a copy ("the book is a mess") of Babe Ruth's Own Book of Baseball, 1928. sg Feb 1 (28) $650

**Rutherford, Ernest, 1st Baron Rutherford of Nelson, 1871-1937**

**ALs,** 8 Jan 1921. 3 pp, 8vo. To an unnamed physicist. Requesting some information about radioactivity for a projected lecture course. Illus in cat. star Mar 21 (606) DM3,000

**Rutter, Owen, 1889-1944**

**Autograph Ms,** The Vindication of William Bligh. 1933. 26 pp, 8vo, in small school book, in purple ink. Sold with proof copy with corrections of The Quarterly Review, No 518, Oct 1933, in which this article appeared & with 3 Ls s of C. Lawrence, Ed of The Quarterly Review. b Mar 20 (182) £280

# S

**Sackville, Thomas, 1st Earl of Dorset**

**Ds,** 23 Oct & 30 Nov 1599. 1 p, 200mm by 105mm. Authorization as Lord Treasurer for investigation into a claim by Capt. Anthony Hawes. Sgd as "T. Buckhurst". b May 30 (354) £190

**Sackville-West, Victoria, 1892-1962**

**Autograph Ms,** gardening book for 1951-52, containing holograph drafts of her In Your Garden articles for the Observer, with related material. About 80 leaves, folio, in bds. S Dec 18 (420) £3,000 [Gekoski]

**Photograph, sgd & inscr,** Jan 1931. 12.5 by 10 inch port. Inscr to Nancy Pearn. With soiled margins & holes. Illus in cat Ck Nov 17 (156) £480

**Sage, Russell, 1816-1906**

**ADs,** 3 Feb 1868. 1 p, 8vo. Receipt for payment for bonds of the Galveston, Houston & Henderson Rail Road Company. Including other transactions relating to these bonds on recto & verso. Illus in cat. rms June 6 (372) $650

**Saint-Gaudens, Augustus, 1848-1907**

**Photograph, sgd,** [c.1890]. 354mm by 277mm, mtd. Half length, by G. C. Cox. Illus in cat. Marans collection. CE Apr 17 (218) $1,000

**Saint-Saens, Camille, 1835-1921**

**ALs,** 19 Oct 1910. 3 pp, 8vo. To Rene Doire. Protesting the ommission of his Ouverture de fete: "...It is a strange way of thanking me for my work. The Courrier had to talk about the approach which itself will not be useful to send to me: It is a...sad chapter in our acquaintance..." With translation. rms Oct 11 (341) $400

— 12 Feb 1916. 4 pp, 8vo, on 1 sheet folded. To a friend. Giving news of his work & concert schedule. sg Feb 1 (211) $325

**Autograph quotation,** 3 bars of music from his work Elena, 1904. 1 p, 8vo. Sgd. Illus in cat. rms June 6 (225) $325

**Sakharoff, Alexander**

**Photograph, sgd,** [1968]. 5.5 by 4 inch bust photo. Sgd in Cyrillic. Signature smeared. sg Sept 28 (244) $300

**Salinger, Jerome David**

**Ds,** 25 Feb 1964. 2 pp, folio. Contract for publication of the Catalan Ed of Franny & Zooey. Typescript carbon copy with ink revisions. Also sgd by the Spanish pbr. CE May 22 (416) $1,000

**Salisbury, Robert Arthur Talbot Gascoyne-Cecil, 3d Marquess**

**ALs,** 30 Nov 1883. 12 pp, 8vo. Recipient unnamed. About housing for working men in the suburbs. rms Nov 30 (292) $300

**Salk, Jonas**

**Ms,** Report entitled Vaccination Against Paralytic Poliomyelitis Performance and Prospects. [12 Apr 1955]. 37 pp, 4to. With spring spine binding. Sgd on title page. Detail in cat rms Oct 11 (342) $475

**Ls,** 6 July 1959. 2 pp, 4to. To Frederick R. Lachman. About a visit of the medical faculty of Hebrew University. HN May 15 (2697) DM320

**Signature,** [n.d.]. No size given. With photo of Salk holding up his anti-polio vaccine & related material. Signature light. Framed. Over-all size 22 by 25.5 inches. Illus in cat rms Oct 11 (16) $475

**Salm-Neuburg, Nikolaus III, Graf zu, d.1580**

**Ls,** [1579]. 2 pp, folio. To the estates in Lower Austria. Requesting them to defray the costs for the completion of the fortifications at Raab. Illus in cat. HN Nov 24 (2854) DM1,800

**Samosch, Gertrud, 1892-1978.** See: Gert, Valeska

**San Francisco**

**Document,** 31 Jan 1887. 1 p, 5.5 by 10.24 inches. Stock Certificate No. 341 in the California Street Cable Railroad Co. In plastic holder. Sgd by Charles Mayne & made out to J. B. Stetson. Also sgd by Thomas W. Hinchman. Larson collection pba Feb 12 (259) $225

— SAN FRANCISCO PRESIDIO. - Ms, sealed-paper petition of Juan Coopea, an artillery soldier in the company of Miguel Benevides, 23 June 1831. 1 p, 12.5 by 8.5 inches. Sgd by the commandante, Ignacio Martinez in 2 places. Larson collection pba Sept 24 (219) $1,000

### San Martin, Jose de, 1778-1850
**Ds,** 4 Dec 1821. 1 p, folio. Military appointment for Jose Andres Odiaga. With related material. rms Oct 11 (344) $330

— 7 Jan 1822. 1 p, folio. Appointment of Ambrosio Marquez as "Ayudante" in Lima. star Mar 22 (1639) DM750

### Sand, George, 1804-76
**ALs,** [28 Aug 1844]. 1 p, 8vo. To Marie de Rosieres. Discussing Chopin & his sister's travel plans, & announcing the completion of her novel. Address panel in Chopin's hand. S Dec 1 (125) £1,100

— 14 Aug 1852. 2 pp, 8vo. To Dr. Philips. Concerning Mme Fleury, who wants to consult an opthalmologist. star Mar 21 (324) DM550

— 3 Jan 1876. 2 pp, 8vo. To Zacharie Maulmond. Thanking for a letter & sending family news. star Mar 21 (325) DM460

**AL,** [c.1840s]. 4 pp, 8vo. To Pauline Viardot. Looking forward to seeing her on her return from London & mentioning Chopin. S May 15 (223) £700

### Sandburg, Carl, 1878-1967
**Autograph Ms,** Copy of his poem "Chicago." 1913. 2 pp, 4to. Sgd & dated "Carl Sandburg, Chicago Illinois, U.S.A. 1913 A.D." CNY Oct 27 (122) $18,000

**Sander, Johann Daniel, 1759-1825.** See: Forster, Georg

### Sandow, Eugene, 1867-1925
**Photograph,** sgd & inscr, [n.d.]. 7.5 by 4.5 inches mtd to 9.5 by 6.5 inches. Inscr to H. T. Jordan. rms Nov 30 (295) $340

### Sanskrit Manuscripts
**Ms,** Bhagavata-purana. [Kashmir, c.1800]. 258 leaves, 100mm by 155mm. Contemp silk over paper wraps. In devanagari script. With 12 pages of ilumination & 22 full-page miniatures. HH Nov 14 (93) DM4,200

— Ms, the legend of Krishna. [Kashmir, c.1800]. 42 leaves, 130mm by 160mm. Contemp lea. With 41 miniatures in colors. Imperf. HH Nov 14 (99) DM320

### Santa Anna, Antonio Lopez de, 1794-1876
**Ds,** 28 June 1861. 1 p, folio. Mortgage bond for $500. CNY May 17 (302) $800

— 28 June 1866. 1 p, folio. $500 bond. Aged. Mtd. Over-all size 13 by 17.5 inches. rms Oct 11 (345) $800

— 28 June 1866. 1 p, folio. Mortgage bond. rms Nov 30 (296) $900

### Saphir, Moritz Gottlieb, 1795-1858

**ALs,** 16 May 1832. 3 pp, 4to. To Louis Schneider. Inquiring about the arts & the theater in Berlin. star Mar 21 (326) DM220

### Sarasate y Navascues, Pablo de, 1844-1908
**ALs,** 26 Sept [n.y.]. 1 p, 8vo. Recipient unnamed. Declining a dinner invitation. HN May 15 (2698) DM220

### Sargeant, Frederick
[An archive of material from 1860-1905 relating to Sargeant & the Alaska Commercial Company. Sold at Pacific on 11 Oct 1995, lot 125 for $1,700.]

### Sargent, John Singer, 1856-1925
**ALs,** 24 Feb [1924]. 1 p, 8vo. To Rev. Charles Russell Peck. Accepting an unspecified offer. rms June 6 (316) $325

— 17 Nov [n.y.]. 2 pp, 8vo. To his friend Abbott. Thanking for suggesting that his name be on the Whistler Monument Committee. Including autograph postcript. Framed with a port. Illus in cat. rms June 6 (315) $575

— [n.d.]. 2 pp, no size given. Regretfully declining a dinner invitation. pba Feb 22 (93) $110

### Sartre, Jean Paul, 1905-80
**Autograph Ms,** draft for part of Les Mots, with extensive revisions. [before 1964] 24 pp, 270mm by 213mm. With typed version of the draft with corrections in a secretarial hand, 24 pp, & typed concordance showing the relationship of the draft to the pbd version. All bound in half mor. P June 5 (329) $3,000

### Sassoon, Siegfried, 1886-1967
**ALs,** 1 Nov 1957. 1 p, no size given. To Mr. Deval. About Trollope: " I find Trollope so much pleasanter to read in the original editions..." Creased & soiled. Ck Nov 17 (157) £90

### Satie, Erik, 1866-1925
**ALs,** 11 Mar 1916. 1 p, 16mo. To Ricardo Vines. Declining invitations & inquiring about performing some music. S Dec 1 (309) £400

— 1 June 1920. 2 pp, 8vo. To Maria Freund. Informing her that he has given her address to the Comte de Beaumont, mentioning a fee, & sending his address. star Mar 22 (1030) DM2,200

### Savigny, Friedrich Karl von, 1779-1861
**ALs,** 21 Jan 1812. 3 pp, 8vo. To an unnamed colleague. About some scholarly publications. HN May 15 (2699) DM600

### Sayers, Dorothy L., 1893-1957
**Collection** of 12 A Ls s & Ls s & 7 Christmas cards, sgd, Dec 1948 to Feb 1950. To Dr. S. J. Curtis. Mainly about the philosophy of Dante. pn June 13 (248) £1,300

### Sayn-Wittgenstin, Wilhelm, Fuerst zu, 1770-1851
**Collection** of ALs & Ls, 22 June 1845 & 10 June 1850. 3 pp, 4to. To Herr Esperstedt. Contents not stated. FD May 14 (1127) DM210

**Scammell, Alexander, 1747-81**
ALs, 13 Aug 1779. 1 p, folio. To Col. Ezra Badlam. Giving orders concerning arms & recruits. P Dec 13 (335) $500

**Scarlatti, Alessandro, 1660-1725**
ALs, 16 Dec 1702. 1 p, folio. To the Viceroy of Naples. Asking to be allowed to appear before him with the fruit of his musical labors when he returns to Naples the next day. Illus in cat. S May 15 (482) £10,000

**Schadow-Godenhaus, Wilhelm von, 1789-1862**
ALs, 18 Dec 1827. 2 pp, 4to. To Michael Beer. About colors for his paintings & their friend Immermann. star Mar 21 (713) DM350

**Scharnhorst, Gerhard von, 1755-1813**
Ls, 17 Aug 1809. 2 pp, 4to. To his landlord. Responding to a demand for payment of rent due for the past three years. star Mar 22 (1640) DM400
— 7 Jan 1810. 1 p, 4to. To a department of the army. Returning newspaper reports. star Mar 22 (1641) DM250
— 23 Jan 1810. 1 p, 4to. To Friedrich Karl Heinrich von Wylich und Lottum. Inviting him to a meeting. star Mar 22 (1642) DM360

**Schefer, Leopold, 1784-1862**
Autograph Ms, 3 poems, [n.d.]. 6 pp, 8vo; paginated 7 - 12. HH May 9 (2557) DM400
— Autograph Ms, poem, Des Teufels Testament; [n.d.]. 3 pp, 8vo. 10 stanzas. HH May 9 (2558) DM400

**Scheffel, Joseph Victor von, 1826-86**
ALs, 24 Oct 1880. 1 p, 8vo. To O. Schimmler. Concerning the German trans of Ekkehard IV casus sancti Galli. HH Nov 17 (3311) DM320
Autograph sentiment, sgd, [25 Dec] 1877. 1 p, 8vo. Praising honesty & hard work. HN May 15 (2701) DM200

**Scheuren, Johann Kaspar Nepomuk, 1810-87**
ALs, 18 Feb 1852. 3 pp, 4to. To Christian Hohe. Asking for a sketch of the university in Bonn. Including 2 pen-&-ink sketches. star Mar 21 (714) DM450

**Schieber, Anna, 1867-1945**
Collection of 5 A Ls s, 3 Ls s, & 8 postcards, sgd (6 autograph), 13 Dec 1926 to 18 Dec 1937. 17 pp, various sizes, & cards. To Dr. August Heisler. About personal & literary matters. star Mar 21 (329) DM850

**Schiller, Friedrich von, 1759-1805**
ALs, 7 Dec 1785. 1 p, 8vo. To Friedrich & Wilhelmine Kunze. Chatting about friendship & poetical works. Illus in cat. star Mar 21 (330) DM34,000
— 12 Nov [1804]. 2 pp, 8vo. To Wilhelm von Wolzogen. Asking him to present his new work to Grand Duchess Maria Paulowna & reporting about a recent conversation with her. star Mar 21 (331) DM22,000
— BECKER, HEINRICH. - ALs, 21 Mar 1801. 2 pp, 4to. To Franz Kirms. Informing him about a quarrel between two actresses about roles in Schiller's Wallenstein & Schiller's position in the matter. star Mar 21 (332) DM1,500

**Schindelmeisser, Louis, 1811-64**
ALs, 18 Oct 1860. 3 pp, 8vo. To Richard Wagner. Speculating about the performance of Tannhaeuser in Paris. star Mar 22 (1032) DM450

**Schinkel, Karl Friedrich, 1781-1841**
ALs, 29 July [1827]. 1 p, 8vo. To Karl Begas. Informing him of the commission to paint an altarpiece. Illus in cat. star Mar 21 (715) DM1,100

**Schlegel, August Wilhelm von, 1767-1845**
ALs, 12 Mar 1806. 20 pp, 8vo. To Fouque. Important letter discussing literature in Germany, recipient's works, & his travels in Italy. star Mar 21 (335) DM6,500
— [1817]. 1 p, 8vo. To Wilhelm Ternite. Asking for his opinion about some Italian paintings. Fold tear. star Mar 21 (336) DM550

**Schlegel, Friedrich von, 1772-1829**
ALs, 8 May 1805. 4 pp, 8vo. Recipient unnamed. Referring to his work at the Bibliotheque Nationale, discussions with recipient, etc. HH Nov 17 (3313) DM900
— 5 Sept 1806. 2 pp, 8vo. Recipient unnamed. Thanking for his hospitality & asking him to forward some letters. HN May 15 (2705) DM750

**Schmid, Carlo, 1896-1979**
Collection of 2 A Ls s & 5 Ls s, 22 Aug 1973 to 26 Aug 1979. 7 pp, various sizes. Recipient unnamed. Mostly concerning the publication of his memoirs. star Mar 22 (1205) DM550

**Schmidt, Heinrich von, 1850-1928**
[An archive of 30 documents relating to personal matters & his profession as architect, 1883 to 1925, sold at Granier on 29 Sept 1995, lot 333, for DM1,900.]

**Schmidt, Johann Philipp Samuel, 1779-1853**
ALs, 13 July 1809. 1 p, 4to. To Friedrich Rochlitz. Discussing the art scene in Berlin in a time of war. star Mar 22 (1033) DM550

**Schmidt von Werneuchen, Friedrich Wilhelm August, 1764-1838**
ALs, 25 Nov 1830. 1 p, 4to. Recipient unnamed. Requesting that a student be informed about his father's death. star Mar 21 (337) DM420

**Schmidt-Isserstedt, Hans, 1900-73**
Collection of 6 A Ls s & 6 autograph postcards, sgd, 26 Aug 1924 to [Sept 1936]. 13 pp, folio & 4to, & cards. To Alfred Morgenroth. About his Sinfonia concertante, his work as a conductor, & family matters. star Mar 22 (1034) DM750

**Schmidt-Rottluff, Karl, 1884-1976**

**ALs,** 25 Nov 1952. 2 pp, 8vo. To Rosemarie Lehmann-Haupt. Thanking for her report from Mexico. HN Nov 24 (2858) DM340

### Schmitt, Florent, 1870-1958

**Autograph music,** song, Tristesse au jardin, to a text by Laurent Teilhade, 1 or 2 Mar [18]97. 14 pp, folio. Scored for voice & piano; sgd F. S. star Mar 22 (1035) DM1,200

### Schnitzler, Arthur, 1862-1931

**Autograph Ms,** poem, beginning "Gefahrvoll ist's der Vaeter Weisheit traun...'", 15 May 1907. 1 p, 8vo. 12 lines, sgd. star Mar 21 (339) DM1,100

**Collection** of ALs & autograph postcard, sgd, 11 Nov 1904 & 16 May 1905. 2 pp, 8vo, & card. To Adolf Crombach. About a contribution to recipient's journal Heim der Jugend. star Mar 21 (341) DM320

— Collection of c.50 A Ls s, Ls s, & postcards, sgd, 1909 to 1929. About 60 pp, various sizes. To Dr. Robert Adam Pollak. Commenting on recipient's works. S May 15 (226) £8,500

**ALs,** 31 Dec 1913. 2 pp, 4to. To Theodor Reik. Hoping to see him to discuss Reik's conclusions about the psychological background of Schnitzler's works. HN Nov 24 (2859) DM1,600

**Ls,** 10 July 1903. 1 p, folio. Recipient unnamed. Commenting on Frank Wedekind's work Erdgeist. star Mar 21 (340) DM380

— 17 July 1924. 2 pp, 4to. To Nathan Ausubel. Expressing doubts that he can influence young people in America with his writings. star Mar 21 (342) DM450

### Schnorr von Carolsfeld, Ludwig von, 1836-65

**ALs,** 9 Jan 1862. 1 p, 4to. To Bernhard Friedel. Declining an invitation. HN May 15 (2707) DM520

### Schnorr von Carolsfeld, Malvina von, 1825-1904

**ALs,** 21 Mar 1866. 1 p, 8vo. Recipient unnamed. Sending two compositions previously in her husband's possession. HN May 15 (2708) DM520

### Schnyder von Wartensee, Xaver, 1786-1868

**Autograph quotation,** Palindromus; 9 Aug 1858. 1 p, 8vo. 12 bars on 4 systems; sgd. star Mar 22 (1037) DM650

### Schoenberg, Arnold, 1874-1951

**Ls,** 5 Dec 1927. 1 p, 4to. To Fritz Hirt. Discussing financial arrangements for a concert. wa Oct 28 (133) $650

— 21 Dec 1944. 1 p, 4to. To Gottfried Bermann Fischer. Concerning a contribution to a special Ed of the Neue Rundschau honoring Thomas Mann. star Mar 22 (1039) DM1,800

**Autograph quotation,** 4 bars from his Chamber Symphony in E major, 31 Dec 1933. 1 p, 4to. Sgd & inscr to Roaz Piller. Inscr by Sir George Henschel on verso. star Mar 22 (1038) DM3,000

### Schopenhauer, Johanna, 1766-1838

**ALs,** [n.d.]. 1 p, 8vo. To Karoline Bertuch. Inquiring about some missing newspapers. star Mar 21 (151) DM800

### Schott, Gaspar

**Ms,** Pantometrum Kircherianum. [Wuerzburg, c.1660] 206 leaves, 4to, in contemp vellum bds. With explanations & diagrams in ink, 1 in color, with worked examples. Madsen Ms S Mar 14 (207) £5,200

### Schroeder, Friedrich Ludwig, 1744-1816

**ALs,** 5 July 1812. 1 p, 4to. To Friedrich August Werdy. Referring to the theater in Hamburg. star Mar 22 (1158) DM650

### Schroeder, Rudolf Alexander, 1878-1962

**Autograph Ms,** poem, beginning "Horch, Bacchus, ruft dich nicht in grauer Weite...", [n.d.]. 1 p, 4to. 14 lines, including revisions. Illus in cat. star Mar 21 (343) DM750

### Schroedinger, Erwin, 1887-1961

**ALs,** 16 Jan 1955. 2 pp, 4to. To Rolf Hosemann. Criticizing recipient's Ms. star Mar 21 (612) DM3,200

### Schubert, Ferdinand, 1794-1859

— DRECHSLER, JOSEPH. - Ds, 23 Dec 1819. 1 p, 4to. Report on Ferdinand Schubert's examination as a choral director. C Nov 29 (249) £350

### Schubert, Franz, 1797-1828

**Autograph music,** Overture in C minor for string instruments, scored for string quartet, [summer 1811]. 15 pp, folio. star Mar 22 (1040) DM58,000

— STADLER, ALBERT. - ALs, 4 Jan 1853. 4 pp, 8vo. To an unnamed lady. Reminiscing about his friend Schubert. star Mar 22 (1041) DM3,000

### Schubert, Gotthilf Heinrich von, 1780-1860

**ALs,** 20 Sept 1838. 1 p, 4to. To the bookseller Oehmigke. Thanking for fees. star Mar 21 (613) DM500

### Schulz, Charles M.

**Ls,** 7 Apr 1966. 1 p, 4to. To unnamed recipient. An invitation to discuss a book. With envelope. pba Feb 22 (94) $170

### Schumann, Clara, 1819-96

**Series** of 4 A Ls s, 25 June 1868 to 2 Sept 1895 & [n.d.]. 18 pp, 8vo. To her daughter Elise. Family letters. star Mar 22 (1047) DM3,000

**ALs,** 5 June 1844. 3 pp, 4to. Recipient unnamed. Thanking for a present, referring to musical life in Leipzig, & urging him to proceed with his plans for a music festival in St. Petersburg. S May 15 (487) £600

— 1 Apr 1860. 2 pp, 8vo. To Frau Ritter. Discussing the program for a concert in Dresden. star Mar 22 (1044) DM1,100

— 10 Sept 1862. 3 pp, 8vo. Recipient unnamed. Concerning a projected concert in Wroclaw. star Mar 22 (1045) DM900

— 14 June 1868. 2 pp, 8vo. Recipient unnamed. Sending congratulations on his daughter's engagement to be married. star Mar 22 (1046) DM700

— 5 Sept 1869. 8 pp, 8vo. To her son Felix. Advising him not to choose music as a profession. star Mar 22 (1048) DM3,400

— 30 Sept 1872. 4 pp, 8vo. To Ferdinand Breunung. Discussing dates for a concert. star Mar 22 (1049) DM600

— 1 Sept 1895. 4 pp, 8vo. To Novello's About the English publication of Robert Schumann's Studies and Sketches. With a check made out to & endorsed by her. S May 15 (137) £520

**Autograph quotation,** opening 5 bars from Robert Schumann's Piano Quintet, Op.44, 17 Apr 1884. 1 p, 15cm by 25cm. Sgd & inscr to Arthur Chappell. S May 15 (488) £550

**Photograph, sgd,** June [18]88. 162mm by 106mm, mtd. Seated at her piano; by Franz Hanfstaengl. Illus in cat. Marans collection. CE Apr 17 (259) $800

— Anr, Dec [18]91. 136mm by 97mm (image). By Hanfstaengl. star Mar 22 (1050a) DM2,400

### Schumann, Robert, 1810-56

**Autograph music,** Laendliches Lied, from his Album fuer die Jugend, Op.68 no 20, [1848]. 1 p, c.19cm by 23cm. Notated on 5 two-stave systems & including some corrections. Stichvorlage. With autograph inscr, sgd, by Clara Schumann at head. Illus in cat. S Dec 1 (312) £17,000

— Autograph music, Thema mit Variationen fuer das Pianoforte, [1854]. 6 pp, various sizes. Complete score of his last composition; inscr to his wife Clara on tp & sgd at end. star Mar 22 (1051) DM155,000

**ALs,** [Nov 1837]. 1 p, 8vo. To Friedrich Hofmeister. Asking for some compositions by Adolf Henselt & Valentin Alkan. star Mar 22 (1052) DM4,000

— 28 July 1840. 1 p, 8vo. To Ferdinand David. Inviting him to a concert at his house. star Mar 22 (1053) DM3,500

— 27 June 1844. 3 pp, 4to. To Ignaz Moscheles. Asking for his help in planning concerts in England. star Mar 22 (1055) DM7,500

— 17 Dec 1853. 1 p, 8vo. To his children. Informing them of their projected return. star Mar 22 (1056) DM2,000

### Schumpeter, Joseph, 1883-1950

**ALs,** [n.d.]. 2 pp, 8vo. Recipient unnamed. Regretting that he is not able to accept an invitation to the opera. star Mar 21 (615) DM750

### Schurz, Carl, 1829-1906

**ALs,** 7 July 1904. 2 pp, 8vo. Recipient unnamed. Explaining elections & party conventions in the United States. star Mar 22 (1645) DM600

**Ls,** 10 Nov 1905. 1 p, 8vo. To R. U. Johnson. Approving of the election of W. M. Sloane "as a member of the Academy of Arts and Letters". star Mar 22 (1646) DM180

**Autograph sentiment,** 21 Jan 1873. "Truly yours." Framed with photo & engraving of the Battles at Chancellorsville. rms Nov 30 (26) $370

### Schuyler, Philip, 1733-1804

**Ls,** 7 Feb 1777. 1 p, 4to. To John Barclay. Thanking for efforts in garrisoning Ticonderoga with NY militia. P Dec 13 (337) $4,750

### Schwab, Gustav, 1792-1850

**ALs,** 16 June 1824. 1 p, 4to. To the Ed of the Berlinischer Taschen-Kalender. Sending contributions for the next year. star Mar 21 (344) DM500

— Sept 1837. 3 pp, 8vo. Recipient unnamed. Regretting that he was not able to meet the pbr Georg Wigand. HN May 15 (2711) DM420

### Schwarzenberg, Karl Philipp, Fuerst zu, 1771-1820

**Ls s** (2), 14 Mar & 1 June 1810. 4 pp, folio. To Gen. Clarke. Inquiring about 2 prisoners of war. star Mar 22 (1647) DM250

### Schwatka, Frederick, 1849-92

**ALs,** 5 Feb 1877. 3 pp, 8vo. To his father. Reporting from Nebraska during the Sioux uprising. CNY May 17 (303) $2,200

### Schweitzer, Albert, 1875-1965

[An Archive of materials from 1913 to the 1970s. relating to Albert Schweitzer. Sold at Swann on Sept 28, 1995, as lot 248 for $2,200.]

**Typescript,** Draft of a speech or article entitled "Friede oder Atomkrieg; Verzicht auf Atomwaffen." 22 Feb 1958. 50 pp, 4to. Unsgd. With holograph corrections & additions. Bound loosely with string. Worn. sg Sept 28 (247) $325

**A Ls s** (2), 26 July 1961 & 5 Feb 1963. 2 pp, 8vo. To the Rev. Klaus Thomas. Sending news from Lambarene, & expressing thanks. 1 ALs as postscript to ALs by his secretary Mathilde Neumann. HH Nov 17 (3316) DM650

**ALs,** 15 Mar 1934. 1 p, 8vo. To Daniel Halevy. Thanking him for a book: "Thank you for sending me the book about Father Angonard, who has always been very nice to me. The volume...will be particularly precious to me too because it bears a dedication to you..." Letter is on the second page of a letter by his assistant Guy Martin to Halevy. pba Oct 26 (123) $800

— Jan 1937. 2 pp, 8vo. To Mr. Daniel Halevy. Trying to arrange a meeting in Paris & lamenting a toothache. pba Oct 26 (124) $700

— 15 Apr 1945. 1 p, 8vo. To Winifred Troup. Thanking for a donation for his hospital. star Mar 21 (616) DM400

— 1 May 1954. 2 pp, 4to. To Dr. Max A. Goldzicher. In German, about his own medical condition. wa Oct 28 (157) $500

— 22 Jan 1957. 1 p, oblong 8vo. To Dr. Max A. Goldzicher. In German, thanking him for birthday greetings. wa Oct 28 (158) $300

**ANs,** 22 July 1953. 8vo. To J. R. James. Thanking for a donation. At foot of a 2-page letter by Ali Silver, expressing thanks & reporting about Lambarene. HN Nov 24 (2861) DM380

— 9 Nov 1960. 1 p, 4to. To Dr. & Mrs. Emery. A thank you note written in the hand of Miss Ali Silver in

English with a holograph sentiment from Schweitzer in French. Not translated. pba June 13 (170) $350
— 26 Mar 1965. 1 p, 12mo. To Samuel Edgar Worth. Sending best wishes. Framed with photo. cb June 25 (2575) $225

**Photograph, sgd,** [n.d.]. 12mo. Framed under glass. Over-all size 7.5 by 5.75 inches. rms Oct 11 (346) $285

**Photograph, sgd & inscr,** July 1955. 218mm by 136mm. Inscr to Richard Charles Nalven(?). Illus in cat. Marans collection. CE Apr 17 (55) $700
— Anr, 24 May 1957. 105mm by 146mm. Inscr to Col. Robert E. Carter on margin. CE June 12 (111) $500

### Schwerin, Kurt Christoph, Graf von, 1684-1757

**ALs,** 30 Sept 1722. 1 p, 4to. To the merchant de Vigne. Expressing his displeasure that some tapestry has not been furnished yet. Illus in cat. star Mar 22 (1656) DM550

### Scopes, John T., 1900-70

**Photograph, sgd,** [c.1925]. 247mm by 198mm. Half length. Marans collection. CE Apr 17 (175) $1,300

### Scott, Blanche Stuart, 1891-1970

**Photograph, sgd & inscr,** [c.Sept 1910]. 205mm by 253mm. Seated in her plane. Marans collection. CE Apr 17 (25) $480

**Scott, John,** Secretary to Lord Nelson. See: Nelson, Horatio Nelson

### Scott, Paul Mark, 1920-78

**ALs,** 21 Oct 1964. 2 pp, 4to. To Christopher Hibbert. Complaining about the writer's lot: "you can write your arm off in this world & nobody seems to notice unless you happen to get raped by a giraffe in Regent's Park as well." S Dec 18 (419) £340 [Davids]

### Scott, Capt. Robert Falcon, 1868-1912

**Ls,** 4 Apr 1910. 1 p. To A. Cockrane. Acknowledging a subscription to the 1910 expedition, with receipt attached. With a typed list of donations received. b Sept 20 (28) £300

### Scott, Sir Walter, 1771-1832

**ALs,** "Thursday". 2 pp. To Mr. Ballantyne. About the Lady of the Lake & some verses. Ck Apr 12 (112) £350
— [n.d.]. 1 p, no size given. To his daughter Anne. Concerning family news: "...how delighted Mama and I are to hear from your letters that Walter continues better - Mama is very well and in excellent spirits..."Trimmed. With a torn corner. Ck Nov 17 (160) £290

**Ds,** 26 Nov 1819. 1 p, oblong 4to. "Accept. Walter Scott" on front of a promissory note sgd by James Ballantyne. rms Nov 30 (297) $340

### Scott, Walter ("Death Valley Scotty")

**ALs,** 26 May 1935. 1 p, 4to. To Mr. Willard of the Los Angeles Examiner. On various matters. sg June 6 (285) $120

### Scott, Winfield, 1786-1866

**Check,** accomplished & sgd, 20 Apr 1830. Drawn on the Bank of the U.S. for $20.57 payable to himself. Illus in cat. rms June 6 (50) $150

### Scriabin, Aleksandr Nikolaevich, 1872-1915

**Autograph music,** Poeme for piano, Op.69 no 1, [1913]. 3 pp, folio. Notated on 3 or 4 systems per page, 2 staves each. Sgd at head. Stichvorlage, but with divergences from pbd version. S Dec 1 (336) £4,700

**Autograph quotation,** main theme of the Introduction to the 1st movement of his 3d Symphony, sgd; 2 Dec 1912. 1 p, 23cm by 18cm. On hand-drawn stave. S Dec 1 (335) £850

— Anr, opening 8 bars of his Piano Sonata No 10, sgd; [n.d.]. 1 p, 4to. Framed. S Dec 1 (334) £2,100

### Seaborg, Glenn Theodore

**Autograph Ms,** preface to an article, From Mendeleev to Mendelevium - and beyond; 14 Dec 1971. 3 pp, 4to. Sgd. star Mar 21 (617) DM360

### Searle, Humphrey, 1915-82

**Autograph quotation,** 6 bars from his 5th Symphony, Andante; [n.d.]. 1 p, 8vo. Sgd. star Mar 22 (1057) DM280

### Sebastiani, Horace Francois Bastien, Comte de la Porta, 1772-1851

**ALs,** 4 Feb 1813. 1 p, 4to. To Gen. Clarke. Concerning the promotion of officers. With engraved port. star Mar 22 (1472) DM260

### Sedgwick, Theodore, 1746-1813

**ALs,** 11 Feb 1801. 1 p, 4to. To W. Williams. As Speaker of the House of Representatives, reporting about the balloting for the Presidential election. CNY May 17 (256) $4,000

### Segal, George

**Typescript carbon copy,** Master's thesis, submitted at Rutgers University in May 1963. 28 pp plus 7 mtd photographic reproduction of his works. Segal's own copy. sg Jan 11 (388) $325

### Segner, Johann Andreas von, 1704-77

**ALs,** 2 July 1770. 3 pp, 4to. To the Rev. Grosse. Encouraging him to trans Euclid's Elementa. star Mar 21 (618) DM380

### Seidel, Heinrich, 1842-1906

**Collection** of 15 A Ls s & 3 postcards, sgd, 24 Oct 1896 to 21 June 1906. 48 pp, 8vo, & cards. To Paul Warncke. About meetings, personal news, his work, friends, etc. Partly in Low German. star Mar 21 (345) DM7,000

### Seifert, Jaroslav, 1901-86

**Autograph Ms,** novel, Hvezdy nad Rajskov zahradov [Stars over the Tomato Garden], dated 18 July 1929. About 150 pp, 4to, in cardboard folder. In ink; ptr's copy. S Dec 1 (51) £1,600

**Seipel, Ignaz, 1876-1932**
ALs, 8 Dec 1931. 3 pp, 4to. Recipient unnamed. Discussing the attitude of the Catholic church towards other sects & denominations. star Mar 22 (1657) DM480

**Selous, Frederick Courteney, 1851-1917**
ALs, 14 June 1900. 4 pp, 8vo. To B. Knowles. Comparing British racial attitudes in South Africa with those of the Boers. pn Nov 9 (370) £130

**Selznick, David O., 1902-65**
Collection of 2 ALs s & 7 Ls s, 31 July 1958 to 20 Aug 1964. 18 pp, 8vo & 4to. To L. Arnold Weissberger. Concerning plays, films & the actress Jennifer Jones [Mrs. Selznick]. Detail in cat rms Oct 11 (348) $2,500

— Collection of ALs & Ls 18 July & 11 July 1964, 5 pp & 3 pp, 8vo. To Arnold Weissberger. ALs Discussing a potential project involving the possibility of making James Baldwin's play Blues for Mr. Charlie into a film. rms Oct 11 (349) $1,500

**Semmes, Raphael, 1809-77**
Ds, 1 Sept 1861. 1 p, folio. Approving payment to Auguste Silvia Rios for 255 pounds of beef & 255 pounds of vegetables for the C. S. Steamer Sumter. On ptd form of "Confederate States Navy Department." With a paymaster's receipt for $31.90 sgd by Rios at the bottom of the form. sg Sept 28 (64) $1,400

**Sendak, Maurice**
ANs, [n.d.]. 1 p, 8vo. To Arthur. saying that "a small boy says Sorry". With ink drawing sgd Maurice below. sg Feb 1 (213) $300

**Seneca, Lucius Annaeus, 54? B.C.-39 A.D.**
Ms, Epistolae, [Milan, c.1440] 228 leaves including 4 blanks, on vellum, 228mm by 164mm, in contemp blind-tooled calf over wooden bds with 3 brass catches. Written by 2 scribes in brown ink in a cursive humanist bookhand. With 3 historiated initials of St. Paul writing, Seneca handing a letter to a messenger & Seneca reading a scroll, by the Master of the Vitae Imperatorum C Apr 3 (6) £28,000

**Serra, Junipero**
ADs, [n.d.]. 1 leaf, 11.75 by 7.9 inches, written on both sides, 90 lines total. Confirmation record of the Missions of Santa Barbara, San Antonio de Padua, San Buenaventura & San Luis Obispo. Sgd in 3 places. Larson collection pba Sept 24 (222) $19,000

**Seton, Ernest Thompson, 1860-1946**
Photograph, sgd, 1915. 3.5 by 5 inch sepia oval port. Sgd as " Ernest Thom. Seton as chief scout B. S. A. 1915". Illus in cat pba June 13 (223) $180

**Seuse, Heinrich, 1295?-1366.** See: Suso, Heinrich

**Seuss, Dr.**
Original drawing, Cat in the hat in pen & ink. [n.d.]. 1 p, 8vo. Mtd & framed under glass. Over-all size 8.75 by 10.75 inches. Illus in cat rms Oct 11 (351) $800

**Seve, Jacques de, 1742-88.** See: Buffon, Georges Louis Marie Leclerc & Seve

**Seward, William, d.1740**
Ms, journal kept as Methodist preacher in America, 13 Aug 1739 to 1 Apr 1740. 235 pp, 317mm by 203mm, disbound. P Dec 13 (338) $14,000

**Seward, William Henry, 1801-72**
Ms, Entitled "United States and Ch R 15th July 1868, to the Secretary of State of the United States, from Jos. S. Wilson, Commissioner." 15 July 1868. 67 pp, folio. Representing correspondence between Seward & Commissioner Joseph S. Wilson of the General Land Office, Dept of the Interior about treaty negotiations with China. Illus in cat pba Oct 26 (315) $850

ALs, 28 Sept 1840. 1 p, 4to. To John H. Goulie. Offering congratulations: "When I was in New York a friend put into my hands the letter of Paul Inglis to the Workingmen of the United States...I could not deny myself the pleasure of congratulationg you upon success in this timely appeal to our countrymen..." pba Oct 26 (314) $170

— 28 Dec 1851. 1 p, 4to. To Leonard Bacon. On the demoralization of the "public mind." rms Nov 30 (298) $350

— 11 June 1852. 1 p, no size given. To William S. De Zeng. Thanking him for a note. With port of Lincoln & his Cabinet. Framed. Over-all size 15.5 by 25.5 inches. Illus in cat rms Oct 11 (18) $350

Franking signature, on envelope postmarked 11 June [n.d.]. Addressed in anr hand to William S. DeZeng at Manhattan Life Insurance Company in NY. Framed with port & image of the execution of 4 Lincoln Assassination conspirators. rms Nov 30 (27) $280

Photograph, sgd, [c.1867]. 100mm by 65mm. Profile port. Marans collection. CE Apr 17 (176) $650
See also: Lincoln, Abraham & Seward

**Seyffer, Karl Felix, 1762-1822**
ALs, [c.June 1804]. 1 p, 4to. To [P. Lingemann]. Informing him that he has accepted a position in Munich. star Mar 21 (619) DM260

**Shackleton, Sir Ernest Henry, 1874-1922**
ALs, 5 Nov 1912. 3 pp, 8vo, laid down on card. To Mr. Spicer. Content not given. b May 30 (143) £130

**Shaler, William**
ALs, 29 Apr 1815. 1 p, 4to. To Tobias Lear. About embarking with his squadron. rms Nov 30 (95) $1,500

**Shamil, Imam of Dagestan, 1797?-1871**
AL, [n.d.]. 1 p, 12mo. To Naib Idris Effendi. Requesting a safeguard for his sister-in-law. Sgd with his seal. With related material. Illus in cat. HN May 15 (2616) DM750

**Shapiro, Karl**
Autograph Ms, poem, Israel. 5 stanzas of 6 lines each, 1 p, 4to. Sgd. Dated in anr hand, 15 May 1948. sg Feb 1 (214) $110

### Sharpe, Horatio, 1718-90
**Ds,** 27 Nov 1762. 1 p, on vellum, folio. Land grant to Charles Pen in Frederick County MD. bbc June 24 (50) $110

### Shatalov, Vladimir
**Autograph Ms,** cosmonaut trainee notebook, Feb 1963 to Nov 1964. About 170 pp, 279mm by 203mm, in plastic notebook. P Mar 16 (156) $1,700

### Shaw, George Bernard, 1856-1950
**Collection** of ALs & Ls, 26 July & 29 Nov 1912. 2 pp, 4to & 12mo. To Harry Nicholls. Criticising recipient's performance in Captain Brassbound's Conversion. With ALs by Nicholls, 2 Dec 1912, draft of return letter, & the copy of Shaw's Captain Brassbound's Conversion, L, 1907, used by Nicholls as prompt book. CNY May 17 (109) $2,400

**ALs,** 10 Sept 1905. 1 p, 4to. To Philip Snowden. Concerning the proposed use of his photograph in a publication. C Nov 29 (187) £350

— 16 Jan 1915. 1 p, 12mo. To George R. Wormald. Insisting that Dickens's "collection of real women is one of the most terribly truthful portrait galleries in literature." Illus in cat. rms June 6 (121) $875

— 25 June 1928. 1 p, 8vo. To unnamed recipient. Requesting grammar corrections in the manuscript of his Intelligent Woman's Guide. Illus in cat rms Oct 11 (352) $750

— 23 June 1929. 1 p. Recipient unnamed. Bluntly refusing to contribute to a forthcoming book. Sgd with initials. wad Oct 18 (158) C$420

— 27 Nov 1930. 1 p, 12mo. To F. B. Czarnowski. Apologizing for not having been able to come on Friday. rms Nov 30 (300) $500

— 15 Feb 1932. 1 p, 8vo. To unnamed recipient. In full: " Your wire has just arrived. So you did it in one day after all! Pure swank, I call it, but if I had been with you I should have stood in if I could have got you out of bed in time. Charlotte is venturing out for her first drive this afternoon at 5/ GBS" With a portrait. Framed. Over-all size 17.75 by 13.75 inches. Illus in cat rms Oct 11 (243) $450

**Ls,** 20 Mar 1891. 1 p, 4to. To W. H. Dircks, pbr's reader at Walter Scott & Co. Angrily demanding that The Quintessence of Ibsenism be published in decent cloth & on good paper. pn Mar 14 (413) £820

**Autograph postcard, sgd,** [18 Feb 1926]. To Ernest Belfort Bax. Concerning a book about Giordano Bruno. star Mar 21 (346) DM600

— 19 July 1950. To Alfredo Benedetti in Buenos Aires. Recommending that Argentinians export all their beef in order to live as long as Shaw has. On verso is a ptd statement headed Vegetarian Diet. wd Nov 15 (19) $900

**ANs,** [n.d.]. On card, 2 by 3.5 inches. Saying he will make another appointment. Framed with photo. wa Oct 28 (53) $260

**Note,** 2 Oct 1944. 1 p, 8vo, on card. Printed message of refusal to speak. With holograph addendum, sgd with initials, regretting that he cannot become vice president of the N.A.-V.S. pn Nov 9 (451) £320 [Wilson]

**Autograph sentiment,** 25 May 1936. On 7 pp, 4to Ms. " This is a childish forgery obviously G.B.S...." MS presents itself as a letter for "My dear David." pba Oct 26 (67) $350

**Photograph, sgd,** [c.1925]. 228mm by 154mm. Shoulder-length port; by H. J. Whitlock & Sons. Illus in cat. Marans collection. CE Apr 17 (90) $1,300

— Anr, [n.d.]. 9.5 by 6.5 inch port photo. By Claude Harris. Mtd. Soiled. Ck Nov 17 (161) £650

**Photograph, sgd & inscr,** 9 June 1925. 11.8 by 9 inches. Inscr & sgd on lower right of image to Frank Reilly. wd Nov 15 (20) $900

— Anr, 16 Jan 1928. 5.75 by 7.75 port photo. By Raphael. Mtd. Over-all size 11 by 14 inches. Illus in cat pba Oct 26 (68) $1,800

### Shelley, Percy Bysshe, 1792-1822
**Check, sgd,** 6 Mar 1818. Payable to Mr. Brown on Shelley's account with Messrs Brookes, for £2 17s. Entirely in Shelley's hand illus in cat S Dec 18 (206) £1,000 [Silverman]

### Shepard, Ernest Howard, 1879-1976
**Original drawing,** "It was a special pencil case," showing Pooh and Piglet & inscr in pencil "Winnie the Pooh p 156". 120mm by 90mm. In pencil, pen & black ink. Sgd with initials. Ck Dec 8 (336) £13,000

### Sheridan, Ann, 1915-67
**Photograph, sgd & inscr,** [n.d.]. 13.25 by 10.37 inches. Seated, in an elaborate gown; by Hurrell. Inscr to "Dear Boy". Illus in cat. rms June 6 (159) $400

### Sheridan, Philip Henry, 1831-88
**ALs,** 28 Apr 1888. 3 pp, 8vo. To William T. Sherman. Explaining that his wife's illness prevents him from attending a banquet. rms June 6 (53) $700

**Signature,** [n.d.]. On 4 by 5 inch page. Sgd as " P. H. Sheridan/ Lt. General/ U. S. A." Mtd. Soiled. pba Feb 22 (178) $80

— Anr, [n.d.]. No size given. With engraved port & an early VI corps badge. Framed. Over-all size 15.5 by 19.5 inches. Detail in cat rms Oct 11 (113) $550

### Sherman, James S., 1855-1912
**Ls,** 8 Jan 1894. 3 pp, 4to. To Gov. Levi P. Morton of NY. Recommending Thomas Wheeler for Superintendant of Public Buildings. rms Nov 30 (301) $200

### Sherman, Roger, Signer from Connecticut
**ALs,** 6 Mar 1790. 3 pp, 4to. To Gov. Samuel Huntington. Informing him about Congressional business, the national debt, etc. Illus in cat. P Dec 13 (339) $24,000

— 12 Aug 1790. 2 pp, 4to. To Samuel Huntington. Reporting on the acts of the 1st Congress. With engraved port. Forbes Magazine collection. CNY May 17 (183) $6,000

**ADs,** 12 Nov 1783. 1 p, oblong 8vo. Receipt "of Pay Table Committee, an Order on Treasurer For Two Hundred Pounds lawful Money for which I am to Acct." With 3-line holograph notation referring to

"Act of Assembly passed in Octobr. 1783 Respecting the Delegates appointed to attend Congress." rms Nov 30 (302) $550
— 9 May 1786. 1 p, oblong 16mo. Order to CT Treasurer John Lawrence to pay funds. sg Feb 1 (216) $225

**Sherman, William Tecumseh, 1820-91**

ALs, 30 Sept 1861. 4 pp, 4to. To Philemon Ewing. Lamenting the lack of discipline among his volunteer soldiers & worrying about his weak military situation. Forbes Magazine collection. CNY May 17 (184) $17,000
— 8 Jan 1862. 1 p, 4to. To Dr. D. L. McGugin of the 3d Iowa Cavalry. About letting Sherman know when there is neglect of the sick. bbc June 24 (53) $2,100
— 20 Jan 1862. 1 p, 4to. To Philemon Ewing. Discussing with his brother-in-law whether or not he is suitable for command. With tear at signature. Illus in cat CNY Dec 15 (234) $7,000
— 20 Jan 1883. 3 pp, 8vo. To Alexander Hamilton Stephens. On various laws governing the acceptance of candidates to a special military school. sg Oct 26 (59) $450
— 7 July 1890. 3 pp, 8vo. To Lloyd Bryce. Discussing an article he is writing for the North American Review. rms Mar 21 (333) $435

Ls, 26 Sept 1878. 5 pp, 4to. To General David G. Colton. Praising the railroad: " Having just arrived from the East...I cannot honestly neglect the opportunity to thank you and your associates personally and officially for having built a first class Steel Rail Road across the great desert..." Sgd as " W. T. Sherman/ General ". Illus in cat pba Feb 22 (179) $3,500

Photograph, sgd, [c.1865]. 153mm by 100mm, mtd. Seated, in uniform; by Brady. Illus in cat. Marans collection. CE Apr 17 (177) $3,200
— Anr, [n.d.]. 9 by 7.5 inches (image); framed, overall size 18 by 20.5 inches. Bust pose, in uniform; by Tensfeld & Kuhn. Illus in cat. rms June 6 (55) $3,500
— Anr, [n.d.]. 4.5 by 6.5 inch sepia cabinet photo. By L Powers. Sgd on verso. sg Sept 28 (249) $900

Signature, [n.d.]. No size given. pba Feb 22 (180) $130

**Shippen, William**

ALs, 17 Jan 1777. 2 pp, 8vo. To Elbridge Gerry. Submitting names of prominent surgeons for appointment in the medical department of the Continental Army. Docketed on verso by Gerry. rms Nov 30 (56) $700

**Shirley, William, 1694-1771**

Ds, 21 Dec 1744. 1 p, folio. Appointing George Gardmer as Judge probate in the name of George II. Toned, dampstained & with numerous fold breaks. pba June 13 (45) $300

**Sholem Aleichem, 1859-1916**

ALs, 14 Dec 1904. 1 p, 8vo. To friends. Letting them know that he has returned home & that everyone is reasonably well. Illus in cat. sg Feb 1 (217) $1,800
— [n.d.]. 4 pp, 8vo, on a single folded sheet. To a friend, referred to as Leonid Tikhonovich. About the month he has just spent in Warsaw, where his 4-act play is having great success. sg June 6 (165) $2,200

Autograph postcard, sgd, 26 Jan 1905. To the Levins in St. Petersburg. Inquiring about his daughter, Ernestina, who is visiting their daughter. sg June 6 (166) $1,400

**Shostakovich, Dimitri, 1906-75**

Autograph music, Byelinsky No 12/Moderato; comprising a passage of 20 bars of his music for the film biography of Vissarion Byelinsky, Op.85, [c.1950]. 1 p, 4to. Full score, notated for strings on 2 five-stave systems. Sgd. Illus in cat. S Dec 1 (324) £1,900

Ms, Suite for 2 Pianos, Op.6; 1922. 68 pp, folio. Notated on 3 systems per page, 4 staves each. In a scribal hand, with autograph corrections & annotations throughout. Inscr on tp; sgd. S Dec 1 (322) £1,700

Series of 6 A Ls s, 1944 to 1960. 9 pp, 8vo. To Kara Karayev. About his compositions, financial problems, political forces, recipient's works, etc. S Dec 1 (314) £20,000

ALs, 23 Aug 1924. 4 pp, 8vo. To Valerian Mikhailovich Bogdanov-Berezkovsky, here addressed as "Dear and greatly respected little prick". About accosting a woman in the street. sg Feb 1 (218) $1,700
— 4 Apr 1925. 2.5 pp on half-sheet torn from book of minutes, 4to. To Valerian Mikhailovich Bogdanov-Berezkovsky, here addressed as "Red Critic". Reproaching him for missing an appointment; goes on about his loneliness & sexual frustration. sg Feb 1 (219) $1,300
— [1958]. 1 p, 16mo. To the Registrar of Oxford University. Thanking him for the award of an honorary doctorate. S May 15 (492) £460

Autograph postcard, sgd, 26 Nov 1965. To the composer Lobkovsky. wa Oct 28 (134) $200

Autograph quotation, 9 bars from the finale of his 8th Symphony, sgd; 26 Jan 1944. 1 p, 23cm by 18cm. Inscr in other hands on verso. Illus in cat. S Dec 1 (325) £1,000
— Anr, 9 bars from the finale of his 8th Symphony, 26 Jan 1944. 1 p, 23cm by 18cm. Sgd. Illus in cat. S May 15 (493) £2,000
— Anr, opening 10 bars of the 1st movement of his 10th Symphony, sgd; 23 June 1969. 1 p, 11cm by 21cm. Inscr by Franz Schreker on verso. Illus in cat. S Dec 1 (323) £1,400

**Shtemenko, Sergei Matveevich, 1907-76**

Ls, 17 May 1943. 2 pp, 8vo & folio. To Marshal Voronov. Sending a list of code names (included). rms June 6 (636) $1,300

**Sibelius, Jean, 1865-1957**

Collection of ALs & autograph quotation, 21 & 23 Jan 1931. 2 pp, 8vo. Recipient unnamed. About Beethoven. Laid down on musical quotation, sgd, beginning 20 bars of the violin part of the slow movement of his Violin Concerto, Op.47. Illus in cat. S Dec 1 (326) £2,400

ALs, 5 July 1906. 2 pp, folio. To Robert Lienau. About his symphonic poem Pohjola's Daughter & plans for performances of some other works. S Dec 1 (332) £550

# SIBELIUS

— 19 Oct 1913. 1 p, 4to. In German, to an unidentified friend. Agreeing that his Fourth Symphony might be called a Nature Symphony. sg June 6 (167) $600
— 18 Oct 1931. 1 p, 4to. To Poul Knudsen. Returning an opera. With a port. Illus in cat. rms Mar 21 (334) $650
Ls, 14 Feb 1940. 1 p, 4to. Recipient unnamed. About the invasion of Finland by the Soviet Union. In English. Framed. S Dec 1 (331) £360
Autograph postcard, sgd, 18 Mar 1904. To Herr Kistner. Stating his age & birthdate. CE May 22 (427) $130
Ds s (2), 4 & 22 June 1907. 2 pp, 8vo. Contracts with the pbr K. E. Holm. star Mar 22 (1059) DM950
Autograph quotation, 11 bars of music, notated in short score on 3 systems of 2 staves each, 3 Feb 1933. 1 p, c.16cm by 13cm, cut from larger sheet. Laid down with ptd visiting card & other material. Illus in cat. S Dec 1 (328) £1,000
— Anr, opening 9 bars of his 4th Symphony, [n.d.] 1 p, 8vo.In short score; sgd & inscr at head. With a photograph. Illus in cat. S Dec 1 (329) £1,300
— Anr, 10 bars from his 1st Symphony, scored for solo clarinet & timpani, [n.d.]. 1 p, c.13cm by 26.5cm, cut from larger sheet. S May 15 (494) £450
Photograph, sgd, [c.1930]. 226mm by 165mm. Half length, looking out of the window, by Fred Runeberg. Marans collection. CE Apr 17 (260) $600

## Sibley, John
ALs, 15 Aug 1804. 9 pp, folio. Recipient unnamed. Describing the anxiety of the inhabitants of the area of the Louisiana Purchase at the change in government & his own efforts to calm their fears. Sang - Engelhard collections. CNY Jan 26 (181) $5,000
— 2 Apr 1805. 10 pp, folio. To Sir William Dunbar. Written from Natchitoches, Louisiana, setting forth his observations on the Red River and its adjacent country & the inhabitants. Illus in cat CNY Jan 26 (183) $16,000

## Siegbahn, Karl Manne Georg, 1886-1978
Ls, 13 May 1946. 1 p, 4to. To Rudolf Ladenburg. Inquiring about a conference on nuclear physics at Princeton. star Mar 21 (620) DM240

## Siemens, Werner von, 1816-92
ALs, 24 Apr 1862. 1 p, 8vo. To Heinrich Kiepert. Concerning the organization of an upcoming election. star Mar 21 (621) DM650

## Sigismund I, King of Poland, 1467-1548
Document, [24 Jan] 1525. 1 p, vellum, folio. Confirmation of privileges for 2 manors granted by King Wenceslaus in 1404. HN May 15 (2714) DM4,000

## Sigismund I, Emperor, 1368-1437
Document, 31 Oct 1427. 1 p, vellum, 255mm by 525mm. Permission to the City of Nuremberg to receive various rights & properties from the Burggraf of Nuremberg, Markgraf Friedrich von Brandenburg. Including confirmation of receipt of the grant by Heinrich, Abbot of St. Egidius in Nuremberg, 31 May 1432. C Nov 29 (4) £750

## Signac, Paul, 1863-1935
ALs, [1891]. 2 pp, 8vo. To Camille Pissaro. Asking for a painting in his possession for an exhibition. star Mar 21 (718) DM480

## Silbermann, Andreas, 1678-1734
ADs, 27 Dec 1719. 1 p, 4to. Bill for repairs on a church organ in Strasbourg. Including autograph receipt, sgd, at foot. Illus in cat. star Mar 22 (1062) DM5,500

## Silbermann, Gottfried, 1683-1753
— ALBRECHT, JOHANN LORENZ. - Ms, preface for Michael Praetorius's Kurzer Entwurf derjenigen Dinge, welche Bey Probirung ... eines neuen Orgelwerks in Acht zu nehmen, & appendix containing detailed descriptions of organs built by Silbermann & others, [1760s]. About 135 pp, various sizes, in 19th-cent bds. Presumably unpbd; partly probably autograph. S May 15 (497) £8,800

## Silesia
— KNOCHENMEISTER, CAPT. HANS. - Document, [21 Sept] 1414. 1 p, vellum, folio. Confirmation of a document of 1371 granting Weigel Zachinkirch an annual rent from the village of Kletschkau. Including seal of King Wenceslaus IV of Bohemia. star Mar 22 (1643) DM1,400

## Silliman, Benjamin, 1816-85
ALs, 10 Jan 1828. 1 p, 8vo. To Josiah Whitney. Advising Whitney to find out about a new work that might aid his brother's illness. With docket in anr hand identifying Eli Whitney as the subject of the letter. Toned & with tears in the margin. rms Oct 11 (353) $250

## Simrock, Fritz, 1837-1901
ALs, 4 Nov 1877. 3 pp, 8vo. To [Hedwig von Holstein]. Inquiring about the cancellation of a performance of Brahms's 2d Symphony. star Mar 22 (982) DM900

## Sinatra, Frank
Ds, 21 Sept 1960. 3 pp (carbon copy). Contract between Sinatra & Fred Kohlmar Productions for The Devil at Four O'Clock. Also sgd by Catherine Bennett for Kohlmar. Sold with photo of Sinatra. Ck Dec 14 (183) $280
— 12 Dec 1973. 1 p, 4to. "Certification of Winding Up and Dissolution." Concerning Cal Jet Airways. Also sgd by Milton A. Rudin & Nathan Golden. Stamped. With folds & staple holes. sg Sept 28 (251) $250

## Sitwell, Dame Edith, 1887-1964
Photograph, sgd & inscr, [c.1930]. 195mm by 239mm (image). At her desk in medieval dress; by Howard Colts(?). Inscr to Evelyn. Mount imperf. Marans collection. CE Apr 17 (91) $400

## Sitwell, Sacheverell
Autograph Ms, essay, The Sleeping Beauty [pbd 1948]. 16 leaves, folio, in a notebook. S Dec 18 (422) £650 [Ritchie]

**Sivori, Camillo, 1815-94**
**Autograph quotation,** Allegro Cantabile, 6 Nov 1841. 1 p, 8vo. 15 bars, sgd. star Mar 22 (1064) DM210

**Skorzeny, Otto, 1908-75**
**Ls,** 5 May 1959. 1 p, 4to. To Norman E. Heilman. Responding to a request for weapons used by the Legion Condor. rms June 6 (633) $135

**Skroup, Frantisek Jan, 1801-62**
**Autograph quotation,** Trio pour le Piano, Violon et Violoncelle, Oeuv.27, 16 June 1846. 1 p, folio. 7 bars, sgd. star Mar 22 (1066) DM280

**Slavery**
**ADs,** 10 Mar 1856. 1 p, 7.75 by 5.25 inches. Concerning the fate of slaves of the estate of Erasmus Culpepper: " deed the following named Negroes allotted and set off to Mrs. Harriet Pate wife of F. Pate...." Dar Oct 19 (43) $100

**Ds,** 16 Apr 1799. 1 p, 8vo. "note of hand for one hundred and fourteen pounds for which when paid will be in full for a negro man sold him". With break. pba June 13 (35) $90

**Document,** 1 Nov 1812. 1 p, 4to. Manifest of slaves on board the schooner Fanny & Maria, sgd by the ship's Master, Stephen Miller. sg Feb 1 (221) $550

— 24 Jan 1826. Bill of sale for the slave Judy & her child Ann, for $300, to Robert Tweedy, in Washington. 1 p, 4to. sg Mar 28 (315) $275

— 19 Aug 1844. 1 p, folio. Bill of sale for the slave Judson Diggs, for $100, to Elisha D. Owen. sg Mar 28 (317) $150

— 10 Feb 1851. 1 p, 8vo. Bill of sale for the mulatto slave William Mathews, for $400, to Brooke Mackall. sg Mar 28 (318) $150

— 7 Dec 1852. 1 p, 4to. Bill of sale for the slave Theodore Bowe, for $234.50, to Brooke McKall. sg Mar 28 (315) $275

— 12 Dec 1856. 1 p, 8 by 10 inches. Listing the details and value of the personal estate of Mrs. Susan McDuffie. Dar Oct 19 (44) $100

— KNIGHT, SARA. - ADs of Manumission, 7 Mar 1797. 1 p, 4to. Executed by Sarah Knight of Maryland, allowing the eventual freedom of her 3 slaves. sg Mar 28 (325) $500

**Smeaton, John, 1724-92**
**Ms,** The Report of John Smeaton Engineer upon the Harbour of Christchurch in Hampshire.... [Ansthorpe, 13 Aug 1764]. 10 pp, folio, sewn into wraps. b May 30 (40) £300

**Smetana, Bedrich, 1824-84**
**ALs,** 16 Apr 1873. 1 p, 8vo. Recipient unnamed. Announcing his visit. Illus in cat. star Mar 22 (1067) DM3,600

**Smith, Adam, 1723-90**
**ALs,** 6 Oct 1783. 4 pp, 4to. To his pbr. Informing him that the revisions for a new Ed of his book are almost finished & that he will have to postpone his visit in London, & discussing political matters. star Mar 21 (622) DM44,000

**Smith, Edward E., 1890-1965**
**Autograph Ms,** Cloud and the Boneheads [pbd as The Vortex Blaster Makes War]. [1942] 21 leaves, 278mm by 214mm. Minor corrections. cb Oct 17 (566) $1,500
See also: Campbell, John W. & Smith

**Smith, Joseph, 1805-44**
**Ds,** 10 Apr 1844. 1 p, 55mm by 200mm. Certifying that "The City Treasurer [of Nauvoo] will pay...one dollar for service as City watch" to Warren Smith. Sgd as Mayor of Nauvoo. CNY Dec 15 (120) $3,800

**Smith, Samuel F., 1808-95**
**Autograph Ms,** 4 stanzas of "America". 13 March 1888. Smith has added "Written in 1832". Penned in 2 columns. Darkened with age and stained. Illus in cat sg Sept 28 (252) $800

— Autograph Ms, 4 stanzas of "America". 15 Apr 1885. 2 pp, 8vo. Sgd & dated at the end: "S. F. Smith Written Feb 1832. Apr. 15, 1885." Text light. Top margin torn. pba Oct 26 (71) $850

**Autograph transcript,** the opening words of America. Sgd 23 Oct 1895 & with note "Written in 1832". rms Nov 30 (304) $300

**Transcript,** sgd, America. 1 p, 4to, sgd & dated 22 May 1895. Framed in lacquered display case with 2 brass plaques. cb June 25 (2577) $900

**ALs,** 21 Oct 1808. 1 p, 8vo. To David Pell Secor. About the house where he was born and his education. Sgd as " S. F. Smith". Tipped to larger page. Illus in cat pba Feb 22 (97) $150

— 20 Dec 1892. 3 pp, 8vo. To David Pell Secor. About his visit to the World's Fair. Tipped to a larger page. With a sketch by Secor mentioned in the letter & also with an ANs by Secor. pba June 13 (225) $300

— 28 May 1895. 1 p, 8vo. To David Pell Secor. Concerning a plaster cast of his hand: " This certfies that the plaster cast of my right hand - the hand which wrote the hymn ' My country, 'tis of thee' was Taken, at your suggestion by Mr. Cavolti in Bridgeport, Conn., May 11, 1895." Tipped to a larger sheet, With transcription. Illus in cat rms Oct 11 (356) $750

— 8 Oct 1895. 4 pp, 8vo. To David Pell Secor. Thanking him for a gift & mentioning singing his hymn, My Country 'tis of Thee in memory of President Grant. Tipped to a larger page. pba June 13 (224) $550

**Photograph, sgd,** [n.d.]. 4.5 by 8 inch sepia portrait photo. Overall size 8 by 11 inches. Illus in cat pba Feb 22 (98) $450

**Signature,** 27 Mar 1895. On a folio engraved port. Featuring an engraved facsimilie of a stanza from his hymn, America. Foxed. Tipped to a larger sheet which is torn & missing a corner. rms Oct 11 (355) $325

**Smith, Stevie, 1902-71**
**Autograph transcript,** of her poem, Scorpion. On a postcard to Jean MacGibbon, postmarked 8 Oct 1970, sgd. S Dec 18 (423) £280 [Davids]

Collection of 3 Ls s & 2 ALs s, 3 Jan 1946 to Nov 1969, Various lengths, no size given. To Polly Hill. About poetry. Margins creased. Ck Nov 17 (163) £400

**Smith, Gerrit, 1797-1874**
Photograph, sgd & inscr, 5 Sept 1862. Carte size, mtd on larger sheet. Inscr to Mary R. Smith. Illus in cat. rms Mar 21 (335) $210

**Smits, Jimmy —&**
**Bernsen, Corbin —& Others**
Signature, 3 Mar 1986. On 118 p, 4to LA Law Script. With cast photo. rms Oct 11 (370) $260

**Smuts, Jan Christiaan, 1870-1950**
ALs, 2 Feb 1927. 2 pp, 8vo. Recipient unnamed. Explaining the intentions of his book Holism and Evolution. star Mar 22 (1383) DM250

**Snow, W. R.**
Autograph Ms, Gammer Gurton Illustrated. 1868. 16 leaves, comprising frontis of a clown, pictorial tp, 13 large illusts of nursery rhyme subjects & final leaf with 2 words formed by contortionists. Each page sgd with monogram & dated 1868. S Nov 2 (566) £750 [Hirsch]

**Solms-Braunfels, Johann Albrecht, Graf von, 1563-1623**
ALs, 8 Sept 1618. 3 pp, folio. To an unnamed prince. Wondering about the attitude of the Bohemians in the current war. star Mar 22 (1239) DM650

**Solomon, Simeon**
Original drawings, (10) to illus One Two Come Buckle my Shoe. [1860s or 1870s] 4to, in mor extra by Zaehnsdorf. Colored crayon drawings, each captioned & sgd with initials. S May 16 (509) £3,600

**Sontag, Henriette, 1806-54**
ALs, 6 Feb 1827. 3 pp, 16mo. To an unnamed lady. Sending a theater ticket. star Mar 22 (1068) DM300

**Soong Mei-ling (Mme. Chiang Kai-shek).** See: Chiang Kai-shek & Soong Mei-ling (Mme. Chiang Kai-shek)

**Sophie, Kurfuerstin von Hannover, 1630-1714**
ALs, 19 Feb [1656]. 4 pp, 4to. To her mother. Interesting letter discussing relatives & other members of royal & aristocratic households. In French. HN May 15 (2584) DM5,000

— 20 Jan 1663. 1 p, 4to. To an unnamed princess. Assuring her of her good will & devotion. Illus in cat. star Mar 22 (1352) DM2,200

**Soult, Nicolas Jean, Duc de Dalmatie, 1769-1851**
Series of 45 A Ls s, 23 Jan to 25 Dec 1811. About 127 pp, 4to. To his wife, Louise. Describing important battles during the Peninsular War. C June 26 (341) £2,500

**Sousa, John Philip, 1854-1932**
Autograph transcript, 5 bars of music from the Jack Tar march. Sgd & dated 1904. wa Oct 28 (135) $300

Ds, 28 Aug 1908. 1 p, 4to. Payment voucher from Willow Grove Park for music furnished from 23 Aug to 29 Aug 1908. Sgd as received at bottom. Framed with sgd photo, 1905. cb June 25 (2578) $700

Autograph quotation, Aug 1900. On verso 1 p, 3.75 by 6.5 inch album leaf. Trimmed. sg Sept 28 (253) $250

— Anr, 16 Nov 1922. No size given. On verso of a Flag Custodian's calling card featuring the American flag. 3 bars of music from The Stars and Stripes Forever. Illus in cat rms Oct 11 (357) $600

— Anr, 5 bars from "The Stars and Stripes Forever". [2 Dec 1930]. 1 p, 3.75 by 5.1 inches. Paper aged & stained. With pencil note on verso dating it at 2 Dec 1930. Illus in cat sg Sept 28 (254) $425

Photograph, sgd & inscr, sgd & inscr, 1928. 7 by 9.5 inches. wa Oct 28 (136) $220

**Southey, Robert, 1774-1843**
ALs, 26 Apr 1819. 3 pp, 4to. To Maj. Gen. Peachy. About seeing the publisher Ticknor & the health of Walter Scott, & his own wife & baby. pn June 13 (249) £460

— 14 Nov 1825. 2 pp, 4to. To an author who had written on Coleridge's Aids to Reflection & on phrenology. Giving advice on writing. pn Mar 14 (414) £260

**Soyer, Raphael**
Christmas card, [n.d.]. No size given. With anr similar card. pba June 13 (226) $50

**Space Program, Soviet**
Typescript carbon copy, Taetigkeits-Bericht, report on the organization of the Soviet's top secret rocket development facility in Germany. Bleicherode, 1 Nov 1945. Booklet in paper covers, with foldout diagrams & charts. Sgd on authorization leaf by Gherman, Reitz & Chertok. Boris Chertok's copy P Mar 16 (10) $700

— COSMONAUTS. - Group photograph of all 11 flown cosmonauts from the Vostok and Voshkod Programs. Sgd by all. Circa 1966. Oblong 4to, 5.5 by 7.75 inches. sg June 6 (47) $4,600

— FEOKTISTOV, KONSTANTIN. - Autograph Ms, history of the Vostok missions. 11 pp plus 2 drawings, sgd & dated 12 Jan 1996. P Mar 16 (33) $1,200

— GROETTRUP, HELMUT. - Das Geraet A9. Bleicherode, 20 Feb 1946. Typescript copy of early technical report on the A9 rocket & its flight control system. With diagrams & folding plate. Boris Chertok's copy P Mar 16 (11) $900

— LUNA-8. - 2 handwritten algorithms for the control of the Luna spacecraft, 4 & 6 Dec 1965. 2 strips of paper, 603mm by 89mm, in ink & pencil. Boris E. Chertok Collection P Mar 16 (119) $1,600

— LUNAKHOD-2. - Collection of 4 Ms descriptions of Lunakhod-2, prepared by the engineers who created & guided the Lunakhod-2. About 40 pp, with photographs & graphs. [1971-76] With a statement by Oleg G. Ivanovsky concerning this material [c.1994]. With a copy of a book in Russian, A Moving Laboratory on the Moon - Lunakhod-1, Moscow, 1971. P Mar 16 (141) $900

— SALYUT 3. - Ms leaf from the log book of Salyut 3, containing the 1st message to be transmitted from the space station. Sgd by Pavel Popovich & Yuri Artyukhin & with postscript added after landing. 24 June - 24 Aug 1975. P Mar 16 (171) $2,250

— SOYUZ 26, SALYUT 6. - Autograph Ms notes on the scientific observation of the earth & its atmosphere from Salyut 6, by Georgy M. Grechko, with drawings by Yuri V. Romanenko, 1977. 46 pp, various sizes. With explanatory notes written by Grechko in 1994. P Mar 16 (237) $3,000

— SOYUZ 32, SALYUT 6. - Acrylic sketch on nylon by Andrei Sokolov, with notes concerning its accuracy by cosmonauts V. Lyakhov & V. Ryumin. 419mm by 314mm. [1979]. P Mar 16 (246) $4,000

— SOYUZ 32, SALYUT 6. - Acrylic sketch on nylon of the Black Sea from outer space, with notes concerning its accuracy by cosmonauts V. Lyakhov & V. Ryumin. 410mm by 308mm. [1979]. P Mar 16 (247) $4,000

— SOYUZ 32, SALYUT 6. - Pocket cyclogram describing the operation of Salyut-6 from 25 Feb to 20 Aug 1979. 83mm by 1,740mm, in 2 sections joined with tape. Photomechanically ptd, highlighted with colored inks, portions amended with white paint & relabled in ink, with pencil notes. Mtd into folding cardbd cover with sgd 5-page statement by Gen. Kerim A. Kerimov. P Mar 16 (251) $300

— SOYUZ 39, SALYUT 6. - Pocket cyclogram describing the operation of Soyuz 39 from launch to docking with the Salyut 6 Space Station, 22-30 Mar 1981. 13 folds (each representing an orbit or group of orbits), 95mm by 622mm, lettered in a calligraphic hand, with many colored diagrams. Presented to Gen. Kerim A. Kerimov by the mission's launch engineers. Kerim A. Kerimov collection P Mar 16 (255) $200

— SOYUZ 9. - On-Board Flight Manual & Logbook, 1-19 June 1970. About 700 pp, 235mm by 178mm, in cloth-backed bds with arms & cipher of Soviet Union, spiral-bound in 3 rings. Partly in the hand of Andrian G. Nikolayev. P Mar 16 (161) $4,000

— SOYUZ 9. - Ptd map of the world embellished in black & colored inks with the daily orbital trajectories of Soyuz 9. 629mm by 1,410mm, sgd by Nikolayev & Sevastyanov, 10 June 1970. With 2 sgd Ms statements about the map by Nikolayev. Andrian G. Nikolayev collection P Mar 16 (163) $6,500

— SOYUZ T-14. - Group of notebooks & papers kept by cosmonaut-researcher Vladimir V. Vasyutin during his training period, c.1977-80. Together, 7 notebooks & 21 loose leaves. With related material. P Mar 16 (321) $1,500

— SOYUZ T-5, SALYUT-7. - 6 annotated leaves from the logbook of cosmonaut Anatoly N. Berezovoy, 13 May to 10 Dec 1982. Each 317mm by 222mm, in various felt-tip inks & pencil. About his life on Salyut-7 obital station. P Mar 16 (270) $1,500

— SOYUZ T-5, SALYUT-7. - Space correspondence between Anatoly N. Berezovoy & his wife, Lida Berezovaya, 13 May to 10 Dec 1982. With related material. P Mar 16 (273) $4,250

— SOYUZ T-5, SALYUT-7. - Space correspondence between Anatoly N. Berezovoy & his daughter, Tanya, comprizing 2 drawings by Tanya & 2 letters by Berezovoy with signatures of other members of the crew, 13 May to 10 Dec 1982. P Mar 16 (274) $2,400

— SOYUZ T-5, SALYUT-7. - Space correspondence between Anatoly N. Berezovoy & his son, Sergei, comprizing 2 letters to his son & 3 letters from his son, 13 May to 10 Dec 1982. With related material. P Mar 16 (275) $3,250

— SOYUZ T-5, SOYUZ T-6, SALYUT-7. - Cartoon drawing by Jean Loup Chretien depicting 4 French candidates for the flight, brought on board Salyut 7. Inscr to the Russian crew on 2 July 1982. Sgd & inscr by Anatoly Berezovoy "Space mail. Delivered to Salyut 7 aboard SS Soyuz T-6 on 26 June 1982". P Mar 16 (277) $1,100

— SOYUZ T-5, SOYUZ T-6, SALYUT-7. - Special edition of Izvestia ptd for the crew of Salyut 7, 16 June 1982. 4 pp, 597mm by 419mm. Inscr by Vladimir A. Dzhanibekov & sgd by cosmonauts Berezovoy, Lebedev, Ivanchenkov & Chretien. Anatoly N. Berezovoy collection P Mar 16 (281) $1,400

— SOYUZ T-5. - Draft cyclogram of the 1st mission aboard the space station, ending 22 Oct 1982. Roll of computer printout paper, 1,219mm by 419mm, hand-colored in yellow & green with orbital periods. Some fold breaks. Valery I. Rozhdestvensky collection P Mar 16 (266) $800

— SOYUZ T-5. - Time chart cyclogram program for the mission & spacecraft, 13 May to 2 Nov 1982. 1,511mm by 397mm, on continuous roll computer paper. Printout with color pencil added by hand in purple, blue & yellow & captioned in multicolor felt-tipped pens. Some annotations in ballpoint pen. Sgd by the Soyuz T5 crew: A. N. Berezovoy & A. Lebedev; also sgd by the crew of the joint French-Soviet mission Soyuz T7: V. Dzhanibekov, A. Ivanchenkov & J. L. Chretien. Anatoly N. Berezovoy collection P Mar 16 (268) $2,000

— SOYUZ TM-2. - Graphite & color pencil drawing of Mir spacewalk, 11 Apr 1987, by Yuri V. Romanenko. 190mm by 260mm, inscr, 12 Apr 1987. With related material. Yuri V. Romanenko collection P Mar 16 (336) $1,100

— SOYUZ TM-2. - Ptd map of the Earth with projects of the orbit of the Mir Space Station. 660mm by 1,010mm. Sgd by cosmonauts Yuri Romankeno & A. Alexandrov, & used by Romanenko in space, 5 Feb to 29 Dec 1987. Yuri V. Romanenko collection P Mar 16 (335) $500

— SOYUZ-APOLLO / APOLLO-SOYUZ. - Joint Operating Instructions Log Book for Spacecraft Apollo-Soyuz, 1975. 34 ptd leaves, 187mm by 149mm, in 2-ring notebook. Unflown. Sgd by cosmonaut Alexei A. Leonov. P Mar 16 (181) $2,250

— SOYUZ-APOLLO / APOLLO-SOYUZ. - Cyclogram on 7 3-fold graph paper sheets, each describing 1 day of the mission. Each sheet 6 by 16 inches, sewn into paper cover with drawing of the Soyuz-Apollo insignia, sgd by Gen. Kerim A. Kerimov, 11 July 1975.

With Kerimov's sgd 3-page statement. P Mar 16 (183) $600
— SOYUZ-APOLLO / APOLLO-SOYUZ. - Flown log book for the Russian commander of the mission, Alexei A. Leonov. 135 leaves including blanks, 219mm by 156mm, in cloth-backed bds stamped with arms & cipher of the Soviet Union, spiral bound with 3 rings. Includes numerous sketches & pencil drawings. P Mar 16 (186) $7,500
— SOYUZ-SALYUT PROGRAM. - Autograph notes with sketches & diagrams on the urgent repair of Orlan Spacesuit Shell-7, 28-29 Oct 1983. 6 pp, various sizes. On Salyut-7 Station. Working draft of engineer Oleg F. Gerasimenko-Kartenko. P Mar 16 (137) $1,100
— VOSKHOD 1. - ANs of Sergei Korolev, 1 June 1963. 7 lines on a 1-page autograph memorandum sgd by his deputy, Mikhail Tikhonravov, 1 June 1963. About a group of aerospace engineers being considered for cosmonaut training. Valery Kubasov collection P Mar 16 (86) $1,200
— VOSKHOD 1. - Program of the Impact of the Descent Apparatus of the Voskhod Object. 4 map 1964. Blueprint document of the report, 9 pp, in notebook. Valery Kubasov collection P Mar 16 (90) $200
— VOSKHOD 1. - Typed list of 10 scientists to be considered as candidates for Voskhod 1. 27 Dec [1963?]. 2 pp, 203mm by 289mm. With additions & correction in blue pencil in the hand of Sergei Korolev. Valery Kubasov collection P Mar 16 (87) $1,000
— VOSKHOD 2. - Emergency Escape Order for Voskhod 2, 16 Mar 1965. 1 p, 289mm by 203mm. Sgd by Sergei Korolev & with related statement by Korolov concerning the order. P Mar 16 (97) $2,000
— VOSKHOD 2. - Notebooks containing daybook notations by workers & managers preparing the Voskhod prototype & the Voskhod 2 mission itself. Baikonur, 1 Dec 1964 to 17 Mar 1965. In 2 ruled notebooks, c.170pp, sgd & dated by various participants in the projects. P Mar 16 (96) $1,000
— VOSKHOD 2. - Program for Conducting Independent and Complex Tests of the Ejection Seats of Elbrus Pilots and Berkut Spacesuits. Blueprint document, 87 pp. Nov 1964. P Mar 16 (94) $200
— VOSKHOD 2. - Report of the Strength Test of the Volga Airlock. Blueprint document, 15 pp in a notebook, 302mm by 232mm. 1 Mar 1965. P Mar 16 (95) $600
— VOSTOK & VOSKHOD PROGRAMS. - Autograph Ms of Alexei A. Leonov about the origins of the Soviet Space Program. 4 leaves. With accompanying typescript, sgd & dated 15 June 1994. P Mar 16 (111) $800
— VOSTOK & VOSKHOD PROGRAMS. - Group photograph of all flown cosmonauts, c.1965-67. 140mm by 194mm, sgd by Gagarin, Titov, Nikolayev, Popovich, Bykovsky, Tereshkova, Leonov, Belyayev, Feoktistov, Komarov & Yegorov; inscr on reverse by Nikolayev. Andrian G. Nikolayev collection P Mar 16 (102) $5,500
— VOSTOK & VOSKHOD PROGRAMS. - Group photograph of the 11 Vostok & Voskhod cosmonauts, 1965-67. 194mm by 235mm. Sgd by Gagarin, Tereshkova,
Bykovsky, Nikolayev, Popovich, Titov, Leonov, Feoktistov & Belayev. Inscr in a calligraphic hand to Georgy S. Shonin. P Mar 16 (103) $1,700
— VOSTOK & VOSKHOD PROGRAMS. - Group photograph of the 11 Vostok & Voskhod cosmonauts, 1965-67. 140mm by 225mm. Sgd by Kerimov, Leonov, Gagarin, Titov, Bykovsky, Tereshkova, Nikolayev, Yegorov, Popovich, Feoktistov & Belayayev. Mtd on cardbd. With sgd holograph statement by Leonov. P Mar 16 (109) $4,000
— VOSTOK & VOSKHOD PROGRAMS. - Resolution of birthday congratulations to General Karpov. [2 Feb 1971]. Typed in blue ink & sgd by N. Kuznetsov, N. Somsonov, V. Popov & cosmonauts Beregovoy & Nikolayev. Mtd on large folding card ptd incolors & sgd by cosmonauts Volkov, Leonov, Kubasov, Filipchenko, Krunov, Shatalov, Yeliseyev, Bykovsky & Gorbatko. In folder. P Mar 16 (110) $500
— VOSTOK PROGRAM. - Autograph Ms notes of Evgeny A. Karpov on the flight of Vostok 1 [n.d.]. 10 pp, 289mm by 203mm. Karpov family collection P Mar 16 (38) $11,000
— VOSTOK PROGRAM. - Autograph Ms by Alexei Leonov about the first squad of cosmonauts. [c.1994] 2 pp. Yuri M. Baginsky collection P Mar 16 (84) $800
— VOSTOK PROGRAM. - Blueprint of the pressurized inner shell of the Sk-1 spacesuit, sgd by Chief Designer Alekseyev, 6 Dec 1960. 1 p, cyanotype, 17 by 30.75 inches. Galina I. Afanasenko's copy P Mar 16 (31) $1,100
— VOSTOK PROGRAM. - Collection of 3 autograph Ms s by Evgeny A. Karpov relating to cosmonaut Valentina Tereshkova & the Vostok cosmonauts. 76 pp, removed from notebooks, stapled & sewn together. P Mar 16 (71) $4,250
— VOSTOK PROGRAM. - Ignition control schedule for the launch of Vostok 6, sgd by many of those present at the launch & later by the first cosmonauts. 1 p, 200mm by 292mm. Karpov family collection P Mar 16 (73) $3,000
— VOSTOK PROGRAM. - Photograph of Yuri Gagarin with State officials & cosmonauts taken 9 Apr 1961, 3 days before the flight of Vostok 1. 5 by 7 inches, sgd on recto by Gagarin & on verso with notes by K. A. Kerimov, M. V. Keldysh, Kuznetsov & N. A. Pilyugin. Yuri M. Baginsky collection P Mar 16 (35) $3,000
— VOSTOK PROGRAM. - Photograph of the 1st 4 cosmonauts, sgd by all on lower left margin. 105mm by 152mm. Karpov family collection P Mar 16 (44) $1,600
— VOSTOK PROGRAM. - Photograph of the 1st "Gagarin" Cosmonaut Corps, c.May 1961. 178mm by 241mm. Sgd by Korolev, Gagarin, Titov, Nikolayev, Popovich, Bykovsky, Shonin & others. With the pennant designed for the Military Space Forces, as shown in the photo. Yuri M. Baginsky collection P Mar 16 (46) $3,750
— VOSTOK PROGRAM. - Photograph of the Earth from space, taken from Vostok-2 on 7 Aug 1961 by cosmonaut Gherman Stepanovich TItov. 222mm by

165mm. Captioned & sgd by Titov. Yuri M. Baginsky collection P Mar 16 (60) $6,500

— VOSTOK PROGRAM. - Protocol for Inspection of the First Woman's Space Suit.... 1 July 1963. 6 pp, 298mm by 203mm. Sgd by 17 members of the Zvezda Inspection Team. P Mar 16 (75) $800

— VOSTOK PROGRAM. - Protocol of 14 Apr 1961 on Spacesuit SK-1 inspection after flight of Vostok 1. 3 pp, 302mm by 216mm, carbon copy. Sgd by all 8 members of the commission that made the inspection. P Mar 16 (42) $600

— VOSTOK PROGRAM. - Protocol of 29 Mar 1961 on the inspection of the space suit emergency kit, etc. 9 pp, 302mm by 216mm. P Mar 16 (27) $500

— VOSTOK PROGRAM. - Report on Debriefing of Cosmonaut Pilots Bykovsky & Tereshkova on the results of flights on Vostok-5 & Vostok-6 in space on 14 to 19 June 1963. Typed document, 6 pp. Dated 24 Sept 1963. P Mar 16 (74) $2,250

— VOSTOK PROGRAM. - Report on Results of Recovery Mission of Vostok 3KA-2 space capsule to the Chief Designer of Zvezda Plant 918, Comrade Alexeev. 26 Mar 1961. 3 pp, carbon copy with signatures of 2 members of the rescue team at foot of 3d page. P Mar 16 (26) $800

— VOSTOK PROGRAM. - Technical diaries kept by the manufacturer's group responsible for the pilots' seats on the Vostok flights, 1 Apr to 27 June 1961 & 22 Feb to 17 June 1963. In 2 half-cloth notebooks. Boris Mikhailov collection P Mar 16 (58) $1,000

— VOSTOK PROGRAM. - Typed document, 2-22 Dec 1960. 20 pp, 276mm by 197mm. Temporary technical terms for the SK-1 space suite flown on Vostok 3KA-2. Sgd by 4 members of the design team. P Mar 16 (29) $400

— VOSTOK PROGRAM. - Typescript carbon copy of the draft copy of the Records File for Vostok 2, made by Gherman Stapanovich Titov, for submission to the International Aeronautical Federation for new records set for flightduration & orbital flight range. 25 leaves in Russian & 22 in English, 311mm by 222mm. Tp sgd in pencil by Sergei Korolev, 25 Aug 1961. Konstantin P. Feokistov collection P Mar 16 (61) $17,000

— YEFIMOV, VIKTOR P. - Autograph working draft containing extensive notes & diagrams in ink & pencil of specifications for system designs for portions of spacesuits, with photographs of the completed designs. 40 pp, 298mm by 206mm, in notebook. Illus in cat P Mar 16 (32) $700

— ZOND 3. - Typed memorandum produced by Zond-3 Control Group to Sergei P. Korolev reporting on probe photographs of a portion of the dark side of the moon on 16-17 August 1965, with autograph commentary by Korolev written in pencil diagonally across text of document. 17 Aug 1965. 1 p, 279mm by 197mm. Greb Y. Maksimov collection P Mar 16 (113) $1,900

— ZOND 3. - Typed memorandum produced by Zond-3 Control Group to Sergei P. Korolev reporting on probe photographs of the dark side of the moon on 9-10 November 1965, with autograph commentary by Korolev written in pencil diagonally across text of document. 10 Nov 1965. 1 p, 279mm by 197mm. Greb Y. Maksimov collection P Mar 16 (116) $2,000

## Spain

**Document,** 11 Dec 1246. 1 p, vellum, 290mm by 187mm, in fitted case. Agreement between Jeronimo Aznar, Bishop of Calahorra & the Benedictine Abbey of St. Emilia de Cuculla settling a long-term dispute about some churches. Including 2 massive seals. S June 18 (37) £1,000

— [1543]. 52 pp, folio. Draft of a notarial document concerning the sale of the towns of Baltanzas & Guaza by Charles V to the Order of Santiago to defray the costs of his expeditions against Barbarossa in Tunis. S Dec 1 (2) £350

— JACA, ARAGON. - Document, 6 Jan 1440. 1 leaf, vellum, 330mm by 466mm. Contract between the Jews of the Great Synagogue of Jaca & Don Sancho Latras. Drawn up according to Jewish custom by Martin de Rayca, notary public to the Kings of Aragon & Valencia. S Dec 5 (23) £2,600 [Leftly]

— RELIGIOUS ORDERS. - Ms, Tratado metodico judicial para las visitas y causas de los Regulares, segun derecho, [c.late 17th cent?]. About 150 pp, 4to, in contemp vellum wraps. Rules for canonical visitations of religious houses. S Dec 1 (52) £550

## Spare, Austin Osman

**Autograph Ms,** The Arcana of AOS & the Consciousness of Kia-Ra. 10 leaves containing 20 ink drawings, 5 on mtd sheets, all but the last in watercolor, a few heightened with gold, mostly captioned. 217mm by 140mm, in contemp vellum gilt Pickford Waller's copy, with his first book plate designed by Spare, 1905 S Nov 21 (411) £3,200

— Autograph Ms, The Focus of Life and the Papyrus of Amen A.O.S. 11 leaves containing 21 ink & watercolor drawings, mostly heightened with gold, with additional ink drawing pasted in, sgd & dated 1905-6. In notebook, contemp vellum gilt Pickford Waller's copy, with his first bookplate designed by Spare, dated 1905 S Nov 21 (410) £1,000

**Autograph sketchbook,** of automatic drawings (45) of grotesque figures, elemental entities & the qliphoth, 1924-27. 255mm by 195mm, orig bds. With additional drawing by Spare pasted in & inscr to Oswell Blakeston, 1932. S Nov 21 (412) £700

## Sparks, Jared, 1789-1866

**ALs,** 7 Jan 1864. 1 p, 8vo. To "My Dear Anna". Responding to a request for 12 signatures by agreeing to send 6 & a photo. Repaired on verso. With the photo, which is soiled. rms Oct 11 (358) $260

## Speer, Albert, 1905-81

**ALs,** [c.1 Jan 1937]. 1 p, 8vo. To [Philipp & Helli] Bouhler. Sending New Year's wishes. Illus in cat. rms Mar 21 (368) $490

— [Jan 1968]. 2 pp, 4to. To a former guard of his from Spandau. Discussing books & magazines. With original holograph envelope. pba Feb 22 (309) $200

## Speke, John Hanning, 1827-64
ALs, 30 June [1864]. 4 pp, 8vo. To [the Rev. James Stewart]. Discussing possible areas of missionary activity in Africa. Illus in cat. C Nov 29 (188) £1,400

## Spencer, Sir Stanley, 1891-1959
Collection of 5 A Ls s, 3 Ls s (1 jointly with Cyril Connolly) & 1 autograph postcard, sgd, [1938-89]. 13 pp, 4to & 8vo. To Desmond Hawkins. S July 11 (292) £1,700

## Spender, Stephen
Autograph Ms, Notebook entitled Poems July 1939 Stephen Spender & Fair copy of Poems, from July 20 1939. Written for Peter Watson. 1939-[c.1942]. 55 pp, 4to, Canvas. With 2 leaves cut out by poet. With deletions & corrections. Illus in cat S June 28 (213) £5,800

Collection of 3 ALs s & 1 Ls, [c.1930-56], 7 pp, 4to. To Harold Nicolson. Inviting Nicolson to give a talk & other matters. S June 28 (199) £420

Proof copy, [13 Dec 1962]. No size or length given. Corrected galley proofs for The Struggle of the Modern. With 13 Dec 1962 ALs presenting the proofs to Anthony Hobson. Illus in cat S June 28 (214) £460

## Spener, Johann Karl Philipp, 1749-1827
ALs, 20 Sept 1805. 1 p, 4to. To an unnamed pbr. Concerning etchings for Marpurg's work about the fugue. star Mar 22 (983) DM250

## Spohr, Louis, 1784-1859
Autograph music, song, Gondelfahrt, [n.d.]. 6 pp, 4to. Draft. Including authentication by his daughter. HN May 15 (2718) DM2,400

ALs, 23 Apr 1840. 1 p, 4to. Recipient unnamed. Sending payment for a copying job. Repaired. star Mar 22 (1070) DM300

— 11 May 1852. 1 p, 4to. To an unnamed conductor. Congratulating him on his appointment & saying he is not able to recommend any of his students at this point. Illus in cat. star Mar 22 (1071) DM650

## Spontini, Gaspare, 1774-1851
ALs, 23/24 Nov 1838. 1 p, 4to. To Domenico Barbaia. Asking him to find lodgings for him in Naples. star Mar 22 (1072) DM300

## Squibb, Edward Robinson, 1819-1900
ALs, 9 Oct 1875. 1 p, 8vo. To E. P. Hitchcock. Politely declining to make a loan. Illus in cat rms Oct 11 (363) $800

Check, accomplished & sgd, 28 Jan 1868. Drawn on the Long Island Bank for $18.00 payable to John F. Baker. Illus in cat. rms June 6 (333) $375

## Stadler, Albert, 1794-1888. See: Schubert, Franz

## Stael-Holstein, Anne Louise Germaine, Baronne de, 1766-1817
ALs, 20 Jan 1813. 4 pp, 8vo. To [Princess Lieven]. About Napoleon, & expressing enthusiasm for England. S May 15 (227) £500

— 12 Dec 1815. 3 pp, 4to. Recipient unnamed. Requesting his help in a financial matter & sending personal news. star Mar 21 (350) DM1,300

— 22 Nov [n.y.]. 3 pp, 8vo. To Louis Secretan. Inquiring about a legal case & remembering her father. star Mar 21 (351) DM1,100

A Ls (2), 10 Apr 1804 & 22 July [1808]. 7 pp, 8vo. To Claude Hochet. About personal & political news, her work, etc. star Mar 21 (349) DM1,700

Ls, 19 Feb 1812. 2 pp, 4to. To Messrs. Le Roy, Bayard & Evers. Discussing financial matters. HN Nov 24 (2866) DM600

## Stainer, Sir John
Ds, 2 Feb 1892. 2 pp, 8vo. Contract for publication of The Crucifixion. With related ALs. S May 15 (144) £150

## Stalin, Joseph, 1879-1953
Autograph endorsement, sgd, [c.15 Aug 1944]. On a report addressed to him by Marshall Voronov regarding anti-aircraft forces for the Ukrainian front, 8 pp, folio; agreeing with his suggestions. rms June 6 (635) $6,500

Endorsement, sgd, 27 Sept 1944. On a report addressed to him by Marshal Voronov outlining various forms of defensive armaments, 4 pp, folio. Illus in cat. rms June 6 (634) $8,000

Photograph, sgd & inscr, [c.1926]. 5.75 by 4.4 inches, mtd. Inscr to Jerome Davis. With related material. sg June 6 (170) $5,000

## Stanford, Sir Charles Villiers, 1852-1924
Series of c.70 A Ls s, 1876-1915 & [n.d.]. Over 180 pp, 8vo. To Henry & Alfred Littleton of Novello's. On musical matters. Annotated by the recipients. S May 15 (143) £1,500

## Stanford, Leland, 1824-93
ALs, 23 Feb 1876. 1 p, 4to. To J. R. McConnell. Concerning upcoming legislation. pba Feb 22 (149) $1,200

## Stanhope, Lady Hester Lucy, 1776-1839
ALs, 15 Nov 1815. 4 pp, 12mo. Recipient unnamed. Thanking her for a gift; warns of travel to Baghdad. sg June 6 (171) $550

## Stanhope, Philip Henry, 5th Earl, 1805-75
A Ls s (2), 24 Dec 1831 & [n.d.]. 14 pp, 4to. To King Ludwig I of Bavaria. Discussing Kaspar Hauser. star Mar 22 (1358) DM2,200

## Stanislavski, Konstantin Sergeevich, 1863-1938
Ptd photograph, [n.d.]. Mtd on postcard. Bust port, sgd on mount. Illus in cat. rms June 6 (125) $375

## Stanley, Sir Henry Morton, 1841-1904
ALs, 10 Feb 1897. 2 pp, 8vo. To B. Knowles. About In Darkest Africa. pn Nov 9 (371) £190

AL, 13 Mar 1900. 1 p, 8vo. In 3d person. To B. Knowles. About how to purchase How I Found Livingstone. pn Nov 9 (372) £130

**Photograph,** sgd, 11 Oct 1886. 181mm by 125mm. Shoulder-length vignette port, by E. Plassingham. Marans collection. CE Apr 17 (26) $1,000

**Photograph,** sgd & inscr, [c.1875]. Carte size. Inscr on verso to Lieut. L. Dawson. b Jan 31 (21) £170

### Stanton, Edwin M., 1814-69

**ALs,** 4 July 1858. 1 p, 8vo. To P. H. Watson. Sending on letters [not present]: "I have addressed several letters to Mrs. Stanton at Washington to your care. Not knowing myself where she may be please send them to her..." pba Oct 26 (316) $150

— 14 June 1864. 1 p, 4to. Warrant asking that $1,000,000 be issued to the paymaster at N. Y. sg Oct 26 (60) $140

### Star Trek

**Group photograph,** [n.d.]. Oblong 4to publicity still of the cast of the original series. Sgd by cast members Shatner, Nimoy, Kelley, Takei, Koenig, Barret, Nichols & Doohan. wa Oct 28 (497) $375

**Starhemberg, Gotthard von, 1563-1624?.** See: Leopold V, Regent of Tirol, 1586-1632

### Stark, Freya

**Typescript,** Alexander's Path from Caria to Cilicia [c.1957]. About 350 pp, 4to. With extensive holograph corrections. With ANs to Sir Michael Stewart & with 19 related photographs. b Sept 20 (358) £650

**Series** of c.35 A Ls s, 1954-82. Various sizes. To Sheridan Russell. About her writing, travel plans, health & friends. b Sept 20 (375) £170

### Steichen, Edward, 1879-1973

**Photograph,** sgd, [c.1960]. 233mm by 172mm. By Jean Miller. Illus in cat. Marans collection. CE Apr 17 (219) $700

### Stein, Gertrude, 1874-1946

**A Ls s** (2), 20 Jan & 6 Mar 1937. 3 pp on 2 sheets, 8vo. To Margaret Lucha, Associate Editor of the Academic Observer, a high-school literary magazine. Agreeing to be the dedicatee; acknowledges receipt & asks that a copy be sent to Carl van Vechten. With a copy of the magazine & an Ls from Van Vechten to Lucha asking for anr copy. sg June 6 (173) $1,600

**ALs,** [postmarked 22 Nov 1922]. 8 pp, 8vo. To Mrs. J. Moses. Detailing her life in Paris to a relative in Baltimore. CNY Oct 27 (128) $2,400

### Stein, Karl, Freiherr vom und zum, 1757-1831

**ALs,** 3 May 1788. 3 pp, 4to. To Franz von Reden. Discussing a financial matter. star Mar 22 (1667) DM2,600

— 22 Jan 1830. 4 pp, 4to. To Field Marshal von Gneisenau. Discussing the revision of the Prussian municipal statutes. HN May 15 (2721) DM5,000

**Ls,** 23 Apr 1814. 2 pp, folio. To Freiherr von der Horst. About the use of waterways in the Netherlands for military transports. star Mar 22 (1668) DM700

### Steinbeck, John, 1902-68

**ALs,** [c.25 Aug 1937]. 2 pp, 4to. To Harry T. Moore. Literary letter, responding to questions from Moore relating to his book about Steinbeck. CNY Oct 27 (133) $2,400

— 20 Feb 1949. 1 p, folio. To his his former wife, Gwyn. About their divorce. With a photo of the 2 on their wedding day. CE Feb 21 (248) $1,400

— 13 Nov 1953. 2 pp, folio. To Harold Otis Bicknell & Grant McLean. About finishing Sweet Thursday. CE Feb 21 (249) $2,400

— 3 July 1956. 2 pp, folio, on 1 sheet. To his son Thom. Sending news to summer camp about his work & his coming wedding to Elaine. CE Feb 21 (250) $1,600

**Signature,** [n.d.]. Framed with port & first-day issue cover. CE Feb 21 (251) $220

— Anr, [n.d.]. On 11 by 14 inch movie poster for The Wayward Bus. Inscr. With some tape bits & adhesion residue. Lacking small piece from right side. pba Feb 22 (101) $250

— Anr, [n.d.]. No size given. With 1960s wire photo of the author, a 1940s newspaper article conerning his Pulitzer Prize for The Grapes of Wrath, and 2 photos of the dust bowl. Framed. Over-all size 17.5 by 27.5 inches. Illus in cat rms Oct 11 (242) $450

### Steinheil, Karl August von, 1801-70

**Series** of 4 A Ls s, 6 Sept 1847 to 28 Feb 1849. 7 pp, 4to & 8vo. To Ernst von Bibra. Giving advice regarding recipient's expedition to South America. star Mar 21 (624) DM1,100

**Stendhal, 1783-1842.** See: Beyle, Marie Henri ("Stendhal")

### Stengel, Charles Dillino ("Casey"), 1889-1975

**Signature,** [n.d.]. No size given. On verso of a souvenir card. pba June 13 (177) $60

### Stephanie, Crown Princess of Austria, 1864-1945

**ALs,** 6 Mar 1940. 3 pp, 4to. To Ambassador Nieuwenburg. Asking for tickets to a celebration at the Vatican. star Mar 22 (1493) DM440

### Stephanie, Grossherzogin von Baden, 1789-1860

**A Ls s** (2), 4 Mar & 18 July [1830]. 3 pp, 8vo. To the Duchesse de Decres. Inviting her, & sending condolences. star Mar 22 (1424) DM850

### Stern, Julius, 1820-83

**Autograph quotation,** old Hebrew melody, 14 May 1846. 1 p, 4to. Scored for voice & wind instruments; sgd. star Mar 22 (1073) DM450

### Sternberg, Johann Heinrich, 1772-1809

**ALs,** 17 June 1803. 2 pp, 4to. To the bookseller Keil. Offering a plan for a hospital in Goslar for print. star Mar 21 (625) DM210

### Steuben, Friedrich Wilhelm von, 1730-94

**Ds,** 11 June 1791. 2 pp, 4to. Agreement with William Colbarth regarding the sale of his lands in NY State. Also sgd by 3 others. P Dec 13 (350) $850

**Stevens, Thaddeus, 1792-1868.** See: Morrissey, John & Others

**Stevenson, Jonathon**
Ds, 1 Nov 1849. 4 pp, 12.5 by 7.75 inches. Articles of Copartnership between Jonathon D. Stevenson and William C. Parker. Larson collection pba Sept 24 (680) $550

**Stevenson, Robert Louis, 1850-94**
ALs, 5 Dec 1885. 1 p, 8vo. To his father. Discussing their health. CE Sept 27 (27) $800
**Autograph quotation,** [n.d.]. 1 p, 3.5 by 4.3 inches. "The Man who cannot imagine any mortal thing is a green hand in life." Illus in cat sg Sept 28 (257) $1,200
**Check,** 17 June 1892. Payable to Arrick for £2 2s. cb June 25 (2580) $600
**Photograph, sgd & inscr,** [c.1890]. 170mm by 119mm, mtd. Half length, seated; inscr to Mrs. Frank Hume. Illus in cat. Marans collection. CE Apr 17 (92) $3,800

**Stewart, Walter, c.1756-96**
ALs, 20 Feb 1788. 3 pp, 4to. To Gen. William Irvine. Discussing the opposition to the new Constitution in Pennsylvania. P Dec 13 (351) $500

**Stiles, Ezra, 1727-95**
ALs, 11 Jan 1785. 1 p, 8vo. To John Fry. Evicting a public house. sg June 6 (174) $175

**Stobwasser, Johann Heinrich, 1740-1829**
ALs, 9 Nov 1793. 1 p, 4to. To the Rev. Sievers. Sending some lacquered boxes. star Mar 21 (720) DM620

**Stockton, Richard, Signer from New Jersey**
ALs, 3 May 1771. 2 pp, 4to. To Mr. Hunt. Counseling a client on a pending suit. P Dec 13 (352) $900

**Stoker, Bram, 1847-1912**
ALs, 14 Feb 1899. 1 p, 8vo. To Willie. Sending (not present) tickets for Henry Irving Saturday evening performance. CE May 22 (441) $280
Ls, 2 Feb 1893. 1 p, 8vo. Recipient unnamed. Giving information about rehearsals but requesting that nothing is to be pbd until after the performance. Including autograph postscript. rms June 6 (126) $375

**Stone, Harlan Fiske, 1872-1946**
**Photograph, sgd & inscr,** 27 Nov 1941. 7.1 by 11 inch profile port photo. By Harris & Ewing. Insct to John A. Blomgren. Sgd as "Harlan F Stone". pba Oct 26 (341) $130
— BARMORE, CHARLES. - Engraving, bust port of Stone, [n.d.]. Framed; overall size 23.75 by 17.75 inches. Sgd by Stone & Barmore. Illus in cat. rms Mar 21 (343) $280

**Stone, Thomas, Signer from Maryland**
ADs, [c.10 Mar 1779]. 1 p, size not stated. Complaint brought by Patrick & Elizabeth Graham against Martha Portons for theft of a slave. Sgd 4 times. P Dec 13 (354) $1,300

**Story, Joseph, 1779-1845**
ALs, 9 Dec 1823. 2 pp, 4to. To Judge John Davis. Concerning the fact he is to "call a final meeting of the Committee of the Over seers [sic] on the state of Harvard College."Franked & docketed. Damp-stained. Illus in cat pba Oct 26 (342) $325
**Signature,** [n.d.]. No size given. With engraved port. Mtd & framed under glass. With moisture defects on mat. Over-all size 12.25 by 9.25 inches. rms Oct 11 (364) $210

**Stowe, Harriet Beecher, 1811-96**
ALs, 12 Apr 1869. 20 pp, 8vo. To Elizabeth, Duchess of Argyll. Saying that she is dedicating her latest & best novel to her mother, the Duchess of Sutherland. pn Nov 9 (452) £2,300
**Cut signature,** 1882. Cut from a letter, with sentiment, mtd on card. bbc June 24 (54) $100
**Photograph, sgd,** [c.1876]. 165mm by 108mm, mtd. Bust-length profile port, by Hastings. Illus in cat. Marans collection. CE Apr 17 (93) $1,400
**Signature,** 12 Nov 1875. On 4 by 6 inch page. pba Feb 22 (184) $75

**Strachey, Lytton, 1880-1932**
ALs, 5 May 1909. 2 pp, 8vo. To A. H. Clough's sister, Annie, founder of Newnham. Effusion about her cottage. pn June 13 (317) £240

**Stradivari, Antonio, 1644-1737**
ALs, 12 Aug 1708. 1 p, 8vo, cut from larger sheet. To an unnamed nobleman. Concerning repairs to a violin. Illus in cat. S Dec 1 (337) £28,000

**Strauss, Franz Joseph, 1822-1905**
**Autograph music,** 4 choruses for soprano, alto, tenor & bass, settings of poems by Hammer, Moerike, & others; [n.d.]. 17 pp, 8vo. Notated on 5 two-stave systems per page. Including autograph tp & numerous corrections. S Dec 1 (340) £1,600

**Strauss, Johann, 1825-99**
**Autograph music,** sketches for the 1st 16 bars of the concert coda of the waltz Nordseebilder, Op.390, scored for full orchestra, [n.d.]. 2 pp, folio, framed. Including authentication by Adele Strauss, 1925. Illus in cat. C Nov 29 (255) £3,400
— Autograph music, sketches of various vocal & instrumental sections, [n.d.]. 2 pp, folio. Including note of authenticity in his wife's hand, at foot. Illus in cat. S May 15 (503) £700
ALs, [1864]. 2 pp, 8vo. To a journalist. About a concert to benefit wounded soldiers. b Sept 20 (30) £160
— 12 Nov 1882. 3 pp, 8vo. To Herr Schosberg. Wondering why he did not hear from him, & confirming that he will be pleased to read a good libretto. star Mar 22 (1075) DM1,200
**Photograph, sgd & inscr,** 14 Oct [18]94. Carte size. Waist-length pose, by Rudolf Krzinanek. Inscr to Th. Kretschmann. Illus in cat. rms June 6 (195) $1,500
— Anr, [1890s]. Framed, overall size 19.5cm by 15cm. By Victor Ingerer; inscr to Amalie Eisenberg with a

musical quotation from his opera Ritter Pazman. Illus in cat. S Dec 1 (338) £950

**Signature,** [n.d.]. On engraved port; detached tp of The Festival, 35cm by 25cm. S May 15 (501) £500

**Strauss, Richard, 1864-1949**
[A collection of A Ls s & postcards, sgd, 1892 & 1893, c.140 pp, various sizes, written to his parents & his sister Johanna during his year of travels in Southern Europe & Egypt, giving details of travels, concerts & compositions, with related material, sold at Sotheby on 1 Dec 1995, lot 342, for £7,000.]

**Ms,** Serenade Op.7, [c.1881-82]. 38 pp, 8vo, in bds. Full score, notated on 11 staves per page. In the hand of his father Franz Joseph Strauss; sgd by Richard Strauss & inscr to F. W. Meyer on tp. S Dec 1 (343) £1,800

**ALs,** 1 Jan 1875. 3 pp, 4to, on embossed stationery. To his parents. 20-line poem; New Year's greetings. S Dec 1 (341) £1,200

— 4 Jan [1886?]. 1 p, 8vo. To Otto Lessmann. Thanking for a favorable review. star Mar 22 (1076) DM1,300

— 13 Sept 1897. 2 pp, 8vo. To Herr Curtius. About the instrumentation of Till Eulenspiegel & Tod und Verklaerung. S Dec 1 (346) £320

— 7 Nov [1898]. 1 p, 8vo. To Fritz Simrock. Asking him to forward a letter. star Mar 22 (1077) DM550

— 30 Dec 1910. 2 pp, 4to. To [Willy Levin]. Discussing arrangements for the premiere of Der Rosenkavalier in Dresden. Illus in cat. star Mar 22 (1079) DM3,300

— 19 June 1915. 3 pp, 8vo. To Hermann Kutzschbach. Making plans for the premiere of his Alpensinfonie. star Mar 22 (1080) DM3,600

— 18 Sept 1916. 3 pp, 8vo. To Hermann Kutzschbach. About performances of his works in Vienna & Dresden. star Mar 22 (1081) DM1,700

— 6 Dec 1917. 1 p, 8vo. To L. Sache. About a concert schedule. Illus in cat pba Feb 22 (103) $425

— 5 [Apr?] 1921. 1 p, 8vo. Recipient unnamed. Providing information about his birth & his parents. HH May 9 (2564) DM600

— [c.1923]. 1 p, 8vo. To Sir Thomas Beecham. Offering congratulations & felicitations for the founding of a new English national opera. C June 26 (287) £280

— 10 Aug 1929. 1 p, 8vo. To [George Sylvester] Viereck. Declining the offer of a libretto. star Mar 22 (1084) DM700

— 9 Mar 1934. 1 p, 8vo. To [Raoul Gunsbourg]. About arrangements on the day of a performance of Arabella. star Mar 22 (1086) DM540

— 16 Mar [19]42. 2 pp, 8vo. To Emil von Sauer. Congratulating him on a recent performance. S Dec 1 (351) £520

— 29 Oct 1947. 2 pp, 8vo. To Sir Thomas Beecham. Thanking him for the Strauss festival that Beecham organized. C June 26 (286) £360

— 8 Oct 1949. 3 pp, 4to. To Eugen Antosch. Discussing his financial situation. star Mar 22 (1088) DM3,500

**Autograph postcard, sgd,** 12 Aug 1920. To Barbara Kemp. Taking leave. star Mar 22 (1082) DM650

**Autograph quotation,** 2 bars from Till Eulenspiegel, 11 June 1906. 1 p, 11cm by 18cm. Sgd. Illus in cat. S May 15 (508) £500

— Anr, Salomes Tanz, [n.d.]. 1 p, 4to. 7 bars from his opera Salome, sgd. Illus in cat. star Mar 22 (1078) DM2,400

**Lithographed port,** 13 Oct 1933. 38cm by 29cm. By Hanfstaengl; sgd by Strauss & inscr to [Enrico] Mainardi. star Mar 22 (1085) DM1,100

**Photograph, sgd,** 24 March 1904. No size given. Cabinet photo by Charles L. Ritzmann. Place and date have been added in anr hand. pba Feb 22 (102) $500

— Anr, [1921]. Postcard. Knee-length; by Barakovich. star Mar 22 (1083) DM500

**Photograph, sgd & inscr,** 22 June [19]49. Postcard. Inscr on verso with ANs to his sister Johanna, thanking for birthday wishes. Illus in cat. S Dec 1 (352) £1,200

— KOLB, ALOIS. - Engraving, port of Strauss, 1926. 495mm by 325mm. Sgd by Strauss & Kolb. With Kolb's orig drawing for the engraving, sgd by Kolb. FD May 14 (1137) DM2,100

**Stravinsky, Igor, 1882-1971**

**Autograph music,** early version of the 1st part [here described as 2d part] of Les noces, [1914-15]. 17 pp, 4to & folio, in vellum bdg handpainted by Stravinsky. Working Ms in full & short score, with extensive revisions. S May 15 (513) £12,000

**Ms,** orig piano reduction of Apollon Musagete, in the hand of & sgd for him by his 1st wife, Katerina Nossenko, 9 Jan 1928. 38 pp, folio. C June 26 (288) £5,000

**Ls,** 24 June 1954. 4 pp, 4to. To Arnold Weissberger. Discussing "the renewal of [his] recording contract with Columbia". Including autograph addition. rms June 6 (226) $700

**Autograph postcard, sgd,** [16 Aug 1921]. To Sofia Kochanska. Hoping to see them, mentioning friends, his work on an opera, etc. In Russian & French. Illus in cat. star Mar 22 (1089) DM1,600

**Ds,** 7 Feb 1966. On memo from Irwin Beckman of CBS requesting his Social Security number. Supplying the number. Sold with his ASCAP membership certificate. rms Nov 30 (309) $275

**Autograph quotation,** one bar from The Firebird, sgd; 1933. 1 p, 10cm by 11cm. With a photograph. Illus in cat. S Dec 1 (354) £460

— Anr, 2 bars from his ballet Jeu aux Cartes, 20 Oct 1937. 1 p, 8vo. Sgd. HN Nov 24 (2868) DM1,000

— Anr, 4 bars from the 2d Air de Danse of his Orpheus, 1955. 10cm by 22cm. In piano score, sgd & inscr to Torsten Carlander. Illus in cat. S Dec 1 (357) £700

**Photograph, sgd,** 1947. 7 by 9 inch b&w photo. Sgd in upper right quadrant. bbc Sept 18 (94) $210

**Photograph, sgd & inscr,** 1950. 235mm by 171mm. Seated; inscr to Sybil Janson. Marans collection. CE Apr 17 (262) $500

— Anr, Oct 1966. 33cm by 24cm. Sgd & inscr to E. Maurice Bloch with a musical quotation from The Firebird. S May 15 (511) £1,300

**Self-caricature,** Dec 1953. Framed with a photograph, overall size c.39.5cm by 20.5cm. Sgd & inscr to Alexis Haieff. S Dec 1 (356) £850

— RAMUZ, CHARLES FERDINAND. - Autograph Ms, Noces et autres histoires d'apres le texte russe Igor Strawinsky, [c.1943]. 36 leaves, 4to, in full cream mor by Denise Stravinsky. Including autograph musical quotation by Igor Stravinsky, sgd & inscr to R. Heyd; & 30 leaves of mtd ink drawings by Theodore Stravinsky. Marked for the ptr. S Dec 1 (355) £8,000

**Streicher, Julius, 1885-1946**

**Ls,** 23 Dec 1935. 1 p, 4to. To Philipp Bouhler. Sending some cakes to share with his wife. Illus in cat. rms June 6 (619) $300

**Stresemann, Gustav, 1878-1929**

**Ls,** 8 July 1919. 4 pp, 4to. To Antonie Hoffmann. Responding to insinuations that he is profiting from the income of a party publishing venture. star Mar 22 (1670) DM750

**Strickland, Charlotte, 1759-1833 —&**
**Strickland, Juliana Sabina, 1765-1849**

**Ms,** Specimens of British Plants, [c.1800]. 3 vols. 144 hand-colored botanical studies, most interleaved with descriptive text in ink, folio size (not uniform), in mor gilt. C Oct 25 (88) £5,500

**Strickland, Juliana Sabina, 1765-1849.** See: Strickland, Charlotte & Strickland

**Strindberg, August, 1849-1912**

**Autograph quotation,** sgd, 14 words from his Till Damaskus, vol 2; Apr 1901. Below an orig pen-&-ink port of him by Robert Kastor, sgd by the artist. Overall size 12 by 9.5 inches. Illus in cat. rms June 6 (127) $950

**Photograph,** sgd, [c.1890]. 167mm by 110mm. By Herman Anderson. Marans collection. CE Apr 17 (94) $950

**Stroud, Robert**

[Archive of material relating to Robert Stroud. Sold at Pacific on 13 June 1996 as lot 172 for $12,000.]

**Strungk, Nicolaus Adam, 1640-1700**

**Ms,** memorandum recording undertakings given by the Imperial court organist in Vienna during his visit there in 1686, [1692-97]. 1 p, folio. Sgd. Illus in cat. S May 15 (514) £1,400

**Stuart, James Ewell Brown, 1833-64**

**ALs,** 30 June 1855. 1 p, 4to. To the Editor of the Lierty Tribune in Liberty Mo. Sending an ad (present) for insertion which offers to purchase in gold horses for the First Regiment of Cavalry. Sgd JEB Stuart. cb June 25 (2476) $6,000

**Stueve, Johann Karl Bertram, 1798-1872**

**ALs,** [25] Aug 1827. 2 pp, 4to. To his family. Reporting from his travels & mentioning a meeting with Goethe. star Mar 21 (152) DM750

**Suchet, Louis Gabriel, Duc d'Albufera, 1770-1826**

**Ls,** [16 Sept 1801]]. 1 p, 8vo. To the commissioner Jullien. Asking him to forward two packages. star Mar 22 (1473) DM250

**Sullivan, Sir Arthur, 1842-1900**

**Autograph quotation,** music to the text The sun whose rays Are all ablaze With ever living glory, Mar 1887. 1 p, 8vo. Sgd. Inscr in anr hand on verso. star Mar 22 (1091) DM1,550

**Photograph, sgd,** [c.1890]. 167mm by 108mm, mtd. Bust vignette port, by J. C. Schaarwaechter. Illus in cat. Marans collection. CE Apr 17 (263) $850

**Sullivan, John, 1740-95**

**Ls,** 23 Aug 1778. 1 p, 4to. To Gen. William Whipple. Discussing military options at Newport after the French retreat & requesting advice. P Dec 13 (355) $2,750

**Sully, Thomas, 1783-1872**

**ALs,** 31 May 1869. 1 p, 4to. To an unnamed gentleman in England. About a painting. Illus in cat pba June 13 (230) $275

**Sumner, Charles, 1811-74**

**ALs,** 6 Oct 1863. 3 pp, 8vo. To Mrs. A. H. Gibbons. Responding to a plea: "...If I were in Washington, I should plead at once with the Secy & Surgeon Genl. " pba Oct 26 (318) $225

— 21 Feb 1867. 1 p, 8vo. To Sec of War E. M. Stanton. Expressing support. Bound with related material. P Dec 13 (356) $1,000

**Autograph quotation,** 2 March 1866. 1 p, 8vo. " Equality in rights is the first of rights. Charles Sumner/ Senate Chamber/ 2nd March '66 ". Illus in cat pba Feb 22 (186) $150

**Sun Yat-sen, 1866-1925**

**Photograph, sgd,** [c.1910]. 250mm by 175mm, mtd. Half length, by Burr. Illus in cat. Marans collection. CE Apr 17 (183) $2,200

**Supreme Court**

**Group photograph,** [1940s]. 11.25 by 16.25 inch photo of the Harlan Stone Supreme Court. By Harris & Ewing. Sgd by all 9 justices. Some smudged. Illus in cat pba Oct 26 (343) $1,500

— Anr, sgd, of Chief Justice William H. Rehnquist's Court [c.1995]. Folio size, framed. rms Nov 30 (316) $950

**Suso, Heinrich, 1295?-1366**

**Ms,** Dialogus de Arte Moriendi, with De Meditatione Mortis, attributed to St. Peter Damian, & 2 chapters from the Meditations of St. Bernard. [Netherlands, 15th cent]. 46 leaves, vellum, 147mm by 101mm. Modern black mor. In black ink in a gothic bookhand. With 6 large decorated initials. Ownership inscr of Cardinal Francis Spellman. S June 18 (65) £2,400

**Suter, Hermannn, 1870-1926**
**Autograph quotation,** 3 bars from his Symphony in D minor, Op.17, July 1920. 1 p, 8vo. Sgd. star Mar 22 (1092) DM340

**Sutter, John A., 1803-80**
**ALs,** 8 Sept 1856. 2 pp, 10.5 by 8.25 inches. To Col. Warren. About selling him produce. With related material. Larson collection pba Sept 24 (691) $2,750
**Ls,** 26 Apr 1847. 3 pp, 4to. To John C. Fremont. Requesting payment for the use of Fort Sacramento by the U.S. Volunteers & their families between July 11, 1846 & Feb 26, 1847. cb June 25 (2382) $15,000
**Photograph, sgd,** [1868]. 108mm by 61mm, mtd. Seated, by Ulke. Sgd on verso. Illus in cat. Marans collection. CE Apr 17 (184) $1,700

**Suttner, Bertha von, 1843-1914**
**Autograph postcard, sgd,** 27 May 1906. Recipient unnamed. Appeal to lay down the arms everywhere. JG Sept 29 (311) DM320

**Swedenborg, Emanuel, 1688-1772**
**Ls,** 17 Mar 1747. 4 pp plus blank leaf, sewn, folio. To the King. Petition in letter form in recommendation of baron Nils Reuterholm. Sgd as assessor of the Swedish board of mines. Also sgd by 6 others. S Mar 14 (351) £900

**Swift, Johnathan, 1667-1745**
**AL,** [n.d.]. 4 fragments of a letter. To an unnamed recipient. Concerning the weather. pba Oct 26 (75) $425

**Synge, John Millington, 1871-1909**
**ALs,** 5 Feb 1906. 2 pp on 1 sheet, 4to. To Karel Musek. About his production in Prague of The Shadow of the Glen. CNY Oct 27 (136) $1,100

**Syriac Manuscripts**
**Ms,** The New Testament, in the Peshitta trans. [Syria, 9th - 12th cent]. About 200 leaves, vellum, 230mm by 170mm. Def contemp[?] bdg of wooden bds elaborately carved on inside of upper cover. In a well-formed estrangelo hand. With full-page carpet-page frontis in red & black. Dampstained; many leaves stuck to each other. S Dec 5 (29) £4,800 [Assad]

**Szyk, Arthur, 1894-1951**
**Original drawings,** (10) in watercolor to illus The Ten Commandments. 200mm by 150mm, each with text, large initial incorporated in illust, & decoration above & below. Sgd & dated 1946. Framed S Nov 21 (521) £14,200

# T

**Taft, William Howard, 1857-1930**
**Ls,** 11 Nov 1898. 1 p, 8vo. To W. D. Guilbert. Acknowledging receipt of laws sent to him. rms Mar 21 (110) $220
— 6 May 1904. 1 p, 8vo. To Mr. Lewis Haupt. Acknowledging the receipt of Haupt's letter. pba June 13 (84) $120

— 26 Feb 1907. 1 p. Declining an invitation. Framed with port. Signature smudged. rs Nov 11 (45) $300
— 3 Feb 1910. 1 p, 4to. To the Rev. Newell Dwight Hillis. Responding to his letter about Gen. H. C. King. Signature light & slightly smudged. wa Oct 28 (233) $120
— 3 Apr 1911. 1 p, 4to. To Gov. O. B. Colquitt. Referring to border disagreements between Mexico, Texas & New Mexico. CNY May 17 (308) $900
— 20 July 1911. 2 pp, folio. To the President of Honduras. Informing him that Fenton R. McCreery has resigned his position as U.S. Minister to Honduras. Countersgd by P. C. Knox. Illus in cat. rms Mar 21 (108) $650
— 11 Dec 1911. 1 p, 4to. To Elmer J. Burkett. Thanking him for a supportive note: "...thank you for taking the trouble to let me know of your approval of my anti-trust message." pba Oct 26 (320) $225
— 29 June 1912. 2 pp, 4to. Copy of a testimonial letter given to the family of Gen. Edward S. Bragg. rms Nov 30 (310) $360
— 18 Jan 1914. 1 p, 4to. To" Mr. Justice Clark". Making arrangements for a dinner for the Class of '78. With port. Mtd & framed under glass. Over-all size 19.5 by 8.3 inches. rms Oct 11 (367) $210
— 28 Jan 1917. 1 p, 4to. To Elmer J. Burkett. Concerning a speaking engagement he has accepted. pba Oct 26 (321) $150
— 11 Apr 1922. 1 p, 4to. To H. S. Boutell. Thanking for an article. Illus in cat. rms June 6 (479) $160
— 2 July 1924. 1 p, 4to. To Judge C. A. Woods. Regretfully declining to join him & other judges on a trip to England. With holograph postcript. sg Sept 28 (262) $275
— 20 Mar 1925. 1 p, 4to. To Elmer Burkett. Writing the Nebraska Senator about an appointment: "I tried to do what I could to get Munger appointed. I think that your Senators can not exercise any particular influence with this Administration..." With holograph marking "personal". Illus in cat pba Oct 26 (345) $225
— 17 Sept 1927. 1 p, 4to. To Walter Pratt. Saying that his name can be used for a dinner of the Mass. Society of Mayflower Descendants but that he cannot attend. wa Oct 28 (234) $190
**Ds,** 12 Mar 1910. 1 p, folio, on vellum. Appointment of Ormond L. Cox as a Naval Lieutenant, jg. Countersgd by Sec of War George Meyer. CE June 12 (116) $350
— 24 June 1910. 1 p, folio. Appointment of Charles Gerhard as Major of Infantry. Illus in cat. rms Mar 21 (111) $400
**Autograph quotation,** 1 June 1914. No size given. In full: "Sincerely yours/ Wm. H. Taft/ New Haven/ June 1st 1914." With a sepia-toned reprint photo of Taft golfing & a Yale leather banner. Framed. Over-all size 15.5 by 19.5 inches. Illus in cat rms Oct 11 (324) $350
**Autograph sentiment,** 7 July 1927. 1 p, 4to. Extending greetings to the graduates of a high school in NY. Framed with photo & 1908 campaign button. rms Nov 30 (41) $370

# TAFT                                    AMERICAN BOOK PRICES CURRENT

**Cut signature,** [n.d.]. No size given. Cut from letter. pba Feb 22 (282) $95

**Photograph, sgd & inscr,** 17 June 1909. 9 by 6 inch portrait full-face bust photo. By Harris & Ewing. Inscr for Paul Benson. On 14 by 10 inch sheet. sg Sept 28 (261) $250

— Anr, 15 Dec 1909. 10.5 by 13.5 inch sepia port photo. Inscr to A. G. Foster. Illus in cat pba Oct 26 (319) $300

— Anr, 31 Dec 1925. 9.25 by 11.25 inch photo. Of Taft & Justice Pierce Butler at the White House. By Harris & Ewing. Inscr "With warm wishes of goodwill for John Butler, and gratitude for the good fortune of the country and myself that Pierce is in the Court." Also inscr by Pierce Butler to his brother. Backed with board. sg Sept 28 (259) $375

— Anr, 23 Nov 1927. 9.5 by 7.5 inches. Inscr on bottom blank margin. sg June 6 (176) $200

— Anr, [n.d.]. 4to. In judicial robes, by Harris & Ewing. Inscr to Alexander A. Tomaky. Framed. Illus in cat. rms Mar 21 (344) $340

**Talleyrand-Perigord, Charles Maurice de, 1754-1838**

**ALs,** [4 June 1798]. 1 p, 4to. To Elbridge Gerry. Assuring him that he will regard the information provided as confidential. star Mar 22 (1474) DM660

**Ls,** [18 Mar 1799]. 2 pp, size not stated. To Jean Lamarre. Informing him that he has sent an inquiry concerning his brother to the embassy in Madrid. HN May 15 (2725) DM290

— 7 Mar 1804 [15 Ventose an 12]. 1 p, folio. To Robert R. Livingston. About the Louisiana Purchase Treaty. CNY Jan 26 (179) $1,900

— 23 Mar 1804. 2 pp, 4to. To Robert Livingston. Sending a report regarding a British Minister guilty of a conspiracy plot. P Dec 13 (357) $450

— [c.May 1805]. 1 p, folio. To Louis Bignon. Asking him to forward two documents. star Mar 22 (1475) DM390

**Tammen, H. H.**

**Ls,** 6 Oct 1913. 1 p, 4to. To W. J. Langer. Offering a contract for performances in the Sells-Floto 1914 productions. With ANs on verso from Langer, accepting the offer. sg June 6 (295) $325

**Tartini, Giuseppe, 1692-1770**

**ALs,** 31 Oct 1764. 1 p, 4to. To Gottlieb Neumann. Expressing satisfaction about the success of recipient's compositions in Dresden. Illus in cat. star Mar 22 (1094) DM4,600

**Tate, Allen, 1899-1979**

**Collection** of 7 A Ls s & 7 Ls s, 7 July 1936 to 10 Jan 1973. 22 pp, 8vo & 4to. To Desmond Hawkins. With copies of Hawkins's letters to Tate. S July 11 (294) £900

**Taylor, Zachary, 1784-1850**

**ALs,** 28 Sept 1824. 1 p, 4to. To Col. George Gibson. Testimony for 2 businessmen. CNY May 17 (309) $800

— 25 Mar 1838. 4 pp, 4to. To Major Gen. T. S. Jesup. Making plans for actions against the Seminole Indians in Florida. Forbes Magazine collection. CNY May 17 (188) $14,000

**Ls,** 11 Mar 1835. 1 p, 4to. To General R. Jones. Letter of transmittal for the Return and Recruiting Return of his unit for January past. Sgd as " Z. Taylor. Col., 1st Regt U. S. Infy." Framed. pba Oct 26 (322) $1,200

— 18 Sept 1835. 1 p, 4to. To Adjutant General R. Jones. Forwarding his return of his troops. Text pale. CNY Dec 15 (121) $1,400

— 21 Mar 1839. 3 pp, 4to. To Col. William Davenport. Making plans "to drive every Indian from Middle Florida before the ensuing summer." Forbes Magazine collection. CNY May 17 (189) $14,000

— 8 Apr 1839. 3 pp, 4to. To Colonel William Davenport. Concerning military strategy during the Second Seminole War. CNY Dec 15 (238) $3,800

— 24 May 1850. 2 pp, 251mm by 200mm, on bifolium. To Mrs. Phillippa W. B. Carothers. Denying a request for a military land grant. P June 5 (102) $3,250

**ADs,** 14 Apr 1812. 1 p, 8vo. Receipt for $23.00 from Taylor for ferrying soldiers across the Ohio. Sgd by Margaret Geiger & Jas. T. Pendleton; sgd by Taylor in text. Illus in cat. rms Mar 21 (39) $1,100

**Cut signature,** [n.d.]. No size given. Cut from letter addressed to J. J. Crittenden. pba Feb 22 (283) $600

**Tchaikovsky, Peter Ilyich, 1840-93**

**Autograph music,** working Ms of 5 bars of the 3d movement of his Piano Concerto No 1 in B flat minor, Op.23, in the version for 2 pianos, [c.1875?]. 1 p, 21cm by 26.5cm, cut from larger sheet. Illus in cat. S Dec 1 (366) £16,500

**Tcherepnin, Alexander Nikolayevich, 1899-1977**

**Ls,** [c.1930]. 3 pp, 4to. To Gerhard Tischer. Sending biographical information for a forthcoming article. star Mar 22 (1099) DM280

**Teller, Edward**

**Ls,** 24 Aug 1959. 1 p, 4to. To Frederick R. Lachman. Responding to a request for his participation in campaign dinners. HN May 15 (2726) DM380

**Telschow, Otto**

**Autograph Ms,** diary of his daily life & professional career, Mar 1941 to 16 Apr 1945. Illus in cat rms Nov 30 (248) $5,100

**Tenniel, Sir John, 1820-1914**

**ALs,** 2 Feb 1878. 1 p, 8vo. To Southey. Declining an invitation. sg Feb 1 (45) $100

**Tennyson, Alfred, Lord, 1809-92**

**ALs,** [n.d.]. 1 p, 8vo. To a lady. Thanking her for a gift. Framed with photograph & plaque. cb June 25 (2583) $375

**Check,** sgd, 28 May 1864. 1 p, 8vo. Payable to Jonathan Webb. Accomplished in his wife's hand. rms Mar 21 (256) $195

Corrected proof, for his poem, Sea Dreams: an Idyll. 8 pp, 4to. Extensively marked up by Tennyson. pn June 13 (318) £1,800

Photograph, sgd, [c.1892]. 164mm by 107mm, mtd. Seated; by Reynold's Photo Co. Illus in cat. Marans collection. CE Apr 17 (95) $1,300

### Terentius Afer, Publius, 185-159 B.C.

Ms, Comoediae. [Italy, mid-15th cent] 117 pp, on vellum. With 7 large illuminated initials in burnished gold. 245mm by 159mm, in 18th-cent mor gilt. Gladstone copy C Apr 3 (7) £25,000

### Tereshkova, Valentina

Autograph Ms, reply to a journalist's query about what feelings & thoughts are evoked in her by the word "Mother". 4 Mar 1964. On 2 index card mtd on a stub. Aleksandr P. Romanov collection P Mar 16 (77) $2,500

Transcript, copy of her official press conference given at Moscow, 1 July 1963. 28 pp, 292mm by 203mm. Sgd by Gen. Nikolai Kamanin. With photograph sgd by Valery Bykovsky & Tereshkova. Aleksandr P. Romanov collection P Mar 16 (76) $1,700

### Termoulet, Bernardo

Ds, 19 July 1796. Petition to construct a bathhouse, addressed to the Governor-General of Louisiana, with ink map of a riverfront block in New Orleans & Ms map of a section of the New Orleans waterfront sgd by Carlos Trudeau. 3 pp, folio & 4to. Endorsed by Baron de Carondelet approving the petition. Illus in cat CNY Jan 26 (166) $4,200

### Terry, Ellen, 1847-1928

Photograph, sgd & inscr, 26 June 1889. 14 by 12 inches. Inscr to Lady Dorothy Nevill. Ck Apr 12 (13) £70

### Teschner, Gustav Wilhelm, 1800-83

ALs, 1 Aug 1839. 3 pp, 4to. To Joseph Klein. About the Ed of the works of Bernhard Joseph Klein & the musical scene in Berlin. star Mar 22 (1096) DM250

### Tesla, Nikola, 1856-1943

Ls, 4 Feb 1895. 1 p, 4to. To Richard Watson Gilder, editor of Century Magazine. Asking that a forthcoming article be sent to Edward D. Adams. sg June 6 (179) $1,400

Photograph, sgd & inscr, sgd, 5 Sept 1934. 9.5 by 7.5 inches. Inscr in New York. sg Feb 1 (224) $1,700

Signature, [n.d.]. On card. sg June 6 (178) $250

### Tetens, Johannes Nikolaus, 1736-1807

ALs, 30 July 1798. 3 pp, 4to. To Abbe Giacomo Pacchetti. Thanking for his election as corresponding member of the Academy in Siena. star Mar 21 (626) DM320

### Thackeray, William Makepeace, 1811-63

Autograph Ms, Part 2 of "Codlingsby. By B. De Shrewsbury, esq." [1847?]. 8 pp, 8vo. A parody of Disraeli's Coningsby. Not sgd. With 3 pen & ink sketches. In half mor slipcase. CNY Dec 15 (39) $2,600

ALs, 19 Oct [n.y.]. 2 pp, 8vo. To Brown. Comparing his family with the Merdles. Sgd with initials. Bound into a bound vol of ptd & Ms letters by Thackeray. pn Nov 9 (453) £220

Ds, [25 Jan 1847]. 2 pp, 4to. Memorandum of agreement with Bradbury & Evans for the publication of his novel Vanity Fair. With small ink stain in margin. CNY May 17 (111) $7,000

### Thalberg, Sigismund, 1812-71

ALs, 14 Aug 1838. 2 pp, 4to. To Breitkopf & Haertel. Promising to send his Andante Op.32 for publication. star Mar 22 (1097) DM380

### Thatcher, Margaret. See: Carter, James Earl ("Jimmy") & Thatcher

### Theological Manuscripts

Ms, Introductio in theologiam christianam theticam & character obiecti theologici studii. Pars prima: Propedeutica. [Germany, c.1780]. 224pp, 199mm by 175mm. Contemp bds. HH Nov 14 (16) DM280

### Thibaut, Anton Friedrich Justus, 1772-1840

Ms, Pandekten, [1837-38]. 690 pp, 4to, in contemp bds. Extensive lecture notes, in the hand of W. von Trott. HN Nov 24 (2871) DM220

### Thiess, Frank, 1890-1977

ALs, 1 Feb 1940. 2 pp, 4to. To Erich Ebermayer. About affairs at the Zsolnay Press & the publication of recipient's new novel. star Mar 21 (358) DM360

### Thirty Years' War

— BRIAUMONT, JEAN PAUL. - Ls, 23 Oct 1639. 2 pp, folio. To the magistrates in Upper Austria. Reporting about the military situation. star Mar 22 (1248) DM220

— GORDON, JOHN. - Ls, 1 Mar 1640. 2 pp, folio. To magistrates in Trier. Referring to the Emperor's orders to establish winter quarters for his regiment in Trier. star Mar 22 (1244) DM2,200

### Thoma, Hans, 1839-1924

ALs, 14 July 1903. 1 p, 8vo. To Otto Julius Bierbaum. Concerning illusts for recipient's poems. star Mar 21 (723) DM220

### Thoma, Ludwig, 1867-1921

[A collection of 35 documents, 31 Mar 1902 to 2 Mar 1939, various lengths & sizes, 10 sgd by Kubin, 25 by his heiress Maidi von Liebermann, contracts with publishing houses & related matters, sold at Hartung & Hartung on 17 Nov 1995, lot 3323, for DM5,500.]

Autograph Ms, play, Christnacht 1914, [1914]. 29 pp, 4to. Including numerous autograph corrections. With related material. HH Nov 17 (3319) DM9,000

Series of 13 A Ls s, 25 Aug 1887 to Aug 1902. 56 pp, 8vo. To Ludwig von Raesfeld. Important correspondence about personal & family affairs. HH Nov 17 (3320) DM5,000

ALs, 7 Nov 1906. 3 pp, 8vo. To Georg Hirth. From Stadelheim Prison, requesting books. HH Nov 17 (3321) DM1,200

— 5 Aug 1921. 1 p, 4to. To Gottfried Boehm. Giving instructions for his funeral. With related material. HH Nov 17 (3322) DM1,000

**Autograph postcards** (2), 10 May 1911 & 27 Apr 1915. To Marion Thoma. Sending greetings from Kellerbach & from the eastern front. HH May 9 (2565) DM320

— LIEBERMANN, MAIDI VON. - Collection of 115 Ls s & 45 autograph postcards, sgd, 17 Feb 1930 to 7 July 1941. 425 pp, 4to & 8vo. Correspondence with the Albert Langen Press regarding the publication of Thoma's works, fees, copyright matters, etc. With carbon copies of replies. HH Nov 17 (3324) DM1,600

### Thomas, Dylan, 1914-53

**Autograph Ms,** early working draft of Do Not Go Gentle into That Good Night. [May 1951] 2 pp on 1 sheet, 8vo. Illus in cat CNY Oct 27 (140) $28,000

— Autograph Ms, working notes for the poem On a Wedding Anniversary. 12 pp, 4to, in pen & pencil on 9 sheets. With a fair copy of the poem. The last working version is dated July 1940. Illus in cat CNY Oct 27 (139) $7,500

**Collection** of 26 A Ls s & 7 Ls s, 1935-40. 48 pp, 4to & 8vo. To Desmond Hawkins. Some of the illustrated. Includes an 8-page letter discussing poems in The Map of Love. S July 11 (296) £18,500

**Series** of 7 A Ls s & 1 Ls, 4 May to 22 August 1939, 9 pp, 8vo & 4to. To Richard Church & other members of the publishing firm J. M. Dent & Sons. About many aspects of the publication of his book Map of Love. With some holes in the margins & some marginal notes. With carbon copies of 9 letters from those at Dent to Thomas. Illus in cat CNY Dec 15 (40) $6,000

— Series of 4 A Ls s, 1947 to 7 May 1953 & [n.d.]. 13 pp, 4to & 16mo. To his wife, Caitlin. With an autograph verse acrostic spelling her name, together with his black wallet, containing passport-size photo of Caitlin. S July 11 (350) £11,000

**ALs,** 12 Apr 1947. 1 p, 8vo. To John Davenport. Apologizing for missing a lunch, hoping to be invited again & discussing his family's arrival in Italy: "It is difficult to abuse officials in a language one does not know...." In half mor album. With a b&w photo of Thomas. S June 28 (220) £820

**Ptd photograph,** [n.d.]. 5 by 3 inches. With clipped signature mtd. Ck Apr 12 (118) £110

### Thomas, George H., 1816-70

**ADs,** [n.d.]. 1 p, 2 by 4.5 inches. In full: "I cheerfully endorse the foregoing application" With a port & a 69 caliber roundball from the woods of Chickamuga. Framed. Over-all size 13.5 by 14.5 inches. Illus in cat rms Oct 11 (114) $425

### Thomas, Lorenzo, 1804-75

**Ds,** 3 Feb 1863. 1 p, 4to. To Lewis Taylor. Notifying him that he is granted a 20-day leaves of absence. Framed with photo & 2 19th-cent stereographs. rms Nov 30 (29) $340

### Thompson, Francis, 1859-1907

**Autograph Ms,** poem, The Poppy. 80 lines, 4 pp, folio, sewn in wraps. 8 July 1895. Dediction Ms, illuminated in watercolor, to Monica Meynell. Sold with a collection of letters about the poem & his love for her. pn Mar 14 (415) £4,400

### Thompson, Jacob, 1810-85

**Ds,** 30 Mar 1858. 1 p, folio. Patent to John C. F. Solomon for an improvement in railroad brakes. Framed. P Dec 13 (358) $350

### Thomson, Charles, 1729-1824

**ALs,** 28 Mar 1785. 2 pp, folio. Recipient unnamed. Sending a report dealing with forged certificates for settling army accounts. P Dec 13 (361) $3,000

**Ls,** 7 June 1788. 1 p, 12.75 by 8 inches. Circular letter of transmittal. rs Nov 11 (46) $200

**Ds,** 9 Mar 1781. 3 pp, 4to. Congressional resolution commending Gen. Daniel Morgan & other officers for their victory at Cowpens. P Dec 13 (360) $4,500

— 27 July 1785. 1 p, 4to. Congressional resolution requesting the thirteen states to submit copies of their legislation; ptd. Evans 19285. P Dec 13 (362) $2,500

— 22 May 1788. 1 p, 4to. Congressional resolve adopting a Committee report "relative to public and unsettled Accounts"; ptd. Evans 21534. P Dec 13 (363) $1,800

**Check,** accomplished & sgd, 24 June 1819. Drawn on the Bank of Pennsylvania for $100 to Mary Thomson. Stained. Sang collection. P Dec 13 (364) $200

— Anr, 7 Nov 1820. 1 p, 4to. $80 payable to Mary Shoster [sic, Shoester] or Bearer. With ANs on verso by J. Thomson dated 27 Nov 1822 explaining why Shoester delayed in cashing the check. rms Oct 11 (373) $350

### Thomson, Virgil, 1896-1989

**Collection** of 44 A Ls s or Ls s, 1959-77. Mostly 1 p, 8vo or 4to. To Arnold Weissberger. Concerning his works, business & legal transactions. rms Nov 30 (312) $4,000

### Thornton, Matthew, Signer from New Hampshire

**ALs,** 7 Aug 1775. 1 p, folio. To Philip Schuyler. Abut a planned attack on Canada. With marginal edge breaks. rms Oct 11 (31) $4,500

**A Ds s** (2), 1 & 3 Feb 1766. 2 pp, 8vo. Legal writs in a paternity suit. P Dec 13 (365) $550

### Thornycroft, Sir William Hamo

**Series** of c.20 A Ls s, 1878-1914. About 40 pp, 8vo, in bds. To Theodore Blake Wirgman. pn Nov 9 (430) £100

### Thorpe, James Francis, 1888-1953 —& Williams, Theodore Samuel ("Ted")

**Group photograph,** [c.1950]. 253mm by 206mm. 3-quarter length, sgd by both. Illus in cat. Marans collection. CE Apr 17 (284) $1,000

## 1995 - 1996 · AUTOGRAPHS & MANUSCRIPTS TOWN

**Thurston, Howard, 1869-1936**
Signature, 22 Oct 1928. On program for a reception in his honor by Assembly No 4 of the Society of American Magicians in Philadelphia. Inscr above his port. CE June 12 (117) $100

**Tichatschek, Josef, 1807-86**
ALs, 14 Apr 1868. 1 p, 8vo. To the pbr N. Simrock. Ordering the piano reduction of Wagner's Meistersinger. HN May 15 (2727) DM320

**Tieck, Ludwig, 1773-1853**
ALs, 2 Jan 1829. 1 p, 4to. To Joseph Schreyvogel. Recommending the actor Blumenau. Illus in cat. HN May 15 (2728) DM740
— [c.1840]. 1 p, 8vo. To Ferdinand Johann Wit von Doerring. Postponing a lecture. HN May 15 (2729) DM700
— 2 Nov 1842. 1 p, 4to. To the bookseller Jonas. Ordering Voss's poems. star Mar 21 (359) DM520
— 21 Oct 1844. 1 p, folio. Recipient unnamed. Expressing reservations about his plans for a wandering troupe of players. S May 15 (230) £260

**Tiedge, Christoph August, 1752-1841**
ALs, [9 Aug 1823]. 2 pp, 8vo. To "Amalia". Expressing condolences. Including related ALs by Elisa von der Recke on integral leaf. star Mar 21 (360) DM280

**Tieftrunk, Johann Heinrich, 1760-1837**
ALs, 19 May 1802. 1 p, 4to. To Christian Gotthilf Herrmann. Sending a review. star Mar 21 (627) DM240

**Tiemann, Walter, 1876-1951**
[His guest book, 1920 to 1938, 18 pp & blanks, folio, in red lea gilt, containing entries by numerous printers, publishers & artists in Leipzig, sold at Hartung & Hartung on 17 Nov 1995, lot 3325, for DM700.]

**Tilly, Johann Tserclaes, Graf von, 1559-1632**
Ls, 21 Apr 1628. 2 pp, folio. To the mayor & council of the town of Stendal. Responding to a complaint about the Imperial army. With engraved port. star Mar 22 (1266) DM1,650
— 16 May 1630. 1 p, folio. To Maximilian von Trautmannsdorff. Discussing problems between Denmark & Hamburg regarding the payment of duties. HH May 9 (2449) DM1,300
Ds, 19 June 1630. 1 p, folio. Safeguard for the Jew Selsche Scheya. HN Nov 24 (2872) DM1,200

**Titov, Gherman S.** See: Gagarin, Yuri & Titov

**Titov, Gherman Stepanovich**
Autograph Ms, statement about his space flight, giving details of his mission. 1 p, 298mm by 210mm. With snapshot photo of Titov & Akulinichev, sgd by both. Yuri M. Baginsky collection P Mar 16 (63) $1,200
Ls, 21 Feb 1965. 1 p. 289mm by 203mm. To Galya Matinchenko. Sending congratulations on the birth of her daughter Elena. Sgd in pencil. Text in the hand of G. T. Dobrovolsky & with signatures of other cosmonauts from the Cosmonaut Training Center.
With related material. Sergei Zaytsev collection P Mar 16 (64) $300

**Tojo, Hideki, 1884-1948**
Photograph, sgd, [c.1945]. 95mm by 40mm, clipped from larger photograph. Full-length profile port. Illus in cat. Marans collection. CE Apr 17 (185) $1,200

**Toklas, Alice B., 1877-1967**
Collection of 41 A Ls s & 3 Ls s, 1950-67. To Arnold Weissberger. rms Nov 30 (313) $3,100

**Tolkien, John Ronald Reuel, 1892-1973**
ALs, 7 Dec 1946. 2 pp, 4to. To Miss. M. Standeven. About the coming completion of The Lord of the Rings. pn Mar 14 (416) £2,100
— 22 Oct 1955. 1 p on both sides. Framed. To Miss Judson. About her interest in his languages such as Quenya & Sindarin. b Jan 31 (24) £600

**Toller, Ernst, 1893-1939**
ALs, [n.d.]. 2 pp, 8vo. To Mr. & Mrs. Kapp. Announcing his departure. star Mar 21 (361) DM420

**Tolstoy, Leo, 1828-1910**
Photograph, sgd, 12 Dec 1905. 139mm by 88mm. Half length; by R. Thiele. Illus in cat. Marans collection. CE Apr 17 (96) $2,200

**Tompkins, Charles H., 1830-1915**
Ds s (2), 6 July & 21 Sept 1863. 2 pp, 4to. Lists of Quartermaster's Stores transferred to Washington. rms June 6 (57) $150

**Toombs, Robert Augustus, 1810-55**
Signature, [n.d.]. No size given. Sgd as " R. Toombs/ Washington, Ga." pba Feb 22 (187) $100

**Torgau, Friedrich von, Prince Bishop of Merseburg**
Document, [17 Oct] 1275. 1 p, vellum, 4to. Sale of property at Sitzenroda belonging to the cathedral at Merseburg to the Benedictine nuns at Sitzenroda. Illus in cat. star Mar 22 (1332) DM2,300

**Torstenson, Lennart, Count, 1603-51**
Ds, 29 Sept 1646. 1 p, folio. Order addressed to the Mayor of Grimmen to supply provisions for some servants & horses. star Mar 22 (1267) DM560

**Toscanini, Arturo, 1867-1957**
Autograph quotation, 2 bars. 28 Apr 1932. 1 p, 6 by 4.25 inches. Sgd. Illus in cat pba Oct 26 (77) $325
Photograph, sgd, 8 Mar 1938. 5.5 by 9.25 inch photo. Inscr to Thomas Sarnoff. Mtd. Illus in cat pba June 13 (232) $600
Photograph, sgd & inscr, 10 Aug 1931. 136mm by 84mm. Bust profile port, inscr with 2 musical quotations. Marans collection. CE Apr 17 (264) $700

**Tournachon, Gaspard Felix, 1820-1910.** See: Nadar

**Town, Thomas H.**
Autograph Ms, Nostalgia in the Army of the Potomac: Its Discovery, Cause and Effect by the late.... Introduction and Thesis by Capt. J. P. Russell. Harrison's

211

Landing VA, Aug 1862. 30 pp & title leaf, folio, unbound. F Mar 28 (680) $1,200

**Tracy, Spencer, 1900-67**
ALs, 6 July 1936. 1 p, 4to. To Mr. LeVino. Sending thanks for a thoughtful message. sg June 6 (183) $120
See also: Hepburn, Katharine & Tracy

**Tralles, Johann Georg, 1763-1822.** See: Humboldt, Alexander von

**Travis, William B., 1809-36**
ALs, 6 Feb 1835. 3 pp, 4to. To David G. Burnet. Discussing events & politicians in Texas, business matters, his slaves, immigrants to Texas, etc. Illus in cat. CNY May 17 (313) $18,000

**Trczka, Adam Erdmann, Count, 1599-1634**
Ls, [n.d.]. 1 p, folio. To [the estates of Lower Austria?]. Responding to a complaint about contributions requested by the Marchese de Granna. star Mar 22 (1268) DM2,000

**Trojan, Johannes, 1837-1915**
Autograph Ms (2), poems, Die 88er Weine, & Der leidende Raeuberhauptmann, [n.d.]. 7 pp, folio & 4to. Both sgd. star Mar 21 (362) DM400

**Trotsky, Leon, 1879-1940**
ALs, 22 Nov 1936. 4 pp, 4to. To Gerard Rosenthal. About his desperate situation in Norway & the theft of his papers in France, & requesting help in finding a safe country to stay. Illus in cat. star Mar 22 (1671) DM3,400
Ls, 14 May 1940. 1 p, 4to. To Suzanne La Follette. Explaining why he cannot publish in the same journal as [Herny Noel] Brailsford. star Mar 22 (1672) DM1,750

**Troup, Robert, 1757?-1832**
ALs, 4 Mar 1777. 3 pp, folio. To John Jay. Expressing doubts about the conquest of Canada. P Dec 13 (367) $800

**Truebner, Wilhelm, 1851-1907**
ALs, 24 June 1904. 2 pp, 8vo. To the pbr Cassirer. Sending a Ms. HN May 15 (2732) DM280

**Truman, Bess Wallace, 1885-1982**
ALs, [23 Jan 1952]. 3 pp, 8vo. To Cobina Wright. Mentioning a photo & the Duke of Windsor: " I am perfectly delighted to have the beautiful and interesting photograph of you. It was extremely nice of you to send it and I shall enjoy having it. I do hope the Duke called you while he was here - he told me he surely would. I think their visit was a great success..." With dampstained original holograph envelope. rms Oct 11 (374) $325

**Truman, Harry S., 1884-1972**
Typescript (duplicated), mimeographed address to the Indiana Democratic Editorial Association, 27 Aug 1955. 4 pp, folio. Criticizing the Eisenhower administration; sgd. P Dec 13 (369) $1,100

Series of 4 Ls s, 12 May 1947 to 7 Jan 1949. 1 p, 4to each. To James Pendergast. About a variety of matters. The last letter sgd by Rose A. Conway, the President's assistant. CNY Dec 15 (245) $650

Ls, 4 Nov 1939. 1 p, 4to. To Mr. W. L. Bryson. About his son & a possible appointment for him: "...i cannot offer you any encouragement...I have hundreds of applications on file for this appointment [US Naval Academy] from boys all over the State..." pba Oct 26 (323) $200

— 11 Dec 1941. 1 p, 4to. To Mr. A. Loyd Collins. Suggesting Collins offer to work for the War Department. pba Oct 26 (324) $225

— 28 Feb 1945. 1 p, 4to. To Mrs. Ollie Hatner. About her soldier son: "...When the boy returns to the States [from the war]. I will, of course, be glad to be of any assistance to him that I can. However....the army greatly resents what they call Congressional interference, as they rightly should..." With ptd free frank on enevlope. Illus in cat CNY Dec 15 (240) $650

— 15 May 1946. 1 p, 8vo. To Richard R. Nacy. Criticizing Gov. Harwood's actions as Governor of the Virgin Islands. P Dec 13 (368) $850

— 30 Dec 1946. 1 p, 4to. To John W. Carrothers. Thanking for news & photographs, & sending New Year's wishes. Illus in cat. rms Mar 21 (144) $500

— 20 March 1947. 1 p, 4to. To Edward McKim. Thanking him for his comments on his message to Congress. With handwritten postscript. With original envelope. pba Feb 22 (285) $350

— 12 Dec 1949. 1 p, 4to. To Frank L. Weil, Chairman of the President's Committee on Religion and Welfare in the Armed Forces. Suggesting a special appeal to all communities to extend friendship & hospitality to those members of the armed forces "who must stand duty and cannot be with their families." rms Nov 30 (314) $2,200

— 29 Aug 1953. 1 p, 4to. To Frederick R. Lachman. Agreeing to attend a meeting regarding Hebrew University. HN May 15 (2733) DM480

— 2 Dec 1953. 1 p, 4to. To Phil Kerby. Thanking him for a telegram: "It was worded just right". pba June 13 (86) $75

— 28 May 1954. 1 p, 8vo. To the Secretary General of the Institute of Pacific Relations. Sending thanks for a book. Framed with photo. rms Nov 30 (42) $420

— 4 Oct 1956. 1 p. To Wilmer Stanley Roberts. Thanking him for a note and "the Critic Kit." rms Nov 30 (315) $325

— 26 June 1957. 1 p, 4to. To Arnold M. Grant. About whether or not he can come to New York for the Human Rights Award Dinner. sg Feb 1 (231) $175

— 14 Aug 1957. 1 p, 4to. To Stacy Keach (the elder). Thanking him for a phonograph recording on the Constitution. wa Oct 28 (239) $90

— 31 Mar 1959. 1 p, 4to. To Mr. Lurge. About the right to vote. pba Oct 26 (325) $450

— 28 Mar 1960. 1 p, 4to. To Phil Kerby. Thanking him for sending an article. pba Oct 26 (326) $110

— 21 Nov 1961. 1 p, 4to. To David J. Oestreicher. Defending the bombing of Hiroshima & Nagasaki. Illus in cat. P Dec 13 (370) $25,000
— 12 June 1962. 1 p, folio. To Paul Nachtman. Thanking for congratulations on his birthday. star Mar 22 (1678) DM750
— 28 May 1963. 1 p, 4to. To Stacy Keach (the elder). Thanking him for a phonograph recording on the Bill of Rights. wa Oct 28 (237) $120
— 12 Aug 1963. 1 p, 4to. To Stacy Keach (the elder). Commenting on Keach's project to set to music portions of the Constitution. wa Oct 28 (238) $230
— 12 Mar 1965. 1 p, 4to. To Paul Nachtman. Sending a photograph (not present) for a young man. rms June 6 (483) $140
— 21 Oct 1970. 1 p, 4to. To Peter J. Tayer. Concerning history: "You will find the study of history a fascinating subject and one that will help guide you in your future life and judgements you will be making..." With port. Mtd & framed under glass. Frame chipped. Over-all size c. 13.3 by 17.1 inches. rms Oct 11 (375) $400
**ANs**, 13 Feb 1945. On ALs of an autograph collector requesting a sgd photo. "Out of pictures Here's an autograph. Harry S Truman". wa Oct 28 (236) $160
— 24 Oct 1955. 2 pp, 12mo. To D. R. Sutphia. Confirming that he has read Progress and Poverty. Illus in cat. rms Mar 21 (146) $155
**Ds s (2)**, 10 Jan & 8 March 1927. 1 p each, 4to. Approved purchase orders for Jackson County, Mo. sg Sept 28 (267) $350
**Check**, sgd, Feb 1934. Drawn on the Treasurer of Jackson County, Missouri for $24.84 payable to Southside Supply Co. rms June 6 (336) $250
**Group photograph**, sgd, 10 Aug 1945. Oblong folio. Showing Truman in session with his Cabinet & others, sgd by all 15 others. With key to the photo & pencilled numbers on the photo. wa Oct 28 (235) $1,900
**Photograph, sgd & inscr**, 22 Sept 1966. On 8 by 10 inch port photo. Inscr to Mrs. Gaye Boyer. Illus in cat pba Oct 26 (329) $350
**Signature**, 16 Dec 1958. At the bottom of a note asking him for an autograph. "Best wishes & good luck". sg Feb 1 (232) $200
— Anr, [n.d.]. On 9 by 12 inch ptd engraving. Inscr to Catherine E. Breslin. Illus in cat pba Oct 26 (330) $225

## Truman, Harry S., 1884-1972 —& Barkley, Alban William
**Signature**, [n.d.]. No size given. On separate cards. With a 1949 inauguration button & 2 first-day stubs from the 1948 Democratic National Convention. Framed. Over-all size 10.5 by 14 inches. Illus in cat rms Oct 11 (325) $285

## Trumbull, Jonathan, 1710-85
**Ls**, 30 Apr 1780. 1 p, 4to. To Nehemiah Hubbard. Writing the Deputy Quartermaster General about provisions: "This moment received a letter from Major General Howe at the Highlands, dated the 27th instant expressing the distress of that department of the army for want of provisions...That they have had no fresh beef for three weeks, and desiring salted provisions to be forwarded..." pba Oct 26 (150) $850
**ADs**, 4 July 1777. 1 p, 8vo. Warrant to Sheriff Jabez Huntington of Windham County to "deliver to Mr. Gamalid Babcock Two Thousand pounds weight of Coffee belonging to this State, for the Continental Army..." Sgd as Governor of Connecticut. Illus in cat rms Oct 11 (32) $475
**Ds**, 20 Jan 1742. 1 p, 8vo. Summons from Daniel Huntington's suit against Samuel Raymond for 4 pounds, 15 shillings & interest. Browned & offset. pba June 13 (46) $100

## Tshombe, Moise, 1919-69
**Ls**, 25 May 1964. 2 pp, folio. To Senator Jacob Javits. Reporting on the situation in the Congo Dar Oct 25 (239) $110

## Tucker, Thomas Tudor, 1745-1828
**Ds**, 8 Feb 1814. 1 p, 4to. Receipt for Peter Gordon, Treasurer of New Jersey for $92, 541.06 as "the net amount of the quota of the State of New Jersey of the Direct Tax imposed by the Act of Congress of the 2d of August 1813..." Offset. rms Oct 11 (376) $350

## Tudor, William, 1750-1819
**ALs**, 23 June 1775. 5 pp, folio. To Stephen Collins. Patriot account of Bunker Hill. Tape-reinforced. P Dec 13 (36) $14,000

## Tuerk, Daniel Gottlob, 1750-1813
**ALs**, 23 Dec 1786. 2 pp, 4to. To [Friedrich Gottlieb Busse]. Referring to a subscription & to an unpleasant letter by recipient's brother. star Mar 22 (1100) DM400

## Tufts, Cotton, 1732-1815
**ALs**, 15 Oct 1772. 1 p, oblong 8vo. To his daughter. Thanking her for a letter. CE June 12 (124) $100

## Turgenev, Ivan, 1818-83
**Photograph, sgd**, [c.1870]. 103mm by 58mm, mtd. 3-quarter length, standing; by Carjat. Marans collection. CE Apr 17 (97) $1,100

## Turgot, Anne Robert Jacques, Baron de l'Aulne, 1727-81
**Series** of 28 A Ls s, 6 Apr 1770 to 16 Oct [1776]. About 85 pp, mostly 8vo, in mor-backed cloth. To the Marquis de Condorcet. Discussing scientific, literary & political matters. C Nov 29 (190) £4,500
**Ls**, 14 Jan 1775. 1 p, folio. Recipient unnamed. Sending thanks for New Year's greetings. With port. sg June 6 (185) $300

## Turkish Manuscripts
**Ms**, Muntahab natigat as-sa... [Ottoman, c.1825]. 200 leaves, 275mm by 152mm. Contemp lea. In nastaliq script. Imperf. HH Nov 14 (106) DM220
— ALI BEN SULTAN MUHAMMAD AL-QUARI AL-HEREWI. - Raf' al-hafa' an dat as-Sifa. [Ottoman, 18th cent]. 403 leaves (incomplete), 210mm by 150mm. Contemp

lea gilt. In naskhi script. With illuminated tp. HH Nov 14 (91) DM340

**Turner, Joseph Mallord William, 1775-1851**
**Ds,** 18 Apr 1820. 1 p. Authorization, on behalf of the Royal Academy, for the importation of plaster casts from Italy for F. L. Chantry. Also sgd by Sir Thomas Lawrence & H. Bone. wad Oct 18 (155) C$400
**Cut signature,** [n.d.]. No size given. pba June 13 (233) $120

**Twain, Mark.** See: Clemens, Samuel Langhorne

**Tweed, William Marcy, 1823-78**
**Photograph, sgd,** [c.1873]. 82mm by 60mm, mtd. Shoulder-length port. Marans collection. CE Apr 17 (27) $850
**Signature,** May 1853. 1 p, 4to. On a petition of Patrick Highland to Greene C. Bronson for a Custom House position. Also sgd by 9 others. rms June 6 (488) $200

**Two Guns White Calf, Chief, 1872-1934**
**Photograph, sgd,** [c.1927]. 324mm by 250mm. Profile port, by Hileman. Sgd with totem signature (2 guns & a calf). Illus in cat. Marans collection. CE Apr 17 (186) $1,800

**Tyler, John, 1790-1862**
**ALs,** 21 Mar 1834. 1 p, 4to. Recipient unnamed. About an inquiry about a pension claim under the Act of June 1832. In passable condition. sg Feb 1 (235) $250
— 10 Apr 1841. 1 p, 8vo. To William C. Johnson. About "a memorial of a large number of Master Mariners...representing the great necessity of establishing certain Light Houses for the security of vessels [sic] navigating the Gulf of Mexico...the Government can never feel otherwise than deeply interested in whatever shall advance the interests of trade,and that the subject of the memorial will receive all the attention to which its merits entitle it..." Withport. Mtd & framed. Over-all size 16.75 by 12.75 inches. Illus in cat rms Oct 11 (377) $550
— 23 Nov 1843. 1 p, 4to. To Mrs. Benson. Agreeing to a request. CE June 12 (125) $750
— 11 Oct 1844. 2 pp, folio. To John Y. Mason. Responding to a letter from Mason about contracts for building docks in Brooklyn & Pensacola & other places with the Sceretary of the Navy. With Mason's letter to the President. CNY Dec 15 (125) $1,800
— 12 Nov 1849. 3 pp, 4to. To John Y. Mason. Elaborating on his financial difficulties to the former Secretary of the Navy. CNY Dec 15 (249) $1,600
— 24 June 1852. 1 p, 4to. To Charles Wayne. Apologizing for being unable to supply Wayne with Gen. Harrison's autograph & suggesting he contact the Harrison family. pba Oct 26 (331) $1,500
**Ls,** 29 June 1826. 2 pp, 4to. To Sec of War James Barbour. Requesting the return of 2 military deserters. Forbes Magazine collection. CNY May 17 (193) $700

**Ds,** 4 May 1826. 1 p, 4to. Appointment of Stephen Sanders as Lieut. in the 35th Regiment, 19th Brigade. cb June 25 (2385) $650
— 22 Mar 1842. 1 p, 4to. Order to affix the U.S. Seal to a letter of credence for Washington Irving as Minister to Spain. Mtd to a detached cover of a Washington Irving book. First 2 letters of signature light. sg Feb 1 (236) $425
— 12 Nov 1842. 1 p, folio, parchment. Ship's passport for the ship America. Countersgd by Secretary of State Daniel Webster. With envelope featuring holograph free frank. CNY Dec 15 (250) $900
— 11 Aug 1843. 1 p, folio. Land grant to Joseph Vidal. P Dec 13 (371) $550
— 25 Aug 1843. 1 p, on vellum, oblong 4to, mtd to modern vellum. Appointment of William K. Mayo as a midshipman in the Navy. CE June 12 (126) $650
— 24 June 1844. 1 p, on vellum, 15 by 11.75. Ship's passport. Countersgd by John C. Calhoun. rs Nov 11 (48) $650
— 29 June 1844. 1 p, folio. Four-language ship's papers for the whaler Mitten. Countersgd by Secretary of State John C. Calhoun. CNY Dec 15 (248) $750
— 18 Dec 1844. 1 p, folio. Ship's passport for the barque Pilgrim. Countersgd by H. S. Legare. rms Mar 21 (36) $1,200
**Envelope,** 7 Jan 1846. 3-line address on 4to address leaf. With related materials. sg Sept 28 (270) $500

# U

**Udet, Ernst, 1896-1941 —& Others**
[The signatures of Udet & 5 other aviators, Oct 1928, on verso of a postcard photograph of a Dornier airplane, sold at Granier on 29 Sept 1995, lot 260, for DM200.]

**Uhland, Ludwig, 1787-1862**
**ANs,** 18 Apr 1837. 1 p, 8vo. Recipient unnamed. Ordering books. HN May 15 (2734) DM340
**ADs,** 11 Sept 1855. 1 p, 4to. Postal receipt. star Mar 21 (365) DM450

**United States**
— SUPREME COURT. - Group photograph, [26 Nov 1963]. 280mm by 355mm. The justices of the Warren Court during the funeral of President Kennedy; sgd by all 9. Illus in cat. Marans collection. CE Apr 17 (191) $4,500

**United States of America**
— LOUISIANA PURCHASE. - Ds, [23 May 1803], 1 p, folio. Statement that the Louisiana Treaty & 2 related conventions, now ratified by Napoleon, have been delivered to the US envoys. Sgd by Francois de Barbe-Marbois, Robert R. Livington & James Monroe. With Ls, [28 May 1803], 1 p, 4to, from Barbe-Marbois to Livingston & Monroe. Requesting them to temporarily return the ratified treaties so that further copies can be made & to briefly delay the departure of Peter A. Jay for the US. Sang - Engelhard collections CNY Jan 26 (172) $18,000

— U.S. ARMY SIGNAL CORPS. - Ms notes documenting the technology of balloon construction during the First World War. Akron, 1917-18. 86 leaves, 8vo, in loose-leaf binder. Including technical drawings by Lieut. Howard A. Scholle. With c.50 leaves of related material laid in. sg May 16 (7) $500

**Unold, Max, 1885-1964**
Autograph postcards (2), sgd, 27 Sept 1919 & 26 Sept 1923. To Alfred Kubin. About visits. HH Nov 17 (3283) DM400

**Unsworth, Barry**
Autograph Ms, workbook for his novel, Sacred Hunger. About 140 pp, folio, spiral-bound. Sgd & inscr on upper cover. S Dec 18 (427) £1,600 [Gordon]

**Upward, Edward**
Series of 5 A Ls s, 1933-62. 8 pp, 8vo. To Olive Mangeot. S Dec 18 (357) £300 [Quaritch]

**Urban VIII, Pope, 1568-1644**
Document, 22 June 1629. 1 p, 4to. Papal brief addressed to William Ogilby, sending him & 8 monks to Scotland as missionaries. star Mar 22 (1498) DM650

**Usher, John Palmer, 1816-89**
ALs, 20 Nov 1864. 1 p, no size given. To Mrs. H. W. Tilton. Apologizing for being slow to respond to her. With orig cover featuring his franking signature. pba June 13 (30) $375

# V

**Valentino, Rudolph, 1895-1926**
Photograph, sgd & inscr, [n.d.]. 9 by 7 inches. Inscr to Mr. & Mrs. Paul Lawrence. sg Feb 1 (237) $750

**Vallejo, Mariano G.**
ALs, 5 June 1871. 2 pp, 8 by 5 inches, on single folded sheet. To his son Platon. Depressed letter. With related material. Larson collection pba Sept 24 (265) $150

— 10 May 1887. 4 pp, 11 by 8.5 inches. To his nephew, Guillermo Carrillo. Sending news of his life and health. Larson collection pba Sept 24 (263) $325

— 1889. 4 pp, 6 by 5 inches, on single folded sheet. To his nephew. About the funeral of a relative. Larson collection pba Sept 24 (264) $275

**Van Buren, Martin, 1782-1862**
ALs, [c.Dec 1818]. 2 pp, 8vo. To John Henry. Promising to support him in a suit. star Mar 22 (1679) DM600

— 15 Dec 1827. 2 pp, 4to. To Abraham Beninger. About buying some of Beninger's pale sherry. rms Nov 30 (318) $900

— 20 Feb 1830. 2 pp, 4to. To Mr. Wilde. About the Consulship at Gibraltar. sg Feb 1 (238) $550

— 27 Apr 1839. 4 pp, 4to. To B. F. Butler. About candidates for the position of Surveyor for the Port of New York & a diplomatic Matter in Central America. Illus in cat sg Sept 28 (271) $2,800

— 26 July 1839. 2 pp, 4to. To Levi Woodbury. Sending a blank paper with his signature to be used for an appointment. rms Mar 21 (32) $1,600

— 29 Apr 1840. 3 pp, 4to. To B. F. Butler. About possible appointments & political matters. rms Nov 30 (319) $1,100

— 15 Oct 1844. 3 pp, 4to. To John D. Mendenhall. Declining to attend a Democratic party meeting but expressing confidence in the Democratic cause. Including franking signature. rms June 6 (489) $1,500

— 13 Sept 1860. 1 p, 8vo. To E. G. Chapman. Sending his autograph. wa Oct 28 (240) $290

— [n.d.]. 1 p, 8vo. To Mr. Everett. About a dinner. pba Feb 22 (288) $250

AL, 2 Feb [n.y.]. 1 p, 4to. Accepting an invitation to the Ball to be given by the Albany Burgettes Corps. In 3d person. CE June 12 (129) $70

Ds, 9 Mar 1838. 17 by 13.75 inches, on vellum. Appointment of John C. Long as Commander in the Navy. rs Nov 11 (50) $675

— 10 Oct 1840. 1 p, 14.75 by 11.25 inches, on vellum. Countersgd by John Forsyth. rs Nov 11 (49) $475

— [c.1840]. 1 p, folio. Ship's passport for the Haeline of New Bedford. P Dec 13 (377) $450

Cut signature, [n.d.]. Cut from Envelope. pba Feb 22 (289) $190
See also: Jackson, Andrew & Van Buren

**Van Gogh, Vincent, 1853-90**
ALs, [c.Aug 1886]. 6 pp, 8vo. To H. M. Levens. Explaining his views on color & his initial encounter with the work of the French Impressionists. In English. Illus in cat. S Dec 1 (55) £37,000

— [February 1890]. 2 pp, 270mm by 210mm. To Albert Aurier. Thanking an art critic for a rave review: "Many thanks for your article...I like it very much as a work of art in itself, in my opinion, your words produce color, in short, I rediscover my canvases in your article, but better they are, more full of meaning..." Browned. With frayed margins & some paper loss, including a few words at the top left corner. Illus in cat P Dec 12 (172) $95,000

**Vanbrugh, Sir John, 1664-1726**
Autograph Ms, proposals for the rebuilding of part of Hamton Court Palace. 3 pp, folio. With a scribal copy of same, sgd by Vanbrugh. S Dec 18 (543) £2,000 [Maggs]

**Vance, Dazzy, 1891-1961.** See: Johnson, Walter Perry & Vance

**Vanderbilt, Cornelius, 1794-1877**
ADs, 21 July 1824. 1 p, 4to. Receipt by Noah Mostman for $6.50 from Vanderbilt "for keeping horses". Illus in cat. rms June 6 (490) $1,000

Photograph, sgd, [c.1865]. 100mm by 60mm, mtd. 3-quarter length, by D'Utassy. Sgd on verso. Illus in cat. Marans collection. CE Apr 17 (188) $2,400

**Vangerow, Karl Adolf von, 1808-70**

**Vangerow**

**Ms,** Pandecten-Vorlesung, [1854-55]. About 675 pp in 2 vols, in contemp bds. Lecture notes, in the hand of Bodo von Buelow. HN Nov 24 (2876) DM400

**Varese, Edgard, 1883-1965**
**ALs,** 31 Oct 1928. 1 p, 4to. To an unnamed Ed. Planning a concert in Paris & inquiring about news from Paris. star Mar 22 (1101) DM310
**Autograph postcard, sgd,** [7 May 1955]. To Fred Gruenfeld. Thanking for a card & hoping to see him. star Mar 22 (1102) DM240

**Varnhagen von Ense, Karl August, 1785-1858**
**Autograph Ms,** 7 poems, each sgd, [n.d.]. 2 pp, 8vo. HN May 15 (2736) DM480
— Autograph Ms, poem addressed to Wilhelm Neumann, beginning "Vom Blumenhuegel ist herabgeflossen...", & 2 other poems, [n.d.]. 4 pp, 8vo. HN May 15 (2737) DM420
**ALs,** 3 Sept 1849. 4 pp, 8vo. To an unnamed lady. About old age, the political situation, travels, new books, etc. HN May 15 (2735) DM600

**Vasarely, Victor de**
**Autograph Ms** (2), Preface, Vasarely Inconnu, & Dessins Spatiaux 1942, [n.d.]. 2 pp, 4to. star Mar 21 (724) DM360

**Vaughan Williams, Ralph, 1872-1958**
**ALs,** [9 June 1935]. 1 p, 4to. To the Rev. Greville Cooke. Responding to an inquiry about his composition On Wenlock Edge. star Mar 22 (1103) DM650

**Venice**
**Document,** census of the inhabitants, [16th cent]. 18 pp, 4to. Listed in 6 groups by sestiero & classified according to rank or profession; with list of monasteries at end. S Dec 1 (56) £480

**Veniero, Antonio, Doge of Venic, d.1400**
**Letter,** 1 Sept [1386]. 1 p, vellum, folio. To Jacobutio Portia. Referring to a report by Leonardo Dandolo & Marino Maripetro about recipient's activities "ad honorum nostrum et bonum... libertatis patrie". star Mar 22 (1376) DM580

**Verdi, Giuseppe, 1813-1901**
**Autograph music,** draft of the orig version of the Willow Song & the Ave Maria from Act 4 of his opera Otello, with drafts for the drinking song in the 1st Act of the opera; [c.1885]. 20 pp (1 blank), folio, in fitted black calf case. Differing in many respects from final version. Including presentation inscr by Maria Carrara Verdi. Previously unrecorded. Illus in cat. S Dec 1 (375) £170,000
**ALs,** 23 Oct 1856. 2 pp, 8vo. To Ercolano Balestra. About various business matters. star Mar 22 (1104) DM2,400
— 15 Dec 1872. 1 p, 4to. To the chairman of the Comitato presso l'Accademia Filarmonico-Drammatica at Ferrara. Sending a contribution for a charity. star Mar 22 (1105) DM1,500
— 28 Oct 1873. 2 pp, 8vo. To Francesco Florimo. Thanking for some cantatas by Scarlatti & reporting about his stay in the country. star Mar 22 (1106) DM2,000
— 2 Jan 1887. 2 pp, 8vo. To Domenico Morelli. Asking him to send a photograph of a painting to Milan. star Mar 22 (1107) DM1,750
— 22 Mar 1894. 2 pp, 8vo. To Paul Solanges. Expressing his determination to attend the production of Falstaff in Paris. S May 15 (523) £2,800
— 22 Aug 1894. 3 pp, 8vo. To Paul Solanges. Remarking that he has heard no reports about the success of Falstaff & Aida at Paris. S May 15 (524) £3,200
— 2 [Jan?] 1896. 1 p, 8vo. To unnamed recipient. In full: "Thanks to a distinguished artist for having remembered the old maestro, who thanks you also on the part of his wife and wishes you every happiness." Foxed & toned. Withport. Mtd & framed under glass. Over-all size 16.75 by 10.3 inches. rms Oct 11 (380) $650
**ANs,** 31 Mar 1862. 1 p, c.12cm by 18cm. Recipient unnamed. Requesting the forwarding of his correspondence to Turin. In French. S May 15 (522) £1,200
**Autograph telegram,** sgd, [n.d.]. 1 p, 4to. To Teresa Stolz. Inquiring whether he must come to Borgo. Including ALs, draft, to an unnamed recipient on verso. star Mar 22 (1108) DM1,250
**Photograph, sgd,** 18 May 1897. 163mm by 110mm, mtd. Bust port, by Ricordi. Illus in cat. Marans collection. CE Apr 17 (265) $5,200
— Boito, Arrigo. - 4 A Ls s, 1887 to 1893. 16 pp, 8vo. To Paul Solanges. About Verdi's Otello & Falstaff. S May 15 (525) £550
— Verdi, Giuseppina Strepponi. - ALs, 9 May 1872. 3 pp, folio. To [Cesare Vigna]. Discussing her husband's character. star Mar 22 (1109) DM900

**Verdi, Giuseppina Strepponi, 1815-97.** See: Verdi, Giuseppe

**Verlaine, Paul, 1844-96**
**Collection** of 2 A Ls s & autograph Ms, 30 Jan 1894 to [1 June 1894]. 7 pp, 8vo. To Emile Bally. Sending a poem (included, Toast a S.Em. Bally), & expressing condolences & inquiring about a painting. C Nov 29 (191) £1,300

**Verne, Jules, 1828-1905**
**ALs,** 14 Sept 1897. 1 p, 16mo. Recipient unnamed. Sending his autograph. star Mar 21 (367) DM800
**Photograph, sgd & inscr,** 16 Aug 1900. 153m by 100mm, mtd. Bust-length profile port, by Nadar. Inscr to Dudley Payne Lewis. Illus in cat. Marans collection. CE Apr 17 (98) $1,500

**Vernon, Edward, 1684-1757**
**Ds,** 12 Oct 1745. 1 p, 4to. Warrant addressed to Lieut. John Eeles to discharge David Coulton. P Dec 13 (378) $250

**Viardot, Louis, 1800-83.** See: Viardot, Pauline & Viardot

**Viardot, Pauline, 1821-1910 —&**
**Viardot, Louis, 1800-83**
ALs, 7 Jan 1859. 4 pp, 8vo. To George Sand. Joint letter, concerning Pauline's visit to Hungary & Leipzig, Franz Liszt, an article in the Gazette des Beaux-Arts, etc. S May 15 (526) £750

**Victoria, Queen of England, 1819-1901**
**Autograph Ms,** memorial written in favor of James Pristo, former farm manager at Osborne. 4 pp, 8vo. Dated 21 Apr 1873. pn June 13 (218) £170
ALs, 28 June 1839. 2 pp, 8vo. To "Alexandre". Wishing he could visit. HN May 15 (2739) DM750
— 7 Nov 1855. 4 pp, 8vo. To His Serene Highness Prince Edward of Saxe Weimar. Requesting new ports of relatives. Sgd "VR." With autograph envelope sgd "The Queen." Stained. sg Feb 1 (240) $450
AL, 21 Mar 1839. 1 p, 8vo. In 3d person, approving the appointment of a consul & granting Mr. Bligh an audience. CE June 12 (130) $110
— 8 Jan 1857. 2 pp, 8vo. To Sir George Grey. In 3d person, returning his dispatches & commenting on British policy in South Africa. star Mar 22 (1346) DM950
Ds, 3 July 1854. 1 p, 4to. Approval of appointments submitted by the Lord Chancellor. rms Nov 30 (321) $300
— 27 June 1862. 1 p, folio. Appointment of John Hill as Lieutenant of Engineers. rms Mar 21 (347) $320
— 19 July 1881. 2 pp, folio. Appointing Sir Hardinage Stanley Gifford as Counsel for George Tydell Rowley. pba Feb 22 (311) $150
**Document,** 1856. 50cm by 48cm, vellum, in wooden box. Confirmation of arms for the Rev. Jameson. Including 3 large achievements of the arms in gold & colors. JG Sept 29 (317) DM480
**Signature,** [n.d.]. On routing slip. Sgd "The Queen". Countersgd by Prime Minister Russell. Framed with port photo. rms Nov 30 (47) $450

**Victoria, Queen of England, 1819-1901 —&**
**Albert, Prince Consort of Victoria of England, 1819-61**
[A pair of matched photographs, sgd, [c.1861], 95mm by 63mm, mtd, by Mayall & Silvy respectively, sold at Christie's East on 17 Apr 1996, lot 189, for $22,200.]

**Viertel, Berthold, 1885-1953**
[A collection of 27 typescripts of poems (15 carbon copies), 28 Oct 1944 & [n.d.], 29 pp, 4to, 6 sgd, sold at Hauswedell & Nolte on 24 Nov 1995, lot 2879, for DM2,000.]

**Villa, Francisco ("Pancho"), 1877-1923**
**Ptd photograph,** [c.1915]. 138mm by 95mm (image). With 2 children; sgd by Villa. Illus in cat. Marans collection. CE Apr 17 (28) $3,200

**Villa Lobos, Heitor, 1887-1959**
**Autograph music,** ballet, Uirapuru (O passaro encantado) (Bailado Brasileiro), [c.1934?]. 84 pp, folio, in red cloth gilt. Fair copy of the full score in the revised version of 1934, sgd on tp & at head; inscr to Serge Lifar. Including 2 pp in typescript. star Mar 22 (1110a) DM11,000

**Villard, Henry, 1835-1900**
ALs, 21 Aug 1893. 1 p, 8vo. To Mr. Bullitt. Thanking him for a note. Detail in cat rms Oct 11 (381) $300

**Virchow, Rudolf, 1821-1902**
ALs, 17 Mar 1878. 2 pp, 4to. To an unnamed physician. Responding to an article offered for print in his journal. star Mar 21 (631) DM900
**Autograph postcard, sgd,** 9 Jan 1894. To Karl Weinhold. Declining a dinner invitation. star Mar 21 (632) DM700
Ds, 1876. 1 p. Admission card for Mr. Brant to the lectures relating to the anatomy of muscles & bones at the University of Berlin. rms Nov 30 (322) $400

**Vishinsky, Andrei —&**
**Litvinov Maxim**
**Menu,** sgd by both, 13 Feb 1945. On an 8vo official embossed menu card. rms Nov 30 (323) $500

**Vittorio Emanuele III, King of Italy, 1869-1947**
Ls, 22 July 1940. 1 p, folio. To King George II of Greece. Offering condolences on the death of his uncle. S Dec 1 (57) £300
Ds, 22 Sept 1927. 1 p, folio. Transfer of Lieut. Marco Todeschini to the Engineer Corps. Countersgd by Mussolini. Illus in cat. rms June 6 (425) $375
— 3 Nov 1927. 1 p, folio. Military promotion for Lieut. Adriano Bacula. Countersgd by Mussolini. Illus in cat. rms Mar 21 (322) $520
— 21 Nov 1938. 1 p, folio. Military discharge. Countersgd by Mussolini. star Mar 22 (1371) DM320
See also: Mussolini, Benito & Vittorio Emanuele III

**Vlaminck, Maurice de, 1876-1958**
ALs, 19 Feb 1920. 1 p, 4to. To "cher Carco". Requesting the return of some notes. star Mar 21 (725) DM400

**Vogt, Karl, 1817-95**
A Ls s (2), 19 & 30 June 1871. 3 pp, 8vo. To Robert Oppenheim. Discussing a projected trans of a work by James D. Dana. star Mar 21 (633) DM320

**Voight, Hans Henning**
**Autograph Ms,** poem, Endymion. 41 lines on 2pp, 4to. S Nov 21 (3) £450

**Voigtmann, Caspar**
Ms, Beschreibung dieses neuen Artilleriebuchs.... 1686. 100 leaves, 322mm by 192mm, in contemp calf. With dedication to Heinrich, Duke of Saxony in watercolor, 47 colored plates (6 large & folding) 6 pen & wash plates, 9 diagrams & 2 pen & wash titles of flags & arms. Dedication inscr within cartouche on 1st illuminated leaf. C June 26 (24) £8,000

**Volta, Alessandro, 1745-1827**
ALs, 19 May 1801. 1 p, 4to. To Pietro Pulli. Sending some information about his "nouvel Appareil elec-

trique, ou galvanique". Illus in cat. star Mar 21 (634) DM7,300

**Voltaire, Francois Marie Arouet de, 1694-1778**
ALs, 6 [May 1761]. 2 pp, 8vo, in mor gilt bdg. To [Ponce Denis Ecouchard Le Brun]. Discussing various accusations & intrigues. star Mar 21 (368) DM6,500

Ls, 5 June 1772. 2 pp, 8vo. To the Marquise Dudeffant. About the influence of health on a person's disposition, medical experiments, etc. Illus in cat. rms June 6 (494) $1,500

— 16 Apr 1778. 2 pp, 8vo. To Coun.d. Rochefort. About his health & arrangements for his funeral & burial. With translation. Illus in cat rms Oct 11 (382) $925

ANs, [n.d.]. 1 p, 8vo. Recipient unnamed. Concerning a text which he will send to M. Cramer. HN Nov 24 (2880) DM1,800

**Vulpius, Christian August, 1762-1827**
ALs, 17 Feb 1814. 1 p, 8vo. To [F. A. Brockhaus]. Offering contributions for print. star Mar 21 (153) DM320

# W

**Wagner, Cosima, 1837-1930**
Ms, diary, 29 Dec 1928 to 31 Mar 1930. 46 pp, 12mo, in black calf. Thoughts on her father Franz Liszt, her husband Richrd Wagner, & others, in the hand of her daughter Eva. With earlier matter in anr hand. S May 15 (533) £1,500

**Wagner, Ernst, 1769-1812**
ALs, 13 Feb 1810. 1 p, 4to. To his pbr [Goeschen]. About a 2d Ed of his novel Die reisenden Maler. star Mar 21 (369) DM560

**Wagner, Richard, 1813-83**
Autograph Ms, draft of a prose essay, Music and Music of the Soul. [c.1870s] 9 pp, 4to. Illus in cat sg Feb 1 (241) $2,000

Autograph music, Ankunft bei den schwarzen Schwaenen, paraphrase in A flat major of the aria Sei mir gegruesst, from his opera Tannhaeuser; 29 July 1861. 3 pp, 4to. Scored for piano; sgd on tp & inscr to the Countess Pourtales. star Mar 22 (1111) DM37,000

— Autograph music, sketches comprising c.100 bars for the opening orchestral prelude to Act 2 of Siegfried & c.40 bars for the opening of the Prologue to Goetterdaemmerung, 20 May [18]57. 2 pp, c.17cm by 25.5cm, cut from larger leaf. In short score, with numerous revisions. Differing significantly from final versions. Framed. Illus in cat. S Dec 1 (388) £11,000

ALs, 13 Oct [18]39. 1 p, 4to. To Gottfried Engelbert Anders. About Luigi Lablache's refusal to include an aria written by Wagner in a production of Bellini's Norma. Illus in cat. S Dec 1 (382) £1,800

— 29 Aug 1845. 3 pp, 8vo. To Johann Kittl. Thanking for recipient's compositions, discussing Der fliegende Hollaender, & inviting Kittl to a performance of Tannhaeuser in Dresden. star Mar 22 (1112) DM4,000

— 14 Jan 1852. 2 pp, 8vo. To Franz Brendel. Protesting against an article by August Hitzschold in the Neue Zeitschrift fuer Musik. star Mar 22 (1113) DM4,600

— 13 Aug 1853. 5 pp, 8vo. To [Louis Schindelmeisser]. Expressing dissatisfaction about the public discussion of his libretto Der Ring des Nibelungen & discussing changes in Tannhaeuser. star Mar 22 (1114) DM11,000

— 23 Sept 1853. 4 pp, 4to. To [Robert Franz]. Discussing his own & recipient's compositions, the conflict between modernism & traditionalism, & the impossibility of separating form & content in music. S Dec 1 (385) £3,200

— 23 Mar 1857. 3 pp, 8vo. To an unnamed theater director. Promising to have the score of Tannhaeuser sent to him & expressing his confidence that the projected production will be the best in Germany. S Dec 1 (384) £1,500

— 31 Dec 1857. 3 pp, 8vo. To [Eduard Liszt?]. Asking for his help in obtaining monies due him for performances of Tannhaeuser in Vienna. S May 15 (531) £2,900

— 5 Sept 1858. 3 pp, 8vo. To an unnamed theater director. About the success of Lohengrin at recipient's theater, & requesting a payment of 500 florins. S Dec 1 (386) £1,500

— 4 Mar 1859. 1 p, 8vo. Recipient unnamed. Urging him to send 2,000 florins. S Dec 1 (380) £1,000

— 12 Feb 1863. 1 p, 8vo. To [Matteo Salvi]. Concerning problems in finding singers for a projected performance of Tristan und Isolde in Vienna. star Mar 22 (1115) DM3,400

— 26 Feb 1864. 1 p, 8vo. Recipient unnamed. Asking for help in settling a debt. S May 15 (529) £1,000

— 31 May 1864. 1 p, 8vo. Recipient unnamed. Referring to a disappointing response to a request for a loan & his good relations with the King of Bavaria. S Dec 1 (387) £2,600

— 9 June 1864. 2 pp, 8vo. Recipient unnamed. Making arrangements to buy back from Herr Rebel the effects from his house in Penzing. S May 15 (530) £1,700

— 18 Oct 1868. 4 pp, 4to. To Oswald Marbach. Venting his frustrations about the times & doubting that true art will be appreciated. star Mar 22 (1116) DM6,200

— 15 Oct 1871. 5 pp, 8vo. To Ernst Wilhelm Fritzsch. Discussing fees for his collected works. star Mar 22 (1117) DM5,200

— 27 Dec 1872. 4 pp, 8vo. Recipient unnamed. Inquiring about the financial situation of the Wagner Society in Vienna. star Mar 22 (1118) DM6,200

— 16 Feb 1873. 2 pp, 8vo. To [Karl Batz]. Sending a power of attorney for a suit in Leipzig & discussing financial matters. star Mar 22 (1119) DM2,900

— 21 Mar 1873. 2 pp, 8vo. To Herr Lieblein. Insisting that he must decline his invitation to give a concert in Prague. star Mar 22 (1120) DM2,100

— 30 Apr 1875. 3 pp, 8vo. To Adolf Fuerstner. Stating conditions for the publication of some revised scenes of Tannhaeuser. star Mar 22 (1121) DM4,500

— 18 May 1877. 1 p, 12mo. To Dr. Bernhard Schnappauf. Asking him to forward a parcel with some silk textiles. C Nov 29 (264) £1,100

**Ls,** 21 Aug 1867. 1 p, 8vo. To Giovan Gualberto Guidi. Looking forward to hearing his business conditions. S May 15 (528) £600

— 1 Nov 1881. 1 p, 8vo. To the director of the theater in Frankfurt. Giving instructions for payments. star Mar 22 (1123) DM900

**Autograph quotation,** the Shepherd's pipe tune from Act 3 of Tristan und Isolde, 26 Sept 1861. 1 p, 4to. Four bars, sgd. Illus in cat. S Dec 1 (379) £3,600

### Wagner-Warmbronn, Christian, 1835-1918

**Autograph Ms,** poem, Romanze vom Siegelberg, 13 May 1898. 2 pp, 8vo. 8 stanzas, sgd at head. star Mar 21 (370) DM900

### Walewski, Alexandre Florian Joseph Colonna, Comte de, 1810-68

**Ls s** (2), 3 July 1855 & 1 June 1858. 3 pp, folio. To the Vicomte de l'Espine. Concerning his appointment & his discharge as secretary of the legation in St. Petersburg. star Mar 22 (1434) DM350

### Walker, Mary Edwards, 1832-1919

**ALs,** [n.d.]. 1 p, 12mo. To unnamed recipient. Thanking them for a " your early decision". With trimmed carte-de-visite photo. Mtd. Illus in cat rms Oct 11 (383) $475

**Autograph quotation,** [n.d.]. Beginning "We leave the print of every thought on some mind every day...." Sgd Mary E. Walker, M.D. With related material. rms Nov 30 (324) $400

**Photograph, sgd,** [c.1877]. 165mm by 105mm, mtd. 3-quarter length, by Bell. Marans collection. CE Apr 17 (190) $3,800

### Wallace, Alfred Russel, 1823-1913

**ALs,** 2 Dec 1897. 2 pp, 8vo. To B. Knowles. Setting out the theory of evolution as discovered by himself & Charles Darwin. pn Nov 9 (417) £2,100

### Wallace, Edgar, 1875-1932

**Photograph, sgd & inscr,** [c.1915]. 213mm by 126mm, mtd. 3-quarter-length port; by Horace W. Nicholls. Marans collection. CE Apr 17 (99) $250

### Wallenda, Karl, 1905-78

**Group photograph,** [c.1945]. 259mm by 200mm. With his 2 brothers & sister, doing one of their acts, with NY skyline in the background; sgd & inscr by Karl Wallenda. Illus in cat. Marans collection. CE Apr 17 (29) $700

### Wallenstein, Albrecht von, Herzog von Friedland & Mecklenburg, 1583-1634

**Ls,** 23 Dec 1627. 1 p, folio. To the city of Greifswald. Requesting them to prevent the Danish from returning to northern Germany. Illus in cat. star Mar 22 (1269) DM3,700

**Letter,** 13 June 1625. 3 pp, folio. To the Imperial chancellery. Draft; concerning his elevation to the dukedom. HH May 9 (2449a) DM1,600

### Waller, Thomas ("Fats"), 1904-43

**Photograph, sgd & inscr,** [c.1940]. 254mm by 199mm. Seated at the piano in a radio studio; inscr to Maurice Holland. Marans collection. CE Apr 17 (239) $400

### Walser, Martin

**Autograph Ms,** book review, Die Ortliebschen Frauen, by Franz Nabel; [n.d.]. 19 pp, 4to, on verso of photocopies. Including revisions; sgd. star Mar 21 (372) DM1,100

### Walter, Bruno, 1876-1962

**ALs,** 27 Aug 1925. 4 pp, 4to. On 2 sheets. To "Liebe Justi". [Justine Rose, sister of Mahler]. Decrying her actions & warning her that she is putting their friendship in jeopardy: "I warn you to remember what it means to gamble with a friendship of over thirty years...to say nothing and to fret and grumble for years...Else has adored Gustav deeply, and was very attached to him. She was and is attached to you..." sg Sept 28 (273) $150

**Photograph, sgd,** 2 Oct 1917. 6.25 by 4.25 inches. Sepia photo by Joseph Paul Bohm. Mtd on 8vo sheet. Nicked. pba June 13 (235) $140

### Walton, George, Signer from Georgia

**ALs,** 28 Oct 1779. 3 pp, 8vo. To Benjamin Lincoln. On military matters. Illus in cat. Sang collection. P Dec 13 (379) $3,750

**Ds,** 27 Jan 1783. 1 p, folio. Legal summons in a trespass case. In hand of & also sgd by Nathaniel Pendleton. sg Feb 1 (242) $300

— 20 June 1789. 1 p, folio. Land grant in Washington County to John Gardner. Tied together with Ms map of the grant. sg Feb 1 (243) $325

### Walton, Sir William, 1902-83

**A Ls s** (2), 28 Mar 1939 & 2 Sept [n.y.]. 5 pp, 8vo. To Leslie Heward. Stating that the premiere of his Violin Concerto has been postponed because Heifetz is unavailable, mentioning a performance of his 1st Symphony, & congratulating him on a performance of Elgar's Falstaff. S Dec 1 (389) £400

### Ward, Thomas

**Autograph Ms,** diary of a bibliographical tour of the Coninent in 1733. About 100 pp, 8vo, in contemp calf pn Nov 9 (437) £650 [Marlborough]

### Warner, Charles Dudley, 1829-1900. See: Clemens, Samuel Langhorne & Warner

### Warren, Francis E.

[An archive of letters & other material, 1884-1915, to & from Warren as President of the Warren Live Stock Co. & relating to its failing state sold at Pacific on 8 August 1996 for $1,100.]

### Warren, James, 1726-1808

**ALs,** 27 Apr 1775. 1 p, 4to. To [Elbridge Gerry?]. Reporting about deliberations in the Rhode Island legislature regarding a cooperation with Massachusetts. Illus in cat. P Dec 13 (380) $3,000

**Warren, Joseph, 1741-75**

ADs, 1773. 1 p, 8vo. Receipt for payment of "Medicines and Attendance for himself from May 16, 1772 to January, 1773." Silked. With port. Detail in cat rms Oct 11 (385) $2,300

Ds, 14 May 1775. 1 p, 12mo. Order addressed to the Commissary General to supply provisions. Illus in cat. Sang collection. P Dec 13 (381) $4,000

**Washburne, Elihu B., 1816-87**

ALs, 16 Aug 1881. 2 pp, 8vo. Letter of Introduction for Levi Z. Leiter. rms Oct 11 (386) $185

**Washington, Booker T., 1856-1915**

Ls, 8 June 1897. 1 p, 4to. Recipient unnamed. Recruiting teachers for the coming year. sg Mar 28 (369) $375

— 10 June 1897. 1 p, 4to. Recipient unnamed. Asking about an address. sg Mar 28 (370) $130

— 21 Feb 1902. 1 p, 4to. Recipient unnamed. Saying that there no present vacancies that could be offered Mr. Doane. sg Mar 28 (371) $275

— 22 Apr 1904. 1 p, 4to. To C. B. Smith. About a position that has already been filled. Illus in cat pba Feb 22 (109) $275

— 7 Apr 1913. 1 p, 4to. To a resident of Owego NY. Seeking a donation. bbc June 24 (55) $130

— 23 Feb 1915. 1 p, 4to. To James B. Forgan. Trying to raise funds for the Tuskegee Institute: "...There are few institutions in the country where students do more to help themselves than is true here: they provide the cost of their board, books, travelling expenses, clothing etc, but are unable to pay the cost of tuition, which is $50.00 a year...Any amount, however small will be helpful to us..." Illus in cat pba Oct 26 (128) $350

Photograph, sgd, 7 June 1909. 199mm by 149mm, mtd. Seated, by Rockwood. Illus in cat. Marans collection. CE Apr 17 (192) $1,300

**Washington, Bushrod, 1762-1829**

ADs, 1 Apr 1806. 1 p, 8vo. Pay order in favor of Charles Simms. Inscr in anr hand on verso. Illus in cat. rms Mar 21 (345) $700

Cut signature, 11 July 1903. Framed with photo. sg Mar 28 (373) $130

**Washington, George, 1732-99**

Autograph Ms, Leaf from his First Inaugural Address, beginning "But until the people of America shall have lost all virtue" on side numbered 35 & "of the people of that Country. To embrace this object the mind must dilate with the dimensions of a Continent, and extend with the revolutions of futurity." [Apr 1789] With note by Jared Sparks "Washington's handwriting, but not his composition". Illus in cat pn June 13 (225) £180,000

— Autograph Ms, Map & survey of 40,000 acres in the Dismal Swamp belonging to the Potomac Company; [c.late 1780س]. 1 p, folio. Docketed in Washington's hand on verso. Illus in cat. rms Mar 21 (2) $9,000

— Autograph Ms, Portion of his First Inaugural Address. [1789]. Pages 59 & 60. About developing the country. Illus in cat. Sparks - Stein - Engelhard Ms CNY Jan 26 (155) $50,000

ALs, 22 Aug 1775. 3 pp, 4to. To Joseph Palmer. Discussing fortifications around Boston. Illus in cat. P Dec 13 (384) $22,000

— 7 May 1778. 1 p, 229mm by 187mm. To Maj. Gen. Benjamin Lincoln. Sending [not present] Lincoln & Benedict Arnold sets of epaulets given Washington by Lafayette. Illus in cat P June 5 (115) $57,500

— 9 July 1787. 1 p, 4to. To [Michael-Guillaume Saint Jean de Crevecoeur]. Thanking the recipient for a letter and a copy of his book, Letters from an American Farmer. Left margin worn. Illus in cat CNY Dec 15 (255) $27,000

— 8 May 1788. 2 pp, 4to. To [James McHenry]. Referring to the ratification of the Constitution by Maryland, a shipment of peas, & M. Campion's request for money. Illus in cat. rms Mar 21 (1) $21,000

— 8 June 1788. 2 pp, 232mm by 190mm. To Oliver Pollock. Apologizing for the belated acknowledgment in responding to Pollock's request. P June 5 (117) $21,000

— 18 Mar 1789. 2 pp, 4to. To James Mercer. Requesting payment of money owed to him by recipient's brother John. P Dec 13 (391) $16,000

— 27 July 1794. 4 pp, 4to. To Col. Burgess Ball. About the purchase of land for a federal arsenal & the work habits of a former overseer at Mount Vernon. Forbes Magazine collection. CNY May 17 (198) $19,000

— 23 Dec 1795. 1 p, 4to. To Edward Carrington. Acknowledging several letters & informing him about problems with administrative appointments. CNY May 17 (316) $16,000

— 1 Feb 1796. 2 pp, 4to. To Oliver Wolcott, Sr. Referring to the death of Samuel Huntington & Wolcott's succession as Governor of Connecticut. Illus in cat. P Dec 13 (393) $37,500

— 8 July 1796. 1 p, 4to. To John Marshall. Offering him the appointment as Minister to France. Silked. Illus in cat. Forbes Magazine collection. CNY May 17 (199) $26,000

— 20 July 1796. 1 p, 4.5 by 7.5 inches. To Oliver Wolcott, Jr. Writing his Secretary of the Treasury about his own finances. Docketed by Wolcott on verso. With some show through. Lacking upper & lower left corners of address leaf. Detail in cat Dar Oct 19 (10) $15,000

— [1799]. 1 p, 4to. To William [B.] Harrison. Portion of letter only. Negotiating for a neighbour's property. Spotted & with losses at folds. With holograph free frank. Missing a portion of blank margin. CNY Dec 15 (257) $13,000

Ls, 13 Aug 1776. 1 p, 175mm by 181mm, inlaid to larger sheet. To Richard Derby, Jr. Thanking him for a dispatch. P June 5 (113) $9,000

— 14 Apr 1777. 1 p, folio. To Col. John Patton. Complaining of recruiting officers under recipient's command who "spend a great deal of time in Idleness & Dissipation". Illus in cat. Forbes Magazine collection. CNY May 17 (195) $13,000

— 26 Apr 1777. 1 p, folio. To Brigadier General John Glover. Trying to persuade Glover to rejoin the Revolution. With free frank. Reapairs on versos. Illus in cat CNY Dec 15 (251) $42,000

— 1 Aug 1777. 1 p, 4to. To Lieut. Col. Anthony Walton White. Instructing him to send unreliable soldiers to headquarters. P Dec 13 (385) $18,000

— 28 Dec 1777. 1 p, folio. To Major Gen. William A. Stirling. Approving of his suggestions for measures against persons "furnishing the Enemy with Provisions." Forbes Magazine collection. CNY May 17 (196) $14,000

— 14 July 1779. 1 p, folio. To [Col. John Lamb]. Instructing him to supply the militia with ammunition. Including autograph postscript. Forbes Magazine collection. CNY May 17 (197) $13,000

— 15 Feb 1780. 1 p, folio. To Colonel Stephen Moylan. Asking his Chief of Calvary for "an Exact Return of the number of Non Commissioned Officers and privates of your Regiment ...You cannot be too expeditious in forwarding me this Return..." Dampstained & spotted, affecting words in the text. CNY Dec 15 (127) $9,000

— 31 Jan 1781. 1 p, folio. To [the Officer Commanding at Charlottesville, N. C.]. About the exchange of prisoners of war. In the hand of Alexander Hamilton as Washington's Aide-de-Camp. Docketed. Browned & silked. With a defective upper left-hand corner and losses at folds. Backed with linen. CNY Dec 15 (128) $8,500

— 5 Aug 1781. 2 pp, folio. To Brigadier General James Clinton. Directing the Yorktown campaign: "I have also prevailed on Major General Lincoln to set out tomorrow Morning for Berkshire & Hampshire Counties to urge on the Levies with all possible expedition: from General Lincoln's high reputation...I cannot but flatter myself that this measure will be attended with success..." Stained. Mtd & Framed with an engraved port of Brigadier General Clinton. Illus in cat CNY Dec 15 (129) $27,000

— 21 Nov 1796. 1 p, 4to. To the President of the Council & the Speaker of the House of Assembly of the State of New Jersey. About his retirement from public life; acknowledging their Resolution approving his conduct in the administration of the government of the US. F Mar 28 (697A) $40,000

— 16 Dec 1798. 4 pp, 4to. To Sec. of War James McHenry. Planning for the possibility of war with France. Illus in cat wd May 8 (30) $65,000

ADs, 22 Oct 1750. 1 p, 308mm by 184mm. Survey of 203 acres made for Isaac Foster, with plat. Framed with port. P June 5 (111) $8,000

— 7 June 1775. 1 p cut from a larger sheet, 41mm by 114mm, backed. Reciept for 32 pounds from John Ross on account of Andrew Litch. P June 5 (112) $7,500

— 18 May 1785. 1 p, folio. Exchange of lands between Washington & William Triplett. Sgd twice by Triplett; sgd by Washington in endorsement. Illus in cat. P Dec 13 (388) $23,000

— 22 Sept 1786. 1 p, folio. Purchase of lands owned by the late Harrison Manley. Also sgd by others. P Dec 13 (389) $18,000

— 16 - 19 Dec 1797. 8 pp, folio. Lease of lands on the Great Kanawha River to James Welch; Washington's copy. P Dec 13 (396) $40,000

— 26 Nov 1799. 1 p, 4to. Order addressed to John Gill to supply blankets & cloth for his slaves. Silked. Illus in cat. rms Mar 21 (3) $12,000

Ds, [1768]. 1 p, 32mm by 128mm. Ticket no 372 for the Mountain Road Lottery. CNY May 17 (315) $4,500

— 19 Mar 1791. 295mm by 368mm, framed. Commission of James Stephenson as a Lieutenant in the First Regiment of Levies. P June 5 (118) $5,500

— 8 June 1783. 1 p, 4to. Military discharge for John List. Framed with a port. Illus in cat. P Dec 13 (387) $6,500

— 8 June 1783. 1 p, folio. Army discharge for Jacob Bennett. Countersgd by Jonathan Trumbull, Jr. Fold through signature. Framed. sg Feb 1 (244) $5,800

— 13 June 1783. 2 pp, folio. Discharging soldier John Meachem after his service in the war. Countersgd by Jonathan Trumbull Jr. Small stain affecting 1 letter of Washington's signature. cb June 25 (2386) $6,500

— 13 June 1783. 2 pp, folio. Discharging soldier Moses Bushman after his service in the war. Countersgd by Jonathan Trumbull Jr. Dampstained. With discolored edges & repairs to verso. CNY Dec 15 (130) $4,800

— 30 June 1783. 1 p, 10.75 by 8.3 inches. Discharge of James Grindall Dummer. rs Nov 11 (51) $6,500

— 24 May 1784. 1 p, 360mm by 510mm, parchment. Certificate of membership to the Society of Cincinnati for Jonathan Holmes. Engraved by Jean-Jacques Andre Le Veau. Handcolored. Stained. CNY Dec 15 (131) $4,500

— 31 Oct 1785. 1 p, on vellum, oblong folio. Document issued by the Society of the Cincinnati to Bartholomew von Hees. Also sgd by Henry Knox. Washington signature faded but legible. F June 20 (769) $2,100

— 24 May 1794. 1 p, folio. Three-language ship's papers for the vessel Marshall. Countersgd by Secretary of State Thomas Jefferson, Collector of the Port of Alexandria John Fitzgerald, and Mayor Robert Mease. Browned & brittle & cracked. With worn edges & repairs on verso. Illus in cat CNY Dec 15 (256) $9,000

— 8 Feb 1797. 1 p, folio. Land grant to John Jameson. Countersgd by Timothy Pickering. Illus in cat. P Dec 13 (394) $6,500

— 21 Jan 1799. 1 p, 32mm by 197mm, cut from larger sheet. Acknowledgment that a plan in deeds made for George Mercer's lands is correct. Also sgd by others. P Dec 13 (397) $2,250

Document, 5 Dec 1794. 1 p, 108mm by 200mm. Written & sgd by William Deakins. Receipt given to Washington for his 2d payment towards the purchase of a water lot property in Washington. Mtd with supporting materials. P June 5 (119) $1,200

Check, 26 Aug 1797. 1 p, 4to. $762.50 payable to Dr. James Craik. Check No.1. Aged. Left corner repaired. Illus in cat rms Oct 11 (387) $20,000

# WASHINGTON

**Cut signature,** [n.d.]. On 4.5 by 2 inch slip of paper. Dampstained. Illus in cat pba Oct 26 (334) $4,000

**Franking signature,** on address panel clipped from a letter addressed in hand of Tench Tilghmen to Richard Derby, [13 Aug 1776]. Inlaid to larger sheet. P June 5 (114) $4,000

**Lottery ticket,** 1768. 1 p, 40mm by 115mm. Ticket for the Mountain Road Lottery. Sgd. CNY Dec 15 (126) $5,000

— MOUNT VERNON. - ALs each by Robert Toombs & John A. Washington, & Ds by Edward Everett, 11 Aug 1856 to 30 July 1859, 4 pp, size not stated; relating to the sale of Mount Vernon to the Mount Vernon Ladies' Association. P Dec 13 (289) $1,200
See also: Hancock, John

## Waterhouse, Benjamin, 1754-1846

**ALs,** 5 Jan 1799. 1 p, 4to. To Congressman Christopher Grant Champlin. Asking for help in gaining an Army commission for George Waterhouse: " Genl. Knox appears very partial to George & spoke of his success with confidence but as there are so many applicants I thought that your influence would go a great way towards rendering the matter certain..." With integral holohgraph address leaf. Illus in cat rms Oct 11 (388) $1,000

— 9 June 1812. 4 pp, 4to. To Caleb Strong. About his trouble at Harvard: "I have moreover felt no small repugnance at the very idea of exposing to the view of the public the unhappy differences that have taken place in the medical department of our University, which department I have been labouring to build up the greatest part of my life..." pba Oct 26 (129) $1,400

## Watson, Thomas Augustus, 1854-1934

**Photograph,** sgd & inscr, Feb 1927. 247mm by 201mm, mtd. Shoulder-length port. Illus in cat. Marans collection. CE Apr 17 (57) $1,600

## Watt, James, 1736-1819

**ALs,** 10 Apr 1785. 3 pp, 4to. To Jean Andre de Luc. About his son & his new inventions. star Mar 21 (635) DM3,000

## Watts, Thomas Hill

**ALs,** 9 Nov 186(2-3). 1 p, 4to. To Confederate Congressman H. Cruikshank. Giving an endorsement for a Captain Oden. Illus in cat pba June 13 (31) $750

## Waugh, Evelyn, 1903-66

**Autograph Ms,** A Layman's Hopes of The Vatican Council. [1962]. 6 pp, folio. With corrections & revisions & an added paragraph on verso of a leaf. Also with an APS from 30 Jan 1964 to [Simon Nowell Smith] presenting the manuscript. S June 28 (268) £2,500

**Typescript,** Decline & Fall. [1928]. 210 pp, folio. With some pencil corrections. Also with a general title & title pages. S June 28 (238) £11,000

**Series** of 19 ALs s & 8 APs s, 1928-30, 1931 & 1951, 29 pp, 8vo. To Thomas Balston. Concerning his books,

his marriage to Evelyn Gardner & travel. S June 28 (236) £6,200

**ALs,** [c.1929]. 1 p, 8vo. To Lord Hastings. Thanking him for 2 vols on Selina, Countess of Huntington. S Dec 18 (431) £260 [Lenygon]

— 27 Dec 1945. 2 pp, 8vo. To G. D. Hobson. Concerning Hobson's letter published in the Times about a Picasso exhibition at the Tate. S June 28 (255) £520

— 22 June 1963. 1 p, 8vo. To Mrs. Frederick Stopp. About the beauty of his character; congratulates her on her election as FRSL. S Dec 18 (429) £360 [Henry]

**Ds,** 18 Oct 1932. 1 p, 8vo. Wager concerning John Julius Cooper (later Viscount Norwich), in the hand of A. Windham Baldwin & sgd by both he & Waugh ("Boaz"). S July 11 (353) £360

## Wayne, Anthony, 1745-96

**Autograph Ms,** notes & observations on the Constitution of Pennsylvania, [1787]. 15 pp, folio. P Dec 13 (404) $6,500

**ALs,** 29 Sept 1777. 4 pp, 4to. Recipient unnamed. Angry letter about the fall of Philadelphia to the British. P Dec 13 (402) $15,000

— 25 Dec 1780. 4 pp, 8vo. To George Washington. Discussing movements of the British fleet. P Dec 13 (403) $14,000

— 20 May 1789. 3 pp, 4to. To James Wilson. Congratulating him on his appointment to the Supreme Court. P Dec 13 (406) $5,500

**ADs,** 21 July 1780. 1 p, folio. Minutes of a "Council of War held in the field..."at Bull's Ferry. Soiled. With worn edges & a separation at the horizontal fold. CNY Dec 15 (132) $13,000

## Wayne, John, 1907-79

**Ds,** 26 May 1947. 16 pp. Contract between Wayne & Argosy Pictures Corporation for 1 film. Illus in cat. Ck Dec 14 (224) £1,500

**Photograph,** sgd & inscr, [n.d.]. 9 by 7 inches. Inscr to Myrna & sgd in black felt pen. Ck Dec 14 (223) £300

## Webb, Alexander Stewart

**ALs,** 12 Aug 1881. To an editor. About difficulties in writing about the campaign in the Peninsula. Framed with photo & related material. rms Nov 30 (30) $600

## Weber, Bernhard Anselm, 1766-1821

**ALs,** 22 Apr 1809. 2 pp, 4to. To Ambrosius Kuehnel. Sending some compositions for publication. star Mar 22 (1128) DM650

## Weber, Carl Maria von, 1786-1826

**ALs,** 6 Dec 1819. 2 pp, 4to. To Count Bruehl. Discussing plans for the premiere of his opera [Der Freischuetz] in Berlin. Illus in cat. star Mar 22 (1129) DM9,500

## Webern, Anton von, 1883-1945

**ALs,** 2 May 1922. 1 p, 8vo. To Paul Koeniger. Promising to contact Schoenberg on his behalf. S May 15 (535) £650

— 12 Mar 1927. 2 pp, 8vo. To Paul Koeniger. Discussing his conducting commitments & mentioning Berg's Chamber Concerto. S May 15 (536) £700

**Autograph postcard, sgd,** 8 Aug 1934. To Egon Wellesz. Discussing the festschrift for Dr. Bach. S May 15 (556) £500

### Webster, Daniel, 1782-1852

**ALs,** 28 May 1818. 1 p, 9.75 by 15.5 inches. To Thomas W. Thompson. About giving President Brown a few copies of the Blue Book. rs Nov 11 (53) $200

— 8 Feb 1847. 4 pp on 1 folded 8vo sheet. Recipient unnamed. Defending then-Senator Jefferson Davis over an amendment concerning the issue of secession. CE Sept 27 (29) $700

**Ds,** 4 Apr 1841. 1 p, folio. To an unnamed dignitary. Letter of State announcing the death of President William Henry Harrison. Soiled. rms Oct 11 (187) $8,500

**Engraving,** [c.1830]. 257mm by 205mm. Shoulder-length port of Webster by Cheney & R. W. Dodson; sgd by Webster & inscr to Mr. Brown. Illus in cat. Marans collection. CE Apr 17 (193) $600

### Wedekind, Frank, 1864-1918

**ALs,** 7 June 1904. 2 pp, 4to. To Bruno Cassirer. Concerning a publishing contract. star Mar 21 (374) DM630

— 24 Aug 1909. 2 pp, 8vo. To Jacques Mahler. Discussing the possible performance of his plays in Riga. With other letters to Mahler. S Dec 1 (58) £650

— [c.8 May 1914]. 2 pp, 8vo. To Adolf Weisse. Accepting an invitation to a performance of his play Musik. star Mar 21 (375) DM750

### Weill, Kurt, 1900-50

**Autograph quotation,** 4 bars from Der Jasager, to the text "Er hat ja gesagt...", [25 Dec] 1931. 1 p, 11cm by 11cm. Sgd. Illus in cat. S Dec 1 (390) £520

### Weinheber, Josef, 1892-1945

**Collection** of ALs & lithographed port, sgd, 28 Sept 1944. 2 pp, 4to. To the soldier Leb. Sending 2 books & expecting to be drafted into the army. HN May 15 (2746) DM400

**ALs,** 23 Nov 1936. 2 pp, 4to. Recipient unnamed. Responding to an invitation to lecture in Bonn. star Mar 21 (376) DM420

### Weizmann, Chaim, 1874-1952

**Collection** of 2 ALs s & 1 typed file copy, sgd, 4 June 1930 to 8 June 1931. 8 pp. To Lewis Namier as political secretary to the Jewish Agency for Palestine. With related material. S July 11 (376) £4,600

**Ls,** 14 nov 1928. 1 p, 4to. To David Freiberger, president of the American Zion Commonwealth. About repayment of a $250,000 loan. sg June 6 (188) $950

— 7 Apr 1930. 1 p, folio. To the Ed of the Weekend Review. Complimenting him on an article. S May 15 (234) £800

### Weizsaecker, Julius, 1828-89

[A group of 12 documents & letters relating to his career as a scholar, 1846 to 1887, sold at Stargardt on 21 Mar 1996, lot 636, for DM440.]

### Welch, Lew

**ALs,** 20 Mar 1971. 1 p, no size given. To Stephen Vincent. Concerning an offer to teach a class at the San Francisco Art Institute. With mailing envelope. pba Jan 25 (375) $425

### Welles, Gideon, 1802-78

**Ls,** 19 Dec 1863. 1 p, 4to. To Lt. Comm John G. Walker. Informing him that he is " hereby detached from temporary duty at the Navy Yard, Boston, and you will hold yourself in readiness for the command of the U. S. Steamer Saco..." pba June 13 (32) $250

— 13 June 1865. 1 p. To Paymaster James C. Graves of the U.S.S. Shawmut. About the cancellation of a requisition. Framed with port 7 2 stereographs. rms Nov 30 (31) $400

**Ds,** 6 July 1861. 1 p, 4to. Orders for surgeon Albert Schriver to report for duty on the U. S. Sloop of war Marion. pba Feb 22 (195) $130

### Welles, Orson, 1915-85

**Collection** of 2 Ls s & 2 inscr Christmas cards, 21 Nov 1951 & [n.d.]. 2 pp & cards. To Arnold Grant. sg Feb 1 (246) $450

**Ls,** [c.1962). 1 p, 8vo. To his lawyer, Arnold M. Grant. About a lawsuit. sg Feb 1 (245) $350

### Wellington, Arthur Wellesley, 1st Duke, 1769-1852

**Collection** of 183 A Ls s & documents, 14 Nov 1807 to 12 Sept 1851. Over 350 pp. To Sec. to the Admiralty John Wilson Croker. With Wellington's holograph notes for Croker's pamphlet "Military Events of the French Revolution 1830", 18 pp plus 2 pp of Croker's holograph notes & 5 Croker A Ls s, 1828-30 to Wellington. All inlaid to larger sheets & bound in mor extra by Riviere. P June 5 (345) $23,000

**ALs,** 29 July 1816. 2 pp, 4to. Recipient unnamed. Renting recipient's house. star Mar 22 (1681) DM550

— 2 Mar 1817. 1 p, 4to. To George Canning. Recommendation of Montague Corby. rms Nov 30 (327) $400

— 18 Feb 1821. 3 pp, 12mo. To Lord Burghersh. Introducing Capt. and Mrs. Bligh. sg Feb 1 (247) $175

— 18 Oct 1825. 1 p, 8vo. To Samuel Smith. About preparation & delivery of various papers. Ink light throughout. sg June 6 (189) $130

— 7 Aug 1833. 1 p, 4to. To Bartholomew Lloyd. Referring to measures "recommended to the House of Lords on behalf of Trinity College Dublin". star Mar 22 (1683) DM250

— 24 Nov 1834. 1 p, 8vo. To Richard Dawson. Expressing thanks. HH May 9 (2567) DM200

— 6 July 1847. 1 p, 8vo. To unnamed recipient. About the train schedules in the Bishopgate area. pba Feb 22 (208) $170

— 4 Apr 1848. 8 pp, 8vo. To Gen. Sir Edward Blakeney. About the threat of the Chartist uprisings. S July 11 (371) £1,600

**ADs,** 20 Nov 1826. 1 p, 8vo. Order to admit 2 ladies to the House of Lords. star Mar 22 (1682) DM220

**Wellington, James**

**ALs,** 8 Nov 1777. 3 pp, 4to. To Thomas Clarke. Giving a full account of Clinton's attack on Fort Clinton. Sang collection. P Dec 13 (407) $2,000

**Wells, H. G., 1866-1946**

**ALs,** 27 May [19]20. 1 p, 8vo. To an unnamed recipient. Agreeing to take part in a gathering. With mounting remnants on verso. rms Oct 11 (390) $250

— 3 Apr 1929. 1 p, 4to. To Mr. Crowden. Declining to lecture because of the pressures of work. rms Nov 30 (328) $250

— 11 Feb 1943. 1 p. To Mr. Thornhill. About listening to a discussion group from anr room. Ck Apr 12 (120) £140

**Photograph, sgd & inscr,** May 1926. 345mm by 247mm, mtd. Half-length port, seated; by Harris & Ewing. Inscr to Harold Wheeler. Illus in cat. Marans collection. CE Apr 17 (100) $900

**Wells, Henry, 1805-78 —& Fargo, William George, 1818-81**

**Ds,** 22 Mar 1860. 1 p, 4to. Stock certificate no 508 in the American Express Company issued to Crommelin Goodwin Curtis. CNY May 17 (233) $1,800

— 29 Sept 1863. 1 p. Stock certificate of the American Merchants Union Express Co. Filled out to W. Y. Frost for 50 shares. cb June 25 (2325) $375

**Werfel, Franz, 1890-1945**

**Series** of 3 Ls s, 30 Mar to 2 Aug 1944. 4 pp, 4to. To Miss Sparr at Viking Press. About the publication of his work Between Heaven and Earth. star Mar 21 (377) DM1,000

**Werth, Jan van, c.1600-52**

**Ls,** 6 June 1648. 1 p, folio. To Gen. Luther von Boennighausen. Asking him to discharge an officer. star Mar 22 (1270) DM850

**Wesley, John, 1703-91**

**ALs,** 24 Mar 1782. 1 p, 4to. To Mr. Walton. Agreeing to his proposal about the refitting of a "Scare-crow House"; outlines his own YOrkshire itinerary. S June 12 (233) £1,100

**Wesley, Samuel, 1766-1837**

**Series of Ds s,** 7 Ds s, 1830-34. 7 pp. Assigning copyright of works to J. Alfred Novello. S May 15 (148) £550

**Wesley, Samuel Sebastian, 1810-76**

**Collection** of 11 A Ls s & 6 Ds s, 1832-70 & [n.d.]. About 40 pp. To the publisher Novello. On musical matters. S May 15 (147) £1,200

**West, Rebecca, 1892-1980**

**Collection** of 6 A Ls s, 10 Ls s & 3 Ds s, 4 Nov 1962 to 29 July 1974. About 20 pp, various sizes. To L. Arnold Weissberger. About personal & professional matters. rms June 6 (128) $1,000

**Weston, Edward.** See: Jeffers, Robinson & Weston

**Westpoint Military Academy**

**Group photograph,** graduating class of 94 cadets in uniform, [n.d.]. 7.37 by 9.37 inches (image). Each cadet identified by no; sgd by each on verso. Illus in cat. rms June 6 (497) $200

**Wetzel, Friedrich Gottlob, 1779-1819**

**Autograph Ms,** 3 poems, Das Paradies der Tiere, Die Wunderblume, & anr; [n.d.]. 2 pp, folio. Including revisions; poem on verso cancelled. Illus in cat. star Mar 21 (378) DM4,400

**Whaling Manuscripts**

**Ds,** 15 Nov 1822. 14 pp, folio. An act "to incorporate a company for carrying on the Whale and seal fisheries from the Port of Perth Amboy." Sgd by Jesse Upson & David Thompson. With orig cords. sg Sept 28 (274) $475

**Wharton, Edith, 1862-1937**

**ALs,** 23 Oct [after 1904]. 3 pp, 8vo. To Fred. Congratulating him on his engagement to Miss Satterlee. CE May 22 (465) $1,000

**Whipple, Joseph**

**Ds,** 26 Apr 1777. 1 p, folio. Land deed to Moses Little. rms Nov 30 (58) $260

**Whipple, William, Signer from New Hampshire**

**ALs,** 18 Mar 1777. 3 pp, 4to. To John Langdon. Discussing naval matters & sending news of Benjamin Franklin. Repaired. P Dec 13 (409) $2,750

**Whistler, James Abbott McNeill, 1834-1903**

**Photograph,** of his painting, The Little White Girl, inscr to Swinburne. [N.d.] Size in frame c.14 by 10.75 inches. With Swinburn's related poem ptd on gold paper & pasted on the frame by Whistler. S July 11 (236) £2,000

**White, Joseph Blanco**

**Autograph Ms,** 3 poems. 1825-6. 2 pp, 4to. All entitled "Night and Death". Ck Nov 17 (174) £240

**Whitman, Walt, 1819-92**

**Autograph Ms,** draft for a press announcement of Whitman's 1880 address on the Lincoln Assassination. 1 p, 3 by 7.5 inches, cut from larger sheet. Framed with 1887 photogravure port by George C. Cox. With instruction to printer at head. Jacqueline Bouvier Kennedy Onassis collection P Apr 23 (165) $16,000

**Autograph postcard, sgd,** 7 July [1889]. 1 p, 3 by 5.1 inches. On Government postcard. To Sloane Kennedy. " Nothing new or different--keep up-go out in the wheel chair-a bad spell the last week & am (gradually declining)-a letter from Mrs. O'C[onnor], Wash'n. She is gloomily poorly, left without means. The little dinner book is being put in type." Stained. Illus in cat sg Sept 28 (275) $1,100

**Cut signature,** [n.d.]. 0.62 by 3.62 inches, mtd to larger card. With a port. Illus in cat. rms Mar 21 (350) $540

**Photograph, sgd,** 1880. 3.75 by 6 inch sepia tone photo port. Illus in cat pba Oct 26 (82) $1,300

**Photograph, sgd & inscr,** [Sept 1872]. 188mm by 110mm, mtd. With white Stetson hat; by G. F. E. Pearsall. Inscr with his birthdate. Illus in cat. Marans collection. CE Apr 17 (101) $2,800

**Signature,** [n.d.]. On 1 by 4 inch slip of paper. pba Feb 22 (113) $300

### Whittier, John Greenleaf, 1807-92

**ALs,** 16 Sept 1872. 3 pp, 8vo. To Dr. Holland. Declining a request to write for a magazine. Torn. pba June 13 (238) $50

— 31 Aug 1891. 1 p, 12mo. To Nellie Joseph. Sending his autograph. rms June 6 (498) $125

— 18 Aug [n.y]. 1 p, 6.25 by 4.75 inches. Sending a corrected piece (not included). With orig cabinet photo. Repaired. pba Oct 26 (83) $110

**Autograph quotation, sgd,** 2 Jan 1883. 8 lines beginning "I know not what the future hath" on verso of carte photo. sg Feb 1 (248) $250

### Widmann, Joseph Viktor, 1842-1911

**ALs,** 2 Nov 1874. 4 pp, 8vo. To an unnamed composer. Making suggestions for a libretto. star Mar 21 (379) DM320

### Wieck, Friedrich, 1785-1873

**ANs,** 25 Oct 1865. 1 p, 8vo. To "Marie". Sending a birthday present. star Mar 22 (1134) DM750

### Wieland, Christoph Martin, 1733-1813

**ALs,** 29 June 1801. 1 p, 4to. To the pbr Weidmann. Offering to revise his Horazens Briefe for a new Ed. star Mar 21 (380) DM9,000

### Wigman, Mary, 1886-1973

**Collection** of 27 A Ls s & 3 autograph postcards, sgd, 13 Mar 1968 to 5 July 1971. About 63 pp, various sizes. To Tilly Meyer. About her travels, health problems & old age, etc. With related material. star Mar 22 (1160) DM1,400

### Wigner, Eugene Paul

**Autograph Ms,** essay about scholarly methods, [n.d.]. 6 pp, 4to. Fragment of a larger work; sgd & inscr at head. star Mar 21 (640) DM480

— Autograph Ms, Reduction of Direct Products and Restriction of Representations to Subgroups: the Everyday Tasks of the Quantum Theorists, [1971]. 34 pp, 4to. Including numerous corrections; sgd at head. star Mar 21 (639) DM750

### Wilde, Oscar, 1854-1900

**Autograph Ms,** poem, Autumn. 12 lines, 1 p, 4to. S Dec 18 (220) £3,500 [Gekoski]

**Ms,** Stanza XXII of Garden of Eros. Mar [18]82. 1 p, no size given. Beginning "Nay, when Keats died, the Muses still had left..."With Sgd photo from 1895?

Framed together. Overall size 229mm by 190mm. Photo cracked and with light mat burn. Illus in cat P Dec 12 (177) $4,750

**ALs,** 8 Aug 1887. 1 p, 8vo. To Arthur Clifton. Inviting him Drury Lane the following evening. Sgd with initials. S Dec 18 (241) £600 [Edwards]

— [c.13 Oct 1888]. 3 pp, 8vo. To Robert Ross. Congratulating him on going to university. S July 11 (237) £3,200

— [c.1889]. 1 p, 8vo. To Richardson. Making a date to have tea on Fricay. pn June 13 (251) £920

— [watermarked 1893]. 2 pp, 4to. To a Countess. Asking to postpone a visit to the following week because of his mother's illness. S Dec 18 (221) £1,400 [Maggs]

— [n.d.]. 2 pp, 8vo. To Anthony John Mundella. Asking for an interview. rms June 6 (129) $1,200

— [n.d.]. 3 pp, 8vo. Written from 16 Tite Street. To an editor. Saying that Wilde's letters for publication should be signed as they are written. S Dec 18 (218) £1,100 [Maggs]

**ANs,** [n.d.]. 1 p. "Tommorrow. 7.45. here. no dress. O.W." S Dec 18 (219) £550 [Levin]

**Photograph, sgd,** July [18]91. 165mm by 108mm, mtd. Seated, by W. & D. Downey. Illus in cat. Marans collection. CE Apr 17 (102) $3,000

— Anr, [n.d.]. 2.5 by 4 inch carte-de-visite profile port. By Elliot & Fry. Creased in upper right corner. Illus in cat pba Oct 26 (84) $3,500

### Wildenbruch, Ernst von, 1845-1909

**A Ls s** (2), 30 Mar 1882 & 23 Feb 1896. 5 pp, 8vo. To his pbr. Concerning corrections to his works. HN May 15 (2750) DM420

### Wilder, Thornton, 1897-1975

**ALs,** 6 Mar 1960. 1 p, 8vo. To Mr. Van Delinder. Protesting that he never gave him "permission to cut or alter Our Town or play any portion of it." rms June 6 (130) $350

**Photograph, sgd & inscr,** 7 May 1943. 6.5 by 5 inches (image). In uniform; inscr to Mary & Curt. rms June 6 (131) $210

### Wilhelm I, Deutscher Kaiser, 1797-1888

**ALs,** 16 July 1871. 3 pp, 8vo. To his niece Marie of the Netherlands. Congratulating her on her marriage with Wilhelm zu Wied. HN May 15 (2751) DM960

— 29 Dec 1878. 1 p, 8vo. Recipient unnamed. Asking him to a meeting to discuss an unpleasant affair. star Mar 22 (1214) DM550

**ANs,** 9 Oct 1871. 1 p, 8vo. To the Rev. Wilhelm Hoffmann. Responding to an invitation to attend a general synod the next day. On fragment of letter addressed to him. star Mar 22 (1213) DM300

### Wilhelm II, Deutscher Kaiser, 1859-1941

**ALs,** 2 Feb 1903. 2 pp, no size given. On a royal correspondence card. To Edward VII of England, his uncle. About peace: " ...I fervently hope & pray that the sword may never be recurred to! With regard to the pen - which is certainly more desirable - in settling international difficulties, I am under the impression that in some cases it is in the act of doing a great deal of mischief..." Illus in cat pba Feb 22 (312) $4,500

— 18 Nov 1939. 1 p, 8vo, on verso of picture postcard. To Poultney Bigelow. Hoping that Germany will win the war. star Mar 22 (1222) DM750

**Ls,** 17 Oct 1885. 1 p, 4to. To a military unit in Berlin. Informing them of the sale of some horses. star Mar 22 (1219) DM230

**Ds,** 18 Jan 1901. 1 p, folio. Decoration for Max Grubitz. HN May 15 (2753) DM270

— 14 June 1905. 1 p, folio. Bestowing on Dr. Adolf Cohn the title of "Privy Councillor of the Board of Health...trusting that he will continue to serve US and Our Royal Household with unswerving loyalty and that he will contribute to the general public's benefit..."With full translation. Illus in cat rms Oct 11 (391) $425

### Wilhelm V, Herzog von Bayern, 1548-1626

**Ls,** 15 Dec 1590. 1 p, folio. To Cardinal Montelboro. Announcing that he is sending an envoy to the new Pope. star Mar 22 (1164) DM540

### Wilhelmina, Queen of William I of The Netherlands, 1774-1837

**ALs,** 25 Sept 1824. 2 pp, 4to. To her son Frederick. Chatting about her relatives in Prussia. HN May 15 (2761) DM400

### Wilken, Friedrich, 1777-1840

**ALs,** 8 Apr 1799. 2 pp, 4to. To Professor [Rosenmueller]. Sending a paper & asking for his comments. star Mar 21 (641) DM220

### Wilkinson, Norman

**Original drawing,** for the d/j of Compton Mackenzie's Carnival [pbd 1912]. 8 by 5 inches. Title lettering slightly blurred; mtd on bd. pn Mar 14 (412) £130

### Wille, Pierre Alexandre, 1748-1821

**ALs,** 12 May 1765. 1 p, 4to. To Johann Wilhelm Meil. Thanking for some of his etchings. star Mar 21 (726) DM250

### William, Comte de Champagne, Cardinal, 1135-1202

**Document,** 1182. 1 p, vellum, 237mm by 232mm. Confirmation of land grants in Flanders to the church at Messines. Including seal (restored). Illus in cat. S June 18 (32) £3,800

### William I, Prince of Orange, 1533-84 —& August, Kurfuerst von Sachsen, 1526-86

**Ls,** [7 Oct 1561]. 2 pp, folio. To Emperor Ferdinand. Interceding in favor of Lorentz von Kuhdorff. HH May 9 (2569) DM1,100

### William II, King of The Netherlands, 1792-1849

**ALs,** 9 Apr 1824. 1 p, 4to. To Princess Luise of Prussia. Announcing the birth of a daughter & asking her to be a godmother. HN May 15 (2756) DM300

### William III, King of England, 1650-1702

**Ds,** 3 Feb 1696. 1 p. folio. Warrant for the Privy Purse to pay his cousin William, Earl of Portland. Ck Apr 12 (121) £450

### William IV, Prince of Orange, 1711-51

**ALs,** 13 Feb 1740. 2 pp, 4to. To [Count Virmond]. Congratulating him on his appointment as president of the Imperial appellate court. HN May 15 (2757) DM800

### William V, Prince of Orange, 1748-1806

**Ls,** 7 Jan 1770. 2 pp, folio. To Markgraf Karl Friedrich of Baden-Durlach. Responding to an inquiry about some mortgaged property at Ebernburg. HN Nov 24 (2743) DM700

— 28 Nov 1770. 2 pp, folio. To Clemens Wenzeslaus of Saxony & Poland, Archbishop & Elector of Trier. Informing him about the birth of his daughter. Kuenzel collection. HN Nov 24 (2875) DM720

— 22 Feb 1786. 4 pp, folio. Recipient unnamed. Fragment, discussing claims of the House of Orange at Hadamar. HN Nov 24 (2790) DM680

### Williams, Otho H.

**Ls,** 4 Jan 1793. 1 p, 4to. To Gov. Henry Lee of Virginia. Letter of transmittal as Collector at Baltimore. With port. sg Feb 1 (249) $250

### Williams, Ralph Vaughan, 1872-1958

**ALs,** [n.d.]. 1 p, no size given. To C. R. Perkins. Thanking him for a letter & discussing music. Creased. With ANs & portion of original envelope. Ck Nov 17 (169) £110

### Williams, Tennessee, 1911-83

**Collection** of 13 Ls s & 1 ALs, 22 Aug to 12 Dec 1970. 18 pp, 4to. To David Lobdell. About his writing and his health and his travels. Illus in cat CNY Dec 15 (41) $7,500

### Williams, Theodore Samuel ("Ted"). See: Thorpe, James Francis & Williams

### Williams, William, Signer from Connecticut

**ALs,** [12] Aug 1776. 2 pp, folio. To Jabez Huntington. Summarizing affairs in the first weeks of independence. Illus in cat. P Dec 13 (410) $20,000

**ADs,** 20 Jan 1783. 1 p, 8vo. Receipt. With endorsement on verso by Committee of the Connecticut Pay-Table. Addressed to Treasurer John Lawrence. Also sgd by Eliza Wales & Finn Wadsworth. Detail in cat rms Oct 11 (34) $200

**Ds,** 30 Apr 1792. 1 p, oblong 8vo. Certification that school has been kept in the town of Lebanon CT for 11 months of the year 1791. Also sgd by John Clark. sg Feb 1 (250) $140

### Williams, William Carlos, 1883-1963

**ALs,** 16 Sept 1915. 1 p, 4to. To "Dear People". Thanks for $100 & some pictures sent. Sgd as "Bill". pba Oct 26 (85) $500

**Series** of 3 Ls s, 9 Mar 1957 to 12 May 1958. 3 pp, 8vo & folio. Two granting permission to dramatize In the

American Grain; the 3d about Ezra Pound. CE May 22 (477) $1,150

**Ls,** 26 May 1944. 2 pp, 4to. To Fred. Discussing religion, various authors, & other matters. CE May 22 (476) $650

— 20 Apr 1948. 2 pp on 1 sheet, 4to. To Charles Olson. Sternly criticizing T. S. Eliot. CNY Oct 27 (148) $3,800

**Williamson, Jack**
**Typescript,** And Searching Mind. [Pep NM, c.1948] 85 leaves, 278mm by 214mm, loose sheets, sgd. cb Oct 17 (574) $800

**Willkie, Wendell Lewis, 1892-1944**
**Ls,** 30 Nov 1940. 1 p, 4to. To Mr. Demauriac. Thanking him for a message: " It conveys to me not only your good will, but also a heartening faith in the principles for which I stand". pba June 13 (88) $70

**Wilson, Edith Bolling, 1872-1961**
**ALs,** [n.d.]. 1 p, 8vo. To Mrs. Warren. Inviting her to lunch. pba June 13 (89) $180

**Wilson, R. D.**
**Autograph Ms,** bound vol of journal-letters written to his mother while touring the Middle East, 1861-63. About 300 pp, 8vo, in calf. Some leaves cut away. pn June 13 (198) £1,700

**Wilson, Woodrow, 1856-1924**
**Ls,** 19 Apr 1910. 1 p, 8vo. To J. Hartford Chidester. Thanking for a letter of approval. rms June 6 (499) $350

— 11 July 1912. 1 p, 4to. To Herman Bernstein. Sending a line in reply to convey his appreciation. Framed with photo. rms Nov 30 (49) $320

— 7 Sept 1916. 1 p, 4to. To Martyn Johnson. About his inability to recall a member of the National Guard from the Mexican Border: " ...It gives me a real pain to say that I cannot recall Mr. Kitchell from the border unless his battery is itself ordered home again..." rms Oct 11 (393) $425

— 12 July 1920. 1 p, 4to. To Hamilton Holt. Declining "to make any definite engagements with regard to [his] future work." rms Mar 21 (114) $260

— 15 Apr 1922. 1 p, 4to. Recipient unnamed. Thanking for recipient's good wishes. rms June 6 (500) $200

— 26 Dec 1923. 1 p, 4to. To Louis Pennington. Thanking for books. Illus in cat. rms Mar 21 (115) $470

**ANs,** 11 Dec 1917. 1 p, 8vo. To Baker. Sending thanks for summaries. Sgd with initials. sg Feb 1 (251) $150

**Ds,** 27 Feb 1911. 1 p, 4to. Extradition warrant to the Gov. of Pennsylvania requesting the arrest of William Jefferson for burglary. sg June 6 (190) $130

— 19 July 1916. 1 p, folio. Appointing Gaston Ernest Liebert as Consul General of France at New York. Countersgd by the Acting Secretary of State. With folds. rms Oct 11 (408) $210

— 11 Dec 1917. 1 p, folio. Appointing Eugene H. MacLachlen as Notary Public for the District of Columbia. Countersgd by Attorney General Thomas W. Gregory. With worn folds. rms Oct 11 (394) $260

— 1 Dec 1919. 1 p, oblong folio. Appointment of William C. Saunders as Postmaster at Waterford CT. Countersgd by Postmaster General Albert S. Burleson. CE June 12 (134) $250

**Endorsement,** 14 June 1918. On 1 p, 4to. 12 June 1918 Ls of H. A. Garfield. Approve & authorize expenditure for "an addition to the Fuel Administration Building." sg Sept 28 (280) $275

**Envelope,** 2 Nov 1898. No size given. Addressed to his wife. pba Feb 22 (292) $150

**Lithographed port,** 1922. 10 by 14.5 inches . Sgd & dated. Numbered #20 of 200. Also sgd by artist. Illus in cat pba Oct 26 (337) $275

**Photograph, sgd,** [c.1915]. 204mm by 145mm. 3-quarter length, seated at his desk; by Underwood. Marans collection. CE Apr 17 (194) $700

— Anr, [n.d.]. 4to. Half length, by Harris & Ewing. Framed. Illus in cat. rms June 6 (502) $500

**Photograph, sgd & inscr,** [c.27 Jan 1922]. 7.4 by 10.75 inches. Inscr to William J. Patterson. With mtd Ls of J. R. Bolling, Wilson's secretary, transmitting photo. sg June 6 (191) $300

**Ptd photograph,** [n.d.]. 12.5 by 9.5 inches. By G. Prints & ptd by Atlantic Publishing. Framed under glass. Over-all size c. 19.5 by 15.5 inches. Illus in cat rms Oct 11 (326) $350

**White House card,** sgd, [n.d.]. rms Nov 30 (330) $400
See also: George V & Wilson

**Wilson, Woodrow, 1856-1924 — &**
**Baker, Newton D.**
**Ds,** 27 Nov 1916. 1 p, folio, vellum. Appointing William Roberts as "Major on the Retired List of the Army". Framed with 2 photos. Over-all size 28.5 by 32.25 inches. Illus in cat rms Oct 11 (19) $625

**Winchester, Oliver F., 1810-80**
**Ls,** 12 Nov 1875. 1 p, 4to. To Nelson King, Superintendent of the Sharps Rifle Company. Informing him that he cannot tell the costs of an order in advance. Framed. CNY May 17 (318) $4,500

**Windsor, Edward, Duke of, 1894-1972**
**ALs,** "Monday". 2 pp, 8vo. To Harry Preston. Sending thanks for cigars. Sgd as Prince of Wales. sg Feb 1 (83) $225

**Cut signature,** 27 Apr [19]32. 1 by 3.37 inches. Matted with a photograph. Illus in cat. rms Mar 21 (285) $350

**Photograph, sgd,** 13 July 1911. 12 by 8 inches. Sgd as Prince of Wales. With a medal commemorating his investiture. Ck Apr 12 (51) £380

— Anr, 1912. 200mm by 150mm. In naval cadet uniform. Sgd on mount Edward P. 1912. b May 30 (365) £130

— Anr, 1912. 7 by 5 inches. Port photo by Rose K. Durrant & Son. Of the Duke in his Royal Naval College uniform. Sgd as " Edward P." Browned. Ck Nov 17 (69) £110

**Windsor, Edward, Duke of, 1894-1972** —&
**Windsor, Wallis Simpson, Duchess of, 1896-1986**
Group photograph, [c.1965]. 252mm by 203mm. Walking together. Sgd by both & inscr to William H. Wray in the Duke's hand. Marans collection. CE Apr 17 (133) $550

**Windsor, Wallis Simpson, Duchess of, 1896-1986**
ALs, 13 Aug 1960. 4 pp, 4to. To Major Gray Phillips. Arrangin.d.tes for a visit & about what she & the Duke have been doing. With orig envelope. Worn. sg Sept 28 (281) $375
See also: Windsor, Edward & Windsor

**Winterhalter, Franz Xaver, 1805-73**
ALs, [1 Oct 1848]. 1 p, 8vo. To Wilhelm Metzler. Asking him to forward his mail. star Mar 21 (727) DM230

**Wise, Henry Alexander, 1806-76**
ALs, 26 Mar 1856. 1 p, 8vo. To John Glancy Jones. Discussing the presidential election & expecting Buchanan to win. rms Mar 21 (49) $1,500

**Wistar, Caspar, 1761-1818**
Ds, 8 Mar 1816. 1 p, 12mo. Receipt for $49 for medical services to Norton Pryor. Illus in cat. rms June 6 (503) $325

**Witherspoon, John, Signer from New Jersey**
ALs, 21 Mar 1787. 1 p, 4to. To St. George Tucker. About Tucker's sons & their care at Princeton: " ...Your Opinion respecting their Education is the same with mine...please to know that I accept the Charge of them & will direct every thing with respecting them myself. This offer I have done for many Gentlemens [sic] sons..." Docketed by Tucker on vberso. Illus in cat rms Oct 11 (396) $3,000

**Wodehouse, Pelham Grenville, 1881-1975**
Typescript, entitled "Bring on the Earls". [n.d.]. 15 pp, no size given. Concerning his time in New York in 1909. Ck Nov 17 (186) £240
Series of 4 Ls s, 25 Aug 1965 to 11 Jan 1975, 4 pp, 4to & 8vo. To Arnold Weissberger. The first letter is carbon concerning a New York corporation interested in attaining the stage, screen & tv rights to Jeevs & Bertie Wooster. rms Oct 11 (397) $300
Ds, 4 Jan 1917. 4 pp, 4to. Contract for the lyrics to "a new theatrical representation, at present entitled O Boy, the music whereof is by Jerome D. Kern". sg June 6 (192) $550

**Woehler, Friedrich, 1800-82**
Autograph postcard, sgd, 25 June 1878. To Otto Janke. Thanking for a journal & requesting anr. star Mar 21 (643) DM320

**Woelfflin, Heinrich, 1864-1945**
Autograph Ms, Fuehrung durch die Pinakothek, [n.d.]. 300 leaves in 2 vols, 223mm by 183mm, in half lea. Draft of lectures on art history, based on paintings in the museum in Munich. HH May 7 (24) DM5,500

**Wolcott, Oliver, Signer from Connecticut**
ALs, 26 Oct 1776. 2 pp, 8vo. To Samuel Lyman. Referring to the military situation at NY & Ticonderoga, his health problems, & other Connecticut Signers. P Dec 13 (413) $2,750
Ls, 5 Nov 1794. 2 pp, 4to. To the President, Directors & Company of the Bank of the United States. Concerning "unexpected demands upon the Treasury for the support of the Militia Army..." that "render it necessary for me to request the consent of your board for postponing one or two Months the payment of the Installment of two hundred thousand Dollars which fell due to the Bank on the first Instant, upon condition that the United States pay interest for the prolonged term..." rms Oct 11 (35) $5,500
— 3 July 1797. 1 p, 4to. To Sylvanus Bourne. Asking him to deliver whose propositions to Mr Jones in Wolcott's absence. sg Feb 1 (253) $140
ADs, certification of sums from the Estate of David Baldwin paid by the administrator. sg Feb 1 (252) $175

**Wolcott, Oliver, 1760-1833**
Ds, 28 Nov 1797. Circular to Customs Collectors & Revenue Supervisors. An act concerning foreign coins. pba Oct 26 (338) $700

**Wolf, Hugo, 1860-1903**
Autograph music, fragment of his opera Der Corregidor, [1895/96]. 2 pp, folio. 15 bars in full score, comprising the final bars of the 1st act. Illus in cat. star Mar 22 (1135) DM24,000
ALs, [16 Apr 1891]. 3 pp, 8vo. To Heinrich Rauchberg. About his stay in Mannheim, performances of his works, etc. star Mar 22 (1136) DM3,600
— 17 July 1891. 2 pp, 8vo. To Heinrich Rauchberg. Hoping for a performance of his work Christnacht in Cologne, & announcing his departure for Bayreuth. star Mar 22 (1137) DM2,800

**Wolfgang Wilhelm, Pfalzgraf von Neuburg, 1578-1653**
Ls, 23 Apr 1610. 2 pp, folio. To Count Friedrich von Solms-Roedelheim. Giving instructions regarding Austrian troop movements. star Mar 22 (1272) DM950

**Wolfskehl, Karl, 1869-1948**
Ls, 8 July 1933. 1 p, 4to. To Dr. Zeitz. Declining a request for a contribution to the Berliner Tageblatt. HN May 15 (2764) DM200

**Woodward, William M.**
Ls, 17 Sept 1945. 1 p, 4to. To I. I. Rabi. Encouraging his participation in the movement for solely peaceful development of atomic energy by scientists. With related material. bbc Dec 18 (76) $300

**Wool, John Ellis, 1784-1869**
Ls, 3 July 1863. 3 pp, 4to. To George Opdyke. Listing the number of forts & soldiers in NY State & noting that this is a "very small force for the defence of this great emporium." rms June 6 (58) $800

## Woolf, Virginia, 1882-1941

**A Ls s** (2), 13 Apr 1934 & [n.d.]. 4 pp, 4to. To Lady Southorn. Thanking her for a gift of teas & other matters. Tipped into a volume & with a photo of Woolf by Cecil Beaton. S June 28 (281) £1,100

**ALs,** 19 Dec 1920. 1 p, 8vo. To Chatto & Windus. Thanking them for sending her a copy of Roger Fry's book. S Dec 18 (436) £480 [Dupre]

— 24 Apr 1931. 2 pp on 1 sheet, 8vo. To Claudian. Reporting on John Mayanrd Keynes, Clive & Julian Bell & others. Sgd "V". Framed with photo. wa Oct 28 (60) $250

— 29 Apr 1932. 2 pp, 8vo. To Miss McAfee. Returning proofs of an article & quoting some sources. Illus in cat. rms June 6 (504) $1,300

**Collection** of 8 ALs s, 1 ALs, 7 Ls s, 8 letters, 15 autograph postcards & 1 typed postcard, Mar 1927 to 14 Nov 1936. 67 pp, 8vo & 4to. To Julian Bell. Writing her nephew about her work, his poetry, their family & the Bloomsbury Circle. Many featuring holograph revisions & additions. Creased & with torn repairs. Illus in cat CNY Dec 15 (42) $14,000

**Ls,** [2 Jan 1931]. 1 p, 4.5 by 7 inches. To Julian [Bell]. Concerning Christmas present: "I meant to get you a book for a Christmas present but since I don't know what you want I send you a chque [sic] instead, which can be spent on anything--dog, drink, what you like." Illus in cat pba Oct 26 (86) $400

## Wordsworth, William, 1770-1850

**Autograph Ms,** sonnet, The Trossacks, 20 Oct 1831. 1 p, 4to, in 19th-cent album. Sgd & inscr to [Alicia] Allen. With ALs by Mary Wordsworth to Miss Allen, [n.d.], 2 pp, 4to; enclosing the poem & sending news. Illus in cat. C Nov 29 (192) £2,200

**ALs,** [n.d. but docketed 8 Apr 1841]. 4 pp, 8vo. To his future son-in-law, Edward Quillinan. Replying to Quillinan's letter concerning Dora's portion in relation to their forthcoming marriage. S Dec 18 (247) £900 [Maggs]

— 17 Feb 1846. 4 pp, 8vo. To Earl de la Warr. Commenting on the death of his own brother; belatedly thanking him for presenting his volume to the Queen. S Dec 18 (248) £460 [Stodolski]

## World War II

— ENOLA GAY CREW. - Group photograph, [n.d.]. 4to. Sgd by Paul Tibbets, Tom Ferebee, & Theodore J. Van Kirk. Framed with wirephoto of the devastation at Hiroshima. rms Nov 30 (7) $300

— LEOPOLD, ADOLF. - ALs, 3 Nov 1940. 1 p, size not stated. To his mother. From the concentration camp at Sachsenhausen/Oranienburg, thanking for presents & hoping for an end of the war. On ptd letterhead of the camp; with censor's stamp. JG Sept 29 (275) DM200

— PAUL W. TIBBETS. - Signature. [n.d.]. 11 by 14 inch reroduced color painting of the Enola Gay. Mtd. Dar Oct 19 (18) $100

— POSTDAM CONFERENCE. - Ds. 23 July 1945. 8vo. Ptd seating plan & music progam for a dinner in Potsdam. Sgd by 13 guests including Winston Churchill, Joseph Stalin, Harry Truman and Bernard Law Montgomery. With a sgd port photo of General Zhulov. Illus in cat Ck Nov 17 (42) £19,000

## Wrangel, Friedrich Heinrich Ernst, Graf von, 1784-1877

**ALs,** 6 May 1835. 2 pp, 4to. To James Booth. Discussing the purchase of plants. star Mar 22 (1685) DM380

## Wright, Frank Lloyd, 1869-1959

**Ls,** [1933?]. 2 pp, 4to. To Lewis Mumford. Praising Mumford for a recent talk & as a critic, questioning the recognition accorded to him, & referring to his book. rms June 6 (305) $4,750

— 19 July 1945. 1 p, oblong 4to. To Samuel L. Scher. Saying that paper relating to his project will be along soon. wa Oct 28 (63) $850

— 29 Aug 1945. 1 p, oblong 4to. To Mrs. Samuel L. Scher. About a delay in her project. With holograph insertion. wa Oct 28 (62) $1,100

— 5 Dec 1952. 1 p, oblong 4to. To John Ford. Asking him to use his influence so that a little playhouse can play The Quiet Man on Christmas Day. Framed with photo & plaque. cb June 25 (2590) $1,800

**Photograph, sgd,** [1957]. 11.25 by 8.5 inches (image). At his drafting table, by Al Krescanko. Illus in cat. rms June 6 (306) $750

**Photograph, sgd & inscr,** [c.1935]. 300mm by 231mm. Shoulder-length port, inscr to Judith & Frank Sanders. Illus in cat. Marans collection. CE Apr 17 (220) $1,800

## Wright, Orville, 1871-1948

**Ls,** 11 June 1913. 1 p, 4to. To Albert LeVino. Commenting on an article on the Wright Brothers that has some errors. sg June 6 (196) $750

**Check,** sgd, 13 June 1941. Payable to Mabel Beck for $60.96. CE June 12 (135) $420

**Photograph, sgd & inscr,** [c.1910]. 188mm by 122mm. Shoulder-length port. With signature on card, [n.d.]. Marans collection. CE Apr 17 (31) $1,100

**Signature,** 1909. At bottom of unused German picture postcard showing "Orville Wright mit seiner Flugmaschine in Berlin". sg Feb 1 (254) $1,300

— Anr, [n.d.]. On 3.5 by 5.5 inch piece of paper. With orig enevlope. Illus in cat pba Oct 26 (131) $400

## Wright, Wilbur, 1867-1912

**Group photograph,** [c.1910]. 90mm by 139mm. With an unnamed friend, sgd & inscr by Wright. Illus in cat. Marans collection. CE Apr 17 (30) $6,000

## Wuertenberger, Ernst, 1868-1934

**Series** of 3 autograph postcards, sgd, 10 Sept 1926 to [25 Sept 1929]. To an unnamed married couple. Sending greetings from travels with Hans Sturzenegger. Including 2 pen-&-ink sketches. star Mar 21 (728) DM550

## Wyeth, N. C.

**ALs,** [c.1930]. 1 p, 4to. To Sessler's Book Store. Concerning 2 of his paintings which are for sale. Framed with related material. rms June 6 (317) $650

**Wyman, Jane.** See: Reagan, Ronald & Wyman

**Wythe, George, Signer from Virginia**
ADs, [c.1747]. 1 p, 8vo. Brief for a suit brought by Anthony Strother against Christopher Zimmerman. Framed with a port. P Dec 13 (414) $600

# Y

**Yamashita, Tomoyuki, 1885-1946**
Signature, [c.1945]. On Philippine one-peso banknote, "victory" issue. Sgd in English & Japanese. sg June 6 (195) $750

**Yeats, William Butler, 1865-1939**
ALs, 14 Oct [n. y.]. 1 p, 8vo. To unnamed recipient. Thanking them for "your little book which I look forward to reading." Toned. rms Oct 11 (412) $300

**Yorck von Wartenburg, Ludwig, Graf, 1759-1830**
Ls, 10 Mar 1812. 1 p, folio. To an unnamed prince. Informing him that Lieut. Friedrich Zeugmeister has been sent to Pillau for the execution of the sentence of the court martial. star Mar 22 (1690) DM320

**Young, Ann Eliza, b.1844**
ALs, 23 Jan 1882. 7 pp, 8vo. To the Chicago Chairman of an Anti-Mormon Meeting: " I have noticed with great satisfaction the movement to hold meetings throughout the country...for the purpose of arousing the government and the people...to the threatening nature of that political, social and religious monstrosity - Polygamous Mormonism..." With related material. CNY Dec 15 (103) $4,200

**Young, Brigham, 1801-77**
Ls, 14 Apr 1863. 1 p, 4to. To Samuel L. Avery. Sending his signature for sale at a fair for the benefit of wounded soldiers. CNY May 17 (319) $3,000
Ds, 20 Jan 1849. Gold dust note. rs Nov 11 (55) $425
Cut signature, [n.d.]. 2 by 4.25 inches. Illus in cat. rms Mar 21 (346) $400
Photograph, sgd, [1864]. 100mm by 60mm. Bust port, by C. R. Savage. Illus in cat. Marans collection. CE Apr 17 (195) $3,200
Signature, [n.d.]. On a 2 by 4 inch card. pba Feb 22 (150) $300

**Ysaye, Eugene, 1858-1931**
ALs, 17 Apr 1892. 4 pp, 8vo. Recipient unnamed. Making plans for a concert. star Mar 22 (1139) DM380

# Z

**Zach, Franz Xaver von, 1754-1832**
ALs, 25 Apr 1801. 1 p, 8vo. To [J. B. Trommsdorf]. Thanking for some chemical specimens & discussing J. W. Ritter's experiments. star Mar 21 (154) DM380

**Zaharias, Mildred Didrikson ("Babe"), 1914-56**
Photograph, sgd & inscr, [c.1950]. 235mm by 189mm. Playing golf; inscr to Sybil. Illus in cat. Marans collection. CE Apr 17 (285) $750

**Zaharoff, Basil, 1849-1936**
Photograph, sgd & inscr, 1919. 265mm by 178mm, mtd. Full length, seated, by Numa Blanc Fils; inscr to Daniel. Marans collection. CE Apr 17 (196) $1,300

**Zedlitz, Karl Abraham, Freiherr von, 1731-93**
ALs, 18 Sept 1775. 1 p, 4to. To Moses Mendelssohn. Inquiring about Johann Georg Buesch & hoping to see him more often. star Mar 21 (557) DM600

**Zelter, Karl Friedrich, 1758-1832**
ALs, 6 May 1813. 1 p, 4to. Recipient unnamed. Requesting a ticket for the opera. Kuenzel collection. star Mar 22 (1141) DM850

**Zemlinsky, Alexander von, 1871-1942**
Autograph sentiment, inscr to Frau Schwarz, sgd, June 1927. 1 p, folio. On lithographed caricature. HN Nov 24 (2885) DM520
Photograph, sgd & inscr, [n.d.]. 8vo. Inscr to Frau Schwarz. HN Nov 24 (2886) DM650

**Zeppelin, Ferdinand von, 1838-1917**
Photograph, sgd & inscr, [1910]. 149mm by 98mm (image). Shoulder-length port, inscr to B. v. Woenke. Marans collection. CE Apr 17 (32) $900
— Anr, May 1914. 3.5 by 5.3 inch photo. Of zeppelin at mooring. In anr hand at lower right "Card carried by me in flight arranged by Count Zeppelin, May 1914. Thomas S. Baldwin." Also with note about a biplane in the picture. Outer margins worn. sg Sept 28 (283) $550

**Zick, Januarius, 1730-97**
Ds, 27 Apr 1781. 1 p, 4to. Receipt for 50 talers in partial payment for paintings executed by his father in 1755. Illus in cat. Kuenzel collection. star Mar 21 (729) DM1,700

**Ziegfield, Florenz, 1869-1932**
Ls, 17 March 1915. 1 p, 4to. To Charles Dillingham. About negotiations with Maurice Farkoa. pba Feb 22 (117) $350

**Zilcher, Hermann, 1881-1948**
Autograph quotation, opening bars of his Suite for String Quartet Op.77, Jan 1936. 1 p, 8vo. Sgd. star Mar 22 (1142) DM320

**Zille, Heinrich, 1858-1929**
ALs, [n.d.]. 1 p, 8vo. Recipient unnamed. Fragment, promising to write when he is feeling better. HN Nov 24 (2887) DM240

**Zincgref, Julius Wilhelm, 1591-1635**
Autograph sentiment, Quantum est quod ignoramus!, 8 May 1621. 1 p, 8vo. Sgd. HN May 15 (2770) DM960

**Zola, Emile, 1840-1902**
ALs, 6 Feb 1884. 1 p, 8vo. To E. Lepelletier. Subscribing to a newspaper. HH May 9 (2570) DM200
— 27 Dec 1889. 2 pp, 8vo. To a group of young ladies. Responding to an invitation to lecture. star Mar 21 (381) DM420

— 25 May [1895?]. 1 p, 8vo. Recipient unnamed. Giving permission to reprint one of his works. star Mar 21 (382) DM300
— 4 Oct [year unreadable]. 1 p, 8vo. To Leon Hennique. Making plans to meet; sends a message through Hennique to his publisher. Framed with port. CE June 12 (136) $400
— Mardi soir. 1 p, 8vo. Recipient unnamed. Suggesting that they have dinner together; mentions that Mme Daudet is bedridden. wad Oct 18 (159) C$260
**ADs,** [n.d.]. 1 p, 12mo, on engraved visiting card. Admission to his play Ventre de Paris. Illus in cat. rms June 6 (132) $450
**Photograph, sgd,** 10 Aug 1900. 145mm by 106mm. Bust port, by Nadar. Illus in cat. Marans collection. CE Apr 17 (103) $1,800

### Zuckmayer, Carl, 1896-1977

**Collection** of ALs & 3 Ls s, 16 June to 9 July 1950. 5 pp, 8vo & 4to. To his secretary. About his workload, proofreading, family matters, etc. HH May 9 (2575) DM300
**ALs,** 21 Apr 1935. 2 pp, 4to. To Rudolf Joseph. Suggesting that he write to Alexander Korda regarding a movie about Liszt. star Mar 21 (383) DM400
**Ls s** (2), 27 May & 16 June 1950. 4 pp, 4to. To his secretary. About his correspondence, negotiations with a pbr, theatrical & personal matters. HH May 9 (2574) DM360

**Ls,** 20 Oct 1943. 4 pp, folio. To Dr. Bondy. Important letter concerning a Free Germany Movement, German re-education, & hopes for a complete eradication of nationalism in the world. HH May 9 (2571) DM700

### Zweig, Stefan, 1881-1942

**Collection** of ALs & autograph postcard, sgd, [1 Aug 1937] & [n.d.]. 2 pp, 8vo, & card. To Alexander Muskat. Making plans for meetings, & requesting medical advice for Joseph Schmidt. star Mar 21 (387) DM580
**ALs,** 18 May 1908. 4 pp, 8vo. To Maximilian Harden. Discussing a misunderstanding about the ptg of an essay on Balzac. star Mar 21 (384) DM1,500
**Ls s** (2), 14 Nov 1934 & 23 Oct 1935. 2 pp, 4to. To Cyril Lakan. Expressing thanks, & agreeing to review Freud's autobiography. star Mar 21 (386) DM460
**Ls,** 11 Nov 1936. 1 p, 4to. To Berthold Viertel. Introducing Willi Maass. HN Nov 24 (2888) DM220
**Autograph postcard, sgd,** [7 Jan 1921]. To Noel Charavay. Ordering an autograph by St. Beuve. star Mar 21 (385) DM550

# PART II

# Books

### ATLASES, BOOKS, BROADSIDES, AND MAPS & CHARTS ARE REPORTED IN THIS SECTION

## A

A., T.B. See: Aldrich, Thomas Bailey

**Aalborg, Niels Mikkelsen**
— Ny Hussholdings Callender.... Copenhagen, 1638 [1636]. 8vo, contemp vellum. H4 with tear; some fraying, staining & soiling; contemp annotations at ends. S Mar 14 (1) £280

**Abbadie, Jacques, 1654?-1733**
— The History of the late Conspiracy against the King and Nation.... L, 1696. 8vo, later half calf. Trimmed. pba June 20 (1) $130

**Abbey, Edward**
— Black Sun. NY, [1971]. 1st Ed. In dj. pba Jan 25 (1) $100
— Desert Solitaire: A Season in the Wilderness. NY, [1968]. 1st Ed. In dj. Inscr, 1988. pba Oct 5 (1) $325
— The Fool's Progress. NY: Henry Holt, [1988]. In dj. Inscr. pba Aug 22 (1) $120
— Jonathan Troy. NY, [1954]. Orig cloth; tape residue to covers & free endpapers. pba Dec 7 (2) $55
— The Journey Home. NY, [1977]. In dj. Sgd on front free endpaper. pba Jan 25 (2) $180
— Vox: Clamantis in Deserto - Some Notes from a Secret Journal. Santa Fe: Rydal Press, 1989. One of 250. pba May 23 (1) $120

**Abbey, John R.**
— Life in England in Aquatint and Lithography, 1770-1860. L, 1953. 1st Ed, One of 400. 4to, orig cloth in dj; top & bottom edges chipped. sg Apr 11 (2) $75
— [Sale Catalogue] Catalogue of Valuable Printed Books and Fine Bindings.... L, 1965-78. 10 vols. 4to, orig bds & wraps. ds July 27 (1) $200
Anr copy. 10 parts in 10 vols. 4to, bds or wraps. With price lists inserted in all but parts 1 &-10. sg Apr 11 (14) $150

— Scenery of Great Britain and Ireland in Aquatint and Lithography. L, 1952. One of 500. 4to, orig cloth, in soiled dj. S Mar 28 (29) £150
1st Ed. 4to, cloth in dj; top & bottom edges worn. sg Apr 11 (1) $425
— Travel in Aquatint and Lithography. L, 1956-57. 1st Ed, One of 400. 2 vols. 4to, orig cloth in dj; worn. sg Apr 11 (3) $650
2d Ed. L, 1972. 4 vols. 4to, orig cloth in djs. S Oct 27 (1009) £270 [Sagen]

**Abbott, Berenice**
— Faces of the 20's. NY: Parasol Press, 1981. One of 60. Folio, loose as issued in portfolio. P June 5 (147) $3,250
— The World of Atget. NY, [1964]. 1st Ed. 4to, cloth, in chipped dj. pba Mar 7 (1) $50
Anr copy. Orig cloth, in rubbed dj. sg Feb 29 (22) $80

**Abbott, Carlisle S.**
— Recollections of a California Pioneer. NY, 1917. 1st Ed. Orig cloth. With frontis port. Larson copy. pba Sept 28 (290) $120

**Abbott, Edwin Abbott**
— Flatland. San Francisco: Arion Press, 1980. One of 275. 4to, ptd aluminum covers & aluminum case. sg Sept 14 (24) $650; sg Feb 15 (8) $425

**Abbott, Henry, b.1850**
— Fish Stories. NY: Pvtly ptd, 1919. Bds; spine ends worn, extremities rubbed. Inscr. pba July 11 (1) $75
— Fishing Brook. NY: Pvtly ptd, 1925. Inscr. pba July 11 (2) $140

**ABC...**
— Li-bel-lus Abc-da-ri-us. Halle: Christoph Salfelden, [c.1705]. 12mo, contemp half sheep gilt; contemp Latin annotations in ink on endpapers. S Nov 2 (329) £500 [Schiller]; S Mar 14 (15) £1,100

# ABDULLAH

**Abdullah bin Abdulkadir, Munshi**
— Translations from the Hakayit Abdulla.... L, 1874. 8vo, orig cloth; recased. b May 30 (194) £280

**A'Beckett, Gilbert Abbott, 1811-56**
— The Comic History of England. [L]: Punch Office, 1855-53. Illus by John Leech. 2 vols. 8vo, half mor; front joint of of Vol I splitting, extremities worn. With 23 hand-colored plates. sg Sept 21 (56) $150

Anr Ed. L, 1864. 2 vols. 8vo, later 19th-cent half mor gilt; extremities scuffed. With 10 hand-colored plates. F June 20 (508) £110

— The Comic History of Rome. L, [1860s]. Illus by John Leech. 8vo, contemp half calf. With 10 hand-colored plates. wa Dec 14 (363) $55

**Abel, Clarke**
— Narrative of a Journey in the Interior of China. L, 1818. 1st Ed. 4to, calf; rebacked. With 4 maps & 18 plates, 8 of them hand-colored. Hole in lower margin of plate facing p. 185. b Sept 20 (321) £520

Anr Ed. L, 1819. 4to, contemp calf; rebacked, worn. With 4 maps & 18 (of 19) hand-colored plates. The hand-coloring is modern. S June 13 (629) £240

**Abelin, Johann Philipp, d. c.1634**
— Archontologica Cosmica. Frankfurt: Matthaeus Merian, 1649. Vol II only. Contemp calf; def. With 52 maps & 134 plates & plans & 7 large folding plans & panoramas. Lacking tp & Plate 74 but with duplicate 21; 1st few leaves detached; panoramas of Nuremberg & Prague damaged; some cropping, staining & creasing. S June 27 (77) £11,000

— Newe Welt und Americanische Historien.... Frankfurt, 1655. 3d Ed. Folio, contemp vellum over pastebd; dampstained, corner of lower cover damaged. With engraved title, 3 folding maps, 1 double-page map & folding plate. Some browning & fold tears. Sometimes attributed to Johann Ludwig Gottfried. C Oct 25 (125) £2,600

**Abercrombie, John, 1780-1844**
— Inquiries Concerning the Intellectual Powers and the Investigation of Truth. Edin., 1832. 8vo, half calf. Some foxing. bba July 18 (224) £70 [Therese]

**Abercrombie, Lascelles, 1881-1938.** See: Gregynog Press

**Abercromby, Patrick**
— The Martial Atchievements of the Scots Nation. Edin., 1711-15. 2 vols. Folio, contemp calf; rebacked. CG June 12 (21) £180

**Abert, James W.**
— Through the Country of the Comanche Indians.... [San Francisco], 1970. 4to, cloth, in dj. pba Apr 25 (260) $55; pba July 25 (84) $50

— Western America in 1846-1847. San Francisco, 1966. Folio, cloth. pba Apr 25 (261) $65

# AMERICAN BOOK PRICES CURRENT

**Abney, Capt. William de W.**
— Thebes and its Five Greater Temples. L, 1876. 4o, orig cloth; extremities worn, front hinge starting. With 40 Woodburytypes in ptd mounts. Foxed, affecting some plates. sg Feb 29 (5) $1,200

**Aboab, Imanuel**
— Nomologia o discursos legales. [Amst., 1629]. 4to, modern lea. Tp & some other margins patched; some staining & browning. CE Dec 6 (194) $420

**Abrizzi, Isabella, Countess**
— The Works of Antonio Canova in Sculpture and Modelling.... L, 1849. 3 vols. 4to, later half calf gilt; spines scuffed. Foxing affecting some plates. sg Jan 11 (76) $225

Anr Ed. Bost., 1876-78. 2 vols. 4to, mor gilt; extremities worn. sg June 13 (73) $250

**Academie Royale de Chirurgie**
— Observations on Surgical Diseases of the Head and Neck. Selected from the Memoirs of the Royal Academy of Surgery of France. L: Sydenham Society, 1848. Trans by Drewry Ottley. 8vo, orig cloth. sg May 16 (466) $60

**Academy...**
— Academy of Pacific Coast History: Publications. Berkeley, 1910-19. Orig cloth; covers slightly worn. Larson copy. pba Sept 28 (36) $225

**Accoramboni, Girolamo, 1469-1537**
— Tractatus de Lacte. Venice: Arrivabene, 1536. 1st Ed. 8vo, modern bds. Title stained; quire E browned; light spotting. Ck Mar 22 (2) £850

**Accum, Friedrich Christian, 1769-1838**
— Culinary Chemistry; Exhibiting the Scientific Principles of Cookery. L: R. Ackerman, 1821. 1st Ed. 12mo, contemp cloth; spine restored, worn. With hand-colored frontis & title vignette. Some browning & spotting; prelims thumb-soiled. Ck Mar 22 (3) £220

Anr copy. Modern half calf. With hand-colored frontis & title vignette. Ck Mar 22 (4) £240

— A Practical Essay on Chemical Re-Agents or Tests. L, 1816. 1st Ed. 2 parts in 1 vol. 12mo, contemp bds; corners bumped. With title vignette. Some spotting. Ck Mar 22 (5) £350

— A Practical Essay on the Analysis of Minerals. Phila., 1809. 1st American Ed. 12mo, orig bds; spine lacking, front flyleaves missing. With 2 plates. Stained & foxed. Met Feb 24 (303) $200

— A System of Theoretical and Practical Chemistry. Phila., 1808. 1st American Ed. 2 vols. 8vo, contemp calf; worn & foxed. With 7 plates. Some foxing. wa Feb 29 (145) $130

— A Treatise on Adulterations of Food.... L, 1820. 1st Ed. 12mo, contemp half calf; joints cracked, extrems worn. With title vignette. Title spotted. Ck Mar 22 (8) £240

Anr copy. 8vo, later half cloth; worn. Some spotting. F June 20 (611D) $260

234

— A Treatise on the Art of Brewing. L, 1820. 1st Ed. 12mo, contemp bds; rebacked, spine head & tail bumped. With hand-colored frontis & title vignette by W. Read, & 2 folding tables. Spotted; margins damspatined.   Ck Mar 22 (6) £280

**Acerbi, Giuseppe, 1773-1846**
— Travels through Sweden, Finland, and Lapland, to the North Cape.... L, 1802. 1st Ed. 2 vols. 4to, half calf; rubbed, spine of Vol I reglued. Marginal stains; foxed.   K Feb 11 (1) $375

**Achebe, Chinua**
— Things Fall Apart. NY, [1959]. In dj. pba Aug 22 (3) $90

**Acheson, Dean.** See: Onassis copy, Jacqueline Bouvier Kennedy

**Ackermann Publications, Rudolph—London**
— Cambridge. 1815. ("A History of the University of Cambridge.") 2 vols. 4to, lev gilt by Morrell. With port & 95 hand-colored plates. Some browning. C Oct 5 (353) £2,200
Anr copy. Contemp mor gilt; scuffed, hinges & edges rubbed. With port & 79 hand-colored plates. Port spotted. Without the Founder's plates. S Apr 23 (341) £2,500
— The History of the Abbey Church of St. Peter's Westminster.... 1812. 1st Ed, 2d Issue. 2 vols. 4to, 19th-cent calf gilt; extremities scuffed & worn. With port, plan & 81 colored plates. Some foxing. pba Nov 30 (1) $550
— The Microcosm of London. 1808-10. 3 vols. 4to, contemp calf gilt; rubbed, hinges weak, upper cover of Vol II detached, spine of Vol III repaired. With 104 hand-colored plates. Some browning. C Oct 5 (357) £4,800
Anr Ed. L, 1904. 3 vols. 4to, orig half vellum; worn & soiled.   F Mar 28 (387) $50
— Oxford. 1814. ("A History of the University of Oxford.") 2 vols. 4to, contemp calf gilt with Chancellor of Oxford's seal; rebacked. With port & 97 hand-colored plates. C Oct 5 (355) £1,500
Anr copy. Mor gilt. With port, 70 hand-colored aquatints on 64 sheets & 17 hand-colored costume plates. Browned & spotted. C Oct 25 (99) £2,200
Anr copy. Contemp mor gilt; scuffed, hinges & edges rubbed. With port & 81 hand-colored plates. Without the Founders' ports. S Apr 23 (340) £2,400
— Winchester, Eton & Westminster. 1816. ("The History of the Colleges of Winchester, Eton, and Westminster....") 4to, contemp russia; rebacked. With 48 hand-colored plates. Some browning. C Oct 5 (351) £2,000

**Acosta, Cristoval de, 1597-1676?.** See: Orta & Acosta

**Actius, Thomas**
— De Ludo Scacchorum in legali methodo tractatus.... Pesaro, 1583. 4to, contemp vellum. With port. Tear in A1; some leaves wormed in lower margin; some foxing & marginal dampstaining. sg Oct 19 (1) $700

**Acton, Eliza, 1799-1859**
— Modern Cookery in all its Branches. Phila., 1858. 8vo, orig cloth; worn, repaired, new endpapers. Old clippings & recipes mtd on front matter. F June 20 (599) $50
— Poems. Ipswich, 1826. 8vo, contemp bds with cloth spine.   b Dec 5 (352) £190

**Acuna, Christoval, 1597-1676?**
— Nuevo Descubrimiento del gran rio de las Amazonas. Madrid, 1641. 4to, contemp Spanish vellum. Some underlining & dampstaining. S June 27 (179) £22,000

**Adair, Arthur H.** See: Toye & Adair

**Adair, James, 1709?-83?**
— The History of the American Indians.... L, 1775. 1st Ed. 4to, contemp half calf with vellum corners; scuffed, spine worn. With folding map. Half-title creased.   C May 31 (78) £600

**Adalbert, Prince of Prussia, 1811-73**
— Travels in the South of Europe and in Brazil. L, 1849. 2 vols. 8vo, contemp cloth; rubbed, recased. With frontis & 4 folding maps. b May 30 (140) £100

**Adam, Melchior**
— Vitae Germanorum Medicorum: qui Seculo Superiori.... Heidelberg, 1620. 8vo, new vellum. Browned.   CE Nov 8 (60) $260

**Adam, William, d.1748**
— Vitruvius Scoticus; being a Collection of Plans, Elevations and Sections of Public Buildings. Edin.: A. Black, [1810]. Folio, modern half calf. With 179 plates, 16 of them double-page, 7 folding. Fold tear to 1 plate; some dampstaining. C Nov 29 (80) £8,500

**Adams, Ansel Easton**
— Ansel Adams. Hastings-on-Hudson, [1972]. 4to, cloth, in dj with tear to rear panel. Sgd on half-title. pba Nov 16 (4) $50
Anr copy. Cloth, in dj with minor soiling. With 117 photographic reproductions. Sgd on half-title. sg Feb 29 (6) $140
One of final galley proofs. Wraps. ANs on half-title, 13 Oct 1972 & with sgd photograph laid in. pba June 20 (2) $650
— My Camera in the National Parks.... Yosemite National Park & Bost., 1950. 4to, ptd bds, spiral bound, in dj. With 30 photo reproductions. Sgd. pba June 20 (3) $180
Anr copy. Ptd bds, spiral bound, in dj. Sgd. sg Feb 29 (9) $300
— The Pageant of History in Northern California.... San Francisco, [1954]. Text by Nancy Newhall. 4to, spiral-bound wraps; scratched. pba Nov 16 (3) $50
Anr copy. With 56 plates. wa Feb 1 (228) $95
— Sierra Nevada: The John Muir Trail. Berkeley: Archetype Press, 1938. One of 500. Folio, cloth. pba June 20 (4) $1,700

## ADAMS

— Yosemite and the Range of Light. Bost.: New York Graphic Society, 1979. Intro by Paul Brooks. Oblong 4to, cloth, in dj. Sgd on half-title. sg Feb 29 (12) $110

— Yosemite and the Sierra Nevada: Selections from the Works of John Muir. Bost., 1948. 4to, cloth, in dj. With 64 plates. pba Aug 8 (1) $200

**Adams, Edgar Holmes**

— Private Gold Coinage of California, 1849-55. [N.p., n.d.]. Reprint Ed. Orig mor. With 11 full-page illus & five dollar gold piece. Larson copy. pba Sept 28 (472) $850

**Adams, Emma H.**

— To and Fro in Southern California.... Cincinnati, 1887. Orig cloth; spine ends rubbed. pba Apr 25 (263) $100

**Adams, George, 1750-95**

— Astronomical and Geographical Essays.... Whitehall, 1800. 8vo, contemp sheep; front joint cracked. With 16 folding plates. Browned, with traces of mold. sg May 16 (106) $100

— An Essay on Electricity.... L, 1784. 12mo, contemp half calf; joints cracked. With frontis & 6 folding plates. CE May 22 (1) $320

Anr copy. Contemp calf; rebacked retaining orig backstrip. With 6 folding plates. sg May 16 (105) $275

— Geometrical and Graphical Essays. L, 1791. 8vo, old calf; rebacked. With frontis & 32 folding plates. Some browning; some plates with old misfolds; some wear & chipping; frontis foxed; 1 plate with small hole. bbc Dec 18 (376) $200

**Adams, Henry, 1838-1918**

See also: Fore-Edge Paintings; Limited Editions Club

— Memoirs of Arii Taimai E Marama of Eimeo Teriirere.... Paris, 1901. 4to, orig cloth; rebacked retaining backstrip, stains on rear cover. With double-page map having institutional stamp on verso. sg Apr 18 (1) $800

— Mont Saint Michel and Chartres. Wash., 1904. 1st Ed. 4to, cloth, orig cloth laid down. Marginal paper cracks or chipping on 1st several leaves. Inscr on inserted leaf. sg Apr 18 (2) $650

**Adams, Herbert Mayow**

— Catalogue of Books Printed on the Continent of Europe, 1501-1600, in Cambridge Libraries. Cambr., 1967. 2 vols. 4to, orig cloth in dj; frayed, crudely taped. sg Apr 11 (4) $650

Anr Ed. Cambr., 1987. 2 vols. 4to, orig cloth. Ck Apr 12 (180) £260

**Adams, John, Riding Master**

— The Analysis of Horsemanship.... L, 1805. 3 vols. 8vo, contemp half calf; worn, Vol I spine chipped. Some foxing. O Jan 9 (1) $300

**Adams, John, 1735-1826**

— A Defence of the Constitutions of Government of the United States of America. L, 1787-88. 3 vols. 8vo, contemp calf; worn, repaired, rebacked. Inscr to Charles Maurice de Talleyrand-Perigord, 21 May 1794. CNY Dec 15 (43) $26,000

Anr Ed. L, 1787. 8vo, old calf; worn & dry, front bd detached. Lacking prelim blanks; tape residue to gutter of pastedown & detached title; Some foxing. wa Feb 29 (264) $550

**Adams, John Stowell**

— The Story of Aleck, or Pitcairn's Island.... Amherst, Mass., 1829. 1st Ed. 16mo, orig wraps; soiled. b Mar 20 (5) £1,300

**Adams, Ramon F.**

— The Cowboy and His Humor. Austin, 1968-69. Bound with: The Cowboy and His Code of Ethics 1st Eds, One of 850. 2 vols, Bds. Robbins copy. pba Mar 21 (1) $225

**Adams, Ramon F. —&
Britzman, Homer Elwood**

— Charles M. Russell: The Cowboy Artist. Pasadena, 1948. In dj. pba Apr 25 (639) $180

**Adams, Richard, Novelist**

— The Girl in a Swing. [L, 1980]. 1st Ed, Uncorrected proof of suppressed issue, book Ed of suppressed issue & censored issue. 3 vols. Ptd wraps & cloth, in djs. Censored issue sgd. sg Dec 14 (1) $90

— Watership Down. L, 1972. 1st Ed. Minor insect damage to cloth. In rubbed & repaired d/j. pba May 4 (97) $425

Anr Ed. L, 1976. Illus by John Lawrence. In dj. Sgd & dated by Lawrence. pba Aug 22 (5) $95

One of 250. Lev gilt by Sangorski & Sutcliffe. cb Oct 17 (347) $400

**Adams, William**

— A Disquisition of the Stone and Gravel.... L, [1773]. 8vo, bds. Tp soiled. b May 30 (7) £70

**Adamson, Alistair Beaton**

— Allan Robertson, Golfer: His Life and Times. Worcestshire: Grant Books, 1985. 1st Ed, One of 1,055. Cloth. Sgd. pba Apr 18 (1) $120

**Adanson, Michel, 1727-1806**

— Histoire naturelle du Senegal.... Paris, 1757. 1st Ed. - Illus by Marie-Therese Reboul. 4to, contemp half calf. With folding map by P. Buache, & 19 folding plates.. S Oct 27 (686) £700 [Ghyoot]

— A Voyage to Senegal.... L, 1759. 8vo, contemp sheep; needs rebdg. Library stamp on tp. sg Mar 7 (1) $500

**Addams, Charles, 1912-88**

— My Crowd. NY, [1976]. 4to, pictorial cloth, in dj with repairs. Sgd & dated. sg June 20 (1) $80

## Addison, Joseph, 1672-1719
See also: Spectator
— Works. Birm.: Baskerville, 1761. 4 vols. 4to, contemp calf; small piece missing from spine head of Vol IV. Lacking 2 blanks but with the Directions to the Binder; Hh2 in Vol II with tear; Vol IV with some staining, affecting top edge of upper cover. S Dec 18 (119) £400 [Woods]

Anr Ed. NY, 1854. 6 vols. 12mo, contemp half calf gilt. sg Feb 8 (2) $90

## Address...
— Address, on the Opening of the Warrington Theatre, December 1818. Warrington, 1818. 4to, sewn as issued. Some spotting. b Dec 5 (176) £80

## Adelphi
— The Adelphi. L, 1923-25. Ed by John Middleton Murry. 21 vols. Pictorial wraps; spines browned, extremities chipped. Ck Nov 17 (104) £180

## Adelphus, Johannes
— Die Tuerckisch Chronica.... Strassburg: Martin Flach, 1508. Folio, modern calf-backed wooden bds with brass clasps. Minor staining & soiling throughout; marginal repairs at ends. C Apr 3 (11) £2,400

## Adhemar, Jean
— Toulouse-Lautrec: his Complete Lithographs and Drypoints. NY, [1965]. 4to, cloth, in dj. F June 20 (252) $60; pba Aug 8 (631) $50; sg Jan 11 (430) $50

## Adventurer...
— The Adventurer. L, 1762. Ed by John Hawkesworth. 4 vols. 12mo, calf; glue to spine heads & upper joints. pba Nov 30 (174) $170

## Adventures... See: Clemens, Samuel Langhorne

## Advertisement...
— Broadside advertising the goods sold at Lawes & Co., No. 115 Regent Street.... L, 1825. Torn at lower corner. S Oct 12 (83) £100

## Advertisseur Haytien...
— L'Avertisseur Haytien, journal politique, commercial et litteraire. Port-au-Prince, 1818. 4to, wraps; chipped. sg Mar 28 (93) $225

## Aegidius Romanus, d.1316
— De regimine principum. Seville: Meinard Ungut & Stanislaus Polonus for Johannes de Alemano & Melchior Gorricio, 20 Oct 1494. ("Regimiento de los principes.") Folio early vellum; upper joint loose. 44 lines & headline; double column; types 4:144G (incipit, headlines), 2:111G (chapter headings, colophon), 5:98G (text). With full-page woodcut on title. British Museum stamp & cancelled stamp; last leaf with minor paper repairs; ends with soiling & waterstaining. 254 (of 256) leaves; lacking blanks H10 & AA6. Goff A-91. Schaefer copy. P Nov 1 (1) $14,500

## Aeneas Sylvius Piccolomini, Pope Pius II, 1405-64
— Abbrevatio supra Decades Blondi. Rome: D.D.L.D.S.P.V., 1481. Folio, old bds; rebacked in 19th-cent calf. 32 lines; roman letter. Some worming at ends. 156 leaves. Goff P-654. Kloss - Amherst of Hackney copy. S June 27 (359) £1,050
— De Bohemorum origine ac gestis historia.... Solingen: Joannes Soter, 1538. 8vo, modern mor. bba Sept 7 (199) £240 [Robertshaw]
— Epistolae familiares. Nuremberg: Anton Koberger, 16 Sept 1481. Folio, 18th-cent half calf with unidentified illuminated arms on flyleaf. 52 lines; gothic letter. With contemp German miniature & full-page border on fol. 7r. Some worming at ends; 2 repairs in margins of fol. 7 with minor damage to border; ownership note on fol. 1 erased with minor damaged; a few Ms notes in margins. 244 (of 246) leaves; lacking 1 blank. Goff P-717. S June 27 (360) £5,800

Anr Ed. Louvian: Johann de Paderborn, 1483. Folio, recent calf. 31 lines; roman letter. Marginal annotations & underscoring in an early hand; a2-3 cropped & mtd on guards & probably from anr copy; last leaf cut round & laid down; repair to upper margin of penultimate leaf; marginal dampstaining. 302 (of 304) leaves; lacking initial blank & m5. Goff P-718. S Dec 18 (75) £500 [Rix]

Anr Ed. Milan: Uldericus Scinzenzeler, 10 Dec 1496. Folio, 18th-cent vellum; loose. 59 lines; roman letter. Tp stained & repaired in lower margin; text dampstained at foot throughout causing fraying. 188 leaves. Goff P-721. S Dec 18 (76) £480 [Zioni]
— Epistolae in Pontificatu editae. Milan: Antonius Zarotus for Johannes de Legnano, 31 May 1481. Folio, old bds formerly covered in rough calf; rebacked in calf, upper bd broken. 34 lines; roman letter. Tear in fore-margin of d7 touching text; contemp annotations. 164 leaves. Goff P-725. S Dec 18 (74) £800 [Zioni]

## Aepinus, Franciscus Maria Ulricus Theodorus
— Tentamen theoriae electricitatis et magnetismi, accedunt dissertationes duae. St. Petersburg, [1759]. 4to, contemp half calf. With 8 folding plates. Some spotting & discoloration; Ss1 & Ss4 with repair to lower margins. S Mar 14 (6) £2,100

## Aeschylus, 525-456 B.C.
See also: Limited Editions Club
— Opera. Venice: Aldus, 1518. ("Tragoediae.") 8vo, modern mor. In Greek. C Apr 3 (12) £3,200
— The Oresteian Trilogy. Greenbrae: Allen Press, 1982-83. One of 140. Orig cloth. bba May 9 (442) £75 [Collinge & Clark]

## Aesop, c.620-560 B.C.
See also: Golden Cockerel Press; Gregynog Press; Limited Editions Club

### Fables
— 1609. - Fabulae. Lyons: Joannes Jullieron. 16mo, contemp vellum; front joint cracked. Dampstaining throughout; front corner off m2 causing slight text loss; marginal tears. sg Mar 21 (1) $225

# AESOP

— 1651. - The Fables. L. Trans by John Ogilby. 4to, contemp calf; corners rubbed, rebacked. With port & 81 plates. Some plates repaired or with portion of margin torn away; Plate 66 with rust-hole; some staining. S July 11 (108) £1,800

— 1664. - Fabulae. Treviso: Franciscus Righettinus. 12mo, old vellum. Some browning; hole in 1 leaf affecting woodcut. sg Mar 21 (2) $120

— 1666. - Fables.... L. Folio, contemp calf; joints repaired. Minor discoloration. In English, French & Latin. Schaefer copy. P Nov 1 (2) $13,000

— 1668. - The Fables. L. Bound with: Aesopics, or a Second Collection of Fables. L, 1668. 2 parts in 1 vol. 2d Ed of 1st part; 1st Ed of 2d part. Paraphrased in verse by John Ogilby. Folio, contemp half calf. With port, frontis & 81 plates in 1st part & 67 plates in 2d part. pba Nov 30 (6) $3,250

— 1699. - Fables of Aesop and Other Eminent Mythologists. L. Ed by Sir Roger L'Estrange. 2 vols in 1. Folio, contemp calf; rubbed. With port & frontis. Some discoloring. b Sept 20 (81) £130

— 1700. - Esope en belle humeur.... Brussels: Foppens. 2 vols in 1. 8vo, 18th-cent mor gilt in the style of Derome; lower joint starting. With frontis & 163 half-page engravings. Some spotting & browning; repaired hole on tp. Schaefer copy. P Nov 1 (3) $2,000

— 1793. - Fables. L: John Stockdale. 2 vols. 8vo, modern mor. With 112 plates, including engraved titles. Some spotting & rubbing. b Sept 20 (594) £170

Anr copy. Contemp half calf. With engraved vignettes on titles (cropped at lower margin) & 110 plates. b Jan 31 (45) £150

Anr copy. Contemp calf; covers of Vol I detached. With engraved titles & 112 plates. CE Sept 27 (30) $280

Anr copy. Contemp calf gilt; rebacked, sides rubbed. With 2 engraved titles & 110 plates, 6 within gilt borders, 2 within blue borders. Titles, headings & initials all heightened in gold, with 75 hand-painted headpieces & 90 tailpieces added to margins; a few other small hand-painted ornaments in margins, with additional hand-painted illuminated title added to Vol I; 16 pp with hand-painted borders. Margins of both titles cropped with slight shaving of text in Vol II; some browning & spotting. S Nov 2 (275) £620 [Stone]

Anr copy. 2 vols. 8vo, later calf; dry & rubbed, hinges weak. With 112 plates, including engraved titles. Z June 28 (1) $450

— 1807. - Select Fables of Esop and Other Fabulists. Phila.: Mathew Carey. 12mo, contemp sheep; worn. Browned throughout; some tears. sg Oct 26 (97) $50

— 1818. - The Fables of Aesop and Others. Newcastle Illus by Thomas Bewick. 8vo, lev extra by Worefold. Inserted is a receipt sgd by Thos. Bewick. L.p. copy. sg Sept 21 (80) £425

— 1912. - Fables. L. One of 1,450, sgd by the artist. Trans by V. S. Vernon Jones; illus by Arthur Rackham. 4to, orig cloth; soiled. With 13 colored plates. b Jan 31 (210) £160

Anr copy. Mor extra by Bayntun-Riviere, with onlaid design of a scene from The Hare & the Tortoise. CE Sept 27 (233) $1,800

Anr copy. Orig cloth; soiled, endpapers foxed. Met Dec 5 (345) $350

Anr copy. Orig cloth; upper cover stained. S Nov 2 (116) £260 [Bayntuns]

Anr copy. Orig cloth; recased, hinges reinforced. sg Sept 14 (301) $850

Anr copy. Later mor gilt. With 13 colored plates. Exhibition announcement mtd on back of frontis. sg Oct 19 (197) $800

— 1928. - Twenty Four Fables.... L: Alcuin Press One of 50. Ed by Sir Roger L'Estrange. 4to, half lev by Bumpus. pba June 20 (6) $170

— [1931]. - Fables. Paris: Harrison of Paris One of 495 on Auvergne handmade paper. Illus by Alexander Calder. 4to, orig bds, in dj. sg Sept 14 (85) $600

— 1936. - L. One of 525, sgd by the artist. Trans by Sir Roger L'Estrange; illus by Stephen Gooden. 4to, orig vellum gilt. Additional sgd proof of A Smith and his Dog loosely inserted. b Sept 20 (592) £450

Anr copy. Orig vellum gilt. Additional sgd proof of tp loosely inserted. b Sept 20 (593) £350; S May 16 (115) £400

Anr copy. Orig vellum gilt; binder's blanks foxed. sg Oct 19 (2) $325

— 1954. - 12 Fables of Aesop. NY Ltd Ed. Illus by Antonio Frasconi. 4to, half cloth. Sgd by Frasconi, Wescott & Joseph Blumenthal, the ptr. sg Sept 14 (136) $225

— 1968. - Fables. L. One of 250, sgd by the artist. Illus by Elizabeth Frink. Folio, orig mor gilt. Lacking the 4 sgd lithos. sg Sept 14 (137) $275

— 1973. - The Fables: The First Three Books of Caxton's Aesop. Verona: Officina Bodoni One of 160. 2 vols. Orig half mor. sg Oct 19 (188) $2,200

— 1980. - Thomas Bewick's Fables of Aesop. L: Florin Press Illus by Thomas Bewick. 4to, half calf. sg Sept 14 (134) $200

**Aflalo, F. G.**
— A Book of Fishing Stories. L, 1913. Cloth; spots to upper front cover. Foxed. pba July 11 (4) $90

**Agapios, Monk of Crete**
— Biblion oraiotaton kaloumenon amartolon sotiria meta pleistes epimeleias. Venice: Andrea Giuliani, 1681. 4to, contemp bds. Dampstaining at end, with traces of mold. sg Mar 21 (3) $600

**Agee, James, 1909-55**
— A Death in the Family. NY, [1957]. In dj. sg Dec 14 (2) $60
— A Way of Seeing. NY, [1965]. Illus by Helen Levitt. In rubbed dj; some soiling to bdg. sg Feb 29 (183) $250

**Agg, John**
— A Consolatory Epistle to a Noble Lord on the Sudden and Unexpected Close of his Political Career. By Humphrey Hedgehog. Evesham, 1805. 4to, sewn as issued. b Dec 5 (412) £260

**Aglio, Augustine.** See: Kingsborough, Edward

**Agostini, Leonardo**
— Le gemme antiche figurate di Leonardo Agostini. Rome, 1657-69. 2 vols. 4to, contemp mor gilt bound for Ferdinando & Flavio Orsini, Dukes of Bracciano, with their crowned arms. C Apr 3 (10) £2,400

**Agricola, Georgius, 1494-1555**
— De ortu & causis subterraneorum.... Basel, 1558. Folio, modern mor. Marginal worming in 1st few leaves. C Apr 3 (14) £1,600
— De re metallica. Basel: Froben, 1556. 1st Ed. Folio, 19th-cent blind-tooled mor; extremities rubbed. Tears at inner margins of a1 & 2. C Apr 3 (13) £9,500
2d Ed. Basel, 1561. Folio, 17th-cent half blind-stamped pigskin over paste-paper bds covered in vellum; some wear. Some contemp marginalia. P June 5 (150) $6,500
Anr Ed. Basel, 1657. Folio, contemp vellum. Browned. S Mar 14 (9) £2,000
Anr copy. Contemp sheep gilt; extremities worn, crack to front joint. Lacking 2 prelim leaves & final blank. sg Oct 19 (220) $1,900
Anr Ed. L, 1912. Trans by Herbert C. & Lou Hoover. Folio, orig vellum; joint split, minor wear. Inscr to Edgar Richard. cb Feb 14 (2623) $1,000
Anr copy. Orig half vellum. S Mar 14 (10) £360
Anr copy. Orig bds; rear cover scratched. Inscr by Herbert Hoover to Harry Howard Webb. sg Oct 19 (221) $500
Anr copy. Orig half vellum. Library markings. Inscr by Herbert Hoover to Charles Edison. sg May 16 (107) $225
Anr Ed. Rome: Societa Finanziaria Siderurgica, 1959. One of 1,000. Folio, vellum. With booklet by Alberto Mondini laid in. Facsimile of 1561 Ed. pba Nov 30 (7) $250

**Agrippa, Henricus Cornelius, 1486?-1535**
— De occulta philosophia libri tres. [Cologne: Johannes Soter], July 1533. Folio, contemp pigskin laid down on modern mor, lower pastedown & front endpapers from contemp Ms fragments laid down on modern paper. P June 5 (151) $3,000
— Of the Vanitie and Uncertantie of Arts and Sciences. L, 1684. ("The Vanity of Arts and Sciences.") 8vo, contemp calf; worn, covers detached. sg May 16 (108) $400

**Agunti, Anna**
— Tapies. The Complete Works. NY, 1988. 2 vols. 4to, cloth, in djs. sg Jan 11 (413) $250

**Ahmad I, Sultan**
— True Copies of the Insolent, Cruell... Letter Lately Written by the Great Turke.... L, 1621. 4to, half mor. Lacking initial blank; last leaf wormed, affecting 2 letters. STC 208. Phillipps copy. b May 30 (238) £700

**Ahmad ibn Muhammad ibn Ahmad ibn Yaha**
— The History of the Mohammedan Dynasties in Spain. L, 1840-43. Trans by Pascual de Gayangos. 2 vols. 4to, 19th-Century half calf; slightly rubbed. Some spotting. S Oct 26 (2) £750 [Bruschettini]

**Aiguino, Illuminato**
— La Illuminata de tutti tuoni di canto fermo.... Venice: Antonio Gardano, 1562. 1st Ed. 4to, 18th-cent "carta rustica". Some dampstaining at beginning. S Dec 1 (60) £950

**Aikin, Arthur, 1773-1854**
— Journal of a Tour through North Wales and Part of Shropshire.... L, 1797. 8vo, 19th-cent half lev gilt by Blackwell. With folding diagram. Some soiling. sg May 16 (109) $375

**Aikin, John, 1747-1822**
— A Description of the Country from Thirty to Forty Miles round Manchester. L, 1795. 4to, half calf. With frontis & 69 (of 71) plates. Lacking folding map & plan; some spotting. b Sept 20 (298) £160
Anr copy. Contemp tree calf; lower cover scratched, joints broken. With additional title, & 65 plates, maps & plans (3 folding). Top 3d of additional title lacking; 2 plates loose & laid down. S Oct 26 (379) £180 [Smith]
— England Delineated.... L, 1804. 2 vols. 8vo, orig bds; needs rebdg. With 148 plates. Library stamp on each plate verso & on titles & some text leaves. sg Mar 7 (73) $200

**Aikin, Lucy, 1781-1864**
— Memoirs of the Court of King Charles the First. L, 1838. 2 vols in 3. 8vo, half mor gilt by Bayntun; hinges rubbed. Extra-illus with plates. ALs to her niece tipped in. wd Nov 15 (25) $300

**Ainsworth, Edward**
— The Cowboy in Art. NY & Cleveland, 1968. Calf. pba Apr 25 (264) $110

**Ainsworth, Henry**
— Annotations upon the Five Books of Moses.... L: John Haviland for John Bellamie, 1622. Folio, disbound. Blank margin of tp for Annotations on Exodus torn away. K June 23 (67) $375

**Ainsworth, William Harrison, 1805-82**
— Jack Sheppard. L, 1839. 1st Ed. - Illus by George Cruikshank. 3 vols. 12mo, half calf. With 27 plates. pba Aug 22 (536) $100
— Windsor Castle. L, 1844. 8vo, Half mor gilt, orig cloth bound in. With 19 plates, 14 by George Cruikshank. sg Feb 8 (3) $100

**Ainsworth's...**
— Ainsworth's Magazine. L, 1842-50. Vols I-XVII, lacking Vol IX. 8vo, contemp half calf. Sold w.a.f. b Jan 31 (46) £160

### Akenside, Mark, 1721-70
— The Poems. L, 1772. 1st Collected Ed. 4to, contemp calf gilt; spine ends worn. pba Mar 7 (4) $140

### Alain-Fournier, Henri, 1886-1914
— Le Grand meaulnes. Paris, [1930]. One of 166. Illus by Hermine David. 4to, mor extra by Paul Boney, 1941 [Carnets, 538]. S Nov 21 (5) £13,000

### Alamanni, Luigi, 1495-1556
— La Coltivatione. Florence: Giunta, 1546. Anr Ed. 8vo, later calf. pba June 20 (5) $275

### Alaska
— Alaska Herald. San Francisco, 1871-72. Vol IV, Nos 76-99, bound in 1 vol. Modern half mor. pba Nov 16 (9) $1,800
— The Official Guide to the Klondyke Country and the Gold Fields of Alaska. Chicago: W. B. Conkey, 1897. 8vo, orig wraps; minor wear, chipped. bbc Feb 26 (383) $180

### Albanis de Beaumont, Jean Francois, Viscount, 1753?-1811?
— Travels through the Rhaetian Alps. L, 1792. Folio, contemp calf; rebacked preserving spine. With map & 10 plates. Some spotting. b Dec 5 (111) £450

### Albanus, Franciscus
— Picturae Francisci Albani in aede verospia. Rome, 1704. Folio, 19th-cent russia gilt by Kalthoeber; rebacked with spine laid down. With engraved title & 16 plates, 5 of them double-page, all on guards. Some spotting; 1 ceiling view trimmed & mtd. Sir Joshua Reynolds's sgd copy. Beckford - James copy. C June 26 (180) £1,600

### Albemarle, George Thomas Keppel, Earl of, 1799-1891. See: Keppel, George Thomas

### Albers, Josef, 1888-1976
— Interaction of Color. New Haven, 1963. 2 vols. 4to, text orig cloth, commentary in orig wraps & boxed with plates, unbound as issued. With 80 double-page plates. sg Jan 11 (1) $1,100

### Alberti, Leon Battista, 1404-72
— Della pittura.... Venice: Gabriel Giolito de Ferrara, 1547. 8vo, 19th-cent mor gilt by Quinet. Some browning. C Apr 3 (16) £1,100
— Opera. [Florence: Bartolommeo de Libri, c.1497-99]. 4to, 16th-cent vellum. 33 lines; type 1C:97R. Contemp Ms corrections. 52 leaves. Goff A-211. Sussex - Redgrave - Clark of Saltwood copy. C Apr 3 (15) £5,200

### Albertus Magnus, 1193?-1280
— Compendium Theologicae Veritatis. Ulm: Johann Zainer, [c.1478-80]. 4to, 19th-cent bds. 40 lines; gothic letter. 32 leaves from anr Zainer Ed inserted after fol. 14; fols. 2-7 def at upper outer corners with loss; all but 1 of missing leaves supplied in photofacsimile. 148 (of 162) leaves only. Goff A-233. S Dec 18 (1) £600 [Rix]
— Historia Alexandri Magni.... Strassburg: Printer of the 1483 Jordanus de Quedlinburg (Georg Husner), 17 Mar 1489. Bound with: Columna, Guido de. Historia destructionis Troiae. Strassburg: Printer of the 1483 Jordanus de Quedlinburg (Georg Husner), c.25 May 1489. Folio, 16th-cent pigskin over paper bds, blindstamped; rubbed, small stain on back cover. 1st work: 43 lines; double column; types 1:160G & 3 [2a]:91G. 2d work: 43 lines & headline; double column; same types. Initials, paragraph marks, headline & capital strokes in red. Small piece replaced from top of tp; minor stain on tp & i2. 1st work: 38 leaves. Goff A-398. 2d work: 88 leaves. Goff C-774. C Nov 29 (22) £1,500

### Albin, Eleazar, fl.1713-59
— Birds. L, 1731-38. ("A Natural History of Birds.") 1st Ed, 1st Issue. 3 vols. 4to, 19th-cent half calf; scuffed. With 306 hand-colored plates. With 3 hand-colored impressions of a plate from Albin's Spiders showing him on horseback mtd as frontises in each vol. Browning to c.6 text leaves in Vol II; a few plates shaved into image area; 2 plates with smudging or soiling; frontis & 1 plate with small tears in upper margins. Fattorini copy. C Oct 25 (1) £8,000
— Songbirds. L, 1737. ("A Natural History of English Songbirds....") 1st Ed. 8vo, contemp calf; rubbed. With hand-colored frontis & 23 hand-colored plates. Some plates cropped. Evelyn copy. b Sept 20 (453) £400

### Albinus, Bernard Siegfried, 1697-1770
— Icones ossium foetus humani.... Leiden, 1737. 1st Ed. 4to, modern half mor. With 32 plates. F4 torn, scattered foxing & soiling, some plates browned. CE Nov 8 (61) $600
— Tables of the Skeleton and Muscles of the Human Body. L, 1749. Folio, modern half mor. With 48 plates. Tp soiled, stained & repaired; dampstained & stained throughout. Sold w.a.f. CE Nov 8 (62) $1,500
— Tabulae ossium humanorum. Leiden, 1753. Folio, contemp half vellum; rubbed & soiled. With 34 finished life-size plates & 34 corresponding outline plates with explanatory text. Last few leaves stained; some creasing to centerfolds. C June 26 (182) £1,500
— Tabulae sceleti et musculorum corporis humani. Leiden, 1747. Bound in 2 vols. Folio, modern half calf. With engraved dedication & 28 plates, of which the 1st 12 have key plates. About 20 plates damaged by damp & restored in margins; 1 text leaf torn & repaired in lower margin. S Nov 30 (311) £2,000

### Album...
— Album pintoresco de la isla de Cuba. [Havana: B. May, c.1850]. Oblong folio, orig cloth; new endpapers. With colored engraved title, 2 folding colored maps & 27 colored plates. Some plates smudged. S Nov 30 (173) £2,600
Anr Ed. Havana: B. May, [1851]. Oblong 4to, orig cloth; spine worn, hinges & sewing weak. With chromolitho title partly ptd in gold & 27 chromolitho

plates & folding maps of Cuba & of Havana. Some spotting & soiling; 3 plates loose with margins soiled & torn. C May 31 (87) £2,200

**Albumasar, 805-886**
— De magnis conjunctionibus. Augsburg: Ratdolt, 31 Mar 1489. 1st Ed. - Ed by Johannes Angelus. 4to, 19th-cent half vellum. 40 lines; gothic letter. Some astrological woodcuts inexpertly hand-colored. Soiling at beginning & end; o1 & 6 from a shorter copy; 1 leaf stained. 117 (of 118) leaves; lacking last leaf. Goff A-360. S Mar 14 (11) £2,200

**Alcaforado, Marianna**
— Les Lettres portugaises. Paris, [1946]. One of 190. Illus by Henri Matisse. 4to, unbound as issued in orig wraps. wad Oct 18 (322) C$3,400
One of 270. Half mor, orig wraps bound in. S Nov 21 (4) £1,400

**Alchabitius**
— Libellus isagogicus. Venice: Erhard Ratdolt, 1485. 4to, modern velvet gilt by C. Casavalle. 32 lines; types 3:91G, 4:75G, 9:130G, 10:65G, 6:56(75)G. Minor worming; stab hole in last 4 leaves affecting 3 letters. 98 leaves. Goff A-363. C Nov 29 (21) £1,300

**Alciatus, Andreas, 1492-1550**
— Emblemata. Madrid, 1781. 8vo, contemp vellum. With 211 woodcut emblems in text Some staining. S Oct 27 (1039) £160 [Zioni]
— Emblematum.... Lyons, 1548. ("Emblemata Andreae Alciati jurisconsulti clarissimi.") 8vo, mor gilt by Hardy; a few scuff marks to upper cover. Tp with closed tear along inner margin of border; some soiling; a few leaves cut close at head. Schaefer copy. P Nov 1 (4) $1,500
Anr Ed. Lyons: Jean de Tournes & C. Gazeau, 1549. ("Clarissimi viri d. Alciati Emblematum libri duo.") 8vo, contemp mor gilt, with Roemer supralibros on front vellum flyleaf; inner hinges weak. With 113 woodcuts in text by Bernard Salomon. Roemer - von Nostitz - Hoe - Coolidge - Schaefer copy. P Nov 1 (5) $8,000

**Alcock, Charles William**
— Famous Cricketers and Cricket Grounds.... L, [1895]. 18 parts in 1 vol. Folio, orig cloth; extremities worn. pn Oct 12 (169) £70; pn Oct 12 (271) £65

**Alcock, Sir Rutherford, 1809-97**
— The Capital of the Tycoon. L, 1863. 1st Ed. 2 vols. 8vo, orig cloth; joints & corners rubbed. With 2 frontises, 2 folding maps & 14 chromolitho plates. S June 27 (218) £800

**Alcoholics Anonymous**
— Alcoholics Anonymous: The Story of How More than Fourteen Thousand Men and Women Have Recovered from Alcoholism. NY: Works Publishing, 1942. 1st Ed, 3d Ptg. sg Dec 14 (269) $275
— The Story of How More Than One Hundred Men and Women Recovered from Alcoholism. NY, 1939.
1st Ptg. Orig cloth; rubbed & soiled, spine ends & corners frayed. Pencil underlining & marginal markings. bbc June 24 (205) $1,900
— The Story of How More Than Two Thousand Men and Women Recovered from Alcoholism. NY, 1944. 2d Ptg. In soiled & chipped dj. bbc June 24 (206) $900

**Alcott, Louisa May, 1832-88**
[A set of Little Women, 1st State, 1868, 2d State 1869, Part Second, 1869 & Little Men, 1871, all Bost.: Roberts Brothers, sold at Christie's New York on 27 Oct 1995 for $17,000 in the Engelhard collection]; Limited Editions Club

**Aldam, W. H.**
— A Quaint Treatise on "Flees...." L, 1876. 4to, orig cloth; worn. With 2 colored plates & the series of 22 specimen flies on sunken mounts. Some foxing; flies in last 2 mounts loose. O Feb 6 (1) $1,000
Anr copy. Some foxing. O Feb 6 (2) $1,500

**Alden, John.** See: Brown Library, John Carter

**Alden, John Eliot**
— Rhode Island Imprints, 1727-1800 NY, 1949. O Dec 5 (1) $50

**Aldin, Cecil, 1870-1935**
— Farm Yard Puppies. L, [c.1910]. 4to, orig pictorial bds; hinges weak. Inscr, with 2 colored drawings. bba Sept 7 (379) £320 [Demetzy]
— Old Inns. L, 1925. 4to, mor by Sangorski & Sutcliffe. NH July 21 (40) $155
— Ratcatcher to Scarlet. L, [1926]. One of 100 with a sgd pencil sketch. 4to, orig half vellum gilt. O Jan 9 (2) $425
— Time I Was Dead. L, 1934. One of 100. Orig half mor. O Jan 9 (3) $350

**Aldine...**
— Aldine: The Art Journal of America. NY, 1871-74. Vols IV-VII, No 23, in 5 vols. Folio, half lea; some bds detached. Library markings. O July 9 (5) $120
Anr Ed. NY, 1875. Vol VII. Folio, contemp half mor; rubbed. F Mar 28 (739) $60

**Aldington, Richard, 1892-1962**
— Death of a Hero. Paris, 1930. One of 300. 4to, orig wraps. sg June 20 (2) $150
— Images of War. L, 1919. 1st Ed, One of 30 on japon. Illus by Paul Nash. Orig half vellum. Desmond Coke's copy. S May 16 (120) £900

**Aldrich, Henry, 1647-1710**
— The Elements of Civil Architecture.... Oxford, 1789. 1st Ed in English. 4to, modern cloth. With 55 plates. pba June 20 (7) $150

**Aldrich, Thomas Bailey, 1836-1917**
— The Bells: a Collection of Chimes, by T.B.A. NY, 1855. 8vo, cloth, in protective cloth dj. ALs tipped in, 10 Apr 1893. sg Sept 21 (59) $450

# ALDRICH

— Margorie Daw and Other People. Bost., 1873. 8vo, cloth; rubbed. Inscr to Charles H. Webb. sg Sept 21 (60) $175
— Pansy's Wish. Bost., 1870. 4to, orig wraps; minor chips to corners. sg Sept 21 (61) $1,500

### Aldrovandi, Ulisse, 1522-1605
— Monstrorum historia.... Bologna, 1642. Folio, 18th-cent calf; joints cracked, worn. Browned & water-stained. S June 12 (234) £2,200

### Alechinsky, Pierre
[-] Pierre Alechinsky. NY, [1977]. One of 100 with sgd litho laid in. Intro by Eugene Ionesco. 4to, cloth. sg Sept 7 (93) $100

### Alegria, Ricardo E.
— Los Renegados. San Juan, [1962]. One of 200. Illus by Lorenzo Homar. Cloth; bowed. Inscr by Alegria & Homar. sg Feb 15 (1) $60

### Aleichem, Sholem, 1859-1916. See: Sholem Aleichem

### Alembert, Jean le Rond d', 1717?-83
See also: Diderot & Alembert
— Traite de l'equilibre.... Paris, 1745. 4to, contemp calf; rubbed. With 10 folding plates. Some spotting. S Oct 27 (796) £500 [Pressley]

### Alence, Joachim d'
— Abhandlung dreyer so nothwendig- als nuetzlichen Instrumenten.... Mainz: Ludwig Bourgeat, 1688. 4to, bds. With 35 plates. Some browning. S Mar 14 (14) £1,100
— Magnetologia curiosa. Mainz: Christoph Kuechler, 1690. 4to, bds; worn. With 34 plates. Frontis misbound after Plate 3; some browning. S Mar 14 (13) £850

### Aleni, Giulio, 1582-1649
— T'ien-chu chiang-sheng ch'u-hsiang ching-chieh. [Peking, n.d.]. 28 leaves only, folio, modern fabric, orig wraps bound in. Ptd xylographically on native paper; with 49 (of 56) woodcut illusts. S June 27 (229) £2,000

### Alexander, David
— The Arts of War. L, 1992. Folio, cloth, in dj. sg Jan 11 (2) $60

### Alexander de Ales
— Summa theologica. Venice: Johannes de Colonia & Johannes Manthen, 1475. ("Super tertium sententiarum.") Folio, 19th-cent blind-stamped pigskin; rubbed, upper joint split at head. 52 lines; gothic letter. Some worming. 379 (of 380) leaves; lacking 1st blank. Goff A-385. S Dec 18 (2) £1,500 [Zioni]

### Alexander II, Emperor of Russia, 1818-81
— Opisanie svashchenn'shago koronovia ikh' Imperatorskikh' velichestv' gosudaria imperatora Aleksandravtorago i gosudariyii imperatirtritsi Mariyaliksandrovna vsei Rossii. [Paris: Lemercier for Imperatorskoy Akademii nauk in St. Petersburg, 1856]. Folio, orig half mor; joints repaired. With color title ptd partly with gold, cholor frontis, color double port, dedication & 17 plates & folding tinted panorama of Moscow. b June 28 (1) £7,000

### Alexander, Sir James Edward, 1803-85
— Travels from India to England. L, 1827. 4to, modern half cloth. With 2 maps, 14 plates & port in india-proof state. b May 30 (239) £400

### Alexander Library, L. D.
— [Sale Catalogue] Catalogue of the Large and Valuable Library.... NY: Bangs & Co., 1895. Parts 1 & 2 bound in 1 vol. Contemp half mor, orig wraps bound in. Prices in ink or pencil. pba Aug 22 (540) $130

### Alexander, Lloyd
— My Five Tigers. NY, [1956]. In dj with rubbing to spine ends. pba May 23 (3) $60

### Alexander the Great, 356-323 B.C.
[-] Cy commence lhystoire du tres vaillant noble preux et hardy roy Alixandre le grant. Lyon: Olivier Arnoullet, [c.1530]. 4to, 18th-cent mor janseniste by Bauzonnet. 35 lines; gothic type. Lacking H8. Prince d'Essling - Yemeniz - Schaefer copy. P Nov 1 (6) $6,500

### Alexander VI, Pope, 1431?-1503
— Bulla. [Rome?, after 28 Mar 1499]. ("Consueverunt Romani pontifices praedecessores nostri ad retinendam puritatem religionis christianae.") 4to, vellum wraps from a Hebrew Ms. 4 leaves. Goff A-372. S Dec 18 (3) £300 [Schiff]

### Alexander, William, 1767-1816
— Russians. L, [1819]. ("Picturesque Representations of the Dress and Manners of the Russians....") 8vo, contemp half mor; extremities rubbed, hinges reinforced, later endpapers. With 64 hand-colored plates. cb June 25 (1898) $325
Anr Ed. L, [c.1823]. 8vo, contemp mor gilt; broken. With 64 hand-colored plates. Met Feb 24 (463) $300

### Alexander, Sir William, 1567-1640
— Recreations with the Muses. L, 1637. 1st Ed. Folio, calf gilt; joints cracked, spine worn. Lacking port. pba Nov 30 (8) $150

### Alexandre, Arsene
— L'Art decoratif de Leon Bakst. Paris, 1913. Folio, orig half vellum gilt; worn, spine heel chipped. With port, 27 plain & 50 colored plates. Stain on index leaves & rear endpaper. sg Sept 7 (32) $400
— Jean-Francois Raffaelli, peintre, graveur.... Paris, 1909. 4to, cloth. Library markings. Inscr to Robert William Vonnoh & with inscr etching to Vonnoh & ALs from Alexandre to Raffaelli, which the latter forwarded to Vonnoh with an ANs. sg Sept 7 (287) $375

Anr copy. Half mor, orig wraps bound in; rubbed. sg June 13 (326) $300
— Paul Gauguin. Paris, 1930. 4to, wraps, unopened. sg Jan 11 (190) $110

**Aleyn, John.** See: Morris's copy, Lewis

**Algarotti, Francesco, Count, 1712-64**
— Saggio sopra l'opera in musica. lIvorno: Marco Coltellini, 1763. 8vo, contemp vellum. Some spotting. S June 12 (4) £300

**Alger, Horatio, 1832-99**
— Bertha's Christmas Vision. Bost., 1856. 8vo, orig cloth; tear in head of spine. First few leaves with some dampstaining. O Sept 12 (1) $300
— Digging for Gold: A Story of California. Phila., [1892]. 1st Ed. Orig cloth; shelf worn. With 4 plates. Larson copy. pba Sept 28 (296) $90
— The Young Miner; or, Tom Nelson in California. Bost., [1879]. 1st Ed. Orig cloth; extremities faded & worn; 1 corner bumped. With frontis & half-title. Larson copy. pba Sept 28 (294) $130
  Anr Ed. San Francisco: Book Club of California, 1965. One of 450. Half bds. With frontis. Larson copy. pba Sept 28 (295) $70

**Alghisi, Galasso**
— Delle Fortificationi.... [Venice], 1570. Bound with: Barozzi, Giacomo. Regola delle Cinque Ordini d'Architettura. Venice: Francesco Ziletti, 1582. And: Besson, Jacques. Theatrum instrumentorum et machinarum. Lyons: Bartholomaeus Vincentius, 1578. Folio, contemp blind-tooled pigskin over wooden bds with the arms of Prince Bishop Julius Echter von Mespelbrunn stamped in black with traces of red & green enamel, fore-edges gilt lettered with title & owner's name. Most margins waterstained; Besson lacking Plate 27; lower half of Plate 26 torn out. sg Oct 19 (3) $3,200

**Algren, Nelson**
— The Man with the Golden Arm. NY, 1949. 1st Ed. In dj. With tipped-in sheet, sgd. sg June 20 (3) $175
— Nelson Algren's Own Book of Lonesome Monsters. NY: Bernard Geis, [1962]. In dj with minor defs. Inscr, with colored drawing of a cat. pba Aug 22 (6) $120
— Never Come Morning. NY, [1942]. In def dj. Inscr, 1947. pba May 23 (4) $250

**Algue, P. Jose**
— Atlas de Filipinas. Manila, 1899. Folio, cloth; extremities worn. With 30 maps. sg Dec 7 (40) $250

**Ali Sharaf Al-Din**
— The History of Timur-Bec. L, 1723. 2 vols. 8vo, old calf; loose. sg Mar 7 (5) $300

**Alison, Sir Archibald, 1792-1867**
— History of Europe from the Commencemnet of the French Revolution in 1789 to the Restoration of the Bourbons [from the Fall of Napoleon in 1815 to the Accession of Louis Napoleon in 1852]. Edin. & L, 1849-59. 24 vols. 8vo, contemp half calf gilt. sg Sept 21 (1) $2,000

**Alison, C. H.** See: Colt & Alison

**Alix, Edmond**
— Essai sur l'appareil locomoteur des oiseaux. Paris, 1874. 8vo, modern cloth, orig wraps bound in. With 3 double-page plates. Foxed. sg May 16 (2) $175

**Alken, Henry, 1784-1851**
— Ideas, Accidental and Incidental to Hunting, and other Sports.... L [plates dated 1826-30]. Folio, orig half lea gilt. With 42 hand-colored plates. Marginal foxing. sg Oct 19 (4) $5,000
— The National Sports of Great Britain. L, 1821. 1st Ed, Issue not given. Folio, half lea; bumped. with 42 hand-colored plates. In French & English. Met Feb 24 (426) $400
— Symptoms of Being Amused. L, 1822. Vol I (all pbd). Oblong folio, contemp half lea; worn 7 soiled, spine chipped, rear cover detached. With 42 hand-colored plates. Some foxing & soiling. O Jan 9 (6) $425

**All...**
— All Men are Brothers. NY: John Day, [1933]. Trans by Pearl Buck. 2 vols. Pearl Buck's own copy with corrections in pencil throughout & sgd in Vol I. cb Oct 17 (352) $225

**Allacci, Leone.** See: Allatius, Leo

**Allard, Carolus**
— Nieuwe Hollandse scheeps-bouw. Amst., 1705. Vol II only. 4to, old half sheep; needs rebacked. With 105 plates. Plates & tp stamped. Sold w.a.f. sg Mar 7 (235) $250

**Allatius, Leo**
— De Symeonum scriptis diatriba.... Paris: Simeon Piget, 1664. 2 parts in 1 vol. 4to, vellum. Some browning. b May 30 (240) £120

**Alldridge, Lizzie**
— By Love and Law. L, 1877. 3 vols. 8vo, contemp half calf; rubbed. Library markings. O Mar 5 (2) $60

**Allemagne, Henry Rene d'**
— Les Cartes a jouer du XIVe au XXe siecle. Paris, 1906. 2 vols. 4to, orig bds; worn & stained, spine detached, endpapers foxed. O Sept 12 (5) $600
— Du Khorassan au pays des Backhtiaris. Paris, 1911. 4 vols. 4to, cloth; worn & shaken, spine of Vol I partly detached. Library markings of Universal Pictures Co. Research Dept. Inscr. cb Oct 17 (178) $900
— Histoire des jouets. Paris, 1902. 4to, pictorial bds; stained & soiled, pine detached, endpapers foxed. O Sept 12 (6) $300
— Le Novle jeu de l'oie en France.... Paris, 1950. One of 700. 4to, pictorial bds; soiled & shaken. O Sept 12 (7) $180
— La Toile imprimee et les indiennes de traite. Paris, 1942. One of 500. Vol II only. Bds; spine lacking. Met Dec 14 (239) $475

### Allen...

— The Allen Press Bibliography. [Greenbrae, 1981]. One of 140. Folio, Orig half cloth. cb June 25 (1899) $425
Anr copy. Half cloth. pba Mar 7 (10) $850
Anr copy. Library of Congress copyright stamp on copyright page. sg Sept 14 (2) $475
Anr Ed. San Francisco: Book Club of California, 1985. One of 750. bba May 9 (444) £130 [Collinge & Clark]; sg Sept 14 (3) $90

### Allen, Harris Stearns

— The Trial of Beauty. San Francisco: Allen Press, 1940. One of 100. Offset from glue of tipped-in illust to preceding few leaves; p. 9 foxed. pba Mar 7 (5) $950

### Allen, Hervey, 1889-1949. See: Limited Editions Club

### Allen, Ira

— Particulars of the Capture of the American Ship, Olive Branch. [Phila., 1804]. Vol II. Orig bds; with new paper backstrip, worn & stained. Some foxing & staining. wa Feb 29 (272) $85

### Allen, Jay. See: Quintanilla, Luis

### Allen, Nathan

— The Opium Trade.... Lowell, 1853. 8vo, orig wraps; top of backstrip chipped. sg May 16 (360) $50

### Allen, Thomas, 1803-33

— A New and Complete History of the County of York. L, 1828-31. 3 vols. 4to, modern cloth, Vol III in half mor. bba Nov 1 (255) £380 [Wallis]

### Allen, W. W. —& Avery, R. B.

— California Gold Book: First Nugget, Its Discovery and Discoverers and Some of the Results Proceeding Therefrom. San Francisco, 1893. 1st Ed. Orig cloth; spine dull. With 11 plates. Larson copy. pba Sept 28 (297) $130

### Allen, Capt. William.

— The Dead Sea, a New Route to India. L, 1855. 1st Ed. - Plates by Hullmandel. 2 vols in 1. 8vo, cloth; repaired. With 2 folding maps, & 9 plates. S Oct 26 (139) £600 [Folios]

### Allerton, Reuben G.

— Brook Trout Fishing. NY, 1869. 8vo, orig cloth; front endpaper lacking. Folding plate loose. O Feb 6 (3) $450

### Allestree, Richard, 1619-81

— The Government of the Tongue. Oxford, 1674. 8vo, calf gilt; 1 corner & head of spine repaired. Old ink to Imprimatur leaf. pba Nov 30 (12) $190
— The Ladies Calling. Oxford, 1673. 2d Ed. 8vo, calf; lower rear joint starting, new endpapers. Lacking prelims to tp. pba Nov 30 (13) $85
— Works. Oxford & L, 1684. 2 parts in 1 vol. Folio, contemp mor gilt to a cottage-roof design; scuffed, minor damage to lower cover. C June 26 (181) £450

### Alley, Ronald

— Francis Bacon. L, [1964]. Intro by John Rothenstein. 4to, orig cloth; rubbed. With 27 mtd colored plates. bba July 18 (29) £150 [Sims]

### Alliaco, Petrus de

— Imago mundi et tractatus alii. [Louvain: Johann de Paderborn (Westphalia), c.1483]. Folio, contemp blind-stamped over wooden bds by the Rood & Hunte binder, used as sewing guards in 3 quires are vellum strips from a Sixtus IV indulgence to benefit the Knights of Rhodes ptd by William Caxton in 1480. 41 lines; types 1B:89G (text), 2:118G (headings) & 5:79G (captions). With 8 large woodcut geographical & meteorological diagrams, including a mappamundi. 172 leaves. Goff A-477. Weld - Schaefer copy. P Nov 1 (172) $42,500

### Allibone, Samuel Austin, 1816-89

— A Critical Dictionary of English Literature and British and American Authors. Phila., 1870-71. 3 vols. 4to, orig cloth; spine ends worn. sg Apr 11 (6) $50

### Allies'...

— The Allies' Fairy Book. L, [1916]. 1st Issue, with pictorial endpapers. Illus by Arthur Rackham. Orig cloth. With 12 colored plates. Some spotting 7 staining. Inscr by Rackham to Marion Ballantyne, Sept 1919, with an ink sketch. Ck May 31 (145) £600
One of 525, sgd by artist. Ck May 31 (144) £280

### Allioni, Carlo, 1725-1804

— Flora Pedemontana. Turin, 1785. 3 vols in 1. Folio, contemp half calf; worn. With port & 92 plates. Library stamp at foot of tp; lacking half-titles; some spotting; a few plates with ink stains. S June 27 (1) £1,800

### Allison, Dorothy

— Bastard Out of Carolina. NY, [1992]. In dj. pba Dec 7 (5) $60

### Allison, William

— The British Thoroughbred Horse. L, 1901. Cloth, unopened; some wear. Some foxing. O Jan 9 (7) $100

### Allnatt, Charles A.

— Poverty: a Poem. Shrewsbury, 1801. 8vo, contemp mor gilt. b Dec 5 (311) £140

### Allom, Thomas, 1804-72

— Views in the Tyrol. L, [1836]. 4to, orig cloth; spine def. With 1 map & 45 plates. Some cropping & staining. b Sept 20 (238) £130

### Allsop, Robert

— California and Its Gold Mines. L, 1853. 1st Ed. Orig cloth; covers soiled, worn at edges, spine cloth split & repaired. Robbins copy. pba Mar 21 (3) $900

### Allut, Paul

— Recherches sur la vie et sur les oeuvres du P. Claude-Francois Menestrier.... Lyon, 1856. 8vo, mor by

Martin; rubbed, split at head of upper joint. O Mar 26 (2) $200

**Allyn, A.**
— A Ritual and Illustrations of Free-Masonry.... Shebbear [Devon]: S. Thorne, 1848. 8vo, orig cloth; worn. With 24 woodcut illusts. b Sept 20 (43) £50

**Almack, Edward, 1852-1917**
— Fine Old Bindings. L, 1913. One of 200. Folio, orig cloth; marked. bba May 9 (135) £170 [Bosley]

**Almanacs**
See also: Stoddard, W. L.
— Almanacco imperiale reale per le provincie del regno Lombardo-Veneto... per l'anno 1829. Milan, [1828]. 8vo, contemp red mor gilt with arms of Archduke Rainer. C May 1 (1) £1,100
— Almanach chantant de parodies nouvelles.... Paris: Duchesne, [1765]. 24mo, contemp calf gilt. Silvain copy. sg Apr 18 (4) $325
— Almanach royal. Paris, 1756. 8vo, contemp citron mor gilt, painted arms in center, spine with armorial mallet of Phelypeaux, comte de St. Florentin. Fuerstenberg - Schaefer copy. S Dec 7 (4) £4,200
Anr Ed. Paris, 1760. 8vo, contemp mor extra with arms of Micault d'Harvelay. Fuerstenberg - Schaefer copy. S Dec 7 (5) £1,800
Anr Ed. Paris, 1762. 12mo, contemp mor extra, with arms of the marquise d'Epinay. Fuerstenberg - Schaefer copy. S Dec 7 (6) £3,800
Anr Ed. Paris, 1767. 8vo, contemp red mor gilt with arms of Louis Jean Marie de Bourbon, duc de Penthievre. Fuerstenberg - Schaefer copy. S Dec 7 (7) £1,300
Anr copy. Contemp mor gilt, with arms of Charles, comte de Coblenz; upper cover detached. S Mar 28 (498) £300
Anr Ed. Paris, [1771]. 8vo, contemp mor extra with arms of Rene Nicolas Charles Augustin de Maupeou; small restoration to spine. Fuerstenberg - Schaefer copy. S Dec 7 (8) £1,300
Anr Ed. Paris, [1783]. 8vo, contemp red mor gilt with arms of Charles Pierre Savalette de Magnanville. Fuerstenberg - Schaefer copy. S Dec 7 (9) £1,300
Anr Ed. Paris, 1785. For 1786. 8vo, contemp red mor gilt with arms of Jacques Mathieu Augeard, marquis de Buzancy; spine chipped & repaired. Fuerstenberg - Schaefer copy. S Dec 7 (10) £1,400
Anr Ed. Paris, [1788]. 8vo, contemp mor gilt with arms of Louis Claude Goyon de Matignon, called comte de Vaudreuil. Fuerstenberg - Schaefer copy. S Dec 7 (11) £2,400
Anr Ed. Paris, [1792]. 8vo, contemp red mor gilt with gilt crowned escutcheon with initials L. B. at center of covers. With map. Fuerstenberg - Schaefer copy. S Dec 7 (12) £1,400
— Almanach utile et agreable de la loterie de l'ecole royale militaire, Amst., 1759 Brussels, 1779. 18mo, contemp calf. With frontis & 90 plates by Gravelot. Some plates soiled. Fuerstenberg - Schaefer copy. S Dec 7 (13) £1,700

— Almanack 1929 with Twelve Designs Engraved on Wood by Eric Ravilious. Lanston Monotype Corporation, 1929. Some foxing. bba May 9 (413) £200 [Rush]
— The Angler's Almanac and Pocket-Book for 1853. L, 1853. 8vo, contemp cloth. pba July 11 (227) $110
— The Angler's Almanac for 1849. NY, 1849. 8vo, later half mor, orig wraps bound in; rubbed, joints worn. Copy has 2 sets of the parts from Jan to June only. O Feb 6 (41) $160
— An Anglo-Chinese Calendar for the Year 1846. Canton, 1846. 8vo, orig wraps; stained & chipped. Sold w.a.f. sg Mar 7 (6) $120
— Le Calendrier de la Cour.... Paris, 1716. 18mo, contemp calf extra with onlaid panels of silver & red foil under mica & large center panel of floral emproidery in silk, with 2 metal bosses. Silvain copy. sg Apr 18 (5) $950
— The East India Kalendar; or, Asiatic Register... For the Year 1794. L, 1794. 12mo, disbound. sg Mar 7 (7) $200
— Entrennes galantes des promenades et amusemens de Paris.... Paris: Boulanger, [1783]. 24mo, contemp mor gilt; loose. Engraved throughout. Silvain copy. sg Apr 18 (6) $700
— Entrennes mignonnes, curieuses et utiles. Paris, 1754. For 1754. 32mo, contemp calf gilt with gouache miniatures of floral bouquets under mica. Silvain copy. sg Apr 18 (7) $600
— Entrennes mignonnes... pour l'Annee de Grace 1762. Paris: Durand, 1762. 32mo, contemp wraps; loose. Tp & last leaf soiled. sg Mar 21 (7) $120
— Entrennes mignons pour l'an de grace de notre seigneur MDCCXCIV. Liege: H. Dessain & Soeurs, [1794]. 32mo, contemp embroidered bdg with gouache-on-paper centerpiece of a shepherd on front cover & shepherdess on rear cover. Silvain copy. sg Apr 18 (8) $800
— Era Almanack, Dramatic & Musical, 1868-84. L, [1867-85]. Ed by Edward Ledger. 18 parts in 3 vols. 8vo, mor gilt, some upper wraps bound in. S Apr 23 (221) £380
— Etat actuel de la musique du Roi et des trois spectacles de Paris.... Paris, 1773. 12mo, contemp red mor with Mlle Clairon lettered on upper cover. With engraved title, frontis & 4 plates. Fuerstenberg - Schaefer copy. S Dec 7 (196) £1,500
— Etrennes nationales, curieuses et instructives.... Paris: Cailleau, [1787]. 24mo, contemp embroidered bdg with inset gouache miniature paintings under mica showing a young man & 2 young women in country settings, doublure inside cover with inset mirror (cracked). Silvain copy. sg Apr 18 (9) $700
— The Gentleman and Citizen's Almanack... 1743. Dublin: S. Powell for John Watson, 1743. 12mo, contemp mor gilt with English royal arms. Contemp owner's notes on blanks at end. sg Mar 21 (13) $250
— The Gentleman and Citizen's Almanack... 1768. Dublin: S. Powell for John Watson, 1768. Bound with: The Gentleman's and Tradsman's Memorandum-Book, for... 1768. 12mo, contemp vellum gilt with expanding cover pockets. sg Mar 21 (14) $250

# ALMANACS

— The Gentleman and Citizen's Almanack... 1782. Dublin: Samuel Watson & Thomas Stewart, 1782. Bound with: The English Registry, for... 1782. John Exshaw, [1782]. 12mo, contemp mor gilt with expanding cover pockets; spine chipped. sg Mar 21 (16) $400
— Hand-Book Almanac of the Pacific States...for the Year 1862. San Francisco: H. H. Bancroft, 1862. Ed by William Henry Knight. Orig cloth; soiled. pba Aug 8 (91) $50
— The Liberty Almanac for 1852. NY: American Anti-Slavery Society, [1851]. 8vo, pictorial wraps. Stained. sg Mar 28 (298) $1,200
— Martin's Sportsman's Almanack, Kalendar, and Traveller's Guide for 1819. L, 1819. 8vo, modern calf. With half-title, & 43 hand-colored maps (1 folding). S Oct 26 (376) £450 [Baskes]
— The New Sporting Almanack. L, 1845. 12mo, orig cloth. With engraved title & 10 plates. O Jan 9 (171) $80
— The New-York Pocket Almanack, for the Year 1764. NY: H. Gaine, [1763]. 24mo, bdg not described. Interleaves with blanks. Some fraying, stains & coiling, corners curled. O Nov 14 (125) $225
— The Oracle of Rural Life; an Almanack for Sportsmen and Country Gentlemen [continued as The Sporting Oracle and Almanac of Rural Life]. L, 1839-41. 3 vols. 8vo, pictorial wraps; 2d vol rebacked in paper facsimile. Alfred B. Maclay's set. sg Mar 7 (508) $600
— Rider's British Merlin for MDCCLXXVIII. L, 1778. Bound with: A New Edition... of the Court and City Register... for the year 1778. 12mo, contemp mor gilt; front joint starting. Tax stamp on 1st title. sg Mar 21 (9) $140
— The Treble Almanack for the Year MDCCLXXXVIII.... Dublin: W. Wilson, [1788]. 3 parts in 1 vol. 12mo, contemp sheep. With engraved title & folding plan of Dublin. sg Mar 21 (11) $200
— Le Tresor des almanachs, entrennes nationales... our l'annee bissextile 1784. Paris: Cailleau, [1784]. 18mo, contemp mor gilt with gilt balloon at center & legend Glove enleve par Mrs Robert et Charles [Montgolfier]. Fuerstenberg - Schaefer copy. S Dec 7 (369) £2,200
— The Universal Scots Almanack for... M,DCC,LXXXIII. Edin.: John Robertson, [1783]. 12mo, contemp bds; spine ends chipped, front joint cracked. With folding frontis map of Scotland. Tax stamp on tp. sg Mar 21 (12) $200

**Alonso de Madrid**
— A Breefe Methode or Way of Teachinge all sorts of Christian People, how to serve God.... St. Omers: C. Boscard for John Heigham, 1625. 24mo, contemp calf; spine repaired. STC 535.7. b Dec 5 (180) £750

**Alphand, Jean Charles Adolphe**
— Les Promenades de Paris.... Paris, 1867-73. 2 vols. Folio, later cloth. With frontis & 126 plates, 22 chromolithographed, the others on india paper. b Sept 20 (454) £900

# AMERICAN BOOK PRICES CURRENT

**Alston, Charles**
— A Dissertation of Quick-Lime and Lime-Water. Edin., 1754. Bound with: A Second Dissertation.... Edin., 1755; A Third Disseration.... Edin., 1757 3 works in 1 vol. 8vo, modern calf. Ck Mar 22 (10) £190

**Alta California**
— Alta California. San Francisco, 25 Jan 1849. Vol I, No 4. 2 pp With related material. Larson copy. pba Feb 12 (529) $425

**Alter, J. Cecil**
— James Bridger. Salt Lake City, [1925]. Ltd Ed, sgd. pba Apr 25 (269) $225

**Alvarez y Baena, Joseph Antonio**
— Hijos de Madrid.... Madrid, 1789-91. 4 vols. 4to, contemp calf gilt; joints & extremities rubbed. CE Sept 27 (32) $350

**Amadis de Gaul**
— Le Premiere Livre de Amadis de Gaule.... Paris, 1543-50. Books 1-41 (of 12) in 1 vol. Folio, modern mor gilt by McLeish. Book 1: 1st 4 leaves wormed in upper blank margin; tp repaired; tear to margin of X1; Book 2: hole in G4 with loss of a few characters; Book 4: browned at beginning; A3 shaved with loss to marginal illusts on verso; lower outer corner of blank margin of P2 torn away. C Nov 29 (23) £1,100
— The Third [Fourth] Booke of Amadis de Gaule.... L: Nicholas Okes, 1618. 2 vols in 1. Calf; rebacked, corners repaired. Lacking pp. 143-44 (replaced with facsimile); last 2 leaves trimmed & with margins replaced. STC 543. pba Mar 7 (136) $600

**Amar, Antonio —& Others**
— Informe sobre la Majora y Aumento de la Cria de Caballos. Barcelona, 1818. 4to, contemp mor gilt. With frontis & folding plate. b May 30 (327) £500

**Amaral, Anthony A.**
— Comanche: The Horse That Survived the Custer Massacre. Los Angeles, 1961. In dj. pba June 25 (1) $120

**Amateur Angler.** See: Marston, Edward

**Ambassades...** See: Nieuhoff, Jan

**Ambler, Eric**
— The Care of Time. NY, 1981. 1st American Ed, One of 300. pba Aug 22 (8) $65

**Ambros, August**
— Der Dom zu Prag. Prague, 1858. 16mo, orig half cloth; spine ends chipped. With 13 plates. sg Sept 7 (6) $60

**Ambrosius, Saint, 340?-397**
— Commentarii in omnes Diui Pauli Epistolas. Antwerp: Johann Stellsius, 1540. 8vo, contemp blind-stamped calf; rubbed. Some browning & staining. bba Sept 7 (184) £400 [Hubert]

— De Officiis. Milan: Valdarfer, 7 Jan 1774. Folio, old calf; worn, spine chipped, remnant of clasp. Lacking leaves 99-114. Goff A-560. O Mar 5 (5) $450
— Epistolae. Milan: Antonius Zarotus, 1 Feb 1491. Folio, modern mor. 40 lines; type 5:110R. Worming occasionally affecting letters; repaired tear in 1st 2 leaves. 192 leaves. Goff A-553. C Apr 3 (17) £1,000
— Les trois livres des offices.... Paris: Guillaume Chaudiere, 1588. 12mo, contemp olive mor gilt, possibly from the atelier of Clovis Eve. Burton copy. C May 1 (2) £1,400

**American...**
— American and British Chronicle of War and Politics.... L, [1783]. 1st Ed. 8vo, half mor by Sangorski & Sutcliffe. Some soiling; last leaf rubbed. wa Feb 29 (296) $400
— The American Annual Cyclopedia and Register of Important Events of the Year 1862. NY, 1866. Half calf. pba Apr 25 (169) $80
— American Archives. Wash., 1837-53. Ed by Peter Force. 4th Series, Vols I-VI & 5th Series, Vols I-III. Folio, later cloth; some wear. Library markings. O Mar 5 (6) $1,400

Anr copy. Modern cloth. Some staining. wa Feb 29 (294) $650
— The American Athletic Journal. NY, 1877. Vol I, No 1. 8 pages, folio. Creases from folding. pba Aug 22 (546) $300
— American Book Prices Current. NY, 1895-1994. Vols 1-100. ds July 27 (5) $1,800

Vols 16-81. NY, 1910-76. Orig cloth. With extra copy of the 1954-55 vol. O May 7 (13) $360

Anr Ed. NY, 1976-94. Vols 82-93, 95-99, & indexes for 1970-83. 8vo, orig cloth; index bindings defective. sg Apr 11 (8) $850

Anr copy. Vols 87-99 & indexes for 1970-91. 8vo, sg Apr 11 (9) $900

Anr Ed. NY, 1982-95. Vols 87-100. 8vo, orig cloth. sg Apr 11 (7) $550

Index vols for 1979-83. NY, 1984. bbc Dec 18 (103) $140

Vols 90-97. NY, 1985-1991. bbc Dec 18 (105) $550

Vols 91-95. NY, 1986-90. wa June 20 (2) $130

Anr Ed. NY, 1988. Index vols for 1979-83. 2 vols. 8vo, orig cloth. sg Apr 11 (12) $275

Vol 96-100. NY, 1990-94. Cloth. wa June 20 (3) $350

Index vols for 1987-91. NY, 1992. bbc Dec 18 (104) $225; wa June 20 (6) $350
— American Museum, or Repository of Ancient and Modern Fugitive Pieces.... Phila.: Mathew Carey, 1787-88. Vol II, Nos I-VI & Vol IV, Nos I-VI. 2 vols. contemp sheep; spine titles reversed. pba June 13 (250) $200
— American Race Horses. A Review.... NY, 1936-54. 19 vols. 4to, cloth; soiled. O Jan 9 (10) $275

— The American Review: a Whig Journal. NY, 1845. Vol I, Jan-Dec. Bound in 2 vols. 8vo, contemp half calf. CE May 22 (377) $450
— The American Traveller, being a New Historical Collection.... L, 1741. 1st Ed. 12mo, half calf; spine ends & joints worn. With frontis & 4 plates. Text & plates trimmed. CE May 22 (8) $280
— American Turf Register and Sporting Magazine. Balt. & NY, 1829. Vol I, Nos 1-12, bound in 1 vol. 8vo, contemp half calf; worn & broken. Some stains & foxing. O Jan 9 (11) $180

**American Angler**
— The American Angler: a Weekly Journal of Angling. NY, 1883-84. Vol IV. 26 issues in 1 vol. Folio, modern half cloth; some wear. O June 25 (3) $120

**American Bibliopolist**
— The American Bibliopolist. NY, 1869-75. Vol I, No 1 to Vol VII, No 78, bound in 7 vols. Half mor gilt, last in later cloth; worn & scuffed, some covers detached. Library markings. bbc Dec 18 (140) $275

**American Kennel Club**
— The National American Kennel Club Stud Book. St. Louis, 1879. Vol I, 1878. 12mo, cloth. sg Mar 7 (439) $110

**Ames, Joseph, 1689-1759 —& Herbert, William, 1718-95**
— Typographical Antiquities. L, 1785-90. 3 vols. 4to, contemp calf; rubbed, joints broken or with early repairs. With 2 ports & 8 plates. Minof foxing & soiling. O Mar 26 (5) $300

Anr Ed. L, [1810]-19. Ed by Thomas Frognall Dibdin. Vols I-IV (all pbd). 4to, contemp calf; rebacked in later lea, rubbed. Some foxing; Vol III lacks the Directions to the Binder. O Mar 26 (6) $200

Anr copy. Contemp calf gilt; rubbed. With 14 ports & 25 other plates. Some spotting. S Apr 23 (185) £650

**Ames, Richard**
— A Farther Search after Claret. L, 1691. 4to, 19th-cent half mor; edges worn. Lacking F2; tp backed; some corners renewed; lower margins cut close, affecting a few catchwords. CE Sept 27 (35) $260

**Amico, Bernardino**
— Trattato delle piante & immagini de sacri edifizi di Terra Santa. Florence: Pietro Cecconcelli, 1620. Plates engraved by Jacques Callot. 4to, 18th-cent calf; joints weak, spine ends chipped. With engraved title & 34 double-page plates showing 46 plans & views. Mtd on guards throughout. C Nov 29 (81) £1,700

**Amis...**
— Amis et Amille. Paris: Le Nouveau Cercle Parisien du Livre, 1957. One of 30 for members of the family & those involved in the production. Illus by Andre Derain. 4to, unsewn in orig wraps. With 22 colored illusts. S Nov 2 (9) £150 [Landau]

## Amis de Livres
— Portraits graves par MM. Abot, Paul Avril, Gaston Manchon et Rodolphe Piguet. Paris, 1899. 8vo, contemp half mor; rubbed, joints worn. With 87 ports. Minor foxing. O Mar 26 (7) $90

## Amis, Martin
— Dead Babies. NY, 1976. In dj. Sgd on tp. pba Jan 25 (3) $75
— The Information. L: Flamingo, [1995]. One of 356. pba Jan 25 (4) $85
— Other People: A Mystery Story. L, [1981]. In dj. Inscr. pba Jan 25 (5) $50
— The Rachel Papers. NY, 1974. 1st American Ed. In dj. Sgd on tp. pba Jan 25 (6) $95
— Success. L, [1978]. In dj. Inscr on tp. pba Jan 25 (7) $75

## Amman, Jost, 1539-91
— Kuenstliche und wolgerissene Figuren der fuernembsten Evangelien. Frankfurt, 1579. 1st Ed. 4to, 19th-cent bds; extremities worn, upper joint split. Type impression across the woodcut on D4r. P June 5 (154) $4,500
— Kunstbuechlein. Frankfurt, 1599. 4to, 18th-cent mor gilt; split to spine head & joints. With 289 (of 293) full-page woodcuts. Walpole - Beckford copy. C June 26 (31) £4,000

## Ampere, Andre Marie, 1775-1836
— Essai sur la philosophie des sciences.... Paris, 1834. 8vo, contemp half calf; rubbed. Some foxing. S Mar 14 (16) £320

## Amsden, Charles Avery
— Navaho Weaving: its Technic and History. Santa Ana, 1934. 8vo, cloth. pba July 25 (249) $190
  Anr Ed. Albuquerque, 1949. Met Dec 14 (236) $55

## Amuchastegui, Axel
— Some Birds and Mammals of South America. L, 1966. One of 50 with an orig drawing. Text by Carlos Selva Andrade. Folio, vellum gilt by Zaehnsdorf. With orig watercolor. S Nov 30 (2) £1,000
  Anr copy. Vellum gilt by Zaehnsdorf. With orig watercolor. S Nov 30 (3) £750

## Amundsen, Roald, 1872-1928
— The South Pole: an Account of the Norwegian Antarctic Expedition in the "Fram." L, 1912. 2 vols. Orig cloth; bumped. Minor foxing to titles & half-titles. pba July 25 (2) $500

## Amundsen, Roald, 1872-1928 —& Ellsworth, Lincoln
— Our Polar Flight: The Amundsen-Ellsworth Polar Flight. NY, 1925. Orig cloth; rear hinge starting. pba Apr 25 (138) $75

## Anacreon, 572?-488? B.C.
— 1785. - Odaria. Parma: Bodoni. 4to, early 19th-cent mor gilt. S Nov 30 (253) $800

— 1791. - Parma: Bodoni Press. 8vo, mor gilt by Riviere. Several leaves of late 19th-cent Ms excerpts from ancient Greek works bound at ends. Edward Gordon Duff's copy, inscr by him to H. D. Owen, 1886. sg Mar 21 (60) $600
— 1802. - L. 4to, contemp calf gilt; rebacked preserving orig spine. In Greek. bba May 30 (136) £80 [Unsworth]
— 1810. - Odes. Paris 8vo, contemp mor extra a la Anacreon. A few leaves spotted or stained at edges. Beckford copy. S July 11 (134) £260

## Anacreon, 572?-488? B.C. —& Others
— Oeuvres. Paphos, 1773. 8vo, mor gilt by Chambolle-Duru. b May 30 (515) £280
  Anr Ed. Paris: Le Boucher, 1773. 8vo, contemp mor gilt, with suite of plates in modern mor gilt. With frontis & 25 head- & tailpieces; suite with 19 of the head- & tailpieces.. Rahir - Fuerstenberg - Schaefer copy. S Dec 7 (16) £3,000

## Analectic...
— Analectic Magazine. Phila., 1813-18. Vols I-XII. 8vo, half mor gilt; worn, some vols becoming disbound. Contains 1st magazine appearance of The Star-Spangled Banner, here called Defence of Fort M'Henry. wa Feb 29 (494) $500

## Anatomy...
— Anatomy Epitomized and Illustrated.... Edinburgh, [c.1840?]. 8vo, half lea; rebound. With 16 (of 17) folding plates. Some foxing & soiling, 1 plate torn. Sold w.a.f. CE Nov 8 (66) $130

**Ancient...** See: Lockhart, John Gibson

## Ancillon, Charles
— Eunuchism Display'd, Describing all the different Sorts of Eunuchs.... L, 1718. 8vo, 18th-cent calf; joints split, hinges repaired. Lacking a prelim leaf; some spotting. S May 15 (270) £600

## Ancona, Mirella Levi d'
— Miniatura e miniatori a Firenze dal XIV al XVI secolo. Florence, 1962. 4to, cloth. sg June 13 (243) $110

## Andersen, Hans Christian, 1805-75
See also: Limited Editions Club
— Fairy Tales. L, [1916]. Illus by Harry Clarke. 4to, mor gilt pictorial bdg by Bayntun. CE Feb 21 (7) $280
  Anr Ed. L, [1924]. Illus by Kay Nielsen. 4to, orig cloth. S May 16 (129) £240
  One of 500. Orig vellum gilt; soiled & stained. With 12 tipped-in colored plates. Some browning. pn Dec 7 (92) $360 [Shapero]
  Anr Ed. L, [1932]. Illus by Arthur Rackham. 4to, orig cloth, in dj. Ck May 31 (167) £350
  Anr copy. Cloth, in dj with chip to spine. sg Feb 15 (244) $140
  One of 525. Orig vellum gilt. With 12 colored plates. bba May 9 (411) £850 [Baring]

Anr copy. Orig vellum gilt; spotted. Ck May 31 (166) £750; sg Oct 19 (208) $1,300

Anr Ed. L, 1935. ("Fairy Tales and Legends.") One of 150. Illus by Rex Whistler. bba May 9 (279) £50 [Adelman]

— Images de la Lune. Paris, 1942. One of 995. Illus by Alexander Alexieff. Folio, loose as issued in orig wraps. bba May 9 (175) £140 [Roe & Moore]

— Stories. L, 1911. ("Stories from Hans Andersen.") One of 100. Illus by Edmund Dulac. 4to, mor extra with onlay design from The Snow Queen, by Bayntun-Riviere. With 28 colored plates. CE Sept 27 (108) $3,200

One of 750. Orig vellum gilt. With 28 colored plates. b Sept 20 (614) £180; b Jan 31 (154) £360; sg Oct 19 (78) $1,400

**Anderson, Adam, 1692?-1765**

— An Historical and Chronological Deduction of the Origin of Commerce.... L, 1764. 2 vols. 4to, contemp sheep; worn, dry, joints split. Some foxing. wa Feb 29 (150) $600

**Anderson, Edward L.**

— Modern Horsemanship. Edin., 1884. 8vo, half lea; some wear. O Jan 9 (12) $60

**Anderson, Eustace**

— Chamouni and Mont Blanc. L, 1856. 8vo, orig cloth; recased, soiled. With folding chromolitho frontis & 1 plate. Frontis frayed & soiled. bba Nov 1 (527) £190 [Gonzalez]

**Anderson, George William**

See also: Cook, Capt. James

— A New, Authentic, and Complete Collection of Voyages Round the World.... L: Alex. Hogg [1784-86]. 2d Ed. Folio, contemp calf; worn. With frontis port & 156 plates. Some worming at beginning, affecting plates & text. S Mar 28 (418) £700

Anr Ed. L, [1784-86]. Folio, modern bds. With frontis port, folding map, & 74 maps & plates. Lacks titles. S Oct 26 (450) £400 [Ostby]

2d Ed. L: Alex. Hogg, [1784-86]. Folio, contemp calf; hinges strengthened, joints cracked, lower bd rubbed. With port, folding map & 155 maps & plates. Some dampstaining; a few plates remargined & repaired & some frayed. Schaefer copy. P Nov 1 (69) $1,600

Anr copy. Contemp calf, rubbed, rebacked, lower cover almost detached. With port & 155 maps & plates. Some imprints cropped. S June 13 (563) £460

**Anderson, James, 1680?-1739**

— Constitutions of the Antient Fraternity of Free and Accepted Masons. L, 1756. 4to, contemp calf; worn & broken. b Sept 20 (50) £300

Anr Ed. L, 1767. 4to, contemp calf; joints worn. b Sept 20 (51) £360

Anr Ed. L, 1784. 4to, contemp calf; rebacked. Tp foxed. b Sept 20 (52) £300

Anr copy. Contemp calf gilt with mor inlay & masonic tools; joints split. Frontis shaved; some spotting. b May 30 (320) £370

— The Constitutions of the Free-Masons. L, 1723. 4to, contemp calf; rubbed. With frontis. Discoloration throughout. b Jan 31 (244) £400

**Anderson, Joseph**

— The Artless Muse; or, Attempts in Verse.... Peterhead, 1818. 12mo, contemp half mor; rubbed. b Dec 5 (511) £90

**Anderson, Joseph, 1832-1916 —& Drummond, James, 1816-77**

— Ancient Scottish Weapons. L, 1881. One of 500. 4to, orig half mor. With 54 plates. pnE Sept 20 (149) £230

**Anderson, Sherwood, 1876-1941**

See also: Limited Editions Club

— Home Town. NY, [1940]. 4to, cloth, in torn dj; bdg & endpapers stained. sg Feb 29 (130) $110

— The Triumph of the Egg. NY, 1921. 1st Ed, 1st Issue. Orig cloth; some soil. Goodwin - Engelhard copy. Inscr to Gertrude Stein. CNY Oct 27 (4) $1,200

— Windy McPherson's Son. NY, 1916. 1st Ed. Inscr to Gertrude Barnes. Engelhard copy. CNY Oct 27 (2) $1,400

— Winesburg, Ohio. NY, 1919. 1st Ed, 1st Ptg. Orig cloth; spine ends worn, endpapers with some discoloration. Inscr to Van Wyck Brooks. Goodwin - Engelhard copy. CNY Oct 27 (3) $2,100

Anr copy. Cloth. pba May 23 (5) $90

**Anderson, William, 1805-66**

— The Scottish Nation. Edin., 1860-63. 3 vols. 4to, half sheep; extremities worn. Some dampstaining. sg Mar 7 (10) $70

Anr Ed. Edin., 1863. 3 vols. 4to, half calf; 1 joint starting. pba Apr 4 (293) $250

**Anderson, William, 1842-1900**

— Japanese Wood Engravings. L, 1895. Folio, cloth; spot to front cover, front free endpaper lacking. pba Aug 8 (226) $50

**Anderson-Maskell, Mrs. A. E.**

— Children with the Fishes. Bost.: D. Lothrop, [1887]. Pictorial cloth; spine head chipped. pba July 11 (6) $120

**Andersson, Johan Gunnar.** See: Nordenskjold & Andersson

**Andre, George Guillinane**

— The Draughtsman's Handbook of Plan and Map Drawing.... L, 1891. 8vo, orig cloth; rubbed at edges. pba July 25 (87) $150

**Andre, Johann Anton**

— Catalogue thematique de toutes les compositions de W. A. Mozart.... Offenbach, [1805]. 1st Ed. 8vo, wraps. Lithographed throughout. Tp browned. S May 15 (106) £2,000

### Andrea, of Modena
— Canto harmonico.... Modena: heirs of Cassiani, 1690. 1st Ed. 4to, modern half mor. With 3 plates. Some repairs; 1 plate def; few burn holes; browning. S Oct 27 (912) £320 [Schneider]

### Andree, John, the Younger
— Observatons upon a Treatise on the Virtue of Hemlock.... L, [1761]. 8vo, bds. Ink-spill on tp & at end. b May 30 (8) £80

### Andreini, Giovanni Batista
— L'Adamo, sacra rapresentatione. Milan, 1617 [reissue of sheets of 1613 Ed]. 4to, mor by Clarke & Bedford; extremities rubbed. cb June 25 (1915) $600

### Andres, Glenn
— The Art of Florence. NY, 1987. 2 vols. 4to, cloth; worn. O May 7 (27) $130

### Andres, Glenn —& Others
— The Art of Florence. NY: Abbeville Press, 1988. 2 vols. Folio, cloth. pba Jan 4 (228) $250

### Andresen, Andreas —& Weigel, Rudolph
— Der Deutsche Peintre-Graveur.... [N.p., n.d.]. 5 vols. 8vo, cloth. Reprint of Leipzig, 1864-78, Ed. sg June 13 (43) $80

### Andrewes, Margaret Hamer. See: Browne, Maggie

### Andrews, C. C. See: Pierce's copy, Franklin

### Andrews, James, 1801?-76
— The Parterre, or Beauties of Flora. L, 1842. Folio, orig cloth; spine laid down. With 11 (of 12) hand-colored plates. Dampstaining to outside edge. Met Feb 24 (427) $1,500

### Andrews, John, Geographer —& Dury, John
— A Topographical Map of the County of Kent.... L, 1 Jan 1768. Folio, contemp bds; rebacked & recornered, rubbed. With engraved title & dedication leaf, & 23 double-page sectional maps colored in outline, & a plan of Canterbury. Some marginal soiling & fraying. S Nov 30 (47) £1,200

Anr Ed. L, 1769. Folio, contemp half calf; worn. With engraved title & dedication leaf, & 24 double-page sectional maps, many colored in outline, plus a plan of Canterbury. S Mar 28 (125) £1,600

### Andrews, John, 1736-1809
— History of the War with America, France, Spain, and Holland.... L, 1785-86. 4 vols. 8vo, contemp sheep with onlaid mor gilt spines; some wear. With engraved titles, 7 maps hand-colored in outline (all but 1 folding) & 25 ports. S Mar 28 (310) £260

Anr copy. Contemp calf; Vol I bds detached, joints splitting. With 31 maps & plates, 7 of the maps colored in outline. wa Feb 29 (286) £600

### Andrews, W. S.
— Illustrations of the West Indies. L: Day & Son, [n.d.]. 2 vols. Oblong 4to, orig cloth; def & loose. With 30 plates, 22 of them tinted, 2 double-page. Some spotting. b Jan 31 (429) £2,200

### Andrews, William Loring, 1837-1920
— Bibliopegy in the United States and Kindred Subjects. NY, 1902. One of 141. Mor by the French Binders. b May 30 (516) £170

— An English XIX Century Sportsman, Bibliopole, and Binder of Angling Books. NY, 1906. One of 125. Orig vellum gilt. With 17 plates. bba May 9 (233) £70 [Laywood]

— The Heavenly Jerusalem: a Mediaeval Song.... NY, 1908. One of 120 on Arches. Mor gilt by Birdsall. b Sept 20 (595) £65

### Andry de Boisregard, Nicolas, 1658-1742
— Vers solitaires et autres de diverses especes.... Paris, 1718. 4to, contemp calf; worn. With 22 plates, 16 folding, the 1st 4 ptd as pairs on 2 sheets. b May 30 (9) £150

### Andueza, Jose Maria de
— Isla de Cuba, pintoresca, historica, politica, literaria.... Madrid, 1841. Folio, contemp half mor; spine ends worn. With 12 plates. Library markings partly erased from tp & spine; lacking map. cb Feb 14 (2573) $700

### Aneau, Barthelemi
— Picta poesis. Lyons: Mace Bonhomme, 1552. 8vo, mor gilt by Cape. Some soling; faded annotations; 1 marginal note trimmed. Daspect - Double - de Vertot - Burton - Schaefer copy. P Nov 1 (7) $2,500

### Anecdotes...
— Anecdotes and Adventures of Fifteen Gentlemen. L, 1821. Illus by Robert Cruikshank. 8vo, orig wraps; worn & marked, front cover def. With 15 hand-colored plates. Repaired tears, affecting 1 illust & with 1 word of text supplied by hand; first few leaves frayed; some staining. bba May 30 (339) £180 [Wise]

— Anecdotes of a Croat; or the Castle of Serai. L, 1823. 2 vols. 12mo, orig bds; Vol I loose. sg Mar 7 (11) $100

### Angel, Myron
— History of Nevada. Oakland, 1881. 1st Ed. 4to, later half mor. Robbins copy. pba Mar 21 (264) $1,300

— History of San Luis Obispo County.... Oakland, 1883. 1st Ed. 4to, orig half calf; spine & extremities worn. Some foxing & soiling; a few tears & pieces missing; ink stamp on front free endpaper. cb Feb 14 (2576) $550

### Angelo, Henry Charles William, 1760-1839?
— Reminiscences. L, 1828-30. 2 vols. 8vo, contemp half calf. Lowther copy. S June 13 (666) £160

### Angelo, Valenti
— Valenti Angelo: Author, Illustrator, Printer. San Francisco: Book Club of Calif., 1976. One of 400. pba June 20 (30) $375

### Angelou, Maya
See also: Limited Editions Club
— I Know Why the Caged Bird Sings. NY, [1969]. In dj. sg Mar 28 (3) $120

Anr copy. In repaired dj. sg June 20 (5) $150

### Angelus de Clavasio, 1411-95?
— Summa angelica de casibus conscientiae. Venice: Georgius Arrivabenus, 22 Oct 1487. 4to, contemp blind-stamped pigskin over wooden bds with metal fittings; wormed. 53 lines & foliation; double column; types 1:110bG, 7:65G. Small wormholes occasionally touching text; some browning. 370 leaves. Goff A-714. C Apr 3 (19) £1,300

Anr Ed. Strassburg: Martin Flach, 31 Oct 1489. Folio, modern cloth. 53 lines; double column; gothic letter; initials in red & blue Dampstained throughout; several leaves inkstained at head; some worming affecting text; piece torn from upper margin of tp. 387 (of 388) leaves; lacking last blank. Goff A-719. S Dec 18 (4) £550 [Zioni]

### Anghiera, Pietro Martire d'. See: Martyr, Peter

### Angiolieri, Cecco
— Sonette. Verona: Officina Bodoni, 1944. One of 165. Orig bds. bba May 9 (612) £360 [Marks]

### Angler, An. See: Davy, Sir Humphry

### Angler's...
— The Angler's Guide Book and Tourists' Gazetteer of the Fishing Waters of the United States and Canada, 1885. NY: The American Angler, [1884]. Orig cloth. pba July 11 (136) $200
— Angler's Notebook and Naturalist's Record. L, 1880. 4to, half mor, orig cloth bound in. John Gerard Heckscher's copy. pba July 11 (11) $300

### Anglers' Club of New York
— The Anglers' Club Story. Our First Fifty Years, 1906-1956. NY: Pvtly ptd, 1956. One of 750. 4to, cloth; worn. Inscr to Pete Hidy from Sparce Grey Hackle on front endpaper & from Hidy to Flyfisher's Club of Oregon on front pastedown. O Feb 6 (5) $475; O June 25 (4) $110
— The Best of the Anglers' Club Bulletin 1920-1972. NY, 1972. One of 1,000. O Feb 6 (6) $90; O June 25 (5) $100
— Well Dressed Lines Stripped from the Reels of Five New Englanders. NY: Anglers' Club, 1962. One of 500. O Feb 6 (7) $100

### Anglo-Saxon...
— The Anglo-Saxon Review. L, 1899-1900. Ed by Lady Randolph S. Churchill. In 10 vols. 4to, orig calf gilt. b Jan 31 (68) £190

### Anker, Jean Thore Hojer Jensen
— Bird Books and Bird Art. Copenhagen, 1990. One of 300. 4to, cloth. Reprint of 1938 Ed. sg Dec 7 (194) $175

Anr Ed. Copenhagen, [1990]. One of—300. 4to, orig cloth. sg Apr 11 (277) $300

### Annabel, Russell
See also: Derrydale Press
— Hunting and Fishing in Alaska. NY, 1948. 4to, cloth, in chipped & frayed dj. O Oct 10 (32) $225

### Annals...
— The Annals of Philosophy; or, Magazine of Chemistry, Mineralogy, Mechanics.... L, 1813-26. 28 vols. 8vo, orig half cloth; chipped. Sold w.a.f. S Mar 29 (679) £520
— The Annals of Sporting and Fancy Gazette. L, 1822-28. 15 vols. 8vo, contemp half mor. With 153 plates, 50 of them hand-colored. Some foxing. b Dec 5 (144) £1,300

1st Ed. 78 issues in 13 vols. 8vo, contemp half calf; bds detached, rubbed. With 156 plates (53 hand-colored). Some spotting & offsetting. S Oct 27 (837) £1,300 [Chelsea Gal.]

### Anne...
— Anne of Brittanny; An Historical Romance. L, 1810. 3 vols. 12mo, contemp half calf. Ck Sept 8 (193) £500

### Annuaire...
— Annuaire des ventes de livres. Paris, [1920-30]. Ed by Leo Delteil. 12 vols. 8vo, half mor; orig wraps bound in, joints worn. O Mar 26 (74) $120

### Annual...
— The Annual Register; or, a View of the History, Politics.... L, 1776-83. 8 vols. 8vo, Vol I in russia-backed bds, remainder in old calf bds with later calf spines; worn & scuffed. wa Feb 29 (495) $325

### Ansaldi, Ansaldo
— Decisiones sacrae rotae romanae. Rome: Camera Apostolica, 1711. Folio, contemp mor gilt with arms of Pope Clement XI. Dedication copy. C Apr 3 (20) £2,500

### Anson, George, Baron Anson, 1697-1762
— A Voyage Round the World.... L, 1748. 1st Ed. 4to, contemp calf; front joints & lower rear joint cracked, spine worn. With folding frontis map, 29 folding plates, & 13 folding maps. Some spotting & tears. Ck Mar 22 (12) £750

Anr copy. Contemp calf; rebacked with modern calf. With frontis & 42 folding maps, charts & plates. A few plates repaired; chart of Philippines with short central tear. pba Feb 13 (1) $1,400

Anr copy. Contemp russia gilt; rebacked retaining orig spine. With 42 folding maps, charts & plates. some plates shaved to just within neatline; 1 tear repaired; some spotting. S June 27 (244) £1,050

Thick-paper Issue. Contemp calf; worn. With 42 folding maps, charts & plates. Wormed towards end,

mostly marginal. bba Nov 16 (277) £550 [Remington]
2d Ed. 4to, contemp calf; worn. With 3 folding maps only. Tear to 1 map; some browning. Ck Feb 14 (307) £150
5th Ed. L, 1749. 4to, modern lea by Dr. Craig Alden Burns. With frontis & 42 maps & plates. Pacific & frontis with some dampstaining; tip of South America with tear; Philippines with short central tear. pba Oct 9 (1) $650
Anr Ed. L, 1762. 8vo, contemp calf; scuffed & worn, hinges cracked. With 2 charts. Browned; tape repair to frontis map. pba July 25 (375) $225

**Ansrasy, Mano, Count —& Others**
— Les chasses et le sport en Hongrie. Pest, [1857]. Folio, contemp half cloth with large portion of orig upper ptd wrap laid down; extremities & upper cover scuffed. With 25 plates (13 full-page). C May 31 (1) £4,500

**Anstey, Christopher, 1724-1805**
— The Poetical Works. L, 1808. 1 vol extended to 2. 4to, calf gilt by Zaehnsdorf. With 2 ports, 4 plates & 8 illusts in text. Extra-illus with 53 plates. S Apr 23 (1) £550

**Anstey, F.**
— The Cambridge Tatler, No 1. Cambr., 6 Mar 1877. Contemp half lea. Inscr to Horace Pym. S Apr 23 (63) £160
— Vice Versa, or A Lesson to Fathers. L, 1882. 2 vols. 8vo, orig cloth. With 2 A Ls s tipped in. Pym copy. S Apr 23 (68) £1,050

**Antarah ibn Shaddad**
— Antar: poeme heroique arabe.... Paris, 1898. Out-of-series copy on japon with 3 extra suites of the illusts, this copy with anr set of the 1st 2 suites separately bound. Trans by L. Marcel Devic; illus by E. Dinet. 4to, mor extra by G. Crette, extra set of suites in half mor by Mercier. Kettaneh copy. S Nov 21 (114) £1,700

**Anthoensen, Fred**
— Types and Bookmaking. Portland, 1943. One of 500. O Dec 5 (9) $100

**Anthoine-Legrain, Jacques —& Others**
— Pierre Legrain, Relieur.... Paris, 1965. One of 620. Folio, orig wraps in slipcase & sleeve; loose as issued. With 250 plates, 7 in color. sg Apr 11 (47A) $375

**Anthon, Charles**
— A Classical Dictionary. NY, 1852. 8vo, calf. pba Aug 8 (228) $100

**Anthony, Gordon**
— Russian Ballet: Camera Studies. L, 1939. 4to, orig cloth; traces of removed bookplate to front pastedown. With 91 tipped-in plates. pba Aug 8 (229) $50

**Antichrist...**
— Der Antichrist und die fuenfzehn Zeichen. [Munich, 1970]. One of 650. 2 vols. 4to, half vellum. sg Sept 14 (21) $70

**Antient...**
— The Antient and Present State of the Empire of Germany. L, 1702. 8vo, contemp calf; loose. With engraved title & folding map by Herman Moll Tp stamped. sg Mar 7 (83) $300

**Antoine, Francois, Baron de Betti**
— Relation veritable des cruautes faites dans le Monastere du Mont Saint Athos.... Cologne, [c.1680?]. 8vo, unbound. S Oct 26 (175) £520 [Maggs]

**Antoni, Alessandro Vittorio Papacino d'**
— A Treatise of Gun-Powder.... L, 1789. 1st Ed in English. 8vo, contemp calf; worn, spine ends chipped, front cover detached. With 24 folding plates. wa Feb 29 (195) $400

**Antoninus, Brother.** See: Everson, William

**Antoninus Florentinus, Saint, 1389-1459**
— Summa confessionum. Memmingen: Albrecht Kunne, 1483. ("Confessionale: Defecerunt scrutantes scrutinio...."). 4to, 19th-cent half calf. 32 lines; double column; types 1:82G, 2:115G. With uncorrected colophon giving Kunne's Christian name as Abertum. Upper margin of 1st leaf cut away; 2 small wormholes in text of 1st leaf; some spotting in margins. 95 (of 96) leaves; lacking the blank. Goff A-811. S Dec 18 (5) £880 [Zioni]

Anr Ed. Louvain: Johann de Paderborn, [c.1485]. Folio, early 19th-cent half calf; rubbed. 41 lines; double column; gothic letter; initials & paragraph marks in red & blue. Large strip torn from lower margin of c2; tear in outer margin of e2; some staining & soiling. 69 (of 114) leaves; lacking initial blank & Tractatus de septem sacrementis. Goff A-816. S Dec 18 (6) £500 [Maggs]

Anr Ed. Strassburg: Martin Flach, 1499. 4to, contemp blind-stamped calf over wooden bds; lacking 1 clasp. 35 lines & headline; gothic letter. Wormed; marginal dampstaining; annotations at beginning. 148 leaves. Goff A-833. S Dec 18 (7) £900 [Zioni]

— Summa moralis. Nuremberg: Anton Koberger, 1478-79. 4 vols. Folio, contemp blindstamped calf over wooden bds, possibly by Joerg Schapf; spines & sides repaired, lacking some cornerpieces. 59 lines & headline; double column; types 3:110G (text) & 4:160G (titling). Elaborately rubricated & with illuminated initials Lower margins of Fols. 80 & 298 (Vol II) cut away without loss; dampstaining in Vol II, which has a few leaves partly detached; 1st initial of Vol III excised with loss of 10 lines of text & knife-cuts in following leaves; tear in final leaf of Vol III repaired; some marginal worming & contemp annotations. 254 leaves, 322 leaves, 462 (of 464) leaves (lacking 2 blanks) & 337 (of 338) leaves (acking final blank). Goff A-871. Madsen copy. S Mar 14 (17) £4,800

— Summa theologica. Venice: Johannes de Colonia & Johannes Manthen, 1477. ("Summa theologica, pars II.") Folio, half vellum; wormed, pastedowns from 12th-cent Ms. 53 lines & headline; double column; gothic letter; 1st initial supplied in blue on panel of red & blue penwork. Worming at ends; some staining. 365 (of 366) leaves; lacking initial blank. Goff A-868. S Dec 18 (8) £1,800 [Zioni]
Anr Ed. Venice: Leonardus Wild, 1480. Vol III only. Folio, modern half vellum. 59 lines; double column; gothic letter. Last leaf of Part 2 repaired in lower margin; some staining. 430 (of 432) leaves; lacking q5-6 in Part 2. Goff A8-73. S Dec 18 (9) £700 [Aspin]

**Antonio, Nicolas**
— Bibliotheca Hispana vetus [Hispana nova].... Madrid, 1788. 4 vols. Folio, contemp sheep gilt. With 2 ports. sg Apr 18 (10) $1,300

**Antonius de Bitonto**
— Sermones dominicales per totum annum. Strassburg: Johann (Reinhard) Greuninger, 20 Feb 1495. 8vo, modern bds. 34 lines & headline; double column; gothic letter. First gathering supplied form a shorter copy; repairs in margins of 1st & last few leaves; browned in margins. 277 (of 280) leaves; lacking g4-5 & final blank. Goff A-891. S Dec 18 (10) £420 [de Palol]

**Antonius de Raymundia**
— Libellus contra beneficiorum reservationes.... Paris: Jean Petit, [c.1498]. 4to, modern calf. Gothic letter. Some annotations in margins. 8 leaves. Goff A-916. S Nov 30 (245) £900

**Antuiano, Mateo de**
— Epitome historial y conquista espiritual del Imperio Abyssino, en Etiopia la alta.... Madrid: Antonio Goncalez de Reyes, 1706. 4to, recent half calf gilt. Repair to 1 corner. S Nov 30 (145) £700

**Anville, Jean Baptiste Bourguignon d', 1697-1782**
— Atlas general de la Chine, de la Tartarie Chinoise et du Tibet. Paris, [1737]. Folio, 19th-cent bds; rebacked. With engraved title & 64 maps & plates, the general maps hand-colored in outline. S June 27 (219) £4,000
— Compendium of Ancient Geography. L, 1791. 2 vols. 8vo, contemp vellum gilt. With 10 folding maps. b May 30 (127) £160
— A Complete Body of Ancient Geography. L, 1818. Folio, contemp half sheep; worn. With 13 maps, hand-colored in outline. Several maps trimmed to image border. Sold w.a.f. sg May 9 (49) $200
— Geographie ancienne et abregee. Paris, 1769. Folio, later half mor. With 10 maps hand-colored in outline, 8 of them double-page. Tp trimmed & laid down; some marginal tears; 1 map cropped; guarded throughout. Sold w.a.f. b May 30 (122) £400
Anr copy. Contemp calf; worn, joints cracked. With 8 (of 9) double-page maps. S Oct 26 (426) £170 [Zioni]

**Apes, William**
See also: Snelling, William Joseph
— A Son of the Forest. NY, 1831. 2d Ed. Contemp half mor; extremities rubbed. Frontis lacking. pba July 11 (366) $85

**Apianus, Petrus, 1495-1552**
— Cosmographicus liber. Antwerp: G. Bontius, 1550. ("Cosmographia....") Ed by Gemma Frisius. 4to, bdg not described. Fragment only, but has double-page woodcut cordiform world map. S Mar 14 (375) £1,150
Anr Ed. Venice: Petrus de Nicolinis for Melchior Sessa, [1551]. ("Cosmographiae introductio: cum quibusdam geometriae....") 8vo, 19th-cent half lea; needs rebacking. sg May 16 (111) $550
Anr Ed. Antwerp, 1581. ("Cosmographie....") 4to, 18th-cent calf; worn. Lothian - Davies copy. P June 5 (155) $3,750

**Apicius Coelius, fl.14-37 A.D.**
— De opsoniis et condimentis.... Amst., 1709. 8vo, modern half bds. With frontis by J. Goeere. S Oct 12 (4) £560
— De re coquinaria libri decem. [Venice: Joannem de Cereto de Tridino, 1503]. 4to, later half calf. Goff A-921. pba Nov 30 (97) $5,000
— De re culinaria libri decem.... Lyons: S. Gryphus, 1541. 8vo, later calf; rebacked. With title device. Title soiled; light dampstaining; some browning & spotting. Ck Mar 22 (13) £460

**Apollinaire, Guillaume, 1880-1918**
— Calligrammes. Paris, 1918. 8vo, orig wraps, unopened; spine cracked. Browned. sg Apr 18 (88) $1,200
— Les Epingles. Paris, [1928]. One of 835. Orig wraps. With port. sg June 20 (7) $80
— Le Poete assassine. Paris, 1926. One of 20 on Japon with 2 additional suites of plates on Hollande & Chine. Illus by Raoul Dufy. 4to, orig wraps. With 36 lithos. sg Apr 18 (89) $2,000
One of 470. Orig wraps in board folder with design by Dufy; joint broken. With 36 lithos. Ck Sept 8 (1) £1,100; S Mar 28 (499) £360

**Apollonius of Tyre.** See: Golden Cockerel Press

**Apollonius Rhodius, 240-186 B.C.**
See also: Limited Editions Club
— Argonautica. Florence: [Laurentius (Francisci) de Alopa], 1496. 4to, 19th-cent calf; edges worn. Types 114Gk & 111Gk. Modern decoration added to renewed margins of 1st leaf; dampstaining to most fore-edges, with repairs. 171 (of 172) leaves; lacking final blank. Goff A-924. C June 26 (30) £2,500
1st Ed. Florence: [Laurentius (Francesci) de Alopa, Venetus] 1496. 4to, later 18th-cent mor gilt. 33 & 29 lines; type 5a,b:114Gk, 5c:111Gk. Wormhole in last few leaves mended, with a few letters in ink facsimile. 172 leaves. Goff A-924. Fitzwilliam - Mersey copy. C Apr 3 (21) £9,500

**Apology...** See: Pratt, Samuel Jackson

**Apperley, Charles J., 1777?-1843**
— The Chace, the Turf, and the Road. L, 1837. 1st Ed. - Illus by Henry Alken. 8vo, orig cloth; some wear. Some foxing & stains. O Jan 9 (13) $60
— Hunting Reminiscences. L, 1843. 1st Ed. 8vo, orig cloth; recased. Some foxing. O Jan 9 (14) $80
— The Life of a Sportsman; by Nimrod. L, 1842. 1st Ed, 1st Issue. 8vo, mor by Morrell; minor rubbing. With engraved title, port & 34 plates, all hand-colored. O Jan 9 (15) $750

Issue not indicated. Later half mor; minor rubbing. With engraved title, port & 34 plates, all hand-colored. Outer margins trimmed, affecting imprint in some cases; 1 plate with further loss to margins; some soiling. pn Dec 7 (102) £600

— Memoirs of the Life of the Late John Mytton, Esq. L, 1837. 2d Ed. - Illus by Henry Alken. 8vo, orig cloth. Some foxing, 2 signatures sprung. O Jan 9 (16) $275

Anr copy. Modern calf; spine rubbed. With engraved title & 18 hand-colored plates. Margin of C2 repaired with loss. S Mar 29 (783) £100

Anr copy. Mor by Morrell; joints rubbed, upper joint cracked. Marginal tears repaired; a few imprints cropped. S June 13 (455) £150

Anr copy. Later calf extra by Riviere, orig cover & spine bound in. With engraved title & hand-colored plates. sg Mar 7 (389) $475

Anr copy. Later mor, orig cloth bound in; extremities rubbed, joints cracked. With engraved title, frontis & 18 hand-colored plates. Some fraying, affecting captions; a few leaves repaired. Z June 28 (5) $200

— Nimrod Abroad. L, 1842. 1st Ed. 2 vols. 8vo, orig cloth. Some foxing & soiling. O Jan 9 (17) $80
— Nimrod's Northern Tour. L, 1838. 8vo, orig cloth; worn. O Jan 9 (19) $130

**Appert, Nicholas, 1750-1841**
— L'Art de Conserver pendant plusieurs annees toutes les substances animales et vegetales. Paris, 1810. 1st Ed. 8vo, recent half mor. With half-title & folding plate. Plate soiled; text spotted. Sgd by Appert on half-title. Ck Mar 22 (14) £450
— Le Livre de Tours les Menages.... Paris, 1813. 3d Ed. 8vo, orig wraps. With folding plate. Some browning & spotting. Sgd by Appert on verso of title. Ck Mar 22 (16) £100

**Appia, Louis Amedee**
— The Ambulance Surgeon; or, Practical Observations on Gunshop Wounds. Edin., 1862. 8vo, orig cloth. John Watts De Peyster's annotated copy. sg May 16 (363) $120

**Appian of Alexandria**
— The History.... L, 1690. Trans by John Davies. Folio, contemp calf; broken, spine chipped. Library stamps on title. sg Mar 21 (18) $130

**Appleton & Co., Daniel**
— Appleton's Cyclopaedia of American Biography. NY, 1888-89. Ed by J. G. Wilson & John Fiske. 6 vols. 4to, cloth. pba Oct 26 (360) $350
— Appleton's Journal of Literature, Science, and Art. NY, 1869. Vols 1-2. 4to, half lea; extremities worn. With 9 (of 10) steel-engraved plates & 12 (of 15) folding wood-engraved plates. NH June 1 (160) $440

**Appleton, Tony**
— The Writings of Stanley Morison: A Handlist. Brighton, 1976. One of 600. Orig half vellum, in dj. bba May 9 (25) £60 [Mandl]

**Apuleius, Lucius**
See also: Ashendene Press; Golden Cockerel Press; Limited Editions Club
— De Cupidinis et Psyches amoribus. L: Vale Press, 1901. One of 310. Illus by Charles Ricketts. Folio, half cloth; backstrip def. sg Sept 14 (336) $130

Anr copy. Half cloth, unopened. sg Feb 15 (304) $375

— Metamorphose, autrement l'asne d'or. Lyon: Jean de Tournes & Guillaume Gazeau, 1553. 16mo, mor gilt by Hardy; upper joint starting. Rust spot on c5. Schaefer copy. P Nov 1 (8) $3,000
— Works. L, 1822. ("The Metamorphosis, or Golden Ass, and Philosophical Works....") Trans by Thomas Taylor. 8vo, modern half lev by Bradstreet's; rubbed. With 5 leaves of "Passages Suppressed" at end. pba June 20 (328) $325

**Aquino, Carlo d'**
— Sacra exquialia in funere Jacobi II.... Rome, 1702. Folio, contemp half mor; edges worn. With title arms, folding frontis, 3 folding plates, & 15 full-page plates. Frontis weak at fold, with some tears. S Oct 26 (382) £500 [Borison]

**Arabia**
— L'univers pittoresque. Arabie. Paris, 1847. 8vo, wraps. S Oct 26 (4) £460 [Map House]

**Arabian Nights**
— 1802. - The Arabian Nights. L. Edward Forster's trans. 5 vols. 8vo, mor gilt. With 24 proof plates. L.p. copy. Ck Sept 8 (169) £1,400
— 1825. - L. Illus by Richard Westall. 4 vols. 8vo, contemp calf; 2 vols rebacked with orig spines laid on, front hinge of Vol I tight. Foxed. pba Dec 14 (206) $120
— 1839-41. - The Thousand and One Nights.... L. Edward William Lane's trans. 3 vols. 8vo, mor gilt by Riviere. pba Sept 14 (232) $550
— 1840-41. - L. Trans by Edward William Lane. 3 vols. 8vo, contemp half calf. ALs of Lane tipped in. S Apr 23 (100) £240
— [1885-88]. - The Book of the Thousand Nights and a Night, with Supplemental Nights. L.Benares Ed. 17 vols. 8vo, orig half mor. b Sept 20 (559) £1,700

Anr copy. Cloth. pnE Sept 20 (28) £340

— 1897. - Library Ed. L. Sir Richard F. Burton's trans. 12 vols. 8vo, contemp half mor; scuffed. F June 20 (719) $325
— 1899-1904. - Le Livre des mille nuits et une nuit. Paris One of 75 on hollande. J. C. Mardrus's trans; illus by A. Robida. 16 vols. 8vo, Vols I-VII in calf by Charles Meunier, the remainder in orig wraps. With 618 ink & watercolor drawings, 43 full-page on inserted sheets, the remainder drawn directly in margins & other blank areas. S Nov 21 (259) £4,700
— 1900-1. - The Book of the Thousand Nights and a Night, with Supplemental Nights. [Denver: Burton Society] One of 1,000. Sir Richard F. Burton's trans. 16 vols. 8vo, half mor by Phister; some joints cracked. pba Mar 7 (46) $550
— 1919. - Contes des 1001 Nuits. Paris: Les Editions de la Sirene One of 310. Illus by Kees Van Dongen. 4to, mor extra by Charles de Samblanx, orig wraps bound in. S Nov 21 (208) £450
— 1926-32. - Le Livre des mille nuits et une nuit. Paris One of 50 on japon imperial with 2 additional suites of the plates & orig watercolour. J. C. Mardrus's trans; illus by Leon Carre. 12 vols. 4to, half vellum with spines gilt & painted, by Devauchelle, orig wraps bound in. With 24 sgd orig watercolors, 12 inserted into the books & the others mtd on card & in a fitted box. S Nov 21 (261) £7,000
— [n.d.]. - The Book of the Thousand Nights and a Night, with Supplemental Nights. L: Burton Club One of 1,000. Sir Richard F. Burton's trans. 17 vols. 8vo, orig cloth. b Jan 31 (67) £220
Anr copy. 16 vols. 8vo, bba Oct 19 (275) £240 [Sotheran]
Anr copy. 17 vols. 8vo, cb Feb 14 (2750) $900
Anr copy. Half mor gilt. pnE Mar 20 (110) £1,100

— Aladdin and his Wonderful Lamp. L, [1920]. One of 250. Illus by Thomas Mackenzie. 4to, cloth. With 12 colored plates tipped in. b May 30 (454) £300
— The Arabian Nights: Their Best-Known Tales. NY, 1916. Ed by K. D. Wiggin & Nora Smith; illus by Maxfield Parrish. 4to, orig cloth; worn, frayed. Marginal dampstaining affecting several plates. F Mar 28 (563) $150
— Hassan Badreddin el Bass Raoui. Conte des 1001 nuits. Paris: Editions de la Sirene [1919]. One of 10 on japon imperial. J. C. Mardrus's trans; illus by K. van Dongen. 4to, unsewn in orig wraps; spine ends chipped, extremities rubbed. cb Oct 17 (626) $650
— Persian Stories from the Arabian Nights. Kentfield, CA: Allen Press, 1980. One of 140. Folio, wraps. pba June 20 (13) $425; sg Sept 14 (5) $350; sg Sept 14 (15) $225
— Princess Badoura. Retold by Laurence Housman. [L, 1913]. Illus by Edmund Dulac. 4to, lev extra exhibition bdg by Zaehnsdorf, dated 1898 [sic]. sg Oct 19 (79) $800
One of 750, sgd by artist. Orig cloth. sg Sept 14 (110) $600; sg Feb 15 (95) $350
— La Princesse Badourah. Paris, 1914. Illus by Edmund Dulac. 4to, orig bds; joints & spine ends worn. With 10 colored plates. sg Feb 15 (96) $100

— Sinbad the Sailor. [L, 1914]. Illus by Edmund Dulac. 4to, orig cloth; frayed, corners bumped. Met Dec 5 (160) $225

**Aragon, Louis, 1897-1982.** See: Limited Editions Club

**Arber, Agnes**
— Herbals. Their Origin and Evolution. Cambr., 1938. sg Sept 7 (5) $70

**Arber, Edward, 1836-1912**
— The Term Catalogues, 1668-1709 L, 1903-6. 4to, orig cloth; worn. O Mar 26 (8) $150

**Arbus, Diane**
— Diane Arbus. Rome: Electa Editrice, 1979. One of 1,000. Folio, loose in orig folding dj. With 12 plates. sg Apr 24 (575) $1,200
— Diane Arbus: Magazine Work. NY: Aperture, [1984]. Folio, photo-pictorial bds, in rubbed dj with tear to rear panel. sg Feb 29 (15) $80

**Arcadelt, Jacob, c.1505-67**
— Il Primo Libro de Madrigali a Quatro Voci.... Venice: Alessandro Gardane, 1581. Oblong 8vo, contemp paper backed by early Ms. Tenor & bass parts. C June 26 (245) £900

**Archiconfrairie Royale du Saint-Sepulchre de Jerusalem**
— Discours prononce a l'assemblee nationale, par la deputation de l'archiconfrairie royale du Saint-Sepulchre de Jerusalem, a la seance du soir, le samedi 10 avril 1790. Paris, [1790]. 2 parts in 1 vol. 8vo, contemp red mor gilt with arms of Marie Antoinette; upper cover bumped. Fuerstenberg - Schaefer copy. S Dec 7 (298) £1,100

**Archimedes, 287?-212 B.C.**
— Opera. Paris, 1615. Ed by David Rivault. Folio, 17th-cent blind-stamped vellum; backstrip def, front joint cracked, turn-ins sprung. Library stamp on tp & next leaf. In Greek & Latin. sg May 16 (112) $1,300

**Archipenko, Alexander, 1887-1964**
[-] MA. Aktivista Folyoirat. Vienna, [1921]. Vol VI, No 6. 4to, wraps; spine chipped. With essay on Archipenko by Ival Goll, poem dedicated to him by Blaise Centrars & illusts of his sculptures. Sgd by Lajos Kossak & by Hanna Hoech. sg June 13 (281) $350

**Architectural Iron Works Company**
— Illustrations of Iron Architecture. NY, 1865. Folio, orig cloth. With 102 lithos, c.45 of them tinted or hand-colored Some foxing. K Oct 1 (15) $4,500

**Ardemanio, Giulio Cesare, d.1650**
— Musica a piu voci con il basso continuo per l'organo. Milan: Gratiado Ferioli, 1628. 4to, later bds. Alto part. C June 26 (246) £800

## Ardizzone, Edward, 1900-79
— Lucy Brown and Mr. Grimes. L, 1937. 1st Ed. Folio, orig bds, in chipped & worn dj. Inscr. O Sept 12 (9) $650

## Arents Collection, George, Jr.
— Tobacco: Its History Illustrated in the...Library. NY, 1958-69. Supplementary Catalogue, Parts I-VII, compiled by Sarah A. Dickson & Parts VIII-X compiled by Perry H. O'Neil. 4to, wraps. O Mar 26 (9) $160

## Aretino, Pietro, 1492-1556
— Del Primo Libro de le lettere. Paris, 1609. Vols 3-6. 8vo, contemp vellum. pba Mar 7 (13) $75
— Geschichten. Siena, 1907. Ltd Ed. 8vo, orig vellum. With 15 plates. b May 30 (332) £80
— Talanta comedia. Venice: Francesco Marcolini, Mar 1542. 8vo, old vellum; resewn, modern endpapers. Tp & A2 with repaired marginal tears. C Apr 3 (22) £2,200

## Argens, Jean Baptiste de Boyer, Marquis d', 1704-71
— Les enchainemens de l'amour et de la fortune.... The Hague, 1746. 2 parts in 1 vol. 12mo, contemp calf with arms of Antoine-Pierre de Courtins, comte d'Ussy. Fuerstenberg - Schaefer copy. S Dec 7 (18) £110

## Argento, Gaetano, 1661-1730
— De re beneficiaria dissertationes tres.... Naples, 1709 [1709]. 4to, contemp mor elaborately gilt. C Apr 3 (23) £1,100

## Argenville, Antoine Joseph Dezallier d'. See: Dezallier d'Argenville, Antoine Joseph

## Arias, P. E.
— A History of 1000 Years of Greek Vase Painting. NY: Abrams, [n.d.]. 4to, cloth. sg June 13 (45) $150

## Ariosto, Ludovico, 1474-1533
— Bellezze del furioso...scielte da Oratio Tascanella. Venice: Pitro dei Franceschi &nepotii, 1574. 4to, 18th-cent calf; rubbed, joints split. With title device. Title stained. S Oct 27 (1041) £260 [Zioni]
— Orlando furioso. Venice: Francesco de Franceschi Senese, 1584. 2 parts in 1 vol. Folio, 19th-cent mor gilt. With 46 full-page plates. Plate 34 suppressed & replaced by a repetition of Plate 33; marginal tears repaired; tear in K1 repaired; 1st title on a stub; 8 leaves from a shorter copy; small hole from ink burn in tp. C Apr 3 (24) £380
— Orlando Furioso.... L, 1634. English trans by William Stewart Rose. 2 vols. 19th-cent lev gilt by Bickers; rubbed. With 12 plates. Extra-illus with c.66 plates from earlier Eds. pba Nov 30 (16) £160
Anr copy. English trans by Sir John Harington. Folio, later calf. Tp margin trimmed; at least 1 page with piece lacking. pba Mar 7 (14) $350
— Orlando furioso. Paris: Prault, 1746. 4 vols. 12mo, contemp red mor gilt with arms of David Pierre Perrinet, seigneur de Pezeau; spines of Vols I & II chipped. Fuerstenberg - Schaefer copy. S Dec 7 (21) £800
Anr Ed. Birm.: Baskerville, 1773. 4 vols. 4to, contemp red mor extra by Richard Wier. Bound at beginning is the 4-page 4to issue of the proposal of 1772. With port & 46 plates. MacCarthy Reagh - Furstenberg - Schaefer copy. S Dec 7 (22) £10,000
Anr Ed. Birm., 1773. 4 vols. 8vo, contemp mor gilt, attributed to Johann Baumgarten, with arms of Michael Wodhull. With 46 plates. Some staining & browning. Fuerstenberg - Schaefer copy. S Dec 7 (23) £2,200
Anr Ed. Birm.: Baskerville, 1773. 4 vols. 8vo, contemp mor gilt. Marginal foxing throughout. sg Apr 18 (11) $600
Anr Ed. Paris: Delalain, 1777. 4 vols. 12mo, contemp red mor gilt by Derome le jeune. With engraved titles, frontis, & port. Fuerstenberg - Schaefer copy. S Dec 7 (24) £600
Anr Ed. L, 1799. Illus by William Blake. 5 vols. 8vo, contemp calf gilt; joints weak. sg Feb 8 (4) $90
— Orlando Furioso.... L, 1807. English trans by John Hoole. 6 vols. 8vo, contemp calf; rubbed. With frontises. Marginal waterstaining; some foxing. bba May 30 (137) £95 [Carter]
— Roland furieux. Paris, 1775-83. 4 vols. 8vo, red mor gilt by Derome le jeune, with his ticket. With port & 46 plates. L.p. copy on papier d'hollande. Fuerstenberg - Schaefer copy. S Dec 7 (25) £2,600

## Aristides, Aelius
— Logoi. Orationes. Florence: Filippo Giunta, 20 May 1517. Folio, 18th-cent calf; joints split, tear to front cover, corners rubbed. Tp soiled & with 1 corner worn; some dampstaining; last quire wormed in margin. C Apr 3 (25) £1,100

## Aristophanes, 448?-380? B.C.
See also: Limited Editions Club
— Comoediae undecim. Leiden: J. Maire, 1624. Ed by Joseph Scaliger. 3 vols. 12mo, contemp mor; rubbed & faded. S Oct 27 (1042) £300 [Theotoky]
— The Eleven Comedies. NY, 1928. Illus by Jean de Bosschere. 2 vols. In djs. With 12 plain & 12 colored plates. pba June 20 (33) $90
— Komodiai ennea. Comoedia novem. Venice: Aldus, 15 July 1498. Folio, early 19th-cent half sheep; rubbed. Preface in Latin; text in Greek Some worming, affecting letters; 2 sets of Ms glosses in margins. 347 (of 348) leaves; lacking final blank. Goff A-958. C Apr 3 (26) £9,000
— Lysistrata. L, 1896. One of 100. Illus by Aubrey Beardsley. 4to, orig bds. S Nov 2 (70) £1,900 [Zioni]
— Praxagora, adaptation de L'Assemblee des femmes par Maurice Donnay. Paris: Les Centraux Bibliophiles, 1932. One of 130. Illus by Pierre Bouchet after Kuhn-Regnier. Unsewn in orig wraps. With 65 colored wood-engravings & 2 added orig gouache designs. S Nov 21 (8) £400

**Aristotle, 384-322 B.C.**
See also: Limited Editions Club
— Aristotle's Ethics and Politics.... L, 1797. 2 vols. 4to, contemp calf gilt; covers detached or starting. sg Mar 21 (21) $500
— De interpretatione. Paris: Chretien Wechel, 1531. 4to, bds. Roman, italic & Greek types. P Dec 12 (19) $800
— The Metaphysics. L, 1801. Trans by Thomas Taylor. 4to, contemp calf gilt with Signet crest; rebacked, orig spine strip laid on. pba Nov 30 (18) $900
Anr copy. Contemp calf gilt; spine ends chipped, covers detached. sg May 16 (113) $350
— Oeconomicorum.... Siena: Simeone Nardi, 1 Feb 1508. 4to, recent half sheep. Roman types. P Dec 12 (8) $800
— Opera. Venice: Aldus, 1495-98. 1st Ed in Greek. 5 vols. Folio, 16th-cent half pigskin with clasps & catches, arms of Zurich on upper covers. 30 lines & head-line; Greek letter; woodcut initials & headpieces. Small wormholes in all vols, many repaired; 1st 17 lines of text on yx2 (Vol II) have not ptd. Library stamp on titles. 1,852 leaves. Goff A-959. C Apr 3 (27) £145,000
Anr Ed. Venice: Joannes & Gregorius de Gregoriis de Forlino, for Benedictus Fontana, 13 July 1496. Folio, contemp blind-stamped pigskin over wooden bds, spine painted; bds wormed, lacking 2 clasps & catches. 44 lines & headline; roman letter. Worming at beginning & end. 506 (of 508) leaves; lacking x4-5. Goff A966. Madsen copy. S Mar 14 (18) £2,700
Anr Ed. Venice: [Joannes & Gregorius de Gregoriis, de Forlivio] for Octavianus Scotus, 26 Apr 1496. Folio, half sheep. 56 lines & headline, double column, gothic types Some worming at end; marginal staining. 375 (of 376) leaves; lacking final blank. Goff A-965 (II). Soudek copy. P Dec 12 (1) $4,500
Anr Ed. Venice: Aldus, June 1498. Vol V, Parts 1-2 only, in 2 vols. Folio, contemp calf with traces of 4 pairs of thong ties; rebacked, corners repaired. 31 lines & headline; Greek & Roman types. 222 (of 330) leaves; comprising Nicomachean Ethics, Oeconomica & Politica. Goff A-959. Soudek copy. P Dec 12 (2) $9,000
Anr Ed. Basel: J. Bebel & M. Isingrinius, 1550. Folio, contemp pigskin over wooden bds, dated 1565, with brass clasps. P Dec 12 (27) $2,750
Anr Ed. Frankfurt: Andreas Wechel, 1584-87. 10 vols. 4to, 18th-cent mor gilt. P Dec 12 (33) $1,300
— Politicorum libri octo.... Paris: Henri Estienne, 1511. Bound after: In politica Aristotelis introductio.... Paris: Henri Estienne, 22 Nov 1516. Folio, recent calf. Roman types. Some worming. P Dec 12 (14) $900
Anr Ed. Paris: Simon de Colines, 1543. Folio, 19th-cent half calf; lower joint split. Some dampstaining & soiling; contemp annotations on tp. S June 12 (5) £520
— Politicorum Libri VIII. Paris: Simon de Colines, 30 Apr 1526. Folio, 18th-cent goatskin; rebacked. Roman types. Tp soiled & strengthened at inner margin; repaired tear entering tp border; early annotations. P Dec 12 (17) $350
— Textus ethicorum ad Nicomachum.... Paris: Antoine Bonnemere for Denis Roce, 17 Sept 1509. 4to, contemp calf over wooden bds with remains to 2 brass clasps; upper joint split. Gothic types; partially rubricated. Some worming. P Dec 12 (9) $1,100

**Arizona**
— Memorial and Affidavits showing Outrages Perpetrated by the Apache Indians, in the Territory of Arizona, during the Years 1869 and 1870. San Francisco, 1871. 8vo, disbound. sg Oct 26 (5) $275

**Arkham...**
— The Arkham Collector. Sauk City: Arkham House, 1967-71. Nos 1-10 Orig self-wraps. pba Aug 22 (12) $100
— The Arkham Sampler. Sauk City: Arkham House, 1948-49. 8 issues from Spring 1948 to Winter 1949. Wraps; rust marks from staples. pba Aug 22 (13) $160

**Arkus, Leon**
— John Kane, Painter. Pittsburgh, 1971. 4to, cloth, in dj. O May 7 (37) $60

**Arkwright, Francis**
— Gossip and Glory of Versailles, 1692-1701. NY: Brentano's, [n.d.]. 6 vols. Half mor by Whitman Bennett; spine ends & joints rubbed. pba Dec 14 (2) $120

**Arlanibaeus, Philippus.** See: Abelin, Johann Philipp

**Armor, Samuel**
— History of Orange County California.... Los Angeles, 1921. 2d Ed. pba Nov 16 (12) $110

**Armour, George Denholm**
— Humour in the Hunting Field. L, 1928. One of 100. Folio, orig cloth. With 20 colored plates, all sgd in pencil. b Jan 31 (129) £380
— Pastime with Good Company.... L: Country Life, [1914]. Folio, orig half cloth; worn, stained. With 54 tipped-in plates. bba July 18 (101) £110 [Stacpoole]

**Armroyd, George**
— A Connected View of the Whole Internal Navigation of the United States.... Phila., 1826. 8vo, orig half cloth; soiled, edges worn. With 10 folding maps with waterways hand-colored. Library stamp on tp. S June 27 (174) £1,900

**Arms and Armor Club**
— A Miscellany of Arms and Armor. NY: Pvtly ptd, 1927. One of 115. 4to, cloth; worn. Sgd by Bashford Dean & by 15 of the 32 contributors. O June 4 (33) $160

**Armstrong, Ambrose N.**
— Oregon.... Chicago, 1857. 12mo, orig cloth; spine ends & corners worn, discolored. Foxed; dampstaining near end. wa Feb 29 (471) $210

## Armstrong, Edmund Archibald
— Axel Herman Haig and his Work. L, 1905. 4to, orig half mor. L.p. copy. pba June 20 (189) $300

## Armstrong, Nevill Alexander Drummond
— After Big Game in the Upper Yukon. L, [1937]. Some foxing. O Oct 10 (35) $100

## Arnal, Juan Pedro
— Descubrimiento de los pavimentos de Rielves. Madrid, [1787-88]. Folio, contemp bds; repaired. With 21 hand-finished plates. S June 27 (274) £4,000

## Arnaud d'Agnel, G. —& Isnard, Emile
— Monticelli, sa vie et son oeuvre.... Paris, 1926. One of 550. Folio, wraps; shaken. With 52 plates, 4 of them in color. sg Sept 7 (253) $70

## Arnauld, Antoine, 1612-94 —& Nicole, Pierre, 1625-95
— Logica, sive ars cogitandi. L, 1687. 8vo, contemp calf. sg May 16 (114) $275

**Arndt, Julius.** See: Horn & Arndt

**Arnold, Sir Edwin, 1827-92.** See: Limited Editions Club

## Arnold, Isaac Newton
— The Life of Abraham Lincoln. Chicago, 1885. One of 375. 8vo, cloth. With port. sg Oct 26 (211) $140

## Arnold, Matthew, 1822-88
— Empedocles on Etna, and Other Poems. L, 1852. 1st Ed. 8vo, orig cloth; hinge cracked, extremities rubbed. ALs, 24 Jan 1864, to J. Estlin Carpenter, laid in. CE Sept 27 (39) $200
— Geist's Grave. I., 1881. 8vo, orig wraps; detached. Wise forgery. Todd 4f. S Dec 18 (245) £200 [Jarndyce]
— The Scholar Gipsy and Thyrsis. L, 1910. One of 100. Illus by W. Russell Flint. 4to, orig vellum gilt. b Sept 20 (617) £190

## Arnold, Richard, d.1521?
— Chronicle of London. [Antwerp: Adrian van Bergen, c.1503]. ("In this Booke is Conteyned the Names of ye Baylifs....") Folio, modern cloth. Lacking several leaves at beginning, including tp (supplied in photofacsimile), & with contents supplied in facsimile; lacking leaves at end. Sold w.a.f. pba Nov 30 (20) $800

Anr Ed. L, 1811. ("The Customs of London.") 4to, 19th-cent calf gilt; joints rubbed. pba Nov 30 (21) $120

## Arnold, Sir Thomas Walker, 1864-1930 —& Grohmann, Adolf
— The Islamic Book. L, 1929. One of 375. 4to, cloth. With 104 plates. sg Sept 7 (25) $425

## Arnoldi, Henricus, c.1407-87
— De modo perveniendi ad veram Dei et proximi dilectionem. Basel: Michael Wenssler, [not after 1 Dec 1472]. 4to, modern mor antique. 25 lines; type 1a:121aG. Small tear in 1/2 repaired affecting letters; hole in fo. 29 affecting letters; marginal dampstaining. 125 (of 126) leaves; lacking initial blank. Goff A-1061. C Nov 29 (24) £2,400

## Arnoldus de Geihoven
— Gnotosolitos, sive speculum conscientiae. 25 May Brussels: [Fratres Vitae Communis] 1476. Folio, modern calf over wooden bds by Claessens; extremiteis rubbed. 50 lines & headline; double column; type 1:101G. With 33 initials in contemp blue with red penwork decoration & green highlights & in red with blue penwork. Small tears in 1st 3 leaves repaired with partial loss of 2 letters. 474 leaves. Goff A-1063. C June 26 (149) £32,000

## Arnott, David
— The Witches of Keil's Glen.... Cupar, 1825. 8vo, half mor; rubbed. b Dec 5 (544) £70

## Arntzen, Etta —& Rainwater, Robert
— Guide to the Literature of Art History. Chicago, 1980. 4to, orig cloth. sg Apr 11 (13) $110

## Aron, Pietro
— Compendiolo di molti dubbi segreti et sentenze intorno al canto fermo, et figurato.... Milan: Juan Antonio da Castellono, [c.1549]. 1st Ed. 4to, later "carta rustica". Browning on outer leaves; 2 small wormholes in 1st 3 leaves. S Dec 1 (65) £2,300
— Lucidario in musica.... Venice: Girolamo Scotto, 1545. 1st Ed. 4to, modern calf. Some worming in 1st 3 leaves; made-up copy; some foxing. S Dec 1 (66) £3,600
— Toscanello in musica.... Venice: Bernardio & Matheo de Vitali, 5 July 1529. Bound with: Aron. [Supplement to] Trattato di tutti gli tuoni di canto. Venice: Bernardino de Vitali, 1531 Folio, contemp vellum; partly misbound. Tp of Toscanello laid down & with strip cut away from margin; F2-3 browned; some worming at inner margin; Supplement lacking final blank. C Apr 3 (153) £1,050

**Arp, Jean (or Hans), 1887-1966.** See: Lissitzky & Arp

**Arrillaga, Jose.** See: California

## Arrowsmith, Aaron
— An Atlas of Ancient Geography. L, 1829. 8vo, contemp half mor; def. With 25 double-page mapsheets, hand-colored in outline. Some foxing & browning. sg May 9 (50) $300
— Atlas to Thompson's Alcedo or Dictionary of America.... L, 1816. Folio, contemp half mor; worn, disbound. With 6 maps & 19 folding mapsheets. Some tears, soiling, & marginal fraying. S Oct 26 (473) £8,500 [Map House]

## Arrowsmith, John, 1790-1873
— The London Atlas of Universal Geography. L, 1842. Folio, 19th-cent half calf; def. With 50 double-page maps, hand-colored in outline. Tp & 1st 2 maps loose & frayed. S June 13 (507) £2,200

## Ars Memorandi
— Ars Memorandi. Reproduit en fac-simile sur l'exemplaire de la Bibliotheque Nationale.... Paris, 1883. One of 100. 4to, unbound, later bd folder; worn. Inscr to Alexander Archipenko by J. B. Neumann, NY, Christmas 1925. sg Apr 11 (140A) $100

## Ars Moriendi
— Ars moriendi. [Lyons: Printer of the Ars moriendi, c.1488-89]. 4to, 16th-cent deerskin with armorial supralibros & medalion of Gottfried Troilo; minor repairs. 36-38 lines; type 105G (title) & 82G (text). With 12 full-page woodcuts. 20 leaves. Goff A-1096. Schaefer copy. P Nov 1 (11) $65,000

## Art...
— Art et Decoration: Revue mensuelle d'art moderne. Paris, 1897-1903. Vols 1-14. 4to, orig half cloth; some rubbing. wa Feb 1 (302) $1,100

— Art in Federal Buildings: an Illustrated Record of the Treasury Department's New Program in Painting and Sculpture. Wash., 1936. Vol I: Mural Designs. Oblong folio, half cloth. pba June 20 (79) $190

— The Art Journal. L, 1849-56. Vols XI-XXV in 31. 4to, contemp half calf; scuffed. bba Oct 19 (42) £1,600 [Pagan]

Anr Ed. L, 1849-1906. Vols I-L. 4to, mor or calf. Ck Feb 14 (311) £3,000

— Art of the Sixties / Kunst der Sechzinger Jahre. Cologne: Wallraf-Richartz Museum, 1971. 5th Ed. - Ed by Gerd von der Osten & Horst Keller. Plastic covers with metal screws; soiled. With 209 tipped-in color plates. pba June 20 (351) $225

— Art populaire. Paris, [1931]. 2 vols. 4to, buckram. On European folk art as shown at the First International Congress of Popular Arts held in Prague in 1928. sg Jan 11 (27) $120

## Artaud, Thibault, d.1499
— La tresample et vraye exposition de la reigle Monsieur Sainct Benoist. Paris: Pierre Didoue par Simon Vostre, [c.1510]. Folio, late 19th-cent blinstamped mor by G. Vignal. Batarde & gothic types. Woodcut of Crucifixion on tp verso; 6- & 9-line ornamented & historiated crible initials throughout. Marginal tear to xxx-xxxi, touching text. C June 26 (35) £1,300

## Arthur, King of Britain
— La Deuise des armes des Cheualiers de la Table Ronde.... Paris: F. Regnault, [1525?]. 16mo, mor gilt by Bauzonnet; extremities worn. With 179 heraldic woodcuts in text, most with pochoir color. Tp with tiny tear. P June 5 (285) $5,000

## Artists...
— The Artist's London. As Seen in Eighty Contemporary Pictures. L, 1924. Ltd Ed. 4to, half lea. With litho by Brangwyn & etching by W. P. Robins, each sgd. Some foxing. pba Mar 7 (35) $275

— Artists of the Italian Renaissance. L, 1907. Ed by E. L. Seeley. 8vo, velluccnt bdg by Cedric Chivers, with large painted panel of Madonna & Child. With 34 plates, 13 of them in color. sg Oct 19 (240) $475

## Artists Equity Fund
— Improvisations -- Artists Equity Masquerade Ball 1953. NY, 1953. 4to, pictorial wraps by Vertes, spiral bound; some wear at edges. sg Sept 7 (26) $250

## Arts...
— Arts et metiers graphiques. Paris, 1930. No 16: Numero Special Consacre a la Photographie. Ptd wraps, spiral-bound; covers creased & chipped. Marginal pencil notations. sg Feb 29 (17) $150

## Artzybasheff, Boris
— As I See. NY, 1954. 1st Ed. 4to, orig cloth, in worn & soiled dj; front endpaper discolored. F Mar 28 (381) $110

## Arundell, Francis Vyvyan Jago, 1780-1846
— Discoveries in Asia Minor. L, 1834. 2 vols. 8vo, calf, glit-lettered Head Master's LIbrary; minor wear. With folding map & 10 plates. Map mtd on linen. b May 30 (241) £200

## Asbjornsen, Peter Christen, 1812-85 —& Moe, Jorgen I., 1813-82
— East of the Sun and West of the Moon. L, [1914]. Illus by Kay Nielsen. 4to, orig cloth, in dj with colored illust mtd on upper cover. With 24 mtd colored plates. Ck May 31 (26) £510

Anr copy. Orig cloth, in dj. With 25 colored plates. Plate facing p.88 positioned unevenly. sg Feb 15 (209) $110

Anr Ed. NY: Doran, [1927?]. In dj. With 25 colored plates. Plate facing p.88 positioned unevenly. sg Feb 15 (210) $175

## Ascham, Roger, 1515-68
— The Scholemaster.... L: A. Jeffes, 1589 [colophon dated 1573]. ("The Schoolemaster....") 4to, 19th-cent calf gilt. Black letter. N4 holed with loss; colophon leaf laid down. Ck Sept 8 (162) £550

## Asconius Pedianus, Quintus
— Commentarii in orationes Ciceronis [& other works]. Venice: Johannes de Colonia & Johannes Manthen, after 2 June [1477]. Folio, Bound c.1725 by Thomas Elliott for the Earl of Oxford in gilt-panelled russia; rebacked. 33-36 lines; types 8*:109R (text), De Spira type: 110GK (a few words). Unrubricated. Stained. 184 leaves. Goff A-1154. Doheny copy. S Nov 30 (246) £2,500

## Ash, Charles Bowker
— The Poetical Works. Market-Drayton, 1831. 2 vols. 8vo, modern half calf. b Dec 5 (312) £70

## Ash, Edward Cecil
— Dogs: their History and Development. Bost., [1927]. 2 vols. 4to, orig cloth. Last leaf of Vol I torn.  bba May 30 (428) £110 [R. Edwards]
 Anr copy. Half cloth. Tape-stain at foot of tp in Vol I.  O Jan 9 (22) $275

## Ashbee, Charles Robert
— Modern English Silverwork. L: Essex House Press, 1909. Out-of-series copy. Illus by C. R. Ashbee. 4to, orig cloth. With 100 plates, some hand-colored.  W Nov 8 (1) £520

## Ashby, Thomas Almond
— The Valley Campaigns, being the Reminiscences of a Non-Combatant...during the War of the States. NY, 1914. Minor foxing; pencil markings in margin.  bbc Apr 22 (62) $250

## Ashe, Thomas, 1836-89
— Travels in America.... L, 1809. 8vo, modern cloth; spotted.  sg Oct 26 (6) $100

## Ashendene Press—London
— A Book of Songs and Poems from the Old Testament and the Apocrypha. 1904. One of 150.  sg Oct 19 (11) $950
— A Descriptive Bibliography of the Books... 1935. One of 390.  J. R. Abbey's annotated copy, with Ls to him from C. H. St. J. Hornby.  sg Oct 19 (23) $800; sg Feb 15 (12) $900; sg Apr 18 (18) $1,300
— [Ecclesiasticus] The Wisdom of Jesus, the Son of Sirach... 1932. One of 328. Bernard Berenson's copy.  Met Sept 28 (31) $1,000; sg Oct 19 (21) $850; sg Apr 18 (16) $1,500
— Hymns and Prayers for Use at the Marriage of Michael Hornby and Nicolette Ward. 1928.  sg Sept 14 (42) $110
Apuleius, Lucius. - The Golden Asse. 1924. One of 165.  sg Sept 14 (40) $700
 Anr copy. Inscr to Sydney Cockerell by C. H. St. J. Hornby, 24 Oct 1924.  sg Oct 19 (17) $1,100; sg Apr 18 (13) $500
Berners, Dame Juliana. - A Treatyse of Fysshynge wyth an Angle. 1903. One of 150.  sg Sept 14 (41) $700; sg Oct 19 (9) $600
Cervantes Saavedra, Miguel de. - Don Quixote. 1927-28. One of 225. 2 vols.  sg Oct 19 (19) $1,600; sg Apr 18 (14) $2,200
Dante Alighieri. - La Vita Nuova. 1895. One of 45 on Japanese vellum.  sg Oct 19 (8) $1,000
Francis of Assisi. - I Fioretti... 1922. One of 240.  sg Oct 19 (15) $500
Horace. - Carmina Alcaica. 1903. One of 150. Inscr by Sydney Cockerell to George Bernard Shaw.  bba Nov 16 (218) £440 [Sotheran]
Horace. - Carmina Sapphica. 1903. One of 150.  sg Oct 19 (10) $500
Longus. - Les Amours pastorales de Daphnis et Chloe. 1933. One of 20 on vellum.  P June 5 (160) $9,500
 One of 290.  sg Oct 19 (22) $950; sg Apr 18 (17) $750
Malory, Sir Thomas. - Le Morte Darthur. 1913. One of 145.  sg Oct 19 (13) $2,800
More, Sir Thomas. - Utopia. 1906. ("A Fruteful and Pleasaunt Worke...") One of 100.  sg Oct 19 (12) $500; sg Apr 18 (12) $1,100
Spenser, Edmund. - The Faerie Queene. 1923. One of 180.  sg Oct 19 (16) $1,400
Spenser, Edmund. - Minor Poems. 1925. One of 200.  sg Sept 14 (43) $650; sg Oct 19 (18) $475
Thucydides. - The History of the Peloponnesian War. 1930. One of 20. Saks copy.  S May 16 (61) £10,500
 One of 260.  sg Oct 19 (20) $1,400; sg Apr 18 (15) $1,400
Todhunter, John. - Ye Minutes of ye CLXXVIIth Meeting of Ye Sette of Odd Volumes.... 1896. One of 37 for the ptr.  S Nov 2 (50) £150 [Leichti]
Tolstoy, Leo. - Where God is Love Is. 1924. One of c.200. Trans by Louise & Aylmer Maude.  sg Sept 14 (44) $110
Verino, Ugolino. - Vita di Santa Chiara Vergine. 1921. One of 236.  sg Oct 19 (14) $400; sg Feb 15 (13) $250

## Asher, Georg Michael
— A Bibliographical and Historical Essay on the Dutch Books and Pamphlets Relating to New Netherland.... Amst., 1854-67. 4to, contemp half mor; rubbed. With folding map.  Ck Apr 12 (194) £100

## Ashley, Clifford Warren
— Whaleships of New Bedford. Bost. & NY, 1929. One of 1,000. 4to, cloth. With 60 plates.  sg Mar 7 (201) $120
— The Yankee Whaler. Bost. & NY, 1926. 1st Ed. 4to, half cloth; extremities worn. Some foxing.  sg Mar 7 (11A) $225

**Ashley, William H.** See: Morgan, Dale Lowell

## Ashmole, Elias, 1617-92
— The Institution, Laws & Ceremonies of the most Noble Order of the Garter. L, 1672. 1st Ed. Folio, contemp calf; joints repaired. With title, port, & 31 plates (17 double-page). 1 plate & p. 9 torn; small flaw at p. 271; pp. 269 & 469 torn & repaired. R. B. Honeyman Sr. copy.  S Oct 26 (304) £300 [Marlborough]

## Ashworth, Edmund & Thomas
— A Treatise on the Propagation of Salmon.... Stockport: E. H. King, 1853. Orig bds; rebacked, hinges reinforced. Stamp to folding plate.  pba July 11 (21) $90

## Asimov, Isaac
— The Asimov Chronicles. Arlington Heights: Dark Harvest, 1989. One of 52. Illus by Ron Lindahn & Val Lakey Lindahn. 4to, syn.  O Dec 5 (154) $90
— Foundation. NY: Gnome Press, 1951. In dj. Inscr to Marty Greenberg. Gnome Press file copy.  cb Oct 17 (502) $1,100
 Anr copy. In 2d bdg, in 2d dj; chipping to d/j & short tears. Browned.  pba Aug 22 (14) $75
— The Gods Themselves. Garden City, 1972. In dj with spine ends rubbed.  pba May 4 (100) $60

— I, Robot. NY: Gnome Press, 1950. In dj. cb Oct 17 (503) $650
— Only a Trillion. L & NY, [1957]. In torn & soiled dj. pba May 23 (6) $90
— Pebble in the Sky. Garden City, 1950. In nicked dj with spine head crinkled. sg June 20 (11) $150
 Limited Fortieth Anniversary Ed. NY, [1990]. Printer's copy. pba May 4 (99) $55
— The Rest of the Robots. Garden City, 1964. 1st Ed. In dj with spine ends chipped. pba May 4 (101) $80

**Askew Library, Anthony**
— [Sale Catalogue] Bibliotheca Askeviana.... L, 1775. 8vo, disbound. Priced throughout in a contemp hand. O Mar 26 (10) $140
 Anr Ed. L, [1775]. 8vo, later half calf. Some waterstaining. S Oct 27 (1011) £300 [Mauss]
 Anr copy. Later half calf; spine chipped. Browned; red rule in margins. S Oct 27 (1012) £150 [Maggs]

**Aspin, Jehoshaphat**
— A Picture of the Manners, Customs... Inhabitants of England.... L, 1825. 1st Ed. 12mo, period half calf; hinge cracked, book broken in two. pba Apr 18 (2) $85

**Aspiotis, Marie —& Puaux, Rene**
— Corfou.... Paris, [1930]. One of 570. Illus by Lycidas Logevinas. 4to, wraps. With half title, frontis, litho plate, 7 color plates, 32 illus, & 13 other reproductions. S Oct 26 (38) £800 [Chelsea Rare]

**Asplund, Karl**
— Anders Zorn, his Life and Work. L, 1921. 4to, half vellum gilt; backstrip spotted. sg Sept 7 (357) $90
— Zorn's Engraved Work. Stockholm, 1920. One of 325. 2 vols. 4to, cloth. sg Jan 11 (475) $400

**Asprey**
— Asprey Reference Library. L, [1924]. 8 vols. 8vo, mor by Asprey. CE Nov 8 (171) $320

**Asquith, Lady Cynthia, 1887-1960**
— The Flying Carpet. NY: Scribner's, [1925]. pba Aug 22 (676) $80

**Assemani, Giuseppe Simone**
— Saggio sull' origine culto letteratura e costumi degli arabi avanti il pseudoprofeta Maometto. Padua, 1787. Text in Italian & Arabic 1st Ed. 8vo, contemp bds. Some foxing; p.65 soiled; last leaf stained; lacking prelim pages 3-8. sg Mar 7 (12) $60

**Assize of Bread...**
— The Assize of Bread Together With Sundry Good and Useful Ordinances for Bakers, Brewers, Inholders, Victualers.... L, 1626. 4to, recent half calf. Some old stains to edges; F3r soiled. Ck Mar 22 (20) £1,000

**Aste, T.**
— The Pier and Bay or Douglas; or, Forget Me Not.... Douglas, 1825. 12mo, orig wraps with cloth spine. b Dec 5 (138) £160

**Astell, Mary, 1668-1731**
— An Essay in Defence of the Female Sex.... L, 1696. 8vo, contemp calf; worn. Tear on tp touching a letter. CE May 22 (36) $500

**Astesanus de Ast**
— Summa de casibus conscientiae. [Strasbourg: Johann Mentelin, not after 1469]. Folio, contemp pigskin over wooden bds, sides painted; rebacked. 60 lines, double column, gothic letter, 4 initials in green & pink on panels; rubricated. Some worming at ends; repaired tears with small loss in fols. 1, 58 & 159. 233 (of 443) leaves only. Goff A-1160. S June 27 (293) £2,500
 Anr Ed. Venice: Johannes de Colonia & Johannes Manthen, 18 Mar 1478. Folio, contemp oak bds; rebacked in calf. 54 lines & headline; double column; types 10:160G2, 11c:76G. Initials & paragraph marks in red. Stain in text of M10-Y5 & in upper margin at ends; worming to margins at ends. 587 (of 589) leaves; lacking 2 blanks. Goff A-1165. S June 27 (294) £2,200
— Textus canonum penitentionalium. [Nuremberg: Peter Wagner, c.1495]. 4to, 19th-cent vellum. 33 lines; gothic letter. Marginal repairs. 8 leaves. Goff A-1158. S Mar 28 (466) £320

**Astle, Thomas, 1735-1803**
— The Origin and Progress of Writing. L, 1803. 2d Ed. 4to, contemp calf; worn, needs rebdg. Some foxing. sg Dec 7 (190) $100

**Astor, John Jacob**
— A Journey in Other Worlds. NY, 1894. Orig cloth; extremities worn. Z June 28 (9) $120

**Astronomica...**
— Astronomica veterum scripta isagogica Graeca & Latina. [Heidelberg], 1589. 8vo, contemp calf; lacking endleaves, spine repaired. Tp cut round & mtd; old Greek Ms notes; Radcliffe Observatory stamps; dampstain at top. pba June 20 (36) $250

**Astruc, Jean, 1684-1766**
— L'Art d'accoucher reduit a ses principes.... Paris, 1766. 1st Ed. 12mo, contemp sheep gilt; spine top chipped. sg May 16 (364) $375

**Atget, Eugene**
— Atget: Photographe de Paris. Paris, 1930. 4to, cloth; bowed & worn. Frontis with 1-inch tear. sg Feb 29 (18) $250
— A Vision of Paris. NY, 1963. Text by Marcel Proust. 4to, cloth; front cover dampstained, marginal stains on front pastedown & free endpaper. sg Feb 29 (21) $90

**Atherton, Faxon Dean**
— The California Diary of Faxon Dean Atherton, 1836-1839. San Francisco: CA Historical Society, 1964. One of 325. Ed by Doyce B. Nunis. Orig cloth. With frontis port, folded map, 5 folded facsimiles, & 9 illus. Larson copy. pba Sept 28 (39) $140

## Atherton, Gertrude
— The Splendid Idle Forties. NY, 1902. Illus by Harrison Fisher. Orig cloth; spine ends & corners rubbed. Hole at foot of tp from erasure. pba July 25 (90) $85

1st Ed. Orig cloth; shelf worn. With 8 plates. Robbins copy. pba Mar 21 (5) $180

Anr Ed. Kentfield: Allen Press, 1960. One of 150. Folio, cloth. pba June 20 (10) $170

## Athias, Isaac
— Tesoro de preceptos a donde se encierran las joyas de los seys cientos y treze preceptos.... Venice: Giovanni Caleoni, 1627. 4to, modern lea. Tp & final 2 leaves with fore-margins worn & reinforced with cellotape; gutter margin of tp pasted close along new flyleaf; some gatherings with wormtracks affecting text near inner margins; some worming, staining & soiling; leaves R1-R2 in duplicate. CE Dec 6 (195) $3,200

Anr Ed. Amst., [1649]. 4to, contemp calf over wooden bds; joint cracked, lacking clasps, new endpapers. Wormholes in gutter margin penetrating text block & affecting a few letters; lower corner on Ii3 chipped affecting shoulder note; some staining & browning. CE Dec 6 (196) $950

## Atkins, Anna
— Photographs of British Algae. Halstead Pace near Sevenoaks, [1843-53]. 3 vols. 4to, contemp mor; 1 bd detached. With 424 cyanotypes (general title, 3 sub-titles, decation leaf, intro leaf, 7 leaves of Contents & 411 images of algae). Bliss - Eton College copy. b June 28 (5) £120,000

## Atkins, Henry Martin
— Ascent to the Summit of Mont Blanc.... L, 1838. 8vo, orig cloth. With 8 litho plates. Some waterstaining. Inscr but name of recipient erased. bba Nov 1 (565) £400 [Gonzalez]

## Atkins, John, 1685-1757
— A Voyage to Guinea, Brasil, and the West-Indies.... L, 1737. 8vo, contemp calf; spine restored. Some staining & soiling; wormed in outer margins towards end. S Mar 28 (324) £180

## Atkinson, George Francklin
— "Curry & Rice" on Forty Plates.... L, [1859]. 4to, contemp half mor gilt; extremities scuffed. With 40 chromolitho plates, including title. sg Mar 7 (13) $325

## Atkinson, John Augustus, 1775-1831 —& Walker, James, 1748-1808
— A Picturesque Representation of the Manners...of the Russians. L, 1803-4. 3 vols in 1. Folio, recent half mor. With port & 100 hand-colored plates. Staining to Vol II Plate 5; library stamp on each plate. S Nov 30 (94) £700

## Atkinson, Thomas Witlam, 1799-1861
— Oriental and Western Siberia. L, 1858. 8vo, orig cloth. Tear to map; stamp on tp. sg Mar 7 (14) $90

1st American Ed. NY, 1858. 8vo, orig cloth; spine ends frayed. sg Mar 7 (268) $140

## Atkyns, Arabella, Pseud.
— The Family Magazine. L, 1741. 2 parts in 1 vol. 8vo, contemp calf; rubbed, upper cover def. b Sept 20 (121) £320

## Atkyns, Sir Robert, 1647-1711
— The Ancient and Present State of Glostershire. L, 1712. 1st Ed. Bound in 2 vols. Folio, later calf; rubbed. With frontis, port, map & 72 plates. S Mar 28 (31) £3,400

Anr copy. Folio, 19th-cent russia gilt; rebacked retaining backstrip, spine chipped, front cover detached. With frontis, port, map & 72 plates. Early marginalia; port foxed & repaired. sg Apr 18 (19) $4,600

2d Ed. L, 1768. Folio, cloth. With 8 plates of arms, double-page map & 64 double-page plates. Library stamps to text only; frontis from anr work mtd at beginning; some soiling. bba Nov 1 (80) £2,800

Anr copy. Contemp russia; rebacked, corners rubbed. With folding map & 64 plates & 8 plates of arms. Folding map repaired with loss to margin; other repairs, with loss to plate at p. 448 & index leaves. S June 27 (85) £3,800

## Atl, Doctor, Pseud.
— El Paisaje. Mexico, 1933. Oblong 4to, loose as issued in cloth with text booklet laid in. Inscr to Witter Bynner. sg Jan 11 (32) $90

## Atlas
See also: Neptune...
— Adolf Stieler's Handatlas.... Gotha: Justus Perthes, [1882]. Folio, half mor; spine lacking, broken. With 94 double-page hand-colored maps. wa Feb 29 (598) $375

— The American Military Pocket Atlas. L, [1776]. 8vo, later calf; extremities worn, spine ends worn away, front cover detached. With 6 folding maps, outlined in color by a contemp hand. Perforated library stamp to tp; ink stamp to anr leaf. cb Oct 17 (160) $7,000

— Asher & Adams' New Commercial, Statistical and Topographical Atlas.... NY, [1872]. 2 vols. Folio, orig half sheep; worn, loose. Some dampstaining & soiling. Sold w.a.f. sg Dec 7 (1) $900

— Atlas des anciens plans de Paris.... Paris, 1880. Vol I (of 2). Folio, loose in contemp half mor; rubbed. With 20 (of 23?) plans on 32 sheets. Last 2 sheets spotted. S Oct 26 (258) £280 [Orssich]

— An Atlas of the United States of North America, Corrected to the Present Period.... L & Phila., 1832. 4to, orig bds; def, covers loose. With 17 hand-colored maps (1 folding). Lacking title & prelims; text & maps loose. S Oct 26 (472) £440 [Map House]

— Atlas to Accompany the Official Records of the Union and Confederate Armies. Wash., 1891-95. Parts

1-35 plus index. Folio, loose as issued in orig ptd wraps; chipped, stained, worn, some lacking. With 178 double-page color & chromolitho plates. bbc Apr 22 (156) $700

— Atlas to Adam's Geography. Bost., 1832. 12mo, pictorial wraps; spine reinforced with cloth. With 11 maps hand-colored in outline. wa Feb 29 (599) $170

— Bradley's Atlas of the World. NY, 1891. Folio, old half sheep; spine lacking, covers worn & detached. With 62 double-page & 13 full-page hand-colored maps. bbc Feb 26 (11) $180

— The California Water Atlas. Sacramento, 1979. Folio, cloth. pba Apr 25 (488) $95

— Colton's Atlas of the World. NY, 1856. Vol II only. Orig half sheep; worn, spine lacking, loose. With frontis & 43 hand-colored maps, some double-page. Some chipping. bbc Feb 26 (13) $400

— Colton's General Atlas.... NY, 1858. Folio, half mor; worn & def, upper cover detached. With frontis & 96 hand-colored maps. Some spotting & discoloration; some pp. loose. S Oct 26 (425) £750 [Smith]

— Colton's Illustrated Cabinet Atlas and Descriptive Geography. NY, 1859. Folio, orig half mor; extremities worn. sg Dec 7 (15) $950

— The Consular Atlas. L: Letts & Son, 1883. Folio, half mor; extremities worn. With 80 color map sheets. sg Dec 7 (26) $275

— Cornell's Companion Atlas to Cornell's High School Geography. NY, 1870. Folio, orig pictorial bds; worn & soiled. With 27 maps, 25 of them hand-colored. Tp chipped at top. pba July 25 (378) $60

— Cram's Modern Atlas.... Atlanta, [1901]. Folio, orig cloth; worn, hinges weak. Some foxing. wa Feb 29 (600) $210

— Cram's Unrivaled Family Atlas of the World. Chicago, [1883]. Folio, orig cloth; worn, becoming disbound. Some soiling & tears. wa Feb 29 (601) $110

— Erster Typometrischer Atlas, oder Austria.... Vienna, 1843. Folio, orig half cloth; worn. With tp & 15 chromolitho maps. pba Oct 9 (29) $350

— Fisher's County Atlas of England and Wales. L & Manchester, [1842-45]. 4to, modern half mor; rubbed. With 48 maps. S Oct 26 (372) £460 [Baskes]

— Il Gazzettiere Americano contenente un distinto regguaglio di tutte le parti del Nuovo Mondo.... Livorno, 1763. 3 vols. 4to, orig bds; lacking backstrips, need resewing, soiled. With 39 maps & plans & 39 plates. Some dampstaining, mainly in margins; occasional wormholes repaired; repair to verso of 1 folding map. wa Feb 29 (381) $2,800

— A General Atlas. Phila.: Warner & Carey, 1818. 4to, contemp half sheep; extremities worn. With 52 maps, some folding. Some browning & foxing. sg May 9 (104) $900

— Johnson's New Illustrated Family Atlas. NY, 1861. Folio, disbound. With 62 hand-colored maps, 28 of them double-page. Dampstaining to margins, map of Europe & some text leaves; map of Ohio & Indiana torn at centerfold. wa Feb 29 (602) $800

Anr Ed. NY, 1866. Folio, orig cloth; worn, corner broken. With 105 plates. Dampstain affecting top edge. Met Sept 28 (337) $500

Anr copy. Orig mor; def. Some chips & edge-tears. sg May 9 (74) $1,200

Anr copy. Half mor; scuffed. With engraved title, 40 double-page & 21 single-page color maps. Dampstained at bottom edge throughout; 1 map separated. wa Feb 29 (603) $500

Anr Ed. NY, 1867. Folio, half sheep; spine lacking with upper cover detached. With 26 full-page & 34 double-page hand-colored maps. Some chipping; a few text leaves torn. bbc Feb 26 (16) $675

Anr Ed. NY, 1868. Folio, orig cloth. Foxed & browned; emblem plate def. Sold w.a.f. Met Sept 28 (338) $400

Anr Ed. NY: Johnson & Ward, 1874. Folio, orig half sheep; needs rebdg. Some leaves at beginning chipped. sg May 9 (75) $1,200

— Johnson's New Illustrated (Steel Plate) Family Atlas. NY, 1862. Folio, orig half mor gilt; soiled & worn, spine ends worn away, joints starting, hinges cracked. With engraved title & 59 colored plates. Some soiling & staining; lacking 4 maps. cb Feb 14 (2572) $850

Anr copy. Orig half mor; extremities worn. With 98 hand-colored maps. Some dampstaining to text at beginning. sg Dec 7 (22) $1,200

Anr copy. Remains of half mor bdg. With engraved title, 40 full-page & 26 double-page colored maps. Some foxing; a few closed tears at margins; long split at center of Ohio-Indiana. wa Feb 29 (604) $800

Anr copy. Half mor; shabby & taped, becoming disbound. With engraved title, color time diagram & 62 colored maps, 32 of them double-page. Some soiling & smudging, occasionally affecting images; 1 map detached & in tatters. wa Feb 29 (605) $450

Anr Ed. NY, 1863. Folio, orig half sheep; needs rebdg. Some leaves chipped. sg May 9 (76) $950

Anr Ed. NY, 1864. Folio, orig half mor; extremities worn, hinges cracked. Lacking 2 double-page maps. sg Dec 7 (23) $1,600

Anr copy. Disbound. With 38 double-page & 23 full-page maps. Browned; dampstained at bottom edge; Pennsylvania-New Jersey halved with loss. wa Feb 29 (606) $550

— Memorial Atlas of Ireland.... Phila., 1901. Folio, half calf; edges scuffed. With 33 doublepage hand-colored maps. bbc Feb 26 (18) $400

— Mitchell's New General Atlas. Phila., 1864. Folio, half calf; worn, joints weak. With 85 hand-colored maps on 50 sheets. 1st pp. becoming loose, frayed; world map creased; some staining. S Oct 26 (439) £900 [Smith]

Anr Ed. Phila., 1867. Folio, orig half lea; rubbed. With 47 full-page & 5 double-page hand-colored maps. Some foxing. NH June 1 (50) $875

— Mitchell's New Universal Atlas. Phila., 1863. ("Mitchell's New General Atlas.") Folio, orig half mor; extremities rubbed, soiled. With maps numbered 1-84, hand-colored. sg Dec 7 (31) $1,200

Anr Ed. Phila., 1869. Folio, half lea; worn, spine fragmented, loose. With 99 hand-colored maps. Corner lacking on Plate 5; Plates 27 & 28 chipped. Met May 22 (294) $675

Anr Ed. Phila., 1871. Folio, orig half lea; needs rebdg. With 47 full-page & 9 double-page hand-colored maps. New York loose with tears into text; marginal stains. Sold w.a.f. bbc Feb 26 (21) $400

Anr Ed. Phila., 1874. Folio, orig half lea; spine & corners rubbed. With hand-colored maps throughout. pba Nov 16 (289) $850

Anr Ed. Phila., 1885. Folio, half sheep gilt; worn, upper cover detached, tp loose. With 43 full-page & 29 double-page hand-colored maps. Contents leaf with insect damage. bbc Feb 26 (19) $550

— The National Atlas; Containing Elaborate Topographical Maps of the United States and the Dominion of Canada.... Phila., 1883. Folio, half lea; worn & rubbed, covers detached. K June 23 (50) $500

— Neues Kriegs-Theater oder Sammlung der Merkwuerdigsten Begebenheiten des gegenwaertigen Krieges in Teutschland. Leipzig, 1757-[62]. Oblong 4to, contemp bds; worn. With engraved title & 80 town & battle-plans, several hand-colored. Marginal dampstaining. sg Dec 7 (298) $1,100

— Nieuwe Atlas, van de Voornaamste gebouwen en gezigten der stad Amsterdam. Amst.: Maaskamp, [c.1800]. Folio, contemp bds; worn, needs rebacking. With double-page city plan & 101 (of 102) views, 3 of them folding, the rest double-page. Plates foxed towards beginning; dampstained in lower margins in 2d half of vol. sg May 9 (275) $2,600

— The Official Atlas of the Civil War. NY: Thomas Yoseloff, [1958]. Intro by Henry Steele Commager. Folio, cloth; worn & frayed, stained. pba June 13 (259) $60

— Pigot's & Co.'s British Atlas. L, [1840]. Folio, modern half calf. With 4 folding general maps & 40 county maps, hand-colored. Folding maps linen-backed; Hampshire repaired & restored. S Nov 30 (60) £800

— Rand, McNally & Co's Indexed Atlas of the World.... Chicago, 1883. Folio, half lea; rubbed & broken. NH July 21 (25) $325

— Rand, McNally & Co's New Indexed Business Atlas.... Chicago, 1881. Folio, half cloth. With numerous maps with highlights ptd in colors; 6 large folding color maps ptd on onion skin paper & inserted on stubs. bbc Feb 26 (23) $350

— The Republican Advocate's Universal Atlas of the World. Willsborough, 1900. Folio, cloth; extremities worn, hinges cracked. sg Dec 7 (42) $100

— The Royal Illustrated Atlas. L, [1862]. Folio, contemp half mor; worn, upper hinge broken. With engraved title & 25 double-page maps & plans, hand-colored. A few maps split; some fraying & discoloration. S Mar 28 (175) £620

— The Royal Illustrated Atlas of Modern Geography. L & Edin., [1864]. Folio, disbound. With 74 hand-colored maps. Some soiling; some text damaged. S Oct 26 (429) £700 [Map House]

— School Atlas: Cummings' Ancient & Modern Geography. Bost., 1817. Orig wraps. With 8 double-page maps, hand-colored in outline. pba Oct 9 (31) $100

— The Sea-Coasts of France from Calais to Bayonne. L: for W. Mount & T. Page, [1715]. Folio, half calf; worn. With engraved title & 15 double-page or folding charts. S June 13 (555) £450

— Smith's Atlas Designed to Accompany the Georgaphy, by R. C. Smith. Hartford: John Paine, [1839]. 4to, ptd wraps; worn & soiled. With 17 colored maps. Library markings, but maps unstamped. O Nov 14 (167) $800

**Attaway, William**
— Let Me Breathe Thunder. NY, [1939]. 1st Ed. In dj split along rear joint, taped & chipped. pba May 23 (7) $75

**Attic...**
— The Attic Miscellany; or, Characteristic Mirror of Men and Things.... L, 1789-91. Vols I-III in 2 vols. 8vo, 19th-cent calf gilt by W. Pratt. With 49 plates, 24 of them folding. Some soiling. S Mar 28 (581) £380

**Atwater, Caleb**
— Writings. Columbus, 1833. 8vo, contemp calf; worn. With 10 plates. Some foxing. wa Feb 29 (312) $80

**Aubert Dupetit-Thouars, Abel, 1758-1831**
— Voyage autour du monde sur la Fregate la Venus.... Paris, 1840-46. 10 vols of text plus 4 vols Atlas bound in 3; lacking text of Botanique. 8vo & folio, half mor. All plates present plus 2 extra mollusques plates; 2 plates torn & repaired without loss; minor spotting; 4 orig watercolor costume subjects tipped in at beginning of Atlas pittoresque. S June 27 (267) £13,000

**Aubier, Dominique**
— Seville en fete. Paris: Robert Delpire, [1954]. Illus by Brassai. 4to, cloth, in chipped dj. bbc Apr 22 (203) $250

**Aubigne, Theodore Agrippa d'**
— L'Histoire universelle. Maille: Jean Moussat, 1616-20. 3 parts in 2 vols. Folio, contemp calf, with arms of Nicolas le Provost du Parc; worn, joints weak. S Mar 28 (467) £600

**Aubrun, Marie Madeleine**
— Henri Lehmann.... Nantes, [1984]. One of 300. 2 vols. Folio, cloth. sg Sept 7 (214) $120

**Aucassin & Nicolette**
— Aucassin & Nicolette, a Love Story.... L: Kegan Paul, 1887. 8vo, orig cloth; upper hinge cracked. Aubrey Beardsley's copy, sgd on front free endpaper. CE Feb 21 (6) $240

**Auctoritates Aristotelis**
— Auctoritates Aristotelis et aliorum philosophorum. [Cologne: Cornelis de Zierikzee, c.1499]. 4to, half sheep; worn. Gothic types; rubricated. Piece torn

from upper margin of tp. 58 leaves. Goff A-1197. P May 5 (16) $1,400
— Auctoritates Aristotelis, Senece. Boetij Platonis. Apulei.... [Cologne: sons of Heinrich Quentell], 24 Dec 1503. 4to, recent mor. Gothic types. Reprint of Quentell's 1498 Ed. P Dec 12 (5) $850

**Auden, Wystan Hugh, 1907-73**
— About the House. NY, [1965]. In dj. Sgd & with 15 holograph corrections; ALs to Mr Corfield, Ns of authorization to B. C. Bloomfield & photograph inserted. Hobson copy. S June 28 (21) £850
[-] The Badger. Colwall, 1934-37. Nos II,4; III,5; III,6; V,10. Folio, orig wraps. Hobson copies. S June 28 (10) £480
— But I Can't. Cambr. MA: Ptd for Svatava Pirkova Jakobson by Laurence Scott, Mar 1966. One of 10. Illus by Laurence Scott. Unbound as issued. Hobson copy. S June 28 (25) £320
— The Dance of Death. L, 1933. Orig bds, in chipped & soiled dj. F June 20 (468) $50
— Epithalamion Commemorating the Marriage of Giuseppe Antonio Borgese and Elisabeth Mann at Princeton, New Jersey November 23, 1939. NY, [1939]. Folio, unbound. Hobson copy. S June 28 (17) £1,800
— Look, Stranger! L, 1936. 8vo, orig cloth, in chipped & soiled dj; bdg worn & soiled. F June 20 (467) $50
— On This Island. NY: Random House, [1937]. Sgd by Joseph Blumenthal. Harold J. Corbin's copy. sg June 20 (12) $200
— The Orators, an English Study. L, 1932. 1st Ed. In dj with small tears. John Hayward's copy, with holograph corrections by Auden. Hobson copy. S June 28 (6) £550
— Our Hunting Fathers. L: Pvtly ptd, 1935. 1st Ed, one of 5 on Normandie. 76mm by 52mm, orig wraps. Hobson copy. S June 28 (12) £380
— Poem. [N.p.]: ptd for Frederic Prokosch, 1933. One of 5 on Fabriano. Orig wraps. Inscr by T. S. Eliot. Hayward - Hobson copy. With ALs from Auden to Eliot, 5 Feb 1934. S June 28 (8) £4,000
— Poems. L: Stephen Spender, 1928. 1st Ed, one of c.45. 16mo, orig wraps. Inscr 3 times & with c.25 holograph corrections. Hayward - Hobson copy. S June 28 (4) £9,500
1st Trade Ed. L, 1930. 4to, orig wraps; rebacked with orig backstrip laid down. Some soiling. CE Sept 27 (45) $160
Anr copy. Orig wraps. Hobson copy. S June 28 (5) £380
Anr Ed. NY: Random House, [1934]. In worn & chipped dj. sg June 20 (13) $100
Anr Ed. NY, 1937. Library markings. sg Sept 28 (20) $150
— River Profile. Cambr. MA, 1967. One of 50. Illus by Laurence Scott. Unbound as issued. Hobson copy. S June 28 (26) £100
— Sonnet. L: Pvtly ptd, 1935. one of 5 on Normandie. 76mm by 57mm, orig wraps. Hobson copy. S June 28 (13) £350

— Three Songs for St. Cecilia's Day. [NY]: Pvtly Ptd, 1941. One of 250. Orig wraps. Inscr by Caroline Newton to Mabel Zahn & by Mabel Zahn to Anthony Hobson. S June 28 (18) £250
— Two Poems. [N.p.]: ptd for Frederic Prokosch, 1934. Proof copy, sgd by Auden & initialed by Prokosch. 16mo, orig wraps. Hobson copy. S June 28 (11) £420

**Audsley, George Ashdown, 1838-1925**
— The Art of Chromolithography. L, 1883. Folio, orig cloth; loose. Some foxing. cb June 25 (1916) $700
Anr copy. Cloth; worn & broken. With 44 color plates. Some soiling & smudging. wa Nov 16 (289) $75
— Guide to the Art of Illuminating on Vellum. L, 1911. 3d Ed. Cloth. With 16 plates, including chromolitho frontis. pba Aug 8 (306) $55
— The Ornamental Arts of Japan. L, 1882-[85]. 2 vols in 4 parts. 4to, loose as issued in half cloth portfolios; worn, separated at spine panels. Soiled & brittle with marginal tears & chipping; plates for Section 4 trimmed & stapled to bds with text on verso; Section 5 with text stapled at top edge to verso of plates. Sold w.a.f. wa Dec 14 (529) $130

**Audsley, George Ashdown, 1838-1925 —& Bowes, James Lord, 1834-99**
— Keramic Art of Japan. L, 1881. 4to, modern cloth, orig front cover & backstrip laid down. sg June 13 (85) $80

**Audubon, John James, 1785-1851**
— The Birds of America. NY & Phila., 1840-44. 1st 8vo Ed. Orig parts 1-5 only (of 100). Orig wraps; spines perished, 1 front cover detached, some wear. With 19 hand-colored plates. Text & guards foxed; minor foxing to plates. cb Feb 14 (2609) $3,000
Anr copy. 7 vols. Mor by Sangorski & Sutcliffe. Text & plates cleaned but many plates still foxed & a few with dampstains; Plates 296, 310, 341, 363, 442 & 465 cropped; lacking half-titles; Vols III-IV & VI-VII lacking subscribers' lists. CNY May 17 (49) $19,000
Anr Ed. NY, 1856-57. 7 vols. 8vo, half lea; hinges cracked, bumped. With 500 hand-colored plates. Some leaves torn; browned; dampstained. Met Sept 28 (391) $17,000
Anr Ed. NY, 1859-60. 7 vols. 8vo, orig mor; minor wear, corners bumped, split to spine head of Vol VI. With 500 hand-colored plates. Minor spotting. cb Oct 17 (120) $15,000
2d Folio Ed. NY, 1860. Atlas of plates only. With 99 (of 105) sheets of chromolitho plates. Library stamps & penciled call-numbers in margins of most plates; marginal tears repaired; some soiling & browning; a few plates linen-backed; a few plates with tears & closed tears into image. P Dec 12 (192) $50,000
Anr Ed. NY, [1870-71]. 8 vols. 8vo, contemp half mor; extremities worn, some bds detached. With 100 hand-colored plates. cb Oct 17 (144) $1,900

## AUDUBON

Anr Ed. NY & Amst., 1971-72. One of 250. Folio, orig half calf gilt. With 435 colored plates. CNY Dec 15 (3) $13,000

Anr copy. Loose in paper portfolios in 6 wooden flat files. P Dec 12 (193) $14,000

— Birds of America. NY: Abbeville Press, [1981]. Folio, lea gilt. Sgd by R. T. & V. M. Peterson. sg May 16 (284) $140

— The Birds of America: A Selection of Plates. L: Ariel Press, 1973. One of 750. Vol II (of 2). Folio, orig half cloth. S Oct 27 (687) £620 [Fonseca]

— Journal Made While Obtaining Subscriptions...1840-1843. Bost., 1929. One of 225. pba Aug 8 (7) $50

— The Original Water-Colour Paintings by John James Audubon for the Birds of America. NY & L, 1966. 2 vols. 4to, cloth. b Sept 20 (456) £80

— A Synopsis of the Birds of North America. Edin., 1839. 1st Ed. 8vo, orig cloth; rebacked. sg Oct 26 (7) $90

**Audubon, John James, 1785-1851 —& Bachman, John, 1790-1874**

— The Viviparous Quadrupeds of North America. NY, 1845-48. 1st Ed. The 3 plate vols only. Folio, half cloth; library markings on spine & endpapers, Vol III with inner hinge split & some plates shaken. With 150 hand-colored plates. Some soiling; marginal tears; Plate V with 2-inch glassine tape repair, Plate VI with 1-inch glassine tape repair; Plate XI with marginal tear into image; a few plates with faint discoloration. P Dec 12 (194) $125,000

Anr Ed. NY, 1849-51-54. ("The Quadrupeds of North America.") 3 vols. 8vo, half calf; extremities worn, Vol II starting.. With 155 hand-colored plates. Some foxing & staining; a few plates shaved, affecting captions. P June 5 (11) $6,000

Anr copy. Modern half calf gilt; Vol I slightly taller. Some chipping; Plates 7 & 8 with marginal repairs; half-title in Vol III only; stamp removed from tp of Vol I. S June 27 (4) £2,600

1st 8vo Ed. 3 vols. Contemp half mor; rubbed. With 155 colored plates. Some browning & foxing. cb Feb 14 (2610) $4,750

Anr copy. Half lea; worn. With 155 colored plates. T. M. Brewer's copy. Met May 22 (411) $6,600

Anr Ed. NY, 1851-51-54. 3 vols. 8vo, lea gilt, orig wraps bound in. With 155 hand-colored plates. Met Sept 28 (392) $8,000

Anr Ed. NY, 1852-51-54. 3 vols. 8vo, 19th-cent mor gilt; worn, Vol II loose, spine & upper cover of Vol III detached but present. With 154 (of 155) colored plates. Lacking Yellow-Cheeked Meadow Mouse. P June 5 (12) $3,750

**Audubon, John Woodhouse, 1819-62**

— The Drawings of John Woodhouse Audubon Illustrating his Adventures Through Mexico.... San Francisco: Book Club of California, 1957. One of 400. pba June 20 (37) $120

— The Drawings of John Woodhouse Audubon Illustrating his Adventures through Mexico.... San Francisco: Book Club of California, 1957. One of 400. Ed by Carl S. Dentzel. Half bds. With 34 plates. Larson copy. pba Sept 28 (300) $180

— Western Journal, 1849-50. Cleveland, 1906. 1st Ed. Orig cloth; front cover edge bumped. With 6 illus & folded map. Larson copy. pba Sept 28 (299) $120

**Auel, Jean**

— The Clan of the Cave Bear. NY, 1980. In dj with wear to spine ends. Sgd on pbr's label mtd to half-title. pba May 23 (8) $55

**Augustine, Saint, 354-430**
See also: Limited Editions Club

— Confessiones. Milan: Johannes Bonus, 21 July 1475. 4to, 19th-cent half calf. 26 lines; type 1:105R; initials in red. Some staining at beginning. 164 leaves. Goff A-1251. S Dec 18 (11) £4,800 [Quaritch]

Anr Ed. [Cologne: Bartholomaeus de Unkel], 9 Aug 1482. 4to, modern mor gilt. Writing on blank recto of 1st leaf washed with resulting staining; some penwork decoration cropped. 177 (of 178) leaves; lacking final blank. Goff A-1252. S June 27 (295) £1,900

— De civitate Dei. Venice: Nicolaus Jenson, 2 Oct 1475. Folio, 19th-cent half lea; stamp removed from front cover. 46 lines & headlines; double column; types 4:84G & 4:110R. Illuminated by the Master of the Rimini Ovid, with 11-line initial opening the text, forming part of architectural border with armorial of the Lampugnani family. Some spotting. 304 (of 306) leaves; lacking 2 blanks. Goff A-1235. C Apr 3 (28) £9,000

Anr Ed. Venice: Bonetus Locatellus for Octavianus Scotus, 18 Feb 1489. Folio, modern vellum. 51 lines of text & 65 lines of commentary; types 4:92G (text), 1:74G (commentary), 2:130G (titles & headlines); double column. Some dampstaining; all but 1 of missing leaves supplied in photo-facsimile. 255 (of 264) leaves; lacking A gathering & B1. Goff A-1245. S Dec 18 (12) £450 [Norlis]

— De la cita di Dio. [Venice: Antonio di Bartolommeo, not after 1483]. Folio, later vellum; repaired. Tape repair to 1 leaf; some staining; last 6 leaves with small portions of text in handwritten facsimile. 322 (of 324) leaves; lacking blanks. Goff A-1248. cb June 25 (1758) $1,400

— De la Cite de Dieu. Abbeville: Pierre Gerard & Jean du Pre, 1486-87. 2 vols. Folio, 19th-cent calf. 47 lines & headline; double column; type 1:109B. With 23 woodcuts. Marginal repairs to 2 leaves; some marginal waterstaining. 339 (of 340) leaves in Vol I; lacking blank a1. 327 (of 330) leaves in Vol II; lacking g3 & 2 blanks. Goff A-1247. Schaefer copy. P Nov 1 (12) $40,000

— Enchiridion de fide, spe et caritate. [Cologne: Ulrich Zel, c.1467]. Lacking final blank. Bound with: Sermo super orationem dominicam.... [Cologne: Ulrich Zel, c.1470] Lacking initial blank. And: De vita christiana.... Cologne: Ulrich Zel, 1467. Lacking 4 leaves. And: Alphabetum divini amoris. [Cologne: Ulrich Zel, c.1466-67]. 4to, contemp calf over wooden bds with remains of 2 clasps, front flyleaf with contemp contents list; rebacked in calf, endpapers renewed. Goff A-1265, A-1303, A-1355, A-525. C June 26 (150) £18,000

— Of the Citie of God.... L, 1620. 2d Ed in English. Folio, old calf; rebacked, orig spine retained. Tp torn & chipped & repaired; some leaves missing marginal pieces; 2 leaves at end repaired; some creases & chips. bbc June 24 (209) $475

— Opuscula. Parma: Angelus Ugoletus, 31 Mar 1491. ("De academicis.") Folio, 19th-cent half vellum. 41 lines & headline; roman letter. Stained at top throughout; last gathering wormed in outer margins. 305 (of 306) leaves; lacking last blank. Goff A-1220. S Dec 18 (13) £750 [Zioni]

— Sermones. Basel: Johann Amerbach, 1494. Parts 1-5 (of 7). Folio, contemp calf over wooden bds by the Octagonal Rose Binder. Headline & 52 lines; types 1b:180G, 5:106(88)G, 13:124G, 14:285G, 17:87R, 19:62; 24:75R, 87G. Full-page woodcut touched with red, 2 7-line initials. Writing partially deleted from title; dampstaining at fore-edge, repaired in 1st few leaves; last leaf torn & repaired with some loss. 304 leaves. Goff A-1308. C Nov 29 (25) £2,200

— Sermones ad heremitas. Brescia: Jacobum Britannicum, 5 Jan 1486. 8vo, 19th-cent half calf. 26 lines; roman letter. Short tear at head of a3 with minor loss; repair in final leaf with letters supplied in Ms on verso; some staining at ends. 171 (of 172) leaves; lacking a1, b1; r gathering & x10. Goff A-1313. S Dec 18 (14) £360 [de Palol]

**Augustinus, Pseudo-**

— Dieci gradi al perfezione. Florence, 20 June 1489. 4to, modern calf. 26 lines; type 1:110R. 48 leaves. Goff A-1328. Landau copy. C June 26 (36) £1,600

**Auldjo, John, d.1857**

— Narrative of an Ascent to the Summit of Mont Blanc. L, 1828. 4to, contemp blind-stamped calf; rebacked, rubbed. L.p. copy. bba Nov 1 (522) £600 [Gonzalez]

Anr copy. Orig bds; worn & broken, backstrip def. With 2 maps, folding panorama, folding table & 18 plastes, some on India paper; table & 1 plate hand-colored, 1 map hand-colored in outline & frayed. L.p. copy. bba Nov 1 (566) £300 [Astill]

— Sketches of Vesuvius.... L, 1833. 8vo, orig cloth; backstrip repaired. With folding hand-colored map & 16 plates. Foxing on some plates. sg May 16 (115) $250

**Aurora...**

— Aurora Australis. Bluntisham: Paradigm, 1986. One of 375. Ed by Ernest Shackleton; illus by George Marston. 4to, orig wraps. With pamphlet containing intro by John Millard. Facsimile reprint. pba July 25 (12) $250

**Ausonius, Decimus Magnus**

— Opuscula varia. Lyons: Sebastian Gryphius, 1540. 8vo, contemp pigskin, elaborately blindstamped; def at foot, pastedowns parting. Browned; bottom margin of tp def. wd May 8 (35) $150

**Austen, Jane, 1775-1817**

See also: Limited Editions Club

— Emma. L, 1816. 1st Ed. 3 vols. 8vo, modern mor gilt by Wood. Half-titles in facsimile; Vol I lacking blank at end; Vol III tp tipped in. P June 5 (162) $3,750

— Mansfield Park. L, 1814. 1st Ed. 3 vols. 12mo, later half calf; rubbed. Lacking half-titles, final blank in Vol II & final ad leaf in Vol III; some spotting; 1 marginal def. bba May 30 (146) £3,400 [Pickering & Chatto]

Anr copy. Modern half calf gilt. Lacking half-titles. CE Sept 27 (46) $2,200

Anr copy. Modern mor gilt by Wood. Half-titles in facsimile or from other copies; Vol II lacking blank at end; Vol III lacking ad leaf at end; marginal tears repaired. P June 5 (161) $3,500

Anr copy. Contemp calf; joints cracked. Lacking half-titles, final blank in Vol II & final ad leaf in Vol III; some foxing. sg Feb 8 (164) $1,900

— Northanger Abbey and Persuasion. L, 1818. 1st Ed. 4 vols. 12mo, modern mor gilt by Wood. Lacking half-title in Vol II; lacking 2 terminal blanks in Vol IV; a few marginal tears repaired. P June 5 (163) $3,500

— Pride and Prejudice. L, 1813. 1st Ed. 3 vols. 12mo, old half calf; rubbed, upper joint of Vol I split. Lacking half-titles; foxed; marginal defs. bba May 30 (145) £5,500 [Heritage]

— Works. L, 1872-77. 6 vols. 8vo, contemp half calf; worn, 1 cover detached. bba May 30 (173) £110 [Classic Bindings]

Anr Ed. Edin., 1906. 10 vols. Half mor. b Sept 20 (557) £380

Winchester Ed. Edin., 1911-12. 12 vols. Mor gilt. Library markings. cb Oct 17 (259) $2,500

Anr Ed. Oxford: Clarendon Press, 1926. 5 vols. Contemp half mor gilt by Hatchards. C July 1 (324) £550

**Austen, John**

— Rogues in Porcelain: a Miscellany of Eighteenth Century Poems. L, 1924. Compiled by Austen. Mor extra with inlays picturing an 18th-cent couple. sg Sept 14 (45) $425

**Austin, Gabriel.** See: Grolier Club

**Austin, Mary Hunter, 1868-1934**

— The Flock. Bost., 1906. 1st Ed. - Illus by E. Boyd Smith. Orig cloth. Robbins copy. pba Mar 21 (6) $110

— The Land of Little Rain. Bost & NY, 1903. 4to, cloth; corners rubbed, insect damage, chipped. pba Nov 16 (16) $60

Anr Ed. Bost., 1950. Illus by Ansel Adams. 4to, cloth, in rubbed dj. pba Apr 25 (262) $100

Anr copy. Cloth, in repaired dj. sg Feb 29 (7) $120

— Taos Pueblo. Bost., 1977. One of 950. Illus by Ansel Adams. K June 23 (3) $500; pba Mar 7 (2) $600; sg Feb 29 (10) $700

**Austin, Stephen F., 1793-1836**
— The Austin Papers. Wash., 1924-28. Ed by Eugene C. Barker. 2 vols in 3. ds July 27 (17) $125

**Australasian...**
— Australasian Antarctic Expedition, 1911-14. Scientific Reports. Sydney & Adelaide, 1916-47. Series A, Vol I. Part 1, Narrative. Part 2, Cartography. Folio, orig wraps; small edge tear. pba July 25 (43) $80

**Australia**
— Historical Records of New South Wales. Sydney, 1895-1901. Vol III-VII. 8vo, contemp half mor; worn. Inscr by the Ed, F. M. Bladen. b Mar 20 (107) £130

**Austria**
— Austria and the Austrians. L, 1837. 2 vols. 8vo, cloth; 2 joints splitting. With port frontises. sg Mar 7 (16) $70

**Authville des Amourettes, Charles Louis**
— Essai sur la cavalerie tant ancienne que moderne. Paris: Jombert, 1756. 4to, contemp calf; rubbed. Fuerstenberg - Schaefer copy. S Dec 7 (28) £160

**Auzoles a La Peyre, Jacques d'**
— Le Mercure Charitable.... Paris: Gervais Alliot, 1638. Folio, contemp citron mor gilt & painted, bound for presentation to the dedicatee, Charles de Schomberg, Mareschal de France, with arms & emblems of Auzolles & Schomberg. C May 1 (7) £4,000

**Avedon, Richard**
— Avedon Photographs 1947-1977. NY: Farrar, Straus & Giroux, [1978]. Intro by Harold Brodkey. Folio, bds; ink notes to rear pastedown. pba Aug 22 (633) $110

Anr copy. Bds, in ptd plastic dj; rubbed. sg Feb 29 (27) $250

— In the American West. NY, [1985]. Folio, orig cloth, orig acetate outer wrap. sg Feb 29 (24) $110

— Nothing Personal. NY, 1964. Text by James Baldwin. Bds; minor wear. sg Feb 29 (25) $200

— Observations. NY, [1959]. Text by Truman Capote. Folio, bds; minor soiling. F Mar 28 (40) $150

Anr copy. Bds; spine stained. Some soiling. sg Feb 29 (26) $275

— Portraits. NY, 1976. In dj. sg Feb 29 (28) $225

**Avensohar**
— Liber Teisir sive rectificatio medicationis et regiminis.... Venice: Joannes & Gregorius de Gregoriis, de Forlivio, 4 Jan [1490/91?]. 1st Ed. Folio, modern vellum. With 107 (of 108) leaves, doubel column. Some marginal spotting. Ck Mar 22 (21) £1,800

**Avery Architectural Library.** See: Columbia University

**Avery, R. B.** See: Allen & Avery

**Avicenna, 980-1037**
— Canon medicinae. Venice, 1608. 3 vols in 2. Folio, 19th-cent half lea gilt; extremities rubbed, Vol I front cover detached. Titles stamped. sg May 16 (365) $900

— De animalibus. Venice: Gregoriis de Forlivio, [c.1500]. Bound after: Celsus, Aulus Cornelius. Medicinae libri octo. Venice: Luc Antonio Giunta, 10 Mar 1524. Folio, 19th-cent half vellum. Some worming & staining to margins, occasionally affecting text. S June 27 (296) £8,500

**Avila y Zuniga, Luis de, c.1500-64**
— Commentariorum de bello Germanico.... Antwerp: Juan Steelsius, 1550. 8vo, contemp calf gilt with port stamp of Elector Frederick the Wise of Saxony on upper cover & of Elector John the Constant of Saxony on lower cover; spine & corners repaired. With folding woodcut map & 3 woodcut plans & views. Plan after Q1v cropped along left margin; 2 short tears in plan after E4v; some soiling, dampstaining, marginalia & underlining. Schaefer copy. P Nov 1 (14) $3,750

**Aviler, Augustin Charles d', 1653-1700**
— Ausfuehrliche Anleitung zu der gantzen Civil Baukunst von J. Bar. de Vignola. Amst., 1699. 4to, 18th-cent sheep gilt; rubbed. sg Apr 18 (20) $1,100

— Cours d'architecture. Paris, 1750. 4to, contemp calf; rebacked, spine worn, joints cracked. Some soiling & staining; engraved title with tears & backed; some leaves extended or reattached with guards. cb Oct 17 (3) $325

**Axe, John Wortley**
— The Horse: Its Treatment in Health and Disease. L, 1905. 9 vols. 4to, orig cloth. Frontis loose & frayed in Vol I. O Jan 9 (24) $140

Anr Ed. L, 1906. 9 vols. 4to, orig cloth. C July 1 (332) £100; Z Jan 30 (512) $125

**Axelson, G. W.**
— "Commy". The Life Story of Charles A. Cominsky.... Chicago, 1919. In chipped dj. Z June 14 (390) $160

**Axsom, Richard**
— The Prints of Frank Stella. NY, [1983]. 4to, wraps. sg June 13 (349) $50

**Ayers, James J.**
— Gold and Sunshine: Reminisces of Early California. Bost., [1922]. 1st Ed. - Illus by Charles B. Turrill. Orig cloth. With frontis & 15 illus. Larson copy. pba Sept 28 (301) $900

**Ayers, John G.** See: Howard & Ayers

**Aykroyd, Joseph**
— Original Poems; Sacred, Natural and Moral. Bradford, 1832. 12mo, orig cloth; worn. b Dec 5 (423) £75

**Aymon**
— Les quatre fils aymon. Lyons: Jaques Arnollet, 10 Jan 1502. Folio, modern mor with metal clasps. 45 lines; types 1:180G (beginning of text), 2:110G (heading on a4r), 3:94G (text). With 29 woodcuts (10 are repeats). Some worming throughout; 1st 2 leaves

repaired in outer margins; some staining.  122 leaves.  Schaefer copy.   P Nov 1 (15) $9,000

**Ayres, Philip, 1638-1712**
— Emblems of Love....  L, [1683].  2d Ed. 8vo, contemp mor gilt; rebacked.  Some soiling; plate margins trimmed.  CE Sept 27 (47) $500

**Ayrouard, Jacques**
— Recueil de plusieurs plans des ports et rades...de la Mer Mediterranee.  Paris, 1746.  4to, half calf; worn.  With 79 maps.  sg May 9 (52) $1,100

**Azeglio, Massimo d'**
— Niccolo de' Lapi; ovvero, I Palleschi e i Piagnoni. Florence, 1850.  12mo, contemp vellum gilt.  Inscr by Elizabeth Barrett Browning to Edith M. Story, 25 Dec 1859.  sg Apr 18 (33) $1,600

# B

**B., A.** See: Britaine, William de

**B., R.** See: Crouch, Nathaniel

**Babb, James Tinkham.** See: Onassis copy, Jacqueline Bouvier Kennedy

**Babbit, Edwin D.**
— The Principles of Light and Color.  NY, 1878.  8vo, cloth; spine ends rubbed, pieces of rear free endpaper lacking.  Tp with owner's stamp.  pba Mar 7 (15) $80

**Babcock, Louis L.**
— The Tarpon.  [N.p.: Pvtly ptd], 1930.  One of 250. Wraps with edge-wear.  Inscr.  O Feb 6 (17) $375

Anr copy.  Wraps.  Inscr to Charles H. Bredin, 1932. pba July 11 (22) $250

**Babcock, Philip H.** See: Derrydale Press

**Babie, F.**
— Voyages ches les peuple sauvages, ou l'homme de la nature.  Paris, 1801.  3 vols. 8vo, contemp half lea. Without plates.  sg Mar 7 (18) $130

**Babson, Grace K.**
— A Descriptive Catalogue of the Collection of the Works of Sir Isaac Newton.  NY, 1950.  2 vols, including supplement. 8vo, orig cloth.  sg Apr 11 (278) $150

**Babson Collection, Grace K.**
— A Descriptive Catalogue of the Grace K. Babson Collection of the Works of Sir Isaac Newton....  NY, 1950.  2 vols, including Macomber's 1955 Supplement.  wa Feb 29 (7) $95

**Bach, Carl Philipp Emanuel, 1714-88**
— Sei Sonate per Cembalo....  Nuremberg: Schmid, [1742].  34 pp, engraved throughout.  Some staining; trimmed.  S Dec 1 (67) £1,100

**Bach, Johann Christian, 1743-1814**
— Six Sonates pour le clavecin....  [L, 1766].  Oblong folio, contemp bds.  Engraved throughout; tp by Bartolozzi after Cipriani.  Some staining.  S May 15 (273) £1,000

**Bach, Johann Sebastian, 1685-1750**
— Werke.  Leipzig, 1851-97.  57 (of 60) vols; lacking Vols 44-46.  4to, half mor.  S May 15 (4) £650

**Bache, Alexander D.**
— Notices of the Western Coast of the United States.... Wash., 1851.  8vo, later half mor, orig front wrap bound in.  Trimmed during rebdg; tp stamped.  Inscr by Washington Allon Bartlett to Capt. L. L. Young. pba July 25 (91) $350

**Bachman, John, 1790-1874.** See: Audubon & Bachman

**Bachman, Richard.** See: King, Stephen

**Back, Sir George, 1796-1878**
— Narrative of the Arctic Land Expedition....  L, 1836. 8vo, half mor gilt.  With folding map & 15 plates. Some foxing & browning.  sg Oct 26 (8) $200

Anr copy.  Early calf; rebacked.  With folding map & 16 plates.  Some foxing.  sg Mar 7 (269) $275

**Backer, Alois de.** See: Backer & Backer

**Backer, Augustin de —&**
**Backer, Alois de**
— Bibliotheque de la Compagnie de Jesus....  Louvain, 1960.  12 vols. 4to, orig cloth.  Reprint of 1890 Ed. bba Oct 5 (45) £1,200 [Maggs]

**Backhouse, Edward, Jr.**
— Original Etchings of Birds.  Ashburne, 1840.  Folio, contemp mor gilt, the upper cover stamped in gilt Edward Backhouse Junr. to Edward and Emily Mounsey, 1847; hinges scuffed.  With etched title & 56 plates, some from other works.  Presentation copy, given by the author to his sister & brother-in-law on the occasion of their marriage.  Fattorini copy.  C Oct 25 (55A) £3,000

**Bacon, Sir Francis, 1561-1626**
See also: Cresset Press; Eragny Press; Limited Editions Club
— Baconiana.  L, 1679.  1st Ed. 4to, contemp calf; rebacked.  With port.  Imprimateur on A4 recto.  pba June 20 (38) $170

Issue not indicated.  8vo, modern calf.  pba June 20 (39) $90

— Cases of Treason.  L, 1641.  1st Ed. 4to, early calf; sides cracked, rubbed.  Browned.  Z June 28 (12) $250

— Considerations Touching a Warre with Spaine.  L, 1629.  1st Ed. 4to, modern mor gilt.  CE May 22 (41) $750

— The Historie of the Raigne of King Henry the Seventh. L, 1622.  1st Ed. Folio, calf; front joint cracked through.  Lacking frontis; pp. 248-48 def & repaired; minor marginal worming.  Gibson 116a; STC 1159. pba Nov 30 (27) $275

Mixed State. Folio, contemp calf with gilt monogram of Sir William Bentinck, 1st Earl of Portland; re-backed, corners repaired. Has reading "souldiers" on line 12 of p. 3, but errata partly corrected elsewhere. Dampstained; port holed; some foxing. S Mar 28 (469) £260
— History Naturall and Experimentall, of Life and Death. L, 1638. 2d Ed of Wm. Rawley's authorised trans. 12mo, 18th-Cent calf; joints splitting, letter-piece lacking. C5 torn with loss & repaired; D5v & D6r smudged. Ck Mar 22 (22A) £360
2d Ed of Wm. Rawley's authorized trans. L, 1650. 12mo, old calf; rubbed, edges worn, rebacked. K Feb 11 (37) £375
— [Novum organum] Instauratio magna. L, 1620. 1st Ed, 1st Issue. Folio, contemp vellum gilt, with Bacon's crest on both covers; lacking ties, spine repaired. L.p. copy. Lacking initial blank. Houghton - Hefner copy. CNY May 17 (3) $350,000
— Novum organum scientiarum. Amst.: Adrianus Wyngaerden, 1650. 12mo, 17th-cent mor gilt; joints & spine ends worn. sg Mar 21 (23) $175
— Resuscitatio.... L, 1671. 2 parts in 1 vol. Folio, contemp calf; worn, covers detached. Library stamp on tp; 2d title foxed. sg May 16 (117) $100
— Sylva Sylvarum. L, 1635. Folio, contemp calf. pba Nov 30 (25) $500
7th Ed. L, 1658. Folio, contemp calf; def. sg May 16 (285) $250
— The Twoo Bookes of Francis Bacon. Of the Proficience and Advancement of Learning.... L, 1629. Bound with: The Essays or Counsels.... L, 1629. 4to, mor gilt by Macdonald; extremities rubbed. 1st work with tp frayed; marginal holing in upper left corner; 2d work lacking A1 & Ccc4; corner of E3 lacking, affecting border; Yy1-4 from anr copy; last 3 leaves tattered at margins. Z June 28 (14) $600
1st Ed in English of the Expanded Ed. Oxford, 1640. ("Of the Advancement and Proficience of Learning....") 2d Issue with colophon dated 1640. Folio, contemp calf; rebacked, new endpapers, rubbed. cb Feb 14 (2627) $700
Anr Ed. L, 1674. Folio, calf; rebacked. pba Sept 14 (9) $375
— Works. L, 1765. Ed by Thomas Birch. 5 vols. 4to, contemp calf; minor wear & scuffing, joints cracked, Vol I lacking front free endpaper & flyleaf. With 4 frontises & 2 folding tables. pba Nov 30 (26) $600
Anr Ed. L, 1819. 10 vols. 8vo, contemp calf gilt with arms of Trinity College, Dublin; rebacked in mor. cb June 25 (1798) $325
Anr Ed. L, 1825-36. 16 vols in 17. 8vo, calf gilt by Tout; scuffed, joints & extremities rubbed. Front matter of Vol I dampstained. F Sept 21 (400) $375

## Bacon, Thomas, 1700?-68
— Laws of Maryland at Large, with Proper Indexes. Annapolis, 1765 [1766]. 1st Collected Ed. Folio, recent half calf. Some browning; old worming in bottom margin. bbc June 24 (413) $475
— Six Sermons.... L, 1751. 2 parts in 1 vol. 12mo, bds; worn. Slight staining. S Oct 26 (482) £170 [Felco]

## Badcock, John
— The Groom's Oracle. L, 1830. 8vo, calf; rubbed. With colored folding frontis by Alken. Minor foxing. O Jan 9 (143) $110
— Sportsman's Slang; a New Dictionary.... L, 1825. 8vo, old half cloth; worn, shaken. With folding colored frontis & 4 plates. Browning & soiling. O Jan 9 (25) $425

## Baddeley, John Frederick
— Russia, Mongolia, China. NY: Burt Franklin, [n.d.]. 2 vols. Folio, cloth. Reprint of 1919 Ed. pba Nov 16 (342) $60

## Bade, William Frederic
— The Life and Letters of John Muir. Bost., 1924. 1st Ed. 2 vols. Buckram. Robbins copy. pba Mar 21 (253) $95
— A Manual of Excavation in the Near East. Berkeley, 1934. Inscr. pba Aug 8 (10) $50

## Badeslade, Thomas —&
## Toms, William Henry
— Chorographia Britanniae, or a Set of Maps of all the Counties in England and Wales. L, 1742. 3d Issue. 8vo, disbound. With 46 maps, each with table. Lacking title. S Oct 26 (368) £550 [Ingol Maps]
1st Ed, Maps plain. Issue not stated. 8vo, contemp calf. With double-page dedication & 45 (of 46) double-page maps. Map of Middlesex def. pnE Mar 20 (53) £370

## Badger, George Percy, 1815-88
— The Nestorians and their Rituals. L, 1852. 1st Ed. 2 vols. 8vo, contemp calf. With 2 plans, 2 folding maps, & 13 plates. Some spotting. S Oct 26 (10) £650 [Loman]

## Badham, Charles David
— Prose Halieutics or Ancient and Modern Fish Tattle. L, 1854. 1st Ed. 8vo, orig cloth. pba July 11 (23) $130
Anr copy. Contemp calf; cover detached, extremities rubbed. S Oct 12 (5) £100

## Baer, Elizabeth
See also: Fowler & Baer
— Seventeenth Century Maryland: a Bibliography. Balt., 1949. One of 300. 4to, cloth, in frayed & soiled dj. O Dec 5 (10) $110
Anr copy. Cloth, in plain-paper dj glued to paste-downs. O Mar 26 (13) $110

## Baerentzen, E.
— Danmark. Copenhagen, 1856. Folio, recent half calf. With litho frontis & 77 tinted views. Some spotting or staining. S June 13 (533) £900

## Bage, Robert, 1728-1801
— Hermsprong; or Man as he is Not. L, 1796. 1st Ed. 3 vols. 12mo, contemp half calf. Some marginal defs; lacking half-title to Vol III. Ck Sept 8 (196) £1,800
— Man as he Is. L, 1796. 2d Ed. 4 vols. 12mo, contemp half calf. Some marginal staining in Vol II; 1 line on

H6r of Vol II erased; half-title, title & B1-2 of Vol IV with deep tear at inner margin. Ck Sept 8 (195) £380

**Bagehot, Walter, 1826-77**
— The English Constitution. L, 1867. 8vo, orig cloth; spine ends worn, front endpaper stained, upper hinge fragile. Foxing at ends. S Dec 18 (481) £450 [Quaritch]

**Bagellardo, Paolo, d.1492?**
— Opusculum recens natum de morbis puerorum.... Lyons: Germanum Rose, 1538. 8vo, old vellum; backstrip damaged, corners worn through. Dampstaining & minor worming in margins; tp soiled. sg May 16 (366) $275

**Baglivius, Georgius, 1669?-1707**
— The Practice of Physick Reduc'd.... L, 1704. 8vo, contemp calf; spine ends chipped, covers detached. Marginal dampstaining throughout. sg May 16 (367) $130
   Anr Ed. L, 1723. 8vo, modern cloth. Browned; stamp on tp. sg May 16 (368) $50

**Bagnold, Enid**
— National Velvet. NY, 1935. In chipped dj. pba May 23 (9) $75

**Bagrow, Leo**
— History of Cartography. Chicago, [1985]. Revised by R. A. Skelton. 4to, orig cloth, in dj. pba Apr 25 (151) $110
— A History of the Cartography of Russia.... Wolfe Island: Walker Press, [1975]. 2 vols. 4to, cloth. sg May 9 (5) $100

**Baigell, Matthew**
— Thomas Hart Benton. NY: Abrams, [1973]. Oblong folio, cloth, in dj. sg Jan 11 (42) $120
   Anr Ed. NY, [1973?]. One of 350. Orig lea. sg Sept 7 (40) $225

**Bailey, Henry**
— Travel and Adventures in the Congo Free State.... L, 1894. 8vo, orig cloth; worn, spine discolored. Library markings. O June 4 (37) $140

**Bailey, Liberty Hyde, 1858-1954**
— Cyclopedia of American Agriculture. NY, 1907-9. 4 vols. 4to, half mor; rubbed. O Jan 9 (26) $225

**Baillet, Adrien, 1649-1706**
— Auteurs deguisez. Sous des noms etrangers.... Paris, 1690. 12mo, contemp calf; rubbed, joints worn. Some browning & foxing. O Mar 26 (14) $200
— Jugemens des savans sur les principaux ouvrages des auteurs. Paris, 1722. 7 vols. 4to, contemp calf; worn, some joints broken, spine tips chipped or repaired. O Mar 26 (15) $375

**Baillie, Marianne**
— Guy of Warwick.... Kingsbury, 1817. 8vo, orig bds; spine def. Inscr to the Bishop of Ely & Mrs. Sparke. b Dec 5 (237) £70

**Baillie-Grohman, William Adolph**
— Sport in Art. L, [1920]. 2d Ed. 4to, half mor; rubbed. O June 25 (18) $90

**Baily, John**
— Central America.... L, 1850. 1st Ed. 8vo, orig cloth; worn & soiled. With 3 plates. Some dampstaining to plates & front matter. F Mar 28 (457) $110

**Baily's Magazine...**
— Baily's Magazine of Sports and Pastimes. L, 1860-64. Vols 1-10. 8vo, contemp half calf gilt; 1 spine worn, rubbed. C July 1 (327) £150

**Bainbridge, George Cole**
— The Fly Fisher's Guide.... Liverpool, 1816. 1st Ed. 8vo, half cloth; worn. With 8 hand-colored plates. Some foxing & soiling. ALs tipped to front endpaper. O Feb 6 (19) $2,200
   Anr copy. Modern half calf by Aquarius of London. With 8 hand-colored plates. W Nov 8 (358) £420

**Bainbridge, Henry Charles**
— Peter Carl Faberge.... L, 1949. 4to, orig cloth, in dj. sg Sept 7 (31) $60
   De Luxe Ed, one of 250. 4to, half lev gilt. Library stamp at foot of tp. S June 12 (319) £200
   Anr Ed. NY & L, 1949. One of 100. 4to, orig half mor; spine discolored. CE Nov 8 (166) $160

**Baird, Bill**
— The Art of the Puppet. NY, [1965]. Folio, cloth, in dj. pba Aug 8 (575) $80

**Baird, Joseph Armstrong.** See: Grabhorn Printing

**Baird, Joseph Armstrong —& Evans, Edwin Clyve**
— Historic Lithographs of San Francisco. San Francisco: Steven A. Waterson, 1972. Ltd Ed. Folio, cloth. With 11 color & 35 monochrome or partly colored plates. Larson copy. pba Feb 12 (340) $1,800

**Baird, Robert, 1798-1863**
— View of the Valley of the Mississippi.... Phila., 1834. 12mo, orig cloth; spine ends chipped, stain to lower cover, front hinge split. Some foxing & browning; library markings; piece missing from bottom margin of 1 leaf. bbc Dec 18 (429) $240

**Baird, Spencer Fullerton, 1823-87 —& Others**
— The Birds of North America. Phila., 1860. 2 vols. 4to, orig cloth; frayed, front free endpaper in Vol I clipped, stamps to endpapers & front blank in Vol I. With 100 colored plates. bbc June 24 (282) $1,100

**Baird Warner, Inc.**
— A Portfolio of Fine Apartment Homes. Evanston, 1928. Folio, half cloth. sg June 13 (1) $375

**Baker, Charles H., Jr.** See: Derrydale Press

**Baker, Edward Charles Stuart**
— The Indian Ducks and their Allies. L, 1908. 8vo, half lea; spine heel bumped. With litho title & 30 colored plates. Some foxing. Met Feb 24 (429) $200

**Baker, Ezekiel**
— Remarks on Rifle Guns. L, 1825. 9th Ed. 8vo, contemp half lea; worn. With 5 plain & 6 hand-colored plates & tables. Marginal browning & dampstaining; foxed; marginal tears. Sold w.a.f. O Oct 10 (38) $160

11th Ed. L, 1835. 8vo, contemp bds; rebacked, worn. With 17 plates & tables, 8 of them hand-colored. O June 4 (38) $200

**Baker, George, 1781-1851**
— The History and Antiquities of the County of Northampton. L, 1822-41. Parts 1-4 plus "Towcester Hundred" in 5 vols. Folio, contemp half calf. worn. With 39 plates, 2 hand-colored. Extra-illus with 8 plates. bba Apr 11 (339) £300 [Cizdyn]

**Baker, Henry, 1698-1774**
— An Attempt towards a Natural History of the Polype.... L, 1743. 8vo, contemp calf gilt; rebacked. S June 12 (236) £220

**Baker, Sir Richard, 1568-1645**
— A Chronicle of the Kings of England.... L, 1741. 2 vols in 1. Later half calf; lacking front flyleaves. Last leaf of text adhered to ad page. pba June 20 (137) $50

**Baker, Sir Samuel White, 1821-93**
— The Albert N'yanza. L, 1866. 1st Ed. 2 vols. 8vo, half mor gilt. Frontises foxed; some nicks; folding map repaired on verso. CE June 12 (147) $300
— Ismailia. L, 1874. 1st Ed. 2 vols. 8vo, orig cloth. b Sept 20 (403) £200
— The Rifle and the Hound in Ceylon. L, 1884. 8vo, half calf extra. sg Mar 7 (394) $150

**Baker, William S., 1824-97**
— Bibliotheca Washingtoniana: A Descriptive List.... Phila., 1889. One of 400. 4to, orig cloth; shaken. Library markings. Inscr to the Pennsylvania Historical Society. F June 20 (404) $50

**Bakewell, Thomas, Weaver**
— The Moorland Bard.... Hanley, 1807. 2 vols in 1. 12mo, modern half calf. Some spotting. b Dec 5 (344) £70

**Bakst, Leon, 1866?-1924**
— The Inedited Works. NY: Brentano's, 1927. One of 600. Oblong folio, hand-colored pictorial bds; rubbed, hinge cracked. pba June 20 (40) $700

**Balanci, Bernard**
— Charles Lapicque: Catalogue raisonne.... Paris, [1972]. One of 1,000. 4to, cloth. sg Jan 11 (253) $60

**Balbinus, Bohuslaus Aloysius, 1621-88**
— Epitome Historica Rerum Bohemicarum.... Prague, 1677. 4to, old calf; rebacked, bookplate removed from pastedown. Some browning. wd May 8 (37) $250
— Vita Venerabilis Arnesti (Vulgo Ernesti) Primi Archiepiscopi Pragensis.... Prague, 1664. 4to, old vellum; rebacked with calf, soiled & scuffed, spine chipped. With 3 plates, 1 folding. Browned; erasure on tp affecting letters. wd May 8 (36) $125

**Balbus, Joannes**
— Catholicon. [Strassburg: R-Press type 2 (Johann Mentelin & Adolf Rusch), not after 1475]. 4th Ed. Folio, contemp calf over wooden bds, blindstamped, with 2 brass catches, bound at Augsburg, Kyriss shop 92, stamps 1-3, 5, 7; extremities worn, spine repaired. 67 lines; double column; type 2:100G. Marginal foxing; browning in quire 21; dampstain in extreme right margin; some marginal tears repaired. 369 (of 372) leaves; lacking 1st & final blanks & with fo. 1/2 supplied in facsimile with painted initials. Goff B-23. C Nov 29 (26) £3,000

**Baldacchino, Filippo**
— Ad... Silvium Passerium Corytanum pontificalem secretarium. Perugia: Cosmus Blanchinus, 1514. 4to, 19th-cent floral bds; spine worn. C Apr 3 (29) £1,800

**Baldaeusm Phillippus, 1632-72**
— Naauwkeurige beschryvinge van Malabar en Choromandel. Amst., 1672. 1st Ed. 3 parts in 1 vol. Folio, contemp calf; worn, joints weak, upper spine repaired. With additional title, 2 ports, 32 (of 35) doubel-page folding maps, & 52 illus in text. Some maps frayed with loss; some staining & soiling. S Oct 26 (568) £550 [Baskes]

**Baldry, Alfred Lys**
— Albert Moore: His Life and Works. L, 1894. 2 vols. 4to, cloth; extremities rubbed. Some foxing. sg Jan 11 (292) $250

**Balduinus, Benedictus**
— De Calceo Antiquo, et jul. nigronus de caliga veterum.... Amst.: Andreae Frisl, 1667. 2 vols in 1. 12mo, old vellum. With 7 folding plates & 21 full-page plates. sg Mar 21 (24) $400

**Baldung, Hieronymus**
— Aphorismi compunctionis theologicales. [Strassburg:] Johann Grueninger, 6 Jan 1497. 1st Ed. 4to, old bds covered with part of an old Ms. A few leaves stained; repair in outer margin of a4. 39 (of 40) leaves; lacking final blank. Goff B-36. S Nov 30 (247) £1,700

**Baldwin, Alice Blackwood**
— Memoirs of the late Frank D. Baldwin.... Los Angeles, 1929. Sgd & with 2 inscr cards. pba June 25 (4) $250

**Baldwin, C. C.** See: Maclay & Baldwin

## Baldwin, James
— Blues for Mister Charlie. NY, 1964. In worn dj with short tears. Sgd. wa Feb 1 (29) $160
— Little Man Little Man. NY, [1976]. Illus by Yoran Cazac. 4to, pictorial bds, in dj. sg Mar 28 (12) $50
— Nobody Knows My Name. NY, 1961. In dj. sg Mar 28 (13) $175
— Notes of a Native Son. NY, [1955]. In worn & repaired dj. sg Mar 28 (14) $200
— Tell Me How Long the Train's Been Gone. NY, [1968]. In dj; bdg shaken. Sgd. sg Mar 28 (15) $175

## Baldwin, William, fl.1547
— A Myrrour for Magistrates. L: Felix Kingston, 1609-10. 4to, later calf; rebacked. Oo4 lacking; some corners repaired at beginning; marginal soiling 7 staining; early marginalia throughout. STC 13446. CE June 12 (148) $650

## Balfour, James
— Reminiscences of Golf on St. Andrews Links. Carlinville, IL, 1982. Reprint of 1887 Ed, One of 300. Wraps. pba Apr 18 (3) $95

## Balinghem, Antoine de
— Apres dinees et propos de table contre l'excez av boire et av manger.... St. Omer: Charles Boscart, 1624. 2d Ed. 8vo, recent vellum. Title soiled. Ck Mar 22 (23) £400

## Ball, John, 1818-89
— Peakes, Passes, and Glaciers. L, 1859. 8vo, orig cloth; hinges weak, rubbed, spine ends frayed. bba Nov 1 (567) £380 [Chessler]
— Series I-II. L, 1859-62. 3 vols. 8vo, orig cloth; rubbed. bba Nov 1 (500) £450 [Cavendish]

## Ball, Nicholas
— The Pioneers of '49.... Bost., 1891. 1st Ed. 8vo, cloth. With 100 illus. Larson copy. pba Sept 28 (304) $90

## Ballantine, James
— The Life of David Roberts.... Edin., 1866. 4to, orig cloth; blistered, worn & repaired. Foxing affecting 3 of the 9 plates. sg June 13 (51) $700

## Ballard, James Graham
— The Drowned World. L, 1962. In dj. Inscr. b Jan 31 (138) £150
— The Unlimited Dream Company. L, [1979]. In dj. Inscr. sg Dec 14 (4) $60
— Why I Want to Fuck Ronald Reagan. Brighton: Unicorn Bookshop, 1968. One of 50. Orig ptd stapled wraps. b Jan 31 (139) £120

## Ballard, Robert
— The Solution of the Pyramid Problem.... NY, 1882. 8vo, orig cloth; later cloth shelf labels. With 8 plates. sg May 16 (118) $80

## Balston, Thomas
— The Cambridge University Press Collection of Private Press Types. Cambr., 1951. One of 350. Orig cloth. pba Nov 30 (29) $70

## Baltimore
— Baltimore City Directory for 1897. Balt., 1897. Orig half cloth; upper joint & front hinge repaired, lower hinge cracked, old brass stud punched through bottom corner of lower cover. bbc Dec 18 (434) $250
— A History of the City of Baltimore.... Balt., 1902. 4to, orig cloth; worn & frayed, shaken. Tp worn & soiled. F June 20 (433) $70

## Baltz, Lewis
— Candlestick Point. Tokyo, 1989. One of 45. 4to, bds; rubbed. sg Feb 29 (30) $225
— Park City. Albuquerque, 1980. 4to, cloth, in chipped & abraded dj. sg Feb 29 (31) $90

## Balzac, Honore de, 1799-1850
See also: Limited Editions Club
— Droll Stories. L: Hotten, [c.1874]. Illus by Gustave Dore. 8vo, mor gilt by L. Broga. b Dec 5 (3) £60
— The Hidden Treasures.... Kentfield: Allen Press, 1953. One of 160. Illus by Malette Dean. Bds. pba June 20 (11) $180
— Works. Bost., 1899. ("Comedie Humaine.") Edition Grand Format, one of 40. 41 vols. Mor gilt. With hand-colored frontises & plates throughout by Jeanniot. cb Oct 17 (260) $4,350

## Balzac, Jean Louis Guez, Sieur de, 1597?-1654
— Lettres familieres... a M. Chapelain. Amst.: Elzevier, 1661. 12mo, early 20th-cent mor extra a caissons dores sgd Joly fils. Washed copy. Schaefer copy. P Nov 1 (16) $1,500

## Bancroft, Anne
— The Memorable Lives of Bummer & Lazarus.... Los Angeles: Ward Ritchie Press, 1939. One of 500. In dj. Sgd on half-title. pba Feb 12 (245) $60

## Bancroft, George, 1800-91
— History of the United States.... Bost., 1890. 6 vols. 8vo, half calf; worn, 2 vols lacking front free endpaper. wa Feb 29 (314) $160

## Bancroft, Hubert Howe, 1832-1918
— Some Cities and San Francisco and Resurgam. NY, 1907. 5 vols. 8vo, orig cloth. Inscr. pba Feb 12 (246) $65
— Works. San Francisco, 1882. 1st Ed. 8vo, cloth. Larson copy. pba Sept 28 (1) $180
Anr Ed. San Francisco, [1882]-90. 39 vols. 8vo, orig mor; spines faded & worn. Robbins set. pba Mar 21 (8) $2,500

## Bancroft, Laura. See: Baum, L. Frank

## Bandelier, Adolph Francis, 1840-1914
— The Delight Makers. NY, [1890]. 12mo, orig cloth; rubbed, crease to front cover. pba Nov 16 (19) $75
1st Ed. 12mo, orig cloth; front cover stained, some shelf wear. Robbins copy. pba Mar 21 (9) $85

## BANDELIER

— The Gilded Man. NY, 1893. 1st Ed. Orig cloth; spine ends & corners rubbed. Robbins copy. pba Mar 21 (10) $225

— Historical Introduction to the Studies among the Sedentary Indians of New Mexico. Bost., 1881. Orig bds; spine ends chipped, reglued. Library markings. pba Aug 8 (13) $50

— Report of an Archaeological Tour in Mexico, in 1881. Bost., 1884. Orig wraps; extremities worn, spine perishing, stamps on front cover. Library markings; soiling; 1 signature detached. cb Oct 17 (179) $160

**Bandelier, Adolph Francis, 1840-1914 —& Bandelier, Fanny R.**

— Historical Documents relating to New Mexico.... Wash., 1923-37. 1st Ed. - Ed by Charles Wilson Hackett. 3 vols. Orig wraps; worn. Texts in Spanish & English. Robbins copy. pba Mar 21 (11) $225

**Bandelier, Fanny R.** See: Bandelier & Bandelier

**Bandini, Ralph.** See: Derrydale Press

**Bankes, Thomas —& Others**

— A New Royal Authentic and Complete System of Universal Geography. L, [c.1790]. 2 vols in 1. Folio, later calf; rubbed. With 20 maps & 88 plates only. Lacking text at beginning. Sold w.a.f. b May 30 (124) £450

**Banks, Sir Joseph, 1743-1820**

— Banks' Florilegium. L, 1980-85. One of 100. Parts 1, 2, 4-20 (of 34). Folio, loose in portfolios. With 405 plates ptd a la poupee in up to 10 colors. P Dec 12 (195) $25,000

Anr Ed. L, 1986. Part 23 only. Folio, loose in portfolio. With 22 color plates. b May 30 (171) £950

— The Endeavour Journal of Joseph Banks 1768-1771. Sydney, 1963. 2d Ed. - Ed by J. C. Beaglehole. 2 vols. 8vo, in djs. pba Feb 13 (4) $190

Anr copy. Orig cloth. Vol I sgd by Beaglehole. wa Feb 29 (170) $220

— The Journal of.... Guildford: Genesis Publications, 1980. One of 500. 2 vols. Orig half calf. Sgd by the Duke of Edinburgh on p 9. pba Feb 13 (5) $475

**Bannerman, David Armitage**

— The Birds of West and Equatorial Africa. Edin. & L, 1953. 2 vols. Cloth, in djs with minor defs. pba Mar 7 (16) $225

**Bannerman, David Armitage —& Bannerman, Winifred Mary**

— Birds of Cyprus. Edin., 1958. 1st Ed. 8vo, pictorial dust wrap. With half title, map, & 29 color plates. Inscr. S Oct 22 (43) £420 [Karides]

**Bannerman, David Armitage —& Lodge, George Edward**

— The Birds of the British Isles. L, 1953-63. 12 vols. In djs. b Sept 20 (457) £180; S Mar 29 (723) £260

**Bannerman, Helen**

— Histoire du Petit Negre Sambo. NY: Frederick A. Stokes, [1921]. 24mo, orig pictorial bds, in dj. F Mar 28 (509) $60

— The Story of Little Black Sambo. Chicago: Reilly & Britton, 1905. ("Little Black Sambo.") Intro by L. Frank Baum. 4 by 3 inches, pictorial bds; rear cover creased. Christmas Stocking Series. pba Jan 18 (145) $225

**Bannerman, Winifred Mary.** See: Bannerman & Bannerman

**Bannet, Ivor.** See: Golden Cockerel Press

**Banning, Kendall.** See: Hiller & Banning

**Banville, Theodore de, 1823-91**

— Trente-six ballades joyeuses. Paris, 1873. 8vo, mor gilt by Amand, orig wraps bound in. With orig variant drawing of the frontis & holograph poem, sgd on front free endpaper. b May 30 (518) £130

**Baradere, H.**

— Antiquites Mexicaines, relation des trois expeditions du Capitaine Dupaix.... Paris, 1834-44. 2 vols in 1 of text & Atlas. Folio, modern half calf. With pictorial title to Atlas & 166 plates on 161 sheets & map. Repairs to foremargin of Vol I tp with minor loss; some upper margins renewed; repairs in some other margins. S June 27 (191) £5,000

**Barbeau, Charles Marius**

— Cornelius Krieghoff.... Toronto, 1934. 4to, orig cloth, in chipped dj. Inscr. wad Oct 18 (185) C$240

**Barber, Edward C.**

— The Crack Shot. NY, [1873]. Orig cloth; extremities rubbed, hinges cracking. pba Aug 8 (14) $55

**Barber, Joel D.** See: Derrydale Press

**Barber, John Warner, 1798-1885**

— History and Antiquities of New Haven.... New Haven, 1831. 1st Ed. 12mo, orig cloth; worn & frayed. With 2 maps & 6 plates, all hand-colored. Some foxing. Inscr. wa Feb 29 (355) $130

**Barber, John Warner, 1798-1885 —& Howe, Henry, 1816-93**

— Historical Collections of the State of New York. NY, 1841. Orig sheep; worn. sg Oct 26 (276) $110

**Barberis, Philippus de**

— Discordantiae sanctorum doctorum Hieronymi et Augustini. [Rome: Georgius Teutonicus & Sixtus Riessinger, c.1482]. 4to, modern mor gilt. 28 lines; type 2:75G, 3:109R, 4:93G. With 13 woodcuts. Damage to corner of woodcut border repaired; 1st leaf repaired with lower margin renewed; repair at upper inner margin of final 11 leaves touching text but with loss of 3 characters only. 68 leaves (1st leaf supplied from anr copy). Goff B-120. C Nov 29 (27) £1,200

Anr Ed. Venice: Bernardinus de Benali, [after 1500]. 4to, 19th-cent vellum. With 12 full-page woodcuts Minor staining. 28 leaves. Goff B-121. C June 26 (37) £1,250

**Barbey d'Aurevilly, Jules, 1808-89**
— Les Diaboliques. Paris, 1874. 1st Ed. 12mo, mor janseniste by Marius Michel, orig wraps bound in. S Nov 21 (17) £3,000

**Barbie du Bocage, Jean Denis.** See: Barthelemy, Jean Jacques

**Barbier, Antoine Alexandre, 1765-1825**
— Dissertation sur soixante traductions francaises de l'Imitation de Jesus-Christ.... Paris, 1812. 8vo, contemp red mor by Bozerian jeune with the arms of the Empress Marie Louise. Dedication copy. Fuerstenberg - Schaefer copy. S Dec 7 (31) £2,600

**Barbier, Georges**
— Le Bonheur du jour.... Paris, [1924?]. Oblong folio, unsewn in orig wraps. With 16 plates & hand-colored cover illust. Outer edges of each leaf slightly discolored. S Nov 21 (18) £4,600
— Designs on the Dances of Vaslav Nijinsky.... L, 1913. One of 400. 4to, orig wraps; small loss on spine. Met Dec 5 (19) $500
— Falbalas et fanfreluches. Paris, 1922-26. 6 vols in 1. 8vo, half mor gilt by Gruel, orig wraps bound in. S Nov 21 (134) £3,200

**Barbiere, Joe**
— Scraps from the Prison Table. Doylestown, 1868. 8vo, orig cloth; front joint & spine ends frayed, spotted. Some browning & dampstaining. sg Oct 26 (45) $110

**Barbieri, Giovanni Francesco, 1591-1666.** See: Guercino

**Barbour, George M.**
— Florida for Tourists, Invalids, and Settlers. NY, 1887. Revised Ed. pba July 25 (379) $85

**Barbour, Ralph Henry**
— The Secret Play. NY, 1915. Illus by Norman Rockwell. In dj. CE Sept 27 (48) $240

**Barcia, Andres Gonzalez de.** See: Gonzalez de Barcia, Andres

**Barckley, Sir Richard**
— A Discourse of the Felicitie of Man. L: for W. Ponsonby, 1598. 4to, contemp calf; worn, bds showing. Lower corner gnawed; lacking 1 leaf. Sold w.a.f. STC B1381. CE June 12 (149) $375

**Barclay, Edgar**
— Stonehenge and its Earth-Works. L, 1895. 4to, orig cloth. With 29 plates & plans. sg Jan 11 (37) $110

**Barclay, James**
— A Complete and Universal Dictionary of the English Language. Bungay, 1812. 4to, contemp calf. Some foxing & soiling; a few leaves loose. bba July 18 (213) £85 [Puliti]

Anr Ed. L, [c.1840]. ("A Complete and Universal English Dictionary....") 4to, contemp half calf; worn, hinges split. With frontis, engraved title & 60 maps. Some spotting & soiling; a few maps cropped, affecting surface on Cornwall, Gloucester & Isle of Wight. S Mar 28 (73) £460

Anr Ed. L: Virtue, [c.1850]. 4to, contemp calf; rubbed. With engraved title, frontis, 11 plates & 72 maps, many hand-colored in outline. Sold w.a.f. b Sept 20 (377) £320

**Barclay, Robert, 1648-90**
See also: Franklin Printing, Benjamin
— An Apology for the True Christian Divinity.... Newport, 1729. Old sheep; rebacked retaining orig backstrip. Washed; some sidenotes cropped. sg Oct 26 (10) $500

**Bardi, Giovanni de', conte di Vernio, 1534-1612**
— Discorso sopra il giuoco del calcio fiorentino. Florence: Giunta, 1580. 4to, 19th-cent half mor. With double-page plate (mtd). Worming in margins of tp repaired. S June 27 (298) £2,100

**Barduzzi, Bernardino**
— A Letter in Praise of Verona (1489). Verona: Officina Bodoni, 1974. One of 150. Half vellum. bba May 9 (617) £170 [Blackwell]

**Baret, Michael**
— An Hipponomie or the Vineyard of Horsemanship.... L: George Eld, 1618. 3 parts in 1 vol. 4to, contemp bds; loose. Some soiling, foxing & edge stains. O Jan 9 (28) $850

**Bargos, Abraham de**
— Pensamientos sagrados y educaciones morales. Florence: Isaac de Moise de Pas, 1749. 8vo, modern lea. Some staining & browning. CE Dec 6 (198) $300
— Traduccion de la oracion del ajuon de los temblores de tierra. Pisa: Evangelista Pugli, 1746. 8vo, rebound in modern lea gilt. Some staining & browning. CE Dec 6 (197) $650

**Barham, Richard Harris, 1788-1845**
See also: Fore-Edge Paintings
— The Ingoldsby Legends. L, 1863. 4to, modern half calf antique. sg Feb 8 (6) $200

Anr Ed. L, 1864. 8vo, mor gilt by Bayntun. With 60 illusts. pba Dec 14 (3) $350

Anr Ed. L, 1868. 8vo, contemp calf gilt. With 60 illusts. sg Sept 21 (229) $110

Anr Ed. L, 1877. 8vo, mor gilt; scuffed. wa Feb 1 (18) $75

Anr Ed. L, 1898. Illus by Arthur Rackham. Cloth; spine ends rubbed. With 12 color plates. pba Nov 30 (270) $60

Anr copy. Orig cloth. sg Feb 15 (246) $175

Anr Ed. L, 1905. With 12 colored plates. sg Feb 15 (247) $90

# BARHAM

Anr Ed. L & NY, 1907. 4to, half lev gilt. With 24 colored plates. Corner of frontis chipped. sg Feb 15 (248) $175

One of 560, sgd by Rackham. Mor gilt with onlaid mor design depicting an enraged Lord Brougham, by Bayntun-Riviere. With 24 colored plates. CE Feb 21 (12) $1,200

Anr copy. Orig vellum; bowed. Ck May 31 (130) £300

Anr copy. Orig vellum gilt; discolored & bowed. With 24 tipped-in colored plates. Some spotting. S Nov 2 (124) £260 [Miles]

Anr Ed. L, 1910. 4to, mor gilt by Asprey. CE Sept 27 (234) $800

Anr Ed. L, 1919. 4to, orig cloth. With 24 colored plates. b Sept 20 (635) £70

Anr copy. Half calf gilt by Bayntun. sg Feb 15 (250) $100

**Baring, Daniel Eberhard**
— Clavis diplomatica tradens specimina veterum scripturarum.... Hanover, 1737. 1st Ed. 4to, contemp vellum; worn. With 32 plates. Some browning & foxing; tp cut close, shaving imprint date. O Mar 26 (17) $180

Anr copy. Contemp half vellum; rubbed. 2 plates at end repaired & strengthened on verso; some foxing. O Mar 26 (18) $100

**Baring-Gould, Sabine, 1834-1924**
— A Book of Fairy Tales. NY, 1894. 8vo, orig cloth. pba Aug 22 (773) $65

**Barker, Clive**
— Books of Blood. Santa Cruz: Scream Press, 1985. One of 250. Vols IV-VI in 3 vols. Syn. O Dec 5 (159) $100
— The Damnation Game. L: Weidenfeld & Nicolson, [1985]. One of 250. O Dec 5 (161) $80
— The Great and Secret Show. L, 1989. 1st Ed, one of 500. Syn. O Dec 5 (164) $50
— Imagica. NY, [1991]. One of 500. Half cloth; worn. O Dec 5 (163) $130
— Shadows in Eden. Lancaster PA: Underwood-Miller, 1991. 1st Ed, one of 52 lettered copies with orig sgd drawing. Half lea with snakeskin. O Dec 5 (166) $100
— Weaveworld. NY: Poseidon Press, [1987]. One of 500. In dj. O Dec 5 (167) $90

**Barker, Lucy D. Sale**
— Kate Greenaway's Birthday Book for Children. L, [1880]. 1st Ed. 16mo, cloth; spotted. Inscr to Lady Dorothy Nevill, 10 Feb 1881 (detached) & sgd at appropriate birth dates by c.150 friends of Lady Dorothy, including Oscar Wilde, Charles Darwin, Edward VII & Alexandre Dumas. Ck Apr 12 (9) £3,600

**Barker, Matthew Henry, 1790-1846**
— Greenwich Hospital, a Series of Naval Sketches.... L, 1826. Illus by George Cruikshank. 4to, mor; hinges weak, scuffed. With 12 hand-colored plates. Browned. wd May 8 (48) $450

# AMERICAN BOOK PRICES CURRENT

**Barker, Nicolas**
See also: Roxburghe Club
— Aldus Manutius and the Development of Greek Script & Type in the Fifteenth Century. Sandy Hook CT: Chiswick Book Shop, 1985. One of 200. With 4 orig specimen leaves at end. bba May 9 (27) £85 [Fogelmark]
— The Printer and the Poet. Cambr.: Pvtly ptd, 1970. One of 500. bba May 9 (14) £95 [Mandl]

**Barker, Thomas, fl.1651**
— Barker's Delight: or, the Art of Angling. L, 1657 [but 1820]. One of 100. 12mo, modern cloth; worn, cracked behind 1st signature; tp soiled & browned. O Feb 6 (20) $200

**Barker, William Burckhardt**
— A Practical Grammar of the Turkish Language. L, 1854. 8vo, orig cloth. sg Mar 7 (21) $70

**Barlaam...**
— Barlaam and Josaphat: A Christian Legend of the Buddha. Kentfield CA: Allen Press, 1986. One of 140. sg Sept 14 (4) $130

**Barlet, Annibal**
— Le Vray et methodique cours de la physique resolutive vulgariement dite chymie.... Paris, 1653. 1st Ed. 4to, modern vellum. Some dampstaining & worming; 1 leaf remargined. S Nov 30 (312) £2,200

**Barletius, Marinus**
— Historia de vita et gesti Scanderbegi.... Rome: Bernardus Venetus de Vitalibus, [1510?]. Folio, later vellum; lower cover split. With port. Roman letter. Lacking final blank; tp & last leaf holed but repaired, with loss to tp; 1 leaf with marginal hole. C Apr 3 (31) £1,200

**Barlow, Chester**
— The Story of the Farallones. Alameda, 1897. Orig wraps. pba July 25 (93) $80

**Barlow, John**
— The Loss of the Earl of Abergavenny...a Poem.... Weymouth, [c.1805]. 4to, disbound. Small stain on tp. With contemp Ms account of attempts to salvage the cargo, using a diving bell. b Dec 5 (94) £360

**Barlow, John W. —&**
**Heap, D. P.**
— Letter from the Secretary of War, Accompanying an Engineer Report of a Reconnoissance of the Yellowstone River in 1871. Wash., 1871. 8vo, modern half cloth. With folding map. Tears to map. 42d Contress, 2d Session, Senate Exec. Doc. 66. pba June 25 (5) $80

**Barnard, George, 1807-90**
— Elementary Studies of Trees. Rowney, 1844. Oblong 4to, orig cloth; rebacked. With litho title & 24 plates. b May 30 (519) £60
— The Theory and Practice of Landscape Painting in Water-Colours. L, 1855. 8vo, orig cloth; rebacked. Marginal tears. pba June 20 (41) $120

**Barnard, John Gross, 1815-82**
— Report on the Defenses of Washington.... Wash., 1871. 4to, contemp half sheep; scuffed, spine ends worn, joints split. With folding frontis & 30 folding plates. Marginal dampstaining at ends; some map folds affected by damp or splitting. wa Feb 1 (95) $150

**Barnard, Osbert H.** See: Biorklund & Barnard

**Barnard Library, Thomas Allen**
— [Sale Catalogue] A Catalogue of the Genuine Library of.... L: Egerton, 1789. 8vo, contemp wraps. b Jan 31 (58) £380

**Barnes, Djuna**
— A Book. NY, [1928]. pba Aug 22 (20) $65

**Barnes, James M.**
— Picture Analysis of Golf Strokes.... Phila., [1919]. 5th Ed. - Illus with photos by L. F. Deming. 4to, cloth. Inscr from Andre Edward Lee to Capt. Asterhouse. pba Apr 18 (6) $110

**Barnes, Joseph K.**
— The Medical and Surgical History of the War of the Rebellion. Wash., 1870-88. Parts 2 & 3 of Vol II. 4to, orig cloth; rubbed & shaken, extremities worn. Sold w.a.f. sg May 16 (371) $350

Vols I-VI. 4to, orig cloth; Medical Part I front cover stained & shaken, Surgical Part I rear cover stained, Surgical Part III front hinge cracking. cb Oct 17 (162) $1,700

**Barnes, Joshua, 1654-1712**
— The History of that most Victorious Monarch Edward IIId. Cambr., 1688. Folio, modern calf. pba Sept 14 (11) $225

**Barnes, Julian**
— Metroland. L, [1980]. 1st Ed. In dj. pba Jan 25 (15) $80

**Barnes, William C.**
— Tales from the X-Bar Horse Camp. Chicago, 1920. Half cloth; tape residue to pastedowns. pba Apr 25 (279) $130

**Barneveld, Willem van**
— Medizinische Elektrizitaet. Leipzig, 1787. 8vo, contemp bds; soiled. With 3 folding plates. Some browning & spotting. S Mar 14 (25) £260

**Barnum, Phineas Taylor, 1810-91**
— Thirty Years of Hustling, or How to Get On. Rutland IL, [1891]. 8vo, pictorial cloth; rubbed. sg Feb 8 (166) $80

**Baronio, Giuseppe, 1759-1811**
— Degli innesti animali. Milan: Stamperia e Fonderia del Genio, [1804]. 8vo, contemp sheep gilt; spine chipped & wormed. Library stamp on tp. S Nov 30 (313) £1,800

**Barozzi, Francesco, 1528-1612**
— Cosmographia in quator libros distributa. .. Venice: G. Perchacini, 1598. 8vo, old calf; worn. Some defs (not specified). F Mar 28 (592) $250

**Barozzi, Giacomo, called Vignola, 1507-73**
— Le Due Regole della prospettiva practica.... Rome, 1611. Folio, 18th-cent vellum gilt. Several leaves browned; lacking final blank. sg Jan 11 (4) $550

— Livre nouveau ou regles des cinq ordres d'architecture.... Paris, 1767. Folio, later half mor; spine abraded, joints starting. Foxing & soiling; some margins reinforced. cb Oct 17 (4) $1,400

— Regola delli cinque ordini d'architettura. [N.p., c.1600]. Folio, modern half vellum; spine damaged at foot. Engraved throughout, with title, dedication & 42 plates. last plate with repair to lower outer corner, affecting surface; some browning & staining, especially to last few plates. C Apr 3 (254) £800

**Barr, Alfred H. —&
Hugnet, Georges**
— Fantastic Art, Dada, Surrealism. NY, 1936. 1st Ed. 4to, orig cloth, in dj with tears; bdg cocked. sg June 13 (125) $50

**Barra, E. I.**
— Tale of Two Oceans: New Story by an Old Californian. San Francisco, 1893. 1st Ed. Orig wraps; worn & soiled, spine chipped, covers backed with silk. With 2 plates. Larson copy. pba Sept 28 (306) $50

**Barraband, Jacques**
— Exotic Birds. NY, [1963]. Folio, orig cloth, in dj. sg May 16 (287) $90

**Barratt, Joseph.** See: Teneleses, Nicola

**Barre, Louis, 1799-1857**
— Herculaneum et Pompei. Paris, 1840-39-40. Vols I-VI (of 8). 8vo, orig bds; extremities rubbed. sg May 9 (278) $90

**Barrett, Ellen C.**
— Baja California: A Bibliography.... Los Angeles, 1957-67. One of 550. 2 vols plus 1965-66 Supplement by Katharine M. Silvera, 1968. pba Apr 25 (280) $110

**Barrett, Joseph O.**
— History of "Old Abe", the Live War Eagle of the Eighth Regiment Wisconsin Volunteers. Madison WI, 1876. 8vo, orig wraps. With port of the bird & map. sg Oct 26 (46) $60

**Barrett, Timothy**
— Nagashizuki: the Japanese Craft of Hand Papermaking. North Hills, Pa.: Bird & Bull Press, 1979. One of 300. Half mor by Grey Parrot. sg Sept 14 (60) $275

# BARRETT

**Barrett, Walter**
— Old Merchants of New York. NY, 1866. 4 vols. 8vo, half mor gilt with City of NY seal. sg Feb 8 (17) $175

**Barrie, Sir James Matthew, 1860-1937**
— The Admirable Crichton. L, [1914]. One of 500, sgd by Thomson. Illus by Hugh Thomson. 4to, orig vellum gilt. sg Sept 14 (330) $425
— The Little White Bird. NY, 1902. 1st American Ed. pba Aug 22 (21) $60

Anr copy. Foxed. pba Aug 22 (677) $55
— Peter Pan in Kensington Gardens. L, 1906. Illus by Arthur Rackham. 4to, orig cloth; rubbed. bba May 9 (401) £340 [Johnstone]

Anr copy. Mor gilt by Bayntun-Riviere with onlaid design of Peter Pan seated upon a goat; lacking orig free endpapers with map. With 50 colored plates. CE Sept 27 (235) $1,200

Anr copy. Orig cloth. Ck May 31 (126) £550

Anr copy. Orig cloth. With 50 colored plates. Prelims foxed. Sgd by Arthur Rackham on half-title. sg Sept 14 (302) $450

Anr copy. Orig cloth; rubbed. With 50 colored plates. sg Sept 21 (280) $650

One of 500. Orig vellum gilt; some spotting. With 50 mtd color plates. Crease to p.5. P Dec 12 (150) $2,250

One of 500, sgd by Rackham. Orig vellum gilt; front cover soiled. With 50 colored plates. Ck May 31 (176) £1,200

Anr copy. Orig vellum gilt; covers marked. With 50 colored plates. Some crumpling throughout. S Nov 2 (129) £650 [Vallejo]

Anr copy. With 50 colored plates. sg Oct 19 (194) $3,200

Anr Ed. L, [1909]. ("The Peter Pan Calendar 1910 by Arthur Rackham. Selections from Peter Pan in Kensington Gardens.") 4to, loose in orig wraparound card portfolio with mtd color illust after Rackham; worn & browned. With 6 colored plates mtd on 6 cards decorated in gilt secured at top by modern pink silk tie. Ck May 31 (137) £500

Anr Ed. L, 1910. 4to, calf. With 50 colored plates. b Dec 5 (45) £200

Anr copy. Orig cloth. b May 30 (448) £200

Anr Ed. L, [1912]. 4to, orig cloth. With 50 colored plates. Some leaves frayed & loose. b Jan 31 (212) £130

Anr copy. Orig cloth; spine foot chipped. With 50 colored plates. b May 30 (449) £150

Anr copy. Orig cloth; some staining. Ck May 31 (141) £250
— Quality Street. [L, 1913]. One of 1,000, sgd by Thomson. Illus by Hugh Thomson. 4to, orig vellum gilt. With 22 colored plates. sg Sept 14 (331) $225
— Works. NY, 1929-31. One of 1,030. 14 vols. Half mor. ALs tipped in. pba June 20 (42) $275

## AMERICAN BOOK PRICES CURRENT

**Barrington, Daines, 1727-1800**
— Miscellanies. L, 1781. 1st Ed. 4to, contemp calf. With 2 ports, 5 tables & 2 maps. pba Feb 13 (7) $800

Anr copy. Old calf; rebacked preserving backstrip, worn & bumped, spine head torn. With 2 ports, 5 tables & 2 maps. Some spotting. wa Feb 29 (472) $800
— The Possibility of Approaching the North Pole Asserted. L, 1818. 8vo, 19th-cent half mor; extremities worn. With frontis map. Ink marginalia. sg Mar 7 (270) $150

**Barron, Stephanie.** See: Tuchman & Barron

**Barron, William**
— History of the Colonization of the Free States of Antiquity.... L: T. Cadell, 1777. 4to, recent wraps. K June 23 (13) $300

**Barrow, Albert Stewart**
— Shires and Provinces. L, 1926. Illus by Lionel Edwards. 4to, orig cloth; rubbed. O Jan 9 (29) $275

**Barrow, John, F.R.S.**
— A Visit to Iceland by Way of Tronyem. L, 1835. 12mo, contemp half lea; needs rebdg. sg Mar 7 (271) $175

**Barrow, Sir John, 1764-1848**
— The Eventful History of the Mutiny and Piratical Seizure of H.M.S. Bounty. L, 1831. 1st Ed. 8vo, modern cloth. Library stamp on tp & frontis. sg Mar 7 (23) $150

**Barry, Martin, 1802-55**
— Ascent to the Summit of Mont Blanc.... L: Pvtly ptd, 1835. 8vo, orig bds; spine worn, corners rubbed. With 2 litho plates on india paper & loosely inserted folding map. bba Nov 1 (568) £500 [Gonzalez]

Anr Ed. Edin. & L, 1836. 8vo, orig cloth; soiled, stain to upper cover. With 2 hand-colored plates & folding panorama. Foxed. bba Nov 1 (302) £300 [Gonzalez]

**Barry, Theodore Augustus, 1825-81 —& Patten, B. A.**
— Men and Memories of San Francisco.... San Francisco, 1873. 12mo, orig cloth; worn & soiled. Lacking the double-frontis. pba Nov 16 (20) $50

Anr copy. Orig cloth; joints & spine ends rubbed. pba Feb 12 (247) $150

**Barry, W. J.**
— Up and Down; or Fifty year's Colonial Experiences.... L, 1879. 1st Ed. Orig cloth; worn & soiled; spine chipped. With frontis port, 4 plates, & 6 illus. Some foxing. Larson copy. pba Sept 28 (307) $50

**Barten, Sigrid**
— Rene Lalique: Schmuck und Objets d'Art, 1890-1910. Munich, [1989]. 4to, cloth, in dj. sg June 13 (227) $100

**Barthe, Edouard.** See: Fore-Edge Paintings

**Barthelemy, Jean Jacques, 1716-95**
— Maps, Plans, Views and Coins Illustrative of the Travels of Anacharsis.... L, 1791. 4to, contemp half calf; extremities worn. With 30 double-page maps 7 plates, some hand-colored in outline. Browned throughout. sg May 9 (53) $130
  Anr Ed. L, 1806. 4to, modern cloth; worn. With hand-colored map & 38 plates, many double-page, 9 of the maps hand-colored. Library markings. F June 20 (822A) $160
  Anr copy. Recent half calf. With frontis, folding map & 38 maps & plates, hand-colored in outline. Map with repair; some discoloration. S Mar 28 (280) £150
— Travels of Anacharsis the Younger in Greece.... L, 1793-94. 4th Ed. 7 vols, plus atlas ("Maps, Views....by M. Barbie du Bocage"). Together, 8 vols. 8vo & 4to, contemp calf, Atlas in half calf; worn, some spines def, most plates in Atlas detached. With 31 double-page plates, several hand-colored in outline. bba Oct 19 (252) $80 [Macdonnell]
— Voyage du jeune Anacharsis en Grece. Paris, 1788. 5 vols, including Atlas vol. 4to, contemp red mor extra. With 31 double-page maps, plates & plans, some of the maps hand-colored in outline. Fuerstenberg - Schaefer copy. S Dec 7 (32) £1,800
  Anr Ed. Amst., 1799. 8 vols, including Atlas. 4to, Atlas in contemp half mor, text in contemp mor. With port & 39 plates & maps, 10 of them hand-colored in outline. b May 30 (242) £650

**Barthelemy Library, Jean Jacques**
— [Sale Catalogue] Catalogue des livres.... Paris, 1800. 8vo, contemp wraps. Minor foxing; without supplement but with Table Alphabetique in duplicate. O Mar 26 (19) $140

**Barthelme, Donald**
— Sixty Stories. Putnam NY, 1981. One of 500. sg Dec 14 (6) $90

**Barthes, Roland**
— Erte. Parma, 1972. 4to, cloth; tear to spine. pba June 20 (155) $120; sg Jan 11 (166) $200

**Bartholinus, Caspar, 1650-1705.** See: Bartholinus, Thomas

**Bartholinus, Thomas, 1616-80**
— Acta medica & philosophica Hafniensa. Copenhagen, 1673. 4to, buckram; rebound. With 15 plates. Some plates def, browned & soiled; margins frayed & worming on 1st & last pp. Sold w.a.f. CE Nov 8 (68) $210
— Anatomia, ex Caspari Bartholini.... Leiden, 1674. 8vo, contemp calf; rebacked, rubbed. With additional title, 14 plates (12 folding), & 101 full-page illus. Lacking title-page; additional title & other pp. frayed at edges; some worming, soiling, & damstaining. S Oct 27 (1043) £100 [Zioni]
— De armillis veterum schedion.... Amst., 1676. Bound with: Antiquitatum veteris puerperii synopsis a filio Casparo Bartholini commentario illustrata. Amst., 1676. And: Bartholinus, Caspar. De inauribus veterum syntagma. Amst., 1676. 12mo, contemp vellum. S Mar 14 (31) £150
— De cometa, consilium medicum, cum monstrorum nuper in Dania natorum historia. Copenhagen, 1665. 8vo, modern vellum. Browned. S Mar 14 (29) £650
— De unicornu observationes novae. Amst., 1678. 2d Ed. 12mo, contemp calf with M. Le Petit stamped in gilt on upper cover; spine worn. With engraved title & folding plate (backed). S Mar 14 (30) £360

**Bartholomaeus Anglicus, fl.1230-50**
— De proprietatibus rerum. Cologne: Johann Koelhoff the Elder, 1481. Folio, contemp blind-stamped calf over wooden bds; sides rubbed, rebacked. 39 lines; gothic letter. Dampstaining; tears & repairs; some worming at ends. 456 (of 458) leaves; lacking 2 blanks. Goff B-133. S Dec 18 (15) £1,200 [Zioni]
— El Libro de propietatibus rerum. Toulouse: Henricus Mayer, 18 Sept 1494. Trans into Spanish by Vicente de Burgos. Folio, 19th-cent calf. 46-47 lines & headline; type 6:280G (title), 7:140 (headlines) & 8:101G (text). With woodcut arms on tp & 17 page-width woodcuts. Sheet d3 bound before d2; tp remargins; last few leaves repaired, affecting letters; early annotations & underlinings; some soiling & water-staining. 320 leaves. Goff B-150. Schaefer copy. P Nov 1 (18) $18,000
— Van den proprieteyten der Dinghen. Haarlem: Jacob Bellaert, 24 Dec 1485. Folio, contemp calf over wooden bds with 2 brass clasps; rubbed. 40 lines; double column; type 1:98G. With 11 full-page woodcuts. Leaves a1, a2, a8 & b1 supplied from anr copy. Marginal tears; repair to 1 woodcut; some soiling & staining. 466 leaves. Goff B-142. Schaefer copy. P Nov 1 (17) $40,000

**Bartholomew, Ed**
— The Biographical Album of Western Gunfighters. Houston, 1958. Inscr. pba Aug 22 (884) $160

**Bartholomew, John**
— Philips' Atlas of the Counties of England. L, 1873. 8vo, cloth; rubbed. With 40 double-page color maps. bbc Feb 26 (9) $180

**Bartlet, William Henry, 1809-54.** See: Wright, Thomas

**Bartlett, Dana W.**
— The Better City. Los Angeles, 1907. With 32 plates. Inscr. pba Feb 12 (390) $50

**Bartlett, Edward Everett**
— The Typographic Treasures in Europe. NY & L, 1925. One of 585. Folio, orig half cloth; extremities rubbed. sg Feb 8 (166A) $50

**Bartlett, Henrietta Collins —&
Pollard, Alfred William**
— A Census of Shakespeare's Plays in Quarto...(1594-1709). New Haven, 1916. 4to, half cloth; worn & soiled, corners bumped. O Mar 26 (20) $60

### Bartlett Library, John
— Catalogue of Books on Angling.... Cambr. MA, 1882. 4to, bds; worn & soiled. Library markings. Inscr. O Feb 6 (21) $150

### Bartlett, John Russell, 1805-86
— The Literature of the Rebellion.... Bost. & Providence, 1866. One of 60 L.p. copies. 4to, half mor; extremities worn, spine ends chipped. With ALs. sg Oct 26 (47) $275
— Personal Narrative of Explorations and Incidents in Texas.... NY, 1854. 1st Ed. 2 vols. 8vo, orig cloth; spine ends rubbed. With 2 folding frontises, 14 tinted litho plates & folding map. Lacking 2 woodcut plates; foxed & stained. K June 23 (61) $275
Anr copy. Cloth; frayed & bumped. With folding map & 16 plates. Lacking 1 plate in Vol II but with unlisted view of Tucson; some foxing. Met Feb 24 (368) $475
Anr copy. 2 vols in 1. 8vo, orig cloth; worn, spine tips chipped. Library markings. O Nov 14 (17) $325
Anr copy. With: ALs to Lt. Col. Sir Jas. E. Alexander, 4pp 2 vols. 8vo, orig cloth in half mor slipcase. With 2 folding frontises, 1 folding map, & 14 illus. Inscr to Alexander. Robbins copy. pba Mar 21 (12) $3,250

### Bartlett, N. Gray
— Mrs. Mother Goose of '93. Bost., 1893. Oblong folio, cloth, with remains of dj. With 10 mtd photogravures. With 2-page handwritten identification of all children in each photo. bbc Feb 26 (311) $190

### Bartlett, William Henry, 1809-54
— Walks about the City and Environs of Jerusalem. L, [c.1845]. 2d Ed. 4to, orig cloth; worn. Library markings. sg Mar 7 (25) $90

### Bartok, Bela, 1881-1945
— La Musique populaire des Hongrois.... Budapest: Edmond Stemmer, 1937. 4to, modern half mor gilt. Inscr to M. & Mme. Paul de Kleyn. S Dec 1 (74) £360

### Bartoli, Daniello, 1608-85
— Geographia Moralibus et Politicus. Constance, 1674. 8vo, later calf; joints cracked, rubbed. With halftitle map, & 5 folding maps. Some browning. S Oct 26 (420) £580 [Antiquariat]

### Bartoli, Francesco. See: Bartoli & Bartoli

### Bartoli, Pietro Santi, c.1635-1700
— Le Antiche Lucerne sepolcrali figurate. Rome, 1729. Folio, contemp calf; rebacked preserving spine, rubbed. With 116 plates. S Mar 14 (32) £240
— Colonna Traiana.... Rome, [1667?]. Folio, contemp half calf; worn, covers detached. With 125 plates. Some marginal soiling. S Oct 26 (263) £400 [Zioni]
Anr Ed. [Rome, 1673]. Oblong folio, modern cloth. With engraved dedication & 107 plates only. Marginal dampstaining with traces of mold; index leaf creased & torn; lacking title & plates 5, 50-65 & 118-19. Sold w.a.f. sg Dec 7 (300) $425
Anr Ed. [Rome, c.1700]. Oblong folio, contemp calf gilt; worn, lower hinges split. With engraved title & dedication & 132 plates. Marginal browning. pn Dec 7 (24) £340 [Burden]
— Lucernae veterum sepulchrales iconicae.... Berlin, 1702. 3 parts in 1 vol. Folio, old vellum; warped. With 118 plates. sg June 13 (52) $350
— Museum Odescalchum, sive Thesaurus antiquarum gemmarum. Rome, 1751-52. 2 vols. Folio, old half vellum; soiled. With 104 plates. S June 12 (312) £360
— Recueil de peintures antiques. Paris, 1783-87. One of 100 L.p. copies. 3 vols. Folio, contemp English mor calf gilt with arms of Louis XVIII. With 54 plates in plain & hand-colored states & 1 plain plate. Abdy - Peyrefitte copy. S Nov 30 (232) £10,500

### Bartoli, Pietro Santi, c.1635-1700 —& Bartoli, Francesco
— Picturae antiquae cryptarum Romanorum. Rome, 1791. Folio, contemp half calf; rubbed, foot of spine def. With 94 (on 57) plates. b Sept 20 (74) £300

### Bartolozzi, Francesco, 1727-1815 —& Others
— Eighty-Two Prints.... L, [c.1800]. 2 vols. Folio, later half mor gilt. With 43 (of 82) plates ptd in sepia. Some browning. C Oct 25 (101) £1,900
— Italian School of Design. L, 1835. 2 vols. Folio, half mor; rubbed. Some foxing. rs Nov 11 (64) $375

### Barton, William Paul Crillon, 1786-1856
— A Flora of North America. Phila., 1821-23. 1st Ed. Vol II only. Orig bds; broken. With 33 plates. Folding plate 63 torn & creased; some foxing. Met Feb 24 (430) $300
Anr copy. 3 vols. 4to, half calf; spine split, rubbed, hinges weak. With 106 hand-colored plates. Some foxing. Met Feb 24 (431) $1,100
— Florae Philadelphia Prodromus.... Phila., 1815. 4to, old bds; detached, corners gone, edges worn. Dampstained in upper right corner; some pages bent. Met Feb 24 (306) $500

### Bartram, William, 1739-1823
— Botanical and Zoological Drawings, 1756-1788. Phila., 1968. Folio, orig cloth, in dj. F Mar 28 (247) $100
Anr copy. Cloth, in dj with wear. sg May 16 (288) $80
— Travels through North and South Carolina, Georgia.... Phila.: James & Johnson, 1791. 1st Ed. 8vo, contemp calf; worn & broken. With 8 plates & folding map. Frontis chipped, affecting port border; map with fold break; dedication with tears & creases; 1 plate missing piece in margin. bbc June 24 (374) $4,400
Anr copy. Contemp sheep; extremities worn. Folding map def; lacking 3 of the 8 plates; some plates def. Sold w.a.f. sg Oct 26 (11) $375

Anr Ed. Dublin, 1793. 8vo, contemp calf; rubbed. With frontis, 7 plates (1 folding), & folding map. Tear in map repaired; small hole in title. S Oct 26 (484) £360 [Maggs]

**Barzun, Jacques**
— Lincoln: the Literary Genius. Evanston, 1960. One of 120. Lea. Sgd. sg Oct 26 (213) $130

**Basan, Pierre Francois, 1723-97**
— Collection de cent-vingt estampes, gravees d'apres les tableaux & dessins...de M. Poullain. Paris, 1781. 4to, 18th-cent mor gilt. With engraved title & headpiece, tp by Lebrun engraved by Dambrun & 118 plates on 114 sheets. Some marginal spotting; a few leaves browned. Fuerstenberg - Schaefer copy. S Dec 7 (33) £1,100
— Receuil d'estampes gravees d'apres les tableaux du Cabinet de Monseigneur le Duc de Choiseul. Paris, 1771 [but c.1850]. 4to, 19th-cent half lea; worn, lacking backstrip & lower cover. With engraved title, port & 128 plates. bba June 6 (2) £240 [Finney] Anr Ed. Paris, 1771. 4to, contemp red mor gilt; recased, with new endpapers. With engraved title, port & 128 plates on 125 sheets. Repair in lower margin of tp; dampstain in plates 68 & 69. Fuerstenberg - Schaefer copy. S Dec 7 (34) £850

**Bascom, Louise Rand**
— The Bugaboo Men. NY, [1914]. pba Aug 22 (678) $95

**Basilius Valentinus**
— The Triumphant Chariot of Antimony.... L, 1678. ("His Triumphant Chariot....") 8vo, contemp sheep; worn, needs rebacking. With 5 plates. Some foxing & marginal dampstaining; marginalia. sg May 16 (119) $700

**Baskin, Leonard**
— Ars Anatomica: A Medical Fantasia. NY, [1972]. Folio, loose as issued in portfolio. With 13 plates. sg Feb 15 (22) $50
— Caprices & Grotesques. Northampton, Mass.: Gehenna Press, 1965. One of 500. 4to, wraps. Inscr. sg Feb 15 (18) $100
— Castle Street Dogs. Worcester: Gehenna Press, 1952. One of 20. Inscr. sg Feb 15 (19) $1,700
— Demons, Imps & Fiends. Northampton: Gehenna Press, 1976. One of 450. 4to, bds; extremities worn. sg Feb 15 (20) $100
— Drawings for the Iliad. NY, 1962. One of 90. Folio, loose as issued. With 60 etchings. rs Nov 11 (65) $350
— Figures of Dead Men. Amherst MA, 1968. One of 200, sgd. Preface by Archibald MacLeish. Laid in is an orig sgd woodcut by Baskin. sg Feb 15 (25) $250
— A Gehenna Alphabet. Northampton, 1982. One of 110, this copy an artist's proof. Text by Sidney Kaplan. 4to, syn. Inscr by Baskin & his wife. sg Feb 15 (28) $450
— The Wood Engravings of Leonard Baskin, 1948-1959. Northampton: The Gehenna Press, 1961. One of 24.

Folio, loose as issued in portfolio. sg Feb 15 (36) $4,400

**Bassani, Giovanni Battista**
— La moralita armonica.... Bologna: Giacomo Monti, 1683. 1st Ed. Basso continuo part only (of 3 parts). 4to, contemp wraps. Light dampstain at end. S Oct 27 (913) £150 [Schneider]

**Bassegoda Nonell, Juan.** See: Collins & Bassegoda Nonell

**Baston, Thomas**
— Twenty Two Prints of Several Capital Ships of His Majies Royal Navy.... L: T. Bowles, [c.1721]. Folio, recent half calf. With engraved title & 21 plates. Restoration at foot of engraved title affecting image; plates all cut round & mtd, some 2 to a leaf. S Nov 30 (225) £2,600

**Bateman, James, 1811-97**
— The Orchidaceae of Mexico and Guatemala. L, [1837]-43. One of 125. Folio, contemp half mor gilt; extremities worn, soiled. With litho title & 40 hand-colored plates. C May 31 (5) £30,000

**Bates, Craig D. —&**
**Lee, Martha J.**
— Tradition and Innovation. A Basket History of the Indians of the Yosemite-Mono Lake Region. Yosemite National Park: Yosemite Association, [1990]. In dj. Larson copy. pba Feb 12 (5) $50

**Bates, Ely.** See: Fore-Edge Paintings

**Bates, Henry Walter, 1825-92**
— The Naturalist on the River Amazons. L, 1863. 1st Ed. 2 vols. 8vo, orig cloth; hinges of Vol II weak. With frontises, 1 folding map & 7 plates. S June 13 (372) £700

**Bates, Herbert Ernest.** See: Golden Cockerel Press

**Bates, John**
— Menai Bridge, an Episodic Poem. Holyhead, 1826. 8vo, modern half mor; rubbed. Some foxing. b Dec 5 (503) £280

**Bates, Joseph D.**
— The Art of the Atlantic Salmon Fly. Bost., [1987]. One of 250. 2 vols. 4to, cloth. O June 25 (20) $170
— The Atlantic Salmon Treasury. Montreal: Atlantic Salmon Association, 1975. One of 1,000. Mor gilt, unopened. O June 25 (17) $180
Anr copy. Mor gilt. O June 25 (21) $160; sg Mar 7 (397) $200

**Bates, William, d.1884**
— George Cruikshank.... L & Birm., 1879. 2d Ed. 4to, lea-backed cloth. sg Jan 11 (128) $60

**Batten, John H.**
— Skyline Pursuits. Clinton: Amwell, [1981]. One of 1,000. Lea. sg Mar 7 (398) $130

**Batteney, M.** See: Lemoine & Batteney

### Battershall, Jesse P.
— Food Adulteration and Its Detection. NY, 1887. 8vo, orig cloth; rubbed. sg May 16 (120) $130

### Batteux, Charles
— Les Quatre Poetiques: d'Aristote, d'Horace, de Vida, de Despreaux. Paris, 1771. 2 vols. 8vo, contemp mor gilt; rubbed. Some browning at beginning of Vol I. L.p. copy on hollande. Furstenberg - Schaefer copy. S Dec 7 (36) £400

### Batty, Elizabeth Frances
— Italian Scenery. L, 1820. 4to, contemp calf; spine lacking. With engraved title & 59 (of 60) plates. b Jan 31 (433) £480

Anr copy. Contemp half mor; rubbed. With engraved title & 60 plates. S June 13 (536) £600

Anr copy. Contemp half mor gilt; worn, spine chipped, needs recased. With engraved title & 60 plates. Lacking tp; foxed; 1 signature misbound. wa Nov 16 (383) $500

### Batty, J. H.
— How to Hunt and Trap.... NY, 1878. 12mo, orig cloth; spine ends frayed, lacking front free endpaper. sg Mar 7 (399) $50

### Batty, Robert, d.1848
— Campaign of the Left Wing of the Allied Army in the Western Pyrenees.... L, 1823. 4to, half sheep; needs rebdg. With 25 plates. Stamp on tp & each plate. sg Mar 7 (163) $300
— French Scenery. L, 1822. 4to, orig cloth; joints split, loose. With frontis, pictorial title & 64 plates. Foxed. bba June 6 (39) £100 [Eurobooks]
— Hanoverian and Saxon Scenery. L, 1829. Folio, contemp mor elaborately gilt; upper cover detached, text loose. With engraved title, engraved dedication leaf & 61 full-page plates. bbc June 24 (181) $1,200
— Scenery of the Rhine, Belgium and Holland. L, 1826. 4to, contemp half lea; rubbed, upper joint cracked, spine extremities chipped. With engraved title, frontis & 60 plates. Library markings; verso of tp stamped. pn Dec 7 (136) £440

Anr copy. Contemp half mor; rubbed. Some spotting. S June 13 (535) £550
— Welsh Scenery. L, 1823. 4to, late 19th-cent half mor gilt. With 35 plates. sg May 9 (280) $300

### Baudartius, Wilhelmus, 1565-1640
— Pourtraits en taille douce, et descriptions des sieges, battailles... durant les guerres des Pays bas.... Amst., 1616. 2 parts in 1 vol. 4to, contemp vellum with von Auhalt arms; soiled. With 280 plates, including general map & 23 ports. Plate 5 at B3 pasted over a duplicate of Plate 6; Vol II, Plate 205 at V4 pasted over a duplicate subject; minor creasing. S Nov 30 (95) £2,200

### Baudelaire, Charles, 1821-67
See also: Limited Editions Club
— Douze poemes. Paris: Philippe Gonin, 1939. One of 25. Illus by Jean Berque. Folio, mor extra with design of large revolving nebula in gilt & palladium,

orig wraps bound in, by Therese Moncey. With 12 hand-colored plates. Bound in are 21 drawings, 4 in ink, the rest in ink & watercolor or gouache, each sgd, including all 12 designs for the plates. S Nov 21 (28) £7,000
— Les Fleurs du mal. Paris, 1857. 1st Ed, 1st Issue, with the 6 condemned poems. 12mo, mor gilt by Cuzin, orig wraps bound in. Tipped in are ALs to Victor Hugo, autograph draft by Hugo of letter of condolence to Baudelaire's mother; corrected proof of L'Albatros with stanza added in Baudelaire's hand; ANs of Baudelaire to Gustave Chaix d'Est-Ange. Inscr to Chaix d'Est-Ange in pencil. Paillet - Rodocanachi - Duche - Du Bourg de Bozas copy. S June 27 (299) £50,000

Anr Ed. Paris: Pour les Cent Bibliophiles, 1899. One of 115, this copy for Adolphe Bordes with 7 orig watercolor drawings, 2 menus, & additional vol with 17 etchings & 6 lithos by various artists. Illus by Armand Rassenfosse. 4to, mor extra (orig wraps bound in) by Marius Michel with inset panel of a nude woman & cresent moon in calf, with robe & hair in gilt & watercolor, sgd G. Guetant; suite vol in half mor. S Nov 21 (24) £6,500

Anr Ed. Paris: G. Boutitie, 1923. One of 1,000. Illus by Raphael Drouart. 4to, wraps, in glassine dj. sg Feb 15 (37) $100

Anr Ed. Paris, 1947. One of 320, sgd by Matisse. Illus by Henri Matisse. Half mor, orig wraps bound in. P May 18 (137) $800
— Fleurs du mal in Pattern and Prose. L, 1929. One of 500. Illus by Beresford Egan. 4to, orig cloth; spine head chipped. b Dec 5 (4) £50
— Intimate Journals. NY & L, 1930. One of 400. Trans by Christopher Isherwood; intro by T. S. Eliot. Orig cloth; marked. Inscr by Christopher Isherwood to Cyril Connolly. Hobson copy. S June 28 (162) £500
— Petits poemes en prose. Paris, 1932. ("Le Spleen de Paris.") One of 55 on Hollande. Illus by J. L. Boussingault. 4to, mor extra by Paul Bonet [Carnets, 885]. Orig receipt in Bonet's hand loosely inserted. S Nov 21 (26) £10,000

### Baudrier, Henri
— Bibliographie Lyonnaise. Paris, 1964-65. 13 vols. 4to, cloth. sg Apr 11 (32) $750

### Baudry des Lozieres, Louis N.
— Voyage a la Louisiane. Paris, 1802. 8vo, early sheep; extremities worn. With folding map. sg Oct 26 (12) $500

### Baudu, Rene
— Agora. Paris, 1925. One of 25 sur papier japon ancien with plates in 4 states & orig design in pencil & chalk. Illus by Almery Lobel-Riche. 4to, contemp mor, with inlaid panel of lighter green. b Sept 20 (598) £400

### Bauer, Aleck
— Hazards. Worcestershire, 1993. 1st Ed, One of 750. Foreword by Peter Thomson. Inrto by Fred Hawtree.

Ed by H. R. J. Grant. Cloth. Sgd by Shirley Grant. pba Apr 18 (7) $95

**Bauer, Ferdinand.** See: Stearn, William T.

**Bauer, Max Hermann, 1844-1917**
— Precious Stones. L, 1904. 4to, half mor; rubbed, scuffed, front hinge cracked. Some foxing. wa Nov 16 (309) $240

**Bauer, Rudolf**
— Das Geistreich I. Charlottenburg-Westend, [1930]. One of 1,000. Illus by Aubrey Beardsley. Folio, wraps. sg Feb 15 (38) $400

**Baughman, Robert W.**
— Kansas in Maps. Topeka, 1961. Folio, cloth, in dj. sg May 9 (6) $150

**Baum, Frank Joslyn**
— The Laughing Dragon of Oz. Racine: Whitman, [1934]. Illus by Milt Youngren. Pictorial bds; rubbed. pba Jan 18 (3) $550

**Baum, L. Frank, 1856-1919**
See also: Thompson, Ruth Plumly
— American Fairy Tales. Chicago: George M. Hill, 1901. Pictorial cloth; rubbed & scratched. pba Jan 18 (4) $225

Anr copy. Pictorial cloth; soiled, hinges cracked, front hinge repaired. pba Jan 18 (14) $500

Anr Ed. Indianapolis, [c.1920s]. ("Baum's American Fairy Tales.") 4to, orig cloth; cover bumped. With 8 color plates. pba Jan 18 (8) $180

— The Army Alphabet. Chicago: Hill, 1900. 1st Ed. 4to, half cloth; corners & extremities rubbed, scratched, spine ends repaired. pba Jan 18 (6) $1,100

— The Art of Decorating Dry Goods Windows and Interiors. Chicago, 1900. 1st Ed. 4to, cloth; spine rubbed, hinges cracked. pba Jan 18 (7) $1,300

— Aunt Jane's Nieces and Uncle John. Chicago, [1911]. 1st Ed, 1st State. Some soiling. pba Jan 18 (103) $120

— Aunt Jane's Nieces in Society. Chicago, [1910]. 1st Ed, 1st State. pba Jan 18 (112) $100

— Aunt Jane's Nieces in the Red Cross. Chicago, [1915]. 1st Ed, 1st State. Orig cloth. pba Jan 18 (109) $95

Anr copy. Orig cloth; some spotting. pba Jan 18 (110) $70

2d Ed. Chicago, [1918]. pba Jan 18 (111) $120

— Aunt Jane's Nieces on the Ranch. Chicago, [1913]. 1st Ed, 1st Ptg. pba Jan 18 (113) $60

— Aunt Jane's Nieces on Vacation. By Edith Van Dyne. Chicago: Reilly & Britton, [1912]. 1st Ed, 1st State with ad on verso of half-title listing 7 titles. In soiled dj. pba Jan 18 (115) $90

— Aunt Jane's Nieces Out West. Chicago, [1914]. 1st Ed. pba Jan 18 (118) $75

— Babes in Birdland. Chicago, [1911]. 1st Ed. Cloth-backed pictorial bds; insect discoloration to spine, corners rubbed. pba Jan 18 (92) $190

— Bandit Jim Crow. Chicago, [1906]. Orig cloth; soiled, new endpapers. pba Jan 18 (93) $160

— Baum's Own Book for Children. Chicago, [1912]. 1st Ed. 4to, pictorial bds; rubbed. sg Feb 8 (172) $375

— The Boy Fortune Hunters in Alaska. Chicago, [c.1911]. 1st Ed, 3d State. Orig cloth; some rubbing; spot to lower extremities of front endpapers & following 2 pages. pba Jan 18 (87) $100

— The Boy Fortune Hunters in China. Chicago, [1909]. 1st Ed. Orig cloth; spine ends frayed, rubbed. Frontis lacking. pba Jan 18 (88) $110

— The Boy Fortune Hunters in Egypt. Chicago, [c.1911]. 1st Ed, 3d State. Orig cloth; spine ends chipped & with tears, corners rubbed. pba Jan 18 (89) $110

— The Boy Fortune Hunters in Panama. Chicago, [c.1911]. 1st Ed, 2d State. Orig cloth; mold damage to cover extremities. pba Jan 18 (90) $110

— The Boy Fortune Hunters in Yucatan. Chicago, [1910]. 1st Ed. Soiled. Pbr's File Copy. pba Jan 18 (91) $600

— By the Candelabra's Glare. Chicago, 1898. One of 99. 8vo, pictorial cloth; soiled & discolored, hinge cracked, loose. Inscr to Harrison Rountree. pba Jan 18 (11) $5,000

Anr copy. Orig cloth; soiled, hinges cracked, front endleaves loose. William H. Ellis's copy. sg Oct 19 (26) $2,600

— The Daring Twins. Chicago, [1911]. 1st Ed. In 1st bdg; spine ends rubbed. pba Jan 18 (12) $160

— Daughters of Destiny. Chicago, [1906]. 1st Ed. In 1st bdg; spine ends & corners worn, hinges weak, stamp on pastedowns. pba Jan 18 (101) $150

— Dorothy and the Wizard in Oz. Chicago, [1908]. 1st Ed, 1st Issue. Orig cloth; spine ends rubbed, covers scratched. Lacking 1 plate. pba Jan 18 (13) $375

Anr copy. Orig cloth 2ndary bdg, in torn & chipped dj. sg Oct 19 (28) $2,200

— Dot and Tot of Merryland. Chicago, 1901. 1st Ed. 4to, pictorial cloth; hinges cracked, rear joint repaired. sg Feb 8 (167) $425

Anr Ed. Indianapolis, 1902 [but later]. Pictorial cloth; spine ends & hinges rubbed. pba Jan 18 (15) $225

Anr copy. Pictorial cloth; rubbed. Marginal tears & spotting to a few leaves. pba Jan 18 (32) $50

3d Ed. Chicago, [c.1913]. 4to, pictorial cloth. sg Feb 8 (173) $200

— The Emerald City of Oz. Chicago, [1910]. 1st Ed, 1st State. Bdg extremities rubbed. pba Jan 18 (16) $700

2d State. pba Jan 18 (17) $300

— The Enchanted Island of Yew. Indianapolis, [1903]. 1st Ed, 1st State. Cloth; extremities worn, spine ends chipped. Some soiling; piece lacking from p.11. pba Jan 18 (19) $75

Anr copy. Orig cloth; extremities rubbed, minor bubbling to front cover, inner hinge cracked. sg Feb 8 (168) $325

— The Fate of a Crown. Chicago, [c.1912]. 2d Ed. Orig cloth; spine worn. pba Jan 18 (102) $90

## BAUM

— Father Goose: His Book. Chicago: Hill, [1899]. 1st Ed, 1st Ptg. 4to, pictorial bds; rebacked in cloth, rubbed, hinges repaired. Marginal soiling. pba Jan 18 (20) $110

— Father Goose's Year Book. Chicago, [1907]. 1st Ed. Orig cloth; spine lettering worn off. pba Jan 18 (21) $130

— Glinda of Oz. Chicago, [1920]. 1st Ed. Orig cloth; worn & soiled, 1 plate loose. With 12 color plates. F June 20 (663) $180; K Feb 11 (43) $325

Anr copy. With 10 (of 12) color plates. pba Jan 18 (22) $250

Anr copy. Orig cloth. With 8 (of 12) color plates. pba Jan 18 (23) $75

Anr copy. Orig cloth, in dj with small repair to front & tiny hole on rear panel. With 12 colored plates. Folding color map of Oz laid in. Dick Martin copy. sg Oct 19 (33) $1,800

Anr Ed. Toronto: Copp, Clark, [1920]. Canadian issue with Reilly & Lee sheets but integral title-leaf & lower spine imprinted for Copp Clark. Insect spotting to spine & extremities. pba Jan 18 (24) $110

Anr copy. Hinge cracked, bdg edges worn. sg Jan 14 (285) $500

— John Dough and the Cherub. Chicago, [1906]. 1st Ed, 1st State. Orig cloth; upper part of rear cover discolored, spine rubbed. With the detachable contest blank. pba Jan 18 (25) $500

— The Jolly Giraffe of Jomb. NY: Butterick Publishing, 1905. Orig wraps. In: The Delineator, Vol LXVI, No 1, July 1905. pba Jan 18 (27) $70

— Juvenile Speaker. Chicago, [1912]. ("Baum's Own Book for Children.") Half cloth; bumped. pba Jan 18 (9) $550

Anr copy. Half cloth; extremities rubbed, covers scratched. pba Jan 18 (10) $100

— L. Frank Baum's Juvenile Speaker. Chicago, [1910]. 1st Ed. 4to, orig cloth; spine head rubbed & foot frayed, darkening to upper extremities. Amateur hand-coloring to several illusts. pba Jan 18 (28) $170

— The Land of Oz. Chicago, [1904 but c.1914]. Spine ends & extremities rubbed, rear hinge starting. With 12 color plates. Some tears & chipping to plates. pba Aug 22 (680) $65

— The Last Egyptian. Phila., 1908. 1st Ed, 1st State. Orig cloth; spine relettered in white. Baughman copy. pba Jan 18 (86) $80

— The Life and Adventures of Santa Claus. Indianapolis, [1902]. 1st Ed, 1st State. Bdg with front hinge cracked. pba Jan 18 (29) $400; pba Jan 18 (30) $110

4th Ed. Chicago: M. A. Donohue, [c.1913]. Orig cloth. pba Jan 18 (31) $95

— Little Bun Rabbit.... Chicago, [1916]. 1st Ed, 2d State. 4to, pictorial bds; upper corners rubbed. pba Jan 18 (33) $300

Anr Ed. Chicago, [1920]. Bds, in partial dj; bdg with soiling & spine ends worn. pba Jan 18 (34) $170

— Little Wizard Stories of Oz. Chicago, [1914]. 1st Ed, 1st State. Orig cloth; bowed. pba Jan 18 (35) $300

— The Lost Princess of Oz. Chicago, [1917]. 1st Ed, 1st State. Orig cloth; spine ends rubbed. pba Jan 18 (36) $550

Anr copy. Spot to upper spine. pba Jan 18 (37) $325

Anr copy. Orig cloth, in dj with minor wear & repair. With 12 colored plates. Dick Martin copy. sg Oct 19 (31) $2,600

— The Magic of Oz. Chicago, [1919]. 1st Ed, 1st State. Orig cloth; spot on rear cover. K Feb 11 (45) $350

Anr copy. Spine soiled & faded. pba Jan 18 (38) $275

Anr copy. Orig cloth, in dj. With 12 colored plates. Dick Martin copy. sg Oct 19 (32) $2,000

Anr Ed. Toronto, [1919]. Orig cloth; insect damage to spine & extremities. pba Jan 18 (39) $170

— The Marvelous Land of Oz. Chicago, 1904. 1st Ed, 2d State. Illus by John R. Neill. 4to, pictorial cloth; spine ends rubbed, spot to front cover, front hinge cracked. pba Jan 18 (40) $475

— Mary Louise. Chicago, [1916]. 1st Ed, 1st State. Orig cloth; spine foot rubbed, rear hinge starting. Tp foxed. pba Jan 18 (122) $130

— The Master Key. Indianapolis, [1901]. 1st Ed, 1st State. Orig cloth; spine ends rubbed, front hinge starting. Tear along lower gutter of tp; stains to upper edges. pba Jan 18 (41) $120

— Mother Goose in Prose. Chicago: Way & Williams, [1897]. 1st Ed, 1st State. 4to, cloth; spine ends chipped, scratched, some soiling. pba Jan 18 (43) $2,000

— Mr. Woodchuck. Chicago, [1906]. 2d Ed. In chipped & creased d/j. pba Jan 18 (94) $375

3d Ed. In chipped d/j. pba Jan 18 (95) $400

— The Musical Fantasies of L. Frank Baum: With Three Hitherto Unpublished Scenarios.... Chicago: Wizard Press, 1958. One of 50 bound by Dick Martin. Inscr by Alla Ford to George M. Breslin. pba Jan 18 (154) $180

— The Navy Alphabet. Chicago, 1900. 1st Ed. 4to, pictorial bds; rebacked, orig spine strip laid own, rubbed, new endpapers. Soiling to a few plates; copyright page chipped. pba Jan 18 (44) $425

— A New Wonderland. NY, 1900. 1st Ed, 2dary bdg. 4to, cloth; soiled, chipped. With 15 (of 16) color plates. Staining to bottom corners of several pages in middle of book, affecting plates. pba Jan 18 (5) $650

— Ozma of Oz. Chicago, [1907]. 1st Ed, 1st State. Pictorial cloth; covers dampstained, hinges weak. pba Jan 18 (50) $100

Anr Ed. Chicago, [c.1911]. 2d State. F Mar 28 (80) $80

Variant with missing "O" on p 11. Orig cloth, in chipped dj; bdg edges spotted. sg Oct 19 (27) $600

Anr Ed. Chicago: Reilly & Lee, [c.1923]. Spine ends rubbed. pba Jan 18 (51) $80

— The Patchwork Girl of Oz. Chicago, [1913]. 1st Ed, 1st State. Orig cloth, 1st bdg; minor finger-soiling. bbc June 24 (461) $210; K Feb 11 (52) $425

Anr copy. 1st bdg; spine ends frayed, corners & extremities rubbed.  pba Jan 18 (52) $190

Anr copy. 1st Bdg; soiled, spine rubbed.  pba Jan 18 (53) $130

— Phoebe Daring. Chicago, [1912]. 1st Ed. In 1st bdg; rubbed.  pba Jan 18 (54) $75

— Policeman Bluejay. Chicago, [1907]. 1st Ed. Half cloth; corners bumped, insect damage to spine.  pba Jan 18 (96) $425

Anr copy. Half cloth; corners rubbed, soiled.  pba Jan 18 (97) $275

— Prairie-Dog Town. Chicago: Reilly & Britton, [1906]. 3d Ed, 1st Issue. Pictorial bds; rubbed.  pba Jan 18 (98) $170

— Prince Mudturtle. Chicago: Reilly & Britton, [1906]. 2d Ed. Pictorial bds, in spotted & chipped dj.  pba Jan 18 (99) $275

— The Purple Dragon of Oz and other Fantasies. Lamont GA: Fictioneer Books, 1976. One of 1,500. Orig cloth; joints & spine ends rubbed. Some soiling & foxing.  pba Jan 18 (56) $130

— Rinkitink in Oz. Chicago, [1916]. 1st Ed, 1st State. Orig cloth.  K Feb 11 (53) $425; pba Jan 18 (59) $375

Anr copy. Orig cloth; soiled, spine leaning.  pba Jan 18 (60) $190

Anr copy. Orig cloth, in dj. Dick Martin copy.  sg Oct 19 (30) $3,200

— The Road to Oz. Chicago, [1909]. 1st Ed, 1st State. Piece lacking from upper corner of p.129.  K Feb 11 (54) $325

Anr copy. Later cloth; orig spine strip & covers laid-on, rubbed.  pba Jan 18 (61) $250

Anr Ed. Chicago, [1918]. 4th Issue. Cloth.  pba Jan 18 (62) $110

— The Scarecrow of Oz. Chicago, [1915]. 1st Ed, 1st State. Orig cloth; spine head rubbed.  pba Jan 18 (63) $200

Anr copy. Orig cloth, in dj. With 12 colored plates. Dick Martin copy.  sg Oct 19 (29) $3,200

— The Sea Fairies. Chicago, [1911]. 1st Ed, Chicago Issue. In 1st bdg; stain on rear cover, rubbed.  K Feb 11 (56) $200

Anr copy. In 2d bdg; spine soiled & rubbed.  pba Jan 18 (65) $180

2d Ed. Chicago, [c.1920]. Orig cloth; worn & soiled.  F Mar 28 (87) $60

— Sky Island. Chicago, [1912]. 1st Ed. Orig cloth; tear to top of spine.  K Feb 11 (57) $275

Anr copy. 4to, orig cloth; spine soiled, rear hinge cracked. With 12 colored plates.  pba Jan 18 (66) $180

Anr copy. Orig cloth; soiled, front hinge starting, rear free endpaper chipped.  pba Jan 18 (67) $80

— The Songs of Father Goose. Chicago, 1900. 1st Ed. 4to, half cloth; new endpapers, spine ends & corners rubbed, hinges starting.  pba Jan 18 (68) $150

Anr copy. Half cloth; spine torn, frayed, hinges cracked. Browned; repaired tear to tp.  wa Dec 14 (423) $75

— The Story of the Wizard of Oz. Racine, 1939. Illus by Henry E. Vallely. Folio, pictorial wraps.  pba Jan 18 (70) $85

— Strange Tale of Nursery Folk. Douglasville GA: Pamani Press, 1978. 1st Ed in Book form, one of 150. Pictorial wraps.  pba Jan 18 (71) $140

— The Surprising Adventures of the Magical Monarch of Mo. Indianapolis, [1947]. In chipped dj.  pba Jan 18 (72) $55

— Tamawaca Folks. [Macatawa, Mich.:] Tamawaca Press, [1907]. 1st Ed. Orig cloth; spine ends & corners bumped.  pba Jan 18 (100) $1,100

— Tik-Tok of Oz. Chicago, [1914]. 1st Ed, 1st State.  pba Jan 18 (73) $375

Anr copy. Orig cloth; extremities worn, hinges cracked.  pba Jan 18 (74) $160

— The Tin Woodman of Oz. Chicago, [1918]. 1st Ed, 1st State. Orig cloth; worn & soiled, corner bumped, hinges weak.  F Mar 28 (84) $140

Anr copy. Orig cloth; spine ends & corners rubbed.  pba Jan 18 (75) $475

1st Canadian Ed from American sheets. Toronto, [1918].  sg Feb 8 (174) $100

— The Wizard of Oz. Chicago & NY, 1900. With: The New Wizard of Oz. Indiannapolis, [1903], 8vo, orig cloth, 8 color plates, 5th Ed 1st Ed, 1st State. Illus by W. W. Denslow. 8vo, orig pictorial cloth; spine age-darkened, frayed at ends, shaken. With 24 tipped-in color plates. Some soiling.  CE Nov 8 (167) $5,000

— The Wizard of Oz Waddle Book. NY, [1934]. 2d state. With 8 color plates Lacking the 6 "waddle toys".  pba Jan 18 (80) $110

— The Woggle-Bug Book. Chicago, 1905. 1st Ed, 2d State. 4to, cloth-backed pictorial wraps; soiled, lower corner of front wrap lacking, edge-tears.  pba Jan 18 (81) $1,000

— The Wonderful Wizard of Oz. Chicago & NY, 1900. 1st Ed, 2d State. 8vo, cloth; rubbed & soiled, hinges cracked, lacking front free endpaper. A few plates scratched; 1 plate torn & repaired on verso; 2 plates detached. Sold w.a.f.  pba Jan 18 (84) $425

Anr copy. Orig cloth; soiled, extremities worn, inner hinges cracked, lacking front free endpaper. Plate facing p. 20 scratched & torn; plate facing p. 44 with incision; Plate facing p. 112 detached, torn & repaired.  wad Oct 18 (58) C$450

2d Ed, 3d State. Indianapolis, [1903]. ("The New Wizard of Oz.") Orig cloth; spine ends & joints rubbed, hinges weak.  pba Aug 22 (681) $75

5th Ed. Indianapolis, [c.1922]. ("The Wizard of Oz.") Orig cloth; rear cover dampstained. Some foxing & marginal worming.  pba Jan 18 (77) $60

Photoplay Ed. Indianapolis, [1925]. ("The New Wizard of Oz.") With 8 plates.  pba Jan 18 (47) $180

Anr Ed. Indianapolis, [1939]. In chipped d/j. With 8 color plates.  pba Jan 18 (48) $95

Anr Ed. L, [1939]. ("The Wizard of Oz.") In chipped dj; bdg extremities worn.  pba Jan 18 (78) $90

Anr Ed. [Racine: Whitman, 1939]. ("The Wizard of Oz Picture Book.") Wraps.  pba Jan 18 (79) $70

Anr Ed. West Hatfield MA: Pennyroyal Press, 1985. One of a few copies with a pencil drawing by Moser, sgd. Folio, bds. With 62 wood-engraved illusts. P June 5 (167) $1,900

One of 350. Bds; some wear. O Sept 12 (20) $400

**Baum, L. Frank, 1856-1919 — &
Denslow, William Wallace**

— Two Songs of Father Goose. Chicago, 1900. Folio, pictorial wraps; spines dampstained. Christmas Music Supplement of the Examiner. pba Jan 18 (125) $375

**Baum, L. Frank, 1856-1919 — &
Hough, Emerson, 1857-1923**

— The Maid of Athens: A Musical Comedy in Three Acts. Chicago: Pvtly ptd, 1903. Folio, unbound sheets, stapled at top (as issued). Last leaf detached; tp lacking corner. Library of Congress Duplicate, so stamped on tp, dated 27 Nov 1903. pba Jan 18 (124) $3,750

**Baum, Roger S.**

— Long Ears and Tailspin in Candy Land. NY: Exposition Press, [1968]. In dj. Sgd on front free endpaper. pba Jan 18 (143) $90

**Baumann, Gustave**

— Frijoles Canyon Pictographs.... Los Angeles: William & Victoria Dailey, 1980. In dj. pba Mar 7 (18) $120

**Baur Collection—Geneva**

— Chinese Ceramics. Geneva, 1968-77. One of 50 on Arches. Compiled by John G. Ayers. Vol I only. Orig pigskin, in dj. pn Dec 7 (68) £240

— Japanese Sword-Fittings and Associated Metalwork. Geneva, 1980. Ltd Ed. Compiled by B. W. Robinson. 4to, orig cloth, in dj. sg June 13 (331) $175

**Baur, Johann Wilhelm**

— Iconographia.... Augsburg, [c.1680?]. Illus by melchior Kysell after baur. Folio, contemp vellum. With 141 (of 148) plates. 1st 2 plates crudely hand-colored. S Oct 27 (1102) £900 [Chelsea Gal.]

Anr Ed. Augsburg, 1682. 4 vols in 1. Folio, contemp vellum. With general title, 4 divisional titles, & 142 (of 146) plates. Lacking plates 19-20 & 24 in vol I, & 14 in vol IV; some plates torn & repaired; some worming in margins. S Oct 27 (1101) £900 [D'Arte]

**Bausch & Lomb**

— The Bausch & Lomb Lens Souvenir.... Rochester, 1903. 4to, orig wraps with mtd photo on cover; extremities worn. sg Feb 29 (263) $120

**Baxter, Andrew, 1686?-1750**

— An Enquiry into the Nature of the Human Soul. L, 1745-50. 3 vols, including Appendix. 8vo, contemp calf; worn, covers detached, library stamps on front endpapers. sg Mar 21 (27) $300

**Baxter, William, 1787-1871**

— British Phaenogamous Botany.... Oxford, 1834-43. Vols I-IV (of 6). 8vo, contemp half cloth; worn. With 320 hand-colored plates. Some browning. bba June 6 (3) £260 [Neptune Gallery]

2d Ed. Oxford, 1834-40. Vols I-V only. 8vo, orig cloth; chipped & shaken. With 396 (of 400) hand-colored plates. Some spotting; few leaves loose. S Oct 27 (619) £300 [Squire]

**Bayer, Johann, 1572-1625**

— Uranometria. Augsburg: C. Mangus, 1603. 1st Ed. Folio, 18th-cent calf. With engraved title & 51 double-page star maps. Repair to engraved title; reguarded throughout; lacking prelims; leaves inserted at end with Ms tables & annotations, probably by Folkmar Danchel; 3 plates repaired without loss. Madsen copy. S Mar 14 (35) £6,000

**Bayer, Peter**

— Tavrinensis de Medenis Humani.... Frankfurt, 1612. 8vo, contemp vellum. Marginal chipping on 1st pp; worming throughout. Sold w.a.f. CE Nov 8 (70) $100

**Bayle, Pierre, 1647-1706**

— Dictionaire historique et critique. Rotterdam, 1720. 3d Ed. 4 vols. Folio, contemp calf; hinges cracked, corners bumped, some front free endpapers torn. Occasional worming & dampstaining. S June 12 (9) £170

— Dictionnaire historique et critique. Amst. & Leiden, 1730. 4th Ed. 4 vols. Folio, contemp calf; worn & repaired, corners covered with cloth. O Mar 5 (12) $325

**Bayliss, Marguerite F.** See: Derrydale Press

**Baynard, Edward**

— Health; A Poem... by Dabry Dawne M.D. L: John Taylor, [1716]. 8vo, contemp wraps; dog-eared, backstrip chipped. Some soiling & dampstaining. sg May 16 (373) $100

**Bayne, Samuel G.**

— On an Irish Jaunting Car Through Donegal and Connemara. NY, [1902]. Inscr. pba May 23 (179) $80

**Baz, Gustavo, 1852-1904 — &
Gallo, Edouardo L.**

— History of the Mexican Railway. Mexico, 1876. 1st Ed in English. - Trans by G. F. Henderson. Folio, cloth. With folding litho map & 24 9of 32) tinted litho plates. Also lacking litho title; library stamps on tp. b Dec 5 (110) £400

**Bazin, Gilles Augustin, d.1754**

— The Natural History of Bees.... L, 1744. 8vo, old calf; front bd detached, rubbed, inside hinges split. Some index leaves lacking. Met Feb 24 (307) $250

**Bazincourt, Mlle Thomas de**

— Abrege historique et chronologique des figures de la Bible. Paris, 1768. 8vo, contemp red mor gilt with arms of Charles X as comte d'Artois. Fuerstenberg - Schaefer copy. S Dec 7 (37) £650

**Beach, Spencer Ambrose, 1860-1922**
— Apples of New York. Albany, 1905. 2 vols. Cloth; Vol I cover spotted. NH July 21 (158) $240

**Beach, William Nicholas.** See: Derrydale Press

**Beadle, John Hanson, 1840-97**
— Polygamy or the Mysteries and Crime of Mormonism.... [N.p., 1904]. pba Nov 16 (21) $60

**Beagle, Peter S.**
— A Fine and Private Place. NY, 1960. In dj with tear to spine. Inscr, 1982. pba May 23 (13) $160
— The Last Unicorn. NY: Viking, [1968]. In dj with tear to front panel. pba May 4 (104) $50

**Beale, Joseph Henry**
— A Bibliography of Early English Law Books. Buffalo, 1966. 2 vols, including Supplement, in 1. Cloth; worn. Facsimile of 1926-43 Ed. O Mar 26 (21) $120

**Beale, Reginald**
— Lawns for Sports. L: Simpkin, Marshall, Hamilton, Kent, 1924. 1st Ed. Bds; covers spotted, rear joint chipped. pba Apr 18 (8) $150

**Beall, Karen F.**
— American Prints in the Library of Congress. A Catalogue of the Collection. Balt., [1970]. 4to, cloth, in soiled dj. wa Nov 16 (370) $110

**Bean, Percy**
— The Chemistry and Practice of Finishing. Manchester, 1912. Vol II only. With 48 cards with 2 swatches each. Met Dec 14 (229) $300

**Beard, Peter Hill**
— The End of the Game. NY, [1965]. 4to, cloth, in dj; some wear. O June 25 (22) $70

**Beardsley, Aubrey, 1872-98**
— The Early Work. L, 1912. With: The Later Work. L, 1912. Together, 2 vols. 4to, half mor gilt. sg Jan 11 (38) $110

**Beasley, Norman.** See: Penney, James Cash ("J. C.")

**Beaton, Cecil, 1904-80**
— The Best of Beaton. L, [1968]. 4to, cloth, in rubbed & torn dj. sg Feb 29 (32) $90

**Beattie, Ann**
— Chilly Scenes of Winter. Garden City, 1976. In dj with spine ends rubbed. pba Aug 22 (27) $50

**Beattie, William, 1793-1875**
— The Castles and Abbeys of England. L, [c.1860]. 2 vols. 8vo, 19th-cent half lea gilt; extremities rubbed. Dampstain in blank margin of some plates. sg Dec 7 (192) $140
— The Danube. L, [1844]. Illus by W. H. Bartlett. 4to, contemp calf gilt; worn, front bd detached. With engraved title, 1 map & 78 plates. Some foxing. wa Nov 16 (385) $325

Anr Ed. L, [c.1860]. 4to, orig cloth; worn. With engraved title, port, 2 maps & 80 plates. b Sept 20 (240) £300

— Scotland Illustrated.... L, 1838. 2 vols. 4to, contemp half calf; corners bumped, affecting interior of Vol II. Some foxing. pba Mar 7 (19) $90

Anr copy. 4to, contemp half calf; spines faded. With folding map & 118 plates. Stained in margins. S Oct 26 (383) £190 [Map House]

Anr copy. 2 vols. 4to, contemp half mor; worn. With 2 engraved titles, folding map & 118 plates. Some foxing. wa Nov 16 (384) $140

— Switzerland Illustrated.... L, 1836. Illus by W. H. Bartlett. 2 vols. 4to, half calf; rebacked, rubbed, 2 corners detached. With engraved titles, folding map & 106 plates. Library markings; some spotting. bba June 6 (40) £140 [Eurobooks]

Anr copy. Half calf gilt; spines worn. With engraved titles, folding map & 105 (of 106) plates. bbc June 24 (171) $300

Anr copy. Contemp mor gilt; front covers detached. Some plates browned or stained. CE May 22 (51) $170

Anr copy. Contemp half mor. With 106 plates & folding map. S Oct 26 (264) £350 [Kammer]

Anr copy. Contemp half calf; rubbed & stained. With engraved titles, folding map & 106 plates. Stain to lower inner corner in Vol I. S June 13 (537) £260

Anr copy. Contemp half mor; rubbed. With engraved titles, folding map & 105 (of 106) plates. S June 13 (539) £250

— The Waldenses. L, 1838. 4to, contemp half mor. With port, folding map, engraved title & 70 plates. S Apr 23 (343) £220

**Beatty Library, Sir A. Chester**
— A Catalogue of the Indian Miniatures. L, 1936. 3 vols. Folio, orig cloth. With 103 plates, 19 in gold & colors. Ck Sept 8 (25) £420

**Beaubourg, Maurice**
— Nouvelles Passionnees. Paris, 1893. Out-of-series copy. Illus by Edouard Vuillard. Later cloth. sg Feb 15 (307) $70

**Beauclerk, George Robert**
— A Journey to Morocco in 1826.... L, 1828. Bound with: Blaquiere, Edward. Narrative of a Second Visit to Greece.... L, 1825. 8vo, half mor gilt. pba July 25 (382) $130

**Beaufort, Emily Anne, Viscountess Strangford**
— The Eastern Shores of the Adriatic in 1863.... L, 1864. 1st Ed. - Illus by Hanhart. 8vo, contemp half mor. With 4 color plates & 1 photo. Some plates discolored. S Oct 26 (13) £150 [Scott]

**Beaufort, Francis, 1774-1857**
— Karamania, or a Brief Description of the South Coast of Asia-Minor. L: R. Hunter, 1817. 8vo, half calf; rebacked preserving orig spine. With 7 plates &

maps. Some discoloration to plates; extra plate inserted facing p. 21.   b Sept 20 (324) £700

Anr Ed. L, 1818.  8vo, half calf. With 7 maps & plates. Neatline of 1 chart cropped; some foxing to plates.   b Sept 20 (325) £500

**Beaufoy, Mark, 1764-1827**
— Mexican Illustrations Founded upon Facts.... L, 1828. 4to, lea gilt; rubbed, spine split, residue of library pocket on rear flyleaf. Some foxing; tp stamped. Met Feb 24 (333) $525
— Nautical and Hydraulic Experiments.... L, 1834. Vol I (all pbd). 4to, orig cloth; inner joint broken, front endpaper lacking, shaken. With port, 16 plates & 8 double-page tables. Tipped in is presentation leaf to the Grand Duke of Oldenburg.   O Mar 5 (13) $200

**Beauharnais, Hortense Eugenie de, 1783-1837**
— Romances, mises en musique.... L: Dobbs, [c.1825]. Oblong 4to, contemp mor-backed lea gilt. With engraved title & port & engraved music with 12 plates on facing leaves. Minor foxing.   S May 15 (7) £120

**Beaulieu, Sebastien de Pontault de.** See: Maps & Charts

**Beaumarchais, Pierre Augustin Caron de, 1732-99**
— Le Barbier de Seville. Paris, 1963.   One of 270. Illus by Andre Derain. Folio, unsewn in orig wraps. With 2 plain & 54 colored illusts.   sg Apr 18 (91) $500

**Beaumont, Adalbert de**
See also: Collinot & Beaumont
— Sketches in Denmark, Sweden, Lapland & Norway. L: Thomas McLean, 1840. Illus with plates by C. Bentley after Beaumont. Folio, 19th-cent half mor; worn. With hand-colored litho title, litho dedication & 24 hand-colored plates, some heightened with gum arabic. Blindstamp to each plate, touching image.   S Nov 30 (96) £1,900

**Beaumont, Francis, 1584-1616 —&**
**Fletcher, John, 1579-1625**
— Fifty Comedies and Tragedies. L, 1679. 2d Ed. Folio, contemp calf; rubbed, rebacked. With frontis. Stained; Ccc4 torn; lacking final blank leaf.   S Oct 27 (1044) £400 [Cherryman]
— Works. L, 1647. ("Comedies and Tragedies.") 1st Collected Ed, 1st State of port. Folio, modern mor. Frontis & tp remargined & repaired; ff. A2-4 torn at corners with loss to catchwords; some staining & edge-wear; ^c-^L cropped; some leaves torn at bottom edges; last leaf with ragged edges.   S July 11 (109) £1,000
2d State of port. Old bds; rebacked with modern calf. Port laid on backing sheet & lacking piece from bottom, 2 pieces supplied from anr engraving; lacking last leaf; tp & following leaves chipped. Sold w.a.f.   pba Nov 25 (30) $300
2d Collected Ed. L, 1679. ("Fifty Comedies and Tragedies.") Folio, contemp calf; def. Tp remargined. Sold w.a.f.   CE June 15 (251) $220

Anr Ed. L, 1750.   10 vols. 8vo, contemp calf; rebacked, worn.   sg Feb 8 (7) $250

Anr Ed. Edin., 1812.   14 vols. 8vo, contemp calf gilt. pba Mar 7 (20) $350

**Beaumont, William, 1785-1853**
— Experiments and Observations on the Gastric Juice.... Plattsburgh, 1833. 1st Ed. 8vo, orig half cloth; broken, worn & stained. Some foxing & dampstaining. CE May 22 (52) $950
Anr copy. Old bds; rebacked, old spine relaid, extrems rubbed. With 3 illus. Spotted; 1 gathering browned.   Ck Mar 22 (26) £480
Anr copy. Orig cloth; parts of spine perished. Some soiling.   P Dec 12 (42) $800
Anr Ed. Edin., 1838.   8vo, contemp half cloth; broken, front cover stained.   sg May 16 (375) $275

**Beauties...** See: Goldsmith, Oliver

**Beauvau, Henri de**
— Relation journaliere du voyage du Levant. Nancy, 1615. 1st Illus Ed. 4to, recent half calf. With title, & 49 illus. Title damaged with loss, backed; some staining & browning; last 42 pp. with small whole affecting text & illus.   S Oct 26 (44) £2,300 [Karides]

**Beauvilliers, Antoine, 1754-1817**
— The Art of French Cookery. L, 1826.   12mo, contemp half calf; rubbed, spine ends worn.   bba May 30 (125) £65 [Bib. Gastronomica]

**Beazley, Charles Raymond, 1868-1955**
— Prince Henry the Navigator. NY, 1895. 8vo, contemp calf gilt, prize bdg with certificate on front pastedown. With 28 maps & plates.   sg Mar 7 (26) $70

**Becanus, Guglielmus.** See: Ferdinand

**Beccanuvoli, Lucrezio**
— Tutte le donne vicentine, maritate, vedove, e dongelle. [Bologna, 1539].   4to, modern vellum; 1st gathering loose. Trimmed at top.   C Apr 3 (32) £1,800

**Beccaria, Cesare Bonesana di, 1738-94**
— Dei Delitti e delle pene. [Livorno: Tipografia Coltellini], 1764.   4to, contemp vellum over paper bds. Some foxing.   C Apr 3 (34) £8,500

**Beccaria, Giovanni Battista, 1716-81**
— Dell' elettricismo artificiale e naturale.... Turin, 1753. 4to, contemp vellum; upper cover warped. Half-title soiled; some browning & marginal stains.   S Mar 14 (34) £260
— Experimenta, atque observationes quibus electricitas vindex late constituitur atque explicatur. Turin, 1769.   4to, modern calf gilt, orig wraps bound in. With folding plate & table. D2v soiled. Tp inscr: "Ex dono Don Alexandri Voltae liber Comitis Jo. Bap. Jovii 1771". Madsen copy.   S Mar 14 (33) £1,000

**Becher, Johann Joachim, 1635-82**
— Chymischer Rosen-Garten. Nurembert: heirs of J. D. Tauber, 1717. 8vo, contemp vellum. S Mar 14 (36) £800

**Beck, Christian Daniel**
— Specimen historiae bibliothecarum Alexandrinarum. Leipzig, 1779. 4to, contemp wraps; worn & soiled. Munby - Kraus copy. O Mar 26 (22) $170

**Beck, Theodoric Romeyn**
— Elements of Medical Jurisprudence. Albany, 1823. 1st Ed. 2 vols. 8vo, modern half mor. Foxed throughout. CE Nov 8 (71) $380

**Becker, Felix.** See: Thieme & Becker

**Becker, George Ferdinand, 1847-1919**
— Geology of the Comstock Lode and the Washoe District.... Wash., 1882. 2 vols, including Atlas. Half lea; bds chipped. With 7 litho plates in text vol & 19 litho maps in Atlas, all but 2 double-page. Some stains. Z June 14 (206) $130

**Becker, Joseph Ernest de.** See: De Becker, Joseph Ernest

**Becker, Robert H.** See: Grabhorn Printing

**Becker, Wilhelm Adolf, 1796-1846.** See: Fore-Edge Paintings

**Beckett, Samuel, 1906-89**
See also: Limited Editions Club
— Au loin un oiseau. NY, 1973. One of 120, sgd by author & artist. Illus by Avigdor Arikha. 4to, unsewn in wraps as issued. sg Dec 14 (8) $650
— From an Abandoned Work. L, 1958. Wraps. sg Dec 14 (7) $60
— Malone Dies. NY, [1956]. One of 500. pba Jan 25 (17) $140
— Murphy. NY: Grove Press, [c.1957]. One of 100. Half cloth. b Jan 31 (140) £280
— Quatres Poems. Four Songs NY: Gunnar A. Kaldewey, 1986. One of 50, sgd by author & artist & with 45rpm record inserted. Music by Bun-Ching Lam. Folio in triangular shape, bds. Schaefer copy. P Nov 1 (20) $600
— Whoroscope. Paris: The Hours Press, 1930. 1st Ed, One of 100. Orig wraps. S June 28 (149) £1,200

**Beckford, Peter, 1740-1811**
See also: Fore-Edge Paintings
— Thoughts on Hunting. Salisbury, 1781. 1st Ed. 4to, contemp calf; rebacked, rubbed. Some foxing & soiling. O Jan 9 (30) $200
Anr copy. Contemp half calf; worn. Inscr to Thomas Bowen. O Jan 9 (31) $225
Anr copy. Contemp half calf; rubbed, spine chipped. O Jan 9 (32) $180

**Beckford, William Thomas, 1760-1844**
See also: Limited Editions Club
— Recollections of an Excursion to the Monasteries of Alcobaca and Batalha. L, 1835. 8vo, later half calf. Tear to fore-edge of 1st 4 leaves. bba May 30 (370) £100 [Devitt]

**Beckford Library, William Thomas**
— [Sale Catalogue] The Valuable Library of Books in Fonthill Abbey. L, 1823. 8vo, bds; broken. Z Jan 30 (47) $100

**Beckmann, Johann, 1739-1811**
— A History of Inventions and Discoveries. L, 1846. 4th Ed. 2 vols. 12mo, orig cloth. Institutional stamp on bottom edges & in upper margin of the 2 ports. sg May 16 (123) $60

**Beddie, M. K.**
— Bibliography of Captain James Cook.... Sydney, 1970. 2d Ed. 8vo, orig cloth in dj. sg Apr 11 (32A) $80

**Bede, The Venerable, 673-735**
— Commentationum in sacras literas.... Paris, 1545. 3 vols in 1. Folio, modern half mor. S July 11 (1) £300
— The History of the Church of Englande. Oxford: Shakespeare Head Press, 1930. One of 475. Trans by Thomas Stapleton. Folio, bds, unopened. sg Sept 14 (321) $350
Anr copy. Half calf. sg Feb 15 (273) $225

**Bede, Cuthbert.** See: Bradley, Edward

**Bee, Jon.** See: Badcock, John

**Beebe, Charles William, 1877-1962**
— A Monograph of the Pheasants. L, 1918-22. One of 600. 4 vols. Folio, contemp mor gilt by Groschupf; upper corner of Vol III rubbed. With 90 color plates, 88 photogravures & 20 distribution maps. C May 31 (4) £3,600
— Pheasants, their Lives and Homes. Garden City, 1926. 2 vols. Orig cloth; worn & soiled. F June 20 (325) $60
Anr Ed. Garden City, 1931. 2 vols. Orig cloth; owners' stamps to front endpapers. pba Nov 16 (343) $55

**Beebe, Frank L. —&**
**Webster, Harold M.**
— North American Falconry and Hunting Hawks. [Denver, 1964]. 4to, orig cloth, in dj with wear; lower portion of covers & contents dampstained. Sgd by Beebe & Webster. sg May 16 (289) $50

**Beebe, Lucius Morris, 1902-66 —&**
**Clegg, Charles M.**
— Cable Car Carnival. Oakland, 1951. 1st Ed. In dj. Sgd by both authors. pba Feb 12 (257) $110
— Virginia & Truckee: A Story of Virginia City and Comstock Times. Oakland, 1949. One of 950. In dj. pba Feb 12 (491) $130

**Beechey, Frederick William, 1796-1856**
See also: Grabhorn Printing
— Narrative of a Voyage to the Pacific and Beering's Strait.... L, 1831. 2 vols. 8vo, later half calf. With 23 plates & 3 maps. Larson copy. pba Sept 28 (42) $325

# BEECHEY

1st Ed. 2 vols. 4to, contemp calf; bindings worn, vol I front joint cracking. With 23 plates & 3 maps. Some plates foxed; 1 leaf torn, anr repaired. Larson copy.   pba Sept 28 (41) $2,250

Anr copy. Modern bds, fragments of orig spine laid on. Some foxing & discoloration to plate margins. pba Feb 13 (10) $2,500

2d Ed. 2 vols. 8vo, contemp half calf; rubbed. With 3 folding charts & 23 plates, 4 of them double-page. Some spotting.   b Mar 20 (10) £340

1st American Ed. Phila., 1832.  8vo, orig half cloth; backstrip damaged, front cover loose. Tp stamped; foxed.   sg Mar 7 (272) $120

— The Zoology of Captain Beechey's Voyage.... L, 1839. 1st Ed. 4to, modern calf. With 44 hand-colored plates & 3 folding charts, hand-colored in outline. Some soiling to text.   pba Feb 13 (12) $7,500

## Beeck, J.
— The Triumphs of William III, King of England.... L: H. Rhodes, 1702. 8vo, contemp calf; worn, covers detached. With frontis & 61 plates. Text browned; lacking Plate 22.   sg Mar 21 (28) $275

## Beeckman, Daniel
— A Voyage to and from the Island of Borneo.... L, 1718. 1st Ed. 8vo, contemp calf; worn, rebacked. With 2 maps & 5 plates. Some discoloration. S Mar 28 (381) £1,100

## Beedham, Ralph
— Wood Engraving. Ditchling: St. Dominic's Press, 1925. 2d Ed. - Intro by Eric Gill; illus by Eric Gill & Desmond Chute. Orig half cloth; rubbed & spotted. bba May 9 (339) £70 [Cox]

## Beerbohm, Sir Max, 1872-1956
— A Book of Caricatures. L, 1907. Folio, half cloth; upper corner bumped, edges worn, hinges cracked. With frontis & 48 mtd plates. Prelims foxed.   wa Nov 16 (276) $80

— Fifty Caricatures. L, 1913. 4to, orig cloth.   bba July 18 (264) £55 [Ginnan]

— Heroes and Heroines of Bitter Sweet. L, 1931. One of 900. Folio, loose as issued.   bba July 18 (271) £65 [Bell, Book & Radmall]

— Observations. L, 1925. 1st Ed. 4to, orig cloth. With colored frontis & 51 plates.   bba July 18 (270) £65 [Sotheran]

— A Peep into the Past. [NY]: Privately Printed, 1923. One of 300 on japan vellum. Half cloth.   S Nov 2 (76) £120 [Zioni]

— Rossetti and his Circle. L, 1922. Orig cloth.   bba July 18 (268) £80 [Ginnan]

One of 350.   bba July 18 (267) £140 [Sotheran]

— Works. L, 1896. 1st Ed. 4to, orig cloth. Inscr by John Lane.   sg Sept 21 (76) $250

Anr Ed. L, 1922-28.  One of 780, sgd.  10 vols. Half calf gilt by Sotheran.   sg Sept 21 (2) £1,400

— Zuleika Dobson. L, 1911. 1st Ed, Issue not stated. sg Sept 21 (77) $200; sg June 20 (16) $325

## Beers, D. G.
— Atlas of Franklin County New York. Phila., 1876. Folio, modern cloth retaining panels of orig cloth. sg Dec 7 (34) $425

## Beethoven, Ludwig van, 1770-1827
— 4me Grande Simphonie en Sib majeur...Op:60. Bonn & Cologne, [1823]. Bound with: Beethoven. Cinquieme Sinfonie en ut mineur... Oeuvre 67. Leipzig, [1826] And: Beethoven. Sixieme Sinfonie Pastorale en fa majeur... Oeuvre 68. Leipzig, [1826]. 8vo, half cloth; def. A few stains. S May 15 (284) £1,300

— Diabelli Variations. Vienna: Cappi & Diabelli, [1823]. ("33 Veraenderungen ueber einen Walzer fuer das Pieno-Forte....") Bound after: Schubert, Franz, Sonate...Oeuvre 120 [in A major, D.664]; 2 vols of J. S. Bach's Noch wenig bekannte Orgelcompositionen [RISM B474]; 4 vols of Grandes Suites dites Suites angloises [BWV 807, 809, 806, 810]; Pastorella, Berlin [c.1824] [BWV 590] & W. A. Mozart's La Fantasie et Sonata [K475 & 457], Offenbach, [c.1814]; & other works. Together, 10 works bound in 1 vol. 4to, contemp half calf; worn. S May 15 (282) £3,200

— Fantaisie pour le pianoforte... Oeuv. 77. Leipzig: Breitkopf & Haertel, [1810]. Oblong folio. Lithographed throughout. Tp border trimmed; paper label reading St. Petersbourg pasted to foot of title.   S May 15 (569) £800

— Fidelio, drame lyrique in trois actes. Paris: Aristide Farrenc, [c.1831]. 3d Issue. Full score in 3 vols. 4to, cloth bds. Engraved throughout. Some spotting & staining at the beginning. Early Ms of Florestan's aria in Act 2 tipped in. S May 15 (8) £360

— Grande Sonate pour le Clavecin ou Piano-Forte... Oeuvre 7. Vienna: Artaria, [1797]. Oblong folio, in modern cloth chemise. Engraved throughout. Washed. S May 15 (565) £1,000

— Grande Sonate pour le Pianoforte... Oeuvre XXVIII. Vienna: au Bureau d'Arts et d'Industrie, [1802]. Oblong folio, modern cloth folder; disbound. Engraved throughout. Some staining. S May 15 (566) £1,000

— LIme sonate pour le pianoforte... Op.54. Vienna: au Bureau d'Arts et d'Industrie, [1806]. Oblong folio, modern cloth folder; disbound. Engraved throughout. Washed. S May 15 (568) £850

— Overture No 2 zur Oper Leonore.... Leipzig: Breitkopf & Haertel, [n.d.]. 4to, half cloth. Wilhelm Furtwaengler's annotated performing copy, sgd. S May 15 (287) £2,400

— Quatuor pour deux Violons, Alto et Violoncelle... Oeuvre 127. Mainz & Paris: A. Schott, [1826]. Complete parts. Bound with: Op. 18, Nos 1-3. Paris & Bon: N. Simrock, [c.1802]. And: Op. 18, Nos 4-6. Mainz: Schott, [n.d.]. And: quartets by Haensel & Fodor. Contemp bds. S Dec 1 (75) £950

— Sestetto Pour 2 Clarinettes, 2 cors et 2 bassons [Op. 71]. Leipzig: Breitkopf & Haertel, [1810]. Folio, complete parts. Tp repaired, affecting 2 letters; some dust-staining. S Dec 1 (79) £1,100

— Sonate fuer Pieno-forte und Violin... Op. 96 [parts for violin & piano]. Vienna: Steiner, [1816]. Folio, unbound; some wear at hinge. S Dec 1 (76) £950

— Terzetto originale (Tremate, empi, Tremate!), per il soprano, tenor e basso con accompagnamento dell'orchestra... Op. 116. Vienna: S. A. Steiner, [1826]. Oblong folio, Unbound in modern cloth folder. Engraved throughout. With additional Ms copy of the 2d bassoon part; some fraying & spotting. S May 15 (573) £700

**Beeton, Isabella Mary, 1836-65**
— The Book of Household Management. L, 1861. 1st Ed. 2 vols. 8vo, modern half calf. With color frontis, additional title, & 12 plates. Spotted. S Oct 12 (85) £650

Anr copy. 2 parts in 2 vols. 8vo, contemp half calf; worn. With color frontis, additional color title, & 12 plates.. S Oct 12 (86) £250

**Beeverell, James**
— Les Delices de la Grand Bretagne et de l'Irlande. Leiden, 1707. Vols I-VIII in 7. Contemp vellum. With 9 double-page engraved titles, 194 double-page plates & 3 double-page views. Writing washed out of half-titles, staining following prelims in Vol IV. sg May 9 (281) $325

**Behan, Brendan, 1923-64**
— Brendan Behan's Island.... NY, [1962]. Illus by Paul Hogarth. In dj. Sgd by Behan & Hogarth on tp. pba May 23 (16) $120

**Behrens, Conrad Berthold, 1660-1736**
— Selecta diaeetica.... Frankfurt, 1710. 1st Ed. 4to, contemp bds; rebacked in calf, lower front corner bumped. Leaves browned throughout. Ck Mar 22 (27) £190

**Bekhterev, Vladimir Mikhailovich**
— Provodjashchie puti spinnogo i golovnogo mozga. St. Petersburg, 1896-98. 2 vols in 1. 8vo, contemp half lea; spine rubbed with puncture at bottom, joints worn, lacking front free endpaper. sg May 16 (376) $110

**Belanger, Charles**
— Voyage aux Indes-orientales.... Paris, [1831]-34. 21 livraisons: 9 Historique, 4 Botanique, 8 Zoologie. 4to & 8vo, unsewn & folded in orig wraps; some wraps torn & soiled. Historique with 42 lithos, 15 of them hand-finished, & 2 maps; Botanique with 31 plates, 3 of them ptd in colors; Zoologie with 40 hand-colored plates. Some spotting & browning. S June 27 (5) £3,000

**Belcher, Edward.** See: Simpkinson & Belcher

**Belcher, Sir Edward, 1799-1877**
— Narrative of a Voyage Round the World.... L, 1843. 1st Ed. 2 vols. 8vo, orig cloth; rubbed, Vol I shaken. Plates foxed; library markings. CE June 12 (151) $600

Anr copy. Orig cloth; worn. With 19 plates & 3 folding charts in end pocket. Library markings. S June 13 (565) £350

**Belcher, John, d.1913 —& Macartney, Mervyn Edmund, 1853-1932**
— Later Renaissance Architecture in England. L, 1901. 2 vols. Folio, half mor; front cover lacking some lea, Vol I with hinge cracked, gutta percha perished. With 170 photographic plates. pba Sept 14 (14) $180

**Beldam, George W.**
— Great Golfers: Their Methods at a Glance. L: Macmillan, 1904. 1st Ed. Cloth; joints & spine ends chipped, corners bumped, rear hinge starting. With 268 photos. pba Apr 18 (9) $100

— The World's Champion Golfers: Their Art Disclosed by the Ultra-Rapid Camera. L, [1924]. 1st Ed. 9 (of 11) vols, bds; spines chipped, vol I spine stained. pba Apr 18 (10) $450

**Beldam, George W. —& Fry, C. B.**
— Great Batsmen.... L, 1905. pn Oct 12 (279) £210
— Great Bowlers & Fielders.... L, 1906. pn Oct 12 (280) £200

**Beldam, George W. —& Taylor, John H.**
— Golf Faults Illustrated. L, [c.1900]. Cloth; spine ends rubbed. pba Nov 9 (2) $150

**Belden, David**
— Souvenir of the Carnival of Roses... 1901. Santa Clara: Carnival of Roses, [1901]. Half mor. Inscr by A. Greeninger, Director General of the Rose Bowl Committee. pba Nov 16 (23) $50

**Belden, Frank A.** See: Haven & Belden

**Belgique...**
— La Belgique horticole, journal des jardins de serres et des vergers. Liege, 1851-62. Ed by C. & E. Morren. Vols I-XII (of 35). 12 vols in 6. 8vo, contemp half mor. With 269 hand-colored plates by G. Severyns. Some discoloration & offsetting. Sold w.a.f. S Oct 27 (760) £1,650 [Walford's]

**Belidor, Bernard Forest de, 1693?-1761**
— Architecture hydraulique.... Paris, 1737-53. 4 vols. 4to, contemp calf; repaired. With 2 frontises & 219 folding plates. Plate 57 from anr copy; Worming in Vols II-IV; some discoloration. S June 12 (295) £650

Mixed Eds. Paris, 1737-39-88-90. 4 vols. 4to, contemp vellum or calf. Lacking port of author & plates 7 & 30 ; some discoloration. Sold w.a.f. S Mar 14 (38) £340

**Beljakov, Aleksandr Vassilevich —& Others**
— Navigator's Log Book Airplane No 25. Moscow, 1939. 2 vols. 4to, facsimile in orig cloth, explanatory text in orig wraps. sg May 16 (8) $90

**Bell, Alexander Graham, 1847-1922**
— Improvement in Telegraphy... Letters Patent No. 174,465. Wash.: United States Patent Office, 7 Mar 1876. Folio, unbound. Upper blank forecorner of 1st leaf torn away; chip to fore-edge of last leaf. CNY May 17 (4) $12,000

**Bell, Andrew**
— Anatomia Britannica: A System of Anatomy. Edin., 1798. Parts 1 & 2 only in 1 vol. Disbound. With 38 plates only. Foxing & staining. Sold w.a.f. sg Dec 7 (183) $225

**Bell, Sir Charles, 1774-1842**
— A Series of Engravings, Explaining the Course of the Nerves.... Phila., 1818. 1st American Ed. 4to, contemp half lea; worn, front cover detached. With 9 plates. Some foxing. sg May 16 (377) $150

**Bell, Ellis.** See: Limited Editions Club

**Bell, George**
— Rough Notes of an Old Soldier.... L, 1867. 2 vols. 8vo, cloth; worn. O Nov 14 (19) $250

**Bell, Horace, 1830-1918**
— Reminiscences of a Ranger, or Early Times in Southern California. Los Angeles, 1881. 1st Ed. 8vo, cloth. Larson copy. pba Feb 12 (392) $1,900
Anr copy. Cloth; worn, hinges cracked & 1 tape-repaired. Bell's annotated copy. Larson copy. pba Feb 12 (393) $250
Anr copy. Orig cloth; spine faded, joints rubbed. Robbins copy. pba Mar 21 (14) $450

**Bell, Isaac**
— Foxiana. L: Country Life, 1929. One of 150. Illus by G. D. Armour. 4to, lea; rubbed. O Jan 9 (33) $160

**Bell, James Stanislaus**
— Journal of a Residence in Circassia.... L, 1840. 2 vols. 8vo, orig cloth; spine ends chipped, hinges cracked. With folding map hand-colored in outline & 12 plates, 3 colored. Dampstained in margins. sg Mar 7 (27) $275

**Bell, John, 1745-1831**
— Bell's British Theatre. L, 1776-84. Vols I-XX. 20 vols. 8vo, contemp calf gilt; worn. S Apr 23 (219) £120

**Bell, William Abraham**
— New Tracks in North America. L, 1869. 1st Ed. 2 vols. 8vo, contemp half calf. With 20 color lithos, 3 botanical plates & 1 map. Lacking the folding map but with facsimile laid in; dampstain to frontis of Vol I & to margins of some plates. pba Nov 16 (24) $750
Anr copy. Orig cloth; spine ends & edges worn, corners bumped, spines soiled, front hinge of Vol II cracked. With 24 plates & 2 maps. Short tear to folding color map. wa Feb 29 (511) $400

**Bellamy, Edward, 1850-98**
See also: Limited Editions Club
— Looking Backward.... Bost., 1888. 1st Ed, 1st State. 12mo, orig cloth. pba May 4 (105) $200
Anr copy. Orig cloth; soiled, library bookplate on front pastedown. sg Sept 21 (79) $70

**Bellani, Luigi Vittorio Fossati**
— I Libri di viaggio e le guide della raccolta. Rome, 1957. 3 vols. Orig bds, in djs. bba Oct 5 (11) £380 [Cartiglio]
Anr Ed. Mansfield, [n.d.]. One of 300. 3 vols. Orig cloth. bba July 18 (1) £150 [Ritchie]

**Bellarmine, Roberto Francesco Romolo, Saint, 1542-1621**
— De scriptoribus ecclesiasticis. Cologne, 1684. 4to, contemp vellum; worn. Some browning. O Mar 26 (23) $225

**Bellepierre de Neuve-Eglise, Louis Joseph de**
— Le patriot artesien. Paris, 1761. 8vo, contemp red mor gilt with arms of Chauvelin; upper joint worn at head. Lower outer corner of I4 torn away. Fuerstenberg - Schaefer copy. S Dec 7 (41) £550

**Bellew, Henry Walter, 1834-92**
— Kashmir and Kashghar. L, 1875. 8vo, orig cloth; rubbed & stained, hinges weak. Inscr. bba Nov 1 (430) £350 [Randall]

**Belli, Melvin**
— Ready for the Plaintiff! NY, 1956. Inscr. pba June 13 (136) $50

**Bellin, Jacques Nicolas, 1703-72**
— Description geographique du golfe de Venise.... Paris, 1771. 1st Ed. 4to, contemp calf; spine head & tail & corners worn, rubbed. With addition title by Arrivet, & 47 (of 49) maps & plans (13 folding). Some dampstaining in foremargins. S Oct 26 (15) £700 [Frew]
— Le Petit Atlas Maritime. Paris, 1764. 5 vols. 4to, contemp calf gilt; rubbed, some spines chipped. With engraved general title, 6 engraved divisional titles, engraved dedication & indexes & 581 maps & plans. Some dampstaining. S Nov 30 (66) £9,000
— Teatro della guerra marittima, e terrestre. Venice, 1781. Folio, contemp half sheep; spine wormed. With engraved title, 2 views & 41 maps. Gulf of Mexico shaved with minor loss. C Apr 3 (35) £2,800

**Bellini, Lorenzo, 1643-1704**
— De urinis et pulsibus, de missione sanguinis.... Leiden, 1717. 4to, contemp vellum; worn. Library stamp on tp; some browning & foxing. O Mar 5 (14) $140
— Excercitationes anatomicae duae de structura et usu renum ut et de gustus organo.... Leiden, 1726. Bound with: Opuscula aliquot.... Leiden, 1737. 2 works in 1 vol. 4to, contemp vellum. Together, 7 folding plates. 1 plate with whole; lacking 1 half-title; some dampstaining & spotting. Ck Mar 22 (28) £200

### Bellini, Vincenzo, 1801-35
— La Straniera.... Milan: Antonio Fontana, 1829. 8vo, later wraps. Some foxing & creasing. Libretto for the premiere. S Dec 1 (86) £850

### Belloc, Hilaire, 1870-1953
— Beasts from Belloc: A Selection of Poems.... [Portland OR], 1982. 1st Ed, One of 125. Illus by Sarah Chamberlain. Orig half mor. bba May 9 (365) £150 [Marks]
— The Highway and its Vehicles. L, 1926. One of 1,250 numbered copies. 4to, cloth; rubbed & soiled. Some foxing. sg Feb 15 (41) $60

### Bellori, Giovanni Pietro, 1636?-1700
— Veteres arcus Augustorum triumphis insignes. Rome, 1690. Folio, contemp vellum; worn & soiled. Some foxing & soiling. O Mar 5 (15) $600
— Veterum illustrium philosophorum poetarum.... Rome, 1685. Folio, contemp calf gilt. With 95 (of 96) plates. Lacking frontis; some browning. sg Jan 11 (39) $600

### Bellow, Saul
— Dangling Man. NY, 1944. 1st Ed. Orig cloth, in tape-repaired dj; bdg sloth soiled, spine leaning. pba Oct 5 (5) $425
— The Dean's December: a Novel. NY, 1982. One of 500 specially bound. sg Dec 14 (10) $80
— The Victim. NY, [1947]. In dj with spine head chipped & rear panel stained at bottom. pba Oct 5 (6) $95

### Bellows, George Wesley, 1882-1925
— The Paintings. NY, 1929. Folio, bds; extremities worn. Library markings. sg Sept 7 (38) $80; sg Jan 11 (40) $100
  Anr copy. Half vellum; corners worn. sg June 13 (55) $140

### Belsham, William
— History of Great Britain.... L: Richard Phillips, 1806-12. 12 vols. Calf gilt; spine tops pulled. K June 23 (81) $525

### Beltaine
— Beltaine. L, 1899-1900. Ed by William Butler Yeats. 3 Nos in 1 vol. 4to, brown bds; extremities rubbed. pba Aug 22 (528) $225

### Beltrami, Giacomo Constantino, 1779-1855
— La decouverte des sources du Mississippi et de la Riviere Sanglante. New Orleans, 1824. 8vo, contemp calf; extremities rubbed. Last 13 text leaves wormed, with loss. sg Oct 26 (13) $450

### Beman, David
— The Mysteries of the Trade.... Bost., 1825. 8vo, contemp calf; rubbed. Some foxing & soiling. O Nov 14 (21) $250

### Bemelmans, Ludwig, 1898-1962
  See also: Onassis copy, Jacqueline Bouvier Kennedy
— The Donkey Inside. NY, 1941. One of 175. pba June 20 (53) $225

— Father, Dear Father. NY, 1953. One of 151. Sgd on the orig drawing & inscr on the limitation page & on the slipcase. sg Sept 28 (36) $200
— Madeline's Rescue. NY, 1953. In frayed dj. O Sept 12 (21) $400

### Benacci, Vittorio
— Descrittione de gli apparati fatti in Bologna par la venuta di N. S. Papa Clemente VIII. Bologna: Vittorio Benacci, 1598. Illus by Guido Reni. 4to, 18th-cent half vellum. With 8 plates. Tp soiled. C Apr 3 (37) £2,600

### Benardin de Saint Pierre, Jacques Henri, 1737-1814
— Paul et Virginie. Paris, 1876. One of 70 on Whatman. Illus by P. E. A. Hedouin. 12mo, mor; orig vellum wraps bound in. With port & 6 plates. Port in 4 states; plates in 2 states. S Oct 27 (1162) £650 [Chelsea Rare]

### Benavides, Alonso de
— Fray Alonso de Benavides' Revised Memorial of 1634. Albuquerque, 1945. Annotated by Frederick Webb Hodge, George P. Hammond, & others. Orig cloth in dj; d/j spine ends chipped, some rubbing, spine faded. Robbins copy. pba Mar 21 (16) $90
— The Memorial of Fray Alonso de Benavides, 1630. Chicago: Pvtly ptd, 1916. One of 300. Trans by Mrs. Edward E. Ayer. 8vo, orig cloth. Robbins copy. pba Mar 21 (15) $375

### Benedictus
— Variations.... Paris, [c.1925]. Folio, loose as issued in orig portfolio. With 20 pochoir colored plates. Minor marginal soiling & tears. pn Dec 7 (70) £420

### Benedictus de Nursia
— De conservatione sanitatis. [Rome: Stephan Plannck, c.1487-88]. 4to, vellum. With 54 leaves. Light spotting; marginal staining; outer bifolia & last quire rehinged; fol.2 & final 2 leaves marginally renewed. Ck Mar 22 (29) £2,400

### Benedictus, Edouard
— Variations. Paris, [1923]. 4to, loose in orig half cloth portfolio; bowed, discolored. With 20 plates & cover design, colored through stencils. Minor wear to plates. cb June 25 (1921) $1,000

### Benesch, Otto
— The Drawings of Rembrandt. L, 1954-57. 6 vols. 4to, cloth. sg Jan 11 (374) $500

### Benet, Stephen Vincent, 1898-1943. See: Limited Editions Club

### Benezit, Emmanuel, 1854-1920
— Dictionnaire critique.... Paris, 1966. 8 vols. bba July 18 (57) £200 [Rozman]; S Mar 28 (428) £230
  Anr Ed. Paris, 1976. 10 vols. bba Oct 5 (12) £260 [Gutenberg]; bbc Dec 18 (152) £260

### Ben-Gurion, David, 1886-1973. See: Onassis copy, Jacqueline Bouvier Kennedy

**Bening, Simon**
— Le Livre d'heures aux fleurs. Lucerne, [1991]. 2 vols. 8vo, velvet in slipcase. sg Apr 11 (215) $650

**Benjamin, Asher, 1773-1845**
— The Practical House Carpenter.... Bost., 1830. 4to, contemp half sheep; worn. Browned throughout. sg Jan 11 (41) $285
— Practice of Architecture.... Bost., 1840. 4to, orig sheep; extremities rubbed. With 60 plates. Some foxing affecting plates. sg Jan 11 (5) $200

**Benjamin ben Jonah, of Tudela**
— Itinerarium.... Leiden, 1633. 8vo, later calf gilt, with Nedonchel arms. In Hebrew. CE Dec 6 (10) $1,200
Anr copy. 24mo, later mor with Nedonchel arms. In Latin. CE Dec 6 (11) $500

**Benjamin, Marcus**
— John Bidwell, Pioneer. Wash., 1907. 1st Ed. Wraps; darkened & dampstained. With frontis port. Some dampstaining. Inscr & sgd by Cowan. Larson copy. pba Sept 28 (315) $50

**Bennet, Abraham**
— New Experiments on Electricity. Derby, 1789. 8vo, orig bds; spine def. With folding frontis & 3 folding plates. S Mar 14 (39) £600

**Bennett, James**
— Overland Journey to California.... NY: Edward Eberstadt, [1932]. One of 200. Orig wraps; minor soiling. pba Aug 8 (16) $140

**Bennett, Melba Berry**
— Robinson Jeffers and the Sea. San Francisco, 1936. One of 300. Half mor, in def dj. pba Oct 5 (193) $50

**Benoit, Pierre Andre, 1886-1962**
— Le Puits de Jacob. Paris, [1927]. One of 15 with orig illuminated miniature. Illus by Arthur Szyk. Wraps. Minature framed & separate. sg Feb 15 (283) $1,800
One of 300. Wraps. sg Feb 15 (284) $325

**Benoit, Pierre Jacques, 1782-1854**
— Voyage a Surinam. Brussels, 1839. Folio, half cloth; extremities worn. With litho title & 49 plates on india paper mtd, 14 of them on tinted paper. Some spotting. C Nov 29 (82) £800
Anr copy. Contemp mor gilt stamped "AP" in center; rubbed. With pictorial litho title & 49 tinted litho plates. Small spot in lower margin at Plate XVIII. S Nov 30 (146) £1,300

**Bensen, D. R.**
— Irene, Good Night. NY, 1982. One of 250. Illus by Edward Gorey. Silk, in pictorial glassine designed by Gorey. sg June 20 (90) $350

**Benson, Arthur Christopher, 1862-1925**
— The Book of the Queen's Dolls' House. [The Book of the Queen's Dolls' House Library]. L, 1924. One of 1,500. 2 vols. 4to, half cloth, with remains of djs. pba June 20 (54) $375

**Benson, E. F. —& Miles, Eustace H.**
— A Book of Golf. L: Hurst & Blackett, 1903. 1st Ed. - Illus with photos by A. Gandy. Cloth; spine ends chipped, soiled, rear hinge starting. pba Apr 18 (13) $225

**Benson, Richard**
— Morni; an Irish Bardic Story.... Dublin, 1815. 8vo, orig bds; worn. b Dec 5 (596) £80

**Bentivoglio, Guido, Cardinal, 1579-1644**
— Della Guerra di Fiandra. Venice, 1645. 3 parts in 1 vol. 4to, contemp vellum. sg Mar 21 (29) $140
— The History of the Wars of Flanders.... L, 1654. Folio, 19th-cent calf gilt; front cover detached. With 24 ports & double-page map. Text browned. sg Mar 21 (30) $475
Anr Ed. L, 1678. Folio, contemp calf. pba Sept 14 (15) $450
Anr copy. Contemp calf; joints cracked. sg Mar 21 (31) $400

**Bentley, Harry C. —& Leonard, Ruth S.**
— Bibliography of Works on Accounting by American Authors.... Bost., 1934-35. 2 vols. Cloth; worn, 1 joint strengthened. Vol II lacking tp. O Mar 26 (25) $50

**Bentley, Wilder**
— The Poetry of Learning. Berkeley: Archetype Press, 1973-85. Ltd Ed. 25 scrolls, each in cardbd tube covered with decorated paper or unbleached linen. pba June 20 (55) $300

**Bentley's Miscellany**
— Bentley's Miscellany. L, 1837-39. Vols I-XX bound in 10. 8vo, contemp half calf; worn, some spines def. S Apr 23 (4) £780

**Benton, Joseph Augustine, 1818-92**
— The California Pilgrim.... Sacramento, 1853. 1st Ed. - Illus by Charles Nahl. 8vo, orig cloth; cover extremities worn, joints & hinges cracked. With 6 plates. Larson copy. pba Sept 28 (309) $120

**Benton, Thomas Hart, 1782-1858**
— In Senate of the United States. February 9, 1829...[concerning the fur trade]. [Wash., 1829]. Senate Issue. 8vo, modern half mor. pba July 25 (253) $325

**Benton, Thomas Hart, 1889-1975**
— An Artist in America. NY: Robert McBride, [1937]. In dj. Sgd on half-title. sg Sept 7 (39) $120

**Benzenberg, Johann Friedrich, 1777-1846**
— Versuche ueber das Gesetz des Falls, ueber den Widerstand der Luft.... Dortmund, 1804. 8vo, near-contemp half calf; worn, head of spine torn. With frontis, engraved title & 6 plates on light blue paper.

Library stamps on tp. Honeyman - Hefner copy. CNY May 17 (5) $1,200

**Benzing, Joseph**
— Die Buchdrucker des 16. und 17. Jahrhunderts im Deutschen Sprachgebiet. Wiesbaden, [1982]. 8vo, orig wraps. sg Apr 11 (34) $150
— Lutherbibliographie. Baden-Baden, 1966. 8vo, orig wraps. sg Apr 11 (33) $250

**Beraldi, Henri.** See: Portalis & Beraldi

**Beraldi Library, Henri**
— [Sale Catalogue] Bibliotheque. Paris, 1934-35. 5 vols. Recent cloth, orig wraps bound in. bba May 9 (112) £100 [Maggs]

**Berard, Auguste Simon Louis**
— Essai bibliographique sur les editions des Elzevirs.... Paris, 1822. 8vo, contemp bds; spine chipped. O Mar 26 (26) $150

**Berchoux, Joseph**
— La Gastronomie, Poeme.... Paris, 1805. 4th Ed. 12mo, contemp calf; spine worn. With frontis & 3 plates. sg Sept 21 (120) $80

**Berckelars, Ferdinand Louis.** See: Seuphor, Michel

**Berenson, Bernard, 1865-1959**
— The Drawings of the Florentine Painters. L, 1903. One of 300. 2 vols. Folio, half lea; worn, rubbed & chipped. O May 7 (51) $300
   Anr Ed. Chicago, 1938. 3 vols. 4to, cloth. sg June 13 (56) $300

**Berg, R.** See: Nielsen & Berg

**Berger, Thomas**
— Crazy in Berlin. NY, [1958]. In chipped dj. pba Oct 5 (7) $110
— Little Big Man. NY, 1964. In rubbed dj. pba Aug 22 (29) $85

**Berghauer, Johann Thomas Adalbert**
— Bibliomaxeia, das ist: Biblischer Fledzug und Musterung vieler jaemmerlich-verfaelschten Bibeln. Oberammergau: Wagner, 1746. 4to, contemp calf; rubbed. Some browning & foxing. Kraus copy. O Mar 26 (27) $500

**Berghaus, Heinrich**
— Kleiner Geographisch-Statischer Atlas der Preusischen Monarchie. Gotha, 1842. 8vo, half cloth. With 10 double-page maps, hand-colored in outline. Last map dampstained. sg May 9 (54) $70

**Bergman, Ray**
— Just Fishing. Phila., [1932]. In dj with pieces lacking. Sgd on half-title. pba July 11 (27) $55
— Trout. NY, 1952. Joint cracked. Ns to Bill Kaufmann laid in. pba July 11 (28) $120

**Bergstraesser, J. A. B.**
— Nomenclatur und Beschreibung der Insecten in der Graffschaft Hanau-Muenzenberg.... Hanau, 1778-79. Vols I-III (of 4) in 1 vol. 4to, contemp half sheep gilt. With 72 hand-colored plates, captioned in contemp hand. Some soiling & staining to plates. sg May 9 (355) $600

**Berhaut, Marie**
— Caillebotte, sa vie et son oeuvre. Paris, 1978. Folio, cloth, in dj. sg Jan 11 (73) $250

**Berkeley, G. C. Grantley F., 1800-81**
— Fact against Fiction... Hydrophobia and Distemper. L, 1874. 2 vols. Cloth; soiled. O June 4 (39) $50

**Berkeley, George, 1685-1753**
— Works. Dublin, 1784. 2 vols. 4to, contemp calf; rubbed, Vol I covers detached. Port lacking port; small hole in folding plate. bba May 30 (121) £190 [Cathach]

**Berkenmeyer, Paul Ludolph**
— Le curieux antiquaire ou recueil geographique et historique des choses les plus remarquables. Leiden, 1729. 3 vols. 8vo, 19th-cent bds; rubbed. With 2 maps & 23 folding plates. S Mar 28 (223) £150

**Berlin**
— Berlin and its Treasures. A Series of Views.... Leipzig & Dresden, [c.1854]. 4to, orig cloth; rubbed, joints of Vol I worn. bba June 6 (41) £240 [Garwood & Voigt]
— Katalog der Ornamentstichsammlung der Staatlichen Kunstbibliotek Berlin. Berlin & Leipzig, 1939. 4to, orig cloth; inner hinges weak. Ck Apr 12 (196) £160

**Berlioz, Hector, 1803-69**
— Grande Messe des Morts... Op. 5. Paris: Schlesinger, [1838]. Contemp bds; worn. Engraved throughout. Some spotting, browning & staining; Ms index in German on initial blank. Inscr to J. Maurel Temoignage. S Dec 1 (88) £3,800

**Bernacchi, L. C.**
— Saga of the "Discovery". L: Blackie, [1938]. Edges foxed. pba July 25 (14) $75

**Bernal, Ignacio**
— Bibliografia de arqueologia y etnografia Mesoamerica y Norte de Mexico, 1514-1960. Mexico City, 1962. Folio, orig cloth. ds July 27 (21) $150

**Bernanos, Georges**
   See also: Limited Editions Club
— Jeanne, relapse et sainte. Paris: Le Livre Contemporain, 1951. One of 23, this copy ptd for Albert Malle. Illus by Jacques Vallery-Radot. 4to, calf extra with semi-abstract design & monogram of Jeanne d'Arc, by Rose Adler, 1953. Bound in are orig watercolor drawing, various related ephemera & a separate suite of 5 plates, 4 of them with their color progressions. C May 1 (11) £24,000

## Bernard, Saint (Bernardus Claravallensis), 1091-1153

— Homiliae super evangelium "Missus est angelus Gabriel." Antwerp: Gerard Leeu, 1487-89. 4to, 19th-cent half vellum. Lower margins of leaves B2, B3 & E6 repaired; 3 letters of last line, B2v, supplied in facsimile; tp soiled. 30 leaves. Goff B-400. Schaefer copy. P Nov 1 (21) $4,250

— Modus bene vivendi. Florence: L. Morgiani & J. Petri for Pietro Pacini, 27 Jan 1495/6. 4to, modern mor. 30 lines & foliation; type 1:110R. With 1 woodcut. Sheet h1.8 reversed in bdg; tear into text in k6 repaired without loss; hole affecting a few letters in several leaves. 124 leaves. Goff B-418. C Nov 29 (28) £1,600

— Sermones de tempore et de sanctis. Mainz: Peter Schoeffer, 14 Apr 1475. Folio, modern calf. 47 lines; double column; gothic letter. Last leaf repaired with loss; 1st leaf browned & with library stamp; some dampstaining in 1st few leaves; some staining; marginal repairs. 206 (of 235) leaves; lacking 1st 28 leaves (supplied in photofacsimile) 7 final blank. Goff B-436. S Mar 29 (641) £1,300

## Bernard, Auguste Joseph

— Geofroy Tory: Painter and Engraver.... Bost. & NY, 1909. One of 370. Folio, bds. sg Sept 14 (48) $350

## Bernard, Claude, 1813-78

— Introduction a l'etude de la medicine experimentale. Paris & NY, 1865. Bound with: Lecons sur la chaleur animale sur les effets de la chaleur et sur la fieve. Paris, 1876; Lecons sur le diabete et la glycognese animale. Paris, 1877. 1st Eds. 3 works in 1 vol. 8vo, modern half calf; orig wraps bound in, with repaires. With 3 separate half-titles. Some spotting. Ck Mar 22 (30) £270

— Lecons de physiologie operatoire. Paris, 1879. 1st Ed. 8vo, later cloth. sg May 16 (378) $140

— Memoire sur le pancreas.... Paris, 1856. 1st Separate Ed. 4to, modern half mor; orig wraps bound in, extrems brittle. With 9 plates (4 hand-colored). Some spotting; 1st 7 leaves with closed hole; 1 plate misbound. Ck Mar 22 (33) £900

— Nouvelle Fonction du Foie considere comme organe producteur de matiere sucree chez l'homme et les animaux. Paris, 1853. 1st Monograph Ed. 4to, orig wraps; spine brittle. With half-title & illus. Inscr on upper cover. Ck Mar 22 (34) £2,800

— L'Oeuvre. Paris, 1881. 8vo, modern bds; orig wraps bound in, with repairs to margin. With frontis port. Some spotting. Ck Mar 22 (36) £150

## Bernard, Pierre —& Others

— Le Jardin des plantes. Paris, 1842-43. 2 vols. 4to, contemp half calf; rubbed & chipped. With 2 ports, 1 double-page plate, 1 folding map & 145 plates, 37 of them colored. Some foxing. S Mar 29 (724) £160

## Bernard, Pierre Joseph

— Oeuvres. Paris: Didot, 1797. One of 150. Illus by Pierre Paul Prud'hon. 4to, red mor gilt by Bozerian. With 4 plates before letters. Fuerstenberg - Schaefer copy. S Dec 7 (43) £2,000

## Bernard, Tristan, 1866-1947

— Tableau de la boxe. Paris, [1922]. Ltd Ed. Illus by A. D. de Segonzac. 4to, contemp mor gilt by Leveque, orig wraps bound in. With 29 etchings. b Sept 20 (599) £250

## Bernardino de Laredo

— Subida del Monte Sion; por la via contemplativa. Seville: Juan Cromberger, 1538. 4to, 16th-cent blind-tooled calf; rebacked with orig spine laid down, endpapers renewed, orig front endpaper laid down. With 27 woodcuts. Gothic type. Writing on tp verso scratched out leaving 3 small repaired holes; 1 sheet in 1st quire strengthened in inner margin; 2 leaves with Ms notes bound in at end. Schaefer copy. P Nov 1 (140) $4,000

## Bernardus Carthusiensis

— Dialogus Virginis Mariae misericordiam elucidans. Leipzig: [Conrad Kachelofen], 1493. 4to, modern vellum bds. With 50 (of 56) leaves, 40 lines 7 headline. Lacking gathering A. S Oct 27 (1045) £350 [Gabinete]

## Bernardus Parmensis

— Casus longi super quinque libros decretalium. Basel: Michael Wenssler, [not after 1479]. Folio, contemp blind-stamped calf over wooden bds, pastedowns from early service book. 45 lines & headline; double column; gothic letter. Some worming at beginning; a few leaves browned; Ms annotations in margin & list of contents on front flyleaf. Leaf count not given. Goff B-455. S Dec 18 (19) £1,800 [Zioni]

**Bernatz, Johann Martin.** See: Schubert & Bernatz

## Berners, Dame Juliana, b.1388?

See also: Ashendene Press

— Book of St. Albans. L: for Humfrey Lownes, 1595. ("The Gentlemans Academie. Or, the Book of S. Albans....") 4to, remboitage of early calf; rebacked, spine rubbed. Tp & next 2 leaves supplied; lacking 3 blanks; library markings. sg Mar 21 (32) $2,000

Anr Ed. L: Elliot Stock, 1899. ("The Boke of Saint Albans....") 4to, parchment-covered wraps; spine chipped. Facsimile of the 1486 Ed. pba July 11 (31) $500

— A Treatyse of Fysshynge wyth an Angle. NY, 1875. 8vo, cloth. Marginal dampstain throughout. O Feb 6 (23) $90

Anr Ed. L, 1883. ("An Older Form of the Treatyse of Fysshynge wyth an Angle.") One of 200. 4to, half mor gilt; joints rubbed. pba July 11 (29) $160

Anr copy. Orig bds; backstrip def. Inscr by the Ed, Thomas Satchell. sg Mar 7 (400) $275

## Bernhard, Karl, Duke of Saxe-Weimar-Eisenach

— Reize naar dn Door Noord-Amerika. Dordricht, 1829. 2 vols. 8vo, contemp wraps; some wear. Minor foxing. O Mar 5 (17) $170

— Travels through North America.... Phila., 1828. 2 vols in 1. 8vo, half sheep; spine & joints tape-repaired. bbc Dec 18 (436) $210

**Bernhardt, Sarah, d.1923**
— Ma Double Vie. Memoires de Sarah Bernhardt. Paris, 1907. 8vo, half mor. Inscr to Juliette Ford, 1 Jan 1918. S June 12 (165) £180

**Berni, Francesco, 1497-1536**
— Il primo [secondo] Libro dell'opere burlesche.... Florence: Heredi di Bernardo Giunti, 1548-55. 2 vols. 8vo, 18th-cent vellum & 19th-cent vellum gilt. Minor flaws in lower margin of A2 in Vol II; some spotting. C June 26 (38) £1,200

**Bernier, Francois, 1620-88**
— Voyages de Francois Bernier contenant le description des etats du Grand Mogol, de l'Hindoustan.... Amst., 1711. 2 vols. 12mo, later calf gilt; joints weak. With 2 frontises, 3 folding maps & 1 folding plate. wa Dec 14 (195) $500

**Bernonville, P. de**
— Nouvelle decouverte d'une langue universelle, pour les negocians, et le secret de lire l'hebreu sans points. Paris: Charles Fosset, 1687. 12mo, early wraps; spine def. 1st plate cut round & mtd with loss; some staining. CE Dec 6 (12) $700

**Bernoulli, Jean, 1667-1748**
— Opera. Lausanne & Geneva, 1742. 4 vols. 4to, disbound. With 91 folding plates. Library markings; lacking engraved titles & 2 ports. Sold w.a.f. O Mar 5 (18) $150
Anr copy. Contemp calf; worn. With engraved title,1 port & 91 folding plates. Lacking port of author. S Mar 14 (41) £440
Anr copy. 19th-cent half mor gilt; worn. With 90 (of 93) plates. Some foxing; Plate 28 bound upside-down; library markings. sg May 16 (125) $500

**Berquin, Arnaud, 1749?-91**
— Pygmalion. Paris, 1775. 2 parts in 1 vol. 8vo, modern mor gilt. Fuerstenberg - Schaefer copy. S Dec 7 (47) £300
Anr copy. 2 parts in 1 vol plus anr copy of Part 2 inserted. 8vo, orig wraps. Fuerstenberg - Schaefer copy. S Dec 7 (48) £400
— Romances. Paris, 1801. 12mo, contemp calf gilt. Fuerstenberg - Schaefer copy. S Dec 7 (51) £150

**Berquin-Duvallon, —**
— Vue de la colonie espagnole du Mississipi.... Paris, 1803 [An XI]. 1st Ed. 8vo, contemp calf gilt; joints & extremities rubbed. With 2 hand-colored folding maps. Tear to gutter edge of 1 map; each map with tear at mount. Engelhard copy. CNY Jan 26 (170) $3,000

**Berr de Turique, Marcelle**
— Raoul Dufy. Paris, 1930. 4to, orig wraps. sg Sept 7 (132) $175
Anr copy. Orig wraps; rebacked with cloth. With frontis etching. sg Jan 11 (155) $140

**Berretini da Cortona, Pietro.** See: Ottonelli & Berretini da Cortona

**Berry, John J.**
— Life of David Belden. NY, 1891. Orig cloth; front hinge cracking, tp split at top of gutter margin. pba Apr 25 (287) $50

**Berry, William, 1774-1851**
— The History of the Island of Guernsey. L, 1815. 4to, 19th-cent half mor gilt; rubbed. With folding map & 29 plates. Browned & foxed. bba Nov 1 (23) £320 [Mandl]

**Bertarelli, Achille.** See: Caproni Guasti & Bertarelli; Caproni & Bertarelli

**Berthold, Victor M.**
— The Pioneer Steamer California, 1848-1849. Bost., 1932. One of 550. pba Feb 12 (503) $75; pba Apr 25 (288) $55

**Berthollet, Claude Louis, Comte, 1748-1822**
— Elements of the Art of Dyeing.... L, 1824. 2 vols. 8vo, contemp sheep; extremities rubbed. Some text browned. sg May 16 (126) $80

**Berthoud, Ferdinand, 1727-1807**
— Essai sur l'horlogerie. Paris, 1786. 2 vols. 4to, contemp calf; rubbed, corners worn, joints rubbed, library numbers on spines. With 38 folding plates. Library stamps to titles; some browning. bba Sept 7 (73) £700 [Penney]

**Bertius, Petrus, 1565-1629**
— Commentariorum rerum germanicarum, libri tres. Amst.: J. Jansen, 1616. Oblong 4to, contemp lea gilt; worn, joints cracked. Some marginalia & underscoring; lacking tp. Sold w.a.f. sg May 9 (55) $3,600

**Bertotti-Scamozzi, Ottavio, 1719-90**
— Les Batimens et les desseins d'Andre Palladio. Vicenza: Giovanni Rossi, 1786. 4 vols in 2. 4to, contemp half sheep gilt; extremities worn. With 210 plates on 209 leaves. Dampstaining in inner corners. sg Sept 7 (17) $3,600

**Bertrand, Aloysius, 1807-41**
— Gaspard de la nuit. Paris: Le Livre et l'Estampe, 1903. Out-of-series copy on japon with etchings in 2 states & an ink & watercolor drawing by Fontanez. Illus by J. Fontanez. 8vo, calf extra incised bdg by Charles Meunier, 1905, orig wraps bound in. S Nov 21 (41) £500

**Bertrand du Guesclin.** See: Guesclin, Bertrand du

**Beruete, A. de**
— Velazquez. Paris, 1898. Folio, half lev gilt, orig wraps bound in. O May 7 (52) $80

**Besant, Sir Walter, 1836-1901 —& Others**
— Survey of London. L, 1902-27. Vols 1-11. 4to, cloth; worn & soiled. Some soiling. cb Oct 17 (29) $500
Anr Ed. L, 1906-25. 10 vols. 4to, orig cloth. b Jan 31 (340) £160

**Besler, Basilius, 1561-1629**
— Hortus Eystettensis sive diligens et accurata omnium plantarum.... Eichstatt & Nuremberg, 1613. Issue without text on reverse of plates. Bound in 1 vol. Folio, contemp pigskin gilt with arms & 1636 ownership stamp of joachim Entzmueller, Reichgraf von & zu Windhaag; some worming. With 4 engraved titles & 365 (of 367) plates. General title supplied in Ms; without port; titles to Spring & Winter grazed & Winter repaired at lower outer corner; some plates trimmed to plate line at outer edge; some worming in lower margins at end; some staining. S Nov 30 (6) £130,000

**Bessel, Friedrich Wilhelm, 1784-1846**
— Astronomische Untersuchungen. Koenigsberg, 1841-42. 2 vols. 4to, contemp half calf. Library stamp on tp. Inscr to Sir John Herschel. b May 30 (12) £850

**Besson, Jacques**
— Il Theatro de gl'instrumenti & machine. Lyons: Barth. Vincentium, 1582. Folio, 18th-cent half calf; spine repaired. Some waterstaining throughout; Gi with loss to margin. b June 28 (6) £1,800

**Best, Thomas**
— A Concise Treatise on the Art of Angling.... L: C. Stalker, [1789?]. 2d Ed. 12mo, old calf; rebacked, new endpapers. Some staining, soiling & foxing. O Feb 6 (24) $225

**Bestall, A. E.**
— The New Adventures of Rupert. L, 1936. 4to, orig pictorial cloth, in remains of dj; endpapers spotted. S Nov 2 (278) £340 [Mills]

**Besterman, Theodore**
— Old Art Books. L, 1975. Folio, orig cloth. sg Apr 11 (36) $225
— A World Bibliography of Bibliographies.... Lausanne, [1965]. 4th Ed. 5 vols. 4to, orig cloth; worn. sg Apr 11 (35) $400

**Bestiaries.** See: Destructiorum...

**Bethelot, Marcellin, 1827-1907**
— Combinaisons de la Glycerine avec les Acides et Reproduction artificielle des Corps gras neutres. Paris, 1854. 1st Ed. 8vo, contemp wraps; chipped. Inscr on title. Ck Mar 22 (39) £480

**Betjeman, Sir John, 1906-84**
See also: Onassis copy, Jacqueline Bouvier Kennedy
— Collected Poems. L, 1958. One of 100. Orig lea gilt. Ck Apr 12 (127) £320
— Continual Dew. L, 1937. 1st Ed. Orig cloth; rubbed. bba May 30 (278) £95 [Rigneil]
— Mount Zion, or, In Touch with the Infinite. L: James Press, [1931]. 1st Ed. Orig bds; spine head def. Sgd on tp. Ck Apr 12 (126) £320

**Bettelheim, B. J.**
— Letter from Rev. B. J. Bettelheim, M.D. of Lewchew, giving an Account of His Labors there during the last Three Years. Canton: Office of the Chinese Repository, 1850. 8vo, orig wraps; chipped & brittle. sg Mar 7 (28) $400

**Betussi, Giuseppe**
— Della Geneologia de gli dei Dim. Giovanni Boccaccio. Venice: Giorgio Valentini, 1627. 8vo, contemp vellum. Ink note to leaf facing tp. pba Mar 7 (28) $200

**Beveridge, Albert J., 1862-1927**
— The Life of John Marshall. Bost., 1929. ("The Life and Times of John Marshall.") 4 vols in 2. Half mor gilt. pba June 13 (252) $70

**Beveridge, Thomas J.**
— English Renaissance Woodwork.... L: Technical Journals, 1921. Folio, orig cloth. With 80 plates. pba June 20 (56) $160
Anr copy. Half cloth; tips bumped with loss, extermities rubbed, soiled. sg June 13 (58) $60

**Bevers, Holm —& Others**
— Rembrandt: The Master & his Workshop. New Haven, [1991]. 2 vols. In djs. pba Nov 30 (272) $90

**Bewick, Thomas, 1753-1828**
— A General History of Quadrupeds. Newcastle, 1791. 2d Ed. 8vo, 19th-cent russia; front joint rubbed. Inscr by Frederick Locker-Lampson to his daughter, 1889. sg Dec 7 (187) $150
4th Ed. Newcastle, 1800. 8vo, contemp half sheep; rebacked, corners worn. Prelim ad leaf rehinged. sg Feb 8 (188) $110
— A History of British Birds. Newcastle, 1797-1804. 1st Ed. With: Supplement. Newcastle, 1821. 1st Ed. 4 vols in 2. 8vo, calf gilt, supplement in orig bds. pnE Mar 20 (174) £300
2d Ed of Vol I, 3d Ed of Vol II. Newcastle, 1798-1805. 2 vols. 8vo, contemp russia gilt. Land Birds with 110 of the illusts & 44 of the decorations colored by a contemp hand. Fattorini copy. C Oct 25 (2) £900
2d Ed of Vol I; 1st Ed of Vol II. Newcastle, [1798]-1804. 2 vols. 8vo, contemp calf gilt; extremities rubbed, spines & joints dry & worn, hinges split, front free endpaper of Vol I torn. Some foxing or spotting. Schaefer copy. P Nov 1 (23) $225
3d Ed of Vol I; 1st Ed of Vol II. Newcastle, 1804 [1805]-1804. demy 8vo Issue of Vol I. 2 vols. 8vo, contemp half mor; some wear. b May 30 (483) £200
3d Ed of Vol I, 2d Ed of Vol II. Newcastle, 1805. 2 vols. 8vo, 19th-cent mor gilt. sg Sept 21 (81) $250
Anr Ed. Newcastle, 1826. 2 vols. 8vo, mor gilt by Mansell. Prelims foxed. pba Sept 14 (18) $225
— A Memoir of Thomas Bewick. Newcastle & L, 1862. 8vo, orig cloth. With 1 copper engraving & numerous wood-engravings. pba July 11 (32) $120
— Select Fables. Newcastle, 1784. 2d Ed. 12mo, mor gilt by Riviere. pba Mar 7 (24) $850

**Bey, Pilaff.** See: Greene, Graham

**Beyle, Marie Henri ("Stendhal"), 1783-1842**
See also: Limited Editions Club
— La Chartreuse de Parme. Paris, 1883. Unique copy on japon a la forme for Leon Rattier, with each illust accompanied by the pencil and/or wash drawing & with 2 additional suites & a further impression of the frontis & 6 orig drawings for unused illusts. 2 vols in 4. 8vo, mor extra by Marius Michel, orig wraps bound in; upper cover of Vol I, Part 2 with traces of stain. S Nov 21 (415) £2,500

**Bhushan, Jamila Brij**
— Indian Jewellery, Ornaments, and Decorative Designs. Bombay, [1935]. 4to, half cloth; shaken. sg Sept 7 (192) $200

**Bianchi, Giovanni Paolo de**
— Nouvelle Instruction et remonstration de la... science du liure de compte.... Antwerp: Gilles Copyns de Diest for Anne Swinters, 1543. 4to, 16th-cent vellum; spine damaged. With tp woodcut & borderpieces colored in red Tp with fingersoiling. Schaefer copy. P Nov 1 (25) $8,000

**Bianchini, Francesco, 1662-1729**
— De tribus generibus instrumentorum musicae veterum organicae dissertatio. Rome, 1742. 4to, later half vellum. With 8 plates Some spotting. S Dec 1 (92) £500

**Bianco, Margery Williams, 1881-1944**
— Poor Cecco. NY, 1925. One of 105. Illus by Arthur Rackham. 4to, orig bdg, in dj. With 7 colored plates. CE May 22 (394) $3,800

Anr copy. Orig vellum-backed bds; front free endpaper detached. With 7 colored plates. Repair to p. 173, affecting 1 word; a few minor marginal tears. P Dec 12 (153) $3,000
— The Skin Horse. NY, [1927]. Illus by Pamela Bianco. 4to, pictorial bds, in dj with closed tears. pba Aug 22 (692) $130

**Bibiena, Ferdinando Galli, 1657-1743**
— L'Architettura civile preparata sulla geometria.... Parma, 1711. Folio, modern half calf. With 72 plates & port. Marginal soiling & dampstaining with trace of mold; blank corner of tp repaired. sg June 13 (2) $6,000

**Bibiena, Giuseppe Galli, 1696-1756**
— Architettura, e prospettive. Augsburg, 1740-[44]. Folio, 19th-cent half mor; rubbed. With engraved title & dedication leaf & 50 plates. Lacking port. Bound with 6 (of 7) double-page plates for Teatro i Proscenio della festa Teatrale intitolata Constanza e Fortezza rappresentata nel Reale Castello di Prago.... Some small tears repaired. C May 31 (77) £3,200

Anr copy. Recent mor gilt. 2 suites in 1 vol. First suite with engraved title, frontis, port, engraved dedication & 40 (of 50) plates; 2d suite with same prelims & 50 plates. Repair to Plate 7 in Part 3 of Suite II. S Nov 30 (234) £5,100

**Bible in Arabic**
— Ahad al-Fash al-Mujid [Commentary on the Epistles of Paul]. Dair as-Shuwait, [n.d., c.1810?]. 4to, contemp mor; worn. 1st few leaves repaired; lacking 1 leaf at end; some discoloration. S Oct 26 (138) £600 [Brunt]
— Kitab al Oktoihos [Octateuch]. Dair as-Shuwait, [n.d., c.1816?]. 8vo, contemp mor; worn. Discolored & stained. S Oct 26 (136) £280 [Brunt]

— Kitab al-ingil as-sarif at-tahir wal-misbah.... [Book of the Liturgical Gospels. Melchite Use] Dair as-Shuwair, 1776. Folio, orig goatskin gilt; lower cover damaged. With 4 ports of the Evangelists. Some foxing & staining. S June 27 (150) £3,800

**Bible in Cherokee**
— 1860. - [New Testament]. NY 12mo, orig sheep; extremities worn. Some dampstaining. D & M 2448. sg Oct 26 (14) $250

**Bible in Chinese (High Wen-Li)**
— 1814]. - [New Testament] [Canton: ptd for the trans, Robert Morrison. 1st Ed of New Testament in Chinese, one of 2,000. 8 parts in 1 vol. Folio, 19th-cent bds; rebacked. Minor marginal tears; embossed stamp on tp. Text ptd in Chinese characters from woodblocks. sg Oct 19 (38) $2,800

**Bible in Danish**
— 1550. - Copenhagen: L. Dietz. Folio, modern blind-stamped calf over wooden bds, with 2 clasps & catches. Lacking 2 prelims & 2 blanks; 2 leaves from anr copy; tears & repairs, with loss at ends. Darlow & Moule 3156. S June 27 (300) £1,500
— 1632-33. - Biblia det er den gannste hellige Scrifft. Copenhagen 3 parts in 1 vol. Folio, contemp mor over wooden bds with metal cornerpieces, 2 clasps & catches, with initials G.S.H. & date 1668 stamped on upper cover; a few knife cuts on both covers, rubbed. Tp repaired in lower margin; other marginal tears; early annotations. D & M 3160. Madsen copy. S Mar 14 (47) £2,600

**Bible in Dutch**
— [c.1635]. - Biblia, dat is: De Gantsche H. Schrifture.... Leiden: Paulus Aertz. Folio, contemp calf over wooden bds with metal cornerpieces & clasps; backstrip def. b Sept 20 (197) £300
— 1729. - Biblia, dat is, de gantsche heylige Schrift.... Dordrecht: Pieter & Jacob Keur. Folio, contemp calf over wooden bds with metal fittings; lacking 1 clasp, joints cracked. Foxed; some stains & tears; the 6 double-page maps cropped in outer margins with loss. Sold w.a.f. sg Mar 21 (38) $900

**Bible in Dutch Creole**
— 1818. - Die Nywe Testament... ka set over in die Creols Tael.... Copenhagen 8vo, needs rebdg. Worming in 1st half, with loss. D & M 3458. sg Oct 26 (15) $275; S Oct 27 (1177) £180 [Albert]

# BIBLE

## Bible in English

— 1537. - [Miles Coverdale's version]. Southwarke: J. Nycolson. 4to Ed. 17th-cent calf over wooden bds; rebacked preserving most of spine. Lacking prelims & all leaves up to a8; also lacking b2, b4, er-e8, f4-f5, P8 & Q5-Q6; several leaves torn, some with loss; small holes affecting text on 6 leaves; a few leaves soiled or shaved; incomplete Metrical Psalter bound in at end. STC 2065; Herbert 33. S July 11 (42) £6,800

— 1539. - L: John Byddell for Thomas Barthlet. Folio, 19th-cent calf gilt; rubbed. Lacking general title & 1 other leaf from prelims; also lacking A6, Nnn4 & R6-R8; XX4 bound before XX3; worming at beginning & end; tears, some with loss; some browning & soiling; some cropping. Herbert 45; STC 2067. S July 11 (48) £26,000

— 1540. - The Byble in Englyshe. L.2d or 3d Ed. Folio, 19th-cent mor gilt by Isaac Nichols of Leeds, with Masonic emblems & gilt lettering "The Gift of Brother and Companion James Manks, to the Alfred Lodge, No. 571, Leeds"; rebacked preserving spine. Lacking c.5 prelim leaves, Cranmer's prologue, Q4 blank & last 3 leaves; tp mtd with hole & tear repaired; bottom half of l4 & RR6 restored & the latter leaf remtd; some leaves remargined or torn; marginal dampstaining; some cropping. S Dec 18 (96) £3,800 [Aspin]

— 1541. - Byble in Englyshe.... L: Grafton. 5 parts in 1 vol. Folio, 18th-cent calf; rebacked, repaired. Black letter. Leaf CC1 from anr copy; Cromwell's arms erased; general title repaired & completed with fragments from other copies; 9 leaves with headlines shaved; marginal restoration to last 2 gatherings. STC 2075; Herbert 62. S July 11 (44) £6,000

— 1541, Nov. - [Great Bible] L: Edward Whitchurch. 6th Ed of this version. Folio, modern half calf. Black letter Lacking both titles (supplied in facsimile), the 6 prelim leaves & the first 10 leaves of Genesis; also lacking Ee3 & Ff5 & 12 leaves at end from NT. Herbert 62; STC 2075. S July 11 (45) £1,800

— 1549. - [Matthew's version] L: Thomas Raynalde & William Hyll. 2 parts in 1 vol. Folio, contemp blind-stamped calf over oak bds, with metal fittings; rebacked, corners restored, worming near base of spine. Black letter. Lacking all before Y1 & all after a4; also lacking Ddd8 in OT & 6 leaves including title in NT; H7 of NT torn with loss of most text; dampstained; repairs. Herbert 75; STC 2078. S July 11 (43) £1,600

— 1551. - L: Thomas Petyt. 5 parts in 1 vol. Folio, 19th-cent half calf; worn, spine repaired with tape. Repaired, sometimes affecting text; lacking a2 & final leaf (supplied in facsimile); Kalendar lacking 2 leaves; bottom half of NN6 cut away without loss. bba Apr 11 (276) £3,200 [Thomas]

— 1553. - The Byble in English.... L.9th folio Ed of the Great Bible, the "Queen Mary Bible". Folio, modern russia. Black letter. Lacking 1st 2 leaves, L7 & L8; tears to C1 & M4; loss affecting text on 3 leaves;
marginal repairs; minor worming & shaving. Herbert 102; STC 2091. S July 11 (47) £2,600

— 1553. - [Great Bible - O.T. only]. L: R. Grafton. 4to, disbound. Black letter Lacking all before b1, including tp; tears & creases; some stains & worming; some cropping. Herbert 103; STC 2092. S July 11 (39) £300

— 1560. - [Geneva version] Geneva: Rouland Hall. Bound with: The Booke of Common Prayer, 1623 [STC 16316] & The Booke of Psalmes, 1628 [STC 2604.5]. 4to, modern calf by Middleton. Lacking tp (supplied in facsimile), Adddress leaf after the Epistle & 5 map leaves; repairs or tears to 3 leaves; loss to Kk3 & Lll1; some marginal worming, dampstaining & headline-shaving. STC 2093; Herbert 107. S July 11 (51) £5,200

— 1566. - [Great Bible]. Rouen: R. Carmarden. Folio, 17th-cent blind-stamped calf; rebacked, repaired. Partly misbound; tp & 2 other missing prelims supplied in facsimile; repairs, stains & other defs. Herbert 119. bba Apr 11 (278) £2,400 [Hopkins]

— [1566?]. - The Newe Testament of Our Lord Jesus Christ. L: Richard Jugge. 4to, modern mor. Black letter; with 2 woodcut maps Lacking 14 leaves at beginning (including title) & lacking last leaf; repairs with loss; some cropping. STC 2873; Herbert 121. S July 11 (37) £3,600

— [1568]. - [Bishops' Bible] L: R. Jugge. 1st Ed of this version. Folio, modern calf. Lacking c.81 leaves; made-up copy; some leaves repaired with loss; some tears with loss. S July 11 (40) £1,300

Anr copy. Old calf over wooden bds; def, upper cover detached, torn. Black letter. Lacking 8 leaves from prelims & 2 at end; also lacking ff.91-96; some dampstaining, worming & fraying; NT tp torn & repaired. STC 2099; Herbert 125. S July 11 (103) £1,700

— 1569. - [Great Bible] L: J. Cawood. 4to, old calf with brass cornerpieces & bosses; rebacked, later clasps. Tp def & supplied from anr Ed; lacking other leaves; some leaves repaired. Sold w.a.f. CE June 12 (153) $3,200

Anr copy. Modern half calf. Lacking the 24 prelim leaves, XX8 & LLll10 & last 2 leaves; NT title cut down & from anr copy; some other leaves from other copies; Yyy1 & Lll19 remargined, the lastter restored in Ms facsimile; repairs & restoration to G2, M3, D5 & R3; some worming & repairs; leaves at end cropped. STC 2103; Herbert 128. S July 11 (50) £1,600

— [1573?]. - The Holie Byble. L: R. Jugge. 2d quarto Ed of the Bishops' version. 17th-cent mor gilt with silver clasps; spine worn. Black letter. Lacking al prelims except general title; lacking Apocrypha; last leaf in Revelations in facsimile; general title remtd & The holie Byble inked over; cropped affecting commentaries. Extra-illus with 92 hand-colored woodcuts by Sigmund Feyerabend from the Lutheran Bible of 1567. STC 2108; Herbert 135. S July 11 (46) £1,150

— 1576. - [Geneva version] L: Christopher Barker. Bound with: The Whole Booke of Psalms. L: John Day, 1576. Folio, 18th-cent calf; rebacked. Marginal dampstaining; browned; inserted plan repaired; map inserted in NT. STC 2118; Herbert 144. S July 11 (41) £620

— 1578. - [Geneva Version]. L: C. Barker. Folio, 18th-cent calf; rebacked, spine worn. Minor defs, tears or repairs, occasionally affecting text; some waterstaining & worming. Herbert 154. bba Apr 11 (279) £1,600 [Breece]

Anr copy. Old calf; rebacked. Black letter. Lacking 15 prelim leaves; tp torn & repaired; 1 leaf of Cranmer's Preface torn; also lacking 10 leaves of table & Suppatation at end; loss to several leaves; other repaired tears. STC 2123; Herbert 154. S July 11 (38) £550

— 1582. - [1st Ed of the Douai New Testament] Rheims: John Fogny. 4to, contemp calf; worn. A1-A4 with marginal paper repairs not affecting text; imperf at end. Sold w.a.f. b Sept 20 (86) £350

Anr copy. Contemp calf; rubbed, rebacked preserving orig spine. Some leaves at beginning with small tears; some staining & browning. Herbert 177. S Dec 18 (93) £1,400 [Ohlhausen]

Anr copy. Early 19th-cent calf; rebacked, endpapers renewed. Hand-colored throughout in the 19th-cent, with some initials in gold. Herbert 177; STC 2883. sg Apr 18 (23) $2,200

— 1585. - L: Christopher Barker. Fragment from Genesis 44 to Haggai 2. Folio, disbound. Sold w.a.f. D & M 188. b May 30 (380) £740

— 1589. - [New Testament] L: Deputies of Christopher Barker. Folio, contemp calf gilt; corners restored, rebacked. Some Ms notes in a contemp hand. Herbert 202; STC 2888. S July 11 (49) £850

— 1592. - L: Christopher Barker. Folio, modern mor gilt by Birdsall. Extremities worn Some browning, soiling & staining; cut close at top with loss to running heads; some underlinings & marginal notes. cb June 25 (1922) £850

— 1599]. - Amst.: J. F. Stam, 1633 [but imprint reads L: Deputies of Christopher Barker. 4to, later calf; new endpapers. Small tears throughout; browned. STC 2177. bba Oct 19 (214) £160 [Brake]

— 1611. - [Authorized version] L: Robert Barker With reading "he" in Ruth III, 15. Folio, 17th-cent sheep; joint cracked, some edge wear, later endpapers. Black letter. Lacking Speed's map; waterstaining to margins at beginning; tp creased & torn at margin; tear in 5B1 affecting 5 lines. STC 2216; Herbert 309. C June 26 (186) £57,000

Anr copy. 17th-cent calf gilt; rebacked, some restorations, clasps removed. 1st title & 1st leaf of dedication in facsimile; last 2 leaves replaced from later Eds; lacking Speed's map; some fraying. Bishop Richard Bagot's copy. STC 2216; Herbert 309. S July 11 (63) £28,000

— 1613. - L: Robert Barker. Folio, modern calf. Black letter. Lacking general title & final leaf Nnnn4 (supplied in photofacsimile); loss to margin of NT title, affecting border; leaves from Lll3 to end remargins; ink stains to Fff1 & Nnnn3; some dampstaining; tp of Speed's genealogies torn & repaired with loss. Herbert 322; STC 2226. S July 11 (59) £1,050

Anr copy. Contemp calf with brass fittings. General title laid down, dated 1614 & possibly from anr copy; leaves of calendar & almanack torn & repaired with loss; other prelim leaves torn; worming to margins at ends; repaired tears to Ggg3; wormholes affecting text on Hhhh2-Hhhh5; lacking Nnnn3; last leaf laid down. S July 11 (110) £1,600

Anr copy. Contemp mor over wooden bds; worn & flaking, spine lacking, covers detached. Lacking NT title; without Speed's genealogies; many leaves frayed; several leaves torn, affecting text; soiling & dampstaining; leaves at end of NT torn & creased with loss sometimes affecting text. Herbert 322; STC 2226. S July 11 (111) £1,100

— 1613-11. - L: Robert Barker With "she" reading in Ruth III, 15. Folio, contemp calf over wooden bds, with brass fittings; rebacked, 1 cornerpiece on lower cover missing, lacking front lower clasp. Black letter. General title repaired & remtd with slight loss; some dampstains; a few leaves remargined; loss to corners of Kkk4 & D2. S July 11 (60) £6,500

Anr copy. Contemp bds; very worn, fragments of calf remaining, rebacked with mor. Lacking 1st title, A6, X3, X4 & 5 leaves at end (partially replaced by leaves from anr Ed); prelims & genealogies torn & partially restored with loss; Speed's map missing 2 pieces at corners. Herbert 319; STC 2224. S July 11 (61) £6,200

Anr copy. Early 18th-cent calf, superimposed are 18th-cent silver stamp of Resurrection & 4 large embossed silver corner stamps; edges worn. General title remtd with loss & possibly from anr copy; lacking last 2 leaves & Speed's map; some headlines shaved; short tears to G1 & S2 in OT & L6 & M2 in NT; 2 leaves loose. STC 2224; Herbert 319. S July 11 (113) £6,800

— 1615. - L: Robert Barker. Bound with: The Booke of Psalmes. L, 1615. And: Speed's Genealogies. [STC 23039d.9] with the double-page map trimmed & laid down. And: The Book of Common Prayer, 1615 [STC 16344], with tp torn with major loss. 4to, contemp mor gilt; rubbed. Herbert 340. b Sept 20 (198) £300

— 1616. - [Authorized version] L: Robert Barker. Bound with: The Booke of Common Prayer. L, 1616. Folio, old calf; extremities rubbed. Loss to margin of tp of 2d work. STC 2244. b Sept 20 (196) £550

Anr copy. Bound with: Speed's Genealogies, [n.d.] And: Psalms, 1624. And: a def Book of Common Prayer. contemp calf; worn. Sold w.a.f. STC 2244. b May 30 (381) £280

Anr copy. Modern half calf; upper hinge split. Some soiling & dampstaining at ends; marginal loss to a prelim leaf; inner margin of map repaired with tape; A1 margin repaired with loss; some tears & staining. Herbert 349; STC 2245. S July 11 (56) £750

— 1617. - L: R. Barker. Folio, 17th-cent calf. Black letter; double-column. Lacking tp & genealogies; lower margins of Calendar & some leaves at end def, with loss of letters in Revelation; single wormhole through most leaves of NT. Sold w.a.f. Herbert 353; STC 2245. b Dec 5 (182) £5,000

Anr copy. Modern calf. Black letter. Lacking Cc3, Cc4, Xxxx6 & final leaf, the last supplied in photofacsimile; some leaves repaired. Herbert 353; STC 2247. S July 11 (58) £4,200

Anr copy. 19th-cent half calf; worn. Lacking A2-B2, Eeeee3, Eeeee4 & all leaves after Rrrrr6; early leaves torn with loss, soiled & repaired with black tape at inner margin; some leaves torn with loss. Herbert 353; STC 2247. S July 11 (112) £3,800

— 1631. - ["Wicked" Bible] L: Robert Barker. Bound with: The Book of Common Prayer (lacking A1, A2 & A5); The Way to True Happiness; and The Whole Book of Psalmes (incomplete). 8vo, contemp blind-tooled calf over wooden bds with remains of clasps & brass fittings; later brass strips on covers holding felt protective cover for spine. Lacking Mm1, Mm8 & Nn1; restoration to Zz5 & to Zz8 with loss; without genealogies or map. Herbert 444; STC 2296. S July 11 (66) £17,500

— 1634. - L: Barker. Folio, disbound. Black letter. Lacking all before C, NT title & 6D2-6; some leaves repaired with loss at beginning; some tears to lower margin & corners throughout, with loss on c.8 leaves. STC 2312; Herbert 487. S July 11 (57) £5,000

— 1637. - Cambr. Bound with: a def Psalms, 1637. And: Speed's Genealogies, [n.d.]. 4to, contemp calf; def & loose. Sold w.a.f. b May 30 (383) £110

— 1637. - Cambr.: Robert Barker & Assigns of John Bill. Bound with: The Whole Book of Psalmes. L: E. G. for the Company of Stationers, 1638. 24mo, contemp embroidered dos-a-dos bdg; rubbed, extremities worn, some embroidery worn away. Some worming, affecting letters on c.50 leaves; cut close, affecting tp border & text on a few leaves. STC 2953.3 & 2681.3. Schaefer copy. P Nov 1 (29) $1,500

— 1639. - L. Folio, old mor with silver catches & clasps, front cover with later gilt stamp "George Bland the gift of E. Dunelm 1856". Some ink & pencil scrawls; extensive notes on endleaves; bound with Book of Common Prayer & Whole Booke of Psalmes. Herbert 542. sg Mar 21 (39) $500

— 1653. - L: John Field. 24mo, contemp calf with pewter medallion of the arms of the Commonwealth mtd on upper cover. Some shaving affecting text. S July 11 (116) £360

— 1703. - Oxford 4to, contemp mor gilt; rebacked retaining backstrip, front joint cracked. Book of Common Prayer & Whole Booke of Pslams, both 1703, bound in. Extra-illus with c.140 plates. sg Mar 21 (40) $500

— 1717-16. - ["Vinegar" Bible]. Oxford: John Baskett. 2 vols in 1. Folio, contemp calf gilt; rubbed. Remargined at end; pen restoration to part of R6; repaired tears or marginal restoration to c.20 leaves. Herbert 942, Variant A. S July 11 (69) £1,300

— 1725. - Edin.: A. Anderson. 4to, ornate Scottish bdg. pnE May 15 (57) £1,100

— 1763. - Cambr.: Baskerville. Folio, contemp calf gilt; rebacked preserving orig spine, corners restored. Herbert 1146. S July 11 (72) £500

— 1772-71. - Birm.: Baskerville. Folio, contemp calf; foot of spine worn, lacking front free endpaper, rear endpaper torn. With 8 plates. Some worming to margins; some staining. Gaskell 53. S July 11 (76) £280

— 1772. - Birm.: Baskerville 2d State of tp. Folio, calf gilt; rebacked, orig spine laid down, extremities worn. With 10 plates. Some foxing throughout. NH June 1 (56) $475

— 1775-76. - L: John Archdeacon. 4to, contemp mor gilt lettered at center of upper cover Mary Provis to Mary Whitmarsh; damage to corner of upper cover, rubbed, lacking clasps, lower cover bowed, Ms notes relating to Langford family on prelim & final leaves & pasted to rear endpaper. With frontis, additional title, 127 plates & 6 folding maps. Tears to maps. Herbert 1247. S July 11 (70) £400

— 1791. - Trenton: Isaac Collins. 4to, contemp sheep; worn & broken, endpapers detached. Some foxing & spotting; early family records written on blanks. CE May 22 (56) $550

Anr copy. Contemp sheep; worn, front cover detached, loose. Lacking Ostervald's Observations. F June 20 (107) $350

— 1791. - Worcester, Mass.: Isaiah Thomas. 2 vols in 1. Folio, contemp sheep; worn, covers detached. Some browning. sg Oct 26 (16) $450

— 1795. - L. 4 vols. 4to, contemp mor gilt; rubbed, some staining. pn Dec 7 (4) £280

— 1800. - The Holy Bible... Embellished with Engravings.... L. 7 vols in 6. Folio, contemp mor gilt; rebacked preserving orig spine of Vol VII. Some foxing & dampstaining. Herbert 1445. S July 11 (74) £1,400

— 1824. - The Holy Bible. NY 12mo, contemp calf; rubbed. Some staining at beginning. Herbert 1740. Z June 28 (4) $300

— 1846. - The Illuminated Bible. NY 4to, orig mor gilt; worn & loose, joints repaired. O Mar 5 (119) $110

Anr copy. Orig mor. sg Feb 8 (8) $325

— c.1904. - The Holy Bible. BostLibrary Ed, one of 1,000. 14 vols. 8vo, half pigskin; lightly rubbed. sg Feb 8 (10) $475

— 1913. - L: Ballantyne Press. 3 vols. Later mor gilt by Cedric Chivers; some hinges starting. cb Oct 17 (317) $300

— 1965. - Cleveland: World Publishing Co.. Folio, calf. Facsimile reprint of the 1st Ed of the King James version, 1611. Z June 28 (156) $900

— The Book of Job. Leigh-on-Sea, 1948. One of 110. Illus by Frank Brangwyn. 4to, half vellum gilt. S May 16 (102) £400

Anr copy. With 33 sgd etchings. sg Feb 15 (61) $650

— The Book of Jonah. L: Clover Hill Editions, 1979. One of 300. Illus by David Jones. Half cloth. bba May 9 (161) £110 [Cox]

— The Book of Ruth. L, 1896. Intro by Ernest Rhys; illus by W. B. MacDougal. 4to, half mor by Bumpus. pba June 20 (71) $120

— Ecclesiastes. L, [1902]. ("Ecclesiastes; or, The Preacher, and the Song of Solomon.") Ltd Ed. Designed by Charles Ricketts. Folio, mor extra sunburst bdg by Fritz Eberhardt. sg Sept 14 (337) $1,100

Anr Ed. Paris: Trianon Press, 1967. One of 200. Illus by Ben Shahn. 4to, mor. sg Feb 15 (272) $375

— The Epistles and Gospelles.... L: R. Banks, c.1540. STC 2968. Bound with the same, STC 2969 4to, 17th-cent calf; worn & broken. Some cropping & dampstaining to 1st work. S Dec 18 (99) £2,100 [Smith]

— The First Tome or Volume of the Paraphrase of Erasmus upon the Newe Testamente. L: E. Whitchurche, [1549]. Vol I. Folio, 18th-cent calf; rebacked. Lacking tp & all before C1v of Preface; lacking all after kkk8; some worming; repairs with some loss. Herbert 73; STC 2854.5. S July 11 (36) £550

— The Four Gospels from William Tyndale's Translation of the New Testament 1526. Lexington: Anvil Press, 1954-55. One of 300. Illus by Victor Hammer. 4 vols. sg Sept 14 (22) $500

— The Holy Gospel According to Matthew, Mark, Luke and John. Verona: Officina Bodoni, 1962. One of 320. Folio, orig mor gilt. Ck May 31 (2) £850

— The Song of Solomon. [Jerusalem, 1930]. One of 125. Illus by Zeev Raban. 4to, mor with brass plaque; front cover soiled & stained. sg Sept 14 (236) $275

Anr Ed. Cambr.: Rampant Lions Press, 1937. One of—125. Illus by Harry Hicken. 4to, half lev. pba June 20 (278) $75

— The Song of Songs which is Solomon's. L: J. Dodsley, 1781. ("A Poetical Translation of the Song of Solomon....") Trans & ed by Ann Francis. 4to, contemp sheep; joints cracked. sg Mar 21 (41) $500

— St. Luke's Life of Christ. L: Curwen Press, 1956. One of 150. Orig half mor. bba May 9 (355) £75 [Clancey]

**Bible in French**

— c.1525. - Le nouveau testament.... Turin: Pour Francoys Cavillon [but Lyon: Francois Carcan & Claude Neurry]. 4 parts in 1 vol. 16mo, 19th-cent vellum. Title in red with woodcut arms in red & black of Savoy. Tear in lower margin of tp; some waterstaining. "One of only four known copies.". C June 26 (41) £24,000

— 1535. - La Bible qui est toute la Saincte Escripture. Neuchatel [but pbd in Serrieres]: Pierre de Wingle. Folio, 18th-cent French red mor gilt; extremities rubbed, spine head chipped. Hole in bb5 with loss; marginal tears to a few leaves repaired; some worming, occasionally affecting letters. D & M 3710. C Apr 3 (41) £8,000

— 1554. - Lyon: Jean de Tournes. 3 vols in 1. Folio, modern blind-stamped mor. Lacking bb5 of Vol I; small hole in margin of r5 of Vol III; prelim leaf & tp torn & repaired; wormhole in margin of Vol I to p. 158, touching text; library stamp on tp; some staining. S June 12 (11) £1,300

— Le Cantique des cantiques. Paris, 1886. One of 10 on china with an additional impression of the frontis etching on velin. Illus by Alexandre Bida. Folio,

mor extra with onlays in an Art Nouveau design by Marius Michel, from his early period. C May 1 (21) £11,000

Anr Ed. Paris, 1925. One of 110 on velin d'Arches. Trans by Ernest Renan; illus by F.-L. Schmied. 8vo, mor extra by G. Schroeder. b Sept 20 (638) £3,500

Anr copy. Mor extra sgd F.L.S. with interlocking linear design in gilt, orig wraps bound in. Inscr to Jean Borderel with orig watercolor & gouache drawing, heightened with silver, sgd by Schmied. Bound at end is suite of proof impressions ptd in black only of 11 of the illusts or borders, with holograph note sgd by Schmied. S Nov 21 (58) £10,000

One of 6 for collaborators with 2 additional suites, in black & in color. Red lacquer bdg sgd & dated Canape et Corriez 1930, 1 lacquered panel sgd Dunand after Schmied, the upper cover with elaborate design of 2 doves in lacquer, crushed eggshell, gilt & watercolor, spine of snakeskin, orig wraps bound in; suite vols in calf sgd Canape & Corriez; 1 corner of the red lacquer cracked. With 80 pages each with wood-engraved illust, pictorial or decorative initial or borders ptd in color, many heightened with gold or silver, 6 with additional hand-coloring by Schmied (so attested by 1 of the 2 holograph notes by Schmied bound in). S Nov 21 (59) £22,000

— Ruth et Booz. Paris, 1930. One of 162. Trans by J. C. Mardrus. 4to, half cloth. With 28 plates plus 2 extra suites in black & in color. Inscr by F. L. Schmied. Ck Sept 8 (13) £1,100

**Bible in German**

— Die heilige Schrift der Israeliten. Stuttgart, 1854. Illus by Gustave Dore. 2 vols in 1. Folio, publisher's mor; rubbed. S Oct 26 (92) £150 [Albert]

— 1567. - Biblia, das ist die gantze Heilige Schrift.... Frankfurt: S. Feyerabent Rab & Weygand Hanen Erben. 2 vols. Folio, contemp blind-stamped pigskin over wooden bds, the upper cover stamped with name of Cecilia Schadnerin & date 1573; lacking mettal fittings, rubbed. Some tears & holes; minor staining. Darlow & Moule 4209. S June 27 (302) £1,900

— 1574. - Frankfurt: Kilan Han for the heirs of Hans Weigand. 3 parts in 1 vol. Folio, 17th-cent blind-stamped pigskin over wooden bds with brass fittings; lacking 2 cornerpieces, rebacked, both covers detached. S Nov 30 (248) £600

— 1596. - Nuremberg: Paul Kauffmann. Folio, early lea; worn, clasps lacking. Tp. NH Sept 16 (51) $800

— 1641. - Lueneburg: Johann & Heinrich Stern. 3 parts in 1 vol. Folio, contemp mor gilt over wooden bds with names Bodo Leporinus & Anna Meiers, & date 1645; rubbed & wormed, edges worn, lacking 2 clasps & catches. Lacking 1 port & 7 plates; portion of 1 double-page map torn away but retained, anr map backed; worming at ends. Sold w.a.f. S Mar 14 (48) £520

— 1752. - Das ganze Neue Testament. Zurich: David Gessner. Bound with: Die CL. Psalmen Davids.... Zurich: Gessner, 1749. And: Geistreiches Fest- und Nachtmahl Buechlein. [N.p., n.d.]. And: Die Kleine

# BIBLE

Bibel.... Zurich: Gessner, 1749. 8vo, contemp Swiss black velvet with elaborate silver-gilt mounts; some nap worn. Abbey copy. C May 1 (19) £1,800

— Das Buch Ruth. Berlin, 1924. One of 200. Illus by Max Liebermann. Folio, orig half mor, in orig plain dj. CE May 22 (309) $650

**Bible in Gothic.** See: Codex

**Bible in Greek**
— 1516. - [New Testament] Basel: Froben Ed by Desiderius Erasmus. Folio, contemp blind-stamped pigskin over later wooden bds, new endpapers. Tp remargined; last leaf largely cut away; some worming & browning. S July 11 (14) £16,300
— 1516. - Novum Instrumentum omne [New Testament]. Basel: Froben Ed by Desiderius Erasmus. 2 parts in 1 vol. Folio, later vellum bds. Border on A1 shaved at fore-margin; 2 small tears in tp repaired with loss of letters; portion of upper margin of q4 cut away without loss; small wormholes at end; light staining, mostly in margins; lacking t6 blank; some early Ms notes & textual corrections. Chatsworh copy. D & M 4591. S Nov 30 (250) £4,000
— 1549. - Paris: Robert Estienne. NT only. 16mo, old mor; spine chipped at top, spine rubbed. Lacking 2 final blanks; some staining at end. sg Mar 21 (42) $500
— 1549. - [New Testament]. Paris: R. Estienne. 2 vols. 16mo, 17th-cent mor gilt. Tp in Vol I a facsimile & cropped. Sold w.a.f. S July 11 (13) £550
— 1550. - Paris: Robert Estienne. 2 parts in 1 vol. Folio, old vellum; spotted. Marginal dampstaining at beginning. sg Apr 18 (25) $4,000
— 1553. - Geneva: Jean Crispin. 8vo, 18th-cent calf; worn, rebacked. Worming in lower margin of 1st few leaves; lacking last leaf; fore-margin of last 2 leaves repaired; some cockling towards end; minor dampstains. S July 11 (16) £260
— 1757. - He Kaine Diatheke. Berlin 12mo, contemp mor gilt, armorial bdg. sg Sept 21 (82) $100

**Bible in Greek & Latin**
— 1519. - [New Testament]. Basel: Froben. Folio, contemp pigskin over wooden bds with remnants of clasps. Without the additional vol of annotations; lacking index; tp torn, as is leaf p3; some marginal dampstaining & tears; old annotations. D & M 4597. F Mar 28 (165) $4,400
— 1565. - [Geneva]: H. Estienne Ed by Theodorus Beza. Folio, modern half mor with gilt centerpiece from earlier bdg pasted onto covers. Dampstained throughout. S July 11 (12) £600
— 1600. - Lyon: Antoine de Harsy. 16mo, contemp German gold-tooled calf with animals in foliage & upper cover with centerpiece of haloed Christ holding an orb; small repairs to spine. C June 26 (42) £950

**Bible in Hawaiian**
— Ka Palapala Hemolele a Iehova Ko Kakou Akua.... Honolulu: Missionary Press, 1843. 8vo, later half mor by Kaufmann. Tp soiled with small hole at lower margin; pp. 15-16 with small holes affecting text. S Apr 23 (286) £700

**Bible in Hebrew**
— 1551. - Torat Hamashiach. Paris: Martin Juven. 8vo, contemp gilt; rebacked, corners repaired. Some soiling; ruled in brown ink throughout. D & M 5095. CE Dec 6 (14) $550
— 1565-66. - Antwerp: Plantin. 4to, old calf; upper cover detached, spine ends worn. Tp reinforced on verso; margins trimmed affecting marginalia; last leaf loose. D & M 5099. CE Dec 6 (15) $1,300
— 1573-74. - Antwerp: Christopher Plantin. 4 parts in 2 vols, 105mm by 45mm, contemp sharkskin with metal clasps; upper cover of Vol II cracked. Browning & staining. D & M 5102. CE Dec 6 (16) $2,600

Anr copy. 8vo, contemp vellum gilt. Some browning & staining. St. 227. CE Dec 6 (17) $1,700
— 1587. - Hamburg: Elian. Folio, contemp vellum with bronze bdg protectors, clasps; rubbed, bumped, clasps & hinges def. D & M 5108. Met Sept 28 (203) $2,100
— 1610. - Leiden: Franciscus Raphelengius. 16mo, rebound in modern mor. Some staining & browning. D & M 5114. CE Dec 6 (21) $650
— 1611-12. - Basel: Konrad Waldkirch. 8vo, contemp sharksin over bds; upper join & spine ends worn. Lacking blank prelims; library stamp on tp; some staining & browning. St. 395. CE Dec 6 (22) $800
— 1630-31. - Amst.: Menasseh ben Israel. Bound with New Testament in Greek. L: R Whittaker, 1633. 8vo, contemp calf; spine & corners worn. D & M 5123. CE Dec 6 (25) $850

Issue with Latin imprint. Contemp vellum gilt. Some browning & staining. D & M 5123. CE Dec 6 (26) $1,600
— 1631-35. - Amst.: Menasseh ben Israel. 4 parts in 1 vol. 4to, modern calf. General title soiled & frayed; marginal repairs. D & M 5124. CE Dec 6 (27) $1,300
— 1637-39. - Amst.: Menasseh ben Israel. 8vo, mor gilt. Some browning & staining. D & M 5127. CE Dec 6 (30) $1,500
— 1659. - Amst.: Joseph Athias. 8vo, contemp sharkskin with 1 remaining brass clasp. Tp soiled; some browning & staining. St. 525. CE Dec 6 (34) $800
— 1666-67. - [Pentateuch with Haftarot & Calendario] Amst.: Joseph Athias. 12mo, contemp mor gilt; worn. D & M 5134. CE Dec 6 (39) $2,400
— 1670-71. - [Pentateuch with Five scrolls & Readings from the Prophets'. Amst.: Uri Fayvesh Ha-levi. 16mo, later sheep; spine ends & corners rubbed, hinges cracked. Margins cut close, affecting running heads & shouldernotes; marginal repairs; some soiling & staining. St. 567. CE Dec 6 (40) $220
— 1699. - Berlin: Daniel Ernst Jablonski. 4 vols. 4to, later half vellum. Browned throughout; 1st 4 gatherings inlaid to size (from 8vo issue). D & M 5138. CE Dec 6 (41) $600
— 1699-1700. - Sefer Ha-maggid. Amst.: Caspar Steen. 10 vols. 12mo, contemp calf; spine ends & corners

worn. Former Prophets without own tp; some foxing & browning. St. 703, 703a. CE Dec 6 (42) $900

— 1700-1. - Amst.: Immanuel ben Joseph Athias. 12mo, contemp calf gilt; worn. Some staining; marginal repairs affecting letters on 2 leaves; some holes affecting letters. Sold w.a.f. St. 745. CE Dec 6 (43) $120

Anr copy. Contemp mor gilt; spine ends & corners worn. Zedner 101. CE Dec 6 (44) $1,300

— 1701. - Amst. 12mo, contemp mor; rebacked with sheep, worn. D & M 5139. CE Dec 6 (45) $300

Anr copy. Contemp mor gilt; hinges cracked. Corner of 1st few leaves brittle; engraved title chipped. D & M 5139. CE Dec 6 (46) $320

Anr copy. Contemp sharkskin; spine head torn. Minor staining & soiling. D & M 5139. CE Dec 6 (47) $240

— 1705. - Amst. & Utrecht 2 parts in 4 vols. 8vo, contemp calf; spine ends chipped, corners worn. D & M 5141. CE Dec 6 (49) $280

— 1710-11. - Berlin: D. E. Jablonski. 4 parts in 1 vol. 16mo, contemp sheep gilt. St. 791. CE Dec 6 (50) $400

— 1719. - Amst.: Solomon ben Joseph Proops. 8vo, 19th-cent half vellum. Some staining & soiling. St. 830. CE Dec 6 (52) $350

— 1720. - Halle Ed by Johann Heinrich Michaelis. 2 vols in 1. 4to, orig pigskin. F Sept 21 (356) $200

— 1726. - Amst. 5 vols. 12mo, w8th-cent mor gilt, with arms of the De Pinto family; extremities scuffed, inner hinges weak. Bound in each vol is Seder hatefillot, Amst., 1726.. St. 7492. CE Dec 6 (53) $6,500

— 1762. - Berlin: D. E. Jablonski. 4 parts in 1 vol. 12mo, contemp calf; rebacked. Some staining. CE Dec 6 (55) $190

— 1767-69. - Amst.: Gerard Janson & Israel Mondovy. 5 vols. 8vo, contemp calf gilt. Bound in is Jehuda Pisa's Luchot Ha-ibbur, Amst. 1769. Some browning & staining. CE Dec 6 (58) $1,000

Anr copy. Marginal browning & staining. CE Dec 6 (59) $1,300

— 1818-21. - Roedelheim: Wolf Heidenheim. 5 vols. 8vo, contemp half calf; spine ends worn. St. 952. CE Dec 6 (60) $380

— Mishlei Shelomoh, Kohelet ve-Shir Ha-shirim. Strasbourg, [1519]. 16mo, contemp calf; covers detached, spine ends & corners worn. Some staining & browning. CE Dec 6 (20) $1,600

Anr Ed. Strasbourg: Typis Schadaeanis, [1591]. 16mo, contemp calf gilt; joints cracked, worn. Some soiling. St. 300. CE Dec 6 (19) $1,600

— [Psalms & the book of Daniel]. Hamburg, 1662. Folio, contemp vellum. Some staining & browning. CE Dec 6 (37) $1,200

— Targum Shir Ha-shirim im mikra ha-pasuk. Amst.: Immanuel ben Joseph Athias, 1705. 12mo, old vellum. Some staining & browning. St. 749. CE Dec 6 (48) $260

**Bible in Hebrew & English**

— 1984. - The Five Scrolls, Hebrew Text and English Translations. NY: CCAR Press One of 175. Illus by Leonard Baskin. 8vo, half mor gilt by Gray Parrot. sg Feb 15 (26) $250

**Bible in Hebrew & Latin**

— Aseret ha-devarim. Basel: Froben, 1527. 8vo, contemp vellum. Some dampstaining; library markings. CE Dec 6 (13) $750

— Samuelis libri duo Ebraice et Latine. Leiden: Johannes Le Maire, 1521 [but 1621]. 12mo, contemp vellum; upper hinge cracked. Some staining. St. 435. CE Dec 6 (23) $480

**Bible in Hebrew & Spanish**

— 1664. - Paraphrasis caldaica en los cantares de Selomoh con el Texto Hebrayco y Ladino traduzido en lengua Espanolla.... Amst.: David de Crasto Tartaz. 8vo, 18th-cent mor gilt; corners worn. Some staining. St. 540. CE Dec 6 (38) $1,300

— 1762. - Biblia en dos Colunas Hebrayco y Espanol. Amst. 4 parts in 1 vol. Folio, contemp goatskin gilt for Isaac de Elias Lindo, 1768. Some foxing. D & M 5156. CE Dec 6 (56) $7,500

**Bible in Icelandic**

— 1644. - Biblia Pad er, Oll Heilog Ritning.... Hoolum 3 parts in 1 vol. Folio, 18th-cent vellum over wooden bds; rubbed, spine torn at head, lacking 1 cornerpiece, pastedowns from Icelandic ptd material. Tp & next leaf cut down with loss; K3-4 & M3-4 detached; tear in foremargin of N2 repaired with loss to ptd sidenote: Aa6 lacking upper portion of fore-margin, repaired with loss of sidenote & foliation; many margins at beginning & in Part 3 repaired with loss to sidenotes & headlines. D & M 5491. S Nov 30 (251) £3,200

**Bible in Ladino**

— 1873. - El Libro de la Ley, Los Profetas, y la Escrituras.... Constantinople: A. H. Boyagian. 8vo, modern lea. Browned; minor marginal worming. CE Dec 6 (204) $380

**Bible in Latin**

— c.1450-55. - Mainz: Gutenberg. Single leaf, comprising Proverbs, Chapters 24:5-26:28, mtd in mylar mat. Trier- Houghton copy. CNY Dec 15 (24) $15,000

— c.1450-55. - [Mainz: Gutenberg. Single leaf, Exodus 38:11-40:3. Mor gilt. In: Newton, A. Edward. A Noble Fragment. NY, 1921. Inscr by Newton to R. L. Taylor. P June 5 (173) $19,000

Anr copy. Single leaf, comprising Exodus 16:23-18:25. Modern calf. Previously used as binder's waste with loss of last 25mm of each line (supplied in modern facsimile); some tears & stains. S Dec 18 (20) £10,000 [Quaritch]

— 1475, 9 Dec]. - [Nuremberg: Johann Sensenschmidt & Andreas Frisner. Folio, 18th-cent deerskin gilt; extremities worn. Gothic type. Marginal soiling & dampstaining at ends; minor marginal tears; several

headlines cropped towards end; some underscoring & marginalia. 458 leaves. Goff B-544. sg Apr 18 (26) $10,000
— 1480. - Venice: Franciscus Renner de Heilbronn. 4to & 8vo, 19th-cent vellum. 53 lines & headlines (rectos only); types 6:65G (text) & 7:130G (headline, incipits); rubricated throughout in yellow, with lombard initials in red & blue. Extensive repairs to 1st quire with some text in pen-facsimile; D11 remargined with loss. 469 (of 470) leaves; lacking final blank. Goff B-566. P June 5 (172) $3,250
— not after 1480]. - [Strassburg: Adolf Rusch for Anton Koberger. 4 vols. Folio, bdgs not uniform: Vols I & III with contemp pigskin over wooden bds with later onlay having gilt arms of Marie Augusta of Sulzbach, Vol II in contemp pigskin over wooden bds & Vol IV in early 16th-cent pigskin over wooden bds with unidentified roll-tooling. 72-73 lines of commentary; double column; types 1:180G, 2:106G, 3:92G & 4:68G. Initial B opening Psalms with painted miniature of David playing the harp. Marginal dampstaining; worming at end of Vol II affecting letters & in Vol IV touching letters. 1,210 (of 1,211) leaves; lacking final blank. Goff B-607. C June 26 (40) £8,500
Anr copy. Vol I only. Folio, contemp calf over wooden bds; rebacked with lea, worn. Some staining; 1st 2 leaves with marginal repairs & staining; some worming. 253 (of 254) leaves; lacking 1 leaf in Leviticus. Goff B-607. pba June 20 (58) $3,000
— 1483. - Venice: Franciscus Renner de Heilbronn. 4to, contemp blindstamped doeskin over wooden bds; rebacked, lacking 2 clasps. 50 lines & headline, double column, gothic letter. First initial in red on blue panel within silver border, smaller initials in red or blue. Some worming & marginal staining; marginal notes. 476 leaves. Goff B-578. S July 11 (29) £3,200
— 1484, 30 Apr. - Venice: Johannes Herbort de Seligenstadt. 4to, old mor. Worming at beginning; holes in last few leaves of Register; old stains at end. 407 (of 408) leaves; lacking 1st leaf. Goff B-580. K Feb 11 (228) $2,700
Anr copy. 17th-cent calf; rubbed. Last leaf repaired; some staining; minor worming at beginning & end. 407 (of 408) leaves; lacking 1st leaf. Goff B-580. S Mar 29 (642) £2,200
— 1485-87. - Nuremberg: Anton Koberger. Mixed Ed. 4 vols. Folio, contemp Nuremberg blind-stamped pigskin-backed bds, Kyriss 113; upper bd of Vols I & IV renewed, lacking some clasps & catches. Some staining & wormholes; lacking final blank in Vol IV; General Theological Seminary Library plates & stamps. Goff B-613 & 614. S Dec 18 (21) £5,500 [Zioni]
— 1489. - Venice: [Bonetus Locatellus for] Octavianus Scotus. Vol III only. Modern vellum. Worming in outer margins, affecting text; annotated throughout in a contemp hand. 244 leaves. Goff B-616. S Dec 18 (22) £620 [Zioni]
— 1491, 9 Jan. - Basel: Nicolaus Kesler. Folio, later blindstamped pigskin over bds; front joint starting. Some dampstaining & foxing; marginal repairs; last

c.25 leaves with dark stains to lower corner; some worming to margins at end. 436 leaves. Goff B-591. pba Sept 14 (21) $1,500
— 1492]. - Strassburg: [Johann (Reinhard) Grueninger. Vol II (of 4) only. Folio, modern calf with old calf sides. 53 lines text & 67 lines of commentary & headline, double column, gothic letter. some worming at ends; tears & stains. 370 leaves (plus 6 additional leaves of Incipit libellus). Goff B-617. S July 11 (25) £580
— 1492, 7 Sept. - Venice: Hieronymus de Paganinis. 8vo, modern calf. 50 lines & headline; double column; gothic letter Wormed at ends; some dampstaining; some notes 7 headlines shaved. 544 (of 552) leaves; lacking A1-2 & 10, a1-2 & 5/8-10. Goff B-594. S July 11 (27) £520
— 1495, 27 Oct. - Basel: Froben. 8vo, later vellum. AA2-8 & E1 from anr copy; Cc3 with lower corner def, touching text; Dd3 torn; some shaving; last leaf laid down; some repairs. 505 (of 508) leaves; lacking tp, BB4 & A1 blank. Goff B-598. bba Apr 11 (288) £1,250 [A. Stewart]
— 1497, 6 Sept. - Nuremberg: Anton Koberger. 4 vols. Folio, 17th-cent vellum; joints dry & cracking, some spine ends perished, corners bumped. 52 lines & headlines; types 14:130G, 15:91G, 19:71G, 21:75G; with 43 woodcuts in text; rubricated. Cd6 in Part 1 with marginal repair; scattered closed tears; some stains. 1,432 leaves. Goff B-619. P June 5 (171) $6,500
Anr copy. Part 4 (of 4) only. contemp English blind-stamped calf over wooden bds; rebacked, lacking clasps. 70 lines & headline, double column, gothic letter, initials supplied in red Ms annotations on front free endpapers, single leaf at end & tp verso. 352 leaves. Goff B-619. William Smyth's copy. S June 27 (351) £1,000
— 1498, 1 Dec. - Basel: Johann Froben & Johann Petri. Part 6 (of 6) only. Folio, contemp pigskin over wooden bds; worn & blistered, soiled. Wormed with minor loss. 280 leaves. Part of Goff B-609. F Mar 28 (166) $875
— 1511, 28 May. - Venice: Lucantonio Giunta. 4to, contemp goatskin with central medallion port & monogram AC; rebacked. Some soiling; marginal dampstaining & cropping; last leaf repaired with some damage. S July 11 (30) £750
— 1512. - Paris: Philippe Pigouchet for Simon Vostre. Folio, late 16th-cent calf; repaired & wormed. Lacking C4-5, with duplicates of D4-5 misbound in their place; also lacking final leaf; marginal browning; repaired tear at foot of s1. S June 12 (142) £550
— 1522, 24 Mar. - Lyons: J. Moyli al's de Cambray. 4to, 18th-cent calf; rebacked. Early annotations (many cropped); dampstained at ends. S July 11 (24) £700
— 1526, Aug. - Sacra Biblia ad LXX interpretum.... Basel: A. Cratander. 4to, modern calf. Some soiling, browning & dampstaining. S July 11 (22) £500
— 1530, Apr. - Cologne: Johannes Prael. 16mo, 16th-cent calf gilt, with name & arms of Baron Sigismund von Wolkenstein und Rodnegg. S July 11 (21) £850
— 1534, Jan. - Antwerp: Martinus Caesar. Folio, 18th-cent calf over wooden bds; rebacked. Lacking NN6

& final blank; dampstaining at ends; marginal repairs at beginning with occasional loss of notes; last few leaves frayed; marginal worming; some tears; 5 leaves with foremargins torn away.   S July 11 (28) £420

— 1538. - Lyons: M. & G. Trechsel Illus by Hans Holbein.  Folio, 19th-cent calf; worn. Rust holes costing a few letters; some soiling, browning & marginalia; minor repairs; 1st few leaves with marginal worming & dampstaining.  Schaefer copy.   P Nov 1 (26) $4,750

— 1540. - Novum testamentum Latinum.... L: J. Mayler. 4to, 19th-cent mor by Lambert, edges diapered, colored & gilt; rebacked, rubbed. Lll6 blank & lacking; marginal worming at beginning; 1 opening soiled; some upper margins cropped; dampstaining towards end.   STC 2799.   S July 11 (18) £4,000

— 1542-46. - Lyons: Sebastian Gryphius. 5 vols. 16mo in 8s, contemp calf gilt painted & stained mosaiquee en cire bdgs, with initials A.B.. Tear to lower margin of Q6 of the Pentateuch.   C Nov 29 (30) £19,000

— 1562. - Biblia Sacra.  Lyons: Sebastian Honoratis. Folio, later vellum; scratched. Some worming, heavier in last 12 leaves; some dampstaining to upper & lower margins.   S June 12 (13) £300

— 1669. - Biblia sacra. Venice: Nicolaum Pezzana. 4to, later half sheep; rubbed. Marginal repairs.   b Sept 20 (199) £140

— 1961. - Paterson & NY: Pageant Books One of 1,000. 2 vols. Folio, orig mor. Facsimile of the Gutenberg Bible of c.1450-55.  CE Feb 21 (111) $1,300

— 1985. - Paris: Les Editions des incunables. 4 vols, including commentary. Folio, mor gilt. Facsimile of the Mazarin Library copy of the Gutenberg Bible.   P Dec 12 (43) $3,000

### Bible in Latin & English

— 1538. - The New Testament both in Latine and Englyshe.  Southwark: James Nicolson. 4to, modern mor.  Title in facsimile; lacking 4 leaves; last leaf def & repaired, with loss of lower portion of text; other repairs; some stains & soiling.   Harmsworth copy. S July 11 (19) £6,000

— 1538. - The Newe Testament in Englyshe and Latyn. L: Robert Redman. 4to, 18th-cent calf; rebacked. Lacking 1st title & last leaf; almanac leaves heavily repaired; cropped with loss of some headlines; some dampstaining.   S July 11 (17) £6,500

### Bible in Latin & French

— 1793-98. - Le Nouveau Testament. Paris 5 vols. 8vo, 19th-cent mor gilt.  With 5 frontises & 108 plates. Fuerstenberg - Schaefer copy.   S Dec 7 (53) £1,500

### Bible in Massachuset

— 1663-61. - The Holy Bible.... Cambr. MA: Samuel Green & Marmaduke Johnson. ("Mamusse wunneetupanatamwe up-biblum God....") 1st Ed of Eliot's Indian Bible. - Trans by John Eliot. Group of 34 leaves.   P June 5 (36) $6,500

### Bible in Mongolian

— [St. John's Gospel]. St. Petersburg, 1819. Folio, contemp sheep; worn & brittle, needs rebacked. Sold w.a.f.   sg Mar 7 (29) $225

### Bible in Russian

— c.1878. - [New Testament] [N.p.] Folio, velvet over wooden bds with bas-relief silver panel with 5 figures of Christ; central figure of Christ with right arm lacking, lacking 1 corner boss on rear cover. Lacking general title & possibly other leaves.   pba Nov 30 (284) $900

— Apostol. Moscow: Synodal Press, July 1910. Folio, contemp velvet over wooden bds, upper cover with icon of 2 Evangelists painted on copper under repousse chased & engraved silver gilt oklad, by P. I. Olovianishnikov & Sons, St. Petersburg. C May 1 (4) £400

### Bible in Slavonic

— Evangelie [Gospels]. Moscow, 1796. Folio, contemp repousse, chased & engraved brass bdg over wooden bds, the upper cover with oval enamel plaques of the Resurrection, cornerpieces of the Evangelists with 4 scenes from the Passion, lower cover with plaques of God the Father & the Archangels Michael & Gabriel; some wear to the plaques, 1 lacking mount, 1 damaged. Some browning, minor tears & wormholes; some stains. Sold w.a.f.   C June 26 (238) £1,800

### Bible in Spanish

— 1553. - Biblia en Lengua Espanola. Ferrara: Duarte Pinel for Jeronimo de Vargas. Folio, later mor with clasps; lacking 1 catch. Wormed; lacking last leaf; tp soiled & def & probably supplied & cut round & mtd, with loss to border; wormed; B4 def, with 8 lines of text in Ms facsimile; repaired tear to B5; closed tear to Gg4 with old repair between text columns; some traces of white powder in gutters.   CE Dec 6 (199) $20,000

— 1630. - Amst. Folio, later half vellum. Wormed; wear to corners & spine ends; tp def & laid down; heavy worming; 1 leaf def.   CE Dec 6 (201) $600

— 1646. - Amst.: Gillis Ioost. Folio, contemp calf; worn, rebacked, lacking clasps, new endpapers. Worming near gutter margin throughout, sometimes affecting text; tp soiled & frayed; marginalia; staining & browning; Bbb6 with fore-margin chip tape-repaired; some discoloration.   CE Dec 6 (202) $1,200

— Humas de Parasioth & Aftaroth. Amst.: Imanuel Beneveniste, 1643.  8vo, contemp calf over wooden bds with 2 brass clasps; spine ends & corners worn, rubbed. Some staining; early marginalia.   CE Dec 6 (31) $1,600

— Humas de parasioth y aftharoth, traduzido palabra por palabra de la verdad Hebraica en Espanol. Amst.: Menasseh ben Israel, 1627. 8vo, modern calf. Lacking 3 leaves at end; tp & Z3 def; wormed &

# BIBLE

chipped with loss; browned & stained. Sold w.a.f. CE Dec 6 (200) $6,500
— Humas o cinco libros de la ley divina. Amst.: Menasseh ben Israel, 1655. 12mo, contemp calf; extermities worn, upper hinge cracked. Tp repaired; cut close; some browning & staining. CE Dec 6 (33) $1,900

**Bible in Syriac**
— 1555. - Liber Sacrosancti Evangelii de Jesu Christo Domino & Deo Nostro. Vienna1st Ed, 1st Issue. 4to, modern mor gilt. Some repairs; marginal worming; without prelims to Parts 2 & 3. D & M 8947. C Nov 29 (32) £1,100; S Oct 27 (1048) £280 [Pearson]

**Bible, Polyglot**

— [New Testament]. [Geneva]: Henri Estienne, 1569. Folio, orig presentation [to Queen Elizabeth I] bdg of pierced calf over velvet, elaborately tooled, gilt & painted; rebound in mor, preserving original sides, restored & def, new endpapers. Title remargined; corner of some leaves strengthened. The Dedication copy. In Greek, Latin & Syriac. S July 11 (34) £18,000
— 1528. - Biblia. Paris: Robert Estienne. Folio, 18th-cent calf; rebacked retaining spine. Lower margins wormed throughout; some textual worming; staining, especially in text of D6-E6; Dd6 with repaired tear; lower margin of fff7 torn away with loss; early annotations. D & M 6109. S July 11 (26) £1,000
— 1586. - Biblia sacra, hebraice, graece & latine. Geneva: Officina Sanctandreana. Bound in 2 vols. Folio, contemp blind-stamped calf over wooden bds, medieval Ms leaves used as front pastedowns; rubbed & worn. Some staining. bba Nov 16 (16) £450 [Solmi]
— 1728. - Figures de la Bible. The Hague: Pierre de Hondt. 2 parts in 1 vol. 4to, 19th-cent mor gilt. Engraved throughout; with 2 titles, 2 dedications & 212 plates. Fuersternberg - Schaefer copy. S Dec 7 (52) £2,400

— Besorot Me-Ha-Torah Ha-Hadashah... Quatuor Evangelia Novi Testamenti. Prague, 1746. Folio, contemp calf; spine painted gray & lettered in black. In Hebrew, Yiddish, German & Latin. sg Mar 21 (37) $425
— Revelation. Leiden: Elzevier, 1627. 4to, 19th-cent vellum over pastebd. Some foxing. In Syriac, Aramaic, Latin & Greek. D & M 1438. CE Dec 6 (24) $900

**Biblia Pauperum**
— Biblia Pauperum. [Low Countries, c.1465]. Folio, late 18th-cent mor gilt with Carysford arms added; rubbed. 40 leaves. Sheets ptd on inner side only, now divided & each leaf remargined with Whatman paper. Each woodcut page comprises 3 pictures, 4 ports & Latin text. Division affecting the outermost frame replaced in Ms; a few small wormholes repaired slightly affecting text or illust in c.12 leaves; minor defs repaired; minor rubbing to some leaves; def in center of fo. 8 restored with missing lines of illust replaced in Ms. Schreiber xyl. ed. III. Ashburnham - Carysfort - Proby copy. C Nov 29 (19) £240,000

**Bibliofilia**
— La Bibliofilia. Raccolta di scritti sull'arte antica in libri.... Florence, 1900-89. 91 vols bound in 65 plus 4 vols of indices to Vols 1-80. Half mor. Sold w.a.f. Ck Apr 12 (198) £2,600

**Bibliographica...**
— Bibliographica: Papers on Books, their History and Art. L, 1895-97. 12 parts in 12 vols. 8vo, orig half mor; rubbed, covers detached. F Sept 21 (265) $210

**Bibliophile...**
— Le Bibliophile francais. Gazette illustree des amateurs de livres. Paris, 1868-73. Vols I-VII. 4to, half lea. Library markings. Sold w.a.f. O Mar 26 (30) $160

**Bibliotheca...**
— Bibliotheca Parisiana. L, 1791. 8vo, modern cloth. With half-title. S Oct 27 (1014) £260 [Guedroitz]
— Bibliotheca Philosophica Hermetica. Christ, Plato, Hermes Trismegistus. The Dawn of printing: Catalogue of the Incunabula. Amst., 1990. Vol I, parts 1 & 2, in 2 vols. Folio, orig cloth in slipcase. sg Apr 11 (143) $100

**Bibliotheque...**
— Bibliotheque universelle des Romans. Paris, [1776]. 2 parts in 1 vol. 12mo, contemp mor gilt with arms of the comtesse du Barry. Margins of 4 leaves in Part 1 torn away; repair in margin of E12; rusthole in text of F11. Fuerstenberg - Schaefer copy. S Dec 7 (55) £750

**Bibliotheque du Roi**
— Catalogue des volumes d'estampes dont les planches sont a la bibliotheque du Roi. Paris, 1743. Folio, contemp red mor gilt in the style of the cabinet du Roi. Fuerstenberg - Schaefer copy. S Dec 7 (91) £6,800

**Bichat, Marie Francois Xavier, 1771-1802**
— Anatomie generale appliquee a la physiologie et a la medecine. Paris, 1801. 1st Ed. 2 parts in 4 vols. 8vo, modern half calf. With 2 folding tables. 16 leaves torn & 30 leaves stained in vol III; other soiling, dampstaining & foxing. CE Nov 8 (72) $260

**Bichurin, Nikita Jakovlevich, 1777-1853**
— Zapiski o Mongolii. St. Petersburg, 1828. 2 vols in 1. 8vo, contemp half mor gilt; corners worn. With 5 hand-colored plates & folding map. Old stamp on titles & verso of map. sg Apr 18 (66) $600

**Bickham, George, the Elder, d.1769**
— The British Monarchy.... L, 1743. Folio, later half calf. Engraved throughout, with tp, dedication & 159 leaves only. Sold w.a.f.  pn Dec 7 (25A) £360

Anr Ed. L, [leaves dated 1743-49]. Folio, modern calf. With frontis, folding map, folding chart, 2 unnumbered charts & 45 full-page maps. Some browning & spotting; folding map tape-repaired; folding chart following leaf 161 with tape repairs in margins; some chipping.  wa Feb 29 (349) $3,750

— The Musical Entertainer. L: Charles Corbett, [c.1739]. 2 vols in 1. Folio, red mor by Bretault; upper joint split. Engraved throughout. 12 plates apparently added from anr copy; repairs in margins of 1st e leaves; tear at head of Plate 8; some tears & repairs. Fuerstenberg - Schaefer copy.  S Dec 7 (56) £2,400

— The Universal Penman.... L, 1743. Folio, contemp calf gilt; front cover detached, rubbed. Some soiling & foxing.  cb June 25 (1923) $1,100

**Bicknell, Ralph Edmund**
— Ralph's Scrap Book.... Lawrence MA: Pvtly ptd, 1905. Ltd Ed ptd by the Andover Press. Mor gilt.  pba Feb 12 (6) $300

**Bicot de Morogues, Sebastien Francois, Vicomte**
— Naval Tactics; or, a Treatise of Evolutions and Signals.... L, 1767. 4to, later half mor; extremities worn. With 8 folding plates & folding table. Small portion excised from tp, affecting 1 word.  sg Mar 7 (224) $400

— Tactique Navale, ou traite des evolutions et des signaux. Paris, 1763. 4to, contemp red mor gilt with monogram of Czar Paul I; covers spotted. With engraved title & 49 plates. Fuerstenberg - Schaefer copy.  S Dec 7 (445) £1,100

**Bidwell, Frederick D.**
— History of the Forty-Ninth New York Volunteers. Albany, 1916. Orig cloth; spine numbers & removed bookplate.  NH July 21 (60) $150

**Bidwell, John, 1819-1900**
— Echoes of the Past: an Account of the First Emigrant Train to California.... Chico, Calif., [1914]. 1st Ed. Orig wraps; front cover stained. With tp port, & 3 illus. Larson copy.  pba Sept 28 (312) $55

Anr Ed. Chico, California, [1914]. Wraps; extremities worn. With 3 photos.  pba Apr 25 (290) $75

— General Bidwell's Letter of Acceptance. N.p., n.d. [1891]. Bound with: Original Prohibition Party ticket with John Bidwell listed as the candidate for president Together, 2 items, wraps; stained, chipped at edges. Larson copy.  pba Sept 28 (322) $250

— A Journey to California.... San Francisco: John Henry Nash, 1937. One of 650. 4to, half bds. Inscr to Eleanor Bancroft. Larson copy.  pba Sept 28 (313) $50

Anr Ed. Berkeley: Friends of the Bancroft Library, 1964. Designed & printed by Lawton Kennedy. Orig cloth. With 1 folded map. Larson copy.  pba Sept 28 (314) $60

**Bie, Oskar**
— Hollaendisches Skizzenbuch. Berlin, 1911. One of 500. Frontis litho by Max LIebermann. Oblong folio, cloth.  sg Sept 7 (220) $350

**Bieber, Ralph B. —&**
**Hafen, Le Roy R.**
— The Southwest Historical Series. Glendale: Arthur H. Clark, 1931-43. 12 vols.  pba Nov 16 (25) $1,100

**Bienvenu, —.** See: Launoy & Bienvenu

**Bierbaum, Otto Julius, 1865-1910**
— Das schoene Maedchen von Pao. Munich, 1910. One of 600. Illus by Franz von Bayros. Folio, orig mor gilt by Huebel & Denck to a design by Paul Renner, pictorial doublures & endleaves ptd in gold. With 7 lithos.  S Nov 21 (42) £340

**Bierce, Ambrose, 1842-1914?**
See also: Limited Editions Club
— Black Beetles in Amber. San Francisco, 1892. 1st Ed. 8vo, orig cloth; spine ends rubbed. Inscr to Walter Blackburn Harte, 1892.  pba Mar 7 (26) $375

— The Cynic's Word Book. NY, 1906. 1st Ed, BAL state A. H. L. Mencken's copy.  wa Feb 29 (67) $450

— The Shadow on the Dial and Other Essays. San Francisco, 1909. 1st Ed. Cloth, in glassine dj.  pba Dec 14 (5) $50

— Tales of Soldiers and Civilians. San Francisco, 1891. 1st Ed. 12mo, orig cloth; rubbed.  pba Dec 14 (4) $70

Anr copy. Orig cloth; extremities rubbed, corners bumped, library bookplate.  sg Sept 21 (83) $90

**Bigelow, Jacob, 1787-1879**
— American Medical Botany.... Bost., 1817-20. 3 vols. 8vo, half lea. With 60 hand-colored plates. Plate 1 with old blindstamp on upper corner.  Met May 22 (378) $2,000

**Bigelow, John, 1817-1911**
— The Campaign of Chancellorsville. Dayton: Morningside House, 1984. Photofacsimile of 1910 Ed.  bbc Apr 22 (65) $260

**Biggers, Earl Derr, 1884-1933**
— Keeper of the Keys. Indianapolis, [1932]. In creased & repaired dj.  sg Dec 14 (37) $70

**Bigland, Ralph**
— Historical, Monumental and Genealogical Collections relative to the County of Gloucester. L, 1791-1819. 3 vols in 2. Mor gilt by Hollings. Some foxing.  pba Nov 30 (33) $800

Anr Ed. L, 1791. 2 vols. Folio, later calf gilt; rubbed.  S Mar 28 (33) £260

**Bigler, John**
— Speech of Gov. Bigler, Delivered at Shasta City.... [Shasta City?, 1855]. Removed from larger vol. Darkening & soiling; last leaf chipped. Robbins copy.  pba Mar 21 (18) $400

## Bigot, Georges
— O-Ha-Yo Album. [N.p., c.1890]. 4to, orig wraps; soiled, edges frayed. With etched title & 30 plates plus 10 woodcut plates possibly fro anr work at end. Sold w.a.f. bba June 6 (4) £1,000 [Fine Books Oriental]

## Bilberg, Johan
— Refractio solis inoccidui, in septemtrionalibus oris. Stockholm: B. N. Wankifius, [1695]. 4to, 19th-cent half calf gilt. With 5 woodcut plates, each with diagram on recto & verso. S Mar 14 (50) £550

## Bill, Max
— 16 Constellations. Paris, 1974. One of 25 horse commerce on velin d'Arches. Folio, loose as issued in portfolio. With 16 color lithos. sg May 23 (492) $1,300

## Billings, LeMoyne. See: Onassis copy, Jacqueline Bouvier Kennedy

## Bilson, Thomas
— The True Difference betweene Christian Subjection and Unchristian Rebellion. Oxford: Joseph Barnes, 1585. 1st Ed. 8vo, modern bds; backstrip def. Marginal dampstaining; contemp underscoring & marginalia; last index leaf imperf. sg Mar 21 (48) $275

## Bindley, Charles
— Bipeds and Quadrupeds. L, 1848. 8vo, half mor by Zaehnsdorf; rubbed. O Jan 9 (35) $80
— Hints to Horsemen. L, 1856. 8vo, half mor by Zaehnsdorf, orig cover bound in at end; rubbed. O Jan 9 (36) $80
— The Hunting-Field. L, 1850. 8vo, half mor by Zaehnsdorf, orig cover bound in; rubbed. O Jan 9 (37) $80
— The Pocket and the Stud.... L, 1848. 8vo, half mor by Zaehnsdorf, orig cover bound in; rubbed. O Jan 9 (38) $170
— Practical Horsemanship. L, 1850. 8vo, half mor by Zaehnsdorf, orig cover bound in; rubbed. O Jan 9 (39) $80
— Precept and Practice. L, 1857. 8vo, half mor by Zaehnsdorf, orig cover bound in; rubbed. Small stain on tp. O Jan 9 (40) $80
— Sporting Facts and Sporting Fancies. L, 1853. 8vo, half mor by Zaehnsdorf; rubbed. O Jan 9 (41) $80
— The Sporting World. L, 1856. 8vo, half mor by Zaehnsdorf, orig cover bound in at end; rubbed. O Jan 9 (42) $80
— The Sportsman's Friend in a Frost. L, 1857. 8vo, half mor by Zaehnsdorf; rubbed. O Jan 9 (43) $80
— Stable Talk and Table Talk.... L, 1845-46. 2 vols. 8vo, half mor by Zaehnsdorf, orig covers bound in; rubbed. O Jan 9 (44) $140
— The Stud, for Practical Purposes and Practical Men. L, 1849. 8vo, half mor by Zaehnsdorf, orig cover bound in; rubbed. O Jan 9 (45) $120
— Things Worth Knowing About Horses. L, 1859. 8vo, half mor by Zaehnsdorf, orig cover bound in at end; rubbed. O Jan 9 (46) $100

— A Treatise on the Proper Condition for all Horses. L, 1852. 8vo, half mor by Zaehnsdorf, orig cover bound in; rubbed. O Jan 9 (47) $120
— The World: How to Square It. L, 1850. 8vo, half mor by Zaehnsdorf, orig cover bound in; rubbed. O Jan 9 (48) $80

## Bindman, David
— The Complete Graphic Works of William Blake. NY, [1978]. Folio, cloth, in dj. O May 7 (54) $110

Anr copy. Rupperstamp on bottom edges. sg Jan 11 (46) $50

## Bingham, Hiram, 1789-1869
— A Residence of Twenty-One Years in the Sandwich Islands. Hartford & NY, 1848. 2d Ed. 8vo, orig cloth; lacking spine strip, spine split, corners & edges showing. With port, folding map & 6 plates. Tp soiled. pba July 25 (383) $90

## Bingham, Hiram, b.1875
— Machu Picchu: a Citadel of the Incas. New Haven, 1930. One of 500. Folio, half cloth; bumped. Met Feb 24 (64) $450

Anr copy. Half cloth; front bd & endpapers stained. Met May 22 (80) $375

## Bini, Pietro
— Memorie del calcio fiorentino. Tratte da diverse scritture.... Florence, 1688. 4to, vellum. With engraved arms on tp & 2 double-page plates. b June 28 (8) £1,300

## Binion, Samuel Augustus
— Ancient Egypt, or Mizraim. NY, 1887. One of 800. 2 vols. Folio, orig half mor; soiled, joints cracked, spines def, front cover of Vol II detached but present, endpapers reinforced. With 49 chromolitho & 23 uncolored plates. Library stamps; some soiling. cb Oct 17 (181) $1,100

## Binyon, Laurence, 1869-1943
— The Drawings and Engravings of William Blake. L, 1922. One of 200. Folio, orig vellum. K Oct 1 (55) $200

## Binyon, Laurence, 1869-1943 —& Others
— Persian Miniature Painting. L, 1933. Folio, cloth; worn, spine scuffed. O May 7 (55) $275

## Biographie...
— Biographie universelle, ancienne et moderne. Paris, 1811-55. Ed by J. F. Michaud. Vols 1-85 (First Series, Vols 1-52; Partie Mythologique, Vols 53-55; Supplement, Vols 56-85) Contemp half calf. bba Oct 5 (15) £650 [Sander]

## Bion —& Moschus
— Idylles.... Paris: Didot jeune, 1795. 18mo, contemp mor gilt. With port & 3 plates, each in 2 states. Fuerstenberg - Schaefer copy. S Dec 7 (58) £550

**Bion, Nicolas, 1652-1753**
— L'usage des globes celestes et terrestres et des spheres. Paris, 1699. 1st Ed. 8vo, contemp calf; upper joint cracked, upper cover split, extremities rubbed. With 26 plates. Some worming in 1st 40 leaves lower margins; browned; 1st 8 leaves moldstained; title soiled. S Oct 27 (797) £340 [Arader]

**Biorklund, George —&
Barnard, Osbert H.**
— Rembrandt's Etchings True and False. L, 1968. 2d Ed, one of 600. 4to, orig half cloth, in dj; bdg shaken. sg Sept 7 (290) $300

**Biot, Jean Baptiste, 1774-1862**
— Traite de physique experimentale et mathematique. Paris, 1816. 4 vols. 8vo, 19th-cent half cloth; worn. With 22 folding plates. sg May 16 (129) $325

**Birch, A. G.**
— The Moon Terror and Other Stories.... Indianapolis: Popular Fiction Co., [1927]. In dj with tear to front panel & piece lacking from back. pba May 4 (106) $60

**Biringuccio, Vannoccio**
— De la pirotechnia libri X. [Venice: Comin da Trino di Monferrato, 1559] 1558. ("Pirotechnia.") 4to, 19th-cent half vellum. Lower portion of last leaf cut away with loss to last line of colophon; 1st 12 leaves stained. S Mar 14 (52) £520
— Pirotechnia. NY: American Institute of Mining and Metallurgical Engineers, 1943. 4to, half vellum; worn, spine soiled. wa Dec 14 (168) $55

**Birkbeck, Morris, 1764-1825**
— Notes on a Journey in America. L, 1818. 8vo, later cloth. With folding map colored in outline, possibly from anr copy, laid-in & with trimmed margins. sg Oct 26 (18) $120

**Birnbaum, Solomon**
— The Hebrew Scripts. Leiden, 1971. 2 vols. Folio, orig cloth. sg Apr 11 (171) $275

**Bischoff, Jan de.** See: Episcopius, Johannes

**Bishop, J. Leander**
— History of American Manufactures from 1608 to 1860. Phila., 1866. 3 vols. 8vo, orig cloth, both covers of Vol III nearly detached; cocked, worn, ends chipped. wa Feb 29 (424) $210

**Bishop, Nathaniel Holmes, 1837-1902**
— Four Months in a Sneak-Box: a Boat Voyage...down the Ohio and Mississippi Rivers. Bost., 1879. 1st Ed. 8vo, orig cloth. sg Oct 26 (20) $395
— Voyage of the Paper Canoe.... Bost., 1878. 8vo, orig cloth; worn, rear inner joint starting. O July 9 (33) $100
  Anr copy. Orig cloth; repaired. pba Aug 22 (889) $65

**Bishop, Richard Evett**
— Bishop's Birds. Phila., 1936. One of 135. 4to, vellum gilt; small tape marks to upper cover edges. With 73 plates & 1 orig etching, sgd. pba Nov 30 (40) $250
— Bishop's Wildfowl. St. Paul, 1948. 4to, lea; rubbed. O June 25 (24) $60
  Anr copy. Lea; worn. O June 25 (26) $110; pba July 11 (367) $85
  Anr copy. Orig lea. sg Mar 7 (401) $110
  Anr copy. Lea. wa Feb 1 (197) $110

**Bisland, Elizabeth, 1861-1929**
— The Life and Letters of Lafcadio Hearn. Bost., 1906. 1st Ed, One of 200 L.p. copies. 2 vols. sg Dec 14 (142) $1,600

**Bissell, Alfred Elliott**
— Tuscarora Recollections. Wilmington DE, 1965. O Feb 6 (25) $700

**Bisset, James**
— Bisset's Magnificent Guide, or Grand Copperplate Directory, for the Town of Birmingham. Birm., 1803. 8vo, contemp half lea; extremities worn, joints starting. With frontis map, additional title & 51 plates. Extra-illus with 18 contemp proofs of bank notes. sg Mar 7 (30) $400
— The Origin, Rise and Progress of Leamington Spa.... Leamington, 1828. 12mo, orig ptd wraps; worn. With 16 plates & 1 woodcut illust. b Dec 5 (395) £150
— A Poetic Survey round Birmingham.... Birm., [1800]. 12mo, modern half calf. With map & 27 plates. b Dec 5 (10) £260

**Bisset, Robert, 1759-1805**
— Douglas; or, The HIghlander.... L, 1800. 1st Ed. 3 vols. 12mo, contemp half calf. Lacking half-titles to Vols I-II; some soiling & staining. Ck Sept 8 (197) £480

**Bitaube, Paul Jeremie**
— Guillaume. En dix chants. Amst.: M. Magerus, 1773. 8vo, 18th-cent mor. S Dec 7 (59) £220

**Bitting, Katherine Golden**
— Gastronomic Bibliography. San Francisco, 1939. pba Aug 8 (358) $225
  Anr Ed. [L, 1981]. One of 500. 8vo, orig cloth in dj. sg Apr 11 (42) $225

**Bizot, Pierre, 1630-96**
— Histoire metallique de la Republique de Hollande. Paris, 1687. Folio, contemp sheep; corners worn, covers detached. With 12 numismatic plates (the 6th bound upside down). sg Mar 21 (53) $250
— Medalische Historie der Republyk van Holland. Amst., 1690. 4to, contemp calf; warped, needs rebacked. Marginal dampstaining affecting plates; lacking 1 plate; lower margin of tp restored. sg Mar 21 (54) $120

## BLAAUW

**Blaauw, Frans Ernst**
— A Monograph of the Cranes. Leiden & L, 1897. One of 170. Folio, orig cloth; corners bumped, spine ends chipped. With 22 colored plates. C May 31 (6) £2,600

**Black, Adam —&**
**Black, Charles**
— Black's New Large Map of England and Wales.... L, [1864 or later]. Folio, contemp half mor; worn, joints weak. With 15 litho sheets, hand-colored. S Oct 26 (369) £150 [Baskes]
— General Atlas of the World. Edin., 1857. Folio, contemp half mor; worn, upper cover detached. With 56 colored maps. Some discoloration. S Mar 28 (169) £130

**Black, Charles.** See: Black & Black

**Black Elk.** See: Neihardt & Black Elk

**Black, George Fraser**
— Gypsy Bibliography. Liverpool: Gypsy Lore Society, 1909. Provisional Issue. Ptd wraps; some wear & soiling. O Mar 26 (32) $50
Anr Ed. Edin., 1914 [1913]. Orig wraps; some wear. pba Aug 8 (309) $55

**Black Hills Engineer**
— The Black Hills Engineer: Custer Expedition Number. Rapid City SD: South Dakota State School of Mines, 1929. Vol XVII, No 4. Orig wraps. Inscr by the president of the School, Cleophas O'Harra. pba June 25 (185) $110

**Black, Joseph, 1728-99**
— Experiments upon Magnesia alba.... Edin., 1782. 12mo, calf. sg May 16 (130) $950

**Black, William**
— Game at Golf: William Black's Poem of 1791. [Glasgow]: Patrick Press, 1987. One of 70. Commentary by David Hamilton. Half mor. With 2 sgd notes from hamilton to Conefry. Sgd & inscr to Hal Conefry. pba Apr 18 (11) $300

**Blackburn, Jane**
— Birds Drawn from Nature. Edin., 1868. One of 6 colored under Blackburn's personal supervision. Folio, orig half mor; recased, modern endpapers. With litho title dated 1862, title to 2d part dated 1865 & 43 hand-colored plates. Most outer margins affected by damp; lacking ad leaf. Fattorini copy. C Oct 25 (3) £1,700

**Blackburn, Philip C.** See: Spiller & Blackburn

**Blacker, Valentine, 1778-1823**
— Memoir of the Operations of the British Army in India during the Mahratta War.... L, 1821. 2 vols. 4to, orig bds; rebacked. With 2 folding color frontises, & 46 maps & plans. S Oct 26 (554) £320 [Miles]

## AMERICAN BOOK PRICES CURRENT

**Blacker, William**
— Art of Angling, and Complete System of Fly-Making. L, 1855. ("Art of Fly Making....") 12mo, orig cloth; worn. With frontis, engraved title & 20 plates, most of them hand-colored. Some foxing; piece clipped from blank margin of engraved title. O Feb 6 (26) $650
Anr copy. Contep mor; rebacked. W Nov 8 (361) £500

**Blackmore, Sir Richard, 1654-1729**
— Prince Arthur. An Heroick Poem. L, 1695. 1st Ed. Folio, contemp calf; rubbed. b Sept 20 (90) £110

**Blackmore, Richard Doddridge, 1825-1900**
— Fringilla.... Cleveland, 1895. Review copy. Illus by Will H. Bradley. 8vo, bds. Foxed. K Feb 11 (105) $225

**Blackstone, Sir William, 1723-80**
— Commentaries on the Laws of England. Oxford, 1765-69. 1st Ed. 4 vols. 4to, contemp half mor; rebacked retaining portions of spines, some rubbing. Browning & foxing. cb Feb 14 (2628) $5,500
Anr copy. Early 19th-cent calf; spines rebacked. Vol III marginaly dampstained in front. Epstein copy. CNY Dec 15 (5) $5,500
2d Ed of Vols I & II; 3d Ed of Vol III; 1st Ed of Vol IV. Oxford, 1766-67-70-69. 4 vols. 4to, contemp calf; rubbed. b Sept 20 (92) £750
Anr Ed. Dublin, 1771. 4 vols. 4to, contemp calf; lower cover of Vol I detached, rubbed, joints cracked. cb June 25 (1781) $475
Anr Ed. Dublin, 1788. 4 vols. 12mo, contemp calf; spines worn, ends chipped, covers starting, stamps on front endpapers. Some browning. sg Mar 21 (182) $110
Anr Ed. L, 1825. 4 vols. 8vo, contemp calf; Vol I spine def. pba Jan 4 (153) $200

**Blackwell, Elizabeth, c.1700-58**
— A Curious Herbal. L, 1739. 2d Ed. 2 vols. Folio, contemp calf; extremities worn, joints split. Engraved throughout, with 2 titles, 7 dedicatory leaves & 500 uncolored plates. Margin of Plates 249-52 wormed; index leaf adhering to rear free endpaper of Vol I. C May 31 (8) £2,200

**Blackwell, Thomas, Principal of the Marischal College**
— Memoirs of the Court of Augustus. L, 1764. 3 vols. 4to, contemp calf gilt; some joints tender. sg Feb 8 (62) $90

**Blackwood, Lady Alicia**
— Scutari, the Bosphorus and the Crimea. Ventnor, Isle of Wight, 1857. 2 vols. Folio, orig wraps; soiled. With 2 litho titles & 19 litho plates, 4 of them in 2 sections & folded. b May 30 (244) £400

**Blaes, Gerard.** See: Blasius, Gerardus

**Blaeu, Jan, 1596-1673.** See: Blaeu & Blaeu

**Blaeu, Willem, 1571-1638**
— Institution astronomique de l'usage des globes et spheres celestes et terrestres. Amst., 1642. 2 parts in 1 vol. 4to, contemp calf; worn. Wormed; some spotting. S Oct 27 (798) £800 [Arader]

**Blaeu, Willem, 1571-1638 —&
Blaeu, Jan, 1596-1673**
— Atlas major, sive cosmographia Blaviana. Amst., 1662. 1st Ed. Vol VI only [Scotland & Ireland]. Folio, contemp vellum gilt; worn. With 55 hand-colored maps. Lacking engraved title; library stamp of Principality of Monaco Library. pnE May 15 (265) £4,600
— Le Grand Atlas, ou cosmographie Blaviane. Amst., 1667. Vol II only (Northern & Eastern Europe). Folio, contemp vellum gilt; worn. With 40 maps & plans in contemp hand-coloring, title & cartouches heightened with gold. Moscow with repaired tear; browned. S June 27 (93) £3,000
2d Ed with French text. 12 vols. Folio, orig vellum gilt with yapp edges; minor staining, lacking some ties. With 13 frontises (most with overslips) hand-colored & heightened with gold & occasionally silver & 599 maps & plates, all finely colored in a contemp hand, plus 21 additional hand-colored double-page maps by Visscher & de Wit with some capital cities dotted with gold. All leaves guarded, minor soiling & browning. "A superb luxury copy". P June 5 (174) $230,000
2d French text Ed. Vol VI [Scotland & Ireland]. Contemp vellum gilt. With 55 maps finely colored in a contemp hand & heightened with gold. Browned. S June 27 (86) £2,600
Anr copy. Vol V [England & Wales]. With frontis & 58 double-page maps, hand colored in a contemp hand, titles & cartouches heightened in gold. Hereford stuck together; some browning. S June 27 (87) £11,000
Anr copy. Vol III [Germany]. With 97 double-page maps in contemp hand-coloring, title 7 cartouches heightened with gold. Ducatus Silesia Iavrani torn. S June 27 (94) £5,300
Anr copy. Vols VII & VIII [France & Switzerland]. Contemp vellum gilt; some wear. With frontis & 73 double-page maps, hand colored in a contemp hand. S June 27 (95) £3,800
Anr copy. Vol IX [Italy]. With frontis & 60 double-page maps, hand colored in a contemp hand, titles & cartouches heightened in gold. Liguria torn; some browning & waterstaining. S June 27 (96) £7,500
Anr copy. Vol IV [Netherlands]. With frontis & 63 double-page maps, hand colored in a contemp hand, titles & cartouches heightened in gold. Hollandiae Pars Septentrionalis with wear at fold; some green cracked; browned; worming & waterstaining at edges. S June 27 (97) £7,200
Anr copy. Vol X [Spain & Africa]. Contemp vellum gilt; some soiling. With 41 double-page maps, hand colored in a contemp hand, titles & cartouches heightened in gold. Some cracking of green; general map of Africa with splitting at fold. S June 27 (98) £6,500

Anr copy. Vol XI [Asia]. Contemp vellum gilt; joints split, spine def. With engraved title & 28 maps, hand colored in a contemp hand, titles & cartouches heightened in gold. Browned throughout. S June 27 (2121) £3,600
Anr Ed. Amst., 1967-68. Out-of-series set. 12 vols. Folio, orig lea. With reproductions of orig engraved titles, 598 maps & plates. A reprint of the 1st French Ed (1663) of Blaeu's Atlas Major. CE June 15 (297) $1,900
— Grooten Atlas, oft werelt-beschryving, in welcke 't aerdryck.... Amst., 1664. Vol II only (of 9): Tweede Stuck der Aedrycks-Beschriving, 't welck vervat Duytslandt, en d'aengegrensde Landtschappen. Folio, contemp calf gilt; abraded, spine & corners repaired. With 107 full-sheet maps (3 of them inserted as plates, 2 of these composed of 2 joined sheets) & with variant prelim setting with variant map of quire M. Tp creased & with closed marginal tear; some creasing & fold breaks & repairs; c.5 maps shaved at neatline; wormhole at bottom edge of Ll6-Ss. Schaefer copy. P Nov 1 (38) $12,000
Anr copy. Vol VI only: Derde Stuk der Aardrijks-Beschrijving, welk vervat Vrankyrk. Folio, orig vellum gilt; soiled, spine repaired at foot. With 63 full-sheet engraved maps (variant with 15 inserted as plates & without the descriptive letterpress on outside of mapsheet) & 20 woodcut illusts of coins. With 2 additional contemp maps inserted. Tp border colored by a contemp hand & heightened with gold; maps partially colored in outline, with cartouches fully colored & often heightened with gold. Schaefer copy. P Nov 1 (39) $6,500
— Novum ac magnum theatrum urbium Belgicae.... Amst., [1649]. Vol II: Belgium Contemp vellum gilt; soiled. With letterpress title on slip pasted within engraved armorial border & 92 plates showing 143 views, plans, etc, all in contemp hand-coloring, the title heightened in gold. Creasing to title; fore-edges stained, affecting 2 images. S June 27 (92) £13,000
— Novus Atlas.... Amst., [1655, or later]. Vol VI only [China]. Folio, orig vellum gilt; rebacked. With engraved title, hand-colored & heightened with gold, & 17 maps, hand-colored in outline. Minor discoloration; 1 map with tears repaired. Latin text. b Dec 5 (57) £2,500
— Le Theatre du monde, ou nouvel atlas.... Amst., 1643-[46]. Vols I-IV. Folio, contemp vellum gilt; worn. With 6 engraved titles (5 with overslips) & 334 (of 336) mostly double-page maps hand-colored in outline, with titles & cartouches fully colored, titles heightened in gold. Print crease to Europa & Suecia; Lithuaniae torn without loss; Francofurtensis with Ms annotations; waterstaining to upper edges at end of Vol II; maps 63-66 in Vol III waterstained; Vol IV waterstained affecting 1st 14 maps & 4 at end; Northantonensis with abrasion at fold; some browning. S June 27 (71) £52,000
Anr Ed. Amst., 1647-50. Part 1 only. 2 parts in 1 vol. Folio, contemp vellum gilt. With engraved title & 120 maps, hand-colored in outline. Westphalia cut down & from anr copy; some fold repairs; browned

throughout; lacking engraved title to Part 2; Maps 1 & 3 replaced by general maps by Janvier, both backed with text in Ms from the Blaeu vol. S June 27 (99) £12,000

— Theatrum orbis terrarum. Amst., 1635. ("Novus Atlas....") 2 vols. Folio, orig vellum gilt over bds; soiled, extremities worn & repaired, new endpapers. With 205 full-sheet maps (5 ptd on 2 joined sheets & inserted as plates), 3 engraved text maps, 1 engraved & 5 woodcut astronomical diagrams, 20 woodcut illusts of coins & 2 additional contemp maps inserted. Titles colored by a contemp hand & heightened with gold; maps partly hand-colored in outline, with cartouches & decorations fully hand-colored. Tp of Vol II extended & repaired; 1 map with burn hole in cartouche; some fold breaks repaired; marginal tears & repairs; some creasing, soiling & marginal dampstaining. Schaefer copy. P Nov 1 (37) $47,500

Vol III only: Italy & Greece. Milan, 1958. one of 1,000. Folio, loose as issued in half calf. Italy maps on 20 double-page color maps. Facsimile of 1640 Ed. pba Aug 22 (926) $200

**Blagdon, Francis William, 1778-1819**
— Authentic Memoirs of the late George Morland. L, 1806 [but 1824 or later]. Folio, mor gilt by Morrell, orig backstrip & lettering-piece bound in. With 19 (of 20) colored plates & facsimile of his writing plate mtd at end. C Oct 25 (102) £2,000

**Blaine, Delabere Pritchett**
— An Encyclopaedia of Rural Sports. L, 1852. 2d Ed. 8vo, half calf; front joint starting. pba July 11 (368) $275

**Blair, Dorothy**
— A History of Glass in Japan. [NY, 1973]. 4to, cloth, in mylar dj. sg June 13 (168) $200

**Blair, Eric Arthur, 1903-50.** See: Orwell, George

**Blair, Hugh, 1718-1800**
— Lectures on Rhetoric and Belles Lettres. L, 1818. 3 vols. 8vo, half calf. pba Dec 14 (10) $100

**Blair, John, d.1782**
— The Chronology and History of the World. L, 1768. Folio, contemp mor gilt; worn, repaired. Some plates repaired. With presentation leaf to the Prince of Wales, 1773. CE June 15 (284) $1,100

Anr copy. Illus by Thomas Kitchin. Contemp calf; rebacked, lower bds detached. With title, dedication, & 14 folding maps. Some spotting. S Oct 26 (421) £500 [Storey]

**Blair, Robert, 1699-1746**
— The Grave.... L, 1808. Folio, later calf. With engraved title & 11 plates after William Blake & port after T. Phillips, all engraved by Schiavonetti. Foxing on frontis & engraved title; stains at bottom of a few plates. K Oct 1 (68) $800

Anr copy. Later half mor; rubbed & stained. Port & pictorial title with dampstaining. O Mar 5 (21) $750

Anr Ed. L, 1813. Proof copy Issue. Folio, contemp mor gilt by C. Smith. With engraved title & 11 plates after William Blake & port after T. Phillips, all engraved by Schiavonetti. Pbr's name reads Davis on plates 1, 3-4, 7-8, 10-11; Caption of Plate 2 reads The Valley of Death; caption titles without quotations from the poem. Marginal soiling & foxing. Schaefer copy. P Nov 1 (40) $3,250

**Blair, Walter A.**
— A Raft Pilot's Log. Cleveland, 1930. Orig cloth; lower corner of front cover bumped. pba Nov 16 (27) $60

**Blake, Thomas**
— Vindiciae foederis; or a Treatise of the Covenant.... L: Abel Roper, 1653. 4to, modern calf. Prelims with browned & ragged edges. sg Mar 21 (55) $200

**Blake, William, 1757-1827**
See also: Limited Editions Club; Nonesuch Press
— All Religions are One. L: Trianon Press, 1970. One of 662. 4to, half lev. With 10 facsimile plates. K Oct 1 (56) $110
— Dante. NY, 1968. ("Illustrations to the Divine Comedy of Dante.") One of 1,000. Folio, half mor. wa Nov 16 (270) $90
— Designs for Gray's Poems. Clairvaux: Trianon Press, 1972. ("Water-Colour Designs for the Poems of Thomas Gray.") One of 100 for Paul Mellon. Ed by Geoffrey Keynes. Loose as issued in vellum wrap. sg Oct 19 (42) $500
— Illustrations of Dante. L: Trianon Press, 1978. One of 376. Oblong folio, half mor. With 12 plates. sg Oct 19 (43) $300
— Illustrations of the Book of Job. L, 1825 [1826]. Folio, 19th-cent mor gilt; rebacked, corners repaired. With engraved title & 21 plates, about 210mm by 163mm, marked Proof in lower right corner & ptd on india paper mtd on wove paper with J Whatman Turkey Mill 1825 watermark. Tp mount soiled. Schaefer copy. P Nov 1 (31) $26,000

Anr Ed. L, 1825 [label dated 1826]. Folio, loose in portfolio. With engraved title and 21 plates, all proof impressions. Spotting to tp & 4 plates. S Apr 23 (264) £31,000

Anr Ed. L & NY, 1902. One of 1,000. Folio, loose in individual mats. With engraved title & 21 plates. Sold w.a.f. sg Sept 7 (45) $200
— Illustrations to the Bible. L: Trianon Press, 1957. One of 506. Folio, orig half mor. With 9 colored plates. pba Sept 14 (61) $375; S Nov 21 (228) £250
— Jerusalem. L: Trianon Press, 1974. One of 516. Half mor. K Oct 1 (59) $250
— The Marriage of Heaven and Hell. [L: Trianon Press, 1960]. One of 526. Folio, half mor. With 27 colored plates. Facsimile of the Rosenwald Ms.. K Oct 1 (60) $225

Anr copy. Half mor. Facsimile of the Rosenwald Ms.. pba Sept 14 (57) $250
— Milton, a Poem. Paris: Trianon Press, 1967. One of 380. 4to, half mor gilt. K Oct 1 (61) $250

— Songs of Innocence and Experience. [L: Trianon Press, 1955]. One of 526. Orig mor; covers soiled. S May 16 (101) £150

— Visions of the Daughters of Albion. [L: Trianon Press, 1959]. Out-of-series copy. Folio, bds. With 11 hand-colored plates. K Oct 1 (65) $225

— Works. L, 1893. Ed by Ellis & Yeats. 3 vols. 8vo, orig half mor gilt; corners of Vol III worn. S Apr 23 (261) £820

**Blake, William O.**
— The History of Slavery and the Slave Trade.... Columbus, Ohio, 1858. 8vo, contemp calf; extremities worn. Some foxing. sg Mar 28 (271) $60

**Blakeney, Thomas S.**
— Sherlock Holmes: Fact or Fiction? L, 1932. In dj. sg Dec 14 (38) $70

**Blakey, Robert, 1795-1878**
— Historical Sketches of the Angling Literature of all Nations.... L, 1856 [1855]. 1st Ed. 12mo, recent cloth; worn. O Feb 6 (27) $100

Anr copy. Cloth. pba July 11 (37) $90

— Old Faces in New Masks. L, 1859. Illus by George Cruikshank. 8vo, later mor, orig backstrip with gilt design by Cruikshank bound in; joints cracked, some leaves loose. sg Sept 21 (142) $80

**Blakston, W. A. —& Others**
— The Illustrated Book of Canaries and Cage-Birds.... L, [1877-80]. 4to, contemp half calf; rubbed. With 56 chromolitho plates. b Jan 31 (289) £130

Anr copy. Orig cloth. b May 30 (523) £170

Anr copy. Orig cloth; recased with new endpapers. O Mar 5 (22) $375

**Blanc, Charles, 1813-82**
— L'Oeuvre de Rembrandt.... Paris, 1873. 2 vols. 4to, contemp half mor; spotted, extremities rubbed. pba Aug 22 (638) $100

**Blanchan, Neltje**
— The American Flower Garden. NY, 1909. 4to, cloth. Some foxing. pba Aug 8 (430) $80

— Birds that Hunt and are Hunted. NY, 1898. 8vo, cloth; front hinge cracked. pba Aug 8 (296) $100

**Blanck, Jacob Nathaniel**
— Bibliography of American Literature. New Haven, 1955-73. Vols I-VI [Adams through Parsons]. 4to, orig cloth. Ck Apr 12 (205) $220

Anr Ed. New Haven, 1955-92. Vols I-IX. ds July 27 (27) $600

Anr copy. Vols I-III only. Cloth. F June 20 (523A) $90

1st Ed. New Haven, 1955-91. Vols I-IX (of 10). 9 vols. 4to, orig cloth. Lacks index. sg Apr 11 (43) $800

**Blanco, Amanda**
— Type-Faces: A Photographic Study of Ward Ritchie. Northridge: Santa Susana Press, 1988. One of 65. Loose in clamshell box. With 12 mtd photographs. pba June 20 (344) $160

**Blanco, Manuel, 1778-1845**
— Flora de Filipinas. Manila, 1837. 4to, modern vellum. S Nov 30 (8) £1,000

Anr Ed. Manila, 1877-80-[83]. 4 vols of text in 5 portfolios & 3 portfolios of plates. Folio, unbound in 8 modern half-calf cases. With litho title, dedication plate, port, plate of ms facsimile & 177 chromolitho plates. Some edge defs; pp. 213-16 in Vol IV on different paper; pp. 26-27 in Vol I stained. S Nov 30 (9) £32,000

**Blanford, William Thomas, 1832-1905 —& Others**
— Scientific Results of the Second Yarkand Mission.... Calcutta or L, [1870s-90s]. 15 parts. 4to, orig wraps; some spines torn. With 71 plates, 46 of them hand-colored; folding colored maps. Some spotting & marginal tears. Fattorini copy. C Oct 25 (87) £2,500

**Blarrorvio, Petrus de**
— Insigne nanceidos opus de bello nanceiano. Saint Nicolas du Port: Petrus Jacobi, 5 Jan 1518 [1519]. Bound with: Guntherus, Ligurinus. Opus de Rebus gestis Imp. Caesaris Friderici. And: Bartholinus, Richardus. De bello Norico, Austriados. Strassburg: Johann Schott, 1531. 1st Issue, with privilege dated 4 Sept 1518. Folio, 16th-cent mor gilt with supralibros of Jacques Auguste de Thou; lower joint worn, minor rubbing. Chatsworth - Abbey - Schaefer copy. P Nov 1 (41) $15,000

**Blasche, Bernhard Heinrich —&
Boileau, Daniel**
— The Art of Working in Pasteboard.... L, 1827. 16mo, orig bds; rubbed. Some foxing. bba May 30 (327) £140 [Black]

**Blasius, Gerardus, 1626?-92?**
— Anatome animalium. Amst., 1681. 1st Ed. 4to, 19th-cent half mor; rubbed. With frontis & 65 plates. Piece torn from outer margin of Plate 46; lower margin of R4 torn; some upper blank forecorners damaged; some soiling. S June 12 (241) £450

— Observationes medicae rariores; accedit monstri triplicis historia. Amst., 1677. 8vo, 18th-cent half calf; some wear. With 12 plates. Some plates trimmed within platemark; lower margins stained at end. S June 12 (240) £320

**Blatty, William Peter**
— The Exorcist. NY: Harper & Row, [1971]. Advance Reading Copy. Wraps. pba May 4 (108) $65

**Bleackley, Horace William, 1868-1931**
— More Tales of the Stumps. L, 1902. Illus by Arthur Rackham & by "Rip". Orig cloth; extremities rubbed. Ck May 31 (119) £500

**Bledsoe, Anthony J.**
— Indian Wars of the Northwest.... San Francisco, 1885. 1st Ed. 8vo, orig calf; covers rubbed; joint tender.

Errata slip tipped in. Robbins copy. pba Mar 21 (19) $600

**Bleeker, Capt. Leonard**
— The Order Book of.... NY, 1865. One of 50 L.p. copies. 4to, half mor, orig wraps bound in. wa Feb 29 (404) $200

**Blegny, Nicolas d**
— Le bon Usage du the, du caffe et du chocolat.... Paris, 1687. Illus by Hainzelman. 12mo, contemp calf; rebacked, restored. With frontis, & 13 full-page illus. Frontis with closed tear; browned & stained. Ck Mar 22 (43) £600

**Blew, William C. A.**
— Brighton and its Coaches. L, 1894 [1893]. 1st Ed. 8vo, orig cloth; worn, spine scuffed. With 20 hand-colored plates. Minor foxing. O Jan 9 (49) $180
— A History of Steeple-Chasing. L, 1901 [1900]. Orig cloth; spotted, spine frayed. O Jan 9 (50) $70
   Anr Ed. L, 1901. Illus by Henry Alken. Orig cloth; shaken. With 12 color plates. sg Mar 7 (403) $60

**Blewitt, Mary**
— Surveys of the Seven Seas.... L, 1957. Folio, cloth. pba Feb 13 (16) $75

**Bligh, William, 1754-1817**
   See also: Golden Cockerel Press; Limited Editions Club
— An Account of the Dangerous Voyage, Performed by Captain Bligh.... L, 1818. 12mo, modern calf. b Mar 20 (36) £140
[-] An Account of the Mutinous Seizure of the Bounty.... L: for Robert Turner, July 1791. 8vo, modern half mor. Lacking 1st blank; with early stamp "Carne, 96" at head of tp. b Mar 20 (15) £9,500
   Anr Ed. L: for E. Bentley, [1792]. 8vo, contemp bds; later calf spine. Corner torn from c2. b Mar 20 (22) £2,800
— The Bligh Notebook.... Canberra, 1986. 2 vols. Half lea gilt. pba Feb 13 (18) $425
— Capitainens vid Engelske Ammiralitetet William Bligh's Resa i Soderrhafvet.... Nykoping, 1795. 8vo, early wraps. b Mar 20 (30) £330
[-] The Dangerous Voyage of Captain Bligh.... L, 1818. 12mo, contemp half mor. With woodcut frontis & 4 woodcut illusts. b Mar 20 (35) £220
— The Dangerous Voyage Performed by Captain Bligh.... Dublin, 1824. 12mo, contemp calf. b Mar 20 (39) £180
   Anr copy. Orig ptd wraps; spine worn. b Mar 20 (40) £250
[-] The Extraordinary Account and Wonderful Preservation of Captain Bligh, and Eighteen Seamen.... L, 1804. 12mo, bound with 2 other tracts in red mor. Tp soiled; last leaf torn with minor loss to text. b Mar 20 (34) £260
[-] Legislative Assembly. New South Wales. William Henry (Petition of...). Sydney, 1860. 4to, modern half calf. b Mar 20 (42) £100

— Memoir to Accompany a Chart of the Coast of Blankenberg to the Walcheren Island, in the Month of October, 1803. L: Admiralty Hydrographical Office, 3 Dec 1803. 4to, framed with the engraved chart. b Mar 20 (33) £1,300
[-] The Mutiny of the Bounty; or, the Marvellous Adventures of Christian and his Comrades. L: Cheerful Visitor Office, [c.1820]. 16mo, bound with 5 other chapbooks in contemp half mor. b Mar 20 (38) £200
— A Narrative of the Mutiny on Board His Majesty's Ship Bounty.... Dublin, 1790. 8vo, modern half calf. Minor staining. b Mar 20 (18) £350
   1st Ed. L, 1790. 4to, contemp half calf. With folding plate & 3 charts. Plates laid down; some staining. Francis Hayward's inscr copy. b Mar 20 (16) £9,000
[-] A Poem on a Voyage of Discovery, Undertaken by a Brother of the Author's.... L, 1792. 4to, sewn as issued. Lacking 2 leaves at end; some soiling & creasing at ends. b Mar 20 (23) £300
— Reise in das Sudmeer, welche mit dem Schiffe Bounty.... Berlin, 1793. 8vo, bds; rebacked. b Mar 20 (29) £220
— Relation de l'enlevement du navire le Bounty. Paris, 1790. 8vo, later mor. With 3 folding maps. b Mar 20 (17) £300
[-] Statements of the Loss of His Majesty's new Ship the Bounty.... L: Thomas Tegg, [c.1809]. 8vo, disbound. With folding frontis (browned at edges). b Mar 20 (195) £240
— Verhaal van de Muitery, aan boord van het Engelsch Konigsschip de Bounty.... Rotterdam, 1790. Bound with: Echtrelaas wegens het gesmeede oproer, op het uytgaande E.E. Oost-Indische Compagnie Schip Duynenburg.... Rotterdam, [c.1770]. 4to, contemp half calf. b Mar 20 (19) £800
— Voyage a la Mer du Sud, entrepris par ordre de S. M. Britannique pour introduire, aux Indes Occidentales, l'arbre a pain.... Paris, 1792. 8vo, half mor. Folding plate trimmed with loss to text at foot; some waterstaining. b Mar 20 (24) £160
   Anr copy. Contemp half mor; spine repaired. With folding plate & 2 folding maps. Minor spotting. b Mar 20 (25) £260
— A Voyage to the South Sea.... Dublin, 1792. 4to, contemp calf. Lacking port & plate. b Mar 20 (26) £200
   1st Ed. L, 1792. 4to, contemp calf; rebacked using orig spine. With 7 plates & maps, 6 of them folding. Owen Rutter's copy. b Mar 20 (27) £3,600
   Anr copy. Contemp calf gilt; rebacked, corners worn. With frontis, 4 engraved charts (3 folding), 2 folding plans & 1 plate. Gutter margin of frontis reinforced. Hefner copy. CNY May 17 (6) $3,800
   Anr copy. Modern mor gilt. With frontis & 8 plates. Frontis, tp & some other leaves foxed; 4 plates mtd on linen & repaired; 1 leaf with small burnhole. pba Feb 13 (17) $3,750
   Anr Ed. Honolulu: Rare Books, [n.d.]. 4to, cloth. Facsimile of 1792 Ed. pba Apr 25 (141) $50

**Bligh Collection, William**
SWAINSON, WILLIAM. - [Sale Catalogue] A Catalogue of

the Rare and Valuable Shells.... L: W. Smith for Dubois' Auction Rooms, [c.1822]. 8vo, contemp half mor. With 2 hand-colored lithos. Some ink annotations. Sold with 3 shells believed to be part of the collection.   b Mar 20 (196) £1,900

**Blin de Sainmmore, Adrien Michel Hyacinthe**
— Joachim, ou le triomphe de la piete filiale. Amst., 1775. 8vo, contemp red mor gilt. Marginal staining at beginning. Fuerstenberg - Schaefer copy.   S Dec 7 (61) £150

**Bliss, Douglas Percy**
— Border Ballads selected & decorated with woodcuts.... L, 1925. 4to, Goatskin extra by Jen Lindsay, 1985.   C May 1 (23) £580
— Edward Bawden. Godalming: Pendomer Press, [1979]. One of 200. 4to, orig half mor, litho loose in a paper folder.   bba May 9 (198) £160 [Sims Reed]; bba May 9 (358) £200 [Scott]

**Bliss, Frank C.**
— St. Paul, Its Past and Present.... St. Paul, 1888. Orig cloth; covers rubbed.   pba Apr 25 (295) $55

**Bliss Collection, Robert Woods**
— Pre-Columbian Art. NY, 1957. Folio, cloth.   sg Sept 7 (47) $250; sg June 13 (59) $120
Anr copy. Orig cloth, in mylar dj.   wa Feb 1 (377) $130

**Blixen-Finecke, Bror von**
— African Hunter. NY, 1938. 1st American Ed. In dj with scrape; both d/j & lower extremities of bdg dampstained.   pba May 23 (444) $60

**Bloch, Robert**
— The Opener of the Way. Sauk City: Arkham House, 1945. 1st Ed, Ltd Ed. In dj with soiling to rear panel.   K June 23 (37) $225; sg June 20 (17) $300
— Psycho. L, [1960]. In dj.   sg Dec 14 (14) $60
— The Scarf. NY, 1947. Advance copy. In dj.   sg June 20 (18) $110

**Block Book.** See: Biblia Pauperum

**Block Books.** See: Ars Moriendi

**Blogie, Jeanne**
— Repertoire des catalogues de ventes de livres imprimes. Brussels, 1982-92. 4 vols. 4to, orig buckram.   S Oct 27 (1015) £320 [Sawyer]
Anr Ed. Brussels, 1982. Bound with: Blechet, Francoise, Les Ventes Publiques des livres en France, 1630-1750; Oxford, 1991 4 vols. 4to, Blogie in orig cloth, Blechet in wrappers.   sg Apr 11 (15) $250

**Blome, Richard, d.1705**
See also: Cox & Blome
— Britannia: or a Geographical Description.... L, 1673. 1st Ed. Folio, 18th-cent calf; worn. With 50 maps (5 folding) plan of London & 12 leaves with 24 plates of arms, colored throughout by a contemp hand. Margin of Berkshire strengthened; folding maps at margins; fold splits.   S Nov 30 (48) £4,400

Anr copy. 18th-cent calf; rebacked, worn. With 50 maps, full-page plan of London & 24 plates on 12 leaves, showing arms. Waterstaining to map edges.   S Mar 28 (74) £3,000
— The Present State of His Majesties Isles and Territories in America.... L, 1687. 8vo, contemp sheep. Lacking port & maps.   sg Oct 26 (21) $250

**Blondel, Jacques Francois, 1705-74**
— Architecture Francoise.... Paris, 1752-56. 7 vols in 4. Folio, contemp calf gilt. With 499 plates numbered to 500 with the number 496 omitted. Some spotting; lower margins wormed in Vol III; hole to 1 headpiece; ink spot in upper margin of Plate 300; a few margins extended; part of Plate 453 washed; tear repaired in Plate 490. Fuerstenberg - Schaefer copy.   S Dec 7 (63) £5,000
— De la distribution des maisons de plaisance et de la decoration des edifices en general. Paris, 1737-38. 1st Ed. 2 vols. 4to, contemp calf gilt. With frontis & 155 plates. Lacking half-title; tear through center of Plate 22; some browning. Fuerstenberg - Schaefer copy.   S Dec 7 (64) £1,400
Intermediate Issue. Contemp vellum gilt; some soiling. With frontis & 155 plates. Some browning to text; 1 plate loose.   C Mar 17 (367) £160
— Reimpression de l' Architecture Francaise. Paris, [c.1950s]. 4 vols. Folio, recent cloth.   bba Oct 19 (109) £360 [Bernett]
Anr copy. Later half mor; extremities worn, spine heads worn, Vol III rear cover detached, hinges cracked, endpapers brittle. With 499 plates. Tear into image of 1 plate.   cb Oct 17 (7) $375

**Blondus, Flavius, 1388-1463**
— Historium ab inclinatione Romanorum imperii decades. Venice: Octavianus Scotus, 16 July 1483. Folio, contemp half pigskin chained bdg. 42 lines; roman letter. Worming at beginning & end; marginal stains. 372 leaves. Goff B-698. Madsen copy.   S Mar 14 (56) £4,200

**Bloomfield, Robert, 1766-1823**
— The Farmer's Boy: a Rural Poem. L, 1800. 1st Ed. 4to, orig front bd only. Thomas Park's L.p. copy, with related material, some of it holograph.   bba July 18 (203) £1,200 [Quaritch]
— Wild Flowers; or, Pastoral and Local Poetry. L, 1806. Half mor.   pba June 20 (57) $160

**Blossfeldt, Karl**
— Art Forms in Nature. NY, [1930s]. Folio, cloth; worn & stained, hinges cracked. With 96 plates.   sg Feb 29 (36) $175
Anr Ed. L, 1932. 2d Series. Folio, cloth; worn, shaken, endpapers & half-title foxed. With 120 plates. Marginal loss to Plate 29.   sg Feb 29 (37) $1,000
— La Plante. Berlin: Ernst Wasmuth, [n.d.]. Folio, cloth; worn & soiled, front hinge split, endpapers foxed. With 120 plates.   sg Feb 29 (38) $200
— Urformen der Kunst. Berlin, [c.1929]. Folio, cloth; worn & soiled. With 120 photogravures. Soiling at beginning.   sg Feb 29 (40) $475

# BLOSSFELDT

Anr Ed. Berlin, 1929. Intro by Karl Nierendorf. 4to, orig cloth; minor wear. With 120 plates. Tp repaired at gutter. cb Oct 17 (124) $375

Anr copy. Orig cloth; joint starting, backstrip soiled, hinges starting, shaken. With 120 plates. sg Apr 24 (577) $750

Anr Ed. Berlin, [1935]. Folio, cloth; minor wear to extremities. With 96 photogravures.. sg Feb 29 (39) $250

— Wunder in der Natur. Berlin, [1942]. 4to, cloth; extremities worn, split to front hinge, endpapers stained. sg Feb 29 (41) $350

### Blouet, Guillaume Abel
— Expedition scientifique de Moree. Paris, 1831-38. 3 vols. Folio, contemp half calf; spines worn, 1 chipped. With engraved titles & 262 plates, 5 colored. Blackmer copy. S Nov 30 (119) £4,000

### Blount, Thomas, 1618-79
— Nomo-Lexicon: A Law-Dictionary. L, 1670. 1st Ed. Folio, contemp calf; worn. Hole at foot of tp; dampstained. S Mar 29 (753) £300

### Bloxam, John Francis
— The Priest and the Acolyte. L: Pvtly ptd, [c.1902]. Half mor, orig front wrap bound in; spine head chipped, joints rubbed. Richard Le Gallienne's copy. sg June 20 (107) $275

### Blue...
— The Blue Review; Literature, Drama, Art, Music. L, May to July 1913. Ed by John Middleton Murry. 3 parts (all pbd). 4to, orig wraps. Ck Nov 17 (107) £650

### Bluett, Thomas
— Some Memoirs of the Life of Job...a Slave about Two Years in Maryland.... L, 1734. 8vo, disbound. Lacking port. sg Mar 28 (326) $3,000

### Blumauer, Alois
— Vergils Aeneis. Travestiert.... Munich, 1910. One of 990. Illus by Heinrich Kley. 4to, bds. sg Sept 14 (249) $80

### Blume, Friedrich
— Die Musik in Geschichte und Gegenwart. Allgemeine Enzyklopaedie der Musik.... Kassel, 1949-69. Vols I-XIV (of 16) in 74 parts. 4to, wraps in 14 cloth casings; worn, few covers loose. sg Apr 11 (238) $275

### Blume, Karl Ludwig, 1796-1862
— Collection des orchidees les plus remarquables de l'Archipel Indien et du Japon. Amst., 1858-[59]. Vol I (all pbd). Folio, modern half mor. With litho title, 14 plain & 56 hand-colored plates. Library stamps on plates; some foxing; Chrysoglossum oxidized. S Nov 30 (10) £3,800

**Blunt, Lady Anne, 1837-1917.** See: Gregynog Press

### Blunt, Sir Anthony Frederick
— The Paintings of Poussin. L & NY, 1967-68. Vols I-II (of 3). Folio, orig cloth, in djs. sg Jan 11 (363) $60; sg Jan 11 (364) $60

**Blunt, Edmund March.** See: Furlong, Laurence

### Blunt, Wilfrid Jasper Walter
See also: Sitwell & Blunt
— Tulips and Tulipomania. L: Basilisk Press, 1977. One of 500. Illus by Rory McEwen. 4to, half mor. With 16 mtd colored plates & 8 large colored plates. sg Sept 14 (46) $130

**Blunt, Wilfrid Scawen, 1840-1922.** See: Gregynog Press; Kelmscott Press; Lawrence's copy, T. E.

### Bly, Robert
— Ducks. [N.p.]: Ox Head Press, 1968. One of 150. Inscr & with autograph postcard, sgd, laid in. pba Jan 25 (26) $130

### Boate, Gerard, 1604-50
— Irelands Naturall History.... L, 1652. 8vo, contemp sheep; worn, front joint cracked. sg May 16 (290) $950

### Bob...
— Bob Buffon's Naturalist's Cabinet. L: Hodgson, [watermarked 1821]. 12mo, orig wraps. Engraved & hand-colored throughout. Ink marks on 2 leaves, pencil on anr; some soiling & spotting. S May 16 (154) £260

**Bobbin, Tim.** See: Collier, John

### Boccaccio, Giovanni, 1313-75
See also: Limited Editions Club
— De casibus virorum illustrium. Bruges: Colard Mansion, 1476. ("De la ruine des nobles hommes et femmes.") Folio, later vellum. 33 lines; double column; type 1:162B. With 8 (of 9) pasted-on plates; rubricated. Outer margins cropped; 1st engraving trimmed at top; Goettingen University stamp & deaccession notice. 289 (of 292) leaves; lacking 3 blanks. Goff B-711. Schaefer copy. P Nov 1 (42) $625,000

Anr Ed. Lyons: Matthias Huss & Johann Schabeler, 1483. ("De la ruyne des nobles hommes et femmes.") Folio, 18th-cent calf gilt; rubbed, upper joint worn. 37 lines; double column; types 2:180G (headings) 1:106GB (text). With 9 half-page woodcuts. Some waterstaining at ends; tear in lower margin of p2 into text; margins at end wormed without loss. 227 (of 228) leaves; lacking initial blank. Goff B-712. Schaefer copy. P Nov 1 (43) $30,000

Anr Ed. L: Richard Tottel, 1554. ("A Treatise Excellent and Compendious, Shewing the Falles of Sondry Most Notable Princes....") Folio, 19th-cent calf gilt; spine repaired, joints cracked. Gothic type. Lydgate's Daunce Machabree present. With 12 woodcuts. Minor dampstaining; 6 leaves remargined along bottom & fore-edge. Schaefer copy. P Nov 1 (44) $2,750

— Genealogie deorum gentilium. Venice: Bonetus Locatellus for Octavianus Scotus, 23 Feb 1494/95. Folio, modern half calf with older front wooden bd & 3 remaining clasps. Roman & Greek types. With 13 full-page woodcut genealogical diagrams. Dampstained; worming, some repaired, at end touching text; repairs to tears in 1st & last leaves. 162 leaves. Goff B-753. C Apr 3 (47) £850

— The Nymphs of Fiesole. Verona: Bodoni, 1952. One of 225. 4to, orig half vellum. Ck May 31 (3) £600

— Vita di Dante Alighieri. Rome: Francesco Priscianese, 1544. 8vo, 18th-cent citron mor gilt. Lacking 2 blanks; early ink marginalia. C Nov 29 (34) £1,100

### Decameron in English

— 1625-20. - The Decameron.... L.2d Ed in English of Vol I, 1st Ed of Vol II. 2 vols in 1. Folio, early 19th-cent mor gilt, with Abdy arms; small repair to upper cover. Lacking 3 blanks; some leaves may be from anr copy; last leaf in facsimile; hole in Ll3; some repairs; some soiling. STC 3173 & 3172. S July 11 (114) £750

— 1741. - L. 8vo, calf; front cover detached. wd May 8 (40) $100

— 1906. - L. Illus by Louis Chalon. 2 vols. Contemp half mor. CE Feb 21 (23) $200

— 1934-35. - The Decameron. Oxford: Shakespeare Head Press One of 325. 2 vols. 4to, orig mor. S May 16 (62) £460

### Decameron in French

— 1548. - Paris: for Estienne Roffet Trans by Antoine Le Macon. 8vo, 19th-cent calf gilt; upper joint cracked. Tp trimmed at lower margin; early writing partially erased from tp. S June 12 (14) £380

— 1580. - Lyons: Barthelemy Honoratus. 16mo, 19th-cent calf; worn, front joint restored. Marginal dampstaining; tp heavily soiled & stained; lacking last 8 leaves. Sold w.a.f. sg Mar 21 (58) $110

— 1697. - Contes et nouvelles. Amst.: G. Gallet Illus by Romein de Hooghe. 2 vols. 8vo, late 18th-cent mor gilt; upper hinge of Vol I split. With frontis in Vol I & 100 half-page plates. Some spotting. Fuerstenberg - Schaefer copy. S Dec 7 (66) £1,500

— 1757-61. - Le Decameron. L [but Paris] 5 vols. 8vo, contemp red mor gilt; some joints rubbed, small hole piercing upper bd of Vol IV. With 5 engraved titles & 110 plates with the paraph mark on verso. Fuerstenberg - Schaefer copy. S Dec 7 (67) £3,000

### Decameron in Italian

— 1516, 29 July. - Il Decamerone. Florence: Filippo Giunta. 4to in 8's, late 18th-cent red mor gilt. C June 26 (46) £4,000

— 1522, Nov. - Venice: Aldus. 4to, 19th-cent lea gilt. Owner's stamp to tp. C June 26 (47) $5,500

— 1527. - Florence: Giunta. 4to, 19th-cent mor extra in the style of Derome, commissioned by Sir George Holford & possibly by Francis Bedford. Abbey copy. C May 1 (24) $5,000

— 1573. - Florence: Giunti. 4to, contemp vellum. Some foxing throughout; partial dampstaining, mainly towards end. sg Mar 21 (56) $225

### Boccioni, Umberto, 1882-1916

— Pittura, scultura futuriste. Milan, 1914. Orig wraps; chipped & creased. With port & 51 plates. Foxing to opening leaves & covers. Inscr to the Contessa Salasco. sg Apr 18 (92) $500

### Boccone, Paolo, 1633-1704

— Icones et descriptiones rariorum plantarum Siciliae, Melitiae... Oxford, 1674. 4to, disbound. Some stains & soiling; frayed. Sold w.a.f. O Mar 5 (23) $300

### Bochart, Samuel, 1599-1667

— Opera. Leiden & Utrecht, 1692. 3 vols. Folio, contemp vellum. WIth port, frontis & 13 maps, 4 of them double-page. b May 30 (245) £130

### Bochius, Joannes, 1555-1609

— Descriptio publicae gratulationis spectaculorum et ludorum in adventu...Ernesti, Archiducis Austriae...An. MDXCIIII. Antwerp: Plantin, 1595. 1st Ed. Folio, vellum gilt with supralibros of Ferdinand Hoffman, yapp edges; rebacked, cockled & warped, color restoration. Schaefer copy. P Nov 1 (45) $5,500

— Historica narratio profectionis et inaugurationis serenissimorum Belgii Principum Alberti et Isabellae, Austriae Archiducum. Antwerp: Plantin, 1602. Folio, contemp calf gilt; stained, extremities repaired. With 4 engraved title borders & 28 plates. Lower platemark edge of general title repaired; edge tear on c3 affecting text. Schaefer copy. P Nov 1 (46) $6,000

### Bock, C. E.

— Atlas of Human Anatomy. NY, 1879. Folio, orig cloth; front hinge cracked. With 38 hand-colored plates. sg May 16 (380) $250

### Bock, Carl A.

— The Head-Hunters of Borneo. L, 1882. 2d Ed. 8vo, later cloth; rubbed. With folding map & 30 plates, 28 of them chromolithos. S Mar 28 (383) £160

### Bock, Hieronymus, 1489?-1554

— Kraeuterbuch. Strassburg: Wendel Rihel, 1539. ("New Kreueter Buch.") Bound with: Ryff, Walther Hermann. Das new gross Distillier Buech. Frankfurt: C. Egenolff, 1545. Folio, contemp blind-stamped calf over wooden bds; worn, rebacked. 1st work: tp repaired with loss on verso; marginal repairs to other prelims;d3-4 in Part 2 in facsimile; corner torn from #34; i1 repaired; some browning & staining. 2d work: some marginal staining, repairs, browning & staining; lacking final blank. Madsen copy. S Mar 14 (54) £3,400

— Teuetsche Speisskammer. Strassburg: Wendel Rihel, 1555. 4to, modern vellum; stitching weak. With printer's device. Title browned; O2 marginally torn; dampstained in margins; block split; title & final leaf marked. Ck Mar 22 (46) £1,100

**Bode, William**
— Lights and Shadows of Chinatown. San Francisco: Kate Bode, 1896. Folio, wraps. pba Apr 25 (297) $100

**Bode, Winston**
— A Portrait of Pancho—The Life of a Great Texan: J. Frank Dobie. Austin: Pemberton Press, 1965. One of 150. Lea. Sgd on half-title. pba Aug 22 (890) $110

**Bodin, Jean, 1530-96**
— De la Demonomanie des sorciers. Paris: Jacques du Puys, 1580. 1st Ed. 4to, modern half calf; lacking front free endpaper. Hole on last leaf, not affecting text; some dampstaining. S June 12 (15) £420
— The Six Bookes of a Common-weale.... L, 1606. Trans by Richard Knolles. Folio, contemp calf gilt, with arms of Queen Elizabeth within the Garter; spine ends chipped, rubbed, marked & scratched. Worming at ends; fragment of Ms on vellum bound in at beginning. S June 12 (17) £950
— Les Six Livres de la Republique. Lyons: Jacques de Puys, 1579. Folio, 17th-cent calf. Glue stain from bookplate on tp verso; wormed at ends; tp ragged at fore-edge; some dampstaining. S June 12 (16) £260

**Bodmer, Karl, 1809-93**
[-] Karl Bodmer's America. Lincoln, [1984]. Intro by William H. Goetzmann, annotations by David C. Hung & Marsha V. Gallagher, biography by William J. Orr. Folio, cloth, in dj. pba Apr 25 (298) $60

**Bodoni, Giovanni Battista, 1740-1813**
— Le Piu insigni pitture Parmensi.... Parma: Bodoni, 1809 [1816]. 4to Ed. Orig bds; soiled, spine repaired. With frontis & 59 plates. Marginal foxing. CE Sept 27 (58) $1,000
Anr copy. Modern half mor. With engraved title & 59 plates. Some spotting. S June 13 (375) £280
— Serie di maiuscole e caratteri cancellareschi. [Parma, 1788]. 113 leaves, 505mm by 345mm, unbound. Tp & last leaf foxed. sg Apr 18 (29) $22,000

**Boeckler, Georg Andreas**
— Architectura curiosa nova. Nuremberg, 1664. 4 parts in 1 vol. Folio, contemp half vellum; spine def. With engraved & 231 plates on 200 leaves. Some soiling & spotting; hole in Plates 109 & 112 with loss. S June 27 (276) £2,200
— Theatrum machinarum novum.... Nuremberg, 1662. Folio, contemp vellum. With engraved title & 154 plates. Stains to 1st few pages; possibly washed. pba Nov 30 (59) $3,250
Anr Ed. Nuremberg, 1703. Bound with: Architectura curiosa nova. Nuremberg, [1673]. Folio, modern pigskin. 1st work with the engraved title def in margins & backed; 2d work with repairs to outer margin of 1st title & following 2 leaves & with Plate 83 having partly failed to print. Madsen copy. S Mar 14 (55) £1,600

**Boeckler, Johann Heinrich**
— Bibliographia Historico-Politico-Philologica.... Germanopoli, 1696. 8vo, contemp calf; rubbed. Some foxing & browning. O Mar 26 (34) $225

**Boecklin, Arnold, 1827-1901**
— Neben Meiner Kunst. Flugstudien.... Berlin, [1909]. 4to, orig bds. sg May 16 (10) $50

**Boehme, Jacob, 1575-1624**
— The Third Booke of the Authour Being the High and Deepe Searching out of the Threefold Life of Man.... L, 1650. 4to, later half calf. pba Sept 14 (72) $850

**Boelker, Homer H.**
— Portfolio of Hopi Kachinas. Hollywood, [1969]. One of 1,000. 4to, cloth plus 16 loose plates in wraps. pba Aug 22 (891) $250

**Boerhaave, Hermann, 1668-1738**
— Elementa chemiae. Paris, 1733. 2 vols. 4to, contemp calf; worn, covers detached. With 17 folding plates. Library stamp on titles. sg May 16 (131) $175
Anr copy. Contemp calf; extremities worn, Vol I joints cracked. With 17 folding plates. sg May 16 (132) $175
— Elements of Chemistry. L, 1735. 2 vols in 1. 4to, disbound. With 17 folding plates. Tp stamped. sg May 16 (133) $225

**Boethius, Anicius Manlius Torquatus Severinus, 480?-524?**
— De Consolatione philosophiae. Nuremberg: Anton Koberger, 12 Nov 1476. Folio, 19th-cent mor gilt; extremities scuffed. 34 lines, table & commentary in 2 columns, type 2:115G. Folio 1/6 supplied form anr copy; some worming touching text; marginal tears repaired. 135 (of 140) leaves; lacking blanks. Goff B-771. Sykes - Syston Park copy. C Nov 29 (35) £9,000
— De consolatione philosophiae. Venice: Gregorius de Gregoriis, 12 Aug 1516. ("De philosophiae consolatione.") 8vo, old vellum. sg Mar 21 (63) $400
— Della Consolazione della Filosofia.... Parma: Reale Tipografia [Bodoni], 1798. 4to, contemp half sheep; spine ends chipped, front joint cracked, lacking rear free endpaper. sg Mar 21 (61) $175

**Boethius, Gerda**
— Anders Zorn, his Life and Work. Stockholm, 1954. One of 1,200. 4to, lea gilt. sg June 13 (390) $375

**Boetticher, Jacob Gottlieb, 1754-92**
— A Geographical, Historical, and Political Description of the Empire of Germany, Holland.... L, 1800. 4to, cloth; shelf numbers on backstrip. With 3 folding maps, folding index map & 23 city maps. Library stamps; folding maps strengthened on versos. sg Mar 7 (32) $250

**Bofa, Gus**
— Slogans. Paris: LIbrairie des Champs-Elysees, 1940. One of 25 on Arches. Orig wraps. With Ms preface, drawings for the 60 pbd illusts & drawings for 5 others suppressed by the censor. S Nov 21 (45) £500

**Boffito, Giuseppe**
— Biblioteca Aeronautica Italiana Illustrata.... Florence, 1929-37. 2 vols, including Supplement. 4to, contemp half cloth (shaken) & orig wraps (broken). sg May 16 (11) $800

Anr copy. Supplement only. Orig wraps; broken, rear cover torn & repaired. sg May 16 (12) $300

**Bogatzky, Carl Heinrich von, 1690-1774.** See: Fore-Edge Paintings

**Bogeng, Gustave Adolf Erich**
— Die Grossen Bibliophilen. Leipzig, 1922. 3 vols. 4to, orig cloth; spine ends frayed, hinges cracked. sg Apr 11 (45) $120

**Boggs, Mae Helene Bacon**
— My Playhouse was a Concord Coach.... Oakland, CA [1942]. 4to, cloth. With 8 folded maps inserted & 13 text maps. Larson copy. pba Sept 28 (326) $200

1st Ed. Oakland, Calif., [1942]. 4to, buckram; spine sunned. Robbins copy. pba Mar 21 (20) $150

**Boileau, Daniel.** See: Blasche & Boileau

**Boileau-Despreaux, Nicolas, 1636-1711**
— Explication des vignettes de la second edition des oeuvres de Boileau. Amst.: B. Picart, 1729. Oblong 8vo, contemp calf. Some soiling to margins. Fuerstenberg - Schaefer copy. S Dec 7 (69) £360

— Le Lutrin; poeme heroi-comique. Lyon: N. Scheuring, 1862. One of 25 on hollande with extra suite. Illus by Ernest & Frederic Hillemacher. 4to, mor gilt; upper cover rubbed. With 8 drawings comprising the preliminary designs for the frontis & 1 of the headpieces, an unused port of the author & finished designs for the headpieces (sgd by E. Hillemacher) & with ALs by the author, 4 Mar 1703, & an ALs of Carlo Botta. S Nov 21 (48) £1,000

— Oeuvres. Amst., 1718. 2 vols. Folio, contemp calf; worn, rebacked. With frontis & 7 plates & port. Some rust-marks. S June 12 (18) £250

Anr Ed. Paris, 1747. 5 vols. 8vo, 18th-cent red mor gilt. With port & 6 plates before letters. A few leaves browned; note of ownership washed from head of titles. Fuerstenberg - Schaefer copy. S Dec 7 (70) £800

**Boillot, Joseph**
— Nouveaux Pourtraitz et figures de termes pour user en l'architecture.... Langres: J. Des Preyz, [1592]. Folio, modern calf gilt. With port & 55 plates. Repair with loss of part of ornaments to C1v. S June 27 (277) £10,000

**Boisgelin de Kerdu, P. M. Louis de, 1758-1816**
— Feldzeuge des Marschalls von Luremburg.... Potsdam, 1783-86. 4 vols. 4to, early calf, orig front wrap bound in; needs rebdg. With 63 folding battleplans, some with troop positions in color. sg May 9 (56) $600

**Boissard, J. J. Francois Marin**
— Fables. [Paris], 1777. 2 vols. 8vo, contemp calf gilt; lower joint of Vol II split at head. With engraved titles & 9 plates. L.p. copy on hollande. Rahir - Langlois - Fuerstenberg - Schaefer copy. S Dec 7 (72) £340

**Boissard, Jean Jacques, 1528-1602**
— Icones quinquaginta virorum.... Frankfurt, 1597-99. 4 parts in 4 vols. 4to, 17th-cent vellum; dampstain to lower cover of Vol II, worming at inner hinges. With 4 engraved titles, 3 ports of author & 198 full-page ports. Marginal worming in Vols II & IV; Some repairs & staining. CNY May 17 (51) $4,500

**Bok, Hannes.** See: Merritt & Bok

**Bokelburg Collection, Werner**
— Happy Birthday Photography. Zurich, 1989. 4to, cloth, in dj. With 136 plates. sg Feb 29 (43) $175

**Bolio, Antonio Mediz**
— The Land of the Pheasant and the Deer. Mexico City, 1935. One of 900. Illus by Diego Rivera. Pictorial bds; extremities rubbed. pba Nov 30 (275) $140

**Bolivia**
— Mission scientifique francaise en Amerique du Sud. Travaux et fouilles de Tiahuanaco. [N.p.], 1903. Oblong folio, mtd in half mor album. With 61 photographs, all mtd. S June 27 (180) £700

**Bolton...**
— Bolton Abbey. [Halifax: Holden, c.1817]. 4to, folded half-sheets as issued. b Dec 5 (425) £100

**Bolton, Henry Carrington, 1843-93**
— A Select Bibliography of Chemistry.... Wash., 1893-1901. 4 vols. 8vo, 1st 3 vols disbound, 4th in wrappers. sg Apr 11 (279) $200

**Bolton, Herbert Eugene**
— Anza's California Expeditions. Berkeley, 1930. 5 vols. In djs. pba Feb 13 (21) $475; pba Apr 25 (142) $275; pba Apr 25 (303) $400

1st Ed. 5 vols, orig cloth. Larson copy. pba Sept 28 (44) $425

Anr copy. 5 vols. Orig cloth; shelf worn. Robbins copy. pba Mar 21 (21) $650

— Athanase de Mezieres and the Louisiana-Texas Frontier, 1768-1780. Cleveland, 1914. 1st Ed. 2 vols. Orig cloth. With folded map. Robbins copy. pba Mar 21 (22) $700

— Coronado on the Turquoise Trail. Albuquerque, 1940. Frontis by Margaret Fearnside. Orig cloth in dj; d/j spine ends worn. With frontis, 3 folding map, & 4 stamps tipped in. Robbins copy. pba Mar 21 (23) $140

— Font's Complete Diary: A Chronicle of the Founding of San Francisco. Berkeley, 1933. 2d Ed. - Ed by Bolton. pba Feb 13 (23) $70

— Fray Juan Crespi: Missionary Explorer.... Berkeley, 1927. Orig cloth; extremities rubbed, rear hinge repaired. pba Feb 13 (24) $100

## BOLTON

1st Ed. Orig cloth; corner bumped. Larson copy. pba Sept 28 (45) $170
— Fray Juan Crispi, Missionary Explorer on the Pacific Coast, 1769-1774. Berkeley, 1927. 1st Ed. Orig cloth. Robbins copy. pba Mar 21 (24) $150
— New Spain and the Anglo-American West. Historical Contributions Presented to.... Los Angeles, [1932]. 1st Ed, One of 500. 2 vols. Orig cloth; shelf worn. With frontis port. Frontis partially detached. Robbins copy. pba Mar 21 (27) $225
— The Padre on Horseback: A Sketch of Eusebio Francisco Kino, S.J. San Francisco: Sonora Press, 1932. 1st Ed. - Frontis by Will Wilke. Half cloth in dj; d/j worn at extremities. Robbins copy. pba Mar 21 (25) $110
— Pageant in the Wilderness. Salt Lake City: Utah State Historical Society, 1950. In dj. pba Feb 13 (25) $95
— The Rim of Christendom.... NY, 1936. 1st Ed. With 8 folding maps. pba Nov 16 (29) $55

Anr copy. In dj. Sgd on tp. pba Feb 13 (26) $110

Anr copy. Orig cloth in dj; d/j chipped 7 torn, covers stained. Robbins copy. pba Mar 21 (26) $90; pba Apr 25 (299) $60
— Spanish Explorations in the Southwest.... NY, 1916. pba Feb 13 (27) $250

### Bolton, James, d.1799
— Harmonia Ruralis, or, an Essay towards a Natural History of British Song Birds. Stannary & L, 1794-96. 1st Ed. 2 vols in 1. 4to, contemp mor gilt. With frontis & 80 hand-colored plates. Fattorini copy. C Oct 25 (4) £5,800

Anr Ed. L, 1845. 2 vols in 1. 4to, contemp half mor; scuffed. With frontis & 80 hand-colored plates. Fattorini copy. C Oct 25 (5) £1,300

### Bolton, Theodore
— Early American Portrait Draughtsmen in Crayons. NY, 1923. One of 325. Half cloth; worn. O Dec 5 (15) $80; sg Jan 11 (51) $50
— Early American Portrait Painters in Miniature. NY, 1921. One of 300. Half cloth. One leaf torn without loss. O Dec 5 (16) $70

### Bolts, Willem, 1740?-1808
— Etat civil, politique et commercant du Bengale. Maastricht, 1775. 2 vols. 8vo, orig bds; rubbed. With frontises & folding map. sg Mar 7 (33) $175

### Bolus, Harry, 1835-1911
— The Orchids of the Cape Peninsula. Cape Town, 1888. 8vo, orig cloth. With 36 plates, partially hand-colored. Offprint from Transactions of the South-African Philosophical Society, 1888, Vol V, Part 1. pba June 20 (253) $600

### Bon Genre
— Le Bon Genre: A Selection.... Paris, [c.1922]. Folio, tipped onto guards as issued, in orig half cloth; rubbed, spine chipped. With 100 pochoir-colored plates. cb Feb 14 (2763) $1,000

## AMERICAN BOOK PRICES CURRENT

### Bonacini, Claudio
— Bibliografia delle arti scrittorie e della calligrafia. Florence, 1953. 1st Ed, One of 666. 8vo, orig wraps; edges worn. sg Apr 11 (46) $140

### Bonacossi, Pinamonte
— Relazione del torneo a'piedi fatto in Mantova l'anno 1674. Per festeggiare... Leopoldo Cesare e di Claudia.. arciduchessa d'Austria. Mantua: the Osanna family, [1674]. 8vo, 19th-cent mor gilt. With frontis & 5 folding plates. Some spotting; 2 folding plates with repaired tear at inner margin. C Apr 3 (49) £4,400

**Bonafous, Louis Abel de.** See: Fontenai, Abbe de

### Bonaparte, Charles Lucien, 1803-57
See also: Wilson & Bonaparte

**Bonaparte, Charles Lucian, 1803-57.** See: Wilson & Bonaparte

### Bonaparte, Charles Lucien, 1803-57. See: Wilson & Bonaparte
— Iconographie des pigeons. Paris, 1857-[58]. Folio, modern half mor. With 55 colored plates, many with added blue was backgrounds. Library blindstamps on plates; marginal repairs. S Nov 30 (11) £2,600

### Bonaparte, Lucien, 1775-1840
— Charlemagne, ou l'eglise delivree. Paris, 1815. 2 vols. 8vo, red mor gilt by Bozerian jeune; upper cover of Vol II spotted. Fuerstenberg - Schaefer copy. S Dec 7 (73) £300

### Bonaventura, Saint, 1221-74
— Breviloquium et Biblia pauperum. Strassburg: Printer of Henricus Arminensis, [c.1473-74]. 4to, half calf; spine perished, broken. Some staining; last leaf repaired. 82 leaves. Goff B-856. cb June 25 (1760) $2,000
— De triplici via. Montserrat: Johann Luschner, 27 May 1499. 8vo, mor by Brugalla, 1949. 27 lines; gothic types. Some spotting; dampstain to final leaf; a1.8 rehinged. 31 (of 32) leaves; a1 in facsimile. Goff B-972. C Apr 3 (50) £1,300
— The Life of Saint Francis of Assisi. San Francisco: John Henry Nash, 1931. One of 385. Trans by E. Gurney Salter. Folio, mor-backed vellum leaves of 16th-cent music. sg Sept 14 (264) $175
— Die Nachtwachen des Bonaventura. Munich: Der Buecherwinkel, [1923]. One of 275. Illus by Bruno Goldschmitt. 4to, unsewn as issued, text unopened. With 17 etchings. Some soiling. wa Nov 16 (311) $150
— Opuscula. Strassburg: [Printer of the 1483 Jordanus de Quedlinburg (Georg Husner)], 1495. Vol II only. Contemp nuremberg bdg by Kyriss 113 of blind-stamped calf over wooden bds, with brass fittings; upper bd split & repaired, rebacked, lacking 2 clasps. 368 (of 370) leaves; lacking c6 & final blank. Goff B-928. S Dec 18 (23) £1,200 [Zioni]
— Sermones de tempore et de sanctis. Ulm: Johann Zainer, 1481. Folio, contemp pigskin over wooden bds; worn. 40 lines & headline; types 4:96aG,

5:136G. Initials & paragraph marks in red. Some browning 7 staining; qq3 holed in inner margin. 427 (of 428) leaves; lacking first blank. Goff B-949. S Dec 18 (24) £1,500 [Zioni]

Anr Ed. Reutlingen: [Johann Otmar], 1485. Folio, old calf; broken. Marginal repairs; some dampstaining; 1st leaf laid down; 1st signature loose. 285 leaves. Goff B-951. cb Feb 14 (2509) $1,100

— Soliloquium. Antwerp: Claes Leeu, 17 Dec 1487. ("Boek van de vier oefeninghen.") 8vo, 16th-cent pigskin, remboitage. 18 lines; type 1:100G. With 7 woodcuts. First 2 leaves with paper repairs in margins & soiled. 106 leaves. Goff B-957. Schaefer copy. P Nov 1 (47) $4,750

### Bond, Catherine
— Goldfields and Chrysanthemums: Notes of Travel in Australia and Japan. L, 1898. Orig cloth. Inscr. bba July 18 (340) £140 [Sotheran]

### Bonelli, Renato —&
### Portoghesi, Paolo
— Trattati di Architettura. Milan: Il Polifilo, 1966-90. 8 vols in 11. Orig half mor. Ck Apr 12 (207) £140

### Bonet, Theophile
— A Guide to the Practical Physician.... L, 1684. 1st Ed in English. Folio, contemp calf; front joints cracked, spine & 1 corner repaired. With half-title. 1st few leaves dampstained; 4O2 torn; some stains. Ck Mar 22 (48) £650

### Bonfils, Winifred Black
— The Life and Personality of Phoebe Apperson Hearst. San Francisco: John Henry Nash, 1928. One of 1,000. Vellum. Ls from John Henry Nash tipped in. pba Apr 25 (450) $60

### Bonfons, Pierre
— Les Antiquitez et choses plus remarquables de Paris. Paris, 1608. 8vo, contemp calf; worn. S Oct 26 (268) £160 [Robertshaw]

### Boni, Albert
— Photographic Literature. NY, [1962]. 2 vols. Cloth & wraps, both vols in djs. pba Aug 8 (553) $110

Anr copy. 4to, cloth, in torn & chipped dj. sg Feb 29 (267) $60

### Boniface VIII, Pope, 1235?-1303
— Liber sextus decretalium. Paris: Thielmann Kerver for Jean Petit & Jean Cabiller, 24 Sept-30 Nov 1511. ("Sexti libri materia cum capitulorum numero....") 4 parts in 1 vol. 4to, old pigskin over wooden bds; spine chipped, remains of clasps, upper joint split. Gothic type. With 4 large woodcuts. Small marginal tears to Part 1; A8 in 4th part torn & repaired. C Nov 29 (36) £1,500

### Bonnard, Camille
— Costumes des XIIIe, XIVe et XVe siecles.... Paris, 1829-30. 2 vols. 4to, contemp cloth; 1 vol rebacked. With 200 plates on india proof paper. b Dec 5 (9) £85

### Bonnard, Pierre, 1867-1947
— Correspondances. Paris, 1944. 1st Ed, One of 1,025. Folio, loose in wraps as issued. sg Sept 7 (50) $225

### Bonnefoy, Yves
— Alberto Giacometti. Paris, 1991. Folio, cloth, in dj. sg Jan 11 (193) $60

### Bonner, James
— A New Plan for Speedily Increasing the Number of Bee-Hives in Scotland.... Edin., 1795. 8vo, disbound. Old stamp on tp. Sgd by David Hosack on tp. sg May 16 (291) $60

### Bonner, T. D.
— The Life and Adventures of James P. Beckworth, Mountaineer.... NY, 1856. 1st Ed. 12mo, orig cloth; spine ends & corners worn. With frontis. Robbins copy. pba Mar 21 (28) $400

### Bonnet, Charles, 1720-93
— Considerations sur les corps organises.... Amst., 1762. 2 vols. 8vo, contemp calf; lower cover of Vol II repaired. Vol I badly dampstained & with last leaf torn & def; Vol II slightly dampstained. S June 12 (242) £150

### Bonney, Benjamin Franklin
— Across the Plains by Prairie Schooner. Eugene, OR, n.d.. Orig wraps; some creases & abrasions. Inscr & sgd to Carl Wheat. Larson copy. pba Sept 28 (580) $65

### Bonney, Thomas George, 1833-1923
— English Lake Scenery. L, 1876. Illus by Elijah Walton. Folio, orig cloth; rubbed. With 22 colored plates. b Jan 31 (352) £60

### Bononcini, Giovanni Battista
— Messe brevi a otto voci, Op. 7. Bologna: Giacomo Monti & Marino Silvani, 1688. Canto secondo choro only. 4to, old card wraps. Small tear in C1. S June 13 (683) £240

### Bonpland, Aime J. A., 1773-1858. See: Humboldt & Bonpland

### Bontemps, Arna. See: Hughes & Bontemps

### Bonvalot, Gabriel
— Through the Heart of Asia. L, 1889. 2 vols. 8vo, orig cloth; rubbed. b Jan 31 (434) £70

### Bonvoisin, Maurice
— Oeuvre grave de Felicien Rops. Brussels, 1879. One of 10. 8vo, contemp half mor, orig wraps bound in. With additional etched leaf with port of Rops & fool's head by Courboin. Inscr by Bonvoisin. Offprint from Bibliophile Belge, Vol XIV. S June 12 (352) £440

### Bony, Anne
— Les Annees 10. Paris, 1991. 2 vols. 4to, cloth, in djs. sg June 13 (60) $250

## Book, Booke, or Boke

— Book Auction Records. L, 1964-94. Vols 60-91. bba Oct 5 (21) £800 [Cizdyn]

Anr Ed. L, 1966-83. Vols 62, 63-60, & 7th Index for vols 57-60. 4to & 8vo, orig cloth. S Oct 27 (1016) £200 [Stavrovski]

Vols 69-91 plus General Index 1979-1984 (pbd in 1985). [L, 1973-94). Ck Apr 12 (208) £350

— The Book of the Bench. L, [1909]. Folio, orig vellum. With 39 mtd colored plates. NH Sept 16 (245) $220

— Book of Trades, or Library of the Useful Arts. L, [1805-15]. 6th Ed of Vols II-III, 1st Ed of Vol I. 3 vols. 12mo, orig half lea, later paper jackets. Minor tears; some browning. S May 16 (155) £150

## Book of Common Prayer

— 1664. - L. Bound with: The Whole Book of Psalms. L, 1655. 4to, modern calf gilt. Marginal dampstaining. sg Mar 21 (64) $350

— 1665. - Cambr.: J. Field. 2 parts in 1 vol. 12mo, contemp calf; joints weak, front free endpaper gone. Worming in upper corner at end, affecting text. In Greek. sg Mar 21 (65) $250

— 1669. - L: Assigns of John Bill & Christopher Barker. Folio, contemp mor gilt from the workshop of Samuel Mearne, with royal cypher of Charles II; minor staining to rear cover, corners worn, front joint tender, endpapers soiled. cb June 25 (1931) $1,000

— 1687. - L. Folio, mor gilt for King James II; rubbed. Marginal tears; some soiling. bba Apr 11 (293) £550 [E. V. Phillips]

— 1760. - Cambr.: Baskerville. 1st 8vo Ed. Contemp mor gilt; minor wear. Gaskell 12. S Dec 18 (120) £400 [Finch]

— 1761. - Cambr.: Baskerville. 8vo, Scottish wheel bdg in mor gilt; rubbed. Sold as a bdg, w.a.f. S July 11 (83) £280

— 1785. - Dublin: George GriersonContemp calf. A few leaves torn. pba Mar 7 (25) $60

— 1787. - Ne Yakawea Yondereanayendaghkwa Oghseragwegouh. L. 4to, disbound. Met May 22 (359) $1,300

— 1842. - Hamilton Bound with: [Song of David in Mohawk] Trans by John Hill into Mohawk. Contemp mor; worn & scuffed, spine def & with label. Some leaves reattached with cloth tape; annotations to several leaves including tp; some foxing & soiling. cb Oct 17 (163) $200

— 1844. - L: William Pickering. Folio, mor gilt by Riviere; raised bands scuffed, endpapers foxed. sg Sept 21 (93) $750

— 1903. - L: Essex House One of 400. Folio, half lea over wooden bds. S July 11 (86) £460

Anr copy. Half lea over wooden bds with wrought-iron clasps; 1 clasp lacking lea strap. sg Sept 14 (117) $650

— [c.1915]. - Book of Common Prayer.... OxfordMor gilt by Katherine Adams, with initials M. H. on upper cover. b Dec 5 (6) £60

— 1930. - Bost.: Merrymount Press One of 500. Folio, mor. sg Sept 14 (335) $1,340

## Bookman's...

— Bookman's Price Index. Detroit, [1977-81]. Vols 12-22. Cloth. NH July 21 (355) $190

## Bookwalter, Thomas E.

— Honor Tarnished: The Reno Court of Inquiry. West Carrolton OH: Little Horn Press, [1973]. One of 10. Intro by John M. Carroll. Orig lea; cut close in bdg, front hinge repaired. Inscr by Carroll. pba June 25 (11) $150

## Boole, George, 1815-64

— An Investigation of the Laws of Thought.... Cambr. & L, 1854. Later Issue, with cancel title & errata on last prelim leaf. 8vo, orig cloth; spine ends chipped, corners frayed, hinges starting. sg May 16 (135) $3,600

**Boon, Karel G.** See: White & Boon

## Boone & Crockett Club

— North American Big Game. A Book of the Boone and Crockett Club.... NY & L, 1939. Orig cloth; worn & soiled. F June 20 (125) $120

Anr copy. In chipped & frayed dj. O Oct 10 (45) $325; O Oct 10 (47) $130

Anr copy. In chipped & frayed dj; some wear. O Oct 10 (202) $250

— North American Big Game Competitions. NY, [c.1940]. Pictorial wraps. Related material laid in. O Oct 10 (46) $150

— North American Big Game. Official Measurement Records Compiled...for the Boone and Crockett Club.... Bridgeport CT: Remington Arms Co, 1934. Pictorial wraps. O Oct 10 (92) $800

— Records of North American Big Game.... NY: Boone & Crockett Club, 1952. In tattered dj. O Oct 10 (48) $180

Anr copy. In frayed dj. Inscr by 3 of the editors or contributors. O Jan 9 (52) $250

Anr copy. In chipped dj. Sgd on half-title by 6 contributors. O Jan 9 (185) $275

Anr copy. In tattered dj. Sgd on half-title by 3 contributors. O Jan 9 (186) $190

Anr copy. Cloth; worn. Inscr. O June 25 (29) $130

Anr Ed. NY: Boone & Crockett Club, 1958. In frayed dj. O Oct 10 (49) $130

Anr copy. In chipped & repaired dj. O Oct 10 (50) $140

Anr copy. In frayed & worn dj. Inscr by the Ed, Samuel B. Webb. O Jan 9 (53) $175

Anr Ed. NY: Boone & Crockett Club, 1964. In frayed dj. O Jan 9 (54) $100

Anr Ed. Alexandria, 1981. One of 750. 4to, syn gilt. O Oct 10 (52) $60

Anr Ed. Missoula, 1993. One of 100. 4to, half lea. O Oct 10 (53) $225

— The Wild Sheep in Modern North America. [N.p.]: Boone & Crockett Club, 1975. One of 100. Syn gilt; some wear. O Oct 10 (266) $150

**Boone, Nicholas**
— Military Discipline. The Newest Way and Method of Exercising Horse & Foot. Bost.: John Allen for Nicholas Boone, 1718. 12mo, orig calf; worn, spine head chipped, lacking front flyleaf. Small hole at bottom of tp affecting imprint; tear in 1 leaf; portion of pp. 17-18 torn away with loss. Bristol B539. NH Sept 16 (283) $10,100

**Boosey, Thomas**
— Piscatorial Reminiscences and Gleanings, by an Old Angler and Bibliopolist. L, 1835. 2 parts in 1 vol. 8vo, cloth; stamp to free endpaper. pba July 11 (39) $180

**Booth, Edward Thomas**
— Rough Notes on the Birds.... L, 1881-87. 3 vols. Folio, orig half mor gilt by R. H. Porter. With 2 colored maps & 114 hand-colored plates. Fattorini copy. C Oct 25 (6) £3,500

**Booth, Stephen**
— The Book Called Holinshed's Chronicles.... San Francisco: Book Club of California, 1968. Ltd Ed. 4to, half cloth; stained. With orig leaf from the 1587 Ed. pba June 20 (73) $90
Anr copy. Half cloth. With orig leaf from the 1587 Ed. sg Sept 14 (81) $110

**Booth, William, 1829-1912**
— In Darkest England and the Way Out. L, [1890]. 1st Ed. 8vo, orig cloth. b May 30 (1) £60

**Booth, William Beattie, 1804?-74.** See: Chandler & Booth

**Borchgrevink, Carsten Egeberg, 1864-1934**
— First on the Antarctic Continent. L, 1901. 1st Ed. Orig cloth; spine ends & corners frayed. With port & 3 colored folding maps & photographic illusts. Some pencil marks & notes; frontis detached. pba July 25 (15) $375

**Borcht, Petrus van der**
— Imagines et figurae Bibliorum. L, [1582?]. Folio, 19th-Cent half mor; rubbed. With 60 (of ?) plates, & additional watercolor title. 1 plate torn with loss. Sold w.a.f. S Oct 27 (1107) £420 [D'Arte]

**Borde, Andrew**
— The Breviary of Healthe.... L: William Powell, 1557. 3d Ed. 2 parts in 1 vol. 4to, modern mor. With 2 titles & 1 full-page illus. Some leaves repaired at edges & corners; C1v soil-marked. Ck Mar 22 (49) £3,400

**Borden Collection, Matthew Challoner Durfee**
— A Catalogue of the Printed Books, Manuscripts.... NY: Pvtly Ptd, 1910. One of 50. 2 vols. 4to, half mor by Stikeman; rubbed. O Mar 26 (37) $300

**Borderlands...**
— Borderlands 2: Anthology of Imaginative Fiction. Balt.: Borderlands Press, 1991. One of 750. In dj. pba Dec 7 (135) $50

**Bordone, Benedetto**
— Libro de Benedetto Bordone nel qual si ragiona de tutte l'isole del mondo. Venice: [Francesci di Leno, c.1540]. ("Isolario....") Folio, modern half mor; front joint worn. Some dampstaining along bottom edges; stain on tp & next few leaves. sg Apr 18 (30) $5,600

**Borelli, Giovanni Alfonso, 1608-79**
— De motu animalum.... The Hague, 1743. 2 parts in 1 vol. 4to, contemp half calf; spine worn, joint cracked, corners worn. With frontis & 19 folding plates. Some browning & staining. CE Nov 8 (74) $250
— De Vi Percussionis. Leiden, 1686. 4to, contemp vellum. With engraved title & 20 folding plates. Tp stamped; some spotting. S June 12 (296) £300

**Borellus, Pierre, 1620?-89**
— Historiarum, et observationum medicophysicarum, centuriae IV.... Frankfurt, [1670]. 8vo, contemp vellum dated 1679 & with gilt initials F.C.M.M.D.; worn & soiled. Tp damaged at foot & repaired with loss of imprint; frontis & 1st leaf of text repaired with loss; some dampstains. Sold w.a.f. O Mar 5 (25) $225

**Boreman, Thomas**
— A Description of a Great Variety of Animals and Vegetables.... L, 1736. 1st Ed. 12mo, modern half calf. With frontis & 90 plates on 53 leaves. Spotted. S Nov 2 (158) £1,100 [Schiller]

**Borg, Carl Oscar**
— The Great Southwest; Etchings. Santa Ana: Fine Arts Press, 1936. Ed by E. C. Maxwell. 4to, half cloth. Sgd on tp by Borg. pba Apr 25 (308) $140
Anr copy. Sgd on tp by Borg. sg Jan 11 (56A) $150

**Borges, Jorge Luis, 1899-1986.** See: Limited Editions Club

**Borget, Auguste, b.1809**
— La Chine et les chinois. Paris, [1842]. Folio, contemp half mor. With additional litho title, 32 tinted litho plates on 25 sheets & 2 engraved dedication leaves. Spotted; mtd on new guards throughout. S June 27 (222) £8,500

**Borie, Victor, 1818-80**
— Animaux de la ferme. Espece bovine. Paris, 1863-67. 4to, orig bds; soiled, rebacked. With 46 chromolitho plates. Marginal repair to 1 plate; minor staining. b May 30 (484) £700

**Borja y Aragon, Francisco, Prince of Esquilache, 1582-1658**
— Las Obras en verso. Madrid, 1648. 1st Ed. 4to, 18th-cent calf, with arms of James Hamilton as Baron Claneboye & Viscount Limerick. Lacking tp. S Nov 30 (255) £500

## Borlase, William, 1695-1772
— Observations of the Antiquities Historical and Monumental, of the County of Cornwall. L, 1769. ("Antiquities Historical and Monumental of the County of Cornwall.") 2d Ed. Folio, contemp calf; worn, rebacked in library mor. With 25 plates & 1 folding map Extra-illus with 8 plates.  bba Nov 1 (33) £600 [Tambuyser]

Anr copy. Contemp russia gilt; joints starting.  pba Sept 14 (75) $300

## Borneman, Henry Stauffer
— Pennsylvania German Bookplates. Phila., 1953. Orig bds.  F June 20 (521A) $50

## Borras, Maria Lluisa
— Picabia. NY, [1985]. 4to, cloth, in dj.  sg Jan 11 (341) $225

## Borrichius, Olaus, 1626-90
— De ortu et progressu chemiae. Dissertatio. Copenhagen, 1668. 4to, contemp vellum. Browned.  S Mar 14 (58) £550
— Metallische Probier-Kunst.... Copenhagen, 1680. 8vo, modern bds. Some staining & soiling.  S Mar 14 (59) £280

## Borroni, Fabia
— Bibliographia dell'archeologia classice dell'arte italiana. Florence, 1954-67. One of 666. In 12 vols.  bba Oct 5 (23) £320 [Parikian]

## Borrow, George Henry, 1803-81
— Celebrated Trials...: L, 1825. 1st Ed. 6 vols. 8vo, orig bds; chipped, Vol V spine foot def. With 35 plates. Some waterstaining at end of Vol III.  S Apr 23 (7) £600
— Works. L & NY, 1923-24. One of 775. 16 vols. Half mor.  cb Oct 17 (261) $950

## Borsi, Franco
— Leon Battista Alberti. NY, [1977]. 4to, orig cloth, in dj.  sg Jan 11 (6) $50

## Borthwick, John Douglas
— Three Years in California. Edin. & L, 1857. 8vo, orig cloth; rebacked with orig spine strip laid on. Marginal stains; tp & following leaf repaired.  pba Nov 16 (31) $170

1st Ed. 8vo, orig cloth; some wear. With 8 plates. Frontis foxed, some pencil notations. Larson copy.  pba Sept 28 (327) $1,100

## Bory de Saint-Vincent, Jean Baptiste G. M., 1778?-1846
— Essais sur les Iles Fortunees et l'Antique Atlantide... Archipel des Canaries. Paris, [1802]. 4to, contemp sheep; needs rebdg. With 10 maps & plates.  sg Mar 7 (35) $275

## Bory de Saint-Vincent, Jean Baptiste G. M., 1778?-1846 —& Schneider, Antoine
— Histoire et description des Iles Ioniennes.... Paris, 1823. 2 vols, including Atlas. 8vo & 4to, contemp half mor gilt; rubbed. With 16 plates & maps & 2 plates of coins. Some foxing.  S June 27 (133) £1,200

**Bos, Lambert van den.** See: Bosch, Lambert van den

## Boscana, Geronimo, 1776-1831
— Chiingchinich-Chi-ni ch-nich. A Revised... Version of Alfred Robinson's Translation of... Boscana's Historical Account of... the Indians of... San Juan Capistrano.... Santa Ana, 1933. Ed by Phil Townshend Hanna. Illus by Jean Goodwin. Foreword by Frederick Webb Hodge. Half cloth; bd edges rubbed. With 11 plates (5 color). Robbins copy.  pba Mar 21 (30) $435

## Bosch, Lambert van den
— Leeven en daden der doorluchtighste zee-helden en ontdeckers van landen, deser eeuwen. Amst., 1676. 1st Ed. 2 parts in 1 vol. 4to, vellum. With engraved title & 26 plates only. Soiling & staining. Sold w.a.f.  CE June 12 (157) $100

## Boschini, Marco, 1613-78
— L'Arcipelago. Con tute le Isole, Scogli secche, e Bassi fondi.... Venice: Francesco Nicolini, 1658. 4to, contemp vellum; upper hinge broken, lower hinge weak, some wear. With plate of arms & 49 maps & charts. Inkstain on A2.  S June 27 (134) £4,600
— Il Regno tutto di Candia.... Venice, 1651. 4to, old calf; spine chipped at head, joints weak. With engraved title, allegorical plate & 60 plates & maps numbered to 61, 9 of them folding. Some old dampstaining; 3 folding plates with repairs at folds.  C Oct 25 (103) £3,200

## Bosio, Antonio, 1575-1629
— Rome Sotterranea. Rome, 1632. Folio, 17th-cent goatskin gilt; spine worn. Dampstain to upper margin, sometimes affecting text; some browning.  C Apr 3 (53A) £900

## Bosman, Willem
— A New and Accurate Description of the Coast of Guinea.... L, 1705. 8vo, contemp calf; corners rubbed, rebacked, new endpapers. With folding map & 7 plates.  S June 27 (245) £400

## Bosphorus
— Bosphorus and the Danube.... L, [c.1845]. 4to, 19th-Cent half calf. With 163 plates. Some plates detaching. Sold w.a.f.  S Oct 26 (19) £450 [Mertturkmen]

**Bosqui, Edward.** See: Grabhorn Printing

**Bosschere, Jean de.** See: De Bosschere, Jean

## Bossert, Helmuth Theodor
— Das Ornamentwerk.... Berlin, 1924. Folio, bdg not described. With 120 color plates.  F Mar 28 (354) $80

## Bossius, Donatus
— Chronica. Milan: Antonius Zarotus, 1 Mar 1492. Folio, later vellum bds. 45 lines; types 5:111R, 7:76G. Some staining; wormholes occasionally touching text; genealogical chart trimmed at bottom. 168 leaves. Goff B-1040.   C Apr 3 (54) £2,400

## Bossu, Jean Bernard, 1720-92
— Nouveaux Voyages aux Indes occidentales.... Paris, 1768. 1st Ed. 2 parts in 2 vols. 12mo, contemp sheep; repaired, scraped. With 4 plates. Engelhard copy.   CNY Jan 26 (163) $800
— Nouveaux Voyages dans l'Amerique septentrionale. Amst. [Paris], 1777. 1st Ed. 8vo, late 18th-cent half calf; rubbed, upper inner hinge weak, tears to free endpapers. With 4 plates, 1 of them folding. Engelhard copy.   CNY Jan 26 (165) $850

Anr copy. Contemp calf. With 4 plates. Fuerstenberg - Schaefer copy.   S Dec 7 (74) £650

## Bossuit, Francis
— Beeld-Synders Kunst-Kabinet. Amst., 1727. Illus by Mattys Pool. 4to, later half lea gilt. With 103 plates. CE Sept 27 (60) $450

## Boston
— Catalogue of Books in the Theological Library in the Town of Boston. Bost., 1808. 12mo, unbound. Browned & foxed; some chipping & fraying.  O Mar 26 (38) $70

## Boswell, James, 1740-95
See also: Fore-Edge Paintings; Limited Editions Club
— An Account of Corsica. Dublin, 1768. 12mo, modern mor gilt. Lacking half-title. sg Mar 21 (66) $600

2d Ed. L, 1768. 8vo, contemp calf; joints cracked, spine ends & edges rubbed, hinge cracked, bookplate removed from front pastedown. Half-title creased; tear to map.  pba June 20 (74) $110

[-] Everybody's Boswell. L, 1930.  Ltd Ed.  Illus by E. H. Shepard. Mor gilt with onlaid mor design depicting a waving Dr. Johnson, by Bayntun-Riviere. CE Feb 21 (17) $400

— The Life of Samuel Johnson.... L, 1791. 1st Ed, Issue not indicated.  2 vols. 4to, old calf gilt; broken & def. wd May 8 (41) $850

With the "give" reading on p. 135 of Vol I. Contemp calf gilt; rebacked, worn. With port, 2 facsimiles & 7 cancels. Repair to fore-edge tear on Yyy3 in Vol II; foxed.   P June 5 (177) $1,300

With the "gve" reading. Modern half calf gilt. Lacking initial blank in Vol II.  b Jan 31 (60) £1,400

Anr copy. Contemp calf gilt; lower joints renewed but cracked, upper joints cracked, upper cover of Vol II, endpapers renewed. Lacking some ads in Vol I & front blank in Vol II; some foxing. CE Feb 21 (24) $3,000

Anr copy. Later half russia. Some spotting & staining; corner of R2 in Vol I remargined; repaired tears to plate facing Fff1v in Vol II, with the sheet mtd. P June 5 (176) $1,400

Anr copy. Contemp calf; rebacked. Vol II lacking initial blank.  sg Oct 19 (47) $2,200

2d Ed. L, 1793. 3 vols. 8vo, calf gilt; lower joint of Vol I starting, rubbed. With port & 2 folding plates. CE Sept 27 (61) $380

Anr Ed. Bost., 1807.  3 vols. 8vo, calf; repaired & rebacked, spine def. Waterstain in top portion of text throughout Vols II & III.   Z June 28 (35) $300

6th Ed. L, 1811. 4 vols. 8vo, calf; joints cracked. With frontis & folding facsimile plate. pba June 20 (75) $95

Anr Ed. L, 1824. 4 vols. 8vo, calf gilt.  pba Sept 14 (77) $275

Anr Ed. L, 1831. 5 vols. 8vo, lev extra by Larkin. Extra-illus with c.200 plates.  sg Sept 21 (141) $1,000

Anr Ed. L, 1839. 10 vols. 8vo, calf gilt by Riviere. sg Sept 21 (3) $475

Anr copy. Half calf gilt. sg Sept 21 (4) $300

Anr Ed. NY, 1841.  2 vols. Contemp calf.  Some foxing.  pba Aug 22 (565) $90

Anr Ed. L, 1874. 3 vols. 8vo, contemp calf; rebacked, extremities scuffed. With hand-colored frontis. Extra-illus with c.35 plates.  F June 20 (497) $210

Temple Bar Ed. NY, 1922.  Ed by Clement Shorter. 10 vols. 8vo, mor gilt. cb Oct 17 (262) $850

— Private Papers from Malahide Castle in the Collection of Ralph Heyward Isham. L, 1928-37.  One of 570. Ed by Geoffrey Scott.  18 vols. Orig bds. sg Sept 14 (83) $650

## Bosworth, Newton, d.1848
— The Accidents of Human Life.... L, 1813. 1st Ed. 12mo, modern half mor. With frontis & 5 plates. Some plates foxed.  CE Nov 8 (75) $100

## Botanic...
— The Botanic Garden.... L, 1825-[51]. Vol I-IX. Contemp half lea; rubbed, stitching def in Vols II & IX. Sold w.a.f.  S Nov 30 (38) £1,900

Vol IV. Contemp half lea; corners showing, rubbed, soiled. With 24 hand-colored plates. Engraved title foxed; other foxing.  Met Feb 24 (456) $350

Vols II-XII. Cloth. With engraved titles & 266 hand-colored plates. wa Nov 16 (168) $2,900

Vols I-V. - Ed by Benjamin Maund. Half mor gilt. With 121 hand-colored plates. A few plates with some oxidation.  P June 5 (293) $3,000

Vols I-XIII (complete set), plus the Auctarium, the Fruitist & the Floral Register. Contemp half calf; rubbed, 1 cover detached.  b Sept 20 (480) £2,200

## Botanical... See: Loddiges, Conrad & Sons

## Botanist...
— The Botanist: Containing Accurately Coloured Figures of Tender and Hardy Ornamental Plants. L, [1837-42].  Ed by Benjamin Maund & J. S. Henslow. 5 vols. 4to, orig cloth; rebacked preserving orig spines. With engraved & ptd title in each vol & 250 hand-colored plates. Minor spotting.  b Sept 20 (481) £700

Anr copy. Contemp half mor gilt; spines rubbed. With engraved & ptd title in each vol & 249 (of 250) hand-colored plates. Lacking Plate 75 & its text; additional titles spotted or browned; 2 plates misbound. C May 31 (33) £1,800

Anr copy. Early half mor; extremities rubbed. With 237 hand-colored plates only. sg May 9 (309) $2,200

**Botero, Giovanni, 1540-1617**
— Aggiunta alla quarta parte dell'Indie.... Venice: Alessandro Vecchi, 1622. 8 parts in 1 vol. 4to, contemp vellum; waterstained. With tp woodcut, 30 full-page & 2 half-page woodcut illusts. C Nov 29 (85) £3,600
— Dell ragion di stato libri dieci. Ferrara: Vittorio Baldini, 1590. 3d Ed. 8vo, modern half calf. With title vignette. 1st & last few leaves with brittle margins; ink annotations; some dampstaining & marginal tears. Ck Mar 22 (50) £170

**Botticelli, Sandro**
— Drawings by Sandro Botticelli for Dante's Divina Commedia. L, 1896. Ltd Ed. Intro by Friedrich Lippmann. 4to, mor by Hoyt; rubbed. O Mar 5 (26) $100

**Bottomley, Gordon, 1874-1948**
— Frescoes from Buried Temples. L: The Pear Tree Press, 1928. One of 55. Illus by James Guthrie. Folio, unbound as issued in orig wraps, endpapers & wraps ptd in silver & gold. With 35 intaglio plates of text, cover design, endpapers, 3 subtitles & 17 illusts ptd from blocks or woodcuts & 2 illusts ptd from plates. S Nov 21 (50) £1,500

**Bottomley, Samuel**
— Greenfield, a Poem. Manchester, [c.1820]. 16mo, contemp mor gilt. With 11 plates. b Dec 5 (180) £70

**Bottoni, Albertino, d.1596?**
— De vita conservanda. Padua: Jacob Bozzam, 1582. 1st Ed. 4to, later half vellum. With title device. Title stained; A4 repaired; some browning. Ck Mar 22 (51) £450

**Bouchardon, Edme**
— Etudes prises dans le bas peuple, ou les cris de Paris.... Paris, 1737-46. 5 parts in 1 vol. 4to, 19th-cent red mor by Hardy-Mennil. With 60 plates. Fuerstenberg - Schaefer copy. S Dec 7 (75) £9,000

**Bouche, Henri.** See: Dollfus & Bouche

**Bouche, Louis.** See: Yarrow & Bouche

**Boucher, Francois**
— Le Pont-Neuf. Paris, 1925-26. 2 vols. 4to, wraps. sg Sept 7 (7) $80

**Boucher, Francois, 1703-70**
[A bound collection of plates by Bouchard, from the Fuerstenberg-Schaefer collection, sold at Sotheby's on 7 Dec 1995, lot 76, for £5,500]
— Recueil de fontaines. Paris, [1736]. 2 parts in 1 vol. Folio, 19th-cent calf gilt. With 14 plates. Marginal repairs; small pinholes on upper margins of some plates. Fuerstenberg - Schaefer copy. S Dec 7 (78) £1,400
— [Sale Catalogue] Catalogue... des tableaux, desseins, estampes, bronzes, terres cuites... porcelaines... meubles curieux... madrepores, coquilles... de feu M. Boucher. Paris, 1771. 8vo, 19th-cent half mor by Lemardeley. Outer margins of tp frayed but repaired. Fuerstenberg - Schaefer copy. S Dec 7 (77) £2,200

**Boucher, Juste Francois, 1736-82**
— Arabesques. Paris, [c.1760]. 8 parts in 1 vol. Folio, half sheep. With 8 suites of plates on 12 leaves, lettered & numbered A-H 1-6. Soiled; plate margins worn. Fuerstenberg - Schaefer copy. S Dec 7 (79) £360
— Nouveau Livre de vases. Paris, [n.d.]. Bound with: Houdan, J. Premier Cahier de petits vases. Paris, [n.d.]. Folio, 19th-cent calf gilt by Pagnant. Engraved throughout. Fuerstenberg - Schaefer copy. S Dec 7 (80) £600

**Bouchet, Jean, 1476-c.1550**
— Les Annales d'Aquitaine. 1 June Paris 1537. 2 vols, including Les corectes et additionnees, Poitiers, 1531. Folio, old calf (rebacked) & 18th-cent calf. Lettre batarde. Repair on tp with loss on verso; 2 leaves misbound; some dampstaining & soiling; some worming. Vol I is Phillipps copy. S Mar 29 (643) £300
— Le lugement poetic de l'honneur femenin & seiour des illustres claires et honnestes Dames. Poitiers: Jean & Enguilbert Marnef freres, 1 Apr 1538. 4to, 18th-cent mor; rubbed, tear at spine head. Civilite type with shoulder notes in italic, titling types in Roman. P Nov 1 (49) $7,500

**Bouchot, Henri Francois Xavier Marie, 1849-1906**
— Les Reliures d'art a la Bibliotheque Nationale. Paris, 1888. 1st Ed. 8vo, calf, orig wraps preserved. bba May 9 (136) £110 [Maggs]

**Boudinot, Elias, 1740-1821**
— A Star in the West. Trenton, NJ, 1816. 8vo, early half sheep; scuffed, upper joint cracked. Some browning & foxing. bbc Feb 26 (385) $140

**Bougainville, Hyacinthe Yves Philippe Potentien, Baron de, 1781-1846**
— Album pittoresque de la Fregate la Thetis.... Paris, 1828. 6 parts in 1 vol. Folio, contemp half sheep; worn. With 28 uncolored plates. Marginal foxing. sg Oct 19 (48) $5,000
— Journal de la navigation autour du globe.... Paris, 1837. 2 text vols only. 4to, half mor; extremities rubbed. sg Mar 7 (36) $425

**Bougard, R.**
— The Little Sea Torch. L, 1801. Folio, recent half mor. With 20 hand-colored plates of coastal profiles & 24 hand-colored plates of ports on 13 leaves. S Mar 28 (170) £1,150

— Le Petit Flambeau de la Mer. Havre, 1694. 4to, modern mor. Some margins repaired; dampstaining at ends. S Mar 28 (224) £480

**Bouilhet, Henri**
— L'Orfevrerie Francaise aux XVIIIe & XIXe Siecles. Paris, 1908-12. 3 vols. 4to, modern half calf. bba Apr 11 (43) £440 [Sims Reed]

**Boulard, A. M. H.**
— Catalogue des livres de la bibliotheque. Paris, 1828. 4 vols. 8vo, contemp half sheep; spines brittle & worn. sg Apr 11 (16) $300

**Boulmier, Joseph**
— Estienne Dolet. Paris, 1857. 8vo, contemp half mor; scuffed. F June 20 (523B) $50

**Bourcard, Gustave**
— A travers cinq siecles de gravures.... Paris, 1903. One of 250. Contemp half mor; rubbed, spine foot stained & singed. O Mar 26 (39) $120

**Bourdigne, Charles**
— La Legende de maistre Pierre Faifeu, mise en vers. Paris, 1723. 12mo, 18th-cent green mor gilt, with arms of Claude Henri Watelet; damage to head of spine. Fuerstenberg - Schaefer copy. S Dec 7 (81) £340

**Bourgelat, Claude, 1712-79**
— Le Nouveau Newcastle; ou, Nouveau Traite de Cavalerie. Lausanne, 1744. 8vo, contemp calf; rubbed, joints worn. Some foxing & soiling. O Jan 9 (55) $250

**Bourgeois, Louis**
— Observations diverses sur la sterilite perte de fruiet, fercondite.... Rouen, 1626. 2 vols in 1. 8vo, modern mor. With title vignette & port. S Oct 27 (799) £550 [Antiquarian]

**Bourgeois, Thomas Louis**
— Les Amours deguisez, ballet. Paris: Christophe Ballard, 1713. Oblong 4to, contemp calf; worn. Inscr. S Dec 1 (98) £380

**Bourgery, Marc Jean, 1797-1849 —& Others**
— Traite complet de l'anatomie de l'homme.... Paris, 1867-71. Vol II-V (of 8). Folio, contemp half lea gilt; covers detached or starting. With 359 (of 407) hand-colored plates. Sold w.a.f. sg May 16 (381) $1,800

**Bourges, Elemir**
— Les Oiseaux s'envolent et les fleurs tombent. Paris: E. Plon, [1893]. 12mo, mor extra by Noulhac, orig wraps bound in. Inscr. b Sept 20 (602) £60

**Bourguignon Anville, Jean Baptiste.** See: Anville, Jean Baptiste Bourguignon d'

**Bourke, John Gregory, 1843-96**
— Bourke's Diary.... La Mirada CA: James Willert, [1986]. One of 180. Notes & annotations by James Willert. Syn decorated in silver. Inscr by Willert. pba June 25 (14) $80
— On the Border with Crook. NY, 1891. 1st Ed. 8vo, orig cloth. With 7 photo plates. Robbins copy. pba Mar 21 (31) $400

Anr copy. Orig cloth; extremities rubbed, front hinge repaired. Stain to dedication page from newsclipping. pba June 25 (12) $250
— The Snake-Dance of the Moquis of Arizona. L, 1884. 8vo, orig cloth; new endpapers. With 33 plates. bbc June 24 (377) $320

Anr copy. Cloth; bumped, spine head chipped, library stamp on flyleaf. With 33 plates, of which 15 are colored. Tp foxed. Met May 22 (331) $250

**Bourke-White, Margaret**
— The Photographs.... Greenwich, 1972. Ed by Sean Callahan. 4to, cloth, in dj. Bottom corner of last few leaves creased. sg Feb 29 (47) $100
— Shooting the Russian War. NY: Simon & Schuster, 1942. 8vo, orig cloth. Inscr to Richard Simon, 20 June 1942. CE Feb 21 (206) $320
— Twelve Soviet Photo-Prints [First and Second Series]. [N.p., 1940s]. 1st Series only. Folio, loose in paper portfolio. With 12 photogravures. pba Mar 7 (33) $350

**Bourke-White, Margaret —& Caldwell, Erskine, 1903-87**
— Say, Is This the U.S.A. NY, [1941]. 1st Ed. Folio, pictorial cloth; rubbed. Some foxing. sg Feb 29 (45) $100

**Bourne, John C. —& Britton, John, 1771-1857**
— Drawings of the London and Birmingham Railway. L, 1839. Folio, disbound. With pictorial litho title, map & 27 (of 29) tinted litho plates. Some staining, mainly marginal; lacking text. S June 27 (88) £600

**Boutet, Henri**
— Les Modes feminines du XIX siecle. Paris, 1902. One of 600. 2 vols. 4to, contemp half mor; joints & spine rubbed. With 100 hand-colored plates. CE Nov 8 (172) $380

**Boutillier, Jean**
— La somme rurale. Abbeville: Pierre Gerard, 1486. 2 vols. Folio, 18th-cent calf gilt. 47 lines & headline, double column, type 1:109B. Rubricated; full-page woodcut colored in yellow, blue & violet. Tear on n1 crudely repaired, with lower margin backed; upper margin of 1st leaf cut out; early marginalia on G7v & G8r, that on f7v cropped. 253 (of 254) leaves; lacking final blank. Goff B-1052. Schaefer copy. P Nov 1 (50) $40,000

**Bouvet de Cresse, A. J. B.**
— Histoire de la Catastrophe de Sainte Domingue.... Paris, 1824. 12mo, modern half calf, orig wraps bound in. Last 2 leaves dampstained; library stamps. sg Mar 28 (96) $275

**Bouvier, A.** See: Naumann & Bouvier

**Bova, Ben**
— The Star Conquerors. Phila.: Winston, [1959]. 1st Ed. In chipped dj. pba May 4 (112) $140

**Bowditch, Nathaniel, 1773-1838**
— The New American Practical Navigator.... Newburyport, MA: Edmund M. Blunt, 1802. 1st Ed. 8vo, period sheep; cover edges worn, rebacked. With 9 plates. Light foxing. Robbins copy. pba Mar 21 (32) $3,500
25th New Stereotype Ed. NY, 1855. 8vo, orig sheep; rubbed, spine creased & ends chipped, half of front flyleaf torn off. With 13 plates. Frontis map creased; pencil notes or scribbles. pba July 25 (98) $85

**Bowen, Emanuel, d.1767.** See: Owen & Bowen

**Bowen, Emanuel, d.1767 —&**
**Kitchin, Thomas, d.1784**
— The Maps and Charts to the Modern Part of the Universal History. L, 1766. Folio, 19th-cent half calf; worn, upper cover detached. With 37 maps. Some staining; world map with small holes & soiling in right margin; some shaving at lower margin. C May 31 (48) £1,800
Anr copy. Contemp sheep; worn, rebacked with cloth. With 39 maps. Tp & map list trimmed & possibly from anr copy; library markings, but maps unmarked; marginal notations to maps. sg Dec 7 (4) $1,600

**Bower, B. M.**
— The Lure of the Dim Trails. NY: Dillingham, [1907]. Orig cloth; some wear. pba July 25 (347) $85

**Bowes, James Lord, 1834-99.** See: Audsley & Bowes

**Bowles, Paul**
— The Delicate Prey and Other Stories. NY: Random House, [1950]. In chipped dj. pba May 23 (22) $70
— Let It Come Down. NY, [1952]. In dj with spine wear. sg Dec 14 (15) $60
— Next To Nothing. Kathmandu: Starstreams 5, 1976. One of 500. Orig pictorial wraps. Sgd on tp. pba Aug 22 (34) $100
Anr Ed. Santa Barbara: Black Sparrow Press, 1981. One of 300. Half cloth. wa Feb 29 (23) $60
— Things Gone and Things Still Here. Santa Barbara: Black Sparrow Press, 1977. 1st Ed, One of 250. wa Feb 29 (24) $90

**Bowles, Samuel, 1826-78**
— The Switzerland of America. Springfield MA, 1869. 1st Ed. 8vo, orig cloth; rubbed. pba Aug 8 (20) $50

**Bowlker, Charles, d.1779**
— The Art of Angling.... Birm., 1786. 12mo, old calf; worn & broken. Some soiling, foxing & staining. O Feb 6 (28) $170
Anr Ed. Ludlow, 1826. 12mo, later half calf; rubbed. With hand-colored frontis. Some soiling & foxing. O Feb 6 (29) $160

Anr Ed. Ludlow, 1854. Unique copy with 28 hand-tied tlies tipped in. 16mo, cloth. With hand-colored frontis. Some soiling or browning. O Feb 6 (30) $550

**Bowman, Henry, 1814-83**
— The Churches of the Middle Ages. L, [c.1850]. 2 vols. Folio, half mor. Some foxing. pba Sept 14 (78) $200

**Bowman, S. M. —&**
**Irwin, R. B.**
— Sherman and his Campaigns.... NY, 1865. 8vo, contemp half calf; rubbed. Margins of tp darkened. pba June 13 (295) $85

**Bowness, Alan**
— The Complete Sculpture of Barbara Hepworth 1960-69. L, 1971. 1st Ed, One of 150, with an orig screenprint, sgd by Hepworth. 4to, orig cloth, in dj. sg Sept 7 (181A) $350

**Bowring, Sir John, 1792-1872**
— The Kingdom and People of Siam. L, 1857. 2 vols. 8vo, orig cloth; spines worn. With port, 8 colored plates, 7 uncolored plates, 2 facsimile letters & folding map. Some spotting. S Mar 28 (373) £340

**Bowyer, Robert, 1758-1834**
— An Illustrated Record of Important Events in the Annals of Europe.... L, 1816. Folio, recent half calf. With map, facsimile plate & 10 hand-colored views, some folding. S Mar 28 (225) £650
— An Impartial Historical Narrative.... L, 1823. Folio, orig bds; spine def. With 5 plates, 3 hand-colored. S Apr 23 (345) £150
— The Triumphs of Europe.... L, 1814. Bound with: Bowyer. An Illustrated Record of Important Events in the Annals of Europe. L, 1815. And: Bowyer. The Campaign of Waterloo. L, 1816. Folio, contemp half mor; extremities scuffed. Lacking 1st tp & 2 leaves of Appendix; 4 plates spotted. C May 31 (80) £1,200

**Box, Michael James**
— Adventures and Explorations in New and Old Mexico. NY, 1869. 12mo, orig cloth; worn & chipped, pencil scribbling to endpapers. Dampstain to lower edges & some gutters. wa Feb 29 (512) $150

**Boyce, William**
— Cathedral Music. L, [c.1849]. 3 vols. Contemp mor gilt; rebacked, extremities worn, bowed. Some foxing, soiling & marginal dampstaining; tp repaired. cb Oct 17 (351) $1,500
— Twelve Sonatas for Two Violins.... [N.p., 1747]. Complete parts with subscribers' list L-Z only [RISM B 4174]. Bound with: Locatelli: VI sonatas... opera Terza. [after 1736] [RISM L 2612]. And: Festing: Twelve Sonatas in Three Parts... Opera Secunda. 1731 [RISM F 668]. And: Fisher. Six Sonatas... Opera Prima. [1753]. [RISM F 1049]. Contemp bds. S May 15 (298) £600

**Boyd, E.**
— Popular Arts of Spanish New Mexico. Santa Fe, 1974. 4to, cloth, in soiled dj. pba Apr 25 (311) $75

**Boydell, John —&**
**Boydell, Josiah**
— Boydell's Picturesque Scenery of Norway.... L, 1820. Folio, contemp half calf gilt; rebacked, extremities rubbed. With 80 hand-colored plates. Some spotting to text leaves. L.p. copy & with additional contents leaf in Norwegian. C May 31 (82) £11,400
— Graphic Illustrations of the Dramatic Works of Shakespeare. NY, 1852. ("Illustrations of the Dramatic Works of Shakespeare....") 2 vols. Folio, later half mor; extremities worn, corners showing, Vol I spine perishing & bds detached, endpaper in Vol II replaced with kraft paper. Some foxing & dampstaining. cb Oct 17 (336) $2,500
Anr copy. 2 vols. 8vo, contemp half mor; def. With 100 plates. CE June 12 (160) $1,900
Anr Ed. L, 1874. ("The Boydell Gallery. A Collection of Engravings Illustrating the Dramatic Works of Shakespeare.") Folio, half mor gilt. With 97 Woodburytype plates. b Sept 20 (641) £140
— An History of the River Thames. L, 1794-96. 2 vols. Folio, contemp half russia; worn. With frontis, 74 hand-colored plates & 2 folding maps. Series title & vol titles lightly creased. Sold with vol containing 30 orig watercolor views & 14 other views, 12 in aquatint. C May 31 (83) £8,500
— A Set of Prints Engraved after the most Capital Paintings in the Collection of...the Empress of Russia.... L, 1787-88. 2 vols. Folio, 19th-cent half mor. With 2 ports, 28 plans & elevations on 19 sheets & 76 (of 127) plates on 60 sheets. Lacking tp; some spotting. bba Nov 30 (84) £420 [Bifolco]

**Boydell, Josiah.** See: Boydell & Boydell

**Boyer, Abel, 1667-1729**
— Le Grand Theatre de l'honneur et de la noblesse. L, 1729. 4to, contemp calf; rubbed, front joint cracked. In French & English. Some browning & spotting. F June 20 (318) $90

**Boyer, Jean Baptiste de, Marquis d'Argens.** See: Argens, Jean Baptiste de Boyer

**Boyer, Mary G.**
— Arizona in Literature: A Collection of the Best Writings of Arizona Authors.... Glendale, Calif., 1934. 1st Ed. Orig cloth; spine faded. With color frontis. Robbins copy. pba Mar 21 (33) $80

**Boyle, Frederick**
— About Orchids: A Chat. L, 1893. Orig cloth; spine head chipped, front hinge weak. With 8 chromolitho plates. pba June 20 (254) $60
— The Culture of Greenhouse Orchids.... L, 1902. Orig cloth; soiled, spine ends rubbed. With 3 chromolitho plates. pba June 20 (255) $50
— The Woodlands Orchids Described and Illustrated.... L, 1901. Half lea. With 16 chromolitho plates. Met Feb 24 (433) $200

**Boyle, John, Earl of Cork & Orrery, 1707-62**
— The First Ode of the First Book of Horace. Dublin, 1741. Fine paper issue. 8vo, contemp mor gilt by John Brindley; head of spine chipped. Author's interleaved & annotated copy. C Nov 29 (120) £2,000

**Boyle, Robert, 1627-91**
— Certain Physiological Essays. L, 1669. 2d Ed. 4to, contemp sheep; worn. Title & prelims affected by damp; later leaves dampstained; T1 holed with loss; 2L1-2P2 soiled. Ck Mar 22 (53) £280
— A Disquisition about the Final Causes of Natural Things. L, 1688. 1st Ed, 1st Issue. 8vo, contemp sheep; rubbed. Minor dampstaining; hole in P1 affecting text. S Mar 14 (64) £950
— Experiments and Considerations about the Porosity of Bodies.... L, 1684. 1st Ed. 8vo, contemp calf. B2 corner torn away; D8 with burn-hole. Inscr to John Wentworth. Ck Mar 22 (55) £2,800
— Experiments and Considerations Touching Colours.... L, 1664. 1st Ed. 8vo, modern vellum. Some 18th-cent annotations; tp soiled. S Mar 29 (644) £220
— Medicinal Experiments, or a Collection of Choice and Safe Remedies.... L, 1693. 2d Ed of Vol I; 1st Ed of Vol II. 12mo, contemp calf; worn. Some browning. b Sept 20 (96) £160
— New Experiments Physico-Mechanicall, Touching the Spring of the Air and its Effects.... Oxford, 1662. Bound with: A Defence of the doctrine Touching the Spring and Weight of the Air. L, 1662. And: An Examen of Mr. T. Hobbes his Dialogus Physicus de Nature Aeris. L, 1662. 4to, modern calf. Brittle; 1 leaf in 1st work reattached & lacking folding plate; 2 leaves in 2d work misbound; 3d work with repeat in pagination of pp. 85-86. K Feb 11 (104) $800
2d Ed of New, 1st Ed of Defence. Bound with: A Defence of the Doctrine touching the Spring and Weight.... L, 1662 4to, old calf; rebacked, worn & broken. Lacking the plate; marginal pencil marks; some chipping. Sold w.a.f. pba Nov 30 (64) $350
— The Philosophical Works. L, 1725. 3 vols. 4to, contemp calf; rubbed. With 21 folding plates. bba Nov 16 (384) £300 [Wheeler]
2d Ed. L, 1738. 3 vols. 4to, contemp half calf; joints cracked, spines chipped. With frontis & 13 plates. S Mar 29 (688) £420
— Some Considerations Touching the Usefulnesse of Experimental Naturall Philosophy. Oxford, 1663. 1st Ed. 2 parts in 1 vol. 4to, contemp mor; extrems rubbed, spine & cover edges blackened. With frontis port. A1a misbound; 2n1 & 2o1 with holes. Ck Mar 22 (54) £700
2d Ed. Oxford, 1664. Fulton's "A" Issue. 2 parts in 1 vol. 4to, contemp calf. Tp stamped; some spotting. S Mar 14 (62) £150
— Tentamina quaedam physiologica diversis temporibus & occasionibus conscripta. Geneva: S. de Tournes, 1680. 3 parts in 1 vol. 4to, modern vellum bds. Some browning. bba May 30 (408) £140 [Poole]
— Tracts Containing I. Suspicions about some Hidden Qualities of the Air.... L, 1674. 1st Ed. 8vo, contemp sheep; partly misbound. With the bookbinder

leaf; both title pages to the tract on Suction present. S Mar 14 (63) £950
— Works. L, 1699-1700. Vols I-III (of 4). 8vo, contemp calf; worn, 1 cover detached, Vol II spine broken. With 20 plates. Lacking port in Vol I. S Mar 29 (687) £325

**Boynton, Charles Brandon, 1806-83 —& Mason, Timothy B.**
— A Journey through Kansas: with Sketches of Nebraska. Cincinnati, 1855. 6th Thousand. 12mo, orig wraps; spine ends worn. Minor staining. CE May 22 (10) $190

**Boys, Thomas Shotter, 1803-74**
— Architecture pittoresque dessine d'apres nature. Paris, 1835. Illus by Boys & A. Rouargue. Folio, contemp half calf; rubbed. With title vignette & 48 plates. Spotted. S Oct 26 (341) £300 [Sotheran]
— Original Views of London.... L, 1842. Folio, orig half mor; rubbed & soiled, loose. With litho title, dedication & 25 plates. Some spotting; marginal tears, occasionally touching image. S June 27 (89) £2,600
— Picturesque Architecture in Paris, Ghent, Antwerp, Rouen. L, 1839. Folio, half mor; def. With 17 chromolitho views on 15 sheets only. Lacking prelims & other letterpress matter; plates foxed & chipped. sg May 9 (321) $500

**Boze, Claude Gros de, 1680-1753.** See: Gros de Boze, Claude

**Brabant**
— El Lustre y la gloria del ducado de Brabante.... [Brussels, 1699]. Folio, contemp calf; spine ends chipped, covers detached. Folding plates browned; marginal dampstains. sg Mar 21 (292) $550

**Bracken, Henry, M.D.**
— Farriery Improved. Phila., 1796. 12mo, contemp half calf. With 10 full-page & folding plates. Some foxing & soiling; piece of 1 folding plate torn off but present. O Jan 9 (56) $250

**Brackenridge, Hugh Henry**
— Incidents of the Insurrection in the Western Parts of Pennsylvania.... Phila., 1795. Old bds; later endpapers, front hinge almost detached. Browned. Z June 28 (38) $170

**Brackett, Leigh, 1915-78**
— The Starmen. NY: Gnome Press, [1952]. In dj with chip to spine head. pba Dec 7 (17) $60

**Bradbury, Ray**
See also: Limited Editions Club
— About Norman Corman. Northridge: California State University, 1979. One of 60. Illus by Amanda Blanco. Loose in orig folding cloth portfolio. With 12 photographs, sgd & numbered by Blanco. cb Oct 17 (510) $200
— Fahrenheit 451. NY: Ballantine Books, [1953]. In dj with tears to extremities. pba May 4 (113) $500

Anr copy. In rubbed & soiled dj. Sgd & with full-page drawing by Bradbury on front free endpaper, 1985. pba Aug 22 (40) $450
— The Halloween Tree. NY, [1972]. Illus by Joseph Mugnaini. In dj with closed tear. Inscr. pba Aug 22 (41) $90
— The Martian Chronicles. Garden City, 1950. 1st Ed. In dj. K June 23 (124) $375
Anr copy. In rubbed dj with repaired tear. Sgd. pba Aug 22 (43) $750
— Old Ahab's Friend, and Friend to Noah, Speaks his Peace. [N.p., 1971]. One of 485. String-bound wraps. pba May 23 (26) $85
— R is for Rocket. Garden City, [1962]. In dj. pba Dec 7 (18) $180
— Something Wicked This Way Comes. NY, 1962. In dj with stain on bottom panel. pba Aug 22 (44) $225
2d Ptg. In dj with spine wear. Inscr to Tim Seldes, his agent. sg Dec 14 (17) $150

**Bradbury, Ray —& Mitchell, Lisa**
— Ready When You Are, Mister Fabian!: An Outline for a Screenplay. Hollywood, [1990]. Wraps. Inscr by Bradbury & with ANs of Mitchell. pba Aug 22 (38) $170

**Braddock, James J.**
[-] Relief to Royalty: The Story of James J. Braddock.... [N.p., 1936]. Orig cloth. Inscr by Braddock, 1936. pba Apr 4 (96) $225

**Bradford, Thomas Gamaliel, 1802-87**
— A Comprehensive Atlas.... Bost., 1834. Folio, contemp half lea; extremities worn. Maps hand-colored in outline; some foxing & browning. sg Dec 7 (5) $1,100
Anr Ed. Bost. & NY, 1835. 4to, contemp half calf; worn, spine repaired. With title, hand-colored frontis, 9 plates, & 60 (of 66) maps & plans. Spotted & discolored; map of U.S. badly stained; some pp. frayed at edges. S Oct 26 (423) £460 [Map House]

**Bradford, William, c.1779-1857**
— Sketches of the Country, Character, and Costume in Portugal and Spain. L, [1813-20]. Folio, mor gilt; worn. With 51 hand-colored plates. Lacking Plate 7 & Plate 40. S Mar 28 (226) £800

**Bradley, David**
— South Street. NY, 1975. In dj. pba Dec 7 (19) $75

**Bradley, Edward, 1827-89**
— Photographic Pleasures, Popularly Portrayed with Pen & Pencil. L, 1855. 1st Ed. 8vo, orig cloth; some wear. With 24 plates, including litho title & frontis. b May 30 (43) £300

**Bradley, John Hodgdon**
— Farewell, Thou Busy World. Los Angeles: Primavera Press, 1935. Illus by Paul Landacre. Half cloth; soiled. pba July 11 (172) $50

**Bradley, John William, 1830-1916**
— A Dictionary of Miniaturists, Illuminators, Calligraphers.... L, 1887-89. 3 vols. 8vo, orig half mor; worn. O Mar 5 (29) $300

**Bradley, Richard, d.1732**
— A Complete Body of Husbandry. L, 1727. 8vo, contemp calf; rubbed. b Sept 20 (97) £160
— A Philosophical Account of the Works of Nature. L, 1721. 1st Ed. 4to, contemp calf; scraped, spine repaired & wormed at ends. With 28 hand-colored plates. S Mar 29 (755) £440

**Bradley, Will H.**
— Bradley: His Book. Springfield Mass., 1896-97. Vol I & Vol II, Nos 1-3. Half mor, orig wraps bound in; worn, front cover of Vol II detached. sg Feb 15 (60) $450

**Brady, Cyrus Townsend**
— Indian Fights and Fighters. NY, 1904. pba June 25 (16) $60
— Northwestern Fights and Fighters. NY, 1907. Orig cloth. Pages 85-86 torn across center. pba Apr 25 (313) $50

**Brady, Robert, 1627?-1700**
— A Complete History of England.... L, 1685. 1st Ed. Folio, old calf; rebacked, old notes to pastedown. pba Nov 30 (65) $425

**Brady, William**
— The Kedge-Anchor; or, Young Sailors' Assistant.... NY, 1872. 18th Ed. 8vo, orig cloth; front hinge cracked, spine rubbed. Tp & frontis foxed. pba July 25 (99) $65

**Bragdon, Dudley A.** See: Denslow & Bragdon

**Brahe, Tycho, 1546-1601**
— Astronomiae instauratae mechanica. Nuremberg, 1602. 2d Ed. Folio, modern mor gilt. Tp & following 3 leaves guarded; marginal repairs; minor worming, affecting text; tp stained. Madsen copy. S Mar 14 (67) £5,000
 1st Ed. Uraniberg & Prague, 1602. Folio, contemp vellum, with arms of the Duke of Abaltemps. Some browing & staining. Madsen copy. S Mar 14 (66) £12,000
— De mundi aetherei recentioribus phaenominis liber secundus. [Uraniborg, 1588] & Prague, 1603. 4to, contemp vellum with arms of the Duke of Abaltemps; rebacked retaining part of orig spine. Some browning; tear at head of 3N1. Madsen copy. S Mar 14 (68) £6,200
— Opera. Frankfurt, 1648. 2 parts in 1 vol. 4to, modern vellum. Some worming at ends, affecting text, that in 1st title repaired with loss of 1 character. Madsen copy. S Mar 14 (69) £1,200

**Braid, James**
— Advanced Golf or, Hints and Instruction for Progressive players. Phila.: George W. Jacobs, [1908]. 1st American Ed. Cloth; cover with insect damage. With frontis. pba Apr 18 (12) $120

**Braim, Thomas Henry, 1814-91**
— A History of New South Wales.... L, 1846. 2 vols. 8vo, orig cloth; rebacked. b Mar 20 (67) £120

**Brainard, C. H.**
— Brainard's Portrait Gallery of Distinguished Americans. Bost., 1855. Folio, orig half sheep; upper cover detached, worn & warped, lower cover with cloth peeling, shaken. With 19 mtd oval litho ports on india paper Some dampstains to portions of text & ports; some foxing at beginning; front blanks creased & torn. bbc Dec 18 (440) $450

**Brainard, Mary**
— Campaigns of the One Hundred and Forty-Sixth Regiment New York State Volunteers. NY, 1915. 1st Ed. Orig cloth; library markings to bdg only. Inscr. NH July 21 (61) $160

**Braislin Collection, William C.**
— [Sale Catalogue] The Important American Library.... NY: Anderson Galleries, 1927. 2 vols. Cloth, orig wraps bound in. Priced in ink. ds July 27 (37) $80

**Braithwaite, John**
— The History of the Revolutions in the Empire of Morocco.... L, 1729. 8vo, calf; worn, hinges cracked. With folding map. NH July 21 (115) $170

**Braive, Michel Francois**
— The Photograph: A Social History. L, [1966]. 1st English Ed. 4to, cloth, in torn & repaired dj; pastedowns & endpapers foxed, fore-edge stained. sg Feb 29 (48) $80

**Bramah, Ernest**
— The Eyes of Max Carrados. L, 1923. Orig cloth; bumped, spine rubbed. sg Dec 14 (39) $110

**Bramsen, Johannes**
— Letters of a Prussian Traveller. L, 1818. 2 vols. 8vo, 19th-Cent half calf. S Oct 26 (47) £500 [Bank of Cyprus]

**Branch, Edward Douglas**
— The Cowboy and his Interpreters. NY & L, 1926. Orig cloth. Inscr with ink sketch on half-title verso, 10 Dec 1926. pba Nov 16 (82) $375

**Brand, Hannah, 1760-1821**
— Plays and Poems. Norwich, 1798. 8vo, orig bds; worn. b Dec 5 (245) £150

**Brand, Max.** See: Derrydale Press

**Brandt, Bill**
— Perspective of Nudes. NY, 1961. 4to, bds, in worn & chipped dj; bdg extremities worn. sg Feb 29 (49) $300
— Shadow of Light. NY, [1966]. 4to, Cloth, in crimped & torn d/j. Wrinkling throughout at bottom. sg Feb 29 (50) $120

**Brandt, Geeraert, 1626-85**
— Het leven en bedryf van Michiel de Ruitter. Amst., 1687. Folio, contemp blind-stamped vellum. With 7 double-page plates & single plate. sg Apr 18 (32) $700
— La Vie de Michel de Ruiter.... Amst., 1698. Folio, later bds; hinges cracked, worn. With engraved title, frontis (both in duplicate) & 8 plates. Text browned. wd Nov 15 (33) $400

**Brandt, Joseph van den**
— Catalogue des principaux ouvrages sortis des presses des Lazaristes a Pekin de 1864 a 1930. Paking, 1933. Ltd Ed. Half lea, orig wraps bound in; rubbed. O Mar 26 (283) $200

**Brangwyn, Frank, 1867-1956**
— Catalogue of the Etched Work.... L: The Fine Art Society, 1912. 4to, orig half vellum; front hinge cracked. sg Sept 7 (56) $90

**Brannon, George**
— Vectis Scenery.... Wooton-Common, Isle of Wight, 1860. Oblong folio, orig cloth; rubbed. With engraved title & 40 plates; folding map at end. Some foxing; tp loose. bba June 6 (59) £150 [Ventnor]

**Brannt, William T.**
— A Practical Treatise on the Raw Materials and the Distillation and Rectification of Alcohol.... Phila., 1885. 8vo, orig cloth; stains on covers. sg May 16 (137) $175

**Brant, Sebastian, 1458-1521**
— Stultifera Navis...The Ship of Fooles. L: John Cawood, [1570]. Trans by Alexander Barclay. Folio, mor gilt. Tp in facsimile; 1st 5 leaves with repairs to margins & portions in facsimile; some staining at end. cb Feb 14 (2510) $2,250

   Anr copy. Contemp calf gilt; rehinged. Tp restored in top margin & washed; Y2 & Vv4 supplied from a smaller copy. STC 3546. Martin - Hefner copy. CNY May 17 (7) $7,000

   Anr copy. 17th-cent calf; rebacked, endpapers renewed. Some dampstaining & worming at ends. Wollascott - Major - Schaefer copy. P Nov 1 (51) $7,000

   Anr copy. Mor gilt by the French Binders. Tp soiled & discolored; B3 with small rust hole; S4 & 2T2 with marginal tear; marginal dampstains. P June 5 (179) $6,000

   Anr Ed. Seal Harbor: High Loft, [1982]. ("The Shyp of Fooles....") One of 200. Folio, half cloth. sg Sept 14 (84) $120

**Brantome, Pierre de Bourdeille, Sieur de, 1535?-1614**
   See also: Golden Cockerel Press
— Oeuvres. The Hague, 1740. 15 vols. 12mo, contemp mor gilt. Fuerstenberg - Schaefer copy. S Dec 7 (82) £600

**Braque, Georges, 1882-1963**
   See also: Vallier, Dora
— Cahier de G. Braque 1917-1947. Paris, 1948-[55]. One of 750 on velin du Marais. 4to, unsewn in orig wraps; chipped & tattered. cb Oct 17 (609) $200
— Carnet intimes. Paris, 1955. Folio, orig bds. Verve Nos 31/32. sg Jan 11 (63) $225
— Catalogue de l'oeuvre de Georges Braque, 1916-1957. Paris: Maeght, 1959-73. 6 vols. 4to, orig cloth binders. wad Oct 18 (173) C$3,600
— Espaces. Paris, 1957. One of 300. Folio, unsewn as issued in orig portfolio. With 13 plates. Marginal staining; stains to top extemities of text. pba Mar 7 (36) $750
— The Intimate Sketchbooks. NY, 1955. Folio, orig bds, in worn & chipped dj. Verve Nos 31/32. wa Feb 1 (308) $190

**Brasher, Rex, 1869-1960**
— Birds and Trees of North America. NY, 1961-62. 4 vols. Oblong folio, cloth. With 875 colored plates. sg Dec 7 (239) $140

**Brassai, Pseud. of Gyula Halsz**
— Brassai. NY: Museum of Modern Art, [1968]. Intro by Lawrence Durrell. In dj; library stamp on front free endpaper. sg Feb 29 (51) $100
— Paris de nuit. Paris: Arts et Metiers Graphiques, 1933. Spiral bound; worn, front cover creased. Some soiling. sg Feb 29 (53) $400

**Brathwaite, Richard, 1588-1673**
— Ar't Asleepe Husbande? A Boulster Lecture.... L, 1640. 1st Ed, tp Issue reading "R. Bishop"; dedication leaf Issue "To all modest dames.". 8vo, mor gilt; joints rubbed, corners bumped. Engraved title with repairs. P June 5 (178) $1,900

**Braun, Georg —&**
**Hogenberg, Franz**
— Civitates orbis terrarum. Antwerp & Cologne, 1572-75. Parts I & II in 1 vol. Folio, 18th-cent half calf; worn. With engraved titles, dedications & 115 (of 118) maps & plates, all mtd on guards. First engraved title cut down & mtd as frontis; some spotting & dampstaining; 2 plates shaved with loss, many def in margins; some fold tears. C May 31 (47) £18,000
   Anr Ed. Cologne: H. von Aich, 1574. ("Contrafactur und Beschreibung von den vornembsten Stetten der Welt.") Vol I only. Folio, contemp vellum; worn. With engraved title & 59 double-page maps on guards plus 6 additional plates inserted. Engraved title torn with minor loss; soiled; tears affecting maps, some with loss. C Oct 25 (104) £9,500

**Braun, Johann**
— Vestitus Sacerdotum Hebraeorum.... Amst., 1698-97. 2 vols in 1. 4to, contemp vellum; front joint worn, bowed. Some browning. pba Nov 30 (200) $800

**Brauns, Reinhard**
— Das Mineralreich. Stuttgart, 1903. Folio, orig half cloth. With 91 plates, most in color. Tissue guard partly adhered to Plate 66. sg May 16 (138) $600

**Brautigan, Richard**
— A Confederate General from Big Sur. NY, 1964. In dj. Sgd on half-title, 11 Sept 1966, with small drawing of a fish. CE Feb 21 (25A) $220
— Rommel Drives on Deep Into Egypt. NY, [1970]. In dj. pba Aug 22 (45) $70
— The Tokyo-Montana Express. NY, 1979. One of 350. pba May 23 (28) $130
— Trout Fishing in America. San Francisco: Four Seasons Foundation, 1967. Orig wraps. 1st several leaves detached. Ls laid in. pba Aug 22 (47) $300

**Bray, William.** See: Manning & Bray

**Brayley, Edward Wedlake, 1773-1854**
See also: Britton & Brayley
— The History and Antiquities of the Abbey Church of St. Peter, Westminster. L, 1818-23. L.p. copy. 2 vols. 4to, contemp half mor gilt; rubbed. With 2 engraved titles & 59 plates. Some spotting. S Apr 23 (366) £200

**Breakenridge, William M.**
— Helldorado: Bringing the Law to the Mesquite. Bost., 1928. pba Nov 16 (34) $50

**Breasted, James Henry, 1865-1935**
— The Edwin Smith Surgical Papyrus.... Chicago, 1930. 2 vols. 4to, orig cloth; spine of plate vol rubbed. sg May 16 (382) $225

**Brebeuf, Jean de, 1593-1649.** See: Golden Cockerel Press

**Brecht, Bertolt, 1898-1956.** See: Limited Editions Club

**Bree, Charles Robert, 1811-86**
— A History of the Birds of Europe. L, 1859-63. 4 vols. 8vo, later half mor gilt; extremities worn. With 238 colored plates. sg Dec 7 (195) $300
Anr Ed. L, 1863-67. 4 vols. 4to, orig cloth; worn & soiled, spines chipped. With 238 hand-colored plates. Some foxing. F June 20 (567) $350
Anr Ed. L, 1866-67. 2d Issue. 4 vols. 8vo, contemp half mor; extremities worn. With 238 hand-colored plates. Some browning & foxing; 2 plates in Vol IV detached. cb Feb 14 (2613) $700
2d Ed. L, 1875-76. 5 vols. 8vo, orig cloth; spine ends frayed. Ck Feb 14 (322) £320
Anr copy. Orig cloth; spines faded. With 252 hand-colored plates. S Oct 27 (624) £330 [Shapero]
Anr Ed. L, 1875. 5 vols. 8vo, contemp mor; rubbed. With 252 hand-colored & 1 plain plates. Marginal tear in vol IV frontis. S Oct 27 (704) £460 [Egglishaw]

**Breeds...**
— The Breeds of our Different Domestic Animals, Part First (all pbd). Edin., 1830. Oblong folio, orig wraps; worn. With 4 plates. Some spotting & creasing; repairs to text leaves. bba June 6 (25) £150 [Kennedy]

**Breen, Patrick, d.1868**
— The Diary of.... San Francisco: Book Club of California, 1946. One of 300. pba June 20 (12) $50
— The Diary of Patrick Breen... the Ordeal of the Donner Party.... San Francisco: Book Club of California, 1946. One of 300. Intro by George R. Stewart. Half bds. Larson copy. pba Sept 28 (422) $75

**Breeskin, Adelyn D.**
— The Graphic Work of Mary Cassatt. A Catalogue Raisonne. NY, 1948. One of 550. 4to, half cloth, in dj with stain. sg Sept 7 (69) $350
— Mary Cassatt.... Wash., 1970. 4to, cloth; worn. Ink stamp on contents leaf. ds July 27 (52) $1,500

**Brehm, Alfred, 1829-84**
— Cassell's Book of Birds.... L, [1869-73]. 4 vols in 2. 4to, half mor; extremities rubbed. Plates foxed. sg Dec 7 (196) $110

**Bremer Press—Toelz, Munich, etc.**
— Ballads and Songs of Love. 1930. One of 280. pba Mar 7 (37) $80
DANTE ALIGHIERI. - La Divinia commedia. 1921. One of 300. sg Oct 19 (50) $550
PASCAL, BLAISE. - Pensees. 1930. One of 270. CE May 22 (63) $350
Anr copy. Tear across 1 text leaf. Sold w.a.f. sg Oct 19 (51) $650
SCHULTE-STRATHAUS, E. - Die echten Ausgaben von Goethes Faust. 1932. One of 85. O Mar 26 (40) $400
VESALIUS, ANDREAS. - Icones anatomicae. 1934. One of 615. With 277 plates. Lacking portfolio; pencil markings on 1 plate; 1st index leaf creased. sg May 16 (520) $2,400

**Brenni, Vito**
— Bookbinding: a Guide to the Literature. Westport, Conn., [1982]. 8vo, orig cloth. sg Apr 11 (48) $70

**Bres, Paschalis**
— Ad I. U. Prolysin, die XXI Jun. hora X matutina.... Turin: Typus Regiis, 1783. 4to, contemp white glazed calf with outer border of mor in ribbon pattern with background of green tinsel; central oval miniature (Justice on upper cover, Athena on lower cover) under mica within elaborate frame. Sold as a bdg. C Apr 3 (43) £5,500

**Breslauer, Bernard.** See: Grolier Club

**Breton, Andre, 1896-1966**
— Manifeste du surrealisme. Paris, [1929]. Orig wraps; tears to front joint. sg June 20 (367) $110
— Yves Tanguy. NY: Pierre Matisse, [1946]. One of 1,150. Designed by Marcel Duchamp. Folio, bds. sg Jan 11 (412) $425

**Breton, Nicholas, 1545?-1626?**
See also: Golden Cockerel Press
— The Twelve Moneths and Christmas Day. NY, 1951. One of 100 on handmade paper & bound in mor. pba Aug 22 (568) $170

**Breve...**
— Breve relacion de las cosas mas admirables en la Gran China.... [Manila?], 1705. 4to, recent vellum gilt. Minor marginal margins. S Nov 30 (195) £2,200

**Brewer, David J.**
— The World's Best Essays.... St. Louis, 1900. Connoisseur Ed, one of 250. 10 vols. Half mor. pba Aug 8 (270) $250

**Brewer, E. Cobham.** See: Fore-Edge Paintings

**Brewer, William H., 1828-1910**
— Such a Landscape!... Yosemite: Yosemite Association, 1987. One of 500 printed by Susan Acker at Feathered Serpent Press. Intro & photographs by William Alsup. Folio, half cloth. pba Feb 12 (8) $50
— Up and Down California in 1860-1864. New Haven, 1930. In dj. With related material, including ALs. pba Feb 12 (7) $650
Anr copy. In worn & soiled dj. With folding map & 32 plates. wa Feb 29 (324) $110
1st Ed. - Ed by Francis P. Farquhar. Orig cloth. Robbins copy. pba Mar 21 (34) $140

**Brewington, Dorothy.** See: Brewington & Brewington; Peabody Museum

**Brewington, Marion Vernon.** See: Peabody Museum

**Brewington, Marion Vernon —&**
**Brewington, Dorothy**
— Kendall Whaling Museum Paintings. Sharon MA, 1965. 4to, cloth; worn. O Dec 5 (23) $70
— Kendall Whaling Museum Prints. Sharon MA, 1969. 4to, cloth; minor wear. O Dec 5 (24) $70

**Brewster, Anna Richards**
— Sketches from the British Isles.... NY: Marchbank Press, [c.1954]. One of 250. 4 vols. 4to, cloth. Met Feb 24 (6) $200

**Breydenbach, Bernhard von**
— Viaje dela tierra sancta. Saragossa: Paulus Hurus, 16 Jan 1498. Folio, early 19th-cent mor antique by V. Arias. 43 lines & headline; double column; types 2*:145G, 3:100G, 4:156G. With full-page allegorical woodcut & 64 (of 67 - 3 supplied in rough facsimile) woodcuts of the life of Christ & 13 woodcuts with narrow borders of alphabets and scenes of the Near East, woodcut of the Holy Sepulchre, woodcut of animals & woodcut initials, some cuts touched with yellow. First 7 last leaves repaired; margial wormholes repaired; small hole in k8 affecting 2 woodcuts; tear into text in b3 repaired without loss. 171 (of 205) leaves; i4 in ink facsimile & all folding views lacking. Goff B-1196. Dyson Perrins copy. C Nov 29 (37) £3,500

**Briand, P. C.**
— Les jeunes voyageurs en Asie.... Paris, 1829. 8 vols. 8vo, calf gilt by Thouvenin. With 7 folding maps hand-colored in outline & 16 plates. b May 30 (246) £250

**Bricker, Charles**
— Landmarks of Mapmaking. Amst., 1968. Folio, cloth, in repaired dj. pba Oct 9 (22) $90
Anr Ed. NY, [1976]. Folio, cloth, in dj. sg May 9 (7) $225

**Bridge, Horatio**
— Journal of an African Cruiser... by an Officer of the U.S. Navy. NY, 1845. Ed by Nathaniel Hawthorne. 12mo, modern half mor. F June 20 (412A) $170

**Bridges, Robert, 1844-1930**
See also: Gregynog Press
— Poems. L, 1873. 1st Ed. 8vo, orig cloth. S Apr 23 (8) £200
— Shorter Poems. Oxford: Daniel Press, [1894]. One of 150. 8vo, mor gilt by Zaehnsdorf. CE Sept 27 (92) $380
— The Tapestry. L, 1925. One of 150. bba May 9 (13) £260 [Quaritch]

**Bridges, Robert, 1844-1930 —&**
**Wooldridge, H. Ellis, 1845-1917**
— Hymns. Oxford, 1899. Ed by Bridges & Wooldridge. 8vo, contemp vellum bds by Morley of Oxford, orig 4 part wraps bound in at end. bba May 9 (16) £100 [Collinge & Clark]

**Brieger, Peter H. —& Others**
— Illuminated Manuscripts of the Divine Comedy. L, 1970. 2 vols. 4to, cloth. sg June 13 (244) $150

**Briere, Gaston**
— Le Chateau de Versailles. Paris, [1907-9]. 3 vols. Folio, cloth; worn. With 200 plates. Foxed, affecting plates. sg Sept 7 (8) $325

**Briggs, Clare**
— Golf: The Book of a Thousand Chuckles. Chicago: P. F. Voland, [1916]. 1st Ed. Half cloth; cover fore-edges rubbed, front hinge starting. pba Apr 18 (14) $150

**Briggs, Ernest E.**
— Angling & Art in Scotland. L, 1908. With 32 color plates. pba July 11 (41) $160

**Briggs, Walter**
— Without Noise of Arms. Flagstaff: Northland Press, [1976]. One of 100 bound in lea. Illus by Wilson Hurley. pba Feb 13 (28) $140

**Brigham, Clarence Saunders**
— Paul Revere's Engravings. NY, 1969. 4to, cloth. wa Dec 14 (580) $50

**Brigham, William Tufts**
— A Catalogue of Works Published at, or Relating to, the Hawaiian Islands. Bost., 1868. 8vo, orig cloth; worn. In: Hawaiian Club Papers. Edited by a Committee of the Club. October 1868.. O Mar 26 (42) $100

**Brill, Charles J.**
— Conquest of the Southern Plains. Oklahoma City, 1938. Some tape-repaired tears. pba June 25 (18) $75

**Brillat-Savarin, Anthelme, 1755-1826**
See also: Limited Editions Club
— Physiologie du gout. Paris, 1826. 1st Ed. 2 vols. 8vo, contemp bds; rubbed. Some spotting & staining. Ck Mar 22 (57) £650

Anr copy. Some spotting & soiling; 6.5 torn at margin; quire 25 in vol II heavily stained. Ck Mar 22 (58) £420

Anr Ed. Paris, 1864. 8vo, orig wraps; spine ends chipped, tears at corners of front cover. pba Nov 30 (98) $150

**Brin, David**
— The River of Time. Niles IL: Dark Harvest, 1986. One of 400. In dj. O Dec 5 (157) $50

**Brindesi, Jean**
— Elbicei atika; musee des anciens costumes Turcs de Constantinople. Paris, [1955]. Folio, modern half mor. With chromolitho title & 22 chromolitho costume plates within gold borders. Library blindstamp on each plate touching borders; title cut round & mtd. S Nov 30 (120) £2,400

**Brininstool, Earl Alonzo**
See also: Hebard & Brininstool
— Crazy Horse. Los Angeles, 1949. In chipped dj. pba June 25 (20) $85
— Fighting Red Cloud's Warriors. Columbus OH: Hunter-Trader-Trapper Co., 1926. Library stamps. pba June 25 (21) $180

**Brinkley, Frank, 1841-1912**
— Japan. Described and Illustrated by the Japanese. Bost. [1897-98]. Empress Ed, One of 25. 10 vols. Folio, each vol in a different-colored pictorial silk with silk tassels. P Apr 18 (132) $8,000

Anr Ed. Bost., [1897-98]. Orig 15 parts. Folio, orig wraps with reinforced cloth spines; chipped, lower cover of Section 1 missing large chunk & taped. With 30 hand-colored albumen prints, 15 color calotypes & c.200 halftone reproductions in text & 15 full-page woodcuts. bbc June 24 (184) $325

Edition De Luxe, One of 750. 10 vols. Folio, bds; minor wear. Some foxing throughout. sg Oct 7 (519) $1,400

Yedo Ed, One of 1,000. 10 vols. Folio, each vol bd in different Japanese cloth; some wear & fraying. Some smudging. wa Feb 1 (246) $475

— Oriental Series: Japan and China. Bost. & Tokyo, 1901-2. Lotus Ed, one of 26 on Japan vellum. 12 vols. 4to, mor extra. cb Oct 17 (263) $2,500

**Brinton, Daniel Garrison, 1837-99**
— The Lenape and Their Legends. Phila., 1885. 8vo, orig cloth; wear & soiling. Tp browned. F June 20 (385) $70

Anr copy. Orig cloth; corner bumped. Trace from removed bookplate & tp erasure. pba Apr 25 (145) $80

**Brion de la Tour, Louis**
— Atlas general.... Paris, 1786-[1790]. Folio, contemp half calf; def. With title & 51 hand-colored double-page maps Maps with splits at folds, several repaired; world map torn with abrasion; creased & soiled throughout. S Oct 26 (424) £650 [Franks]

**Brion, Marcel**
— Ernst Fuchs. NY, [1979]. Oblong 4to, cloth, in dj. sg Jan 11 (188) $50

**Brioys, Jean**
— Nouvelle Maniere de fortification.... The Hague: Guillaume de Voys, 1711. 12mo, later calf gilt; edges worn, upper joint split. With 12 folding charts & plans. Tp detached & trimmed. bbc June 24 (223) $300

**Briquet, Charles Moise, 1839-1918**
— Les Filigranes. Hildesheim, 1984. 4 vols. 8vo, orig cloth. sg Apr 11 (57) $275

**Briscoe, J. Potter**
— Tudor and Stuart Love Songs. L, 1902. Vellucent bdg by Cedric Chivers, the painted center panel showing a seated cupid playing a lyre. Some soiling. CE Sept 27 (53) $550

**Briseux, Charles Etienne**
— Traite du beau essentiel dans les parts.... Paris, 1752. 2 vols. Folio, contemp sheep; worn, lower cover of Vol II detached. With port & 138 plates. Stamps on verso of titles; some marginal marking & foxing; 1 plate torn at fold. bba Nov 16 (45) £800 [Hetherington]

**Brissart-Binet, Charles A.**
— Cazin, sa vie et ses editions. Par un Cazinophile. Cazinopolis, 1876. 8vo, contemp half mor, orig wraps bound in; rubbed, upper cover detached. O Mar 26 (43) $50

**Brisson, Mathurin Jacques, 1723-1806**
— Ornithologie.... Paris, 1760. 1st Ed. 6 vols. 4to, contemp calf; worn, some covers detached. Library markings. O Mar 5 (32) $1,800

**Brissot de Warville, Jacques-Pierre, 1754-93**
— Nouveau Voyage dans les Etats-Unis. Paris, 1791. 1st Ed. 3 vols. 8vo, contemp calf; spines scuffed, joints cracked. Some browning & underlining; library markings. bbc Dec 18 (441) $290

**Bristed, John, 1778-1855**
— The Resources of the United States of America.... NY, 1818. 1st Ed. 8vo, modern pigskin. Last leaf with chip affecting text. pba June 13 (255) $80

**Bristol...**
— Bristol: A Satire. L, 1794. 4to, disbound. Some spotting. Ck Sept 8 (241) £1,700

## BRITAINE

**Britaine, William de**
— Humane Prudence, or, the Art by which a Man may Raise Himself...by A. B. L: Richard Sare, 1702. ("Human Prudence, or the Art....") 9th Ed. 12mo, contemp calf; glue along joints. pba Nov 30 (69) $140

**British...**
— The British Essayists. L, 1823. Ed by Alexander Chambers. 38 vols. 12mo, contemp calf. sg Sept 21 (5) $850
— British Hunts and Huntsmen.... L, 1908-11. 4 vols. Folio, half mor; rubbed, corner of 3 vols chewed (mice or puppy). O Jan 9 (59) $300
— The British Plutarch. L, 1816. 6 vols. 8vo, contemp half mor; corners bumped, edges scuffed. F Mar 28 (168) $90
— British Sports and Sportsmen. L: Sports and Sportsmen Ltd., [1908-33?]. Royal Ed, One of 250. 12 (of 15) vols. Folio, orig mor gilt. S Mar 29 (786) £600

**British American Land Company**
— Views in Lower Canada. L, 1836. Illus by Robert Shore Milnes Bouchette. Oblong 4to, orig wraps; upper cover marked. With litho title & 7 uncolored plates. S Nov 30 (135) $900

**British Library.** See: British Museum

**British Museum—London**
— The Art of Central Asia. The Stein Collection.... 1982. One of 550. Compiled by Roderick Whitfield. 3 vols. b May 30 (187) £1,200
— The Book of the Dead. L, 1894. 2d Ed. - Ed by E. A. Wallis Budge. Folio, contemp half mor; extremities rubbed. sg Sept 7 (136) $250

Anr Ed. 1895. Folio, contemp half mor. Library stamps. pba Nov 30 (71) $225

Anr Ed. 1899. By E. A. Wallis Budge. Folio, later cloth; worn & scuffed. Library markings; some repairs; perforated stamp on tp. cb Oct 17 (188) $800

— Quarterly. 1926-40. Vols 1-14. Cloth. Library markings. sg Sept 7 (61) $150

### Catalogues
— Artificial Curiosities from the Northwest Coast of America.... 1981. In dj. pba Feb 13 (96) $120
— Books Printed in the XVth Century.... L, 1908-63. Vols I-IX in 10 vols. Folio, cloth & cloth over bds; some loose. Sold w.a.f. ds July 27 (42) $400

Anr Ed. 1963-85. Vols I-X & 2 vols of facsimiles. Folio, half cloth. bba Oct 5 (25) £650 [Bosio]

Anr Ed. 1963-[62]. 12 vols, including 2 vols of facsimiles. Folio, half cloth. Ck Apr 12 (210) £700

— Catalogue of Books printed in the XVth Century. L, 1908-71. Vols I-X. Folio, half cloth; vol II-X rebacked in buckram, vol I shaken. sg Apr 11 (144) $800

— Catalogue of Seventeenth Century Italian Books. [L, 1988]. 3 vols. 8vo, orig cloth. sg Apr 11 (65) $140

## AMERICAN BOOK PRICES CURRENT

— Drawings by Dutch and Flemish Artists.... 1915-32. Compiled by Arthur M. Hind & A. E. Popham. 5 vols. bba Oct 5 (224) £340 [Sims]
— Early German and Flemish Woodcuts.... Vaduz, 1980. Compiled by Campbell Dodgson. 2 vols. Orig cloth. Reprint. sg June 13 (135) $140
— Early Italian Engravings.... 1910-9. Compiled by Arthur M. Hind. 2 vols. bba Oct 5 (225) £220 [Bologna]; sg Sept 7 (184) $350
— Engraved British Portraits.... 1908-25. Compiled by Freeman O'Donoghue & Henry M. Hake. 6 vols, including Supplements & Indexes. Orig cloth & later cloth; rubbed, some joints split. Library markings. bba Oct 5 (226) £180 [Simon]
— General Catalogue of Printed Books. NY: Readex, 1967-69. 27 vols plus 5 Supplements. 4to, cloth. bba Oct 5 (340) £540 [Cizdyn]

Anr Ed. NY: Readex, 1967. 27 vols. 4to, orig cloth. ds July 27 (38) $325

— The Harleian Manuscripts in the British Museum. 1808-12. 4 vols. Contemp half calf; rebacked. R. W. Hunt's copy. bba May 9 (78) £110 [Bennett & Kerr]
— List of Catalogues of English Book Sales, 1676-1900. L, 1915. 8vo, orig cloth; spine faded. sg Apr 11 (17) $90
— Political and Personal Satires. 1870-1978. Vols 1-11 in 12. bba Oct 5 (227) £1,200 [Schffler]

Anr copy. Vol V only. F Mar 28 (33) $100

— Reproductions of Drawings by Old Masters. L, 1888-1894. 4 parts in 1 vol. Folio, contemp half mor; rubbed. With 84 plates on 77 leaves. Some spotting. S Oct 27 (960) £150 [Reiden]
— A Short Title Catalogue of French Books, 1601-1700.... Folkestone, 1973. Compiled by V. F. Goldsmith. 4to, orig cloth. sg Apr 11 (64) $175
— Short-Title Catalogue of Books Printed in Italy and Italian Books Printed in Other Countries from 1465 to 1600. L., 1958. 8vo, orig cloth; spine faded. sg Apr 11 (59) $80
— Short-Title Catalogue of Books Printed in the German-Speaking Countries..... L, 1958. 8vo, orig cloth; spine faded. sg Apr 11 (60) $100
— Short-Title Catalogue of Books printed in the Netherlands and Belgium and of the Dutch and Flemish Books printed in Other Countries from 1470 to 1600. L, 1965. 8vo, orig cloth in dj. sg Apr 11 (61) $150
— STC French. 1966. ("Short-Title Catalogue of Books Printed in France....") ds July 27 (39) $80
— STC German. 1962. ("Short-Title Catalogue of Books Printed in the German-Speaking Countries.....") ds July 27 (40) $60
— STC Spanish. 1966. ("Short-Title Catalogues of Spanish, Spanish-American, and Portuguese Books printed before 1601.") In dj. ds July 27 (41) $70

**British Musical Miscellany...**
— The British Musical Miscellany, or, the Delightful Grove.... L, 1734-37. 6 vols in 3. 8vo, contemp calf; some wear, a few leaves loose. Engraved through, with 3 frontises. S Dec 1 (104) £750

## British Poets
— The Poets of Great Britain. Edin., 1776-92. Ed by John Bell. 105 vols only. 18mo, calf. Sold w.a.f. b Sept 20 (165) £350

**Britten, Benjamin, 1913-76.** See: Plomer & Britten

## Britten, James, 1846-1924
— European Ferns. L, [1879-81]. 4to, half calf; extremities worn. With 30 colored plates. sg Dec 7 (214) $90

## Britton, John, 1771-1857
See also: Bourne & Britton
— Picturesque Antiquities of the English Cities. L, 1836. Illus by W. H. Bartlett. 4to, orig cloth; spine def. With 60 plates. b May 30 (95) £320

## Britton, John, 1771-1857 —& Brayley, Edward Wedlake, 1773-1854
— The Beauties of England and Wales.... L, 1801-18. 19 vols in 26. 8vo, contemp calf gilt; rubbed, a few spines torn. C July 1 (329) £550
— Devonshire & Cornwall Illustrated. L, 1832-31. 2 vols in 1. 4to, contemp half calf; def: With engraved titles, 2 maps & 116 views on 67 plates. Some staining. b Sept 20 (301) £150
— A Topographical and Historical Description of the County of Cumberland. L, [1802]. 4 vols. 4to, recent half mor. With 10 plates. Sold w.a.f. Extra-illus with 120 plates & with text from The Beauties of England and Wales. S Mar 28 (37) £680

## Britwell Court Library
— The Britwell Handlist, or Short-Title Catalogue.... L, 1933. 2 vols. 4to, cloth; soiled, upper cover & front endpapers of Vol I stained. bba May 9 (113) £50 [Brinded]

**Britzman, Homer Elwood.** See: Adams & Britzman

## Brizard, Gabriel, 1744?-93
— Analyse du voyage pittoresque de Naples et de Sicile.... Paris, 1787. 8vo, orig wraps. Fuerstenberg - Schaefer copy. S Dec 8 (562) £280

## Brize-Fradin, C. A.
— La Chimie pneumatique appliquee aux travaux sous l'eau.... Paris, 1808. 8vo, contemp half russia; spine ends chipped, joints cracked. Marginal stains in text; plates foxed. sg May 16 (141) $140

## Broadsides
— [California] Decree of the Republic of Mexico regarding representation of Alta and Baja California in the National Congress. Mexico, Oct 26 1835. 11-1/2in by 8in Single sheet in Spanish, with holograph notations. Larson copy. pba Sept 28 (54) $190
— A Comparative View of the Natural Small-Pox, Inoculated Small-Pox & Vaccination in their Effects on Individuals & Society. Phila.: Jane Aitken, 1803. 17.6 by 10 inches. Repaired on verso, affecting a few letters. K Feb 11 (266) $1,900
— Disputatio medica.... Louvan: [1750]. 475mm by 390mm, framed & glazed. Ck Mar 22 (100) £300

— Donner Party. Sacramento: H.S. Crocker, [c.1879]. ("Terrible! Thrilling! True! History of the Donner Party [advertisement for his book by C. F. McGlashan].") 11in by 14in Soiled. Larson copy. pba Sept 28 (420) $350
AFRICAN-AMERICAN MILITARY. - The Military and Historical Portrait Group of the Officers of the Third North Carolina U. S. V. Infantry in the War with Spain.... Ashville: Capt. Thomas L. Leatherwood, [c.1899]. 23.75 by 35.25 inches. Foxed. sg Mar 28 (204) $2,600
AMERICAN REVOLUTION. - In Congress, June 6, 1778 [resolving that subsistence money be extended to all troops called into the Continental service]. Yorktown: John Dunlap, 1778. 4to size. rms Nov 30 (59) $1,900
BIRTH CONTROL. - Mothers! Can you afford to have a large family? [Announcement for the clinic at 46 Amboy Street, Brooklyn]. [NY, 1920s]. 309mm by 233mm. In English, Yiddish & Italian. Sold w.a.f. Sgd by Margaret Sanger. sg Oct 26 (19) $400
BOSTON. - Declaration of Sentiments of the Colored Citizens of Boston on the Fugitive Slave Bill!!! Bost, [1850]. 575mm by 410mm. Some foxing & fold creases. P June 5 (40) $2,750
CALIFORNIA. - The Names of the President and Senators of the First Senate of the State of California Convened at the Capitol at San Jose, December the 15th, One Thousand Eight Hundred and Forty Nine. [San Francisco, 1849]. 20.7cm by 26.8cm. 2 small splits at former fold repaired with archival tape. pba Feb 12 (542) $130
CALIFORNIA GOLD RUSH. - Acts of the Congress... Seamen, Merchants [agreement for shipping aboard the Bark Josephine of NY to San Francisco & other ports]. NY, 1849. 595mm by 460mm. Fold breaks; marginal staining. cb June 25 (1705) $425
CIVIL WAR, AMERICAN. - The Eighty-First Ohio [honoring a Union victory in Oct 1862]. Cincinnati: Time Print, 1862. 355mm by 430mm. Minor creasing. sg Oct 26 (63) $225
CIVIL WAR, AMERICAN. - "Let Us Forgive, But Not Forget" [Andersonville, with detailed sketch of the prison]. Chicago, [n.d.]. 27 by 20.5 inches, Framed. cb June 25 (2422) $600
CIVIL WAR, AMERICAN. - "The Surrender of Fort Sumter!" [N.p.]: Morning Herald Extra, 14 Apr 1861. 21 by 8 inches, framed. cb June 25 (2477) $1,000
CONFEDERACY. - Proclamation. To the Inhabitants of Kentucky! [by Gen. John Hunt Morgan, calling Kentuckians to the cause of the Confederacy]. Monticello TN: Morgan's Press Print, 22 Aug 1862. 430mm by 223mm, mtd. CNY Dec 15 (102) $7,000
COPENHAGEN. - Eigentiche Abbildung (und wahrhaffter Bericht) der kon:Dennem. Residentz Stadt Kopenhagen, sampt dero Fortification, wie auch welcher gestald der Koenig von Schweden An. 1658 den 9 Augusti St. Vet dieser Stadt zu belagern anfangen. [Danzig?], 1659. 3 sheets joined, 755mm by 418mm, mtd. Engraving sgd Jo. Benshiemer. Mtd & restored. S June 13 (518) £350
DICKENS, CHARLES. - Free Trade Hall, Manchester. On Wednesday Evening, February 11th, 1852 [for Bulwer-Lytton's Not So Bad as We Seem & for Mr.

# BROADSIDES

Nightingale's Diary by Dickens & Mark Lemon, the whole directed by Dickens]. [Manchester, 1852]. 480mm by 246mm, framed. Patch with facsimile to c.1-inch hole. Sold w.a.f. CE Feb 21 (90) $480

GENOA. - Convenzione stipulata in Montebello presso a Milano li 5 e 6 Giugno 1797....[creation of the Ligurian Republic]. Genoa, [1797]. Folio size. b Dec 5 (170) £90

HANNIBAL & ST. JOSEPH RAIL ROAD. - The Hannibal & St. Joseph Rail Road Co Offers for Sale over 500,000 Acres.... Bost., [c.1860s]. 13.5 by 45 inches. Showing the lands throughout Missouri. wa Feb 29 (645) $325

HOSMER, HEZEKIAH LORD. - Charge of Chief Justice Hosmer, to the Grand Jury of the First Judicial District, M.T., Delivered, December 5th, 1864. [Virginia, 1864]. Folio size, triple column. Tear & ship in upper margin, affecting 2 words. sg Oct 26 (264) $950

JACKSON, ANDREW. - Bill of Fare. 1st Division Pa. Militia [menus with relief cuts, including the affray involving Jackson & Thomas hart Benton in a Nashville tavern in 1813 & Jackson whipping his slaves] [Pennsylvania, c.1828]. 23 by 12 inches. Some fold breaks with minor loss; marginal tear near bottom edge; some foxing. K June 23 (33) $1,700

KANE, ELISHA KENT. - Dr. Kane's Arctic Voyages. Phila., 1857. 555mm by 205mm. sg Mar 7 (274) $200

KEARNEY, STEPHEN WATTS. - Proclamation. Proclama. To the People of California. The President of the United States... [inaugural address]. Monterey, 1 Mar, 1847. 12-1/2in by 8-1/2in, chemise folder & cloth slipcase. Larson copy. pba Sept 28 (546) $9,000

LINCOLN, ABRAHAM. - Ford's Theatre...Night 191...Friday evening, April 14th, 1865. This Evening the Performance will be honored by the presence of President Lincoln...Tom Taylor's Celebrated Eccentric Comedy...Our American Cousin.... [N.p., n.d.]. Later ptg. 455mm by 130mm. Repaired. sg Oct 26 (214) $325

LINCOLN, ABRAHAM. - Proclamation!! The remains of our late lamented President [arrival in York PA en route to Springfield] York PA, 1865. 230mm by 140mm. Issued by Chief Burgess David Small, dated 21 Apr with year added in later typewriter type. sg Oct 26 (219) $300

LOS ANGELES. - Martin Tract! Fifty Lots for Sale. Los Angeles: T. E. Rowan, [before 1888]. 18.25 by 11.5 inches, corner-mtd on stiff bd. pba Feb 12 (427) $140

LOUISIANA. - E Pluribus Unum. United America. Louisiana. By William C. C. Glaiborne, Governor of the Mississibbi, exercising the powers of Governor-General and Intendant of the Province of Louisiana [shipping regulations for vessels anchoring at New Orleans]. New Orleans, 29 Dec 1803. 430mm by 315mm. Posting holes at corners; old tape repairs to margins. Schwartz - Parsons - Engelhard copy. CNY Jan 26 (175) $12,000

LOUISIANA. - Proclamation au nom de la Republique Francaise. Laussat, prefet colonial, aux Louisianais. New Orleans, 6 Apr 1803. 556mm by 403mm. Some small holes. P June 5 (79) $2,500

MASSACHUSETTS. - Commonwealth of Massachusetts... a Proclamation, for a Day of Public Thanksgiving. Bost., 1802. 565mm by 455mm. Loss at intersecting folds, not affecting text; some fold breaks. sg Oct 26 (24) $150

MONSTROUS SERPENT. - Description of a Monstrous Serpent, which was Discovered Near the Banks of the Ohio River, in Kentucky, January 1815, and Killed by Three Soldiers. [Phila., 1815]. 533mm by 441mm. Ink burn holes to 2 letters of headline. P June 5 (64) $1,700

NATIONAL ASSOCIATION FOR THE ADVANCEMENT OF COLORED PEOPLE. - "For the Good of America" [about lynching & mob violence & aid to the NAACP]. NY, 1922. 15 by 10.75 inches. Edges rippled; lacking top right corner; bottom left corner torn. bbc Dec 18 (505) $270

NORTHERN PACIFIC RAILROAD. - New 7-30 Gold Loan of the Northern Pacific Railroad Co. Secured by First Mortgage on Railroad and Land Grant.... Quincy IL, [c.1880]. 15.75 by 8.75 inches. Double column of text on recto; map on verso. Minor tears. pba Apr 25 (610) $60

PACIFIC COAST MAIL. - To Persons Mailing Letters for California and the Territories of Oregon and Washington. Wash., 5 Mar 1856. 14 by 8.25 inches. Some soiling & staining; piece cut out of lower margin, affecting last line of text; 2 marginal holes. pba Apr 25 (324) $120

PIOUS FUND. - Primera Secretaria de Estado Departamento del Interior... Art. 1. El gobierno procedera al arrendamiento de las fincas rusticas pertenecientes al fondo piadoso de Californias.... [Mexico, 1832]. 11-3/4 in by 8-1/4 inches. Robbins-Streeter copy. pba Mar 21 (282) $225

SLAVERY. - Injured Humanity, being a Representation of what the unhappy Children of Africa endure.... NY: Samuel Wood, [c.1830]. 16.5 by 17 inches. Chipped, affecting border. sg Mar 28 (274) $450

TEXAS & ARKANSAS. - Cheap Land. Easy Terms. Good Climate. Rich Soil. Choice Markets. Free Range. Central Homes. Chicago, [c.1876]. Below advertising is a 16.25 by 15.25 inch map. wa Feb 29 (684) $270

TITANIC. - "One of the Two Largest Steamers in the World". [N.p.], Dec 1911. 40 by 30 inches. cb June 25 (2585) $450

TORNEL, JOSE MARIA. - Decree of the President of the United States of mexico to secularize the missions and open California to colonization. Mexico, Dec 2 1833. English trans by Christian Devaux. 12-1/2in by 7-3/4in Larson copy. pba Sept 28 (186) $180

WASHINGTON, GEORGE. - Ode on Washington and Days of Absence. Bost., [1789]. 220mm by 200mm. With 3 small holes, affecting 2 letters of text; wrinkled. K June 23 (503) $325

Anr copy. With 3 small holes, affecting 2 letters of text. sg Oct 26 (386) $2,400

WHITE STAR LINE. - Leaving New York Every Saturday...[White Star Line, New York & Liverpool]. [N.p., 19th cent]. 16 by 24.5 inches. With center oval of a ship, surrounded by 4 smaller views of accomodations.. rce July 25 (90) $1,600

**Brock, Alan St. H.**
— A History of Fireworks. L, [1949]. In rubbed dj with closed tear. With 8 color plates. pba Aug 8 (408) $60

**Brockedon, William, 1787-1854**
— Illustrations of the Passes of the Alps.... L, 1828-29. 2 vols. 4to, old cloth; rebacked in calf. With double-page map & 108 plates. L.p. copy. bba Nov 1 (306) £700 [Valentine]
Anr copy. Contemp half mor; some wear, some hinges cracked, front free endpaper of Vol I detached. With 96 plates & 12 maps with hand-colored highlights. Some foxing. bbc Feb 26 (460) $650
Anr copy. Contemp half mor; rubbed. With 96 plates & 12 (of 13) maps. Some marginal dampstaining in Vol I. S June 13 (541) £520
Anr Ed. L, [1877]. 2 vols. 4to, contemp half calf; rebacked preserving orig spines, rubbed. With double-page map & 108 plates. Some foxing. bba June 6 (42) £600 [Frew]

**Brockett, Paul**
— Bibliography of Aeronautics, 1925. Wash., 1928. 4to, cloth. sg May 16 (14) $250

**Brocklesby, Richard, 1722-97**
— Oeconomical and Medical Observations in Two Parts.... L, 1764. 1st Ed. 8vo, contemp calf; extrems rubbed. Browned. Inscr. Ck Mar 22 (59) £680

**Brockway, Thomas**
— The Gospel Tragedy: an Epic Poem.. Worcester: James R. Hutchins, 1795. Frontis by Amos Doolittle. 12mo, contemp calf; rubbed. Some browning & foxing. Isaiah Thomas Jr.'s copy, sgd. O Nov 14 (31) $250

**Brockwell, Maurice W.**
— A Catalogue of some of the Paintings of the British School in the Collection of Henry Edwards Huntington at San Marino, Ca. NY, 1925. 4to, orig cloth. Inscr by Joseph Duveen. bba May 30 (6) £180 [Mandl]

**Brodie, Walter**
— Pitcairn's Island and the Islanders in 1850.... L, 1851. 8vo, orig cloth; rubbed. b Mar 20 (164) £120
2d Ed. 8vo, orig cloth; spine faded, ends frayed. With 3 plates. Some foxing. Robbins copy. pba Mar 21 (35) $170

**Bromley, A. Nelson**
— A Fly Fisher's Reflection 1860-1930. L: The Fishing Gazette, 1930. pba July 11 (43) $110

**Bronson, William**
— How to Kill a Golden State. Garden City, 1968. In d/j Larson copy. pba Feb 12 (56) $60

**Bronte, Charlotte, 1816-55**
— Jane Eyre. L, 1847. 1st Ed. 3 vols. 8vo, orig cloth; bdg a little loose, corners worn. Some foxing & spotting. Parsons - Engelhard copy. CNY Oct 27 (6) $19,000
Anr Ed. Bost., 1848. 8vo, orig cloth; spine ends worn, hinges repaired. Some foxing. CE May 22 (64) $1,100
Anr Ed. L, 1898. 2 vols. 8vo, half mor. sg Feb 8 (64) $90
— The Professor. L, 1857. 1st Ed. 2 vols. 8vo, later mor, orig cloth back covers & spine of Vol I bound in; soiled. Lacking ads in Vol I; pp. 83-94 supplied in facsimile. Sold w.a.f. F June 20 (453) $140
Anr copy. Orig cloth; bumped, upper hinge to Vol I cracked. S July 11 (136) £580
1st American Ed. NY, 1857. 8vo, modern cloth. sg Feb 8 (190) $200
— Shirley. L, 1849. 1st Ed. 3 vols. 8vo, orig cloth; repaired, hinges cracked. Marginal soiling; some spotting. CE May 22 (65) $2,200
Anr copy. Orig cloth; spine ends worn. Jones - Newton - Doheny - Manney copy. S Dec 18 (163) £3,000 [Copus]
Anr copy. Orig cloth; hinges repaired, joints to Vol I split. Edges of Vol I dampstained. S July 11 (137) £1,100
1st American Ed. NY, 1850. 8vo, half mor. Foxed. pba Aug 8 (347) $70
— Villette. L, 1853. 1st Ed. 3 vols. 8vo, orig cloth; Vol I rebacked with orig spine strip laid on, spine ends chipped. pba Nov 30 (70) $1,000

**Bronte, Charlotte, Emily & Anne**
— Poems by Currer, Ellis, and Acton Bell. L, 1846. 1st Ed, 2d Issue. 8vo, orig cloth. Tp with owner's stamp; some foxing; without errata slip. S July 11 (135) £980
— Works. L, 1899-1900. Haworth Ed. 7 vols. 8vo, half mor. b Jan 31 (62) £350
Thornton Ed. Edin., 1907. Ed by Temple Scott. 12 vols. Half mor. b Sept 20 (558) £800
Anr Ed. L, 1909. 12 vols. Half mor; rubbed. cb Oct 17 (320) $1,300
Anr Ed. Edin., 1911. Ed by T. Scott. 12 vols. 8vo, mor gilt. cb Oct 17 (264) $1,600
Anr Ed. Edin., 1924. Ed by Temple Scott. 12 vols. Orig cloth. b Jan 31 (61) £100

**Bronte, Emily, 1818-48**
See also: Limited Editions Club
— Wuthering Heights. NY, 1848. 2 vols. 8vo, orig ptd wraps; spine of Vol II chipped. Some foxing. sg Sept 21 (97) $2,400

**Bronte, Patrick, 1777-1861**
— Cottage Poems. Halifax, 1811. 1st Ed. 8vo, orig bds. b Dec 5 (428) £620

**Brook, Stephen**
— A Bibliography of the Gehenna Press, 1942-1975. Northampton MA, 1976. One of 50 specially bound by Carolyn Coman & with extra, sgd impression of the Barry Moser port of Leonard Baskin. sg Feb 15 (24) $200

**Brooke, Henry, 1703?-83**
— Three Silver Trouts from the Fool of Quality. Westport, 1947. One of 125. Half cloth; some wear. O June 25 (33) $70

**Brooke, Sir James, Rajah of Sarawak, 1803-68**
— Narrative of Events in Borneo and Celebes.... L, 1848. 1st Ed. - Ed by Capt. Rodney Mundy. 2 vols. 8vo, recent cloth. With port & 5 folding maps, 1 colored, & 5 tinted litho plates. Minor discoloration. S Mar 28 (401) $200

Anr copy. Orig cloth; recased, new endpapers. With 5 folding maps, 6 litho plates & 12 wood-engraved plates. Short tear to 1 folding map. S June 27 (250) £400

Anr copy. Early half calf; needs rebdg. With port, 5 maps & 17 plates. Titles & plates stamped. sg Mar 7 (195) $325

Anr copy. Later half mor; rubbed, spines chipped. With port, 17 plates & 5 folding, linen-backed maps. Signature & 1 plate in Vol II detached but present; 1 leaf in Vol I torn at gutter; some foxing. wa Nov 16 (140) $210

**Brooke, L. Leslie**
— The Story of the Three Bears. L: Frederick Warne, [n.d.]. Pictorial bds. pba Aug 22 (705) $50

**Brooke, Ralph, 1553-1625**
— A Catalogue and Succession of the Kings, Princes...of England.... L, 1619. Folio, 19th-cent calf gilt; worn, joints starting. Marginal foxing. sg Mar 21 (67) $325

2d Ed. L, 1622. Folio, 19th-cent calf; upper cover rubbed. Tp border trimmed; tear in upper margin of B1; fore-margin of C6 & S2 repaired. S Mar 28 (474) £260

**Brooke, Rupert, 1887-1915**
— Democracy and the Arts. L, 1946. 1st Ed, one of 240. Half mor. With port. sg June 20 (20) $80
— Poems. L, [1950]. Contemp half mor gilt by Sangorski & Sutcliffe. Cs & inscr by Stanley Bray inserted. F June 20 (724) $70
— Selected Poems. L, 1917. 1st Ed. In nicked dj. sg Dec 14 (18) $140

**Brookes, Richard**
— The Art of Angling, Rock and Sea-Fishing. L, 1740. 1st Ed. 12mo, contemp calf; rubbed. Some soiling & browning. O Feb 6 (39) $300

**Brookes, Richard, M.D.**
— Brookes's General Gazetteer Improved.... Phila., 1812. 8vo, orig sheep; spine heel frayed. With 11 maps. Some dampstaining. sg Oct 26 (25) $130
— A New and Accurate System of Natural History. L, 1763. 6 vols. 12mo, mor, gilt by Lloyd, Wallis & Lloyd; hinges worn; Vol IV cover detached. CE Nov 8 (173) $220

Anr copy. Contemp calf gilt; joints def. With 148 plates. S Nov 2 (165) £220 [Bickersteth]

**Brooks, Charles E.**
— The Henry's Fork. Piscataway: Winchester Press, [1986]. One of 500. 4to, syn. O Feb 6 (40) $170

**Brooks, Elisha**
— A Pioneer Mother of California. San Francisco, 1922. Orig cloth. With frontis & 1 port. Larson copy. pba Sept 28 (330) $80

**Brooks, J. Tyrwhitt**
— Four Months Among the Gold-finders in Alta California.... L, 1849. 1st English Ed. Orig cloth; some wear. With frontis map. Some foxing. Larson copy. pba Sept 28 (331) $850

**Brooks, Juanita**
— The Mountain Meadows Massacre. Stanford, [1950]. In dj. pba Apr 25 (314) $75

**Brooks, Van Wyck, 1886-1963.** See: Limited Editions Club

**Brooks, Van Wyck, 1886-1963 —& Wheelock, John Hall**
— Verses by Two Undergraduates. [Cambr., Mass.: Privately ptd], 1905. 1st Ed. Orig wraps; spine cracked & mended. Inscr by Wheelock. Goodwin - Engelhard copy. CNY Oct 27 (7) $400

**Brookshaw, George**
— Groups of Flowers [Groups of Fruit... Six Birds...]. L, 1819. 2d Ed. 3 parts in 1 vol. 4to, half lea gilt; rubbed, edges worn. With 18 plates, each in 2 states, plain & hand-colored. Met Feb 24 (435) $1,700

Anr copy. Calf gilt. pnE Sept 20 (230) £1,100

Anr copy. 3 parts in 1 vol. Folio contemp mor; rubbed, joints repaired. With 18 plates. Some spotting & offsetting. S Oct 27 (706) £1,000 [Kennedy]
— The Horticultural Repository.... L, [1820]-23. 2 vols. 8vo, modern half calf. With 98 (of 104) hand-colored plates. C May 31 (11) £6,200
— A New Treatise on Flower Painting.... L, 1816. 1st Ed. 4to, orig cloth; rebacked with spine laid down. With 22 (of 24) plates, 14 colored. Some foxing; 1 plate torn & repaired. Met Feb 24 (434) $350

Anr Ed. L, 1818. 4to, orig bds, in modern cloth wraps. With 25 plates, 12 in both hand-colored & uncolored states. C May 31 (10) £1,600
— Pomona Britannica. L, [1804]-12. 1st Ed in Book form. Folio, contemp mor gilt; spine rubbed, joints strengthened, corners repaired, modern doublures & endleaves. With 90 colored plates, finished by hand. Vertical crease to tp & last leaf, both laid down; vertical crease to dedication leaf; lower outer corner of tp & 1st 6 leaves repaired; tear in lower blank margin of Plate XVI. C May 31 (12) £58,000

**Brosamer, Hans**
— Biblia veteris testamenti et historiae artificiosis picturis effigiata. Frankfurt: Hermann Guelfferich, 1553. 3 parts in 1 vol. 8vo, contemp blind-stamped pigskin gilt; spine wormed at head. With 274 woodcuts in text. Bb7 of Part 3 torn out; small portion of outer margin of I7 in Part 1 burnt away without loss;

small portion of woodcut on Bb1 recto in Part 3 rubbed with loss; staining in margins. S Nov 30 (249) £2,500

— Ein new kunstbuechlein von mancherly schoenen Trinckgeschiren zu gut der yebenden jugend der Goldschmidt.... Nuremberg: Jobst Gutnecht, [c.1538]. 4to, modern calf. With 38 full-page woodcuts. Tp with small slip pasted on correcting Godschmidt misprint; retouching to 5th & 15th designs. C June 26 (50) £8,000

**Brossa, Joan —& Others**
— Miro: Obra inedita recent. Barcelona, 1964. One of 1,000. 4to, unsewn in orig wraps. pba Aug 22 (810) $80

**Brosses, Charles de, 1709-77**
— Catalogues et armoiries des gentilhommes qui ont assiste a la tenue des Etats generaux... de Bourgogne. Dijon: Jean Francois Durand, 1760. Folio, contemp calf; joints cracked. With frontis & 36 plates plus additional plate for the years 1760 & 1763, plus 2 loose plates for the years 1766, 1769 & 1772. Fuerstenberg - Schaefer copy. S Dec 7 (84) £220

**Brothers, Richard**
— A Revealed Knowledge of the Prophecies and Times.... L, 1794. Bound with: Halhead, Nathaniel Brassey. Testimony of the Authenticity of the Prophecie of Richard Brothers. L, 1795. And: The Prophecy of Humphrey Tindal.... L, 1795. 8vo, 19th-cent calf gilt; soiled. Some leaves stained. Robert Southey's copy. S Apr 23 (10) £360

**Brough, Robert Barnabas, 1828-60**
— Shadow and Substance. L, 1860. Illus by Charles Bennett. 8vo, contemp mor gilt; rebacked. With 30 hand-colored plates. CE Sept 27 (51) £220

**Broughton, William Robert, 1762-1821**
— A Voyage of Discovery to the North Pacific Ocean. L, 1804. 1st Ed. 4to, modern half calf. With 9 plates & maps. Some soiling & dampstaining; the 2 large charts & 1 folding plate backed & repaired. pba Feb 13 (3) $4,250

**Brown, Abbie Farwell, d.1927**
— The Lonesomest Doll. Bost., 1928. Illus by Arthur Rackham. With colored title, 3 colored plates & 26 illusts. Ck May 31 (160) £320

**Brown, Alan K.** See: Stanger & Brown

**Brown, Bob**
— Words. Paris: Hours Press, 1931. One of 150. Orig bds with lea spine; soiled. Hobson copy. S June 28 (152) £320

**Brown, Charles Brockden, 1771-1810**
— Wieland: or the Transformation. An American Tale. NY: T. & J. Swords, for H. Caritat, 1798. 12mo, contemp sheep; worn, spine ends chipped, joints starting. Foxed; ink numbers on verso of rear blank. wa Feb 29 (25) $230

**Brown, Dee.** See: Schmitt & Brown

**Brown, Fredric**
— Angels and Spaceships. NY, 1954. In dj. pba May 4 (115) $160
— Space on my Hands. Chicago: Sasta Publishers, [1951]. In dj with small tears. Sgd. pba May 4 (116) $150
— What Mad Universe. NY, 1949. In dj with short tears. pba May 4 (114) $150

**Brown, Glenn**
— History of the United States Capitol. Wash., 1900-2. 2 vols. Folio, orig cloth; spine ends worn & frayed, hinges cracked. wa Feb 1 (96) $110

**Brown, J. Lewis**
— Golf at Glens Falls. Glens Falls, NY: Glens Falls Country Club, [1923]. 1st Ed. Bds. With frontis map. pba Apr 18 (15) $100

**Brown, James S.**
— California Gold... History of the First Find.... Salt Lake City, 1894. 1st Ed. 12mo, orig wraps in folder & slipcase. With frontis port. Larson copy. pba Sept 28 (332) $800

**Brown, Jane**
— Fulbrook...The Sketchbook, Letters, Specification... House by Edwin Lutyens, 1896-1899. Marlborough: Libanus Press, 1989. 2 vols. Half mor. sg June 13 (3) $130

**Brown, John, of Osawatomie, 1850-59**
— The Life and Letters of Captain John Brown.... L, 1861. Ed by Richard Webb. 12mo, orig cloth; spine ends chipped, 1 signature sprung. With albumen print of Brown as frontis. wa Feb 29 (321) $950

**Brown Library, John Carter**
— European Americana: A Chronological Guide.... NY, 1980-87. Ed by John Alden & Dennis C. Landis. 3 vols. 4to, cloth. ds July 27 (4) $300

**Brown, John Henry, 1810-1905**
See also: Grabhorn Printing
— Reminiscences and Incidents, of "The Early Days" of San Francisco. San Francisco, [1886]. 8vo, cloth; front cover soiled, front hinge cracked. pba Feb 12 (253) $325

**Brown, Leslie.** See: Fennessy & Brown

**Brown, Margaret Wise**
— Little Pig's Panic and Other Stories. Bost., [1939]. Illus by Walt Disney Studio. pba Mar 7 (92) $75

**Brown, Dr. O. Phelps**
— The Complete Herbalist, or the People Their Own Physicians.... Jersey City, 1865. Cloth; covers spotted. pba Aug 8 (348) $120

**Brown, Paul.** See: Derrydale Press

**Brown, Peter, fl.1776**
— New Illustrations of Zoology. L, 1776. 4to, mor gilt with stamp of the house of Commons Library; rebacked. With 50 hand-colored plates. Spotting on margin of 3 plates; some marginal waterstaining. C May 31 (14) £15,000

**Brown, R. N. Rudmore —& Others**
— A Naturalist at the Poles. The Life, Work & Voyages of Dr. W. S. Bruce the Polar Explorer. Phila., 1924. 1st American Ed. pba July 25 (17) $100

**Brown, Samuel R., 1775-1817**
— The Western Gazetteer, or Emigrant's Directory.... Albany, 1817. 1st Ed, 3d Issue. 8vo, contemp calf; worn, joints weak. Browned. wa Feb 29 (391) $80

**Brown, Capt. Thomas**
— Illustrations of the Recent Conchology of Great Britain and Ireland. L, 1844. 2d Ed. 4to, contemp half mor; rubbed. With 62 colored plates. Some foxing & soiling. O Mar 5 (33) $700

**Brown, William Robinson.** See: Derrydale Press

**Browne, Belmore**
— Guns and Gunning. Chicopee Falls MA: J. Stevens Arms & Tool, [1908]. Ed by Dan Beard. Inscr by Beard to Frederick W. Skiff. pba July 11 (370) $120

**Browne, Edgar Athelstane**
— Phiz and Dickens as they Appeared.... L, 1913. One of 175. In torn dj. bba May 30 (172) £90 [Devitt]

**Browne, Edward, 1644-1708**
— Durch Niederland, Teutschland, Hungarn, Servien, Bulgarien, Macedonien... gethane gantz sonderbare Reisen.... Nuremberg: Zieger, 1711. 4to, contemp calf; rubbed, upper joint broken, upper cover wormed. With engraved frontis & 18 plates, some folding. Some foxing & browning; marginal repairs to a few plates. O Mar 26 (45) $400

**Browne, G. Lathom —& Stewart, C. G.**
— Reports on Trials for Murder by Poisoning.... L, 1883. 8vo, orig cloth; fornt hinge cracked. sg May 16 (384) $175

**Browne, George, A.M.**
— Arithmetica infinita; or the Accurate Accomptant's Best Companion.... [Edin., 1718). Oblong 12mo, contemp calf; notes on front free endpapers, scuffed. pba Sept 14 (81) $275

**Browne, John, 1642-1700**
— Myographia Nova: or, a Graphical Description of all the Muscles in the Humane Body. L, 1698. Folio, contemp calf gilt; rebacked, corners rubbed. With port & 41 plates. Lacking G1; damage to verso of F2; some browning & rust-holes. Subscriber's copy of Peirce Dent. C June 26 (185) £500

**Browne, John Ross, 1817-75**
— Adventures in Apache Country.... NY, 1869. 1st Ed. 12mo, orig cloth; spine ends frayed, hinges tender. Robbins copy. pba Mar 21 (36) $600
— Adventures in the Apache Country.... NY, 1869 [1868]. 1st Ed. 12mo, orig cloth; soiled, spine & edges worn. wa Feb 29 (309) $110
— Relacion de los debates de la Convencion de California.... NY, 1851. 1st Spanish Ed. 8vo, orig calf; scuffed, spine top chipped, front joint cracked, rear joint starting. Some darkening. Larson copy. pba Sept 28 (345) $50
— Report of the Debates in the Convention of California, on the Formation of the State Constitution.... Wash., 1850. 1st Ed. 8vo, orig cloth; spine ends & corners worn, hinges repaired. Marginal stain to 1st 44 pages. Robbins copy. pba Mar 21 (37) $400
1st English Ed. 8vo, orig cloth; spine top chipped. Larson copy. pba Sept 28 (344) $550

**Browne, Maggie, Pseud.**
— The Surprising Adventures of Tuppy and Tue. L, 1904. Illus by Arthur Rackham. Orig cloth; extremities rubbed. With 4 colored plates. Light marginal staining. Ck May 31 (122) £140
— Two Old Ladies, Two Foolish Fairies and a Tom Cat. L, 1897. Illus by Arthur Rackham. 8vo, modern cloth, orig cloth & spine labels laid down; new endpapers. With 4 colored plates. Tear at margin of 1 plate; some stains. Ck May 31 (110) £170

**Browne, Mary Ann**
— Ignatia, and other Poems. Liverpool, 1838. 8vo, orig cloth. b Dec 5 (182) £65

**Browne, Moses**
— Piscatory Eclogues: An Essay to Introduce New Rules, and New Characters into Pastora. L, 1729. 8vo, half calf; rebacked with corners replaced. Thomas Westwood's copy. pba July 11 (45) $600

**Browne, Sir Thomas, 1605-82**
See also: Limited Editions Club
— Certain Miscellany Tracts. L, 1684. 1st Ed, 2d Issue. 8vo, contemp calf; worn, broken. Tp stamped; lacking port. sg Mar 21 (70) $120
— Hydriotaphia, Urne-Buriall.... L, 1932. ("Urne Buriall and the Garden of Cyrus.") One of 215. Ed by John Carter; illus by Paul Nash. Folio, orig vellum with mor panel with gilt & inlaid design by Nash. Inscr by Carter & Nash to Richard Smart. S May 16 (124) £2,000
Anr copy. Inlaid vellum by Sangorski & Sutcliffe. sg Sept 14 (265) $1,700
— Pseudodoxia Epidemica.... L, 1646. 1st Ed. Folio, contemp calf; spine def, rear joint cracked. Ink blot on p. 1; marginal tears in b2 & 2P1. sg Mar 21 (68) $350
4th Ed. L, 1658. 4to, contemp calf; broken. sg Mar 21 (69) $150

**Browne, William, 1591-1643?.** See: Golden Cockerel Press

### Browne, William George
— Travels in Africa, Egypt, and Syria.... L, 1799. 1st Ed. 4to, contemp tree calf; repaired preserving orig spine, worn. With half title, frontis, & 2 folding maps. 1st few pp. stained; frontis repaired; 1st map repaired, maps spotted & offset.  S Oct 26 (21) £300 [Zioni]

### Brownell, Henry
— The Pioneer Heroes of the New World. Cincinnati, 1856. 8vo, orig mor; extremities worn.  sg Oct 26 (26) $60

### Browning, Elizabeth Barrett, 1806-61
See also: Browning & Browning; Fore-Edge Paintings; Limited Editions Club
— Poems. L, 1850. 2 vols. 12mo, modern half mor; new endpapers & binder's blanks. Stain at top edge of Vol II.  Z June 28 (40) $450
— Poems Before Congress. L, 1860. 1st Ed. 8vo, orig cloth; soiled. pba Dec 14 (15) $90

Anr copy. Orig cloth; extremities rubbed with loss of cloth to head. sg Feb 8 (191) $60
— Sonnets from the Portuguese. L: Vale Press, 1897. One of 300. 4to, mor extra to an abstract design by Sybil Pye, 1921. C May 1 (25) £4,200

Anr Ed. L: Riccardi Press, 1914. One of 1,000. pba Dec 14 (16) $90

Anr Ed. Montagnola: Officina Bodoni, 1925. One of 225. 4to, orig vellum. Ck May 31 (4) £240

### Browning, Robert
— A History of Golf, the Royal and Ancient Game. L, [1955]. 1st Ed. Cloth in dj; d/j chipped & torn. pba Nov 9 (3) $160

Anr Ed. L: Aldine Press for Sportsmans Book Club, 1956. Cloth. pba Apr 18 (16) $140

### Browning, Robert, 1812-89
See also: Doves Press; Eragny Press; Fore-Edge Paintings; Limited Editions Club
— Christmas-Eve and Easter-Day. L, 1850. 1st Ed. 8vo, orig cloth; rubbed & cocked. Z June 28 (41) $150
— Paracelsus. L, 1835. 1st Ed. 8vo, later half mor gilt; new endpapers & binder's blanks, front hinge weak. Z June 28 (42) $800
— The Pied Piper of Hamelin. L, [1934]. One of 410. Illus by Arthur Rackham. Orig vellum. With 4 colored plates. CE Sept 27 (236) $550; sg Oct 19 (210) $650
— Selections from the Poetical Works. L, 1896. 12mo, hand-painted & illuminaged vellum by the Royal School of Art Needlework. pba Nov 30 (36) $425
— Works. NY, [1898]. 12 vols. 8vo, contemp half calf gilt. sg Sept 21 (6) $650

### Browning, Robert, 1812-89 —&
### Browning, Elizabeth Barrett, 1806-61
— Two Poems. L, 1854. 8vo, mor gilt by Riviere. b Jan 31 (64) £110

### Bruce, C. G.
— Kulu and Lahoul. L, 1914. Orig cloth; spine head nicked. With folding map & frontis. bba Nov 1 (375) £450 [Boyes]
— Twenty Years in the Himalaya. L, 1910. 1st Ed. 8vo, orig cloth; spine head nicked. bba Nov 1 (374) £350 [Barnby]

### Bruce, James, 1730-94
— Cartes et figures du Voyage en Nubie et en Abyssinie. Paris, 1792. 4to, modern cloth; worn & soiled. With 4 folding maps & 77 (of 84) plates, 19 of them folding. Soiled throughout; some browning; 2 maps with tape repairs. wa Dec 14 (114) $230
— Travels to Discover the Source of the Nile. Edin., 1790. 1st Ed. 5 vols. 4to, contemp calf; rebacked with orig backstrip. With 3 hand-colored maps & 58 plates. Some discoloration. b May 30 (247) £1,300

Anr copy. Contemp calf; spines & edges worn, joints weak. With 3 folding maps & 58 plates. CE June 12 (161) $1,400

Anr Ed. Dublin, 1791-90. 6 vols (including Appendix vol). 8vo, contemp calf; repaired. With 62 plates & maps. Writing erased from Vol I title. S Mar 28 (356) £650

2d Ed. Edin., 1805. 8 vols, including Atlas. 8vo & 4to, contemp half calf; rubbed. With 3 folding maps & 79 plates. Some spotting. S June 13 (376) £320

3d Ed. Edin., 1813. 8 vols, including Atlas. 8vo & 4to, contemp calf gilt, Atlas in matching half calf; joints & corners worn, 1 folding map loose. 2 maps lined; all 3 with repairs & wear. CE June 12 (162) $600

### Bruce, Peter Henry, 1692-1757
— Memoirs.... Dublin, 1783. 8vo, modern sheep. sg Mar 7 (38) $90

### Brue, Adrien Hubert
— Atlas universel de geographie.... Paris, 1822. Folio, contemp half lea; worn. With engraved title & 35 (of 36) double-page maps, hand-colored in outline. Tp & plate leaf chipped; marginal repair to 1 map; folding map tape-repaired on verso. sg May 9 (57) $700

### Bruehl, Anton
— Photographs of Mexico. NY, [1933]. One of 1,000. Folio, half lea; spine worn. sg Feb 29 (56) $200

Anr Ed. NY, [1945]. Folio, cloth, in separated dj. sg Feb 29 (57) $80

### Bruehl Library, Heinrich
— Catalogues Bibliothecae Bruhlianae. Pars Quarta. Dresden, 1756. Folio, contemp calf; rebacked, rubbed. Some foxing & soiling. O Mar 26 (46) $350

### Bruele, Gualtherus
— Praxis Medicinae, or, the Physicians Practise. L, 1639. 2d English Ed. 4to, modern calf; rebound. Ccc2 torn & chipped; table misbound; marginal darkening & wear; some soiling. CE Nov 8 (76) $320

**Bruff, Joseph Goldsborough**
— Gold Rush. NY, 1944. 4to, half cloth. pba Aug 8 (22) $180
   1st Ed. - Ed by Georgia Willis Read and Ruth Gaines. 2 vols. 4to, bds; lacking slipcase. Larson copy. pba Sept 28 (333) $170
   Anr copy. Ed by Georgia Willis Read & Ruth Gaines. 4to, half cloth in slipcase; slipcase edges worn. Robbins copy. pba Mar 21 (38) $275
   Anr Ed. NY, 1949. Ed by Georgia Willis Read and Ruth Gaines. Orig cloth in dj; d/j worn. Larson copy. pba Sept 28 (334) $95

**Bruguiere, Francis**
— San Francisco. San Francisco, 1918. Bds; spine chipped. Foxed. pba Nov 16 (35) $55

**Bruin, Cornelis de.** See: Le Brun, Cornelius

**Brulliot, Franz, 1780-1836**
— Dictionnaire des monogrammes, marques figurees, lettres initiales.... Munich, 1817-20. 2 vols, including Table Generale. 4to, 19th-cent half sheep; rebacked with cloth. Some foxing. sg Sept 7 (62) $200

**Brummer Collection, Ernest**
— [Sale Catalogue] The Ernest Brummer Collection. Zurich, 1979. 2 vols. Folio, cloth, in djs. sg Jan 11 (35) $50

**Brummer Gallery**
— Brancusi Exhibition. NY, 1926. 4to, wraps. sg Sept 7 (55) $225

**Bruna...**
— La Bruna & la Biancha. [Bologna: de Bazaleris, c.1495]. 4to, modern bds. 32 lines; double column; type 3:83R. With title woodcut within decorative border. Wormhole affecting a few letters; outer bifolium strengthened at hinge. 4 leaves. Sander 1411. C Apr 3 (55) £11,000

**Brune, Johannes de, 1589-1658**
— Emblemata of Zinne-werck; voorghestelt in Beelden.... Amst.: Hans van der Hellen for J. E. Kloppenburch, 1624. 4to, contemp vellum; soiled, cockled, inner hinge weak, duplicate stamp on lower pastedown. With 51 emblems. Corner torn from Ee1; minor spotting. Schaefer copy. P Nov 1 (53) $1,300

**Brunet, Gustave, 1807-96**
— Dictionnaire de bibliologie catholique. Paris, 1860. 4to, modern buckram; orig wrappers bound in. sg Apr 11 (66) $175
— Imprimeurs imaginaires et libraires supposes. Paris, 1866. 8vo, later cloth; worn. Some foxing. O Mar 26 (47) $100
— La Papesse Jeanne. Paris, 1862. One of 54. 12mo, contemp half cloth; some wear. O Mar 26 (51) $375

— Recherches sur diverses editions Elzeviriennes.... Paris, 1866. One of 250. 8vo, half cloth, orig wraps bound in. O Mar 26 (48) $170

**Brunet, Jacques Charles, 1780-1867**
— Manuel du libraire et de l'amateur de livres. Paris, 1810. 1st Ed. 3 vols. 8vo, contemp bds; worn & chipped. Minor dampstaining in Vol I. O Mar 26 (49) $675
   Anr Ed. Paris, 1838-45. 5 vols. 8vo, later half cloth; worn. Some foxing. O Mar 26 (50) $130
   Anr Ed. Paris, 1842-44. 5 vols plus the 1878-80 Supplement in 2 vols. 8vo, contemp half sheep; rubbed, worn, some covers detached. Sold w.a.f. ds July 27 (43) $200
   Anr Ed. Paris, 1860-65. 6 vols plus supplement in 2 vols & Deschamps, Dictionnaire de Geographie. Together, 9 vols. 8vo, later half calf, Vol IX in contemp half mor gilt; rubbed. bba Oct 5 (28) £450 [Banzhaf]
   Anr Ed. Paris, 1860-80. 8 vols, including 2 Supplements. 8vo, later half mor. Ck Apr 12 (214) £450
   Anr copy. Contemp half mor, Supplements in orig wraps; rubbed, wraps broken. F Sept 21 (268) $230
   Anr copy. Half mor; hinges cracked. pba June 20 (80) $160
   Anr Ed. Berlin, 1921. Vols I-VI (of 9). 8vo, half vellum; shaken. sg Apr 11 (67) $225

**Brunet, Patrick J.** See: Clark & Brunet

**Bruni, Leonardo, Aretinus, 1369-1444**
— Aquila Volante. Venice: Peregrino Pasquale, 6 June 1494. Folio, 16th-cent bds; spine torn & def. 43 lines; roman type; large woodcut title. Tp & lower leaves stained; upper margins of later leaves affected by damp; small wormholes to lower margin. 126 leaves. Goff B-1232. C Apr 3 (56) £2,500

**Brunner, Johann Conrad A.**
— Experimenta nova circa pancreas. Leiden, 1722. 8vo, contemp sheep; restored. With frontis, title, & 4 plates (2 folding). Title soiled; some creasing; M5 torn at head. Ck Mar 22 (60) £190

**Bruns, Henry P.**
— Angling Books of the Americas. Atlanta, 1975. 4to, cloth; worn. O June 25 (34) $130
   Anr copy. Cloth; worn, front hinge weak, spine creased. O June 25 (35) $60

**Brunus Aretinus, Leonardus.** See: Bruni, Leonardo

**Brussel, Isidore Rosenbaum**
— Anglo-American First Editions. L, 1935-36. One of 500. Vol I: East to West, only. pba Aug 8 (312) $50

**Bruyerinus Campegius, Joannes Baptista**
— De re cibaria libri XXII. Lyons: Sebastian de Honoratis, 1560. 1st Ed. 8vo, modern calf; spine faded. With device on title. Title margins repaired in lamination; other corners with laminated repairs;

some marginal dampstaining. Ck Mar 22 (61) £1,000

**Bry, Johann Israel de.** See: Bry & Bry

**Bry, Johann Theodor de, 1561-1623**
See also: Bry & Bry
— Atalanta fugiens, hoc est, emblemata nova de secretis natura chymica. Oppenheim, 1617. Illus by Matthias Merian. 4to, 19th-cent sheep. With 50 plates. Lacking port; 2 plates corrected with new plates pasted over. P Dec 12 (47) $11,000

**Bry, Johann Theodor de, 1561-1623 —&**
**Bry, Johann Israel de**
— [Little Voyages] Frankfurt, 1598-1613. ("Indiae orientalis navigationes.") Parts 1-8 in 2 vols. Recent half mor gilt. Sold w.a.f. S Nov 30 (196) £8,000

**Bry, Theodor de —&**
**Bry, Johann Theodor de, 1561-1623**
— Emblemata nobilitati et vulgo scitu digna singulis historiis symbola adscripta & elegantes. Frankfurt, 1593. 4to, mor gilt with supralibros of Frederick Perkins; joints dry & starting. With engraved title & 87 leaves of plates, a few with central space blank. Lacking emblem plates but with additional heraldic plates inserted. Perkins - Wilmerding copy. P June 5 (183) $3,250

**Bryan, Daniel**
— The Mountain Muse. Comprising the Adventures of Daniel Boone.... Harrisonburg, [Va.]: Davidson & Bourne, 1813. 12mo, contemp sheep; worn, scuffed, front joint starting. Browned; some dampstaining; lacking subscriber's list; pp. 41-44 bound upside down. wa Feb 29 (315) $130

**Bryan, Michael, 1757-1821**
— Dictionary of Painters and Engravers. L, 1816. ("A Biographical and Critical Dictionary of Painters and Engravers.") 2 vols in 4. 4to, mor; some covers detached, rubbed. Minor staining. CE Sept 27 (65) $800

Anr Ed. L, 1918-19. 5 vols. 4to, orig cloth. b May 30 (462) £60

**Bryant, Edwin, 1805-69**
— What I Saw in California. NY & Phila., 1848. 1st Ed. 8vo, orig cloth; spine faded. Slight discoloration & foxing. Larson copy. pba Sept 28 (335) $425

Anr copy. Orig cloth; spine slightly faded. Title foxed. Robbins copy. pba Mar 21 (39) $900

Anr Ed. Santa Ana, 1936. Illus by Dorothy Smith Sides. Bds. With frontis. Larson copy. pba Sept 28 (336) $110

**Bryant, Jacob, 1715-1804**
— A Dissertation concerning the War of Troy.... L, 1799. 2d Ed. 4to, orig wraps; needs rebdg. sg Mar 7 (164) $175

**Bryant, William Cullen, 1794-1878**
See also: Limited Editions Club; Picturesque...
— Poems. Cambr. MA, 1821. 1st Ed, One of 750. 12mo, orig bds; soiled, spine chipped, pastedowns foxed. sg Sept 21 (99) $700

**Buchon, Jean Alexandre, 1791-1846**
— Atlas geographique, statistique, historique et chronologique des deux Ameriques.... Paris, 1825. Folio, contemp half lea; worn. With 51 double-page hand-colored maps, 2 double-page hand-colored plates & 2 double-page hand-colored tables. Tp & 4 maps browned. C May 31 (49) £2,600

**Buchotte, Ingenieur du Roi**
— Les regles du dessin et du lavis.... Paris, 1721. 8vo, contemp citron mor gilt with arms of Henri, comte de Calembourg. Fuerstenberg - Schaefer copy. S Dec 7 (85) £1,100

Anr Ed. Paris, 1743. 8vo, contemp mor gilt with arms of the marquis d'Argenson; marked. Fuerstenberg - Schaefer copy. S Dec 7 (86) £1,500

**Buc'hoz, Pierre Joseph, 1731-1807**
— Les Secrets de la Nature et de l'Art.... Paris, 1769. 1st Ed. Vols I-II only. 12mo, modern half bds. Ck Mar 22 (64) £90

**Buck, Franklin A.**
— A Yankee Trader in the Gold Rush. Bost. & NY, 1930. 1st Ed. - Compiled by Katherin A. White. Orig cloth in dj; d/j chipped. With 8 illus. Larson copy. pba Sept 28 (337) $55

**Buck, Nathanael.** See: Buck & Buck

**Buck, Pearl S., 1892-1973**
— The Good Earth. NY, [1931]. 1st Ed, 1st Issue. In chipped dj. Z June 28 (46) $325

Advance copy. Orig wraps; spine def. Z June 28 (45) $330

**Buck, Samuel —&**
**Buck, Nathanael**
— Antiquities; or Venerable Remains of Above Four Hundred Castles, Monasteries.... L, 1774. 3 vols. Folio, contemp calf gilt, Vol III in mor-backed calf; all rubbed & recased. With 1 engraved title only, port from a smaller copy, double-page map, 427 (of 428) engraved views & 83 double-page perspective views. Some plates creased or with minor tears, occasionally affecting surface, a few repaired. C Oct 25 (105) £18,000

**Buck, Samuel D.**
— With the Old Confeds: Actual Experiences of a Captain in the Line. Balt., 1925. 8vo, orig cloth; rubbed, endpapers foxed. Sgd by Buck's widow. bbc Dec 18 (454) $700

**Buck, Walter J.** See: Chapman & Buck

**Buckbee, Edna Bryan**
— The Saga of Old Tuolumne. NY: Press of the Pioneers, 1935. pba Apr 25 (317) $90
— The Saga of the Old Tuolomne. NY: Press of the Pioneers, 1935. 1st Ed. Orig cloth in dj. With 16 photo plates. Larson copy. pba Sept 28 (338) $180

**Bucke, Richard Maurice, 1837-1902**
— Notes and Fragments: Left by Walt Whitman.... [Ontario]: Pvtly ptd, 1899. One of 255. 4to, orig cloth; minor rubbing. sg Feb 8 (364) $140

**Buckell, George Teasdale Teasdale.** See: Teasdale-Buckell, George Teasdale

**Buckingham, James Silk, 1786-1855**
— Canada, Nova Scotia, New Brunswick, and the Other British Provinces in North America.... L, [1843]. 8vo, orig cloth; spine ends frayed. Plates foxed. sg Oct 26 (30) $50
— Travels among the Arab Tribes Inhabiting the Countries East of Syria and Palestine. L, 1825. 4to, half calf. Stark - Stewart copy. b Sept 20 (326) £1,100
— Travels in Palestine. L, 1821. 1st Ed. 4to, contemp calf; joints repaired. With frontis port, 1 folding map, & 7 full-page maps. Some spotting & offsetting. S Oct 26 (23) £650 [Baring]

**Buckingham, Nash.** See: Derrydale Press

**Buckland, William, 1784-1856**
— Geology and Mineralogy. L, 1836-37. 2 vols. 8vo, early calf gilt; rubbed. With 87 plates numbered 1-69 plus 1 plate in Supplement. wa Nov 16 (194) $180
1st American Ed. Phila., 1837. 2 vols. 12mo, orig cloth; stamps on front endpapers. With 90 plates, including hand-colored double-page folding diagram. Foxed. sg May 16 (142) $50
— Reliquiae diluvianae. L, 1823. 1st Ed. 4to, contemp half calf; rubbed. With 27 plates, 3 hand-colored. Spotted. S June 13 (377) £300

**Buckle, Richard**
— Jacob Epstein Sculptor. L, 1963. 4to, cloth, in chipped dj. sg Jan 11 (164) $60

**Bucknill, Sir John Charles, 1817-97.** See: Dickens's copy, Charles

**Bucovich, Mario**
— Paris. Paris, [1928]. Folio, bdg not described; worn & soiled, endpapers foxed, penciled notations on tp & rear pastedown. sg Feb 29 (58) $90

**Budge, Sir Ernest Alfred Wallis, 1857-1934**
— The Book of the Dead. L, 1901. 3 vols. Calf prize bdg by Baker & Son, Clifton. wa Nov 16 (66) $210
— The Gods of the Egyptians. L, 1904. 2 vols. 4to, orig cloth. Lacking 1 plate. bba May 30 (363) £330 [Braham]
— The Life and Exploits of Alexander the Great. L, 1896. 1st Ed, small paper Issue. One of 500. Trans by Budge. 8vo, orig half mor gilt. sg Mar 7 (4) $175

— Osiris and the Egyptian Resurrection. L, 1911. 2 vols. b May 30 (249) £120
Anr copy. In djs. bba May 30 (362) £190 [Braham]
— Some Account of the Collection of Egyptian Antiquities in the Possession of Lady Meux. L, 1893. One of 200. 4to, orig cloth. bba May 30 (364) £220 [Braham]; British Museum

**Buel, Clarence Clough.** See: Johnson & Buel

**Buenting, Heinrich, 1545-1606**
— Itinerarium Sacrae Scripturae, Or, The Travels of the Holy Patriarchs. L, 1619. 1st English Ed. 4to, recent old-style calf. Fol.3 holed; final lead 204 laid down; few water-stains & discoloration. S Oct 26 (48) £400 [Sophoclides]

**Buerger, Gottfried August, 1747-94**
— The Chase, and William and Helen. Edin., 1796. Trans by Sir Walter Scott. 4to, contemp bds; re-backed in vellum, related matter mtd on pastedowns. Accession stamp on tp verso. sg Sept 21 (291) $325

**Buffet, Bernard**
— Lithographs, 1952-1966. NY, [1968]. Text by Fernand Mourlot. 4to, orig wraps. sg Jan 11 (67) $450
Anr copy. Orig wraps, in dj; both with tears. wa Nov 16 (274) $280
Anr copy. Orig wraps. With 11 plates. wa June 20 (326) $400

**Buffier, Claude, 1661-1737**
— Geographie universelle. Paris, 1759. Bound with: Buffier. Nouveau Traite de la Sphere. Paris: Marc Bordelet, 1738. 12mo, calf; extermiteis worn, inner hinges broken. With 18 folding maps. Inner margin of last leaf damaged with loss of letters; map of both hemispheres crumpled. NH June 1 (213) $250
Anr Ed. Paris, 1783. 12mo, contemp sheep gilt; extremities worn, spine chipped. With 17 folding maps. sg May 9 (58) $350

**Buffon, Georges Louis Marie Leclerc, Comte de, 1707-88**
— Eaux-fortes originales pour des textes de Buffon. Paris, 1942. One of 30 on japon Imperial, with an extra suite of the etchings on chine. Illus by Pablo Picasso. Folio, lev extra with semi-abstract design of a bull's head, designed by Paul Bonet [Carnets 1017], bound by Rene Desmules & finished by Cochet, 1952. With 31 plates. C May 1 (128) £45,000
— Histoire naturelle, generale et particulier. Amst.: H. Schneider, 1766-99. 22 vols only (of 38). 4to, contemp calf; worn. S Mar 29 (645) £2,000
— Natural History.... L & York, 1812. 20 vols. 8vo, contemp calf; rubbed, some spines def. With port & 679 (of 680) plates. b Jan 31 (290) £180
— Oeuvres. Paris, 1848. 11 vols, including Buffon. Histoire de ses travaux et sus idees, 1844. Contemp le gilt stamped "Ste. Barbe" inside wreath ornament in center panels of upper covers. O Mar 5 (34) $350

Anr Ed. Brussels, 1852. 9 vols. 8vo, contemp half mor; rubbed. Slight soiling & spotting. S Oct 25 (707) £360 [Walford's]
— Oiseaux. Paris, 1770-86. ("Histoire naturelle des oiseaux.") 10 vols. Folio, mor gilt by Kalthoeber; minor bumping, inner hinges with worming. With 1,008 hand-colored plates, including the 35 plates of insects. Lacking blanks in Vols I, II & IX; Vol V with minor damage to margin of Plate 7; Plate 747 with repaired tear along plate mark; Plates 565-68 with repaired hole or tear in upper margin. Fattorini copy. C Oct 25 (7) £44,000
— Le petit Buffon des enfants.... Avignon: Chaillot, 1805 [An XIII]. 12mo, half calf; rebacked. With 12 plates, 1 folding Library stamp on tp. S Nov 2 (166) £180 [Schiller]

**Buffum, Edward Gould**
— Six Months in the Gold Mines.... L, 1850. 12mo, orig cloth; spine ends torn. pba Nov 16 (36) $250

Anr Ed. Phila., 1850. 12mo, orig cloth; spine ends chipped. Some foxing. wa Feb 29 (325) $400

1st Ed. 12mo, orig cloth; spine top chipped, corner worn. Streeter-Larson copy. pba Sept 28 (339) $550

Anr Ed. Los Angeles, [1965]. Ed by John W. Caughey. Bds. With 6 daguerrotype illus. Larson copy. pba Sept 28 (340) $60

**Buisson, Sylvie & Dominique**
— La Vie et l'oeuvre de Leonard-Tsuguharu Foujita. [Paris, 1987]. 4to, cloth, in dj. sg Jan 11 (178) $175

**Bukowski, Charles**
— Barfly: The Continuing Saga of Henry Chinaski. Sutton West: Paget Press, [1984]. One of 200. Half cloth. pba Jan 25 (32) $150
— Crucifix in a Deathhand. NY, [1965]. 4to, wraps, with wrap-around band laid in loose. Ptd on paper of various weights & colors. pba Jan 25 (34) $170
— Goint Modern. Fremont: Ruddy Duck Press, [n.d.]. One of 500. Wraps. pba Jan 25 (36) $55
— Love is a Dog from Hell. Santa Barbara: Black Sparrow Press, 1977. One of 750. Sgd on tp, with drawing. pba Jan 25 (37) $150
— Mockingbird Wish Me Luck. Santa Barbara: Black Sparrow Press, 1972. 1st Ed, One of 250. pba Jan 25 (38) $100
— Play the Piano Drunk Like a Percussion Instrument.... Santa Barbara: Black Sparrow Press, 1979. One of 300. pba Jan 25 (39) $120
— Poems Written Before Jumping out of an 8 Story Window. Glendale: Poetry X Change, [1968]. Pictorial wraps. sg on tp, with drawing. pba Jan 25 (40) $225

Anr copy. Pictorial wraps; tape along spine. Bookstore stamp on front pastedown. Inscr & with a sketch on dedication page. pba Aug 22 (50) $75
— The Roominghouse Madrigals. Santa Rosa: Black Sparrow Press, 1988. One of—150. pba Jan 25 (41) $140

— War All of the Time. Santa Barbara: Black Sparrow Press, 1984. One of 176, with tipped-in painting. Half cloth. pba Jan 25 (42) $400
— You Get So Alone at Times.... Santa Barbara: Black Sparrow Press, 1986. One of 400. Half cloth. pba Jan 25 (44) $95

**Bula N'Zau, Pseud.** See: Bailey, Henry

**Bulfinch, Thomas, 1796-1867.** See: Limited Editions Club

**Bulkeley, John —&**
**Cummins, John**
— A Voyage to the South Seas.... L, 1743. 8vo, contemp half calf; joints cracked. Lacking prelims to tp; staining at beginning. pba July 25 (385) $425

**Bulkeley, John —&**
**Cummings, John**
— A Voyage to the South Seas.... Phila., 1757. 2d Ed. 8vo, half mor. S Oct 26 (606) £480 [Bennell]

**Bull, George, 1634-1710**
— Some Important Points of Primitive Christianity Maintained and Defended.... L: W. B. for Richard Smith, 1713. 3 vols. 8vo, contemp mor gilt to a cottage roof design, with arms of Queen Anne. Marriott - Furstenberg copy. C May 1 (28) £1,500

**Bull, Henrik Johan**
— The Cruise of the "Antarctic" to the South Polar Regions.... L & NY, 1896. 8vo, orig cloth; rubbed, corner stained. With 12 plates. Some soiling & wear; stamp to half-title & verso of front free endpaper. pba July 25 (18) $1,200

**Bullart, Isaac, 1599-1672**
— Academie des sciences et des arts. Paris, 1682. 2 vols. Folio, contemp calf; worn, spines dried, joints cracked. Some browning; marginal tears & stains. Sold w.a.f. CE Sept 27 (67) $110

Anr copy. Later calf; spine ends worn. CE June 12 (163) $1,200

**Bullen, Frank Thomas, 1857-1915**
— The Cruise of the "Cachalot". L, 1898. 1st Ed. 8vo, orig cloth; shaken. pba Apr 25 (148) $60; sg Sept 21 (100) $90

**Bulwer, John**
— Extracts from My Journal. Norwich: Pvtly ptd, 1853. 8vo, orig cloth. With 4 plates. bba Nov 1 (309) £700 [Atlas]

Anr copy. Orig cloth; spine head def, corners rubbed. Inscr to Arthur G. Sandberg. bba Nov 1 (569) £650 [Atlas]

**Bulychev, Ivan Dem'ianovich**
— Voyage dans la Siberie Orientale...Premier Partie. Voyage au Kamchatka. [St. Petersburg, 1855]. Folio, modern half mor preserving earlier cloth bds. With tinted litho title & 63 plates only, some colored. Some leaves spotted, a few with marginal dampstains. C May 31 (84) £1,400

### Bunbury, Sir Charles James Fox, 1809-86
— Journal of a Residence at the Cape of Good Hope.... L, 1848. 8vo, orig cloth; soiled, spine ends frayed. sg Mar 7 (40) $150

### Bunbury, Henry W., 1750-1811
— An Academy for Grown Horsemen. L, 1812. Bound with: Annals of Horsemanship. Illus by Thomas Rowlandson. 8vo, old calf; worn & broken, most of spine gone. Some foxing & soiling. O Jan 9 (63) $400

### Bunn, Alfred
— The Stage. L, 1840. 1st Ed. 3 vols. 8vo, contemp half mor; scuffed, extremities rubbed. F Mar 28 (439) $170

### Bunnell, Lafayette Houghton, 1824-1903
— Discovery of the Yosemite and the Indian War of 1851.... Chicago, [1880]. 1st Ed. 12mo, orig cloth; extremities worn, hinges cracked. Owner's stamp on front free endpaper. pba Feb 12 (9) $1,000

Anr copy. Orig cloth; spine darkened, head frayed, foot & corners rubbed, front hinge cracked. With frontis port & 6 plates. Robbins copy. pba Mar 21 (40) $200

2d Ed, 1st ptg. 12mo, orig cloth; spine ends worn, rear cover stained. pba Feb 12 (10) $75

2d Issue. Orig cloth; extremities worn. pba Feb 12 (11) $100

3d Ed. Chicago, [1892]. 12mo, orig cloth; front cover waterstained, hinge repaired. pba Feb 12 (12) $110

Anr Ed. NY, [1892]. Orig cloth. With frontis port & double-page map. Inscr to L. P. Hunt, June 23, 1893. Robbins copy. pba Mar 21 (41) $400

4th Ed. Los Angeles, 1911. 12mo, cloth. pba Feb 12 (13) $95

### Bunyan, John, 1628-88
See also: Cresset Press; Limited Editions Club
— The Doctrine of the Law and Grace Unfolded.... L, 1765. 6th Ed. 12mo, modern calf. Old notes on bottom & verso of tp; repairs to gutters of title & following leaf. pba Nov 30 (72) $110

— The Pilgrim's Progress. L, 1860. Illus by Charles Bennett. 8vo, mor gilt with pictorial cartouche, by Charles Bennett. sg Feb 8 (18) $110

Anr Ed. L: Essex House Press, 1899. One of 750. 16mo, vellum. sg Sept 14 (118) $150

— Solomon's Temple Spiritualiz'd.... L: for James Schofield in Middlewich, 1756. 8vo, contemp sheep; upper cover detached. With frontis. b Jan 31 (250) £95

### Buonanni, Filippo, 1638-1725
— Ordinum equestrium et militarium catalogus.... Rome, 1724. 3d Ed. 4to, contemp vellum. With engraved title & 166 plates. Italian tp stamped; opening leaves frayed & dampstained along fore-edge; some browning. sg May 9 (328) $650

### Burbank, E. A.
— Portraits of American Indians. Chicago: Arts & Crafts, [c.1900]. Folio, orig half cloth portfolio,; worn. With 32 color plates, 16 of them mtd. F Mar 28 (761) $625; F June 20 (831) $190

### Burbank, Luther, 1849-1926
— His Methods and Discoveries and their Practical Application. NY & L, 1914-15. 12 vols. Orig calf; scuffed. Foxing. F June 20 (631) $190; pba Aug 22 (569) $110

### Burbidge, Frederick William Thomas, 1847-1905
— Cool Orchids and How to Grow Them. L, 1874. 8vo, orig cloth; spotted. pba June 20 (256) $70

### Burchett, Josiah, 1666-1746
— A Complete History of the most Remarkable Transactions at Sea. L, 1720. 1st Ed. Folio, contemp calf; needs rebdg. With frontis & 9 maps. sg Mar 7 (204) $400

### Burckhard, Jacob
— Historia Bibliothecae Augustae que Wolffenbutteli est.... Leipzig, [1744]-46. 2 (of 3) parts in 1 vol. 4to, contemp vellum; some wear & soiling. Some browning. O Mar 26 (52) $110

### Burckhardt, Johann Ludwig, 1784-1817
— Notes on the Bedouins and Wahabys. L, 1830. 1st Ed. 4to, contemp calf. With map. Some discoloration. S Oct 26 (20) £2,100 [Quaritch]

Anr copy. Orig bds, unopened; rubbed & soiled, rebacked. With engraved map. Tears in 2B4; last 2 leaves torn & repaired. Wilfred Thesiger's copy. S June 27 (135) £1,700

— Travels in Arabia. L, 1829. 2 vols. 8vo, half calf; new endpapers. With 5 folding maps. Short tear in Vol II tp. S June 27 (136) £900

— Travels in Syria and the Holy Land. L, 1822. 4to, modern half mor; new endpapers. bba Apr 11 (330) £560 [Joppa]

### Burckhardt, John Lewis, 1784-1817. See: Burckhardt, Johann Ludwig

### Burdett, Charles
— The Life and Adventures of Kit Carson. NY, 1860. 1st Ed. Orig cloth; spine faded. With 6 plates. Frontis foxed; marginal darkening. Robbins copy. pba Mar 21 (42) $250

### Burdett-Coutts, W.
— The Brookfield Stud of Old English Breeds of Horses... L, 1891. 4to, pictorial cloth; worn & soiled. O Jan 9 (64) $150

### Burdick, Arthur Jared
— The Mystic Mid-Regions: The Deserts of the Southwest. NY, 1904. 1st Ed. Orig cloth; covers soiled. Robbins copy. pba Mar 21 (43) $110

**Burdick, Usher**
— The Last Battle of the Sioux Nation. Stevens Point WI: Worzalla Publishing, [1929]. pba June 25 (28) $130
— Tales from Buffalo Land.... Balt.: Wirth Brothers, 1940. pba June 25 (29) $55

**Burdick, Usher —& Hart, Eugene D.**
— Jacob Horner and the Indian Campaigns of 1876 and 1877.... Balt.: Wirth Brothers, 1942. Orig wraps. Owner's stamps. pba June 25 (27) $70

**Burdon, Capt. William**
— The Gentleman's Pocket-Farrier. L, 1735. 8vo, disbound. Some soiling & foxing. sg May 16 (292) $175

**Bure, Guillaume Francois de.** See: De Bure, Guillaume Francois

**Burger, John**
— Horned Death. Huntington, 1947. Orig cloth; rubbed. O June 4 (61) $110

**Burgess, Anthony**
— A Clockwork Orange. L: Heinemann, [1962]. In dj with chips & tear to upper cover. Ck Apr 12 (130) £140
— Coaching Days of England. L, 1966. Oblong folio, cloth, in chipped & soiled dj; bdg soiled. O Jan 9 (65) $50

**Burgess, Capt. F. F. R.**
— Sporting Fire-Arms for Bush and Jungle. L, 1884. 8vo, cloth; worn. O Oct 10 (57) $120
 Anr copy. Bdg not described but worn. O June 4 (62) $90

**Burgess, Gelett, 1866-1951**
— The Lark. San Francisco, 1895-97. 1st Book Ed. 2 vols including Epilark. Orig cloth; Vol II top corner bumped. With orig ink sketch & sgd inscr laid in. Robbins copy. pba Mar 21 (45) $400
 1st Eds. San Francisco, 1895-1897. Nos 1-24 plus Epilark in 2 vols. Orig wraps; fore-edges worn, some darkening, stitching loose. Robbins copy. pba Mar 21 (44) $200

**Burgess, Nathan G.**
— The Ambrotype Manual.... NY, 1856. 8vo, orig cloth; rubbed & buped. Some foxing. Met Feb 24 (270) $200

**Burgess, Thornton W.**
— The Adventures of Johnny Chuck. Bost., 1923. Illus by Harrison Cady. Some soiling. Sgd on front free endpaper, 1923. pba Mar 7 (43) $70
— The Burgess Sea Shore for Children. Bost., 1929. Some foxing. pba Aug 22 (708) $50
— Tommy and the Wishing Stone. NY, 1915. Illus by Harrison Cady. In chipped dj. pba Aug 22 (709) $130

**Burgoyne, John, 1722-92**
— A State of the Expedition from Canada.... L, 1780. 2d Ed. 4to, half calf; taped backstrip, front bd detached. With folding chart & 6 folding maps having troop distribution hand-colored. Some foxing & soiling; cut close; Saratoga repaired. wa Feb 29 (321) $950

**Burgundia, Antonius a**
— Mundi lapis lydius.... Antwerp, 1639. 4to, modern mor. With engraved title & 50 plates. Engraved title cropped & laid down. b Sept 20 (33) £280

**Burke, Edgar**
— American Dry Flies and How to Tie Them. NY: Derrydale Press, 1931. One of 500. O June 25 (54) $275

**Burke, Edmund, 1729-97**
 See also: Limited Editions Club
— An Impartial History of the War in America, between Great Britain and her Colonies. L, 1780. 1st Ed. 8vo, contemp calf; rebacked. With folding map & 11 ports only. Some foxing & edge tears to map. bbc Feb 26 (386) $975
— Reflections on the Revolution in France. L, 1790. Bound with: Burke. An Appeal from the New to the Old Whigs.... L., 1796. 1st Ed. 8vo, contemp mor. Inscr. Lacking leaf G3. Margins stained. 1st Ed. Inscr to Mrs. Crewe. Houghton - Hefner copy. CNY May 17 (8) $4,500
— Three Memorials on French Affairs.... L, 1797. 1st Ed, 1st Impression. 8vo, later bds. Lacking half-title. Todd 69A. pba Nov 30 (73) $250
— Works. L, 1803. 8 vols. 8vo, contemp mor gilt; joints rubbed. pba Sept 14 (87) $250

**Burke, James Lee**
— Dixie City Jam. NY: Hyperion, [1994]. One of 1,525. pba Aug 22 (52) $85
— To the Bright and Shining Sun. [Huntington Beach: James Cahill, 1992]. One of 400. Illus by Joe Servello. pba Oct 5 (9) $60; pba Dec 7 (21) $65; pba Aug 22 (54) $85
— Two for Texas. [Huntington Beach: James Cahill, 1992]. One of 400. Illus by Joe Servello. pba Oct 5 (10) $80; pba Aug 22 (55) $75; wa Feb 29 (27) $120
— Winter Light. [Huntington Beach: James Cahill, 1992]. One of 326. Illus by Phil Parks. pba Aug 22 (56) $75; wa Feb 29 (26) $80; wa Feb 29 (28) $50

**Burke, Thomas, 1886-1945**
— Limehouse Nights. L, 1916. pba Aug 22 (57) $100

**Burley, Walter, 1275-1345?**
— Expositio in octo libros Aristotelis physica. Venice: Bonetus Locatellus for Octavianus Scotus, 2 Dec 1491. Folio, contemp vellum wraps; spine def. 68 lines & headline; gothic letter. Staining & browning, with fraying & loss at lower outer corners of 1st few leaves; some worming & short tears; contemp Ms annotations. 234 leaves. Goff B-1305. Madsen copy. S Mar 14 (74) £950

# BURLINGTON

**Burlington, Charles —& Others**
— The Modern Universal British Traveller. L, 1779. Folio, contemp calf gilt; worn, lower joint split. With frontis, 2 folding maps & 105 plates. S Mar 28 (38) £500

**Burlington Fine Arts Club—London**

### Catalogues of Exhibitions
— Collection of Objects of Chinese Art. 1915. 4to, orig cloth. sg June 13 (68) $110
— Early Chinese Pottery and Porcelain.... 1911. Folio, orig cloth; rubbed, endpapers spotted. bba May 30 (41) £130 [Angelini]
— English Embroidery. 1905. Folio, orig cloth. bba Oct 19 (185) £85 [Axe]
— Specimens of Japanese Lacquer and Metal Work. 1894. 4to, contemp half sheep gilt; joints worn. sg Jan 11 (68) $50

**Burma**
— An Account of the Burman Empire.... Calcutta, 1839. 8vo, contemp half mor; bds rubbed. S Oct 26 (570) £200 [Morrel]

**Burmannus, Johannes, 1706-79**
— Thesaurus Zeylanicus.... Amst., 1737. 2 parts in 1 vol. 4to, bds; worn, spine def. With port & 111 plates. Met Feb 24 (437) $1,600

**Burmeister, K. H. von**
— Sebastian Muenster; Eine Bibliographie. Wiesbaden, 1964. 8vo, orig wraps. sg Apr 11 (68) $140

**Burnaby, Arthur —& Wain, Louis**
— Days in Catland.... L: Raphael Tuck, [n.d.]. 4to, orig pictorial bds; broken. With 4 chromolitho plates with 14 numbered slots & 14 cut-out cat figures in pocket at end. Sold w.a.f. Ck May 31 (31) £95

**Burnaby, Frederick Gustavus, 1842-85**
— On Horseback through Asia Minor. L, 1877. 2 vols. 8vo, orig cloth; library bookplate. With port & 3 folding maps. b May 30 (250) £90

**Burnand, Sir Francis Cowley**
— Records and Reminiscences, personal and general.... L, 1904 [1903]. 2 vols. 8vo, mor extra by Root. Extra-illustrated with 28 plates & 5 A Ls s. b Sept 20 (604) £110

**Burne-Jones, Sir Edward Coley, 1833-98**
— The Flower Book. L, 1905. One of 300. 4to, mor gilt; spine ends scuffed, endpapers browned. C June 26 (187) £2,500; Ck May 31 (32) £2,400

**Burnet, Gilbert, 1643-1715**
— An Exposition of the Thirty-Nine Articles of the Church of England. L: R. Roberts for Richard Chiswell, 1699. Folio, contemp calf; joints cracked, lea partly loose, corner torn from front free endpaper. sg Mar 21 (71) $80

— History of his Own Time. L, 1724-34. 1st Ed. 2 vols. Folio, calf; joints cracked, spine ends worn. pba Sept 14 (88) $250

**Burnet, Thomas, 1635?-1715**
— The Theory of the Earth. The Two First Books. L, 1684. 2 parts in 1 vol. Folio, contemp calf; worn, top spine compartment off, covers detached. Stamp on general title. sg May 16 (143) $250

**Burnett, Frances Hodgson, 1849-1924**
— Little Lord Fauntleroy. NY, 1886. 1st Ed, Issue not indicated. 4to, orig cloth; bdg askew. sg Sept 21 (101) $90

Anr copy. Orig cloth; extremities rubbed, spine ends frayed, hinges cracked. sg Sept 21 (102) $140
— Piccino and Other Child Stories. NY, 1894. 1st Ed. 8vo, cloth; spine ends rubbed. pba Dec 14 (21) $80

**Burnett, Peter Hardeman, 1807-95**
— An Old California Pioneer. Oakland, 1946. One of 675. Orig cloth. With 1 facsimile & 2 folded maps. Sgd. Larson copy. pba Sept 28 (342) $80
— Recollections and Opinions of an Old Pioneer. NY, 1880. With: A.L.S. of Peter Burnett to Mrs. Louise Muir, Oct 29, 1883 1st Ed. 12mo, orig cloth; hinges slightly cracked. Larson copy. pba Sept 28 (341) $500

Anr copy. Orig cloth; hinges split. Robbins copy. pba Mar 21 (46) $170

Anr copy. Orig cloth; rebacked with orig spine strip laid down, new endpapers. Library markings; tp browned, remargined & tape-repaired. pba Apr 25 (318) $70

**Burnett, William Hickling**
— Views of Cintra.... L: J. Dickinson, [1836]. Folio, orig wraps; soiled & chipped. With 14 plates on india paper. S June 13 (543) £1,050

**Burnett, William Riley**
— The Asphalt Jungle. NY, 1949. In dj. sg June 20 (21) $130

**Burney, Charles, 1726-1814**
— The Present State of Music in France and Italy. L, 1771. 1st Ed. 8vo, calf; front cover detached. pba Mar 7 (44) $120
— The Present State of Music in Germany, the Netherlands, and United Provinces. L, 1773. 1st Ed. 2 vols. 8vo, contemp calf; joints cracked. Wormed. pba Mar 7 (45) $150

Anr copy. Wormed; tear to pp. 161-62 of Vol II, with brown stain from earlier tape repair. pba June 20 (83) $140

**Burney, Frances, 1752-1840**
— Evelina, Or, A Young Lady's Entrance into the World. L, 1794. 2 vols. 12mo, modern calf extra. sg Feb 8 (65) $200

**Burney, Sarah Harriet, 1770?-1844**
— Clarentine; A Novel. L, 1796. 2d Ed. 3 vols. 12mo, contemp half calf; spines scuffed. Some leaves affected by damp; E9 with small piece torn from outer margin; L6 with large tear at inner margin; G5 of Vol II torn with loss to a few words. Ck Sept 8 (198) £500

**Burnouf, Eugene, 1801-52 —& Jacquet, Eugene, 1811-38**
— L'Inde Francaise, ou collection de dessins lithographies.... Paris, 1827-35. 25 livraisons in 2 vols. Folio, orig half calf. With 225 hand-colored plates, a few heightened with gum arabic or gold. Minor discoloration. S Nov 30 (193) £6,500

**Burns, John, 1774-1850**
— Obstetrical Works.... NY, 1809. 8vo, contemp sheep; extremities rubbed. Some browning. sg May 16 (386) $90

**Burns, Robert, 1759-96**
See also: Limited Editions Club
— The Jolly Beggars. Edin., 1802. Half lev. Pages badly trimmed & somewhat stained. pba Aug 8 (350) $190
— Poems, Chiefly in the Scottish Dialect. Dublin: William Gilbert, 1787. Piracy. 12mo, 18th-cent calf. pnE May 15 (273) £320

2d (1st Edin.) Ed. Edin., 1787. Issue with "skinking" on p.263. 8vo, orig sheep. pnE May 15 (267) £490

Issue with "stinking" on p.263. Contemp calf; rebacked using much of orig backstrip, worn, joints cracking. Some foxing & soiling. pba June 20 (84) $350

3d (1st London) Ed. L, 1787. 8vo, mor gilt by Bayntun. CE Sept 27 (68) $500

Anr copy. Contemp half calf. pnE May 15 (268) £260

Anr Ed. L, 1797. 2 vols in 1. 8vo, later half calf gilt; spines frayed, covers stained. pnE May 15 (269) £250

— The Poems, Letters, and Land of Robert Burns. L: Virtue, [plates dated 1838-40]. 2 vols. 4to, mor gilt. pba June 20 (64) $180
— Reliques.... L, 1808. 8vo, calf with older front & rear calf panels laid on. pba Nov 30 (74) $160
— Tam O'Shanter. NY: W. J. Widdleson, 1868. Illus by Alexander Gardner. 8vo, orig half cloth; hinges cracked. With mtd frontis & 7 mtd albumen photos of drawings. bbc Apr 22 (216) $550

Anr Ed. L: Essex House Press, 1902. One of 150. 8vo, orig vellum. S May 16 (55) £220
— Works. L, 1801. 4 vols. 8vo, contemp calf; rebacked. sg Sept 21 (7) $250

Anr Ed. L, 1834. 8 vols. 8vo, contemp calf. b Jan 31 (66) £140

Anr Ed. Phila., 1875. Mor gilt. pba Dec 14 (22) $170

Edition De Luxe. Phila: Gebbie & Co, [1886]. one of 1,000. 6 vols. 8vo, half mor. cb Oct 17 (266) $325

**Burr, David H., 1803-75**
— An Atlas of the State of New York.... NY, 1829. Folio, modern half mor; extremities rubbed. With 52 maps hand-colored in outline. Some marginal finger-soiling. sg Dec 7 (38) $4,600

Anr copy. Later half calf; extremities rubbed, front free endpapers creased. With 52 colored maps. Tp browned. sg May 9 (91) $5,000
— A New Universal Atlas. NY, 1836. Folio, orig cloth; rebacked. With engraved title & 63 colored maps. Some foxing & soiling. sg Dec 7 (6) $4,000

**Burrard, Sir Gerald**
— The Modern Shotgun. L & NY, 1931-32. 3 vols. Orig cloth; worn. Ownership stamps. O Oct 10 (58) $200

Anr copy. Cloth; worn, edges foxed. O June 4 (63) $150

**Burritt, Elijah H., 1794-1838**
— Atlas, Designed to Illustrate the Geography of the Heavens. Hartford, 1835. Folio, orig ptd wraps; def. Maps browned, some with bent corners, 1 crudely remargined affecting image. Sold w.a.f. sg Dec 7 (9) $275

Anr Ed. NY, 1835. Folio, orig wraps; edge-tears. With 8 maps, all but 1 hand-colored. Some foxing. sg Dec 7 (7) $475

Anr copy. Orig wraps; edges worn. Some soiling & browning to maps; pencil notes on some maps. sg Dec 7 (8) $325

Anr Ed. NY, 1850. Folio, orig wraps; spine chipped, stained, repaired. With 8 plates. Met May 22 (380) $225

Anr copy. Orig wraps; soiled & frayed, covers detached. With 7 star maps (1 double-page) & 1 double-page chart. Maps frayed at edges. NH Sept 16 (392) $280

**Burroughs, Edgar Rice, 1875-1950**
— I Am a Barbarian. Tarzana, [1967]. In dj. pba May 4 (86) $90
— Apache Devil. Tarzana, [1933]. In dj. pba May 4 (79) $300
— At the Earth's Core. Chicago, 1922. In soiled dj with tears, some repaired. K Oct 1 (77) $1,600

Anr copy. In dj with chips to spine. pba May 4 (54) $1,800
— Back to the Stone Age. Tarzana, [1937]. In dj; stamp to front pastedown, minor wear to spine ends. pba May 4 (58) $650

1st Ed. In backed dj. sg June 20 (22) $700
— The Bandit of Hell's Bend. Chicago, 1925. 1st Ed. In restored dj. Library stamps to back of frontis & rear free endpaper. pba May 4 (71) $1,800
— The Beasts of Tarzan. Chicago, 1916. In restored dj with some painting. pba May 4 (6) $2,500

Anr copy. Orig cloth; spine ends rubbed, creasing to front cover cloth. pba May 23 (33) $100
— Beyond Thirty and the Man-Eater. South Ozone Park NY, 1957. In dj. pba May 4 (83) $65

# BURROUGHS

— Carson of Venus. Tarzana, [1939]. In dj. pba May 4 (63) $250
— The Cave Girl. Chicago, 1925. In dj with piece lacking from lower left corner of front panel. pba May 4 (70) $2,000
— The Chessmen of Mars. Chicago, 1922. Illus by J. Allen St. John. In tape-repaired dj. pba May 4 (47) $1,800
— The Deputy Sheriff of Comanche County. Tarzana, [1940]. In dj with smoke damage to flap. pba May 4 (82) $300
[-] The Edgar Rice Burroughs Library of Illustration. West Plains, 1976. 4to, pictorial covers; spine heels rubbed. pba May 4 (93) $325
— The Efficiency Expert. Kansas City MO: House of Greystoke, 1966. 1st Ed in Book form. Pictorial wraps; minor wear. pba May 4 (85) $130
— The Eternal Lover. Chicago, 1925. In chipped dj. pba May 4 (72) $1,600
Anr copy. Orig cloth; soiled, spine ends rubbed. Foxed. pba Aug 22 (60) $50
— A Fighting Man of Mars. NY: Metropolitan, [1931]. In dj with rubbing & chipping. pba May 4 (49) $1,200
— The Girl from Farris's. Tacoma WA: Wilma Co., [1959]. 1st Ed in Book form, one of 250. Orig wraps. pba May 4 (65) $190
Anr Ed. Kansas City MO: House of Greystoke, 1965. Frontis by Frank Frazetta. Orig wraps. pba May 4 (66) $130
— The Girl from Hollywood. NY: Macaulay, [1923]. Cloth, Currey's A bdg, in dj with chips & extremities worn, tape repairs. pba May 4 (68) $2,250
Anr copy. Cloth, Currey's A bdg, in dj with closed tears, pieces lacking, staining to spine. pba Aug 22 (61) $275
— The Gods of Mars. Chicago, 1918. In chipped dj with splits at folds. pba May 4 (41) $4,250
Anr copy. Cloth; spine ends rubbed, stamp to front free endpaper. pba May 4 (42) $130
— The Illustrated Tarzan. Book No. 1. NY, [1929]. Orig half cloth; rubbed. pba May 4 (3) $400
— Jungle Girl. Tarzana, [1932]. In dj with faint crease along spine. pba May 4 (78) $1,500
Anr Ed. L, [1933]. In repaired dj. sg June 20 (25) $110
— Jungle Tales of Tarzan. Chicago, 1919. Illus by J. Allen St. John. In chipped dj & 1st bdg. pba May 4 (12) $750
Later ptg. Inscr, 26 Apr 1928. pba May 4 (13) $900
— The Lad and the Lion. Tarzana, [1938]. In dj. pba May 4 (81) $350
— Land of Terror. Tarzana, 1944. In backed & repaired dj. sg June 20 (27) $150
— The Land That Time Forgot. Chicago, 1924. In dj with minor rubbing; bdg with lower corner bumped. pba May 4 (69) $5,500
— Llana of Gathol. Tarzana, [1948]. In dj. pba May 23 (34) $180
— Lost on Venus. Tarzana: Burroughs, [1935]. Illus by J. Allen St. John. In dj. pba May 4 (62) $325

## AMERICAN BOOK PRICES CURRENT

— The Mad King. Chicago, 1926. Bdg spine rubbed. In d/j with edge tears & repairs. pba May 4 (74) $1,600
Anr Ed. NY: Grosset & Dunlap, [1927]. In dj with chips & tears. pba May 4 (2) $130
— The Master Mind of Mars. Chicago: McClurg, 1928. Orig cloth, in chipped dj with folds repaired. pba May 4 (48) $1,100
Anr copy. Orig cloth; spine ends rubbed, some soiling. pba May 23 (35) $130
— The Monster Men. Chicago, 1929. In dj with some rubbing. Blindstamp to title. pba May 4 (77) $1,300
— The Moon Maid. Chicago, 1926. 1st Ed. In dj with piece missing, repairs on verso, minor stains. pba May 4 (73) $1,900
— The Mucker. Chicago: McClurg, 1921. In dj with minor defs. pba May 4 (67) $4,000
— The New Adventures of Tarzan "Pop-Up." Chicago: Pleasure Books, [1935]. Color pictorial bds; minor rubbing to extremities & spine. With 3 full-color double-page pop-up illusts. pba May 4 (30) $350
— The Oakdale Affair - The Rider. Tarzana, [1937]. In dj with spine ends rubbed. pba May 4 (80) $400
Anr copy. In chipped & peeling & repaired dj. Inscr, 22 May 1937. pba May 23 (36) $850
Anr copy. In backed & restored dj. sg June 20 (28) $250
— Official Guide of the Tarzan Clans of America. Tarzana, 1939. 1st Ed. Ptd wraps. pba May 4 (34) $300
— The Outlaw of Torn. Chicago, 1927. In chipped dj. pba May 4 (75) $1,300
— Pellucidar. Chicago, 1923. In restored dj. pba May 4 (55) $1,900
Anr Ed. NY: Grosset & Dunlap, [1924]. In dj with spine soiled & chips. pba May 4 (56) $170
— Pirates of Venus. Tarzana, [1934]. In dj. pba May 4 (61) $325
— A Princess of Mars. Chicago, 1917. Cloth; possibly recased. Old tape repairs to pp. 155-56 along marginal tear; marginal dampstaining. pba May 23 (37) $70
Anr copy. Illus by Frank E. Schoonover. Cloth; corners bumped. With 5 plates. Duplicate of 5th plate substituted for the 4th plate. pba May 4 (40) $400
— The Return of Tarzan. Chicago, 1915. Advance review copy. Orig wraps; minor creasing to spine. pba May 4 (4) $5,500
Anr Ed. NY: A. L. Burt, [1916]. In dj by N. C. Wyeth. pba May 4 (5) $110
— Savage Pellucidar. NY: Canaveral Press, 1963. In dj. pba May 4 (60) $85
— The Son of Tarzan. Chicago, 1917. 1st Ed. - Illus by J. Allen St. John. 8vo, orig cloth, in rubbed & repaired dj; stamp to rear pastedown, bdg rippled along rear cover. pba May 4 (8) $2,250
— Swords of Mars. Tarzana: Burroughs, [1936]. In repaired dj. Inscr to Raleigh Evans, 3 Mar 1937. cb June 25 (1805) $750
— Synthetic Men of Mars. Tarzana, [1940]. 1st Ed. In dj. pba May 4 (51) $350

## BURROUGHS

— Tales of Three Planets. NY: Canaveral Press, 1964. In dj.  pba May 4 (84) $110
— Tanar of Pellucidar. NY, [1930]. 1st Ed. In dj; bdgs with spine ends & corners rubbed.  pba May 4 (57) $1,800
— Tarzan and the Ant Men. Chicago, 1924. 1st Ed. In dj with small tears at extremities.  pba May 4 (18) $1,300
— Tarzan and the Castaways. NY: Canaveral Press, 1965. In dj.  pba May 4 (39) $100
— Tarzan and the City of Gold. Tarzana, [1933]. In dj with short tears & with creasing to front panel.  pba May 4 (26) $1,300
— Tarzan and the Forbidden City. Tarzana: Burroughs, [1938]. In dj with thin line of smoke damage at edge of front flap.  pba May 4 (33) $300
Anr copy. In backed & restored dj.  sg June 20 (30) $500
— Tarzan and the Foreign Legion. Tarzana, [1947]. In dj with chip.  pba May 4 (36) $75
— Tarzan and the Golden Lion. Chicago, 1923. In repaired dj; insect damage to spine.  pba May 4 (16) $1,200
Anr copy. In backed & restored dj.  sg June 20 (31) $800
Photoplay Ed. NY: Grosset & Dunlap, [1924]. In dj with a few tiny edge-tears.  pba May 4 (17) $500
— Tarzan and the Jewels of Opar. Chicago, 1918. In chipped dj.  pba May 4 (9) $1,600
Anr copy. Orig cloth; front hinge starting.  pba May 4 (10) $160
Anr Ed. NY: Grosset & Dunlap, 1918 [but later]. In dj with wear & repairs.  pba May 4 (11) $170
— Tarzan and the Leopard Men. Tarzana, [1935]. 1st Ed. In the laminated d/j with rubbing to spine head.  pba May 4 (28) $300
Anr copy. In d/j with wear to extremities.  pba May 4 (29) $150
— Tarzan and the Lion Man. Tarzana, [1934]. 1st Ed. In dj.  pba May 4 (27) $450
— Tarzan and the Lost Empire. NY: Metropolitan, [1929]. 1st Ed. In dj with minor rubbing.  pba May 4 (22) $900
Anr copy. In backed & restored dj.  sg June 20 (35) $800
— Tarzan and the Madman. NY: Canaveral Press, 1964. In dj; bdg bumped.  pba May 4 (38) $75
— Tarzan and the Tarzan Twins. NY: Canaveral Press, 1963. In dj with chip to spine foot.  pba May 4 (37) $85
— Tarzan and the Tarzan Twins with Jad-Bal-Ja, the Golden Lion. Racine: Whitman, [1936]. Pictorial bds, with only number 4056 on spine; joints & edges worn & abraded, snowman sticker on front pastedown. A few leaves with short tears; brittle.  pba May 4 (31) $100
— Tarzan at the Earth's Core. NY: Metropolitan, [1930]. In d/j with chips & tiny tears.  pba May 4 (23) $1,180
— Tarzan, Lord of the Jungle. Chicago: A. C. McClurg, 1928. In dj with small split. 1 plate detached but present.  pba May 4 (21) $140

Anr copy. In backed & restored dj.  sg June 20 (37) $800
— Tarzan of the Apes. Chicago, 1914. 1st Ed, 1st Ptg. Orig cloth, Curray's A bdg.  b May 30 (428) £800
Anr copy. Orig cloth, in pictorial dj with minor wear to spine head & corners & chip to spine foot; bdg leaning. Copy in orig d/j.  pba May 4 (1) $17,000
Ptg not stated. Orig cloth, in facsimile dj; bdg leaning.  sg June 20 (29) $800
— Tarzan the Invincible. Tarzana, [1931]. In chipped dj with foxing to verso & tear to crease.  pba May 4 (24) $475
Anr copy. In supplied remainder dj.  sg June 20 (32) $200
— Tarzan the Magnificent. Tarzana, [1939]. In laminated dj.  pba May 4 (35) $300
— Tarzan the Terrible. Chicago, 1921. In worn & chipped dj with adhesion damage to front panel, affecting letters (repaired on verso); bdg leaning.  pba May 4 (15) $550
Anr copy. Orig cloth; hinges cracked.  pba May 23 (41) $60
— Tarzan the Untamed. Chicago, 1920. In rubbed dj. Some soiling to tp.  pba May 4 (14) $900
Anr copy. In backed & restored dj.  sg June 20 (36) $800
— Tarzan Triumphant. Tarzana, [1932]. 1st Ed. In dj.  pba May 4 (25) $450
Anr copy. In backed & restored dj.  sg June 20 (38) $150
— The Tarzan Twins. Joliet, 1927. 1st Ed. Pictorial bds; extremities worn.  pba May 4 (20) $500
2d Ed. Pictorial bds; rubbed. Half-title with spots of adhesion damage.  pba May 4 (19) $700
— Tarzan's Quest. Tarzana, [1936]. In chipped dj; dampstain at edges of lower cover.  bbc Feb 26 (268) $290
Anr copy. In dj with minor rubbing & crease to front flap.  pba May 4 (32) $350
— Thuvia, Maid of Mars. Chicago, 1920. Orig cloth, in chipped dj; bdg with spine ends rubbed. With 10 plates.  pba May 4 (45) $1,300
Anr copy. Orig cloth, in soiled & chipped & silked dj.  pba Aug 22 (63) $450
Anr copy. In backed & restored dj.  sg June 20 (39) $800
Anr Ed. NY: Grosset & Dunlap, [c.1921]. Orig cloth, in dj with edge wear. With 4 plates.  pba May 4 (46) $150
— The War Chief. Chicago, 1927. In creased d/j.  pba May 4 (76) $1,300
— The Warlord of Mars. Chicago, 1919. 1st Ed, 1st Issue. In dj with chip to spine & small tear to rear panel.  pba May 4 (43) $3,000
Anr copy. Orig cloth; spine ends rubbed.  pba May 4 (44) $50; pba May 23 (44) $110

**Burroughs, John, 1837-1921**
— Camping & Tramping with Roosevelt. Bost., 1907. Inscr slip, 13 Jan 1915, laid in.  pba Aug 22 (896) $60

# BURROUGHS

**Burroughs, Stephen**
— Memoirs.... Albany, 1811. 2 vols in 1. 12mo, contemp sheep. Browned. sg Oct 26 (28) $80

**Burroughs, William S.**
— Junkie. NY: Ace Books, 1953. 1st Ed. Wraps, bound dos-a-dos with anr work on drug addiction, Narcotic Agent, by Maurice Helbrant. sg Dec 14 (19) $90
— Naked Lunch. NY, [1962]. In chipped dj with crease along spine. pba Aug 22 (64) $50
— Nova Express. L, [1966]. In chipped & rubbed dj. pba Aug 22 (65) $80

**Burrus, Ernest J.**
— Kino and the Cartography of Northwestern New Spain. [Tucson], 1965. One of 750. Folio, cloth. pba Nov 16 (37) $170; pba Feb 13 (32) $225
 Anr copy. Orig cloth. pba Apr 25 (320) $180
 Anr copy. Cloth. pba Aug 22 (897) $150
 1st Ed. Folio, orig cloth. Robbins copy. pba Mar 21 (47) $375
 Anr Ed. Rome: Jesuit Historical Institute, 1971. pba Feb 13 (31) $80

**Burt, Edward, d.1755**
— Letters from a Gentleman in the North of Scotland.... L, 1754. 1st Ed. 2 vols. 8vo, contemp calf; rubbed, rebacked. With 9 plates. Some spotting; p.120 & facing plate in vol II stained. S Oct 26 (387) £150 [Map House]

**Burt, William Austin —& Hubbard, Bela**
— Report on the Geography, Topography, and Geology of...the South Shore of Lake Superior. Detroit, 1845. 12mo, orig cloth. With folding map. A few small holes & tears. sg Oct 26 (258) $600
 Anr Ed. Detroit, 1846. 12mo, orig cloth; worn & stained. With 2 maps on 1 folding sheet. Text foxed. wa Feb 29 (414) $230

**Burtin, Francois Xavier de, 1743-1818**
— Memoire sur la Question quels sont les vegetaux.... Brussels, 1784. 1st Ed. 4to, contemp wraps; upper wrap worn away. Title with hole & tear; margins soiled; T1v & T2r spotted. Ck Mar 22 (65) £50
— Oryctographie de Bruxelles.... [Brussels], 1784. Folio, orig bds; backstrip lacking, stitching weak. With engraved title & 32 hand-colored plates. C Nov 29 (86) £450

**Burton, Mrs. General**
— The Squatter and the Don.... San Francisco, 1885. 1st Ed. Orig cloth; rear joint & spine foot gouged. Robbins copy. pba Mar 21 (207) $50

**Burton, Sir Richard Francis, 1821-90**
See also: Limited Editions Club
— First Footsteps in East Africa. L, 1856. 1st Ed. 8vo, later half mor. With 2 maps & 4 colored plates. With the inserted leaf cancelling Appendix IV. Marginal dampstaining throughout. CE Feb 21 (30) $750

# AMERICAN BOOK PRICES CURRENT

 Anr copy. Modern mor. With 2 maps & 4 colored plates. Without the 4th Appendix; a few leaves loose. S Mar 28 (357) £400
— Goa, and the Blue Mountains. L, 1851. 1st Ed. 8vo, modern half calf. With 4 plates & 1 folding map. Some foxing. CE Nov 8 (174) $650
— The Lake Regions of Central Africa. L, 1860. 1st Ed. 2 vols. 8vo, orig cloth; spine ends repaired. Vol II lacking pp. 155-56 & ads at end. bba Nov 16 (275) £550 [Maggs]
— The Land of Midian Revisited. L, 1879. 1st Ed. 8vo, modern cloth. With folding map, & 36 plates. Some discoloration. S Oct 26 (24) £250 [Scott]
— Personal Narrative of a Pilgrimage to El-Medinah and Meccah. L, 1855-56. 1st Ed. 3 vols. 8vo, contemp calf; joints & extremities worn. With 14 plates (5 colored), & 3 maps & plans. Lacks half-titles; final text page in vol I browned. CE Nov 8 (175) $1,600

**Burton, Sir Richard Francis, 1821-90 —& Drake, Charles F. T.**
— Unexplored Syria. L, 1872. 1st Ed. 2 vols. 8vo, modern cloth. With 2 frontises, folding map, & 25 plates (11 folding). Some discoloration. S Oct 26 (25) £360 [Marins]

**Burton, Robert, 1577-1640**
See also: Nonesuch Press
— The Anatomy of Melancholy. L, 1676. 8th Ed. Folio, contemp calf; rebacked, corners replaced, hinges repaired. pba Sept 14 (89) $275
 Anr Ed. L, 1804. 2 vols. Later half mor; joints rubbed. sg Feb 8 (66) $90
 Anr copy. Contemp calf; rebacked, worn, rear cover of Vol II dampstained. wa Nov 16 (142) $70
 Regency Ed. L, 1826. 2 vols. 8vo, contemp half mor; joints & extremities rubbed. F Mar 28 (575) $140

**Burton Library, William Evans**
— [Sale Catalogue] Bibliotheca Dramatica. Catalogue of the Theatrical and Miscellaneous Library of.... [NY, 1860]. Bound with: Shakspeariana Burtonensis: Being a Catalogue...Shakespeariana of the late W. E. Burton.... Compiled by Joseph Sabin. 4to, contemp half mor, orig wraps bound in; scuffed. Frontis foxed. pba Aug 22 (541) $70

**Burton, William Kinninmond.** See: Milne & Burton

**Bury, Richard de, 1287-1345.** See: Grolier Club

**Bury, Thomas Talbot, 1811-77**
— Coloured Views of the Liverpool and Manchester Railway. Oldham, [1977]. One of 250. 4to, contemp calf by Zaenhsdorf. S Oct 26 (388) £160 [Levitt]

**Bush, George**
— A Grammar of the Hebrew Language.... NY, 1835. 12mo, orig cloth; spine ends frayed with loss. sg Oct 26 (175) $350

356

**Bush, Richard J.**
— Reindeer, Dogs and Snow-Shoes. NY: Harper, 1871. Orig cloth; spine ends frayed, corners showing. Long tear to folding map.  pba July 25 (386) $130

**Busoni, Ferruccio B., 1866-1924**
— Arlecchino. Ein theatralisches Capriccio. Berlin, 1932. One of 20 on japon. Illus by Rafaello Busoni. Folio, vellum-backed pictorial bds; worn & soiled.  O Mar 5 (37) $170

**Butcher, David**
— The Stanbrook Abbey Press 1956-1990 Andoversford: Whittington Press, 1992. One of 350. 4to, half cloth.  sg Feb 15 (278) $150
— The Whittington Press: A Bibliography 1971-1981. Andoversford: Whittington Press, 1982. One of 95 specially bound & with additional specimens. Folio, orig half vellum.  bba May 9 (351) £550 [Thomsen]

**Butler, Alban**
— The Lives of the Fathers, Martyrs, and Other Principal Saints. L, 1812-13. 12mo, contemp calf; rebacked, rubbed. Minor stains.  b Jan 31 (48) £80

**Butler, Arthur Gardiner, 1844-1925**
— Foreign Finches in Captivity. L, 1894-[96]. 1st Ed. 4to, orig cloth; some wear. With 60 hand-colored plates.  O Mar 5 (38) $100

**Butler, Henry**
— South African Sketches. L, 1841. Folio, orig cloth. With litho title & 10 hand-colored plates (of 15). Tear to 1 plate.  b Sept 20 (410) £120

**Butler, Joseph, 1692-1752**
— The Analogy of Religion, Natural and Revealed, to the Constitution and Course of Nature. L, 1736. 1st Ed. 4to, contemp calf; scuffed, soiled. Marginal dampstaining.  F Mar 28 (300) $140

**Butler, Robert Olen**
— They Whisper. Huntington Beach: James Cahill, 1993. One of 150. Half mor.  pba Oct 5 (11) $55

**Butler, Samuel, 1612-80**
— Hudibras. L, 1732. Illus by William Hogarth. 12mo, contemp calf; joints cracked, new endpapers. With port & 9 plates.  sg Mar 21 (72) $80
Anr Ed. L, 1764. 2 vols. 8vo, contemp calf; joints starting.  pba Mar 7 (47) $130
Anr Ed. L, 1806. Ed by Zachary Grey; illus by Wm. Hogarth. 2 vols. 8vo, recent half mor gilt; worn. With port & 16 plates. Tape to verso of folding plate.  wa Feb 29 (10) $55
Anr Ed. L: Baldwyn, 1819. 3 vols. 8vo, later 19th-cent mor gilt; ends worn. With 11 plates, including additional titles. Some foxing; engraved titles trimmed; several text leaves trimmed & inlaid to size. Extra-illus with 60 hand-colored ports separately pbd to accompany this Ed.  sg Sept 21 (103) $150
Anr copy. Later half lea; rebacked preserving old backstrips, edges worn. with 68 plates & 2 engraved titles. L.p. copy with many plates on india paper.  wa Nov 16 (143) $210
Anr Ed. L, 1822. Illus by J. Clark. 2 vols. 8vo, later half calf. With 12 hand-colored plates.  wa Feb 1 (19) $120

**Butler, Samuel, 1774-1839**
— Atlas of Antient Geography. Phila., 1841. 8vo, half sheep; worn. With 21 maps, hand-colored in outline. Some foxing.  sg Dec 7 (11) $200
Anr Ed. L, [c.1850]. 8vo, half leaf lea; extremities rubbed. With engraved title & 22 double-page maps, hand-colored in outline.  sg Dec 7 (10) $90

**Butler, Samuel, 1835-1902.** See: Gregynog Press; Limited Editions Club

**Butlin, Martin**
— The Paintings and Drawings of William Blake. New Haven, 1981. 2 vols. 4to, orig cloth, in djs.  sg Jan 11 (47) $130

**Butlin, Martin —&**
**Joll, Evelyn**
— The Paintings of J. M. W. Turner. New Haven, 1984. 4to, orig cloth, in dj.  O May 7 (77) $110
Anr copy. Revised Ed. 2 vols. 4to, orig cloth, in djs.  sg Jan 11 (436) $80

**Butter, William, 1726-1805**
— A Treatise on the Disease commonly called Angina Pectoris. L, 1791. 1st Ed. 8vo, modern calf. Half-title with smudge; preface leaf misbound; E2 browned.  Ck Mar 22 (66) £65

**Butterworth, Benjamin**
— The Growth of Industrial Art. Wash., 1888. 1st Ed. Folio, cloth; worn & scuffed, hinges split, free endpapers chipped. Lacking Plates 135-42; some wear & chipping. Sold w.a.f.  bbc Feb 26 (427) $350

**Butterworth, James**
— Manchester, a Poem. Manchester, 1803. 8vo, modern half mor. Tp repaired.  b Dec 5 (186) £190

**Buxton, Sir Thomas Powell, 1837-1915**
— The African Slave Trade. L, 1839. 8vo, orig cloth; spine heel chipped.  sg Oct 26 (339) $130

**Bybelsche...**
— Bybelsche Historien des Ouden en des Nieuwen Testaments. Dordrecht, 1702. Folio, contemp bds; worn. With 51 plates. Minor marginal soiling; small stains on tp.  P Dec 12 (44) $850

**Byne, Arthur —&**
**Stapley, Mildred**
— Decorated Wooden Ceilings in Spain. NY, [1920]. Folio, unbound. With 50 plates. Tp soiled & torn; plates stamped recto & verso.  sg June 13 (69) $80
— Majorcan Houses and Gardens. NY, 1928. Library markings.  sg June 13 (4) $350

**Bynner, Witter.** See: Ford & Bynner

### Byrd, Richard Evelyn, 1888-1957
— Alone. NY, 1938. Illus by Richard E. Harrison. In dj. Sgd on front flyleaf (which has been cut diagonally to remove recipient's name). pba June 13 (138) $60
— Discovery: the Story of the Second Byrd Antarctic Expedition. NY, 1935. One of 500. 8vo, half cloth. pba Nov 30 (75) $140
— Little America: Aerial Exploration in the Antarctic.... NY, 1930. Sgd, 1931. pba July 25 (19) $60
Anr copy. Sgd. wa Dec 14 (120) $70
One of 1,000. sg Mar 7 (275) $175; sg May 16 (15) $175

### Byron, George Anson, Baron Byron
— Voyage of H.M.S. Blonde to the Sandwich Islands. L, 1826. 1st Ed. 4to, contemp half calf; joints cracked, spine scuffed. With 15 maps & plates. Some foxing. bbc June 24 (172) $1,350

### Byron, George Gordon Noel, Lord, 1788-1824
See also: Fore-Edge Paintings
— Beppo, a Venetian Story. [Kentfield, Calif.]: Allen Press, 1963. ("A Venetian Story.") One of 150. Oblong folio, loose as issued. With 35 plates. cb June 25 (1900) $350; pba June 20 (14) $275
Anr copy. Cloth. sg Feb 15 (3) $140
— The Corsair. L, 1814. 1st Ed, 2d Issue. 8vo, 19th-cent half calf; joints & extremities rubbed. Some spotting; port inserted. F Mar 28 (586) $70
— Don Juan. L, 1820-24. 1st Foolscap 8vo Ed. Cantos I-XVI in 6 vols. 8vo, 19th-cent calf gilt. S July 11 (144) £900
— Don Juan. Cantos I & II. L, 1819. 1st Ed. 4to, orig bds; rebacked badly. Tp & half-title from anr copy; foxed. wd Nov 15 (36) $150
— English Bards and Scotch Reviewers. L, [1809]. 1st Ed, 2d Issue. 12mo, orig bds; joints & corners worn. CE Sept 27 (70) $800
Issue not stated. Later calf by Zaehnsdorf. sg Sept 21 (105) $250
— Hebrew Melodies. L, 1815. 1st Ed, 1st Issue. 8vo, orig wraps, unopened. CE Sept 27 (72) $1,100
2d Issue. Later calf by Riviere. sg Sept 21 (107) $110
— Hours of Idleness. Newark, 1807. 1st Ed. 8vo, 19th-cent calf; rebacked, extremities worn, front cover loose. CE Sept 27 (69) $700
Anr Ed. L, 1820. 8vo, calf gilt by Zaehnsdorf. Prelims from anr copy; facsimile half-title; some browning. wd Nov 15 (37) $70
— The Island, or Christian and his Comrades. L, 1823. 1st Ed. 8vo, contemp half calf; rebacked. b Mar 20 (68) £180
Anr copy. Orig wraps; soiled. b Mar 20 (69) £260
Anr copy. Orig wraps; spine ends chipped. CE Sept 27 (73) $400
— Letters and Journals of.... L, [c.1880]. 2 vols. 8vo, contemp half mor; joints & extremities scuffed. Some browning & foxing. F Mar 28 (581) $60

— Marino Faliero.... L, 1821. 1st Ed, 1st Issue. 8vo, orig bds; worn & soiled, spine gone. Some spotting. F Mar 28 (584) $120
— Monody on the Death of the Right Honourable R. B. Sheridan.... L, 1817. 2d Ed. 8vo, calf by Riviere; spine def. Half-title repaired. wd Nov 15 (38) $125
— Poemi di... Byron recati in italiano.... Milan: Giuseppe Crespi, 1834. Copy on blue paper specially ptd for Conte Gaetano Melzi. Trans by Giuseppe Nicolini. 8vo, orig bds covered with carta marocchinata, unopened; some rubbing to extremities. C Apr 3 (57) £1,500
— Sardanapalus, a Tragedy. The Two Foscari, a Tragedy. Cain, a Mystery. L, 1821. 1st Ed. 8vo, 19th-cent half mor gilt; joints & extremities scuffed, minor soiling. Some spotting. F Mar 28 (583) $70
— The Siege of Corinth.... L, 1816. 1st Ed. 8vo, later calf by Riviere. Lacking final ads. sg Sept 21 (111) $90
— Werner, a Tragedy. L, 1823. 1st Ed, 1st Issue. 8vo, 19th-cent half mor gilt; soiled & scuffed. F Mar 28 (582) $90
— Works. L, 1832-33. 17 vols. 8vo, contemp half mor; extremities scuffed, bowed. Some leaves detached, dampstained or browned. F Mar 28 (578) $425
Anr copy. Half mor gilt; joints tender, some spine heads chipped. Some dampstaining & browning; lacking 3 half-titles. Extra-illus with c.90 additional plates. wa June 20 (33) $325
Anr Ed. L, 1847. 17 vols. 8vo, half mor. pba Sept 14 (92) $375
Anr Ed. L, 1898-1904. 13 vols. 8vo, orig cloth. bba May 30 (263) £280 [Katrina]

### Byron, George Gordon Noel, Lord, 1788-1824 —& Rogers, Samuel, 1763-1855
— Lara, a Tale; Jacqueline, a Tale. L, 1814. 1st Ed. 8vo, later calf gilt, by Zaehnsdorf. sg Sept 21 (108) $80

### Byron, John, 1723-86
— The Narrative of the Honourable John Byron.... Dublin, 1768. 1st Dublin Ed. 8vo, contemp calf. Fore-edge stained; B4 fore-edge sgd. S Oct 26 (607) £190 [Bennell]

### Bytemeister, Heinrich Johann, 1698-1745
— Bibliothecae appendix, sive catalogus apparatus curiosorum artificialium et naturalium.... Helmstedt, 1735. Folio, modern half calf. With engraved title & 28 plates. Plates 17 & 18 cut down & mtd; inner margins of tp repaired; 1st gathering reattached; duplicate from Royal LIbrary, Munich. Madsen copy. S Mar 14 (75) £1,200

# C

### Cabala...
— Cabala, sive Scrinia sacra, Mysteries of State and Government.... L, 1663. 2d Ed. Folio, later calf; rebacked, edges rubbed. CE June 12 (164) $50
Anr copy. Modern half calf with older spine strip laid on; endpapers foxed. Some soiling; tear to tp. pba Nov 30 (76) $225

**Cabell, James Branch, 1879-1958.** See: Golden Cockerel Press; Limited Editions Club

**Cabeus, Nicolaus**
— Philosophia magnetica.... Ferrara: Francesco Succhi, 1629 [Ptd title: Cologne: Johann Kinck, 1629]. 1st Ed. Folio, 18th-cent calf; rubbed. Tp & dedication leaf with browning. Madsen copy. S Mar 14 (76) £2,000

**Cabinet...**
— Cabinet du Roi: Fetes de Versailles. Paris, [c.1720]. 3 parts in 1 vol. Folio, contemp red mor gilt with gilt arms of France & monograms at corners & on spine; minor staining. With 20 plates. Some marginal defs. S June 27 (306) £7,000

**Cable, George Washington, 1844-1925**
— The Grandissimes. A Story of Creole Life. NY, 1880. 1st Ed. 8vo, cloth; spine ends rubbed. pba Dec 14 (27) $120
— Old Creole Days. NY, 1879. 1st Ed, 1st Issue. 12mo, cloth; spine ends & corners rubbed. pba Mar 7 (49) $100

**Cacciatore, Leonardo**
— Nuovo Atlante Istorico.... Florence, 1831-33. 4th Ed. 3 parts in 2 vols. Oblong 4to, contemp mor gilt; Vol I front joint starting. With 86 (of 143) maps & plates. Severe ink blot on 1 text leaf in Part 2; Part 3 imperf. sg Dec 7 (12) $375

**Caddy, Lieut. J. H.**
— Scenery of the Windward and Leeward Islands. L: Ackermann, 1837. Oblong folio, loose in cloth case. With 12 colored plates. 2 plates chipped in upper outer corners. sg Apr 18 (34) $3,600

**Cadman, S. Parkes**
— The Parables of Jesus. Phila.: David McKay, [1931]. Illus by N. C. Wyeth. Orig cloth; spine ends frayed. wa June 20 (307) $220

**Cadogan, William**
— A Dissertation on the Gout.... L, 1781. 8vo, bds. b May 30 (13) £280

**Caen, Herb**
— Only in San Francisco. Garden City, 1960. In dj. Inscr. pba Apr 25 (322) $50

**Caen, Herb —&**
**Kingman, Dong**
— San Francisco: City on Golden Hills. Garden City, 1967. One of 350. pba Feb 12 (264) $85

**Caesar, Caius Julius, 100-44 B.C.**
See also: Limited Editions Club

### The Commentaries
— 1482. - Venice: Octavianus Scottus. 8vo, calf; spine ends chipped, joint cracked. Minor worming; last 2 leaves repaired. 148 leaves. Goff C-22. cb Feb 14 (2511) $2,250

— 1635. - Leiden: Elzevir. 12mo, contemp calf; rebacked, scuffed. With engraved title & 3 folding maps. bbc June 24 (214) $225
— 1661. - Opera. Amst.: Elzevir. 8vo, later half calf; worn. Folding map lacking piece from lower right corner, which is replaced with plain paper. pba Mar 7 (50) $75
— 1753. - L. Folio, lea; covers detached. rs Nov 11 (84) $425
— 1790. - L. 2 vols. 8vo, 19th-cent mor extra; rubbed. sg Feb 8 (67) $80

**Caffin, Charles Henry**
— Photography as a Fine Art. NY, 1901. 1st Ed. 4to, cloth; worn & soiled. Soiling & penciled notations on several leaves. sg Feb 29 (264) $90

**Cahen, Gustave**
— Eugene Boudin, sa vie et sone oeuvre. Paris, 1900. One of 300. 4to, orig wraps; broken. Lacking 1 plate (of 10); foxed. sg Sept 7 (53) $225

**Cahiers...**
— Cahiers d'art. Paris, 1948. Nos 23. 4to, wraps. sg Jan 11 (342) $90
  Anr Ed. Paris, 1951. Nos 26. 4to, cloth, orig wraps bound in. With lithos by Miro & Giacometti. sg Jan 11 (71) $250

**Cahill, Holger**
— George O "Pop" Hart. Twenty-Four Selections from his Work. NY: The Downtown Gallery, 1928. One of 250. Orig bds; backstrip def. With an orig litho, sgd by Hart. sg Sept 7 (175) $150
— Max Weber. NY: Downtown Gallery, 1930. Bds; front joint repaired. With 32 plates. sg Jan 11 (462) $110
  One of 250, sgd by Weber. Cloth; spine ends rubbed. With orig sgd litho as frontis. sg Sept 7 (347) $375
  Anr copy. Cloth; rubbed. sg Feb 15 (311) $250

**Cahill, James**
— Ten Tales. Huntington Beach: James Cahill, 1994. One of 250. Foreword by Lawrence Block; into by Poppy Brite. pba Dec 7 (26) $60

**Cahusac, Louis de, 1706-59**
— Zeneide, comedie en un acte.... Paris, 1744. 8vo, contemp red mor gilt with arms of the duc de la Vrilliere. Fuerstenberg - Schaefer copy. S Dec 7 (93) £600

**Cailler, Pierre**
— Catalogue raisonne de l'oeuvre lithographie et grave de Hans Erni, 1930-1970. Geneva, 1969-71. 2 vols. 4to, cloth, in djs. sg Jan 11 (165) $175

**Caillet, Albert Louis**
— Manuel bibliographique des sciences psychiques ou occultes. Nieuwkoop, 1964. One of 300. 3 vols. Reprint of Paris 1912 Ed. sg May 16 (143A) $275

**Cain, James M.**
— Mildred Pierce. NY, 1941. 1st Ed, Advance copy. 8vo, orig wraps; edges worn. F June 20 (17) $120
— Our Government. NY, 1930. In chipped dj. sg June 20 (40) $90
— Three of a Kind. NY, 1944. In dj. Inscr. pba Aug 22 (72) $75

**Cain, Julien**
[-] Humanisme actif. Melanges d'art et de litterature offerts a Julien Cain. Paris, 1968. 2 vols. 4to, orig wraps; soiled & scuffed. With etched frontis by Dunoyer de Segonzac & other illusts. Review copy, with Ls requesting a review from Pierre Beres to Lawrence Thompson. O Mar 26 (55) $130

**Caldas, Francisco Jose de, 1768-1816**
— Ensayo de una Memoria sobre un Nuevo Metodo de medir las Montanas.... Burdeos, 1819. 4to, contemp wraps; backstrip def. sg Oct 19 (223) $1,000

**Calder, Alexander, 1898-1976**
— Calder. Paris: Galerie Maeght, 1973. Folio, loose as issued in wraps; extremities worn. Derriere le Miroir, No 201. sg Sept 7 (64) $175

**Calderon de la Barca, Pedro, 1600-81**
— Primera parte de comedias. Madrid: Maria de Quinones for Pedro Coello & Manual Lopez, 1636. 4to, contemp vellum upper cover only; worn. Last leaf detached, affecting inner margin; some browning. C Apr 3 (58) £3,200

**Caldwell, Erskine, 1903-87**
See also: Bourke-White & Caldwell
— Journeyman. NY, 1935. 1st Ed, one of 1,475. pba Jan 25 (46) $55

**California**
— Atlas of Maps and Seismographs Accompanying the Report of the State Earthquake Investigation Commission upon the California Earthquake of April 18, 1906. Wash., 1908. Folio, orig cloth; worn & soiledd. Accession number on tp verso. cb June 25 (1725) $450
— Bel-Air, a Picturesque Domain of Homes. Los Angeles: Alphonzo E. Bell Corporation, [1927]. Pictorial wraps in color. pba Feb 12 (391) $80
— Bishop's Oakland Directory for 1876-7. Oakland: B. C. Vandall, 1876. Orig half lea; worn, spine head chipped. Tears to early leaves, including tp. pba Nov 16 (201) $275
— California Gold Discovery. San Francisco, 1947. 1st Ed. Orig cloth. Robbins copy. pba Mar 21 (120) $90
— Chinese Immigration: Its Social, Moral, and Political Effect. Report of the California State Senate of its Special Committee on Chinese Immigration. Sacramento, 1878. 1st Ed. 19th-cent mor; spine faded. Robbins copy. pba Mar 21 (57) $275
— City and County Directory of San Joaquin, Stanislaus, Merced, and Tuolumne.... San Francisco, 1881. 8vo, orig half lea; stained, edge-worn, spine rubbed. pba Nov 16 (242) $900

— History of Merced County.... Fresno: California History Books, 1974. Reprint of 1881 Ed. pba Feb 12 (460) $50
— History of Placer County.... Oakland, 1882. Folio, later cloth, orig cloth & lea spine laid in; partly misbound. This copy taken apart for reprint Ed & reassembled afterwards; some tears & chipping & tape-repairs. pba Feb 12 (467) $170
— History of Santa Barbara County, California.... Oakland, 1883. Folio, orig half calf; extremities worn, new endpapers. With 2 litho titles, 83 litho plates & 13 port plates. Some soiling, foxing & marginal dampstaining; some fraying; a few tears into text; lacking 8 pages. cb Feb 14 (2577) $600
— Napa City and County Portfolio and Directory. Napa: H. A. Darms, [1908]. Folio, orig cloth; spine worn & chipped. pba Feb 12 (465) $425
— Official Historical Atlas Map of Alameda County, California. Oakland, 1878. Folio, orig half lea; spine perished, covers worn, front cover detached along with front free endpaper, tp & 1 double-page map. Marginal tears & soiling. pba Nov 16 (8) $700
— Report of the Board of Commmissioners on the Irrigation of the San Joaquin, Tulare, and Sacramento Valleys of the State of California. Wash., 1874. Bound with: Report of the Board of Commissioners of the West Side Irrigation District... Report of the Engineer on the Result of the Reconnaisance of Tulare Lake and Report of the Engineer of the Sacramento Valley. Sacramento, 1877. Calf; worn & scuffed. Some fold tears to charts; foxed. William Hammond Hill's annotated copy. pba Feb 12 (34) $60
— Report of the Commission on Roads in Yosemite National Park, California. Wash., 1900. Disbound from larger vol, with a few leaves loose. With 2 folding profiles & large folding map. 56th Congress, 1st Session, Senate Exec. Doc. 155. pba Aug 8 (219) $50
— Santa Catalina Island, Winter and Summer. Los Angeles: Wilmington Transportation Co., [1895]. 12mo, pictorial wraps; small stain on front cover. With bank compliments stamp. pba Feb 12 (400) $110
— A Short Account of the Big Trees of California. Wash., 1900. Ptd wraps. Prepared by the USDA Division of Forestry for the U.S. Senate Committee on the Public Lands. pba Feb 12 (168) $60

ARRILLAGA, JOSE. - Recopilacion de Leyes, Decretos, Bandos.... Mexico, 1838. 1st Collected Ed. Half bds; spine dry & scuffed, bds rubbed. Larson copy. pba Sept 28 (205) $300

JOHNSON, KENNETH M. - Pious Fund. Los Angeles, 1963. One of 225. Half bds. Folded facsimile of letter of Don Antonio Bucareli to Father Serra in 1775. Larson copy. pba Sept 28 (190) $55

JUNTA DE FOMENTO DE CALIFORNIAS. - Coleccion de los Principales Trabajos... para promover el progresso de.... Mexico, 1827. 8 pamphlets bound together. 8vo, contemp wraps; outer wraps soiled & aged. Robbins copy. pba Mar 21 (175) $1,800

MIDWINTER INTERNATIONAL EXPOSITION. - California Educational Series. Colored Art Series. Midwinter Fair and the Golden State. San Francisco, 1894. 2 vols. Folio, ptd wraps; spine chipped, some discoloration. With 24 chromolitho plates. pba Feb 12 (306) $50

SONOMA COUNTY. - Sonoma County and Russian River Valley, Illustrated. San Francisco, [1888]. Folio, pictorial wraps; foxed. With color litho supplement of Verano & with large folding map of Sonoma County. pba Apr 25 (671) $475

**California Column...**
— The California Column: Its Campaigns and Services in New Mexico, Arizona and Texas.... Santa Fe, 1908. Orig wraps. Historical Society of New Mexico, No 11. pba Apr 25 (556) $150

**California Letter Sheets**
— Assassination of James King of William. San Francisco: Britton & Rey, [1856]. ALs by member of the vigalantes. Double sheet, 10.875 by 8.4 inches. With 4 litho illusts. Worn with small defs at folds & blank margins. Larson copy. Baird 5. pba Feb 12 (552) $2,750

Anr Ed. San Francisco: Britton & Rey, 14 May 1856. Double sheet, 10.875 by 16.75 inches. With 4 litho illusts. Laid on backing sheet, with tears repaired. Baird 5. pba Nov 16 (214) $75

— Commandments to California Wives. San Francisco: James M. Hutchings, 1855. Drawn by W. C. Butler. Double sheet, 11.25 by 9 inches. With 2 wood-engraved vignettes, & 3 small illusts. Chip to right upper corner; repaired tears. Larson copy. Baird 42. pba Feb 12 (550) $250

Anr copy. AL sgd by P. S. Tappen, 28 Apr 1856 to Miss C. Van Allen. Double sheet, 11 by 9 inches. With 2 wood-engraved vignettes, & 3 small illusts. Baird 42. pba July 25 (336) $475

— Crossing the Plains. Sacramento: Barber & Baker,1853. Engraved by George H. Baker. Double sheet, 11 by 8.75 inches. With 13 wood-engraved vignettes Old creases & breaks from folding; indecipherable pencil writing on rear blank sheet. Baird 47. pba Nov 16 (215) $325

— Downieville; Sierra County, Cal. San Francisco: Sam W. Langton & Bro., 1852. Litho by Cooke & LeCount. 9-1/4in by 12-1/2in Larson copy. pba Sept 28 (432) $600

— Fire in San Francisco. Jn [sic] the Night from the 3d.- 4th May, 1851. Loss $20,000,000. San Francisco: Justh & Quirot, 1851. Double sheet, 8-9/16 by 10-7/16 inches. With 1 litho illust. Worn & silked. Larson copy. Baird 77. pba Feb 12 (547) $140

Anr Ed. San Francisco, 1851. Litho by Justh & Co.. 11.25 by 9 inches, folded to 4 pp. With 1 litho illust. with contemp hand-coloring. Silked. Larson copy. Baird 77. pba Feb 12 (546) $650

— The First Trial and Execution in S. Francisco on the Night of 10th of June at 2 O'Clock. San Francisco: Justh & Quirot, 1851. Drawn by W. C. K.. 8.1 by 10.7 inches. With 1 litho illust. Larson copy. Baird 79. pba Feb 12 (553) $250

— Great Fire in San Fransisco. [sic] May 4th, 1850. 400 Buildings Burned! Loss $5,000,000!. San Francisco: W. B. Cooke & Co., [1850]. Double sheet, 10.5 by 8.75 inches. With 1 litho illust & map.. Larson copy. Baird 96a. pba Feb 12 (548) $200

— Hutching's California Scenes. The California Indians. San Francisco: J. M. Hutchings, [1854?, 1861?]. Drawn by Charles Nahl; wood-engraved by Anthony & Baker. Double sheet, 11.35 by 9.1 inches. With 8 wood-engraved vignettes. Repaired fold breaks. Larson copy. Baird 105. pba Feb 12 (554) $250

— Miners at Work with Long Toms. San Francisco: Britton & Rey, [1852]. Litho by Quirot & Co.. 10.75 by 8.75 inches. With 3 litho illusts. Edge tears. Larson copy. Baird 159. pba Feb 12 (544) $350

— Miner's Life Illustrated. Sacramento: Barber & Baker, 1854. 11.25 by 8.75 inches, folded to 4 pp. With 13 wood-engraved illusts.. Contains ALs of a miner dated 23 Nov 1854. Larson copy. Baird 165. pba Feb 12 (543) $1,400

— The Miner's Ten Commandments. San Francisco: J. M. Hutchings, 1854. Engraved by Harrison Eastman, and Anthony & Baker. 11 by 9.25 inches. With 11 wood-engraved vignettes. Tiny holes at old folds. Larson copy. Baird 167b. pba Feb 12 (549) $750

— Pavilion, for the First Industrial Exhibition of the Mechanics' Institute, of the City of San Francisco, Cal., commencing on September 7th, 1857. San Francisco, 1857. Lithograph by Kuchel & Dresel, ptd by Britton & Rey. On blue paper, with lined integral leaf, 9 by 11.25 inches With view of the domed pavilion with a gathering before the entrance. Some creasing; short tear at lower edge. Baird 194. pba Apr 25 (594) $425

— San Francisco, 1854. San Francisco: Britton & Rey, 1854. ALs from "your affectionate brother Napoleon" to his sister, 16 May 1854, with 2 x's marking spots. Double sheet, 10.5 by 16.75 inches. With 1 litho illust. Creased at folds & with short tears repaired. Baird 239. pba Nov 16 (217) $325

— San Francisco Upper California, in November 1851. San Francisco: Quirot & Co., 1851. Variant with Lith. Britton & Rey at lower left below image. Double sheet, 10.5 by 16.25 inches. With 1 litho illust. Baird 252. pba Apr 25 (596) $250

Anr Ed. San Francisco: Justh, Quirot & Co., 1851. AL sgd by D. C. Stockny[?], dated at Sacramento, 17 Nov 1851, to Susan DeWitt Engraved by C. Quirot. Double sheet, 10-11/16 by 17 inches. With 1 litho illust. Creased & worn at old folds; some holes & loss; discolored. Clifford copy. Baird 252. pba Apr 25 (595) $500

— Sundry Amusements in the Mines. San Francisco: Britton & Rey, [1850s]. Double sheet, 8.25 by 10.5 inches. With 4 litho illusts. Larson copy. Baird 268. pba Feb 12 (545) $250

— View of Agua Fria Town. San Francisco: Quirot & Co., [1850s]. Double sheet, 8.5 by 10.5 inches. With 1 litho illust. Larson copy. Baird 281. pba Feb 12 (551) $375

— View of Nevada. Pub. by A. W. Potter, Miners Book Store, Main Street. San Francisco: Britton & Rey, [n.d.]. 10.5 by 16.5 inches, hinged to mat. With view of Nevada City, from a daguerreotype by Kilbourn. Chip to lower left corner & short edge tear. Baird 308. pba Apr 25 (597) $500

**California Star**
— The California Star: Yerba Buena and San Francisco. Volume I, 1847-48. Berkeley, 1965. pba Feb 12 (533) $75

**Californian...**
— The Californian. Monterey, 10 Oct 1846. Vol I, No 9. 32cm by 21.3cm, disbound. Trimmed at top; sewing holes visible; staining in right margin. Sgd by Capt. Wm. Mervine (cropped). Larson copy. pba Feb 12 (531) $900
— The Californian, Volume I. Facsimile Reproductions of Thirty-eight Numbers.... San Francisco: Howell, 1971. Folio, cloth. pba Feb 12 (530) $75

**Call, Johann van**
— Admirandorum quadruplex spectaculum, delectum, pictum, et aeri incisum. Amst.: Petrus Schenk, [c.1700]. 4 parts in 1 vol. 4to, contemp calf, armorial bdg. With engraved title, engraved dedication, 4 engraved part titles, port, 71 plates & engraved list of plates. Repaired tears to lower margins of 2 plates. b May 30 (334) £1,000

**Callahan, Harry**
— Callahan. NY, 1976. Ed by John Szarkowski. Folio, cloth; bumped. sg Feb 29 (60) $80
— Photographs. Santa Barbara: El Mochuelo Gallery, [1964]. One of 1,500. 4to, orig bds; endpapers stained. sg Feb 29 (61) $375

**Callander, John**
— Terra Australis Cognita, or Voyages to the Terra Australis, or Southern Hemisphere. Edin., 1766-68. 3 vols. 8vo, contemp calf; worn, loose. sg Mar 7 (37) $5,200

**Callimachus**
— Inni di Callimaco Cirenese cogli epigrammi.... Parma: Bodoni, 1792. One of 6 on carta d'anonnay. 4to, half vellum; rubbed. In Italian only. C Nov 29 (117) £1,100

**Callis, Robert**
— The Reading of Robert Callis upon the Statute of...Sewers. L, 1685. 2d Ed. 4to, calf; rebacked & recornered. K June 23 (165) $225

**Callot, Jacques, 1592-1635**
— Das gesamte Werk. Munich, [1971]. 2 vols. In djs. sg June 13 (70) $100

**Callotto...**
— Il Callotto Resusciato, oder Neii eingerichtes Zwerchen Cabinet. Amst.: Wilhelm Engelbert Koning, [c.1716-20]. ("Dwergen Tooneel of Geschakelde Samenspraak van des zelfs Personagien. Le Monde plein de fols....") Folio, 19th-contemp calf elaborately gilt. With 78 plates within elaborate historiated borders. Plate 40 repaired, affecting surface; a few other marginal repairs; small rusthole in Plate 24. S June 27 (307) £5,000

**Calvo, Marco Fabio**
— Antiquae urbis Romae cum regionibus simulachrum. Rome: Valerio Dorico, Apr 1532. Folio, later half cloth. Marginal soiling & fraying. C Apr 3 (60) £8,000

**Cambray, —— de, Chevalier**
— Maniere de fortifier de Mr. de Vauban. Paris: Cramoisy, 1694. 2 parts in 1 vol. 8vo, old calf; worn & chipped, backstrip lacking fragments. With frontis & 31 folding plates. Wormed at bottom edge; title of Vol I with "Tome Premier" erased. wa Feb 29 (196) $180

**Cambridge...**
— The Cambridge Bibliography of English Literature. Cambr., 1966. 5 vols. 8vo, orig cloth. sg Apr 11 (70) $100
— Cambridge History of China. Cambr., [1986]. Ed by Denis Twitchett & Michael Loewe. 9 vols. In djs. pba Jan 4 (181) $275
— The Cambridge History of English Literature. Cambr., 1908-16. 2d Ptg of Vol I. Ed by A. W. Ward & A. R. Waller. 14 vols. Half mor. cb Oct 17 (327) $325
— Cambridge History of Iran. Cambr., 1968. 8 vols. pba Jan 4 (287) $250
— The Cambridge Medieval History. NY, 1924-36. Ed by J. B. Bury & others. 8 vols. Orig cloth. pba Sept 14 (90) $160

**Camden, William, 1551-1623**
— Annals. L, 1625-29. ("Annales. The True and Royall History of the Famous Empresse Elisabeth [i.e., Parts 1-3] * Tomus Alter & Idem; or, the History of...that Famous Princesse, Elizabeth [i.e., Part 4].") Vol I only. Contemp calf gilt; rebacked with orig backstrip laid down, corners repaired. With the port of Darcie inserted at end; later state of tp. Lacking Kkk4; To the Reader from anr copy; inkstain on Pp4. STC 4497. CE June 12 (165) $2,200
— Britain.... L, 1637. 2d Ed of Philemon Holland's trans. - Maps by William Kip or William Hole after Christopher Saxon or John Norden. Folio, modern half calf; worn, upper cover becoming detached. With title map, 8 plates, & 57 maps (2 full-page). Title soiled & torn; waterstained along upper edge; small hole in Warwick map; 1 map with split; East Riding loosely inserted. S Oct 26 (370) £3,200 [Franks]

Anr copy. Half sheep; worn, spine broken. With title map, 8 plates, & 55 (of 57) maps (2 full-page). Lacking preliminary leaf *3; Middlesex holed; a few light marks; some creasing. S Oct 26 (371) £2,500 [Franks]
— Britannia: or a Chorographical Description.... L, 1637. ("Britain....") 2d Ed of Holland's trans. Folio, contemp calf; rebacked. With engraved title & 57 double-page maps, colored throughout by a contemp hand. Several maps shaved; Cornwall torn with minor loss; Gloucester & Hereford holed; other minor defs. S Nov 30 (50) £5,200

Anr copy. 18th-cent russia gilt, with arms in lower compartment on spines. With engraved title & 57 double-page maps & 8 plates of coins. Repair in 1 plate of coins; Lincolnshire duplicated. S Nov 30 (51) £4,000

Anr copy. Contemp calf; rebacked. With engraved title & 57 double-page maps & 8 plates of coins, partly colored in outline by a contemp hand. Essex & Rutland shaved at fore-margins; Stafford repaired; some rustholes & creasing. S Mar 28 (75) £2,600

1st Ed of Gibson's trans. L, 1695. ("Britannia....") Folio, later calf; worn, covers detached. Port torn with loss & loose; 2 maps torn affecting surface & repaired; 5 maps torn along fold; 4 folding maps soiled at outer edges; some leaves trimmed with loss. C May 31 (50) £1,200

Anr copy. Contemp calf; rebacked. With port, 50 double-page or folding maps & 9 plates of coins & antiquities. A few maps split at lower fold; 2 general maps & Hertfordshire cut close; a few holes. S Nov 30 (52) £1,800

Anr copy. Contemp calf; some wear. With port, 50 maps & 9 plates of coins & antiquities. Port torn; some maps cropped at margins (9 affecting engraved surface); some worming to edges of Mmm2-Yyy, affecting map of Ireland. S June 27 (90) £1,400

Anr copy. Contemp sheep; needs rebdg. With frontis, 9 plates & 46 (of 50) double-page maps. Some staining. sg May 9 (60) $900

Anr copy. Contemp calf; rebacked, worn & frayed. Lacking map of Derbyshire; some maps trimmed on leading edges; Surrey & East Riding of Yorkshire repaired & laid down, the latter with loss; Hertfordshire repaired at edges. W Nov 8 (311) £1,000

2d Ed of Gibson's trans. L, 1722. 2 vols. Folio, contemp calf; worn. b Sept 20 (100) £1,200

Anr copy. Contemp calf; def, loose. With port & 50 double-page or folding maps & 9 plates of coins & antiquities. Worming at centerfolds, especially in Vol I. S Apr 23 (346) £850

Anr copy. Contemp sheep; needs rebdg. With port, 9 single-page plates & 50 double-page plates. Frontis & both titles rebacked; 1 text leaf def & imperf; library stamps on titles. sg May 9 (59) $1,000

2d Ed of Gough's trans. L, 1806. 4 vols. Folio, contemp calf gilt, with small crest on sides; several joints split. With port, 57 maps & 105 plates. b Dec 5 (58) £660

Anr copy. Contemp half calf; def. With port, 49 maps & 109 plates. Browning & discoloration. Sold w.a.f. Extra-illus with c.prints, lithos, sketches & watercolors. S Mar 28 (76) £800

## Camera Work

— 1903. - Camera Work. NY No 1. sg Feb 29 (62) $2,150
— 1904. - NY No 7. sg Apr 24 (579) $375
— 1906. - NY No 15. sg Feb 29 (64) $800
— 1907. - NY No 19. sg Feb 29 (66) $750
— 1909. - NY No 25. sg Feb 29 (67) $1,300
— 1910. - NY No 29. sg Apr 24 (584) $500
— 1911. - NY No 33. sg Apr 24 (585) $600
 No 34/35. sg Feb 29 (69) $1,100
 No 36. sg Feb 29 (70) $9,000
— 1912. - NY No 37. sg Feb 29 (71) $650
 No 38. sg Feb 29 (72) $1,400
— 1913. - NY No 42/43. sg Feb 29 (75) $2,200
— 1914. - NY No 45. sg Apr 24 (586) $550
 No 46. sg Feb 29 (77) $325
— 1916. - NY No 48. sg Feb 29 (78) $4,000

**Cameron, Elizabeth**
— A Book of White Flowers. L, 1980. One of 250. Folio, orig half cloth. bba May 30 (426) £90 [Lloyd]

**Cameron, John**
— Our Tropical Possessions in Malayan India.... L, 1865. 8vo, orig cloth; rubbed. With 7 chromolithos, 1 of them double-page. Some spotting. b May 30 (195) £400

**Cameron, Verney Lovett, 1844-94**
— Across Africa. L, 1877. 2 vols. 8vo, contemp half calf; joints weak. With folding map & 32 plates. b May 30 (145) £80

**Camers, Giovanni**
— C. J. Solini Polyhistor.... [Cologne: E. Cervicornum & H. Fuchs, 1520]. 4to, later bds. Early annotations. CE May 22 (73) $150

**Camilli, Camillo**
— Imprese illustri di diversi coi discorsi. Venice: Francesco Ziletti, 1586. 3 parts in 1 vol. 4to, old vellum. Some soiling; a few leaves stained. sg Mar 21 (73) $650

**Camouflet**
— Histoire de Camouflet, souverain potentat de l'empire d'Equivopolis. Equivopolis, 1751. 12mo, contemp red mor gilt with arms of Nicolas Rene Berryer; arms worn. Fuerstenberg - Schaefer copy. S Dec 7 (96) £280

**Camp, Charles L.**
— James Clyman, American Frontiersman. San Francisco, 1928. 1st Ed. Orig cloth in dj; d/j sunned, soiled, chipped 7 torn; rear cover with residue. With 2 ports, 1 facsimile, & 3 maps (1 folding). Inscr to Bob Long. Robbins copy. pba Mar 21 (51) $350

Anr Ed. Portland OR: Champoeg Press, 1960. ("James Clyman, Frontiersman.") One of 1,450. Unopened copy. pba Nov 16 (44) $100

Anr Ed. Portland OR: Champoeg Press, [1960]. One of—1,450. Orig cloth; spine head bumped. pba Apr 25 (328) $85

Definitive Ed. Portland OR: Champoeg Press, 1960. Orig cloth. With 4 maps (2 folding). Robbins copy. pba Mar 21 (52) $130

**Campan, Jeanne Louise Henriette, 1752-1822**
— Memoirs of the Private Life of Marie Antoinette.... Phila., 1823. 8vo, contemp half calf. Prelim blank detached. pba Dec 14 (7) $85

**Campano, Giovanni Antonio, 1429-77.** See: Campanus, Johannes Antonius

**Campanus, Johannes Antonius, 1429-77**
— Opera. Rome: Eucharius Silber, 31 Oct 1495. Folio, 19th-cent calf gilt with John Rylands monogram added. 56 lines & headline; roman letter; illuminated initial & three-quarter illuminated border on a2 recto consisting of a red & blue bar with floral extensions & a coat-of-arms surmounted by a bishop's mitre inside a wreath in the lower margin. Ff 16-18 misbound after a1; fore-edge of tp repaired; tears in tp, e4, A1 & [G]1 partly repaired without loss; inner margins of final few leaves wormed; some spotting; early Ms annotations. 304 leaves. Goff C-73. Spencer-Rylands copy. S June 27 (308) £2,000

**Campbell, Archibald, United States Commissioner —& Twining, William J.**
— Reports upon the Survey of the Boundary between the Territory of the United States and the Possessions of Great Britain from the Lake of the Woods to the Summit of the Rocky Mountains.... Wash., 1878. 4to, orig cloth; worn, soiled, broken. With 15 tinted lithos, 7 large folding maps & 7 other maps & charts. Prelims chipped; some soiling. wa Feb 29 (468) $150

**Campbell, Colin, d.1720 —& Others**
— Vitruvius Britannicus. L, [1715]-17-31-67-71. Vols I-III only. Contemp calf; scuffed. Plate 37 in Vol I loosely inserted & with frayed margins; Vol III without engraved title, dedication & final plate. C Nov 29 (87) £4,000

Anr copy. Vols I-IV bound in 2 vols. Later half mor; joints starting. cb Oct 17 (8) $4,500

Anr Ed. L, [1715-25]. Vols I-III (of 5) in 1 vol. Folio, mor; spine ends & joint worn. With 2 titles, dedication, & 230 (of 233?) plates. CE Nov 8 (176) $3,400

Anr Ed. L, 1717. Vols I-II (of 5) only. Folio, contemp calf; rubbed, upper cover of vol I detached. With 158 plates (27 double-page & 4 folding). S Oct 26 (331) £1,400 [Wascom]

Anr Ed. L, 1967-72. 4 vols. 4to, cloth; soiled. bba Oct 19 (114) £390

**Campbell, J. F.**
— My Circular Notes. L, 1876. 8vo, calf gilt prize bdg. pba Aug 8 (28) $120

**Campbell, John, Baron Campbell, 1779-1861**
— The Lives of the Lord Chancellors and Keepers of the Great Seal of England. L, 1848. 7 vols. 8vo, contemp calf gilt; joints weak. sg Sept 21 (8) $175

**Campbell, John, 1766-1840**
— Travels in South Africa [2d Journey].... L, 1822. 2 vols in 1. 8vo, contemp calf; edges worn. Some foxing & dampstaining. Met Feb 24 (338) $500

**Campbell, John W., 1910-71**
— Islands of Space. Reading: Fantasy Press, 1956. In dj with spine ends rubbed. pba Dec 7 (27) $55

Anr copy. In dj with smudge to bottom edge at rear. pba May 23 (62) $50

— The Mightiest Machine. Providence: Hadley, [1947]. In tape-repaired dj. pba Dec 7 (28) $75

**Campbell, Marinus Frederik Andries Gerardus**
— Annales de la typographie neerlandaise au XVe siecle. The Hague, 1874. 8vo, buckram; rebound. Lacking supplements. sg Apr 11 (144A) $60

**Campbell, Roy, 1901-57**
— The Wayzgoose. L, 1928. 1st Ed. In dj. Inscr to Frank Wyndham Goldie. b Jan 31 (147) £100

**Campbell, Thomas, 1777-1844**
See also: Fore-Edge Paintings
— Specimens of the British Poets.... L, 1819. 1st Ed. 7 vols. 8vo, contemp calf gilt; marked. bba May 30 (149) £160 [Classic Bindings]

**Campillo, J.** See: Castro Casimiro & Campillo

**Campora, Giacomo**
— Dell'immortalita dell'anima. Milan: Ulrich Scinzenzeller, 6 Sept 1497. 12mo, modern vellum. 30 lines; types 4:186G & 13:75R. Wormholes touching letters; writing washed form 1st leaf. 38 leaves. IGI 2397. C June 26 (52) £1,000

**Campra, Andre**
— L'Europe galante ballet en musique. [Paris: Ballard, 1699]. 3d Ed. Oblong 4to, contemp calf; upper joint split. Part of tp torn away; some browning. S Dec 1 (110) £320

**Camus, Albert, 1913-60**
See also: Limited Editions Club
— Albert Camus and the Men of the Stone. San Francisco: Greenwood Press, 1972. One of 750. Ed by Robert Proix; trans by Gregory H. Davis. Pictorial stiff wraps. pba May 23 (63) $85
— L'Envers et L'Endroit. Algers: Editions Edmond Charlot, [1937]. 1st Ed, One of 300. Orig wraps; spine repaired, sides scratched. Engelhard copy. CNY Oct 27 (8) $600
— L'Etranger. Paris: Gallimard, 1942. Mor, orig wraps bound in, by by Tchekeroul. Engelhard copy. CNY Oct 27 (9) $4,000
— The Fall. Kentfield: Allen Press, [1966]. One of 140. Folio, ptd bds. CE Feb 21 (3) $160

Anr copy. Ptd bds. ANs of Lewis Allen laid in & prospectus with holograph note form Allen. pba June 20 (15) $325
— L'Homme revolte. [Paris]: Gallimard, [1951]. One of 10 lettered copies hors commerce. Orig wraps, unopened. Inscr to Jacques Lecat. Engelhard copy. CNY Oct 27 (12) $900
— Le Malentendu, Caligula. Paris, 1944. 1st Ed, one of 13 on van Gelder. Orig bds, unopened. Inscr to Raymond Gallimard. Engelhard copy. CNY Oct 27 (10) $1,900

— Oeuvres. Paris, [1962]. 6 vols. 4to, wraps, unopened. Accession no on verso of titles. sg Dec 14 (21) $110
— La Peste. [Paris]: Gallimard, [1947]. One of 200. Orig wraps, unopened. Inscr to Yves Breton & later (1952) to Jacques Lecat. Engelhart copy. CNY Oct 27 (11) $4,500

### Canada
— Report on the Exploration of the Country between Lake Superior and the Red River Settlement. Toronto, 1858. 8vo, half lea. With 1 folding map in rear. Z Jan 30 (413) $120

### Candolle, Augustin Pyramus de, 1778-1841
— Plantarum succulentarum historia, ou Histoire naturelle des plantes.... Paris, [1799-1805]. 3 vols. Folio, contemp half calf; extremities rubbed. With 144 color-ptd plates. Titles with creases & with overslips removed from imprint; marginal dampstains; last part imperf; 1st plate almost detached & creased. P Dec 12 (221) $9,000
— Plantes grasses... Paris: Chez Garnery, [1802-3]-4 [An IX-XIII]. ("Plantarum historia succulentarum, ou plantes grasses.") Illus by Pierre Redoute. Nos 1-28 (of 31) orig parts bound in 2 vols. 4to, 19th-cent half calf gilt by E. Wettstein; worn. With 169 hand-finished colored plates. Tears repaired in margins of Plates 28 & 57. S June 27 (59) £4,500

### Canfield, Thomas H.
— Northern Pacific Railroad. Partial Report to the Board of Directors, of a Portion of a Recommoissance Made in the Summer of 1869, between Lake Superior and the Pacific Ocean.... NY: Pvtly ptd, May 1870. 8vo, contemp half lea; worn. With 2 folding maps. Some dampstain & mildew, affecting text & maps. With related photographic material & ANs of Canfield. CE May 22 (28) $1,000

### Cangiullo, Francesco
— Piedigrotta, parole in liberta. Milan, 1916. 8vo, orig wraps; recased. sg Apr 18 (95) $500

### Canney, Margaret. See: Goldsmiths' Library of Economic Literature

### Cannibale
— Cannibale. Paris, 25Apr & 25 May 1920. Ed by Francis Picabia. Nos 1 & 2 in 2 vols. Orig wraps. sg Apr 18 (127) $2,500

### Cannon, George Quayle, 1827-1901
— The Life of Joseph Smith.... Salt Lake City, 1888. 8vo, mor; joints cracked, spine repaired. Library markings. Inscr to L. C. Hopkins, 1895. pba Nov 16 (251) $95

### Canova, Antonio, 1757-1822
— Works. L, 1824. Vols I-II. 4to, contemp mor gilt, armorial bdg; joints rubbed. With ports & 99 plates, all mtd india-proofs. sg Sept 7 (67) $200

### Canova, Antonio, 1757-1822 —& Visconti, Ennio Quirino, 1751-1818
— A Letter from the Chevalier Antonio Canova and Two Memoirs... Sculptures in the Collection of the Earl of Elgin by the Chevalier E. Q. Visconti.... L, 1816. 8vo, contemp half calf; spine rubbed. S Mar 28 (294) £240

### Cantica...
— Cantica Canticorum. [Berlin, 1921]. One of 220. 4to, half vellum. Color facsimile of Dutch block book. sg Apr 11 (145) $140

### Cantrel, Emile
— Nouvelles a la main sur la Comtesse du Barry.... Paris: Henri Plon, 1861. Half mor. Sgd by Aubrey Beardsley. pba June 13 (189) $250

### Cantzler, Bernhard —& Trew, Abdias
— Summa geometricae practicae.... Nuremberg, 1673. 8vo, contemp blind-tooled armorial pigskin. Stained; frontis & tp mtd; Plate P torn & restored with image loss. Sold w.a.f. sg May 16 (144) $250

### Capa, Robert
— Images of War. NY, [1964]. Illus with images by Capa. Folio, cloth, in chipped dj. pba Aug 8 (555) $60

Anr copy. Cloth, in dj. ALs of Cornell Capa laid in. sg Feb 29 (82) $90

### Capel, Rudolf
— Norden, oder zu Wasser und Lande im Eise und Snee. Hamburg: J. Naumann, 1678-76. 2 parts. Bound with: Frobisher, Martin. Historia navigationis.... Hamburg, 1675. 4to, contemp vellum. Rusthole in armorial plate before A1 of 1st work. S June 27 (256) £2,600

### Capilli, Giovanni Battista. See: Egnatius, Johannes Baptista

### Capivaccio, Girolamo
— Opera. Frankfurt, 1603. Bound with: Medendi methodus universalis tabulis comprehensa. Frankfurt, 1606 Folio, contemp blind-stamped vellum; worn. Browned; marginal dampstaining & worming; tp frayed; bottom edge frayed. sg May 16 (387) $300

### Capodistrias, Joannis, 1776-1831. See: Kapodistrias, Ioannos Antonios

### Caponigro, Paul
— Megaliths. Bost., [1986]. 4to, cloth, in dj; ink stamp on bottom edge, some wear to extremities. sg Feb 29 (84) $70
— Sunflower. NY, [1974]. One of 400. 4to, cloth. With silver print of sunflower, ptd 1985, sgd. sg Feb 29 (85) $550

### Capote, Truman, 1924-84
See also: Onassis copy, Jacqueline Bouvier Kennedy
— In Cold Blood. NY, [1965]. In worn dj. Inscr. sg Dec 14 (23) $150
One of 500. In mylar dj with closed tear. sg Dec 14 (24) $275
— Local Color. NY, 1950. Half cloth. Inscr to Mildred Natwick, 27 Mar 1952. wd Nov 15 (39) $250
— Other Voices, Other Rooms. NY, [1968]. Anniversary Issue. In repaired dj. Sgd by Capote on tipped-in leaf. sg June 20 (42) $200
— The Thanksgiving Visitor. NY, [1967]. One of 300. sg Dec 14 (25) $225

### Capra, Alessandro
— La Nuova Architettura Famigliare. Bologna: Giacomo Monti, 1678. 4to, old vellum; crack across backstrip, fore-edge of covers worn through. Marginal dampstaining at ends. sg June 13 (5) $225

### Capron, Elisha S., 1806-83
— History of California, from its Discovery to the Present Time. Bost., 1854. 12mo, orig cloth; rebacked with orig spine seal laid on. Tape-repaired tear to map. pba Apr 25 (331) $80

### Caproni Guasti, Timina —& Bertarelli, Achille
— Francesco Zambeccari, Aeronauta.... Milan, 1932. One of 600. Folio, orig wraps. sg May 16 (19) $120

### Caproni, Timina Guasti —& Bertarelli, Achille
— L'Aeronautica Italiana nell'immagine, 1487-1875. Milan, 1938. One of 500. Folio, half vellum gilt. Tp creased. pba Nov 30 (23) $160
One of 600. Orig bds. With 174 plates, some colored. bba Oct 5 (90) £240 [Weiner]
Anr copy. Half vellum; rear joint cracked, fore-edges foxed. sg May 16 (20) $500

### Caraccioli, Louis Antoine de, 1721-1803. See: Livre...

### Caracciolus, Robertus, 1425-95
— Opera varia. Venice: Joannes & Gregorius de Gregoriis de Forlivio, 15 Mar 1490. 4to, later vellum bds. 51 lines & foliation; double column; gothic letter. Some worming at ends. 338 leaves. Goff C-134. S Dec 18 (25) £750 [Zioni]
— Sermones quadragesimales de poenitentia. Venice: Johannes de Colonia & Johannes Manthen, 1476. 4to, 17th-cent vellum. 40 lines, double column, type 9:76Gb. Opening initial rubbed. 295 (of 296) leaves; lacking 1st blank. C June 26 (159) £2,000

### Caradeuc de la Chalotais, Louis Rene de
— Essai d'education nationale.... [N.p.], 1763. 8vo, contemp wraps; worn. sg Mar 21 (74) $150

### Caradoc of Llancarfan, Saint
— The Historie of Cambria, now called Wales. L: Rafe Newberie & Henrie Denham, 1584. 1st Ed. 4to, contemp vellum; repaired. Mostly black letter. Small rust holes affecting a letter each to H3 & Dd2; lower forecorner of Ee5 with tear. CNY May 17 (55) $1,500
Anr copy. Modern lea; front joint rubbed. Marginal dampstaining, mainly at end; some underscoring; I1 & 2G1 supplied from shorter copy; lacking final blank. sg Oct 19 (54) $1,000
Anr Ed. L, 1811. Folio, modern cloth. Library stamp to tp verso. pba Nov 30 (322) $110

### Caravia, Alessandro, 1503-68
— Il sogno dil Caravia. Cenice: da Sabbio, May 1541. 4to, mor gilt by Duru. Some browning. Huth copy. C June 26 (54) £3,800

### Caravita, Nicolo, 1647-1717
— Nullum jus Pontificis Maximi in Regno Neapolitano dissertatio historica-juridica. Alithopoli [Naples], 1708. 4to, mor extra presentation copy to Charles III, King of Spain & Sicily. With 4-page Ms dedication to Charles III bound before title. C Apr 3 (61) £700

### Carburi, Marin, Comte
— Monument eleve a la gloire de Peirre-le-Grand.... Paris, 1777. Folio, contemp red mor gilt with arms of King Victor Amadeus III of Sardinia. With 12 plates. Some browning. C May 1 (29) £2,400

### Carcano, Michael de
— Sermonarium de decem praeceptis per quadragesimam. Venice: Joannes & Gregorius de Gregoriis de Forlivio for Alexander Calcedonius, between 18 Jan & 1 Mar 1492/3. 4to, modern mor. 51 lines & headline; double column; type 22:130G, 21:92aG, 19:64G. Washed; marginal annotations in a contemp hand. 231 (of 232) leaves; lacking final blank. Goff C-193. C Nov 29 (38) £700

### Carco, Francis
— L'Ami des filles. Paris, 1921. One of 25 on van gelder, with extra suite in color & 2 other illusts in color not used. Illus by Charles Laborde. 8vo, mor extra by Paul Bonet [Carnets, 89], orig wraps bound in; silk doublures & endleaves frayed with some loss. With 10 illusts. S Nov 21 (60) £4,200
— L'Amour venal. Paris, 1926. One of 25 on japon imperial, with additional suite on chine, 67 further etchings & an ink drawing. Illus by Marcel Vertes. 4to, mor extra by Durvand - L. Pinard, orig wraps bound in. With 48 etchings, 21 full-page. Plesch copy. S Nov 21 (61) £600
— La Boheme et mon coeur. Paris, 1929-30. One of 105. Illus by J. G. Daragnes. 4to, mor extra to an Art Deco design by Pierre Legrain, orig wraps bound in. S Nov 21 (64) £4,000
— L'Homme traque. Paris, 1929. One of 33 on hollande with 3 additional suites. Illus by Charles Laborde. 4to, mor extra by Franz, orig wraps bound in. S Nov 21 (63) £500
— La Legende et la vie d'Utrillo. Paris: Seheur, 1927. One of 100. Illus by Maurice Utrillo. 4to, mor extra by Erse. With 31 illusts, 11 of them full-page, the frontis ptd in color. With 2 additional suites of

the illusts & a further cancelled suite of the full-page illusts. S Nov 21 (62) £2,200
— Montmartre vecu par Utrillo. Paris, 1947. One of 240. Illus by Maurice Utrillo. Folio, mor extra with onlays by Creuzevault, orig wraps bound in. With 22 chromoliths, 12 full-page. S Nov 21 (66) £3,000
— Quelques-unes. Paris, 1931. One of 142. Illus by Louis Legrand. 4to, mor gilt by Semet & Plumelle, orig wraps bound in. With 46 etchings. S Nov 21 (65) £600

**Carcopino-Tusoli, Francois, 1886-1958.** See: Carco, Francis

**Cardanus, Hieronymus, 1501-76**
— De subtilitate libri XXI. Basel: Ludovicus Lucius, Mar 1554. Folio, contemp blind-stamped pigskin over wooden bds with 2 clasps & catches. Minor dampstaining. Madsen copy. S Mar 14 (78) £2,800
Anr Ed. Lyons: G. Roville, 1559. 8vo, contemp calf; library numbers on spine. Inkstamp on title; bookplate on verso of last leaf; some browning & waterstaining; remains of 16th-cent work bound as endpapers. bba Sept 7 (74) £2,500 [Walker]

**Cardim, Antonio Francisco**
— Fasciculus e Japponicis floribus suo adhuc madentibus sanguine. Rome, 1646. 2 parts in 1 vol. 4to, cotnemp sheep gilt; spine wormed. With 86 plates. Lacking map & 1 plate; tp with tear; Plate 7 with marginal repair; stamps to tp & B4. Ck Sept 8 (78) £550

**Careme, Marie Antonin, 1784-1833**
— L'art de la cuisine fancaise au dix-neuvieme siecle. Paris, n.d.-1843-44. 5 vols. 8vo, contemp half bds & orig wraps. With 24 plates. Vols 1-3 spotted & dampstained. S Oct 12 (10) £1,150
— Le cuisiner parisien. Paris, 1842. 3d Ed. 8vo, later half calf. With additional title & 24 (of 25?) plates. Spotted. S Oct 12 (9) £450

**Carew, Thomas, 1595?-1645?.** See: Golden Cockerel Press

**Carey, David, 1782-1824**
— Life in Paris. L, 1822. 1st Ed in Book form. - Illus by George Cruikshank. 8vo, contemp calf gilt; joints & extremities scuffed. With engraved title & 20 hand-colored plates. Lacking half-title. F Sept 21 (411) $150
Anr copy. Contemp calf gilt by Riviere; rebacked. With engraved title & 20 hand-colored plates. pba Sept 14 (114) $225

**Carey, Jacques —& Omont, Henri**
— Athenes au XVIIe siecle. Paris, 1898. Folio, loose in modern half cloth. With 46 plates. Lightly dustsoiled. A. C. Lascarides copy. S Oct 26 (27) £420 [Dellarokas]

**Carey, Mathew, 1760-1839**
— Carey's American Pocket Atlas.... Phila., 1814. 4th Ed. 12mo, contemp lea; worn, rear cover detached, spine perished. With 23 maps & 2 folding tables. Foxing & dampstaining affecting a few maps. cb Feb 14 (2548) $1,700

**Carey, William**
— Adventures in Tibet. NY: Baker & Taylor, [1901]. pba July 25 (387) $75

**Caricature...**
— La Caricature [politique], morale, religieuse, litteraire et scenique. Paris, 1830-35. Ed by Charles Philipon. Nos 1-251 in 10 vols. 4to, half mor. With 466 plates, numbered to 524, 97 hand-colored, 14 partly colored & 2 ptd in 2 colors, 7 of the partly colored plates & 341 of the uncolored plates in 2 states; 5 plates with lifting flap or sliding panel; poster in No 124. Together with the 24 double-page plates issued to subscribers & a later impression of Plate 57. Some text leaves browned; some plates spotted or stained; a few marginal tears to subscription plates, the last with tear affecting ptd surface; title pages in Vols 5, 8 & 9 reprints; lacking table for Vols 1, 5 & 8. S Nov 21 (69) £16,000

**Carleton, George, 1559-1628**
— A Thankfull Remembrance of God's Mercie. L, 1627. 3d Ed. 4to, contemp calf; worn. Minor marginal soiling. CE June 12 (166) $650

**Carletti, Giuseppe**
— Vestigia delle Terme di Tito e loro interne pitture. Rome: L. Mirri, [1776-78]. Folio, contemp half calf; worn. With 60 double-page plates, including title, 8 of them folding. S Apr 23 (231) £5,200

**Carlevariis, Luca, 1663-1730**
— Le Fabriche e vedute di Venetia designate.... Venice, [1705?]. Oblong folio, contemp red mor gilt with arms of Cardinal Barberini; stained, corners rubbed, minor worming. With engraved title, dedication & 101 plates in 2d state. S June 27 (100) £15,000

**Carlisle, Donald Thompson.** See: Derrydale Press

**Carlyle, Thomas, 1795-1881.** See: Doves Press; Limited Editions Club

**Carmichael, James Wilson**
— Views on the Newcastle and Carlisle Railway.... Newcastle, 1837. Folio, modern wraps with orig ptd upper wrap laid down. With 23 plates in india-proof paper. Lacking engraved title. b Jan 31 (308) £140

**Carmichael, Richard, 1779-1849**
— An Essay on the Venereal Diseases, and the Uses and Abuses of Mercury in their Treatment. Phila., 1825. 2d American Ed. 8vo, modern half calf. With 5 hand-colored plates (3 folding). Some browning. CE Nov 8 (77) $100

### Carmina...
— Carmina ethica ex diversis auctoribus collegit. Paris, 1795 [An III]. Ed by Antoine Auguste Renouard. 18mo, contemp mor gilt by Bozerian jeune. Fuerstenberg - Schaefer copy. S Dec 7 (99) £1,300

### Carmontelle, Louis de, 1717-1806
— Jardin de Monceau pres de Paris. Paris, 1779. Folio, half calf. With 18 plates. Fuerstenberg - Schaefer copy. S Dec 7 (100) £3,200

### Carne, John, 1789-1844
— Syria, the Holy Land, Asia Minor.... L, [1836-38]. 3 vols in 2. 4to, contemp roan; worn. With 2 maps, & 117 plates. Some spotting. S Oct 26 (26) £230 [Mola-Mauto]

Anr copy. Illus by W. H. Bartlett. Contemp mor gilt. With 3 engraved titles, 2 maps & 118 plates. b May 30 (251) £220

Anr copy. 3 vols. 4to, contemp half mor; chipped & worn. With 3 engraved titles, 2 maps & 117 plates. S Mar 28 (285) £300

Anr Ed. L, [1842]. Vol I only. Later bds. With 35 plates. b Sept 20 (364) £70

Anr copy. 3 vols. 4to, contemp half calf; rubbed. With 123 plates & maps. S June 13 (588) £320

### Carnegie, Andrew
— An American Four-in-Hand in Britain. NY, 1883. 1st Ed. 8vo, orig cloth; worn. Inscr as from the author. F June 20 (543) $150

### Carnegie, David Wynford
— Spinifex and Sand... Pioneering and Exploration in Western Australia. L, 1898. 1st Ed. 8vo, orig fawn cloth; dust-stained, lower hinge weak. With half-title, port frontis, 4 folding maps, & 13 plates. S Oct 26 (609) £960 [Morrel]

### Carnicero, Antonio
— Coleccion de la principales suertes de una corrida de toros. Madrid, 1790. Oblong folio, modern bds. With hand-colored title & 12 hand-colored plates. F June 20 (840A) $1,900

Anr Ed. Madrid, [c.1935]. Oblong folio, modern lea gilt; stained, rear binder's blank & free endpaper gnawed. Reprint of 1792 Ed. sg May 9 (323) $550

### Caroso, Fabritio
— Il Ballarino.... Venice: Francesco Ziletti, 1581. 2d Issue, with Ziletti's device on tp & with title reset. Illus by Giacomo Franco. 4to, 19th-cent vellum. With port & 22 plates. Small repaired hole in margin of last few leaves; tp strengthened. C June 26 (56) £6,000

### Carpenter, Charles
— Tiffany Silver. NY, [1978]. F Mar 28 (142) $90

### Carpenter, Ralph E.
— Arts and Crafts of Newport, Rhode Island.... Newport, 1954. Advance copy. 4to, wraps; worn. O Dec 5 (25) $225

### Carpenter, Robert Ruliph Morgan
— Game Trails from Alaska to Africa. [N.p., n.d.]. One of 50. Lea. Inscr to Bill Beach. O Oct 10 (64) $700

### Carpenter, William
— The Angler's Assistant. L, 1848. 12mo, orig cloth; worn. O Feb 6 (44) $200

### Carpentier, Alejo. See: Limited Editions Club

### Carpentras
— Liber primus missarum.... Avignon: Jean de Channey for the composer & Stephan Bellon, 15 May 1532. Folio, modern bds overlaid with fragments of Ms. Type-set music with oval noteheads, ptd by double impression. Last leaf repaired at hinge; O2-3 misbound; some browning. S Dec 1 (113) £18,500

### Carr, John, 1827-96
— Pioneer Days in California.... Eureka, Calif., 1891. 1st Ed. 8vo, orig cloth. With frontis port. Tp partially detached. Larson copy. pba Sept 28 (354) $170
— A Vulcan Among the Argonauts.... San Francisco, 1936. One of 500. Ed by Robin Lampson. Orig cloth. Sgd by ed. Larson copy. pba Sept 28 (355) $80

### Carr, Sir John, 1772-1832
— The Stranger in Ireland. L, 1806. 1st Ed. 4to, contemp half sheep; needs rebdg. With hand-colored map & 15 (of 16) plates. Foxing & browning. sg Mar 7 (42) $325

### Carr, Larry
— Four Fabulous Faces. New Rochelle, 1970. Folio, orig cloth; minor soiling. F Mar 28 (138) $60

### Carra, Carlo
— Guerrapittura. Futurismo Politico, Dinamismo Plastico. Milan, 1915. 8vo, orig wraps; foxed. With photograpic port, 12 plates & 2 broadsides. sg Apr 18 (96) $650

### Carracci, Annibale, 1560-1609
— Diverse figure... dagli originali da Simone Guilino Parigino. Rome, 1646 [but later]. Folio, later bds. With port & 80 plates. Some foxing. bba Sept 7 (202) £110

Anr Ed. Rome, 1646. Folio, wraps; dampstained. With port & 80 plates. Dampstained, affecting prelims & c.15 plates. pn Dec 7 (26) £3,600

### Carre de Montgeron, Louis Basile
— La Verite des miracles operes par l'intercession de M. de Paris, demontree contre M. l'Archeveque de Sens. Cologne, 1739. 4to, modern half lea. With 20 plates. sg Mar 21 (75) $90

### Carrington, Frances C.
— My Army Life and the Fort Phil. Kearney Massacre.... Phila., 1910. Orig cloth; worn & soiled. Some spotting. F Mar 28 (47) $120

Anr copy. Inscr by Gen. Henry B. Carrington. pba June 25 (32) $350

**Carrington, Margaret Irvin, 1831-70**
— Ab-Sa-Ra-Ka Home of the Crows.... Phila., 1868. 12mo, orig cloth; rubbed, spine ends frayed. With folding map. Tears & tape-repairs to map. pba June 25 (33) $130

**Carroll, Bartholomew R.**
— Historical Collections of South Carolina.... NY, 1836. 1st Ed. 2 vols. 8vo, orig cloth; library numbers on spines. With folding map. NH Sept 16 (375) $260

**Carroll, John M.**
— 4 on Custer by Carroll. [N.p., 1976]. One of 100. Half cloth. pba June 25 (38) $60
— The Black Military Experience in the American West. NY, [1971]. One of 300. In dj. Ls to John Popovich laid in. pba June 25 (42) $300
— Buffalo Soldiers West. [Fort Collins, 1971]. One of 50, with orig pencil drawing by Lorence Bjorklund. Oblong 4to, lea gilt; spine ends rubbed. pba Sept 14 (96) $400; pba June 25 (34) $475
— Custer in Texas. NY, 1975. One of 30, sgd on sheet bound in at rear. Orig half lea with spine imprint "LBHA San Antonio, 1981". Dampstaining to margins of leaves at end. pba June 25 (37) $300
— Custer in the Civil War.... San Rafael: Presidio Press, [1977]. Ed by Carroll. In dj. pba June 25 (44) $55
— The Grand Duke Alexis in the United States of America. NY: Interland Publishing, 1972. One of 100. Illus by Joe Grandee. Lea gilt. ALs of Carroll laid in. pba June 25 (47) $225
— The Two Battles of the Little Big Horn. NY, [1974]. One of 1,000. pba June 25 (56) $75
— The Unpublished Papers of the Order of Indian Wars. New Brunswick NJ: Pvtly ptd, [1977]. One of 100. 10 booklets. pba June 25 (57) $100

**Carroll, John M. —&**
**Steinberger, Irene**
— A Graphologist Looks at Custer and Some of his Friends.... Bryan TX: Pvtly ptd, [1977-78]. One of 100. Illus by Lorence Bjorklund. 3 vols. Pictorial wraps. pba June 25 (48) $90

**Carroll, Lewis.** See: Dodgson, Charles Lutwidge

**Carroll, W.**
— The Angler's Vade Mecum.... Edin., 1818. 1st Ed. 8vo, later calf gilt; front hinge with old glue-stain. With 12 hand-colored plates. pba July 11 (47) $250

**Carron du Villards, Charles Joseph Frederic**
— Recherches pratiques sur les causes qui font echouer l'operation de la cataracte selon les divers procedes. Paris, 1835. 8vo, contemp half calf; joints rubbed. With 2 folding plates. Browned. sg May 16 (388) $80

**Carryl, Guy Wetmore**
— Fables for the Frivolous. NY, 1898. Illus by Peter Newell. Orig cloth; spine ends chipped. pba Aug 22 (820) $70

— Mother Goose for Grown-Ups. NY, 1900. Illus by Peter Newell & Gustave Verbeek. Orig cloth; spine ends rubbed, hinges tight. pba Aug 22 (821) $90

**Carson, Christopher ("Kit"), 1809-68**
— Kit Carson's Own Story. Taos, NM, 1926. 1st Ed. - Ed by Blanche C. Grant. Orig wraps; spine top chipped & torn. With frontis port & 12 illus. Larson copy. pba Sept 28 (350) $120

**Carson, James H.**
— Recollections of the California Mines.... Oakland, 1950. One of 750. Illus by Henry Shire. Cloth. With 2 folded maps. Larson copy. pba Sept 28 (352) $70

**Carson, Rachel**
See also: Limited Editions Club
— Silent Spring. Bost., 1962. 1st Ed, Illus by Lois & Louis Darling. In dj with extremities rubbed. pba Jan 25 (49) $80

**Carstensen, Georg Johann Bernhard —&**
**Gildemeister, Charles**
— New York Crystal Palace. NY, 1854. Orig cloth; corners & extremities worn, dampstaining, endpapers soiled. With chromolitho frontis & 6 folding plates. Library markings; plates foxed & with a few dampstains; most of 1 plate lacking. cb Oct 17 (102) $200

**Cartari, Vincenzo**
— Le Imagini de i Dei degli antichi.... Venice: Giordano Ziletti, 1567. Bound with: Le Imagini con la Spositione de i Dei degli antichi.... Venice: Francesco Rampazetto, 1566 4to, old vellum; 19th-cent endpapers. pba Mar 7 (52) $750

**Carter Collection, Amon G.**
RENNER, FREDERIC G. - Charles M. Russell: Paintings, Drawings, and Sculpture in the...Collection. Austin: Univ. of Texas, [1966]. Folio, cloth, in dj. With 36 colored plates. ds July 27 (173) $80
One of 250, with extra suite of plates in portfolio. Cloth. With 36 colored plates. ds July 27 (172) $275

**Carter, Charles**
— The Complete Practical Cook.... L, 1730. 1st Ed. 4to, contemp calf. With 60 plates. pba Nov 30 (99) $2,750
— The London and Country Cook.... L, 1749. 8vo, modern lea. With frontis & 48 plates. Some staining, soiling, browning & repairs. Sold w.a.f. O Mar 5 (40) $275

**Carter, Harry.** See: Morison & Carter

**Carter, James Earl ("Jimmy")**
— Keeping Faith, Memoirs of a President. NY: Bantam, [1982]. Ltd Ed. pba June 13 (49) $100

**Carter, James Earl ("Jimmy") —&**
**Carter, Rosalynn**

## CARTER

— Everything to Gain. NY, [1987]. In dj. Sgd by both Carters on front free endpaper. pba June 13 (50) $120

**Carter, John Waynflete, 1905-75 —& Muir, Percy H.**
— Printing and the Mind of Man. L, 1967. 4to, orig cloth, in dj. bba May 9 (55) £110 [Ritchie]
Anr copy. Orig cloth. bbc Dec 18 (115) $150
Anr Ed. NY, 1967. 4to, cloth; worn. wa Feb 29 (2) $80

**Carter, John Waynflete, 1905-75 —& Pollard, Graham**
— An Enquiry into the Nature of Certain Nineteenth Century Pamphlets. L & NY, 1934. Cloth; rubbed. pba Dec 14 (28) $130
Anr copy. Cloth, in stained & chipped dj. pba Aug 8 (313) $110
Anr copy. Orig cloth; bdg askew. sg Sept 21 (325) $80

**Carter, Rosalynn.** See: Carter & Carter

**Carter, Susannah**
— The Frugal Housewife, or Complete Woman Cook.... Phila., 1796. 12mo, contemp half calf; upper cover nearly detached. With 2 plates Lower margin of K6 trimmed affecting last line on recto. CE June 12 (176) $1,200
Anr Ed. L: J. Newberry, [c.1800]. 12mo, contemp half calf; cover detached, worn. With 3 plates. S Oct 12 (89) £200

**Carter, T. Donald.** See: Mochi & Carter

**Carter, William H.**
— Old Army Sketches. Balt., 1906. 1st Ed. - Illus by Howard Chandler Christy & others. Orig cloth. With 4 plates. Robbins copy. pba Mar 21 (53) $275

**Carteret, Leopold**
— Le tresor du bibliophile romantique et moderne, 1801-1875. [Breuil-en-Vexin], 1976. 4 vols. 4to, orig wraps. sg Apr 11 (72) $175

**Cartier-Bresson, Henri**
— The Decisive Moment. NY, [1952]. Folio, bds, in chipped dj. With separate pamphlet of captions laid in. bbc Apr 22 (207) $310
Anr copy. Bds, in worn & chipped dj. F Mar 28 (39) $160
Anr copy. Bds, in def dj. K Oct 1 (306) $225
Anr copy. Pictorial bds with design by Matisse; in torn & soiled dj; bdg soiled, foxed & bowed, cellotape on spine. sg Feb 29 (88) $500
— Les Europeens. Paris: Verve, [1955]. Folio, bds with design by Miro; extremities rubbed. Ck May 31 (35) £190
— Images a la sauvette. Paris, 1952. Folio, orig bds; spine browned, hinges split. Ck May 31 (34) £180
Anr copy. Color litho bds by Matisse; lacking front free endpaper, broken & worn. wa Dec 14 (565) $110

**Cartoons...**
— Cartoons Magazine. Chicago, 1912-21. Vols 1-20. 4to, cloth; worn. O July 9 (43) $300

**Cartwright, Edmund.** See: Fore-Edge Paintings

**Caruso, Enrico, 1873-1921**
— Caricatures. NY, 1908. Folio, half mor gilt. Some wear to tp. S Dec 1 (117) £600

**Carvajal, Bernardino de**
— Oratio in die Circumcisionis.... Rome: Stephan Planck, 1484. 8vo, modern half vellum. Foxed; partially eradicated stamp in lower margin of 1st leaf. 8 leaves. Goff C-222. pba June 20 (87) $1,600

**Carver, Jonathan, 1732-80**
— Travels through the Interior Parts of North America.... L, 1778. 1st Ed. 8vo, contemp sheep. With 4 plates & 2 folding maps. sg Oct 26 (34) $1,600

**Carver, Raymond**
— At Night the Salmon Move. Santa Barbara: Capra Press, 1976. One of 100. pba Aug 22 (74) $200
— Will You Please Be Quiet, Please? NY: McGraw-Hill, [1976]. In chipped dj with foxing to edges. pba Aug 22 (75) $150
— Winter Insomnia. Santa Cruz, CA: Kayak Books, 1970. Wraps. Inscr on tp. pba Jan 25 (51) $180

**Cary, G. T.** See: Lower...

**Cary, John, c.1754-1835**
— Cary's New English Atlas. L, 1811. Folio, contemp half mor; rebacked, worn. With engraved title & 42 maps on 44 double-page sheets, hand-colored in wash & outline. Marginal soiling; contents cut out & pasted on tp verso. S June 13 (481) £920
— New and Correct English Atlas. L, 1787. 4to, contemp fold-over calf. With 47 maps, hand-colored in outline. Library markings. S Mar 28 (78) £400
Anr copy. Contemp calf; rubbed. Some spotting. S June 13 (482) £520
Anr Ed. L, 1793. 4to, contemp half calf; rebacked, repaired. With engraved title & 47 maps, hand-colored in outline. Some spotting. S Mar 28 (79) £380
Anr copy. Contemp half calf; rebacked. With engraved title & 47 maps, hand-colored in outline. S Mar 28 (80) £400
— New Map of England and Wales.... L, 1794. 4to, contemp half calf; worn. With engraved title & dedication, hand-colored general map & map in 77 sections, numbered to 81, hand-colored in outline. S Mar 28 (84) £220
Anr copy. Contemp half calf; minor wear. S Mar 28 (105) £150
Anr copy. Recent half calf. S June 13 (480) £150
Anr copy. Contemp half calf; rebacked & recornered. With engraved title & dedication, hand-colored general map & map in 77 sections, numbered to 81, hand-colored in outline. Some spotting. S June 13 (483) £120

— New Universal Atlas. L, 1808. Folio, contemp half calf; def. With engraved title & 56 colored double-page or folding maps. Some maps torn or repaired. CE May 22 (75) $2,000

**Cary, Joyce**
— The Horse's Mouth. L, 1957. One of 1,500.  sg Sept 14 (96) $150

**Casalius, Joannes Baptista**
— De profanis et sacris veteribus ritibus. Frankfurt, 1681. 3 parts in 1 vol. 4to, contemp vellum.  b Sept 20 (411) £150

**Casanova de Seingalt, Giacomo Girolamo, 1725-98**
See also: Limited Editions Club
— Memoires.... Paris, [1950].  Illus by Umberto Brunelleschi.  2 vols. 4to, orig pictorial wraps; spine ends frayed.  wa Feb 1 (310) $100

**Casas, Bartolome de las, 1474-1566**
[A complete collection of the 1st Eds of his 9 tracts sold at Sotheby's on 27 June 1966, lot 195, for £54,000]
— An Account of the First Voyages and Discoveries made by the Spaniards in America. L, 1699. 1st English Ed. 8vo, calf; worn, rebacked. With 1 double-page plate. Lacks A4 & p.1 plate; F4 torn; some browning.  S Oct 26 (514) £320 [Dalleggio]
— Istoria o brevissima relatione della distruttione dell' Indie occidentali.... Venice, 1630.  Bound with: Il supplice schiavo indiano.... Venice, 1636. 4to, contemp calf. S Mar 28 (332) £340
— Narratio regionum indicarum per Hispanos quosdam devastatarum verissima.... Oppenheim: T. de Bry, 1614. 4to, 18th-Cent mor; rubbed & soiled. With illus. Pp. 20-21 stained; title fore-margin restored.  S Oct 26 (515) £1,500 [Fernandez-Holman]

**Case, John, d.1600**
— Sphaera civitatis. Oxford: Joseph Barnes, 1588. Bound with: Thesaurus oeconomiae, seu commentarius in oeconomica Aristotelis. Oxford: Joseph Barnes, 1597. 4to, contemp blind-stamped calf; rebacked. Folding diagrammatic plates backed with linen & trimmed, with a few letters lacking. P Dec 12 (34) $350

**Cashin, Hershel V. —& Others**
— Under Fire with the Tenth U. S. Cavalry... Negro's Participation in the Wars of the United States.... Chicago: American Publishing House, [1902]. 2d Ed, Salesman's dummy.  sg Mar 28 (30) $300

**Casillas y Cabrera, Francisco**
— Coleccion de las Ordenanzas, que para el Gobierno de el Opispado de Michoacan. Mexico: Felipe de Zuniga y Ontiveros, 1776. Contemp vellum; chewed, black stain to fore-edges & margins. Some pencil annotations.  pba Mar 7 (53) $130

**Cassas, Louis Francois**
— Portion de l"arneca, dans l'Isle de Cypre. [Paris, 1779]. Bound with: Vue d'une mosquee, de Famagouste, en Cypre. 2 engraved views. 295 by 460mm Some marginal soiling.  S Oct 26 (49) £360 [Sofianus]

**Cassin, John, 1813-69**
— Illustrations of the Birds of California.... Phila., [1853]-56. 1st Ed. 8vo, half lea. With 50 hand-colored plates. Some browning & foxing.  Met Sept 28 (397) $2,500
Anr Ed. Austin: Texas State Historical Association, [1991]. One of 250. Half syn. Facsimile of the 1856 Ed, with Plate II from that Ed included.  pba Feb 12 (17) $50
— United States Exploring Expedition. During the Years 1838-42. Mammalogy and Ornithology. Phila., 1858. Atlas vol. Folio, disbound. With 53 hand-colored plates. bbc Feb 26 (59) $3,800
Anr copy. 2 vols, including Atlas vol. Folio, cloth; library markings on spine & inside covers. With 53 hand-colored plates. Plate 20 with marginal soiling; some discoloration to edges.  P Dec 12 (198) $3,250

**Cassirer, Ernst**
— Substance and Function and Einstein's Theory of Relativity. Chicago, 1923. 4to, cloth. Sgd by Einstein on front free endpaper.  sg Sept 28 (96) $1,300

**Casson, A. J.**
— Watercolours. Don Mills: M. B. Loates Publishing, 1980. One of 60. Folio, calf. With 3 color plates, 40 sgd & numbered plates & 1 orig litho. wad Oct 18 (192) C$8,000

**Castaneda, Carlos**
— Our Catholic Heritage in Texas, 1519-1936. NY, 1976. 7 vols. Reprint of 1936-58 Ed.  ds July 27 (53) $400

**Castanedo, Pedro de.** See: Grabhorn Printing

**Castarede, J.** See: Onassis copy, Jacqueline Bouvier Kennedy

**Castellan, Antoine Laurent, 1772-1838**
— Lettres sur la Moree et les isles de Cerigo, Hydra et Zante. Paris, 1808. 2 vols in 1. 8vo, contemp bds. With 2 folding maps & 24 plates. S June 13 (590) £400

**Castelnau, Francis de, 1812-80**
— Expedition dans les parties centrales de l'Amerique du Sud. Paris, 1852-57. 9 (of 15) vols in 7; without the 6-vol Histoire du Voyage. Late 19th-cent half lea, Itineraire & Geographie in modern half lea. Some foxing & dampstaining; institutional stamps. Sold w.a.f.  sg Dec 7 (246) $3,800
Anr Ed. Paris, 1855-59. Part 7: Zoologie, ou animaux nouveaux ou rares.... 3 vols. 4to, contemp half calf. With 172 (of 176) plates, 141 of them hand-colored. Some foxing.  S June 27 (13) £2,100

**Castiglione, Baldassare, 1478-1529**

*Il Cortegiano*

— Il libro del cortegiano. Florence: heirs of Philippo di Giunta, [1529?].  8vo, 19th-Cent half calf; rubbed.

## CASTIGLIONE

With 219 leaves. Lacking final blank leaf. S Oct 27 (1052) £520 [Kunkler]
— 1531, Apr. - Parma: Antonio di Viota. 8vo, contemp calf gilt; scuffed, spine worn, joints cracked. C Apr 3 (62) £1,900
— 1742. - Il Cortegiano; or The Courtier.... L. 8vo, contemp calf; front cover nearly detached, lacking rear free endpaper. pba Nov 30 (79) $160

**Castro, Alfonso de**
— De potestate legis poenalis libri duo. Salamanca: Andreas de Portonariis, 1551. Folio, old vellum. Foxed; opening leaves dampstained in outer margins. sg Mar 21 (183) $600

**Castro Casimiro —&**
**Campillo, J.**
— Mexico y sus alrededores, colleccion de monumentos, trajes y paisajes.... Mexico, 1855-56. Folio, orig half cloth; worn, corners & extremities chipped, free endpapers creased. With 42 tinted litho plates including litho title & 1 duplicate plate (Abbey 13), the Spouting Fountain plate without the title ptd on the plate & 7 plates partly colored. Minor marginal worming; foxing to about half the plates. CNY May 17 (56) $4,000

**Catalogo...**
— Catalogo colletivo della libreria italiana. Milan, 1881. 4 vols. 8vo, later cloth; worn. Some foxing. O Mar 26 (57) $100
— Catalogo delle edizioni Bodoniane eseguite in Parma. Parma: presso la vedova Bodoni, 1830. 16mo, unbound. Late spotting on the last 2 leavesf. S Nov 30 (254) £850

**Cataneo, Pietro**
— I Quattro Primi Libri di architettura. Venice: Aldus, 1554. 1st Ed. Folio, contemp bds; backstrip def, hinges repaired, sewing weak. Tp from anr copy; some browning; worming at inner blank margins of leaves M1 to end. C Apr 3 (63) £900

**Catesby, Mark, 1679?-1749**
— The Natural History of Carolina, Florida, and the Bahama Islands.... L, 1771. 3d Ed. 2 vols. Folio, half mor; extremities worn, Vol II rebacked with cloth, hinges split in Vol I, shaken. With folding colored map & 220 hand-colored plates. Split at fold of map; some discoloration & spotting to plates. P Dec 12 (199) $35,000

**Catharina Senensis.** See: Catherine of Siena

**Cathecuminum...**
— Cathecuminum secundum ordinem Romane Ecclesie: necnon morem Ecclesie Fauentine. Faenza: Giovanni Maria Simonetta, 25 May 1524. 4to, mor gilt by Lortic. Essling copy. C Apr 3 (191) £1,400

**Cather, Willa, 1873-1947**
See also: Limited Editions Club
— Alexander's Bridge. L, 1912. 1st English Ed. In dj with creases & short tears. pba Oct 5 (13) $1,200

New Ed. Bost., [1922]. In soiled & chipped dj. pba Oct 5 (14) $100
— April Twilights. Bost., 1903. 1st Ed. Orig bds. Inscr to Jessie B. Rittenhouse, 19 Mar 1913. Engelhard. CNY Oct 27 (13) $2,500

Anr copy. Orig bds; spine chipped. Inscr to Mrs. Robert Burns Peattie, 3 July 1903. pba Oct 5 (15) $3,250; pba Oct 5 (16) $2,250
— The Bookkeeper's Wife. NY, 1916. Orig wraps; broken, insect damage to rear cover. In: Century Magazine, May 1916. pba Oct 5 (18) $95
— Death Comes for the Archbishop. L, [1927]. In chipped dj. pba Aug 22 (77) $275

1st Ed. NY, 1927. In creased & repaired dj. pba Oct 5 (20) $550

Advance Review copy. Orig wraps; broken, small piece lacking from lower corner of front wrap. pba Oct 5 (19) $900

Anr Ed. NY, 1929. One of 170 L.p. copies. 4to, in dj with piece lacking from spine. pba Oct 5 (21) $800

Anr copy. Vellum; discolored. sg Feb 1 (53) $400
2d Ed. Inscr to Gertrude Lane. pba Oct 5 (22) $850
— A Lost Lady. NY, 1923. In 3 issues of Century Magazine. Orig wraps. In: Century Magazine, Vol 105, No 6 & Vol 106, Nos 1-2. pba Oct 5 (28) $140

1st Ed, One of 20 lettered copies. Half cloth; some rubbing. pba Oct 5 (29) $3,250

One of 200 L. p. copies, sgd. pba May 23 (64) $475

One of 200 L. p. copies, this copy with number eradicated. Library markings. sg Sept 28 (47) $100
— Lucy Gayheart. NY, 1935. 1st Ed, one of 749. In dj with piece lacking from lower front panel. pba Oct 5 (32) $250; wd Nov 15 (40) $200
— My Antonia. L, 1919. 1st English Ed. In dj. pba Oct 5 (34) $1,100

New Ed. Bost., [1926]. Inscr, 1927. pba Oct 5 (35) $800
— My Autobiography, by S. S. McClure. L, 1914. 1st English Ed. In dj. pba Oct 5 (38) $850

1st Ed. NY, [1914]. In later dj. Inscr by McClure to his wife, Harriet Hurd. pba Oct 5 (36) $250
— My Mortal Enemy. NY, 1926. In dj. pba Oct 5 (42) $160; pba May 23 (65) $130

One of 220 on Japanese vellum, sgd. cb Oct 17 (354) $450

Anr copy. Half cloth. pba Oct 5 (40) $300
— Not Under Forty. NY, 1936. 1st Ed, One of 333 on Japan vellum, sgd. In oversize dj. pba Oct 5 (43) $425
— O Pioneers! Bost., 1913. 1st Ed. pba Oct 5 (46) $325
— Obscure Destinies. NY, 1932. 1st Ed. In dj. pba Oct 5 (48) $55

One of 260 copies on Japan vellum, sgd. pba Oct 5 (47) $375; pba May 23 (66) $475

One of 260 copies on japan vellum. Half vellum; worn. wa Feb 29 (30) $210
— The Old Beauty and Others. NY, 1948. In dj. With 3 A Ls s to Miss Chapin laid in. cb June 25 (1808) $800

— One of Ours. NY, 1922. 1st Ed, One of 310 L.p. copies, sgd. Bds; spine head bumped. pba Oct 5 (49) $350

— The Professor's House. NY, 1925. 1st Ed. In dj. pba Oct 5 (51) $425

One of 185 L.p. copies. Half cloth, unopened. pba Oct 5 (50) $700

— Sapphira and the Slave Girl. NY, 1940. 1st Ed. In trimmed & soiled dj. Advance copy. pba Oct 5 (53) $95

Anr copy. In dj. one of—520. pba Oct 5 (54) $450

— Shadows on the Rock. NY, 1931. 1st Ed. In dj with repair. Inscr to Alice M. Dodge, 24 Aug 1931. pba Oct 5 (57) $800

Anr copy. In dj. pba Aug 22 (81) $75

Advance Review copy. Orig wraps; chipped, rear wrap creased, some soiling. pba Oct 5 (55) $120

One of 619. Cloth, in dj with spine repaired. pba Oct 5 (56) $300

— The Song of the Lark. Bost., 1915. 1st Ed, 1st Issue. pba Oct 5 (58) $375

Later Issue. pba Oct 5 (59) $130

— The Troll Garden. NY. 1905. 1st Ed, 1st Issue. In dj with spine head chipped. pba Oct 5 (60) $7,000

Anr copy. Cloth; spine ends & corners worn. Inscr to Isabelle McClung, the dedicatee. pba Oct 5 (61) $1,900

— Works. Bost., 1937-41. One of 970. 13 vols. Orig half lev. pba Oct 5 (45) $4,250

— Youth and the Bright Medusa. NY, 1920. 1st Ed, One of 35, sgd. Sgd on front free endpaper. pba Oct 5 (62) $3,500

Anr Ed. L, 1921. In chipped dj. pba Oct 5 (63) $600

**Cather, Willa, 1873-1947 —&
Fisher, Dorothy Canfield**

— The Fear that Walks by Noonday. Lincoln, Neb.: Pbd by the Junior Class of the University of Nebraska [1894], in The Sombrero [for 1895]. 1st Ed. 4to, orig cloth; minor soiling. pba Oct 5 (25) $650

1st Ed in Book form. NY, 1931. One of 30. Orig bds, unopened. Goodwin - Engelhard copy. CNY Oct 27 (14) $7,500

**Catherine of Siena, Saint, 1347-80**

— Epistole. Venice: Aldus, 15 [i.e.19?] Sept 1500. Folio, 18th-cent vellum. 40 lines & foliation; types 115R (text), 10:82R (dedication, inscriptions on woodcut illusts), 80 Italic cut by Francesco Griffo (2 inscrs on illustration). One woodcut illust; numerous woodcut initials from 7 sets. Minor staining; 1 wormhole in 1st 3 leaves & end, touching letters. 422 leaves. Goff C-281. Sneyd copy. C Apr 3 (64) £5,500

**Catholic...**

— Catholic Anthology 1914-1915. L, 1915. 1st Ed, one of 500. Ed by Ezra Pound. Orig bds; rubbed. Containing the 1st Ed in Book form of The Love Song of J. Alfred Prufrock & 4 other poems by T. S. Eliot. Hobson copy. S June 28 (40) £850

**Catlin, George, 1796-1872**

— Letters and Notes on the Manners, Customs, and Condition of the North American Indians. L, 1841 [but c.1892]. ("The Manners, Customs, and Condition of the North American Indians.") 2 vols. 8vo, orig cloth. cb Feb 14 (2579) $750

1st Ed. L, 1841. 2 vols. 8vo, early calf; worn & scuffed, spines soiled. With 309 plates & 3 maps Lacking errata slip. wa Feb 29 (332) $650

2d English Ed. 2 vols. 8vo, early half calf; cover panels detached, spines worn & def, scuffed. First few leaves of Vol I detached; some foxing; plates foxed. bbc Dec 18 (448) $300

5th Ed. L, 1845. ("Illustrations of the Manners, Customs, and Condition of the North American Indians....") 2 vols. 8vo, orig cloth. With 177 uncolored plates & 3 maps. sg Oct 26 (36) $350

Anr Ed. Phila., 1860. 2 vols in 1. 8vo, orig pictorial cloth; rubbed & cracked. Some foxing & spotting. Sold w.a.f. NH July 21 (186) $170

Anr Ed. L, 1866. ("Illustrations of the Manners, Customs, and Condition of the North American Indians.") 2 vols. 8vo, contemp half mor gilt; rubbed. With 313 hand-colored illusts on 180 plates, including large folding map. S Apr 23 (347) £5,200

Anr Ed. L, 1876. 2 vols. 8vo, contemp half calf; extremities rubbed, joints of Vol I starting; some foxing. With 180 colored plates & 1 map. cb Feb 14 (2578) $1,100

Anr copy. Orig cloth; worn, backstrips tape-repaired. With 180 colored plates. Tear to 1 plate margin taped on verso. wa Feb 29 (331) $1,000

Anr Ed. Edin., 1926. ("North American Indians.") 2 vols. 4to, pictorial cloth; corners bumped on Vol I. cb Oct 17 (148) $600

— Nord-Amerikas Indianer. Stockholm, 1848. 8vo, contemp half sheep gilt; extremities rubbed, rear joint cracked. Text foxed; frontis & title loose; plate facing p.154 cropped in upper margin. sg Oct 26 (37) $250

— North American Indian Portfolio. L, 1844. 1st Ed. Folio, half calf; corners bumped, extremities worn, joints rubbed. With 25 hand-colored lithos, heightened with gum arabic. Tp with crease & soiling; minor soiling to plate margins. Colored copy. P June 5 (26) $70,000

Anr Ed. L: Geo Catlin, [c.1845]. Folio, 19th-cent half mor; extremities scuffed. With 31 hand-colored plates. Frontis cracked, split at foot; last plate detached; sky portion of plate 3 dusty; frontis guard creased. Robbins copy with his pencil notes. pba Mar 21 (54) $80,000

— O-Kee-pa: A Religious Ceremony.... L, 1867. 1st English Ed. 8vo, orig cloth; extremities rubbed. With 13 plates. Scattered foxmarks. Robbins copy. pba Mar 21 (55) $2,750

**Catlin, Mark**

— Fly Fishing for Trout. Appleton WI: Badger, 1930. O Feb 6 (45) $160

**Cato, Marcus Porcius, 234-149 B.C.**
— Cato: Disticha de moribus. Basel: [Johann Amerbach], 14 June 1486. ("Disticha de moribus ad filium....") 4to, 19th-cent half sheep. 32 lines; types 1:185G, 6:108G, 5:106(92)G, 3:92a*(83)G, 9:63G. Woodcut on tp. Library stamp on tp. 48 leaves. Goff C-297. C Nov 29 (40) £1,600

— Cato's Moral Distichs. San Francisco: Book Club of California, 1939. One of 250. Facsimile of the Benjamin Franklin Ed of 1735, with an orig leaf from a Franklin-ptd work tipped in. pba Oct 26 (135) $200

**Cats, Jacob, 1577-1660**
— Werke. Amst., 1712. ("Alle de Wercken.") 2 vols in 1. Folio, lea gilt; worn. NH Sept 16 (168) $650

Anr copy. 2 vols. Folio, old half calf; extremities worn, needs rebacking. With 3 ports & 5 plates, 3 double-page. Inscr by Samuel Putnam Avery in Vol I. sg Mar 21 (77) $700

**Catullus, Caius Valerius, 84?-54 B.C.**
— Catulli Carmina. The Poems of Catullus. L: Piazza Press, 1929. One of 500. Trans by F. C. W. Hiley; illus by Vera Willoughby. Vellum. sg Sept 14 (97) $50

**Catullus, Tibullus & Propertius**
— Opera. Paris: Simon Colines, 1543. 16mo, later calf; rubbed & scuffed. Trimmed affecting tp border. pba Aug 22 (571) $100

Anr Ed. Paris: A. U. Coustelier, 1743. 2 vols. 12mo, contemp calf gilt; joints rubbed, frontis nearly detached in Vol I. Ptd on vellum. Powis - Fuerstenberg - Schaefer copy. S Dec 7 (134) £3,000

Anr Ed. Birm.: Baskerville, 1772. With A2 cancelans & H3 cancelandum. 4to, contemp mor gilt. bba May 9 (7) £360 [Quaritch]

**Caulfield, James, 1754-1826**
See also: Wilson & Caulfield

— Portraits, Memoirs, and Characters, of Remarkable Persons from the Revolution in 1688 to the End of the Reign of George II. L, 1819-20. 4 vols. 8vo, contemp half mor; rubbed, joints rubbed. With 118 plates Vol III with 1 plate cut down & mtd & anr loosely inserted; Vol IV with a couple of plates waterstained; some annotations, foxing & browning; some leaves loose. bba May 30 (150) £65 [Young]

Anr copy. Later half calf; marked. Spotted. S Oct 27 (841) £110 [Person]

**Caus, Salomon de, 1576-1626?**
— La pratique et demonstration des horloges solaires. Paris, 1624. 1st Ed. Folio, contemp vellum; rebacked using part of orig spine, new endpapers. Badly dampstained; some leaves reinforced in margins; worming affecting text. Sold w.a.f. S Mar 14 (79) £800

**Causley, Charles**
[A collection of 33 items, his works, 1 ALs & 3 Ls s to John Middleton Murry, sold in the Hobson sale at Sotheby's on 28 June 1996 for £650]

**Cauvet, Gilles Paul**
— Recueil d'ornemens a l'usage des jeunes artistes qui se destinent a la decoration des batimens.... Paris, 1777. Broadsheets, 550mm by 370mm, contemp vellum. With frontis & 98 plates on 65 leaves only. Fuerstenberg - Schaefer copy. S Dec 7 (102) £1,250

**Cavalca, Domenico, d.1342**
— Frutti della lingua. Florence, [Bartolommeo di Libri, c.1494]. 4to, 19th-cent half mor. 33 lines; types 1:97R1, 3:114G. With woodcut. Some spotting or staining, mainly to margins. 142 leaves. Goff C-332. C Apr 3 (65) £1,100

— Pungi lingua. Venice: Baptista de Tortis, 9 Oct 1494. 4to, 19th-cent mor gilt by Lloyd. 38 lines; double column; type 10:82G; spaces for initials with guide letters. Crucifixion woodcut on tp. Lower margin of last leaf renewed; words deleted by early reader on b2v. 80 leaves. Goff C-342. Fairfax Murray - Manhattan College copy. C Apr 3 (66) £1,500

Anr copy. 19th-cent half calf. 38 lines; double column; type 10:82G; spaces for initials with guide letters. Crucifixion woodcut on tp. 80 leaves. Goff C-342. C June 26 (57) £1,800

**Cavalieri, Giovanni Battista, 1525-97**
— Antiquarum statuarum urbis Romae. Rome, 1585-94. 2 vols in 1. Folio, 19th-cent bd; worn. With 2 engraved titles & 203 plates. Foxed; scored early writing on tp. sg Sept 7 (72) $950

Anr copy. 19th-cent bds; worn. Foxed; early scored writing & heavy spotting on tp. sg May 9 (325) $750

**Cavallo, Tiberius, 1749-1809**
— A Complete Treatise of Electricity in Theory and Practice. L, 1795. 4th Ed. 3 vols. 8vo, contemp calf; rebacked, joints starting. sg May 16 (146) $225

**Cave, William, 1637-1713**
— Scriptorum ecclesiasticorum historia literaria. Geneva: de Tournes, 1694. 2 parts in 1 vol. Folio, contemp vellum; worn & soiled. Bound at end are Gerio's Appendix ad Partem Alteram HIstoriae Literarae, Geneva, 1699 & Cave Dissertationes Tres, 1699. O Mar 26 (58) $225

**Cavendish, George, 1500?-62**
See also: Kelmscott Press

— The Negotiations of Thomas Wolsey, the great Cardinall of England.... Chipping Camden: Alcuin Press, 1930. ("The Life and Death of Cardinal Wolsey.") One of a few specially bound with illuminated initials & decorations by Mabel Scriven. 4to, mor gilt. bba May 9 (296) £400 [Marks]

**Cavendish, William, Duke of Newcastle.** See: Newcastle, William Cavendish

**Cavendish, William, 7th Duke of Devonshire.** See: Devonshire Collection, William Cavendish

**Cavigioli, Giovanni Battista**
— Livre des Proprietes du vinaigre. Poitiers: [Jehan & Engelbert de Marnef], 1541. 1st Ed. 16mo in 8s, 19th-Cent mor. Ck Mar 22 (69) £2,400

**Caxton Club—Chicago**
KENYON, FREDERIC G. - Ancient Books and Modern Discoveries. 1927. One of 350. Inscr by Bruce Rogers to T. M. Cleland. sg Sept 14 (89) $375
LA SALLE, NICOLAS DE. - Relation of the Discovery of the Mississippi River. 1898. One of 269. sg Oct 26 (202) $200
LA SALLE, RENE ROBERT CAVELIER. - Relation of the Discoveries and Voyages.... 1901. One of 227. sg Oct 26 (203) $175
STEELE, JOHN. - Across the Plains in 1850. 1930. One of 350. Ed by Joseph Schafer. Orig cloth. With port, 1 folded map, & 6 sketches. Larson copy. pba Sept 28 (676) $80

**Caxton, William, 1422?-91.** See: Kelmscott Press

**Caylus, Anne Claude Philippe, Comte de, 1692-1765**
— Memoires de l'Academie des Colporteurs. Paris, 1748. 8vo, contemp calf; spine ends repaired. With engraved title & 8 plates.. Fuerstenberg - Schaefer copy. S Dec 7 (104) £150
— Le Pot-pouri, ouvrage nouveau de ces dames et de ces messieurs. Amst., 1748. 5 parts in 1 vol. 12mo, contemp red mor gilt. With frontis. Fuerstenberg - Schaefer copy. S Dec 7 (105) £300

**Cayton, Horace R.** See: Drake & Cayton

**Cazotte, Jacques, 1720-92**
See also: Laboureur & Cazotte
— Le Diable amoureux. Naples [but Paris: Legay], 1772. 8vo, citron mor gilt by Chambolle-Duru. With 6 plates. (Leaf of engraved music not mentioned). Fuerstenberg - Schaefer copy. S Dec 7 (105) £900

**Cazzone, Doctor, Pseud.** See: Nerciat, Andrea de

**Ceccherelli, Alessandro**
— Descrizione di tutte le feste, e mascherate fatte in Firenze per il carnovale.... Florence: L. Torrentino, 1567. 8vo, 19th-cent half lea. C June 26 (58) £600

**Celine, Louis Ferdinand Destouches, 1894-1961**
— Voyage au bout de la nuit. Paris, 1932. 1st Ed, Out-of-series copy. Orig wraps, unopened. Some minor stains. CE May 22 (76) $1,200

**Celiz, Francisco**
— Diary of the Alarcon Expedition into Texas.... Los Angeles: Quivira Society, 1935. One of 600. With 10 plates Library markings. pba Aug 8 (30) $85

**Cellarius, Andreas**
— Harmonia Macrocosmica seu atlas universalis et novus. Amst.: J. Jansson, 1660. Folio, 17th-cent vellum gilt over bds with yapp edges; soiled, minor repair to spine. With frontis & 29 double-page maps, all colored & some heightened in gilt by a contemp hand. Marginal repair to Chart 9; Chart 4 creased & abraded; some fold breaks & chipping; some damp-staining at lower margin; ff1 & Qq2 with short tears at lower margin. P June 5 (188) $80,000
— Regni Poloniae magnique docatus lituaniae.... Amst.: J. Jansson, 1659. 12mo, contemp calf covered in later cloth; upper hinge cracked. With engraved title, folding map & 20 folding views. b June 28 (83) £450

**Cellarius, Christoph, 1638-1707**
— Geographia antiqua.... Rome, 1774. 4to, half calf. With 33 double-page maps. b Sept 20 (378) £160
— Geographica antiqua. Rome, 1774. Oblong folio, later cloth; rubbed. With engraved title, frontis & 35 double-page or folding maps. Some spotting. bba June 6 (290) £450 [Frew]
— Notitia orbis antiqui sive Geographia Plenior.... L, 1703. Vol I (of 2). 4to, contemp vellum; worn & soiled, rejointed, pastedowns pulling loose. With engraved title, port, plate & 20 maps. Some foxing. cb Oct 17 (248) $300

**Cellarius, Christoph, 1638-1707 —& Others**
— Kratkoe rukovodstvo k' drevnei geografii. St. Petersburg, 1788. 4to, contemp calf; spine worn, lacking front flyleaf. With 28 folding maps. A2-3 loose & frayed; Map 16 torn without loss; small library stamps on tp. S Nov 30 (74) £2,600

**Cellini, Benvenuto, 1500-71**
See also: Limited Editions Club
— The Life of Benvenuto Cellini.... NY & L, [1906]. Trans by J. A. Symonds. 2 vols. 8vo, half mor bilt by Brentano's. sg Jan 11 (83) $50
— The Treatises of Benvenuto Cellini on Goldsmithing and Sculpture. L: Essex House Press, 1898. Out-of-series copy for C. R. Ashbee. 4to, mor gilt by Douglast Cockerell, 1899. Minor foxing. sg Oct 19 (57) $1,600

**Celsus, Aurelius Cornelius**
— De medicina. Venice: Philippus Pincius for Benedictus Fontana, 6 May, 1497. Folio, modern mor. With 94 leaves & Fontana device on final verso. H1.8 browed. Ck Mar 22 (70) £2,000
— De re medica libri octo. Venice: Aldus, 1528. ("Medicinae libri viii."). 8vo, later vellum. Holes in 8 text leaves; other marginal worming; erasures on tp & flyleaf. S Nov 30 (316) £750

**Celtis, Conrad**
— Septenaria sodalitas litteraria Germaniae. Vienna: [Johann Winterburg], 1500. 4to, modern blind-stamped pigskin. 39 lines; spaces for Greek filled in; types 1:78G, 6:78G, 6:79G, 5:104G. 8 leaves. Goff C-374. C Nov 29 (41) £4,400

**Cendrars, Blaise, 1887-1961**
— La Fin du monde, filmee par l'Ange N.D. Paris, 1919. One of 1,225. Illus by Fernand Leger. 4to, orig wraps. Half-title spotted. Ck Sept 8 (7) £1,400 Anr copy. Marginal repair to 1 leaf; half-title spotted. Ck May 31 (36) £380

## CENDRARS

— Panama, or the Adventures of my Seven Uncles. NY, 1931. One of 300, sgd by author & artist. Trans & illus by John Dos Passos. Pictorial wraps. sg June 20 (85) $175
— Petits Contes Negres pour les Enfants des Blancs. [Paris]: Sans Pareil, [1929]. One of 12 on japon imperial with an extra suite of plates. 4to, mor extra by Paul Bonet, orig wraps bound in; spine chipped. b Sept 20 (607) £2,000

### Cent...
— Les Cent Nouvelles. Paris: Javal et Bourdeaux, 1931. One of 40 hors commerce on japon, this copy with orig watercolor drawing sgd by Carlo Farneti & 4 additional suites of the plates by Malassis, with remarques & additional suite of 25 plates by Carlo Farneti (this 1 of 40 in 3 states). Illus by C. Lorraine after Edmond Malassis. 4to, mor extra pictorial bdg sgd Mercher Doreur, orig wraps bound in, the additional suites loose as issued in orig wraps. S Nov 21 (70) £2,000

### Cent Nouvelles...
— Les cent nouvelles nouvelles. Cologne [but Amst.]: P. Gaillard, 1701. 2 vols. 8vo, later 18th-cent calf; spines repaired. With frontis & 100 half-page vignettes & 1 tailpiece. Fuerstenberg - Schaefer copy. S Dec 7 (451) £180

### Century...
— The Century Dictionary and Cyclopedia. NY, [1906]. 10 vols. 4to, half mor. wa Dec 14 (28) $120
— The Century Guild Hobby Horse. L, 1886-94. Second No 1 - No 28. 4to, orig wraps; soiled, No 9 rear cover creased & torn, No 21 with corner off. wad Oct 18 (428) C$550

### Ceremonials
— 1622. - Caeremoniale continens ritus electionis romani pontificis. Rome: Typographia Camerae Apostolicae. 4to, contemp mor gilt, by Baldassarre Sorensino; rebacked retaining part of spine. S Mar 28 (505) £750

### Cervantes Saavedra, Miguel de, 1547-1616
See also: Ashendene Press; Limited Editions Club; Nonesuch Press; Onassis copy, Jacqueline Bouvier Kennedy
— The Dialogue of the Dogs. Kentfield: Allen Press, 1969. One of 140. 4to, cloth. sg Sept 14 (6) $175

#### Don Quixote in French
— Pages choisies de Don Quichotte de La Manche. Paris, 1957. One of 25 for the Libreria l'Amateur, Buenos Aires. Illus by Salvador Dali. Folio, orig wraps in folder & slipcase. Orig sgd etching by Dali laid in. P June 5 (209) $3,000

#### Don Quixote in English
— 1620. - L.2d Ed in English of Part 1; 1st Ed in English of Part 2. 2 vols. 4to, mor gilt by Riviere. Small repair to dedication leaf; Vol II without engraved titles; lacking 2K4 blank; browned throughout. Honeyman copy. bba Nov 16 (128) £2,500 [Thorp]

## AMERICAN BOOK PRICES CURRENT

Anr copy. Modern half calf; 1 cover detached, some scuffing. Some cropping, affecting heads, catchwords & signature marks; old stamp to 1st ptd page. pba Sept 14 (101) $2,500
— 1687. - L. Trans by John Phillips. Folio, half lev gilt by H. Jackel. With 8 plates. Marginal replacements to tp; stains to tp & extremities of following few pages. pba Nov 30 (80) $600

Anr copy. Old sheep; worn, needs rebacked. With frontis & 8 plates. Frontis & tp trimmed & mtd. sg Mar 21 (294) $1,100

#### Don Quixote in French
— 1723-24. - Paris: Jacques Francois Chereau. Folio, half mor; soiled. With 25 plates reproducing the cartoons of Charles Coypel for a series of Gobelin tapestries.. Fuerstenberg - Schaefer copy. S Dec 7 (109) £3,200

#### Don Quixote in Spanish
— 1738. - L. 4 vols. 4to, contemp turkey; rebacked in calf, affected by damp. With port & 68 plates. Some browning. L.p. copy. Ck Sept 8 (180) £850

#### Don Quixote in English
— 1742. - L. Trans by Charles Jarvis. 2 vols. 4to, lea gilt; broken, worn. Plates trimmed. rs Nov 11 (75) $275

#### Don Quixote in French
— 1746. - Les Principales Avantures de l'admirable Don Quichotte. The Hague 4to, contemp red mor gilt with arms of Comte Henri de Calenberg; rubbed. With 31 plates in 1st state. Bound in are 12 orig drawings in sanguine, some with wash. Fuerstenberg - Schaefer copy. S Dec 7 (110) £14,500

#### Don Quixote in English
— 1774. - The History of the renowned Don Quixote de la Mancha. L. Trans by Charles Henry Wilmot. 2 vols. 4to, contemp calf; spine ends worn. Few closed tears. Sold w.a.f. CE Nov 8 (178) $120

#### Don Quixote in Spanish
— 1780. - Madrid: Joaquin Ibarra. 4 vols. 4to, contemp calf gilt; rubbed. With hand-colored double-page map, frontises & 31 plates. Marginal dampstaining to 1st few leaves of Vol I. C Nov 29 (121) £2,300

Anr copy. Contemp mor gilt by Gabriel de Sancha; extremities rubbed, repaired tear on lower cover of Vol I. With double-page folding map & 36 plates before letters. Marginal foxing to plates. Wilmerding - Schaefer copy. P Nov 1 (56) $44,000

Anr copy. Contemp sheep gilt; spines & extremities worn. With 4 engraved titles, port, 31 plates & double-page map. Some foxing & dampstaining. Inscr in Spanish by Jose Ferrer to Paul Robeson, 25 Dec 1943. P Dec 12 (50) $1,800
— 1797-98. - Madrid 5 vols. 8vo, contemp sheep with FNL cypher; spine ends wormed with small loss. With 35 plates, including map. Some spotting; tear just into image of map. Schaefer copy. P Nov 1 (57) $2,000

## Don Quixote in English
— c.1798. - L: Cooke's Edition Trans by Tobias Smollett. 5 vols. 16mo, contemp calf; worn. sg Sept 21 (116) $120

## Don Quixote in French
— 1799. - Don Quichotte de la Manche.... Paris: Didot l'aine. 3 vols. 8vo, mor gilt by Chambolle-Duru. With 24 plates in 3 states Lacking port of Cervantes. Fuerstenberg - Schaefer copy. S Dec 7 (111) £800

## Don Quixote in English
— 1810. - L. Trans by Charles Jarvis. 4 vols. 8vo, contemp calf gilt; rubbed, front cover of Vol I detached. Foxed. F June 20 (495) $110
— 1818. - L. Trans by Mary Smirke; illus by Robert Smirke. 4 vols extended to 8. 8vo, mor gilt. Extra-illus with c.320 plates. CE May 22 (82) $650
— 1819. - L. Illus by J. Clark. 4 vols. 8vo, calf gilt; hinges weak, Vol III spine def. With 24 hand-colored plates. wd May 8 (42) $125
— 1833. - The History and Adventures of the Renowned Don Quixote.... L. Illus by George Cruikshank. 3 vols. 8vo, calf gilt. pba June 20 (110) $225
— 1906-7. - NY One of 140. 5 vols. 4to, bds. With extra suite of illusts before letters in bd portfolio. sg Feb 15 (67) $200

## Cesalpino, Andrea
— Quaestionum Peripateticarum Lib. V. Venice: Giunta, 1593. 1st Complete Ed. 8vo, old bds; covers damp-stained, joints & corners worn. Some foxing. CE Nov 8 (78) $5,000

## Cesaris, Angelo. See: Strassoldo-Grafenberg & Cesaris

## Cescinsky, Herbert —& Gribble, Ernest
— Early English Furniture and Woodwork. L, 1922. 2 vols. Folio, orig half mor; rubbed. bba May 30 (33) £100 [Lobo]
Anr copy. Half lea; rebacked retaining most of orig backstrips, hinges reinforced. sg June 13 (153) $60
Anr copy. Orig mor. wa Dec 14 (460) $80

## Chacon, Alonso. See: Ciaccone, Alfonso

## Chadourne, Louis
— Le pot au noir, scenes et figures des tropiques. Paris, 1922. One of 79 hors commerce on hollande. Illus by P. Falke, colored by pochoir by J. Saude. 4to, half mor with onlays by Paul Bonet [Carnets, 5], orig wraps bound in. With 81 woodcuts. Tp with stains. S Nov 21 (71) £1,200

## Chadwick, Sir Edwin, 1800-90
— Report from the Poor Law Commissioners on an Inquiry into the Sanitary Condition of the Labouring Population of Great Britain. L, 1842-43. 2 vols, including Supplementary Report. 8vo, orig cloth. With 2 folding maps, folding chart & 20 plates. Stamps on title versos. b May 30 (2) £650

## Chagall, Marc, 1887-1985
— The Biblical Message. NY, [1973]. 4to, cloth, in dj. sg June 13 (108) $80
— Chagall. Paris, 1957. Folio, unsewn as issued in orig wraps. Derriere le Miroir, No 99-100. sg Jan 11 (93) $425
— Chagall lithographe. Monte Carlo: Andre Sauret, 1960-63-69-74-84. Vol III only. Orig cloth, in dj. sg Jan 11 (101) $275
Anr copy. In dj. Copy with German text. sg June 13 (107) $175
Anr copy. Text by Fernand Mourlot. Vols I-III. 4to, orig cloth, in djs. cb Oct 17 (614) $1,900
— Contes de Boccace. Paris, 1950. Folio, orig wraps; torn, lacking piece on rear panel. Verve, No 24. Inscr. pba June 20 (88) $425
Anr copy. Orig wraps. Verve, No 24. sg June 13 (113) $200
— Dessins pour la Bible. Paris, 1960. Folio, bds; worn, lower joints starting. Minor waterstaining at ends. Verve No 37/38. sg Sept 7 (82) $3,000
Anr copy. Orig bds. Verve No 37/38. wad Oct 18 (228) C$3,800
— Drawings for the Bible. NY, 1960. Folio, bds; spine ends & corners worn, spine split. Some foxing. Verve No 37/38. cb June 25 (1935) $3,000
— Illustrations for the Bible. NY, 1956. Folio, orig bds; worn, spine def, covers detached. Verve No 33/34. sg June 13 (106) $2,800
Anr copy. Orig bds. Verve No 33/34. wad Oct 18 (229) C$4,400
— The Jerusalem Windows. NY, 1962. Text by Jean Leymarie. Folio, orig cloth, in dj. P Dec 12 (51) $1,100
Anr copy. Orig cloth, in dj with minor wear. P June 5 (191) $1,200
Anr copy. Cloth, in dj with adhesive traces on rear panel. sg Sept 7 (83) $1,200
Anr copy. Cloth, in dj. sg Oct 19 (60) $1,100
Anr copy. Cloth, in repaired dj. sg Jan 11 (95) $1,100
Anr copy. Orig cloth in dj with minor fraying. wa Nov 16 (280) $950
— The Lithographs of Chagall. Monte Carlo & NY or Bost., 1960-86. Vol III In dj. bbc June 24 (121) $240
Anr copy. 6 vols. 4to, orig cloth, in djs. P June 5 (189) $3,000
Anr copy. Vols III-VI. In djs. P June 5 (190) $600
Anr copy. Vol III In dj. pba June 20 (89) $275
Anr Ed. Monte Carlo & NY or Bost., 1960-84. Vol I. Orig cloth, in dj. bbc June 24 (119) $1,300
Anr copy. Orig cloth, in chipped dj; minor tears to front free endpaper. F Mar 28 (558) $1,600
Anr copy. In dj. sg Sept 7 (84) $1,400; sg Jan 11 (102) $1,400
Anr copy. Orig cloth, in dj. wad Oct 18 (230) C$1,900
Vol II. In dj lacking flaps. bbc June 24 (120) $650
Anr copy. In dj. pba Nov 30 (82) $550; sg Sept 7 (85) $750; sg Sept 7 (86) $750; sg Jan 11 (103) $650

Anr Ed. Monte Carlo & NY or Bost., 1960-86. Vol IV. In frayed dj; upper hinge of bdg cracked. CE Feb 21 (33) $110
Anr copy. In dj. pba Aug 22 (718) $225
Anr Ed. Monte Carlo & NY or Bost., 1960-84. Vol IV. In dj. sg Jan 11 (104) $425
Vol VI. In dj. bbc June 24 (122) $90
— Marc Chagall: Life and Works. See: Meyer, Franz

**Chain, Ernest Boris —& Others**
— Penicillin as a Chemotherapeutic Agent. L, 24 Aug 1940. 4to, sewn as issued. Minor stains. In: The Lancet, Vol CCXXXIX, No 6104, pp. 226-28. sg May 16 (388A) $150

**Challamel, Augustin, 1818-94**
— The History of Fashion in France.... NY, 1882. 8vo, orig half cloth; shaken. With 21 color plates. sg Jan 11 (117) $140
Anr copy. With 21 colored plates. sg Jan 11 (117) $140

**Chalmers, Alexander, 1759-1834.** See: British...; Fore-Edge Paintings

**Chalon, Renier Hubert Ghislain, 1802-89**
— Catalogue d'une tres-riche mais peu nombreuse collection de livres provent da la bibliotheque de feu le Comte J.-N.-A. de Fortsas.... Brussels: Van Trigt, [n.d.]. 8vo, orig wraps; dampstained. O Mar 26 (59) $170

**Chamberlain, Newell D.**
— The Call of Gold: True Tales on the Gold Road to Yosemite. Mariposa CA: Gazette Press, 1936. Orig cloth; front cover stained. pba Apr 25 (336) $55

**Chamberlin, Everett**
— Chicago and its Suburbs. Chicago, 1874. 8vo, orig cloth; worn. sg Oct 26 (149) $950

**Chamberlin, Harry D., 1887-1944.** See: Derrydale Press

**Chambers, Charles Edward Stuart**
— Golfing: A Handbook to the Royal and Ancient Game.... Edin.: W. & R. Chambers, 1887. 1st Ed. - Illus by Ranald M. Alexander. Cloth. With color frontis port of Tom Morris. pba Apr 18 (17) $950
Anr Ed. Edin., 1887. Illus by Ronald M. Alexander. Cloth. With color frontis port. pba Nov 9 (5) $800

**Chambers, E. T. D.**
— The Ouananiche and its Canadian Environment. NY, 1896. 8vo, cloth. sg Mar 7 (409) $120

**Chambers, Ephraim, d.1740**
— Cyclopaedia: or, an Universal Dictionary of Arts and Sciences. L, 1741. Plate vol only. Calf; worn & rubbed, covers & 1st few leaves detached. Sold w.a.f. K Feb 11 (117) $350
Anr Ed. L, 1778-83. 4 vols. Folio, contemp russia gilt; most covers detached, some later free endpapers. With engraved frontis & 138 plates only. Sold w.a.f. bba Oct 19 (188) £200 [Dyson]

**Chambers, Robert William, 1865-1933**
— The Maker of Moons. NY, 1896. sg Feb 8 (252) $90

**Chambers, William**
— American Slavery and Colour. L, 1857. 8vo, orig cloth; spine ends worn. With chromolitho map. sg Mar 28 (277) $80

**Chambers, Sir William, 1726-96**
— A Treatise on Civil Architecture. L, 1759. 1st Ed. Folio, later half mor; worn, spine ends chipped, joints starting. With 50 plates. Browned; some foxing & staining; marginal tears repaired; 4 plates with tap repair to versos; 1 plate lacking corner, affecting image. wa Feb 29 (86) $600
2d Ed. L, 1768. Folio, modern half calf. With 50 plates. Some spotting; single stabmark in margins of text only. b Sept 20 (75) £450

**Chambliss, William H.**
— Chambliss' Diary; or, Society As It Really Is. NY, 1895. 1st Ed. 8vo, orig cloth; extremities rubbed, rear joint rubbed. Robbins copy. pba Mar 21 (56) $190

**Chamisso, Adelbert von, 1781-1838.** See: Grabhorn Printing

**Champier, Symphorien**
— Liber de quadruplici vita Theologia Asclepii.... Lyon: Jannot de Campis for Staphanus Gueynardus & Jacobus Huguetannus, 31 July 1507. 4to, 19th-cent half calf. Gothic type. With 7 woodcuts & 2 metalcuts. Tear in a1 & a2 without loss; early marginalia; some staining. Schaefer copy. P Nov 1 (58) $7,500
— Le Recueil ou croniques des hystoires des royaulmes d'austrasie. Lyon: Vincent de Portunaris, 11 July 1510. Folio, calf gilt by Bauzonnet-Purgold. Gothic & bastarda types. With 37 woodcuts. Washed; finger-soiling. Schaefer copy. P Nov 1 (59) $8,000

**Champlain, Samuel de, 1567-1635**
— Les Voyages de la Nouvelle France Occidentale.... Paris, 1632. 3d Issue with Collet imprint. 4to, recent calf gilt; corners worn. Folding map in facsimile laid in at rear; library stamp on tp; some dampstains & tears. bbc Dec 18 (450) $3,300

**Champollion, Jean Francois, 1792-1832**
— Precis du systeme hieroglyphique des anciens Egyptiens. Paris, 1824. 1st Ed 2 vols. 8vo, orig wraps; spines worn, Vol I spine split. With 48 plates. C Apr 3 (68) £1,900

**Chandler, Alfred, 1804-96 —&
Booth, William Beattie, 1804?-74**
— Illustrations and Descriptions of the Plants which Compose the Natural Order Camellieae.... L, 1831. Vol I (all pbd). Folio, contemp half mor gilt; worn & loose. With 40 hand-colored plates. Some varnish corrosion to plant foliage; some plates trimmed to plate line. S June 27 (7) £12,000

### Chandler, Francis
— Municipal Architecture in Boston...Designs by Edmund M. Wheelwright, City Architect.... Bost., 1898. One of 500. 2 vols. Folio, half mor; joints splitting. With 100 mtd photographic plates. Library markings. cb Oct 17 (9) $300

### Chandler, Melbourne C.
— Of GarryOwen and Glory: The History of the Seventh United States Cavalry. Annandale VA: Turnpike Press, [1960]. In dj. pba June 25 (58) $80

### Chandler, Raymond, 1888-1959
— The Big Sleep. NY, 1939. In repaired dj. CE Feb 21 (34) $3,900

Anr copy. Orig cloth; soiled, library stamp on front pastedown. sg June 20 (43) $275

Anr Ed. NY, [1946]. In worn dj. With plates from the Warner Brothers film. sg Dec 14 (40) $110

Anr Ed. San Francisco: Arion Press, 1986. One of 425. sg Sept 14 (25) $400

— Farewell, My Lovely. NY, 1940. In dj with light wear at ends. CE Feb 21 (35) $2,200

Anr copy. In backed & restored dj. sg June 20 (44) $850

— Killer in the Rain. Bost., 1964. 1st American Ed. In dj. sg June 20 (45) $175

— The Lady in the Lake. NY, 1943. In backed & restored dj; bookplate & writing removed from pastedown. sg June 20 (46) $700

— The Little Sister. Bost., 1949. 1st American Ed, 1st Issue. In dj with closed tears & soiling to rear panel. wa Dec 14 (32) $250

— The Smell of Fear. L, [1965]. In dj. sg Dec 14 (41) $275

— Spanish Blood. Cleveland, [1946]. 1st Ed, Review copy. In dj. sg June 20 (49) $100

### Chandler, Richard, 1738-1810
— The History of Ilium or Troy.... L, 1802. 4to, modern mor. With folding map. Browned throughout. b May 30 (252) £160

— Travels in Asia Minor.... Oxford, 1775. 1st Ed. In 2 vols. 4to, contemp calf; rebacked. With folding map. b May 30 (253) £380

### Chanlaire, Pierre Gregoire —& Herbin, P. C.
— Atlas de la republique francaise. [Paris], 1802 [An X]. 4to, half lea; extremities worn. With engraved title & 101 maps colored in outline. Ink stamp on verso of each map. sg May 9 (62) $600

### Chanslor, Roy
— The Ballad of Cat Ballou. Bost., [1956]. In dj. Inscr. pba May 23 (68) $80

### Chansonnier...
— Chansonnier Normand. Paris, 1905. One of 125, this copy for the typographer. Illus by Adolphe Giraldon. Folio, contemp mor extra by Canape. With extra suite of the ports on velin bound at end. Lacking pp. 35-38, 49-50 & 89-90; marginal tear to 1 leaf. Bound in are various examples of Giraldon's orig artwork for the book. Ck May 31 (45) £190

### Chants...
— Chants et chansons populaires de la France. [Paris], 1843. 3 vols. 4to, mor gilt by Chambolle-Duru. b Sept 20 (608) £450

### Chapman, Abel, 1851-1929 —& Buck, Walter J.
— Wild Spain (Espana Agreste): Records of Sport with Rifle.... L, 1893. Cloth. Foxed. O June 4 (69) $80

### Chapman, Hay
— Law of the Links: Rules, Principles and Etiquette of Golf. San Francisco, 1922. 1st Ed. Orig bds; spine & extrems sunned, spine ends chipped. pba Apr 18 (18) $130

### Chapman, Hilary
— The Wood Engravings of Ethelbert White. Wakefield: Fleece Press, 1992. One of 200 with 2 separate mtd wood-engravings. 4to, orig ptd wraps. bba May 9 (488) £70 [Besley]

### Chapman, John Ratcliffe
— Instructions to Young Marksmen.... NY, 1848. 12mo, orig cloth; worn, spine ends torn, rear joint chipped. Some foxing. wa Feb 29 (179) $130

### Chapman, Maria Weston
— Right and Wrong in Massachusetts. Bost., 1839. 12mo, orig cloth; spine heel chipped. sg Oct 26 (340) $90

### Chapman, Thomas
— A Narrative of the Case of... who discovered the means of making the Fur of the Seal available.... Southwark, [1810]. 8vo, orig wraps. b May 30 (152) £400

### Chapman, William
— Observations on the Various Systems of Canal Navigation.... L, 1797. 4to, cloth. With map & 3 plates. b May 30 (15) £200

### Chappe d'Auteroche, Jean, 1728-69
— A Journey into Siberia. L, 1770. 4to, contemp calf. With folding map & 9 plates. pba July 25 (388) $250

Anr copy. Contemp calf; upper cover loose. With folding map (partly hand-colored) & 9 plates. Map shaved at lower neat-line. S Mar 14 (80) £180

Anr copy. Modern cloth. With folding map & 11 plates. Inked library stamps on tp & plate versos. sg Mar 7 (276) $425

### Chappe, Ignace
— Histoire de la telegraphie. Paris, 1824. 1st Ed. 2 vols. 8vo, contemp half sheep; spine ends worn. With 34 double-page plates. Some foxing. sg May 16 (148) $225

### Chappuis, Adrien
— Album de Paul Cezanne. Paris, 1966. One of 550. 2 vols. Facsimile notebook in cloth, text in orig wraps. bba Oct 19 (5) £130 [Kunkler]
— Die Zeichnungen von Paul Cezanne im Kupferstichkabinett Basel. Olten, 1962. 2 vols. 4to, cloth, in djs. sg Sept 7 (80) $250; sg Jan 11 (90) $90

### Char, Rene
— L'Inclemence lointaine. Paris, 1961. One of 130. Illus by de Vieira da Silva. Folio, loose as issued in orig folder. S Nov 21 (73) £1,000
— Le Monde de l'Art n'est pas le Monde du Pardon. Paris: Maeght, 1974. One of 75 on velin de Lana. Folio, unsewn in orig cloth portfolio. With 3 color lithos, 2 aquatints & 1 etching by Mirl, Lam, Charbonnier, Szenes, Wou-Ki & Vieira de Silva. sg May 23 (423) $1,800
— Poemes. Paris, 1952. One of 90. Illus by Nicolas de Stael. 4to, unsewn in orig wraps. With colored litho & 14 plates. S Nov 21 (74) £6,200
— Retour amont. [Paris], 1966. One of 188. Illus by Alberto Giacometti. 4to, unsewn in orig wraps. With 4 aquatints. S Nov 30 (338) £1,000

### Charaka Club
— The Proceedings of the Charaka Club. NY, 1902-10. One of 300 & 315. Vols I-III. 8vo, orig half cloth; worn. sg May 16 (389) $140

### Charcot, Jean Baptiste A. E., 1867-1936
— The Voyage of the "Why Not?" in the Antarctic. Toronto: Musson Book Co., [1911]. Rebound with most of orig bdg laid on. pba July 25 (24) $180

**Charles, C. J.** See: Duveen, Charles Joel

### Charles I, King of England, 1600-49
— Eikon Basilike. The Pourtraicture of His Sacred Majestie.... [L], 1649. 8vo, 19th-cent mor gilt; old writing to front free endpaper. Wing E-307. Madan 25. pba Nov 30 (84) $130

Anr Ed. L: De la More Press, 1904. One of 290. Mor gilt by Bumpus; mar to rear cover, some foxing to endpapers. pba Nov 30 (85) $180
— Works. L, 1662. ("Basilika. The Workes of....") 2 vols in 1. Folio, old calf; rebacked preserving orig spine. With 1 (of 2) frontis, engraved title & 2 (of 3) folding plates. Minor tears; a few burn-holes; some leaves stained. bba May 30 (84) £100 [Unsworth]

### Charles II, King of England, 1630-85
— An Account of the Preservation of King Charles II after the Battle of Worcester...by himself. L, 1803. 8vo, contemp calf gilt. pba June 20 (90) $60

**Charles V, Emperor, 1500-58.** See: Clement VII & Charles V

### Charles VI, King of France, 1368-1422
— Inventaire de la bibliotheque du Roy Charles VI.... Paris, 1867. Ed by L. C. Douet-d'Arcq. 8vo, half mor; rubbed. O Mar 26 (60) $110

### Charleton, T. W.
— The Art of Fishing. North Shields, 1819. 8vo, modern half cloth. b Dec 5 (271) £100

Anr copy. Contemp parchment-backed wraps; old label to bottom of front wrap, small pieces of spine lacking. Some foxing. pba July 11 (48) $100

### Charleton, Walter, 1619-1707
— Onomasticon Zoicon plerorumque animalium.... L, 1668. 4to, later calf; recased, rubbed & dry. With 8 folding plates. Library markings; some foxing. O Mar 5 (41) $550

### Charlevoix, Pierre Francois Xavier de, 1682-1761
— Histoire et description generale du Japon. Paris, 1736. 1st Ed. 2 vols, including Supplement. 4to, 18th-cent calf gilt with later monogram of the Empress Josephine; spine & joints repaired, sides rubbed. Some spotting & staining; lacking privilege leaf at end of Vol II. Fuerstenberg - Schaefer copy. S Dec 7 (113) £1,900
— Letters to the Dutchess of Lesdiguieres.... L, 1763. 8vo, contemp calf gilt; joints & edges worn. With folding map. Some browning. bbc Dec 18 (451) $1,150

Anr copy. Mor gilt. With folding map. sg Oct 26 (38) $425

### Charlot, Jean
— Dance of Death. NY, 1951. In torn & rubbed dj. Inscr & with double-page ink drawing on half-title. bba May 9 (203) £90 [Breitfeld]

### Charnay, Desire
— Cites et Ruines Americaines. Paris, 1863. 8vo, orig wraps; spine cracked. Some foxing. sg Oct 26 (39) $50

### Charriere, Gerard
— Utah Reader. NY, 1986. One of 40. Oblong 4to, mor extra by Mark Beard. CE June 12 (229) $1,600

### Chase, J. Smeaton
— Yosemite Trails. Bost., 1911. 1st Ed, 2d ptg. With 16 plates from photos & double-page map. With ALs. pba Feb 12 (18) $150

**Chase, Owen.** See: Golden Cockerel Press

### Chase, Salmon P., 1808-73
— Speech of Salmon P. Chase, in the Case of the Colored Woman Matilda.... Cincinnati, 1837. 12mo, disbound. Foxed. sg Mar 28 (278) $400

### Chassepol, Francois de
— The History of the Grand Visiers.... L, 1677. 1st Ed in English. 8vo, contemp calf; rebacked. With frontis. b May 30 (254) £220

### Chastellain, Georges
— Histoire du bon chevalier, Messire Iacqves de Lalain.... Brussels: Chez la veuve d'Hubert Anthoine Velpius, 1634. 4to, 17th-cent calf gilt; rubbed, mottling on endpapers, front free endpaper repaired.

With port. Lacking 1 leaf; tp soiled; some browning. Schaefer copy. P Nov 1 (60) $850

**Chastellux, Francois Jean, Marquis de, 1734-88**
— Travels in North America in the Years 1780, 1781, and 1782. L, 1787. 1st Ed in English. 2 vols. 8vo, contemp calf; spine ends & joints worn. Marginal browning. CE May 22 (12) $280

Anr copy. Modern half mor. With 2 maps & 3 plates. sg Oct 26 (40) $425

**Chateau de Mouchy Library**
— Catalogue de la Bibliotheque du Chateau de Mouchy. Paris: Techener, 1872. One of 100. 8vo, contemp calf; rubbed & dried, upper cover detached. Inscr by the Duc de Mouchy to the Baron d'Aldenbourg. O Mar 26 (192) $225

**Chateaubriand, Francois Rene de, 1768-1848**
— Genie du christianisme ou Beautes de la religion chretienne. Paris, [1802]. 5 vols in 4. 8vo, contemp calf gilt; minor defs. Spotting & marginal soiling in outer margins of gatherings R-X in Vol II. Fuerstenberg - Schaefer copy. S Dec 7 (117) £750
— Lettres sur Rome. Paris, 1935. One of 25 on rives with orig gray wash over pencil drawing & an additional suite of 23 of the engravings on thinner paper, this copy with a planche refusee. Illus by Albert Decaris. Folio, mor extra by Paul Bonet to an architectural trompe l'oeil design (Carnets, No 386). Chevalier copy. C May 1 (34) £18,000
— Les martyrs, ou le troimphe de la religion chretienne. Paris, 1809. 1st Ed. 2 vols. 8vo, modern mor. S Oct 27 (1110) £180 [Fonseca]
— Travels in Greece, Palestine, Egypt and Barbary.... L, 1812. 2 vols. 8vo, contemp calf gilt; rubbed, Vol I wupper cover detached. bba May 30 (346) £60 [Trotter]

**Chatelain, Henri Abraham**
— Atlas historique, ou nouvelle introduction a l'histoire.... Amst., 1705. Vol I (of 7) only. Folio, contemp half calf; worn, upper cover detached. bba June 6 (291) £550 [Faupel]

**Chatelain, Jean.** See: Chagall, Marc

**Chater Collection, Sir Catchick P.**
— The Chater Collection, Pictures Relating to China, Hongkong, Macao.... L, 1924. One of 750. 4to, cloth; upper cover dampstained. S Oct 26 (559) £250 [Wattis]

**Chatto, William Andrew, 1799-1864**
See also: Jackson & Chatto
— Scenes and Recollections of Fly Fishing.... L, 1834. 12mo, half mor; rubbed. Some foxing & soiling. O Feb 6 (46) $150
— A Treatise on Wood Engraving. L, [1861]. 8vo, cloth; spine ends worn, front hinge cracked. sg June 13 (115) $60

**Chatwin, Bruce**
— On the Black Hill. L, [1982]. In dj. sg Dec 14 (28) $70

**Chaucer, Geoffrey, 1340?-1400**
See also: Golden Cockerel Press; Kelmscott Press; Limited Editions Club
— Canterbury Tales. [Westminster: William Caxton, c.1484]. 2d Ed. Folio, 18th-cent calf; rebacked. 38 lines & headline; types 2*:135B (headlines) & 4*:100B (text). With 47 woodcuts. Soiled & repaired. 276 (of 314) leaves; lacking 35 text leaves. Goff C-432. Channour - Buxton - Schaefer copy. P Nov 1 (61) $250,000

Anr Ed. Oxford, 1798. Ed by T. Tyrwhitt. 2 vols. 4to, later mor gilt; rubbed, lower joints cracked. S Apr 23 (21) £200

Anr Ed. L: Pickering, 1822. 5 vols. 8vo, lev gilt by Bayntun. sg Sept 21 (9) $850

Anr Ed. L, 1830. 5 vols. 8vo, later mor gilt. rs Nov 11 (76) $400

Anr Ed. L: Riccardi Press for the Medici Society, 1913. One of 500. Illus by W. Russell Flint. 3 vols. 4to, vellum. sg Sept 14 (127) $650

Anr copy. Half cloth; worn & spotted. sg Feb 15 (111) $275

Anr Ed. NY, 1930. One of 924. Illus by Rockwell Kent. 2 vols. Folio, cloth; worn. sg Feb 15 (176) $225

Out-of-series copy. Half mor. F Mar 28 (188) $130

Out-of-series copy, with extra suite of the plates. Mor. Inscr by Kent to Audrey. wd Nov 15 (78) $1,700

Anr Ed. Waddington, 1972. One of 50. Illus by Elizabeth Frink. Folio, cloth. With 19 plates. S May 16 (111) £360
— Poetical Works. L, 1782. 14 vols. 18mo, contemp calf; joints weak, spine extremities worn. sg Feb 8 (69) $200
— The Prologue to the Canterbury Tales.... [Verona: Officina Bodoni, 1988]. One of 15 specially bound in mor. Modernized by Nevill Coghill. 4to, lev. sg Sept 14 (292) $400
— The Romaunt of the Rose. L, 1908. One of 12 on vellum. Orig vellum. Some foxing. bba May 9 (489) £420 [De Beaumont]

One of 500. Orig vellum. bba May 9 (305) £85 [Deighton Bell]; sg Sept 14 (90) $350
— Works. L: J. Kyngston for J. Wight, 1561. Folio, contemp calf; rebacked. Lacking general title; title leaf for Canterbury Tales lacking large piece from lower margin intruding into illust & laid on backing sheet; 1 leaf torn & shaved; more wear to preface leaves than to rest of text; some staining. pba Nov 30 (86) $1,600

Anr Ed. L: Adam Islip, 1598. Folio, later half calf; upper hinge weak. Lacking all before A3, A5; B1-6, C2-4 & all after Uuu5; some margins def; title & imprint supplied in Ms by 19th-cent owner. Sold w.a.f. bba Sept 7 (256) £380 [Rix]

# CHAUCER

Anr Ed. L, 1687. Ed by Thomas Speght. Folio, 19th-cent mor gilt; covers detached. Sold w.a.f. CE Sept 27 (78) $650

Anr Ed. L, 1721. Folio, later calf extra; minor rubbing. Some soiling. cb June 25 (1925) $550

Anr Ed. Cleveland: World Publishing Co., [1958]. Folio, orig cloth, in dj. Facsimile of the Kelmscott Chaucer. pba Aug 22 (572) $75

Anr Ed. L: Basilisk Press, 1974. 2 vols. Folio, orig cloth. Facsimile of the Kelmscott Ed. sg Oct 19 (135) $700

## Chauvin, Etienne

— Lexicon rationale sive thesaurus philosophicus. Rotterdam, 1692. Folio, contemp vellum. With engraved title, port & 30 folding plates. Marginal worming; 1 leaf stained. S Mar 14 (81) £600

## Cheadle, Walter Butler, 1835-1910. See: Fitzwilliam & Cheadle

## Cheek, Elizabeth

— Miscellaneous Poems. Manchester, [1801]. 12mo, orig bds; spine def. b Dec 5 (188) £120

## Cheeseman, Bruce S. —& Lowman, Al

— "The Book of All Christendom": Tom Lea, Carl Hertzog, and the Making of "The King Ranch". Kingsville TX, 1992. One of 50 specially bound. Half mor. pba July 25 (268) $90

## Cheetham, Robert Farren

— Odes and Miscellanies. Stockport, 1796. 8vo, contemp calf; rubbed. Library stamp on tp. b Dec 5 (42) £120

— Poems. Stockport, 1798. 8vo, 19th-cent cloth; soiled. With 64 pages of orig Ms bound in at front & notes by William Ford of Manchester about Cheetham. b Dec 5 (43) £280

## Chekhov, Anton, 1860-1904. See: Limited Editions Club

## Chemitz, Johann Hieronymus

— Kleine Beytraege Testaceotheologie oder zur Erkaentniss Gottes aus den Conchylian. Nuremberg, 1760. 4to, bds. b May 30 (16) £80

— Von einem Geschlechte vielschalichter Conchylien.... Nuremberg, 1784. 4to, bds. With 2 hand-colored plates heightened with varnish. b May 30 (17) £80

## Cheney, A. Nelson. See: Orvis & Cheney

## Chenu, Charles Maurice

— My Canoe. L, 1931. One of 25. pba July 11 (372) $140

## Cherry-Garrard, Apsley, 1886-1959

— The Worst Journey in the World. L, 1922. 2 vols. Orig half cloth; cocked, spines frayed, 1 def. With 6 colored plates, 10 folding plates & 5 maps (4 folding). wa Feb 29 (133) $550

# AMERICAN BOOK PRICES CURRENT

1st Ed. L, 1922-23. 1st Issue. 2 vols. Orig cloth; recased, new endpapers, soiled. Foxing to page edges. pba July 25 (25) $600

## Cheselden, William, 1688-1752

— The Anatomy of the Human Body. L, 1741. 6th Ed. 8vo, contemp calf; joints cracked. With 40 engraved plates. CE Nov 8 (79) $150

Anr Ed. L, 1792. 8vo, contemp calf; rubbed. With engraved title, frontis & 40 plates. Signature on tp abraded with resulting hole; plates browned; tear in Q5. sg May 16 (390) $120

## Chesterfield, Philip Dormer Stanhope, 4th Earl of, 1694-1773

— The Poetical Works. L [ptd at Officina Bodoni, Montagnola], 1927. Ltd Ed. bba May 9 (607) £240 [Collinge & Clark]

## Chesterton, Gilbert Keith, 1874-1936

— The End of the Roman Road. L, 1924. Orig cloth, in amateur dj. ANs on front endpaper. bba May 30 (281) £140 [Mandl]

## Chetham, James, 1640-92

— The Angler's Vade Mecum.... L, 1681. 1st Ed. 8vo, modern calf antique. O Feb 6 (47) $1,900

## Chetwood, William Rufus, d.1766

— The Voyages, Dangerous Adventures and Imminent Escapes of Captain Richard Falconer.... L, 1734. 4th Ed. 12mo, modern cloth. sg Oct 26 (41) $60

5th Ed. L, 1764. 12mo, contemp sheep; front cover loose. sg Oct 26 (42) $120

## Chevalier, Francois —& Taglang, Jacques

— America's Cut Yacht Designs, 1851-1986. [Paris, 1987]. Oblong folio, cloth, in dj. Sgd by both. sg Mar 7 (410) $275

## Chevalier, Nicolas, 1650-1720

— Histoire de Guillaume III Roy d'Angleterre, d'Ecosse, de France... Amst., 1692. Illus by Romeyn de Hooghe. Folio, contemp vellum; needs rebacked, front endpapers wormed. With frontis & 12 full-page plates. Browned. sg Mar 21 (80) $175

## Chevreul, Michel Eugene, 1786-1889

— Recherches chimiques sur les corps gras d'origine animale. Paris, 1823. 1st Ed. 8vo, modern half calf. With half-title, 3 folding tables, & 1 plate. Dampstained; some spotting; pp.348-49 adhering to one another; half-title repaired at margin. Ck Mar 22 (73) £100

— Theorie des effets optiques qui presentent les etoffes de soie. Paris, 1846. 1st Ed. 8vo, contemp half calf. With half-title & folding color plate. Some discoloration. S Oct 27 (800) £220 [Lyon]

## Chiabrera, Gabriello

— Il rapimento di Cefalo rappresentato nelle nozze della... regina di Francia e Navarra Maria Medici. Florence: Giorgio Marescotti, 1600. 4to, contemp vellum. Minor spotting. C Apr 3 (69) £600

**Chiarello, Giovanni Battista**
— Historia degli avenimenti dell' armi imperiali contro a' ribelli et ottomani.... Venice: Steffano Curti, 1687. Carta rustica wraps; worn. With 7 folding maps & plans. Some worming, browning & dampstianing. S Mar 28 (286) £280

**Chiarenza, Carl**
— Aaron Siskind: Pleasures and Terrors. Bost., 1982. Illus by Aaron Siskind. 4to, cloth, in rubbed dj. Sgd by Siskind. sg Feb 29 (288) $150

**Chicago...**
— Chicago American League Base Ball Score Book...1900. Chicago, [1900]. 6 leaves. 8vo, pictorial wraps; worn, adhesion affecting rear wrap. O July 9 (25) $130

CHICAGO TRIBUNE TOWER. - The International Competition for a New Administration Building for the Chicago Tribune.... Chicago, [1923]. Folio, orig cloth. With 282 plates. sg Sept 7 (12) $900

Anr copy. Later cloth. sg Jan 11 (10) $375

**Chicago Tribune Tower.** See: Chicago

**Chidren's...**
— The Children's Cabinet or a Key to Natural History consisting of Beasts, Birds & Insects. L, 1798. Oblong 12mo, orig wraps; soiled, creased. With 25 plates. S Nov 2 (176) £500 [Hirsch]

**Child, Andrew**
— Overland Route to California: Description of the route via Council Bluffs, Iowa.... Los Angeles, 1946. One of 35. Intro by Lyle Wright. Half mor. Sgd by Wright & John B. Goodman. Larson copy. pba Sept 28 (358) $170

**Child's...**
— The Child's Own Book of Animals. L: Darton, [c.1846]. Folio, orig cloth; stained. With 12 colored plates. S Nov 2 (172) £320 [Schiller]

— A Child's Rosary Book. Ditchling: St. Dominic's Press, 1924. Illus by David Jones. Loose in orig wraps; small piece missing from backstrip. S May 16 (58) £240

**Chile**
— Constitucion politica del estado di Chile promulgada en 20 de diciembre de 1923. Santiago de Chile: Imprenta Nacional, [1823]. Folio, wraps. L.p. copy. S June 27 (182) £700

**Chinese...**
— The Chinese Repository. Vaduz: Kraus Reprint, [c.1970]. 20 vols. b May 30 (196) £420

**Chipiez, Charles.** See: Perrot & Chipiez

**Chipman, W. F.**
— General M. G. Vallejo of California: Soldier, Statesman, Patriot. San Francisco, 1931. Wrapps. Larson copy. pba Sept 28 (267) $140

**Chippendale, Thomas, 1718?-79**
— The Gentleman and Cabinet-Maker's Director. L, 1754. 1st Ed. Folio, half calf; rubbed. With 159 plates only. Some discoloration at beginning. b Sept 20 (76) £2,000

2d Ed. L, 1755. Folio, mor gilt by Riviere. Lacking half-title; repaired marginal tear to 1 plate. Harewood - Schaefer copy. P Nov 1 (63) $3,750

**Chiquet, J.**
— Le Nouveau et curieux Atlas geographique et historique.... Paris, [c.1720]. Oblong 4to, contemp vellum; soiled, spine ends worn. With engraved title, 4 plain & 23 colored maps. Dampstaining throughout occasionally affecting images; tears with paper repairs; 2 leaves partially backed; small holes & abrasions. cb Oct 17 (249) $1,300

**Chirico, Giorgio de**
— L'Apocalisse. Milan, 1941. One of 150. 4to, unsewn in orig wraps. With plates in colored & uncolored states. P June 5 (195) $8,000

**Chisolm, John Julian**
— A Manual of Military Surgery for the Use of Surgeons in the Confederate Army.... Richmond, 1862. 12mo, orig cloth; worn. Lacking pp. 507-8 & part of the folding form. NH July 21 (63) $875

Anr Ed. Richmond, 1863. 12mo, disbound. Some staining, soiling & foxing; dog-eared; browned. O Mar 5 (164) $950

**Chittenden, Newton H.**
— Health Seekers', Tourists' and Sportsmen's Guide to the...Health and Pleasure Resorts of the Pacific Coast. San Francisco, 1884. 2d Ed. Orig cloth rear cover stained. pba Apr 25 (338) $150

**Choderlos de Laclos, Pierre A. F.** See: Laclos, Pierre A. F. Choderlos de

**Choiseul, Etienne Francois, Duc de.** See: Basan, Pierre Francois

**Choiseul-Gouffier, Marie Gabriel F. A., Comte de, 1752-1817**
— Voyage pittoresque de la Grece. Paris, 1782-1822. 3 parts in 3 vols. Folio, mor gilt. With engraved titles, port, 2 folding maps & 285 plates on 168 leaves. Some staining in 3d vol. b May 30 (255) £5,500

**Choris, Louis, 1795-1828**
— Voyage pittoresque autour du monde.... Paris: Firmin Didot, 1822. Folio, modern half cloth. With 99 (of 104) hand-colored plates & 2 maps. Some foxing & dampstaining. P June 5 (196) $9,000

1st Ed, 2d Variant. Folio, contemp calf in half mor slipcase; rubbed, stained & worn. With 104 litho plates & 103 hand-colored plates. Marginal dampstaining; foxing & soiling; tissue guard chipped, torn & lacking. Robbins copy, formerly in Library of Imperial Academy of Arts & Sciences. pba Mar 21 (58) $40,000

**Chosen...**
— Chosen Koseki Zufu. [N.p.]: Seiun-do, 1925-35. 15 vols. Folio, orig cloth; soiled. Some stains & wear. wa Dec 14 (539) $3,250

**Choukri, Mohamed**
— Tennessee Williams in Tangier. Santa Barbara: Cadmus Editions, 1979. One of 26. Trans by Paul Bowles. pba Aug 22 (36) $50

**Christ, Yvan**
— Atget: Photographe de Saint German des pres 1900. Paris, 1930. Pictorial wraps; minor wear. sg Feb 29 (19) $60

**Christensen, Lars**
— Such is the Antarctic. L, 1935. Orig cloth, with portion of dj; spine ends bumped. pba July 25 (26) $70

**Christian, Arthur, 1838-1906**
— Debuts de l'imprimerie en France. Paris, 1905. 4to, orig wraps. bba May 9 (29) £55 [O'Keefe]

**Christian, Fletcher**
[-] Letters from Mr. Fletcher Christian, Containing a Narrative of the Transactions on Board His Majesty's Ship Bounty.... L, 1796. 8vo, modern sheep. Leaves at ends chipped. A spurious work. b Mar 20 (78) £3,000
[-] The Voyages and Travels of Fletcher Christian, and a Narrative of the Mutiny.... L, 1798. 8vo, orig bds; rebacked in cloth. With frontis. Owen Rutter's copy. b Mar 20 (79) £3,200

**Christian Woman's Exchange**
— The Creole Cookery Book. New Orleans, 1885. Orig half lea; lower joints cracking, extremities rubbedf. pba Aug 8 (359) $190

**Christie, Agatha, 1891-1976**
— The Murder of Roger Ackroyd. L, [1926]. Orig cloth; extremities rubbed, staining to upper cover. Some staining, mainly marginal. Ck Apr 12 (131) £110
— The Mysterious Affair at Styles. L, [1920]. 1st English Ed. Orig cloth; bumped, some leaves poorly opened, stain on upper cover. bba Oct 19 (306) £700 [Drovanti]
Anr Ed. NY, 1927. In dj with spine ends chipped. b Jan 31 (150) £110
— N or M? NY, 1941. 1st American Ed. In chipped dj; adhesion residue to front pastedown. pba Jan 25 (52) $80
— A Pocket Full of Rye. L, [1953]. Galleys. Stapled into wraps. K Feb 11 (119) $250

**Christie, James, 1730-1803**
— A Disquisition upon Etruscan Vases.... L, 1806. Folio, 19th-cent russia gilt, with Northumberland arms. With engraved title & 17 plates. Inscr to Richard Gough. Dawson Turner's annotated copy with ALs from Christie to Turner. Blackmer copy. S June 27 (101) £1,700

**Christina, Queen of Sweden's copy**
MENESTRIER, CLAUDE FRANCOIS. - La Devise du Roy justifiee.... Paris, 1679. 4to, contemp vellum. With c.150 annotations on 54 pp in French in the hand of Queen Christina & with Ls by her in Italian inserted. C Apr 3 (70) £4,800

**Christmas...**
— Christmas at Little America. Mount Vernon NY: Pvtly ptd, 1930. One of 250. Orig bds; rubbed & discolored. Inscr by Willard Vander Veer, cinematographer of the Byrd Antarctic Expedition, to Lawrence Smith, 1938. pba July 25 (27) $55

**Christomanos, Constantin**
— Das Achilles-Schloss auf Corfu. Vienna, 1896. 4to, pictorial bds. S Oct 26 (39) £230 [Theotoky]

**Christy, Howard Chandler**
— Men of the Army and Navy. NY, 1899. Folio, orig bds; worn. With 6 plates. Some wear. F Mar 28 (763) $110

**Christy, Thomas**
— Thomas Christy's Road Across the Plains. Denver, 1969. 1st Ed. - Ed by Robert Becker. Orig cloth in dj. With frontis port, 3 route maps, & 94 detail maps. Larson copy. pba Sept 28 (360) $55; pba Apr 25 (339) $65

**Chromolithograph...**
— The Chromolithograph: a Journal of Art, Decoration, and the Accomplishments. L, 1868 [1867-69]. Ed by William Day. Vols I & II (all pbd). 4to, contemp half calf (Vol I) & orig cloth; Vol I bdg broken. Vol I lacking tp & all to B1 & 1 plate. Sold w.a.f. bba May 30 (331) £65 [Besley]

**Chronicles**
— Chronicles of England [St. Alban's Chronicle]. L: Wynken de Worde, 1520. Part 2 only: The Descrypcyon of Englande. 4to, 18th-cent calf. 18 leaves only; 4 leaves at end supplied in ink black letter; title margin & corner of B1 restored; 2 wormholes affecting letters. S July 11 (104) £420
— Die Cronica van der hilliger Stat van Coellen. [Cologne]: Johann Koelhoff the Younger, 23 Aug 1499. Folio, 17th-cent vellum. 49 lines & headline; types 4:96G (text), 5:140G, 2:290G (headings); with 92 woodcuts; title cut hand-colored. Lacking 2d titleleaf; tp with extended margins & repaired marginal tear; other leaves of Register with extended margins; some soiling; quires ii-mm supplied from a shorter copy. 365 (of 368) leaves; lacking A1 & 2 blanks. Goff C-476. P June 5 (201) $7,000
— Cronike van Brabant. Antwerp: Roland van den Dorp, 28 Feb 1497. Folio, 19th-cent bds; rubbed. 40 lines; double column; type 1:98G. With xylographic title & 96 woodcuts (including repeats). Quire RR bound before cc; erased library stamp on a1v; 1st & final leaf soiled; some worming to inner margin of quire C & D. 216 leaves. Goff C-475. Liechtenstein - Schaefer copy. P Nov 1 (71) $70,000

— Rudimentum novitiorum. Paris, 1488-89. ("La mer des histoires.") 2 vols. Folio, 19th-cent calf blind-stamped to a 15th-cent style & incorporating Arenberg supralibros, by Claessens. 50 lines & headline; double column; types 2:117B (text), 3:236G (titles & headlines). With 383 woodcuts, 2 full-page woodcuts, 2 maps, 65 genealogical stemmae, all colored by an early hand. Some repaired tears without loss; a few leaves remargined, with slight loss to lower border of a2. 299 (of 310) leaves only. Goff R-346. C June 26 (173) £40,000

## Chrysanthos, of Madytos

— Great Theory of Music. Trieste, 1832. 1st Ed. 8vo, contemp half calf. With half title & table. Some foxing; hole in title without loss. S Oct 26 (29) £1,200 [Antiquaria]

## Church, A. H.

— Josiah Wedgwood, Master Potter. L, 1903. 4to, cloth; spine ends worn. Pencil notes on recto of frontis. sg Sept 7 (74) $50

## Church Library, Elihu Dwight

— A Catalogue of Books Relating to the Discovery and Early History of North and South America.... NY, 1907. Out-of-series copy. Compiled by George W. Cole. 5 vols. 4to, later half mor. Ck Apr 12 (217) £850

Anr Ed. NY, 1951. Compiled by George Watson Cole. 5 vols. 4to, cloth. ds July 27 (57) $300

Anr Ed. Mansfield CT: Martino, [n.d.]. One of 100. 5 vols. 4to, cloth; some wear. O May 7 (87) $125

## Church, George Earl

— Mexico. Its Revolutions.... NY, 1866. 8vo, orig wraps; soiled & worn, corners chipped. pba Aug 8 (32) $50

## Church, Henry

— Les Clowns. Paris: Editions des Deux Amis, 1922. One of 240. Illus by Georges Rouault. Wraps, in dj. With cover & 3 hand-colored pochoir illusts. sg Sept 14 (320) $850

## Church, John

— A Cabinet of Quadrupeds. L, 1805. Illus by J. Tookey after J. Ibbetson. 2 vols. 4to, contemp russia; joinst cracked. With 84 plates. Some spotting & offsetting. S Oct 27 (710) £320 [Alden]

## Church, Percy W.

— Chines Turkestan with Caravan and Rifle. L, 1901. Orig cloth; spine tips frayed, front cover discolored, white markings on spine. Library markings. O June 4 (70) $180

## Church, Thomas

— The History of King Philip's War.... Exeter, 1834. 12mo, contemp sheep. Piece excised from upper margin of tp. sg Oct 26 (43) $175

## Churchill, Charles, 1731-64

— The Duelist: A Poem in Three Books. L, 1764. Bds; spine ends worn, later endpapers. Half-title spotted. pba Nov 30 (89) $100

— Poems. L, 1766. 3d Ed. 2 vols. 8vo, contemp calf. pba Mar 7 (57) $130

**Churchill, Randolph Spencer, 1911-68.** See: Onassis copy, Jacqueline Bouvier Kennedy

## Churchill, Randolph Spencer, 1911-68 —& Gilbert, Martin

— Winston S. Churchill. L, 1975-90. 20 vols, including Companion vols. Orig cloth, in djs. b Dec 5 (197) £220

## Churchill, Sir Winston, 1620-88

— Divi Britannici: Being a Remark upon the Lives of all the Kings of this Isle. L, 1675. 1st Ed. Folio, contemp calf. Early marginalia. CE June 12 (171) $160

Anr copy. Old calf; worn, broken. Tp soiled & stained; lacking initial blank or license leaf. sg Mar 21 (81) $375

## Churchill, Sir Winston L. S., 1874-1965

— The Collected Works. L, 1973-76. 34 vols. With: The Collected Essays. L, 1976. 4 vols. Together, 38 vols. Orig vellum gilt. b Dec 5 (191) £1,000

— First Journey. L, 1964. Ltd Ed. Calf. rs Nov 11 (77) $700

— Great Contemporaries. L, 1937. 1st Ed. Orig cloth, in frayed dj. b Dec 5 (203) £200

— The Great War. L, [1933]. 1st Ed in Book form. 3 vols. 4to, orig cloth. sg June 20 (52) $225

— A History of the English-Speaking Peoples. L, 1956-58. 1st Ed. 4 vols. Mor gilt by Zaehnsdorf. CE Sept 27 (81) $600

Anr copy. Half mor gilt by Asprey. Ck Nov 17 (26) £650

Anr copy. In repaired djs. sg June 20 (53) $140

— Ian Hamilton's March. L, 1900. 1st Ed. 8vo, orig cloth; rubbed, library bookplate. b Dec 5 (205) £150

Anr copy. Half mor gilt by Aspreys. Ck Nov 17 (9) £240

Anr copy. Half mor gilt by Hatchards. Ck Nov 17 (11) £280

— India. Speeches and an Introduction. L, 1931. 1st Ed. Orig wraps. b Dec 5 (206) £100

— Into Battle. L, 1941. Orig cloth. Inscr in the month of publication. S July 11 (397) £900

— Liberalism and the Social Problem. L, 1909. 1st Ed. Orig cloth. Minor spotting. b Dec 5 (208) £280

Anr copy. Orig cloth; inner hinges weak, extremities rubbed & bumped. Ck Nov 17 (14) £320

— London to Ladysmith via Pretoria. L, 1900. 1st Ed. 8vo, orig cloth; minor soiling. b Dec 5 (210) £240

Anr copy. Half mor gilt by Sangorski & Sutcliffe. Ck Nov 17 (10) £280

— Lord Randolph Churchill. L, 1906. 1st Ed. 2 vols. b Dec 5 (211) £60

Anr copy. Orig cloth; rubbed. b Jan 31 (72) £60

Anr copy. Dampstaining affecting top edge of Vol II; some spotting. Ck Nov 17 (12) £110
Review copy with blind-stamped "Presentation Copy" on titles. sg June 20 (54) $250
— Marlborough, his Life and Times. L, 1933-38. 1st Ed. 4 vols. b Dec 5 (213) £100
Anr copy. Orig cloth. Ck Nov 17 (20) £180
One of 155. Orig cloth. Inscr to his private sectetary Eddie Marsh. S July 11 (402) £13,000
2d Ed of Vol I, 1st Ed of Vols II-IV. 4 vols. bba Oct 19 (310) £70 [Weber]
1st American Ed. NY, 1933-38. 6 vols. Orig cloth; minor defs. wa Dec 14 (33) $120
— My African Journey. L, 1908. 1st Ed. Minor spotting. b Dec 5 (215) £150
Anr copy. Orig cloth; small stains on upper cover. bba Oct 19 (309) £120 [de Freitas]
Anr copy. Some spotting throughout. Ck Nov 17 (13) £180; S July 11 (392) £620
— My Early Life. L, 1948. Inscr to John Gibson, 1948. pn Mar 14 (366) £340
— My Early Life. A Roving Commission. L, 1930. 1st Ed. In dj with small tears. Minor spotting. b Dec 5 (216) £520; Ck Nov 17 (16) £60
Anr Ed. L, 1948. Orig cloth; worn & stained. Inscr. S Dec 18 (488) £700 [Spencer]
Anr Ed. L, 1958. Orig cloth; stained & with upper cover partially detached. Sgd on half-title & with Christmas card from Clementine Churchill loosely inserted. S Mar 28 (621) £180
— The People's Rights. L, 1910. 1st Ed. Orig wraps; backstrip chipped. b Dec 5 (230) £1,300
— The River War. L, 1899. 1st Ed. 2 vols. 8vo, orig cloth. Copy of Lt. Col. James Grove White. b Dec 5 (231) £2,400
Anr copy. Mor gilt by Sangorski & Sutcliffe. Ck Nov 17 (8) £1,250
Anr copy. Calf by Bickers; some rubbing & soiling. Foxing. pba Nov 30 (90) $800
— Savrola. L, 1900. 1st English Ed. 8vo, orig cloth; spine rubbed. Minor spotting. b Dec 5 (224) £320
Anr copy. Orig cloth; rubbed. Inscr, 16 Feb 1928. S Dec 18 (483) £1,700 [Levine]
— The Second World War. L, 1948-54. 1st English Ed. 6 vols. In chipped djs. CE Feb 21 (38) $300
Anr copy. In chipped djs. Inscr to Lord Dufferin & Ava, 1955. Ck Nov 17 (23) £650
Anr copy. Half mor gilt by Sangorski & Sutcliffe. With: The Second World War and an Epilogue on the Years 1945 to 1957. L, 1959.. Ck Nov 17 (24) £850
Anr copy. Orig cloth, in djs with tears. Inscr in each vol. S July 11 (399) £3,000
Anr copy. In djs with edge-wear. sg June 20 (56) $130
One of 100 specially bound in mor. b Jan 31 (74) £400
— The Story of the Malakand Field Force. L, 1898. 1st Ed. 8vo, orig cloth. Minor spotting. b Dec 5 (233) £1,100

Anr copy. Some spotting at beginning. Ck Nov 17 (7) £1,500
Anr copy. Orig cloth; soiled. Foxed. S July 11 (398) £1,000
— Thoughts and Adventures. L, 1932. 1st Ed. Minor spotting. b Dec 5 (236) £50
Anr copy. Inscr to the 4th Marquis of Salisbury, Nov 1932. Ck Nov 17 (18) £1,200
— The World Crisis. L, 1923-31. 1st Ed. 5 vols in 6. b Dec 5 (235) £440; Ck Nov 17 (15) £480; S July 11 (394) £2,400

**Churchman's...**
— The Churchman's Monthly Magazine. New Haven; Oliver Steele & Co., 1806. Vol III, No 4. 8vo, ptd wraps; spine def. Sgd on front cover by Richard Allen. sg Mar 28 (267) $800

**Churilin, Tikhon**
— Vesna Posl Smerti. Moscow, 1915. One of 240. 4to, orig wraps; soiled, tears in spine. C June 26 (216) £650

**Ciaccone, Alfonso**
— Columnae Trajani ortographia... utriusque belli Dacici historiam consistens. Rome, 1773. Oblong folio, modern half vellum. With 137 plates on 134 leaves. Some plates foxed. sg Apr 18 (36) $650
— Historia utriusque belli Dacici a Traiano Caesare gesti.... Rome, 1616. Oblong folio, old calf; worn & broken. With 130 double-page plates. Last plate stained, frayed & repaired. O Mar 5 (45) $1,700
— Vitae, et res gestae pontificum Romanorum et S.R.E. Cardinalium. Rome, 1677. 4 vols. Folio, old vellum; splayed, spines def. With 9 plates. Browned. wd May 8 (43) $325

**Ciardi, John**
— A Genesis. NY: Touchstone, 1967. One of 50. Illus by Gabor Peterdi. Folio, loose as issued in cloth portfolio; front cover rubbed & soiled. sg May 23 (416) $900

**Ciceri, Eugene**
— Les Pyrenees. L, [1871]. 2 vols. Folio, orig cloth; discound, worn. With 3 maps & plans (2 folding), & 56 plates. Some duplicate plates; 1 plate torn & soiled. S Oct 26 (270) £400

**Cicero, Marcus Tullius, 106-43 B.C.**
See also: Franklin Printing, Benjamin; Limited Editions Club
— De amicitia, sive Laelius de amicitia. L, 1904. ("De Amicitia or Book of Friendship.") One of 150. sg Sept 14 (119) $225
— De officiis. L, 1680. ("Tully's Offices.") Trans by Roger l'Estrange. 8vo, contemp calf. pba Nov 30 (92) $300
— De philosophia. Lyon: Symphorien Barbier for Antoine Vincent, 1562. Vol I (of 2). 16mo, contemp calf gilt with plaquette stamp of Emperor Philip II, initials LS & date 75; some wear. Lower corner dampstained; browned. Schaefer copy. P Nov 1 (64) $1,100

— Epistolae ad Brutum, ad Quintum fratrem, ad Atticum. Venice: Aldus, 1548. ("Epistolae ad Atticum....") 8vo, 18th-cent vellum. Ownership mark removed from tp; some spotting; minor dampstaining.  P June 5 (197) $400

Anr Ed. Venice: Aldus, 1553. 8vo, modern mor. Some ink annotations; spotting & staining. H. W. Poor copy.  b Sept 20 (32) £140

— Epistolarum familiarum. Lyon: Jean Frellon II, 1560. ("Epistolae familiares.") 16mo, 16th-cent calf with gilt & painted strapwork design; hinges & edges restored.  S June 12 (28) £750

— Epitres choisies de Ciceron, latines et francoises. Rouen: chez R. Lallemant, 1773. 12mo, contemp red mor gilt with arms of Marie Christine de Lorraine, Archduchess of Austria. Fuerstenberg - Schaefer copy.  S Dec 7 (123) £420

— Opera. Lyon: Sebastian Gryphius, 1540. 9 vols. 18th-cent vellum; extremities worn. Some soiling; ink notations on tp.  cb Oct 17 (322) $425

— Orationes. Lyons: Jean de Tournes & Guillaume Gazeau, 1554. ("In omnes M. Tullii Ciceronis orationes...doctissimorum virorum enarrationes.") Folio, contemp bilnd-stamped pigskin, 1572; rubbed & bumped, lacking clasps & catches. Annotations in an early hand; Ee1 of Vol II torn; corner of Pp4 torn away; library stamp on tp verso.  S June 12 (29) £500

— Der Teutsch Cicero. Augsburg: Heinrich Steyner, 1535. Folio, modern half lea. 44 lines; gothic letter. First quire laid down; Cc3 sgd Dd3 & misfoliated; soiled.  C Apr 3 (71) £900

— Those Fyve Questions which M. T. Cicero Disputed in his Manor of Tusculanum.... L: T. Marshe, 1561. 8vo, mor gilt by Riviere. Trimmed; some browning. CE May 22 (87) $1,500

— Tusculanae disputationes. Venice: Nicolaus Jenson, 1472. 4to, 18th-cent calf; spine ends rubbed. 33 lines, type 1:115R. Stain on fo.5/8.  85 (of 88) leaves; lacking 2 blanks. Goff C-631.  C Nov 29 (42) £7,000

**Cicogna, Emmanuele Antonio, 1789-1868**
— Saggio di bibliografia Veneziana. NY, [1967]. 3 vols, includes supplement. 8vo, orig cloth. sg Apr 11 (82) $225

**Cicognara, Leopoldo, 1767-1834**
— Catalogo ragionato dei libri d'arte e d'antichita. Pisa, 1821. 2 vols. 8vo, orig bds; rubbed. Some foxing. bba May 9 (56) £280 [Quaritch]

**Cid, Ruy Diaz de Vivar**
[-] Chronica del Famoso Cavallero Cid Ruy Diez Campeador. Burgos: Philippe de Junta & Juan Baptista Varesio, 1593. Folio, old vellum; spine wormed. Browned & dampstained; tp torn & repaired with loss; lacking last leaf.  sg Mar 21 (295) $2,200

**Cieca di Lione, Pietro de.** See: Cieza de Leon, Pedro de

**Cieza de Leon, Pedro de, 1518-60**
— Parte primera de la chronica del Peru. Seville, 1553. 1st Ed. Part 1 (all pbd). Folio, 19th-cent calf. Library stamp washed from tp & last leaf; some dampstains; 4 lines of text pasted to foot of *2r; name of Juan de Samano pasted in at end of privilege.  S June 27 (190) £18,000

**Cigongne Library, Bernard Armand**
— Catalogue des Livres, Manuscrits et Imprimes.... Paris, 1861. 8vo, contemp half cloth. Some soiling & foxing.  O Mar 26 (61) $100

**Cinderella...**
— Cinderella and the Sleeping Beauty. Chicago: Reilly & Britton, 1905. Intro by L. Frank Baum. 4 by 3 inches, cloth-backed pictorial bds; rear cover creased. Christmas Stocking Series. pba Jan 18 (144) $225

— Cinderella, or the Little Glass Slipper. Albany: Horsford, 1810. 12mo, stiff wraps; worn. Some stains & soiling; 2 leaves torn.  O July 9 (7) $160

Anr Ed. L, 1814. Sq 16mo, orig wraps. With separate folding coach, 6 cut-out figures & 2 hand-colored heads. Lacking hats.  S Nov 2 (279) £360 [Hirsch]

**Cino da Pistoia.** See: Sinibuldi, Guittone

**Cioranescu, Alexandre**
— Bibliographie de la litterature francaise.... Paris, 1969. 3 vols. 4to, imitation lea.  sg Apr 11 (83) $200

**Ciotti, Vittorio Fani**
— Archi Voltaici. Parole in liberta e sintesi teatrali. Milan, 1916. 8vo, orig wraps; tears in backstrip. Inscr by Bruno Corra.  sg Apr 18 (137) $550

**Cipelli, Giovanni Battista.** See: Egnatius, Johannes Baptista

**Cipriani, Giovanni Battista, 1727-85.** See: Navone & Cipriani

**Cirici Pellicer, A.**
— El Arte Modernista Catalan. Barcelona, 1951. Folio, cloth, in chipped dj. sg Sept 7 (71) $175

**Cirillo, Domenico Maria Leone, 1739-99**
— Traite complet et observations pratiques sur les maladies veneriennes.... Paris, 1803. 19th-cent bds. pba Mar 7 (179) $150

**Civil War, American**
— A Digest of the Military and Naval Laws of the Confederate Sates. Columbia, 1864. 8vo, contemp half cloth; broken. Brittle.  O Nov 14 (108) $200

**Cladera, Christobal, 1760-1816**
— Investigaciones historicas sobre los principales descubrimientos de los espanoles en el mar oceano en el siglo XV.... Madrid, 1794. 1st Ed. 8vo, contemp calf; spine ends worn. With folding map & 5 ports. CE May 22 (89) $280

**Clampitt, Amy**
— A Homage to John Keats. [N.p.]: Sarabande Press, 1984. One of 250. Folio, stiff paper wraps in dj. Z June 28 (55) $90

**Clan Chisholm...**
— The Clan Chisholm and Allied Clans. NY: Pvtly ptd, 1935. Compiled by Harriette F. Thrasher for H. J. Chisholm. 3 vols. 4to, cloth; worn. O Dec 5 (27) $90

**Clancy, Tom**
— The Hunt for Red October. Annapolis: Naval Institute Press, [1984]. In dj with tears to spine head. pba Dec 7 (30) $225

Anr copy. In chipped dj. pba Aug 22 (88) $225

**Clapcott, C. B.**
— The Clapcott Papers. Edin., 1985. 1st Ed, One of 400. Ed by Alastair J. Johnston. Cloth. pba Apr 18 (20) $225
— The Rules of Golf of the Ten Oldest Golf Clubs from 1754 to 1848.... Edin., [1935]. 1st Ed, One of 500. Orig half buckram in glassine; glassine chipped. pba Apr 18 (19) $550

**Clappe, Louise A. K. S., 1819-1906**
See also: Grabhorn Printing
— The Shirley Letters from California Mines.... San Francisco, 1922. One of 450. Half cloth, in rubbed dj. With 8 colored plates. Tear to 1 plate. pba Aug 8 (184) $200

1st Book Ed. With: The Pioneer Magazine, May 1855 One of 200 on buff California Bond paper. Ed by Thomas C. Russell. Orig cloth; covers spotted, magazine wrapper missing. With 8 hand-colored illus. Sgd by Russell. Larson copy. pba Sept 28 (362) $350

One of 200 on Exeter Book Paper. Half bds; front hinge cracked. With 8 hand-colored illus. Inscr & sgd by Russell. Larson copy. pba Sept 28 (363) $325

1st Ed in book form, One of 200 on Buff California Bond paper. Orig cloth; cloth soiled. With 8 hand-colored plates. Robbins copy. pba Mar 21 (60) $300

**Clare, John, 1793-1864**
— The Village Minstrel. L, 1821. 1st Ed. 2 vols. 12mo, orig bds, uncut. S Dec 18 (123) £420 [Blackwell]

**Clarendon, Edward Hyde, 1st Earl of, 1609-74**
— The History of the Rebellion and Civil Wars in England.... Oxford, 1702-4. 1st Ed. 3 vols. Folio, contemp calf; rebacked, Vol I front cover detached, Vol II joints starting. Tp dampstained in outer margin & with tear in gutter. sg Mar 21 (82) $300

Anr Ed. Oxford, 1707. 3 vols in 6. Folio, contemp calf; rebacked. b Jan 31 (75) £120

Anr Ed. L, 1717. 3 vols in 6. Contemp calf; spine heads chipped. sg Feb 8 (71) $150

Anr Ed. Oxford, 1732. 3 vols in 6. 8vo, contemp calf; joints & extremities worn. pba Sept 14 (104) $225

Anr Ed. Oxford, 1816. 3 vols in 6. Folio, half calf; rubbed. Some foxing & staining. O Mar 5 (46) $325

Anr Ed. Oxford: Clarendon Press, [1969]. 6 vols. 8vo, cloth, in frayed djs. Top edges foxed. wa Feb 1 (153) $130
— The Life of Edward Earl of Clarendon... Written by himself. Oxford, 1759. 1st Ed. Folio, modern half calf. With frontis port & title vignette. Hole in port; wax stains on 5 leaves; some spotting & offsetting. Ck Mar 22 (76) £100

**Clark, Carol —& Others**
— Maurice Brazil Prendergast. Charles Prendergast. A Catalogue Raisonne. Williamstown & Munich, 1990. Folio, cloth, in dj. sg Jan 11 (365) $120; sg Jan 11 (366) $100

**Clark Library, Clarence H.**
THOMSON, JOHN. - A Descriptive Catalogue of the Books forming the Library. Phila., 1888. One of 75. 2 vols. 8vo, half mor; rubbed. Owner's stamps; some soiling & staining. Inscr by Clark to Clark Zantzinger. O Mar 26 (62) $180

**Clark Collection, F. Ambrose**
— The F. Ambrose Clark Collection of Sporting Paintings. NY: Pvtly ptd, 1958. One of 250. 4to, lea; rubbed, plate before title detached & frayed. O Jan 9 (68) $190

**Clark, Francis D.**
— The First Regiment of New York Volunteers.... NY: George S. Evans, 1882. With: A.L.S. to Captain Naglee, [July 29, 1850] 1st Ed. Orig cloth; cover extremities worn. With 2 ports. Larson copy. pba Sept 28 (677) $450

**Clark, Galen, 1814-1910**
— Big Trees of California. Yosemite Valley, 1910. 2d Ed. 8vo, orig wraps; front free endpaper removed. pba Feb 12 (21) $70; pba Apr 25 (344) $50
— Indians of Yosemite Valley. Yosemite Valley, 1904. Orig cloth. Sgd & with ALs to T. G. Pool. pba Feb 12 (20) $1,800

**Clark, John Heaviside, 1770-1863**
— A Practical Illustration of Gilpin's Day.... L, 1811. 1st Ed, 1st Issue. Folio, orig bds; chipped. With 30 hand-colored plates. Duplicate of plate 4 inserted. S Oct 27 (845) £1,000 [Harley-Mason]

**Clark, Larry**
— Teenage Lust. NY, [1983]. 4to, orig wraps; lower corner bumped, abrasions on rear cover. With related material, including 8 mtd silver prints of photographs from the work & other material in 2 folio-size cloth clamshell boxes. sg Feb 29 (95) $2,600

Anr Ed. NY, [1987]. 4to, pictorial wraps. Sgd. sg Feb 29 (96) $400
— Tulsa. NY: Lustrum Press, 1971. Orig bds, in dj. Sgd with star on half-title. pba June 20 (94) $600
One of 400, with orig silver print. In dj. sg Feb 29 (97) $950

## Clark, Robert, 1825-94
— Golf; a Royal and Ancient Game. L, 1875. 8vo, cloth. pnE Sept 20 (51) £610

1st Ed. 8vo, cloth; spine ends & corners worn. With T.L.s. from Edward Clark, 1922, tipped in. pba Nov 9 (6) $4,500

Anr copy. Cloth; spine rubbed; rear joint torn, front hinge starting. pba Apr 18 (22) $2,750

2d Ed. L, 1893. 8vo, cloth; spine ends & corners, front cover discolored. With tp etching. Endpapers dampstained in gutter. pba Nov 9 (7) $275

3d Ed. Cloth; spine ends rubbed. Plates foxed. pba Apr 18 (23) $275

## Clark, Robert A. —& Brunet, Patrick J.
— The Arthur H. Clark Company: A Bibliography and History.... Spokane: Arthur H. Clark, 1993. One of 500. pba Feb 13 (38) $140

## Clark, Roland
See also: Derrydale Press
— Pot Luck. West Hartford, [1945]. One of 460. O June 25 (37) $170

## Clark, Samuel, 1810-85
— Reuben Ramble's Travels through the Counties of England. L: Darton & Clark, [c.1845]. 5 parts in 1 vol. 8vo, orig cloth upper cover; lower cover from anr book, spine is binder's tape. With color frontis, pictorial title & 40 maps with colored inset views. O Sept 12 (46) $1,000

## Clark, Thomas Blake
— Omae, First Polynesian Ambassador to England. San Francisco: Colt Press, 1940. One of 500. Half cloth & bark. With frontis. pba Nov 16 (350) $120

## Clark, William, 1770-1838. See: Lewis & Clark; Limited Editions Club

## Clarke, A. Ross. See: James & Clarke

## Clarke, Arthur C.
— 2001: A Space Odyssey. NY: New American Library, [1968]. In dj tears to extremities. pba Dec 7 (32) $110

Anr copy. In dj with offset from former protector & bumps to spine ends. pba May 23 (75) $110

— Against the Fall of Night. NY: Gnome Press, [1953]. In dj with spine ends rubbed & small tear at front. pba May 4 (119) $90

Anr Ed. L, [1956]. ("The City and the Stars.") In chipped & creased dj with piece lacking from spine head. pba May 23 (73) $110

— Interplanetary Flight: An Introduction to Astronautics. L: Temple Press, [1950]. In dj. pba Dec 7 (33) $110

— The Sands of Mars. NY, [1952]. In dj with chip & tear. pba Dec 7 (34) $140

Anr copy. In rubbed dj. pba May 23 (74) $70

## Clarke, Asa B.
— Travels in Mexico and California.... Bost., 1852. 1st Ed. 12mo, orig wraps in modern folding case; soiled & chipped at edges. Larson copy. pba Sept 28 (366) $800

Anr copy. Orig wraps; lower front wrap scuffed & curled. Robbins copy. pba Mar 21 (61) $3,250

Anr copy. Modern cloth, orig wraps bound in. Inscr "by Clarke's daughter(?)" on inserted leaf before title. sg Oct 26 (73) $275

## Clarke, Edward Daniel, 1769-1822
— Greek Marbles Brought from the Shores of the Euxine.... Cambr., 1806. Bound with: Hamilton, William Richard. Memorandum on the Subject of the Earl of Elgin's Pursuits in Greece. 1st & 2d Ed. 2 works in 1 vol. 8vo, 19th-Cent calf. With frontis, 3 plates, & 2 illus by H. Moses. Inscr to R. Crawley. S Oct 26 (32) £260 [Dellarokas]

— Travels in Various Countries of Europe, Asia and Africa. L, 1810-23. 1st Ed. Vols I-IV (of 6). 4to, contemp half calf; rubbed. b May 30 (256) £420

## Clarke, H. Savile
— Alice in Wonderland, a Dream Play for Children. L, 1886. 8vo, orig wraps; front cover detached. Some foxing. sg Feb 8 (223) $950

## Clarke, Hermann Frederick
— John Hull. Portland, 1940. One of 500. 4to, cloth, unopened; some wear. O Dec 5 (28) $225

## Clarke, J.
— A Series of Twenty-Four Views Illustrative of the Holy Scriptures.... L, [c.1817?]. Illus by Luigi Mayer & others. Folio, bds; rebacked. With 24 hand-colored plates. S Oct 26 (170) £320 [Hollin]

Anr Ed. L, 1833. 4to, contemp half cloth. With 24 plates. Some tears. b May 30 (286) £220

## Clarke, James, Surveyor
— A Survey of the Lakes of Cumberland, Westmorland, and Lancashire.... L, 1787. Folio, cloth. With 2 plates & 11 folding maps. Some tears & repairs; last leaf def & repaired without loss; soiled & foxed. bba Nov 1 (42) £320 [Burden]

2d Ed. L, 1789. Folio, contemp russia gilt; joints weak, edges rubbed. With 2 plates & 11 folding maps. Some discoloration & creasing. S Mar 28 (41) £750

Anr copy. Orig bds; worn, 1 hinge broken. Tp & 1 plate repaired; a few folds repaired or strengthened. S Mar 28 (42) £480

## Clarke, Joseph Thacher —& Others
— Investigations at Assos: Drawings and Photographs of the Buildings and Objects Discovered.... L, etc., 1902-[21]. One of 525. Folio, loose in ptd board folder; worn. sg June 13 (118) $175

## Clarke, Kit
— Where the Trout Hide. NY & L, 1889. 16mo, contemp half mor; rubbed. Dampstained in lower margin throughout; lacking ads. O Feb 6 (48) $100

# CLARKE

**Clarke, Samuel, 1675-1729.** See: Leibnitz & Clarke

**Clarke, William Barnard**
— Narrative of the Wreck of the "Favorite" on the Island of Desolations...Privations of John Nunn.... L, 1850. 8vo, orig cloth; rubbed, 1 gathering loose. With folding map Some soiling. bba Nov 16 (283) £250 [Fabicant]

**Clarkson, Thomas, 1760-1846**
— The History of the Rise, Progress and Accomplishment of the Abolition of the African Slave Trade. L, 1839. 8vo, cloth; worn. With port & 2 folding charts. sg Mar 28 (279) $110
— Thoughts on the Necessity of Improving the Condition of the Slaves in the British Colonies.... NY, 1823. 8vo, disbound. sg Mar 28 (280) $110

**Claude Lorrain (Claude Gelee), 1600-82**
— Liber Veritatis, or a Collection of Prints.... L, 1777-1819. 3 vols. Folio, 19th-cent mor gilt with vellum doublures with Buckingham & Chandos stamp & endleaves, in the style of Charles Lewis; spine edges & corners worn, upper joint of Vol I broken. With 2 ports & 300 plates. With: vol of 172 outline proofs from the work, with tp & 8 text leaves from Boydell Ed of Vol I, port of Earlom by Lupton & ports of John Boydell & Claude (proof before letters), bound to match & lettered Etchings on spine. CNY May 17 (57) $6,500

Anr copy. 18th-cent calf gilt; rebacked in mor in 19th-cent. With ports of Earlom & Boydell & 300 plates. Lacking port of Lorrain; some foxing, spotting & discoloration; 1 plate with small hole in image. Schaefer copy. P Nov 1 (146) $7,000

**Claudel, Paul, 1868-1955**
— L'Annonce faite a Marie. Paris: Auguste Blaizot & fils, [1940]. One of 200. Illus by Maurice Denis. 4to, mor extra with star design by G. Grette; bookplate removed from free endpaper. S Nov 21 (78) £2,800
— Tete d'Or. Paris, [1950]. One of 5 sgd by Claudel & with extra suite of illusts. Illus by Roger de la Fresnaye. 2 vols. 4to, loose as issued in vellum bd wraps; soiled. With 12 wood engravings. CE Sept 27 (83) $550

**Claudin, Anatole, 1833-1906**
— Histoire de l'imprimerie en France au XVe et au XVIe siecle. Paris, 1900-4. Vols I-III (of 4). 4to, half mor gilt; rubbed. b Dec 5 (11) £260

**Claus, Hugo**
— Karel Appel, Painter. NY, 1962. One of 250. 4to, pictorial bds, in dj. wad Oct 18 (162) C$475

**Clavell, Robert, d.1711**
— His Majesties Propriety, and Dominion of the Brittish Seas Asserted. L, 1665. 1st Ed. 4to, contemp sheep; rebacked, worn, covers detached. Lacking map. sg Mar 7 (206) $100

**Clavigero, Francisco Saverio, 1731-87**
— The History of Mexico. Collected from the Spanish and Mexican Historians.... L, 1807. 2d Ed. 2 vols. 4to, contemp calf; joints cracked. With folding map & 24 plates. Some pencil annotations. S Oct 26 (503) £200 [Butcher]

**Clay, Enid.** See: Golden Cockerel Press

**Clayton, William**
— The Latter-Day Saints' Emigrants' Guide.... Salt Lake City, n.d. [1921]. Orig cloth. Larson copy. pba Sept 28 (367) $120

**Clayton, Sir William**
— A Treatise on Greyhounds.... L, 1819. 12mo, orig bds; backstrip renewed. Ms veterinary recipies in Ms in lower margins of pp. 118-19. b Sept 20 (498) £100

**Cleaver, Eldridge**
— Soul on Ice. NY, [1968]. Cloth, in dj; bdg worn. Inscr to Dr. Shapiro, 16 Mar 1968. sg Mar 28 (32) $500

**Clegg, Charles M.** See: Beebe & Clegg

**Cleland, Robert Glass**
— The Place Called Sespe. [N.p.: Pvtly ptd], 1940. Inscr by Keith Spalding (who owned the Sespe ranch) to Hullett C. Merritt & with Ls from Spalding to Merritt. pba Apr 25 (345) $65

**Clemens, Samuel Langhorne, 1835-1910**
See also: Grabhorn Printing; Limited Editions Club
— The £1,000,000 Bank-Note. NY, [1917]. 1st Separate Ed. 8vo, cloth; extremities rubbed. pba Dec 14 (171) $55
— The £1,000,000 Bank-Note and Other Stories. NY, 1893. 1st Ed. 8vo, orig cloth. pba Dec 14 (170) $275
— The Adventures of Huckleberry Finn. L, 1884. 1st English Ed. 8vo, orig cloth; rubbed & soiled, torn at spine head & base. Prelims foxed; some leaves creased; contents leaves torn. S Oct 27 (1230) £380 [Hearn]
— The American Claimant. NY, 1892. 1st Ed. 8vo, orig cloth. pba Dec 14 (154) $350
— Be Good, Be Good. NY: Pvtly ptd, 1931. 1st Ed. Single sheet, ptd in green & folded to form 4 pp, folded again for mailing, with orig envelope with Merle Johnson's return address. K June 23 (201) $250
— The Celebrated Jumping Frog of Calaveras County.... NY, 1867. 1st Ed, 1st Ptg. 12mo, half mor. Dedication leaf in facsimile; hole in tp. K Oct 1 (106) $750

Anr copy. Later half lea; front cover nearly detached, edges dented. K June 23 (202) $1,500

Anr copy. Orig green cloth, with frog in lower left corner; minor wear, fading & dampstaining. P June 5 (139) $2,750

Later ptg. Orig brown cloth, with frog in lower left corner. O Sept 12 (188) $400

— The Christmas Fireside. [N.p.]: Allen Press, [1949]. One of 75. cb June 25 (1903) $250; pba Mar 7 (11) $325
— Concerning Cats. Two Tales by Mark Twain. San Francisco: Grabhorn Press for the Book Club of California, 1959. One of 450. 4to, half cloth. pba June 20 (340) $100
— A Connecticut Yankee in King Arthur's Court. NY, 1889. 1st Ed. 8vo, orig cloth; rubbed. sg Feb 8 (349) $225
1st Issue. Orig cloth; spine ends worn, bumped, hinge repaired. K Oct 1 (108) $275
2d Issue. Orig cloth. pba Aug 22 (457) $275
Salesman's dummy. Orig composite bdg. With prelims, excerpts, pbr's announcement & blank register. CE May 22 (98) $1,300
— Eve's Diary. L & NY, 1906. In repaired dj. sg Sept 21 (314) $325
— Following the Equator. Hartford, 1897. 1st Ed. 8vo, cloth; extremities rubbed. sg Feb 8 (350) $110
1st Issue. Orig cloth. pba Dec 14 (159) $275
One of 250. Orig cloth; front endpapers renewed, newspaper clippings pasted to lower endpapers. With related material, most concerning a photograph of Clemens in a cart. Somervell - Bingham copy. P June 5 (145B) $2,250
— How To Cure a Cold. San Francisco: Cloister Press, 1937. Ltd Ed. Orig vellum. K June 23 (207) $130
— Huckleberry Finn. L, 1884. ("The Adventures of Huckleberry Finn.") 1st Ed. 8vo, orig cloth; rubbed, joints splitting, spine head torn, loose. Ink stamps on half-title & frontis verso. bba May 30 (181) £80 [Mead]
Anr copy. Orig cloth; spine with minor rubbing. bbc Dec 18 (223) $1,350
Anr copy. Orig cloth. Parsons - Engelhard copy. CNY Oct 27 (16) $4,200
Anr copy. Orig cloth; spine ends bumped. S July 11 (149) £650
1st American Ed. NY, 1885. 1st Issue. 8vo, orig sheep; minor wear. P June 5 (143) $4,250
Early issue. Mor gilt, the front cover set with oval port miniature of Clemens, orig cloth bound in. CE Sept 27 (84) $1,800
Anr copy. Calf gilt, orig cloth bound in. Lacking final blank; some browning. CE May 22 (96) $800
Anr copy. Orig sheep; front joint cracked, minor wear. Engelhard copy. CNY Oct 27 (17) $3,200
Anr copy. Orig cloth. "The finest copy one is likely to ever see". pba Dec 14 (151) $8,000
Anr copy. Cloth; spine ends & corners worn, leaning. Foxed. pba Dec 14 (152) $700
Anr copy. Orig cloth; rubbed, shelf numbers on front pastedown. sg Sept 21 (312) $1,000
Anr copy. Orig cloth; ownership stamp on front free endpaper, scratch to front cover. Pp 243-46 with outer margins shorter. sg Feb 8 (345) $4,000
Anr copy. Orig cloth; rubbed, cloth bubbled on spine. With a Clemens "grasshopper" signature laid in. sg Feb 8 (346) $1,700

Later Issue. Orig cloth; extremities rubbed. cb Feb 14 (2649) $1,700
Anr copy. Orig cloth; spine & corners frayed & worn, front hinge cracked. F Mar 28 (296) $90
Anr copy. Orig sheep; rubbed, front joint cracked. Some dampstaining to lower margins at end. pba Sept 14 (354) $1,200
Mixed Issue. Orig cloth; front hinge cracked, rubbed, spine ends worn. CE May 22 (97) $400
Anr copy. Orig cloth; spine tips restoried. Some foxing & staining. O Sept 12 (187) $600
Anr copy. Orig cloth; worn, bumped, stained, writing partially erased from front free endpaper. wd Nov 15 (42) $800
Anr Ed. West Hatfield MA: Pennyroyal Press, 1985. One of 350 with an extra suite of plates in separate portfolio. Illus by Barry Moser. Folio, orig mor gilt. CE Sept 27 (219) $400
— The Innocents Abroad. Hartford, 1869. 1st Ed, 1st Issue. 8vo, orig half calf; edges rubbed. CE May 22 (90) $450
3d Issue. Orig cloth; spine foot worn, shaken. pba Dec 14 (161) $180
Salesman's dummy. Orig cloth. Sample strips of cloth laid down on front pasedown & calf spine laid down on rear pastedown; subscriber's list, with 1 page filled out, at end. pba June 20 (343) $1,700
Anr Ed. Hartford, 1876. 8vo, orig cloth; spine ends & corners worn. Inscr to Charles Warren Stoddard, Oct 1877, as Twain. CNY May 17 (58) $2,000
— Is Shakespeare Dead? NY & L, 1909. 1st Ed, 1st Issue. Orig cloth; rubbed & bumped. pba Dec 14 (163) $55
— Life on the Mississippi. Bost., 1883. 1st American Ed, 1st State. 8vo, orig cloth; spot to lower spine. pba Dec 14 (166) $1,400
Anr copy. Orig cloth; rubbed, corners & spine ends worn, hinge cracked before title, frontis & front endpaper nearly detached. pba Apr 25 (248) $140
Intermediate A State. Orig cloth; hinge cracked. Frontis nearly detached. K Oct 1 (110) $375
1st Ed. L, 1883. 1st Issue. 8vo, orig cloth; spine ends & joints rubbed. CE May 22 (95) $480
— The Love Letters of Mark Twain. NY, 1949. 1st Ed, one of 155. In dj. cb June 25 (1809) $900
— The Man that Corrupted Hadleyburg.... L, 1900. 1st English Ed. Some foxing at beginning. K June 23 (210) $90
— Mark Twain on Simplified Spelling. NY: Simplified Spelling Board, 1906. 1st Ed, 2d Issue. Single leaf folded to 4 pp with integral title. Crease near spine fold; short tear from spine fold at center. bbc Dec 18 (226) $170
[-] Mark Twain's 70th Birthday. [NY], 23 Dec 1905. 4to, orig wraps; soiled & worn, repaired along inside of spine, loose in bdg. pba Dec 14 (194) $160
— Mark Twain's Autobiography. NY, 1924. 1st Ed. 2 vols. In djs; bdg spine rubbed, lower corners bumped. Blindstamp to tp. pba Dec 14 (168) $190; pba May 23 (435) $70
— Mark Twain's (Burlesque) Autobiography and First Romance. NY, [1871]. 1st Ed, 1st State. 12mo,

## CLEMENS

orig cloth. Early childish pencil ownership scribblings. sg Sept 21 (315) $140
— Mark Twain's Sketches. NY, [1874]. 1st State of wraps. 8vo, wraps; chipped. K June 23 (214) $300
— The Prince and the Pauper. L, 1881. 1st Ed, 1st Issue. 8vo, orig half mor, bdg state B. Minor staining at ends. CE May 22 (93) $280
1st American Ed. Bost., 1882. 8vo, orig cloth; spine ends worn, rear cover marked, front inner hinge broken. Clemens's copy with his alterations & additions, sgd "Mark Twain". Engelhard copy. CNY Oct 27 (15) $10,000
Anr copy. Orig cloth, bdg state A; extremities rubbed. sg Feb 8 (351) $450
1st Issue. Orig cloth; extremities worn. CE May 22 (94) $650
— Pudd'nhead Wilson. NY, 1893-94. 7 parts in 2 vols. 8vo, contemp half mor gilt; joints & extremities rubbed. Some dampstaining. In: The Century Illustrated Monthly Magazine, Vols XXV & XXVI. pba Dec 14 (173) $120
1st American Ed in Book form. Hartford, 1894. 8vo, cloth. pba Dec 14 (179) $550
Anr copy. Orig cloth. sg Sept 21 (316) $250
Anr copy. Orig cloth; signs of bookplate removal. sg Feb 8 (352) $325
— Punch, Brothers, Punch! and other Sketches. NY, [1878]. 1st Ed in Book form, 2d Issue. 16mo, orig cloth; worn & frayed. Some browning; a few leaves smudged. bbc Dec 18 (225) $110
— The Quaker City Holy Land Excursion.... NY: M. Harzof, 1927. One of 200. Wraps. K June 23 (218) $250
— Roughing It. Hartford, etc., 1872. 1st American Ed. 8vo, orig half mor; spine with 2 tiny holes, corners rubbed. pba Dec 14 (174) $1,600
— Saint Joan of Arc. NY & L, [1919]. Illus by Howard Pyle. Orig cloth. pba Dec 14 (175) $55
— S.L.C. to C.T. NY: Pvtly ptd, 1925. One of 100. Orig ptd wraps. K June 23 (219) $225
— Tom Sawyer. Hartford, 1876. ("The Adventures of Tom Sawyer.") 1st American Ed, 1st Ptg. 8vo, orig cloth; shaken. O Mar 5 (229) $6,300
Anr copy. Orig cloth; spine & extremities with wear. P June 5 (140) $4,500
Anr copy. Orig cloth; recased, spine ends chipped, hinges reinforced, later endpapers. Half-title stained. pba June 20 (342) $1,600
2d Ptg, Issue A. Orig cloth; extremities rubbed. P June 5 (141) $1,600
Anr copy. Orig cloth; rebacked, orig spine strip laid on, new endpapers. pba Dec 14 (153) $110
Anr copy. Orig cloth; rubbed, tape marks on pastedowns & endpapers. sg Sept 21 (313) $425
2d Ptg, Issue C. Later half mor. sg Feb 8 (347) $600
— A Tramp Abroad. Hartford, 1879. Salesman's dummy for the 1st Ed. 8vo, orig brown cloth; hinges starting, spine ends with some wear. With binding samples, prelims, frontis & excerpts, with pbr's announcement & register (listing 5 subscribers' names on 1st leaf). CE May 22 (92) $1,200

## AMERICAN BOOK PRICES CURRENT

1st Ed. Hartford & L, 1880. 8vo, orig cloth, BAL's State A; front cover stained. Frontis foxed. pba Dec 14 (180) $190
Anr copy. Calf gilt by Bayntun; spine scraped. pba Aug 8 (634) $50
— A True Story, and the Recent Carnival of Crime. Bost., 1877. 1st Ed, 1st State of bdg. 8vo, orig cloth; minor wear. P June 5 (142) $1,000
— What is Man? NY, 1906. 1st Ed, one of—250. Orig bds. Foxing at ends. CE May 22 (100) $800
— Works. Hartford, 1899-1907. Autograph Ed, one of—512. 23 (of 25) vols; lacking vols XXIV & XXV. Half mor; some hinges cracked. pba Mar 7 (258) $800
Author's Edition de luxe. L, 1899-1907. one of 620. 25 vols. 8vo, contemp half calf by Bayntun; rubbed. b Sept 20 (562) £1,600
Ed de Luxe. 24 (of 25) vols. 8vo, orig cloth; rubbed. Sgd. S Oct 27 (1201) £360 [Hearn]
Hillcrest Ed. NY: Harper, [1907]. 25 vols. Contemp half mor. sg Sept 21 (52) $900
**Clemens's copy, Samuel Langhorne**
LOWELL, JAMES RUSSELL. - Letters. NY, 1893. 2 vols. 8vo, orig cloth; inner hinges of Vol I cracked, 1 leaf loose. With Clemens's inscr & extensive annotations, including long note comparing his suicide attempt with Lowell's. Engelhard copy. CNY Oct 27 (18) $8,500

**Clement, of Alexandria**
— Opera. Florence: Lorenzo Torrentino, 1551-50. ("Omnia quae quidem extant opera....") 2 vols (Vol I: Latin; Vol II: Greek). Folio, old vellum; soiled, inner hinges split. Tp repaired; D5 wormed; some browning or spotting. L.p. copy. C Apr 3 (72) £900

**Clement, Denis Xavier**
— La journee du chretien, sanctifee par la priere et la meditation.... Lyon: B. M. Mauteville, [c.1760]. 18mo, contemp mor gilt; loosening. Fuerstenberg - Schaefer copy. S Dec 7 (124) £150
— Meditations sur la passion de Jesus Christ notre Seigneur. Paris, 1765. 3 vols. 12mo, contemp red mor gilt with arms of Pope Clement XIII. Fuerstenberg - Schaefer copy. S Dec 7 (125) £500

**Clement, Hal, Pseud.**
— Needle. Garden City, 1950. In chipped dj with short tears. pba May 4 (122) $75

**Clement VII, Pope, 1478-1534 —&**
**Charles V, Emperor, 1500-58**
— [Entry of Pope Clement VII & Emperor Charles V after the coronation at Bologna, 23 Feb 1530]. Antwerp?: for Jan Nicolas Hogenberg & Engelbert Bruning, [c.1530]. 371mm by 310mm, broadsheets, 19th-cent vellum gilt plaque bdg; soiled, lower cover rubbed. With 39 (of 40) plates; lacking engraved title. Some soiling; tear repaired on Plate 36. Launoit - Moszynki - Schaefer copy. P Nov 1 (80) $22,000

**Clericus, Johannes.** See: Le Clerc, Jean

**Cleveland, Grover, 1837-1908**
— Fishing and Shooting Sketches. NY, 1907. pba July 11 (51) $55

**Cleveland, Richard, 1773-1860**
— A Narrative of Voyages and Commercial Enterprises. Cambr., 1842. 2 vols. 8vo, orig cloth; extremities worn. Some dampstaining to gutter margin at beginning of Vol II; foxed. pba Feb 13 (39) $425
— Voyages of a Merchant Navigator.... NY, 1886. 8vo, cloth. Tp detached. pba July 25 (112) $50

**Clichtoveus, Jodocus, d.1543**
— De vera nobilitate opusculum.... Paris: Simon de Colines, 15 Mar 1520. 4to, 18th-cent calf; rebacked, corners restored. Roman types. Wodhull copy. P Dec 12 (15) $600

**Climent, Enrique**
— 10 Grabados en Linoleo a Color / Linoleum Engravings in Color. Mexico City, 1951. One of 300. Text by Carlos Merida. Folio, loose in cloth portfolio. pba Nov 30 (93) $170

**Clinton, Hillary Rodham**
— It Takes a Village. NY, 1995. In dj. Sgd on front flyleaf. pba June 13 (54) $110

**Clissold, Frederick**
— Narrative of an Ascent to the Summit of Mont Blanc.... L, 1823. 8vo, modern wraps. bba Nov 1 (570) £650 [Atlas]

**Clive, Robert**
— Sketches of Nineveh and the Hold Land. L, [c.1852]. Parts I-III in 2 portfolios. Folio, cloth; def. With 18 (of 24?) hand-colored illus on 17 sheets. Some dustsoiling. S Oct 26 (31) £6,500 [Jaidah]

**Clodius, Johann Christian**
— Compendiosum lexicon latino-turcico-germanicum.... Leipzig, 1730. 2 parts in 1 vol. 8vo, contemp vellum; With frontis; 2 errata leaves at end. S Mar 28 (288) £200

**Clouet, Jean Baptiste Louis**
— Geographie moderne.... Paris, 1787. Folio, later half calf. Some foxing & soiling; some edges trimmed to neatline; corner of 1 map torn off but reattached; some ink & pencil doodling; a few ink droplets. cb Oct 17 (250) $1,000

**Clouzot, Henri**
— Ferronnerie moderne. Nouvelle Serie. Paris: A. Morance, [c.1928]. 2 vols. Folio, loose in half cloth portfolios as issued. With 72 plates. Some plates soiled, margins chipped; 2 plates tape-repaired. sg June 13 (197) $235

**Clutterbuck, Robert, 1772-1831**
— The History and Antiquities of the County of Hertford. L, 1815-27. 1st Ed. 3 vols. Folio, modern cloth. With folding map & 52 plates, 2 in color. Some foxing. bba Nov 1 (100) £300 [Clarke]

Anr copy. Mor gilt by Bedford. With 54 plates & maps, 3 hand-colored, several marked Proof. Some discoloration. S June 13 (496) £600

**Cluverius, Philippus, 1580-1622**
— Introductio in omnen geographiam. Wolffenbuetel, 1694. 4to, contemp vellum. With additional title, title, 43 maps, & 5 plates. Spotted throughout. S Oct 26 (452) £520 [Zioni]
— Introductionis in universam geographiam.... Amst.: Elzevir, 1661. 12mo, old half calf; rebacked in cloth. With engraved title & 32 folding maps only. bbc Feb 26 (463) $600

Anr Ed. Leiden: Elzevir, 1672. 12mo, contemp sheep; needs rebdg. Short tears to several maps. sg May 9 (62A) $400

Anr Ed. Amst., 1676. 4to, old half calf; scuffed. With folding plate & 45 double-page maps. Lacking tp; 5 maps cut down & mtd, 3 others torn at fold; with 1-page Ms list of the maps. C May 31 (52) £1,500

**Clyde, Norman**
— Norman Clyde of the Sierra Nevada. San Francisco: Scrimshaw Press, 1971. Ltd Ed. Foreword by Francis Farquhar; prologue by Jules Eichorn. Larson copy. pba Feb 12 (27) $200

**Clymer, W. B. Shubrick —&**
**Green, Charles R.**
— Robert Frost: A Bibliography. Amherst, 1937. One of 650. pba Oct 5 (127) $70

**Clyne, Geraldyne**
— The Jolly Jump-Ups on Vacation. Springfield: McLoughlin Bros., 1948. 4to, pictorial bds. pba Aug 22 (829) $50

**Coan, Charles F.**
— History of New Mexico. Chicago, 1925. 3 vols. 4to, cloth; worn. NH June 1 (8) $250

**Cobb, Humphrey**
— Paths of Glory. NY, [1935]. Advance uncorrected proof. Ptd wraps; tips dog-eared. sg Dec 14 (33) $60

**Cobbold, Richard, 1797-1877**
— Valentine Verses: or, Lines of Truth, Love and Virtue. Ipswich, 1827. 8vo, orig half cloth; rubbed. With litho frontis, ports & 101 plates. b Dec 5 (361) £120

**Cobden-Sanderson, Thomas James, 1840-1922**
See also: Doves Press
— Ecce Mundus. Industrial Ideals and the Book Beautiful. Hammersmith, 1902. 8vo, orig half vellum bds, unopened. Z June 28 (56) $200

**Cobham, Claude Delaval**
— Excerpta Cypria. Materials for a history of Cyprus. Cambr., 1908. 4to, cloth. With half-title. S Oct 26 (50) £320 [Karides]

## Coburn, Alvin Langdon
— Alvin Langdon Coburn, Photographer: An Autobiography. NY, [1966]. Ed by Helmut & Alison Gernsheim. 4to, cloth, in worn dj. sg Feb 29 (98) $110
— Men of Mark. L, 1913. 4to, orig cloth; worn & soiled. With 33 tipped-in photogravures. CE May 22 (107) $650
— New York. L & NY, [1910]. Folio, orig half mor; rebacked, front cover bowed. With 20 mtd photogravures. sg Feb 29 (100) $5,800

## Coburn, Walt
— Mavericks. NY, [1929]. 1st Ed. Orig cloth; front cover stained. With sgd watercolor on front free endpaper by Ross Santee. Robbins copy. pba Mar 21 (327) $275

## Cocchi, Antonio, 1695-1758
— Del Vitto Pitagorico per uso della Medicina. Florence, 1743. 1st Ed. 4to, contemp bds; spine worn away. With title vignette. Ck Mar 22 (77) £220

## Cochin, Charles Nicolas, 1715-90
See also: Gravelot & Cochin
— Boutiques du Pont Neuf. Paris, [c.1750]. Oblong folio, half mor by Noulhac. With 3 plates. Minor spotting on Plate 1. Fuerstenberg - Schaefer copy. S Dec 7 (129) £900
— Suite de seize estampes representant les conquestes de l'Empereur de la Chine. Paris, [1775]. Broadsheets, over-all 635mm by 495mm, contemp calf gilt; rubbed. All plates with new guards; marginal repairs to versos of 2 plates. Fuerstenberg - Schaefer copy. S Dec 7 (127) £40,000

## Cockburn, Sir George, 1772-1853
— A Voyage to Cadiz and Gibraltar. L, 1815. 1st Ed. 2 vols. 8vo, early half calf; worn, several covers loose. With engraved title, 6 maps & plans & 23 hand-colored plates. Library stamp on titles. sg Mar 7 (47) $325

## Cockburn, John, Mariner
— A Journey over Land from the Gulf of Honduras, to the Great South Sea. L, 1735. 1st Ed. 8vo, contemp calf; worn. With folding map. Some soiling & spotting. S Oct 26 (504) £1,100 [Maggs]

## Cockburn, William, 1669-1739
— The Symptoms, Nature, Cause and Cure of a Gonorrhoea. L, 1715. 1st Ed. 8vo, contemp calf; rebacked. Minor discoloration. b Jan 31 (291) £110

## Cockerell, Sir Sydney Carlyle, 1867-1962
— Old Testament Miniatures: a Medieval Picture Book.... NY, [1969]. Folio, cloth, in chipped dj. pba June 20 (95) $160

## Cockings, George
— War: an Heroic Poem, from the Taking of Minorca.... Bost., 1762. 8vo, contemp sheep; lacking free endpapers. sg Oct 26 (100) $850

## Cockton, Henry, 1807-53
— The Life and Adventures of Valentine Vox, the Ventriloquist. L, 1840. 1st Ed. - Illus by T. Onwyhn. 8vo, calf gilt by Riviere; covers discolored. With 60 plates. Some foxing; lacking half-title. pba June 20 (96) $100

## Cocteau, Jean, 1889-1963
— L'Ange Heurtebise, Poeme. Paris, 1925. One of 25 on van Gelder. Folio, unsewn as issued in orig wraps; soiled along backstrip. S May 16 (6) £480
— Le Cap de bonne esperance. Paris, 1919. One of 510. 16mo, orig wraps. Inscr to Blaise Cendrars. S Nov 21 (79) £1,600
— Le Dragon des Mers. Paris, 1955. One of 25 on Arches with a suite on Auvergne. Illus by Tsuguharu Foujita. 4to, loose as issued in wraps. S Nov 21 (81) £3,000
— Le Livre blanc. Paris, 1928. Out-of-series copy. 4to, orig wraps, unopened. S May 16 (7) £1,000
— Le Mystere laic: essai d'etude indirecte. Paris, 1928. 1st Ed, One of 10 on japon imperial, sgd & 1 of 100 in 4to with 2 etchings sgd in pencil by de Chirico. Illus by Giorgio de Chirico. Orig wraps; soiled. With 2 orig page proofs with Ms corrections by Coctear loosely inserted. Sold with the autograph manuscript, illus with ink sketches, on c.60 leaves. S Nov 21 (84) £21,000
— Pegase. Paris, [1965]. One of 150 , this copy for Jean Popelin. Illus by Leopold Survage. Folio, loose as issued in orig wraps. S May 16 (29) £260
— Romeo et Juliette. Paris, 1926. One of 350 on velin Montgolfier. Illus by Jean Hugo. Folio, mor extra by Marianne, with handmade flyleaves in watercolor & gouache heightened with gold. Some leaves discolored with spotting at lower edge. S Nov 21 (83) £1,100

## Cocteau, Jean, 1889-1963 —& Hugnet, Georges
— La nappe du Catalan. Paris, 1952. One of 80, with 2 watercolor drawings sgd & dated by Hugnet & ink sketch by Hugnet captioned & dated on half-title. 4to, orig wraps. With 16 colored lithos by Cocteau. S May 16 (8) £800

## Codex
— Codex Argenteus Upsaliensis. Upsala & Malmo, [1927]. 4to, cloth; soiled. Library markings, but plates unmarked. sg Sept 7 (230) $200
— Codex Cryptensis. Rome: Libreria dello Stato for Monumenta Musicae Byzantinae, 1951. ("Hirmologium e codice cryptensi.") 2 vols, including commentary. 4to, modern vellum gilt. S June 13 (692) £120
— Codex Gerundensis. Beato de Liebana. Comentario al Apocalipsis Edicion Facsimil del Codice de Gerona.... Madrid, 1975. Folio, lea. sg Apr 11 (216) $325
— Codex Mendoza. The Mexican Manuscript.... L, 1938. 3 vols. Folio, orig vellum. S Oct 26 (505) £700 [Lands Beyond]

**Cody, William F. ("Buffalo Bill"), 1846-1917**
— An Autobiography.... NY, 1920. Illus by N. C. Wyeth.  pba Aug 22 (878) $120
— Buffalo Bill's Wild West and Congress of Rough Riders of the World. NY, 1895. 4to, orig wraps; chipped, worn, lacking top corner of front wrap.  pba Apr 25 (346) $120
  7th Ed. Buffalo: Courier Company, [c.1900]. 4to, orig wraps; spine torn, chip to lower corner of front cover.  pba Nov 16 (54) $160

**Coe, Michael D.** See: Grolier Club

**Coedes, George**
— Bronzes Khmers. Paris, 1923. Folio, cloth. With 51 plates. Library markings.  sg Sept 7 (109) $60

**Coehorn, Menno de, Baron, 1641-1704**
— Nouvelle fortification. Utrecht, 1741. 8vo, contemp calf; rubbed. With 14 folding plates.  b Sept 20 (102) £180

**Coelson, Lancelot**
— The Poor-Man's Physician and Chyrurgion. L, 1656. 1st Ed. 8vo, modern mor. Wormed at foot throughout; title & last leaf frayed & strengthened; soiled & stained.  S Oct 27 (801) £550 [Antiquarian]

**Coetlogon, Denis de**
— A Tour through the Animal World.... L, 1746. 8vo, contemp calf; worn. With frontis & 153 (of 155) plates. Prelim & final leaves browned; the missing 2 plates present in facsimile.  S Nov 2 (178) £150 [Schiller]

**Coffin, George**
— A Pioneer Voyage to California and Round the World, 1849-1852. Chicago, 1908. 1st Ed. Orig cloth; rear hinge broken, front hinge weak, covers' bottom damaged. With frontis port & 12 plates. Larson copy.  pba Sept 28 (374) $50

**Cogan, Thomas, 1545?-1607**
— The Haven of Health, Chiefly Gathered for the Comfort of Students.... L, 1605. 4th Ed. 4to in 8s, 18th-Cent calf; rebacked in 19th-Cent sheep, spine rubbed. Title torn & repaired; quire B browned; L6 creased & miscut; marginal stains.  Ck Mar 22 (78) £850

**Cogniat, Raymond**
— Paul Gauguin: A Sketchbook. NY, 1962. One of 1,000. 3 vols. Facsimile sketchbook in cloth, separate text vols in French & English in orig wraps.  bba Oct 19 (7) £100 [Chichester Gallery]

**Cohen, Arthur A.**
— Herbert Bayer: The Complete Work. Cambr., 1984. One of 100, with sgd photo by Bayer laid in. In dj.  sg Sept 7 (36) $350

**Cohen, Henri, 1808-80**
— Guide de l'amateur de livres a gravures du XVIIIe siecle. Paris, [n.d.]. 7th Ed. - Revised by Seymour de Ricci. 8vo, half cloth. Reprint of 1912 edition.  sg Apr 11 (85) $175

**Cohn, Albert Mayer**
— George Cruikshank: a Catalogue Raisonne. L, 1924. One of 500. 4to, cloth.  sg Jan 11 (129) $250

**Cohn, David L.**
— New Orleans and its Living Past. Bost., 1941. One of 1,000. Illus by Clarence John Laughlin. 4to, cloth.  wa Dec 14 (560) $270

**Cohn, Louis Henry**
— Bibliography of the Works of Ernest Hemingway. NY, 1931.  pba Aug 22 (233) $50

**Coigney, Rodolphe L.**
— Izaak Walton. A New Bibliography.... NY, 1989. One of 540. In dj.  O June 25 (38) $90

**Coit, Daniel Wadsworth, 1787-1876.** See: Grabhorn Printing

**Coke, Henry John**
— A Ride Over the Rocky Mountains to California.... L, 1852. 1st Ed. 8vo, orig cloth; rebacked with orig spine laid down. Tp partially separated. Larson copy.  pba Sept 28 (378) $275
— A Ride Over the Rocky Mountains to Oregon and California.... L, 1852. 1st Ed. 8vo, orig cloth; spine repaired, recased, covers rubbed. With frontis. Darkening. Robbins copy.  pba Mar 21 (62) $200

**Coker, John, d.1635?**
— A Survey of Dorsetshire. Containing the Antiquities and Natural History.... L, 1732. Folio, later cloth; spine rubbed. With folding map & 6 plates. With 6 Ms pp of notes bound in at beginning.  bba Nov 1 (58) £400 [Austin]

**Colacello, Bob.** See: Warhol & Colacello

**Colardeau, Charles Pierre**
— Oeuvres choises. Paris, 1811. One of 2 on vellum. 12mo, orig vellum. Fuerstenberg - Schaefer copy.  S Dec 7 (130) £900

**Colas, Rene**
— Bibliographie generale du costume et de la mode. Paris, 1933. 1st Ed. 2 vols. Cloth; rubbed.  bba Oct 5 (244) £220 [Sims]
  Anr copy. Orig wraps, unopened.  sg Sept 7 (111) $110
  One of 1,000. 2 vols. 8vo, orig cloth; spines faded, labels worn.  sg Apr 11 (86) $150

**Colbert, Charles Eleonor**
— [Sale Catalogue] Bibliotheca Colbertina. Paris, 1728. Vol I (of 3). 12mo, contemp calf; rubbed, upper joint broken. Partly priced in Ms Sold w.a.f. Munby copy.  O Mar 26 (64) $100

**Colchen, Jean Victor, Comte, 1751-1830**
— Memoire statistique du departement de la Moselle adresse au Ministre de l'Interieur d'apres ses instructions. Paris, 1802. Folio, contemp red mor gilt with

arms of Napoleon I [Olivier 2652 fer 7]; upper joint cracked near head, small tear on lower cover. Some spotting. Fuerstenberg - Schaefer copy. S Dec 7 (131) £750

**Colden, Cadwallader, 1688-1776**
— The History of the Five Indian Nations of Canada.... L, 1747. 2 parts in 1 vol. 8vo, contemp calf. With folding map. sg Oct 26 (75) $1,300

**Colden, Cadwallader David, 1769-1834**
— Memoir Prepared at the Request of a Committee of the Common Council at the Celebration of the Completion of the New York Canals. NY, 1825 [1826]. 4to, old bds with mtd label "Presented by the City of New York, to David Hosack by the hands of the recorder R. Riker"; hinges reinforced with tape. With 47 maps & plates & 8 pages of facsimiles. Some foxing. Met Feb 24 (376) $800

Anr copy. Becoming disbound. With 47 plates & 8 facsimiles. Repair to geological profile; 1 plate laid in. With 2 cut signatures of DeWitt Clinton laid in. NH July 21 (255) $400

— Memoir...Presented to the Mayor of the City at the Celebration of the Completion of the New York Canals. NY, 1825-26. 4to, early calf; rebacked, extremities worn, hinges weak. With the Appendix. Inscr by Richard Riker to Charles G. Ferris. sg Oct 26 (32) $650

**Coldewey, Jan.** See: Keulemans & Coldewey

**Cole, Alan S.**
— Ancient Needlepoint and Pillow Lace.... L, 1875. Orig half mor; rubbed & bumped, spine ends perished, several leaves detached, dampstained, bowed. With 20 mtd photographic plates. cb Oct 17 (107) $325

**Cole, G. —& Roper, J.**
— The British Atlas. L, 1810. Folio, contemp half calf; worn. With 58 maps, colored in outline & 19 (of 21) city plans. Marginal staining & soiling; 1 plan loose. S June 13 (484) £780

**Coleman, William, 1766-1829**
— A Collection of the Facts and Documents, relative to the Death of...Alexander Hamilton. NY, 1804. 8vo, contemp sheep; rebacked. sg Oct 26 (129) $70

**Coleridge, Samuel Taylor, 1772-1834**
See also: Kelmscott Press; Limited Editions Club; Nonesuch Press; Wordsworth & Coleridge
— Aids to Reflection in the Formation of a Manly Character. L, 1825. 8vo, half calf. Inscr to Hartley Coleridge. S Apr 23 (26) £700
— Biographia Literaria; or, Biographical Sketches.... L, 1817. 1st Ed. 2 vols in 1. 8vo, contemp calf; rebacked, rubbed. S Dec 18 (250) £200 [Duncan]
— Christabel; Kubla Khan, a Vision; the Pains of Sleep. L, 1816. 1st Ed. 8vo, contemp calf gilt. b Jan 31 (76) £380

Anr copy. Later calf. CE May 22 (109) $1,700
— The Rime of the Ancient Mariner. NY, 1877. Illus by Gustave Dore. Folio, orig cloth; spine chipped. F Mar 28 (752) $120

Anr Ed. East Aurora: Roycrofters, 1899. ("So This Then is ye Rime of ye Ancient Mariner.") One of 910. Illus by W. W. Denslow. 8vo, orig suede. O July 9 (55) $50

Anr Ed. L, 1903. One of 150. Vellum. sg Sept 14 (120) $475

Anr Ed. L, [1910]. Illus by Willy Pogany. 4to, orig cloth. Sgd on half-title by Pogany. b May 30 (444) £220

Anr copy. Orig cloth; worn. With 20 colored plates. F June 20 (526) $220

Anr copy. With 20 colored plates. Tear to half-title. pba Mar 7 (207) $170

Anr Ed. Bristol: Douglas Cleverdon, 1929. One of 400. Illus by David Jones. 4to, half cloth. sg Sept 14 (235) $425

One of 60, sgd by Jones & with an extra suite of the engravings. Orig cloth. S May 16 (117) £800

Anr Ed. L: Corvinus Press, 1944. One of 21. 4to, orig half cloth. sg Sept 14 (92) $425

Anr Ed. NY: Chilmark Press, 1964. One of 115 with portfolio containing an extra suite of plates & 5 additional plates. Illus by David Jones. 4to, half paper-parchment. With 10 engravings. sg Sept 14 (234) $500

— Sibylline Leaves. L, 1817. 1st Ed. 8vo, 19th-cent mor gilt. Some foxing. S Apr 23 (25) £580

Anr copy. Orig bds; front cover detached. wd Nov 15 (44) $200

— Works. L, 1877. 4 vols. 8vo, half vellum. Note on pastedown states that this 1 of 24 ptd on Whatman. S Apr 23 (27) £380

**Coles, William, 1626-62**
— Adam in Eden. L, 1657. Folio, calf; scuffed, stain on front cover, spine top chipped, hinges partly open. Some browning. K June 23 (310) $950

**Colette, Sidonie Gabrielle, 1873-1954**
See also: Limited Editions Club
— Claudine a l'ecole * Claudine a Paris * Claudine en menage * Claudine s'en va. Paris, 1947. One of 72 with extra suite of plates in black only. Illus by Grau Sala. 4 vols. Half mor, orig wraps bound in. With 1 orig watercolor in each vol. S Nov 21 (88) £250
— L'Envers du music-hall. [Paris], 1926. One of 30 on Holland with an extra suite of the illusts. Illus by J. E. Laboureur. 4to, wraps, in dj. sg Sept 14 (251) $800
— Paradis terrestre. [Lausanne, 1932]. One of 25 on Japan imperial, with an orig charcoal drawing by Jouve. Illus by Paul Jouve. 4to, mor extra by George Crette with inlaid lacquer & mother-of-pearl by Dunand depicting a jungle scene, orig wraps bound in. With 2 additional suites of the illusts, 19 additional plates at various stages of color decompo-

sition & 5 prelim crayon sketches by Jouve.  S Nov 21 (87) £15,000

— Le Voyage egoiste.  Paris, 1922.  1st Ed, one of 35 on Japon.  Illus by Charles Guerin.  4to, mor extra by P. L. Martin, orig wraps bound in.  With 12 chromolithos.  Inscr to Maurice Crick.  With an additional suite of the illusts in 4 or 5 states.  S Nov 21 (85) £3,600

### Colle, Charles, 1709-83

— Chansons qui n'ont pu etre imprimees et que mon censeur n'a point du me passer.  [Neufchatel?], 1784.  12mo, red mor gilt by Thouvenin for Charles Nodier.  Fuerstenberg - Schaefer copy.  S Dec 7 (132) £650

### Collection...

— Collection de vues des principaux palais, eglises, batimens publies, campagnes & jardins tant de Vienne que de ses environs....  Vienna: Marie Geisler, [n.d.].  Oblong folio, orig bds; soiled.  With engraved title & 50 hand-colored plates (of 100).  Interleaved throughout; Plate 27 discolored.  S Mar 28 (228) £1,700

— Collection des moralistes anciens. Paris: Didot l'Aine, 1782-83.  One of 12 on vellum.  Menander vol only.  Mor gilt by Derome, with his ticket.  Fuerstenberg - Schaefer copy.  S Dec 8 (608) £3,400

— A Collection of Interesting, Authentic Papers Relative to the Dispute between Great Britain and America....  L: J. Almon, 1777.  1st Ed. 8vo, later calf; chipped, joints worn, trimmed.  wa Feb 29 (307) $160

### Collie, John Norman

— Climbing on the Himalaya and other Mountain Ranges.  Edin., 1902.  With 3 folding maps.  Some waterstaining.  Freya Stark's copy.  b May 30 (163) £170
 Anr copy.  Orig cloth; hinges weak.  Library markings.  bba Nov 1 (379) £300 [Davies]

### Collier, Jeremy, 1650-1726

— A Defence of the Short View of the Profaneness and Immorality of the English Stage.  L, 1699.  1st Ed. 8vo, contemp calf; front cover almost detached.  Some spotting.  pba June 20 (334) $130

**Collier, John.** See: Nonesuch Press

### Collier, John, 1708-86

— Human Passions Delineated, by Timothy Bobbin, Esq.  L, 1773 [but Manchester, c.1860].  Folio, orig cloth; worn, backstrip def.  With engraved title, port & 44 plates on 25 sheets.  bba June 6 (5A) £110 [Pope]

**Collier, John Payne, 1789-1883.** See: Limited Editions Club

### Collier le Cityoyen

— Contes a rire d'un nouveau genre et des plus amusants.  Brussels, 1881.  One of 500.  8vo, mor gilt by Rene Kieffer.  With 4 full-page watercolors & over 50 marginal watercolors, sgd by A. Beer.  b May 30 (531) £550

**Collin, Jonas.** See: Kjaerbolling & Collin

### Collinot, Eugene —& Beaumont, Adalbert de

— Encyclopedie des arts decoratifs de l'Orient.  Paris, 1883.  One of 100.  Folio, loose in recent cloth portfolio.  With half-title, & 30 plates (24 color) by Lemercier after Beaumont.  2 short tears repaired.  S Oct 26 (34) £650 [Folios]

### Collins, Arthur, 1690?-1760

— The Peerage of England.  L, 1779.  5th Ed. 8 vols. 8vo, disbound from orig lea.  NH June 1 (144) $240

### Collins, Charles

— Icones avium cum nominibus anglicis.  L, 1736.  Oblong folio, framed.  With 12 plates.  Some browning & tears.  Fattorini copy.  C Oct 25 (9) £3,800

### Collins, David, 1756-1810

— An Account of the English Colony in New South Wales.  L, 1804.  2d Ed. 4to, half lea; rubbed.  With 34 maps, plans & plates.  Some foxing.  Met Sept 28 (350) $1,200

### Collins, Edward

— Tintern Abbey; or, the Beauties of Piercefield.  Chepstow, [1825].  8vo, contemp bds; spine def.  b Dec 5 (241) £140

### Collins, Francis

— Voyages to Portugal....  L, 1807.  1st Ed. 8vo, later half calf.  With frontis.  Few leaves remargined & annotated.  S Oct 26 (35) £240 [Shapero]

### Collins, George R. —& Bassegoda Nonell, Juan

— The Designs and Drawings of Antonio Gaudi.  Princeton, [1983].  Folio, cloth, in dj.  sg June 13 (6) $60

### Collins, Victor

— Attempt at a Catalogue of the Library of the Late Prince Louis Lucien Bonaparte.  [L], 1894.  4to, buckram; rebound.  Half-title repaired & rehinged, last 2 leaves facsimiles.  sg Apr 11 (87) $50

### Collins, Wilkie, 1824-89

See also: Dickens & Collins; Limited Editions Club

— The Life of William Collins....  L, 1848.  2 vols. 8vo, orig cloth; spine heads torn.  Charles Dickens's copy.  P June 13 (22) $4,500

— The Woman in White.  L, 1860.  1st English Ed. 3 vols. 8vo, contemp half calf; rubbed.  With 2 A Ls s to Nina Lehmann tipped in & with letter of Frederick Lehmann sending them on to Horace Pym.  S Apr 23 (33) £850

**Collins, William, 1721-59.** See: Fore-Edge Paintings

### Collis, Maurice

— Quest for Sita.  L, 1946.  Illus by Mervyn Peake.  4to, orig cloth, in dj.  b Jan 31 (198) £130

### Collodi, Carlo, Pseud., 1826-90

See also: Limited Editions Club

## COLLODI

— Le Aventure di Pinocchio. Milan, [1944]. One of 999. Illus by Vsevolod Nicouline. 4to, silk over bds. pba Nov 30 (95) $350
— The Story of a Puppet, or the Adventures of Pinocchio. NY: Cassell, 1892. 8vo, orig cloth; recased, discolored. S May 16 (171) £500
  Anr Ed. NY, 1932. ("The Pop-Up Pinocchio.") Illus by Harold Lentz. 4to, orig bds; minor wear. O Sept 12 (110) $200
  Anr copy. Orig bds; worn. Some foxing. Sold w.a.f. O July 9 (163) $300

**Collyer, Joseph, d.1776.** See: Fenning & Collyer

**Collyns, Charles Palk, 1793-1864**
— Notes on the Chase of the Wild Red Deer. L, 1902. Some foxing. O June 4 (71) $50

**Colnett, James, 1755?-1806**
— The Journal of.... Toronto, 1940. Ed by F. W. Howay. Champlain Society Publications, No 26. pba Feb 13 (40) $160
— A Voyage to the South Atlantic and Round Cape Horn. L, 1798. 1st Ed. 4to, contemp russia; rebacked in lea. With port, 6 folding charts, & 3 plates. Maps with some tears. Peter Decker & Robbins copy. pba Mar 21 (63) $10,000
  Anr copy. Old half calf. With port, 6 folding charts, 2 engraved coastal profiles & 1 plate. S Nov 30 (216) £3,200

**Colom, Arnold**
— Zee-Atlas ofte Water-Wereldt. Amst.:, [c.1658]. Folio, contemp vellum with gilt arms of the Seven Provinces. With hand-colored world map & 14 (of 16) charts, the cartouches & decorations heightened with gold, all double-page & on think paper mtd on thicker paper. Lacking North Sea & English Channel; lower corners of 1st 3 maps damaged; some fold breaks. C Oct 25 (106) £19,000

**Colombia**
— Edicto para manifestar al publico el indulto general, concedido por... Don Carlos III a todos los comprehendidos en las revoluciones acaecidas en el ano pasado de mil setecientos ochenta y uno. Santa Fe de Bogota, 1782. Folio, disbound. Stain towards end. S Nov 30 (150) £400

**Colombo, Fernando, 1488-1539**
— Historie del S. D. Fernando Colombo.... Venice: Giuseppe Tramontin, 1685. 12mo, old bds. Dampstains on tp & some other prelims. CE June 12 (173) $100

**Colombo, Michele**
— Catalogo di alcune opere attinenti alle scienze alle arti e ad altri bisgni dell'uomo. Milan, 1812. 8vo, contemp wraps, unopened; spine torn, corners curled. Some foxing. O Mar 26 (65) $110

**Colonial...**
— Colonial Families. A De Lux Volume of Genealogy, Biography and Heraldry. NY: American Historical Society, 1931. 4to, half mor; extremities worn. NH July 21 (162) $140

**Colonna, Francesco, d.1527**
— Hypnerotomachia Polophili. Venice: Aldus, 1545. ("La Hypnerotomachia di Poliphilo.") Folio, later vellum. Ownership markings cut from tp with loss on verso; worming to 1st few leaves partly repaired with loss; ink highlighting & additions in woodcuts on K4v, l2r, t4v & t5r. S Nov 30 (256) £3,400

**Colonna, Vittoria, 1492-1547**
— Rime de la divina Vittoria Colonna. Parma: A. de Viottis, 1538. 8vo, 18th-cent vellum; spine wormed. C Apr 3 (73) £1,200

**Colophon...**
— The Colophon: A Book Collector's Quarterly. NY, 1930-50. First Series, 20 parts. Bds. bbc Dec 18 (118) $375

**Colorado**
— Instructions to U.S. Deputy Mineral Surveyors, for the District of Colorado, May 1, 1886. [N.p.], 1886. Orig lea; soiled & worn. With folding map. pba Aug 8 (36) $50
— Over the South Park to Leadville. Denver: Chain & Hardy, [c.1880]. Cloth; rubbed. With 18 glossy litho panels folding accordian-style. pba Aug 8 (37) $90

**Colquhoun, Patrick, 1745-1820**
— A Treatise on the Police of the Metropolis.... Phila., 1798. ("A Treatise on the Police of London.") 8vo, contemp sheep; rubbed. Tear in folding table; lacking some index leaves. F June 20 (437) $100

**Colquitt, William**
— Poems. Chester, 1802. 4to, orig bds; worn. b Dec 5 (44) £140

**Colt, Armida Maria-Theresa**
— Weeds and Wild Flowers. L: Two-Horse Press, 1965. One of 220. Ptd by Will Carter at Rampant Lions Press. 4to, Orig half cloth & orig bd portfolio. With 11 wood-engravings in 2 suites. bba May 9 (391) £280 [Gray]

**Colt, H. S. —& Alison, C. H.**
— Some Essays on Golf Course Architecture. Worcestershire: Grant Books, 1990. One of 700. Intro & commentary by Geoffrey Cornish & Fred Hawtree. Cloth. Sgd by Shirley Grant. pba Apr 18 (25) $170

**Colt, Samuel, 1814-62**
— Armsmear: the Home, the Arm, and the Armory of Samuel Colt: a Memorial. NY: Pvtly ptd, 1866. 4to, orig mor presentation bdg by Matthews. Some staining to margin. cb June 25 (1710) $900

**Colton, Calvin, 1789-1857**
— A Voice from America to England. L, 1839. 8vo, orig bds. sg Oct 26 (76) $375

**Colton, Charles**
— Hypocrisy. A Satire. Tiverton, 1812. 8vo, mor gilt. b Dec 5 (78) £60

**Colton, George Woolworth, 1827-1901.** See: Atlas

**Colton, Joseph H., 1800-93**
— Colton's Traveler and Tourist's Guide-Book Through the United States.... NY, 1852. 12mo, orig cloth; worn & soiled. With 2 folding color maps. wa Feb 29 (389) $260

**Colton, Walter, 1797-1851**
— Deck and Port. NY, 1850. 1st Ed, 2d Issue, with the map. 12mo, orig cloth; spine ends lacking. With frontis & 4 colored plates. Some foxing & staining. sg Oct 26 (77) $60
2d Issue. Plates by Sarony & Major. Orig cloth; front cover spotted. With frontis port & 4 color plates. Robbins copy. pba Mar 21 (64) $120
Anr Ed. NY, 1852. Orig cloth; spine faded, water spots on covers. With frontis port, map, & 4 plates. Some foxing. Larson copy. pba Sept 28 (383) $50
— Three Years in California. NY 1850. 1st Ed. 12mo, orig cloth; covers rubbed, worn in extremities. With 12 plates, 1 map, & folding facsimile of Declaration of Rights. Facsimile torn & repaired; marginal darkening. Robbins copy. pba Mar 21 (65) $225
Anr Ed. NY, 1850. 12mo, orig cloth. With frontis port, map, folded facsimile, & 11 plates. Some foxing; facsimile torn & repaired. Larson copy. pba Sept 28 (385) $375

**Columbia University**
AVERY ARCHITECTURAL LIBRARY. - The Catalogue. NY, 1895. 4to, contemp half lea; joints & extremities worn. sg Apr 11 (29) $250

**Columbus, Christopher, 1451-1506**
— His Own Book of Privileges.... L, 1893. Folio, early half calf over wooden bds, with brass clasps; spine ends & edges worn. Facsimile of the Ms. CE June 12 (174) $100
One of 20. Orig half pigskin; worn & scuffed. Facsimile of the Ms. Inscr by Henry Harrisse to his nephew. bbc June 24 (174) $280
— The Voyages of Christopher Columbus: being the Journals.... L: Argonaut Press, 1930. One of 1,050 on Japon vellum. 4to, orig half vellum. pba Feb 13 (42) $175

**Columna, Guido de.** See: Albertus Magnus

**Colvin, Sir Sidney, 1845-1927**
— Drawings of the Old Masters in the University Galleries and in the Library of Christ Church Oxford. Oxford, 1907. 3 vols. Folio, half mor; worn. O May 7 (92) $200

**Combe, William, 1741-1823**
— The Dance of Life. L: R. Ackermann, 1817. Illus by Thomas Rowlandson. 8vo, calf gilt by Bartlett & Gibeston; shelf label at foot of spine, bookplate on pastedown. Stamps on ad leaf. sg Sept 21 (283) $550

— The English Dance of Death. L, 1815-16. 1st Ed. - Illus by Thomas Rowlandson. 2 vols. 8vo, contemp half calf; joints rubbed & cracked. With 72 hand-colored plates. Lacks frontis & additional title; some spotting & staining. S Oct 27 (852) £280 [Elliott]
1st Ed in Book form. L: R. Ackermann, 1815-16. 2 vols. 8vo, contemp calf; spines rubbed & stained. With engraved title, frontis & 74 plates, all colored. Ck Sept 8 (81) £300
Anr copy. Calf gilt by Tout, restored by J. Macdonald. With engraved title & 72 plates. pba June 20 (97) $800
Anr copy. Calf gilt by Bartlett & Gibeston; shelf labels at foot of each spine. With 74 hand-colored plates. Library stamps. sg Sept 21 (284) $1,200
Anr copy. Later calf; worn, covers off. With engraved titles & 72 plates. sg Feb 8 (332) $850
Anr copy. Half mor; def, front cover of Vol II lacking. With 72 hand-colored plates only. wd May 8 (45) $300
— English Dance of Death * Dance of Life. L, 1815-17. 1st Eds. 3 vols. 8vo, cloth by Remnant & Edmonds; bumped, Life with upper hinge weak & small discoloration on cover. With hand-colored engraved titles & 100 colored plates including titles. Laid in are 24 proof impressions of plates in various states, 1 watercolor sgd & 1 ink sketch. Some spotting & soiling; a few tiny tears. Schaefer copy. P Nov 1 (65) $9,000
— A History of Madeira. L: Ackermann, 1821. 4to, modern half mor gilt. With 27 colored plates. Some soiling. S Nov 30 (97) £900
— The Tour[s] of Doctor Syntax in Search of [1] the Picturesque; [2] Consolation; [3] a Wife. L, 1819-20-21. 9th Ed of 1st Tour; 3d Ed of 2d Tour; 1st Ed of 3d Tour. 3 vols. 8vo, orig cloth; rebacked, orig spine strips laid on, bumped. With 2 engraved titles & 78 colored plates. pba Nov 30 (282) $225
Miniature Ed. L: Ackermann, 1823. Illus by Thomas Rowlandson. 3 vols. 12mo, later calf gilt by Morell; some corners off, chipped. sg Feb 8 (333) $200
"9th" Ed. L, 1855. 3 vols. 8vo, later calf gilt; joints cracked, joints & spine ends worn. With 81 hand-colored plates. CE Sept 27 (247) $160
Anr copy. Orig cloth; spine ends chipped & frayed. Minor foxing & soiling. O Mar 5 (49) $200
Anr copy. 19th-cent calf gilt; rebacked preserving orig spines. With 2 engraved titles & 78 hand-colored plates. S Mar 28 (548) £200

**1st Tour**
— [c.1812]. - Phila.: Wm. Charles. 2d American Ed. - Illus by Thomas Rowlandson. 8vo, calf; worn. With 30 hand-colored plates. Some gatherings pulled; some foxing. NH Sept 16 (213) $475

**Syntax Imitations, not by Combe**
— The Grand Master or Adventures of Qui Hi in Hindostan. L, 1816. Illus by Thomas Rowlandson. 8vo, later half calf; extremities rubbed. With engraved title, 1 plain & 25 (of 26) colored plates. sg Sept 21 (286) $425

Anr copy. Calf gilt; scuffed, hinges weak. With folding frontis, engraved title & 29 hand-colored plates Browned. wd May 8 (47) $300
— The Life of Napoleon. L, 1815. 1st Ed. - Illus by George Cruikshank. 8vo, mor extra by Canape; back cover detached. With 30 colored plates, plus an uncolored set from the 1817 Ed. wd Nov 15 (45) $450
— The Tour of Doctor Prosody. L, 1821. 1st Ed. 8vo, half calf; joints & corners rubbed. With 20 colored plates. pba Dec 14 (30) $180
— The Tour of Doctor Syntax through London. L, 1820. 8vo, 19th-cent half mor; scuffed. With 20 hand-colored plates. Minor spotting. F June 20 (842) $150
— The Wars of Wellington. L, 1819. Illus by William Heath. 4to, half mor; scuffed, corners bumped, spine head repaired. With 30 colored plates. Foxed. wd May 8 (46) $550

**Comber, Thomas**
— A Companion to the Temple. L, 1676. Parts 1 & 2 in 2 vols. 8vo, contemp turkey mor, covers gilt-tooled with a flower & bird roll border enclosing a cottage roof of volutes with clusters of volutes hanging from the eaves & with contemp fore-edge painting of flowers, birds, butterflies & the initials A. B. & J. F., bdg by Roger Bartlett of Oxford. Doheny - Schaefer copy. P Nov 1 (66) $4,750

**Comenius, John Amos, 1592-1670**
See also: Golden Cockerel Press
— Opera didactica omnia. Prague, 1957. 3 vols. Folio, half pigskin. sg Sept 21 (119) $60
— Orbis sensualium pictus.... L: for J. Kirton, 1659. 8vo, 18th-cent calf gilt; rebacked, rubbed. Staining & spotting; minor shaving occasionally touching text; small marginal tears; corner tear with loss at F3; burnhole touching plate on E6; some worming sometimes affecting text. Schaefer copy. P Nov 1 (67) $17,000
Anr Ed. St. Petersburg, 1793. ("Zrelische vselennyia.") 8vo, contemp sheep; erubbed, upper hinge split. In Russian, French & German. C June 26 (240) £1,300

**Comines, Philippe de, Seigneur d'Argenton**
— Les Memoires.... Lyon: Jean de Tournes, 1559. Folio, English Restoration bdg of mor gilt by Queen's Binder A (William Nott); color restoration to spine & edges, minor repairs to spine ends. Some staining; last leaf reinforced. Sunderland - Perkins - Crocker - Abbey - Furstenberg - Schaefer copy. P Nov 1 (68) $8,000
Anr Ed. Leiden: Elzevir, 1648. 12mo, mor gilt fanfare bdg by Cape. C May 1 (35) £850
Anr Ed. L & Paris, 1747. 4 vols. 4to, contemp calf; rubbed, joints cracked. Some soiling. S Oct 27 (864) £180 [Zioni]

**Commager, Henry Steele**
— Freedom of Religion & Separation of Church and State. Mount Vernon: A. Colish, [1985]. Folio, loose in cloth portfolio, with booklet inserted in front pocket. pba Nov 30 (94) $130

**Commelin, Caspar, 1636-93**
— Beschryvinge van Amsterdam.... Amst., 1694-93. 2 vols. Folio, contemp blind-stamped vellum; spotted & discolored. With engraved title & 52 plates, plans & maps. Piece torn from margin of Stock Exchange plate; some leaves loose. sg Apr 18 (39) $2,000

**Commelin, Isaac, 1598-1676**
— Frederick Hendrick van Nassauw, Prince van Orangien, zyn Leven en Bedryf. Utrecht, 1652. 2 parts in 1 vol. Folio, contemp blind-stamped vellum. With engraved title, port & 20 (of 34) plates. Lacking tp. sg May 9 (326) $300

**Commercial...**
— The Commercial Bulletin. Richmond VA, 6 May 1865. Vol I, No 1. Folio, unbound. sg Oct 26 (68) $350

**Compania de Filipinas**
— Nueva Real Cedula de la Compania de Filipinas de 12 de Julio de 1803. Madrid, 1803. Contemp mor gilt. L.p. copy. S Nov 30 (211) £1,000

**Compania Guipuzcoana de Caracas**
— Instruccion y ordenanzas, que deberan observar los oficiales y gente, que sirviere en los navios de la Compania.... [Madrid, 1728]. 4to, later wraps. G1 repaired; some discoloration. S Nov 30 (188) £2,500

**Compendious...**
— A Compendious Geographical and Historical Grammar.... L, 1795. 12mo, contemp mor; extremities rubbed. sg Dec 7 (16) $400

**Compleat...**
— The Compleat Geographer: or, the Chorography and Topography.... L, 1723-22. 2 parts in 1 vol. Folio, contemp calf gilt; front bd detached but present, extremities rubbed. With 48 maps & 1 folding map. Some worming at beginning. cb June 25 (1737) $1,400

**Compton-Burnett, Ivy, 1884-1969**
— Works. L, 1972. One of 500. In djs. bba Oct 19 (315) £240 [Makrosky]

**Comstock, Francis Adams —& Fletcher, William Dolan**
— The Work of Thomas W. Nason. Bost., 1977. Folio, cloth, in rubbed & stained dj. O May 7 (96) $110

**Comstock Lode**
— Statement and Reports Concerning the Uncle Sam Senior and Gold Canon Silver Lodes, in Nevada. Bost., 1865. 8vo, orig ptd wraps; spine reglued. pba Nov 16 (61) $80

**Comte, Auguste, 1798-1857**

— The Positive Philosophy. L, 1853. Trans by Harriet Martineau. 2 vols. 8vo, half calf. pba Sept 14 (106) $250

**Concordia**
— Concordia Christliche Widerholete einmuetige Bekentnues nachbenanter Churfuersten, Fuersten und Stende Augspurgischer Confession. Frankfurt, 1581. Folio, contemp calf; rebacked with pigskin, worn, catches & part of clasps lacking, front joint cracked, new endpapers. Tp backed; some worming & chips repaired throughout; dampstain to top edges. wa June 20 (177) $325

**Conder, Josiah, 1789-1855**
— The Modern Traveller. L, 1830-34. 33 vols. 12mo, contemp half calf. With 128 (of 133) plates. Some spotting & dampstaining. S June 13 (566) £620

**Conder, Josiah, b.1852**
— Landscape Gardening in Japan. Tokyo, 1893. 2 vols, including Supplement. Folio, orig half cloth; soiled, corners worn. With 77 plates. Library markings. wa Dec 14 (487) $650
— Paintings and Studies by Kawanabe Kyosai. L, 1911. Folio, orig cloth; bumped & soiled. With 61 uncolored & 10 color plates. Met May 22 (6) $210

**Condillac, Etienne Bonnot de, 1715-80**
— Oeuvres. Paris, 1795-[98]. 23 vols. 8vo, contemp calf; extremities rubbed. Lacking half-titles in Vols 1-17; Vol 17 with lower corner of tp torn away; some foxing. S June 12 (33) £650

**Condivi, Ascanio, b. c.1520**
— Vita di Michelangelo Buonarroti. Rome: Antonio Blado, 16 July 1553. 1st Ed, 1st Issue. Folio, contemp vellum; worn & loose. Tear in D4; lacking final blank; some staining; Ptr's device at end partly colored by a child. C June 26 (61) £5,000

2d Issue. Contemp vellum; spine worn. Waterstaining at beginning; hole in foremargin of last 5 leaves. C June 26 (62) £4,000

**Condorcet, Marie Jean Antoine Nicolas Caritat, Marquis de, 1743-94**
— Outlines of an Historical View of the Progress of the Human Mind. L, 1795. 8vo, old calf; covers detached, spine ends chipped, spine cracked. Some foxing. bbc Feb 26 (428) $220

**Confucius**
See also: Limited Editions Club
— The Morals. L, 1691. 8vo, calf. Library stamps. pba Nov 30 (96) $1,300

**Congreve, William, 1670-1729**
See also: Nonesuch Press
— Works. Birm.: Baskerville, 1761. 3 vols. 8vo, contemp calf gilt; rubbed. With port & 5 plates. S June 12 (34) £250

**Conklin, E.**
— Picturesque Arizona: Being the Result of Travels and Observations in Arizona During the Fall and Winter of 1877. NY, 1878. 1st Ed. Orig cloth; spine sunned, ends & corners rubbed. Robbins copy. pba Mar 21 (67) $225

**Conkling, Margaret.** See: Conkling & Conkling

**Conkling, Roscoe —& Conkling, Margaret**
— The Butterfield Overland Mail, 1857-1869. Glendale, 1947. 1st Ed. 3 vols. Orig cloth; spines sunned, heads bumped. With 2 frontis, 3 folding maps, & 77 plates. Robbins copy. pba Mar 21 (68) $700

**Connelley, William Elsey, 1855-1930.** See: Root & Connelley

**Connelly, Marc**
— The Green Pastures. NY, 1930. One of 550, sgd. 4to, vellum bds. Inscr to Hal Wallis, 1936. pba Jan 25 (54) $50; sg June 20 (57) $50

**Connelly, William Elsey, 1855-1930**
— Doniphan's Expedition and the Conquest of New Mexico and California. Kansas City, MO, 1907. 1st Ed. 8vo, orig cloth. With 8 maps (2 folded). Larson copy. pba Sept 28 (414) $85

**Connett, Eugene V.** See: Derrydale Press

**Connick, Charles Jay**
— Adventures in Light and Color. NY, [1937]. One of 300. 4to, half lea, with remnants of dj. Inscr. O Mar 5 (50) $90

**Connoisseur, Madam, Pseud.**
— The Complete Fortune-Teller.... L, 1812. 12mo, half calf; rubbed. Some spotting. pba June 20 (162) $120

**Conrad, Howard Louis**
— "Uncle Dick" Wootton. Chicago, 1890. 1st Ed. Orig cloth; marginal browning. Robbins copy. pba Mar 21 (66) $300

**Conrad, Joseph, 1857-1924**
See also: Limited Editions Club
— Almayer's Folly. L, 1895. 1st Ed. 8vo, orig cloth; spine cocked, split to top of spine & hinge. cb Feb 14 (2650) $325
— Last Essays. Toronto & L, 1926. In dj. sg June 20 (58) $110
— Laughing Anne. L, 1923. One of 200. bbc June 24 (479) $200
— Lord Jim. Edin. & L, 1900. 1st Ed. 8vo, orig cloth; front hinge starting. sg Sept 21 (121) $500
— The Mirror of the Sea. L, 1906. 1st Ed. Cloth; rubbed, ink spot on front cover. sg Dec 14 (34) $175
— The Nigger of the "Narcissus". L, 1898. 1st English Ed. 8vo, orig cloth; nick to front cover, bumped, spine rubbed. sg Sept 21 (122) $100

## CONRAD

— Notes on my Books. L, 1921. One of 250. O Mar 5 (51) $170
  Anr copy. Currie copy. sg Sept 21 (123) $175
— An Outcast of the Islands. L, 1896. 1st Ed. sg June 20 (60) $140
— The Rescue.... L & Toronto, 1920. 1st English Ed. In dj. sg Sept 21 (124) $50
— The Rover. L, 1923. 1st English Ed. In nicked & soiled dj. sg June 20 (61) $90
— The Secret Agent. L, 1907. 1st Ed, 1st Issue. Orig cloth; edges foxed. bbc June 24 (483) $450
  1st American Ed. NY, 1907. Inscr by Jack Lemmon. pba May 23 (80) $90
  Anr Ed. L, 1923. One of 1,000. Half vellum. pba June 20 (100) $85
— A Set of Six. L, 1908. 1st Ed, Later issue. sg Sept 21 (126) $60
— Tales of Unrest. L, 1898. 1st Ed. 8vo, orig cloth; spine bumped. sg Sept 21 (127) $90
— Typhoon and Other Stories. L, 1903. 1st English Ed in Book form. Orig cloth; rubbed. sg Sept 21 (128) $150
— Under Western Eyes. NY, 1911. 1st American Ed. Orig cloth. sg Sept 21 (129) $90
— Victory. L, [1915]. In orig pictorial dj; torn & repaired. Inscr to the dedicatees. Goodwin - Engelhard copy. CNY Oct 27 (21) $25,000; sg Sept 21 (130) $150
— Within the Tides. L, 1915. sg Sept 21 (131) $150
— Works. L, 1921-27. One of 780. 18 (of 20) vols. Orig half cloth. cb Oct 17 (267) $900
  Memorial Ed. Garden City, 1925-26. one of 99. 23 vols. Vellum gilt; Vol XI front hinge cracked, some extremities worn & soiled. Some dampstaining to front & rear leaves. cb Oct 17 (324) $1,300
— Youth. Edin. & L, 1902. 1st Ed. Orig cloth; rubbed & soiled. Inscr to Arnold Bennett, 20 Nov 1902. Engelhard copy. CNY Oct 27 (20) $5,500
  Anr Ed. Kentfield, Calif., [1959]. One of 140. Bds. pba June 20 (16) $375
  Anr copy. Bds; soiled. sg Sept 14 (7) $375
— Youth and Two Other Stories. NY, 1903. Orig cloth; spine head rubbed with loss. sg Sept 21 (132) $250
  Anr copy. Orig cloth; corner bumped, stain on rear cover, inner hinge cracked. sg June 20 (62) $140

## Conradi, Johann Michael
— Der dreyfach geartete Sehe-Strahl. Coburg, 1710. 4to, 18th-cent bds; spine soiled & chipped. With engraved title & 24 folding plate. Piece cut form tp; some spotting & browning. S Mar 14 (87) £900

## Conroy, Pat
— The Boo. Verona VA: McClure Press, 1971. 2d Ptg. In dj with ring stain. Inscr to Clyde & Pluma, 1 Mar 1972 & with ALs. Z June 28 (62) $400

## Considerations...
— Considerations on the Impropriety and Inexpediency of renewing the Missouri Question... By a Pennsylvanian. Phila., 1820. 8vo, disbound. sg Mar 28 (300) $425

## Constable, John, 1776-1837
— English Landscape Scenery. L, 1855. Folio, contemp mor gilt. With 40 plates. S June 12 (317) £540
  Anr copy. Contemp half mor gilt. Prelims foxed; some plates with marginal foxing. sg June 13 (119) $700

## Constant, Samuel Victor
— Calls, Sounds and Merchandise of the Peking Street Peddlers. Newtown: Bird & Bull Press, 1993. One of 200. Illus by Rosemary Covey. 4to, half mor. With 25 tipped-in wood-engraved plates & with proof plate laid in. sg Feb 15 (44) $275

## Constitution of the United States of America
— The Constitution of the United States of America.... Salt Lake City, 1852. 12mo, disbound. pba Apr 25 (709) $600
— Constitution of the United States Published for the Bicentennial of its Adoption in 1787. San Francisco: Arion Press, 1987. One of 500. Preface by Warren Burger; intro by Daniel J. Boorstin. Vellum laced with red vellum strips & lettered in blue. sg Sept 14 (26) $375

## Constitutions...
— The Constitutions of the Several Independent States of America.... L, 1783. 2d Ed. - Ed by William Jackson. 8vo, modern cloth. Tp loose & with perforated library stamp. sg Oct 26 (370) $225

## Const-Thoonende Juweel...
— Const-Thoonende Juweel, by de loflijcke Stadt Haerlem. Zwolle: Zacharias Heyns, 1607. Bound with: Haerlems Juweel. Zwolle, 1608. 4to, old vellum. 3A1.4 with blank outer margins repaired. Sold w.a.f. sg Mar 21 (83) $1,100

## Continental Congress
— Extracts from the Votes and Proceedings...5th of September, 1774. Phila.: William & Thomas Bradford, 27 Oct 1774. 8vo, disbound. Foxed & browned; 1 leaf lacking. Met Sept 28 (341) $475
  Anr copy. Wraps; stained & bumped. Dampstained & foxed. Met May 22 (334) $575

## Conway, James
— Forays Among Salmon and Deer. L, 1861. Half lev gilt by Birdsall. With litho frontis. pba July 11 (53) $275

## Conway, Sir William Martin, 1856-1937
— The Alps. L, 1904. One of 300. Illus by A. D. McCormick. 4to, orig cloth; soiled. With 70 colored plates. bba Nov 1 (312) £300 [Highton]
— The Bolivian Andes. NY & L, 1901. Orig cloth; bumped. pba July 25 (391) $150

## Cook, Clarence, 1828-1900
— Art and Artists of Our Time. NY: Selmar Hess, [1888]. 3 vols. 4to, half mor gilt; worn, hinges starting. wa Nov 16 (295) $95
— The House Beautiful: Essays.... NY, 1878. 4to, orig cloth; rubbed, front hinge split, frontis detached.

With color frontis by Walter Crane. bbc June 24 (127) $210

**Cook, Eliza.** See: Fore-Edge Paintings

**Cook, Elliott Wilkinson**
— Land Ho! The Original Diary of a Forty-Niner. Balt., [1935]. 1st Ed. - Ed by Jane James Cook. Half bds. Larson copy. pba Sept 28 (379) $75

**Cook, Everett & Pennell**
— Catalogue of Drugs, Chemicals, Proprietary Medicines.... Portland ME, 1896. 8vo, cloth; some wear & staining. O Dec 5 (36) $225

**Cook, Frederick**
— General John Sullivan's Indian Expedition 1779. NY, 1887. 8vo, cloth; worn. Some foxing. O July 9 (59) $130

**Cook, Frederick Albert, 1865-1940**
— My Attainment of the Pole. NY, 1911. 1st Ed. 4to, orig cloth; soiled. Inscr. NH July 21 (325) $350
— Through the First Antarctic Night.... NY, 1900. 8vo, orig cloth; minor wear. pba July 25 (28) $300

**Cook, Capt. James, 1728-79**
See also: Limited Editions Club
— James Cook, Surveyor of Newfoundland. Being a Collection of Charts.... San Francisco, 1965. One of 365. 2 vols. Folio, loose as issued in box. With 10 charts. Facsimile of the 1769-70 Ed. pba Nov 16 (348) $375
Anr copy. Loose as issued in box. Facsimile of the 1769-70 Ed. pba Nov 30 (152) $300
— The Journals.... Cambr.: Hakluyt Society, 1955-74. 5 vols in 6, including portfolio of charts & views. 8vo & folio, orig cloth, 3 vols in djs. pba Feb 13 (46) $1,000
Anr Ed. Cambr.: Hakluyt Society, 1967-74. 5 vols in 6, including portfolio of charts & views. 8vo & folio, cloth, text vols in djs. sg Apr 18 (41) $850
Anr copy. Cloth. wa Feb 29 (171) $600
— [Set of Hawkesworth, South Pole & Pacific Ocean]. L, 1773-77-84. 1st Eds. 9 vols, including Atlas. 4to & folio, 19th-cent half calf; bds rubbed, worn, Vol I head repaired. With 24 folding maps, 1 folding table, 1 folding chart, 1 double-page chart, & 61 plates. Some staining; paper mildly aged in atlas. Robbins set. pba Mar 21 (69) $17,000

### First Voyage
HAWKESWORTH, JOHN. - An Account of the Voyages.... Dublin, 1773. 1st Dublin Pirated Ed. 3 vols. 8vo, contemp calf; worn. Lacks folding chart in vol I. S Oct 26 (610) £100 [King]
1st Ed. L, 1773. 3 vols. 4to, contemp half calf; extremities worn, joints cracked, lacking all free endpapers. With 51 (of 52) plates & maps. Some pencil notations; minor foxing; some fold splits. bbc June 24 (175) $1,950
2d Ed. 3 vols. 4to, modern half calf. With 52 plates & maps. Tear in 1 map; some spotting; tp of Vol II torn. b Sept 20 (415) £650

Anr copy. Later calf gilt; rebacked, corners bumped, tips worn through. With 52 maps & plates. Small marginal or fold-line tears to a few plates; 1 chart backed. cb Oct 17 (182) $2,000
"3d" Ed. L, 1785. 4 vols. 8vo, orig bds; rebacked with calf. With 2 folding maps & 9 folding plates. sg Mar 7 (50) $400
HAWKESWORTH, JOHN. - Cartes et figures des voyages.... Paris, 1774. Atlas vol only. 4to, contemp half lea; scuffed & insect-damaged, spine ends chipped. With 52 plates & charts. Some foxing; a few plates with crease tears or marginal wormholes. pba Feb 13 (49) $475
PARKINSON, SYDNEY. - A Journal of a Voyage to the South Seas.... L, 1773. 1st Ed. 4to, contemp half calf; rebacked, spine laid down, rubbed. With port & 27 plates. Some foxing, affecting a few plates. cb June 25 (1718) $4,000
Anr copy. Modern calf. With port, map & 26 plates. Some foxing & spotting; soiling to frontis & tp; marginal repair to frontis; lacking final blank. pba Feb 13 (148) $4,000
Anr copy. Contemp calf; worn, upper cover detached. With port, 27 plates, & folding chart. Some spotting & offsetting. S Oct 26 (613) £2,100 [Stern]

### Second Voyage
— A Voyage towards the South Pole and Round the World. L, 1777. 2 vols. 8vo, contemp calf; rebacked. With 44 plates. Some staining. Sold w.a.f. S Oct 26 (453) £250 [Pordes]

### Third Voyage
— A Voyage to the Pacific Ocean. L, 1785. 2d Ed. 3 vols, lacking the Atlas. 4to, early calf; extremities worn. With 24 maps & charts. sg Mar 7 (49) $650
3d Ed. 3 vols (lacking Atlas). 4to, later calf; worn & dry, Vol III with text block split. With 24 maps & charts & 2 frontis ports. Some soling & foxing. wa Feb 29 (473) $800
RICKMAN, JOHN. - Journal of Captain Cook's Last Voyage.... L, 1785. 8vo, contemp calf; rebacked. With folding frontis, folding chart & 6 (of 10) plates. S Mar 28 (424) £1,000

### Third Voyage Abridged
— A Voyage to the Pacific Ocean. L, 1785-88. 4 vols. 8vo, contemp calf; joints cracked. With port, folding map & 49 plates. Tp in Vol I trimmed at head. b May 30 (148) £550

### Three Voyages
— [Set of Hawkesworth, South Pole & Pacific Ocean]. L, 1773-77-84. 1st Eds. 10 vols. 4to & folio, various contemp calf or half calf or mor bdgs. cb Oct 17 (183) $19,000
Anr copy. 11 vols. 4to (8 vols) & folio (3 vols), lev gilt in Robert Adam Style by Aquarius of London. 1st Voyage with plates in Atlas format & is early issue without chart of Strait of Magellan & directions to the binder; 35 of the plates are without folds, some with deckle edges. 2d Voyage with plates bound apart & in Atlas format, with 58 of them without folds, some with deckle edges. Atlas to 3d Voyage with

plates 11, 12, 26 & 59 torn & repaired & some old staining. Hefner copy. CNY May 17 (9) $56,000
Anr copy. 9 vols. 4to & folio, contemp calf; rebacked in modern calf, Atlas in modern half calf. pba Feb 13 (45) $18,000
2d Ed of 1st Voyage; 4th Ed of 2d Voyage; 2d Ed of 3d Voyage. L, 1773-84-85. 9 vols. 4to & folio, text vols in half calf; Atlas in modern half calf. C Oct 25 (107) £6,000
— The Three Voyages.... L, 1821. 7 vols. 8vo, contemp calf gilt; some covers loose. Folding map torn with loss; later annotations. S Mar 28 (419) £150
ANDERSON, GEORGE WILLIAM. - A Collection of Voyages round the World. L, 1790. 6 vols. 8vo, contemp calf; re-backed. With 25 folding maps & 180 plates. Some duplicates; some repairs & browning. Sold w.a.f. S Oct 26 (449) £600 [Ostby]

**Cook, James H.**
— Fifty Years on the Old Frontier as Cowboy, Hunter.... New Haven, 1923. pba June 25 (59) $75

**Cook, Col. John**
— Observations on Fox-Hunting.... L, 1826. 8vo, orig bds. With 3 plates. some foxing & soiling. O Jan 9 (71) $160
Anr copy. Contemp calf; rubbed. Some foxing & soiling. O Jan 9 (72) $80

**Cook, Samuel**
— The Jenolan Caves. L, 1889. 8vo, orig cloth; backstrip def. sg Mar 7 (15) $50

**Cook, Sir Theodore Andrea, 1867-1928**
— Old Touraine. L, 1898. 3d Ed. 8vo, half calf gilt; scuffed. F Mar 28 (433) $80

**Cooke, Edward William, 1811-80**
— Fifty Plates of Shipping and Craft. L, 1829. 4to, contemp mor; rubbed. With title, vignette, & 63 plates. 2 plates loose, foxed. S Oct 26 (319) £420 [Hearn]
— Sixty Five Plates of Shipping and Craft. L, 1829. 4to, contemp half mor; rubbed. With title, vignette, & 63 plates. Title torn, some marginal spotting. S Oct 26 (320) £420 [Hearn]

**Cooke, Edward William, 1811-80 —& Rennie, George, 1791-1866**
— Views of the Old and New London Bridges. L, 1833. Folio, contemp half mor. With 12 plates, most in india-proof state. Marginal tears & waterstains. b Sept 20 (305) £200

**Cooke, George, 1781-1834.** See: Cooke & Cooke

**Cooke, John, 1738-1823 —& Maule, John**
— An Historical Account of the Royal Hospital for Seamen at Greenwich. L, [1789]. 4to, contemp calf; spine ends worn. With 4 plates, including double-page folding frontis. sg May 16 (395) $200
Anr Ed. Greenwich: sold only at the Hospital, 1803. 8vo, disbound. Tp soiled. sg May 16 (396) $80

**Cooke, John Estes.** See: Baum, L. Frank

**Cooke, Philip St. George, 1809-95**
— Report from the Secretary of War Communicating...Official Journal of Cooke, from Santa Fe to San Diego.... [Wash., 1849]. 8vo, modern cloth. wa Feb 29 (572) $160

**Cooke, William Bernard, 1788-1855 —& Cooke, George, 1781-1834**
— Views on the Thames. L, 1822. Atlas vol only. Folio, contemp half mor; extremities rubbed. With 75 plates only. b Jan 31 (315) £280

**Cookson, C.**
— Glastonbury Abbey; a Poem. Taunton, 1828. 12mo, orig bds; backstrip def. b Dec 5 (327) £70

**Coolidge, Calvin, 1872-1933**
— Autobiography. NY, 1929. 1st Ed, one of 1,000 L.p. copies. NH July 21 (106) $160

**Coomaraswamy, Ananda Kentish, 1877-1947.** See: Nivedita & Coomaraswamy

**Cooney, Loraine M.**
— Garden History of Georgia, 1733-1933. Atlanta: Peachtree Garden Club, 1933. One of 1,500. 4to, cloth; worn & soiled, cracked after title. Library markings. wa Dec 14 (465) $85

**Cooper, Abraham**
— Impressions of a Series of Animals, Birds.... L, 1821. 8vo, contemp half calf; rubbed. With engraved title & 16 mtd india-proof plates. O Jan 9 (73) $200

**Cooper, Charles Henry**
— Memorials of Cambridge. Cambr., 1860. 4to, contemp half mor; rubbed, joints cracked, 1 cover detached. Some soiling. bba Nov 1 (17) £400 [Barford]

**Cooper, Douglas**
— Les Dejeuners. Paris: Cercle d'Art, [1962]. Illus by Pablo Picasso. Folio, pictorial cloth. sg Jan 11 (343) $60
— Picasso theatre. Paris, 1967. One of 100. 8vo, orig cloth. wad Oct 18 (349) C$1,700
— Picasso Theatre. NY, [1968]. 4to, cloth. sg Jan 11 (344) $100

**Cooper, James Fenimore, 1789-1851**
See also: Limited Editions Club
— The Deerslayer. Phila., 1841. 2 vols. 12mo, orig cloth. sg Sept 21 (138) $1,100
— The Headsman: or, the Abbaye des Vignerons. L, 1833. 1st Ed. 3 vols. 12mo, orig bds; rebacked, lacking front free endpaper in Vol I. Z June 28 (65) $200
— Homeward Bound. L, 1838. 1st Ed. 3 vols. 12mo, orig half cloth. sg Apr 18 (44) $700
— The Last of the Mohicans. Phila., 1826. 1st Ed. 2 vols. 12mo, modern half mor. Some browning & foxing; last leaf of Vol II creased; tp with short tear to top. pba Mar 7 (65) $1,200
— Lionel Lincoln, or the Leaguer of Boston. Paris, 1825. 3 vols. 12mo, orig wraps; backstrips chipped,

Vol I front cover partly detached. Some foxing. sg Apr 18 (42) $200
— The Monikins. Phila., 1835. 1st American Ed. 2 vols. 12mo, orig half cloth. Some foxing. sg Apr 18 (43) $800
— Notions of the Americans. L, 1828. 1st English Ed. 2 vols. 8vo, orig bds; worn. sg Oct 26 (80) $175
— Pages and Pictures from the Writings of James Fenimore Cooper. NY, 1865. Notes by Susan Fenimore Cooper. 4to, mor gilt; rubbed, some discoloration. pba June 20 (102) $85
— The Prairie. Paris, 1827. 3 vols. 12mo, contemp calf. Foxed. sg Sept 21 (139) $750
— The Spy. Paris, 1825. 3 vols. 12mo, contemp mor gilt with arms of Wilhelm, Duke of Braunschweig. Lacking half-titles. sg Oct 19 (61) $2,200
— Works. NY, 1861. 30 vols. Cloth; minor wear. sg Sept 21 (11) $300

**Cooper, Susan**
— The Dark is Rising. NY, 1973. 1st American Ed. In dj. pba May 23 (82) $190
— Greenwitch. NY, 1974. In dj. pba May 23 (83) $130
— Over Sea, Under Stone. L, [1965]. In dj with spine ends rubbed. pba May 23 (81) $850

**Cooper, Thomas, 1759-1840**
— Some Information Concerning Gas Lights. Phila., 1816. 8vo, modern lea; worn. Some stains & browning. O Nov 14 (50) $400

**Cooper, William, Judge**
— The History of North America. Albany, 1815. 8vo, contemp sheep; rubbed. Some soiling. pba Apr 25 (172) $55

**Coote, William**
— The Western Pacific.... L, 1883. 8vo, pictorial cloth, unopened. sg Mar 7 (51) $90

**Copernicus, Nicolaus**
— De revolutionibus orbium coelestium. Basel: Henricpetrina, 1566. 2d Ed. Folio, modern vellum; spotted. Foxed throughout; marginal dampstaining at ends; minor worming; old scored writing on tp. sg Apr 18 (45) $16,000

**Copia...**
— Copia de una letters venuta dal campo d'Africa che narra dal principio infino ala uenuta di Dragut & sur rotta. [Rome: A. Blado, 1550]. 8vo, calf gilt by Bedford; rubbed. Woodcut on tp depicting part of coastline of North Africa with cities; large woodcut arms of Charles V on verso. C June 26 (65) £1,600

**Copleston, John Gaius**
— Lynmouth, or Sketches and Musings in North Devon, by a Sojourner. Awlescombe, 1835. 8vo, half mor. b Dec 5 (79) £140

**Copp, Johann.** See: Kopp, Johann

**Coppard, Alfred Edgar, 1878-1957.** See: Golden Cockerel Press

**Coppier, Andre Charles**
— Les Eaux-fortes authentiques de Rembrandt. Paris, [1929]. 2 vols. 4to, wraps; joints torn. sg Jan 11 (375) $130

**Copway, George, 1818-63**
— The Life, History and Travels of Kah-Ge-Ga-Gah-Bowh. Phila., 1847. 8vo, orig cloth; spine ends worn, front joint cracked. Some foxing. Inscr to Sterling Thomas, 30 Nov 1847. cb Feb 14 (2582) $425

**Coqueley de Chaussepierre, Charles Georges, 1676-1754**
— Le Roue vertueux.... Lauzanne [but Paris], 1770. 2 parts in 1 vol. 8vo, contemp calf; recased, 2 wormholes in spine heel. Short tear in upper margin of A6 in 2d part; repair in outer margin of half-title. With orig drawing loosely inserted. Fuerstenberg - Schaefer copy. S Dec 7 (138) £550

**Coquiot, Gustave, 1865-1926**
— En Suivant la Seine. Paris, 1926. One of 235. 4to, half mor gilt with art deco patterns by Paul Bonet [not in Carnets], orig wraps bound in. With 8 double-page & 33 full-page illusts. S Nov 21 (93) £3,200

**Coral, Lenore.** See: Munby & Coral

**Corancez, Louis Alexandre Olivier de, 1770-1832**
— Histoire des Wababis.... Paris, 1810. 8vo, orig bds; spine worn. Library stamp on tp verso; minor worming at inner margins; some spotting. S June 27 (138) £950

**Corbett, Col. Edward**
— An Old Coachman's Chatter. With some Practical Remarks on Driving.... L, 1891. 8vo, half mor by Riviere, orig covers & spine bound in. With 8 plates. Some dampstaining, affecting plates. O Jan 9 (74) $130

**Corbett, Sir Julian**
— Naval Operations: History of the Great War Based on Official Documents. L, 1920-31. 5 vols in 9 including 4 separate map cases. 8vo, orig cloth; rubbed & soiled. With maps throughout, including 111 loose in cases or pockets. Library markings. pn Dec 7 (128) £440

**Cordier, Henri, 1849-1925**
— Bibliotheca Indosinica. NY: Burt Franklin, [1967]. 6 vols in 4. 4to, cloth; some wear. O May 7 (95) $130

**Cordiner, James**
— A Description of Ceylon. L, 1807. 2 vols. 4to, contemp calf. With 25 maps & plates. bba Nov 16 (289) £750 [Waggett]

**Cordoba, Antonio de**
— Relacion del ultimo viage al Estrecho de Magallanes.... Madrid, 1788. 2 vols in 1, including Appendix. 4to, contemp sheep gilt; rubbed, corners worn.

# CORDUS

With port, 4 folding maps & 4 folding tables. Some staining & browning. CE May 22 (113) $480

**Cordus, Valerius, 1515-44**
— Il Dispensario di Vaerio Cordo. Venice: Pietro Dosello, 1558. 12mo, old bds; spine def. Some headlines shaved; dampstained. S Mar 28 (480) £90

**Corelli, Arcangelo, 1653-1713**
— Parte prima sonate a violino e violone o cimbalo... opera quinta. Rome, [1700]. 1st Ed, 2d Issue. 2 parts in 1 vol. Oblong folio, contemp vellum; soiled. Engraved throughout; frontis bound before title. Some staining, mainly in margins; Ms musical additions to p. 61. S Dec 1 (133) £700

**Corinth, Lovis, 1858-1925**
See also: Schwarz, Karl
— Das Leben Walter Leistikows. Berlin, 1910. 4to, orig bds. sg Feb 15 (187) $175
— Die Liebschaften des Zeus. [N.p.]: Fritz Gurlitt, 1920. One of 100. Folio, loose as issued in orig portfolio. With 8 colored lithos, mtd. S May 16 (37) £1,200

**Corle, Edwin, 1906-56**
— Burro Alley. NY, [1938]. In dj. Inscr & with Ls. pba Aug 22 (94) $140
— Death Valley and the Creek Called Furnace. Los Angeles: Ward Ritchie Press, [1962]. Illus by Ansel Adams. In dj. pba Feb 12 (43) $140; pba Aug 22 (881) $90

**Corlieu, Francois de**
— Briefve instruction pour tous estats. Paris: Philippe Danfrie & Richard Breton, 1558. 4to, mor by Chambolle-Duru. S June 27 (381) £1,350

**Corneille, Pierre, 1606-84**
— Le Theatre.... [Geneva], 1764. 12 vols. 8vo, contemp calf gilt; some spine ends with tears. With frontis & 34 plates. Fuerstenberg - Schaefer copy. S Dec 7 (140) £650

**Corneille, Thomas, 1625-1709**
— Oeuvres. Paris, 1665. 5 vols. 12mo, mor gilt by Trautz-Bauzonnet. Hoe copy. b Dec 5 (12) £220

**Cornelius, Brother (Herman Emanuel Braeg)**
— Keith: Old Master of California. NY, [1942]-56. 2 vols. In djs. Inscr to Elinor B. Nichols. pba July 25 (305) $180
 Anr copy. In djs. Sgd in Vol I. sg Jan 11 (238) $175

**Cornelius, Charles Over**
— Furniture Masterpieces of Duncan Phyfe. NY, 1922. One of 150. Bds; worn. rce Nov 18 (748A) $50

**Cornelius Nepos**
— Vitae imperatorum. Venice: Bernardinus Venetus de Vitalibus, [c.1498-1500]. 4to, modern vellum. 29 lines & headline; type 3:111R. Wormhole at inner margin affecting a few letters. 50 leaves. Goff C-918. C Apr 3 (74) £420

**Cornet, Severin**
— Cantiones musicae 5, 6, 7 & 8 vocum * Madrigali... * Chansons Francoyses.... Amst.: Christopher Plantin, 1581. Parts for Tenor & Bass only (of 6), each 3 vols in 1. Together, 2 vols. 4to, contemp vellum. S Dec 1 (134) £5,600

**Corney, Peter**
— Voyages in the Northern Pacific.... Honolulu, 1896. 8vo, orig wraps; worn & soiled. A few leaves dog-eared. pba Feb 13 (53) $375

**Cornhill Magazine**
— The Cornhill Magazine. L, 1874-76. Vols 29-34. 6 vols in 3. 8vo, half calf; rubbed. Contains Thomas Hardy's Far from the Madding Crowd & The Hand of Ethelberta. Z June 28 (107) $450

**Cornwallis, Charles Cornwallis, 1st Marquis, 1738-1805**
[-] As Great a Man as Nelson.... L, [n.d.]. 12mo, modern cloth. sg Oct 26 (81) $275

**Coronelli, Vincenzo Maria, 1650-1718**
— Epitome cosmografica. Venice, 1693. 8vo, contemp calf; joints cracked. With frontis & 32 (of 37) mostly double-page plates, 1 having 6 volvelles. Lacking 3 celestial charts & 2 double-page plates; Western Hemisphere repaired with loss; some worming at top affecting a few plates; some discoloration. S June 27 (72) £2,000
— An Historical and Geographical Account of the Morea.... L, 1687. 12mo, contemp calf; worn, covers pitted, spine worn. With 41 folding plates. Marginal dampstains throughout; marginal pencil notes; 2 plates with long repaired tears. cb Oct 17 (184) $1,300
— Memoires, historiques et geographiques du royaume de la Moree.... Amst., 1686. 8vo, contemp calf; worn. With 41 double-page maps & plates. Some shaving. b May 30 (257) £600

**Corpus...**
— Corpus codicum Americanorum medii aevi. Copenhagen, 1942-52. Ed by Ernst Mengin. 4 vols in 6. Folio, half vellum. ds July 27 (59) $550

**Corraro, Angelo**
— Rome Exactly Describ'd.... L, 1668. 8vo, contemp sheep; worn, needs rebacking. Old stamp on tp; some worming in lower outer corners; lacking initial blank or license leaf. sg Mar 7 (52) $100

**Correll, J. Lee**
— Through White Men's Eyes: A Contribution to Navajo History.... Window Rock: Navajo Heritage Center, 1979. Oblong 4to, cloth; joint ends rubbed. pba Apr 25 (550) $200

**Correspondance...**
— Correspondance litteraire, philosophique, et critique par Grimm, Diderot, Raynal, Meister.... Nendeln: Kraus Reprint, 1968. 16 vols. Facsimile of 1877-82 Ed. P Dec 12 (64) $700

**Correspondence...**
— Correspondence on the Subject of Removal of Inhabitants of Pitcairn's Island to Norfolk Island. L, 1857. 3 parts in 1 vol. 4to, contemp half calf. b Mar 20 (166) £170

**Corrette, Michel**
— Le Maitre de clavecin.... Paris, 1753. 4to, modern half calf. Engraved throughout. A few marks at beginning & end. S Dec 1 (135) £1,000

**Corrigan, Sir Dominic John**
— Lectures on the Nature and Treatment of Fever. Dublin, 1853. 8vo, contemp half calf; extremities rubbed. Old stamp on tp. sg May 16 (397) $130

**Corrigan, Douglas ("Wrong Way")**
— That's My Story. NY, 1938. 1st Ed. In chipped dj. Inscr. sg May 16 (23) $50

**Corsettus, Antonius**
— Tractatus de re militari & duello. Lyon: Benedictus Bonnyn, 8 Sept 1543. 4to, old vellum. With title & printer's device Some margins repaired; some discoloration. S Oct 26 (321) £550 [Zioni]

**Corsini, Bartolommeo, d.1675**
— Il Torracchione desolato.... Londra [Paris], [1768]. 2 vols. 12mo, contemp red mor gilt. With 2 engraved titles, port & folding table in Vol II. Fuerstenberg - Schaefer copy. S Dec 7 (141) £300

**Corte, Claudio**
— Il Cavallerizzo nel qual si tratta della natura de cavalli.... Venice: Ziletti, 1573. 4to, contemp vellum; front hinge cracked. Lacking 4 leaves. sg Mar 7 (413) $225

**Cortes, Hernando, 1485-1547**
— La Preclara Narratione di Ferdinando Cortese della Nuova Hispagna del Mare Oceano.... Venice, 1524. 1st Ed in Italian. 4to, contemp vellum; frayed. Lacking R6 with ptr's device & the folding plan of Mexico. C Apr 3 (76) £1,600

**Cortesao, Armando**
— History of Portuguese Cartography. Coimbra, 1969-71. 2 vols. 4to, cloth. sg May 9 (9) $350
— The Nautical Chart of 1424 and the Early Discovery and Cartographical Representation of America. Coimbra: University Press, 1954. Ltd Ed. Folio, orig lea over cloth. ds July 27 (47) $425

**Cortesao, Armando —&**
**Teixeira da Mota, Avelino**
— Portugaliae monumenta cartographica. Lisbon, 1960-[62]. 5 folio vols plus 4to Index vol. Orig vellum gilt. CE June 12 (182) $900

**Cortese, Ferdinando.** See: Cortes, Hernando

**Cortissoz, Royal**
— Monograph of the Work of Charles A. Platt. NY, 1913 [but 1919]. Folio, cloth; rubbed, spine ends

worn, some soiling, shaken. Tp foxed; some marginal dampstains. wa Dec 14 (388) $160

**Corvisart des Marets, Jean Nicolas, Baron, 1755-1821**
— An Essay on the Organic Diseases, and Lesions of the Heart and Great Vessels. Phila., 1812. Trans by Jacob Gates. 8vo, contemp tree calf; rebacked, extrems rubbed. Title browned; browned & spotted throughout. Ck Mar 22 (82) £140

**Coryate, Thomas, 1577?-1617**
— Coryats Crudities.... L, 1611. 1st Ed. 2 parts in 1 vol. 4to, mor gilt by Bedford; partly misbound, extremities worn; joints dry & starting; bookplate removed from upper pastedown. With engraved title & 6 engravings, including 2 in text; full-page woodcut of Prince of Wales feathers inserted as issued. Marginal corrections, doodles on the verso of last leaf; engraved title repaired; folding plate of vessel repaired; Strasbourg clock plate trimmed at head & tail; some repairs. STC 5808. P June 5 (205) $3,000

**Cosentino, Frank J.**
— Edward Marshall Boehm, 1913-1969. Chicago, 1970. Folio, syn gilt with imitation ceramic crest on front cover. sg June 13 (86) $90

**Costaguti, Giovanni Battista**
— Architettura della Basilica di S. Pietro in Vaticano. Rome, 1684. Folio, contemp vellum bds. With engraved title & 32 plates. Some spotting. S June 27 (278) £1,000

**Costakis Collection, George**
— Russian Avant-Garde Art. NY, [1981]. Folio, cloth, in dj. sg Sept 7 (303) $150

**Costalius, Petrus.** See: Coustau, Pierre

**Coste, Pascal**
— Architecture Arabe ou monuments du Kaire. Paris, [1837]-39. Folio, half mor; front joint splitting, spine torn & loose, front hinge repaired, also reattaching tp, rear hinge cracked. With half title, 70 litho plates & 29 more detailed litho plates. Lacking Plate 3; plate numbering confused; some edges foxed. cb Oct 17 (185) $4,250
— Monuments modernes de la Perse. Paris, 1867. Plates by Muguet & others. Folio, contemp half mor; joints repaired. With half title, title, & 56 plates (8 color). Fore-corner of some plates waterstained. S Oct 26 (40) £4,200 [Wishiewski]

**Costo, Tomaso**
— Memoriale delle cose piu notabili accadute nel regno di Napoli. Naples, 1639. 2d Ed. 8vo, modern vellum. Spotted; few early leaves repaired. S Oct 26 (272) £260 [Zioni]

**Costume...**
— The Costume of the Russian Empire. L, 1803. Folio, mor; rear free endpaper folded & tape-repaired, front hinge cracked, extremities worn. With 73 hand-colored plates, including title. cb Oct 17 (112) $425

## COSTUME...

Anr copy. Mor gilt. pba Mar 7 (77) $500

Anr copy. Contemp mor gilt. S June 13 (630) £550

Anr Ed. L, 1804 [some plates watermarked 1823]. Folio, modern half mor gilt. With 73 colored plates. sg Dec 7 (258) $400

Anr Ed. L, 1810. Folio, contemp mor; worn, cover & 1st gathering loose. With engraved colored title & 71 colored plates. Minor marginal staining to some plates; Plate 22 with marginal tear repaired. CE June 12 (141) $900

— Costume of the Russian Empire. L, 1810. Folio, contemp half calf; rebacked, rubbed. With hand-colored additional title & 72 plates. Text in English & French. Some offsetting. S Oct 26 (567) £500 [Dennistoun]

— The Costume of the Russian Empire. L, 1811. Folio, disbound. With engraved title & 72 colored plates. Lacking text to Plate 14; 1 leaf tape-repaired; some foxing & browning. wa Feb 29 (98) $220

— The Costume of Yorkshire. L, 1814. Folio, contemp mor; worn. With 40 colored plates. Frontis lacking; some soiling & foxing. F June 20 (838) $975

### Costumes...

— Costumes of British Ladies from the Time of William 1st to the Reign of Queen Victoria.... L, 1843. Folio, contemp mor gilt; rubbed. With 48 mtd hand-colored litho plates. Minor foxing to text. With hand-colored Ms title. F June 20 (836) $425

### Costumi...

— Costumi religiosi adobbamenti delle cappelle e palazzi pontifici. Rome: Presso il Deposito di Stampe, [c.1830]. 4to, half lea; rubbed, recornered. With 2 hand-colored titles & 83 hand-colored plates. Piece cut from margin of tp; marginal foxing. K June 23 (236) $900

### Cottafavi, Gaetano

— Raccolta delle principali vedute di Rome e suoi contorni. L, [1843]. Oblong folio, half lea. With engraved title & 53 plates. sg Sept 7 (300) $600

### Cottin, Marie, called Sophie

— Malvina. Par Madame ***, Auteur de Claire d'Albe. Paris, 1800. 4 vols. 12mo, contemp wraps; some wear. With 4 frontises. Minor soiling & foxing. O Mar 5 (53) $70

### Cotton, Arthur Disbrowe. See: Grove & Cotton

### Cotton, Charles, 1630-87

See also: Limited Editions Club; Nonesuch Press; Walton & Cotton

— The Genuine Works. Dublin, 1770. ("The Genuine Poetical Works.") Contemp calf; rebacked in modern calf, corners worn, hinges reinforced. Wreden copy. pba June 20 (104) $85

### Cotton, Henry

— Golf: Being a short treatise.... L: Eyre & Spottiswoode, 1931. 1st Ed. - Foreword by Bernard Darwin. Cloth. pba Apr 18 (27) $120

— Hints on Play with Steel Shafts. Liverpool, [c.1893]. 1st Ed. Wraps; soiling, lower front wrap scraped. Center signature detached. pba Nov 9 (8) $80

### Cotton, John, d.1850

— The (Resident) Song Birds of Great Britain. L, 1836. ("The Song Birds of Great Britain.") 2 parts in 1 vol. 8vo, contemp mor gilt. With 33 hand-colored plates. Fattorini copy. C Oct 25 (8) £1,200

### Cotton, Sir Robert Bruce, 1571-1631

— Cottoni Posthuma: Divers Choice Pieces.... L, 1651. 1st Ed. 2 parts in 1 vol. 8vo, calf; front cover almost detached. pba June 20 (105) $75

### Couch, Jonathan, 1789-1870

— A History of the Fishes of the British Islands. L, 1864-65. 4 vols. 8vo, orig cloth; Vol IV spine chipped at foot. With 252 colored plates. ALs tipped in. S Apr 23 (306) £460

Anr Ed. L, 1868-69. 4 vols. 8vo, orig cloth; vol IV spine head chipped. With 252 color plates. Soiled; 1 plate loose & soiled. S Oct 27 (630) £400 [Mondo Sas]

### Coughlin, Jack

— Impressions of Bohemia. Carmel: Pacific Rim Galleries, 1986. One of 125. 4to, loose in wraps with text pamphlet in box. With 12 sgd etchings. pba June 20 (106) $150

### Coulter, Edith M. —& Van Nostrand, Jeanne

— A Camera in the Gold Rush. San Francisco: Book Club of California, 1946. One of 600. Together, 13 folders. Half mor. pba Feb 12 (516) $70

### Couplet, Philippe

— Kien kia sin tcheng. Catalogus patrum Societatis Jesu qui ab anno 1581 usque ad 1681 in Sina Jesu Christi fidem propagarunt ubi singulorum nomina, patria, praedicatio, mors, sepultura libri sine editi recensentur. Peking, [n.d.]. Folio, modern fabric, orig wraps bound in. Ptd xylographically in Chinese on 1 side of folded leaves, with ptd Chinese title pasted to front wrap with Latin title. S June 27 (224) £2,000

### Courieres, Edouard des

— Van Dongen. Paris, 1925. 4to, contemp half mor gilt by Trinckvel, Viau & Zona, orig wraps bound in. sg Sept 7 (129) $175

### Courmacel, Victor. See: Fore-Edge Paintings

### Courtauld, Samuel Augustine —& Jones, Edward Alfred

— Some Silver Wrought by the Courtauld Family of London Goldsmiths in the Eighteenth Century. Oxford: Shakespeare Head Press, 1940. 1st Ed, one of 100. Folio, orig vellum. With port & 64 plates. W Nov 8 (78) £700

**Coustau, Pierre**
— Pegma. Lyons: Matthiam Bonhomme, 1555. 8vo, 19th-cent mor gilt by Chambolle-Duru; rubbed. With 95 woodcuts within woodcut architectural borders. Schaefer copy. P Nov 1 (70) $3,400
— Le pegme. Lyons: Matthiam Bonhomme, 1560. 8vo, 16th-cent calf; rebacked, rubbed, new rear endpapers. Underlinings & annotations in text in red; tp stained & frayed at fore-edge; tape-mark at inner edge; repaired hole on lower corner of E2; some dampstaining. S June 12 (35) £240

**Coustos, John**
[-] The Sufferings of John Coustos for Free-Masonry...in the Inquisition at Lisbon. Dublin, 1746. 8vo, bound with an unidentified work in an unidentified bdg. With port & 3 folding plates. soiled. b Sept 20 (54) £85

**Couts, Cave Johnson**
— Hepah, California! The Journal of Cave Johnson Couts.... [Tucson], 1961. One of 750. Ed by Henry F. Dobyns. Orig cloth. With frontis port, 4 illus plates, & 9 maps (1 folding). Larson copy. pba Sept 28 (389) $65

**Covarrubias, Miguel**
— The Eagle, the Jaguar, and the Serpent.... NY, 1954. 4to, cloth. pba Nov 16 (67) $75
— Indian Art of Mexico and Central America. NY: Knopf, 1957. Illus by Covarrubias. Inscr. sg Sept 7 (118) $225
— Negro Drawings. NY, 1927. In dj. With frontis & 56 plates. sg Mar 28 (34) $950
— The Prince of Wales and other Famous Americans. NY, 1925. 8vo, half cloth. sg Sept 14 (93) $175; sg Feb 15 (76) $140

**Coventry, Francis, d.1759?.** See: Golden Cockerel Press

**Cowan, Robert Ernest**
— A Bibliography of the History of California and the Pacific West 1510-1906. Columbus, 1952. 4to, cloth. pba Feb 13 (54) $90

**Cowan, Robert Ernest —&**
**Cowan, Robert G.**
— A Bibliography of the History of California, 1510-1930. San Francisco, 1933. 1st Ed. 3 vols. 4to, half cloth; spines soiled, corners rubbed. cb Oct 17 (151) $300
Anr Ed. San Francisco, 1964. 4 vols in 1. 4to, cloth. ds July 27 (61) $150

**Cowan, Robert G.** See: Cowan & Cowan

**Cowen, Nell Barrow.** See: Parker & Cowen

**Cowley, Arthur Ernest, 1861-1931**
— A Concise Catalog of Hebrew Printed Books in the Bodleian Library. Oxford, 1929. 8vo, orig cloth; worn. sg Apr 11 (172) $200

**Cowley, Malcolm.** See: Limited Editions Club

**Cowling, George H.** See: Tolkien's copy, John Ronald Reuel

**Cowper, Lancelot**
— A Collection of Poems, on Various Subjects. Bishop Auckland, 1819. 12mo, orig wraps; def. Some tears with loss. b Dec 5 (100) £55

**Cowper, William, 1666-1709**
See also: Fore-Edge Paintings
— Anatomia corporum humanorumcentum et quatordecim tabulis.... Leiden, 1739. Folio, contemp calf; worn, covers detached. With 2 titles & 114 plates. 1st title detached & frayed; 2d title soiled; plate 23 torn 7 repaired; plate 58 torn; plate 56 stained; several small tears; soiled & spotted; several leaves detached at end. Sold w.a.f. S Oct 27 (802) £1,400 [Antiquarian]

**Cowper, William, 1731-1800.** See: Fore-Edge Paintings

**Cox, Charles E., Jr.** See: Derrydale Press

**Cox, David, 1783-1859**
— A Treatise on Landscape Painting.... L, 1813-14 [plates watermarked 1818]. 2d Issue. Oblong folio, contemp half mor gilt; extremities rubbed, lacking 1 cornerpiece, front inner hinge split. With 24 etched plates, 16 aquatint plates & 16 hand-colored aquatint plates. Marginal repairs to 2 plates; etched plates spotted. C May 31 (86) £550

**Cox, Edward Godfrey**
— A Reference Guide to the Literature of Travel. [Cambr.: Martino, n.d.]. One of 350. 3 vols. 8vo, orig cloth. sg Apr 11 (87A) $150
Anr Ed. Seattle, 1935-49. Vols I-III. 4to, cloth; rebound. O May 7 (97) $100

**Cox, Isaac**
— The Annals of Trinity County. Oakland, Calif.: John Henry Nash, 1940. One of 350. Half cloth. Inscr by Harold C. Holmes. pba Feb 12 (486) $70

**Cox, Jacob D.**
— The Battle of Franklin, Tennessee, November 30, 1864.... NY, 1897. Orig bdg; rubbed. With 4 maps, 2 folding. Inscr by Ellison Capers. K June 23 (187) $350

**Cox, Nicholas —&**
**Blome, Richard, d.1705**
— The Gentlemans Recreation. L, 1686. 2 parts in 1 vol. Folio, modern calf gilt by Sangorski & Sutcliffe. Engraved title browned; lacking 2 plates; some shaving; 1 plate dampstained, anr with closed tears. Wing B-3213. Ck Feb 14 (312) £2,200
Anr copy. Contemp calf; rebacked, worn. With frontis & 86 plates. Some soiling; few tears; slight worming in lower margins. S Oct 27 (713) £2,700 [Squire]
Anr Ed. L [Oxford], 1686. 2 parts in 1 vol. Folio, old calf; rebacked, worn. Most of p.91-92 torn away; some soiling & staining. Sold w.a.f. Wing C-6704. O Feb 6 (51) $225

**Cox, Palmer, 1840-1924**
— Another Brownie Book. NY: Century, [1890]. 8vo, chromolitho bds. Sgd card mtd to front free endpaper, with small orig drawing by him of a Brownie. pba Jan 4 (22) $300

**Cox, Ross, 1793-1853**
— Adventures on the Columbia River.... L, 1831. 1st Ed. 2 vols. 8vo, modern half mor. Some foxing. Robbins copy. pba Mar 21 (71) $1,100

**Cox, Samuel S.**
— Miscegention or Amalgamation. Wash., 1864. 8vo, self-wraps, unopened; dusty & creased at edges. sg Mar 28 (35) $90

**Cox, Sidney**
— Robert Frost, Original "Ordinary Man." NY, 1929. One of 1,000. In chipped dj. Inscr by Frost to James & Hilda Wells, 3 Mar 1929. pba Oct 5 (128) $75

**Coxe, Daniel, 1673-1739**
— A Collection of Voyages and Travels.... Cornhill: Olive Payne, 1741. 8vo, orig bds; worn & bumped. Dampstained & foxed. Met May 22 (335) $4,500

**Coxe, Tench, 1755-1824**
— The Federalist: containing Some Strictures upon a Pamphlet. Phila., 1796. 8vo, modern wraps. sg Oct 26 (82) $60
— A View of the United States of America. L, 1795. 8vo, later half calf; worn & scuffed, joints weak. With 3 folding charts. Some foxing. wa Feb 29 (357) $160

**Coxe, William, 1747-1828**
— Account of the Russian Discoveries Between Asia and America. L, 1780. 1st Ed. 4to, modern half calf. Some foxing. pba Feb 13 (55) $1,400
3d Ed. L, 1787. 8vo, contemp calf; rebacked with modern calf. With 5 maps & plates. Some staining to top margins. pba Feb 13 (56) $450
Anr copy. Contemp bds; rebacked with paper. Fire-damaged. pba Apr 25 (173) $160
4th Ed. L, 1804. L.p. Issue. 4to, contemp russia gilt; rebacked with orig spine strip laid on, extremities worn, top of front cover discolored. With 5 maps & 1 plate. Foxing to plates. pba Feb 13 (57) $1,900
— Travels into Poland, Russia, Sweden, and Denmark. L, 1784-90. 3 vols. 4to, contemp calf; rubbed. With 12 plates & 14 maps & plans, some folding. Some foxing & soiling. O Mar 5 (54) $550
1st Ed. L, 1784. Illus by Thomas Kelly & Tscherchaskoy. 2 vols. 4to, recent half calf. With 12 plates, 13 maps, & 2 illus. Lacking map of Moscow; p.101 in vol. I torn; some maps torn; spotted. S Oct 26 (273) £200 [Waggett]
Anr Ed. L, 1792. 8vo, calf; worn, reattached. With 9 (of 10) plates & 5 folding charts 7 tables. K Oct 1 (116) $250
Anr Ed. L, 1802. 5 vols. 8vo, contemp sheep; worn, 2 hinges cracked, the others weak. With 15 folding maps & plans, 3 folding tables & 13 plates. Folding maps repaired; some foxing. wa Nov 16 (232) $200

**Coy, Owen Cochran**
— Pictorial History of California. Berkeley, [c.1915]. 4to, cloth. pba Apr 25 (355) $130

**Coyne, Joseph Stirling, 1803-68.** See: Willis & Coyne

**Cozzens, Frederic Schiller —& Kelley, James Douglas Jerrold, 1847-1922**
— American Yachts. NY: Scribner's, [1884-85]. Proof copy with each mount sgd by the Cozzens. Text vol & folder, Folio, text disbound, plates in half lea portfolio. With 26 chromolitho plates & 25 reproductive outline plates. Plate 13 remtd; some scuffing; mounts soiled & brittle. P June 5 (207) $19,000

**Cozzens, Samuel Woodworth, 1834-78**
— The Marvellous Country. Bost., [1874]. 8vo, orig cloth; worn, possibly recased. With map & 27 plates. pba Nov 16 (70) $275
Anr Ed. Bost., [1876]. Orig cloth. With 27 plates. Robbins copy. pba Mar 21 (72) $110

**Craddock, Harry**
— The Savoy Cocktail Book. NY, 1930. Half cloth; rubbed, rear hinge cracked. pba Jan 4 (185) $100

**Crahl, Regina**
— Chinese Ceramics in the Topkapi Saray Museum, Istanbul. L, 1986. One of 1,500. 3 vols. Folio, orig cloth, in djs. bba Oct 19 (201) £180 [Kelly]

**Craig, Edward Gordon, 1872-1966**
— Paris Diary, 1932-1933. North Hills: Bird & Bull Press, 1982. One of 350. Orig half mor. sg Sept 14 (61) $80; sg Feb 15 (45) $140

**Craig, William**
— The Complete Instructor in Drawing. L, 1806. Bound with: The Complete Instructor in Drawing Figures. 2 vols in 1. Folio, contemp half calf; rubbed. With 2 pictorial titles, & 72 plates. Some spotting & waterstaining. S Oct 27 (842) £420 [Barker]

**Craigie, Sir William**
— Scandinavian Folk-Lore. Illustrations of the Traditional Beliefs. L, 1896. 8vo, mor extra by Ethel Taunton, 1902. b Sept 20 (610) £170

**Craik, George Lillie, 1798-1866 —& MacFarlane, Charles, 1799-1858**
— The Pictorial History of England. L, 1841. 6 vols. Mor gilt. pba Aug 8 (272) $275

**Crais, Robert**
— Sunset Express. Huntington Beach: James Cahill, 1996. One of 200. pba Aug 22 (95) $70

**Cramer, Johann Andreas, 1710-77**
— Angfansgrunde der propierkunst...aus dem Lateinischen ins Deutsche uebersetzt.... Stockholm, 1746. 8vo, contemp calf. With 6 folding plates. S Mar 14 (88) £550

### Cranach Press—Weimar
SHAKESPEARE, WILLIAM. - Hamlet. 1928. One of 230. sg Apr 18 (131) $2,600
Anr Ed. 1930. Out-of-series copy for Wilma, Marquise de Brion, bound in red mor. P Dec 12 (54) $6,000
VERGILIUS MARO, PUBLIUS. - The Eclogues. 1927. One of 225 on papier de chanvre. Illus by Aristide Maillol; trans by J. J. Mason. cb Oct 17 (653) $2,500
Anr copy. Orig half cloth, unopened. sg Oct 19 (62) $3,600
Anr copy. Unopened copy with library markings. sg Feb 15 (79) $900

### Crandall, Marjorie Lyle
— Confederate Imprints: A Check List Based Principally on the Collection of the Boston Athenaeum. Bost., 1955. 1st Ed. 2 vols. O Dec 5 (37) $130

### Crane, Hart, 1899-1932
See also: Limited Editions Club
— The Bridge. Paris: Black Sun Press, 1930. 1st Ed, One of 200 on Holland. 4to, orig wraps; some discoloration. S June 28 (29) £1,400
One of 50 on japan vellum. Engelhard copy. CNY Oct 27 (23) $4,000

### Crane, Joan
— Willa Cather: A Bibliography. Lincoln: University of Nebraska Press, [1982]. In dj. pba Oct 5 (64) $70

### Crane, John
— An Address to the Bachelors by a Bird of Bromsgrove. Birm., [c.1799]. Single sheet folder to 24mo, orig wraps. Small tear. b Dec 5 (17) £120

### Crane, Leo
— California Golf Directory. Fresno, 1953. 1st Ed. Wraps. pba Apr 18 (29) $50

### Crane, Stephen, 1871-1900
See also: Grabhorn Printing; Limited Editions Club
— Active Service. NY, [1899]. 1st Ed. 8vo, orig cloth; stamp to front pastedown, front hinge reinforced, spine ends rubbed. pba Dec 14 (31) $55
— The Black Riders and Other Lines. Bost., 1895. 1st Ed, one of 50 on Japan vellum. 12mo, orig bds, unopened; dust-soiled. Fletcher - Engelhard copy. CNY Oct 27 (25) $1,500
— Maggie, a Girl of the Streets. [NY, 1893]. 1st Ed. 8vo, orig wraps; some fraying, chip gone from top of spine. Dampstain at upper left corner of front cover & c.25 leaves. Engelhard copy. CNY Oct 27 (24) $6,000
— The Monster & Other Stories. NY, 1899. 1st Ed. 8vo, orig cloth. sg Feb 8 (260) $120
— The Open Boat.... NY, 1898. 16mo, orig cloth. sg Feb 8 (261) $250
— The Red Badge of Courage. NY, 1895. 1st Ed, 1st Issue. 8vo, orig cloth; some wear, head of spine frayed, small stains to lower cover. Small stain at top margin of tp & 1st few leaves; spot of adhesion to 2 leaves; adleaves with short tears. bbc Apr 22 (82) $450

Anr copy. Orig cloth, in dj with small split repaired. Engelhard copy. CNY Oct 27 (26) $4,000
— The Third Violet. NY, 1897. 1st Ed. 12mo, orig cloth, in dj. sg Feb 8 (264) $375
— War is Kind. NY, 1899. 1st Ed. 8vo, orig bds; spine soiled. S Nov 2 (78) £340 [National Gallery of Australia]
Anr copy. Orig bds; spine ends worn, browning to backstrip. sg Feb 8 (265) $325
— Wounds in the Rain.... NY, [1900]. 2d Ed. 8vo, cloth. Extra-illus with c.65 photographs, notes, & 4 mtd clipped signatures of Fitzhugh Lee, Wm. R. Schaftner, Nelson Miles & Russell Alger. pba June 20 (156) $700

### Crane, Thomas —& Houghton, Ellen
— Abroad. L, [c.1884]. Half cloth; extremities rubbed. pba Aug 22 (737) $60

### Crane, Walter, 1845-1915
— The First of May, a Fairy Masque. L, 1881. One of 200. Oblong folio, loose as issued in orig cloth portfolio. With 56 proof plates on india paper. b Jan 31 (151) £110
Anr copy. Bound along top edge in contemp half or gilt; covers soiled. With 57 proof plates on india paper. Some foxing. sg Feb 15 (80) $200
— Of the Decorative Illustration of Books Old and New. L, 1896. One of 130 on Japan vellum. 8vo, half mor gilt; extremities worn. CE Sept 27 (90) $220

### Cranmer, Thomas, 1489-1556
— Reformatio Legum Ecclesiasticarum.... L: John Day, Apr 1571. 4to, later vellum. STC 6006. Thomas Saltern's copy. C Nov 29 (45) £700

### Crantz, David, 1723-77
— The History of Greenland. L, 1767. 2 vols. 8vo, contemp calf; needs rebdg. Library markings. sg Mar 7 (277) $100

### Crary, Mary
— The Daughters of the Stars.... L: Hatchards, 1939. One of 300. Illus by Edmund Dulac. 4to, orig half vellum. With 2 colored plates.. Inscr & with 1 A Ls & 2 Ls s to Dr. Phelps. S May 16 (107) £200

### Craven, E. S.
— A Legend of Mona.... Douglas, 1825. 16mo, disbound. b Dec 5 (139) £180

### Craven, Lady Elizabeth, 1750-1828
— A Journey through the Crimea to Constantinople. L, 1789. 4to, 19th-cent half calf. With folding map & 6 plates. Plate 2 trimmed at foot; portion of foremargin of F5-6 torn away. S June 13 (591) £260

### Craven, Tunis Augustus Macdonough
— A Naval Campaign in the Californias...Journal of.... San Francisco: Book Club of California, 1973. One of 400. pba Apr 25 (357) $50

## Crawford, Capt. Jack
— The Bronco Book. East Aurora: Roycrofters, 1908. Lea gilt. Inscr with poem, Sept 1908, to "My Friend Mark Twain". pba Apr 25 (358) $170

## Crawford, James Ludovic Lindsay, 26th Earl of, 1847-1913
— Bibliotheca Lindesiana. Collations and Notes No. 7. Catalogue of a Collection of Fifteen Hundred Tracts by Martin Luther and his Contemporaries 1511-1598. Aberdeen, 1903. One of 150. Folio, loose in sheets, in half mor box. O Mar 26 (31) $100

## Crawford, John M.
— Chinese Calligraphy and Painting.... NY, 1962. One of 850. 4to, orig cloth. sg Sept 7 (119) $150

## Crawford, Lewis F.
— Rekindling Camp Fires: The Exploits of Ben Arnold...as Indian Fighter.... Bismark, [1926]. Orig cloth; rubbed & soiled. pba June 25 (60) $50

## Crawfurd, George —& Robertson, George, 1750?-1832
— A General Description of the Shire of Renfrew.... Paisley, 1818. 2 parts in 1 vol. 4to, contemp calf. pnE Sept 20 (229) £150

## Crawhall, Joseph, b.1821
— A Collection of Right Merrie Garlands for North Country Anglers. Newcastle, 1864. 8vo, orig half lea; soiled, spine ends rubbed. pba July 11 (55) $250

— "Impresses Quaint." Newcastle, 1889. 4to, orig bds; rubbed. pn Dec 7 (84) £120

## Crease, Francis
— Thirty-Four Decorative Designs.... L, [1927]. One of 60. Preface by Evelyn Waugh. Folio, orig bds; minor damage. Lower margins dampstained. Hobson copy. S June 28 (235) £340

## Creasy, Sir Edward Shepherd, 1812-78. See: Limited Editions Club

## Creation...
— La Creation Les trois premiers livres de Genese suivis de la Genealogie Adamique.... Paris, 1928. One of 175 with plates in 2 states. Illus by F. L. Schmied. Folio, mor extra with lacquer panel by F. L. Schmied & Jean Dunand. S May 16 (28) £17,000

## Crebillon, Claude Prosper Jolyot de, 1707-77
— Tanzai et Neadarne. Histoire Japonoise. Pekin [i.e., Paris], 1740. 2 vols. 12mo, contemp mor gilt. With 5 plates. Fuerstenberg - Schaefer copy. S Dec 7 (145) £800

## Crebillon, Prosper Jolyot de, 1674-1762
— Oeuvres. Paris, 1818. 2 vols. 8vo, contemp half mor by Thouvenin. With port & 9 plates, all in 3 states. L.p. copy on papier velin. Fuerstenberg - Schaefer copy. S Dec 7 (144) £460

## Creeley, Robert
See also: Olson & Creeley
— A Day Book. L, 1972. One of 295. Illus by R. B. Kitaj. Folio, orig cloth; hinges weak. With 12 plates, all sgd & numbered by Kitaj. Dampstaining affecting final leaves & last print. CE May 22 (299) $620

— The Gold Diggers. Mallorca: Divers Press, 1954. Ptd wraps. Inscr on front free endpaper. pba Jan 25 (63) $110

— The Kind of Act of. Mallorca: Divers Press, 1953. Ltd Ed. Ptd wraps; front wrap torn along joint. Clayton Eshleman's copy. pba Jan 25 (64) $65

## Cremer, Wilhelm Hubert —& Wolffenstein, Richard
— Der inner Ausbau. Berlin: Ernst Wasmuth, [n.d.]. 4 vols. Folio, later half sheep; worn & scuffed. With 400 photographic plates. Library markings; some soiling, affecting a few images. cb Oct 17 (74) $275

## Crenius, Thomas
— De furibus librariis dissertatio. Leiden, 1716. 8vo, modern half calf. O Mar 26 (66) $325

## Crescentiis, Petrus de, 1230?-1310?
— Commodorum ruralium. Augsburg: Johann Schuessler, c.16 Feb 1471. ("Ruralia commoda.") Folio, modern vellum bds. 2 initials supplied on Folio 1. 209 (of 212) leaves; lacking 3 blanks at end. Goff C-965. Hopkinson - Beauchamp - Hefner copy. CNY May 17 (10) $23,000

Anr Ed. Vicenza: Leonardus Achates de Basilea, 17 Feb 1490. Folio, 19th-cent half calf. 52 lines & headline; double column; type 6:88R. Some staining; e4.5 laid in from anr copy; marginal worming in 1st quire. 142 (of 146) leaves; lacking initial blank, final index leaf & with duplicate k3.6 substituted for k4.5. Goff C-974. C June 26 (112) £800

## Crespelle, Jean-Paul
— Terechkovitch. Geneva, 1958. One of 120. 4to, pictorial bds; extremities rubbed. CA Oct 5 (236) AU55

## Cresset Press—London
— The Apocrypha. 1929. One of 450. sg Feb 15 (81) $200

BACON, SIR FRANCIS. - The Essayes or Counsels, Civill and Morall. 1928. One of 250. sg Sept 14 (95) $225; sg Feb 15 (82) $120

BUNYAN, JOHN. - The Pilgrim's Progress. 1928. One of 195. 2 vols. bba May 9 (473) £280 [Rush]

LAWRENCE, DAVID HERBERT. - Birds, Beasts, and Flowers. 1930. One of 500. bba May 9 (475) £150 [Thomsen]

MARKHAM, GERVASE. - The Pleasures of Princes, or Good Men's Recreations. 1927. One of 600. Half mor by Bayntun. pba July 11 (57) $140

Anr copy. Half vellum. pba July 11 (58) $50

SPENSER, EDMUND. - The Shepheards Calendar. 1930. One of 350. pba Mar 7 (69) $400

WARNER, SYLVIA TOWNSEND. - Elinor Barley. 1930. One of 350. bbc Dec 18 (229) $110

**Cresswell, Beatrix Feodore**
— The Royal Progress of King Pepito. L: S.P.C.K., [1889]. 1st Ed. - Illus by Kate Greenaway. 8vo, half mor, orig wraps bound in. pba Aug 22 (775) $80

**Crevecoeur, Michel Guillaume St. Jean de, 1735-1813**
— Letters from an American Farmer.... L, 1783. 8vo, modern half calf. With 2 folding maps. b Jan 31 (442) £360
— Lettres d'un Cultivateur Americain.... Paris, 1784. 2 vols in 1. 8vo, contemp calf gilt; joints & corners worn. CE Feb 21 (41) $300

**Crevenna, Pietro Antonio**
— Catalogue raisonne.... [Amst.], 1775-76. 6 vols. 4to, contemp wraps; spine chipped & browned. Ck Apr 12 (221) £650

**Crews, Harry**
— This Thing Don't Lead to Heaven. NY, 1970. 1st Ed. In dj. Inscr. pba Aug 22 (97) $85

**Crichton, Arthur**
— The Festival of Flora, a Poem with Botanical Notes. L, 1815. 8vo, contemp calf; corners worn, re-backed, new endpapers. With 6 watercolor drawings. S Nov 2 (182) £130 [Sotheran]

**Crichton, Michael**
— Eaters of the Dead. NY, 1976. In dj. pba May 4 (124) $60

**Cripps-Day, Francis Henry**
— A Record of Armour Sales, 1881-1924. L, 1925. Folio, cloth; extremities rubbed. sg Mar 7 (414) $175

**Crispolti, Enrico.** See: Marck & Crispolti

**Critics...**
— The Critics and the Scribblers of the Day: A Satire. By a Scribler. Skipton, 1827. 8vo, early half calf; rebound. Marginal tear in tp. b Dec 5 (436) £150

**Croall, Alexander.** See: Johnstone & Croall

**Croft-Murray, Edward Frederick**
— Decorative Painting in England 1537-1837. L, [1962-70]. 2 vols. 4to, orig cloth, in djs. bba Oct 19 (47) £220 [Pagan]

**Crofts Library, Thomas**
— [Sale Catalogue] Bibliotheca Croftsiana. A Catalogue of the Curious and Distinguished Library.... [L, 1783]. 8vo, modern half mor. Priced in ink. Some browning. bba May 9 (43) £150 [Maggs]
Anr copy. Old calf; rebacked, worn & singed, joints strengthened with tape. Priced in margins throughout & with 2 pages of Ms notes at end. Some browning & soiling. O Mar 26 (67) $225

**Crofutt, George A.**
— Crofutt's Grip-Sack Guide of Colorado. Omaha, 1881. 4to, pictorial cloth; worn, cocked. With 2 maps, 1 in color. Folding map repaired at margin & with 1 short fold split. wa Feb 29 (351) $450

**Croker, Temple Henry —& Others**
— The Complete Dictionary of Arts and Sciences. L, 1766. 3 vols. Folio, contemp calf gilt; worn joints cracked, Vol I dampstained & mildewed. sg May 9 (333) $325

**Crombie, Charles**
— Motoritis, or Other Interpretations of the Motor Act. L: Perrier, [1906]. Oblong folio, orig bds. With 12 colored litho plates. pnE Sept 20 (101) £320

**Crome, Robert**
— The Fiddle New Model'd or a Useful Introduction for the Violin.... L: David Rutherford, [c.1730]. 8vo, contemp wraps. Engraved throughout, with 8 folding plates. S May 15 (527) £650

**Cromwell, Thomas Kitson, 1792-1870**
— Excursions through Ireland. L, 1820. 2 vols. 8vo, orig half cloth; backstrips worn. sg Mar 7 (53) $120

**Cronau, Rudolf**
— Von Wunderland zu Wunderland. Leipzig, 1886. Folio, orig cloth. With 24 (of 25) mtd plates. sg Oct 26 (84) $650

**Cronise, Titus Fey**
— The Natural Wealth of California. San Francisco, 1868. 8vo, orig cloth. Larson copy. pba Feb 12 (29) $300
Anr copy. Orig cloth; front hinge cracked. pba Apr 25 (360) $80

**Crosby, Caresse**
— Crosses of Gold. Paris, 1925. One of 100. Orig pigskin. pba Nov 30 (44) $650
New Ed. Bds, variant with The Poetry Publishing Co, Haven Road, Exeter ptd in gilt on front cover; spine head chipped. Inscr with verse by Caresse Crosby. pba Nov 30 (45) $350
— Painted Shores. Paris, 1927. One of 221. Illus by Francois Quelvee. 4to, painted wraps. pba Nov 30 (46) $300
— The Passionate Years. L: Alvin Redman, [1955]. Sheet of paper inscr tipped to front free endpaper, with Ls laid in. pba Aug 22 (98) $130

**Crosby, Harry**
— Chariot of the Sun. Paris: Black Sun Press, 1928. 1st Ed, One of 44. Half calf, orig wraps bound in. Caresse Crosby's copy, with related ANs. pba Nov 30 (47) $750
Anr Ed. Paris: Black Sun Press, 1931. One of 500. Intro by D. H. Lawrence. 4to, ptd wraps; spine chipped. sg Dec 14 (11) $140
— Mad Queen: Tirades. Paris: Black Sun Press, 1929. Ltd Ed. Wraps. pba Nov 30 (54) $450
— Shadows of the Sun. Paris: Black Sun Press, 1928-29-30. One of 44. 3d Series only. Orig wraps. pba Nov 30 (48) $800

**Crosby, Henry Grew**
— War Letters. Paris: Black Sun Press, 1932. One of 125. Half calf; spine & extremities rubbed. pba Nov 30 (50) $400

**Cross, Ira B.**
— Financing an Empire: History of Banking in California. San Francisco: S. J. Clarke, 1927. 4 vols. pba Nov 16 (71) $110; pba Apr 25 (361) $150

**Crouch, Donald E.**
— Carl Rungius: The Complete Prints. Missoula, [1989]. One of 250. Oblong 4to, syn. O Oct 10 (73) $200
  Anr copy. Syn; some wear. O Oct 10 (236) $200

**Crouch, Nathaniel, 1632?-1725?**
— A Journey to Jerusalem.... Hartford CT, 1796. 12mo, half sheep; worn. sg Oct 26 (176) $350

**Crow, William**
— The Banks of the Hudson, a Poem.... Leith, 1821. 8vo, contemp half mor. b Dec 5 (538) £450

**Crowder, Henry**
— Henry Music. Paris: Hours Press, 1930. 1st Ed, One of 100. Folio, orig bds; rubbed, bubbling to rear cover. Laid in is additional title with colophon & limitation on verso, sgd by Crowder. sg Mar 28 (36) $3,600
  One of 100, sgd. Orig bds with photomontage by Man Ray. Hobson copy. S June 28 (150) £1,600

**Crowley, Aleister, 1875-1947**
— The Argonauts. Inverness, 1904. Orig wraps. pba Mar 7 (70) $150
— The Book of Thoth. [L], 1944. One of 200, sgd. 4to, orig half mor by Sangorski & Sutcliffe. Inscr to Viscount Tredegar, 21 July 1944. S July 11 (268) £1,500
— The City of God, a Rhapsody. L, 1943. Orig wraps. pba Mar 7 (71) $120
— The Fun of the Fair. L, 1942. One of 200, but this copy unsgd. Wraps. pba Mar 7 (72) $120
— Hymn to Pan. L, 1980. One of 75. Illus by Andre Durand. Folio, loose in orig cloth case. With 10 prints. S May 16 (36) £300
— Olla: An Anthology of Sixty Years of Song. L, [1947]. One of 500. Orig cloth, in soiled dj. pba Mar 7 (73) $140

**Crowquill, Alfred.** See: Forrester, Alfred Henry

**Crozat, Joseph Antoine, Marquis de Tugny**
— Recueil d'estampes d'apres les plus beaux tableaux...qui sont en France. Paris, 1729-42. 2 vols. Folio, contemp red mor gilt. With 182 plates. Fuerstenberg - Schaefer copy. S Dec 8 (518) £6,800

**Cruikshank, George, 1792-1878**
— The Comic Almanack. L, 1835-53. 19 vols (all pbd) in 4. 8vo or 12mo, half mor by Bayntun. Some foxing. NH June 1 (57) $230
— Omnibus. L, 1842. 1st Ed in Book form. 8vo, calf gilt by Riviere; spotted. Some foxing. pba June 20 (107) $180
— Points of Humour. L, 1823-24. 2 parts in 1 vol. 8vo, calf gilt by Riviere. With 20 plates. Lacking ads; some foxing. pba June 20 (109) $140
— Table-Book. L, 1845. Ed by G. A. a Beckett. 12 orig parts bound in 1 vol. 8vo, mor gilt by Worsfold, orig wraps for No 4 bound at rear; scuffed. With 12 plates. Marginal tear to pp. vii-viii & 1-2; minor foxing. pba June 20 (108) $250

**Cruikshank, Isaac Robert, 1789-1856**
— Cruikshank at Home.... L: Henry Bohn, 1845. First-Fourth Series. Bound in 2 vols. Orig cloth; spine ends rubbed, front hinges cracked, front cover of Vol II coming off. pba Mar 7 (74) $140

**Cruise...**
— A Cruise in the Pacific from the Log of a Naval Officer. L, 1860. Ed by Fenton Aylmer. 2 vols in 1. 8vo, modern cloth; shelf numbers on backstrip. sg Mar 7 (17) $100

**Crumb, Robert**
— The Yum Yum Book. San Francisco: Scrimshaw Press, 1975. In dj. pba Aug 22 (100) $50

**Crumley, James**
— The Mexican Tree Duck. Huntington Beach: James Cahill, 1993. One of 150. Half mor. pba Oct 5 (73) $70
— One to Count Cadence. NY: Random House, [1969]. In dj. bbc Dec 18 (231) $160; pba Aug 22 (102) $250
— The Pigeon Shoot. Santa Barbara: Neville, 1987. One of 350. pba Aug 22 (103) $55
— Whores. Missoula: Dennis McMillan, 1988. One of 501. pba Aug 22 (105) $60
— The Wrong Case. NY: Random House, [1975]. In dj. pba Aug 22 (104) $225

**Crunden, John**
— Convenient and Ornamental Architecture.... L, 1791. Folio, lea; worn & bumped, hinges split. With 70 plates. Some staining. Met Sept 28 (398) $400

**Cruttwell, Clement**
— Atlas of Cruttwell's Gazetteer. L: for G. C. & J. Robinson, [1799]. 8vo, modern half cloth over old bds. With 22 (of 26) double-page maps, hand-colored in outline. sg Dec 7 (17) $550

**Cruveilhier, Jean, 1791-1874**
— Traite d'Anatomie Descriptive. Paris, 1843-45. 4 vols. Half mor. Some browning. CE Nov 8 (82) $120

**Cruz, Martin de la**
— The Badianus Manuscript. Balt., 1940. Ed by Emily W. Emmart. 4to, orig cloth, in dj. sg May 16 (399) $275

## 1995 - 1996 · BOOKS

**Crysostome, Dion**
— Le Chasseur ou histoire Eubeenne. Paris, 1943. One of 136. Illus by Paul-Emile Colin. 4to, contemp mor by Rene Kieffer with orig woodblock by Colin inset into upper cover, orig wraps bound in. b Sept 20 (611) £260

**Csoma de Koros, Alexander**
— Essay towards a Dictionary, Tibetan and English.... Calcutta: Baptist Mission Press, 1834. 4to, contemp half calf. Library stamp on half-title & English title; pp. 182-83 foxed. S June 27 (231) £1,200

**Cuala Press—Churchtown & Dublin**
— A Broadside. 1908-13. One of 300. 1st Year, No 1 to 5th Year, No 12. 58 (of 60) nos. P Dec 12 (56) $1,500
YEATS, WILLIAM BUTLER. - In the Seven Woods. 1903. One of 325. Hobson copy. S June 28 (297) £700
YEATS, WILLIAM BUTLER. - Poems Written in Discouragement 1912-1913. 1913. One of 50. Unsewn in orig wraps. S June 28 (303) £1,700

**Cualnge**
— The Tain. Dublin, 1969. Illus by Louis Le Brocquy; trans by Thomas Kinsella. Mor extra by Gemma O'Connor. P Dec 12 (132) $550

**Cuba**
— Album Vascongado. Relacion de los festejos publicos hechos por la cuidad de la Habana en los dias 2, 3 y 4 de junio de 1869.... Havana, 1869. Folio, contemp bds; rebacked. With litho & 3 plates. S June 27 (185) £750
— En la cuidad de la Havana en diez y seis de Octubre de mil setecientos ochenta y tres anos: el Senor D. Luis de Unzaga y Amezaga [stating that sons & daughters over 25 years of age must ask for and obtain parental consent before engaging in matrimony]. Havana: la Imprenta de la Capitania General, 1799. 4to, modern wraps. S June 27 (187) £380

**Cubley, L. M.**
— The Hills and Plains of Palestine. L, 1860. Illus by F. Jones, T. Picken, & others. 4to, cloth. With hand-colored title vignette, hand-colored frontis, & 28 hand-colored plates. Some discoloration. S Oct 26 (42) £380 [Pollack]

**Cudworth, Warren H.**
— History of the First Regiment (Massachusetts Infantry). Bost., 1866. 12mo, orig cloth; spine ends chipped. With 16 plates. NH July 21 (64) $135

**Cuitt, George, 1779-1854**
— Wanderings and Pencillings amongst Ruins of the Olden Time. L, 1855. Folio, half mor; cover detached. rs Nov 11 (79) $250

**Cullen, Countee, 1903-46**
— The Black Christ & Other Poems. NY, 1929. In repaired dj. sg Mar 28 (37) $80
— The Lost Zoo.... NY, [1940]. 1st Ed. Orig cloth; frayed. Inscr to "Pa". sg Mar 28 (38) $375

## CUMINGS

— My Lives and How I Lost Them. NY, [1942]. ILlus by Robert Reid Macguire. In chipped & repaired dj. sg Mar 28 (39) $120

**Cullen, William, 1710-90**
— Lectures on the Materia Media. L, 1772. 1st Ed. 4to, contemp half calf; worn. Title torn in margin; some spotting & soiling. Ck Mar 22 (83) £280

**Culleton, James**
— Indians and Pioneers of Old Monterey. Fresno: Academy of California Church History, 1950. In soiled dj. pba Nov 16 (72) $60

**Culloden...**
— Culloden Papers comprising an Extensive and Interesting Correspondence from the Years 1625 to 1748. L, 1815. 4to, contemp half calf; rubbed. With engraved title & 3 plates. Some spotting. Simon Fraser of Lovat's copy. CG June 12 (36) £200
Anr copy. Contemp mor gilt; rubbed. CG June 12 (37) £300

**Culpeper, Nicholas, 1616-54**
— The English Physician Enlarged. L, 1822. ("Culpeper's Complete Herbal.") 4to, old calf; rebacked. With frontis & 40 hand-colored plates. pba Nov 30 (177) $850
— The English Phystian.... L, 1850. ("The Complete Herbal.") 4to, contemp calf; rebacked. With port & 20 hand-colored plates. Port foxed & dampstained in margins. sg May 9 (296) $325
— Semeiotica Uranica: or, an Astological Judgement of Diseases. L, 1671. 4th Ed. 8vo, contemp calf; worn. Marginal staining. b Sept 20 (106) £130

**Culs...**
— Culs de Lampe. Northhampton MA: Gehenna Press, [1968]. One of 250. Half vellum. Inscr by Leonard Baskin. sg Feb 15 (115) $100

**Culver, Henry Brundage**
— Contemporary Scale Models of Vessels of the Seventeenth Century. NY, [1926]. One of 1,000. Folio, cloth. With 50 plates. sg Mar 7 (207) $100

**Cuming, Edward William Diron**
— The British Sport, Past and Present. L, 1909. Illus by G. Denholm Armour. 4to, cloth; shaken. With 31 colored plates. sg Mar 7 (415) $100

**Cuming, Fortescue, 1762-1828**
— Sketches of a Tour to the Western Country.... Pittsburgh, 1810. 12mo, orig half cloth; front hinge cracked. Dampstains in gutter margins at front; some foxing & spotting. CNY Jan 26 (186) $1,600
Anr copy. Contemp sheep; rebacked, lacking free endpapers. sg Oct 26 (85) $1,200

**Cumings, Edward M.**
— Fly Fishing. Flint MI, [1934]. Pictorial cloth; worn. O Feb 6 (53) $90

415

## CUMMING

**Cumming, Alexander, 1733-1814**
— The Elements of Clock and Watch-work.... L, 1766. 4to, orig half cloth; rubbed, lacking lower free endpaper, other endpapers later. With 16 plates. Library stamp on tp; some browning. bba Sept 7 (75) £450 [Rogers Turner]

**Cumming, Constance Frederica Gordon**
— Granite Crags of California. Edin., 1886. Orig cloth; spine sunned, rear cover corner stained. With 5 autotype plates. Robbins copy. pba Mar 21 (122) $90
New Ed. Edin. & L, 1886. 8vo, cloth. pba Feb 12 (66) $110

**Cumming, Roualeyn G. Gordon, 1820-66**
— Five Years of a Hunter's Life in the Far Interior of South Africa. L, 1850. 1st Ed. 2 vols. 8vo, orig cloth; worn. Some foxing. O Oct 10 (74) $70
Anr Ed. NY, 1850. 2 vols. 12mo, orig cloth; spine ends with small cracks. Foxed. sg Mar 7 (416) $175

**Cumming, William P.**
— The Discovery of America. NY, [1972]. 4to, cloth, in dj. pba Feb 13 (58) $85
— The Southeast in Early Maps. Chapel Hill, [1962]. 4to, cloth. sg May 9 (10) $475
Anr Ed. Chapel Hill, [1973]. 4to, cloth. pba Apr 25 (153) $250

**Cummings, Edward Estlin, 1894-1962**
— 50 Poems. NY, [1940]. One of 150. sg June 20 (64) $200
— Ciopw. NY, 1931. One of 391, sgd. 4to, burlap. Sgd on tp in green watercolor. pba Aug 22 (108) $250
— The Enormous Room. NY, [1922]. 1st Ed, p 219 censored. In chipped & repaired dj. Inscr to Ingle Barr, 18 Nov 1959. CE Sept 27 (91) $200
P 219 uncensored. Orig cloth; worn & soiled. Inscr to John Cage, 25 Apr 1951. CE May 22 (121) $750

**Cummings, John.** See: Bulkeley & Cummings

**Cummins, Ella Sterling**
— The Story of the Files: a Review of Californian Writers and Literature. San Francisco, 1893. 1st Ed. 8vo, orig bds; extremities rubbed. pba Apr 25 (363) $225

**Cummins, John.** See: Bulkeley & Cummings

**Cunard, Nancy**
— Negro. L, 1934. 1st Ed. - Ed by Cunard. With contribs by Beckett, Langston Hughes, Pound, W. C. Williams & Dreiser. 4to, orig cloth. With copy of the orig prospectus addressed to Yves Tanguy, sgd by Cunard, 1931. sg Mar 28 (42) $6,000

**Cundell, John**
— Rules of the Thistle Golf Club. Far Hills, NJ: Thistle Press for U.S.G.A., 1983. Bound with: Robert Chambers. A Few Rambling Remakrs on Golf.... One of 1,900. Forewords by Joseph C. Dey. 2 vols, half cloth in slipcase. pba Apr 18 (31) $225

## AMERICAN BOOK PRICES CURRENT

**Cuneo**
— La vera discrittione dell'assedio et impresa di Connio.... MIlan: Stampa Moscheniana, [1557]. 4to, 19th-cent vellum. With woodcut arms of Savoy on tp, partly hand-colroed red; double-page woodcut view of the siege of Cuneo. Minor spotting & staining. C June 26 (66) £1,600

**Cuningham, William**
— The Cosmographical Glasse, Conteinyng the Pleasant Principles of Cosmographie.... L, 1559. 1st Ed. Folio, rebound in modern calf. Tp chipped; A3 in facsimile; lower margins dampstained, sometimes touching catchwords; folding view soiled & with fold breaks. CE June 12 (183) $3,800

**Cunningham, Daniel John, 1850-1909**
— Stereoscopic Studies of Anatomy prepared under authority of the University of Edinburgh. NY, [c.1910]. Bound with: Keystone View Co. Stereographic Library. Tour of the World. 2 vols. 4to. 8 vols. 4to, loose in slipcases. With wood & metal stereoscope with folding handle. Sold w.a.f. CE Nov 8 (150) $240

**Cunningham, Eugene**
— Triggernometry: a Gallery of Gunfighters. NY, 1934. 1st Ed. 8vo, cloth; extremities rubbed. Robbins copy. pba Mar 21 (73) $225

**Cunningham, Imogen**
— Imogen! Imogen Cunningham Photographs 1910-1973 Seattle & L, [1974]. In soiled dj. Inscr. sg Feb 29 (105) $140

**Cunningham, Peter, 1816-69**
— The Story of Nell Gwyn. L, 1852. 8vo, later mor gilt by Sangorski & Sutcliffe. F June 20 (451) $50
Anr Ed. L, 1892. One of 250. 8vo, mor extra by P. Ruban. With orig watercolor tp by Ostolle replacing ptd title & 21 hand-colored plates before letters. b Sept 20 (612) £450

**Cunnington, Cecil Willett**
— English Women's Clothing in the Nineteenth Century. L, 1937. 1st Ed. Folio, orig bds. bba Oct 19 (192) £60 [Attias]

**Cureau de la Chambre, Marin**
— Nouvelles observations et coniectures sur l'iris. Paris: Pierre Rocolet, 1690. 4to, contemp red mor gilt pointille bdg by the Pierre Rocolet-Antoine Padeloup Atelier. C May 1 (41) £14,000

**Curie, Marie, 1867-1934**
— Pierre Curie. NY, 1923. One of 100. NH Sept 16 (121) $575
— Untersuchungen ueber die Radioaktiven Substanzen.... Braunschweig, 1904. 8vo, orig cloth. CE Nov 8 (82A) $80

**Currey, L. W.**
— Science Fiction and Fantasy Authors. Bost., 1979. pba May 23 (88) $85

416

**Currier...** See: Peters, Harry Twyford

**Currier, Thomas Franklin**
— A Bibliography of Oliver Wendell Holmes. NY, 1953. 4to, cloth. ds July 27 (91) $50

**Cursham, Mary Ann**
— Martin Luther, a Poem. Nottingham, 1825. 8vo, orig bds; worn. b Dec 5 (300) £70

**Curtis, Edward S., 1868-1952**
— The North American Indian. Norwood, 1926. One of 500. Ed by F. W. Hodge. Vol XV only, half mor. With 75 photos. Larson copy. pba Sept 28 (2) $2,250
— [Prospectus for The North American Indian] Cambr. MA, 1908. 20 pp, 4to, wraps; worn & shaken. With 1 photogravure. bbc Apr 22 (211) $270

**Curtis, John**
— Shipwreck of the Stirling Castle.... L, 1838. 8vo, contemp half calf; scuffed, hinge cracked. With 6 (of 7) plates. Lacking frontis. pba July 25 (392) $95

**Curtis, John, 1791-1862**
— British Entomology. L, 1823-40. 8 vols. 8vo, 19th-Cent half calf; rubbed. With 770 hand-colored plates. Some spotting & offsetting. S Oct 27 (631) £2,400 [Rigout]
Anr Ed. L, 1824-39 [1823-40]. 8 vols. 8vo, orig cloth; joints worn. With 752 hand-colored plates only. b Sept 20 (462) £1,050
Anr copy. Contemp half mor gilt; rubbed. With 770 hand-colored plates. Plate 334 inverted; some browning. S June 27 (15) £1,400

**Curtis, Paul A.** See: Derrydale Press

**Curtis, Samuel, 1779-1860**
— Monograph on the Genus Camellia. L: J. & J. Arch, 1819. Illus by Clara Maria Pope. Folio, loose as issued in mor box. With 5 hand-colored plates in card window mounts. Lacking tp; text a modern reprint on a single smaller format leaf; pbr's imprint indistinct on Plate 1. Fattorini copy. C Oct 25 (50) £36,000

**Curtis, William, 1746-99**
— The Botanical Magazine; or Flower Garden Displayed. L, 1787-1808. Vols 1-27 in 9 vols. Contemp half lea; worn, covers detached or missing. With 1,103 plates, all but 2 hand-colored. Lacking tp to Vol 19. Sold w.a.f. S June 27 (16) £5,000
Vols 1-35 plus index to Vols 1-20, in 34 vols. L, 1787-1812. Half calf; many spine ends worn & lacking, most joints cracked, some covers detached. With 1,460 hand-colored plates. cb Oct 17 (125) $11,000
Vols 1-17 bound in 8. L, 1793-88-1803. Various bdgs. With 644 plates, all but 1 hand-colored; plus duplicates of Plates 286-88. Sold w.a.f. S June 27 (17) £3,200
Vols 1-20. L, 1793-88-1805. Contemp half calf; lettering piece to spine of Vol XI lacking, scuffed. With port, 1 uncolored & 785 hand-colored plates, 3 of them folding. Some browning. C May 31 (15) £4,400
Vols 7-9 in 1 vol. L, 1794-95. Later cloth; soiled. With 108 hand-colored plates. sg Dec 7 (216) $950
Vols 31-48. L, 1810-21. Bound in 12 vols. Contemp calf; worn. With 1,038 hand-colored plates, 1 uncolored plate. Some browning. pnE Sept 20 (133) £3,100
Vols 43-44. L, 1816-17. Early calf; needs rebdg. With 173 hand-colored plates. Plates heavily browned. Sold w.a.f. sg Dec 7 (215) $650
Vols 13-14. L, 1840-41. Half lea; worn. With 169 hand-colored plates. Met Feb 24 (441) $1,000
Vol 86. L, 1860. Later half mor; some wear. With 66 hand-finished color plates. Minor foxing & soiling. cb Feb 14 (2611) $800
Vol 94. L, 1868. Half mor. Met Sept 28 (401) $650
Vol 96. L, 1870. Half mor. Met Sept 28 (402) $650
Vol 98. L, 1872. Half mor. Met Sept 28 (403) $650
Vol 99. L, 1873. Half lea; scuffed. With 65 hand-finished color plates. bbc June 24 (303) $700
Vol 114. L, 1893. Half lea. With 60 hand-colored plates. Met Feb 24 (442) $300
Vol 120. L, 1894. Half lea. Met Sept 28 (404) $600
Vol 136. L, 1910. Half lea. Met Sept 28 (405) $600
Anr copy. Half lea; spine splitting. With 60 hand-colored plates. Met Feb 24 (439) $300
Vol 138. L, 1912. Later half calf; hinges starting. With 60 hand-colored plates. Some spotting & soiling. cb Feb 14 (2612) $700
Anr copy. Half lea. With 60 hand-colored plates. Met Feb 24 (440) $300
— Flora Londinensis. L, [1775]-77-[88]. Parts 1-5 (of 6). Folio, contemp half calf; worn. With 360 (of 432) plates (75 hand-colored). Sold w.a.f. S Oct 27 (632) £2,300 [Shapero]
Anr Ed. L, [1775]-77-98. 6 parts in 4 vols. Folio, 19th-cent half calf; rubbed, joints with splits. With 435 (on 432) hand-colored plates, arranged systematically. Plate 163 stained; Plate 321 with repaired tear; some discoloration. S June 27 (19) £4,900
— Lectures on Botany. L, 1805. 3 vols. 8vo, later calf gilt; rubbed. With 119 hand-colored plates. Plate 33 shaved; text browned in Vol III; port in facsimile. S June 27 (18) £1,100

**Curtiss, Daniel S.**
— Western Portraiture, and Emigrants' Guide.... NY, 1852. 1st Ed. 12mo, orig cloth; rebacked with most of spine strip laid on, damage to front pastedown. With folding map. Library stamps. pba Apr 25 (364) $70
Anr copy. Orig cloth; worn. With folding map, attached to rear pastedown & stained from glue. wa Feb 29 (392) $160

**Curtius (Quintus Curtius Rufus)**
— Historia Alexandri magni Regis Macedonum.... Lyon: Antoine Gryphius, 1582. ("De rebus gestis Alexandri Magni.") 16mo, contemp mor elaborately gilt by Soresino for Federico Gentile; joints restored. Furstenberg copy. C Apr 3 (79) £1,200

# CURTIUS

Anr Ed. Utrecht: Frans Halma, 1685. ("De rebus Alexandri magni....") 8vo, contemp calf; worn. With frontis, map & 12 plates. Some waterstaining. b May 30 (295) £90

**Curwen Press—London**
— The Curwen Press Miscellany. L, 1931. One of 275. S Nov 2 (51) £420 [Banks]
— A Specimen Book of Pattern Papers.... L, 1928. One of 210. Intro by Paul Nash. Library markings. bba May 9 (476) £800 [Gatteno]

**Cussans, John Edwin, 1837-89**
— History of Hertfordshire. L, 1870-81. Bound in 7 vols. 4to, modern syn; stained. With port & 20 plates, 4 in color, 14 tinted. S Mar 28 (43) £100
One of 75 L.p. copies. 3 vols. Folio, half mor gilt; repaired, minor stains. S Mar 28 (44) £380

**Custer, Elizabeth Bacon, 1842-1933**
— "Boots and Saddles." NY, 1885. 1st Ed. 8vo, orig cloth; spine & corners rubbed, bookplate removed from front pastedown. With port & map. pba Apr 25 (365) $100
— Tenting on the Plains, or General Custer in Kansas and Texas. NY, 1895. 8vo, orig cloth; front hinge repaired. pba June 25 (65) $80

**Custer, George Armstrong, 1839-76**
— Battling with the Sioux on the Yellowstone. [N.p., 1876]. 8vo, modern cloth. Some highlight marks in text; pp. 91-102 removed from Galaxy Magazine, July 1876. pba June 25 (68) $50
— My Life on the Plains.... NY, 1874. 1st Ed. 8vo, orig cloth; extremities rubbed. With 8 plates. pba June 25 (69) $1,100

**Cutbush, Edward, 1772-1843**
— Observations on the Means of Preserving the Health of Soldiers and Sailors.... Phila., 1808. 1st Ed. 8vo, modern half calf. With 3 folding tables. Dampstaining & water damage throughout; wormholes on title & last 2 leaves; some browning. CE Nov 8 (83) $150

**Cutcliffe, H. C.**
— The Art of Trout Fishing on Rapid Streams. L: Sampson Low, [c.1883]. 12mo, cloth; some wear. O Feb 6 (54) $140

**Cuthell, John**
— A Catalogue of Books, in Physic, Surgery, Anatomy.... L, [c.1785]. 8vo, disbound. Lower edge trimmed with loss; some tears & holes; minor staining. bba May 9 (81) £90 [Wellcome Institute]

**Cutright, Paul Russell**
— A History of the Lewis and Clark Journals. Norman, 1976. 1st Ed. In torn dj. Robbins copy. pba Mar 21 (199) $120

**Cutter, Donald C.**
— Malaspina in California. San Francisco, 1960. One of 1,000. Unopened. Sgd on tp. pba Feb 13 (128) $50

# AMERICAN BOOK PRICES CURRENT

Anr copy. Inscr to Irving Robbins. pba Aug 22 (935) $65

**Cutter, William Richard, 1847-1918**
— Genealogical and Family History of Northern New York.... NY, 1910. 3 vols. 4to, orig half lea; edge wear. NH July 21 (163) $150

**Cutts, James M.**
— The Conquest of California and New Mexico. Albuquerque, [1965]. Simulated lea in dj. With 2 ports & 4 maps. Larson copy. pba Sept 28 (391) $55

**Cuvier, Frederic Georges, 1773-1838.** See: Geoffroy Saint-Hilaire & Cuvier

**Cuvier, Georges L. C., Baron, 1769-1832**
— The Animal Kingdom. L, 1827-35. Vols I-VIII (of 16). Contemp half mor; scuffed. S June 13 (436) £600
Anr copy. 17 vols including duplicate of Vol 11. 8vo, 19th-cent half mor; rubbed. With 797 (of 803) plates not counting the duplicate volume, 12 of them hand-colored. Some foxing. S June 27 (14) £2,800

**Cuvillies, Francois de**
— Morceaux de caprice a divers usages. Munich & Paris, [1770]. Tp & 7 plates only. Folio, 19th-cent half mor. Fuerstenberg - Schaefer copy. S Dec 7 (147) £1,000

**Cyprus**
— The Cyprus Gazette. Nicosia, 1931. Nos. 2104-2189. Folio, bds; worn. Few marginalia. S Oct 26 (82) £1,400 [Karides]

**Czwiklitzer, Christophe**
— Picasso's Posters. NY, [1971]. In dj. sg Jan 11 (346) $50

# D

**Dabney, W. P., 1865-1952**
— Cincinnati's Colored Citizens. Cincinnati: Dabney Publishing Company, [1926]. sg Mar 28 (43) $275

**Dacre, Lady Barbarina.** See: Fore-Edge Paintings

**Dahl, Roald**
— [Children's Books] L: Harper Collins, 1991. Commemorative Ed, One of 500. 15 vols. Orig half mor, each in slipcase, set in further slipcase. S Nov 2 (280) £220 [Sotheran]
— The Gremlins.... L: Collins, [1944]. 1st English Ed. - Illus by Walt Disney Studios. 4to, orig half cloth; soiled. Some edge-tears. bbc Dec 18 (233) $200

**D'Albertis, Luigi Maria**
— New Guinea: What I did and what I saw. L, 1880. 2 vols. 8vo, orig cloth; rebacked retaining orig spine. S June 13 (655) £420

**Dale, Edward Everett**
— The Range Cattle Industry. Norman: U of Oklahoma Press, 1930. Some foxing. pba Apr 25 (368) $300

**Dale, Harrison Clifford**
— The Ashley-Smith Explorations, and the Discovery of a Central Route to the Pacific. Cleveland, 1918. 1st Ed. pba Feb 13 (61) $300
Anr copy. Orig cloth; spine faded. With 4 plates & double-page color frontis map. Robbins copy. pba Mar 21 (74) $375

**Dale, Samuel, 1659?-1739.** See: Taylor & Dale

**Dale, Thomas Francis, 1858-1923**
— Polo at Home and Abroad. L, 1915. One of 100. 4to, orig vellum. S Oct 27 (826) £460 [The Barn]

**Dali, Salvador, 1904-89**
See also: Halsman & Dali
— Aliyah. NY: Shorewood, 1968. One of 250. Folio, orig cloth & silk portfolio box; covers worn & soiled. With 25 color lithos, loose as issued. Marginal foxing on plates. sg May 23 (300) $7,500
— La Conquete de l'irrationnel. Paris, [1935]. One of 35 with orig drawing. Orig bds. Inscr to Mlle. Andwruss, 1935. pn June 13 (197) £820
— An Exhibition of Drawings & Paintings by Dali. NY, [1943]. 4to, orig wraps. Sgd on cover. sg June 13 (127) $130
— Salvador Dali 1939. NY: Julien Levy Gallery, 1939. 4to, cloth-backed pictorial wraps; edge-wear. sg June 13 (126) $300
— The Secret Life. NY, 1942. 1st Ed. 4to, orig cloth. Inscr to Alexandre, 1963, & with full-page watercolor drawing. P June 5 (208) $2,250
One of 119 with orig ink drawing. Half cloth; extremities worn. sg Sept 7 (120) $1,300

**Dali, Salvador, 1904-89 —&**
**Halsman, Philippe**
— Dali's Mustache: A Photographic Interview. NY: Simon & Schuster, [1954]. Orig bds; spine lacking. Inscr by Dali. bba July 18 (290) £130 [Roe & Moore]

**Dall, William H., 1845-1927**
— Alaska and its Resources. Bost., 1870. 1st Ed. 4to, cloth; worn, hinges split. With folding map & 15 plates. Closed tear in map. wa Feb 29 (268) $160

**Dallas, Robert Charles, 1754-1824**
— Aubrey; A Novel. L, 1804. 1st Ed. 4 vols. 12mo, contemp half calf; rubbed. Marginal tears; G10 of Vol IV with burnhole at margin; some spotting & staining. Ck Sept 8 (201) £1,000

**Dallaway, James, 1763-1834**
— Anecdotes of the Arts in England. L, 1800. 8vo, half calf. With engraved title. bba Oct 19 (48) £55 [Graves-Johnston]
— Inquiries into the Origin and Progress of the Science of Heraldry in England. Gloucester, 1793. 2 parts in 1 vol. 4to, early sheep; worn, rebacked. Some foxing & browning. sg Feb 8 (304) $90

**Dallimore, William**
— Poisonous Plants, Deadly, Dangerous and Suspect. L, 1927. One of 350. Illus by John Nash. Folio, orig cloth; spine discolored. sg Feb 15 (208) $200

**Dalrymple, Alexander, 1737-1808**
— A Collection of Charts and Memoirs. L, 1771-72. 4to, contemp sheep; needs rebdg. With 11 folding maps or charts. Piece excised from top edge of each map. sg Mar 7 (54) $1,800
— An Historical Collection of the Several Voyages and Discoveries in the South Pacific Ocean. L, 1770-71. 2 vols in 1. 4to, old bds; rebacked & repaired. With 15 plates only. Minor worming to 1 map affecting image; edges soiled; some browning & soiling. cb Oct 17 (186) $3,750

**Dalrymple, Sir John, 1726-1810**
— Memoirs of Great Britain & Ireland. Edin & L, 1771-73-82. Vols I-II (of 3). Contemp calf; Vol II joints restored. sg Mar 21 (84) $130

**Dalrymple, William**
— Travels through Spain and Portugal.... L, 1777. 4to, modern cloth. With folding map & 1 plate. Some browning & soiling; library stamps. sg Mar 7 (55) $120

**Dalton, Emmett, 1871-1937**
— When the Daltons Rode. Garden City, 1931. pba Nov 16 (75) $120

**Dalton, John, 1766-1844**
— Meteorological Observations and Essays. L, 1793. 1st Ed, Issue not indicated. 8vo, cloth. sg May 16 (152) $175

**Dalton, Ormonde Maddock**
— East Christian Art: A Survey of the Monuments. Oxford, 1925. 4to, cloth; top of spine panel torn, joints tender. With frontis & 69 plates. sg June 13 (128) $50

**Dalvimart, Octavien**
— The Costume of Turkey. L, 1802 [watermarked 1796-1811]. Folio, contemp russia gilt by Charles Hering, with his ticket; joints repaired. With 60 colored plates. Fuerstenberg copy. C May 1 (42) £750
Anr Ed. L, 1804 [some plates watermarked 1818]. Folio, mor; extremities worn & scuffed. With 30 hand-colored plates. cb Oct 17 (109) $400
Anr Ed. L, 1804 [some plates watermarked 1811]. Folio, mor gilt. With 60 colored plates. pba Mar 7 (78) $850
Anr Ed. L, 1804 [plates watermarked 1817-20]. Folio, mor gilt; worn & broken. With 60 colored plates. Library markings. wa Feb 29 (99) $425

**Daly, Cesar, 1811-94**
— L'Architecture privee au XIXme siecle sous Napoleon III... Paris, 1877. 3d Series. 2 vols. Folio, contemp

half mor; corners & spine edges rubbed. With 156 chromolithos. Some foxing. cb Oct 17 (10) $1,500

**Dalyell, Sir John Graham, 1775-1851**
— Fragments of Scottish History. Edin., 1798. 4to, contemp russia gilt; corners worn. pba Nov 30 (104) $140

**Dalziel, Gavin**
— A Selection of Poetical Pieces. Paisley, 1825. 16mo, half calf. Inscr to David Laing. b Dec 5 (578) £80

**Damascus**
— Histoire veritable de quatre Peres Capucins cruellement tyrannisez.... Lyon, 1620. 8vo, modern half vellum. 6 leaves. Some dampstaining. S Oct 26 (87) £240 [Folios]

**Dame...**
— Dame Wiggins of Lee and her Seven Wonderful Cats.... Orpington: George Allen, 1885. Ed by John Ruskin. 8vo, later half mor; extremities worn. Library markings. sg Sept 21 (210) $200

**Damhouderius, Jodocus, 1507-81**
— La Practicque et enchiridion des causes criminelles. Louvain: Estienne Wauters & Jean Bathen, 1554. 4to, 19th-cent mor gilt. Italic type, with some lines in roman. With 56 woodcuts, all but 2 within integral architectural borders. Washed & pressed, with residual stains. Paillet - Hoe - Schaefer copy. P Nov 1 (73) $5,500
— Practycke ende handbouck in criminele zaeken. Antwerp: Steven Wouters & Jan Bathen for Hans de Laet, 1555. 4to, disbound. Tp soiled; repairs at end, affecting text on 2 leaves. sg Mar 21 (184) $800

**Damon, Samuel Chenery, 1814-85**
— A Journey to Lower Oregon and Upper California.... San Francisco, 1927. One of 250. pba July 25 (271) $75

**Dampf...**
— Dampf und Elektricitaet: Die Anfang des Zwanzigsten Jahrhunderts. Laipzig: Otto Maier, [c1910]. Oblong folio, cloth. With 12 chromolitho moveable machinery models. pba Nov 30 (235) $600

**Dampier, William, 1652-1715**
— A Collection of Voyages. L, 1729. 4 vols. 8vo, contemp calf; rebacked, corners rubbed. With 65 plates & maps. World map renewed in margin; A2 of Vol II from anr copy; rusthole in 1 leaf. S June 27 (246) £2,500
— A New Voyage Round the World. L, 1699. 4th Ed of Vol I; 1st Ed of Vol II. 2 vols. 8vo, contemp calf; front joint cracked, rubbed. cb Feb 14 (2534) $950
— Voyages and Discoveries. L: Argonaut Press, 1931. Out-of-series copy. 4to, orig half vellum; bumped. pba Apr 25 (174) $95

**Dana, C. W.** See: Old Settler

**Dana, Charles Anderson, 1819-97**
— The United States Illustrated; in Views of City and Country. NY: H. J. Meyer, [c.1855]. Illus by W. H. Bartlett. 2 vols. 4to, orig half mor. Some foxing. pba Nov 16 (49) $750

**Dana, Edmund**
— Geographical Sketches on the Western Country. Cincinnati, 1819. 1st Ed. 12mo, contemp calf; worn. Browned, spotted, & dampstained; U1 torn. CE Nov 8 (183) $180

**Dana, James Dwight, 1813-95**
— A System of Mineralogy. New Haven, 1837. 1st Ed. 8vo, orig sheep; upper spine eroded & rubbed. With 4 plates. Foxing to text. NH June 1 (149) $625

**Dana, Richard Henry, Jr., 1815-82**
See also: Grabhorn Printing; Limited Editions Club
— To Cuba and Back. Bost., 1859. 1st Ed. 12mo, cloth; spine ends frayed. Some foxing; stain to top margin. pba July 25 (120) $55
— Two Years Before the Mast. NY, 1840. 2d Issue. 12mo, lev gilt by Sangorski & Sutcliffe, orig cloth bound in. sg Feb 8 (273) $750
1st Ed. 12mo, orig cloth. Larson copy. pba Sept 28 (71) $500
Anr Ed. NY, 1841. 12mo, orig cloth; spine ends chipped, frayed, corners showing. Some foxing. pba July 25 (121) $90
2d True English Ed. L, 1842. Orig cloth; covers faded. With frontis. Larson copy. pba Sept 28 (72) $190
New Ed. Boston, 1869. 8vo, orig cloth. With 1 headpiece, & sgd blank tipped in. Larson copy. pba Sept 28 (73) $225
Anr Ed. Bost.: Houghton Mifflin, 1911. Orig cloth. ALs, 7 Oct 1841. pba July 25 (122) $250
Anr Ed. NY, 1911. Illus by Charles Pears. In dj with 1 short tear. pba July 25 (124) $180
Anr Ed. Chicago, 1930. One of 1,000. Illus by Edward A. Wilson. Cloth. pba Aug 22 (875) $50
Anr Ed. Los Angeles, 1964. Illus by R. A. Weinstei. Ed by John H. Kemble. 2 vols, orig cloth in slipcase. With 8 color illus. Larson copy. pba Sept 28 (75) $80
Anr copy. Illus by Robert A. Weinstein. 2 vols. pba Nov 16 (76) $95; pba Feb 13 (63) $60; pba July 25 (128) $95
Anr Ed. Cambr., MA, 1968. Ed by Robert F. Lucid. 3 vols, orig cloth in slipcase. With 7 charts of family trees. Larson & Lawrence Clark Powellcopy. pba Sept 28 (74) $100

**Danckwerth, Caspar —&**
**Mejer, Johannes**
— Newe Landesbeschreibung der zweye hertzogthuemer Schleswich und Holstein. [Husum], 1652. Folio, later lea. With 40 double-page or folding plates. Heavily repaired with occasional loss; library markings. Sold w.a.f. CE June 15 (286) $2,200

**Dandelion...**
— The Dandelion Chain, by Margaret. Glasgow, 1838. 8vo, orig cloth. b Dec 5 (553) £80

**Dandini da Cesena, Girolamo, 1554-1634**
— Missione apostolica al patriarcha, e Maroniti del Monte Libano.... Cesena, 1656. 1st Ed. 4to, loose in contemp vellum. With additional title. Some waterstains. S Oct 26 (140) £1,300 [Dessy]

**Daniel, William**
— A Journal or Account of William Daniel, His late Expedition or Undertaking to go from London to Surrat in India. L, 1702. 1st Ed. 8vo, half calf. Title remounted, affecting border; contemp ms. corrections; some discoloration & worm-holes. S Oct 26 (88) £550 [Folios]

**Daniel, William Barker, 1753?-1833**
— Rural Sports. L, 1807. 3 vols. 8vo, contemp calf gilt; joints cracked. With engraved titles & 67 plates, 1 double-page. S June 13 (457) £220

Anr Ed. L, 1812. 3 vols. 4to, contemp calf; worn or broken. Staining, foxing, soiling. Sold w.a.f. O Jan 9 (76) $160

Anr copy. Modern half lea gilt. With engraved titles & 74 plates. Some foxing. sg Mar 7 (417) $375

Anr copy. Old half calf; becoming disbound. Foxed. wa Feb 1 (198) $200

Anr copy. Calf gilt; needs rebacked. Some foxing. wa Feb 29 (229) $170

**Daniele, Francesco**
— Le Forche Caudine illustrate. Naples: Angelo Trani, 1811-12. Folio, orig half calf; worn & scuffed, with some peeling, hinges cracked. With folding plate & 5 copperplate text illusts. bbc June 24 (183) $290

**Daniell, Thomas, 1749-1840 —& Daniell, William, 1769-1837**
— A Picturesque Voyage to India.... L, 1810. Oblong folio, half calf; spine perished. With 50 colored plates. wd May 8 (49) $850

**Daniell, William, 1769-1837**
See also: Daniell & Daniell
— Sketches representing the native Tribes, Animals and Scenery of Southern Africa. L, 1820. Oblong 4to, half cloth; bumped. With 40 (of 46) plates. Sold w.a.f. Met Sept 28 (406) $350

**D'Annunzio, Gabriele, 1863-1938**
— Opere. Verona: Bodoni, 1927. One of 300, this copy for Otto H. Kahn. Folio, orig wraps. bba May 9 (608) £95 [Taro]

**Danreiter, Franz Anton**
— Die Garten Prospect von Hellbrun. Augsburg: J. A. Pfeffel, [c.1730]. Oblong folio, modern half vellum. With engraved title & 19 plates. Repaired tears to 6 plates, affecting image of Plate 16. C Apr 3 (80) £2,400

**Dansdorf, Chrysilla von**
— Heart's Desire. Pvtly ptd [n.d.]. One of 70. Illus by John Buckland Wright. 4to, orig cloth. S May 16 (105) £1,100

**Danse Macabre...**
— La Grande Danse Macabre des hommes et des femmes historiee .... [Lyon: Mathias Huss], 18 Feb 1499-1500. 4to, mor janseniste. 46 lines; double column; types 10:120G (title, headings), 17:97B (text) & 60G (on 4 cuts); large calligraphic historiated initial on a1r. With 67 (of 69) woodcuts, including repetitions. Washed; outer & lower margin of a1 repaired affecting large initial; repaired tears in a2 without loss. 40 (of 42) leaves; lacking b2 & g6 (supplied in photofacsimile). GW 7954. Lignerolles - Guyot de Villeneuve - Essling - Schaefer copy. P Nov 1 (74) $150,000

Anr Ed. Troyes: Jean Antoine Garnier, [1728]. 4to, unbound in paper chemise. With 58 woodcuts. tear with loss to C3; some fraying. Fairfax Murray, no 108. Schaefer copy. P Nov 1 (75) $800

**Dante Alighieri, 1265-1321**
See also: Ashendene Press; Bremer Press; Limited Editions Club; Nonesuch Press
— De la volgare eloquentia. Vicenza: Tolomeo Ianiculo, Jan 1529. Bound with: Trissino, Giovanni Giorgio. La Poetica. Vicenza, Apr 1529. And: Trissino. Epistola de le lettere nuovamente aggiunte ne la lingua italiana. Vicenza, Feb 1529. And: Trissino. Dialogo... intitulato il Castellano nel quale si tratta de la lingua italiana. Vicenza, [1529]. Folio & 4to, contemp vellum from a 14th-cent Bible bifolium, with vellum strip pasted over spine; worming to spine. Cosimo Bartoli's copy. C June 26 (67) £4,000
— The New Life. L, [1915]. One of 150. Illus by Evelyn Paul; trans by Dante Gabriel Rossetti; music by Alfred Mercer. Vellum gilt. K Oct 1 (124) $250
— La Vita nova. Paris, 1907. One of 130. Illus by Maurice Denis; trans by Henry Cochin. 4to, mor extra by Joly to a Grolieresque design, orig wraps bound in. With additional suite of 68 color decompositions of the woodcuts on chine & japon. S Nov 21 (101) £700
— La Vita nuova. Bergamo, 1921. One of 1,321. Illus by Vittorio Grassi. Folio, cloth. sg Sept 14 (98) $90

Anr Ed. Montagnola: Officina Bodoni, 1925. One of 225. Folio, vellum. Minor foxing. bba May 9 (20) £880 [Heritage]

Anr copy. Vellum, unopened. Ck May 31 (6) £650

Anr copy. Vellum. pba Aug 8 (378) $250

**Divina Commedia in Italian**
— 1481, 30 Aug. - Florence: Nicolaus Laurentii Alamanus. Folio, modern blind-stamped mor. 45 lines of text, 60 lines commentary & headline; types 4b:115R (text), 5:91R (commentary). Made-up copy, with C3.8 inserted & mtd, a5, D2 & L2 from smaller copy; 1st engraving cropped & restored; repairs & worming; some sheets washed; repaired tears; spotting at ends. 366 (of 373) leaves; lacking 6 blanks. Goff D-29. S June 27 (311) £10,000

— 1491, 18 Nov. - Venice: Petrus de Plasiis Cremonensis called Veronensis. Folio, 19th-cent mor janseniste. 45 lines of text, 61 lines of commentary; types 6:109R (text) & 7:80R (commentary); 100 woodcut illusts. Tear to 1st leaf repaired; small stain on B1; some leaves rehinged; contemp marginal annotations washed. 324 leaves. Goff D-33. C June 26 (160) £4,000

— 1502. - Le Terze Rime. Venice: Aldus Issue with the anchor on last page. 8vo, 19th-cent mor. Tp extended at margins; 3-line initial & armorial device washed from a2; 1st leaf repaired, obscuring the Aldine device, which has been replaced in facsimile; some staining. Early annotations attributed to Celio Calcagnini by Giuseppe Cav. Antonelli in 1852. C Apr 3 (81) £5,200

Anr copy. Mor gilt by Trautz-Bauzonnet. C Apr 3 (82) £3,500

— 1529. - Comedia. Venice: Jacopo da Borgofranco for Luc' Antonio Giunta. Folio, orig vellum; tear at head of spine. Stamp & writing on A2; tp border rubbed; some worming & staining. S June 12 (37) £550

— 1768. - Paris: Prault. 2 vols. 12mo, contemp red mor gilt by Derome le jeune. With port, engraved title & folding plate. Holford - Fuerstenberg - Schaefer copy. S Dec 7 (148) £1,200

### Divina Commedia in English

— 1900. - L. Trans by Henry Wadsworth Longfellow. 8vo, vellum gilt by Giulio Giannini, with goal-leaf initial D on upper cover enclosing hand-painted miniature of Danti with multi-colored floriated rubrication. sg Sept 21 (84) $475

— 1906. - Bost. & NY One of 650 L.p. copies. Trans by Henry Wadsworth Longfellow; illus by Flaxman. 6 vols. cloth. sg Feb 8 (274) $110

### Divina Commedia in Italian & German

— 1921. - Vienna, etc. One of 1,100. Illus by F. von Bayros. 3 vols. 4to, half vellum gilt; hinges cracked on Vol I, worn, soiled. wa Dec 14 (590) £210

### Divina Commedia in English

— 1929. - San Francisco: John Henry Nash One of 250 on handmade paper. 4 vols, including The Florence of Dante. Folio, vellum. sg Oct 19 (64) $1,500

— 1931. - The Inferno. NY One of 1,200. Illus by William Blake. Folio, lev. With 7 plates. pba Sept 14 (63) $200

— 1983. - L: Talfourd Press One of 185. Illus by Tom Phillips. Folio, unsewn as issued in 2 fitted silk cases. With 140 plates. S Nov 2 (100) £800 [Fluhmann]

## Dapper, Olfert, d.1690

— Asia.... Antwerp, 1672. Folio, contemp vellum; soiled. With additional title, title, 31 plates (15 double-page), & 28 illus in text. Lacking map of Persia; many plates frayed; some worming, soiling, & staining. S Oct 26 (575) £400 [Al-Ankavy]

Anr Ed. Nuremberg, 1681. 2 parts in 1 vol. Folio, contemp calf; worn. With engraved title, 1 double-page map only (of 11), 22 double-page plates & 8 full-page plates showing 11 subjects. Some plates frayed or torn; worming or staining affecting letters. S June 13 (592) £340

— Naukeurige beschryving der Eilanden, in de Archipel der Middelantische Zee.... Amst., 1688. Folio, early calf gilt; backstrip loose. With engraved title & 17 maps & plates. sg Mar 7 (56) $2,400

## Daran, Jacques

— Anatomie des parties de la generation de l'homme et de la femme.... Paris, 1778. Illus by Jacques Gautier d'Agoty. Folio, 19th-cent half calf; spine def. With 9 plates ptd in 4 colors. S Nov 30 (324) £5,000

## Darbee, Harry

— Catskill Flytier. My Life, Times and Technique. Phila., [1977]. One of 125. 4to, lea. With a salmon fly, "Little Inky Boy," tipped to limitation leaf. Inscr to Sparse Grey Hackle. O Feb 6 (55) $1,600

## Darby, William, 1775-1854

— The Emigrant's Guide to the Western and South-Western States and Territories. NY, 1818. 8vo, contemp half lea; extremities worn, numbers on backstrip. Inked stamp on tp. sg Oct 26 (87) $850

Anr copy. Contemp calf; edges worn, joints weak, spine heel chipped. With 3 maps & 2 tables. Some foxing. wa Feb 29 (393) $800

— A Tour from the City of New-York, to Detroit, in the Michigan Territory.... NY, 1819. 1st Ed. 8vo, disbound. With 3 maps. Final text leaf lacking corner with loss of words. sg Oct 26 (88) $100

**Dares Phrygius.** See: Dictys Cretensis & Dares Phrygius

## Dark...

— Dark at Heart. Arlington Heights: Dark Harvest, 1992. One of 400. Ed by Joe R. & Karen Lansdale. In dj. pba Dec 7 (120) $80

## Darley, Felix Octavius Carr, 1822-88

— The Cooper Vignettes. NY, 1862. L.p. Ed. Folio, mor gilt; worn, ends chipped, joints starting. With 64 plates, all mtd India-proofs before letters. wa Feb 29 (103) $220

## Darlow, Thomas Herbert —& Moule, Horace Frederick

— Historical Catalogue of the Printed Editions of Holy Scripture.... Cambr. MA: Martino, [n.d.]. One of 350. 4 vols. 4to, cloth; some wear. Facsimile reprint of the 1903 Ed. O Mar 26 (68) $160

Anr copy. Cloth; some wear. Facsimile reprint of the 1903 Ed. O May 7 (99) $150

## Darlow, Thomas Herbert —& Moule, Herbert Frederick

— Historical Catalogue of the Printed Editions of Holy Scripture.... L, [n.d.]. One of 350. 2 vols in 4. 8vo, orig cloth. Reprint of 1903-11 Ed. sg Apr 11 (88) $200

## Darmon, J. E.
— Dictionnaire des estampes & livres illustres sur les ballon & machines volantes.... Montpellier, 1929. One of 1,000. Wraps. sg May 16 (26) $175

## Darmstaedter, Ludwig
— Handbuch zur Geschichte der Naturwissenschaften und der Technik. Berlin, 1908. 8vo, half cloth; spine top chipped, joints cracked. sg Apr 11 (281) $90

## Darrow, Clarence, 1857-1938
— Fannington. NY, [1928]. Sgd, with clipped picture of him mtd above. pba Sept 14 (119) $225
— Farmington. NY, 1932. Inscr to Col. & Mrs. Bailey by Darrow & by Jessie Darrow Brownlee & with Ls from Paul Darrow to Col. Bailey laid in. pba Sept 14 (120) $300
— The Story of My Life. NY & L, 1932. Cloth, in chipped dj; dent in upper cover. Inscr to Clarence Higgins, 17 Oct 1932. bbc Dec 18 (466) $800

Anr copy. Orig cloth; spine ends rubbed with tear at head. Inscr to Col. & Mrs. Bailey, 1933. pba Sept 14 (121) $350

**Dart, Robert Paul.** See: Hoyt Collection, Charles B.

**Darton, Frederick Joseph Harvey.** See: Sawyer & Darton

## Darwin, Bernard
See also: Duncan & Darwin
— Golf Between Two Wars. L, 1944. 1st Ed. Cloth. pba Apr 18 (32) $140
— The Golf Courses of Great Britain. L: Jonathan Cape, [1925]. Cloth; spine area & extrems rubbed, rear hinge cracked. With color frontis illus. pba Apr 18 (37) $325
— The Golf Courses of the British Isles. L, [1910]. 1st Ed. - Illus by Harry Rountree. Cloth. With 64 color plates. Foxed. pba Nov 9 (10) $750

Anr Ed. L, 1910. Cloth. pba Apr 18 (36) $1,100
— Golf; Pleasures of Life Series. L, [1954]. 1st Ed. In dj; d/j chipped. pba Nov 9 (11) $160
— Green Memories. L, [1928]. 1st Ed. Cloth; spine ends rubbed, lower front joint torn, spine cloth creased. With frontis port. pba Apr 18 (33) $225
— Second Shots: Casual Talks About Golf. L, 1930. 1st Ed. Cloth; front cover spotted. pba Nov 9 (13) $190

Anr copy. Cloth; spine ends rubbed. pba Apr 18 (35) $275

## Darwin, Bernard —& Others
— A History of Golf in Britain. L, [1952]. 1st Ed. - Foreword by Robert T. Jones. Cloth in dj; d/j spine ends chipped & creased, spine & corners torn, small piece lacking from d/j upper panel. pba Nov 9 (9) $200

Anr Ed. L: Cassell, [1952]. Cloth in dj; d/j chipped. pba Apr 18 (38) $250

## Darwin, Charles, 1809-82
See also: Limited Editions Club
— The Different Forms of Flowers on Plants of the Same Species. L, 1877. 1st Ed. 8vo, orig cloth. Tp spotted. S Apr 23 (310) £320
— The Effects of Cross and Self Fertilisation in the Vegetable Kingdom. L, 1876. 1st Ed. 8vo, orig cloth, unopened; extremities rubbed. With errata slip. S Apr 23 (309) £300
— The Formation of Vegetable Mould through the Action of Worms. L, 1881. 1st Ed. 8vo, orig cloth; upper cover marked. S Apr 23 (312) £240
— Journal of Researches into the Geology and Natural History of the Various Countries.... L, 1839. 1st Ed. 8vo, orig cloth; rebacked retaining orig spine, marked. With 2 folding maps. Tear in 1 map. S Nov 30 (319) £900

Anr copy. Orig cloth; spine def at head. With 2 folding maps. Edward Stanley's copy. S Apr 23 (311) £1,300

Anr copy. Orig cloth. With 2 folding maps. Lacking ads. Freeman 11b. S June 13 (384) £3,200

Anr Ed. NY, 1846. 2 vols. 12mo, orig cloth; spine ends worn. Some foxing. sg Mar 7 (57) $350

Anr copy. Orig cloth; spines chipped. sg May 16 (298) $130
— The Life and Letters of Charles Darwin. NY, 1887. 2 vols. 8vo, orig cloth; spine head of Vol I rubbed. pba Aug 8 (380) $90
— On the Origin of Species.... L, 1859. 1st Ed. 8vo, orig cloth; minor wear & inkstain on upper cover, spine discolored, abrasion on upper joint. C Nov 29 (123) £3,000

Anr copy. Orig cloth, Freeman's A bdg; lower corners bent, spine ends rubbed, upper joint split after 1st quire, lower joint cracked. Publisher's catalogue in Freeman's state 3, dated June 1859. Some foxing. Hefner copy. CNY May 17 (11) $21,000

Anr copy. Orig cloth; spine ends worn, stain on rear free endpaper. With 32 pp of Murray's ads dated June 1859 at end. S June 12 (245) £13,000

Anr copy. Orig cloth; rebacked retaining orig backstrip. With 32 pp of Murray's ads dated June 1859 at end. Minor marginal repairs. sg Apr 18 (144) $7,000

Anr Ed. NY, 1860. 2d Issue. 8vo, orig cloth; spine end chipped with crack at bottom of upper joint, some signatures sprung. Some browning & foxing; old pencil notes & markings in margins. bbc Feb 26 (430) $230

1st American Ed. 8vo, orig cloth; spine ends chipped, front cover & free endpaper loose, rear hinge cracked. sg May 16 (299) $130
— On the Various Contrivances by which British and Foreign Orchids are Fertilised by Insects. L, 1862. 1st Ed. 12mo, orig cloth; rubbed, spine ends & corners frayed. pba June 20 (257) $450; S June 13 (438) £600
— The Power of Movement in Plants. L, 1880. 1st Ed. 8vo, orig cloth. b Sept 20 (218) £150
— The Variation of Animals and Plants under Domestication.... L, 1868. 1st Ed, 1st Issue. 2 vols. 8vo,

orig cloth. Tipped-in Vol I is AN of Emma Darwin on behalf of her husband Charles. S Apr 23 (308) £400
— The Zoology of the Voyage of H.M.S. Beagle. L, 1840-43. 5 vols in 3. 4to, 19th-cent russia gilt; 1 cover detached, others coming loose, 2 spines damaged. With 84 plain & 82 colored plates. Lacking half-titles to Parts 3 & 4; some foxing; some corners damaged in Part 2. S June 27 (20) £28,000

**Darwin's copy, Charles**
— New Testament in Greek. L, 1820. ("Novum Testamentum; juxta exemplar millianum... editio Secunda.") 8vo, contemp sheep backed in calf by Broadbere; rubbed, inner hinge split. Sgd by Darwin on front flyleaf. With related material. CNY May 17 (65) $24,000

**Darwin, Charles, 1809-82 —& Others**
— Narrative of the Surveying Voyages of his Majesty's Ships Adventure and Beagle.... L, 1839. 1st Ed. 4 vols, including Appendix to Vol II. 8vo, orig cloth, variant a with author's names on spines; spines worn. With 9 maps & plans & 47 plates. Bodleian library release stamps. S Nov 30 (320) £5,200

Anr copy. Orig cloth, variant with authors' names on spines; Vol II def at head of spine, other spine heads with small tears. With 55 plates & maps, including 7 (of 8) loose in pockets. Lacking Track Chart in Appendix to Vol II; tears to 2 maps; some foxing. S Apr 23 (307) £2,600

**Darwin, Erasmus, 1731-1802**
— The Botanic Garden. L, 1791-90. 2d Ed. 2 vols in 1. 4to, contemp calf; worn. Some cropping & spotting. b Sept 20 (108) £350
— Zoonomia; or, the Laws of Organic Life. L, 1794-96. 1st Ed. 2 vols. 4to, contemp calf; rebacked & repaired. With 10 plates, 6 of them colored. Stain in margin of 1 plate; some foxing. S June 12 (248) £650

**Darwin, Sir George Howard**
— Scientific Papers. Cambr., 1907-16. 5 vols. 4to, orig cloth. sg May 16 (153) $250

**Dasent, George Webbe, 1817-96**
— Popular Tales from the Norse. Edin., 1869. 2d Ed. 8vo, early 20th-cent half calf. F June 20 (713) $100

**Dash, Mary**
— Sacred and Moral Pieces. Brighton, 1827. 8vo, half calf. b Dec 5 (378) £160

**Dater, Judy**
— Imogen Cunningham: A Portrait. Bost., [1979]. 4to, cloth, in dj with small tears. sg Feb 29 (106) $50

**Dauberville, Jean & Henry**
— Bonnard... Catalogue raisonne de l'oeuvre peint. Paris, 1965-74. Vol II only. In dj. sg Jan 11 (55) $650

Anr Ed. Paris, 1966-74. One of 1,000. 4 vols. 4to, orig cloth; shaken. sg Jan 11 (54) $2,600

**Daudet, Alphonse, 1840-97**
— Aventures prodigieuses de Tartarin de Tarascon. Paris, 1937. One of 130. Illus by Raoul Dufy. 4to, mor extra by Paul Bonet with lion's head, orig wraps bound in. S May 16 (18) £17,000
— Lettres de mon moulin. Monte Carlo: Editions Le Parnasse, [n.d.]. One of 188 with orig sgd watercolor. Illus by Hubert Clerissi. 8vo, loose as issued in fabric-covered box. wd May 8 (50) $100
— Sapho. Paris: Collection Charpentier Maison Quantin, 1888. One of 50 L.p. copies on Japon with plates in 2 states. 8vo, mor extra by Yvert, orig wraps bound in. Limitation number erased. CNY May 18 (203) $400
— Sapho: Parisian Customs. Paris, 1897. One of 38 on chine extra-fort, with 3 extra suites of the plates & 2 extra suites of the illusts. 8vo, mor extra pictorial bdg by Charles Meunier, orig wraps bound in. S Nov 21 (104) £2,200

**Dautert, Erich**
— Big Game in Antarctica. L, [1937]. Orig cloth; spot to rear cover, lacking front free endpaper. pba July 25 (29) $50

**Davenant, Charles, 1656-1714**
— Discourses on the Publick Revenues.... L, 1698-[97]. Bound in 1 vol. 8vo, contemp calf; rubbed. With 4 folding plates. b Sept 20 (110) £850
— An Essay upon the Probable Methods of Making a People Gainers in the Ballance of Trade. L, 1699. 1st Ed. 8vo, calf; spine rubbed. With 6 folding tables. S July 11 (117) £500
— An Essay upon Ways and Means of Supplying the War. L, 1695. 2d Ed. 8vo, contemp calf; worn. Tear to folding plate. b Sept 20 (109) £250

**Davenant, Sir William, 1606-68**
— Works. L, 1673. 1st Collected Ed. Folio, contemp calf; rubbed, rebacked. Some leaves worn or torn. CE June 12 (184) $260

**Davenport, Cyril**
— Cameos. L, 1900. 8vo, orig cloth. With 8 color plates. Library markings. sg Sept 7 (121) $50
— The English Regalia. L, 1897. One of 500. Folio, orig cloth. With 12 color plates. pba Mar 7 (79) $55

**Davenport, John, 1789-1877**
— Curiositates eroticae physiologiae. L, 1875. 4to, contemp bds; rebacked with cloth, extremities rubbed, half-title loose. sg May 16 (400) $50

**Davenport, W.**
— Historical Portraiture of Leading Events in the Life of Ali Pacha, Vizier of Epirus.... L, 1823. Folio, contemp russia; rebacked, scuffed. With 6 handcolored plates. Smear to 1 plate; anr mtd to size. C Oct 25 (109) £1,000

1st Ed. - Plates by G. Hunt. Folio, orig bds; dust-soiled, inner hinges strengthened, worn. With half title, & 6 hand-colored plates. S Oct 26 (89) £1,050 [Bankes]

### Davey, Neil K.
— Netsuke: A Comprehensive Study Based on the M. T. Hindson Collection. L, [1974]. 4to, cloth, in dj. sg June 13 (130) $130

### David, Saint, c.500-600. See: Gregynog Press

### David, Andrew
— The Charts & Coastal Views of Captain Cook's Voyages. L: Hakluyt Society, 1988-92. 2 vols. Folio, cloth, in djs. pba Feb 13 (48) $400

### David, Jan
— Duodecim specula deum aliquando videre desideranti concinnata. Antwerp: Plantin, 1610. 8vo, contemp calf gilt, with Jesuite device; rebacked, new endpapers. With engraved title & 12 plates. sg Mar 21 (85) $425

### David, Robert B.
— Malcolm Campbell, Sheriff.... Casper WY, [1932]. Later cloth. pba Aug 8 (40) $50

### Davidov, V. P.
— Atlas k putevym zapiskam Davidova.... Paris & St. Petersburg, 1839. Part 1 only. Folio, contemp half mor; some wear. With 13 hand-colored lithos heightened with gum arabic (1 double-page with short split in fold) & 10 plans, 1 with details hand-colored. General title & list of plates for the complete 1840 Ed loosely inserted. Some spotting & marginal staining; some plates mtd & not uniform in size. S June 27 (141) £8,000

### Davidovitch, David
— The Ketuba: Jewish Marriage Contracts through the Ages. Tel-Aviv, [1968]. Folio, orig cloth in dj & slipcase; worn. With 18 tipped-in color plates. Inscr & sgd. sg Apr 11 (173) $90

### Davidson, Bruce
— East 100th Street. Cambr., 1970. 4to, photo-pictorial stiff wraps; soiled. sg Feb 29 (111) $250

### Davidson, George, 1825-1911
— The Alaska Boundary. San Francisco, 1903. 1st Ed. 4to, orig cloth; extremities slightly rubbed. With 2 folding maps & frontis port. Robbins copy. pba Mar 21 (75) $300
— Coast Pilot of California, Oregon, and Washington Territory. Wash., 1889. 4th Ed. 4to, half lea; rebacked with orig spine laid on, worn, front free endpaper reattached. Larson copy. pba Feb 12 (32) $375
— Directory for the Pacific Coast of the United States.... [Wash., c.1862]. 4to, orig wraps; worn, chipped, tape-repaired. Dampstained. pba July 25 (130) $140
— An Examination of Some of the Early Voyages of Discovery and Exploration on the Northwest Coast of America, from 1539 to 1603. Wash., 1887. 4to, half mor. With 1 folded map. Larson copy. pba Sept 28 (79) $120

Anr copy. Orig wraps. U.S. Coast & Geodetic Survey, Appendix No. 7 -- Report for 188. Larson copy. pba Feb 12 (30) $65

Anr copy. Mor; spine foot stained. U.S. Coast & Geodetic Survey, Appendix No. 7 -- Report for 1886. Inscr to Mrs. Thomas B. Bishop & with holograph corrections. pba July 25 (132) $170
— Francis Drake on the Northwest Coast of America in the Year 1579. [San Francisco], 1908. Wrappers. Larson copy. pba Sept 28 (80) $50
— Identification of Sir Francis Drake's Anchorage on the Coast of California in the Year 1579. [San Francisco]: California Historical Society, [1890]. Orig cloth; corners bumped. Inscr by Davidson & with related material. pba July 25 (131) $300
— The Origin and Meaning of the Name California. San Francisco, 1910. Orig wraps. Geographical Society of the Pacific: Transactions and Proceedings. Larson copy. pba Feb 12 (31) $65
— Pacific Coast: Coast Pilot of California, Oregon, and Washington Territory. Wash., 1869. 4to, orig cloth; torn & glue-repaired. pba July 25 (133) $140

### Davie, Oliver
— Methods in the Art of Taxidermy. Columbus, 1894. 4to, orig cloth; hinges reinforced. pba Aug 8 (613) $55

### Davies, Edward William Lewis
— Algiers in 1857. L, 1858. 8vo, cloth. sg Mar 7 (58) $175

### Davies, George R.
— Collection of Old Chinese Porcelains. L, 1913. 4to, orig cloth; needs rebacked. With 25 color plates. Some text leaves foxed. sg Sept 7 (75) $100

### Davies, Llywelyn
— Hanes Mod-daith y Brig Albion.... Caernarvon, 1820. 8vo, contemp canvas; soiled. Soiled. S Oct 26 (488) £800 [Maggs]

### Davies, Nina M. —&
### Gardiner, Alan Henderson
— Ancient Egyptian Paintings. Chicago, 1936. Vols I-II (of 3, lacking text vol). Cloth; worn & loose, some plates nearly detached. With 104 color plates. Library markings to plates & covers. wa Nov 16 (293) $600

### Davies, Richard, 1635-1708. See: Gregynog Press

### Davies, William Henry, 1871-1940
See also: Gregynog Press
— The Hour of Magic. L, 1922. One of 100. 4to, orig half cloth; soiled. bba May 9 (246) £60 [Blackwell]

### Daviler, A. C.
— Ausfuehrliche Anleitung zu der gantzen Civil Baukunst von J. Bar. de Vignola. Augsburg: heirs of Jeremias Wolff, 1725. 4to, contemp sheep; worn. With 149 (of 151) plates, 52 of them folding. Plates 73 & 91 def; tears in many other folding plates; lacking Plates 115 & 116. Sold w.a.f. sg Jan 11 (3) $300

**Davillier, Jean Charles, Baron, 1823-83**
— Spain. L, 1881. Trans by J. Thomson; illus by Gustave Dore. 4to, orig cloth; spine ends chipped. pba Mar 7 (95) $250

**Davin, Nicholas Flood**
— The Irishman in Canada. L, [1877]. 8vo, orig cloth; worn & shaken. F June 20 (80) $100

**Davis, Charles G.**
— Shipping & Craft in Silhouette. Salem, 1929. In dj. O Dec 5 (38) $50; O Dec 5 (39) $50
— Ships of the Past. Salem, 1929. With 12 folding plans. Prelims dampstained in gutter. O Dec 5 (40) $50

**Davis, Ellis A.**
— Davis' Commercial Encyclopedia of the Pacific Southwest.... Berkeley, 1911. Folio, orig cloth; extremities rubbed. pba Nov 16 (77) $140

**Davis, Jefferson, 1808-89**
— Message of the President. [Montgomery, 29 Apr 1861]. 12mo, modern wraps. Some marginal chips. pba Apr 25 (167) $150

**Davis, John, 1774-1854**
— Travels of Four Years and a Half in the United States of America.... Bost.: The Bibliophile Society, 1910. ("Travels in the United States of America....") One of 487. Ed by J. V. Cheney. 2 vols. 8vo, bds. sg Oct 26 (90) $130

**Davis, Lavinia**
— A Bibliography of the Writings of Edith Wharton. Portland ME, 1933. One of 325. Cloth, unopened. O Dec 5 (41) $80

**Davis, Raymond Cazallis, b.1836**
— Reminiscences of a Voyage Around the World. Ann Arbor, 1869. 12mo, orig cloth; rubbed, extremities worn, rear cover cloth rippling. Dampstaining & foxing. pba Aug 8 (41) $100

**Davis, Tenney L.**
— The Chemistry of Powder and Explosives. NY, 1941-43. Pencil notations on free endpapers in Vol I. bbc June 24 (296) $225

**Davis, William Heath, 1822-1909**
— Seventy-Five Years in California.... San Francisco, 1929. Illus by Douglas Rodger. 4to, orig cloth in dj; d/j chipped, front flap lacking, soiled. With 68 chapter headings, 40 plates, 1 facsimile, & prospectus. Larson copy. pba Sept 28 (395) $55
California Collector's Ed, One of 22. 4to, half bds in dj & clamshell box; d/j soiled, creased & torn. With 68 chapter headings, 40 plates, 1 facsimile, & 22 embellishments. Sgd by Douglas Watson, ed, & John Howell. Larson copy. pba Sept 28 (394) $900
— Sixty Years in California: Events and Life.... San Francisco, 1889. 1st Ed. 8vo, orig cloth in later slipcase; spine faded. Larson copy. pba Sept 28 (393) $225

Anr Ed. San Francisco, 1929. ("Seventy-Five Years in California....") Ed by Douglas S. Watson. 4to, cloth. pba Apr 25 (370) $65
Argonaut Ed, one of 100. 4to, half cloth; worn. With related material inserted. Larson copy. pba Feb 12 (273) $1,400

**Davis, Winfield J**
See also: Illustrated...
— History of the Political Conventions in California, 1849-1892. Sacramento, 1893. 1st Ed. 8vo, orig calf; covers scuffed. Robbins copy. pba Mar 21 (76) $450

**Davy, G. Burton**
— Saga of the Rockies. Manchester NH: Lew A Cummings, [n.d.]. Cloth; worn. O June 25 (40) $350

**Davy, Sir Humphry, 1778-1829**
— Elements of Agricultural Chemistry. L, 1813. 1st Ed. 4to, contemp calf; joints cracked, spine & lettering piece chipped, rubbed. With frontis & 19 plates (1 folding). Some offsetting; plates dampstained in inner margins; some leaves spotted. Ck Mar 22 (86) £70
— On the Safety Lamp for Coal Miners.... L, 1818. 1st Ed. 8vo, orig bds. With folding plate. A few leaves waterstained. b May 30 (18) £950
Anr copy. Half calf; scuffed. Library stamps to front pastedown, front flyleaf & tp. pba Sept 14 (124) $800
— Salmonia: or, Days of Fly Fishing. Phila., 1832. 1st American Ed. 12mo, orig cloth. Library markings. sg Mar 7 (418) $175

**Davy, John, 1790-1868**
— Notes and Observations on the Ionian Islands and Malta. L, 1842. 1st Ed. 2 vols. 8vo, orig cloth, unopened; front joint splitting on 1 vol. With 6 plates. sg Mar 7 (59) $175

**Dawson, George, 1813-83**
— Pleasures of Angling with Rod and Reel for Trout and Salmon. NY, 1876. 1st Ed. 8vo, orig cloth; spine ends frayed. Small tape-stain on tp. O Feb 6 (56) $200
Anr copy. Cloth; inner joints starting. O June 25 (41) $110
Anr copy. Orig cloth; spine ends chipped, soiled, corners rubbed, front hinge cracked. Inscr, 1879. pba July 11 (65) $250

**Dawson, Nicholas, 1819-1903.** See: Grabhorn Printing

**Dawson, Warren Royal.** See: Smith & Dawson

**Dawson, William Leon**
— The Birds of California. San Diego, 1923. 4 vols. 4to, orig cloth. pba Apr 25 (372) $200
One of 100. Lev gilt with hand-carved birds of hard wood. Larson copy. pba Feb 12 (40) $1,700
One of 350. Bds; extremities worn & scuffed, spine ends rubbed, 2 tears to top of Vol III spine, some joint tears. cb Oct 17 (126) $800

Anr copy. Orig lev gilt with hand-colored birds. With orig watercolor, sgd by Allan Brooks, framed. cb June 25 (1715) $700

**Dawson's Book Shop**
— Baja California Travel Series. Los Angeles: Dawson's Book Shop, 1965-86. One of 500. Ed by Doyce B. Nunis. 48 vols, Orig cloth; shelf worn. Robbins set. pba Mar 21 (7) $550

— Early California Travel Series. Los Angeles, 1951-61. Ltd Ed. 50 vols (complete). Cloth & bds; minor shelf wear. Robbins copy. pba Mar 21 (92) $1,500

**Day, Charles Russell, 1860-1900**
— The Music and Musical Instruments of Southern India. L, 1891. One of 700. 4to, vellum gilt, in wrap. With 17 chromolitho plates. S May 15 (21) £200; S May 15 (23) £240

**Day Lewis, Cecil.** See: Lewis, Cecil Day

**Day, Richard, 1552-1607?**
— A Booke of Christian Prayers.... L, 1590. 4to, 18th-cent mor gilt; rubbed, joints split. Gothic & roman type; title within wide woodcut border of Jesse's dream, with full-page woodcut borders of Elizabeth I on verso; text within elaborate woodcut borders. Some foxing at beginning & end; some lower borders cropped; a few leaves dampstained in upper portion. CNY May 17 (66) $1,900

Anr copy. Contemp calf gilt; rebacked. Roman & black letter types. Some ink stains; early pen trials on O3v. Davis - Schaefer copy. P Nov 1 (48) $4,250

**Daye, Eliza**
— Poems, on Various Subjects. Liverpool, 1798. 8vo, 19th-cent half calf. b Dec 5 (191) £240

**Days...**
— Days of the Dandies. L: Grolier Society, [after 1900]. One of 100. 15 vols. 8vo, mor gilt; joints rubbed. CE Sept 27 (251) $1,000

**Dayton, Edson C.**
— Dakota Days, May 1886-August 1898. Hartford: Pvtly ptd, 1937. One of 300. wa Feb 29 (359) $190

**De Andrea, Miguel.** See: Onassis copy, Jacqueline Bouvier Kennedy

**De Becker, Joseph Ernest, 1863-1929**
— The Nightless City, or, the History of the Yoshiwara Yukwaku. Yokohama: Max Nossler, [c.1905]. pba Mar 7 (82) $300

**De Bosschere, Jean**
— Folk Tales of Flanders. NY, 1918. 4to, orig cloth; corners bumped. With 12 color plates. Some browning. F June 20 (547) $70

**De Britaine, William.** See: Britaine, William de

**De Bure, Guillaume Francois, 1731-82**
— Musaeum typographicum.... Paris, 1755. One of 12. 12mo, contemp citron mor gilt, with arms of Michel de Leon; Vol X not uniform and with joints cracked.

B4 torn at edge of text area. Fuerstenberg - Schaefer copy. S Dec 7 (88) £3,200

— [Sale Catalogue] Catalogue des livres de la bibliotheque de feu M. de Duc de La Valliere. Paris, 1783. 3 vols. 8vo, contemp calf gilt; rubbed, some joints cracked. Price list at end of Vol III; with port & 4 folding plates. Fuerstenberg - Schaefer copy. S Dec 7 (89) £110

**De Camp, L. Sprague**
— The Tritonian Ring and Other Pusadian Tales. NY: Twayne, [1953]. In dj with piece lacking from upper front panel. pba May 4 (129) $60

**De Camp, L. Sprague —& Pratt, Fletcher**
— The Incomplete Enchanter. NY: Holt, [1941]. In chipped dj. pba May 4 (126) $120

Anr copy. In dj by Artzybasheff. sg June 20 (317) $130

— Land of Unreason. NY, [1942]. In dj by Artzybasheff. sg June 20 (318) $150

**De Carava, Roy —& Hughes, Langston, 1902-67**
— The Sweet Flypaper of Life. Munich, [1956]. ("Harlem Story.") 1st German Ed. Pictorial bds; rubbed & soiled. sg Feb 29 (112) $250

**De Casseres, Benjamin**
— Robinson Jeffers: Tragic Terror. [N.p.]: John Mayfield, [1928]. One of 49. Orig string-bound wraps. Inscr by Paul Jordan-Smith to Phil La Vie. pba Oct 5 (194) $500

— When Huck Finn Went Highbrow. NY, 1934. One of 125. Half vellum. O Dec 5 (43) $70

**De Chair, Somerset.** See: Golden Cockerel Press

**De Chelus, D.**
— Histoire naturelle du cacao et du sucre. Paris, 1719. 1st Ed. 12mo in 8s & 4s, contemp calf; extrems rubbed. With 6 plates (4 folding). Lower margins stained; plate 1 crumpled. Ck Mar 22 (87) £220

2d Ed. Amst., 1720. 8vo, contemp calf; rubbed, upper joint split. With title, 6 plates (4 folding). Plate 2 repaired & torn; plate 4 torn in margin. Ck Mar 22 (88) £300

**De Creux, Francois**
— Historiae Canadiensis, seu Novae-Franciae libri decem.... Paris, 1664. 4to, contemp calf; rebacked, worn. With title device & 13 plates (1 folding). Lacking folding map; some discoloration. S Oct 26 (489) £1,000 [Faupel]

**De Forest, John W., 1826-1906**
— History of the Indians of Connecticut.... Hartford, 1851. 1st Ed. 8vo, orig cloth; extremities frayed. Folding map creased; some dampstaining. F June 20 (386) $70

**De Freitas, Leo John**
— Tenniel's Wood-Engraved Illustrations to Alice's Adventures Underground and Through the Looking Glass. Oxfordshire: Macmillan, 1988. One of 250. 2 folding cases & vol of text. With 93 plates. sg Feb 8 (248) $2,400; sg Feb 15 (298) $1,300

**De Gouy, Louis Pullig.** See: Derrydale Press

**De Grey, Thomas**
— The Compleat Horse-Man, and Expert Ferrier. L, 1639. Folio, contemp calf; needs rebacking. Hole in corner of 2Y2. sg May 16 (301) $600

**De Jure...** See: Molloy, Charles

**De Kay, Charles**
— Bird Gods. NY, [1898]. Review copy. Illus by George Wharton Edwards. Pictorial cloth; spine heel rubbed. pba Mar 7 (83) $80

**De La Gray, Thomas.** See: De Grey, Thomas

**De la Mare, Walter, 1873-1956**
— Songs of Childhood. L, 1902. 1st Ed. Orig half vellum. S Nov 2 (281) £230 [Sotheran]
Anr copy. Orig half vellum. Inscr, 17 June 1925. S Nov 2 (282) £480 [Sotheran]

**De La Porte du Theil Library, Jean Gabriel**
— [Sale Catalogue] Catalogue des livres de la bibliotheque de feu.... Paris, 1816. 8vo, contemp half calf; rubbed. Priced throughout. Library stamps. O Mar 26 (69) $130

**De La Rue, Warren, 1815-89 —& Others**
— Researches on Solar Physics. L, 1865-66-68. 3 parts in 1 vol. 4to, modern bds. With 5 plates. Soiling to 1st title & to fore-margin of Plate IV; marginal tears; Plate 5 creased. CNY May 17 (12) $2,500

**De Long, George Washington**
— The Voyage of the Jeannette. Bost., 1884. 2 vols. 8vo, orig cloth; Vol I hinges cracked. With folding map in Vol I rear cover pocket. sg Mar 7 (278) $150

**De Massey, Ernest**
— A Frenchman in the Gold Rush. San Francisco: California Historical Society, 1927. pba Nov 16 (79) $75
Anr copy. Copy of the appendix, Some Phases of French Society in San Francisco in the Fifties, laid in. pba Feb 12 (495) $110

**De Quille, Dan.** See: Wright, William

**De Quille, Dan, Pseud.** See: Wright, William

**De Quincey, Thomas, 1785-1859**
— Confessions of an English Opium-Eater. L, 1822. 1st Ed. 12mo, contemp half mor. Lacking half-title & ads. b Jan 31 (106) £160
— Klosterheim; or, the Masque. By the English Opium-Eater. Edin. & L, 1832. 8vo, orig cloth; spine head chipped. S Apr 23 (37) £150

— Works. Bost., 1856-59. 21 vols. 8vo, half mor. Dampstaining to several vols. pba Dec 14 (37) $110
Anr Ed. Edin., 1862-63. Vols I-XV (of 16). 8vo, orig cloth; some covers waterstained. b Jan 31 (78) £70
Anr Ed. Bost.: Houghton Mifflin, [1877]. 6 vols. 8vo, half mor by Roach. pba Aug 8 (274) $250
Anr Ed. Edin., 1889-90. 14 vols. 8vo, half mor gilt. wa Dec 14 (13) $475

**De ritibus Sinensium...**
— De ritibus Sinensium erga Confucium philosophum, et progenitores mortuos Alexandri Papeae VII decreto permissis.... Liege, 1700. 12mo, contemp vellum. Ed with 620 pp. b Sept 20 (412) £300

**De Russailh, Albert B.** See: Grabhorn Printing

**De Soto, Hernando.** See: Grabhorn Printing

**De Tolnay, Charles**
— Pierre Breugel l'Ancien. Brussels, 1935. 2 vols. 4to, wraps. With 116 plates. sg June 13 (65) $100

**De Trafford, Sir Humphrey Francis**
— The Horses of the British Empire. L, [1908]. 2 vols. 4to, orig mor gilt; rubbed. C July 1 (330) £500
Anr copy. Orig cloth; some wear, corners frayed. O Jan 9 (77) $190

**De Vinne, Theodore Low, 1828-1914.** See: Grabhorn Printing

**De Voto, Bernard, 1897-1955**
— Across the Wide Missouri. Bost., 1947. 1st Ed, One of 265. Illus by A. J. Miller, Charles Bodmer, & George Catlin. Orig cloth. Robbins copy. Inscr & sgd to Herbert M. Evans. pba Mar 21 (77) $350
— The Year of Decision: 1846. NY: Book-of-the-Month Club, [1984]. In dj. pba Apr 25 (374) $65

**De Vries, Hugo, 1848-1935**
— Die Mutationstheorie. Versuche und Beobachtungen ueber die Entstehung von Arten im Pflanzenreich. Liepzig, 1901-3. 2 vols. 8vo, old half lea; cracked & worn, Vol I lacking spine, Vol II spine loose & cracked. With 12 colored plates. Met May 22 (406) $250

**De Wint, Peter, 1784-1849.** See: Light & De Wint

**Deakin, Edwin**
— The Twenty-one Missions of California. Berkeley, 1901. Bound with: A Gallery of California Mission Paintings by Edwin Deakin. Los Angeles, 1966; and The Golden Era of the Missions. San Francisco, [1974] 4th Ed. Together, 3 vols, orig cloth; front & rear hinge cracking. With 21 b&w plates & 1 map. 3 leaves detached in Golden Era. Larson copy. pba Sept 28 (151) $90

**Bashford Collection, Dean**
— The Bashford Dean Collection of Arms and Armor, in the Metropolitan Museum of Art. Portland ME, 1933. One of 250. 4to, half cloth. Laid in is an ink

drawing by W. A. Dwiggins for the ornamental letter T on p. 12.  O Dec 5 (42) $350
— Catalogue of European Daggers.  NY, 1929.  One of 900.  2 vols. 4to, half cloth.  sg Mar 7 (420) $175

**Dean, Henry**
— The Whole Art of Legerdemain....  NY, 1817. ("Hocus Pocus, or the Whole Art....") 17th Ed. 12mo, disbound.  Browned.  sg Sept 21 (146) $1,900

**Dear, Joseph**
— The Converted Arabs, a Poetical Fragment....  Bath, [c.1818].  8vo, contemp calf gilt.  b Dec 5 (328) £130

**Death...**
— The Death and Burial of Cock Robin. Lichfield & Stafford: A. Morgan, [c.1797].  Orig wraps.  With 15 woodcut illusts.  S Nov 2 (283) £360 [Hirsch]
Anr Ed. York: J. Kendrew, [n.d.].  32mo, orig wraps; soiled.  With 14 hand-colored illusts.  Met Dec 5 (88) $200

**Debs, Eugene V., 1855-1926**
— Walls and Bars.  Chicago: Socialist Party, [1927]. Orig cloth.  Irving Stone's annotated copy.  pba May 23 (421) $110

**DeBussy, Claude, 1862-1918**
— La boite a joujoux, ballet pour enfants.  Paris: A. Durand & Fils, [c.1919].  Illus by Andre Helle.  4to, modern half mor.  With pictorial tp, 5 preliminary leaves with illusts in text, 5 pictorial subtitles, 12 plates & tailpiece ptd in color.  Also with musical notation.  S June 13 (699) £200

**DeCasseres, Benjamin.** See: De Casseres, Benjamin

**Decker, P.**
— Chinese Architecture.  L, 1759.  In 2 parts. With 36 plates.  Bound with: Decker. Gothic Architecture.  L, 1759. In 2 parts.  With 24 plates.  Together, 4 parts in 1 vol.  Oblong 4to, modern half calf incorporating early bds.  First title torn & repaired; some old dampstaining & marginal soiling.  C Nov 29 (91) £900

**Decker, Peter**
— The Diaries of Peter Decker....  Georgetown CA: Talisman Press, 1966.  One of 100.  pba Nov 16 (83) $140

**Declaration...**
— Declaration by the Representatives of the United Colonies of North-America....  Phila: Hall & Sellers, 12 July 1775.  Single sheet, 410mm by 251mm.  Some browning & chipping.  Postscript to the Pennsylvania Gazette, No 2429.  P June 5 (31) $31,000

**Declaration of Independence**
— In Congress. July 4, 1776. A Declaration....  York-Town Pa: John Dunlap, 1778.  8vo, later cloth; broken, spine lacking.  In: Journals of Congress, Containing the Proceedings from January 1, 1776 to January 1, 1777, Vol II, pp 241-46.  bbc June 24 (391) $5,500

Anr Ed. N.p.: E. Huntington, [c.1829]. ("In Congress July 4th, 1776. Unanimous Declaration of the thirteen United States of America.") 22.75 by 18.75 inches.  Paper soft with some deterioration; short tears; shrink-wrapped.  Sold w.a.f.  pba June 13 (263) $475

**Dee, Arthur**
— Fasciculus Chemicus: or Chymical Collectoins....  L, 1650.  8vo, modern lea.  Library stamps; frontis chipped & mtd.  sg Oct 19 (224) $2,600

**Dee, John, 1527-1608**
— A True and Faithful Relation of what Passed...between Dr. John Dee...and some Spirits....  L, 1659.  Folio, later calf; upper bd detached, lower joint cracked. Some staining; Z2 with hole affecting text; minor rust-stains; some browning.  S July 11 (272) £1,300

**Defensorium...**
— Defensorium Immaculatae Virginitatis.  Leipzig, 1925.  One of 500.  4to, half vellum.  Color facsimile of Dutch block book.  sg Apr 11 (146) $100

**Defoe, Daniel, 1659?-1731**
See also: Limited Editions Club
— King William's Affection for the Church of England Examin'd.  L, 1703. 1st Ed. 4to, old wraps; backstrip chipped.  Page 2 soiled.  sg Mar 21 (86) $90
— The Life, Adventures and Pyracies, of the Famous Captain Singleton. L, 1720. 1st Ed. 8vo, contemp calf gilt; joints cracked, spine head chipped. sg Oct 19 (65) $475
— A New Voyage Round the World.  L, 1725.  8vo, contemp calf gilt; front joint starting.  With 4 plates. Some browning.  sg Oct 19 (66) $600
— The Novels. Edin., 1810.  12 vols. 8vo, calf; hinges worn.  CE Nov 8 (184) $320
— Reflections upon the Late Great Revolution. L, 1689. 4to, floral wraps. L.p. copy.  b May 30 (397) £380
— Robinson Crusoe. Frankfurt, 1773. ("Des weltberuehmten Engellaenders Robinson Crusoe....") 2 vols in 1. 8vo, contemp bds; rubbed.  With 2 frontises & 12 plates.  Lacking 1 prelim leaf in Vol II.  S Mar 28 (507) £260
Anr Ed. L, 1831. ("The Life and Surprising Adventures of Robinson Crusoe.") Illus by George Cruikshank.  Parts 1 & 2 in 2 vols. 8vo, 19th-cent half calf gilt; front joint of Vol II starting.  sg Sept 21 (143) $130
Anr Ed. L, 1884.  One of 100.  Parts 1 & 2 in 2 vols. 8vo, half mor gilt by Fazakerley.  Extra-illus with 11 plates.  rs Nov 11 (80) $350
Anr Ed. L: Basilisk Press, 1979.  One of 25 specially bound & with 10 orig plates.  Illus by Edward Gordon Craig.  4to, orig mor by Tony Miles.  sg Sept 14 (47) $650
One of 515.  Orig half mor.  With 2 plates & an orig etching by Craig.  bba May 9 (449) £120 [Sutherland]; bba May 9 (450) £130 [Bankes Books]
— The Storm.  L, [after 1704]. ("A Collection of the most remarkable Casualties and Disasters....") 8vo, contemp calf; rebacked.  Browned, stained &

wormed; some upper margins cropped, touching page numerals.  CE May 22 (122) $130
— 1st Ed. L, 1704.  8vo, contemp calf; front joint restored but cracked.  sg Apr 18 (45A) $250
— A True Collection of the Writings of the Author of the True Born Englishman. L, 1703.  1st Authorized Ed. Vol I only. 8vo, contemp calf; rebacked with orig backstrip.  sg Mar 21 (87) $250
— Works. Oxford: Shakespeare Head Press, 1927-28. ("Novels and Selected Writings.") One of 750.  14 vols. In djs, unopened.  wd Nov 15 (51) $350

### DeGolyer, Everett Lee, 1886-1956
— Across Aboriginal America: The Journey of Three Englishmen Across Texas in 1568. El Paso, 1947. One of 465.  Frontis & maps by Jose Cisneros; designed & ptd by Carl Hertzog.  4to, bds, in dj.  Inscr to Fred Sealey.  Z June 28 (70) $180

### DeGrazia, Ted
— The Rose and the Robe.... Los Angeles, 1968.  One of 500.  Half cloth in dj. Sgd. Larson copy.  pba Sept 28 (229) $85

### DeGroot, Henry
— Recollections of California Mining Life. San Francisco, 1884.  1st Ed. 8vo, orig wraps; wraps chipped, soiled, reinforced at spine. With 5 full-page illus. Larson copy.  pba Sept 28 (398) $1,000

### Deidier, ——, Abbe, 1696-1740
— L'Arithmetique des geometres.... Paris, 1739.  2 vols in 1. 4to, old calf gilt; worn, spine ends chipped, bdg wormed. With 2 folding charts. Dampstain to upper right corners; stamp to tp.  wa Feb 29 (185) $160

### Deiman, Johann Rudolph
— Von den guten Wuerkungen der Elektricitat.... Copenhagen, 1793.  2 vols. 8vo, contemp bds; worn.  S Mar 14 (95) £150

### DeKay, James E., 1792-1851
— Zoology of New-York. Part II—Birds. Albany, 1844. 4to, orig cloth; some wear. With 141 hand-colored plates. Foxed.  bbc June 24 (283) $400
Anr copy.  Cloth; needs rebdg.  sg Dec 7 (197) $375
Anr copy.  Bound in 2 vols. 4to, 19th-cent cloth; worn. Foxed; contemp plate captions in ink.  sg Dec 7 (198) $300
Anr copy.  4to, later half mor by Trow. Some foxing; some smudges.  wa Dec 14 (123) $450
Anr copy.  Orig cloth; frayed. Foxed; some closed tears.  wa Feb 29 (209) $400
— Zoology of New-York. Part III- Reptiles and Amphibia. Albany, 1842.  Plate vol only. Orig cloth; corners rubbed, spine ends chipped.  With engraved title & 102 plates.  pba Nov 30 (106) $80
Anr copy.  2 vols. 4to, orig cloth; worn & chipped. With 2 engraved titles & 102 plates. Some foxing. wa Feb 29 (211) $130
— Zoology of New-York. Parts V (Mollusca) & VI (Crustacea). Albany, 1843-44.  4to, cloth; def. With 50 (of 53) hand-colored plates. Some dampstaining.  sg May 9 (327) $140

Anr copy. Orig cloth; frayed. With 53 hand-colored plates. Minor foxing.  wa Feb 29 (210) $300

### Del Rey, Lester
— And Some Were Human. Phila.: Prime Press, 1948. Pictorial wraps; spine ends repaired.  pba Dec 7 (39) $110

### Delafield, John, 1812-65
— An Inquiry into the Origin of the Antiquities of America. NY, L & Paris, 1839.  1st Ed. 4to, orig cloth. With folding frontis, 5 plain & 5 hand-colored plates. Frontis wrinkled; library markings.  bbc Dec 18 (484) $210

### Delafosse, Jean Charles, 1734-89
— Nouvelle iconologie historique ou attributs hieroglyphiques. Paris, 1771-[68].  24 parts in 1 vol. Old bds. With 200 subjects on 144 plates. Some thumbmarks & a few stains.  S Nov 30 (257) £600
— Receuil des fontaines, frontispieces, pyramides, cartouches.... Paris, [c.1770].  2 vols in 1. Folio, disbound. With 97 (of 103) plates.  sg Dec 7 (264) $900

### Delalain, Paul Adolphe, 1840-1924 —& Others
— Catalogue de la Bibliotheque Technique. Paris: Cercle de la Librairie, Sept 1894.  8vo, contemp half mor; rubbed.  O Mar 26 (70) $160

Delalause, L'Abbe. See: Parmentier & Delalause

### DeLand, Charles E.
— The Sioux Wars. Pierre SD: State Publishing Co., 1934.  Cloth; front hinge starting.  In: South Dakota Historical Collections, Vol XVII, pp. 177-551.  pba June 25 (75) $75

### Delandine, Antoine Francois, 1756-1820
— Memoires bibliographiques et litteraires. Paris, 1810. Out-of-series copy. 8vo, contemp half calf; rubbed.  O Mar 26 (71) $350

### Delaney, Beauford
— A Retrospective. NY: The Studio Museum in Harlem, 1978.  Orig wraps. With A Ls of Henry Miller to Delaney, 21 Jan 1946 & Ls of Jean Harlow to Delaney [n.d.].  CE May 22 (123) $1,000

### Delano, Alonzo, 1806-74
See also: Grabhorn Printing
— Life on the Plains and among the Diggings. Auburn, 1854.  1st Ed. 12mo, orig cloth; spine faded, binding & extremities worn. With frontis & 3 plates. Some foxing. Larson copy.  pba Sept 28 (399) $250
Anr copy. Orig cloth; covers faded, spine ends & corners worn. With 4 plates. Robbins copy.  pba Mar 21 (78) $100
3d Thousand. Orig cloth; extremities worn, spine faded. With frontis & 3 plates. Larson copy.  pba Sept 28 (400) $140
— A Live Woman in the Mines or Pike County Ahead: A Local Play in Two Acts. NY, [1857].  1st Ed. Wraps; separated at spine & reglued. Larson copy. pba Sept 28 (402) $75

1995 - 1996 · BOOKS

DELTEIL

— The Miner's Progress; or, Scenes in the Life of a California Miner. Sacramento, 1853. 1st Ed. - Illus by Charles Nahl. 12mo, orig wraps in modern double cloth case. With 11 illus. Larson copy. pba Sept 28 (403) $1,000
— Old Block's Sketch Book. Santa Ana: The Fine Arts Press, 1947. Illus by Charles Nahl. Orig cloth. Larson copy. pba Sept 28 (404) $80

**Delano, Amasa, 1763-1823**
— A Narrative of Voyages and Travels in the Northern and Southern Hemispheres.... Bost., 1817. 8vo, modern half calf. With 3 plates. Browned throughout. b Mar 20 (81) £240

**Delany, Patrick, 1685?-1768**
— Reflections upon Polygamy, and the Encouragement given to that Practice in the Scriptures of the Old Testament...by Phileleutherus Dubliniensis. L, 1737. 1st Ed. 4to, orig front wrap only; detached. pba Mar 7 (86) $110

**Delaplaine, Joseph**
— Delaplaine's Repository of the Lives and Portraits of Distinguished American Characters. Phila., 1815. 3 parts i 1 vol. 4to, later 19th-cent mor; scuffed, rubbed. With engraved titles, frontis & 18 ports. Some foxing. F June 20 (432) $80

**Delaunay, Robert**
— Les Tours Eiffel de Robert Delaunay. Paris, 1974. One of 1,000. 4to, pictorial bds, in plastic outer wrap. sg June 13 (132) $150

**Delaunay, Sonia**
— Compositions couleurs idees. Paris: Editions d'Art Charles Moreau, [c.1930]. Folio, loose as issued in portfolio. Some plate edges discolored. sg Feb 15 (85) $275

**Delavan, James**
— Notes on California and the Placers... By One Who Has Been There. Oakland, 1956. With: The Gold Rush: Letters of Dr. James Delevan..., Mount Pleasant, MI, 1976 One of 700. 2 vols, orig cloth. With 2 illus. Larson copy. pba Sept 28 (408) $75

**Delen, Adrien Jean Joseph**
— Histoire de la gravure dans les anciens pays-bas & dans les provinces Belges. Paris & Brussels, 1924-35. 2 vols in 3. Folio, Needs rebinding. sg Apr 11 (90) $200

**Delevoy, Robert L. —& Others**
— Fernand Khnopff: Catalogue de l'Oeuvre. [Brussels, 1979]. 4to, cloth, in dj. sg Jan 11 (240) $50

**Delfino, Federico**
— De fluxu et reflexu aquae maris.... Venice: Aldus, 1559. Folio, 19th-cent half cloth; partly misbound. Tp browned; corner of D2 lacking. Liechtenstein - Horblit copy. C Apr 3 (83) £1,200

**Delille, Jacques Montanier, 1738-1813**
— L'Homme des champs, ou les georgiques francoises. Paris, 1805. 8vo, contemp calf gilt by Thouvenin; minor rubbing, joints split at head, front endpaper partly detached. With 4 plates & 8 headpieces, all with contemp hand-coloring. Fuerstenberg - Schaefer copy. S Dec 7 (152) £600
— Les Jardins ou l'art d'embellir les paysages. L, 1801. 4to, contemp mor gilt. Some margins soiled. Fuerstenberg - Schaefer copy. S Dec 7 (154) £750

**Delisle, Guillaume, 1675-1726**
— Atlante novissimo che contiene tutte le parti del mondo. Venice, 1740-50. 2 vols in 1. Folio, later half lea; extremities rubbed. With engraved titles & 78 double-page maps; mtd on guards. C May 31 (55) £6,500
Anr copy. 2 vols. folio, later half vellum. With engraved titles & 78 double-page maps, 10 hand-colored. Persia repaired; 4 maps repaired at fold; some staining at end of both vols. S June 27 (75) £7,200
— Atlas. Paris, 1700-31. Folio, later half mor; extremities worn, corners showing. With 94 maps, all but 2 with contemp hand-coloring in outline. Some soiling & staining; library stamp & ink stamp in margins of 1 map. cb Oct 17 (251) $13,000

**Delisle, Leopold**
— Le Cabinet des manuscrits de la Bibliotheque Imperiale. NY, 1973. 4 vols. 4to, cloth; worn. Facsimile of 1868-81 Ed. O Mar 26 (72) $130
— Catalogue des livres imprimes ou publies a Caen avant le milieu du XVIe Siecle. Caen, 1903-4. 2 vols in 1. 8vo, later half lea, orig front wrap bound in. In: Bulletin de la Societe des Antiquaires de Normandie, Tome XXIII & XXIV. O Mar 26 (73) $90

**Dellenbaugh, Frederick Samuel**
— A Canyon Voyage. NY, 1908. 1st Ed. Orig cloth. With color frontis. Some foxing. Robbins copy. pba Mar 21 (79) $250
— Fremont and '49: the Story of a Remarkable Career.... NY, 1914. 1st Ed. Orig cloth; spine sunned. With color frontis. Robbins copy. pba Mar 21 (80) $225
— The North Americans of Yesterday. NY, 1901. 1st Ed. Orig cloth. Robbins copy. pba Mar 21 (81) $140
— The Romance of the Colorado River. NY, 1903. 2d Ptg. 8vo, orig cloth; worn, front hinge cracked, bookplate removed. pba July 25 (135) $65

**Delpech, Jacques**
— Precis elementaire des maladies reputees chirurgicales. Paris, 1816. 2 vols. Half calf. pba June 20 (240) $180

**Delteil, Loys, 1869-1927**
— Catalogue Raisonne of the Etchings of Charles Meryon. NY, 1924. 4to, half cloth. With addenda-errata booklet laid in. sg Sept 7 (243) $225
— Le Peintre-graveur illustre. Paris, 1925-30. Vols XX-XXIX: Honore Daumier. 10 vols plus Index in 11 vols. Orig wraps; worn, some covers detached,

431

Vol XX lacking backstrip. bba Oct 5 (251) £380 [Rinsen]

**Demeuse, Nicolas**
— Nouveau traite de l'art des armes. Liege: F. J. Desoer, 1778. 12mo, contemp calf. With half-title, headpiece by Godin, & 14 folding plates. S Oct 27 (1111) £150 [Robertshaw]

**Demidoff, Anatole de, 1813-70**
— Voyage dans la Russe meridonale et la Crimee. Paris, [1848]. Plates by Auguste Bry. Atlas only. Folio, recent half calf. With half title, additional title, wrap as title, 9 divisional titles, & 90 plates. Some discoloration; plate #100 torn at margin. S Oct 26 (90) £600 [Schuster]

**Demidov, Elim Pavlovich, Prince of San Donato**
— After Wild Sheep in the Altai and Mongolia. L, 1900. Cloth; worn & shaken. O Oct 10 (77) $550

**Demijohn, Thom.** See: Disch & Sladek

**Deminne, Edouard**
— Le Probleme de la Navigation Aerienne. Namur, 1868. 8vo, modern bds, orig wraps bound in. With folding wood-engraved plate. sg May 16 (28) $350

**Demosthenes, 385?-322 B.C.**
— Orationes quatuor contra Philippum. Venice: Aldus, 1549. 4to, modern bdg by Becher & Eitel of Hartford; extremities rubbed. Tp rehinged; soiled. NH Sept 16 (148) $210
— The Three Orations of Demosthenes Chiefe Orator among the Grecians in Favour of the Olynthians...with those his Fower Orations...against King Philip of Macedonia. L: Henrie Denham, 1570. 1st Ed in English. 4to, calf gilt. Largely black letter. STC 6578. Downshire - Hefner copy. CNY May 17 (13) $2,600
Anr copy. Modern cloth. Marginal dampstaining at ends; hole in tp affecting top 2 lines of text; minor worming, affecting letters; some sidenotes cropped; library markings. sg Mar 21 (88) $1,100

**Dempster, Thomas, 1579?-1625**
— De Etruria regalia libri VII. Florence, 1723-24-26. Vol I only. Folio, 18th-cent half sheep; spine ends damaged, loose. Lacking 4 plates; 2L1 torn & repaired. sg June 13 (133) $150

**Demus, Otto**
— The Mosaics of San Marco in Venice. Chicago, 1984. 4 vols. 4to, cloth. sg June 13 (266) $300

**Den, Petr**
— Petkrat Kolin, Muj Kolin. Prague, [1947]. Illus by Jaromir Funke. 4to, wraps, in chipped & worn dj; spine cracked. sg Feb 29 (143) $200

**Denesle, —**
— Les prejuges du public sur l'honneur. Paris, 1766. 2d Ed. 3 vols. 8vo, contemp mor gilt with arms of the dedicatee, Antoine de Saartine, comte d'Alby; upper joints of Vols I & II repaired. Fuerstenberg - Schaefer copy. S Dec 7 (158) £1,300

**Denham, Sir James Steuart, 1712-80**
— An Inquiry into the Principles of Political Oeconomy. L, 1767. 1st Ed. 2 vols. 4to, contemp calf; joints split. Lacking intial blank in Vol I. C June 26 (210) £4,000

**Denis, Alberta Johnson**
— Spanish Alta California. NY, 1927. 1st Ed. - Illus by Loren Barton. Orig cloth; With frontis. Larson copy. pba Sept 28 (81) $50

**Denison, E. S.**
— E. S. Denison's Yosemite Views. San Francisco: Sam Miller, [1881]. 12mo, pictorial wraps; repaired, soiled, chipped. Some upper marginal wear. Larson copy. pba Feb 12 (52) $1,000

**Denmark**
— Judske Lowbog. Copenhagen: Jorgen Holst, 1642-43. 10 parts in 1 vol. 4to, contemp blindstamped calf, upper cover stamped F R P & with cipher of Christian IV. S Mar 14 (9) £170

**Dennis, Faith**
— Three Centuries of French Domestic Silver. NY: Metropolitan Museum of Art, 1960. 2 vols. 4to, cloth. W Nov 8 (127) £520

**Dennis, Jack H.**
— Western Trout Fly Tying Manual. Volume II Jackson Hole: Snake River Books, [1980]. Unique copy with the actual fly that was tied for the photography in the book tipped to limitation leaf. 4to, half syn; some wear. Inscr. O Feb 6 (57) $275

**Denon, Dominique Vivant, Baron, 1747-1825**
— Egypt Delineated. L, 1819. Folio, contemp mor gilt; rubbed. With port, folding map & 198 plates, 8 folding or double-page. Tears to 2 plates & folding map. S June 27 (142) £800
— Travels in Upper and Lower Egypt. L, 1803. 3 vols, including Atlas vol. 4to & 8vo, old calf; some covers detached, worn & scuffed. Library markings to bdgs & titles. bbc June 24 (177) $375
Anr copy. 3 vols. 8vo, contemp calf gilt; joints cracked or starting. With 60 plates. Lacking Plate 39; some dampstaining. sg Mar 7 (165) $400
— Voyage dans la basse et la haute Egypte.... Paris: Didot l'aine, 1802 [An X]. 2 vols. Folio, contemp bds, uncut; worn, spines def or missing. With 141 plates & 1 map. b Sept 20 (365) £2,400
Anr copy. Half calf. With 143 plates on 142 leaves. b June 28 (15) £2,200
— Voyages dans la basse et la haute Egypte.... L, 1807. 3 vols. 4to & folio, contemp calf, Atlas in half-calf. With frontises, folding map & 106 plates. Vol II frontis with headline cropped. b May 30 (258) £1,600

## Denslow, William Wallace
See also: Baum & Denslow; West & Denslow
— Johnnie Johnston's Air Ship. Batavia: Johnston Harvester Company, 1909. 8vo, pictorial wraps, stapled; some dampstaining & smudging, ring stain on rear cover. With 1 double-page & 4 full-page color illusts. bbc Feb 26 (285) $400

Anr copy. Pictorial wraps. pba Jan 18 (148) $90
— Pictures from the Wonderful Wizard of Oz. Chicago: George W. Ogilvie, [c.1903]. Text by Thomas Russell. Orig cloth-backed pictorial wraps; re-backed. Lower front corner of cover, tp & following 2 pages lacking; repaired tear to tp. pba Jan 18 (149) $275

## Denslow, William Wallace —& Bragdon, Dudley A.
— Billy Bounce. Chicago: M. A. Donohue, [c.1910-13]. Orig cloth with mtd color illust; minor rubbing. With 16 inserted color plates. bbc Feb 26 (286) $120

2d Ed. Spine ends & lower corners rubbed. pba Jan 18 (150) $95

## Department of Agriculture. See: United States of America

## Depero, Fortunato
— Depero Futurista. Milan, 1927. One of 1,000. 4to, bds with leaves held by large aluminum bolts; bumped, lower outer corner chipped. sg Apr 18 (98) $3,200
— Liriche Radiofoniche. Milan, 1934. 8vo, orig wraps; extremities worn, front cover dampstained. sg Apr 18 (99) $800

## Depping, G. B.
— L'Angleterre, ou description historique et topographique. Paris, 1828. 6 vols. 8vo, contemp half calf gilt. With 57 miniature county maps, hand-colored in outline, folding general map, ptd folding table & 19 plates. S Nov 30 (53) £1,100

## Depping, George Bernhard. See: Rechberg & Depping

## Derbec, Etienne
— A French Journalist in the California Gold Rush. Georgetown, 1964. One of 75 on Ticonderoga India text. Ed by A. P. Nasatir & others. Half bds in orig slipcase. With frontis port & 2 full-page illus. Sgd by ed. Larson copy. pba Sept 28 (409) $110

## Derby, George Horatio, 1823-61
See also: Grabhorn Printing
— Phoenixiana, or Sketches and Burlesques. NY, 1873. pba Apr 25 (376) $120

## Dereme, Tristan
— Le Zodiaque ou les etoiles sur Paris. Paris, 1927. One of 225. Illus by Hermine David. 4to, mor extra with zodiac design by Paul Bonnet [not in Carnets]; minor wear to spine. S Nov 21 (109) £11,000

## Derham, William, 1657-1735
— The Artificial Clock-Maker. L, 1714. 8vo, contemp calf; def. With 3 folding plates & 2 folding tables. Cropped; 1 table with tear. b Jan 31 (239) £140

## Dering, Edward
— A Sermon Preached Before the Queenes Majestie...25 Day of February, Anno 1569. L, 1578. 3d Ptg. 12mo, calf; spine dampstained. Trimmed at top. pba June 20 (123) $170

## Derleth, August William
See also: Lovecraft & Derleth
— Here on a Darkling Plain Phila., 1940. In dj with some soiling. Inscr to O. Kirsch, with 3-line quote, 1940. pba Jan 25 (73) $100
— The Solar Pons Omnibus. Sauk City: Arkham House, [1982]. 2 vols. pba Dec 7 (44) $50
— Something Near. Sauk City: Arkham House, 1945. Review copy. In dj. sg June 20 (66) $225

## Dernieres... See: Matisse, Henri

## Derriere le Miroir—Paris
— Derriere le Miroir. 1966. Nos 156-62. 4to, unsewn in orig wraps. Sold w.a.f. sg June 13 (282) $80

## Derrydale Press—New York
— A Decade of American Sporting Books & Prints by the Derrydale Press 1927-1937. 1937. One of 950. O June 25 (59) $110

Anr copy. Inscr to Warren Howell. sg Mar 7 (426) $175

ANNABEL, RUSSELL. - Tales of a Big Game Guide. 1938. One of 950. O Oct 10 (78) $160; O Oct 10 (79) $250; O Oct 10 (80) $170; sg Mar 7 (421) $250

BABCOCK, PHILIP H. - Falling Leaves: Tales from a Gun Room. [1937]. One of 950. O Oct 10 (81) $110; pba July 11 (374) $60

BAKER, CHARLES H. - The Gentleman's Companion. 1939. One of 1,250. 2 vols. O June 25 (46) $110

BANDINI, RALPH. - Veiled Horizons... [1939]. Review Copy. pba July 11 (67) $130

BARBER, JOEL D. - 'Long Shore. [1939]. One of 750. O June 25 (47) $375; pba July 11 (68) $450; wa Feb 1 (200) $65

BAYLISS, MARGUERITE F. - Bolinvar. 1937. One of 950. 2 vols. O Oct 10 (82) $50

BEACH, WILLIAM NICHOLAS. - In the Shadow of Mount McKinley. 1931. One of 750. O Oct 10 (83) $400; O Oct 10 (84) $325

BRAND, MAX. - The Thunderer. 1933. One of 950. O Oct 10 (85) $50

BROWN, PAUL. - Aintree: Grand Nationals—Past and Present. 1930. One of 850. O Jan 9 (78) $325; O Jan 9 (79) $180

BROWN, PAUL. - Hits and Misses. 1935. One of 950. O June 25 (50) $130

Anr copy. Sold w.a.f. sg Mar 7 (423) $90

BROWN, WILLIAM ROBINSON. - The Horse of the Desert. 1929. One of 750. sg Mar 7 (423A) $225

BUCKINGHAM, NASH. - Blood Lines... [1938]. One of 1,250. O June 25 (51) $130; rce Nov 16 (34) $160

BUCKINGHAM, NASH. - De Shootinest Gent'man and Other

# DERRYDALE

Tales. [1934]. One of 950. O June 25 (52) $250
BUCKINGHAM, NASH. - Mark Right! [1936]. One of 1,250. K Feb 11 (149) $225; O June 25 (53) $170; pba July 11 (375) $140; rce Nov 16 (35) $160
BUCKINGHAM, NASH. - Ole Miss'. 1937. One of 1,250. O Oct 10 (86) $180
CARLISLE, DONALD THOMPSON. - The Belvidere Hounds. 1935. One of 1,250. O June 25 (55) $50; sg Mar 7 (424) $80
CHAMBERLIN, HARRY D. - Riding and Schooling Horses. 1934. One of 950. sg Mar 7 (408) $50
CLARK, ROLAND. - Etchings. 1938. One of 800. Met Sept 28 (35) $350; sg Mar 7 (425) $550
CLARK, ROLAND. - Gunner's Dawn. 1937. One of 900. K Oct 1 (128) $350
CONNETT, EUGENE V. - American Big Game Fishing. [1935]. One of 950. O Oct 10 (87) $425
CONNETT, EUGENE V. - Random Casts. 1939. One of 1,075. Inscr. O June 25 (56) $225
CONNETT, EUGENE V. - Upland Game Bird Shooting in America. 1930. One of 850. O Oct 10 (110) $375; sg Mar 7 (427) $275
COX, CHARLES E. - John Tobias, Sportsman. [1937]. One of 950. O Oct 10 (88) $60; O June 25 (57) $225
CURTIS, PAUL A. - Sportsmen All. [1938]. One of 950. O Oct 10 (90) $80
DE GOUY, LOUIS PULLIG. - The Derrydale Cook Book of Fish and Game. 1937. One of 1,250. 2 vols. O June 25 (60) $140
FOOTE, JOHN TAINTOR. - Jing. [1936]. Review copy. O June 25 (61) $100
GRAND, GORDON. - Colonel Weatherford and his Friends. 1933. One of 1,450. Inscr. O Jan 9 (80) $130
GRAND, GORDON. - Colonel Weatherford's Young Entry. 1935. One of 1,350. Inscr. O Jan 9 (81) $70
GRAND, GORDON. - Old Man, and other Colonel Weatherford Stories. 1934. One of 1,150. Inscr. O Jan 9 (82) $150
Anr copy. Inscr. O June 25 (63) $70
GRAND, GORDON. - The Silver Horn and Other Sporting Tales of John Weatherford. 1932. One of 950. Sgd on half-title. O Jan 9 (83) $90
GRAND, GORDON. - The Southborough Fox, and Other Colonel Weatherford Stories. 1939. One of 1,450. O Jan 9 (84) $70
GRAY, DAVID. - Sporting Works. 1929. One of 750. 3 vols. O Oct 10 (93) $600; O June 25 (66) $70; O June 25 (67) $80
HAIG-BROWN, RODERICK L. - The Western Angler.... 1939. One of 950. 2 vols. Sgd on half-title. pba July 11 (69) $650
HARKNESS, WILLIAM HALE. - Temples and Topees. 1936. One of 200. O June 25 (69) $70
HERBERT, HENRY WILLIAM. - Sporting Novels. 1930. One of 750. 4 vols. O Jan 9 (134) $160
HERBERT, HENRY WILLIAM. - Trouting Along the Catasauqua. NY, 1927. One of 423. O Feb 6 (58) $225; O June 25 (70) $160
KIRMSE, MARGUERITE. - Dogs. 1930. One of 750. sg Mar 7 (429) $500
KIRMSE, MARGUERITE. - Dogs in the Field. 1935. One of 685. Inscr to Sheldon Prentice. rs Nov 11 (81) $375; sg Mar 7 (430) $700
LANIER, HENRY W. - A. B. Frost: the American Sportsman's Artist. [1933]. One of 950. O Jan 9 (86) $180; O June 25 (73) $130; sg Mar 7 (431) $140
LEE, AMY FREEMAN. - Hobby Horses. 1940. One of 200. O June 25 (74) $70
LYTLE, HORACE. - Point! A Book about Bird Dogs. [1941]. One of 950. O Oct 10 (94) $170
MANCHESTER, HERBERT. - Four Centuries of Sport in America, 1490-1890. 1931. One of 850. O Jan 9 (87) $90; O June 25 (75) $110; O June 25 (192) $60; sg Mar 7 (432) $200
MARKLAND, GEORGE. - Pteryplegia: The Art of Shooting-Flying. 1931. One of 300. O June 25 (76) $60
MONTGOMERY, RUTHERFORD G. - High Country. 1938. One of 950. O Oct 10 (96) $70; O Oct 10 (97) $90; O Oct 10 (98) $90; O Oct 10 (99) $80
O'CONNOR, JACK. - Game in the Desert. [1939]. One of 950. Unopened copy. O Oct 10 (101) $750; O Oct 10 (102) $275; O Oct 10 (103) $275; O Jan 9 (89) $275
PAGE, HARRY S. - Between the Flags. 1929. One of 850. O Jan 9 (90) $60
PHAIR, CHARLES. - Atlantic Salmon Fishing. 1937. One of 950. O Feb 6 (59) $375; O June 25 (78) $325; wa Feb 1 (199) $400
PICKERING, HAROLD G. - Dog-Days on Trout Waters. 1933. One of 199. O Feb 6 (60) $475; pba July 11 (70) $150
PICKERING, HAROLD G. - Merry Xmas. Mr. Williams. 20 Pine St. N.Y. 1940. One of 267. Inscr to the illus, Harry L. Timmins. pba July 11 (376) $250
POOR, CHARLES LANE. - Men against the Rule. 1937. One of 950. pba Mar 7 (208) $60
REEVE, J. STANLEY. - Red Coats in Chester County. 1940. One of 570. Inscr. O Jan 9 (91) $180
RIVES, REGINALD W. - The Coaching Club.... 1935. One of 30. O Jan 9 (92) $1,900
One of 300. O Jan 9 (93) $350; O Jan 9 (94) $300
SANTINI, PIERO. - Riding Reflections. 1932. One of 850. O June 25 (80) $60
SHEPPERD, TAD. - Pack & Paddock. [1938]. One of 950. O June 25 (81) $130; O June 25 (82) $70
SIMMONS, ALBERT DIXON. - Wing Shots. [1936]. One of 950. pba July 11 (377) $60
SMITH, EDMUND WARE. - Tall Tales and Short. [1938]. One of 950. Inscr. O June 25 (83) $130
SMITH, EDMUND WARE. - A Tomato Can Chronicle.... [1937]. One of 950. O June 25 (84) $130
SOMERVILLE, EDITH & MARTIN, VIOLET. - Sporting Works. 1927. Hitchcock Ed, One of 500. 7 vols. O Jan 9 (95) $325
SPILLER, BURTON L. - Firelight. [1937]. One of 950. O Oct 10 (104) $190; rce Nov 16 (40) $100
One of 950, this a Review Copy. pba July 11 (378) $160
SPILLER, BURTON L. - Grouse Feathers. 1935. rce Nov 16 (41) $100
One of 950. O Oct 10 (105) $200; O June 25 (85) $130
Review copy. Ben Hur Lampman's copy, sgd on front pastedown. O Oct 10 (106) $200
SPILLER, BURTON L. - More Grouse Feathers. [1938]. One of 950. O Oct 10 (107) $225; rce Nov 16 (42) $80

SPILLER, BURTON L. - Thoroughbred. 1936. One of 950.
O Oct 10 (108) $160; O Oct 10 (109) $160; rce Nov 16 (43) $100

STURGIS, WILLIAM B. - New Lines for Flyfishers. [1936]. One of 950. O Feb 6 (62) $60; O June 25 (86) $50

THOMAS, JOSEPH B. - Hounds and Hunting through the Ages. 1928. One of 750. Inscr. O Jan 9 (240) $200

Anr copy. Inscr. O June 25 (87) $70; sg Mar 7 (433) $225

VAN DYKE, HENRY. - The Travel Diary of an Angler. 1929. One of 750. Sgd by R. L. Boyer (illus) on frontis. pba July 11 (71) $110

VAN URK, JOHN BLAN. - The Story of American Foxhunting.... 1940-41. One of 950. 2 vols. O Jan 9 (96) $225

Anr copy. Inscr. sg Mar 7 (434) $175

VOSBURGH, WALTER S. - Cherished Portraits of Thoroughbred Horses from the Collection of William Woodward. 1929. One of 200. Mor gilt by Sangorski & Sutcliffe. Inscr by Woodward. O Jan 9 (97) $1,400

WALDEN, HOWARD T. - Big Stony. 1940. One of 550. O June 25 (88) $140

WALDEN, HOWARD T. - Upstream & Down. 1938. One of 950. O June 25 (89) $140

WILLIAMS, BEN AMES. - The Happy End. [1939]. One of 1,250. O June 25 (68) $70

Anr copy. With tipped-in presentation sheet to the Clove Valley Rod and Gun Club. O June 25 (90) $90; O June 25 (91) $90

**Desaguliers, John Theophilus, 1683-1744**

— A System of Experimental Philosopy, prov'd by Mechanicks.... L, 1719. 4to, contemp calf; rubbed. With 10 plates. Some spotting. b Sept 20 (112) £280

**Desarnod, A.** See: Sayger & Desarnod

**Descamps-Scrive Library, Rene**

— [Sale Catalogue] Bibliotheque.... Paris, 1925. 3 vols. 4to, wraps; frayed. Priced in margins throughout. O Mar 26 (75) $180

**Descargues, Pierre**

— Hartung. NY, [1977]. 4to, cloth, in dj. Some dampstaining at beginning. sg Jan 11 (212) $50

**Descartes, Rene, 1596-1650**

— De homine. Leiden, 1662. 1st Ed. 4to, contemp calf; spine head chipped, spine heel & lower cover repaired. With 9 (of 10) plates. S Mar 29 (689) £420

Anr Ed. Amst., 1686. ("Tractatus de homine, et de formatione foetus.") 4to, contemp vellum gilt. S June 12 (249) £360

— Geometria.... Amst., 1683. 2 vols. 4to, contemp vellum. S June 12 (299) £220

— Opera philosophica. Amst., 1664. 4th Ed. 3 parts in 1 vol. 4to, contemp calf; worn. With port & frontis (frayed). b Sept 20 (113) £300

— Les Principes de la philosophie.... Paris, 1724. Contemp calf. pba Nov 30 (109) $120

**Descourtilz, Jean Theodore**

— Ornithologie Bresilienne, ou histoire des oiseaux du Bresil.... Rio de Janeiro [L ptd]: Thomas Reeves, [1854-56). Folio, 19th-cent half mor gilt, orig wraps bound in; extremities worn. With 48 color plates. Foxed. sg Dec 7 (199) $9,500

**Description...**

— Description de l'Egypte ou recueil des observations et des recherches...pendant l'expedition de l'armee francaise. Paris, 1821-29. 2d Ed. 11 plate vols & 23 text vols bound in 25; lacking final vol of text & portfolio of large-format plates, contemp half mor. Most plate vols with light dampstaining; 1 port holed torn & repaired; other minor tears. Sold w.a.f. C Oct 25 (108) £6,000

— Description des festes donnees par la ville de Paris a l'occasion du mariage de Madame Louise-Elisabeth de France, & de Dom Philippe, Enfant...d'Espagne. Paris, 1740. Folio, contemp mor gilt, with arms of the City of Paris; repaired. With 13 plates. Fuerstenberg - Schaefer copy. S Dec 7 (65) £1,600

Anr copy. Contemp red mor gilt armorial bdg; rubbed, recased preserving orig spine, corners repaired, wormholes in spine. With 13 plates & 22 engraved plates of text. Tear in lower margin of Plate 2 affecting caption; tears at extremities of central crease on 4 double-plates, affecting surface in 2. S Mar 28 (513) £1,350

— The Description of a Course; A Poem, Addressed to the Patroness of the Harlech Hunt. Dolgelley, 1805. 8vo, contemp wraps. A contemp inscr attributes the poem to Evan Vaughan Esq., late member for Merionethshire. b Dec 5 (504) £200

— A Description of a Remarkable Vision, seen by Thomas Webster, while speaking over a Corpse at the Grave's side.... L: G. Riebau, 1798. 8vo, later half calf; rubbed. With folding hand-colored frontis (stained at fold). S June 12 (39) £150

**Descrizione...**

— Descrizione delle feste celebrate in Parma l'anno MDCCLXIX per...nozze di...Don Ferdinando colla Reale Arciduchessa Maria Amalia. Parma, [1769]. Folio, contemp bds; worn, covers detached. With 36 plates. Old stamp on verso of plates & on recto of both titles & 1 double-page plate. sg Apr 18 (46) $2,600

**Deseine, Francois Jacques, d.1715**

— Beschryving van oud en nieuw Rome. Amst., 1704. With 3 engraved titles & 99 (of 102) maps, plans & plates. Bound with: Kennett, Basil. De Aaloudheden van Rome. Amst., 1704. With engraved title & 19 maps, plans & views. Folio, contemp calf gilt; spines def. Some discoloration. Sold w.a.f. S Nov 30 (98) £2,200

**Desgraviers, Auguste Claude Leconte, 1749-1822**

— Le Partait Chasseur.... Paris, 1810. 8vo, modern cloth. sg Mar 7 (435) $60

### Deshayes, P. B.
— Physique du monde. Versailles & Paris, 1775. 8vo, contemp mor. Some spotting. S Oct 27 (803) £220 [Antiquarian]

### Desmonceaux, —, Abbe
— Traite des maladies des yeux et des oreilles.... Paris, 1786. 2 vols. 8vo, contemp sheep gilt; spine ends chipped. sg May 16 (401) $375

### Desnos, Louis Charles
— Almanach geographique ou petit atlas elementaire. Paris, 1770. 24mo, mor gilt; corners worn, joints & hinges starting, wormholes in front joint. With 32 double-page hand-colored maps. cb Feb 14 (2551) $325
— Atlas general methodique et elementaire. Paris, 1770-[71]. Folio, contemp half calf gilt. With 7 double-page diagrams & 56 double-page maps, hand-colored in wash & outline Lacking 2 regional maps of France; some fold splits. S Nov 30 (68) £1,600

### Despreaux, Jean Etienne
— Mes passe-temps: Chansons suivies de l'art de la danse, poeme.... Paris, 1807. 8vo, contemp calf gilt; rubbed. With 47 pp of engraved music, frontis & 2 plates. Some spotting. With 2 orig ink & wash drawings by Moreau le jeune, both sgd & dated 1805. Fuerstenberg - Schaefer copy. S Dec 7 (163) £1,000

### Desprez de Boissy Library, Charles
— [Sale Catalogue] Bibliotheque.... Paris, 1803. 8vo, wraps; rebacked. Some wear & soiling. O Mar 26 (76) $110

### Desroches, Jean, 1740-87
— Histoire ancienne des Pays-Bas autrichiens. Antwerp: chez J. Grange, 1787. 2 vols. 8vo, contemp calf gilt with stamp of Empress Josephine at foot of spines & Malmaison stamped in gilt on upper covers. With frontis & folding map. Short tear in map; a few leaves browned. Fuerstenberg - Schaefer copy. S Dec 7 (164) £850

### Destouches, Andre Cardinal
See also: Lalande & Destouches
— Isse, pastorale heroique representee devant sa Majeste a Trianon, le 17 Decembre 1697 [full score]. Paris, 1724. 4to, contemp calf gilt; joints splitting, def at head & foot; tp & last leaf stamped. S Dec 1 (140) £500

### Destouches, Philippe Nericault. See: Nericault-Destouches, Philippe

### Destructiorum...
— Destructiorum vitiorum ex similtudinum creaturarus exemplorum. Lyons: Claude Nourry, 11 June 1509. 4to, mor janseniste by Rene Aussourd. Gothic type. With 154 woodcuts (1 full-page). Tp stained; A3 & G3 with marginal tears. 61 (of 62) leaves; lacking final blank. Schaefer copy. P Nov 1 (77) $8,500

### Devonshire Collection, William Cavendish
— Catalogue of the Library at Chatsworth.... L: Chiswick Press, 1879. 4 vols. 8vo, orig cloth, unopened. bba Oct 5 (48) £500 [Forest Books]

### Devotion...
— La Devotion au coeur de Jesus. Strasbourg: Jean Francois Leroux, 1767. 8vo, contemp mor gilt with arms of Antoinette de Ricouart d'Herouville. With frontis & 2 plates. Fuerstenberg - Schaefer copy. S Dec 7 (166) £300

### Dewar, George Albemarle Bertie, 1862-1934
— The Book of the Dry Fly. L, 1897. 1st Ed. 8vo, cloth; front hinge starting, soiled. With 6 plates, 4 of them hand-colored. pba July 11 (72) $55

### Dewees, William Potts
— A Treatise on the Physical and Medical Treatment of Children. Phila., 1825. 8vo, contemp sheep; worn, needs rebacking. Browned. sg May 16 (402) $300

### Dewey, Sherman
— Account of a Hail Storm.... Walpole NH, 1799. 8vo, unbound. Tp stained; some chipping. sg Oct 26 (93) $175

### Dexter, F. Theodore
— Forty-Two Years' Scrapbook of Rare Ancient Firearms. Los Angeles: Warren F. Lewis, [1954]. In dj. pba July 11 (379) $60; sg Mar 7 (436) $80

### Deyeux, Nicolas. See: Parmentier & Deyeux

### Dezallier d'Argenville, Antoine Joseph, 1680-1765
— Abrege de la vie des plus fameux peintures. Paris, 1762. 4 vols. 8vo, 19th-cent citron mor gilt. With frontis & 254 ports. Tear at head of D2 in Vol II & N2 in Vol III. Fuerstenberg - Schaefer copy. S Dec 7 (20) £600
— L'Histoire naturelle eclaircie dans deux de ses parties principales, la lithologie et la conchyliologie.... Paris, 1742. 4to, contemp red mor gilt with arms of Henri Francois d'Aguesseau. With frontis (2d state) & 32 (of 35) plates. Some spotting. Fuerstenberg - Schaefer copy. S Dec 7 (19) £2,600

### D'Hauterive, Borel
— Annuaire de la pairie et de la noblesse de France et des maisons souveraines de l'Europe. Paris, [1843-92]. 48 vols. 8vo, contemp half lea; rubbed. Some foxing. O Mar 26 (129) $475

### D'Hebrail, Jacques —& La Porte, Joseph de, 1713-79
— La France litteraire.... Paris: La Veuve Duchesne, 1769-84. 4 vols, including Supplement & Nouveau Supplement. 8vo, contemp calf. O Mar 26 (77) $425

### Dhormoys, Paul
— Une Visite avec Soulouque d'un Voyage dans l'Ile d'Haiti. Paris, 1859. 8vo, ptd wraps; cocked. Some foxing. sg Mar 28 (101) $175

**Dialogues...**
See also: Lyttelton, George
— Dialogues of Creatures Moralised. Kentfield: Allen Press, 1967. One of 130. Folio, cloth. pba June 20 (17) $475; sg Sept 14 (9) $225

**Dialogus...** See: Nicolaus Pergamenus

**Dialogus Creaturarum.** See: Destructiorum...

**Diaz Arquer, Graciano**
— Libros y Folletos de Toros: Bibliografia Taurina.... Madrid, 1931. One of 400. Later half mor, orig wraps bound in. Ck Apr 12 (224) £200

**Diaz del Castillo, Bernal, c.1492-1581?.** See: Limited Editions Club

**Dibble, Sheldon, 1809-45**
— A Voice from Abroad. Lahainaluna: Press of the Missionary Seminary, 1844. 8vo, contemp half roan; rubbed & chipped. S Oct 26 (608) £360 [Baring]
Anr copy. Half lea; rubbed, front cover detached. Z Jan 30 (314) $200

**Dibdin, Thomas Frognall, 1776-1847**
— Aedes Althorpianae.... L, 1822. 2 vols. 8vo, mor gilt; rubbed. Ck Feb 14 (306) £140
— A Bibliographical, Antiquarian and Picturesque Tour in France and Germany. L, 1821. 1st Ed. 3 vols. 8vo, modern half calf. With 84 plates; errata slip in Vol I. Library stamp on verso of titles. b Jan 31 (30) £210
Anr copy. Contemp mor gilt; covers detached, needs rebdg. Some foxing & offsetting. CE Sept 27 (96) $350
Anr copy. 3 vols. 4to, contemp calf gilt by Hering, armorial bdg; rebacked with orig spine, rubbed, cover of Vol III detached. S July 11 (93) £160
Anr copy. 3 vols. 8vo, mor gilt; front cover of Vol I detached, backstrip loose, Vol II loose in bdg. wd Nov 15 (54) $200
— The Bibliographical Decameron. L, 1817. 3 vols. 8vo, contemp calf; backstrips rubbed. b Jan 31 (31) £130
Anr copy. Orig bds; recased, Vol I joints cracked. With 37 plates; many of illusts are mtd india-proofs. Sarolea - Smith - Garden copy. sg Oct 19 (67) $500
Anr copy. Contemp mor gilt. With 37 plates, many in mtd india-proof state. sg Apr 18 (47) $450
Anr copy. 3 vols. 4to, russia. Some foxing & browning. L.p. copy.. wd May 8 (51) $200
— Bibliophobia. Remarks on the Present Languid and Depressed State of the Book Trade...by Mercurius Rusticus. L, 1832. 1st Ed. 8vo, modern half cloth; new endpapers. L.p. copy. ds July 27 (65) $225
— An Introduction to the Knowledge of Rare and Valuable Editions of the Greek and Latin Classics. L, 1827. 4th Ed. 2 vols. 8vo, contemp half calf; worn. Foxed. wa Nov 16 (4) $210
— An Introduction to the Knowledge of Rare and Valuable Editions of the Greek and Roman Classics. Gloucester, 1802. 1st Ed. 8vo, contemp bds; needs rebacking. sg Apr 11 (91) $120

— Lettre neuvieme relative a la bibliotheque publique de Rouen. Paris, 1821. One of 100 L.p. copies. 8vo, contemp calf; scuffed, spines rubbed. Some foxing. F Mar 28 (418) $650
— The Library Companion. L, 1825. 2d Ed. 8vo, mor gilt; edges rubbed & worn. Clare copy. wa Nov 16 (5) $190
— Typographical Antiquities: or, the History of Printing in England.... L, 1810-19. 4 vols. 4to, later calf; spines lacking, covers detached. Some edges smoke-damaged; a few leaves with minor creases. bbc June 24 (65) $200
Anr copy. Vols I-II (of 4). Contemp calf. pba Sept 14 (127) $300
One of 65 L.p. copies. 4 vols. 4to, orig bds. Some spotting. S Mar 28 (455) £600

**Diccionario...**
— Diccionario de Marinha Portuguez - Francez - Inglez.... Rio de Janeiro: E. Dupont, 1872. Contemp half cloth; cards affixed to front pastedown, writing to front free endpapers, hinges repaired. Pencil corrections in text. pba July 25 (183) $180

**Dick, Philip K.**
— The Man in the High Castle. NY: Putnam, [1962]. 1st Ed, with code D36 at base of p 239. In dj with closed tears & corners rubbed. pba Aug 22 (112) $275
— A Scanner Darkly. Garden City, 1977. Bds, in dj with spine ends rubbed. pba May 4 (133) $75

**Dickens, Charles, 1812-70**
See also: Fore-Edge Paintings; Limited Editions Club; Nonesuch Press
— American Notes for General Circulation. L, 1842. 1st Ed, 1st Issue. 2 vols. 8vo, mor gilt by Riviere, orig cloth bound in. Final prelim leaf with repaired tear; top corner of final ad leaf torn off. pba June 20 (124) $450
2d Issue. Half calf by Mansell. Dickens postage stamp affixed to front flyleaves of each vol. pba Dec 14 (39) $65
— Barnaby Rudge. L, 1841. 1st Ed in Book form. 8vo, variant bdg of orig mauve fine-diaper cloth with covers stamped in blind with borders & stem-leaf in curtain-like designs. S July 11 (170) £1,600
— The Battle of Life. L, 1846. 1st Ed, 2d Issue. 8vo, orig cloth; extremities worn. pba June 20 (125) $250
— Bleak House. L, 1852-53. 1st Ed in orig 20/19 parts. 8vo, orig wraps; most rebacked or with spines repaired, some wear & soiling. Some foxing to plates; lacking some ads. CE Feb 21 (74) $1,000
Anr copy. Orig wraps; rebacked, soiled. Lacking some slips. P Dec 12 (60) $550
Anr copy. Wraps; some torn or chipped on spine. S July 11 (154) £380
1st American Ed. NY, 1852-53. 4 vols. 8vo, contemp half calf; rubbed, some joints weak. Bound from serialization in Harper's New Monthly Magazine, 1852-53. sg Feb 8 (72) $120

1st Ed in Book form. L, 1853. 8vo, orig cloth; hinges cracked. Some plates foxed. CE Feb 21 (75) $1,100

Anr copy. Orig cloth, 2ndary bdg; hinges cracked. CE Feb 21 (76) $1,100

Anr copy. Orig cloth; some staining, spine ends worn, hinges cracked. CE May 22 (152) $550

Anr copy. Old half mor; front cover detached. pba Dec 14 (40) $80

Anr copy. Orig cloth; lower hinge starting. S July 11 (161) £2,300

Anr copy. Mor gilt by Delrue. Minor staining. sg Sept 21 (147) $150

Anr copy. Later calf gilt by Sangorski & Sutcliffe. Lacking half-title; minor foxing to plates. sg Sept 21 (148) $275

Anr copy. Half calf gilt by Zaehnsdorf; spine & joints worn. Marginal dampstain on frontis & additional title; marginal browning to other plates. sg Feb 8 (275) $175

1st American Ed. NY: Harper, 1853. 2 vols. Contemp half mor; Vol I rear joint & hinges repaired. pba Dec 14 (41) $80

— A Child's History of England. L, 1852-54. 1st Ed. 3 vols. 16mo, orig cloth; spine head of Vol I worn. Suzannet copy. CE Feb 21 (77) $900; CE May 22 (154) $2,400

Anr copy. Orig cloth; spot on Vol I upper cover. sg Feb 8 (276) $2,200

— The Chimes. L, 1845. 1st Ed, 1st Issue. 8vo, orig cloth. CE Feb 21 (66) $850

— [Christmas Books]. L, 1843-48. 1st Eds. 5 vols. 12mo, orig cloth; worn, hinges cracked. cb June 25 (1811) $3,750

Anr Ed. L, 1886-[88]. 5 vols. 12mo, orig cloth; marked. bba May 30 (168) £110 [Williams]

— A Christmas Carol. L, 1843. 1st Ed, 1st Issue. 8vo, mor gilt with mor onlay design depicting Mr. Fezziwig's Ball, by Bayntun, orig covers bound in. With 4 hand-colored plates. CE Sept 27 (99) $1,800

Anr copy. Orig cloth; backstrip def at ends; some staining & soiling, rear endpapers dampstained. CE June 12 (185) $1,600

1st Issue; Smith 2:4. Orig cloth; endpapers cracked at inner hinges, becoming loose, some staining & soiling to covers, corners bumped. CE Feb 21 (63) $4,000

Anr copy. Orig cloth; hinges cracked, corners bumped, some staining & soiling. CE May 22 (137) $4,000

Anr copy. Orig cloth; stained & soiled, corners bumped, cocked endpapers stained & cracked, loose. Some browning & staining. CE May 22 (138) $1,500

Anr copy. Mor gilt by Sangorski & Sutcliffe. CE May 22 (139) $1,800

3d Issue. Orig cloth; worn & slightly stained. S July 11 (174) £650

Eckel's 3d state. 1st Issue. Orig cloth. A. Edward Newton copy. P June 5 (210) $5,000

Anr Ed. L, 1844. 8vo, orig cloth; minor stains, inner joints cracked. A few leaves with stains. CNY Dec 15 (10) $7,000

Anr Ed. L & Phila., 1915. Illus by Arthur Rackham. 4to, orig cloth. With orig watercolor & ink drawing on half-title. P Dec 12 (152) $4,250

Anr Ed. Phila., 1938. Illus by Everett Shinn; intro by Lionell Barrymore. With 4 hand-colored plates. Sgd by Shinn & Barrymore & with extra set of 6 mtd plates laid in. sg Feb 15 (274) $150

Anr Ed. L, [1948]. Illus by Arthur Rackham. Calf by Bayntun. O Mar 5 (57) $300

— The Cricket on the Hearth. L, 1846 [1845]. 1st Ed. 8vo, mor gilt by Sangorski & Sutcliffe. sg Sept 21 (150) $225

— A Curious Dance Round a Curious Tree. L, [1860]. 1st Separate Ed, 2d Issue. 8vo, orig wraps; some soiling, faint vertical crease from accompanying mailing envelope. CE May 22 (163) $1,600

— David Copperfield. L, 1849-50. 1st Ed in orig 20/19 parts. 8vo, orig wraps; some parts rebacked, some worn & repaired. A few marginal tears; lacking some ads. CE Feb 21 (71) $2,000

Anr copy. Orig wraps; most rebacked or repaired. Ad leaves repaired; some plates foxed; lacking some ads. CE May 22 (148) $3,800

1st Ed in Book form. L, 1850. 8vo, orig cloth; spine extremities rubbed, 1 gathering loose, 1 plate detached. bba Oct 19 (237) £320 [Axe]

Anr copy. Orig cloth; spine ends & joints split. Some plates foxed. CE Feb 21 (72) $1,100

Anr copy. Orig cloth; hinges repaired. CE May 22 (149) $2,900

Anr copy. Contemp half calf; rubbed. Minor foxing. O Mar 5 (63) $475

Anr copy. Orig cloth. S July 11 (168) £3,200

Anr copy. Contemp half calf gilt; extremities rubbed. With 40 plates. sg Sept 21 (165) $225

Anr Ed. NY, [1850]. 8vo, orig cloth. CE May 22 (150) $1,300

— Dombey and Son. L, 1846-48. 1st Ed in orig 20/19 parts. 8vo, orig wraps; most rebacked or repaired, some soiled. Later issue of Parts 11 & 14; with 12-line errata slip in Part 5, the Advertiser in each part & most other ads. CE Feb 21 (69) $300

Anr copy. Orig wraps; mostly rebacked or repaired, some soiling. Lacking some ads. CE May 22 (144) $850

Anr copy. Orig wraps; some rebacked or repaired, spine ends worn, a few covers soiled. CE May 22 (145) $750

1st Ed in Book form. L, 1848. 8vo, orig cloth; lower cover detached. Frontis & tp browned. CE Feb 21 (70) $160

Anr copy. Orig cloth; hinges cracked. Marginal browning to frontis & tp. CE May 22 (146) $1,300

Anr copy. Orig cloth; recased. Plates foxed. CE May 22 (147) $500

Anr copy. Orig cloth; joints broken, shaken. O Mar 5 (58) $300

Anr copy. Modern half mor. Washed at beginning; some browning, staining & soiling. O Mar 5 (59) $130

Anr copy. Half calf. Plates foxed. pba Dec 14 (43) $95

Anr copy. Contemp half calf. pba Aug 22 (113) $90

Anr copy. Variant bdg of orig olive green fine-diaper cloth with covers stamped in blind. S July 11 (166) £3,400

Anr copy. Mor gilt by the Old Court Bindery. sg Sept 21 (151) $225

Anr copy. Modern half calf gilt. sg Feb 8 (277) $150

— Great Expectations. L, 1861. 1st Ed in Book form. 3 vols. 8vo, modern half calf. bba May 30 (169A) £6,500 [Velentine]

Anr copy. Lev; back cover of Vol I detached. Half-titles in facsimile. wd Nov 15 (55) $900

Anr Ed. NY, 1861. 2 vols. 8vo, orig cloth. CE May 22 (166) $1,700

— Hard Times. L, 1854. 1st Ed in Book form. 8vo, orig cloth; minor staining to covers, leaning. Suzannet copy. CE Feb 21 (78) $800

Anr copy. Orig cloth; spine head worn. CE May 22 (155) $320

Anr copy. Orig cloth; spine ends worn, cocked, hinges cracked. CE May 22 (156) $260; S July 11 (169) £750

Anr copy. Later calf gilt by Wallis. sg Sept 21 (153) $300

— The Haunted Man and the Ghost's Bargain. L, 1848. 1st Ed. 12mo, orig cloth; rebacked, orig spine strip laid on. pba Dec 14 (45) $110

[-] The Library of Fiction. L, 1836-37. 2 vols. 8vo, contemp half mor gilt; edges rubbed. Includes 2 Dickens stories. CE Feb 21 (44) $1,900

Anr copy. Orig cloth; recased, new endpapers, 1 flyleaf lacking. Includes 2 Dickens stories. CE May 22 (124) $1,200

— The Life of Our Lord... NY: Simon & Schuster, 1934. In dj. Minor soiling. pba Aug 8 (383) $55

— Little Dorrit. L, 1855-57. 1st Ed in orig 20/19 parts, 1st Issue. 8vo, orig wraps; most rebacked, some repairs & soiling. With the 60 individual ad inserts, the Little Dorrit Advertiser in each vol & the errata slip in Part XVI. A few plates foxed. CE Feb 21 (79) $450

Anr copy. Orig wraps; a few spines rebacked, spine ends worn, some repairs & soiling. With the 60 individual ad inserts, the Little Dorrit Advertiser in each vol & the errata slip in Part XVI. CE May 22 (157) $850

Anr copy. Orig wraps; most spines rebacked, some repairs & soiling. Lacking some inserts. CE May 22 (158) $650

Anr copy. Bound together in half mor; rubbed. sg Sept 21 (156) $120

1st Ed in Book form. L, 1857. 8vo, orig cloth; spine tightened, hinges cracked, some rubbing & staining. Envelope addressed by Dickens to Caroline Le Grand pasted to front free endpaper. CE Feb 21 (80) $1,600

Anr copy. Orig cloth; minor wear to spine ends, recased. Foxing & browning to plates. CE May 22 (159) $800

Anr copy. Orig cloth; spine ends worn & scuffed. Some foxing & browning to plates. CE May 22 (160) $900

Anr copy. Half calf; front hinge cracked. Foxed. pba Dec 14 (47) $120

Anr copy. Orig cloth. Lacking errata slip on p.481. S July 11 (165) £2,000

Anr copy. Later calf gilt by Sangorski & Sutcliffe; corner of front cover with crackling. sg Sept 21 (157) $275

Anr copy. Mor gilt by Riviere. Some spotting. sg Sept 21 (158) $130

Anr copy. Early half calf; needs rebdg. sg Feb 8 (280) $60

Anr copy. Later half calf. Some foxing. wa Dec 14 (14) $200

— Martin Chuzzlewit. L, 1843-44. 1st Ed in orig 20/19 parts, 1st Issue. 8vo, orig wraps; rebacked or with spine repaired. CE Feb 21 (64) $650

1st Ed in Book form. L, 1844. 8vo, orig cloth; joints repaired, endpapers renewed. CE Feb 21 (65) $750

Anr copy. Half calf gilt. sg Sept 21 (154) $200

Issue not indicated. Orig cloth; hinges cracked. Some browning & foxing to plates. CE May 22 (141) $750

Anr copy. Orig cloth; spine ends & joints repaired, covers stained, hinges repaired. CE May 22 (142) $270

Anr copy. Contemp half mor; extremities rubbed. Lacking 6 plates; 1 plate torn. F June 20 (102) $50

Anr copy. Later calf gilt by Wallis. sg Feb 8 (282) $325

Issue not stated. Modern half calf; front cover scraped. pba Dec 14 (46) $160

Anr copy. Variant bdg of orig brown horizontally-ribbed cloth stamped in blind. S July 11 (167) £4,200

— Master Humphrey's Clock. L, 1840-41. 1st Ed, 1st Issue, in 88 weekly parts. 8vo, orig wraps; light soiling & chipping. CE Feb 21 (58) $850

Anr copy. Orig wraps; chipped & soiled, some spines repaired. CE May 22 (134) $900

In 20 monthly parts. Orig wraps; some parts repaired or chipped. Marginal tears repaired. CE Feb 21 (59) $480

Anr copy. Some soiling. CE May 22 (135) $850

1st Ed in Book form. 3 vols. 8vo, orig cloth. b Jan 31 (80) £280

Anr copy. Orig cloth, marbled endpapers; extremities with minor wear. CE Feb 21 (60) $600

Anr copy. Orig cloth, plain endpapers; minor wear to spine ends & corners. CE Feb 21 (61) $150

Anr copy. Orig cloth; worn & loose. Foxed, some staining & soiling. O Mar 5 (61) $60

Anr copy. Contemp half mor; rubbed. Some foxing. O Mar 5 (62) $180

## DICKENS

Anr copy. Contemp half mor; spine & corners scuffed. pba Dec 14 (48) $90

Anr copy. Lev gilt by Riviere, orig cloth bound in; lower corners of Vol III bumped. Some soiling. pba June 20 (127) $375

Anr copy. Orig cloth; stained, corners worn. sg Sept 21 (160) $90

Anr copy. Sheep-backed early cloth; scuffed. Some foxing, affecting plates; a few text leaves in Vol II detached. Extra-illus with Thomas Sibson's Illustrations of Master Humphrey's Clock, 1842, with 72 plates & 8 pages of letterpress. wa Nov 16 (78) $260

[-] Memoirs of Joseph Grimaldi. L, 1838. 1st Ed, 1st Issue. Ed by Dickens; illus by George Cruikshank. 2 vols. 8vo, orig cloth; later endapers. CE Feb 21 (53) $550

Anr copy. With port & 12 plates. K Oct 1 (135) $1,150

Anr copy. Lev gilt by Riviere, orig cloth bound in. With port & 12 plates. Some foxing; lower corner of frontis nicked. pba June 20 (128) $325

2d Issue. Orig cloth, 2d bdg. Minor staining to Vol II. CE May 22 (129) $700

Anr copy. Half lev. Some foxing. sg Sept 21 (161) $350

1st Issue. Illus by George Cruikshank. Mor; orig cloth bound in. With port, 12 plates, & 17 extra hand-colored plates. Spotted. S Oct 27 (1187) £500 [Baring]

— The Mudfog Papers. L, 1880. 1st Collected Ed. 8vo, cloth. Tp creased. pba Dec 14 (49) $95

— The Mystery of Edwin Drood. L, 1870. Bound with: Jackson, Henry. About Edwin Drood. Cambr., 1911 8vo, mor gilt by Cedric Chivers with hand-painted central medallion with arms of the city of Rochester; upper joint worn. Extra-illus with 24 plates containing 16 watercolors. Tipped at front is 2-page ALs sgd by the artist, S. L. Fildes to Maurice Clifford & other related material. S Dec 18 (178) £900 [Heritage]

1st Ed in Book form. 8vo, contemp half calf. pba Aug 22 (114) $200

Anr copy. Contemp half calf gilt; joints rubbed. sg Sept 21 (163) $80

1st Ed, in orig 6 parts. 8vo, orig wraps; spinew worn. Lacking 2 back ads in No 1 & all back ads in Nos 2, 5 & 6. Some foxing. pba Mar 7 (88) $160

Anr copy. Wraps; backstrips repaired, some soiling & tears. sg Sept 21 (162) $350

6 orig parts. 8vo, orig wraps; all rebacked. CE Feb 21 (85) $240

Anr copy. Orig wraps; each part rebacked. CE May 22 (168) $600

— Nicholas Nickleby. L, 1838-39. 1st Ed, in orig 20/19 parts. 8vo, orig wraps; spines rebacked or repaired, some covers repaired or soiled. Some text margins repaired; corner of Advertiser in Part 2 torn away affecting text. CE Feb 21 (51) $850

Anr copy. Orig wraps; some spines rebacked or repaired, some soiling. CE May 22 (130) $950

## AMERICAN BOOK PRICES CURRENT

1st Ed in Book form. L, 1839. 8vo, orig blue cloth, 2ndary bdg; joints split, hinges cracked. CE Feb 21 (52) $1,100

1st Issue. Orig purple cloth; hinges repaired. Some browning & staining. CE May 22 (132) $1,100

Anr copy. Modern half calf gilt. Plates browned. sg Feb 8 (278) $100

Early Issue. 2 vols. 8vo, orig cloth, Smith's 1st bdg; worn, inner joints broken. Last leaf torn & reinserted; some browning, soiling & staining. O Mar 5 (60) $350

Issue not indicated. 8vo, orig cloth; lower joint repaired, spine ends worn. CE May 22 (131) $2,200

Anr copy. Contemp mor; upper joint repaired, rubbed, hinges cracked. Some foxing & browning. CE May 22 (133) $450

Later issue. Mor gilt by the Old Court Bindery. Some spotting. sg Sept 21 (155) $150

— The Old Curiosity Shop. L, 1841. 8vo, orig cloth, variant in mauve fine-diaper cloth with covers stamped in blind with borders & stem-leaf. S July 11 (164) £2,200

— Oliver Twist. L, 1838. 1st Ed in Book form, 1st Issue. Illus by George Cruikshank. 3 vols. 12mo, orig cloth. CE Sept 27 (98) $1,900

Anr copy. Orig cloth; minor rubbing & staining. CE Feb 21 (54) $6,000

Anr copy. Orig cloth, variant blindstamped with less intricate arabesque design on sides; possibly recased with endpapers renewed, extremities rubbed, front inner hinge of Vol I cracked & stained. Plates foxed or spotted. CNY May 17 (68) $3,500

Anr copy. Orig cloth; tear along spine of Vol II, all spine ends rubbed, some discoloration to covers. Foxed. pba Dec 14 (50) $2,750

Anr copy. Lev gilt by Riviere, orig cloth bound in. Imprint of 1 plate in Vol I shaved. pba June 20 (129) $2,250

Anr Ed. L, 1841. 3 vols. 8vo, orig cloth; hinge of Vol I cracked. CE Feb 21 (55) $220

Anr Ed. L, 1846. 8vo, orig cloth; some rubbing, hinges renewed. Plates with some staining & browning. CE Feb 21 (57) $320

Anr Ed. L, Jan-Oct 1846. In 10 monthly parts. 8vo, wraps; some supplied, worn & soiled, spines restored. Some foxing. CNY Dec 15 (11) $3,000

New Ed. L, 1846. 8vo, orig cloth. S July 11 (162) £1,300

— Our Mutual Friend. L, 1864-65. 1st Ed, in orig 20/19 parts. 2 vols. 8vo, orig wraps; spine ends worn or repaired. Some soiling & wear at edges. CE Feb 21 (83) $850

Anr copy. 8vo, orig wraps; some lacking or def. Lacking some ads. Sold w.a.f. pba June 20 (130) $450

1st Ed in Book form. L, 1865. 2 vols. 8vo, contemp half calf; rubbed, spine lea crackled. Some foxing. pba Aug 22 (115) $150

Anr copy. Orig cloth. Without the slip tipped in to page [1] of Vol I of some copies. S July 11 (163) £1,700

Anr copy. Later half calf. Scuffed. wa Dec 14 (15) $280

[-] The Pic Nic Papers. L, 1841. 1st Ed. - Ed by Dickens. 3 vols. 8vo, orig cloth; some joints repaired, endpapers renewed, stains on covers. Some foxing & browning to plates. CE Feb 21 (62) $220

Anr copy. Orig cloth; spine ends worn, endpapers renewed. CE May 22 (136) $140

— [Pickwick Papers]. L, 1836-37. 1st Ed, in orig 20/19 parts. 8vo, orig wraps; spines torn or repaired, 1 wrap cut close. Some marginal repairs; plates loose in Part 1; lacking all inserted ads in Parts 1 & 3-8; Advertiser in Part 9 from anr part & that in Part 11 lacking a leaf; an inserted 4-page ad in Parts 13 & 15 lacking; also lacking Dickens Address leaf in Part 2 & pbr Address leaf in Part 3. CE Feb 21 (47) $500

Anr copy. Orig wraps; some rebacked or repaired, a few short tears, later issues of wraps to some parts (that on Part 17 & 18 dated 1837). Mixed 1st & 2d states of plates; lacking Advertisers in 5 parts & some other inserted ads. CE Feb 21 (48) $1,400

1st Ed in Book form. L, 1837. 8vo, contemp mor; recased. With 43 plates. Some browning & foxing. CE May 22 (127) $900

1st English Ed in Book form, 1st Issue. 8vo, later mor gilt by Riviere. sg Feb 8 (281) $850

Early issue. Later half calf; worn. Some foxing & soiling. O Mar 5 (64) $400

Early Issue with all but 1 of the 7 first-issue points. Mor gilt by Bayntun; minor rubbing. With 43 plates plus 12 duplicate plates by Phiz, a set of the 1837-38 plates by Newman & 1 extra plate by Leslie. Some foxing to plates. S July 11 (160) £320

Issue not indicated. Calf. Some discoloration. Tipped in are poem An Athenian Describes Athens, sgd & dated by Thomas Talfourd, 23 Dec 1846 & an ALs by Robert W. Buss. b May 30 (398) £220

Later Issue. Orig cloth; back cover cracked with pastedown torn. A few plates creased. CNY Dec 15 (9) $6,500

Anr copy. Calf extra by Birdsall. Repair to Plate 36; lacking half-title. sg Sept 21 (167) $140

Anr copy. Mor. Some spotting. sg Sept 21 (168) $80

Anr Ed. L, 1910. One of 250. Illus by Cecil Aldin. 2 vols. Folio, orig vellum gilt; soiled & foxed. With 24 colored plates. wa Nov 16 (244) $350

Anr Ed. L, [1910]. ("Mr. Pickwick.") One of 350. Illus by Frank Reynolds. 4to, orig vellum gilt; stained, hole in spine. Ck May 31 (39) £55

Anr Ed. L, 1930. Illus by Charles E. Brock. Lev gilt extra with lea inlays illustrating Mr. Pickwick holding the fainting Mrs. Bardell, by Bayntun-Riviere. CE Feb 21 (8) $800

— Pictures from Italy. L, 1846. 1st Ed. 8vo, orig cloth; rubbed. bba May 30 (166) £100 [Frew]; CE Feb 21 (68) $350; CE May 22 (143) $350

Anr copy. Orig cloth; endpapers cracked at inner hinges. Inscr to the Countess of Blessington, 19 May 1846. CNY Dec 15 (12) $30,000

— Sketches by "Boz." L, 1836-37. 1st Ed in Book form of First Series; 1st Ed of 2d Series. 3 vols. 12mo, various orig cloth bdgs; that of 2d Series rebacked. With 3 frontises, 1 additional title & 22 plates. 1st Series Vol I inscr to Thomas Beard. Suzannet copy. CNY Dec 15 (7) $20,000

Anr copy. Lev gilt by Riviere. Some soiling or foxing. pba June 20 (132) $2,500

Anr Ed. L, 1837. 2d Series only. 12mo, orig cloth; spine repaired, recased. Some staining & browning to plates. CE May 22 (126) $260

Anr Ed. L, 1837-39. In 20 monthly parts. 8vo, orig wraps; No 20 lacking wraps & supplied with reprint of front wrap, 4 nos lack back wraps with others supplied, 3 wraps def, 1 torn, some rebacking. Some plates foxed or stained. CNY Dec 15 (8) $3,500

Anr Ed. L, 1839. 8vo, orig cloth; spine ends worn, front hinge cracked. Tp margin strengthened. CE Feb 21 (45) $600

Anr copy. Orig brown cloth; front hinge cracked, spine ends worn. CE Feb 21 (46) $3,200

Anr copy. Calf gilt by Riviere. ANs from the dedicatee, Lord Russell, tipped to dedication leaf. sg Sept 21 (170) $850

Anr Ed. L, 1856. 8vo, contemp half mor; extremities rubbed. With 40 plates. Edges soiled. F June 20 (524) $60

— Speeches: Literary and Social. L, [1870]. 8vo, contemp half mor; rubbed. With a collection of sheets for the 1st Ed, with some autograph corrections & markings in various hands. S July 11 (151) £360

— Sunday under Three Heads. L, 1836. 1st Ed. 8vo, orig wraps; upper cover detached, lower cover splitting along joint, some rubbing & soiling. Marginal soiling & wear. CE Feb 21 (50) $1,500

Anr copy. Orig wraps; worn, with chips & splits. CE May 22 (125) $650

— A Tale of Two Cities. L, 1859. 1st Ed in Book form. 8vo, later calf; joints & edges rubbed. CE May 22 (162) $750

1st Issue. Later half calf; spine ends & edges worn. Browning & staining to plates. CE May 22 (161) $600

Later Issue. Half mor, orig cloth bound in. Lacking plate list. K Feb 11 (154) $375

— The Uncommercial Traveller. L, 1861 [1860]. 1st Ed in Book form. 8vo, orig cloth; edges rubbed. Suzannet copy. CE Feb 21 (82) $1,000; CE May 22 (164) $950

Anr copy. Orig cloth; faded, writing on front free endpaper. CE May 22 (165) $900

— The Village Coquettes: A Comic Opera. L, 1836. 1st Ed. 8vo, unbound. Minor foxing at ends. CE Feb 21 (49) $1,400

— Works. L, 1863-66. 26 vols. 8vo, later 19th-cent half calf, spine with spelling "Dicken's Works" throughout. S July 11 (175) £2,100

Anr Ed. L, [c.1870]. 30 vols. 8vo, contemp half calf; spines worn & age-darkened. CE Nov 8 (185) $450

Illustrated Library Edition. L: Chapman & Hall, [1880s]. 30 vols. 8vo, contemp calf gilt by Sotheran's; rubbed, rear endpapers on 1st 2 vols affected by silverfish. S Dec 18 (177) £1,300 [Sotheran]

# DICKENS

Anr Ed. L, 1881-82. One of 1,000. 30 vols. 4to, orig cloth. S Apr 23 (42) £420

Ed de Luxe. 30 vols. 4to, contemp mor. Offset & foxed. S Oct 27 (1185) £700 [Harrington]

People's Ed. Phila.: J. B. Lippincott, 1886. 15 vols. 8vo, half calf; 1 front joint cracked & cover bent forward. pba Mar 7 (89) $140

Anr Ed. Bost., 1892. One of 1,000. 48 vols. 8vo, half lev; spines browned, joints & extremities rubbed. pba Dec 14 (52) $1,100

Anr Ed. Bost. & NY, 1894. One of 500. 32 vols. 8vo, mor gilt. Check, sgd, bound into Vol I. Met May 22 (109) $5,750

Gadshill Ed. L, 1897-1903. Vols 1-34 only. Half calf by Bayntun Riviere. b Sept 20 (564) £2,000

Anr copy. 36 vols. 8vo, half lev gilt; spine heads nicked. pba Sept 14 (130) $2,500

Broadstairs Ed. L, 1900. One of 250. 40 vols. 8vo, half mor gilt. cb Oct 17 (268) $2,750

**Dickens's copy, Charles**

BUCKNILL, SIR JOHN CHARLES. - The Psychology of Shakespeare. L, 1859. 1st Ed. 8vo, orig cloth; bumped, splits along joints. Inscr to Dickens by Bucknill & with marginal notes by Dickens in pencil on p. 27 about Macbeth. cb Oct 17 (359) $2,500

PARKMAN, FRANCIS. - Pioneers of France in the New World. Bost., 1865. 8vo, orig cloth; spine ends & edges rubbed. With bookplate & the Gadshill Place, June 1870, sale book label. CE May 22 (174) $700

**Dickens, Charles, 1812-70 — & Collins, Wilkie, 1824-89**

— The Wreck of the Golden Mary.... Kentfield, Calif.: Allen Press, 1956. One of 200. pba Nov 30 (9) $180; pba Feb 12 (500) $55; sg Sept 14 (10) $425

**Dickerson, Fannie M.**

— Mary had a Little Lamb. Akron: Saalfield, [c.1910]. Cloth book, ptd on muslin. pba Aug 22 (725) $65

**Dickeson, Montroville Wilson**

— American Numismatical Manual.... Phila., 1865. 3d Ed. 4to, cloth; extremities worn. sg Oct 26 (281) $110

**Dickinson, Emily, 1830-86**

See also: Limited Editions Club

— Acts of Light. Bost: New York Graphic Society, [1980]. One of 750. Illus by Nancy Ekholm Burkert. sg Feb 15 (63) $175

— Letters of.... Cambr. MA, 1958. Ed by Thomas H. Johnson. 3 vols. pba Dec 14 (55) $110

— Poems by Emily Dickinson Edited by Two of her Friends.... Bost., 1890. 1st Ed. - Ed by Mabel Loomis Todd & T. W. Higginson. 12mo, orig cloth; soiled, extremities rubbed. CE Sept 27 (102) $3,800

— Poems of.... Cambr. MA, 1955. 3 vols. pba Dec 14 (56) $140

— The Single Hound. Poems of a Lifetime. Bost., 1914. Orig half cloth. CE Sept 27 (103) $480

**Dickinson, Henry Winram —& Jenkins, Rhys**

— James Watt and the Steam Engine. L, 1927. 4to, cloth; worn. O Mar 5 (66) $170

**Dickinson, John, 1732-1808**

— Letters from a Farmer in Pennsylvania. L, 1768. 8vo, later wraps. Inscr by Dickinson's daughter, Maria Logan, to her son-in-law, Thomas Betton. K Oct 1 (137) $3,000

Anr Ed. NY, 1903. One of 260. Half vellum, in dj. pba Aug 8 (385) $50

— The Letters of Fabius, in 1788, on the Federal Constitution.... Wilmington, 1797. Later wraps. K Oct 1 (136) $900

**Dicks, John**

— The New Gardener's Dictionary, or Whole Art of Gardening. L, 1771. Folio, modern bds; worn & broken. With 6 colored & 8 uncolored plates. 3 plates def. Sold w.a.f. O July 9 (74) $130

**Dickson, Albert Jerome**

— Covered Wagon Days. Cleveland, 1929. 1st Ed. Orig cloth; spine ends rubbed, bumped. pba Nov 16 (84) $110

**Dickson, R. W.**

— A Complete System of Improved Live Stock and Cattle Management. L, 1824. 2 vols. 4to, contemp tree calf. With additional title, port, & 32 plates. Some plates with marginal tears repaired; slightly wormed at beginning vol I. S Oct 27 (720) £180 [The Barn]

— Practical Agriculture; or, a Complete System of Modern Husbandry. L, 1805. 2 vols. 4to, early half calf; needs rebdg. With 87 plates, 27 of them hand-colored. sg May 9 (297) $400

**Dickson, William**

— Letters on Slavery. L, 1789. 1st Ed. 8vo, contemp calf. Stain at fore-margin of tp. S Mar 28 (340) £220

**Dictionary...**

— Dictionary of American Biography. NY, 1928-73. 24 vols, including Index & 3 Supplements. 4to, orig cloth; not uniform. S June 12 (362) £440

Anr Ed. NY, 1943-44. 22 vols, including Index & Supplement One. 4to, cloth. sg Sept 28 (92) $700

— Dictionary of National Biography. L, [1965]. 22 vols. Orig cloth, in frayed djs. bba Oct 5 (50) £500 [Brinded]

— The Dictionary of National Biography. Oxford, 1968-76. 28 vols, including Supplements. All but 1 in djs. bba May 9 (58) £400 [Ginnan]

Anr Ed. L, 1972-76. 28 vols, including 6 vols Supplements for 20th-Cent. 8vo, orig cloth in djs. S Oct 27 (1021) £750 [Baring]

Anr Ed. L, 1973. 22 vols plus Twentieth Century in 6 vols. In djs. bba Oct 5 (323) £650 [Forest]

Compact Ed. L, 1975. 2 vols. Folio, cloth, boxed with magnifying glass. b Jan 31 (32) £220

— A Dictionary of Natural History, or Complete Summary of Zoology.... L, 1802. 8vo, orig lea gilt;

rubbed. With frontis & 47 hand-colored plates. S Nov 2 (183) £220 [Schiller]

**Dictionnaire...**
— Dictionnaire abrege du Surrealisme. Paris, 1938. Orig wraps with design by Yves Tanguy; front joint rubbed, ink blot at bottom of front cover. sg Apr 18 (101) $400

**Dictys Cretensis —&**
**Dares Phrygius**
— Historia Troiana. Venice: Christophorus de Pensis, de Mandello, 1 Feb to 20 Mar 1499. ("De Historia belli Troiani et Dares Phrygius de eadem....") 4to, 18th-cent half vellum. 61 lines & headline; type 7:109R. Some old soiling & dampstaining. 74 leaves. Goff D-187. C Nov 29 (46) £700

**Diderot, Denis, 1713-84**
See also: Grimm & Diderot
— Les Bijoux indiscrets. Au Monomotapa [Paris, c.1775]. 2 vols in 1. 12mo, contemp calf; worn, shelf label on spine. With 7 plates. b May 30 (532) £350

**Diderot, Denis, 1713-84 —&**
**Alembert, Jean le Rond d', 1717?-83**
— Encyclopedie.... Paris, Neuchatel & Amst., 1751-80. 1st Ed. Complete set, consisting of: Encyclopedie, ou dictionnaire raisonne des sciences et des arts. 17 vols. Paris, 1751-57 & Neuchatel, 1765. Supplement a l'encyclopedie. 4 vols. Amst., 1776-77. Table analytique et raisonne des matieres. 2 vols. Paris & Amst., 1780. Recueil de planches. 11 vols. Paris, 1762-72. Suite de recueil de planches. Paris & Amst., 1777. Together, 35 vols. Folio, contemp calf, some vols with Palatinate Library arms, Vol VII of tables with other arms; Vol VI of the plates with Palatinate arms added; the 2 vols of tables without arms; some staining, some spines damaged & repaired. Some vols with Munich Royal library stamp on tp verso. S Nov 30 (321) £11,000

**Didion, Joan**
— Play It as It Lays. NY, [1970]. 1st Ed, Review copy. In dj. pba Oct 5 (75) $55
— Run, River. NY, [1963]. 1st Ed. In chipped dj; bdg spine ends rubbed. pba Oct 5 (76) $70
— Slouching Towards Bethlehem. NY, [1968]. 1st Ed. In dj. With ALs & Ls. pba Oct 5 (77) $90

**Diehl, Edith**
— Bookbinding: its Background and Technique. L & NY, 1946. 2 vols. O Dec 5 (44) $110; O May 7 (108) $70
Anr Ed. NY, 1946. 2 vols. 8vo, orig cloth; rubbed. sg Apr 11 (49) $50

**Diemerbroeck, Isbrandus de, 1609-74**
— The Anatomy of Human Bodies.... L: W. Whitwood, 1694. Folio, contemp calf; worn, needs rebacking. With 15 folding plates only. Some tears; lacking frontis port & Plate 6; tp stamped. sg May 16 (403) $275

**Dienst, Alex**
— The Navy of the Republic of Texas, 1835-1845. Fort Collins CO: Old Army Press, [n.d.]. One of 150. Inscr by the pbr, Mike Koury. pba June 25 (76) $70

**Dietrich, Dr.**
— The German Emigrants or Frederick Wohlgemuth's Voyage to California. Guben: F. Fechner, [c.1852]. With: a reprint, Stanford University, 1949 1st Ed. - Trans by Leopold Wray. 12mo, orig bds; paper spine perished. With 8 color plates. Larson copy. pba Sept 28 (412) $400

**Dieuaide, Emmanuel**
— Tableau d'Aviation.... Paris, [n.d.]. Single sheet, 554mm by 720mm. Partly separated along folds & reinforced on verso. sg May 16 (29) $225

**Digby, Sir Kenelm, 1603-65**
— The Closet of the Eminently Learned Sir Kenelme Digby Kt. Opened.... L, 1677. Bound with: Choice and Experimented Receipts in Physick and Chirurgery, L, 1675 3d & 2d Eds. 2 works in 1 vol. 8vo, contemp calf; rubbed. With frontis. Soiled. S Oct 12 (90) £400
— Two Treatises. In the one of which, the Nature of Bodies.... Paris, 1644. 1st Ed. Folio, old calf; upper cover detached. Tp soiled & frayed; some browning & staining; 1 leaf with tear affecting a few letters. CE May 22 (198) $650
Anr Ed. L, 1669. ("Of Bodies, and of Mans Soul....") 4to, contemp calf; rebacked. Some dampstaining. S June 12 (250) £340

**Digges, Sir Dudley, 1583-1639**
— The Compleat Ambassador, or Two Treaties.... L, 1655. 1st Ed. Folio, 19th-cent mor gilt; extremities rubbed. Internal tear on Cc touching letters. CE June 12 (186) $480

**Digges, Leonard, d.1571?**
— A Boke named Tectonicon.... L, 1634. 4to, modern half mor. Lacking 2 folding tables; tp repaired with loss & foot trimmed with loss of date; C3 corner def with loss; some cropping with loss of text or catchwords. Sold w.a.f. bba May 30 (411) £80 [Denniss]

**Dilke, Charles Wentworth**
— Greater Britain. L, 1868. 2 vols. Orig cloth; extremities rubbed, Vol I cracked at endpapers. pba Aug 22 (911) $90

**Dillard, Annie**
— An American Childhood. NY, [1987]. One of 250. pba Aug 22 (118) $60

**Dillaye, Blanche.** See: Pennell & Dillaye

**Dilley, Arthur Urbane**
— Oriental Rugs and Carpets: A Comprehensive Study. L & NY, 1931. 4to, cloth; extremities rubbed, bumped. With 79 plates. sg June 13 (75) $60

**Dillin, John G. W.**
— The Kentucky Rifle. Wash., 1924. 4to, cloth; worn. O June 4 (83) $60

**Dillon, John B.**
— The History of Indiana. Indianapolis, 1843. Vol I [all pbd]. 8vo, recent cloth. Some foxing. sg Oct 26 (94) $325

**Dillon, Peter, 1785?-1847**
— Narrative and Successful Result of a Voyage in the South Seas.... L, 1829. 2 vols. 8vo, 19th-cent calf; rebacked, corners showing. With 2 folding litho frontises, 1 hand-colored, folding litho chart & litho plate. Foxing to half-titles; small stains to 1st title. pba Feb 13 (64) $1,900

**Dilworth, W. H.**
— The History of the Bucaniers of America.... [L], 1758. 12mo, contemp sheep; worn, joints split. With 4 plates. Annotated in pencil; some browning & soiling. S Nov 2 (284) £950 [Schiller]

**Dimsdale, Thomas, d.1866**
— The Vigilantes of Montana, or Popular Justice in the Rocky Mountains. Virginia City, 1866. 1st Ed. 12mo, orig wraps in mor slipcase; lacking spine strip & rear wrap, front wrapper chipped. Lower corners of first pages chipped & torn. Robbins & Peter Decker copy. pba Mar 21 (83) $9,500

**Dindorf Library, Gottlieb Immanuel**
— [Sale Catalogue] Verzeichniss der Bibliothek.... Leipzig, 1813. 8vo, contemp paper spine only. Outer leaves frayed & dusty; some foxing & browning. O Mar 26 (78) $180

**Dinesen, Isak**
— Out of Africa. NY: Random House, [1938]. In chipped dj with closed tear. Insect damage to rear gutter; shaken. pba May 23 (96) $60
Anr copy. In dj. sg Dec 14 (81) $140
Anr copy. In dj with chip to rear panel. sg June 20 (76) $70
— Seven Gothic Tales. NY, 1934. One of 1,010. Illus by Majeska. sg Dec 14 (80) $90

**Dinsdale, Alfred**
— Television. Seeing by Wireless. L: for Sir Isaac Pitman & Sons, 1926. Orig stiff wraps, in soiled & repaired dj. With 10 plates & frontis photo. Foremargin caption of 1 plate cropped. Hefner copy. CNY May 17 (14) $4,800

**Dio Cassius, b.155?**
— Des faictz & gestes insignes des romains.... Paris: Arnoul & Charles les Angeliers, 1542. Folio, contemp calf gilt; rubbed & repaired. Some holes & 1 marginal tear; tp & last 2 leaves loose. P June 5 (212) $1,300

**Diogenes Laertius**
— Compendio delle vite de filosofi antichi. Venice: G. Brugmuolo, 1598. 4to, 19th-cent bds. Some browning & dampstaining. S Mar 28 (481) £220

— Vitae et sententiae philosophorum. Venice: Nicolaus Jenson, 14 Aug 1475. ("Vitae et sententiae eorum qui in philosophia probati fuerunt.") Folio, modern half pigskin over old wooden bds, with 2 new clasps. 34 lines; types 1:115(111)R, 115Gk; Ms initials in red & blue. Marginal annottions. 186 (of 187) leaves; lacking last blank. Goff D-220. Kloss - Trapnell - Hornby - Rattey copy. C Nov 29 (47) £7,500

**Dionis du Sejour, ——, Mlle**
— Origine des graces.... Paris, 1777. Illus by Cochin. 8vo, orig wraps. With frontis, plate for chant II in 3 states, plates for chants I, III & V in 2 states, plate for chant IV in 3 states. Fuerstenberg - Schaefer copy. S Dec 7 (171) £360

**Dionis, Pierre, d.1718**
— The Anatomy of Humane Bodies Improv'd.... L, 1703. 1st Ed in English. 8vo, contemp calf; rebacked, endpapers renewed. Soiling & marginal dampstaining; corner off Y7 with loss. sg May 16 (404) $140
— A Course of Chirurgical Operations, Demonstrated in the Royal Garden at Paris. L, 1710. 1st Ed in English. 8vo, contemp calf; spine ends & rear joint chipped, front cover detached. Dampstained; old scrawls on tp & front endleaves. sg May 16 (405) $140
2d Ed in English. L, 1733. 8vo, contemp calf; worn, covers detached. Tp stamped. sg May 16 (406) $60

**Dionysius, Saint, the Aeropagite**
— Opera. Antwerp: Plantin, 1634. 2 vols. Folio, contemp blind-stamped pigskin over wooden bds with arms of Count Sternberg, with clasps & catches; clasps def on Vol II. With frontis by C. Galle after P. P. Rubens. S Mar 29 (651) £420

**Dionysius Areopagiticus.** See: Dionysius

**Dionysius Halicarnassus**
— Opera. Frankfurt: Weschel, 1586. 2 vols in 1. Folio, contemp vellum; spine ends repaired. Tear & minor repair to 1st title. b May 30 (330) £240

**Dionysius Periegetes**
— De situ orbis. Oxford, 1710. ("Orbis descriptio: Commentario critico & geographico.") 8vo, modern bds. With 4 folding maps. Repaired tear to Asia Minor. pba Mar 7 (90) $70
— Geographia, emendata et locupletata. Oxford, 1704. 8vo, contemp calf. With 15 maps. Some worming at extreme edges. S June 13 (513) £220

**Dioscorides, Pedacius**
— De materia medica. Frankfurt: C. Egenolph, 1543. ("De medicinali materia libri VI.") 2 parts in 1 vol. Folio, contemp vellum; recased. With 595 hand-colored woodcuts in text. Tp holed & restored in margins; marginal repairs throughout, some affecting text; a3-4 transposed; lacking final blank; library stamp removed from tp & last page. S June 27 (22) £6,000

— Opera. [Frankfurt]: A Wechel, 1598. Bound with: De facile parabilibus tam simplicibus quam compositis medicamentis.... Folio, old half vellum; front joint cracked. Browned & dampstained; tp creased & stamped; early owner's Ms index leaf bound in. sg May 16 (407) $500

**Disch, Thomas — & Sladek, John**
— Black Alice. Garden City, 1968. In dj. sg Dec 14 (82) $100

**Disher, Maurice Willson**
— Clowns & Pantomimes. Bost. & NY, 1925. 4to, cloth. Foxed. pba Aug 8 (618) $60

**Dismond, Binga**
— We Who Would Die and Other Poems. NY, 1943. Orig bds, in dj; spine ends rubbed. sg Mar 28 (46) $80

**Disney, John**
— Museum Disneianum, being a Collection of Ancient Marbles.... L, 1849-48. 2d Ed of Part 1, 1st Ed of parts 2-3. 4to, half mor; extremities rubbed. With 130 plates. sg Sept 7 (4) $225

**Disney Studios, Walt**
— The Adventures of Mickey Mouse. L, 1931. Orig bds; rubbed. bbc June 24 (492) $550

Anr copy. Orig bds; children's markings on inside of front cover. NH June 1 (100) $400

Anr Ed. Phila.: David McKay, [1931]. Orig bds; rubbed. sg Dec 14 (83) $650

— Mickey Mouse in King Arthur's Court. NY: Blue Ribbon Books, [1933]. Pictorial bds; soiled, backstrip chipped. With 4 pop-up illusts. Some discoloration. S Nov 2 (286) £280 [Sotheran]

— Mickey Mouse Movie Stories. L, [1932]. 4to, orig half cloth; spine frayed. O July 9 (138) $160

— Mickey Mouse Stories, Book No 2. Phila.: David McKay, [1934]. Cloth with pictorial label. pba June 20 (135) $170

— The Pop-up Mickey Mouse. NY, [1933]. pba Apr 4 (493) $350

— The Pop-up Minnie Mouse. NY: Blue Ribbon Books, [1933]. Bds; soiled. Some soiling. pba June 20 (136) $170

— The Pop-Up Silly Symphonies Containing Babes in the Woods and King Neptune. NY: Blue Ribbon Books, [1933]. Orig pictorial bds; spine damaged. Some defs to pop-ups. NH June 1 (102) $525

— "Sketch-Book" [for Snow White]. L, [1938]. 4to, orig cloth; soiled, endpapers spotted. With 12 colored plates. S Nov 2 (287) £200 [Heritage]

— The Tortoise and the Hare. Racine: Whitman Publishing, [1935]. In dj with smudge. pba Aug 22 (753) $100

— Walt Disney's Snow White and the Seven Dwarfs. NY, 1937. Pictorial wraps; soiled & creased. pba Apr 4 (499) $400

**Disraeli, Benjamin, 1st Earl of Beaconsfield, 1804-81**
— Henrietta Temple: A Love Story. L, 1880. 8vo, contemp mor; rubbed. Inscr to James Daly. CE May 22 (199) $320

— Works. L, 1866. 6 vols. 8vo, half mor. pba Aug 8 (276) $130

Crown Ed. NY & L, 1904. One of 999. 20 vols. Mor gilt with different color for each vol, by Saint Dunstan bindings; spines def. pba Mar 7 (93) $475

Bradenham Ed. L, 1926-27. ("Novels and Tales.") 12 vols. wa Nov 16 (79) $160

**D'Israeli, Isaac, 1766-1848**
— An Inquiry into the Literary and Political Character of James the First. L, 1816. Orig bds, in modern cloth dj; hinges reinforced. Inscr to William Harris. pba Aug 22 (576) $160

**Distances**
— Distances. Brussels, 1928. Ed by Rene Magritte. Nos 2-3 Orig wraps. sg June 13 (290) $225

**Disturnell, John, 1801-77**
— A Trip Through the Lakes of North America; Embracing a Full Description of the St. Lawrence River.... NY, 1857. 12mo, orig cloth. Fold breaks to the large folding map. NH July 21 (256) $350

**Disturnell, William C.**
— Disturnell's Strangers' Guide to San Francisco and Vicinity.... San Francisco, 1883. 12mo, orig cloth; worn & soiled, stain to rear cover. With folding map. wa Feb 29 (504) $200

**Divertissemens...** See: Cabinet...

**Dix, Ernest Reginald McClintock**
— Printing in Dublin Prior to 1601. Dublin, 1932. 2d Ed, One of 200. In dj. ds July 27 (66) $100

**Dixon, Charles, 1858-1926**
— The Game Birds and Wild Fowl of the British Islands. Sheffield, 1900. 2d Ed. 4to, orig cloth. Ck Feb 14 (324) £220

**Dixon, Capt. George, 1755?-1800**
— A Voyage Round the World.... L, 1789. 2d (L.p.) Issue. 4to, modern calf. With 6 folding maps, 9 plain & 7 colored plates. Worming to lower margin of frontis chart; minor stains to some lower margins. pba Feb 13 (65) $1,900

1st Ed, Issue not stated. 4to, contemp calf with blind crest of Lord Grenville on both bds; front cover detached, some wear. Some spotting; half-title partly detached. wa Feb 29 (474) $1,300

**Dixon, Joseph Kossuth**
— The Vanishing Race.... Garden City, 1914. Illus by R. Wanamaker. 4to, cloth. pba June 25 (78) $160

**Dixon, Maynard, 1875-1946**
— Rim-Rock and Sage: The Collected Poems. San Francisco: California Historical Society, [1977]. One of 1,300. 4to, half cloth, in dj. pba May 23 (97) $65; pba Aug 8 (387) $60

## Dizionario...

— Dizionario Biografico degli Italiani. Rome, 1960-89. Vols 1-37. bba Oct 5 (52) £1,000 [Bosio]

**Dobai, Johannes.** See: Novotny & Dobai

**Dobell, Bertram, 1842-1914**
— Catalogue of Books Printed for Private Circulation. L, 1906. 8vo, cloth; worn. O Mar 26 (79) $50

**Dobie, James Frank, 1888-1964**
— Apache Gold & Yaqui Silver. Bost., 1939. One of 265 but this copy without extra suite of plates. Illus by Tom Lea. Orig half cloth; scratched, edges rubbed. pba Aug 8 (43) $300
— Coronado's Children; Tales of Lost Mines.... Dallas, [1930]. 1st Ed, 1st Issue. Orig cloth, in chipped & worn dj; insect damage to covers. pba Aug 8 (45) $50
   Later Issue. In repaired dj; bdg bumped. pba Nov 16 (86) $160
   Anr Ed. Dallas: Neiman-Marcus, 1980. One of 300. 4to, orig half goatskin with handmade Mexican bark paper bds. sg Oct 26 (95) $275
— The Flavor of Texas. Dallas, 1936. Illus by Alexandre Hogue. pba Nov 16 (87) $80
— John C. Duval, First Texas Man of Letters. Dallas, 1939. pba Nov 16 (89) $55
— Juan Oso. Bear Nights in Mexico. Dallas, 1933. One of 250. Wraps; extremities creased. Inscr to Carlton Mead ("Ben"). pba Nov 16 (90) $250
   Anr copy. Wraps; tear to rear wrap. pba Aug 8 (46) $100
— The Longhorns. Bost., 1941. Illus by Tom Lea. In dj with edge-tears. pba Nov 16 (91) $75
   1st Ed, one of 265. Orig lea, in soiled & chipped dj. wa June 20 (125) $800
— The Mustangs. Bost., [1952]. 1st Ed. - Illus by Charles Banks Wilson. In chipped dj. pba Nov 16 (92) $65
— Mustangs and Cow Horses. Austin: Texas Folk-lore Society, 1940. In soiled & worn d/j. pba Nov 16 (93) $90
— The Seven Mustangs. Austin, 1948. Orig wraps. pba Aug 8 (48) $55
— Tales of the Mustang. Dallas, 1936. One of 300. Illus by Jerry Bywaters. Modern mor by Dan Sanders. Library stamps. pba Aug 8 (47) $250
— A Vaquero of the Brush Country. Dallas, 1929. 1st Ed. - Illus by Justin Gruelle. Fake snake, with 1st endpapers reading Rio Grande River on pastedown; lower corners & edges rubbed. pba Nov 16 (99) $350
   Anr copy. In def & repaired dj. Sgd & with hand-inked brands on dedication page. pba Apr 25 (382) $85
   Anr copy. Fake snake, with 1st endpapers reading Rio Grande River on pastedown; hinges cracked, piece missing from spine head. pba Aug 8 (49) $60
— The Voice of the Coyote. Bost., 1949. In dj. pba Nov 16 (100) $95

**Doble, John**
— John Doble's Journal and Letters from the Mines.... Denver: Old West Publishing Co., [1962]. One of 1,000. Unopened. With 5 plates & 3 folding maps. pba Nov 16 (103) $85
   Anr copy. Orig cloth. Robbins copy. pba Mar 21 (84) $75
   Anr copy. Unopened copy. pba July 25 (274) $50

**Dobson, Austin, 1840-1921**
— The Ballad of Beau Brocade. L, 1892. One of 450 L.p. copies. Illus by Hugh Thomson. 8vo, mor gilt with onlaid mor design of Hogarth "jotting her down on the spot" by Bayntun. CE Feb 21 (20) $500
— Eighteenth Century Vignettes. L, 1892-94. 1st Series only. 4to, cloth, in cloth dj; hinge cracked. Inscr. sg Sept 21 (174) $60
— William Hogarth. NY, 1891. 1st American Ed. 8vo, mor extra. Extra-illus with engravings, including 1 by Hogarth  sg Sept 21 (176) $375
   Anr Ed. L, 1902. Copy without the duplicate plate vol. 4to, cloth; worn. Dampstained at bottom edges. wa Feb 1 (353) $55

**Doctorow, E. L.**
— Drinks Before Dinner. NY, [1979]. In dj. Sgd on half-title. sg June 20 (77) $70
— Ragtime. NY, [1975]. One of 150. sg Dec 14 (84) $200

**Dodd, James Solas**
— The Ancient and Modern History of Gibraltar.... L, 1781. 8vo, half calf; needs rebdg. sg Mar 7 (166) $90

**Dodge, Richard Irving, 1827-95**
— Our Wild Indians.... Hartford, 1883. Orig cloth. pba June 25 (79) $110
— The Plains of the Great West and their Inhabitants. L, 1877. ("The Hunting Grounds of the Great West....") 8vo, contemp calf; rebacked. sg Oct 26 (96) $80

**Dodgson, Campbell**
See also: British Museum
— A Catalogue of Etchings by Augustus John.... L, 1920. One of 325. 4to, half cloth; extremities worn. sg Jan 11 (231) $225
— The Etchings of James McNeill Whistler. L, 1922. Folio, half vellum. pba Mar 7 (265) $200
   Out-of-series copy of Ltd Ed. Vellum gilt. sg Sept 7 (349) $200
— An Iconography of the Engravings of Stephen Gooden. L, 1944. One of 160 with frontis sgd by Gooden. 4to, orig half vellum gilt. b May 30 (546) £180
   One of 500. Ed by Campbell Dodgson. sg Sept 14 (172) $250

**Dodgson, Charles Lutwidge, 1832-98**
See also: Limited Editions Club; Williams, Sidney Herbert
— Alice's Adventures in Wonderland. L, 1866 [1865]. 2d (1st Pbd) Ed. 8vo, orig cloth; rebacked with orig spine laid down, 2 corners renewed. Some finger-

soiling & staining; tears in some margins. cb June 25 (1812) $850

Anr copy. Orig cloth, this copy with pale blue endpapers & gilt edges; rubbed, joints & spine ends worn, some stitching def. S Nov 2 (290) £2,300 [Temperley]

Anr copy. Orig cloth; recased & rebacked, preserving orig spine, hinges repaired. sg Feb 8 (196) $1,400

1st American Ed, comprising the sheets of the 1st (suppressed) English Ed with a cancel title. NY: D. Appleton & Co., 1866. 8vo, orig cloth; frayed, corners bumped, black mark across lower spine, leaning. CE Sept 27 (105) $5,500

Anr copy. Mor gilt with mor onlays to design of Alice and Dodo, by Bayntun-Riviere. CE Sept 27 (106) $2,200

Anr copy. Orig cloth; water-damaged, soiled, spine frayed, hinge cracked, bumped. Crease to 1st few corners of text from bump. CE Feb 21 (92) $3,200

Anr copy. Orig cloth; rebacked & recased with new endpapers, 1 signature partially sprung. sg Feb 8 (195) $5,200

Anr Ed. L, 1869. 8vo, mor gilt by Riviere after designs by John Stonehouse, with circular miniature of the end of the tea party by Miss Currie inlaid in upper cover. P Dec 12 (67) $3,000

Anr Ed. L, 1886. ("Alice's Adventures Under Ground.") 8vo, orig cloth; rubbed, hinge cracked. bba May 30 (230) £140 [Clancey]

Anr copy. Later half calf. Inscr to Margaret Langton Clarke, Feb 1887. sg Feb 8 (222) $2,200

Anr Ed. L, [1907]. One of 1,130. Illus by Arthur Rackham. 4to, orig pictorial cloth gilt; soiled, spine browned. With 13 colored plates. pn Dec 7 (97) £380

Anr copy. Orig cloth; soiled, 1 plate loose. S Nov 2 (105) £340 [Miles]

Anr copy. Orig cloth, in later dj. Inscr by Austin Dobson to his son, Alban, & again by his son, Christopher for his daughter Rosemary. Poem by Austin Dobson on p. v is sgd by him. Loosely inserted are 3 early versions of Austin Dobson's poem, 1 typed, the other 2 being early printer's proofs with Ms Corrections by Dobson. Also with related material, including Ls s of William Heinemann & an ALs of Arthur Rackham. S Nov 2 (125) £3,000 [Fogg]

Anr copy. Orig pictorial cloth gilt; soiled. S May 16 (137) £220

Anr copy. Orig cloth; spine soiled, free endpapers browned. sg Oct 19 (195) $1,000

Anr Ed. NY, 1969. Ltd Ed. Illus by Salvator Dali. Folio, half mor. rs Nov 11 (74) $1,600

Anr copy. Unsewn in orig wraps; ties broken. With etched frontis & 12 colored plates, each overprinted with a "remarque" by Dali. sg Apr 18 (97) $2,000

Anr Ed. West Hatfield MA: Pennyroyal Press, 1982. One of 350. Illus by Barry Moser. 4to, half mor over bds. rs Nov 11 (73) $1,600

— Aventures d'Alice au pays des merveilles. L, 1869. Illus by Sir John Tenniel. 8vo, orig cloth; lacking front endpaper. sg Feb 8 (200) $1,000

— La Chasse au Snark. Chapelle-Reanville: Hours Press, 1929. One of 15 on japon. Trans by Louis Aragon. 4to, orig bds; joints splitting. Annotated by Nancy Cunard inside front cover in pencil "Hours Press Copy 1945". Hobson copy. S June 28 (143) £280

— Elisa Katika Nchi Ya Ajabu. L: Sheldon Press, 1940. 1st Ed in Swahili. sg Feb 8 (204) $900

— The Game of Logic. L, 1886. 8vo, orig cloth; front hinge starting. With the card board & 9 counters in orig loosely inserted envelope. Dampstaining to lower extremities. Inscr to W. H. Laverty, Mar 1887 & with related material. pba June 20 (85) $2,000

Anr copy. Orig cloth; minor soiling. With the card board & 7 (of 9) counters in orig loosely inserted envelope. Inscr to his nephew, Stuart D. Collingwood, Mar 1887. sg Feb 8 (225) $3,000

2d Ed. L, 1887. 8vo, orig cloth. With the envelope containing the diagram & 9 colored counters. Inscr to Edith Rix, Mar 1887. sg Feb 8 (224) $4,000

Anr copy. Orig cloth. Inscr to Bessie Badcock, 23 Feb 1894 & with ALs laid in. sg Feb 8 (226) $3,600

— The Hunting of the Snark. Bost., 1876. 1st American Ed. 12mo, pictorial bds; extremities rubbed. sg Sept 21 (114) $550

1st Ed. L, 1876. 12mo, orig gilt-pictorial blue cloth in dj which lacks spine panel. Inscr on the day of publication to H. P. Liddon. sg Feb 8 (216) $7,000

— Notes of an Oxford Chiel. Oxford: James Parker & Co., 1872-74. 1st Eds of Blank Cheques & Facts, Figures and Fancies, later Eds of the other 4 pamphlets. 6 pamphlets plus a anr Ed of The New Belfrey bound in 1 vol. Bdg not described but contents loose, orig wraps all present; rear wrap of last pamphlet detached. Falconer Madan's copy. sg Feb 8 (212) $2,600

— Phantasmagoria, and Other Poems. L, 1869. 1st Ed. 8vo, orig cloth; spot to lower front cover, spine ends & joints rubbed. pba Aug 22 (715) $200

Anr copy. Orig cloth; extremities worn with some loss, rear joint repaired with cellotape. Inscr to the Rev. G. W. Kitchin & his wife, Jan 1869. sg Feb 8 (208) $2,400

— Rhyme? and Reason? L, 1883. 1st Ed. 8vo, orig cloth; rubbed & shaken. Falconer Madan's annotated copy. sg Feb 8 (218) $275

Anr copy. Orig cloth; rubbed, some discoloration to upper cover. sg Feb 8 (219) $60

— Six Letters by Lewis Carroll. L: Pvtly ptd 1924. One of 26. Ed by Wilfred Partington. Cloth, orig wraps bound in. sg Feb 8 (247) $225

— The Songs from "Alice's Adventures in Wonderland." L, [1870]. Music by William Boyd. 4to, wraps; spine perished, some foxing to covers. Variant with tp in dark brown ink rather than gold. sg Feb 8 (209) $1,400

— Supplement to Euclid and his Modern Rivals. L, 1885. 1st Ed. 8vo, ptd wraps; front joint repaired,

chipped. Inscr "R. E. B. from C. L. D.". sg Feb 8 (221) $1,400
— Sylvie and Bruno Concluded. L: Macmillan, 1893. 1st Ed. 8vo, orig cloth. With the ad leaf preceding the preface. sg Feb 8 (230) $100
— Symbolic Logic. Specimen-Syllogisms. Premises. [N.p.], Feb 1894. Single sheet, 8.75 by 8.65 inches, ptd on both sides. sg Feb 8 (235) $850
— Through the Looking-Glass. L, 1872 [1871]. 1st Ed, 1st Issue, with "wade" on p. 21. 8vo, later half mor; joints & corners rubbed. bba May 30 (174) £330 [Franklin]
Anr copy. Mor gilt by Riviere, orig cloth bound in. S Nov 2 (291) £450 [Hirsch]
Issue not indicated. Orig cloth; recaed & rebacked, hinges repaired. sg Feb 8 (211) $400
Anr Ed. NY, 1912. Illus by Peter Newell. With port & 40 plates. sg Sept 21 (268) $60
Anr Ed. West Hatfield MA: Pennyroyal Press, 1982. One of 350. Illus by Barry Moser. Folio, orig half mor. P June 5 (214) $1,300
— To All Child-Readers of "Alice's Adventures in Wonderland". Oxford, 1871. Single sheet, folded 4 pp & ptd on 3 sides. sg Feb 8 (210) $200
— The Walrus and the Carpenter. Los Angeles: Wheeler & Scofield, 1932. One of 60. Illus by John Belmar Hall. sg Feb 8 (240) $200

**Dodgson's copy, Charles Lutwidge**
— Geometry Without Axioms. Or the First Book of Euclid's Elements. L, 1834. 8vo, orig bds; dampstained, upper joint split, portions of spine worn away. Sgd on front pastedown. S Dec 18 (184) £750 [Lindseth]

**Dodgson presentation copy, Charles Lutwidge**
SHUTE, E. L. - Jappie-Chappie and How He Loved a Dollie. L: Warne, [c.1885]. 4to, pictorial wraps; spine perished, some chipping. Inscr by Dodgson to "Edith - from CLD". sg Feb 8 (238) $750

**Dodoens, Rembert, 1518-85**
— Cruydt-Boeck.... Leiden: Plantin, 1608. Folio, later wooden bds; spine lacking. Some browning & dampstaining; lacking 5 leaves; tp loose & frayed; tears without loss. Sold w.a.f. pn Dec 7 (104) £550 [Bifolco]
— Frumentorum leguminum, palustrium et aquatilium herbarum...historia. Antwerp: Plantin, 1556. Bound with: Florum et coronariarum odoratarumque nonnullarum herbarum historia. Antwerp: Plantin, 1568. 8vo, early vellum. With 84 full-page woodcuts in 1st work & 108 full-page woodcuts in 2d work. Some dampstaining to a few leaves. S June 27 (25) £2,500

**Dodsley, Robert, 1703-44.** See: Oeconomy...

**Dodsley, Robert, 1703-64**
— A Collection of Poems by Several Hands. L, 1770. 6 vols. 8vo, contemp calf; spine ends worn, some joints weak. sg Mar 21 (89) $110
— A Select Collection of Old Plays. L, 1874-76. One of 10 on Whatman. Ed by W. Carew Hazlitt. 15 vols. 8vo, contemp calf. S Apr 23 (51) £750

**Dodsworth, Roger, 1585-1654.** See: Dugdale & Dodsworth

**Dodwell, Edward, 1767-1832**
— A Classical and Topographical Tour through Greece.... L, 1819. 2 vols. 4to, contemp mor. With 1 folding map & 66 plates, 2 hand-colored. Fold tear to map. b May 30 (259) £850
— Views in Greece, from Drawings by... L, 1821. Folio, contemp mor gilt; worn, upper joint split. With 30 hand-colored plates. Blackmer copy. S Nov 30 (122) £3,100
1st Ed. - Illus by R. Havell, T. Fielding, F.C. Lewis. Folio, 19th-cent half mor; rubbed. Text in French & English. With color vignette on title, & 30 hand-colored plates. Margins lightly discolored; some spotting. S Oct 26 (91) £5,800 [Frew]

**Doede, Werner**
— Bibliographie deutsche Schreibmeisterbuecher von Neudoerffer bis 1800. Hamburg, [1958]. One of 600. Folio, orig cloth. sg Apr 11 (92) $130

**Doesburg, Theo van**
— Drie Voordrachten over de Nieuwe Beeldende Kunst. Amst., 1919. sg June 13 (136) $120

**Doglioni, Giovanni Nicolo, d.1629.** See: Franco, Giacomo

**Dogma...**
— Dogma moralium philosophorum. Paris: Badius Ascensius & Jean Petit, after 7 Mar 1511. 8vo, 19th-cent half sheep. Roman types Patched tear on tp. P Dec 12 (11) $1,400

**Doheny Collection, Estelle**
— [Sale Catalogue] The Estelle Doheny Collection.... NY: Christie's, 1987-89. 7 vols. Folio, orig cloth. Price lists laid in. ds July 27 (69) $225
Anr copy. With 3 price lists laid in. O May 7 (109) $180
Anr copy. Parts 3-5 only. Orig cloth. Price lists loosely inserted. pba Aug 8 (318) $80

**Doisneau, Robert**
— 1, 2, 3, 4, 5. Lausanne, [1955]. 4to, pictorial bds; extremities worn, front free endpaper partly detached. sg Feb 29 (116) $130
— Paris. NY, [1956]. 4to, pictorial bds; front cover detached. sg Feb 29 (115) $250

**Doiteau, Victor —&**
**Leroy, Edgar**
— La Folie de Vincent Van Gogh.... Paris: Editions Aesculape, 1928. One of 150 on velin d'Arches. 4to, mor extra to a geometric Art Deco design by J. Augoyat, finished by Adolphe Cuzin. Sickles copy. C May 1 (46) £1,400

**Dolaeus, Johann, M.D.**
— Dolaeus upon the Cure of the Gout by Milk Diet. L, 1732. 1st Ed in English. - Trans by William Stephens. 8vo, contemp calf; joints cracked. Ck Mar 22 (101) £160

**Dolce, Lodovico, 1508-68**
See also: Ovid
— Il primo libro di Sacripante. Venice: F. Bindoni & M. Pasini, June 1536. 4to, 18th-cent vellum. C June 26 (70) £1,100
— La Vita di Giuseppe. Venice: Gabriel Giolito, 1561. 4to, later half mor; worn. CE May 22 (202) $130

**Dollfus, Charles —& Bouche, Henri**
— Histoire de l'aeronautique. Paris, 1942. Folio, orig half cloth; shaken, rear joint cracked. sg May 16 (31) $225

**Domenech, Emmanuel, 1825-86**
— Journal d'un Missionnaire au Texas et au Mexique. Paris, 1857. 8vo, modern half mor; new endpapers & flyleaves, library numbers, stamps & pocket. With folding map. pba Apr 25 (385) $80
— Seven Years' Residence in the Great Deserts of North America. L, 1860. 2 vols. 8vo, orig cloth. With 58 plates & folding map. pba Aug 8 (50) $275
Anr copy. Contemp calf. With 58 plates & 1 folding map. S June 13 (386) £460

**Dominguez Bordona, Jesus**
— Exposicion de codices miniados espanoles. Madrid, 1929. Ltd Ed. 4to, cloth. sg June 13 (245) $90

**Dominguin, Luis Miguel**
— Toros y Toreros. Paris, 1961. Illus by Pablo Picasso. Folio, orig cloth. sg Jan 11 (349) $60

**Dominicus de Sancto Geminiano**
— Super sexto decretalium. Pavia: Franciscus Girardengus & Johannes Antonius Birreta, [c.1490]. Folio, 18th-cent calf over wooden bds blindstamped in 15th-cent style; scuffed, split in upper hinge. 90 lines; type 4:130G, 9:68G. Initial blank detached; minor repairs to extreme margins of final leaves. 262 leaves. Hain 7528. C Nov 29 (48) £2,000
Anr Ed. Venice: Andreas Torresanus de Asula, 1491. Folio, contemp blind-stamped goatskin-backed wooden bds; rebacked. 68 lines; double column; gothic letter. Some dampstaining in margins; some corners repaired; some worming. 317 (of 318) leaves; lacking last blank. IGI 3538. S Dec 18 (28) £1,900 [Sokol]

**Domselaer, Tobias van**
— Het Ontroerde Nederlandt, door de Wapenen des Konings van Vrankryk. Amst., 1674. Vol I (of 2). 4to, contemp vellum; cracks at bottom corners of fornt cover, a few plates loose. With engraved title & 22 plates, 6 double-page, & double-page map. sg Mar 21 (90) $225

**Donaldson, Alfred Lee, 1866-1923**
— A History of the Adirondacks. NY, 1921. 1st Ed. 2 vols. Worn. orig cloth. NH July 21 (5) $130

**Donaldson, Thomas, Weaver of Glanton**
— Poems, Chiefly in the Scotish Dialect.... Alnwick, 1809. 8vo, contemp calf; rubbed. With 34 wood-engravings by Thomas Bewick. Some discoloration throughout. b Dec 5 (272) £70

**Donaldson, Thomas Leverton, 1795-1885**
— Architectural Maxims and Theorems. L, 1847. 8vo, contemp half mor; rubbed. Library stamp on tp verso. bba Oct 19 (118) £70 [Pagan]

**Doncker, Hendrik**
— De Zee-Atlas of Water-Werelt. Amst., 1669 [or later]. Folio, old bds; almost disbound. With 34 double-page maps colored in a contemp hand. Some color faded; some maps frayed; some soiling; most maps backed; several text leaves & charts becoming detached from guards. S Nov 30 (69) £18,000

**Donders, Frans Cornelis, 1818-89**
— On the Anomalies of Accomodation and Refraction of the Eye. L, 1864. 1st Ed. 8vo, orig cloth; top of spine chipped. sg May 16 (408) $50

**Doni, Antonio Francesco, 1513?-74**
— I Marmi. Venice: Francesco Marcolini, 1552-53. 1st Ed. 4 parts in 1 vol. 4to, 19th-cent vellum. Staining to a few margins. S June 27 (312) £850

**Donizetti, Gaetano**
— L'Elisir d'amore..... Milan: G. Truffi e Comp., [1832]. Bound with 4 other early librettos 8vo, 19th-cent bds. S May 15 (340) £350

**Donn, Benjamin, 1729-98**
— A Map of the County of Devon, with the City and County of Exeter. L, 1765. Folio, 19th-Cent half calf; worn, upper cover detached. With title, double-page index map, & 12 double-page map sheets. S Oct 26 (351) £600 [Baskes]
Anr copy. Modern half calf. With general map & 12 sectional maps. Small inkstain on sheet 2; some spotting. S Mar 28 (108) £420

**Donne, John, 1573-1631.** See: Limited Editions Club

**Donnelly, Ned**
— Self-Defence; or, The Art of Boxing. L, 1879. Orig cloth. pba Aug 8 (342) $130

**Donovan, Edward, 1768-1837**
— Birds. L, 1794-1815-1797-1820-1809-1819. ("The Natural History of British Birds.") New Ed of Vols III & V, 1st Eds of others. 10 vols in 5. 8vo, 19th-cent calf gilt. With 244 hand-colored plates. Some spotting to text. C Oct 25 (10) £5,000
— The Natural History of British Birds. L, 1794-1820. 10 vols in 5. 8vo, modern half mor. With 244 hand-colored plates. Some browning & offsetting; lacking title in vol VI. S Oct 27 (722) £1,900 [Shapero]
— The Natural History of the Nest and Eggs of the British Birds. L, 1826. 8vo, modern buckram; orig wraps preserved. With 14 (of 17) hand-colored plates. S Oct 27 (721) £200 [Kafka]
— The Naturalist's Repository, or Monthly Miscellany of Exotic Natural History.... L, 1823-27. 5 vols (all pbd). 8vo, mor; rebacked. With 180 hand-colored plates. pnE Mar 20 (103) £2,100

**Dooley, Mrs. James H.**
— Dem Good Ole Times. NY, 1906. 4to, pictorial cloth. wa Feb 29 (83) $100

**Doran, John, 1807-78**
— Monarchs Retired from Business. L, 1857. 2 vols extended to 4. Later half mor gilt by Morrell. Extra-illus with c.170 plates. pba Nov 30 (111) $275
— "Their Majesties' Servants." Annals of the English Stage. L, 1888 [1887]. One of 300. 3 vols. 8vo, half mor; rubbed. With 50 ports, each in 2 states, on Japan vellum & in mtd India-proof. O Mar 5 (67) $325

**Dorat, Claude Joseph, 1734-80**
— Les Baisers.... The Hague & Paris, 1770. Issue on grand papier de hollande with title in red & black. 8vo, mor extra by S. David, gilt by Benard. Fuerstenberg - Schaefer copy. S Dec 7 (175) £1,100
— La declamation theatrale, poem didactique en quatre chants.... Paris: Sebastien Jorry, 1767. 8vo, contemp calf gilt with Mlle. Clarion stamped in gilt on upper cover. With frontis & 4 plates. Copy of Claire Joseph Leris (Mlle Clarion). Fuerstenberg - Schaefer copy. S Dec 7 (174) £300
— Fables nouvelles. The Hague & Paris, 1773-[75]. 2d Ed, 1st Issue. 2 vols in 1. 8vo, red mor gilt by David. With 2 frontises & plate. Fuerstenberg - Schaefer copy. S Dec 7 (173) £1,100

**Dorgeles, Roland**
— Le Cabaret de la belle femme. Paris, [1924]. One of 640. Illus by Andre Dunoyer de Segonzac. 4to, wraps; chipped. sg Feb 15 (102) $225

**Doria, Arnauld, Comte**
— Louis Tocque. Paris, 1929. 4to, wraps; spine chipped, front cover loose. sg Jan 11 (425) $70

**Dormoy, Marie**
— Dentelles de l'Europe Centrale. Paris, [1926]. 4to, loose in bd folder; spine def. Owner's signature on front cover & 2 plates. sg June 13 (221) $200

**Dorr, David**
— A Colored Man Round the World. By A Quadroon. Cleveland, 1858. 8vo, bdg not described; rubbed. sg Mar 28 (48) $275

**D'Ors, Eugenio**
— Pablo Picasso. Paris, 1930. One of 1,250. 4to, orig wraps; backstrip def. sg June 13 (317) $325
Anr copy. Orig wraps; loose. sg June 13 (318) $400

**Dortous de Mairan, Jean Jacques**
— Traite physique et historique de l'aurore boreal. Paris, 1733. 1st Ed. 4to, contemp calf; worn. With 15 folding plates. Some browning & shaving; tp stamped. S Mar 14 (101) £280

**Dortu, M. G.**
— Toulouse-Lautrec et son oeuvre. NY, 1971. One of 1,450. 6 vols, cloth. bba Oct 5 (256) £460 [Farfouille]

— Toulouse-Lautrec et son Oeuvre. NY, 1971. One of 1,450. 6 vols. 4to, orig cloth in djs. S Oct 27 (994) £350 [Schmidt & Grunth]
— Toulouse-Lautrec et son oeuvre. NY, 1971. One of 1,500. 6 vols. 4to, orig cloth, in djs. cb Feb 14 (2756) $475

**Dos Passos, John, 1896-1970**
— 1919. NY, [1932]. In dj. pba Oct 5 (82) $140
— The 42nd Parallel. NY, 1930. In torn & chipped dj. pba Oct 5 (80) $160
Anr copy. Half cloth. Cs tipped to front free endpaper. pba Aug 22 (121) $120
Anr copy. In rubbed & repaired dj. sg June 20 (79) $175
— Airways, Inc. NY, [1928]. In worn & repaired dj. sg June 20 (78) $150
— The Big Money. NY, [1936]. 1st Ed. In dj with spine ends chipped. pba Oct 5 (79) $110
— The Garbage Man. NY, 1926. In chipped dj; endpapers foxed. sg June 20 (80) $175
— Manhattan Transfer. NY, 1925. In dj with chips to spine. sg June 20 (81) $225
— One Man's Initiation - 1917. L, [1920]. 1st Issue. In dj. CE May 22 (203) $250
— Orient Express. NY, 1927. In dj. sg June 20 (82) $250
— A Pushcart at the Curb. NY, [1922]. In dj. sg June 20 (83) $200
— Rosinante to the Road Again. NY, [1922]. In chipped dj. sg June 20 (84) $110
— U.S.A. NY, 1930-36. ("The 42nd Parallel * 1919 * The Big Money.") 3 vols. In chipped djs. cb Oct 17 (360) $450
Anr Ed. Bost., 1946. One of 365, sgd by author & artist. Illus by Reginald Marsh. 3 vols. pba Oct 5 (91) $475
Anr copy. In djs. pba May 23 (101) $450

**Dostoevsky, Fyodor, 1821-81**
See also: Limited Editions Club
— Byesy. St. Petersburg, 1873. 1st Ed. 3 vols. 8vo, contemp half calf, orig ptd upper wrap to Vol I bound in; rubbed, inner hinges weak. Spotted & soiled; 3 leaves in Vol II torn into text without loss; 1 leaf reinserted. C Nov 29 (125) £1,200
— A Gentle Spirit, a Fantastic Story. Paris, 1931. One of 50. Half vellum, in dj. sg Sept 14 (224) $130
— The Grand Inquisitor. L, 1930. One of 300. Intro by D. H. Lawrence. Pigskin with abstract geometrical design of onlays; rubbed. sg Dec 14 (196) $90
— Stavrogin's Confession and the Plan of the Life of a Great Sinner. NY, 1947. ("Stavrogin's Confession: Suppressed Chapters from The Possessed.") Trans by Virginia Woolf & S. S. Koteliansky. In browned dj. pba Jan 25 (103) $80

**Double, Francois Joseph, 1776-1842**
— Traite du croup.... Paris, 1811. 8vo, mor gilt with arms of Nicolas Jean de Dieut Soult, the dedicatee. Fuerstenberg - Schaefer copy. S Dec 7 (178) £1,400

**Doubleday, Neltje, 1865-1918.** See: Blanchan, Neltje

**Doubleday, Thomas**
— The Coquet-Dale Fishing Songs, now first collected and edited by a North-Country Angler. Edin., 1852. Orig cloth; spine ends frayed, insect damaged to pastedowns. Some foxing. pba July 11 (54) $80

**Doucet, Jacques, 1853-1929**
— [Sale Catalogue] Collection.... Paris, 1912. 3 vols. 4to, cloth; worn. O Mar 26 (80) $50

**Dougal, William H.**
— Off for California: The Letters, Log, and Sketches.... Oakland: Biobooks, 1949. 1st Ed. - Ed by Frank Stanger. Orig cloth. With port, 20 illus (1 folded, 1 color paintinng. Larson copy. pba Sept 28 (429) $85

**Doughty, Charles Montagu, 1843-1926**
See also: Limited Editions Club
— Travels in Arabia Deserta. L & Bost., 1921. One of 500. Intro by T. E. Lawrence. 2 vols. 8vo, cloth. Sgd by Doughty, Lawrence & King Feisal on front endpapers. S July 11 (328) £8,000
Anr Ed. L, [1949]. Intro by T. E. Lawrence. 2 vols. In djs. pba Aug 22 (912) $85

**Doughty, Dorothy**
— The American Birds of Dorothy Doughty. Worcester MA, [1962]. One of 1,500. Folio, lea, in dj. With 70 mtd color plates. sg June 13 (87) $250

**Douglas, Aaron.** See: Hughes & Douglas

**Douglas, Norman, 1868-1952**
— Three Monographs. L, 1906. One of 250. bba July 18 (293) £95 [Bell, Book]

**Douglas, Robert, 1594-1674**
— A Phenix, of the Solemn League and Covenant. Edin., 1651. 12mo, old calf; rebacked, upper cover nearly detached, tape repairs at hinges. Some pencil underlining. bbc June 24 (222) $200

**Douglass, Frederick, 1817-95**
— Narrative of the Life of.... Wortley: Joseph Barker, 1846. 8vo, orig cloth; lacking endpapers. sg Mar 28 (328) $700
Anr Ed. Hartford, 1882. ("The Life and Times of....") 8vo, orig cloth. sg Mar 28 (327) $200
— Works. NY, 1950-55. ("The Life and Writings....") Ed by Philip S. Foner. 4 vols. In djs. sg Mar 28 (49) $150

**Dousa, Georgius**
— Die itinere suo Constantinopolitano, epistola. Leiden: Plantin, 1599. 1st Ed. 8vo, orig bds; worn. Waterstained; part torn from title lower margin. S Oct 26 (93) £220 [Christodolou]

**Doves Press—London**
— Catalogue Raisonne of Books Printed and Published at the Doves Press. 1908. One of 150. No. III only Mor gilt by the Doves Bindery, 1917. sg Oct 19 (74) $1,100
One of 300. No. I only sg Sept 14 (100) $120; sg Feb 15 (88) $225
— The English Bible. 1903-5. One of 500. 5 vols. cb Oct 17 (627) $2,500; S July 11 (79) £1,900
BROWNING, ROBERT. - Dramatis Personae. 1910. One of 250. Mor extra by C. & C. McLeish in the style of the Doves Bindery. sg Oct 19 (70) $750; wd Nov 15 (56) $250
BROWNING, ROBERT. - Men and Women. 1908. One of 250. 2 vols. Flourished in red and blue & sgd by Edward Johnston. sg Sept 14 (99) $1,200
CARLYLE, THOMAS. - Sartor Resartus. 1907. One of 300. Inscr by T. J. Cobden-Sanderson, Nov 1911. O Mar 5 (69) $180; sg Sept 14 (101) $275
Anr copy. Mor gilt by the Doves Bindery, 1917. sg Oct 19 (68) $1,700
Anr copy. With tipped-in hand-written slip "with Cobden-Sanderson's compliments". sg Feb 15 (87) $225
COBDEN-SANDERSON, THOMAS JAMES. - Amantium Irae. 1914. One of 150. sg Oct 19 (73) $500
COBDEN-SANDERSON, THOMAS JAMES. - The City Planned. 1910. Inscr by Cobden-Sanderson, 1914. sg Sept 14 (102) $110
COBDEN-SANDERSON, THOMAS JAMES. - The Ideal Book or Book Beautiful. 1900. One of 300. sg Sept 14 (103) $500
COBDEN-SANDERSON, THOMAS JAMES. - London: An Address Given at a Sitting of the Art Workers Guild.... 1906. One of 300. Orig vellum. sg Sept 14 (104) $175; sg Feb 15 (90) $120
EMERSON, RALPH WALDO. - Essays. 1906. One of 300. sg Sept 14 (105) $450
Anr copy. Later mor gilt. sg Feb 15 (91) $325
GOETHE, JOHANN WOLFGANG VON. - Faust. 1906-10. One of 25 on vellum. 2 vols. lev extra by the Doves Bindery, 1911. Paul Hirsch's copy, with related ephemera. C May 1 (64) £13,000
One of 3 on vellum with gilt initials. The Garden - Schaefer copy. P Nov 1 (99) $13,000
One of 300 & 250. Vol II only. bbc June 24 (494) $260
GOETHE, JOHANN WOLFGANG VON. - Torquato Tasso ein Schauspiel.... 1913. Retree copy on vellum without initials, so stated by Cobden-Sanderson. Mor gilt by Doves Bindery, 1921; rubbed. b May 30 (530) £800
MACKAIL, JOHN WILLIAM. - William Morris: an Address.... 1901. One of 300. sg Sept 14 (106) $120
MILTON, JOHN. - Paradise Lost. 1902. One of 300. In 1929 mor bdg by Sybil Pye gilt to a cubist design with green & tan mor onlays. Schaefer copy. P Nov 1 (156) $6,000
SHAKESPEARE, WILLIAM. - Anthony and Cleopatra. 1912. One of 200. sg Oct 19 (71) $400
SHAKESPEARE, WILLIAM. - Julius Caesar. 1913. One of 200. Inscr by Cobden-Sanderson to Margaret & Jack. sg Oct 19 (72) $750
SHAKESPEARE, WILLIAM. - Lucrece. 1915. One of 175. bba Nov 16 (222) £280 [Thorp]
SHAKESPEARE, WILLIAM. - Sonnets. 1909. One of 250. S May 16 (57) £230; sg Oct 19 (69) $425

## DOW

**Dow, Alexander**
— The History of Hindostan. L, 1768-72. 3 vols. 4to, 19th-cent half calf; worn. Some staining. pba June 20 (138) $350

**Dow, George Francis, 1868-1936**
— Every Day Life in the Massachusetts Bay Colony. Bost., 1935. One of 100. 4to, half cloth. O Dec 5 (45) $90
— Whale Ships and Whaling. Salem, 1925. O Dec 5 (46) $110

**Downie, William**
— Hunting for Gold: Reminiscences.... San Francisco, 1893. 1st Ed. 8vo, orig cloth; spine & covers faded, covers spotted. With frontis port. Larson copy. pba Sept 28 (431) $350

**Downing, Andrew Jackson, 1815-52**
— The Architecture of Country Houses.... NY, 1859. 6th Ed. 8vo, orig cloth; frayed. F June 20 (629A) $80
— The Fruits and Fruit-Trees of America. NY, 1869. 2d Ed. 4to, orig cloth; some wear. Library markings. F Mar 28 (474) $130
— A Treatise on the Theory and Practice of Landscape Gardening.... NY, 1856. 8vo, orig cloth. Some foxing. pba Mar 7 (96) $110

**Downing, Clement**
— A Compendious History of the Indian Wars.... L, 1737. 12mo, contemp calf; worn, front cover loose. Library stamps. sg Mar 7 (209) $250

**Downman, Hugh**
— Poems, Sacred to Love and Beauty. Exeter, 1808. 2 vols in 1. 12mo, contemp calf; rebacked. Inscr. b Dec 5 (80) £80
— Poems to Thespia. Exeter, 1792. 8vo, mor gilt. Inscr with 16-line poem. b Dec 5 (82) £170

**Downs, Joseph**
— American Furniture. NY, 1952. 1st Ed. 4to, cloth, in dj. O May 7 (110) $60
Anr copy. Cloth, in dj with chips & tears; bdg spine ends bumped. pba Mar 7 (97) $90
Anr copy. Cloth. pba Aug 8 (388) $90

**Dowson, Ernest C., 1867-1910**
— Verses. L, 1896. One of 300. 8vo, vellum gilt; soiled. S Nov 2 (72) £120 [Zioni]

**Doy, John**
— The Narrative of John Doy, of Lawrence, Kansas. Bost., 1860. 12mo, orig wraps; worn & soiled, stained, spine chipped. wa Feb 29 (410) $140

**Doyle, Sir Arthur Conan, 1859-1930**
See also: Limited Editions Club
— The Adventure of the Blue Carbuncle. NY: The Baker Street Irregulars, 1948. Ed by Edgar W. Smith. In dj. sg June 20 (86) $50
— The Adventures of Sherlock Holmes. L, 1892. With: The Memoirs of Sherlock Holmes. L, 1894. 1st Ed in Book form. - Illus by Sidney Paget. 8vo, orig cloth; hinges partly broken in 2d work. S Dec 18 (183) £400 [Levine]
1st American Ed. NY, 1892. 8vo, orig cloth. pba Aug 22 (124) $65
— The Complete Sherlock Holmes. Garden City, 1953. One of 147. 2 vols. Half mor; spine ends scuffed. pba May 23 (103) $900
— The Exploits of Brigadier Gerard. L, 1896. 1st Ed, Issue not indicated. 8vo, cloth. sg Dec 14 (87) $70
— His Last Bow. L, 1917. 1st Ed. Mor. sg Dec 14 (44) $150
— The Hound of the Baskervilles. L, 1902. 1st Ed. cb June 25 (1815) $1,500
Anr copy. Pictorial cloth; minor abrading at the extremities. sg Sept 21 (177) $850
Anr copy. Orig cloth; extremities worn, 1 gathering loose. sg June 20 (87) $550
Anr Ed. San Francisco: Arion Press, 1985. One of 400. bba May 9 (448) £75 [Marks]; sg Sept 14 (27) $150; sg Sept 14 (28) $150
— The Land of Mist. NY: George H. Doran, [1926]. 1st American Ed. In chipped dj, lacking lower 3d of spine, stain to rear panel; bdg spine warped. pba May 4 (134) $160
— The Last Galley: Impressions and Tales. L, 1911. 1st Ed. sg June 20 (88) $110
— The Memoirs of Sherlock Holmes. L, 1894 [1893]. Illus by Sidney Paget. 8vo, orig cloth. Library stamp on tp verso. S June 12 (185) £240
— Memories and Adventures. Bost., 1924. 1st American Ed. Lower extremities of frontis & tp stained. pba Jan 25 (76) $60
— My Friend the Murderer and Other Mysteries and Adventures. NY, [1893]. 1st Ed in Book form of 5 stories, 1st American Ed of remainder. 12mo, pictorial cloth; spine skewed & nicked. sg Feb 8 (283) $60
— The Refugees. L, 1893. 1st Ed. 3 vols. 8vo, half mor gilt. Lacking ads in Vol I; foxed. S Dec 18 (182) £260 [Hawthorn]
— The Return of Sherlock Holmes. NY, 1905. 1st American Ed. - Illus by C. H. Macauley. Orig cloth; rubbed, spine lettering worn off, hinges cracked. pba Aug 22 (125) $50
— A Study in Scarlet. L, 1888. 1st Ed in Book form. - Illus by Charles Doyle. 8vo, contemp half mor; rubbed, bumped, tears to spine with loss. Lacking all ads; browned. bba Oct 19 (242) £2,600 [Williams]
— Uncle Bernac: A Memory of the Empire. L, 1897. 12mo, orig cloth; skewed. sg Dec 14 (88) $70
— The Valley of Fear. L, 1915. 1st Ed in Book form. Orig cloth; bdg skewed. sg June 20 (89) $200
— Works. L, 1903. Author's Ed, One of 1,000. 12 vols. Inscr by the illust, Arthur Twidle, to his wife, 22 Oct 1903. S Dec 18 (180) £750 [Sandstrom]
One of 1,000, sgd. Half calf. b Sept 20 (565) £1,800
Anr Ed. Garden City, 1930. One of 760. 24 vols. Orig half cloth, in tan wraps; some wraps soiled, 1 repaired. cb Oct 17 (325) $2,250
Anr copy. Half cloth; corners bumped, 1 hinge weak. pba June 20 (139) $2,250; rs Nov 11 (82) $1,700

**Doyle, Richard, 1824-83**
— The Foreign Tour of Messrs. Brown, Jones and Robinson.... NY, 1877. 4to, cloth; lacking front free endpaper & following flyleaf, spine ends rubbed. pba Aug 8 (389) $50
— Richard Doyle's pictures of Extra Articles and Visitors to the Exhibition. L, [1851]. 8vo, orig bds; creased, spine chipped. With 8 double-page hand-colored plates. sg Feb 8 (284) $200

**Doyle, Roddy**
— Paddy Clarke Ha Ha Ha. L, [1993]. In dj. pba Jan 25 (78) $50

**Doze...**
— Doze Comedias famosas de quatro poetas naturales.... Madrid, 1614. 3d Ed. 4to, contemp vellum; soiled. Some browning. S June 27 (375) £2,300

**Drago, Harry Sinclair**
— Outlaws on Horseback. NY, [1964]. One of 150. Mor. pba Apr 25 (386) $120

**Drake, Charles F. T.** See: Burton & Drake

**Drake, Daniel, 1785-1852**
— A Systematic Treatise, Historical, Etiological, and Practical, on the Principal Diseases of the Interior Valley of North America. Cincinnati, 1850 & Phila., 1854. 1st Series only. 8vo, orig sheep; joints broken. Some foxing throughout. O Nov 14 (56) $400

**Drake, Edward Cavendish**
— A New Universal Collection of Authentic and Entertaining Voyages and Travels. L, 1768. Folio, contemp calf; rebacked. With title, frontis, 8 maps (1 folding), & 54 plates. S Oct 26 (454) £550 [Webb]
Anr Ed. L, 1770. Folio, contemp calf; rebacked, endpapers renewed but retaining the bookplate of Joseph Banks. With frontis & 63 (of 64) plates & maps. Marginal tears; 1 map stained on verso. b Sept 20 (416) £320

**Drake, Sir Francis, 1540?-96**
— Le Voyage curieux faict autour du monde. Paris, 1641. 8vo, contemp vellum bds; stained. Dampstained throughout; tp & 1st 10 leaves with wormtracks at gutter margin, affecting letters; without map. CE May 22 (204) $400
— The World Encompassed. L: Argonaut Press, 1926. 1st Ed. - Ed by N. M. Penzer. 4to, half cloth. With tp by William Monk, & 5 maps. Larson copy. pba Sept 28 (88) $75

**Drake, Milton**
— Almanacs of the United States. NY, 1962. 2 vols. sg Oct 26 (98) $60

**Drake, Samuel Gardner, 1798-1875**
— Indian Biography.... Bost., 1833. ("The Book of the Indians of North America.") 5 parts in 1 vol. 8vo, contemp calf; rubbed. Port trimmed; some foxing, dampstaining & tears. F Mar 28 (412) $50

**Drake, St. Clair — & Cayton, Horace R.**
— Black Metropolis, A Study of Negro Life in a Northern City. NY, [1945]. 2d Ptg. Intro by Richard Wright. In dj. sg Mar 28 (50) $50

**Draud, George**
— Bibliotheca librorum germanicorum Classica: Das ist: Verzeichnuss aller und jeder Buecher.... Frankfurt, 1611. 1st Ed. 8vo, contemp pigskin with blind-tooled arms in center panels; small piece torn from spine. Some foxing & browning. Kraus copy. O Mar 26 (81) $1,300

**Drayton, Michael, 1563-1631**
— Nymphidia and the Muses Elizium. L, 1896. One of 210. Ed by John Gray. 8vo, lev gilt by Sangorski & Sutcliffe. sg Oct 19 (249) $850

**Dreams...**
— Dreams and Derisions. NY, 1927. One of 200. Illus by Rockwell Kent. 4to, half mor. sg Sept 14 (247) $150

**Dred Scott Case.** See: Howard, Benjamin C.

**Dreiser, Theodore, 1871-1945**
See also: Limited Editions Club
— An American Tragedy. NY, 1925. 1st Ed, 1st Issue. 2 vols. In chipped djs, that of Vol I with tears & creases along spine. pba Oct 5 (93) $190
One of 795. Half cloth. pba Oct 5 (92) $300; sg June 20 (92) $600
— Epitaph: a Poem. NY, [1929]. One of 800. sg June 20 (93) $130
— Sister Carrie. NY, 1900. 1st Ed. 8vo, orig cloth; endpapers cracking at inner hinge. Inscr to John Kendrick Bangs, 19 Apr 1907. Parsons - Engelhard copy. CNY Oct 27 (27) $9,500

Anr copy. Orig cloth; rubbed, small puncture on spine. K June 23 (267) $1,800

**Dresden Royal Gallery**
— Recueil d'estampes d'apres les plus celebres tableaux de la Galerie Royale de Dresde. Dresden, 1753-57. 2 vols. Folio, contemp half calf; rebacked, repaired. With 1 (of 2) engraved plan & 85 (of 100) plates. Plate 49 with tear repaired; some browning. bba Nov 30 (88) £3,400 [Etching]
— Recueil d'estampes d'apres les plus celebres tableaux de la Galerie Royale de Dresden. Dresden, 1753-47-1874. 3 vols. Folio, contemp Dresden red mor with electoral arms. With 3 ports, 2 plates of the plan & elevation & 150 plates of pictures, 9 double-page. Plates 7 & 12 in Vol II from smaller copy. Fuerstenberg - Schaefer copy. S Dec 7 (179) £8,000

**Dresser, Henry Eeles, 1838-1915**
— A History of the Birds of Europe. L, 1871-96. 9 vols, including Supplement. 4to, half mor gilt, orig wraps to Supplement bound in. With 721 hand-colored plates & 2 plain plates. Fattorini copy, with 3 loosely inserted uncolored proof plates, 1 titled & initialled by Dresser. C Oct 25 (11) £7,200

Anr copy. Contemp half mor. With 721 hand-colored plates & 2 plain plates. About 100 plates spotted or browned. Fattorini copy. C Oct 25 (62) £4,200

Anr copy. Without Supplement. 8 vols. 4to, contemp half mor gilt; worn. With 2 plain & 632 hand-colored plates. Marginal tears; c2 torn in Vol I; some soiling, mainly to text. S Nov 30 (17) £4,200

**Dressler, Albert**
— California Chinese Clatter. San Francisco, 1927. One of 525. In dj with short tear. pba Aug 8 (51) $55

**Dreyfus, John.** See: Nonesuch Press

**Drinkwater, John, 1762-1844**
— A History of the Late Siege of Gibraltar. L, 1786. 2d Ed. 4to, later half calf; worn. Some foxing; closed tears to most maps. wa Nov 16 (212) $160

Anr Ed. L, 1790. 4to, calf. With 4 folding maps & 6 folding plates. Tears to 2 maps; lower outside corners throughout wormed. pba Nov 30 (112) $120

**Drinkwater, John, 1882-1937 —& Rutherston, Albert**
— Claud Lovat Fraser. L, 1923. One of 450, sgd by both authors. 4to, orig cloth, in dj with spine panel def. sg Jan 11 (183) $225

Anr Ed. NY, 1923. One of 50. 4to, orig cloth; stained. Some staining. Sgd by both authors. bba Oct 19 (49) £75 [Cross]

**Drugulin, W.**
— Historischer Bilderatlas. Verzeichnis einer Sammlung von Einzelblaettern.... Hildesheim, 1964. 2 vols in 1. 8vo, orig cloth. sg Apr 11 (93) $50

**Drummond, Alexander, d.1769**
— Travels through Different Cities of Germany, Italy, Greece.... L, 1754. 1st Ed. Folio, 19th-Cent half mor; worn. With frontis & 34 maps. Some browning, & tears with repairs. S Oct 26 (54) £1,000 [Severis]

**Drummond, James.** See: Fore-Edge Paintings

**Drummond, James, 1816-77.** See: Anderson & Drummond

**Drummond, William Hamilton**
— The Giant's Causeway, a Poem. Belfast, 1811. 8vo, contemp calf. With map & 4 plates, 3 of them folding. Some cropping. b Dec 5 (599) £80

**Drury, Clifford Merrill**
— Marcus and Narcissa Whitman and the Opening of Old Oregon. Glendale, 1973. 2 vols Vol I sgd on tp. pba Apr 25 (388) $85

**Drury, Dru, 1725-1803**
— Illustrations of Natural History. L, 1770-82. Vol III only. 4to, contemp calf; rebacked preserving orig spine. With 50 colored plates. Pencil annotations in lower margins. S Mar 29 (726) £2,100

**Dryden, John, 1631-1700**
See also: Golden Cockerel Press
— Alexander's Feast. L: Essex House Press, 1904. One of 140 on vellum. Orig vellum. sg Sept 14 (121) $300
— All for Love: or, the World Well Lost. Kentfield: Allen Press, 1976. One of 140. Folio, cloth. pba June 20 (18) $130
— Fables Ancient and Modern.... L, 1700. Bound with: Poems on Various Occasions; and Translations from Several Authors. L, 1701. 1st Ed. Folio, contemp calf; joints repaired, corners worn. Some browning & foxing. CE June 12 (187) $100
— Original Poems and Translations. L, 1743. 2 vols. 12mo, calf gilt; spine ends scuffed. pba Nov 30 (113) $225
— Troilus and Cressida. L, 1679. 1st Ed of Dryden's adaptation. 4to, modern wraps. Dampstained; foxed & smudged throughout. Perry - R. W. Martin copy. wd Nov 15 (57) $100
— Works. L, 1808. Ed by Sir Walter Scott. 18 vols. 8vo, contemp half calf; rubbed. S Apr 23 (52) £460

**Du Bartas, Guillaume de Saluste, 1544-90**
— His Devine Weekes and Workes. L, [1613]. 4th Ed. 4to, contemp calf; rebacked. bba Oct 19 (213) £200 [Page]

Anr Ed. L, 1621. ("His Divine Weekes and Workes") Folio, contemp calf; waterstained, worn, upper cover reattached with tape. STC 21653. bba May 30 (77) £50 [Humber Books]

**Du Bellay, Guillaume, 1491-1543**
— Instructions sur le faict de la guerre. Paris: Michel de Vascosan, 1549. Bound with a copy of the 1559 De Tournes Ed of Commines. 8vo, 17th-cent calf; worn. S June 12 (10) £1,500

**Du Bois, William Edward Burghardt, 1868-1963**
— Black Reconstruction; an Essay toward a History.... NY: Harcourt Brace, [1935]. 8vo, cloth, in worn & chipped dj. Inscr, 22 June 1935. sg Mar 28 (54) $800
— The Gift of Black Folk. Bost., 1924. In chipped dj. sg Mar 28 (56) $120
— The Quest for the Silver Fleece. Chicago, 1911. sg Mar 28 (58) $175
— The Souls of Black Folk. NY, 1953. Ltd Ed with commemorative label, sgd by Du Bois. sg Mar 28 (59) $250
— The World and Africa. NY, 1947. 2d Ptg. Library markings. Sgd. sg Mar 28 (60) $225

**Du Buisson, Paul Ulric**
— Le Tableau de la volupte.... Cythere [Paris], 1771. 8vo, red mor gilt by Joly fils. Fuerstenberg - Schaefer copy. S Dec 7 (181) £240

**Du Chesne, Joseph, c.1544-1609**
— Quercetanus Redivivus hoc est Ars Medica Dogmatico-Hermetica.... Frankfurt, 1648. 4to, contemp vellum; worn & soiled. Wormed with minor losses; some dampstaining & spotting. F June 20 (192) $150

**Du Choul, Guillaume**
— Discorso della religione antica de Romani.... Lyons, 1559. 2 parts in 1 vol. Folio, vellum; browned, front spine edge cracked, bumped & scuffed. Foxed, dampstained & browned; marginal repairs; tp repaired; folding diagram torn & with small hole. cb June 25 (1762) $475
— Discours sur la castrametation et discipline militaire des romains.... Wesel: Andre de Hoogenhuyse, 1672. ("Discours de la religion des anciens Romains....") 2 parts in 1 vol. 4to, contemp vellum; soiled, wormed. Some browning, spotting & soiling; some worming at end; some leaves cut close; marginal tears & repairs. cb June 25 (1782) $150
Anr copy. 4to, 18th-cent calf gilt. Tp soiled. sg Mar 21 (92) $425

**Du Crest, Charles Louis, Marquis**
— Essais sur les machines hydrauliques.... Paris, 1777. 8vo, contemp red mor gilt with arms of Emperor Joseph II. With 5 folding plates. Fuerstenberg - Schaefer copy. S Dec 7 (182) £600

**Du Halde, Jean Baptiste, 1674-1743**
— A Description of the Empire of China.... L, 1738-41. 2 vols. Folio, contemp calf; rebacked, cover of Vol I detached, endpapers renewed. Sold w.a.f. CE May 22 (205) $2,600
Anr copy. Contemp calf; hinges cracked, spine ends worn. With folding map hand-colored in outline, 23 plates, 1 engraved sheet of music & 30 (of 40) folding maps. Short tears to folding map. S June 13 (387) £650

**Du Hamel, Jean Baptiste, 1624-1706**
— Operum Philosophicorum. Nuremburg: Johannis Ziegeri, 1681. 2 vols. 4to, 18th-cent calf. Vol II lacking pp. 617-24 & 687-96; small piece lacking from p. 200; marginal staining at end of Vol II. pba Mar 7 (180) $150

**Du Laurens, Andre, 1558-1609**
— De mirabili strumas sanandi vi solis Galliae regibus...liber unus et de strumarum natura.... Paris: M. Orry, 1609. 8vo, brown mor gilt with arms of Marie de Medicis surrounded by the widow's cordeliere, by Clovis Eve; repaired. C May 1 (47) £18,000
— Historia anatomica humani corporis. Frankfurt: Matthew Becker, [1599]. Folio, contemp calf; upper cover detached, worn. With tp & 26 plates. Title soiled & frayed; lacks final Nnn4; some worming; 2 plates torn & chipped, others dampstained & soiled; some margins repaired. CE Nov 8 (84) $750

**Du Maurier, Daphne, 1907-89**
— Rebecca. NY, 1938. 1st American Ed. Orig cloth with silver wrap-around label. Sgd on flyleaf. pba May 23 (106) $170

**Du Maurier, George, 1834-96**
— Trilby. [NY, 1894]. 8vo, half lev. Page [168] in facsimile; last pages of each part clipped & laid down on paper. Orig ptg extracted from Jan-Aug issues of Harper's New Monthly Magazine. With ALs from Du Maurier & other related matter bound in. pba June 20 (143) $150
Anr Ed. L, 1895. One of 250 L.p. copies. 4to, half vellum; extremities rubbed. bbc Feb 26 (289) $160

**Du Moncel, Theodore Achille Louis, Count**
— De Venise a Constantinople.... Paris, [1845?]. Oblong folio, contemp half mor; rebacked retaining orig spine, rubbed. With tinted litho title & half-title, map & 51 plates, 2 of them double-page. Tear to 1 double-page plate; some foxing & minor creasing. S June 27 (144) £14,000

**Du Mont, John S.**
— Custer Battle Guns. [Fort Collins: Old Army Press, 1974]. One of 50. Folio, lea gilt. pba June 25 (83) $120

**Du Pinet, Antoine, 1515-84**
— Historia plantarum.... Lyons, 1567. 12mo, contemp vellum; soiled, hinges detached. Tp soiled; margins of tp & 1st leaves def with some loss to border of title; some staining. b Sept 20 (463) £500

**Du Rosoi, B.-F.**
— Les Sens, poeme en six chants. L [i.e. Paris], 1766. 1st Ed. 8vo, mor gilt by Cuzin; front cover starting. With 7 engravings. wd Nov 15 (58) $150

**Du Vair, Guillaume**
— La Saincte Philosophie.... Chalons-sur-Marne: Claude Guyot, 1603. 12mo, contemp vellum; worn & soiled. Repaired with minor losses; tp browned; some dampstaining. F June 20 (191) $140

**Dube, Annemarie —&**
**Dube, Wolf Dieter**
— Erich Heckel: Das Graphische Werk. NY, 1964-65. One of 600. 2 vols. 4to, cloth. sg Sept 7 (180) $500

**Dube, Jean Paul**
— Let's Save our Salmon. Ottawa: Dube, [1972]. One of 850. O June 25 (95) $300

**Dube, Wolf Dieter.** See: Dube & Dube

**Dublin Harbour Improvements.** See: Ireland

**Dubliniensis, Phileleutherus.** See: Delany, Patrick

**Dubois, Emile Bernard.** See: Dubois & Dubois

**Dubois, Urbain —&**
**Dubois, Emile Bernard**
— La Cuisine classique. Etudes pratiques.... Paris, 1874. 6th Ed. 2 vols. 4to, contemp half roan; vol. I lower corner eaten away. With additional title. Vol I badly damaged at end. Sold w.a.f. S Oct 12 (91) £220

**Dubos, Jean Baptiste**
— Reflexions critiques sur la poesie et sur la peinture. Paris, 1755. 6th Ed. 3 vols. 4to, 18th-cent calf gilt; Vol I upper joint split, sides rubbed. A few leaves browned. Fuerstenberg - Schaefer copy. S Dec 7 (180) £320

**Dubourg, Matthew**
— Views of the Remains of Ancient Buildings in Rome. L, 1820. Folio, orig cloth; later mor backstrip. With 26 colored plates. Marginal spotting. b Sept 20 (245) £1,000

**Dubuffet, Jean, 1901-85**
— Coucou Bazar: Bal de l'Hourloupe. NY, [1973]73. One of 500. Folio, wraps. sg June 13 (138) $50

**Dubuisson, Pierre Paul**
— Armorial des principales maisons et familles du royaume.... Paris, 1757. 2 vols. 12mo, contemp red mor gilt with arms of Andre Hercule de Rosset, duc de Fleury. Fuerstenberg - Schaefer copy. S Dec 7 (184) £3,000

**Duchamp, Marcel, 1887-1968**
[-] Marcel Duchamp. Antwerp: Ronny Van de Velde, 1991. One of 850. Wooden box containing list of exhibits; portfolio of reproductions; copy of H. Vuibert's Les anaglyphes geometriques, Paris 1912 with 3D glasses; reproduction of page from The Blind Man, No 2; booklet with articles on Duchamp by Andre Breton & Arturo Schwarz which includes reproduction of The Large Glass; audiocassette of Duchamp speaking in velvet-covered plastic case with mtd rubber nipple; photographic postcard of Duchamp; & acknowledgment & colophon folder. CE May 22 (206) $950

**Duchow, Charles John**
— The Duchow Journal: A Voyage from Boston to California, 1852. [Kentfield, Calif.], 1959. One of 200. Illus by Mallette Dean. Folio, half cloth. With frontis port. Larson copy. pba Sept 28 (433) $60

**Duclos, Charles Pinot, 1704-72?**
— Acajou et Zirphile. [Paris, 1744]. 4to, contemp mor gilt with arms of Prince Louis Joseph de Bourbon-Conde. With frontis & 9 plates. Fuerstenberg - Schaefer copy. S Dec 7 (185) £600

**Dudin, ——**
— The Art of the Bookbinder and Gilder. Leeds: Elmete Press, 1977. One of 490. Folio, half lea gilt. sg Feb 15 (92) $175

**Dudley, Sir Robert, self-styled Duke of Northumberland, 1574-1649**
— Dell'Arcano del mare...libri sei. Florence: Francesco Onofri, 1646-48. ("Dell'Arcano del mare.") 2 (of 6) parts in 1 vol. Folio, contemp mor gilt; hinges worn. With 29 (of 30) plates in Part 1 & 14 plates & 14 (of 15) maps in Part 2. Some dampstaining; tear across 1 plate repaired; lacking 1 volvelle; 18th-cent Ms essay on navigation inserted after tp. Osterley Park - Franks - Horblit copy. C Oct 25 (110) £12,000

**Duennhaupt, Gerhard**
— Bibliographisches handbuch der barockliteratur. Stuttgart, 1980-81. 1st Ed. 3 vols. 4to, orig cloth. sg Apr 11 (94) $450

**Duerer, Albrecht, 1471-158**
— [Series of engraving after] Little Passion. N.p., n.d. [late 16th-Cent?]. 4to, 17th-Cent vellum; recipe in 18th-Cent English written on inside upper cover. With 36 engravings. Some marginal staining. S Oct 27 (1058) £600 [Quarlitch]

**Duflot de Mofras, Eugene, 1810-84**
— Exploration du territoire de l'Oregon.... Paris, 1844. Atlas vol only (of 3). Folio, contemp half lea; worn. With folding voyage map hand-colored in outline mtd on cloth & disbound & with 25 plates numbered 2-26 on 17 sheets. Tp & last plates spotted by soot. CNY May 17 (76) $7,500

Anr copy. 2 vols (of 3, lacking Atlas) in 4. 8vo, orig ptd bds; rubbed, corners worn, some soiling. pba Oct 9 (4) $1,000

Anr copy. 2 vols plus Atlas. 8vo & folio, period half calf & bds; text spine ends rubbed, joints tender. With 8 plates in text; 22 maps & charts on 14 sheets (1 hand-colored folding, 1 double-page), 3 plates & 1 plan in atlas. Text darkened & discolored; atlas marginally dampstained & foxed, large folding map torn & repaired. Robbins copy. pba Mar 21 (85) $11,000

1st Ed. 3 vols. 8vo, half mor; vol I front joint repaired & rear joint cracking, text covers & atlas extremities worn. With 8 engravings, 25 maps, & 1 folded map. Some foxing. Larson copy. pba Sept 28 (92) $9,500

— Travels on the Pacific Coast. Santa Ana, 1937. 1st English Ed. - Trans & ed by Margaurite E. Wilbur. 2 vols, half mor. With 4 maps, 1 folding. Larson copy. pba Sept 28 (93) $300

**Dufour, Adolphe Hippolyte**
— Atlas universel physique, historique et politique de geographie.... Paris, 1860-[61]. Folio, orig half mor; some wear. With 40 double-page mapsheets hand-colored in outline. 2 maps becoming loose on guards. S Mar 28 (172) £380

**Dufour, Adolphe Hippolyte —& Duvotenay, T.**
— Atlas de l'Histoire de Consulat et de l'Empire.... Paris, 1866. Folio, orig half mor; scuffed. With 66 maps. bbc Feb 26 (24) $230

**Dufour, Philippe Sylvestre, 1622-87?**
— De l'usage du caphe, du the, et du chocolate. Lyon, 1671. 1st Ed. 12mo, contemp calf; spine head & foot restored. With 1 full-page woodcut. S Oct 12 (92) £900

— The Manner of Making of Coffee, Tea, and Chocolate. L, 1685. 3 parts in 1 vol. 12mo, contemp calf; worn. Some browning. CE June 12 (177) $1,100

**Dufresne, Frank**
— Alaska's Animals & Fishes. West Hartford VT, [1946]. One of 475. Illus by Bob Hines. O Oct 10 (120) $80

## Dugdale, James
— The New British Traveller. L, 1819. 4 vols. 4to, contemp calf; worn. Spotted & soiled. S Oct 26 (390) £180 [Adams]

## Dugdale, Sir William, 1605-86
— The Antient Usage in Bearing of such Ensigns of Honour as are commonly call'd Arms. Oxford, 1682. 2d Ed. 8vo, calf. Some mold spotting; plate torn & backed on later paper. pba Nov 30 (175) $140
— The Antiquities of Warwickshire.... L, 1656. 1st Ed. Folio, contemp calf; worn. With port, 5 double-page maps & 9 plates. Frontis & tp laid down at margins; 3A2 torn; some leaves torn at margins. S Nov 30 (54) £750
 2d Ed. L, 1730. 2 vols. Folio, modern half calf. With port & 24 maps & plates. Some soiling, mostly marginal. bba Nov 1 (241) £420 [Sparkes]
— The Baronage of England. L, 1675-76. 3 parts in 2 vols. Folio, calf gilt, armorial bdg; rubbed, 1 cover detached. With 5 double-page tables. Some staining; tear in Vol II repaired with old paper. K Feb 11 (156) $225
— The History of St. Paul's Cathedral.... L, 1658. 1st Ed. Folio, 19th-cent mor gilt; rubbed. With port & 15 plates. S July 11 (118) £480
— A Short View of the late Troubles in England. Oxford, 1681. Folio, old calf; rebacked. pba Nov 30 (114) $425

## Dugdale, Sir William, 1605-86 —&
## Dodsworth, Roger, 1585-1654
— Monasticon Anglicanum. L, 1718. ("Monasticon Anglicanum, or the History of the Ancient Abbeys....") 3 parts in 1 vol. Folio, contemp calf; rubbed, upper joint split. With engraved title & 103 plates, some of them folding. Last folding plate torn at fold, anr torn; foot of Xx torn without loss. bba May 30 (319) £300 [Williamson]
 Anr Ed. L, 1817-30. 6 vols in 8. Folio, contemp calf; rubbed. Sold w.a.f. b Sept 20 (307) £200

## Duguay-Trouin, Rene, 1673-1736
— Memoires. Amst., 1740. 4to, contemp vellum. With frontis, 5 plates (4 folding) & 1 folding map. CE May 22 (14) $420
— Memoires de Monsieur Dugue-Trouin. Amst. [Paris], 1730. 12mo, modern calf. S Mar 28 (509) £190
 Anr copy. Contemp calf; worn, spine ends chipped, joints cracked, corner of front free endpaper excised. Some browning. sg Mar 7 (210) $200
— Recueil des Combats de Duguay-Trouin. Paris, [mid-18th-cent]. Folio, later 19th-cent half sheep gilt; joints worn. Engraved throughout; with port, 10 plates & 2 double-page maps. Port trimmed & mtd & from anr work. sg Apr 18 (49) $850

## Duhamel du Monceau, Henri Louis, 1700-81?
— Art de Raginer le Sucre. [Paris], 1764. Folio, contemp calf; worn. With 10 plates. Dampstained; marginal browning; 1 plate soiled; spotted. Ck Mar 22 (1) £140

— The Elements of Agriculture. L, 1764. 2 parts in 2 vols. 8vo, contemp calf; extremities worn, stained. With 14 folding plates. Some staining. pba June 20 (144) $130
— La Physique des arbres; ou il est tratie de l'anatomie des plantes.... Paris, 1758. 2 vols. 4to, contemp calf gilt; spine & corners rubbed, joints cracked. With 50 folding plates. bba Sept 7 (143) £400 [Heuer]
— Traite des arbres et arbustes. Paris, 1755. 1st Ed. 2 vols. 4to, contemp calf gilt; rubbed. With 250 woodcut illusts & 4 folding plates. Tears to 1 leaf. bba Sept 7 (142) £1,700 [Libreria Naturalistica]

## Duhaut-Cilly, Auguste Bernard, 1790-1849
— Viaggio Intorno al Globo Principalmente alla California.... Turin, 1841. 1st Foreign Language Ed. - Trans into Italian by Carlo Botta. 2 vols. 8vo, later cloth; some wear. Some foxing. Larson copy. Inscr by W. H. Crocker to Pacific-Union Club Library. pba Sept 28 (95) $700

## Dulac, Edmund, 1882-1953
See also: Fairy...
— Fairy Book: Fairy Tales of the Allied Nations. L, [1916]. One of 350. 4to, orig cloth. With 15 colored plates. sg Oct 19 (80) $600
— Lyrics, Pathetic and Humorous, from A-Z. L & NY, 1908. 4to, bds; soiled. O Sept 12 (61) $225

## Dulac, Jean
— Les Dessous de demi siecle. Lyons, 1956. One of 1,500. Folio, unsewn in orig wraps. sg Jan 11 (118) $120

## Dulaurens, Henri Joseph, 1719-97
— Le Compere Matthieu.... [Paris], 1796. 3 vols. 8vo, contemp mor gilt. On papier velin with illusts before letters. Hoe - Fuerstenberg - Schaefer copy. S Dec 7 (183) £600

## Dulwich...
— Dulwich Gallery. Dulwich: R. Cockburn, [c.1830]. Later half mor. With 39 hand-colored plates mtd on 35 mats. CE May 22 (108) $1,600

## Dumas, Alexandre, 1802-70, pere
See also: Limited Editions Club
— Celebrated Crimes. L, 1895. 8 vols. 8vo, half mor by Bayntun. pba Aug 22 (550) $450
— A Gil Blas in California. [Santa Ana]: Fine Arts press, 1948. With: Wilbur's ms. of translation 1st English Ed. - Trans by Marguerite Eyer Wilbur. 2 items, orig cloth; spine discolored. Larson copy. pba Sept 28 (434) $250
— Grand dictionnaire de cuisine. Paris, 1873. 1st Ed. 4to, orig cloth; worn. With frontis & 1 plate. S Oct 12 (93) £260
— La Tour de Nesle. Paris, 1901. One of 115, this for Adrien Lachenal. Illus by A. Robida. 8vo, mor extra by Charles Meunier, with insent panels of calf dapicting the Tour de Nesle & Marguerite de Bourgogne & the lower depicting Buridan framed by a dragon & crossed swords. Inserted is a menu for the Societe des Amis des Livres with etched illust by A.

## DUMAS

Dezarrois, sgd by 4 members of the society plus engraved copperplate of the upper cover design.  S Nov 21 (126) £3,000

— Les Trois Mousquetaires. Paris, 1894. one of 100 with separate suite of all the wood-engravings, to which are added 12 preparatory drawings including 6 finished ink & wash studies.  Illus by Maurice Leloir.  2 vols. Folio, half mor by Rene Aussourd, orig wraps bound in; spines discolored.  S Nov 21 (123) £550

### Dumas, Alexandre, 1824-95, fils
See also: Limited Editions Club

— La Dame aux camelias. Paris, 1872.  One of 526, with plates in 2 states. Illus by R. de los Rios.  2 vols in 1. 8vo, mor extra with camelia design by Rene Kieffer after J. Chadel, orig wraps bound in. Autograph statement, sgd, inserted at beginning.  S Nov 21 (124) £950

Anr Ed. Paris: Maison Quantin, [1886}.  One of 100 on japon with plates & illusts in 2 states.  Illus by Albert Lynch. 4to, mor gilt by Charles Meunier, orig wraps bound in.  Watercolor of Marguerite painted by E. Loire on half-title, sgd & dated 1889.  S Nov 21 (125) £1,000

### Dumont d'Urville, Jules Sebastien Cesar, 1790-1842
— An Account in Two Volumes of Two Voyages to the South Seas....  Melbourne, 1987.  Trans by Helen Rosenman.  2 vols.  pba July 25 (140) $75

### Dumont, Jean, Baron de Carlscroon
— Batailles gagnees par le Prince Eugene de Savoye. The Hague, 1720.  Folio, contemp calf gilt with princely crown at each corner; spine repaired at head, heel scratched. With port, 4 double-page maps & 10 plates. Crease in inner margin of half-title; short tear repaired in lower margin of H1.  Fuerstenberg - Schaefer copy.  S Dec 7 (188) £2,200

— Corps universel diplomatique du droit des gens. Amst. & The Hague, 1726-39.  8 vols. Without Supplement. Folio, contemp vellum; joints split, tears to spines.  S Mar 8 (510) £650

### Dumont, Jean, Baron de Carlscroon —& Rousset de Missy, Jean
— Histoire militaire du Prince Eugene de Savoye, du Prince et Duc de Marlborough....  The Hague, 1729. 3 vols. Folio, early red mor bound for Pope Pius VI; spines & corners repaired, small damage to surface, 4 free endpapers lacking. With 98 plates & maps only. Some repairs & browning.  C Apr 3 (85) £5,200

— The Military History of the late Prince Eugene of Savoy and of the late John, Duke of Marlborough. L, 1736-37.  2 vols. Folio, contemp calf; rebacked, worn, covers detached. With 2 ports & 11 plates only.  sg May 9 (341) $350

Anr copy. Vol I only. Old calf; hinges cracked, spine & corners damaged. Browned & waterstained. wd May 8 (53) £125

Anr Ed. L, 1742. ("Memoirs of the Lives and Conduct....") 2 parts in 1 vol. Folio, contemp sheep; worn, joints cracked, endpapers renewed.  With frontis, port & 12 plates. Library stamp on tp & next leaf; some plates repaired in margins.  sg May 9 (340) $350

### Dunbar, Edward E.
— The Romance of the Age; or, the Discovery of Gold in California. NY, 1867.  1st Ed.  Orig cloth; binding lightly worn, rear joint cracking at spine top. With frontis port & 2 plates. Larson copy.  pba Sept 28 (435) $70

### Dunbar, Paul Laurence, 1872-1906
— Candle-Lightin' Time. NY, 1901. 1st Ed. Cloth; joints damaged by insects. Some foxing.  pba Jan 25 (79) $55; pba May 23 (108) $120

Anr copy. Cloth; minor wear.  sg Mar 28 (63) $110

— Folks From Dixie. NY, 1898. 1st Ed. - Illus by E. W. Kemble.  8vo, pictorial cloth; rubbed.  sg Mar 28 (64) $130

— Howdy Honey Howdy. NY, 1905. Orig cloth; spine top frayed, hinges starting, 1 signature loose, endpapers foxed.  sg Feb 29 (120) $50

— Lyrics of Love and Laughter. NY, 1903.  F June 20 (479) $150; sg Mar 28 (66) $60

— Lyrics of Lowly Life. NY, 1908.  sg Mar 28 (67) $175

Anr copy. Orig cloth; stained.  sg Mar 28 (68) $130

— Majors and Minors: Poems. Toledo, [1895].  8vo, orig cloth. Lacking frontis.  sg Mar 28 (69) $650

— Speakin' O' Christmas and Other Christmas and Special Poems. NY, 1914.  In Blanck's A bdg.  sg Mar 28 (70) $225

— The Strength of Gideon.... NY, 1900. 1st Ed. - Illus by E. W. Kemble.  8vo, orig cloth; newspaper clippings affixed to endpapers.  sg Mar 28 (71) $100

— The Uncalled, a Novel.... NY, 1898. 1st Ed in Book form. 12mo, orig cloth, 2d bdg; front hinge cracked. sg June 20 (94) $100

— When Malindy Sings. NY, 1903.  sg Mar 28 (73) $150

### Dunbar, Seymour
— A History of Travel in America. Indianapolis, [1915]. One of 250.  4 vols. Half cloth, in frayed djs. With 2 double-page maps & 12 mtd colored plates.  wa Feb 29 (361) $190

### Duncan, David Douglas
— Picasso's Picassos. NY, [1961]. 1st American Ed. 4to, cloth, in dj.  Library markings.  sg Sept 7 (273) $100

### Duncan, Francis, 1836-88
— History of the Royal Regiment of Artillery. L, 1872-73.  2 vols. 8vo, orig cloth; Vol I worn, cloth along joint of Vol II partly torn with corners worn, spines soiled.  wa Feb 29 (197) $150

### Duncan, George —& Darwin, Bernard
— Present-Day Golf. NY: George H. Doran, 1921. 1st American Ed. - Illus with photo by G. W. Beldam. Cloth; lower covers spotted.  pba Nov 9 (14) $85

Anr copy. Illus with photos by G. W. Beldam. pba Apr 18 (39) $75

**Duncan, Robert Edward**
— My Mother Would Be a Falconress. Berkeley: Oyez, 1968. Single sheet, 28 by 20 inches. Sgd, 1982. pba Jan 25 (80) $130

**Duncumb, John, 1765-1839**
— Collections towards the History and Antiquities of the County of Hereford. Hereford, 1804-13. 1st Ed. 9 parts in 6 vols. Later half mor; rubbed. With frontis, 15 plates & 8 maps. Sold w.a.f. bba Nov 1 (97) £300 [Ross]

**Dundass, Samuel Rutherford**
— Journal of.... Steubenville, Ohio, 1857. 1st Ed. Stitched. Soiled & foxed; dog-eared towards end; corners of last two leaves gone. Robbins & C. G. Lytell copy. pba Mar 21 (86) $12,000

**Dunkel, Johann Gottlob Wilhelm**
— Historisch-Kritische Nachrichten von verstorbenen Gelehrten und deren Schriften. Hildesheim, 1968. 3 vols. 12mo, orig cloth. sg Apr 11 (95) $100

**Dunkin, Robert**
— The Roedeer. A Monograph. By "Snaffle." Southampton: Ashford Press, 1987. One of 50 with an orig watercolor painting tipped in. Illus by Neil McReddie. 4to, lea gilt. O June 25 (101) $110

**Dunlap, William, 1766-1839**
— A History of the American Theatre. NY, 1832. 8vo, orig half cloth; spine perished. pba June 20 (335) $50

Anr copy. Orig cloth; joints starting, stain to rear bd, endpapers foxed, closed tear to front free endpaper. Errata slip glued to front pastedown. wa Feb 29 (363) $100

— History of the Rise and Progress of the Arts of Design in the United States. NY, 1834. 1st Ed. 2 vols. 8vo, orig half cloth; worn & frayed. Foxed. wa Feb 29 (364) $120

**Dunlop, R. H. W.**
— Hunting in the Himalaya. L, 1860. 8vo, cloth; spine tips rubbed, markings on front flyleaf. Some foxing. O June 4 (84) $400

— Service and Adventure with the Khakee Ressalah.... L, 1858. 8vo, cloth; front free endpaper loose. With 8 plates, including color litho costume plates. sg Mar 7 (167) $200

**Dunn, Jacob Piatt, 1855-1924**
— Massacres of the Mountains. A History of the Indian Wars of the Far West. NY, 1886. 1st Ed. 8vo, orig cloth; soiled, edges worn, corners bumped. wa Feb 29 (405) $170

**Dunn, John Duncan**
— A-B-C of Golf. NY: Harper, [1919]. Cloth in dj; d/j piece lacking. pba Apr 18 (42) $80

**Dunn, John Duncan —& Jessup, Elon**
— Intimate Golf Talks. NY: G. P. Putnam's, 1920. 1st Ed. Cloth. Inscr & sgd by Dunn to W. G. Hamilton, 1920. pba Apr 18 (40) $130

Anr copy. Cloth; spine ends rubbed. pba Apr 18 (41) $60

**Dunn, Katherine**
— Attic. NY, [1970]. In rubbed dj. pba Aug 22 (128) $90

**Dunn, Seymour**
— Golf Fundamentals. Saratoga Springs: Saratogian Printing Services, [c.1922]. 1st Ed. Cloth; spotted, spine head frayed, corners rubbed. With folding chart. pba Apr 18 (43) $120

**Dunning, John**
— Tune In Yesterday. Englewood Cliffs, [1976]. In dj. pba Aug 22 (130) $160

**Dunraven, Edwin Richard Windham Quin, 3d Earl of.** See: Quin, Edwin Richard Windham

**Duns Scotus, Johannes, 1265?-1308?**
— Quaestiones in quattuor libros sententiarum. Venice: Johannes Herbert de Seligenstadt for Johannes de Colonia & Nicolaus Jenson et Socii, 10-22 Nov 1481. 3 (of 4) vols; lacking Vol III. 4to, 19th-cent mor or contemp calf over wooden bds. Gothic type. Lower margin of 1st leaf in Vol I cut short; some browning & tears. 279 (of 282), 177 (of 178), & 300 leaves. Goff D-381. S Dec 18 (29) £800 [de Palol]

**Dunsany, Edward Plunkett, 18th Baron, 1878-1957**
— The Chronicles of Rodriguez. L & NY, 1922. One of 500. Illus by S. H. Sime. 4to, half vellum, in chipped dj. pba Jan 25 (81) $160

— Fifty-One Tales. L, 1915. 4to, orig half cloth; tips rubbed, edges browned. sg Feb 8 (285) $100

— Jorkens Remembers Africa. NY, 1934. In dj with initials in ink to front panel. pba May 4 (135) $120

— Time and the Gods. L, 1922. One of 250. Illus by S. H. Sime. 4to, orig half vellum, in dj with tears. With 10 plates. S May 16 (145) £220

— Unhappy Far-Off Things. Bost., 1919. 1st American Ed. In chipped dj. pba May 23 (111) $65

**Dunthorne, Gordon**
— Flower and Fruit Prints of the 18th and Early 19th Centuries. Wash., 1938. 4to, orig cloth. bba Oct 19 (88) £110 [Page]

Anr Ed. L, 1970. 4to, orig cloth, in worn dj. Small stain at foot. bba July 18 (8) $150 [Sotheran]

Anr Ed. NY, 1970. Folio, orig cloth. sg Apr 11 (282) $175

**Dunton, John, 1659-1753**
— Athenian Sport. L, 1707. 8vo, calf; rebacked retaining orig backstrip. bba Oct 19 (221) £160 [Page]

Anr copy. Contemp calf. pba June 20 (147) $110

# DUNTON

— The Life and Errors of John Dunton.... L, 1705. 8vo, contemp calf; rebacked. Last 50 pages misnumbered, as are some other pages. pba Aug 8 (391) $425

**Dupaix, Guillielmo.** See: Baradere, H.

**Dupetit-Thouars, Abel Aubert.** See: Aubert Dupetit-Thouars, Abel

**Duplessis, Georges V. A. Gratet, 1834-99**
— Bibliographie Paremiologique. Paris, 1847. 1st Ed. 8vo, contemp half calf; needs rebacking. Foxed. sg Apr 11 (96) $60
— Costumes historiques des XVIe, XVIIe et XVIIIe siecles.... Paris, 1867. 4to, loose as issued in orig bd folder; worn & taped. With 125 (of 150) colored plates. some soiling & foxing; stamp to versos of plates. wa Feb 29 (100) $260

**Dupont de Nemours, Pierre Samuel, 1739-1817**
— Quelques Memoires sur differens sujets.... Paris, 1807. 8vo, contemp calf; extremities worn, needs rebacking. With plate & folding map. sg May 16 (302) $425

**Duppa, Richard, 1770-1831**
— Illustrations of the Lotus of the Ancients.... L, 1816. One of 25. Folio, cloth; soiled. With 12 hand-colored plates. All plates with library blindstamps; 1 plate-mark cropped; frontis & tp backed with linen; some discoloration. S June 27 (24) £800

**Dupre de Saint-Maur, Nicolas Francois**
— Essai sur les monnoies.... Paris, 1746. 2 parts in 1 vol. 4to, contemp calf. b June 28 (17) £600

**Dupre, Jean**
— Le palais des nobles dames [Dialogue auquel sont introduitz Iupiter et Cupido disputans de leurs puissances]. [Lyons, c.1534]. 2 parts in 1 vol. 8vo, 19th-cent mor gilt by Trautz-Bauzonnet. Bastarda type. With 16 woodcuts. Washed & pressed; last leaf repaired & with missing letters supplied; some staining. Lignerolles - Dubois - Fairfax Murray - Brunschwig - Radoulesco - Schaefer copy. P Nov 1 (78) $4,500

**Dupuis, Charles Francois**
— Origine de tous les cultes ou religion universelle. Paris: Agasse, [1795]. Atlas vol only. Contemp wraps. With frontis & 22 plates. sg Dec 7 (14) $300

**Dupuis-Delcourt, Jules Francois**
— De l'art aerostatique.... Paris, 1847. 4to, orig wraps; piece missing from backstrip. sg May 16 (32) $110

**Durade, J. Georges**
— Traite physiologique et chimique sur la nutrition. Paris, 1767. 1st Ed. 12mo, contemp half calf. Title browned. Ck Mar 22 (103) £360

**Durand-Brager, Jean Baptiste Henri, 1814-79**
— Voyage dans la Mer Noire, le Bosphore.... Paris, [c.1855]. Folio, orig half mor gilt. With litho title

# AMERICAN BOOK PRICES CURRENT

on india paper & 24 litho plates. Plates with blind-stamp below caption. S Nov 30 (123) £1,800

**Durante, Castore, 1520-90**
— Herbario nuovo. Rome, 1585. Folio, contemp vellum; restored. Some browning. S June 27 (26) £2,800
— A Treasure of Health.... L, 1686. 1st Ed in English. 12mo, modern calf. Page edges browned; I6 & L2 torn in lower margin. Ck Mar 22 (104) £1,000

**Duranti, Gulielmus, 1237?-96**
— Rationale divinorum officiorum. Vicenza: Hermannus Leichtenstein, 1478. Folio, modern vellum; lacking backstrip. 56 lines; double column; types 5:74G, 6:150G; initials & paragraph marks in red. Some worming touching letters at beginning & repaired in last leaf. 227 (of 228) leaves; lacking initial blank. Goff D-417. C Apr 3 (86) £1,100

Anr Ed. Nuremberg: Koberger, Nov 1481. Folio, 18th-cent half calf. Stained heavily in gutter margin; other stains & soiling. Sold w.a.f. 193 (of 197) leaves; lacking the 1st 4 leaves (present in facsimile). Goff D-425. O Mar 5 (70) $600

— Repertorium aureum iuris canonici. [Cologne: Ulrich Zel, c.1475]. Folio, contemp calf over wooden bds, with vellum Ms pastedowns; worn, lacking central boss on front cover & 4 corner brasses on rear cover, wooden feet attached to lower bd edges. 35 lines; double column; type 2:115G. repraired tears with loss. 237 (of 238) leaves; lacking 22/6. Goff D-443. C June 26 (69) £1,000

**Duret, Theodore, 1838-1927**
— Histoire d'Edouard Manet et de son oeuvre.... Paris, 1902. One of 600. 4to, half mor, orig wraps bound in. Minor foxing. sg June 13 (141) $900
— Histoire des peintres impressionnistes. Paris, 1906. 4to, contemp half lev gilt, orig wraps bound in; joints rubbed, hinges split. With 2 etchings by Renoir & 1 each by Pissarro, Cezanne, Guillaumin & by P. M. Roy after Sisley. sg Sept 7 (133A) $2,800

Anr Ed. Paris, 1919. 8vo, orig wraps; spine repaired with tape. Includes 2 orig etchings by Renoir & 1 by Guillaumin. Some foxing. wad Oct 18 (259) C$1,750

— Lautrec. Paris, 1920. Contemp half lev gilt, orig front wrap bound in; spine repaired. sg Sept 7 (333) $425
— Manet and the French Impressionists. L & Phila., 1910. With 4 etchings by Manet, Morisot & Renoir (2).. sg Sept 7 (134) $1,300

Anr copy. Orig cloth; joints rubbed. sg Jan 11 (157) $2,000

**Durrell, Lawrence**
— The Alexandria Quartet. L, 1962. 1st Collected Ed, one of 500. Ck Nov 17 (65) £200
— Transition: Poems. L: Caduceus Press, 1934. Inscr to Joseph Allen. bba Oct 19 (320) £1,600 [Ulysses]

**Durrenmatt, Friedrich.** See: Limited Editions Club

460

**Dury, Andrew**
— A New General and Universal Atlas. L, 1761. 8vo, contemp calf; lower cover edge repaired. With title, dedication, 32 maps on 39 sheets. S Oct 26 (428) £1,100 [Smith]

Anr Ed. L, [c.1763]. Oblong 8vo, contemp calf; rebacked. With engraved title & 45 maps on 38 plates, hand-colored in outline. World map with some discoloration at fold. S Mar 28 (173) £420

**Dury, John.** See: Andrews & Dury

**Dussler, Luitpold**
— Die Incunabeln der Deutschen Lithographie (1796-1821). Heidelberg, 1955. 8vo, orig cloth. sg Apr 11 (97) $80

**Dutch...**
— Dutch Cruelty Exemplified; or, a True Relation of the Unjust, Cruel and Barbarous Proceedings against the English, at Amboyna.... L, 1762. 12mo, 19th-cent sheep; joints weak, spine rubbed. Marginal dampstaining towards end; lacking half-title. sg Mar 7 (68) $110

**Dutch Flat Swindle**
— The Great Dutch Flat Swindle!!.... [San Francisco, n.d., c.1864]. 1st Ed. Orig wraps; rear wrapper darkened & foxed. Robbins copy. pba Mar 21 (88) $1,600

**Duties...**
— Duties of Masters to Servants: Three Premium Essays. Charleston, 1851. 8vo, orig cloth. sg Oct 26 (341) $325

**Dutrone de la Couture**
— Vues generales sur l'importance du commerce de colonies.... [N.p.], 1790. 8vo, wraps. Browned. sg Mar 28 (103) $250

**Dutton, Capt. Clarence Edward**
— Atlas to Accompany the Monograph on the Tertiary History of the Grand Canyon District. Wash., 1882. Folio, orig cloth; worn, spine ends & corners worn, rear pastedown foxed. With 23 plates & maps, some colored. 2 small surface peels to 1 sheet. cb Feb 14 (2585) $2,500

1st Ed. - Lithos by W. H. Holmes & Thomas Moran. Folio, orig cloth; extremities worn; spine top stained. With 22 double-page plates. Plate VXI adhered along gutter with damage. Robbins copy. pba Mar 21 (89) $2,500

— Report on the Geology of the High Plateaus of Utah. Wash., 1880. 1st Ed. 4to, orig cloth; spine faded, rubbed at ends. With 12 heliotype plates (1 folding) & 3 folding geologic plates. Lacks atlas vol. Robbins copy. pba Mar 21 (91) $150

— Tertiary History of the Grand Canyon District. Santa Barbara, 1977. 2 vols. 4to & folio, half cloth. With 12 folded maps & 10 folded panoramas. Robbins copy. pba Mar 21 (90) $350

**Dutuit, Auguste**
— La Collection Dutuit. Livres et manuscrits. Paris, 1899. One of 350. Folio, orig bds; rebacked in cloth, new endpapers, soiled. Library markings; dampstain to some lower corners. O Mar 26 (82) $425

**Duval, John C.**
— The Adventures of Big-Foot Wallace, the Texas Ranger and Hunter. Phila., 1871. 12mo, orig cloth; recased, spine laid down, new endpapers with orig free endpapers retained. bbc June 24 (395) $500

Anr copy. Orig cloth; rebacked, new endpapers with earlier chipped endpapers bound in. With frontis & 6 plates. Some foxing & smudging. wa Feb 29 (521) $325

— Early Times in Texas. Austin, 1892. 8vo, early cloth; rubbed. Browned; some marginal tears. wa Feb 29 (522) $160

**Duval, Paul**
— A. J. Casson, a Tribute. Toronto, [1980]. One of 150, with orig sgd litho. Folio, half calf. wad Oct 18 (191) C$800

**Duvall, Marius**
— A Navy Surgeon in California, 1846-1847. San Francisco, 1957. One of 600. Ed by Fred Blackburn Rogers. Orig cloth. With frontis port, 2 illus & 4 facsimiles. Larson copy. pba Sept 28 (437) $55

**Duveen, Charles Joel**
— Elizabethan Interiors, by C. J. Charles. L, [1912]. One of 800. Folio, half mor. sg June 13 (191) $60

**Duverney, L.** See: Gautier d'Agoty & Duverney

**Duvotenay, T.** See: Dufour & Duvotenay

**Duyckinck, Evert Augustus, 1816-78**
— History of the War for the Union. NY, [1862-65]. 3 vols. 4to, half mor; worn. wa Feb 29 (341) $180

— National History of the War for the Union. NY, [1862-65]. 3 vols. 4to, orig half lea; rubbed. NH July 21 (67) $130

— National Portrait Gallery of Eminent Americans. NY, [1846]. 4 vols. 4to, contemp mor gilt; edges worn. CE Sept 27 (213) $550

Anr Ed. NY, [1864-67]. 2 vols. 4to, half mor; worn & weak. wa Feb 29 (239) $160

— Portrait Gallery of Eminent Men and Women of Europe and America. NY, [c.1873]. 2 vols. 4to, bdg not described but def. F Mar 28 (542) $80

**Dwiggins, Clare Victor**
— Toast Book. Phila: John C. Winston, [1905]. Bds in shape of a skull; rubbed. pba Aug 8 (392) $55

**Dwight, Timothy, 1752-1817**
— The Conquest of Canaan: a Poem.... Hartford, 1785. 1st Ed. 8vo, orig sheep; rubbed. F June 20 (389) $60

## DWINELLE

**Dwinelle, John Whipple**
— The Colonial History of the City of San Francisco. San Francisco, 1866. 8vo, half lea; hinges weak. Tp repaired. Met Feb 24 (382) $300
3d Ed. 8vo, contemp half mor; back cover rubbed. Library numbers in pencil on tp verso. Larson copy. pba Feb 12 (281) $500

**D'Wolf, John**
— A Voyage to the North Pacific.... Bristol RI: Rulon-Miller, 1983. One of 225. Folio, half cloth. pba Feb 13 (60) $110

**Dyer, Anthony**
— Classic African Animals. NY: Winchester Press, [1973]. One of 375. Illus by Bob Kuhn. Folio, half syn bd portfolio with 6 extra color plates in front cover pocket. O Jan 9 (99) $700

**Dyer, Frederick Henry**
— A Compendium of the War of the Rebellion.... NY: Thomas Yoseloff, [1959]. 3 vols. 4to, orig cloth. NH July 21 (68) $130

**Dyer, George, 1755-1841**
— History of the University and Colleges of Cambridge. L, 1814. 2 vols. 8vo, contemp mor gilt; spines rubbed. With engraved title & 31 plates. Extra-illus with 61 plates. S Apr 23 (348) £200

**Dyer, Isaac Watson**
— A Bibliography of Thomas Carlyle's Writings and Ana. Portland, 1928. One of 600. With 2 extra copies of frontis laid in. O Dec 5 (47) $70

**Dykes, William Rickatson**
— The Genus Iris. Cambr., 1913. Folio, orig half mor gilt; spine ends rubbed, spotting & blistering on front cover. With 48 colored plates. sg Oct 19 (161) $600

**Dyl, Yan-Bernard**
— La Petit Ville. Paris, [n.d.]. One of 150 on velin. 4to, mor extra with snakeskin design by unknown binder, orig wraps bound in. S Nov 21 (129) £2,200

## E

**Eadmer, Monk of Canterbury, d.1124?**
— Historiae novorum sive sui saeculi libri VI.... L, 1623. Folio, old sheep; worn, needs rebacking. Marginal dampstains on opening leaves. sg Mar 21 (95) $200

**Eames, Wilberforce, 1855-1937.** See: Eliot, John

**Earhart, Amelia, 1897-1937**
— Last Flight. NY, [1937]. 1st Ed. - Arranged by George Palmer Putnam. In dj with minor wear. sg May 16 (33) $90

**Earl, George Windsor**
— The Eastern Seas. L, 1837. 8vo, modern cloth. With 4 maps, 1 of them folding. Brittle; library stamps. b May 30 (199) £110

## AMERICAN BOOK PRICES CURRENT

Anr copy. Contemp calf gilt; rebacked preserving spine. With 4 folding maps & ad leaf. Institutional stamp. S Mar 28 (388) £260

**Early...**
— Early Western Travels, 1748-1846. Cleveland, 1904-7. Ltd Ed. Ed by Reuben G. Thwaites. 32 vols. Orig cloth. sg Oct 26 (366) $3,200
Ltd Ed. Cleveland, 1904-6. 32 vols. With 81 plates by Charles Bodmer. Top margins dampstained. Robbins copy. pba Mar 21 (361) $3,250

**Easterby, J. H.**
— The South Carolina Rice Plantation.... Chicago, [1945]. pba Aug 8 (412) $50

**Eastman, Mary Henderson, b.1818**
— Chicora and Other Regions. Phila., [n.d.]. ("The American Annual: Illustrative of the Early History of North America.") 4to, orig cloth; worn. With 19 (of 21) plates. Some staining. pba July 25 (278) $225

**Eastman, Max**
— Enjoyment of Laughter. NY, 1936. Inscr to Richard Simon, Nov 1936. CE Feb 21 (207) $150

**Eastman, Ralph M.** See: Forbes & Eastman

**Easton, John**
— A Narrative of the Causes which led to Philip's Indian War.... Albany, 1858. One of 110. 4to, bds. With folding litho map (tear repaired). S Nov 30 (136) £300

**Eates, Margot**
— Paul Nash: the Master of the Image.... L, 1973. 4to, cloth, in dj. sg Jan 11 (309) $50

**Eaton, Elon Howard**
— Birds of New York. Albany, 1910-14. 1st Ed. 2 vols. 4to, orig cloth; worn & shaken. With 106 colored plates. NH July 21 (46) $90
Anr copy. Cloth. sg Dec 7 (201) $100

**Eaton, Seymour**
— The Roosevelt Bears. Their Travels and Adventures. Phila.: Edward Stern, 1906. 1st Ed. - Illus by V. Floyd Campbell. 4to, orig bds; worn, corners chipped, shaken. With 16 color plates. F June 20 (582) $110
— Shakespeare Rare Print Collection. Phila.: R. G. Kennedy, [1900]. Connoisseur Ed, Ltd Ed. 12 parts. Folio, loose as issued in paper folders & orig chemise. pba Aug 22 (577) $180

**Eban, Abba.** See: Onassis copy, Jacqueline Bouvier Kennedy

**Ebendorfer, Thomas**
— Sermones dominicales super epistolas Pauli. [Strassburg]: Heinrich Knoblochtzer, 13 Dec 1478. Folio, contemp blindstamped pigskin over wooden bds with vellum pastedown at end from early 15th-cent Ms; wormed, clasps & bosses lacking, stitching weak. 38 lines; type 114G & 2:102G. Old damp-

staining; some worming. 355 (of 356) leaves; lacking 1 blank. Goff E-2. C Nov 29 (49) £1,600

**Eberlein, Harold Donaldson**
See also: Richardson & Eberlein
— Villas of Florence and Tuscany. Phila., 1922. 4to, cloth; cocked, 1st gathering becoming loose. With 300 plates. Inscr. sg June 13 (7) $140

**Ebers, Georg Moritz, 1837-98**
— Egypt: Descriptive, Historical and Picturesque. L, NY, etc., [1881-82]. 2 vols. Folio, half mor; bumped & scuffed. wd Nov 15 (59) $300
— L'Egypte Alexandrie et le Caire. L, 1880. Bound with: L'Egypte du Caire a Philae. Paris, 1881. Later half sheep; worn, label on front cover & lower spine, front hinge cracked. Library markings, including ink stamps on several plate images. cb Oct 17 (187) $170

**Ebers, Georg Moritz, 1837-98 —&**
**Guthe, Hermann**
— Palaestina in Bild und Wort. Stuttgart & Leipzig, 1883-84. 2 vols. Folio, orig half cloth; worn, part of 1 spine lacking. Sold w.a.f. bbc Feb 26 (473) $290

**Eberstadt, Edward**
— The Annotated Eberstadt Catalogues of Americana. NY, 1965. One of 90 including an orig leaf from Venegas's Noticia de la California, 1757. Nos 103-138 (1935-1956). 4 vols. Half mor. sg Oct 26 (104) $275

**Ebert, Friedrich Adolf, 1791-1834**
— Allgemeines Bibliographisches Lexikon. Hildesheim, 1965. 2 vols. 4to, orig cloth. sg Apr 11 (98) $100
— Die Bildung des Bibliothekars. Leipzig, 1820-25. 1st Ed. 2 vols in 1. 4to, half cloth; worn. Some foxing. Kraus copy. O Mar 26 (84) $130
— A General Bibliographical Dictionary. Oxford, 1837. 4 vols. 8vo, half cloth; 1 spine torn. Some foxing. O Mar 26 (85) $160

**Ebony**
— Ebony. NY, Nov 1945. Vol I, No 1. Folio, pictorial wraps; worn. sg Mar 28 (75) $175

**Eby, Kerr**
— War. New Haven, 1936. 4to, cloth, in dj. With 28 plates. Inscr. sg Jan 11 (160) $140

**Eccleston, Robert**
— The Mariposa Indian War, 1850-1851.... Salt Lake City, 1957. pba Feb 12 (54) $85
1st Ed, One of 500. Ed by C. Gregory Crampton. Orig cloth. With frontis port & folding map. Robbins copy. pba Mar 21 (93) $55
— Overland to California on the Southwestern Trail.... Berkeley, 1950. One of 750. Ed by George P. Hammond & Edward H. Howes. Orig cloth in dj. With frontis port & 2 folded maps. Larson copy. pba Sept 28 (438) $50
1st Ed. Orig cloth. With frontis port & 2 folding maps. Robbins copy. pba Mar 21 (94) $110

**Echague, Jose Ortiz, 1886-1980**
— Spanish Koepfe. Berlin, [1929]. 4to, half cloth, in chipped & worn dj. Some foxing. sg Feb 29 (122) $140

**Echanove Trujillo, Carlos A.**
— Enciclopedia Yucatanese.... Merida, 1944-45. 8 vols. Cloth; some front hinges cracked, pastedowns browned. Some worming affecting a few letters; Vol VII tp lacking. ds July 27 (73) $650

**Eck, Johann von, 1486-1543**
— Chrysopassus. Augsburg: ex officina Millerana, 1514. Folio, contemp blind-tooled half pigskin & wooden bds, with brass catches & 1 remaining clasp; front cover detached, both covers wormed. Some staining; wormed, affecting letters. sg Mar 21 (96) $375

**Eckel, John C.**
— The First Editions of the Writings of Charles Dickens. L, 1913. One of 250. 4to, orig half vellum; spine soiled. O Mar 5 (73) $160

**Economy...** See: Oeconomy...

**Eddison, Eric Ruecker**
— Mistress of Mistresses, a Vision of Zimiamvia. L, 1935. Illus by Keith Henderson. In soiled dj with closed tears. sg June 20 (96) $60
1st American Ed. NY, [1935]. In soiled dj. pba May 4 (136) $90
— The Worm Ouroboros. L: Jonathan Cape, [1922]. 1st Ed. In chipped & rubbed dj. pba May 4 (137) $200; sg June 20 (97) $60

**Eddy, Mary Baker Glover, 1821-1910**
— Science and Health. Lynn, 1882. 3d Ed. 2 vols. 8vo, mor gilt. pba Sept 14 (136) $225

**Eddy, Richard**
— History of the Sixtieth Regiment New York State Volunteers. Phila., 1864. 12mo, orig cloth; worn. NH July 21 (69) $110

**Eddy, Thomas, 1758-1827**
— An Account of the State Prison or Penitentiary House, in the City of New York. NY, 1801. 8vo, later half mor; scuffed. With 2 folding plates. Some leaves repaired. F Mar 28 (452) $140

**Edgar, J. Douglas**
— The Gate to Golf. St. Albans: Edgar & Co., 1920. 1st U.K. Ed. Cloth. pba Apr 18 (44) $225

**Edgeworth, Maria, 1767-1849**
See also: Golden Cockerel Press
— Belinda. L, 1801. 1st Ed. 3 vols. 12mo, contemp half calf; rubbed & flaked. Some staining & marginal defs; dead fly in Vol III obscuring 2 words of text on verso; P12 of Vol III with hole through 2 letters on recto; last leaf soiled. Ck Sept 8 (202) £450
— Patronage. L, 1814. 1st Ed. 4 vols. 12mo, contemp half calf; rubbed. Lacking half-title in Vol I; marginal doodles in Vol I; some staining & soiling. O Mar 5 (74) $130

# EDGEWORTH

— Tales and Miscellaneous Pieces. L, 1825. 14 vols. 8vo, mor gilt. Foxed. pba Aug 22 (551) $350

**Ediciones...**
— Ediciones Poligrafa. L, [1979]. One of 1,000. Wraps by Miro. sg Sept 7 (248) $200

**Edinburgh...**
— The Edinburgh Advertiser.... Edin., 1802-13. Vols 78-100. Contemp half calf. Sold w.a.f. pnE May 15 (121) £600
— The Edinburgh Journal of Natural History and of the Physical Sciences. Edin., [1835-40]. Ed by William Macgillivray. 6 parts only. Folio, bds; stained & bumped, library stickers. With 89 hand-colored plates only. Some foxing. Met Feb 24 (444) $1,100

**Edinburgh Angling Club**
— Songs and Selections from the Album of the Edinburgh Angling Club.... Edin.: David Douglas, 1900. Orig cloth. pba July 11 (78) $85
— Songs of the Edinburgh Angling Club. Edin.: Pvtly ptd, 1879. 2d Ed. Orig cloth; front joint rubbed, later endpapers. Some foxing. pba July 11 (77) $100

**Edinburgh Circulating Library**
— A New Catalogue of the Edinburgh Circulating Library.... Edin.: [c.1790]. Bound with: Ferrers, Edmund. Catalogue of the Curious and Extensive library... which will be sold... by Mr. Evans... Monday May 8th 1826. And: Catalogue of... books... sold at auction by Mr. C. B. Tait... on Monday January 30, 1837. [Edin., 1837] 8vo, Bdg not described. Some staining. S Apr 23 (188) £1,700

**Edison...**
— The Edison Light. [NY, 1883]. 8vo, orig wraps; soiled, edges worn, stab hole in upper left corner through pamphlet leaves. sg Oct 26 (333) $150

**Edkins, Diana E.** See: Newhall & Edkins

**Edmonds, Harfield H. —&
Lee, Norman N.**
— Brook and River Trouting. Bradford: Pvtly ptd, [1916]. 4to, cloth; shaken. Henry A. Siegel's copy. O Feb 6 (70) $110

**Edward, David B.**
— The History of Texas, or the Emigrant's, Farmer's and Politician's Guide.... Cincinnati, 1836. 1st Ed. 12mo, modern lea. Map lacking, facsimile supplied; some stamps. pba Apr 25 (390) $425

**Edward VIII, King of England, 1894-1972.** See: Windsor, Edward

**Edwards, Bryan, 1743-1800**
— The History, Civil and Commercial, of the British Colonies in the West Indies. Dublin, 1793. 2 vols. 8vo, early sheep; several covers loose. With folding map & 5 folding tables. sg Oct 26 (105) $90

**Edwards, Edwin**
— Old Inns. L, 1880. Part 2 (of 3) only. Folio, loose. With 55 etchings. S Oct 12 (95) £80

**Edwards, Elza Ivan**
— Desert Voices: A Descriptive Bibliography. Los Angeles: Westernlore Press, 1958. One of 500. In dj. ds July 27 (75) $50
— The Valley Whose Name Is Death. Pasadena: San Pasqual Press, 1940. One of 500. pba Feb 12 (45) $110

**Edwards, George, 1694-1773**
— Natural History of Birds. L, 1743-51. 4 vols in 2. 4to, contemp calf gilt; rubbed, 1 spine with extermities worn. With frontis & 205 (of 210) hand-colored plates. Some corners repaired. bba Sept 7 (145) £4,200
— A Natural History of Uncommon Birds. L, 1743-64. ("A Natural History of Birds * Gleanings of Natural History.") 7 vols. 4to, 19th-cent half mor gilt; worn. With 361 (of 362) hand-colored plates, port of Edwards & port of a Samojeed. Lacking American Kingfisher; some browning; Plate 146 torn in inner margin; Plate 172 stained; Plate 195 mtd; Plate 213 repaired in lower margin; last 2 leaves in Vol VII def with loss. S June 27 (27) £7,000
  Bound into 1st work are: Some Memoirs of the Life and Works of George Edwards, 1776. And: Linnaeus. A Catalogue of the Birds, Beasts...contained in Edwards's Natural History, 1776. One of 12 sets colored by Edwards. 7 vols. Folio, contemp mor gilt. With 363 hand-colored plates; French title & text at back of each vol in 1st work; port in 1st work; 2 copies of the uncolored Samoyed plate. Lacking port in 2d work; Vol III with 2 text leaves & 3 plates having margins torn & repaired. Fattorini copy. C Oct 25 (12) £16,000
  Anr Ed. L, 1802-6. One of 25. 7 vols in 4. Folio, contemp mor gilt by Staggemeier & Welcher; rubbed & chipped. With 362 hand-colored plates. Golitsyn - Fattorini copy. "Unique Large Paper copy". C Oct 25 (13) £26,000

**Edwards, John**
— The Tour of the Dove.... Derby, [c.1825]. 2d Ed. 12mo, orig bds; upper cover detached. b Dec 5 (68) £100

**Edwards, Jonathan, 1703-58**
— An Account of the Life of the late Reverend David Brainerd.... Bost., 1749. 1st Ed. 8vo, orig calf; worn & rubbed, lacking front free endpaper. Tp trimmed at top with loss of 1st word; browned; marginal tear. K June 23 (270) $275
  Anr copy. Old calf; worn, front free endpaper torn & nearly detached. Browned. wa Feb 29 (366) $220
— A Careful and Strict Enquiry into the Modern Prevailing Notions of that Freedom of Will.... Bost.: S. Kneeland, 1754. 1st Ed. 8vo, contemp calf; scuffed. With bookplate of Lord Kames. pba Sept 14 (139) $1,200
— The Great Christian Doctrine of Original Sin Defended.... Bost., 1758. 8vo, contemp calf; rebacked.

Lacking 1 leaf of subscribers. bbc June 24 (397) $310
— A Treatise concerning Religious Affections. Bost., 1746. 8vo, contemp calf; front cover detached. K Feb 11 (159) $550

**Edwards, Lionel**
— My Hunting Sketch Book. L, 1928. Vol I (of 2) only. 4to, cloth, in dj with wear at corners. Some foxing. sg Mar 7 (442) $130
— My Scottish Sketch Book. L, 1929. One of 250. 4to, half vellum. With 16 colored plates. O Jan 9 (101) $550
— A Sportsman's Bag. L, [1926]. One of 650. Folio, orig cloth, in frayed dj. With 18 colored plates. bba Sept 7 (159) £350 [McEwan]

**Edwards, Ralph.** See: Macquoid & Edwards

**Edwards, S. J. Celestine**
— From Slavery to a Bishopric, or the Life of Bishop Walter Hawkins.... L: John Kensit, 1891. 8vo, cloth; waterstains on front cover, hinges cracked. With port. sg Mar 28 (76) $100

**Edwards, Samuel E., b.1810**
— The Ohio Hunter. Battle Creek MI, 1866. 16mo, orig cloth; spine ends & corners frayed. Text with some foxing & staining. bbc Dec 18 (469) $375

**Edwards, Sydenham Teak, 1769?-1819**
— The Botanical Register. L, 1816. Vol 2. Half lea; worn & abraded, hinge starting. With 86 hand-colored plates (of 87). Met May 22 (427) $875
Vol 4. L, 1818. Half lea; worn, abraded, hinge starting. With 84 hand-colored plates (of 86). Met May 22 (424) $875
Vol 5. L, 1819. Half lea. With 81 hand-colored plates only. Met May 22 (428) $875
— Botanical Register. L, 1842. New Series, Vol 5 only. 8vo, half mor; worn. Lacking 5 plates. O Mar 5 (75) $650
New Series, Vol 8 only. L, 1845. 8vo, half mor; some wear. Lacking 4 plates. O Mar 5 (76) $700

**Edwards, William**
— Art of Boxing and Science of Self-Defense.... NY: Excelsior Publishing, [1888]. Orig half cloth; corners rubbed. pba Aug 8 (343) $120

**Egan, Pierce, 1772-1849**
— Boxiana; or Sketches of Antient & Modern Pugilism. L, 1818-29. 5 vols. 8vo, mor gilt by Root; spine bands & joints rubbed, 2 covers detached. pba Nov 30 (116) $450
— Life in London. L, 1821. 1st Ed, Issue not indicated. 8vo, later 19th-cent mor gilt; rebacked retaining most of backstrip. With 36 hand-colored plates & 3 folding leaves of engraved music. Lacking To the Subscribers. sg Feb 8 (286) $110
1st Issue, with no footnote on p. 9. Illus by I. R. & George Cruikshank. Later lev extra by Birdsall. With 36 hand-colored plates & 3 folding leaves of engraved music. sg Sept 21 (178) $700

**Egerton, Daniel Thomas**
— Borough Election: A Serio-Comic Poem. By Peter Quiz. Huntington, 1824. 12mo, half mor. Ms annotations on tp verso. Lord Esme S. Gordon's copy. b Dec 5 (137) £70
— The Necessary Qualifications of a Man of Fashion. L, 1823 [some plates watermarked 1824]. Oblong folio, later 19th-cent half calf. With 12 hand-colored plates. sg Oct 19 (83) $1,500

**Egnatius, Johannes Baptista, Pseud. of G. B. Capilli**
— Summaire chronique contenans les vies, gestes et cas fortuitz de tous les Empereurs.... Paris: Geoffroy Tory, 13 Apr 1529. Trans by Geoffroy Tory. 8vo, contemp deerskin over pastebd; rubbed & loose. Roman type Very small wormhole in final 28 leaves affecting a few letters. Abrams copy. C June 26 (73) £1,800

**Ehrenberg, Ralph E.** See: Schwartz & Ehrenberg

**Eichenberg, Fritz**
— The Wood and the Graver.... NY, [1977]. One of 150 with sgd wood engraving laid in. 4to, cloth, in dj. sg Jan 11 (161) $150
One of 500. Cloth, in dj. With sgd engraving laid into rear pocket. sg Jan 11 (162) $110

**Eickemeyer, Carl**
— Over the Great Navajo Trail. NY, 1900. Inscr. wa Feb 29 (513) $240

**Einstein, Albert, 1879-1955**
— About Zionism: Speeches and Letters. NY, 1931. In chipped dj with def spine. pba Nov 30 (118) $110
— Die Grundlage der allgemeinen Relativitaetstheorie. Leipzig, 1916. Presentation issue. Orig wraps; top of spine restored. The Garden - Hefner copy. CNY May 17 (15) $15,000
1st Separate Ed. Leipzig, 1916 [c.1919?]. Orig wraps; front joint stained, rear joint starting. sg Oct 19 (225) $1,200
— Ueber die spezielle und die allgemeine Relativitaetstheorie Gemeinverstaendlich. Braunschweig, 1917. Wraps; cover nearly detached. In: Sammlung Vieweg, Vol 38. pba Sept 14 (142) $1,700

**Eisen, Charles Dominique Joseph**
— [Suite of engravings for Pygmalion] Paris: chez Naudet marchand d'estampes, [n.d.]. Image size 140mm by 95mm, paper in various sizes, loose in folder. I in 2 states, (2d with title Pigmalion & Aliamet direxit added in center); II in states; III in 4 states, IV in 2 states; V in 2 impressions of same state; VI in 2 states; plus 1 plate of Pygmalion kneeling before Galathea. Fuerstenberg - Schaefer copy. S Dec 7 (191) £180

**Eisenberg, ——, Baron d'**
— Description du manege moderne dans sa perfection. The Hague, 1737. ("L'art de monter a cheval ou description du manege moderne....") Folio, half mor gilt; front joint restored, bottom of spine chipped,

endpapers & opening leaves creased. With 55 (of 59) plates. Lacking last 4 plates & related text leaves. sg Mar 7 (442A) $1,600

Anr Ed. Amst., 1759. ("L'Art de monter a cheval ou description du manege moderne....") 3 parts in 1 vol. Oblong folio, contemp calf gilt; spine ends chipped, joints cracked. With 59 plates. Some browning. sg Apr 18 (50) $2,600

**Eisenhower, Dwight D., 1890-1969**
— Crusade in Europe. Garden City, 1948. Inscr. sg Sept 28 (99) $375

Anr copy. In dj with minor wear. Inscr. sg Feb 1 (87) $325

Anr Ed. L, [1948]. In dj. Inscr to Ricard Simon & sgd with initials, Christmas 1948. CE Feb 21 (208) $300

— Mandate for Change, 1953-56. NY, 1963. One of 1,434. pba June 13 (57) $350

Anr copy. Inscr by George Friedland. wa Feb 29 (238) $325

— Peace with Justice. NY, 1961. In dj. Inscr to Art Neff. pba Oct 26 (224) $375

**Eisenmenger, Johann Andreas, 1654-1704**
— Entdecktes Judenthum. Frankfurt, 1700. 2 vols. 4to, later half lea; rubbed & bumped. Library markings. Met Sept 28 (197) $250

**Eisenstaedt, Alfred**
— Witness to our Time. NY, [1967]. Folio, cloth, in dj with small tears. sg Feb 29 (123) $200

**Elder, David Paul**
— California the Beautiful. Camera Studies by California Artists.... San Francisco, [1911]. 4to, half cloth. pba Aug 22 (913) $70

**Elderfield, John**
— Frankenthaler. NY, [1989]. Folio, cloth, in plastic dj. sg Jan 11 (180) $90

**Eldredge, Zoeth Skinner**
— The Beginnings of San Francisco.... San Francisco, 1912. 1st Ed. 2 vols. With 15 maps (8 folding) & 29 plates. pba Feb 12 (301) $60

**Eldridge, Elleanor**
— Elleanor's Second Book. Providence, 1839. 18mo, orig half cloth; chipped. Some foxing. sg Mar 28 (330) $350

— Memoirs. Providence, 1843. 18mo, orig half cloth; rubbed. Some foxing. sg Mar 28 (329) $100

**Eldridge, Paul.** See: Viereck & Eldridge

**Eldridge, Zoeth Skinner**
— The March of Portola and the Discovery of the Bay of San Francisco. San Francisco, 1909. 1st Ed. Orig cloth; slight chipping. With 4 illus, 1 facsimile & 1 map. Larson & Robert Cowan copy. pba Sept 28 (96) $70

**Elgar, Sir Edward, 1857-1934**
— Concerto for Violoncello and Orchestra. L: Novello, 1921. Folio, orig bds. With holograph dedication to the cellist Felix Salmond. Also inscr by Salmond's widow to Pierre Fournier. S May 15 (347) £1,800

**Elimithar, Elluchsam**
— Tacuini sanitatis Elluchasem Elimithar medici de Baldath, de sex rebus non naturalibus.... Strassburg: J. Schottus, 1531. Bound with: Mesue, Joannes. Tacuini aegritudinum et morborum ferme omnium corporis humani.... Strassburg: J. Schottus, 1532. 1st Eds. 2 works in 1 vol. Folio, 18th-Cent calf; spine restored, extrems rubbed. Dampstained; hole through lower margin; Mesue lacking final blank. Vicaire copy. Ck Mar 22 (155) £3,200

**Eliot, George, 1819-80**
— Daniel Deronda. NY, 1876. 1st American Ed. 2 vols. 8vo, cloth; spine ends chipped. Owner's stamp to titles. pba Aug 8 (395) $55

— Middlemarch. Berlin: A. Asher, 1872. Copyright Ed. 4 vols. 8vo, half calf. pba Dec 14 (61) $140

— Scenes of Clerical Life. Edin., 1858. 1st Ed. 2 vols. 8vo, orig cloth; spines worn, tear to lower joint of Vol I, both vols shaken. CNY Dec 15 (20) $3,000

— Silas Marner. L, 1953. sg Nov 9 (170) $70

— Works. Edin., [c.1901]. 10 vols. Half mor. pba June 20 (152) $225

**Eliot, John, 1604-90**
— John Eliot and the Indians, 1652-1657: Being Letters Addressed to the Rev. Jonathan Hanmer.... NY, 1915. One of 150. Ed by Wilberforce Eames. Bds; spine abraded. Library markings. O Mar 26 (88) $180

**Eliot, Thomas Stearns, 1888-1965**
See also: Catholic...
— Animula. [L, 1929]. 1st Ed, one of 400 L.p. copies. Orig bds. sg June 20 (98) $300

Anr copy. Orig bds; spine head chipped. wa Feb 29 (33) $140

— Ara vus prec. L: Ovid Press, [1920]. One of 220. 4to, orig half cloth (1st bdg). cb Oct 17 (363) $700

Out-of-series copy. Orig half cloth (1st bdg). Hobson copy. S June 28 (45) £750

Recension of Ara Vos Prec. NY, 1920. ("Poems.") Orig bds, in chipped dj. Hobson copy. S June 28 (46) £750

— Ash Wednesday. L & NY, 1930. One of 600. sg June 20 (99) $550

— Dante. L, [1929]. 1st Ed. Orig bds, in dj. sg Dec 14 (91) $250; sg June 20 (100) $110

One of 125. Ck Nov 17 (71) £190

— Ezra Pound: His Metric and his Poetry. NY, 1917 [pbd Jan 1918]. 1st Ed. Orig bds. Hobson copy. S June 28 (42) £320

— Four Quartets. NY: Harcourt Brace, [1943]. 1st Ed, 1st ptg, with the words "first American edition" on verso of tp. bbc Dec 18 (246) $210

Anr Ed. L, [1960]. One of 290, sgd. Folio, orig parchment-backed bds. With related material by the printer, Officina Bodoni. Hobson copy. S June 28 (56) £950

— Marina. [L, 1930]. 1st Ed, one of 400. Orig bds. sg June 20 (103) $300

— Old Possum's Book of Practical Cats. L, 1939. 1st Ed. In dj. Inscr to Violet Smyth. bba Oct 19 (322) £650 [Ogino]

Anr copy. In creased dj. bba Oct 19 (323) £160 [Sotheran]

— Poems. L: Hogarth Press, 1919. 1st Ed, 1st State, with "capitaux" on p. 13. Orig blue burlap-like cloth backed with paper, with label ptd in red; extremities with wear. Goodwin - Engelhard copy. CNY Oct 27 (28) $8,500

Anr copy. Orig wraps; separated along hinge. Clive Bell's copy. Hobson copy. S June 28 (44) £3,800

— Poems 1909-1925. L, 1925 [1926]. Out-of-series copy, sgd. Orig cloth, unopened. Hobson copy. S June 28 (51) £3,200

— Poetry and Drama. L, [1951]. 1st English Ed. In dj. Inscr to Christopher Sykes. sg June 20 (104) $500

— Prufrock and Other Observations. L: The Egoist, 1917. 1st Ed, one of 500. Orig wraps; spine & extremities affected by creasing & rubbing. Ck Apr 12 (134) £1,600

Anr copy. Orig wraps. Hobson copy. S June 28 (41) £5,500

— Selected Essays, 1917-1932. L, [1932]. One of 115. Orig half vellum. Hobson copy. S June 28 (53) £650

— Sweeney Agonistes: Fragments of an Aristophanic Melodrama. L, 1932. 1st Ed. In nicked dj. sg Dec 14 (90) $60

— Thoughts After Lambeth. L, [1931]. 1st Ed. Orig wraps; chipped. Inscr to Aldous Huxley. Goodwin - Engelhard copy. CNY Oct 27 (30) $2,000

— Two Poems. [N.p.: ptd for Frederic Prokosch], 1935. 1st Ed, One of 5 on Normandie. Orig wraps. Hobson copy. S June 28 (57) £1,800

— The Waste Land. L, Oct 1922. 1st Ed. Orig wraps; spine repaired. In: The Criterion, Vol I, No 1. Goodwin copy. Z June 28 (81) £200

1st Ed in Book form, 1st State, with "mountain" spelled correctly. NY, 1922. One of 1,000. In dj split along front outer joint. Laid in is Boni & Liveright royalty check, endorsed on verso by Eliot. Engelhard copy. CNY Oct 27 (29) $12,000

1st State. Z June 28 (82) $900

Mixed state. Hobson copy. S June 28 (48) £1,900

1st English Ed in Book form. L: Hogarth Press, 1923. Orig bds, 1st state of label; rubbed. Sgd. Ck Nov 17 (70) £1,200

Anr copy. Orig bds, label with border of asterisks; extremities rubbed. Hobson copy. S June 28 (49) £900

Anr copy. Orig bds; rubbed, backstrip torn. Foxed. S July 11 (282) £750

Anr Ed. NY, [1971]. ("The Waste Land: a Facsimile and Transcript of the Original Drafts.") One of 250. 4to, cloth. pba Aug 22 (136) $80

**Elizabeth I, Queen of England, 1533-1603**
[-] A True Report of sundry horrible Conspiracies of late time detected to have (by Barbarous murders) taken away the life of the Queenes most excellent Majestie.... L: Charles Yetsweirt, 1594. 4to, modern mor gilt; rebacked. Lacking D1; browned & dampstained. STC 7603.5. S Dec 18 (102) £750 [Schiff]

**Ellacombe, Rev. H. N.**
— Shakespeare as an Angler. L: Elliot Stock, 1883. Vellum gilt; soiled. With frontis woodcut. pba July 11 (79) $55

**Ellenberger, Jean Marie**
— Le Minotaure d'Octobre. Lausanne: Gonin, 1978. One of 38 hors commerce, with an additional suite of the illusts. Illus by Hans Erni. 4to, unsewn as issued in orig wraps. S Nov 21 (127) £320

**Elling, Christian —&**
**Fisker, Kay**
— Monumenta Architecturae Danicae. Copenhagen, 1961. Folio, half vellum. With 181 plates. Text in Danish & English. sg June 13 (8) $275

**Elliot, Daniel Giraud, 1835-1915**
See also: Wolf & Elliot
— The New and heretofore Unfigured Species of the Birds of North America. NY, [1866]-69. 2 vols. Folio, half mor; extremities worn. With 73 hand-colored plates. cb Oct 17 (128) $12,000

— Paradiseidae. NY & Amsterdam, 1977. ("A Monograph of the Paradiseidae, or Birds of Paradise.") One of 250 hand-bound copies. sg Apr 18 (145) $650

— Tetraoniae. NY, [1864]-65. ("A Monograph of the Tetraoninae, or Family of Grouse.") Folio, mor gilt by Stikeman; some wear, edges nicked, spine heel scuffed. With 27 hand-finished colored plates. Minor soiling. P June 5 (220) $7,000

— The Wild Fowl of the United States.... NY, 1898. One of 100. 4to, cloth, in cloth dj; moderate wear. O June 25 (102) $250

Anr copy. Orig cloth; lacking front free endpaper. sg Mar 7 (443) $325

**Elliot, Ebenezer**
— Corn Law Rhymes. Sheffield, 1831. 12mo, contemp half calf. W. E. Gladstone's copy. b Dec 5 (441) £75

**Elliot, George H.**
— Report on a Tour of Inspection of European Light-House Establishments.... Wash, 1874. Modern half calf. pba Aug 8 (498) $80

**Elliot, Capt. Robert**
— Views in the East Comprising India, Canton, and the Shores of the Red Sea. L, 1833. 2 vols in 1. Folio, contemp calf. With 60 plates. S June 13 (631) £360

**Elliott, E. N.**
— Cotton is King, and Pro-Slavery Arguments. Augusta GA, 1860. 8vo, contemp calf; rebacked. With

frontis & 4 ports. Prelims foxed. sg Mar 28 (284) $400

**Elliott, Henry W.**
— Our Arctic Province: Alaska and the Seal Islands. NY, 1887. 1st American Ed. Orig cloth; spine ends chipped. Stamp to front free endpaper & tp. pba July 25 (394) $130

Anr copy. Pictorial cloth; spine ends & edges worn. wa Feb 29 (269) $55

**Elliott, Mary Belson**
— The Book of Birds, beautifully coloured.... L: William Darton, 1826. 12mo, orig ptd wraps; soiled, backstrip worn. With 24 hand-colored plates. Some spotting. S Nov 2 (187) £380 [Schiller]
— Rustic Excursions, to Aid Tarry-at-Home Travellers. L, [c.1825-27]. 2 vols, including Continuation. 12mo, 19th-cent calf. With frontis & 11 hand-colored plates in each vol. S Nov 2 (186) £480 [Elizabeth Gant]

**Elliott, Maud Howe**
— Art and Handicraft in the Women's Building... Columbian Exposition. Paris & NY, 1893. 4to, orig cloth; scuffed, edges worn. F Mar 28 (102) $130

**Elliott, William, 1788-1863**
— Carolina Sports by Land and Water.... NY, 1859. 8vo, orig cloth. pba July 11 (80) $80

**Ellis, H. D.**
— A Short Description of the Ancient Silver Plate Belonging to the Worshipful Company of Armourers and Brasiers.... L, 1892-1910. 2 vols, including supplement. 4to, orig mor with arms of the company gilt. Author's copies with related material inserted. W Nov 8 (94) £440

**Ellis, Havelock, 1859-1939.** See: Golden Cockerel Press

**Ellis, Henry, 1721-1806**
— Reise nach Hudsons Meerbusen.... Goettingen, 1750. 8vo, contemp vellum. With 2 maps & 9 plates. O Nov 14 (63) $225
— Reize naar de Baai van Hudson.... Leiden, 1750. 1st Ed in Dutch. 8vo, contemp half calf; rubbed, joints worn, spine ends chipped. With folding map & 9 folding plates. Some foxing & soiling. O Nov 14 (64) $180
— Voyage a la Baye de Hudson.... Leiden, 1750. 8vo, old calf gilt; leaning, some wear & minor repair, joints cracked. With folding map & 9 folding plates. bbc Feb 26 (393) $230
— A Voyage to Hudson's Bay.... L, 1748. 1st Ed. 8vo, contemp calf; upper cover almost detached, rubbed. With folding map & 9 plates, 5 of them folding. Folding map becoming loose with marginal wrinkling. CE May 22 (15) $480

Anr copy. Early calf; rebacked. sg Oct 26 (106) $750

**Ellis, Sir Henry, Principal Librarian of the British Museum**
— A Catalogue of Books on Angling 1811. Twickenham: Honey Dun Press, 1977. One of 50. Half mor; worn. O Feb 6 (71) $350

**Ellis, Sarah Stickney**
— Family Secrets. L, 1841. 1st Ed. 3 vols. 8vo, calf gilt; worn & soiled. With engraved titles & 28 plates. wa Dec 14 (142) $100

**Ellis, William, 1794-1872**
— A Journal of a Tour Around Hawaii.... Bost., 1825. 12mo, old calf; hinges weak, rear endpaper def. With folding map & 4 plates. Foxed. Met May 22 (306) $1,000

Anr copy. Contemp half sheep; spine & corners rubbed. Some foxing. pba July 25 (395) $225

Anr copy. Modern half mor. With folding map & 5 plates. Dampstained. sg Oct 26 (132) $100
— Narrative of a Tour through Hawaii. Honolulu, 1917. 8vo, cloth; worn & soiled. Reprint of 1827 Ed. wa Feb 1 (99) $50
— Polynesian Researches.... NY, 1833. 4 vols. 12mo, orig cloth. sg Mar 7 (72) $175

**Ellison, Ralph**
— Invisible Man. Franklin Center, 1980. Syn gilt. Sgd. sg Mar 28 (77) $225

**Ellroy, James**
— Because the Night. NY, [1984]. In dj. Inscr. sg June 20 (106) $50

**Ellsworth, Lincoln**
See also: Amundsen & Ellsworth
— The Last Wild Buffalo Hunt. NY: Pvtly ptd, 1916. Samuel Webb's copy. O Oct 10 (122) $800

**Ellsworth, Robert**
— Chinese Furniture: Hardwood Examples of the Ming and Early Ching Dynasties. NY, 1971. Folio, cloth. sg June 13 (154) $600

**Ellwanger, George H.**
— In Gold and Silver. NY, 1892. One of 200. pba July 11 (380) $60

**Elman, Robert**
— The Great American Shooting Prints. NY, 1972. Hors commerce copy, specially bound & with envelope containing 4 additional color plates. Oblong folio, half lea. With 72 colored plates. sg Mar 7 (444) $60

One of 450, specially bound, sgd by Elman & with a suite of 4 additional colored plates. Half lea. O Jan 9 (102) $190

**Elmes, James, 1782-1862**
See also: Shepherd & Elmes
— Memoirs of the Life and Works of Sir Christopher Wren.... L, 1823. 4to, contemp half calf; rubbed. With 12 plates, some folding. Tp reinforced at hinge & browned; some pencil annotations. bba Oct 19 (122) £80 [Axe]

**Elphinstone, Mountstuart, 1779-1859**
— An Account of the Kingdom of Caubul.... L, 1815. 1st Ed. 4to, 19th-cent cloth; worn. With 2 maps & 14 plates, all but 1 hand-colored. Tear without loss to tp.  S June 13 (633) £480

**Elsholtz, Johann Sigismund, 1623-88**
— The Curious Distillatory, or the Art of Distilling Coloured Liquors.... L, 1677. 8vo, modern mor gilt by Marcus Crahan. Lacking frontis; browned & dampstained. Sold w.a.f.  Crahan copy.  sg May 16 (155) $450
— Diaeteticon. Berlin, 1682. 4to, contemp half calf; spine head chipped, corners bumped. With title & 9 plates. Plates & title dampstained; Rr4 repaired; Tt3 with hole in margin; Xx4 with printing flaw.  Ck Mar 22 (105) £2,600

**Elton, Richard**
— The Compleat Body of the Art Military. L, 1650. 1st Ed. Folio, contemp calf; worn. With port. Some fraying, browning & marginal worming.  CE May 22 (212) $950

**Eluard, Paul, 1895-1952**
— Repetitions. Paris: Au Sans Pareil, 1922. One of 350. Illus by Max Ernst. Orig wraps; spine worn, ends chipped.  sg Apr 18 (100) $1,600

**Eluard, Paul, 1895-1952 —& Ernst, Max, 1891-1976**
— Misfortunes of the Immortals. [NY]: Black Sun Press, 1943. Ltd Ed. Trans by Hugh Chisholm. 4to, bds.  bba May 9 (212) £280 [Brocchi]

**Elwes, Henry John, 1846-1922 —& Henry, Augustine**
— The Trees of Great Britain and Ireland. Edin., 1906-13. 7 vols. 4to, orig wraps.  S June 13 (439) £500

**Elwood, Louis Butler.** See: Grabhorn Printing

**Elworthy, Frederick Thomas**
— The Evil Eye. L, 1895. Orig cloth.  pba Aug 8 (397) $85

**Elyot, Sir Thomas, 1490?-1541**
— The Castell of Health Corrected.... L: Thomas Berthelet, 1541. 4to, recent mor. With title & coat-of-arms. Title soiled & frayed; early leaves stained in lower margin; f1 with paper fault & tear.  Ck Mar 22 (106) £1,500

**Emanuel, Walter**
— A Dog Day. NY, [1919]. Illus by Cecil Aldin. Pictorial bds; lower corners rubbed.  pba Aug 22 (668) $30

**Embree, Edwin R.**
— Brown Americans. The Story of a Tenth of the Nation. NY, 1943. Orig cloth; shelf number at base of spine. Inscr to & sgd by W. E. B. Du Bois.  sg Mar 28 (79) $175

**Emerson, Ralph Waldo, 1803-82**
See also: Doves Press; Limited Editions Club
— Essays. With: Essays. Second Series. Bost., 1841 & 1844. 1st Eds. 2 vols. 8vo, orig cloth, BAL bdg C & bdg A; minor loss to front pastedown of 2d Series. Some foxing to Essays; some staining to 2d Series.  P June 5 (221) $1,300
— Letters and Social Aims.... Bost., 1876. 1st Ed. 12mo, orig cloth. Inscr to William Ellery Channing, 19 Dec 1875. Wakeman - Henry - Engelhard copy.  CNY Oct 27 (31) $4,000
— Nature. Bost., 1836. 12mo, orig cloth. Some foxing. Inscr to Rebecca Baldwin by Lidian Emerson, July 1841.  CE May 22 (213) $2,600
— Nature: An Essay. To which is added, Orations, Lectures, and Addresses. L, 1845. Orig cloth.  pba Dec 14 (62) $130
— An Oration delivered before the Phi Beta Kappa Society, at Cambridge, August 31, 1837. Bost., 1837. 1st Ed. 8vo, later wraps. Lacking final blank.  sg Sept 21 (180) $200
— Representative Men: Seven Lectures. L, 1850. 8vo, orig cloth. Inscr on Emerson's behalf by the pbr to Arthur Hugh Clough.  pn June 13 (288) £260
— Success, Greatness, Immortality. Bost., 1877. 1st Ed. 32mo, cloth; spine ends rubbed with loss.  sg Sept 21 (181) $80
— Works. Bost., [1883-93]. Riverside Ed. 12 vols. 12mo, contemp half calf gilt.  sg Sept 21 (15) $800
Concord Ed. Cambr. MA, 1903-4. 12 vols. Cloth; spine ends rubbed.  pba Aug 8 (398) $75
Autograph Centenary Ed. Cambr., Mass., 1903-4. one of 600. 12 vols. Half mor. With 1 leaf of autograph Ms tipped into Vol I.  cb Oct 17 (269) $3,000
Anr Ed. Phila.: John D. Morris, [1906]. One of 1,000. 6 vols. Half mor; tears to 2 spine heads.  pba Aug 22 (552) $80
Edition DeLuxe. Phila.: Nottingham Society, [n.d.]. 6 vols. 8vo, half mor; spine ends rubbed, Vol I with clippings mtd to front flyleaves.  pba Dec 14 (63) $150

**Emerson, William, 1701-82**
— The Doctrine of Fluxions.... L, 1768. 3d Ed. 8vo, contemp calf; front joint cracked, ends chipped, stamps on front endpaper. With 12 folding plates.  sg May 16 (156) $50

**Emmons, Ebenezer, 1799-1863**
— Agriculture of New-York. Albany, 1846-54. 4 (of 5) vols; lacking Vol IV. Orig cloth; spine ends cropped. Foxed.  wa Feb 29 (212) $150
Anr Ed. Albany, 1851. Vol III (of 5) only. 4to, orig cloth; worn. With 99 hand-colored plates. Some foxing; stained.  F June 20 (850) $250
Anr copy. Vol III. 4to, contemp half mor; extremities scuffed. Lacking 3 hand-colored plates; stained.  F June 20 (852) $240
Vol V: Insects. Albany, 1854. 4to, cloth; some wear. With 50 hand-colored plates. Some foxing.  F June 20 (851) $100
Anr copy. Half mor; extremities scuffed. Lacking 1 plate; some foxing.  F June 20 (853) $160

### Emmons, Richard, b.1788
— The Fredoniad.... Bost., 1827. 4 vols. 12mo, contemp calf gilt; worn & soiled, lacking 4 flyleaves, 1 signature in Vol I sprung. wa Nov 16 (128) $110

### Emory, William H.
See also: Fremont & Emory
— Lieutenant Emory Reports: A Reprint of Lieutenant Emory's Notes of a Military Reconnoissance. Albuquerque, 1951. Intro by Ross Calvin. Half bds. With facsimile tp & 6 maps. Larson copy. pba Sept 28 (443) $55
— Notes of a Military Reconnoissance, from Fort Leavenworth...to San Diego.... Wash., 1848. 8vo, orig cloth; spine & joints repaired. With 3 battle plans, 2 folding maps & 64 plates. Map from Senate issue in pocket attached to outside of rear cover Large map with minor tears; 1 text leaf loose; library markings. pba Apr 25 (391) $800
Anr copy. Orig cloth; becoming disbound. With 64 plates & 6 maps, 3 of them folding. Large map with tears along folds. 30th Congress, 1st Session H of R Ex. Doc No 41. wa Feb 29 (367) $425
House Issue. Bdg not described but worn, loose & lacking front free endpaper. With 64 plates, 3 battle plans & 2 folding maps. Lacking some leaves. 30th Congress, 1st Session, H of R Exec. Doc 41. CE May 22 (16) $320
1st Ed. With: Envelope to Kenneth Johnson, with photo of Emory & sgd 8vo, orig cloth; backstrip worn, paper spine chipped. With 2 folded maps, 3 plates of plans, & 63 litho plates. 1 folded map detached and laid in. Larson copy. pba Sept 28 (441) $650
Senate Issue. Orig cloth; rear joint & hinge broken & repaired, spine worn & partly illegible. With 40 litho plates, 3 battle plans, & 1 folded map. Dampstaining to map & plates; map torn at folds & repaired. Larson copy. pba Sept 28 (442) $275
— Report on the United States and Mexican Boundary Survey.... Wash., 1857-59. House Issue. Vol I only. Later cloth preserving orig covers. Some foxing & soiling. O Mar 5 (77) $140
Senate Issue. 2 vols. 4to, recent calf. bbc Feb 26 (394) $2,100
Anr copy. Modern cloth. With 2 maps, folding chart, folding profile & 346 plates (37 in color). Some foxing; frontis & a few other leaves tape-repaired; library markings. cb Feb 14 (2588) $1,700
Anr copy. Vol I only. Orig cloth; spine rubbed, front joint repaired. With 1 plain & 1 hand-colored folding map, 9 plates of views, 12 color lithos of Indians & views, 33 plates with 66 engraved outline sketches & 2 folding diagrams or sections. Stub tears to maps. Sold w.a.f. pba Aug 8 (52) $850
Anr Ed. Austin, [1987]. 3 vols. Facsimile of the 1857-59 Ed. pba July 25 (142) $225

### Emparan, Madie Brown
— The Vallejos of California. San Francisco, 1968. 1st Ed. Cloth. With 12 ports. Sgd. Larson copy. pba Sept 28 (268) $300

### Emporium...
— The Emporium of Arts & Sciences. Phila., 1812-14. Vols I-II & New Series, Vols I-III. 8vo, contemp half lea gilt; worn. Foxed, affecting plates; library markings. sg May 16 (158) $120

### Enault, Louis, 1824-1900
— L'Inde pittoresque. Paris, 1861. Half mor; front joint cracked. Foxed. pba July 25 (408) $130
— La Mediterranee, ses iles et ses bords. Paris, 1863. 8vo, orig cloth; spine rubbed. With 21 (of 24) plates, 3 hand-colored costume plates. b May 30 (261) £60

### Enciclopedia...
— Enciclopedia dell'arte antica. Rome, [1958-73]. 9 vols, including Supplement & Atlas. 4to, orig half mor. sg Sept 7 (141) $650
— Enciclopedia italiana di scienze, lettere ed arti. Milan & Rome, 1929-61. 36 vols. Orig cloth or half lea, Index in cloth. bba Oct 5 (62) £400 [Crimt]

### Encyclopaedia Britannica
— Encyclopaedia Britannica. L, 1910-11. 11th Ed. 29 vols, including Index Mor gilt. bbc June 24 (92) $800
Anr copy. 29 vols, including Index. Half mor. NH July 21 (120) $310
Anr copy. 28 vols. Mor. pba Nov 30 (121) $350
Anr Ed. L, 1911-22. 31 vols, including Supplement, but without Index. Mor gilt; spine ends scuffed. wa Nov 16 (6) $180

### Encyclopedia...
— Encyclopedia of World Art. NY, 1959-68. 15 vols. 4to, orig cloth. Met Feb 24 (23) $225
Anr copy. Orig cloth; worn & soiled. wa June 20 (313) $425

### Encyclopedie...
— Encyclopedie methodique. Paris, 1786-1824. 22 vols only: Arts et metiers macaniques, 8 vols; Marine, 3 vols; Art militaire, 3 (of 4) vols; Recueil de planches, 8 vols. 4to, contemp half calf. Plates stamped with a number in margin; a few tears & stains. Sold w.a.f. S Mar 14 (106) £2,000

### Enfant...
— L'Enfant naturaliste, ou petites lecons sur les trois regnes de l'histoire naturelle. Lille: Blocquel, [c.1810]. 16mo, orig ptd pictorial bds; rebacked, soiled. With frontis, pictorial title & 9 hand-colored plates. Browned. S Nov 2 (188) £300 [Schiller]

### Enfield, William, 1741-97
— The History of Philosophy.... L, 1791. 2 vols. Folio, orig bds; rebacked in modern calf, extremities rubbed. pba Nov 30 (122) $200

### Engbeck, Joseph H., Jr.
— State Parks of California from 1864 to the Present. Portland: Charles H. Belding, [1980]. One of 1,000. In dj. pba Feb 12 (61) $65

### Engelhardt, Zephyrin, 1851-1934
— The Franciscans in California. Harbor Springs MI, 1897. 8vo, orig cloth; spine repaired, joints & corners worn. pba Apr 25 (393) $100
1st Ed. Harbor Springs, MI, 1897. 8vo, later cloth. Larson copy. pba Sept 28 (97) $55
— The Missions and Missionaries of California. San Francisco, 1908-16. 1st Ed. 5 vols. 8vo, orig cloth. Larson copy. pba Sept 28 (98) $300
2d Ed of Vol I, 1st Ed of others. San Francisco, 1912-29. 5 vols. 8vo, orig cloth. pba Nov 30 (106) $225

### Engestroem, Gustaf von
— Guide du voyageur aux carrieres et mines de Svede.... Stockholm, 1796. 8vo, contemp wraps; worn, needs rebacking. Stain in lower margin of last few index leaves. sg May 16 (159) $140

### Engineering Research Associates
— High Speed Computing Devices. NY, 1950. Orig cloth, in soiled & creased dj. F Mar 28 (487) $60

### England
— A Complete Collection of State Trials, and Proceedings for High Treason L, 1730-66. 10 vols. Folio, contemp sheep; worn. F June 20 (730) $130
— England Illustrated.... L, 1764. 2 vols. 4to, contemp calf; worn. With 54 maps & 27 (of 29) plates. Tears to folding maps. Sold w.a.f. b May 30 (103) £1,000
Norwich. - Notices and Illlustrations of the Costume, Processions, Pageantry, &c., Formerly Displayed by the Corporation of Norwich. Norwich: Charles Muskett, 1850. Folio, contep half mor; rubbed, new endpapers. With hand-colroed frontis, 2 tinted plates & 19 hand-colored litho plates. Repair to 1 plate affecting plate-mark. bba Nov 30 (105) £700 [Norwich Library]
World War I. - Official History of the War: Naval Operations. L, 1920-31. Ed by J. S. Corbett & H. Newbolt. 9 vols. 8vo, cloth; rubbed & frayed. With 112 maps. wa Nov 16 (206) $600

#### Laws & Statutes
— An Act for allowing further Time for the Exportation of, or Payment of the Duties upon, Bugles.... L, 1776. Folio, disbound. pba June 13 (296) $100
— An Act for Repealing Certain Duties [amending the customs provision of the Revenue Act of 1764]. L, 1766. Folio, calf; worn & rubbed. 6 George III, cap. 52. K June 23 (18) $500
— An Act to Prevent the Importation of Slaves... into... America. L, 1803. Folio, disbound. First leaf chipped. 46 George III, cap. 52. sg Oct 26 (338) $200

#### Parliament
— A Collection of Debates in the House of Commons, in the Year 1680. L, 1725. 8vo, contemp calf; rebacked in lea. wa Feb 29 (158) $130

#### Proclamations
— A Booke of Proclamations. L: Robert Barker, 1609. Folio, 17th-cent calf; rebacked, later endpapers. Tp & last leaf cut down & mtd; A2 lacking. STC 7760. bba Oct 19 (212) £460 [Cizdyn]

### Englefield Collection, Sir Henry Charles
— Vases from the Collection.... L, 1819. By Henry Moses. 4to, half mor; lacking backstrip, tape-repaired. With engraved title, frontis port & 39 plates. Some spotting; tape repairs to inside edges of tp & frontis. bba June 6 (29) £320 [Kafka]

### English... See: Sowerby & Smith

### English, Harriet
— Conversations and Amusing Tales. L, 1799. 4to, contemp russia gilt; extremities worn, old catalogue entry mtd to verso of front free endpaper. pba Nov 30 (87) $350

### English Opium-Eater. See: De Quincey, Thomas

### English Poets
— The Works of the English Poets. L, 1790. Prefaces by Samuel Johnson. 75 vols. 8vo, contemp calf gilt. S Dec 18 (130) £3,200 [Osborn]
Anr copy. Contemp calf gilt; some spines split or cracked. S Mar 28 (611) £2,300

### Enlart, Camille, 1862-1927
— Les Monuments des croises. Paris, 1925-28. 2 vols. 4to, half vellum. With 4 ports of Richard the Lion Heart & a pamphlet loosely inserted. S June 27 (145) £800

### Enschede, Charles, 1855-1919
— Typefoundries in the Netherlands.... Haarlem, 1978. Folio, orig half calf. bba May 9 (30) £130 [Collinge & Clark]

### Ensor, James, 1860-1949
— Les Ecrits. Brussels, 1921. One of 500. 4to, pictorial wraps; browned & soiled. With 36 plates. sg Sept 7 (143) $110
— Scenes de la vie du Christ. Brussels, 1921. One of 285. Oblong 4to, unsewn as issued in cloth folder; worn. With 21 (of 32) colored lithos. Sold w.a.f. sg Sept 7 (144) $325

### Entick, John, 1703?-73
— The General History of the late War. L, 1765-63-66. 5 vols. 8vo, old calf; spine worn & chipped, joints weak, Vol I rebacked with unmatching lea. With 39 (of 41) ports & 8 folding maps. Some ink annotations in margins. wa Feb 29 (368) $160
— A New Naval History.... L, 1757. Folio contemp sheep; worn, front cover loose. Worming in lower margin to several leaves at beginning. sg Mar 7 (211) $225

### Entrecasteaux, Antoine R. J. de B., 1737-93
— Voyage de Dentrecasteaux, envoye a la recherche de La Perouse. Paris, 1807-8. Atlas only. Folio, 19th-cent half calf; worn. With engraved title, engraved contents list & 37 (of 39) plates. Contents leaf cropped at lower margin; margin of 1st chart with

small cut; library stamps on tp. S June 27 (260) £1,700

**Entzelt, Christoph**
— De re metallica hoc est de origine.... Frankfurt: Heirs of Christian Egenolf, 1557. 8vo, modern vellum. With title device, 3 double-page tables, & 5 illus. Lacking R8; wormholes, some repaired & affected text restored; final leaf with loss. S Oct 27 (804) £440 [Zioni]

**Ephemera.** See: Fitzgibbon, Edward

**Epictetus.** See: Limited Editions Club

**Epicurus, 342?-270 B.C.** See: Limited Editions Club

**Episcopius, Johannes, 1646-86**
— Signorum veterum icones. [N.p., c.1670]. With 100 plates. Bound with: Episcopius. Paradigmata graphices variorum artificum.... The Hague, 1671. With 57 plates. Folio, contemp mor gilt; rebacked. C Nov 29 (84) £1,400

**Epistolae...**
— Epistolae diversorum philosophorum, oratorum, rhetorum. Venice: Aldus, [29] Mar & [not before 17 Apr] 1499. 2 parts in 1 vol. 4to, 19th-cent mor by Petit. 26 lines; types 2:114Gk & 2:114R. One quire short; some spotting. 404 leaves. Goff E-64. C Apr 3 (87) £5,800
— Epistolae et Evangelia ad usum congregationis Sancti Mauri ordinis Sancti Benedicti.... Paris, 1708. Folio, mor extra bound for Baron Arundell of Wardour by Padeloup, le jeune. C May 1 (50) £4,800

**Epistolai...** See: Epistolae...

**Epitomes...**
— Epitomes des roys de France en Latin & en Francoys. Lyon: Balthasar Arnoullet, 1546. Issue with tp engraved. 8vo, mor janseniste by Thibaron-Echaubard. Roman & italic types. With engraved title & 58 medallion ports by the Master CC. Some soiling & marginal tears, sometimes affecting pagination, affecting text on V3-4. Rahir - Bullrich - Schaefer copy. P Nov 1 (81) $3,500

**Epstein, Jacob, 1880-1959**
— Let There be Sculpture. L, 1940. One of 100. Orig vellum. b May 30 (467) £100

**Eragny Press—London**
BACON, SIR FRANCIS. - Of Gardens: an Essay. 1902. One of 226. b Dec 5 (14) £240
BROWNING, ROBERT. - Some Poems by Robert Browning. 1904. One of 10 on vellum. sg Oct 19 (85) $1,500
FLAUBERT, GUSTAVE. - Un Coeur Simple. 1901. One of 226. Marked "File copy, not to be taken away". b Dec 5 (17) £100
FLAUBERT, GUSTAVE. - Herodias. 1901. One of 226. b Dec 5 (15) £110
FLAUBERT, GUSTAVE. - La Legende de Saint Julien l'Hospitalier. 1900. One of 226. Marked "File Copy, not to be taken away". b Dec 5 (16) £100
MOORE, T. STURGE. - A Brief Account of the Origin of the Eragny Press. 1903. One of 235. b Dec 5 (23) £340
PERRAULT, CHARLES. - Deux Contes de ma Mere L'Oye. 1899. One of 220. b Dec 5 (20) £340
PERRAULT, CHARLES. - Histoire de peau d'ane. 1902. One of 230. b Dec 5 (19) £200
ROSSETTI, CHRISTINA GEORGINA. - Verses by Christina G. Rossetti. 1906. One of 175. Mor extra by De Sauty with 6 mother-of-pearl bosses, paper from orig bds bound in. sg Oct 19 (86) $1,300
VILLON, FRANCOIS. - Autres Poesies. 1901. One of 222. b Dec 5 (21) £180
VILLON, FRANCOIS. - Les Ballades. 1900. One of 222. b Dec 5 (22) £260

**Erasmus, Desiderius, 1466?-1536**
See also: Limited Editions Club
— Apothegmatum.... Lyon: Jean Marcorel for Barthelemy Vincent, 1573. ("Apophthegmatum ex optimis utriusque linguae scriptoribus....") 8vo, contemp German vellum tooled in silver, with yapp edges, with large panel with sea-monsters in the 4 corners, panel attributed by Schunke to a Strassburg bindery. C May 1 (49) £1,300
— Brevissima maximeque compendiaria conficiendarum epistolarum formula. Paris: Christian Wechel, 1541. Bound with: Aphthonius, Sophista. Declamationis prae-exercitamenta.... Paris, 1539. And: Vives, Juan Luis. De conscribendis epistolis.... Paris, 1542. 8vo, needs rebdg. sg Mar 21 (127) $600
— The Colloquies, or Familiar Discourses.... L, 1671. 1st Ed in English. 8vo, contemp calf; new endpapers. pba Nov 30 (123) $200
— De Contemptu Mundi. L: Thomas Berthelet, 1533. 8vo, 19th-cent mor gilt by Bedford. Black letter. Lacking M1 table at end. STC 10471. C Nov 29 (50) £1,100
— De recta Latini Graecique sermonis pronuntiatione.... Basel: Froben, Mar 1528. 8vo, contemp blind-tooled pigskin; 3 endpapers detached, some scuffing. Marginal notes; rust-hole in e3; ptr's device on tp colored by an early hand. C Apr 3 (88) £2,400
— L'Eloge de la Folie. [Paris], 1751. Illus by Charles Eisen. 4to, contemp calf gilt. With frontis & 13 plates. Fuerstenberg - Schaefer copy. S Dec 7 (194) £680
— Epitome adagiorum. Cologne: Martinus Gymnicus, 1545. 8vo, contemp blind-tooled pigskin over pastebd. Upper outer corner of last few leaves damp-stained & corroded with slight text loss; lacking last leaf. sg Mar 21 (128) $250
— The First [Seconde] Tome or Volume of the Paraphrase of Erasmus upon the Newe Testamente. L: Edwarde Whitechurche, 1548-49. 2 vols. Folio, modern cloth. Black letter. Lacking final blank in Vol I; Fol. 58 in Vol I replaced by 2 leaves from anr copy; some headlines shaved; tp in Vol I trimmed & shorter; worming in Vol II to tp; some staining; a few repairs; 1 leaf lacking lower corner. STC 2854. pba Sept 14 (156) $1,900
— In evangelium Lucae paraphrasis per autorem recognita. Basel, 1523. 8vo, contemp calf over wooden bds with blind-stamped panels [Oldham Misc 12 & 13];

clasps lacking, spine def. Some worming & waterstaining. Sold as a bdg. b Sept 20 (35) £850
— Moriae encomium.... Basel, 1780. ("Morias enkomion. Stultitiae laus.") 8vo, contemp sheep gilt. Tp stamped. sg Feb 8 (288) $30
— Moriae Encomium... Lob der Torheit. Basel, 1931. Illus by Hans Holbein; intro by H. A. Schmid. 2 vols. 8vo, bds in slipcase. Text in German. sg Apr 11 (101) $175
— Moriae Encomium; or, The Praise of Folly.... Basel, 1931. Illus by Hans Holbein; intro by H. A. Schmid. 2 vols. 8vo, bds in slipcase. Text in English. sg Apr 11 (100) $175
— Paraphraseon in Novum Testamentum.... Basel: Froben, 1535. Bound with: Tomus secundus continens paraphrasin in omneis epistolas apostolicas. Basel: Froben, 1532. Folio, contemp blind-stamped calf over wooden bds; rebacked & repaired, rubbed. Lacking final leaf to 2d part; some marginal tears; wormhole through several leaves at beginning. bba Apr 11 (297) £380 [Pinfield]
— A Playne and Godly Exposytion or Declaration of the Commune Crede.... [N.p., c.1726]. 8vo, early 19th-cent sheep; worn, covers detached. Some foxing; pencil marginalia. Reprint of 1533 Ed. sg Mar 21 (130) $90
— Precatio dominica in septem portiones distributa. [Basel: Froben, 1523?]. Bound with: De libero arbitrio diatribe, sive collatio. Basel: Froben, Sept 1524. And: De immensa dei misericordia.... Antwerp: Michael Hoochstraten, 1524. And: Exomologesis, sive modus confitendi. Basel: Froben 1524. 8vo, disbound. Some staining; marginalia in ink. Sold w.a.f. sg Mar 21 (126) $2,800
— Twenty-Two Select Colloquies. L, 1711. 8vo, contemp calf; rebacked, endpapers renewed. With port. Dampstaining on opening leaves. sg Mar 21 (129) $225
— Witt against Wisdom.... Oxford, 1683. 8vo, calf; new endpapers. Lacking prelims to tp, which has contemp notes. pba Nov 30 (124) $170

**Ercolani, Giuseppe Maria.** See: Neralco, Pastore Arcade

**Erikson, Erik H.** See: Newton & Erikson

**Erlaeuterte Merkwuerdigkeiten der Natur**
— Erlaeuterte Merkwuerdigkeiten der Natur. Dresden, 1737. Ed by M. C. Hanow. 52 issues in 1 vol. 4to, bdg not described. S Mar 14 (108) £220

**Erman, Wilhelm —&**
**Horn, Ewald**
— Bibliographie der deutschen Universitaeten. Hildesheim, 1965. 3 vols. 8vo, orig cloth. sg Apr 11 (102) $175

**Ernst, Max, 1891-1976**
See also: Eluard & Ernst
— La Femme 100 tetes. Paris, 1929. One of 1,000. 4to, half mor. S Nov 2 (11) £500 [Seragnoli]
[-] Hommage a Max Ernst. Paris, 1971. 4to, orig cloth,

in dj. Special No of Vingtieme Siecle. sg June 13 (305) $70
— Reve d'une petite fille qui volut entrer au Carmel. Paris, 1930. One of 950. 4to, orig wraps. sg Apr 18 (102) $2,000

**Erotisme...**
— L'Erotisme au Cinema par Lo Duca. Paris, 1957-68. Ed by Jean Jacques Pauvert. 4 vols, including Supplement. Cloth or wraps, in rubbed & chipped djs. sg Feb 29 (93) $175

**Ersch, Johann Samuel**
— Allgemeines Repertorium der Literatur fuer die Jahre 1785 bis... 1795. Jena or Weimar, 1793-1800. 4to, contemp bds; worn. Some foxing. O Mar 26 (89) $190

**Erskine, Esme Steuart**
— Isabel, a Tale, in Two Cantos.... Romford, 1814. 8vo, contemp mor gilt; rubbed. b Dec 5 (114) £70

**Erskine, John Elphinstone, 1806-87**
— Journal of a Cruise...The Western Pacific. L, 1853. 8vo, orig cloth; rebacked retaining orig spine, recased, new endpapers. Folding map repaired & laid down; lacking ads & errata slip. S June 13 (656) £220

**Eruditorium...**
— Eruditorium poenitentiale. [Paris: Antoine Caillaut, c.1488]. 4to, modern mor gilt by Bedford. 24-26 lines; type 8:111B. With 17 woodcuts. Tp strengthened & repaired. 76 leaves. Goff E-107. Fairfax-Murray copy. C June 26 (162) £18,000

**Escarmouche...**
— L'Escarmouche. Paris, 1893-94. Vol I, Nos 1-8 & Vol II, Nos 1-2. Folio, half cloth. With 33 illusts. S Nov 21 (130) £500

**Escobar, Juan de**
— Hystoria del muy noble, y valeroso cavallero, El Cid Ruy Diez du Biuar.... Lisbon: Antonio Alvarez, 1605. 8vo, contemp vellum; spine worn. Lacking *8, A1 & last 8 or so leaves; tp torn & repaired; corner torn from A3 with loss; some soiling, tears, repairs & marginal worming. "Apparently the only extant copy". C Apr 3 (89) £4,600

**Eslaba, Sebastian de**
— Diario de todo lo ocurrido en la expugnacion de los Fueres de Bocachica.... [Madrid], 1741. 4to, recent vellum. Tp repaired without loss. S Nov 30 (148) £950

**Esmerian Library, Raphael**
— [Sale Catalogue] Bibliotheque Raphael Esmerian. Paris, 1972-74. 5 vols in 7. 4to, orig cloth or orig wraps. bba Oct 5 (64) £280 [Heuer]
Anr copy. 6 vols, including the extra vol for part 2. 4to, cloth. P June 5 (223) $400
Anr Ed. Paris, 1972-73. Part 3 only. pba Aug 8 (319) $50

## ESMERIAN

— [Sale catalogue] Bibliotheque Raphael Esmerian. Paris, 1972-74. 5 vols in 6. 4to, orig cloth. S Oct 27 (1023) £340 [Sawyer]

**Esnault-Pelterie, Robert A. C.**
— L'Astronautique. Paris, 1930. Bound with: L'Astronomique. Complement. Paris, 1935. Later half mor, orig wraps bound in. sg May 16 (36) $2,300
— L'Exploration par fusees de la tres haute atmosphere.... Paris, 1928. Later half mor, orig wraps bound in. Ls to the Tresorier General des Ailes Brisees laid in. sg May 16 (35) $550

**Esparbes, Georges d'**
— La Legende de l'Aigle. Paris, 1893. One of 15 on Holland. 12mo, mor extra by Mercier, orig wraps bound in. Each story with orig watercolor on its sectional tp. S Nov 21 (100) £520

**Espinosa, J. Manuel**
— First Expedition of Vargas into New Mexico, 1692. Albuquerque, 1940. Orig cloth, in dj; d/j faded, spine head worn, rear panel torn. With frontis port. Robbins copy. pba Mar 21 (97) $90

**Espinosa y Tello, Jose, 1763-1815**
— Relacion del viage hecho por las goletas sutil y mexicana...para reconocer el Estrecho de Fuca. Madrid, 1802. 2 vols. 4to & folio, contemp sheep, atlas in later calf rebacked with orig spine strip laid on. With 9 folding maps in text vol; Atlas vol with 9 maps & 8 plates, some folding. Tp foxed; maps in text vol with edge tears; light staining to maps in Atlas. pba Feb 13 (70) $11,000
   1st Ed. 2 vols. 4to & small folio, 19th-century half mor & half sheep; Minor rubbing, extremities worn. With 9 maps (4 folding) & 8 plates (2 color folding). Pp. 103-104 in text vol creased; some maps with stub tears, marginal stains & darkening to 5 plates. Robbins & W. J. Holliday copy. pba Mar 21 (98) $11,000
— A Spanish Voyage to Vancouver and the North-West Coast of America. L: Argonaut Press, 1930. One of 525. 4to, half vellum. pba Feb 13 (71) $190
   Anr copy. Half vellum, unopened; soiled & bumped. pba Apr 25 (181) $130
   Anr Ed. L, 1930. One of—525. Trans by Cecil Jane. Half vellum. With 6 plates (1 folding) & folding map. Robbins copy. pba Mar 21 (99) $150

**Esquemeling, Alexandre Olivier.** See: Exquemelin, Alexandre Olivier

**Esquivel, Laura**
— Like Water for Chocolate. NY, 1992. 1st American Ed. In dj. pba Dec 7 (48) $70

**Essay...**
— An Essay on Civil Government. In Two Parts. L, 1743. 8vo, old calf; broken, worn. Some browning & foxing; some leaves dampstained at gutter. bbc June 24 (300) $220

**Essling, Victor Massena, Prince d', 1836-1910**
— Les Livres a figures venetiens de la fin du XVe siecle.... Paris & Florence, 1907-14. One of 300. 3 parts in 4 vols. 4to, contemp half mor; worn. bba Oct 5 (65) £950 [Franks]
— Les livres a figures venetiens de la fin du XVe siecle.... Venice, 1907-09. 1st Ed, One of 300. 4 (of 6) vols. Folio, vol 1/2 in buckram, rest half lea; lea vols rebacked in buckram & worn, some hinges split. Sold w.a.f. sg Apr 11 (103) $550
— Les Livres a figures venetiens de la fin du XVe siecle.... Torino, 1967. 3 parts in 6 vols. 4to, orig half lea. Ck Apr 12 (226) £380
   Anr Ed. Mansfield CT: Martino, [n.d.]. One of 350. 3 parts in 6 vols. 4to, cloth. bba July 18 (9) £220 [Seydi]
   Anr copy. Cloth; worn. O May 7 (128) $160

**Estampas...**
— Estampas de la Revolucion. Mexico, 1947. One of 500. Folio, loose as issued in wraps. With 85 wood-engraved plates. sg Sept 7 (244) $275

**Estampe...**
— L'Estampe et l'affiche. Paris, 1897-99. Vols I-III. 4to, contemp half mor. S Nov 21 (131) £6,500

**Estcourt, T. H. S. Bucknall**
— Alhambra. L, 1832. Oblong folio, 19th-cent half mor; repaired. With 14 litho plates plus an extra plate of entrance to the Generalife at end. S June 27 (103) £2,600

**Estienne, Henri, 1528?-98**
— Conciones sive orationes ex Graecis latinisque historicis excerptae. [Geneva], 1570. 2 parts in 1 vol. Folio, 18th-cent vellum; rebacked, hinge cracked. Joseph "Consul" Smith's copy. bba May 9 (50) £220 [O'Keefe]
   Anr copy. Contemp vellum with yapp edges; shelf mark on spine. Abrams copy. P June 5 (224) $800
— Dictionarium medicum, vel, expositiones medicinalium.... [Geneva]: H. Estienne, 1564. 1st Ed. 8vo, 18th-cent mor; joints & corners worn, lea treated. A8 torn, repaired, & discolored; marginal foxing & soiling. CE Nov 8 (88) $600
— Francofordiense Emporium, sive Francofordienses Nundinae. [Geneva], 1574. 1st Ed. 8vo, modern vellum with yapp edges. Roman, italic & a few greek types. Tp soiled; some spotting & staining; British Museum stamps on tp verso & k4 verso. Schaefer copy. P Nov 1 (82) $3,250
— Medicae artis principes, post Hippocratem & Galenum.... [Geneva]: H. Estienne, 1567. 5 parts in 2 vols. Folio, old vellum. General title with small hole in margin; a few outer margins damaged towards end of Vol I; Vol II with final leaf def; some index leaves wormed. S Nov 30 (322) £950

**Estienne, Robert, 1503-59**
— Hebraea, Chaldaea, Graeca, et Latina nomina virorum, mulierum.... Paris: Robert Estienne, 1549. Bound with: Clenardus, Nicolas. Luach Ha-dikduk. Paris:

Carolus Stephanus, 1556. 4to, later vellum. Some browning & staining. CE Dec 6 (74) $1,600

Anr Ed. Antwerp: C. Plantin, 1560. 16mo, 19th-cent calf; spine & extremities rubbed. Some dampstaining. sg Apr 18 (51) $900

**Etat...** See: Almanacs

**Etchison, Dennis.** See: Lord John Press

**Etchison, Dennis —& Others**
— The Complete Masters of Darkness. Novato: Underwood-Miller, 1990. One of 345 sgd by Etchison & 39 of the 45 contributors. Half lea, in dj. O Dec 5 (173) $80
— Lord John Ten: A Celebration. Northridge: Lord John Press. Presentation copy of half mor issue sgd by all contributors. pba May 23 (116) $130

**Etherege, Sir George, 1635?-91?**
— She Wou'd if She Cou'd. L, 1693. 3d Ed. 4to, mor gilt by Kaufmann. Margins trimmed, affecting last line of G2 & some catchwords. CE June 12 (192) $320

**Eton, William**
— A Survey of the Turkish Empire. L, 1799. 8vo, orig bds; needs rebdg. sg Mar 7 (74) $150

**Ettenhard y Abaca, Francisco Antonio de**
— Compendio de los fundamentos de la verdadera destreza, y filosofia de las armas.... Madrid: Antonio de Zafra, 1675. 4to, mor extra with onlays, by Noulhac. With engraved title & 18 full-page illusts. Tp shaved at lower & outer margins; repaired tear to V3; some shaving. C Apr 3 (90) £1,300
— Diestro italiano y espanol, explican sus doctrinas... y filosofia de las armas. Madrid: Manuel Ruiz de Murga, 1697. 4to, mor extra by Noulhac. With 4 plates, 3 of them folding. Repaired tears. C Apr 3 (91) £1,100

**Eucharistic Controversy**
[A Collection of 7 works, including the 1st Latin Ed of Martin Luther's Libellus... de sacramento eucharistae, Wittemberg, 1526, sold at Sotheby's on 11 July 1996, lot 3, for £2,400]

**Euclid**

**Elementa**
— 1559. - Strassburg: Josias Rihel. 8vo, modern bds. Early scrawls on title; marginalia. sg May 16 (161) $125
— 1570. - L: John Daye. 1st Ed in English. - Trans by H. Billingsley. Folio, 19th-cent half calf; rebacked, corners restored, inner hinges reinforced, extremities rubbed. With 2 copies of Yy3.4 bound in; lacking Ll2.5 & with duplicate of Ii2.5 bound in its place; lacking at least 1 overslip; 5 overslips or parts of them detached; lacking final blank; soiling at beginning & end; marginal worming throughout, with repair grazing title border; wormhole through text in quires O-P; repaired tear to folding chart; last leaf creased; perforated library stamps; inkstain to Gg4; some dampstaining. CNY May 17 (77) $3,500

Anr copy. Disbound with old calf bdg present. Groundplat repaired & restored, with a few words in facsimile; lacking some overslips; staining & soiling; some repairs with loss. Sold w.a.f. O Mar 5 (79) $5,100
— 1591. - Cologne: J. B. Chiotti. 2 vols in 1. Folio, contemp calf gilt; spine ends repaired, new endpapers. Lacking q2 & 5 in Vol I; some dampstaining; first few leaves frayed; tp repaired in margins; a few margins wormed. S Mar 14 (111) £550
— 1847. - L. 4to, mor gilt by Bayntun-Riviere. Some dampstaining; library stamp on tp. S June 12 (252) £900

**Euler, Leonhard, 1707-83**
— Introductio in analysin infinitorum. Lyons, 1797. 2 vols. 4to, 19th-cent half cloth; spine ends chipped. With folding table & 16 plates. sg May 16 (162) $200

**Euripides**
See also: Gregynog Press
— Opera. Venice: Aldus, Feb 1503. ("Tragoediae septendecim.") 2 vols. 8vo, 19th-cent mor gilt; Vol I rebacked with old spine laid down, Vol II joints weak, corners rubbed. Lacking 1 blank. C Apr 3 (92) £3,800

**Eusebius Pamphili, 260?-340?**
— Autores historiae ecclesiasticae. Basel: Froben, 1535. Folio, later half calf; worn. Soiling & staining; 1st 2 leaves def in margins & repaired. Sold w.a.f. O Mar 5 (80) $250
— Chronicon. Venice: Erhard Ratdolt, 13 Sept 1483. 4to, old vellum. 41 lines; gothic & roman letter; ptd in red & black throughout Some dampstaining in upper margins; early marginalia; 2 wormholes in blank outer margins towards end. 179 (of 182) leaves; lacking 2 blanks. Goff E-117. sg Oct 19 (87) $4,200
— De Evangelica preparatione. Treviso: Michael Manzolus, 12 Jan 1480. Folio, modern bds; spine ends worn. Soiling to 1st & last leaf; marginal notes. 107 (of 108) leaves; lacking final blank. Goff E-121. cb Feb 14 (2512) $1,100

**Eustratius, Archbishop of Nicaea**
— Eustratii et aliorum insignium peripateticorum commentaria in...Artistotelis de moribus ad Nicomachum.... Venice: Aldus, 1536. Folio, 19th-cent half sheep; loose. Minor staining. P Dec 12 (22) $2,250

Anr copy. Early 19th-cent russia gilt. Marginal worming at ends; marginal stains on last leaves; annotations at beginning. P Dec 12 (23) $550

**Euthemia...**
— Euthemi; or, the Power of Harmony. A Poem.... L, 1756. 4to, disbound. Tp soiled; Ms alterations to pp 4-5. Inscr to "Ric. Graves 1764" but with 1st part cropped away. Ck Sept 8 (233) £200

**Evangelista, Giovanni**
— Apocalisse. Milan: Carlo E. Bestetti, 1977. One of 1,125. Illus by Giorgio de Chirico. Folio, orig mor with metal fittings. Ck Apr 12 (227) £90

**Evans, Albert S.**
— A la California. San Francisco, 1873. 1st Ed. - Illus by Ernest Narjot. 8vo, orig cloth. Larson copy. pba Sept 28 (444) $50

**Evans, Ambrose**
— The Adventures, and surprizing Deliverances, of James Dubourdieu and his Wife.... L, 1719. 4to, contemp calf; worn. Lacking prelims & endpapers. CE May 22 (223) $850

**Evans, Arthur Humble.** See: Wilson & Evans

**Evans, Sir Arthur John, 1851-1941**
— The Palace of Minos at Knossos. NY: Biblo & Tannen, 1964. Vols I-IV in 6 vols plus Index vol. 4to, orig cloth. wad Oct 18 (5) C$400

**Evans, Charles, 1850-1935**
— American Bibliography. Chicago, 1903-34. 12 vols plus Shipton's continuation & Bristol's Index. Vols I-XII sgd by Evans. Ck Apr 12 (228) £270
Anr Ed. NY, 1941-67. 14 vols, including Index. Z Jan 30 (143) $220
Anr Ed. Chicago, 1903-34 & Worcester, 1955-59. 14 vols. 4to, cloth; several vols need rebdg. Sold w.a.f. sg Oct 26 (107) $375
Mini-Print Ed. Metuchen, N.J., 1967. 13 vols in 1. 4to, orig cloth. bbc Dec 18 (122) $250

**Evans, Charles ("Chick")**
— Chick Evans' Golf Book.... Chicago: Thomas E. Wilson, [1921]. Cloth; spine ends rubbed. With 65 illus. pba Nov 9 (17) $80
1st Ed. Chicago: Thos. E. Wilson, [1921]. Cloth; spine spotted. With 65 illus. pba Apr 18 (48) $180
Anr Ed. NY: Thomas E. Wilson, [1924]. One of 999. Cloth; spine ends & joints rubbed. With 65 illus. Sgd. pba Nov 9 (16) $1,600
Uncorrected proofs. NY: Thomas E. Wilson, 1969. Wraps. Inscr. pba Nov 9 (18) $120

**Evans, Charles Seddon**
— Cinderella. L, 1919. One of 325 on Japan vellum, with an extra plate. Illus by Arthur Rackham. 4to, orig half vellum; spine discolored & bumped, small mark on upper cover. S Nov 2 (132) £520 [Hirsch]
Anr Ed. Phila. & L, 1919. One of—325 on Japan vellum, with an extra plate. 4to, mor gilt by Sangorski & Sutcliffe for Asprey, with onlaid design of the glass slipper on a cushion. CE Sept 27 (237) $1,300
One of 525 on handmade paper. Orig half cloth; corners rubbed. Ck May 31 (147) £450
— The Sleeping Beauty. L, [1920]. One of 625, with an extra plate. Illus by Arthur Rackham. 4to, orig half vellum; minor soiling. CE May 22 (395) £650
Anr copy. Orig half vellum; stained & rubbed. Ck May 31 (152) £240

Anr copy. Orig half vellum; corners worn, bookplate removed. sg Sept 14 (303) $550; sg Oct 19 (200) $550

**Evans, Edwin Clyve.** See: Baird & Evans

**Evans, George Bird**
— An Affair with Grouse. [N.p.]: Old Hemlock, 1982. One of 1,000. 4to, syn. O Oct 10 (11) $140; O Oct 10 (12) $140; O Oct 10 (123) $140; O Oct 10 (124) $160; O Oct 10 (125) $160
— The Bird Dog Book. Clinton NJ: Amwell Press, [1979]. One of 1,000. 4to, syn. O Oct 10 (126) $190
— Opus 10: Men Who Shot and Wrote About It. [N.p.]: Old Hemlock, 1983. One of 990. Inscr. O Oct 10 (127) $200
— Recollections of a Shooting Guest. Clinton NJ: Amwell Press, [1978]. One of 1,000. 4to, syn. O Oct 10 (13) $300; O Oct 10 (128) $300; O Oct 10 (129) $350
— The Ruffed Grouse Book. Clinton NJ: Amwell Press, [1977]. One of 1,000. 4to, cloth. O Oct 10 (130) $300
— The Upland Gunner's Book. Clinton NJ: Amwell Press, [1979]. One of 1,000. 4to, syn. O Oct 10 (131) $180
— The Woodcock Book. Clinton NJ: Amwell Press, [1977]. Publisher's Presentation copy. 4to, cloth. O Oct 10 (132) $200

**Evans, Patricia**
— The Mycophagists' Book. San Francisco, 1951. One of 175. Some soiling. pba Aug 8 (361) $80

**Evans, Peter**
— Goodbye Baby & Amen: A Saraband for the Sixties. NY, [1969]. 1st American Ed. - Illus by David Bailey. Folio, cloth, in chipped dj; shaken. sg Feb 29 (29) $175

**Evans, Walker**
— Many are Called. NY, 1966. 1st Ed. Ptd wraps; minor wear & soiling. sg Feb 29 (127) $110
— Message from the Interior. NY, [1966]. Folio, cloth. With 12 photos. sg Apr 24 (589) $275
— Walker Evans First and Last. NY, [1978]. 1st Ed. 4to, orig cloth. wa Feb 1 (240) $85

**Evelyn, John, 1620-1706**
— The Diary. Oxford, 1955. 6 vols. 8vo, cloth, in djs. wa Feb 29 (168) $130
— Memoirs.... L, 1819. 2d Ed. 2 vols. 4to, contemp half calf. With 12 plates, including 1 pedigree. b Jan 31 (84) £90
Anr copy. Contemp mor gilt. pba Sept 14 (158) $225
Anr Ed. L, 1827. 5 vols. 8vo, half mor. Extra-illus with c.200 plates. sg Sept 21 (182) $400
— Sculptura.... L, 1662. ("Sculptura: or the History and Art of Chalcography and Engraving in Copper....") 1st Ed. 8vo, 19th-cent mor gilt; bumped, dry. With frontis, folding port & plate. Some spotting & soiling; mezzotint with small abrasion affecting image. Schaefer copy. P Nov 1 (83) $2,750

— Sylva.... L, 1729. 5th Ed. Folio, contemp calf; rubbed. b Sept 20 (120) £170

Anr Ed. York, 1786. 2 vols. 4to, contemp calf; joints worn. H3 in Vol I torn & repaired; some browning & staining. CE May 22 (225) $280

Anr copy. 2 vols in 1. 4to, contemp mor. With port frontis, & 42 plates. Some spotting. S Oct 27 (726) £280 [Cumming]

Anr Ed. York, 1812. 2 vols. 4to, half calf. With port & 45 plates. Some foxing. K Feb 11 (162) $300

**Everard, Harry Stirling Crawfurd**
— Golf in Theory and Practice. L: George Bell & Sons, 1898. 3d Ed. Cloth; soiled, hinges cracking. pba Apr 18 (50) $130
— A History of the Royal & Ancient Golf Club St. Andrews from 1754-1900. Edin., 1907. 1st Ed. Cloth; corners bumped, spine ends worn. pba Nov 9 (20) $1,000

Anr Ed. Edin.:, 1907. Cloth; spine ends rubbed. pba Apr 18 (49) $1,100

**Everitt, Graham**
— English Caricaturists and Graphic Humourists of the Nineteenth Century. L, 1886. 4to, orig cloth; rear inner joint broken. Some soiling & foxing. O Mar 26 (90) $80

**Evers, Myrlie B.**
— For Us The Living. NY, 1967. In dj. Sgd. sg Mar 28 (81) $140

**Everson, William**
— Black Hills. San Francisco: Didymus Press, [1973]. One of 285. 4to, half cloth. pba Aug 22 (138) $80
— Blame it on the Jet Stream! [Santa Cruz, Calif.]: Lime Kiln Press, 1978. One of 150, sgd. Oblong 8vo, half mor. Inscr to George Houle. pba Aug 22 (139) $80
— The Blowing of the Seed. New Haven, 1966. 1st Ed, one of 218. 4to, bds. Inscr as Brother Antoninus. pba Aug 22 (140) $110
— A Canticle to the Waterbirds. Berkeley, 1968. 1st Ed, one of 200. pba Aug 22 (141) $60
— In Medias Res: Canto One of an Autobiographical Epic.... San Francisco: Adrian WIlson, 1984. 1st Ed, one of 226. Folio, half mor. pba Jan 25 (85) $160

Anr Ed. San Francisco: Adrian Wilson, 1984. one of—226. Folio, half mor. pba Aug 22 (143) $140
— In the Fictive Wish. [Berkeley]: Oyez Press, [1967]. One of—200. pba Aug 22 (144) $85
— The Last Crusade. Berkeley: Oyez Press, [1969]. One of 165. Half cloth. Inscr as Everson to the pbrs. pba Aug 22 (145) $90
— The Masks of Drought. Santa Barbara: Black Sparrow Press, 1980. One of 50. Half cloth. With holograph poem, sgd, bound in. bbc June 24 (498) $250
— On Printing. San Francisco: Book Club of California, 1992. One of 400. pba Jan 25 (87) $110
— Poems of Nineteen Forty Seven. [Reno]: Black Rock Press, [1967]. One of 180. Folio, cloth. pba Aug 22 (146) $60

— The Poet Is Dead: a Memorial for Robinson Jeffers. San Francisco, 1964. One of 205. Half mor, in dj. pba Oct 5 (96) $160

One of 205, sgd. Half mor, in dj. Inscr to John Knight by Everson & by the ptr, Andrew Hoyem. pba Aug 22 (147) $140

Anr Ed. Santa Cruz: Good Book Press, 1987. One of 140. pba Aug 22 (148) $95
— Rattlesnake August. [Northridge, Calif.]: Santa Susana Press, 1978. One of 50, sgd by author & artist. Illus by Hans Burkhardt. 4to, sheets loose in folding case, as issued. With 4 colored plates. pba Aug 22 (149) $90
— River-Root: A Syzygy for the Bicentennial of these States. Berkeley: Oyez Press, 1976. One of 250. 4to, half lea by Cardoza-James. Inscr. pba Jan 25 (88) $90
— San Joaquin. Los Angeles: Ward Ritchie Press, 1939. One of 100. 4to, half cloth. ALs to Hildegarde Flanner laid in. pba Jan 25 (89) $750
— Tendril in the Mesh. [N.p.]: Cayucos Books, 1973. One of 250. Half lea. Inscr to John Knight. pba Aug 22 (151) $60
— The Tongs of Jeopardy: A Meditation on the Death of President Kennedy. [N.p., c.1965]. Proof copy. Script-bound in acetate. pba Jan 25 (90) $75
— Who is She That Looketh Forth as the Morn. Santa Barbara: Capricorn Press, 1972. One of 250. Folio, Half cloth. pba Aug 22 (153) $65

**Everson, William —& Others**
— Out of the West. Northridge CA: Lord John Press, 1979. One of 350. Half cloth. pba Jan 25 (196) $100

Anr copy. Half cloth. Sgd by all 5 contributors on pages preceding their poems. pba Aug 22 (159) $55

**Ewart, Joseph, 1831-1906**
— The Poisonous Snakes of India. L, 1878. 4to, orig cloth; stained & worn, lower bd pulling. With 2 uncolored & 19 color plates. bba May 30 (431) £240 [Vercruysse]

**Ewers, Hanns Heinz, 1871-1908**
— Blood. NY, 1930. One of 750. Illus by Edgar Parin d'Aulaire. sg Dec 14 (93) $60

**Ewert, Theodore**
— Private Theodore Ewert's Diary of the Black Hills Expedition of 1874. Piscataway NJ: CRI Books, [1976]. Ed by John M. Carroll & Lawrence A. Frost. In dj. Inscr by Carroll. pba June 25 (87) $65

**Ewing, Thomas**
— Ewing's New General Atlas. Egin., [1862]. 4to, contemp half mor; rubbed. With engraved title & 27 maps, hand-colored in outline. Soiling to margins. S Mar 28 (174) £220

**Exact...**
— An Exact Relation of the Several Engagements...of His Majesties Fleet, under the Command of...Prince Rupert. L, 1673. 1st Ed. 8vo, later half calf; needs rebdg. sg Mar 7 (212) $120

## Exercises...

— Exercises journaliers de piete a l'usage de l'auguste Imperatrice et...Reine de Hongrie et de Boheme. Prague, 1776. 8vo, contemp mor gilt with enamel painting. With 8 plates. Some foxing. Schaefer copy.   P Nov 1 (84) $2,500

## Expedicion...

— La Expedicion Malaspina, 1789-1794. Madrid: Lunwerg Editores, [1987-92]. 4 vols in 5. Folio, orig cloth, in djs. pba Apr 25 (206) $400

## Exquemelin, Alexandre Olivier, 1645?-1707

— Bucaniers of America.... L, 1684-85. 2d Ed in English of Vol I, 1st Ed in English of Vol II. 2 vols in 1. 4to, calf; joints weak, spine dry, rebacked. Small tears; H2 with repaired tear; a1 with tear through text; American map with tear.   P June 5 (225) $2,750

Anr Ed. L, 1704. ("The History of the Bucaniers of America.") 8vo, later mor; some folds repaired; browned. With 20 folding & mostly full-page engravings.. wa Nov 16 (116) $475

5th Ed. L, 1771. 2 vols. 12mo, contemp calf; worn, rebacked.  S Oct 26 (507) $200 [Fernandez-Holman]

— Histoire des avanturiers.... Paris, 1688. 12mo, contemp calf; rubbed, backstrip wormed at ends. Some worming at end, partly restored.   bba July 18 (131) £440 [Maggs]

— Historie der Boecaniers, of Vrybuyters van America. Amst., 1700. 4to, contemp vellum. With engraved title, folding map & 7 plates. Some staining & browning.   CE May 22 (17) $420

## Eyb, Albrecht von, 1420-75

— Margarita poetica de arte dictandi ac practicandi epistolas. Basel: Johann Amerbach, 1495. Folio, contemp blind-stamped pigskin-backed wooden bds; upper bd split. 55 lines; roman letter. Tp soiled & wormed in margins; marginal dampstaining; piece torn from upper inner margin of last leaf. 244 leaves. Goff E-178. S Dec 18 (30) £800 [Frew]

## Eydoux, Andre Honore

— Instructions Generales en Changes sontenant un cours suivi et complet de la banque. Turin, 1797. 1st Ed. 8vo, contemp sheep gilt; extremities worn, spine chipped. Marginal dampstaining. sg Mar 21 (99) $110

## Eyton, Robert William, 1815-81

— Antiquities of Shropshire. L, 1854 [1853]-60. One of 300. 12 vols. 8vo, contemp half calf; rubbed. bba Nov 1 (191) £680 [Candle Lane]

## Eyton, Thomas Campbell, 1809-80

— A Monograph of the Anatidae, or Duck Tribe. L, 1838. 1st Ed. 4to, orig cloth; covers marked, spine ends worn. With 18 plain plates by G. Scharf & 6 hand-colored plates by Edward Lear. Inscr to William Kenyon, 1847. S June 27 (28) £1,900

# F

## Faber du Faur, Kurt von

— German Baroque Literature: A Catalogue of the Collection in the Yale University Library. New Haven, 1958-69. 2 vols. 4to, orig cloth. sg Apr 11 (104) $475

## Faber, Petrus, 1540-1600

— Agonisticon. Lyons: F. Faber, 1592. 1st Ed. 4to, 19th-Cent half calf. With woodcut device. S Oct 27 (920) £160 [Edwards]

## Fabre, Jean Henri, 1823-1915

— Book of Insects. L, [n.d.]. Illus by Edward J. Detmold. 4to, modern goatskin gilt by the Ashley Bindery, 1980. bba May 9 (151) £200 [James]

## Fabre, Pierre Jean

— Alle in zwei Theile verfassete Chymische Schriften.... Hamburg, 1713. 4to, contemp vellum; stain on upper cover, soiled. Dampstaining at foot of leaves at beginning & end; tear in 3K1; marginal worming. S Mar 14 (113) £650

## Fabri, Andrea

— Celaryus Polski, oder nach der Methode des Lateinischen LIbri Memoralis Cellarii.... Brieg: Gottfried Tramp, [c.1740]. 8vo, contemp bds. Tp torn without loss; library stamps on title. S Mar 28 (511) £150

**Fabricius ab Aquapendente, Hieronymus.** See: Fabrizzi, Girolamo

**Fabricius, Hieronymus, ab Aquapendente.** See: Fabrizzi, Girolamo

## Fabricius, Johann Albert, 1668-1736

— Bibliographia antiquaria.... Hamburg, 1716. 4to, contemp half vellum. O Mar 26 (91) $150
— Bibliotheca Latina.... Hamburg, 1712. Vol I (of 2). 8vo, contemp vellum. With engraved frontis. Browned & lightly stained. sg Apr 11 (105) $50

## Fabris, Salvator

— Scienza e pratica d'arme. Copenhagen: Henrico Waltkirch, 1606. Folio, later half vellum. Tp & some other leaves supplied from anr copy; some staining & browning. Sold w.a.f. CE May 22 (226) $1,000

## Fabrizzi, Girolamo, 1537-1619

— De Chirurgicale Operatien.... The Hague, 1630. 2 parts in 1 vol. 4to, contemp vellum; dust-soiled. S Mar 29 (691) £200
— Heelkonstige Werkingen. Rotterdam: Joannes Naeranus, 1661. 4to, contemp vellum. Black letter. Marginal dampstaining; old stamp on half-title; scored writing on tp. sg May 16 (411) $175

## Fabyan, Robert, d.1513

— The Chronicle.... L: John Kingston, Apr 1559. 2 parts in 1 vol. Folio, early calf bds with pastedowns of 15th-cent Ms in Latin, spine reinforced with fragment from a 15th-cent breviary; rebacked, upper joint split, extremities worn. In black letter & italic. Minor tears; a few ptd marginal notes shaved; early annotations & corrections in a contemp hand. STC 10664. P June 5 (226) $2,750

Anr Ed. L: John Kynston, 1559. Folio, old calf; rebacked using orig spine strip, rubbed & scuffed. Margins trimmed affecting shoulder notes & running headings; marginal ink notations. Sold w.a.f. STC 10663. pba Nov 30 (126) $1,100

— The New Chronicles of England and France.... L, 1811. Folio, 19th-cent half mor; rubbed, spine scuffed. Lacking leaf before title; minor foxing. pba Nov 30 (127) $100

**Faden, William**
— Atlas minimus universalis. L, 1798. Oblong 8vo, contemp calf; rebacked. With engraved title & 55 hand-colored plates. b May 30 (123) £650

**Fages, Pedro.** See: Grabhorn Printing

**Fahey, Herbert.** See: Grabhorn Printing

**Fahey, Herbert & Peter**
— Parchment and Vellum. San Francisco, 1940. One of 50. Orig vellum bds gilt. With frontis & 8 mtd vellum samples. pba Nov 30 (128) $600

**Fairbanks, George R.**
— The History and Antiquities of the City of St. Augustine, Florida.... NY, 1858. 4to, pictorial cloth. NH July 21 (149) $140

**Fairfield, Asa Merrill**
— Fairfield's Pioneer History of Lassen County, California.... San Francisco, [1916]. With folding map & 4 plates. Underlining in red pencil. pba Feb 12 (459) $100

**Fairy...**
— A Fairy Garland. L, [1928]. One of 1,000. Illus by Edmund Dulac. 4to, orig half vellum; spine soiled, foxing to endpapers & margins of prelims. With 12 colored plates. sg Sept 14 (109) $350

Anr copy. Orig half vellum; stained. sg Feb 15 (93) $350

**Faithorne, William, 1616-91**
— The Art of Graveing, and Etching.... L, 1662. 1st Ed. 8vo, contemp half calf; rebacked, orig spine laid down. With engraved title & 10 plates. Some soiling & marginal ink stains. Glanville - Davies - Schaefer copy. P Nov 1 (85) $3,250

**Falconer, C. M.**
— Specimens of a Bibliography of the Works of Andrew Lang. Dundee: Pvtly ptd, 1889. One of 75. 8vo, orig wraps. Inscr by Lang to Horace Pym & with ALs to Pym, 23 Dec 1889. S Apr 23 (109) £220

**Falconer, Thomas, 1805-82**
— Letters and Notes on the Texan Santa Fe Expedition.... NY, 1930. Half cloth; soiled, corners showing, removed bookplates & spine label. With frontis. pba Aug 8 (54) $70

**Falconer, William, 1732-69**
— The Shipwreck, a Poem. L, 1808. 4to, modern half sheep. Some foxing; stamp on tp & plate margins, occasionally touching image. CE May 22 (227) $90
— A Universal Dictionary of the Marine. L, 1784. 4to, contemp sheep; worn, front cover detached. With 12 folding plates. Foxing affecting plates; tear on Plate 2 tape-repaired on verso. sg Mar 7 (213) $200

**Falconer, William, 1744-1824**
— Remarks on the Influence of Climate.... L, 1781. 1st Ed. 4to, contemp calf; upper rear joint cracked. Lacking index; spotted. Ck Mar 22 (107) £130

**Falda, Giovanni Battista.** See: Ferrerio & Falda; Rossi & Falda

**Falteri, Orazio**
— Lunario perpetuo, overo calculo astronomico. Florence: G. A. Caneo, 1600. 4to, modern bds; a few leaves misbound. Some browning; tp soiled & with short tear repaired in outer margins. S Mar 14 (114) £460

**Family...** See: Atkyns, Arabella

**Famin, A.** See: Grandjean de Montigny & Famin

**Fanelli, Francesco, fl.1707**
— Atene Attica descritta da suoi principii sino all' acquisto fatti dall' armi Venete nel 1687. Venice, 1707. 8vo, contemp vellum. With frontis, 8 ports & 5 folding plates. Some discoloration. Blackmer copy. S Nov 30 (124) £2,600

**Faraday, Michael, 1791-1867**
— Faraday's Diary. L, 1932-36. 8 vols, including Index. Library markings. sg May 16 (163) $700

**Fargo, Frank**
— A True and Minute History of the Assassination of James King of Wm. at San Francisco.... San Francisco, 1856. 8vo, orig wraps; spine perished, dried glue on spine margins of wraps. Lower right corners of last 5 leaves clipped. pba Feb 12 (570) $160

1st Ed. 8vo, orig wraps; wraps torn at front & rear. Marginal soilmarks. Robbins & Plath copy. pba Mar 21 (100) $2,750

**Fargue, Leon Paul, 1878-1947**
— Pour la musique, poemes. Paris, 1914. Ltd Ed, this copy for Mme Judith Gautier. 8vo, mor extra with radiating interlocking gilt fillets, by P. L. Martin, orig wraps bound in. Inscr to Mme Judith Gautier. Laid in is autograph postcard, sgd by Paul Valery to the author. Later Paul Eluard's copy, with his bookplate designed by Max Ernst. S Nov 21 (135) £4,000

**Farington, Joseph, 1747-1821**
— Views of the Lakes. L, 1789. Oblong folio, disbound. With 20 plates. Some foxing. S Dec 18 (254) £320 [Duncan]

## FARISH                  AMERICAN BOOK PRICES CURRENT

**Farish, Thomas Edwin**
— The Gold Hunters of California. Chicago, 1904. 1st Ed. - Illus by F. I. Wetherbee. Orig cloth. With frontis & 12 illus. Larson copy. pba Sept 28 (446) $170

**Farman, D.**
— ABC du Conducteur d'Automobiles. Paris, 1898. Cloth; spine ends rubbed. pba Aug 8 (237) $190

**Farmer, Fannie Merritt, 1857-1915**
— Chafing Dish Possiblities. Bost., 1898. 1st Ed. 8vo, orig cloth; spine ends & corners rubbed. pba Aug 8 (362) $65

**Farmer, John —&**
**Moore, Jacob**
— A Gazetteer of the State of New-Hampshire. Concord, 1823. 12mo, contemp sheep; rubbed. With folding map hand-colored in outline & 10 plates. Some foxing. F June 20 (112) $60

Anr copy. Contemp sheep; rebacked, hinges reinforced. With folding map hand-colored in outline & 9 plates. sg Oct 26 (275) $275

**Farnham, Eliza W.**
— California, In-Doors and Out. NY, 1856. 1st Ed. Orig cloth; cover extremities worn & water spotted. Tp separated & repaired; 2 marginal text tears repaired; some foxing. Larson copy. pba Sept 28 (451) $160

**Farnham, Thomas Jefferson, 1804-48**
— Life, Adventures and Travels in California.... NY, 1850. Pictorial Ed. 8vo, orig cloth; worn. Larson & Jean Hersholt copy. pba Sept 28 (447) $70
— Travels in the Californias.... NY, 1849. ("Life, Adventures, and Travels in California....") 8vo, cloth. sg Oct 26 (108) $90

**Farnie, Henry Brougham**
— The Golfer's Manual. L: Dropmore Press, 1947. One of 750. Intro by Bernard Darwin. Illus by John O'Connor. Half cloth in dj; d/j browned & rubbed. pba Apr 18 (51) $425

**Farnol, Jeffery**
— The Broad Highway: A Romance of Kent. L, [1910]. Illus by C. E. Brock. 8vo, calf gilt by Sangorski & Sutcliffe. pba Aug 8 (251) $140

**Farova, Anna**
— Andre Kertesz. Prague: Odeon, [1966]. 4to, pictorial wraps. sg Feb 29 (173) $120
— Robert Capa. Prague: Odeon, [1973]. 4to, ptd wraps; some wear. sg Feb 29 (83) $110
— Werner Bischof 1916-1954. Prague: SNKLHU, [1960]. 4to, ptd wraps; rubbed. sg Feb 29 (35) $110

**Farquhar, Francis Peloubet**
— History of the Sierra Nevada. Berkeley, 1965. In dj. pba Feb 12 (62) $65

Anr copy. In dj with tear. Sgd. pba Apr 25 (396) $60

— Place Names of the High Sierra. San Francisco, 1926. Orig wraps; spine ends worn. 1 leaf of intro detached but present. pba Apr 25 (397) $85
— Yosemite, the Big Trees and the High Sierra: A Selective Bibliography. Berkeley, 1948. 1st Ed. Orig cloth in dj; d/j soiled & torn. Robbins copy. pba Mar 21 (101) $100

**Farquhar, George, 1678-1707.** See: Nonesuch Press

**Farrago**
— Farrago. Oxford: Simon Nowell Smith, 1930-31. Ed by Peter Burra. Nos 1-6 (all pbd). 8vo, orig pictorial wraps. Hobson copy. S June 28 (58) £320

**Farrer Collection, William Francis**
— Catalogue of the Collection of Old Plate.... L, 1924. Out-of-series copy. Compiled by Edward Alfred Jones. 4to, later half mor by C. Fox. With frontis & 93 plates. W Nov 8 (200) £2,500

**Farris, John**
— Fiends. Arlington Heights: Dark Harvest, 1990. One of 52. Illus by Phil Parks. Syn, in dj. O Dec 5 (174) $70

**Fashionable...**
— Fashionable Tours from London, to the Pleasant Parts of Lancashire, Yorkshire, Westmoreland, Cumberland.... L, 1802. 8vo, contemp calf; worn, front cover detached. With 17 plates. sg Feb 8 (256) $150

**Fassam, Thomas**
— An Herbarium for the Fair. L, 1949. One of 250, sgd. 4to, lev gilt with onlays, by Deborah Evetts. sg Sept 14 (49) $800

Anr copy. Mor extra with onlays, by Denise Lubett; With engraved title by A. R. Lane & 20 plates by Betty Shaw-Lawrence, each sgd in pencil. sg Sept 14 (50) $850

**Fassbender, Adolf**
— Pictorial Artistry. NY, [1937]. One of 1,000. Orig spiral-bound cloth; bumped. sg Feb 29 (132) $300

**Faujas de Saint-Fond, Barthelemi, 1741-1819**
— Description des experiences de la machine aerostatique de M. de Montgolfier.... Paris, 1783-84. 1st Ed. 2 vols, including suite of plates. 8vo, contemp calf; corners bumped, 1 corner of Vol I bdg chipped. With 14 plates. Vol I has 4-page Supplement at end. Minor marginal staining; 1 border-rule shaved. Hefner copy. CNY May 17 (16) $3,200

Anr Ed. Paris, 1784. 8vo, contemp half vellum; rubbed & soiled. With frontis & 7 folding plates. S Mar 14 (116) £650
— Descrizione delle esperienze della macchina aerostatica. Naples: Vincenzo D'Aloysio, 1784. 8vo, contemp bds; joints cracked. With 9 plates. Tear to last plate. P Dec 12 (80) $1,500

**Faulkner, William, 1897-1962**
See also: Limited Editions Club
— Absalom, Absalom! NY, 1936. sg June 20 (113) $450

2d Ptg. In dj. CE May 22 (230) $170

One of 300, sgd. Orig half cloth; spine soiled. cb Feb 14 (2660) $1,700

Anr copy. Orig half cloth. Engelhard copy. CNY Oct 27 (36) $1,500

Anr copy. Orig half cloth; corners worn. Met Feb 24 (194) $600

— As I Lay Dying. NY, [1930]. 1st Ed, 1st State. Orig cloth, in soiled & chipped dj. Tape repair to 1 leaf. cb Feb 14 (2661) $1,100

— Doctor Martino and other Stories. NY, 1934. One of 360 L.p. copies. Orig cloth. Tear to tp margin. cb Feb 14 (2662) $450; CE May 22 (229) $650

Anr copy. Orig cloth; spine ends chipped, extremities rubbed, smudge to front cover, shaken. pba Jan 25 (92) $550

Anr copy. Orig cloth; extremities rubbed, front cover with smudge, shaken. pba Jan 25 (93) $120

— A Fable. NY, [1954]. 1st Ed. In dj with 2 short tears to front panel. pba Oct 5 (97) $75

One of 1,000. In frayed dj. CE May 22 (232) $380

Anr copy. In repaired dj. sg Dec 14 (97) $50

1st Trade Ed. NY, 1954. Cloth, in dj. pba Aug 22 (160) $50

— Faulkner on Truth and Freedom. [Manila: Philippine Writer's Association, 1955]. Orig wraps. cb Feb 14 (2664) $425

— Go Down, Moses. NY, [1942]. One of 100. Orig half cloth; some abrasion to rear cover. Engelhard copy. CNY Oct 27 (37) $6,000

— A Green Bough. NY, 1933. In dj. cb Feb 14 (2665) $550

— Idyll in the Desert. NY, 1931. 1st Ed, one of 400. Orig bds; stained. cb Feb 14 (2666) $550

Anr copy. Orig bds; extremities rubbed. CE Feb 21 (93) $400

— Intruder in the Dust. NY, [1948]. 1st Ed. In chipped dj. F June 20 (478) $50

— Knight's Gambit. NY, [1949]. 1st Ed. Cloth, in chipped dj. bbc June 24 (500) $250

— Light in August. [NY, 1932]. 1st Ed. In rubbed dj. sg June 20 (114) $550

1st Issue. In dj. cb Oct 17 (365) $425

Anr copy. In dj with minor defs. pba Aug 22 (161) $375

— The Marble Faun. Bost.: The Four Seas Company, [1924]. 1st Ed. Orig bds; spine cracked. Inscr to Anita Loose, 12 Feb 1925. Stockhausen - Engelhard copy. CNY Oct 27 (32) $5,000

— Miss Zilphia Gant. [Dallas]: The Book Club of Texas, 1932. 1st Ed, one of 300. cb Feb 14 (2667) $1,000

— Mosquitoes. NY, 1927. 1st Ed. In dj with pencil notes across front panel. cb Feb 14 (2668) $1,100

Anr copy. In 1st dj with repaired tear to spine. CNY Oct 27 (33) $900

— Notes on a Horsethief. Greenville, Miss.: The Levee Press, 1950. 1st Ed, one of 975. Orig cloth; spine bumped. Library bookplate. cb Feb 14 (2669) $375; CE May 22 (231) $420

Anr copy. Cloth; rubbed. sg Dec 14 (95) $475

— The Reivers. NY, [1962]. 1st Ed, one of 500, sgd. CE May 22 (233) $600

— Requiem for a Nun. NY, 1951. In dj. pba May 23 (121) $50

One of 750. In dj. cb Feb 14 (2671) $425

Anr copy. In dj; bookplate removed from bdg. sg Dec 14 (96) $425

— Salmagundi; and a Poem ["Ultimately"] by Ernest M. Hemingway. Milwaukee, 1932. 1st Ed, One of 525. Wraps; spine worn, library bookplate. cb Feb 14 (2672) $275

2d state of bdg. CE Feb 21 (94) $320

— Sanctuary. NY, [1931]. 1st Ed. In dj. cb Feb 14 (2673) $1,300

— Sartoris. NY, [1929]. 1st Ed. Orig cloth, in chipped & repaired dj. cb Feb 14 (2674) $1,000

Anr copy. Orig cloth, in dj frayed at spine head. Engelhard copy. CNY Oct 27 (34) $2,400

— Soldiers' Pay. NY, 1926. 1st Ed. In dj with chipped spine. cb Feb 14 (2675) $4,500

Anr Ed. L, 1930. In chipped & soiled dj; spine cocked. cb Feb 14 (2676) $650

— The Sound and the Fury. NY, [1929]. 1st Ed. In worn dj. cb Feb 14 (2677) $3,250

Anr copy. Orig half cloth, in dj; spine faded. Goodwin - Engelhard copy. CNY Oct 27 (35) $2,400

Anr Ed. L, 1931. In dj. b Jan 31 (157) £75

— Tandis que j'agonise. Paris, 1946. One of 175. Folio, loose in wraps. sg Dec 14 (94) $120

— This Earth: a Poem. NY, 1932. Illus by Albert Heckman. Wraps; creased. sg June 20 (115) $130

— The Town. NY, [1957]. In dj. cb Feb 14 (2679) $500

One of 450. sg Dec 14 (98) $500

1st Ed. Cloth, in rubbed dj. sg June 20 (116) $120

— The Unvanquished. NY, [1938]. One of 250, sgd. cb Feb 14 (2680) $750

1st Ed, ptg not given. In dj laid on paper backing. pba Oct 5 (100) $110

— The Wild Palms. NY, [1939]. 1st Ed. In chipped & rubbed dj; rear hinge of bdg cracked. pba Oct 5 (101) $80

Advance copy. In ptd wraps made from dj; cocked. K Feb 11 (166) $350

**Faure, Giambattista**
— Congetture fisiche intorno alle cagioni de' fenomeni osservati in Roma nella macchina elettrica. Rome: presso il Bernabo, 1747. 4to, contemp vellum. Some dampstaining in margins. S Mar 14 (117) £190

**Favier, J.**
— Tresor du Bibliophile Lorraine. Nancy, 1889. One of 130. Folio, loose in pictorial bds as issued; rebacked, worn & soiled. With frontis & 100 plates of facsimiles. O Mar 26 (92) $90

**Favre, Joseph**
— Dictionnaire universel de cuisine et d'hygiene alimentaire. Paris, n.d.. 4 vols. 4to, orig half mor; rubbed, hinges weak. Slightly browned. S Oct 12 (20) £420

## FAVRE

— Dictionnaire universel de cuisine pratique. Paris, n.d.. 2d Ed. 4 vols. 4to, orig half mor; spines rubbed. With 4 plates. S Oct 12 (19) £420
10th Ed. Paris, 1902. 4 vols. 4to, orig bds; extremities rubbed. S Oct 12 (96) £220

**Favre, P. J. D. G.**
— Parallele de la France et de l'Angleterre a l'Egard de la Marine. [N.p.], 1779. 8vo, contemp half sheep; front joint cracked. Bookseller's stamp. sg Mar 7 (214) $400

**Fearing, Daniel Butler**
— A Catalogue of an Exhibition of Angling Book Plates.... NY: Pvtly ptd, 1918. One of 500. 4to, ptd bds, unopened; spine ends bumped. pba July 11 (83) $80

**Fearing, Kenneth Flexner, 1902-61**
— Angel Arms. NY, 1929. In chipped dj. K June 23 (280) $85

**Fearnside, William Gray.** See: Tombleson & Fearnside

**Feather, John**
— English Book Prospectuses: An Illustrated History. Newton PA: Bird & Bull Press, 1984. One of 300. Bds. With 14 folding facsimiles loose in paper folder as issued. bba May 9 (453) £80 [Sabin]; bba May 9 (454) £90 [Cox]; bba July 18 (11) £110 [Devitt]; NH July 21 (43) $55; sg Sept 14 (62) $130

**Federation Francaise de Golf**
— Les Golfs de France et d'Afrique du Nord. Paris, 1952. 1st Ed. Wraps; piece of wraps lacking. Corner of last half of pp. lacking. pba Apr 18 (52) $160

**Feijoo de Sosa, Miguel**
— Relacion descriptiva de la Ciudad, y Provincia de Truxillo del Peru.... Madrid, 1763. Folio, recent calf. With port, folding view ptd in blue, folding hand-colored map & folding uncolored plan. S Nov 30 (155) £1,000

**Feild, Robert D.**
— The Art of Walt Disney. L, 1945. 4to, orig cloth, in remains of dj. K Oct 1 (140) $350

**Felbinger, Jeremias**
— Christliches Hand-Buechlein.... Balt.: Samuel Saur, 1799. 12mo, early calf. sg Oct 26 (109) $175

**Felbien, Andre, 1619-95.** See: Cabinet...

**Felibien, Jean Francois, 1656-1733**
— Description de l'Eglise royale des Invalides. Paris, 1706. Folio, contemp calf gilt with arms of Heinrich, Graf von Bruehl; spine repaired at head, 2 small tears on upper cover, recased. Trace of rust on 2K. Fuerstenberg - Schaefer copy. S Dec 7 (208) £950
— The Tent of Darius Explain'd.... L, 1703. Folio, contemp calf; rubbed. Tear at foot of vertical fold of double-page plate. b Sept 20 (203) £100

## AMERICAN BOOK PRICES CURRENT

**Feliciano, Felice**
— Alphabetum Romanum. Verona: Officina Bodoni, [1960]. One of 400. Orig mor gilt. bba May 9 (23) £320 [Collinge & Clark]

**Felix, N.** See: Wanostrocht, Nicholas

**Feller, Francois Xavier**
— Biographie Universelle des hommes qui se sont fait un nom. Nevers, 1845. 4 vols. 4to, contemp half roan. Stamp of Joseph Brunet. sg Apr 11 (106) $80
— Dictionnaire historique.... Lyon, 1821-23. 10 vols. 8vo, contemp half lea; rubbed. Library markings; some foxing & soiling. O Mar 26 (93) $90

**Fellows, Sir Charles, 1799-1860**
— An Account of Discoveries in Lycia. L, 1841. Calf; joints worn. With 2 maps & 37 plates, 1 colored, several folding or double-page. b Sept 20 (334) £380
— A Journal Written During an Excursion in Asia Minor. L, 1839. 4to, orig cloth. With frontis, folding double-page map & 20 plates. Inscr by William Fraser Rae. b Sept 20 (333) £200
— Narrative of an Ascent to the Summit of Mont Blanc. L, 1827. 4to, contemp half lea; worn. With litho vignette title, facsimile, 10 litho & 1 engraved plate. Some foxing. Inscr. bba Nov 1 (571) £1,700 [Gonzales]
— A Narrative of an Ascent to the Summit of Mont Blanc. L: Pvtly ptd, 1827. One of 50 L.p. copies. 4to, orig bds; rebacked, corners rubbed. Repair to corner of tp; some soiling. bba Nov 1 (525) £1,600 [Chalon]

**Fels, Florent**
— Henri Matisse. Paris, 1929. One of 500. 4to, cloth, orig wraps bound in. sg Jan 11 (273) $325

**Feltham, Owen, 1602?-68**
— Resolves Divine, Morall, Politicall. L, 1631. ("Resolves, a Duple Century.") 4th Ed. 4to, 19th-cent mor gilt. CE June 12 (195) $400

**Fenelon, Francois de Salignac de la Mothe, 1651-1715**
— The Adventures of Telemachus. L, 1795. 2 vols. 4to, contemp calf; rebacked, worn. With 12 plates. Spotted. b Jan 31 (242) £65
— Les Avantures de Telemaque.... Paris, 1730. 2 vols in 1. 4to, 18th-cent mor gilt with crowned dolphins; spine ends repaired. With frontis, folding map & 24 plates. Repaired dear in margin of Ii4 in Vol II. Fuerstenberg - Schaefer copy. S Dec 7 (209) £500
Anr Ed. Amst. & Rotterdam, 1734. One of 150. Folio, 18th-cent red mor gilt with arms of Emmanuel Pinto de Fonseca; joints repaired. With frontis, port & 29 plates. Lacking the suppressed "Examen de la conscience d'un roi.". Fuerstenberg - Schaefer copy. S Dec 7 (210) £3,400
— Les Aventures de Telemaque. Paris: Drouet, 1781. ("Les Avantures de Telemaque....") Vol I (all pbd). 4to, contemp red mor gilt, with arms of Maria Feodorovna of Russia. Fuerstenberg - Schaefer copy. S Dec 7 (211) £1,100

Anr Ed. Paris, 1785. 2 vols. 4to, 18th-cent mor gilt by Bozerian jeune; cracked & scuffed. With port, orig drawing of royal coat-of-arms, half-title & engraved title, 24 engraved chapter summaries with tailpiece & 72 plate (66 before letters). Laid in are 4 states of a port of Fenelon by Vivien. C May 1 (51) £2,000

— Refutations des erreurs de Benoit de Spinosa.... Brussels [but Amst.]: Francois Foppens, 1731. 12mo, 18th-cent mor gilt with Renouard stamped in upper cover. Renouard - Fuerstenberg - Schaefer copy. S Dec 8 (580) £800

**Fenn, Eleanor, 1743-1813**
— A Short History of Insects.... L, [1797]. 12mo, contemp half lea gilt. With frontis & 7 hand-colored plates. S Nov 2 (191) £220 [King]
— A Short History of Quadrupeds.... L, [1796]. 2 vols. 12mo, contemp lea gilt. Small hole in margin of 1 plate; short tears in margin of 2 others. S Nov 2 (190) £440 [Schiller]

**Fenn, John**
— Original Letters, Written during the Reigns of Henry VI, Edward IV and Richard III. L, 1787-1823. Vols I-IV, in 2. Contemp calf; rebacked with orig spines used. Some browning. b May 30 (114) £120

Anr copy. 5 vols. 4to, 19th-cent calf; front cover of Vol I stained, rubbed. Some spotting. Ck Feb 14 (333) £150

Mixed Ed. L, 1787-1825. 5 vols. 4to, early 19th-cent calf gilt; rejointed. Some foxing & staining; some repairs with loss. sg Mar 21 (131) $250

**Fennell, Samuel**
— Original Poems, Corrected and Revised. Clonmel, 1811. 12mo, modern half calf. With frontis. b Dec 5 (601) £85

**Fennessy, Rena —&**
**Brown, Leslie**
— Birds of the African Bush. Tryon Gallery, [1975]. One of 295. Folio, orig mor gilt. With 24 color plates. b Dec 5 (147) £130

**Fenning, Daniel —&**
**Collyer, Joseph, d.1776**
— A New System of Geography.... L, 1773. 2 vols. Folio, contep calf; rubbed, spine ends worn. Some foxing & staining. cb Feb 14 (2553) $750

**Fenollosa, Ernest F., 1853-1908**
— Epochs of Chinese & Japanese Art. NY, [1913]. 2 vols. 4to, half cloth; extremities worn. Some foxing. sg Sept 7 (150) $175
— Epochs of Chinese and Japanese Art. L, [1912]. 2 vols. Half cloth; 1 spine wormed. sg June 13 (147) $175

**Fer, Nicolas de, 1646-1720**
— Atlas curieux, ou le monde represente dans les cartes. Paris, 1705-[16]. 2 parts in 1 vol. Oblong folio, 19th-cent half lea; worn. With 2 diagrams, 222 maps & views & 155 text plates & tables. Some leaves frayed or creased; some discoloration. S Nov 30 (71) £5,800

Anr Ed. Paris, 1705. 2 parts in 1 vol. Oblong folio, contemp sheep; extremities worn. With 186 (of 188) plates, including title & table of contents. Tp soiled; 1 leaf of description def. sg May 9 (64) $11,000

— Introduction a la geographie.... Paris, 1717. 8vo, contemp calf; spine ends worn. With 6 folding maps. Maps repaired on verso; ink stains & notations to tp & following leaf. CE June 15 (287) $200

**Ferdinand, Infant of Spain, Cardinal**
BECANUS, GUGLIELMUS. - Serenissimi Principis Ferdinandi Hispaniarum Infantis S.R.E. Cardinalis Infroitus in Flandriae Metropolim Gandavum. Antwerp: Johannes Meursius, 1636. 535mm by 380mm broadsheets, contemp vellum gilt with arms of Ghent; spine repaired, some staining to lower cover. With 42 plates. Some dampstaining; Plate 5 with marginal tear prepaired. Schaefer copy. P Nov 1 (19) $7,500

**Ferguson, Adam, 1723-1816**
— An Essay on the History of Civil Society. Edin., 1768. 3d Ed. 8vo, contemp calf; rubbed. b Sept 20 (122) £170

**Ferguson, J. B.**
— Spirit Communications: A Record.... Nashville, 1854. 8vo, orig cloth; warped, some wear. F Mar 28 (478) $150

**Ferguson, James, 1710-76**
— Astronomy Explained upon Sir Isaac Newton's Principles. L, 1772. 5th Ed. 8vo, contemp calf; hinges cracked, worn & bumped. With 18 folding plates. Some worming in rear index. Met May 22 (384) $200
— Select Mechanical Exercises. L, 1773. 1st Ed. 8vo, contemp calf; rebacked. With 9 folding plates. S Mar 14 (118) £360

**Ferguson, John, 1837-1916**
— Bibliotheca Chemica: a Catalogue of...the Collection of the late James Young. L, 1954. ("Bibliotheca Chemica. A Bibliography of Books on Alchemy, Chemistry and Pharmaceutics.") 2 vols. Reprint of the Glasgow 1906 Ed. ds July 27 (55) $70

Anr copy. 2 vols. 8vo, orig cloth. Reprint of the Glasgow 1906 Ed. sg Apr 11 (283) $110

**Ferguson, John Alexander, 1881-1969**
— A Bibliography of Australia.... Sydney & L, 1976-86. Vols I-VII. In djs (except for Vol IV). O May 7 (138) $350

Anr Ed. Canberra, 1977-86. Facsimile Ed. 7 vols. bba July 18 (12) £130 [Layward]

**Fergusson, David**
— Letter of the Secretary of War, Communicating...Report of Major D. Fergusson on the Country...between Tucson and Lobos Bay. Wash, 1863. 8vo, sewn. With 2 folding maps. Fold tears & stain

to 1 map; some foxing; final blank with repaired tear. 37th Congress, Special Session, Senate Exec. Doc 1. pba July 25 (282) $170

**Fergusson, W. N.**
— Adventure, Sport and Travel on the Tibetan Steppes. NY, 1911. 4to, cloth; worn. O Oct 10 (133) $225

**Ferrandis, Jose**
— Marfiles arabes de occidente. Madrid, 1935. One of 800. 2 vols. Wraps. sg June 13 (198) $700

**Ferrarius, Octavius**
— De re vestiaria libri septem. Padua, 1654. 2 parts in 1 vol. 4to, contemp vellum; turn-ins sprung, front hinge split. With 2 engraved titles, 4 plates & 19 illusts, all but 1 full-page. Tear in 1 engraved title. sg Mar 21 (132) $200

**Ferraro, Piero Antonio de**
— Cavello Frenato.... Venice, 1620. Folio, contemp vellum; spine wormed. Minor worming; some browning; tear to margin of L3; hole in M2. C Apr 3 (94) £900

**Ferree, Barr, 1862-1924**
— American Estates and Gardens. NY, 1904. Folio, orig cloth; worn, shaken. F Mar 28 (771) $80
Anr Ed. NY, 1906. Folio, orig cloth; worn & soiled, hinges cracked. wa Dec 14 (361) $150
Anr copy. Orig cloth; spine ends chipped, hinges cracked. Some soiling at beginning. wa Dec 14 (389) $160

**Ferrerio, Pietro —&**
**Falda, Giovanni Battista**
— Nuovi disegni dell'architetture, e piante de' palazi di Roma.... Rome, [c.1670]. 2 parts in 1 vol. Oblong folio, old calf gilt; rebacked & recornered, part of old spine laid down. Engraved throughout, with titles & 101 plates. First title creased & repaired in lower margin. C Apr 3 (96) £1,300

**Ferrero, Guglielmo**
— The Greatness and Decline of Rome. NY, [1909]. 5 vols. Contemp half calf; scuffed. F Mar 28 (429) $170

**Ferriar, John, 1764-1815**
— The Bibliomania, an Epistle to Richard Heber. Warrington, 1809. 4to, half calf. b Dec 5 (194) £250

**Ferris, Samuel, 1760-1831**
— A Dissertation on Milk. L & Edin., [1785]. 8vo, contemp tree calf; rebacked. With title vignette & halftitle. Prelims with singed fore-margins; repaired; spotted. Ck Mar 22 (108) $240

**Fesulanus, Prosperus.** See: Inghirami, Curzio

**Fete or Fetes...**
— Fetes publiques donnees par la ville de Paris a l'occasion du mariage de Monseigneur le Dauphin...le 23. et 26. Fevrier 1745. [Paris, 1745]. Folio, contemp red mor gilt by Padeloup, with arms of the city of Paris; joints of upper cover split. Engraved throughout, with tp, allegorical plate, 9 leaves of calligraphic text within ornamental borders & 19 plates, 10 of them double-page. Fuerstenberg - Schaefer copy. S Dec 7 (221) £2,400
Anr copy. 19th-cent half sheep; spine & corners worn, joints cracked. Engraved throughout, with allegorical plate & 19 plates, including 10 double-page. Old stamp on tp & image side of plates; stain in lower outer corner throughout. sg May 9 (342) $1,800

**Fetridge, W. Pembroke**
— The Rise and Fall of the Paris Commune in 1871. NY, 1871. 12mo, cloth; some wear. F Mar 28 (19) $50

**Feustking, Friedrich Christian**
— Das geoeffnete Antiquitaten-Zimmer.... Hamburg, 1704. 12mo, unbound. Some wear. O Mar 26 (95) $160

**Feyjoo y Montenegro, Benito Jeronimo.** See: Fore-Edge Paintings

**Fibbleton, George.** See: Greene, Asa

**Ficino, Marsilio, 1433-99**
— Contro alla peste. Florence: Giunta, 1576. 8vo, contemp vellum; soiled. With title device. Margins stained. S Oct 27 (805) £320 [Zioni]
— De triplici vita.... [Basel: Johann Amerbach, c.1498]. 4to, modern half vellum. With 100 leaves. Some browning & marginal repairs. Ck Mar 22 (109) £1,700
Anr Ed. Basel: [Cratandrus & Bebelius], 1532. Ed by Andreas Leennius. 8vo, modern calf. Lacking Y4; 1st few leaves dampstained in upper margin; Q8 torn; Y1 torn & closed. Ck Mar 22 (110) £480
— Epistolae. Nuremberg: Anton Koberger, 24 Feb 1497. 4to, contemp goatskin over wooden bds; worn, rebacked retaining part of orig spine. 42 lines & headline; roman letter. Some staining & spotting; a few short tears. 254 leaves. Goff F-155. S Dec 18 (32) £1,700 [Quaritch]

**Fictuld, Hermann**
— Der laengst gewuenschte und versprochene chymisch-philosophische Probier-Stein.... Frankfurt, 1740. 8vo, contemp half vellum. With frontis. Browned. S Mar 14 (121) £650

**Fidanza, Paolo**
— Continuazione delle teste scelte di personnagi illustri in lettere.... Rome, 1763. Vols III-IV only. Folio, half calf. With 66 plates only. Sold w.a.f. b May 30 (478) £550

**Field...**
— The Field of Mars.... L, 1781. 2 vols. 4to, old calf; worn & dry, joints split or starting. With 58 maps & plates. Some foxing. wa Feb 29 (193) $400

### Field, Eugene, 1850-95
— Poems of Childhood. NY, 1904. Illus by Maxfield Parrish. Orig cloth; corners bumped. With frontis & 8 colored plates. F June 20 (539) $90

Anr copy. Orig cloth; frayed & worn, front hinge cracked. wa Dec 14 (559) $85

— Works. NY, 1920. 12 vols. 8vo, mor, unopened. Vol VI dampstained. pba June 20 (157) $170

### Field, M.
— City Architecture; or, Designs for Dwellings.... NY, 1853. Cloth; spine ends chipped. pba Aug 8 (230) $225

### Field, Stephen Johnson, 1816-99
— Personal Reminiscences of Early Days in California.... [Wash.: Privately ptd, c.1893]. 8vo, orig cloth; edges worn, rear inner hinge starting. wa Feb 29 (326) $200

2d Ed. [Wash.: Privately ptd., 1893]. Later Issue. 8vo, cloth; extremities & joints rubbed. Robbins copy. Inscr & sgd. pba Mar 21 (103) $75

### Field, Thomas W., 1820-81
— An Essay towards an Indian Bibliography.... Columbus, 1951. 8vo, cloth. pba Apr 25 (400) $70

### Fielding, Henry, 1707-54
See also: Golden Cockerel Press; Limited Editions Club

— The History of the Adventures of Joseph Andrews.... L, 1742. 2d Ed. 2 vols. 12mo, contemp calf gilt; rubbed. S Dec 18 (126) £650 [Quaritch]

— The History of Tom Jones.... L, 1749. 1st Ed. 6 vols. 12mo, contemp calf; rebacked & cornered, joints weak, upper cover of Vol III detached. Lacking final blanks in Vols I & III; some browning or dampstaining. C Nov 29 (127) £600

Anr Ed. L, 1759. 6 vols. 12mo, contemp calf gilt; worn & rubbed, front free endpaper of Vol I loose. Some foxing; tears in at least 3 leaves. K Feb 11 (168) $1,600

Anr Ed. Paris, 1780. 4 vols. 8vo, contemp mor gilt; extremities rubbed. F June 20 (496) $200

— Works. L, 1784. 10 vols. 8vo, later calf gilt; scuffed. F Sept 21 (422) $375

Anr Ed. L, 1893. One of 150. Ed by George Saintsbury. 12 vols. 8vo, half lev. pba Sept 14 (160) $300

Autograph Ed. NY, [1902-3]. one of 75. 16 vols. 8vo, half mor gilt. Ck Sept 8 (94) £850

Anr Ed. L: Navarre Society, [c.1910]. 12 vols. Half calf by Ramage. b Sept 20 (566) £300

Anr Ed. Oxford: Shakespeare Head Press, 1926. One of 520. 10 vols. Half cloth. bba May 9 (636) £200 [Sotheran]

### Fielding, Mantle
— Dictionary of American Painters, Sculptors and Engravers. Phila., [1945]. One of 700. 4to, cloth; rubbed. sg Jan 11 (172) $90

Anr Ed. NY, 1965. Ed by James F. Carr. 4to, cloth; some wear. F Mar 28 (246) $55

### Fielding, Sarah, 1710-68
— The Governess: or, Little Female Academy. Phila.: Dobson, 1791. 16mo, contemp calf; worn, loose. Some browning & soiling. O Mar 5 (82) $450

— The Lives of Cleopatra and Octavia. L, 1757. 1st Ed. 4to, contemp sheep; spine ends & corners chipped, joints cracked. Some foxing. sg Mar 21 (133) $250

### Fielding, Theodore Henry, 1781-1851
— Picturesque Description of the River Wye. L, 1841. Folio, cloth; stained. With 12 hand-colored plates, each titled in pencil by a contemp hand. L.p. copy. S Mar 28 (47) £1,300

### Fielding, Theodore Henry, 1781-1851 —& Walton, J.
— A Picturesque Tour of the English Lakes. L, 1821. 4to, recent half mor; rubbed. With hand-colored vignette & 45 (of 48) hand-colored plates. S Oct 26 (392) £460 [Map House]

Anr Ed. L: Ackermann, 1821. 4to, 19th-cent half mor; rubbed. With pictorial title & 48 hand-colored plates. Some discoloration. S Mar 28 (46) £850

### Fierabras
— Fierabras. Lyon: Jacques Maillet, 21 July 1489. Prose text by Jean Bagnyon. Folio, mor gilt to a grolieresque pattern by A. Motte. 38 lines; type 1:114B. With 53 woodcuts, 2 of them full-page. Washed & pressed; Repairs with ink facsimile to a1; a few tiny holes. 86 leaves. Goff F-169. Fairfax Murray - Schaefer copy. P Nov 1 (87) $60,000

### Figueroa, Jose, 1792-1835
— Manifesto a la Republica Mejicana que hace el General del Brigada Jose Figueroa.... Monterrey: Imprenta del C. Agustin V. Zamorano, 1835. 1st Ed. 12mo, old sheep. Robbins-Plath copy. pba Mar 21 (104) $35,000

### Figuier, Louis
— Reptiles and Birds. L, [1869]. Ed by Parker Gilmore. Contemp half mor. pba Aug 8 (258) $170

### Filheul Library
— [Sale Catalogue] Catalogue des livres rares et singuliers. Paris, 1779. 8vo, contemp calf; rubbed, joints worn, spine-ends chipped. Priced & blank spaces for prohibited books filled in. O Mar 26 (96) $350

### Filhol, Antoine Michel
— Galerie du Musee Napoleon.... Paris, 1804-15. 10 vols. 8vo, contemp calf gilt with arms of Prince Eugene de Beauharnais, Herzog von Leuchtenberg; spine ends rubbed. With port, frontis & 720 plates. Fuerstenberg - Schaefer copy. S Dec 7 (354) £6,000

### Filippi, Filippo de, 1869-1938
— The Ascent of Mount St. Elias, Alaska, by H.R.H. Prince Luigi Amadeo de Savoia.... L, 1900. 8vo, orig cloth. bba Nov 1 (411) £380 [Chessler]

— Karakoram and Western Himalaya. L, 1912. 2 vols, including Atlas vol. 4to, orig cloth. Ink stamp on tp & plate versos. bba Nov 1 (390) £700 [Atlas]

# FILIPPI

1st Ed. 2 vols. 4to, orig half cloth; vol II spine head cracked. With half-title, 50 plates (18 folding, 5 double-page, 25 photogravure), & 3 folding maps. Inscr by S. M. Fraser.  S Oct 26 (575) £700 [Morrel]

**Fillmore's copy, Millard**
HAMMOND, JABEZ D. - Life and Times of Silas Wright.... Syracuse, 1848.  8vo, orig cloth; spine ends worn, color retouched, hinges tightened. Sgd by Fillmore on front pastedown, 26 Aug 1848, & inscr by him to the Rev. Dr. Choules.  CE Feb 21 (95) $500

**Filson, John, 1747?-88**
— Histoire de Kentucke.... Paris, 1785. 1st Ed in French. 8vo, old bds; rebacked, lacking backstrip. With folding map. Dampstaining at end; map with fold-wrinkles.  CE May 22 (18) $800

**Finch-Davies, C. G.**
— The Bird Paintings of C. G. Finch-Davies. Johannesburg: Winchester Press, [1984]. Folio, orig cloth. sg May 16 (303) $300

**Finden, William, 1787-1852 & Edward Francis, 1791-1857**
— Findens' Tableaux of National Character.... L, 1843. 2 vols. Folio, orig cloth, rebacked. With hand-colored additional titles & 51 (of 58) hand-colored plates. Some plates repaired with loss.  S Mar 28 (549) £500
— Illustrations to the Life and Works of Lord Byron. L, 1833-34. 3 vols. 4to, contemp half mor, Vol III in modern half mor. With port & 121 plates. Some foxing.  bba June 6 (46) £240 [Frew]

Anr copy. Contemp mor stamped in gilt & blind; worn, joints starting. With 3 engraved titles & 123 plates.  wa Nov 16 (302) $240
— Portraits of the Female Aristocracy of the Court of Queen Victoria. L, 1849. 2 vols. Folio, later half mor gilt. With frontis & 94 ports.  S Apr 23 (485) £620
— Views of Ports and Harbours, Watering Places, Fishing Villages...on the English Coast. L, [1874]. ("Finden's Views of the Ports, Harbours & Watering Places....") 2 vols. 4to, orig cloth. With 142 plates. S Apr 23 (349) £680

**Finden, William, 1787-1852 & Edward Francis, 1791-1857 —&**
**Horne, Thomas Hartwell, 1780-1862**
— Landscape Illustrations of the Bible.... L, 1836. 2 vols. 4to, contemp lea gilt. Some plates foxed.  sg Dec 7 (268) $275

**Findlay, Alexander G.**
— A Directory for the Navigation of the South Pacific Ocean.... L, 1877. 3d Ed. 8vo, orig cloth; stamp to front free endpaper & tp foot, front cover with stain & other defs. With 3 plates & 4 folding maps.  pba July 25 (143) $120

**Findley, William, 1751-1821**
— History of the Insurrection, in the Four Western Counties of Pennsylvania. Phila., 1796. 1st Ed. 8vo, con-

temp calf; worn & scuffed, joints starting. Top edge of tp torn with loss in margin; browned throughout.  wa Feb 29 (488) $350

**Fine, Oronce, 1494-1555**
— Arithmetica practica. Paris: Simon de Colines, 1535. ("Arithmetica practica, libris quatuor....") Folio, modern half calf; upper hinge cracked. Ink underlinings on tp; annotations on verso of final leaf; tear on tp repaired; inner corner of final leaf torn away without loss; some soiling.  S June 12 (49) £1,100

**Finerty, John Frederick, 1846-1908**
— War-Path and Bivouac, or the Conquest of the Sioux. Chicago, [1890]. 8vo, orig cloth; spine ends & corners rubbed.  pba June 25 (88) $100

**Finlayson, Duncan.** See: Grabhorn Printing

**Finlayson, George, 1790-1828**
— The Mission to Siam, and Hue.... L, 1826. 8vo, orig bds; rebacked. Some spotting.  S Mar 28 (375) £440

**Finley, Anthony**
— A New General Atlas. Phila., 1830. Folio, disbound. With 58 hand-colored maps & 2 hand-colored charts, 2 double-page. Some chipping; lacking tp.  bbc Feb 26 (15) $2,000

**Finney, Charles Grandison, b.1905.** See: Limited Editions Club

**Finney, Jack**
— Time and Again. NY: Simon & Schuster, [1970]. In dj. Dampstaining to upper edges of covers & text. Inscr on tp.  pba Aug 22 (163) $130

**Fior...**
— Fior di Vertu historiato. Venice: Giovanni Padovano, Apr 1542. 8vo, early 19th-cent half lea. Some worming at beginning & end, affecting a few letters; cut close; some discoloration.  C Apr 3 (97) £1,100

**Firdausi**
— Histoire de Minoutchehr selon le livre des rois. Paris, 1919. One of 25 on japon with 2 additional suites of the illusts, this copy also with a watercolor by Simonidy. Illus by M. Simonidy. Mor extra with a mosaic design, orig wraps bound in.  S Nov 21 (140) £1,200

**Firenzuola, Agnolo, 1493-1545**
— Prose. Florence: Lorenzo Torrentino, 1552. 8vo, contemp vellum with initials HC gilt on covers. Light marginal staining at end.  Fletcher of Saltoun—Jeudwine copy.  bba May 9 (2) £90 [O'Keefe]

**Firestone, Harvey S.**
— The Romance and Drama of the Rubber Industry. [N.p., n.d.]. 8vo, ptd wraps. Library markings. Inscr to Charles Edison, 8 Dec 1932.  sg Sept 28 (101) $150

**Firmicus Maternus, Julius**
— Astronomicon. Venice: Aldus, June & [17] Oct 1499. ("De Nativitatibus [with other tracts].") Bound in 2 vols. Folio, late 18th-cent mor gilt with Spencer arms, by Kalthoeber, with his ticket. 38 lines & head-line; greek & roman letter. Facsimile half-title inserted at beginning of Vol II; recent ruling in red throughout; capital spaces with guide-letters; *5-6 in Vol I supplied from a shorter copy; small hole in a7 touching 1 letter; ink underlinings on a10-b3 removed; text of dd-ee8 inlaid; smal stains in foremargins of 2 leaves. 374 (of 376) leaves; lacking 2 blanks. Goff F-191. Spencer-Rylands copy. S June 27 (317) £5,200

**Firmicus Maternus, Julius —& Others**
— Astronomicon. Venice: Aldus, June & [17] Oct 1499. ("De nativitatibus. Astronomicorum libri octo....") Folio, mor extra by Bozerian jeune. 1st leaf from anr copy; tear in T7 without loss; some spotting. 375 (of 376) leaves; last leaf in facsimile. Goff F-191. C June 26 (163) £7,000

**Firmin-Didot Library, Ambroise**
— [Sale Catalogue] Catalogue illustre des livres precieux, manuscrits et imprimes.... Paris, 1878-84. One of 500. 6 vols. 4to, half mor; rubbed. C. Fairfax Murray's copy. O Mar 26 (97) $900

**First...**
— First Steamship Pioneers. Edited by a Committee of the Association. San Francisco, 1874. One of 100. 4to, orig mor; scuffed. Without the photos for tipping in. pba Feb 12 (502) $600

**Fisher, Albert Kenrick, 1856-1948**
— The Hawks and Owls of the United States.... Wash., 1893. 8vo, orig cloth; worn & spotted. With 26 chromolitho plates. O Mar 5 (84) $160
Anr copy. Orig cloth; worn, some leaves detached. With 26 chromolitho plans. Some foxing. wa Dec 14 (124) $120

**Fisher, Dorothy Canfield.** See: Cather & Fisher

**Fisher, George Thomas**
— Photogenic Manipulation: Containing the Theory and Plain Instructions in the Art of Photography.... Phila.: Carey & Hart, 1845. 16mo, orig cloth; soiled & scuffed. Pencil notations & underlinings; library markings. bbc Apr 22 (214) $900

**Fisher, James.** See: Philip & Fisher

**Fisher, Jonathan, d.1812**
— A Picturesque Tour of Killarney. L, 1789. Oblong folio, half cloth; def. With hand-colored map & 20 hand-colored plates. Some waterstaining; margins frayed. b June 28 (24) £1,400

**Fisher, Thomas, 1781?-1836**
— Collections Historical, Genealogical, and Topographical for Bedfordshire. [L], 1812-1836. Folio, contemp half lea; rubbed. With engraved title & 116 plates, some hand-colored. S Apr 23 (350) £150

**Fisher, Vardis, 1895-1968**
— City of Illusion. Caldwell: Caxton Printers, 1941. One of 100. Mor gilt. pba Jan 25 (96) $70

**Fisk, James L.**
— Expedition of Captain Fisk to the Rocky Mountains.... Wash., 1864. 8vo, sewn. Soiling to 1st plate. pba Aug 8 (56) $160

**Fiske, John, 1842-1901**
— Works. Bost.: Houghton Mifflin, [1902]. Standard Library Ed. 12 vols. 8vo, half mor; spine ends worn. pba Dec 14 (64) $375

**Fisker, Kay.** See: Elling & Fisker

**Fitch, Elijah**
— A Discourse, the Substance of which was delivered at Hopkinton, on the Lord's-Day, March 24th, 1776.... Bost.: John Boyle, [1776]. 8vo, contemp wraps; worn & frayed. Some staining & soiling. O Mar 5 (85) $275

**Fitch, Franklin Y.**
— Life, Travels, and Adventures of an American Wanderer.... NY, [1883]. 1st Ed. 8vo, orig cloth; covers worn, front hinge cracked. Light soiling. Larson copy. pba Sept 28 (453) $80

**Fite, Emerson D. —&
Freeman, Archibald**
— A Book of Old Maps, Delineating American History.... Cambr. MA, 1926. 1st Ed. Folio, cloth; 1 corner frayed. With 75 plates, including color frontis. sg Oct 26 (110) $120

**FitzGerald, Edward, 1809-83**
— Polonius; a Collection of Wise Saws and Modern Instances. L, 1852. 1st Ed. 16mo, orig cloth. Foxed. S Apr 23 (55) £240

**Fitzgerald, F. Scott, 1896-1940**
See also: Limited Editions Club
— All the Sad Young Men. NY, 1926. 1st Ed. In dj with minor wear; spine cocked. cb June 25 (1818) $900
Anr copy. In dj. Inscr to J. Stuart Groves. Engelhard copy. CNY Oct 27 (43) $3,500
— The Beautiful and Damned. NY, 1922. 1st Ed, 1st Ptg. In dj with spine crease & some dust-soiling; orig cloth bdg with some soiling. Inscr to Harry Hansen. Engelhard copy. CNY Oct 27 (40) $4,200
Anr copy. In repaired dj. sg June 20 (117) $2,600
Ptg not stated. Orig cloth. pba Jan 25 (97) $150
— The Great Gatsby. NY, 1925. 1st Ed, 1st Ptg. Orig cloth; endpapers with pencil notes, edge-wear. Tear in 1 leaf. bbc June 24 (501) $260
Anr copy. Orig cloth, in frayed dj. Inscr to Zelda's sister & her husband. Goodwin - Engelhard copy. CNY Oct 27 (42) $55,000
Anr copy. Orig cloth, in dj lacking front interior flap & with losses on spine. Met Feb 24 (195) $5,000
Anr copy. Orig cloth; spine ends rubbed, newspaper article mtd to front pastedown. pba Jan 25 (98) $130

# FITZGERALD

Anr Ed. NY, 1926. 5 parts. 8vo, orig wraps; minor wear. CE June 12 (196) $130

Anr Ed. San Francisco: Arion Press, 1984. One of 400. Illus by Michael Graves. bba May 9 (447) £90 [Marks]; sg Sept 14 (30) $175

— Tales of the Jazz Age. NY, 1922. 1st Ed. Inscr to Kenneth Brightbill, 27 Sept 1922. Goodwin - Engelhard copy. CNY Oct 27 (41) $3,800

— Taps at Reveille. NY, 1935. 1st Ed, 1st State. Orig cloth, in soiled dj. cb Feb 14 (2683) $750

Anr copy. Orig cloth, in worn dj. Minor wear to bdg. CE Feb 21 (97) $380

Anr copy. Orig cloth, in dj. Hansen - Engelhard copy. CNY Oct 27 (45) $3,200

2d State. In worn & chipped dj. NH June 1 (130) $230

— Tender is the Night. NY, 1934. 1st Ed. Orig wraps; spine with wear. Advance copy. Engelhard copy. CNY Oct 27 (44) $4,200

Advance copy. Pictorial wraps made from a trial dj; repaired & rubbed. sg Dec 14 (102) $1,800

— This Side of Paradise. NY, 1920. 1st Ed, 3d Ptg. Orig cloth. With the tipped-in "The Author's Apology", sgd. CE Feb 21 (96) $1,800

Anr copy. Orig cloth; spine repaired. sg June 20 (118) $1,000

**Fitzgerald, Percy Hetherington, 1834-1925**

— Chronicles of a Bow Street Police-Office. L, 1888. 2 vols. 8vo, cloth; spine heads worn. sg Feb 8 (344) $225

— The Life of David Garrick. L, 1868. 2 vols extended to 4. Half calf; spines chipped & split along hinges. Extra-illus with plates, an ALs & "autographed notes". CE June 12 (197) $220

**Fitzgerald, S. J. Adair**

— The Zankiwank and the Bletherwitch. L, 1896. Illus by Arthur Rackham. 8vo, orig cloth. Some spotting. Ck May 31 (106) £280

**Fitzgibbon, Edward, 1803-57**

— The Book of the Salmon.... L, 1850. 8vo, orig cloth. With 9 hand-colored plates. W Nov 8 (369) £550

**Fitzwilliam, James Wentworth**

— Parham in Sussex. L, 1947. One of 250 on handmade paper. Folio, orig half vellum gilt. C May 13 (508) £380; C May 13 (509) £380; C May 13 (510) £260; C May 13 (512) £280

**Fitzwilliam, William Wentworth —& Cheadle, Walter Butler, 1835-1910**

— The North-West Passage by Land. L, [1865]. 1st Ed. 8vo, orig cloth; recased with spine ends repaired. With 2 folding maps with some hand-coloring in outline & 22 plates. pba Aug 8 (139) $750

**Flanagan, Sue**

— Trailing the Longhorns. Austin: Madrona Press, [1974]. One of 250. Folio, half lea. pba Apr 25 (405) $120

# AMERICAN BOOK PRICES CURRENT

**Flaubert, Gustave, 1821-80**

See also: Eragny Press; Limited Editions Club

— La Legende de Saint Julien l'Hospitalier. Paris, 1906. One of 170 on japon. Illus by H. Malatesta. 4to, mor extra by G. Mercier, orig wraps bound in. S Nov 21 (141) £400

— Madame Bovary. Paris, 1857. 1st Ed in Book form. 2 vols. 12mo, orig wraps; lower wraps with creasing, small hinge tears. Engelhard copy. CNY Oct 27 (48) $7,500

— Novembre. [Paris, 1928]. One of 150 with separately bound additional suite of the illusts with remarques, 4 etchings not used & the colophon illust, all sgd, 1 with note by the artist. Illus by Edgar Chahine. 4to, mor gilt by Creuzevault, orig wraps bound in. With 21 plates. S Nov 21 (144) £1,500

— Salammbo. Paris, 1900. One of 600. 2 vols. 8vo, calf gilt by Root. pba Aug 22 (578) $140

Anr Ed. Paris, [1923]. One of 850. Illus by F. L. Schmied. 8vo, contemp half mor gilt, orig wraps bound in. bbc Dec 18 (88) $450

Anr Ed. Paris: Maison Quantin, [n.d.]. One of 50 L.p. copies on japon. 4to, mor extra by Canape. With 10 etchings. With additional suite of the plates & 17 orig drawings by "Mes" including 5 watercolors. S Nov 21 (143) £500

— The Temptation of Saint Anthony. Kentfield: Allen Press, 1974. One of 140. 4to, cloth. bba May 9 (440) £65 [Deighton Bell]

— La Tentation de Saint Antoine. Paris, 1907. one of 60 on japon imperial with 2 additional suites, this copy with over 100 further impressions in various states. 4to, mor extra by G. Levitzky. S Nov 21 (142) £450

Anr Ed. Paris: Reynaud, 1926. One of 250 on Arches. Illus by Arthur Szyk. Orig wraps, in glassine dj. With 20 colored plates. sg Feb 15 (288) $425

Anr Ed. Paris, 1935. Out-of-series copy for G. Jacquart. Illus by Odilon Redon. Folio, half mor, orig wraps bound in. S Nov 21 (145) £650

**Flaxman, John, 1755-1826**

— Compositions...from the Divine Poem of Dante Alighieri.... L, 1807. 4to, contemp half mor; extremities worn. With engraved title and 110 plates. Foxed. sg Sept 7 (152) $150

**Flechier, Valentin Esprit, Bishop of Nimes, 1632-1710**

— The Life of the Emperour Theodosius the Great.... L, 1693. 8vo, contemp calf. pba Sept 14 (162) $200

**Fleischer, Esaias**

— Forsog til en Natur-Historie.... Copenhagen: Gyldendals Forlag, 1786-1804. 10 vols in 20. 8vo, contemp half calf. S Mar 14 (122) £140

**Fleming, Sir Alexander, 1881-1955**

— Penicillin: its Practical Application. Phila., 1946. 1st American Ed. In chipped dj. O Mar 5 (86) $160

**Fleming, Ian, 1908-64**

— Casino Royale. L, 1953. 1st Ed. In dj. Some wear slightly soiled. cb June 25 (1819) $5,000

Anr copy. In dj. Fine copy. Ck Nov 17 (74) £3,400
Anr copy. Orig cloth; library marking to spine. Outer margins spotted. Ck Nov 17 (75) £240
Anr copy. In dj. pnE Mar 20 (185) £2,500
Anr copy. In dj with creases. S Dec 18 (297) £340 [Jonkers]
— Diamonds Are Forever. L, 1956. In dj. Ck Nov 17 (80) £240; Ck Nov 17 (81) £220
Anr copy. In chipped dj. pba May 23 (124) $350
— Dr. No. L, [1958]. 1st Ed. In dj. Ck Nov 17 (82) £120
— For Your Eyes Only. L, [1960]. 1st Ed. In dj with spine browned. Sgd on tp. Ck Nov 17 (88) £900
— Goldfinger. L, 1959. 1st Ed. Orig cloth; hinges week, bumped, soiling to lower cover. Sgd on tp. Ck Nov 17 (86) £1,200
— Live and Let Die. L, 1954. 1st Ed. Orig cloth, in dj. Inscr to William Plomer. Ck Nov 17 (76) £5,500
Anr copy. In browned & chipped dj. Endpapers & half-title spotted. Ck Nov 17 (77) £300
Anr copy. In browned & chipped dj. Copy belonging to Julia who "rolled Ian Fleming's hand-made cigarettes". Ck Nov 17 (78) £380
Anr copy. In dj nicked at spine ends. S Dec 18 (299) £240 [Hawthorn]
— The Man with the Golden Gun. L, [1965]. Variant bdg in black cloth with gun design blocked in gilt on upper cover, in dj. S Dec 18 (294) £950 [Williams]
— Moonraker. L, [1955]. 1st Ed. In dj. Fine copy. Ck Nov 17 (79) £800
Anr Ed. L, 1964. Orig cloth, in dj; bdg rubbed, spine block twisted. Ck Apr 12 (136) £800
— You Only Live Twice. [L, 1964]. In dj. Inscr to Alan Ross. cb June 25 (1820) $2,750
Anr copy. In chipped dj; spotting to upper cover. Inscr to Julie (on leaf with stain & ink scribble). Ck Nov 17 (89) £1,400
Anr copy. Inscr to the real James Bond, 5 Feb 1964. S July 11 (283) £11,000
Uncorrected proof. Ptd wraps; rubbed. sg Dec 14 (47) $200

**Fleming, John F.** See: Wolf & Fleming

**Fletcher, John, 1579-1625.** See: Beaumont & Fletcher

**Fletcher, William Dolan.** See: Comstock & Fletcher

**Fleurieu, Charles Pierre Claret de, Comte, 1738-1810**
— Voyage autour du monde, pendant...1790-92.... Paris, 1798-1800 [Ans VI-VIII]. Presentation Issue. 4 vols. 4to, 19th-cent half calf with Admiralty Library emblem giltstamped on front cover; rebacked. With 15 folding maps, plate and folding table. Some foxing; 1st title with edge chip. Inscr to Alexander Dalrymple. pba Feb 13 (75) $4,220

**Fleurimont, G. R.**
— Medailles du regne de Louis XV. [Paris, c.1749]. Folio, contemp red mor gilt with arms of Louis XV [Olivier 2495, fer 2]; recased. With engraved title & dedication leaf & 78 leaves with engraved border, 54 of them with text & medallion & 24 before letters.

With extra plate by Vasse of the birth of the Dauphin. Plates 53 & 54 pasted in engraved border. Fuerstenberg - Schaefer copy. S Dec 7 (224) £300

**Fleuron...**
— The Fleuron: A Journal of Typography. L & Cambr., 1923-30. Ed by Oliver Simon & Stanley Morison. Nos 1-7 (all pbd). 4to, orig cloth or half cloth, in soiled & frayed djs. bba May 9 (31) £320 [Morris]

**Flinders, Matthew, 1774-1814**
See also: Golden Cockerel Press
— A Voyage to Terra Australis.... L, 1814. 1st Ed. 2 vols only, lacking Atlas vol. 4to, contemp half calf; rebacked preserving spines. With 9 plates. L.p. copy. b May 30 (150) £900
Anr copy. Orig bds; backstrips torn, repaired. With 9 plates. Some discoloration. S Nov 30 (218) £1,000
Facsimile Ed. Netley, 1989. One of 500. 3 vols, including Atlas vol. 4to & folio, orig half mor. b Mar 20 (90) £220

**Flint, Ralph**
— Contemporary American Etching. NY, [1930-31]. sg Jan 11 (174) $110

**Flint, Thomas**
— Diary of Thomas Flint: California to Maine and Return, 1851-1855. Los Angeles, 1923. Wraps. With folding map & 1 plate. pba Apr 25 (406) $55

**Flint, Timothy, 1780-1840**
— The History and Geography of the Mississippi Valley. Cincinnati, 1833. 3d Ed. 2 vols in 1. 8vo, contemp calf. Foxed. pba Aug 22 (916) $50
— Indian Wars of the West.... Cincinnati, 1833. 1st Ed. 12mo, remains of orig calf bdg. Lacking front blank; browned & stained. wa Feb 29 (370) $75
— Recollections of the Last Ten Years.... Bost., 1826. 8vo, orig bds; front cover loose, spine cracked. sg Oct 26 (111) $120

**Flint, Violet, Pseud**
— A Golfing Idyll.... [Worcestershire: Grant Books, 1978]. One of 250. Illus by A. Islay Bannerman. Cloth; upper corners bumped. Sgd by H. R. & Shirley Grant. pba Apr 18 (53) £110

**Flint, Sir William Russell, 1880-1969**
See also: Golden Cockerel Press
— Breakfast in Perigord. L, 1968. One of 25 bound in mor. Folio. sg Sept 14 (126) $750
— Drawings. L, 1950. Folio, cloth, in chipped dj. sg Jan 11 (175) $150
— In Pursuit. L, 1970. One of 150 specially bound. 4to, orig mor gilt. sg Jan 11 (176) $300
— Models of Propriety. L, 1951. One of 500. 4to, pba Mar 7 (107) $140

**Florence**
— Uffici della citta di Firenze. [Florence: Nicolaus Laurentii alamanus, c.1485-86]. 4to, unbound in folder covered with vellum Ms antiphonal leaf. 26

lines; type 7:111R 1st leaf detached; some spotting. 6 leaves. IGI 3974.   C Apr 3 (98) £3,000

**Florence, William Jermyn**
— The Gentlemen's Hand-Book on Poker. L, 1892. 8vo, orig cloth; rubbed. With port.   bba May 30 (239) £50 [Burgess Browning]

**Flores, Juan de**
— Histoire de Aurelio et Isabelle.... Brussels, 1608. 8vo, old calf; rebacked. Some browning.   CE May 22 (236) £450

**Florian, Jean Pierre Claris de, 1755-94**
— Galatee. Paris, 1793. 4to, contemp mor gilt; joints & edges rubbed. With 4 color-ptd plates before letters.   S Nov 30 (259) £850

Anr copy. Contemp mor gilt; corners repaired, spine rubbed at foot. With 4 color-ptd plates before letters. Marginal repairs in K2. L.p. copy.   S June 27 (319) £1,500

— Numa Pompilius, second Roi de Rome. Paris: Didot l'aine, 1786. 2 vols. 18mo, contemp red mor gilt in the style of Derome le jeune. With frontis & 12 plates. Fuerstenberg - Schaefer copy.   S Dec 7 (227) £220

**Florio, John, 1553?-1625**
— Florios Second Frutes. L: Thos. Woodcock, 1591. 1st Ed. 2 parts in 1 vol. 4to, 18th-cent calf. Lacking final blank; upper margin cropped; general title soiled; last leaf creased.   S July 11 (106) £1,300

**Flosculi...**
— Flosculi Sententiarum: Printers Flowers Moralised. [Northampton: Gehenna Press, 1967]. One of 250. Folio, half vellum.   sg Feb 15 (27) $225

**Flowerdew, Henry**
— The Parr, Salmon, Whitling & Yellowfin Controversy. Manchester, 1883. 2d Ed. Orig cloth; spine ends rubbed.   pba July 11 (92) $100

**Floyd's copy, William**
RAYNAL, GUILLAUME THOMAS FRANCOIS. - A Philosophical and Political History of the Settlements...in the East and West Indies. Edin., 1782. Vol IV (of 6). Calf gilt. Sgd by Floyd on tp.   sg Sept 28 (102) $475

**Floyer, Sir John, 1649-1734**
— Medicina Gerocomica, or the Galenic Art of Preserving Old Men's Healths. L, 1724. 1st Ed. 8vo, modern bds. Browned.   Ck Mar 22 (112) £180

**Fludd, Robert, 1547-1637**
— Tomus secundus de supernaturali.... Oppenheim, 1619. Bound with: Tomi secundi tractatus primi, sectio secunda, de technica microcosmi historia.... [Oppenheim, 1620?] And: Brunn, Lucas. Praxis perspectivae das ist: von Verzeichnungen ein ausfuehrlicher Bericht. Leipzig: L. Rober, 1615. Folio, contemp blind-stamped pigskin; rubbed & soiled. Sold w.a.f. Madsen copy.   S Mar 14 (123) £2,800

**Fly Fisherman...**
— Fly Fisherman. The Magazine for the Complete Angler. St. Louis, 1969-91. 22 vols. 4to, half syn, orig pictorial wraps bound in; some wear.   O Feb 6 (81) $900

**Fly-Fishers' Club**
— The Book of the Flyfishers Club 1884-1934. [L, 1934]. 4to, cloth; worn.   O June 25 (114) $160

Anr copy. Half mor gilt. Foxed.   pba July 11 (93) $170

**Flying Hawk, Chief.** See: McCreight & Flying Hawk

**Foa, Moses Benjamin**
— Catalogus librorum qui venales prostant Mutinae.... Modena, 1770. 8vo, orig bds; rubbed. Some foxing.   bba May 9 (45) £260 [Maggs]

**Foan, Gilbert A.**
— The Art and Craft of Hairdressing. L: New Era Publishing, [1958]. 4to, half mor.   pba Jan 4 (232) $80

Anr Ed. L: New Era Publishing, [n.d.]. 4to, lea; rubbed.   Met Dec 14 (248) $125

**Fodere, Francois Emanuel**
— Traite de medecine legale et d'hygiene publique.... Paris, 1813. 6 vols. 8vo, orig bds, unopened; backstrips gnawed, Vol I fore-edges dampstained with traces of mold.   sg May 16 (413) $175

**Fogazzaro, Antonio.** See: Grabhorn Printing

**Fogg Museum of Art**
— Drawings in the Fogg Museum.... Cambr. MA, 1946. 2d Ed. - Compiled by Agnes Mongan & Paul J. Sachs. 2 vols. 4to, cloth, in frayed djs; stain at bottom of Vol I front cover.   sg June 13 (263) $200

**Folengo, Teofilo, 1496?-1544**
— Macaronicorum opus. Amst., 1692. ("Opus Merlini Cocaii poetae Mantuani macaronicorum.") 8vo, mor extra by Kalthoeber, with his ticket. Beckford - Avery copy.   C May 1 (53) £900

**Foley, Edwin**
— The Book of Decorative Furniture. L, 1910-11. 2 vols. 4to, orig cloth; upper cover of Vol II stained, shaken.   b May 30 (468) £80

**Follot, Paul**
— Documents de bijouterie et orfevrerie modernes. Paris, [c.1895]. Folio, loose in orig cloth portfolio; worn. With 24 plates. Sold w.a.f.   CE June 12 (198) $300

**Folnesics, Josef**
— Alte Innenraeume Oesterreichischer Schloesser, Palaeste und Wohnhaeuser.... Vienna, [1926]. Folio, unbound in half cloth folder; backstrip def. With 68 plates.   sg Sept 7 (44) $130

**Folter, Roland.** See: Grolier Club

**Fonseca, Damiano**
— Del giusto scacciamento de moreschi da Spagna.... Rome: Bartholomeo Zannetti, 1611. 4to, 18th-cent calf; upper cover detached. Dampstain at head of last few leaves. Chatsworth copy. S June 27 (320) £700

**Fontaine, Nicolas, Sieur de Royaumont**
— The History of the Old and New Testament. L, 1705. Trans by Robert Blome. Bound in 2 vols. Folio, contemp mor gilt; broken. Dampstained in outer margins; lacking 2 maps. sg Mar 21 (33) $750

**Fontaine, Pierre Francois Leonard, 1762-1853.** See: Percier & Fontaine

**Fontana, Niccola**
— Osservazioni intorno alle Malattie.... Livorno, 1781. 1st Ed. 8vo, contemp bds; spine shelf-marked. With vignette title & cancel G2. Ck Mar 22 (113) £350

**Fontanini, Giusto, Archbishop of Ancyra**
— Bibliotheca dell' eloquenza Italiana.... Venice, 1753. 2 vols. 4to, contemp vellum; worn & soiled, 1 joints starting. Library stamps. O Mar 5 (89) $130

**Fontenai, Abbe de**
— Galerie du Palais Royal. Paris, 1786-1808. Illus by J. Couche. Vol I only. contemp half calf; upper cover detached. Sold w.a.f. S Apr 23 (237) £650

**Fontenelle, Bernard le Bovier de, 1657-1757**
— Oeuvres. The Hague, 1728-29. 3 vols. Folio, contemp calf; spine ends chipped, tear on upper cover of Vol II, lower cover of Vol I bumped, joints cracked. With 6 plates. S June 12 (50) £320

**Foot, Mirjam M.**
— The Henry Davis Gift; a Collection of Bookbindings. L, 1982-83. One of 250 & 750. 2 vols. 4to, orig cloth. O Mar 26 (98) $130

**Foote, Henry Stuart, 1804-80**
— Pen Pictures from the Garden of the World, or Santa Clara County.... Chicago, 1888. Folio, later cloth; soiled. With port & 78 plates & double-page map. Perforated stamp on tp; library markings; some soiling; hole in 1 leaf; 1 plate & page with adhesion damage. cb Oct 17 (170) $200

**Foote, John Taintor.** See: Derrydale Press

**Forbes, Alexander, 1778-1862**
— California; a History of Upper and Lower California.... L, 1839. 1st Ed. 8vo, orig cloth; unopened, 1 corner bumped. With 10 lithographed plates, & 1 folded map. Larson copy. pba Sept 28 (103) $1,900
Anr copy. Orig cloth; spine faded, ends chipped, covers stained & extremities worn. With 10 plates & 1 folding map. Pp. 105-6 chipped. Robbins copy. pba Mar 21 (105) $350
Anr Ed. San Francisco, 1937. Half bds. With 10 lithographed plates, 1 facsimile, & 1 folded map. Larson copy. pba Sept 28 (104) $150

One of 650. 4to, bds, in dj with piece lacking from front panel. pba Apr 25 (408) $50

**Forbes, Allan —&**
**Eastman, Ralph M.**
— Yankee Ship Sailing Cards.... Bost., [1948-52]. 3 vols, wraps. With 107 sailing ship cards reproduced. Larson copy. pba Sept 28 (368) $100

**Forbes, Charles**
— Iceland; its Volcanoes, Geysers, and Glaciers. L, 1860. 8vo, orig cloth; hinges weak, numbers on backstrip. sg Mar 7 (279) $90

**Forbes, Edward, 1815-54.** See: Spratt & Forbes

**Forbes, Frederick E.**
— Dahomey and the Dahomans. L, 1851. 1st Ed. 2 vols. 8vo, early half calf; needs rebdg. Library markings. sg Mar 7 (77) $100

**Forbes, James, 1749-1819**
— Oriental Memoirs. L, 1813. 1st Ed. Vols I-II only. Later half mor. Lacking 5 plates; Plate 14 torn & repaired. S June 13 (634) £360

**Forbin, Louis, Comte de, 1777-1841**
— Voyage dans le Levant en 1817 et 1818. Paris, 1819. 2 vols, including Atlas. 8vo & folio, contemp calf & orig bds. With 80 plates & plans. Some spotting; staining in upper margin of some plates. S June 27 (146) £2,800

**Forbonnais, Francois Veron Duverger de**
— Recherches et considerations sur les finances de France.... Basel: Freres Cramer, 1758. 2 vols. 4to, contemp calf gilt; joints cracked. Titles stamped; portion of blank upper margins torn away. sg Mar 21 (100) $475

**Forbush, Edward Howe, 1858-1929**
— Birds of Massachusetts.... [Bost.], 1925-29. 3 vols. 4to, cloth; some wear. O July 9 (84) $120

**Ford, Charles Henri**
— Spare Parts. [Athens, 1966]. One of 850. Pictorial bds; extremities rubbed. sg Dec 14 (104) $50

**Ford, Gerald R.**
— A Time to Heal. NY, [1979]. One of 250. pba June 13 (61) $250
— A Vision for America. Northridge, CA: Lord John Press, 1980. One of 100. Lea gilt. pba June 13 (62) $85

**Ford, Henry Chapman**
— An Artist Records the California Missions. San Francisco: Book Club of California, 1989. One of 450. Folio, cloth. pba Feb 13 (77) $50
— Etchings of California. [Santa Barbara], 1961. Orig cloth. With 36 illus. Larson copy. pba Sept 28 (105) $60

**Ford, James W.**
— The Negro and the Democratic Front. NY, [1938]. Sgd. sg Mar 28 (85) $130

**Ford, John, 1586-c.1640**
— Works. L, 1869. Ed by Alexander Dyce. 3 vols. 8vo, mor gilt by Alfred Matthews. wa Feb 29 (12) $200

**Ford, Julia Ellsworth — & Bynner, Witter**
— Snickerty Nick and the Giant. NY, 1919. Illus by Arthur Rackham. 4to, orig cloth, in dj with tears; With 3 colored plates. Ck May 31 (148) £260
Anr copy. Orig cloth, in frayed dj; With 3 colored plates. O Sept 12 (67) $375

**Ford, Paul Leicester, 1865-1902**
— The Great K. & A. Train-Robbery. NY, 1897. 1st Ed, 2d Ptg. 12mo, orig cloth, in dj with chips. sg Sept 21 (183) $175
— The New England Primer: a History of its Origin and Development. NY, 1897. One of 425. 4to, orig half lea; spine ends worn. Some soiling. O Mar 26 (99) $60

**Ford, Richard, 1796-1858**
— A Hand-Book for Travellers in Spain. L, 1845. 2 vols. 8vo, half calf by J. Larkins. With 2 folding maps. ANs mtd to front flyleaf. pba Aug 8 (57) $225

**Fore-Edge Paintings**
— [Bible in Japanese] The New Testament. Kobe, 1937. 16mo, orig lea gilt with vertical painting of the Holy Family. sg Oct 19 (88A) $450
— Book of Common Prayer. Cambr.: John Baskerville, 1761. 8vo, 19th-cent mor gilt with painting of the Tower of London from across the Thames. sg Oct 19 (88) $850
Anr Ed. Derby: T. Trimmer, 1777. 8vo in 4s, contemp mor gilt with painting of Worcester Cathedral. sg Feb 8 (103) $550
Anr Ed. L, 1813. 8vo, later mor gilt with painting of river scene with cathedral in background, sgd MK. sg Feb 8 (102) $550
Anr Ed. Oxford, 1845. 8vo, contemp mor with painting of a country estate. sg Sept 21 (184) $175
— The Comprehensive Bible. Hartford, 1832. 4to, sheep gilt with painting of a city street; edges & joints scuffed. pba Mar 7 (109) $350
— Les Evangiles de Notre Seigneur Jesus-Christ. Paris, 1837. 4to, orig mor gilt with painting of a Parisian street scene. wa June 20 (338) $280
— Favourite English Poems of Modern Times. L, 1862. 8vo, contemp mor gilt with painting of 2 couples picking fruit from an orchard. pba Nov 30 (132) $450
— The Gentleman's Diary... Almanac for the Year 1839. L, [1838]. 8vo, contemp mor gilt with painting of a hunting scene. sg Feb 8 (118) $375
— Gleanings from the English Poets, Chaucer to Tennyson. Edin., [c.1860]. 12mo, contemp mor gilt with painting of 2 18th-cent lovers, entitled Autumn. pba Nov 30 (134) $500
— The Holy Bible.... Oxford, 1812. Bound in 2 vols. 8vo, contemp mor gilt with paintings of English coastal views. sg Sept 21 (190) $500
— Order of the Administration of the Last Supper.... L, 1718. 8vo, contemp mor extra with double painting of The Last Supper after da Vinci & the Deposition from the Cross after Fra Bartolomeo; worn, front cover detached. sg Feb 8 (140) $600
— Specimens of Sonnets from the Most Celebrated Italian Poets. L, 1827. 8vo, later mor extra with painting of Spoleto. sg Feb 8 (152) $475
— Thirty Illustrations of Childe Harold... produced expressly for the Art-Union of London. L, 1855. 4to, contemp lea gilt with painting of a battle scene; front joint & corners rubbed. Some foxing. sg Sept 21 (185) $175

ADAMS, HENRY. - Letters of.... Bost., [1930]. Calf gilt by Sangorski & Sutcliffe with painting of George Washington crossing the Delaware. pba Nov 30 (130) $350

BARHAM, RICHARD HARRIS. - The Ingoldsby Legends. L, 1877. 8vo, later gilt-pictorial mor with painting of fishermen. sg Feb 8 (124) $500

BARTHE, EDOUARD. - Litanies de la tres Saint Vierge. Paris, 1853. 8vo, contemp mor with multicolored onlays, with painting of Notre Dame. sg Feb 8 (98) $275

BATES, ELY. - Rural Philosophy. L, 1811. 8vo, contemp calf with painting of 6 men fishing. pba Sept 14 (164) $550

BECKER, WILHELM ADOLF. - Charicles: or Illustrations of the Private Life of the Ancient Greeks. L, 1866. 8vo, later mor gilt prize bdg with painting of temple ruins; extremities scuffed. F Mar 28 (298) $400

BECKFORD, PETER. - Thoughts on Hunting. L, [1820]. Illus by Thomas Bewick. 8vo, contemp mor extra with double-painting of the hounds meeting at Whitewell near Wenwyn & The Death. sg Feb 8 (99) $600

BOGATZKY, CARL HEINRICH VON. - A Gold Treasury for the Children of God.... L, [c.1840]. 12mo, contemp mor extra with painting of Scottish highlanders around an outdoor cooking pot. sg Feb 8 (101) $110

BOSWELL, JAMES. - The Life of Samuel Johnson.... L, 1853. ("Boswell's Life of Johnson....") Ed by John Wilson Croker. 8vo, contemp mor extra with painting of Johnson with London street scenes on either side of him. sg Feb 8 (114) $275

BREWER, E. COBHAM. - Character Sketches of Romance, Fiction and Drama. NY, 1902. 6 vols. Orig cloth, each vol with painting of putti in central oval & decorative motifs on either side. pba Sept 14 (169) $550

BROWNING, ELIZABETH BARRETT. - Aurora Leigh. L, 1859. 8vo, mor gilt by Hayday with painting of Newstead Abbey. pba Mar 7 (110) $225

BROWNING, ROBERT. - The Poetical Works. L, 1924. 2 vols in 1. Calf gilt by Riviere with painting of butterflies; rubbed, front joint starting. pba Nov 30 (131) $225

BYRON, GEORGE GORDON NOEL. - Poetical Works. L, [c.1860]. 8vo, contemp mor extra with painting of the Palace of Brighton. sg Feb 8 (104) $325

CAMPBELL, THOMAS. - The Poetical Works. L, 1851. 8vo, contemp mor with painting of a golf scene. sg Feb 8 (106) $250

CAMPBELL, THOMAS. - Poetical Works. Edin., 1863. 8vo, contemp mor gilt with ice-skating scene. sg Feb 8 (105) $200

CARTWRIGHT, EDMUND. - Armine and Elvira. A Legendary Tale. L, 1802. 9th Ed. 8vo, contemp mor gilt with split double-paintings showing 4 London views. sg Feb 8 (108) $700

CHALMERS, ALEXANDER. - A History of the College...University of Oxford. L, 1810. 8vo, contemp mor gilt with painting of Oxford. sg Feb 8 (109) $450

COLLINS, WILLIAM. - The Poetical Works.... L, 1798. 8vo, mor gilt with painting of a church & landscape. pba Sept 14 (165) $275

COOK, ELIZA. - Poems. L, 1866. 8vo, contemp mor with painting of a pony being fed by 2 girls. sg Feb 8 (110) $250

COURMACEL, VICTOR. - Les Paquerettes. Calais, 1842. 8vo, contemp mor extra with painting of a river scene. Inscr to Mme Hepper of Gibraltar. sg Feb 8 (111) $275

COWPER, WILLIAM. - Cowper's Poems. L, 1841. 2 vols. 8vo, contemp mor with paintings of New York from Weehawken & of Boston & Bunker Hill from the East; front hinges cracked, extremities rubbed. sg Feb 8 (112) $200

COWPER, WILLIAM. - Poems. L, 1798-1815. 3 vols. Mor with paintings of scenes from Alice in Wonderland, after Tenniel. cb Oct 17 (634) $650

COWPER, WILLIAM. - Poems. L, 1833. 2 vols. 8vo, contemp mor gilt with 2 paintings of a coach & horses. CE May 22 (238) $700

DACRE, LADY BARBARINA. - Tales of the Peerage and the Peasantry. L, 1835. 3 vols. 12mo, contemp mor gilt with double paintings of Hastings from White Rocks & Yarmouth from the Roads in Vol I; Conway Castle in North Wales & Brough Castle in Westmoreland in Vol II; & Whitby & Windermere in Vol III; rebacked retaining backstrips. sg Sept 21 (186) $3,200

DICKENS, CHARLES. - Pickwick Papers. L, 1887. 8vo, half calf with painting of Mr. Pickwick addresses the club. cb Oct 17 (635) $275

DRUMMOND, JAMES. - Letters to Young Naturalist. L, 1832. 2d Ed. 8vo, contemp mor extra by Clarke & Bedford with painting of 2 field mice at play. sg Feb 8 (115) $200

FEYJOO Y MONTENEGRO, BENITO JERONIMO. - Teatro critico universale.... Rome, 1744. 4to, contemp vellum with arms of Vincenzo Canonico Fucci & painting of St. Peter's & the castle of St. Angelo; rebacked retaining orig backstrip. sg Feb 8 (116) $425

GEORGE, HENRY. - Protection or Free Trade. An Examination of the Tariff Question.... NY, [1886]. 12mo, half mor with painting of the three-masted ship Cosmos; painting slightly cut off at top. pba Mar 7 (111) $180

GILPIN, WILLIAM. - Observations Relative Chiefly to Picturesque Beauty Made in 1776...the High-Lands of Scotland.... L, 1808. 3d Ed. 2 vols. 8vo, contemp mor gilt with double paintings of Dundee & an unidentified view in Vol I & Aberdeen & Glannis Castle in Vol II. sg Sept 21 (187) $950

GOLDSMITH, OLIVER. - Works. L, 1846. 8vo, mor gilt by Root, with painting of Westminster Abbey. pba Nov 30 (133) $375

GRAY, THOMAS. - Poems. L, 1814. 8vo, contemp mor extra with double painting of Gray inserted into a view of Westminster from the terrace of Somerset House & with Horace Walpole & the entrance to the Grand Canal in Venice; 2d side shows Strammongate Bridge & Caernavon Castle. sg Feb 8 (120) $750

GRAY, THOMAS. - Works. L, 1807. 2 vols. 8vo, contemp mor gilt with paintings of Gray's monument in Stoke Park & West End Green at Stoke. sg Sept 21 (188) $650

Anr Ed. L, 1825. 2 vols. 8vo, contemp mor gilt with paintings of Eton Hall & Stoke Poges Churchyard. sg Feb 8 (119) $550

HEMANS, FELICIA. - Songs of the Affections. L, 1845. 8vo, contemp calf gilt with painting of a street scene. sg Feb 8 (122) $375

HERBERT, GEORGE. - Poetical Works.... L, 1856. 8vo, later calf gilt with painting of Stapleford on the Wiley. sg Feb 8 (123) $200

HOMER. - The Iliad. L, 1871. 2 vols. 8vo, contemp mor gilt with 2 erotic paintings. CE May 22 (239) $600

HOOD, THOMAS. - Poems. L, 1852. 12mo, contemp mor gilt with painting of Badminton House; joints & ends scuffed. wa Nov 16 (305) $210

Anr Ed. L, 1855. Calf gilt with painting of Shanbally Castle in Tipperary. pba Apr 4 (176) $190

JUSTINIANUS I. - Corpus juris civilis Justinianei. Amst., 1664. 2 vols. 8vo, later mor richly gilt with paintings of floral motifs surrounding the motto & crest of Lord Minto. sg Oct 19 (89) $4,400

LASKER, EMANUEL. - Common Sense in Chess. NY, [1917]. Later mor gilt gift bdg with "Harvard Club 1936-1937. Godfrey L. Cabot Champion" on upper cover, with painting of Harvard College. sg Feb 8 (125) $400

LEWES, GEORGE HENRY. - The Life of Maximilian Robespierre. L, 1849. 8vo, contemp calf gilt with painting of a rural fishing scene; joints & corners rubbed. sg Feb 8 (127) $175

LONGFELLOW, HENRY WADSWORTH. - Ballads and Other Poems. L, 1886. 8vo, orig mor with painting of Regent Street. pba Aug 8 (416) $325

LONGFELLOW, HENRY WADSWORTH. - Hyperion. L, 1853. Mor gilt with painting of Chatsworth; joints rubbed. pba Nov 30 (135) $170

LONGFELLOW, HENRY WADSWORTH. - The Poetical Works. L, 1853. 8vo, contemp mor gilt with painting of Richmond House. pba Sept 14 (166) $325

MARCUS AURELIUS ANTONINUS. - Meditations. L, 1926. ("To Himself.") 16mo, contemp mor by Sangorski & Sutcliffe with painting of an English landscape; front joint cracked. sg Feb 8 (128) $140

MATHIAS, THOMAS JAMES. - The Pursuits of Literature. A Satirical Poem.... L, 1801. 8vo, contemp mor gilt with double painting with ports of Plato, Virgil & Dante on one side & ports of Chaucer, Goethe & Voltaire on the other. sg Feb 8 (129) $800

MAVOR, WILLIAM FORDYCE. - The British Tourists.... L, 1800. 5 vols. 12mo, contemp mor gilt with paintings of views of Glasgow, Loch Katrine, Killarney Castle, Windermere & the Wye Valley. With engraved allegorical title in Vol I & 4 folding maps hand-colored in outline. sg Oct 19 (90) $1,200

MEROU, MARTIN GARCIA. - Poesias.... Buenos Aires, 1885. 8vo, lev gilt with painting of a scene at Fiji. Inscr. sg Feb 8 (130) $800

MILLER, E. - Scripture History.... L: Kelly, 1824. 3 vols in 1. 8vo, contemp calf gilt with painting done vertically of David slaying Goliath; rebacked. sg Feb 8 (131) $1,300

MILNE, ALAN ALEXANDER. - When We Were Very Young. L, [1928]. Contemp calf with Pooh characters in gilt on upper cover, with painting of the Pooh characters in a field. sg Feb 8 (132) $750

MILNER, JOSEPH. - The History of the Church of Christ. L, 1827. New Ed. 3 vols. 8vo, 19th-cent mor gilt, armorial bdg, with paintings of nautical sceens; 2 vols rebacked retaining backstrips. sg Sept 21 (191) $500

MILTON, JOHN. - Paradise Lost. L, 1808. 8vo, contemp mor gilt with painting of the Garden of Eden with Adam & Eve holding an inserted port bust of Milton. sg Feb 8 (133) $1,200

Anr Ed. L, 1817. 8vo, contemp mor gilt with split painting showing views of St. Paul's Cathedral from Bankside (left half) from Waterloo Bridge (top right quarter) & from Southwark Bridge (bottom right quarter). sg Sept 21 (193) $600

MILTON, JOHN. - Poetical Works. L, 1826. 3 vols. 8vo, contemp mor gilt with paintings of London scenes; bdgs worn. O Mar 5 (92) $375

Anr Ed. L, 1846. 8vo, orig lea gilt with paintings of exterior of St. Paul's School; rebacked retaining orig backstrip. sg Sept 21 (194) $325

Anr Ed. L, 1874. 2 vols. 16mo, contemp calf gilt with bust of Milton on upper covers & coat-of-arms on lower, with paintings of Cambridge with inset port of Milton & of Milton's cottage. sg Feb 8 (135) $425

Anr Ed. L, [c.1880]. 8vo, contemp mor with painting of a ferry crossing a river, after Rowlandson. sg Feb 8 (134) $450

MOORE, THOMAS. - Lalla Rookh. L, 1817. 8vo, mor with painting of a town on a river with people sitting on near bank. pba Sept 14 (167) $600

Anr copy. Contemp mor gilt with double painting, 1st side with inset port of Moore with harp & view of Tholsel; the reverse shows Chatsworth. sg Feb 8 (136) $2,200

Anr Ed. L, 1846. 8vo, mor gilt with painting of Bantry. pba Nov 30 (136) $275

MOORE, THOMAS. - Poetical Works. L, [c.1875]. 8vo, contemp mor with painting of an Irish castle scene. sg Feb 8 (137) $100

MORRISON, JOHN. - Family Prayers for Every Morning and Every Evening. L, [1837]. 4to, contemp embossed mor with painting of Boston harbor filled with boats flying the American flag. sg Feb 8 (138) $325

MOSES, HENRY. - A Collection of Vases.... L, [1814]. 8vo, contemp mor extra with painting of figures in the style of an Etruscan vase. sg Dec 7 (188) $650

NELSON, ROBERT. - The Great Duty of Frequenting the Christian Sacrifice. L, 1750. 12th Ed. 12mo, contemp mor gilt with painting of Salisbury. sg Sept 21 (189) $425

POUCHET, FELIX ARCHIMEDE. - The Universe; or the Infinitely Great and the Infinitely Little. L, [c.1900]. 8vo, mor gilt with painting of a herd of elephants. sg Feb 8 (141) $450

ROGERS, SAMUEL - Italy. A Poem. L, 1842. 8vo, contemp lea gilt, armorial bdg, with painting of the Aventine Hill in Rome; spine & extremities rubbed. sg Sept 21 (195) $325

ROGERS, SAMUEL. - Poems. L, 1834. 8vo, contemp mor gilt with painting of a castle flying the British flag as seen from a river. L.p. copy. sg Feb 8 (142) $1,100

Anr Ed. L, 1846. 12mo, orig mor gilt, with painting of 5 putti; joints & ends scuffed. wa Nov 16 (306) $210

RUSKIN, JOHN. - Frondes Agrestes. Readings in Modern Painters.... Orpington, 1876. 8vo, 19th-cent mor gilt with painting of Rhuddlan in Wales. sg Sept 21 (196) $325

SAXE, JOHN GODFREY. - Poems. Bost., 1873. 8vo, contemp blindstamped mor with painting of an American whaling ship & whales. sg Feb 8 (143) $650

SCOTT, SIR WALTER. - Marmion. L, 1808. 8vo, early vellum gilt with painting of Penhurst. sg Feb 8 (144) $140

SCOTT, SIR WALTER. - Poetical Works. L, 1862. 8vo, contemp calf gilt prize bdg stamped St. John's School. 1863, with painting of Elgin, Scotland. sg Feb 8 (146) $400

Anr Ed. L: Charles Daly, [c.1880]. 8vo, mor gilt with painting of ladies with umbrellas & a young man with topcoat & hat; painting rubbed. pba Mar 7 (113) $200

SCOTT, SIR WALTER. - Rokeby, a Poem. L, 1813. 8vo, contemp mor gilt with painting of Barnard Castle; extremities rubbed. sg Feb 8 (145) $300

SELLAR, W. Y. - The Roman Poets of the Augustan Age. Oxford, 1899. 8vo, contemp calf gilt with painting of the Roman amphitheater at Verona. sg Feb 8 (147) $175

SHAKESPEARE, WILLIAM. - The Oxford Shakespeare. L, 1913. 8vo, half calf with painting of a scene from Othello. sg Feb 8 (149) $500

SHAKESPEARE, WILLIAM. - The Songs of Shakespeare. L, 1872. 12mo, contemp mor gilt with painting of Shakespeare's birthplace; joints scuffed, corners worn. Some foxing. wa Nov 16 (304) $200

SHAKESPEARE, WILLIAM. - Works. L, 1821. 8vo, contemp calf gilt with painting of buildings & people with port of Shakespeare inset. sg Feb 8 (150) $1,200

Anr Ed. Phila., 1873. 8vo, orig mor gilt, with painting of Charleston harbor. sg Feb 8 (148) $500

SOUTHEY, ROBERT. - Thalaba the Destroyer. L, [c.1860]. 8vo, contemp mor gilt with painting of Derwentwater & Skiddaw. sg Feb 8 (151) $375

STANLEY, ARTHUR PENRHYN. - Lectures on the History of the Eastern Church.... L, 1869. 8vo, contemp lea gilt with painting of Canterbury; rebacked retaining backstrip. sg Sept 21 (197) $600

TENNYSON, ALFRED. - Idylls of the King. L, 1859. 8vo,

contemp mor gilt with painting of the castle at Knowle, with fox-hunting scene. sg Feb 8 (154) $700

Anr Ed. L, 1869. 8vo, contemp mor extra with painting of High Street in Oxford. sg Feb 8 (153) $500

TENNYSON, ALFRED. - In Memoriam. L, 1862. 8vo, mor with painting of Saffron Walden, Essex. pba Mar 7 (115) $300

Anr Ed. L, 1867. Mor gilt with painting of Cornwell Terrace. pba Aug 8 (417) $325

TENNYSON, ALFRED. - Locksley Hall Sixty Years After.... L, 1886. 8vo, mor with painting of Piccadilly Circus. pba Aug 8 (418) $325

TENNYSON, ALFRED. - Poems. L, 1865. 8vo, contemp mor with vertical painting of a girl by a church. sg Feb 8 (155) $500

TENNYSON, ALFRED. - The Princess: A Medley. L, 1860. 12mo, contemp mor gilt, armorial bdg with painting of London bridge scene. sg Feb 8 (156) $275

THACKERAY, WILLIAM MAKEPEACE. - The Four Georges.... L, 1862. 8vo, later lev with painting of Windsor Castle. sg Sept 21 (198) $700

THOMAS A KEMPIS. - De l'imitation de Jesus-Christ. Paris, 1820. 12mo, contemp mor gilt with painting of Blois. sg Feb 8 (126) $325

THOMSON, JAMES. - The Seasons and The Castle of Indulgence. L, 1830. 8vo, mor gilt with painting of Kylemore Abbey. pba Nov 30 (137) $250

TIGHE, MARY. - Psyche, with Other Poems. L, 1811. 3d Ed. 8vo, contemp mor. With port frontis. S Oct 27 (844) £200 [The Barn]

TODD, JOHN. - The Daughter at School. L, 1853. 8vo, contemp mor extra with painting of people dancing in front of an English Inn. sg Feb 8 (157) $300

TRENCH, RICHARD CHENEVIX. - Poems. L, 1899. 8vo, later mor gilt by Riviere, with painting of Burton Dasset Church. sg Feb 8 (158) $225

TUPPER, MARTIN FARQUHAR. - Proverbial Philosophy. L, 1854. 8vo, calf gilt with painting of Warrworth Castle, Northumberland. pba Mar 7 (116) $200

Anr Ed. L, 1855. 8vo, contemp blindstamped mor with painting of St. Paul's as seen from the Thames. sg Feb 8 (159) $375

TYTLER, ALEXANDER FRASER. - An Historical and Critical Essay on...Petrarch. Edin., 1810. 8vo, contemp mor gilt with painting of a city. sg Feb 8 (159A) $650

WHITE, HENRY KIRKE. - Poetical Works. L, 1853. 8vo, later mor by Edmonston & Douglas with painting of Canterbury Cathedral. sg Feb 8 (160) $275

WHITE, HENRY KIRKE. - The Poetical Works. L, 1857. 8vo, mor gilt with painting of Nottingham. O Mar 5 (93) $170

WORDSWORTH, WILLIAM. - Poetical Works. L, 1866. 12mo, orig mor gilt with painting of Penhurst. wa Nov 16 (307) $260

Anr Ed. L, 1895. 8vo, contemp mor with painting of a fox-hunting scene. sg Feb 8 (161) $700

YOUNG, EDWARD. - The Complaint: or, Night Thoughts.... L, 1822. 8vo, contemp mor extra with painting of a man aiming a rifle at a love-making couple. sg Feb 8 (162) $700

ZIMMERMANN, JOHANN GEORG. - Solitude considered with Respect to its Influence upon the Mind and the Heart.... L, 1798-99. 2 vols. 8vo, contemp mor, with paintings of the King's entance to the House of Lords & of Parliament House; spine ends & corners rubbed, Vol I rear cover discolored. sg Sept 21 (199) $800

**Foreest, Pieter Van, 1522-97**
— Observationum et curationum medicinalium.... Leiden: Plantin, 1596. 1st Ed. 8vo, contemp calf; rebacked. CE Nov 8 (90) $150

**Foreign...**
— Foreign Field Sports: Fisheries, Sporting Anecdotes.... L, 1814 [but 1818]. 4to, contemp mor gilt; extremities scuffed, later endpapers. With 110 colored plates. Inner margin of title torn; Plate 64 torn in half & repaired; some soiling throughout; lacking half-title. C May 31 (116) £1,000

1st Ed. L, 1814-13. 4to, modern half mor. With 110 hand-colored plates. S June 27 (261) £1,400

Anr Ed. L: Edward Orme [c.1823]. Folio, contemp mor; scuffed, hinges broken. With 110 colored plates. bbc June 24 (368) $4,000

**Fores's...**
— Fores's Sporting Notes & Sketches. L, 1885-1902. Vols 1-28, lacking Vol 26. 8vo, orig cloth; worn. O Jan 9 (104) $325

**Forest, Louis**
— Monseigneur le Vin. Paris, 1924-27. Illus by Charles Martin & others. 5 vols. 8vo, orig wraps; backstrips worn. With 7 mounted plates, 8 maps (3 folding, 3 color), & 5 folding plates. S Oct 12 (81) £160

Anr Ed. Paris, 1927. Illus by Charles Martin. 5 vols. 8vo, orig stiff wraps. pba Apr 4 (447) $325

**Forestier, J. C. N.**
— Gardens: A Note-book of Plans and Sketches. NY: Scribner's, 1924. Folio, cloth; spine ends worn. Owner's seal on tp. wa Dec 14 (488) $65

**Forkel, Johann Nicolaus, 1749-1818**
— Life of Johann Sebastian Bach. L, 1820. 8vo, orig bds; lacking rear free endpaper. pba Aug 22 (545) $150

**Forman, Henry Chandlee**
— The Virginia Eastern Shore.... Easton, [1975]. 4to, cloth, in dj with dampspots. wa Dec 14 (390) $140

**Forman, Samuel S.**
— Narrative of a Journey Down the Ohio and Mississippi in 1789-90. Cincinnati, 1888. 8vo, wraps. sg Oct 26 (112) $80

**Formey, Jean Henri Samuel**
— Conseils pour former une bibliotheque peu nombreuse, mais choisie. Berlin, 1756. Issue with xx, 352 pages. 8vo, contemp calf; rubbed. Some foxing & browning. O Mar 26 (101) $190

Issue with xxiv, 380, (4) pages. Contemp calf; rubbed, some lea gone from upper cover. O Mar 26 (100) $160

## FORMEY

— Entwurf aller Wissenschaften. Zum Gebrauche der Juenglinge.... Berlin, 1765-72. 8 vols in 5. 8vo, contemp calf, Vol VIII half calf; 2 covers wormed. Last vol wormed at end, affecting text. S Mar 14 (124) £220

### Forrest, Charles Ramus

— Viage pintoresco a las orillas de los rios Ganges y Jumna en la India oriental. L, 1827. 4to, 19th-cent half calf with later mor gilt lettering-piece & later endpapers. With 24 hand-colored plates. S Nov 30 (197) £1,300

### Forrest, Earle Robert

See also: Milner & Forrest
— Missions and Pueblos of the Old Southwest. Cleveland, 1929. 1st Ed, One of 100. 2 vols. Orig cloth. With 1 folding map. Robbins copy. pba Mar 21 (106) $650

### Forrest, John, 1847-1918

— Explorations in Australia. L, 1875. 8vo, modern half mor. With 4 folding maps & 8 ports & plates. S June 13 (657) £360

### Forrest, Capt. Thomas, 1729?-1802?

— A Voyage to New Guinea and the Moluccas.... Dublin, 1779. 1st Irish Ed. 8vo, contemp calf; rebacked. With folding map & 3 plates. Some discoloration. S Mar 28 (390) £260

1st Ed. L, 1779. 4to, 19th-cent half calf; rubbed. With port & 31 plates & maps. Some browning. S Mar 28 (389) £1,000

### Forrester, Alfred Henry, 1804-72

— Phantasmagoria of Fun. L, 1843. 1st Ed. 2 vols. 8vo, modern half lev, orig cloth backstrips bound in. Tp versos stamped. sg Sept 21 (200) $90

### Forrester, Alfred Henry, 1804-72 & Charles Robert, 1803-50

— The Pictorial Grammar. L, [1842]. 8vo, orig cloth; spine ends rubbed, front cover with spot. pba Dec 14 (33) $70

### Forrester, Alfred Henry, 1804-72 & Charles Robert, 1803-50

### Forrester, Robert, 1803-50. See: Kosewitz, W. F. von

### Forsius, S. A.

— Een beraettelse, och eenfallight judicium.... Stockholm: Anund Olufsson, 1615. 4to, modern bds. Some staining; browned; margins framed at ends. S June 12 (301) £230

### Forster, Edward

— Prospectus of the British Gallery of Engravings.... L, 1807. Folio, contemp half mor; rubbed. With 52 plates. b Sept 20 (523) £300

Anr copy. Half calf; rubbed, upper hinge loose. With 48 plates. Some foxing. wad Oct 18 (271) C$500

### Forster, Edward Morgan, 1879-1970

— Battersea Rise. NY: Harcourt Brace, [1955]. Sgd & with 1 textual correction by Forster. bbc Feb 26 (295) $280
— The Eternal Moment and other Stories. NY, [1928]. Sgd on tp. wa Feb 29 (34) $90
— Howard's End. NY, 1921. In chipped dj with flaps reattached with tape. pba May 23 (125) $225
— A Passage to India. L, 1924. 1st Ed. Orig cloth; extremities rubbed. sg June 20 (119) $150

2d impression. Cloth; rubbed. With 3 typed pages of Author's notes & an introduction for the Everyman Ed, sgd in type. sg Dec 14 (106) $1,600

1st American Ed. NY, [1924]. pba Aug 22 (170) $50

### Forster, Georg, 1754-94

— A Voyage Round the World.... L, 1777. 2 vols. 4to, contemp calf; rebacked with modern calf. With folding chart. Blindstamps to titles; ink number to bottom of 1st tp. pba Feb 13 (78) $1,600

### Forster, Johann Reinhold, 1729-98

— Observations Made during a Voyage Round the World.... L, 1778. 1st Ed. 4to, contemp vellum; rubbed & soiled. With 2 folding plates of the same chart, 1 on thinner paper & with 2 tables. Corners of last 5 leaves gnawed off, not affecting text. Bradley Martin copy. pba Feb 13 (79) $2,000

Anr copy. Contemp calf; rebacked with modern calf, endpapers & flyleaves discolored. With folding chart & 2 tables. Foxing to chart. pba Feb 13 (80) $1,000

### Forster, John

— Englands Happiness Increased, or a Sure and Easy Remedy.... L: A. Seile, 1664. 19th-cent vellum gilt. S Mar 29 (757) £460

### Forster, John, 1812-76

— The Life of Charles Dickens. L, 1872-74. 3 vols. 8vo, calf gilt by Sangorski & Sutcliffe. sg Sept 21 (17) $1,300

### Forsyth, George A.

— The Story of the Soldier. NY, 1900. Illus by Rufus Zogbaum. Orig cloth; spine ends rubbed. Owner's stamps. pba June 25 (90) $85

### Forsyth, Robert, 1766-1846

— The Beauties of Scotland. Edin., 1805-8. Vols I-II (of 5). 8vo, contemp calf; needs rebdg. sg Mar 7 (331) $100

### Forsyth, William, 1737-1804

— A Treatise on the Culture and Management of Fruit-Trees. L, 1802. 1st Ed. 4to, contemp half calf; rubbed. With 13 folding plates. With ALs of William North about a hothouse for vines. S Mar 29 (758) £180

### Forsythe, Lieut. James

— The Sporting Rifle and its Projectiles. L, 1863. 8vo, orig cloth; worn. With 3 plates, 2 folding. O Oct 10 (135) $190

### Fort, Paul, 1872-1960
— Le Livre des ballades. Paris: H. Piazza, [1921]. One of 1,300. Illus by Arthur Rackham. 4to, pictorial wraps; worn, spine chipped. Soiling & marginal stains. O Mar 5 (94) $100

### Fortescue, Sir John William, 1858-1933. See: Gregynog Press

### Fortsas...
— The Fortsas Catalogue. North Hills: Bird & Bull Press, 1970. One of 225. 4to, half cloth; some wear. F June 20 (165G) $80

### Fortune, Robert, 1813-80
— A Journey to the Tea Countries of China.... L, 1852. 8vo, cloth. With additional title, 3 plates & 2 tinted lithos. b Sept 20 (417) £300
— A Residence among the Chinese. L, 1857. 8vo, orig cloth; rubbed. b Sept 20 (418) £280; b May 30 (151) £130
— Two Visits to the Tea Countries of China and the British Tea Plantations.... L, 1853. 3d Ed. 2 vols. 8vo, orig cloth; worn. b Sept 20 (336) £200

### Foscolo, Ugo, 1778-1827
— Dei sepolcri. Montagnola: Bodoni, Nov 1924. One of 225. Folio, orig cloth. Ck May 31 (7) £480

### Fossati, Gaspard, 1809-83
— Aya Sophia, Constantinople, as Recently Restored.... L, [1852]. Folio, contemp half mor. With chromolitho title & 25 tinted litho plates. Each plate trimmed to image & mtd; some repairs to text leaves. b May 30 (264) £5,000

### Fossati, Giorgio
— Memorie della vita del glorioso patriarca San Giuseppe. Venice, 1750. Folio, contemp bds backed with marbled paper. With engraved title, frontis & 19 plates, ptd in various shades of red, brown, sepia, green & black. C Apr 3 (99) £5,000

### Fosse, Charles Louis Francois
— Idees d'un militaire pour la disposition des troupes.... Paris, 1783. Illus by L. M. Bonnet. 4to, later vellum gilt. With 11 color plates. P Dec 12 (82) $1,400

### Fossett, Frank
— Colorado: its Gold and Silver Mines, Farms, and Stock Ranges.... NY, 1879. 12mo, orig cloth; rebacked with orig spine laid on, worn, new endpapers. pba Apr 25 (411) $80
2d Ed. NY, 1880. 12mo, orig cloth; spine head bumped. A few leaves dog-eared. pba Aug 8 (58) $50

### Foster, Andrew. See: Lester & Foster

### Foster, George G., d.1850
— The Gold Regions of California. NY, 1848. 2d Issue. 8vo, modern cloth & bds. With frontis map. Margins chipped. Larson copy. pba Sept 28 (456) $400

### Foster, S. Conant
— Wheel Songs. Poems of Bicycling. NY, 1884. 4to, orig pictorial cloth; soiled, corners & spine ends worn. Some foxing. wa Feb 29 (141) $85

### Foster, Stephen Collins, 1826-64
— Foster Hall Reproductions. Songs, Compositions and Arrangements by.... Indianapolis, 1933. 3 vols. 4to, loose in portfolios set in 3-shelf metal case; rubbed. Facsimile reproductions of c.225 pieces of sheet music. Some library stamps. pba Aug 22 (579) $350

### Fotografie...
— Fotografie 1928-58. Prague, 1959. Intro by Josef Kainar. 4to, pictorial cloth portfolio; bumped. With 20 photographs. sg Feb 29 (134) $800

### Foucault, Leon
— Demonstration physique du mouvement de rotation de la terre au moyen du pendule. Paris, 1851. 4to, orig wraps; backstrip gone, chipped. In: Comptes rendus hebdomadaires des Seances de l'Academie des Sciences, Vol XXXII, No 5. sg May 16 (165) $600

### Fougasses, Thomas de
— The General Historie of the Magnificent State of Venice.... L, 1612. 1st English Ed. 2 vols in 1. Folio, contemp calf; repaired. With title view & 90 ports. Some rust-holes & natural paper flaws, affecting letters; some repairs & soiling. S Oct 26 (52) £1,800 [Knohl]

### Foulis, Henry, 1638-69
— The History of Romish Treasons & Usurpations. L, 1671. Folio, contemp sheep; extremities worn, rebacked, covers detached. sg Mar 21 (134) $175

### Fouque, Victor
— The Truth Concerning the Invention of Photography, Nicephore Niepce.... NY, 1935. Cloth; endpapers dampstained. sg Feb 29 (224) $225

### Four...
— Four Fictions. Kentfield, CA: Allen Press, 1973. One of 137. Folio, bds. pba Mar 7 (7) $375; sg Sept 14 (8) $250

### Fournier, Francois Ignace
— Nouveau Dictionnaire portatif de bibliographie. Paris, 1809. 8vo, contemp bds. Minor foxing. O Mar 26 (102) $120

### Fournier, Pierre Simon, 1712-68
— Fournier on Typefounding. The Text of the Manuel Typographique. L, 1930. One of 260. bba May 9 (32) £55 [Collinge & Clark]
— Manuel typographique, utile aux gens de lettres. Paris, 1764-66. 2 vols. 8vo, contemp calf; 1 spine head worn. With 2 frontises & 13 plates in Vol I. Fuerstenberg - Schaefer copy. S Dec 7 (235) £1,500

### Fourquevaux, Raimond de Beccarie de Pavie, Baron de. See: Du Bellay, Guillaume

## Fowler, Gene
— Beau James. The Life and Times of Jimmy Walker. NY, 1949. Final proof of folded & gathered sheets. In proof dj. Holograph note stating that this is 1 of 2 sets, sgd & dated Apr 1949. cb Oct 17 (392) $300
— Timber Line: A Story of Bonfils and Tammen. NY, 1933. One of 99. Inscr to Rowland Brown & with 42-line Ls. pba May 23 (127) $50

## Fowler, Harlan D.
— Three Caravans to Yuma. Glendale: Arthur H. Clark, 1980. One of 750. pba Apr 25 (413) $50

## Fowler, Laurence Hall —& Baer, Elizabeth
— The Fowler Architectural Collection of the Johns Hopkins University: Catalogue. Balt., 1961. One of a few copies with Fowler's name spelled Lawrence. 4to, orig cloth. With cancel title tipped in. bbc Feb 26 (141) $100
Anr Ed. San Francisco, 1991. 4to, orig cloth in dj. sg Apr 11 (107) $80

## Fowles, John
— The Collector. Bost., [1963]. 1st American Ed. In rubbed dj. sg Dec 14 (107) $100
Anr Ed. L, [1963]. Bds in dj. Some lower edges spotted. pba Jan 25 (99) $325
Anr copy. In dj. pba May 4 (139) $350
— Daniel Martin. L, 1977. In dj. Inscr, 1981. b Jan 31 (162) £75
— The French Lieutenant's Woman. Bost., [1969]. In dj. Sgd on front free endpaper. pba Aug 22 (173) $110
Anr Ed. L, 1969. Advance proof copy. Orig wraps, in dj. b Jan 31 (163) £90

## Fowles, John —& Pinter, Harold
— The French Lieutenant's Woman: A Screenplay. Bost., 1981. One of 360. sg Dec 14 (111) $110

## Fox, Charles K.
— Rising Trout. Carlisle, [1967]. Ltd Ed. In worn dj. O Feb 6 (92) $90; O June 25 (126) $110
— This Wonderful World of Trout. Carlisle, [1963]. In frayed dj. Sgd. O June 25 (127) $60
Anr Ed. Rockville Centre, [1971]. One of 350. Syn gilt. O Feb 6 (93) $100

## Fox, George, 1624-91
— The Great Mystery of the Great Whore Unfolded.... L, 1659. Bound with: Fox & others. A Battle-Door for Teachers & Professors to Learn Singular & Plural.... L, 1660. And with 10 broadsides about Quakers: Wing C6816, F1871B, R1494, B6041, M1447, H3233, S128, S4080, F1888A. Folio, old calf; broken, covers detached, worn & scuffed. Tp soiled & chipped; some short tears 7 foxing. bbc June 24 (224) $2,900
— A Journal, or Historical Account of the Life, Travels.... L, 1765. 3d Ed. Folio, contemp calf; worn, joints cracked. sg Mar 21 (135) $150

## Fox, George Henry
— Photographic Illustrations of Skin Diseases. NY, 1887. 4to, contemp half lea gilt; joints cracked. With 48 plates by Edward Bierstadt. sg May 16 (414) $100

## Fox, Gustavus Vasa
— Confidential Correspondence of Gustavus Vasa Fox. NY: Naval History Society, 1918. One of 1,200. Ed by Robert Thompson & Richard Wainwright. Half vellum. wa Feb 1 (89) $70

## Fox, John William, 1863-1919
— The Little Shepherd of Kingdom Come. NY, 1931. One of 500. Illus by N. C. Wyeth. 4to, half pigskin. sg Sept 14 (344) $1,200
Anr copy. Half vellum. sg Feb 15 (315) $750

## Fox, Joseph
— The Natural History and Diseases of the Human Teeth. Phila., 1846. 4to, orig sheep; broken, spine worn. With 30 plates. sg May 16 (415) $140

## Foxe, John, 1516-87
— Book of Martyrs. L: John Day, 1570. 2 vols. Folio, later half calf; worn, 3 covers detached. Vol I lacking d3-4 & s1; margins frayed or cropped affecting text; Vol II lacking all before T1, CCc1-MMm1 & DDD1-OOO1; 6 leaves def; some worming. Sold w.a.f. bba May 30 (72) £300 [Lachman]
Anr Ed. L, 1776. ("The Book of Martyrs....") Folio, 19th-cent calf; rebacked with cloth, some defs to surface of covers. Tear in pp 75-80 affecting text; lacking plate of The Burning of Rose Allin but with plate of deaths of John Wycliffe & George Scherter not called for. sg Mar 21 (136) $350

## Foxhound...
— The Foxhound Kennel Stud Book. L, 1886-1948. Vols 3-34. 8vo,. half lea various defs. Sold w.a.f. O Jan 9 (105) $300

## Foxon, D. F.
— English Verse 1701-1750. Cambr., 1975. 2 vols. 4to, cloth, in djs. bba May 9 (85) £120 [Bedford]

## Foyer, Archibald
— Scotland's Present Duty.... Edin., 1700. 4to, 19th-cent sheep; needs rebacked. Tp soiled, with early crude decorations in ink. sg Mar 21 (137) £110

## Fracassini, Antonio, 1709-77
— Naturae morbi hypochondriaci ejusque curationis mechanica investigatio. Verona, 1756. 1st Ed. 8vo, contemp bds. With frontis port & title vignette. Frontis torn; hole in title; A8 lower corner torn away. Ck Mar 22 (123) £180

## Fraccus, Ambrosius Novidius
— Sacrorum fastorum libri XII. Rome: Ant. Bladus Asulanus, 1547. 4to, contemp mor by Maestro Luigi, panelled in silver & blind; spine & corners repaired. C Apr 3 (100) £800

**Franc, Martin**
— Le Champion des dames. [Lyon: Ptr of the Champion des dames (Jean du Pre), before 20 May 1488]. Folio, 19th-cent mor janseniste. 36 leaves; double column; type 1:119B. With full-page woodcut, page-width presentation woodcut & 61 column-width woodcuts. Some soiling; minor marginal repairs; word on a5r overwritten. 186 leaves. Goff F-277. Schaefer copy. P Nov 1 (88) $50,000

**Francais...**
— Les Francais peints par eux-memes. Paris, 1840-42. 9 vols. 8vo, half mor by David, orig wraps bound in. Lacking the additional plate to Gavarni's Maitre d'etude. S Nov 21 (149) £2,200

**France**
— Constitution de la Republique Francaise.... Paris: Chez David, [c.1800]. Illus by F. A. David. 4to, contemp mor gilt. With 7 plates. Stain to 1st plate. pba Aug 22 (573) $75
— Constitution Francaise. Nancy: widow of Leclerc & Bontoux, [1791]. 12mo, contemp inlaid Revolutionary bdg by Dufey fils of mor gilt; hinges rubbed. C May 1 (58) £2,000
— De Franse Merkurius, vertoonende Alle de Steden.... Amst.: Jacob van Meurs, 1679. Oblong 4to, contemp calf; needs rebacked. Lacking frontis & numerous leaves with illusts. Sold w.a.f. sg May 9 (345) $650

**France, Anatole, 1844-1924**
See also: Limited Editions Club
— Memoires d'un Volontaire. Paris, 1902. One of 20 with etchings in 3 states & orig watercolor bound in. Illus by Xavier Lesueur after Adrien Moreau. 8vo, lev extra by Rene Kieffer, orig wraps bound in. pba Nov 30 (35) $600
— La Rotisserie de la Reine Pedauque. Paris, 1911. One of 34 for M & Mme Rene Helleu, with orig drawing, additional suite of the illusts on chine & separations for those in color. Illus by Auguste Leroux. 4to, mor extra by Marius Michel, orig wraps bound in. Limitation statement leaf loose. S Nov 21 (152) £6,000
— Works. NY, 1924. Autograph Ed, one of 1,075. 30 vols. Half mor. cb Oct 17 (270) $1,800
Anr copy. Half cloth, in djs (a few with stains). pba Aug 8 (421) $65

**Franchere, Gabriel, 1786-1863**
— Narrative of a Voyage to the Northwest Coast of America.... NY, 1854. 1st American Ed. 8vo, cloth. With 3 plates. Met May 22 (344) $210

**Francis, Austin M.**
— Catskill Rivers. Birthplace of American Fly Fishing. NY: Beaverskill Press, 1983. Out-of-series copy, unsgd. 4to, mor; minor wear. O Feb 6 (94) $300

**Francis, Dick**
— Blood Sport. NY, 1967. 1st American Ed. In soiled dj. wa Dec 14 (37) $95
— Flying Finish. L: Michael Joseph, [1966]. In rubbed dj. pba Aug 22 (174) $120
— Knock Down. NY, [1974]. 1st American Ed. In dj; blindstamp to lower rear joint. Inscr. pba Aug 22 (175) $50

**Francis, Francis**
— A Book on Angling: a Complete Treatise.... L, 1867. 1st Ed. 8vo, orig cloth; loose. O Feb 6 (95) $450
Anr copy. Later cloth; worn. Some soiling & foxing. O June 25 (131) $375
2d Ed. 8vo, cloth; shaken, front endpaper missing. Some foxing & soiling. O Feb 6 (96) $110
5th Ed. L, 1880. 8vo, orig cloth; 1 signature detached, front hinge starting. With 17 plates, 6 of them hand-colored. pba July 11 (104) $200
— The Practical Management of Fisheries. L, 1883. 1st Ed. 8vo, orig cloth. pba July 11 (106) $50

**Francis I, King of France**
— Coppia della risposta che fa il... Re di Francia alle parole dalla... Maesta Cesarea alla presentia... di... Paulo.... Bologna: Giovanni Battista di Phaelli, [1536]. 4to, 19th-cent cloth; spine worn. Hole in tp; A2-3 becoming loose; some waterstains. C June 26 (76) £600

**Francis, John**
— Annals, Anecdotes and Legends: A Chronicle of Life Assurance. L, 1853. 1st Ed. 8vo, orig cloth. S Apr 23 (284) £130

**Francis of Assisi, Saint, 1182-1226**
See also: Ashendene Press
— Petites fleurs. Paris, 1913. One of 120. Illus by Maurice Denis. 4to, mor extra by L. Leveque, orig wraps bound in. A few short tears at lower edge. S Nov 21 (151) £2,000

**Franciscus de Mayronis, c.1285-after 1328**
— Super primo libro sententiarum. Basel: Nicolaus Kesler, 15 Oct 1489. Folio, contemp blind-stamped pigskin over wooden bds; wormed, 2 clasps renewed, lacking metal fittings, partly misbound. 55 lines & headline; gothic letter; initials supplied in red. Stamp washed from lower margin of a2; some letters rubbed in 1st heading; wormholes at ends, affecting text. 226 leaves. Goff M-90. S June 27 (342) £500

**Franck, Richard**
— Northern Memoirs.... Edin., 1821. Ltd Ed. Preface & notes by Sir Walter Scott. 8vo, orig bds; spine perished, needs rebdg. M. G. Watkins' copy. pba July 11 (107) $95

**Franco, Giacomo**
— Habiti d'huomini et donne venetiane.... [Venice, c.1610]. Bound with, Doglioni, Giovanni Nicolo. La Citta di Venetia con l'origine e governo di quella.... Venice: A. Turini, 1614. Folio, modern calf gilt. Part 1 with engraved title, map & 25 plates; Part 2 with map & 15 plates, 2 of them double-page. Some staining; a few plates just shaved. C June 26 (74) £8,800

### Franco, Nicolo
— Le Postole vulgari. Venice: Antonio Gardane, 20 Apr 1539. 8vo, 19th-cent half calf. Tp wormed, affecting border; worming to last 3 leaves, affecting letters. C Apr 3 (101) £1,000

### Franco-British Exhibition
— Souvenir of the Fine Art Section Franco-British Exhibition 1908. L, 1908. 4to, cloth; extremities rubbed. sg Jan 11 (179) $110

### Francois de Neufchateau, Nicolas Louis, comte, 1752-1828
— Anthologie morale, ou choix de quatrains et de distiques.... Paris, 1784. 12mo, contemp mor gilt with arms of the Dauphin (the dedicatee). Fuerstenberg - Schaefer copy. S Dec 7 (236) £320

### Frank, Ann, 1929-45
— Diary of a Young Girl: Het Achterhuis. West Hatfield MA: Pennyroyal Press, [1985]. One of 350. Illus by Joseph Goldyne. 4to, mor; some discoloration. sg Feb 15 (227) $900

Out-of-series copy with extra suite. Mor, suite in half mor portfolio. CE Sept 27 (220) $650

### Frank Leslie's...
— Frank Leslie's Illustrated Newspaper. NY, 1865. Vol XIX, Nos 484-535, lacking No 500. Folio, contemp half sheep; worn & broken, loose. Sold w.a.f. bbc Feb 26 (292) $240

— Frank Leslie's Illustrations. The American Soldier in the Civil War. NY, [1895]. Folio, orig cloth; shaken. Some soiling & tears. Clipped signature of Henry E. Seiders on front pastedown. pba June 13 (257) $170

### Frank, Robert
— Les Americains. Paris, 1958. Texts by Alain Bosquet. Pictorial bds; soiled, joints cracked, corners bumped, some leaves detached, endpaper foxed. sg Apr 24 (591) $1,000

— The Americans. NY, 1969. Photo-pictorial stiff wraps; rubbed & soiled. Thumbed; 1 plate with printing def; foxed. sg Feb 29 (135) $80

Anr Ed. NY, [1978]. In soiled dj; front free endpaper creased, as is half-title. sg Feb 29 (136) $100

— The Lines of My Hand. [Tokyo, 1972]. 4to, pictorial wraps; extremities worn. sg Feb 29 (137) $250

### Frankau, Julia, 1864-1916
— An Eighteenth Century Artist and Engraver, John Raphael Smith.... L, 1902. Folio, lev extra by Morrell. With 30 photogravure plates. pba Nov 30 (34) $225

Anr copy. 2 vols. 8vo & folio, contemp mor gilt. With 79 plates. S June 12 (320) £1,100

### Frankfurter, Felix, 1882-1965
— The Case of Sacco and Vanzetti. Bost., 1927. In repaired dj. sg June 20 (122) $140

### Frankl, Paul Theodore
— Form and Re-Form. A Practical Handbook of Modern Interiors. NY, 1930. Cloth; shaken, spine rubbed. sg June 13 (192) $150

### Frankland, Charles Colville
— Travels To and From Constantinople. L, 1830. 2d Ed. 2 vols. 8vo, contemp mor. With 31 plates, including 2 hand-colored frontises. Minor tears to 2 plates. S June 13 (593) £550

### Franklin, Alfred
— Les Anciens Bibliotheques de Paris. Paris, 1867-73. 3 vols. Folio, orig bds; worn & repaired. O Mar 26 (103) $350

— Les Sources de l'Histoire de France. Paris, 1877. 8vo, half lea, orig wraps bound in; rubbed. O Mar 26 (104) $160

### Franklin, Benjamin, 1706-90
See also: Limited Editions Club

— Autobiography. L, 1793. ("The Private Life of the Late...."). 1st Ed in English. 8vo, contemp half calf with vellum corners; spine ends worn, rubbed. CE Feb 21 (102) $700

— Briefe von der Elektricitat. Leipzig: for Gottfied Keisewetter, 1758. 8vo, later calf; rubbed. Some browning; tp stamped. S Mar 14 (127) £400

— The Examination of Doctor Benjamin Franklin...relating to the Repeal of the Stamp-Act. [Phila.: Hall & Sellers, 1766]. 1st Ed. 8vo, 19th-cent half cloth. Some foxing. P June 5 (20) $4,750

— Experiments and Observations on Electricity. L, 1751-53. 1st Ed. 3 parts in 1 vol. Bound with: Colden, Cadwallader. The Principles of Action in Matter.... L, 1751. And: The Pancronometer, or Universal Georgian Calendar. L, 1753. Old calf; corners eroded, edges rubbed, rebacked. K Oct 1 (189) $42,000

4th Ed. L, 1769. 4to, half mor; rubbed. With 7 plates. cb Oct 17 (154) $2,000

Anr copy. Later calf; joints repaired. With 7 plates. B4 torn; 2 plates with margins cropped, others cut close; some staining at beginning. CE Feb 21 (100) $2,200

Anr copy. Contemp calf; rebacked, worn. Wormed throughout, affecting text & plates. CE June 12 (199) $1,000

— An Historical Review of the Constitution...of Pennsylvania from its Origin. L, 1759. 1st Ed. 8vo, early calf; extremities worn. Owner's name excised from upper margin of tp. sg Oct 26 (295) $375

— Kleine Schriften. Weimar, 1802. 2 parts in 1 vol. 8vo, contemp half calf. S Mar 14 (126) £320

— Memoires de la vie privee.... Paris, 1791. 1st Ed. 2 parts in 1 vol. 8vo, contemp bds; spine lacking, edges worn. Library markings. CE Feb 21 (101) $850

— New Experiments and Observations on Electricity. L, 1754. 2d Ed of Parts 1-2; 1st Ed of Part 3. 3 parts in 1 vol. 4to, half cloth; worn & stained. Some soiling at ends; old library stamp on titles; contemp notes in margins; plate reinforced on verso. cb Feb 14 (2589) $4,500

— The Way to Wealth.... [L: J. Johnson, 1779 or 1780]. Single sheet, 422mm by 292mm. Mtd. Backed, closing a few tears & holes; browned. P June 5 (38) $4,000

— The Way to Wealth, or Poor Richard Improved.... [L, 1774]. ("The Way to Wealth, As Clearly Shewn in the Preface of an old Pennsylvania Almanack, Intitled, Poor Richard Improved.") Later calf; hinge cracked. pba June 13 (264) $850

— Works. Charlestown MA: John Lamson, 1798. 16mo, contemp sheep; worn. Lacking port. F June 20 (105) $60

Anr Ed. L, 1799. 2 vols. 8vo, half lev by Sangorski & Sutcliffe. pba Nov 30 (138) $200

**Franklin Printing, Benjamin**

— The Psalms of David.... Phila., 1740. 8vo, orig calf; becoming disbound. Some soiling; brittle. Met Feb 24 (385) $3,000

BARCLAY, ROBERT. - The Anarchy of the Ranters, and other Libertines.... Phila., 1757. 8vo, contemp sheep; covers refurbished, wormhole in spine. Some soiling & marginal dampstains; 1 marginal tear. pba June 13 (265) $375

CICERO, MARCUS TULLIUS. - Cato Major. Phila., 1744. 1st Ed, 2d State, with "only" on p.27. 8vo, later half sheep. Tp laid down with loss; 1 leaf repaired. cb Oct 17 (155) $1,700

HALL, DAVID. - A Mite into the Treasury.... Phila., 1758. 8vo, later half mor; extremities rubbed. Top margin short touching numerals; tp frayed; D7-8 lacking corner with loss, the latter tattered at outside margin. Z June 28 (91) $200

**Franklin, Colin**

— The Ashendene Press. Dallas, 1986. One of 750. 4to, half cloth. sg Sept 14 (135) $60; sg Feb 15 (11) $80

— Themes in Aquatint. San Francisco: Book Club of Calif., 1978. One of 500. pba Mar 7 (117) $70

**Franklin, Sir John, 1786-1847**

— Narrative of a Journey to the Shores of the Polar Sea.... L, 1823. 1st Ed. 4to, contemp half mor; rubbedted. With 4 maps & 30 plates, 11 of them handcolored. S June 13 (391) £680

Anr Ed. L, 1829. ("Journey to the Shores of the Polar Sea...with a Brief Account of the Second Journey....") 4 vols. 12mo, contemp calf. With folding map & 23 plates. S Apr 23 (351) £120

**Franzke, Andreas**

— Dubuffet. NY, [1981]. Oblong 4to, cloth, in dj. sg Jan 11 (145) $100

**Frasca, Albert —& Hill, Robert**

— The .45-70 Springfield. Northridge, 1980. One of 1,000. 4to, syn. sg Mar 7 (447) $100

**Frasconi, Antonio**

— Birds from my Homeland. [NY], 1958. Artist's copy. Oblong folio, bds; rubbed, dent to spine. bba May 9 (369) £130 [Collinge & Clark]

**Fraser, James, 1713-54**

— The History of Nadir Shah.... L, 1742. 2d Ed. 8vo, contemp calf; front cover loose. Library stamp on tp. sg Mar 7 (78) $110

**Fraser, James Baillie, 1783-1856**

— The Dark Falcon. L, 1844. 4 vols. 8vo, contemp half sheep; needs rebacked. sg Mar 7 (80) $600

**Fraser, Sir William, 1816-98**

— The Book of Carlaverock. Edin., 1873. One of 150. 2 vols. 4to, cloth. pnE Sept 20 (126) £260

**Fraunhofer, Joseph von**

— Bestimmung des brechungs- und farbenzerstreuungs-vermoegens verschiedener Glasarten.... Munich, [1817]. 4to, 19th-cent half calf; rubbed. With 2 other papers bound in. Madsen copy. S Mar 14 (129) £2,100

**Frazer, Sir James George, 1854-1941**

See also: Limited Editions Club

— The Golden Bough. L, 1922. 12 vols. Lev gilt by Harcourt Bindery; 1 raised band broken. pba Nov 30 (139) $550

Anr Ed. NY, 1935. 12 vols. Orig cloth; worn & soiled. Part 7 suplied from L, 1913, Ed. F Mar 28 (315) $130

**Frederick, Sir Charles**

— Foxhunting. L, 1930. One of—375. With sgd colored frontis by Lionel Edwards. O Jan 9 (114) $150

**Frederick, James Vincent**

— Ben Holladay: the Stagecoach King. Glendale, Calif., 1940. 1st Ed. Orig cloth. With 1 folding map. Robbins copy. pba Mar 21 (107) $160

**Frederickson, A. D.**

— Ad Orientem. L, 1889. 8vo, orig cloth; corners bumped. With colored frontis, folding map, facsimile & 24 plates. F June 20 (559) $70

**Frederik III, King of Denmark, 1609-70**

— Lex regia det er: Den Souveraine Konge lov.... Copenhagen, 1709. Folio, contemp mor gilt Danish royal presentation bdg by Johann Boppenhausen. With 2 engraved titles & calligraphic port. With 16 leaves of engraved text, each within elaborate engraved borders. Some tears repaired without loss; a few leaves with marginal soiling. Abbey - Schaefer copy. P Nov 1 (143) $6,500

Anr copy. Contemp mor gilt Danish royal presentation bdg by Johann Boppenhausen; later endpapers. With engraved title & 18 plates, including a 2d engraved title & an equestrian calligraphic port. Some staining throughout touching surface; marginal tears; tp soiled. S June 27 (321) £1,600

**Freeman, Archibald.** See: Fite & Freeman

## FREEMAN

**Freeman, Don**
— Don Freeman's Newsstand: A Journal of One Man's Manhattan. NY, 1941. Vol I, Nos 1-4. 4to, orig wraps. sg Sept 7 (154) $225

**Freeman, Douglas Southall, 1886-1953**
— George Washington: a Biography. NY, 1948-54. 6 vols. wa Feb 1 (127) $130
— Lee's Lieutenants; a Study in Command. NY, 1942-44. 3 vols. In worn djs. Inscr. wa Feb 29 (342) $160

**Freeman, Edward Augustus.** See: Jones & Freeman

**Freeman, Richard Austin, 1862-1943**
— Death at the Inn. NY, 1937. 1st American Ed. In rubbed dj. sg Dec 14 (51) $150
— The Mystery of 31, New Inn. NY, 1937. 1st American Ed. In dj with spine wear. sg Dec 14 (52) $110

**Freeman, Strickland**
— The Art of Horsemanship Altered and Abbreviated.... L, 1806. 4to, 19th-cent half calf. With 16 plates. S Apr 23 (285) £240

**Freen, Henry, Pseud.**
— Nothing. L, 1950. In dj. F Mar 28 (385) $50

**Freer Gallery of Art—Washington**
— A Descriptive and Illustrative Catalogue of Chinese Bronzes.... 1946. Ed by A. G. Wenley. Folio, orig cloth. sg Sept 7 (155) $80

**Freire de Andrade, Jacinto, 1597-1657**
— The Life of Dom John de Castro, the Fourth Vice-Roy of India. L, 1664. 1st Ed in English. Folio, early half sheep; needs rebdg. With 2 plates. Lacking port frontis; double-page plate chipped at edges; several leaves including tp with tears; library stamps. sg Mar 7 (81) $250

**Freire, Francisco de Brito**
— Nova Lusitania, historia da guerra Brasilica. Lisbon, 1675. 2 parts in 1 vol. Folio, contemp calf. Minor waterstaining & discoloration; slight worming at end; last leaf damaged near inner margin. S Nov 30 (156) £1,000

**Freman, G.** See: Kip & Freman

**Fremont, Jessie Benton, 1824-1902**
— Mother Lode Narratives. Ashland: Lewis Osborn, 1970. One of 650. Ed by Shirley Sargent. In dj. Inscr by Sargent. pba Feb 12 (149) $90

**Fremont, John Charles, 1813-90**
— Geographical Memoir upon Upper California.... Wash., 1848. 1st Ed. 8vo, modern half mor. With 1 folding map. Map stub-torn, tp darkened. Robbins copy. pba Mar 21 (108) $900
— Memoirs of My Life. Chicago, 1887. 1st Ed in Book form. Vol I (all pbd). 8vo, orig mor; spine faded. Robbins copy. pba Mar 21 (109) $1,000
— Report of the Exploring Expedition to the Rocky Mountains.... Wash., 1845. 1st Ed, House Issue. 8vo, orig mor gilt presentation bdg. Lacking folding map. pba Nov 16 (108) $250
Anr copy. Contemp half calf; spine rubbed & chipped. With 22 tinted litho plates & 4 maps, 2 of them folding. sg Oct 26 (115) $350
Senate Issue. Orig cloth; minor shelf wear. With 22 plates & 5 maps (3 folding). Dampstained, darkened & foxed. Robbins copy. pba Mar 21 (110) $850
Anr copy. Orig cloth; worn, spotting & staining, endpapers foxed. With 23 plates & 2 maps, lacking that in pocket. Foxed. wa Nov 16 (117) $150
Anr copy. Orig cloth; edge wear. With 22 plates & 5 maps, including large folding map in rear pocket. Some spotting; large map with some fold tears. wa Feb 29 (375) $700

**Fremont, John Charles, 1813-90 —& Emory, William H.**
— Notes of Travel in California. NY, 1849. Contemp half bds; corners bumped. With frontis map. Slight darkening. Larson copy. pba Sept 28 (458) $140

**French, John, 1616?-57**
— The Art of Distillation.... L, 1651. 1st Ed. 4to, contemp calf; worn, rebacked. Some staining. S Mar 29 (694) £850

**French, John C.**
— The Passenger Pigeon in Pennsylvania. Altoona, 1919. Pictorial wraps. pba Aug 8 (424) $130

**Frere, George**
— A Short History of Barbados.... L, 1768. 1st Ed. 8vo, half calf; rebacked. sg Oct 26 (117) $175

**Freshfield, Douglas W., 1845-1934**
— Across Country from Thonon to Trent. L, 1865. 1st Ed. 8vo, orig cloth; rubbed & soiled. Freshfield's mother's annotated copy, with her name in his hand. bba Nov 1 (534) £2,000 [Hunter]
— Across the Country from Thonon to Trent. L, 1865. 8vo, orig cloth. Ink stamp on tp verso. bba Nov 1 (316) £1,500 [Hunter]
— The Exploration of the Caucasus. L, 1896. 1st Ed. 2 vols. 4to, orig cloth; spines def. Lacking map in pocket at end of Vol II; pencil scribbling on some tissue guards. b May 30 (165) £100
Anr copy. Cloth; rubbed. With 76 plates, 3 folding panoramas & 4 folding colored maps. Library markings. pn Dec 7 (145) £380

**Freshfield, Mrs. Henry**
— A Summer Tour in the Grisons and Italian Valleys of the Bernina. L, 1862. 1st Ed. 8vo, contemp half calf. With 2 folding maps & 4 plates. bba Nov 1 (320) £300 [Astengo]

**Freud, Sigmund, 1856-1939**
— Inhibition, Symptom, and Anxiety. L: Hogarth Press, 1936. 1st English Ed. In chipped dj. pba Aug 22 (178) $60
— Die Traumdeutung. Leipzig & Vienna, 1900. 8vo, modern half mor gilt. Marginal dampstaining. sg Apr 18 (54) $5,000

**Freytag, Friedrich Gotthilf, 1723-76**
— Analecta litteraria de libris rarioibus. Leipzig, 1750. 1st Ed. 8vo, contemp calf; rebacked. Browned. sg Apr 11 (110) $110

**Frezier, Amedee Francois, 1682-1773**
— Reise nach der Sued-See.... Hamburg, 1745. 8vo, old bds. With frontis & 10 plates & maps. Some staining & browning. CE May 22 (19) $800
— La Theorie et la pratique de la coupe des pierres et des bois.... Strassburg, 1737-39. 3 vols. 4to, calf gilt; rubbed, 2 vols with joints splitting, 1 with hinges reinforced. With engraved plate facing dedication & 113 folding plates. Some spotting or staining. bba Oct 19 (124) £130 [Cudia]
— A Voyage to the South-Sea, and Along the Coast of Chili and Peru. L, 1717. 4to, modern sheep antique. With 37 maps, plans & views. Small piece missing from margin of 1 leaf. pba Feb 13 (81) $2,500

Anr copy. Contemp calf; joints cracked, rubbed. With 36 (of 37) maps, plans & views. S Mar 28 (327) £350

Anr copy. Contemp calf; rebacked. With 37 maps, plans & views. Some foxing. sg Mar 7 (82) $900

**Frezza dalle Grotte, Giuseppe**
— Il Cantore ecclesiastico. Padua: Stamperia del seminario, 1698. 4to, old vellum; new liners. Worming affecting text in E-H; tp repaired at foot; some browning. S Dec 1 (154) £500

**Frick Collection, Henry Clay**
— The Frick Collection. An Illustrated Catalogue.... Pittsburgh, 1968-77. 6 vols. 4to, cloth. Library markings; d/j blurbs & pockets glued to pastedowns. wa Nov 16 (261) $55

**Fricker, Carl, of Leipzig**
— The Antarctic Regions. L, 1900. American Issue. Orig cloth; soiled. Some foxing to page edges. pba July 25 (35) $200

**Fried, Michael**
— Morris Louis. NY, [1980?]. Oblong 4to, cloth, in dj. sg Jan 11 (259) $70

**Friedlaender, Johnny**
— Oeuvre 1961-1965. NY & Stuttgart: Touchstone, [1967]. Folio, cloth. With 14 tipped-in color plates. With orig litho, sgd in pencil, laid in. sg Jan 11 (185) $80
— Un Petit Bestiare. Stuttgard: Manuspresse, 1963. One of 50 but without the drawing & color etching. Folio, loose as issued in cloth portfolio. With 11 etchings with aquatint. Some browning to extreme sheet edges. sg May 23 (315) $1,700

**Friedlaender, Max J., 1852-1934**
— Early Netherlandish Painting. Leiden: A. W. Sijthoff, [1967-76]. 10 parts in 12 vols only. In djs. sg June 13 (150) $1,100

**Friedlander, Lee**
— The American Monument. NY: Eakins Press, [1976]. Oblong 4to, cloth. Sgd. sg Feb 29 (139) $400
— Factory Valleys: Ohio and Pennsylvania. NY, 1982. 4to, cloth, in dj with minor wear. Sgd. sg Feb 29 (140) $225
— Letters from the People. NY: Distributed Art Publishers, [1993]. Folio, cloth. With silver print sgd on verso, 1993. sg Feb 29 (141) $600
— Self Portrait. New City: Haywire Press, [1970]. One of 100 hard-bound & with orig silver print bound in. Oblong 4to, orig cloth with mtd photo on front cover. sg Feb 29 (142) $2,400

**Friend...**
— The Friend; a Monthly Journal, Devoted to Temperance, Seamen.... Honolulu, 1861-68. Ed by Samuel C. Damon. Vols XVIII-XXV. 96 issues, each 4 leaves. Contemp half sheep; worn & broken. Browning, foxing & library stamps. P June 5 (52) $1,600

**Fries, H. de**
— Frank L. Wright: Aus dem Lebenswerke eines Architekten. Berlin, 1926. Half cloth; shaken, soiled. sg Jan 11 (8) $400

**Frigerio, Ambrogio, 1537-98**
— Vita e Miracoli del Gloriosissimo S. Nicola di Tolentino. Rome: Stamperia della Cam. Apostolica, 1610. 4to, early 19th-cent half calf gilt; spine chipped. Some staining; tp with abraded writing; tear in H1 repaired. sg Mar 21 (140) $200

**Frink, Elisabeth**
— Etchings Illustrating Chaucer's Canterbury Tales. L, 1972. One of 50. Orig mor gilt. With 19 plates. bba May 9 (495) £460 [Finbar Macdonnell]

**Frisch, Jodocus Leopold**
— Die Welt im Feuer, oder das Wahre Vergehen und Ende der Welt.... Sorau, 1746. 1st Ed. 4to, contemp calf; worn, upper joint split, spine ends torn. With 12 hand-colored plates. Some dampstaining. Madsen copy. S Mar 14 (133) £1,100

**Frisch, Johann Leonhard**
— Vorstellung der Voegel Deutschlandes.... Berlin, 1734-63. 2 vols. Folio, modern vellum. With frontis, 23 (OF 24) section titles & 253 (of 255) hand-colored plates. Repaired tear to Plate 8; supplementary Plate 31 torn with loss of most of folded section. Extra-illus with 2 plates of pheasants. C May 31 (19) £18,000

**Frisi, Antonio Francesco**
— Memorie storiche di Monza e sua corte. Milan: Gaetano Motta, 1794. 4to, 19th-cent half calf; worn. With 19 plates. S Mar 28 (227) £420

**Frith, Francis**
— Lower Egypt, Thebes, and the Pyramids. L, [c.1862]. Bound in 2 vols. Folio, contemp half mor; rubbed. With 37 mtd photos. b May 30 (46) £1,400

— Sinai and Palestine. L: William Mackenzie, [1862 or later]. Folio, orig half lea. With litho title & 37 mtd plates. Some spotting. W Nov 8 (318) £750

**Froger, Francois**
— Relation d'un voyage de la mere de sud.... Amst., 1715. 12mo, contemp calf; repaired, some wear. With 28 plates & maps, some folding. CE May 22 (20) $450

**Frohawk, Frederick William**
— Natural History of British Butterflies. L, [1914]. 2 vols. Folio, orig cloth; minor wear. With 60 color plates only. F June 20 (845) $190

**Froissart, Jean, 1333?-1400?**
See also: Limited Editions Club
— Chronicles. L: Richarde Pynson, 1523-25. ("Here begynnith the first Volum of Syr John Froyssart....") 1st Ed in English. 2 vols in 1. Folio, early 20th-cent velvet over wooden bds, with metal fittings. Lacking Vol I tp (supplied in photofacsimile); last leaf in Vol II & its conjugate restored with portions in facsimile; the 2 inner sheets of quire d in Vol I & a quire in Vol II ptd on different paper stock & possibly supplied; some dampstaining, marginal tears or repairs, worming & staining; last few leaves in Vol II heavily soiled; washed & pressed; a few wormholes. CNY May 17 (78) $3,500

Anr Ed. L, 1842. Trans by Thomas Johnes. 2 vols. 8vo, contemp vellum gilt. Some spotting. bba July 18 (229) £140 [Page]

Anr Ed. Paris, 1881. 4to, contemp mor gilt. S Apr 23 (56) £150

Anr Ed. Stratford: Shakespeare Head Press, 1927-28. ("Froissarts Cronycles....") One of 350. 8 vols. 4to, bds; scuffed & scratched. pba June 20 (300) $650

— Le Premier volume des croniques de France, Dangleterre...Le Second...Le Troisieme...Le Quart.... Paris: Antoine Verard, [c.1495-1500]. Vols I-III (of 4). Folio, 18th-cent red mor gilt, Vol III similarly bound in 1860s by Clyde for Lord Ashburnham; joints worn. 46 lines; double column; batarde type 12:106. With full-page miniature on a8v by an artist in the circle of Jacques de Besancon(this leaf from anr copy); 166 smaller column-with miniatures painted in the Verard atelier over the ptd chapter-headings; many illuminated initials in gold, red & blue. Leaves e.2.7, ii3.6 & ii4.5 are orig Ms replacement sheets. Ptd on vellum. 279 leaves (including Ms replacements) in Vol I; 287 leaves in Vol II; lacking AA8; 237 leaves in Vol III; lacking aaa6. Goff F-322-3. C June 26 (26) £100,000

Anr Ed. Paris: Pierre l'Huillier, 1574. ("Histoire et cronique memorable....") 4 vols in 1. Folio, 18th-cent calf; rebacked, lower cover detached, damage from removal of bookplates. Strip torn from top of tp of Vol I & small tear at lower margin; 2 corners torn away; 1 leaf in Vol III repaired at lower corner; wormhole throughout. S June 12 (51) £280

Anr Ed. Paris, 1574. 4 vols in 2. Folio, later half calf; spine ends worn, Vol II front cover almost detached. Some leaves repaired. wa Nov 16 (175) $260

**Frolov, I. —&**
**Mokshin, S.**
— [Flying Amid Stars, in Russian]. Moscow: Political Literature Publishers, 1963. 8vo, orig wraps. Sgd by Valery Bykovsky & Valentina Tereshkova. P Mar 16 (79) $900

**Fromm, Hans**
— Bibliographie deutscher Uebersetzungen aus dem Franzoesischen, 1700-1948. Baden-Baden, [1981]. 6 vols. 8vo, orig cloth. Reprnt of 1950-63 Ed.. sg Apr 11 (111) $200

**Frost, A. B., 1851-1928**
— A Book of Drawings. NY, [1904]. Intro by Joel Chandler Harris; verse by Wallace Irwin. Folio, orig pictorial bds; worn & soiled. F Mar 28 (355) $60
— Shooting Pictures. NY: Winchester Press, [1972]. One of 750. Folio, loose in cloth portfolio with accompanying text bound in, as issued; some wear. With 12 color plates. Some staining & spotting. O Feb 6 (97) $225

**Frost, Donald McKay**
— Notes on General Ashley, the Overland Trail, and South Pass. Worcester, Mass., 1945. 1st Ed. 4to, orig wraps; rear wrap corner bumped. With folding map. Robbins copy. pba Mar 21 (111) $150

**Frost, H. Gordon**
— Blades and Barrels. El Paso, [1972]. One of 300. 4to, syn. Inscr. sg Mar 7 (448) $150

**Frost, John, 1800-59**
— History of the State of California.... Auburn, 1850. 1st Ed. 8vo, mor; worn. With 16 plates. NH July 21 (52) $170

Anr copy. Orig lea; spine faded. With 16 full-page illus. Light foxing; some creases. Larson copy. pba Sept 28 (460) $800

**Frost, Lawrence A.**
— Boy General in Bronze.... Glendale: Arthur H. Clark, 1985. One of 350. No IX in the Hidden Springs of Custeriana series. pba Aug 8 (59) $50
— Custer's 7th Cav and the Campaign of 1873. El Segundo: Upton & Sons, 1986. In dj. Inscr to John Popovich. pba June 25 (94) $50

**Frost, Robert, 1874-1963**
[His "Class Hymn" in the Order of Exercises for the Forty-First Anniversary of the Lawrence High School (1st appearance & sgd) & in The Lawrence Daily American, for Friday, 1 July 1892 (3d appearance) sold at Christie's New York on 27 Oct 1995 as lot 50 of the Engelhard Collection for $3,500]; Limited Editions Club
— A Boy's Will. L: David Nutt, 1913. 1st Ed, 1st Issue. Orig cloth, 1st bdg, unopened; blistered in some places. CE Sept 27 (121) $400

Anr copy. Unopened copy. pba Oct 5 (102) $4,500
2d Issue. Orig wraps, Bdg C. Inscr. CE Sept 27 (122) $1,100
1st American Ed. NY, 1915. 2d Ptg. With holograph poem on front free endpaper, sgd & dated 5 Mar 1917. wa Feb 29 (35) $850
— Class Hymn. Lawrence MA, June or July 1892. 2d Appearance. Orig wraps. In: High School Bulletin, Vol XIII, No 10. Sgd twice. Stockhausen - Engelhard copy. CNY Oct 27 (51) $1,300
— Collected Poems. NY, 1930. One of 1,000. Sgd on tp. pba Oct 26 (23) $750
1st Ed. pba Oct 5 (103) $275
— Collected Poems, 1939. NY, [1939]. Sgd. sg June 20 (124) $175
— A Fountain, A Bottle, Donkey's Ears and Some Books [excerpt]. [N.p., n.d.]. 7 lines (rearranged from pbd version), 233mm by 157mm, single sheet. Inscr to Earl Bernheimer, sgd with initials. cb Feb 14 (2684) $375
— A Further Range. NY, [1936]. One of 803. Orig cloth, in chipped dj. CE Feb 21 (104) $240
— Hard Not to be King. NY: House of Books, 1951. 1st Ed, one of 300. pba Oct 5 (107) $275
— In the Clearing. NY, [1962]. In dj. Sgd on front free endpaper. bbc Feb 26 (296) $150
One of 1,500. pba Oct 5 (108) $250
— The Lone Striker. NY: Knopf, 1933. Pictorial wraps, in envelope. Inscr, 1933. pba Oct 5 (120) $100
— A Masque of Mercy. NY, [1947]. 1st Ed. In dj. Inscr. pba Oct 5 (110) $130
One of 751. Half cloth. pba Oct 5 (109) $225
Anr copy. Half cloth. Photograph of Frost tipped to front pastedown. sg June 20 (125) $225
— A Masque of Reason. NY, [1945]. 1st Ed, One of 800. Half cloth. pba Oct 5 (111) $225
— Mountain Interval. NY, [1916]. 1st Ed, 1st Issue. In repaired dj. pba Oct 5 (112) $500
— New Hampshire. NY, 1923. 1st Trade Ed. Half cloth, in dj. Inscr to Harold Baily. pba Oct 5 (113) $450
Ptg not indicated. Half cloth. pba May 23 (131) $65
Anr Ed. Hanover, NH, 1955. One of 750. Inscr to Harold Baily. pba Oct 5 (114) $225
— La Noche Triste. Lawrence, Mass., Apr 1890. 4to, orig wraps; spine split. In: High School Bulletin, Vol XI, No 8. Engelhard copy. CNY Oct 27 (49) $9,500
— North of Boston. L, [1914]. 1st Ed, 1st Issue. Orig cloth, Bdg A. CE Sept 27 (123) $550
Anr Ed. L: David Nutt, [1914]. 1st Issue. Cloth. pba Oct 5 (115) $1,600
Anr Ed. L, [1914]. Issue not indicated. Inscr to Charles C. Auchincloss. sg June 20 (126) $1,200
— October. Bost., 1939. Pictorial wraps. In: The Old Farmer's Almanac 1939. Inscr. pba Oct 5 (116) $110
— The Poetry. Barre, 1971. Ltd Ed. Ed by E. C. Lathem. 2 vols. pba Jan 25 (104) $55
— The Road Not Taken. NY, [1951]. Ed by Louis Untermeyer. In dj. Inscr to Harold Baily, 1952. pba Oct 5 (121) $120

— Several Short Poems. NY, [1924]. 1st Ed. Single folded sheet. Wraps. Sgd. pba Oct 5 (117) $225
— Steeple Bush. NY, 1947. 1st Ed. In dj. Inscr to Harold Baily. pba Oct 5 (119) $170
One of 751. pba Oct 5 (118) $300
— A Way Out. NY, 1929. 1st Ed, one of 485, sgd. Inscr. pba Oct 5 (122) $275
— West-Running Brook. NY, [1928]. One of 1,000 L.p. copies, sgd by author & artist. Illus by J. J. Lankes. Inscr. sg June 20 (127) $500
— A Witness Tree. NY, 1942. In dj. Inscr to Harold Baily, 1942. pba Oct 5 (123) $250
One of 735. F June 20 (481) $200
— You Come Too. NY, [1959]. Half mor specially bound for Edgar Rigg, president of Holt. Inscr to Rigg, 21 Jan 1960. sg Dec 14 (114) $1,100
Anr Ed. NY, [1961]. 4th Ptg. In dj. Sgd. wa Feb 1 (42) $120

**Frothingham, Alice Wilson**
— Lustreware of Spain. NY, 1951. 8vo, cloth. sg Sept 7 (76) $50

**Froude, James Anthony, 1818-94**
— The English in Ireland in the Eighteenth Century. L, 1887. 3 vols. 12mo, contemp calf gilt by Grieve. pba Nov 30 (38) $190
— Works. L, 1856-96. 28 vols. 8vo, half mor; chipped. Met Feb 24 (222) $550

**Frutaz, Amato Pietro**
— Le Piante di Roma. Rome, 1962. 3 vols, including 2 Atlases. Folio, cloth. With 684 facsimile illusts. bba Oct 5 (345) £340 [Casali]

**Fry, C. B.** See: Beldam & Fry

**Fry, Edmund, 1754-1835**
— Pantographia, Containing Accurate Copies of all the Known Alphabets.... L, 1799. 1st Ed. 8vo, contemp blind-stamped calf; rubbed, spine ends chipped. S June 12 (199) £220

**Fry, Francis, 1803-86**
— A Bibliographical Description of the Editions of the New Testament. L, 1878. 4to, orig cloth; backstrip detached. sg Apr 11 (112) $110

**Fry, Lewis G.**
— Oxted, Limpsfield and Neighbourhood. Oxted, 1932. Illus by Arthur Rackham. Orig half cloth. Ck May 31 (168) £170

**Fryer, Mary Ann, b.1791.** See: Golden Cockerel Press

**Fuchs, Eduard**
— Geschichte der Erotischen Kunst. Munich, [1922-24]. 2 vols. 4to, orig cloth; rubbed. b May 30 (533) £70
— Die Karikatur der europaischen Voelker vom Altertum bis zur Neuzeit. Berlin, [c.1920]. 2d Ed. 4to, bds; rebacked with cloth, extremities worn. sg Jan 11 (77) $70

## Fuchs, Leonhard, 1501-66
— De historia stirpium.... Lyons: B. Arnoullet, 1549. 8vo, contemp calf with mor onlay frames & central medallions outlined in gilt, with Hoffmann arms gauffered on fore-edge, by Jakob Krause; extremities & joints rubbed, corners bumped & restored. Roman & italic types, with a few words in Greek & gothic types. With port & 510 text woodcuts. Some foxing. Hoffmann - Bullinger - Firmin-Didot - Lauder - Fairfax Murray - Schaefer copy. P Nov 1 (89) $42,500

## Fuell, Melissa
— Blind Boone, His Early Life and His Achievements. Kansas City, 1915. Half lea; spine rubbed, front hinge cracked. sg Mar 28 (88) $175

## Fuentes, Carlos
— The Good Conscience. NY: Ivan Obolensky, [1961]. In dj. pba Oct 5 (133) $90

## Fuerst, Julius
— Bibliotheca Judaica. Hildesheim, 1960. 3 vols in 2. 8vo, orig cloth. sg Apr 11 (174) $250

## Fulignati, Giuntino, (Pseud.)
— Della Famosissima Compagnia della lesina dialogo. Treviso: Fabritio Zanetti, 1601. 4to, 19th-cent half vellum. Some foxing or soiling. sg Mar 21 (141) $250

## Fuller, Metta Victoria
— Lives of Female Mormons.... Phila., 1860. Orig cloth; some wear. pba July 25 (286) $100

## Fuller, Peter
— Robert Natkin. NY, 1981. Oblong 4to, cloth, in dj. sg Jan 11 (311) $90

## Fuller, Thomas, 1608-61
— The Church-History of Britain. L, 1655. 1st Ed. Folio, modern half mor; worn. With 3 (of 5) plates. Sold w.a.f. O Mar 5 (97) $100
— The Historie of the Holy Warre. Cambr., 1651. 4th Ed. Bound with: Fuller. The Holy State. L, 1663. Folio, later calf; joints split, spine rubbed. Inscr to Violet Dickinson by Virginia Woolf, sgd as "Sparroy". Ck Apr 12 (124) £320
— The Holy State. Cambr., 1642. 1st Ed. Folio, contemp calf; rubbed. With engraved title & 20 ports. Tear in Ccc2; margin of 1st 2 leaves frayed; marginal worming & staining. bba May 30 (80) £180 [Scott] Anr copy. Contemp calf; rebacked. Corner of 2 leaves repaired. CE June 12 (201) $160

## Fuller, William, 1670-1717?
— A Brief Discovery of the True Mother of the Pretended Prince of Wales...Mary Grey. L, 1696. 8vo, later calf gilt. CG June 12 (20) £70

## Fulton, Robert, 1765-1815
— Torpedo War, and Submarine Explosions. NY, 1810. Oblong 4to, loose in orig wraps; lacking backstrip & stitching. With 5 plates. sg Apr 18 (55) $8,500

## Fulvio, Andrea
— Illustrium imagines. Rome: Jacobus Mazochius, 15 Nov 1517. 8vo, later calf; extremities worn, wormed. Leaves at end remarginated; part of tp border in Ms; tear through text of 2d leaf; soiling & browning. cb Feb 14 (2513) $900
Anr copy. 19th-cent calf gilt with gauffering; torn at head. Tp frayed & with wormhole in border; worming in lower margins repaired just touching edge of textf. S Nov 30 (262) £1,600

**Fumagall, Giuseppe.** See: Ottino & Fumagall

## Fumagalli, Giuseppe
— L'Arte della legatura alla corte degli estensi.... Florence, 1913. 1st Ed. 4to, later cloth, orig wraps bound in; rubbed. bba May 9 (137) £190 [Page]
— Lexicon typographicum italiae. Dictionnaire geographique d'Italie. Florence, 1905. 4to, modern cloth. bba May 9 (60) £85 [Tosi]

## Fumee, Martin, Sieur de Genille
— The Historie of the Troubles of Hungarie.... L: Felix Kyngston, 1600. 1st Ed in English. Folio, modern cloth. Tear in C5 repaired; tp & last 2 index leaves laminated; repair in corner of last index leaf affecting text; lacking 2A6 & initial & final blanks. sg Mar 7 (169) $200

## Fumet, Stanislas
— Sculptures de Braque. [N.p.], 1951. Orig wraps with plates loose in rear cover pocket as issued. With 35 plates. sg Jan 11 (65) $60

## Funck, M., b.1870
— Le Livre Belge a gravures. Paris, 1925. 8vo, orig cloth; orig front wrapper bound in. sg Apr 11 (113) $110

## Funk, Casimir, 1884-1967
— Die Vitamine.... Wiesbadenm 1914. 1st Ed. 4to, modern cloth; orig wraps bound in. With half-title & 2 plates. Ck Mar 22 (124) £300

## Funke, Jaromir
— Jaromir Funke Fotografie. Prague: Odeon, [1970]. 4to, cloth; minor soiling. sg Feb 29 (144) $130

## Funnell, William
— A Voyage Round the World.... L, 1707. 8vo, contemp calf; rebacked, new endpapers. With 5 folding maps & 10 plates. Spotted & soiled. S June 27 (247) £750

## Furber, Robert
— Twelve Months of Flowers. L, 1730. Folio, contemp calf; minor wear. With engraved list of subscribers within hand-colored floral border serving as tp & 12 hand-colored plates. Some soiling & marginal tears. Fattorini copy. C Oct 25 (64) £20,000

## Furhange, Maguy
— Carzou: Graveur et Lithographe.... Nice, [1971]. 4to, cloth, in dj. sg Jan 11 (79) $60; sg Jan 11 (80) $50

**Furlong, Laurence**
— The American Coast Pilot.... Newburyport, 1804. 4th Ed. 8vo, contemp sheep; recornered, ink writing & pencil scribbles to endpapers. With 10 (of 11) charts. Some foxing.  pba July 25 (146) $350
  16th Ed. NY, 1850. 8vo, orig sheep; rear flyleaf lacking, front flyleaves torn & lacking portions. With 17 plates. Some staining & edgewear.  pba July 25 (97) $200

**Furmerus, Bernardus**
— De rerum usu et abusu. Antwerp: Plantin, 1575. 4to, mor gilt by Lortic; scuff on lower cover. With 25 engravings in text. Hoe - Harth - Schaefer copy.  P Nov 1 (90) $5,000

**Furness, William Henry**
— The Home-Life of Borneo Head-Hunters. Phila., 1902. One of 500. Inscr by H. H. Furness.  S Mar 28 (391) £440

**Furst, Herbert Ernest Augustus**
— The Decorative Art of Frank Brangwyn. L & NY, 1924. 4to, cloth; corners bumped, hinge cracking. With 33 color plates.  pba Nov 30 (67) $50
— The Modern Woodcut. L, 1924. 1st Ed, One of 75. 4to, orig half cloth. With 3 orig woodcuts.  bba May 9 (215A) £180 [Breckenridge]

**Fux, Johann Joseph, 1660-1741**
— Gradus ad Parnassum.... Vienna: J. P. Van Ghelen, 1725. Folio, modern half vellum. Burn hole in 1st few leaves; tp & following leaf repaired & remargined.  S Dec 1 (155) £850

**Fyler, Arthur Evelyn**
— The Development of Cyprus, and Rambles in the Island. L, [1899]. 8vo, cloth; spine faded. With 21 plates.  S Oct 26 (53) £620 [Christodoulou]

# G

**Gaboriau, Emile, 1832-73**
— Works. NY, 1909-13. 12 vols. Half mor gilt.  sg Sept 21 (18) $650

**Gadbury, John, 1627-1704**
— Ephemerides of the Celestial Motions and Aspects, Eclipses... for XX Years. Beginning Anno 1682. L, 1680. 4to, later calf; rubbed.  O Mar 5 (99) $180
— Ephemerides of the Celestial Motions for X. Years, Beginning Anno 1672.... L, 1672. 4to, old calf; rebacked, rubbed. Some foxing & soiling; license leaf lacking.  O Mar 5 (98) $140

**Gaddis, William**
— The Recognitions. NY, [1955]. Advance copy. Orig wraps; some wear. Inscr.  K June 23 (295) $350

**Gadolin, Johan, 1760-1852**
— Inledning til Chemien. Abo [Turku], 1798. 8vo, contemp half calf. With errata leaf.  S Mar 14 (134) £950

**Gaffarel, Jacques, 1601-81**
— Iacobi Gaffarelli... quaestio pacifica, num orta in religione dissidia componi et conciliari possint. Paris: Charles du Mesnil, 1645. 4to, contemp red mor gilt with arms of Cardinal Mazarin. Dedication copy.  C May 1 (59) £1,400

**Gag, Wanda**
— Millions of Cats. NY, 1928. 1st Ed, one of 250. Bds. With orig woodblock print, sgd & dated (stained in upper margin).  Met Dec 5 (180) $625

**Gage, Thomas, d.1656**
— The English-American his Travail, by Sea and Land.... L, 1648. 1st Ed. Folio, contemp calf; worn & rubbed, spine ends chipped, corners showing, joints cracked. Dampstained & soiled; marginal tears & scribbling to tp.  pba July 25 (397) $700
  3d Ed. L, 1677. ("A New Survey of the West-Indies.") 8vo, contemp calf; lacking front free endpaper. Tear in folding map repaired; tear at foot of Q1; some staining & soiling.  S June 13 (611) £220
— A New Survey of the West Indias.... L, 1655. 2d Ed. Folio, contemp calf; worn, rebacked. With 4 maps (3 folding). Tear in title margin; T5 misbound; some browning.  S Oct 26 (509) £460 [Remington]
— Nouvelle relation, contenant les voyages... dans la Nouvelle Espagne.... Amst., 1721. 4 vols in 2, orig calf; worn, stained, vol I front cover badly chipped. With 4 folded frontis illus & 3 folded maps. Larson copy.  pba Sept 28 (52) $100

**Gaiani, Giovanni Battista**
— Arte di maneggiar la espada a piedi et a cavallo. Loano: Francesco Castello, 1619. 4to, mor gilt by V. Krafft.  C June 26 (75) £3,200

**Gailhabaud, Jules, 1810-88**
— L'Architecture du Vme au XVIIme Siecle.... Paris, 1858. 4 vols in 2. 4to, later half mor; worn, spine ends def, joints starting. With 223 uncolored & 35 chromolitho plates. Foxed; ink stamps.  cb Oct 17 (77) $190

**Gailhard, Jean**
— The Present State of the Republic of Venice. L, 1669. 12mo, contemp sheep; worn. Tp stamped.  sg Mar 21 (142) $225

**Gaillot, Bernard**
— Les Arts et les metiers, recueil de carricatures. Paris: Bernard, [c.1820]. Folio, loose in contemp wraps with ptd title mtd on upper cover. With 12 lithos ptd by Senefelder.  bba June 6 (10) £850 [Marlborough]

**Gaines, Ernest J.**
— The Autobiography of Miss Jane Pittman. NY, 1971. In dj with some wear. Inscr by Gaines.  sg Mar 28 (89) $225

**Gale, George**
— Upper Mississippi; or Historical Sketches of the Mound Builders.... Chicago, 1867. 12mo, orig cloth; worn & frayed, split to spine head. With port, 4 maps & 9 plates.  wa Feb 29 (456) $80

**Gale Collection, Mr. & Mrs. Richard P.**
HILLIER, JACK RONALD. - Catalogue of the Japanese Paintings and Prints.... Rutland & Tokyo, [1970]. 2 vols. 4to, cloth; bookplate removed. Stamp on prelim leaf in each vol. sg June 13 (165) $90

**Gale, T.**
— Electricity or Ethereal Fire.... Troy, 1802. 1st Ed. 12mo, modern half mor; rebound. Lacks M3-M4; tp reinforced; some browning & dampstaining. CE Nov 8 (92) $130

**Galenus, Claudius**
— Libri aliquot Graeci partim hactenus non visi.... Basel: Froben & Episcopius, 1544. 2 vols in 1. 4to, contemp calf; rebacked, worn & chipped. With 4 woodcut diagrams; text in Greek. Some soiling. CE Nov 8 (93) $200
— Opera. Venice: Giunta, 1576-77. 14 parts in 7 vols. Folio, 17th-cent calf; spines with worming, 2 ends chipped. Some dampstaining & browning; minor worming to margins in 2 vols; cropped marginalia. sg May 16 (416) $2,400
— Opera omnia. Basel: Froben & Episcopius, 1542. Vol I only. Contemp calf over wooden bds, with roll-border dated 1536; rebacked, both bds wormed. Some worming. S Mar 29 (655) £140

**Galerie...**
— Galerie contemporaine des illustrations francaises. Paris: Paul de Lacroix, [after 1885?]. 8 vols. Folio, contemp half mor by Magnier; rubbed. With 200 full-page photographs mtd on thick paper 7 many smaller photographic ports mtd in text. Some spotting & staining. S Nov 21 (155) £3,000
— Galerie de Florence. Tableaux, Statues, Bas-Reliefs et Camees. Paris, 1819. 4 vols in 2. Folio, half calf; worn. Some spotting. bba Nov 30 (86) £850 [Bifolco]
Anr copy. Vol II only. Folio, contemp mor gilt; rubbed. bba June 6 (11) £220 [Bell]
— Galerie meridionale: monumens & paysages, portraits historiques & costumes. Marseilles: Charavel, [c.1836]. Oblong folio, contemp bds; needs rebacked, front endleaves creased. Lithographed throughout, with 24 plates. Some foxing affecting plates. sg Apr 18 (56) $650

**Galerie Van Diemen**
— Erste Russische Kunstaustellung Berlin 1922. Berlin, 1922. 8vo, wraps with design by El Lissitzky. sg June 13 (166) $700

**Galiani, Ferdinand, 1728-87**
— Dialogues sur le commerce des bleds. L [but Paris], 1770. 8vo, contemp calf gilt; rubbed. Ink stains on pp. 198-99. Fuerstenberg - Schaefer copy. S Dec 7 (241) £550

**Galilei, Galileo, 1564-1642**
— Dialogo di Galileo Galilei Linceo matematico...sopra i due massimi sistemi del mondo Tolemaico e Copernico. Florence, 1632. 1st Ed. 4to, early limp paper bds, entirely untrimmed; new sewing & endpapers. Repaired tears to B4, B5 & C1; minor marginal tears to 3 leaves; a few leaves with minor foxing. Hefner copy. CNY May 17 (17) $21,000
Anr copy. 18th-cent half calf; spine worn. Some leaves flawed or short in lower margins; final blank torn & holed; some browning; hole in Q1. Madsen copy. S Mar 14 (135) £8,000
— Opere. Bologna, 1656-55. 2 vols. 4to, contemp vellum; discolored, stained & wormed. With frontis, port & folding plate. 2d vol smaller; folding plate adhered at fold. pba Nov 30 (142) $3,500
Anr Ed. Florence, 1718. 3 vols. 4to, 18th-cent calf with arms of von Closen und Arnstorff at spine foot; spine torn at head. Lacking 8 leaves in Vol II (replaced with blanks) & a port (19th-cent litho port loosely inserted); tear in C6 of Vol II repaired with small loss. S Mar 14 (136) £480
— Il Saggiatore nel quale con bilancia equisita e giusta si ponderano le cose contenute nella libra astronomicae filosofica di Lotario Sarsi. Rome, 1623. 1st Ed, 1st Issue. 4to, contemp vellum gilt. Some waterstaining; without the 4 leaves of introductory verses. C Apr 3 (103) £6,000
— Systema cosmicum.... Lyons, 1641. 4to, contemp calf, with arms of the Signet Library; corners worn, rebacked. Foxed. S Mar 29 (656) £2,800

**Gall, Alice Crew**
— Mother McGrew and Gerald Giraffe. NY, [1917]. Illus by Lee Wright. Pictorial bds; extremities rubbed, soiled. pba Aug 22 (767) $60

**Gallaeus, Servatius, 1627?-1709**
— Dissertationes de Sybillis, earumque oraculis.... Amst., 1688. 4to, contemp half vellum; worn. With folding port, added title & 14 plates. Minor dampstain to corner of quire c. Schaefer copy. P Nov 1 (91) $1,000

**Gallandius, Petrus —& Turnebus, Adrianus**
— De agrorum conditionibus & constitutionibus limitum.... Paris, 1554. 4to, contemp vellum. Early marginalia. CE June 12 (202) $260

**Gallatin, Albert Eugene, 1881-1952**
— Aubrey Beardsley's Drawings; a Catalogue.... NY, 1903. One of 30 interleaved & specially bound. Folio, orig vellum gilt; soiled. Inscr to Frederick H. Evans. Extra-illus with 19 platinotype facsimiles by F. H. Evans of Beardsley drawings, various proof & unpbd drawings, a clipped signature & the orig Beardsley drawings for the full-page border of p 879 of Le Morte Darthur inset with a platinum print of Evans's port of Beardsley, sgd by Evans on mount. S Nov 21 (157) £7,500

**Galle, Servaticus.** See: Gallaeus, Servatius

**Gallery...**
— The Gallery of Mezzotints: An Annual for 1849. NY, 1849. 8vo, half mor gilt; joints rubbed. pba Dec 14 (108) $55

# 1995 - 1996 · BOOKS

# GANS

**Galli da Bibiena, Giuseppe.** See: Bibiena, Giuseppe Galli

**Gallico, Paul**
— The Adventures of Hiram Holliday. L, [1939]. In dj. b Jan 31 (165) £80

**Gallo, Agostino, of Brescia**
— Le Vinti Giornate dell'Agricoltura et de' piaceri della villa. Venice: Domenico Imberti, 1603. 4to, contemp vellum; tear in spine. First few leaves frayed; some staining & browning. S Mar 14 (137) £300

**Gallo, Edouardo L.** See: Baz & Gallo

**Gallois, Emile**
— Costumes Espagnols. NY, [1939]. Preface by Jacques Soustelle. Folio, loose as issued in portfolio with pochoir-colored plate laid down on front cover; spine ends & corners worn, spine scufed. With 40 pochoir-colored plates. cb Oct 17 (111) $275

**Gallonio, Antonio, d.1605**
— De SS. Martyrum Cruciatibus.... Paris, 1660. 4to, 17th-cent calf gilt; spine chipped, front joint cracked. Old ink blots on titles; some soiling & dampstaining; lacking port. sg Mar 21 (143) $350
— Trattato de gli instrumenti di martirio.... Rome: Ascanio e Girolamo Donangeli, 1591. 1st Ed. 4to, 18th-cent vellum gilt; rubbed. With 46 plates. C June 26 (78) £1,300

**Gallucci, Giovanni Paolo, 1538-1621?**
— Coelestium corporum et rerum ab ipsis pendentium accurata explicatio per instrumenta, rotulas & figuras. Venice: G. B. Somasco, 1605. 4to, contemp calf gilt; spine ends worn, upper hinge broken. With 49 woodcuts in text with total of 65 volvelles (some possibly in facsimile). Folding table torn along fold; woodcut port pasted inside upper cover. S Nov 30 (323) £820

**Galsworthy, John, 1867-1933**
See also: Limited Editions Club
— The Forsyte Saga. L, 1922. 1st Ed, One of 275, sgd. Orig lea; extremities scuffed. pba May 23 (132) $90
— A Man of Devon. L, 1901. 1st Ed. 12mo, orig cloth. Inscr to Ford Madox Hueffer. CE Sept 27 (127) $600
Anr copy. Spotted. sg June 20 (128) $110
— Villa Rubein. L, 1900. 1st Ed. 8vo, orig cloth; hinges starting. Inscr to Ford Madox Hueffer, 9 Nov 1900. CE Sept 27 (126) $550
— Works. L, 1923-36. Manaton Ed, one of 530. 30 vols. Calf gilt; rubbed. b Sept 20 (567) £1,400

**Galtier-Boissiere, Jean**
— La Bonne Vie. Paris, 1928. One of 29 on japon. Illus by Andre Dignimont. 4to, mor extra by Vermorel - H. Hugonet, with illustrated doublures, orig wraps bound in; spine with discoloration. S Nov 21 (156) £400

**Galvez, J. de**
— Reales Ordenanzas para la direcion regimen, y gobierno del important Cuerpo de la Mineria de Nueva Espana. Madrid, 1783. Folio, contemp mor gilt with royal arms; some staining on lower cover, corners rubbed. Wormed in lower margins; a few holes repaired. S June 27 (192) £1,800

**Gamba da Bassano, Bartolommeo, 1776-1841**
— Delle Novelle Italiane in Prosa Bibliografia. Florence, 1835. 2d Ed. 8vo, contemp half vellum; some wear. O Mar 26 (107) $170
— Serie de' testi di lingua usati a stampa nel vocabolario degli Accademice della Crusca. Bassano, 1805. 8vo, later half lea; rubbed. Some soiling & foxing. O Mar 26 (108) $90

**Gamba, Pietro, Count, 1801-26**
— A Narrative of Lord Byron's Last Journey to Greece. L, 1825. 1st Ed. 8vo, contemp half calf; rubbed. Lacking half-title; library stamps erased. b May 30 (265) £150

**Gamboa, Francisco Xavier, 1717-94**
— Commentaries on the Mining Ordinances of Spain. L, 1830. 2 vols. 8vo, orig bds; spine ends chipped, joints starting, endpapers & titles foxed. With 3 folding plates. sg May 16 (168) $175

**Gamelin, Jacques**
— Nouveau Recueil d'osteologie et de myologie.... Toulouse: J. F. Desclassan, 1779. 2 parts in 1 vol. Folio, modern half chamois. With frontises, port & 82 plates, including some in 2 states. Some soiling frontis for Part 1 cut round & mtd; plate of musician skeletons remargined; repairs to 3 marginal tears on plates. Schaefer copy. P Nov 1 (92) $6,000

**Gandara, Felipe de la**
— Armas, y Triunfos. Hechos Heroicos de los Hijos de Galicia. Madrid: Pablo de Val, 1662. 4to, contemp vellum; loose in bdg. Some browning; old scored writing on tp. sg Mar 21 (296) $1,000

**Gandellini, Giovanni Gori**
— Notizie istoriche degl' intagliatori. Siena, 1808-16. 15 vols. 8vo, 19th-cent half lea with Astor Library lettered in gilt at base of spines; rubbed. Library markings. Wilberforce Eames's set. O Mar 26 (109) $275

**Gandhi's copy, Mohandas K.**
— The Bhagavadgita. Oxford, 1898. Front hinge cracked, shaken. With passages marked by Gandhi in pencil. pn Nov 9 (395) £19,000

**Gans, A. I.**
— Catalogue of Mexican Pamphlets in the Sutro Collection 1623-1888. San Francisco: California State Library, 1939-40. 5 vols of photocopied typescript plus 1946 Supplement, contemp calf, orig wraps bound in. Ck Apr 12 (278) £260

### Gans-Ruedin, E.
— The Splendor of Persian Carpets. NY, 1978. 4to, cloth, in dj. wa Dec 14 (586) $55

### Gantez, Annibal
— L'entretien des musiciens. Paris, 1878. One of 6 ptd on vellum. 8vo, mor gilt by Emile Rouselle. With frontis in 8 states. b May 30 (542) £200

### Gantillon, Simon. See: Golden Cockerel Press

### Garces, Francisco
— On the Trail of a Spanish Pioneer: The Diary and Itinerary.... NY, 1900. One of 950. 2 vols. 8vo, orig cloth; previous owner's stamps on front pastedowns. pba Feb 13 (82) $225

Anr copy. Trans & ed by Elliott Coues. Orig cloth; extremities worn, hinges cracked. 1 folded map detached in vol I. Larson copy. pba Sept 28 (109) $160

Anr copy. Orig cloth; spine ends frayed. pba Aug 8 (38) $250

1st Ed. - Trans & Ed by Elliott Coues. 2 vols. 8vo, orig cloth. Robbins copy. pba Mar 21 (70) $350

### Garcia Bermejo, Antonio
— Oracion funebre... en las solemnes exequias celebradas... en la Real Iglesia de S. Isidro de Madrid... por el alme del Rey de las Dos Sicilias Francisco Primero. Madrid: Eusebio Aguado, 1831. One of 12 specially bound. 4to, contemp purple mor gilt with arms of King Ferdinand VII of Spain, by Antonio Suarez. C May 1 (60) £3,200

### Garcia Icazbalceta, Joaquin, 1825-94
— Bibliografia mexicana del siglo XVI.... Mexico, 1954. 4to, cloth. ds July 27 (96) $100

Anr copy. Orig half lea; rubbed. O Mar 26 (110) $100

### Garcia Icazbalceta, Joaquin, 1825-94 —& Wagner, Henry Raup
— Nueva bibliografia del siglo XVI.... Mexico 1940 [1946]. Folio, wraps. ds July 27 (95) $150

### Garcia Marquez, Gabriel
See also: Limited Editions Club; Marquez, Gabriel Garcia
— One Hundred Years of Solitude. NY, [1970]. In later dj, chipped. pba Jan 25 (107) $170

1st Issue. In dj with minor rubbing & short closed tear. pba Aug 22 (179) $475

### Garden, Alexander, 1757-1829
— Anecdotes of the Revolutionary War in America. Charleston, 1822. 8vo, contemp calf; worn. wa Feb 29 (298) $170

### Gardiner, Alan Henderson
See also: Davies & Gardiner
— Egyptian Grammar. Oxford, 1927. 4to, orig cloth. pba Aug 22 (582) $80

### Gardiner, Howard C.
— In Pursuit of the Golden Dream.... Stoughton, MA: Western Hemisphere, 1970. One of 100. Ed by Dale Morgan. Folio, half mor in cloth slipcase. With 2 maps (1 folded) & 8 plates. Sgd by Morgan. Larson copy. pba Sept 28 (461) $275

### Gardiner, Samuel Rawson, 1829-1902
— Oliver Cromwell. L, 1899. One of 1,475. Folio, half mor. With hand-tinted frontis. pba Nov 30 (103) $140

### Gardner, Alexander, 1821-82
— Gardner's Photographic Sketch Book of the War. Wash., 1866. 2 vols. Oblong folio, orig mor gilt. With 50 albumen prints in each vol. P Oct 5 (69) $30,000

### Gardner, J. D.
— Ascent and Tour of Mont Blanc.... Chiswick, 1851. 1st Ed. 16mo, orig half mor, unopened. bba Nov 1 (322) £320 [Atlas]

### Gardner, John, 1933-82
— Grendel. NY, 1971. In dj. pba May 4 (140) $85

### Gardner Library, John Dunn
— [Sale Catalogue] Catalogue of the Principal Portion of the Valuable Library. L, 1854. 8vo, half mor gilt, orig wraps preserved. Priced throughout. bba July 18 (13) £190 [Braham]

### Gardner, Robert W.
— The Parthenon: Its Science of Forms. NY, 1925. One of 700. Folio, half cloth; corners worn, some soiling. With 11 plans. sg June 13 (167) $50

### Gargiulo, Raffaele
— Collection of the Most Remarkable Monuments of the National Museum. Naples, 1872. 4 vols in 1. 4to, later half mor, orig wraps bound in. bba May 30 (43) £75 [Classic Bindings]

### Garland, Hamlin, 1860-1940
— The Book of the American Indian. NY, 1923. 1st Ed. - Illus by Frederic Remington. Folio, half cloth in dj; d/j chipped & torn, corners worn. With 35 plates. Robbins copy. pba Mar 21 (295) $200
— Forty Years of Psychic Research. NY, 1936. With 3 Ls s & responses from John Davidson laid in. pba Apr 25 (418) $85

### Garland, James A.
— The Private Stable: its Establishment, Management and Appointments. Bost., 1903. 8vo, cloth; spotted. O Jan 9 (115) $200

### Garland's copy, Judy
THORNDYKE, HELEN LOUISE. - Honey Bunch: Her First Visit to the City. NY, 1923. Orig cloth-backed pictorial cover; worn & rubbed, front hinge cracked at tp. Sgd "Frances Gumm from St. Paul's Church School" on front free endpaper & with Ns of Liza Minelli. cb Oct 17 (412) $350

### Garlick, Theodatus
— A Treatise on the Artificial Propagation of Fish. NY, 1858. 2d Issue. 8vo, cloth; endpapers removed, some wear. Minor foxing & soiling. O Feb 6 (101) $50

### Garnett, Porter
— Papers of the San Francisco Vigilance Committee of 1851. Berkeley, 1910. Wraps. Vol I, No 7 of Publications of the Academy of Pacific Coast History. Inscr on front wrap. pba Aug 8 (204) $50

### Garnier, Charles, 1825-98
— Le Nouvel Opera de Paris. Paris, 1880. Vols I-II only. Loose in portfolio. Lacking 1 double plate & 1 single plate in Vol I & 4 chromolitho plates in Vol II; stamp partly erased on Vol I tp; Universal Pictures stamp on each plate verso. cb Oct 17 (80) $1,100

Anr copy. Vols I-II in 1. Later half mor; some peeling, scuffed, spine ends worn & torn, numbers at lower spines. With port & 76 leaves of plates Library markings; ink stamp on tp. cb Oct 17 (81) $1,400

### Garnier, Edouard
— La Porcelaine tendre de Sevres. Paris, [n.d.]. Folio, disbound. With 50 plates ptd in colors & gold. Marginal soiling & thumbing with small closed tears. wa Feb 29 (92) $2,200

— The Soft Porcelain of Sevres. L, 1892. Folio, orig cloth; rubbed. With 50 chromolitho plates heightened with gold. Some foxing. bba May 30 (47A) £1,300 [A. Cumming]

### Garrard, George, 1760-1826
— A Description of the Different Varieties of Oxen, Common in the British Isles. L, 1800. Oblong folio, half calf; rebacked, old spine laid down. With 39 (of 52) hand-colored plates. Some creasing at beginning; marginal staining. S Nov 30 (21) £1,500

### Garrard, Lewis Hector, 1829-87
— Wah-to-Yah & the Taos Trail.... Cincinnati, 1850. 12mo, orig cloth; rebacked in syn, new endpapers, corners worn. wa Feb 29 (576) $500

1st Ed. 12mo, orig cloth; spine foot frayed, front cover top corner lightly bumped. Some foxing, hinge weak. Robbins copy. pba Mar 21 (112) $4,250

### Garrett, Pat F.
— The Authentic Life of Billy, the Kid.... Santa Fe, 1882. 1st Ed. Orig wraps; wraps torn & chipped at edges, spine chipped, rear wrapper lacking corner. With 6 plates. Few pages chipped; several printed on smaller paper. Robbins copy. pba Mar 21 (113) $13,000

Anr Ed. NY, 1927. ("Pat F. Garrett's Authentic Life of Billy the Kid.") Ed by Maurice Garland Fulton. pba Apr 25 (294) $75

### Garrick, David, 1717-79
— Garrick ou les Acteurs Anglois.... Paris, 1771. 8vo, contemp calf; rubbed. Some browning. bba July 18 (182) £65 [Seydi]

### Garrigou, Marcel
— Georges Crette. Toulouse, 1984. One of 500. Folio, orig wraps in slipcase; loose as issued. Includes errata leaf. sg Apr 11 (50) $275

### Garrison, Wendell P. & Francis J.
— William Lloyd Garrison. The Story of his Life. NY, 1885. 4 vols. 8vo, half mor; rubbed. With holograph leaf of Garrison's autobiography tipped in. rs Nov 11 (89) $500

### Garrison, William Lloyd
— Juvenile Poems for the Use of Free American Children, of Every Complexion. Bost.: Garrison & Knapp, 1835. 12mo, orig ptd wraps; chipped, spine def. Top edge of initial signature chewed; foxed. Emily Howland's copy. sg Mar 28 (287) $3,600

### Garrulous Man...
— The Garrulous Man. A Parody upon L'Allegro of Milton address'd to Mr. and Mrs. Miller. Bath: S. Hazard, 1777. 4to, disbound. Ck Sept 8 (234) £650

### Garsault, Francois Alexandre Pierre de
— Le Nouveau Parfait Marechal, ou la connoissance generale...du cheval. Paris, 1755. 4to, contemp calf gilt; joints cracked. With 29 (of 48) folding plates; lacking the botanical plates. sg Mar 7 (450) $250

### Garton, Ray
— Crucifix Autumn. Arlington Heights: Dark Harvest, 1988. One of 26 lettered copies. Syn. O Dec 5 (175) $100

— Methods of Madness. Arlington Heights: Dark Harvest, 1988. One of 52 lettered copies. Syn, in dj. O Dec 5 (178) $60

### Gaskell, Elizabeth Cleghorn, 1810-65
— Cranford. L, 1923. Illus by Hugh Thomson. Calf with pictorial inlays; front joint rubbed. sg Feb 8 (20) $130

### Gasparini, Quirino
— L'Inno Stabat Mater. [The Hague, c.1770]. 1st Ed. 4to, stitched but unbound. Some staining. Inscr "A. Stechway & Comp.". S Oct 27 (922) £200 [Palazzolo]

### Gaspey, William
— Tallis's Illustrated London. L, [c.1852]. 2 vols. 12mo, later cloth. Some foxing. bba July 18 (69) £200 [Sims Reed]

### Gass, Patrick, 1771-1870
— Gass's Journal of the Lewis and Clark Expedition. Chicago, 1904. Intro & indexed by James K. Hosmer. Orig cloth. Robbins copy. pba Mar 21 (115) $250

— A Journal of the Voyages and Travels.... Pittsburgh, 1807. 1st Ed. 12mo, contemp half lea; worn. Some leaves cut close; several leaves with old creases; tear to 1 leaf. pba Nov 16 (161) $1,800

Anr copy. Period half lea & bds; bds rubbed & scuffed. Pp.101-104 slightly smaller & askew; darkened & soiled; pages at rear marginally stained. Robbins copy. pba Mar 21 (114) $2,000

### Gassendi, Pierre, 1592-1655
— Institutio astronomica juxta hypotheses tam veterum.... L, 1653. 3 parts in 1 vol. 8vo, contemp calf; worn, front free endpaper torn. Minor waterstains. b Sept 20 (124) £550

Anr copy. Contemp calf; worn. b Sept 20 (125) £850

Anr copy. Contemp calf; rebacked. S Mar 14 (138) £800

Anr Ed. The Hague: Adrian Vlacq, 1656. 5 parts in 1 vol. 8vo, contemp vellum. Lacking port & with modern port tipped in at beginning; A4 cropped at foot. S Mar 14 (140) £320

— Tychonis Brahei vita.... The Hague, 1655. ("Tychonis Brahei, equitis Dani...vita....") 2d Ed. 4to, contemp vellum. Library markings; the 2 ports & divisional title to life of Copernicus in facsimile. sg May 16 (169) $300

### Gastineau, Henry, 1791-1876
— South Wales Illustrated. L, [c.1832]. 4to, 19th-cent half lea; worn, front cover detached. With engraved title & 110 mtd india-proof plates. Plate mounts foxed. sg May 9 (346) $150

### Gates, Eleanor
— Good-Night (Buenas Noches). NY, 1907. Illus by Arthur Rackham. Orig cloth. With 5 color plates. Some staining. Ck May 31 (129) £300

### Gattine, Michel Ange de
— Relation curieuse et nouvelle d'un voyage de Congo.... Lyon, 1680. 12mo, contemp calf gilt; needs rebacked. sg Mar 7 (93) $850

### Gatty, Charles Tindal
— Catalogue of a Loan Collection of the Works of Josiah Wedgwood, Exhibited at the Liverpool Art Club. Liverpool, 1879. 4to, modern half cloth, orig wraps bound in. bba Oct 19 (195) £65 [Mayer]

### Gau, Francois Chretien
— Antiquites de la Nubie.... Stuttgart & Paris, 1822-23. Folio, contemp half mor gilt. With 64 plates, 4 of them hand-colored. Some foxing throughout. sg Apr 18 (57) $4,200

### Gaudier-Brzeska, Henri, 1891-1915
— Henri Gaudier-Brzeska 1891-1915. L: Ovid Press, [1919]. One of 250. Folio, unbound as issued in orig portfolio; soiled. With 20 facsimile drawings. bba May 9 (216) £280 [Goddard]

### Gauffecourt, Jean Vincent Capperonnier de, 1691-1766
— Traite de la relieure des livres. La Motte: Pvtly ptd, [1762]. 8vo, bds; some wear. Fuerstenberg - Schaefer copy. One of 6 known copies. S Dec 7 (243) £4,800

### Gauguin, Paul, 1848-1903
— The Intimate Journals. NY, 1921. One of 530. Trans by Van Wyck Brooks. 4to, pictorial bds. sg Sept 7 (160) $150
— Noa Noa. Tahiti & NY, [1987]. Folio, cloth. sg Sept 7 (161) $70

### Gaunt, William
— The Etchings of Frank Brangwyn. A Catalogue Raisonne. L, 1926. 4to, half vellum. sg Sept 7 (57) $175

One of 125 with an orig etching by Brangwyn, sgd. Vellum. S May 16 (103) £200

### Gauthier, M. P.
— Les Plus Beaux Edifices de la ville de Genes et de ses environs. Paris, 1818-31. Part 1. Folio, later half mor; front joint cracked, endpapers brittle. With 108 plates. Library accession stamp. cb Feb 14 (2631) $1,200

### Gautier d'Agoty, Jacques, 1717-85 — & Duverney, L.
— Myologie complette en couleur et grandeur naturelle. Paris, 1746-[78]. 2 vols in 1. Folio, contemp bds; calf backstrip renewed. With 20 color plates, 11 double-page & mtd on guards. Letterpress to the last double-page plate repaired; lacking sectional titles. b June 28 (27) £12,000

Anr Ed. Paris, 1746-[48]. Bound in 1 vol. Folio, contemp vellum. With 20 plates ptd in 4 colors & varnished, 11 of them double-page. Text leaf [6] & its attached plate 2 detached & with edges frayed; right side of Plate 20 & lower margin of its text leaf with tear affecting surface & slight stain. CNY May 17 (79) $15,000

### Gautier d'Agoty, Jean Fabien
— Histoire naturelle ou exposition generale.... Paris: Moutard, 1777. Prospectus. 4to, contemp olive mor gilt with arms of Louis Antoine Sophie de Vignerot du Plessis de Richelieu. With 8 sample plates with Ms captions & ptd explications. Fuerstenberg - Schaefer copy. S Dec 7 (244) £9,000

### Gautier de Chatillon, Philippe
— Alexandreidos libri decem.... Lyons: Robert Granjon, 1558. 4to, mor gilt by Cape. In civilite type Rusthole in text of f3; tp & flyleaves washed. S Nov 30 (263) £2,000

### Gautier, Theophile, 1811-72
See also: Golden Cockerel Press
— L'Eldorado ou Fortunio. Paris, 1880. One of 115. 8vo, mor extra by Durvand, orig wraps bound in. With 12 plates in 2 proof states by Milius & etched vignettes in 2 proof states by Avril. b Sept 20 (620) £170

Out-of-series copy with all but 1 of the plates in 2 states & 2 additional suites on chine of the letters & vignettes. Illus by Milius, with vignettes & letters by Paul Avril. Mor extra by Lortic fils, orig wraps bound in. S Nov 21 (158) £300

— Une Nuit de Cleopatre. Paris, 1894. One of 200 with etchings in 2 states, this copy with 3 states. Illus by Paul Avril. 8vo, mor gilt by Lortic. b Dec 5 (26) £130
— One of Cleopatra's Nights, and Other Fantastic Romances. NY, 1882. Trans by Lafcadio Hearn. 8vo, cloth, 1st bdg; extremities stained, number to spine, library bookplate. pba Dec 14 (76) $250
— Le Roman de la momie. Paris, 1929. One of 834. Illus by Georges Barbier. 4to, mor extra by Jeanne Huck, orig wraps bound in. With 5 fan-shaped watercolor drawings & 4 additional suites of the illusts. S Nov 21 (160) £1,050

**Gay, John, 1685-1732**
See also: Limited Editions Club
— Fables. L, 1727-38. 1st Ed. 2 vols. 4to, contemp calf; rebacked. With frontis & 66 plates. Tear to 1 plate; Vol I discolored. b Jan 31 (166) £120
Anr Ed. L: for J. Tonson & J. Watts, 1729. 8vo, contemp calf; hinges worn. With 51 half-page engravings in text. Upper margins wormed, repaired in last few leaves. bba Oct 19 (224) £55 [Corke]
Anr Ed. L, 1738-42. 2 vols. 4to, contemp calf; upper half of front cover of Vol II cracked. pba Aug 8 (433) $140
Anr Ed. L, 1793. 2 vols. 8vo, contemp calf gilt; Vol I rubbed. With 66 (of 67) plates. Tear in 1 plate, anr with pencil scribbles in margin; marginal tears. bba May 30 (129) £120 [Breckenridge]
Anr Ed. L: Darton & Harvey for Rivington & others, 1793. 2 vols in 1. 8vo, modern calf gilt; front cover detached. With 36 plates, including frontis & title. Institutional stamps on tp verso. sg Sept 21 (203) $80
— Polly: an Opera.... L, 1729. 4to, mor gilt by Riviere; front hinge weak. Z June 28 (92) $250
Anr Ed. L, 1923. One of 380. Illus by William Nicholson. With 9 mtd colored plates. b Jan 31 (193) £60
— Rural Sports.... NY, 1930. One of 225. Illus by Gordon Ross. 4to, calf. pba July 11 (382) $85

**Gay, Jules, b.1807**
— Bibliographie des ouvrages relatifs a l'amour.... Turin & L, 1871-73. 6 vols in 3. 12mo, contemp half lea; vol 1/2 front hinge split, vol 3/4 backstrip loose. sg Apr 11 (114) $275

**Gay, Theresa**
— James W. Marshall: the Discoverer of California Gold. Georgetown, Calif., 1967. One of 250. Half mor in slipcase; slipcase soiled. With 2 color ports, 5 facsimile inserts, & 25 illus. Sgd. Larson copy. pba Sept 28 (464) $65

**Gaztaneta Iturrivalzaga, Antonio de**
— Norte de la navegacion hallado por el quadrante de reduccion. Sevilla: Juan Francisco de Blas, 1692. Folio, contemp calf. With 13 plates & 2 folding tables. Minor repairs at lower margin. S Nov 30 (158) £4,000

**Gazzettiere.** See: Atlas

**Gebeden...**
— Gebeden der Portugeesche Jooden, door een Joodsch Genootschap uit het Hebreeuwsch vertaalt. The Hague: Lion Cohen, 1791-93. 4 vols. 8vo, contemp calf gilt with arms of the De Pinto family; spines worn, a few backstrips partially detached, marginalia on endpapers & prelims of 1st vol. CE Dec 6 (142) $2,000

**Gebhart, Emile, 1839-1908**
— Cloches de Noel et de Paques. Paris: Champenois & Piazza, [1900]. One of 35 on japon, with additional suite of the illusts. Illus by Alphonse Mucha. 4to, orig wraps. With 78 color plates. S Nov 21 (164) £800

**Gee, Ernest Richard**
— The Sportsman's Library. NY, 1940. One of 600. Folio, cloth; some wear. O Dec 5 (49) $100; pba July 11 (383) $85

**Gee, Joshua, 1698-1748**
— The Trade and Navigation of Great-Britain Considered.... L, 1730. 8vo, disbound. Tp soiled; last leaf from anr copy. sg Mar 21 (101) $70

**Geel, Pierre Corneille van —& Others**
— Encyclographie du regne vegetal. Brussels, 1827-32. 95 (of 100) orig parts; lacking libraisons 1, 17, 25, 84 & 92. Unbound as issued in orig ptd wraps; wraps to libraison 60 lacking, others soiled, some tears. With 1 uncolored & 569 hand-colored plates. Some staining. C Nov 29 (109) £4,500

**Geffroy, Gustave, 1855-1926**
— Charles Meryon. Paris, 1926. 4to, wraps; spine partly cracked. sg Jan 11 (278) $120

**Gehler, Johann Samuel Traugott**
— Physikalisches Woerterbuch. Leipzig, 1825-45. Vols 1-10 & 2 Atlas vols bound in 23. 8vo & oblong 4to, text in orig bds, Atlas in half calf; rubbed, Atlas lacking section of 1 spine. S Mar 14 (141) £600

**Geiger, Maynard J.**
— The Life and Times of Fray Junipero Serra.... Wash., 1959. Bound with: Francis Weber, A Bicentennial Compendium of Maynard J. Geiger's the Life and Times of... 1st Ed. 2 works in 3 vols, orig cloth. With 6 maps. Inscr & sgd to Kurt Baer. Larson copy. pba Sept 28 (233) $75

**Geiger, Vincent —&**
**Wakeman, Bryarly**
— Trail to California.... New Haven, 1945. 1st Ed. - Ed by David Morris Potter. Orig cloth; cover worn. With frontis port & folded map. Marginal page tear & repair. Larson copy. pba Sept 28 (465) $50

**Geiler von Kaisersberg, Johann, 1445-1510**
— Das Irrigschafe.. Strassburg: Johann Greiniger, 1514. Folio, 19th-cent half lea; rubbed. Some soiling & browning. cb Feb 14 (2514) $2,750
— Navicula sive speculum fatuorum prestantissimi sacrarum literarum.... Strassburg: [J. Preuss], 16 Jan

# GEISEL

1511. 4to, 19th-cent mor gilt by C. Smith; upper hinge cracked. With woodcut on title & 111 woodcuts in text. Marginal waterstaining; corner of a few leaves repaired; minor browning. Beckford-Rosebery copy. CNY Dec 15 (23) $5,500

**Geisel, Theodor Seuss, 1904-91.** See: Seuss, Dr.

**Geissler, Johann Gottlieb**
— Der Drechsler. Leipzig, 1795-1801. 3 vols in 5. 4to, contemp calf; worn & rubbed. With 152 folding plates. Some spotting & browning. S Mar 14 (143) £1,200

**Geistliche...**
— Geistliche Auslegung des Lebens Jesu Christi. Leipzig, 1922. One of 200. Afterword by Albert Schramm. 8vo, vellum. Illus hand-colored. sg Apr 11 (148) $80

**Gekoski, R. A. —& Grogan, P. A.**
— William Golding. A Bibliography 1934-1993. L, 1994. One of 26 for authors & pbr, sgd by Golding. Half mor. S Dec 18 (388) £140 [Finch]

**Geldner, Ferdinand**
— Die deutschen Inkunabeldrucker. Stuttgart, 1970. 2 vols. 4to, orig cloth in djs. sg Apr 11 (149) $200

**Gell, Sir William, 1777-1836**
— Itinerary of the Morea....the Morea. L, 1817. 8vo, half calf. With folding map. b Sept 20 (337) £160
— Narrative of a Journey in the Morea. L, 1823. 8vo, cloth; worn. With 9 plates. b Sept 20 (367) £150
— Pompeiana: the Topography, Edifices and Ornaments of Pompeii. L, 1832. 2 vols. 8vo, contemp half mor; rubbed. With port & 85 plates, 1 hand-colored. b Jan 31 (447) £90

Anr copy. Mor gilt. With 88 plates with later hand-coloring. pba Sept 14 (173) $225
— The Topography of Troy and its Vicinity. L, 1804. 1st Ed. Folio, contemp half mor; rubbed. With colored title & 28 hand-colored plates & 2 maps. Some browning. b Sept 20 (366) £1,200

**Gelli, Jacopo**
— Bibliografia generale della scherma. Milan, 1895. 2d Ed. 4to, half cloth; some wear. NH July 21 (136) $100

**Gellius, Aulus**
— The Attic Nights. L, 1795. Trans by W. Beloe. 3 vols. 8vo, contemp calf gilt, prize bdg; joints cracking. pba Mar 7 (21) $90

**Gelman, Georg**
— Chirurgiae tripartita flora. Frankfurt, 1680. 4to, contemp vellum. With port, frontis & 36 plates. Browned; some worming; repairs in margins of 1st 3 leaves. S Mar 29 (695) £300

**Geminus, Thomas**
— Anatomes Totius, aere Insculpta Delineatio.... Paris: Andreas Wechel, 1564. Folio, bds; worn. With 38 (of 40) plates. Browned throughout; few plate margins frayed; some plates reinforced. CE Nov 8 (94) $2,000
— Compendiosa totius anatomie delineatio. L, 1545. Trans by Nicolas Udall. Folio, modern vellum. With 45 plates on 39 sheets & engraved title with arms of Henry VIII. Tp remargined at lower right corner; some staining & soiling, affecting text & images; small hole in Quinta musculorum tabula. Alferi - Rota - Schaefer copy. P Nov 1 (93) $17,000

**General...**
— A General Collection of Treatys, Declarations of War, Manifestos, and Other Publick Papers... from 1648 to the Present Time.... L, 1710. 8vo, contemp calf. Old ink notes to tp & several other leaves. pba Mar 7 (263) $160
— A General Collection of Voyages and Discoveries made by the Portuguese and the Spaniards. L, 1789. 1st Ed. 4to, orig bds with parchment spine; worn & soiled. With 4 plates & 4 (of 5) maps, 3 folding. Some foxing. pba July 25 (447) $500

**Genet, Elzear, c.1470-1548.** See: Carpentras

**Genet, Jean, 1910-86**
— Querelle de Brest. [Paris, 1948]. One of 525. Illus by Jean Cocteau. Half mor, orig wraps bound in. Prelim leaf torn & repaired. S May 16 (34) £850

**Genga, Bernardino, 1655-1734**
— Anatomia per uso et intelligenza del disegno recercata non solo su gl'ossi e muscoli del corpo humano. Rome, 1691. Folio, half lea; rebound. With 40 plates & 16 engraved leaves. Some staining, marginal soiling. CE Nov 8 (95) $2,000

**Genius...**
— Genius: Zeitschrift fuer werdende und alte Kunst. Munich, 1919-20-21. Vols I-III (all pbd). 3 vols. 4to, orig wraps. Met Feb 24 (27) $750
Anr copy. Various bdgs. Lacking 3 plates. Sold w.a.f. sg June 13 (287) $550

**Genlis, Stephanie de, 1746-1830**
— Les Chevaliers du Cygne. Paris, 1795. 3 vols. 8vo, contemp calf gilt; backstrips partly detached. sg Mar 21 (144) $90
— Theatre a l'usage des jeunes personnes. Paris, 1779-80. 4 vols in 5. 12mo, contemp citron mor gilt with a dentelle design made up of small tools. C May 1 (61) £13,000

**Genovesi, Antonio, 1712-69**
— Lettere familiari.... Naples, 1788. 2 vols in 1. 8vo, contemp vellum. Foxed; marginal dampstaining at end. sg Mar 21 (102) $175

**Genthe, Arnold**
— As I Remember. NY, [1936]. 1st Ed. 4to, cloth; corners bumped, notations on front free endpaper, rear

hinge cracked. With 112 photographic plates. sg Feb 29 (145) $70

One of 250. Half mor. Inscr to Betty Walter, 1940. pba Apr 4 (187) $275

— The Book of the Dance. NY, 1916. 1st Ed, Out-of-series copy. 4to, bds; soiled & rubbed. sg Feb 15 (128) $130

— Impressions of Old New Orleans. NY, [1926]. 1st Ed. 4to, half cloth; worn. With 101 plates. Tp soiled. sg Feb 29 (146) $90

— Isadora Duncan. NY, 1929. 4to, cloth; worn, soiled, spine cracked. sg Feb 29 (147) $50

— Pictures of Old Chinatown. NY, 1908. 1st Ed. - Text by Will Irwin. Orig cloth; covers rubbed. Robbins copy. pba Mar 21 (116) $110

Anr Ed. L, 1913. ("Old Chinatown.") Cloth; rubbed. Prelims foxed. Text by Will Irwin. sg Feb 29 (148) $130

### Gentil, ——

— Dissertation sur le caffe.... Paris, 1787. 1st Ed. 8vo, contemp half calf; spine worn. With frontis by O. Michel. Some spotting. Ck Mar 22 (126) £500

Anr copy. Contemp wraps; rubbed, spine foot chipped. With frontis by O. Michel. S Oct 12 (98) £200

### Gentleman...

— The Gentleman Angler: Containing Short, Plain and Easy Instructions.... L, 1726. 1st Ed. 12mo, 19th-cent calf; lacking free endpapers. Some staining. pba Mar 7 (12) $325

### Gentry, Thomas George, 1843-1905

— Nests and Eggs of Birds of the United States. Phila., 1882. 4to, orig cloth; worn, 1st few leaves detached. With port, color title & 54 colored plates. K June 23 (117) $400

### Geoffroy Saint-Hilaire, Etienne, 1772-1844 —& Cuvier, Frederic Georges, 1773-1838

— Histoire naturelle des mammiferes. Paris, [1819]-24-[16?]. 3 vols in 4. Folio, half mor; rubbed & soiled. With 240 hand-colored plates only. Plates stamped; titles & last leaf of Vols I-III backed with linen. Sold w.a.f. S Nov 30 (22) £3,000

### Geoffroy Saint-Hilaire, Isidore, 1805-61

— Histoire Generale et particuliere des anomalies de l'organisation chez l'homme et les animaux. Paris, 1832-36. 4 vols including Atlas. 8vo, orig wraps; stitching broken in Vol I; upper covers of Vol I & Atlas detached. With 20 litho plates. S June 12 (258) £260

### George, Henry, 1839-97

See also: Fore-Edge Paintings

— Progress and Poverty. San Francisco, 1879. 1st Ed. 8vo, orig cloth; rebacked, some cover wear. Robbins copy. pba Mar 21 (117) $450

### George III, King of England, 1738-1820

[-] The Pedigree of King George the Third. L, 1812. 8vo, half mor with monogram of William Sterling Maxwell. sg Sept 21 (239) $100

### Georgi, Theophilus

— Allgemeines europaisches Buecher-Lexicon. Leipzig, 1742-58. Parts 1-4 (of 5) & Supplements 1 & 2 (of 3) bound in 1 vol. Folio, modern vellum; worn. Some soiling & foxing; library perforation stamps. O Mar 26 (111) $130

### Geraldy, Paul, Pseud.

— La guerre, Madame. Paris, 1918. Illus by Bernard Naudin. 8vo, mor extra by Pierre Legran, orig wraps bound in. S Nov 21 (205) £1,400

— Toi et moi. Paris, [1939]. One of 25 on japon nacre with 2 additional suites. Illus by A. E. Marty. 8vo, mor extra by Bellevalle, orig wraps bound in. S Nov 21 (206) £650

### Gerard, John, 1545-1612

— The Herball.... L, 1597. 1st Ed. Folio, old half calf; rebacked. Some repairs; engraved title lacking; last leaf of text torn & repaired with loss; colophon leaf def. Sold w.a.f. W Mar 6 (194) £510

2d Ed. L, 1633. Folio, modern bds; spines lacking. Lacking engraved title & c.32 leaves; marginal repairs; some leaves mtd on guards. Sold w.a.f. pn Dec 7 (105) £340 [Bifolco]

3d Ed. L, 1636. Folio, contemp calf; rebacked, worn. Engraved title laid down with marginal losses; some browning & rust spots; lacking 1st 3 leaves of prelims. Sold w.a.f. b Dec 7 (149) £500

Anr copy. Later half calf; worn. Lacking initial & final blanks; some repairs at end; browned & soiled. Sold w.a.f. CE June 12 (212) $850

Anr copy. Modern mor. Lacking 1st & last blanks; lower outer margins stained at end. S Nov 30 (23) £1,150

Anr copy. 18th-cent sheep; extremities worn, front cover loose. Tp lacking lower right corner with loss to border & backed; dampstaining at end; last 3 leaves repaired & with some text in facsimile. Sold w.a.f. sg Dec 7 (220) $1,200

### Gerard, Philippe Louis, 1737-1818

— Le comte de Valmont.... Paris, 1807. 6 vols. 8vo, contemp half mor. With 5 orig drawings for this Ed by Moreau & with 7 drawings by Monnet for an Ed of Gerard's works. Fuerstenberg - Schaefer copy. S Dec 7 (246) £3,000

### Gerardus de Zutphania

— Tractatus de spiritualibus ascensionibus. Montserrat: Johann Luschner, 16 May 1499. 8vo, mor by Riviere. 27 lines; type 1:136G (title, 1st lines of paragraphs), 2:100G (paragraph, headings, colophon), 3:78G (text). Early foliation cropped; some dampstaining, marks & underlinings. 84 leaves. Goff G-179. Schaefer copy. P Nov 1 (94) $7,500

## GERBER

**Gerber, Ernst & Mary**
— The Photo Journal Guide to Comic Books. Minden, 1989. One of 900. 2 vols. Folio, syn. sg Dec 7 (249) $130

**Gerdes, Daniel**
— Florilegium historico-criticum librorum rariorum. Groningen & Bremen, 1763. 3d Ed. 8vo, contemp calf; spine ends chipped, joints cracked. sg Apr 11 (115) $200

**Gerlach, Martin**
— Allegorien.... Vienna, [c.1900]. Folio, unsewn in orig cloth portfolio. With pictorial tp & 120 plates, many ptd in color, some heightened with gold. Stamp on each sheet. S Nov 21 (163) £1,000
— Allegorien und Embleme. Vienna, 1882. 4 parts in 2 vols. Folio, loose as issued in bd folders. With 353 plates. Sold w.a.f. sg Sept 7 (1) $500

**Germain, Pierre**
— Elements d'orfevrerie. Paris, 1748. 2 parts in 1 vol. 4to, 19th-cent mor gilt by Lloyd. With engraved titles & 100 plates. Fuerstenberg - Schaefer copy. S Dec 7 (247) £1,700

**German...**
— The German Classics: Masterpieces of German Literature. NY: The German Publication Society, [1913]. 20 vols. Mor gilt with gilt-stamped German shields to front covers; spine ends rubbed. pba Aug 8 (290) $180

**Gerning, Johann Isaak von, 1767-1837**
— A Picturesque Tour along the Rhine.... L, 1820. 4to, 19th-cent half mor gilt. With double-page map & 24 hand-colored plates. Marginal tear to Plate 10. Schaefer copy. P Nov 1 (95) $4,000

**Gernsback, Hugo, 1884-1967**
— Ralph 124C41+: A Romance of the Year 2660. Bost., 1925. sg June 20 (130) $300

**Gernsheim, Helmut**
— Lewis Carroll, Photographer. NY, 1949. 1st Ed. In worn dj. With 64 plates. sg Feb 29 (87) $120

**Gernsheim, Helmut & Alison**
— The History of Photography from the Camera Obscura.... NY, 1969. In worn & torn dj. sg Feb 29 (149) $150

**Gerrit van der Goude**
— Boexken van der missen. Antwerp: Hendrik Eckert van Homberch, 8 June 1520. 8vo, 19th-cent calf over wooden bds. 21 lines; gothic type. With 72 woodcuts. Brown stain to 1st 5 leaves; marginal waterstain on last leaves; some soiling. Capuchins de Velp - Louis Napoleon - Meeus - Schaefer copy. P Nov 1 (96) $1,600

**Gersaint, Edme Francois, d.1750**
See also: Lorangere & Lorangere Collection
— Catalogue raisonne considerable de diverses curiosites en tous genres.... Paris, 1744. Bound with: Catalogue raisonne des coquilles et autres curiosites naturelles. Paris, 1736. 12mo, contemp calf with arms of Jean Claude Fauconnet de Vilde; spine chipped at head, corners rubbed, 1st half-title & tp detaching. Fuerstenberg - Schaefer copy. S Dec 7 (249) £850

**Gershwin, George, 1898-1937**
See also: Heyward & Gershwin
— Rhapsody in Blue. NY: Harms, [1927]. Folio, orig wraps; chipped, spine split. Piano solo score. Inscr to Molly King. CE June 12 (42) $6,500

**Gerson, Johannes, 1362-1428?**
— Opera. [Strassburg: J. Gruninger?], 1488. Part 3 (of 3), only. Folio, bdg not described. Worming at beginning & end; lower margin of tp repaired; some dampstaining; tear at head of Ee2; library stamp on 1st 2 leaves. 360 leaves. Goff G-186. S Mar 29 (657) £450

Anr Ed. [Nuremberg: Georg Stuchs], 22 Nov 1489. Part 3 (of 3) only. Folio, contemp blind-tooled goatskin over wooden bds; lacking 8 metal bosses & 2 clasps & catches, spine ends repaired. 50 lines & headline; double column; gothic type. Some browning & worming; occasional short tears. 400 leaves. Goff G-188. S Dec 18 (33) £700 [Zioni]

**Gerstaecker, Friedrich, 1816-72**
See also: Grabhorn Printing
— Narrative of a Journey Round the World.... L, 1853. 1st English Ed. 3 vols. 8vo, orig cloth; two spots on vol I cover. Larson copy. pba Sept 28 (466) $1,400
1st American Ed. NY, 1853. Orig cloth; rear cover water spotted, spine worn at top & bottom. Light foxing; 1 page torn & repaired. Larson copy. pba Sept 28 (467) $85
— Scenes de la vie californienne. Geneve, 1859. 1st French Ed. - Trans by Gustave Revilliod. 12mo, orig cloth. With 6 plates. Inscr by trans. Larson copy. pba Sept 28 (468) $50
— Wild Sports in the Far West. Bost., 1859. 12mo, orig cloth; rubbed. With 8 color lithos. sg Oct 26 (120) $50

**Gerstinger, Hans**
— Die griechische Buchmalerei. Vienna, 1926. Folio, half cloth, plates loose in matching half cloth folder. With 28 plates. sg Jan 11 (265) $550

**Gertanni, Giovanni Battista**
— I tormenti amorosi favola pastorale... rappresentata in Padova da l'Accad. dei Disuniti l'anno 1641. Padua: Julio Crivelari, [c.1641]. Bound with: a copy of Il Maometto extracted from anr Ed. 12mo, contemp vellum. S May 15 (293) £800

**Gervais, Stephen.** See: King, Stephen

**Gesamtkatalog...**
— Gesamtkatalog der Wiegendrucke. Leipzig, 1925-92. Vols I-IX & Vol X, Parts 1 & 2. bba Oct 5 (82) £420 [Maggs]
Anr Ed. Stuttgart & NY, 1968-78. Vols I-II & IV-V only. Cloth; some wear. O Mar 26 (112) $120

### Geschichte...
— Zur Geschichte der Kostueme. Munich, [c.1890]. Folio, half cloth; spine def, worn & rubbed. With 95 double-page color costume plates. Sold w.a.f. K Feb 11 (143) $300

Anr copy. Cloth; spine frayed, crack in front joint. With 125 hand-colored double-page plates. sg Jan 11 (119) $175

### Gesner, Conrad, 1516-65. See: Grabhorn Printing

### Gessi, Berlingiero
— La Spada di Honore.... Venice: Paolo Balioni, 1672. 12mo, contemp vellum; rear joint chipped, slit in rear cover. With 11 plates. Marginal staining. sg Mar 21 (145) $300

### Gessner, Salomon, 1730-88
— Contes moraux et nouvelles idylles.... Zurich, 1773. 1st Ed. Vol I (of 2). 4to, contemp red mor gilt. With engraved title & 10 plates. Subscribers' list bound at end. Fuerstenberg - Schaefer copy. S Dec 7 (257) £1,700

— Idylles et poems champetres. Paris, 1762. Bound with: Macpherson, James. Carthon, poeme, traduit de l'anglois. Londres [Paris], 1762. 8vo, contemp red mor gilt with arms of Simon Pierre Merard de St.-Just. Fuerstenberg - Schaefer copy. S Dec 7 (258) £2,400

— La Mort d'Abel. Paris, 1793. 4to, contemp red mor gilt; spine heel rubbed. With engraved port & 5 colored plates. Tp soiled & with minor damage; some margins soiled. Fuerstenberg - Schaefer copy. S Dec 7 (260) £300

— La morte d'Abelle.... Paris, 1782. 12mo, contemp mor gilt with name of A. A. Renouard stamped on upper cover. With port, 2 plates before letters by Moreau inserted & 5 plates by Marillier. Fuerstenberg - Schaefer copy. S Dec 7 (259) £300

— New Idylles. L, 1776. Trans by W. Hooper. 4to, mor gilt by Bayntun. With hand-colored additional title & 9 hand-colored plates. b Sept 20 (621) £250

— Oeuvres. [Paris: Cazin, 1778]. 3 vols. 18mo, 19th-cent mor gilt by Chambolle. With port & 14 plates in 2 states plus plates by Marillier for anr Ed. Fuerstenberg - Schaefer copy. S Dec 7 (251) £1,050

Anr Ed. [Paris, 1780-93]. 3 vols. 4to, calf gilt with monogram LD of Prince Louis Demidov; spines repaired. With 3 engraved titles, 2 frontises & 72 plates. Date added in ink to tp of Vol I. Fuerstenberg - Schaefer copy. S Dec 7 (252) £300

Anr Ed. [Paris: Cazin, 1785?]. 3 vols. 18mo, contemp calf by Kalthoeber, with his ticket; worn, Vol I broken. With port 3 titles & 14 plates. Fuerstenberg - Schaefer copy. S Dec 7 (254) £220

Anr Ed. Paris: Renouard, 1799. One of 20 on thin papier de hollande. 4 vols in 1. 8vo, contemp mor extra by Bozerian jeune. With plates on papier velin or japon & before letters. Renouard's copy. Fuerstenberg - Schaefer copy. S Dec 7 (256) £1,800

### Gesta...
— Gesta Romanorum.... Nuremberg: Anton Koberger, 20 Jan 1497. 4to, contemp blindstamped calf over wooden bds by the Antwerp binder, with Oldham stamps 98, 99, 106 & 107; spine chipped, hinges splitting. 43 lines 7 headline; double column; 14:130G, 19:71G, 21:74G. Some stains & soiling; tp partly detached. 132 leaves. Goff G-295. Saville LIbrary - Fitzwilliam copy. C Nov 29 (51) £3,000

### Gettysburg...
— Gettysburg Battlefield Directory. Hyde Park MA, [1868]. 8vo, orig wraps; chipped. With large folding litho battleplan. Some fold breaks to map. sg Dec 7 (66) $375

### Gevartius, Joannes Casparus
— Pompa introitus honori serenissimi principis Ferdinandi Austriaci. Antwerp, 1641. Folio, contemp vellum; 1 headband sprung. With 42 plates & maps & 45 text illusts. Plates discolored; tears at crease folds or guard mounts; 1 plate cropped at right margin; some leaves loose; with stamps of Bostom Museum of Fine Arts. Schaefer copy. P Nov 1 (97) $8,000

### Geymuller, Heinrich von. See: Stegmann & Geymuller

### Ghent, William james. See: Hafen & Ghent

### Ghent, William James
— The Road to Oregon: A Chronicle of the Great Emigrant Trail. L, 1929. In chipped dj. pba Apr 25 (419) $70

### Gheyn, Jacob de, 1565-1615
— Waabenhandling om Ror Musketter, oc Spedser. The Hague, 1608. 3 parts in 1 vol. Folio, 17th-cent calf gilt; extremities worn, corners & spine ends repaired, spine worn, joints weak. With 110 (of 117) plates with contemp hand-coloring & highlighted with gold & silver. P June 5 (235) $6,000

### Ghose, Sudhin N. See: Golden Cockerel Press

### Giacometti, Alberto, 1901-66
— Giacometti: The Complete Graphics and Fifteen Drawings. NY, [1970]. 4to, cloth, in dj. sg Jan 11 (196) $175

Anr Ed. NY, 1970. 4to, cloth, in dj. sg Jan 11 (196) $175

### Giafferri, Paul Louis de
— L'Histoire du costume feminin.... Paris, [1922-23]. Orig 10 parts. Folio, loose in pochoir part wraps as issued; last 4 wraps need rebacking. With 120 pochoir-colored plates. sg Jan 11 (120) $300

### Gibb, William
— The Royal House of Stuart. L, 1890. Folio, orig half mor; rubbed. With 40 colored plates. bba May 30 (235) £70 [Lobo]

### Gibbings, Robert. See: Golden Cockerel Press

# GIBBON

**Gibbon, Edward, 1737-94**
See also: Limited Editions Club
— An Essay on the Study of Literature.... L, 1764. 1st Ed in English. 8vo, contemp calf gilt. Hefner copy. CNY May 17 (18) $1,200
— The History of the Decline and Fall of the Roman Empire. L, 1776-88. 1st Ed, 1st state. 6 vols. 4to, 19th-cent calf; worn, corners bumped. With port & 3 maps, 2 of them folding. Lacking half-titles; some browning. S Mar 29 (658) £4,200
2d State of Vol I. Contemp calf gilt; upper joint of Vol I repaired, some joints cracked, spine ends chipped, corners worn. With port & 3 folding maps. Lacking half-titles; errata leaves in Vols I & II repaired; lacking 3 final blanks; O2 & Zz2 in Vol III torn & repaired; some browning. Downshire - Hefner copy. CNY May 17 (19) $7,500
Anr copy. One map cut close; lacking final blanks in Vol VI. S Dec 18 (127) £1,700 [Woods]
Anr copy. Contemp calf; rebacked, endpapers renewed. Some foxing. sg Oct 19 (91) $2,000
3d Ed of Vol I, 1st Ed of Vols II-VI. L, 1777-88. 6 vols. 4to, calf. With port & 3 folding maps. Some foxing; Vol V, Sigs. 3Q & 3R bound in reverse order. K June 23 (297) $1,600
3d Ed of Vol I, New Ed of Vols II-III, 1st Ed of Vols IV-VI. 6 vols. 4to, contemp calf; rebacked, spines & extremities worn, Vol I front joint started. With port & 3 folding maps. sg Feb 8 (288A) $650
Anr Ed. Dublin, 1789. 6 vols. 8vo, contemp calf; joints weak. Old stencilled name to tops of titles. pba June 20 (169) $425
Anr Ed. L, 1797. 12 vols. 8vo, contemp calf; rebcked. sg Sept 21 (19) $600
Anr Ed. L, 1813. 12 vols. 8vo, contemp calf; rebacked, rubbed. b Sept 20 (568) £180
Anr Ed. L, 1838-39. 12 vols. 8vo, half mor. b Jan 31 (87) £170
Anr Ed. L, 1854-55. 8 vols. 8vo, contemp calf gilt by Sangorski & Sutcliffe; part of spine replaced. pba June 20 (170) $225
Anr Ed. L, 1862. 8 vols. 8vo, contemp calf. b Jan 31 (86) £280
Anr Ed. L, 1900. 7 vols. 8vo, cloth. Foxed. pba Aug 22 (583) $100

**Gibbon, Lardner.** See: Herndon & Gibbon

**Gibbons, Alfred St. Hill, 1858-1916**
— Exploration and Hunting in Central Africa 1895-96. L, 1898. 8vo, cloth; inner joint cracked, edges rubbed. O June 4 (140) $650

**Gibbs, James, 1682-1754**
— Rules for Drawing.... L, 1736. 2d Ed. Folio, contemp calf; worn, back cover reinforced. With 63 (of 64) plates. Lacks plate 47; dampstained. Sold w.a.f. CE Nov 8 (195) $750

**Gibbs, Mifflin Wistar**
— Shadow and Light: An Autobiography.... Wash., 1902. 1st Ed. Orig cloth. With 39 illus. Larson copy. pba Sept 28 (291) $450

**Gibbs, William, Artist**
— Decorative Alphabets for the Chisel, the Brush, the Pen, and the Needle. L, [c.1865]. 4to, orig cloth; soiled, some leaves loose or frayed. O Mar 5 (103) $130

**Gibson, C. D'W.**
— Shoot If You Must. NY, [1950]. One of 250. Inscr. O June 4 (141) $90

**Gibson, Charles Dana, 1867-1944**
— Drawings. NY, 1894. Oblong folio, half cloth; stained, soiled & rubbed, front joint cracked. pba Aug 8 (437) $60
— Eighty Drawings, Including the Weaker Sex. NY & L, 1903. Oblong folio, orig pictorial bds; spine soiled. wa Feb 29 (111) $80
— Sketches in Egypt. L & NY, 1899. 8vo, orig cloth; soiled. pba Nov 30 (143) $55
— The Social Ladder. NY, 1902. 1st Ed. Oblong folio, orig pictorial bds; some soiling to cloth. wa Feb 29 (112) $80
— A Widow and her Friends. NY, 1901. Oblong folio, pictorial bds; soiled. wa Feb 29 (110) $120

**Gibson, J. Watt**
— Recollections of a Pioneer. [St. Joseph, 1912]. 1st Ed. Orig cloth; worn & spotted. With frontis port. Larson copy. pba Sept 28 (470) $300

**Gibson, John, Engineer**
— Atlas Minimus, or a New Set of Pocket Maps.... L, 1792. 24mo, disbound. With engraved title & 59 (of 52) maps, hand-colored in outline & with most borders hand-colored. Some foxing & soiling. wa Feb 29 (607) $800

**Gibson, Walter B.**
See also: Grant, Maxwell
— Magician's Manual. NY: Magician's League of America, [1933]. 2d Ed. Bds; soiled. pba Aug 22 (613) $80

**Gibson, William, fl. c.1720**
— New Treatise on the Diseases of Horses.... L, 1754. 2 vols. 8vo, contemp calf; rubbed. Some foxing & soiling. O Jan 9 (117) $225

**Giddings, Joshua Reed, 1795-1864**
— The Exiles of Florida: or, the Crimes Committed by Our Government against the Maroons who Fled from South Carolina. Columbus, 1858. 1st Ed. 8vo, cloth. sg Mar 28 (288) $150

**Gide, Andre, 1869-1951**
— Les Caves du Vatican. Paris, 1929-30. One of 372. Illus by J. E. Laboureur. 8vo, mor gilt by Paul Bonet [Carnets 197], orig wraps bound in. With 5 frontises & 32 illusts in black & sanguine. S Nov 21 (166) £5,000
— Charles-Louis Philippe. Paris, 1911. 1st Ed. Orig wraps; front joint splitting, spine ends frayed. Inscr. sg June 20 (131) $120

— Paludes. Paris, 1921. One of 300. Illus by Roger de La Fresnaye. 4to, half mor gilt with geometric designs, by Paul Bonet [not in Carnets], orig wraps bound in. With 6 lithos. S Nov 21 (165) £3,200
— Prometheus Illbound. L, 1919. One of 100. Orig vellum; soiled & bowed. Repaired tear to top edge of tp, limitation & preface leaves. wa Feb 29 (36) $90
— La Tentative Amoureuse ou le traite du vain desir. Paris, 1921. One of 410. Illus by Marie Laurencin. 4to, half mor, orig wraps bound in. With orig Caron D'Ashe remarque sgd by Laurencin on front free endpaper. sg Sept 14 (254) $1,300
— Theseus. Verona: Officina Bodoni, 1949. One of 200. Illus by Massimo Campigli. 4to, orig wraps. With 12 lithos. sg Feb 15 (222) $1,300
— Le Voyage d'Urien. Paris, 1893. 1st Ed, One of 300. Illus by Maurice Denis. 4to, half mor, orig wraps bound in. With cover woodcut design & 29 tinted lithos. S Nov 21 (167) £3,200

**Gidney, C. M. —& Others**
— History of Santa Barbara, San Luis Obispo, and Ventura Counties, California. Chicago, 1917. 2 vols. Later half mor; worn & soiled, joints cracked, call numbers. Library markings, including perforated stamps, occasionally affecting text. cb Oct 17 (147) $275

**Giffard, James, Vicar of Wootton**
— Thornton Abbey.... Louth, 1823. 8vo, contemp half calf. b Dec 5 (233) £65

**Gifford, John, 1758-1818**
— A History of the Political Life of...William Pitt. L, 1809. 3 vols. 4to, contemp calf gilt; rubbed. b Sept 20 (126) £130

**Gilbert & George**
— Dark Shadows. The Sculptors. L: Art for All, 1974. With thumbprint signatures. b Jan 31 (168) £65

**Gilbert, Grove Karl —& Others**
— The San Francisco Earthquake and Fire of April 18, 1906 and Their Effects on Structures and Structural Material. Wash., 1907. Ptd wraps; spine frayed. With 55 photographic plates & 2 folding maps. pba Feb 12 (283) $50

**Gilbert, Martin.** See: Churchill & Gilbert

**Gilbert, Olive**
— Narrative of Sojourner Truth, a Northern Slave.... Bost., 1875. 8vo, orig cloth; tape remnants at head of spine. sg Oct 26 (342) $175

**Gilbert, William, 1540-1603**
— De Magnete. L, 1600. 1st Ed. Folio, modern calf with calf panels from orig bdg; spine scuffed. Rusthole in R5 with loss to 2 letters; old dampstaining to upper outer corner of S3 & 4. Inscr by Lancelot Browne as received from Gilbert. C Apr 3 (106) £20,000
Anr copy. 17th-cent vellum. With 89 woodcuts, 4 of them full-page & 1 of them folding. Some worming from quire Q, affecting text & some illusts; some dampstaining at front. Schaefer copy. P Nov 1 (98) $14,000
Anr copy. Later calf gilt; rubbed, rebacked preserving most or orig spine. Tp repaired in lower margin where library stamp removed; minor worming & repairs; some spotting. Madsen copy. S Mar 14 (144) £4,400

**Gilbert, Sir William Schwenck, 1836-1911**
See also: Limited Editions Club
— Fifty "Bab" Ballads.... L, 1877. 8vo, mor gilt with onlays forming 7 of the characters, orig cloth bound in. S Nov 21 (169) £460
— Trial by Jury. L, 1875. 1st Issue. 8vo, orig wraps; spine chipped & split, foxed. Foxing at ends. CE June 12 (204) $240

**Gilbert, Sir William Schwenck, 1836-1911 —& Sullivan, Sir Arthur, 1842-1900**
— The Sorcerer. L, [1877]. 4to, orig wraps; joints splitting. Full score; Sullivan's name stamped on tp. Some wear. CE Feb 21 (109) $190

**Gilchrist, Alexander, 1828-61**
— Life of William Blake. L, 1880. 2 vols. 8vo, orig cloth; endpapers browned. sg Jan 11 (48) $225
Anr copy. Later half mor extra; Vol I front joint started. sg Feb 8 (189) $300

**Gildemeister, Charles.** See: Carstensen & Gildemeister

**Gill, Emlyn Metcalf**
— Practical Dry-Fly Fishing. L, 1912. 1st English Ed. pba July 11 (112) $55
Anr Ed. NY, 1912. O June 25 (137) $80
Anr Ed. NY, 1915. Orig cloth. Marginal pencilmarks. Inscr to Birket "Kit" Clarke. pba July 11 (111) $160

**Gill, Eric, 1882-1940**
See also: Golden Cockerel Press
— 25 Nudes. NY, 1950. In spotted dj. With 26 plates. bba May 9 (221) £100 [Virgo Books]
— Beauty Looks After Herself. L, 1933. Orig cloth; spine rubbed, worn. Inscr to Elizabeth Pepler by Douglas Pepler. S Nov 2 (86) £280 [Bankes]
— Emblems Engraved on Wood. Ditchling, 1916. Out-of-series copy. 4to, orig wraps; short tear at fore-edge of both covers. S Nov 21 (172) £850
— Engravings.... Bristol: Douglas Cleverdon, 1929. One of 10 on Japan vellum, with extra set of engravings & 4 sgd proofs of port. 4to, orig mor gilt by Sangorski & Sutcliffe. Some spotting. S Nov 21 (171) £3,800
One of 400. Cloth; hinges weaked, rubbed, bumped. With pencil drawing of lettering for a memorial to Mary Constance Wemyss, sgd with initials & dated 4.7.38. S Nov 21 (170) £950
Anr Ed. L, 1934. 4to, orig cloth, unopened. With 133 woodcuts. Some spotting. S Nov 2 (87) £550 [Manheim]
Anr Ed. Wellingborough: Christopher Skelton, 1983. One of 85 with additional portfolio of 8 wood-

engravings. 2 vols. Folio, orig half mor & cloth portfolio. bba May 9 (377) £600 [Thomas] Anr copy. Orig half mor. sg Oct 19 (92) $750
— Sculpture. Ditchling: Douglas Pepler, 1918. 1st Separate Ed. Cloth; soiled. sg Feb 15 (130) $70
— Wood-Engravings. Ditchling: St. Dominic's Press, 1924. One of 150. 4to, orig cloth; rubbed & spotted. With 32 plates. bba May 9 (632) £600 [Ginnan]

**Gillett, James B.**
— Six Years with the Texas Rangers.... Austin, [1921]. Orig cloth; spine ends frayed, corners bumped, shaken. With 8 plates. pba Aug 8 (60) $85

**Gilliss, James Melville, 1811-65**
— The U. S. Naval Astronomical Expedition to the Southern Hemisphere. Wash., 1855-56. Vols I-II (of 4). 4to, orig cloth; hinges repaired, minor wear. With folding panorama with some hand-tinting, 5 maps (4 folding), 15 color litho plates of birds, 4 other color lithos, 5 duotone lithos & 17 steel-engraved plates. pba Feb 13 (84) $250

**Gillmore, Joseph.** See: Steele & Gillmore

**Gillmore, Parker**
— Gun, Rod, and Saddle. Personal Experiences. By Ubique. NY, [1869]. 12mo, orig cloth. With frontis. sg Mar 7 (453) $100
— Prairie and Forest. NY, 1874. 8vo, cloth. pba July 11 (384) $70

**Gillmore, Quincy Adams**
— Official Report to the United States Engineer Department, of the Siege and Reduction of Fort Pulaski.... NY, 1862. 8vo, orig wraps; def. With 4 folding maps 7 plans 7 8 litho views. Foxed. Inscr by Maj. Gen. Joseph Gilbert Totten. CE June 12 (118) $500

**Gillot, Claude**
— Nouveaux desseins d'habillements a l'usage des balets, operas, et comedies. Paris, [c.1725]. 8vo, contemp calf; worn. Engraved throughout, with title & 72 plates. Lacking Plates 73-84; some browning. Fuerstenberg - Schaefer copy. S Dec 7 (261) £750

**Gillray, James, 1757-1815**
— The Caricatures of Gillray. L, [1818]. Oblong 4to, half mor; rubbed. With 22 hand-colored plates only. Lacking tp, 10 plates & some text; 1st plate creased, 2 torn with loss. bba Nov 30 (96) £1,100 [George]
— Works. L, 1847. Folio, half mor gilt by Hammond; rubbed, extremities worn. With port & 582 plates on 152 sheets. wad Oct 18 (278) C$1,300

**Gilmore, Jene C.**
— Art for Conservation: the Federal Duck Stamps. Barre, 1971. One of 300. 4to, half calf. Inscr to John Howell. pba Mar 7 (121) $110

**Gilpin, Laura**
— The Mesa Verde National Park. NY, 1927. 4to, orig wraps. pba Apr 25 (420) $275

— The Pueblos: A Camera Chronicle. NY: Hastings House, [1941]. 4to, orig cloth, in dj. F Mar 28 (227) $130

**Gilpin, William, 1724-1804**
See also: Fore-Edge Paintings
— Remarks on Forest Scenery.... L, 1791. 1st Ed. 2 vols. 8vo, contemp calf gilt. With double-page map & 31 plates. b Jan 31 (320) £80

**Gilpin, William, 1822-94**
— Mission to the North American People.... Phila., 1873. Orig cloth. With folding hand-colored maps. Maps with few stub-tears. Robbins copy. pba Mar 21 (119) $225

**Gilpin, William Sawrey, 1762-1843**
— Practical Hints upon Landscape Gardening. L, 1832. 8vo, calf; broken, most of spine lacking. With 16 plates. Some dampstain at top; foxing affecting plates, which are cut close. wa Nov 16 (308) $150

**Ginanni, Marc Antonio**
— L'Arte del blasone. Venice, 1756. 4to, contemp vellum. bba Oct 5 (83) £320 [Franks]

**Gingrich, Arnold**
— The Fishing in Print. A Guided Tour through Five Centuries.... NY, 1974. In dj. O June 25 (138) $60

**Ginguene Library, P. L.**
— [Sale Catalogue] Catalogue des livres de la bibliotheque de feu.... Paris: Merlin, 1817. 8vo, contemp wraps; corners curled. Some foxing. O Mar 26 (113) $500

**Ginsberg, Allen**
— Planet News 1961-1967. San Francisco, 1968. 1st Ed, One of 500. pba Jan 25 (111) $85

**Gioacchino da Fiore, c.1145-1202**
— Interpretatio... in Hieremiam Prophetam.... Venice: Barnardinus Benalius, 20 Nov 1525. 4to, modern calf gilt. C June 26 (80) £1,000

**Giono, Jean, 1895-1970**
— Recherche de la purete. Paris, 1953. One of 30 with an orig pencil drawing by Buffet & a suite of the plates on velin with 4 orig etchings not used. Illus by Bernard Buffet. 4to, calf extra by Pierre-Lucien Martin, orig wraps bound in. With 21 plates. S Nov 30 (342) £12,000

**Giovannoli, A.**
— Roma antica.... Rome, 1619. 3 parts in 1 vol. Oblong folio, contemp vellum; soiled. With etched title to each part & 138 plates. Lacking plates 31-32, 42, 44 & 48; also lacking a map in Part 1; Plate 34 torn affecting image; Part 3 torn at lower corner with loss; some soiling & fraying. S Nov 30 (01) £1,200

**Giovio, Paolo.** See: Jovius, Paulus

### Girardin, Stanislas Xavier de
— Promenade ou itineraire des Jardins d'Ermenonville. Paris, 1788. 8vo, early 19th-cent calf. With 25 plates. Fuerstenberg - Schaefer copy. S Dec 7 (262) £1,600

### Giraud, I. E.
— The Flowers of Milton. L, [1846]. Folio, orig bds; broken. With colored title & 28 plates. pnE Mar 20 (141) £240

### Giraudoux, Jean, 1882-1944
— Le Sport. Paris: Editions d'Auteuil, 1962. One of 27 on japon imperial with 10 further etchings not used in the book, a suite of the etchings on japon ancien, a suite of the wood engravings & an ink drawing. Illus by Andre Dunoyer de Segonzac. 4to, unsewn in orig wraps. S Nov 21 (177) £750
— Suzanne et le Pacifique. Paris, 1921. 1st Ed. 12mo, modern half mor; orig wraps bound in. Inscr. S Oct 27 (1121) £200 [Guichard]
  Anr Ed. Paris, 1927. Out of series copy for M. Pierre Babouot with additional suite of the illusts & pencil drawing for 1 engraving. Illus by J. E. Laboureur. 4to, mor extra by Henri Creuzevault, suite in half vellum. Kettaneh copy. S Nov 21 (176) £2,800

### Giraudoux, Jean, 1882-1944 —& Others
— Les Sept Peches capitaux. Paris: Kra, 1926. One of 300. Illus by Marc Chagall. 4to, halr mor gilt with onlays by Virinand, orig wraps bound in. With 15 etchings. S Nov 21 (175) £1,800

### Girault de Prangey, Joseph Philibert
— Choix d'ornements Moresques de l'Alhambra. Paris, [1842]. Folio, loose in orig ptd wraps. With litho title & 29 plates. Tp & several plates with short tears in margins repaired. S June 27 (105) £1,300

### Gironi, Robustiano, 1769-1838
— Le Danze dei Greci. Milan, 1820. Folio, mor gilt by Sangorski & Sutcliffe. With frontis & 5 plates. S Nov 21 (221) £600

### Gist, Christopher, 1706?-59
— Journals.... Pittsburgh, 1893. 8vo, cloth. With 7 maps. sg Oct 26 (89) $175

### Giustiniano, Bernardo, 1408-89
— Historie Chronologiche dell'Origine degl'Ordini Militari.... Venice: Combi & LaNou, 1692. Folio, later 18th-cent calf gilt; spine & joints cracked, tape remnants on rear endpapers. sg Mar 21 (147) $400

### Givry, Grillot de
— Witchcraft, Magic & Alchemy. L, 1931. 4to, orig cloth, in dj. With 10 color plates. b Jan 31 (285) £70

### Glaeser, Ludwig. See: Museum of Modern Art

### Glaser, Curt
— Gotische Holzschnitte. Berlin, [1923]. One of 100. Folio, half vellum; bowed & soiled. With 55 plates, some in color. pba June 20 (171) $100

### Glasgow, Ellen, 1874-1945
— Works. NY, 1938. Ltd Ed, sgd. 12 vols. Half vellum. cb Oct 17 (329) $300

### Glass, E. L. N.
— The History of the Tenth Cavalry 1866-1921. Tucson, 1921. Foreword by John J. Pershing. Syn; rubbed & bumped, lacking small piece of rear pastedown. Library stamp at bottom right corner of tp. cb Oct 17 (141) $600

### Glasscock, Amnesia. See: Steinbeck, John

### Glasse, Hannah, fl.1747
— The Art of Cookery, Made Plain and Easy.... L, 1796. 8vo, orig lea; rebacked. NH June 1 (92) $290

### Glauber, Johann Rudolf, 1604-62
— A Description of New Philosophical Furnaces.... L: R. Coats & T. Williams, 1651. 1st English Ed. 7 parts in 1 vol. 4to, modern mor by Fiona Anderson. Spotted & soiled; burn-hole in E4; lacking Qq1; Vv2 torn & repaired. S Oct 27 (807) £750 [Zioni]
— Furni novi philosophici, sive descriptio artis destillatoriae novae. Amst., 1651. 6 parts in 1 vol. Bound with: Libellum ignium, oder Feuer-Buechlein. Prague, 1703. And: De tribus lapidibus ignium secretorum. Prague, 1703. 8vo, vellum. Lacking 1 plate; tp & frontis of 1st work repaired with small loss. S Mar 14 (145) £650

### Gleason, J. Duncan & Dorothy
— Windjammers. NY: Bernhardt Wall, 1922. One of 325. Folio, half cloth; warped. Etched throughout. pba July 25 (457) $375

### Gleichen, Wilhelm Friedrich von
— Decouvertes les plus nouvelles dans le regne vegetal.... [Nuremberg & Paris], 1770. 3 parts in 1 vol, including Supplement. Folio, contemp calf gilt; repaired. With 51 hand-colored plates & with additional tp dated 1763. S June 27 (323) £3,400

### Gleig, George Robert, 1798-1888
— Lives of the Most Eminent British Military Commanders. L, 1832. 8vo, later 19th-cent calf gilt. sg Sept 21 (20) $550

### Gleizes, Albert, 1881-1953 —& Metzinger, Jean, 1883-1956
— Cubism. L, 1913. sg Jan 11 (197) $175

### Glenn, Thomas Allen
— Some Colonial Mansions and Those Who Lived in Them. Phila., 1899-1900. 2 vols. 8vo, orig cloth; worn, front hinges cracked. wa Feb 29 (382) $80

### Glisson, Francis, 1597-1677
— De rachitide.... L, 1650. 1st Ed. 8vo, contemp calf; restored. Ck Mar 22 (127) £4,400
  2d Ed. L, 1660. 8vo, modern vellum. Some dampstains. Ck Mar 22 (128) £650

**Gloedon, Wilhelm von**
— Taormina. [Pasadena]: Twelvetress Press, 1986. Folio, cloth, in soiled dj. sg Feb 29 (331) $90

**Gloucester, Massachusetts**
— The Fishermen's Own Book, comprising the List of Men and Vessels lost from the Port of Gloucester, Mass., from 1874 to April 1, 1882.... Gloucester: Procter Brothers, [1882]. 8vo, orig cloth; top corner of front free endpaper missing. pba July 25 (149) $70

**Gluck, Jay —& Hiramoto, Sumi**
— A Survey of Persian Handicraft. Tehran, 1977. 4to, cloth, in dj. sg June 13 (194) $130

**Glushko, V. P.** See: Langeman & Glushko

**Gmelich, Karl.** See: Kolb & Gmelich

**Godard, Andre**
— Les Bronzes du Luristan. Paris, 1931. Folio, cloth. sg Sept 7 (163) $90

**Godard d'Aucour, Claude, 1716-95**
— Memoires turcs, par un auteur turc de toutes les academies mohametanes.... Amst., 1776. 2 vols. 12mo, contemp calf gilt with arms of Maria Feodorovna of Russia. Fuerstenberg - Schaefer copy. S Dec 7 (264) £360

**Godart de Beauchamps, Pierre Francois, 1689-1761**
— Histoire du Prince Apprius.... Constantinople [i.e., Lyons], 1728. 12mo, old calf; worn. Some foxing & soiling. O Mar 5 (104) $100

**Goddard, Frederick B.**
— Where to Emigrate, and Why.... NY, 1869. Orig cloth; dampstained & worn, cloth on rear cover becoming loose. Some marginal dampstaining. Inscr. pba Aug 8 (61) $95

**Godeau, Antoine**
— Oeuvres chretiennes. Paris, 1633. 8vo, contemp red mor gilt a la fanfare with each of the 39 compartments containing the mirror monogram of Noel de Bullion, Marquis de Gallardon, probably from the atelier of Mace Ruette; spine ends repaired. C May 1 (63) £15,000

**Godey's**
— Godey's Lady's Book. Phila., 1849. 8vo, mor gilt; rebacked. pba Aug 22 (771) $160

**Godfrey, Edward Settle**
— The Field Diary of Lt. Edward Settle Godfrey ... Battle of the Little Big Horn.... Portland OR: Champoeg Press, 1957. One of 1,000. pba Apr 25 (421) $85
Anr copy. Inscr by Edgar Stewart to John & Natalie Popovich. pba June 25 (98) $50

**Godfrey, Masters John**
— Monograph & Iconograph of Native British Orchidaceae. Cambr., 1933. 4to, cloth; worn. Met May 22 (386) $200

**Godwin, Thomas, d.1642**
— Romanae historiae anthologia recognita et aucta. An English Exposition.... Oxford: John Lichfield for Henry Cripps, 1633. 4to, contemp vellum; recased. Old stamp on tp. sg Mar 21 (148) $140

**Godwin, William, 1756-1836**
— An Enquiry Concerning Political Justice. L, 1793. 1st Ed. 2 vols. 4to, contemp sheep; worn, endpapers stamped. sg Mar 21 (149) $375
— Essay on Sepulchres: or, a Proposal for Erecting Some Memorial.... L, 1809. 8vo, contemp calf gilt by J. Larkins; pieces lacking from spine, joints cracked. pba Nov 30 (145) $140
Anr copy. Orig half cloth; worn. S Apr 23 (59) £380
— Of Population. An Enquiry concerning the Power of Increase...an Answer to Mr. Malthus. L, 1820. 1st Ed. 8vo, half calf. Lacking half-title. b May 30 (3) £1,150
Anr copy. Orig bds; spine head chipped, joints worn. With half-title. Light spotting; x & xi stained. Ck Mar 22 (129) £1,300

**Goedeke, Karl, 1814-87**
— Grundriss zur Geschichte der deutschen Dichtung.... Nendeln, 1979. Index by Hartmut Rambaldo. Volumes I-V in 11, includes index. Together, 12 vols. 8vo, orig wraps, index in cloth; vol 4/1/2 rear cover detached. sg Apr 11 (120) $400

**Goeldi, Emil August, 1859-1917**
— Album de aves amazonica. Rio de Janeiro, 1900-6. 4to, cloth. With 48 chromolitho plates. Met May 22 (429A) $250

**Goethe, Johann Wolfgang von, 1749-1832**
See also: Doves Press; Limited Editions Club
— Faust. Berlin, 1924. One of 1,000. 4to, vellum. Limitation number clipped out. pba Mar 7 (122) $90
Anr Ed. L, [1925]. One of 1,000, sgd by the artist. Trans by John Anster; illus by Harry Clarke. 4to, orig half vellum. b May 30 (429) £200
Anr copy. Half vellum. sg Feb 15 (73) $375
Anr Ed. NY, 1930. One of 501. Illus by Lynd Ward. pba Apr 4 (436) $275
Anr Ed. Berlin, 1932. 4to, orig half vellum. sg Feb 8 (289) $80
Anr Ed. Paris, [1943]. One of 400 with 2 extra suites of the plates. Illus by Louis Icart. 2 vols. 4to, wraps, unopened. With 24 color plates. sg Apr 18 (103) $1,000
[-] Goethe Galerie. NY, 1870. Illus by Frederick Pecht & Arthur von Ramberg. 4to, mor gilt. With 50 plates. pba Aug 22 (772) $75
— Die Leiden des Jungen Werthers.... Freystadt, 1775. 2 vols in 1. 8vo, modern half calf. sg Feb 8 (290) $60
— Promethee. Paris, 1950. One of 165. Trans by Andre Gide, illus by Henry Moore. Folio, wraps. Inscr by Henry Moore, Oct 1972. wad Oct 18 (337) C$3,100

— Reineke Fuchs. Stuttgart & Tuebingen, 1846. 1st Issue. 4to, lev gilt by Cape, with 1 part wrap bound in. With 38 plates including additional title & leaf of pictorial instructions to the bookbinder. sg Oct 19 (94) $850
— Saggio sulla Metamorfosi delle Piante di... Goethe. Milan, 1842. 4to, contemp mor extra bound for presentation to Archduke Rainer, with his arms. Dedicatee's copy. L.p. copy. C May 1 (66) £1,500
— Werke. Stuttgart & Tuebingen, 1850-51. 30 vols in 20. 8vo, contemp half calf; joints & edges rubbed. With 2 plates. Some spotting. S Oct 27 (1123) £100 [Zioni]

**Goetzmann, William H.**
— Army Exploration in the American West, 1803-1863. New Haven, [1960]. 2d Ptg. In dj; bdg with corners bumped, hinge cracking before title, small stain to rear endpaper. pba Apr 25 (422) $80
— Exploration and Empire. NY, 1966. In dj. Errata slip laid in. pba Nov 16 (110) $120

**Goeurot, Jean**
— Le Sommaire et entretenement de vie tressingulier.... N.p., [1516]; [?Poitiers: Jacques Bouchet, ca. 1540]. 8vo, 18th-Cent bds; extrems rubbed, upper joints splitting. Includes Regime singulier de sancte by Nicolas de Houssemaine, & Le traicte du regime de sancte by Pierre de Tuviganes. D4 holed with loss; G8 torn. Ck Mar 22 (130) £1,200

**Goff, Frederick R.**
— Incunabula in American Libraries: A Third Census. NY, 1964-72. 2 vols, including Supplement Ls to Warren F. Skillings of Anthoensen Press & related material laid in. O Dec 5 (50) $160; O Mar 26 (115) $190
Anr Ed. NY: Kraus, 1973. 4to, orig cloth. Facsimile of Goff's copy with his annotations. sg Apr 11 (150) $150

**Gogol, Nikolai Vasil'evich, 1809-52**
See also: Limited Editions Club
— Les Ames mortes. Paris, 1948. One of 285. Illus by Marc Chagall. 2 vols. Folio, unsewn in orig wraps. Copy with 74 (of 96) plates only. C June 26 (188) £7,200
Anr copy. Marginal ink smudges. sg May 23 (283) $21,000
— Tarass Boulba.... Paris, 1931. One of 110. Illus by A. Grinevsky. 4to, mor extra by Nicolet, the vellum doublures with ink & pencil drawings, orig wraps bound in. S Nov 21 (184) £550

**Gold**
— Gold and Silver Tables.... San Francisco, 1867. Half bds; covers varnished. Larson copy. pba Sept 28 (473) $300

**Golden...**
— The Golden Hind, a Quarterly Magazine of Art and Literature. L, 1922-24. Ed by Clifford Bax & Austin Spare. Vol I, No 1-Vol II, No 8. 4to & folio, orig wraps; some soiling. sg Feb 15 (147) $140

**Golden Cockerel Press—Waltham Saint Lawrence, Berkshire**
— The Birth of Christ from the Gospel according to Saint Luke. 1925. One of 370. bba May 9 (308) £90 [Collinge & Clark]; sg Feb 15 (134) $100
— The Book of Jonah. 1926. One of 175. bba May 9 (510) £720 [Marks]; S May 16 (63) £650
— Chanticleer, a Bibliography of the Golden Cockerel Press. 1936. One of 300. bba May 9 (567) £200 [Sotheran]
— The Chester Play of the Deluge. 1927. One of 275. bba May 9 (519) £450 [Poetry Bookshop]; S May 16 (64) £550
— Ecclesiastes, or the Preacher. 1934. One of 247. S Nov 2 (35) £400 [Gateway]; sg Sept 14 (145) $350
— The Four Gospels. 1931. One of 488. C Nov 29 (128) £900; S July 11 (78) £2,100; sg Oct 19 (95) $4,400
— The Golden Cockerel Greek Anthology. 1937. One of 74. sg Sept 14 (152) $375
— Harriet and Mary. 1944. One of 450. sg Sept 14 (155) $90
— Homeric Hymn to Aphrodite. 1948. One of 650. bba May 9 (554) £50 [Deighton Bell]
— Mabinogion. 1948. One of 475. Trans by Gwyn Jones & Thomas Jones. Inscr by Gwyn Jones, 1964. bba May 9 (556) £220 [Bankes Books]; S Nov 2 (36) £180 [Sotheran]; sg Oct 19 (100) $275
— The Ninety-First Psalm. 1944. One of 350. bba May 9 (546) £100 [Sotheran]
— Passio Domini Nostri Jesu Christi. 1926. One of 250. Illus by Eric Gill. bba May 9 (515) £640 [Sotheran]
— Pertelote. 1943. One of 200. bba May 9 (569) £110 [Sotheran]
— Samson and Delilah. 1925. One of 325. bba May 9 (508) £310 [Rush]
— Shelley at Oxford. 1944. One of 470. sg Feb 15 (143) $50
— Sir Gawain and the Green Knight. 1952. One of 60 specially bound. Trans by Gwyn Jones. S May 16 (74) £180; sg Sept 14 (165) $375
— The Song of Songs... 1925. One of 720. bba May 9 (505) £500 [Collinge & Clark]
Anr Ed. 1936. One of 140. sg Feb 15 (146) $250
One of 64 with 6 extra plates specially bound. bba May 9 (536) £190 [Brook]
AESOP. - The Fables. 1926. One of 350. bba May 9 (309) £160 [Ginnan]; sg Sept 14 (146) $120
APOLLONIUS OF TYRE. - Historia. 1956. One of 75 with an extra set of the plates. sg Sept 14 (138) $425
APULEIUS, LUCIUS. - The XI Bookes of the Golden Asse. 1923. One of 450. cb Oct 17 (638) $225
BANNET, IVOR. - The Amazons. 1948. One of 500, but in the special bdg. sg Feb 15 (133) $175
BATES, HERBERT ERNEST. - Flowers and Faces. 1935. One of 325. sg Sept 14 (139) $475
BLIGH, WILLIAM. - The Log of the Bounty. 1936-37. One of 300. 2 vols. b Mar 20 (46) £550
BLIGH, WILLIAM. - Voyage in the Resource. 1937. One of 350. b Mar 20 (44) £380; b Mar 20 (45) £280
BRANTOME, PIERRE DE BOURDEILLE. - The Lives of Gallant Ladies. 1924. One of 625. 2 vols. bba May 9

(502) £80 [Rush]

BREBEUF, JEAN DE. - The Travels & Sufferings...Among the Hurons of Canada. 1938. One of 300. sg Sept 14 (142) $300

BRETON, NICHOLAS. - The Twelve Moneths. 1927. One of 500. bba May 9 (517) £280 [Rush]; bba May 9 (518) £150 [Ginnan]

BROWNE, WILLIAM. - Circe and Ulysses, the Inner Temple Masque. 1954. One of 100 specially bound in mor gilt & with 4 extra illusts. bba May 9 (561) £150 [Bankes Books]

CABELL, JAMES BRANCH. - Jurgen. 1949. One of 500. bba May 9 (557) £80 [Cox]

CAREW, THOMAS. - A Rapture. 1927. One of 375. sg Sept 14 (140) $70

CHASE, OWEN & OTHERS. - Narratives of the Wreck of the Whale-Ship Essex. 1935. One of 275. bba May 9 (532) £340 [Collinge & Clark]

CHAUCER, GEOFFREY. - The Canterbury Tales. 1929-31. One of 485. 4 vols. S Nov 2 (33) £1,700 [Blackwell]

CLAY, ENID. - The Constant Mistress. 1934. One of 300. S Nov 2 (34) £240 [Bankes]; sg Feb 15 (135) $275

CLAY, ENID. - Sonnets and Verses. 1925. One of 450. bba May 9 (506) £120 [Brook]

COMENIUS, JOHN AMOS. - The Labyrinth of the World.... 1950. One of 70 specially bound. sg Feb 15 (136) $375

Out-of-series copy specially bound. bba May 9 (559) £160 [Deighton Bell]

COPPARD, ALFRED EDGAR. - Clorinda Walks in Heaven. 1922. One of 770. Inscr. bba May 9 (499) £85 [Collinge & Clark]

COPPARD, ALFRED EDGAR. - Hips & Haws. 1922. One of 480. bba May 9 (500) £120 [Finch]

COVENTRY, FRANCIS. - The History of Pompey the Little. 1926. One of 400. bba May 9 (17) £55 [Dowdell]

DE CHAIR, SOMERSET. - The First Crusade. 1945. One of 100 specially bound. sg Sept 14 (143) $250; sg Sept 14 (148) $300

One of 500. bba May 9 (310) £75 [Sotheran]; sg Sept 14 (144) $90

DRYDEN, JOHN. - Songs and Poems. 1957. One of 100 specially bound in mor gilt & with a duplicate set of illusts. b Dec 5 (27) £300; cb Oct 17 (639) $170

EDGEWORTH, MARIA. - Letters of Maria Edgeworth & Anna Letitia Barbauld. 1953. One of 60 specially bound. bba May 9 (560) £120 [Wilkins Jones]

ELLIS, HAVELOCK. - Kanga Creek, an Australian Idyll. 1922. One of 1,375. sg Feb 15 (137) $50

FIELDING, HENRY. - A Journey from this World to the Next. 1920. Copy with colophon scribbled over in ink & lettered "xyz". Copy bound in mor gilt with instructionsfor the placement of the plates in pencil on each engraving. sg Sept 14 (147) $325

FIELDING, HENRY. - The Life of Mr. Jonathan Wild the Great. 1932. One of 350. sg Feb 15 (138) $75

FLINDERS, MATTHEW. - Narrative of his Voyage in the Schooner "Francis." 1946. One of 100 specially bound. b Sept 20 (622) £450

One of 750. bba May 9 (552) £240 [Bankes Books]; sg Sept 14 (149) $400

FLINT, SIR WILLIAM RUSSELL. - Minxes Admonished, or Beauty Reproved. 1955. One of 150 specially bound. sg Oct 19 (101) $425

Out-of-series copy. sg Feb 15 (139) $250

FRYER, MARY ANN. - John Fryer of the Bounty. 1939. One of 300. b Mar 20 (93) £230

GANTILLON, SIMON. - Maya. 1930. One of 500. bba May 9 (524) £80 [Collinge & Clark]

GAUTIER, THEOPHILE. - Mademoiselle de Maupin. 1938. One of 50 specially bound. b Sept 20 (623) £480

GHOSE, SUDHIN N. - Folk Tales and Fairy Stories from India. 1961. One of 100 specially bound. sg Sept 14 (151) $325

GIBBINGS, ROBERT. - The Seventh Man, a True Cannibal Tale of the South Seas. 1930. One of 500. bba May 9 (525) £120 [Blackwell]

GILL, ERIC. - Art & Prudence. 1929. One of 500. bba May 9 (523) £80 [Blackwell]

GRAY, THOMAS. - An Elegy Wrote in a Country Churchyard. 1946. One of 750. bba May 9 (550) £160 [Bankes Books]

One of 80 specially bound. sg Sept 14 (153) $500

GRIMM BROTHERS. - Grimm's Other Tales.... 1956. One of 75 specially bound. sg Sept 14 (154) $375

HARTNOLL, PHYLLIS. - The Grecian Enchanted. 1952. One of 360. sg Feb 15 (140) $80

HERRICK, ROBERT. - One Hundred and Eleven Poems. 1955. One of 445. pba Mar 7 (123) $225

JONES, GWYN. - The Green Island. 1946. One of 400. bba May 9 (551) £50 [Deighton Bell]

KEATS, JOHN. - Lamia, Isabella, the Eve of Saint Agnes and Other Poems. 1928. One of 485. sg Sept 14 (157) $450

LACOMBE, JEAN DE. - A Compendium of the East. 1937. One of 300. bba May 9 (538) £50 [Deighton Bell]; sg Mar 7 (135) $175

LASCARIS, EVADNE. - The Golden Bed of Kydno. 1935. One of 60 specially bound in mor but this without extra plates. Inscr by Lettice Sandford. bba May 9 (533) £190 [Brook]

One of 60 specially bound in mor & with an extra sgd set of the prints. S May 16 (68) £400

Anr copy. With folder containing 3 A Ls s of Christopher Sandford to Guy Littell, 1935. sg Oct 19 (96) $1,200

One of 60 specially bound in mor but lacking extra sgd set of the prints. sg Feb 15 (141) $200

LAWRENCE, THOMAS EDWARD. - Crusader Castles. 1936. One of 1,000. 2 vols. b Jan 31 (169) £480; S July 11 (311) £600; sg Oct 19 (97) $1,100

LAWRENCE, THOMAS EDWARD. - Men in Print. 1940. One of 470. S May 16 (71) £240

LAWRENCE, THOMAS EDWARD. - Secret Despatches from Arabia. 1939. One of 970. bba May 9 (543) £240 [Baring]; S May 16 (69) £260; S July 11 (322) £600

LAWRENCE, THOMAS EDWARD. - Shaw-Ede...Letters to H. S. Ede. 1942. One of 470. S May 16 (72) £240

LONGUS. - Daphnis and Chloe. 1930. One of 450. bba May 9 (526) £80 [Collinge & Clark]

LUCAS, FRANK LAURENCE. - Gilgamesh, King of Erech. 1948. Out-of-series copy. bba May 9 (311) £220 [Bankes Books]

LUCIAN OF SAMOSATA. - The True Historie.... 1927. One of 275. sg Sept 14 (158) $300; sg Sept 14 (159)

$225; sg Feb 15 (142) $300
MALLARME, STEPHANE. - L'Apres-Midi d'un faune. 1956. One of 100 specially bound. bba May 9 (564) £400 [Baring]
MARSTON, JOHN. - The Metamorphoses of Pigmalion's Image 1926. One of 325. bba May 9 (513) £55 [Blackwell]
MILTON, JOHN. - Paradise Lost. 1937. One of 200. bba May 9 (539) £200 [Marks]
MONCRIF, FRANCOIS AUGUSTIN PARADIS DE. - Moncrif's Cats. 1961. One of 100 specially bound. sg Sept 14 (160) $300
MORRISON, JAMES. - The Journal of Boatswain's Mate of the Bounty. 1935. One of 325. b Mar 20 (131) £300
MUSAEUS. - Hero and Leander. 1949. One of 100 specially bound & with extra plate. S May 16 (73) £340
One of 500. bba May 9 (558) £85 [Deighton Bell]
OMAR KHAYYAM. - The Golden Cockerel Rubaiyat. 1938. One of 270. bba May 9 (541) £400 [Marks]; S Nov 2 (38) £550 [Marks]; sg Sept 14 (161) $375
PHILBY, HARRY ST. JOHN BRIDGER. - A Pilgrim in Arabia. 1943. One of 350. sg Oct 19 (99) $325
POWYS, LLEWELYN. - Glory of Life. 1934. One of 275. bba May 9 (531) £340 [Blackwell]
RUTTER, OWEN. - The First Fleet. 1937. One of 370. bba May 9 (540) £320 [Collinge & Clark]
SHAKESPEARE, WILLIAM. - The Poems & Sonnets. 1960. One of 100. sg Sept 14 (163) $375; sg Feb 15 (144) $275
One of 470. sg Feb 15 (145) $130
SHELLEY, PERCY BYSSHE. - Zastrozzi. 1955. One of 60 specially bound, with an extra set of the illusts. sg Sept 14 (164) $90
SMITH, AARON. - The Atrocities of the Pirates. 1929. One of 500. bba May 9 (414) £100 [Rush]
SPARRMAN, ANDERS. - A Voyage Round the World with Captain James Cook... 1944. One of 300. pba Feb 13 (177) $350; pnE Sept 20 (87) $220; S May 16 (75) £250; sg Sept 14 (166) $500
STRONG, LEONARD ALFRED GEORGE. - The Hansom Cab and the Pigeons. 1935. One of 212. bba May 9 (534) £170 [Bankes Books]
SUCKLING, SIR JOHN. - A Ballad Upon a Wedding. 1927. One of 375. bba May 9 (520) £130 [Collinge & Clark]
SWIFT, JONATHAN. - Directions to Servants. 1925. One of 30. S May 16 (76) £1,200
One of 350. bba May 9 (509) £80 [Dowdall]; S May 16 (77) £350; wd Nov 15 (63) $125
SWIFT, JONATHAN. - Gulliver's Travels. 1925. One of 450. 2 vols. bba May 9 (509A) £300 [Bankes Books]; sg Sept 14 (167) $400
SWINBURNE, ALGERNON CHARLES. - Hymn to Proserpine. 1944. One of 50 specially bound. bba May 9 (547) £380 [Sotheran]
Anr copy. Inscr by John Buckland-Wright to Lilian Burtinshaw. sg Sept 14 (168) $700
SWINBURNE, ALGERNON CHARLES. - Lucretia Borgia. [1942]. One of 30 specially bd in mor gilt with facsimile plates of chapter 6 of Ms. S May 16 (78) £150

Anr Ed. 1942. One of 320. bba May 9 (165) £60 [Sotheran]
SWINBURNE, ALGERNON CHARLES. - Pasiphae. 1950. One of 100 specially bound. S May 16 (79) £150
SWIRE, HERBERT. - The Voyage of the "Challenger." 1938. One of 300. 2 vols. bba May 9 (542) £220 [Heritage]

**Golden Gate Park.** See: San Francisco

**Golder, Frank Alfred, 1877-1929**
— Bering's Voyages; an Account of the Efforts of the Russians to Determine the Relation of Asia and America. NY, 1922-25. 2 vols. pba Feb 13 (13) $120; pba Apr 25 (140) $100
— Russian Expansion on the Pacific, 1641-1850. Cleveland, 1914. 1st Ed. Orig cloth. Robbins copy. pba Mar 21 (121) $475

**Golding, Arthur**
— A Moral Fable-Talk. San Francisco: Arion Press, 1987. One of 425. sg Sept 14 (31) $130

**Golding, William**
— Lord of the Flies. L, 1954. 1st Ed. In dj with spine ends rubbed. pba Aug 22 (187) $1,400
— Nobel Lecture 7 December 1983. Leamington Spa: Sixth Chamber Press, 1984. One of 50 bound in mor. bba Oct 19 (332) £110 [Rees]

**Goldman, Joan M.**
— The School in our Village. L: Batsford, [1957]. Illus by Edward Ardizzone. In soiled & repaired dj. Inscr by Ardizzone on half-title with sketches of children at play. O Sept 12 (8) $2,100

**Goldman, Marcus Selden**
— In Praise of Little Fishes. Bost.: David Godine, 1977]. One of 300. Illus by Craig Ronto. Half cloth. pba July 11 (113) $80

**Goldman, William**
— The Princess Bride. L, 1975. In dj with extremities rubbed. Warping to pages in middle. pba May 23 (138) $70

**Goldschmidt, Ernst Ph.**
— Gothic & Renaissance Bookbindings.... Nieuwkoop & Amst., 1967. 2d Ed, one of 600. 2 vols. 4to, orig cloth. b May 30 (545) £110
Anr copy. With 50 plates not in 1st Ed. sg Apr 11 (51) $300

**Goldschmidt, Lucien.** See: Grolier Club

**Goldsmith, Oliver, 1728-74**
See also: Fore-Edge Paintings
— The Beauties of English Poesy.... L, 1767. 1st Ed. 2 vols. 12mo, contemp calf; rebacked with orig spine laid on. Lacking half-titles. Met Feb 24 (197) $325
— An History of the Earth and Animated Nature. L, 1856 [1857]. 2 vols. 8vo, half lea; extremities worn. With port, 2 colored titles & 71 color plates. NH June 1 (71) $230

# GOLDSMITH

Anr Ed. L, [c.1856]. 4to, contemp half mor; worn. With port, 2 hand-colored titles & 72 hand-colored plates. Frontis port foxed. wa Nov 16 (195) $150
— The Life of Richard Nash of Bath. L, 1762. 8vo, contemp calf; extremities worn. F Mar 28 (415) $50
— Miscellaneous Works. Paris, 1825. Ed by Washington Irving. 4 vols. 8vo, calf gilt; rubbed. Some staining. Z June 28 (98) $250
— The Roman History.... L, 1769. 1st Ed. 2 vols. Half calf; rubbed. Z June 28 (99) $450
— She Stoops to Conquer. L, 1773. 1st Ed, Variant 2 state. 8vo, contemp half calf; corners bumped. E4 with short tear to lower margin; some staining; bound with 5 other 18th-cent comedies & operettas. Ck Sept 8 (230) £550
— A Survey of Experimental Philosophy. L, 1776. 1st Ed. 2 vols. 8vo, contemp half vellum. bba Sept 7 (125) £370 [Axe]
— The Vicar of Wakefield. L, 1792. 2 vols in 1. 12mo, contemp calf gilt. pba Mar 7 (125) $180
Anr Ed. L, [c.1910]. Contemp calf gilt by Sangorski & Sutcliffe. pba Aug 8 (250) $65
Anr Ed. L, 1929. Illus by Arthur Rackham. 4to, mor gilt with onlays forming the design of the frontis plate. bbc Dec 18 (96) $210
One of 575. Orig vellum gilt. b Sept 20 (636) £380
One of 775. Orig vellum gilt. Some spotting. bba May 9 (409) £520 [M. Edwards]
Anr copy. With 12 colored plates. S Nov 2 (131) £300 [Toledano]; sg Oct 19 (204) $325; sg Feb 15 (251) $325

## Goldsmith, Oliver, 1728-74 —& Parnell, Thomas, 1679-1718
— Poems. L, 1795. Illus by Thomas Bewick & John Bewick. 4to, 19th-cent half mor. With 5 full-page & 8 smaller wood-engravings. S Apr 23 (267) £480

## Goldsmiths' Library of Economic Literature
— Catalogue of the Goldsmiths' Library.... Cambr., 1970-83. Vols 4 vols. 4to, orig cloth, in soiled dj. bba Oct 5 (193) £340 [Cody]

## Goldston, Will
— Great Magicians' Tricks. L, [1931]. Ltd Ed. 4to, orig cloth. pba Mar 7 (170) $325
— Will Goldston's Exclusive Magical Secrets. L, [1912]. 4to, orig mor with name of George Wetherald stamped on lower cover; joints worn & cracking. pba Mar 7 (171) $275

## Goldstone, Adrian H. —& Payne, John R.
— John Steinbeck: A Bibliographical Catalogue of the Adrian H. Goldstone Collection. Austin, [1974]. pba Oct 5 (353) $275

## Golf
— American Annual Golf Guide. NY: Golf Guide Co., 1928-1931. 1st Eds. 3 vols, cloth; spines faded, spine ends chipped, hinges cracked. Some pp. detached. pba Apr 18 (59) $160

— Motor Guide to Golf Links About Chicago. Chicago, [1918]. 1st Ed. Wraps. With folding map. 2 pp. with residue; 1 p. torn. pba Nov 9 (4) $800
— Program of the 41st Losa Angeles Open, Pro-Amateur at the Rancho Park Golf Course. Los Angeles, 1967. Wraps; rear wrap pieces missing. Dampstained. Sgd by Arnold Palmer, Jack Nicklaus, Gary Brewer, Chichi Rodriguez, Doug Sanders, Gene Littler, & Bill M. Pieces. pba Nov 9 (25) $120

## Goll, Claire
— Diary of a Horse. Brooklyn, [1946]. One of 320. With 4 illusts by Marc Chagall. 4to, bds. sg Feb 1 (54) $250

## Goll, Ivan, 1891-1950
— Die Chapliniade. Eine Kinodichtung. Dresden, 1920. Illus by Fernand Leger. 4to, orig pictorial bds. sg Apr 18 (104) $475
— Elegie d'Ihpetonga, suivi di masques de Cendre. Paris, 1949. One of 180. Illus by Pablo Picasso. 4to, unsewn in orig wraps. Ck Sept 8 (10) £1,400
— Four Poems of the Occult. Kentfield: Allen Press, 1962. One of 130. Folio, 5 folded fascicles, each with wraps. cb June 25 (1904) $950; pba Mar 7 (8) $1,400

## Goltzius, Hubert, 1526-83
— C. Iulius Caesar, sive historiae Imperatorum Caesarumque Romanorum.... Bruges, 1562 (but Sept 1563). Folio, contemp calf gilt, presentation bdg to Gaspar Schetz; rebacked & restored. Roman & greek types. With engraved title & 54 numismatic plates in text. Tp soiled, foxed & with erasures; H1 repaired in margin; some spotting. Schaefer copy. P Nov 1 (101) $10,000
— Fastos magistratum et triumphorum Romanorum...restitutos. Bruges, 1566. Folio, contemp calf gilt with supralibros of Du Verdier, yapp edges; bumped, spine ends worn. With engraved title, 162 engravings in text & 72 woodcut borders. Some foxing & soiling. Schaefer copy. P Nov 1 (102) $18,000
Anr copy. 18th-cent calf gilt; joints weak. Repair in fore-margin of a1 just touching edge of plate. S Nov 30 (264) £1,400
— Vive omnium fere imperatorum imagines.... Antwerp, 1557. Folio, mor gilt over wooden bds with Laurinus supralibros within a gilt wreath; some stains & worming, joints worn. With engraved title in green & gold & 131 cuts in text ptd on rectos only from an engraved plate & 2 color (tan & gold) woodblocks. Some worming throughout, occasionally affecting images; some spotting & discoloration. Schaefer copy. P Nov 1 (100) $60,000

## Gombert, Nicolas
— Cantiones quinque vocum. [Strassburg: P. Schoeffer, 1539]. ("Mutetarum liber primus.") 1st Ed. Alto part only (of 5). Oblong 4to, contemp calf gilt with fleuron in center & ALTUS at top, over pastebds; wormed with some loss at foot, spine ends repaired. 40 leaves; type-set music by double impression. S Dec 1 (166) £2,700

### Gomez de la Serna, Ramon
— Le Cirque. Paris: Pierre Tremois, [1927]. One of 33 on Arches, with 2 extra suites in uncolored state, 1 with remarques. Illus by Marcel Vertes. Folio, half mor, orig wraps bound in. A few leaves at ends with spotting or stains. S Nov 21 (182) £400

### Gondar, Jacques
— Chroniques Francoises.... Paris: Louis Janet, [1830]. One of a few hand-colored copies bound in velvet. 2 parts in 1 vol. 8vo, orig velet; edges worn through, loose. With tp, 4 plates, borders & initials all hand-colored. sg Feb 8 (22) $110

### Gonse, Louis
— L'Oeuvre de Jules Jacquemart. Paris, 1876. One of 10 with the engravings before text. 2 vols in 1. 4to, mor extra by Charles Meunier, orig wraps bound in; joints rubbed. Bound in are 6 A Ls s by M. Desboutin, Louis Gonse, Jules Jacquemart, Armand Quesroy & H. Giacomelli. S Nov 21 (186) £350

### Gonzalez de Barcia, Andres
— Ensayo cronologica, para la historia general de la Florida.... Madrid, 1723. 1st Ed. Folio, contemp vellum. Lacking 1 prelim leaf; a few margins torn; tp stamped & patched. CE May 22 (9) $950

### Gonzalez de Salas, Jose Antonio
— Nueva idea de la tragedia antigua [Tragedia Practical]. Madrid, 1778. 2d Ed. 2 vols. 8vo, contemp tree calf; spine head & foot chipped. With 3 plates. S Oct 27 (1124) £100 [Pearson]

### Gonzalez, Tirso
— Veritas religionis Christianae manifeste demonstrata adversus omnes infideles. Naples, 1702. 2 vols. 8vo, contemp red mor gilt presentation bdgs for Pope Clement XI, with his arms; minor abrasion upper cover of Vol I. C Apr 3 (108) £1,600

### Gooch, Rebecca
— Original Poems on Various Subjects. Southwold, 1821. 8vo, orig bds; worn. b Dec 5 (363) £140

### Good...
— The Good Boy's Aviary, being a Collection of Birds, chiefly Foreign. L: William Cole, 1825. 12mo, orig wraps with hand-colored pictorial label on upper cover. With pictorial title & 12 leaves, each with hand-colored illust. Engraved throughout. S Nov 2 (196) £550 [Schiller]

### Goodall, Nelson & Perkins Company
— Frieght Tariff to Take Effect July 1, 1875. San Francisco, [1875]. 8vo, cloth. pba Feb 12 (373) $150

### Goode, George Brown, 1851-96
— The Fisheries and Fishery Industry of the United States. Wash., 1884-87. 5 parts in 5 vols. 4to, cloth & half mor; worn, 1 joint split. Sold w.a.f. pba July 25 (151) $170

### Gooden, Mona
— The Poet's Cat. L, 1946. One of 110, sgd by author & artist. Illus by Stephen Gooden. Orig half calf. sg Sept 14 (171) $110

### Goodhue, Bertram Grosvenor, 1869-1924
— A Book of Architectural and Decorative Drawings. NY, 1924. 2d Ptg. Folio, half cloth; rebacked retaining backstrip. Library markings. sg June 13 (11) $90

### Goodison, Jack Weatherburn
— Reynolds Stone: His Early Development as an Engraver on Wood. Cambr., 1947. One of 200. Orig half cloth; rubbed. bba May 9 (424) £280 [Marks]

### Goodman, John Bartlett
— The Key to the Goodman Encyclopedia of the California Gold Rush Fleet. Los Angeles, 1992. One of 275. Ed by Daniel Woodward. Wraps in cloth box. With 17 folded sheets of tables. Larson copy. pba Sept 28 (369) $90

### Goodrich, Lloyd
— Edward Hopper. NY: Abrams, [1978]. Oblong folio, cloth, in dj. sg Sept 7 (189) $80
— Raphael Soyer. NY, [1972]. Folio, cloth, in dj. Bookplate sgd by Soyer mtd to tp. sg June 13 (347) $200
— Reginald Marsh. NY: Abrams, [1972]. Oblong folio, cloth, repaired dj. sg June 13 (329) $200
— Thomas Eakins. His Life and Work. NY, 1933. 4to, cloth. sg Jan 11 (158) $110
 Anr Ed. Cambr. MA, 1988. 2 vols. 4to, cloth. O May 7 (147) $90

### Goodrich, Samuel Griswold, 1793-1860
— General Atlas of the World. Bost., [1841?]. Folio, disbound. With engraved title & 51 hand-colored maps. Waterstains to tp; some foxing to maps; frayed. Met Sept 28 (336) $1,600
— Peter Parley's Universal History on the Basis of Geography. Bost., 1837. 1st Ed, 2d Ptg. 2 vols. 16mo, orig cloth. CE May 22 (252) $1,200

### Goodridge, Charles Medyett
— Narrative of a Voyage to the South Seas.... Exeter, 1841. 4th Ed. 8vo, cloth; dampstained, worn & bumped. With frontis & 2 plates. Met Feb 24 (342) $310

### Goodspeed, Charles Eliot
— Nathaniel Hawthorne and the Marine Museum of the Salem East India Marine Society.... Bost.: Club of Odd Volumes, 1946. One of 99. In frayed dj. O Dec 5 (51) $100
— Yankee Bookseller: Reminiscences. Bost., 1937. One of 310. Half lea; spine ends rubbed. F June 20 (515) $80

### Goodwin, Francis, 1784-1835
— Rural Architecture. L, 1835. 2d Ed. 2 vols. 4to, orig cloth; spine repaired, orig backstrip laid down. With 99 plates & plans. bba Sept 7 (30) £300 [Arnold]

Anr copy. Orig cloth; 1 spine tightened & frayed. bbc Dec 18 (164) $400

**Gordan, John D.**
— The Ghost at Brede Place. NY, 1953. Laid in is a program for the play given at Brede School House (Crane's home) on 28 Dec 1899, inscr by Stephen Barr as to its origin. Met May 22 (130) $1,600

**Gordon, Adam Lindsay**
— Poems: Sea Spray and Smoke Drift.... Melbourne: A. H. Massina, 1880. Contemp mor gilt. Some foxing. pba July 11 (386) $60

**Gordon, Arthur Charles Hamilton, 1st Baron Stanmore**
— Fiji Records of Private and Public Life 1875-1880. Edin.: Pvtly ptd, 1897-1912. 4 vols. 8vo, orig cloth; spine heads worn. S Nov 30 (217) £3,000

**Gordon, Patrick, fl.1700**
— Geography Anatomized: or, the Geographical Grammar. L, 1693. 1st Ed. 12mo, later mor gilt; extremities worn, front joint rubbed. With 18 double-page maps, hand-colored in outline. Some browning & foxing; library stamps on text leaves. cb June 25 (1731) $425
Anr Ed. L, 1737. 8vo, early calf; extremities rubbed. With 17 folding maps. sg Dec 7 (18) $375

**Gordon, Theodore, 1854-1915**
— The Complete Fly Fisherman: The Notes and Letters.... NY, 1947. Ed by John McDonald. pba July 11 (115) $70
Anr Ed. NY, 1970. One of 50. 4to, calf gilt. pba July 11 (114) $750
[-] The Gordon Garland: A Round of Devotions by his Followers. NY, 1965. Ed by Arnold Gingrich, One of 1,500. 8vo, half lea, unopened; spine ends worn. O Feb 6 (103) $110

**Gordon, Thomas**
— The Independent Whig. Phila: S. Keimer, 1724. 4to, contemp sheep stamped in blind; spine head gouged, scuffed. Pages 21-94 only. pba June 13 (272) $190

**Gorey, Edward**
— Amphigorey Also. NY, [1983]. One of 250. In dj. sg Dec 14 (115) $80
— The Dancing Rock. The Floating Elephant. [N.p.], 1993. Wraps. Sgd as Ogdred Weary & Dogear Wryde. pba Aug 22 (189) $50
— The Pointless Book.... [N.p.]: Fantod Press, 1993. Wraps. Sgd as Garrod Weedy. pba Aug 22 (190) $50
— The Vinegar Works: Three Volumes of Moral Instruction. NY, [1963]. 3 vols. Bds. bbc Dec 18 (251) $160; sg June 20 (133) $150

**Gori, Antonio Francisco, 1691-1757**
— Dactyliotheca Smithiana. Venice, 1767. 2 vols. 4to, contemp calf; rebacked, corners repaired. With engraved titles, frontis & 100 plates. Some soiling. bba May 9 (5) £550 [Nibris]

**Gorringe, Henry H., 1841-85**
— Coasts of the Mediterranean Sea. Wash., 1875-79. 3 vols. 8vo, cloth; worn. S Oct 26 (141) £440 [Folios]

**Gorse, Andre**
— Les Pyrenees monumentales et pittoresques...Premiere partie: Luchon et ses environs. Luchon, [c.1850]. Oblong folio, contemp cloth; worn, bds detached. With litho title & 24 tinted litho plates. Some spotting; a few plates loose. bba June 6 (47) £65 [Bell]

**Gorsen, Peter —&**
**Molinier, Pierre**
— Pierre Molinier, Lui-Meme. Munich: Rogner & Bernhard, 1972. Cloth, with clear outer wrap; tear at spine end. sg Feb 29 (213) $750

**Gosse, Pierre —&**
**Pinet, D.**
— A collection of 20 military maps and plans. The Hague, [1763]. Engraved by J.V. Schley. 4to, backed on linen in 2 cases. S Oct 26 (250) £250 [Antiquariat]

**Gosselman, Carl August**
— Resa i norra Amerika. Nykoeping, 1835. 2 vols. 8vo, contemp half calf. O Mar 5 (105) $120

**Gossip, Robert**
— Turkey and Russia.... Edin., 1879. 4to, orig cloth; rubbed. With 28 litho plates. b May 30 (266) £85

**Gostling, George**
— Extracts from the Treaties between Great-Britain and other Kingdoms...as relate to the Duty and Conduct of the Commanders of His Majesty's Ships of War. L, 1792. 4to, contemp calf; rebacked in cloth. b Sept 20 (204) £70

**Gotendorf, Alfred N.** See: Hayn & Gotendorf

**Gottfried, Johann Ludwig.** See: Abelin, Johann Philipp

**Gouffe, Jules, b.1807**
— Le livre de cuisine. Paris, 1881. 5th Ed. 4to, orig cloth; worn. With color plates. Pp. 817-824 torn, no loss; spotted. S Oct 12 (23) £320

**Gould, John, 1804-81**
— The Birds of Asia. L, 1850-83. 7 vols. Folio, orig half mor; library markings on spine & pastedowns, hinges weak, some rubbing & repairs. With 530 hand-colored plates. Plates 66, 68 & 69 in Vol II spotted; Plate 1 in Vol III with tp abraded, Plate 2 discolored, Plates 19 & 20 with marginal soiling; Plates 45-46 in Vol IV with foxing; Plate 3 in Vol 7 nicked, Plate 71 with soiled fingerprints affecting image. P Dec 12 (209) $55,000
— The Birds of Australia. L, [1840]-48. 7 vols, plus the Supplement, [1851]-69. Folio, 19th-cent half mor; spine & extremities worn, library labels at feet of spines. With 681 hand-colored plates. Minor foxing & browning; minor marginal dampstaining in Supplement. P Dec 12 (204) $85,000

Facsimile Ed. Melbourne, 1972. 8 vols. Folio & 8vo, orig cloth. Fattorini copy. C Oct 25 (65A) £1,200
— The Birds of Europe. L, [1832]-37. 5 vols. Folio, contemp mor gilt with onlaid marbled-paper panels; joints & extremities scuffed. With 448 hand-colored plates. Plate 35 shaved into image area; Plate 51 creased; text to Plate 350 with margin repaired. William Busfield Ferrand's subscriber's copy. Fattorini copy. C Oct 25 (14) £36,000

Anr copy. Orig half mor; extremities worn, library labels at spine feet. With 448 hand-finished colored plates. Some spotting & foxing. P Dec 12 (202) $45,000
— The Birds of Great Britain. L, [1862]-73. 5 vols. Folio, contemp half mor; refurbished. With 367 hand-colored plates, most heightened with gum arabic. Spotting to 1 plate & adjacent text leaf. b June 28 (29A) £29,500

Anr copy. Calf gilt; extremities rubbed. With 367 hand-colored plates, most heightened with gum-arabic. Henry Charles Sturt's subscriber's copy. Fattorini copy. C Oct 25 (15) £28,000

Anr copy. Orig half mor gilt; extremities worn, library markings on spine. With 367 hand-colored plates. Lower right corner of tp of Vol I chipped; minor soiling, mainly marginal. P Dec 12 (212) $42,000

Anr copy. Contemp half mor gilt; rubbed. Some spotting; Peregrine Falcon reinserted on guard. S June 27 (31) £29,000
— The Birds of New Guinea and the Adjacent Papuan Islands.... L, 1875-88. 5 vols. Folio, modern mor gilt. With 320 hand-colored plates. Some spotting, affecting plates. b Dec 5 (153) $20,000

Anr copy. Orig half mor; extremities worn, joints rubbed, Vol I bds detached, Vol III with upper bd detached. A few plates with discoloration. P Dec 12 (213) $40,000
— A Century of Birds from the Himalaya Mountains. L, [1831]-32. 2d Issue. Folio, half mor; library label at foot of spine. With 80 hand-colored plates. Minor soiling; subscriber list, plate list & 1st plate with crease. P Dec 12 (201) $10,000
— Humming-Birds. L, [1849]-61. ("A Monograph of the Trochilidae or Family of Humming-Birds.") Orig 25 parts. Folio, orig half cloth; worn. With 354 (of 360) hand-colored plates, many heightened with gold, overpainted with transparent varnish & oil colors by Gould & H. C. Richter. 10 plates extracted & framed; marginal tears & soiling to a few leaves. C May 31 (21) £50,000

Anr copy. 5 vols, plus Supplement, [1880]-87. Together, 6 vols. Folio, orig half mor; some hinges split, endpapers weak along inner edge, library markings on spine & inner bds. With 418 hand-finished colored plates. P Dec 12 (208) $50,000
— Macropodidae. 1841-42. ("A Monograph of the Macropodidae or Family of Kangaroos.") 2 orig parts in 1 vol. Folio, modern mor gilt, front wrap of Part 2 bound in. With 30 hand-colored plates.. sg Oct 19 (162) $18,000

— The Mammals of Australia. L, [1845]-63. 3 vols. Folio, orig half mor; spine heads chipped on Vols II & III, front cover of Vol II detached. With 182 hand-colored plates. Some foxing, affecting a few plates; marginal tear on 1st 3 plates of Vol III. P Dec 12 (207) $26,000
— A Monograph of the Odontophorinae, or Partridges of America. L, [1844]-50. Folio, half mor; extremities rubbed, library label at foot of spine. With 32 hand-colored plates. P Dec 12 (205) $5,000

Anr copy. Half mor; extremities worn, library markings on tp & rear pastedown. With 32 hand-colored plates. Some foxing. P Dec 12 (206) $5,000
— A Synopsis of the Birds of Australia. L, 1837-38. 8vo, contemp half mor gilt; library call numbers in white on spine, extremities worn. With 73 hand-finished color plates. Foxing to 2 platesn. P Dec 12 (203) $2,500
— Toucans. L, 1852-54. ("A Monograph of the Ramphastidae, or Family of Toucans.") 2d Ed. Folio, 19th-cent mor gilt; rebacked. With 1 plain & 51 hand-colored plates. Extra-illus with suite of plates from the 1st Ed. Fattorini copy. C Oct 25 (64A) £21,000

Anr copy. 19th-cent half mor; extremities rubbed, corners scuffed. With 51 hand-colored plates & 1 uncolored plate. Plate 6 with bloom; some foxing. P Dec 12 (210) $21,000
— Trogons. L, [1836]-38. ("A Monograph of the Trogonidae or Family of Trogons.") Folio, half mor; spine worn. With 36 hand-colored plates. Some foxing; library stamp on tp; 1 folding plate with tape repairs. cb Oct 17 (131) $20,000

2d Ed. L, [1858]-75. Folio, 19th-cent mor gilt; rebacked, bumped. With 47 hand-colored plates. Fattorini copy. C Oct 25 (65) £12,000

Anr copy. Contemp mor gilt; rubbed, central panels on covers replaced. With 47 hand-colored plates, most heightened with gum arabic. C May 31 (22) £12,500

Anr copy. Half mor; library markings on spine, extremities rubbed. With 47 hand-colored plates. P Dec 12 (211) $16,000

**Gould, Robert Freke, 1836-1915**
— The History of Freemasonry.... L, 1883-87. 3 vols. 4to, contemp mor gilt; rubbed. b Jan 31 (253) £130

Anr Ed. L, 1886-87. 3 vols. 4to, orig half mor, in worn dj. bba May 30 (226) £260 [Jackson]

**Gourmont, Remy de, 1858-1915**
— Un Coeur Virginal. Paris: Les Cent Bibliophiles, 1937. One of 120, this copy for A. Givaudan. 8vo, mor extra by Marot-Rodde with design in calf onlays of a nosegay, orig wraps bound in. With 28 orig watercolor illusts.. Bound in are 6 added pencil drawings for the illusts & & menu for the society dinner. S Nov 21 (188) £2,300
— Litanies de la rose. Paris: Kieffer, 1919. One of 50 on japon with a suite in uncolored state on japon pelure. Illus by Andre Domin. 4to, mor extra by Rene Kieffer, pictorial bdg, orig wraps bound in. With autograph agreement & 3 letters relating to the

book, 23 preparatory drawings for the illusts in pencil & ink & watercolor & 8 ink drawings for the ornamental lettering, 5 double-page ink designs for the borders, a set of sheets with 27 of illusts colored by the artist as a model & 6 proofs of borders ptd on satin. S Nov 21 (189) £1,100

**Goury, Jules.** See: Jones & Goury

**Gouvea, Antonio de, 1505-65**
— Histoire orientale des grans progres de l'eglise Cathol.... Antwerp, 1609. 8vo, contemp mor, with royal arms. Some discoloration; small reinforcements to several margins. b Dec 5 (119) £520

**Gove, Capt. Jesse A.**
— The Utah Expedition, 1857-58. Letters of Capt. Jesse A. Gove...to Mrs. Gove.... Concord NH, 1928. Ed by Otis G. Hammond. 4to, orig cloth; stained. pba Nov 16 (115) $90

**Gowin, Emmet**
— Emmet Gowin: Photographs. NY, 1976. In dj with tears. sg Feb 29 (152) $90

**Graaf, Reiner de, 1641-73**
— De vivorum organis generationi inservientibus.... Leiden & Rotterdam, 1668. 1st Ed. 8vo, contemp calf; joints & spine ends worn. With tp & 11 folding plates. Some soiling. CE Nov 8 (97) $250

**Graah, Wilhelm August, 1793-1863**
— Undersogelses-Reise till Ostkysten af Gronland. Copenhagen, 1832. 4to, contemp calf gilt. With 8 hand-colored plates. Lacking map; some discoloration. S June 13 (653) £340

**Grabhorn, Jane B.** See: Grabhorn Printing

**Grabhorn Printing—San Francisco, etc.**
— The Book of Job. 1926. One of 210. pba Nov 30 (164) $170
— California as it is.... 1933. 4th Ed, One of 500. Larson copy. pba Sept 28 (740) $50
— California in 1846.... 1934. One of 550. pba July 25 (313) $50
— A Leaf from the 1611 King James Bible. With "The Noblest Monument of English Prose" by J. L. Lowes & "The Printing of the King James Bible" by L. I. Newman. 1937. One of 300. Inscr by Alfred Bender & with related material laid in. sg Sept 14 (182) $350
— An Original Leaf from Francisco Palou's Life of... Father Junipero Serra. 1958. One of 177. Larson copy. pba Sept 28 (244) $190
— Original Leaves from the First Four Folios of...Shakespeare. 1935. One of 65, with an inserted leaf from each of the four folios. cb Feb 14 (2771) $1,200
— Regulations for Governing the Province of the Californias Approved by His Majesty by Royal Order, dated October 24, 1781. 1929. One of 300. 2 vols. Larson copy. pba Sept 28 (206) $75; pba July 25 (294) $60

— The Sermon on the Mount. [1924]. One of 190. pba Nov 30 (165) $60
— The Treaty of Guadalupe Hidalgo.... 1949. One of 500. Larson copy. pba Sept 28 (720) $85
Anr copy. With matching map folder. pba Apr 25 (439) $160
— The Voyage of Sebastian Vizcaino to the Coast of California.... 1933. One of 240. Inscr to Keith Spaulding. Larson copy. pba Sept 28 (279) $120

BAIRD, JOSEPH ARMSTRONG. - California's Pictorial Letter Sheets 1849-1869. 1967. One of 475. pba Nov 16 (17) $140

BECKER, ROBERT H. - Designs on the Land, Disenos of California Ranchos and Their Makers. 1969. One of 500. pba Feb 13 (9) $100; pba Apr 25 (285) $75

BECKER, ROBERT H. - Disenos of California Ranchos.... 1964. One of 400. cb June 25 (1948) $225
Anr copy. Larson copy. pba Sept 28 (40) $150; pba Feb 13 (8) $250

BEECHEY, FREDERICK WILLIAM. - An Account of a Visit to California.... [1941]. One of 350. Larson copy. pba Sept 28 (43) $130
Anr Ed. 1941. pba Nov 16 (22) $150; pba July 25 (252) $140

BOSQUI, EDWARD. - Memoirs. 1952. One of 350. pba Nov 16 (33) $55

BROWN, JOHN HENRY. - Reminiscences and Incidents, of "The Early Days" of San Francisco. 1933. One of 500. pba Apr 25 (316) $50

CASTANEDO, PEDRO DE. - The Journey of Francisco Vazquez de Coronado. 1933. One of 550. pba July 25 (267) $75

CHAMISSO, ADELBERT VON. - A Sojourn at San Francisco Bay 1816.... 1936. One of 250. Larson copy. pba Sept 28 (58) $375

CLAPPE, LOUISE A. K. S. - California in 1851 [1852]. The Letters of Dame Shirley. 1933. 2 vols. Larson copy. pba Sept 28 (364) $100

CLEMENS, SAMUEL LANGHORNE. - Letter to William Bowen... 1938. One of 400. K June 23 (213) $300; pba July 25 (359) $65

CLEMENS, SAMUEL LANGHORNE. - Letters from the Sandwich Islands. 1937. One of 550. pba June 20 (181) $150

COIT, DANIEL WADSWORTH. - An Artist in El Dorado.... 1937. One of 325. Larson copy. pba Sept 28 (376) $50

CRANE, STEPHEN. - The Red Badge of Courage. 1931. One of 980. pba Dec 14 (32) $55; sg Sept 14 (179) $120

DANA, RICHARD HENRY. - Two Years Before the Mast. NY, 1936. One of 1,000. Larson copy. pba Sept 28 (76) $50
Anr Ed. NY: Random House, 1936. One of—1,000. pba July 25 (127) $130; pba Aug 8 (444) $50; sg Feb 15 (149) $100

DAWSON, NICHOLAS. - Narrative. 1933. One of 500. pba Nov 16 (78) $60; pba Apr 25 (371) $70

DE RUSSAILH, ALBERT B. - Last Adventure. 1931. One of 475. Larson copy. pba Sept 28 (410) $70

DE SOTO, HERNANDO. - The Discovery of Florida. 1946. One of 280. pba Nov 16 (80) $130; sg Oct 26 (92) $90

DE VINNE, THEODORE LOW. - Aldus Pius Manutius... 1924. One of 250 with an orig leaf from the Hypnerotomachia Poliphili. pba June 20 (179) $75; sg Feb 15 (150) $325

DE VINNE, THEODORE LOW. - The Plantin-Moretus Museum. 1929. One of 425. pba June 20 (121) $110; pba June 20 (180) $80
Out-of-series copy. sg Sept 14 (180) $90

DELANO, ALONZO. - Pen-Knife Sketches.... 1934. One of 550. Larson copy. pba Sept 28 (405) $80

DERBY, GEORGE HORATIO. - Phoenixiana: a Collection of the Burlesques...of John Phoenix. 1937. One of 550. pba Aug 8 (446) $70

ELWOOD, LOUIS BUTLER. - Queen Calafia's Land: An Historical Sketch of California. 1940. One of 325. Robbins copy. pba Mar 21 (96) $50

FAGES, PEDRO & SERRA, JUNIPERO. - Letters... 1936. One of 110. pba July 25 (280) $60

FAHEY, HERBERT. - Early Printing in California.... 1956. One of 400. Larson copy. pba Sept 28 (194) $170; pba Aug 8 (53) $150

FINLAYSON, DUNCAN. - Traits of American Indian Life & Character, by a Fur Trader. 1933. One of 500. pba Apr 25 (402) $100; pba Aug 8 (453) $80

FOGAZZARO, ANTONIO. - Eden Anto. 1930. One of 250. pba July 25 (285) $50

GERSTAECKER, FRIEDRICH. - Scenes of Life in California. 1942. One of 500. Robbins copy. pba Mar 21 (118) $100

GESNER, CONRAD. - On the Admiration of Mountains. 1937. One of 325. pba July 25 (398) $120

GRABHORN, JANE B. - A California Gold Rush Miscellany.... 1937. One of 550. Larson copy. pba Sept 28 (495) $75

GRABHORN, JANE B. - The Compleat Jane Grabhorn... 1968. One of 400. pba Nov 30 (168) $85

GRABHORN, ROBERT. - Nineteenth Century Type Displayed in 18 Fonts.... 1959. One of 300. Sgd by Edwin & Robert Grabhorn. pba June 20 (185) $85

HALE, JOHN. - California As It Is. 1954. Reprint of 1851 Ed, One of 150. Larson copy. pba Sept 28 (507) $70
Reprint of the 1851 Ed. pba July 25 (297) $50

HARLOW, NEAL. - The Maps of San Francisco Bay from the Discovery...to the American Occupation. 1950. One of 375. cb Feb 14 (2770) $200; cb June 25 (1949) $375
Anr copy. Larson copy. pba Sept 28 (117) $500; pba Oct 9 (7) $550; pba Feb 13 (91) $700

HELLER, ELINOR R. & MAGEE, DAVID. - Bibliography of the Grabhorn Press, 1915-1940. 1940. One of 210. cb June 25 (1950) $250; sg Sept 14 (181) $425

HUTTON, WILLIAM RICH. - California 1847-1852. 1942. One of 700. pba Apr 25 (465) $70

IDE, SIMON. - The Conquest of California. 1964. One of 500. Robbins copy. pba Mar 21 (163) $200

JEFFERS, ROBINSON. - The Beaks of Eagles. 1936. One of 135. Inscr by Albert M. Bender to Jake Zeitlin & twice by Zeitlin. pba Oct 5 (163) $225

JEFFERS, ROBINSON. - Hungerfield. 1952. One of 32. pba Nov 30 (195) $3,500

JEFFERS, ROBINSON. - Return: An Unpublished Poem. 1934. One of 250. pba Oct 5 (181) $120

JEFFERS, ROBINSON. - Solstice and Other Poems. NY: Random House, 1935. One of 320. pba Oct 5 (183) $150; pba Jan 27 (274) $150; pba May 23 (184) $120
Anr copy. Half cloth. sg June 4 (234) $100
Anr copy. Sgd. sg June 20 (180) $90

KANE, THOMAS LEIPER. - The Private Papers and Diary of.... San Francisco, 1937. 1st Ed, One of 500. Robbins copy. pba Mar 21 (177) $75

LAWRENCE, DAVID HERBERT. - Fire and Other Poems. 1940. One of 300. pba Mar 7 (160) $170

LEIGHLY, JOHN. - California as an Island.... 1972. One of 450. Copy with large oily footprint stain on rear cover. pba Nov 16 (160) $400; pba Nov 30 (220) $700; pba Feb 13 (116) $700
Anr Ed. San Francisco, 1972. One of—450. Larson copy. pba Sept 28 (48) $450

LEWIS, OSCAR. - Hearn and his Biographers. 1930. One of 350. Inscr by Edwin Grabhorn. sg Dec 14 (143) $300

LITTLEJOHN, DAVID. - Dr. Johnson and Noah Webster. 1971. One of 500. sg Sept 14 (185) $150

LYMAN, GEORGE D. - The Book and the Doctor. 1933. One of 50. pba Nov 16 (165) $160; pba Feb 12 (525) $110

MACARTHUR, MILDRED YORBA. - California-Spanish Proverbs. 1954. One of 450. pba Nov 16 (166) $50; pba Aug 8 (104) $55

MAGEE, DAVID. - Catalogue of Some Five Hundred Examples of the Printing of Edwin & Robert Grabhorn. [1961]. One of 350. pba Aug 8 (443) $85

MAGEE, DAVID. - The Hundredth Book: a Bibliography of the Publications of the Book Club of California... 1958. One of 400. O Mar 26 (116) $110
Anr copy. In dj. pba Apr 4 (54) $225

MAGEE, DAVID. - In Memoriam Edwin Grabhorn. 1969. One of 150. pba Aug 8 (440) $90

MARTIN, DON JOSE. - Memorial and Proposals of... on the Californias.... 1945. One of 250. Larson copy. pba Sept 28 (142) $50

METZGAR, JUDSON D. - Adventures in Japanese Prints. [1943]. One of 300. pba Nov 30 (154) $130

MEYERS, WILLIAM H. - Journal of a Cruise to California and the Sandwich Islands.... 1955. One of 400. Larson copy. pba Sept 28 (145) $120; pba Nov 16 (173) $100; pba Apr 25 (531) $120

MEYERS, WILLIAM H. - Naval Sketches of the War in California. NY, 1939. One of 1,000. Larson copy. pba Sept 28 (146) $75; pba Nov 30 (155) $225

MEYERS, WILLIAM H. - Sketches of California and Hawaii.... 1970. One of 450. Larson copy. pba Sept 28 (147) $120

MILLER, HENRY. - Account of a Tour of the California Missions.... 1952. One of 375. Larson copy. pba Sept 28 (159) $50; pba July 25 (323) $55

NUNEZ CABECA DE VACA, ALVAR. - Relation...of What Befel the Armament in the Indias... 1929. One of 300. pba Nov 30 (156) $350

OLDFIELD, OTIS. - Aboard the Three Masted Schooner Louise.... 1969. One of 400. sg Feb 15 (152) $140

PARSONS, GEORGE F. - The Life and Adventures of James W. Marshall. 1935. pba Apr 25 (584) $140
Anr Ed. San Francisco, 1935. One of 47 containing orig Gold Rush letter. Larson copy. pba Sept 28

(632) $850

PATTISON, MARK. - The Estiennes: A Biographical Essay... 1949. One of 390. sg Sept 14 (183) $225

PHILLIPS, CATHERINE COFFIN. - Coulterville Chronicle.... 1942. One of 500. pba Apr 25 (590) $65; pba July 25 (332) $60

1st Ed. Larson copy. pba Sept 28 (643) $100

POWELL, H. M. T. - The Santa Fe Trail to California. [1931]. One of 300. cb June 25 (1951) $800; sg Oct 26 (122) $650

Anr copy. Ed by Douglas S. Watson. Larson copy. pba Sept 28 (645) $1,200

ROBERTSON, JOHN WOOSTER. - Francis Drake and Other Early Explorers Along the Pacific Coast. 1927. One of 1,000. Inscr. pba Feb 13 (158) $225; pba July 25 (206) $130

Anr copy. Inscr by Ed Grabhorn to F. W. Dewart, 1937. pba July 25 (342) $190

ROBERTSON, JOHN WOOSTER. - Francis Duke and Other Early Explorers Along the Pacific Coast. 1927. 1st Ed, One of 1,000. Larson copy. Inscr & sgd. pba Sept 28 (211) $160

ROBERTSON, JOHN WOOSTER. - The Harbor of St. Francis.... 1926. One of 100. Larson copy. pba Sept 28 (86) $100

ROGERS, FRED B. - Soldiers of the Overland.... 1938. One of 1,000. Robbins copy. pba Mar 21 (303) $55

SANDELS, G. M. - A Sojourn in California by the King's Orphan.... 1945. One of 300. Sgd by Ed & Robert Grabhorn. Larson copy. pba Sept 28 (217) $50

SAWYER, EUGENE T. - The Life and Career of Tiburcio Vasquez.... 1944. One of 500. Robbins copy. pba Mar 21 (329) $60; pba July 25 (349) $70

SCAMMON, L. N. - Spanish Missions, California: A Portfolio of Etchings.... 1926. One of 10 with the edchings sgd & limitation leaf sgd by artist & pbr. 10 orig etchings tipped into individual paper folders, loose as issued, in parchment portfolio with satin back, lined in satin cb June 25 (1952) $600

SHAKESPEARE, WILLIAM. - [Henry IV]. The First Part of Henry the Fourth. 1961. One of 180. pba Nov 30 (163) $75

SHAKESPEARE, WILLIAM. - Julius Caesar. 1954. One of 180. pba Nov 30 (160) $40

SHAKESPEARE, WILLIAM. - King Lear. [1959]. One of 180. pba Nov 30 (158) $160

SHAKESPEARE, WILLIAM. - Othello. 1956. One of 185. pba Nov 30 (157) $60; pba Nov 30 (161) $85

SHAKESPEARE, WILLIAM. - Richard the Third. 1953. One of 180. pba Nov 30 (159) $75; pba Nov 30 (162) $85

SHAKESPEARE, WILLIAM. - The Tempest. 1951. One of 160. sg Feb 15 (153) $100

STEVENSON, ROBERT LOUIS. - Silverado Journal. 1954. One of 400. pba July 25 (354) $65

SUTTER, JOHN A. - The Diary of Johann August Sutter. 1932. 1st Ed, One of 500. pba Sept 28 (687) $120

SUTTER, JOHN A. - New Helvetia Diary... 1939. One of 950. Larson copy. pba Sept 28 (689) $75; pba Apr 25 (695) $55

SUTTER, JOHN A. & OTHERS. - Pioneers of the Sacramento. 1953. One of 400. Larson copy. pba Sept 28 (690) $50

TOKE, MONROE TSA. - The Peyote Ritual.... 1957. One of 325. pba Nov 16 (266) $275

VESPUCCI, AMERIGO. - Letter...describing his Four Voyages to the New World... 1926. One of 250. pba July 25 (456) $120; sg Oct 26 (374) $110

VIZCAINO, SEBASTIAN. - The Voyage of...to the Coast of California.... 1933. One of 240. Book Club of California, No 45. pba July 25 (361) $85

WAGNER, HENRY RAUP. - The Plains and the Rockies.... 1937. One of 600. O May 7 (290) $100; pba Apr 25 (719) $95; pba July 25 (362) $95

WASEURTZ, G. M. - A Sojourn in California by the King's Orphan.... 1945. One of 300. pba Apr 25 (721) $90

WASHINGTON, GEORGE. - Washington's Farewell Address. 1922. One of 125. pba Aug 8 (454) $60

WATSON, DOUGLAS S. - The Spanish Occupation of California... 1934. One of 550. pba July 25 (295) $50

WESTON, BRETT. - White Sands. 1949. One of 50. pba Nov 30 (326) $10,000

WHEAT, CARL I. - Mapping the Transmississippi West. 1957-63. One of 1,000. 5 vols in 6. bbc June 24 (450) $1,600; pba Feb 13 (197) $3,500

WHEAT, CARL I. - The Maps of the California Gold Region. 1942. One of 300. pba Feb 13 (198) $1,200; sg May 9 (48A) $1,800

WHEAT, CARL I. - The Pioneer Press of California. 1948. One of 450. pba Apr 25 (728) $120

WHITMAN, WALT. - Leaves of Grass. NY, 1930. One of 400. pba Nov 30 (166) $650; sg Sept 14 (184) $1,500

WIERZBICKI, FELIX PAUL. - California as it is.... 1933. One of 500. pba Apr 25 (733) $90

WILDE, OSCAR. - The Fisherman and his Soul. 1939. One of 200. pba July 11 (335) $100

WILDE, OSCAR. - Salome. 1927. One of 195. pba Aug 22 (674) $60

WILTSEE, ERNEST A. - Gold Rush Steamers of the Pacific. 1938. One of 500. Larson copy. pba Sept 28 (742) $150; pba June 20 (182) $80

WOOD, ELLEN LAMONT. - George Yount, the Kindly Host of Caymus Rancho. 1941. One of 200. Robbins copy. pba Mar 21 (392) $80

**Grabhorn, Robert.** See: Grabhorn Printing

**Gracchus Babeuf**
— The Defence of Gracchus Babeuf before the High Court of Vendome. Northampton MA: Gehenna Press, 1964. One of 50 on Mirabeau with an additional suite. Illus by Thomas Cornell. Folio, loose as issued in lea folder & linen-covered folder. sg Feb 15 (116) $475

**Graeff, Werner**
— Es Kommt der Neue Fotograf. Berlin, 1929. 4to, cloth; worn, backstrip detached, hinges cracked. Some soiling. sg Feb 29 (206) $175

**Graesse, Johann Georg Theodor, 1814-85**
— Tresor de livres rares et precieux.... Milan, 1950. 8 vols, including Supplement. 4to, orig cloth. bba Oct 5 (88) £440 [Franks]; bba Oct 5 (199) £320 [Burden]; Ck Apr 12 (232) £300

Anr Ed. Milan, [1950]. 8 vols. 4to, orig cloth; spines rubbed, vol IV loose. sg Apr 11 (122) $250

Anr Ed. Cambr. MA: Martino, [n.d.]. One of 275. 8 vols, including Supplement, in 4. orig cloth. O May 7 (148) $190

**Graff Collection, Everett Dwight**
— A Catalogue of the Everett D. Graff Collection of Western Americana. Chicago, 1968. Compiled by Colton Storm. 4to, cloth, in dj. With index pamphlet laid in. pba Nov 16 (116) $65

**Graffigny, Francoise P. H. de, 1695-1758**
— Lettres d'une Peruvienne.... Paris, 1797. 2 vols. 18mo, mor by Chambolle Duru, 1866. With port with caption & before letters & triple suite of the 8 plates. Fuerstenberg - Schaefer copy. S Dec 7 (268) £400

**Grafton, Richard, d.c.1572**
— A Chronicle at Large and Meere History of the Affayres of Englande.... L: Denham for R. Tottle & H. Toye, 1569. 2d Ed. 2 vols in 1. Folio, later lea. Tp & 1st few leaves remargined; some worming; 2Q1 torn afffecting letters; some other tears repaired. CE June 12 (207) $650

**Grafton, Sue**
— "B" is for Burglar. NY: Holt Rinehart & Winston, [1985]. In dj. Inscr. sg June 20 (134) $450

**Graham, R. B.**
— Photographic Illustrations with Description of Mandalay & Upper Burmah. Birm., 1887. 4to, orig cloth; worn at foot of spine. With 59 mtd photos & litho plan of Mandalay. b Dec 5 (120) £460

**Graham, Ron —& Others**
— A Study of the Colt Single Action Army Revolver. Texas, 1976. 4to, cloth; worn. Sgd by Graham & co-author John Kopec. O June 4 (142) $110

**Graham, Tom.** See: Lewis, Sinclair

**Graham, William A.**
— Abstract of the Official Record of Proceedings of the Reno Court of Inquiry...to Investigate his conduct at the Battle of Little Big Horn.... Harrisburg: Stackpole, [1954]. Preface by Graham. In dj. pba June 25 (103) $50
— The Story of the Little Big Horn.... NY: Century, [1926]. pba June 25 (102) $110

**Grahame, Kenneth, 1859-1932**
See also: Limited Editions Club; Milne, Alan Alexander
— The Wind in the Willows. L, 1908. 1st Ed. Orig cloth; dampstained, spine & corners rubbed. S May 16 (159) £340

Anr copy. Orig cloth; rubbed, base of spine abraded. sg Sept 21 (204) $1,100

Anr Ed. NY, 1940. Illus by Arthur Rackham. In dj with short tears. Ck May 31 (171) £350

Anr Ed. L, 1950. Illus by E. H. Shepard. Calf gilt by Bayntun of Bath. Inscr by Shepard & with ANs by him laid in. sg Sept 21 (205) $425

Anr Ed. L, 1951. One of 500. Illus by Arthur Rackham. 4to, orig lea gilt. With 12 colored plates. S Nov 2 (108) £650 [Sotheran]; sg Oct 19 (214) $1,100

**Graham's...**
— Graham's Magazine of Literature & Art. Phila., 1841-42. ("Graham's Lady's and Gentleman's Magazine.") Vols 19 & 20. 8vo, contemp half mor. Foxed. sg Feb 8 (330) $175

Vol XX. Phila., 1842. ("Graham's American Monthly Magazine.") 8vo, orig half calf; rear joint cracked. pba Aug 22 (635) $120

Vol XXIV. Phila., 1844. ("Graham's Lady's and Gentleman's Magazine.") 8vo, contemp half calf. Contains 1st ptg of Hawthorne's Earth's Holocaust & Poe's Review of Orion. pba June 20 (270) $140

Anr Ed. Phila., Mar 1846. 8vo, contemp mor gilt. Foxed; tape repair to prelim blank. pba Oct 5 (294) $120

**Grancsay, Stephen V.** See: Bashford Collection, Dean

**Grand, Gordon.** See: Derrydale Press

**Grand-Carteret, John, 1850-1927**
— Les Almanachs francais: bibliographie, iconographie des almanachs.... Paris, 1896. One of 1,200. 4to, contemp half mor, orig wraps bound in. b Dec 5 (28) £120
— XIXe Siecle en France. Paris, 1893. 8vo, half mor gilt. Some foxing. pba Dec 14 (68) $75

**Grandjean de Montigny, Auguste Henri Victor —& Famin, A.**
— Architecture Toscane, ou palais, maisons et autres edifices.... Paris, 1806-15. Folio, contemp half sheep; rebacked. With engraved title & 102 (of 109) plates. Half-title & tp creased; lacking plates 98-103. sg June 13 (12) $175

**Grandjean, Serge.** See: Musee du Louvre

**Grandville, 1803-47**
— The Flowers Personified, being a Translation of Les Fleurs Animees. NY, 1847-49. 2 vols. 4to, mor gilt; extremities rubbed, hinges cracked, Vol I lacking flyleaf. With 2 engraved hand-colored titles & 50 hand-colored plates. cb Feb 14 (2773) $850

Anr copy. Vol I bound in 2 vols. Orig lea gilt; joints cracked, rebacked. Some soiling & foxing. sg May 9 (302) $850

Anr Ed. NY, 1849. Bound with: Modern Botany for Ladies by Foelix Trans by N. Cleveland, Esq.. 8vo, orig lea. With 2 uncolored & 25 hand-colored plates. sg Dec 7 (221) $550
— Scenes de la vie privee et publique des animaux. Paris, 1842. 1st Ed in Book form. 2 vols. 8vo, orig half mor. S Mar 29 (731) £580

Anr copy. Contemp half calf; spine ends worn, front joint starting. sg Sept 21 (206) $175

Anr copy. Contemp half calf gilt; front joint starting on Vol II, library label at foot of spines. Library markings. sg Sept 21 (207) $300
Anr Ed. Paris, 1844. 2 vols. 8vo, contemp half mor; worn. S Nov 2 (13) £190 [Stone]

**Granet, Jean Joseph**
— Histoire de l'Hotel Royal des Invalides. Paris, 1736. Illus by Cochin & Chauveau. Folio, contemp calf; worn. With title, half-title, frontis, 16 vignettes, & 103 plates (27 double-page). Stained in upper margin. S Oct 26 (332) £900 [Chelsea Gal.]

**Granger, Lewis**
— Letters of Lewis Granger: Reports of the Journey from Salt Lake to Los Angeles in 1849.... Los Angeles, 1959. One of 250. Ed by LeRoy Hafen. Orig cloth. With frontis & folded facsimile. Sgd by ed. Larson copy. pba Sept 28 (496) $55

**Grant, Anne, 1755-1838**
— Memoirs of an American Lady. L, 1808. 1st Ed. 2 vols. 12mo, calf; rubbed. Z June 28 (103) $180

**Grant, Blanche C.**
— Taos Indians. Taos, 1925. Bound with: Taos Today. 1st Eds. 2 vols. Orig wraps; wraps edges worn. Robbins copy. pba Mar 21 (123) $100

**Grant, Donald**
— Personal Reminiscences of Royal Dornoch Golf Club, 1900-1925. [L, 1979]. 1st Ed. - Foreword by Herbert Warren Wind. Wraps. Inscr & sgd by Grant to Hal Conefry. pba Apr 18 (67) $85

**Grant, James, 1822-87**
— The Tartans of the Clans of Scotland. Edin., 1886. Folio, orig cloth; worn. CG June 12 (9) £280

**Grant, Maxwell, Pseud.**
— The Shadow Laughs. NY, [1931]. Pictorial bds; spine ends worn. pba May 4 (143) $100

**Grant, Ulysses S., 1822-85**
— Personal Memoirs. NY, 1885-86. 2 vols. 8vo, orig cloth. F June 20 (411) $60

**Granville, Augustus Bozzi, 1783-1872**
— Graphic Illustrations of Abortion and the Diseases of Menstruation. L, 1834. 4to, orig cloth; rebacked retaining backstrip. With 14 uncolored plates. sg May 16 (418) $325

**Grapaldus, Francescus Marius, 1465?-1515**
— De partibus aedium. Venice: A. de Bindonis, 31 Jan, 1517. 4to, contemp limp vellum; lower cover foreedge damaged. Margins water-stained. S Oct 12 (73) £1,000

**Grapheus, Cornille**
— La Tresadmirable, tresmagnificque & triumphante entree du treshault...Prince Philipes.... Antwerp: Gillis van Diest, 1550. Folio, contemp vellum. With 29 woodcut illusts & plans, 4 of them folding, 20 of them full-page. Some soiling & spotting. Schaefer copy. P Nov 1 (103) $7,500

**Graphic...**
— The Graphic, an illustrated weekly newspaper. L, 1875. Vol 12. Bdg not described but worn. Z Jan 30 (407) $130
Vol 13. Bdg not described but worn. Z Jan 30 (408) $130
Vol 18. L, 1878. 4to, contemp cloth; spines faded. S Oct 26 (83) £420 [Lepanto]

**Grass, Guenter**
See also: Limited Editions Club
— Die Blechtrommel. Neuwied, [1968]. One of 500. Illus by Heinrich Richter. Half vellum. With sgd litho by Richter laid in. sg Dec 14 (116) $225

**Grasse, Francois J. P., Comte de**
— The Operations of the French Fleet.... NY: Bradford Club, 1864. One of 150. 4to, orig cloth; worn. wa Feb 29 (297) $170

**Grassi, Girolamo**
— Tractatus de tumoribus praeter natural, de solutione continui, de ulceribus. Venice: J. Ziletti, 1562. 4to, modern vellum. With title device. 1st & last leaf washed. S Oct 27 (809) £340 [Zioni]

**Grastorf, Dennis J.**
— Wood Type of the Angelica Press. Brooklyn: Angelica Press, 1975. One of 220. Folio, loose in wraps, in specially designed wooden case, as issued. bba May 9 (445) £110 [Collinge & Clark]

**Gratarolus, Gulielmus**
— A Direction for the Health of Magistrates and Students.... L: W. How, 1574. 1st Ed in English, Variant with the "Veale" imprint. 8vo in 4s, 18th-Cent calf; rebacked & repaired. H2 stained in margin. Ck Mar 22 (133) £2,600

**Grateloup, Jean Baptiste, 1735-1817**
— L'Oeuvre grave de J. B. de Grateloup de 1765 a 1771. [N.p., n.d.]. 312mm by 256mm, modern mor gilt. With 8 plates on various papers, hinged, within mats, engraved & sgd by Grateloup, plus 3 plates engraved by his nephew, J.P.S. de Grateloup. Fuerstenberg - Schaefer copy. S Dec 7 (270) £1,100

**Gratianus, the Canonist, d.c.1150**
— Decretum. Venice: Thomas de Blavis de Alexandria, 28 July 1486. 4to, contemp vellum; soiled. Some staining & browning; contemp annotations; a few passages inked through. 520 leaves. Goff G-376. cb Feb 14 (2515) $1,700
Anr Ed. Venice: Luc'Antonio Giunta, 20 May 1514. 4to, modern calf. Tp & last leaf rehinged; minor stains. sg Mar 21 (185) $400

**Grattan, Thomas Colley, 1792-1864**
— Civilized America. L, 1859. 1st Ed. 2 vols. 8vo, orig cloth; minor wear. With 2 folding color maps. wa Feb 29 (386) $120

**Gravell, T. L. —&**
**Miller, G.**
— A Catalogue of American Watermarks, 1690-1835. NY, 1979. 4to, cloth. ds July 27 (85) $70

**Gravelot, Hubert Francois, 1699-1773 —&**
**Cochin, Charles Nicolas, 1715-90**
— Iconologie par figures ou traite complet des allegories.... Paris, [1791]. 4 vols. 12mo, contemp calf gilt. With 4 engraved titles, 2 ports & 202 plates before letters, with a proof state of 10 plates added. Some spotting. Fuerstenberg - Schaefer copy. S Dec 7 (272) £1,600

**Graves, Charles —&**
**Longhurst, Henry**
— Candid Caddies. L, [1935]. 1st Ed. - Intro by Bernard Darwin. Illus by Bert Thomas. Bds; pencil mustache on front cover figure. Soiled. pba Nov 9 (27) $75

**Graves, George, fl.1777-1834**
— British Ornithology. L, 1811-13. Vols I-II (of 3). 8vo, modern half calf. With 96 hand-colored plates. Some spotting & soiling; plate 74 stained. S Oct 27 (731) £280 [Shapero]
  1st Ed. L, 1811-21. 3 vols. 8vo, modern half calf by Bernard Middleton. With 144 hand-colored plates. Some browning or spotting of text. Fattorini copy. C Oct 25 (16) £1,500

**Graves, Robert, 1895-1985**
— At the Gate: Poems. [L: Bertram Rota] Hatfield: Stellar Press, 1974. One of 536. In dj. pba Jan 25 (114) $85
— Beyond Giving: Poems. L: Pvtly ptd, 1969. 1st Ed, one of 536. Bds, in dj. pba Jan 25 (115) $75
— Colophon to "Love Respelt." L, 1967. One of 350. In dj. pba Jan 25 (116) $75
— Country Sentiment. L, 1920. 1st Ed. Orig bds. Inscr to Robert Nichols. Hobson copy. S June 28 (69) £300
— Fairies and Fusiliers. L, 1917. 1st Ed. Inscr, 1920. Hobson copy. S June 28 (65) £280
  Anr copy. 1st bdg of red cloth. Sgd by Graves & inscr by William Nicholson. sg Dec 14 (117) $225
— The Feather Bed. L: Hogarth Press, 1923. 1st Ed, one of 250. Orig bds; rubbed. K Feb 11 (184) $225
  Anr copy. Orig bds; spine rubbed. Hobson copy. S June 28 (73) £120
— The Golden Fleece. L, 1944. In repaired dj. ALs to his mother laid in. Hobson copy. S June 28 (85) £380
— Goliath and David. L, [1917]. One of 200. Orig wraps. Inscr to Sir Sydney Cockerell & with variant autograph Ms of Not Dead. Hobson copy. S June 28 (64) £1,600
— Good-bye to All That. L, 1929. 1st Ed, 1st Issue. In chipped dj. Review copy. bba Oct 19 (335) £320 [Springer]
  Anr copy. In dj. pnE Mar 20 (133) £340
  Anr copy. In dj with 2 small tears on lower cover. Hobson copy. S June 28 (82) £600

— The Green-Sailed Vessel. L, 1971. One of 500. In dj. pba Jan 25 (117) $75
— The Isles of Unwisdom. NY, 1949. 1st Ed. In dj. ALs to his mother inserted. Hobson copy. S June 28 (87) £160
— John Kemp's Wager. Oxford: Shakespeare Head Press, 1925. 1st Ed, one of 100. Half vellum. Hobson copy. S June 28 (76) £170
— Lars Porsena. L, 1972. One of 100. pba Jan 25 (118) $120
— The Marmosite's Miscellany. L: Hogarth Press, 1925. 1st Ed. Orig bds; soiled at top. S June 28 (78) £190
— Over the Brazier. L, 1916. 1st Ed, 1st Issue. Orig wraps. With incomplete ALs to Edward Marsh laid in. Hobson copy. S June 28 (63) £850
— The Person From Porlock. Madrid, 1959. One of 50. Single sheet folded to form 4 pp, ptd in 3 sides Pictorial wraps. Inscr to Harris Williams. sg June 20 (136) $600
— The Pier-Glass. L, [1921]. 1st Ed. Orig bds, in dj. Hobson copy. S June 28 (70) £120
— Poems, 1914-1927. L, 1927. 1st Ed. In dj with minor soil. Hobson copy. S June 28 (80) £220
— Poems 1929. L, 1929. 1st Ed, one of 225. Margin of pp 27-28 def. Hobson copy. S June 28 (193) £160
— Seventeen Poems Missing from "Love Respelt." L, 1966. 1st Ed, one of 330. Orig bds, unopened, in dj. pba Jan 25 (120) $85
— The Shout. L, [1929]. One of 530, sgd. 4to, orig bds, in dj. pba Jan 25 (121) $225
— Ten Poems More. Paris: Hours Press, 1930. 1st Ed, one of 200. Orig half calf, the bds with photomontages by Len Lye; lower bd & spine rubbed. Hobson copy. S June 28 (146) £250
— Timeless Meeting: Poems. L, 1966. 1st Ed, one of 536. In dj. pba Jan 25 (122) $85
— To Whom Else? Majorca: Seizin Press, 1931. One of 200. Orig half cloth; glassine d/j stuck to bds. Hobson copy. S June 28 (196) £80
— Treasure Box. L, [1919]. Illus by Nancy Nicholson. Orig wraps. Inscr to Mr & Mrs Sydney Cockerell by Nicholson for both, with address in Graves's hand. Hobson copy. S June 28 (68) £700
— Welchman's Hose. L: The Fleuron, 1925. 1st Ed, one of 525. 4to, orig half cloth. S Nov 2 (96) £240 [Temperley]; S May 16 (123) £230
— The White Goddess. L, 1948. In dj. ALs to his mother, 15 Apr 1944, inserted. Hobson copy. S June 28 (86) £420

**Graves, Robert, 1895-1985 —&**
**Riding, Laura**
— No Decency Left. L, 1932. Illus by James Metcalf. In dj. Hobson copy. S June 28 (83) £1,500

**Gravesande, Willem Jakob Storm van 's, 1688-1742**
— Elemens de physique. Paris, 1747. 2 vols. 8vo, contemp mor gilt with arms of C. F. P. le Normand de Tournehem. With headpiece & 49 folding plates. Sheet I in Vol I browned. Fuerstenberg - Schaefer copy. S Dec 7 (273) £2,300

**Gravures...**
— Gravures sur bois tirees des Livres Francais du XVe Siecle. Paris, 1868. 4to, half mor; joints cracked, spine worn. pba June 20 (72) $85

**Gray, Asa, 1810-88**
— Plates Prepared between the Years 1849 and 1850 to Accompany a Report on the Forest Trees of North America. Wash., 1891. Folio, disbound. With 23 hand-colored plates. Marginal chipping & tears. P Dec 12 (86) $2,000

**Gray, David.** See: Derrydale Press

**Gray, Harold**
— Little Orphan Annie and Jumbo, the Circus Elephant. Chicago: Pleasure Books, [1935]. Pictorial bds; soiled, piece of front cover lacking. With 3 pop-ups. Last pop-up lacking animal that stood on center piece. pba Mar 7 (209) $70

**Gray, John Edward, 1800-75.** See: Richardson & Gray

**Gray, Thomas, 1716-71**
See also: Fore-Edge Paintings; Golden Cockerel Press; Limited Editions Club
— Designs by Mr. R. Bentley for Six Poems. L, 1753. 1st Ed, 1st Ptg. Folio, 18th-cent calf; rebacked with sheep, spine rubbed. Foxed throughout. sg Mar 21 (150) $225
— An Elegy Wrote in a Country Church Yard. NY: Harper, [1940]. ("Elegy Written in a Country Churchyard.") Illus by J. J. Lankes. pba Aug 8 (457) $55
— Poems. Parma: Bodoni, 1793. 4to, 19th-cent calf gilt with arms of George Agar Ellis; minor rubbing. bba May 9 (10) £220 [B. Franklin]
— Works. L, 1768. ("Poems.") 8vo, later mor gilt by Roger de Coverly. B7 torn & repaired with small loss; foxed. bba July 18 (193) £100 [Cox]

**Gray, Sir Thomas, d.1369?**
— Scalacronica. Glasgow, 1907. One of 95. 4to, orig half vellum. Inscr by the pbr. pba Mar 7 (126) $55

**Graydon, Alexander, 1752-1818**
— Memoirs of a Life, Chiefly Passed in Pennsylvania.... Harrisburg, 1811. 8vo, contemp sheep; loose. sg Oct 26 (123) $90

**Grayson, Andrew Jackson**
— Birds of the Pacific Slope. San Francisco, 1986. One of 425. 2 vols. Folio & 4to, cloth, plates loose as issued in orig cloth folding case. CE June 12 (208) $1,100

**Grayson, William John, 1788-1863**
— The Hireling and the Slave. Charleston, S.C., 1856. 3d Ed. 12mo, orig cloth; extremities worn. sg Mar 28 (91) $120

**Graziani, Antonio Maria, 1537-1611**
— De casibus virorum illustrium.... Paris, 1680. 1st Ed. 4to, contemp red mor extra with arms of Charles de Sainte-Maure, Duc de Montausier & his wife, Julie Lucie d'Angennes de Rembouillet. C May 1 (68) £1,800

**Great...**
— The Great Britain, Atlantic Steam Ship of 3500 Tons. L, 1847. Folio, cloth-backed wraps; worn. With 14 folding plates numbered 1-25. Dampstain in lower margins throughout. Sold w.a.f. sg Mar 7 (236) $200
— Great Exhibition, 1851. L, [1851]. ("The Art Journal Illustrated Catalogue: The Industry of All Nations.") 4to, contemp calf gilt; scuffed. sg June 13 (174) $110

**Gree, Jonathan**
— Camera Work: A Critical Anthology. Millerton, NY: Aperture, 1973. 1st Ed. 4to, cloth, in dj. sg Feb 29 (79) $130

**Greek Anthology**
— Anthologia epigrammatura graecorum libri VII... Geneva: H. Estienne, 1566. ("Florilegium diversorum epigrammatum veterum in septem libros divisum.") 4to, old calf; rebacked, soiled, bumped. Browned & dampstained. wd May 8 (56) $125

**Greeley, Horace, 1811-72**
— The American Conflict: A History of the Great Rebellion. Hartford, 1864-66. 2 vols. 8vo, contemp half calf; front joint of Vol II cracked through. pba Apr 25 (168) $140
— An Overland Journey from New York to San Francisco.... NY, 1860. 1st Ed. 12mo, orig cloth; spine head worn. Robbins copy. pba Mar 21 (124) $2,250

**Green, Charles R.** See: Clymer & Green

**Green, F. H.**
— Old English Clocks: being a Collector's Observations.... Ditchling: St. Dominic's Press, 1931. One of 300. 4to, half cloth, in dj lacking small piece. bba Sept 7 (91) £320 [Penney]
Anr copy. Orig half mor. bba May 9 (634) £360 [Whyte]

**Green, John, Geographer**
— A Journey from Aleppo to Damascus.... L, 1736. 8vo, modern cloth. With folding map. Map backed with minor loss at edges; tp backed with loss in margins affecting several words of text; repairs to 1st & final gatherings; last leaf silked; library stamp on tp. sg Mar 7 (88) $325

**Green, Philip James**
— Sketches of the War in Greece. L, 1828. 8vo, contemp calf; extremities worn. sg Mar 7 (170) $100

**Green, Robert B.**
— On the Arkansas Route to California in 1849: The Journal.... Lewisburg, 1955. Ed by J. Orin Oliphant. Sgd by Oliphant. pba Apr 25 (566) $85

**Green, Seth, 1817-88.** See: Roosevelt & Green

**Green, Thomas, Botanist**
— The Universal Herbal, or Botanical, Medical and Agricultural Dictionary.... L, [1824]. ("The Universal Herbal.") 2 vols. 4to, contemp calf; covers of Vol II lacking. With 2 hand-colored frontises & 107 hand-colored plates. 1 plate loose.  b May 30 (490) £450

**Green, William**
— The Art of Living in London. Walsall, [c.1811]. 8vo, contemp bds; rebacked in calf. With engraved title & 3 maps.  b Dec 5 (346) £110

**Greenaway, Kate, 1846-1901**
— Almanack for 1883. L, [1882]. 24mo, orig half cloth; rubbed.  sg Feb 8 (292) $150
— Almanack for 1886. L, [1885]. 24mo, orig half cloth.  pba Mar 7 (127) $85
— Almanacks for 1883-1895 & 1897. L: Routledge, [1882-96]. 14 vols. 24mo & 32mo, orig bdgs, 3 with orig ptd mailing wraps; some soiling & scuffing, 1893 with stitching loose. 1990 inscr to Miss Norman Shaw.  CNY May 17 (82) $2,800
— Book of Games. L: Routledge, [1889]. 4to, pictorial cloth; worn.  O Sept 12 (80) $225
— A Day in a Child's Life. L: Routledge, [1881]. 1st Ed. 4to, orig half cloth, in def & soiled dj. Inscr to John Ruskin, Dec 1881.  CNY May 17 (81) $3,500
Anr copy. Orig half cloth; corners worn.  F June 20 (672) $140
— Kate Greenaway Pictures from Originals Presented...to John Ruskin.... L, 1921. 4to, orig cloth, in torn dj.  b Sept 20 (587) £80
Anr copy. Orig cloth. With port & 20 tipped-in color plates.  b May 30 (434) £60
Anr copy. Minor foxing.  F June 20 (669) $140
— Language of Flowers. L: Routledge, [1884]. 1st Ed. 12mo, orig half cloth; worn & soiled. Foxed.  wa Feb 1 (324) $50
— Marigold Garden. L, [1885]. 1st Ed. 4to, orig bds; worn.  F June 20 (671) $100
— Under the Window. L: Routledge, [1878]. 1st Ed, Issue not indicated. 4to, pictorial bds; chipped.  sg Feb 8 (293) $150

**Greene, Asa, 1788-1837**
— Travels in America, by George Fibbleton, Esq.... NY, 1833. 12mo, orig cloth; extremities worn.  sg Oct 26 (124) $120

**Greene, Graham, 1904-91**
— Babbling April. Oxford, 1925. 1st Ed. Orig bds, in dj. Inscr "A book of juvenilia which I prefer to forget." Engelhard copy.  CNY Oct 27 (54) $3,800
Anr copy. Disbound with orig bds present; stained & rubbed. Inscr to Gwendoline Howell & with 2 A L s inserted, 1 to her & 1 to her husband after her death.  S Dec 18 (310) £1,600 [van Gelder]
Anr copy. Orig bds, in soiled & chipped dj. Inscr to Eric Quayle.  S Dec 18 (312) £1,200 [Mandl]
Anr copy. Orig bds, in dj. Inscr to Anthony Hobson.  S June 28 (93) £1,900

— The Basement Room and Other Stories. L: Cresset Press, 1935. 1st Ed. Orig cloth, 2d bdg, in dj. Inscr to Anthony Hobson.  S June 28 (103) £480
— The Bear Fell Free. L, 1935. One of 285. Orig cloth, in frayed dj. Hobson copy.  S June 28 (102) £480
[-] The Berkhamstedian. Berkhamsted, 1920-22. New Series, Vol XL, No 215; Vol XLI, Nos 216 & 128; Vol SLII, Nos 219-20. Orig wraps. These contain Greene's earliest ptd work. Hobson copies.  S June 28 (91) £420
— Brighton Rock. L, 1938. 1st English Ed. Inscr to Reginald Addyes-Scott; with later note, 1945, saying "a book that suffers from over-writing & a too explicit theme". Hobson copy.  S June 28 (106) £800
Continental Ed, one of 12 specially bound, this copy ptd for the author. Half mor.  S July 11 (285) £800
— The Confidential Agent. L, 1939. 1st Ed. Orig cloth. Inscr to Anthony Hobson.  S June 28 (108) £420
— England Made Me: A Novel. L, [1935]. 1st Ed. Inscr to Anthony Hobson.  S June 28 (101) £300
— A Gun for Sale. L, [1936]. Orig cloth, in frayed dj. Hobson copy.  S June 28 (104) £6,200
— It's a Battlefield. L, 1934. 1st Ed. Orig cloth; marked. Inscr to Anthony Hobson.  S June 28 (99) £250
1st American Ed. NY, 1934. In dj with edge wear.  CE May 22 (246) $260
— The Little Fire Engine. L, [1950]. Oblong 4to, orig bds, in dj. Inscr to Anthony Hobson.  S June 28 (114) £600
— The Little Train. L, [1946]. 1st Ed. - Illus by Dorothy Craigie. In dj. Inscr to Anthony Hobson.  S June 28 (111) £550
— The Man Within. L, 1929. 1st Ed. Inscr to Eric Quayle.  S Dec 18 (313) £380 [van Gelder]
Anr copy. Inscr to Lady Ottoline Morrell, 23 Oct 1930 & with ALs from her to him. Hobson copy.  S June 28 (94) £1,700
Anr copy. In rumpled dj. Inscr to Anthony Hobson.  S June 28 (95) £1,800
Anr copy. In soiled, rubbed & creased dj; bdg repaired at spine head.  S July 11 (287) £650
— The Ministry of Fear. L, 1943. 1st Ed. In repaired dj.  b Jan 31 (172) £160
— The Potting Shed. NY, 1957. 1st Ed. In dj with dust-soiling. Inscr to his wife. Engelhard copy.  CNY Oct 27 (58) $1,200
— The Power and the Glory. L, 1940. 1st Ed. In dj. Inscr to Anthony Hobson. "A remarkably fine copy".  S June 28 (109) £4,500
— Rumour at Nighfall. L, [1931]. 1st Ed. Orig cloth; spine creased. Inscr to Anthony Hobson & with ALs from Lady Ottoline Morrell to Greene.  S June 28 (97) £1,600
— Stamboul Train. L, 1932. 1st Ed. Inscr to Greene's mother-in-law, 1932. Engelhard copy.  CNY Oct 27 (55) $900
Anr copy. In repaired dj. Inscr to R. A. Addyes-Scott. With ALs to Lady Ottoline Morrell & with 5-line autograph quotation, sgd. Hobson copy.  S June 28 (98) £2,500

Anr copy. Bdg skewed. sg Dec 14 (54) $100
— The Third Man and the Fallen Idol. L, [1950]. In frayed dj with chip. Inscr to his brother, Herbert. Engelhard copy. CNY Oct 27 (56) $1,600
— The Virtue of Disloyalty. L: Pvtly ptd, 1972. 1st Ed, one of 300. Orig wraps. Inscr to John Carter. Hobson copy. S June 28 (128) £180
— A Visit to Morin. L, [1959]. 1st Ed in English, one of—250. In dj. Hobson copy. S June 28 (121) £160
— Yes and No and For Whom the Bell Chimes. L, 1983. One of 750. wa Feb 29 (38) $120
BEY, PILAFF. - Venus in the Kitchen. L, 1952. 1st Ed. - Intro by Graham Greene. In dj. Inscr by Greene to John Hayward, 30 Dec 1952. Hobson copy. S June 28 (117) £420

### Greene, Max
— The Kanzas Region: Forest, Prairie, Desert.... NY, 1856. 1st Ed. 12mo, orig cloth; front bd spotted. wa Feb 29 (577) $325

### Greene, William Thomas
— Parrots in Captivity. L, 1884-87. 3 vols. 8vo, orig cloth; rebacked retaining backstrips. With 81 colored plates. sg Apr 18 (147) $2,800
— The Science of Gunnery. L, 1846. 8vo, modern cloth; rubbed. O Oct 10 (142) $150

### Greener, William
— The Gun: or, a Treatise on the Various Descriptions of Small Fire-Arms. L, 1835. 1st Ed. 8vo, modern cloth; worn. With 4 plates. Some foxing & soiling. O Oct 10 (140) $250
— Gunnery in 1858. L, 1858. 1st Ed. 8vo, modern cloth; worn. With 4 plates. Some foxing. O Oct 10 (141) $120
Anr copy. Orig cloth; worn & soiled, inner hinges cracked, spine ends torn. With 5 plates. wa Feb 29 (199) $80

### Greener, William Wellington
— The Gun and its Development.... NY, 1899. 8vo, cloth; spine ends rubbed, front cover bumped. pba Aug 8 (463) $75

### Greenewalt, Crawford H.
— Hummingbirds. Garden City, [1960]. 4to, cloth, in dj. Sgd on tp. sg May 9 (284) $90
Anr copy. With 70 mtd color photos. sg May 16 (304) $80

### Greenhill, Elizabeth
— Elizabeth Greenhill Bookbinder: A Catalogue Raisonne. L, 1986. One of 500. 4to, goatskin extra by Flora Ginn to Elizabeth Greenhill's design, sgd by both, 1994. bba May 9 (158) £1,000 [Page]

### Greenhill, Thomas, 1681-1740?
— Nekrokedeia: or the Art of Embalming.... L, [1705]. 4to, modern half mor gilt; extremities worn, joints rubbed. With 13 plates (1 folding) plus folding frontis & folding map. Lacking 3 leaves; frontis & map repaired on verso; other marginal repairs; some plates spotted. pba June 20 (187) $300

### Greenhouse...
— Greenhouse Favorites. L: Groombridge, [c.1850]. 4to, half mor gilt by Bayntun. With 36 hand-colored plates. sg Dec 7 (222) $500

### Greenhow, Robert T., 1800-54
— The History of Oregon and California.... Bost., 1844. 1st Ed. 8vo, 19th-cent half mor; extremities worn. With 1 folded map. Map torn 7 repaired. Larson copy. pba Sept 28 (113) $250
Enlarged Ed. 8vo, 19th-century half calf; scuffed. With 2 folding maps. Robbins copy. pba Mar 21 (125) $2,250

### Greenwood, Charles & John
— Atlas of the Counties of England. L, 1834. Folio, contemp half bds; def, covers loose. With title index map, & 44 (of 46) maps. Slight fraying & soiling; last map dampstained. S Oct 26 (373) £1,100 [Hepner]
Anr copy. Contemp half mor; stained. With engraved title & 46 hand-colored maps. Lincolnshire split & frayed; Ms index on front flyleaf. S Nov 30 (55) £1,300

### Greenwood, Jeremy
— The Wood-Engravings of John Nash. Liverpool: The Wood Lea Press, 1987. One of 750. 4to, orig half cloth. sg Jan 11 (308) $150

### Greenwood, Robert
— California Imprints, 1833-1862. Los Gatos, 1961. One of 750. In frayed & soiled dj. O Mar 26 (117) $60
Anr copy. In dj. Metzdorf copy. pba Nov 16 (118) $50
Anr copy. In soiled & torn dj. pba Apr 25 (429) $55
— The California Outlaw, Tiburcio Vasquez.... Los Gatos, 1960. One of 750. Half cloth, in dj. pba Nov 16 (117) $60

### Greg, E. H.
— A Narrative of the Cruise of the Yacht Maria among the Feroe Islands.... L, 1855. 8vo, orig cloth. With 10 tinted litho plates. b May 30 (154) £650

### Greg, Sir Walter Wilson, 1875-1959
— A Bibiography of the English Printed Drama to the Restoration. L, 1970. 4 vols. 4to, orig cloth. bba Oct 19 (174) £55 [Makroski]

### Gregen, Archibald
— A Dictionary of the Manks Language.... Doublas, 1835. 8vo, half calf. b May 30 (106) £80

### Gregg, John Robert
— Gregg Shorthand. NY, [1929]. Vellum. Library markings. Inscr to Helge Kokeritz, with message in shorthand. sg Sept 28 (118) $60

**Gregg, Josiah, 1806-50?**
— Commerce of the Prairies, or the Journal of.... NY, 1844. 1st Ed, 1st Issue. 2 vols. 12mo, orig cloth; shelf wear. With frontises, 4 plates, 2 maps (1 folding), & 5 illus. Some foxing. Robbins copy.  pba Mar 21 (126) $3,250
Anr Ed. NY & L, 1844. 2d Issue. 2 vols. 12mo, orig cloth; cocked, spine ends chipped. With 6 plates & 2 maps. Closed tear to folding map.  wa Feb 29 (388) $800
— Diary & Letters of.... Norman, Okla., 1941 & [1958]. 1st Ed. - Ed by Maurice Garland Fulton. 2 vols. Orig cloth in djs. Robbins copy.  pba Mar 21 (127) $85

**Gregoire, Henri Baptiste, 1750-1831**
— Lettre au Philanthropes.... Paris, Oct 1709. 8vo, disbound; stitching replaced by staples. Browned.  sg Mar 28 (110) $250
— Memoire en faveur des gens de couleur ou sangre meles de Saint Domingue.... Paris, 1789. 8vo, disbound. First signature browned; some penciled annotations; worming to margins of Sig. C.  sg Mar 28 (111) $550

**Gregory, B.**
— Short Poems on Various Religious Subjects. Belper, 1838. 12mo, contemp cloth.  b Dec 5 (73) £50

**Gregory, George, 1754-1808**
— A Dictionary of Arts and Sciences. NY, 1821-22. 3 vols. 4to, contemp sheep; rubbed. Foxing & dampstaining.  F Mar 28 (544) $80
— The Economy of Nature.... L, 1798. 2d Ed. 3 vols. 8vo, later half calf; worn & soiled. With 56 plates. Some foxing. Inscr to Maryann Black.  wa Feb 29 (224) $170

**Gregory I, Saint, Pope, 540-604**
— Dialogorum libri quattuor. Cologne: Bartholomaeus de Unkel, [c.1484]. 4to, modern mor. 27 lines; type 1:103G.. 152 leaves. Goff G-404.  C Nov 29 (52) £1,100
— Epistolae. Venice: Lazzaro de Soardi, 1505. Folio, contemp Spanish Mudejar wallet bdg of mor, with eyelets.  C May 1 (69) £3,600
— Homiliae super Ezechielem. [Paris, c.1490]. Bound after: Pastorale. [Paris, c.1490] 4to, contemp blind-stamped calf; rebacked, lacking clasp & catch. Roman letter. Margins of last 4 leaves repaired; some dampstaining; repairs to text of last 2 leaves with minor loss. Homilae: 173 (of 176) leaves; lacking 3 final leaves; Pastorale: 66 (of 74) leaves; lacking 1st 8 leaves. GKW 11426 & 11445.  S Nov 30 (266) £650
— Moralia, sive Expositio in Job. Paris: Ulrich Gering & Berthold Rembolt, 31 Oct 1495. Folio, modern calf. 50 lines & headlines; double column; gothic letter. Some worming at ends affecting text; tp soiled & flawed in margin; a few letters erased on verso of tp & on a2. 380 (of 382) leaves; lacking 2 blanks. Goff G-431.  S Dec 18 (34) £1,000 [Frew]
— Sopra la vita di Job. Florence: Nicolaus Laurentii Alamanus, 15 June 1486. Vol I only. Later vellum bds. 362 leaves only. Goff G-435.  S June 12 (145) £580

**Gregory IX, Pope, d.1241**
— Decretales. Nuremberg: Anton Koberger, 14 July 1482. Folio, 16th-cent blindstamped calf over wooden bds, armorial stamp of Hubertus Govaerts; rebacked & restored. 78 lines of commentary; double column; gothic letter. Worming at ends; some staining & soiling; large ink-stain in text of q6r; tear in text of D4; other marginal tears.  S Dec 18 (35) £750 [Zioni]
Anr Ed. Speyer: Peter Drach, 16 Aug 1486. Folio, contemp blind-stamped calf over wooden bds, with remains of 2 clasps; worn, spine ends renewed. 78 lines (varies) of commentary surrounding double-column text & headline; types 9:78G, 11:90G, 12*:180G. Rubricated, with some Maiblumen initials in red & blue, flourished lombard initials in blue, capital strokes in red. Some soiling, browning & marginal dampstaining; some leaves wormed affecting letters. 304 leaves; lacking all 32 leaves before d3. Goff G-461. Donau 254.  S June 27 (322) £950
Anr Ed. Basel: Johann Froben & Johann Amerbach, 7 Oct 1500. 4to, contemp Erfurt bdg from Kyriss shop 93 of blind-stamped pigskin over wooden bds. 67 lines of commentary & headline; double column; gothic letter. Some staining & worming. 508 leaves. Goff G-479.  S Dec 18 (36) £850 [Frew]

**Gregory, Montgomery.** See: Locke & Gregory

**Gregory of Nazianzus, Saint, 329-389**
— Orationes novem. Venice: Aldus, 1536. 8vo, early 19th-cent mor gilt with Aldine device on covers; extremities worn. Greek text. Tp browned. Syston Park copy.  sg Mar 21 (151) $750

**Gregynog Press—Newtown, Wales**
— [Ecclesiastes] Llyfr y Pregeth-wr. 1927. One of 223.  sg Sept 14 (200) $120
— The Lamentations of Jeremiah. 1933. One of 110 bound in mor.  sg Apr 18 (58) $2,200
One of 250.  S Nov 21 (242) £800; sg Oct 19 (106) $2,400
— Psalmau Dafydd.... 1929. One of 200.  sg Sept 14 (205) $175
— The Revelation of St. John the Divine. 1932. One of 250.  S May 16 (82) £900; sg Sept 14 (206) $900
ABERCROMBIE, LASCELLES. - Lyrics and Unfinished Poems. 1940. One of 175.  sg Sept 14 (189) $200
AESOP. - Fables. 1931. One of 250.  sg Oct 19 (104) $2,400
BLUNT, LADY ANNE & BLUNT, WILFRID SCAWEN. - The Celebrated Romance of the Stealing of the Mare. 1930. One of 275.  sg Sept 14 (190) $400
BRIDGES, ROBERT. - Eros and Psyche. 1935. One of 300.  sg Oct 19 (108) $700
BUTLER, SAMUEL. - Erewhon. 1932. One of 300.  sg Sept 14 (191) $650
DAVID. - The Life of Saint David. 1927. One of 175.  sg Oct 19 (102) $650
DAVIES, RICHARD. - An Account of...that Ancient Servant

of the Lord. 1928. One of 175. sg Sept 14 (192) $90

DAVIES, WILLIAM HENRY. - Selected Poems. 1928. One of 310. sg Sept 14 (193) $90

EURIPIDES. - The Eight Plays. 1931. One of 500. cb Feb 14 (2774) $250; sg Sept 14 (194) $325

FORTESCUE, SIR JOHN WILLIAM. - The Story of a Red-Deer. 1935. One of 15 specially bound. sg Oct 19 (110) $1,100

HABERLY, LOYD. - Anne Boleyn and Other Poems. 1934. One of 300. sg Sept 14 (195) $175

HARTZENBUSCH, JUAN EUGENIO. - The Lovers of Teruel. 1938. One of 175. b Jan 31 (173) £220

HERBERT OF CHERBURY, EDWARD. - Autobiography. 1928. One of 300. sg Sept 14 (197) $225

JOINVILLE, JEAN. - The History of Saint Louis. 1937. One of 200. b Sept 20 (624) £400; sg Oct 19 (111) $1,000; sg Apr 18 (59) $1,600

LAMB, CHARLES. - Elia and the Last Essays of Elia. 1929-30. One of 285. 2 vols. sg Sept 14 (199) $100

MILTON, JOHN. - Four Poems. 1933. One of 250. S May 16 (81) £440

MILTON, JOHN. - On the Morning of Christ's Nativity. 1937. One of 250. sg Sept 14 (202) $100

OMAR KHAYYAM. - [The Rubaiyat in Welsh] Penillion. 1928. One of 285. sg Sept 14 (203) $300

SAMPSON, JOHN. - XXI Welsh Gypsy Folk-Tales. 1933. One of 250. sg Oct 19 (105) $650

SHAW, GEORGE BERNARD. - Shaw Gives Himself Away. 1939. One of 275. sg Oct 19 (112) $325

THOMAS, RONALD STUART. - Laboratories of the Spirit. 1976. One of 175. Hobson copy. S June 28 (228) £160

VANSITTART, ROBERT. - The Singing Caravan. 1932. One of 250. sg Sept 14 (207) $100; sg Feb 15 (157) $150

VEGA CARPIO, LOPE FELIX DE. - The Star of Seville. 1935. One of 175. sg Oct 19 (107) $375

XENOPHON. - Cyropaedia. 1936. One of 150. sg Sept 14 (208) $650; sg Oct 19 (109) $900

**Greig, John.** See: Storer & Greig

**Grenier, Jean**
— Bores. NY, [1961]. Illus by Francisco Bores. 4to, pictorial bds. With 8 color lithos. sg Sept 7 (52) $150

**Greppo, J. G. H.**
— Essay on the Hieroglyphic System of M. Champollion, Jun.... Bost., 1830. 12mo, orig half cloth; spine ends chipped, front joint cracked. sg Mar 7 (89) $80

**Gresset, Jean Baptiste Louis, 1709-77**
— Oeuvres. Paris, [1794]. 18mo, contemp red mor gilt. With 5 plates. Spotting in margins of plates. Fuerstenberg - Schaefer copy. S Dec 7 (275) £180

Anr Ed. Paris, 1811. In 2 vols. 8vo, red mor by Doll. With port & 8 plates, all but 1 in 2 states. Fuerstenberg - Schaefer copy. S Dec 7 (277) £320

**Greuze, Jean Baptiste, 1725-1805**
— Divers Habillements suivant le costume d'Italie.... Paris, 1768. Folio, contemp half calf; rubbed, paper label on lower corner of upper cover. With etched title & 24 etched plates. Repaired tear in lower margin of Plate 11. Fuerstenberg - Schaefer copy. S Dec 7 (279) £3,200

— Tetes de differents caracteres dediees a Mr. J.G. Wille.... Paris, 1766. 4 parts in 1 vol. 4to, red mor gilt by Taffin. With port, engraved title & 18 plates pasted on thick paper at left outer margin. Some spotting on C2 & C3. Fuerstenberg - Schaefer copy. S Dec 7 (278) £3,200

**Greville, Robert Kaye, 1794-1866.** See: Hooker & Greville

**Grevin, Jacques, 1538-70**
— De venenis, libri duo. Antwerp: Plantin, 1571. 8vo, disbound in cloth slipcase. Tp soiled; lacks Y4. CE Nov 8 (98) $320

**Grew, Nehemiah, 1641-1712**
— Cosmologia Sacra: or a Discourse of the Universe.... L, 1701. 1st Ed. Folio, contemp calf; worn, broken. Tp & next leaf stamped. sg May 16 (172) $120

— Musaeum Regalis Societas, or a Catalogue.... L, 1681. 1st Ed. Folio, contemp calf. With frontis port & 31 plates (1 folding). Some marginalia. CE Nov 8 (99) $650

**Grey, Edward, Viscount Grey of Fallodon, 1866-1933**
— Fly Fishing. L & Toronto, 1930. One of 150, sgd & with an extra wood-engraving sgd by the artist. Illus by Eric Daglish. 4to, orig vellum bds. sg Mar 7 (457) $600

**Grey, Sir George, 1812-98**
— Journals of Two Expeditions of Discovery in North-West and Western Australia.... L, 1841. 2 vols. 8vo, contemp calf gilt; rebacked. Pencilled marginalia; lacking ads. bba Nov 16 (280) £450 [Dunsheath]

Anr copy. Orig cloth; rubbed, Vol I recased & with new endpapers. With 22 litho plates (6 of them colored); 2 folding maps in pocket at end. Short split at folds of folding maps. S June 27 (249) £400

**Grey, James T., Jr.**
— Salmon Rivers of Cape Breton Island. Yardley PA, 1984. One of 50. O June 25 (141) $110

**Grey, John S.**
— Centennial Campaign: The Sioux War of 1876. Fort Collins CO: Old Army Press, [1976]. Maps by John A. Popovich. In dj. pba June 25 (104) $95

One of 3. Inscr by the pbr, Michael J. Koury to John Popovich. pba June 25 (106) $600

**Grey, Romer C.**
— Adventures of a Deep-Sea Angler. NY, 1930. 4to, cloth, in dj with edge-tears. pba July 11 (118) $1,200

**Grey, Zane, 1875-1939**
— Betty Zane. NY: Charles Francis Press, [1903]. 2d Ed. Cloth; rubbed & spotted.  bbc Dec 18 (252) $210
— The Last of the Plainsmen. NY, 1908.  pba Jan 25 (124) $50
— Tales of Fishes. NY: Harper, 1919.  pba July 11 (120) $180
— Tales of Fishing Virgin Seas. NY & L, 1925. 4to, cloth, in dj. With Grey's library blindstamp.  cb June 25 (1845) $650
— Tales of Fresh-Water Fishing. NY & L, 1928. 4to, half mor. Some leaves discolored. With Grey's library blindstamp.  cb June 25 (1846) $1,800
  Anr copy. Cloth; worn & stained, inner hinges weak. O June 25 (143) $225; pba Apr 25 (430) $120
  Anr copy. In worn dj.  wa Feb 1 (210) $55
— Tales of Lonely Trails. NY: Harper, [1922].  pba Jan 25 (126) $50
  Anr copy. In chipped dj. Inscr.  sg June 20 (138) $275
— Tales of Swordfish and Tuna. NY, 1927. 1st Ed. 4to, cloth. Inscr by Romer Grey to Hal Wallis.  pba Mar 7 (129) $250
— Tales of Tahitian Waters. NY, 1931. Orig cloth; spine head rubbed.  pba Mar 7 (130) $275
— Tales of the Angler's Eldorado, New Zealand. NY & L, 1926. 4to, half mor gilt. With Grey's library blindstamp.  cb June 25 (1847) $1,000
  Anr copy. Cloth, in dj. With Grey's library blindstamp.  cb June 25 (1848) $800
— Tales of the Southern Rivers. NY, [1924]. 4to, cloth, in soiled dj. With Grey's library blindstamp.  cb June 25 (1849) $450
— Tappan's Burro and Other Stories. NY: Harper, [1923].  pba Aug 22 (194) $90

**Gribble, Ernest.** See: Cescinsky & Gribble

**Gribbon, William Lancaster, 1879-1940.** See: Mundy, Talbot

**Grierson, James**
— Saint Andrews as it Was and as it Is. Cupar, 1838. 3d Ed. Modern half calf; joints starting. With 12 plates.  pba Nov 9 (28) $2,500
  Anr copy. Later calf.  pba Apr 18 (68) $2,250

**Griffen, John S.**
— A Doctor Comes to California: The Diary of.... San Francisco, 1943. 1st Ed. - Intro by George Walcott Ames. Orig cloth. With frontis & 4 maps. Larson copy.  pba Sept 28 (500) $60
  Anr copy. Orig cloth.  pba Apr 25 (431) $55

**Griffin, John, 1769-1834**
— Memoirs of Captain James Wilson. L, [1818]. 2d Ed. 8vo, half mor.  b Mar 20 (94) £80

**Griffith, George**
— The Devil's Spadeful; a Traditional Poem. Bewdley, 1839. 12mo, orig wraps; worn. Inscr to Miss Puckey.  b Dec 5 (414) £120

**Griffiths, Arthur George Frederick, 1838-1908**
— Mysteries of Police and Crime. L, 1912. Illus by Arthur Rackham. 3 vols. 8vo, orig cloth; rubbed & soiled.  Ck May 31 (118) £80

**Grimaldi, Stacey, 1790-1863**
— The Toilet. L, 1821. 2d Ed. 16mo, mor gilt; front cover detached, rubbed. With engraved title & 9 hand-colored plates with moveable flap.  rs Nov 11 (134) $250
  3d Ed. 16mo, bds; worn. With 9 hand-colored plates with moveable flap.  rs Nov 11 (135) $350

**Grimeston, Edward**
— A Generall History of the Netherlands. L, 1608. 1st Ed, 1st Issue. Folio, 19th-cent calf gilt; extremities worn. Tp soiled; lacking initial blank.  sg Mar 21 (152) $475

**Grimm Brothers**
See also: Golden Cockerel Press; Limited Editions Club
— Das blaue Licht. [Berlin: Bruno Cassirer, 1924]. Illus by Max Slevogt. Folio, orig vellum-backed case. With separate set of 15 lithos, each sgd by Slevogt.  S Nov 21 (198) £300
— Fairy Tales. L, 1909. Illus by Arthur Rackham. 4to, orig cloth. With 40 colored plates. 1 plate loose.  b Jan 31 (215) £580
  Anr copy. Orig cloth; spine ends rubbed. With 40 mtd color plates. A few plates creased.  bba May 9 (259) £360 [Clancey]
  Anr copy. Orig cloth; rubbed, upper joint repaired.  bba May 9 (404) £260 [Clancey]
  One of 750. Mor gilt by Sangorski & Sutcliffe for Asprey, with onlaid design of a fairy.  CE Sept 27 (238) $2,800
  Anr copy. Orig vellum gilt; stained. With 40 colored plates.  Ck May 31 (136) £800
  Anr copy. Orig vellum gilt; spine soiled.  rs Nov 11 (113) $1,500
  Anr copy. Orig vellum gilt; marked.  S Nov 2 (126) £850 [Hirsch]
— German Popular Stories. L, 1823-26. 1st English Ed, 1st Issue. Illus by George Cruikshank. 2 vols. 12mo, loose mtd sheets, in folding cloth chemise. With 22 plates on 11 sheets of india paper; with 1st state of the vignette title (without the diaeresis). Bruten - Bement - Pforzheimer - Schaefer copy.  P Nov 1 (72) $4,750
— Hansel and Gretel. L, [1925]. One of 600. Illus by Kay Nielsen. Orig cloth; browned & worn, spine repaired at ends.  S Nov 2 (98) £700 [Hirsch]; sg Feb 15 (211) $1,700
  Anr Ed. NY, [c.1927]. Orig cloth. With 12 plates.  K Oct 1 (289) $325

**Grimm, Friedrich Melchior, 1723-1807 — & Diderot, Denis, 1713-84**
— Memoires historiques, litterraires et anecdotiques tires de la correspondance.... Londres, 1814. 4 vols. 8vo, contemp calf. With port. Bedford - Fuerstenberg - Schaefer copy.  S Dec 7 (280) £380

## Grimm, Heinrich
— Deutsche Buchdruckersignete des XVI. Jahrhunderts. Wiesbaden, 1965. 4to, bds in dj. sg Apr 11 (123) $50

## Grimod de la Reyniere, Alexandre Balthazar Laurent, 1758-1838
— Almanach des Gourmands. Paris, 1804-1807. 3d Ed of Vol. I, 1st Eds of Vols. II-V. Vols. I-V (of 8) only. 12mo, contemp half calf; rubbed. Spotted; lacking half-titles; 1 leaf in Vol. III torn. S Oct 12 (99) £250

— Manuel de Amphitryons, contenant un traite de la dissection des viandes.... Paris, 1808. 3 parts in 1 vol. 8vo, contemp half bds; worn. With frontis & 16 plates. Dampstained. S Oct 12 (28) £420

Anr copy. Contemp half bds; rubbed & faded. 3 pp. torn; letter from title moved to frontis. S Oct 12 (29) £380

## Grimshaw, William Robinson
— Grimshaw's Narrative: Being the Story of Life and Events in California.... Sacramento, 1964. One of 310. Ed by J. R. K. Kantor. Orig cloth in dj. With frontis port. Larson copy. pba Sept 28 (502) $95

## Grindlay, Robert Melville
— Scenery, Costumes and Architecture, Chiefly on the Western Side of India. L, 1826-30. 2 vols in 1. 4to, mor; both covers detached, spine worn. With 36 hand-colored plates. K Feb 11 (186) $4,300

## Grinnell, George Bird, 1849-1938
See also: Roosevelt & Grinnell
— American Big Game in its Haunts. NY, 1904. Ed by Grinnell. Orig cloth; some wear. O Oct 10 (145) $60

— The Cheyenne Indians: Their History and Ways of Life. NY, 1962. 2 vols. Orig cloth in djs; d/j spines sunned. Robbins copy. pba Mar 21 (128) $65

— The Fighting Cheyennes. NY, 1915. Orig cloth; worn, rubbed & soiled. O Jan 9 (120) $100; pba June 25 (107) $70

1st Ed. Orig cloth; spine sunned. Robbins copy. pba Mar 21 (129) $180

— Hunting and Conservation. New Haven, 1925. Orig cloth; worn. O Jan 9 (121) $120

— Hunting at High Altitudes. NY & L, 1913. Orig cloth; worn. O Oct 10 (147) $50

Anr copy. In tattered dj. O Jan 9 (119) $375

## Grinnell, Joseph, 1877-1939
— Report on the Birds Recorded During a Visit to the Islands of Santa Barbara, San Nicolas.... Pasadena, 1887. Orig wraps; chipped. Pasadena Academy of Sciences Publication No 1. pba July 25 (154) $85

## Grinnell, Joseph, 1877-1939 —& Others
— Fur-Bearing Mammals of California. Berkeley, 1937. 1st Ed. 2 vols. in djs. Robbins copy. pba Mar 21 (131) $75

## Grinnell, Joseph, 1877-1939 —& Storer, Tracy
— Animal Life in the Yosemite. Berkeley, 1924. Orig cloth; rubbed. pba Feb 12 (67) $140

## Grinnell, Joseph, 1877-1939 —& Storer, Tracey
— Animal Life in the Yosemite. Berkeley, 1924. 1st Ed. Orig cloth in dj; sunned & worn. Robbins copy. pba Mar 21 (130) $150

## Grisenthwaite, William
— Sleep, a Poem in Two Books.... Lynn, [1812]. 8vo, mor gilt. Inscr, with 2 pages of Ms poems, sgd with initials. b Dec 5 (251) £90

## Grisham, John
— The Firm. NY, [1991]. 1st Ed. In dj. Sgd on front free endpaper. pba Aug 22 (195) $130

## Grison, Theophile
— La Teinture au Dix-Neuvieme Siecle en ce qui concerne la Laine et les Tissus.... Paris, 1884-1908. 2 vols. 4to, contemp half lea; rubbed, Vol I needs rebacked. With 22 plates & 459 dyed fabric specimens mtd on 63 leaves. sg May 16 (173) $60

## Grisone, Federico
— Ordini di cavalcare, et modi di conoscere le nature de cavalli. Naples, 1550. 4to, 17th-cent sheep; worn, top of spine chipped. Blank portions of title excised & restored; early owner's notes on blank 3G4. sg Mar 7 (458) $500

Anr Ed. [N.p.], 1561. 8vo, old vellum. Early Ms annotations. S Mar 28 (484) £340

## Griswold, Frank Gray, 1854-1937 —& Hume, R. D.
— The Life-History of the Atlantic and Pacific Salmon of Canada. NY, 1930. 12mo, half cloth; some wear. O June 25 (145) $120

## Griswold, Martin van Buren
— Murder of M.V.B. Griswold.... Jackson, Calif., 1859. 1st Ed. Orig wraps; edges frayed, split up spine foot, rear wrap stained. With 3 illus. Robbins copy. pba Mar 21 (132) $2,750

## Griswold, N. W.
— Beauties of California.... San Francisco, 1883. Orig color litho wraps; minor wear to spine, small stain on back wrap. With 26 color plates on 13 leaves. pba Feb 12 (69) $400

## Gritsch, Johannes
— Quadragesimale. Cologne: Heinrich Quentell, 11 July 1481. Bound with: Voragine, Jacobus de. Sermones de sanctis. Augsburg: Hermann Kaestlin, 10 Apr 1484. Folio, contemp pigskin over wooden bds; spine worn, 1 thong missing, early repairs on back cover. Partially misbound; small hole & stain on f.43; some worming. 198 leaves in 1st work. Goff G-497. 206 leaves in 2d work. Goff J-188. C June 26 (167) £3,200

## Grivas, Theodore
— Military Governments in California, 1846-50.... Glendale, Calif., 1963. 1st Ed. Orig cloth in dj. With 10 ports. Larson copy. pba Sept 28 (503) $65

## Groeber, Karl
— Children's Toys of Bygone Days.... NY, 1928. 4to, cloth, in dj. sg June 13 (370) $110

## Groenen, Lievin
— Illustrated Marine Encylopedia. Antwerp, 1890. 4to, cloth; front free endpaper lacking. Some foxing. pba July 25 (426) $160

## Grogan, P. A. See: Gekoski & Grogan

## Grohmann, Adolf. See: Arnold & Grohmann

## Grohmann, Johann Gottfried
— Ideenmagazin fuer Liebhaber von Gaerten.... Leipzig, 1796-1806. No of parts not given, but from 1796 only. Modern paper over bds. With 70 plates, 7 of them hand-colored. Some foxing & dampstaining; a few guards lacking. cb Oct 17 (82) $800

Anr Ed. Leipzig, 1798-1802. 9 issues in 1 vol. 4to, old half calf; worn. With 90 plates. Foxed. Sold w.a.f. CE Nov 8 (194) $350

## Grohmann, Will
— Wassily Kandinsky: Life and Work. NY, [1958]. Folio, cloth, in dj. Library markings. sg Sept 7 (199) $80

Anr copy. Cloth. sg Jan 11 (233) $60

## Grolier Club—New York
— A Decree of Star Chamber concerning Printing... 1884. One of 150. sg Sept 14 (212) $325
— The History of Helyas, Knight of the Swan. 1901. One of 325. sg Sept 14 (214) $175
— One Hundred Books Famous in English Literature. Intro by George E. Woodberry* Kent, H.W.-Bibliographical Notes on One Hundred Books... 1902-3. Each, One of 305. 2 vols. sg Sept 14 (218) $60; sg Sept 14 (219) $100
— A Selection of American Press Books, 1968-1978. Printer's Choice... 1983. One of 325. Intro by Ruth Fine & William Matheson; bibliographical descriptions & notes by W. Thomas Taylor. sg Sept 14 (341) $175; sg Feb 15 (109) $140

AUSTIN, GABRIEL. - The Library of Jean Grolier... 1971. One of 1,000. sg Sept 14 (209) $50

BRESLAUER, BERNARD & FOLTER, ROLAND. - Bibliography: its History and Development. 1984. One of 600. O Mar 26 (118) $100; O May 7 (68) $60; sg Sept 14 (210) $50; sg Feb 15 (62) $130

BURY, RICHARD DE. - The Philobiblon. 1889. One of 297. 3 vols. sg Sept 14 (211) $130

COE, MICHAEL D. - The Maya Scribe and his World. 1973. One of 1,000. sg Oct 26 (74) $100

GOLDSCHMIDT, LUCIEN & NAEF, WESTON. - The Truthful Lens: a Survey of the Photographically Illustrated Book, 1844-1914. 1980. One of 1,000. O May 7 (152) $225; sg Feb 29 (151) $400

HALSEY, RICHARD T. H. - The Boston Port Bill as Pictured by a Contemporary London Cartoonist. 1904. One of 325. F Mar 28 (435) $80; sg Sept 14 (213) $50

HENDERSON, ROBERT W. - Early American Sport: a Chronological Check-list... 1937. One of 400. O June 25 (146) $120; O June 25 (158) $130

HOE, ROBERT. - A Lecture on Bookbinding as a Fine Art... 1886. One of 200. Copy bound in mor gilt by David. b May 30 (552) $550

HORBLIT, HARRISON D. - One Hundred Books Famous in Science. 1964. One of 1,000. Inscr. sg Oct 19 (229) $425

IRVING, WASHINGTON. - A History of New York. 1886. One of 175. 2 vols. sg Oct 26 (165) $550

KENNEDY, EDWARD GUTHRIE. - The Etched Work of Whistler. 1910. 6 vols. S Nov 21 (227) £1,150

Anr copy. Text vol & 5 vols of plates. Lacking 3 plates & with a few additional plates loosely inserted. S Mar 28 (437) £300

MATTHEWS, WILLIAM F. - Modern Bookbinding Practically Considered. 1889. One of 300. Inscr. bba May 9 (159) £110 [Maggs]; sg Sept 14 (216) $100

MORES, EDWARD ROWE. - A Dissertation upon English Typographical Founders and Foundries. 1924. One of 250. Ed by D.B. Updike. bba May 9 (36) £65 [Collinge & Clark]; sg Sept 14 (217) $50

MORISON, STANLEY. - Fra Luca de Pacioli of Borgo S. Sepolcro. 1933. One of 390. bba Oct 5 (213) £300 [Franks]; bba May 9 (19) £460 [Marks]; Ck May 31 (52) £380; sg Oct 19 (150) $750; sg Apr 18 (138) $900

RUZICKA, RUDOLPH. - New York. 1915. One of 250. sg Sept 14 (221) $550

STAUFFER, DAVID MCNEELY. - American Engravers upon Copper and Steel. 1907. One of 350. 2 vols. O May 7 (277) $225

TORY, GEOFROY. - Champ Fleury. 1927. One of 390. sg Oct 19 (248) $200

WROTH, LAWRENCE C. - The Colonial Printer. 1931. One of 300. Unopened. O Dec 5 (151) $110

## Grollier de Serviere, Nicolas
— Recueil d'ouvrages curieux de mathematique et de mecanique.... Lyons, 1719. 1st Ed. 4to, contemp calf. With 85 plates. b May 30 (21) £850

## Gromort, Georges
— L'Art des jardins. Paris, 1934. 2 vols. 8vo, later cloth; joints of Vol II just starting. wa Dec 14 (497) $300

## Gronow, Rees Howell, 1794-1865
— Reminiscences: Being Anecdotes of the Camp, the Court, and the Clubs. L, 1892. ("The Reminiscences and Recollections of Captain Gronow.") 2 vols. 8vo, lev gilt by Bayntun. Extra-illus with c.100 plates. sg Sept 21 (211) $425

## Groom, G. Laurence
— The Singing Sword. Leeds: The Swan Press, 1927. Countee Cullen's sgd copy. sg Mar 28 (41) $150

## GROOME

### Groome, F. H.
— Ordnance Gazetteer of Scotland.... Edin., 1882-85. 6 vols. 4to, orig cloth; free endpapers lacking, hinges cracked. Library markings. sg May 9 (67) $175

### Gropius, Walter, 1883-1969
— Bauhausbuecher 12: Bauhausbauten Dessau. Munich, 1930. 4to, orig wraps in def dj. bba Oct 19 (129) £280 [W. English]

### Groppo, Antonio
— Catalogo di tutti i drammi per musica recitati ne' teatri di Venezia dall'anno 1637.... Venice: Antonio Groppo, 1745. 12mo, carta rustica; new liners. A7-B5 repaired. S Dec 1 (169) £1,700

### Gros de Boze, Claude, 1680-1753
— Catalogue des Livres du Cabinet.... Paris, 1753. 1st Ed. 8vo, contemp calf; joints rubbed. With headpiece. S Oct 27 (1018) £240 [Guedroitz]
— [Sale Catalogue] Catalogue des Livres du Cabinet.... Paris, 1753. 8vo, contemp calf; rebacked preserving orig spine, rubbed. Priced in a contemp hand; contemp Ms copies of accounts of the library bound at end. bba May 9 (44) £160 [Mauss & Kreker]

Anr copy. 19th-cent calf; rubbed, tips & edges worn. O Mar 26 (120) $200

### Grose, Francis, 1731?-91
— The Antiquities of England and Wales. L, [1783]-97. 8 vols, including Supplement. 8vo, contemp half mor; rubbed. With frontis & 43 hand-colored maps. Lacking 1 map in Vol VIII; sold w.a.f. b Sept 20 (309) £250
— The Antiquities of Ireland. L, 1791-95. 2 vols. 4to, early calf; extremities worn, rebacked with non-uniform calf. Library markings; plates unstamped. sg Dec 7 (274) $400
— The Antiquities of Scotland. L, 1797. 2 vols. 4to, contemp mor gilt; joints & corners rubbed. With 190 plates, including titles. Some foxing, affecting plates. sg Mar 7 (90) $200
— Military Antiquities Respecting a History of the English Army. L, 1812. 2 vols. 4to, contemp mor gilt; rubbed. With 3 engraved titles & 141 plates. Library markings. S Mar 28 (160) £200

### Grose, Francis, 1731?-91 —& Others
— The Antiquarian Repertory: a Miscellaneous Assemblage of Topography.... L, 1807-9. 4 vols. 4to, contemp calf with stamps of the Signet Library; rubbed, some covers detached. bba May 30 (139) £200 [Finch]

### Grose-Smith, Henley —& Kirby, William F., 1844-1912
— Rhopalocera Exotica, Being Illustrations of...Butterflies. L, 1887-92. 3 vols. 4to, modern half calf gilt. With 180 hand-colored plates. Piece removed from upper outer corner of title pages; 4 other marginal excisions. Fattorini copy. C Oct 25 (66) £2,800

## AMERICAN BOOK PRICES CURRENT

### Grosvenor, Edwin Augustus
— Constantinople. Bost., 1895. 2 vols. 8vo, cloth. sg Mar 7 (91) $90

### Grosz, Georg, 1893-1959
— 30 Drawings & Watercolours. NY, 1944. 4to, orig wraps. pba Aug 8 (462) $50
— Drawings, with an Introduction by the Artist. NY, 1944. Folio, cloth, in dj. sg June 13 (176) $90
— Ecce Homo. Berlin, [1923]. 1st Ed, Ausgabe C. Folio, wraps; tear in lower inner corner of front free endpaper. With 84 plain & 16 colored plates. sg Apr 18 (105) $900

Anr copy. Orig wraps; soiled. wa Dec 14 (499) $750

Anr Ed. NY, 1965. Folio, bds. pba Aug 8 (461) $50
Anr copy. Bds, in dj. sg Jan 11 (204) $110
Anr copy. Bds. sg June 13 (178) $60
— Das Gesicht der Herrschenden Klasse. Berlin, [1921]. 3d Ed. Cloth; worn & foxed. sg Feb 15 (159) $175
— Die Gezeichneten: 60 Blaetter aus 15 Jahren. Berlin, 1930. 4to, wraps; chipped & soiled, front panel separated. wa Feb 1 (350) $95
— Interregnum. NY: Black Sun Press, 1936. Ltd Ed. Folio, half cloth. With orig sgd colored litho. CE May 22 (247) $1,400
— A Little Yes and a Big No. NY, 1946. In dj. sg Sept 7 (169) $100
— Das neue Gesicht der Herrschenden Klasse. Berlin, 1930. 4to, cloth, in soiled dj. sg Sept 7 (168) $250

### Grote, George, 1794-1871
— A History of Greece. L, 1888. 10 vols. 8vo, calf gilt, prize bdg. pba Sept 14 (185) $300

### Grotius, Hugo, 1583-1645
— De jure belli ac pacis. Amst., 1631. Folio, contemp calf; worn. Last leaf frayed; dampstained; tp torn & laid down. S June 13 (393) £350
— De Rebus Belgicis: or, the Annals.... L, 1665. Trans by Thomas Manley. 8vo, contemp calf; backstrip def, front cover detached. sg Mar 21 (154) $225
— Le Droit de la guerre, et de la paix. Paris, 1687. 2 vols. 4to, calf; spines needing repair. pba Mar 7 (131) $150
— Of the Law of Warre and Peace. L, 1654. 1st Ed in English. 8vo, contemp calf; spine ends chipped, corners worn, front endpaper renewed. Some dampstaining. Downshire - Hefner copy. CNY May 17 (20) $2,100

Anr Ed. L, 1682. ("His Three Books Treating of the Rights of War & Peace.") Folio, contemp calf; rebacked. pba Sept 14 (186) $950

Anr copy. Contemp calf; brittle, covers detached. Old stamp on tp. sg Mar 21 (186) $500

### Grouse...
— The Grouse in Health and Disease; being the Final Report of the Committee of Inquiry on Grouse Disease. L, 1911. 2 vols. 4to, cloth, in frayed djs; Vol I hinges cracked. sg Dec 7 (203) $175

544

## Grove, Arthur —& Cotton, Arthur Disbrowe
— A Supplement to Elwes' Monograph of the Genus Lilium. L, 1933-[34]-62. Parts 1-9. Folio, orig wraps. With 40 hand-colored plates. Fattorini copy. C Oct 25 (51) £2,200

## Grove, Harriet
— The Calendar of Nature, or the Seasons of England. L, [1849-50]. Folio, modern half mor. With colored litho title & 24 colored plates. Some foxing & discoloration; marginal staining at beginning. S June 27 (32) £1,000

## Gruber, F.
— Illustrated Guide and Catalogue of Woodward Gardens.... San Francisco, 1879. 8vo, ptd wraps; soiled, 1 corner chipped. With frontis. pba Feb 12 (386) $150

## Gruel, Leon, 1841-1923
— Manuel historique et bibliographique de l'amateur de reliures. Paris, 1887-1905. One of 1,000 & one of 700. 2 vols. 4to, modern half calf, orig wraps bound in, rubbed. bba May 9 (137A) £350 [Maggs]

One of 1,000; vol II is one of 600 on rives. Modern mor. S Oct 27 (1027) £600 [Mauss]

## Gruelle, Johnny
— Marcella Stories. NY: P. F. Volland, [1929]. Pictorial bds. Inscr to H. Spenser Lewis with drawing of Raggedy Ann, 26 Dec 1930. cb Feb 14 (2691) $2,750

## Gruner, Ludwig, 1801-82
— Fresco Decorations and Stuccoes of Churches and Palaces in Italy. L, 1844. Folio, contemp half mor; scuffed. With hand-colored title & 50 plates, of which 11 are fully or partially colored. Descriptive text & last 4 plates inlaid to size; some spotting. bba June 6 (15) £320 [Lester]

— Specimens of Ornamental Art. L, 1850. 2 vols. Folio, half mor. With 80 color plates & 8 additional uncolored plates. Some foxing. wad Oct 18 (281) C$1,400

## Guadacerius, Agathius
— Alphabetum hebraicum accedunt Obadiah. Paris: Chr. Wechel, 1553. 8vo, modern half mor. CE Dec 6 (80) $550

## Gualdo Priorato, Galeazzo, Count, 1606-78
— Historia di Leopoldo Cesare. Vienna, 1670-74. 2 (of 3) vols. Folio, contemp vellum bds; soiled. With frontis, 153 ports & 71 maps & plans, some folding. 3 plates shaved with loss. Sold w.a.f. b Dec 5 (121) £360

— Historia di Lepoldi Cesare. Vienna, 1670-74. 1st Ed. 3 vols. Folio, contemp half vellum. With 3 frontis ports, 163 ports, & 81 folding maps, plans, & views. Some portraits browned; some tears. Sold w.a.f. S Oct 26 (282) £1,600 [Zioni]

## Gualterotti, Rafaello, 1543-1638
— Feste nelle nozze del serenissimo Don Francesco Medici gran Duca di Toscana.... Florence, 1579. 4to, 18th-cent gilt paper; spine rubbed. With 16 plates, 6 ptd in red & 10 in green. Dampstaining to upper corner; some plates with platemark shaved, not affecting image. C Apr 3 (110) £9,500

## Gualtieri, Niccolo, 1688-1747
— Index testarum conchyliorum.... Florence, 1742. Folio, half calf; worn, broken. With frontis, port & 110 plates. Marginal dampstain throughout, occasionally affecting images; Plate 98 with marginal tear. P June 5 (240) $4,250

## Guarini, Camillo Guarino
— Architettura civile...opera postuma.. Turin, 1737. Folio, bds; spine gone 7 supplied in binder's tape. With frontis & 79 plates. K June 23 (34) $2,000

— Modo di misurare le fabriche. Turin, 1674. 8vo, old vellum. C Apr 3 (111) £950

**Guarnati, G. F.** See: Pallucchini & Guarnati

## Guastalla, Giorgio & Guido
— Marino Marini. Rome, 1993. In dj. sg Sept 7 (234) $350; sg June 13 (246) $300

**Guay-Trouin, Rene du, 1673-1736.** See: Duguay-Trouin, Rene

## Guazzo, Francesco Maria
— Compendium maleficarum. Milan, 1608. 8vo, contemp vellum. Some dampstains in margins. S June 27 (325) £2,400

## Guccioli, Teresa, Countess, 1801-73
— My Recollections of Lord Byron. L, 1869. 8vo, contemp half mor gilt; joints & extremities rubbed. With mtd port. Some browning. F Mar 28 (580) $130

## Gudde, Erwin G.
— California Gold Camps.... Berkeley, [1975]. 1st Ed. - Ed by Elizabeth K. Gudde. Orig cloth in dj. Larson copy. pba Sept 28 (504) $50

## Gudlaugsson, Sturla J.
— Geraert Ter Borch. The Hague, 1959-60. 2 vols. 4to, orig cloth, in djs. sg Jan 11 (415) $375

## Guercino, 1591-1666
— Raccolta di alcuni disegni. Rome, 1764. Bound with: Raphael Sanzio d'Urbino. Picturae Raphaelis Sancti Urbinatis ex aula et conclavibud palatii Vaticanici. Rome, 1722. Folio, contemp calf gilt; spine def. 1st work with frontis & 28 plates; 2d work with double-page engraved title & 18 plates. S Apr 23 (238) £6,000

## Guericke, Otto von, 1602-86
— Experimenta nova (ut vocantur) Magdeburgica de vacuo spatio. Amst., 1672. 1st Ed. Folio, 18th-cent bds with Luxdorph supralibros o elephant head supporting a coronet with its trunk. With frontis, port, 7

full-page plates, 2 double-page plates & 24 engraved textual diagrams & figures. Some dampstaining; corner off 1 leaf. Schaefer copy. P Nov 1 (104) $4,250

Anr copy. Contemp vellum. Lacking port & final errata leaf; some browning. Madsen copy. S Mar 14 (150) £1,900

**Guerin, Leon**
— Histoire maritime de France. Paris, 1852. 6 vols. 8vo, half sheep gilt; extremities rubbed. Browned & foxed. sg Mar 7 (216) $150

**Guerin, Maurice de, 1810-39**
— The Centaur. Montague, Mass., 1915. One of 135. Trans by George B. Ives; designed by Bruce Rogers. Bds; rebacked. With sgd port of Rogers & related material. sg Sept 14 (317) $650
— Poemes en prose. Paris, 1901. One of 23 on japon, this copy for Leon Rattier. Illus by E. Florian. 4to, mor extra by Gruel, orig wraps bound in. S Nov 21 (203) £1,200

Anr Ed. [Paris], 1928. Out-of-series copy for Georges Barbier. Illus by Georges Barbier. 4to, mor extra by Pierre Legrain, orig wraps bound in. Bound in is watercolor inscr by Barbier to Mme Pierre Legrain & ALs to her. S Nov 21 (202) £7,000

**Gueroult, Guillaume, d.c.1570**
— De virtutibus herbarum. Geneva: Ptr of the 1495 Fardelet du temps (Jean Belot), [c.1495]. ("Herbarum varias qui vis cognoscere vires....") Bound with: Eaux artificielles. Vienne en Dauphine: Peter Schenck, [c.1484]. 4to, early vellum Ms leaf over pastebd. 1st work: 33 lines; gothic types; woodcut on tp of author (also repeated ) & 66 text woodcuts of plants. 2d work: 24 lines; type 1:116G; with 4 woodcuts, 1 of them full-page. Some marginalia cropped; small 17th-cent engraving pasted onto title cut of 1st work; some soiling & staining. 1st work: 52 leaves; Goff M-6. 2d work: 49 (of 52) leaves, lacking leaves b2.7 & f10; H 6524. Schaefer copy. P Nov 1 (149) $35,000

**Guerra, Francisco**
— Iconografia Medica Mexicana. Mexico, 1952. One of 550. 4to, orig wraps; some wear. ds July 27 (88) $70

**Guerry, Andre Michel**
— Essai sur la statistique morale de la France. Paris, 1833. 4to, half calf. With 7 maps & tables ptd in color. b Sept 20 (40) £300

**Guesclin, Bertrand du**
— Le Livre des faits de messire Bertrand du Guesclin. [Lyons: Guillaume Le Roy, c.1487]. Folio, mor gilt with grolieresque interlace incorporating the monogram of Yemeniz, probably by Trautz-Bauzonnet. A35 lines, double column; type 9:112B. With full-page port cut used twice & 27 page-width cuts. Washed & pressed. 88 leaves. Goff G-541. Yemeniz - Seilliere - Bauchard - Maus - Schaefer copy. P Nov 1 (105) $47,500

**Gueulette, Thomas Simon, 1683-1766**
— Memoires de Mademoiselle Bontemps.... Amst., 1738. 12mo, mor gilt armorial bdg by Belz-Niedree. b Sept 20 (625) £60

**Guggenheim, Peggy**
— Art of this Century. NY, 1946. 4to, orig cloth, in rubbed dj. sg Jan 11 (205) $175

**Guibert, Albert Jean**
— Bibliographie des oeuvres de Rene Descartes.... Paris, 1976. 8vo, orig cloth. sg Apr 11 (124) $60

**Guicciardini, Francesco, 1483-1540**
— La Historia de Italia. Livorno: Niccolo Capurro, 1819. ("Istoria d'Italia....") 10 vols in 5. 8vo, contemp blindstamped calf by Martin. sg Feb 8 (21) $300
— The Historie of Giucciardin, Containing the Warres of Italie.... L: Thomas Vautrollier, 1579. Folio, later calf; spine head def. Tp repaired; lacking 1 prelim leaf; tear in 5F6 with loss; last few leaves of Table lacking or with loss. bba May 30 (73) £280 [Rix]

Anr Ed. L: Richard Field, 1599. Folio, old vellum; worn & soiled. Tp soiled & frayed; some dampstaining; library markings. Sold w.a.f. O Mar 5 (107) $300

Anr copy. Half calf; rubbed, joints & hinges cracked. Z June 28 (105) $400

**Guicciardini, Lodovico, 1521-89**
— Commentarii... delle cose piu memorabili seguite in Europa. Venice: Nicolo Bevilacqua, 1565. 4to, contemp vellum. With device on title. 1st few leaves water-stained. S Oct 26 (106) £280 [Zioni]
— Description de touts les Pais-Bas.... Antwerp: Silvius, 1567. Folio, contemp calf gilt attributed to Jacob Bitner; spine ends def, corners rubbed & bumped. Roman & italic types. With double-page engraved map, 4 double-page woodcut maps, 10 double-page woodcut plans & views & 1 engraving in text, all hand-colored. Fugger - Schaefer copy. P Nov 1 (106) $50,000

Anr Ed. Amst., 1609. Folio, contemp sheep gilt; worn, joints cracked. With 91 (of 95) double-page maps & views. Half-title masked & rehinged; some browning; some plates dampstained in margins; views of Louvain & Leiden crudely hand-colored. sg May 9 (68) $3,600
— Descrittione...di tutti i Paesi Bassi.... Antwerp, 1588. Folio, contemp vellum gilt; soiled. With frontis, port & 78 plates & maps. Some fold tears; most plates browned. C Apr 3 (112) £2,100
— Omnium Belgii, sive Inferioris Germaniae.... Arnhem: J. Jansson, 1616. Folio, contemp vellum; warped, front joint stained. With 10 maps, armorial illust & 91 views only. Lacking 2T2.3, 2V1.4 & rear free endpaper. Sold w.a.f. sg May 9 (70) $2,800
— Omnium Belgii sive inferioris Germaniae regionum descriptio.... Amst.: Jansson, 1613. Folio, old half sheep; worn, needs rebacked. With 75 (of 99) double-page maps & views. Stamp on image of armorial engraving; some plates dampstained in margin; Ant-

werp gnawed in corner; titles & some plate versos stamped. Sold w.a.f. sg May 9 (69) $1,600

**Guichard, Kenneth M.**
— British Etchers 1850-1940. L, 1977. Illus by Robin Tanner. 4to, half calf; rubbed. wa Nov 16 (374) $200

**Guidi, Guido, c.1500-69**
— Les Anciens et renommes aucteurs de la medicine et chirurgie.... Lyons: G. Roville, 1555. 16mo, modern vellum. Upper margins shaved with loss of 1st line of tp & several headlines; some dampstaining. S Mar 29 (697) £360

**Guido de Monte Rocherii**
— Manipulus curatorum. Strassburg: Printer of the 1483 Jordanus de Quedlinburg (Georg Husner), 20 Nov 1490. 4to, modern bds. 35 lines & headline; gothic letter. Some browning & staining. S Dec 18 (38) £750 [Zioni]

**Guigard, Joannis, 1852-92**
— Armorial du bibliophile. Paris, 1870-73. 8vo, contemp half mor; spine faded, ends worn. sg Apr 11 (52) $130

**Guilbert, Aline**
— Prieres Fac-simile du 9 an 15 Siecle. Paris, 1838. 8vo, mor gilt with painting of a medieval woman grasping prayer book inset in front cover, with raised metal bezel; joints & spine ends rubbed. Some foxing. pba Nov 30 (88) $325

**Guillaume de Deguilleville, b. c.1295**
— Boeck van den pelgrim. Delft: Hendrik Eckert van Homberch, 5 Apr 1498. 4to, 19th-cent calf over wooden bds with older metal fittings. 30 lines; types 1:145G (y6v titling) & 2:97G (text). With 58 (of 61) woodcuts. Some soiling; last leaf repaired with ptr's device touched up in pen; small tear in inner margin of a1. 125 (of 132) leaves; lacking c1.6, e1, i1.6, k1.6. Schaefer copy. P Nov 1 (107) $9,000

**Guillie, Sebastien, 1780-1865**
— Essai sur l'instruction des aveugles. Paris, 1820. 3d Ed. 8vo, contemp bds; worn, spine chipped. With 23 plates. O Mar 26 (121) $130

**Guillim, John, 1565-1621**
— A Display of Heraldrie. L, 1632. 2d Ed. Folio, contemp calf; rebacked, bound tight. Marginal soiling; last leaves frayed. CE June 12 (209) $220
Anr Ed. L, 1638. Bound with: Guillim. A Most Exact Alphabetical Table.... L, 1640. Folio, contemp sheep with later brass catches & clasps; recased. Arms, initials & decorations throughout hand-colored in the 19th-cent. Leaves at ends gnawed along edges; corners off P1 & X1 affecting text; 2G4 & 2K1 torn & restored in ink facsimile. sg Mar 21 (156) $500
4th Ed. L, 1660. Folio, calf; rebacked, worn. K Feb 11 (217) $275
Anr copy. Modern half mor; new endpapers. Lacking tp; following leaf reconstructed; typed index added at end; stains at beginning. pba June 20 (188) $75

**Guinness, Arthur, Son & Co.**
— Songs of our Grandfathers, Re-set in Guinness Time. Dublin, 1936. Illus by Rex Whistler. 8vo, orig wraps; rubbed. bba May 9 (280) £85 [Astor]

**Guirlande...**
— La Guirlande: Album mensuel d'art et de litterature. Paris, 1919-20. One of 800. 2 vols. 4to, half mor, orig wraps bound in. With 53 pochoir-colored plates. S Nov 21 (200) £9,000

**Guiteras, Pedro J., 1814-90**
— Historia de la conquista de la Habana. Phila., 1856. 1st Ed. 8vo, half mor; rebound, edges rubbed. Some worming. CE Nov 8 (198) $100

**Guldahl, Ralph**
— Groove Your Golf. [Indianappolis, 1939]. 1st Ed. - Foreword by Bobby Jones. Cloth. pba Nov 9 (29) $200

**Gumpeltzhaimer, Adam**
— Lustgaertlins teuetsch und lateinischer geistlicher Lieder. Augsburg: Johann Ulrich Schoenigk, 1619. Complete parts for Cantus, Tenor & Bassus, each 2 vols in 1. Together 3 vols, 4to, fragments of old vellum over pastebd; worn, some worming in hinges. Tear to A1-2 in Tenor; some leaves trimmed; some stains. S Dec 1 (170) £6,000

**Gumuchian & Cie, Kirkor**
— Catalogue de reliures du XVe au XIXe siecle.... Paris, [1930]. 4to, orig cloth; shaken. Library markings. sg Sept 7 (51) $140
One of 1,000. Half vellum, orig wraps bound in. S Mar 22 (195) £55 [Quaritch]
One of 100 on Hollande. Later half mor gilt by Sangorski & Sutcliffe, orig wraps bound in. bba May 9 (137B) £320 [Maggs]
— Les Livres de l'enfance du XVe au XIXe siecle. Paris, [1930]. One of 900. 2 vols. 4to, orig cloth; worn & soiled. O Mar 26 (123) $225
Anr Ed. L, [1979]. One of 600. 2 vols. 4to, orig cloth in djs. sg Apr 11 (75) $175

**Gun...**
— The Gun at Home and Abroad. L, 1912-15. One of 500. Vol IV only: The Big Game of Asia and North America. Lea gilt; rubbed, spine head chipped. O June 25 (36) $425

**Gunn, Douglas**
— Picturesque San Diego, with Historical and Descriptive Notes. Chicago, 1887. Orig lea; worn & scuffed, joints repaired. pba Apr 25 (432) $80

**Gunn, Thom**
— A Geography. Iowa City: Stone Wall Press, 1966. One of 220. Orig wraps. pba Jan 25 (127) $90
— Mandrakes. Cambr.: Rainbow Press, [1974]. One of 150. Illus by Leonard Baskin. Half vellum by San-

gorski & Sutcliffe. Hobson copy. S June 28 (138) £160

**Gunning, Peter**
— The Paschal or Lent-fast, Apostolical & Perpetual. L: R. Norton, 1662. 4to, contemp mor with onlays, gilt-tooled to a cottage-roof pattern with floral volutes; short repair to upper joint. Doheny - Schaefer copy. P Nov 1 (109) $6,000

**Gunnison, John W.**
— The Mormons, or Latter-Day Saints.... NY: George Munro's Son, [1887]. 12mo, orig pictorial wraps. Browned & brittle; 2-inch tear to tp. pba Apr 25 (433) $65

**Gunsaulus, Helen Cowen**
— Japanese Sword-Mounts in the Collections of the Field Museum. Chicago, 1923. Wraps. With 61 plates. sg Sept 7 (172) $80

**Guptill, A. B.**
— Yellowstone Park Guide: A Practical Hand-Book. St. Paul, 1894. 8vo, cloth; spine rubbed. With folding map tipped to rear pastedown. pba Apr 25 (434) $85

**Guptill, Arthur Leighton**
— Norman Rockwell, Illustrator. NY, 1946. Folio, cloth. Inscr to H. H. Grady by Rockwell. pba Mar 7 (222) $300
Anr copy. Cloth in dj with wear to spine ends. Sgd by Rockwell on front free endpaper. pba June 20 (286) $150

**Gurdjieff, G.**
— The Herald of the Coming Good.... Paris, 1933. Orig ptd suede wraps; extremities chipped, spine repaired. Subscription pages lacking from rear. pba Nov 30 (170) $400

**Gurney, Joseph John, 1788-1847**
— The House of Bishops of the Protestant Episcopal Church of the United States. NY, 1862. 8vo, mor gilt; disbound, with 1 leaf detached. With 24 mtd ovel albumen ports. Foxed. sg Feb 29 (154) $150
— Observations on the Religious Peculiarities of the Society of Friends.... L, [1819]. Proof copy. Folio, orig bds. With numerous pencil annotations in Gurney's hand. S Apr 23 (198) £160

**Gutbir, Aegidius**
— Lexicon Syriacum. Hamburg, 1706. Bound with: Notae criticae in Novum Testamentum Syriacum; Novum Domini Nostri Jesu Christi Testamentum Syricae.... Hamburg, 1664. 3 work in 1 vol. 8vo, contemp vellum; soiled. S Oct 26 (219) £150 [Folios]

**Gutenberg Printing, Johann.** See: Bible in Latin

**Guthe, Hermann.** See: Ebers & Guthe

**Guthrie, Alfred Bertram**
— The Big Sky. NY, 1947. In chipped & repaired dj. Sgd. pba Oct 5 (137) $180
— Murders at Moon Dance. NY, 1943. Inscr. pba Oct 5 (135) $140
— These Thousand Hills. Bost., 1956. 1st Ed. In dj with chips & short tears to spine & tape repairs. pba Oct 5 (139) $80
— The Way West. NY: William Sloan, [1949]. In dj with chip to spine head. pba Oct 5 (138) $90

**Guthrie, Maria**
— A Tour performed in the Years 1795-6 through the Taurida, or Crimea.... L, 1802. 1st Ed. 4to, contemp half calf; rubbed. With 2 folding maps & 11 plates. Some spotting. b May 30 (268) £180

**Guthrie, Thomas Anstey, 1856-1934.** See: Anstey, F.

**Guthrie, William, 1708-70**
— An Atlas to Guthrie's Geographical Grammar. L, 1809. 4to, contemp half sheep; front cover abraded, front joint cracked. With uncolored plate & 31 hand-colored double-page plates. Some foxing. sg May 9 (71) $800
— The Atlas to Guthrie's System of Geography. L, [1785]. Folio, half calf; becoming disbound, worn. With 24 maps, hand-colored in outline, plus plate of armillary sphere. Folding map of Germany & Switzerland halved & repaired but lacking large fragment; World torn & taped on verso. wa Feb 29 (608) $350
— A New Geographical, Historical and Commercial Grammar.... L, 1770. 8vo, contemp calf; loose. sg Dec 7 (20) $300
New Ed. L, 1777. 8vo, contemp calf; rubbed. With 20 plates & maps. b Sept 20 (422) £80
Anr copy. Contemp calf; upper cover detached. With 20 plates & maps. Tear with loss to 1 map. b May 30 (128) £70
Anr Ed. L, 1795. 8vo, orig sheep; front cover loose. sg May 9 (72) $225

**Gutierrez, Diego**
— Historia del Origen, y Soberania del Condado, y Reino de Castilla. Madrid: Miguel Escribano, 1785. 4to, contemp vellum. sg Mar 21 (297) $325

**Gutman, Judith Mara**
— Lewis W. Hine and the American Social Conscience. NY, 1967. In soiled dj. sg Feb 29 (155) $50

**Guy, Joseph**
— Birmingham, and its Vicinity. A Poetic Fragment.... Birm., 1821. 4to, orig ptd wraps. b Dec 5 (22) £340

**Guyot, Charles**
— La Toison d'or. Paris, 1921. One of 1,300. Illus by Edmund Dulac. 4to, mor extra with inlays, by Susan Spring Wilson, orig wraps bound in. sg Sept 14 (52) $850

**Guyot, Guillaume Germain**
— Histoire de France representee par figures.... Paris, 1787-96. Illus by Francois Anne David. 5 vols. 4to, later half mor gilt. Fuerstenberg - Schaefer copy. S Dec 7 (282) £320

**Guyton de Morveau, Louis Bernard, 1737-1816 —& Lavoisier, Antoine Laurent, 1743-94**
— A Translation of the Table of Chemical Nomenclature. L, 1799. 4to, contemp half calf; rebacked preserving old spine, rubbed. Tp & 1st few leaves with marginal waterstains; lacking dedication leaf; some soiling & spotting. bba July 18 (78) £120 [P & P Books]

**Guzman, Jose Maria**
— Breve Noticia que de al Supremo Gobierno del Actual Estado del Territorio de la Alta California.... Mexico, 1833. 8vo, orig wraps in folder & slipcase. With folded table. Some dampstains. Larson copy. pba Sept 28 (114) $700

**Guzman, Luis de**
— Historia de las missiones...los reynos de la China y Japon. Alcala, 1601. 2 vols. Folio, contemp vellum; new endpapers. Staining in lower margins of Vol I; titles repaired; hole in text of Z1 in Vol I with minor loss; repairs in last leaf of Vol II with a few words in pen facsimile. S June 27 (232) £12,500

**Guzman, Sancho de**
— Panegirico ad Andres de la Torre y Leon.... Malaga: Mateo Lopez Hidalgo, 1664. 4to, recent vellum bds. S Mar 28 (229) £150

**Gwinett, Ambrose**
— The Life and Adventures of Ambrose Gwinett.... Norwich: John Trumbull, 1784. 8vo, later half lea. Some foxing. Met May 22 (345) $250

**Gwynn, John**
— Liber Ardmachanus. The Book of Armagh. Dublin, 1913. One of 400. 4to, orig cloth-backed wraps. S Mar 28 (4) £420

**Gyldendalske Samling**
— Samling af de bedste og nyeste Reisebeskrivelser i et udforligt Udtog.... Copenhagen, 1789-98. 16 vols. 8vo, bds. Sold w.a.f. S Mar 14 (152) £220

# H

**H., H.** See: Jackson, Helen Hunt

**H., N.**
— The Compleat Tradesman; or, the Exact Dealers Daily Companion. L: John Dunton, 1684. 12mo, contemp calf; broken. Some staining & soiling. Sold w.a.f. sg Mar 21 (103) $600

**Haak, Bob**
— The Golden Age: Dutch Painters of the Seventeenth Century. NY, 1984. Folio, cloth, in dj. wa Dec 14 (438) $50

**Haberly, Loyd**
See also: Gregynog Press
— Mediaeval English Pavingtiles. Oxford: Shakespeare Head Press, 1937. One of 425. 4to, orig half mor gilt. Library stamp on half-title; erased stamp at foot of tp. Pamphlet of Floriated Initials by Haberly loosely inserted. bba May 9 (346) £150 [Besley]

**Hackett, Charles Wilson**
— Revolt of the Pueblo Indians of New Mexico.... Albuquerque, 1942. 2 vols, orig cloth in djs; extremities worn & d/js soiled. Robbins copy. pba Mar 21 (133) $275

**Hackle, Sparse Grey.** See: Miller, Alfred W.

**Haddock, J. A.**
— A Souvenir. The Thousand Islands of the St. Lawrence River.... Alexandria Bay NY, 1895. 4to, bdg not described; label removed from base of spine. NH July 21 (385) $150

**Haebler, Konrad**
— Rollen- und Plattenstempel des XVI. Jahrhunderts. Nendeln & Wiesbaden, 1968. 2 vols in 1. 8vo, orig cloth. sg Apr 11 (53) $800
— Typenrepertorium der Wiegendrucke. Halle & Leipzig, 1905-22. Vols I-V (of 6). 8vo, half cloth. Lacks 2d supplement. sg Apr 11 (151) $200

**Haecht Goidtsenhoven, Laurens van**
— Chroniicke vande Hertoghen van Brabant. Antwerp, 1612. Folio, later calf; worn, joints & hinges cracked. With frontis & 42 ports. Lacking blanks & half-title; tp trimmed & repaired, affecting imprint date; some browning & dampstaining. wa Dec 14 (129) $350

**Haedo, Diego de**
— Topographia, e historia general de Argel. Valladolid: Diego Fernandez de Cordova y Oviedo, 1612. Folio, contemp vellum. Tp soiled, with old pencil notes; some dampstaining; wormholes through c.40 leaves towards end with loss. sg Mar 21 (298) $1,700

**Haentzschel, Walter**
— Die Praxis des modernen Maschinenbaues. Elfte Auflage. Berlin, 1919. 3 vols. 8vo & folio, orig cloth. Atlas with 10 chromolitho plates with multiple die-cut overlays. sg May 16 (217) $130
— Die Praxis des modernen Maschinenbaues. Modell-Atlas. Berlin, 1909. Folio, orig half cloth. With 8 sectional models. Sold w.a.f. sg May 16 (218) $80
Anr Ed. [Berlin, c.1915-20]. Folio, orig half cloth; rubbed & bumped. With 8 sectional models. cb Oct 17 (670) $425
Anr copy. Orig half cloth; shaken, extremities worn, joints torn & frayed. With 8 chromolitho plates with multiple die-cut overlays. Sold w.a.f. sg May 16 (219) $80

**Haesaerts, Paul**
— James Ensor. NY, [1959]. 4to, cloth, in torn dj. sg Sept 7 (145) $100

**Haestens, Henrik van.** See: Orlers & Haestens

**Hafen, Ann W.** See: Hafen & Hafen

**Hafen, Anne W.** See: Hafen & Hafen

**Hafen, Le Roy R.**
See also: Bieber & Hafen
— The Mountain Men and the Fur Trade of the Far West. Glendale, 1965-72. 10 vols. pba Nov 16 (124) $375

**Hafen, Le Roy R. —&**
**Ghent, William James**
— Broken Hand: The Life Story of Thomas Fitzpatrick.... Denver, 1931. 1st Ed, One of 100. Half cloth & bds; bds sunned. With 8 plates & 1 double-page map. Robbins copy. Inscr to Francis H. Hagner. pba Mar 21 (136) $250

**Hafen, Le Roy R. —&**
**Hafen, Ann W.**
— The Far West and the Rockies.... Glendale, Calif., 1954-61. 15 vols. pba Nov 16 (122) $1,100

**Hafen, Le Roy R. —&**
**Hafen, Anne W.**
— Old Spanish Trail: Santa Fe to Los Angeles.... Glendale, 1960. 1st Ed. Orig cloth. With 1 folding map. Robbins copy. pba Mar 21 (134) $100
  Anr Ed. Glendale, Calif., [1960]. 2d printing. Orig cloth. With frontis, 1 folded map, & 16 plates. Larson copy. pba Sept 28 (506) $60

**Hafen, Le Roy R. —&**
**Young, Francis Marion**
— Fort Laramie and the Pageant of the West, 1834-1890. Glendale, 1938. 1st Ed. Orig cloth. With 1 folding map Bumped. Robbins copy. pba Mar 21 (135) $180

**Haftmann, Werner**
— Wols: Watercolors, Drawings, Writings. NY, [c.1965]. 4to, cloth. sg Jan 11 (468) $100

**Hagelgans, Johann Georg**
— Architectura cosmica eclectica & enucleata. Frankfurt, 1736. 8vo, later half vellum. With 10 charts & 10 plates & folding table at end. S Mar 14 (154) £900

**Hagen, Karl.** See: Schott & Hagen

**Haggard, Sir Henry Rider, 1856-1925**
— Allan and the Ice-Gods. Garden City, 1927. In backed & restored dj. sg June 20 (139) $110
— Belshazzar. Garden City, 1930. In backed & restored dj. sg June 20 (140) $70
— Marion Isle. Garden City, 1929. In backed & restored dj. sg June 20 (141) $80
— Queen of the Dawn. Garden City, 1925. In backed & restored dj. sg June 20 (143) $80
— She: a History of Adventure. L, 1887. 1st Ed. 8vo, orig cloth. With 2 tinted litho frontises. Cut signature inserted. b Jan 31 (88) £90
  1st Issue, with Godness me on p 269, line 38. Orig cloth. sg June 20 (142) $600
— Treasure of the Lake. Garden City, 1926. In backed & restored dj. sg June 20 (144) $100

**Hahnemann, Samuel, 1755-1843**
— Der Kaffee in seinen Wirkungen. Leipzig, 1803. Bound with: Vogel, Samuel Gottlieb von. Historisch-medizinische Abhandlung.... Berlin, 1781 8vo, later bds; spines rubbed. Severe worming in gutter. Ck Mar 22 (136) £320

**Haig-Brown, Roderick L.**
See also: Derrydale Press
— Alison's Fishing Birds. Vancouver: Colophon Books, 1980. One of 500. O Feb 6 (110) $100
— Return to the River; a Story of the Chinook Run. NY, 1941. One of 520. Illus by Charles DeFeo. Half lea. Inscr. O Feb 6 (114) $450; O June 25 (152) $200

**Hailey, Clarence**
— Stallions.... Newmarket, [1910]. 10 parts in 2 vols. 4to, cloth; some wear. O Jan 9 (122) $425

**Hain, Ludwig, 1781-1836**
— Repertorium bibliographicum in quo libri omnes ab arte typographica inventa usque ad annum MD. Stuttgart, Tuebingen & Paris, 1826-38. 4 vols. 8vo, later half mor. Ck Apr 12 (235) £160
  Anr Ed. Milan, [1948]-1950. 7 vols, including Copinger plus Burger's 1908 supplement. 8vo, orig cloth; spines faded. sg Apr 11 (152) $500

**Hainault, Comte**
— Les chartes nouvelles du pays et comte de Haynau. Mons, 1642. Old limp vellum. S Oct 27 (1063) £100 [Culot]

**Haines, Elijah M.**
— Historical and Statistical Sketches of Lake County, Illinois. Waukegan, 1852. 16mo, orig wraps; front joint splitting. With folding frontis & errata leaf. sg Oct 26 (150) $900

**Haining, Peter**
— Movable Books. An Illustrated History. L, [1979]. 4to, cloth, in dj; some wear. O July 9 (96) $70

**Haiti**
— Correspondance de M. le General avec l'Assemblee Generale de la partie francois de Saint Domingue. Port-au-Prince, 1790. 16 pp, 8vo, wraps. sg Mar 28 (125) $550
— Deputation de 24 Membres de L'Assemblee legislatif au Roi.... Paris: De l'Imprimerie des Patriotes, [1791]. 8vo, disbound. Browned. sg Mar 28 (100) $90
— Dissertation et observations sur le tetanos. Cap-Francois: Chez Dufours de Rians, 1786. 8vo, disbound. Browned; stamp on tp. sg Mar 28 (102) $2,800
— Extrait de archives de l'Assemblee Provinciale de Nord de Saint Domingue. Au Cap: De L'Imprimerie Royale, 1790. 8vo, wraps; spine def. Browned. sg Mar 28 (107) $350
— Extrait des registres de la Municipalite du Cap. De la seance extraordinaire du 15 juillet 1790.... Au Cap:

De L'Imprimerie, 1790. 4 pp on 1 leaf. Library markings. sg Mar 28 (108) $325
— Extrait d'une lettre authentique du Cap Francois. Saint Domingue, 1789. 8vo, disbound. Some curling; lacking half-title. sg Mar 28 (109) $375
— Justification de M. Milscent, Creole, a L'Assemblee Coloniale de Saint Domingue. [N.p., c.1790]. 8vo, sewn. Browned, edges curled. sg Mar 28 (116) $750
— Loi. Portant que tout homme est libre en France, & que, quelle soit de sa couleur, il y jouit de tous les droits de Citoyen, s'il a les qualites prescrites par la Constitution. Rennes: Chez Robiquet, 16 Oct 1791. 4 pp on 1 leaf, ptd on 3 sides, folio. Sgd & dated by provincial director, Corbeaux. sg Mar 28 (118) $110
— No 4 Suite de la Correspondance de Monsieur le Gouverneur General. Port-au-Prince, 1790. 8 pp on 1 leaf, unopened. Some foxing. sg Mar 28 (124) $325
— Le Propagateur Hatien. Port-au-Prince, 1 June 1825. No 3. 4to, resewn, stamp on front cover. Browned. sg Mar 28 (129) $110
— La Republique d'Haiti et les Races Africaines, en General Premier Congres Universel des Races, tenu a Londres du Juillet 1911. Port-au-Prince, 1911. 8vo, later half cloth. sg Mar 28 (132) $225
— Republique d'Hayti. Loi sur les Patents. Port-au-Prince, 1829. 8vo, wraps; chipped. sg Mar 28 (131) $200

**Haji Khalfah.** See: Katib Chelebi

**Hake, Henry M.** See: British Museum

**Hakewill, James, 1778-1843**
— A Picturesque Tour of Italy.... L, 1820. Folio, contemp half mor, orig wraps bound in. With engraved title, 63 plates & an additional 36 proofs on chine. Some browning. S June 27 (108) £1,500
— A Series of Views of the Neighbourhood of Windsor. L, 1820. Folio, half mor. With frontis & 33 plates & plans. Some foxing. rs Nov 11 (92) $200

**Hakluyt, Richard, 1552?-1616**
— The Principall Navigations.... L, 1599-1600. 2d Ed, 2d Issue of Vol I. 3 vols plus Supplement of 1812. Folio, 19th-cent mor gilt. Several leaves remargined; some stains affecting letters. S Nov 30 (137) £7,000
  Anr Ed. L, 1809-12. ("Collection of the Early Voyages, Travels and Discoveries of the English Nation.") One of 75. 5 vols. 4to, contemp calf gilt; worn, corners bumped & worn through, hinges cracked, front endpapers in 3 vols & tp in Vol IV detached. Some soiling & foxing; notes in ink. cb Feb 14 (2536) $2,250
  Anr Ed. NY, 1927. 8 vols. sg Mar 7 (94) $130
  Anr Ed. Cambr.: Hakluyt Society, 1965. 2 vols. Folio, cloth, in djs. pba Feb 13 (86) $160
  Anr copy. Cloth. wa Feb 29 (172) $120

**Hakluyt Society**
[A collection of 58 titles in 87 vols from the Second Series of Hakluyt Society Publications, 1957-94, sold at Pacific on 13 Feb 1996, lot 87, for $1,700]

**Hale, Edward Everett, 1822-1909**
— Kanzas and Nebraska.... Bost., 1854. 1st Ed. 12mo, orig cloth. With folding map. sg Oct 26 (126) $90

**Hale, John.** See: Grabhorn Printing

**Hale, John Henry**
— How to Tie Salmon Flies. L, 1892. 8vo, cloth; minor soiling. O Feb 6 (115) $250

**Hale, Lucretia Peabody, 1820-1900**
— The Peterkin Papers. Bost., 1880. 1st Ed. 8vo, cloth; spine base rubbed. With 8 plates. sg Sept 21 (213) $200

**Hale, Sir Matthew, 1609-76**
— The Primitive Origination of Mankind. L, 1677. 1st Ed. 4to, old calf gilt; extremities worn, covers detached. Old stamp on title; lacking initial blank or license leaf. sg Mar 21 (158) $225

**Hale, Sarah Josepha, 1788-1879**
— The Ladies' New Book of Cookery.... NY, 1852. 5th Ed. 12mo, orig cloth; spine torn & chipped. wa Feb 1 (145) $75

**Hale, Thomas, Writer on Husbandry**
— Eden: or, a Compleat Body of Gardening.... L, 1773. Folio, contemp calf; broken, needs rebdg, frontis detached & frayed. With port, frontis & 72 (of 80) plates. Sold w.a.f. wa Feb 29 (177) $3,200

**Halen, Juan van, Count de Perecamps, 1788-1864**
— Narrative of Don Juan van Halen's Imprisonment in the Dungeons of the Inquisition at Madrid.... L, 1827. 1st Ed. 2 vols. 8vo, half calf; Vol I with both bds reattached with tape. With 2 frontis ports, 3 folding facsimile plates, & 2 folding views & folding map. Tape-repair to 1 folding view. wa Dec 14 (153) $80

**Hales, John Groves**
— Maps of the Street-Lines of Boston, 1819 and 1820. Bost. 1894. Folio, orig cloth; spine ends worn. sg Dec 7 (3) $400
— Survey of Boston and its Vicinity. Bost., 1821. 12mo, orig bds; backstrip def. sg Oct 26 (246) $275

**Hales, Stephen, 1677-1761**
— A Description of Ventilators.... L, 1743. 1st Ed. 8vo, wraps. With 2 folding plates. CE Nov 8 (100) $240
— Statical Essays: containing Vegetable Staticks. L, 1738-40. Vols I & II only. 2 vols. 8vo, modern calf. With 19 plates. K6 in vol I torn; some spotting; vol II browned. Ck Nov 22 (137) £160

**Halevy, Ludovic, 1834-1908**
— L'Abbe Constantin. Paris, 1887. One of 200. 4to, lev extra by J. Kauffmann with initial D in center

cartouch of front cover & M on rear cover. Plates in 3 states.  sg Oct 19 (113) $1,600
— La Famille Cardinal. Brussels, 1893.  One of 1 or 2 L.p. copies, with 3 ports in 9 states, 2 frontises in 9 states, 26 engravings in 4 states & 28 wood-engravings in 2 states.  Illus by Charles Leandre.  4to, contemp anacreontic bdg by Charles Meunier in lev gilt with polychrome mor inlays, orig wraps bound in.  C May 1 (75) £2,600
— Trois Coups de Foudre. Paris, 1886.  One of 150.  Illus by T de Mare after Kauffmann.  Mor extra by Marius Michel, orig wraps bound in.  Bound in is a watercolor drawing, sgd by Kauffmann & an ANs of Halevy.  S Nov 21 (207) £450

**Haley, Alex**
— Roots. NY, 1976. 1st Ed.  In dj.  Sgd.  pba May 23 (145) $85

**Haley, Bart.**  See: Morley & Haley

**Haley, C. S.**  See: Price & Haley

**Halford, Frederic M., 1844-1914**
— Dry Fly Entomology: a Brief Description.... L., 1897.  One of 100.  2 vols. 4to, orig mor.  With 18 plain & 28 hand-colored plates & with 100 flies in 12 sunken mounts.  Joseph D. Bates's copy.  O Feb 6 (66) $2,600
 Anr copy. Orig mor; worn.  O Feb 6 (116) $2,400
— Dry-Fly Fishing in Theory and Practice. L., 1902.  Orig cloth; spine leaning. Some foxing.  pba July 11 (126) $50
— The Dry-Fly Man's Handbook. L., 1913.  One of 100.  Half calf; rubbed.  Minor foxing.  O Feb 6 (117) $900
— Floating Flies and How to Dress Them. L., 1886.  8vo, cloth.  With 9 colored plates.  Joseph D. Bates's copy.  O Feb 6 (118) $280
— Making a Fishery. L., 1895.  4to, orig cloth; some mold damage to covers.  pba July 11 (127) $95
— Modern Development of the Dry Fly. L., 1910.  One of 75.  2 vols. 4to. Includes album of 33 flies.  O Feb 6 (120) $1,600
 Anr Ed. NY, 1910.  One of 50.  2 vols. 4to. Includes album of 33 flies.  O Feb 6 (119) $2,600

**Hali...**
— Hali: The International Journal of Oriental Carpets and Textiles. L, 1978-88.  Vol II, No 3 through Vol XI, No 2; lacking Vol V, No 3. Together, 37 issues.  4to, orig wraps; minor wear.  sg June 13 (78) $950

**Halkett, John, 1768-1852**
— Statement Respecting the Earl of Selkirk's Settlement of Kildonan upon the Red River.... L, 1817. 1st Pbd Ed. 8vo, orig bds; bumped & chipped, hinges starting, flyleaf loose.  With folding map with tear.  Met May 22 (303) $235

**Halkett, Samuel, 1814-71 —&
Laing, John, 1809-80**
— Dictionary of Anonymous and Pseudonymous English Literature. L., 1926-62.  9 vols, including Index,

Supplements & Addenda. 4to, orig cloth, in torn djs.  bba Oct 5 (95) £480 [Forest]
 Anr copy. Cloth; worn.  O Mar 26 (124) $425

**Hall, Anna Maria**
 See also: Hall & Hall
— The Book of Royalty. L: Ackermann, 1839.  Folio, contemp mor gilt by Westley, Son & Jarvis; some rubbing & soiling.  With frontis & 12 colored plates.  cb Feb 14 (2775) $200

**Hall, Basil**
— The Great Polyglot Bibles: Including a Leaf from the Complutensian of Acala, 1514-17. San Francisco: Book Club of Calif., 1966.  One of 400.  Folio, unbound.  pba June 20 (20) $250
 Anr copy. Unbound in wraps.  pba Aug 22 (591) $225

**Hall, Basil, 1788-1844**
— Account of a Voyage of Discovery to the West Coast of Corea.... L, 1818.  4to, modern half calf.  With 9 hand-colored plates, 1 uncolored plate & 5 maps.  Minor foxing.  Half title reads "From the Author".  sg Mar 7 (95) $900
— Extracts from a Journal.... Edin., 1824. ("Extracts from a Journal, Written on the Coasts of Chili, Peru, and Mexico.") 2d Ed. 2 vols. 8vo, contemp calf gilt.  Folding map foxed & torn.  pb Oct 9 (6) $170
— Travels in North America in the Years 1827 and 1828. Edin., 1829. 1st Ed. 3 vols. 12mo, later calf; worn, joints rubbed, cut close.  With folding table & folding hand-colored map. Prelims foxed; short tear in map.  wa Feb 29 (396) $210

**Hall, Carroll Douglas**
— Donner Miscellany.... San Francisco, 1947.  One of 350.  Half bds.  With 2 facsimiles & 2 illus.  Larson copy.  pba Sept 28 (423) $75
 Anr copy. Wraps.  pba June 20 (21) $55

**Hall, Charles Francis, 1821-71**
— Narrative of the Second Arctic Expedition.... Wash., 1879.  4to, orig cloth; extremities worn.  sg Oct 26 (128) $110

**Hall, David.**  See: Franklin Printing, Benjamin

**Hall, Edwin**
— Sweynheym & Pannartz and the Origins of Printing in Italy. McMinnville: Bird & Bull Press, 1991.  One of 275. Half mor.  With folding case with leaf from the 1471 Ed of the Postilla of Nicolaus de Lyra.  sg Feb 15 (46) $300

**Hall, Frederic, 1873-1930**
— The History of San Jose and Surroundings.... San Francisco, 1871. 1st Ed. 8vo, orig cloth; spine head chipped & frayed, front hinge split.  With 1 folding map & 4 plates.  Robbins copy.  pba Mar 21 (137) $140

**Hall, Harrison**
— The Distiller. Phila., 1818. 8vo, contemp calf. With folding frontis & 5 plates. CE May 22 (250) $90

**Hall, James, 1793-1868.** See: McKenney & Hall

**Hall, James, 1811-98**
— Palaeontology of New York. Albany, 1847-59. 6 vols in 8; lacking Vol II. 4to, orig cloth; Vol I backstrip detached & taped. With 4 engraved titles & 536 plates. Part of Natural History of New-York series. wa Feb 29 (214) $180

**Hall, James Norman, 1887-1951.** See: Limited Editions Club

**Hall, Linville**
— Around the Horn in '49: The Journal of the Hartford Union Mining and Trading Company. San Francisco: Book Club of California, 1928. One of 250. Inscr by Oscar Lewis. cb Oct 11 (135) $60

**Hall, Manly P.**
— An Encyclopedic Outline of Masonic, Hermetic, Qabbalistic and Rosicrucian Symbolical Philosophy. San Francisco, 1928. One of 800. Folio, half vellum. CE Sept 27 (132) $260

Anr copy. Half vellum; spine soiled. pba Sept 14 (187) $450

**Hall, Samuel Carter, 1800-89**
— The Baronial Halls and Ancient Picturesque Edifices of England. L, 1858. 2 vols. Folio, contemp mor gilt; joints worn, some leaves loose at beginning of Vol I. CE Sept 27 (133) $150

Anr copy. Later 19th-cent lea gilt; joints & extremities worn. With 71 tinted plates. Some foxing to margins. sg Sept 7 (10) $300

Anr Ed. L, 1881. 2 vols. Folio, half mor. Foxed. pba Sept 14 (188) $300

**Hall, Samuel Carter, 1800-89 —&**
**Hall, Anna Maria**
— The Book of the Thames from its Rise to its Fall. L, 1867. 8vo, orig cloth. With 15 mtd photographs. b May 30 (48) £120

— Ireland, its Scenery, Character.... L, 1841-43. 3 vols. 8vo, contemp calf gilt; rubbed. sg Feb 8 (74) $425

Anr Ed. L, [c.1850]. 3 vols in 10 orig parts. 8vo, cloth. pnE Sept 20 (39) £230

**Hall, Sidney**
— A New British Atlas. L, 1833. 4to, 19th-cent half mor. With 47 hand-colored maps. With 4 double-page & the Inland Navigation map in 4 sheets backed on linen; some spotting. S June 13 (485) £340

Anr Ed. L, 1834. 4to, contemp half mor; rubbed. With 50 maps, 3 of them folding, 1 partly hand-colored. Some browning. pn Dec 7 (178) £300

Anr copy. 19th-cent half mor; worn. With 47 colored maps. Inland Navigation map & 4 double-page maps backed on linen; spotting on last few maps. S June 13 (486) £400

— A New General Atlas. L, 1835. Folio, contemp half mor; covers detached. With title, index, & 53 hand-colored maps. Marginal soiling. S Oct 26 (434) £600 [Sharpe]

**Hall, William Henry**
— The New Royal Encyclopaedia. L, [1788?]. 2 (of 3) vols; lacking Vol II. Folio, old calf; worn & scuffed, joints cracked. Some creasing. wa Dec 14 (154) $250

**Halle, Johann Samuel, 1727-1810**
— Fortgesestzte Magie, oder, Die Zauberkrafte der Natur. Vienna, 1788-1803. 12 vols in 9. 8vo, contemp half calf; worn. With 84 folding plates. Sold w.a.f. Madsen copy. S Mar 14 (155) £1,000

— Magie; oder, Die Zauberkraefte der Natur. Berlin: Joachim Pauli, 1784-86. 4 vols. 8vo, contemp half calf; rubbed. With 29 folding plates. vol III tp stained in inner margin. S Mar 14 (156) £380

**Halleck, Fitz Greene, 1790-1867**
— The Poetical Works. NY, 1858. 3d Ed. Folio, with 8vo contents inlaid to size contemp mor gilt by Pawson & Nicholson; joints rubbed. Extra-illus with c.60 ports & plates relating to NY. sg Apr 18 (60) $450

**Hallenbeck, Cleve —&**
**Williams, Juanita H.**
— Legends of the Spanish Southwest. Glendale, 1938. 1st Ed. Orig cloth. With 1 folding map & 8 plates. Robbins copy. pba Mar 21 (138) $180

**Haller, Albrecht von, 1708-77**
— Allgemeine Historie der Natur. Hamburg & Leipzig, 1750-72. Vols V-VIII (of 8). Half calf. pba Mar 7 (40) $400

— Deux memoires sur la formation des os.... Lausanne, 1758. 8vo, contemp calf. Inscr by the recipient, Charles Bonnet. S June 12 (260) £340

— Historia morborum.... Lausanne & Geneva, 1746. 4to, old half vellum; backstrip damaged. sg May 16 (420) $80

— Opuscula sua botanica. Goettingen, 1749. 8vo, contemp half calf. Library markings. S Mar 14 (158) £130

**Halliday, A. B.** See: Martin & Halliday

**Hallock, Charles, 1834-1917**
— An Angler's Reminiscences. A Record of Sport.... Cincinnati, 1913. Orig cloth; spine ends rubbed. Inscr by Fred E. Pond to John P. Holman. pba July 11 (128) $150

— The Fishing Tourist. NY, 1873. Orig cloth; spine head rubbed. ALs tipped in, calling Charles Bradford a plagarist. pba July 11 (129) $300

— The Salmon Fisher. NY, 1890. 16mo, cloth; worn & soiled. O June 25 (153) $50

**Halpin, Warren T.**
— Hoofbeats: Drawings and Comments. Phila., 1938. One of 1,500. Folio, cloth; worn & spotted. O Jan 9 (123) $50

## Halsey, Richard T. H.
See also: Grolier Club
— Pictures of Early New York on Dark Blue Staffordshire Pottery.... NY, 1899. One of 268. 8vo, cloth, in soiled cloth dj. Z Apr 19 (109) $200

## Halsman, Philippe
See also: Dali & Halsman
— Jump Book. NY, 1959. 1st Ed. Half cloth, in stained & worn dj; bdg bumped, some wear, endpapers soiled. Cut signature & inscr affixed to front free endpaper. sg Feb 29 (156) $90

## Halsman, Philippe —& Dali, Salvador, 1904-89
— Halsman/Dali. NY: Neikrug Press, 1981. One of 250. Intro by Yvonne Halsman. With 10 photographs. sg Oct 7 (175) $2,000

**Halsz, Gyula.** See: Brassai

## Hamel, Joseph
— Der gegenseitige Unterricht. Paris, 1818. 8vo, contemp mor gilt. With 2 ports & 12 folding plates. Inscr to the "Prince Regent of Great Britain & Ireland". b Sept 20 (626) £250

## Hamerton, Philip Gilbert, 1834-94
— The Art of the American Wood Engraver. NY, 1894. One of 100. 8vo, half mor; loose. sg Sept 7 (173) $150
— Etching and Etchers. L, 1868. 8vo, orig half lea. Some spotting & discoloring. S Apr 23 (240) £460

Anr Ed. L, 1876. 8vo, mor by Worsfold; spine age-darkened, front joint starting; orig cover & spine bound in. CE Nov 8 (199) $120

Anr Ed. Bost., 1878. 8vo, orig cloth; worn. F June 20 (314) $50

3d Ed. L, 1880. 4to, orig half lea gilt; spine ends chipped, joints worn, front hinge cracked. sg Jan 11 (208) $750

Anr copy. Orig half mor; hinges cracked, spine rubbed. wd Nov 15 (68) $550

Anr Ed. Bost., 1892. 8vo, cloth; worn, spine nicked. wa Feb 1 (351) $50
— The Graphic Arts. L, 1882. 4to, vellum gilt. sg Jan 11 (209) $225
— Landscape. L, 1885. One of 525. Folio, orig half lea; extremities rubbed, hinges starting. sg Jan 11 (210) $150

Anr copy. Orig syn gilt; soiled, hinges cracked. Foxing at ends. sg June 13 (179) $200
— Man in Art: Studies in Religious and Historical Art.... L, 1892. 4to, vellum gilt. sg Jan 11 (211) $175

## Hamilton, Alexander, d.1732?
— A New Account of the East Indies. Edin., 1727. 1st Ed. 2 vols. 8vo, contemp calf; rubbed, rebacked. With 10 plates (1 folding), & 8 folding maps. Browned; few marginal tears. S Oct 26 (580) £1,200 [Dessy]

## Hamilton, Alexander, 1757-1804
— Observations on Certain Documents Contained in..."The History of the United States for the Year 1796".... Phila., 1797. 1st Ed. 8vo, contemp bds; rebacked in calf, rubbed. Tp foxed. K Feb 11 (206) $300
— Sundry Statements by the Secretary of the Treasury in Conformity with the Resolution of the House of Representatives of the 23d of January, 1793. [NY]: Childs and Swaine, [1793]. Folio, orig bdg; loose. rms Nov 30 (178) $2,200

## Hamilton, Anthony, 1646?-1720
— Memoirs of Count Grammont. L, [1794]. One of 5 extra-illus copies on largest paper. 4to, contemp mor gilt extra by Staggemeier & Welcher; joints rubbed & starting. With 98 ports, including 83 in color & 2 orig watercolor miniatures. Schaefer copy. P Nov 1 (111) $7,000

Anr Ed. L, 1889. 2 vols in 4. 8vo, mor. Extra-illus with numerous plates & Mss. b May 30 (314) £320

## Hamilton, David
— Earl Golf at St. Andrews. Glasgow & Oban: Patrick Press, [1986]. One of 350. Bds. pba Apr 18 (71) $140
— Early Aberdeen Golf: Golfing Small-talk in 1636. Glasgow & Oxford: Patrick Press, 1985. 1st Ed, One of 450. Bds. Sgd. pba Apr 18 (69) $130
— Early Golf at Edinburgh & Leith. Glasgow: Patrick Press, 1988. 1st Ed, One of 350. Cloth. Sgd. pba Apr 18 (70) $110
— Early Golf in Glasgow, 1589-1787. Oxford: Patrick Press, 1985. 1st Ed, One of 250. Bds. Inscr & sgd to Hal Conefry. pba Apr 18 (72) $130
— John Kerr, the Sporting Padre.... Glasgow: Patrick Press, 1989. One of 90 deluxe-bound. Half mor. With booklet laid in. Sgd. pba Apr 18 (73) $250
— Souvenirs. NY, [1974]. Folio, cloth with mtd color reproduction, contents loose as issued. With 67 mtd plates. With an orig silver print, sgd in 1974. sg Feb 29 (157) $450

## Hamilton, Edward
— Recollections of Fly Fishing for Salmon.... L, 1884. 1st Ed. 8vo, cloth. Dampstain to frontis. Inscr & with ALs. O June 25 (154) $110

## Hamilton, Frank Hastings, 1818-86
— A Treatise on Military Surgery. NY, 1865. 1st Ed. 8vo, later cloth. Author's signature & scored inscr on tp; newspaper cuttings mtd on facing blank. sg May 16 (422) $350

## Hamilton, G. D.
— Trout-Fishing and Sport in Maoriland. Wellington, N.Z., 1904. pba July 11 (207) $180

## Hamilton, George, Surgeon
— A Voyage Round the World in his Majesty's Frigate Pandora.... Berwick, 1793. 8vo, modern half calf. Lacking port & 1st 2 leaves; some spotting. b Mar 20 (96) £280

## Hamilton, Myra
— Kingdoms Curious. L, 1905. Illus by Arthur Rackham & others. 8vo, orig cloth; spine spotted. Some spotting. Ck May 31 (125) £180

## Hamilton, Sinclair
— Early American Book Illustrators and Wood Engravers, 1670-1870. Princeton, 1958, 1968. 2 vols, including Supplement. 4to, cloth. sg Sept 14 (222) $300

Anr Ed. Princeton, 1968. 2d Ptg. 2 vols. 4to, cloth. ds July 27 (89) $250

Anr copy. Orig cloth. NH July 21 (356) $175

## Hamilton, Sir William, 1730-1803
— Campi Phlegraei.... Naples, 1776-79. 2 vols & Supplement in 1 vol. Folio, contemp mor gilt; spine ends chipped, library label at foot of spine. With double-page map & 59 hand-colored plates. Minor soiling & staining; crease in lower right margin of Plate 54. P Dec 12 (214) $27,000

— Collection of Engravings from Ancient Vases.... Naples, 1791-95. Vol II only. Recent half mor. Stain at inside edge affecting titles & 1st 4 plates; some surface dirt; trimmed at right edge. bba June 6 (17) £750 [L'Acquaforte]

— Collection of Etruscan, Greek and Roman Antiquities. Naples, 1766-67. Vols I only. Recent half mor. Double & folding plates detached from stubs; dampstaining in margins; some creases & finger-soiling. bba June 6 (16) £2,600 [L'Acquaforte]

— Memorandum on the Subject of the Earl of Elgin's Pursuits in Greece. L, 1811. 2d Ed. - Illus by H. Moses. 8vo, contemp half calf. With 1 plate & 2 illus. S Oct 26 (108) £220 [Zioni]

— Outlines from the Figures and Compositions upon the Greek, Roman and Etruscan Vases. L, 1814. 2d Ed. 8vo, contemp mor; rubbed. With half title, & 62 plates. S Oct 26 (122) £300 [Antique]

### Hamilton Collection, Sir William
Anr copy. 4to, contemp half calf; rubbed. b May 30 (276) £70

HANCARVILLE, PIERRE FRANCOIS HUGUES D'. - Antiquites etrusques, grecques et romaines.... Naples, 1766-67. 4 vols. Folio, contemp mor gilt. With 8 hand-colored titles, 5 dedication leaves & 437 plates, 184 hand-colored. Titles in Vols I & IV creased. Horace Walpole's copy. Fuerstenberg - Schaefer copy. S Dec 7 (283) £33,000

Anr copy. Contemp russia gilt; rebacked retaining orig spines. With 8 colored titles, 5 engraved dedications, 254 plain & 183 hand-colored plates. A few plates marked. S June 27 (147) £28,000

Anr Ed. Paris, 1785-88. 5 vols. 4to, Contemp red mor gilt. With engraved titles & 360 plates. Fuerstenberg - Schaefer copy. S Dec 7 (284) £4,600

## Hamilton, William Richard, 1777-1859
— Remarks on Several Parts of Turkey. L, 1809. 2 vols. 4to & folio contemp calf calf; front cover detached, spine perished. With folding map & 24 folding plates. Some browning & foxing. Robert Southey's copy. cb Feb 14 (2537) $900

Anr copy. Part I: Aegyptica (all pbd). 2 vols. 4to & folio, contemp calf gilt. With map & 24 plates. Blackmer copy. S Mar 28 (290) £2,600

## Hamilton, William T., b1822
— My Sixty Years on the Plains.... NY, 1905. 1st Ed. - Illus by Charles M. Russell. Orig cloth; extremities rubbed, front cover stained. With 8 plates. Robbins copy. pba Mar 21 (139) $170

## Hamley, Edward Bruce
— The Story of the Campaign of Sebastopol written in the Camp. L, 1855. 8vo, contemp half calf. With folding map & 9 litho plates, some in color. Some foxing to plates. b Sept 20 (338) £80

**Hammer, Armand.** See: Onassis copy, Jacqueline Bouvier Kennedy

## Hammer Library, Christian
— Catalogue de la Bibliotheque Hammer a Stockholm. Stockholm, 1886-88. 9 vols, including Supplement & plate vol. 8vo, orig wraps; frayed, some soiling. O Mar 26 (125) $300

## Hammer, Kenneth
— Men With Custer: Biographies of the 7th Cavalry, 25 June 1876. Issued with: The Reno Court of Inquiry: The Chicago Times Account. Fort Collins CO: Old Army Press, [1972]. One of 250. 2 vols. Inscr to John Popovich in Vol I; inscr to Popovich by Robert Utley in Vol II; with related material. pba June 25 (109) $275

## Hammer-Purgstall, Joseph von, 1774-1856
— Histoire de l'ordre des Assassins. Paris, 1833. 8vo, half mor. Old Cyrillic library stamp on tp. b Sept 20 (339) £320

— The History of the Assassins. L, 1835. 12mo, cloth. sg Mar 7 (97) $110

## Hammett, Dashiell, 1894-1961
— The Battle of the Aleutians. [Adak, Alaska, Oct] 1944. Oblong 8vo, wraps; crease along center from folding. 12 leaves. Ptd on a mobile press, in a truck. pba Aug 22 (200) $75

— Dashiell Hammett Omnibus. NY, 1935. In chipped & rubbed dj. pba May 23 (146) $75

— The Glass Key. L, 1931. 1st Ed. In dj with some loss of paper at spine extremities. sg June 20 (145) $600
1st American Ed. NY, 1931. Orig cloth; worn & soiled. F June 25 (137) £110

— The Maltese Falcon. San Francisco: Arion Press, 1983. One of 400. Half mor with black bird onlay. sg Sept 14 (32) $450

— The Thin Man. NY, 1934. 1st Ed. In 1st dj with short tears & chipping. pba Aug 22 (201) $1,500

Anr copy. In dj with chip at head of spine panel. sg June 20 (148) $2,000

## Hammett, Samuel Adams.
— A Stray Yankee in Texas. By Philip Paxton. NY, 1853. Orig cloth; joints cracking & repaired, lacking front free endpapers. With frontis & pictorial

title. Foxing, especially to prelims.  pba Aug 8 (76) $95

**Hammond, Daryn**
— The Gold Swing: The Ernest Jones method. NY: Brentano's, [c.1920]. 1st American Ed. Cloth; spine ends rubbed.  pba Apr 18 (75) $95

**Hammond, George P.**
— Adventures of Alexander Barclay, Mountain Man. Denver, 1976. 1st Ed. Lea in dj;  d/j sunned, soiled, slightly torn. With 3 folding maps. Robbins copy.  pba Mar 21 (140) $50
— Noticias de California: First Report of the Occupation by the Portola Expedition, 1770.... San Francisco: Book Club of California, 1958. One of 400. Half cloth in dj. With 2 folded maps, 2 facsimiles, & 1 illus. Larson copy.  pba Sept 28 (191) $70

**Hammond, George P. —& Morgan, Dale Lowell**
— Captain Charles M. Weber.... Berkeley: Friends of the Bancroft Library, 1966. One of 700. Folio, cloth. General Publication No 1.  pba Nov 16 (275) $50

**Hammond, George P. —& Rey, Agapito**
— Don Juan de Onate: Colonizer of New Mexico.... Albuquerque, 1953. 2 vols, orig cloth in djs;  d/js spines faded. Vol I with stain. Robbins copy.  pba Mar 21 (141) $250
— Narratives of the Coronado Expedition, 1540-1542. Albuquerque, 1940. Orig cloth in djs;  d/j faded, ends chipped. With frontis. Robbins copy.  pba Mar 21 (142) $130

**Hammond, Jabez D.** See: Fillmore's copy, Millard

**Hammond, Samuel H., 1809-78**
— Hunting Adventures in the Northern Wilds.... Phila., 1865. 8vo, cloth;  spine ends chipped, extremities rubbed.  pba July 11 (392) $50

**Hamst, Olphar.** See: Thomas, Ralph

**Hanbury, Frederick Janson**
— An Illustrated Monograph of the British Hieracia. L, July 1889-March 1898. Illus by Miss G. Lister & Mrs. F. J. Hanbury. 8 parts in 1 vol. Folio, modern cloth;  orig wraps bound in. With 24 hand-colored plates. S Oct 27 (637) £480 [St. Anns]

**Hancarville, Pierre Francois Hugues d'.** See: Hamilton Collection, Sir William

**Handel, George Frederick, 1685-1759**
— Alcina, an Opera.... L: Walsh, [1737]. 1st Ed. Folio, contemp bds;  broken, calf spine & cornerpieces mostly worn away. Engraved throughout. Small tear on p. 41. S Dec 1 (172) £850
— Alexander Balus, an Oratorio.... L: Walsh, [1748). Bound with: Joseph and his Brethren. L, [c.1747-53] Folio, contemp bds; rebacked in calf, upper cover detached. Engraved titles & music. S Dec 1 (173) £700

Anr Ed. L: Walsh, 1748-49. 2 vols in 1. Folio, disbound. Engraved throughout.. Inscr to Vincent Novello.  S May 15 (75) £550
— Alexander's Feast. L: Walsh, [c.1743]. Bound with: Acis and Galatea, a Mask.... Folio, calf;  restored with orig covers. Small tear on p. 49.  S May 15 (373) £550
— Porus an Opera.... L: Walsh, [1731]. 1st Ed. Folio, modern bds. Engraved throughout. Browning on tp & final page; some corners stained.  S Dec 1 (175) £1,100
— The Triumph of Time and Truth an Oratio. L, [1757]. 1st Ed. Folio, stitched but unbound. With table of songs. Title frayed & torn; few leaves marginally creased.  S Oct 27 (925) £180 [Palazzolo]
— Works. Leipzig, 1858-1902. 96 vols in 57. 4to & oblong folio, half lea;  rubbed. Engraved throughout. S May 15 (76) £3,200

**Handjeri, Alexander, Prince Hospodar of Moldavia**
— Dictionnaire francais-arabe-persan et turc. Moscow, 1840-41. 1st Ed. 3 vols. 4to, later half calf. S Oct 26 (109) £280 [Hakimzadeh]

**Hands, Elizabeth**
— The Death of Amnon. A Poem. Coventry, 1789. 8vo, contemp calf. Some staining.  b Dec 5 (397) £320

**Handy, W. C.**
— Blues: An Anthology. NY, 1926. In dj with wear to spine. Inscr.  cb Oct 17 (400) $1,000
— Father of the Blues. NY, 1941. In dj with crimp at top of rear panel. Sgd.  sg Mar 28 (167) $300

Anr Ed. NY, 1942. In chipped dj. Inscr.  sg Mar 28 (168) $130
— A Treasury of the Blues. NY, 1949. Inscr to Emory Lewis.  pba Oct 26 (28) $250

**Handzeichnungen...**
— Handzeichnungen Alter Meister der Hollaendischen Schule. Harrlem, [c.1900]. 6 vols. Folio, loose in orig half mor portfolios. With 384 plates. S Oct 27 (975) £130 [Reiden]

**Hangest, Hieronymus de**
— Introductorium Morale. Lyons: Joannis Gormontii, 1515. 8vo, later vellum gilt;  bowed. With 1 initial & 1 (of 5) woodcut illust hand-colored. Some soiling & foxing; underlinings & marginal notes.  cb Feb 14 (2516) $750

**Hanley, James**
— Boy. L: Boriswood, [1931]. One of 145. Orig cloth. ANs laid in.  pba Aug 22 (203) $50

**Hanna, Charles A.**
— The Wilderness Trail or the Ventures and Adventures of the Pennsylvania Traders on the Allegheny Path. NY, 1911. 1st Ed, One of 1,000. 2 vols. sg Oct 26 (130) $150

Anr copy. In chipped djs.  wa Feb 29 (489) $220

**Hanneman, Audre**
— Ernest Hemingway: a Comprehensive Bibliography. Princeton, 1969. pba Aug 22 (234) $70

**Hannon, Theo**
— La Toison de Phyrne. Paris: Dorbon Aine, [1913]. One of 100. Illus by Henri Thomas. Half mor, orig wraps bound in; corners bumped, extremities rubbed. cb Oct 17 (631) $550

**Hans, Fred M.**
— The Great Sioux Nation. Chicago: M. A. Donohue, [1907]. Cloth; extremities worn. pba Apr 25 (440) $120

**Hansen, Harvey J. —& Others**
— Wild Oats in Eden. Sonoma County in the 19th Century. Santa Rosa: Pvtly ptd, 1962. pba Feb 12 (485) $55

**Hanway, Jonas, 1712-86**
— An Essay on Tea.... L, [28 Feb, 1756]. 1st Ed. 8vo, modern bds. Title soiled & frayed at margins. Ck Mar 22 (139) £300
— A Journal of Eight Days Journey from Portsmouth to Kingston upon Thames.... L, 1756. 1st Ed. 4to, contemp calf gilt; joints split & repaired at hinges, spine ends chipped. bbc June 24 (182) $240
 2d Ed. L, 1757. 2 vols. 8vo, early sheep; needs rebdg. With 2 engraved frontises. sg Mar 7 (98) $200
— Solitude in Imprisonment, with Proper Profitable Labour.... L, 1776. 8vo, contemp mor gilt with initials G. P. on both covers, by Hanway's 2d binder. Abbey-Martin copy. C May 1 (73) £3,500

**Happe, Andreas Friedrich**
— Botanica pharmaceutica exhibens plantas.... Berlin, 1785. Vols I-IV bound in 2 vols, plus a single part containing plates 401-30. Folio, 19th-cent bds; worn. With 430 hand-colored plates. Some leaves detached; a few plates stained or spotted; lacking engraved title to Vol I. S June 27 (33) £4,600

**Happel, Eberhard Werner, 1647-90**
— Groeste Denkwuerdigkeiten der Welt.... Hamburg, 1683-91. 5 vols. 4to, contemp calf; worn. With 200 (of 202) plates. S Mar 14 (161) £1,900

**Haraszthy, Agostin, 1812-69**
— Grape Culture, Wines, and Wine-Making. NY, 1862. 8vo, orig cloth. P Dec 12 (89) $1,100
 Anr copy. Orig cloth; spine ends rubbed, lacking rear free endpaperg. Stamp on tp; hand-written 1867 list of vines tipped in. pba June 20 (190) $1,100

**Harbaugh, Henry**
— The Birds of the Bible. Phila., 1854. 8vo, orig calf; rebacked. With 12 chromolitho plates. pba Aug 8 (297) $65

**Harbin, Robert**
— Magic of Robert Harbin. Pvtly ptd, 1970. Ltd Ed. Folio, orig cloth. With 3 letters to Rae Hammond & other material inserted. S May 16 (320) £440

**Harbour, Henry**
— Where Flies the Flag. L, [1904]. Illus by Arthur Rackham. With 6 colored plates. Ck May 31 (121) £90

**Hardcastle, Ephraim.** See: Pyne, William Henry

**Hardenbrook, William Ten Eyck**
— Financial New York. NY, 1897. One of 1,200. Folio, half lea; worn, 1 cover detached. Some foxing. O Mar 5 (108) $130

**Hardie, James, 1758-1826**
— The American Remembrancer, and Universal Tablet of Memory. Phila., 1795. 1st Ed. 12mo, old sheep; worn, endpapers browned. wa Feb 29 (397) $70

**Hardie, Martin**
— The British School of Etching. L, [1921]. One of 110. 4to, orig cloth. With frontis etching by Frank Short. sg Sept 7 (174) $120
— Frederick Goulding: Master Printer.... Stirling, 1910. One of 250. 4to half vellum. sg Jan 11 (200) $60
— Water-Colour Painting in Britain. L, 1966-68. 3 vols. Cloth; worn, wormhole in foot of 1 spine. O May 7 (154) $170

**Hardie, Martin —&**
**Sabin, Arthur K.**
— War Posters Issued by Belligerent and Neutral Nations 1914-19. L, 1920. 1st Ed. 4to, cloth; worn. Some foxing, a few plates loose. O July 9 (97) $110

**Hardin, A. N.**
— The American Bayonet. Phila., 1964. 4to, cloth, in chipped dj. sg Mar 7 (464) $120

**Harding, George L.**
— Do Agustin V. Zamorano: Statesman, Soldier, Craftsman, and California's First Printer. Los Angeles, 1934. 1st Ed. Orig cloth; spine top & cover edges faded. With front port. Robbins copy. Inscr & sgd to Garfield D. Merner. pba Mar 21 (143) $140
— Don Agustin V. Zamorano: Statesman, Soldier, Craftsman, and California's First Printer. Los Angeles, 1934. One of 325. Orig cloth in dj. With Harding's prospectus & business card. Larson copy. pba Sept 28 (195) $110

**Harding, John**
— The Chronicle.... L, 1812. 2 parts in 1 vol. 4to, half mor; rubbed. Lacking leaf before title; prelims foxed. pba Nov 30 (172) $80

**Hardouin, Ernest, 1820-54 —&**
**Ritter, Wilhelm Leonard, 1799-1862**
— Java tooneelen uit het leven karakterschetsen en kleederdrachten van Java's bewoners in afbeeldingen naar de natuur geteekend.... Leiden, 1855. 1st Ed. 4to, orig cloth; worn, joints cracked. With engraved title, folding map (outlined in color) & 26 colored plates. Inner margins of title & endpapers damp-stained. C Apr 23 (13) £320 [Ad Orientem]
 Anr copy. Orig cloth; joints rubbed, stain at foot of lower cover. With engraved title & 26 hand-colored

plates, some heightened with gum arabic. Some spotting.  S June 27 (233) £900

**Hardy, Joseph**
— A Picturesque and Descriptive Tour in the Mountains of the High Pyrenees.  L, 1825.  8vo, contemp cloth; worn, spine head gone, front free endpaper loose.  With 24 colored plates, mtd as issued, & map (loose).  F June 20 (843) $350

Anr copy.  Contemp mor gilt; rebacked.  With map & 24 mtd hand-colored tinted plates.  S Mar 28 (230) £520

**Hardy, Robert William Hale, d.1871**
— Travels in the Interior of Mexico.  L, 1829.  1st Ed.  8vo, contemp calf; rubbed.  With 7 plates & folding map.  Some foxing.  S Oct 26 (511) £300 [Remington]

**Hardy, Thomas, 1840-1928**
See also: Limited Editions Club
— The Dynasts.  L, 1927.  One of 525.  3 vols. 4to, orig half vellum in djs; d/js chipped.  S Oct 27 (1219) £300 [Way]
— The Dynasts: a Drama of the Napoleonic War.  L, 1927.  ("The Dynasts.") One of 525.  3 vols. 4to, orig half vellum.  bba May 9 (464) £320 [Blackwell]
— Far from the Madding Crowd.  NY, 1895.  1st American Ed.  Orig cloth; spine head torn, lower front cover rubbed.  pba May 23 (147) $100
— The Hand of Ethelberta.  L, 1876.  1st Ed in Book form.  2 vols. 8vo, half mor, orig cloth bound in.  b Jan 31 (90) £350
— Life's Little Ironies.  L, 1894.  1st Ed. 8vo, cloth.  sg Feb 8 (295) $90
— Poems of the Past and the Present.  L, 1902.  Inscr to George Doublas, Nov 1901.  P Dec 12 (90) $2,000
— The Return of the Native.  L, 1929.  Ltd Ed.  Illus by Clare Leighton.  Orig half cloth; extremities rubbed, corner of front free endpaper lacking.  pba Aug 22 (804) $50
— Selected Poems.  L: Medici Society, 1921.  One of 1,025.  4to, half cloth, in dj.  Inscr to Lacy & Samuel Chew.  With Ns from Florence Hardy laid in.  CE Sept 27 (136) $950
— Tess of the D'Urbervilles.  NY, 1892.  1st American Ed.  Orig cloth; spine ends worn, front hinge starting.  pba Aug 22 (207) $95
— The Trumpet-Major.  L, 1880.  1st Ed.  3 vols. 8vo, orig cloth; rebacked with orig backstrips laid down, soiled, new endpapers.  CE Sept 27 (135) $200
— Wessex Tales.  L, 1888.  1st Ed in Book form.  2 vols. 8vo, early half mor.  b Jan 31 (91) £280
— The Woodlanders.  L, 1887.  1st Ed in Book form.  3 vols. 8vo, orig cloth; minor wear & rubbing, Vol II rebacked, some hinges starting.  P June 5 (242) $1,200
— Works.  L, 1912-17.  Mixed Ed.  21 vols.  Contemp half calf; rubbed.  S Dec 18 (396) £180 [Harrington]
Anniversary Ed.  NY & L, 1920.  21 vols.  Orig cloth, unopened.  pba June 20 (191) $550

**Hargrave, Catherine Perry**
— A History of Playing Cards and a Bibliography....  Bost & NY, [1930].  1st Ed.  4to, orig cloth; scuffed.  Ck Apr 12 (236) £90

**Hargrett, Lester**
— Oklahoma Imprints, 1835-1890.  NY, 1951.  1st Ed.  O Dec 5 (54) $80

**Harington, Sir John, 1561-1612**
— The Metamorphosis of Ajax....  Chiswick: C. Whittingham, 1814.  One of 100.  Half mor; scratched.  pba June 20 (192) $130

**Harkness, William Hale.**  See: Derrydale Press

**Harlan, Robert D.**
— Bibliography of the Grabhorn Press....  San Francisco: John Howell, 1977.  One of 225.  Folio, half mor.  bba May 9 (572) £120 [Collinge & Clark]; sg Sept 14 (178) $425

**Harleian...**
— Harleian Miscellany: A Collection of Scarce, Curious, and Entertaining Pamphlets and Tracts.  L, 1744-46.  1st Ed. 8 vols. 4to, contemp calf; rebacked, hinges repaired.  Some soiling.  S June 12 (128) £380

Anr Ed. L, 1808-13.  12 vols. 4to, contemp half russia gilt; worn, joints weak.  wa Feb 29 (11) $500

**Harley, J. B. — &
Woodward, David**
— The History of Cartography.  Chicago & L, [1987-92].  2 vols. In djs.  sg May 9 (13) $225

**Harlow, Neal**
See also: Grabhorn Printing
— Maps and Surveys of the Pueblo Lands of Los Angeles.  Los Angeles, 1976.  One of 375.  Half cloth.  pba Feb 13 (89) $150; pba Apr 25 (185) $75
— Maps of the Pueblo Lands of San Diego, 1602-1874.  Los Angeles: Dawson's Book Shop, 1967.  One of 375.  Half cloth.  pba Feb 13 (90) $130

**Harman, Samuel W.**
— Hell on the Border; He Hanged Eighty-Eight Men.  Fort Smith AK: Phoenix Publishing Company, [1898].  8vo, orig ptd wraps; spine tender, split along front spine edge, pulling loose.  cb Feb 14 (2590) $750

**Harmon, Daniel Williams, 1778-1845**
— A Journal of Voyages and Travels....  Andover, 1820.  1st Ed. 8vo, orig calf; extremities rubbed, errata slip mtd to rear pastedown.  With port & folding map.  Some staining, mainly to prelims; map detached & laid in.  cb Feb 14 (2591) $700

**Harnsworth, Vyvyan G.**
— Nisbet's Golf Year Book.  L, 1913.  9th Ed.  Cloth; spine darkened, front cover warped, some bleeding.  pba Apr 18 (137) $110

**Harper's...**
— Harper's Bazaar. A Repository of Fashion, Pleasure and Instruction. NY, 1867-68. Vol I, Nos 1-61. Bound in 1 vol. Folio, half leaf; worn, spine reinforced with tape, inner hinges broken. Some fraying at ends. NH June 1 (161) $320
— Harper's New Monthly Magazine. NY, 1850-75. Vols 1-50. 8vo, 45 vols in orig cloth, 5 in orig half mor; minor defs. pba Apr 25 (186) $2,500

Anr Ed. NY, May 1866. No 192. Ptd wraps. Yosemite article with 13 wood-engravings on pp 681-816. pba Feb 12 (219) $65
— Harper's Pictorial History of the Great Rebellion. Chicago, [1866-68]. Ed by Alfred H. Guernsey & Henry M. Alden. 2 vols in 1. Folio, cloth; spine taped. Folding hand-colored map broken in folds. NH July 21 (76) $275

Anr copy. 2 vols. Folio, orig cloth; worn & soiled, a few leaves detached. Folding map torn. wa Feb 29 (343) $150
— Harper's Weekly: A Journal of Civilization. NY, 1857-80. Vols 1-24. Later cloth; a few leaves misbound. Some foxing & dampstaining; portions of a few leaves removed; a few leaves lacking; library markings; a few leaves remargined, extended or folded. Vol II lacking Nos 105, 106, 108 & 116; Vol XXIV lacking No 1230. cb Oct 17 (156) $3,000

Anr Ed. NY, 1858. Vol II. Orig sheep; spine lacking, broken. With 16 full-page & half-page wood-engravings by Winslow Homer. bbc June 24 (403) $260

Vol III. NY, 1859. Orig half sheep; broken, spine lacking. With 9 double-page to half-page wood-engravings by Winslow Homer. bbc June 24 (404) $300
— Harper's Weekly: a Journal of Civilization. NY, 1861-65. Vols V-IX. Modern cloth. sg Oct 26 (51) $3,200

Vols V-VII. Early half mor. sg Oct 26 (52) $1,200
— Harper's Weekly: A Journal of Civilization. NY, 1862. Vol VI Cloth; minor wear & scuffing. With 13 Winslow Homer illusts. bbc Apr 22 (104) $490

Vol VII. NY, 1863. Early half mor; extremities rubbed. sg Oct 26 (53) $750

Vol X. NY, 1866. Folio, orig half sheep; scuffed & worn. bbc June 24 (405) $325

**Harral, Thomas, d.1853**
— Picturesque Views of the Severn.... L, 1824. 2 vols. 4to, contemp mor; scuffed. With 52 hand-colored plates. Some spotting. S Oct 26 (394) £440 [Antique Map]

**Harrington, Charles**
— Summering in Colorado. Denver, 1874. Illus by J. Collier. 12mo, cloth. With 10 mtd albumen prints only. Z Jan 30 (427) $300

**Harrington, John W.**
— The Jumping Kangaroo and the Apple Butter Cat. NY, 1900. 1st Ed. - Illus by J. W. Conde. Orig half cloth in dj; d/j ends & corners chipped, rear d/j torn, spine head soiled. pba Nov 9 (30) $110

**Harris, Chapin A.**
— The Dental Art, a Practical Treatise.... Balt., 1839. 8vo, contemp sheep; covers detached. Tp foxed & detached; other foxing. F Mar 28 (410) $80

**Harris, Elizabeth M.**
— The Art of Medal Engraving. Newton: Bird & Bull Press, 1991. One of 230. 4to, silk. sg Feb 15 (47) $60

**Harris, Gwinn Harris, 1817-87**
— Central Route to the Pacific.... Phila., 1854. 1st Ed. 8vo, orig cloth; spine faded, central spine gouged. With 13 plates. Some foxing. Robbins copy. pba Mar 21 (144) $650

**Harris, Joel Chandler, 1848-1908**
See also: Limited Editions Club
— Little Mr. Thimblefinger and his Queer Country. Bost., [1894]. 1st Ed. - Illus by Oliver Herford. Orig cloth; 1 plate detached. pba Aug 22 (210) $110
— Mingo and Other Sketches in Black and White. Bost., 1893. Orig cloth; inner hinges weak, rubbed. Inscr & with ALs. K Feb 11 (210) $375
— Nights with Uncle Remus.... Bost., 1883. 1st Pbd Ed. 12mo orig cloth; extremities rubbed. Dampstained throughout in lower margin. Sold w.a.f. sg Sept 21 (214) $70

Anr Ed. L: George Routledge, [c.1884]. 8vo, cloth. sg Mar 28 (147) $120
— On the Plantation. NY, 1892. 8vo, orig cloth; some soiling. NH July 21 (166) $95
— The Tar-Baby and Other Rhymes.... NY, 1904. 1st Ed. Some soiling. pba May 23 (149) $140

Anr copy. Orig cloth; extremities worn. sg Sept 21 (215) $300
— Uncle Remus and his Legends of the Old Plantation. L, 1881. 8vo, orig cloth; edges rubbed, front free endpaper chipped at margins & partially detached. Gutter cracked between pp. 112 & 113. Z June 28 (109) $225
— Uncle Remus: his Songs and his Sayings. NY, 1881. ("Uncle Remus and his Legends of the Old Plantation.") 8vo, orig cloth. Met Dec 5 (214) $275

1st Ed, 1st Issue. 8vo, orig cloth; extremities rubbed, front hinge cracked. cb Feb 14 (2693) $750

Anr copy. Cloth. sg Sept 21 (216) $1,300

Anr copy. Cloth; spine worn at top. sg Mar 28 (149) $700

Anr copy. 8vo cloth; rubbed, front hinge starting, rear hinge repaired. sg Mar 28 (150) $400

Anr copy. 8vo, orig cloth; extremities rubbed, shaken. Z June 28 (108) $700

Anr Ed. NY, 1895. One of 250 L.p. copies, sgd. Illus by A. B. Frost. 8vo, vellum. sg Mar 28 (151) $850
— Uncle Remus, or Mr. Fox, Mr. Rabbit, and Mr. Terrapin. L, [1882]. 8vo, pictorial cloth. sg Mar 28 (148) $250
— Uncle Remus Returns. Bost., 1918. Illus by A. B. Frost & J. M. Conde. Orig cloth. sg Feb 8 (296A) $90

# HARRIS

— Wally Wanderoon and his Story-Telling Machine. NY, 1903. Illus by Karl Moseley. Pictorial cloth; spine ends frayed, extremities rubbed. pba Dec 14 (71) $50; pba Aug 22 (780) $55

**Harris, John, 1667?-1719**
— The History of Kent. L, 1719. 1st Ed. Vol I (all pbd). Folio, modern cloth. With port, folding map, & 42 plates. Some foxing. bba Nov 1 (124) £1,400 [Marrin]
— Navigantium atque Itinerarium Bibliotheca; or, a Compleat Collection of Voyages and Travels.... L, 1744-48. 2d Ed. Vol I only. contemp calf; free endpapers detached, rubbbed, hinges cracked. pba Oct 9 (8) $1,000

**Harris, Joseph, 1702-64**
— An Essay upon Money and Coins. L, 1757-58. 2 parts in 1 vol. 8vo, contemp calf; worn & broken, split to spine. Library markings to front pastedown & copyright page. bbc June 24 (295) $220

**Harris, Moses, 1731?-85?**
— The Aurelian. A Natural History of English Insects.... L, 1778 [watermarked 1794]. Folio, contemp mor gilt; laid down, rubbed, corners repaired. With additional French title within hand-colored border, hand-colored diagram plate & 44 hand-colored reversed plates. Some browning & soiling; English title creased. Fattorini copy. C Oct 25 (67) £2,400

Anr Ed. L, 1778 [watermarks 1810]. Folio, 19th-cent mor gilt; rubbed. With frontis & 45 hand-colored plates. S June 27 (34) £3,600

Anr Ed. L, 1840. 4to, contemp half mor gilt; worn. With key plate & 44 hand-colored plates. Engraved title shaved; without frontis. S June 27 (35) £3,000
— An Exposition of English Insects. L, 1782. 2d Ed. 4to, later half cloth. With 50 hand-colored & 1 uncolored plate. Fore-edges fragile & nicked; library stamp in upper margin of most leaves. Met May 22 (433) $600

Anr copy. Contemp half lea; worn. With hand-colored frontis, 1 plain & 51 hand-colored plates. Lower margin of G1-G2 torn. S June 13 (395) £300

**Harris, Robert**
— Sixty Years of Golf. L: Batchworth Press, [1953]. 1st Ed. Cloth. pba Apr 18 (76) $60

**Harris, Stanley**
— The Coaching Age. L, 1885. 8vo, half mor by Larkins; rubbed. Some foxing. O Jan 9 (125) $130
— Old Coaching Days.... L, 1882. 8vo, orig cloth. Some foxing. O Jan 9 (126) $110

**Harris, Thaddeus Mason, 1768-1842**
— The Journal of a Tour into the Territory Northwest of the Alleghany Mountains.... Bost., 1805. 8vo, contemp calf; rebacked. With plan, view & 3 maps. Maps browned. sg Oct 29 (131) $475

Anr copy. Orig bds; worn & soiled, spine labels, stamp on endpaper. Tp repaired. wa Feb 29 (481) $290

# AMERICAN BOOK PRICES CURRENT

**Harris, Thaddeus William, 1795-1856**
— A Treatise on Some of the Insects Injurious to Vegetation. Bost., 1862. 3d Ed. 8vo, half mor; worn, chipped. With 8 color plates. wa Nov 16 (196) $90

**Harris, Tomas**
— Goya: Engravings and Lithographs. Oxford, [1964]. 1st Ed. 2 vols. Folio orig cloth, in rubbed & torn djs. bba Oct 5 (261) £340 [Franks]

**Harris, Sir William Cornwallis, 1807-48**
— The Wild Sports of Southern Africa. L, 1839. 1st Ed. 12mo, orig cloth; bumped & worn. With map & 7 plates. Tp stained; library sticker on tp verso; some wrinkling. Met May 22 (304) $200

3d Ed. L, 1841. 8vo, modern half mor. With colored frontis, map & 24 colored plates. S June 13 (396) £340

**Harrison, Fairfax**
— The Background of the American Stud Book. Richmond: Pvtly ptd at the Old Dominion Press, 1933. O Jan 9 (127) $120
— The Belair Stud 1747-1761. Richmond: Pvtly ptd at the Old Dominion Press, 1929. O Jan 9 (128) $120
— The Equine F. F. Vs. A Study.... Richmond: Pvtly ptd at the Old Dominion Press, 1928. O Jan 9 (130) $100
— The John's Island Stud (South Carolina) 1750-1788. Richmond: Pvtly ptd at the Old Dominion Press, 1931. O Jan 9 (131) $130
— The Roanoke Stud 1795-1833. Richmond: Pvtly ptd at the Old Dominion Press, 1930. O Jan 9 (132) $90

**Harrison, Gabriel**
— John Howard Payne, Dramatist, Poet, Actor.... Phila., 1855. 2 vols. 4to, orig cloth, in chipped dj. F Mar 28 (443) $60

**Harrison, Jim**
— Warlock. NY, [1981]. 1st Ed, One of 250. sg Dec 14 (119) $50

**Harrison, John, 1693-1776**
— The Principles of Mr. Harrison's Time-Keeper. L, 1767. 4to, modern mor gilt. With 10 folding plates. Hefner copy. CNY May 17 (21) $12,000

**Harrison, John, fl.1740-50**
— A Short Comparative View of the Practice of Surgery in the French Hospitals. L, 1750. 8vo, bds. Tp soiled & def. b May 30 (22) £90

**Harrison, Joseph**
— The Floricultural Cabinet, and Florist's Magazine. L, 1833-59. Vols I-XXVII in 14. 8vo, later half mor; rubbed. With additional titles to 20 vols & 352 colored or hand-colored plates & 19 uncolored plates, 3 folding. Some browning, soiling & staining. Sold w.a.f. Fattorini copy. C Oct 25 (68) £1,000

**Harrison, William Henry, 1773-1841**
— A Discourse on the Aborigines of the Valley of the Ohio. Cincinnati, 1838. 8vo, later half mor. With

folding map. Some foxing; library markings. bbc Dec 18 (474) $200

**Harrisse, Henry, 1830-1910**
— Bibliotheca Americana Vetustissima: A Description of Works relating to America.... NY, 1866 & Paris, 1872. One of 400. 2 vols, including Supplement. 4to, mor by Bedford & mor by Petit; both rubbed. 1st vol is Kraus copy; 2d vol in Harrisse's own copy, inscr by him. O Mar 26 (126) $1,500
— Bibliotheca Americana Vetustissima... Additions. Paris, 1872. 4to, later cloth, orig wraps bound in, unopened; worn. Kraus copy. O Mar 26 (127) $80
— L. L. Boilly: Peintre, Dessinateur et Lithographe. Paris, 1898. 8vo, contemp half mor, orig wraps bound in; front joint worn. sg Sept 7 (49) $225
— Notes pour servir a l'histoire, a la bibliographie et a la cartographie de la Nouvelle-France et des pays adjacents, 1545-1700.... Paris, 1872. 8vo, half lea, orig wraps bound in; rubbed, joints worn. Inscr by the Ed, Edwin Tross, to J. Petzholdt. O Mar 26 (128) $140

**Harrop, Dorothy A.**
— A History of the Gregynog Press. Pinner, 1980. 4to, cloth. sg Sept 14 (230) $70

**Hart, Clive —&**
**Knuth, Leo**
— A Topographical Guide to James Joyce's Ulysses. Colchester: A Wake Newslitter Press, [1976]. 2 vols. Wraps. pba Aug 22 (265) $60

**Hart, Dorothy**
— Thou Swell, Thou Witty: The Life and Lyrics of Lorenz Hart. NY, [1976]. 4to, orig cloth, in dj. F June 20 (595) $50

**Hart, Eugene D.** See: Burdick & Hart

**Hart, Fred H.**
— The Sazerac Lying Club. A Nevada Book. San Francisco, 1878. 8vo, orig cloth; spine ends chipped, corners rubbed, front hinge starting. pba Apr 25 (444) $75

**Hart, James**
— Klinike, or the Diet of the Diseased. L, 1633. 1st Ed. 8vo, contemp calf; repaired. Title repaired at margin; dampstained; some ink smudges. Ck Mar 22 (140) £650

**Hart, Joseph C.**
— Miriam Coffin, or the Whale-Fishermen, a Tale. L, 1834. 3 vols. 12mo, orig cloth; spines weak. rce July 25 (29) $350

**Hart, Mary Kerr**
— Health Blossoms: or, Poems Written in Obscurity.... Ballingdon, [c.1830]. 8vo, half cloth. With frontis. Some discoloration. b Dec 5 (364) £70

**Harte, Bret, 1836-1902**
— The Heathen Chinee.... San Francisco: John Nash, 1934. One of 300. Folio, bds. pba Nov 30 (250) $130
— A Millionaire of Rough-and-Ready. Kentfield, Calif., 1955. One of 220. Bds. pba Nov 30 (10) $110
— The Queen of the Pirate Isle. L, [1886]. Illus by Kate Greenaway. 8vo orig pictorial cloth. sg Feb 8 (294) $120
  Anr Ed. Bost. & NY, 1887 [1886]. 8vo, pictorial cloth; rubbed. sg Sept 21 (209) $200
— Works. L, 1882. 5 vols. 8vo, contemp half mor gilt. sg Sept 21 (23) $200
  Standard Library Ed. Bost. & NY, [c.1906]. 20 vols. 8vo, half mor gilt. Library stamp on bottom edges. cb Oct 17 (274) $650

**Harting, James Edmund, 1841-1928**
— Hints on Shore Shooting. L, 1871. 8vo, orig cloth. With frontis & errata slip. b Sept 20 (469) £70
  Anr copy. With frontis. S Mar 29 (789) £200

**Hartley, Cecil B.**
— Life and Times of Colonel Daniel Boone.... Phila., 1859. Orig cloth; rubbed, recased. pba June 13 (253) $100

**Hartley, Marsden**
— Twenty-Five Poems. Paris: Contact, [1923]. Ltd Ed. Orig wraps. Std on tp. sg June 20 (151) $650

**Hartnoll, Phyllis.** See: Golden Cockerel Press

**Hartshorne, Albert**
— Hanging in Chains. L, 1891. Vellum. Inscr on front free endpaper. pba Apr 4 (420) $120

**Hartt, Frederick**
— Michelangelo. NY, [1960s]. 3 vols. Folio, cloth, in djs. sg June 13 (256) $150

**Hartung, Hans**
— Hans Hartung: Oeuvres de 1920 a 1939. [Paris, 1960-61]. 2 vols. 4to, pictorial wraps. sg Sept 7 (176) $100

**Hartzenbusch, Juan Eugenio, 1806-80.** See: Gregynog Press

**Harvard University**
— The Canadian Collection at Harvard University. Bulletins I-V. Cambr. MA, 1944-48. Compiled by William Inglis Morse. 5 vols. Inscr in 2 vols. O Mar 26 (178) $60
— The Houghton Library, 1942-1967. Cambr. MA, 1967. Folio, cloth, in dj; some wear. O May 7 (162) $60
— Kress Library of Business and Economics. Catalogue. Bost., [1940]-67. Vols II-III & Supplement. Smoke-stained. Jenkins copy. ds July 27 (74) $100
— WALSH, JAMES E. - A Catalogue of Fifteenth-Century Printed Books. Binghamton, 1991. Vol I only. 8vo, orig cloth. sg Apr 11 (153) $100

### Harvey, George B.
— How Science Won the Game. NY, 1886. 4to, cloth; rubbed. In: The Boy's Book of Sports. sg Mar 7 (395) $60

### Harvey, William, 1578-1657
— The Anatomical Exercises.... L, 1653. 1st Ed in English. 8vo, modern mor. Minor worming at front; lower outer portions of some leaves stained; a few leaves shaved or cut close. Honeyman - Hefner copy. CNY May 17 (22) $13,000

Anr Ed. L, 1673. 3 parts in 1 vol. 12mo, 19th-cent russia gilt; later endpapers, rebacked with earlier spine strip laid on. Some staining; pages trimmed. pba Nov 30 (173) $2,500

— Exercitatio anatomica de motu cordis et sanguinis in animalibus. Rotterdam, 1660. ("Exercitationes anatomicae de motu cordis et sanguinis circulatione.") 2 parts in 1 vol. 12mo, contemp calf; worn. b Sept 20 (129) £450

— Exercitationes anatomica de motu cordis et sanguinis circulatione. Rotterdam, 1660. Bound with: Jacobus De Back, Dissertatio de corde. 2 works in 1 vol. 12mo, 19th-cent mor; worn. With additional title & 2 plates. Title darkened, chipped, & split along gutter; 6 leaves loose; some chips & dampstains in fore-margins. CE Nov 8 (104) $260

— Exercitationes de generatione animalium. Amst.: Elzevir, 1651. 12mo, contemp calf; def. With engraved title. Sold w.a.f. CE Nov 8 (102) $150

Anr Ed. Amst.: Jansson, 1651. 12mo, contemp half vellum; edges rubbed. Stained. CE Nov 8 (103) $220

Anr copy. Contemp sheep; worn, rebacked, new endpapers. Lacking blank before title; text browned; frontis def & restored at inner edge; tp holed in inner margin. S Mar 29 (699) £1,300

— Observations et historiae omnes.... Amst., 1674. 12mo, 18th-cent half vellum; rubbed. With engraved title & 8 plates. Lacking 1 blank. S June 12 (261) £280

— Opera. [L], 1766. 4to, contemp calf; rubbed, rebacked. Prelims foxed; pencil marginalia. sg May 16 (424) $800

### Harwell, Richard
— Confederate Hundred: a Bibliophilic Selection of Confederate Books. [Urbana], 1964. O Dec 5 (55) $100

### Haselbach, Thomas de. See: Ebendorfer, Thomas

### Haskell, Daniel Carl
See also: Stokes & Haskell
— Manhattan Maps -- A Cooperative List. NY, 1930. Orig wraps. In: Bulletin of The New York Public Library, Vol 34, Nos 4, 5, 7-10. sg May 9 (25) $130

### Haskell, Grace R. See: Latimore & Haskell

### Haskins, Charles Waldo, 1852-1908
— The Argonauts of California, being the Reminiscences of Scenes and Incidents that Occurred in California in Early Mining Days. NY, 1890. 1st Ed. 8vo, orig cloth; front & rear joints cracking, front hinge repaired. Larson copy. pba Sept 28 (516) $375

Anr copy. Cloth; soiled, extremities worn, hinge cracked, removed spine label & bookplates. pba Nov 16 (125) $140

### Hassal, Mary
— Secret History; or The Horrors of St. Domingo.... Phila., 1808. 12mo, contemp sheep; worn. Browned & dampstained; owners' stamps. sg Mar 28 (114) $150

### Hassall, William Owen
— The Holkham Bible Picture Book. L, 1954. One of 100 specially bound. Folio, mor. bba May 9 (87) £200 [Cox]

### Hasse, Johann Adolph
— Solos for German Flute or Violin... Opera Seconda ... Quinta.... [N.p.: Walsh, n.d.]. Bound with: Sammartini, Giuseppe. Six Solos... Opera Seconda ... Quarta..... And: Vinci, Leonardo. Twelve Solos. Size not given. S May 15 (351) £780

### Hassell, John
— Aqua Pictura Illustrated by a Series of Original Specimens.... L, [plates dated 1818]. Oblong folio, contemp mor gilt; joints repaired. With 19 plates, each in 4 states. b June 28 (32) £1,600

— Tour of the Grand Junction. L, 1819. 8vo, modern half cloth. With 24 hand-colored plates. b Sept 20 (310) £280

### Hasselquist, Frederik, 1722-52
— Reise nach Palaestina in den Jahren von 1749 bis 1752.... Rostock: Johann Christian Koppe, 1762. 8vo, modern wraps; a few gatherings sprung. Opening leaves dog-eared. sg Mar 7 (99) $90

— Voyages and Travels in the Levant.... L, 1766. 1st English Ed. 8vo, contemp calf; rebacked. With half title & folding map. Browned, some worming at fore-margins affecting letters. S Oct 26 (55) £260 [Chelsea Rare]

### Hasted, Edward, 1732-1812
— The History and Topographical Survey of the County of Kent. Canterbury, 1778-99. 1st Ed. 4 vols. Folio, contemp half calf; upper cover of Vol II detached. With 60 plates & plans & 37 (of 38) maps, most of them folding. b May 30 (107) £850

Anr copy. Modern cloth. With 100 (of 101) plates, 1 hand-colored in outline. bba Nov 1 (125) £650 [Swift]

1st Eds. 4 vols. Folio, modern calf by Caterbury Bookbinders. With hand-colored folding map, title arms, 95 maps, & 66 text vignettes. 2 maps cut loose; vol II prelims torn & repaired. S Oct 26 (395) £1,150 [Black]

### Hasting, Susannah Willard Johnson
— A Narrative of the Captivity of.... Windsor VT, 1807. 2d Ed. 12mo, lea; rubbed & chipped at head of spine, front hinge broken. Some staining. Z Apr 19 (389) $200

**Hastings, Lansford Warren**
— The Emigrant's Guide to Oregon and California.... Princeton, 1932. Facsimile of 1845 Ed. Orig cloth. With frontis port. Larson copy. pba Sept 28 (621) $110

**Hatch, Benton L.**
— A Check List of the Publications of Thomas Bird Mosher 1891-1923. Northampton, Mass.: Gehenna Press, 1966. One of 500. 4to, orig half cloth. pba June 20 (167) $160

**Hatton, Anne**
— Poetic Trifles by Ann of Swansea. Waterford, 1811. 12mo, orig bds. b Dec 5 (602) £170

**Hatzfeld, Adolf von**
— Sommer. Duesseldorf, 1920. One of 35. Illus by Marie Laurencin. Folio, loose as issued in folder; With 4 lithos. S Nov 21 (209) £500

**Hauch, Adam Wilhelm von**
— Det physiske Cabinet..... Copenhagen, 1836-38. 2 vols in 1. 4to, later half calf. With 64 plates. S Mar 14 (163) £440

**Haudicquer de Blancourt, Francois**
— The Art of Glass.... L, 1699. 8vo, contemp calf; joints cracked, spine ends chipped. With 9 plates. Some worming to lower margin. Ck Sept 8 (36) £700

**Hauksbee, Francis, d.1713?**
— Physico-Mechanical Experiments on Various Subjects.... L, 1709. 4to, contemp goatskin gilt; joints & extremities rubbed, spine chipped at head. With 8 plates. Small holes to Plate 2; lacking 1st & last blanks as usual; 5 plates with short tears at mounts; minor spotting. Hefner copy. CNY May 17 (23) $3,800

Anr Ed. L, 1719. 8vo, contemp calf; worn. With 8 folding plates. S Mar 14 (164) £420

**Haultain, Arnold**
— The Mystery of Golf. Bost., 1908. 1st Ed, One of 440. Half cloth. pba Nov 9 (31) $1,100

**Haultain, Theodore Arnold**
— The Mystery of Golf. Bost. & NY, 1908. 1st Ed, One of 440. Half cloth; spine ends & corners rubbed. Soiled. pba Apr 18 (77) $1,400

2d Ed. NY, 1914. Cloth; spine rubbed, front cover discolored. pba Apr 18 (78) $130

Anr Ed. NY: Serendipity Press, 1965. Foreword by Herbert Warren Wind. Half cloth. pba Apr 18 (79) $110

**Hauptmann, Gerhart, 1862-1946**
— Das Meerwunder. Frankfurt, [1969]. One of 125 in Series B. Illus by Paul Delvaux. 4to, Half vellum. sg Sept 7 (126) $350

— Die Weber. Frankfurt: Erich Steinthal, [1917]. One of 200. Illus by Kaethe Kollwitz. Orig ptd wraps, with tattered remains of dj. With 9 heliogravures

with additional hand-finishing (including cover, tp vignette & tailpiece). cb Oct 17 (649) $425

**Haven, Charles T. —&**
**Belden, Frank A.**
— A History of the Colt Revolver.... NY, 1940. 1st Ed. O Feb 6 (121) $50

Anr copy. In dj with tears & chips. pba Nov 16 (126) $95

**Hawaii**
— Na Haiao i Kakauia e na Misionari ma Hawaii nei. Honolulu, 1841. 12mo, half lea; worn. Z Jan 30 (315) $275

**Hawes, William Post**
— Sporting Scenes and Sundry Sketches. NY, 1842. 1st Ed. - Ed by Frank Forester. 2 vols. 12mo orig cloth; worn. Some foxing. O Feb 6 (122) $150

**Hawk, Dave**
— Eighty Years on Bass. Corpus Christi, [1958]. Pictorial wraps. O Feb 6 (123) $50

**Hawker, Peter, 1786-1853**
— Instructions to Young Sportsmen.... L, 1824. 3d Ed. 8vo, half lea; worn, front hinge starting, newer endpapers. With 10 plates, 4 hand-colored. O June 4 (157) $240

Anr copy. 8vo recent cloth. Z June 14 (365) $180

1st American Ed. Phila., 1846. 8vo, modern cloth. Foxed. sg Mar 7 (467) $150

Anr Ed. Phila., 1853. 8vo, 19th-cent half lea gilt. With 10 plates. Browned. sg Mar 7 (468) $150

**Hawker, Robert Stephen, 1803-75**
— Poems. Stratton, 1836. 8vo, canvas wraps; rebound. b Dec 5 (58) £360

— The Quest of the Sangraal. Chant the First [all written]. Exeter, 1864. 4to, contemp half mor; worn. ALs tipped onto stub at beginning. Lionel Johnson's copy with 4-line Latin prayer & Ms of his poem Hawker of Morwenstow on verso of 1st blank, sgd & dated 1895. S Dec 18 (191) £1,000 [Edwards]

**Hawkesworth, John, 1715?-73.** See: Adventurer...; Cook, Capt. James

**Hawkins, Sir Anthony Hope, 1863-1933**
See also: Limited Editions Club
— The Dolly Dialogues. L, 1894. 20th thousand. Illus by Arthur Rackham. 8vo, orig wraps with remains of calf bdg on spine. Ck May 31 (100) £150

— The Prisoner of Zenda. Bristol, [1894]. 2d Issue. 8vo, orig cloth; bdg askew. sg Sept 21 (227) $80

**Hawkins, Henry, 1571?-1646**
— Partheneia Sacra, or the Mysterious and Delicious Garden of the Sacred Parthenes. [Rouen]: John Cousturier, 1633. 1st Ed. 4to, modern mor gilt. Tiny hole in margin of S3; some soiling & dampstaining in margins at beginning. S Dec 18 (104) £1,200 [Edwards]

# HAWKINS

**Hawkins, J. B.**
— The Al Tajir Collection of Silver and Gold. L, 1983. One of 200. In dj. W Nov 8 (198) £560
 Out-of-series copy. In dj. bba Apr 11 (82) £450 [Greenbalgh]

**Hawkins, Sir John, 1719-89**
— A General History of the Science and Practice of Music. L, 1776. 1st Ed. 5 vols. 4to, half calf; Vol V rebacked, others worn with spines detaching. S May 15 (377) £450

**Hawkins, William G.**
— Lunsford Lane, or Another Helper from the North. Bost., 1864. 8vo, cloth; extremities rubbed. sg Mar 28 (332) $250

**Hawksmoor, Nicholas**
— A Short Historical Account of London-Bridge; with a Proposition for a New Stone-Bridge at Wetsminster. L, 1736. 3 vols. 4to, contemp calf; rubbed. With 2 plates. Some spotting & browning. bba Sept 7 (246) £480 [Bilteliffe]

**Hawthorne, Nathaniel, 1804-64**
See also: Graham's...; Limited Editions Club
— The Celestial Rail-Road. Bost.: Wilder & Co., 1843. 32mo, orig wraps; soiled, frayed, sewn by an amateur hand. Some staining & soiling; pp 17-22 def at bottom. wa Feb 29 (49) $150
— Doctor Grimshawe's Secret. Bost., 1883. 8vo, mor gilt by The Club Bindery. Hoe copy. bbc June 24 (622) $200
 Anr copy. Pictorial cloth; worn & soiled, cocked, cloth rippled. wa Feb 29 (41) $50
— Fanshawe, a Tale. Bost., 1828. 1st Ed. 8vo, orig half cloth; tear in spine, some wear, shaken. Chrysler - Engelhard copy. CNY Oct 27 (62) $18,000
— The Gentle Boy.... Bost., 1839. Oblong 4to, orig wraps; sewn. Some foxing. sg Sept 21 (217) $1,700
— Grandfather's Chair.... Bost., 1841. 1st Ed. 12mo, orig cloth, in worn & frayed dj. Some foxing & staining. wa Feb 29 (42) $60
— The House of the Seven Gables. Bost., 1851. 1st Ed. 8vo, cloth, bdg B; bdg skewed, bookplate & remnants of anr on front patedown. sg Feb 8 (300) $400
 Anr copy. Orig cloth, bdg A; spine ends & corners chipped. wa Feb 29 (50) $160
— The Marble Faun. Bost., 1860. 1st American Ed. 2 vols. 12mo, orig cloth. b Jan 31 (93) £100
 1st Issue. Orig cloth; spine ends chipped, corners rubbed, residue to front pastedowns from removed bookplates. pba Aug 22 (592) $95
— Mosses from an Old Manse. NY, 1846. 1st Ed, Mixed Issue. 2 parts in 1 vol. 12mo, orig cloth; edges worn. wa Feb 29 (43) $120
— Our Old Home: a Series of English Sketches. Bost., 1863. 1st Ed. 12mo, orig cloth; minor wear. wa Feb 29 (44) $65
 Anr copy. Orig cloth; spine ends defyed. Foxed. wa Feb 29 (45) $50

## AMERICAN BOOK PRICES CURRENT

— The Scarlet Letter.... Bost., 1850. 1st Ed, 1st Issue. 8vo, later mor gilt with onlaid mor A. CE May 22 (253) $1,100
 Anr copy. Orig brown cloth. Minor wear, sides slightly marked. Engelhard copy. CNY Oct 27 (63) $8,000
 Anr copy. Orig cloth; corners worn, spine ends frayed. wa Feb 29 (51) $1,700
 Issue not stated. Mor extra with inlaid mor A; minor rubbing. Clipped signature mtd to inserted blank. O Mar 5 (109) $1,200
 Anr copy. Orig cloth; spine ends chipped, corners rubbed, recased but front hinge recracked & front ads detached. pba Dec 14 (73) $700
 2d Ed, 1st ptg. 8vo, orig cloth; spine ends chipped. sg Sept 21 (218) $225
 Anr Ed. Bost., 1892. In dj. pba Dec 14 (74) $140
— Septimius Felton; or, the Elixir of Life. Bost., 1872. 1st American Ed. 8vo, orig cloth. wa Feb 29 (47) $50
— Tanglewood Tales.... L, [1918]. One of 500. Illus by Edmund Dulac. 4to, orig half vellum gilt. sg Oct 19 (81) $700
— Twice-Told Tales. Bost., 1837. 1st Ed. 12mo, orig cloth; worn, cocked, rear joint frayed, spine ends repaired. Some foxing. wa Feb 29 (54) $900
— A Wonder-Book for Girls and Boys. Bost., 1852. 1st Ed. 8vo, orig cloth, 1st bdg; worn. Some spotting. wa Feb 29 (40) $325
 Anr Ed. L, 1922. Illus by Arthur Rackham. In dj. sg Sept 14 (304) $200
 One of 600. Ck May 31 (155) £550; S Nov 2 (109) £580 [Squire]
 Anr copy. 4to, orig cloth. With 16 colored plates. sg Oct 19 (201) $650
— Works. Bost., [1882-84]. Standard Library Ed. 15 vols. 8vo, half mor; joints rubbed. pba Sept 14 (193) $425
 Riverside Ed. Bost., 1890. 13 vols. 8vo, half calf. pba Aug 22 (554) $425
 Anr Ed. Bost., 1897-98. 13 vols. 8vo, contemp half calf gilt. sg Sept 21 (24) $650
 Autograph Ed. Bost., 1900-2. one of 500. 22 vols plus G. E. Woodberry's biography. 12mo, half mor. cb Oct 17 (275) $1,600
— The Young Provincial. Bost., 1830. 16mo, orig cloth; tips worn. In: The Token; a Christmas and New Year's Present. sg Feb 8 (302) $250

**Hawtree, Fred**
— Colt & Co., Golf Course Architects.... Oxford: Cambuc Archive, [1991]. 1st Ed, One of 1,000. Foreword by Sir Denis Thatcher. In dj. Sgd. pba Apr 18 (81) $75

**Hay, John Milton, 1838-1905**
See also: Nicolay & Hay
— Jim Bludsoe of the Prairie Belle.... Bost., 1871. 12mo, ptd wraps; stitching loose, 2 small stains. sg Feb 8 (303) $60

**Hay, William, 1789-1859**
— A Review of the Causes and Consequences of the Mexican War. Bost., 1849. With: Speech of Mr. Truman Smith of Connecticut... Wash., 1848 1st Ed. 8vo, calf. Inscr to Augusta Jay "from her Affectionate Father". Larson copy. pba Sept 28 (538) $180

**Hayashi Collection, Tadamasa**
— [Sale Catalogue] Collection Hayashi. Paris, 1902-3. 2 vols. 4to, pictorial wraps; worn, backstrips reinforced with cloth tape. Some leaves loose. sg Sept 7 (29) $275

**Hayden, Arthur**
— Old English Porcelain. The Lady Ludlow Collection. L, 1932. One of 100. Folio mor; spine cracked, hinges worn. wd Nov 15 (69) $275
— Spode and his Successors. L, 1925. In frayed & soiled dj. wa Dec 14 (569) $85

**Hayden, Ferdinand V., 1829-87**
— Geological and Geographical Atlas of Colorado. NY, 1877. Folio, orig cloth. With litho title & 20 double-page litho plates, 10 of them colored. Final plate foxed; waterstaining at foot. b Dec 5 (122) £260

**Haydn, Franz Joseph, 1732-1809**
— Cantata per un soprano con accompagnamento. Vienna: Artaria, [1782]. 4to, later half vellum. Full score only, without separate instrumental parts; some foxing; library markings. S May 15 (380) £550
— Eco per quatro voilini e due violoncelli.... Naples: Luigi Marescalchi, [c.1793]. Folio, unbound. Complete parts. C June 26 (261) £520
— Gioco Filarmonico o sia maniera facile per comporre un infinito numera di inuetti.... Naples: Luigi Marescalchi, [before 1790]. Folio, sewn. C June 26 (260) £450

**Hayes, Charles, 1772-1826**
— Portraits of British Birds. L, [watermarked 1808-21]. 4to in 6's, early half mor gilt by H. Brockmann of Hannover; minor discoloration to spine. With 144 orig watercolor drawings. Without tp. Ernst August I, King of Hannover's copy. Fattorini copy. C Oct 25 (17) £40,000

**Hayes, Charles W.**
— Galveston: History of the Island and the City. Austin, 1974. 2 vols. Reprint of 1879 Ed. pba Apr 25 (448) $75

**Hayes, Isaac Israel, 1832-81**
— The Open Polar Sea.... NY & Cambr. MA, 1867. 8vo, half calf. Inscr. pba July 25 (402) $225

**Hayes, James Gordon**
— Antarctica; A Treatise on the Southern Continent. L, 1928. Orig cloth; rubbed. pba July 25 (37) $130

**Hayes, John**
— The Drawings of Thomas Gainsborough. L, 1970. 2 vols. 4to, orig cloth, in djs. bba Oct 19 (89) £80 [Breckenridge]

**Hayes, Matthew Horace**
— Points of the Horse. L, 1904. 3d Ed. 4to, cloth. Foxing at ends. pba Mar 7 (139) $85

**Hayes, William, fl.1794**
— The Portraits of British and Exotic Birds.... L, 1778. Folio, contemp half russia; worn. With engraved dedication & 60 hand-colored plates only, 15 of them with Ms titles dated 1773 & sgd by Hayes. 4 plates shaved; small tears to dedication; 1 plate shaved with loss to landscape, anr with partial loss of title & signature. C May 31 (23) £6,200

**Hayley, William, 1745-1820**
— The Life of George Romney. Chichester, 1809. 4to, 19th-cent half mor gilt; worn. Tp & some margins soiled. CE Sept 27 (138) $50
— The Triumph of Music.... Chichester, 1804. 4to, modern half calf. b Dec 5 (382) £80
— The Triumphs of Temper. Chichester, 1803. 12th Ed. - Illus by William Blake after Maria Flaxman. 8vo, cloth; front bds bowed, soiled. wa Feb 1 (307) $60

**Hayn, Hugo, 1843-1923 —&**
**Gotendorf, Alfred N.**
— Bibliotheca Germanorum erotica & curiosa.... Hanau, 1968. 9 vols. 8vo, half sheep; extremities worn. sg Apr 11 (127) $275

**Hayward, Sir John, 1564?-1627**
— The Life and Raigne of King Edward the Sixt. L, 1636. 2d Ed. 12mo, contemp calf; joints & corners rubbed. CE June 12 (210) $280

**Hazard, Samuel, 1784-1870**
— Santo Domingo, Past and Present.... NY, 1873. 1st Ed. 12mo, pictorial cloth; spine ends worn. sg Mar 28 (115) $140

**Hazart, Cornelius, 1617-90**
— Kirchen-Geschichte, das ist: Catholisches Christenthum.... Vienna: Leopold Voigt, 1678. Folio, later vellum over bds; rebacked, minor wear. Some foxing. NH June 1 (250) $350

**Hazelton, William C.**
— Wildfowling Tales from the Great Ducking Resorts of the Continent. Chicago, 1921. O June 25 (156) $225

**Hazlitt, William Carew, 1834-1913**
— Shakespeare Jest Books. L, 1864. Edges rubbed, hinges cracked. Half calf. Z June 28 (251) $200

**Headlam, Cecil**
— Calendar of State papers, Colonial Series, America and West Indies, 1699-1703 L, 1908-13. 5 vols. Orig cloth; some dampstaining. bba July 18 (256) £65 [Neale]
— Ten Thousand Miles Through India & Burma. L, 1903. Foxed; 1 leaf torn without loss. pn Oct 12 (304) £130

**Headsman...** See: Cooper, James Fenimore

**Heal, Sir Ambrose**
— The London Furniture Makers.... L, 1953. 4to, orig cloth, in dj. sg June 13 (155) $80

**Healy, Michael A.**
— Report of the Cruise of the...Corwin in the Arctic Ocean. Wash., 1887. 1 (of 2) vols. 4to, orig sheep; worn. With 38 wood-engraved plates, 4 color litho plates & 2 folding charts. Frontis detached; stub tear to 1 map. pba July 25 (155) $110

**Heaney, Howell J.**
— Thirty Years of Bird & Bull. A Bibliography, 1958-1988. Newtown, 1988. One of 300 with folder of specimen leaves. 4to, half mor. sg Sept 14 (63) $425; sg Feb 15 (48) $375

**Heaney, Seamus**
See also: Limited Editions Club
— After Summer. Old Deerfield & Dublin: Deerfield Press & Gallery Press, [1978]. One of 250. In dj. pba Jan 25 (128) $180
— Death of a Naturalist. L, [1966]. In dj. Sgd on tp. pba Aug 22 (211) $425
— The Haw Lantern. NY, 1987. One of 15 sgd "Artist's copy 5/15. Seamus Heaney". Illus by Barrie Cooke. 4to, orig cloth. S Dec 18 (392) £220 [Kunkler]
— Preoccupations. L, 1980. Proof copy. Ptd wraps. Sgd on tp. sg Dec 14 (120) $175

**Heap, D. P.** See: Barlow & Heap

**Heap, Gwinn Harris, 1817-87**
— Central Route to the Pacific.... Phila., 1854. 8vo, orig cloth; corners bumped & chipped. With folding map & 13 plates. Map mtd to back bd & split into 2 pieces. Met May 22 (346) $600

**Hearn, Lafcadio, 1850-1904**
See also: Limited Editions Club
— Chita; a Memory of Last Island. NY, 1889. 8vo, orig cloth; skewed. sg Dec 14 (124) $400
— Complete Lectures. Tokyo: Hokuseido, 1932-34. 4 vols. In djs. wa Nov 16 (92) $120
— Exotics and Retrospectives. Bost., 1898. sg Dec 14 (129) $175
— Gleanings in Buddha Fields. Bost., 1897. Orig cloth; spine rubbed, front hinge cracked. sg Dec 14 (128) $200
— Glimpses of Unfamiliar Japan. Bost., 1894. 1st Ed. 2 vols. 8vo, cloth; lacking blank following endpaper in Vol II. sg Dec 14 (126) $275
— In Ghostly Japan. Bost., 1899. 8vo, cloth; rubbed. sg Dec 14 (130) $175
— Japan: An Attempt at Interpretation. NY, 1904. Orig cloth; spine ends worn. pba Aug 22 (212) $60; sg Dec 14 (134) $175
— Japanese Fairy Tales. Tokyo, [1905]. 5 vols. Wraps. Ptd in color by hand from Japanese wood blocks. Met Dec 5 (218) $850
— Japanese Goblin Poetry... Tokyo: Oyama, 1934. one of 500. Trans into English & illus by Hearn. Compiled by Kazuo Koizumi. Folio, ptd cloth. English & Japanese text on facing pages. Met May 22 (11) $280
— A Japanese Miscellany. Bost., 1901. 1st Ed, State not indicated. Cloth. sg Dec 14 (132) $225
— Kokoro. Hints and Echoes of Japanese Inner Life. Bost.: Houghton Mifflin, [1896]. 8vo, orig cloth; corners rubbed. sg Dec 14 (127) $175
— Kotto. NY & L, 1902. 1st Ed, 1st Issue. Cloth. sg Dec 14 (133) $225
— Kwaidan. Bost., 1904. Orig cloth. sg Dec 14 (135) $175
— Letters to a Pagan. Detroit, 1933. One of 550. Half cloth, in dj. sg Dec 14 (140) $225
— The Romance of the Milky Way.... Bost. & NY, 1905. 1st Ed. Cloth; extremities abraded. sg Dec 14 (136) $140
— Shadowings. Bost., 1900. 12mo, cloth. sg Dec 14 (131) $225
— Some Chinese Ghosts. Bost., 1887. 1st Ed. 12mo, orig cloth, in dj with spine ends chipped. pba May 23 (154) $100
Anr copy. Orig cloth. sg Sept 21 (220) $175; sg Sept 21 (220) $175
Anr copy. Orig cloth; rubbed. sg Dec 14 (123) $300
— Some New Letters and Writings. Tokyo, 1925. 1st Ed. - Ed by Sanki Ichikawa. Cloth; discolored. 2 copies of the errata slip inserted at rear. sg Dec 14 (138) $225
— Stray Leaves from Strange Literature. Bost., 1884. 1st Ed. 8vo, cloth. Dampstain to upper right margin, not affecting text. sg Dec 14 (121) $400
— Two Years in the French West Indies. NY, 1890. 1st Ed. 12mo, cloth. pba Aug 22 (213) $100
Anr copy. Orig cloth; rubbed. sg Dec 14 (125) $225
— Works. Bost. & NY, 1922. One of 750. 16 vols. Half cloth. pba June 20 (193) $800

**Hearne, Samuel, 1745-92**
— A Journey from Prince of Wales's Fort in Hudson's Bay to the Northern Ocean.... L, 1795. 1st Ed. 4to, old half calf. With 9 folding plates & maps;, 1 with route outlined in color. Some foxing throughout. Met Sept 28 (354) $550

**Heartman, Charles F.**
— The Cradle of the United States, 1765-1789.... Metuchen NJ, 1922-23. One of 100. 2 vols. 4to, orig bds. Lathrop Harper's copy. Ck Apr 12 (238) £85

**Heath, Charles, 1785-1848.** See: Pugin & Heath

**Hebard, Grace Raymond**
— Sacajawea: a Guide and Interpreter of the Lewis and Clark Expedition. Glendale, Calif., 1933. Orig cloth. Robbins copy. pba Mar 21 (146) $350
— Washakie: An Account of Indian Resistance of the Covered Wagon.... Cleveland, 1930. 1st Ed. Orig cloth. Robbins copy. pba Mar 21 (147) $325

**Hebard, Grace Raymond —&
Brininstool, Earl Alonzo**
— The Bozeman Trail. Cleveland, 1922. 2 vols, orig cloth. Robbins copy. pba Mar 21 (145) $375

Anr Ed. Glendale: Arthur H. Clark, 1960. 2 vols. Reprint of 1922 Ed. pba Nov 16 (127) $65

**Heberden, William, 1710-1801**
— Commentaries on the History and Cure of Diseases. L, 1802. 1st English Ed. 8vo, modern half calf. Title creased; outer margin with wormholes; lightly damp-stained. Ck Mar 22 (145) £180

**Hebrew Books**
— The Barcelona Haggadah. [L, 1992]. One of 500. 2 vols. 4to, mor in slipcase. sg Apr 11 (214) $950
— Haggadah. Prague: Gershom Cohen, 1526. ("[The Prague Haggadah.]") Folio, mor by Sangorski & Sutcliffe. Woodcuts, borders & initials all hand-colored.F Marginal worming at beginning & end, affecting vignettes; some soiling. Yaari 6. Schaefer copy. P Nov 1 (110) $250,000

Anr Ed. Amst., 1765. 4to, later half lea. Some fraying, chipping, soiling & staining. Yaari 155. CE Dec 6 (81) $900

Anr Ed. Amst., 1781. 4to, contemp calf gilt; spine repaired, worn, endpapers renewed. With double-page folding map mtd on flyleaf. Lacking engraved title; map repaired. Yaari 199. CE Dec 6 (82) $1,200

Anr Ed. Vienna, 1813. 4to, contemp calf; rebacked, corners renewed, new endpapers. Browned & stained; some corners chipped or repaired; lacking plates & maps. CE Dec 6 (206) $1,100

Anr Ed. L: Beaconsfield Press, [1939]. One of 125, ptd on vellum. Illuminated by Arthur Szyk; ed by Cecil Roth. 4to, orig mor gilt extra by Sangorski & Sutcliffe. P June 5 (241) $6,000

Anr Ed. Jerusalem, 1956. Ed by Cecil Roth; illus by Arthur Szyk. 4to, orig velvet gilt. wa Nov 16 (373) $140

Anr Ed. Tel Aviv, 1962. Illuminated by Arthur Szyk; ed by Cecil Roth. 4to, orig velvet gilt. wa Dec 14 (583) $70

Anr Ed. NY, 1974. ("A Passover Haggadah.") One of 500. Illus by Leonard Baskin. Folio, orig half lea. With orig sgd litho laid in. cb Oct 17 (599) $300; cb Feb 14 (2740) $300; cb June 25 (1919) $300

— Machzor Sfaradim Mi'Yamim Noraim. Amst.: Uri Fayvesh Ha-levi, 1679. 8vo, contemp mor gilt, with arms of the de Pinto family; spine ends & corners worn, lacking 1 clasp. Leaf 9/1 torn along gutter margin, affecting text; some soiling & staining. St. 7490. CE Dec 6 (108) $500

— Minhagim. Frankfurt, 1729. 8vo, contemp half calf; worn. Some staining & browning. CE Dec 6 (160) $1,400

Anr Ed. Amst., 1775. 8vo, later half mor; upper cover detached. Browning & staining throughout. CE Dec 6 (161) $1,800

Anr copy. Contemp half lea; some wear to edges, lower cover broken. Browning & staining throughout; leaf 38 with burn-hole, affecting 2 letters. CE Dec 6 (162) $1,600

— Minhagim. Birkat ha-Mazon. Amst.: Isaac de Cordova, 1723. Bound with: Sefer Minhagim. Amst., 1723. 4to, half sheep; worn & tape-repaired. Tp patched at lower gutter margin affecting border & letters; a few leaves loose; margins trimmed affecting running titles; marginal flaws & repairs with minor loss. CE Dec 6 (159) $2,200

— Mishnayot. Amst., 1697. 12mo, contemp calf with metal fittings; lacking 1 cornerpiece & 1 clasp, spine def. Some leaves loose. CE Dec 6 (163) $320

— The Rothschild Miscellany. L, 1989. One of 500. 2 vols. 4to, mor in slipcases. sg Apr 11 (226) $3,200

— Secer tefillot le'chodashim u-le-mo'adim. Amst.: Abraham ben Rafael Hezekiah Athias, 1740. 4 vols. 32mo, contemp mor gilt; extremities worn. Upper fore-corner cut from each tp, affecting text; some browning. CE Dec 6 (134) $950

— Seder Arba Ta'aniot. Amst.: Menasseh ben Israel, 1644. 8vo, contemp calf gilt; spine ends & corners worn. Tp border shaved. St. 2140. CE Dec 6 (104) $320

Anr Ed. Amst.: Joseph Athias, 1689. 8vo, contemp calf with 2 catches; spine ends def, hinges cracked. Some staining & browning. CE Dec 6 (114) $130

— Seder Berachot-Orden de las Bendiciones. Amst.: Albertus Magnus, 1687. 12mo, contemp sharkskin with 1 remaining brass clasp; minor wear. Lacking front blank prelims; frontis obscured along gutter margin; rear gathering loose; spotting & staining. In Hebrew & Spanish. CE Dec 6 (113) $3,800

Anr copy. Modern lea. Worming on tp & engraved title tape-repaired; some other worming. In Hebrew & Spanish. CE Dec 6 (212) $800

— Seder Berakhot. Amst.: Albertus Magnus, 1687. 12mo, contemp sharkskin over wooden bds; worn. Some staining. CE Dec 6 (111) $1,700

Anr copy. Contemp sharkskin over wooden bds; spine ends def, endpapers wormed. Some foxing. CE Dec 6 (112) $1,800

— Seder Chamicha Ta-Aniot. Amst.: Joseph Athias, 1659. 16mo, 18th-cent mor gilt; lower hinge cracked. Some staining & browning. St. 2154. CE Dec 6 (106) $110

— Seder Leshalosh Regalim Ke'Minhag Carpentras. Amst., 1759. 8vo, contemp sheep; worn. Some running heads shaved; stained & browned. CE Dec 6 (135) $480

— Seder tefillot keminhag Askhenaz u-Folin. Hanau: Hans Jacob Hanau, 1628. Bound with: Zot torat ha-chatat. Hanau: Hans Jacob Hanau, 1628. 8vo, contemp vellum; head of spine worn. Tp frayed, corners frayed; some browning; fore-margins trimmed close; last 6 leaves of 2d work def. Sold w.a.f. CE Dec 6 (103) $1,300

— Seder tefillot ke-minhag k'k Sefarad. Amst.: Uri Fayvesh ben Aaron Ha-levi, 1682. Bound with: Calandario de Ros Hodes fiestas y ayunos que los Hebreos celebran cada anno (1675-1700). Amst.: Giiiles

# HEBREW

Joosten Zangman, 1675. 12mo, contemp calf; piece missing from head of spine. Calendario trimmed, affecting text. CE Dec 6 (109) $1,000
— Seder Tefilot Mikol Hashanah.... Amst., 1766. 16mo, contemp mor gilt peackck bdg; rubbed. Some staining & browning. CE Dec 6 (138) $1,200 Anr Ed. Amst., 1780. 32mo, late 18th-cent mor gilt; spine ends worn, upper hinge cracked. Some browning; a few leaves partially detached; fraying affecting some catchwords. CE Dec 6 (141) $1,200
— Seder Tefilot Mikol Hashanah Keminhag Ashkenaz. Amst: Jochanan Levi Rofe & his son Benjamin, [1797?]. 32mo, late 18th-cent mor gilt; spine worn & chipped, corners worn, hinges cracked. Stained & browned throughout. CE Dec 6 (143) $1,300
— Sefer Lev Tov. Livorno: Anton Santini for Isaac de Moses di Paz, 1753. With Spanish trans by Isaac Nieto. 8vo, modern lea. Some staining. CE Dec 6 (222) $500
— Sefer Raziel. Amst.: Moses ben Abraham Mendes Coutinho, 1701. 4to, later half calf; worn, rubbed. Dampstained. St. 4042. CE Dec 6 (178) $3,000
— Sefer Yetzirah. Mantua, 1562. 4to, lea. Staining & browning; lacking volvelles & unnumbered page of diagrams betweene ff. 102 & 103. CE Dec 6 (179) $1,000
— Siddur Tefillot mi-kol ha-Shanah.... Prague: Judah Bak's Sons, [1682-88]. 24mo, contemp calf; spine wormed. Minor staining. CE Dec 6 (110) $3,800
— [Talmud Babli]. The Babylonian Talmud Seder Nezikin.... L: Soncino Press, 1935-52. One of 1,000. Trans by Isidore Epstein. 51 (of 52) vols; lacking index. Mor. S July 11 (347) £400
— Tikkun keri'ah le-khol laylah va-yom. Amst.: David de Castro Tartas, 1666. 2 parts in 1 vol. 12mo, contemp vellum; front hinges cracked. Some browning & staining. St. 3035. CE Dec 6 (107) $2,000
ABRAHAM BEN MORDECHAI. - Sepher Yair Nethiv. Constantinople, 1718. Bound with: Manoach of Narbonne. Perushim ve-Chiddushim al ha-Rambam. Constantinople, 1718 4to, contemp calf; def. Minor marginal soiling. Yaari 293 & 295. CE Dec 6 (2) $240
BEN-JACOB, ISAAC. - Otzar Ha-Sepharim. Vilna, 1880. 2 vols. 8vo, half lea, orig upper wraps bound in; rubbed. O Mar 26 (24) $160
BENJAMIN BEN JONAH. - Masa'ot Shel Rabi Benjamin.... Ferrara: Samuel ibn Usque, 1556. 8vo, modern lea, old wraps bound in. Tp patched with some letters in facsimile; minor marginal worming; some staining. St. 4570.2. CE Dec 6 (9) $7,000
BONAFOS, MENACHEM BEN ABRAHAM OF PERPIGNAN. - Sefer ha-Gedarim. Salonika, 1567. 4to, later half vellum. Wormed throughout; some tracks patched. St. 6341,1. CE Dec 6 (63) $1,900
CANTARINI, ISAAC VITA HA-KOHEN. - Pachad Yitzhak. Amst.: David de Castro Tartas, 1685. 4to, later bds; rubbed, new endpapers, repaired. Patch to 1 corner; some staining & browning. CE Dec 6 (64) $1,000
CONQUE, ABRAHAM BEN LEVI. - Avak Sopherim. Amst: Nethaneal Foa, 1704. 3 parts in 1 vol. Folio, 18th-cent russia over wooden bds, with 2 brass clasps; joints & corners worn, endpapers browned. St. 4210. CE Dec 6 (65) $800

# AMERICAN BOOK PRICES CURRENT

DAVID BEN SOLOMON IBN YACHYA. - Leshon Limmudim. Constantinople: David & Samuel ibn Nachmias, 1506. 4to, later half vellum. Margins trimmed, affecting some notations & upper & inner margin of of border on opening page; some browning & staining. Sgd by censor in 1590. St. 4812,2. CE Dec 6 (89) $8,500
DUSHNIT, GEDALIAH BEN JACOB. - Safa berurah. Prague: Heirs of Moses Katz, 1704. 8vo, modern wraps. Tp frayed & repaired; margins shaved affecting letters; some browning & staining. St. 5121. CE Dec 6 (67) $900
ELIJAH BEN ASHER LEVITA. - Masoret Ha'masoret. Basel: Froben, 1539. Bound with: Tuv Ta'am. Basel, 1539. And: Sefer ha-Ta'amim. Basel, 1539. And: Reuchlin, Johannes. In septem psalmos poenitentiales hebraicos Grammatico explanatio. Tuebingen: Thomas Anselm, 1512. 8vo, 18th-cent sheep; broken, front free endpaper detached, lower endpaper loose. Tp lacking tp; some soiling, staining & marginal repairs. CE Dec 6 (101) $1,600
ELIJAH BEN ASHER LEVITA. - Pirkei Elijah. Pesaro: Girolamo Soncino, 1520. 4to, modern half vellum. Interleaved with heavy paper; tp border shaved at bottom; some soiling & staining. St. 4960,35. CE Dec 6 (100) $6,500
ELIJAH BEN ASHER LEVITA. - Tishbi. Isni: Pail Fagius, 1541. 4to, later russia; rebacked in modern mor. Staining & browning. St. 4960,46. CE Dec 6 (102) $850
EMDEN, JACOB. - Megillat Sefer Yetziv pitgam.... Altona, [1740]. 4to, later bds. Some running heads shaved; browned & stained. St. 5527,1. CE Dec 6 (70) $750
EMDEN, JACOB. - Sefat Emet Ve'lashon Zehorith. [Altona], 1752. 4to, contemp half lea; extremities worn. Some staining. CE Dec 6 (72) $2,800
FRANKFURTER, SIMEON ISRAEL BEN JUDAH. - Sefer sha'ar sime'on. Amst., 1749. 16mo, later half claf. Cut close, afecting some running heads. Zedner 256. CE Dec 6 (76) $220
GABIROL, SHLOMO IBN. - Keter Malkhut. Livorno, 1769. 8vo, modern lea. Some worming, affecting letters & tailpiece; some staining & foxing. CE Dec 6 (205) $400
GIKATILA, JOSEPH. - Sha'arei Zedek. Riva di Trento: Yakov Mercaria, 1561. Bound with: Carmoly. E. Annalen der hebraischen Typographie von Riva di Trento. Frankfurt, 1868. 4to, modern half vellum. Some soiling & staining; library stamp on tp. CE Dec 6 (79) $2,200
HANAU, SOLOMON BEN JUDAH LEIB KOHEN. - Sefer sha'arei tefillah. Amst.: Leib Soesmans, 1766. 8vo, contemp calf; spine def. Some staining & browning. CE Dec 6 (83) $220
ISAAC BEN ELIA SCHENI. - Me'ah She'arim. Saloniki: [Soncino], 1543. 4to, later calf gilt; spine ends & joints worn. Some staining & soiling. CE Dec 6 (180) $1,300
ISAAC BEN MORDECAI GERSHOM. - Shelom Esther. Constantinople, [c.1575]. 8vo, modern half vellum. Tp & anr leaf cut round & inlaid to size; tp with a few letters suppiled in Ms on verso; some staining & soiling. St. 5388. CE Dec 6 (78) $1,500

JACOB D'ILLESCAS. - Imre Noam. Cremona: Vicenzo Conti, 1565. 4to, modern half vellum. Marginal foxing & spotting. CE Dec 6 (90) $2,400

JEDAIAH BEN ABRAHAM. - Bechinat Olam. Mantua, 1556. 8vo, modern half vellum. Some dampstaining. St. 5670,5. CE Dec 6 (8) $2,100

JOSEPH SHEM TOV BEN SHEM TOV. - Kevod Elohim. Ferrara: A. Usque, 1555-56. 4to, contemp calf gilt; broken, a few leaves loose. Some staining & soiling, mostly marginal. St. 6003,1. CE Dec 6 (88) $3,800

KOPPELMAN, JACOB BEN SAMUEL. - Omek halakhah. Amst., 1710. 4to, 18th-cent half calf. Marginal repairs affecting diagram; some tears affecting text; stained & soiled; some running heads shaved; early marginalia. St. 5612. CE Dec 6 (96) $500

LEVI BEN GERSHON. - Milchamot Hashem. Riva di Trento, 1560. Folio, contemp vellum. To trimmed at foremargin; marginal chips to tp; some staining & browning. St 6138,2. CE Dec 6 (99) $1,300

LIWA YEHUDA BEN BEZALEL. - Netivot Olam. Prague, 1596. Folio, old calf; joints & spine ends worn. Tp margin & a few other leaves patched; erased stamp on tp; some repairs, stains & burnholes, affecting a few letters. St. 6153,13, col 1622. CE Dec 6 (92) $1,900

LIWA YEHUDA BEN BEZALEL. - Netsach Yisrael. Prague, 1599. Folio, modern mor gilt. Some staining & browning. St. 6153,11. CE Dec 6 (93) $1,500

LIWA YEHUDA BEN BEZALEL. - Or Chadash. Prague, 1600. Folio, modern mor. Some staining & browning; library stamp & ink notations on tp. St. 6153,1. CE Dec 6 (94) $1,500

MAARSEN, JOSEPH BEN JACOB. - Tikkun Socharim ve-Tikkun Chillufim. Amst., 1714. 8vo, contemp vellum. Frayed, affecting pagination; running titles gnawed; some staining & browning. St. 5954,7. CE Dec 6 (149) $1,000

MEIR IBN GABAI. - Derech Emunah. Padua: Lorenzo Pasquato, 1562. 4to, modern half calf. Some staining. CE Dec 6 (77) $2,800

MENASSEH BEN ISRAEL. - Dissertatia de la fragilidad humana. Amst., 1642. 8vo, modern lea. Stained throughout; B3 & B4 misbound before B1. CE Dec 6 (218) $2,800

MENASSEH BEN ISRAEL. - Mikveh Israel. Amst., 1650. 8vo, old vellum; repaired, hinges reinforced. Marginal burnhole, affecting some numerals; staining & browning. CE Dec 6 (219) $4,700

MENASSEH BEN ISRAEL. - Nishmat Chaim. Amst., 1651. 4to, contemp calf; rebacked, new endpapers. Tp shaved; lacking 1 leaf; some staining. St. 6205,1. CE Dec 6 (156) $550

MENASSEH BEN ISRAEL. - Thesoro dos Dinim. Amst.: Elijahu Aboab, 1645. 4 (of 5) parts in 1 vol. 8vo, later vellum. Tp laid down; some staining & soiling; margins shaved; title borders shaved along lower edges. CE Dec 6 (155) $1,800

MENASSEH BEN ISRAEL. - Zeror ha-Hayyim. De termino vitae libri tres. Amst., 1639. 12mo, vellum. Tp shaved; some browning. St. 6205.10. CE Dec 6 (154) $2,400

NATHAN BEN JEHIEL OF ROME. - He'aruch. Constantinople: Samuel ibn Nachmias, 1511. 4to, calf. Some old worming to spine ends & upper cover, corners worn;

early marginalia. CE Dec 6 (165) $7,500

NISSIM BEN REUBEN GERONDI. - She'eilot U'Teshuvot. Rome, 1545-46. 4to, contemp vellum. Some staining throughout; early marginalia on title; sgd by censors. St. 6676.11. CE Dec 6 (166) $3,000

PENSO DE LA VEGA, JOSEPH. - Pardes Shoshanim. Amst.: Joseph Athias, 1673. 12mo, later bds. Some dampstaining. St. 5975, col 1518. CE Dec 6 (170) $900

PEREZ BEN ISAAC COHEN. - Ma'arechet Elohut. Ferrara: Samuel ibn Usque, 1557. 4to, mor extra. Some staining & browning. St. 6719,1. CE Dec 6 (171) $3,800

RECANATI, MENAHEM. - Piskei Halachot. Bologna, 1538. 1st Ed. 4to, contemp vellum cut from a 16th-cent French document, with lining consisting of fragments from 3 12-13cent Ms s. CE Dec 6 (173) $1,800

SHAM TOV BEN JOSEPH FALAQUERA. - Tsori ha-yagon. Cremona: Vincenzo Conti, 1557. 4to, modern half vellum. Some running heads trimmed; staining & browning. St. 7101,1. CE Dec 6 (75) $950

SHEMTOB BEN SHABRUT. - Pardas Remonim. Sabbioneta: Tubia Foa, 1554. 4to, half vellum. Some corners patched; some browning & staining. CE Dec 6 (87) $3,000

SOLOMEN BEN JACOB ALMOLI. - Pitron chalomot. Amst.: Menasseh ben Israel, 1637. 12mo, modern mor gilt. Some spotting & soiling. St. 6896.6. CE Dec 6 (3) $1,500

SOLOMON BEN ABRAHAM PENIEL. - Or Enayim. Cremona: Vincenzo Conti, 1557. 4to, contemp vellum. Some soiling & staining; early marginalia on tp; some text censored. St. 6965.2. CE Dec 6 (169) $1,700

TYRNAU, ISAAC. - Minhagim. Amst.: at the Establishment of Elijah Aboab [by Menassah ben Israel], 1645. Bound with: Buxtorf, Johannes. Dissertatio fe Sponsalibus et divortiis. Basel, 1652. Lacking U2-3. 4to, contemp vellum; lower joints split, broken. Tp shaved; 2 leaves with lower margins trimmed; leaf 4/1 with square cut from lower fore-center affecting text & corner of woodcut, reattached in margin; some dampstaining throughout. St. 3822. CE Dec 6 (158) $30,000

**Hecco, Joseph**

— The Narrative of a Japanese.... San Francisco, n.d.. With: Hutching's California Magazine, Feb 1859 Ed by James Murdoch. 2 vols, orig cloth. Larson copy. pba Sept 28 (517) $275

**Hecht, Anthony**

— Aesopic. Twenty Four Couplets...to Accompany the Thomas Bewick Wood Engravings for Select Fables. Northampton: Gehenna Press, [1967]. One of 50 on Arches. Afterword by Philip Hofer. 8vo, bds; worn. With an extra suite of 24 plates on Sekishu paper in portfolio. pba June 20 (168) $375

— A Bestiary. Los Angeles: Kanthos Press, 1962. One of 100. Illus by Aubrey Schwartz. Folio, loose in cloth. With 20 sgd lithos. sg Sept 14 (231) $600

— The Seven Deadly Sins: Poems. Northampton MA.: Gehenna Press, 1958. One of 300. Illus by Leonard Baskin. 4to, orig half cloth; extremities rubbed. CE Feb 21 (107) $160

**Hecker, Genevieve**
— Golf for Women. NY, [1904]. 1st Ed. Cloth; spine ends rubbed, front cover spotted & rubbed. With chapter by Rhona K. Adair. pba Nov 9 (32) $475

**Heckle, Augustin**
— The Lady's Drawing Book: consisting of about an Hundred Different Sorts of Flowers. L: C. Bowles, 1764. Oblong folio, old wraps; some loss at corners. With 1 uncolored & 23 hand-colored plates. Pages curled; some foxing. Met Feb 24 (452) $1,500

**Hedderwick, Peter**
— A Treatise on Marine Architecture.... Edin., 1830. 2 vols. 4to, contemp half calf; rubbed. With 28 plates. Some spotting & staining. S June 12 (201) £340

**Hedrick, Ulysses Prentice**
— The Cherries of New York. Albany, 1915. sg Dec 7 (269) $100

Anr copy. Cloth; back hinge cracked. Z Oct 27 (168) $140
— The Peaches of New York. Albany, 1917. sg Dec 7 (270) $140
— The Plums of New York. Albany, 1911. 4to, cloth; rubbed. With frontis & 107 colored plates. Z Oct 27 (167) $120

**Heerup, Henry**
— Flojte Huggas Billedbog. [N.p.], 1953. One of 600. 4to, pictorial wraps. sg Sept 7 (97) $140

**Hefter, Joseph**
— The Army of the Republic. Bellevue NE: Old Army Press, [1971]. Syn. With 6 loose plates & facsimile booklet, Uniform of the Army of the Republic of Texas. pba June 25 (111) $80

**Heger, Jens Stephan**
— Naturens og Kunstens Tempel. Copenhagen, [1829]. 4to, later half calf gilt. With 35 hand-colored plates plus added map. Minor discoloration. Sold with a small number of loose plates from anr work. S Mar 14 (166) £500

Anr copy. Contemp half calf; some wear. S Mar 14 (167) £480

**Hegesippus**
— Historia de bello judaico. Paris, 1510. Folio, recent mor. Lacking last leaf; writing at foot of tp obliterated, affecting last line of text on verso. bba Nov 16 (4) £380 [Maggs]

**Heggen, Thomas**
— Mister Roberts. Bost., 1946. 1st Ed. Orig cloth; stain from adhesive at hinges, splash stain at upper cover. Inscr by Henry Fonda. bbc Feb 26 (303) $175

**Heidmann, Johann Anton**
— Vollstaendige auf Versuche und Vernunftschluesse gegruendete Theorie der Elektricitaet.... Vienna, 1799. 2 vols. 8vo, contemp half calf; rubbed. With 5 folding plates. Titles stamped; some spotting. S Mar 14 (168) £650

**Heimbinder, Barney A.**
— White Conquest (An Epic of Antarctic). [N.p., c.1930-34]. Folio, mor gilt with "To Admiral Richard E. Byrd" giltstamped on front cover; rebacked with mor. Typescript on rectos only. Inscr with poem to Adm. Richard E. Byrd. pba July 25 (38) $150

**Heine, Heinrich, 1797-1856**
See also: Limited Editions Club
— Aus den Memoiren des Herrn von Schnabelewopsky. Berlin, 1910. One of 250. Illus by J. Pascin. 4to, orig silk; soiled & spotted. bba May 9 (179) £550 [Preissler-Kahan]
— Ausgewaehlte Lieder. L: Essex House Press, 1903. One of 250. Illus by Reginald Savage. Orig bds; rubbed, stain on upper cover, split to upper joint. bba May 9 (486) £160 [Blackwell]
— The Book of Songs. East Aurora, 1903. One of 100, sgd by Elbert Hubbard. Half lea. K Oct 1 (333) $250
— Gedichte. Berlin, 1822. 1st Ed. 8vo, later calf. Lower portion of tp reinforced on verso; some foxing & browning. CE May 22 (258) $1,200
— The North Sea and Other Poems. L: Allan Wingate, [1947]. One of 70. Illus by Jules Pascin. pba Jan 25 (130) $65
— Works. NY: Groscup & Sterling, [190?]. Ed de Luxe, one of 250 on handmade paper with plates in 2 states. 20 vols. Contemp half mor; spines rubbed, some scratched, 2 chipped. bba May 30 (265) £280 [Katrina]

**Heine, Wilhelm, 1817-85**
— Reise um die Erde nach Japan.... Leipzig & NY, 1856. 2 vols. in 1. 8vo, early half mor; needs rebdg. sg Oct 26 (135) $450

**Heinemann, Ernest**
— Collection a vendre de monumens typographiques.... Offenbach am Main, 1840. 8vo, later wraps; worn. Some soiling, staining & foxing. O Mar 26 (131) $160

**Heinlein, Robert A.**
— Between Planets. NY: Scribner's, 1951. 1st Ed. In rubbed dj. pba May 23 (155) $180
— Farmer in the Sky. NY, 1950. In dj. pba May 4 (146) $140

Anr copy. In rubbed dj. pba May 23 (156) $140
— Have Space Suit - Will Travel. NY: Scribner's, [1958]. In chipped dj with inadequately tape-repaired tear. pba May 4 (147) $170
— Rocket Ship Galileo. NY: Scribner's Sons, [1947]. Cloth, in dj with tear to lower rear joint, crease. pba May 4 (148) $425
— The Star Beast. NY: Scribner's, [1954]. In dj with inked number to spine. pba May 4 (151) $150
— Starman Jones. NY: Scribner's, [1953]. In chipped dj, with discoloration to lower rear panel. pba May 4 (149) $150

1st English Ed. L, 1954. In dj. Inscr, 11 Feb 1958. pba May 4 (150) $250
— Starship Troopers. L: New English Library, [1965]. In dj. Sgd on tp & inscr on front free endpaper, with corrections by him on flaps of d/j & comment on rear pastedown about dust jacket blurbs.  K Feb 11 (214) $600

**Heins, Henry Hardy**
— A Golden Anniversary Bibliography of Edgar Rice Burroughs. West Kingston, Rhode Island: Grant, 1964. In soiled dj. pba May 4 (94) $250

**Heisenberg, Werner, 1901-76**
— Das Naturgesetz - Natural Law. [Stuttgart, 1967]. Out-of-series copy with orig pencil drawing, full-page dedicatory pencil drawing, inscr by Erni & a laid-in pencil drawing. Illus by Hans Erni.  4to, half mor.  With 4 plates on silk paper.  cb Oct 17 (630) $350

**Heliodorus, Bishop of Tricca**
— Historiae Aethiopicae libri decem.... Paris, 1619. ("Aethiopicorum, Libri X.") 8vo, 19th-cent mor gilt by Simier. bba May 9 (3) £360 [Quaritch]

**Heller, Elinor R.** See: Grabhorn Printing

**Heller, Joseph**
— Catch-22. NY, 1961. In dj with crimp at top of spine panel. sg June 20 (152) $375
  Advance copy. Wraps; worn. Sgd. cb Oct 17 (402) $600
  Anr copy. Wraps; soiled & spotted. wa Feb 29 (56) $200
  1st English Ed. L, [1962]. In dj. bbc Dec 18 (256) $120; sg Dec 14 (152) $90
— God Knows. NY, 1984. 1st Ed, One of 350. In dj. sg Dec 14 (155) $50
— Good as Gold. NY, 1979. 1st Ed, One of 500. sg Dec 14 (154) $50

**Hellman, George**
— Original Drawings by the Old Masters. [N.p.]: Pvtly ptd, 1915. One of 50. Folio, half cloth; worn. O May 7 (155) $130

**Hellman, Lillian**
— Three. Bost., [1979]. One of 500. sg Dec 14 (156) $100

**Hellwig, Christoph von, 1663-1721**
— Der accurate Scheider und kuenstliche Probierer. Frankfurt & Leipzig, 1717. Bound with: Sparmann, Johann Wilhelm. Anguis in herba, oder das bey vielen unbekandte und dennoch an seinem Leibe habende Ubel. Chemnitz, 1725. Folio, contemp vellum; soiled. S Mar 14 (219) £340
— Nosce te ipsum, vel anatomicum vivum, oder kurtz gefastes...anatomisches Werck. Frankfurt & Leipzig, [1720]. Folio, contemp vellum; worn & loose. With 4 plates, each with numerous overlays. Some browning, soiling, staining & marginal tears. Sold w.a.f. sg May 16 (425) $650

**Helm, H. J.**
— American Roadsters and Trotting Horses. Chicago, 1878. 8vo, modern half mor. With 15 plates. sg Mar 7 (469) $150

**Helman, Isidore Stanislas Henri**
— Abrege historique des principaux traits de la vie de Confucius. Paris, [1788]. 4to, old calf; worn, covers detached, lacking spine panel. With engraved title & 24 plates. Some foxing. wa Nov 16 (148) $130

**Helmont, Jan Baptista, 1577-1644**
— Ortus medicinae.... Lyons, 1655. 2 parts in 1 vol. Folio, modern calf. With half-title & 2 titles B2 verso stained; dampstained; some worming & browning. Ck Mar 22 (148) £180

**Helmuth, John Henry Christian**
— A Short Account of the Yellow Fever in Philadelphia.... Phila., 1794. 8vo, contemp wraps; rebacked. Browned; dampstaining in outer corners. sg May 16 (428) $120

**Helper, Hinton Rowan, 1829-1909**
— The Land of Gold: Reality Versus Fiction. Balt., 1855. 1st Ed. 8vo, orig cloth. Larson copy. pba Sept 28 (519) $170
  Anr copy. Orig cloth; spine faded, covers stained. Some foxing. Robbins copy. pba Mar 21 (148) $400

**Helvetius, Claude Adrien, 1715-71**
— De l'Esprit. Paris: Durand, 1758. 2 vols. 8vo, contemp calf; worn. O Mar 5 (111) $110
  2d Ed. 4to, 18th-cent calf; spine with library number at head. S June 12 (57) £360

**Hemans, Felicia, 1793-1835**
See also: Fore-Edge Paintings
— Poems. Liverpool, 1808. 4to, orig bds; worn. b Dec 5 (181) £80
— Works. Edin., 1857. 7 vols. 8vo, contemp calf gilt. b Sept 20 (569) £350

**Hemenway, Charles W.**
— Memoirs of My Day in and out of Mormondon.... Salt Lake City, 1889. Orig cloth; stamp to front pastedown, hinges cracked. pba Nov 16 (128) $70

**Hemingway, Ernest, 1899-1961**
See also: Limited Editions Club; Men at War...
— Across the River and Into the Trees. L, 1950. 1st Ed. In dj with short tears to extremities & spine ends. pba Oct 5 (142) $70
  Anr copy. Orig cloth, in dj with spine ends rubbed. sg Dec 14 (163) $90
  1st American Ed. NY, 1950. Inscr to A. E. Hotchner. P June 5 (258) $3,500
  Anr copy. In 1st dj. pba Oct 5 (141) $110
  Anr copy. In unidentified state of dj, creased. sg June 20 (154) $100
— Banal Story. NY, 1926. Wraps. In: The Little Review, Spring/Summer 1926. pba Aug 22 (9) $170

# HEMINGWAY

— Death in the Afternoon. L, 1932. 1st English Ed. Orig cloth, in dj with chips & closed long tears, spine def. pba Aug 22 (218) $70

1st Ed. NY, 1932. In repaired dj. CE Feb 21 (118) $1,000

Anr copy. Cloth, in chipped dj. Inscr to Gweneth P. Beam, 1933. Engelhard copy. CNY Oct 27 (70) $4,800

Anr copy. In def dj; stain to front free endpaper. pba Oct 5 (143) $90

Anr copy. Orig cloth; spine ends rubbed. pba Aug 22 (216) $100

Anr copy. In chipped dj lacking a piece from spine head & lower corner of front panel. pba Aug 22 (217) $120

Anr copy. In dj with wear & repair. Inscr by Sidney Franklin. sg Dec 14 (159) $800

— En Avoir ou pas. Paris, [1945]. One of 100. Orig wraps. pba Aug 22 (228) $70

— Ernest Hemingway Selected Letters 1917-1961. NY, [1981]. One of 500. Ed by Carlos Baker. pba Aug 22 (226) $55

— A Farewell to Arms. NY, 1929. 1st Ed, 1st Issue, without the legal disclaimer. In chipped dj; endpapers browned. bbc June 24 (519) $375

Anr copy. In dj. Inscr to C. W. Meyers, Jr. Gindi - Weiner copy. CNY May 17 (85) $6,500

Anr copy. In chipped dj. pba Oct 5 (144) $300

Anr copy. In chipped & repaired dj. pba May 23 (158) $350

Anr copy. In rubbed & chipped dj. pba Aug 22 (219) $130

Anr copy. In chipped dj. pba Aug 22 (593) $275

Anr copy. In dj chipped & browned & with discard stamp on rear, covers spotted, bdg skewed, free endpapers browned. sg June 20 (156) $275

Later issue. Inscr to A. E. Hotchner. P June 5 (259) $2,000

One of 510 L.p. copies, sgd. Orig half vellum. sg June 20 (155) $7,000

One of 510, sgd. Orig bds, with glassine dj & pbr's box. CNY May 17 (86) $4,000

Anr Ed. NY, 1948. In later dj, with tears & wear. Inscr to A. E. Hotchner. Annotated by Hemingway for performance by Marlene Dietrich. P June 5 (260) $4,750; pba Aug 22 (220) $100

— The Fifth Column. NY, 1940. 1st Separate Ed. Orig cloth; foxed, small stain to lower rear cover. pba Oct 5 (150) $250

— The Fifth Column and the First Forty-Nine Stories. NY, 1938. 1st Ed. In dj with small tears & soiling. Inscr to Elizabeth Youngstrom. P June 5 (268) $2,750

Anr copy. In dj with chips & a tear. pba Oct 5 (149) $400

— For Whom the Bell Tolls. NY, 1940. 1st Ed. In 1st Issue dj, with photographer unnamed; bdg spine with minor rubbing. Inscr to Elizabeth P. French. CE Feb 21 (124) $4,500

Anr copy. In 1st Issue dj, with photographer unnamed; repaired on verso. CE May 22 (263) $850

# AMERICAN BOOK PRICES CURRENT

Anr copy. In 1st Issue dj, with photographer unnamed; spine ends & corners worn. CE May 22 (264) $230

Anr copy. In 1st dj, which is heavily chipped. pba Jan 25 (131) $85

Anr copy. In 1st Issue dj, with photographer unnamed, spine head of dj replaced. pba Aug 22 (221) $120

Anr copy. In 1st dj (repaired). sg Dec 14 (160) $650

Anr copy. In 1st dj. sg June 20 (157) $375

Unrevised proof ptd on rectos only for Book-of-the-Month Club judges. Orig wraps. Consisting of all but the last 2 chapters, as noted by the Ed in a typed not attached to last leaf. cb Oct 17 (404) $4,000

1st Separate Ed. In 1st Issue dj, with photographer unnamed; with tear to rear jacket panel, with crease. pba Oct 5 (146) $140

1st English Ed. L, 1941. In frayed dj; endpapers browned. bba Oct 19 (339) £70 [Sotheran]

— God Rest You Merry Gentlemen. NY, 1933. 1st Ed, one of 300. CE Feb 21 (120) $320; K Feb 11 (215) $850

Anr copy. Variant bdg of red cloth lettered in black. pba Oct 5 (147) $600

— Green Hills of Africa. NY, 1935. 1st Ed. In frayed dj. NH June 1 (155) $350

Anr copy. In dj with spine head chipped. pba Oct 5 (148) $300

Anr copy. In chipped dj with creases. pba Aug 22 (222) $650

— In Our Time. Paris: Three Mountains Press, 1924. 1st Ed, one of 170. Orig bds; rubbed & soiled. Inscr to Dr. Don Carlos Guffey. Engelhard copy. CNY Oct 27 (67) $14,000

Anr copy. Orig bds; upper bd warped, spine ends worn. Marginal soiling at beginning & end. P June 5 (265) $6,000

1st American Ed. NY, 1925. Orig cloth; spine ends & corners worn. CE May 22 (260) $600

1st English Ed. L, [1926]. Orig cloth; spine ends worn, stain on rear cover. Inscr to Harry Sylvester & with holograph revisions on 7 pp in pencil. Engelhard copy. CNY Oct 27 (68) $7,000

2d American Ed. NY, 1930. In dj with minor chips & repairs. CE Feb 21 (117) $350

— Men without Women. NY, 1927. 1st Ed, 1st State. In creased dj. CE May 22 (261) $1,300

Anr copy. In frayed dj. Inscr to Mrs. Don Carlos Guffey. Goodwin - Engelhard copy. CNY Oct 27 (69) $4,200

— A Moveable Feast. L, 1964. In repaired dj. sg Dec 14 (165) $100

Anr Ed. NY, [1964]. In frayed & repaired dj. Inscr by Mary Hemingway to A. E. Hotchner & with Ls of Mary Hemingway to Hotchner. P June 5 (262) $1,600

Anr copy. In dj. sg June 20 (162) $110

— Nobody Ever Dies. NY, 1939. Orig pictorial wraps; front cover detached, spine chipped. In: Cosmopolitan, Mar 1939. Inscr at the beginning of the story on p. 29 to Jane Armstrong, whose porch figures in the

story. With photograph of Jane & Richard Armstrong. CE Feb 21 (123) $3,200
— The Old Man and the Sea. L, [1952]. 1st English Ed. In dj. pba Oct 5 (153) $110

Anr copy. In dj with short tears to extremities. pba Jan 25 (133) $170

1st Ed. NY, 1952. Orig cloth, in dj; affixed to front free endpaper is a Scribners' mailing label addressed to James Jones. sg Dec 14 (164) $350

1st Ed in Book form. In dj with rubbing to spine ends. pba Jan 25 (132) $170

Anr copy. Orig cloth, in dj; stamp to front free endpapers. pba Aug 22 (224) $190

— Short Stories. Copenhagen: Hansen & Nielsens Bogtrykerri, [1948]. One of 175. Illus by Dan Sterup-Hansen. 4to, pictorial bds. sg Dec 14 (162) $60
— Le Soleil de Leve Aussi. Paris, [1964]. Illus by Garbell. Orig wraps. With an extra suite of plates. pba Aug 22 (227) $60
— The Spanish Earth. Cleveland, 1938. 1st Ed, 2d Issue. Orig cloth; covers foxed. pba Oct 5 (154) $140
— The Sun Also Rises. NY, 1926. 1st Ed, 1st Issue. Orig cloth, in dj. Inscr to Dr. Don Carlos Guffey & with note by Hemingway on front free endpaper. P June 5 (266) $7,000

Anr copy. In dj with staining & fraying. P June 5 (267) $6,500

Anr copy. In worn dj with closed tear. sg June 20 (164) $6,000

[-] Tabula. Oak Park, Ill., June 1914. Senior Number, June 1914. Orig wraps; def. Inscr by Hemingway on dedication page. Goodwin - Engelhard copy. CNY Oct 27 (64) $2,600

Vol XXII, No 3; Vol XXIII, No 3; Senior Tabula, June 1917. Oak Park, Ill., 1916-17. 3 vols Orig wraps; rear cover stained. Containing story "A Matter of Color" by Hemingway; 2d vol containing 3 poems by him & 3d containing a Class Prophecy by him & photographs of him. 1st 2 are Goodwin copies. Englehard copies. CNY Oct 27 (65) $1,200

— [The Old Man and the Sea - in Yiddish] L: Der Kval, 1958. Orig cloth. pba Aug 22 (225) $80
— To Have and Have Not. NY, 1937. 1st Ed. In dj. CE May 22 (262) $500

Anr copy. In repaired dj. pba Oct 5 (155) $375

Anr copy. In rubbed dj. sg June 20 (163) $400

— Today is Friday. [Englewood, N.J., 1926]. 1st Ed, one of 300. Orig wraps, with orig envelope; spine with splits. CE Feb 21 (114) $500

Anr Ed. [Englewood NJ, 1926]. one of—300. Orig wraps, in original envelope (flap lackin; tears & soiling). sg Dec 14 (157) $375

— The Torrents of Spring. NY, 1926. 1st Ed. Orig cloth; spine ends rubbed. pba Aug 22 (229) $325; sg June 20 (165) $110

1st English Ed. L, [1933]. Cloth, in dj. Some foxing. sg June 20 (166) $400

Anr Ed. NY, [1933]. Orig cloth, in dj. Goodwin copy. CE Feb 21 (116) $300

[-] The Trapeze. Oak Park, Ill., 1916-1920. 39 issues. Folio, tipped into scrapbook; some folds repaired, some issues wrinkled. With 19 issues containing 31 contribs by Hemingway during his senior year & 3 issues from 1919 with articles concerning Hemingway. Goodwin - Engelhard copy. CNY Oct 27 (66) $9,000

— Winner Take Nothing. NY, 1933. 1st Ed. In dj. pba Oct 5 (156) $425

Anr copy. In rubbed & chipped dj. pba Aug 22 (230) $275

— Works. Moscow, 1959. ("Phect Xemh.") 2 vols. pba Aug 22 (231) $110

**Hemingway's copy, Ernest**

— The New Testament. NY, [1901]. Inscr by the minister of the 1st Congregational Church of Oak Park, and with exhortation by Hemingway's mother: "My Darling Son. If you forget everything else; never forget that Jesus Christ died for you to give you everlasting life." Goodwin - Engelhard copy. CNY Oct 27 (72) $2,600

**Hemon, Louis, 1880-1913**

— Maria Chapdelaine.... Paris, 1933. Illus by Clarence A. Gagnon. 4to, orig wraps. wad Oct 18 (202) C$1,400

**Hemphill, Joseph**

— Speech of Mr. Hemphill, on the Missouri Question. [Wash?, 1819]. 8vo, disbound. sg Mar 28 (302) $50

**Henault, Charles Jean Francois, 1685-1770**

— Abrege chronologique de l'histoire d'Espagne et de Portugal. Paris, 1765. 2 vols. 8vo, orig mor gilt with arms of Henault. Author's copy. Rahir - Fuerstenberg - Schaefer copy. S Dec 7 (295) £3,800
— Nouvel Abrege chronologique de l'histoire de France.... Paris, 1756. 5th Ed. 2 vols. 4to, contemp mor gilt; repair to upper cover of Vol I. Fuerstenberg - Schaefer copy. S Dec 7 (293) £600

**Henckel, Johann Friedrich, 1678-1744**

— Kleine mineralogische und chymische Schrifften. Dresden, 1744. 1st Ed. 8vo, contemp half calf; spine head chipped. With 1 plate; errata leaf at end. S Mar 14 (170) £480

**Henderson, Alexander, 1780-1863**

— The History of Ancient and Modern Wines. L, 1824. 4to, contemp half cloth; tears along spines, joints starting. Added frontis & a few mtd vignettes to tp & tops of chapters. pba June 20 (195) $300

**Henderson, George C.**

— The Discoverers of the Fiji Islands.... L, [1933]. Inscr, 1933. Later inscr by David Bonner-Smith. b Mar 20 (98) £60

**Henderson, Halton**

— Artistry in Single Action. Dallas: Charma Press, [1989]. One of 400. Folio, half mor. pba Mar 7 (133) $190

**Henderson, Harold Gould —& Ledoux, Louis Vernon, 1880-1948**
— The Surviving Works of Sharaku. NY, 1939. 4to, cloth, in soiled & torn dj. wa Dec 14 (520) $100

**Henderson, Robert W.**
See also: Grolier Club
— Early American Sport: a Check-List of Books Published in America prior to 1860. NY, 1953. 2d Ed. Cloth; worn. O June 25 (157) $70

**Henderson, Thomas, Antiquarian**
— Picturesque "Bits" from Old Edinburgh. Edin. & L, 1868. Illus by Archibald Burns. 4to, orig cloth; minor wear. With 15 mtd albumen prints. Some waterstaining. b May 30 (51) £220

**Hendley, Thomas Holbein, 1847-1917**
— Damascening on Steel and Iron, as Practised in India. L, 1892. Folio, orig half lea; spine chipped & def. With 32 colored plates, some heightened with gilt. S June 12 (321) £850

**Hendricks, Gordon**
— The Life and Work of Winslow Homer. NY: Abrams, [1979]. In dj. sg June 13 (187) $60
— The Photographs of Thomas Eakins. NY, 1972. Oblong folio, cloth. sg Feb 29 (121) $100

**Henkel, Arthur —& Schoene, Albrecht**
— Emblemata. Handbuch zur Sinnbildkunst des XVI. und XVII. Jahrhunderts. Stuttgart, [1967]. Folio, half leatherette in dj. sg Apr 11 (128) $275

**Henkel, Carolus**
— Eine Predigt ueber die Kunderzucht, welche gehalten wurde, in Columbus, Ohio, im Jahr unsers Herrn 1821. Newmarket VA: S. Henkel, 1822. 12mo, orig ptd wraps. Browned. K Feb 13 (342) $225

**Henle, Jakob, 1809-85**
— Handbuch der rationellen Pathologie. Braunschweig, 1846-53. 2 vols in 3. 8vo, cloth; rubbed. With 3 plates. Marginal waterstaining. bba July 18 (79) £100 [D. White]

**Henley...**
— Henley. A Poem. Henley-on-Thames, 1827. 8vo, orig bds; spine def. With folding frontis. Some spotting. b Dec 5 (310) £120

**Henley, Louise Miller**
— Letters from the Yellowstone. Grinnell IA, 1914. 1st Ed. Cloth; black spots to front cover. With 3 (of 4) tipped-in photographs. Inscr to E. R. Skelley. pba July 11 (393) $85

**Henley, William Ernest, 1849-1903**
— A Book of Verses. L, 1888. 1st Ed, One of 20 on vellum. Mor gilt. With 4 A Ls s to John W. Gilman, sgd with initials.. CE Sept 27 (139) $580

**Hennepin, Louis, 1640-1705?**
— Description de la Louisiane.... Paris: Sebastien Hure, 1683. 12mo, contemp calf; spine ends & joints worn. With map in photogravure facsimile. CE May 22 (21) $950
— A Description of Louisiana. NY, 1880. One of 250. Trans by John Gilmary Shea. 8vo, half mor. Map torn & lacking lower half. pba Apr 25 (451) $110
— A New Discovery of a Vast Country in America.... L, 1698. 1st Ed in English, "Bon-" Issue. 8vo, contemp calf; bds detached, rubbed. With frontis & 5 plates. Lacking the maps; first few leaves reinforced at gutter; some plate repairs. cb Feb 14 (2592) $450
"Tonson" Issue. Contemp calf; rebacked. With 2 maps & 7 plates, 6 folding. sg Oct 26 (136) $3,800
Anr Ed. Chicago, 1903. 2 vols, half cloth & buckram. With 2 folding maps. Robbins copy. pba Mar 21 (149) $80

**Henrey, Blanche**
— British Botanical and Horticultural Literature before 1800.... L, 1975. 3 vols. 4to, cloth. pba Mar 7 (134) $325

**Henri I, e Bourbon, Prince de Conde**
— Negotiation de la Paix, es mois d'Avril & May 1575. Paris, 1576. 1st Ed. 8vo, old vellum; cockled & stained. Browned & stained. S Oct 27 (1064) £180 [Robertshaw]

**Henri II, King of France, 1519-59**
[-] Cest la deduction du sumptueux ordre plaisantz spectacles et magnifiques theatres... exhibes par les citoiens de Rouen.... Rouen: Jean le Prest pour Robert le Hoy & Robert et Jean dictz du Gord, 9 Dec 1551. 4to, 19th-cent mor gilt. Roman & italic types. With 29 woodcuts. Some staining & soiling; a few tears & repairs; fore-edge of C1 extended; 1 burnhole costing letters; pagination in later hand; facsimile of R4 from 1885 Rouen reprint tipped in at end. Schaefer copy. P Nov 1 (79) $15,000

**Henricks, Gordon**
— Albert Bierstadt.... NY: Harry N. Abrams for the Amon Carter Museum, [1974]. 4to, cloth, in dj. ds July 27 (26) $150

**Henry, Coutelier de la Chambre des Pairs**
— Precis descriptif sur les instrumens de chirurgie anciens et modernes. Paris, 1825. 8vo, modern half syn. With 18 plates. Foxed & dampstained. CE Nov 8 (106) $1,000

**Henry, Alexander, d.1814 —& Thompson, David, 1770-1857**
— New Light on the Early History of the Greater Northwest.... Minneapolis: Ross & Haines, [1965]. One of 1,500. 2 vols. 8vo, cloth; corners bumped. pba Nov 16 (129) $85

**Henry, Augustine.** See: Elwes & Henry

### Henry, John Joseph, 1758-1811

— An Accurate and Interesting Account of the Hardships and Sufferings of that Band of Heroes.... Lancaster, 1812. 1st Ed. 12mo, later 19th-cent half calf; front cover detached, rubbed.  F Mar 28 (449) $100

Anr copy. Contemp sheep. Browned throughout.  sg Oct 26 (137) $250

### Henry VIII, King of England, 1491-1547

— Assertio septem sacramentorum adversus Martin Lutherum.... L: Pynson, 1521. 1st Ed. 4to, modern mor gilt. Roman type. Errata leaf repaired; washed. Broxbourne - Schaefer copy.  P Nov 1 (112) $8,000

— Assertio septem sacramentorum: or, an Assertion of the Seven Sacraments against Martin Luther. L: Nath. Thompson, 1687. 4to, modern bds. Marginal dampstaining throughout; wormhole through opening leaves.  sg Mar 21 (159) $225

### Henry, William, 1774-1836

— An Epitome of Chemistry.... Phila., 1802. 12mo, contemp calf; dry & scuffed. With 8 folding plates.  wa Feb 29 (146) $100

### Henshall, James Alexander, 1844-1925

— Book of the Black Bass. Cincinnati, 1889. 8vo, orig cloth; extremities rubbed.  sg Mar 7 (470) $70

— Camping and Cruising in Florida. Cincinnati: Robert Clarke, 1888. Orig cloth; hinges cracked.  pba July 11 (137) $110

### Henson, Joseph, 1789-1881

— Truth Stranger Than Fiction. Father Henson's Story of his Own Life. Bost. & Cleveland, 1858. Intro by Harriet Beecher Stowe. 8vo, orig cloth; extremities rubbed.  sg Mar 28 (333) $325

### Hepplewhite, Alice

— The Cabinet-Maker and Upholsterer's Guide.... L, 1789. 2d Ed. Folio, half mor; rebacked, rubbed, corners worn. With 127 plates. Stain in margin; a few plates with short tears in margin.  cb Feb 14 (2777) $1,500

### Heraclitus

— The Fragments.... Berkeley: Peter Koch, 1990. One of 113.  Trans by Duy Davenport. Folio, bds. Explanatory text booklet laid in.  sg Sept 14 (232) $200

### Heraldry...

— Heraldry of New Helvetica: With Thirty-Two Cattle Brands and Ear Marks.... San Francisco: Book Club of California, 1945. One of 250. Foreword by Carroll D. Hall. Half calf in dj; spine faded, ends rubbed. With 32 facsimiles of brand certificates. Larson copy.  pba Sept 28 (688) $75

### Herbelot, Barthelemy d', 1625-95

— Bibliotheque orientale, ou dictionnaire universel. Maestricht, 1776. Folio, contemp sheep; needs rebdg. Tp repaired.  sg Mar 7 (102) $275

### Herbert, Agnes

— Two Dianas in Alaska. L, 1909. Orig cloth; spine discolored, edges rubbed. Foxed.  O June 4 (159) $90

### Herbert, Frank

— Dune. NY: Chilton, [1965]. 1st Ed. Cloth, in rubbed dj.  sg Dec 14 (167) $1,100

— Dune Messiah. NY, [1969]. In dj.  pba May 4 (152) $200

### Herbert, George, 1593-1633. See: Fore-Edge Paintings

### Herbert, Henry William, 1807-58

See also: Derrydale Press

— Frank Forester's Fish and Fishing of the United States.... L, 1849. 1st Ed. 8vo, orig cloth; spine head torn.  pba July 11 (138) $95

New Ed. NY, 1859. 8vo, orig cloth.  pba July 11 (139) $60

— Frank Forester's Fugitive Sporting Sketches. Westfield WI, 1879. 8vo, cloth; spotted. Some foxing. Inscr by the Ed, Fred E. Pond, as Pond & as Will Wildwood.  O June 4 (160) $170

Anr copy. Cloth. Inscr by the Ed, Fred E. Pond, as Pond & as Will Wildwood to the Wisconsin Sportsmen's Association.  pba July 11 (394) $180

Anr copy. Cloth; insect damage to covers.  pba July 11 (395) $80

Anr copy. Half mor, orig wraps bound in.  sg Mar 7 (471) $120

— Frank Forester's Sporting Scenes and Characters.... Phila.: Peterson, [1881]. 2 vols. 8vo, orig cloth. Some soiling & foxing.  Inscr by F. E. Pond to Allen B. Palmer, 21 Mar 1881.  O Feb 6 (125) $160

— Hints to Horse-Keepers.... NY, 1859. 1st Ed 12mo, orig cloth; spine ends chipped.  pba July 11 (396) $85

### Herbert of Cherbury, Edward, Lord, 1583-1648. See: Gregynog Press

### Herbert, William, 1718-95. See: Ames & Herbert

### Herbert, William, 1778-1847

— Amaryllidaceae. L, 1837. 4to, old half calf; front bd detached, rear bd weak, residue, flyleaves foxed. With 6 plain & 42 hand-colored plates.  Met May 22 (387) $700

### Herbin, P. C. See: Chanlaire & Herbin

### Herbst, J. F. W. See: Jablonsky & Herbst

### Herculaneum

— Le Antichita di Ercolano esposte. Naples, 1757-92. 9 vols. Folio, 19th-cent half russia gilt, with stamped crest of the Ramsay family, by Carss; Vol I not uniform - in contemp sheep, some scuffing of extremities. With titles in red & black, each with engraved medallion port vignette; engraved general title, port, 1 double-page map, & 610 plates. Minor defs.  C Nov 29 (94) £5,500

# HERCULANEUM

Anr copy. 7 (of 9) vols; Vols VI & VIII. Folio, contemp half calf; def. Sold w.a.f. CE Sept 27 (140) $3,400

Anr copy. 9 vols. Folio, 19th-cent half russia gilt; rebacked retaining orig spines. With engraved title, port, double-page map & 610 plates. Some marginal dampstaining. Blackmer copy. S June 27 (109) £8,500

## Hercules
— Le dodici fatiche di Hercole, tratte da diversi autori, con il suo lamento, & morte. Florence: alle Scalee di Badia, [c.1560]. 4to, modern mor gilt. Woodcut of Herculese on tp & 14 illusts in text. Hole in B1 with minor loss. Landau copy. C June 26 (68) £5,500

## Herd, Richard
— Scraps of Poetry. Kirkby Lonsdale, 1837. 12mo, orig cloth; worn. b Dec 5 (168) £50

## Herd, Sandy
— My Golfing Life. L, 1923. 1st Ed. Cloth. pba Nov 9 (33) $190

Anr copy. Foreword by Earl Haig. Cloth; spine ends worn, rear joint torn. pba Apr 18 (82) $80
1st American Ed. NY, 1923. Cloth; spine soiled, lower front joint stained. pba Apr 18 (83) $95

## Here, Emmanuel
— Recueil des plans, elevations et coupes...qu'en perspectivee, des chateaux, jardins et dependances, que le Roi de Pologne occupe en Lorraine. Paris, [1750-53]. 2 vols. With 2 engraved titles & dedication leaf, 2 engraved Description pp, & 60 plates. One margin frayed. With: Here. Plans et elevations de la Place Royale de Nancy...batie par les ordres du Roy de Pologne.... Paris, 1753. With engraved title, engraved Reflexion page & 13 double-page plates. Together, 3 vols. Folio, uniform contemp calf gilt, with arms of Stanislaus Leszczynski, King of Poland; rubbed, corners strengthened. S June 27 (279) £14,000

## Heredia, Jose Maria de, 1842-1905
— La grece et La Siecle. Paris, 1927. 4to, orig wraps, in soiled & chipped glassine dj. With 20 color etchings by Maurice de Becque. sg Feb 15 (162) $80

## Hering, George Edwards, 1805-79
— Sketches on the Danube, in Hungary and Transylvania. L, 1838. 4to, orig half mor. With litho title & Dedication, & 25 plates. Some spotting; list of plates & ad leaf loosely inserted. b Dec 5 (123) £450

## Hermannidus, Rutgerus, d.1680
— Britannia magna. Amst., 1661. 12mo, contemp vellum. With engraved title, folding map & 31 plans, all but 1 double-page. S Mar 28 (50) £650

## Hermbstadt, Sigismund Friedrich
— Systematischer Grundriss der allgemeinen Experimentalchemie zum Gebrauch seiner Vorlesungen entworfen. Berlin, 1791. 3 vols. 8vo, contemp half calf; 2 prelim leaves misbound at end of Vol I. S June 12 (303) £120

## Hernandez de Cordova & Aguilar, Congalo
— Chronica del Gran Capitan Goncalo Hernandez de Cordova y Aguilar. Alcala de Henares: Hernan Ramirez, 1584-[56]. Folio, 19th-cent mor; spotted. Tp rebacked & with margins repaired; repairs to last 2 leaves with words supplied in pen facsimile; some headlines cropped; lacking final blank. Phillipps copy. S June 27 (309) £1,700

## Herndon, William H., 1818-91 —& Weik, Jesse W.
— Herndon's Lincoln; the True Story of a Great Life. Chicago, [1889]. 1st Ed. 3 vols. 12mo, half mor; extremities worn. sg Oct 26 (215) $225

## Herndon, William Lewis, 1813-57 —& Gibbon, Lardner
— Exploration of the Valley of the Amazon. Wash., 1853-54. Senate Ed. 2 vols. 8vo, orig cloth; rubbed. With folding map & 52 plates. Spotting throughout. S Oct 26 (512) £180 [Fonseca]

## Hernmarck, Carl Gustav Michael
— The Art of the European Silversmith, 1430-1830. L, [1977]. 2 vols. Folio, cloth, in djs. sg June 13 (337) $50

## Hero of Alexandria
— Gli artifitiosi et curiosi moti spiritali.... Bologna, 1647. 4to, contemp vellum; creased, tear in lower cover; stained. Library markings. bba Sept 7 (78) £550 [Whitestone]

Anr copy. 19th-cent cloth. sg May 16 (176) $850
— De gli automati, overeo machine se moventi. Venice, 1589. 1st Ed. 2 parts in 1 vol. 4to, modern bds. Some creasing & browning; ink stamp on tp. bba Sept 7 (77) £500 [Rogers Turner]

## Herodotus
See also: Limited Editions Club; Nonesuch Press
— Egypt. Greenbrae: Allen Press, 1989. One of 120. sg Sept 14 (11) $100; sg Feb 15 (4) $120
— Historiarum libri IX. Venice: Aldus, 1502. ("Libri novem.") Folio, 18th-cent calf; rebacked, worn. First 3 leaves repaired in margin; some staining. Saks - Hefner copy. CNY May 17 (24) $6,000
— Historico della guerre de greci et de persi. Venice: Nicolini di Sabbio, 1533. Trans by Matheo Mario Boiardo. 8vo, 17th-Cent calf. Marginalia. S Oct 26 (110) £150 [Zioni]

## Heroes... See: Kingsley, Charles

## Heron, Robert, 1764-1807
— A New and Complete System of Universal Geography.... Edin., 1796. 2 vols. Contemp calf; worn, joints rubbed, hinges cracked, 1 free endpaper & 1 plate detached. Some maps torn, occasionally affecting images; some dampstaining. cb June 25 (1732) $325

## Herondas
— The Miniambs. L: Fanfrolico Press, [1926]. One of 375. b May 30 (538) £60

**Herr, John K. —&**
**Wallace, Edward S.**
— The Story of the U.S. Cavalry, 1775-1942. Bost., [1953]. In chipped & repaired dj. pba June 25 (112) $50

**Herrera, Antonio de, 1559-1625**
— Historia general de los hechos de los castellanos en las islas y tierra firme del mar oceano.... Madrid, 1601. 1st Ed. Decades 1, 3 & 4 (of 8) only. Bound with: Herrera. Descripcion de las Indias occidentales. Madrid, 1601. Folio, later calf; covers detached. Lacking engraved title to Decade 3 & with engraved title to the Descripcion substituted. Sold w.a.f. b May 30 (155) £1,900

**Herrera, Grabriel Alonso de**
— Agricultura general. Madrid, 1777. Folio, contemp calf. With title & folding plate. Title creased; 2 leaves strengthened at margins; some spotting. S Oct 27 (869) £200 [Berk]

**Herrick, Robert, 1591-1674.** See: Golden Cockerel Press; Kelmscott Press

**Herschel, Sir John Frederick William, 1792-1871**
— Results of Astronomical Observations made during 1834-8.... L, 1847. 4to, orig cloth; front hinge cracked. With frontis & 17 plates. sg May 16 (177) $375

**Herschel, Sir William, 1738-1822**
— Description of a Forty-feet Reflecting Telescope.... L, [1795]. 4to, contemp half mor; rubbed. With 18 folding plates. Tp soiled; 2 plates with short tears. Offprint. S Mar 14 (172) £380

**Hersent, Charles**
— Optati Galli de cavendo schismate.... Paris, 1640. Bound with: Arrest de la Cour de Parlement par lequel il est ordonne, que le Libelle intitule Oprati Galli... sera lacere et brusle. Paris, 1640 8vo, citron mor mosaic bdg, c.1730, by Padeloup le Jeune, presumably for Gaignat, with painted oval on both covers, a miniature of a man on upper cover & of a lady on lower cover. Fuerstenberg - Schaefer copy. S Dec 7 (296) £22,000

**Hersey, John.** See: Limited Editions Club

**Hershberger, H. R.**
— The Horseman; a Work on Horsemanship.... NY, 1844. 1st Ed. 12mo, orig cloth. Some foxing & soiling. O Jan 9 (135) $140

**Hertz, Heinrich, 1857-94**
— Electric Waves; being Researches on the Propagation of Electric Action.... L, 1893. 8vo, orig cloth. b May 30 (23) £150

**Herulus, Bernardus**
— Oratio in funere Cardinalis Spoletani. Rome: Johannes Bulle, 2 Apr 1479. 4to, bds. 36 lines; type 1:83 G. Some staining; several leaves disjunct. 6 leaves. Goff H-129. C Apr 3 (113) £500

**Hervey, Elizabeth**
— The History of Ned Evans.... L, 1797. 2d Ed. 4 vols. 12mo, contemp half calf; 2 spines crinkled. Some soiling & staining; crayon mark on H8 of Vol IV. Ck Sept 8 (205) £650

**Hervey, Frederic**
— The Naval History of Great Britain.... L, 1779. 1st Ed. 5 vols. 8vo, contemp calf; glue to joints & spine ends, 1 plate in Vol V mtd to front free endpaper. pba Nov 30 (178) $200

**Hervey, John, 1870-1947**
— Messenger, the Great Progenitor. NY: Derrydale Press, 1935. One of 500. O Jan 9 (85) $90

**Hervey, John, 1870-1947 —&**
**Vosburgh, Walter S.**
— Racing in America, 1665-1936 NY, [1922-37-44]. One of 800. 4 vols. Folio, half cloth; worn. O Jan 9 (136) $900

**Herzog, Johann Jakob**
— Realencyklopaedie duer protestantische Theologie und Kirche. Hamburg, 1854-68. 22 vols. 8vo, contemp half cloth; worn. Some vols dampstained. sg Apr 11 (129) $175

**Hesiod**
— Opera. Florence: Filippo Giunta, 20 Jan 1515. 8vo, modern bds. Foxing & marginal dampstaining. In Greek. sg Apr 18 (61) $1,000

**Hess, Hans**
— Lyonel Feininger. NY, [1961]. Folio, cloth, in dj. sg Sept 7 (149) $225

Anr copy. Cloth, in chipped dj. sg Jan 11 (169) $275

Anr copy. In dj. Dampstaining at edges of several leaves. sg June 13 (146) $175

**Hessus, Helius Eobanus**
— De tuenda bona valetudine.... Frankfurt: heirs of Christian Egenolph, 1560. Bound with: Katzsch, Johann. De gubernanda sanitate.... Frankfurt: heirs of Christian Egenolph, 1557 1st Ed of Katzsch. 2 works in 1 vol. 8vo, contemp vellum. Title & some gatherings browned; marginally dampstained. Ck Mar 22 (149) £1,600

**Hetherington, Arthur Lonsdale**
See also: Hobson & Hetherington
— The Early Ceramic Wares of China. L, 1922. 4to, orig cloth; remnants of mtd cuttings on front endpapers, owner's pencil notes on rear endpapers. sg Jan 11 (85) $225

**Heusden, Willem van**
— Ancient Chinese Bronzes of the Shang and Chou Dynasties. Tokyo, 1952. Ltd Ed. Folio, orig cloth. Limitation leaf creased. sg Sept 7 (183) $100

**Hevesy, Ivan**
— A Futurizmus, Expresszionizmus es Kubizmus Mueveszete. Gyoma, 1922. Orig pictorial bds after

designe by Imre Szobotka; cocked. Inscr to Josef Csaky. sg June 13 (184) $250

**Hewitson, William Chapman, 1806-78**
— British Oology. Newcastle, [1831-38]. 2 vols. 8vo, contemp calf gilt; rubbed. Ck Feb 14 (330) £350
Anr copy. Contemp half russia. With 155 colored plates. S June 13 (397) £215
1st Ed. 2 vols. 8vo, mor by Sangorski & Sutcliffe. With 155 hand-colored plates. Some browning & spotting. S Oct 27 (735) £340 [Grahame]

**Hewitt, Edward R.**
— Secrets of the Salmon. NY, 1922. 1st Ed, one of 780 L.p. copies. 8vo, half cloth; worn. O June 25 (159) $150

**Hewlett, Esther**
— Scripture Natural History for Youth. L, 1828. 2 vols. 16mo, contemp cloth; worn, later endpapers. With frontis, pictorial tp & 80 hand-colored plates. Some tears & soiling. S Nov 2 (199) £160 [Albert]

**Hey, Rebecca**
— The Spirit of the Woods. L, 1837. 8vo, orig half mor; worn & scuffed. With 26 hand-colored plates. Lacking plae guards; 1 plate with small chip. bbc June 24 (217) $200

**Heyeck, Robin**
— Marbling at The Heyeck Press. Woodside CA, 1986. One of 150. 4to, orig half mor. bba May 9 (579) £130 [Blackett]

**Heyerdahl, Thor**
— American Indians in the Pacific.... L, [1952]. In dj. pba July 25 (156) $65

**Heylyn, Peter, 1600-62**
— Cosmographie.... L, 1665-66. Folio, contemp calf; rebacked with orig spine laid down, corners worn, tape-repaired. With engraved title & 4 folding maps. Engraved title inlaid; some soiling, foxing & browning; marginal worming; a few tears & holes, affecting maps. cb Feb 14 (2593) $750
Anr Ed. L, 1670. Folio, contemp vellum; rebacked. With engraved title & 4 folding maps. Browned throughout; maps shaved within margin. b May 30 (129) £500
— The Historie of that most Famous Saint...St. George of Cappadocia.... L, 1633. 2d Ed. 4to in 8s, late 19th-cent half calf; spine & corners scuffed. Lackin A1. pba Nov 30 (179) $140
— Microcosmus, or a Little Description of the Great World. Oxford, 1629. ("Mikrokosmos. A Little Description of the Great World.") 4th Ed. 4to, contemp calf; worn. A few leaves of tables at beginning misbound; 1 cropped; some soiling & marginalia; stains. CE June 12 (213) $130

**Heyward, Du Bose, 1885-1940 —&**
**Gershwin, George, 1898-1937**
— Porgy and Bess. NY, 1935. One of 250. 4to, orig lea. CE June 12 (43) $3,800

**Heywood, Gerald G. P.**
— Charles Cotton and his River. Manchester, 1928. 4to, cloth; spine head & corners worn. pba July 11 (140) $250

**Heywood, John, 1497?-1580?**
— The Spider and the Flie. L: Tho. Powell, 1556. 1st Ed. 4to, 19th-cent mor gilt, with orig mor bdg of c.1600 mtd as doublures. With woodcut port (repeated) & 98 woodcuts. Houghton copy. C Nov 29 (53) £4,200

**Heywood, Peter**
— Remarks on, and Instructions for Navigating the River Plate. L, [1813]. 4to, contemp half russia. Marginal waterstaining; stamp of the Hydrographical Office. Capt. Frederick Spencer's copy. With related material. b Mar 20 (104) £1,500

**Heywood, Thomas, 1574?-1641**
— Gynaikeion: or, Nine Bookes of Various History Concerninge Women. L, 1624. Folio, 19th-cent mor over bevelled bds, sides panelled in blind. Engraved title shaved at foot & remargined. Inscr by Algernon C. Swinburne to Edward Burne-Jones & sgd by Burne-Jones, 1894. b Sept 20 (205) £750

**Hezlet, May**
— Ladies' Golf. L, 1904. 1st Ed. Cloth; spine ends rubbed, head torn, covers worn, corners bumped. With frontis port. pba Nov 9 (34) $325

**Hibberd, Shirley, 1825-90**
— The Amateur's Rose Book.... L, 1874. 8vo, orig cloth. With 6 folding color plates. sg Dec 7 (223) $50
— Familiar Garden Flowers. L: Cassel, [1895-96]. Illus by F. Edward Hulme. Series 1-5 in 5 vols. 8vo, contemp half lea gilt; spine ends rubbed. sg May 9 (354) $375

**Hichborn, Philip, 1839-1910**
— Report on European Dock-Yards. Wash., 1889. 4to, cloth. pba Nov 16 (353) $50

**Hickes, George, 1642-1715**
— Jovian; or, An Answer to Julian the Apostate. L: Sam. Roycroft for Walter Kettilby, 1683. 8vo, contemp calf gilt; worn, lacking front cover. Tp soiled; tears in genealogical tables. sg Mar 21 (160) $250

**Hieb, Louis A.**
— Tony Hillerman: A Bibliography. Tucson: Press of the Gigantic Hound, 1990. One of 1,000. pba Aug 22 (245) $80

**Hieover, Harry.** See: Bindley, Charles

**Hieronymus, 340?-420**
— Epistolae. Rome: Arnoldus Pannartz, 28 Mar 1476. Vol I only [all pbd]. Folio, 18th-cent russia; worn, rebacked. 46 lines; roman letter; 1st initial supplied in gilt on colored panel of small flowers. Dampstaining affecting illumination on fol. 12; early annota-

tions. 299 (of 302) leaves; lacking register leaf & 2 blanks. Goff H-167.  S Dec 18 (39) £3,600 [Zioni]
Anr Ed. Venice, 12 July 1496. Part 2 (of 2) only. Folio, modern bds. 62 lines; roman letter. Some staining & spotting; minor worming. 398 leaves. Goff H-175.  S Dec 18 (40) £800 [Poole]
Anr Ed. Paris: Chalcographia Ascensiana, 1515. ("Liber epistolarum.") Folio, contemp blind-tooled pigskin over wooden bds with brass catches; lea def, lacking clasps, rear cover wormed. Dampstained & wrinkled; opening leaves corroded in lower margins; 20 extraneous leaves bound at end. Sold w.a.f.  sg Mar 21 (22) $350
Anr Ed. Seville: Juan Cromberger, 1541. ("Epistolas [in Spanish].") Folio, 16th-cent blind-stamped calf over wooden bds; rebacked. Library stamp on label at foot of tp, affecting border; some dampstaining; marginal tears & repairs.  S June 27 (334) £1,400
— A Leaf from the Letters of St. Jerome, First Printed by Sixtus Reissinger, Rome c.1466-1467. Los Angeles: Zeitlin & Ver Brugge, 1981. One of 300. Ed by Bennett Gilbert. Folio, Half vellum. This copy with 3 orig leaves in end pocket.  Ck Apr 12 (240) £75
Anr copy. Half vellum. With orig leaf laid in.  sg Sept 14 (255) $150
— Opera. Basel: Episcopius, 1565. Folio, contemp pigskin over bds; worn, spine head gone. Ink annotations.  F June 20 (193A) $210
— Vitae sanctorum patrum, sive vitas patrum.... Nuremberg: Anton Koberger, 7 May 1478. Folio, old calf; spine head & corners worn. 51 lines 7 headline; double column; type 3:110aG (text), 4:160G (headings & headlines). Some worming; 1st leaf soiled; butnhole in 5 leaves with minor loss; marginal repairs. 246 leaves. Goff H-199.  cb June 25 (1764) $1,300
— Vitas patrum. Ulm: Johann Zainer, [c.1478-80]. Folio, contemp blindstamped calf; worn, rebacked, lacking clasps. 41 lines; gothic letter; some leaves rubricated at beginning. Dampstained throughout. 385 (of 386) leaves; final blank. Goff H-200.  S Dec 18 (41) £1,000 [Gabinete]

**Higgins, Godfrey, 1773-1833**
— Anacalypsis, an Attempt to draw aside the Veil of the Saitic Isis. L, 1836. 2 vols. 4to, contemp half calf; needs rebacked. With 46 plates & plans.  sg Mar 7 (104) $375
— The Celtic Druids, or an Attempt to Show that the Druids were the Priests of Oriental Colonies.... L, 1829 [but later]. 4to, orig cloth; needs rebacking. With 47 plates & plans.  sg Mar 7 (105) $375

**Higginson, Alexander Henry**
— As Hounds Ran: Four Centuries of Foxhunting. NY, 1930. One of 900. Ed by Higginson. 4to, cloth; worn.  O Jan 9 (137) $110
— British and American Sporting Authors.... Berryville, Va., 1949. 4to, cloth; worn, spine heel stained.  O Jan 9 (138) $130
Anr Ed. L, 1951. 4to, cloth, in worn dj.  O June 25 (160) $70
Anr copy. Cloth, in soiled dj with edge-tears.  pba July 11 (398) $150

Anr copy. Cloth, in worn dj.  wa Feb 1 (223) $55
— Letters from an Old Sportsman.... Garden City, 1929. One of 201, sgd. Illus by Lionel Edwards. With colored frontis & 9 plates. Orig sgd etching by Edwards in rear pocket.  O Jan 9 (140) $80

**Hilarius Litomericensis**
— Tractatus contra perfidiam aliquorum Bohemorum. Strassburg: Ptr of the 1483 Jordanus de Quedlinburg (Georg Husner), 15 June 1485. 4to, contemp blind-stamped calf over wooden bds; rebacked & repaired, lacking 1 clasp. 31 lines; gothic letter; initials initial-strokes & underlining in red. Wormholes in foremargins & 1 in text of last few leaves. 112 leaves. Goff H-271. Madsen copy.  S Mar 14 (173) £1,900

**Hildebrandt, Alfred**
— Die Luftschiffahrt nach ihrer geschichtlichen und gegenwaertigen Entwicklung. Munich, 1907. Dampstaining in lower margins.  sg May 16 (43) $130

**Hiler, Hilaire**
— From Nudity to Raiment.... NY, 1930. 4to, wraps; cracked & tape-repaired.  sg Jan 11 (122) $50

**Hiler, Hilaire & Meyer**
— Bibliography of Costume; a Dictionary Catalogue. NY, 1939. 4to, orig cloth.  sg Apr 11 (130) $120

**Hill, Aaron, 1685-1750**
— The Dramatic Works. L, 1760. 2 vols. 8vo, contemp calf.  pba Mar 7 (137) $180

**Hill, Jasper**
— The Letters of a Young Miner.... San Francisco, 1964. Bds. With frontis & folded map. Larson copy.  pba Sept 28 (520) $75

**Hill, Jim Dan**
— The Texas Navy. Chicago 1937 [1950]. In dj. Inscr.  sg Oct 26 (138) $150

**Hill, Sir John, 1716?-75**
— The British Herbal. L, 1756. Folio, orig sheep; rebacked. With frontis & 75 plates. Some dampstianing & browning.  W Mar 6 (198) £760
— The Family Herbal. Bungay, [c.1808]. 8vo, contemp half calf; worn. With 54 colored plates. Some soiling, staining & browning.  O Mar 5 (112) $225
Anr Ed. Bungay, [c.1812]. 8vo, contemp half calf; rubbed. With 124 hand-colored plates.  b Jan 31 (296) £280
— A General Natural History. L, 1751. Vol II (of 3) only. Folio, 19th-cent half lea; rubbed. Some staining & soiling.  O Mar 5 (113) $275
— A Review of the Works of the Royal Society of London. L, 1751. 4to, modern half calf. Lower margin of 1st 2 leaves torn & restored, with loss of a few letters & date from tp; small tear to last leaves; tp browned.  bba July 18 (80) £100 [Price]

**Hill, Jonathan A.**
— The Hill Collection of Pacific Voyages. San Diego, Calif., 1974. 1st Ed, One of 1,000. Vol I (of 3). 8vo, orig cloth. sg Apr 11 (130A) $350

Anr Ed. San Diego, Calif., 1974-83. Vol I is 1 of 1,000; Vol II is 1 of 800 & Vol III is 1 of 950. Ed by De Braganza & Oakes; annotated by Hill. Vols I-II only. ds July 27 (90) $600

Anr copy. 3 vols. pba Feb 13 (92) $800

**Hill, Lewis Webb.** See: Phillips & Hill

**Hill, Oliver, Architect**
— The Garden of Adonis. L, [1923]. 1st Ed. 4to, cloth; spine ends worn, bumped, hinges split, shaken. sg Feb 29 (159) $130

**Hill, Robert.** See: Frasca & Hill

**Hillard, Elias B., 1825-95**
— The Last Men of the Revolution. Hartford, 1864. 12mo, half lea; worn. With 6 colored plates & 6 mtd albumen prints. Some foxing. NH June 1 (297) $875

**Hiller, Lejaren Arthur —& Banning, Kendall**
— Bypaths in Arcady. Chicago: Brothers of the Book, 1915. Folio, half vellum; soiled. Some foxing. sg Feb 29 (160) $200

**Hillerman, Tony**
— The Dark Wind. NY, [1982]. In dj. Sgd. pba Aug 22 (241) $170
— The Jim Chee Mysteries. NY, [1990]. Ltd Ed with orig sgd color frontis & 3 sgd color drawings. Illus by Ernest Franklin. In dj. cb June 25 (1857) $250
— A Thief of Time. NY: Harper & Row, [1988]. One of 250. In dj. cb June 25 (1859) $425

**Hillier, Jack Ronald.** See: Gale Collection, Mr. & Mrs. Richard P.

**Hills, John Waller, 1867-1938**
— A History of Fly Fishing for Trout. L, 1921. 8vo, cloth. Inscr by Eustace Hills, 1921. pba July 11 (141) $140
— A Summer on the Test. L, [1924]. One of 300. Illus by Norman Wilkinson. 4to, half mor; rubbed. With 12 plates. O Feb 6 (128) $850

Anr copy. Cloth. Lacking the etchings. pba July 11 (142) $80

Anr Ed. L, 1930. 4to, orig cloth. pba July 11 (143) $110

**Hills, Louis E.**
— With General George A. Custer on the Northern Pacific Surveying Expedition in 1873. Lamont IA: Reorganized Church of Jesus Christ of Latter Day Saints, 1915. Cloth. In: Journal of History, Vol 8, No 1, Jan 1914, pp. 141-60. pba June 25 (114) $550

**Hills, Robert**
— Sketches in Flanders and Holland. L, 1816. 4to, contemp russia; covers detached, spine lacking. With 36 plates, 5 hand-colored. Marginal spotting. Extra-illus with 18 sheets with 20 orig watercolors by Hills from which Plates 5-16 taken, Hills's passport for the journey & a wash sketch of a medallion & a port of the author mtd as frontis. C May 31 (94) £4,800

**Hilton, Harold H.**
— My Golfing Reminiscences. L: James Nisbet, 1907. 1st Ed. Cloth; spine head rubbed. pba Apr 18 (84) $300

**Hilton, Harold H. —& Smith, Garden G.**
— The Royal and Ancient Game of Golf. L, 1912. One of 100. Orig vellum. bba Nov 16 (419) £1,700 [McEwan]

**Hilton, Harold H. —& Smyth, Garden G.**
— The Royal & Ancient Game of Golf. L, 1912. 1st Ed, One of 900. Mor; soiled & spotted. With frontis, 3 color plates, & 2 photogravures. Pp. 264 & 265 torn. pba Nov 9 (35) $1,400
— The Royal and Ancient Game of Golf. L, 1912. One of 900. Mor; spine ends & extrems scuffed, soiled, lea fading, front hinge cracking. With 3 color plates & 2 photogravures. pba Apr 18 (85) $1,200

**Hilton, James, 1900-54**
— Goodbye Mr. Chips. Bost., 1934. In dj with light soil. sg June 20 (167) $80

Anr Ed. L, 1934. In chipped dj with wrap-around band; minor dampstains to bdg. pba May 23 (163) $55

Birthday Ed. Bost., 1935. one of 600. Illus by H. M. Brock. Half vellum gilt, unopened. wd Nov 15 (70) $125

**Himes, Chester**
— Cast the First Stone. NY, [1952]. Orig cloth, in chipped dj; front bottom corner bumped. bbc Dec 18 (257) $100

**Hind, Arthur Mayger**
See also: British Museum
— Early Italian Engraving: a Critical Catalogue.... L, 1938-48. One of 375. Vols II & III only. sg Jan 11 (215) $325
— Engraving in England in the Sixteenth & Seventeenth Centuries. Cambr., 1952-64. 1st Ed. 3 vols. 4to, orig cloth, in djs. bba Oct 5 (263) £420 [Sawyer]

Anr copy. Orig cloth, 2 vols in djs. bba Oct 19 (90) £260 [Bennett]
— Wenceslaus Hollar and his Views of London.... L, 1922. 4to, orig cloth; some wear. O May 7 (157) $75

**Hind, Charles Lewis, 1862-1927**
— Etchings by Paul Rajon, Furtuny, Unger. L, 1888. One of 250. Folio, half mor; worn & broken. With 17 (of 20) plates. Many text leaves creased, torn or taped. wa Nov 16 (300) $130

**Hind, Henry Youle, 1823-1908**
— Explorations in the Interior of the Labrador Peninsula. L, 1863. 2 vols. 8vo, orig cloth; hinges cracked. With 2 maps, 1 plain & 10 colored plates. CE Sept 27 (142) $600
— Narrative of the Canadian Red River Exploring Expedition.... L, 1860. 2 vols. 8vo, contemp calf. With 8 maps & 20 colored plates. S June 13 (398) £340
— Rapport sur l'Exploration de la Contree Situee entre le Lac Superieur et les Etablissements de la Riviere Rouge. Toronto, 1858. Half lea. Tear at stub of 1st (of 2) map; tp with chip at foot. pba Apr 25 (453) $170

**Hindemith, Paul**
— Konzert fuer Violoncello und Orchester [parts for cello & piano]. Mainz: Schott, [n.d.]. 4to. With holograph additions to the cello part; sgd & inscr to Pierre Fournier, Feb 1962; with Fournier's annotations. S May 15 (383) £1,600

**Hindley, Charles, d.1893**
— The History of the Catnach Press. L, 1886. 8vo, orig bds, in dj. Some soiling. pba Aug 8 (323) $110

**Hindmarsh, Isabella**
— Cave Hoonga, a Tongean Tradition.... Alnwick, 1818. 8vo, contemp calf. b Dec 5 (275) £80

**Hinds, John.** See: Badcock, John

**Hine, Lewis W.**
— Men at Work. [N.p.], 1932. 4to, cloth, in chipped & torn dj with repair. sg Apr 24 (593) $300

**Hines, Gustavus**
— Life on the Plains of the Pacific. NY, 1857. 12mo, orig cloth. sg Oct 26 (139) $60

**Hinman, Charles G.**
— "A Pretty Fair View of the Eliphent" or Ten Letters.... Chicago, 1960. One of 200. Ed by Colton Storm. Half bds. With frontis. Larson copy. pba Sept 28 (522) $60

**Hinton, John Howard, 1791-1873**
— The History and Topography of the United States.... Bost., 1834. 2 vols in 1. 4to, half calf; worn, front bd detached. With 35 plates & map. Corners dampstained throughout, affecting plates. wa Feb 29 (399) $120

**Hipkiss, Edwin James**
— Eighteenth-Century American Arts: the M. and M. Karolik Collection. Bost., 1941. 4to, orig cloth. wa Dec 14 (537) $85

**Hippocrates, 460?-377? B.C.**
— Aphorismi. Lyons, 1549. 8vo, contemp blind-tooled pigskin over pastebd; shaken, opening leaves loose. John Redman Coxe's copy. sg May 16 (429) $275
Anr Ed. Pavia: Francesco Moscheno, 1552. ("Il Giuramento e le Sette Parti degli Aforismi.") 2 parts in 1 vol. 16mo, early 19th-cent bds; front joint cracked. Marginal dampstaining towards end; some blue pencil underscoring. sg May 16 (430) $130
— Opera. Basel: Andreas Cratander, Aug 1526. Folio, 16th-cent blind-stamped pigskin over wooden bds, with 3 (of 4) metal cornerpieces. Early Ms index on verso of front flyleaf. S June 27 (326) £1,400
Anr Ed. Basel: Froben & Episcopius, Sept 1558. Folio, contemp calf gilt with arms of Cardinal Charles II or III de Bourbon on spine; front joint worn, front free endpaper loose. sg May 16 (431) $700

**Hiramoto, Sumi.** See: Gluck & Hiramoto

**Hirsch, August, 1817-94**
— Biographisches Lexikon der hervorragenden Aerzte aller Zeiten und Voelker. Munich & Berlin, 1962. 5 vols. bba Oct 5 (98) £500 [Robertshaw]
Anr Ed. Storrs: Martino, [n.d.]. One of 125. 6 vols. bba July 18 (156) £90 [Tosi]

**Hirschfeld, Christian Cayus Lorenz**
— Theorie de l'art des jardins. Leipzig, 1779-89. Vols I-II (of 5). 4to, contemp half sheep; worn. Foxed; titles stamped. sg Sept 7 (211) $225

**Hirshberg, Leonard Keene.** See: Mencken & Hirshberg

**His...** See: Clavell, Robert

**Historic...**
— The Historic Gallery of Portraits and Paintings. L, 1807-11. 7 vols. 8vo, 19th-cent half calf. Some foxing throughout. pba Aug 22 (793) $55

**Historical...**
— Historical Notes on Slavery and Colonization.... Elizabeth-Town: E. Sanderson, 1842. 8vo, orig wraps. With 2 plates. sg Mar 28 (291) $500

**Historische...**
— Historische-Genealogischer Calender, oder Jahrbuch der Merkwuerdigsten Neuen Weltbegenenheiten fuer 1786. Leipzig: Haude & Spener, [1785]. 32mo, orig bds; needs rebacked. With uncolored engraved title & 2 ports & with 4 costume plates & folding map, all hand-colored. Lacking the 12 plates by Chodowiecki. sg Mar 7 (8) $130

**History...**
— The History of Sam the Sportsman.... L, [c.1910]. Illus by Frank Adams. Folio, half cloth; corners rubbed. pba Aug 22 (730) $80
— History of the 20th (Duke of Cambridge's Own) Infantry, Brownlow's Punjabis. Davenport, [c.1907-10]. 8vo, orig half lea; spine & hinges worn. Presentation copy to H. A. Gwynne by Lieut. Col. L. C.

# HISTORY...

Dunsterville & the Officers. bba May 30 (245) £80 [Clancey]
— History of the Holy Bible.... Bost., 1790. 32mo, old wraps; worn. Piece torn from edge of frontis; early leaves frayed; some foxing. NH Sept 16 (239) $325
— History of the Old Colony Railroad. Bost.: Hager & Handy, 1893. 8vo, cloth. rce Nov 17 (364) $110
— History of the Westminster Election.... L, 1785. 4to, contemp calf; covers detached, later endpapers. Tp creased & torn; browned; frayed. bba July 18 (332) £100 [Maggs]

**History of Beasts...**
— The History of Beasts in Miniature adapted to the Juvenile Capacity. L, [c.1805]. 16mo, orig pictorial wraps; soiled, stitching def. With 22 plates, each with 5 illusts numbered 1-115. S Nov 2 (201) £400 [Hirsch]

**Hitchcock, Edward, 1793-1864**
— Ichnology of New England. Bost., 1858. 4to, cloth; worn & shaken. With 60 plates. Some foxing, staining & soiling. O Mar 5 (115) $150
— Outline of the Geology of the Globe.... Bost., 1854. Orig cloth. With 2 hand-colored folding maps & 5 litho plates. World map with repaired tear with minor loss; both maps creased. pba Nov 16 (354) $120
— Plates Illustrating the Geology and Scenery of Massachusetts. [Bost.: Pentleton's Lithography, n.d.]. Oblong 4to, bds; worn. Map torn in gutter; Plate 2 frayed & loose; some foxing & soiling. O Nov 14 (85) $200
— Report on the Geology of Vermont. Claremont NH, 1861. 2 vols. 4to, orig cloth; rebacked, worn. With 1 uncolored & 6 hand-colored full-page maps, 3 folding hand-colored maps, 5 plates of fossils, 3 folding hand-colored charts & 20 oval litho plates of scenes. Tear into surface of 1 folding map. bbc Feb 26 (412) $260

**Hitchcock, Henry-Russell**
— Early Victorian Architecture in Britain. New Haven, 1954. 2 vols. 4to, cloth, in djs. sg Sept 7 (11) $80

**Hitchcock, Mary E.**
— Two Women in the Klondike. NY, 1899. 1st Ed. Frontis foxed. pba July 25 (404) $110

**Hittell, John Shertzer, 1825-1901**
— A History of the City of San Francisco and Incidentally of the State of California. San Francisco, 1878. 1st Ed. 8vo, orig cloth. Inscr & with ALs. Evans - Larson copy. pba Feb 12 (326) $300
— Marshall's Gold Discovery. A Lecture (The Fourth of the Sixth Annual Course of Lick Lectures) Delivered before the Society of California Pioneers. San Francisco, 1893. Wraps; lower right corner chipped, wraps tanned, spine reinforced. Larson copy. pba Sept 28 (524) $100
Anr copy. Orig wraps. pba Aug 8 (79) $50
— Mining in the Pacific States of North America. San Francisco, 1861. 1st Ed. 8vo, orig cloth; worn & soiled. Library numbers on back of tp. pba Feb 12 (519) $300

**Hittell, Theodore Henry, 1830-1917**
— The Adventures of James Capen Adams. San Francisco, 1860. 12mo, orig cloth; Repaired tear to front free endpaper. Larson copy. pba Feb 12 (1) $1,200
1st Ed. - Illus by Charles Nahl. 12mo, orig cloth; faded, cloth worn & stained. With 12 plates. Robbins copy. pba Mar 21 (150) $375
— History of California. San Francisco, 1885-98. 1st Eds. 4 vols. 8vo, orig half mor & cloth; spines scuffed & stained. Robbins copy. pba Mar 21 (151) $400

**Hitzig, Friedrich**
— Ausgefuehrte Bauwerke. Berlin, [1850-64]. 10 parts in 2 vols, including the 2 Supplements. Folio, 19th-cent half mor. With 68 plates, 25 of them in color or tinted. Blindstamp on each plate. S Nov 30 (235) £1,900

**Hoare, Sir Richard Colt, 1758-1838**
— The Itinerary of Archbishop Baldwin through Wales.... L, 1806. 2 vols. 4to, calf gilt; worn & rubbed, hinges weak. With 55 plates & 5 maps. K Feb 11 (369) $225

**Hoare, Sarah**
— Poems on Conchology and Botany. Bristol, 1831. 8vo, orig cloth. With 5 plates, 2 hand-colored. b Dec 5 (31) £90

**Hobbes, Thomas, 1588-1679**
— Leviathan. L, 1651. 1st Ed, 1st Issue, with "head" ornament on t.p. Folio, modern calf, with Cambridge-style panels laid down & contemp flyleaves with pen trials bound in front & back. Bound at end is: Cock, Charles George. English Law, or a Summary Survey of the Household of God on Earth, 1651. P June 5 (270) $4,750
2d Ed, with "bear" ornament on t.p. L: Andrew Ckooke, 1651 [but Amst., c.1651]. 4to, old calf; covers detached. Some browning; a few leaves torn. CE May 22 (271) $750
— Philosophical Rudiments Concerning Government and Society. L, 1651. 1st Ed in English. 12mo, modern sheep; bound tight. With engraved title & 3 plates. Lacking initial & final blanks; engraved title silked with edge wear. pba June 20 (197) $1,100

**Hobbs, James, b.1819**
— Wild Life in the Far West.... Hartford, 1872. 1st Ed. 8vo, orig cloth; some wear. Frontis & tp frayed at fore-edge. wa Feb 29 (578) $120

**Hobhouse, John Cam, 1st Baron Broughton**
— Historical Illustrations of the Fourth Canto of Childe Harold.... L, 1818. 8vo, contemp mor gilt by Doll. b May 30 (272) £120
— A Journey through Albania and other Provinces of Turkey. L, 1813. 1st Ed. 2 vols. 4to, modern half mor. With frontis, 2 folding maps, & 23 plates (17

hand-colored, 2 folding). Text discolored. S Oct 26 (111) £1,250 [Chelsea Rare]

**Hobson, Anthony Robert Alwyn**
— Great Libraries. NY, [1970]. Folio, orig cloth in dj; worn. sg Apr 11 (131) $120

**Hobson, Geoffrey D.**
— Bindings in the Cambridge Libraries. Cambr., 1929. 1st Ed, one of 230. Folio, orig cloth, in def dj. S Mar 28 (458) £400
— English Bindings 1490-1940 in the Library of J. R. Abbey. L, 1940. One of 180. Folio, orig cloth. Inscr by Abbey to Philip James, 15 Oct 1947. Ck Apr 12 (241) £800
— Maioli, Canevari and Others. Bost., 1926. 4to, orig cloth; spine frayed. With 64 plates. Library markings. O Mar 26 (134) $100
— Notes on the History of Sotheby's. L, 1917. Ltd Ed. Folio, orig wraps. With 2 sgd etchings by Stanley Anderson. bba May 9 (88) £55 [Quaritch]
— Thirty Bindings. L, 1926. Out-of-series copy. 4to, orig cloth; hinge cracked. bba May 9 (138) £80 [Besley]

**Hobson, Richmond Pearson**
— The Sinking of the "Merrimac".... NY, 1899. 8vo, cloth. Inscr. sg Oct 26 (348) $80

**Hobson, Robert Lockhart**
— A Catalogue of Chinese Pottery and Porcelain in the Collection of Sir Percival David. L, 1934. One of 650. Folio, orig silk by Sangorski & Sutcliffe. S June 12 (323) £600
Anr copy. Orig silk by Sangorski & Sutcliffe, in edge-worn dj; wear along bottom edges. sg June 13 (90) $850
— Catalogue of the Leonard Gow Collection of Chinese Porcelain. L, 1931. One of 300, sgd by Gow. 4to, orig cloth. S June 12 (324) £210
— The Later Ceramic Wares of China. L, 1925. One of 250 on handmade paper with 5 extra plates in color. 4to, pigskin; rehinged. Minor foxing on prelims. sg June 13 (89) $175
— Worcester Porcelain. L, 1910. 4to, cloth; worn & shaken. sg Sept 7 (78) $200
Anr copy. Folio, With 109 plates, including 17 in color. sg June 13 (88) $350

**Hobson, Robert Lockhart —& Hetherington, Arthur Lonsdale**
— The Art of the Chinese Potter. L, 1923. One of 1,500. 4to, orig cloth; rear hinge cracked, frontis loose. sg Jan 11 (86) $140; sg June 13 (91) $150

**Hobson, Robert Lockhart —& Morse, Edward S., 1838-1925**
— Chinese, Corean and Japanese Potteries.... NY, 1914. One of 1,500. 4to, half cloth. wa Dec 14 (557) $65

**Hocker, Johann Ludwig**
— Einleitung zur Erkenntnis und Gebrauch der Erd und Himmels-Kugel. Nuremberg: P. C. Monath, 1734. 2 parts in 1 vol. 4to, contemp vellum. With frontis & 10 hand-colored plates. Tear through 1 plate repaired; frontis repaired at inner margin with loss; ptd label pasted in lower margin at end of the Vorrede. S Mar 14 (175) £380

**Hockney, David**
See also: Spender & Hockney
— David Hockney, Photographs. L, [1982]. 4to, cloth, in dj with extremity wear. sg Feb 29 (162) $80
— Paper Pools. L, 1980. One of 1,000. 4to, orig cloth. With orig litho in folder. Ck May 31 (53) £620; wad Oct 18 (287) C$1,900
— Suites No. 8. Geneva: Galerie Krugier & Cie., 1964. Illus by Hockney, Antes, Bertholo, & 3 others. 4to, folder by Uhry; minor wear. Plate corners bumped. sg Sept 7 (324) $50

**Hodge, Hiram C.**
— Arizona As It Is.... NY, 1877. 8vo, cloth; worn. Some foxing. pba Nov 16 (130) $85

**Hodges, James, 1672-1755**
— War Betwixt the Two British Kingdoms Consider'd. L, 1705. 1st Ed. 8vo, calf; rebacked, worn. pba Nov 30 (180) $140

**Hodges, William, 1744-97**
— Travels in India.... L, 1793. 1st Ed. 4to, contemp calf; worn. With folding map & 14 plates. Some soiling & foxing. O Mar 5 (116) £375

**Hodgkin, Thomas, 1798-1866**
— The History of England. L, 1906. 12 vols. Contemp half mor; corners & edges rubbed. CE Feb 21 (148) $800

**Hodgson, William Hope, 1875-1918**
— The House on the Borderland. Sauk City, 1946. In dj with spine ends rubbed. pba May 4 (153) $190
Anr copy. In dj. sg June 20 (168) $200

**Hoe, Robert, 1839-1909**
See also: Grolier Club
— [Sale Catalogue] Catalogue of the Library.... NY, 1911-12. One of 275. Folio, orig wraps; worn. With frontis. S Oct 27 (976) £220 [Sawyer]

**Hoefer, J. C. F.**
— Nouvelle Biographie generale depuis les temps les plus recules jusqu'a nos jours. Paris, 1852-70. 46 vols in 23. 8vo, contemp half mor. sg Apr 11 (132) $425

**Hoehnel, Ludwig von**
— Discovery of Lakes Rudolf and Stefanie. L, 1894. 2 vols. 8vo, orig cloth; joints rubbed, Vol I broken. Library markings. pn Dec 7 (148) £240

**Hoff Library, Grace Whitney**
— Catalogue des manuscrits, incunables.... Paris, 1933. Out-of-series copy on velin d'Arches. 2 vols. 4to, orig wraps. bba May 9 (124) £500 [Maggs]

**Hoffmann, Carl, 1802-83**
— Botanischer Bilder-Atlas nach De Candolle's Natuerlichem Pflanzensystem. Stuttgart, 1884. 4to, orig half cloth; top of spine chipped. With 85 hand-colored plates. sg May 9 (304) $275
— Pflanzen-Atlas nach dem Linneschen System. Stuttgart, 1881. 4to, early half mor; extremities worn. With 80 hand-colored plates. sg May 9 (305) $400

**Hoffmann, Ernst Theodor Wilhelm, 1776-1822**
See also: Limited Editions Club
— Weird Tales. L: Nimmo, 1885 [1884]. One of 50. 2 vols. 8vo, contemp half mor gilt by the Booklover's bindery. With 11 proof etchings by A. Lalauze. bba May 30 (228) £90 [Devitt]

**Hoffmann, Heinrich, 1809-94.** See: Limited Editions Club

**Hoffmann, Peter**
— [In Russian: A Collection Worthy of Curiosity from the Realm of Plants....] Moscow, 1803-[10]. Parts 7-14 in 1 vol. Folio, contemp mor gilt; worn. With engraved dedication & 150 hand-colored plates. Some leaves slightly affected by damp. C May 31 (24) £12,000

**Hofland, Thomas C., 1770-1844**
— The British Angler's Manual. L, 1839. 1st Ed. 8vo, orig cloth. With 14 plates. Some foxing & soiling. O Feb 6 (130) $90

**Hogan, Ben —&**
**Wind, Herbert Warren**
— Five Lessons: The Modern Fundamentals of Golf. NY, [1957]. 1st Ed. - Illus by Anthony Ravielli. In dj; browned. Inscr & sgd. pba Apr 18 (86) $250

**Hogarth, William, 1697-1764**
— The Analysis of Beauty. L, 1753. 4to, contemp calf; joints split, spine torn. With folding frontis & folding plate at end. Repaired tear to frontis. S Mar 28 (610) £460
— Les Satyres. L: R. Sayer, 1768. Folio, contemp bds; rebacked in calf. With 79 plates & the additional March of the Medical Militants & a reduced plate of The Roast Beef ptd above the verse. Tear in tp repaired. C May 1 (78) £1,500
— Works. L & Glasgow, 1821. Ed by John Trusler. 2 vols. Folio, contemp mor gilt; edges worn, hinges cracked. CE Sept 27 (145) $200
Anr Ed. L, 1822. Ed by John Nichols. Folio, contemp calf gilt; joints split, extremities rubbed. With port & 118 leaves of plates showing 154 subjects on 151 plates. 1 leaf shaved with minor loss to caption. C Oct 25 (129) £1,100
Anr copy. Contemp half mor; scuffed. With port & 115 plates.lates. Some leaves spotted & dust-soiled; minor marginal tears. C May 31 (92) £1,100
Anr copy. Contemp calf; worn. Frontis repaired & laid down; library stamp on tp; some soiling & marginal tears. Ck Sept 8 (39) £700
Anr copy. Early half mor; extremities worn, rubbed. With 116 plates. sg May 9 (350) $1,900
Anr Ed. L: Baldwin & Cradock, [1835-37]. Folio, later half mor; rubbed, lea peeling at corners, scuffed, rear pastedown detached. With 154 engravings on 115 plates. Tp creased & with small tears; foxed throughout text & on margins of plates; lacking 1 plate. cb Oct 17 (642) $500
Anr copy. Contemp half mor; front cover detached, spine worn. Sold w.a.f. CE May 22 (272) $800
Anr copy. Contemp half lea; broken, worn. Ck Sept 8 (38) £550
Anr copy. Contemp half lea; worn. With 116 plates. Lacking the suppressed plates; some plates stained, foxed, separated at plate mark, loose & cropped in margins, or frayed. sold w.a.f. O Mar 5 (117) $650
Anr copy. Half mor; covers detached, worn. With 2 suppressed plates smaller & loose. Some tape repairs; 2 plates & tp creased; some foxing & soiling; 4 plates & tp torn. rs Nov 11 (96) $800
Anr Ed. L, 1872. 2 vols. Folio, half russia; front cover of Vol I detached, scuffed & bumped. With photographic plates. Some foxing. wd May 8 (59) $500
Anr Ed. L, [c.1880]. Intro by Janes Hannay. 4to, half mor gilt; worn, hinges cracked. Some foxing. wa Nov 16 (313) $120

**Hogenberg, Franz.** See: Braun & Hogenberg

**Hogg, James, 1770-1835**
— The Jacobite Relics of Scotland.... Edin., 1819-21. Vol I only. 8vo, contemp bds; rebacked with later cloth. Some leaves soiled. CG June 12 (5) £110
Anr copy. 2 vols. 8vo, mor gilt by Toovey; extremities rubbed, spines discolored. Z June 28 (118) $200

**Hogg, Robert, 1818-97 —&**
**Johnson, George William**
— The Wild Flowers of Great Britain. L, 1863-80. 8 vols. 8vo, half lea; bumped & worn. Some foxing. Met May 22 (434) $700

**Hohenemser, Paul**
— Stadtbibliothek Frankfurt am Main. Frankfurt am Main, 1925. 4to, orig cloth. sg Apr 11 (133) $60

**Hohl, Reinhold**
— Alberto Giacometti. NY: Abrams, [1971]. In dj. sg Jan 11 (195) $175

**Hohmann, Walter**
— Die Erreichbarkeit der Himmelskoerper. Munich, 1925 [but after 1945]. Wraps. sg May 16 (45) $475

**Holbach, Paul Henri Thiry, Baron d', 1723-89**
— Ethocratie ou le Gouvernement fonde sur la morale. Amst., 1776. 1st Ed. 8vo, contemp calf; rubbed. Marginal annotations in ink; author's name added in ink below title. Fuerstenberg - Schaefer copy. S Dec 7 (297) £600

**Holbein, Hans, 1497-1543**
— The Dance of Death. L, 1803. 4to, contemp calf; rebacked with mor, sides crackled. Clipping pasted on early blank. Z June 28 (119) $200

Anr Ed. L, 1816. Engraved by Wenceslas Hollar. 8vo, contemp mor gilt; rubbed. With 2 ports & 31 color plates. b May 30 (471) £130

Anr copy. Modern half calf. With 2 ports & 31 hand-colored plates. pba Nov 30 (181) $300

Anr copy. Contemp mor gilt; rebacked retaining backstrip. sg Feb 8 (305) $275

Anr Ed. L, 1892. One of 100. 8vo, orig wraps; stains on front cover. With 49 plates. sg Sept 7 (188) $90

— Facsimiles of Original Drawings in the Collection of his Majesty, for the Portraits of Illustrious Persons of the Court of Henry VIII. L, 1884. Folio, contemp half mor; rubbed, upper hinge broken. bba June 6 (18) £120 [Cherrington]

Anr copy. Half calf gilt. With 88 "colored tinted" plates. pnE Sept 20 (141) £420

— Historiarum veteris instrumenti icones ad vivum expressae. Lyon: Trechel, 1538. 1st Issue. 4to, 19th-cent blind-panelled mor. Roman types. With 92 woodcut illusts. Stamp removed from tp verso; some soiling throughout. P Nov 1 (114) $3,000

— Historiarum veteris testamenti icones.... Lyons: I. & F. Frellon, 1543. 4to, 19th-cent mor; rebacked, rubbed. Repair in fore-margin of A4; some leaves with Latin mottos in an early hand washed; some worming at end; C2 & 3 bound in reverse order. S June 27 (328) £900

Anr Ed. Lyons: Jean Frellon, 1547. ("Icones historiarum Veteris Testamenti....") 4to, modern vellum. Minor foxing. S July 11 (5) £1,000

— Icones mortis duodecim imaginibus praeter priores. Lyons: J. Frellon, 1547. Trans by Gregorius Aemilius. 8vo, modern vellum. Italic with some roman types. With 53 woodcuts in text by Holbein, 42 of them cut in wood by Hans Lutzelburger. Some soiling; worming at head of 1st few leaves; some marginal repairs & dampstains; shaving to some marginalia. Schaefer copy. P Nov 1 (115) $2,750

— Simolachri, historie, e figure de la morte. Lyons: Frellon, 1549. 8vo, modern mor. With 53 woodcuts. Repairs in C7, D5 7 K8-L2 with minor damage to text; some stains; some headlines shaved. S June 27 (327) £900

— Les Simulachres & historieses faces de la mort. Lyons, 1538. 4to, mor with blind-stamped lozenge by Trautz-Bauzonnet; rubbed. Roman types. With 41 woodcuts by Holbein cut by Hans Luetzelburger. Wormholes repaired, costing c.25 characters on B2-F3 (a few characters replaced in pen facsimile); inkstain at lower margin of A2v-3r; tear at foot of M4. Schaefer copy. P Nov 1 (116) $17,000

### Holberg, Ludwig

— Geographie eller Jordbeskrivelse. Copenhagen, 1759-91. 7 vols. 4to, contemp calf; not uniform, rubbed. With 1 plate & 30 maps, 24 of them in contemp body color & 6 in outline color. Wormhole in tp of Vol I. S Mar 14 (176) £720

— A Journey to the World Under-Ground. L, 1742. 8vo, contemp calf; spine cracked, rubbed, lacking rear free endpaper. Some soiling. bba Oct 19 (229) £170 [Axe]

### Holbrook, John Edwards, 1794-1871

— North American Herpetology, or a Description of the Reptiles Inhabiting the United States. Phila., 1842. 2d Ed. 5 vols. 4to, half lea. With 148 hand-colored plates, with variant plate Testudo Carolina. Some foxing & browning; marginal soiling. Met May 22 (434A) $5,000

### Holcroft, Thomas, 1745-1809

— The Theatrical Recorder. L, 1805. 2 vols. 12mo, contemp calf; front cover of Vol I detached. pba Aug 22 (655) $110

### Holden, George H., 1848-1914

— The Idyl of the Split-Bamboo. Cincinnati: Stewart & Kidd, [1920]. Orig cloth. pba July 11 (144) $170

### Holder, Charles Frederick, 1851-1915

— All About Pasadena and its Vicinity. Bost.: Lee & Shepard, 1889. Orig cloth; spine ends & corners rubbed. pba July 25 (159) $250

— Along the Florida Reef. NY, 1892. 1st Ed. 8vo, cloth; front free endpaper lacking, small spot on front joint. pba July 11 (145) $140

Anr copy. Orig cloth; extremities rubbed, front hinge cracked. pba July 25 (160) $110

— The Big Game Fishes of the United States. NY, 1903. One of 100. Contemp half lea; worn. Library markings. sg Mar 7 (472) $90

— The Channel Islands of California. NY, 1910. Orig cloth. pba July 11 (146) $170

Anr copy. Orig cloth; soiled. pba July 25 (162) $180

Anr copy. Orig cloth; some soiling. Foxed. pba Aug 22 (921) $130

— The Game Fishes of the World. NY, [1913]. 4to, cloth; worn & rubbed, spine head torn. pba July 25 (163) $200

— Life in the Open.... NY, 1906. Cloth; rubbed. pba July 11 (399) $70

Anr copy. Cloth; extremities rubbed. Lower corners of prelims creased. pba July 25 (166) $100

— Recreations of a Sportsman on the Pacific Coast. NY, 1910. Orig cloth; endpapers & tp stamped. pba July 25 (168) $200

— Santa Catalina, an Isle of Summer.... San Francisco, 1895. Orig wraps; worn. pba July 25 (169) $800

### Holderman, J. B.

— Grammaire turque; ou, methode courte & facile, pour apprendre.... Constantinople: Ibrahim Mueteferrika, 1730. 1st Ed. 4to, contemp bds; worn. Text in English & Osmanli (Turkish Arabic). With 1 double-page plate. S Oct 26 (113) £1,500 [Mertturkmen]

### Holinshed, Raphael, d.1580?

— The Firste [-Laste] Volume of the Chronicles.... L: [H. Bynneman] for G. Bishop, 1577. 1st Ed, STC13568a. 4 parts in 2 vols. Folio, mor gilt by Bedford; joints & corners rubbed, Vol II upper hinge weak. Black letter; double-column. Errata leaf for Part 1 bound after prelims; errata leaf for Parts 2-3 bound at end of Part 2; general errata bifolium bound at end of Vol II; tp of Vol II from anr copy (repaired) as are fol. 2:3I3 & Edinburgh map (shaved affecting image); repairs; some headlines & shoulder-notes shaved; washed & pressed. CNY May 17 (88) $7,500

Anr Ed. L: [H. Bynneman] for J. Harrison, 1577. STC 13568. 4 parts in 2 vols. Folio, contemp bds; rebacked, rubbed. Some sidenotes shaved; several leaves torn in lower outer corner with minor loss; Vol I lacking contents to 1st part & errata to 2d; last index leaf frayed with loss & mtd; Vol II tp in facsimile; view of Edinburgh repaired along fore-edge. pba Sept 14 (205) $2,500

2d Ed. L, 1587. ("The First and Second [and Third] Volumes of Chronicles.") 3 vols in 4. Folio, old calf; rebacked, rubbed. Titles stamped. O Mar 5 (118) $3,300

Anr Ed. L, 1807-8. ("Chronicles of England, Scotland, and Ireland.") 6 vols. 4to, contemp calf gilt; 1 vol rebacked preserving spine, upper cover of anr vol detached. Some spotting & browning. bba July 18 (211) £310 [Classic Bindings]

**Holland, Henry, 1583-1650?**
— Herologia Anglica hoc est clarissimorum aliquot Anglorum vivae effigies. Arnheim [L?], 1620. Folio, contemp calf; rubbed, upper cover detached, spine split. Engraved title torn, cut down & mtd; 1 leaf torn; several leaves lacking; browned. bba July 18 (161) £60 [Fletcher]

**Holland, Sir Henry, 1788-1873**
— Travels in the Ionian Isles.... L, 1815. 4to, vellum. With map & 12 plates. b May 30 (273) £500

**Holland, John**
— The Village of Eyam. Macclesfield, 1821. 8vo, modern bds. b Dec 5 (45) £70

**Holland, Mary**
— The Economic and Frugal Housewife. L, [n.d.]. 12mo, modern cloth. Repairs to lower edge of frontis & vignette title; 4 plates with marginal worming; lacking prelims & half-title; some foxing & dampstaining. bba Oct 19 (269) £65 [W. English]

**Holland, Ray P.**
— Shotgunning in the Lowlands. West Hartford, [1945]. One of 350. O June 25 (161) $145; sg Mar 7 (473) $200

**Hollander, John**
— Dal Vero. NY: The Library Fellows of the Whitney Museum, 1983. One of 140. Illus by Saul Steinberg. Oblong 4to, half vellum. CE Sept 27 (262) $300

**Hollar, Wenceslaus, 1607-77**
— Animalium Ferarum & Bestiarum, Florum, Fructuum... A New and Perfect Book.... L, 1674 [c.1740]. Folio, modern half calf. With 10 (of 12) plates. S Mar 28 (550) £450

— The Kingdome of England & Principality of Wales, Exactly Described. L, 1676. Folio, contemp sheep; rebacked. With 6 folding maps. Some folds torn. bba June 6 (352) £550 [Baynton-Williams]

Anr copy. 8vo, contemp calf; worn, covers detached. With title & 6 folding map sheets. Sheets loose & damaged with loss. Sold w.a.f. S Oct 26 (354) £260 [Smith]

— Mortalium nobilitas. Antwerp, 1651. 5 mats with 6 engravings mtd within borders on each, 75mm by 54mm blocks, 111mm by 89mm borders. Schaefer copy. P Nov 1 (117) $4,750

— Theatrum mulierum. L: Laurie & Whittle, [1790?]. 12mo, half mor; front free endpaper lacking. K Oct 1 (211) $400

Anr Ed. L, [c.1800]. 8vo, orig wraps. With title & 48 plates. S Oct 26 (307) £180 [Marlborough]

**Hollingsworth, John McHenry**
— The Journal of.... San Francisco, 1923. 1st Ed, One of 300. Orig cloth. With color frontis. Larson copy. pba Sept 28 (679) $60

Anr copy. In def dj; library bookplate. pba Nov 16 (133) $55

One of 50 L.p. copies. Half vellum. pba July 25 (300) $140

**Hollstein, F. W. H.**
— Dutch and Flemish Etchings, Engravings and Woodcuts. Amst., [1949-94]. Vols 1-43 in 40 only [lacking Vols 30, 33 & 34) & Supplement, Parts 1 & 2, 1993-94. 4to, orig cloth, in djs. bba Oct 5 (268) £4,200 [Franks]

Anr copy. Vols 1-38 in 42 only [lacking Vols 4, 25, 26 & 37). 4to, bba Oct 5 (269) £4,000 [Franks]

**Holman, John Paulison**
— Sheep and Bear Trails; a Hunter's Wanderings in Alaska and British Columbia. NY, 1933. 8vo, cloth. Inscr. O Oct 10 (163) $650

Anr copy. Cloth, in frayed dj; worn. Inscr. O Oct 10 (164) $325

One of 75. Orig cloth, unopened; worn & soiled. O Oct 10 (162) $375

**Holman, Louis A., 1866-1939**
— The Graphic Processes: Intaglio, Relief, Planographic. Bost., 1926. Folio, loose as issued in folder. With 32 mtd specimens. O May 7 (160) $275

Anr copy. With 37 specimens. sg Apr 18 (62) $425

**Holme, Charles, 1848-1923**
— Colour Photography and other Recent Developments.... L: The Studio, 1908. 4to, cloth; worn, front hinge cracked. sg Feb 29 (103) $225

Anr copy. Cloth; hinge cracked, worn. sg Feb 29 (103) $225

— English Water-Colour. L: The Studio, 1902. 4to, orig cloth; rubbed. Some scoring. bba July 18 (36) £75 [Classic Bindings]

— Modern Pen Drawings: European and American. L, 1901. Folio, orig cloth; worn. F June 20 (305) $70

## Holme, John Clellon
— The Horn. NY: Random House, [1958]. In chipped dj. pba Oct 5 (157) $55

## Holmes, Eugenia Kellogg
— Adolph Sutro. San Francisco, 1895. Orig cloth. pba Apr 25 (455) $120

## Holmes, Sir Maurice G.
— Captain James Cook...a Bibliographical Excursion. L, 1952. One of 500. pba Feb 13 (50) $170

## Holmes, Oliver Wendell, 1809-94
— The Autocrat of the Breakfast Table. Bost., 1859. L.p. Ed. 8vo, half mor gilt, orig cloth bound in. With ALs to Mr. Hayne inserted. sg Sept 21 (225) $400
State A. Orig cloth; spine ends repaired. With 8 illusts. Inscr to B. R. Curtis. sg Sept 21 (224) $1,000
— Works. Bost., [1892]. Standard Library Ed. 13 vols. 8vo, contemp half mor gilt. sg Sept 21 (25) $650
Artists' Ed. Bost. & NY, [1892]. one of 750. 15 vols, including Morse's 2-vol Life & Letters, 1896. 8vo, mor gilt. With ANs tipped in. cb Oct 17 (276) $1,100

## Holmes, Oliver Wendell, 1841-1935
— The Common Law. Bost., 1881. 1st Ed. 8vo, orig cloth; edges rubbed. K June 23 (318) $950
Anr copy. Cloth; library bookplate. Some leaves chipped. sg Sept 21 (226) $350

## Holroyd, John Baker, 1st Earl of Sheffield, 1735-1821
— Observations on the Commerce of the American States with Europe and the West Indies.... Dublin, 1784. 8vo, contemp calf; worn & soiled. wa Feb 29 (353) $110

## Holt, Ardern
— Fancy Dresses Described; or, What to Wear at Fancy Balls. L, [1882]. 8vo, orig cloth. With 32 litho plates, 16 of them in color shaken. sg Jan 11 (123) $60

## Holt, J. C.
See: Onassis copy, Jacqueline Bouvier Kennedy

## Holt, Luther Emmett, 1855-1924
— The Diseases of Infancy and Childhood. NY, 1897. 1st Ed. 8vo, orig half sheep; spine & corners worn. With 19 plates, 7 of them in color. With errata slip. sg May 16 (432) $200

## Holtzapffel, Charles & John Jacob
— Turning and Mechanical Manipulation. L, 1852-94. Vols I-V (of 6). 8vo, orig cloth; worn. b Jan 31 (267) £340

## Holwell, John Zephaniah, 1711-98
— Interesting Historical Events, Relative to the Provinces of Bengal.... L, 1766-71. 3 parts in 1 vol. 8vo, contemp half calf; worn, joints split. Some foxing & staining. wa Dec 14 (160) $220

## Holywood, John. See: Sacrobosco, Johannes

## Holzworth, John M.
— The Wild Grizzlies of Alaska. L, 1930. 1st Ed. Orig cloth; endpapers foxed. Some foxing to tp & prelims. pba July 25 (405) $110

## Home, Sir Everard, 1756-1832
— Observations on Cancer. L, 1805. 1st Ed. 8vo, contemp calf; rebacked, worn. Tp torn; some marginalia. CE Nov 8 (110) $150

## Home, Henry, Lord Kames, 1696-1782
— Sketches of the History of Man. Edin., 1774. 1st Ed. 2 vols. 4to, contemp calf; Vol I spine chipped. S June 12 (58) £850

## Homer
See also: Fore-Edge Paintings; Limited Editions Club; Nonesuch Press; Southey's copy, Robert

### Iliad & Odyssey in English
— [1611-13]. - L.Trans by George Chapman. 2 parts in 1 vol. Folio, modern mor. Without the unsgd sheet containing sonnets to Viscounts Cranborne & Rochester; B6 marginally def with loss of 1 side-word; I6 torn; Part 2 lacking 3 blanks & engraved title; some worming towards end, occasionally affecting text. Sold w.a.f. bba July 18 (159) £1,200 [Grant & Shaw]

### Iliad in English
— 1715-20. - The Iliad. L. Trans by Alexander Pope. 6 vols. Folio, contemp calf; worn. b Sept 20 (206) £160
— 1891. - L. 8vo, vellum gilt prize bdg with gilt crest of Newton Abbot College; spine soiled, worn. wa Dec 14 (158) $80

### Iliad in French
— 1776. - Iliade. Paris 3 vols. 4to, contemp mor gilt; stain to upper cover of Vol III. Last gathering of Vol II browned; 1 plate foxed. L.p. copy. Fuerstenberg - Schaefer copy. S Dec 7 (299) £950

### Odyssey in English
— 1772. - The Odyssey. Glasgow: Foulis Trans by Alexander Pope. 3 vols. 16mo, contemp calf. Margins trimmed. pba Nov 30 (184) $160
— 1924. - L: Medici Society One of 530. Trans by S. H. Butcher & Andrew Lang; illus by William Russell Flint. 4to, cloth. b Jan 31 (160) £85
Anr copy. Orig cloth. b Jan 31 (161) £70
Anr copy. Cloth, in dj with front panel separated. sg Sept 14 (128) $225
— 1929. - Cambr. MA Illus by N. C. Wyeth. 4to, cloth. sg Feb 15 (316) $175
— 1929. - Cambr., Mass. One of 550 L.p. copies. Illus by N. C. Wyeth. 4to, half pigskin. Without the extra suite of plates; prelims foxed. sg Sept 14 (345) $650
— 1932. - L. One of 530. Trans by T. E. Lawrence. 4to, orig mor. S Dec 18 (341) £700 [Blackwell]; sg Apr 18 (63) $1,100

### Odyssey in Spanish

— 1553. - La Ulyxea. Venice: Gabriel Giolito de Ferrariis & fratelli. 12mo, modern mor. Ptd on blue paper Tp with 2 portions of margins cut away & repaired; some staining at beginning; early marginal annotations. S June 27 (329) £700

### Works in English

— [1616]. - The Whole Works of Homer.... L: Nathaniell Butter Trans by George Chapman. 2 parts in 1 vol. Folio, later half calf; front cover detached. Lacking general title & prelims before Iliad; also lacking 1 leaf from dedication to the Odyssey. Sold w.a.f. pba Nov 30 (183) $200

### Works in Greek

— 1488, 9 Dec. - Florence: Bernardus Nerlius & D. Damilas. 2 vols. Folio, modern calf over bds with metal clasps, in style of Renaissance bdg. Preface repaired with portion in pen facsimile. 438 (of 440) leaves; lacking 2 blanks. Goff H-300. pba Nov 30 (182) $30,000

**Honan, Michael Burke**
— The Andalusian Annual for MDCCCXXXVII. L, 1836. 4to, orig cloth. With 12 hand-colored plates. S June 27 (110) £850

**Hondius, Jodocus, 1563-1611**
See also: Mercator & Hondius
— Theatrum artis scribendi, varia summorum nostri seculi.... Amst.: Johannes Janssonius, 1614. Oblong folio, modern vellum; new endpapers, corner of front flyleaf torn & repaired. With 41 plates of calligraphic specimens within 26 different separately engraved baroque scrollwork borders. Tp soiled & with upper platemark shaved & inner edge of engraving image hidden in gutter; some marginal soiling; stain to upper margin of Plate 13. William Stirling Maxwell's copy. CNY May 17 (54) $750

**Hone, William, 1780-1842**
— The Everyday Book. L, 1826-27. 2 vols. Half mor by Root. With 320 plates, 11 by George Cruikshank. cb Oct 17 (619) $225

**Honey, William Bowyer**
— European Ceramic Art. L, 1949-52. One of 100 & one of 250. 2 vols. 4to, mor gilt; minor defs. pba June 20 (199) $85

**Honeyman Collection, Robert**
— [Sale Catalogue] The Honeyman Collection of Scientific Books and Manuscripts. L, 1978-81. 7 vols. Wraps. ds July 27 (92) $125
Anr copy. Price lists laid in; some prices in ink. O May 7 (161) $200
Anr copy. Orig cloth. sg May 16 (178A) $275

**Honorius, Johannes**
— Epitomata in Valerii Maximi libros.... [Wuerzburg: Jakob Thanner, 1503]. 4to, 19th-cent half sheep; extremities worn. Soiled & dampstained throughout;

marginal repairs. Lacking tp & 3 prelims. Sold w.a.f. sg Mar 21 (325) $300

**Honterus, Joannes, 1498-1549**
— De cosmographiae rudimentis.... Basel: Heinrich Petri, 1561. 8vo, 19th-cent calf. With 24 miniature woodcut maps, 12 of them double-page. Erasure on general title affecting letters. S Nov 30 (72) £2,300

**Hood, John B.**
— Advance and Retreat. New Orleans, 1880. 8vo, later cloth; minor spotting. bbc Apr 22 (106) $200

**Hood, Thomas, 1799-1845**
See also: Fore-Edge Paintings
— Whims and Oddities. L, 1827-29. 2d Ed. 1st & 2d Series. 2 vols in 1. 8vo, 19th-cent half mor; rubbed. Inscr to Edward Moxon on flyleaf before title in each work. S Dec 18 (193) £260 [Roe]

**Hood, Thomas H.**
— Notes on a Cruise in H.M.S. "Fawn".... Edin., 1863. 8vo, orig cloth; some wear. With 9 tinted litho plates & 11 engraved plates. b Mar 20 (108) £190

**Hooft, Pieter Cornelizoon, 1581-1647**
— Mengelwerken. Amst., 1704. Folio, contemp vellum; free endpapers def, juvenile pencil doodles on front pastedowns. Marginal tears. sg Mar 21 (163) $400

**Hooge, Romein de, d.1708**
— Romeyn de Hooghe to the Burgermeisters of Haarlem. Northampton: Gehenna Press, 1971. One of 100 with extra impression of the port sgd by Leonard Baskin. Inscr by Leonard Baskin. sg Feb 15 (32) $300

**Hook, Diana H.** See: Norman & Hook

**Hooke, Andrew**
— An Essay on the National Debt, and National Capital. L, 1750. 8vo, disbound. Margins trimmed. sg Mar 21 (104) $130

**Hooke, Robert, 1635-1702**
— Micrographia, or Some Physiological Descriptions of Minute Bodies Made by Magnifying Glasses. L, 1665. 1st Ed. Folio, contemp calf; joint split, lower cover bumped. Tears to 6 folding plates, 1 of them long & repaired, 3 others repaired; some marginal dampstaining. Phillipps - Hefner copy. CNY May 17 (25) $32,000
— Philosophical Experiments and Observations. L, 1726. 1st Ed. 8vo, contemp calf. With 5 plates. b May 30 (24) £550

**Hooker, Sir Joseph Dalton, 1817-1911**
— The Rhododendrons of Sikkim-Himalaya. L, 1849-[51]. Folio, later half mor. With 30 hand-colored plates. C May 31 (25) £9,500

**Hooker, William, 1779-1832**
— Pomona Londinensis. L, [1813]-18. Vol I (all pbd). 4to, unbound as issued within orig bd portfolio. With

31 hand-colored plates only (of 49). Some soiling to 1st & last leaf. With 6 plates from Pomona Herefordiensis. Sold w.a.f.  C May 31 (26) £3,000

**Hooker, Sir William Jackson, 1785-1865**
— Journal of a Tour in Iceland.... Yarmouth, 1811. 8vo, contemp half sheep; needs rebdg. With hand-colored frontis & 3 plates.  sg Mar 7 (281) $350

**Hooker, Sir William Jackson, 1785-1865 —& Greville, Robert Kaye, 1794-1866**
— Icones Filicum: Ad eas Potissimum Species Illustrandas. Figrues and Descriptions of Ferns.... L, [1827]-31. 2 vols. Folio, contemp half mor gilt; rubbed, upper cover of Vol II off. With 240 hand-colored plates. Lacking subscribers list.  S June 27 (36) £3,200

**Hoover, Herbert, 1874-1964**
— The Challenge to Liberty. NY & L, 1934. 1st Ed. In dj. Sgd on front free endpaper.  pba June 13 (64) $160

Anr copy. Inscr to Walter P. Chrysler.  sg Feb 1 (107) $130

— Fishing for Fun.... NY: Random House, [1963]. One of 200.  O June 25 (162) $190
— The Herbert Clark Hoover Collection of Mining & Metallurgy: Biblioteca de re Metaliica. Claremont, Calif., 1980. 1st Ed, One of 500. 4to, orig cloth in dj.  sg Apr 11 (284) $175
— A Remedy for Disappearing Game Fishes. NY, 1930. One of 990.  pba July 11 (132) $65

**Hope, Anthony.** See: Hawkins, Sir Anthony Hope

**Hope, Thomas, 1770?-1831**
— Anastasius: or, Memoirs of a Greek. L, 1819. 3 vols. Contemp calf gilt; rubbed. Some spotting; lacking half-titles.  S Apr 23 (75) £150
— Costume of the Ancients. L, 1809. 4to, contemp calf gilt. With 196 plates only. Vol number excised from half-title.  sg Dec 7 (259) $90

Anr Ed. L, 1812. 2 vols. 4to, contemp russia gilt; joints weak. With 300 plates.  pba Nov 30 (186) $350

**Hope, Sir William**
— A New, Short and Easy Method of Fencing. Edin., 1707. 4to, modern calf. With folding sheet, & folding plate. Plate & title torn 7 laid down; browned.  S Oct 27 (828) £250 [Way]

**Hopkins, F. Powell**
— Fishing Experiences of Half a Century.... L, 1893. Orig cloth.  pba July 11 (149) $100

**Hopkins, Gerard Manley, 1844-89.** See: Nonesuch Press

**Hopkins, Sarah Winnemucca, 1844-91**
— Life Among the Piutes.... Bost., 1883. Orig cloth; soiled, lacking front free endpaper.  pba Aug 8 (81) $120

**Hopkinson, Cecil**
— Collecting Golf Books. L: Constable, [1938]. 1st Ed. Orig wraps.  pba Nov 9 (37) $1,300

Anr copy. Orig wraps; chipped, corners dogeared, lower rear corner lacking.  pba Apr 18 (87) $950

Anr Ed. Worcestershire: Grant Books, 1980. One of 250. Compiled by H. R. Grant. Cloth; lower corners bumped. With A.N.s. from the Grants & from S. W. Sinclair. Sgd by Shirley Grant & S. W. Sinclair.  pba Apr 18 (88) $300

**Horace, 65-8 B.C.**
See also: Ashendene Press; Limited Editions Club
— Opera. Paris: Badius Ascensius, June 1516. Bound with: Terentius Afer, Publius. Comoedie.... Paris: Badius Ascensius, 15 July 1504. Folio, 18th-cent calf; lower cover scraped, rebacked retaining orig spine. 1st work lacking K6 (supplied in Ms on 2 leaves) & L8; 2d work lacking tp, with repairs in inner margins of 1st gathering & tear in last leaf. Dampstaining & soiling.  S Mar 29 (660) £280

Anr Ed. Cambr., 1711. 2 parts in 1 vol. 4to, modern calf gilt. Some marginal waterstaining.  bba July 18 (175) £130 [Unsworth]

Anr copy. Contemp calf gilt; rebacked retaining most of orig backstrip.  sg Mar 21 (164) $325

Anr Ed. L, 1733-37. Pine's 1st Issue, with "post est" reading on p 108. 2 vols. 8vo, contemp mor gilt. Fuerstenberg - Schaefer copy.  S Dec 7 (300) £1,200

Anr copy. Contemp calf gilt; spine ends repaired.  S June 12 (187) £400

Anr Ed. Paris, 1733. 24mo, 19th-cent lev gilt.  pba Aug 22 (596) $200

Anr Ed. Birm.: Baskerville, 1770. 4to, contemp mor gilt. With frontis & 4 plates. Some browning. Fuerstenberg - Schaefer copy.  S Dec 7 (302) £650

Anr Ed. Paris: Didot l'aine, 1799. One of 100 on papier velin. Folio, contemp red mor extra by Bradel, with his ticket, bound for Napoleon & among the books left behind in Paris, with the arms of Louis XVIII superimposed on covers.  C May 1 (79) £3,000

— Poemata. Rotterdam: Regnus Leers, 1700. 12mo, 19th-cent calf gilt. Margins cut close; edge wear to engraved title; dampstaining.  pba Mar 7 (138) $120
— Works. L: E. C. for W. Lee, G. Bedell, H. Heringman & H. Brome, 1666. ("The Poems.") Trans by Alexander Brome. 8vo, calf gilt; rebacked, preserving bds & backstrip. Cut close; some soiling.  wa Feb 1 (142) $230
— The Works. L, 1849. Illus by Owen Jones. 8vo, modern half mor gilt.  pba Apr 4 (229) $350

**Horae B. M. V.**
— 1499, 20 Mar. - Horae...[Use of Rome]. Lyons: Boninus de Boninis. 8vo, 16th-cent mor gilt over thin bds; joints & spine repaired. Gothic type; ptd on vellum. With 17 metalcuts; all pages surrounded with 6-part metalcut borderpieces. Marginal fingersoiling; 22 pages of the Suffrages censored by scraping to bring prayers into conformity with the mandates of

the Council of Trent. 176 leaves. Goff O-48. Fairfax Murray - Loncle - Schaefer copy. P Nov 1 (118) $6,000
— [1503], 19 Nov. - Paris: Germain Hardouyn. 8vo, early 20th-cent lev gilt. With metalcut borders throughout; 15 larger metalcuts, illuminated & rubricated initials throughout. About 34 leaves with lower margins replaced with vellum, affecting signature marks. Ptd on vellum. 96 leaves. pba Nov 30 (187) $4,000
— [calendar 1507-20]. - Heures a lusaige de Rome. Paris: Hardouin. 8vo, modern mor. With Anatomical Man & 19 full-page miniatures & several smaller metal-cuts, all illuminated. Some shaving. S June 27 (304) £5,800
— 1507. - Horae...[Use of Rome]. Paris: S. Vostre. 8vo, late 16th-cent mor gilt with symbols of a Pope but arms erased. With 27 small & 16 large finely colored woodcut illusts. Minor marginal staining of 1st 6 & final leaves. C June 26 (84) £7,800
Anr copy. Modern calf by Zaehnsdorf. Ptd on vellum; with 10 full-page cuts; initials in gold on red or blue panel. Last 9 leaves stained at lower corner; lacking 1st gathering & c.14 other leaves. Sold w.a.f. S June 12 (19) £950
— [1509]. - Paris: G. Hardouyn. 8vo, 18th-cent mor; worn. Each page with painted outer border; with Anatomical Man & 7 other large miniatures in color. C2 & some other leaves stained. Ptd on vellum. 73 (of 88) leaves; lacking C7-8, D1,3-6,8, E3, F3-6, G4-5. Bohatta 899. C June 26 (85) £2,800
— 1516. - Horae...[Use of Chartres]. Paris: Guillaume Eustace. 16mo in 8s, 19th-cent mor; upper cover detached. With 14 large & 2 small miniatures, all illuminated in colors. Some cropping; some text rubbed. Ptd on vellum. C Nov 29 (55) £3,200
— 1519 [calendar 1519-38]. - Horae...[Second Use of Rome]. Paris: Thielman Kerver. 8vo, 18th-cent calf gilt; foot of spine worn. With anatomical man & 39 three-quarter plates within historiated metal-cut borders. Ptd on vellum. C Apr 3 (115) £1,500
— [c.1520]. - Heures nostre dame a lusige de Romme. Paris: Germain Hardouyn. 8vo, 19th-cent mor gilt; rubbed. Ptd on vellum. With 14 half-page miniatures in gold & colors. Lacking Sig. A; 14 pp with passages scored through; some staining. bba Sept 7 (198) £1,100 [Hildebrandt]
— [calendar dated 1528-45]. - Horae...[Second Use of Rome]. Paris: Gilles Hardouyn. 8vo, 18th-cent sharkskin panelled in blind; rubbed, upper outer joint cracked at foot. Roman type; ptd on vellum. With Anatomical Man metalcut on [A]2r surrounded by 4 small metalcuts of the humours, 15 large mostly oval metalcuts (14 three-quarter or half-page & 1 full-page) & 20 smaller cuts, all fully illuminated in gold & colors. 1st leaf creased & rubbed; some borders & large miniature on B1r rubbed; traces of damp affecting text & borders on F5v-6r & K1; small stain to upper blank margin catching borders of c.10 leaves. CNY May 17 (89) $5,600
— 1570. - Horae...[Use of Rome]. Antwerp: C. Plantin. 8vo, contemp calf gilt to a grolieresque design heightened with silver enamel decoration; rubbed,

lower joint starting. Roman type with index in italic. With 17 full-page plates by Jean Wierix & Pieter Huys after designs by Pieter van der Borcht. Dampstaining to upper corner. Turner - Napoleon Victor Bonaparte - Burrus - Schaefer copy. P Nov 1 (120) $15,000
— 1841. - Le Livre d'heures de la Reine Anne de Bretagne. Paris Out-of-series copy. 2 vols. Folio, mor extra by Cape, the illust vol with arms of Anne de Bretagne. S Nov 21 (107) £550

**Horan, James David**
— The Life and Art of Charles Schreyvogel. NY, [1969]. Folio, orig bdg, in dj with edge-tears. pba Apr 25 (658) $110
One of 249, sgd by Horan & Schreyvogel's daughter. Half syn. sg Sept 7 (307) $130

**Horapollo, the Grammarian**
— De sacris notis & sculpturis libri duo. Paris: J. Kerver, 1551. 8vo, modern cloth. Early marginalia; some soiling; some leaves shaved along fore-edge. sg Apr 18 (64) $1,200

**Horblit, Harrison D.** See: Grolier Club

**Horgan, Paul**
— Great River. The Rio Grande in American History. NY, 1954. One of 1,000. 2 vols. 8vo, cloth. pba Nov 16 (134) $225
— The Return of the Weed. NY, 1936. One of 350. Illus by Peter Hurd. 4to, cloth. Inscr by the dedicatee, Hurd (with orig drawing) & Horgan. sg Feb 15 (164) $325

**Horlock, H. W.**
— Lord Fitzwarine. L, 1861. 3 vols. 8vo, orig cloth; spine ends frayed. Some foxing. O Jan 9 (144) $90
— Recollections of a Fox-Hunter. L, 1861. 8vo, calf by Riviere; rubbed. O Jan 9 (145) $100

**Horman, William, c.1458-1535**
— Vulgaria. L: R. Pynson, 1519. 4to, 19th-cent calf; rebacked. Lacking ff. 184-85 & 297-316; ff.P4-5 inserted form 1530 Ed. S July 11 (105) £400

**Horn, Erna —&**
**Arndt, Julius**
— Schoene alte Kochbuecher. Munich, 1982. One of 680. 8vo, orig cloth in dj. sg Apr 11 (135) $70

**Horn, Ewald.** See: Erman & Horn

**Horn, Georg, 1620-70**
— Accuratissima orbis delineatio, sive geographia vetus. Amst.: Apud Janssonio Waesbergianos, 1677. Folio, contemp vellum; soiled. With 53 double-page mapsheets. A few mapsheets strengthened or repaired without loss; some discoloration. S Nov 30 (73) £2,600

**Horn, Hosea B.**
— Horn's Overland Guide, from the U. S. Indian Sub-Agency...to...Sacramento. NY, 1852. Later Issue. 16mo, orig cloth; covers rubbed. With 1 folding

map. Some dampstaining; map spotted. Robbins copy. pba Mar 21 (152) $2,500

1st Ed, 2d Issue. 16mo, orig cloth. With folding map with hand-colored routes. Small fold breaks; minor foxing. wa Feb 29 (395) $1,500

Anr Ed. NY, 1853. 16mo, orig cloth; rebacked. With folded map tipped in. Larson copy. pba Sept 28 (622) $1,700

**Hornaday, William Temple, 1854-1937**
— Camp-Fires on Desert and Lava. NY, 1908. pba Apr 25 (458) $85

**Hornbooks**
— [Horn book with lower case alphabet engraved on one side of a shaped piece of bone, upper case alphabet on verso] [N.p., late 18th cent]. 105mm by 43mm, With floral decorations on handle & small red circles at top & bottom. S May 16 (198) £300
— [two alphabets, pairs of letters, the Lord's Prayer ptd in red & black] [N.p., early 18th-cent]. 112mm by 53mm, mtd within silver filigree case, faced with mica. S May 16 (199) £920

**Horne, Bernard S.**
— The Complete Angler 1653-1967. A New Bibliography. Pittsburgh, 1970. One of 500. In frayed dj. Vernon Hidy's copy. O Feb 6 (131) $120

Anr copy. In dj. pba July 11 (324) $75

**Horne, Thomas Hartwell, 1780-1862**
See also: Finden & Horne
— An Introduction to the Study of Bibliography. L, 1814. 2 vols. 8vo, contemp calf gilt; rubbed. bba May 9 (63) £110 [Quaritch]

**Horned...**
— Horned Beetles and Other Insects. Northampton, Mass.: Gehenna Press, 1958. One of 30, sgd by the illustrator, Leonard Baskin. Oblong 4to, orig mor gilt, by the Harcourt Bindery. With 8 etchings, ptd in various colors on a variety of handmade papers. b May 30 (520) £2,800; sg Feb 15 (21) $4,800

**Hornor, William MacPherson**
— Blue Book: Philadelphia Furniture, William Penn to George Washington.... Phila., 1935. One of 400. 4to, orig cloth; front hinge weak. Lacking most of errata slip. wa Dec 14 (461) $350

**Horrebow, Niels, 1712-60**
— The Natural History of Iceland. L, 1758. Folio, contemp half sheep; needs rebacked. With folding map. Tear across 1 leaf. sg May 16 (309) $300

**Horrebow, Peder Nielsen**
— Basis astronomiae.... Copenhagen: wido of H. C. Paullus, 1735. 4to, contemp vellum; soiled. With frontis (repeated at p. 16) & 11 folding plates. Madsen copy. S Mar 14 (177) £1,800

**Horsfield, Thomas Walker, d.1837**
— The History, Antiquities, and Topography of the County of Sussex. Lewes, 1835. 2 vols. 4to, contemp half mor; worn, upper cover of Vol I detached.

With 56 plates. Some spotting & discoloration. S Mar 28 (51) £160

**Horst, Gregorius**
— Buechlein von dem Schorbock. Giessen, 1615. Bound with: Giachini, Leonardo. Methodus curandarum febrium. Basel, 1625 2d Ed. 2 works in 1 vol. 8vo, old vellum; spine head chipped. Dampstained throughout; Giachini browned & title detached. Ck Mar 22 (151) £180
— Operum medicorum. Nuremberg, 1660. 1st Ed. 3 vols. 8vo, contemp vellum; upper joints split with damage to spine; soiled. With half-title, frontis, & title by J. Fleischberger. Frontis with hole; lower corner of 2I2, vol I, almost torn away; Y5 in vol II torn & Bb6 with paper fault; some dampstaing & soiling. Ck Mar 22 (152) £180

**Horst, Tieleman van der —&**
**Polley, Jacobus**
— Theatrum machinarum universale.... Amst.: Petrus Schenk, 1736-[43]. 2 vols in 1. Folio, contemp half Dutch vellum; worn. With 54 plates (46 double-page, 8 folding). Some browning; 2 plates & leaves becoming loose. S Oct 26 (334) £600 [Chelsea Gal.]

**Horticultural...**
— Horticultural Society of London. Transactions. L, 1812-30. First Eds of First Series Vols I-VII. 7 vols. 4to, contemp half mor; rubbed, several spines def, new endpapers & flyleaves in Vols VI & VII. With engraved titles & 133 plates, including 69 hand-finished color plates. Some foxing; some dampstaining. F June 20 (854) $2,500

**Hortulus...**
— Hortulus anime cum aliis quam plurimis orationibus.... Lyon: Johannes Clein for Anton Koberger in Nuremberg, 24 Jan 1513. 32mo, 16th-cent vellum. Gothic type. With 74 woodcuts, 13 small woodcuts of initial size. Rubricated in red, with some cuts partly colored in red & yellow. Some foliation cropped; early writing erased from tp; some marginal worming at ends. Schaefer copy. P Nov 1 (121) $6,500

**Hortus...**
— Hortus sanitatis. De herbis et plantis.... Mainz: Jacob Meydenbach, 23 June 1491. ("Hortus sanitatis.") Folio, contemp blindstamped pigskin over wooden bds; wormed & restored. 48 lines & headlines; double column; types 2:155 (headings & headlinesj) & 1:92 (text), with title in woodcut capitals. With 7 full-page woodcuts & 1,066 smaller woodcuts, all colored in a contemp hand. A1.8 reinforced at hinge; some worming, staining & soiling. 454 leaves. Goff H-486. C June 26 (86) £86,000

Anr Ed. Paris: pour Anthoine Verard, [c.1500]. ("Ortus Sanitatis translate de latin en francois.") Part 2 (of 2) only. Folio, 18th-cent vellum. 50 lines, double column, lettre batarde. With full-page woodcut of Anatomical Man on verso of tp; large woodcuts on K5v, R1v & aaa1v. Some dampstaining in margins. 184 leaves. Goff H-490. S June 27 (37) £8,000

**Hose, Charles —& MacDougall, William**
— The Pagan Tribes of Borneo. L, 1912. 2 vols. Orig cloth; marked. S Mar 28 (394) £450.

**Hottenroth, Friedrich**
— Le Costume, les armes, utensiles, outiles des peuples anciens et modernes.... Paris, [1882-92]. 4to, loose in half-cloth portfolio. With 120 color plates Some rubbing to extremities. pba Nov 30 (101) $80

**Houben, H. H.**
— Verbotene Literatur von der klassischen Zeit bis zur Gegenwart. Dessau, 1925; Bremen, 1928. 2d Ed of vol I. 2 vols. 8vo, orig cloth. Pencil underscoring throughout. sg Apr 11 (137) $120

**Houbraken, Arnold, 1660-1719**
— De groote Schouburgh der Nederlantsche Konstschilders en Schilderessen. Amst., 1718-21. 3 vols. 8vo, contemp calf; joints cracked, Vol I spine head def. With engraved title & 47 plates. S Apr 23 (244) £200

**Houbraken, Jacob**
— Verzameling van Omtrent Hondred Portraiten van Vermaarde Persoonaadien. Amst., 1761. 4to, later vellum by Birdsall. With 90 ports. S Apr 23 (245) £300

**Houdart de la Motte, Antoine, 1672-1731**
— Fables nouvelles. Paris, 1719. 4to, 18th-cent olive mor gilt, with ducal arms; joints split, spine chipped. With frontis, tp vignette & 100 vignettes. Some spotting & browning. Fuerstenberg - Schaefer copy. S Dec 7 (348) £1,900
 4th Ed. Amst., 1727. 2 vols in 1. 12mo, mor by Zaehnsdorf. With frontis & 99 plates each with a vignette within a border. Repair on lower margin of tp; lacking half-title; some headlines shaved. Fuerstenberg - Schaefer copy. S Dec 7 (349) £180

**Houdini, Harry, 1874-1926**
— A Magician among the Spirits. NY, 1924. 1st Ed. Inscr to Rachel Reber, 8 June 1924. sg Feb 1 (111) $750

**Houel, Jean Pierre Louis Laurent**
— Voyage pittoresque des isles de Sicile, de Malte et de Lipari. Paris, 1782-87. 4 vols. Folio, contemp red mor gilt; repairs to lower cover of Vol II. With 263 plates. Short tear in margin of Plate CXLII; waterstain in margin of Plate CLXXIV. Fuerstenberg - Schaefer copy. S Dec 7 (304) £11,000

**Hough, Emerson, 1857-1923.** See: Baum & Hough

**Hough, Franklin Benjamin, 1822-85**
— Proceedings of the Commissioners of Indian Affairs...State of New York.... Albany, 1861. 2 vols. 8vo, orig half lea; spines rubbed. With 3 folding maps. NH July 21 (188) $390

**Hough, Walter**
— The Moki Snake Dance. [Chicago]: Published by the Passenger Department, Santa Fe Route, 1899. Bound with: typed poem by Charles F. Lummis, "The Desert Rattle-Snake", and The Works of Charles F. Lummis (pamphlet) Twenty-third thousand. Orig wraps in half mor & cloth bdg; extremities rubbed. Robbins copy. pba Mar 21 (153) $170

**Houghton, Eliza Poor Donner**
— The Expedition of the Donner Party and Its Tragic Fate. Chicago, 1911. 1st Ed. Orig cloth. With 56 illus & news clipping. 1 page torn 7 repaired; some browning. Larson copy. pba Sept 28 (424) $80

**Houghton, Ellen.** See: Crane & Houghton

**Houghton, John, 1640-1705**
— A Collection of Letters for the Improvement of Husbandry & Trade. L, 1728. ("Husbandry and Trade Improv'd....") 4 vols. 8vo, contemp calf; rubbed. b Sept 20 (130) £160

**Houghton, Mary**
— The Border Chieftains. L, 1813. 3 vols. 12mo, contemp half calf; 1 spine with splits. Some browning. Ck Sept 8 (206) £700

**Houghton, W.**
— The Grin of a Moment.... Plymouth-Dock, 1813. 4to, contemp calf gilt; worn. b Dec 5 (84) £100

**Houghton, William, 1829?-97**
— British Fresh-Water Fishes. L, [1879]. 2 vols. Folio, contemp lea; worn. With 40 (of 41) colored plates. Frontis cut away; half-title partly cut; library stamp on each plate. bba Sept 7 (147) £300 [Nepture Gallery]
 Anr copy. Orig cloth; spines chipped. With 41 color plates. Some spotting; few plates loose. S Oct 27 (737) £600 [Colle]
 Anr copy. 2 vols in 1. Folio, contemp half mor. With 41 colored plates. S Mar 29 (792) £680
 Anr copy. 2 vols. Folio, orig cloth. S June 27 (38) £600

**House of Representatives.** See: United States of America

**Household...**
— Household Conveniences. NY, 1884. Pictorial cloth. pba Aug 8 (475) $70

**Housholder, Bob**
— Grand Slam of North American Wild Sheep. Phoenix, [1974]. Cloth; worn. O Oct 10 (166) $90

**Housman, Alfred Edward, 1859-1936**
— A Shropshire Lad. NY, 1897. 1st American Ed, one of 150. Orig half vellum; spine head chipped, tips rubbed. Clarence Stedman's copy. sg June 20 (169) $275

## Housman, Laurence, 1865-1959
See also: Arabian Nights
— Arthur Boyd Houghton. L, 1896. 4to, orig cloth; soiled, spine browned. Edmund J. Sullivan's copy, with related material. bba Oct 19 (91) £130 [Ginnan]
— Stories from the Arabian Nights. L, 1907. One of 350. Illus by Edmund Dulac. 4to, vellum gilt; spine & front cover spotted. With 50 colored plates. sg Sept 14 (113) $350

Anr copy. Mor gilt by Zaehnsdorf. sg Oct 19 (75) $750

## Houssaye, J. G.
— Monographie du the. Description botanique.... Paris, [1843]. 1st Ed. 8vo, orig cloth; cover stained, corners bumped. With half-title, title vignette, & 18 plates. Spotted & dampstained. Ck Mar 22 (153) £190

## Houville, Gerard d'. See: Houville, Marie de Regnier ("Gerard d'Houville")

## Houville, Marie de Regnier ("Gerard d'Houville")
— Le seducteur. Paris, 1926. One of 10 for the collaborators. 4to, mor extra by Marot-Rodde, orig wraps bound in. S Nov 21 (213) £1,200

## Houzeau, Jean Charles —& Lancaster, Albert
— Bibliographie generale de l'astronomie. L, 1964. 2 vols in 3. 4to, orig cloth, in frayed djs. bba Oct 5 (102) £240 [Harris]
— Bibliographie Generale de l'astronomie. L, 1964. 2 vols in 3. 4to, orig cloth. sg Apr 11 (285) $250

## Hovey, Charles Mason
— The Fruits of America.... NY, 1848-56. 2 vols. 4to, contemp lea gilt; spine ends worn, joints cracked. With 2 ports & 96 chromoliths. sg Apr 18 (149) $3,600

## How, George E. P. & Jane P.
— English and Scottish Silver Spoons. L, 1952-57. One of 550. 3 vols. Folio, cloth, in soiled djs. bba Apr 11 (33) £400 [Trace]

Anr copy. Cloth, in djs. W Nov 8 (55) £380

## Howard, Benjamin C.
— Report of the Decision of the Supreme Court of the United States...in the Case of Dred Scott versus John F. A. Sandford. NY, 1857. Bound with: Political Debates... Abraham LIncoln and... Stephen A. Douglas.... Columbus, 1860 8vo, contemp half mor; extremities scuffed. Minor browning. F Mar 28 (108) $170

Anr Ed. Wash.: Cornelius Wendell, 1857. 8vo, orig front wrap only; chipped. Foxing to corner of tp. sg Mar 28 (294) $800

Anr copy. Orig ptd wraps; lacking rear wrap, spine chipped. wa Feb 29 (360) $260

## Howard, David Sanctuary
— Chinese Armorial Porcelain. L, 1974. 4to, cloth, in dj. sg Jan 11 (87) $900

Anr copy. Orig cloth; blotched. wa Feb 1 (376) $450

## Howard, David Sanctuary —& Ayers, John G.
— China for the West.... L, 1978. 2 vols. 4to, cloth, in worn djs. wa Dec 14 (427) $450

## Howard, Frederick, 5th Earl of Carlisle
— The Tragedies and Poems. L, 1801. 8vo, contemp calf; joints rubbed. Minor marking. bba May 30 (135) £60 [Wise]

## Howard, John, 1726?-90
— The State of the Prisons in England and Wales.... Warrington, 1784. 3d Ed. 4to, contemp calf gilt; bumped. pba Sept 14 (209) $225

## Howard, Luke, 1772-1864
— The Climate of London.... L, 1833. 3 vols. 8vo, orig cloth; rebacked. With 7 plates. b May 30 (25) £120

## Howard, Oliver Otis, 1830-1909
— My Life and Experiences among our Hostile Indians. Hartford, [1907]. Orig cloth; spine ends frayed. Tape repairs to front gutters. pba June 25 (117) $80
— Nez Perce Joseph. Bost., 1881. 8vo, orig cloth. wa Feb 29 (401) $250

## Howard, Robert E.
— The Coming of Conan. NY: Gnome Press, [1953]. In rubbed dj. pba May 4 (155) $85

Anr copy. In chipped dj. pba Aug 22 (247) $50
— Conan the Barbarian. NY: Gnome Press, [1954]. In soiled dj. Some browning. pba May 4 (156) $100

Anr copy. In chipped dj. Browned. pba Aug 22 (246) $70
— Conan the Conqueror: The Hyborean Age. NY: Gnome Press, [1950]. In dj. pba May 4 (157) $130
— Etchings in Ivory. Pasadena, Texas: Glenn Lord, 1968. One of 250. pba May 23 (165) $85
— King Conan: The Hyborean Age. NY: Gnome Press, [1953]. In dj with soiled rear panel. pba May 4 (158) $95

Anr copy. In creased dj. pba Aug 22 (248) $60
— Skull-Face and Others. Sauk City, 1946. 1st Ed. In rubbed & chipped dj. cb Oct 17 (535) $700

Anr copy. In chipped dj; insect damage to bdg. pba May 4 (160) $120

Anr Ed. Sauk City, Wisconsin, 1946. In dj. sg June 20 (170) $300
— The Sword of Conan: The Hyborean Age. NY: Gnome Press, [1952]. In dj. pba May 4 (159) $95; pba Aug 22 (249) $50
— Tales of Conan. NY: Gnome Press, [1955]. In repaired dj. pba May 4 (154) $60

Anr copy. In dj. pba Aug 22 (250) $60

## Howard, W. See: Lowe & Howard

**Howard-Bury, Charles Kenneth**
— Mount Everest. The Reconnaissance, 1921. L, 1922. One of 200. Folio, orig half vellum; spine soiled & with tear. With 33 plates, 3 folding colored maps & 14 additional plates. Frontis dampstained. bba Nov 1 (488) £400 [Mountaineering Books]

**Howay, Frederic William**
— The Dixon-Meares Controversy, Containing Remarks.... Toronto: Ryerson Press, [1929]. One of 500. In dj with light dampstain through to covers. pba Feb 13 (93) $225
— Voyages of the "Columbia" to the Northwest Coast 1787-90 and 1790-93. Bost., 1941. With 12 plates. pba Feb 13 (94) $160; wa Feb 29 (475) $130
1st Ed. Half cloth & bds; front cover nicked. Robbins copy. pba Mar 21 (154) $170

**Howe, Henry, 1816-93.** See: Barber & Howe

**Howe, Octavius Thorndike —& Mathews, Frederick C.**
— American Clipper Ships, 1833-1858. Salem, Mass., 1926-27. 1st Ed. 2 vols, orig cloth. Larson copy. pba Sept 28 (370) $190

**Howell, James, c.1596-1666**
— Instructions for Forreine Travell. L, 1642. 1st Ed. 12mo, modern calf by Sangorski & Sutcliffe. With additional title. Some soiling. S Oct 27 (1065) £320 [Clark]

**Howells, John Mead, 1868-1959**
— Lost Examples of Colonial Architecture. NY, 1931. One of 1,100. Folio, cloth; cracked. sg Jan 11 (9) $100

**Howells, William Cooper**
— Recollections of Life in Ohio.... Cincinnati, 1895. 8vo, orig cloth. With port. sg Oct 26 (140) $60

**Howells, William Dean, 1837-1920**
— Indian Summer. Bost., 1886. 8vo, orig cloth. Some insect damage. Willa Cather's sgd copy. pba Oct 5 (68) $325
— Stops of Various Quills. NY, 1895. 8vo, cloth, in dj cracked at front flap, spine chipped. sg Feb 8 (306) $90

**Howes, Wright**
— U.S.A.-iana (1700-1950): a Descriptive Check-list.... NY: Bowker, 1954. 1st Ed. Buckram; shelf wear. Robbins-Camp copy. pba Mar 21 (155) $180
— U.S.-iana (1650-1950); a Selective Bibliography.... NY, 1962. ds July 27 (93) $80
Anr copy. Cloth; extremites worn. sg Oct 26 (141) $50
— U.S.-iana (1700-1950); a Descriptive Checklist.... NY, 1954. 1st Ed. pba Aug 8 (82) $65

**Howitt, Samuel, 1765?-1822**
See also: Williamson & Howitt
— The British Sportsman. L, 1812. 4to, contemp gilt; rubbed. With frontis & 71 plates. S June 13 (399) £1,300

— A New Work of Animals. L, 1811. 4to, contemp half calf; lacks spine, rubbed. With 100 plates. Some spotting & offsetting. S Oct 27 (739) £300 [Chelsea Cal.]
Ed with 100 plates. 4to, contemp mor gilt. Frontis mtd. sg Oct 19 (164) $900
Anr Ed. L, 1818. 4to, contemp mor; rubbed. With 100 plates. Some spotting & offsetting. S Oct 27 (740) £210 [Cherrington]
Anr copy. With 99 (of 100) plates. Somewhat spotted; leaf loose & torn. S Oct 27 (741) £220 [Chelsea Gal.]
Anr copy. Contemp calf; rebacked. With 100 plates. Some foxing to plates. sg Dec 7 (272) $375

**Howitt, William, 1792-1879**
— Homes and Haunts of the Most Eminent British Poets. L, 1877. 2 vols in 1. 8vo, half calf; joints worn. pba Mar 7 (103) $110
— The Rural and Domestic Life of Germany.... Phila., 1843. 2 vols. 8vo, orig wraps; 1 cover loose. sg Mar 7 (106) $50

**Howlett, Robert**
— The Angler's Sure Guide: or, Angling Improved.... L, 1706. 8vo, old calf; upper joint splitting. O Feb 6 (132) $1,500

**Howlett, W. J.**
— Life of the Right Reverend Joseph P. Machebeuf.... Pueblo CO, 1908. Later cloth. Willa Cather's sgd copy. pba Oct 5 (69) $350

**Hoyem, Andrew**
— Shaped Poetry. San Francisco: Arion Press, 1981. One of 300. Folio, loose as issued in wrap & with plexiglas frame for display. With 30 prints. sg Sept 14 (37) $400

**Hoyt Collection, Charles B.**
Tseng Hien-ch'i & Dart, Robert Paul. - The Charles B. Hoyt Collection in the Museum of Fine Arts: Boston. Bost., 1964. Chinese Art: 2 vols. Folio, orig cloth. sg June 13 (189) $120

**Hoyt, Epaphras, 1765-1850**
— Antiquarian Researches, comprising a History of the Indian Wars.... Greenfield, Mass., 1824. 1st Ed. 8vo, half mor; worn, notes mtd to front free endpaper. With folding plate. Foxed. wa Feb 29 (402) $190

**Hubbard, Bela.** See: Burt & Hubbard

**Hubbard, Elbert, 1856-1915**
— Ruskin and Turner. East Aurora: Roycroft Shop, 1896. One of 473. Half cloth; soiled, corners rubbed. pba Aug 22 (785) $60
— Selected Writings.... NY: William H. Wise, [1928]. Memorial Ed. 14 vols. In djs. pba Aug 8 (477) $55

**Hubbard, L. Ron**
— Dianetics: The Modern Science of Mental Health. NY: Hermitage House, [1950]. In dj with piece lacking. pba May 23 (166) $65

Anr copy. In chipped dj. pba Aug 22 (253) $65
Anr copy. In dj. sg June 20 (171) $90
— Final Blackout. Providence: Hadley, [1948]. In rubbed dj. pba May 4 (161) $300
— Two Novels.... NY: Gnome Press, [1951]. In chipped dj. pba May 4 (162) $100

**Hubbard, William, 1621?-1704**
— The Present State of New-England, Being a Narrative of the Troubles with the Indians.... L, 1677. 4to, 19th-cent mor gilt; upper hinge cracked, joints & extremities rubbed. Lacking initial blank; folding map with repaired 3-inch tear & small repair in lower blank corner; washed & pressed. CNY May 17 (90) $38,000

**Huber, Charles**
— Journal d'un voyage en Arabie.... Paris, 1891. 2 parts in 1 vol. 8vo, recent half calf. With half title, 14 maps, & 13 color plates. S Oct 26 (114) £500 [Al-Ankouy]

**Huber, Louisa.** See: Loehr & Huber

**Huber, Michel, 1727-1804**
— Choix de poesies allemandes. Paris, 1766. 4 vols. 8vo, contemp mor gilt. Fuerstenberg - Schaefer copy. S Dec 7 (305) £900
Anr copy. 4 vols. 12mo, contemp mor gilt. With frontis. Fuerstenberg - Schaefer copy. S Dec 7 (306) £450

**Hubert, Saint, Order of**
— Calendarium inclyti ordinis equestris D. Huberto sacri.... [Augsburg, 1781]. 2 parts in 1 vol. 8vo, contemp mor. With 2 titles, & 83 plates. Lacking December pp; some marginal staining. S Oct 27 (1129) £1,000 [Martin]

**Hubert, Pirsson, Architects**
— Where and How to Build. NY, [c.1884]. Oblong 4to, orig cloth; corners worn, spine ends frayed, lacking corner of front free endpaper & half of rear free endpaper. bbc Dec 18 (181) $260

**Huc, Evariste Regis, 1813-60**
— The Chinese Empire. NY, 1855. 2 vols. 8vo, orig cloth. With folding colored map. Foxed. pba July 25 (406) $95
— Travels in Tartary, Thibet, and China during the Years 1844-5-6. L, [1852]. 1st Ed in English. - Trans by William Hazlitt. 2 vols. 8vo, orig cloth. pba Apr 25 (191) $350

**Hudson, Charles, d.1865**
— Where there's a Will there's a Way; an Ascent of Mont Blanc. L, 1856. 8vo, orig cloth; rebacked preserving spine, rubbed. Folding colored map torn; some soiling. bba Nov 1 (538) £350 [Cavendish]
Anr copy. Orig cloth; spine worn. With litho frontis & folding hand-colored map. bba Nov 1 (574) £380 [Gonzalez]

**Hudson, John, of Kendal.** See: Wordsworth presentation copy

**Hudson, William Henry, 1841-1922**
See also: Limited Editions Club; Sclater & Hudson
— The Birds of La Plata. L, 1920. 2 vols. 4to, orig cloth. With 22 colored plates. sg May 16 (310) $100
One of 200 L.p. copies, with duplicate suite of plates. Orig cloth; spine of Vol I bumped, portfolio with extra suite torn along edges. With 22 mtd colored plates. pba Nov 30 (188) $475
— Green Mansions. L, 1926. Illus by Keith Henderson. Calf gilt by Bayntun. pba Aug 8 (248) $55
— Idle Days in Patagonia. L, 1893. 1st Ed, one of 1,750. 8vo, orig cloth; spine head chipped. pba July 25 (407) $95
— A Shepherd's Life: Impressions of the South Wiltshire Downs. L, 1977. One of 100. Illust by Reynolds Stone. 8vo, orig half mor; rubbed. With 10 sgd artist's proof tipped in at end. bba May 9 (427) £190 [Bankes Books]

**Huebner, Johann, the Younger**
— Schul-Atlas aus achtzehen Homannischen landkarten. [Nuremberg or Hamburg], 1754. Folio, contemp calf. With engraved title & 18 double-page maps, hand-colored. Tears at lower centerfold of any maps; Europe cleanly torn along fold; 1 section of Germany torn away; some 18th-cent annotations & doodles; tp stained. Sold w.a.f. C May 31 (57) £900

**Huelsenbeck, Richard**
— Dada Almanach. Im Auftrag des Zentralamts der deutschen Dada-Bewegung. Berlin, [1920]. 12mo, orig wraps; some wear. With 8 photographic plates. sg Apr 18 (106) $400

**Hueso Rolland, Francisco**
— Exposicion de Encuadernaciones Espanolas. Siglos XII al XIX. Madrid, 1934. Folio, cloth; rubbed & shaken. Library markings, including stamps on plates. bba May 9 (139) £180 [Laywood]

**Hugall, J. W.** See: Poole & Hugall

**Hugessen, E. H. K.**
— The Forest Fairy: Christmas in Switzerland. Bost.: Dana Estes, [1896]. 8vo, half cloth; warped spot to rear cover. pba Aug 22 (787) $80

**Hughes, A. W.**
— The Country of Balochistan.... L, 1877. 8vo, orig cloth. With 7 mtd Woodburytypes & map in back pocket. b Sept 20 (340) £650

**Hughes, G. M.**
— A History of Windsor Forest.... L, 1890. One of 400. 4to, orig cloth. Some spotting. bba May 30 (381) £50 [Classic Bindings]

**Hughes, Griffith**
— The Natural History of Barbados. L, 1750. Folio, modern cloth. With folding map & 30 hand-colored plates. sg May 16 (312) $1,600

**Hughes, John T., 1817-62**
— Doniphan's Expedition, Containing an Account of the Conquest of New Mexico. Cincinatti, 1848. 2d Ed, 2d Issue. 12mo, orig cloth; spines chipped & frayed, front cover stained. With 1 folding map. Some foxing. Robbins copy. pba Mar 21 (156) $300

1st Ed. Cincinnati, 1848. "cheap" issue, variant 6. 12mo, orig ptd wraps; edges worn. CE May 22 (22) $260

2d Ed, 2d Issue. 12mo, orig cloth; rebacked. With 2 frontis ports & 1 folded map. Some foxing. Larson copy. pba Sept 28 (416) $250

Anr Ed. Cincinnati, 1850. Orig law calf; front joint, hinge & rear joint cracked; leather scuffed. With 2 frontis ports & 1 folded map. Some foxing, tanning of margins. Larson copy. pba Sept 28 (417) $200

**Hughes, Langston, 1902-67**
See also: De Carava & Hughes
— Don't You Turn Back. NY, [1969]. In dj. sg Mar 28 (154) $150
— Fight for Freedom. NY, 1962. In dj with wear. Inscr to Milton Meltzer. sg Mar 28 (155) $475
— Fine Clothes to the Jew. NY, 1927. Half cloth; spine tips rubbed. sg Mar 28 (156) $175
— A New Song. NY: International Workers Order, 1938. Pictorial wraps; worn. cb June 25 (1862) $225

Anr copy. Pictorial wraps; rubbed. sg Mar 28 (157) $60
— Simple Speaks his Mind. NY, [1950]. In dj. pba May 23 (169) $130
— The Weary Blues. NY, 1926. Inscr to Abbe Niles, 1 Mar 1926. sg Mar 28 (158) $900

Anr Ed. NY, 1931. Inscr. sg Mar 28 (159) $500

Anr Ed. NY, 1945. In dj. Inscr, 1948. pba May 23 (170) $160

**Hughes, Langston, 1902-67 —& Bontemps, Arna**
— The Book of Negro Folklore. NY, 1958. In dj. Milton Meltzer's copy. sg Mar 28 (160) $60

**Hughes, Langston, 1902-67 —& Douglas, Aaron**
— Hughes/Douglas. NY: Opportunity Folio, [1926]. 19 by 13 inches, loose in portfolio; minor wear & staining. sg Mar 28 (161) $2,400

**Hughes, Richard.** See: Limited Editions Club

**Hughes, Robert Edgar**
— Two Summer Cruises with the Baltic Fleet, in 1854-5. L, 1855. 8vo, cloth; 1 gathering loose. With frontis & map. sg Mar 7 (218) $90

**Hughes, Sukey**
— Washi; the World of Japanese Paper. Tokyo, [1978]. One of 1,000. 4to, half cloth. ds July 27 (94) $300

**Hughes, Ted**
— Cave Birds: Ten Poems. L: Scolar Press, 1975. One of 100. Illus by Leonard Baskin. In portfolio. bba Oct 19 (342) £110 [Finch]
— Crow, from the Life and Songs of the Crow. L, 1973. One of 400. Illus by Leonard Baskin. Folio, orig cloth. wa Nov 16 (269) $80
— Pike. Northampton: Gehenna Press, 1959. One of 150. Illus by Robert Birmelin. Single sheet, 530mm by 400mm. Hobson copy. S June 28 (158) £550

**Hughes, Thomas Smart, 1786-1847**
— Travels in Sicily, Greece and Albania. L, 1820. 1st Ed. 2 vols. 4to, contemp half calf; worn, covers becoming loose. With 15 maps, plans & plates. Discolored & spotted. S Oct 26 (115) £400 [Plouviez]

**Hughes, W. C.**
— The Art of Projection and Complete Magic Lantern Manual, by an Expert. L, 1893. 8vo, orig cloth. With 2 folding plates. b May 30 (53) £120

**Hughes, W. E.**
— Chronicles of Black Heath Golfers. L, 1897. 1st Ed. 10 in by 7.25 inches, cloth; spine ends rubbed, hinges cracking. With frontis port. pba Apr 18 (89) $2,500

**Hughman, John**
— Original Poems... By a Traveller. Halesworth, 1834. 16th Ed. 8vo, orig bds. Minor spotting. b Dec 5 (365) £70

**Hughson, David, Pseud. of David Pugh**
— Walks through London. L, 1817. 2 vols. 8vo, contemp mor gilt with Signet Library stamps. With 18 plans & 78 plates, all on laid india paper. Some browning. bba June 6 (61) £160 [Hamilton]

**Hugnet, Georges.** See: Barr & Hugnet; Cocteau & Hugnet

**Hugo, Abel**
— France pittoresque ou description pittoresque.... Paris, 1835. 3 vols. 4to, orig half mor; rubbed. With 102 maps & 374 plates. Lacking titles to Vol II. b Sept 20 (248) £90

**Hugo de Prato Florido**
— Sermones dominicales super evangelia et epistolas. [Reutlingen: Michel Greyff, c.1478]. Folio, contemp blind-stamped pigskin over wooden bds, with 2 clasps & catches; worming & staining in both bds. 61 lines & headline, double column, gothic letter. Some worming at ends; dampstaining at head of some leaves. With full-page Ms diagram on verso of initial blank (illus in cat); Ms annotations. Buxheim Charterhouse stamp. 269 leaves. Goff H-505. Madsen copy. S Mar 14 (179) £4,600

**Hugo, Hermannus, 1588-1629**
— Obsidio Bredana armis Philippi IIII auspiciis Isabellae ductu Ambr. Spinolae perfecta. Antwerp: Plantin, 1626. Folio, contemp vellum. With engraved title

& 13 plates. Closed tears to inner margin of N4; some soiling. Ck Sept 8 (103) £300
— Pia desideria emblematis elegiis.... Antwerp, 1628. 16mo, 18th-cent mor gilt; corners worn. With 45 woodcuts in text by Christoffel van Sichem II. Some dampstaining. Schaefer copy. P Nov 1 (122) $500
— The Siege of Breda. [Ghent], 1627. Folio, contemp calf; very worn, endpapers creased. With engraved title & 20 plates. Some discoloring. STC 13926. b Sept 20 (131) £90

### Hugo Senensis
— Trattato circa la conczervazione della sanita. Milan: Petrus de Corneno, 31 May, 1481. 8vo, later half calf. With 54 leaves, double-column. Some soiling; 1st leaf cut without loss. Ck Mar 22 (154) £9,000

### Hugo, Victor, 1802-85
See also: Limited Editions Club
— Eviradnus. Paris, 1900. One of 40 on velin with additional suite of the engravings & a suite of the wood-engravings on papier pelure. Illus by P. M. Ruty. 8vo, calf extra with upper cover depicting a man in full armor, orig wraps bound in. Hoe copy. S Nov 21 (216) £4,000
— Notre-Dame de Paris. Paris, 1831. 4 vols. 12mo, contemp half sheep; spine ends chipped, covers detached or starting. Inscr to Eugene Delacroix. sg Sept 21 (228) $2,000
— Anr Ed. Paris, 1844. 8vo, mor extra by G. Mercier, orig wraps & cloth bound in. With 55 plates; Plate 15 in 1st issue, With additional suite of 12 engravings, 1 of them in 3 states. With ALs. S Nov 21 (215) £2,400
— Les Orientales. Paris, 1882. One of 135, this copy for M. Dupuich, with each plate in 3 or more states. 4to, mor gilt to Thibaron-Joly, orig wraps bound in; indentations & scuff mark on upper cover. S Nov 21 (214) £500
— Works. Bost.: Colonial Press, [c.1900]. Beacon Ed. 23 vols. 8vo, half mor. pba Dec 14 (77) $250
— Memorial Ed. Bost.., [c.1905]. 30 vols. 8vo, half mor gilt; warped, some scuffing, 1 cover detached. Sold w.a.f. bbc Feb 26 (125) $300

### Hugueras, Maria Dolores
— NW Coast of America: Iconographic Album of the Malaspina Expedition. Madrid, [1991]. Folio, cloth. In Spanish & English. pba Feb 13 (129) $130

**Hugues, P.** See: Jacob & Hugues

### Hulbert, Archer Butler
— Historic Highways of America. Cleveland, 1902-5. 15 vols plus Index. sg Oct 26 (142) $110

### Hulle, Anselm van
— Pronkbeelden der vorsten en vredehandelaars.... Rotterdam: Pieter vander Slaart, 1697. Folio, loose in 19th-cent half mor. With 131 plates, all tipped in on loose sheets. Marginal spotting; repaired tear to margin of final plate repaired. S June 27 (330) £700

### Hulme, Frederick Edward
— Familiar Wild Flowers. L, [c.1875]. Series 1-5 in 2 vols. 8vo, contemp calf gilt. sg Sept 21 (26) $100

### Hulten, K. G. Pontus
— Jean Tinguely. "Meta." Bost., 1975. sg Jan 11 (424) $50
One of 250. Cloth, bound as a suitcase with handle & latch. sg Jan 11 (423) $150
— The Machine as Seen at the End of the Mechanical Age. NY: Museum of Modern Art, 1968. Orig metal cover. sg June 13 (190) $80

### Hulton, Paul Hope —& Quinn, David Beers
— The American Drawings of John White. L, 1964. 2 vols. Folio, orig cloth; spines rubbed. bba Oct 19 (92) £55 [Zwemmer]; CE June 12 (216) $420

### Humbert, B.
— Ferronerie Moderne. Paris, 1900. Folio, half cloth portfolio; spine strip lacking, remaining cloth detaching, worn, soiled 7 dampstained. With 50 hand-colored plates. Laid in are 7 uncolored plates from L'Art to Serrurier. Some soiling & edge-wear; strip of paper with typed note taped to tp. cb Oct 17 (83) $800

### Humboldt, Alexander von, 1769-1859
— Asie Centrale. Recherches sur les Chaines de Montagnes et la Climatologie comparee. Paris, 1843. 3 vols. 8vo, orig wraps, unopened; several covers loose. sg Mar 7 (107) $250
— Cosmos: a Sketch of a Physical Description of the Universe. L, 1849-58. 5 vols. 12mo, contemp calf gilt. pba Sept 14 (212) $250
Anr Ed. NY, 1851. 3 vols. 8vo, cloth. pba Aug 8 (478) $60
— Minerva. Ensayo Politico sobre el Reyno de Nueva Espana. Madrid, 1818. 2 vols. 8vo, modern vellum. Browned. sg Oct 26 (143) $200
— Political Essay on the Kingdom of New Spain. L, 1811. 1st Ed. - Trans by John Black. Vols I-IV (of 5); lacking Atlas vol. 8vo, later half lea. With 11 plates & maps, some folding. A few maps trimmed; some tears & staining. CE June 12 (217) $700
— Sitios de las Cordilleras Monumentos de los Pueblos Indigenas de America. Madrid: Gaspar, 1878. 8vo, contemp half mor. pba Apr 25 (461) $100
— Ueber die unterirdischen Gasarten.... Braunschweig, 1799. 8vo, orig wraps; worn. With 3 folding plates. Spotted, soiled & stained. S Mar 14 (180) £220
— Versuche ueber die chemische Zerlegung des Luftkreises und ueber einige andere Gegenstaende der Naturlehre. Braunschweig, 1799. 1st Ed. 8vo, contemp bds; spine top def, old Ms label on upper cover. With 2 folding plates & 4 tables. Spotted. S Mar 14 (181) £400

### Humboldt, Alexander von, 1769-1859 —& Bonpland, Aime J. A., 1773-1858
— Personal Narrative of Travels to the Equinoctial Regions of the New Continent.... L, 1818-29. 7 vols in

8. 8vo, modern half calf. With 12 maps & diagrams. S June 13 (400) £600

— Voyage aux regions equinoctiales du nouveau continent.... Paris, 1808-34. Part 6, Botanique. nova genera et species plantarum. 7 vols. Folio, half mor. With 2 uncolored & 712 hand-colored plates. Library stamps on plates; a few plates wormed in upper margins; text foxed. S Nov 30 (26) £15,000

Anr Ed. Amst., 1971-73. One of 200. 30 vols plus Personal Narrative in 5 vols. Folio & 4to, cloth, Personal Narrative in djs. Reprint. CE Feb 21 (149) $4,000

**Hume, A.**
— The Learned Societies and Printing Clubs of the United Kingdom. L, 1853. 8vo, orig cloth; spine ends worn. sg Apr 11 (138) $140

**Hume, Allan Octavian —&**
**Marshall, Charles H. T., 1841-1927**
— The Game Birds of India, Burmah, and Ceylon. Calcutta, [1878]-81. 3 vols. 8vo, orig cloth; Vol I def. With 135 chromolitho plates. Some plates def. b Sept 20 (471) £130

**Hume, David, 1711-76**
— Dialogues concerning Natural Religion. L, 1779. 2d Ed. 8vo, contemp calf; minor defs. b Sept 20 (132) £130

— An Enquiry concerning the Principles of Morals. L, 1751. 12mo, contemp calf; lower joint weak, rubbed, lacking front free endpaper. Half-title torn & repaired; F4 torn. S June 12 (59) £450

1st Ed, 1st Issue. 12mo, half calf. Waterstained throughout; stamp on tp verso; 2 leaves chipped. bba May 30 (103) £340 [Price]

Later Issue. Contemp calf; worn, front joint cracked. Marginal spotting towards end. sg Mar 21 (168) $1,600

— The History of England. L, 1767. New Ed. 6 vols. 8vo, contemp mor gilt; rubbed & discolored. Some soiling. S June 12 (62) £550

Anr Ed. L, 1793-94. 13 vols. 12mo, contemp calf; spines repaired. b May 30 (403) £240

Anr Ed. L, [1793-95]. 22 vols, including Smollett's continuation. 12mo, contemp calf; lea worn away in patches on some bds. bba May 30 (266) £680 [Carter]

— The Life of David Hume.... L, 1777. 1st Separate Ed, 1st Issue. 8vo, contemp calf; rubbed, rebacked, new endpapers. S June 12 (63) £240

— Political Discourses. Edin., 1752. 8vo, contemp calf. pnE May 15 (42) £1,900

Anr copy. Contemp calf; rebacked retaining spine, rubbed. Contents leaf with tear; 1st gathering shaken; the Scotticisms & 1 leaf of ads bound at beginning; some ink corrections & stains. S June 12 (61) £2,100

— A Treatise of Human Nature. L, 1739. 1st Ed. Vols I & II only. 8vo, contemp calf; covers detached, spines worn. CE May 22 (273) $4,800

**Hume, R. D.** See: Griswold & Hume

**Humfreville, J. Lee**
— Twenty Years Among Our Hostile Indians.... Hartford, 1897. Orig cloth; worn. Tear to tp. wa Feb 29 (403) $160

2d Ed. NY: Hunter, [1903]. Pictorial cloth; stained, hinges repaired but weak. pba June 25 (118) $50

**Humphreys, Arthur Lee**
— Old Decorative Maps and Charts. L & NY, 1926. One of 1,500. 4to, orig cloth. bba July 18 (14) £60 [Classic Bindings]

**Humphreys, Henry Noel, 1810-79**
— The Illuminated Books of the Middle Ages. L, 1849. Folio, contemp half mor; extremities worn, bumped. With title in red & black, 1 uncolored plate of 13 ornaments, chromolitho title & 39 chromolitho plates. Some spotting. cb Oct 17 (643) $1,700

— Illuminated Illustrations of Froissart.... L, 1844-45. 2 vols in 1. 4to, contemp calf; worn, rebacked preserving spine. Plates hand-colored & heightened in gilt. bba May 30 (320) £200 [C. Smith]

Anr copy. Recent calf with early endpapers. With 2 additional titles & 72 hand-colored plates. bbc June 24 (72) $425

Anr copy. Vol I only. Mor gilt. With 36 hand-colored & chromolitho plates. pba Jan 4 (236) $325

**Humphreys, Henry Noel, 1810-79 —&**
**Westwood, John Obadiah, 1805-93**
— British Butterflies and their Transformations. L, 1841. 4to, 19th-Cent cloth; upper hinge broken. With hand-colored additional title & 41 (of 42) hand-colored plates. Additional title torn; some spotting & rust-marks. S Oct 27 (639) £260 [Dunbar]

Anr Ed. L, 1848. 4to, contemp half mor; rubbed. With hand-colored litho title & 42 hand-colored plates. S June 13 (401) £600

Anr Ed. L, 1849. 4to, half mor; rubbed. With additional hand-colored title & 42 hand-colored plates. b May 30 (491) £280

— British Moths and their Transformations. L, 1843-45. 2 vols. 4to, orig cloth; rebacked. With 124 hand-colored plates. Some fraying; foxed & soiled. bba June 6 (19) £240 [Hamilton]

Anr copy. Contemp half lea; Vol I joints cracked. Some spotting. S Apr 23 (320) £320

Anr Ed. L, 1851. 2 vols. 4to, half lea. With 124 hand-colored plates. b May 30 (492) £250

Anr copy. Orig cloth; spines worn. With 124 hand-colored plates. 2 plates loose & with marginal tear. S June 13 (402) £360

**Humphries, Sydney**
— Oriental Carpets.... L, 1910. Folio, orig cloth; joints splitting. With 24 color plates. sg June 13 (79) $80

**Hungerford, Edward**
— The Story of the Baltimore & Ohio Railroad. NY, 1928. 2 vols. NH July 21 (362) $90

— The Story of the Rome, Watertown and Ogdensburgh Railroad. NY, 1922. 12mo, orig cloth; worn. NH July 21 (363) $160

## Hunt Botanical Library

MACPHAIL, IAN. - A Catalogue of Redouteana exhibited...21 April to 1 August 1963. Pittsburgh, 1963. 4to, wraps. Sgd by Wilfred Blunt, Ian MacPhail & others on front free endpaper. O Dec 5 (58) $80

## Hunt, G. H.

— Outram & Havelock's Persian Campaign. L, 1858. 8vo, later half mor; front free endpaper lacking. sg Mar 7 (171) $150

## Hunt, Henry

— Investigation at Ilchester Gaol.... L, 1821. 8vo, contemp half calf. With hand-colored frontis port by George Cruikshank & 5 hand-colored ports probably by Robert Cruikshank. Offset from former modern jacket to lower extremities of pages; a few leaves def at bottom, slightly affecting text. pba Mar 7 (141) $100

## Hunt, John, Engraver

— British Ornithology. Norwich, 1815-22. 3 vols in 2. 8vo, contemp calf; rubbed. Wtih 180 hand-colored plates & 4 uncolored anatomical plates. With 2 engraved titles only. bba Sept 7 (148) £1,200 [St. Ann's Bookshop]

Anr copy. 3 vols. 8vo, later half mor. With 3 engraved titles, 4 anatomical plates, 8 uncolored plates & 180 hand-colored plates plus a duplicate of the Bee-eater plate & a hand-colored litho of an avocet not by Hunt. Tp to Vol I replaced with Vol II title with numeral altered. Bound in are an ALs of James Reevs & an ALs from Joseph Clarke to Henry Stevenson, both concerning this work. Lilford copy. Fattorini copy. C Oct 25 (19) £1,500

Anr copy. Later half mor gilt. With 3 engraved titles, 4 anatomical plates & 180 hand-colored plates. Lacking the 8 uncolored plates; Vol II with browning to upper margins. Extra-illus with 2 watercolor copies of 2 of the 8 uncolored plates in an unknown hand. Tall copy. Barclay - Fattorini copy. C Oct 25 (20) £1,200

## Hunt, Leigh, 1784-1859

— The Correspondence.... L, 1862. 8vo, half calf. With ALs of Samuel Laurence to Mrs Horace Pym tipped in. S Apr 23 (82) £150

— A Jar of Honey from Mount Hybla. L, 1848. 8vo, calf. With ALs attached to endpaper. S Apr 23 (77) £200

— Poetical Works. L, 1832. 8vo, contemp half calf gilt; extremities rubbed, soiled, bowed. Some soiling. F Mar 28 (577) $60

— The Religion of the Heart. L, 1853. 1st Ed. 8vo, orig cloth. With holograph notes & corrections in ink. S Apr 23 (81) £260

— The Town; its Memorable Characters and Events. L, 1848. 1st Ed. 2 vols. 8vo, orig cloth; soiled. Lacking half-title in Vol I. S Apr 23 (83) £450

## Hunt, R. C.

— Salmon in Low Water. NY: Anglers' Club, 1950. One of 500. With 2 hand-colored plates of flies. O June 25 (163) $250

## Hunt Collection, Rachel McMasters Miller

— Catalogue of Botanical Books.... Pittsburgh, 1958-61. One of 750. 2 vols in 3. 4to, cloth; worn. O Dec 5 (59) $400

## Hunt, Robert, 1807-87

— Photography: a Treatise...on the Chemical Changes Produced by Solar Radiation.... NY, 1852. 1st American Ed. 12mo, cloth; worn, 1 signature detaching. With 2 plates. Fore-edge foxed. sg Apr 24 (594) $475

— Popular Romances of the West of England. L, 1865. 1st Ed. 2 vols. 8vo, orig cloth; spine ends 7 joints chipped. Inscr & with ALs. pba Mar 7 (142) $70

Anr copy. Half mor; spines browned & rubbed. pba Aug 8 (479) $120

— Researches on Light.... L, 1844. 8vo, orig cloth; spine head worn. With folding plate. Library stamp on tp. b May 30 (54) £220

2d Ed. L, 1854. 8vo, orig cloth. With folding plate. Half-title discolored. b May 30 (55) £160

## Hunt, Rockwell Dennis

— John Bidwell: Prince of California Pioneers. Caldwell, Caxton printers, [1942]. 1st Ed. Orig cloth. With frontis port. Sgd. Larson copy. pba Sept 28 (316) $50

— John Bidwell: Prince of Pioneers. Caldwell: Caxton Printers, [1942]. In dj with edge-tears. pba Apr 25 (292) $55

## Hunt, William Holman, 1827-1910

— Pre-Raphaelitism and the Pre-Raphaelite Brotherhood. NY & L, 1905-6. 2 vols. Modern cloth. With 40 plates. Library markings ; tear to 1 margin. wa Nov 16 (356) $120

## Hunt, William Southworth

— Frank Forester: a Tragedy in Exile. Newark, 1933. One of 200. O Dec 5 (60) $150

## Hunter, Alexander, b.1843

— The Huntsman in the South. NY, 1908. Vol I: Virginia & North Carolina (all pbd). Orig cloth; worn. O Oct 10 (167) $390

Anr copy. Orig cloth; worn, spine ends frayed. O June 4 (168) $270

— Johnny Reb and Billy Yank. NY & Wash., 1905. bbc Apr 22 (109) $325

## Hunter, Dard

— The Literature of Papermaking, 1390-1800. [Chillicothe, Ohio, 1925]. One of 190. Folio, loose as issued, in orig portfolio. Some soiling. P Dec 12 (93) $2,200

— Papermaking by Hand in America. Chillicothe, 1950. One of 210. Folio, orig half cloth. With 171 mtd facsimiles & color frontis view. sg Oct 19 (118) $5,400; sg Apr 18 (65) $5,000

— Papermaking: the History and Technique of an Ancient Craft. NY, 1947. 2d Ed. In remains of dj. With folding map. wa Feb 1 (3) $65

— Papermaking through Eighteen Centuries. NY, 1930. bbc Dec 18 (127) $135

Anr copy. Unopened. pba Mar 7 (143) $160
Anr copy. In dj. pba Aug 8 (480) $170
— Primitive Papermaking. Chillicothe, Ohio, 1927. One of 200. Folio, loose as issued in orig portfolio. Some soiling. P Dec 12 (94) $3,250

**Hunter, George Leland, 1867-1927**
— Italian Furniture and Interiors. NY, [1920]. Folio, loose in cloth portfolio as issued. With 200 photographic plates. Tp margins def. sg Jan 11 (223) $375

**Hunter, John Marvin**
— The Trail Drivers of Texas.... Nashville, 1925. One of 100. 2 vols in 1. Dampstained. Inscr by John M. Hunter, 28 Jan 1959. pba Aug 8 (85) $1,700

**Hunter, Richard —& Macalpine, Ida**
— Three Hundred Years of Psychiatry, 1535-1860. Hartsdale, 1982. 8vo, orig cloth in dj. sg Apr 11 (286) $120

**Hunter, Robert**
— The Links. NY: Scribner's, 1926. 1st Ed. Cloth. pba Nov 9 (38) $650
Anr copy. Cloth; front cover soiled & scraped. Some foxing & dampstaining. pba Nov 9 (39) $425
Anr copy. Cloth; spine rubbed. Inscr to Hunter's son, 20 Nov 1935. pba Apr 18 (91) $1,300

**Hunter, Sam**
— Isamu Noguchi. NY: Abrams, [n.d.]. 4to, cloth, in dj. sg Jan 11 (317) $225
— Joan Miro: His Graphic Work. NY, [1958]. 4to, cloth, in dj; some wear. O May 7 (164) $60
Anr copy. Cloth, in worn dj. sg June 13 (258) $150

**Hunter, Samuel J.**
— The Hunters' and Trappers' Illustrated Historical Guide.... St. Louis, 1869. 8vo, orig cloth; edges worn. Some foxing. CE Sept 27 (146) $350

**Hunter, William Stanley**
— Panoramic Guide from Niagara Falls to Quebec. Montreal & Bost., 1857. 12mo, orig cloth. With folding panorama as frontis. sg Oct 26 (146) $100

**Hurd, D. Hamilton**
— History of Hillsborough County, New Hampshire. Phila., 1885. 4to, half lea; extremities scuffed. With colored map & 119 ports. NH June 1 (269) $220

**Hurd, William**
— A New Universal History of the Religious Rites, Ceremonies... of the Whole World. L, [1788]. Folio, contemp calf; worn. With frontis, & 55 (of 60?) plates. S Oct 26 (116) £150 [Landau]

**Hurley, Capt. Frank**
— Argonauts of the South. NY & L, 1925. pba July 25 (39) $140

**Hurston, Zora Neale**
— Moses, Man of the Mountain. Phila., [1939]. In dj with File Copy stamp & in pieces. pba May 23 (172) $180
— Seraph on the Suwanee. NY, 1948. In dj. bbc Dec 18 (260) $240

**Husain, Abu al-Ghazi, Sultan of Shorasan**
— A General History of the Turks, Moguls, and Tatars.... L, 1739-30. 2 vols. 8vo, contemp calf. Staining to covers & pages; edge tear to map in Vol I. pba Apr 25 (247) $200

**Husmann, George**
— The Cultivation of the Native Grape.... NY, [1866]. Orig cloth; spine ends rubbed, spot to front cover. pba Aug 22 (663) $180
Anr copy. Marginal dampstaining. sg Oct 26 (396) $80

**Hussey, Cyrus M.** See: Lay & Hussey

**Hussey, John A.**
— The History of Fort Vancouver.... Washington State Historical Society, [1957]. One of 1,000. pba Nov 16 (137) $70; pba Apr 25 (463) $75

**Huston, John**
— Frankie and Johnny. NY, [1930]. Illus by Miguel Covarrubias. In chipped dj. sg Sept 14 (94) $90

**Husung, Max Joseph**
— Die Drucker- und Velegerzeichen Italiens im XV. Jahrhundert. Munich, 1929. 4to, bds. sg Apr 11 (154) $110

**Hutcheson, Francis, 1694-1746**
— An Essay on the Nature and Conduct of the Passions and Affections.... L, 1728. 8vo, contemp calf; minor wear. b Sept 20 (134) £850

**Hutchings'...**
— Hutchings' Illustrated California Magazine. San Francisco: Hutchings & Rosenfield, 1856-57. Vol I, July 1856 to June 1857, bound in 1 vol. Half mor; scuffed, worn & stained. Some tears. pba Nov 16 (138) $450
Anr Ed. San Francisco: Hutchings & Rosenfield, 1856-61. 60 issues in 5 vols. 8vo, contemp half lea; 3 vols recased. Vol V lacking tp & with damage affecting text of 6 pages. Larson copy. pba Feb 12 (79) $1,000

**Hutchings, James Mason, 1820-1902**
— Hutchings Guide and Souvenir of California. San Francisco, [1900]. 8vo, orig half cloth; rear cover stained; tp with news stand stamp. pba Apr 25 (464) $80
— In the Heart of the Sierras. Yo Semite Valley, 1886. 1st Issue with frontis showing no one seated behind the horse & cabin without a lean-to; frontis port a phototype. Illus by George Fiske. 8vo, half mor gilt; rebacked with cloth, hinge cracked after title, shaken. Port & following 3 leaves detached as a

unit. Inscr to his daughter Gertrude, 5 Oct 1886. pba Nov 16 (139) $1,300

Anr copy. Pictorial cloth. Larson copy. pba Feb 12 (71) $2,250

2d Issue with frontis showing someone seated behind the horse & lean-to added to the cabin & with frontis port engraved. Pictorial cloth; spine & corners worn. pba Feb 12 (72) $130

Anr Ed. Oakland, 1888. Illus by Britton & Rey. 8vo, orig cloth; covers dull, hinge cracked. With 28 phototype plates & 2 maps (1 folding). Robbins copy. pba Mar 21 (159) $75

— Scenes of Wonder and Curiosity in California. NY & San Francisco, [1860]. 1st Ed, 1st Ptg. 8vo, orig cloth; waterstains on front cover. pba Feb 12 (73) $225

Anr Ed. San Francisco, [1860]. 1st Issue. 8vo, orig cloth; covers worn. With 93 illusts. Tp foxed. Robbins copy. pba Mar 21 (160) $300

Anr Ed. San Francisco, 1861. 8vo, orig lea gilt; extremities rubbed. sg Oct 26 (147) $80

2d Ed. San Francisco, 1862. 2d Ptg. Orig cloth; rubbed, extremities worn. Some soiling. pba Feb 12 (75) $150

3d Ed. NY & San Francisco, 1870. 1st Ptg. 8vo, contemp mor gilt. Minor spine wear. pba Feb 12 (76) $120

2d Ptg. Cloth. Spine ends chipped. pba Feb 12 (77) $75

— Seeking the Elephant, 1849.... Glendale: Arthur H. Clark, 1980. One of 750. Ed by Shirley Sargent. In dj. Inscr by Sargent. pba Feb 12 (152) $80

— Souvenir of California: Yosemite Valley and the Big Trees.... San Francisco, [c.1895]. Stiff wraps; spine worn & stained. pba Feb 12 (78) $85

**Hutchins, John, 1698-1773**

— The History and Antiquities of the County of Dorset. L, 1861-70. 3d Ed. 4 vols. Folio, half calf; rubbed. With 103 plates (3 double-page) & 12 maps only. Sold w.a.f. b Jan 31 (323) £340

Anr copy. Contemp half lea; rubbed, Vol IV rebacked, retaining spine. Vol I lacking the 3 "reprints". bba Nov 1 (59) £600 [Proctor]

**Hutchinson, Benjamin**

— Biographia Medica; or, Historical and Critical Memoirs.... L, 1799. 2 vols. 8vo, contemp half calf; worn. Last gathering loose. CE Nov 8 (111) $170

— Cases of Tic Douloureux Successfully Treated. L, 1820. 8vo, orig wraps; backstrip chipped, joints cracked, stains on front cover. sg May 16 (434) $110

**Hutchinson, Francis, 1660-1739**

— An Historical Essay Concerning Witchcraft. L, 1720. 2d Ed. 8vo, modern lea. Some marginalia; 1st blank tattered. Z June 28 (124) $275

**Hutchinson, Horace Gordon**

— Big Game Shooting. L, 1905. 2 vols. pba Apr 4 (213) $225

— The Book of Golf and Golfers. L, 1899. 8vo, orig cloth; rubbed. Foxed. pba Nov 9 (40) $375

Anr copy. Half calf; extrems & spine ends rubbed, spine sunned. Inscr by Cuthbert Blakiston to George Henry Booker. pba Apr 18 (93) $180

— British Golf Links. L, 1897. 1st Trade Ed. 4to, cloth; spine ends & corners rubbed. pba Apr 18 (94) $850

— Fifty Years of Golf. L, [1919]. Cloth. pba Nov 9 (42) $350

1st Ed. L: Country Life, [1919]. Cloth; spine ends rubbed. pba Apr 18 (95) $350

— Golf. L: Longmans, Green, 1890. 1st Ed. Cloth; spine ends rubbed. pba Nov 9 (43) $200

3d Ed. L: Longmans, Green, 1892. Half mor; spine ends scuffed, foot torn. Foxing. pba Nov 9 (44) $250

One of 250 large paper. Illus by Thomas Hodge & Harry Furniss. Half mor; spine lea rubbed & scuffed. Lacking tp & limitation page. pba Apr 18 (96) $800

3d Ed, One of 250 on large paper. Illus by Thoma Hodge & Harry Furniss. Half mor; spine ends & extrems rubbed, spine sunned. pba Nov 9 (45) $2,500

Revised Ed. Phila.: Penn Publishing, 1901. Cloth; insect damage to covers, spine chipped & darkened. pba Nov 9 (46) $95

— Golfing. L: George Routledge, 1893. 1st Ed. Cloth; spine & extrems sunned, spine head repaired, joint ends torn. pba Nov 9 (48) $275

6th Ed. L: George Routledge, 1901. Orig cloth; spine indented. With frontis. pba Nov 9 (47) $130

— Hints on the Game of Golf. Edin., 1893. 8th Ed. Cloth; soiled, spine chipped & rubbed. pba Apr 18 (97) $250

— The New Book of Golf. L: Longmans, Green, 1912. 1st Ed. Cloth; spine ends rubbed, front hinge reinforced. pba Apr 18 (98) $225

**Hutchinson, Walter**

— Hutchinson's Dog Encyclopedia. [L, c.1935]. 3 vols. 4to, cloth; worn & soiled. Prelims foxed. wa Dec 14 (139) $95

**Huth, Frederick H.**

— Works on Horses and Equitation. Hildesheim, 1981. 8vo, bds. sg Apr 11 (139) $80

**Huth Library, Henry**

— Catalogue of the Woodcuts and Engravings in the Huth Library. L: Chiswick Press, 1910. Ltd Ed. 8vo, half lea; spine worn. O Mar 26 (135) $50

**Huttich, Johann, 1480?-1544**

— Imperatorum et Caesarum vitae, cum imaginibus ad vivam expressis. Strassburg: W. Koepfel, 1534. 2 parts in 1 vol. 4to, 17th-cent calf; spine rubbed. C May 1 (80) £600

**Hutton, Alfred**

— Old Sword-Play: the Systems of Fence in Vogue during the XVIth, XVIIth, and XVIIIth Centuries. L & NY, 1892. One of 300. 4to, orig cloth; insect damage. With port & 52 plates. Foxing to prelims. wa Feb 29 (174) $150

**Hutton, Charles, 1737-1823**
— The Principles of Bridges.... Newcastle, 1772. 1st Ed. 8vo, contemp calf. b May 30 (26) £850

**Hutton, James, 1726-97**
— Dissertation upon the Philosophy of Light, Heat and Fire.... Edin., 1794. 7 parts in 1 vol. 8vo, modern cloth. Old stamp on tp; marginal foxing. sg May 16 (181) $400
— Dissertations on Different Subjects in Natural Philosophy. Edin., 1792. 4to, contemp calf; worn, covers detached. With folding plate. sg May 16 (180) $600

**Hutton, William Rich.** See: Grabhorn Printing

**Huxley, Aldous, 1894-1963**
— Along the Road. NY, [1925]. One of 250. Half vellum. pba May 23 (173) $110
— Antic Hay. L, 1923. In chipped dj with edgewear. F Mar 28 (284) $100
— Arabia Infelix, and Other Poems. NY & L, 1929. 1st Ed, One of 692. pba Jan 25 (140) $55
— Brave New World. L, 1932. 1st Ed. In dj with spine ends rubbed. pba Jan 25 (141) $130
   Anr copy. In torn & creased dj. rs Nov 11 (100) $350
— The Burning Wheel. Oxford, 1916. 1st Ed. Wraps; repaired. Inscr to his bride-to-be, Maria, 1917. Engelhard copy. CNY Oct 27 (79) $2,800
— The Defeat of Youth.... Oxford, 1918. 1st Ed. Orig bds; extremities rubbed, spine ends chipped. pba Jan 25 (143) $65
— Essays New and Old. L, 1926. 1st Ed, One of 650. In soiled dj with chipping to spine. pba Jan 25 (144) $65
   Anr copy. Without dj. pba Jan 25 (145) $75
— Holy Face and Other Essays. L: The Fleuron, 1929. One of 300. 4to, orig cloth. bba May 9 (581) £80 [Collinge & Clark]
— Leda. L, 1920. 1st Ed, One of 160. Half cloth; lower cover with stain. pba Jan 25 (147) $50
— Point Counter Point. L, 1928. 1st Ed. Inscr to Charles Wilson, Oct 1930. pba June 13 (210) $130
   Anr copy. Orig cloth, in dj with edge wear. Some soiling. sg June 20 (174) $50
   One of 256. sg June 20 (173) $200
— Prisons. With the "Carceri" Etchings by G.B. Piranesi. L, [1949]. One of 212. Folio wraps; spine bumped. pba Jan 25 (154) $80
   Anr copy. Folio, wraps; upper corners bumped. With 19 plates. pba May 23 (174) $110
— Texts and Pretexts. L, 1932. 1st Ed, One of 214. wa Nov 16 (95) $95

**Huxley, Thomas Henry, 1825-95**
— The Monkey. [Northampton, Mass.]: Apiary Press, 1959. One of 60. Illus by Thomas Brown Cornell. 4to, cloth. sg Feb 15 (5) $400

**Huygens, Christian, 1629-95**
— The Celestial Worlds Discover'd.... L: Timothy Childe, 1698. Ed collating A3, B-L8. 8vo, contemp calf; rebacked, rubbed, lacking rear free endpaper.

With 5 folding plates. Tp reinforced on verso; last leaf lacks corner. sg Oct 19 (230) $800
— Horologium oscillatorium sive de motu pendulorum Paris, 1673. 1st Ed. Folio, contemp calf; worn, back cover detached. Some spotting; smudge on recto of final leaf. C June 26 (194) £9,000

**Hyde, John Alden Lloyd**
— Oriental Lowestoft; Chinese Export Porcelain.... Newport, Monmouthshire, [1954]. 4to, cloth. sg June 13 (94) $100

**Hyde, William Lyman**
— History of the One Hundred and Twelfth Regiment N.Y. Volunteers. Fredonia, 1866. 8vo, orig cloth; worn, library numbers on spine. NH July 21 (77) $150

**Hyginus, Caius Julius**
— De mundi et sphaerae ac utriusque partium. Venice: M. Sessam & P. de Ravanis, 1517. 4to, modern half vellum. Many contemp annotations in Greek & Latin, some touching illusts, some cropped; lacking final blank; stains. sg May 16 (183) $1,900
— Poeticon Astronomicon. Greenbrae CA: Allen Press, 1985. One of 140. 4to, cloth. sg Sept 14 (12) $225

**Hymnal**
— The Yattendon Hymnal. Oxford, 1899. 4to, cloth-backed ptd card wraps. Annotations in pencil. S May 15 (82) £180

**Hyrtl, Joseph, 1810-94**
— Vergleichend-anatomische Untersuchungen ueber das innere Gehoerorgan des Menschen und der Saeugethiere. Prague, 1845. Folio, modern cloth. With 9 plates. Foxed. sg May 16 (435) $110

**Hyslop, Theo. B.**
— Mental Handicaps in Golf. Balt.: Williams & Eilkins, 1927. 1st American Ed. - Forewords by Rolf Creasy & John Henry Taylor. Cloth. pba Apr 18 (99) $70

# I

**Iakinth, Archimandrite.** See: Bichurin, Nikita Jakovlevich

**Ibsen, Henrik, 1828-1906**
   See also: Limited Editions Club
— Peer Gynt. L, 1936. One of 460. Illus by Arthur Rackham. 4to, orig vellum gilt. With 12 colored plates. P Dec 12 (158) $700
   Anr copy. Orig vellum gilt; some discoloration. sg Feb 15 (252) $650
   Anr copy. Orig vellum gilt; spotted & dried. wd Nov 15 (102) $650

**Icazbalceta, Joaquin Garcia, 1825-94.** See: Garcia Icazbalceta & Wagner

**Iciar, Juan de**
— Recopilacion subtilissima: intitulada orthographia practica.... Saragossa, 1550. ("Arte subtilissima por la qual se ensena a escrivir perfectamente.") 2d Ed. 4to, contemp remboitage of blind-tooled pigskin with center medallion stamp of Madonna & child, vellum spine; some worming. With woodcut title, port & 95 plates. Soiled; tp & some other leaves remargined; repairs affecting some plates pen facsimile restorations to quire E; library stamps on B5r & H6r & removed from tp. Pagay - Ford - Schaefer copy. P Nov 1 (124) $8,000

**Ide, Simon**
See also: Grabhorn Printing
— A Biographical Sketch of the Life of William B. Ide.... Claremont, N.H.: Pbd by the Subscribers, [1880]. 1st Ed. 16mo, orig cloth. Robbins copy. pba Mar 21 (161) $1,200

**Ide, William Brown**
— Scraps of California History Never Before Published. Claremont, NH, 1880. 1st Ed. Orig wraps in cloth slipcase. Larson copy. pba Sept 28 (530) $2,000
— Who Conquered California? Claremont, N.H.: Simon Ide, [1880]. 1st Ed. Orig bds; bds stained & worn. Marginal tears to pp.55-6. Robbins copy. pba Mar 21 (162) $900

**Ignotus**
— Golf in a Nutshell. L: Country Life, 1919. 1st Ed. Orig bds. pba Nov 9 (49) $50

**Illingsworth, James**
— A Just Narrative of John Duncalf, whose Hands and Legs rotted off, in the Parish of King's-Swinford.... L, 1757. 8vo, disbound. sg Mar 21 (169) $425

**Illustrated...**
— Illustrated History of Plumas, Lassen & Sierra Counties.... San Francisco, 1882. 1st Ed. 8vo, orig half lea; minor shelf-rubbing & wear. Robbins copy. pba Mar 21 (102) $700
— An Illustrated History of Sacramento County, California. Chicago, 1890. 8vo, later cloth; extremities worn & soiled. Tp detached & with perforated stamp; library markings; lacking pp. 703-6. cb Oct 17 (152) $120
— Illustrated London News. L, 1842-87. Vols 1-91. Folio, contemp half mor; rubbed. Sold w.a.f. S June 12 (202) £8,500
  Vols 73. L, 1878. Folio, contemp half mor; edges library-stamped, rubbed. Chromolitho plate def; lastleaf torn & def. bba June 6 (45) £520 [Severis]
  Anr Ed. L, January-December, 1879. Vols 74-75. Folio, orig cloth; spines faded. P.187 of vol 75 torn, & p.18 poorly printed. S Oct 26 (552) £200 [Chelsea Gallery]

**Ilustracion...**
— Ilustracion Filipina, Periodico Quincenal. Manila, 1859-60. Vol I, No 1 - Vol II, No 24 (all pbd). 4to, modern half calf, 1 orig wrap bound in. Sold w.a.f. S June 27 (237) £6,500

**Imagistes...**
— Des Imagistes: An Anthology. NY: Boni, 1914. 1st American Ed. Orig bds; spine ends rubbed, soiled. pba Jan 25 (174) $160

**Imago...**
— Imago Mundi: The Journal of the International Society for the History of Cartography. Lympne Castle Kent, 1978-83. Vols 30-35. 6 vols. 4to, cloth. sg May 9 (14) $225

**Imbert, Barthelemi, 1747-90**
— Les Bienfaits du Sommeil ou les quatre reves accomplis.... Paris: Brunet, 1776. 8vo, orig wraps. Schiff - Fuerstenberg - Schaefer copy. S Dec 7 (311) £320
— Fables nouvelles. Paris: Delalain, 1773. 8vo, calf gilt by Bozerian. With frontis in 4 states. Browned. Fuerstenberg - Schaefer copy. S Dec 7 (308) £150
— Historiettes ou nouvelles en vers. Amst. & Paris, 1774. 8vo, contemp mor gilt. With engraved title & plate. Fuerstenberg - Schaefer copy. S Dec 7 (309) £360
— Le jugement de Paris. Poeme en IV chants, suivi d'oeuvres melees. Amst. [but Paris], 1774. 8vo, contemp red mor gilt with arms of Leopold Charles de Choiseul-Stainville as Archbishop of Cambrai. With engraved title & 4 plates & 4 headpieces. With tirage a part & eau-forte for all headpieces & 1 plate. Some spotting. Fuerstenberg - Schaefer copy. S Dec 7 (310) £360

**Imlay, Gilbert**
— A Topographical Description of the Western Territory of North America. L, 1797. 3d Ed. 8vo, orig sheep; front joint starting. Repairs to 2 of the 4 maps. sg Oct 26 (155) $600

**Immerito.** See: Browne, Moses

**Imperial...**
— The Imperial Dictionary of Universal Biography. L: William Mackenzie, [n.d.]. 4to, contemp calf gilt; extremities rubbed. wa Nov 16 (64) $425

**Imprint...**
— Imprint: A Typographical Journal. L, 1913. Nos 1-9 (all pbd) in 1 vol. 4to, cloth, upper wrap to Part 1 bound in. Lacking some plates. Sold w.a.f. bba May 9 (33) £50 [Morris]

**Imray, James F.**
— Sailing Directions for the West Coast of North America.... L, 1853. Orig cloth; spine worn, hinges cracked. With chart. Dampstaining at ends. pba July 25 (209) $225
  2d Ed. L, 1868. Orig cloth; some wear, corner bumped. With 10 folding charts. Frontis map with stub tear; some foxing. pba July 25 (170) $225

**Inboden, Gudrun —&**
**Kellein, Thomas**
— Ad Reinhardt. Stuttgart, [1985]. One of 1,500. Oblong 4to, bds. sg Sept 7 (289) $50

## Index Aureliensis
— Index Aureliensis. Catalogus librorum sedecimo saeculo impressorum. Geneva: Fondation Index Aureliensis, 1965-92. 13 vols. Ck Apr 12 (244) £280

## India House
— A Descriptive Catalogue of the Marine Collection.... Middletown, 1973. One of 1,250. 4to, cloth. O May 7 (170) $70

## Indians, North American
— Report of the Secretary of the Interior communicating... the correspondence between the Department of the Interior and the Indian agents and commissioners in California. Wash., 1853. With: George Anderson & others. Treaty Making and Treaty Rejection by the Federal Government in California, 1850-52 2 vols, later mor. Larson copy. pba Sept 28 (23) $50

## Ingalls, Eleazar Stillman
— Journal of a Trip to California by the Overland Route across the Plains in 1850-51. Fairfield, 1979. Reprint of 1851 Ed. - Illus by B. Bluhm & S. M. Luke. Bds. Larson copy. pba Sept 28 (533) $55

## Ingegneri, Angelo
— Della poesia rappresentiva & del modo di rappresentare le favole sceniche. Ferrara: Vittorio Baldini, 1598. 4to, contemp vellum. sg Apr 18 (68) $650

## Ingenhousz, Jan, 1730-99
— Experiments upon Vegetables. L, 1779. 1st Ed. 8vo, contemp calf; rebacked. With folding plate. B8v soiled at lower margin; U2 short tear to outer margin; U3 stained. Ck Mar 22 (156) £950

## Inghirami, Curzio
— Ethruscarum antiquitatum fragmenta. Frankfurt [Florence], 1637. 1st Ed. Folio, old vellum; new endpapers, spine repaired. With 5 double-page or folding plates. Some repairs without loss. S June 13 (549) £220

## Inghirami, Francesco
— Galleria Omerica.... Florence, 1829-26. 6 vols. 8vo, contemp half calf with vellum corners. With 388 plates, many colored. Some spotting. S June 27 (148) £2,600

## Ingholt, Harald
— Gandharan Art in Pakistan. NY, [1957]. 4to, cloth, in dj. sg Jan 11 (224) $200

## Inglis, Henry David, 1795-1835
— The Channel Islands.... L, 1834. 2 vols. 8vo, contemp calf; rebacked. Frontises foxed. pba Oct 9 (9) $50
— Rambles in the Footsteps of Don Quixote. L, 1837. 1st Ed. - Illus by George Cruikshank. 12mo, orig cloth. sg Sept 21 (144) $100

**Ingoldsby, Thomas.** See: Barham, Richard Harris

## Ingraham, Henry Andrews
— American Trout Streams. NY: Ptd at the Derrydale Press, 1926. One of 350. Half cloth; worn. With 5 plates. Inscr. O June 25 (166) $225

## Ingram, James, 1774-1850
— Memorials of Oxford. Oxford, 1837. 3 vols. 4to, contemp half mor. With 98 plates & folding plan. S Apr 23 (353) £300

## Inman, Henry, 1837-99
— Buffalo Jones' Forty Years of Adventure. Topeka, 1899. 8vo, pictorial cloth; worn, spine soiled. wa Feb 29 (406) $95
   1st Ed. Topeka: Crane, 1899. 8vo, orig cloth; rubbed & soiled, front hinge cracked. pba Apr 25 (470) $55
— Tales of the Trail. Topeka, 1898. Orig cloth. pba June 25 (126) $150

## Innocent VIII, Pope, 1432-92
— Bulla 6 Oct 1491 (Sicut bonus pastor). Rome: Stephan Plannck, [after 6 Oct] 1491. 4to, modern bds. 4 leaves. Pellechet Ms 6335. C Apr 3 (116) £1,000

## International...
— International Sport: The Anglo-American Equestrian World. L, [1956-57]. One of 250. Folio, lea gilt; joints cracked. With frontis & 72 ports. Text in English & French. sg Mar 7 (476) $140

## Internationale Buchbinderkunst...
— Internationale Buchbinderkunst Austellung in Frankfurt 1906. Frankfurt: Kunstwerbemuseum, 1906. Mor extra by Reinhold Pfau. b Sept 20 (601) £220

## Interpretationes...
— Interpretationes Hebraeorum, Chaldaeorum, Graecorumque nominum Noui Testamenti. Antwerp: Johann Zeuer; 1528. 8vo, modern half mor. Tp repaired; cut close; soiling. CE Dec 6 (73) $1,700

## Introduction...
— Introduction to View of the Works for the Tunnel under the Thames from Rotherhithe to Wapping. L: Harvey & Darton, 1833. Bds; worn, spine strip lacking. With 10 plates, 2 folding. Tp stamped; some foxing & soiling. cb Feb 14 (2643) $300

**Ionesco, Eugene.** See: Limited Editions Club

## Iowa
— City Charter and Ordinances of Dubuque.... Dubuque, 1861. 8vo, orig cloth; half of backstrip lacking. sg Oct 26 (161) $60
— Dubuque City Directory for 1873-1874. Dubuque, 1873. 8vo, orig cloth; needs rebdg. sg Oct 26 (162) $110

## Iredale, Frank
— 33 Years of Cricket. Sydney, 1920. Orig wraps. pn Oct 12 (308) £130

## Ireland
DUBLIN HARBOUR IMPROVEMENTS. - Reports. [N.p., 1801]. Folio, contemp half calf. Inserted in photocopy of a letter from William Bligh to Banks referring to this work, which includes his report. b Mar 20 (85) £2,600

## Ireland, John, d.1808
— Hogarth Illustrated. L, 1791. 3 vols. 8vo, contemp mor gilt. Bdg & contents stained. Sold w.a.f. pba Aug 8 (473) $75

## Ireland, LeRoy
— The Works of George Innes. An Illustrated Catalogue Raisonne. Austin: Univ. of Texas Press, [1965]. Preface by Donald B. Goodall; Foreword by Robert G. McIntyre. 4to, cloth, in dj. sg Jan 11 (226) $400

## Ireland, Samuel, d.1800
— Picturesque Views on the River Thames. L, 1801-2. 2 vols. 8vo, 19th-cent cloth. With engraved titles, 2 maps & 52 plates. Lacking half-titles; some spotting. S June 13 (403) £180
— Picturesque Views on the Upper, or Warwickshire Avon. L, 1795. 1st Ed. 8vo, modern mor by Hampstead Bindery. With hand-title, hand-colored additional title, 2 ports, & 29 hand-colored plates. S Oct 26 (396) £340 [Hollin]

## Ireland, William Henry, 1777-1835
— Effusions of Love from Chatelar to Mary, Queen of Scotland. L, 1808. 8vo, mor gilt by Cross & Beckwith. b May 30 (405) £100
— England's Topographer: A New and Complete History of the County of Kent. L, 1828-29. 4 vols. 8vo, contemp calf; worn, 1 cover detached. With engraved title in Vol I, folding map & 124 plates. Tear to 1 map; some foxing. bba July 18 (352) £120 [Marlborough]
— The Life of Napoleon Bonaparte. L, 1823-28. 1st Ed. - Illus by George Cruikshank. Vols I-III (of 4). 8vo, 19th-cent half mor. With folding map & 24 hand-colored plates & 1 folding uncolored plate. F June 20 (841) £220
1st Ed in orig 64/53 parts. Bound in 4 vols. 8vo, later mor gilt by Root, with Napoleon's arms. With 26 hand-colored plates, all folding, engraved titles & 1 line engraving with a tint block. Some fold repairs; minor spotting & soiling. P June 5 (303) $1,200
— Miscellaneous Papers and Legal Instruments under the Hand and Seal of William Shakespeare...from the Original Manuscripts. L, 1796. 1st Ed. Folio, 19th-cent half cloth; needs rebacked. Foxing towards end. sg Mar 21 (289) $110

## Iribe, Paul
— Parlons francais: trente-sept dessins de Paul Iribe. Paris, 1934. Folio, pictorial wraps; soiled, corners chipped, plate list coming loose. sg Feb 15 (166) $110
— Les Robes de Paul Poiret. Paris, 1908. One of 250. 4to, orig bds; spine perished, rubbed & soiled. cb June 25 (1955) $1,300

## Irving, John
— The Hotel New Hampshire. NY, 1981. 1st Ed. In dj. Sgd. sg June 20 (175) $60
— A Prayer for Owen Meany. NY, [1989]. One of 250. pba Aug 22 (254) $110
— The Water-Method Man. NY, [1972]. In dj with minor staining to top edges; rubber stamp H to front free endpaper. pba Aug 22 (255) $50
Anr copy. In dj with minor soiling. Sgd on half-title. sg Dec 14 (170) $140

## Irving, Washington, 1783-1859
See also: Grolier Club; Limited Editions Club
— The Angler. Phila., 1931. Out-of-series copy. Bds; worn. O Dec 5 (61) $50
Anr copy. Bds; scuffed, head of spine chipped. O Feb 6 (139) $90
Anr Ed. [N.p.]: Harbor Press, 1933. One of 180. Half cloth. ANs of Roland Wood laid in. pba July 11 (133) $80
— Astoria, or Anecdotes of an Enterprise beyond the Rocky Mountains. Phila., 1836. 1st Ed, 1st State. 2 vols. 8vo, half mor. Folding map inserted at beginning of Vol II. pba Dec 14 (79) $160
Anr copy. Later mor retaining older spine; extremities rubbed. Z June 28 (127) $325
— Bracebridge Hall: or, the Humourists, by Geoffrey Crayon. L, 1877 [1876]. Illus by Randolph Caldecott. 8vo, mor extra by Kelligram. b Sept 20 (628) £280
— A History of New York. NY, 1809. 1st Ed. 2 vols. 12mo, contemp sheep. sg Oct 26 (164) $1,500
Anr Ed. NY, 1850. Illus by F. O. C. Darley. 8vo, half mor. pba Dec 14 (80) $85
— A History of the Life and Voyages of Christopher Columbus. L, 1828. 4 vols. 8vo, orig half cloth; worn; lending label of New Bridge-street Book Society on front cover, with notes on flyleaves & margins by members. With 1 (of 2) folding maps. Some foxing. pba July 25 (409) $130
Anr copy. Half calf; worn, joints weak. With 2 folding maps.. wa Dec 14 (41) $110
— The Legend of Sleepy Hollow. L, [1928]. Illus by Arthur Rackham. 4to, cloth, in rubbed & spotted dj. bba May 9 (408) £110 [Blackwell]
Anr copy. Cloth, in dj with chip to spine. sg Feb 15 (253) $275
One of 375. Orig vellum gilt; minor discoloration. P Dec 12 (155) $1,400; S Nov 2 (114) £1,000 [Hirsch]; sg Oct 19 (203) $800
Anr Ed. NY: Cheshire House, 1931. One of 1,200. Illus by Bernhardt Wall. Folio, half cloth. pba Aug 8 (645) $70
— Life of George Washington. NY, 1855-59. 1st Ed. 5 vols. 8vo, half calf; 1 spine worn. Insect damage to half-title of Vol I. pba Aug 8 (284) $70
— Rip Van Winkle.... L, 1905. One of 250. Illus by Arthur Rackham. 4to, orig vellum gilt; stain to front cover. Ck May 31 (178) £850
Anr copy. Orig vellum gilt; minor soiling. With frontis & 50 color plates. P Dec 12 (149) $2,000; S Nov 2 (121) £380 [Heritage]

Anr Ed. L & NY, 1905. 4to, orig cloth, in wrap. With 50 colored plates. bba May 9 (400) £460 [Sotheran]
Anr copy. Cloth; becoming disbound, spine ends gone. F June 20 (316) $70
Anr Ed. Paris, 1906. Out-of-series copy, unsgd Vellum; soiled & discolored. With 51 mtd color plates. CE May 22 (396) $170
Anr Ed. L, 1907. Illus by Arthur Rackham. 4to, later half mor gilt. With 50 colored plates. sg Feb 15 (254) $225
— Works. NY, 1881. 12 vols. 8vo, contemp calf gilt. sg Sept 21 (27) $600
Author's Autograph Ed. NY, 1895-97. One of 500. 40 vols. 8vo, half mor. With Ms leaf. cb Oct 17 (278) $2,500
Joseph Jefferson Ed. NY & L, 1901. one of 250. 40 vols. Half vellum. pba Sept 14 (216) $350

**Irwin, Eyles, 1751?-1817**
— A Series of Adventures in the Course of a Voyage up the Red-Sea.... Dublin, 1780. 8vo, contemp calf; spine def. With 2 folding maps. b May 30 (274) £130
2d Ed. L, 1780. 4to, contemp half calf; worn, upper cover detached. With plan, 3 folding maps & 2 plates. Some staining; lacking half-title. b Sept 20 (427) £120
Anr copy. Modern cloth. Library stamps on tp & several text leaves. sg Mar 7 (110) $350

**Irwin, R. B.** See: Bowman & Irwin

**Irwin, Will.** See: Genthe, Arnold

**Isaac, Frank**
— English and Scottish Printing Types. Oxford: Bibliographical Society, 1930-32. 2 vols. 4to, half cloth; some wear. ds July 27 (97) $50

**Isaac Medicus**
— De particularibus diaetis. Ladua: Matthaeus Cerdonis, 23 May, 1487. 4to, unbound in half mor box. With contemp annotations & German trans. Ck Mar 22 (157) £8,500

**Iselin, J. C.**
— Allgemeines Historisches Lexicon.... Leipzig, 1730-32. Folio, contemp vellum; soiled. Minor foxing & browning. O Mar 26 (136) $450

**Isherwood, Christopher, 1904-56**
— The Berlin Stories. NY: New Directions, [1945]. In dj with spine ends rubbed. pba May 23 (181) $55
— Goodbye to Berlin. L, 1939. 1st Ed. In frayed dj. b Jan 31 (177) £160
Anr copy. In dj torn at head of spine. ALs to Harold Nicolson laid in. Hobson copy. S June 28 (166) £3,200
— Lions and Shadows. An Education in the Twenties. L: Hogarth Press, 1938. 1st bdg, in frayed dj. Hobson copy. S June 28 (165) £110
— Mr. Norris Changes Trains. L: Hogarth Press, 1935. 1st Ed. In dj. Laid in is autograph postcard, sgd, to Roger Senhouse. Hobson copy. S June 28 (163) £1,300
— Sally Bowles. L: Hogarth Press, 1937. In dj. Sgd on tp. Hobson copy. S June 28 (164) £1,300

**Ishiguro, Kazuo**
— A Pale View of Hills. NY, [1982]. 1st American Ed, Uncorrected proof copy. Ptd wraps; spine leaning. pba Jan 25 (169) $150

**Isla, Jose Fransisco de l'**
— The History of the Famous Preacher Friar Gerund de Campazas. L, 1772. 8vo, contemp calf gilt; scuffed, joints & extremities rubbed. Minor dampstaining. F Mar 28 (438) $140

**Isnard, Emile.** See: Arnaud d'Agnel & Isnard

**Isocrates, 436-338 B.C.**
— Opera. Basel: Officina Oporiniana, 1570. 2 vols in 1. Folio, 17th-cent calf; spine ends chipped, joints cracked. Tp soiled. sg Mar 21 (170) $350

**Israel, August**
— Pestalozzi-Bibliographie.... Hildesheim, 1970. 3 vols. 8vo, orig cloth. sg Apr 11 (163) $140

**It Is**
— It Is. A Magazine for Abstract Art. NY, 1959-60. 6 vols. 4to, wraps; No 6 loose in bdg. sg Sept 7 (191) $425
Anr copy. Nos 1-5 (of 6). Folio, sg Jan 11 (228) $120

**Italy**
— Indice generale degli incunaboli delle biblioteche d'Italia. Rome, 1943-81. 6 vols in 4. 4to, cloth or half cloth, orig wraps bound in. bba Oct 5 (89) £460 [Franks]

**Ito, Kaichi**
— Meihou Ningyou Shu. Kyoto: Rakutou Press, 1937. Folio, orig Japanese-style pictorial bds; rubbed, lacking 1 clasp, insect damage to spine. With 58 leaves of photo-reproductions of Japanese dolls, some full-page. wa Dec 14 (530) $85

**Itoh, Teiji**
— Kura: Design and Tradition of the Japanese Storehouse. Tokyo, [1973]. Folio, cloth, in dj. sg June 13 (13) $90

**Iturbide, Agustin de, 1783-1824**
PACHECO, JOSE RAMON. - Descripcion de la solemnidad funebre con que se honaron la cenizas del heroe de Iguala, Don Agustin de Iturbide, en octubre de 1838. Mexico, 1849. 8vo, contemp calf, orig wraps bound in. With port & 3 litho plates. S Nov 30 (162) £400

**Ives, Edward, d.1786**
— A Voyage from England to India.... L, 1773. 1st Ed. 4to, cloth. Library stamps on tp, rectos of maps & plates & some text leaves. sg Mar 7 (111) $350

### Ives, Joseph Charles
— Report upon the Colorado River.... Wash., 1861. 1st Ed. 4to, orig cloth; rebacked with lea, cover edges worn. With 2 folding maps, 1 profile, 14 views, 7 color plates, 8 folding panoramas, & 3 paleontology plates. Robbins copy. pba Mar 21 (164) $475

### Ives, Joseph Christmas
— Report upon the Colorado River.... Wash., 1861. 4to, modern half mor. With 32 maps & plates only, 8 of them colored. Some maps with tears repaired; tp stamped; some staining. S June 13 (612) £220
Senate issue. Orig cloth; rubbed, spine lacking. With 2 folding maps, 2 folding views, 25 plates (8 in color) & 1 route profile. K June 23 (326) $375

### Ives, Marguerite
— Seventeen Famous Outdoorsmen. Chicago: Canterbury Press, 1929. One of 500. 8vo, cloth; worn. O June 4 (179) $80; O June 25 (167) $90
Anr copy. Orig cloth; insect damage to front cover. pba July 11 (152) $80

# J

### Jablonsky, C. G. —&
### Herbst, J. F. W.
— Natursystem aller bekannten in- und auslaendischen Insekten. Berlin, 1783-1804. 11 text vols, 8vo & 3 plate vols, 4to. 19th-cent bds; worn. With frontis, 11 hand-colored titles & 328 hand-colored plates. Plates 53-54 & 102 short; some soiling & browning. S Nov 30 (27) £5,500

### Jack, Alexander
— Six Views of Kot Kangra.... L, 1847. Folio, contemp mor; rubbed. With tinted litho title & 6 hand-colored plates. Litho title mtd; library blindstamp on each plate. S Nov 30 (200) £3,000

### Jack, Robert Logan, 1845-1921
— Northmost Australia. L, 1921. 2 vols. With 39 plates & 16 folding maps in pockets. b Mar 20 (112) £260

### Jackson, Abraham Valentine Williams, 1862-1937.
See: Onassis copy, Jacqueline Bouvier Kennedy

### Jackson, Donald
— Letters of the Lewis and Clark Expedition with Related Documents, 1783-1854. Urbana, 1962. 1st Ed. Orig cloth in torn dj. pba Feb 13 (118) $60
Anr copy. Orig cloth in torn dj. Robbins copy. pba Mar 21 (200) $80
2d Ed. Urbana, 1978. pba Feb 13 (119) $55

### Jackson, Emily Nevill
— A History of Hand-Made Lace.... L & NY, 1900. 8vo, orig cloth. S Mar 28 (435) £110

### Jackson, Helen Hunt, 1830-85
See also: Limited Editions Club
— A Century of Dishonour. NY, 1881. 1st Ed. 12mo, orig cloth; extremities rubbed, stamp to front pastedown & tp. pba June 25 (128) $70

— Colorado Springs. Bost., 1883. Orig wraps; chipped. First leaf soiled. pba Apr 25 (472) $70
— Ramona: a Story. Bost., 1884. 1st Ed. 12mo, orig cloth. Robbins copy. pba Mar 21 (165) $750

### Jackson, Humphrey, 1717-1801
— An Essay on Bread.... L, 1758. With: Poison Detected, or Frightful Truths and Alarming to the Metropolis in a Treatise on Bread. L, 1757. 1st Eds. 8vo in 4s, Essay in wraps, Poison disbound. Some soiling. Ck Mar 22 (56) £1,000

### Jackson, Jack
— Flags along the Coast.... Austin: David R. Holman for Book Club of Texas, [1995]. One of 350. Folio, cloth over bds. ds July 27 (48) $275

### Jackson, John
— The Practical Fly-Fisher; More Particularly for Grayling or Umber. L, 1854. 8vo, cloth. With 10 plates. O Feb 6 (140) $275
Anr Ed. L, 1880. 8vo, orig cloth. With 10 hand-colored plates. pba July 11 (153) $150

### Jackson, John, Engraver —&
### Chatto, William Andrew, 1799-1864
— A Treatise on Wood Engraving. L, 1839. 8vo, contemp half lea; worn. George Cruikshank's sgd copy. S Apr 23 (272) £190

### Jackson, Joseph Henry
— Anybody's Gold: The Story of California's Mining Towns. NY, 1941. 1st Ed. - Illus by E. H. Suydam. Buckram in dj; d/j worn. With 4 illus. Sgd. Larson copy. pba Sept 28 (536) $70

### Jackson, Shirley
— The Bird's Nest. NY, [1954]. In soiled dj. pba May 4 (163) $60

### Jackson, William Alexander
— An Annotated List of the Publications of... the Reverend Thomas Frognall Dibdin. Cambr., 1965. One of 500. Folio, orig cloth. sg Apr 11 (164) $60

### Jackson, William Henry
— Time Exposure. The Autobiography.... NY, 1940. 1st Ed. In dj with edge wear. Sgd, 16 Aug 1940. pba Nov 16 (144) $170

### Jacob, Alexander, d.1785
— A Complete English Peerage. L, 1767-69. 2 vols in 3. Folio, contemp calf; worn. With frontis & 209 plates, 92 ptd folding genealogical tables. Gathering Pp in Vol II dampstained. S June 13 (404) £480

### Jacob, Giles, 1686-1744
— A New Law-Dictionary. L, 1732. 2d Ed. Folio, contemp calf. b Sept 20 (208) £160

### Jacob, Nicholas Henri —&
### Hugues, P.
— Storia naturale delle scimie e dei maki. Milan, 1812. Part 1 only. Folio, contemp half sheep; scuffed.

With 73 plates. Browning to Italian title. C Apr 3 (117) £4,000
Anr copy. 19th-cent half mor. With 74 plates. S June 27 (39) £3,400

**Jacobaeus, Oligerus**
— Museum regium, seu catalogus rerum, tam naturum quam artificialium...in Basilica Bibliothecae. Copenhagen, [1710]. Folio, later half calf; worn. With frontis & 55 plates. Some cropping at fore-edge; Plate 11 in Part 2, section 4 repaired & backed; hole in 2d Plate 22 in same section; frontis backed. S Mar 14 (185) £650

**Jacobi, Charles Thomas**
— On the Making and Issuing of Books. L: Chiswick Press, 1891. One of 15 on Japanese vellum. 4to, contemp lev extra. With Jacobi's bookplate & his initialed note "Bound by S. T. Prideaux," though bdg stamped-sgd by Kelly & Sons. sg Oct 19 (119) $600

**Jacobi, Johann, of Wallhausen.** See: Wallhausen, Johann Jacobi von

**Jacobson, Yvonne**
— Passing Farms: Enduring Values - California's Santa Clara Valley. Los Altos: William Kaufmann, [1984]. Foreword by Wallace Stegner. In dj. Stain to fore-edge area of half-title. Sgd by Jacobson & by Stegner. pba Jan 25 (348) $130

**Jacobus de Clusa, 1381-1465**
— De valore et utilitate missarum pro defunctis.... Heidelberg: Heinrich Knoblochtzer, [1493]. 4to, 19th-cent half mor. 31 lines; gothic letter. Dampstain at head of leaves; library stamp of Blades Library of St. Brides Foundation. 19 (of 20) leaves; lacking final blank. Goff J-40. S Dec 18 (43) £600 [de Kesel]
— De veritate dicenda aut tacenda. [Basel: Martin Flach, c.1474]. Folio, 18th-cent sheep gilt, armorial bdg. 32 lines; type 1:117G. Wormed. 19 (of 20) leaves; lacking final blank. Goff J-41. C Apr 3 (118) £1,000

**Jacobus de Theramo, 1349-1417**
— Consolation peccatorum, seu Processus Belial. Augsburg: Johann Schuessler, 2 July 1472. Folio, 19th-cent half mor. 33-35 lines; type 1:117G. Final quire rehinged; wormholes affecting letters in final 2 quires; 1st leaf soiled. 115 (of 118) leaves; lacking final 3 blanks. Goff J-64. C Nov 29 (57) £3,200

**Jacobus de Voragine.** See: Voragine, Jacobus de

**Jacoby, Karl**
— Hugo von Hoffmansthal Bibliographie. Berlin, 1936. With: Walsh, James E., The Hofmannsthal [sic] Collection in the Houghton Library, Heidelberg, [1974] One of 400. 8vo, Jacoby in half vellum, Walsh in cloth. sg Apr 11 (165) $70

**Jacquemin, Raphael**
— Iconographie generale et methodique du costume civil et militaire du IV au XIX Siecle.... Paris, [c.1882]. 3 vols. Folio, contemp mor; spine ends torn & lacking, joints starting, partly misbound. With 281 hand-colored plates. cb Oct 17 (113) $600

**Jacquet, Eugene, 1811-38.** See: Burnouf & Jacquet

**Jacquin, Nicolaus Joseph von, 1727-1817**
— Collectanea ad botanicam, chemiam et historiam.... Vienna, 1786-96. 5 vols. 4to, modern half mor. With 8 plain & 98 hand-colored plates. Titles stamped; some spotting. S June 27 (40) £3,200

**Jaehns, Max, 1837-1900**
— Geschichte der Kriegswissenschaften. Munich & Leipzig, 1889-91. 3 vols. 8vo, contemp half lea; backstrips faded, worn, partly detached. Few leaves loose. sg Apr 11 (166) $200

**Jaffe, George**
— Zwei Dialoge ueber Raum und Zeit. Leipzig, 1931. Contemp half lea. Inscr by Jaffe to Einstein & by Einstein to someone named Toni. sg Sept 28 (97) $750

**Jahn, Johann, 1750-1816 —& Oberleitner, Andreas**
— Elementa Aramaicae seu Chaldaeo-Syriacae Linguae. Vienna, 1820. 8vo, contemp half mor gilt. With 3 folding tables. sg Mar 7 (112) $50

**Jahrbuch...**
— Jahrbuch der Auktionspreise fuer Buecher und Autographen. Hamburg, 1961-90. Vols 12-40 in 28 (lacking 36) & 3 Index vols for Vols 11-30. bba Oct 5 (329) £750 [Sawyer]
— Jahrbuch der Original Graphik. Berlin: Wohlgemuth & Lissner, [c.1919]. One of 100. Vol I. Folio, loose as issued in orig wraps; soiled, spine split. sg May 23 (320) $400

**Jalk, Grete**
— 40 Years of Danish Furniture Design. Copenhagen, [1987]. 4 vols. 4to, cloth, in djs. sg June 13 (157) $225

**Jallabert, Jean**
— Experimenta electrica usibus medicis applicata. Basel, 1750. 8vo, contemp half calf; worn. With folding table & 3 folding plates. S Mar 14 (186) £220

**James, G. P. R., 1799-1860**
— The Life of Henry the Fourth, King of France and Navarre. L, 1847. 3 vols. 8vo, half lev by Bayntun. Extra-illus with c.30 ports. sg Feb 8 (77) $375

**James, George Wharton, 1858-1923**
— Arizona the Wonderland. Bost., [1920]. pba Apr 25 (475) $170
— Indian Basketry.... Pasadena, 1903. 3d Ed, Revised & Enlarged. Orig cloth; covers dampstained. Last 20 pp dampstained. Robbins copy. pba Mar 21 (166) $150
— The Indians of the Painted Desert Region.... Bost., 1907. Period half mor; spine faded. Robbins copy.

Inscr to Mrs. Inez Ray Smith.  pba Mar 21 (167) $160
— New Mexico: The Land of the Delight Makers. Bost.: Page, [1920].  pba Apr 25 (476) $190
— Through Ramona's Country. Bost., 1909. Period half mor; spine faded & rubbed, hinge cracked. Robbins copy. Inscr to Mrs. Inez Ray Smith.  pba Mar 21 (168) $150
— What the White Race May Learn from the Indian. Chicago, 1908. Cloth; stain to lower corners of front cover & 1st few leaves.  pba Mar 7 (146) $130
Anr copy. Cloth; front free endpaper & tp stamped. pba Apr 25 (478) $55
— The Wonders of the Colorado Desert.... Bost., 1906. 1st Ed. - Illus by Carl Eytel.  2 vols. Orig cloth; spines sunned. With color frontis. Robbins copy. pba Mar 21 (169) $190
2d Ptg. Bost., 1907.  2 vols. Orig cloth; hinge cracked.  pba Feb 12 (82) $225

**James, H. G.**
— This Work. Comprising a Series of the most interesting Views of Old Halls.... Manchester, [1825]. 4to, contemp half calf; rubbed. With litho title, list of subscribers & 30 (of 36) plates. Marginal discoloration & spotting.  S Mar 28 (55) £200

**James, Henry, 1843-1916**
See also: Limited Editions Club
— The American Scene. L, 1907. One of 800. Orig cloth, 1st bdg; front hinge cracked. Prelims foxed. Inscr to Hugh Walpole, 20 July 1909. Gilvarry - Engelhard copy.  CNY Oct 27 (85) $2,000
— The Author of Beltraffio, Pandora.... Bost., 1885. 8vo, orig cloth; joints & edges rubbed, inner hinges tender.  Inscr to his aunt, Catharine Walsh. Gilvarry - Engelhard copy.  CNY Oct 27 (82) $4,800
— The Beast in the Jungle. Kentfield: Allen Press, 1963. One of 130. Illus by Blair Hughes-Stanton.  pba June 20 (23) $275
— Daisy Miller.... NY, 1879. 1st Ed. 16mo, ptd wraps; broken, portion of spine perished.  sg Sept 21 (232) $200
— Embarrassments. L, 1896. 1st Pbd Ed. 8vo, orig cloth.  Inscr to Edmund Gosse & with ALs. Gilvarry - Engelhard copy.  CNY Oct 27 (83) $4,800
— Notes of a Son and Brother. L, 1914.  1st English Ed. Orig cloth; extremities rubbed.  Inscr to Howard Sturgis, Mar 1914. Gilvarry - Engelhard copy.  CNY Oct 27 (88) $2,900
— The Other House. L, 1896. One of 600.  2 vols. 8vo, orig cloth; rubbed. Some fore-margins in Vol I chipped from careless opening.  Inscr to Edmund Gosse, 12 Mary 1897. Gilvarry - Engelhard copy. CNY Oct 27 (84) $4,500
— The Outcry. L, [1911].  Inscr to Edmund Gosse. Gilvarry - Engelhard copy.  CNY Oct 27 (86) $2,800
— The Portrait of a Lady. L, 1881. 1st Ed. 3 vols. 8vo, orig cloth; tear to 1 outer joint, some wear, most endpapers cracked at inner hinges. Engelhard copy. CNY Oct 27 (81) $9,500
— The Princess Casamassima. L & NY, 1886. 1st Ed. 3 vols. 8vo, half mor.  b Jan 31 (96) £280

— The Reverberator. L & NY, 1888. 1st Ed. 2 vols. 8vo, orig cloth; spine ends & corners rubbed.  pba Dec 14 (83) $85
— Roderick Hudson. Bost., 1876. 1st Ed. 8vo, orig cloth; joints rubbed.  CE May 22 (282) $350
— A Small Boy and Others. L, 1913. 1st Ptg, 2d Issue. 8vo, orig cloth; rubbed. Inscr to Ruth Draper, 27 May 1913. Gilvarry - Engelhard copy.  CNY Oct 27 (87) $2,000
— Transatlantic Sketches. Bost., 1875. 1st Ed. 8vo, contemp half vellum; rubbed. Inscr to Francis Boott. Gilvarry - Engelhard copy.  CNY Oct 27 (80) $2,000
— Washington Square. NY, 1881. 1st Ed. 12mo, orig cloth; tips & edges rubbed.  sg Feb 8 (309) $375

**James, Sir Henry, 1803-77 —&**
**Clarke, A. Ross**
— Ordnance Trigonometrical Survey of Great Britain and Ireland.... L, 1858.  2 vols. 4to, orig cloth.  b Jan 31 (326) £50

**James, Henry Evan Murchison**
— The Long White Mountain; or a Journey in Manchuria.... L, 1888. 8vo, orig cloth; worn & soiled, front hinge cracked. With 10 plates & folding color map. wa Dec 14 (166) $120

**James I, King of Aragon**
— Aureum opus regalium privilegiorum civitatis et regni Valentie cum historia Regis Jacobi ipsius primi conquistatoris. Valencia: Didacus de Gumiel, 30 Oct 1515. 1st Ed. - Compiled by Luis Alanya. Folio, early vellum; worn & mended. 50 lines; double column; gothic type. Minor worming to some inner margins; some browning & marginalia; Early copies of 2 documents on last leaf verso & on an additional leaf. Schaefer copy.  P Nov 1 (13) $7,500

**James I, King of England, 1566-1625**
— An Apologie for the oath of Allegiance.... L: Robert Barker, 1609. 2 parts in 1 vol. 4to, contemp calf; worn, upper cover nearly off. Tp reinforced along gutter with linen.  CE May 22 (280) $400
— Basilikon Doron, or His Majesties Instructions.... L: F. Kyngston for J. Norton, 1603. 8vo, old vellum; worn & soiled. Lacking a prelim leaf. STC 14351. O Mar 5 (121) $275
Anr Ed. L: Richard Field, 1603. 8vo, contemp calf; upper cover detached. Cropped at top; stained throughout; tp laid down. STC 14353. S Apr 23 (85) £110
— A Remonstrance... for the Right of Kings.... Cambr.: Cantrell Legge, 1616. 4to, modern half mor.  Some dampstaining. STC 14369.  CE May 22 (281) $380

**James, Montague Rhodes, 1862-1936**
— The Apocalypse in Latin: Ms. 10 in the Collection of Dyson Perrins.... Oxford, 1927. 4to, contemp half mor.  S June 12 (365) £250

**James, Robert, 1705-76**
— Dictionnaire universel de medecine.... Paris, 1746-48. 6 vols. Folio, orig bds.  S Mar 29 (661) £1,400

### James, Gen. Thomas, 1782-1847
— Three Years among the Indians and Mexicans. St. Louis, 1916. One of 365. NH July 21 (161) $90

### James, William Roderick, 1892-1942
— In the Saddle with Uncle Bill. NY, 1935. 1st Ed. pba Apr 25 (479) $85
— Lone Cowboy; My Life Story. NY, 1930. 1st Ed. In chipped dj. Notes to frontis verso. pba Oct 5 (158) $110

Anr copy. In dj; bdg rubbed. pba Apr 25 (480) $150

Anr copy. Orig cloth; rear cover stained. Sgd. pba July 25 (303) $130

Anr copy. In dj; rear cover of bdg badly waterstained. Ls laid in. pba Aug 8 (87) $95

— Smoky the Cowhorse. NY, 1926. Cloth; worn, hinges cracked at endpapers, lacking rear endpaper, shaken. Inscr to Herndon Davis, 1931. pba Apr 25 (482) $170

Anr copy. In chipped dj; bdg with discoloration. pba Apr 25 (483) $250

Anr copy. Orig cloth; rubbed, front hinge cracked. Inscr to Margaret, Mar 1927. pba July 25 (304) $190

### Jameson, Anna Brownell, 1794-1860
— The Beauties of the Court of King Charles the Second.... L, 1833. 4to, mor gilt; joints & extremities scuffed. Some foxing. F Mar 28 (767) $70
— The Writings on Art of.... Bost., 1896. 5 vols. Contemp half calf gilt; rubbed, 1 spine head chipped. sg Feb 8 (78) $90

### Jameson, Malcolm
— Bullard of the Space Patrol. Cleveland, [1951]. In chipped dj. Some dampstaining. Sgd by Andre Norton on tp. pba May 23 (316) $110

### Jammes, Andre
— Charles Negre, Photographe, 1820-1880. Paris, 1963. One of 300. Oblong folio, pictorial wraps over wraps; outer wrap soiled & torn. With 31 tipped-in collotype plates, ptd from Negre's negatives. sg Feb 29 (166) $375

### Jamot, Paul, 1863-1939
— Dunoyer de Segonzac. Paris, 1929. 4to, wraps; broken. sg Sept 7 (133) $120

### Jamot, Paul, 1863-1939 —& Wildenstein, Georges
— Manet. Paris, 1932. 2 vols. 4to, cloth, orig wraps bound in; some wear, library markings to bdg & endpapers. bbc Dec 18 (175) $190

### Jane's...
— Jane's All the World's Aircraft. NY, 1942. For 1941. Folio, cloth; worn. sg May 16 (46) $150

Anr Ed. L, 1943. 2d Impression. For 1942. Folio, orig cloth; worn. Dampstaining in upper margins throughout. sg May 16 (47) $70

### Janin, Jules Gabriel, 1804-74
— La Normandie. Paris, [1843]. 4to, contemp mor gilt by Giovanni Batta of Parma for Marie Louise, Empress of the French, with her crowned monogram. With port, engraved title, 2 maps & 22 plates. Some browning & spotting. C May 1 (83) £2,000
— Voyage en Italie. Paris, 1839. 4to, orig mor gilt by Boutigny. With 14 plates. Some spotting & browning. C May 1 (82) £350

### Janinet, Jean Francois
— Cahier de Differents Oiseaux Dessinee par Pesotte. Paris: chez Jean, [n.d.]. Folio, modern half mor. With 6 engravings in the crayon manner by Janinet after Pesotte. Fattorini copy. C Oct 25 (71) £400
— Vues pittoresques des principaux edifices de Paris. Paris: chez Lamy, 1792. 8vo, 19th-cent calf gilt. With engraved title & 73 color plates, all pasted on thick paper. Plate 20 spotted; Plate 29 discolored. Fuerstenberg - Schaefer copy. S Dec 7 (317) £2,100

### Janis, Harriet & Sidney
— Picasso: The Recent Years, 1939-1946. NY, 1947. One of 350, sgd by Picasso. 4to, cloth. Some soiling. sg Jan 11 (352) $250

### Jannotius, Donatus
— Dialogi de Repub. Venetorum. Leiden: Elzevir, 1631. Ed with 467 pages. 24mo, contemp vellum bds. With 7 folding plates. Tp to Notae dated 1642. bba July 18 (125) £100 [Unsworth]

### Janson, Charles William
— The Stranger in America: containing Observations Made During a Long Residence.... L, 1807. 1st Ed. 4to, contemp calf; rebacked, extremities rubbed. With engraved title, plan & 8 plates. Browned. cb Feb 14 (2594) $425

Anr copy. Half mor. With hand-colored additional title, & 10 hand-colored plates. Some foxing on plates; some brownings & worming on leaves. CE Nov 8 (202) $1,600

### Janssens, Don Augustin
— The Life and Adventures in California of.... San Marino: Huntington Library, 1953. 1st Ed. - Trans by Francis Price. Ed by William H. Ellison & Price. Half bds in dj. With port photo, 1 etching, & 2 drawings. Larson copy. pba Sept 28 (123) $50

### Janssonius, Joannes
— Cinquiesme Parte du Grand Atlas, contenant une parfaicte description du monde maritime. Amst.: Jansson, 1657. Folio, contemp mor gilt by Albert Magnus, with arms of F. W. van Loon. With engraved historiated tp frame (title on tipped-in letterpress slip), engraved anemometric table & 22 full-sheet maps. Title border & anemometric table colored by a contemp hand & heightened with gold; maps partly hand-colored in outline, with decorative elements hand-colored & heightened in gold. Browning & marginal dampstaining; some breaks at foot of central fold; small gouging in lower margin of Llll2-

Ssss1. Ducard - Schaefer copy. P Nov 1 (127) $85,000
— Nouveau Theatre du Monde. Amst., 1644-39-41. 3 vols. Folio, 18th-cent vellum; corners rubbed. With 3 hand-colored engraved titles, 2 heightened in gold & 319 double-page maps hand-colored in outline, a few with cartouches heightened in gold. Margins with browning & discoloration; tp to Vol III & index leaf of Vol II restored; other repairs. C May 31 (60) £48,000
— Theatrum exhibens Celebriores Galliae et Helvetiae urbes. Amst., 1657. Folio, early vellum gilt; extremities worn, backstrip def. With 40 (of 41) double-page views with later hand-coloring. sg Dec 7 (21) $13,000

**Japanese...**
— Japanese Paper Balloon Bombs: The First ICBM. North Hills PA: Bird & Bull Press, 1982. One of 375. 32mo, orig bds; With separate folder with folding illust. sg May 16 (49) $150

**Jarava, Juan de**
— I Quattro Libri della Filosofia Naturale.... Venice: Andrea Ravenoldo, 1565. 8vo, crude modern vellum. Lacking last leaf; marginal foxing. sg May 16 (185) $300

**Jardine, Alexander**
— Letters from Barbar, France, Spain... by an English Officer. L, 1790. 2d Ed. 8vo, contemp calf; joints weak. Some browning. S Mar 28 (295) £150

**Jardine, Sir William, 1800-74**
— The Naturalist's Library. Edin., 1833-43. 40 vols. 8vo, orig cloth; rubbed. Has hand-colored plates with uncolored backgrounds. b Sept 20 (472) £2,200
Anr copy. Calf. Library stamps. cb Oct 17 (132) $4,750
Anr copy. Modern half mor. P Dec 12 (215) $3,250
Anr copy. 13 vols only: Mammalia. Half mor. pba Mar 7 (147) $600
Anr copy. 40 vols. 8vo, orig cloth; worn & def, front free endpapers lacking in many vols. Lacking 15 plates & some half-titles. Sold w.a.f. S Apr 23 (322) £1,400
Mixed Ed. Edin., 1837-66. 40 vols. 8vo, contemp half calf. P Dec 12 (216) $3,250
Anr Ed. Edin., 1839-58 & [n.d.].. Vols XXXVI-XXXVII: Ichthyology: British Fishes. 2 vols. Cloth; spine chipped, Part 2 with repairs. With 72 hand-colored plates. pba July 11 (154) $300
Anr copy. Vols XXXIX & XL: Ichthyology: The Fishes of British Guiana. 2 vols. Orig cloth; spine ends of Part 1 chipped. With 66 hand-colored plates. pba July 11 (155) $190
Anr Ed. Edin., 1840-41. Entomology only. Vols I-II & IV-VII. 8vo, orig cloth; vols I-II spines cracked & def, other vols chipped. Sold w.a.f. S Oct 27 (640) £200 [Rigout]
Anr Ed. Edin., 1843. 40 vols. 8vo, orig cloth; 2 backstrips lacking, 2 vols with covers detached, some wear. b May 30 (494) £1,600

Anr copy. Orig cloth; some joints or hinges split. S June 13 (405) £1,700
Mixed Ed with various imprints. Edin., [1852-64]. 42 vols. 8vo, orig cloth; spines rubbed. With 40 ports, 42 partly colored engraved titles & 1326 (of 1330) partly colored plates. Lacking 3 insect plates & 1 fish plate. Sold w.a.f. K June 23 (327) $3,100

**Jarves, James Jackson, 1818-88**
— History of the Hawaiian or Sandwich Islands. Bost., 1843. 8vo, orig cloth; rebacked in modern cloth. Some foxing. pba July 25 (412) $300

**Jaume Saint-Hilaire, Jean Henri**
— Plantes de la France. Paris, 1808-09. 1st Ed. 4 vols. 4to, contemp russia; rebacked, old spines laid down, vol II covers detached. With 400 color plates. Some damp-staining & spotting. S Oct 27 (744) £1,000 [Fonseca]

**Jeancon, John A.**
— Pathological Anatomy, Pathology and Physical Diagnosis. Cincinnati, 1885. Folio, cloth; rebound. Marginal age-toning & soiling. CE Nov 8 (113) $120
Anr copy. Orig half lea; worn, backstrip damaged. With 100 plates on 98 leaves, most in color. sg May 16 (436) $50

**Jeanneret, Charles Edouard.** See: Le Corbusier

**Jefferies, Richard, 1848-87**
— The Dewy Morn.... L, 1884. 1st Ed. 2 vols. 8vo, orig cloth. Vol II tp soiled. S Apr 23 (90) £100
— Hodge and his Masters. L, 1880. 1st Ed. 2 vols. 8vo, orig cloth. S Apr 23 (88) £160
— Wood Magic.... L, 1881. 1st Ed. 2 vols. 8vo, orig cloth; upper hinge of Vol I cracked. S Apr 23 (87) £170

**Jeffers, Robinson, 1887-1962**
See also: Grabhorn Printing
— All the Corn in One Barn. San Francisco, 1926. Wraps. In: Lights and Shadows from The Lantern. Inscr. pba Oct 5 (159) $170
— The Alpine Christ & Other Poems. Aramos CA: Cayucos Books, 1973. One of 250. Half lea. pba Oct 5 (160) $80
Anr copy. Half lea. Inscr to Tony Lehman, 1980. pba Aug 22 (256) $70
— Apology for Bad Dreams. San Francisco, 1986. One of 11 ptd by Peter Koch as a gift to the pbr, James Linden. Single sheet, 28.25 by 18.5 inches. pba Oct 5 (162) $200
— An Artist. [Austin, Texas, 1928]. Ltd Ed. 4to, self wraps. Ls from John S. Mayfield to Irving Robbins laid in. pba Oct 5 (161) $600
— Be Angry at the Sun. NY: Random House, [1941]. One of 100. Half cloth, unopened. K June 23 (328) $250
Anr copy. Half cloth. pba Oct 5 (164) $350
— Brides of the South Wind: Poems 1917-1922. [N.p.]: Cayucos Books, 1974. One of 285. Half calf. pba Oct 5 (165) $90

Anr copy. Half calf. Inscr to John Knight, 1795. pba Aug 22 (257) $110
— Californians. NY, 1916. 1st Ed. Orig cloth; spine ends rubbed. pba Oct 5 (167) $190
Advance copy, with pbr's perforated stamp on tp. A few smudges to prelims. pba Oct 5 (166) $500
— Cawdor, and Other Poems. NY, 1928. One of 375. pba Oct 5 (168) $350
Anr copy. Half cloth. sg June 20 (177) $110
— The Collected Poetry of.... Stanford, 1988. 2 vols. In djs. pba Oct 5 (169) $160
— Dear Judas and Other Poems. NY, 1929. One of 375. Half vellum. pba Oct 5 (170) $275
Anr copy. Half vellum. sg June 20 (178) $110
1st Ed. In dj, torn along flap, soiled, insect-damaged. Inscr to John Stuart Groves. pba Oct 5 (171) $170
— Descent to the Dead. NY, [1931]. One of 500. 4to, half vellum; fore-edges spotted. pba Oct 5 (172) $130; sg June 20 (179) $175
— The Double Axe, & Other Poems. NY: Random House, [1948]. In dj. Sgd. pba Oct 5 (173) $275
— Flagons and Apples. Los Angeles, 1912. 1st Ed, one of 500. bbc June 24 (525) $400
— Give Your Heart to the Hawks.... NY, 1933. 1st Ed. In dj. Inscr to Albert Bender, with 4 lines of verse, 1933. pba Oct 5 (176) $225
Anr copy. Inscr to Albert Bender, 5 Oct 1933 & with sgd inscr from Bender. pba Aug 22 (259) $170
One of 200. Half calf. pba Oct 5 (175) $450; pba May 23 (183) $120
— Granite & Cypress. Santa Cruz: Lime Kiln Press, 1975. One of 100. 4to, cloth. pba Mar 7 (102) $6,000
— The Loving Shepherdess. NY, 1956. One of 80. Illus by Jean Kellogg. Merle Armitage's copy, with article about Jeffers by F. B. Drew, inscr, mtd to rear pastedown. pba Oct 5 (177) $600
— Medea. NY, [1946]. 1st Ed. Inscr, 1946. pba Oct 5 (178) $170
— Poems. San Francisco, 1928. One of 310. Frontis by Ansel Adams. CE Feb 21 (152) $480; pba Oct 5 (179) $1,000; pba Mar 7 (149) $375
— Poetry, Gongorism and A Thousand Years. [N.p.]: Ward Ritchie Press, 1949. 1st Ed, One of 200. pba Oct 5 (180) $150
[-] The Robinson Jeffers Newsletter. Occidental & Long Beach, 1962-94. Nos 1-92. In 4 cloth vols & Nos 80-92 loose. pba May 23 (187) $325
— The Selected Poetry of.... NY, 1937 [1938]. pba Jan 25 (171) $90
— Stars. [Pasadena]: The Flame Press, 1930. 1st Ed, one of 110. Single sheet folded to make an 8-page leaflet, unopened pba Oct 5 (184) $600
— Such Counsels You Gave to Me.... NY, [1937]. Inscr to Albert Bender, with 3 lines of verse, 1937; also inscr by Bender, 1938. pba Oct 5 (186) $150 One of 300. Half mor. pba Oct 5 (185) $180
— Tamar, and Other Poems. NY, [1924]. 1st Ed, One of 500. pba Oct 5 (187) $375
— Thurso's Landing and Other Poems. NY, [1932]. One of 200. pba Oct 5 (188) $425

— Tragedy has Obligations. [Santa Cruz, Calif.]: Lime Kiln Press, 1973. One of 200. Folio, half lea. pba Aug 22 (260) $160
— Two Consolations. [San Mateo, Calif.: Quercus Press], 1940. One of 250. 4to, ptd bds; spine head bumped. Inscr to Harry Mielke, 1942 & with related material. pba Oct 5 (189) $325
— The Women at Point Sur. NY, [1927]. Inscr to Albert Bender, with 9 lines of verse, 1927. pba Oct 5 (190) $300
One of 265. sg June 20 (182) $130
Anr Ed. NY, [1935]. Half cloth. Inscr. pba Aug 22 (261) $120

**Jeffers, Robinson & Una**
— Where Shall I Take You: The Love Letters of Una and Robinson Jeffers. [Covello CA]: Yolla Bolly Press, [1987]. One of 245. Ed by Robert Kafka. pba Oct 5 (196) $120

**Jeffers, Una**
— Visits to Ireland. Los Angeles: Ward Ritchie Press, 1954. One of 300. pba Oct 5 (198) $160
Anr copy. Half cloth. pba Aug 22 (264) $150

**Jefferson, George**
— Theatrical Eccentricities.... Northallerton, 1823. 12mo, modern wraps, orig back wrap bound in. Tp repaired. b Dec 5 (457) £50

**Jefferson, Thomas, 1743-1826**
See also: Lafayette & Jefferson; Lewis & Clark; Limited Editions Club
— A Commentary and Review of Montesquieu's Spirit of Laws. phila., 1811. 8vo, bdg not described but in poor condition. Browned; some pencil annotations. rs Nov 11 (102) $550
— Notes on the State of Virginia. L, 1787. 8vo, contemp half calf. With folding map with color outline & folding table. Short tear to map. cb Oct 17 (157) $9,000
Anr copy. Bound with: An Appendix to the Notes on Virginia. Phila., 1800. With map later half mor; joints worn. With 1 folding map & 1 folding table. Map torn & browned. CE Nov 8 (203) $7,500
Anr copy. Orig bds; detached, worn, most of spine lacking. Lacking the folding map; foxed; stamp & slit to 1 leaf. K June 23 (329) $1,800
Anr copy. Contemp sheep; covers loose. Folding map torn & repaired. sg Oct 26 (169) $9,500

**Jefferson, Thomas, 1743-1826 —& Others**
— The Confidential Letters from Thomas Jefferson to William Wirt, being Reminiscences of Patrick Henry. Phila., 1912. One of 10 on Whatman. 4to, orig wraps. sg Oct 26 (167) $350

**Jefferys, Thomas, d.1771**
— The American Atlas. L, 1976. One of 150. Folio, half mor. Maps hand-colored in outline. sg Oct 26 (170) $950
—- A Description of the Spanish Islands and Settlements on the Coast of the West Indies. L, 1762. 4to, recent calf. With 32 folding maps & plans, the 1st

hand-colored in outline. Worming touching image of Plate 1, tp & prelims. S Mar 28 (331) £1,200

**Jeffries, John, M.D.** See: Washington's copy, George

**Jekyll, Gertrude, 1843-1932 —&**
**Weaver, Sir Lawrence**
— Gardens for Small Country Houses. L, 1912. 4to, cloth, extremities rubbed, scratched. sg June 13 (230) $100

**Jelenski, Constantin**
— Leonor Fini. [L & NY: Olympia Press, 1968]. 4to, bds. sg Sept 7 (151) $175

**Jenkins, John H.**
— Basic Texas Books: An Annotated Bibliography.... Austin, [1983]. One of 85. 4to, cloth. Edges soiled. pba Aug 22 (928) $170

**Jenkins, John Stilwell**
— Voyage of the U.S. Exploring Squadron.... Auburn, 1850. 1st Ed. 8vo, orig cloth. With 8 plates, 1 full-page illust, & 1 map. Browned; stamp on half-title. sg Mar 7 (115) $150

**Jenkins, Rhys.** See: Dickinson & Jenkins

**Jennings, Louis J.**
— Rambles Among the Hills in the Peak of Derbyshire and the South Downs. L, 1880. 8vo, mor gilt. Inscr to his daughter, Mabel. b May 30 (554) £110

**Jennings, Otto Emery**
— Wild Flowers of Western Pennsylvania.... Pittsburgh, 1953. 2 vols. Folio, orig cloth, in worn & torn djs. wa Nov 16 (167) $180

**Jennings, Samuel**
— Orchids: and How to Grow Them in India.... L, 1875. 4to, later half mor. With 49 hand-colored plates. pba June 20 (258) $1,700

**Jenyns, Roger Soame —&**
**Watson, William**
— Chinese Art: the Minor Arts. L, 1963-65. 2 vols. Folio, orig cloth, in djs. sg June 13 (208) $100

**Jenyns, Soame, 1704-87**
— A View of the Internal Evidence of the Christian Religion. L, 1776. 4th Ed. 8vo, orig wraps; backstrip def. James Boswell's copy, sgd & dated 1776 on front wrap. CNY May 17 (52) $1,600

**Jerrett, Herman Daniel**
— California's El Dorado, Yesterday and Today. Sacramento, 1915. 1st Ed. Orig cloth in dj. Inscr & sgd. Larson copy. pba Sept 28 (539) $75

**Jesse, Edward, 1780-1868**
— An Angler's Rambles. L, 1836. 8vo, half mor; joints & extremities rubbed. pba July 11 (158) $200

**Jesse, George Richard**
— Researches into the History of the British Dog. L, 1866. 2 vols. 8vo, later half calf gilt. With 20 plates. sg Mar 7 (477) $200

**Jesse, John Heneage, 1815-74**
— London: Its Celebrated Characters and Remarkable Places. L, 1871. 3 vols. 8vo, half mor. Ms indices to plates inserted at beginning of each vol. Extra-illus with 130 plates. S Apr 23 (354) £360
Anr copy. Later half mor. Extra-illus with plates. S June 13 (498) £200
— Works. Bost., 1901-2. ("Historical Memoirs of....") 30 vols. 8vo, orig cloth; worn & frayed. Sold w.a.f. F June 20 (202) $90

**Jessup, Elon.** See: Dunn & Jessup

**Jessup, Henry Harris**
— The Women of the Arabs. NY, 1873. 1st Ed. 8vo, cloth; rubbed. S Oct 26 (143) £340 [Makshaff]

**Jessurun, Isaac**
— Liuro da providencia diuina. Hamburg, 1663. 4to, modern lea. Some staining & browning; M4 repaired, affecting a few words. CE Dec 6 (207) $3,000

**Jesuits**
TORRE Y SEVIL, FRANCISCO DE LA. - El peregrino Atlante S. Francisco Xavier Apostol del Oriente.... Lisbon: Domingos Carneyro, 1674. 4to, contemp vellum; inner hinges weak. With port. Worming at foot of some leaves; some show-through at Y1-4. S Nov 30 (205) £600
TORSELLINI, HORATIO. - Francisci Xaverii epistolarum libri quatuor. Mainz: Balthasar Lippius for Arnold Mylius, 1600. 8vo, contemp vellum. Minor discoloration. S Nov 30 (204) £950
VIVERO, MATIAS. - Vida y milagros del glorioso beato Xavier, Religioso de la Compania de Jesus.... Tarragona: Gabriel Roberto, 1620. Bound with: Satyra al beato Francisco Xavier.... Barcelona: Estevan Lliberos, 1620. 8vo, recent bds. Minor discoloration. S Nov 30 (202) £500

**Jewish...**
— The Jewish Encyclopedia. NY, [1925]. 12 vols. 4to, orig cloth; shaken, vols VI & XI spines chipped. sg Apr 11 (175) $250

**Jewish Museum—London**
— Catalogue of the Jewish Museum London. Hertford, 1974. Edited by R. D. Barnett. Folio, orig cloth in dj. sg Apr 11 (176) $450

**Jewitt, John R., 1788-1821**
— Narrative of the Adventures and Sufferings...among the Savages of Nootka Sound. Middletown: Seth Richards, 1815. Revised by Richard Alsop. 12mo, old calf; worn, lacking some lea, spine repaired. Inscr. Met May 22 (305) $200
Anr copy. Contemp calf; worn & scuffed. Browned & soiled; tape to front free endpaper & recto of frontis. wa Feb 29 (274) $120

Anr Ed. NY, [c.1815]. 12mo, orig cloth-backed pictorial bds; worn. sg Oct 26 (3) $90
Anr copy. Disbound. Cut close. sg Oct 26 (4) $60

## Jimenez, Juan Ramon, 1881-1958
— Poesias escojidas (1899-1917). NY, 1917. One of 600. 8vo, orig cloth. S Mar 28 (515) £220

## Joanellus, Petrus
— Cantus novi thesauri musici liber.... Venice, 1568. 4to, contemp vellum, stained red & with armorial device; front hinges split. Some lower corners repaired. C June 26 (266) £2,600

## Joannes, Glogoviensis
— Computus chirometralis. Cracow: J. Haller, after 11 Feb 1507. 4to, modern mor by the French Binders of Garden City. Some marginalia cropped. Honeyman - Schaefer copy. P Nov 1 (129) $3,500

## Joannides, Paul
— Masaccio and Masolino. NY, [1993]. 4to, cloth, in dj. sg Jan 11 (271) $50

## Johannes Chrysostomus, Saint, 345?-407
— In Sanctum Jesu Christi evangelium.... Paris: C. Guillard, 1543. 4 parts in 2 vol. 8vo, contemp mor gilt, with author's name & titles on front cover & owner's initial F.A.M.G. on back cover. C June 26 (89) £1,700
— XXVI Homilies. Paris: Claude Cramoisy, 1521. 12mo, contemp mor gilt, bound for Henri II, Duc de Montmorency. Lacking 1st leaf of index; annotations in margins. S Mar 28 (478) £700

**Johannes de Sacro Busto.** See: Sacrobosco, Johannes

## Johannes de Sancto Geminiano
— Liber de exemplis ac similitudinis rerum. Venis: Joannes & Gregorius de Gregoriis de Forlivio for Staphanus & Bernardinus de Nallis, 10 Apr 1497. 4to, contemp blind-stamped calf; rebacked, new clasps. 46 lines & headline; double column; gothic letter; white-on-black initials. Some dampstaining. 393 (of 404) leaves; lacking 11 leaves of prelims. Goff J-429. S Nov 30 (271) £400

## John the Baptist, Saint
— La vita & morte di sancto Giovanni Baptista. [Florence, c.1495-1500]. 4to, 19th-cent mor. 36 lines; double column; type 86R. Woodcut on title.. 4 leaves. C Apr 3 (256) £3,340

## Johnson, Alfred Forbes
— One Hundred Title Pages, 1500-1800. L, 1928. 4to, half cloth in dj; worn. sg Apr 11 (168) £110

## Johnson, Alvin Jewett, 1827-84
— Johnson's New Illustrated Family Atlas. See: Atlas

**Johnson, Benjamin F., of Boone.** See: Riley, James Whitcomb

## Johnson, C. Pierpoint, d.1893 —& Sowerby, John E., 1825-70
— British Wild Flowers.... L, [1858]-60. 8vo, orig mor gilt; hinges cracked. With 2 plain & 80 hand-colored plates. b Sept 20 (496) £70

## Johnson, Capt. Charles, Pseud.
— A General History of the Lives and Adventures of Highwaymen.... L, 1839. ("The Lives and Actions of Highwaymen....") Contemp half mor; joints & corners rubbed. pba Dec 14 (85) $85

## Johnson, Eldridge Reeves
— Tarpomania—The Madness of Fishing. NY, 1908. 8vo, orig lev gilt with white mor inlay. Stamps on tp. Inscr to Thomas Edison. sg Mar 7 (478) $1,900

**Johnson, George William.** See: Hogg & Johnson

## Johnson, Jack
— Jack Johnson - in the Ring - and Out. Chicago, 1927. Orig cloth; worn at bottom edge of front cover. Inscr. sg Mar 28 (171) $950

## Johnson, James Weldon, 1871-1938
— The Autobiography of an Ex-Colored Man. Bost., 1912. Orig cloth; spine rubbed with loss of cloth at head. sg Mar 28 (172) $475
— Black Manhattan. NY, 1930. In chipped dj. Inscr. O Mar 5 (134) $400
Anr copy. Inscr. sg Mar 28 (173) $375
— The Book of American Negro Poetry. NY, [1922]. In dj. sg Mar 28 (178) $275
— God's Trombones. NY, 1927. Orig bds; edges worn. Some annotations in pencil. Inscr to Lawrence & Armina Langner, 18 May 1927. sg Mar 28 (175) $400
2d Ptg. Half cloth. Sgd. sg Mar 28 (176) $200

## Johnson, John, 1777-1848
— Typographia, or the Printers' Instructor L, 1824. 2 vols. 12mo, early half cloth; needs rebdg. sg Feb 8 (310) $150

## Johnson, Kenneth M.
See also: California
— Aerial California: An Account of Early Flight.... Los Angeles, 1961. One of 350. pba Apr 25 (484) $75
— The New Almaden Quicksilver Mine.... Georgetown, 1963. One of 75 sgd on Ticonderoga India text. Half bds. With 2 disenos, 1 folded map, 14 illus, & 3 mining ephemera. Larson copy. pba Sept 28 (540) $150

## Johnson, Lyndon B., 1908-73
— A President's Country. A Guide to the Hill Country of Texas. Austin: Alcade Press, [1964]. Orig lea; scuffed. Inscr to Ann Brinkley. wa Dec 14 (78) $210
— The Vantage Points. NY, 1971. In dj. Sgd on front flyleaf. pba June 13 (68) $250
Anr copy. In dj. Sgd bookplate mtd to half-title. Inscr to George W. De Frannaux. wa Feb 29 (241) $200

**Johnson, Overton —& Winter, William H.**
— Route Across the Rocky Mountains, with a Description of Oregon and California. Lafayette, 1846. 1st Ed. 8vo, orig half bds in chemise folder & cloth clipcase; bds soiled & worn. Larson copy. pba Sept 28 (623) $7,500
Anr Ed. Lafayette, IN, 1846. 8vo, orig bds; extremities worn, bds stained, joints rubbed. Light foxing. Robbins copy. pba Mar 21 (171) $6,500
2d Ed (Reprint of 1846 Ed). Princeton, 1932. Orig cloth. With facsimile of orig tp, & 2 plates. Larson copy. pba Sept 28 (624) $120

**Johnson, Richard, 1734-93**
— Rural Felicity; or, the History of Tommy and Sally. Phila.: Francis Bailey, 1793. 16mo, orig wraps; worn. Stains, soiling & foxing. sg Apr 18 (69) $5,400

**Johnson, Robert Underwood, 1853-1937 —& Buel, Clarence Clough**
— Battles and Leaders of the Civil War. NY, [1887-89]. 4 vols. 4to, orig cloth; shaken, some hinges cracked. NH July 21 (78) $90

**Johnson, Ruth & Foster**
— Kelmscott Revisited. Meriden, 1966. Copy marked Printer's extra no. 7. 4to, bds covered in Morris's Acorn pattern wallpaper. Laid in are conjugate leaves from a Kelmscott book. ds July 27 (106) $175

**Johnson, Samuel, 1649-1703**
— A Confutation of a late Pamphlet intituled, A Letter ballancing the Necessity of keeping a Land-Force in Times of Peace.... L, 1689. 4to, early 19th-cent half lea; spine ends worn, front joint cracked. sg Mar 21 (175) $225
— A Second Five Year's Struggle against Popery and Tyranny. L, 1689. 8vo, contemp mor gilt in cottage-roof design; front joint cracked. Dampstained at ends. Corfield copy. sg Apr 18 (70) $800

**Johnson, Samuel, 1709-84**
— A Dictionary of the English Language. L, 1755. 1st Ed. 2 vols. Folio, 19th-cent sheep; extremities scuffed. Some dampstaining & spotting. C Nov 29 (129) £2,800
Anr copy. 19th-cent half calf; rebacked, spine ends, joints & bds rubbed, Vol I joints cracked, small holes in rear bd of Vol I affecting last few signatures. Crease to tp, with staining & tears to margins; preface leaf torn in gutter with minor loss; marginal tears; library stamp to verso of titles; some foxing & staining. cb June 25 (1864) $3,250
Anr copy. Old calf; rebacked & recornered. Tp in facsimile; marginal tear in Sig. 6E. K Feb 11 (230) $2,100
Anr copy. Contemp calf; rebacked, endpapers renewed, corners bumped, spine ends rubbed. Creasing at ends of each vol; repairs to lower margin of 1st 5 pp of Vol I; some foxing or browning; dampstaining in lower margin at end of Vol II. P June 5 (275) $6,000
Anr copy. Contemp calf; rebacked, Vol I front joint starting, Vol front joint cracked. Lacking 3 leaves; Vol II tp creased. Sold w.a.f. sg Apr 18 (71) $2,000
Anr Ed. Dublin, 1768. 8vo, later half calf. Tp frayed. Z June 28 (139) $300
Harrison's Ed. L, 1786. Folio, contemp sheep; rebacked, worn, front joint cracked. Opening leaves soiled; some staining; tp tape-repaired & with corner off; vertical crease in last several leaves. sg Mar 21 (176) $175
10th Ed. L, 1794. 8vo, contemp calf; rebacked in sheep, rubbed. CE May 22 (285) $160
Anr Ed. Phila., 1818. 4 vols. 4to, contemp calf; worn, some hinges weak. Repaired tears in 2 leaves; 1 leaf lacking corner. K Feb 11 (232) $475
Anr Ed. Phila., 1819. 4 vols in 2. 4to, contemp calf; new endpapers. George Putnam's copy. pba Sept 14 (220) $500
Anr Ed. L, 1820. 2 vols. 4to, contemp half calf. sg Sept 21 (235) $475
— Irene. L, 1749. Bound with: Godwin, William. Antonio: A Tragedy. L, 1800. 8vo, contemp halfcalf; spine worn. Ck Sept 8 (231) £800
1st Ed. 8vo, modern calf gilt. Some browning. S Dec 18 (132) £3,200 [Edwards]
[-] Johnsoniana: or Supplement to Boswell.... L, 1836. 1st Ed. 8vo, contemp calf; upper cover nearly off, rubbed. With 45 plates. Marginal staining; some foxing. O Mar 5 (135) $120
— A Journey to the Western Islands of Scotland. L, 1775. 1st Ed, with 12-line errata. 8vo, modern calf. With 4 stamps, 1 on tp. sg Sept 21 (236) $175
— The Lives of the Most Eminent English Poets. L, 1781. 1st Separate London Ed. 4 vols. 8vo, contemp calf; front cover of Vol I detached, spines rubbed. pba Sept 14 (223) $200
Anr copy. Contemp calf gilt; joints cracked, 1 spine cracked. pba Mar 7 (150) $110
— Miscellaneous and Fugitive Pieces. L: for T. Davies, 1784. 3 vols. 8vo, contemp calf; joints rubbed or splitting. Margins browned. bba Oct 19 (248) £340 [Axe]
— Miscellaneous Observations on the Tragedy of Macbeth.... L: E. Cave, 1745. 1st Ed. 12mo, early 19th-cent half calf. With the folding leaf of Proposals (torn at head with loss of 2d O and part of 2d P) Some browning. Bound into The Idler, Dublin, 1762. S Dec 18 (131) £13,000 [Johnson]
— Prayers and Meditations. L, 1785. 1st Ed. 8vo, calf; joints cracked, hinges rubbed. Z June 28 (140) $170
— Taxation no Tyranny: an Answer to the Resolutions and Address of the American Congress. L, 1775. 2d Ed. 8vo, modern cloth. Initial & final gatherings with extensive marginal repairs; last 2 text leaves supplied in facsimile. Joseph Reed's copy. sg Oct 26 (312) $400
— The Vanity of Human Wishes. L, 1749. 1st Ed. 4to, half mor gilt; edges worn. Tp soiled & creased at upper fore-edge. CE Sept 27 (153) $2,200
Anr Ed. L: Rampant Lions Press, [1984]. One of 188. Illus by Denis Tegetmeier. Folio, cloth. sg Sept 14 (329) $110

— Works. L, 1787-88. 14 vols. 8vo, bdg not described but rubbed & Vol I rebacked. bba May 30 (113) £340 [R. Clark]
Anr Ed. L, 1792. 12 vols. 8vo, contemp calf; spines worn, 1 spine head torn. pba Aug 22 (600) $160
Anr Ed. L, 1806. 12 vols. 8vo, contemp russia gilt; joints starting. pba Sept 14 (224) $250

**Johnson, Susannah**
— A Narrative of the Captivity of.... Windsor, Vt., 1807. 2d Ed. 12mo, modern mor. Tp fore-edge repaired on verso. sg Oct 26 (156) $120

**Johnson, Theo**
— Illustrations of British Butterflies. L: Pvtly ptd, 1878. One of 12. 8vo, mor gilt by Tout. With 53 full-page watercolor drawings. S Apr 23 (325) £6,800
— Illustrations of British Hawk Moths and their Larvae.... L, 1874 [but 1876]. 4to, mor gilt by Tout. With 36 orig watercolor drawings. S Apr 23 (323) £3,500
— Illustrations of the Larvae and Pupae of British Lepidoptera.... L, 1878. 8vo, mor gilt by Tout. With 53 full-page watercolor drawings. S Apr 23 (324) £3,200

**Johnson, Theodore T., b.1818**
— Sights in the Gold Region.... NY, 1849. 1st Ed. 12mo, orig cloth; spine top repaired. Light foxing. Larson copy. pba Sept 28 (541) $180
Anr copy. Orig cloth; joints rubbed & split, spine ends frayed. Foxed throughout. sg Oct 26 (172) $150
Anr copy. Orig cloth; edges worn. Some foxing. wa Feb 29 (327) $230

**Johnson, Thomas Burgeland, d.1840**
— The Hunting Directory.... L, 1830. 8vo, half cloth; soiled. Some foxing. O Jan 9 (159) $100
Anr copy. Half calf; rubbed. First few leaves with marginal dampstains. O Jan 9 (160) $70
Anr copy. Modern calf gilt. With 7 plates. sg Mar 7 (479) $150

**Johnson, William, 1771-1834**
— Sketches of the Life and Correspondence of Nathanael Greene.... Charleston, 1822. 1st Ed. 2 vols. 4to, orig bds; worn & soiled, front bd of Vol I detached along with front free endpaper. With port, folding map & 7 plans. Map with closed tear; some foxing. wa Feb 29 (299) $1,600

**Johnston, Alastair J. —&
Murdoch, Joseph S. F.**
— C. B. Clapcott and His Golf Library. Worcestershire: Grant Books, 1989. 1st Ed, One of 300. Cloth. Sgd. pba Apr 18 (21) $100

**Johnston, Alexander Keith, 1804-71**
— The National Atlas of Historical, Commercial, and Political Geography. Edin, 1843. Folio, orig half mor; worn, backstrip torn. With engraved title & 46 maps & charts, hand-colored in outline.. bba June 6 (313) £260 [McKinnon]

— The Physical Atlas.... L, 1856. Folio, contemp half mor; rubbed. Library markings. bba May 30 (416) £140 [Walford]

**Johnston, Edward**
— A Carol and Other Rhymes. L, 1916. Evelyn Waugh's copy, sgd & dated Feb 1921. Hobson copy. S June 28 (230) £550

**Johnston, Lt.-Col. George**
[-] Proceedings of a General Court-Martial for the Trial of Lt.-Col. G. Johnston.... L, 1811. 8vo, half calf. Some discoloration at ends; no errata leaf. b Mar 20 (114) £1,700

**Johnston, Paul**
— Biblio-typographica: A Survey.... NY, 1930. 1st Ed, One of 1,050. In frayed & repaired dj. O Dec 5 (62) $60

**Johnston, William G., b.1828**
— Experiences of a Forty-Niner. Pittsburgh, 1892. With: Life and Reminiscences..., Pittsburgh, 1901; 2p. holograph letter to Alden Hays 1st Ed. 3 items. 8vo, orig cloth. With 6 ports, 8 illus, & folded blue-print map. Some pages creased & soiled. Sgd presentation slip tipped in at tp. Larson copy. pba Sept 28 (542) $1,900
Anr copy. 8vo, orig cloth; spine foot worn. With 14 plates. Robbins copy. pba Mar 21 (172) $400

**Johnstone, William Grosart —&
Croall, Alexander**
— The Nature-Printed British Sea-Weeds. L, 1859-60. 4 vols. 4to, orig cloth; rubbed. With 4 engraved titles & 221 nature-ptd color plates. sg Oct 19 (165) $1,000

**Joinville, Jean, Sieur de, 1224?-1317**
See also: Gregynog Press
— Memoirs. L: Hafod Press, 1807. 2 vols. 4to, contemp half russia gilt. With 3 plates & 3 maps. Some foxing. sg Mar 7 (117) $425

**Jolas, Eugene**
— Secession in Astropolis. Paris: Black Sun Press, 1929. One of 100. Ptd wraps. pba Nov 30 (51) $160

**Joll, Evelyn.** See: Butlin & Joll

**Jolly, David**
— Antique Maps, Sea Charts, City Views, Celestial Charts & Battle Plans. Brookline & Amherst, 1983-92. 10 vols. sg May 9 (15) $650

**Jolly, John**
— Gold Spring Diary: The Journal of John Jolly. Sonora, 1966. One of 500. Ed by Carlo M. De Ferrari. Orig cloth. With frontis port & 1 facsimile. Larson copy. pba Sept 28 (544) $95

**Joly, Henri L.**
— Bibliotheque de Lyon: Exposition de Reliures. Lyon, 1925. One of 311. 4to, contemp cloth; rubbed. Some soiling. bba May 9 (139A) £65 [Maggs]

— Legend in Japanese Art. L, 1908 [1907]. 4to, orig cloth; tear to spine head. pba June 20 (206) $130

Anr copy. Orig cloth; piece missing at top, rear joint cracked. sg June 13 (211) $275

Anr Ed. Rutland VT, [1967]. 4to, cloth, in dj, secured to pastedowns with cellotape. Abraded stamp on tp. sg Sept 7 (197) $80

**Jombert, Charles Antoine, 1712-84**

— Architecture moderne, ou l'art de bien batir. Paris, 1774. 2 vols. 4to, contemp calf with later spine strips & cornerpieces; rubbed, hinges reinforced. Some soiling; foxed; small hole with tears in 1 plate. cb Oct 17 (24) $400

**Jonas, F. M.**

— Netsuke. L, 1928. Sheep gilt; spine split, rubbed. Some foxing & marginal browning. Inscr by the Japanese Minister of Foreign Affairs to Adm. B. W. Decker & with related material. ds July 27 (101) $100

**Jones, Abner Dumont, 1807-72**

— The American Portrait Gallery. Phila., 1859. 4 vols. 4to, blingstamped mor; 1 joint repaired. sg Feb 8 (16) $250

**Jones, Chuck**

— Chuck Amuck. NY, [1989]. Foreword by Steven Spielberg. In dj. Inscr. pba Aug 22 (601) $50

**Jones, Dan Burne**

— The Prints of Rockwell Kent. Chicago, 1974. Folio, orig bdg, in dj. wa Nov 16 (332) $210

Anr copy. Orig bdg, in soiled dj. wa June 20 (356) $120

**Jones, David, 1895-1974**

— The Chester Play of the Deluge. L, 1977. One of 250. 4to, orig half cloth, in dj. With 10 illusts. b May 30 (556) £95

— The Engravings of David Jones. Rampant Lions Press for Clover Hill Eds, 1981. One of 105 with a portfolio containing an additional suite of the illusts on japon. 4to, loose as issued in orig fitted case. P June 5 (276) $800

— In Parenthesis. L, 1937. In dj. b Jan 31 (178) £100

**Jones, Edward, 1752-1824**

— Lyric Airs. L, 1804. 1st Ed. - Frontis by Thomas Rowlandson. Folio, contemp mor; repaired. With hand-colored frontis, & 16 leaves of musical notation. Some water-staining. S Oct 26 (119) £1,100 [Chelsea Rare]

**Jones, Edward Alfred**

See also: Courtauld & Jones

— Catalogue of the Collection of Old Plate of William Francis Farrer.... L, 1924. Out-of-series copy. Folio, later half mor by C. Fox; front hinge weak. W Nov 8 (200) £2,500

— A Catalogue of the Objects in Gold and Silver...in the Collection of the Baroness James de Rothschild. L,

1912. Ltd Ed. Folio, orig half cloth; rubbed, hinges weak. W Nov 8 (199) £440

— The Gold and Silver of Windsor Castle. Letchworth, 1911. One of 285. Folio, orig cloth. Inscr to Sir Schonberg K. McDonnell. W Nov 8 (203) £180

— The Old English Plate of the Emperor of Russia. Letchworth & L, 1909. 4to, orig half mor gilt. W Nov 8 (202) £210

— The Old Silver of American Churches. Letchworth, 1913. One of 506. Folio, cloth; rebacked, endpapers renewed, bookplate & card pocket. sg June 13 (338) $450; W Nov 8 (159) £330

**Jones, Gwyn.** See: Golden Cockerel Press

**Jones, Henry Albert.** See: Raleigh & Jones

**Jones, Herschel V.**

— Adventures in Americana, 1492-1897.... NY, 1928. 1st Ed, One of 200. 3 vols including Check List. 4to, orig cloth. Robbins-Streeter copy. pba Mar 21 (173) $160

**Jones Library, Herschel V.**

Anr copy. 2 vols. 4to, cloth. ds July 27 (102) $100

Anr copy. Cloth; rubbed, portion of front free endpaper excised from 1 vol. sg Oct 26 (174) $50

**Jones, Howard E.**

— Illustrations of the Nests and Eggs of the Birds of Ohio. Circleville, Ohio, 1879-86. 1 vol only. Folio, bdg not described. With 36 (of 68) hand-colored plates. Lacking list of subscribers & list of plates. P Dec 12 (217) $3,250

**Jones, Inigo, 1573-1652**

— Designs of Inigo Jones and others published by I. Ware. [L, 1757?]. 4to, contemp half calf; worn & soiled, spine strip perishing, joints cracked. With engraved title & 48 plates, including 6 double-page, numbered 1-53. Some soiling & foxing. cb Oct 17 (25) $325

— The Designs of Inigo Jones consisting of Plans and Elevations for...Buildings. L, 1727. 1st Ed. 2 vols in 1. Folio, later mor. With 97 plates only. bba June 6 (22A) £1,700 [York Gallery]

Anr copy. Contemp calf; worn. With frontis & 97 plates (28 double-page or folding). CE Nov 8 (205) $3,500

2d Ed. L, 1770. 2 vols. Folio, contemp calf; worn. With frontis & 99 plates. Lower margin of Vol I dampstained affecting most plates; frontis & 4 plates in Vol I shaved into surface; last 2 plates in Vol II creased. C May 31 (93) £1,300

— The Most Notable Antiquity of Great Britain, Vulgarly Called Stone-Heng.... L, 1655. Folio, old bds; modern calf back & tips. With 7 folding woodcut plates. Marginal soiling & dampstaining not affecting plates; lacking frontis port. Ink & wash drawing of Stonehenge bound in. sg Sept 7 (12A) $425

2d Ed. L, 1725. 3 parts in 1 vol. Folio, contemp calf; rebacked with most of orig backstrip, corner of front cover restored. With 14 plates. sg Jan 11 (11) $650

### Jones, James
— From Here to Eternity. NY, 1951. 1st Ed. Orig cloth, in frayed dj. sg June 20 (185) $130

One of 1,500 sgd on tipped-in sheet. Cloth, in nicked dj. sg June 20 (184) $225

### Jones, Judge T. E.
— Leaves from an Argonaut's Notebook: A Collection of Holiday and Other Stories.... San Francisco, 1905. 1st Ed. - Illus by Laura Adams Armer. Orig cloth. Larson copy. pba Sept 28 (545) $140

### Jones, Mary Harris ("Mother Jones"), 1830-1930
— Autobiography. Chicago, 1925. Irving Stone's annotated copy. pba May 23 (422) $110

### Jones, Owen, 1809-74
— The Grammar of Ornament. L, 1856. Folio, orig half mor gilt; corners worn, joints & head of spine rubbed, broken. With chromolitho title & 100 colored plates. Some foxing & soiling. cb Oct 17 (86) $1,800

Anr Ed. L, [1865]. Folio, half cloth; frayed, some wear, hinges cracked. With litho title & 111 chromolitho plates. bbc Feb 26 (233) $260

Anr Ed. L, 1868. Folio, cloth; rebacked with orig backstrip laid down, worn & frayed, later endpapers. With illuminated title & 112 plates. Some plates with ink markins in margins or on plates; some text leaves underlined. bbc June 24 (136) $220

Anr copy. Contemp half mor gilt; joints & edges rubbed. With illuminated title & 112 plates. CE Sept 27 (154) $320

Anr copy. Disbound. With engraved title & 112 plates. Met May 22 (436) $325

Anr copy. Modern mor. With illuminated title & 112 plates. Tp & chromolitho title reinforced with archival tape to versos & the latter chipped. pba Nov 30 (196) $375

Anr Ed. L, 1910. Folio, cloth; scraped, scuffed, spine ends frayed. With 112 colored plates. bbc June 24 (137) $125

Anr copy. Cloth; spine ends starting; library stamp on tp. rs Nov 11 (103) $200

Anr Ed. L, 1928. Folio, orig cloth; later endpapers. With 112 plates. Ck May 31 (55) £130

— Grammatik der Ornamente. L, 1868. Folio, modern cloth; orig backstrip & portion of front cover laid down. With illuminated title & 112 plates. sg Jan 11 (232) $375

### Jones, Owen, 1809-74 —& Goury, Jules
— Plans, Elevations, Sections, and Details of the Alhambra.... L, 1842-45. 2 vols. Folio, contemp half mor; extremities & corners worn. With 30 plates on india-proof paper laid down, 1 hand-colored engraving, 69 chromolitho plates including half-titles & 4 litho plates (1 hand-colored). Some soiling; Vol I with 1 text leaf creased. cb Oct 17 (189) $5,500

### Jones, Owen Glynne
— Rock Climbing in the English Lake District.... L, 1897. 8vo, orig cloth. bba Nov 1 (361) £320 [Cizdyn]

### Jones, Robert T. ("Bobby"), 1902-71
— Rights and Wrongs of Golf. N.p.: A. G. Spaulding, [1936]. 1st Ed. Wraps. pba Apr 18 (100) $160

### Jones, Robert T. ("Bobby"), 1902-71 —& Keeler, O. B.
— Down the Fairway. NY, 1927. One of—300. Foreword by Grantland Rice. Half vellum; front cover dampstained & bowed. 1st 3 pp. dampstained. Sgd by Jones & Keeler on limitation & frontis. pba Apr 18 (102) $3,750

### Jones, Shirley
— Soft Ground Hard Ground. Croydon: Red Hen Press, 1986. One of 40. Folio, mor-backed portfolio by Jen Lindsay. With 12 color etchings. Schaefer copy. P Nov 1 (130) $550

### Jones, Thomas
— The Gregynog Press. Oxford, 1954. One of 750. In dj. sg Sept 14 (198) $140; sg Feb 15 (156) $50

### Jones, Tom
— The Last of the Buffalo.... Cincinnati, 1909. Oblong folio, orig string-bound pictorial wraps, in orig ptd envelope. pba Aug 22 (895) $85

### Jones, Sir William, 1746-94
— Dissertations...relating to the History and Antiquities...of Asia. Dublin, 1793. 8vo, contemp sheep; spine worn, joints cracked. sg Mar 7 (118) $175

— Works. L, 1799-1804. 6 vols, plus 2 vols of Supplement & Life by Lord Teignmouth. Folio, contemp calf; 1st 2 vols with front covers, endpapers & titles detached, other joints cracking or tender. Foxed. pba June 20 (207) $325

Anr Ed. L, 1807. 13 vols. 8vo, orig bds; spine ends lacking pieces, some covers detached or starting. Titles stamped; some plates browned. sg Mar 7 (119) $350

### Jones, William Basil Ticknell —& Freeman, Edward Augustus
— The History and Antiquities of Saint David's. L, 1856. 4to, later 19th-cent half mor; extremities scuffed. With 23 plates. sg June 13 (212) $130

### Jones, William Carey
— Report of... Special Agent to Examine the Subject of Land Titles in California.... [Wash., 1851]. 2d Ed. - Map by William M. Eddy. 8vo, modern wraps. With folding map. Text darkened & map with stub tear. Robbins copy. pba Mar 21 (174) $1,100

### Jonghe, Clement de
— Icones praecipuarum urbium totius Europae. Amst., 1675. Folio, contemp vellum; repaired, new endpapers. With allegorical frontis & 36 full-sheet plates, all colored by a contemp hand. Frontis trimmed to platemark & mtd; some fraying & staining; some

fold breaks & closed tears; Lisbona with marginal rusthole; Paranambuca trimmed to platemark & mtd; Forum Amstelodamense worn with repaired tears & center section rebacked. Schaefer copy. P Nov 1 (131) $85,000

**Jonghe d'Ardoye, Theodore Alexander, Vicomte de —& Others**
— Armorial Belge du Bibliophile. [Brussels], 1930. One of 700. 3 vols in 1. 4to, contemp cloth, orig wraps bound in; rubbed & soiled. bba May 9 (139B) £120 [Laywood]

**Jonson, Ben, 1573?-1637**
See also: Limited Editions Club
— Volpone: or the Fox. L, 1898. One of 1,000. Illus by Aubrey Beardsley. 4to, orig cloth; spine repaierd, tips rubbed. sg Feb 8 (185) $225
— Works. L, 1616-40. 1st Ed. 3 vols in 2. Folio, mor gilt by Riviere. Tp & a few other leaves in facsimile; some browning & repairs. Sold w.a.f. STC 14751 & 14754. CE Sept 27 (155) $550

Vol I only. Folio, modern calf. Lacking 1st 72 pages & added title; some soiling 7 staining; some ink notes; top fifth of pp. 79-80 torn off. Sold w.a.f. STC 14751 or 14752. pba Nov 30 (197) $250

Anr Ed. L, 1640-[41]. 3 vols in 2. Folio, 19th-cent calf; joints worn. Repair with loss to 1 leaf. STC 14753; 14754a. Laid in is flyleaf with 3-line unsgd presentation to Lady Cholmondely. CE May 22 (289) $1,100

Anr Ed. L, 1640. 3 vols in 2. Folio, 18th-Cent calf; rebacked. Lacking M-R4 in vol III; vol II tp torn; leaves soiled; some dampstaining & browning. S Oct 27 (1190) £350 [Clark]

Anr Ed. L, 1692. Folio, contemp calf; hinges cracked, rebacked & recornered. Some dampstaining; last leaf repaired & remargined. cb Oct 17 (410) $275

Anr copy. Modern half mor. Repairs to tp verso & margins at beginning; some worming. pba Mar 7 (152) $275

Anr Ed. L, 1716. 6 vols. 8vo, later calf. Browned. wd May 8 (65) $200

Anr Ed. L, 1816. 9 vols. 8vo, calf gilt; scuffed. Minor soiling. F Sept 21 (419) $250

**Jonston, John, 1603-75**
— Historiae naturalis de quadrupetibus.... Amst., 1657. 6 parts in 2 vols. Folio, 18th-cent calf; scuffed, joints split, spines chipped. With 4 engraved titles & 250 plates. C Apr 3 (121) £1,800

Anr copy. 6 parts in 1 vol. Folio, contemp vellum; lower joint split. With 4 engraved titles & 249 plates. Hole in bird plate 15 repaired. S Nov 30 (28) £2,000

Anr copy. 3 (of 6) parts in 1 vol. Folio, old calf; scuffed & bumped. Sold w.a.f. wd Nov 15 (76) $225

**Joppien, Ruediger —& Smith, Bernard**
— The Art of Captain Cook's Voyages. New Haven, 1985. 2 vols. Folio, cloth, in djs. pba Feb 13 (51) $400

**Jordan, David Starr, 1851-1931**
— The California Earthquake of 1906. San Francisco, 1907. pba Feb 12 (285) $190
— The Days of a Man. Yonkers, 1922. One of 390. 2 vols. Half mor. pba Mar 7 (153) $70

**Jordana y Morera, Ramon**
— Bosquejo geografico e historico-natural del Archipielago Filipino. Madrid, 1885. 4to, half calf. With 12 colored plates. b Dec 5 (125) £550

**Jorden, Edward**
— A Discourse of Naturall Bathes, and Minerall Waters.... L, 1673. 3 parts in 1 vol. 8vo, disbound. Library stamp on tp. sg May 16 (187) $120

**Jorge, Marco, S.J.**
— Tien-chu Sheng-chiao Ch'i-men. China, [c.1620]. Bound with: Da Rocha, Joannes. Nien-chu Kneich'eng. Folio, contemp vellum, bound Chinese style; stained. Printed from wood blocks; text in 8 ruled columns. With 14 line woodcuts. On thin rice paper. Ink staining in margins, not affecting text; some fraying & tears, occasionally affecting text & cuts. Schaefer copy. P Nov 1 (132) $14,000

**Joseph, Marin.** See: Las Cases, Emmanuel

**Josephus, Flavius, 37-100?**
— Des Fuertrefflichen Juedischen Geschicht Schreibers Flavii Josephi Sammliche Wercke. Tuebingen, 1735. 2 parts in 1 vol. Folio, old half vellum. With engraved title & 10 plates & maps. Some repairs & browning. S June 13 (594) £160
— Des Hochberuemten Juedischen Geschichtschreibers. Strassburg, 1581. Bound with: Hegespius. Des Hochberuemten Fuertrefflichen Christlichen Geschichtschreibers Fuenff Buecher. Strassburg, 1581 Folio, late 19th-Century half cloth; rubbed. Some staining & browning. S Oct 27 (1066) £170 [Robertshaw]
— Repuesta de Josepho contra Apion alexandrino. Amst., 1687. 8vo, contemp calf; worn. Lacking into leaf; minor worming in gutter margin affecting letters; some staining & browning. CE Dec 6 (208) $3,000
— Works. L, 1609. Folio, half mor; worn, hinges split. Tp & 4 rear index leaves repaired with marginal pieces replaced; marginal notes to index pages; some closed tears. pba Nov 30 (198) $500

Anr Ed. L, 1693. Folio, modern half calf. Piece torn from lower marign of last leaf & restored with minor loss; frontis cropped & remtd; folding map split & frayed. Sold w.a.f. O Mar 5 (136) $180

## JOSSELYN

**Josselyn, John**
— An Account of Two Voyages to New-England.... L, 1675. Bound with: New-Englands Rarities Discovered. L, 1672. 8vo, disbound with old bdg incorporating orig sheep on upper cover. Rarities lacking last 8 leaves & misbound between 1st & 2d parts of the Account; some edges at ends browned & frayed; Account with rusthole to B3-4 catching a few letters; Rarities with 2 headlines shaved; some worming to upper margins. CNY May 17 (91) $6,500
— New-Englands Rarities Discovered.... L, 1672. 1st Ed. 16mo, early 19th-cent mor gilt; spine chipped, front joint starting. Ink accession no on p.1; tear in outer margin of plate repaired; lacking initial blank, pp 103-14, & final 2 leaves. sg May 16 (313) $2,400

**Joubert, Francois Etienne**
— Manuel de l'amateur d'estampes. Paris, 1821. 1st Ed. 3 vols. 8vo, contemp half mor gilt. Sgd in each vol. b Sept 20 (629) £140

**Jouffroy, Alain**
— Aube a l'Antipode. Paris, 1966. One of 77 in a specially designed case. Illus by Rene Magritte. Wraps, unopened. S Nov 2 (19) £280 [McCulloch] Club du Soleil Ed, One of 100, with additional suite of cards. Wraps. sg Feb 15 (191) £110

**Jouffroy, Alain —&**
**Teixidor, Joan**
— Joan Miro: Sculpture. NY & Paris, [1974]. 4to, cloth, in dj. With 2 double-page color lithos by Miro. sg Jan 11 (286) $100

**Jouffroy, Jean Pierre**
— La Mesure de Nicolas de Stael. Neuchatel, [1981]. 4to, cloth, in dj. sg Jan 11 (142) $100

**Jouhandeau, Marcel, 1888-1979**
— Descente aux enfers. Paris, 1961. One of 170. 4to, loose as issued in wraps. With 4 lithos. pba Nov 30 (68) $1,300
— Petit Bestiaire. Paris, 1944. One of 358. Illus by Marie Laurencin. 8vo, unsewn in orig wraps. Ck Sept 8 (11) £450

**Jouin, M. Henry**
— Ancien Hotel de Rohan. Paris, 1899. Folio, half mor, orig wraps bound in; spine top rubbed. With 62 plates. Some foxing. sg June 13 (16) $150

**Jourdain, Margaret —&**
**Lenygon, Francis**
— English Decoration and Furniture of...1500-1650. L, 1924. Folio, contemp calf. Stamp at foot of tp. bba May 30 (35) £60 [Kingsmill]

**Journal...**
— Journal of Design and Manufactures. L, 1849-50. Vols I-IV (of 6). 8vo, contemp half mor; worn, bds detached, backstrips def. With frontis, folding view of the future Crystal Palace (torn) & with 138 samples of cloth & paper mtd or bound in. Lacking 1 sample, a few loose; some browning. bba June 6 (21) £750 [Pope]
— The Journal of Negro History. NY, [1970]. 53 vols. 4to, orig cloth. Complete reprint through 1968. sg Mar 28 (180) $750
— The Journal of the Indian Archipelago and Eastern Asia. Singapore, 1850-51. Vols IV-V. 8vo, half calf. With 6 folding maps. b May 30 (208) £320 Anr Ed. Nendeln: Kraus Reprint, 1970. Series I, No 1-5 & Series 2, No 1-4 & 6-9, in 12 vols. b May 30 (207) £320

**Journal des Mines...**
— Journal des mines; ou, recueil des memoires sur l'exploitation des mines.... Paris, 1794-1810. Vols 1-28. Orig wraps or contemp sheep gilt; various defs & covers off. Foxed; folding table in Vol 13 separated at fold; Vol 20 with sidenotes & plate margins cropped; Vol 4 lacking Plate 17; Vol 5 lacking Plate 20; Vol 17 lacking Plate 6. Sold w.a.f. sg May 16 (188) $550

**Journeys...**
— Journeys into the Moon, Several Planets and the Sun. Phila., 1837. 12mo, half mor; rubbed. sg Sept 21 (289) $600

**Jovellanos, Gaspar Melchior de**
— Pan y toros. Oracion apologica que en defensa del estado floriente de Espana.... Palma de Mallorca, 1813. 4to, modern wraps. S Oct 26 (283) £170 [Quaritch]

**Jovius, Paulus, 1483-1552**
— Dialogo dell' imprese militari et amorose. Lyons: Guillaume Rouille, 1574. 8vo, modern vellum bds. 3 leaves repaired at lower margin. S June 12 (54) £420
— Historiarum sui temporis.... Florence: Lorenzo Torrentino, 1550-52. 2 vols in 1. Folio, 18th-cent calf gilt with French royal arms; rebacked. Early annotations; 4th leaf torn & repaired at margin; wormed at ends; some soiling. S June 12 (53) £250
— Le vite di dicenove huomini illustri. Venice: Giovan Maria Bonelli, 1561. Trans by L. Domenichi & G. B. Gelli. 4to, later vellum bds. With title device. Some browning. S Oct 27 (1062) £200 [Zioni]

**Joyant, Maurice**
— Henri de Toulouse-Lautrec. Paris, 1926-27. 2 vols. 4to, contemp vellum gilt by Asprey, orig wraps bound in. Ck May 31 (57) £280
Anr copy. Contemp half mor by Riviere, orig wraps bound in. With 20 colored plates, 4 etched ports, many plates in 2 states. Dessins vol is one of 200 & has 2 additional etched ports but lacks the 4 additional lithos. S Nov 2 (23) £260 [Weinbaum]
Anr Ed. Paris, 1927. 2 vols. 4to, orig wraps; soiled, spine panel worn & ends chipped. sg June 13 (367) $140

**Joyce, James, 1882-1941**
See also: Limited Editions Club
— Anna Livia Plurabelle. NY, 1928. One of 800. Ck Apr 12 (139) £850

Anr copy. Spine of bdg bumped. Ck Apr 12 (140) £800; S Dec 18 (321) £750 [Seragnoli]
— The Cat and the Devil. NY, [1964]. 1st Separate Ed. - Illus by Richard Erdoes. In dj. Inscr by Erdoes, 1967, & with orig drawing of a jester with a cat.  pba May 23 (190) $130
— Chamber Music. L, 1907. 1st Ed, 2d bdg variant. one of 509. CE Sept 27 (156) $1,200
3d bdg variant. Foxing to endpapers. S Dec 18 (322) £1,200 [Buddenbrooks]
1st (Unauthorized) American Ed. Bost.: Cornhill, [1918]. 16mo, orig cloth. pba Oct 5 (199) $350; pba Jan 25 (173) $225
— Dubliners. L, [1914]. 1st Ed. Engelhard copy. CNY Oct 27 (100) $2,400
Anr copy. Orig cloth; some wear, spine creased. Hugh Walpole - John Huston copy. S Dec 18 (327) £750 [Essig]
— Exiles. L, 1918. 1st English Ed. Orig half cloth. Epstein copy. CE May 22 (291) $600
— Finnegans Wake. L, 1939. 1st Ed. In frayed & chipped dj; endpapers & tp foxed.  wa Feb 29 (57) $425
One of 425. CE Sept 27 (159) $3,500; Ck Apr 12 (142) £2,200; S Dec 18 (328) £2,600 [Buddenbrooks]
— Haveth Childers Everywhere. Paris, 1930. 1st Ed, one of 100 on japan. Folio, orig wraps, in dj. S Dec 18 (323) £2,300 [Copus]
[-] The Joyce Book. L: The Sylvan Press, [1933]. 1st Ed, one of 450. 4to, orig cloth. S May 16 (86) £340
[-] Our Exagmination round his Factification for Incamination of Work in Progress. Paris, 1929. 1st Ed. Orig wraps. Inscr to Eric Gill by Evan Gill, 22 Feb 1931. Ck Apr 12 (141) £420
— Pomes Penyeach. Paris: Shakespeare & Co., 1927. 1st Ed. Orig bds. With the errata slip. Some foxing. Met Feb 24 (200) $500
Anr copy. Half cloth; soiled. With the errata slip. pba Nov 30 (199) $275
— A Portrait of the Artist as a Young Man. L: Jonathan Cape, 1924. Cloth; spine ends frayed, joints torn. Sgd, 1930. pba Oct 5 (200) $1,600
— Storiella As She Is Syung. [L: Corvinus Press], Oct 1937. 1st Ed, one of 25. 4to, orig vellum; worn. Inscr to Thomas & Anne Wilson, 28 May 1938.  bbc June 24 (528) $5,750
— Tales Told of Shem and Shaun. Paris: Black Sun Press, 1929. 1st Ed, one of 500. Orig wraps. S Dec 18 (326) £450 [Essig]
— Ulysses. Paris, 1922. 1st Ed, One of 100 on Van Gelder Zonen, sgd. 4to, orig wraps, unopened; some fraying to spine, minor soiling to rear cover. Engelhard copy. CNY Oct 27 (101) $35,000
One of 150, on verge d'Arches. Orig wraps. "Superb copy". sg Dec 14 (173) $16,000
One of 750 on handmade paper. Half mor, orig wraps bound in. Some prelims chipped; 2 leaves with marginal repairs; some browning. cb Feb 14 (2696) $1,600
Anr copy. Orig wraps; rubbed, with a few closed tears, spine reinforced. CE Sept 27 (157) $7,500

Anr copy. Modern mor by Michael Wilcox. S Dec 18 (333) £3,600 [Buddenbrooks]
Anr copy. Contemp vellum, orig wraps bound in. S Dec 18 (334) £2,200 [Gekoski]
Anr copy. Orig wraps; spine restored. S July 11 (300) £3,200
2d Ptg (1st English Ed). Paris: Pbd for the Egoist Press, L, by John Rodker, 1922. 4to, orig wraps; frayed.  b Sept 20 (546) £320
Anr copy. Contemp lea. Tp & margins browned. bba Oct 19 (346) £160 [Finch]
Anr copy. Half mor, orig wraps bound in; joints & spine ends worn. Half title with lower corner chipped. CE Sept 27 (157A) $1,700
Anr copy. Wraps; minor rubbing to extremities. With 8 leaves of errata tipped in. pba Mar 7 (155) $3,000
Anr copy. Modern vellum bds, orig wraps bound in. S Dec 18 (332) £500 [Cathach]
Anr copy. Orig wraps; stains on upper cover, edges rubbed. sg June 20 (187) $2,200
Anr copy. Wraps; spine crumpled, small tear on front wrap. Last 2 leaves crumpled at upper corner. wd Nov 15 (77) $950
Anr copy. Modern half mor gilt; lacking 1st & last blanks. Some leaves dog-eared at end; imprint leaf lacking outside corners; errata leaf bound in. Z June 28 (142) $950
9th Ptg. Paris, 1927. 4to, orig wraps; creased, tear along front joint, chipped. F Mar 28 (588) $70
Anr copy. Later half mor, orig wraps bound in; later endpapers & binder's blanks. Z June 28 (143) $150
Anr Ed. Hamburg: Odyssey Press, [1932]. 2 vols. Wraps; extremities framed. Tp torn at top & with small stain at edge; Vol II with stain at corner of half-title. Z June 28 (145) $110
1st Ptg in England. L, 1936. one of 900. In torn & creased dj. bba Oct 19 (347) £360 [Sotheran]
Anr Ed. L, 1937. cb Feb 14 (2787) $950
Anr copy. In dj designed by Eric Gill. CE May 22 (292) $400

**Judson, Clara Ingram**
— Flower Fairies. Chicago, [1915]. Illus by Maginel Wright Enright. pba Aug 22 (797) $60

**Juedisches...**
— Juedisches Lexikon. Ein enzyklopaedisches Handbuch. [Koenigstein, 1982]. 4 vols in 5. 4to, orig cloth; 1st 3 spines discolored. sg Apr 11 (177) $200

**Jukes, Joseph Beete, 1811-69**
— Narrative of the Surveying Voyage of H. M. S. Fly.... L, 1847. 1st Ed. 2 vols. 8vo, orig cloth; spine ends torn, library shelfmarks, rear cover stained, residue of library label on front free endpaper. Foxed; library stamps. cb Oct 17 (193) $900

**Jung, Gertrud.** See: Ziegenfuss & Jung

## JUNGKEN

**Jungken, Johann Helffrich**
— Nach den heutigen... Grund-Regulen der Medicin.... Frankfurt, 1701. 8vo, calf; spines scuffed. With 15 plates. Some browning & marginal dampstaining. sg May 16 (437) $175

**Junta de Fomento de Californias.** See: California

**Jussieu, Antoine Laurent, 1748-1836**
— Genera plantarum.... Zurich, 1791. 8vo, orig bds; spine def, front cover detached. Tp stamped; some foxing. sg May 16 (314) $225

**Just...** See: Kipling, Rudyard

**Justinianus I, Emperor, 483-565**
See also: Fore-Edge Paintings
— Digestum vetus. Nuremberg: Anton Koberger, 22 Nov 1482. Folio, contemp half pigskin over wooden bds with brass clasps; outer half of front cover missing. Wormed at ends; 1st leaf soiled with part of margins excised; a10 & Y1 loose. 402 (of 404) leaves; lacking 1st & last blanks. Goff J-549. sg Mar 21 (187) $1,500
— Institutiones. Lyons: Antoine Vincent, 1552. 8vo, contemp calf over wooden bds with covers tooled in gilt, silver & blind, with outer roll-tooled border of the 4 Evangelists enclosing a large panel stamp, that on upper cover of Christ on the Cross & that on the lower cover of the Resurrection, with initials IM & date 1553 tooled in silver & gilt on upper cover; joints cracking, spine ends chipped, silver tooling oxidized. With folding woodcut of the Arbor Civilis inserted after F1. Marginal dampstaining, extending into text at beginning; text browned. Schaefer copy. P Nov 1 (134) $47,500

**Justinianus, Laurentius, Patriarch of Venice**
— Dottrina della vita monastica. Venice: Bernardinus Benalius, 20 Oct 1494. 4to, modern mor. 35 lines; types Benali 13:130G, 85G. With 3 full-page woodcuts. Some spotting. 114 leaves. Goff J-500. C Apr 3 (120) £3,300

**Justinus, Marcus Junianus**
— Epitome in Trogi Pompeii historias. Basel: Andreas Cratander, 1530. ("In Trogi Pompei historias exordium.") 8vo, contemp blind-tooled calf; rebacked, endpapers renewed. Some underscoring & marginal dampstaining; lacking last leaf. sg Mar 21 (177) $200
— The History of Justine. L, 1606. Bound with: Blackmore, Sir Richard. Eliza: An Epick Poem. L, 1705. Folio, modern half calf. Sold w.a.f. bba May 30 (74) £85 [Rix]

**Juvenalis, Decimus Junius, 60-140 —&
Persius Flaccus, Aulus, 34-62**
— Satyrae. [Venice]: Bonetus Locatellus for Octavianus Scotus, 8 Mar 1492. Folio, 17th-cent bds covered with 15th-cent vellum Ms leaf; spine chipped. 62 lines of commentary surrounding text & headline; types 5:80R, 6:105R, 105Gk, 80Gk. Some browning. 102 leaves. Goff J-658. C Apr 3 (122) £1,400

## AMERICAN BOOK PRICES CURRENT

Anr Ed. Turin: Nicolaus de Benedictis & Jacobinus Suigus, 8 Oct 1494. Folio, contemp half pigskin over wooden bds; worn. 53 lines of commentary & headline; types 6:114R, 7:87R.. 136 leaves. Goff J-660. C Apr 3 (123) £1,800

Anr Ed. Venice: Joannes Tacuinus de Tridino, 18 Aug 1512. Folio, modern lea. Minor worming to corners of opening leaves; marginal traces of mold towards end. sg Mar 21 (178) $425

Anr Ed. Antwerp, 1529. 8vo, later calf; rebacked, rubbed. Some waterstaining. bba July 18 (116) £425 [Unsworth]

**Juvenile...**
— The Juvenile Miscellany, or Magazine of Knowledge and Entertainment of Young Persons of Both Sexes. L, 1808-9. 12 parts in 1 vol bound as 2. 8vo, contemp calf gilt; joints def, corners worn. With 24 plates, 18 of them folding. General title in Vol II in facsimile; some plates torn, 1 split in 2 sections, anr lacking fore-edge margin. S Nov 2 (216) £420 [Schiller]

# K

**K., J.**
— Wieder neu aufgerichtete und vergroesserte in zwei theilen angewiesene curieuse Kunst- und Werck-Schul. Nuremberg: Johann Zieger, 1705-7. 2 vols. 4to, contemp vellum. Frontis in Vol I. Madsen copy. S Mar 14 (187) £1,900

**Kaempfer, Engelbert**
— Amoenitatum exoticarum politico-physico-medicarum. Fasciculi V. Lemgo, 1712. 5 parts in 1 vol. 4to, contemp blindstamped vellum; some soiling. With frontis & 78 plates & maps. Some browning. C Apr 3 (124) £3,800
— Histoire naturelle, civile et ecclesiastique de l'empire du Japon.... The Hague, 1729. 1st Ed in French. 2 vols. Folio, contemp calf; extremities worn, joints weak & partially split. With engraved title & 45 maps & plates. Plates 35-37 browned; some foxing. P June 5 (278) $4,250

**Kafka, Franz, 1883-1924**
See also: Limited Editions Club
— Die Verwandlung. Leipzig: Kurt Wolff, [1915]. Orig wraps; spine head chipped. P Dec 12 (97) $3,000

**Kaftal, George**
— Saints in Italian Art: Iconography of the Saints in Tuscan Painting; ...Central and South Italian Painting; ...the Painting of North East Italy. Florence, [1952]-78. Ltd Eds. 3 vols. 4to, cloth, in torn dj. bba Oct 19 (59) £320 [Sims Reed]

**Kahnweiler, Daniel Henry**
— Juan Gris: his Life and Work. NY, 1947. Trans by Douglas Cooper. 4to, cloth. With 2 mtd color plates. sg Jan 11 (202) $50

**Kallir, Jane**
— Egon Schiele. L, 1990. 4to, orig cloth, in dj. sg Jan 11 (385) $130

**Kallir, Otto**
— Egon Schiele: Oeuvre Catalogue of the Paintings. NY, 1966. 4to, half cloth. Met Sept 28 (22) $300

**Kalm, Peter, 1716-79**
— Travels into North America.... Warrington, 1770 & L, 1771. 1st Ed in English. 3 vols. 8vo, 19th-cent mor with painted edges. P June 5 (63) $2,750
Anr Ed. L, 1772. 2 vols. 8vo, half calf & half cloth; both rebacked. With a map & 6 plates. Met Feb 24 (392) $700

**Kampen, Nicolaas Godfried van, 1776-1839**
— The History and Topography of Holland and Belgium. L, [1837]. Illus by W. H. Bartlett. 8vo, orig mor gilt. sg Mar 7 (120) $275
— Vues de la Hollande et de la Belgique. L, [1837]. Illus by W. H. Bartlett. 8vo, mor extra. sg Mar 7 (121) $300

**Kane, Elisha Kent, 1820-57**
— Arctic Explorations. NY, 1853. ("The U. S. Grinnell Expedition in Search of Sir John Franklin....") 8vo, orig cloth; rebacked with part of spine retained. Inscr to Dr. Benton & with ALs of the author's father, J. K. Kane, to Dr. Benton stating that this copy "is one of the first edition, of which some 20 copies survived the fire". K Feb 11 (24) $425
Anr Ed. Phila., 1857. 2 vols. 8vo, contemp calf. With engraved title, frontis ports, 3 maps (2 of them folding) & 18 plates. b May 30 (158) £220
Anr copy. Contemp half calf gilt; small defs on front covers. sg Mar 7 (282) $50

**Kane, Paul, 1810-71**
— Paul Kane's Frontier, Including Wanderings of an Artist among the Indians.... Austin, [1971]. One of 50 hors commerce. 4to, lea. ds July 27 (103) $275
1st Ed. Austin & L, [1971]. Ed by J. Russell Harper. 4to, orig cloth in dj; d/j repaired. Robbins copy. pba Mar 21 (176) $170

**Kane, Thomas Leiper, 1822-83**
See also: Grabhorn Printing
— The Mormons, a Discourse delivered before the Historical Society of Pennsylvania. Phila., 1850. 8vo, orig string ties but lacking wraps. Tp chipped; rear blank soiled. wa Feb 29 (459) $380

**Kanomi, Takako**
— People of Myth: Textiles and Crafts of the Golden Triangle. Kyoto, [1991]. 4to, orig cloth. sg June 13 (355) $100

**Kant, Immanuel, 1724-1804**
— Critik der reinen Vernunft. Riga, 1781. 1st Ed. 8vo, contemp half calf gilt; upper joint cracked, lower joint starting, corners & extremities rubbed. Some foxing; minor marginal dampstaining to 1st 20 & last 40 leaves; small tear to Ff8; inkstamp to front flyleaf. CNY May 17 (26) $5,500

**Kapodistrias, Ioannos Antonios, Count, 1776-1831**
— Epistolai. Athens, 1841-43. 4 vols. 8vo, contemp mor gilt. With port. Institutional stamp on half-titles; stamps washed out of titles. sg Mar 7 (122) $225

**Kapsner, Oliver L.**
— A Benedictine Bibliography. Collegeville, 1962. 2d Ed. 2 vols. 4to, orig cloth; vol I hinge cracked. sg Apr 11 (185) $70

**Karl, Johann Friedrich**
— Vue et prospect des differentes parties du parc pres du Chateau de Freundenhaim.... Passau, [c.1770]. Oblong 4to, loose. With engraved title & 20 hand-colored plates. Tp repaired & browned. bba June 6 (299) £400 [Preissler]

**Karlstrom, Paul J.**
— Louis Michel Eilshemius. NY, 1978. Oblong 4to, cloth, in dj. sg Jan 11 (163) $90

**Karolik, Maxim**
— The M. & M. Karolik Collection of American Water Colors & Drawings, 1800-1875. Bost., 1962. 2 vols. 4to, cloth. O May 7 (187) $80

**Karolik Collection, M. & M.**
— American Paintings 1815 to 1865. Bost., 1949 [but 1951]. 4to, orig cloth; soiled & bumped, paint blotch to lower spine. wa Feb 1 (296) $130

**Karpel, Bernard**
— Arts in America: A Bibliography. Wash., [1979]. 4 vols. Folio, cloth; worn. sg Jan 11 (236) $120

**Karpinski, Louis C.** See: Spaulding & Karpinski

**Karpinski, Louis Charles**
— Bibliography of Mathematical Works printed in America through 1850. Ann Arbor, 1940. 4to, cloth. bba Oct 5 (201) £90 [Halwas]
Anr copy. Cloth; shaken. sg Oct 26 (193) $120

**Karr, Alphonse, 1808-90**
— Voyage autour de mon jardin. Paris, 1851. 8vo, orig cloth; foxed, spine rubbed. pba Aug 22 (580) $150

**Karsh, Yousuf**
— Faces of Destiny. Chicago, [1946]. 4to, cloth. Inscr to Gabriel Haver & with Haver's annotations. pba Oct 26 (40) $110
Anr copy. Cloth, in dj with tape repairs. Sgd, 1947. pba Jan 25 (176) $55
— Portraits of Greatness. NY, [1959]. Folio, cloth, in partial dj. sg Feb 29 (168) $100

**Karshan, Donald**
— Malevich: The Graphic Work.... Jerusalem, 1975. 4to, cloth, in dj. sg Sept 7 (227) $150

## KARSLAKE — AMERICAN BOOK PRICES CURRENT

**Karslake, Frank**
— Notes from Sotheby's.... L, 1909. 4to, orig cloth; extremities rubbed. sg Apr 11 (186) $110

**Kasket...**
— Die Kasket: Handdruck zur Geschichte der Militaerischen Tracht. Berlin, 1924. Some of the hand-colored plates trimmed. pba Mar 7 (68) $50

**Katalog...**
— Katalog der Ornamentstichsammlung der Staatlichen Kunstbibliotek Berlin. Utrecht, 1986. 2 vols. 8vo, orig cloth. sg Apr 11 (309) $80

**Katib Chelebi**
— Kitab-i Jihannuma li Katib Chelebi. Constantinople: Ibrahim Muterferrikah, 1732. Folio, 19th-cent goatskin; spine splitting. With 13 engraved diagrams & tables & 26 maps, all hand-colored somewhat later. Lacking tp & beginning of the dedication; some staining & repairs;. S June 27 (78) £9,000

**Katzenbach, Lois & William**
— The Practical Book of American Wallpaper. Phila., 1951. 4to, cloth. ds July 27 (104) $60

**Kavanagh, Julia**
— Women in France During the Eighteenth Century. NY, 1893. One of 100 L.p. copies. 2 vols. Mor gilt by the Sobota bindery in Cosway style, with insert circular color port in front cover of Vol I. Plates on india paper mtd. Some foxing. pba Nov 30 (201) $475

**Kay, John, 1742-1826**
— A Series of Original Portraits and Caricature Etchings. Edin., 1837-38. 2 vols. 4to, half mor. With 429 plates & 27 supplementary plates. pnE Mar 20 (150) £560

Anr Ed. Edin., 1877. Vol II only. Disbound. bba June 6 (22) £150 [Baynton-Williams]

Anr copy. 2 vols. 4to, orig half lea; rubbed. With 361 plates. Some soiling. Sold w.a.f. wad Oct 18 (299) C$420

**Kay, Stephen**
— Travels and Researches in Caffraria.... NY, 1834. 12mo, sheep; joints starting. sg Mar 7 (124) $150

**Kaye, Sir John William, 1814-76**
— Poems and Fragments. Jersey, 1835. 8vo, contemp calf. Cecil William Kaye's annotated copy. b Dec 5 (142) £110

**Keane, John F.**
— My Journey to Medinah.... L, 1881. 8vo, contemp half lea. b May 30 (275) £400

**Keate, George, 1729-97**
— An Account of the Pelew Islands. L, 1789. 3d Ed. 4to, contemp sheep; worn, rebacked. With port, folding map & 15 plates. sg Mar 7 (126) $175

**Keating, William H., 1799-1840**
— Narrative of an Expedition to the Source of St. Peter's River.... Phila., 1824. 1st Ed. 2 vols. 8vo, contemp sheep; rebacked, endpapers renewed. sg Oct 26 (194) $650

Anr Ed. L, 1825. 2 vols. 8vo, half calf; front bd of Vol I detached, joints weak. With 7 (of 8) plates, 3 folding tables & folding map with colored route. wa Feb 29 (412) $95

**Keats, John, 1795-1821**
See also: Golden Cockerel Press
— The Eve of St. Agnes. Chicago: Ralph Fletcher Seymour, 1900. One of 20 on japan vellum. Mor extra; minor rubbing. With double-page title & 4 large illusts & several dozen pictorial initials, all hand-colored & with gilt. bbc June 24 (102) $325
— Lamia, Isabella, the Eve of Saint Agnes and Other Poems. L, 1820. 1st Ed. 12mo, orig bds; minor wear. P June 5 (279) $16,000
— Life, Letters, and Literary Remains. L, 1848. Ed by Richard Moncton Milnes. 2 vols. 8vo, contemp calf gilt; extremities rubbed. F Mar 28 (576) $80

Anr copy. Orig cloth; rubbed. With 8-page pbr's ads dated Oct 1851. S Apr 23 (92) $300
— Poems. L, 1817. 1st Ed. 16mo, contemp bds; rebacked. Half-title in facsimile; lacking initial blank. sg Apr 18 (72) $6,500

Anr Ed. L: George Bell, 1898. Illus by Robert Anning Bell. 8vo, mor gilt by Sangorski & Sutcliffe. b Sept 20 (547) £120
— The Poetical Works. L, 1866. 8vo, later calf gilt. sg Feb 8 (79) $90
— Poetical Works. NY, 1938-39. One of 1,050. Intro by John Masefield. 8 vols. Sgd by Masefield. pba June 20 (210) $425

**Keeler, Charles A.**
— Evolution of the Colors of North American Land Birds. San Francisco, 1893. 8vo, modern half calf. With 19 chromolitho or tinted litho plates, 5 of them double-page. Inscr to G. W. Peckham. sg May 16 (315) $275

**Keeler, O. B.**
See also: Jones & Keeler
— The Autobiography of an Average Golfer. NY, 1925. 1st Ed. Cloth. Front free endpaper holed. pba Apr 18 (103) $110
— The Boy's Life of Bobby Jones. NY, 1931. 1st Ed. Cloth. pba Apr 18 (104) $225

**Keeley, Gertrude**
— Story of the Wild Flowers for Young People with Flower Alphabet. NY, [1914]. Half cloth. pba Apr 4 (517) $130

**Keene, J. Harrington**
— Fishing Tackle, its Materials and Manufacture. L, [1886]. Pictorial cloth; some wear. O Feb 6 (142) $250
— Fly-Fishing and Fly-making for Trout.... NY, 1887. 8vo, cloth; worn. O June 25 (168) $275

**Kees, Weldon**
— Poems 1947-1954. San Francisco: Adrian Wilson, 1954. Half cloth; soiled. pba Jan 25 (178) $85

**Keese, John**
— The Floral Keepsake.... NY, 1854. 4to, orig cloth; spine ends chipped. With 30 hand-finished color plates. pba June 20 (211) $180

**Keightley, Thomas, 1789-1872**
— The Crusaders. L, 1833. 8vo, orig cloth; upper cover detached, becoming disbound. Tp, endpaper & 1st few leaves repaired with tape. Inscr to Robert Southey & then below by William Wordsworth to his grandson Henry Curwen Wordsworth. S Dec 18 (257) £1,100 [Quaritch]

**Keim, De B. Randolph**
— Sheridan's Troopers on the Border.... Phila., 1870. 1st Ed. 8vo, orig cloth; spine ends frayed. sg Oct 26 (54) $70

**Keith, E. C.**
— Elmer Keith's Big Game Hunting. Bost., 1948. In chipped & frayed dj; some wear. O Oct 10 (176) $80
— Keith. An Autobiography. NY: Winchester, [1974]. Illus by J. C. Harrison. 4to, cloth, in dj with light wear. Sgd. O June 25 (169) $130
— Keith's Rifles for Large Game. Huntington, 1946. 4to, cloth, in tattered dj; some wear. O Oct 10 (180) $230
  Anr copy. Cloth; some wear. O Oct 10 (181) $160; O Oct 10 (182) $180; O June 4 (182) $190
— Sixgun Cartridges and Loads. Onslow County, [1936]. sg Mar 7 (483) $60

**Keleher, William A.**
— The Fabulous Frontier: Twelve New Mexico Items. Santa Fe, [1945]. 1st Ed, One of 500. Orig cloth. Robbins copy. pba Mar 21 (178) $80

**Kelemen, Pal**
— Medieval American Art.... NY, 1943. 2 vols. Folio, cloth. ds July 27 (105) $125

**Kellein, Thomas.** See: Inboden & Kellein

**Keller, David Henry, 1880-1966**
— Life Everlasting: And Other Tales of Science.... Newark, 1947. One of 1,000. In chipped dj with browned spine. pba May 4 (167) $55
— The Solitary Hunters and The Abyss. Phila., 1948. In chipped dj; owner's stamp & note to front free endpaper. pba May 4 (168) $55

**Keller, Helen, 1880-1968**
— Journal. Garden City, 1938. Inscr to Mr. Swanton, 22 Mar 1939. CE Sept 27 (161) $420

**Kelley, Hall, 1790-1874**
— History of the Colonization of the Oregon Territory. Worcester, 1850. 8vo, sewn as issued. Tp with adhesion damage & stain with short tear & ink spot; last leaf soiled with central crease; dampstain to gutter margins. pba July 25 (306) $1,000

**Kelley, James Douglas Jerrold, 1847-1922.** See: Cozzens & Kelley; Wagner & Kelley

**Kelley, William D.**
— Lincoln and Stanton.... NY, 1885. 8vo, mor extra by Zucker of philadelphia. Extra-illus with 88 ports. sg Oct 26 (216) $450

**Kelly, J. Wells.** See: Nevada

**Kelly, Luther S.**
— "Yellowstone Kelly": The Memoirs of Luther S. Kelly. New Haven, 1926. In repaired dj. pba June 25 (131) $70

**Kelly, William**
— Across the Rocky Mountains from New York to California.... L, 1852. 2d Ed. Contemp half mor; some scuffing. Larson copy. pba Sept 28 (549) $275
— An Excursion to California over the Prairie.... L, 1851. 1st Ed. 2 vols. 8vo, contemp half calf; lea & bds scuffed, edges bumped. Larson copy. pba Sept 28 (548) $1,300

**Kelmscott Press—London**
— The Floure and the Leafe.... 1896. One of 300. b Dec 5 (30) £900
— The History of Godefrey of Boloyne.... 1893. One of 300. S Nov 2 (29) £650 [Sotheran]
  Anr copy. John Henry Middleton's copy. sg Oct 19 (124) $1,600
— Laudes Beatae Mariae Virginis. 1896. One of 10 on vellum. sg Oct 19 (136) $4,400
  One of 250. sg Sept 14 (240) $425
— Of the Friendship of Amis and Amile. 1894. One of 500. Contemp calf cuir-cisele bdg. sg Oct 19 (128) $550
— Psalmi Penitentiales. 1894. One of 300. sg Sept 14 (243) $475
— Syr Ysambrace. 1897. One of 350. sg Sept 14 (245) $500
— The Tale of Beowulf. 1895. One of 300. Inscr to Lady Georgiana Burne-Jones. sg Oct 19 (130) $3,000
— The Tale of the Emperor Coustans and of Over Sea. 1894. One of 525. sg Sept 14 (246) $400
  Anr copy. Lev gilt by Riviere. sg Apr 18 (73) $700
BLUNT, WILFRID SCAWEN. - The Love-Lyrics and Songs of Proteus.... 1892. One of 300. Inscr "Violet Jane from Proteus April 29, 1892". sg Oct 19 (122) $850; sg Feb 15 (169) $650
CAVENDISH, GEORGE. - The Life of Thomas Wolsey. 1893. One of 250. sg Sept 14 (237) $400
CAXTON, WILLIAM. - The History of Reynard the Foxe. 1892. One of 300. sg Sept 14 (238) $1,700
CHAUCER, GEOFFREY. - Works. 1896. One of 425. Pigskin gilt, bound by the Doves Bindery to a special design by William Morris & dated 1897. Radford - Popham - Schaefer copy. P Nov 1 (62) $55,000

# KELMSCOTT

Anr copy. Pigskin gilt, bound by the Doves Bindery to a special design by Cobden-Sanderson, & dated 1896. P Dec 12 (98) $50,000

Anr copy. Terry copy. P Dec 12 (99) $22,000; P June 5 (282) $26,000

Anr copy. Linen-backed bds by Gerhard Gerlach in imitation of orig bdg. sg Oct 19 (134) $22,000

COLERIDGE, SAMUEL TAYLOR. - Poems Chosen out of the Works of Samuel Taylor Coleridge. 1896. One of 300. sg Oct 19 (133) $800

HERRICK, ROBERT. - Poems. 1895. One of 250. sg Sept 14 (239) $550

Anr copy. Pigskin gilt by Katherine Adams, 1914. sg Oct 19 (132) $3,000

MORRIS, WILLIAM. - Child Christopher and Goldilind the Fair. 1895. One of 600. 2 vols. sg Sept 14 (241) $425

MORRIS, WILLIAM. - Gothic Architecture.... 1893. One of 1,500. bba July 18 (325) £180 [Cox]; pba Nov 30 (202) $150; S Nov 2 (31) £220 [Sotheran]; sg Sept 14 (242) $350; sg Feb 15 (170) $400

MORRIS, WILLIAM. - Love is Enough. 1897. One of 300. P June 5 (281) $1,900; sg Oct 19 (138) $1,700; sg Feb 15 (171) $2,600

MORRIS, WILLIAM. - A Note on his Aims in Founding the Kelmscott Press. 1898. One of 525. sg Oct 19 (140) $550

MORRIS, WILLIAM. - Poems by the Way. 1891. One of 300. bba May 9 (582) £520 [Baring]

MORRIS, WILLIAM. - The Story of Sigurd the Volsung. 1898. One of 160. sg Oct 19 (139) $2,000

MORRIS, WILLIAM. - The Story of the Glittering Plain. 1891. One of 200. CE May 22 (294) $1,300

Anr Ed. 1894. One of 250. sg Oct 19 (127) $2,400

MORRIS, WILLIAM. - The Well at the World's End. 1896. One of 350. Library markings. bba Nov 16 (224) £600 [Thorp]; S Nov 2 (30) £1,200 [Blackwell]

ROSSETTI, DANTE GABRIEL. - Ballads and Narrative Poems. 1893. One of 310. pba Nov 30 (203) $425; S Apr 23 (136) £550; sg Oct 19 (126) $900

ROSSETTI, DANTE GABRIEL. - Hand and Soul. 1895. One of 11 on vellum. In mor extra exhibition bdg by Zaehnsdorf, 1900. sg Oct 19 (131) $2,200

One of 525. K Feb 11 (236) $300; sg Sept 14 (244) $425

ROSSETTI, DANTE GABRIEL. - Sonnets and Lyrical Poems. 1891. One of 310. sg Oct 19 (129) $700

Anr Ed. 1894. pba Nov 30 (204) $425; S Apr 23 (137) £580

SHAKESPEARE, WILLIAM. - The Poems of William Shakespeare. 1893. One of 500. Mor gilt by Zaehnsdorf, 1905. cb Oct 17 (338) $700; S Nov 2 (32) £600 [Barnitt]; sg Oct 19 (123) $650

SHELLEY, PERCY BYSSHE. - The Poetical Works. [1894]-95. One of 250. 3 vols. wd May 8 (66) $1,700

SPENSER, EDMUND. - The Shepheards Calendar. 1896. One of 225. Contemp mor gilt by Sarah Prideaux, 1900. C May 1 (165) £2,200; sg Oct 19 (137) $1,500

SWINBURNE, ALGERNON CHARLES. - Atalanta in Calydon. 1894. One of 250. sg Feb 15 (172) $800

TENNYSON, ALFRED. - Maud, a Monodrama. 1893. One of 500. sg Oct 19 (125) $600

VORAGINE, JACOBUS DE. - The Golden Legend. 1892. One of 500. 3 vols. P June 5 (280) $1,600; S July 11 (102) £1,500

## AMERICAN BOOK PRICES CURRENT

**Kelsall, Charles**
— Classical Excursion from Rome to Arpino. Geneva, 1820. 8vo, contemp half mor; extremities scuffed. With folding frontis & 4 plates & maps. Some browning to 2 plates. C Nov 29 (95) £380

**Kelson, George M.**
— The Salmon Fly. L, 1895. 4to, orig cloth. With port & 8 colored plates. S June 13 (458) £360

**Keltie, Sir John Scott, 1840-1927**
— A History of the Scottish Highlands, Clans and Regiments. L, [c.1890]. 5 vols. 4to, orig cloth; worn. Some soiling & foxing. F June 20 (81) $120

**Kelton, J. C.**
— A New Manual of the Bayonet for the Army and Militia of the United States. NY, 1861. 12mo, orig cloth; worn & soiled, lacking front flyleaf. With 30 plates. Some fold wear. NH July 21 (80) $70

**Kemble, Edward Cleveland, 1828-86**
— A History of California Newspapers, 1846-1858. Los Gatos, 1962. One of 50 specially bound. Half mor. With frontis port, 1 plate, & 8 folded facsimiles. Larson copy. pba Sept 28 (550) $110

Anr Ed. Los Gatos, Calif., 1962. One of 750. In dj. pba Feb 12 (535) $75

**Kemble, Edward Windsor, 1861-1933**
— A Coon Alphabet. NY, 1898. 8vo, pictorial bds, in partial dj. With orig drawing, 14 Dec 1898. sg Mar 28 (181) $2,800

**Kendall, George Wilkins, 1809-67**
— Narrative of the Texan Santa Fe Expedition.... NY, 1844. 1st Ed. 2 vols. 12mo, orig cloth; recased preserving backstrips, covers & endpapers. With folding map & 5 plates. Repair to map. wa Feb 29 (514) $450

— The War between the United States and Mexico.... NY, 1851. Illus by Carl Nebel. Folio, orig half cloth; spine split & worn, cloth worn. With 12 color plates & map. Storming of Chapultepec; some foxing to margins. Met May 22 (353A) $5,250

**Keneally, Thomas**
— Schindler's Ark. L, [1982]. In dj. Inscr. sg June 20 (188) $175

Anr Ed. L, [1992]. In dj. pba Jan 25 (179) $70

**Kennedy, Edward Guthrie, 1849-1932.** See: Grolier Club

**Kennedy, Edward M.**
— In Critical Condition. NY, 1979. In dj. Inscr. pba June 13 (69) $60

**Kennedy, John F., 1917-63**
See also: Onassis copy, Jacqueline Bouvier Kennedy

— As We Remember Joe. Cambr. MA, 1945. Orig cloth; stain at foot of spine. Dampstaining to lower margins at ends. CE May 22 (295) $500
— Profiles in Courage. NY, 1956. Inscr to Father George Brennan. CE Feb 21 (154) $1,900
Anr copy. Inscr to Glenn Anderson. pba June 13 (70) $1,500
Anr copy. Inscr to Charlotte Lord. rms Nov 30 (210) $1,600
Inaugural Ed. NY, 1961. In dj. Sgd. CE Feb 21 (155) $1,800

**Kennedy, Robert F., 1925-68**
— The Enemy Within. NY, [1960]. In soiled dj. Inscr to Alice Frein Johnson & with Christmas card, sgd. wa Feb 29 (242) $450

**Kennedy, William**
— The Ink Truck. NY, 1969. In rubbed dj with tear & crease. pba May 23 (191) $120
— Ironweed. NY, 1983. In dj with tear to rear panel. Inscr on tp to John Gill, Mar 1983. pba Jan 25 (180) $150

**Kennett, Basil, 1674-1715.** See: Deseine, Francois Jacques

**Kenney, Louis A.**
— Catalogue of the Rare Astronomical Books in the San Diego State University Library. San Diego, 1988. One of 1,000. 4to, cloth; some wear. O Mar 26 (140) $100

**Kennion, Edward**
— An Essay on Trees in Landscape. L, 1844. 4to, orig cloth; recased with new endpapers, worn. With 62 plates. O Mar 5 (137) $750

**Kennion, R. L.**
— By Mountain, Lake, and Plain.... Edin., 1911. sg Mar 7 (484) $130

**Kenny, D. J.**
— Illustrated Cincinnati: a Pictorial Hand-Book of the Queen City. Cincinnati, 1875. 12mo, orig cloth; spotted. sg Oct 26 (44) $100

**Kent, Rockwell, 1882-1971**
— A Birthday Book. [NY], 1931. One of 1,850. sg Feb 15 (173) $100
— The Bookplates & Marks of Rockwell Kent. NY, 1929. One of 1,250. Cloth, in dj. pba Aug 22 (605) $225
— Greenland Journal. NY, 1962. 1st Ed, One of 1,000. With a suite of 6 orig lithos, 1 sgd. bba May 9 (385) £70 [Breckenridge]
— Later Bookplates & Marks. NY, 1937. One of 1,250. In dj. Loosely inserted is pamphlet "Later Bookplates and Marks of Rockwell Kent". sg Feb 15 (174) $200
— Voyaging Southward from the Strait of Magellan. NY, 1924. 1st Ed. 4to, cloth, in dj. cb Feb 14 (2697) $250

— Wilderness; a Journal of Quiet Adventure in Alaska. Los Angeles, [1970]. Revised Ed. pba July 25 (174) $80
— World-Famous Paintings. NY, 1947. 4to, white pigskin over wooden bds gilt with onlaid leaves & acorns & flowers. b Sept 20 (637) £380

**Kenton, Maxwell.** See: Southern, Terry

**Kenyon, Frederic G.** See: Caxton Club

**Kepler, Johannes, 1571-1630**
— De cometis libelli tres. Augsburg, 1619-[20]. 4to, 19th-cent vellum; warped. Some worming & dampstaining to margins only. sg May 16 (193) $2,000
— Epitome astronomiae copernicanae.... Frankfurt, 1635. 7 parts in 1 vol. 8vo, contemp blind-panelled vellum; soiled. S June 12 (304) £1,200
— Prodromus dissertationum cosmographicarum continens mysterium cosmographicum. Tuebingen, 1596. 1st Ed. 4to, 19th-cent half mor gilt; extremities rubbed. Pages [2], 1-83 (of 181) only. Lacking plates; each leaf trimmed & inlaid. Sold w.a.f. sg May 16 (192) $500

**Keppel, Frederick, 1845-1912**
— The Golden Age of Engraving: a Specialist's Story about Fine Prints. NY, 1910. Ltd Ed. 8vo, orig wraps. sg Jan 11 (465) $225

**Keppel, George Thomas, Earl of Albemarle, 1799-1891**
— Narrative of a Journey Across the Balcan. L, 1831. 8vo, contemp calf; rubbed. With hand-colored frontis & 3 maps, 2 folding. b Sept 20 (341) £200
Anr copy. Contemp calf; spines def. b Jan 31 (453) £220
— Personal Narrative of Travels in Babylonia. L, 1827. 3d Ed. 2 vols. 8vo, orig bds. With folding map, & 4 hand-colored plates. S Oct 26 (120) £250 [Scott]

**Keppel, Sir Henry, 1809-1904**
— The Expedition to Borneo of H.M.S. Dido. L, 1846. 2d Ed. 2 vols. 8vo, orig cloth; worn. With 12 plates & 6 maps & plans. Some spotting. S Mar 28 (396) £320
Anr Ed. NY, 1846. 12mo, orig cloth. With frontis map. Prelim gathering carelessly opened; some foxing. sg Mar 7 (127) $200

**Kern, Edward M.**
— The Fort Sutter Papers. A Transcript... Commentary by Seymour Dunbar. NY: De Vinne Press, 1921. One of 20. Half bds. Inscr by Edward Eberstadt to Mrs. Malcolm Whitman. larson copy. pba Sept 28 (701) $2,250

**Kerouac, Jack, 1922-69**
— On the Road. NY, 1957. 1st Ed. Mor extra in wraparound design of a desert road, by Jonathan Root. pba Nov 30 (37) $650
Anr copy. In repaired dj. sg Dec 14 (178) $850
— The Town and the City. NY, [1950]. 1st Ed. In repaired dj. CE May 22 (297) $900

Anr copy. In worn dj. NH June 1 (185) $320
Anr copy. In photofacsimile dj. pba Aug 22 (266) $90
Advance copy. Wraps. CE May 22 (296) $750

**Kerr, John, 1852-1920**
— The Golf-Book of East Lothian. Edin., 1896. One of 500. 4to, cloth. Sgd. pba Apr 18 (105) $1,500
1st Ed, One of 500 small paper. 4to, cloth; spine & extremities sunned. Sgd. pba Nov 9 (50) $1,500

**Kerridge, Philip Markham**
— An Address on Angling Literature. Fullerton, [1970]. Ltd Ed. Half calf. pba July 11 (161) $180

**Kertesz, Andre**
— Andre Kertesz: Sixty Years of Photography.... NY, 1972. Ed by Nicolas Ducrot. Oblong 4to, cloth, in torn dj. sg Feb 29 (172) $90
— Day of Paris. NY: J. J. Augustin, [1945]. In soiled & worn dj; endpapers soiled. sg Feb 29 (169) $200
— A Lifetime of Perception. Toronto, 1982. 4to, cloth, in rubbed & dampstained dj; bdg with spotting to front cover, rear hinge split. sg Feb 29 (170) $70
— On Reading. NY, 1971. 1st Ed. In rubbed d/j. Small tear on last leaf. sg Feb 29 (171) $60

**Kesey, Ken**
— One Flew Over the Cuckoo's Nest. NY, [1962]. In rubbed dj; ink stamp on front free endpaper. cb Oct 17 (413) $325

**Kessel, Joseph**
— Kisling. NY, [1970s]. In dj. sg Sept 7 (201) $110

**Ketcham, Hank**
— The Merchant of Dennis the Menace. NY: Abbeville Press, [1990]. In dj. Sgd with sketch on half-title. pba Aug 8 (492) $80

**Ketham, Johannes de**
— Fasciculo de medicina collectorio.... [Venice: C. Arrivabeno, 1522]. Folio, modern mor gilt. Lacking final blank; repaired tears in text of 1st 4 gatherings, with some facsimile. S Nov 30 (325) £2,700
Anr copy. Lacking final blank; repaired tears to 1st 4 gatherings, with losses repaired in facsimile. S June 27 (336) £2,700

**Kettell, Samuel, 1800-55**
— Specimens of American Poetry.... Bost., 1829. 3 vols. 12mo, orig cloth. CE May 22 (376) $780

**Keulemans, Tony —& Coldewey, Jan**
— Feathers to Brush. Deventer: Pvtly ptd, [1982]. One of 500. Folio, half lea. pba Apr 25 (192) $160

**Keulen, Joannes van**
— Le Nouveau & Grand Illuminant Flambeau de la Mer. Amst., 1681-89. Part V only. Folio, contemp vellum; soiled. With 28 double-page coastal charts & 5 engraved coastal profiles. Some browning; tp creased & holed. C May 31 (61) £3,000

**Key, Francis Scott, 1779-1843**
— Poems....Spangled Banner. NY, 1857. Orig cloth, B bdg; rubbed. Z June 28 (154) $250
— The Star-Spangled Banner. Phila.: Winkle & Wiley, 1814. ("Defence of Fort M'Henry.") Folio, contemp half calf; spine ends chipped, worn. Foxed; library markings; tp stamped. In: The Analectic Magazine, Vol IV, No 23 (Nov 1814). bbc June 24 (411) $250

**Keyes, Norman, Jr.** See: Stebbins & Keyes

**Keynes, Sir Geoffrey**
— Bibliotheca Bibliographici: A Catalogue of the Library.... L: Trianon Press, 1964. One of 500. 4to, orig half cloth. With loosely inserted pamphlet by David Garnett, 1978, Sir Geoffrey Keynes: A Tribute, one of 50. bba May 9 (64) £110 [Brindel]
— The Complete Portraiture of William and Catherine Blake. L, 1977. Out-of-series copy. 4to, half mor. sg Sept 7 (46) $175
— Engravings by William Blake. The Separate Plates. Dublin, 1956. One of 500. 4to, cloth. pba Sept 14 (66) $325

**Keynes, John Maynard, 1st Baron, 1883-1946**
— How to Pay for the War. L, 1940. b Jan 31 (269) £70

**Keysler, Johann Georg, 1693-1743**
— Travels through Germany, Bohemia, Hungary, Swtizerland, Italy, and Lorrain. L, 1760. 3d English Ed. 8vo, contemp calf; vol I spin broken. With frontis & 7 folding plates. S Oct 26 (284) £250 [Watzlawick]

**Khan, Mohummud Abdullah**
— The Cricket Guide. Lucknow, 1891. 12mo, orig wraps; torn & def. pn Oct 12 (310) £340

**Khrypffs, Nicolaus de Cusa, Cardinal**
— The Idiot in Four Books. L, 1650. 1st Ed in English. 12mo, 19th-Cent calf; spine rubbed. Browned; F2r & G8 soil-marked; I9 torn with loss; I11-12 damaged at margin. Ck Mar 22 (84) £1,800

**Kidder, Frederic**
— The Expeditions of Capt. John Lovewell.... Bost., 1865. 4to, cloth; spine ends chipped. Inscr. pba July 25 (415) $120

**Kidder, Jonathan Edward**
— Japanese Temples: Sculpture, Paintings, Gardens, and Architecture. Tokyo, [1964]. 4to, cloth, in dj. wa Dec 14 (522) $65

**Kiepert, Heinrich**
— Kleiner Atlas der Neueren Geographie. Berlin: Dietrich Reimer, [c.1862]. 8vo, half lea slipcase; worn & broken. With 15 folding maps hand-colored in outline, each c.12.5 by 16.25 inches plus margins & borders. bbc Feb 26 (17) $170

**Kierkegaard, Soren Aabye, 1813-55**
— Afsluttende uvidenskabelig Esterskrift til de philosophische Smuler. Copenhagen, 1846. 8vo, modern half mor. Blank corner lacking fro tp & 1 other leaf; pencil underlinings in text. S June 12 (174) £380

## Kiesler, Frederick
— Contemporary Art Applied to the Store and its Display. NY, [1930]. 4to, cloth; worn. sg Jan 11 (243) $175

## Kijewski, Karen
— Wild Cat. Huntington Beach: James Cahill, 1994. One of 150. Half mor. pba Oct 5 (201) $80
Anr copy. Half cloth. pba Aug 22 (268) $55

## Kilgour Collection, Bayard Livingston
— The Kilgour Collection of Russian Literature, 1750-1920. Cambr. MA, 1959. 4to, orig cloth; spine rubbed. sg Apr 11 (188) $150

## Kilmer, Joyce, 1886-1918
— The Circus and Other Essays. NY, 1916. 1st Ed. Orig cloth; spotted. Inscr, 1916. pba May 23 (192) $60
— Trees and Other Poems. NY, 1914. Orig bds. sg June 20 (190) $50

## Kilner, Elizabeth
— A Visit to a Farm-House.... By S. W. L: Tabart & Co., 1804. 12mo, contemp calf. With frontis & 7 plates. S Nov 2 (215) £220 [James]

## Kimball, Fiske, 1888-1955
— Mr. Samuel McIntire, Carver. Portland ME, 1940. 1st Ed. 4to, cloth. O Dec 5 (64) $160
One of 675. Cloth. Some foxing. sg June 13 (17) $140

## Kimball, J. Horace. See: Thome & Kimball

## Kimball, Maria Brace
— A Soldier-Doctor of Our Army: James B. Kimball.... Bost., 1917. Orig cloth; owner's stamp to front free endpaper. Inscr. pba June 25 (132) $180

## Kimes, Maymie B. See: Kimes & Kimes

## Kimes, William F. —& Kimes, Maymie B.
— John Muir: A Reading Bibliography. Palo Alto: William P. Wreden, 1977. Foreword by Lawrence Clark Powell. 4to, orig bds. Larson copy. pba Feb 12 (128) $170
1st Ed, One of 300. Half cloth. With frontis port. Robbins copy. Sgd. pba Mar 21 (254) $110

## Kindig, Joe, Jr.
— Thoughts on the Kentucky Rifle in its Golden Age. York: Trimmer Printing, 1960. 4to, cloth, in dj. sg Mar 7 (485) $90

## King, Charles, fl.1721
— The British Merchant. L, 1721. 3 vols. 8vo, contemp calf; spine ends rubbed, joints cracked, library stamps on pastedowns. With 2 folding tables in Vol I. cb June 25 (1784) $550

## King, Charles, 1844-1933
— Campaigning with Crook and Stories of Army Life. NY, 1890. 12mo, orig cloth; extremities rubbed. pba June 25 (133) $50
— Indian Campaigns: Sketches of Cavalry Service in Arizona and on the Northern Plains. Fort Collins CO: Old Army Press, [1984]. One of 250. Ed by Harry H. Anderson. 12mo, orig cloth. pba June 25 (135) $85

## King, Clarence, 1842-1901
— Clarence King Memoirs. The Helmet of Mambrino. NY, 1904. Half vellum; worn & discolored. Marginal notations. pba Feb 12 (89) $110
— Mountaineering in the Sierra Nevada. Bost, 1872. 1st Ed, 1st Issue. 8vo, orig cloth; spine ends rubbed, some soiling. pba Feb 12 (85) $300
Anr Ed. Bost., 1872. 8vo, orig cloth; spine ends worn. Owner's stamp on front blank; foxing at end. sg Oct 26 (195) $300
1st Ed, 1st Issue. 8vo, orig cloth; front hinge cracked. Robbins copy. pba Mar 21 (179) $500
Anr Ed. Bost., 1879. 8vo, orig cloth; rear joint nicked, extremities rubbed. Foxed. pba Aug 22 (929) $120
6th Ed. Orig cloth; rear joint nicked, extremities rubbed. With 2 folding maps. Light foxing. Robbins copy. pba Mar 21 (180) $170

## King, Jeff
— Where the Two Came to Their Father: A Navaho War Ceremonial. New York: Pantheon, [1943]. Plates by Maude Oakes from paintings by King. Folio, cloth folder. With 18 plates. Lacking commentary by Joseph Campbell. Robbins copy. pba Mar 21 (181) $700
2d Ed. Princeton, N.J., 1969. Recorded by Maude Oakes; commentary by Joseph Campbell. Folio, unbound in wraps. With 18 colored plates. pba Aug 22 (607) $180

## King, John Lyle
— Trouting on the Brule River.... Chicago: Chicago Legal News Co., 1879. 8vo, cloth; worn, soiled & spotted. With folding map. Inscr. O June 25 (171) $225

## King, Martin Luther, 1929-68
— Nobel Lecture.... NY, 1964. Wraps, in dj. sg Mar 28 (183) $375
— Stride Toward Freedom. NY, [1958]. 1st Ed. In dj with edge wear & repair to spine. sg Mar 28 (184) $110

## King, Peter
— An Enquiry into the Constitution, Discipline, Unity & Worship, of the Primitive Church.... [N.p.], 1712. 2 parts in 1 vol. Contemp calf; rubbed. pba Nov 30 (208) $160

## King, Stephen
— The Bachman Books: Four Early Novels.... NY: New American Library, [1985]. Advance proof copy. pba May 4 (169) $200

— Carrie. Garden City, 1974. In dj. Inscr, 22 Aug 1980. O Dec 5 (180) $475; pba May 4 (170) $500; sg Dec 14 (179) $600
— Christine. NY: Viking, [1983]. In dj. Inscr. sg June 20 (191) $175

Anr Ed. West Kingston: Donald M. Grant, [1983]. One of 1,000. In dj. O Dec 5 (181) $225; sg June 20 (192) $150
— Cujo. NY: Viking, [1981]. In dj. Inscr. sg June 20 (193) $200

Anr Ed. NY: Mysterious Press, [1981]. One of 750. O Dec 5 (182) $130; pba May 4 (172) $325
— The Dark Tower II: The Drawing of the Three. West Kingston RI: Donald M. Grant, [1987]. One of 850. Illus by Phil Hale. In dj with edge tears. O Dec 5 (183) $200
— The Dark Tower III: The Waste Lands. Hampton Falls NH: Donald M. Grant, [1991]. One of 1,250. Illus by Ned Dameron. In dj. O Dec 5 (184) $150
— The Dark Tower: The Gunslinger. West Kingston, Rhode Island: Grant, [1982]. Trade Ed. In dj. pba May 4 (173) $300
— Delores Claiborne. L: Hodder & Stoughton, [1992]. Ltd Ed, with bookplate sgd by King affixed to half-title. O Dec 5 (187) $75
— Different Seasons. NY, [1982]. In worn dj. Inscr. O Dec 5 (185) $100
— Dolan's Cadillac. Northridge CA: Lord John Press, 1989. One of 1,000. O Dec 5 (186) $130
— Firestarter. Huntington Woods MI: Phantasia Press, 1980. In dj. Inscr. sg June 20 (194) $250

One of 725. In dj. This copy sgd on 7 July. cb Feb 14 (2698) $375

Anr copy. In dj with minor edge wear. O Dec 5 (188) $250

Anr copy. In dj. This copy sgd on 6 July. pba May 4 (175) $325
— Letters from Hell. Northridge: Lord John Press, [1988]. Ltd Ed. Single sheet, 17.5 by 23.5 inches, framed. O Dec 5 (191) $50
— My Pretty Pony. NY: Whitney Museum of Art, 1988. One of 200. Illus by Barbara Kruger. Folio, morbacked, stainless steel sheets over bds on covers with mtd digital timepiece on front cover. sg Dec 14 (180) $1,300
— Night Shift. Garden City, [1978]. In rubbed dj. pba May 4 (177) $350; sg June 20 (195) $400
— Nightmares and Dreamscapes. L: Hodder & Stoughton, [1993]. Ltd Ed, with bookplate sgd by King affixed to half-title. O Dec 5 (194) $75
— Salem's Lot. Garden City, 1975. In 2d Issue dj with misprint "Father Cody" and price clipped off. bbc June 24 (557) $240

Anr copy. In worn 2d dj. NH June 1 (187) $250

Anr copy. In 2d Issue dj with misprint "Father Cody" and price clipped off. pba May 4 (178) $350
— The Shining. Garden City, 1977. In frayed & soiled dj. Sgd. O Dec 5 (195) $200

Anr copy. In rubbed & chipped dj. pba May 4 (179) $120

Anr copy. In dj with spine ends rubbed. pba May 23 (194) $110
— Skeleton Crew. [Santa Cruz]: Scream Press, 1985. One of 1,000. Illus by J. K. Potter. In dj. With color fold-out laid in loose, as issued. O Dec 5 (196) $275; pba May 4 (180) $225
— The Stand. Garden City, 1978. In dj. O Dec 5 (198) $50

Anr copy. In dj with extremities rubbed. pba May 4 (181) $120

Anr copy. In dj. pba May 23 (195) $130

Anr copy. In dj with short tears to spine. pba Aug 22 (270) $95

Anr Ed. NY, [1990]. One of 1,250. Lea. O Dec 5 (199) $300
— Thinner. NY: New American Library, [1984]. In dj. pba Aug 22 (271) $60

**King, Stephen —& Straub, Peter**
— The Talisman. West Kingston: Donald M. Grant, 1984. One of 70. 2 vols. O Dec 5 (200) $325

**King, Thomas Butler, 1804-64**
— Report of Hon. T. Butler King on California. Wash., 1850. With: Correspondence on the Subject of Appraisement... 1st Ed. 8vo, disbound. Some stains, chips & creases. Larson copy. pba Sept 28 (553) $50

2d Ed. Orig wraps; spine chipped. Larson copy. pba Sept 28 (554) $100

**King, W. Kent**
— Tombstones for Bluecoats: New Insights into the Custer Mystery. Marion Station MD, 1980-81. Typescript facsimile, folio, wraps. pba June 25 (137) $100

**King, William F.**
— George Davidson: Pacific Coast Scientist.... Claremont: Claremont Graduate School and University Center, 1973. Folio, mimeographed, syn. Inscr to John Kaskle Kemble. pba Feb 12 (35) $70

**Kingdom, John**
— Adieu to Clifton! A Descriptive Poem. Bath, 1824. 8vo, orig bds; spine def. Inscr. b Dec 5 (332) £90

**Kingdome...** See: Hollar, Wenceslaus

**Kinglake, Alexander William, 1809-91**
— Eothen, or Traces of Travel brought Home from the East. L, 1844. 1st Ed. 8vo, contemp half calf; worn. With 2 hand-colored lithos. Lacking half-title; some foxing. b Sept 20 (342) £120
— Eothen, or Traces of Travel brought home from the East. L, 1844. 1st Ed. 8vo, recent half calf. With half title, folding hand-colored frontis, & 1 hand-colored plate. Frontis worn at fold; some discoloration. S Oct 26 (121) £100 [Scott]
— Eothen, or Traces of Travel brought Home from the East. L, 1845. 2d Ed. 8vo, orig cloth; corners worn. pba Oct 9 (10) $75

Anr Ed. L, 1912. One of 100. Illus by Frank Brangwyn. 4to, orig half vellum; rubbed. b Sept 20 (603) £130

**Kingman, Dong.** See: Caen & Kingman

**Kingsborough, Edward, Viscount**
— Antiquities of Mexico: Comprising Facsimiles of Ancient Mexican Paintings and Hieroglyphics.... L, 1830-38. Illus by Augustine Aglio. 9 vols. Folio, half mor; joints & corners renewed, scuffed. With 742 plates. Some foxing & discoloration; marginal pencil notes. P June 5 (284) $10,500

**Kingsley, Charles, 1819-75**
— The Heroes.... L, 1912. One of 500. Illus by W. Russell Flint. 4to, orig vellum gilt. b Sept 20 (618) £250

Anr copy. Vellum, in dj. With 12 mtd color plates. sg Sept 14 (129) $250

— Two Years Ago. Cambr., 1857. 1st Ed. 3 vols. 8vo, later 19th-cent calf; rebacked. F June 20 (452) $90
— The Water-Babies. L, 1909. One of 250. Illus by Warwick Goble. 4to, mor gilt by Bayntun-Riviere. CE Feb 21 (9A) $400

**Kinnell, Galway**
— Flower Herding on Mount Monadnock. Bost., 1964. In dj. Inscr to John Gill, 1964. pba Jan 25 (183) $70
— The Past. Bost., 1985. One of 200. Half mor. sg Dec 14 (181) $100

**Kinney, Troy**
— The Etchings. Garden City, 1929. Folio, half cloth. sg Sept 7 (200) $50

**Kino, Eusebio F.**
— Kino's Historical Memoir of Pimeria Alta: A Contemporary Account of the Beginnings of California, Sonora, and Arizona. Cleveland, 1919. 2 vols. With 7 plates & maps. pba Feb 13 (97) $450; pba Apr 25 (491) $400

1st Ed. - Trans & Ed by Herbert Eugene Bolton. 2 vols in 1. Orig cloth. With 7 plates & maps (1 large folding). Robbins copy. pba Mar 21 (182) $500

Anr Ed. Berkeley, 1948. 2 vols in 1. With 7 plates & maps. pba Apr 25 (492) $60

— Kino's Plan for the Development of Pimeria Alta, Arizona & Upper California. [Tucson], 1961. One of 500. With facsimile frontis. Robbins copy. pba Mar 21 (183) $50

**Kinsella, Thomas**
See also: Cualnge
— A Selected Life. Dublin: Peppercanister, 1972. One of 150. 4to, half mor. pba Jan 25 (184) $120

**Kinsey, William Morgan**
— Portugal Illustrated in a Series of Letters. L, 1828. 1st Ed. 8vo, contemp mor gilt; rubbed. With folding frontis & 26 plates, 9 of them hand-colored & including 4 additional plates; 1 folding map. S June 13 (550) £360

**Kinzie, Juliette A.**
— Wau-Bun, the "Early Days" of the North-West.... NY, 1856. 1st Ed. 8vo, orig cloth; worn. With 6 plates. sg Oct 26 (196) $300

**Kip, Joannes**
— Britannia Illustrata, or Views of Several of the Queens Palaces.... L: Carington Bowles, [c.1760]. ("Britannia Illustrata: or, Perspective Views of the Royal Palaces....") Folio, 19th-cent half mor gilt; worn. With engraved title & 80 double-page views, 2 also folding. Some spotting & discoloration; tp soiled & loose. S Nov 30 (56) £3,800

**Kip, Joannes —&**
**Freman, G.**
— The History of Nature in Two Parts, Emblematically Expressed.... L, 1720. Folio, orig bds with vellum spine; bds tattered, joints split at ends, spine flaking. With 89 plates. Minor soiling & dampstaining. Grantham - Schaefer copy. P Nov 1 (135) $7,000

**Kip, Lawrence**
— Army Life on the Pacific. NY, 1859. 8vo, orig cloth. Peter V. Hagner's copy. wa Feb 29 (476) $170

**Kip, Leonard**
— California Sketches, with Recollections of the Gold Mines. Albany, 1850. 1st Ed. 12mo, period half mor; rebound, wraps missing (facsimile laid in). Last 5 pages in facsimile. Larson copy. pba Sept 28 (556) $1,500

**Kipling, Rudyard, 1865-1936**
See also: Limited Editions Club
— An Almanac of Twelve Sports.... L, 1898. Illus by William Nicholson. 4to, orig half cloth; rubbed. bba June 6 (30) £240 [Kane]

Issue ptd on japan vellum. Half vellum; bumped. sg Sept 21 (240) $500

Anr Ed. L, 1899. 4to, orig half cloth; rubbed. F Mar 28 (380) $220

— American Notes. NY, [1891]. 1st Ed, 1st Issue. 8vo, orig wraps; chipped. Browned. F Mar 28 (461) $50

— The Art of Fiction. L, 1926. Orig wraps. sg June 20 (197) $50

— "Captains Courageous." L, 1897. 1st English Pbd Ed. 8vo, orig cloth; extremities rubbed, leaning. CE Sept 27 (165) $200

— La Chasse de Kaa. Paris, 1930. One of 60 hors commerce for the artist. Illus by Camille Beltrand after Paul Jouve. 4to, mor extra by G. Crette with intertwined snakes on trelliswork, orig wraps bound in. S Nov 21 (230) £21,000

— The Day's Work. L, 1898. 1st English Ed. 8vo, orig cloth. Frederick York Powell's copy. pba Dec 14 (88) $50

— Departmental Ditties and Other Verses. NY, [1890]. ("Departmental Ditties, Barrack Room Ballads, and Other Verses.") 8vo, cloth. Eraser mark to tp at author's name. pba Jan 25 (185) $375; sg Sept 21 (242) $300

# KIPLING

— The Jungle Book. With: The Second Jungle Book. L, 1894-95. 2 vols. 8vo, mor gilt by Bayntun-Riviere. b Sept 20 (549) $800
Anr copy. Orig cloth. Some foxing. cb Oct 17 (415) $700
Anr copy. Mor extra by Bayntun-Riviere, with onlaid design depicting Kala Nag. CE Sept 27 (164) $1,500
Anr copy. Contemp half mor gilt. Ck Nov 17 (93) £200
Anr copy. Orig cloth; bumped & rubbed, 1 spine block twisted. Ck Nov 17 (94) £170
Anr copy. Orig cloth; extremities bumped. Ck Apr 12 (144) £420
Anr copy. Orig cloth; rubbed & bumped. S Mar 28 (626) £280
Anr copy. Lev gilt with inlays of Father Wolf & of Mowgli & Father Wolf. sg Sept 21 (88) $950
— Just So Stories.... L, 1902. 1st Ed. Orig cloth, in def dj. CE Sept 27 (166) $1,200
Anr copy. Orig cloth; bumped, endpapers & half-title foxed. sg Sept 21 (243) $450
— Kim. L, 1901. 1st English Pbd Ed. Orig cloth; skewed. sg June 20 (199) $90
— Letters.... [N.p.: Pvtly ptd], 1936. Out-of-series copy. Half cloth. O Dec 5 (65) $70
— Letters of Marque. Allahabad, 1891. One of 1,000. 8vo, orig cloth; worn & stained. Pbr's stamp on half-title. bba May 30 (237) £50 [Williams]
Anr copy. Orig cloth; spine ends rubbed, front joint & hinge cracked, staining to upper corner of rear cover. pba June 20 (212) $150
Anr copy. Orig cloth; spine head rubbed. sg Sept 21 (244) $140
— Le Livre de la jungle. With: Le Second Livre de la jungle. Paris, 1941. One of 250. Illus by Henri Deluermoz. 2 vols. unbound as issued in orig wraps. cb Oct 17 (595) $250
— Many Inventions. L, 1893. Orig cloth. pba Jan 25 (186) $120; sg Dec 14 (182) $200
— The Outlaws. NY, 1914. One of 50. Single sheet, 10.6 by 7.1 inches. sg June 20 (201) $200
— Plain Tales from the Hills. Calcutta & L, 1888. 1st Ed. 8vo, orig cloth; spine rubbed, tips bumped. sg June 20 (202) $200
— Poems, 1886-1929. Garden City, 1930. 1st American Ed, One of 525. 3 vols. 4to, orig bds. Library markings. sg Dec 14 (185) $350
— Puck of Pook's Hill. NY, 1906. Illus by Arthur Rackham. Orig cloth. sg Sept 14 (305) $110
— Sea and Sussex. Garden City, 1926. One of 150. Illus by Donald Maxwell. 4to, half vellum gilt; bottom panel damaged. sg Feb 8 (311) $200
Anr Ed. L, 1926. One of 500. 4to, half vellum, in chipped dj. sg Dec 14 (183) $275
— The Second Jungle Book. L, 1895. 8vo, orig cloth; spine ends & joints rubbed. pba Nov 30 (209) $110
Anr copy. Cloth. sg Sept 21 (245) $140
— A Song of the English. L, [1909]. Illus by W. Heath Robinson. 4to, orig cloth. sg Sept 14 (314) $175
One of 500, sgd by Robinson. Orig vellum gilt; some discoloration, ink sale stamp to front paste-

# AMERICAN BOOK PRICES CURRENT

down, front hinge cracked. With 30 mtd colored plates. cb Oct 17 (684) $700
— Songs of the Sea. L, 1927. One of 500. Illus by Donald Maxwell. 4to, orig half vellum; free endpapers browned. sg Dec 14 (184) $275
— A Tour of Inspection. NY: Pvtly ptd, 1928. One of 93, this copy marked Printer's Copy. Bds, unopened; worn. O Dec 5 (66) $90
— Under the Deodars. Allahabad & L, [1890]. 1st English Ed. 8vo, orig wraps. Bemis copy. S Dec 18 (335) £800 [Heuer]
— Works. NY, 1898-1919. 27 vols. 8vo, half mor; spines & edges faded. CE Nov 8 (206) $1,800
Seven Seas Ed. Garden City, 1914-26. one of 1,050. 24 (of 27) vols. pba Jan 25 (187) $400
Anr Ed. NY: Scribner's, 1925-37. 32 vols. pba June 20 (213) $250

**Kipling, Rudyard, 1865-1936 —& Others**
— Quartette, the Christmas Annual of the Civil & Military Gazette. By Four Anglo-Indian Writers. Lahore, 1885. 8vo, contemp cloth. sg June 20 (203) $275

**Kippis, Andrew, 1725-95**
— The Life of Captain James Cook. L, 1788. 8vo, modern buckram. With port, 40 maps & plates from other works. S Oct 26 (612) £470 [Baring]

**Kirby, William F., 1844-1912**
See also: Grose-Smith & Kirby
— European Butterflies and Moths. L, 1882. 4to, orig cloth; loose, hinges cracked. With 61 hand-colored pates & 1 uncolored plate. S Apr 23 (327) £230
Anr copy. Contemp half mor; extremities rubbed. With 1 uncolored & 61 hand-colored plates. Some soiling & browning. sg May 9 (357) $600
Anr Ed. L, 1889. 4to, orig cloth. With 1 uncolored & 61 colored plates. S Mar 29 (732) £360

**Kircher, Athanasius, 1602-80**
— Arca Noe. Amst., 1675. Folio, contemp calf, tooled in blind; rebacked, later endpapers. With engraved title, port & 18 maps & plates. Repairs to 5 plates or maps & c.20 leaves of text; some browning. C June 26 (92) £1,000
Anr copy. Contemp vellum; soiled. With engraved title, port & 18 plates & maps, 13 of them double-page or folding. Some browning & spotting; wormhole through 1st few leaves; library stamp on tp. Madsen copy. S Mar 14 (200) £3,200
— Ars magna lucis et umbrae.... Amst., 1671. Folio, 19th-cent calf; rubbed. Frontis, port & folding plate backed; some browning & spotting; some marginal repairs; last leaf of index backed; library stamps on tp. Madsen copy. S Mar 14 (192) £3,600
— Ars magna sciendi, in XII libros digesta. Amst., 1669. 2 vols in 1. Folio, contemp blind-stamped pigskin; def. With 2 engraved titles, port, 3 plates & 4 (of 5) tables. Two plates with volvelles. Port trimmed & with hole at foot; 1 plate & 1 engraved title trimmed; some browning & staining; stamp of Fuerstenberg family on tp. S Mar 14 (199) £1,400

— Ars magnesia, hoc est, disquisitio bipartita-emperica seu experimentalis.... Wuerzburg: E. M. Zinck, 1631. 4to, 18th-cent vellum-backed bds. Browned & dampstained; tp grazed. Madsen copy. S Mar 14 (189) £3,000
— China Monumentis. Amst., 1667. 1st Ed. Folio, 19th-Cent half vellum; rubbed, hinges weak. With title, 2 maps, & 23 plates. Folding plate backed on linen; some soiling & staining; few wormholes. S Oct 26 (586) £500 [Black]
— China monumentis.... Amst., 1667. 1st Ed. Folio, 19th-cent calf. With engraved title, port, 2 folding maps & 23 plates. Plates all backed on linen; washed copy. Madsen copy. S Mar 14 (197) £1,100
Anr copy. Contemp calf; spine damaged. Tear in frontis repaired without loss; tear in K2; marginal tears & worming; some dampstaining. Madsen copy. S Mar 14 (198) £950
— China Monumentis. Antwerp, 1667. Folio, later half calf; rubbed. With title, 2 folding maps, & 23 plates. Lacking port; title repaired; browned; 1st few pp loose. S Oct 26 (587) £520 [Squire]
— Latium, id est nova et parallela Latii.... Amst., 1671. 1st Ed. Folio, contemp calf; joints weak. Some discoloration, mainly to text. b May 30 (159) £1,100
— Magnes, sive de arte magnetica.... Rome, 1641. 1st Ed. 4to, 18th-cent calf; rubbed. With 2 engraved titles & 32 plates, including volvelle at p. 287. Library stamp on tp; some plates shaved at fore-edge; browning. Madsen copy. S Mar 14 (190) £2,800
Anr Ed. Cologne, 1643. 4to, vellum. With frontis & 29 plates. Some browning; a few pencil annotations in margins. S Nov 30 (326) £900
3d Ed. Rome, 1654. Folio, contemp vellum. Some browning. Madsen copy. S Mar 14 (191) £1,800
— Mundus subterraneus.... Amst.: J. Jansson & E. Weyerstraet, 1665. 2 vols in 1. Folio, 17th or 18th-cent vellum over pastebds; upper hinge cracked. With 2 engraved titles, 2 ports & 21 plates & maps. Engraved title repaired at foremargin; Southeast Asia cropped; lunar map detached & with small fold break; Mediterranean with tear; some other fold breaks; minor dampstaining. Hefner copy. CNY May 17 (27) $5,500
3d Ed. Amst., 1678. 2 vols. Folio, contemp vellum. With 2 engraved titles, 6 maps & 13 plates. Lacking port; some browning & spotting. Madsen copy. S Mar 14 (196) £2,800
— Musurgia universalis sive ars magna consoni et dissoni.... Rome, 1650. 2 vols in 1. Folio, contemp calf gilt, with arms of Ernst Guenther, Herzog von Schleswig-Holstein-Sonderburg in Augustenburg. With 2 frontises, port & 21 plates on 20 sheets. Library stamps on tp; wormholes in 1st few leaves. Inscr to the Duke of Holstein Gottorp. Madsen copy. S Mar 14 (194) £8,800
— Neue Hall- und Thon-Kunst.... Noerdlingen: Friderich Schultes, 1684. Folio, contemp calf; worn. Lacking last leaf of index. S Mar 14 (206) £700
— Obelisci Aegyptiaci, Nuper Inter Isaei Romani rudera effossi interpretatio hieroglyphica. Rome, 1666. Bound with: Sphinx mystagoga, sive diatribe hieroglyphica. Amst., 1676. Folio, contemp calf; worn.

1st work lacking frontis & with dampstaining & worming affecting text. 2d work with browning & dampstaining & worming affecting text. S Mar 14 (202) £1,100
Anr copy. Bound after: Kestlerus, Joannes Stephanus. Physiologia Kircheriana experimentalis. Amst., 1680. And: Sepi, Giorgio de. Romani Collegii Societatus Jesu Musaeum celeberrimum... ex legato Alphonsi Donini. Amst., 1678. old vellum; soiled. Madsen copy. S Mar 14 (205) £3,300
— Physiologia Kircheriana Experimentalis. Amst., 1680. Folio, 18th-cent half calf; worn. Tear in frontis repaired; short tear in text of A3 & Cc1; long tear in L4; some other tears & spotting. Madsen copy. S Mar 14 (203) £1,300
— Scrutinium physico-medicum contagiosae luis.... Rome, 1658. 4to, contemp vellum. Browned. Inscr. Madsen copy. S Mar 14 (195) £4,400
— Sphinx mystagoga, sive diatribe hieroglyphica. Amst., 1676. Folio, 18th-cent calf gilt; worn. With 5 plates, 2 of them folding. Some browning; 1 plate lacking outer section. S Mar 14 (201) £700
— Toonneel van China. Amst., 1668. Folio, modern calf. Some leaves damaged in margins, many repaired; bottom of 1 leaf has been torn away with loss. NH June 1 (104) $500
— Turris Babel sive Archontologia. Amst., 1679. Folio, contemp vellum; upper cover def. Library stamp on tp. Madsen copy. S Mar 14 (204) £2,800

**Kirchmann, Johannes, 1575-1643**
— De annulis liber singularis. Accedunt Georgii Longi, Abrahami Gorlaei, et Henr. Kornmanni de iisdem tractatus.... Leiden, 1672. 4 parts in 1 vol. 12mo, contemp vellum. With engraved title. sg June 13 (215) $200

**Kirkaldy, Andra**
— Fifty Years of Golf: My Memories. NY: E. P. Dutton, [1921]. 1st American Ed. Cloth; spine dulled, front cover spotted, rear cover chewed. With frontis. pba Nov 9 (51) $90
Anr Ed. NY, [1921]. Cloth; spine rubbed & darkened. With frontis. pba Apr 18 (106) $140

**Kirkbride, John**
— The Northern Angler. L, 1840. 2d Ed. 8vo, orig cloth. pba July 11 (162) $170

**Kirkman, Frederick Bernuf Beever, 1869-1945**
— The British Bird Book. L & Edin., 1911-13. 4 vols in 12. 4to, contemp half mor. b Sept 20 (474) £50
Anr copy. 4 vols in 12 parts. 4to, orig bds; rubbed & warped. bba May 30 (435) £180 [Greth]

**Kirmse, Marguerite.** See: Derrydale Press

**Kirstein, Lincoln**
— Pavel Tchelitchew Drawings. NY, 1947. 4to, cloth, in dj. sg Jan 11 (414) $130

## KIRSTEIN

**Kirstein, Lincoln —& Newhall, Beaumont**
— The Photographs of Henri Cartier-Bresson. NY, [1947]. 4to, cloth; soiled. Minor foxing. sg Feb 29 (92) $150

**Kirwan, Richard, 1733-1812**
— Essai sur le Phlogistique, et sur la constitution des acides.... Paris, 1788. 1st French Ed. 8vo, contemp calf; worn. With half-title & title vignette. 2 gatherings browned; 1st & last few leaves marginally browned. Ck Mar 22 (158) £130

**Kissinger, Henry**
— White House Years. Bost., [1979]. Ltd Ed, sgd. pba June 13 (73) $80

**Kitab...**
— Kitab al nabu'at al-kanasi [Book of the Prophets]. Dair as-Shuwait, 1833. 3d Ed?. Folio, contemp mor; worn. Double columns in red & black ink. Title repaired; damp-stained & damaged near end. S Oct 26 (137) £200 [Brunt]

**Kitchin, Thomas, d.1784.** See: Bowen & Kitchin

**Kitchin, Thomas, d.1784 —& Others**
— A General Atlas. L: Sayer & Bennett, 1777. Folio, later half mor; spine ends & corners worn, joints rubbed. With 22 maps on 33 plates with contemp hand-coloring in outline & with 1 additional colored map laid in. Piece torn from edge of 1 plate with loss to map area; 2 corners on anr plate torn away with slight loss; tp stamped; fold breaks. cb Oct 17 (252) $3,750

Anr Ed. L, 1782. Folio, contemp half calf; def, covers detached. With title, & 23 maps on 35 double-page mapsheets. Some soiling; all becoming loose; some ms. annotations. S Oct 26 (435) £1,600 [Smith]

Anr Ed. L: Robert Sayer, [c.1788]. Folio, bdg not described; worn. With 23 maps on 35 sheets, with contemp outline color. Fold breaks; 1 map frayed with minor loss. b June 28 (84) £2,400

— A New Universal Atlas.... L: Laurie & Whittle, 1796. Folio, contemp calf; rebacked, worn. With 66 maps, several folding, hand-colored in outline. Some creasing; mapsheet 6 damaged at 1 fold; sheet 28 split at 1 fold without loss. S Nov 30 (75) £5,000

2d Ed. L, 1798. Folio, later half calf; extremities rubbed. With 20 large mapsheets, hand-colored in outline. sg May 9 (78) $12,000

**Kitchiner, William, 1775?-1827**
— The Housekeeper's Oracle; or, Art of Domestic Management.... L, 1829. 1st Ed. 8vo, orig bds; spine repaired, bumped. With frontis by E. Finden. Some spotting. S Oct 12 (32) £200

**Kitto, John**
— The Gallery of Scripture Engravings. L, [1847]. 3 vols. 4to, contemp half calf. With 188 (of 192) engraved plates. K June 23 (278) £225

## AMERICAN BOOK PRICES CURRENT

**Kitty...**
— Kitty Dan. A Poem. Leicester, 1808. 12mo, orig wraps; soiled. b Dec 5 (229) £80

**Kjaerbolling, Niels, 1806-71 —& Collin, Jonas**
— Skandinaviens Fugle, med searligt Hensyn til Danmark og de nordlige Bilande. Copenhagen, 1875-77-79. 2 vols, including 2 supplements. 8vo & folio, half calf gilt. With 107 hand-colored plates. S June 13 (441) £600

**Kjersmeier, Carl**
— Centres de style de la sculpture negre africaine. Paris & Copenhagen, 1935-38. 4 vols. 4to, orig bds, in djs, 1 torn. S Mar 14 (209) £90

**Klaricova, Katerina**
— Frantisek Drtikol. Prague: Pressfoto, [1981]. 4to, loose as issued in pictorial folding jacket. With 12 silver prints. Pamphlet of text laid in. Plate 10 with marginal damage not affecting image. sg Feb 29 (118) $200

**Klein, William**
— Mister Freedom. [Paris, 1970]. 4to, bds; extremities worn. sg Feb 29 (174) $100
— Moscow. NY, [1964]. Folio, cloth; worn, soiled, backstrip shaken, some gatherings split. Last plate creased at upper right corner. sg Feb 29 (175) $250
— Tokyo. NY, [1964]. Folio, cloth, in worn dj. Ink notations on half-title. sg Feb 29 (176) $350

**Kleiner, Salomon, 1703-59**
— Residences memorables de l'incomparable heros de notre siecle.... Augsburg, 1731-40. Bound with: Kleiner. Representation des animaux de la menagerie.... Augsburg, 1734. Oblong folio, contemp half calf; modern endpapers. Engraved throughout, with 11 titles in French & German, dedication in French, 90 plates in 1st work, 12 plates of animals in the 2d work, 9 folding. Repaired tears in lower margins of 3 animal plates; 1 folding plate torn into image & repaired. C Apr 3 (125) £6,500

**Klimius, Nicholas.** See: Holberg, Ludwig

**Klimt, Gustav, 1862-1918**
— Fuenfundzwanzig Handzeichnungen. Vienna: Gilhofer & Ranschburg, [1919]. One of 500. Folio, unbound as issued in bd folder. With 25 plates. S May 16 (21) £750

**Kline, Otis Adelbert, 1891-1946**
— The Planet of Peril. Chicago, 1929. Orig cloth; spine warped. pba May 4 (186) $160
— The Prince of Peril. Chicago, 1930. In dj. pba May 4 (188) $300

**Klinefelter, Walter**
— A Bibliographical Check-List of Christmas Books. Portland ME, 1937. Half cloth, unopened; worn. O Dec 5 (67) $60

**Klipstein, August**
— The Graphic Work of Kaethe Kollwitz. NY, 1955. One of 200. 4to, orig cloth, in soiled & chipped dj. Text in German.  sg June 13 (218) $1,100

**Kloss, Georg Franz Burkhard**
— [Sale Catalogue] Catalogue of the Library of Dr. Kloss of Franckfort.... L, 1835. 8vo, disbound. Sold w.a.f.  pba Aug 22 (543) $70

**Kluegel, Georg Simon**
— Analytische Dioptrik in zwey Theilen.... Leipzig, 1778. 4to, contemp half calf; rubbed. With 4 folding plates.  S Mar 14 (210) £650

Anr copy. Contemp half calf; worn. With 4 folding plates. Foxed.  S Mar 14 (211) £650

**Knecht, Edmund**
— A Manual of Dyeing, for the Use of Practical Dyers.... L, 1916. 4to, orig cloth; extremities frayed.  F Mar 28 (248) $70

**Kneeland, Samuel**
— The Wonders of the Yosemite Valley.... Bost., 1872. Illus by John Soule. 8vo, cloth; extremities worn. With 2 maps & 10 orig mtd photos. With 2 stereoscopic cards by Soule laid in.  pba Feb 12 (91) $250

3d Ed. - Photos by John B. Soule. 8vo, orig cloth; spine ends & corners worn. With 10 orig albumen photos. Robbins copy.  pba Mar 21 (184) $700

**Knickerbocker, Diedrich.** See: Irving, Washington

**Knight, Charles, 1791-1873**
— Half-Hours with the Best Authors. L: Rouledge, [c.1868]. Ed by Knight. 4 vols. 12mo, half calf gilt.  sg Sept 21 (29) $100
— Old England: a Pictorial Museum of Regal, Ecclesiastical, Municipal, Baronial and Popular Antiquities. L, [c.1860]. 2 vols. Folio, contemp half lea gilt. With 24 color plates. Foxed, affecting plates.  sg Dec 7 (276) $175

Anr copy. Orig cloth.  sg Jan 11 (246) $60

Anr copy. Cloth; soiled & worn, hinges cracked.  sg June 13 (217) $50

— The Popular History of England. L, 1856-62. 8 vols. 8vo, 19th-cent calf gilt.  sg Sept 21 (30) $700

Anr Ed. L, [c.1870]. 8 vols. 8vo, contemp half calf; rubbed.  F June 20 (721) $60

**Knight, Dame Laura**
— A Book of Drawings. L, 1923. One of 500. 4to, orig half cloth; extremities rubbed.  Ck May 31 (58) £140

**Knights Templar**
— Pacific Coast Guide and Programme of the Knights Templar Triennial Conclave at San Francisco, August, 1883.... San Francisco: Ira G. Hoitt, 1883. 8vo, cloth. With folding street map, frontis wood-engraving & 5 wood-engraved ports.  pba Feb 12 (327) $120

**Kniphof, Johann Hieronymus**
— Botanica in originali seu herbarium vivum. Erfurt, 1747. Folio, contemp vellum. Calligraphic Ms tp & 686 nature-ptd botanical plates ptd on rectos only, with Ms polynomials & authorities in Latin. With Ms index. Presentation copy to the Leopoldine Academy.  P Dec 12 (130) $3,750

**Knoop, Johann Hermann**
— Fructologie ou description des arbres fruitiers. Amst., 1771. With 19 hand-colored folding plates. Bound with: Knoop. Pomologie. Amst., 1771. With 20 hand-colored folding plates. Some leaves stained. Folio, contemp calf; rebacked, scuffed.  F Mar 28 (768) $3,000
— Pomologia. Fructologia. Dendrologia. Leeuwarden, [1758-63]. 2 vols. Folio, modern cloth. With 39 hand-colored plates. Some browning & spotting. Fattorini copy.  C Oct 25 (73) £1,500

**Knott, David.** See: Goldsmiths' Library of Economic Literature

**Knotts, Benjamin**
— Pennsylvania German Designs.... NY: Metropolitan Museum of Art, [1943]. Folio, loose in bd folder. With 20 color plates.  sg June 13 (310) $225

**Knower, Daniel**
— The Adventures of a Forty-Niner. Albany, 1894. 8vo, orig cloth; spine ends bumped.  pba Nov 16 (152) $55

1st Ed. 8vo, orig cloth; worn. Some darkening. Larson copy.  pba Sept 28 (560) $150

**Knox, Alexander**
— Essays on the Political Circumstances of Ireland...by a Gentleman of the North of Ireland. Dublin, 1798. 1st Ed, Issue not indicated. 8vo, contemp sheep; rubbed. Minor spotting; library markings.  F Mar 28 (467) $150

**Knox, George**
— Giambattista and Domenico Tiepolo. Oxford, 1980. 2 vols. 4to, cloth in djs.  sg Jan 11 (419) $130

**Knox, John, 1505-72**
— The Historie of the Reformatioun of Religioun within the Realm of Scotland. Edin., 1732. Folio, calf; extremities rubbed, spine ends chipped. Minor spotting.  cb Oct 17 (279) $550

**Knox, Robert, M.D.**
— Fish and Fishing in the Lone Glens of Scotland.... L, 1854. 4to, half cloth. Stamp to bottom of contents page.  pba July 11 (163) $160

**Knox, Ronald Arbuthnott, 1888-1957**
— A Selection from the Occasional Sermons. L: Dropmore Press, 1949. One of 500. Ed by Evelyn Waugh. 4to, orig cloth. Inscr by Waugh to Christopher Sykes, July 1949. Hobson copy.  S June 28 (257) £450

**Knuth, Leo.** See: Hart & Knuth

**Koch, Robert, 1843-1910**
— Investigations into the Etiology of Traumatic Infective Diseases. L, 1880. 8vo, orig cloth; spine stained. With 5 plates. CE Nov 8 (114) $110

**Koch, Rudolf, 1876-1934 —& Kredel, Fritz**
— Das Blumenbuch. Leipzig, 1942. Folio, orig half vellum, in dj. With 80 hand-colored plates. sg Oct 19 (167) $300

**Kock, Charles Paul de, 1794-1850**
— Works. Bost., [1902-4]. Author's Ed, one of 1,000. 25 vols. bbc Dec 18 (235) $230

**Koehler, H.**
— Polychrome Meisterwerke der monumentalen Kunst in Italien vom V bis XVI Jahrhundert. Leipzig: Baumgaertner, 1880. Folio, contemp half sheep; worn, covers detached, opening leaves loose. With 12 color plates. sg Dec 7 (266) $750

**Koehler, Johann David, 1684-1785**
— Descriptio orbis antiqui in XLIV tabulis exhibita. Nuremberg: C. Weigel, [c.1720]. Folio, contemp half calf; worn. Engraved throughout, with 44 hand-colored maps. Some browning. C May 31 (59) £1,000

**Koehring, Hans**
— Bibliographie der Almanache, Kalendar und Taschenbuecher fuer die Zeit von ca. 1750-1860. Hamburg, 1929. 8vo, orig cloth. sg Apr 11 (189) $140

**Koeman, Cornelis**
— Atlantes Neerlandici: Bibliography of Terrestrial, Maritime and Celestial Atlases and Pilot Books.... Amst., 1967-71. 5 vols plus Supplement, 1985. Folio, orig cloth; rubbed. Waterstaining to margins of Vol I. bba Oct 5 (351) £700 [Ross]
Anr Ed. Amst., 1967-85. 6 vols. 4to, cloth. S Oct 26 (436) £650 [Asher]
Anr Ed. Amst., 1967-71. 5 vols. Folio, orig cloth. sg May 9 (16) $1,900

**Koenig, Amand**
— Catalogue systematique des livres francois.... Strasbourg, 1801. 8vo, contemp half calf. Some foxing. O Mar 26 (141) $120

**Koenig, Joseph**
— Geist der Kochkunst.... Stuttgart & Tuebingen, 1822. 1st Ed. 8vo, contemp half calf; rebacked, rubbed. Some spotting; title torn & laid down. S Oct 12 (100) £360

**Kohl, Johann Georg, 1808-78**
— Kitchi-Gami. Wanderings round Lake Superior. L, 1860. 8vo, modern mor gilt by Bayntun-Riviere. sg Oct 26 (197) $240

**Kokoschka, Oskar, 1886-1980**
— Handzeichnungen, 1906-1965. NY, [1966]. One of 75 with sgd litho. 4to, cloth. sg Jan 11 (247) $375

**Kolb, Gustav —& Gmelich, Karl**
— Von der Pflanze zum Ornament. Wuerttemberg, [1901]. Folio, loose as issued in portfolio. With 26 (of 30) chromolitho plates. sg May 9 (319) $500

**Koldewey, Karl, 1837-1908**
— The German Arctic Expedition of 1869-70 and Narrative of the Wreck of the "Hansa" in the Ice. L, 1874. 1st Ed in English. 8vo, contemp half calf gilt. With 4 chromolitho plates, 2 ports & 2 colored maps. bba Nov 16 (293) £320 [Berger]

**Koman, Katherine**
— Economic Beginnings of the Far West. NY, 1912. 2 vols. 8vo, bdg not described. With 4 maps & 47 plates. NH July 21 (392) $120

**Kondo, Ichitaro**
— Selected Masterpieces of Ukiyo-e Prints. Tokyo, 1956. Folio, loose in cloth portfolio as issued; With 24 color plates. sg June 13 (207) $350

**Kongow, Iwao**
— The Later Works of the Costume of No Play in Japan. Tokyo, 1935. Folio, cloth. With 50 color plates. sg Sept 7 (114) $100

**Konkyliens...**
— Konkyliens Udstillinger. [N.p., 1966]. One of 600. 4to, wraps. With 12 plates, 10 of them sgd by the artist. sg Sept 7 (101) $110

**Koontz, Dean R.**
— The Bad Place. NY, [1900]. One of 250. In dj. O Dec 5 (202) $60
— Beastchild. Lynbrook: Charnel House, 1992. One of 750. O Dec 5 (203) $60
— The Eyes of Darkness. Arlington Heights: Dark Harvest, 1989. One of 52. Syn. O Dec 5 (205) $100; O Dec 5 (211) $60
— The House of Thunder. Arlington Heights: Dark Harvest, 1988. One of 52 lettered copies. Syn. O Dec 5 (209) $100
— Lightning. NY: Putnam, [1988]. One of 200. Half mor. O Dec 5 (213) $60
— The Servants of Twilight. Arlington Heights: Dark Harvest, 1988. One of 52 lettered copies. Syn. O Dec 5 (214) $60
— Shadowfires. Arlington Heights IL: Dark Harvest, 1990. One of 52. Syn. O Dec 5 (216) $90

**Koop, Albert J.**
— Early Chinese Bronzes. NY, 1924. One of 40. 4to, orig pigskin; extremities rubbed. With 110 plates. sg June 13 (219) $110

**Koops, Matthias**
— Observations on the Political State of the Continent.... L, 1799. Bound with: Thoughts on a Sure Method of annually reducing the National Debt of Great-Britain. L, 1796. 8vo, contemp mor; joints worn. sg Mar 21 (105) $450

**Kopp, Johann**
— Gruntownij a dokonaly regiment, neb zprawa.... Prague: Johann Had, 1535. Folio, contemp blindstamped calf over wooden bds; worn, lacking clasps. Soiled & dampstained; wormed; 1 leaf holed. Broxbourne copy.  S Nov 30 (318) £2,500

**Koran**
— Al-Coranus s. Lex Islamitica.... Hamburg, 1694. 4to, contemp vellum. With Sententia leaf, 2d Arabic half title, & Latin trans. in text. Rust-hole in S2.  S Oct 26 (124) £4,800 [Quaritch]
— The Koran. L, 1649. ("The Alcoran of Mahomet.") 4to, calf; front cover coming off.  pba Mar 7 (172) $350
Anr Ed. L, 1734. Trans by George Sale. 4to, old calf; rebacked. With a folding map & 4 plates (3 folding). Dampstaining in lower outside margin at ends.  Z June 28 (159) $400
Anr Ed. Phila., 1833. 2 vols. 8vo, orig cloth; worn, Vol I rear joint cracked. Library markings; some foxing.  sg Mar 7 (130) $140

**Korolev, Sergei**
— [Rocket Flight in the Stratosphere, in Russian]. Moscow, 1934. Orig wraps, wire-stitched. Alexei Leonov's copy.  P Mar 16 (7) $1,000

**Kosch, Wilhelm — & Others**
— Deutsches Literatur-Lexikon. Bern & Munich, [1968-94]. Vols I-XV, plus supplement. 16 vols. 8vo, orig cloth in djs.  sg Apr 11 (190) $800

**Kosewitz, W. F. von, Pseud.**
— Eccentric Tales. L, 1827. Illus by George Cruikshank. 8vo, mor gilt by Oldach. With 20 hand-colored plates.  sg Oct 19 (63) $475
Anr copy. Later 19th-cent mor gilt.  sg Feb 8 (269) $425

**Kosinski, Jerzy**
— The Painted Bird. Bost., 1976. 2d Ed, Advance copy - uncorrected proofs. Wraps.  Z June 28 (160) $180

**Kosloff, Lou**
— California Bit and Spur. Newport Beach, [1982]. One of 1,000. 4to, lea.  sg Mar 7 (486) $90

**Kotzebue, August von, 1761-1819**
— The Sufferings of the Family of Ortenberg. Dublin, 1799. 12mo, contemp calf. Marginal worming at beginning.  bba Oct 19 (231) £260 [Burmester]
1st American Ed. Phila., 1800. 2 vols in 1. 8vo, contemp sheep; worn.  bba July 18 (206) £180 [Maggs]

**Kotzebue, Otto von, 1787-1846**
— Entdeckungs-Reise in die Sued-See und nach der Berings Strasse.... Weimar, 1821. 1st Ed. 3 vols in 1. 4to, contemp half calf; extremities worn. Tp stamped; some spotting.  cb Oct 17 (194) $8,000
Anr copy. 19th-cent half calf; rebacked with orig spine strip laid on. With 1 plain & 5 folding maps & with 1 plain & 19 colored ports & plates.  pba Feb 13 (98) $6,500
— Enteckungs-Reise en die Sued-See und nach der Berings-Strasse.... Weimar, 1821. 1st Ed. 3 vols in 1. 4to, orig bds; rubbed & stained, extremities & joints worn, hinges cracking, shaken. With 20 plates (19 aquatints, 4 folding, & 15 hand-colored), 6 maps (5 folding), & 2 folding tables. Text darkened; some foxing & spotting. Robbins copy.  pba Mar 21 (185) $4,750
— Neue Reise um die Welt.... Weimar & St. Petersburg, 1830. 2 vols in 1. 8vo, orig cloth; library stamp on front free endpaper. With 2 frontises, 2 folding maps & 1 folding chart. Some foxing.  pba Feb 13 (100) $850
— A New Voyage round the World. L, 1830. 2 vols. 12mo, 19th-cent half mor; joints & spines rubbed. With 2 frontises, 2 folding maps & folding plan. Maps mtd on linen.  pba Feb 13 (101) $1,700
— A Voyage of Discovery into the South Sea and Beering's Straits. L, 1821. 3 vols. 8vo, contemp calf; rebacked with modern calf, some staining. With 8 hand-colored plates, 1 uncolored plate & 7 maps, 4 of them folding. Some foxing; each title with piece cut from lower margin & replaced with paper; 1 map repaired.  pba Feb 13 (99) $1,900
1st English Ed. 3 vols. 8vo, modern half calf. With 9 plates (8 in color), & 7 maps. Some foxing. Larson copy.  pba Sept 28 (124) $2,250
Anr copy. Later 19th-cent half calf; Vol I spine head nicked, light shelf wear. With 8 hand-colored plates, 1 uncolored plate, & 7 maps (4 folding). Lacks half-titles; some foxmarks on tps & charts. Robbins copy.  pba Mar 21 (186) $4,000
Facsimile of 1821 Ed. Amst. & NY, [1967]. 3 vols. 8vo, bds. With 9 plates (8 in color), & 7 maps. Some marginal pencil notes. Larson copy.  pba Sept 28 (125) $130

**Koury, Michael J.**
— Arms for Texas. Fort Collins CO: Old Army Press, [1973]. One of 50. Lea gilt. Inscr to John Popovich.  pba June 25 (138) $120
— Military Posts of Montana. Bellevue NE: Old Army Press, [1970]. One of 50 with orig drawing by Derek FitzJames. Lea gilt. Inscr to John Popovich.  pba June 25 (141) $150

**Kozloff, Max**
— Jasper Johns. NY, [1966]. 4to, cloth, in dj.  sg Sept 7 (196) $375

**Krackhart, Carl**
— Neues Illustriertes Conditiniereibuch.... Nordhausen: Heinrich Killinger, 1908. Pictorial cloth; new endpapers.  pba Mar 7 (64) $350

**Krafft, Johann Carl, 1764-1833**
— Plans des plus beaux jardins pittoresques de France.... Paris, 1809-10. 2 vols. Oblong 4to, contemp half calf; extremities worn. With 194 plates. Some foxing, occasionally affecting image; stain to lower inside corner of Vol I; dampstaining to Vol II.  cb Oct 17 (79) $1,500

**Krafft, Johann Carl, 1764-1833 —& Ransonnette, Nicolas, 1745-1810**
— Plans, coupes, elevations des plus belles maisons et des hotels construits a Paris.... Paris, [1801-2]. Folio, contemp calf gilt; repaired. With frontis & 120 plates. A few plates with Ms notes in margins. Fuerstenberg - Schaefer copy. S Dec 7 (318) £1,600

**Kraft, Jens**
— Forelaesninger over Mekanik med hofoiede Tillaeg. Soro: Jonas Lindgren, 1763-64. 2 vols. 4to, contemp calf; rubbed, 1 joint split. With 61 folding plates. S Mar 14 (216) £480

**Kramer, Hilton**
— Milton Avery Paintings 1930-1960. NY, [1962]. Folio, cloth. Library label on tp. sg Jan 11 (36) $100
— Richard Lindner. Bost.: NY Graphic Society, [1975]. In dj. sg Sept 7 (221) $50

**Krassnigg, Johan Georg**
— Philosophia polemica. Graz, 1690. 4to, contemp half sheep; worn. With frontis by E. C. Heiss, & 18 plates. Some worming to frontis & title. S Oct 26 (335) £170 [Zioni]

**Kraus, Hans P.**
— Sir Francis Drake, A Pictorial Biography. Amst., 1970. 1st Ed. 4to, orig cloth. Larson copy. pba Sept 28 (90) $350

**Krause, Johann Heinrich**
— Olympia; oder, Darstellung der grossen olympischen Spiele.... Vienna, 1838. 8vo, contemp half russia. sg Mar 7 (507) $50

**Krauss, Johann Thomas**
— Augspurgische Garten Lust. Augsburg: Martin Engelbrecht, [c.1750]. Oblong folio, loose in later half-cloth portfolio. With 12 plates. C Apr 3 (126) £3,200

**Krauss, Johann Ulrich**
— Heilige Augen- und Gemueths- Lust vorstellend alle Sonn-Fest- und Feyrtraegliche nicht nur Evangelien.... Augsburg: J. U. Krauss, [1706]. Bound with: Oration Dominica.... 3 vols in 1. Folio, contemp vellum. With 120 plates. Heilige: 3 plates torn, half-title soiled. Oration lacks A1. S Oct 27 (1132) £420 [Stanley]

**Krausz, Sigmund**
— Street Types of Great American Cities. Chicago, 1896. 8vo, orig cloth. K Oct 1 (308) $225

**Krazeisen, Carl**
— Bildnisse augezeichneter Greichen und Philhellenen.... Munich, 1828-31. Folio, contemp half lea, orig lower wrap with litho map bound in; rubbed. With 28 plates. Some spotting, mostly marginal. S June 27 (149) £18,000

**Kredel, Fritz.** See: Koch & Kredel

**Kretschmer, Albert.** See: Rohrbach, Carl

**Krider, John**
— Krider's Sporting Anecdotes, Illustrative of...American Game. Phila., 1853. 8vo, orig cloth. Some foxing. O Feb 6 (143) $100

**Krieg, Michael Otto**
— Mehr Nicht Erscheinen. Ein Verzeichnis unvollendet gebliebner Druckwerke. Bad Bocklet, 1954-58. 2 vols. 8vo, wrappers. sg Apr 11 (192) $200

**Kriss Kringles's...**
— Kriss Kingles's Christmas Tree.... NY, 1846. 8vo, orig cloth. With wood-engraved title & 14 plates. sg Feb 8 (254) $400

**Kroeber, A. L.**
— Handbook of the Indians of California. Wash.: GPO, 1925. 1st Ed. Orig cloth. With 10 maps (7 folding), 73 plates & 78 text illus. Larson copy. pba Sept 28 (25) $120

Anr Ed. Washington: Govt. Ptg. Office, 1925. Orig cloth; spine ends bumped. pba Nov 16 (153) $90

**Kruchenykh, A.**
— Porosyata. St. Petersburg, 1913. Illus by Kasimir Malevich. 8vo, orig wraps; upper wrap creased, with small tear in spine. With 2 lithos, 1 pasted to upper wrap. Some browning. C June 26 (236) £2,400

**Krusenstern, Adam Johann von, 1770-1846**
— Reise um die Welt. St. Petersberg, 1811-12. 2 vols (of 3), lacking Part 1. 16mo, orig wraps. sg Mar 7 (132) $200
— Voyage Round the World.... L, 1813. 2 vols in 1. 4to, orig bds; rebacked & recornered. With folding map & 2 colored plates. Some soiling to tp; marginal hole to contents leaf of Vol II. pba Feb 13 (104) $6,000

**Krusinski, Judas Thaddeus**
— The History of the Revolution of Persia.... L, 1728. 2 vols. 8vo, contemp calf. With folding map. Lacking half-title to Vol I. b Sept 20 (343) £450

**Kubota, Yonezo**
— Saiga Shokunin Burui. Tokyo, 1915. 4to, orig Japanese-style paper covers decorated in silver; rubbed & soiled. With 56 pp of color woodblock prints. wa Dec 14 (517) $210
— Seirou Bijin Gou. Tokyo, 1916. 4to, orig Japanese-style paper covers; rubbed & soiled. With c.200 full-page color woodblock prints. wa Dec 14 (519) $260

**Kuehn, Karl Gottlob**
— Geschichte der medizinischen und physikalischen Elektricitaet. Leipzig, 1783-85. 8vo, contemp calf. With 6 folding plates. S Mar 14 (220) £450

## Kuester, Georg Gottfried
— Bibliotheca Historica Brandenburgica.... Vratislava, 1743. 8vo, contemp bds. Some foxing & browning. O Mar 26 (142) $350

## Kuhlman, Charles
— Legend into History: The Custer Mystery. Fort Collins CO: Old Army Press, [1977]. Intro by Michael J. Koury. Sgd by Koury on tp, 13 Dec 1977. pba June 25 (148) $65

## Kunckel, Johann
— Ars vitraria experimentalis oder Voldkommene Glasmacher-Kunst.... Frankfurt & Leipzig: C. Riegels, 1689. Bound after: Becher, Johann Joachim. Chymischer Gluecks-Hafen.... Frankfurt, 1682. 4to, contemp vellum; stained. 1st work lacking port & with tear in 1 plate repaired; 2 plates shaved at head. 2d work with additional port tipped in & tp frayed. S Mar 14 (221) £1,800

## Kunhardt, Philip B., Jr. See: Onassis copy, Jacqueline Bouvier Kennedy

## Kunz, George Frederick, 1856-1932
— The Book of the Pearl.... NY, 1908. 1st Ed. 4to, orig cloth; worn & soiled. wa Nov 16 (310) $425

Anr copy. Cloth. wd Nov 15 (79) $400

— The Curious Lore of Precious Stones. Phila., 1913. 1st Ed. Orig cloth; shaken, tape stains on free endpapers. sg Sept 7 (207) $60

— Ivory and the Elephant in Art, in Archaeology, and in Science. Garden City, 1916. 4to, orig cloth; spine worn, front endpapers browned from laid-in newspaper clipping. Frontis & tp foxed. Inscr. sg Sept 7 (208) $325

— The Magic of Jewels and Charms. Phila. & L, 1915. 1st Ed. Orig cloth; tape stains on free endpapers. sg Sept 7 (209) $140

## Kunze, Horst
— Werner Klemkes gesammelte Werke. Dresden, [1968]. 4to, cloth, in dj. sg Sept 7 (204) $50

## Kyriss, Ernst
— Verzierte gotische Einbaende im alten deutschen Sprachgebiet. Stuttgart, 1951-58. 4 vols. 8vo, orig wraps. sg Apr 11 (54) $1,700

## Kyster, Anker
— Bookbindings in the Public Collections of Denmark. Copenhagen, 1938. One of 250. Vol I [all pbd]. Folio, half mor. bba May 9 (140) 260 [Brindel]

# L

## L., E.
— Vues de la Grece moderne. Paris, 1824. 1st Ed. - Illus by A.Joly. Folio, orig bds; worn. With title vignette, & 9 plates. 1 plate spotted; lacking pp. 15-16. S Oct 26 (118) £600 [Theotoky]

## La Belle, Christine
— Possibility of an Early Fall. New Rochelle: Elizabeth Press, [1971]. One of 400. Mor extra with inlays, by Susan Spring Wilson. sg Sept 14 (53) $600

## La Borde, Jean Benjamin de. See: Laborde, Jean Benjamin de

## La Branche, George M. L.
— The Dry Fly and Fast Water. NY, 1914. Orig cloth; spine ends rubbed. pba July 11 (164) $150

## La Calprenede, Gautier de Costes, Seigneur de, 1614-63
— Hymen's Praeludia.... L, 1674. Trans by Robert Loveday. Folio, contemp calf; spine ends & corners chipped, front joint cracked, endpapers renewed in 19th-cent. sg Mar 21 (180) $800

## La Chapelle, Georges de
— Recueil de divers portraits des principales dames de la Porte du Grand Turc. Paris, 1648. Folio, modern calf. With engraved title & 12 plates. Margins repaired; frontis shaved. S June 27 (151) £4,000

## La Chapelle, Vincent
— The Modern Cook. L, 1744. 8vo, contemp calf; rubbed. With 6 folding plates. Plate 1 def. b Sept 20 (137) £110

— The Modern Cook's and Complete Housewife's Companion. L, 1751. Last Ed. 8vo, 19th-Cent half mor; rubbed. With 5 folding plates. R5 torn. S Oct 12 (75) £230

## La Condamine, Charles Marie de, 1701-74
— Histoire des Pyramides de Quito. Paris, 1751. 4to, contemp wraps. CE Feb 21 (40) $600

## La Croze, Mathurin Veyssiere de. See: Veyssiere de la Croze, Mathurin

## La Fontaine, Jean de, 1621-95
— Fables choisies mises en vers. Bouillon, 1776. 4 vols. 8vo, contemp calf. With 248 plates. Vol IV marginally stained. S Oct 27 (1133) £800 [Nagara]

— Oeuvres. Paris: Lefevre, 1814. One of 30 on grand papier velin. 6 vols. 8vo, contemp mor gilt by Chilliat; joint of Vol III broken. With port in 3 states & 25 plates before letters, with additional state for plates 7-20 & 22-23 in eau-forte pure & a 3d state for plates 22-24 in eau-forte pure ptd on chine. Fuerstenberg - Schaefer copy. S Dec 7 (326) £1,700

— 1685. - Contes et nouvelles en vers. Amst. 1st Issue. 2 vols. 12mo, 19th-cent mor gilt. With 2 additional ports, frontis (repeated in Vol II) & 58 plates by Romeyn de Hooghe. Spotting to 1 plate in Vol II. S Dec 7 (327) £1,100

— 1743. - Amst. [i.e., Paris] 2 vols. 8vo, contemp mor gilt. With frontis & 70 vignettes. Tp of Vol II dated 1745 but sheets are of 1743 Ed. Fuerstenberg - Schaefer copy. S Dec 7 (328) £1,600

— 1755-59. - Fables choisies mises en vers. Paris 4 vols. Folio, contemp calf; rebacked with spines laid down, some joints starting. Some browning & staining affecting plates. CE Sept 27 (167) $2,950

Anr copy. 18th-cent mor gilt; joints & corners repaired. Some browning; tear in a few lower margins of Vol IV. S Nov 30 (274) £2,600

Anr copy. Contemp red mor gilt. With frontis & 275 plates. Le singe et le leopard without le leopard on signbd. Some browning & spotting; tear in port repaired; some leaves creased. Fuerstenberg - Schaefer copy. S Dec 7 (333) £8,500

Anr copy. Contemp calf gilt; sides rubbed, some prelims in Vol i misbound. With frontis & 275 plates, Le singe et le leopard after letters Some creasing & cockling in Vol IV; some staining; marginal tears. S June 27 (339) £3,600

— 1762. - Contes et nouvelles en vers. Amst. [i.e., Paris]Fermiers-Generaux Ed. 2 vols. 8vo, contemp mor gilt. With 2 ports & 80 plates. CE Sept 27 (168) $1,300

Anr copy. Contemp olive mor richly gilt with tool of a heart inserted in a lozenge by its head; 2 small repairs on lower side of Vol II. Fuerstenberg - Schaefer copy. S Dec 7 (329) £14,000

Anr copy. 18th-cent mor. With 2 ports & 80 plates. Le cas de conscience & Le diable de Papefiguiere in decouvert state; Le cocu battu et content & Les cordeliers de Catalogue engraved by Longueil; Autre imitation d'Anacreon without arrow; Le remede with the ornaments. Some foxing. S Mar 28 (485) £1,200

— 1765-75. - Fables choisies mises en vers. Paris 6 vols in 5. 8vo, contemp calf gilt; spines & hinges repaired. With frontis, 6 engraved titles & 243 plates. Engraved throughout. Dashwood - Fuerstenberg - Schaefer copy. S Dec 7 (334) £1,100

— 1780. - Contes et nouvelles en vers. Londres [but Paris]: Cazin. 2 vols. 18mo, 19th-cent red mor gilt by Lortic, armorial bdg. With port & 24 plates. From the library at Chantilly of the duc d'Aumale. Fuerstenberg - Schaefer copy. S Dec 7 (330) £400

— 1787. - Fables. Paris 1st Issue. 6 vols. 18mo, contemp red mor gilt by Bradel, with his label at end of Vol I; joints weak, upper cover of Vol II detached. With frontis & 274 plates before numbers. Fuerstenberg - Schaefer copy. S Dec 7 (335) £300

— An III [1795]. - Contes et nouvelles en vers. Paris One of 150 on papier velin with plates before letters. 2 vols. 4to, mor gilt by Canape & Corriez, contemp wraps bound in. With port, 18 subjects with plates before letters & eau-forte, 2 subjects with plates before letters only, 3 subjects with eau-forte only, 1 subject with plate after letters, an additional eau-forte for 2 subjects, an additional plate for Le baiser rendu, a later printing of La gageure des trois commeres (Le poirier) & an additional plate & eau-forte by Moreau l'aine for La cruche in Vol II. Some spotting. Fuerstenberg - Schaefer copy. S Dec 7 (331) £3,700

— An VIII [1800]. - Edition stereotype. Paris 2 vols. 18mo, 19th-cent mor gilt by Bauzonnet-Trautz; stain at head of spine of Vol I. Ptd on vellum. Fuerstenberg - Schaefer copy. S Dec 7 (332) £1,900

— 1867. - Fables. Paris Copy ptd on chine. Illus by Gustave Dore. 2 vols in 1. Folio, mor extra by Gruel. With port & 85 plates. C May 1 (89) £2,000

— 1873. - Paris 2 vols. 8vo, contemp half mor by Petitot; scratched, extremities worn. With frontis & 12 plates. Some foxing. cb Oct 17 (318) $130

— 1883. - Contes. Paris One of 100 on Japon. 2 vols bound in 8. 4to, half mor; rubbed. Plates in varying number of states from 1 to 29, to a total number of impressions of c.1,580. S Nov 21 (235) £2,200

— [c.1885]. - Fables. Paris: Garnier Illus by Grandville. 8vo, contemp half mor; corners rubbed. pba Aug 22 (774) $75

— 1931. - The Fables. L. One of 525. Illus by Stephen Gooden. 2 vols. Vellum. sg Sept 14 (173) $275

Anr copy. Vellum; bowed. sg Feb 15 (148) $250

— 1948. - Selected Fables. NY One of 85. Illus by Alexander Calder. 4to, unsewn as issued in half mor folder. sg Sept 14 (86) $450

— Les Amours de Psyche et de Cupidon. Paris, 1791. 4to, contemp calf gilt. With 4 plates. Marginal browning. Fuerstenberg - Schaefer copy. S Dec 7 (337) £750

Anr Ed. Paris, 1795 [An III]. 4to, mor gilt by Chambolle-Duru. With port in 2 states (after letters & reversed after letters hand-colored) & 8 plates, 6 of them in 4 states, 1 in 3 states & 1 in 2 states. With additional port & suite of 8 reduced plates & 6 plates before letters. L.p. copy on papier velin. Fuerstenberg - Schaefer copy. S Dec 7 (338) £4,000

Anr Ed. Paris, 1809. Folio, contemp lea-backed bds; spine ends & corners worn. With 32 plates after Raphael. Some foxing & soiling. pba Nov 30 (14) $325

**La Fosse, Jean Charles de.** See: Delafosse, Jean Charles

**La Garde, Pierre de**

— Journal de musique.... Paris, 1758. 12 vols in 1 (all issued). Oblong 4to, contemp mor gilt; corners worn. Lacking 1 engraved title; tp creased & dustmarked; some creasing at ends. 8 vols inscr at foot of 1st page of music. S Dec 1 (193) £1,300

**La Gueriniere, Francois Robichon de**

— Ecole de cavalerie.... Paris, 1733. Folio, contemp calf; repaired. With engraved title, frontis & 23 plates. 1st folding plate with 3 tears in upper margin, affecting surface; ink sketch in inner margin of H1r; plate facing p. 78 detaching. Fuerstenberg - Schaefer copy. S Dec 7 (343) £1,600

**La Harpe, Jean Francois de, 1739-1803**

— Journal historique de l'etablissement des francais a la Louisiane. New Orleans, 1831. 8vo, contemp calf gilt; repaired. Tear at gutter of quire 7; some foxing. Thomas Winthrop Streeter's annotated copy. Engelhard copy. CNY Jan 26 (188) $2,000

— Tangu et Felime, poeme. Paris: Pissot, 1780. 8vo, 19th-cent mor gilt by Cuzin. With title & 4 plates. Fuerstenberg - Schaefer copy. S Dec 7 (344) £220

## La Loubere, Simon de, 1642-1729

— Du Royaume de Siam. Paris, 1691. 1st Ed. 2 vols. 12mo, 18th-Cent tree calf; worn. With 38 plates (15 double-page), & 2 folding maps. Sir Thomas Phillipps' copy. Inscr MHC.. S Oct 26 (588) £460 [Squire]

## La Maout, Emmanue, d.1877

— Histoire naturelle des oiseaux. Paris, 1853. 4to, contemp half calf; rubbed. With 35 plates (15 hand-colored). Lacks half-title. S Oct 27 (746) £310 [Egglishaw]

## La Marche, Olivier de

— El Cavallero determinado.... Antwerp: Plantin, 1591. 8vo, 19th-cent mor gilt. With 21 full-page etchings. Lacking O4; washed & pressed; some residual soiling & staining. Schaefer copy. P Nov 1 (137) $1,500

— Le Chevalier delibere. Barcelona: Claudio Bornat, 1566. Bound with: Perez de Guzman, Fernan. Exemplo para bien biuir. Lisbon: Widow of German Gallard, Mar 1564. 4to, contemp mor with arms of Aragon; spine ends & corners repaired. 1st work with 20 full-page woodcuts. Some text browning. Schaefer copy. P Nov 1 (136) $8,500

## La Martiniere, Pierre Martin

— Nouveau voyage vers le Septentrion... des Norwegiens, des Lapons.... Amst., 1708. 12mo, contemp sheep; worn. With frontis & 17 plates. sg Mar 7 (283) $325

## La Mesangere, Pierre de, 1761-1831

— Voyages en France. Paris: Chaigneau aine, [1796-98]. 4 vols. 12mo, 19th-cent calf. Ptd on papier velin. With frontis & 31 ports & plates. Salomons - Fuerstenberg - Schaefer copy. S Dec 8 (651) £300

## La Mothe Langon, Etienne Leon de, Baron —& Others

— Biographie Toulousaine, ou dictionnaire historique des personnages.... Paris, 1823. 2 vols. 8vo, contemp calf; rubbed. Minor foxing. O Mar 26 (143) $140

## La Motte-Fouque, Friedrich H. C. de, 1777-1843

— Undine. L, 1909. Illus by Arthur Rackham. 4to, orig cloth, in dj with spine ends repaired; bdg extremities rubbed. Ck May 31 (135) £150

Anr copy. Orig cloth. Sgd & dated 27 Nov 1909 & with ink drawing of a mermaid. P Dec 12 (151) $1,200

One of 1,000. Orig vellum gilt. b Sept 20 (591) £220

Anr copy. Orig vellum gilt; soiled. b May 30 (450) £220; sg Feb 15 (256) $500

## La Noue, Jean Baptiste Sauve de, 1701-60

— La Coquette corrigee, comedie.... Paris: Duchesne, 1757. 12mo, contemp red mor gilt with arms of Mme de Pompadour; corners bumped. Fuerstenberg - Schaefer copy. S Dec 7 (350) £2,800

## La Perouse, Jean Francois Galaup de, 1741-88

— Resa omkring Jorden af.... Stockholm, 1799. Bound with: Johan Hunters Resa til Nya sodra Wallis.... Stockholm, 1797. 8vo, contemp half calf. b Mar 20 (115) £280

— Voyage de la Perouse autor du monde.... Paris, 1797. 1st Ed. 5 vols, including Atlas. 4to & folio, orig bds; joints & extremities worn, spines sunned, atlas spine repaired. With frontis in vol I; atlas with title & 69 illus. Page edges in atlas foxed & darkened; 1 chart creased. Robbins copy. pba Mar 21 (187) $15,000

— Voyage de La Perouse autour du monde.... Paris, 1797. 5 vols, including Atlas. 4to & folio, orig half turkey mor. With frontis in Vol I; Atlas with engraved title & 69 plates & charts. Creases to 2 plates. pba Feb 13 (106) $8,500

Anr Ed. Paris, 1797 [An V]. Atlas vol only. Folio, contemp calf gilt. With engraved title & 69 plates, maps or charts. S Nov 30 (220) £4,200

Anr Ed. L, 1799. 3 vols, including Atlas. 4to & folio, contemp half calf; worn. With port in Vol I & Atlas with engraved title, 31 maps & charts (1 hand-colored in outline) & 33 plates. Text vols lacking half-titles; foxed. S June 27 (264) £1,800

— A Voyage Round the World in the Years 1785.... L, 1798. Atlas vol only. Contemp half calf; worn & broken. With port & 69 plates, many double-page. Some foxing, soiling & dampstaining. cb Oct 17 (238) $2,750

Anr copy. 3 vols. 8vo, later cloth; spine ends worn. With 42 maps & plates. Hole in 1 leaf; 1 plate torn along fold. CE June 12 (220) $700

Anr copy. Lea; rebacked, spines driec, cover of Vol II detached, others starting. With port & 39 (of 41) maps & plates. Library markings. CE June 12 (221) $200

Anr copy. Modern half calf. With 42 plates & maps. Larson copy. pba Sept 28 (128) $1,500

Anr copy. ("The Voyage of M. de la Perouse round the World....") Atlas vol only. Disbound. Lacking 1 plate. S June 13 (568) £950

Anr Ed. L, 1799. 3 vols including Atlas. 4to & folio, contemp calf gilt; rebacked in modern calf. With port, engraved title & 69 plates. Some foxing; lacking half-titles. pba Feb 13 (107) $3,500

Anr copy. Atlas vol only. Early half sheep; worn. With engraved title & 69 plates & maps. Some dampstaining. sg Dec 7 (24) $3,200

Anr Ed. Amst. & NY, 1968. ("A Voyage Round the World Performed in the Years 1785-1788....") 3 vols, including Atlas. 4to & folio, syn. pba July 25 (176) $225

Anr copy. 2 vols, without Atlas. 4to, bds. sg Mar 7 (139) $100

— A Voyage Round the World Performed in the Years 1785-1788.... Amst., [1968]. Facsimile of 1799 4to English Ed. 2 vols & atlas. 4to & folio, bds. With frontis port, & 69 plates & maps (1 folding). Larson copy. pba Sept 28 (129) $95

**La Porte, Joseph de, 1713-79**
See also: D'Hebrail & La Porte
— Nouvelle Bibliotheque d'un Homme de Gout..... Paris, 1777. 4 vols. 12mo, contemp calf; rubbed. O Mar 26 (144) $200

**La Roche Lacarelle Library, J. J. S., Baron de**
— [Sale Catalogue] Catalogue des livres rares. Paris, 1888. Folio, orig wraps; worn & soiled. L.p. copy. O Mar 26 (145) $150

**La Roche-Aymon, A. C. E. P. de**
— Des troupes legeres, ou reflexions sur l'organisation. Paris, 1817. 8vo, contemp mor by Purgold, sgd. With half-title, 2 folding hand-colored plans. Some marginal worming. S Oct 27 (1135) £800 [Bayntun]

**La Rochefoucauld Liancourt, Francois Alexandre Frederic, 1747-1827**
— Voyage dans les Etats-Unis d'Amerique.... Paris, 1799 [An VII]. 8 vols. 8vo, contemp calf gilt; joints & extremities rubbed, upper inner hinge of Vol I cracked. With 3 folding maps. University of Siberia Library inkstamps on titles. Engelhard copy. CNY Jan 26 (168) $2,400

**La Roerie, G. —& Vivielle, J.**
— Navies et Marins de la Rame a l'Helice. Paris, [1930]. 2 vols. Folio, pictorial wraps; worn, spines chipped. pba July 25 (177) $140

**La Salle, Nicolas de.** See: Caxton Club

**La Salle, Rene Robert Cavelier, Sieur de.** See: Caxton Club

**La Serre, Jean Puget de.** See: Puget de la Serre, Jean

**La Valliere, L. C. de la Baume-le-Blanc, Duc de.** See: De Bure, Guillaume Francois

**La Ville sur Illon, Bernard Germain Etienne Lacepede de.** See: Lacepede, Bernard de la Ville sur Illon

**Laar, G. van**
— Magazijn van Tuin-Sieraaden. Amst., [1802]. 4to, bds; needs rebdg. With 190 hand-colored plates. sg June 13 (231) $2,800

**Labadens, J. B.**
— Nouvelle Methode pour apprendre a jouer du violon.... Paris, [c.1770-1800]. Folio, half mor by Perticaroli of Rome, wraps bound in. With 3 plates. Some worming near beginning. S Dec 1 (194) £2,500

**Labbe, Philippe, 1607-67**
— Thesaurus epitaphiorum veterum ac recentium selectorum ex antiquis inscriptionibus.... Paris, 1686. 8vo, contemp vellum; front joint cracked. sg Mar 21 (179) $130

**Labillardiere, Jacques Julien Houton de, 1755-1834**
— Relation du voyage a la recherche de La Perouse.... Paris, An VIII [1800]. 2 vols. 4to, orig half turkey mor. With engraved title, double-page map & 43 plates. Atlas dampstained on lower corners of each page, just touching corners of most images. pba Feb 13 (110) $3,750
— Voyage in Search of La Perouse. L, 1800. 2 vols. 8vo, contemp bds; rebacked in calf. With folding map & 45 plates. Folding chart with repaired tear & crease tear; minor foxing & corner wear. pba Feb 13 (111) $1,300

**Laborde, Alexandre L. J., Comte de, 1774-1842**
— Description des nouveaux jardins de la France.... Westmean: Gregg, 1971. Folio, cloth. Photofacsimile of 1808 Ed. wa Dec 14 (490) $80
— Voyage pittoresque et historique de l'Espagne. Paris: Didot, 1806-20. 2 vols in 4. Folio, 19th-cent half mor gilt; scuffed. With 342 plates only. Vol IV dampstained throughout with maps of Spain mildewed. sg May 9 (361) $5,800

**Laborde, Jean Benjamin de**
— Choix de Chansons, mises en musique. Paris, 1773. 1st Ed. 4 vols. 8vo, contemp red mor gilt by Derome le jeune with his ticket & with added arms of Heraclee Elisabeth Rhingarde de Montboissier-Beaufort-Canillac. Engraved throughout, with port, dedication leaf, 3 frontises & 100 illusts. Fuerstenberg - Schaefer copy. S Dec 7 (322) £2,200

**Laborde, Jean Benjamin de —& Zurlauben, Beat Fidel Antoine, Baron de**
— Tableaux topographiques, pittoresques, physiques, historiques, moraux...de La Suisse. Paris, 1780-86. 5 vols. Folio, 19th-cent mor gilt by Zaehnsdorf. With 1 engraved title, frontis, 328 views on 220 plates, 8 maps & plans, 11 plates of ports & 8 plates of medals, vases, etc. All plates are before letters with Ms captions & with 309 eaux-fortes. Some of the eaux-fortes laid down or inlaid; small repairs in margins; some plates browned in margins. Fuerstenberg - Schaefer copy. S Dec 7 (323) £40,000

**Laborde, Leon de, 1807-69**
— Journey through Arabia Petraea to Mount Sinai.... L, 1836. 8vo, half calf; upper cover detached. With folding map, frontis & 26 plates. Some spotting. b Sept 20 (344) £190
1st English Ed. 8vo, 19th-Cent polished calf. With 2 maps (1 folding), & 26 plates. Some discoloration. S Oct 26 (125) £400 [Zioni]

**Laboureur, Jean Emile**
— Chansons Madecasses. Paris, 1920. One of 400. Vellum gilt with more overlay, by Rose Adler, 1935. With 30 colored wood-engravings. b May 30 (559) £1,200
— Types de l'Armee Americaine en France. Paris, 1918. One of 25. Half mor, orig wraps bound in. With 11 woodcuts, including cover illust. sg Feb 15 (182) $175

**Laboureur, Jean Emile —& Cazotte, Jacques, 1720-92**
— The Devil in Love.... L, 1925. One of 365. 8vo, half cloth. With frontis & 5 plates. sg Feb 15 (181) $60

**LaBree, Ben**
— The Confederate Soldier in the Civil War. Louisville, 1895. Folio, orig cloth; worn & stained, frayed, hinges broken, prelims loose. wa Feb 1 (93) $55

**Lace, T. G.**
— Ode on the Present State of Europe. Liverpool, 1811. 4to, disbound. b Dec 5 (202) £240

**Lacepede, Bernard de la Ville sur Illon, Comte de, 1756-1825**
— Essai sur l'electricite naturelle et artificielle. Paris, 1781. 2 vols. 8vo, contemp wraps; pp. 193-204 in Vol I misbound. Some stains in margins; library stamp on titles. S June 12 (305) £160
— Histoire naturelle de Lacepede. Paris, 1839. 2 vols. 8vo, half mor; extremities rubbed. With 72 (on 36) hand-colored plates. Some foxing. pba Nov 30 (210) $140
— Histoire naturelle des poissons. Paris, 1798-1803. 5 (of 6) vols; lacking Vol 5/1. 4to, contemp sheep; spines worn. With 103 plates only. Text foxed. sg May 9 (343) $700

**Lackington, James, 1746-1815**
— Memoirs of the First Forty-Five Years of the Life of.... L, 1803. 12mo, later mor; joints rubbed. With port & extra hand-colored plate. sg Feb 8 (313) $175
— 13th Ed. L, [n.d.]. 8vo, contemp calf; becoming disbound. bba May 9 (65) £55 [Mandelbrote]

**Laclos, Pierre A. F. Choderlos de, 1741-1803**
— Les Liaisons dangereuses. Londres [Paris], 1796. 2 vols. 8vo, contemp mor gilt. On papier fin verge. With 2 frontises & 12 plates. Some foxing; 3d plate inserted in Vol I; lacking final blank in Vol II; tears in margins of 4th plate; some marginal tears. Fuerstenberg - Schaefer copy. S Dec 7 (352) £480
— Anr Ed. Paris: Black Sun Press, 1929. One of 1,000. Illus by Alastair. 2 vols. 4to, wraps; some soiling. With 14 colored plates. sg Feb 15 (57) $200

**Lacombe, Jean de, Sieur de Quercy.** See: Golden Cockerel Press

**Lacordaire, Henri Dominique**
— Vie de Saint Dominique. Paris, 1919. One of 330. Illus by Maruice Denis. 2 vols. 4to, mor extra with lettered silvered disc pattern designed by Pierre Legrain & executed by Rene Kieffer, for Georges E. Lang, 1920. Vol I with 20 large woodcuts, 19 woodcut headpieces & 7 tailpieces, all ptd in color; Vol II with color progressions of same in 2 to 6 states. C May 1 (87) £9,000

**Lacretelle, Jacques de**
— Lettres espagnoles. Paris, 1926. One of 25 on japon imperiale with 2 suites of the etchings. Illus by Marie Laurencin. Calf extra by Rose Adler, 1928. S May 16 (23) £15,000
— Pressentiments. Paris, 1930. One of 15 on japon imperial with additional suite in black only. Illus by Marie Laurencin. Half mor, orig wraps bound in. With 6 plates. S Nov 21 (237) £2,100

**Lacroix, Frederic**
— Les Mysteres de la Russie. Paris, 1845. 8vo, half mor; extremities rubbed. Some foxing. sg Mar 7 (136) $110

**Lactantius, Lucius Caecilius Firmianus**
— Opera. Venice: Johannes de Colonia & Johannes Manthen, 27 Aug 1478. Folio, vellum bds. Type 8R:109R, 110 Greek, 37 lines. Rubricated. With illuminated floriated initial in gold leaf, blue & green with floral borderpiece in lower margin in colors & gilt highlighting. Epitome bound after quire z. Contemp marginalia in red & violet inks & in brown ink on blank leaves at end. Marginal worming & dampstaining. 228 leaves. Goff L-9. P June 5 (287) $17,000
— Anr Ed. Venice: Bonetus Locatellus for Octavianus Scotus, 11 Oct 1494. Folio, contemp blind-tooled lea over wooden bds with brass catches & clasps; spine pitted & wormed, recased. Worming in gutters through 1st half of vol; last leaf torn & repaired with loss at top. 90 leaves. Goff L-12. sg Mar 21 (181) $900
— Anr Ed. Venice: Simon Bevilaqua, [1497]. Folio, early vellum; worn & soiled, hinges cracked. Some soiling; lacking final blank. 139 (of 140) leaves; lacking final blank. Goff L-13. cb Feb 14 (2519) $1,100

**Lada-Mocarski, Valerian**
— Bibliography of Books on Alaska Published before 1868. New Haven, 1968. 4to, orig cloth, in dj. bba Oct 5 (396) £200 [Forest]; ds July 27 (107) $300; pba Feb 13 (112) $250

**Ladies'...**
— The Ladies' Wreath; an Illustrated Annual.... NY, 1848-49. 8vo, orig cloth. pba Aug 22 (795) $55

**Laennec, Rene Theophile Hyacinthe, 1781-1826**
— De l'auscultation mediate.... Paris, 1819. 1st Ed. 2 vols. 8vo, contemp half calf; joints of Vol I split at head. With 4 folding plates. S Mar 29 (701) £1,600

**Laet, Johannes de, 1593-1649**
— Novus Orbis, seu descriptionis Indiae occidentalis.... Leiden: Elzevir, 1633. 1st Ed in Latin. Folio, contemp calf; library label at foot of spine, rubbed, joints weak. With engraved title & 14 double-page folding maps. Some soiling & browning; Dd5 torn. Essex copy. S June 27 (196) £4,800
— Persia, seu Regni Persici Status, variaque itinera in atque per Persiam. Leiden: Elzevir, 1647. 2d Edd. 8vo, contemp calf; rebacked. With engraved title & 8 woodcuts. b May 30 (160) £130

**Lafayette, Marie Joseph Paul Yves Roch Gilbert du Motier, Marquis de, 1757-1834**
— Memoirs.... NY, 1825. 12mo, contemp sheep; extremities rubbed. sg Oct 26 (199) $225

**Lafayette, Marie Joseph Paul Yves Roch Gilbert du Motier, Marquis de, 1757-1834 —& Jefferson, Thomas, 1743-1826**
— The Letters of Lafayette and Jefferson. Balt. & Paris, 1929. One of 800. Ed by Gilbert Chinard. Bookplate of Monticello Museum. pba Apr 25 (337) $65

**Lafever, Minard**
— The Architectural Instructor.... NY, 1856. 4to, orig cloth; rebacked in calf, edges worn, stain at 1 corner. Some browning & foxing; recent repairs. bbc Dec 18 (169) $500
— The Beauties of Modern Architecture. NY, 1855. 4to, half mor; front cover discolored. With 48 plates. pba Aug 8 (231) $120

**Lafontaine, Gary**
— Trout Flies. Helena, [1993]. One of 250. 4to, half lea, in slipcase with built-in sunken mount containing 3 hand-tied flies; worn. O Feb 6 (144) $250

**Lafont-Pouloti, Esprit Paul de**
— Nouveau Regime pour les Haras. Turin, 1787. 8vo, early 19th-cent half calf gilt. With frontis & folding plate. sg Mar 7 (487) $200

**Lagniet, Jacques**
— Le troisieme livre des proverbes contenant la vie des geux. Paris, [c.1657-63]. 4to, modern half calf. With 41 plates. Some spotting; 1 plate cut down & mtd. S Nov 30 (276) £900

**Lago, Luciano —& Rossit, Claudio**
— Pietro Coppo: Le "Tabulae" (1524-1526). Trieste, [1984-86]. 2 vols. 4to, half syn. sg May 9 (17) $325

**Lahde, Gerhard Ludvig**
— Branden i Kiobenhavn d: 5.6 og 7, Iuny 1795. Copenhagen, 1795. Modern calf gilt. With engraved title having hand-colored vignet, 1 folding plan, 1 hand-colored plan & 7 hand-colored plates. S Nov 30 (03) £800

**Lahontan, Louis Armand, Baron de, 1666-1715**
— New Voyages to North America. L, 1735. 2 vols. 8vo, recent calf. With 4 maps & 16 plates. 1 map bound upside down; stamp on ptg of tp mostly removed; trimmed, affecting neatline of Newfoundland. wa Feb 29 (413) $850

**Laing, Alexander, 1903-76**
— The Cadaver of Gideon Wyck. By a Medical Student. NY, [1934]. In dj with tear & edgewear. sg June 20 (205) $150

**Laing, John, 1809-80.** See: Halkett & Laing

**Lairesse, Gerard de, 1641-1711**
— Principles of Drawing. L, 1773. 4to, cloth; def. With 50 (of 60) plates. Marginal tears; 2 plates with ink stains. Sold w.a.f. b Jan 31 (181) £80

**Lake, Atwell**
— Narrative of the Defence of Kars.... L, 1857. 8vo, contemp calf, armorial bdg; worn. With folding panorama, litho plan & 5 tinted litho plates. Plan torn; some spotting to plates. b Sept 20 (345) £65

**Lalande, Michel Richard de**
— Motets.... Paris, 1729-30-[33]. 1st Issue. 21 vols in 7. Folio, calf; not uniform, Vol I rebacked, worn, some tears. Port browned; Ms annotations to titles; library stamps. S Dec 1 (195) £7,500

**Lalande, Michel Richard de —& Destouches, Andre Cardinal**
— Les Elemens, ballet danse par le Roy, dans son palais des Thuilleries.... Paris, 1742. 2d Ed. Oblong 4to, contemp calf; spine ends def. Engraved throughout. Some staining. S Dec 1 (196) £550

**Lally Tollendal, Thomas Arthur de, Count**
— Discours choisis parmi ceux prononces a la chambre des pairs. Paris, 1820. 8vo, contemp mor gilt with monogram of George IV; extremities worn. CE Sept 27 (55) $400

**Lama, Giuseppe de**
— Vita del Cavaliere Giambattista Bodoni.... Parma, 1816. 2 vols. 4to, later half mor gilt; minor scuff to spine. Some foxing. bba May 9 (11) £280 [O'Keefe]

**Lamarck, Jean Baptiste de, 1744-1829**
— Systeme des animaux sans vertebres.... Paris, 1801. 8vo, orig paper bds; rubbed, corners bumped. With 8 tables, 6 of them folding. Dampstaining to 1st 4 leaves; outer margins spotted; lower blank corners of pp 425-32 & fore-margin of addenda leaf torn away. CNY May 17 (28) $2,600

**Lamartine, Alphonse de, 1790-1869**
— Souvenirs, impressions, pensees et paysages. Paris, 1835. 4 vols. 12mo, contemp half calf. With port, 2 plates, 2 folding maps & 1 folding table. Some foxing. S Oct 26 (126) £300 [Makshaff]

**Lamb, A. C.**
— Dundee, its Quaint and Historic Buildings.... Dundee, 1895. One of 16 on Japanese paper. Folio, orig mor gilt, in mahogany cabinet. pnE May 15 (254) £620

**Lamb, Charles, 1775-1834**
See also: Gregynog Press
— Album Verses.... L, 1830. 1st Ed. 12mo, mor extra by Sangorski & Sutcliffe, 1919. b Dec 5 (31) £520
— A Dissertation upon Roast Pig. Rochester: Printing house of Leo Hart, 1932. One of 950. Illus by Wilfred Jones; typography by Will Ransom; Chinese characters by Sang Ho. Half vellum. pba Aug 22 (796) $55

— Elia. L, 1823. 1st Ed, 2d Issue. 8vo, mor extra by Riviere. wd May 8 (67) $175
— A Masque of Days.... L, 1901. Illus by Walter Crane. 4to, orig half cloth; some wear & soiling. Some soiling. F June 20 (676) $160
 Anr copy. Orig half cloth; worn. sg Sept 21 (140) $120
— Specimens of English Dramatic Poets. L, 1808. 1st Ed. 8vo, mor extra by Sangorski & sutcliffe. b Dec 5 (32) £440
— Works. L, 1870. ("The Complete Correspondence and Works....") 4 vols. 8vo, contemp calf extra; spine heads repaired. sg Feb 8 (80) $130
 Anr Ed. L, 1882. 6 vols. 8vo, half mor by Tout. pba Sept 14 (230) $200
 Mixed Ed. L, 1903-5. Ed by William Macdonald. 12 vols. Half calf. Some foxing. cb Oct 17 (280) $275

### Lamb, Charles & Mary
— Tales from Shakespeare. L, 1909. One of 750, sgd by the artist & with an extra plate. Illus by Arthur Rackham. Ck May 31 (134) £320
 Anr copy. Orig cloth; soiled, endpapers spotted. S Nov 2 (134) £250 [Toledano]

### Lamb, Dana S.
— Bright Salmon and Brown Trout. Barre, [1964]. One of 1,500. O June 25 (172) $90; pba July 11 (165) $140
— Green Highlanders and Pink Ladies. Barre, 1971. One of 1,500. O June 25 (173) $80; O June 25 (174) $90; pba July 11 (166) $140
— Not Far from the River. Barre, 1967. One of 1,500. Inscr. O June 25 (175) $130; O June 25 (176) $95
— On Trout Streams and Salmon Rivers. Barre, 1963. pba July 11 (167) $190
 One of 1,500. Orig cloth; some wear. O June 25 (177) $225; O June 25 (178) $190
— Some Silent Places Still. Barre, 1969. One of 1,500. Half cloth; some wear. O June 25 (179) $90; pba July 11 (168) $140
— Where the Pools are Bright and Deep. NY: Winchester, [1973]. One of 1,500. In dj with tear. pba July 11 (170) $50
— Wood-Smoke and Watercress. Barre, 1965. One of 1,500. Orig cloth; some wear. Inscr. O June 25 (181) $120; O June 25 (182) $100; pba July 11 (169) $140

### Lamb, Peter O. See: West & Lamb

### Lamb, Roger, 1756-1830
— An Original and Authentic Journal of Occurences during the late American War.... Dublin, 1809. 8vo, sheep gilt by J. Larkins; worn, front bd detached, rear joint split. Some foxing. Extra-illus with 30 ports. wa Feb 29 (300) $475

### Lambacher, Phillipp Jacob
— Bibliotheca Antiqua Vindobonensis Civica.... Vienna, 1750. 4to, contemp half vellum; worn. Some soiling & foxing; old library stamp on tp. O Mar 26 (146) $300

### Lambard, William, 1536-1601
— A Perambulation of Kent.... L: H. Middleton for Rafe Newbery, 1576. 1st Ed. 4to, 18th-cent half mor gilt; worn. Lacking beacons map & that of the Heptarchy. STC 15715. S Mar 28 (40) £500

### Lambert, Johann Heinrich
— Beschreibung einer mit dem Calauschen Wachse ausgemalten Farbenpyramide. Berlin, 1772. 4to, contemp bds; rubbed & soiled. With hand-colored plate. Madsen copy. S Mar 14 (227) £1,200
— Beytraege zum Gebrauche der Mathematik. Berlin, 1765-72. 3 vols in 4. 8vo, contemp sheep; spine head of Vol III worn & upper cover marked. With 32 folding plates. Library stamps on titles & some plate versos. Madsen copy. S Mar 14 (226) £2,000
— Photometria sive de mensura et gradibus luminis, colorum et umbrae. Augsburg, 1760. 8vo, contemp half calf; upper joint split. With 8 folding plates. Some browning & spotting. Madsen copy. S Mar 14 (229) £21,000
— Pyrometrie oder vom Maasse des Feuers und der Waerme. Berlin, 1779. 1st Ed. 4to, contemp half sheep; rubbed. With 8 folding plates. Tp browned. S Mar 14 (228) £460

### Lambert, Joseph I.
— One Hundred Years with the Second Cavalry. Fort Rily KS: Capper Printing Co., 1939. Owner's stamp to foot of tp. pba June 25 (151) $225

### Lambert, Samuel W.
— When Mr. Pickering Went Fishing. NY: Brick Row Bookshop, 1924. In dj. Inscr. pba July 11 (171) $55

### Lamberti, Alvise
— Osservazioni sopra alcuni lezioni della Iliade de Omero. Milan, 1813. 4to, red mor gilt with Beauharnais imperial arms, by Lodgiani. Dedication copy. Leuchtenberg copy. C Apr 3 (127) £5,000

### Lambeth...
— Lambert Faire, wherein You Have All the Bishops Trinkets Set to Sale. [L], 1641. 4to, 19th-cent half lea; rubbed & soiled. Trimmed without loss; some staining. wa Feb 29 (221) $180

### Lambeth Palace
— A List of Some of the Early Printed Books in the Archiepiscopal Library at Lambeth. L, 1843. Compiled by Samuel Roffey Maitland. 8vo, contemp half lea. O Mar 26 (169) $50

### Lambton...
— The Lambton Worm. A Legendary Tale. Gateshead, 1830. 12mo, orig ptd wraps. With woodcut frontis. Some discoloration. b Dec 5 (104) £120

**Lamesangere, Pierre**
— Costumes des femmes francaise du XII au XVIII siecle. Paris, 1900. Folio, half mor; spine repaired with contemp spine laid down, slight age-darkening. With 70 color plates. CE Nov 8 (207) $380

**Lamon, Ward Hill**
— The Life of Abraham Lincoln. Bost., 1872. 8vo, orig cloth. sg Oct 26 (217) $130

**Lamont, James, F.G.S.**
— Seasons with the Sea-horses.... NY, 1861. 8vo, orig cloth. sg Mar 7 (284) $120

**Lamotte, Bernard**
— Proust Portfolio: The France of Marcel Proust. NY, 1949. One of 100. Folio, loose as issued in cloth case. With 25 etchings. With Ls of George Macy & Letter from Bernard Lamotte. wa Dec 14 (306) $450

**Lampedusa, Giuseppe Tomasi di.** See: Limited Editions Club

**Lancaster, Albert.** See: Houzeau & Lancaster

**Lancaster, Robert Alexander, Jr.**
— Historic Virginia Homes and Churches. Phila., 1915. 4to, orig cloth; corners bumped, soiled. F Mar 28 (365) $60

**Lancisius, Giovanni Maria**
— De subitaneis mortibus libri duo. Venice: A. Poleti, 1708. 3d Ed. 4to, contemp half calf. S Mar 29 (702) £170

**Lanckoronska, Anna M. I. —& Oehler, Richard**
— Die Buchillustration des XVIII. Jahrhunderts in Deutschland, Oesterreich, und der Schweiz. Leipzig, 1932-34. 1st Ed, One of 800. 3 vols. Folio, bds; rebacked in mor. sg Apr 11 (194) $400

**Lanckoronska, Anna M. I. —& Ruemann, Arthur**
— Geschichte der deutschen Taschenbuecher und Almanach.... Munich, [1954]. One of 700. 8vo, half lea; needs rebacking. sg Apr 11 (195) $110

**Land...** See: Stephens, John

**Landauer Collection, Bella Clara**
— Bookplates from the Aeronautica Collection of Bella C. Landauer. NY, 1930. One of 60. Cloth. pba Nov 30 (24) $120

**Lander, Richard & John**
— Journal of an Expedition to Explore the Course and Termination of the Niger. L, 1832. 3 vols. 12mo, contemp half calf. pnE Sept 20 (74) £260
 1st American Ed. NY, 1832. 3 vols. 12mo, orig cloth; Vol I joints repaired. With 2 maps & 3 plates Foxed. pba Apr 25 (198) $80

**Landi, Giulio**
— L'historia del assedio di Montalcino.... Siena, 13 Nov 1553. 4to, half mor by P. Riach. Woodcut of Virgin on tp. Tp stained & with repair in fore-margin; lacking final blank. C June 26 (94) £900

**Landis, Dennis C.** See: Brown Library, John Carter

**Landon, Harry F.**
— The North Country. Indianapolis, 1932. 3 vols. 8vo, orig cloth. NH July 21 (267) $100

**Landor, A. Henry Savage**
— In the Forbidden Land: An Account of a Journey into Tibet.... NY, 1899. 2 vols. 8vo, orig cloth; worn. F Mar 28 (388) $80

**Landor, Walter Savage, 1775-1864**
See also: Limited Editions Club
— Citation and Examination of William Shakespeare. L, 1834. 1st Ed. 8vo, later mor gilt by Tout. S Apr 23 (99) £200
— Dry Sticks, Fagoted. Edin., 1858. 8vo, orig cloth. Prelims foxed. S Apr 23 (97) £80
— Literary Hours.... Liverpool, 1837. 8vo, orig cloth; spine lacking, endpapers foxed. S Apr 23 (98) £80
— Works. L, 1889. One of 25 bound in vellum. 10 vols. S Apr 23 (96) £360

**Landseer, Thomas, 1795-1880**
— Monkey-ana.... L, 1827. 6 parts in 1 vol. 4to, later half mor; def. With 24 plates in mtd india proof state. Some foxing & browning; library markings, plates unmarked. sg Dec 7 (277) $200

**Landwehr, John**
— Emblem Books in the Low Countries, 1554-1949. Utrecht, [1970]. 4to, orig cloth. sg Apr 11 (196) $120
— French, Italian, Spanish, and Portuguese Books of Devices and Emblems, 1534-1827. A Bibliography. Utrecht, [1976]. 4to, orig cloth. sg Apr 11 (200) $140
— German Emblem Books, 1531-1888: a Bibliography. Utrecht, [1972]. 4to, orig cloth. sg Apr 11 (199) $140
— Romeyn de Hooghe.... Amst., 1970. 8vo, orig cloth in dj. sg Apr 11 (197) $120
— Splendid Ceremonies: State Entries and Royal Funerals in the Low Countries.... Nieuwkoop, Leiden, 1971. 4to, orig cloth in dj; worn. sg Apr 11 (198) $110
— Studies in Dutch Books with Coloured Plates.... The Hague, 1976. 4to, cloth, in dj. Watkinson Library deaccession. sg Jan 11 (252) $100
 Anr copy. Orig cloth in dj. sg Apr 11 (201) $120

**Lane, Charles**
— Sporting Aquatints and their Engravers, 1775-1900. Leigh-on-Sea, 1978-79. One of 500. wa Dec 14 (188) $120

**Lang, Andrew, 1844-1912**
— Angling Sketches. L, 1891. 8vo, orig cloth. pba July 11 (173) $50
— The Animal Story Book. L, 1896. Illus by H. J. Ford. 8vo, orig cloth. sg Sept 21 (247) $110
— The Blue Fairy Book. L, 1889. 1st Ed. 8vo, orig cloth; front hinge starting, tear at top of spine. K Oct 1 (228) $600
— Lost Leaders. L, 1889. 1st Ed, one of 100 L.p. copies. 8vo, vellum. Perforated stamp to tp; rubber-stamps elsewhere. pba July 11 (174) $100
— Prince Charles Edward. L, 1900. One of 1,500. 4to, half vellum. bba May 30 (244) £55 [Cameron]
— The Red True Story Book. L, 1895. 8vo, orig cloth. sg Sept 21 (248) $60

**Lang, Andrew, 1844-1912 —& Others**
— A Batch of Golfing Papers. L: Simpkin, Marshall, Hamilton, Kent, [1892]. 1st Ed. - Ed by R. Barclay. Illus by John Duncan. Cloth. Some foxing to endpapers. pba Nov 9 (52) $150
Anr copy. Ed by R. Barclay. pba Nov 9 (53) $140
Ed by R. Barclay. London: Simpkin, Marshall, Hamilton, Kent, [1892]. 16mo, orig wraps; soiled, backstrip chipped. With frontis & 2 full-page illusts. S Apr 23 (107) £120

**Lang, Herbert O.**
— History of the Willamette Valley.... Portland, 1885. 8vo, orig sheep; rubbed, spine head repaired, joints tender. Tape repairs to 2 prelim leaves. pba Nov 16 (156) $85

**Lang, John D. —& Taylor, Samuel**
— Report of a Visit to Some of the Tribes of Indians located West of the Mississippi River. NY, 1843. 8vo, orig ptd front wrap only. Stamps to tp & front wrap. pba Aug 8 (93) $50

**Langeman, G. E. —& Glushko, V. P.**
— [Rockets, Their Design and Application, in Russian]. Moscow, 1935. Ptd wraps; worn & chipped. Boris Chertok's sgd copy. P Mar 16 (6) $700

**Langford, Thomas**
— Plain and Full Instructions to Raise all sorts of Fruit-Trees. L, 1696. 8vo, contemp calf; rubbed. With 2 plates. Some spotting. b Sept 20 (138) £100

**Langhorne, John, 1735-79**
— The Effusions of Friendship and Fancy. L, 1763. 2 vols. 8vo, contemp calf; rubbed. C1 in Vol I torn affecting text; some foxing & browning. bba July 18 (191) £160 [C. L. Edwards]

**Langland, William**
— The Vision of Pierce Plowman. L: O. Rogers, 21 Feb 1561. 4th Ed. 4to, mor by Sangorski & Sutcliffe. Alexander Pope's copy with 15-line holograph note. b June 28 (42) £8,000

**Langles Library, Louis Mathieu**
— Catalogue des livres, imprimes et manuscrits, composant la bibliotheque.... Paris, 1825. 3 parts in 1 vol. 8vo, half calf; worn. Price list bound in. Olschki copy. O Mar 26 (147) $190

**Langley, Batty, 1696-1751**
— The City and Country Builder's and Workman's Treasury of Designs. L, 1750. 4to, contemp calf; rebacked, worn, library bookplate on front pastedown. With 200 plates. Lacking half-title; tp stained in margin. wa Feb 29 (87) $800
Anr Ed. L, 1756. 4to, old calf; rebacked & restored. With 200 plates. Some soiling. cb Oct 17 (26) $400

**Langley, Batty & Thomas**
— The Builder's Jewel, or the Youth's Instructor and Workman's Remembrancer.... L, 1763. 4to, contemp calf; minor wear. With 99 plates. Lacking frontis; 1 plate def but without loss. Sold w.a.f. b May 30 (317) £110

**Langley, Henry G.**
— The San Francisco Directory for the Year 1860. San Francisco, 1860. 8vo, half lea; backstrip worn, hinges cracked. pba Feb 12 (277) $475
— A Street and Avenue Guide of San Francisco.... San Francisco, 1875. 16mo, cloth; front hinge cracked. Lacking map. pba Feb 12 (278) $110

**Langley, Samuel P.**
— Experiments in Aerodynamics.... Wash., 1891. 4to, orig cloth. sg Oct 19 (232) $250

**Langsdorff, Georg Heinrich von**
— Ansicht des Spanischen Etablissements in St. Francisco. Frankfurt, 1812. 6-1/4in by 7-3/4in, matted, glazed, & framed. Larson copy. pba Sept 28 (126) $500
— Bemerkungen auf einer Reise um die Welt in den Jahren 1803 bis 1807.... Frankfurt, 1812. 2 vols. 4to, orig bds; bds foxed. With 45 plates & folding sheet music. Some foxing; titles stamped. pba Feb 13 (113) $3,250
— Langsdorff's Narrative of the Rezanov Voyage to Nueva California in 1806. San Francisco, 1927. One of 260. Half bds in dj. With 1 folded map, 2 tps, & frontis port. Larson copy. pba Sept 28 (127) $170
Anr copy. Trans by Thomas C. Russell. Half cloth in dj. With folding map, 2 ports, & 5 plates. Robbins copy. Sgd by Russell. pba Mar 21 (188) $225
One of 260, sgd by translator. Half cloth, in dj. pba Apr 25 (199) $160
Anr copy. Half cloth, in dj with spine head chipped. pba Apr 25 (495) $225
Anr copy. Half cloth; stains to bottoms of bds. pba Aug 8 (94) $180
— Voyages and Travels in Various Parts of the World.... L, 1813-14. 2 vols. 4to, contemp calf gilt; rebacked. With 21 plates & folding map. Hole in margin of tp; some foxing. pba Feb 13 (114) $2,000

**Langworthy, Franklin**
— Scenery of the Plains, Mountains, and Mines.... Ogdensburgh, NY, 1855. 1st Ed. 12mo, orig cloth; rebacked & restored, cover worn. Some foxing. Larson copy. pba Sept 28 (564) $900
Anr copy. Orig cloth; corners & spine ends worn. Some fox marks. Robbins copy. pba Mar 21 (189) $1,400
Anr Ed. Princeton, 1932. Ed by Paul C. Phillips. Orig cloth in dj. With 4 plates. Larson copy. pba Sept 28 (565) $55

**Lanier, Henry W.** See: Derrydale Press

**Lankheit, Klaus**
— Der kurpfaelzische Hofbildhauer Paul Egell, 1691-1752. Munich, [1988]. 2 vols. Folio, cloth, in djs. sg Sept 7 (135) $90

**Lanman, Charles, 1819-95**
— Adventures in the Wilds of the United States and British American Provinces. Phila., 1856. 2 vols. 8vo, cloth; spotted, soiled, cloth of Vol I torn along joints. pba July 11 (413) $75
— Adventures of an Angler in Canada.... L, 1848. 8vo, cloth; worn, spine head chipped. O June 25 (183) $190
— Haw-Ho-Noo; or Records of a Tourist. Phila., 1850. 12mo, later half cloth; extremities worn, endpapers renewed. sg Oct 26 (201) $90

**Lansdale, Joe R.**
— The Two-Bear Mambo. Huntington Beach: James Cahill, 1995. One of 100. pba Aug 22 (280) $50; wa Feb 29 (61) $50

**Lanzillo, Vincenzo**
— Navigazione Atmosferica. Turin, 1875. Modern half cloth, orig wraps bound in. sg May 16 (51) $250

**Lapie, Pierre & Alexandre Emile**
— Atlas universel de geographie ancienne et moderne.... Paris, [c.1842]. Folio, half sheep; extremities worn. With 50 double-page maps, hand-colored in outline. sg Dec 7 (50) $700

**Laplace, Cyrille Pierre Theodore**
— Voyage autour du monde, par les mers de l'Inde et de Chine.... Paris, 1833-35. 5 vols text plus Album historique & Atlas hydrographique. 8vo & folio, contemp half calf; folio vols with tear to spines. With 1 folding map in Vol I, 70 plates (61 in color) in Vol V, 72 views in Album historique & 11 maps in Atlas. Some foxing to text. S June 27 (235) £13,500

**Laplace, Pierre Simon de, Marquis, 1749-1827**
— Mecanique Celeste. Bost.: I. R. Butts, 1829-39. Trans by Nathaniel Bowditch. 4 vols. 4to, orig cloth; spine ends worn, Vol I & IV covers detached, Vol III front hinge cracked. sg Oct 19 (233) $1,400

**Larbaud, Valery, 1881-1957**
— 200 Chambres, 200 Salles de Bains. The Hague: Jean Gondrexon, 1927. Ltd Ed, this copy for the Librairie Dorbon-Aine, with additional suite of the illusts. Illus by J. E. Laboureur. Mor extra by Legrain, orig wraps bound in. S Nov 21 (246) £1,300
— Beaute, mon beau souci. Paris, 1920. One of 412. Illus by J. E. Laboureur. Calf extra by Rose Adler, 1952, orig wraps bound in. With 39 plates. S Nov 30 (346) £19,000

**Lardner, Ring, 1885-1933**
— Treat 'Em Rough. Indianapolis: Bobbs-Merrill, [1918]. pba Aug 22 (282) $60

**Larkin, Philip, 1922-85**
— The Whitsun Weddings. L, 1964. In dj with small tears. Inscr to Doreen Deighton. S Dec 18 (337) £460 [Mandl]

**Larkin, Thomas Oliver, 1802-58**
— The Larkin Papers: Personal, Business, and Official Correspondence.... Berkeley, 1951-68. 10 vols (without Index). 8vo, cloth, in djs; some wear & insect damage to covers. pba Aug 22 (930) $500
1st Ed, One of 1,000. Ed by George P. Hammond. 11 vols. 8vo, orig cloth in djs. With 11 frontises. Larson copy. pba Sept 28 (566) $450

**Larrey, Dominique Jean, Baron, 1766-1842**
— Observations on Wounds, and their Complications. Phila., 1832. 8vo, old calf; upper cover detached, worn, some stains. With 2 plates. Some staining. bbc Feb 26 (440) $240

**Lartigue, J. H.**
— Boyhood Photos of J. H. Lartigue: The Family Album of a Gilded Age. [Lausanne]: Ami Guichard, [1966]. Oblong 4to, orig cloth; minor wear. sg Feb 29 (179) $325
Anr copy. Cloth. sg Apr 24 (595) $600

**Las Cases, Emmanuel, Marquis de**
— Le Sage's Historical, Genealogical, Chronological and Geographical Atlas. L, 1818. 2d Ed. Folio, contemp half lea; very worn. With 39 double-page sheets, hand-colored. Some tears & spotting. S Mar 28 (179) £150

**Lasalle, Albert de**
— L'Hotel des haricots. Paris, 1864. Illus by Edmond Morin. 8vo, contemp half mor; extremities rubbed. With title & 70 illus. Spotted. S Oct 12 (78) £200

**Lasater, Laurence M.**
— The Lasater Philosophy of Cattle Raising. El Paso, 1972. One of 295. Half lea, with unused dj to trade Ed laid in. pba July 25 (310) $75

**Lascaris, Constantinus, 1434?-1501**
— Erotemata. Milan: Dionysius Paravisinus, 30 Jan 1476. 4to, contemp half deerskin over wooden bds with orig catch only. 25 lines; type 1:117Gk, 2:118Rf. 76 leaves. Goff L-65. C Apr 3 (128) £170,000

**Lascaris, Evadne.** See: Golden Cockerel Press

648

# LAUMER

**Lasker, Emanuel, 1868-1941.** See: Fore-Edge Paintings

**Lassaigne, Jacques**
— The Ceiling of the Paris Opera. NY, [1966]. Illus by Marc Chagall. 4to, cloth, in dj. Lacking color litho from rear pocket. sg Jan 11 (96) $275; sg June 13 (111) $175
— Chagall. [Paris]: Maeght, [1957]. 4to, wraps, in browned & chipped dj. With 15 lithographs by Chagall. sg Sept 7 (88) $900
   Anr copy. Wraps. sg Jan 11 (97) $600; sg Jan 11 (98) $550; sg Jan 11 (99) $600; sg Jan 11 (100) $500
   Anr copy. Orig bdg, in dj with some loss at top of spine panel. sg June 13 (109) $1,100
— Marc Chagall, Drawings and Water Colors for the Ballet. NY, [1969]. Folio, orig cloth, in dj with wear. sg Sept 7 (89) $175
   Anr copy. Orig cloth, in dj. wa Feb 1 (317) $130
— La Plafond de l'Opera de Paris. L, 1965. Illus by Marc Chagall. 4to, orig cloth, in dj. sg Sept 7 (90) $175
   Anr copy. Orig cloth, in dj; becoming disbound. Sold w.a.f. sg June 13 (110) $130

**Lasso de la Vega, Garcia, 1539?-1616**
— Primera Parte de los Commentarios Reales.... Lisbon: Pedro Crasbeeck, 1609. 1st Ed. Folio, contemp calf; rebacked, worn. With armorial plate. Armorial plate inverted; 2K3 with hole; some brownings. S Oct 26 (510) £1,600 [Quaritch]

**Latassa y Ortin, Felix de**
— Bibliotecas Antigua y Nueva de Escritores Aragoneses.... Zaragoza, 1884-86. 3 vols. 4to, contemp calf; rubbed. O Mar 26 (148) $200

**Latham, Charles**
— In English Homes. L, 1908-9. Mixed Ed. 3 vols. Folio, cloth; extremities worn, 2 back covers loose. sg June 13 (193) $60

**Latham, John, 1740-1837**
— A General Synopsis of Birds. L, 1781-85. 3 vols in 6. Together with: Supplement to the General Synopsis.... L, 1787. And: Supplement II.... L, 1801. And: Index ornithologicus.... L, 1790. 2 vols. Together, 10 vols. 4to. One of 6, this the John North copy. Contemp russia gilt; rebacked, corners rubbed. With 142 etched plates, counter-proofs, hand-colored by Sarah Stone. With orig watercolor by Sarah Stone, Spoonbill, sgd & dated 21 Sept 1777, in accompanying mor folder. Fattorini copy. C Oct 25 (21) £24,000
   2d Ed. Winchester, 1821-28. ("A General History of Birds.") 11 vols. 4to, contemp half mor gilt by Wright. With 193 hand-colored plates. Repaired hole in Plate 9 of Vol I; some spotting. Markree Castle - Cooper - Fattorini copy. C Oct 25 (22) £2,500

**Latham, Simon**
— Falconry. L: Ric. Hodgkinsonne for Thomas Rooks, 1658. ("Lathams Faulconry, or the Faulcons Lure and Cure.") Bound with: Latham's New and Second Book of Faulconry. L: R. H. for Thomas Rooks, 1658. 8vo, 19th-cent calf. 1st work lacking final blank & with minor flaws; 2d work lacking 1st blank; some pentrials at ends. S Dec 18 (108) £700 [Way]

**Latham, Wilfrid**
— The States of the River Plate.... L, 1866. 1st Ed. 8vo, orig cloth, unopened; some wear. O Mar 5 (150) $90

**Lathrop, S. K.**
— Treasures of Ancient America. Geneva: Albert Skira, [1964]. 4to, cloth, in dj, with wrap-around band. pba July 25 (178) $70

**Latimore, Sarah B. —& Haskell, Grace C.**
— Arthur Rackham: a Bibliography. Los Angeles, 1936. One of 550. Bds. Inscr to Charley & Ray. Ck May 31 (173) £120; sg Sept 14 (312) $120

**Latini, Brunetto, 1220-95**
— Il Tesoro.... Venice: G. A. da Sabbio & brothers for N. Garanta & F. da Salo, 20 May 1528. 2d Ed. 8vo, 17th-cent vellum. Port of Latini inserted. Some quires browned & spotted; fore-margin of tp frayed. C June 26 (95) £650

**Latrobe, Charles Joseph**
— The Rambler in North America.... L, 1835. 2 vols. 12mo, orig cloth; worn, spine ends repaired, Vol I inner hinge cracked. Some foxing. wa Feb 29 (415) $110

**Lattre, Jean**
— Atlas moderne.... Paris: Lattre & Delalain, [maps dated 1762 when dated]. 4to, contemp half sheep; extremities scuffed. With engraved title, double-page plate & 35 double-page maps, partly colored in outline. Browning at folds. C Apr 3 (119) £1,300

**Laubin, Reginald & Gladys**
— The Indian Tipi. Norman OK, [1957]. In dj. pba Nov 16 (194) $50

**Lauderdale, James Maitland, 8th Earl of.** See: Maitland, James

**Laufer, Berthold, 1874-1934**
— Jade: A Study in Chinese Archaeology and Religion. Chicago, 1912. Contemp half mor. With 62 uncolored & 6 color plates. sg Sept 7 (212) $120

**Laughlin, Clarence John**
— Ghosts along the Mississippi. NY, 1948. Ltd Autographed Louisiana Ed. Folio, cloth, in worn dj. wa Feb 1 (251) $110

**Laughlin, Ledlie Irwin**
— Pewter in America.... Bost., 1940. 2 vols. Folio, cloth; some wear. O May 7 (190) $90

**Laumer, March**
— The Green Dolphin of Oz. Bellaire: Vanitas Press, [1978]. Illus by Lau Shiu-Fan. pba Jan 18 (155) $75

**Launoy, — —&**
**Bienvenu, —**
— Instruction sur la nouvelle machine...annonce dans le Journal de Paris, le 19 Avril 1784. [Paris, 1784]. 8vo, contemp wraps. sg May 16 (52) $1,000

**Laurencin, Marie, 1885-1956**
— Les Petites Filles. Paris: Paul Rosenberg, 1923. One of 250. sg Feb 15 (183) $900

**Laurens de Reyrac, Francois Philippe de.** See: Reyrac, Francois Philippe de Laurens de

**Lauretum**
— Lauretum. [Florence, c.1513-20]. 4to, 19th-cent half lea; wormhole in lower joint. With woodcut title with scene of young man amidst a group of women, he playing a viol, within border incorporating Medici arms & the title at top. C Apr 3 (129) £7,000

**Laurie, Robert —&**
**Whittle, James**
— Laurie and Whittle's New Juvenile Atlas.... L, 1808. 4to, contemp half lea; spine & corners worn. With 9 colored maps. Some wear to last leaf. CE June 15 (290) $900
— New and Elegant General Atlas. L, 1802. 4to, recent half calf. With pictorial frontis, engraved title & 48 maps, with contemp hand-coloring. S Mar 28 (180) £750

**Laut, Agnes C., 1871-1936**
— The Blazed Trail of the Old Frontier. NY, 1926. Illus by Charles M. Russell. Orig cloth; rubbed, hinges tender. pba Apr 25 (498) $75
1st Ed, One of 200. Orig buckram. Robbins copy. Sgd. pba Mar 21 (190) $340

**Lavater, Johann Kaspar, 1741-1801**
— Essays on Physiognomy. L, 1789-92. 5 vols. 4to, contemp half mor; rubbed, extremities worn, joints cracked. Minor foxing & soiling. pba Nov 30 (213) $550
Anr Ed. L, 1804. 3 vols in 4. 4to, calf gilt; front joint of Vol I cracked. pba Sept 14 (234) $350
Anr Ed. L, 1810. 3 vols in 5. 4to, contemp calf gilt; spine ends & extremities worn. Some foxing. cb June 25 (1785) $600

**Lavater, Ludwig, 1527-86**
— De spectris, lemuribus et magnis atque insolitis frugoribus.... Geneva: Vignon, 1575. 8vo, early 19th-cent half calf; front joint cracked. Margins trimmed. sg May 16 (438) $850

**Laver, Frank**
— An Australian Cricketer on Tour. L, 1905. 2 plates loose. pn Oct 12 (311) £85

**Laver, James, 1899-1975**
— A History of British and American Etching. L, 1929. One of 50. 4to, half lea. wd Nov 15 (81) $175

**Lavoisier, Antoine Laurent, 1743-94**
See also: Guyton de Morveau & Lavoisier
— Elements of Chemistry.... Edin., 1799. 4th Ed. 8vo, contemp calf; worn, spine cracked & crudely repaired with tape; lacking front flyleaves, tape repairs to hinges. With 13 folding plates & 2 folding tables. Old stamps to half-title & tp; plates foxed. pba Nov 30 (214) $95
Anr Ed. Edin., 1802. 2 vols. 8vo, contemp sheep; covers detached, spine ends chipped. With 14 folding plates & 2 folding tables. sg May 16 (198) $60
— Traite elementaire de chimie. Paris, 1789. 1st Ed, 2d Issue. Illus by Marie Lavoisier. 2 vols. 8vo, contemp calf; rubbed. With 2 folding tables, & 13 plates. Laminated repair to vol I half-title; tables & 2 plates browned; plate margins brittle; light spotting. Ck Mar 22 (161) £1,200
"Troisieme Edition". Paris, 1801. 2 vols. 8vo, orig wraps. With 2 folding tables & 13 folding plates. sg May 16 (196) $120

**Lavoisne, C. V.**
— A Complete Genealogical, Historical, Chronological, & Geographical Atlas. Phila, 1820. 2d American Ed. Folio, contemp bds; worn, covers detached. F June 20 (822) $80
Anr copy. Orig half sheep; needs rebdg. With 71 hand-colored double-page maps & tables. sg May 9 (79) $750
Anr Ed. Phila., 1821. Folio, remains of old calf; waterstained & moldy. With 32 colored maps. Sold w.a.f. wa Feb 29 (609) $250
— Lavoisne's Complete Genealogical, Historical...Atlas. L, 1814. Folio, contemp calf; rebacked, corners repaired. With 39 hand-colored tables & 26 double-page hand-colored maps. CE June 15 (291) $180

**Lawler, John**
— Book Auctions in England in the Seventeenth-Century. L, 1898. 4to, cloth; worn. L.p. copy. O Mar 26 (149) $120

**Lawless, Peter**
— The Golfer's Companion. L: J. M. Dent, [1937]. 1st Ed. - Illus by Harry Rountree. Cloth; rear joint torn. pba Nov 9 (54) $60

**Lawrance, Mary**
— A Collection of Roses from Nature. L, 1799 [1796-99]. Folio, contemp mor gilt; extremities worn, minor worming to upper hinge & gutter of front free endpaper & 1st 2 leaves. With 91 hand-colored plates, some heightened with gum arabic. Liechtenstein - Leyel - Schaefer copy. P Nov 1 (141) $47,500

**Lawrence, David Herbert, 1885-1930**
See also: Cresset Press; Grabhorn Printing; Nonesuch Press
— England My England and other Stories. NY, 1922. 1st Ed. In dj. sg Dec 14 (186) $175
— Kangaroo. L, [1923]. 1st Ed. In dj. sg Dec 14 (187) $130

— Lady Chatterley's Lover. Florence, 1928. 1st Ed, one of 1,000. Orig bds, in dj. S Dec 18 (339) £2,400 [Copus]
Anr copy. Orig bds; spine ends perished, scuffed & bumped. Browned & foxed.  wd Nov 15 (82) $225
— Letters.... L, 1932. 1st Ed, one of 525. Vellum with yapp edges.  pba Aug 22 (283) $55
— Pansies. L, 1929. One of 500. 8vo, orig wraps & glassine; torn & discolored. Inscr by Kay Dick to Kathleen Farrell. S Oct 27 (1221) £170 [Sotheran]
1st Ed, one of 250. In soiled dj with tears.  sg June 20 (209) $300
Definitive Ed, one of 500.  bba July 18 (302) £240 [Pearson]; pba June 13 (215) $325
— Psychoanalysis and the Unconscious. NY, 1921. Bds; spine chipped, extremities browned.  pba Jan 25 (189) $80
— Rawdon's Roof. L, 1928. One of 530, sgd. In dj.  sg Dec 14 (188) $300
— Tortoises. NY, 1921. 1st Ed. Bds; spine worn & chipped, front hinge starting.  pba Jan 25 (190) $90
Anr Ed. Williamsburg MA: Cheloniidae Press, 1983. One of 90. Illus by Alan James Robinson. 4to, half vellum, extra suite of plates (sgd) in cloth.  sg Dec 14 (191) $375
Anr copy. Half vellum, extra suite of plates (sgd) in cloth folder.  sg Feb 15 (71) $350
— The Virgin and the Gipsy. Florence, 1930. One of 810. In dj. Litho by Michael Wishart & 2 photos of male nudes loosely inserted.  b May 30 (439) $80
Anr Ed. L, [1930]. In rubbed & soiled dj.  pba Aug 22 (285) $100

**Lawrence, Sir Henry Montgomery, 1806-57**
— Essays, Military and Political, written in India. L, 1859. 8vo, orig cloth; shaken.  sg Mar 7 (173) $175

**Lawrence, Jerome —&**
**Lee, Robert E.**
— Inherit the Wind. NY, [1955]. In dj. Inscr by Lawrence.  sg June 20 (210) $300

**Lawrence, John**
— 45 Wood-Engravers. Wakefield: Fleece Press for Simon Lawrence, 1982. One of 350. 4to, orig half cloth.  bba May 9 (302) £130 [Cox]

**Lawrence, John, 1753-1839**
— British Field Sports. L, 1818. 8vo, contemp half lea; worn, spine chipped. With 34 plates. Foxing, browning & soiling. Sold w.a.f.  O Feb 6 (146) $425
— The History and Delineation of the Horse. L, 1809. 4to, contemp bds; soiled, extremities worn. Some foxing.  O Jan 9 (161) $160
— The Sportsman's Repository. L, 1845. 4to, orig cloth; worn, most of spine gone. Foxing & soiling. Sold w.a.f.  O Jan 9 (162) $425

**Lawrence, Richard, Artist**
— Elgin Marbles from the Parthenon at Athens.... L, 1818. Oblong folio, contemp half mor; scuffed, some scrapes & scratches. With 50 plates.  pba Nov 30 (217) $550
1st Ed. Folio, orig bds; worn, rebacked. With 50 plates. S Oct 26 (127) £650 [Basil]

**Lawrence, S. T. E.**
[-] S. T. E. Lawrence, Boxwood Blockmaker: Wood Engravings Collected in Honour of his Eightieth Birthday. Wakefield: Fleece Press for Simon Laurence, 1980. One of 250. 4to, orig half cloth.  bba May 9 (301) £140 [Cox]

**Lawrence, Sir Thomas, 1769-1830**
— Engravings from the Choicest Works of.... L, 1836. Folio, half mor; joints cracked, rubbed, soiled.  pba June 20 (216) $150

**Lawrence, Thomas Edward, 1888-1935**
See also: Golden Cockerel Press; Woolley & Lawrence
— An Essay on Flecker. L: Corvinus Press, 1937. 1st Ed, one of 30 on Canute paper. 4to, orig cloth. CE Feb 21 (159) $4,600
— The Mint. Garden City, 1936. One of 50. Folio, half vellum. A. W. Lawrence & E. M. Forster's copy. S July 11 (332) £8,000
1st Ed. L, [1955]. one of 2,000. 4to, half mor.  pba Nov 30 (218) $130
— Revolt in the Desert. L, 1927. 1st Ed, one of 315. Half pigskin, in dj. S July 11 (309) £850
Anr Ed. NY, 1927. With folding map.  pba Aug 22 (286) $70
— Seven Pillars of Wisdom. Garden City, 1935. 1st American Trade Ed, one of 750. 4to, half pigskin; rubbed. Some soiling. O Mar 5 (151) $80
Anr copy. Orig half pigskin; spine crackled.  pba Jan 25 (191) $140
1st Trade Ed. L, 1935. 5th impression. 4to, Variant bound in blue crushed mor. S July 11 (312) £240
Anr copy. Variant bound in red crushed mor. S July 11 (314) £260
One of 750. Later half calf.  pba Jan 25 (192) $70
Anr copy. Orig half pigskin. S July 11 (305) £550
Out-of-series copy marked Presentation. Orig half pigskin.  b Jan 31 (182) £320
— Sherifian Co-operation in September * Story of the Arab Movement. Cairo, 1919. Orig wraps; worn & soiled. In: A Brief Record of the Advance of the Egyptian Expeditionary Force... July 1917 to October 1918. H. Pirie-Gordon's copy. S July 11 (316) £300
— Two Arabic Folk Tales. L: Corvinus Press, 1937. One of 30. Trans by Lawrence. Folio, orig cloth. CE Feb 21 (160) $3,200

**Lawrence's copy, T. E.**
— Al-Mu'allaqat al-'ashr. Cairo, [1912]. Orig wraps. With holograph notes on vocabulary. S July 11 (320) £2,000
BLUNT, WILFRID SCAWEN. - A New Pilgrimage, and Other Poems. L, 1889. Orig cloth. Initialled by Lawrence on front endpaper & with Clouds Hill bookplate. S July 11 (326) £620
STEINGASS, F. - The Student's Arabic-English Dictionary. L, 1884. Orig cloth; recased preserving most of orig

bdg, new endpapers. Initialled in pencil on front endpaper & with note by Gerald Clauson attesting that Lawrence gave him the book in 1920. S July 11 (319) £6,100

**Lawrence, Thomas Edward, 1888-1935 —& Others**
— Carchemish. Report on the Excavations at Djerabis on Behalf of the British Museum. L, 1914-21-52. 3 vols. 4to, orig bds. S July 11 (317) £1,500

**Lawrence, William**
— Marriage by the Morall Law of God Vindicated.... L, 1680. 4to, 19th-cent half calf; rubbed. Some soiling & foxing. O Mar 5 (152) $200

**Lawrence, Sir William, 1783-1867?**
— Lectures on Physiology, Zoology, and the Natural History of Man. L, 1819. 8vo, orig bds, unopened. S June 12 (264) £320

**Lawson, John Parker, d.1852**
— Scotland Delineated in a Series of Views.... L, 1854 [engraved title dated 1847]. Folio, early half mor gilt; extremities worn. With 25 plates only. Foxing & soiling; text & prelims lacking. sg May 9 (379) $175

**Lawson, Thomas W.** See: Thompson & Lawson

**Lay, William —&**
**Hussey, Cyrus M.**
— A Narrative of the Mutiny on Board the Ship Globe.... New London, 1828. 1st Ed. 8vo, calf. Foxed; old stain on some leaves. K Feb 11 (241) $750

**Layard, Sir Austen Henry, 1817-94**
See also: Onassis copy, Jacqueline Bouvier Kennedy
— Discoveries in the Ruins of Nineveh and Babylon. L, 1853. 1st Ed. 8vo, contemp calf; worn. With frontis, 2 folding maps & 13 plates & plans. Tear to 1 plate. b May 30 (278) £70

Anr copy. Cloth; discolored. With half title, 5 folding maps, & 11 plates. S Oct 26 (130) £160 [Jaidah] 1st American Ed. NY, 1853. 8vo, orig cloth. Some foxing. pba July 25 (416) $110
— Early Adventures in Persia, Susiana and Babylonia.... L, 1887. 2 vols. 8vo, orig cloth. With frontises, 2 plates & 3 folding maps. b Sept 20 (347) £120

**Layard, George Somes, 1857-1925.** See: Spielmann & Layard

**Lazarnick, George**
— Netsuke & Inro Artists.... Honolulu, [1981]. 2 vols. 4to, cloth, in mylar djs. Inscr. sg June 13 (233) $225

**Le Bas, Philippe, 1794-1860**
— Voyage archeologique en Grece et en Asie Mineure. Paris, 1888. With: Correspondance... Paris, 1898. 2d Ed. 4to & 8vo, half mor & half calf; calf rubbed. S Oct 26 (131) £460 [Tantoulos]

**Le Beau, Charles**
— Eloge de M. le comte d'Argenson. Paris: Panckoucke, 1765. 8vo, contemp red mor gilt with arms of Antoine Rene d'Argenson, marquis de Paulmy. With port. Fuerstenberg - Schaefer copy. S Dec 7 (355) £800

**Le Blanc, Jean Bernard, Abbe, 1707-81**
— Lettres.... Lyons: Aime Delaroche, 1758. 5th Ed. 3 vols. 12mo, contemp red mor gilt with arms of the Marquise de Pompadour. Lacking frontis. Fuerstenberg - Schaefer copy. S Dec 7 (356) £800

**Le Brun, Charles, 1619-90**
— Le Grand Escalier du Chateau de Versailles des Ambassadeurs. Paris, [1725]. Folio, contemp bds; spotted, spine damaged at foot. Engraved throughout, with 24 plates, some double-page. Small stamp VD at foot of tp. S June 27 (281) £1,000

**Le Brun, Charles, 1619-90 —&**
**Le Sueur, Eustache**
— Galerie de Monsieur le President Lambert representant l'apotheose d'Hercule. Paris, [c.1746]. 2 parts in 1 vol. Folio, contemp calf gilt. With double-page frontis, engraved double-page dedication & 36 (of 37) plates, some of them double-page. Lacking frontis & dedication leaf in Part 2 & tp in Part 1. Fuerstenberg - Schaefer copy. S Dec 7 (357) £1,400

**Le Brun, Cornelius**
— Reizen over Moskovie, door Persie en Indie. Amst., 1711. Folio, contemp vellum; joints starting. With port, frontis, 69 folding plates & 42 full-page plates. P June 5 (288) $2,500
— Travels into Muscovy, Persia.... L, 1737. 2 vols. Folio, contemp calf; rebacked. With frontis port, 3 double-page maps & 118 plates. Some staining to lower margins & corners, occasionally intruding into plate or text. pba Feb 13 (115) $1,700
— Voyage au Levant. Delft, 1700. Folio, contemp calf gilt in the style of Albert Magnus; extremities rubbed, lower hinge cracked. With engraved titles, port & 97 plates, ptd in color or a la poupee & finished by hand. Lacking 1 blank; some foxing; lower corner torn from plate 174/175. P Nov 1 (142) $40,000

Collected Ed. Paris, 1725. 5 vols. 4to, contemp calf; joints worn. With port, 5 maps, & 85 plates. Discolored. S Oct 26 (22) £820 [Fisch]

**Le Bruyn, Cornelius.** See: Le Brun, Cornelius

**Le Carre, John**
— A Perfect Spy. L, [1986]. One of 250. Half cloth. sg Dec 14 (55) $130

**Le Cat, Claude Nicolas, 1700-68**
— Traite de la couleur de la peau humaine.... Amst., 1765. 8vo, modern half cloth. With frontis & duplicate retouched plate of the frontis. Small wormholes affecting text sheet D to end. Fuerstenberg - Schaefer copy. S Dec 7 (358) £550

## Le Clerc, Chrestien, 1641-99?
— Nouvelle Relation de la Gaspesie.... Paris, 1691. 12mo, contemp calf; rebacked, orig spine retained. sg Oct 26 (204) $425

## Le Clerc, Jean, 1657-1736
— Histoire des Province-Unies des Pays Bas. Amst., 1737-28-36. 4 vols in 2. Folio, 18th-cent calf. Some browning. S Mar 28 (519) £280

## Le Clerc, Sebastien, 1637-1714
— Pratique de la geometrie.... Paris, 1691. 8vo, contemp calf; rubbed. With frontis & 82 plates. C6 repaired; browning & soiling. S Mar 14 (223) £150

## Le Comte, Louis Daniel, 1655-1728
— Memoirs and Observations Topographical made in a late Journey through the Empire of China. L, 1697. 1st Ed in English. 8vo, contemp calf. With 4 plates & folding table. sg Mar 7 (141) $800

## Le Conte, Joseph, 1823-1901
— The Autobiography.... NY, 1903. 1st Ed, One of 500. Ed by William Dallam Armes. Half mor; spine head torn, chipped, mor rubbed. Robbins copy. pba Mar 21 (191) $75
— A Journal of Ramblings through the High Sierras of California by the "University Excursion Party." San Francisco: Frances & Valentine, 1875. 12mo, cloth. With 9 orig albumen photos laid on captioned leaves. Edwards - Moffitt - Larson copy. pba Feb 12 (96) $7,500

3d Ed. San Francisco: The Sierra Club, 1930. 12mo, half cloth. With port, facsimile of orig tp & 3 other plates. pba Feb 12 (97) $80; pba Apr 25 (501) $85
— A Journal of the Ramblings Through the High Sierras of California by the "University Excursion Party." San Francisco: Francis & Valentine, 1875. 1st Ed. 12mo, orig cloth; spine darkened, spine ends & corners rubbed, cover spotted. With 9 orig albumen photos. Robbins copy. pba Mar 21 (192) $5,500

## Le Corbusier, 1887-1965
— Des Canons, Des Munitions? Merci! Des Logis... S.V.P. Paris, 1938. Oblong 4to, orig pictorial bds; corners worn. sg Apr 18 (110) $850

## Le Dran, Henri Francois, 1685-1770
— Bergleighung der mancherley Manieren den Stein aus der Blasen zu Zeichen. Berlin, 1733. 12mo, contemp wraps; backstrip chipped with fragment lacking at both ends, joints split. With 5 folding plates. Some soiling & foxing; dampstain to gutter at end. wa Feb 29 (191) $100

## Le Fevre, Jacques d'Etaples, d.1537
— Artificialis introductio per modum Epitomatis in decem libros Ethicorum Aristotelis adiectis elucidata commentariis.... Paris: Wolfgang Hopyl & Henri Estienne, 7 May 1502. Folio, recent bdg using a vellum antiphonal leaf. Roman types. Single wormhole affecting an occasional letter. Soudek copy. P Dec 12 (4) $7,000

— In politica Aristotelis introductio.... Paris: Simon de Colines, 1 July 1535. Bound with: Aristotle. Politicorum libri octo.... Paris: Simon de Colines, 1543. Folio, early vellum with yapp edges. Roman types. Stamp on 1st title of the Portuguese royal arms; tear at inner margin of last 10 leaves not affecting text. Soudek copy. P Dec 12 (21) $1,100
— Liber trium virorum & trium spiritualium virginum. Paris: Henri Estienne, 31 May 1513. Folio, modern half mor. Roman types; tp woodcut depicting the 6 authors. Tp margin strengthened & 2 repaired tears entering the woodcut; marginal waterstaining at end. Soudek copy. P Dec 12 (13) $2,250

## Le Fevre, Nicolas, d.1669?
— Neuvermehrter Chymischen Handleiter und Guldnes Kleinod. Nuremberg: J. A. Endter & Sons, 1685. 8vo, later half vellum. With frontis & 14 plates. S Mar 14 (224) £300

## Le Franc de Pompignan, Jean Jacques, 1709-84
— Eloges historique de Monseigneur le duc de Bourgogne. Paris, 1761. 8vo, contemp red mor gilt with crowned monogram & fleurs-de-lis on spine. Some marginal soiling. Copy of Louis de France, Dauphin. Fuerstenberg - Schaefer copy. S Dec 7 (360) £150
— Poesies sacrees divisees en quatre livres. Paris: Chaubert, 1751. 8vo, contemp red mor gilt. Some soiling in lower margin of tp. Fuerstenberg - Schaefer copy. S Dec 7 (359) £360

## Le Gallienne, Richard, 1866-1947
— The Romance of Perfume. NY & Paris, 1928. Illus by Georges Barbier. 4to, bds. pba Aug 8 (542) $110

## Le Grand d'Aussy, Pierre Jean Baptiste
— Histoire de la vie privee des francais. Paris, 1782. 3 vols, contemp calf; spine heads chipped, corners bumped. Some marginal tears. Ck Mar 22 (85) £80

## Le Hay, ——
— Recueil de cent estampes representant differentes nations du Levant. Paris, 1714. Folio, mor gilt. With engraved title, 14 engraved pages, engraved leaf of music & 102 hand-colored plates, 3 of them double-page. b May 30 (279) £7,500

Anr copy. Contemp calf; rubbed. With engraved title, leaf of music & 102 plates, 3 of them double-page. Some browning; a few leaves with marginal spotting. C Oct 25 (133) £3,000

Anr copy. Later half calf; worn, spine ends def. With frontis, tp & 99 plates only. cb Feb 14 (2783) $3,250

## Le Long, Isaac, 1683-1744
— Historische Beschryvinge van der Reformatie der Stadt Amsterdam. Amst., 1729. Folio, contemp blindstamped vellum; pastedowns lifted. With folding plate, 2 double-page plates & 50 views on 27 plates; Tear in 1 plate. sg Mar 21 (196) $500

**Le Long, Jacques, 1665-1721**
— Discours historique sur les principales editions des Bibles polyglottes. Paris, 1713. 8vo, old calf; rubbed & dried, spine chipped, endpapers lacking. O Mar 26 (150) $650

**Le Maingre de Boucicault, Jean**
— Historie de Mre. J. de Boucicant.... Paris, 1620. 4to, contemp vellum. With title & engraved arms. Some annotation & marginalia; Ddd-end wormed; light discoloration. S Oct 26 (58) £2,100 [Christodoulou]

**Le Maire de Belges, Jean, 1473-1513**
— Les Illustrations de Gaule et singularitez de Troye.... [Paris: Francois Regnault, 1528]. 4to, 17th-cent sheep gilt; extremities worn, spine ends damaged. Marginal dampstains; early marginalia. sg Oct 19 (141) $1,100

**Le Mascrier, Jean Baptiste, Abbe**
— Description de l'Egypte.... Paris, 1735. 4to, contemp calf gilt; spine ends & corners worn. With port, folding map & 7 plates. sg Mar 7 (143) $375

**Le Mau de la Jaisse, Pierre**
— Plans des Principales Places de Guerre et Villes Maritimes Frontieres du Royaume de France. Paris: Didot et al., 1736. 8vo, contemp calf gilt; spine heel off, front joint cracked. With 112 mtd engraved medallion city plans, each within ornate woodcut border. Lower portion of 2K3 torn & restored with text supplied in Ms. sg May 9 (80) $1,100

**Le Moine de l'Espine, Jacques**
— Den Koophandel van Amsterdam. Amst., 1715. 8vo, contemp vellum; loose. Tear in 2d folding table. sg Mar 21 (106) $200

**Le Monnier, Guillaume Antoine, 1721-97**
— Fetes des bonnes gens de Canon et des Rosieres de Briquebe.... Avignon, 1777. 2 parts in 1 vol. 8vo, contemp mor gilt; joints rubbed. With frontis. Fuerstenberg - Schaefer copy. S Dec 7 (361) £1,200

**Le Moyne, Louis Valcoulon**
— Country Residences in Europe and America. NY, 1908. Folio, orig cloth; worn, hinge cracked, shaken. wa Dec 14 (393) $120

**Le Noir, Marie Alexandre**
— Nouvelle Collection d'Arabesques, propres a la decoration des appartemens. Paris & Strasbourg, [1810]. Folio, mor gilt by Petit, with arms of Baron Achille Seilliere. With 40 plates. Dampstaining to lower margin. Fuerstenberg - Schaefer copy. S Dec 7 (362) £1,400

**Le Normand D'Etioles, Jeanne Antoinette, Marquise de Pompadour.** See: Pompadour, Jeanne Antoinette

**Le Pelletier, Robert Martin, 1682-1748**
— Histoire des comtes de Champagne et de Brie. Paris, 1753. 2 vols in 1. 12mo, contemp red mor gilt with arms of Charles Philippe d'Albert, duc de Luynes; spine worn, joints repaired. Fuerstenberg - Schaefer copy. S Dec 7 (363) £300

**Le Petit, Jules**
— Bibliographie des principales editions originales d'ecrivains francais du XVe au XVIIIe siecle. Paris, 1888. 8vo, half mor, orig wraps bound in; rubbed. O Mar 26 (151) $130

**Le Plongeon, Augustus**
— Sacred Mysteries among the Mayas and the Quiches.... NY, 1886. 8vo, cloth; spine ends & bottom corners rubbed. pba Aug 8 (97) $75

**Le Pois, Antoine**
— Discours sur les medalles et graveures antiques.... Paris: Mamert Patisson, 1579. 4to, 17th-cent mor gilt. With port & 20 plates. Plate of Priapus unmutilated. Browned in margins; stain in q4-p1; text on G4v rubbed. S Nov 30 (278) £1,600

**Le Prestre de Vauban, Sebastien**
— De l'attaque et de la defense des places. The Hague, 1737-42. Vol I (of 2) only. 4to, contemp calf; worn. With 33 plates. Some foxing, 1 plate misfolded. wa Feb 29 (204) $800

**Le Prince, Jean Baptiste**
— Oeuvres... contenant plus de cdnt soixante planches gravees a l'eau-forte & a l'imitation des dessins laves au bistre.... Paris, 1782. Folio, contemp half sheep; spine repaired. Fuerstenberg - Schaefer copy. S Dec 7 (364) £5,000

**Le Queux, William**
— The Invasion of 1910. L, 1906. 8vo, cloth. sg Dec 14 (198) $110

**Le Quien de la Neufville, Jacques**
— Usage des postes chez les anciens et les modernes.... Paris: Delatour, 1730. 8vo, contemp red mor gilt with arms of Cardinal Jean Andre Hercule de Fleury. Hoe - Fuerstenberg - Schaefer copy. S Dec 7 (365) £500

**Le Rouge Library, Andre Joseph Etienne**
— [Sale Catalogue] Catalogue des livres imprimes et manuscrits.... Paris, 1833. 8vo, contemp half calf; rubbed. Inscr by Le Rouge's son to his uncle, M. Denis, & with accompanying letter. O Mar 26 (152) $140

**Le Rouge, Georges Louis**
— Atlas nouveau portatif.... Paris: Le Rouge, [1756]. Vol I (of 2). 4to, contemp bds; joints & backstrip torn, extremities rubbed. With 4 double-page plates (3 hand-colored) & 87 double-page maps, hand-colored in outline. Some browning. C Apr 3 (135) £1,800
— Recueil des fortifications forts et ports de mer de France. Paris, [1760?]. 8vo, contemp sheep; extremities worn, front cover loose. With 89 mapsheets. Engraved throughout. sg May 9 (82) $350

## 1995 - 1996 · BOOKS

**Le Roy, Julien David**
— Arabesques du Vatican. Paris, 1787. Folio, modern half calf folder. With 14 plates. Fuerstenberg - Schaefer copy. S Dec 7 (366) £650

**Le Royer d'Artezet de la Sauvagere, Felix Francois**
— Recueil d'Antiquites dans les Gaules.... Paris, 1770. 4to, contemp half sheep gilt; spine ends chipped, joints cracked. sg Mar 21 (197) $325

**Le Sage, Alain Rene, 1668-1747**
— The Adventures of Gil Blas of Santillane. L, 1819. Trans by Tobias Smollett. 3 vols. 8vo, half mor gilt by V. Champs. CE May 22 (304) $380
Anr copy. Half mor gilt by Riviere; joints rubbed. pba Mar 7 (162) $130
Anr copy. Lev gilt by Zaehnsdorf. sg Feb 8 (81) $400
— Le Diable boiteux. Paris, 1840. Illus by Tony Johannot. 8vo, contemp half calf. Prelims foxed. sg Sept 21 (249) $50
— Le Diable Boiteux; or, The Devil on Two Sticks. L, 1841. ("Asmodeus, or the Devil on Two Sticks.") Trans by Joseph Thomas; illus by Tony Johannot. 8vo, half mor gilt by Root. Some foxing. pba Nov 30 (219) $65

**Le Sueur, Eustache.** See: Le Brun & Le Sueur

**Le Verrier de la Conterie, Jean Baptiste Jacques**
— L'ecole de la chasse aux chiens courans.... Rouen: Nicolas & Richard Lallemant, 1763. 1st Ed. 2 parts in 1 vol. 8vo, calf; worn. With 14 music plates. S Oct 27 (830) £220 [Way]

**Lea, Tom**
— Bullfight Manual for Spectators. El Paso: Carl Hertzog, 1957. Wraps. Sgd on tp. pba Aug 8 (98) $65
— The King Ranch. Bost., [1957]. 2 vols. pba Apr 25 (502) $80; pba July 25 (311) $100; pba Aug 22 (932) $150; wa Dec 14 (80) $90
— Western Beef Cattle. Austin: Encino Press, [1967]. One of 850. pba Apr 25 (503) $65

**Leach, Bernard**
— A Potter's Portfolio. L, 1951. Folio, orig cloth. With 60 plates. sg June 13 (95) $225

**Leach, Henry**
— Great Golfers in the Making. Phila.: George W. Jacobs, [c.1907]. 1st American Ed. Cloth; soiled, insect damage, spine chipped. With frontis port. pba Apr 18 (111) $120
— The Happy Golfer. L: Macmillan, 1914. 1st Ed. Cloth; upper spine bumped. pba Nov 9 (56) $700
— The Spirit of the Links. L: Methuen, [1907]. 1st Ed. Cloth; front cover extrems discolored. pba Nov 9 (57) $175

**Leach, Jonathan**
— Rough Sketches of the Life of an Old Soldier during a Service in the West Indies.... L, 1831. 8vo, 19th-cent half calf. sg Mar 7 (174) $60

## LEAR

**Leaf, Munro**
— The Story of Ferdinand. NY, 1936. 1st Ed. In later dj. Inscr. Met Dec 5 (251) $300
Anr Ed. NY, 1938. Orig bds; some wear. Inscr to Oscar Lewis. pba Mar 7 (163) $190

**League of American Wheelmen**
— Road Book of New Jersey. [N.p.], 1897. Oblong 12mo, orig cloth; worn. F June 20 (735) $80

**Leake, William Martin, 1777-1860**
— Journal of a Tour in Asia Minor. L, 1824. 8vo, contemp calf; joints worn. With folding map, 2 other maps & 1 plate. Map torn at fold. b Sept 20 (348) £300
— Travels in the Morea. L, 1830. 3 vols. With: Peloponnesiaca: A Supplement to Travels in the Morea. L, 1846. Together, 4 vols. 8vo, tree calf; rebacked. With 13 maps (1 folding) & 17 plates. Leaves slightly brittle. S Oct 26 (132) £1,300 [Basil]

**Leale, John**
— Recollections of a Tule Sailor. San Francisco, 1939. One of 1,000. With 2 maps & 16 photographic plates. pba Feb 12 (335) $50

**Lear, Edward, 1812-88**
— A Book of Nonsense. L: Frederick Warne, [1870]. 4to, contemp half mor; worn, upper cover detached. With title & 112 color illusts. Tp soiled & repaired; anr leaf repaired; some spotting. Ck May 31 (60) £65
— Illustrated Excursions in Italy. L, 1846. 1st Ed, 2d Series. Folio, orig cloth; worn. With 25 plates. Text & plates spotted & loose. S Oct 26 (285) £700 [Harrington]
— Illustrations of the Family of Psittacidae, or Parrots. L: Pion, 1978. One of 530. Folio, half mor gilt; lower edges worn. With 42 color plates. wa Feb 1 (136) $500
— Journal of a Landscape Painter in Corsica.... L, 1870. 1st Ed. 8vo, orig cloth; soiled. With half-title, map, & 40 plates & illus. S Oct 26 (286) £170 [Ministere]
— Journal of a Landscape Painter in Southern Calabria.... L, 1852. 1st Ed. 8vo, orig cloth; soiled, rebacked. With half-title, 2 maps, & 20 plates Soiled. S Oct 26 (287) £340 [Scott]
— The Jumblies. NY: Young Scott Books, [1968]. Illus by Edward Gorey. In dj. Sgd on tp. pba Aug 22 (191) $50
— Views in Rome and Its Environs. L, 1841. 1st Ed. Folio, loose in orig half mor; rubbed & soiled, spine head & foot worn. With title, vignette, & 25 plates. Spotted & soiled. S Oct 26 (288) £950 [Harrington]
— Views in the Seven Ionian Islands. L, 1863. Folio, loose in orig cloth. With litho title & 9 views only. Sold w.a.f. b Jan 31 (454) £720
1st Ed. Folio, loose in org cloth; worn. With title vignette, & 20 plates. Some spotting & soiling. S Oct 26 (135) £2,100 [Theotoky]
Anr Ed. Oldham, 1979. One of 1,000. Folio, orig cloth. S Oct 26 (133) £100 [Theotoky]; S Oct 26 (134) £100 [Theotoky]

655

### Leaves...

— Leaves of Recreation Gathered in the Garden of Knowledge. L, 1803. 12mo, orig wraps; backstrip rubbed. With frontis, pictorial title & 16 leaves, all but the frontis with 2 illusts. S Nov 2 (219) £800 [Schiller]

### Leavitt, Dudley

— Leavitt's Farmer's Almanack and Miscellaneous Year Book for the Year of Our Lord 1853.... Bost.: Edward Livermore, 1852. 8vo, ptd wraps. pba Feb 12 (520) $130

### Lebedev, Valentin

— [211 Days aboard Salyut 7, in Russian]. Moscow, 1983. Sgd 5 times by Anatoly Berezovoy. Also sgd on tp by 46 cosmonauts & astronauts. Anatoly N. Berezovoy's copy. P Mar 16 (289) $1,000

### Lebel, Robert

— Marcel Duchamp. NY, [1959]. Folio, cloth, in def & chipped dj. pba Aug 8 (390) $90

Anr copy. Cloth, in dj with foxing on spine. sg June 13 (139) $250

— Sur Marcel Duchamp. NY, 1959. Text by Andre Breton & H. P. Roche. Wraps; edges rubbed. Duchamp exhibition posted laid in. sg Jan 11 (147) $250

### Leber, Jean Michel Constant

— Plaisantes Recherches d'un homme grave sur in farceur. Paris, 1835. One of 15. 8vo, half mor. Some rubbing & foxing. O Mar 26 (153) $120

### Lebrun, Frederico

— Drawings for Dante's Inferno.... [N.p.]: Kanthos Press, 1963. One of 2,000. Folio, orig cloth; worn & soiled. With 36 plates & 4 orig lithos, sgd in the plate. F June 20 (864) $100

### Leclair, Jean Marie

— Premier Livre de sonates a violin seul avec basse continue [score]. Paris, 1723. Folio, modern half calf. Engraved throughout. Repairs to lower corner of 1st 3 leaves; a few stains; some browning. S Dec 1 (198) £320

### Leclerq, Lena

— Pomme endormie. Paris: Marc Barbezat, 1961. One of 131. Illus by Alberto Giacometti. 4to, half mor, orig wraps bound in. With 8 full-page lithos. S Nov 21 (248) £1,200

### Lecomte, Hippolyte

— Costumes civils et militaires de la monarchie francaise.... Paris, 1820. 2 (of 4) vols. Later half sheep; worn. With 200 hand-colored plates. Some foxing & soiling; light foxing affecting most plates; marginal pencil marks. cb Feb 14 (2784) $650

— Costumes francais, de 1200 a 1715. L: C. Hullmandel, [c.1830]. 8vo, mor gilt. With 100 hand-colored plates, including title. wd Nov 15 (47) $325

### Lecornu, Joseph

— Les Cerfs-Volants. Paris, 1902. 8vo, orig cloth; shaken, discolored. sg May 16 (53) $50

— La Navigation aerienne. Histoire documentaire.... Paris, 1903. 1st Ed. 4to, modern cloth, orig wraps bound in. sg May 16 (54) $130

Anr copy. Contemp half mor gilt. sg May 16 (55) $110

### Lectera...

— Lectera data al sagrestano dOrzamichele. Florence, 12 Oct 1527. 4to, mor gilt by Lloyd, Wallis & Lloyd. With large woodcut. Top margins restored without loss. C Apr 3 (131) £2,000

### Ledermueller, Martin Frobenius, 1719-69

— Mikroskopische Gemueths- und Augen-Ergoetzung.... [Nuremberg], 1761. 4to, contemp half vellum; spine def. With frontis, port & 100 hand-colored plates. F2 misbound after F4; some browning. Madsen copy. S Mar 14 (230) £1,600

— Versuch bey angehender Fruehlings Zeit.... Nuremberg, 1764. Folio, modern bds; extremities scuffed. With hand-colored engraved title & 12 hand-colored plates. Tp & last plate repaired in margin. C May 31 (27) £1,300

### Ledieu, Alcius

— Les Reliures artistiques et armoriees de la Bibliotheque Communale d'Abbeville. Paris, 1891. One of 50. 4to, half mor; rubbed. Blindstamp on tp & at end. bba May 9 (141) £320 [Page]

### Ledoux, Louis Vernon, 1880-1948

See also: Henderson & Ledoux

— An Essay on Japanese Prints. NY, 1938. One of 1,000. Folio, half cloth. sg Sept 7 (213) $110

### Ledyard, Isaac

— An Essay on Matter. Phila., 1784. Bound with 2 other works. 8vo, old calf; worn & scuffed, spines chipped, joints cracked. Browned. bbc June 24 (314) $425

### Lee, Amy Freeman. See: Derrydale Press

### Lee, Bourke

— Death Valley. NY, 1930-32. Bound with: Death Valley Men. 1st Eds. 2 vols. In djs; 1st d/j soiled, both worn. Robbins copy. pba Mar 21 (193) $110

### Lee, Brian North

— Bookplates & Labels by Leo Wyatt. [Wakefield]: Fleece Press, 1988. One of 300. Orig half cloth. bba May 9 (304) £75 [Marks]

### Lee, Chauncey, 1763-1842

— The American Accomptant, Being a Plain...Compendium.... Lansingburgh, 1797. 12mo, contemp sheep gilt; worn & scuffed. Dampstains at fore-edge; lacking initial blank; tear to frontis repaired. wa Feb 29 (420) $220

**Lee, E. G.**
— The Mormons, or Knavery Exposed. Frankfort, 1841. 8vo, self-wraps. Minor staining. sg Oct 26 (267) $6,000

**Lee, Gypsy Rose, 1914-70**
— The G-String Murders. NY, 1941. In dj with rubbing at head of spine. sg June 20 (212) $120

**Lee, Harper**
— To Kill a Mockingbird. NY, [1960]. In dj with minor wear to spine ends. Inscr to Ruth & Bill, sgd Nelle Harper Lee. CE May 22 (305) $11,000
Advance reading copy. Ptd wraps. sg June 20 (213) $1,500
Advance review copy. Wraps; rubbed, wear along spine folds. bbc Dec 18 (301) $1,100

**Lee, Henry**
— Anti-Scepticism; Or, Notes upon each Chapter of Mr. Lock's Essay.... L, 1792. Folio, contemp calf; covers detached. Prelims browned; stamp on tp & next leaf. sg Mar 21 (195) $300
Anr copy. Contemp sheep; spine ends cropped, joints cracked. Worming to front pastedown & 8 leaves at end. wa Feb 29 (219) $350

**Lee, Jack H., "Powder River"**
— West of Powder River. NY, [1933]. 1st Ed. - Illus by Paul Honore. Orig cloth in glassine wrap; glassine chipped. Robbins copy. Inscr. pba Mar 21 (194) $95

**Lee, James, 1715-95**
— An Introduction to Botany. L, 1810. ("An Introduction to the Science of Botany.") 8vo, contemp calf; rubbed. With port & 12 color plates. Some foxing & soiling. F Mar 28 (409) $150

**Lee, James P.**
— Golf in America. NY, 1895. 1st Ed. Cloth. pba Nov 9 (58) $1,600
Anr copy. Cloth; soiled, spine darkened. pba Apr 18 (112) $1,300

**Lee, Martha J.** See: Bates & Lee

**Lee, Norman N.** See: Edmonds & Lee

**Lee, Robert E.** See: Lawrence & Lee

**Lee, Ronald Alfred**
— The Knibb Family Clockmakers. L, 1964. 4to, cloth, in worn dj. bba Sept 7 (95) £450 [Allen]

**Lee, Weyman**
— An Essay to Ascertain the Value of Leases and Annuities.... L, 1738. 8vo, contemp calf; rubbed. b Sept 20 (141) £350

**Lee, William.** See: Burroughs, William S.

**Leech, John, 1817-64**
— The Comic English Grammar. L, 1840. 1st Ed. 12mo, calf gilt by Zaehnsdorf, orig cloth bound in. pba June 20 (219) $325

— Follies of the Year.... [L, 1866]. Oblong 4to, orig half mor; backstrip def, sprung. With hand-colored litho title & 21 hand-colored plates. Some spotting. S Mar 28 (552) £140

**Leeper, David R., 1832-1900**
— The Argonauts of 'Forty-Nine.... South Bend, 1894. 1st Ed. - Illus by O. Marion Elbel. 8vo, orig cloth. Larson copy. pba Sept 28 (573) $400

**Leet, Ambrose**
— A Directory to the Market Towns, Villages, Gentlemen's Seats...in Ireland.... Dublin, 1814. 2d Ed. 8vo, contemp sheep; worn & loose. sg Mar 7 (142) $110

**Leeven...** See: Bosch, Lambert van den

**Lefevre d'Etaples, Jacques.** See: Le Fevre, Jacques d'Etaples

**Lefevre, Paul.** See: Geraldy, Paul

**LeGear, Clara E.** See: Phillips & LeGear

**Legende...**
— Legende de' beati del Terzo Ordine di San Francesco. Vicenza: Henricus de Sancto Ursio, [c.1497]. 4to, early cartone alla rustica with 3 lea thongs. 30 lines; type 111R. Waterstaining, fingersoiling & small inkstains; lower inner margins of quire f reinforced. 98 leaves. Goff L-123. C Apr 3 (132) £1,600

**Leger, Charles**
— Courbet selon les caricatures et les Images. Paris, 1920. One of 400. 4to, half lea. Library markings, but plates unmarked. sg Sept 7 (117) $200

**Legge, William Vincent**
— A History of the Birds of Ceylon. L, [1878]-80. In 3 vols. 4to, modern half mor. With key plate, colored map & 34 hand-colored plates by Keulemans. Fattorini copy. C Oct 25 (74) £2,200
Anr copy. In 1 vol. 4to, modern calf gilt; early spine laid down. With key plate, colored map & 34 hand-colored plates by Keulemans. Browned throughout; 3 plates with spotting; worming through to S4 repaired but affecting 3 plates; repaired tears to inner blank margins of tp & next 2 leaves. C May 31 (28) £1,200

**Legh, Gerard, d.1563**
— The Accedens of Armory. L: Richard Tottill, 1562. 1st Ed. 8vo, later sheep. Lacking the folding plate; trimmed, affecting catchwords & edges of full-page engravings; some dampstaining. pba Sept 14 (198) $375

**Legh, Thomas**
— A Narrative of a Journey in Egypt. L, 1817. 8vo, orig bds; worn & soiled. Tp lacking piece at top margin. wa Feb 29 (156) $210

**Legipont, Oliver**
— Dissertationes Philologico-Bibliographicae.... Nuremberg, 1747. Bound after: Moser, J. Jacob. Bibliotheca Manuscriptorum Mazime Anecdotorum eorumque Historicum. Nuremberg, 1722. 4to, contemp vellum; worn. Some staining & browning. O Mar 26 (154) $350

**Legouve, Gabriel Marie Jean Baptiste**
— La Merite des femmes. Paris: Renouard, 1809. 12mo, mor gilt by Lefebvre. With frontis, 2 plates & 1 wood-engraving. Fuerstenberg - Schaefer copy. S Dec 7 (371) £160

**Legrand, Emile**
— Bibliographie Hellenique des XVe et XVIe Siecles. Paris, 1962. One of 325. 4 vols. bba May 9 (91) £300 [Maggs]

**Legrand, Louis, 1863-1951**
— Le Livre d'heures. Paris, 1898. One of 160. 8vo, mor extra by E. Carayon, the upper cover with pictorial panel by Lucien Rudaux, orig wraps bound in. With additional suite of the cover design & etched illusts ptd in color, 3 ptd proofs & 4 watercolor drawings for the bdg design. S Nov 21 (252) £4,000

**Legrand, Noe**
— Les Collections artistiques de la faculte de medecine de Paris. Paris, 1911. 4to, half mor; rubbed & soiled. With 100 plates. Some foxing. CE Nov 8 (115) $130

**Legrenzi, Giovanni, 1626-90**
— Idee armoniche estese per due e tre voci.... Venice: Francesco Magni detto Gardano, 1678. Folio, contemp vellum. C June 26 (267) £900

**Lehmann, Rosamond**
— Invitation to the Waltz. L, 1932. In dj. Inscr to Roger Senhouse. With ALs from Senhouse inserted. bba Oct 19 (355) £80 [Mandl]

**Lehmann-Haupt, Hellmut —& McCurry, Charles**
— Two Essays on the Decretum of Gratian. Los Angeles, 1971. One of 193 with rubricated vellum leaf from the 1472 Decretum. Folio, half vellum. sg Sept 14 (297) $600

**Leiber, Fritz**
— The Demons of the Upper Air. [N.p.]: Roy A. Squires, [1969]. One of 275. Orig wraps, in envelope. pba May 23 (199) $55
— The Leiber Chronicles. Arlington Heights: Dark Harvest, 1990. One of 52. In dj. O Dec 5 (220) $70
— Night's Black Agents. Sauk City, 1947. In dj. sg June 20 (215) $120
— Two Sought Adventure: Exploits of Fafhrd and the Gray Mouser. NY: Gnome Press, [1957]. 1st bdg, in dj. Browned. pba May 4 (189) $75

**Leibnitz, Gottfried Wilhelm von, 1646-1716 —& Clarke, Samuel, 1675-1729**
[-] A Collection of Papers, which Passed between the Late Learned Mr. Leibnitz and Dr. Clarke in the Years 1715 and 1716.... L, 1717. 1st Ed. 2 parts in 1 vol. 8vo, contemp calf; rebacked. Some discoloration; H4 marked. S June 12 (30) £280

**Leibovitz, Annie**
— Photographs, Annie Leibovitz 1970-90. NY, [1991]. One of 326. Folio, cloth; minor wear on spine. sg Feb 29 (182) $225

**Leigh, Chandos**
— The Spirit of the Age. Warwick, 1832. 8vo, disbound. b Dec 5 (398) £100

**Leigh, Charles, 1662-1701?**
— The Natural History of Lancashire, Cheshire and the Peak in Derbyshire. Oxford, 1700. 1st Ed. 3 parts in 1 vol. Folio, calf; upper cover detached. With port, double-page map hand-colored in outline & 20 (of 22) plates. Sold w.a.f. b Sept 20 (312) £130

**Leigh, William Robinson**
— The Western Pony. NY, [1935]. Later ptg. 4to, cloth. With 6 colored plates. pba Apr 25 (504) $90

**Leighly, John.** See: Grabhorn Printing

**Leighton, John M.**
— Select Views on the River Clyde. Glasgow, 1830. 4to, contemp bds; rebacked. With 42 plates in india-proof state. Waterstaining throughout. b Jan 31 (338) £95

**Leipnik, F. L.**
— A History of French Etching.... L, 1924. One of 100. 4to, cloth, unopened. wd Nov 15 (84) $160

**Leiris, Michel.** See: Miro, Joan

**Leisenring, James E.**
— The Art of Tying the Wet Fly. NY, 1941. 8vo, cloth, in chipped dj. O June 25 (186) $250

**Leiser, Eric**
— The Dettes. Fishkill: Willowkill Press, [1992]. One of 200, with 3 hand-tied flies. 4to, half calf. O Oct 10 (185) $280; O Feb 6 (151) $400

**Leithold, Theodor von**
— Mijn Uitstap naar Brazilie.... Amst., 1821. 8vo, contemp bds; worn. Soiling & foxing. O Mar 5 (156) $50

**Leland, Thomas, 1722-85**
— The History of Ireland. L, 1773. 1st Ed. 3 vols. 4to, calf; scraped, joints of Vol III starting. pba Nov 30 (221) $600

**Lemaire, C. L.** See: Prevost & Lemaire

**Lemaire, Charles, 1801-71 —& Others**
— Flore des serres et des jardins de l'Europe. Ghent, 1845-83. Vol VIII only. Orig cloth; worn & abraded. With 82 hand-colored plates only. Met May 22 (458) $850

Anr copy. Vol X only. With 89 hand-colored plates only. Met May 22 (459) $850

Anr copy. Vol I only. Half mor; corners rubbed. pba Sept 14 (237) $600

Anr copy. Vols I-X only. Contemp half calf; worn. Sold w.a.f. S Nov 30 (29) £4,000

Anr copy. Vol 18 only. Contemp calf gilt; cracked. With 2 tinted lithos & 78 chromolithos, mostly finished by hand, many double-page. S Mar 29 (728) £460

**Lemaitre, Jules, 1853-1914**
— Myrrha, vierge et martyre. Paris, 1903. Unique copy with page stating that it contains the orig drawings following tp. Illus by Xavier Leseur. Mor extra by Chambolle-Duru, orig wraps bound in. With the 13 etchings, the 13 wash drawings, large unpbd watercolor & 3 suites of etchings, including those marked "bon a tiere" by the artist. S Nov 21 (256) £700
— Traite sur les dents. Paris, 1822-24. 3 vols. 4to, contemp mor extra cathedral bdg by Jozon & Chauvet. L.p. copy. C May 1 (92) £3,200

**Lemery, Louis, 1677-1743**
— A Treatise of Foods in General. L, 1704. 1st Ed in English. 8vo, contemp calf; rubbed. Discolored; wormed throughout in lower margin. b Sept 20 (142) £160

Anr copy. Contemp calf; rebacked, tightly resewn. Lacking 1st leaf; browned & affected by damp; C1 to end with wormhole. Ck Mar 22 (165) £140

2d Ed in English. L, 1706. 8vo, contemp calf; rubbed. Some discoloring. b Sept 20 (143) £130

**Lemoine, Pierre Camille —& Batteney, M.**
— Practische Answeisung zur Diplomatik und zu einer guten Einrichtung der Archive. Nuremberg, 1776-77. 4to, contemp bds; worn. With folding table & 52 folding plates. O Mar 26 (155) $180

**Lemoisne, Paul Andre**
— Degas et son oeuvre. Paris, [1946-49]. One of 980. 4 vols. 4to, orig cloth. Deny's Sutton's copy. bba Apr 11 (172B) £600 [Historic Importants]; sg June 13 (131) $2,000

Anr copy. Orig wraps. wad Oct 18 (243) C$1,800
— Les Xylographies du XIVe et du XVe siecle au cabinet des estampes de la Bibliotheque Nationale. Paris & Brussels, 1927-30. 2 vols. Folio, orig wraps. sg June 13 (237) $275

**Lemonnier, Camille, 1844-1913**
— Constantin Meunier, Sculpteur et Peintre. Paris, 1904. 4to, half mor, orig wraps bound in; extremities worn. sg June 13 (255) $110

**Lemonnier, Henry**
— Proces-verbaux de l'Academie Royale d'Architecture 1671-1793. Paris, 1911-26. 10 vols. 8vo, recent cloth with fragment of orig wrap mtd on upper bd. bba Oct 19 (138) £220 [Bernett]

**Lenfant, Jacques**
— Histoire de la Papesse Jeanne.... The Hague, 1720. 2 vols. 12mo, contemp vellum; worn, 1 joint split. With 4 plates, 1 folding. Some foxing & soiling. O Mar 26 (156) $50

**Lenglet du Fresnoy, Pierre Nicolas, 1674-1755**
— Methode pour etudier la geographie.... Paris, 1742. 7 parts in 8 vols. 8vo, contemp vellum. With frontis, 16 folding maps, folding diagram & folding plate. sg May 9 (81) $400
— Methode pour etudier l'histoire.... Paris, 1735. 9 vols. 8vo, contemp calf; rubbed & dried, spine ends worn. Some foxing. O Mar 26 (157) $130

**Lenin, Vladimir Ilyich, 1870-1924**
— Razvitie Kapitalisma v Rosii. St. Petersburg, 1899. 1st Ed. 8vo, contemp half mor, orig front wrap bound in; initials N.T. on spine. Bookseller's stamp on last page. C June 26 (224) £750

**Lenygon, Francis.** See: Jourdain & Lenygon

**Leon & Brother**
— Catalogue of First Editions of American Authors.... NY, 1885. 8vo, orig wraps. O Mar 26 (158) $50

**Leonard, Elmore**
— The Bounty Hunters. NY, 1954. Wraps; worn & skewed. sg June 20 (216) $150

**Leonard, Ruth S.** See: Bentley & Leonard

**Leonard, Zenas**
— Adventures of Zenas Leonard, Fur Trader. Norman, OK, [1959]. Orig cloth in dj; front cover edge bumped, d/j clipped & worn. With 1 map. Larson copy. pba Sept 28 (139) $50
— Leonard's Narrative, Adventures of Zenas Leonard, Fur Trader and Trapper.... Cleveland, 1904. 2d Ed, One of 520. 8vo, orig cloth in dj; d/j rubbed, spine faded, hinge cracked. With folding frontis map, facsimile of orig tp, 2 port plates, 1 map, & 1 other illust. Robbins copy. pba Mar 21 (196) $500
— Narrative of the Adventures.... Clearfield PA, 1839. 1st Ed. 8vo, mor by Zaehnsdorf; rebound. Slight soiling; several marginal repairs; light stain in pp. 11-16. Robbins copy. pba Mar 21 (195) $37,500
— The Narrative of Zenas Leonard, Fur Trader and Trapper, 1831-1836. Cleveland, 1904. Ed by W. F. Wagner. Orig cloth. With 3 maps (1 folded), 2 ports, & 1 sketch. Some foxing. Larson copy. pba Sept 28 (137) $250

**Leonardi, Domenico Felice**
— Le Delizie della Villa di Castellazzo. Milan, 1743. Illus by Marc' Antonio Dal Re. Folio, modern bds. With double-page port & 23 double-page plates, colored by a contemp hand & heightened with gold.

# LEONARDO

Guarded; 2 plates slightly trimmed, not affecting image. C Apr 3 (133) £13,000

**Leonardo da Vinci, 1452-1519**
— Recueil de charges et de tetes de differns caracteres. Paris, 1767. 4to, modern half cloth; front joint cracked & frayed. With 64 (of 67) etchings on 17 (of 20) leaves. Tp in facsimile; marginal foxing & soiling. Sold w.a.f. sg Jan 11 (254) $225
— Trattato della pittura. Paris, 1651. Folio, contemp calf gilt; rebacked, corners restored, rubbed. Lacking final blank; hole to upper margin of frontis; marginal soiling at beginning; fols. G4v-H2r with stains; minor worming at gutters; some browning. Hefner copy. CNY May 17 (29) $8,500
— A Treatise of Painting. L, 1721. 1st Ed in English. 8vo, contemp goatskin gilt; joints restored but upper joint cracked, spine rubbed. With frontis & 33 plates. Some dampstaining. Hefner copy. CNY May 17 (30) $8,500

**Leonard's...**
— Leonard's Annual Price Index of Art Auctions. Newton, 1981-89. Vols 1-9. 4to, cloth. Ink stamps. ds July 27 (109) $500

**Leonardus, Camillus**
— Expositio canonum aequatorii coelestium motuum. Venice: Georgius de Arrivabenis, 21 July 1496. 4to, modern calf gilt. 36 lines; gothic type. Verso of final leaf soiled; repaired wormhole in upper blank margin of last 3 leaves. 41 (of 42) leaves; lacking final blank. Goff L-139. C Nov 29 (59) £3,500
— Lunari al modo de Italia calculato. Venice: Giovanni Andrea Vavassori, 14 Apr 1530. 8vo, modern bdg from part of 17th-cent vellum leaf. Tp with large woodcut; text in roman letter, with 1st 3 lines of title & names of months in text in gothic letter. Quire B misbound; some stains; top margin of last 2 leaves frayed. C June 26 (96) £350

**Leonardus de Matthaei.** See: Leonardus de Utino

**Leonardus de Utino**
— Sermones aurei de sanctis. Venice: Franciscus Renner de Heilbronn & Nicolaus de Frankfordia, 1473. 4to, early 17th-cent sheep; spine ends repaired, later endpapers. 42 lines; double column; type 2:75G. With painted armorial device in lower margin of 2d leaf; 1st initial in red with brown decoration; 2- to 4-line initials in red, some with extensions; some initials in purple. Guarded; small holes in margins of 1st leaf repaired. 313 (of 314) leaves; lacking final blank. Goff L-152. C Apr 3 (134) £3,000
— Sermones de sanctis. Speier: Peter Drach, 9 Feb 1478. Folio, contemp blindstamped calf over wooden bds with remains of 2 fore-edge clasps; rebacked, piece of lea torn from rear bd. 42 lines & headline; double column; types 1:130G (headings & colophon) & 2:94G (text). Marginal tears in 2 leaves; initial blank torn with loss; browned; 2 prelim quires bound at end. 350 leaves. Goff L-160. C Nov 29 (58) £1,200

# AMERICAN BOOK PRICES CURRENT

— Sermones quadragesimales. Lyons: Johannes Trechsel, 5June 1494. 4to, later vellum bds. 53 lines & headline; double column; gothic letter. Some dampstaining. 413 (of 414) leaves; lacking 1st leaf. Goff L-149. S Dec 18 (53) £500 [de Palol]

**Leonowens, Anna Harriette**
— The English Governess at the Siamese Court. Bost., 1870. Orig cloth; spine soiled & rubbed, front hinge starting. pba Dec 14 (97) $225

**Leopold, Rudolf**
— Egon Schiele. Paintings, Watercolors, Drawings. [NY, 1973]. 4to, orig cloth, in dj. With 228 plates, including 84 in color. sg Jan 11 (386) $850

**Lepape, Georges**
— Les Choses de Paul Poiret. Paris, 1911. Out-of-series copy with the 3 additional plates on japon (colored by pochoir). 4to, orig bds; soiled. With 12 colored plates. S Nov 21 (76) £2,600

**Lepsius, Carl Richard**
— Discoveries in Egypt, Ethiopia, and the Peninsula of Sinai.... L, 1852. 8vo, modern half mor gilt. With chromolitho frontis, folding map & uncolored litho plate. sg Mar 7 (144) $225
2d Ed. L, 1853. 8vo, orig mor. With chromolitho frontis, folding map & uncolored litho plate. NH July 21 (22) $140

**Lereboullet, Auguste, 1804-65**
— Zoologie du jeune age.... [Strasbourg], 1858-60. 4to, orig cloth; worn. With engraved title & 33 colored plates. Some foxing. F June 20 (855) $160

**Lermontov, Mikhail Yurievitch, 1814-41**
— A Song about Tsar Ivan Vasilyevitch. L: Aquila Press, 1929. One of 750. Illus by Paul Nash. Orig mor extra by John Nash. Abbey copy. C May 1 (93) £150

Anr copy. Mor with mor onlays. Ck May 31 (62) £75

**Leroux, Gaston, 1868-1927**
— The Phantom of the Opera. NY: Bobbs Merrill, [1911]. Cloth; spine ends rubbed, some soiling. pba Mar 7 (164) $150

**Leroy, Edgar.** See: Doiteau & Leroy

**Lescallier, Daniel, 1743-1822**
— Vocabulaire des termes de marine anglois et francois. Paris, 1797. 3 vols. Contemp mor gilt; repair to upper joint of Vol I. With 20 double-page plates & 3 folding tables. S June 27 (271) £4,000

**Leslie, Alfred Eric, 1866-1925.** See: Satie, Erik

**Leslie, Charles Robert, 1794-1859**
— Life and Times of Sir Joshua Reynolds, with Notices of Some of his Contemporaries. L, 1865. 2 vols in 4. 8vo, calf gilt by Riviere. Extra-illus with c.150 plates. Benz copy. sg Sept 21 (251) $850

**Lesseps, Jean Baptiste Barthelemy, Baron de, 1766-1834**
— Travels in Kamtschatka. L, 1790. 2 vols. 8vo, contemp calf. Lacking the map. sg Mar 7 (285) $175

**Lessing, Gotthold Ephraim, 1729-81**
— Fables et dissertations sur la nature de la fables.... Paris, 1764. 12mo, 18th-cent mor gilt. Tp spotted. Fuerstenberg - Schaefer copy. S Dec 7 (375) £180

**Lessius, Leonard, 1554-1623**
— Hygiasticon: or the Right Course of Preserving Life and Health unto Extream Old Age.... Cambr., 1636. 3d Ed. 2 parts. 24mo in 12s, contemp calf; spine & corners rubbed. Ck Mar 22 (166) £900

**Lesson, Rene Primevere, 1794-1849**
— Histoire naturelle des colibris.... Paris, [1830-32]. 8vo, contemp calf; rubbed & dried, spine chipped, joints broken. With 66 colored plates. Library stamp on each plate. O Mar 5 (157) $500
— Illustrations de zoologie, ou recueil de figures d'animaux peintes d'apres nature. Paris: Arthus Bertrand, [1832-35]. 8vo, half lea; edges worn. With 57 hand-finished color plates. Lacking Part 20, with 3 plates. Met Feb 24 (455) $500

**Lester, Charles Edwards**
— Artists of America: a Series of Biographical Sketches.... NY, 1846. 8vo, cloth. sg Jan 11 (255) $50
— The Life of Sam Houston. NY, 1855. 12mo, cloth; worn & lacquered. Inkstamps at foot of tp & back pastedown; some foxing. Cut signature of Houston mtd on front pastedown. NH July 21 (379) $70

**Lester, Charles Edwards —& Foster, Andrew**
— The Life and Voyages of Americus Vespucius. NY, 1846. 1st Ed. 8vo, orig cloth. pba Apr 25 (251) $75

**Lester, John Erastus**
— The Yo-Semite: Its History, its Scenery, its Development. Providence, 1873. Orig ptd wraps. pba Feb 12 (99) $150

**L'Estrange, Sir Roger, 1616-1704**
— The Observator in Dialogue. L, 1684-87. 2 vols. Folio, contemp calf; very worn, needs rebacked. Some dampstaining; library markings. Sold w.a.f. sg Mar 21 (198) $1,300

**Letarouilly, Paul, 1795-1855**
— Edifices de Rome moderne.... Paris, 1840-74. 3 vols (without text vol). Folio, later half sheep; worn, peeling, spine ends torn. With port, frontis, double-page plan of Rome & 354 plates. Some soiling & foxing; library markings. cb Oct 17 (88) $450
Anr Ed. Paris, 1868-1840-1850-1857. 4 vols. 4to & folio, later half cloth; spine ends & joints repaired. Sold w.a.f. CE Nov 8 (208) $2,000
Anr Ed. Paris, 1874. 3 vols (without text vol). Folio, modern half mor; extremities worn, joints cracked, corners & spine ends worn. With port, frontis, double-page map, & 354 plates. Some soiling; 1 plate tape-repaired on verso. cb Oct 17 (28) $1,600
— Le Vatican et la Basilique de Saint-Pierre de Rome. Cleveland: J. H. Jansen, [n.d.]. Folio, orig cloth; extremities worn, spine end split & worn. With 70 plates. Library markings; ink stamp on verso of each plate. cb Oct 17 (89) $325

**Leth, Hendrik de**
— Nieuwe geographische en historische Atlas van de Zeven Vereenigde Nederlandsche Provintien. Amst.: de Leth, [c.1749]. ("Nieuwe astronomische geographische en historische Atlas....") 8vo, recent half mor. With folding engraved title & 41 folding maps & diagrams, the maps colored in outline in a contemp hand. Some browning; a few thumb-marks. S June 27 (79) £1,400

**Leti, Gregorio, 1630-1701**
— Il Cardinalismo di Santa Chiesa; or, The History of the Cardinals of the Roman Church. L: John Starkey, 1670. Folio, contemp sheep; worn, needs rebacked. Tp stamped. sg Mar 21 (199) $175
— Historia, e memorie recondite sopra alla vita di Olivero Cromuele. Amst.: Pieter & Jan Blaeu, 1692. 2 vols in 1. 8vo, contemp vellum. With 28 plates & folding map. sg Mar 21 (200) $100

**Lettera...**
— Lettera al Sig. Alberico Cibo principe di Massa sopra il giuoco fatto dal Gran Duca intitolato Guerra d'Amore ildi 12 di febraio 1615, in Firenze. Pisa: Giovanni Fontani, 1615. Folio, contemp half vellum. With 26 etchings by Jacques Callot, cut to subject & pasted in spaces left by ptr. Lacking Indian Soldier on A2v; lower margins waterstained. C Apr 3 (136) £2,000

**Letters...**
— Letters writ by a Turkish Spy.... L, 1687. 12mo, contemp calf; rubbed, spine head worn. S Oct 26 (165) £320 [Edwards]

**Letts, John M.**
— California Illustrated. NY, 1852. 1st Ed, 1st Issue. 8vo, orig cloth; spine bottom & corners worn. With 48 plates. Some foxing. Larson copy. pba Sept 28 (575) $1,000
— A Pictorial View of California, including a Description of the Panama and Nicaragua Routes. NY, 1853. 8vo, orig cloth; edges worn, cocked. With 48 plates. Some foxing. wa Feb 29 (323) $350

**Lettsom, John Coakley**
— The Natural History of the Tea-Tress.... L, 1772. 1st Ed. 4to, contemp tree calf; rebacked, corners worn. With folding hand-colored frontis. Frontis torn in margin; C2v soiled; S4r thumb-soiled. Ck Mar 22 (167) £700

**Leupold, Jacob**
— Theatrum machinarum hydrotechnicarum.... Leipzig, 1724. Folio, contemp half vellum. With 51 plates. Some browning & spotting; tp & half-title creased in fore-margin. S Mar 14 (232) £800

— Theatrum machinarum supplementum. Leipzig, 1739. Folio, contemp calf; worn. With 40 (on 36) plates. Some creasing & spotting; text browned; marginal stains. S Mar 14 (231) £480

**Leusden, Johannes, 1624-99**

— Manuale hebraicum & Chaldaicum.... Utrecht, 1668. Bound with: Leusden. Een korte Hebreuse grammatica of taal-konst. Utrecht, 1668. 12mo, contemp vellum; covers stained, hinges starting. CE Dec 6 (98) $420

**Leutmann, Johann Georg**

— Vulcanus Famulans.... Wittenberg, 1723. Bound with: Trifolium Utile. Wittenberg, 1724 8vo, contemp vellum; partly discolored. With 5 folding plates & 2 folding tables. sg May 16 (201) $225

Anr Ed. Wittenberg, 1735. 8vo, contemp half calf. With frontis, 1 table & 55 plates. Tp trimmed at foot. S Mar 14 (233) £240

**Levaillant, Francois, 1753-1824**

— New Travels into the Interior Parts of Africa. L, 1796. 3 vols. 8vo, contemp calf; joints worn. With 1 folding map & 22 plates. Some spotting & offsetting. S Oct 26 (543) £150 [Martin]

— Perroquets. Sydney, 1989. ("Histoire naturelle des perroquets.") One of 200. 2 vols in 4. Folio, orig cloth. With 158 color lithos. C May 31 (29) £1,900; S June 27 (41) £1,800

**Levasseur, Victor**

— Atlas national illustre des 86 Departements et des possessions de la France. Paris, 1852. Orig half mor gilt worn. With engraved title, engraved table & 101 maps, hand-colored in outline. S Nov 30 (77) £1,000

Anr Ed. Paris, 1856. Folio, orig half mor gilt; worn. With statistical table & 99 (of 100) maps, colored in outline. S Nov 30 (76) £700

Anr Ed. Paris, 1866. Folio, orig half sheep gilt; worn, spine strip lacking, rear joint cracked through. With engraved title & 102 partly colored maps. Ink stamps; some soiling. cb Feb 14 (2555) £850

**Lever, Charles James, 1806-72**

— Charles O'Malley, the Irish Dragoon. L, 1897. Illus by Arthur Rackham. 8vo, orig cloth. With 16 plates. Ck May 31 (111) £110

— Nuts and Nutcrackers. L, 1845. Illus by Hablot K. Browne. 8vo, cloth. sg Sept 21 (252) $250

**Levertoff, Denise.** See: Levertov, Denise

**Levertov, Denise**

— Life in the Forest. NY, [1978]. 1st Ed, one of 150. sg Dec 14 (199) $80

**Levine, Bernard R.**

— Knifemakers of Old San Francisco. San Francisco: Badger Books, [1978]. Folio, in dj with short tears. Sgd on front free endpaper. pba Apr 25 (506) $50

**Levine, David**

— Pens and Needles. Bost., 1969. 1st American Ed, One of 300. Intro by John Updike. In dj. sg June 20 (382) $100

**Levine, Philip**

— Red Dust. Santa Cruz: Kayak Press, [1971]. One of 1,200. Orig wraps. pba Jan 25 (197) $65

**Levinson, Andre, 1887-1933**

— Bakst: The Story of the Artist's Life. L, 1923. One of 315. Folio, orig vellum. With 68 colored plates. b Jan 31 (135) £200

— The Designs of Leon Bakst for The Sleeping Princess. L, 1923. One of 1,000. Folio, orig half vellum. b Jan 31 (136) £450

Anr copy. Orig half vellum; small tear to upper cover. S Nov 21 (255) £550; sg Apr 18 (111) $600

Out-of-series copy. Orig half vellum. With port & 54 color plates. S May 16 (3) £280

— Leon Bakst: The Story of his Life. NY, 1922. One of 250. Folio, half vellum; corners worn, spine soiled. pba Nov 30 (28) $550

— Serge Lifar: Destin d'un danseur. [Paris], 1934. Ltd Ed. Folio, wraps; soiled, spine split, loose at backstrip. With frontis by Picasso & 60 plates. wa Dec 14 (568) $90

**Levinson, Orde**

— I Was Lonelyness: The Complete Graphic Works of John Muafangejo.... Capetown, 1987. 4to, cloth, in dj; hinges cracked. sg Sept 7 (255) $100

**Levis, Howard C.**

— A Descriptive Bibliography of the most Important Books in the English Language Relating to...Engraving. L, 1912. 1st Ed, one of 350. 4to, half cloth, unopened; worn & soiled, endpapers foxed, rear inner hinge broken. O Mar 26 (159) $225

**Levy, Julien**

— Surrealism. NY: Black Sun Press, 1936. 1st Ed, one of 1,500. In dj. Some browning. sg Jan 11 (256) $400

Anr copy. In chipped dj. Inscr. sg June 13 (238) $325

**Levy Collection, Julien**

— Photographs from the Julien Levy Collection. NY: Witkin Gallery, 1977. 4to, photo-pictorial wraps, spiral bound; some soiling. sg Feb 29 (184) $80

**Lewes, George Henry, 1817-78.** See: Fore-Edge Paintings

**Lewin, John William**

— A Natural History of the Birds of New South Wales. L, 1822. 4to, 19th-cent half mor gilt; worn, inner hinges repaired. With 26 hand-colored plates. Browned throughout; some marginal worming & tears. S Nov 30 (30) £1,000

**Lewin, William**

— The Birds of Great Britain. L, 1789-94. 7 vols. 4to, contemp mor gilt. With 323 (of 330) colored drawings by the author on peau de velin mtd on paper, the 1st sgd & dated 1788. Lacking 7 paintings; 6 others detached & loosely inserted; light damage to surface of c.26 paintings; single worm-trace through lower margins of about a third of Vol I. Jeanson - Fattorini copy. C Oct 25 (23) £25,000

Anr copy. Vols III-VII bound in 2 vols. 4to, contemp russia gilt; worn & stained. With 221 orig watercolor drawings. S Nov 30 (31) £5,000

One of 60 with orig watercolor drawings. Vols V & VI only, bound in 1 vol. 4to, 19th-cent mor gilt; rubbed, upper cover detached. With 87 (of 90) orig watercolor drawings. Marginal staining at ends. S Mar 29 (733) £1,000

2d Ed. L, 1800-1795-1801. 8 vols in 4. Folio, contemp mor gilt. With 336 hand-colored plates. Some discoloring & minor spotting. b Dec 5 (151) £1,700

**Lewine, J.**

— Bibliography of Eighteenth Century Art and Illustrated Books. L, 1898. One of 1,000. 8vo, cloth; rebound, spine faded. sg Apr 11 (203) $60

**Lewis, Angelo John, 1839-1919**

— Puzzles Old and New. L, 1893. 8vo, orig cloth. pba Apr 4 (207) $120

**Lewis, B. Roland**

— The Shakespeare Documents: Facsimiles, Transliterations, Translations & Commentary. Stanford, [1940-41]. 2 vols. 4to, cloth. wa Dec 14 (186) $50

**Lewis, Cecil Day, 1904-72**

— Dick Willoughby. Oxford, [1933]. 1st Ed. Orig cloth, in dj. S June 28 (31) £300

**Lewis, Charles Thomas Courtney**

— George Baxter, the Picture Printer. L, 1924. 4to, orig cloth. b May 30 (561) £80

— The Picture Printer of the Nineteenth Century, George Baxter, 1804-1867. L, 1911. Cloth; shaken. Some foxing. O Mar 26 (160) $90

**Lewis, Clive Staples, 1898-1963**

— The Horse and his Boy. L: Geoffrey Bles, [1954]. In dj with chip to spine head. pba May 4 (192) $350

Anr copy. In dj. S Nov 2 (303) £260 [Elkins]

— Prince Caspian. L, 1951. In chipped dj with tear along crease of rear flap; spine leaning. pba May 4 (191) $200

1st American Ed. NY, 1951. In soiled & torn dj. wa June 20 (274) $130

**Lewis, James, Architect**

— Original Designs in Architecture.... L, 1797. Mixed Ed. 2 vols in 1. Folio, contemp calf; worn. With 62 plates. C Oct 5 (359) £1,700

**Lewis, James O., 1799-1858**

— The Aboriginal Port-folio. Phila., 1835-36. Folio, half mor; joints rubbed, extremities worn. With 72 hand-colored plates. Tp in facsimile; text soiled, foxed & silked; 7 plates with repaired tears; 12 plates trimmed & inlaid. P June 5 (69) $14,000

**Lewis, John Frederick, 1805-76**

— Illustrations of Constantinople made during a Residence in that City.... L, [1838]. Folio, mor gilt. With litho title & 25 plates. b May 30 (280) £5,000

Anr copy. 19th-cent half mor gilt; worn. With litho title, litho dedication & 27 tinted litho subjects on 25 plates. Library blindstamp on each plate just touching image. S Nov 30 (128) £2,800

**Lewis, John Frederick, 1860-1932**

— Sketches and Drawings of the Alhambra.... L, [1835]. Folio, orig half mor; spine ends chipped, joints cracked. With litho title & 25 plates. Foxing affecting a few images; library bookplate. cb Oct 17 (195) $3,000

Anr copy. Contemp half lea; needs rebacking. Some foxing, affecting plates. sg Sept 7 (14) $1,800

**Lewis, Matthew Gregory ("Monk")**

— Tales of Terror. Dublin, 1801. 8vo, 19th-cent half calf gilt; front cover detached. With engraved title & 3 colored plates. Some foxing. sg Feb 8 (316) $225

**Lewis, Meriwether, 1774-1809.** See: Limited Editions Club

**Lewis, Meriwether, 1774-1809 —&
Clark, William, 1770-1838**

— History of the Expedition.... L, 1814. ("Travels to the Source of the Missouri River and across the American Continent to the Pacific Ocean....") 1st English Ed. 4to, later 19th-cent half lea gilt; rebacked retaining orig backstrip, joints rubbed, hinges reinforced with cloth. With folding map & 5 maps on 3 plates. Blank lower outer corner of 2 text leaves restored. sg Oct 26 (208) $5,000

Anr Ed. Phila., 1814. 2 vols. 8vo, near-contemp sheep; joints & extremities rubbed, upper inner hinges cracked, tears to corners of back flyleaves in Vol II. Tp of Vol I with small holes to upper forecorner; folding map creased & with repaired tear entering border rule; perforation to 2:3E catching a letter; some browning & foxing. Engelhard copy. CNY Jan 26 (187) $25,000

Anr copy. Contemp sheep; recased & reglazed, spines repaired. With folding map & 5 charts. Some foxing; folding map silked & repaired. pba Feb 13 (117) $15,000

Anr copy. Early half calf; needs rebdg. Titles in both vols remargined along upper edge without loss; browning throughout; folding map browned & with repairs & a tear. sg Oct 26 (207) $10,000

1st Ed. 2 vols. 8vo, 19th-cent calf; covers rehinged, rubbed & discolored, vol II spine head chipped; hinge cracked. With 5 maps, 1 folding. Map foxed &

torn; some darkening; prelims of vol I out of order. Robbins copy. pba Mar 21 (197) $19,000
Anr Ed. L, 1817. ("Travels to the Source of the Missouri River and across the American Continent to the Pacific Ocean....") 3 vols. 8vo, modern calf; needs rebdg. Folding map in facsimile; lacking 1 half-title. sg Oct 26 (209) $300
Anr Ed. NY, 1893. One of 200. Ed by Elliott Coues. 4 vols. 8vo, half mor. With 2 ports, 1 facsimile letter, 5 sketches, & 3 folding maps. Robbins copy. pba Mar 21 (198) $850
— The Journals of the Expedition. NY: Heritage Press, [1962]. 2 vols. pba Feb 13 (120) $65
— The Journals of the Lewis and Clark Expedition.... Lincoln: University of Nebraska Press, 1983-93. Ed by Gary E. Moulton. 8 vols. 8vo & folio, cloth, text vols in djs. pba Feb 13 (121) $650
Anr copy. 8 vols, including atlas, Orig cloth in dj; some d/j spines sunned. Robbins copy. pba Mar 21 (201) $850
[-] Message from the President of the United States, Communicating Discoveries made in Exploring the Missouri, Red River, and Washita.... Wash., 1806. Bound with: U. S. Congress. Report of the Committee Appointed...On So Much of the Message of the President...As Relates to the Further Exploring of the Western Waters. December 22, 1806. Wash., 1802. 2 pp. And: U. S. Congress. Documents Accompanying a Bill Making Compensations to Messieurs Lewis and Clarke and their Companions, Presented the 23rd January 1807. Wash., 1807. 8vo, mor gilt. Folding map spotted, with tear crossing border & 3 tissue reinforcements & inserted on a guard; leaf 16/4 torn & repaired at corner with loss of letters; lacking final blank.. Thomas Winthrop Streeter's annotated copy. Engelhard copy. CNY Jan 26 (184) $18,000
— Original Journals of the Lewis and Clark Expedition.... NY, 1904-5. One of 200 on Van Gelder paper. Ed by Reuben G. Thwaites. 8 vols in 15. Folio, orig cloth; worn. with 62 sheets of plates. Library markings; titles stamped. bbc Dec 18 (498) $2,000
Anr Ed. NY, 1904. One of—200 on Van Gelder paper. 8 vols in 15. Folio, orig mor; spines faded & scuffed, corners worn, 1 front cover scratched, some hinges cracking. Vol I front flyleaf loose; page edges darkened. Robbins copy. pba Mar 21 (202) $11,000
Anr Ed. NY, 1904-5. One of—200 on Van Gelder paper. 8 vols in 15. Folio, orig cloth; spine ends worn, some chipped. Frontis of Vol I detached. pba Apr 25 (507) $2,750

**Lewis, Oscar**
See also: Grabhorn Printing
— Bonanza Inn. America's First Luxury Hotel. NY, 1939. In dj. With frontis & 16 plates. Inscr & with related material. pba Feb 12 (337) $55
— Sea Routes to the Gold Fields: The Migration by Water to California in 1849-1952. NY, 1949. With: Report of the Secretary of War, Communicating... the Report of Captain Thomas J. Cram, of November 1856... [Senate Executive Document No. 51, 34th Congress, 3d Session] 1st Ed. Orig cloth in dj; d/j creased. With 1 folded map. Sgd. Larson copy. pba Sept 28 (576) $70

**Lewis, Samella —& Waddy, Ruth G.**
— Black Artists on Art. Los Angeles, 1969-71. 2 vols. 4to, cloth, in djs. sg Mar 28 (23) $250

**Lewis, Samuel, d.1862**
— Atlas to the Topographical Dictionary of England and Wales. L, 1845. 4to, orig cloth; backstrip def. With folding general map, folding plan of London & 43 county maps, hand-colored in outline. S Mar 28 (128) $150
Anr Ed. L, 1847. 4to, orig cloth; stained. With 56 maps, hand-colored in outline. Spotted. S Mar 28 (87) £170
— A Topographical Dictionary of England. L, [c.1840]. Atlas vol only. 4to, orig cloth; foot of spine chipped. With 45 maps, many folding. Sold w.a.f. b Sept 20 (279) £120
— A Topographical Dictionary of Ireland. L, 1849. 2 vols plus Atlas. 4to, cloth; needs rebdg. sg Mar 7 (146) $225

**Lewis, Sinclair, 1885-1951**
See also: Limited Editions Club
— Ann Vickers. NY, 1933. 1st Ed. In dj with closed tear. sg June 20 (220) $120
— Babbitt. NY, [1922]. 1st Ed, 1st State. In repaired dj. Lacking 1st blank. sg Dec 14 (200) $400
— Elmer Gantry. NY, [1927]. 1st Ed, 1st Bdg. In chipped & soiled dj. sg June 20 (221) $200
— Hike and the Aeroplane. By Tom Graham. NY, [1912]. 1st Ed. Orig cloth; worn, hinge repaired. Inscr & with Ls laid in. Goodwin - Engelhard copy. CNY Oct 27 (105) $2,400
— Main Street. NY, 1920. 1st Ed. Inscr to A. S. Le Vino. sg June 20 (222) $475
— Our Mr. Wrenn. NY, 1914. 1st Ed. Orig cloth, in pictorial dj; strengthened. Inscr twice by Lewis. Swann - Goodwin - Engelhard copy. CNY Oct 27 (106) $2,200

**Lewis, William, 1714-81**
— An Experimental History of the Materia Medica.... L, 1761. 1st Ed. 4to, disbound. Old stamp on tp. sg May 16 (441) $250

**Lewis, Wyndham, 1884-1957**
— The Apes of God. L, 1930. 1st Ed, one of 750. 4to, orig cloth, in dj. CE May 22 (306) $400
— The Ideal Giant, the Code of a Herdsman, Cantelman's Spring-Mate. L: Privately ptd, [1917]. 1st Ed. Orig half cloth; rubbed, corners worn. bba May 9 (230) £500 [Poetry Bookshop]

**Leybourn, William, 1626-1700?**
— Cursus Mathematicus: Mathematical Sciences, in Nine Books.... L, 1690. 1st Ed. Folio, disbound. With 44 plates. Marginal dampstaining at end; ink notes on back of plate facing p.701, showing through. Sold w.a.f. sg May 16 (202) $400

**Leyden, John, 1775-1811**
— Tableau historique des decouvertes et etablissemens des Europeens, dans le Nord et dans l'Oeust de l'Afrique. Paris, 1803. 2 vols. 8vo, orig wraps. sg Mar 7 (147) $250

**Leydig, Franz**
— Anatomisch-Histologische Untersuchungen ueber Fische und Reptilien. Berlin, 1853. 4to, orig half cloth; extremities worn, backstrip def. With 4 plates. Foxing to plates. sg May 16 (319) $50

**Leyser, Augustin**
— Meditationes ad Pandectas. Leipzig, 1741-45. 4 vols in 2. 4to, contemp vellum; worn & soiled. F Mar 28 (164) $140

**L'Heritier de Villandon, Marie Jeanne, 1664-1734**
— L'Adroite Princesse, ou les aventures de finette. Paris, 1928. One of 480. Illus by Marie Laurencin. Folio, half mor, orig wraps bound in. With 5 colored lithos. S Nov 21 (219) £1,100

**L'Hopital, Michel de, 1507-73**
— Epistolarum seu sermonum libri sex. Paris: Mamert Patisson, in officina Roberti Stephani, 1585. Folio, contemp mor gilt, elaborately tooled; spine & 2 corners repaired, upper cover wormed & stained. Chatsworth copy. S Nov 30 (279) £1,800

**Libanus Press**
— Daylight Jobbery: Ephemera to 1985 by Libanus Press. L, [c.1986]. One of 75. 4to, loose as issued in orig box. bba May 9 (317) £80 [Deighton Bell]

**Liber...**
— Liber Scriptorum. The First Book of the Author's Club. NY, 1893. One of 251. 4to, orig mor gilt. With 109 contributions, each sgd by its author. CE May 22 (99) $1,300

Anr copy. Orig mor. P June 5 (145A) $2,500

**Liberati, Francesco**
— La Perfettione del Cavallo. Rome: heirs of Francesco Corbelletti, 1639. 4to, old vellum; loose. Some foxing. sg Mar 7 (488) $225

**Liberator**
— The Liberator. Bost., 1834-48. Ed by William Lloyd Garrison. 145 weekly issues K Feb 11 (21) $1,550

**Liberman, Alexander**
See also: Onassis copy, Jacqueline Bouvier Kennedy
— The Art and Technique of Color Photography. NY, 1951. Folio, half cloth, in chipped & repaired dj. sg Feb 29 (102) $120

Anr copy. Half cloth, in chipped dj. sg Feb 29 (102) $120

**Libri, Guillaume, 1803-69**
— Catalogue de la bibliotheque de.... Paris, 1847-48. Bound with: Reponse au rapport de M. Boucly... 2 vols. 8vo, contemp bds. sg Apr 11 (20) $300

**Licetus, Fortunius, 1577-1657**
— De lucernis antiquorum reconditis lib. sex. Udine, 1652. Folio, contemp vellum. With 3 folding plates. Ll4 torn at edge; some browning & soiling; washed ex-libris of an Italian Capuchin library. S Mar 14 (234) £580

— De monstris. Amst., 1665. 4to, vellum; soiled. rs Nov 11 (70) $900

Anr copy. Contemp vellum bds; soiled. With engraved title & 3 plates. Some soiling & spotting. S June 12 (266) £850

Anr copy. Contemp vellum bds; crack across backstrip. Dampstained. sg May 16 (442) $425

**Licht...**
— Lucht und Schatten.... Prague: Artia, [1959]. Intro by Ludvik Vesely. 4to, cloth, in dj with tear on rear panel. sg Feb 29 (108) $110

**Lickbarrow, Isabella**
— Poetical Effusions. Kendal, 1814. 8vo, orig bds; spine def. b Dec 5 (169) £110

**Liebault, Jean, d.1596**
— Secrets de medecine, et de la philosophie chimique. Rouen, 1643. 8vo, 19th-cent half calf. Lacking 1 prelim leaf; a few leaves wormed; last leaf frayed & repaired. S June 12 (302) £300

**Liebmann, Louis —&**
**Wahl, Gustave**
— Katalog der Historischen Abteilung der Ersten Internationalen Luftschiffahrts-Ausstellung.... Frankfurt, 1912. Orig cloth; shaken front joint torn & frayed, pencil notes & mtd postcard on front endpapers. sg May 16 (56) $650

**Liechtenstein, Marie von.** See: Mary

**Lienhard, Heinrich**
— Californien: unmittelbar vor und nach der Entdeckung des Goldes. Zurich, 1898. 1st Ed. 8vo, orig wraps; recased, orig front & rear wraps laid in, wraps chipped. With frontis port. Darkening. Larson copy. pba Sept 28 (577) $190

Anr copy. Orig cloth; cover corners bumped. With frontis port. Robbins copy. pba Mar 21 (203) $275

— A Pioneer at Sutter's Fort, 1846-1850. Los Angeles: The Calafia Society, 1941. Trans & ed by Marguerite Eyer Wilbur. Orig linen. With frontis port. Larson copy. pba Sept 28 (579) $50

1st English Ed. - Trans & Ed by Marguerite E. Wilbur. Orig cloth. With 6 plates. Robbins copy. pba Mar 21 (204) $160

**Lieure, Jules**
— Jacques Callot. NY, 1969. 8 vols. 4to, orig cloth. bba Oct 5 (278) £340 [Fletcher]; S June 12 (326) £200

**Life...**
— Life in the Nursery; The Christmas Tree. Phila.: American Sunday School Union, [c.1865]. 8vo, pic-

torial wraps. With 12 hand-colored illusts. pba Jan 4 (15) $300
— The Life of Takla Haymanot, the Miracles of...& the Book of the Riches of Kings. L, 1906. Out-of-series copy. Trans by E. A. Wallis Budge. Folio, cloth. bba July 18 (59) £360 [Braham]

**Life Magazine**
— Life. NY, 1936-37. Vol I-Vol III, No 22. 54 nos. Folio, orig ptd wraps. bbc June 24 (241) $200

**Light, William, 1785?-1839 — & De Wint, Peter, 1784-1849**
— Sicilian Scenery. L, 1823. 4to, contemp mor gilt. With engraved title & 61 plates. b May 30 (161) £550

**Lighton, Norman**
— The Paintings... for Roberts Birds of South Africa. Capetown, [n.d.]. Folio, orig cloth. With 56 color plates. sg May 16 (320) $200

**Ligne, Charles Joseph, Prince de, 1735-1814**
— Colette et Lucas. Bel-Oeil: P. Charles de Ligne, 1781. 4to, early 19th-cent bds. Dampstaining on the outer margin of F1. Fuerstenberg - Schaefer copy. S Dec 7 (379) £900
— Coup d'oeil sur Beloeil. Bel-Oeil: P. Charles de Ligne, 1781. 8vo, orig half calf; rubbed, spine head repaired. A few margins with crease split. Fuerstenberg - Schaefer copy. S Dec 7 (380) £1,600
— Fantaisies militaires, par un officier autrichien. [N.p., c.1780]. 8vo, 19th-cent bds. Engraved throughout. With 14 plates. Fuerstenberg - Schaefer copy. S Dec 7 (378) £240
— Recueil de six paysages. [N.p., c.1790]. Oblong folio, mor extra by Canape & Corriez. With 13 plates. Fuerstenberg - Schaefer copy. S Dec 7 (377) £2,800

**Ligon, Richard**
— A True & Exact History of the Island of Barbados.... L, 1673. Folio, old calf; rubbed, corners curled, rebacked. Tear repaired; some foxing. Met Feb 24 (349) $1,500

**Lilford, Thomas L. Powys, 4th Baron**
— Coloured Figures of the Birds of the British Islands. L, 1885-97. 7 vols. 8vo, contemp half mor gilt by Birdsall, orig wraps to 7 orig parts bound in. With photogravure port & 421 chromolitho plates. Ink mark to upper margin of p.51 of text in Vol V. Fattorini copy. C Oct 25 (25) £2,200

Anr copy. Contemp half calf; rubbed, 2 covers stained. With port & 421 colored plates, c.60 handcolored. Common Snipe in Vol V frayed; some remnants of tissue guards; some browning of text. S June 27 (43) £1,000

Anr Ed. L, 1891-97. 7 vols. 4to, contemp half mor. With port & 421 chromolitho or hand-colored plates. Marginal spotting, affecting image of c.20 plates. C May 31 (30) £2,000

Anr copy. With port & 421 colored plates, c.60 of them hand-colored. Minor foxing to a few plates. S June 27 (44) £1,350

2d Ed. L, 1891-97 [1898]. ("Figures of British Birds.") 7 vols. 4to contemp mor gilt by R. H. Porter. With port & 421 chromolitho plates. Fattorini copy. C Oct 25 (26) £2,400

**Lilienthal, Otto, 1848-96**
— Birdflight as the Basis of Aviation. L, 1911. Orig bdg; spine ends worn. With 8 folding plates & 94 illusts. pba Nov 30 (224) $150

**Lilly, William, 1602-81**
— Catastrophe Mundi: or, Merlin Reviv'd.... L, 1683. 8vo, contemp calf; worn. With 15 (of 17) woodcut plates. Soiled. S Mar 28 (486) £200
— Christian Astrology. L, 1647. 1st Ed. 3 parts in 1 vol. 4to, contemp calf; rebacked but partially disbound. With frontis port by William Marshall. Some browning, soiling & dampstaining. S Mar 28 (487) £425

**Lillywhite, John**
— Cricketer's Annual. L, 1873-1900. 26 vols; lacking 1878. Orig bdsps; rubbed & soiled. Many margins strengthened with tape. pn Oct 12 (194) £440

**Limborch, Philippus van, 1633-1712**
— Historia inquisitionis; cui subjungitur.... Amst., 1692. 2 parts in 1 vol. Folio, vellum gilt; soiled. K June 23 (345) $300

**Limited Editions Club—New York**
[All entries are one of 1,500 (2,000 from 17 July 1973), sgd by illus or book designer, unless otherwise noted]
[All entries are one of 1,500 (2,000 from 17 July 1973), sgd by illus or book designer, unless otherwise noted]
— All Men are Brothers. 1948. Trans by Pearl Buck. 2 vols. pba Mar 7 (274) $130; sg Nov 9 (70) $110; sg June 27 (58) $120; wa Dec 14 (229) $95
— The Arabian Nights. 1934. Burton's trans. 6 vols. pba Mar 7 (288) $225; sg Nov 9 (19) $200; sg June 27 (401) $90; wa Dec 14 (230) $120
Anr Ed. 1954. 4 vols. sg June 27 (16) $275
— Aucassin and Nicolette. 1931. sg June 27 (21) $100
— Bible (King James Version). 1935-36. 5 vols. sg Nov 9 (46) $140; wa Dec 14 (223) $110
— The Book of Ecclesiastes. 1968. pba Mar 7 (319) $50; sg Nov 9 (168) $70; sg June 27 (146) $70
— Book of Job. 1946. One of 1,950. pba Mar 7 (360) $180; sg Nov 9 (271) $350; sg Feb 15 (285) $250; sg June 27 (233) $200; wa Nov 16 (42) $120; wa Dec 14 (221) $70; wa Feb 1 (7) $80
— The Book of Proverbs. 1963. pba Mar 7 (363) $85; sg Nov 9 (361) $70; sg June 27 (315) $50
— The Book of Psalms. 1960. pba Mar 7 (362) $110; sg Nov 9 (362) $100; sg June 27 (316) $70
— The Book of Ruth. 1947. One of 1,950. pba Mar 7 (361) $190; sg Nov 9 (381) $400; sg Feb 15 (286) $300; sg June 27 (334) $100; wa Dec 14 (222) $110

# 1995 - 1996 · BOOKS

# LIMITED

— The Book of the Dead. 1972.  2 vols.  sg Nov 9 (54) $140
— The Book of the Prophet Isaiah. 1979.  sg Nov 9 (262) $175; sg June 27 (225) $90
— The Dead Sea Scrolls. 1966.  sg Nov 9 (131) $150; sg June 27 (107) $150
— Evergreen Tales. 1949-52.  Series I-V (Nos 1-15). 15 vols.  wa Dec 14 (238) $290
— Evergreen Tales. Group 1. 1948.  3 vols.  sg Nov 9 (178) $110
— Evergreen Tales. Group 2. 1949.  3 vols.  sg Nov 9 (179) $100
— Evergreen Tales. Group 3. 1949.  3 vols.  sg Nov 9 (180) $175
— Evergreen Tales. Group 4. 1949.  3 vols.  sg Nov 9 (181) $100
    Anr Ed. 1952.  3 vols.  sg June 27 (156) $90
— Evergreen Tales. Group 5. 1952.  3 vols.  sg Nov 9 (182) $120; sg June 27 (157) $60
— The Federalist...Papers by Hamilton, Madison and Jay. 1945.  2 vols.  pba Mar 7 (333) $110; sg Nov 9 (184) $225; sg Feb 15 (269) $120; sg June 27 (159) $80
— Fine Books Published by the Limited Editions Club, 1929-1985. 1985.  One of 800.  sg Nov 9 (47) $175
— The First Book of Moses called Genesis. 1989.  One of 400.  Illus by Jacob Lawrence.  sg Nov 9 (206) $1,300; sg Feb 15 (185) $1,400
— The Four Gospels. 1932.  sg June 27 (168) $60
— The Koran; Selected Sutras. 1958.  pba Mar 7 (364) $110; sg Nov 9 (283) $300; sg June 27 (245) $120
— The Living Talmud. 1960.  sg Nov 9 (434) $140
— The Nibelungenlied. 1960.  sg Nov 9 (328) $70
— Quarto-Millenary: the First 250 Publications.... 1959. bba May 9 (320) £80 [Elsmore]; cb Oct 17 (652) $120; pba Mar 7 (392) $300; pba Aug 8 (504) $225; sg Nov 9 (367) $110; sg June 27 (321) $150; Z June 28 (167) $150
— The Saga of Beowulf. 1952.  sg Nov 9 (43) $120; sg June 27 (40) $80
— The Sermon on the Mount. 1977.  One of 1,600.  sg Nov 9 (392) $80
— Sir Gawain and the Green Knight. 1971.  sg Nov 9 (408) $80; sg June 27 (363) $80
— The Song of Roland. 1938.  sg Nov 9 (410) $50
Adams, Henry. - The Education of Henry Adams. 1942.  sg Nov 9 (1) $60
Adams, Henry. - Mont Saint-Michel and Chartres. 1957.  sg Nov 9 (2) $50
Aeschylus. - The Oresteia. 1961.  pba Mar 7 (272) $50; sg Nov 9 (5) $50; sg Nov 9 (5) $50
Aeschylus. - Prometheus Bound. 1965.  With Shelley, P. B. Prometheus Unbound. 1965. pba Mar 7 (271) $50
    Anr copy. With Shelley, P. B. Prometheus Unbound. 1965. sg Nov 9 (6) $70
Aesop. - Fables. 1933.  sg Nov 9 (7) $130
Alcott, Louisa May. - Little Women. 1967.  sg Nov 9 (10) $100; sg June 27 (9) $80
Allen, Hervey. - Anthony Adverse. 1937.  3 vols.  sg Nov 9 (11) $70; sg June 27 (10) $150
Andersen, Hans Christian. - The Complete Andersen.... 1949.  6 vols.  pba Mar 7 (275) $140; sg Nov 9 (12) $200; wa Dec 14 (237) $130
Andersen, Hans Christian. - Fairy Tales. 1942.  2 vols.  sg Nov 9 (13) $150; sg June 27 (11) $150
Anderson, Sherwood. - Winesburg, Ohio. 1978.  sg Nov 9 (14) $70
Angelou, Maya. - Our Grandmothers. 1994.  sg Nov 9 (15) $600
Apollonius Rhodius. - Argonautica. 1958.  sg Nov 9 (16) $100; sg June 27 (12) $120
Apuleius, Lucius. - The Golden Ass. 1932.  sg Nov 9 (17) $90; sg June 27 (13) $120
Apuleius, Lucius. - The Marriage of Cupid & Psyche. 1951.  pba Mar 7 (276) $325; sg June 27 (14) $110
Aragon, Louis. - Le Paysan de Paris. 1994.  One of 300.  sg Nov 9 (20) $425
Aristophanes. - The Frogs. 1937.  sg Nov 9 (22) $70
Aristophanes. - Lysistrata. 1934.  Illus by Pablo Picasso. K Oct 1 (309) $2,100
    Anr copy. Schaefer copy.  P Nov 1 (9) $2,250; sg Oct 19 (7) $2,400; sg Nov 9 (23) $2,400; sg Feb 15 (10) $2,200; sg Apr 18 (90) $2,800; sg June 27 (19) $2,000; wa Dec 14 (215) $1,800
Aristotle. - Politics & Poetics. 1964.  pba Mar 7 (277) $110; sg Nov 9 (24) $100
Arnold, Sir Edwin. - The Light of Asia; or the Great Renunciation. 1976.  sg Nov 9 (25) $60
Augustine. - The Confessions. 1962.  pba Mar 7 (278) $65; sg Nov 9 (26) $50
Austen, Jane. - Emma. 1964.  sg Nov 9 (28) $60; sg June 27 (24) $90
Austen, Jane. - Persuasion. 1977.  One of 1,600.  sg Nov 9 (30) $50
Austen, Jane. - Pride and Prejudice. 1940.  sg Nov 9 (31) $100
Bacon, Sir Francis. - The Essays or Counsels.... 1944.  sg Nov 9 (33) $175
Balzac, Honore de. - Droll Stories. 1932.  3 vols.  O Dec 5 (12) $50; sg June 27 (29) $70
Balzac, Honore de. - Old Goriot. 1948.  sg Nov 9 (35) $60; sg June 27 (31) $100
Baudelaire, Charles. - Les Fleurs du mal. 1940.  Illus by Auguste Rodin.  sg June 27 (33) $450
Baudelaire, Charles. - Flowers of Evil. 1971.  Illus by Pierre Yves Trenois.  2 vols.  sg Nov 9 (36) $60
Beckett, Samuel. - Nohow On. 1989.  One of 550.  sg Nov 9 (37) $1,600; sg June 27 (34) $1,100
Beckford, William Thomas. - Vathek. 1945.  pba Jan 4 (301) $110; sg Nov 9 (38) $50; wa Nov 16 (41) $50
Bellamy, Edward. - Looking Backward. 1941.  sg Nov 9 (40) $60; sg June 27 (37) $60
Benet, Stephen Vincent. - John Brown's Body: a Poem. 1948.  sg Nov 9 (41) $50
Bernanos, Georges. - The Diary of a Country Priest. NY, 1986.  One of 1,000.  sg Nov 9 (44) $150; sg Feb 15 (43) $150; sg June 27 (41) $130; wa Dec 14 (220) $90
Beyle, Marie Henri ("Stendhal"). - The Charterhouse of Parma. 1955.  sg Nov 9 (417) $50
Beyle, Marie Henri ("Stendhal"). - The Red and the Black. 1947.  sg Nov 9 (418) $80
Bierce, Ambrose. - The Devil's Dictionary. 1972.  sg Nov 9 (48) $70
Bierce, Ambrose. - Tales of Soldiers and Civilians. 1943.  sg Nov 9 (50) $70; sg June 27 (45) $60; wa Dec 14

667

(224) $90
BLAKE, WILLIAM. - Poems. 1973.  sg Nov 9 (51) $70
BLIGH, WILLIAM. - A Voyage to the South Seas. 1975.  cb Oct 17 (651) $90; sg Nov 9 (52) $100; sg June 27 (46) $70
BOCCACCIO, GIOVANNI. - Decameron. 1930.  2 vols.  sg Nov 9 (53) $225; wa Dec 14 (225) $75
BORGES, JORGE LUIS. - Ficciones. 1984.  sg Nov 9 (55) $350; sg Feb 15 (59) $550
BOSWELL, JAMES. - The Life of Samuel Johnson. 1938.  3 vols.  sg Nov 9 (58) $120; wa Dec 14 (226) $75
BRADBURY, RAY. - Fahrenheit 451. 1982.  sg Nov 9 (59) $200
BRADBURY, RAY. - The Martian Chronicles. 1974.  cb Oct 17 (514) $250; sg Nov 9 (60) $200; sg June 27 (49) $175
BRECHT, BERTOLT. - The Threepenny Opera. 1982.  sg Nov 9 (61) $110
BRILLAT-SAVARIN, ANTHELME. - The Physiology of Taste. 1949.  pba Mar 7 (281) $150; sg Nov 9 (62) $70; wa Dec 14 (227) $75
BRONTE, EMILY. - Wuthering Heights. 1993.  One of 300.  sg Nov 9 (63) $1,200
BROOKS, VAN WYCK. - The Flowering of New England. 1941.  sg Nov 9 (64) $70
BROWNE, SIR THOMAS. - Religio Medici. 1939.  sg May 16 (385) $50; sg June 27 (53) $80
BROWNING, ELIZABETH BARRETT. - Sonnets from the Portuguese. 1948.  pba Mar 7 (282) $110; sg June 27 (54) $60
BROWNING, ROBERT. - The Poems of Robert Browning. 1969.  sg Nov 9 (67) $60
BROWNING, ROBERT. - The Ring and the Book. 1949.  2 vols.  pba Mar 7 (283) $60
BRYANT, WILLIAM CULLEN. - Poems. 1947.  sg Nov 9 (69) $50; sg June 27 (57) $50
BULFINCH, THOMAS. - The Age of Fable. 1958.  pba Jan 4 (302) $90; pba Mar 7 (285) $80; sg Nov 9 (71) $70
BUNYAN, JOHN. - The Pilgrim's Progress. 1941.  sg Nov 9 (73) $120; sg June 27 (61) $100
BURKE, EDMUND. - On Conciliation with America.... 1975.  sg Nov 9 (74) $70
BURNS, ROBERT. - Poems. 1965.  pba Mar 7 (287) $65; sg June 27 (63) $60
BURTON, SIR RICHARD FRANCIS. - The Kasidah of Haji Abdu el Yezdi. 1937.  sg Nov 9 (76) $70; sg June 27 (64) $50
BUTLER, SAMUEL. - Erewhon. 1934.  pba Jan 25 (181) $75; sg June 27 (65) $130
BUTLER, SAMUEL. - The Way of All Flesh. 1934.  2 vols.  sg Nov 9 (77) $50
CABELL, JAMES BRANCH. - Jurgen: a Comedy of Justice. 1976.  sg Nov 9 (78) $50
CAESAR, CAIUS JULIUS. - The Gallic Wars. 1954.  pba Mar 7 (289) $70; sg Nov 9 (80) $110; sg June 27 (67) $140
CAMUS, ALBERT. - The Stranger. 1971.  sg Nov 9 (81) $80; sg June 27 (68) $80
CARLYLE, THOMAS. - The French Revolution. 1956.  pba Mar 7 (290) $55; sg June 27 (69) $50
CARPENTIER, ALEJO. - The Kingdom of This World. 1987.  One of 750.  sg Nov 9 (83) $120; sg June 27 (70) $100
CARSON, RACHEL. - The Sea Around Us. 1980.  sg Nov 9 (87) $275; sg Feb 15 (65) $175; sg June 27 (73) $100
CASANOVA DE SEINGALT, GIACOMO GIROLAMO. - Memoirs. 1940.  8 vols.  sg Nov 9 (88) $70; wa Dec 14 (233) $65
CATHER, WILLA. - A Lost Lady. 1983.  sg Nov 9 (90) $70
CELLINI, BENVENUTO. - The Life of Benvenuto Cellini Written by Himself. 1937.  sg Nov 9 (91) $150; sg Feb 15 (66) $70
CERVANTES SAAVEDRA, MIGUEL DE. - Don Quixote. 1950.  2 vols.  sg Nov 9 (92) $100; sg June 27 (76) $200; wa Dec 14 (234) $65
CHAUCER, GEOFFREY. - The Canterbury Tales. 1934.  2 vols.  sg Nov 9 (93) $90
Anr Ed. 1946.  pba Mar 7 (291) $130; sg Nov 9 (94) $250; sg June 27 (77) $70; wa Nov 16 (44) $170; wa Dec 14 (236) $100
CHEKHOV, ANTON. - The Short Stories.... 1973.  sg Nov 9 (96) $50
CICERO, MARCUS TULLIUS. - Orations and Essays. 1972.  sg Nov 9 (98) $50
CLEMENS, SAMUEL LANGHORNE. - A Connecticut Yankee in King Arthur's Court. 1949.  pba Mar 7 (417) $50; sg Nov 9 (458) $50
CLEMENS, SAMUEL LANGHORNE. - Huckleberry Finn. 1942.  pba June 20 (225) $160; sg Nov 9 (456) $500; sg June 27 (408) $250; wa Nov 16 (61) $180; wa Dec 14 (352) $200
CLEMENS, SAMUEL LANGHORNE. - The Innocents Abroad. 1962.  sg June 27 (411) $80
CLEMENS, SAMUEL LANGHORNE. - Life on the Mississippi. 1944.  sg Nov 9 (460) $400; sg June 27 (412) $325; wa Nov 16 (60) $190; wa Dec 14 (351) $220
CLEMENS, SAMUEL LANGHORNE. - The Notorious Jumping Frog and Other Stories. 1970.  sg Nov 9 (461) $70
CLEMENS, SAMUEL LANGHORNE. - The Prince and the Pauper. 1964.  sg June 27 (414) $80
CLEMENS, SAMUEL LANGHORNE. - Tom Sawyer. 1939.  sg Nov 9 (457) $325; sg June 27 (409) $225; wa Dec 14 (353) $210
CLEMENS, SAMUEL LANGHORNE. - A Tramp Abroad. 1966.  sg June 27 (415) $120
COLERIDGE, SAMUEL TAYLOR. - The Rime of the Ancient Mariner. 1983.  sg Nov 9 (99) $60
COLETTE, SIDONIE GABRIELLE. - Break of Day. 1983.  sg Nov 9 (100) $120
COLLIER, JOHN PAYNE. - Punch and Judy. 1937.  sg Nov 9 (363) $110
COLLINS, WILKIE. - The Moonstone. 1959.  sg Nov 9 (101) $50
COLLODI, CARLO. - Pinocchio, the Adventures of a Marionette. 1937.  sg Nov 9 (103) $100
CONFUCIUS. - The Analects. 1933.  pba Mar 7 (295) $120; sg Nov 9 (105) $225
Anr Ed. 1970.  sg Nov 9 (106) $175; sg June 27 (84) $200
CONRAD, JOSEPH. - Heart of Darkness. 1992.  One of 300.  sg Nov 9 (109) $800
CONRAD, JOSEPH. - Lord Jim. 1959.  pba Mar 7 (296) $110; sg Nov 9 (110) $110
CONRAD, JOSEPH. - The Nigger of the "Narcissus". 1965.  pba Mar 7 (298) $55; sg Nov 9 (111) $50
CONRAD, JOSEPH. - Nostromo. 1961.  pba Mar 7 (297) $70
CONRAD, JOSEPH. - The Secret Sharer. 1985.  sg Nov 9

(114) $70

CONRAD, JOSEPH. - Youth, Typhoon, The End of the Tether.... 1972.  sg Nov 9 (115) $50

COOK, CAPT. JAMES. - The Explorations in the Pacific. 1957.  pba Mar 7 (299) $170; sg Nov 9 (116) $90; wa Dec 14 (249) $85

COOPER, JAMES FENIMORE. - The Deerslayer. 1961.  sg June 27 (92) $90

COOPER, JAMES FENIMORE. - The Last of the Mohicans. 1932.  sg June 27 (93) $90

COOPER, JAMES FENIMORE. - The Pilot. 1968.  sg Nov 9 (119) $50

COOPER, JAMES FENIMORE. - The Prairie. 1940.  sg June 27 (96) $60

COWLEY, MALCOLM. - Exile's Return. 1981.  sg Nov 9 (122) $90; sg Feb 15 (78) $100; sg Feb 29 (2) $175

CRANE, HART. - The Bridge. 1981.  sg Nov 9 (123) $60

CRANE, STEPHEN. - The Red Badge of Courage. 1944.  sg Nov 9 (125) $130; sg Feb 15 (83) $70; sg June 27 (99) $150; wa Dec 14 (250) $95

CREASY, SIR EDWARD SHEPHERD. - The Fifteen Decisive Battles of the World. 1969.  sg Nov 9 (126) $100

DANA, RICHARD HENRY. - Two Years Before the Mast. 1947.  sg Nov 9 (127) $50

DANTE ALIGHIERI. - The Divine Comedy. 1932.  sg June 27 (102) $80

DARWIN, CHARLES. - The Descent of Man.... 1971.  sg Nov 9 (128) $120; sg June 27 (103) $80

DARWIN, CHARLES. - Journal of Researches...during the Voyage of the HMS Beagle. 1956.  pba Dec 14 (35) $60; pba Mar 7 (304) $110; sg Nov 9 (130) $150; sg June 27 (105) $90; wa Dec 14 (251) $75

DARWIN, CHARLES. - On The Origin of Species. 1963.  pba Mar 7 (305) $120; sg Nov 9 (129) $140; sg June 27 (104) $90

DEFOE, DANIEL. - A Journal of the Plague Year.... 1968.  sg June 27 (110) $60

DEFOE, DANIEL. - Moll Flanders. 1954.  pba Mar 7 (307) $65; sg Nov 9 (132) $175; sg Feb 15 (194) $60; sg June 27 (109) $100

DEFOE, DANIEL. - Robinson Crusoe. 1930.  sg Nov 9 (134) $90

DIAZ DEL CASTILLO, BERNAL. - The Discovery and Conquest of Mexico. 1942.  pba Apr 25 (178) $75; sg Nov 9 (136) $275; wa Nov 16 (45) $130; wa Dec 14 (211) $160

DICKENS, CHARLES. - The Chimes. 1931.  bbc Dec 18 (304) $210

Anr copy.  Copy bound in mor gilt with onlaid mor design depicting Toby Veck, by Bayntun-Riviere. CE Feb 21 (13) $850; K Oct 1 (244) $250

DICKENS, CHARLES. - A Christmas Carol. 1934.  Copy in mor pictorial bdg depicting Scrooge at his desk, by Bayntun-Riviere.  CE Feb 21 (9) $750; sg Nov 9 (138) $80; sg June 27 (113) $100

DICKENS, CHARLES. - The Cricket on the Hearth. 1933.  sg June 27 (114) $80

DICKENS, CHARLES. - Dombey and Son. 1957.  2 vols.  sg June 27 (115) $50

DICKENS, CHARLES. - Great Expectations. 1937.  sg Nov 9 (140) $50; sg June 27 (116) $60

DICKENS, CHARLES. - [Pickwick Papers]. 1933.  2 vols.  sg June 27 (118) $70

DICKINSON, EMILY. - Poems. 1952.  pba Mar 7 (308) $70; sg Nov 9 (143) $100

DODGSON, CHARLES LUTWIDGE. - Alice's Adventures in Wonderland. 1932.  One of 1000.  sg Nov 9 (84) $120

One of 500 sgd by Alice Hargreaves.  sg Feb 8 (207) $475; sg June 27 (71) $650

DODGSON, CHARLES LUTWIDGE. - Through the Looking-Glass. 1935.  One of 1,150 sgd by Alice Hargreaves.  bbc Dec 18 (306) $600; bbc Dec 18 (307) $425; cb Feb 14 (2786) $550

Anr copy.  With carbon copy of Ls from Mrs. Hargreaves's daughter, Cary L. Hargreaves, indicating her mother's willingness to sign 1,150 copies at £2.00 per copy.  sg Nov 9 (85) $500; sg Feb 15 (64) $475; sg June 27 (72) $425; wa Dec 14 (232) $550

DONNE, JOHN. - Poems. 1968.  pba Mar 7 (309) $60; sg Nov 9 (144) $50

DOSTOEVSKY, FYODOR. - The Brothers Karamazov. 1933.  3 vols.  sg Nov 9 (145) $120; sg June 27 (123) $110

Anr Ed. 1949.  2 vols.  pba Mar 7 (310) $100

DOSTOEVSKY, FYODOR. - Crime and Punishment. 1948.  2 vols.  pba Mar 7 (311) $110; sg Nov 9 (146) $120; sg June 27 (124) $150

DOSTOEVSKY, FYODOR. - The Gambler & Notes from Underground. 1967.  pba Mar 7 (312) $55

DOSTOEVSKY, FYODOR. - The House of the Dead. 1982.  sg Nov 9 (148) $70; sg June 27 (126) $60

DOSTOEVSKY, FYODOR. - The Idiot. 1956.  sg Nov 9 (149) $110; sg June 27 (127) $150

DOSTOEVSKY, FYODOR. - The Possessed. 1959.  2 vols.  sg Nov 9 (150) $110; sg June 27 (128) $120

DOSTOEVSKY, FYODOR. - A Raw Youth. 1974.  sg Nov 9 (151) $110; sg June 27 (129) $120

DOUGHTY, CHARLES MONTAGU. - Travels in Arabia Deserta. 1953.  pba Mar 7 (314) $50; sg Nov 9 (152) $130

DOYLE, SIR ARTHUR CONAN. - The Adventures of Sherlock Holmes. 1950.  3 vols. With: The Later Adventures. 1952. 3 vols. And: The Final Adventures. 1953. 2 vols. Together, 8 vols. pba Mar 7 (315) $300

Anr copy.  3 vols.  sg Nov 9 (153) $200; sg June 27 (132) $120

Anr copy. 3 vols. With: The Later Adventures. 1952. 3 vols. And: The Final Adventures. 1953. 2 vols. Together, 8 vols. wa Feb 29 (32) $325

DOYLE, SIR ARTHUR CONAN. - The Final Adventures of Sherlock Holmes. 1952.  2 vols.  sg Nov 9 (155) $130; sg June 27 (134) $150

DOYLE, SIR ARTHUR CONAN. - The Later Adventures of Sherlock Holmes. 1952.  3 vols.  sg Nov 9 (154) $200; sg June 27 (133) $150

DREISER, THEODORE. - An American Tragedy. 1954.  pba Oct 5 (94) $70; sg Nov 9 (156) $130; sg June 27 (135) $250

DREISER, THEODORE. - Sister Carrie. 1939.  pba Oct 5 (95) $100; sg Nov 9 (157) $225; sg Dec 14 (89) $90; sg June 27 (136) $200; wa Dec 14 (257) $60

DUMAS, ALEXANDRE. - The Black Tulip. 1951.  sg June 27 (137) $50

DUMAS, ALEXANDRE. - Camille. 1937.  Mor extra with inlays to form a camillia, by Denise Lubett.  sg Sept 14 (115) $950; sg Oct 19 (82) $350; sg Nov 9 (165) $425; sg Feb 15 (101) $375; sg Feb 15 (184) $225;

sg June 27 (143) $275; wa Dec 14 (258) $325
DUMAS, ALEXANDRE. - The Count of Monte-Cristo. 1941. 4 vols. sg Nov 9 (159) $140; sg June 27 (138) $80
DUMAS, ALEXANDRE. - The Man in the Iron Mask. 1965. sg Nov 9 (160) $90
DUMAS, ALEXANDRE. - Twenty Years After. 1958. sg Nov 9 (164) $50
DURRENMATT, FRIEDRICH. - Oedipus. 1989. One of 650. sg Nov 9 (167A) $175
EMERSON, RALPH WALDO. - Essays, First and Second Series. 1934. sg Nov 9 (171) $70
EMERSON, RALPH WALDO. - Poems. 1945. sg Nov 9 (172) $60
EPICTETUS. - The Discourses. 1966. sg Nov 9 (174) $60
EPICURUS. - [Works]. 1947. pba Mar 7 (322) $70; sg Nov 9 (175) $200; sg June 27 (153) $175; wa Dec 14 (247) $75
ERASMUS, DESIDERIUS. - Moriae Encomium; or, The Praise of Folly.... 1943. sg Nov 9 (176) $200; sg June 27 (154) $60
FAULKNER, WILLIAM. - Hunting Stories. 1988. One of 850. sg Nov 9 (183) $175; sg June 27 (158) $200
FIELDING, HENRY. - The History of the Life of the Late Mr. Jonathan Wild, the Great. 1943. sg Nov 9 (185) $100
FIELDING, HENRY. - The History of Tom Jones. 1931. pba Mar 7 (324) $60
FINNEY, CHARLES GRANDISON. - The Circus of Dr. Lao. 1982. sg Nov 9 (187) $80
FITZGERALD, F. SCOTT. - The Great Gatsby. 1980. sg Nov 9 (189) $90; sg June 27 (163) $70
FITZGERALD, F. SCOTT. - Tender is the Night. 1982. sg Nov 9 (188) $110
FLAUBERT, GUSTAVE. - Madame Bovary. 1938. sg Nov 9 (190) $140; sg June 27 (164) $100
Anr Ed. 1950. sg Nov 9 (191) $140
FLAUBERT, GUSTAVE. - The Temptation of Saint Anthony. 1943. sg Nov 9 (193) $60
FRANCE, ANATOLE. - The Crime of Sylvestre Bonnard. 1937. sg Nov 9 (196) $50
FRANCE, ANATOLE. - Penguin Island. 1947. sg Nov 9 (197) $60
FRANKLIN, BENJAMIN. - Autobiography. 1931. pba Mar 7 (325) $50
FRANKLIN, BENJAMIN. - Poor Richard's Almanacs.... 1964. sg Nov 9 (199) $150; sg June 27 (174) $130
FRAZER, SIR JAMES GEORGE. - The Golden Bough. 1970. 2 vols. sg Nov 9 (200) $80; sg June 27 (175) $80
FROISSART, JEAN. - Chronicles.... 1959. pba Mar 7 (326) $50; sg June 27 (176) $30
FROST, ROBERT. - Complete Poems. 1950. 2 vols. pba Oct 5 (105) $375; pba Mar 7 (327) $425; sg Nov 9 (202) $425; sg Feb 15 (114) $350; sg June 27 (177) $450; wa Dec 14 (291) $375
GALSWORTHY, JOHN. - The Man of Property. 1964. sg Nov 9 (203) $80
GARCIA MARQUEZ, GABRIEL. - One Hundred Years of Solitude. [1983]. sg June 27 (265) $100
GAY, JOHN. - The Beggar's Opera. 1937. sg Nov 9 (205) $100
Anr Ed. 1943. sg June 27 (180) $70
GIBBON, EDWARD. - The History of the Decline and Fall of the Roman Empire. 1946. 7 vols. pba Mar 7 (328) $200; sg June 27 (181) $250; wa Nov 16 (48) $240; wa Dec 14 (293) $170
GILBERT, SIR WILLIAM SCHWENCK & SULLIVAN, SIR ARTHUR. - The First Night Gilbert and Sullivan. 1958. 2 vols. pba Dec 14 (66) $120; pba Mar 7 (329) $80; sg Nov 9 (207) $120; sg June 27 (182) $90; wa Dec 14 (294) $75
GOETHE, JOHANN WOLFGANG VON. - Reynard the Fox. 1954. sg Nov 9 (209) $80
GOETHE, JOHANN WOLFGANG VON. - Wilhelm Meister's Apprenticeship. 1959. sg Nov 9 (210) $60
GOGOL, NIKOLAI VASIL'EVICH. - Dead Souls. 1944. ("Chichikov's Journeys.") 2 vols. sg Nov 9 (211) $50; sg June 27 (186) $60
GOGOL, NIKOLAI VASIL'EVICH. - The Overcoat.... 1976. sg June 27 (187) $400
GRAHAME, KENNETH. - The Wind in the Willows. 1940. One of 2,020. Ck May 31 (172) £420; sg Nov 9 (214) $750
GRASS, GUENTER. - The Flounder. 1985. One of 1,000. 3 vols. sg Nov 9 (215) $175
GRAY, THOMAS. - Elegy Written in a Country Churchyard. 1938. sg Nov 9 (217) $100; wa Dec 14 (295) $70
GRIMM BROTHERS. - Fairy Tales. 1931. pba Mar 7 (332) $120; sg Nov 9 (218) $100
Anr Ed. 1962. 4 vols. sg June 27 (189) $175
HARDY, THOMAS. - Far from the Madding Crowd. 1958. pba Mar 7 (334) $80; sg Nov 9 (221) $90; sg June 27 (191) $120
HARDY, THOMAS. - Jude the Obscure. 1969. sg Nov 9 (222) $80; sg June 27 (192) $120
HARDY, THOMAS. - The Mayor of Casterbridge. 1964. sg Nov 9 (223) $80; sg June 27 (193) $140
HARDY, THOMAS. - Tess of the D'Urbervilles. 1956. sg Nov 9 (224) $80; sg June 27 (194) $140
HARRIS, JOEL CHANDLER. - Uncle Remus: his Songs and his Sayings. 1957. pba Mar 7 (337) $85
HAWKINS, SIR ANTHONY HOPE. - The Prisoner of Zenda. 1966. sg Nov 9 (244) $50
HAWTHORNE, NATHANIEL. - The Marble Faun. 1931. 2 vols. sg June 27 (200) $60
HAWTHORNE, NATHANIEL. - The Scarlet Letter. 1941. sg Nov 9 (230) $110
HAWTHORNE, NATHANIEL. - Twice-Told Tales. 1966. pba Mar 7 (338) $60; sg Nov 9 (231) $100; sg June 27 (200) $60
HEANEY, SEAMUS. - Poems and a Memoir. 1982. sg Nov 9 (232) $225; sg June 27 (201) $175; wa Dec 14 (299) $100
HEARN, LAFCADIO. - Kwaidan. 1932. sg Dec 14 (139) $500
HEINE, HEINRICH. - Poems.... 1957. pba Mar 7 (339) $65; sg Nov 9 (233) $70
HEMINGWAY, ERNEST. - For Whom the Bell Tolls. 1942. sg Nov 9 (234) $175; sg June 27 (203) $175; wa Dec 14 (300) $85
One of 15 out-of-series presentation copies. CE Feb 21 (126) $100
HEMINGWAY, ERNEST. - The Old Man and the Sea. 1990. One of 600. sg Nov 9 (235) $750
HERODOTUS. - The History. 1958. pba Mar 7 (340) $50; sg Nov 9 (236) $90
HERSEY, JOHN. - Hiroshima. 1983. sg Nov 9 (237) $550;

sg June 27 (205) $450
HERSEY, JOHN. - The Wall. sg Nov 9 (238) $60
HOFFMANN, ERNST THEODOR WILHELM. - The Tales of Hoffmann. 1943. sg Nov 9 (240) $90; sg June 27 (207) $100
HOFFMANN, HEINRICH. - Slovenly Peter. 1935. sg Nov 9 (241) $175; sg June 27 (208) $225
HOMER. - The Iliad. 1931. S Nov 2 (43) £180 [Squire]
HOMER. - The Odyssey. 1981. sg Nov 9 (243) $90; sg June 27 (210) $90
HORACE. - Odes and Epodes. With: Pages from Earlier Editions of Horace. 1961. 2 vols. sg Nov 9 (245) $80; sg June 27 (212) $90
HUDSON, WILLIAM HENRY. - Far Away and Long Ago. 1943. sg Nov 9 (247) $60
HUGHES, RICHARD. - The Innocent Voyage. 1944. sg Nov 9 (249) $100; sg Feb 15 (309) $90; sg June 27 (216) $90
HUGO, VICTOR. - Les Miserables. 1938. 5 vols. sg Nov 9 (252) $150; sg June 27 (218) $80
HUGO, VICTOR. - Notre-Dame de Paris. 1930. 2 vols. sg Nov 9 (253) $140
IBSEN, HENRIK. - Three Plays. 1964. sg Nov 9 (257) $70; sg June 27 (221) $70
IONESCO, EUGENE. - Journeys Among the Dead. 1987. One of 1,000. sg Nov 9 (259) $130; sg June 27 (223) $90
IRVING, WASHINGTON. - Rip Van Winkle. 1930. sg Nov 9 (261) $80
JACKSON, HELEN HUNT. - Ramona. 1959. pba Mar 7 (347) $60; sg Nov 9 (263) $80
JAMES, HENRY. - The Ambassadors. 1963. sg Nov 9 (264) $60
JAMES, HENRY. - Daisy Miller. 1969. sg June 27 (228) $80
JAMES, HENRY. - The Turn of the Screw. 1949. sg Nov 9 (267) $50
JEFFERSON, THOMAS. - Writings. 1967. sg Nov 9 (269) $90; sg June 27 (232) $60
JONSON, BEN. - Volpone. 1952. sg Nov 9 (272) $50
JOYCE, JAMES. - Dubliners. 1986. One of 1,000. sg Nov 9 (273) $350; sg June 27 (235) $375
JOYCE, JAMES. - A Portrait of the Artist as a Young Man. 1968. pba Mar 7 (349) $80; sg Nov 9 (274) $90
JOYCE, JAMES. - Ulysses. 1935. One of 250 sgd by Joyce & Matisse. sg Apr 18 (107) $7,000

Anr copy. Illus & sgd by Henri Matisse. P Dec 12 (113) $1,300; sg Oct 19 (121) $2,000; sg Nov 9 (275) $2,200; sg Feb 15 (195) $2,000; sg June 27 (237) $2,400

Anr copy. Illus by H. Matisse. Sgd by Matisse. wa Dec 14 (304) $1,300
KAFKA, FRANZ. - In the Penal Colony. 1987. One of 800. sg Nov 9 (276) $150; sg June 27 (238) $175
KAFKA, FRANZ. - Metamorphoses. 1984. One of 1,500. pba June 20 (222) $120; sg Nov 9 (277) $225; sg June 27 (239) $250
KAFKA, FRANZ. - The Trial. 1975. sg June 27 (240) $100
KIPLING, RUDYARD. - The Jungle Books. 1968. sg Nov 9 (280) $50
LAMPEDUSA, GIUSEPPE TOMASI DI. - The Leopard. 1988. One of 750. sg June 27 (121) $225
LANDOR, WALTER SAVAGE. - Imaginary Conversations.

1936. sg Nov 9 (284) $175; sg June 27 (247) $130
LEWIS, MERIWETHER & CLARK, WILLIAM. - The Journals of the Expedition. 1962. 2 vols. pba Mar 7 (352) $160; sg Nov 9 (287) $110; sg June 27 (250) $100
LEWIS, SINCLAIR. - Main Street. 1937. sg Nov 9 (288) $600; sg June 27 (251) $325; wa Dec 14 (307) $200
LINCOLN, ABRAHAM. - The Literary Works. 1942. sg Nov 9 (289) $110
LIVIUS, TITUS. - The History of Early Rome. 1970. sg Nov 9 (290) $70; sg June 27 (253) $60
LONDON, JACK. - The Call of the Wild. 1960. pba Mar 7 (367) $60; sg Nov 9 (291) $70; sg June 27 (254) $110
LONDON, JACK. - The Sea-Wolf. 1960. pba Mar 7 (368) $55

Anr Ed. 1961. sg Nov 9 (292) $120; sg June 27 (255) $100
LONDON, JACK. - White Fang. 1973. sg Nov 9 (293) $70
LONGFELLOW, HENRY WADSWORTH. - Poems. 1944. One of 1,100 copies. sg Nov 9 (294) $150; sg Feb 15 (188) $90
LONGUS. - The Pastoral Loves of Daphnis and Chloe. 1934. sg June 27 (257) $80
LUCRETIUS CARUS, TITUS. - Of the Nature of Things. 1957. pba Jan 4 (306) $130; pba Mar 7 (369) $95; sg Nov 9 (295) $80
LYTTON, EDWARD GEORGE EARLE BULWER. - The Last Days of Pompeii. 1956. pba Mar 7 (286) $55; sg Nov 9 (72) $60; sg June 27 (60) $90
MACFARLAN, ALLAN A. - American Indian Legends. 1968. sg Nov 9 (258) $100; sg June 27 (222) $80
MACHIAVELLI, NICCOLO. - The Prince. 1954. pba Mar 7 (370) $85; sg Nov 9 (296) $130; sg June 27 (259) $140
MALLARME, STEPHANE. - Un Coup de Des. 1992. One of 300. sg Nov 9 (297) $2,000
MALORY, SIR THOMAS. - Le Morte Darthur. 1936. 3 vols. sg Nov 9 (298) $225; wa Dec 14 (308) $90
MANN, THOMAS. - The Black Swan. 1990. One of 375. sg Nov 9 (299) $500
MANN, THOMAS. - Death in Venice. 1972. sg Nov 9 (300) $80
MANN, THOMAS. - The Magic Mountain. 1962. 2 vols. pba Mar 7 (371) $70; sg Nov 9 (301) $150; sg June 27 (261) $140

Anr Ed. 1972. sg June 27 (260) $110
MARAN, RENE. - Batouala. 1932. sg Nov 9 (303) $100; sg Mar 28 (198) $225; sg June 27 (263) $60
MARQUEZ, GABRIEL GARCIA. - One Hundred Years of Solitude. 1982. sg Nov 9 (305) $200; sg June 27 (265) $100
MASTERS, EDGAR LEE. - Spoon River Anthology. 1942. sg Nov 9 (306) $175; sg June 27 (266) $140; wa Dec 14 (310) $65
MAUGHAM, WILLIAM SOMERSET. - Of Human Bondage. 1938. 2 vols. sg Nov 9 (307) $550; sg June 27 (267) $400; wa Dec 14 (312) $350
MAUPASSANT, GUY DE. - The Tales.... 1963. sg June 27 (269) $110
MELVILLE, HERMAN. - Billy Budd and Benito Cereno. 1965. sg Nov 9 (312) $60
MELVILLE, HERMAN. - Moby Dick. 1943. 2 vols. sg Nov 9 (312) $250; sg June 27 (272) $60; wa Nov 16 (51) $130

# LIMITED          AMERICAN BOOK PRICES CURRENT

MELVILLE, HERMAN. - Omoo. 1961. pba Mar 7 (374) $60; sg Nov 9 (313) $110; sg June 27 (273) $100

MELVILLE, HERMAN. - Typee. 1935. sg Nov 9 (314) $120; sg June 27 (274) $60

MEREDITH, GEORGE. - The Shaving of Shagpat; an Arabian Entertainment. 1955. sg Nov 9 (315) $50

MERIMEE, PROSPER. - Carmen. 1941. sg Nov 9 (316) $150; sg June 27 (276) $110

MILLER, ARTHUR. - Death of a Salesman. 1984. sg Nov 9 (317) $350; sg June 27 (277) $275

MILOSZ, CZESLAW. - The Captive Mind. 1983. One of 1,500. sg Nov 9 (318) $90; sg June 27 (278) $70

MILTON, JOHN. - L'Allegro; Il Penseroso. 1954. One of 1,780. pba Mar 7 (375) $55; sg Nov 9 (319) $100; sg June 27 (279) $70

MILTON, JOHN. - The Masque of Comus. 1954. pba Mar 7 (376) $80; sg Nov 9 (320) $70; sg June 27 (280) $50

MILTON, JOHN. - Paradise Lost and Paradise Regain'd. 1936. sg Nov 9 (321) $100; sg June 27 (281) $60

MITCHELL, JOSEPH. - The Bottom of the Harbour. 1991. One of 250. sg Nov 9 (322) $500; sg Feb 15 (204) $375

MITCHELL, MARGARET. - Gone With the Wind. 1968. 2 vols. pba Mar 7 (377) $150; sg Nov 9 (323) $110; Z June 28 (200) $160

MONTAIGNE, MICHEL EYQUEM DE. - Essays. 1946. 4 vols. pba Mar 7 (379) $60; sg Nov 9 (325) $250

MORE, SIR THOMAS. - Utopia. 1934. sg Nov 9 (326) $60; sg June 27 (283) $90

MORISON, SAMUEL ELIOT. - Journals and Other Documents on...Christopher Columbus. 1963. Trans & Ed by Morison. pba Mar 7 (294) $60

NIETZSCHE, FRIEDRICH WILHELM. - Thus Spake Zarathustra. 1964. pba Mar 7 (381) $75; sg Nov 9 (329) $50; sg June 27 (286) $60

NORDHOFF, CHARLES BERNARD & HALL, JAMES NORMAN. - Mutiny on the Bounty. 1947. pba Mar 7 (382) $75; sg Nov 9 (330) $110

O'HARA, FRANK. - Poems. 1988. One of 550. sg Nov 9 (333) $1,700

OMAR KHAYYAM. - The Rubaiyat. 1935. sg Nov 9 (379) $130; sg June 27 (332) $80

O'NEILL, EUGENE. - Ah, Wilderness! 1972. sg June 27 (290) $80

O'NEILL, EUGENE. - The Iceman Cometh. 1982. sg Nov 9 (335) $110; sg June 27 (291) $80

OVID. - Metamorphoses. 1958. pba Jan 4 (308) $120; pba Mar 7 (383) $85; sg Nov 9 (337) $175; sg June 27 (293) $175

OVIEDO Y VALDES, GONZALO FERNANDEZ DE. - The Conquest and the Settlement of the Island of Boriquen.... 1975. sg Nov 9 (338) $70

PAINE, THOMAS. - Rights of Man. 1961. pba Mar 7 (384) $110; sg Nov 9 (339) $110; sg June 27 (294) $70

PARKMAN, FRANCIS. - The Oregon Trail. 1943. sg Nov 9 (340) $90; sg June 27 (295) $100; wa Nov 16 (56) $90

PASCAL, BLAISE. - Pensees. 1971. sg Nov 9 (341) $90; sg June 27 (296) $90

PASTERNAK, BORIS. - My Sister-Life. 1991. One of 250. sg Nov 9 (342) $275

PATER, WALTER. - The Renaissance. 1976. sg Sept 7 (268) $80; sg Nov 9 (343) $90

PAZ, OCTAVIO. - Three Poems. 1988. One of 750. Illus by Robert Motherwell. sg Feb 15 (207) $1,700

PEPYS, SAMUEL. - Diary. 1942. 10 vols. sg Nov 9 (346) $110; sg June 27 (300) $110; wa Dec 14 (322) $120

PETRARCA, FRANCESCO. - The Sonnets. 1965. sg Nov 9 (347) $80

PETRONIUS ARBITER. - Satyricon. 1964. sg June 27 (302) $90

PLATO. - The Republic. 1944. 2 vols. sg Nov 9 (349) $175; sg Feb 15 (232) $90; sg June 27 (303) $50

PLATO. - Three Dialogues of Plato: Lysis, The Symposium, and Phaedrus. 1968. pba Mar 7 (386) $50; sg Nov 9 (350) $80

PLATO. - The Trial and Death of Socrates. 1962. pba Mar 7 (387) $85; sg Nov 9 (351) $100; sg June 27 (305) $150

PLUTARCH. - The Lives of the Noble Grecians and Romans. 1941. 8 vols. O Dec 5 (117) $80; sg Nov 9 (352) $140; sg June 27 (306) $110

POE, EDGAR ALLAN. - The Fall of the House of Usher. 1985. pba June 20 (271) $350; sg Nov 9 (353) $550; sg Feb 15 (234) $325

POE, EDGAR ALLAN. - The Poems and Essays on Poetry. 1943. sg Nov 9 (354) $130; sg June 27 (308) $110; wa Nov 16 (57) $80; wa Dec 14 (323) $80

POE, EDGAR ALLAN. - Tales of Mystery and Imagination. 1941. sg Nov 9 (355) $110; sg June 27 (309) $110

POLO, MARCO. - The Travels. 1934. 2 vols. sg June 27 (310) $80

PORTER, WILLIAM SYDNEY ("O. HENRY"). - The Voice of the City and Other Stories. 1935. sg Nov 9 (332) $250; sg June 27 (289) $250

POUND, EZRA. - Cathay. 1992. One of 300. sg Nov 9 (357) $1,100

PRESCOTT, WILLIAM HICKLING. - History of the Conquest of Peru. 1957. pba Mar 7 (389) $60; sg Nov 9 (358) $50

PRESCOTT, WILLIAM HICKLING. - The History of the Reign of Ferdinand and Isabella the Catholic. 1967. pba Mar 7 (388) $50

PUSHKIN, ALEKSANDR SERGYEEVICH. - Eugene Onegin. 1943. sg Nov 9 (365) $90; sg June 27 (319) $50

PUSHKIN, ALEKSANDR SERGYEEVICH. - The Golden Cockerel. [1949]. bba May 9 (319) £60 [Heritage]; pba Mar 7 (391) $170; pba June 20 (146) $110; sg Sept 14 (111) $225; sg Nov 9 (366) $110; sg June 27 (320) $110

RABELAIS, FRANCOIS. - Gargantua and Pantagruel. 1936. 5 vols. O Dec 5 (123) $90; sg Nov 9 (368) $130

RASPE, RUDOLPH ERICH. - The Singular Adventures of Baron Munchausen. 1952. sg Nov 9 (369) $70; sg June 27 (323) $50

RASPE, RUDOLPH ERICH. - The Travels of Baron Munchausen. 1929. sg June 27 (324) $80

READE, CHARLES. - The Cloister and the Hearth. 1932. 2 vols. sg June 27 (325) $60

REMARQUE, ERICH MARIA. - All Quiet on the Western Front. 1969. sg Nov 9 (370) $50

RIGGS, LYNN. - Green Grow the Lilacs. 1954. pba Jan 4 (310) $100; pba Mar 7 (394) $150; sg Nov 9 (371) $350; sg June 27 (327) $325; wa Dec 14 (326) $260

RILKE, RAINER MARIA. - The Notebooks of Malte Laurids Brigge. 1987. sg Nov 9 (372) $80; sg June 27 (328) $80

672

1995 - 1996 · BOOKS                                                                                           LIMITED

RILKE, RAINER MARIA. - Selected Poems. 1981. sg Nov 9 (373) $90

RIMBAUD, ARTHUR. - A Season in Hell. 1986. One of 1,000. Illus by Robert Mapplethorpe. sg Nov 9 (374) $1,000

ROSTAND, EDMOND. - Cyrano de Bergerac. 1936. sg Nov 9 (376) $70; sg June 27 (329) $50
Anr Ed. 1954. sg Nov 9 (377) $60

SCOTT, SIR WALTER. - Ivanhoe. 1951. 2 vols. sg June 27 (342) $50

SHAKESPEARE, WILLIAM. - Hamlet. 1933. S May 16 (114) £210; sg Feb 15 (131) $140
Anr Ed. [1944]. sg June 27 (350) $200

SHAKESPEARE, WILLIAM. - Poems. 1967. pba Mar 7 (402) $70; sg June 27 (349) $140

SHAKESPEARE, WILLIAM. - The Poems and Sonnets. 1941. 2 vols. pba Mar 7 (401) $70; sg June 27 (348) $70

SHAKESPEARE, WILLIAM. - Works. 1939-41. 37 vols plus The Poems, in 2 vols. F Mar 28 (189) $180
Anr copy. 37 vols only. Without Poems pba Mar 7 (399) $375
Anr copy. 37 vols plus Preview & Review. sg Nov 9 (393) $650; sg June 27 (346) $475
Anr copy. 37 vols only. Without Poems. wa Dec 14 (332) $375

SHELLEY, MARY WOLLSTONECRAFT. - Frankenstein, or the Modern Prometheus. 1934. sg June 27 (355) $50

SHELLEY, PERCY BYSSHE. - Poems. 1971. sg June 27 (356) $60

SIENKIEWICZ, HENRYK. - Quo Vadis? 1959. pba Mar 7 (404) $65; sg Nov 9 (403) $90

SINCLAIR, UPTON. - The Jungle. 1965. pba Mar 7 (405) $90; sg June 27 (361) $80

SINGER, ISAAC BASHEVIS. - The Gentleman from Cracow. 1979. sg Nov 9 (406) $450

SINGER, ISAAC BASHEVIS. - The Magician of Lublin. 1984. One of 1,500. sg Nov 9 (407) $250; sg June 27 (362) $200

SMOLLETT, TOBIAS. - The Adventures of Peregrine Pickle. 1936. 2 vols. sg June 27 (364) $50

SOPHOCLES. - Oedipus Rex. 1955. sg Nov 9 (412) $110; sg June 27 (367) $110

SPENSER, EDMUND. - The Faerie Queene. 1953. 2 vols. pba Aug 8 (505) $60; sg Nov 9 (414) $130; sg June 27 (369) $150; wa Dec 14 (337) $100

STEINBECK, JOHN. - The Grapes of Wrath. 1940. 2 vols. Insect damage to bdg. pba Oct 5 (331) $250; pba Nov 30 (302) $300; pba Aug 8 (506) $130; sg Nov 9 (415) $600; sg Dec 14 (273) $325; sg Feb 15 (280) $400; sg June 27 (370) $400; wa Dec 14 (338) $500

STEINBECK, JOHN. - Of Mice and Men. 1970. sg Nov 9 (416) $80; sg June 27 (371) $80

STEINBECK, JOHN. - Of Mice of Men. 1970. pba Aug 22 (427) $55

STERNE, LAURENCE. - The Life and Opinions of Tristram Shandy. 1935. 2 vols. sg Nov 9 (420) $60

STERNE, LAURENCE. - A Sentimental Journey.... 1936. bba May 9 (643) £70 [Blackwell]; sg Nov 9 (421) $100; sg Feb 15 (132) $50

STEVENSON, ROBERT LOUIS. - A Child's Garden of Verses. 1944. sg June 27 (377) $70; wa Nov 16 (59) $80; wa Dec 14 (240) $55

STEVENSON, ROBERT LOUIS. - Kidnapped. 1938. sg June 27 (378) $60

STEVENSON, ROBERT LOUIS. - The Master of Ballantrae. 1965. sg Nov 9 (425) $80; sg June 27 (379) $50

STEVENSON, ROBERT LOUIS. - Strange Case of Dr. Jekyll and Mr. Hyde. 1952. sg Nov 9 (427) $100; sg June 27 (380) $50

STEVENSON, ROBERT LOUIS. - Travels With a Donkey in the Cevennes. 1957. sg Nov 9 (428) $60; sg June 27 (381) $50

STEVENSON, ROBERT LOUIS. - Treasure Island. 1941. sg Nov 9 (429) $110; sg June 27 (382) $60

STOKER, BRAM. - Dracula. 1965. pba Mar 7 (408) $110; sg Nov 9 (430) $140; sg June 27 (383) $175

STOWE, HARRIET BEECHER. - Uncle Tom's Cabin. 1938. sg Nov 9 (431) $275; sg Feb 15 (281) $200; sg June 27 (384) $90; wa Dec 14 (342) $120

SUETONIUS TRANQUILLUS, CAIUS. - The Lives of the Twelve Caesars. 1963. pba Mar 7 (409) $60; sg Nov 9 (432) $110

SWIFT, JONATHAN. - Gulliver's Travels. 1929. wa Dec 14 (343) $70

SWIFT, JONATHAN. - Voyage to Lilliput; Voyage to Brobdingnag. 1950. 2 vols. pba Mar 7 (410) $200; sg Nov 9 (433) $225; sg June 27 (387) $200

TENNYSON, ALFRED. - Idylls of the King. 1952. pba Mar 7 (413) $75; sg Nov 9 (437) $100; sg June 27 (391) $60

TENNYSON, ALFRED. - Poems.... 1974. sg Nov 9 (438) $200; sg June 27 (392) $140

THACKERAY, WILLIAM MAKEPEACE. - The History of Henry Esmond, Esq. 1956. sg Nov 9 (439) $70

THACKERAY, WILLIAM MAKEPEACE. - The Newcomes. 1954. 2 vols. sg June 27 (395) $80

THACKERAY, WILLIAM MAKEPEACE. - The Rose and the Ring. 1942. sg Nov 9 (442) $50; sg June 27 (396) $80

THOMAS AQUINAS. - Selections from his Work.... 1969. sg Nov 9 (18) $140

THOREAU, HENRY DAVID. - Cape Cod. 1968. pba Mar 7 (415) $50; sg Nov 9 (444) $60; sg June 27 (398) $70

THOREAU, HENRY DAVID. - Walden. 1936. Illus by Edward Steichen. sg Nov 9 (445) $700; sg Feb 29 (295) $750; sg June 27 (399) $375; wa Dec 14 (348) $325

THOREAU, HENRY DAVID. - A Week on the Concord and Merrimack Rivers. 1974. sg Nov 9 (446) $50

THUCYDIDES. - The History of the Peloponnesian War. [1974]. 2 vols. bba May 9 (24) £55 [Wilson]; sg Nov 9 (447) $140

TOLSTOY, LEO. - Anna Karenina. 1933. 2 vols. pba Mar 7 (416) $80
Anr Ed. 1951. 2 vols. sg Nov 9 (448) $70

TOLSTOY, LEO. - Childhood, Boyhood, Youth. 1972. sg Nov 9 (450) $80

TOLSTOY, LEO. - Resurrection. 1963. sg Nov 9 (451) $80

TOLSTOY, LEO. - War and Peace. 1938. 6 vols. sg Nov 9 (452) $175; wa Dec 14 (349) $95

TROLLOPE, ANTHONY. - Barchester Towers. 1958. sg June 27 (405) $50

TURGENEV, IVAN. - Fathers and Sons. 1951. sg Nov 9 (454) $80; sg June 27 (407) $60

UNTERMEYER, LOUIS. - The Wonderful Adventures of Paul Bunyan. 1945. sg Nov 9 (344) $50

VASARI, GIORGIO. - Lives of the Most Eminent Painters.

**LIMITED**

1966. 2 vols. pba Mar 7 (420) $100; sg Nov 9 (466) $275; sg June 27 (416) $100
VERGILIUS MARO, PUBLIUS. - The Eclogues. 1960. pba Mar 7 (425) $60; sg Nov 9 (474) $50
VERGILIUS MARO, PUBLIUS. - Georgics. 1952. pba Mar 7 (424) $65
VERNE, JULES. - Around the World in Eighty Days. 1962. pba Mar 7 (421) $85; sg Nov 9 (467) $60
VERNE, JULES. - From the Earth to the Moon.... 1970. 2 vols. sg June 27 (418) $70
VERNE, JULES. - A Journey to the Center of the Earth. 1966. sg Nov 9 (469) $70; sg June 27 (419) $70
VERNE, JULES. - The Mysterious Island. 1959. pba Mar 7 (422) $65; sg Nov 9 (470) $50
VERNE, JULES. - Twenty Thousand Leagues Under the Sea. 1956. pba Mar 7 (423) $55; sg Nov 9 (471) $70
VOLTAIRE, FRANCOIS MARIE AROUET DE. - The History of Zadig. 1952. sg Nov 9 (477) $100
WALCOTT, DEREK. - Poems of the Caribbean. 1983. sg Nov 9 (478) $475; wa Dec 14 (355) $120
WALKER, MARGARET. - For My People. 1992. One of 200. sg Nov 9 (479) $650; sg Mar 28 (366) $650
WALLACE, LEW. - Ben-Hur. 1960. sg June 27 (426) $50
WALTON, IZAAK & COTTON, CHARLES. - The Compleat Angler. 1948. pba Mar 7 (427) $120; sg Nov 9 (482) $140; sg June 27 (427) $150; wa Dec 14 (356) $110
WARREN, ROBERT PENN. - All the King's Men. 1989. One of 600. 2 vols. sg Nov 9 (482A) $500; sg June 27 (428) $475
WELLS, H. G. - The War of the Worlds; The Time Machine. 1964. 2 vols. sg Nov 9 (487) $130; sg June 27 (432) $110
WHARTON, EDITH. - Ethan Frome. 1939. O Dec 5 (148) $50; sg Nov 9 (489) $150; sg June 27 (433) $50
WHARTON, EDITH. - The House of Mirth. 1975. sg Nov 9 (490) $50
WHITE, GILBERT. - The Natural History of Selborne. 1972. sg Nov 9 (491) $110
WHITMAN, WALT. - Leaves of Grass. 1929. Mor by William Minter. sg Sept 14 (59) $425
Anr Ed. 1942. 2 vols. cb Feb 14 (2789) $350; sg Nov 9 (492) $400; sg June 27 (434) $400; wa Nov 16 (62) $400; wa Dec 14 (358) $450
WHITMAN, WALT. - Song of the Open Road. 1990. One of 550. sg Nov 9 (492A) $450
WHITTIER, JOHN GREENLEAF. - Poems. 1945. pba Mar 7 (430) $65
WILDE, OSCAR. - The Ballad of Reading Gaol. 1937. sg Nov 9 (494) $70
WILDE, OSCAR. - Lady Windermere's Fan & The Importance of Being Earnest. 1973. sg Nov 9 (495) $110
WILDE, OSCAR. - The Picture of Dorian Gray. 1957. pba Dec 14 (208) $50; pba Mar 7 (431) $70; sg Nov 9 (496) $130
WILDE, OSCAR. - Salome: drame en un acte. * Salome: A Tragedy.... 1938. sg Nov 9 (497) $300; sg June 27 (439) $275
Anr copy. 2 vols. wa Dec 14 (360) $170
WILDE, OSCAR. - The Short Stories. 1968. sg Nov 9 (498) $80; sg June 27 (440) $80
WILDER, THORNTON. - The Bridge of San Luis Rey. 1962. pba Oct 5 (368) $85; pba Mar 7 (432) $65; sg Nov 9

**AMERICAN BOOK PRICES CURRENT**

(499) $120; sg Dec 14 (319) $90; sg June 27 (441) $110
WILDER, THORNTON. - Our Town. 1974. sg Nov 9 (500) $70; sg Dec 14 (320) $70; sg June 27 (442) $100
WILLIAMS, TENNESSEE. - A Streetcar Named Desire. 1982. sg Nov 9 (501) $150
WILLKIE, WENDELL. - One World. 1944. sg Nov 9 (502) $70
WISTER, OWEN. - The Virginian. 1951. sg Nov 9 (503) $50
XENOPHON. - The Anabasis. 1969. sg Nov 9 (506) $90; sg June 27 (446) $120
YEATS, WILLIAM BUTLER. - The Poems. 1970. sg Nov 9 (508) $60

**Limojon de Saint Didier, Alexandre Toussaint, d.1689**

— La Ville et Republique de Venise. [N.p.]: "sur la Copie a Paris chez Guillaume de Lyne", 1680. 12mo, later vellum; spine spotted. sg Mar 21 (201) $225

**Lincoln, Abraham, 1809-65**

See also: Limited Editions Club

— 2d Inaugural Address. Inaugural Address, March 4, 1865.. [Wash., 1865] One of 4 known copies. 4 pp, 8vo, disbound. Streeter - Sonneborn - Engelhard copy. CNY Jan 26 (159) $40,000

[-] The Assassination of Abraham Lincoln...Expressions of Condolence and Sympathy.... Wash., 1867. 4to, half mor; front cover loose, backstrip def. With port. sg Oct 26 (212) $60

— Political Debates between Hon. Abraham Lincoln and Hon. Stephen A. Douglas.... Columbus, 1860. 1st Ed, 1st Issue. 8vo, orig cloth; worn & repaired. Foxed. Horace White's copy. CNY Dec 15 (87) $1,500

Issue not indicated. pba Oct 26 (279) $250

Later Issue. 8vo, orig cloth; worn & repaired. Foxed; dampstains at end. Inscr by Lincoln to I. J. Dyer. Hogan - Sonneborn - Forbes copy. CNY Dec 15 (200) $26,000

Anr copy. Orig cloth; lacking rear free endpaper, shaken, worn. Ink blot to margin of tp & adjacent pages. pba June 13 (275) $150

— Speech of Hon. Abram Lincoln, Before the Republican State Convention, June 16, 1858. Sycamore: O. P. Bassett for Republican Office, 1858. 16mo, loose as issued. Engelhard copy. CNY Jan 26 (158) $30,000

**Lind, James, 1716-94**

— A Treatise on the Putrid and Remitting Marsh Fever.... Edin., 1776. 8vo in 4s, contemp calf; extrems rubbed. Ck Mar 22 (176) £500

— A Treatise on the Scurvy.... L, 1772. 3d Ed. 8vo, contemp calf; spine restored. Title soiled; lower margins dampstained; worm-traces to middle margins; X5r heavily soiled; 2a4 creased; final leaves soiled & stained; final leaf holed. Ck Mar 22 (174) £250

**Lindberg, Pehr.** See: Natrus & Others

**Lindbergh, Anne Morrow**
— North to the Orient. NY, 1935. In dj. Inscr. sg June 20 (224) $90

**Lindbergh, Charles A., 1902-74**
— The Spirit of St. Louis. NY, 1953. Presentation Ed, Ltd Ed, sgd. Red cloth, in clear dj. pba June 13 (153) $550
— The Wartime Journals. NY, [1970]. In dj. Sgd on tp. sg Feb 1 (134) $285

**Linde, Antonius Van Der, 1833-97**
— Benedictus Spinoza. Bibliografie. Nieuwkoop, 1965. 8vo, orig cloth. sg Apr 11 (178) $70

**Linden, Diederick Wessel**
— A Treatise on the Three Medicinal Mineral Waters at Llandrindod.... L, 1756. 8vo, contemp calf; upper cover wormed, rubbed. b Sept 20 (144) £170

**Linden, Joannes Antonides van der, 1609-64**
— Lindenius renovatus, sive Johannis Antonidae van der Linden...de scriptis medicis. Nuremberg, 1686. Revised by G. A. Mercklin. 1 of 2 parts in 1 vol. 4to, contemp vellum; spine top repaired, outer half of front free endpaper excised. Lacking Part 2. Johann Friedrich Blumenbach's sgd & annotated copy. sg May 16 (443) $375

**Linderman, Frank Bird, 1868-1938**
— Indian Old-Man Stories. NY, 1920. Illus by Charles M. Russell. Orig cloth, in djs with soiling & chips. With 8 color plates. pba Aug 8 (100) $300
— Indian Why Stories: Sparks from War Eagles Lodge-Fire. NY, 1915. Illus by Charles M. Russell. With 8 color plates. pba Nov 16 (233) $225

**Lindgren, Waldemer**
— The Tertiary Gravels of the Sierra Nevada of California. Wash., 1911. Folio, orig wraps; soiled & worn, rear wrap detached but present, eradicated stamp to front wrap. pba Apr 25 (509) $85

**Lindley, John, 1799-1865**
— Rosarum Monographia; or, a Botanical History of Roses. L, 1820. 4to, old half lea; spine split. With 1 plain & 18 hand-colored plates. Met May 22 (388) $725

**Lindley, John, 1799-1865 — & Paxton, Sir Joseph, 1801-65**
— Paxton's Flower Garden. L, 1850-53. 3 vols. 4to, half mor; extremities rubbed. With 108 hand-colored plates. Some foxing, mainly to text. sg May 9 (307) $2,200

Anr Ed. L, 1882-84. Vol I only. Half lea; spine lacking corners bumped & worn, hinge split. with 36 color plates. Tp foxed. Met May 22 (445) $400

**Lindner, Kurt**
— Bibliographie der deutschen und der niederlaendischen Jagdliteratur von 1480 bis 1850. Berlin & NY, 1976. 4to, orig cloth. sg Apr 11 (205) $110

**Lindsay, Sir David, fl.1490-1555**
— A Dialogue between Experience and a Courtier.... L: Thomas Purfoote for William Pickering, 1566. 4to, 17th-cent blind-panelled in blind; rebacked with orig spine laid down, worn. Gothic letter, with headlines & subtitles in roman. With 39 woodcut vignettes. Some soiling; minor marginal tears not affecting text. Schaefer copy. P Nov 1 (144) $8,000

**Lindsay, Jack**
— Loving Mad Tom. L: Fanfrolico Press, 1927. One of 375. Illus by Norman Lindsay. 4to, half vellum. Hobson copy. S June 28 (79) £110

Anr copy. Half vellum gilt; spine soiled & spotted. With 5 plates. sg Feb 15 (107) $140

**Lindsay, Norman, 1879-1969**
— The Pen Drawings. Sydney, 1918. One of 35. 4to, orig wraps. S Nov 2 (93) £650 [Marks]

**Lindsay, Vachel, 1879-1931**
— Collected Poems. NY, 1923. One of 400 L.p. copies. Half cloth. F Mar 28 (56) $50

**Linhart, Lubomir**
— Alexandr Rodcenko. Prague, 1964. 4to, pictorial wraps; spine worn. sg Feb 29 (272) $225
— Josef Sudek. Prague, 1956. 4to, cloth, in chipped dj. sg Feb 29 (318) $225

Anr copy. Cloth, in soiled dj. With 232 photogravures. sg Apr 24 (604) $200

**Linnaeus, Carolus, 1707-78**
— Genera plantarum. Stockholm, 1754. 5th Ed. 8vo, contemp sheep; worn, spine ends chipped, covers detached. Browned; some dampstaining in gutters; may lack table or plate. sg May 16 (321) $120
— Hortus Cliffortianus. Amst., 1737. Folio, contemp calf gilt; worn with minor loss at corners, joints dry. With engraved title & 36 plates. Some foxing; Plate 23 with browning. Royal Horticultural Society - Schaefer copy. P Nov 1 (145) $8,000
— Species plantarum exhibentes plantas rite cognitas...secumdum systema sexuale digestas.... Stockholm, 1753. 1st Ed. 2 vols. 8vo, contemp sheep; rubbed, spines repaired. Bound in is prelim matter from 1748 Stockholm Ed of Hortus Upsaliensis; some browning or dampstaining. C Apr 3 (137) £2,400
— A System of Vegetables. Lichfield, 1782-83. 1st Ed in English. 2 vols. 8vo, contemp calf. Vol I tp wormed. b Sept 20 (145) £280

1st English Ed. Litchfield, [1782]-83-[85]. 2 vols. 8vo, contemp calf; joints cracked. With 11 plates. Some spotting. S Oct 27 (646) £280 [Henley]

**Linschoten, Jan Huygen van, 1563-1611**
— Histoire de la navigation.... Amst., 1638. Folio, old calf; rebacked & cornered. With port, 6 folding maps & 32 (of 36) double-page or folding plates & views. Small tears to 5 maps; some browning. C Nov 29 (98) £9,000

## Lion-Goldschmidt, Daisy
— Ming Porcelain. L, [1978]. In dj. sg June 13 (96) $100

## Lion-Goldschmidt, Daisy —& Moreau-Gobard, Jean Claude
— Chinese Art. NY, [1962]. Folio, cloth, in dj. sg June 13 (117) $50

## Lipperheide Library, Franz Joseph von
— Katalog der Freiherrlich von Lipperheide'schen Kostuembibliothek. Berlin, 1965. ("Katalog der Kostuembibliothek.") 2 vols. 4to, orig cloth. bba Oct 5 (245) £350 [Gutenberg]

## Lipperheide, Baron Franz Joseph von
— Katalog der Kostuembibliothek. NY, 1963. 2 vols. 4to, orig cloth. sg Apr 11 (206) $200

## Lipscomb, George, 1773-1846
— The History and Antiquities of the County of Buckingham. L, 1847. 4 vols. 4to, contemp half mor; rubbed, corners worn, Vol III rebacked preserving spine. bba Nov 1 (9) £320 [Norwood]

## Lipsius, Justus, 1547-1606
— Ad C. Cornelium Tacitum curae secundae. Leiden: Plantin, 1588. 8vo, contemp vellum. Inscr to Jacques Augustin de Thou. C Apr 3 (139) £1,800
— Admiranda, sive, de Magnitudine Romana libri quattuor. Antwerp: Plantin, 1598. 1st Ed. 4to, contemp calf gilt with arms of Jacques August de Thou & his 1st wife [Olivier 216 fer 5]; rebacked preserving orig spine, scuffed. Some browning & rust-holes. S Apr 4 (22) £130 [Petten-Rosenthal]

## Lisiansky, Urey, 1773-1837
— A Voyage Round the World.... L, 1814. 4to, old bds; rebacked & recornered in calf. With port, 2 colored aquatints, 3 plates & 10 hand-colored maps on 8 sheets. Some foxing. pba Feb 13 (122) $4,500

## Lisle, Claude de
— Relation historique du royaume de Siam. Paris, 1684. 1st Ed. 12mo, contemp calf; corners worn, rebacked. S Oct 26 (589) £260 [Bankes]

## Lisle, Joe
— Play upon Words. L, [1828]. Oblong 4to, later half mor by Riviere; upper cover dampstained. With 40 hand-colored plates. Lacking tp & text. S Mar 28 (553) £420

## Lissim, Simon
— An Artist's Interpretation of Nature. NY, 1958. One of 25 with separate sgd drawing. Folio, loose as issued in portfolio. sg June 13 (239) $300

## Lissitzky, Eliezer, 1890-1941 —& Arp, Jean (or Hans), 1887-1966
— Die Kunstismen. Zurich, 1925. 4to, orig bds; backstrip worn & fragile. sg Apr 18 (112) $700

List... See: Monroe, James

## Listenius, Nicolaus
— Musica.... Nuremburg: Joannes Montanus & Ulrich Neuber, [c.1544-63]. 8vo, modern vellum bds. A few leaves trimmed at top margin. S Dec 1 (203) £750

## Lister, Martin
— Sanctorii sanctorii de statica medicina. L, 1716. 12mo, contemp half roan; worn. With frontis. S Oct 12 (76) £300

## Lister, Thomas, of Barnsley
— The Rustic Wreath. Poems.... Leeds, 1834. 8vo, contemp mor gilt. With orig ink drawing of Lister inserted as frontis. b Dec 5 (461) £100

## Litchfield Library, Edward S.
— The Edward S. Litchfield Collection. A Catalogue. [N.p.]: pvtly ptd, 1986. Ltd Ed with tipped-in leaves from sporting books. Folio, cloth; some wear. O June 25 (184) $550

## Lithgow, William, 1582?-1645?
— The Totall Discourse of the Rare Adventures.... L, 1640. 4to, old calf; rebacked, new endpapers. Some staining & browning; 1 leaf chipped. CE June 12 (223) $1,300

## Little...
— Little Red Riding Hood... Chicago: Pleasure Books, [1934]. Illus by C. Carey Cloud & Harold B. Lentz. Pictorial bds; remnants stuck to the front & back covers. Illusts include 3 color pop-ups. NH July 21 (329) $100

## Little, Archibald John
— Mount Omi and Beyond.... L, 1901. With folding map & 16 plates. b May 30 (162) £70

## Little, Arthur W.
— From Harlem to the Rhine. NY, [1936]. sg Mar 28 (191) $70

## Little Big Horn Associates
— Compilation of their Newsletter. Great Falls MT & Tacoma WA, 1967-68. Vol I, No 1 to Vol II, No 12, bound in 2 vols. pba June 25 (155) $225

Little, Malcolm. See: Malcolm X

Littlejohn, David. See: Grabhorn Printing

## Littleton, Adam, 1627-94
— Linguae Latinae liber dictionarius quadripartitus. L, 1703. 4th Ed. 4 parts in 1 vol. 4to, modern calf. With frontis, view & map. Wormed at end; 4V4v & 4X1r formerly adhered & separated with loss; marginal repairs at end. sg Mar 21 (203) $110

## Livingston, Jane
— M. Alvarez Bravo. Bost., [1978]. 4to, cloth, in dj with discolored spine. sg Feb 29 (55) $110

**Livingstone, David & Charles**
— Narrative of an Expedition to the Zambesi and its Tributaries.... NY, 1866. 8vo, later cloth; soiled. Soiled; map torn. pba Apr 25 (202) $75

**Livingstone, David, 1813-73**
— Missionary Travels and Researches in South Africa. L, 1857. 1st Ed. 8vo, orig cloth; hinges weak, soiled, spine head & foot worn. With folding frontis, port, 2 folding maps, & 23 plates. Inscr to Thomas Clegg Esq., 29 Oct 1857. S Oct 26 (544) £750 [Remington]

**Livius, Titus, 59 B.C.-17 A.D.**
See also: Limited Editions Club

### Decades

— Le Deche delle historie romane. Venice: Giunti, 1554. Folio, old calf; rebacked, cracked, spine def. Tp mtd on 2d blank & trimmed. wd May 8 (69) $300
— Historiae romanae decades. Venice: M. Sessa & P. Ravani, 3 May 1520. ("Historicus duobus libris auctus.") Folio, contemp Transylvanian blind-tooled calf over wooden bds; lea def in places, clasps removed. With port & 31 woodcuts. Sessa's device removed from tp, affecting letters on verso. C June 26 (100) £800
Anr Ed. Venice: Aldus, 1566. ("Historiarum ab urbe condita.") 2 parts in 1 vol. Folio, contemp calf gilt over wooden bds; spine lea perished, extremities worn. Tp detached with 1st 2 gatherings; index leaves at rear detaching; dampstains to inner margins; dampstaining to outer lower corner of middle leaves & upper margins. cb Oct 17 (417) £275
Anr Ed. Oxford, 1708. 6 vols. 8vo, contemp mor gilt, with arms of Charles Henri, Comte Hoym. Fuerstenberg - Schaefer copy. S Dec 7 (381) £3,800
— Historiarum quod extat. Amst.: Elzevir, 1665. 3 vols. 8vo, contemp mor; faded. Spotted. S Oct 27 (1068) £270 [Zioni]
— The Romane Historie. L, 1659. Folio, 18th-cent calf; rebacked, rubbed. Tp repaired; some rust-holes & stains. S June 12 (68) £180

**Livre...**
— Le Livre de la Marquise. Venice: Cazzo et Coglioni, 1918. Illus by Constantin Somov. 8vo, mor gilt by Sangorski & Sutcliffe, orig wraps bound in. With frontis & 47 illusts, 24 full-page, 12 in color. Some discoloration & spotting. S Nov 21 (262) $750
— Le Livre de quatre couleurs. [Paris: Duchesne, 1760]. 8vo, contemp mor gilt with arms of the marquis de Coislin. Fuerstenberg - Schaefer copy. S Dec 7 (97) £650
— Le Livre des Rois. Lausanne, 1930. One of 25 with 2 extra suites of the illusts. Illus by F. L. Schmied. 4to, unsewn in orig wraps. S Nov 21 (260) £800
Out-of-series copy for the pbr, Philippe Gonin, with additional suite of the illusts on japon. Mor extra by E. Giraldon with 2 silver columns representing the Tables of the Law, orig wraps bound in. S Nov 21 (258) £2,600

— Livre d'or de la conquete de l'air. Brussels, 1909. One of 500. Folio, orig wraps; soiled, spine ends chipped, loose. sg May 16 (58) $250

**Lizars, John**
— A System of Anatomical Plates of the Human Body. Edin.: W.H. Lizars, [c.1840?]. Folio, contemp half mor gilt. With engraved title & 101 colored plates. S June 12 (306) £700

**Ljungstedt, Anders, 1759-1836**
— An Historical Sketch of the Portuguese Settlements in China.... Bost., 1836. 8vo, orig cloth; worn, front free endpaper lacking. With folding frontis, litho view of the landing at Macao, folding facsimile of a broadside & 3 folding maps. Short tears to frontis & 1 map; foxed. pba July 25 (417) $250

**Llewellyn, Richard, 1906-83**
— How Green Was My Valley. L, [1939]. In dj with small loss to top of spine. Inscr to Cecily Shackleton, Apr 1940. b Jan 31 (185) £120

**Llopis, Carlos Ruano.** See: Ruano Llopis, Carlos

**Llosa, Mario Vargas**
— The War of the End of the World. NY, [1984]. One of 250. sg Dec 14 (202) $70

**Lloyd, B. E.**
— Lights and Shades in San Francisco. San Francisco, 1876. 1st Ed. 8vo, contemp mor gilt. With frontis & 18 wood-engraved plates. pba Feb 12 (353) $450

**Lloyd, E.**
— A Visit to the Antipodes, with some Reminiscences of a Sojourn in Australia; by A Squatter. L, 1846. 8vo, orig cloth. With port. S Apr 23 (358) £110

**Lloyd, Llewellyn, 1792-1876**
— The Game Birds and Wild Fowl of Sweden and Norway. L, 1867. 2d Ed. 8vo, orig cloth; stained at 1 corner. Map pocket torn; some spotting. Ck Feb 14 (327) £250
Anr copy. Orig cloth; worn, loose. With 48 chromolitho plates. Tear in 1 leaf. S Apr 23 (328) £110

**Lloyd, William Whitelock**
— Union Jottings. L, [1896]. One of 110. 4to, disbound with orig covers present. Ck May 31 (188) £80

**Llwyd, Richard**
— The Poetical Works. Chester, [1837]. 8vo, contemp mor gilt by Leighton, with arms of the Duke of Westminster. Minor spotting. L.p. copy. b Dec 5 (50) £120

**Lobachevsky, Nikolai Ivanovich**
— Primenie voobrazhaemoj geometrii k nekotorym integralam. Kazan, 1836. 8vo, orig front wrap only; backstrip chipped. sg May 16 (203) $5,000

## L'Obel, Matthias de, 1538-1616 —& Pena, Petrus

— Plantarum, seu stirpium historia. Antwerp: Plantin, 1576. 2 parts in 1 vol. Folio, calf; worn & rubbed, covers detached. Minor worming at end; inserted leaf after PP6 not present; Appendix cut close at top. STC 19595.3. K June 23 (311) $2,100

## Lobera de Avila, Luis

— Libro de pestilencia curativo y preservativo.... [Alcala de Henares: Juan de Brocar, 1542?]. Folio, modern mor gilt. Spanish text in gothic letter; Latin text in italic. Hole in D2 repaired with loss. S June 27 (337) £2,200

## Lobo, Jerome, 1593-1678

— A Voyage to Abyssinia. L, 1789. Trans by Samuel Johnson. 8vo, 19th-cent half calf gilt. sg Mar 7 (116) $400

## Locatelli, Antonio

— Collezione d'Incisioni appartenenti all'Opera del Perfetto Cavaliere. Milan, 1827. 4to, contemp half sheep gilt; joints & spine head worn. sg Mar 7 (489) $325
— Il Perfetto Cavaliere. Milan, 1825-27. 2 vols. 4to, contemp half lea; recased. With 76 plates, 35 of them hand-colored. A few plates just trimmed. pn Dec 7 (109) £800

## Loccenius, Johannes

— De jure maritimo & navali libri tres. Stockholm, 1652. 2d Ed. 24mo, contemp vellum; backstrip def. sg Mar 7 (219) $250

## Locke, Alain —& Gregory, Montgomery

— Plays of Negro Life. NY, 1927. Pictorial bds. Inscr by Locke to Mary Hoyt Wiborg, 2 Oct 1927. sg Mar 28 (192) $275

## Locke, John

— The Voyage of M. John Locke to Jerusalem. L, [c.1599]. Folio, recent bds. With 6 leaves from Hakluyt's Navigations II. Fore-margins wormed. S Oct 26 (59) £340 [Cyprus Pop. BK]

## Locke, John, 1632-1704

— A Collection of Several Pieces Never Before Printed.... L, 1720. 8vo, contemp calf; rebacked retaining spine, joints weak, hinges cracked. S June 12 (69) £220
— Essai philosophique concernant l'entendement humain. Amst., 1742. 4to, contemp calf. Wormhole through lower margin; some foxing or browning. bba May 30 (99) £160 [Mullen]
— An Essay concerning Humane Understanding. L, 1695. 3d Ed. Folio, contemp calf; joints cracked, rubbed. With frontis port. Water-stained. S Oct 27 (1191) £300 [Wheeler]
4th Ed. L, 1700. Folio, half calf; minor scuffing. Marginal annotations. K June 23 (355) $650
— A Letter concerning Toleration. L, 1765. 4to, contemp sheep gilt bound for Thomas Hollis; bumped, spine head worn. Inscr by Thomas Hollis to Consul Joseph Smith. P Dec 12 (92) $4,500
— Several Papers Relating to Money, Interest and Trade. L, 1696. 8vo, old calf; broken & worn, stitching def. bbc June 24 (242) $800
Anr copy. Later half mor; joints rubbed. Trimmed. CE May 22 (316) $1,400
— Some Thoughts concerning Education. L, 1712. 7th Ed. 8vo, contemp calf; joints worn. pba Mar 7 (165) $60
— Two Treatises of Government. L, 1694. 2d Ed. 8vo, contemp calf; rubbed. Minor worming in lower margins. b Sept 20 (148) £400

## Locker, Edward Hawke, 1777-1849

— Views in Spain. L, 1824. 4to, contemp mor gilt; rubbed. With 60 litho plates. b Dec 5 (127) £1,600
Anr copy. Contemp half calf; joints split, corners scraped. With 60 plates. S June 27 (114) £1,300

## Lockhart, John Gibson, 1794-1854

— Ancient Spanish Ballads. Edin., 1823. 4to, later 19th-cent half calf. F June 20 (440) $80
2d Ed. L, 1842. Illus by Owen Jones. 4to, half mor gilt by Root. sg Feb 8 (83) $225
— The Life of Robert Burns. Liverpool, 1914. Ltd Ed. 2 vols. Half vellum. pba Dec 14 (23) $85
— Memoirs of the Life of Sir Walter Scott. Edin., 1837-38. 1st Ed. 7 vols. 12mo, calf. pba June 20 (294) $650

## Lockhart, Sir Robert Hamilton Bruce, 1887-1970

— My Rod my Comfort. L, 1949. One of 500. Illus by J. Gaastra. 8vo, orig half vellum gilt, unopened; owner's stamp to rear free endpaper. pba July 11 (177) $170

## Lockwood, Francis Cummins, 1864-1948

— Pioneer Days in Arizona.... NY, 1932. 1st Ed. Orig cloth. Robbins copy. pba Mar 21 (205) $75

## Lockwood, George

— Hommage to Redon. Northampton: Gehenna Press, 1959. One of 150. 4to, half mor; spine ends worn. With 10 ports. Inscr by Leonard Baskin. sg Feb 15 (122) $150

## Lockwood, James D.

— Life and Adventures of a Drummer-Boy.... Albany: John Skinner, 1893. Orig cloth; rubbed, recased, new endpapers. pba June 25 (157) $150

## Lockwood, R. A.

— Speeches of Rufus A. Lockwood. Speech of R. A. Lockwood, Esq. Delivered in Defense of J. H. W. Frank at the October Term of the Tippicanoe Circuit Court, 1837. Indianapolis, 1837. Bound with: The Vigilance Committee of San Francisco. Metcalf vs. Argenti et al. Speeches of.... San Francisco, 1852. And: Argument of R. A. Lockwood, Esq. Delivered in the Supreme Court of the United States in the Case of Edward Field...vs. Pardon G. Seabury.... San Francisco, 1857. 8vo, mor gilt; spine cracked. With related material. Larson copy. pba Feb 12 (571) $600

**Lockyer, Charles**
— An Account of the Trade in India.... L, 1711. 8vo, contemp calf; spine ends chipped, covers detached. Old stamp on tp. sg Mar 21 (107) $400

**Loddiges, Conrad & Sons**
— The Botanical Cabinet. L, [1817]-33. Vol XVI only. Half lea; worn & bumped, lea cracked along hinges. With 100 hand-colored plates. Foxed. Met May 22 (438) $425

Anr copy. Vols I-VI only, bound in 3 vols. Contemp half russia; rebacked. With engraved titles, 2 uncolored & 600 hand-colored plates. Plates 190-92. Sold w.a.f. S Nov 30 (32) £1,700

Anr copy. Vol XVI only. Orig cloth; needs rebdg. With 100 hand-colored plates. Foxing to c.50 plates. sg Dec 7 (225) $475

Anr Ed. L, 1822. Illus by George Cooke. Vol VII only. 8vo, contemp half calf; rebacked. With 100 hand-colored plates. Title spotted; some offsetting. S Oct 27 (748) £220 [Lloyd]

**Lodge, Edmund, 1756-1839**
— Portraits of Illustrious Personages of Great Britain. L, 1823-34. 12 vols in 6. 4to, contemp half mor gilt; scuffed. Some foxing. F Sept 21 (407) $275

Anr Ed. L, 1835. 12 vols in 6. 8vo, contemp mor gilt; rubbed, 2 upper joints cracked. S June 13 (408) £220

**Lodge, George Edward.** See: Bannerman & Lodge

**Loehneyss, Georg Engelhard von**
— Hof-Staats- und Regier-Kunst.... Frankfurt: G.V.R. in Henning Buchladen, 1679. Bound with: Berward, Christian. Interpres Phraseeologiae Metallurgicae. Frankfurt: Johann David Zunner, 1673. Folio, contemp vellum; soiled. C June 26 (196) £1,300

**Loehr, Max**
— Chinese Bronze Age Weapons: The Werner Jannings Collection in the Chinese National Palace Museum, Peking. Ann Arbor, [1956]. Folio, cloth, in chipped dj. sg Sept 7 (222) $50

**Loehr, Max —&**
**Huber, Louisa**
— Ancient Chinese Jades from the Grenville L. Winthrop Collection in the Fogg Art Museum, Harvard University. Cambr. MA, 1975. 4to, cloth. sg June 13 (201) $150

**Loescher, Carl Immanuel**
— Uibergangsordung bei der Kristallisation der Fossilien.... Leipzig, 1796. 4to, half calf. With 6 folding plates & 3 folding tables. Some spotting. b May 30 (27) £250

**Lofting, Hugh, 1886-1947**
— The Story of Dr. Doolittle. NY, 1920. 1st Ed. Orig cloth; rubbed, spine chipped, soiled. pba Nov 30 (225) $180

Anr copy. In chipped dj. pba Apr 4 (519) $150

— The Voyages of Doctor Dolittle. NY, 1923. Cloth; hinges cracked, date stamps to rear pastedown. Sgd on half-title. pba Aug 22 (806) $80

**Logan, Maria**
— Poems on Several Occasions. York, 1793. 4to, orig wraps; worn. b Dec 5 (462) £100

**Logan, Rayford W.**
— What The Negro Wants. Chapel Hill, [1944]. In dj with edge wear. sg Mar 28 (162) $60

**Loggan, David, 1635-1700?**
— Oxonia illustrata. Oxford, 1675. 1st Ed. Folio, later sheep; worn. With title, dedication, & 40 double-page plates (1 folding). All plates reinforced; some tears, mostly patched; 1 plate repaired; folding plate wrinkled. CE Nov 8 (209) $1,600

**Lom d'Arce, Louis Armand.** See: Lahontan, Louis Armand

**London, Charmian**
— The Book of Jack London. NY, 1921. 1st Ed. 2 vols. Cloth. Both vols inscr to Nellie Holbrook, Dec 1921 & with clipped signature of Jack London mtd to front pastedown of Vol I. With related material. pba Oct 5 (204) $350

— The Log of the Snark. NY, 1915. Inscr by Charmian London to her sister & with photo of Jack & Charmian London tipped to pastedown. cb June 25 (1868) $325; pba Oct 5 (203) $100

**London, Jack, 1876-1916**
See also: Limited Editions Club
— The Abysmal Brute. NY, 1913. 1st Issue. sg Sept 21 (253) $200

Issue not indicated. In olive-green cloth stamped in black & yellow, in chipped & repaired dj; front hinge starting. pba Oct 5 (209) $250

Anr copy. In olive-green cloth stamped in black & yellow; spine rubbed, stamp to front free endpaper. pba Oct 5 (210) $65

Anr copy. Variant bdg of olive-green cloth stamped in black & dark green. pba Jan 25 (201) $70

1st Canadian Ed. Toronto, 1913. In rubbed & chipped dj. cb Oct 17 (420) $180

— The Acorn-Planter: A California Forest Play.... NY, 1916. Orig cloth, BAL A bdg; lettering rubbed. pba Oct 5 (211) $1,200

— Adventure. L, [1911]. 1st Ed. Spine rubbed, front hinge cracked. pba Jan 25 (202) $130

1st American Ed. NY, 1911. Orig cloth; spine ends rubbed. pba Oct 5 (212) $160

Anr copy. Spine ends rubbed, spine lettering worn off, hinges starting. pba Jan 25 (203) $55

Anr copy. Variant bdg in rec cloth lettered in white; spot to front cover. pba Aug 22 (301) $90

Anr copy. Orig cloth; front inner hinge weak. sg June 20 (226) $100

— Before Adam. NY, 1907. 1st Trade Ed. Orig cloth; soiled & rubbed. Check, sgd, tipped in. cb June 25 (1870) $325

Anr copy. In def dj. pba Oct 5 (213) $950

Anr copy. Orig cloth; spine rubbed. Short tear to frontis. Inscr, 1909. pba Oct 5 (214) $600; pba Jan 25 (204) $85

— Brain Beaten by Brute Force.... Hegewisch IL, 1909. Hand-decorated cloth. In: Life, Battles and Career of Battling Nelson, LIghtweight Champion of the World. Inscr by Nelson on front free endpaper. pba Oct 5 (215) $400

— Burning Daylight. NY, 1910. 1st Issue. Orig cloth; bumped, spine ends worn. pba Oct 5 (216) $90

2d Issue. pba Jan 25 (206) $275; pba May 23 (205) $80

Issue not indicated. sg June 20 (228) $150

— The Call of the Wild. NY, 1903. 1st Ed. Orig cloth; rubbed, lower hinge cracked. bbc June 24 (566) $280

Anr copy. In def dj. Inscr by Becky London to Robert Martens. cb Oct 17 (423) $900

Anr copy. Orig cloth, in dj. cb June 25 (1871) $3,000

Anr copy. In chipped dj; bdg bumped at spine head. pba Oct 5 (217) $7,000

Anr copy. Orig cloth; extremities rubbed. sg Sept 21 (254) $325

Anr copy. Orig cloth, in chipped dj with def spine; bdg worn & cocked. wa Nov 16 (97) $700

1st Issue. In dj with spine head & corners chipped & short tears to extremities; bdg with spine ends rubbed. pba Jan 25 (209) $1,500

Anr copy. Orig cloth; white snow in cover & spine designs wearing off, rear hinge weak. pba Jan 25 (210) $110

Anr Ed. NY, [1906]. Cloth; spine ends rubbed & chipped. Inscr to Arnold Genthe. pba Oct 5 (219) $1,400

— Children of the Frost. NY, 1902. 1st Ed. - Illus by Raphael M. Reay. Cloth. pba Oct 5 (220) $275

— The Cruise of the Dazzler. NY, 1902. Wraps; spine ends def. In: St. Nicholas for Young Folks, July 1902. pba Oct 5 (221) $100

1st Ed in Book form. Orig cloth; spine soiled, spine head bumped. pba Oct 5 (222) $1,100

Pbr's Dummy. Sample Copy stamped to front free endpaper & tp; several leaves with Ms text of owner. pba Jan 25 (211) $1,600

— The Cruise of the Snark. NY, 1911. In dj. Inscr to Mary Fisher Quinn, 28 Oct 1916. pba Oct 5 (223) $1,900; pba Oct 5 (224) $400; pba Jan 25 (212) $550

Anr copy. In stained bdg & dj. pba May 23 (206) $300

— A Daughter of the Snows. Phila., 1902. 1st Ed. - Illus by Frederick C. Yohn. Some soiling. pba Jan 25 (213) $140

— Daughters of the Rich. Oakland: Holmes Book Co., 1971. 1st Ed. Wraps. pba Jan 25 (214) $50

— Dutch Courage and Other Stories. NY, 1922. In chipped dj with small pieces lacking, tear to lower front jacket panel. pba Oct 5 (225) $1,400; pba Oct 5 (226) $400

Anr copy. Illus by George Richards. In dj with tears & chipping & spine head def. pba Jan 25 (215) $1,100

Anr copy. In def dj. sg June 20 (230) $450

— The Faith of Men and Other Stories. NY, 1904. pba Oct 5 (227) $350

Anr copy. Cloth; spine lacquered, ends rubbed. pba Jan 25 (216) $250

— The Game. NY, 1905. 1st Ed. With 1/16 inch rubberstamp. Check, sgd, tipped in. cb June 25 (1872) $475

Anr copy. Orig cloth; corners bumped, stamp to upper corner of front pastedown. pba Oct 5 (228) $50

1st Issue, without magazine rubberstamp. Spine ends rubbed. pba Jan 25 (217) $90

Issue not indicated. sg June 20 (231) $60

— The God of his Fathers. NY, 1901. 1st Ed. Cloth; spine ends rubbed. pba Oct 5 (229) $450; pba May 23 (208) $130; sg June 20 (247) $400

— Hearts of Three. L: Mills & Boon, n.d. [1918]. Orig cloth; worn & rubbed. sg June 20 (232) $250

Anr Ed. NY, 1920. In chipped & rubbed dj. pba Oct 5 (230) $2,750

— The House of Pride. NY, 1912. pba Oct 5 (231) $350

Anr copy. Orig cloth; spine ends rubbed. pba Jan 25 (221) $400

— The Human Drift. NY, 1917. Check, sgd, & photo tipped in. Inscr to Charley Peirson by Charmian London. cb June 25 (1873) $450

Advance copy. Cloth. pba Oct 5 (232) $500

1st Ed. pba Oct 5 (233) $300; sg June 20 (233) $300

— The Iron Heel. NY, 1908. Orig cloth; spine ends & corners rubbed, upper corners bumped, front hinge cracked. pba Oct 5 (234) $60

Anr Ed. NY: Macmillan, 1908. Bdg spine ends rubbed. pba Jan 25 (222) $170

Anr copy. Orig cloth; shaken, 1 corner bumped. sg June 20 (234) $200

— Jerry of the Islands. NY, 1917. 1st Ed. In chipped & rubbed dj. pba Oct 5 (235) $2,000; pba Oct 5 (236) $110

Anr copy. Cloth; spine ends rubbed & frayed, extremities rubbed, front hinge cracking. pba Aug 22 (305) $60; sg June 20 (235) $100

Advance Review copy. Cloth; spine ends rubbed. Perforated stamp to tp. pba Jan 25 (224) $550

— John Barleycorn. NY, 1913. 1st Ed, 1st Ptg. In chipped dj. pba Oct 5 (237) $4,500

Anr copy. Cloth; front cover bumped. pba Jan 25 (225) $75

— A Klondike Trilogy: Three Uncollected Stories. Santa Barbara, 1983. One of 300. pba Aug 22 (306) $55

— The Letters.... Stanford, 1988. Ed by Earle Labor, Robert C. Leitz & I. Milo Shepard. 3 vols. pba Oct 5 (239) $300

— The Little Lady of the Big House. NY, 1916. In chipped dj. pba Oct 5 (240) $1,600

— Lost Face. NY, 1910. 1st Ed. Cloth; spine ends worn. With frontis & 5 plates. pba Oct 5 (241) $150

Anr copy. Cloth; minor wear. pba Jan 25 (227) $140; sg June 20 (236) $250
— Love of Life and Other Stories. NY, 1907. Orig cloth, this copy with yellow rule border; upper corners bumped, spine ends rubbed. pba Oct 5 (242) $275

Anr copy. Cloth, variant with yellow rule border on front cover; spine ends rubbed, front hinge weak. pba Jan 25 (228) $225

1st Ed. Cloth. sg June 20 (237) $275

— Martin Eden. NY, 1909. 1st Ed. Sticker on frontis verso; tp with tear along gutter. pba Jan 25 (229) $120; sg June 20 (238) $225

1st Pbd Ed. With check, sgd, laid in. pba Oct 5 (243) $550

Anr copy. ALs to John Meyers O'Hara mtd to front flyleaf; inscr by O'Hara to John Hervey. pba Oct 5 (244) $3,500

Anr copy. Orig cloth; spine chipped. Inscr in pencil to Lute Pease, 23 Nov 1909. sg Sept 28 (170) $225

— Michael, Brother of Jerry. NY, 1917. Cloth; spine ends rubbed. pba Oct 5 (245) $95; pba Jan 25 (230) $160; sg June 20 (239) $110

— Moon-Face and Other Stories. NY, 1906. Blue cloth lettered in cream but with initials RR in center of decoration on front cover in light green, in dj; spine ends bumped. pba Oct 5 (246) $4,250

Anr copy. Blue cloth, but with initials R.R. in center of front cover in light green; spine ends rubbed, endpapers foxed. pba Jan 25 (231) $85

— The Mutiny of the Elsinore. NY, 1914. 1st Ed. Cloth, in chipped dj with soiling & repairs. Lower corner of half-title lacking, with tear to upper half-title. pba Oct 5 (247) $1,400; pba Oct 5 (248) $110

— The Night Born. NY, 1913. 1st Ed, 1st Ptg. pba Oct 5 (249) $170

Anr copy. Orig cloth; spine ends rubbed. pba Jan 25 (233) $75

Anr Ed. L, [1916]. In dj with piece missing from head of spine panel; bdg mildewed. CE Feb 21 (162) $100

— On the Makaloa Mat. NY, 1919. 1st Ed. In chipped dj. pba Oct 5 (250) $2,000

Advance review copy. Orig cloth; rubbed, spotted, hinge cracked. NH June 1 (202) $275

— The People of the Abyss. NY, 1903. 1st Ed. Orig cloth; rubbed. Inscr by Alfred J. Livingston, 1904. pba Oct 5 (251) $400

Anr copy. Cloth; spine ends & corners rubbed, bumped, shaken. pba Jan 25 (234) $225

1st Canadian Ed. Toronto, 1903. Orig cloth; spine ends rubbed. pba May 23 (212) $95

— The Red One. NY, 1918. Pictorial bds; spine ends rubbed. pba Oct 5 (252) $650

Anr copy. In repaired dj lacking part of spine; bdg joints cracked, brown paint to front joint. pba Aug 22 (308) $250

Anr copy. Pictorial bds; spine ends worn. sg June 20 (240) $475

1st Ed. Bds. pba Jan 25 (235) $700

— Revolution and Other Essays. L, [1910]. In chipped dj. pba May 23 (215) $90

Anr Ed. NY, 1910. Cloth; spine foot rubbed, front hinge cracked. pba Oct 5 (253) $375

1st Ed. Variant bdg of brown cloth lettered in gilt, spine reading MACMILLAN. pba May 23 (214) $275

— The Road. NY, 1907. 1st Issue. Cover ptd in gilt & black. pba Oct 5 (254) $300

2d Issue. Cover ptd in black only. Lacking 2 ad pages; some staining to 1 leaf. pba May 23 (216) $60

— The Scarlet Plague. NY, 1915. 1st Ed. In dj with tear. pba Oct 5 (255) $3,500; pba Oct 5 (256) $200

Anr copy. Orig cloth; spine head worn with loss of cloth. sg June 20 (242) $300

— Scorn of Women. NY, 1906. Orig cloth; soiled. pba Oct 5 (257) $800

— The Sea Sprite and the Shooting Star. [N.p., 1932]. One of 35. 4 pp from single folded sheet, as issued. pba May 23 (217) $60

— The Sea-Wolf. NY, 1904. Orig blue cloth lettered in white on front cover & spine, cover illus in dark blue, orange & white; spine ends rubbed. pba Oct 5 (258) $250

Anr copy. Blue cloth, with cover lettering in white & cover illus in dark blue, orange, cream & black, spine lettering in gilt. pba Jan 25 (236) $350

Anr copy. Blue cloth, with cover & spine lettering in white & cover illus in dark blue, orange, cream & black; spine ends & corners rubbed, some wear to white of lettering & front cover design, hinges cracked. Some foxing. pba Jan 25 (237) $55

Anr copy. Blue cloth lettered in white on front cover, in gilt on spine, cover illus in dark blue, orange & white; spine ends & joints rubbed. pba Aug 22 (309) $120

Anr copy. Pictorial cloth. sg June 20 (241) $375

Anr copy. Illus by W. J. Aylward. Orig cloth; extremities rubbed, hinges cracked. With 6 plates. With Ls from Charmian London to Charles Yale describing the actual events. pba May 23 (218) $375

— Smoke Bellew. NY, 1912. 1st Ed. Cloth; spine head rubbed. With frontis & 7 plates. pba Oct 5 (260) $225

Anr copy. With frontis & 7 plates.. pba Jan 25 (238) $250

Anr copy. Cloth; spine ends rubbed. pba May 23 (220) $85

Anr copy. Orig cloth; rubbed. sg June 20 (243) $100

— A Son of the Sun. Garden City, 1912. 1st Ed. Orig cloth, in chipped & soiled dj. With frontis & 3 plates. pba Jan 25 (240) $1,200

Anr copy. Orig cloth. pba Jan 25 (241) $170

1st English Ed. L: Mills & Boon, [1913]. Orig cloth; spine ends rubbed, tear to cloth at spine head. pba Oct 5 (261) $190

— The Son of the Wolf. Tales of the Far North. Bost. & NY, 1900. 1st Ed, 1st Issue. 8vo, cloth, BAL trial bdg B. pba Oct 5 (262) $1,300

## LONDON

Anr copy. Cloth, 1st bdg. pba Oct 5 (263) $650; pba Nov 30 (226) $475

Anr copy. Cloth, 1st bdg; hinges starting, tarnishing of silver stamping on spine & front cover. pba Jan 25 (242) $550

Anr copy. Orig cloth, 1st bdg; rubbed, bdg skewed. sg Feb 8 (317) $300

3d Issue. Variant bdg of gray cloth stamped in silver with no dots in pbr's imprint but with imperfect &. Frontis foxed. cb June 25 (1875) $450

— South Sea Tales. NY, 1911. 1st Ed. Orig cloth; lettering mostly worn off, spine ends & extremities rubbed, endpapers soiled. pba Jan 25 (243) $95

— The Star Rover. L, 1915. ("The Jacket.") 1st Ed. Cloth; spine ends frayed. pba Jan 25 (223) $250

1st American Ed. NY, 1915. pba Oct 5 (264) $375

— The Strength of the Strong. NY, 1914. 1st Ed. In chipped dj with short tears. pba Oct 5 (266) $1,800

Anr copy. Orig cloth; adhesion residue to endpapers. pba Jan 25 (244) $250

Anr copy. Cloth; spine ends rubbed, tear to cloth at bottom of front cover. pba May 23 (221) $50

Anr copy. Bdg rubbed. sg June 20 (244) $225

— Tales of the Fish Patrol. NY, 1905. pba Oct 5 (267) $375; pba Jan 25 (245) $375

Anr copy. Orig cloth; spine ends rubbed. sg June 20 (245) $325

— Theft: A Play in Four Acts. NY, 1910. Later bdg of brown cloth with spine lettered in black; soiled, spine warped. pba Jan 25 (246) $700

Anr copy. Later bdg of brown cloth with spine lettered in black; spine foot chipped, short tear to spine head. pba May 23 (222) $150

1st Issue. Orig cloth; spine soiled, smudges to lower front cover. pba Oct 5 (269) $800

— The Turtles of Tasman. NY, 1916. 1st Ed. pba Oct 5 (268) $250

— The Valley of the Moon. NY, 1913. 1st Ed. pba Oct 5 (270) $450

— War of the Classes. NY, 1905. 1st Ed. pba Oct 5 (271) $325

— When God Laughs. NY, 1911. 1st Ed. In chipped dj with tear to upper rear panel; bdg with spine ends worn. With frontis & 5 plates. pba Oct 5 (272) $3,250

Anr copy. Cloth, gilt-lettered, decorative; spine ends rubbed. pba Jan 25 (247) $170

— White Fang. NY, 1906. 1st Pbd Ed, 2d Issue. Orig cloth; spine ends rubbed. pba Oct 5 (273) $85; pba May 23 (224) $85

## London, Jack, 1876-1916 — & Strunsky, Anna

— The Kempton-Wace Letters. NY, 1903. 1st Ed. Cloth; spine ends rubbed. pba Oct 5 (238) $400

## Lone, Emma Miriam

— Some Noteworthy Firsts in Europe during the Fifteenth Century. NY, 1930. Out-of-series copy. 8vo, bds. O Dec 5 (71) $50

## Long, Frank Belknap

— The Goblin Tower. Denver: New Collector's Group, 1949. One of 500. Pictorial wraps; extremities browned. pba May 4 (195) $80

## Long Island Rail Road

— Long Island and Where to Go!! NY, 1877. Pictorial wraps; dampstaining, tears to joints. With folding frontis map & wood-engravings. pba July 11 (179) $130

## Long, John, Indian Trader

— Voyages and Travels of an Indian Interpreter and Trader.... L, 1791. 1st Ed. 4to, old calf; hinges weak. With folding map. Met Feb 24 (350) $1,000

Anr copy. Contemp calf; front joint cracked. sg Oct 26 (230) $1,300

## Long, Joseph W.

— American Wild-Fowl Shooting. NY, 1874. 8vo, cloth; worn, tear in spine head, covers spotted. O Oct 10 (186) $100

## Long, Margaret

— The Shadow of the Arrow. Caldwell: Caxton Printers, 1950. In dj. With 25 plates & 5 maps. pba Feb 12 (47) $50

## Long, Stephen H.

— Voyage in a Six-Oared Skiff to the Falls of Saint Anthony in 1817. Phila., 1860. 8vo, orig cloth, with gilt imprinted "Collections of the Historical Society of Minnesota"; chipped. wa Feb 29 (445) $80

## Longfellow, Henry Wadsworth, 1807-82

See also: Fore-Edge Paintings; Limited Editions Club

— The Hanging of the Crane. L, 1875. 12mo, orig bds; worn. Dampstained at end. Sgd on tp, 1877. pba Oct 26 (45) $900

— Hyperion. NY, 1839. 1st Ed. 2 vols. 12mo, 19th-cent half mor; worn, upper covers detached. Inscr to Henry R. Cleveland & with photo. CE May 22 (318) $480

Anr copy. Orig half cloth; needs rebdg. sg Feb 8 (318) $90

Anr Ed. L, 1865. 4to, orig cloth. With 24 mtd photos by Francis Frith. b May 30 (57) £150; b May 30 (58) £150

— The Poetical Works. Bost., 1879-80. 2 vols. 4to, orig half sheep; scuffed. Sgd on tp. bbc June 24 (570) $210

— The Song of Hiawatha. Bost., 1855. 1st American Ed, 1st Ptg. 8vo, half mor by Hicks Judd Co.. pba Mar 7 (166) $300

1st English Ed. L, 1855. 8vo, orig cloth; spine faded. Some spotting. S Oct 27 (1192) £200 [Way]

Anr Ed. Bost., 1891. Ltd Ed. Illus by Frederic Remington. 4to, vellum gilt; soiled. With port & 22 plates. K Oct 1 (328) $300

Anr copy. Pictorial sheep gilt; spine ends rubbed, tear along lower front joint. With 22 plates. 19th-cent card with writing mtd to front flyleaf. pba June 20 (282) $180

Players' Ed. Chicago, [1911]. 4to, orig cloth; warped, some wear. F Mar 28 (508) $80
— Tales of a Wayside Inn. Bost., 1863. 1st American Ed, 1st Ptg. 12mo, cloth. sg Sept 21 (255) $60
— Works. Bost., 1871. 4 vols. 8vo, contemp calf gilt. sg Sept 21 (32) $425

Anr Ed. Bost., [1904]. One of 750. 11 vols. 8vo, half mor. cb Oct 17 (281) $950

**Longhurst, Henry.** See: Graves & Longhurst

**Longhurst, Margaret Helen**
— Catalogue of Carvings in Ivory. L: Victoria & Albert Museum, 1927-29. 2 vols. 4to, cloth; front cover of Vol II stained & bowed. sg June 13 (200) $250

**Longman, William, 1813-77 —&**
**Trower, H. F.**
— Journal of Six Weeks' Adventures in Switzerland.... L, 1856. 8vo, orig cloth; lower joint torn. With folding map with routes hand-colored. Inscr by Longman. bba Nov 1 (331) £350 [Atlas]

**Longus**
See also: Ashendene Press; Golden Cockerel Press; Limited Editions Club
— Daphnis and Chloe. L: Zwemmer, 1937. One of 250. Illus by Aristide Maillol. 8vo, orig vellum. b May 30 (441) £300
— Daphnis et Chloe. [Paris], 1745. ("Les Amours pastorales de Daphnis et Chloe.") 4to, modern mor. With engraved title & 28 plates. Fuerstenberg - Schaefer copy. S Dec 7 (383) £1,100

Anr Ed. Paris: chez Lamy, 1787. 4to, contemp mor gilt. With 29 plates. Fuerstenberg - Schaefer copy. S Dec 7 (385) £380

Anr Ed. Paris, 1800. ("Les amours pastorales de Daphnis et Chloe....") 4to, contemp half mor, bound for Duke Albrecht of Saxe-Teschen by Georg Friedrich Krauss. With 9 proof plates. C May 1 (95) £2,500

Anr Ed. Paris, 1937. Hors commerce copy with 2 suites of plates, bound together in a separate vol, 1 a series of proof impressions of 1st state, the 2d in sanguine. Illus by Aristide Maillol. Half mor, orig wraps bound in. S Nov 21 (265) £1,300

One of 250. Unsewn in orig wraps. With an additional suite of the woodcuts. Ck May 31 (63) £480

Anr copy. Unsewn as issued in orig wraps. S Nov 2 (20) £320 [Antiquariat]
— Pastoralium de Daphnide et Chloe. Paris, 1778. 4to, contemp mor gilt. L. p. copy. Fuerstenberg - Schaefer copy. S Dec 7 (387) £800

**Longworth, Maria Theresa, 1827-81**
— Zanita: A Tale of the Yo-Semite. NY, 1872. Orig cloth. C. Hart Merriam's annotated copy. Larson copy. pba Feb 12 (208) $425

1st Ed. Orig cloth; spine ends, corners & joints rubbed. Robbins copy. pba Mar 21 (397) $1,100

**Lonnberg, Einar.** See: Wright & Others

**Loomis, Leander V., 1827-1909**
— A Journal of the Birmingham Emigrating Company.... Salt Lake City, 1928. 1st Ed, One of 1,000. In chipped dj. pba Nov 16 (164) $60

Anr copy. Illus by Frederick Piercy. Orig cloth in dj; front hinge weak, d/j discolored. With 1 folding map 1 plate detached, 1 partially detached; pages slightly darkened. Sgd by author's daughter & daughter of Birmingham Co. captain. Larson copy. pba Sept 28 (581) $100

**Lopes de Castanheda, Fernan, c.1501-60?**
— L'Histoire des indes de Portugal.... Antwerp: Johann Steelius, 1554. 2d French Ed. 8vo, contemp calf; spine worn. With title device. Lacks 2E1; 2E2 with hole affecting text. Inscr "James Leppryngtons bowke bought by me at antwarpe a Dni 1557". S Oct 26 (517) £460 [Rocha]

**Lopes, Duarte —&**
**Pigafetta, Filippo, 1553-1603**
— A Report of the Kingdome of Congo.... L, 1597. 1st Ed in English. 4to, modern wraps. With 10 full-page woodcuts, including 2 repeats. Small piece torn out of blank upper margin of A4; lacking the 3 maps & all prelims except title. Sold w.a.f. sg Mar 7 (150) $850

**Lopez, Moses**
— A Lunar Calendar of the Festivals, and Other Days in the Year, Observed by the Israelites.... Newport, 1806. 8vo, contemp calf; extremities worn, endleaves lacking. Last leaf in pen facsimile. P Dec 12 (117) $800

**Lorangere Collection, Quentin de.** See: Lorangere & Lorangere Collection

**Lorangere, Quentin de —&**
**Lorangere Collection, Quentin de**
— [Sale Catalogue] Catalogue raisonne des diverses curiosites du cabinet de feu M. Quentin de Lorangere.... Paris, 1744. Bound with: Catalogue des livres de feu M. Quentin de Lorangere.... Paris, 1744. Compiled by Edme F. Gersaint. 12mo, contemp calf gilt; joints repaired. Priced. Fuerstenberg - Schaefer copy. S Dec 7 (250) £2,800

**Lord, Eliot**
— Comstock Mining and Miners. Wash., 1883. 4to, orig cloth; covers rubbed, spine ends & corners rubbed. With 3 maps (2 folding, 1 color). 1 map detached & torn. Robbins copy. pba Mar 21 (206) $100

**Lord John Press**
— Lord John Signatures. Northridge CA, 1991. One of 150. Half mor. O Dec 5 (193) $140

ETCHISON, DENNIS. - Lord John Ten: A Celebration. Northridge, 1988. One of 250, sgd by all the contribs. Half cloth. pba May 23 (117) $110

**Lord, Thomas**
— Lord's Entire New System of Ornithology.... L, [1791-96]. Folio, contemp calf gilt; rebacked with orig spine laid down. With engraved title & 114 hand-colored plates. With 8 plates & 9 leaves of text supplied from a smaller copy; repaired tears in blank margins & outer corners of 14 text leaves; Plate 61 creased. Fattorini copy. C Oct 25 (27) £7,800

**Lord's Prayer.** See: Oratio...

**Loreau, Max**
— Cerceaux sorcellent. [Paris, 1967]. One of 750. Illus by Jean Dubuffet. 4to, pictorial wraps. sg Sept 7 (130) $325

**Lorentz, Hendrik Antoon, 1853-1928 —& Others**
— Das Relativitaetsprinzip: Eine Sammlung von Abhandlungen. Leipzig & Berlin, 1913. 1st Ed. 8vo, orig wraps; edges worn. pba June 20 (151) $500

**Lorenzana y Buitron, Francisco Antonio**
— Historia de Nueva-Espana.... Mexico: Joseph Antonio de Hogal, 1770. 3 parts in 1 vol. Folio, contemp calf; some wear. With allegorical plate, folding map of Mexico, folding map of Spanish Southwest & Baja California, folding plate of Aztec temple, calendar plate & 31 full-page plates. Small gash at head of 4O2-5B2 not affecting letters; a few ink corrections in text; allegorical plate with piece missing, touching plate-mark. S Nov 30 (151) £2,600

**Lorenzini, Carlo.** See: Collodi, Carlo

**Lorini, Buonaiuto**
— Le Fortificationi. Venice, 1596. ("Delle fortificationi.") Folio, contemp vellum gilt with central panels having large elaborate central oval arabesque; inner hinges split. Presentation copy for Archduke Rudolf II of Austria, Holy Roman Emperor. C Apr 3 (138) £11,000

**L'Orme, Philibert de**
— Nouvelles inventions pour bien bastir et a petits fraiz.... Paris: Federic Morel, 1561. Folio, old calf; rebacked & recornered. With 34 woodcut illusts, 23 of them full-page. Lacking final blank; some browning. C Apr 3 (140) £2,400

**Lorris, Guillaume de —&
Meung, Jean de**
— Le Roman de la Rose. Lyons: Guillaume Le Roy, [c.1487]. ("Le Rommant de la Rose.") 3d Ed. Folio, citron mor gilt by Trautz-Bauzonnet. 42 lines; double column; type 9:112B. With 91 woodcuts. Washed & pressed; marginal tears in a1-3 repaired. 150 leaves. Goff R-309. Schaefer copy. P Nov 1 (147) $75,000

**Lorry, Anne Charles de**
— Essai sur les Alimens.... Paris, 1757. 2d Ed. 2 vols. 12mo, contemp calf; rubbed, covers flaked. With 2 privilege leaves at end of vol I. Vol I front free endpaper torn; browned & spotted. Vicaire copy. Ck Mar 22 (179) £80

**Los Rios, Francois de.** See: Rios, Francois de los

**Loskiel, George Henry, 1740-1814**
— History of the Mission of the United Brethren Among the Indians in North America.... L, 1794. 8vo, contemp calf; worn, front cover detached, front free endpaper lacking. Lacking map; index def & incomplete; tp browned; some dampstaining. F June 20 (388) $90

**Lostelneau, —— de**
— Le Mareschal de bataille. Paris, 1647. Folio, contemp calf gilt; head of spine worn, hinges split. With 48 full-page illusts; 135 diagrams of battle formations ptd in red & black; 49 battle formations ptd in yellow, red & black, 8 of them folding. Some spotting & browning. C Apr 3 (142) £1,700

**Loti, Pierre**
— Le Mort de Philae. Paris: Rene Kieffer, 1924. One of 460. Illus by Ge Colucci. 4to, mor janseniste by Blanchetiere; rejointed. sg Sept 14 (257) $150
— Pecheur d'Islande. Paris, 1934. One of 25 for collaborators, this on japon with 2 additional suites of the illusts numbered 2/5 & sgd by Pierre Bouchet. Illus by Lucien Simon, wood-engraved by Pierre Bouchet. 8vo, mor extra with waves & onlaid star, by Semet & Plumelle, orig wraps bound in. S Nov 21 (270) £2,000

**Lotti, Lotto**
— L'eta dell'oro, introduzione al balletto della... Principessa Margherita... fatto rappresentare dal... Duca di Parma.... Piacenza: nella stampa ducale del Bazachi, 1690. 4to, 18th-cent wraps. With frontis & 4 double-page plates, all folding. C Apr 3 (143) £4,000

**Lotz, Arthur**
— Bibliographie der Modelbuecher.... Stuttgart, [1963]. 8vo, orig cloth in dj. sg Apr 11 (207) $150

**Loudon, Archibald**
— A Selection of the Most Interesting Narratives, or Outrages, Committed by the Indians.... Harrisburg, 1888. 2d Ed, one of 100. 8vo, orig cloth; worn & shaken, removal stain at each rear pastedown. bbc Dec 18 (502) $280

**Loudon, Jane Webb**
— Annuals. L, 1840. ("The Ladies' Flower-Garden of Ornamental Annuals.") 1st Ed. 4to, contemp half calf; rubbed, spine & upper cover detached. With 48 hand-colored plates. Minor browning. Fattorini copy. C Oct 25 (75) £1,600
Anr Ed. L, 1844. 4to, contemp half mor gilt; rubbed. With 48 hand-colored plates. Lacking halftitle. S June 27 (47) £900
— British Wild Flowers. L, 1846. 1st Ed. 4to, half mor gilt; rubbed. With 60 hand-colored plates. Some plates shaved at fore-edge; Plate 18 stained in inner margin; lacking half-title. S Nov 30 (33) £900
Anr copy. Contemp half calf; rubbed, 1 section becoming detached. S June 27 (48) £500

3d Ed. L, 1859. 4to, orig cloth; rebacked. With half-title & 60 hand-colored plates. S Oct 27 (647) £700 [D'Arte]

— Greenhouse Plants. L, 1848. ("The Ladies' Flower-Garden of Ornamental Greenhouse Plants.") 4to, orig cloth; stained. With 42 hand-colored plates. Some dampstaining in lower outer margins. S June 27 (46) £1,500

2d Ed. L, [1849]. 4to, orig cloth; spine ends & joints worn, hinges cracked. With 42 hand-colored plates. CE May 22 (320) $1,700

— Ornamental Perennials. L, [1849]. ("The Ladies' Flower-Garden of Ornamental Perennials.") 2d Ed. 4to, orig cloth; needs rebdg. With 90 hand-colored plates. Some soiling & foxing. sg Dec 7 (226) $2,400

**Loudon, John Claudius, 1783-1843**

— An Encyclopaedia of Cottage, Farm, and Villa Architecture... L, 1846. 8vo, orig cloth. bba Oct 19 (140) £340 [Sotheran]

— The Magazine of Natural History, or Journal of Zoology, Botany, Mineralogy.... L, 1829-40. Vols I-IX; New Series, Vols I-IV; together 13 vols. 8vo, contemp half lea; rubbed, spine heads chipped. S June 13 (409) £320

— The Mummy, a Tale.... L, 1827. 3 vols. 8vo, old half calf; rebacked, partially restored. S July 11 (235) £1,400

**Louis XIII, King of France, 1601-43**

— Le Soleil au signe du Lyon. D'ou quelques paralleles sont tirez avec...Louys XIII..en son entree triomphante dans sa Ville de Lyon.... Lyons, 1623. 2 parts in 1 vol. Folio, 19th-cent calf gilt by Devauchelle. With 19 plates. C May 1 (94) £2,300

**Louis XIV, King of France, 1638-1715**

[-] Medailles sur les principaux evenements du regne de Louis le Grand. Paris, 1702. Folio, contemp citron mor gilt with French royal arms; sides spotted. Lower margins of Plates 55 & 56 with lower margins shorter & browned. Fuerstenberg - Schaefer copy. S Dec 7 (114) £1,100

Anr Ed. Paris, 1723. Folio, contemp mor gilt; spine cracked at head. C May 12 (76) £900

Anr copy. Contemp red mor gilt with royal cypher on spine; spine ends rubbed. Tear in lower margin of leaf 106 & in outer margin of leaves 291-92, affecting border of leaf 292. Fuerstenberg - Schaefer copy. S Dec 7 (116) £320

— Memoirs. L, 1806. 2 vols. 8vo, half mor; some wear. Extra-illus with plates & Ds. CE Feb 21 (167) $600

[-] Premieres epreuves de la seconde edition des Medailles de l'histoire du Roy. Paris, [1702]. Folio, contemp red mor gilt with arms of Louis XIV; spine rubbed. Engraved throughout; letterpress on 1st 10 leaves only, thereafter only pulls of the engraved borders & medals.. Fuerstenberg - Schaefer copy. S Dec 7 (115) £1,800

**Louis XV, King of France, 1710-74**

— Cours des principaux fleuves et rivieres de l'Europe.... Paris, 1718. 4to, contemp calf gilt with arms of Louis de Rochechouart, duc de Mortemart. With port. Fuerstenberg - Schaefer copy. S Dec 7 (388) £1,600

[-] Fete publique donnee par la Ville de Paris a l'occasion du mariage de Monseigneur le Dauphin avec Marie Josephe de Saxe, le 13 Fevrier 1747. [Paris, 1747]. Folio, contemp mor gilt. With engraved title, frontis & 7 double-page plates. Engraved throughout. Browning to Plate 2. Fuerstenberg - Schaefer copy. S Dec 7 (220) £2,500

— Lettres patentes du Roy, portant reglement pour le commerce des Colonies Francoises. Paris, 1717. 4to, modern wraps. sg Oct 26 (206) $700

[-] Relation de l'arrivee du Roi au Havre-de-Grace, le 19. Septembre 1749. Paris, 1753. Folio, contemp red mor gilt with royal arms. With 6 double-page plates. Fuerstenberg - Schaefer copy. S Dec 8 (522) £2,400

[-] Representation des fetes donnees par la Ville de Strasbourg pour la convalescence du Roi. Paris, 1745. Folio, contemp red mor with arms of Louis XV, by Padeloup, with unidentified arms in the corners; minor rubbing to bands of spine & corners. With engraved title, port & 11 double-page plates. C Nov 29 (83) £10,000

[-] Le Sacre de Louis XV...dans l'eglise de Reims, le XXV Octobre, MDCCXXII. [Paris], 1723. Folio, contemp olive mor gilt by Vente with arms of Louis XV; spine ends repaired. Engraved throughout; with engraved title, 9 double-page plates & 30 plates of costume. Some browning. Fuerstenberg - Schaefer copy. S Dec 8 (552) £7,000

[-] Sacre et Couronnement de Louis XVI, Roi de France. Paris, 1775. 4to, contemp red mor gilt with arms of Louis XVI. With frontis, 9 double-page plates of the ceremony, 39 plates of costume, 1 folding map, 1 folding plate of arms. Small hole in text of sub-title. L.p. copy on hollande. Fuerstenberg - Schaefer copy. S Dec 8 (483) £3,400

**Louisiana**

— An Account of Louisiana, Laid Before Congress by Direction of the President...November 14, 1803.... Providence: Heaton & Williams, [c.1804]. 12mo, orig half sheep; worn, front hinge reinforced. Browned; marginal tear at top of F1. Engelhard copy. CNY Jan 26 (182) $1,700

**Loutherbourg, Philippe Jacques de, 1740-1812**

— The Romantic and Picturesque Scenery of England and Wales. L, 1805. Folio, contemp half or gilt; extremities scuffed. With 18 hand-colored plates. Without frontis. C May 31 (99) £1,600

**Louys, Pierre, 1870-1925**

— Aphrodite. Paris: La Semeuse pour H. Couderc de Saint-Chamant, 1910. Unique copy, containing 43 watercolor drawings by E. Malassis (11 full-page, sgd & dated 1911 or 1912) & titles & ornamental borders by Adolphe Giraldon colored by hand & Giraldon's watercolor design for the covers. Folio, mor extra to Giraldon's design by Rene Kieffer, with upper cover enamel inset by Paul Grandhomme. S Nov 21 (274) £5,500

Anr Ed. Paris, 1937. One of 30 on japon imperial with orig illust & plates in 3 states. Illus by Paul Emile Becat. 4to, mor gilt by Franz. b May 30 (562) £160

Anr Ed. Paris: Les Bibliophiles de l'Amerique Latine, 1954. One of 5 on japon imperial with 2 additional suites, this being No 4 for Georges Crette. Illus by Pierre Bouchet after George Barbier & Georges Lepape. 4to, mor extra with onlays in abstract floral design by Georges Crette. Bound in are 2 watercolors sgd by Georges Barbier & 2 watercolors & pencil drawing sgd by Georges Lepape. Kettaneh copy. S Nov 21 (281) £4,000

— Aphrodite: Moeurs Antiques. Tiflis: Bagration Davidoff, 1928. One of 166. 3 vols in 2. 4to, contemp half lea, orig wraps bound in. With 16 illusts & 4 Ms facsimile plates. Soiling to 1 illust. sg Feb 8 (272) $100

— Les Aventures du Roi Pausole. Paris, 1930. One of 6 on japon. Illus by Umberto Brunelleschi. 4to, mor gilt by Germaine Maubec. Presentation copy from the artist, with additional suite of the full-page illusts on japon in black only, sgd in pencil & 5 additional impressions of the frontis, of which 4 are color decompositions & a watercolor. S Nov 21 (280) £1,100

— Les Chansons de Bilitis. Paris, 1895. One of 10 on japon. 8vo, mor extra by Lortic, with floral borders of hand-painted panels set in & centerpieces, 1 of 2 girls, the other of a trophy with bow, arrows & torch; orig wraps bound in. Added are 8 watercolor drawings heightened with gold, by Adolphe Giraldon for the subtitles & decorations, sgd, & for the upper cover & embroidered border. S Nov 21 (272) £4,250

Anr Ed. Paris, 1925. One of 40 hors commerce with 3 additional suites & a series of 8 additional plates (7 in 4 states, 1 in 3) & 1 planche refusee. Illus by Edouard Chimot. 4to, mor extra by Leon Gruel, orig wraps bound in. Some soiling, mark on lower cover, endpapers spotted. With orig drawing by Chimot. S Nov 21 (277) £700

— La Femme et le pantin. Paris, 1903. One of 300 "of which this is number 304". Illus by P. Roig. Mor extra by Creuzevault, orig wraps bound in. CNY May 14 (450) $480; S Nov 21 (273) £700

Anr Ed. Paris, 1928. One of 20 on japon a la forme with 2 additional suites of the etchings & orig drawing, sgd by Chimot. Illus by Edouard Chimot. 4to, mor extra by Durvand-Pinard, 1929, orig wraps bound in. With 16 color plates. Plesch copy. S Nov 21 (279) £550

— Quatorze Images prose inedites.... Paris, 1925. One of 14 on japon with 2 orig drawing & additional suite of plates. Illus by Andre Dignimont. 8vo, lev extra to an abstract design by Pierre Legrain, orig wraps bound in, the additional suite of plates in wraps. With a 3d orig drawing bound in. C May 1 (96) £14,000

— Trois filles de leur mere. Paris, 1926. One of 50 on Arches. Illus by Marcel Vertes. 4to, mor extra by Pierre Legrain with abstract floral motifs. With 17 etchings. Bound in are 3 drawings by Marcel Vertes. S Nov 21 (278) £2,600

**Love, Rev. Emanuel King**

— History of the First African Baptist Church.... Savannah: The Morning News Print, 1888. 8vo, modern cloth; fore-edge stained. A few leaves at end creased. sg Mar 28 (194) $300

**Lovecraft, Howard Phillips, 1890-1937**

— Beyond the Wall of Sleep. Sauk City: Arkham House, 1943. 1st Ed. In chipped dj with small tears. pba May 4 (197) $800

Anr copy. Orig cloth, in dj with 2 nicks. sg June 20 (249) $800

One of 1,200. Cloth, in chipped dj; newspaper review mtd at front pastedown. bbc June 24 (572) $700

— Dreams and Fancies. Sauk City, WI: Arkham House, 1962. In dj. sg June 20 (250) $90

— Marginalia. Sauk City: Arkham House, 1944. 1st Ed. In dj. sg June 20 (251) $200

— The Outsider and Others. Sauk City: Arkham House, 1939. 1st Ed. In dj with rubbed spine; owner's name stamped on front free endpaper. pba May 4 (198) $1,700

One of 1,200. Cloth, in dj. bbc June 24 (573) $950

— The Shunned House. Athol MA: Pbd by W. Paul Cook/The Recluse Press, 1928. 1st Ed. Orig half cloth; rubbed, light wear. Inscr to Philip Grill by Frank Belknap & with photocopy of letter from August Derleth to Grill offering this copy for sale as 1 of 6 bound copies. cb Oct 17 (549) $8,500

— Something About Cats and Other Pieces. Sauk City: Arkham House, 1949. 1st Ed. In dj. sg June 20 (252) $100

— Supernatural Horror in Literature. NY: Ben Abramson, 1945. Orig cloth; lower extremities stained. pba Aug 22 (315) $85

**Lovecraft, Howard Phillips, 1890-1937 —& Others**

— The Shuttered Room.... Sauk City, Wisc., 1959. In dj. sg June 20 (254) $130

**Lovecraft, Howard Phillips, 1890-1937 —& Derleth, August William**

— The Lurker at the Threshold. Sauk City: Arkham House, 1945. In dj. sg June 20 (253) $100

— The Survivor and Others. Sauk City: Arkham House, 1957. In dj with wear to upper corners. pba May 4 (199) $75

**Lovejoy, Joseph C. & Owen**

— Memoir of the Rev. Elijah P. Lovejoy; who was murdered in Defence of the Liberty of the Press, at Alton, Illinois, Nov. 7, 1837.... NY, 1838. 12mo, orig cloth; lacking backstrip. sg Oct 26 (231) $100

**Lovelace, Richard, 1618-58**
— Lucasta: Epodes, Odes, Sonnets, Songs & c. Chiswick, 1817. Mor by Alfred Mathews; hinges weak, back cover becoming detached. John Payne Collier's annotated copy. Z June 28 (173) $425

**Lovell, Richard Goulburn**
— Home Interiors. [N.p., n.d.]. 5 parts. Folio, loose in half cloth portfolios with shelf markings. With 27 color halftone plates, 2 color charts & 29 engraved plates. Library markings; perforated stamp to each plate, affecting images; marginal dampstaining; Section I incomplete. cb Oct 17 (90) $225

**Lovell, Robert, 1630?-90**
— Panbotanologia sive Enchiridion botanicum or a Compleat Herball. Oxford, 1659. 12mo, contemp calf; loose, backstrip chipped, 1 leaf misbound. bba Sept 7 (149) £360 [Henly]

**Lover, Samuel, 1797-1868**
— Works. NY, 1901. Treasure Trove Ed. 10 vols. Half mor, unopened; spines browned. Extra-illus with plates & hand-colored frontises, some sgd by artists. pba Dec 14 (103) $375

**Low, Charles Rathbone, 1837-1918**
— Her Majesty's Navy. L, 1890-93. 3 vols. 4to, contemp half mor; rubbed. bba May 30 (236) £380 [Cumming]

**Low, David, 1786-1859**
— The Breeds of the Domestic Animals of the British Islands. L, 1842. Illus by W. Nicholson. 2 vols in 1. Folio, half mor; disbound, extremities worn. With 56 hand-finished colored plates. Edge-soiling; frontis cracked along inner edge & with small tear at head; some discoloration. P Dec 12 (219) $4,500

**Low, Sir Hugh, 1824-1905**
— Sarawak. L, 1848. 8vo, orig cloth; rubbed. With 7 plates. S June 13 (659) £240

**Low, John L.**
— F. G. Tait; A Record, Being his Life, Letters, and Golfing Diary. L: J. Nisbet, [1900]. Intro by Andrew Lang. Cloth; spine dulled, soiled. With frontis photo port. pba Nov 9 (59) $250

1st Ed. Cloth; cover spotted, spine rubbed, spine foot smudged. With frontis port photo. pba Apr 18 (117) $85

**Lowe, Edward Joseph, 1825-1900**
— Ferns: British and Exotic. L, 1867-68. 8 vols. 8vo, orig cloth gilt; spines worn & def, old library bookplates, 1 plate detached. With 478 (of 479) plates. Lacking Plate V in Vol I; some plates with minor foxing. cb Oct 17 (133) $325

**Lowe, Edward Joseph, 1825-1900 —& Howard, W.**
— Beautiful Leaved Plants. L, 1865. 8vo, orig cloth. With 60 colored plates. b Sept 20 (476) £80

Anr Ed. L, 1868. 8vo, orig cloth. With 60 colored plates. Some plates loose; 1 foxed. b Sept 20 (475) £50

**Lowell, Amy, 1874-1925**
— Tendencies in Modern American Poetry. NY, 1917. Inscr, 17 Oct 1917. wa Feb 29 (64) $75

**Lowell, Guy**
— More Small Italian Villas and Farmhouses. NY: Architectural Book Publishing Co., [1920]. Folio, cloth; spine ends worn, marked & soiled, sewing cracked. wa Dec 14 (394) $85

— Smaller Italian Villas & Farmhouses. NY, 1922. Folio, cloth; spine ends worn, some marks. wa Dec 14 (395) $110

**Lowell, James Russell, 1819-91**
See also: Clemens's copy, Samuel Langhorne
— The Biglow Papers.... L, 1859. 12mo, orig cloth; some wear, spine frayed at top. With c.50 marginal sketches in ink by Frederick Pollock. With ALs from C. Kegan Paul, presenting this vol to Miss Defell, who was engaged to Frederick Pollock. bbc Feb 26 (323) $180

— Works. Cambr., 1904. Edition de Luxe, One of 1,000. 16 vols. Half mor. ALs & ANs tipped in. cb Oct 17 (282) $650

**Lowell, Robert, 1917-77**
— Land of Unlikeness. [Cummington, Mass.], 1944. 1st Ed, One of 250. Port of Lowell attached to front free endpaper. CE May 22 (321) $750

Anr copy. Ls laid in. Engelhard copy. CNY Oct 27 (107) $1,400

Anr copy. Inscr to his first wife's parents. Hobson copy. S June 28 (171) £1,600

— The Voyage and other Versions of Poems by Baudelaire. L, 1968. One of 200. Illus by Sidney Nolan. 4to, orig cloth. Hobson copy. S June 28 (176) £160

**Lower...**
— The Lower St. Lawrence, or Quebec to Halifax.... Quebec, 1862. 16mo, orig cloth; worn. Some foxing. O Feb 6 (152) $250

**Lowery, Woodbury**
— Lowery Collection: a Descriptive List.... See: Phillips, Philip Lee

**Lowman, Al**
See also: Cheeseman & Lowman
— Printing Arts in Texas. Austin, [1975]. Ltd Ed. 4to, cloth. ds July 27 (150) $100

**Lowndes, William Thomas, d.1843**
— The Bibliographer's Manual of English Literature. L, 1857-64. Ed by Henry G. Bohn. 6 vols. 8vo, contemp half mor; spines rubbed. bba July 18 (16) £70 [Cox]

Anr Ed. L, 1864. 4 vols. 8vo, contemp half calf; rubbed, spine heads chipped. ds July 27 (118) $125

Anr Ed. L, 1871. 4 vols. 12mo, orig half lea; rubbed. O Mar 26 (163) $110

Anr Ed. L, 1883-85. Revised by H. G. Bohn. 6 vols in 4. 8vo, half mor. Sold w.a.f. sg Apr 11 (207A) $100

**Lowry, Malcolm, 1909-57**
— Under the Volcano. NY, [1947]. 1st Ed. Cloth, in chipped dj with spine scrape affecting title. pba Aug 22 (316) $250

**Lowther, George**
— The Adventures of Superman. NY, [1942]. 1st Ed in Book form. In chipped & rubbed dj. pba May 4 (200) $500

**Lowther, Granville**
— The Encyclopedia of Practical Horticulture. North Yakima WA, [1914]. 4to, orig cloth. wa Nov 16 (193) $130

**Loyalist's...**
— The Loyalist's Magazine, Complete.... L, 1821. 8vo, later half lev by Bumpus; tight, scuffed. With 10 plates, 4 of them by George Cruikshank. Salomons copy. bbc Dec 18 (230) $160

**Loysel, Pierre**
— Essai sur l'art de la verrerie. Paris, [1800]. 8vo, contemp half russia; repaired. With folding plate. Boulton copy. S Oct 27 (806) £180 [Antiquarian]

**Lubbock, Basil**
— Bully Hayes, South Sea Pirate. Bost., 1931. 4to, cloth. pba July 25 (179) $75

**Lucanus, Marcus Annaeus, 39-65**
— Pharsalia. Venice: Augustinus de Zanni for Melchior Sessa, 1511. Folio, 19th-cent calf gilt with arms of Ralph Sneyd; front cover detached. Some minor soiling & browning; small repair to f.1, affecting several lines of text; small holes in f.5; last blank missing. Doheny copy. CNY Feb 2 (804) $250 [Parsons Books]

Anr copy. Contemp vellum; hole in backstrip, hinges cracked. Early underscoring & marginalia; some heavy browning; old scored writing on tp; hole in last leaf affecting text; lacking last leaf & rear free endpaper. sg Mar 21 (209) $475

Anr Ed. Paris, 1543. ("Civilis belli.") 8vo, mor gilt. Contemp notes & underlining throughout; pages trimmed. pba Nov 30 (227) $120

Anr Ed. L, 1720. Trans by Nicolas Rowe. 8vo, contemp calf. Ink blots on tp & next leaf. sg Mar 21 (210) $200

Anr Ed. Strawberry Hill, 1760. 4to, modern half calf. Some foxing. bba July 18 (190) £220 [Unsworth]

Anr Ed. Paris: Renouard, 1795 [An III]. One of 5 ptd on vellum. Folio, contemp red mor gilt; rubbed, head of spine worn. Half-title discolored. Fuerstenberg - Schaefer copy. S Dec 7 (390) £2,500

Anr Ed. Vienna: J. V. Degen, 1811. One of 2 on papier velin. 4to, contemp mor gilt with onlays & monograms of Albrecht von Sachsen-Teschen, in neo-classical style. Fuerstenberg - Schaefer copy. S Dec 7 (391) £14,000

**Lucas, Charles**
— The Old Serpentine Temple of the Druids, at Avebury.... Marlborough, 1795. 4to, contemp wraps with cloth backstrip. With 2 folding plates. b Dec 5 (407) £220
— Pharmacomastix: or, the Office, Use and Abuse of Apothecaries explained.... Dublin, 1741. 8vo, bds. Some waterstaining. b May 30 (28) £100

**Lucas, Edward Verrall, 1868-1938**
— Playtime and Company. L, 1925. One of 15 on Japon, sgd by author & artist. Orig vellum; bowed. sg Sept 14 (324) $850

**Lucas, Frank Laurence, 1894-1967.** See: Golden Cockerel Press

**Lucas, Victoria.** See: Plath, Sylvia

**Lucatt, Edward**
— Rovings in the Pacific from 1837 to 1849.... L, 1851. 2 vols in 1. 8vo, contemp half mor. With 4 chromolithos. b Mar 20 (117) £360

**Lucian of Samosata**
See also: Golden Cockerel Press
— Die Hetaerengespraeche. Leipzig, 1907. One of 450. Trans into German by Franz Blei; illus by Gustave Klimt. 4to, orig cloth; hinges cracked. With 15 plates. S May 16 (20) £1,000
One of 50 on japon. Orig cloth; edges worn. With 15 plates. S Nov 21 (282) £700
— Lucian's True History. L, 1894. One of 250. 4to, cloth; extremities worn. With 16 plates. sg Feb 8 (186) $120
One of 54. Orig cloth. S Nov 2 (68) £360 [Zioni]
— Opera. Florence: [Laurentius Francisci de Alopa Venetus], 1496. 1st Ed. Folio, 20th-cent vellum. 42 lines; greek letter. 2 leaves heavily censored on 12 Aug 1708; repairs at beginning affecting a few letters; some staining; browned throughout; Ms marginalia cropped by binder. 263 (of 264) leaves; lacking final blank. Goff L-320. Lyell - Peddie - Mersey copy. C Nov 29 (62) £3,800
Anr Ed. Amst., 1743-44. 4 vols. 4to, contemp mor gilt; joints weak. Fuerstenberg - Schaefer copy. S Dec 7 (392) £500

**Lucretius Carus, Titus, 96?-55 B.C.**
See also: Limited Editions Club
— De rerum natura. Paris & Lyons: G. Rouille, 1563. Ed by Denys Lambin. 4to, contemp blind-stamped pigskin over paper bds, 1566; upper hinge cracked, soiled. Annotations in ink & pencil; 1 gathering misbound; some rust-marks. S June 12 (70) £500
Anr Ed. Paris: Antoine Coustelier, 1744. 2 vols. 12mo, contemp red mor gilt; a2-a4 misbound in Vol I. Ptd on vellum. Fuerstenberg - Schaefer copy. S Dec 7 (135) £5,800
Anr Ed. Amst., 1754. ("Della natura delle cose, libri sei.") 2 parts in 1 vol. 8vo, contemp red mor giltar-

morial bdg; 1 corner of Vol II worn. With engraved titles & 6 plates & 2 frontises. Hoe - Rahir - Fuerstenberg - Schaefer copy. S Dec 7 (393) £5,000

Anr Ed. Londra [but Paris: Prault], 1761. 2 vols. 8vo, contemp olive mor gilt, with added arms of the Duke of Sutherland. With 2 engraved titles & port. Fuerstenberg - Schaefer copy. S Dec 7 (394) £500

— Of the Nature of Things. L: Daniel Browne, 1743. 2 vols. 8vo, contemp calf gilt; Vol I covers detached. Some foxing. sg Mar 21 (211) $175

**Ludewig, Hermann Ernst, d.1856**
— The Literature of American Local History.... L, 1846. 8vo, orig cloth; worn. Some foxing. O Mar 26 (164) $120

**Ludlow Castle...**
— Ludlow Castle; a Brief Historical Poem...By a Resident. Ludlow, 1830. 8vo, contemp calf; upper cover detached. b Dec 5 (318) £80

**Ludlow, William**
— Report of a Reconnaissance of the Black Hills of Dakota. Made in the Summer of 1874. Wash., 1875. 4to, orig cloth; partly erased markings to front pastedown. With 2 large folding maps & plate. Stamp partly erased from tp; other library markings; some tape repairs to maps. pba June 25 (159) $75

**Ludlum, Robert**
— The Scarlatti Inheritance. NY, [1971]. Mor, in dj. Sgd on label mtd to front free endpaper. pba May 23 (227) $70

**Ludolf, Hiob, 1624-1704**
— Dissertatio de locustis.... Frankfurt, 1694. Folio, modern half calf. Some browning. bba May 30 (439) £120 [Poole]

**Ludolphus de Saxonia**
— Vita Christi. Nuremberg: Anton Koberger, 20 Dec 1478. Folio, contemp blind-stamped pigskin over wooden bds; stained, lacking 1 clasp. 61 lines & headline; double column; gothic letter; 1st initial in gilt on colored panel with floral extensions. Repair to 1st initial (which also is rubbed) with loss to text on verso; lower corner of fol. 257 torn away, affecting text; initial cut out of fol. 279 with loss. 182 (of 372) leaves only; lacking all before fol. 190 & final leaf. Goff L-339. S Dec 18 (54) £800 [Zioni]

Anr Ed. Nuremberg: Anton Koberger, 24 July 1483. Folio, 18th-cent half vellum. 56 lines & headline; gouble column; gothic letter. Some dampstaining to margins at end; library stamp. 374 (of 376) leaves; lacking 1st & last blank. Goff L-342. S Dec 18 (55) £1,800 [Tenschert]

Anr Ed. Zwolle: Pieter van Os, 20 Nov [1495]. ("Dat Boeck vanden leven ons Heren Jhesu Cristi anderwerven gheprint.") Folio, contemp blind-stamped calf over wooden bds; rebacked & repaired. 40 lines & headline; double column; type 8:99G. With 157 woodcut illusts. Marginal dampstaining at ends; a few repaired tears; stamp of City Library of Bruges.

355 (of 356) leaves; lacking last blank. Goff L-356. Arenberg - Schaefer copy. P Nov 1 (148) $37,500

**Ludwig Salvator, Erzherzog von Austria, 1847-1915**
— Ueber den Durchstich der Landenge von Stagno. Prague, 1906. 4to, cloth; upper cover marked. With 9 plates (4 color). S Oct 26 (155) £100 [Nebchay]

**Lugt, Frits**
— Inventaire general des dessins des ecoles du nord, ecole hollandais. L, 1929-33. 2 vols. 4to, orig half cloth. sg Jan 11 (305) $200

**Lull, Ramon, 1235?-1315?.** See: Lullus, Raimundus

**Lullus, Raimundus, 1235?-1315?**
— Ars inventiva veritatis. Valencia: Diego de Gumiel, 12 Feb 1515. Folio, 19th-cent half calf. Lacking last 5 leaves; inner margins of gathering A repaired; some dampstaining. Madsen copy. S Mar 14 (236) £5,200

— Testamentum R. Lulli duobus libris universam artem chymicam complectens. Cologne: J. Birckmann, 1573. 8vo, old sheep; spine worn & retouched, joints cracked. Ink blot on tp; ink marginalia & underlining. pba June 20 (228) $275

**Lumiere, Auguste & Louis**
— Sur la Photographie des Couleurs. Lyon: Boulud, [n.d.]. Orig wraps; torn & soiled. Tp soiled; library markings. sg Feb 29 (186) $110

**Lummis, Charles Fletcher, 1859-1928**
— The Land of Poco Tiempo. NY, 1893. 1st Ed. 8vo, orig cloth; extremities & joints rubbed, spine foot frayed, front hinge cracked. With inscr port laid in. Robbins copy. pba Mar 21 (209) $90

Anr Ed. NY, 1902. 8vo, cloth; spine ends rubbed. pba Apr 25 (513) $75

— The Man Who Married the Moon and Other Pueblo Indian Folk-Songs. NY, 1894. 1st Ed. - Illus by George Wharton Edwards. Orig cloth; spine sunned. Robbins copy. pba Mar 21 (210) $375

— Some Strange Corners of Our Country.... NY, 1892. 1st Ed. Orig cloth; light shelf wear. With color frontis. Robbins copy. pba Mar 21 (211) $170

— The Spanish Pioneers. Chicago, 1893. 1st Ed. Orig cloth; light shelf wear. With frontis port & 8 plates. 1 plate detached but present. Robbins copy. pba Mar 21 (212) $50

— A Tramp Across the Continent. NY, 1892. 1st Ed. Orig cloth; covers rubbed. Robbins copy. pba Mar 21 (213) $170

**Lupoldus Bambergensis**
— Germanorum veterum principum zelus et feruor in christainam religionem Deique ministros. Basel: Johann Bergmann de Olpe, 15 May 1497. Folio, 18th-cent half sheep; extremities scuffed, spine ends chipped. 41-42 lines & headline; types 1:109aR, 3:77R, 4:220G. Some staining & spotting; worming touching an occasional letter. 28 leaves. Goff L-399. C Nov 29 (64) £800

## LUSHINGTON

**Lushington, Henry**
— A Great Country's Little Wars.... L, 1844. 12mo, orig cloth; spine chipped at top. sg Mar 7 (175) $110

**Luther, Martin, 1483-1546**
— Colloquia Mensalia: or, Dr. Martin Luther's Divine Discourses. L, 1652. 1st Ed in English. Folio, later mor; new endpapers. pba Sept 14 (251) $700
— A Commentarie upon the Epistle of S Paule to the Galathians. L, 1580. 4to, calf gilt; old notes to endpapers. Notes to margins & spaces of text; paper note mtd to center of tp & verso; hole to center of following leaf, affecting text, repaired with tape; some staining, worming & repairs. pba Nov 30 (228) $400
Anr Ed. L, 1588. 4to, modern lea. F. 295 lacking top corner, affecting text; f.295 def; some ink markings; stamp to front flyleaf; soiled. pba Sept 14 (250) $250
— Von menschen leeren zu meyden. Wittenberg, 1522. Unbound. Crease to lower contents. pba Nov 30 (229) $225

**Lutheran Church.** See: Concordia

**Luthi, Jean Jacques**
— Emile Bernard: Catalogue raisonne de l'oeuvre peint. Paris, [1982]. 4to, cloth, in dj. sg Jan 11 (43) $175

**Luttig, John C., d.1815**
— Journal of a Fur-Trading Expedition on the Upper Missouri. St. Louis, 1920. One of 365. Ed by Stella M. Drumm. Half cloth; rubbed. Inscr. pba Aug 8 (102) $275

**Lyall, Robert, d.1831**
— The Character of the Russians, and a Detailed History of Moscow. L, 1823. 4to, half calf; rubbed. With 23 plates, some hand-colored, & folding map of Moscow. Library stamp on tp verso; map torn without loss. bba May 30 (322) £380 [Besley]

**Lycett, Joseph**
— Views in Australia, or New South Wales.... L, 1824. Oblong 4to, contemp half mor; corners rubbed. With pictorial title & 48 hand-colored views & 2 maps, 1 folding. Short tear in folding map. S June 27 (266) £13,500

**Lycosthenes, Conrad, 1518-61**
— Epitome Bibliothecae Conradi Gesneri. Zurich: Christoph Froschouer, Mar 1555. Folio, 19th-cent pastiche bdg of calf gilt with recessed painted vellum panels. Some worming; short tear in 2 margins. bba Nov 16 (11) £1,200 [Mayer]
— Die Wunder Gottes in der Natur bey Erseheinung der Kometen.... Frankfurt & Leipzig, 1744. 8vo, contemp half calf; worn. With engraved frontis & 83 engravings on 41 plates. S Mar 14 (238) £460

**Lydekker, Richard, 1849-1915**
— The New Natural History. NY, [c.1880]. 6 vols. 8vo, half mor gilt. sg May 9 (363) $175

## AMERICAN BOOK PRICES CURRENT

— The Royal Natural History. L, 1893-96. 6 vols. 8vo, orig cloth. b Sept 20 (477) £60
Anr copy. Contemp half mor; rubbed. Some foxing. bba May 30 (440) £75 [Classic Bindings]
Anr copy. 8 vols. 8vo, orig cloth. Tp & prelims creased. bba May 30 (441) £60 [Frew]

**Lye, Len**
— No Trouble. Deya Majorca, 1930. One of 200. Def in margin of pp. 27-28. S June 28 (194) £80

**Lyell, Sir Charles, 1797-1875**
— Principles of Geology. L, 1830-33. 1st Ed. 3 vols. 8vo, modern half calf gilt. With 3 frontises (2 hand-colored), 5 plates, 3 maps (2 colored) & 2 folding illusts plus a duplicate. Lacking half-title in Vol II & ad leaf at end of Vol III. S June 12 (265) £2,100
1st American Ed. Phila., 1837. 2 vols. 8vo, orig cloth; chipped at spine top, hinges split. With 15 plates. Foxed, affecting plates; library markings. sg May 16 (206) $250
— A Second Visit to the United States. L, 1849. 1st Ed. 2 vols. 8vo, orig cloth; spine ends frayed & chipped. Some foxing. pba Apr 25 (204) $80

**Lyman, Albert**
— Journal of a Voyage to California.... Hartford, 1852. 1st Ed. 12mo, orig wraps in cloth clamshell box; spine top & bottom chipped. With 2 plates & letter from Streeter to grand nephew of Lyman. Some pencil notations. Streeter-Larson copy. pba Sept 28 (582) $4,000

**Lyman, George D.**
See also: Grabhorn Printing
— John Marsh, Pioneer: The Life Story of a Trail-Blazer.... NY, 1930. One of 150. pba Feb 12 (521) $140
— Ralston's Ring. California Plunders the Comstock Lode. NY, 1937. In dj. Alfred Sutro's copy. Larson copy. pba Feb 12 (524) $65
— The Sponge: Its Effect on the Martyrdom of James King of William.... NY, 1928. Folio, mor. Offprint from Annals of Medical History, Vol 10, No 4, pp. 460-79. pba Feb 12 (572) $90

**Lymington, Gerard Vernon Wallop, Viscount**
— Spring Song of Iscariot. Paris: Black Sun Press, 1929. One of 125. 4to, orig wraps. pba Nov 30 (53) $80
Anr copy. Orig wraps, in soiled glassine dj. sg Dec 14 (12) $70
One of 25 on japanese paper. Orig wraps. pba Nov 30 (52) $225

**Lynch, Bohun**
— The Prize Ring. L, 1925. One of 1,000. 4to, half vellum; rubbed. pba Apr 4 (97) $170

**Lynch, Henry Finnis Blosse**
— Armenia Travels and Studies. L, 1901. 1st Ed. 2 vols. 8vo, orig cloth; rubbed. Library markings. pn Dec 7 (159) £240

Anr copy. Buckram; discolored. With folding map, & 197 plates. Some spotting. S Oct 26 (156) £450 [Maggs]

**Lynch, James K.**
— With Stevenson to California, 1846. [N.p.]: Pvtly ptd, 1896. 1st Ed, One of 100. Orig cloth; rear cover stained. Inscr. Larson copy. pba Sept 28 (681) $150

**Lynch, Jeremiah, 1849-1917**
— Three Years in the Klondike. L, 1904. Orig cloth; insect damage to spine, endpapers foxed. pba July 25 (419) $55

**Lynch, William F., 1801-65**
— Narrative of the United States Expedition to the River Jordan and the Dead Sea. L, 1849. 1st English Ed. 8vo, contemp calf; rebacked. With 2 folding maps, & 28 plates. Margins water-stained. S Oct 26 (157) £180 [Wayntraub]

Anr Ed. Phila., 1856. 8vo, orig cloth. sg Mar 7 (151) $100

**Lyndewood, William, 1375?-1446**
— Incipiunt opera super constitutiones provinciales et Othonis. l: Synkyn de Worde, 1526. 8vo, old vellum. Hole in text of penultimate leaf; tear in final leaf repaired with small loss; dampstained throughout; some fraying; early Ms annotations. STC 17111.5. S July 11 (107) £1,400

**Lynes, George Platt**
— Photographs 1931-1955. Pasadena: Twelvetrees Press, [1983]. Folio, wraps; extremities worn. sg Feb 29 (188) $50

**Lyon, Danny**
— The Destruction of Lower Manhattan. Toronto, [1969]. 4to, cloth, in worn dj; bdg corners bumped. sg Feb 29 (190) $110

**Lyon, George Francis, 1795-1832**
— The Sketch Book.... L, 1827. 2 parts. Folio, litho wraps; frayed. With 10 litho plates on india paper. Marginal waterstaining. S Nov 30 (167) £1,050

**Lyrics...**
— Lyrics from the Song-Books of the Elizabethan Age.... L, 1889. Ed by A. H. Bullen. 8vo, mor silver- & gilt-tooled to a design of undulating fillets filled in with Tudor rose, by Irene Nichols. sg Oct 19 (52) $2,600

**Lysons, Daniel, 1762-1834**
— The Environs of London. L, 1800-11. 2d Ed of Vols I-IV, 1st Ed of Vol V. 5 vols including Supplement. 4to, contemp half calf. With 3 engraved titles & 60 maps & plates. bba June 6 (62) £150 [Clarke]

Anr Ed. L, 1811. 3 vols extended to 10. 4to, half calf; def. Sold w.a.f. CE May 22 (322) $1,500

**Lysons, Samuel, 1763-1819**
— A Collection of Gloucestershire Antiquities. L, 1804. Folio, early half calf; worn. With 110 plates. Some foxing. sg Sept 7 (224) $100

**Lytle, Horace.** See: Derrydale Press

**Lyttelton, George, 1st Baron, 1709-73**
— Dialogues of the Dead. L, 1760. 3d Ed. 8vo, contemp calf. pba Mar 7 (167) $75
— Poetical Works. Glasgow: Foulis, 1787. Bound with: Hammond, James. Poetical Works. Gray, Thomas. Poetical Works. Collins, William. Poetical Works. All: Glasgow: Foulis, 1787. Folio, contemp mor gilt with monogram of the Duke of Portland; hinges repaired, rubbed. pn Dec 7 (29) £260

**Lyttelton, Robert Henry —& Others**
— Fifty Years of Sport at Oxford, Cambridge, and the Great Public Schools. Southwood, 1913-22. 3 vols. 4to, orig mor by Cedric Chivers, the upper cover with hand-painted vellucent insert; rubbed. b Jan 31 (238) £130

Anr Ed. Southwood, 1922. 4to, orig mor by Cedric Chivers, the upper cover with hand-painted vellucent insert; rubbed. b Sept 20 (313) £70

**Lytton, Edward George Earle Bulwer, 1st Baron Lytton, 1803-73**
See also: Limited Editions Club
— The Last Days of Pompeii. L, 1834. 1st Ed. 3 vols. 8vo, orig cloth, variant with paper spine labels; extremities rubbed. pba Dec 14 (20) $300
— The Pilgrims of the Rhine. L, 1834. 1st Ed. 8vo, later mor gilt cathedral bdg; minor rubbing. With engraved title & 14 plates. b Dec 5 (10) £50

**Lyungstedt, Anders**
— Contribution to an Historical Sketch of the Portuguese Settlements in China.... Macao, 1832. 8vo, modern calf. b Sept 20 (429) £420

# M

**M., J.** See: Mortimer, John

**MacAllester, Oliver**
— A Series of Letters, discovering the Scheme projected by France...for an Intended Invasion upon England.... L, 1767. 2 vols in 1. 4to, modern cloth. Tp & dedication leaf damaged in outer margin; dampstaining & mold damage. Sold w.a.f. sg Mar 7 (220) $70

**Macalpine, Ida.** See: Hunter & Macalpine

**MacArthur, Douglas, 1880-1964**
— Reminiscences. NY, [1964]. One of 1,750. sg Sept 28 (173) $350; wa Feb 29 (244) $650
— Revitalizing a Nation. Chicago: Heritage Foundation, [1952]. Library markings. Inscr. sg Sept 28 (174) $250

**Macarthur, Mildred Yorba.** See: Grabhorn Printing

**Macartney, Mervyn Edmund, 1853-1932**
See also: Belcher & Macartney
— The Practical Examplar of Architecture.... L: Architectural Review, 1907-28. 6 vols. Folio, loose in half-cloth folders as issued. With 677 plates. sg June 13 (18) $500

**Macaulay, Kenneth**
— The Story of St. Kilda.... L, 1764. 1st Ed. 8vo, contemp calf; worn. With folding map & half-titl. Some foxing. S Oct 26 (397) £240 [Scott]

**Macaulay, Thomas Babington, 1st Baron Macaulay, 1800-59**
— The History of England. L, 1869. 8 vols. 8vo, half calf. b Sept 20 (570) £200
— Lays of Ancient Rome. L, 1863. 8vo, mor gilt by Riviere. pba June 20 (61) $120

**Macbean, Capt. Forbes**
— Sketches of Character & Costume in Constantinople, Ionian Islands.... L, 1854. Folio, recent half mor. With 25 chromolitho plates. Library blindstamp on each plate just touching image; ink spot touching Plate 23 caption. S Nov 30 (129) £1,800

**McCaffrey, Anne**
— The Smallest Dragonboy. Kilquade: Drogonhold Ltd, [1976]. One of 200. In dj. pba May 4 (202) $150

**McCall, George A.**
— A Letter from the Frontiers. Phila., 1868. 8vo, orig cloth; worn, spine ends frayed. Stain in right corner of last 50 pp. wa Feb 29 (379) $400

**McCammon, Robert R.**
— Swan Song. Arlington Heights: Dark Harvest, 1989. One of 52. Syn. O Dec 5 (224) $110
One of 650. In dj. O Dec 5 (225) $50

**McCarthy, Cormac**
— All the Pretty Horses. NY, 1992. In dj. pba Aug 22 (335) $140
— Child of God. NY, [1973]. In dj with rubbing & short tears to spine head. pba Oct 5 (282) $325
— The Stonemason. Hopewell: Ecco Press, [1994]. One of 350. pba Dec 7 (128) $160

**McCarthy, Joe.** See: Onassis copy, Jacqueline Bouvier Kennedy

**McCarthy, John Russell**
— California. Los Angeles, [1928-29]. De Luxe Ed. 9 vols. Orig mor gilt; extremities rubbed. pba Nov 16 (38) $650

**McCarthy, Justin**
— Works L, 1880-1905. 21 vols. 8vo, half calf; scuffed. pba Aug 22 (555) $600

**MacCarthy-Reagh Library, Justin de**
— [Sale Catalogue] Catalogue des livres rares...de la Bibliotheque.... Paris, 1815-16. 2 vols. 8vo, contemp half mor; minor rubbing. Price list bound at end of Vol II. O Mar 26 (165) $900

**McCauley, Lois B.**
— Maryland Historical Prints, 1752-1889. Balt.: Maryland Historical Society, [1975]. 4to, cloth. wa Feb 1 (379) $100

**Maccio, Paolo**
— Emblemata. Bologna, 1628. 4to, modern calf. With engraved title, dedicatory plate & 81 plates. Last leaf with holes affecting text. b Sept 20 (37) £650

**McClellan, Rolander Guy**
— The Golden State. Phila.: William Flint, 1874. Orig calf; covers foxed & rubbed. pba Nov 16 (169) $120

**McClelland, Nancy**
— Duncan Phyfe and the English Regency, 1795-1830. NY, [1939]. 1st Ed, One of 350 L.p. copies, sgd. Folio, cloth; front cover soiled. sg June 13 (158) $150

**M'Clintock, Sir Francis Leopold, 1819-1907**
— The Voyage of the "Fox" in the Arctic Seas. Bost., 1860. 12mo, orig cloth. sg Jan 25 (24) $45

**M'Clung, John A.**
— Sketches of Western Adventure.... Dayton, 1836. 12mo, orig cloth. Foxed. sg Oct 26 (232) $110

**McClure, Floyd Alonzo**
— Chinese Handmade Paper. Newtown: Bird & Bull Press, 1986. One of 325. 4to, half mor. sg Sept 14 (64) $200

**McClure, S. S.** See: Cather, Willa

**M'Collum, William**
— California As I Saw It. Los Gatos, 1960. Reprint of 1850 Ed, One of 750. Ed by Dale Morgan. Half bds in dj. Sgd by Morgan. Larson copy. pba Sept 28 (597) $80

**MacCown, Eugene**
— Paintings - Drawings - Gouaches. Paris, 1930. Orig wraps; mark on upper wrap. Inscr "Number for The Hours Press Own Set" by Nancy Cunard. Hobson copy. S June 28 (145) £420

**McCoy, Joseph G., 1837-1915**
— Historic Sketches of the Cattle Trade.... Columbus, 1951. In worn & soiled dj. pba July 25 (320) $65

**McCracken, Harold**
— Alaska Bear Trails. Garden City, 1931. 1st Ed. pba July 25 (422) $100
— The Charles M. Russell Book. Garden City, 1957. Folio, lea. pba Apr 25 (641) $80
1st Trade Ed. Orig cloth. Inscr to Hal Wallis. pba Apr 25 (640) $60
1st Ed, One of 250. Folio, lea. With tipped-in color plate. Robbins copy. pba Mar 21 (313) $90
— Frederic Remington's Own West. NY, 1960. One of 167. 4to, lea. pba Aug 8 (162) $140
— George Catlin and the Old Frontier. NY, 1959. One of 250. 4to, lea; worn. O May 7 (201) $130

1st Ed. 4to, lea. With color frontis by William H. Fisk. Robbins copy. Sgd. pba Mar 21 (214) $170

**McCreery, John**
— The Press, a Poem, Published as a Specimen of Typography. Liverpool, 1803-27. 1st Ed. 4to, contemp bds; def. b Dec 5 (207) £80

Anr copy. Late 19th-cent bds; edges rubbed. Text browned & foxed. ds July 27 (123) $100

**McCreight, M. I. —&**
**Flying Hawk, Chief**
— Chief Flying Hawk's Tales. NY: Alliance Press, [1936]. In dj. With 11 photo plates. pba June 25 (166) $130

**McCullers, Carson, 1917-67**
— The Heart is a Lonely Hunter. Bost., 1940. 1st Ed. In dj with soiling to rear panel. Inscr to Ralph Colin. CE Sept 27 (175) $260

**McCurry, Charles.** See: Lehmann-Haupt & McCurry

**McDaniel, John M.**
— The Turkey Hunter's Book. Clinton: Amwell, 1980. One of 1,000. Illus by Donald Shoffstall. sg Mar 7 (490) $90

**MacDiarmid, Hugh**
— The Kind of Poetry I Want. Edin., 1961 (ptd at Officina Bodoni, Verona). 1st Ed, One of 300. Folio, orig half vellum; spine soiled. bba May 9 (615) £100 [Cox]

**Macdonald, Charles**
— Scotland's Gift: Golf. NY, 1928. 1st Trade Ed. 8vo, cloth. With color frontis & folding map. pba Apr 18 (118) $500

**MacDonald, George, 1824-1905**
— At the Back of the North Wind. NY, 1871. 1st Ed. 8vo, orig cloth; spine ends chipped, extremities rubbed, stain to flyleaf, shaken. pba June 20 (229) $375

Anr Ed. Phila., 1919. Illus by Jessie Willcox Smith. 4to, orig cloth, in chipped & repaired dj. pba June 20 (307) $275

**MacDonald, John D.**
— Condominium. NY, [1977]. Ltd with on an inserted leaf for patrons of the Libraries of the University of Florida. Half cloth, in dj. sg June 20 (255) $50
— Wine of the Dreamers. NY, [1951]. In dj with spine ends rubbed. pba May 4 (201) $110

**Macdonald, John Ross.** See: Millar, Kenneth

**Macdonald, Ross.** See: Millar, Kenneth

**McDonald, William N.**
— A History of the Laurel Brigade...and Chew's Battery. Balt., 1907. 8vo, orig cloth; shaken. bbc Apr 22 (136) $150

**MacDougall, William.** See: Hose & MacDougall

**M'Dowall, William**
— Poems, Chiefly in the Galloway Dialect. Newton Stewart, 1828. 8vo, orig bds. b Dec 5 (595) £80

**McElroy, John, 1846-1929**
— Andersonville: A Story of Rebel Military Prisons. Toledo, 1879. Salesman's sample book. 8vo, cloth. NH July 21 (81) $125

**Macer, Aemilius, Pseud.** See: Gueroult, Guillaume

**Macfall, Haldane, 1860-1928**
— Aubrey Beardsley: the Clown, the Harlequin, the Pierrot of his Age. NY, 1927. One of 300. 4to, orig cloth; worn & soiled. Soiled. F Mar 28 (321) $80

**Macfarlan, Allan A.** See: Limited Editions Club

**MacFarlane, Charles, 1799-1858**
See also: Craik & MacFarlane
— Constantinople in 1828. L, 1829. 1st Ed. 4to, early calf gilt; worn, spines soiled. With 2 hand-colored frontis & 1 (of 2) folding plates. Some foxing. wa Nov 16 (238) $210

2d Ed. 2 vols. 8vo, contemp half mor. With hand-colored frontises & 2 folding plates. Some foxing to plates. b Sept 20 (349) £260

**McFee, William, 1881-1966**
— Command. Garden City, 1922. 1st Ed, one of 375. Contemp half mor; extremities scuffed. F June 20 (28) $50

**McGaffey, Ernest**
— Poems of Gun and Rod. NY, 1892. Illus by Herbert E. Butler. 8vo, cloth. pba July 11 (199) $50

**Macgillivray, William, 1796-1852.** See: Edinburgh...

**McGillycuddy, Julia B.**
— McGillycuddy Agent: A Biography of Dr. Valentine T. McGillycuddy. Stanford, [1941]. In dj. pba June 25 (167) $50

**McGlashan, Charles F., 1847-1931**
— History of the Donner Party. Truckee, [1879]. 1st Ed. 8vo, orig cloth; spine & covers faded, rubbed, recased, front hinge cracked. Robbins copy. pba Mar 21 (215) $450

Anr Ed. Truckee, CA, [1879]. 8vo, orig cloth. Larson copy. pba Sept 28 (419) $850

**McGowan, Edward, of San Francisco**
— Narrative.... San Francisco, 1857. 1st Ed. 12mo, orig wraps; spine replaced, orig wraps reattached, some soiling. With 9 illus & port on wraps. Dampstained. Robbins copy. pba Mar 21 (216) $1,600

Anr Ed. San Francisco, 1917. One of 200. pba Feb 12 (574) $110

2d Ed. Bds; soiled. Robbins-Evans copy. pba Mar 21 (217) $150

**McGrath, Daniel F.**
— Bookman's Price Index. Detroit, [1983]. Vols 23-25. ds July 27 (33) $50

**McGraw, Eloise Jarvis —& Wagner, Lauren McGraw**
— Merry Go Round in Oz. Chicago: Reilly & Lee, [1963]. 1st Ed. - Illus by Dick Martin. In 2d bdg, in chipped dj. Inscr by McGraw. pba Jan 18 (157) $275

**McGraw-Hill...**
— McGraw-Hill Dictionary of Art. NY, [1969]. Ed by Bernard S. Myers. 5 vols. 4to, cloth; worn. O May 7 (202) $130

**Macgregor, John**
— The Rob Roy on the Jordan, Nile, Red Sea.... NY, 1870. Orig cloth. With 8 maps on 7 plates, 1 folding. pba July 25 (180) $75

**McGuane, Thomas**
— The Sporting Club. NY, [1968]. In dj. pba May 23 (232) $50

**Machiavelli, Niccolo, 1469-1527**
See also: Limited Editions Club
— The Florentine Historie. L, 1674. ("The Florentine History.") 8 parts in 1 vol. 8vo, contemp sheep; worn, needs rebacking. Old stamp on tp & next leaf. sg Mar 21 (213) $300
— Nicholas Machiavel's Prince. L, 1640. 1st Ed in English. 8vo, contemp sheep; rebacked, corners & lower cover abraded. G6 with corner loss affecting rule border; some soiling. Hefner copy. CNY May 17 (31) $9,500
— Opere. Florence, 1818-21. 10 vols in 5. 8vo, contemp half sheep; spine ends worn, joints starting, Vol I front cover detached. sg Sept 21 (256) $500
— Le Prince. Paris, [1921]. One of 10 on Japan imperial with a suite of the port & the initials in black on Japan imperial. Illus by Louis Jou. 4to, lev extra by Pierre Legrain for Louis Barthou, 1929. C May 1 (99) £8,000
One of 310. Mor extra by Pierre Legrain, orig wraps bound in; rubbed. S Nov 21 (285) £1,800
— Works. L, 1675. 1st Ed in English. 4 parts in 1 vol. Folio, modern vellum. Hole on Kk4 & Hhh2; ink correction on ***2. S June 12 (71) £550
Anr Ed. L, 1680. Folio, old calf; worn, covers detached. Some foxing, soiling, fraying & staining. Sold w.a.f. O Mar 5 (162) $325
Anr Ed. L, 1720. Folio, disbound. Minor foxing; tp soiled & with old stamp; pencil notes on last page. sg Mar 21 (214) $350
Anr Ed. L, 1762. 2 vols. 4to, contemp calf; spine ends rubbed, extremities worn, joints splitting, Vol I becoming disbound. Some browning. cb June 25 (1786) $375
Anr Ed. L, 1775. 4 vols. 8vo, contemp calf; stained, spine rubbed. Some waterstaining & browning. bba May 30 (119) £180 [Thoemmes]

**McIlhany, Edward**
— Recollections of a '49er. Kansas City, 1908. 1st Ed. Orig cloth; cover worn. With 2 illus & 3 plates. Larson copy. pba Sept 28 (598) $170

**M'Ilvane, William, Jr.**
— Sketches of Scenery and Notes of Personal Adventure in California and Mexico. Phila., 1850. 1st Ed. 8vo, orig cloth; recased with repairs to spine ends & corners. With 16 plates. Lightly dampstained. Robbins copy. pba Mar 21 (218) $4,250

**McIntosh, Charles, 1794-1864**
— The Book of the Garden. Edin., 1853-55. 2 vols. 8vo, orig cloth; hinges cracked. bbc June 24 (310) $210
— The Greenhouse, Hot House and Stove. L, 1846. 8vo, orig cloth; rubbed. With hand-colored frontis, additional title & 16 plates. bba May 30 (442) £100 [Besley]

**Macintyre, Donald, 1831-1903**
— Hindu-Koh; Wanderings and Wild Sport on and beyond the Himalayas. Edin. & L, 1889. 8vo, cloth; shaken, tips worn. Foxed. O June 4 (185) $100

**Mack, Effie Mona**
— Nevada: a history of the state from the earliest times through the Civil War. Glendale, 1936. 1st Ed, One of 250. Orig cloth; soiled. Robbins copy. pba Mar 21 (219) $250

**Mackail, John William, 1859-1945**
See also: Doves Press
— The Life of William Morris. L, 1899. 1st Ed. 2 vols. 8vo, orig cloth. sg Apr 11 (208) $120

**Mackaness, George**
— The Life of Vice-Admiral William Bligh. Sydney, 1931. In stained dj. b Mar 20 (120) £150
Anr copy. Orig cloth; some wear. wa Feb 29 (173) $150

**Mackay, Alexander, 1849-90**
— The Western World.... L, 1849. 1st Ed. 3 vols. 12mo, later half mor gilt. With 2 folding maps. wa Feb 29 (527) $220

**Mackay, Charles, 1814-89**
— Memoirs of Extraordinary Popular Delusions. L, 1852. 2d Ed. 2 vols. 8vo, contemp half calf; rubbed. Foxing to tp & prelims. pba Dec 14 (104) $70
— The Religious, Social, and Political History of the Mormons. NY, 1858. 8vo, orig cloth; spine ends frayed. sg Oct 26 (268) $130

**McKay, Claude**
— Home to Harlem. NY, 1928. Half cloth. pba Aug 22 (340) $95

**Mackay, George Henry**
— Shooting Journal. Cambr.: Pvtly ptd, 1929. One of 300. Cloth; some wear. O June 4 (186) $150

## McKay, George Leslie
— American Book Auction Catalogues, 1713-1934: a Union List. NY, 1937. 8vo, orig wraps. With 2 supplements laid in. sg Apr 11 (21) $175

Anr copy. Orig wraps; spine darkened, front cover stained. sg Apr 11 (21A) $140

— Bibliography of...Rider Haggard. L, 1930. One of 475. Addenda tipped to limitation page. pba Aug 22 (198) $250

## Mackay, Malcolm S.
— Cow Range and Hunting Trail. NY, 1925. 1st Ed. In frayed dj. Inscr to Daniel Webster Evans II. O Oct 10 (190) $550

## McKay, Richard C.
— Some Famous Sailing Ships and their Builder Donald McKay.... NY, 1928. Orig cloth; some wear. pba July 25 (188) $80

## McKee, Thomas Jefferson
— [Sale Catalogue] Catalogue of the Library.... NY, 1900-6. 6 parts in 2 vols only: American & British Literature & Plays. Half mor gilt by the Adams Bindery. pba Aug 8 (326) $50

## McKelvey, Susan Delano
— Botanical Exploration of the Trans-Mississippi West. Jamaica Plain: Arnold Arboretum, 1955 [i.e. 1956]. 4to, cloth. O Dec 5 (73) $180

## McKenna, Paul. See: Wolfe & McKenna

## McKenney, Thomas L., 1785-1859
— Sketches of a Tour to the Lakes.... Balt., 1827. 1st Ed. 8vo, later half mor. With 29 plates. K Feb 11 (264) $275

Anr Ed. Barre: Imprint Society, 1972. Half cloth. pba July 25 (321) $60

## McKenney, Thomas L., 1785-1859 —& Hall, James, 1793-1868
— History of the Indian Tribes of North America. Phila.: Biddle [Vol I] & D. Rice & J. G. Clark, 1836-42-44. State A of Vol I, State B of Vol II, State A of Vol III. 3 vols. Folio, lea gilt; some wear. With 120 hand-colored plates. Text heavily foxed & dampstained; some dampstaining, mainly to verso of plates; Vol I, p. 105 torn & repaired. Met Feb 24 (457) $36,000

Anr Ed. Phila.: Biddle, 1836, Greenough, 1838, Rice & Clark, 1844. State A. 3 vols. Folio, contemp mor gilt; extremities worn, joints on 2 vols starting, Vol II loose in bdg. With map & 120 hand-finished colored plates. Text & endleaves foxed, affecting a few plates. P Dec 12 (118) $35,000

Anr Ed. Phila., 1855. 3 vols. 8vo, orig mor; upper cover of Vol II detached, other joints breaking, scuffed. With 119 (of 120) colored plates; lacking that of Keokuck. Text badly discolored; plates browned. CNY May 17 (94) $5,500

Anr Ed. Phila: Rice, 1865. 3 vols. 8vo, orig mor. With 121 hand-colored plates. Edges of Plate 17 chipped; Vol III frontis detached & with chipped edges. K June 23 (366) $9,100

Anr Ed. Phila.: D. Rice, 1872. Orig mor; extremities rubbed. With 100 color plates. Robbins copy. pba Mar 21 (220) $5,000

Anr copy. Contemp half mor; rubbed, Vol II partly misbound at beginning, 2 gatherings loose. With 100 plates, most hand-colored but some chromolithos. S June 27 (176) £3,400

Anr Ed. Edin., 1933-34. ("The Indian Tribes of North America.") 3 vols. 4to, orig cloth; worn & soiled. F June 20 (384) $290

Anr copy. Orig cloth, 2 vols in worn djs. K Oct 1 (256) $450

One of 200. Orig cloth. sg Oct 26 (235) $375

## Mackenzie, A., Dr.
— Golf Architecture.... L: Simpkin, Marshall, Hamilton, Kent, [1920]. 1st Ed. - Intro by H. S Colt. Cloth. pba Apr 18 (119) $1,300

Anr Ed. Worcestershire: Grant Books, 1993. One of 700. Intro by Robert T. Jones. Cloth. With frontis port. Sgd by Shirley Grant. pba Apr 18 (120) $85

## Mackenzie, Sir Alexander, 1764-1820
— Voyages from Montreal, on the River St. Laurence.... L, 1801. 1st Ed. 4to, modern half calf. With port & 3 folding maps, 1 with route colored in outline. With errata leaf Library markings; old stamp on tp; text browned; archival repairs & insect damage to maps. K June 23 (360) $900

Anr copy. Modern calf gilt; worn, corners repaired, rebacked. With port & 3 folding maps, 1 hand-colored. Repaired tear to gutter of tp; some repaired crease tears to maps. pba Feb 13 (124) $5,000

Anr copy. Contemp calf; rebacked. With frontis port & 3 folding map (1 hand-colored). Foxed & darkened; dampstained on frontis; torn at map folds. Robbins-Decker copy. pba Mar 21 (221) $6,000

Anr copy. 19th-cent half calf. With port & 3 folding maps, 1 hand-colored. lacking errata leaf; somewhat foxed; marginal marks in pencil; 3G & 3G2 repaired. S July 11 (410) £700

Anr Ed. NY, 1814. 2 vols. 8vo, orig bds; worn. Lacking port & the maps. sg Oct 26 (237) $110

## Mackenzie, Charles, F.R.S.
— Notes on Haiti.... L, 1830. 1st Ed. 2 vols. 12mo, orig half cloth; spines worn & frayed, joints split, some wear. With folding map, 2 plates & folding facsimile. Some leaves roughly opened; some foxing. bbc June 24 (188) $270

## Mackenzie, Sir Edward Montague Compton. See:
Onassis copy, Jacqueline Bouvier Kennedy

## Mackenzie, Sir George Steuart, 1780-1848
— Travels in the Islands of Iceland. Edin., 1812. 2d Ed. 4to, half calf; needs rebdg. With 17 plates & maps, some hand-colored. Library stamps. sg Mar 7 (286) $200

— A Treatise on the Diseases and Management of Sheep. Inverness, 1809. 1st Ed. 8vo, orig bds, unopened; needs rebacking. With 5 plates. Tp stamped. sg May 16 (325) $350

## MACKENZIE

**Mackenzie, Henry, 1745-1831**
— Julia de Roubigne...a Tale. L, 1782. 1st Ed. 2 vols. 12mo, contemp calf. pba Mar 7 (168) $140

**Mackenzie, Roderick**
— A Full and Exact Account of the Proceedings...Company of Scotland...Treaty of Union. Edin., 1706. 4to, 19th-cent half mor; front joint starting. sg Mar 21 (108) $800

**Mackenzie, Roderick, Army Major**
— Strictures on Lt. Col. Tarleton's History of the Campaigns.... L, 1787. 8vo, contemp calf; broken, worn. Library stamp to front free endpaper & tp. Inscr to James Ranken (affected by library stamp). wa Feb 29 (519) $350

**McKim, Mead & White**
— A Monograph of the Work of.... NY, [1915-18]. 4 vols. Folio, orig cloth; joints rubbed, numbers to spines. With 397 plates, 3 of them double-page. Library markings; some soiling occasionally affecting images. cb Oct 17 (91) $900

**McKinnon, Ian**
— Garroot: Adventures of a Clydeside Apprentice. L, 1933. In dj with soiling on spine. S July 11 (330) £880

**McKinstry, Byron N.**
— The California Gold Rush Overland Diary of Byron N. McKinstry.... Glendale CA: Arthur H. Clark, 1975. In dj. pba Nov 16 (170) $70

**Mackintosh, Alexander**
— The Driffield Angler. Gainsborough: Pvtly ptd, 1806. 8vo, modern half mor gilt; scuffed. sg Mar 7 (491) $325

**McKitterick, David**
— A New Specimen Book of Curwen Pattern Papers. [Andoversford, Gloucestershire]: Whittington Press, [1987]. One of 335. sg Feb 15 (178) $175
— Wallpapers by Edward Bawden printed at the Curwen Press. [Andoversford, Gloucestershire]: Whittington Press, [1989]. One of 120. bba May 9 (655) £130 [Sotheran]

**Mackley, George**
— Engraved in the Wood. L: Two Horse Press, 1968. One of 300. 2 vols, including portfolio of plates. Text in orig wraps, plates loose as issued in orig card folder. bba May 9 (392) £240 [Bankes Books]
— Works. Old Woking, 1981. One of 250. 3 vols. 4to, orig half calf. bba May 9 (234) £220 [Cox]

**Mackmurdo, A. H.**
— Wren's City Churches. L, 1883. 8vo, orig half vellum; soiled & worn. S Nov 2 (95) £420 [National Gallery of Australia]

**MacLaren, Archibald, 1819-84**
— The Fairy Family, a Series of Ballads and Metrical Tales.... L, 1857. 1st Ed. - Illus by Burne-Jones.

## AMERICAN BOOK PRICES CURRENT

8vo, orig cloth; lower joint discolored. S Nov 2 (80) £240 [Cheng Yap Seng]

**McLaren, John N.**
— Gardening in California: Landscape and Flower. San Francisco, 1909. Sgd on tp & with related material. pba Feb 12 (321) $70

**Maclaren, Peter Hume**
— Atlas of Venereal Diseases. Phila., 1886. 4to, contemp half mor; joints & edges worn. With 30 color plates. Some soiling. CE Nov 8 (117) $450

**McLaughlin, James**
— My Friend the Indian. Bost., 1910. Orig cloth; rubbed, front hinge cracked. Some foxing; marginal dampstains at rear. pba June 25 (168) $200

**MacLaurin, Colin, 1698-1746**
— An Account of Sir Isaac Newton's Philosophical Discoveries. L, 1748. 1st Ed. 4to, contemp calf; spine ends chipped, joints cracked. With 6 plates. L.p. copy. sg May 16 (208) $275

**Maclay, R. S. —&**
**Baldwin, C. C.**
— An Alphabetic Dictionary of the Chinese Language in the Foochow Dialect. Foochow: Methodist Episcopal Mission Press, 1870. 8vo, cloth-backed batik bds. sg Mar 7 (152) $80

**Maclennon, R. J.**
— Golf at Gleneagles. Glasgow, [1921]. 1st Ed. Orig bds; spine chipped. With color folding map. pba Apr 18 (121) $425

**M'Leod, John, 1777?-1820**
— Voyage of his Majesty's Ship Alceste.... L, 1817. ("Narrative of a Voyage in His Majesty's late ship Alceste to the Yellow Sea.") 1st Ed. 8vo, contemp half cloth; loose. With port & 4 colored plates. sg Mar 7 (153) $275

Anr copy. Contemp calf; rebacked. Some foxing. sg Mar 7 (154) $475

**Maclise, Joseph**
— Surgical Anatomy. Phila., 1857. 4to, cloth; loose. With 68 lithos, hand-finished with color. Most plates browned at edges. sg May 9 (276) $450

**McLoughlin, Maurice E.**
— Tennis As I Play It. NY, [1915]. Cloth; insect damage to spine & joints, spine ends rubbed. Ls laid in. pba Aug 22 (295) $120

**MacMichael, William, 1784-1839**
— The Gold-headed Cane. L, 1827. 1st Ed. 8vo, modern half mor. Some foxing. sg May 16 (445) $80
— Journey from Moscow to Constantinople.... L, 1819. 4to, contemp calf, armorial bdg; rebacked preserving orig spine. With 6 uncolored plates. b Sept 20 (350) £380

Anr copy. Contemp half vellum; soiled. b May 30 (283) £250

**Macmillan, Allister**
— Seaports of the Far East. L, 1925. 4to, orig cloth, in dj. b May 30 (211) £80

**McMillan, Terry**
— Waiting to Exhale. NY, [1992]. Half cloth, in dj; bdg spotted. sg Mar 28 (200) $70

**McMurtry, Larry**
— Horseman, Pass By. NY, [1961]. In dj. CE Feb 21 (170) $450
— In a Narrow Grave: Essays on Texas. Austin, 1968. 1st Ed. In dj. pba Jan 25 (255) $225
   Uncorrected galley proofs. Inscr by the ptr, William D. Wittliff, 22 July 1968. CE Feb 21 (173) $950
— The Last Picture Show. NY, 1966. In dj. CE Feb 21 (172) $220
— Leaving Cheyenne. NY, [1963]. In chipped & repaired dj with minor dampstains; dampstaining to back cover of bdg. CE Feb 21 (171) $320
   Anr copy. In dj with scrape to spine. pba Dec 7 (131) $300
— Lonesome Dove. NY, [1985]. In dj; owner's name embossed on front free endpaper. pba Aug 22 (342) $95
— Moving On. NY, [1970]. In dj; remainder mark to bottom edges. pba Aug 22 (343) $75

**Macomb, John N.**
— Report of the Exploring Expedition from Santa Fe.... Wash., 1876. 4to, recent half calf. With 11 plain & 11 colored plates & folding map. Some foxing; map folds taped with some loss at center. wa Dec 14 (83) $500

**Macomber, Henry P.** See: Babson Collection, Grace K.

**MacPhail, Ian.** See: Hunt Botanical Library

**McPhee, John**
— Alaska: Images of the Country. San Francisco: Sierra Club, [1981]. One of 500. sg Dec 14 (207) $110
— Annals of the Former World. NY, [1981]. One of 450. sg Dec 14 (206) $70

**MacPherson, H. A.**
— A History of Fowling. Edin., 1897. 4to, orig cloth; worn & soiled. O June 4 (187) $100

**Macquer, Pierre Joseph, 1718-84**
— Elements of the Theory and Practice of Chymistry. L, 1768. 3 vols. 8vo, contemp calf; some wear & scuffing. With 6 plates. Crossed-out ink names to top of titles 7 front endpapers; 1 plate lacking top 2 inches. pba Mar 7 (169) $90

**Macquoid, Percy**
— A History of English Furniture. L, 1904-08. 4 vols. Folio, contemp half mor; spine ends worn. CE Nov 8 (211) $160
   Anr Ed. L, 1923. 4 vols. Folio, cloth; spine ends frayed, library markings. bbc June 24 (140) $200
   Anr Ed. L, 1938. 4 vols. Folio, orig cloth. b May 30 (474) £240

**Macquoid, Percy —& Edwards, Ralph**
— The Dictionary of English Furniture. L, 1924-27. 3 vols. Folio, orig cloth, in djs. b May 30 (473) £240
   Anr copy. Orig cloth; holes in 2 upper covers. bba Apr 11 (108) £300 [Graham Gallery]
   Anr copy. Orig cloth, in djs; spine ends & edges worn. bba May 30 (37) £360 [Kelly]
   Anr copy. Orig cloth; corners rubbed, hinge & front endpaper in Vol III reinforced. cb Oct 17 (31) $425
   2d Ed. L, 1954. 3 vols. Folio, cloth, in djs. bba Oct 19 (180) £390
   Anr copy. Orig cloth, in chipped djs. CE Sept 27 (176) $420
   Anr Ed. Woodbridge, 1983. 3 vols. Folio, orig cloth, in djs. bba May 30 (38) £250 [Kelly]

**Macquoid, T. R.** See: Waring & Macquoid

**Macray, William Dunn**
— Annals of the Bodleian Library.... L, 1868. 8vo, orig cloth; worn. Author's annotated copy, with related material. O Mar 26 (166) $375

**Macrobius, Ambrosius Theodosius**
— In Somnium Scipionis.... Cologne: J. Soter, 1527. 12mo, contemp calf over wooden bds, with panel with St. Katherine in upper compartment & possibly St. Roch in lower compartment, 2 clasps; spine lacking some lea, sides lightly worn. C May 1 (100) £1,500

**Macwilliam, H. D.**
— The Official records of the Mutiny in The Black Watch. L, 1910. 4to, orig cloth. CG June 12 (24) £100

**McWilliams, John, b.1832**
— Recollections of John McWilliams, his Youth, Experiences in California.... Princeton, n.d. [1919?]. 1st Ed. Orig cloth; front hinge beginning to crack. With frontis port. Larson copy. pba Sept 28 (601) $95

**Macy, Obed**
— The History of Nantucket.... Bost., 1835. 1st Ed. 8vo, orig cloth; spine ends frayed, front joint starting, lacking front free endpaper. With map & plate. sg Oct 26 (233) $175

**Madden, Richard Robert, 1798-1886**
— Travels in Turkey, Egypt, Nubia, and Palestine.... L, 1829. 2 vols. 8vo, half calf; rubbed. With hand-colored port. Lacking half-titles. b May 30 (284) £280
— The Turkish Empire in its Relations with Christianity and Civilization. L, 1862. 2 vols. 8vo, contemp calf. S June 13 (411) £480
— A Twelvemonth's Residence in the West Indies.... Phila., 1835. 2 vols in 1. 12mo, contemp half sheep; needs rebdg. sg Oct 26 (238) $60

## MADDOW

**Maddow, Ben**
— Edward Weston: His Life in Photographs. [NY]: Aperture, [1979]. sg Feb 29 (346) $70
— Faces. A Narrative History of the Portrait in Photography. Bost., [1977]. 4to, cloth, in rubbed dj. sg Feb 29 (191) $70

**Madison, James, 1751-1836**
— Selections from the Private Correspondence.... Wash., 1859. 4to, later half sheep, unopened. sg Oct 26 (239) $130

**Madol, Roger.** See: Sitwell & Madol

**Madox, Thomas, 1666-1727**
— Firma Burgi, or an Historical Essay Concerning the Cities, Towns and Boroughs of England. L, 1726. 1st Ed. Folio, contemp calf; worn. b Sept 20 (150) £80

**Maeght Editeur**
— Lithographies et Eaux-Fortes Originales, Livres Illustres Originaux, Affiches, Derriere le Miroir. Paris, [1966]. One of 1,500. Wraps with design by Miro; soiled & with spots. With 9 lithos. pba June 20 (231) $180

**Maeterlinck, Maurice, 1862-1949**
— The Life of the Bee. L, 1911. Trans by Alfred Sutro; illus by Edward J. Detmold. 4to, mor gilt with bee ornaments, by Bayntun-Riviere. CE Feb 21 (10) $300
— Le Tresor des humbles. Paris, 1902. Mor gilt by Katherine Adams, 1903. b May 30 (564) £300
— La Vie des abeilles. Paris: Societe des amis du libre moderne, 1908. One of 150, this for Georges Besnard, with decomposition in 10 states of 1 illust & an unused vignette with additional hand-coloring. 4to, mor extra with a pattern of flowers & beas, by Charles Meunier, 1911. S Nov 21 (286) £3,250
— Works. NY, 1901-2. Autograph Ed. 24 vols. Mor gilt; some spines chipped. With 2 leaves of autograph Ms bound in. cb Oct 17 (283) $425

**Maffei, Francesco Scipione, 1675-1755**
— A Compleat History of the Ancient Amphitheatres. L, 1730. 8vo, 18th-cent sheep; worn, covers detached. With 15 plates. Some soiling. Sold w.a.f. sg June 13 (19) $140

**Magdalen Hospital**
— The Rules and Regulations of the Magdalen-charity.... L, 1769. 2 parts in 1 vol. 8vo, contemp mor gilt bound for Jonas Hanway by his 2d Binder. C May 1 (72) £2,000

**Magee, David.** See: Grabhorn Printing

**Magendie, Francois, 1783-1855**
— Precis elementaire de physiologie. Paris, 1816-17. Bound with: Recherches physiologiques et medicales.... Paris, 1818. De l'influence de l'emetique sur l'homme et les animaux. Paris, 1813. Memoire sur l'usage de l'epiglotte dans la deglutition. Paris, 1813. Memoire sur le vomissement. paris, 1813. Memoire sur les proprietes nutritives.... Paris, 1816 1st Eds. 6 works in 2 vols. 8vo, contemp half calf; vol I spine worn, covers rubbed. Vol I, 14.5 & 16.6 margins torn away; 5.8 holed with loss; vol II, 10.3 lower margin cut out. ANs tipped in. Ck Mar 22 (180) £420

**Maggi, Girolamo, d.1572 —& Others**
— Della fortificatione delle citta.... Venice: Rutilio Borgominiero, 1564. Folio, modern calf gilt; detached. Some repairs, not affecting text. b June 28 (40) £1,800

**Magini, Giovanni Antonio.** See: Wytfliet & Magini

**Magistris, Johannes de**
— Summule. Venice: Bonetus Locatellus for Octavianus Scotus, 9 Sept 1490. 4to, early vellum bds; stained, spine wormed. 50 lines & headline; double column; gothic letter. Upper margins trimmed close to headline. 164 leaves. Goff M-34. S Nov 30 (282) £1,500

**Magna Carta**
— Magna Carta. L: at the signe of the Maydens heed by Thomas Petyt, 1542. ("The Great Charter Called in Latyn Magna Carta....") 8vo, 19th-cent calf; worn 7 rebacked, inner hinges reinforced. P June 5 (291) $3,750

**Magnan, Domenico**
— La Ville de Rome.... Rome, 1778. 4 vols. Folio, 19th-cent half russia gilt; joints broken, backstrips def. With 392 plates on 192 leaves. Lacking some leaves; waterstain towards end of Vol IV. S Nov 30 (04) £750

**Magne de Marolles, G. F.**
— An Essay on Shooting, containing the Various Methods of Forging, Boring, and Dressing Gun Barrels.... L, 1789. 8vo, contemp sheep; extremities worn, rebacked, endpapers renewed. A trans of La Chasse au fusil, but attributed to John Acton. sg Mar 7 (445) $150

**Magni, Pietro Paolo**
— Discorsi intorno al sanguinar in corpi humani.... Rome, 1584. 4to, modern calf. With title & 9 (of 11) plates. Lacks 2 leaves with plates; some spotting & soiling. Sold w.a.f. CE Nov 8 (119) $110

**Magninus, Mediolanensis**
— Regimen sanitatis. [Lyons: Francois Fradin, c.1502]. 4to, modern vellum bds. With 130 leaves. Browned; 1st leaf strengthened. Ck Mar 22 (181) £1,700

**Magnus, Olaus, 1490-1558**
— Historia de gentibus septentrionalibus. Rome: Giovanni Maria Viotto, 1555. 1st Ed. Folio, 18th-cent calf laid down over new calf. Map shaved at foot; lacking final leaf with device (supplied in photo-facsimile); long tear in Z5 repaired with minimal loss; writing on tp deleted; some early Ms annotations. S Mar 14 (241) £1,700

— Historia delle genti et della natura delle cose settentrionali. Venice: Domenico Nicolini for Giuntay, 1565. 1st Ed in Italian. Folio, 19th-cent half vellum. Lower outer corner of tp repaired; long tear in M1 repaired with minor loss; browning at foot of all leaves. Madsen copy. S Mar 14 (242) £1,200
— Historia om de Nordiska Folken. Stockholm, 1901-52. One of 200. 5 vols. Folio, vellum. S Mar 14 (243) £260

**Magoffin, Susan Shelby**
— Down the Santa Fe Trail and into Mexico. New Haven, 1926. 1st Ed. Orig cloth; corners bumped. With 7 plates, port, & folding map. Robbins copy. pba Mar 21 (222) $130

**Magri, Gennaro**
— Trattato teorico-pratico di ballo. Naples: Vincenzo Orsini, 1779. 2 vols in 3. 4to, mor gilt by Perticaroli of Rome. With 2 unnumbered folding plates & 29 sheets of engraved music & choreography. Repairs to tp & 2 plates; some leaves trimmed; some staining & creasing on plates & foxing in text. S Dec 1 (223) £3,200

**Magriel, Paul David**
— A Bibliography of Dancing. NY, 1936. 8vo, orig cloth; spine faded. Inscr & sgd. sg Apr 11 (209) $90

**Magritte, Rene, 1898-1967 —& Mesens, Edouard L. T.**
— Oesophage 1. Brussels, Mar 1925. Folio, wraps; partly separated along spine. Foxed. Hannes Meyer's copy. sg Apr 18 (113) $350

**Mahomet II**
— Epistolae magni Turci. Treviso: Geraert van der Leye, [c.1477]. 4to, modern mor. 23 lines; roman letter. Washed; 1st leaf repaired in margins. 22 leaves. Goff M-59. S June 27 (341) £900

Anr Ed. Lyons: Jean Marion for Roman Morin, 30 Mar 1520. 4to, 18th-cent mor gilt. With 34 woodcuts. Some staining; the 2 further books described in the Fairfax Murray catalogue removed & replaced with blanks. Fairfax Murray - Schaefer copy. P Nov 1 (150) $3,000

**Mahood, Ruth I.**
— Photographer of the Southwest: Adam Clark Vroman, 1856-1916. Los Angeles: Ward Ritchie Press, 1961. Intro by Beaumont Newhall. In dj. pba July 25 (237) $110

Anr copy. In dampstained dj. Foxed; top & bottom edges dampstained. sg Feb 29 (333) $50

**Mahr, August**
— The Visit of the "Rurik" to San Francisco in 1816. Stanford, 1932. Cloth. pba Feb 13 (126) $85

**Mahurin, Matt**
— Photographs. Pasadena, [1989]. Folio, cloth, in dj; minor wear on extremities. sg Feb 29 (192) $100

**Maier, Michael, 1568?-1622**
— Secretioris naturae secretorum scrutinium chymicum. Frankfurt, 1687. 4to, contemp calf; worn. Lacking 1 prelim leaf & A2, the latter replaced with 2 leaves from anr Ed; long tear in A3; some browning. S Mar 14 (244) £800

**Maignan, Emanuel**
— Perspective horaria sive de horographia gnomonica.... Rome: P. Rossi, 1648. Folio, contemp vellum; spine repaired, new endpapers, loose. With frontis, engraved dedication, folding table & 43 plates. Frontis frayed & repaired; lst few leaves stained & repaired in upper margins; Tt3-4 flawed affecting text. S Mar 14 (245) £700

**Maigne d'Arnis, W. H.**
— Lexicon manuale ad scriptores mediae et infimae Latinitatis. Paris, 1890. 4to, buckram; rebound. sg Apr 11 (210) $60

Anr copy. Bound with: Lorenz Diefenbach, Glossarium Latino-Germanicum mediae et infimae aetatis, Frankfurt am Main, 1857 Maigne in contemp half lea, Diefenbach in 19th-cent cloth; rubbed. sg Apr 11 (211) $200

**Mailer, Norman**
See also: Onassis copy, Jacqueline Bouvier Kennedy
— The Naked and the Dead. L, [1949]. One of 240. Mor gilt; dampstain to bottom edge, affecting bottom of tp & verso of front free endpaper. sg June 20 (259) $110
— Tough Guys Don't Dance. NY, 1984. 1st Ed, one of 350. sg Dec 14 (209) $100

**Maillard, Leon**
— Etudes sur quelques artistes originaux: Auguste Rodin Statuaire. Paris, 1899. 4to, half mor gilt, orig wraps bound in; joints rubbed. sg June 13 (332) $275

**Maillet, Benoit de**
— Telliamed: or, Discourses Between an Indian Philosopher and a French Missionary. L, 1750. 8vo, modern half calf over old bdg. Lacking prelims to tp, which is repaired; staining to bottom corners at end; repair to p. iv. pba Mar 7 (173) $110

Anr copy. Modern cloth. Old library stamps on title. sg May 16 (210) $225

**Mails, Thomas E.**
— Dog Soldiers, Bear Men and Buffalo Women. Englewood Cliffs, [1973]. 4to, orig bdg, in dj. pba Nov 16 (167) $70

**Maimbourg, Louis, 1620?-86**
— Histoire du Pontificat de S. Gregoire le Grand. Paris: Claude Barbin, 1686. 4to, contemp mor gilt with unidentified arms. L.p. copy. sg Mar 21 (216) $425

**Maimonides, Moses, 1135-1204**
— De idololatria liber. Amst.; J. & C. Blaeu, 1642. Bound with: Vossius, Gerardus Johannes. De Theologia gentili et physiologia Christiana. Amst., 1642. 4to, contemp vellum. CE Dec 6 (150) $120

## Maindron, Ernest, 1838-1908
— Les Affiches illustrees. Paris, 1886. One of 525. 4to, orig wraps; broken. Library markings. Sold w.a.f. sg Sept 7 (282) $550
Out-of-series copy on japon for presentation from the pbrs, with 3 additional chromolithos by Jules Cheret bound in. Half mor, orig wraps (in both plain & colored states) bound in; extremities rubbed. Some soiling. S Nov 21 (290) £2,500
— Les Affiches illustrees 1886-1895. Paris, 1896. One of 1,000. 4to, cloth. Library markings; plates unmarked. sg Sept 7 (283) $1,000

## Maison, Karl Eric
— Honore Daumier: Catalogue Raisonne of the Paintings, Watercolours, and Drawings. L, 1968. One of 1,500. 2 vols. 4to, orig cloth. Ck May 31 (64) £280
One of 500. 4to, cloth. bba Oct 5 (252) £380 [Rinsen]
Anr copy. Library markings. sg Jan 11 (132) $250

## Maitland Club
— Catalogue of the Works Printed for the Maitland Club. Glasgow, 1836. 4to, contemp mor; rubbed. O Mar 26 (168) $110

## Maitland, James, 8th Earl of Lauderdale, 1759-1839
— An Inquiry into the Nature and Origin of Public Wealth.... Edin., 1804. Bound with: Observations by the Earl of Lauderdale on the Review of his Inquiry.... Edin., 1804. 8vo, contemp half calf. pnE May 15 (44) £340
Anr copy. Orig bds. pnE May 15 (81) £380

## Maitland, Samuel Roffey. See: Lambeth Palace

## Maitland, William, 1693?-1757
— The History of London. L, 1756. ("The History and Survey of London.") 2 vols. Folio, contemp calf; worn. With 120 (of 121) plates & maps. Some tears without loss; 7T2 torn & repaired. S Nov 30 (57) £850

## Maitres...
— Les Maitres de l'affiche. Paris, 1896-1900. 5 vols (complete set). Folio, loose as issued in orig cloth portfolios. With 17 lithos & 239 colored reproductions of posters. S Nov 21 (291) £14,000
— Les Maitres Illustrateurs. Paris, 1901-3. One of 50. 12 orig parts bound in 1 vol. 4to, half cloth, orig wraps preserved. Esmerian copy. S Nov 21 (289) £400

## Majors, Alexander
— Seventy Years on the Frontier. Chicago, 1893. 1st Ed. 12mo, orig cloth; extremities rubbed, damage to front pastedown from removed bookplate. pba June 25 (161) $90
Anr copy. Plain wraps. Half-title & read ad leaf torn; 1 marginal tear; some smudges. wa Dec 14 (84) $85
2d Ed. Denver, [n.d.]. Preface by Buffalo Bill Cody. Orig wraps; spine reglued, spine ends chipped, wraps stained. Robbins copy. pba Mar 21 (223) $120

## Makovets...
— Makovets; zhurnal iskusstv. Moscow, 1922. Nos 1-2. 4to, orig wraps; 1 spine repaired. With 10 tipped-in lithos. Vol I inscr by Lev Zhegin to Igor Emmanuilovich Grabar, 30 Nov 1922. C June 26 (227) £180

## Malamud, Bernard, 1914-86
— The Stories of.... NY, [1983]. One of 300. pba Aug 22 (324) $65

## Malaspina, Alejandro
— Viaje Politico-Cientifico Alrededor del Mundo.... Madrid, 1885. 2d Ed. Folio, modern lea, orig wraps bound in. With 7 plates & folding map. Marginal paper restoration at ends; map brittle & tearing at folds; plates with foxing; marginal stain to port. pba Feb 13 (127) $1,100

## Malcles, Louise-Noelle
— Les Sources du Travail Bibliographique. Geneva, 1950-58. 3 vols in 4. 8vo, orig cloth; spines faded. sg Apr 11 (212) $100

## Malcolm, Sir Howard
— Travels in the Burman Empire. Edin., 1840. 8vo, orig front wrap only. Marginal tears. sg Mar 7 (155) $140

## Malcolm, James Peller
— Anecdotes of the Manners and Customs of London during the Eighteenth Century. L, 1808. 4to, contemp half sheep; worn, front cover loose. With 50 plates, including hand-colored costume plates. Tp wrinkled; 1 plate torn into image; library stamps. Sold w.a.f. sg Mar 7 (156) $120

## Malcolm X
— The Autobiography of Malcolm X. NY: Grove Press, [1965]. In dj. pba Aug 22 (325) $60
— Two Speeches by.... NY, 1965. Wraps. sg Mar 28 (195) $100

## Malet, Capt. Harold E.
— Annals of the Road. L, 1876. 8vo, later half mor gilt. With 10 colored plates. sg Mar 7 (492) $130

## Malherbe, Alfred
— Monographie des picidees; ou, histoire naturelle.... Metz: Jules Verronnais for the author, 1861-63. 4 vols in 2. Folio, contemp half mor; rubbed. With 122 (of 123) hand-colored plates. Lacking Plate 13; lacking titles to Vols III & IV & all but the 1st 2 pp of list of plates. S Nov 30 (37) £4,600

## Mallarme, Stephane, 1842-98
See also: Golden Cockerel Press; Limited Editions Club
— L'Apres-midi d'un faune. Paris, 1876. 1st Ed, one of 170 on Hollande. Illus by Edouard Manet. 4to, orig wraps, in calf-backed vellum chemise by the Legrains. Some discoloration of the upper leaf & along fore-edges. With litho frontis on chine loosely inserted & a pictorial bookplate, both ptd in black

with pink added by hand. Sold with a copy of the 1887 Ed of the text. S Nov 21 (293) £5,000
One of 20 on japon. Contemp cloth (trial bdg?) by Pierson, orig wraps bound in. C June 26 (200) £5,000

**Malleson, George Bruce, 1825-98**
— History of the French in India.... L, 1868. Contemp half calf. pba Oct 9 (11) $80

**Mallet, Allain Manesson**
— Beschreibung des ganzen Welt-Kreises. Frankfurt, 1685. Vol 4 only: Europe. 2 parts in 1 vol. Contemp calf. With 2 engraved titles & 274 plates only. sg Dec 7 (279) $3,000
— Description de l'univers. Paris, 1683. 5 vols. 8vo, contemp calf gilt; spine ends chipped, joints cracked or starting. Some browning. sg Apr 18 (78) $5,200
Anr Ed. Frankfurt: J. D. Zunner, 1685-86. Vol V only. Old calf; worn, upper joint reinforced, some plates loose. Sold w.a.f. CE June 15 (292) $600
— La Geometrie pratique. Paris, 1702. 1st Ed. 4 vols. 8vo, contemp vellum; warped. With 2 frontises & 493 plates. sg Apr 18 (80) $1,600
— Les Travaux de Mars.... Paris, 1691. 8vo, contemp calf gilt; spine ends chipped, joints cracked or starting. With 3 engraved titles & 406 full-page illusts. sg Apr 18 (79) $950
Anr Ed. Paris, 1784-85. 3 vols. 8vo, contemp calf; spine ends chipped, corners worn. pba Apr 25 (209) $150

**Mallet, Robert**
— On the Physical Conditions involved in the Construction of Artillery. L, 1856. One of 200. 4to, orig cloth; front cover detached. With 9 plates. Foxing on opening leaves. sg May 16 (211) $225

**Mallet-Stevens, Robert**
— Une Cite Moderne. Paris: Ch. Massin Editeur, [c.1925]. Loose as issued in half cloth; spine taped. With 32 pochoir-colored plates. cb Oct 17 (32) $1,400

**Mallock, William Hurrell**
— In an Enchanted Island or A Winter's Retreat in Cyprus. L, 1889. 2d Ed. 8vo, cloth; rubbed. With half title & frontis. S Oct 26 (60) £150 [Martin]

**Malo, Charles, 1790-1871**
— Histoire des roses. Paris: Louis Chat, [c.1820]. 12mo, mor gilt. With 12 hand-finished colored plates. b Dec 5 (33) £65

**Malory, Sir Thomas, fl.1470.** See: Ashendene Press; Limited Editions Club

### Le Morte Darthur
— 1889-91. - L.Ed by H. Oskar Sommer. 3 vols in 2. 8vo, vellum & half vellum. Vol I with plate mtd to prelim flyleaf. pba Sept 14 (253) $200
— 1893-94. - L. One of 1,500. Illus by Aubrey Beardsley. 2 vols. 4to, cloth; dampstaining to rear covers. Tp reinforced at gutter. sg Feb 8 (187) $600

One of 300 on Dutch handmade paper. 3 vols. 4to, orig vellum gilt. CE May 22 (43) $2,800
Anr copy. Orig vellum gilt; minor soiling. CE May 22 (44) $2,800
Anr copy. In orig 12 parts. Orig wraps; chipped & soiled, spines creased, 1 with tear, stain to cover of Part 7. pn Dec 7 (83) £1,500
Anr copy. 3 vols. 4to, contemp vellum gilt by Birdsall, with designs of medieval knights. S Apr 23 (265) £4,050
— 1909. - L. One of 1,500. Illus by Aubrey Beardsley. 4to, contemp half mor; joints starting, edges rubbed. With frontis. CE Nov 8 (168) £350
— 1910-11. - L: Riccardi Press One of 500. Illus by W. Russell Flint. 4 vols. 4to, vellum. S Nov 2 (85) £360 [Heritage]
— 1917. - L. One of 500. Abridged by A. W. Pollard; illus by Arthur Rackham. 4to, orig vellum. Pages uncut except pp. 23-26 roughly torn open at top fore-edge. cb Oct 17 (679) $750
— [c.1920]. - Bost. Illus by W. Russell Flint. 2 vols. In djs, 1 repaired. With 36 color plates. sg Sept 14 (130) $200
— 1927. - L. One of 1,600. Illus by Aubrey Beardsley. 4to, orig cloth. Some marginal browning. CE May 22 (45) $420
Anr copy. Cloth; joint torn. sg Feb 15 (39) $350
— 1933. - Oxford: Shakespeare Head Press One of 370. 2 vols. 4to, orig mor; 1 spine rubbed. bba May 9 (345) £420 [Sotheran]
Anr copy. Mor gilt. sg Sept 14 (322) $550

**Malpighi, Marcello, 1628-94**
— Opera. Leiden, 1687. 2 vols in 1. 4to, contemp vellum; soiled. With engraved title & 118 plates. Some plates trimmed; K4 in Vol I def; some other tears; marginal dampstaining at beginning; minor worming. S June 12 (270) £340
— Opera posthuma.... Amst., 1698. 4to, contemp vellum. With 19 folding plates. Some plates trimmed at outer edge. S June 12 (267) £250

**Malraux, Andre, 1901-76**
— Les Conquerants. Paris, 1949. One of 125. Illus by Andre Masson. 4to, unsewn as issued in orig wraps. With 33 plates. wd Nov 15 (92) $1,400
— Et sur la Terre.... Paris: Maeght, 1977. One of 205. Illus by Marc Chagall. Folio, loose as issued in cloth portfolio box. With 15 etchings. sg May 23 (287) $3,200
— The Voices of Silence. Garden City, 1953. One of 160. Trans by Stuart Gilbert. 4to, mor by Georges Gauche; joints rubbed, spine scuffed. pba May 23 (228) $50

**Malta**
— L'univers pittoresque. Iles de l'Afrique. Paris, 1848. 8vo, wraps. S Oct 26 (162) £320 [Muscat]

**Malte-Brun, Conrad, 1775-1826**
— Atlas de la Geographie Universelle.... Paris: Garnier Freres, [1837]. Folio, contemp half calf; spine ends

worn. With 71 (of 72) maps, hand-colored in outline. Some staining & browning.  CE June 15 (293) $200

Anr copy. Orig half mor; worn. With 86 on 72 maps, hand-colored in outline.  sg May 9 (83) $900

— A New General Atlas. Phila., 1832. 4to, orig half lea; needs rebdg. With 40 hand-colored maps. Some dampstaining, browning & foxing; burn to fore-edge on several leaves.  sg May 9 (84) $800

**Malthus, Thomas Robert, 1766-1834**
— Additions to the Fourth and Former Editions of an Essay on the Principle of Population. L, 1817. 8vo, contempo half calf; rubbed. Some spotting; L2 with small tear repaired.  bba July 18 (84) £280 [Drury]

Anr copy. Contemp half calf; edges worn, hinges repaired, later endpapers. Lacking half-titles; some foxing; old marginal dampstain in Vol III.  bbc June 24 (318) $525

— An Essay on the Principle of Population.... L, 1798. 1st Ed. 4to, contemp half calf; corners worn, upper joint cracked. Some contemp annotations trimmed. Newton-Borowitz copy.  CNY May 17 (95) $60,000

Anr Ed. L, 1803. 4to, orig bds; rebacked. Dampstain to lower outer corner of front cover & opening leaves; some foxing.  sg Apr 18 (80A) $2,000

— Principles of Political Economy.... L, 1820. 1st Ed. 8vo, later cloth. Marginal staining throughout; lacking half-title. Sold w.a.f.  O Mar 5 (163) $500

Anr copy. Contemp calf gilt; joints cracked. Spotting on leaves in Sig. C; some leaves foxed.  S July 11 (195) £600

**Malton, James, d.1803**
— A Collection of Designs for Rural Retreats.... L, [1802]. Folio, contemp calf gilt; rebacked with orig backstrip laid down. With 34 plates.  CE June 12 (226) $1,400

**Mamerot, Sebastian**
— Les passages doultremer faitz par les francoys. Paris, 27 Sept, 1518. 1st Ed. Folio, 18th-Cent calf; rebacked. With facsimile title illus. Stained & some worming.  S Oct 26 (61) £3,200 [Shapero]

**Manby, George William, 1765-1854**
— An Essay on the Preservation of Shipwrecked Persons. L, 1812. 8vo, modern half cloth.  b Mar 20 (121) £90

**Manchester Anglers' Association**
— Anglers' Evenings: Papers by Members. Manchester & L, 1880-94. Series 1-3 (all pbd). 8vo, orig cloth.  pba July 11 (7) $180

**Manchester, Herbert.** See: Derrydale Press

**Manchester, William.** See: Onassis copy, Jacqueline Bouvier Kennedy

**Mancinellus, Antonius**
— Libellus de figuris. Deventer: Theodoricus de Borne, [early 1500s]. 4to, modern half vellum; worn. Some staining; marginal worming affecting text on last index leaf; lacking last leaf.  sg Mar 21 (218) $500

**Mancinus, Dominicus**
— Tractatus de passione domini. Leipzig: Jacob Thanner, 1508. 4to, disbound, last leaf detached. Tp discolored; contemp annotations.  S Mar 28 (488) £230

**Mandelslo, Johann Albrecht von, 1616-44**
— Voyages celebres et remarquables, faits de Perse aux Indes Orientales.... Amst., 1727. 2 vols in 1. Folio, old calf; rebacked & cornered, old spine laid down, later endpapers. With engraved title, 1 folding plate, 16 double-page plates & 20 maps & plans (13 double-page, 1 folding) & 19 illusts. Some dampstaining & browning; damage to some outer margins.  C Nov 29 (99) £1,400

**Mandeville, Bernard de, 1670?-1733**
— An Enquiry into the Origin of Honour.... L, 1732. 1st Ed. 8vo, contemp calf; spine ends chipped, joints cracked. Prelim leaf loose; b1-2 browned.  S June 12 (74) £300

**Mandey, Venterus —& Moxon, James**
— Mechanick Powers.... L, 1709. ("Mechanick Powers: or the Mystery of Nature and Art Unvail'd....") 4to, contemp calf; rubbed. With 17 plates. Small loss to 1 plates; some others frayed.  b Sept 20 (151) £250

**Mandredini, Vincenzo, 1737-99**
— Regole armoniche o sieno precetti ragionati per apprendere i principi della musica.... Venice: G. Zerletti, 1775. 4to, contemp bds. With port & 20 folding sheets of engraved musical examples.  C Apr 3 (156) £360

**Manet, Edouard, 1832-83**
— Letters with Aquarelles. NY: Pantheon, [n.d.]. One of 345. With 21 facsimile letters colored through stencils.  bba May 9 (235) £55 [Deighton Bell]

**Manifiesto...**
— Manifiesto de los motivos en que se ha fundado la conducta del Rey Christianisimo respecto a la Inglaterra, con la Exposicion de los que han guiado al rey nuestro Senor para su modo de proceder con la misma Potencia. [Madrid: la Imprenta real de la Gazeta, 1779]. 4to, modern cloth. Tp soiled.  b Dec 5 (109) £400

**Manilius, Marcus**
— Astronomicon. Heidelberg: Officina Sanctrandreana, 1590. 8vo, contemp vellum. Some browning.  bbc June 24 (243) $230

— The Five Books...Containing a System of Astrology. L, 1697. 8vo, contemp calf; rebacked. With frontis & 5 plates.  pba Sept 14 (255) $250

Anr copy. Modern half calf. With 5 plates. Some soiling & browning.  sg Oct 19 (234) $500

## Manley, Sir Roger, 1626-88
— The History of the Rebellions in England.... L, 1691. 4to, contemp calf. Tp rubbed & lacking corner. pba Nov 30 (231) $225

## Manly, William Lewis
— Death Valley in '49: Important Chapter of California Pioneer History. San Jose, 1894. 1st Ed. 8vo, orig cloth; extremities rubbed. With port & 3 plates. pba Feb 12 (48) $170

Anr copy. Orig cloth; spine faded. With frontis port & 3 plates. Robbins copy. pba Mar 21 (224) $425

Anr copy. Orig cloth; some wear, inner hinge split. With port & 3 plates. wa Feb 29 (383) $160

## Mann, Franklin W.
— The Bullet's Flight from Powder to Target. NY, 1909. 4to, cloth; tips worn & frayed. Discoloration to bottom edge. O June 4 (188) $70

## Mann, Thomas, 1875-1955
See also: Limited Editions Club
— The Beloved Returns. NY, 1940. 1st American Ed, one of 395. Trans by H. T. Lowe-Porter. 4to, half cloth. sg June 20 (260) $600
— A Sketch of My Life. L, 1930. One of 75. Half vellum; bookplate removed from front pastedown, ink mark to front free endpaper. pba June 20 (233) $500
— The Transposed Heads: a Legend of India. Kentfield, CA: Allen Press, 1977. One of 140. Folio, cloth. bba May 9 (164) £110 [Marks]; pba June 20 (24) $375; sg Sept 14 (13) $375

## Manne, Louis Charles Joseph de, 1773-1832
— Nouveau Recueil d'Ouvrages Anonymes et Pseudonymes. Paris, 1834. 8vo, half mor by David; rubbed. O Mar 26 (170) $60

## Manners, Lady Victoria —& Williamson, George Charles, 1858-1942
— Angelica Kauffmann, R. A., her Life and her Works. L, 1924. One of 75 with 3 extra plates. 4to, half vellum. Library stamps on tp margin & some plates. bba Oct 19 (65) £85 [Sims Reed]

## Manning, Owen, 1721-1801 —& Bray, William
— The History and Antiquities of the County of Surrey. L, 1804-14. 1st Ed. 3 vols. Folio, modern half mor or later half mor; rubbed. With 97 plates only. Vols II & III sgd by Bray & with ALs. bba Nov 1 (220) £360 [Corke]

## Manning, William Ray
— The Nootka Sound Controversy. Wash., 1905. Orig cloth; joints & extremities rubbed, front hinge weak. In: Annual Report of the American Historical Association for the Year 1904, pp. 279-478. pba Feb 13 (134) $50

## Mansfield, Katherine, 1888-1923
— The Doves' Nest and Other Stories. L, 1923. Orig cloth; bumped. John Middleton Murry's copy. Ck Nov 17 (116) £160

— The Garden Party and Other Stories. L, 1922. 1st Ed. Orig cloth in 2d state with lettering stamped in ochre, in chipped & separated dj. Some spotting. Ck Nov 17 (119) £400

Anr Ed. L: Verona Press, 1939 [1947]. One of 1,200. Illus by Marie Laurencin. 4to, bds, in rubbed dj. bba May 9 (611) £1,200 [Sims Reed]

Anr copy. Bds, in chipped dj. Small waterstain at bottom of last 20 pages. cb Oct 17 (650) $1,600

Anr copy. Bds, in dj with short tear to upper cover. Ck Nov 17 (123) £1,100

Anr copy. Bds, in dj with tears & browning. Some spotting at ends. Ck May 31 (65) £950

— In a German Pension. L, [1911]. John Middleton Murry's copy. Ck Nov 17 (135) £2,200

1st impression. Calf gilt by Bayntun-Riviere, orig cloth bound in. Ck Nov 17 (124) £280

2d impression. Contemp cloth for the Times Book Club with its label & date stamp of 18 Feb 1913 to front pastedown; bumped. Ck Nov 17 (125) £400

Anr Ed. L, [Jan 1912]. 2d impression. Orig cloth; bumped. Ck Apr 12 (158) £180

Anr Ed. L, [May or June 1912]. 3d impression. Orig cloth; bumped, rubbed. Some spotting. Ck Nov 17 (126) £160

Later impression. Orig cloth; bumped, rear inner hinges weak. Ck Apr 12 (159) £210

— Je ne parle pas francais. Hampstead: The Heron Press, 1919 [1918]. One of 100. 4to, orig wraps; joints cracked, minor chipping at extremities, lower cover soiled. Ck Nov 17 (129) £1,300

— Letters to John Middleton Murry 1913-1922. L, 1951. Ed by Murry. Orig cloth, in worn dj. With pp. 375-76 removed & cancel inserted. Sgd by Murry. Ck Nov 17 (143) £140

— Poems. NY, 1924. 1st American Ed. Inscr by John Middleton Murry. bba Oct 19 (364) £90 [Kitazawa]

— Prelude. Richmond: Hogarth Press, [1918]. 1st Ed. Orig wraps; inner hinges split, tear to upper cover, spine ends chipped. Ck Nov 17 (136) £1,400

Anr copy. Orig wraps; very worn. Ck Nov 17 (137) £400

Anr copy. Orig wraps in 2d state without line block; edges creased, small tears on edges & spine. Some foxing. S July 11 (340) £380

1st Issue. Orig wraps; worn & broken, spine lacking. Ck Apr 12 (168) £170

— Something Childish and Other Stories. L, 1924. 1st Ed, 1st Issue, without date of publication on verso of tp. Orig cloth, in chipped dj; bdg extremities rubbed. Ck Nov 17 (138) £650

2d Issue. In rubbed & chipped dj. John Middleton Murry's copy. Ck Nov 17 (139) £95

## Manuale...
— Manuale baptisterium secundum morem Romane ecclesie. Venice: heirs of Petrus de Ravanis, Nov 1556. 4to, modern vellum; warped, free endpapers chipped. Some foxing & dampstaining; old scrawls on tp; marginal repairs on verso. sg Mar 21 (219) $800

— Manuale parochialium sacerdotum. Augsburg: Johann Froschauer, Aug 1499. 4to, modern vellum. 31 lines; gothic letter. Tp browned; small wormhole in inner margin of 1st 2 leaves. 18 leaves. Goff M-222. S Dec 18 (58) £500 [Gabinete]

**Manwood, John, d.1610**
— A Treatise and Discourse of the Lawes of the Forrest. L, 1598. 4to, 19th-cent half calf; rubbed. Tp soiled, with tiny hole, extreme corner repaired & Iveah blindstamp. S Mar 29 (765) £440

**Manypenny, George W.**
— Our Indian Wards. Cincinnati, 1880. 8vo, orig cloth. NH July 21 (191) $130

**Manzoni, Alessandro, 1785-1873**
— I Promessi Sposi.... Milan: Vincenzo Ferrario, 1825-26 [but June 1827]. 1st Issue. 3 vols. 8vo, contemp half sheep; extremities scuffed. Old dampstaining in Vol II. C Apr 3 (145) £2,600

**Map...**
— Map Collectors' Circle. L, 1963-75. Ed by R. V. Tooley. Vols I-XI (Nos 1-110). 4to, Nos 1-100 bound in 10 vols in cloth, the remaining issues in orig wraps. sg May 9 (20) $1,900
Anr copy. Wraps. W Mar 6 (19) £430

**Mapei, Camillo**
— Italy: Classical, Historical, and Picturesque. Glasgow, 1864. 4to, orig bds; rubbed, spine def. With engraved title & 60 plates. Some spotting. S June 13 (552) £580
Anr Ed. Glasgow, [c.1890]. 4to, contemp mor gilt. With engraved title & 60 plates.. S June 27 (115) £1,050

**Mapp, Marcus**
— Dissertatio medica de potu chocolatae.... Strassburg, 1695. 1st Ed. 4to, modern cloth. Some spotting. Ck Mar 22 (182) £420

**Mapplethorpe, Robert**
— Black Book. NY, [1986]. 4to, cloth, in soiled dj. F June 20 (693) $50
Anr copy. Cloth, in rubbed dj; front free endpaper soiled. Sgd. sg Feb 29 (197) $225
— Certain People: A Book of Photographs. Pasadena, [1985]. Folio, cloth, in rubbed dj; bdg with minor wear on extremities. Sgd. sg Feb 29 (198) $275
— The Perfect Moment. Phila., [1988]. 4to, photopictorial wraps; rubbed. Sgd. sg Feb 29 (199) $225

**Maps & Charts**

### Africa

ARROWSMITH, AARON. - Africa. L, 1811. Folding map in 4 sheets, joined as 2 parts, 1,248mm by 1,450mm over-all, hand-colored in outline. b Sept 20 (386) £300
BLAEU, JAN. - Aethiopia inferior vel exterior partes.... [Amst., 1662]. 380mm by 495mm, hand-colored. Latin text on verso. b June 28 (119) $300

BLAEU, JAN. - Aethiopia superior vel interior; vulgo Abissinorum. [Amst., 1635, or later]. 390mm by 505mm, hand-colored in outline. Latin text on verso. Browned. sg May 9 (111) $300
BLAEU, WILLEM. - Africae nova descriptio. [Amst., c.1640]. 410mm by 550mm, hand-colored. German text on verso. b June 28 (90) £1,200
Anr Ed. [Amst., c.1650]. 410mm by 545mm, hand-colored in outline, framed. Fold break partially repaired; some browning. Sold w.a.f. sg Dec 7 (57) $900
BRAUN, GEORG & HOGENBERG, FRANZ. - Algerii sarace. [Amst., c.1572]. 350mm by 500mm, hand-colored. Latin text on verso. sg May 9 (123) $250
BUY DE MORNAS, CLAUDE. - Afrique. Paris, 1761. 290mm by 455mm, hand-colored. pba Oct 9 (48) $140
DANCKERTS, JUSTUS. - Novissima et perfectissima Africae descriptio. Amst., [c.1700]. 490mm by 570mm, hand-colored in outline. b Sept 20 (388) £300
DELISLE, GUILLAUME. - Carte du Congo et du pays des Cafres. Paris, 1708. 490mm by 610mm S Oct 26 (537) £150 [Seeling]
FER, NICOLAS DE. - L'Afrique.... Paris, 1700. 463mm by 600mm, hand-colored in outline with later coloring to cartouches, water & borders. Burnhole from ink at upper corners; lower right edge frayed with small tears into border. cb Oct 17 (227) $150
HOMANN'S HEIRS. - Guinea propria. Nuremberg, [1745]. 510mm by 560mm, contemp hand-coloring. Cut close at right; margin added. S Mar 28 (355) £150
MERCATOR, GERARD & HONDIUS, JODOCUS. - Nova Africae tabula. Amst., [1619, or later]. 375mm by 500mm, colored, mtd. CE June 15 (304) $500
MUENSTER, SEBASTIAN. - Aphricae Tabula IIII. Basel, [c.1550]. 255mm by 340mm image size. Latin text on verso. sg Dec 7 (125) $400
MUENSTER, SEBASTIAN. - Totius Africae Tabula. Basel, [1540]. 270mm by 345mm, contemp hand-coloring, framed. S Mar 28 (351) £420
ORTELIUS, ABRAHAM. - Africae propriae tabula.... [Antwerp], 1590. 335mm by 490mm, hand-colored. Margins trimmed; mtd to stiff bd. sg Dec 7 (138) $325
ORTELIUS, ABRAHAM. - Africae tabula nova.... Antwerp, 1570. 370mm by 500mm, contemp hand-coloring, framed. S Mar 28 (352) £320
ORTELIUS, ABRAHAM. - Terra Sancta. [Antwerp, 1584 or later]. 370mm by 470mm, hand-colored in outline. Latin text on verso. Browned; edge tears. Sold w.a.f. sg Dec 7 (144) $375
OTTENS, REGNER & OTTENS, JOSUE. - Tractus littorales Guinaea promontorio Verde usque ad sinum Catenbala. Amst., [1745]. 485mm by 570mm, framed & glazed. Hand-colored. S Oct 26 (538) £140 [Rizzo]
QUADT, MATTHIAS. - Asis partivorbis maxima. Cologne, [c.1600]. 219mm by 295mm. sg May 9 (229) $550
ROBERT DE VAUGONDY, GILLES & DIDIER. - L'Afrique. Paris, 1750. 500mm by 675mm, hand-colored. sg Dec 7 (147) $450
SAYER, ROBERT. - Africa. L, 1772. 4 sheets jointed vertically, 1,070mm by 1,250mm, hand-colored in outline. Folds reinforced on verso; edges restored; some foxing & browning; pencil notations. Sold w.a.f. sg

May 9 (241) $550
SAYER, ROBERT. - A New and Correct Map of Africa. L, [1754]. 530mm by 920mm, hand-colored, framed. S Mar 28 (348) £400
SCHENK, PETER. - Africa elaboratissima. Amst., [c.1708]. 485mm by 580mm, hand-colored. Margins trimmed; closed tears; underlining of some place names. sg May 9 (244) $425
WALDSEEMUELLER, MARTIN. - Tabula Quarta Africae. [Strassburg: J. Schott, 1513]. 335mm by 505mm. sg Dec 7 (176) $900

## Americas

— Alaska and British Columbia Showing the Yukon, Cariboo, Cassiar, with a Portion of the Kootenay Gold Fields. Salt Lake City, 1898. 584mm by 938mm, folded into wraps, both map & wraps on water-resistant paper; wear & woiling & a few minor dampstaining. Small portion of each corner lacking touching surface; marginal tears; 1 tear into map area; some foxing. cb Oct 17 (159) $950
— Carta Esperica que comprehende las costs del Seno Mexicano.... Spain, 1805. 615mm by 940mm. Folds repaired. pba Oct 9 (90) $4,250
— Central America II. Including Texas, California and the Northern States of Mexico. L: Society for the Diffusion of Useful Knowledge, [c.1842]. 317mm by 388mm, hand-colored. pba Apr 25 (75) $140
— A General Map of the Northern British Colonies in America.... L, 1776 [or later]. 470mm by 650mm, partially hand-colored in outline, framed. Chipped; fold breaks. CE June 15 (334) $700
— Watson's New Rail-Road and Distance Map of the United States and Canada, 1869. NY, 1868. 50 by 36 inches, hand-colored, folded to 5 by 7 inches, in orig cloth folder. Some fold tears with minor loss. NH Sept 16 (268) $385
ALLARD, CAROLUS. - Recentissima novi orbis sive Americae septentrionalis et meridionalis tabula.... [Amst., 1690]. 490mm by 570mm, contemp hand-coloring. Repaired tear; some creasing & spotting. S Mar 28 (301) £420
ARCHER, JOSHUA. - Mexico & Texas. L: Grattan & Gilbert, [1838]. 225mm by 282mm, hand-colored. pba Oct 9 (27) $140
ARROWSMITH, AARON. - Map Exhibiting all the New Discoveries in the Interior Parts of North America.... L, [1824]. 1,252mm by 465mm, colored in outline, backed on linen. Browning to 1 panel; linen deteriorating along folds. cb June 25 (1723) $1,600
ARROWSMITH, AARON. - Map of [North & South] America. L, 1804. 1,200mm by 1,440mm, on 4 sheets joined as 2 pairs, hand-colored in outline. b Sept 20 (390) £520
ARROWSMITH, AARON. - A New Map of Mexico and Adjacent Provinces.... L, 1810. 4 sheets joined, 1,290mm by 1,580mm, hand-colored in outline.; Some fraying & soiling. cb June 25 (1724) $6,000
BAKER, JOSEPH. - A Chart shewing Part of the Coast of N.W. America with the Tracks of H.M. Sloop Discovery.... L, 1798. 555mm by 732mm. Crease tear. From the Atlas vol to Vancouver's A Voyage of Discovery to the North Pacific Ocean..... pba Oct 9 (179) $500

BELLIN, JACQUES NICOLAS. - Carte de l'Amerique septentrionale. [Paris], 1755. 575mm by 870mm, hand-colored in outline. Some browning & foxing; marginal tears; tape-staining to upper margin. CE June 15 (305) $450
BELLIN, JACQUES NICOLAS. - Carte de l'isle de Sainte Lucie.... Paris, 1758. 20 by 30.2cm. pba Apr 25 (7) $100
BELLIN, JACQUES NICOLAS. - Carte reduite du Golphe du Mexique.... [N.p., 1806 or later]. 580mm by 830mm, hand-colored in outline, framed. CE June 15 (348) $550
BELLIN, JACQUES NICOLAS. - Karte von dem Ostlichen-Stucke von Neu Frankreich oder Canada. Paris, 1744. 415mm by 565mm, hand-colored. Margins trimmed; some browning. sg May 9 (110) $250
BELLIN, JACQUES NICOLAS. - Karte von Louisiana.... [N.p.], 1744. 15.25 by 21.5 inches, hand-colored. Left margin narrow. wa Feb 29 (591) $700
BERTIUS, PETRUS. - Carte de l'Amerique. Amst., 1646. 385mm by 500mm. Marginal tears & staining to upper portion of image. CE June 15 (306) $750
BLAEU, WILLEM & BLAEU, JAN. - Americae nova tabula. Amst., 1622. 415mm by 555mm, No text on verso. Border vignettes hand-colored, Minor browning along vertical fold. sg May 9 (112) $6,000
BLAEU, WILLEM & BLAEU, JAN. - Chili. Amst., [1630]. 360mm by 480mm, hand-colored in outline. Latin text on verso. Some soiling. sg Dec 7 (58) $250
BLAEU, WILLEM & BLAEU, JAN. - Insulae Americanae in Oceano Septentrionali cum terris adjacentibus. [Amst., 1635, or later]. 380mm by 528mm, contemp hand-coloring in outline with 3 cartouches in full color.. Some foxing & soiling; 2 wormholes in map area & 1 in upper margin; portion of 1 corner torn away. cb Oct 17 (213) $650
BLAIR, JOHN. - A Map of the West Indies. L, [c.1750]. 414mm by 574mm, hand-colored in outline. Some soiling & foxing, remnants from earlier mounting. cb Oct 17 (237) $350
BOISSEAU, JEAN. - Nouvelle Description de l'Amerique. Paris, [c.1653]. 138mm by 190mm, hand-colored, framed. pba Oct 9 (40) $300
BOND, FRANK. - Map of the Territory of Hawaii. Wash., 1904. 600mm by 870mm, in color. Browning along folds. sg May 9 (161) $275
BONNE, RIGOBERT. - Amerique Septentrionale. [Paris, c.1780]. 230mm by 340mm, hand-colored in outline. pba Oct 9 (41) $160
BONNE, RIGOBERT. - Cartes des Isles Antilles et du Golfe du Mexique. Paris, 1782. 3 sheets joined, 660mm by 1,455mm, hand-colored in outline. Margins cut close & supplied in part; loss at edges of image. sg May 9 (117) $1,700
BONNE, RIGOBERT. - Detroit de Magellan.... [Paris, c.1780]. 232mm by 343mm. pba Apr 25 (17) $100
BONNE, RIGOBERT. - Le Nouveau Mexique avec la Partie Septentrionale de l'Ancien ou de la Nouvelle Espagne. [Paris, c.1780]. 225mm by 355mm, hand-colored in outline. sg May 9 (118) $500
BOWEN, EMANUEL. - A Map of the British American plantations.... L, 1754. 22cm by 27.5cm, modern hand-coloring. pba Apr 25 (19) $120
BOWEN, EMANUEL. - A New and Accurate Map of Ameri-

# MAPS

ca. [L, c.1745]. 360mm by 450mm, hand-colored in outline. sg May 9 (120) $425

BRION DE LA TOUR, LOUIS. - Cartes des Isles Antilles et du Golfe du Mexique. Paris, 1782. 520mm by 745mm, hand-colored. Staining & wear at fold. S June 13 (606) £550

BRY, THEODOR DE. - Occidentalis Americae partis, vel earum vel Regionum quas Christophorus Columbus.... [Frankfurt, 1594]. 335mm by 437mm. Borders browned & chipped; minor stains. CE June 15 (310) $4,500

BUACHE, PHILIPPE. - Carte du Golphe du Mexique et des Isles Antilles. Paris, 1780. 500mm by 935mm, 2 sheets joined, hand-colored. Marginal tears; 1 fold tear extending into image. sg Dec 7 (62) $2,400

BUCHON, JEAN ALEXANDRE. - Carte geographique, statistique et historique de l'Amerique. Paris, 1825. 45.5cm by 64.3cm. Marginal tears. pba Aug 8 (113) $130

BUY DE MORNAS, CLAUDE. - Amerique. Paris, 1761. 290 by 455mm plus border, hand-colored. pba Oct 9 (49) $120

CARY, JOHN. - A New Map of Nova Scotia, Newfoundland.... L, 1801. 515mm by 595mm, hand-colored. sg May 9 (139) $150

CHATELAIN, HENRI ABRAHAM. - Carte de la Nouvelle France.... [Amst., c.1708]. 420mm by 385mm. pba Oct 9 (65) $1,800

COLLIN, ETIENNE. - Carte des cotes du Golfe du Mexique. Depot general de la Marine, 1801. 910mm by 600mm. b May 30 (136) £700

COLLIN, ETIENNE. - Carte generale du Golfe Mexique et de l'Archipel des Antilles. Depot general de la Marine, 1807. 582mm by 880mm. b May 30 (135) £700

CONDER, THOMAS. - North America. L, [c.1760]. 345mm by 385mm, hand-colored. Some soiling. sg May 9 (147) $225

COOK, CAPT. JAMES. - A Chart of the Southern Extremity of America 1775. L, 1777. 450mm by 510mm, later crude coloring. Several tears repaired. sg Dec 7 (68) $1,500

CORONELLI, VINCENZO MARIA. - America Meridionale. Venice, [c.1696]. 610mm by 892mm. Repaired tear in Atlantic Ocean. pba Oct 9 (72) $1,400

CORONELLI, VINCENZO MARIA. - America settentrionale. Venice: 1688. 450mm by 594mm, hand-colored in outline. Remargined at left; some creas repairs. pba Oct 9 (71) $4,250

CORONELLI, VINCENZO MARIA. - L'Amerique Septentrionale.... Paris, 1688. 450mm by 594mm, some hand-coloring in outline. pba Oct 9 (75) $6,500

COVENS, JOHANNES & MORTIER, CORNELIS. - Carte particuliere de l'Amerique Septentrionale. Amst., [1735]. 525mm by 490mm, hand-colored in outline. Some spotting on image. sg Dec 7 (69) $2,200

COVENS, JOHANNES & MORTIER, CORNELIS. - Nouvelle Carte particuliere de l'Amerique... la Baye d'Hudson.... Amst., [c.1735]. 605mm by 545mm, hand-colored in outline. sg Dec 7 (70) $1,100

COVENS, JOHANNES & MORTIER, CORNELIS. - Nouvelle Carte particuliere de l'Amerique... la Nouvelle Bretagne.... Amst., [c.1735]. 605mm by 540mm, hand-colored in outline. sg Dec 7 (71) $1,000

COVENS, JOHANNES & MORTIER, CORNELIS. - Nouvelle

## AMERICAN BOOK PRICES CURRENT

Carte particuliere de l'Amerique... les Iles de Bermude.... Amst., [c.1735]. 600mm by 530mm, hand-colored in outline. sg Dec 7 (72) $2,600

COVENS, JOHANNES & MORTIER, CORNELIS. - Nouvelle Carte particuliere de l'Amerique... les Provinces suivantes comme la Caroline Meridionale.... Amst., [c.1735]. 600mm by 530mm, hand-colored in outline. sg Dec 7 (73) $1,900

CRUZ CANO Y HOLMEDILLA, JUAN DE LA. - Mapa geographico de America meridional. L: Wm. Faden, 1 Jan 1799. 6 sheets, hand-colored, mtd on linen & dissected in sections, total dimensions being 1,880mm by 1,320mm, folding into 19th-cent mor case. pba Oct 9 (79) $1,200

DE WIT, FREDERICK. - Tractus australior Americae Meridionalis. Amst., [1715 or later]. 480mm by 555mm, contemp hand-coloring. b Jan 31 (404) £200

DELISLE, GUILLAUME. - L'Amerique septentrionale. Paris, 1700. Quai de l'Horloge issue. 460mm by 605mm, hand-colored in outline. Some soft creases. sg May 9 (152) $1,100

DELISLE, GUILLAUME. - Carte d'Amerique. Paris, 1722. 495mm by 620mm, hand-colored in outline. Marginal browning; tape-staining. CE June 15 (312) $400
Anr Ed. Paris: Dezanche, 1790. 490mm by 615mm, hand-colored. Minor browning along vertical fold. sg Dec 7 (79) $325

DELISLE, GUILLAUME. - Carte de la Louisiane et du cours du Mississippi. Amst.: Covens & Mortier, [1730]. 440mm by 600mm, hand-colored in outline. Browned; tape-repairs on verso. cb June 25 (1728) $700

DELISLE, GUILLAUME. - Carte du Mexique et des Etats Unis d'Amerique. Paris 1703 [but 1718]. 475mm by 650mm, some outline hand-coloring. pba Oct 9 (85) $3,500

DISTURNELL, JOHN. - Mapa de los Estados Unidos de Mejico. NY, 1846. 1st Ed. 1,030mm by 745mm, hand-colored in outline in a contemp hand, folded into 8vo cloth folder. Some splits at folds. cb June 25 (1729) $9,500

DU VAL, PIERRE. - L'Amerique autrement le nouveau monde et Indes occidentales. Paris, 1655. 365mm by 380mm, contemp outline color. Some staining & soiling. S Mar 28 (302) £750

DUDLEY, SIR ROBERT. - Carta particolare del'India Occidentale.... Venice, 1646. 485mm by 745mm, 2 sheets joined. sg Dec 7 (80A) $650

DUFLOT DE MOFRAS, EUGENE. - Mouillage de San Pedro and Mouillage de la Mission de Santa Barbara. Paris, 1844. 13-3/4in by 21-1/4in, backed with linen. Removed from Duflot's Exploration.... Larson copy. pba Sept 28 (94) $50

DUNN, SAMUEL. - A Map of the British Empire in North America. L, 1774. 490mm by 315mm, hand-colored in outline. sg Dec 7 (81) $375

DURELL, PHILIP. - Plan of the Harbour, Town and Forts of Porto Bello.... L, 1740. 525mm by 590mm, hand-colored. Browned. CE June 15 (347) $380

EVANS, LEWIS & POWNALL, THOMAS. - A Map of the Middle British Colonies in North America. L, 1776. 500mm by 815mm, hand-colored in outline but color now faded to brown. Browned; some soiling; repaired on verso. Sold w.a.f. sg Dec 7 (146) $2,000

FADEN, WILLIAM. - A Map of the Inhabited Part of Canada... New York and New England. L, 1777. 595mm by 880mm, hand-colored. Some browning & soiling. sg Dec 7 (85) $900

FER, NICOLAS DE. - L'Amerique, meridionale et septentrionale. Paris, 1705. 464mm by 597mm, later hand-coloring. Ink burn from numerals in upper corners; tear along platemark at lower left; tear along lower centerfold extending into surface; cut close at upper right. cb Oct 17 (228) $1,200

FER, NICOLAS DE. - Le Canada, ou Nouvelle France, le Floride.... Paris, 1702. 235mm by 345mm, hand-colored in outline. Dampstaining in upper margin. sg Dec 7 (87) $750

FER, NICOLAS DE. - Cette carte de Californie et du nouveau Mexique.... Paris, 1700. 224mm by 341mm, hand-colored in outlinebacked & mtd. Some foxing. cb Oct 17 (229) $800

GASTALDI, GIACOMO. - Nueva Hispania Tabula Nova. [Venice, 1548]. 135mm by 170mm. Italian text on verso. sg Dec 7 (87A) $1,200

GASTALDI, GIACOMO. - Tierra Nueva. [Venice, 1561]. 190mm by 260mm, hand-colored. Italian text on verso. sg May 9 (157) $700

GIBSON, JOHN. - New Map of the Whole Continent of America.... L: Sayer, 15 Aug 1786. 2 sheets, each 518mm by 1,188mm, contemp hand-coloring in outline, framed. cb Oct 17 (231) $1,100

GOLDTHWAIT, J. H. - Rail Road Map of New England, Canada & Eastern N.Y. Bost., 1850. 625mm by 495mm, folding to 12mo, hand-colored in outline, in orig cloth case. sg Dec 7 (88) $350

GOOS, PIETER. - Pascaert vande Caribes Eylanden. [Amst., c.1720]. 20 by 20.75 inches plus margins hand-colored. Partial separation at centerfold; mtd; minor tears at margins. bbc June 24 (16) $270

GUESSEFELD, F. L. - Charte von Americe. Leipzig: Homann Heirs, 1796. 595mm by 465mm, hand-colored. Soiling & creasing. sg May 9 (159) $175

GUESSEFELD, F. L. - Charte von den vereinigten Staaten von Nord-America nebst Louisiana. Nuremberg: Homann Heirs, 1784. 460mm by 580mm, colored. CE June 15 (313) $300

HALL, SIDNEY. - Mexico. L, [1841]. 257mm by 366mm, hand-colored. pba Aug 8 (117) $100

HENNEPIN, LOUIS. - Carte d'un tres grand pais nouvellement d'ecouvert dans l'Amerique Septentrionale.... Amst., [c.1704 or later]. 380mm by 450mm, left margin trimmmed close; mtd. CE June 15 (314) $1,800

HERISSON, EUSTACHE. - Carte de l'Amerique septentrionale et meridionale. Paris, 1796. 523mm by 768mm, contemp hand-coloring. Creased, soiled, foxed, lower right edge tattered. cb Oct 17 (232) $450

HERRERA, ANTONIO DE. - Descripcion del Destricto del Audiencia de Nueva Espana. Madrid, [c.1601]. 220mm by 300mm. sg Dec 7 (89) $1,100

HOMANN, JOHANN BAPTIST. - Totius Americae Septentrionalis et Meridionalis. Nuremberg, [c.1710]. 484mm by 568mm, contemp hand-coloring, framed. Some foxing & soiling, 2 tiny wormholes at lower neatline; marginal tear at lower centerfold. cb Oct 17 (233) $1,600

HOMANN'S HEIRS. - America Septentrionalis.... Nuremberg, 1777. 460mm by 510mm, hand-colored in outline. CE June 15 (316) $300

HOMANN'S HEIRS. - Americae. Nuremberg, 1746. 480mm by 570mm, hand-colored in outline. Repair on verso at fold; several extraneous folds; some soiling. sg May 9 (167) $500

HOMANN'S HEIRS. - Charte von America. Nuremberg, 1806. 595mm by 490mm, hand-colored. Some creasing & browning; small hole in cartouche. sg May 9 (169) $175

HOMANN'S HEIRS. - Dominia Anglorum in praecipuis insulis Americae.... [Nuremberg, c.1760]. 505mm by 585mm, hand-colored in outline. Vertical fold repaired on verso affecting surface; closed tear extending into image. sg May 9 (170) $350

HOMANN'S HEIRS. - Indiae Occidentalis... Isthmum Panamensem.... [Nuremberg, c.1750]. 575mm by 485mm, hand-colored in outline. sg Dec 7 (99) $550

HONDIUS, HENRICUS. - America noviter delineata. Amst., 1631. 377mm by 498mm, hand-colored in outline & wash. Marginal tears. pba Oct 9 (103) $1,500

HONDIUS, JODOCUS. - America noviter delineata. [Amst., 1630 or later]. 460mm by 566mm, hand-colored, mtd. Margins repaired on verso; border retouched; some staining. CE June 15 (317) $6,000

JAILLOT, CHARLES HUBERT ALEXIS. - Amerique Septentrionale. Amst.: Pierre Mortier, [1700]. 570mm by 875mm, hand-colored in outline, framed. CE June 15 (318) $1,700

JANSSONIUS, JOANNES. - Accuratissima Brasiliae Tabula. Amst., [c.1630]. Size not given, later hand-coloring. Tape-repaired. pba Apr 25 (41) $160

JANSSONIUS, JOANNES. - America septentrionalis. L, [c.1640]. 470mm by 550mm, hand-colored in outline; mtd. CE June 15 (319) $2,200

JANSSONIUS, JOANNES. - Insulae Americanae in Oceano Septentrionali cum terris adjacentibus. Amst., [c.1640, or later]. 385mm by 525mm, hand-colored in outline. Dutch text on verso. Browning along vertical fold. sg May 9 (179) $800

JANSSONIUS, JOANNES. - Insularum Hispaniolae et Cubae. Amst., [c.1657]. 415mm by 535mm, hand-colored in outline. Some soiling; tear along vertical fold extending into image; left margin trimmed. sg May 9 (180) $425

JANSSONIUS, JOANNES. - Nova Anglia Novum Belgium et Virginia. Amst., [c.1650]. 385mm by 500mm, hand-colored in outline. Closed tears; repairs. CE June 15 (320) $1,200

JANVIER, JEAN. - L'Amerique divisee par Grands Etats. Paris, 1762. 315mm by 455mm, hand-colored in outline. Some foxing & soiling. sg Dec 7 (105) $175

JEFFERYS, THOMAS. - The Bay of Honduras. L, 1775. 500mm by 645mm, hand-colored in outline. sg Dec 7 (107) $175

JEFFERYS, THOMAS. - A Chart of the Gulf of St. Laurence. L, 1775. 630mm by 510mm, hand-colored in outline. sg Dec 7 (108) $425

JEFFERYS, THOMAS. - A Map of the Island of St. John in the Gulf of St. Laurence. L, 1775. 375mm by 710mm, hand-colored in outline. sg Dec 7 (109) $275

# MAPS

JODE, CORNELIS DE. - Americae pars borealis.... Antwerp, [1593]. 365mm by 505mm. Latin text. S June 27 (171) £7,200

JOHNSON, D. G. & A. K. - A New Map of the Union with the Adjacent Islands & Countries. NY, 1857. 1,120mm by 1,380mm, hand-colored, on wooden rollers. Yellowed from orig lacquer; some tears & dampstains. sg Dec 7 (110) $800

KEULEN, GERARD VAN. - Carte nouvelle contenant la partie d'Amerique... le Canada ou Nouvelle France.... Amst., [c.1710]. 520mm by 595mm, hand-colored. Top margin cropped with loss to border. Sold w.a.f. sg May 9 (189) $400

KEULEN, GERARD VAN. - Pas-Kaart van de Zee Kusten in de Boght van Nieuw-Engeland. Amst., 1685. 530mm by 610mm, hand-colored. Margins cut close. sg Dec 7 (112) $7,000

KEULEN, JOANNES VAN. - Nieuwe wassende graade zee kaart over de spaanse zee vant kanaal tot eyland Cuba in Westindia. Amst., [1754]. 600mm by 1000mm, backed. Colored. Some discoloration. S Oct 26 (475) £120 [Yingst]

KEULEN, JOANNES VAN. - Pascaerte van Westindien de Vaste Kusten en de Eylanden. [Amst., 1680]. 445mm by 540mm, hand-colored in outline. Fold repairs. S June 13 (610) £500

LAURIE, ROBERT & WHITTLE, JAMES. - A New and General Map of the Middle Dominions belonging to the United States of America. L, 12 May, 1794. 475mm by 665mm S Oct 26 (478) £380 [Burden]

LE MAIRE, JACOB. - [America]. Amst., 1616. 2 sheets only, each c.410mm by 555mm, colored, with 6 large uncolored vignettes. 1 sheet laid down. Sold w.a.f. CE June 15 (322) $26,000

LE ROUGE, GEORGES LOUIS. - L'Amerique. Paris, 1742. 510mm by 480mm, hand-colored, mtd. Some foxing; closed marginal tears. CE June 15 (323) $750

LE ROUGE, GEORGES LOUIS. - L'Amerique Septentrionale. Paris, 1742. 520mm by 500mm, hand-colored in outline. Some foxing & browning; margins trimmed. sg May 9 (195) $700

LEA, PHILIP. - North America.... L, [1690]. 2d state. 520mm by 570mm, contemp outline color. With 3 small repaired tears at fold. S June 27 (172) £7,200

LEVASSEUR, VICTOR. - Amerique Septentrionale. Paris, [c.1845]. 198mm by 175mm, hand-colored. pba Oct 9 (113) $190

Anr copy. 280mm by 440mm, hand-colored in outline, pictorial engravings hand-colored. pba Nov 16 (300) $170

Anr copy. 198mm by 175mm, hand-colored in outline. pba Apr 25 (48) $190

LEWIS, SAMUEL. - The British Possessions in North America. 395mm by 450mm.. sg May 9 (196) $600

LOTTER, CONRAD. - Regionem Mexicanam et Floridam. Augsburg, [c.1770]. 495mm by 575mm, hand-colored. Some soiling & browning in margins. sg Dec 7 (116) $1,300

LOTTER, MATTHIAS ALBRECHT. - Carte nouvelle de l'Amerique angloise. Augsburg, [c.1763]. 600mm by 490mm, hand-colored. Marginal browning & tears. CE June 15 (325) $380

LOTTER, TOBIAS CONRAD. - Recens Edita totius Novi Belgii.... Augsburg, [c.1730]. 505mm by 585mm, hand-colored. Dampstained along bottom edge, touching image; margins trimmed. sg Dec 7 (118) $1,500

LOWRY, JOSEPH WILSON. - The United States of North America.... Glasgow, [c.1860]. 343mm by 500mm, hand-colored in outline. pba Oct 9 (116) $200

MALLET, ALLAIN MANESSON. - Nouveau Mexique et Californie. Paris, 1683. 143mm by 97mm, hand-colored. pba Oct 9 (117) $200

MAZZA, GIOVANNI BATTISTA. - Americae et proximarum regionum orae descriptio. [Venice, 1590 or later]. 332mm by 460mm, contemp hand-coloring. Wear at fold; some staining. S Mar 28 (304) £8,500

MERCATOR, GERARD. - America. Amst., [1630, or later]. 365mm by 452mm. pba Oct 9 (119) $2,750

MERCATOR, GERARD. - America sive India Nova. [Amst., c.1628]. 350mm by 440mm, hand-colored. French text on verso. S June 27 (165) £1,700

MERCATOR, GERARD. - Nova Hispania et Nova Galicia. Amst., [c.1635]. 350mm by 485mm, hand-colored in outline. Some browning, soiling & repairs. sg Dec 7 (120) $450

MOLL, HERMAN. - Map of South America. L, [c.1720]. 600mm by 970mm, hand-colored in outline. Side margins supplied; other margins repaired; partially separated. sg May 9 (212) $750

MOLL, HERMAN. - A New & Exact Map of the Coast, Countries and Islands within ye Limits of ye South Sea Company. L, [c.1712]. 653mm by 493mm, contemp hand-coloring. b June 28 (120) £150

Anr Ed. L, [c.1720]. 435mm by 485mm, hand-colored in outline. Repaired on verso; 3 smaller Moll maps attached to upper margin. CE June 15 (327) $400

MOLL, HERMAN. - A New and Exact Map of the Dominions of the King of Great Britain on ye Continent of North America. L, 1715. 600mm by 1,010mm, some outline coloring, framed. CE June 15 (326) $5,000

Anr Ed. [L, 1719]. 580mm by 950mm, hand-colored, framed. S Mar 28 (306) £1,700

MOLL, HERMAN. - A New Map of the North Parts of America claimed by France.... L, 1720. 4 half sheets joined in pairs, 622mm by 1,030mm, contemp hand-coloring. b Dec 5 (102) £5,000

MONK, JACOB. - A New Map of that Portion of North America.... Balt., 1854. 1,460mm by 1,580mm, hand-colored, on wooden rollers. Yellow from lacquer. sg Dec 7 (123) $800

MONTANUS, ARNOLDUS. - Chili. Amst., [1671]. 285mm by 365mm. Taped to mat. pba Apr 25 (58) $150

Anr copy. 185mm by 365mm, modern hand-coloring. Trimmed to neatline. pba Aug 8 (130) $100

MORTIER, PIETER. - Cartier nouvelle de l'Amerique angloise. Amst., [c.1700]. 23.75 by 35.5 inches plus margins, hand-colored in outline, mtd. bbc June 24 (14) $825

MORTIER, PIETER. - Les Principales Forteresses, Ports...Amerique Septentrionale. Paris, [c.1735]. 515mm by 620mm, hand-colored in outline. sg Dec 7 (74) $2,400

MOUNT, WILLIAM & PAGE, THOMAS. - A Chart of the Sea Coast of New Foundland New Scotland, New England.... L, [1755]. 455mm by 570mm, hand-colored. S June 27 (169) £750

MOUNT, WILLIAM & PAGE, THOMAS. - A Generall Chart of the Western Ocean. L, [c.1710]. 465mm by 575mm, hand-colored in outline. Soiled. sg Dec 7 (124) $750

MOUNT, WILLIAM & PAGE, THOMAS. - New and Correct Chart of the Trading Part of the West Indies. L, [1780 or later]. 460mm by 810mm image sizes, hand-colored in outline, framed. CE June 15 (349) $600

MUENSTER, SEBASTIAN. - Nie Neuwen Inseln so hinder Hispanien gegen Orient. Basel, [c.1550]. 265mm by 340mm. German text on verso. Browning & soiling. CE June 15 (328) $1,850

MUENSTER, SEBASTIAN. - Tabula novarum insularum.... [Basel, 1540]. 265mm by 340mm. Repaired wormhole at upper fold. S June 13 (603) £1,400

NEELE, S. J. - A Map of...Virginia, Maryland, Delaware.... L, 1787. 590mm by 594mm, hand-colored in outline; laid down, mtd. Some tears. CE June 15 (330) $3,500

NOLIN, JEAN BAPTISTE. - L'Amerique dressee sur les relations les plus recentes. Paris, 1785. 4 sheets joined in 1, with attached border, 1,225mm by 1,425mm, hand-colored by a contemp hand Some restoration & facsimile; laid down & backed on linen. S Nov 30 (134) £3,600

NOLIN, JEAN BAPTISTE. - L'Amerique ou nouveau continent.... Paris, 1754. 468mm by 545mm, hand-colored in outline, mtd. Marginal stains. pba Apr 25 (60) $700

OGILBY, JOHN. - Novissima et accuratissima totius Americae descriptio. L, [1671]. 435mm by 540mm, hand-colored, mtd. Creases with 2 holes at folds. pba Oct 9 (132) $1,100

ORTELIUS, ABRAHAM. - Americae sive novi orbis.... [Antwerp, 1570 or later]. 390mm by 530mm, hand-colored in outline & wash, framed. Small fold breaks. pnE Mar 20 (72) £2,000

Anr copy. 365mm by 505mm, contemp hand-coloring, framed. Wear to lower fold. S Mar 28 (303) £1,800

Anr Ed. [Antwerp, 1584 or later]. 356mm by 497mmm, hand-colored in outline. Small holes in fold repaired on reverse; some repairs & stains. cb June 25 (1742) $1,900

ORTELIUS, ABRAHAM. - Culiacanae, Americae regionis, descriptio; Hispaniolae, Cubae.... [Antwerp, c.1585]. 360mm by 495mm, hand-colored. French text on verso. Browned; margins soiled. sg Dec 7 (139) $700

ORTELIUS, ABRAHAM. - Hispaniae novae sivae magnae recens descripti, 1579. [Antwerp, 1598]. 347mm by 504mm, contemp hand-coloring, framed. Some foxing. cb Oct 17 (241) $650

Anr copy. 348mm by 505mm, hand-colored in outline, cartouches colored in full, framed. Italian text on verso. Lower margin repaired. cb Feb 14 (2563) $550

Anr copy. 348mm by 505mm. French text. Wormed at outer margins. cb June 25 (1744) $550

Anr copy. 345mm by 500mm, hand-colored, mtd. Some closed tears. CE June 15 (344) $650

OVERTON, J. - A New and most Exact map of America.... L, [1668 or later]. 420mm by 537mm, hand-colored. Some tears patched on verso; some soiling. CE June 15 (331) $6,000

POPPLE, HENRY. - A Map of the British Empire in America.... [L, 1733]. In 20 sheets, folded into bds rebacked in calf. With key-map, hand-colored in outline, bound in at front & orig contents leaf pasted to inside front cover. Some foxing; marginal restoration to 6 mapsheets; 3 maps with creases along guards. CNY Dec 15 (35) $19,000

POWNALL, THOMAS & BROENNER, HARRY LODOWICK. - The Provinces of New York...and the Province of Quebec.... Frankfurt, 1777. 2 sheets joined, 1,330mm by 525mm, partially hand-colored. Remargined with minor loss; soiled & creased. Sold w.a.f. sg May 9 (135) $1,600

ROBERT DE VAUGONDY, GILLES & DIDIER. - Carte de la Californie et des Pays Nord Ouest. Paris, [c.1772]. 320mm by 395mm, hand-colored in outline. sg May 9 (231) $250

Anr Ed. Paris, [c.1780]. 293mm by 367mm. pba Oct 9 (88) $500

ROBERT DE VAUGONDY, GILLES & DIDIER. - Carte des parties nord et ouest de l'Amerique.... Paris, 1772. 305mm by 385mm, hand-colored in outline. Top margin trimmed. sg May 9 (232) $130

Anr Ed. Paris, [c.1779]. 29cm by 37.5cm, modern hand-coloring. Some soiling. pba Apr 25 (29) $110

Anr Ed. Paris, [c.1780]. 11 by 14.25 inches plus margins, modern hand-coloring. wa Feb 29 (652) $260

ROBERT DE VAUGONDY, GILLES & DIDIER. - Carte Generale des decouvertes de l'Amiral de Fonte.... Paris, [c.1772]. 330mm by 375mm, hand-colored in outline. sg May 9 (188) $110

ROBERT DE VAUGONDY, GILLES & DIDIER. - Le Nouveau Continent ou l'Amerique.... Paris, 1740. 490mm by 666mm, hand-colored. Repairs. pba Apr 25 (30) $475

RUSCELLI, GIROLAMO. - Terra Nueva. Venice, 1599. 190mm by 265mm. sg Dec 7 (159) $500

SANSON D'ABBEVILLE, NICOLAS. - Amerique septentrionale.... Paris: Pierre Mariette, [1683]. 200mm by 275mm, contemp outline color. Marginal staining & worming. S Mar 28 (307) £300

Anr Ed. Naples, 1700. 395mm by 535mm, colored. Marginal tape-staining; ink notations. CE June 15 (332) $1,100

SANSON D'ABBEVILLE, NICOLAS. - Audience de Guadalajara, nouveau mexique, California.... Paris: Pierre Mariette, [1657]. 204mm by 240mm, hand-colored in outline. pba Aug 8 (133) $425

Anr copy. 203mm by 240mm, contemp outline color. S Mar 28 (305) £220

SAYER, ROBERT & BENNETT, JOHN. - A Chart of the Gulf of St. Laurence. L, 1775. 635mm by 515mm, hand-colored in outline. sg May 9 (243) $300

SAYER, ROBERT & BENNETT, JOHN. - A General Map of America.... L, 1772. 497mm by 540mm, hand-

# MAPS

colored in outline. Some soiling. cb June 25 (1747) $550

SCHERER, HEINRICH. - America Australis. Munich, [c.1720]. 235mm by 360mm. sg Dec 7 (162) $175

SCHERER, HEINRICH. - Idea Naturalis Americae Borealis. Munich, [c.1700-20]. 230mm by 355mm. sg Dec 7 (164) $650

SEALE, R. W. - A Map of North America with the European Settlements.... L, 1745. 469mm by 375mm, contemp hand-coloring in outline, framed. Marginal repairs, 1 touching surface; some soiling. cb Oct 17 (244) $750

SEILE, HENRY. - Americae descriptio nova. L, 1652. 340mm by 420mm, hand-colored in outline, framed. Frayed with some loss of image. CE June 15 (335) $260

SEUTTER, MATTHAEUS. - Novus Orbis sive America meridionalis et septentrionalis. Augsburg, [c.1730, or later]. 499mm by 575mm, hand-colored in outline, cartouches colored in full, mtd. cb Feb 14 (2566) $1,200

SKENE, A. M. - Survey of Baffins Bay taken in the summer of 1818.... L, [1818]. 480mm by 270mm, folded in envelope. S Oct 26 (476) £800 [Sawyer]

SMITH, J. CALVIN. - Map of North America. NY, 1850. 24 by 19.25 inches, archival bd & clear plastic. Marginal wear & darkening; a few chips. Larson copy. pba Sept 28 (584) $150

SONNENSTERN, MAXIMILIAN VON. - Mapa General de la Republica de Guatemala. NY, 1859. 825mm by 870mm, hand-colored in outline, folding into orig cloth covers. Fold tears. pba Oct 9 (167) $350

SONNENSTERN, MAXIMILIAN VON. - Mapa General de la Republica de Salvador. NY, 1859. 552mm by 740mm, hand-colored, folding into orig cloth covers. Fold tears; discolored at left panel from glue. pba Oct 9 (166) $120

SPEED, JOHN. - America.... L, [1676]. 395mm by 440mm, hand-colored. Some discoloration & creasing at fold. S June 27 (166) £2,500

SPEED, JOHN. - America, with those known Parts in that unknown Worlde...discribed.... L: T. Bassett & R. Chiswell, 1626 [but 1676 or later]. 398mm by 522mm, laid down on bd. Some staining. CE June 15 (336) $3,500

TALLIS, JOHN & CO. - Mexico, California and Texas. L, [c.1850]. 220mm by 300mm plus border hand-colored in outline. pba Oct 9 (171) $170

THORNTON, SAMUEL. - A New Chart of the Bahama Islands and the Windward Passages. L, [c.1720]. 420mm by 520mm. S June 13 (608) £620

VALCK, GERARD & SHENK, PETER. - Insulae Americanae in Oceano Septentrionale. Amst., [c.1708]. 380mm by 520mm, hand-colored. Margins soiled & browned; fold break at bottom. sg May 9 (263) $550

VISSCHER, NICOLAUS. - Insulae Americanae in Oceano Septentrionali.... [Amst., c.1670]. 462mm by 563mm, hand-colored. Tears at upper corners; repairs to centerfold & edges. cb Feb 14 (2571) $475

VISSCHER, NICOLAUS. - Novissima et accuratissima totius Americae descriptio. [Amst., 1677 or later]. 490mm by 580mm, hand-colored in outline, cartouche fully colored, framed. Fold tear; marginal soiling. CE June 15 (339) $1,800

WALCH, JOHANNES. - Charte von Nordamerica nach den neuesten Entdeckungen.... Augsburg, 1820. 575mm by 485mm, hand-colored in outline. Some rubbing on verso; fold repair. CE June 15 (338) $300

WALDSEEMUELLER, MARTIN. - Tabula terre nova. Strassburg, [c.1530]. 290mm by 410mm, early hand-coloring. Latin text on verso. sg Dec 7 (176A) $3,000

WELLS, EDWARD. - A New Map of North America.... [Oxford, c.1700). 365mm by 488mm, hand-colored, framed. Some soiling & repairs. pba Oct 9 (184) $700

ZATTA, ANTONIO. - America settentrionale divisa ne' suoi principali stati. Venice:. Zatta, [1785?]. 12 by 16 inches, hand-colored in outline, cartouche fully colored.. Hole just beyond neatline at left. wa Feb 29 (654) $250

ZATTA, ANTONIO. - Nuove Scoperte de' Russi al nord del Mare del Sud si nell' Asia che nell' America. Venice:. Zatta, 1776. 11.75 by 15.5 inches, later hand-coloring. Stains at centerfold. wa Feb 29 (659) $240

ZUERNER, ADAM FRIEDRICH. - Americae tam septentrionalis quam meridionalis... delineatio. Amst.: P. Schenk, [1700 or later]. 505mm by 585mm, hand-colored in outline. Brown spot to Pacific Ocean. sg May 9 (245) $800

ZURNER, ADAM FRIEDRICH. - Americae tam septentrionalis quam meridionalis... delineato. Amst., [c.1709]. 24-3/4in by 21in Removed from Schenk's Atlas Contractus. Larson copy. pba Sept 28 (50) $500

### Asia

— Carte generale de la Mer Rouge. Paris: Depot de la Marine, 1799. 3 sheets, each 595mm by 870mm. b June 28 (117) £700

— Pays de Bassora.... Amst.: Pieter vander Aa, [c.1720]. 100mm by 340mm, hand-colored in outline. b Sept 20 (393) £110

BLAEU, JAN. - Imperii Sinarum nova descriptio. [Amst., 1655]. 465mm by 610mm, contemp outline color. Minor worming infilled. b Jan 31 (370) £150

Anr Ed. [Amst., 1655 or later]. 465mm by 600mm, hand-colored in outline. Margins trimmed. sg May 9 (114) $700

Anr Ed. [Amst., 1662]. 460mm by 600mm, contemp hand-coloring. b Dec 5 (69) £400

BLAEU, JAN & BLAEU, WILLEM. - Natolia quae olim Asia Minor. [Amst., 1635]. 385mm by 500mm, hand-colored in outline. Latin text on verso. sg May 9 (115) $225

BLAEU, WILLEM. - China veteribus Sinarum regio nunc incolis Tame dicta. [Amst., c.1650]. 410mm by 495mm, hand-colored. b Dec 5 (68) £400

BLAEU, WILLEM & BLAEU, JAN. - Asia noviter delineata. [Amst., c.1660]. 411mm by 553mm, hand-colored in outline, with decorations colored. Repair to lower central crease. pba Oct 9 (36) $2,500

BLAEU, WILLEM & BLAEU, JAN. - China veteribus Sinarum regio nunc incolis Tame dicta. Amst., [1640]. 310mm by 500mm Repaired at lower fold; slight spotting. S Oct 26 (556) £420 [Barron]

# 1995 - 1996 · BOOKS

# MAPS

BLAEU, WILLEM & BLAEU, JAN. - Cyprus insula. [Amst., 1635]. 380 by 500mm Double-page, Latin text, hand-colored. Repaired at fold and margins. S Oct 26 (46) £480 [Karides]

Anr Ed. [Amst., c.1645]. 377mm by 495mm, hand-colored. Latin text on verso. S Mar 28 (262) £480

BLAEU, WILLEM & BLAEU, JAN. - Iaponia regnym. [Amst., 1655]. 420mm by 575mm, contemp outline color. b Jan 31 (384) £340

BLAEU, WILLEM & BLAEU, JAN. - Terra Sancta quae in Sacris Terra promissionis olim Palestina. Amst., [1629]. 385mm by 495mm, hand-colored in outline, probably later. French text on verso. Some staining to image; rubbed at fold. Sold w.a.f. sg Dec 7 (59) $325

Anr Ed. Amst., [1640]. 380mm by 500mm, contemp hand-coloring. S Mar 28 (269) £280

BLAIR, JOHN. - Palaestinae sive Terrae Promissionis in duodecim Tribus partitae Facies Vetus. L, 1768. 435mm by 585mm, hand-colored. Browned along vertical fold & in margins; margins trimmed. sg May 9 (116) $250

BONFRERE, J. - Tabula geographica Terrae Sanctae. Amst.: F. Halma, [1717]. 390 by 1,110mm 2 sheets joined. S Oct 26 (185) £350 [Wayntraub]

BRAUN, GEORG & HOGENBERG, FRANZ. - Byzantium, nunc Constantinopolis. [Cologne, 1572]. 330mm by 482mm, contemp hand-coloring in full. Latin text on verso. Repaired hole in centerfold. cb Oct 17 (215) $700

BRAUN, GEORG & HOGENBERG, FRANZ. - Hierosolyma. [Cologne, 1590]. 340 by 480mm, Text in Latin; hand-colored. Repairs & strengthening to cracking. S Oct 26 (117) £150 [Swaifs]

BUY DE MORNAS, CLAUDE. - Asie. Paris, 1761. 290 by 455mm plus border, hand-colored. pba Oct 9 (50) $170

BUY DE MORNAS, CLAUDE. - Conquete de la Terre de Canaan.... Paris, 1761. 290 by 450mm plus border, hand-colored. pba Oct 9 (53) $225

BUY DE MORNAS, CLAUDE. - Histoire-Sainte depuis l'An 2513 jusqu'a l'An 2553. Paris, 1761. 290mm by 450mm, hand-colored. pba Oct 9 (60) $190

CANTELLI DA VIGNOLA, GIACOMO. - Il Regno della China. Rome: G. G. Rossi, 1692. 437mm by 545mm. S June 13 (623) £520

CHATELAIN, HENRI ABRAHAM. - Carte de la Turquie, de l'Arabie et de la Perse. Amst., [1710]. 410mm by 525mm, hand-colored in outline. sg May 9 (146) $275

Anr Ed. Amst., [1740]. 464mm by 574mm, hand-colored in outline. pba Oct 9 (83) $190

CORONELLI, VINCENZO MARIA. - Bosforo Tracio hoggidi Canale di Constantinopoli. Venice, [1691 or later]. 455mm by 610mm. Split at centerfold without loss. b Jan 31 (415) £220

DE WIT, FREDERICK. - Indiae orientalis, nec non insularum adiacentium. Amst., [1690]. 505mm by 594mm, hand-colored. framed. pba Apr 25 (31) £1,200

DE WIT, FREDERICK. - Magnae Tartariae, Magni Mogolis Imperii, Japoniae et Chinae. Amst., [c.1670]. 435mm by 550mm, contemp outline coloring. b Jan 31 (369) £260

DE WIT, FREDERICK. - Terra Sancta, sive Promissionis, olim Palestina recensdelineata. Amst., [1670]. 460 by 550mm Double-page; contemp hand-color. Lower fold repaired. S Oct 26 (187) £160 [Mayersdorf]

DELAMARCHE, CHARLES FRANCOIS. - Asie. Paris, [c.1809]. 500mm by 670mm, hand-colored. Top margin trimmed to platemark. sg Dec 7 (76) $450

DUDLEY, SIR ROBERT. - Carta particolore della Malacca.... [Florence, 1661]. 480mm by 750mm. Some stains. S Mar 28 (370) £2,000

DUDLEY, SIR ROBERT. - Carta prima general dell'Asie. L, [1661]. 460mm by 750mm. Marginal tears. S June 13 (626) £1,050

FULLER, THOMAS. - [Terra Sancta]. [L: John Williams, 1650]. 285mm by 335mm. sg Dec 7 (91) $400

Anr copy. 245mm by 315mm. sg Dec 7 (175) $425

GEELKERKEN, ARNOLDUS & GEELKERKEN, NICOLAAS. - Terrae Sanctae seu Terrae Promissionis nova descriptio. Amst.: Frederik de Wit, [c.1650]. 1,075mm by 1,990mm, 10 sheets joined. Minor damage by abrasion & loss to lower & side borders, affecting a few letters & with some restoration. b June 28 (111) £26,000

HERRERA Y TORDESILLAS, ANTONIO. - Descripcion de la Indias del Poniente. [Amst., 1622 or later]. 215mm by 295mm. b Jan 31 (405) £260

HOLLAR, WENCESLAUS. - Chorographica Terrae Sanctae. L, 1657. 380mm by 500mm. sg May 9 (162) $500

HOMANN, JOHANN BAPTIST. - Vorstellung der Orientalisch-Kayserlichen Haupt- und- Residenz Stadt Constantinopel. Nuermberg, [c.1720]. 490mm by 580mm, contemp color. Minor tears without loss. b Jan 31 (381) £320

HOMANN'S HEIRS. - Asia. Nuremberg, 1744. 475mm by 555mm, hand-colored. Fold tear. CE June 15 (354) $240

Anr copy. 510mm by 585mm, Browned at edges. sg May 9 (168) $250

HONDIUS, HENRICUS. - Asia.... Amst., [1641]. 370mm by 495mm, hand-colored, framed. Some spotting & creasing. S Mar 28 (360) £440

HONDIUS, JODOCUS. - Asiae nova descriptio. [N.p., c.1619 or later]. 380mm by 500mm, hand-colored, mtd. CE June 15 (355) $420

HONDIUS, JODOCUS. - Natoliae sive Asia Minor. [Amst., 1606 or later]. 340mm by 475mm, orig outline color. b Jan 31 (361) £180

Anr Ed. [L, 1636]. 340mm by 475mm, orig outline color. English text on verso. b Jan 31 (360) £200

HONDIUS, JODOCUS. - Situs terrae promissionis.... [Amst., c.1630]. 370mm by 490mm, contemp hand-coloring, framed. Some spotting & staining; laid down. S Mar 28 (271) £220

Anr Ed. [Amst., c.1640]. 375mm by 500mm. German text on verso. Browned; fold break. sg May 9 (171) $550

HUGHES, W. - Palestine with the Hauran.... L, 1858. 390mm by 317mm, backed with linen & sectioned for folding into orig cloth covers. pba Oct 9 (105) $100

JAILLOT, CHARLES HUBERT ALEXIS. - Carte particuliere de la Mer Rouge. Amst.: P. Mortier, [1700 or later]. 518mm by 400mm, contemp hand-coloring. b June 28 (118) £600

711

# MAPS

JAILLOT, CHARLES HUBERT ALEXIS. - Iudaea seu Terra Sancta quae Hebraeorum sive Israelitarum.... Paris, 1709. 460mm by 650mm, hand-colored in outline. Tears at lower centerfold just intruding into map area; marginal dampstaining into map area. cb Oct 17 (235) $250

JANSSONIUS, JOANNES. - China. [Amst., 1650]. 410mm by 500mm, colored in an early hand. S Mar 28 (367) £260

JODE, CORNELIS DE. - China. Antwerp, [1593]. 362mm by 452mm. b Dec 5 (66) £3,000

KOLLER, J. G. - Iudaea seu Terra Sancta.... [Augsburg, c.1700]. 625mm by 1,760mm, 3 sheets joined with added title in German, old color. Minor repairs. S June 27 (153) £2,600

LEVANTO, FRANCESCO MARIA. - Carta maritima dell' isola Cypri. [Genoa, 1664]. 401mm by 523mm. b Dec 5 (79) £1,000

LINSCHOTEN, JAN HUYGEN VAN. - Deliniantur in hac tabula.... [Amst.: C. Claesz, 1595 or later]. 386mm by 536mm. b June 28 (98) £1,200

MARIETTE, PIERRE. - Carte Generalle de l'Empire du Turc. Paris, 1646. 400mm by 510mm. Marginal discoloration. CE Nov 8 (219) $150

MERCATOR, GERARD. - India Orientalis.... Amst., [1606 or later]. 360mm by 490mm, hand-colored in outline. Latin text on verso. Margins trimmed; browned; fold wear; bottom margin reinforced on verso. Sold w.a.f. sg Dec 7 (119) $500

MOLL, HERMAN. - Map of Asia. L, [c.1720]. 580mm by 950mm, hand-colored in outline. Wear, discoloration & strengthening at folds. S Mar 28 (361) £320

MUENSTER, SEBASTIAN. - India Extrema. Basel, 1552. 295mm by 370m image size, hand-colored. Latin text on verso. sg May 9 (214) $950

MUENSTER, SEBASTIAN. - Terra Sancta XXIII.... [Basel, c.1545]. 265mm by 340mm. Latin text on verso. sg May 9 (216) $550

MURILLO VELARDE, PEDRO. - Carta hydrographica y chorographica de las Yslas Filipinas. Manila, 1744. 2 (of 4) double-page sheets, each 565mm by 350mm, contemp outline color. Laid down & repaired. b Jan 31 (402) £650

NOLIN, JEAN BAPTISTE. - L'Asie.... Paris, 1749. 4 sheets joined, over-all 885mm by 1,150mm, hand-colored, mtd on canvas. Minor fold loss. b Jan 31 (365) £1,200

ORTELIUS, ABRAHAM. - Asiae nova descriptio. [Antwerp, 1570 or later]. 370mm by 495mm, contemp hand-coloring, framed. S Mar 28 (363) £650

Anr Ed. [Antwerp, 1579]. 370mm by 480mm Text in French. Margins strengthened. S Oct 26 (553) £500 [Altea]

Anr Ed. [Antwerp, 1595]. 375mm by 480mm. Repaired split at lower fold. Latin text on verso. S Mar 28 (364) £500

ORTELIUS, ABRAHAM. - Indiae orientalis insularumque adiacentium typus. [Antwerp, 1570, or later]. 350mm by 500mm, hand-colored, mtd. Latin text on verso. Repairs to verso; marginal tape-staining & browning. CE June 15 (360) $900

ORTELIUS, ABRAHAM. - Palestinae sive totius terrae promissionis. [Antwerp, 1570 or later]. 345mm by 465mm, contemp hand-coloring. S Mar 28 (272) £340

ORTELIUS, ABRAHAM. - Peregrinationis Divi Pauli Typus Corographicus. Antwerp, 1595. 355mm by 500mm, hand-colored. Latin text on verso. Repair at fold in lower margin; some browning & rubbing at centerfold. sg Dec 7 (142) $700

ORTELIUS, ABRAHAM. - Persici sive sophorum regni typus. Antwerp, [c.1572]. 352mm by 497mm, hand-colored. With Latin text on verso. pba Oct 9 (137) $325

ORTELIUS, ABRAHAM. - Tartariae sive magni Chami Regni typis. [Antwerp, 1570, or later]. 350mm by 475mm, early coloring. With 2 small holes. b Jan 31 (408) £360

Anr copy. Contemp hand-coloring, backed on canvas. b Jan 31 (409) £380

Anr Ed. [Antwerp, 1595, or later]. 352mm by 473mm, contemp hand-coloring, framed. With Latin text on verso. Some soiling; split in centerfold extending into border; 1 repaired hole; brown stain in map area just above lower cartouche. cb Oct 17 (243) $1,100

Anr Ed. [Antwerp, 1570, or later]. 350mm by 460mm, hand-colored. Latin text on verso. Border cropped at 3 sides; lower margin with tear. CE June 15 (358) $400

Anr Ed. [Antwerp, c.1590]. 350mm by 460mm, hand-colored. With Latin text on verso. Single wormhole to each side margin. sg May 9 (221) $600

Anr Ed. [Antwerp, c.1592]. 347mm by 467mm, hand-colored. Latin text on verso. Some soiling; tape stains to margins. pba Oct 9 (139) $500

ORTELIUS, ABRAHAM. - Turcici imperii descriptio. [Antwerp, 1580]. 372mm by 495mm, early coloring. Latin text on verso. b Jan 31 (397) £300

ORTELIUS, ABRAHAM. - Typus Chorographicus, celebrium locorum in regno Iudae et Israhel. [Antwerp, 1586 or later]. 355mm by 465mm, hand-colored. Italian text on verso. Browned; repaired. Sold w.a.f. sg May 9 (222) $325

PALAIRET, JEAN. - le Carte de la Judee ou Terre Sainte. L, 1755. 490mm by 595mm, hand-colored. Some coloring muddied; some staining. Sold w.a.f. sg May 9 (224) $175

PTOLEMAEUS, CLAUDIUS. - Geographica: quarta Asie tabula [Iraq, Syria, Lebanon & Northern Arabia]. [Ulm, 1486]. 375mm by 520mm, hand-colored. Reinforced along fold on verso; minor marginal soiling. Latin text on verso. CE June 15 (356) $3,800

PTOLEMAEUS, CLAUDIUS. - Sexta Asiae tabula. [Basel, 1571]. 270mm by 340mm. b June 28 (93) £420

PTOLEMAEUS, CLAUDIUS. - Sexta Asie tabula. [Strassburg: Johannes Schott, 1513]. 310mm by 555mm. b June 28 (92) £1,400

RAMUSIO, GIOVANNI BATTISTA. - Sumatra. [Venice, 1565]. 265mm by 365mm. Browned. S June 13 (628) £400

ROBERT DE VAUGONDY, GILLES & DIDIER. - Archipel des Indes orientales.... [Paris, 1750]. 495mm by 630mm, later hand-coloring. Some browning. sg Dec 7 (148) $75

ROBERT DE VAUGONDY, GILLES & DIDIER. - L'Empire du

Japon. [Paris], 1750. 480mm by 540mm, handcolored. b Jan 31 (395) £280

ROBERT DE VAUGONDY, GILLES & DIDIER. - Les Indes orientales.... Paris, 1751. 495mm by 575mm, hand-colored. Closed tear into image; browned. sg Dec 7 (151) $325

SANSON D'ABBEVILLE, NICOLAS. - Turcicum Imperium. Amst., [c.1655]. 455mm by 555mm, hand-colored in outline. Browned; marginal tears; repair on verso. sg May 9 (236) $275

SCHERER, HEINRICH. - Asiae status naturalis. [Munich, c.1720]. 235mm by 360mm. sg Dec 7 (163) $400

SCHERER, HEINRICH. - Patriarchatus Ierosolymitanus. [Munich, c.1720]. 235mm by 355mm. sg Dec 7 (166) $425

SENEX, JOHN. - A New Map of Asia.... [N.p., c.1720]. 18.75 by 22 inches, hand-colored in outline Centerfold reinforced. wa Feb 29 (594) $100

SEUTTER, MATTHAEUS. - Deserta Aegypti, Thebaidis Arabiae, Syria.... Augsburg, [c.1745]. 492mm by 570mm, contemp hand-coloring. Fold repair. b Dec 5 (77) £210

SEUTTER, MATTHAEUS. - Imperium Japonicum. Augsburg, [c.1740]. 490mm by 572mm, contemp color. Split in fold. b Dec 5 (96) £2,000

SEUTTER, MATTHAEUS. - Jerusalem, cum suburbiis, prout tempore Christi floruit. Augsburg, [1725]. 575mm by 495mm, hand-colored. Wear & chips to corners; repaired tears. pba Aug 8 (134) $750

SPEED, JOHN. - The Kingdome of Persia.... L, [c.1676]. 15.5 by 20.5 inches, hand-colored in outline, with later coloring to decorations, framed. Browned. wa Feb 29 (682) $325

SPEED, JOHN. - Oxfordshire.... L: Bassett & Chiswell, [1676]. 380mm by 505mm, hand-colored, framed. Wear to fold; some browning; laid down. S Mar 28 (142) £280

STEEL, PENELOPE. - Steel's New and Correct Outline Chart. L, 25 April, 1809. 660mm by 1215mm, in sunk mount. Slight surface dirt. S Oct 26 (558) £420 [Indone]

TIRION, ISAAK. - Carta accurata dell'Imperio del Giappone. [Venice, 1734 or later]. 245mm by 320mm, hand-colored. Corner of border restored in Ms. b Jan 31 (387) £110

VISSCHER, NICOLAUS. - Asiae. Amst., [1670]. 435mm by 540mm, hand-colored in outline. Discoloration at fold. S Mar 28 (362) £380

WYLD, JAMES. - Map of China from Original Surveys. L, [1861]. 615mm by 800mm, backed on linen in orig cloth slipcase. Hand-colored & dissected into 24 sections. S Oct 26 (557) £140 [Bankes]

### Atlantic Ocean

ARROWSMITH, AARON. - Chart of the South Atlantic Ocean. L, [1805]. 4 sheets, each 620mm by 960mm. Frayed. S Mar 28 (319) £260

BELLIN, JACQUES NICOLAS. - Carte reduite du Detroit de Davids Faite au Depost des Cartes, Plans et Journeaux de la Marine.... [Paris], 1765. 54mm by 86mm. pba Apr 25 (11) $300

KEULEN, JOANNES VAN. - Pascaert van Groen-Landt. Amst., [1695]. 510mm by 600mm. S Mar 28 (309) £170

KEULEN, JOANNES VAN. - Pascaerte vande Caribes. Amst., [c.1680]. 515mm by 590mm, colored in a contemp hand. Some cracking of green; fold repairs; lower margin trimmed. S June 13 (609) £330

LINSCHOTEN, JAN HUYGEN VAN. - Vera effigies et delineatio Insula Sanctae Helenae.... Amst., [1644]. 305mm by 475mm, hand-colored. pba Oct 9 (114) $300

### Australasia

BELLIN, JACQUES NICOLAS. - Carte reduite des Terres Australes. Paris, [1753]. 200mm by 275mm S Oct 26 (602) £320 [Baring]

BOWEN, EMANUEL. - A Complete Map of the Southern Continent.... L, 1744. 370mm by 480mm, framed. S Mar 28 (413) £1,400

CANZLER, FRIEDRICH GOTTLIEB. - Karte vom fuenften erdtheil oder Polynaesien-Inselwelt oder Australien od Suedindien. Nuremberg: Homann's Heirs, [1795]. 450mm by 565mm, hand-colored. Some staining & discoloration. S Mar 28 (414) £240

COOK, CAPT. JAMES. - A General Chart Exhibiting the Discoveries made by Captain James Cook.... L, [c.1785]. 595mm by 935mm, hand-colored in outline. Margins cut close; dampstaining to part of image. Sold w.a.f. sg May 9 (233) $500

FLINDERS, MATTHEW. - Chart of Terra Australis. L, 1814. 650mm by 930mm. Covering the coast from Cape Otway to Twofold Bay. b Sept 20 (391) £350

REINECKE, I.C.M. - General-Charte von Australien. Weimar, 1804. 450mm by 605mm, contemp outline color. Creasing. S Mar 28 (415) £260

THEVENOT, MELCHISEDEC. - Hollandia Nova Terre Australe. L, [1663]-72. 2d Ed. 380mm by 590mm With rhumb lines, Tropic of Cancer & genealogical table. S Oct 26 (603) £2,700 [Map House]

### Canada

BELLIN, JACQUES NICOLAS. - Partie orientale de la Nouvelle France ou du Canada.... Paris, 1755. 430mm by 540mm, hand-colored in outline. pba Oct 9 (34) $350

CORONELLI, VINCENZO MARIA. - Partie Occidentale du Canada.... Paris, 1688. 447mm by 603mm. Crease repairs. pba Oct 9 (78) $6,000

DELISLE, GUILLAUME. - Carte du Canada ou de la Nouvelle France. Paris, 1703. 480mm by 555mm, hand-colored in outline. Minor bleeding from linen backing; margins slightly obscured by linen turnovers. sg Dec 7 (78) $325

JAILLOT, CHARLES HUBERT ALEXIS. - Le Canada ou Partie de la Nouvelle France. Paris, 1696. 465mm by 610mm, hand-colored in outline. sg Dec 7 (102) $600

### Celestial

BUY DE MORNAS, CLAUDE. - Centre du Monde. Systemes de Ptolomee et de Ticho-Brahe. Paris, 1761. 290mm by 455mm, hand-colored. pba Oct 9 (52) $550

CASSINI, GIOVANNI MARIA. - Globo terrestre; Globo celeste. Rome: Calcografia Camerale, [1790]-95. 8 double-page mapsheets each with 3 half gores, plus 6 double-page plates containing the calottes & information to be applied to the stand all in contemp

# MAPS

hand-color, each c.490mm by 325mm. b Dec 5 (87) £5,400

CELLARIUS, ANDREAS. - Haemisphaeria Sphaerarum. [Amst., 1660]. 435mm by 515mm, hand-colored. Marginal browning. sg May 9 (141) $1,600

CELLARIUS, ANDREAS. - Hypothesis Ptolemaica. Amst., 1660. 435mm by 510mm, hand-colored. sg May 9 (142) $800

CELLARIUS, ANDREAS. - Theoria Trium Superiorum Planetarum. [Amst., 1660]. 435mm by 515mm, hand-colored. Marginal browning. sg May 9 (143) $1,600

CELLARIUS, ANDREAS. - Theoria Veneris et Mercurii. [Amst., 1660]. 435mm by 515mm, hand-colored. Marginal browning. sg May 9 (144) $1,400

CELLARIUS, ANDREAS. - Tychonis Brahe Calculus, Planetarum Cursus et Altitudines. Amst., 1660. 425mm by 520mm, hand-colored. Minor marginal browning. sg May 9 (145) $1,200

CORONELLI, VINCENZO MARIA. - Planisfero Meridionale, Corretto, et Accresciuto di Molte Stelle. Venice, [1692]. 457mm by 608mm, mtd; mounting hinges detached with small remnants of tape at upper corners. Marginal soiling & foxing across map area. cb Oct 17 (221) $425

DOPPELMAYER, JOHANN GABRIEL. - Tabula selenographica.... Nuremberg, [c.1725]. 490mm by 580mm, orig hand-coloring. bba June 6 (316) £300 [Frew]

HOMANN, JOHANN BAPTIST. - Hemisphaerium Coeli Boreale. Nuremberg, [c.1730]. 500mm by 585mm, hand-colored. Closed tears extending into image; some soiling; backed with paper. sg May 9 (166) $375

HOMANN, JOHANN BAPTIST. - Hemisphaerum Coeli Australe. Nuremberg, [c.1730]. 405mm by 600mm, hand-colored, mtd to bd. Closed tears in margins. sg May 9 (165) $425

### China

CORONELLI, VINCENZO MARIA. - Nanking et Honan.... [Venice, 1695]. 455mm by 605mm, hand-colored in outline. Browning along vertical fold. sg May 9 (150) $400

### Eastern Hemisphere

CORONELLI, VINCENZO MARIA. - Planisfero del Mondo Nuovo. Venice, [c.1690]. 454mm by 604mm, later hand-coloring to cartouches, border, panels & water.. Some worming into border; tiny holes; split along lower centerfold with tear extending across South America to equator, patched on verso. cb Oct 17 (220) $800

DANCKWERTH, CASPAR & MEJER, JOHANNES. - Orbis Vetis.... [Husum], 1651. 432mm by 532mm, decorations partly hand-colored. Remargined at top & bottom. pba Oct 9 (81) $500

### Europe

ANTONELLI, ANTONIO. - Progretto di decorazione per la Piazza Castello di Torino. Rome, 1831. 590mm by 1140mm, 3 sheets, separated dampstained. S Oct 26 (262) £700 [Meyer]

Anr copy. Dampstained. S June 13 (531) £520

BARATERI, M. A. - La Gran Citta di Milan. [Milan, 1638]. 4 sheets joined, 748mm by 795mm. S June 27 (119) £2,900

BARENTS, WILLEM. - Hydrographica descriptio maris Mediterranei.... Amst., [c.1599]. 335mm by 525mm. S Nov 30 (90) £1,500

BARENTS, WILLEM. - Italiae Orae maritime a Portu Herculis dicto.... Amst., [c.1599]. 335mm by 525mm. S Nov 30 (91) £1,600

BARENTS, WILLEM. - Tabula hydrographica, in qua Italiae.... Amst., [c.1599]. 400mm by 540mm. S Nov 30 (89) £4,200

BELL'ARMATO, GIROLAMO. - Tusciae elegantioris Italiae partis Corographiam descripsunus.... Rome: Claudio Duchetti, 1558. 380mm by 525mm. Cut close at side margins; restored at edges; small stamp removed. S Nov 30 (93) £1,200

BELLIN, JACQUES NICOLAS. - Carte reduite des costes de Flandre et de Hollande. [Paris], 1763. 555mm by 850mm, hand-colored in outline. S June 13 (526) £340

BLAEU, WILLEM & BLAEU, JAN. - Stiria/Steyrmarck. [Amst., 1640]. 378mm by 503mm, hand-colored. French text on verso. pba Oct 9 (37) $130

BLAEU, WILLEM & BLAEU, JAN. - Tabula Russiae. [Amst., 1663]. 420mm by 540mm Text in German; contemp handcolored. Small split & stains at fold. S Oct 26 (259) £180 [Weiss]

BOLSTRA, MELCHIOR. - 'T Hooge Heemraed-Schap van Rhynland. Leiden, 1746. 600mm by 376mm, contemp calf gilt; rebacked, corners replaced, joints starting. With engraved tp, hand-colored & heightened in gold; 13 maps & 1 diagram, all with contemp hand-coloring in full or in outline. Some soiling & marginal defs. cb Oct 17 (247) $4,000

BORDIGA, GIOVANNI BATTISTA. - Carte militare del regno d'Etruria e del principato di Lucca. [Milan], 1806. 1080mm by 1075mm backed on linen. 2 small stains. S Oct 26 (244) £270 [Walford's]

BRAUN, GEORG & HOGENBURG, FRANZ. - Antwerpia. Cologne, [c.1590]. 340mm by 480mm Text in Antwerpia. S Oct 26 (242) £280 [MapHouse]

BRAUN, GEORG & HOGENBERG, FRANZ. - Avignon. Amst., [c.1572]. 310mm by 470mm, hand-colored. Latin text on verso. Staining in margins. sg May 9 (124) $400

BRAUN, GEORG & HOGENBERG, FRANZ. - Damascus. [Amst., c.1572]. 320mm by 355mm. French text on verso. Fold browned. sg May 9 (125) $175

BRAUN, GEORG & HOGENBERG, FRANZ. - Elekenforda. [Amst., c.1572]. 355mm by 480mm, hand-colored, mtd to stiff bd. Margins & fold browned. sg May 9 (127) $250

BRAUN, GEORG & HOGENBERG, FRANZ. - Mets. Amst., [c.1572]. 350mm by 480mm, hand-colored. Latin text on verso. sg May 9 (128) $325

BRAUN, GEORG & HOGENBERG, FRANZ. - Mons. Amst., [c.1572]. 355mm by 470mm. French text on verso. sg May 9 (129) $375

BRAUN, GEORG & HOGENBERG, FRANZ. - Saintes. Amst., [c.1572]. 365mm by 460mm, hand-colored. French text on verso. Small tear in bottom margin. sg May 9 (131) $250

BRAUN, GEORG & HOGENBURG, FRANZ. - Urbis Nancei Lotharingiae. [Cologne, 1617]. Double-paged; handcolored. S Oct 26 (256) £160 [Weiss]

BRAUN, GEORG & HOGENBERG, FRANZ. - Vesontio. Amst., [c.1572]. 355mm by 500mm, hand-colored. Latin text on verso. Closed tear extending into image. sg May 9 (132) $275

BUENTING, HEINRICH. - Europa prima pars.... [Magdeburg, 1581]. 230mm by 342mm, hand-colored. Some restoration to margins. b Sept 20 (231) £260

CAMOCIO, GIOVANNI FRANCESCO. - Novo disegno della Forteza della Prevesa. [Venice, 1570]. 242mm by 320mm. Cut close. S Mar 28 (278) £260

CAMOCIO, GIOVANNI FRANCESCO. - Il vero Disegno del sito di Modon et Navarino.... [Venice, 1570]. 280mm by 420mm. Some fold wear & discoloration. S Mar 28 (207) £300

CHOPY, ANTOINE. - Carte du Lac de Geneve.... [1730]. 570mm by 800mm. Trimmed to neatline. S Mar 28 (203) £280

CORONELLI, VINCENZO MARIA. - La Francia Antica e Moderna. Venice, [n.d.]. 2 sheets, each 603mm by 444mm, later hand-coloring. Some soiling; ink & pencil numbering at 2 corners with small holes where ink burned through; repaired tear into surface; separating along centerfold. cb Oct 17 (218) $180

CORONELLI, VINCENZO MARIA. - Parte Occidentale [Parte Orientale] dell'Europa. Venice, [c.1690]. 2 sheets, each 617mm by 460mm, later hand-coloring to cartouches & water. Marginal soiling; small holes & fold breaks; repaired tear to centerfold. cb Oct 17 (219) $300

DE WIT, FREDERICK. - Ducatus Lutzenburgici. Amst., [1670]. 460mm by 555mm. Waterstained along top margin; split at upper fold. S Mar 28 (204) £150

DE WIT, FREDERICK. - Europae. Amst., [c.1680]. 495mm by 595mm, hand-colored in outline. Some foxing. sg May 9 (267) $350

DE WIT, FREDERICK. - Insula Candia. Amst., [c.1750]. 458mm by 545mm, hand-colored. b Dec 5 (74) £400

DE WIT, FREDERICK. - Nova atque emendata descriptio Suydt Hollandiae. Amst., [c.1688]. 450mm by 540mm, hand-colored in outline. Some browning; separation along vertical fold. sg May 9 (269) $150

DE WIT, FREDERICK. - Peloponnesus hodie Moreae regnum. Amst., [c.1680]. 500mm by 757mm, contemp coloring. b June 28 (105) £2,000

DE WIT, FREDERICK. - Tabula Italiae. Amst., [c.1670]. 455mm by 550mm, hand-colored in outline. Some browning along fold; margins trimmed. sg May 9 (270) $325

EYTZINGER, MICHAEL VON. - Leo Belgicus. [Cologne, 1583]. 365mm by 445mm, early hand-coloring. Minor restoration to gutter hinge. sg Dec 7 (84A) $6,000

FINKH, G. S. - Rom. Imp. Circuli et Electoratus Bavariae tabula chorographica.... [Nuremberg, 1671]. 1,185mm by 920mm, dissected into 56 sections & backed on linen. Some staining & edge wear. Sold w.a.f. O Mar 5 (83) $190

HOMANN, JOHANN BAPTIST. - Accurater Grundis der Konigl. Spanischen Haupt und Residentz Stadt Madrit. Nuremberg, [c.1730]. 495mm by 570mm, hand-colored. Tape stains on map verso at edges, showing on recto margins. sg Dec 7 (92) $500

HOMANN, JOHANN BAPTIST. - Belgii pars septentrionalis communi nomine vulgo Hollandia. Nuremberg, [c.1730]. 490mm by 565mm, hand-colored. Closed tears in margin; some soiling. sg May 9 (164) $225

HOMANN, JOHANN BAPTIST. - Comitatus Flandriae. Nuremberg, [c.1730]. 490mm by 585mm, hand-colored. Marginal soiling. sg Dec 7 (94) $175

HOMANN, JOHANN BAPTIST. - Generalis Totius Imperii Russorum novissima tabula. Nuremberg, [1735]. 485mm by 570mm, contemp body color. Browned at fold. S Mar 28 (213) £190

HOMANN, JOHANN BAPTIST. - Insula Creta hodie Candia in sua IV Territoria divisa cum adjacentibus Aegi Maris Insulis.... Nuremberg, [c.1730]. 481mm by 575mm, hand-colored. Marginal foxing; rubbing to neatlines at upper corners. pba Oct 9 (101) $130

HOMANN, JOHANN BAPTIST. - Insularum Maltae et Gozae. Nuremberg, [1715]. 485 by 578mm Double-page, contemp color. S Oct 26 (158) £600 [Melitensia]

HOMANN'S HEIRS. - Bosphorus Thraciscus. Nuremberg, [1764]. 800mm by 505mm, contemp hand-coloring. b June 28 (108) £500

HONDIUS, JODOCUS. - Nova Europae Descriptio. [N.p., c.1619 or later]. 375mm by 505mm, hand-colored, mtd. Repaired along fold with minor loss. CE June 15 (362) $700

JAILLOT, CHARLES HUBERT ALEXIS. - L'Espagne.... Paris, [c.1690]. 450mm by 570mm, hand-colored in outline. Marginal soiling & browning. sg Dec 7 (103) $325

JANSSONIUS, JOANNES. - Damascus. [Amst., c.1657, or later]. 325mm by 360mm, hand-colored. French text on verso. Minor staining in margins. sg May 9 (175) $275

JANSSONIUS, JOANNES. - Moscovia Urbs Metropolis Totius Russiae Albae. [Amst.: Janssonius, c.1657]. 355mm by 465mm, hand-colored. Some creasing & chipping. sg May 9 (182) $500

JANSSONIUS, JOANNES. - Tabula itineraria ex illustri Peutingerorum Bibliotheca. [Amst., 1650]. 2 strips on 4 double-page mapsheets, contemp hand-coloring. S Mar 28 (253) £480

JOLLAIN, GERARD OR FRANCOIS. - Messine. [Paris, 1680]. 400mm by 515mm Text in Latin & French. Edges strengthened; left-hand margin repaired. S Oct 26 (254) £520 [Antiquariat]

KEULEN, JOANNES VAN. - Nieuwe Paskaart vande geheele Oosterze en Norrtze. Amst., [1695]. 510mm by 590mm. Edges stained & frayed. S Mar 28 (209) £220

KEULEN, JOANNES VAN. - Paskaart van een gedeelte der Noort Zee. Amst., [1695 or later]. 510mm by 590mm. Marginal staining & fraying. S Mar 28 (208) £150

KEULEN, JOANNES VAN. - Paskaarte van de Zuyder Zee met alle des Zelfs inkomende. Amst., [c.1700 or later]. 520mm by 600mm, hand-colored in outline. Margins trimmed; some soiling. sg Dec 7 (111) $475

LAFRERI, ANTONIO. - Melita Insula divi Pauli Apostoli.... Rome, [1565 or later]. 375 by 485mm Double-page. Holes & worn at fold; right-hand margin torn with loss; pieced & repaired; margins strengthened. S Oct 26 (160) £2,000 [Potter]

LAURIE, ROBERT & WHITTLE, JAMES. - A New Map of Switzerland. L, 1794. 500mm by 665mm, hand-colored. sg May 9 (194) $225

LE CLERC, JEAN. - Islandia. Paris, 1602 [or later]. 335mm by 480mm, hand-colored. b Jan 31 (379) £750

LEVANTO, FRANCESCO MARIA. - Carta maritima del Levante.... [Genoa, 1664]. 402mm by 518mm. b Dec 5 (84) £700

MARTINON, GIOVANNI. - Desscrizione geografica del Regno di Sicilia.... Paris, 1801. 4 sheets joined, 910mm by 1,190mm, mtd on linen. Minor repairs. S June 27 (128) £800

MERCATOR, GERARD. - Candia cum insulis aliquot circa Graeciam. Antwerp, [c.1574]. 336mm by 475mm, later hand-coloring. Marginal tears & chips; some soiling; 2 stains on reverse showing through. pba Oct 9 (120) $275

MERCATOR, GERARD. - Hella seu Graciae Sophiani. [Amst., 1618]. 365mm by 500mm. S Mar 28 (266) £240

MERCATOR, GERARD. - Islandia. Amst.: Hondius, 1607. 285mm by 435mm. French text on verso. Restored in lower margin. sg May 9 (206) $400

MICHELOT, HENRI & BREMOND, LAURENT. - Nouvelle carte de l'isle de Malthe. Marseilles, [1718]. 465mm by 680mm, hand-colored. Some soiling. S Mar 28 (268) £460

MOLL, HERMAN. - A New and Exact Map of Spain & Portugal. L, [1711]. 2 sheets joined, 615mm by 975mm, hand-colored in outline. Creased in lower margin. sg May 9 (213) $200

MUENSTER, SEBASTIAN. - Nova Graecia XXII. Basel, 1552. 295mm by 370mm image size, hand-colored. sg May 9 (215) $550

NOLIN, JEAN BAPTISTE. - L'Europe dressee sur les nouvelles observations.... Paris, 1789. 4 sheets joined, 1,270mm by 1,400mm, hand-colored. Some restoration. S Nov 30 (88) £2,600

ORTELIUS, ABRAHAM. - Acores insulae. [Antwerp, c.1584]. 325mm by 462mm, early hand-coloring. Creased near fold. b Dec 5 (63) £170

ORTELIUS, ABRAHAM. - Austriae.... [Antwerp, c.1580]. 350mm by 482mm, hand-colored. French text on verso. Some foxing & soiling. pba Oct 9 (136) $130

ORTELIUS, ABRAHAM. - Descriptio Germaniae inferioris. [Antwerp, c.1573]. 370mm by 505mm, hand-colored, framed. Browned. b Jan 31 (401) £100

ORTELIUS, ABRAHAM. - Europae. [Antwerp, 1570 or later]. 340mm by 460mm, contemp hand-coloring, framed. S Mar 28 (196) £220

ORTELIUS, ABRAHAM. - Flandriae Comitatus descriptio. [Antwerp, c.1612]. 380mm by 490mm, hand-colored. Latin text on verso. Closed tear at vertical fold bottom, affecting surface. sg May 9 (219) $150

ORTELIUS, ABRAHAM. - Hollandiae.... [Antwerp, c.1590]. 350mm by 485mm, contemp hand-coloring, framed. Repaired marginal tear; nonarchival backing. Latin text on verso. cb Oct 17 (242) $325

ORTELIUS, ABRAHAM. - Insularum aliquot maris mediterranei descriptio. [Antwerp, 1603]. 365mm by 480mm, hand-colored. Latin text on verso. S Mar 28 (206) £200

ORTELIUS, ABRAHAM. - Islandia. [Antwerp, 1589]. 345mm by 495mm. Latin text on verso. Some dampstaining. sg Dec 7 (140) $2,200

ORTELIUS, ABRAHAM. - Palatinatus Bavariae - Argentoratensis. [Antwerp, 1582 or later]. 305mm by 485mm, partially hand-colored. Some creasing. sg May 9 (220) $120

ORTELIUS, ABRAHAM. - Pontus Euxinus. Amst., [c.1625]. 372mm by 482mm. Centerfold worn & repaired. pba Oct 9 (138) $120

ORTELIUS, ABRAHAM. - Regni Neapolitani. Antwerp, 1612. 365mm by 495mm, hand-colored in outline. Spanish text on verso. sg Dec 7 (143) $500

PONTAULT, SEBASTIEN DE. - Plan de la ville et molle de Taragone. Paris, [c.1650]. 450mm by 545mm, hand-colored. Some foxing. sg May 9 (108) $500

PRESTINO, FRANCESCO. - Descrittione del Rincontro fatto da Francesi all'Armata di Spagna vicino alla Terra di Bolengo. [Turin, c.1631]. 435mm by 625mm plus separate butt-jointed letterpress key b June 28 (121) £1,500

PTOLEMAEUS, CLAUDIUS. - Tabula Secunda Europa. Strassburg, [1513 or 1520]. 380mm by 530mm, early coloring. Small fold breaks; some edge-wear. CE Sept 27 (179) $400

RENARD, LOUIS. - Mare Germanicum ac Tractus Maritimus retro Hiberniam.... Amst., [c.1715]. 490mm by 563mm. Ends of centerfolds split; some soiling. pba Oct 9 (144) $400

ROBERT DE VAUGONDY, GILLES & DIDIER. - Le Royaume de Boheme.... Paris, 1751. 490mm by 580mm, later hand-coloring. Dampstain in right margin; some browning. sg Dec 7 (154) $175

ROBERT DE VAUGONDY, GILLES & DIDIER. - Royaume de Danemarck. Paris, 1750. 500mm by 580mm, later hand-coloring. Browned. sg Dec 7 (155) $100

ROBERT DE VAUGONDY, GILLES & DIDIER. - Royaume de Hongrie. Paris, 1751. 495mm by 570mm, later hand-coloring. Browned. sg Dec 7 (156) $100

ROCQUE, JOHN. - A Plan of Paris.... [1754]. 430mm by 650mm, framed. S Mar 28 (211) £190

SALAMANCA, ANTONIO. - La Dimostratione del luogo dove al presente sitrova l'armat di Barbarossa.... [Rome, 1538]. 295mm by 430mm. Narrow lower margins; 1 small tear; 3 wax stains. S Mar 28 (267) £750

SANSON D'ABBEVILLE, NICOLAS. - Oost-Frise, ou le Comte d'Embden. [Paris]: H. Jaillot, 1692. 435mm by 575mm, hand-colored in outline. Dampstaining to part of image; tear at fold bottom extending into image. sg May 9 (237) $250

SANSON D'ABBEVILLE, NICOLAS. - Parte Septentrional do Reyno de Portugal. Paris, 1654. 425mm by 545mm, hand-colored. Margins trimmed; minor soiling. sg May 9 (239) $140

SANSON D'ABBEVILLE, NICOLAS. - La Seigneurie de Gronigue. Paris: H. Jaillot, 1692. 2 sheets joined, 560mm by 800mm, hand-colored in outline. Minor browning. sg May 9 (240) $325

SCHENK, PETER. - Regni Hungarie, Graeciae et Moreae. Amst., [c.1700]. 490mm by 575mm, hand-colored. Closed tears entering image; unclosed tears in margins; some foxing. sg Dec 7 (161) $350

SENEX, JOHN. - A Map of the Island and Kingdom of Sicily. L, [c.1720, or later]. 495mm by 585mm, hand-colored in outline. Browning at fold & at bottom. sg May 9 (247) $275

SENEX, JOHN. - A New Map of Rome.... L, [c.1720, or later]. 495mm by 585mm. Browned in lower por-

tion of vertical fold. sg May 9 (250) $550
SENEX, JOHN. - A New Map of the City of Amsterdam. L: D. Browne, etc., [1720 or later]. 495mm by 585mm. Margins trimmed; dampstained; tape stains. Sold w.a.f. sg Dec 7 (54) $300
Anr copy. Fold break extending into image. sg May 9 (249) $300
SEUTTER, MATTHAEUS. - Carte des iles de Maiorque, Minorque et d'Yvice. Augsburg, [1741]. 460mm by 560mm, contemp body color. S Mar 28 (190) £240
SPEED, JOHN. - Italia. L: G. Humble, 1626. 395mm by 510mm. Framed. Minor spotting. b Sept 20 (235) £550
SPEED, JOHN. - A New Map of ye XVII Provinces of Low Germanie. L: G. Humble, [1627]. 400mm by 520mm, hand-colored. Margins cropped. S June 13 (527) £420
SPEED, JOHN. - The Turkish Empire. L: T. Bassett & R. Chiswell, 1626. 392mm by 513mm, later hand-coloring, mtd. Repaired; lower margin def; minor worming at bottom; cut close. cb June 25 (1750) $600
TIRION, ISAAK. - Nieuwe Kaart van't Eiland Maltha met Gozo en Comino. Amst., 1761. 280 by 450mm, Double-page; contemp hand-color. S Oct 26 (161) £280 [Fsadni]
VASI, GIUSEPPE. - Prospetto d'Alma Citta di Roma visto dal Monte Gianicolo. Rome, 1765. 6 sheets mtd & dissected on linen in 24 sections, total 1,000mm by 2,260mm. Some edge wear & fraying; piece torn from right edge. Sold w.a.f. O Mar 5 (233) $2,500
VISSCHER, NICOLAUS. - Amstelodami veteris et novissimae urbis.... Amst., [c.1680]. 480mm by 565mm, framed. Some discoloration. b May 30 (133) £450
WAGHENAER, LUCAS JANSZ. - Caerte vande Zee Custen van Acason en Biscaie.... Leiden, [1588]. 325mm by 505mm Text in Dutsch; handcolored. Slight crease at fold; 2 small rustholes. S Oct 26 (243) £260 [MapHouse]
WALDSEEMUELLER, MARTIN. - Tabula Moderna et nova Italie ac Sicilie. [Strassburg: J. Schott, 1513 or later]. 408mm by 549mm. Wormholes at foot of fold; waterstains. b Dec 5 (99) £1,000
WALDSEEMUELLER, MARTIN. - Tabula Moderna Italie. [Strassburg: J. Schott, 1513 or later]. 390mm by 585mm. Waterstaining. b Dec 5 (100) £1,100
WALDSEEMUELLER, MARTIN. - Tabula Moderna Norbegie et Gottie. [Strassburg: J. Schott, 1513 or later]. 320mm by 585mm. Waterstaining. b Dec 5 (101) £2,100
WILL, JOHANN MARTIN. - Kriegs Schauplatz... Russland, Oesterreich und Polen.... Augsburg, [c.1770]. 540mm by 640mm, hand-colored. Margins trimmed to platemark. sg Dec 7 (178) $400
ZATTA, ANTONIO. - Li Contorni de Parigi. Venice, 1776. 315mm by 430mm, partly hand-colored. Browning along vertical fold; minor foxing & soiling. sg May 9 (272) $200

### Great Britain

AINSLIE, JOHN. - Scotland Drawn and Engraved.... Edin. & L: John Ainslie & William Faden, 1 Jan 1789. 1st Ed. 1770mm by 1600mm, backed on linen with orig rollers. In 9 sheets. Soiled, torn at upper edge. S Oct 26 (363) £400 [Smith]
BLAEU, WILLEM & BLAEU, JAN. - Cantabrigiensis Comitatus, Cambridge-Shire. [Amst., 1662]. 16.5 by 20.5 inches, hand-colored in outline, arms fully colored, framed. Browned. wa Feb 29 (612) $375
BLAEU, WILLEM & BLAEU, JAN. - Comitatus Salopiensis; anglice, Shrop shire. [Amst., 1662]. 380mm by 490mm, contemp hand-coloring, framed. Some spotting. S Mar 28 (143) £120
BLAEU, WILLEM & BLAEU, JAN. - Gloucestria Ducatus, vulgo Glocester Shire. [Amst., c.1650]. 440mm by 535mm, hand-colored, framed. Marginal staining. b Jan 31 (321) £110
BLAEU, WILLEM & BLAEU, JAN. - Oxonium comitatus. [Amst., c.1650]. 15 by 19.5 inches, contemp hand-coloring in outline, with later coloring to cartouches & crests, framed. French text on verso. wa Feb 29 (632) $350
BLAEU, WILLEM & BLAEU, JAN. - Somersettensis Comitatus. SomersetShire. [Amst., c.1645]. About 380mm by 500mm, hand-clored, framed. b May 30 (86) £170
BLAEU, WILLEM & BLAEU, JAN. - Suthsexia, vernacule Sussex. [Amst., c.1645]. 380mm by 520mm, framed. b Jan 31 (348) £220
BOWEN, EMANUEL. - An Accurate Map of the County of Sussex. L, [c.1765]. 500mm by 680mm, hand-colored, framed. S Mar 28 (145) £150
BRADSHAW, GEORGE. - Bradshaw's Map of the Railways.... L, [1852]. Size not given, dissected & joined in 2 sections & folded to 4to, in cloth case. Contemp hand-coloring. S Mar 28 (93) £150
BRAUN, GEORG & HOGENBERG, FRANZ. - Londinum feracissimi Angliae Regni metropolis. [Paris, 1575]. Ed by Francois de Belleforest. 320mm by 480mm, hand-colored. b Jan 31 (339) £550
BUY DE MORNAS, CLAUDE. - Insulae - Britannicae. Paris, 1761. 290mm by 455mm plus border, hand-colored. pba Oct 9 (61) $140
CHATELAIN, HENRI ABRAHAM. - Plan de la ville de Londres. [Amst., 1721]. 350mm by 460mm Hand-colored. S Oct 26 (359) £140 [Bankes]
DANCKERTS, CORNELIS. - London. L, 1832. 450mm by 2290mm Litho reproduction of 1647 panorama in 4 sheets, with panorama by N. Whittock. S Oct 26 (358) £750 [Rieden]
DAVIES, BENJAMIN REES. - Davies's New Map of the British Metropolis. L, 1870. 40 sections, 975mm by 1,000mm, hand-colored, orig linen backing, folding into orig 8vo cloth case. Some folds separating. sg May 9 (151) $150
DRAYTON, MICHAEL. - Cornwall. [L, 1612 or later]. 245mm by 320mm, hand-colored, framed. b May 30 (77) £170
FADEN, WILLIAM. - Battle of Guildford. With: Plan of the Battle Fought near Camden. L, 1787. 2 maps on 1 folio sheet, each 230mm by 210mm, troop positions hand-colored. sg May 9 (154) $600
FADEN, WILLIAM. - A New and Accurate Map of the County Twenty-Five Miles Round London. L, [c.1836]. 1200mm by 1300mm backed on linen with orig roller. Soiled & torn. S Oct 26 (360) £150 [Smith]

# MAPS

GREENWOOD, CHARLES & JOHN. - Map of London.... L, 21 Aug 1827. 6 double-page sheets. Bound with: Map of the County of Devon.... L, 20 Feb 1827. in contemp half calf; worn. b May 30 (83) £650

GREENWOOD, CHARLES & JOHN. - Map of...Cornwall.... L, 1 Sept 1827. 6 double-page sheets, folded to folio, in contemp half calf; spine def. Minor waterstains on lower corner margins. b May 30 (82) £260; b May 30 (83) £650

HOMANN, JOHANN BAPTIST. - Magnae Britanniae pars meridionalis.... Nuremberg, [c.1720]. 560mm by 480mm, hand-colored. pba Oct 9 (102) $200

HONDIUS, JODOCUS. - A General Plott and Description of the Fennes.... Amst., 1632. 435mm by 555mm, hand-colored, framed. b May 30 (81) £130

HONDIUS, JODOCUS. - Magnae Britanniae et Hiberniae tabula. Amst., 1631. 375mm by 510mm, hand-colored, framed. Split at fold without loss; some discoloration. b Sept 20 (257) £110

JANSSONIUS, JOANNES. - Edenburgum Scotiae Metropolis. [Amst., 1657, or later]. 345mm by 450mm. French text on verso. Browned in margins; crease parallel to vertical fold. sg May 9 (176) $600

MERCATOR, GERARD. - Eboracum, Lincolnia, Derbia, Staffordia.... [Amst., 1607 or later]. 365mm by 425mm, hand-colored. French text on verso. Margins trimmed with loss to sidenotes on verso. sg May 9 (205) $325

MERCATOR, GERARD. - Irlandiae Regnum. Antwerp, [after 1595]. 328mm by 410mm. pba Oct 9 (121) $500
Anr Ed. [Amst., 1628]. 330mm by 410mm, hand-colored, framed. S Mar 28 (121) £220

MERCATOR, GERARD. - Magnae Britanniae et Hiberniae tabula. [Amst., 1611, or later]. 375mm by 500mm. Dutch text on verso. Wear & repair to folds. S Mar 28 (94) £240

MERCATOR, GERARD. - Scotia Regnum. [Amst.: Hondius, c.1620]. 355mm by 460mm, hand-colored in outline. Dutch text on verso. Creased. sg Dec 7 (120A) $475

MERCATOR, GERARD. - Westmorlandia, Lancastria.... [Amst., 1607 or later]. 365mm by 420mm, hand-colored. French text on verso. Margins trimmed. sg May 9 (207) $325

MUENSTER, SEBASTIAN. - Das Kuenigreich Engellandt mit dem anstossenden Reich Schottlandt. Basel, [c.1550]. 250mm by 340mm image size. German text on verso. Some browning & soiling; marginal hole repaired. sg Dec 7 (128) $250

NOLIN, JEAN BAPTISTE. - Le Royaume d'Irlande. Paris, [1699]. 600mm by 460mm, hand-colored. S Mar 28 (122) £280

OGILBY, JOHN. - The Road from London to Aberistwith...... L, [1675]. 12.5 by 17.5 inches, framed. Some wrinkling. wa Feb 29 (629) £270

OGILBY, JOHN. - The Road from London to the Lands End.... L, [1675]. 320mm by 435mm. Tears & chips around margins; some soiling. pba Oct 9 (133) $200

OGILBY, JOHN. - Map of the Road from York to West-Chester. L, [1675]. With: The Continuation of the Road from York to West-Chester; The Extended Road from Oakham to Richmond. 3 maps. 330mm by 445mm Hand-colored. Some spotting. S Oct 26 (361) £150 [Oak No]

ORTELIUS, ABRAHAM. - Angliae Regni florentissimi nova descriptio.... [Antwerp, 1598]. 380mm by 465mm Text in French. S Oct 26 (353) £300 [Hepner]

ORTELIUS, ABRAHAM. - Angliae, Scotiae, et Hiberniae.... [Antwerp, 1595]. 340mm by 490mm, hand-colored. Latin text on verso. S Mar 28 (96) £260

ORTELIUS, ABRAHAM. - Cambriae typus.... [Antwerp, 1573, or later]. 370mm by 500mm. Spanish text on verso.. b Jan 31 (351) £240

ORTELIUS, ABRAHAM. - Scotiae tabula. [Antwerp, 1573, or later]. 360mm by 485mm, mtd. b Sept 20 (287) £100
Anr Ed. Antwerp, 1584. 360mm by 470mm, hand-colored in outline. Latin text on verso. sg Dec 7 (143A) $550

PRIESTLEY, JOSEPH. - Map of the Inland Navigation, Canals and Rail Roads. Wakefield: R. Nichols, 1830. Map in 54 sections, mtd & dissected on linen, 1,915mm by 1,700mm, hand-colored in outline & folded into contemp calf gilt case. S Mar 28 (149) £180

PTOLEMAEUS, CLAUDIUS. - Tabula Europ. sexta Italiae. [Strassburg, 1513]. 374mm by 575mm. Waterstains; sidenotes shaved on 1 side. b Dec 5 (98) £1,000

PTOLEMAEUS, CLAUDIUS. - Tabulae Europae I. [Strassburg, 1513 or later]. 410mm by 580mm. Restored tear affecting upper centerfold. b Jan 31 (311) £520
Anr Ed. [Lyons, 1535?]. 298mm by 410mm. Latin text on verso. b Sept 20 (258) £200

ROBERT DE VAUGONDY, GILLES & DIDIER. - Le Royaume d'Ecosse. Paris, 1751. 490mm by 625mm, later hand-coloring. Browned, mainly in margins. sg Dec 7 (157) $200

ROBERT DE VAUGONDY, GILLES & DIDIER. - Royaume d'Irlande divise en ses quatre provinces.... Paris, 1750. 495mm by 625mm, hand-colored at a later date. Dampstain in right margin; closed tear which has browned. sg Dec 7 (158) $300

ROCQUE, JOHN. - A Topographical Map of the Count of Surrey. L, [1770]. 9 sheets, dissected & backed on linen; strengthened at folds. Hand-colored. Browned. S Oct 26 (364) £350 [Bankes]

SAXTON, CHRISTOPHER. - Westmorlandie et Cumberlandiae Comit.... L, [1579]. 385mm by 490mm, colored in a contemp hand Some spotting. b Jan 31 (331) £1,100

SAXTON, CHRISTOPHER & LEA, PHILIP. - Devon-Shire Described.... L, [1732 or later]. 380mm by 425mm, contemp hand-coloring. Marginal staining & fraying affecting surface; some spotting. S Mar 28 (109) £340

SCHENK, PETER. - Novissima et accuratissima regni et insulae Hiberniae. Amst., [1690]. 590mm by 490mm, contemp hand-coloring. Some Ms annotations. S Mar 28 (123) £150

SEALE, R. W. - Map of the County of Middlesex. L, [1787]. 510mm by 720mm, hand-colored, framed. S Mar 28 (137) £380

SENEX, JOHN. - A New Map of Ireland. L, [1721]. 565mm by 485mm, hand-colored in outline. Fold

tears extending into image. sg May 9 (248) $550
SPEED, JOHN. - Anno Darbieshire described 1666. L: Bassett & Chiswell, [1676]. 382mm by 510mm, framed & double-glazed. Hand-colored. Some spotting. S Oct 26 (350) £320 [Hepner]
SPEED, JOHN. - Barkshire Described. L: Bassett & Chiswell, [1676]. 380mm by 505mm, hand-colored, framed. Some spotting. S Mar 28 (91) £200
SPEED, JOHN. - The Bishoprick and Citie of Durham. L: T. Bassett & R. Chiswell, [1676, or later]. 385mm by 505mm, hand-colored, framed. S Mar 28 (110) £120
SPEED, JOHN. - Buckingham, both Shyre and Shiretown Described. L, 1610 [1646?]. 380mm by 500mm. Fully colored. Marginal discoloration; small repair to fold on verso. CE Nov 8 (213) $150
SPEED, JOHN. - Cambridgeshire. L: Overton, [1740]. 385mm by 525mm, hand-colored in outline with borders fully colored. Some browning & staining. sg May 9 (254) $600
SPEED, JOHN. - Cambridgeshire Described.... L, 1610 [but 1676, or later]. 15.75 by 21 inches, hand-colored, framed. Frayed along centerfold. wd Nov 15 (91) $600
SPEED, JOHN. - Cornwall. L: T. Bassett & R. Chiswell, 1610 [but 1676, or later]. 395mm by 520mm, hand-colored, framed. b May 30 (78) £380
SPEED, JOHN. - The Countie and Cities of Lyncolne Described. L, 1610. Engraved by Hondius. 380mm by 500mm. Fully colored. Marginal discoloration. CE Nov 8 (216) $150
SPEED, JOHN. - The Countie of Leinster. L: Sudbury & Humble, 1610. 380mm by 510mm. Split at lower central crease without loss; small hole near centerfold; marginal dampstaining. pba Oct 9 (168) $275
Anr Ed. L, [1676]. No size given, hand-colored in outline, with decorations colored in full, framed. cb June 25 (1749) $550
SPEED, JOHN. - The Countie Westmorland and Kendale.... L, [c.1640]. 380mm by 515mm. Minor marginal repairs. b Jan 31 (332) £120
SPEED, JOHN. - The County Palatine of Chester. L: Sudbury & Humble, [1612]. 380mm by 510mm, framed & double-glazed. Hand-colored. Small repair to fold. S Oct 26 (349) £600 [Hepner]
SPEED, JOHN. - The County Pallatine of Lancaster Described. L: Sudbury & Humble, [1612]. 380mm by 510mm, framed & double-glazed. Hand-colored. Repair to fold. S Oct 26 (357) £900 [Hepner]
SPEED, JOHN. - Devonshire with Excester Described. L: J. Sudburi & G. Humble, [1614, or later]. 375mm by 510mm, hand-colored, framed. b May 30 (80) £250
SPEED, JOHN. - Hartfordshire Described. L: G. Humble, [1627 or later]. 380mm by 505mm, hand-colored. b Jan 31 (322) £170
SPEED, JOHN. - Holy Iland; Garnsey; Farne; Iarsey. L, [1676]. 385mm by 510mm, hand-colored. 4 maps on one double page engraved mapsheet. English text on verso. b Jan 31 (314) £160
SPEED, JOHN. - The Invasions of England and Ireland...since the Conquest. L: G. Humble, [1627, or later]. 405mm by 510mm, framed. b Sept 20 (291) £640

Anr Ed. L: T. Bassett & R. Chiswell, [1676 or later]. 375mm by 510mm, hand-colored. Split at fold. S Mar 28 (112) £320
SPEED, JOHN. - Kent. L, [1627]. 370mm by 510mm, framed & glazed. Hand-colored. Worn at fold. S Oct 26 (356) £310 [Hepner]
Anr Ed. L, [c.1650]. 380mm by 485mm, hand-colored, framed. b May 30 (84) £180
Anr Ed. L, [1676 or later]. 370mm by 510mm, hand-colored in outline, framed. Repaired at lower fold. S Mar 28 (126) £380
SPEED, JOHN. - The Kingdome of Great Britaine and Ireland. L, 1610 [but 1614, or later]. 380mm by 510mm, hand-colored in outline, with decorations fully colored. English text on verso. pba Oct 9 (169) $1,000
SPEED, JOHN. - The Kingdome of Irland. L, 1610. Engraved by Hondius. 380mm by 500mm. Fully colored, with 6 vignettes in lower left corner. Marginal discoloration. CE Nov 8 (215) $800
SPEED, JOHN. - The Kingdome of Scotland. L: Rea, [1662 or later]. 400mm by 525mm, hand-colored, framed. Some discoloration. b Sept 20 (288) £420
SPEED, JOHN. - Leicester both Countye and Citie Described. L: J. Sudbury & G. Humble, 1610. 380mm by 515mm, hand-colored, framed. Latin text on verso. b Jan 31 (337) £170
SPEED, JOHN. - Midle-sex Described.... L: Bassett & Chiswell, [1676]. 385mm by 520mm, hand-colored, framed. English text on verso. b Jan 31 (341) £360
Anr copy. 380mm by 510mm, framed. S Mar 28 (138) £420
SPEED, JOHN. - The North and East Ridings of York-shire. L: J. Sudbury & G. Humbell, 1610 [but 1614, or later]. 395mm by 520mm, hand-colored, framed. Fold wear. S Mar 28 (150) £420
SPEED, JOHN. - Somerset-Shire Described.... L: Sudbury & Humble, 1610 [1611]. 375mm by 505mm, hand-colored, framed. Marginal tears & repairs. pn Dec 7 (197) £240
Anr Ed. L: Sudbury & Humble, 1610 [1627]. 375mm by 505mm, hand-colored, framed. Fold repaired. S Mar 28 (144) £220
SPEED, JOHN. - Surrey Described and Divided into Hundreds. L, 1610. Engraved by Hondius. 380mm by 500mm. Fully colored. Tape repair; tear along fold. CE Nov 8 (218) $150
SPEED, JOHN. - Wales. L: Roger Rea, 1650. 385mm by 510mm, framed. b Sept 20 (295) £300
SPEED, JOHN. - Wight Island. L: J. Sudbury & G. Humbell, [1610, or later]. 385mm by 510mm, framed. English text on verso. b Sept 20 (277) £160
SPEED, JOHN. - Wilshire. L, 1610. Engraved by Hondius. 380mm by 500mm. Fully colored. Marginal tape stains & some discoloration. CE Nov 8 (220) $160
SPEED, JOHN. - York Shire. L: J. Sudbury & G. Humble, 1610 [but 1627, or later]. 385mm by 505mm. Centerfold repaired. b Jan 31 (357) £100
Anr Ed. L: Sudbury & Humble, [1612]. 380mm by 510mm, framed & double-glazed. Hand-colored. Repair to lower fold; small flaw at upper fold. S Oct 26 (366) £360 [Hepner]
STRYPE, JOHN. - A New Plan of the City of London, West-

minster and Southwark. L, [c.1720]. 490mm by 670mm, hand-colored, framed. S Mar 28 (132) £350
SYMONSON, PHILIP. - A New Description of Kent. L, 1659. 520mm by 780mm. Small loss of surface affecting left border. b Jan 31 (329) £220
WAGHENAER, LUCAS JANSZ. - Caerte der Noordt custe vu Engelandt... van Robinhodes baij tot Cocket Eijlandt.... Amst., [1588]. 325mm by 510mm Hand-colored. Fold worn; 2 small holes. S Oct 26 (362) £150 [Ingol Maps]

### Pacific Ocean

BELLIN, JACQUES NICOLAS. - Plan de l'isle de France. [Paris, 1753]. 495mm by 715mm S Oct 26 (564) £210 [Chelsea Gal.]
DE WIT, FREDERICK. - Magnum Mare del Zur cum Insula California. Amst., [c.1675]. 490mm by 570mm, contemp hand-coloring. Cartouche repaired. S June 13 (647) £750
GOOS, PIETER. - Paskaerte zynde t'Oosterdeel van Oost Indien met alle de Eylanden daer ontrendt geleegen. Amst., [c.1670]. 440mm by 550mm, hand-colored. Tear at left edge. pba Apr 25 (38) £1,500
JANSSONIUS, JOANNES. - Mar del Zur Hispanis Mare Pacificum. [Amst., 1650]. 440mm by 545mm, hand-colored in outline. Dutch text on verso. Break at top of vertical fold extending into image; minor soiling. sg May 9 (181) £1,200
KEULEN, JOANNES VAN. - Pascaert vande Zuyd See. Amst., [1683]. 520mm by 600mm Browning. S Oct 26 (605) £850 [Potter]
LA PEROUSE, JEAN FRANCOIS GALAUP DE. - Carte des Cotes de l'Amerique et de l'Asie depuis la California jusqu'a Macao.... [Paris, c.1797]. 490mm by 690mm. Some soiling. pba Oct 9 (111) £300
ORTELIUS, ABRAHAM. - Maris Pacifici.... Antwerp, 1589. 345mm by 505mm, hand-colored. Browned & dampstained; some holes; mtd to stiff bd. Sold w.a.f. sg Dec 7 (141) £1,100
Anr Ed. [Antwerp], 1589 [but 1603]. 350mm by 500mm, hand-colored, mtd. CE June 15 (372) $3,500
SCHEUCHZER, J. C. - Imperium Japonicum. L, [1627]. S Oct 26 (561) £1,200 [Map House]
STEURS, FRANCOIS VICTOR ALPHONSE DE. - Ile de Java. [Amst., 1830?]. 620mm by 1278mm, in sunk mount. 2 sheets joined. S Oct 26 (562) £180 [Indone]

### Polar Regions

BLAEU, WILLEM & BLAEU, JAN. - Regiones sub polo arctico. [Amst., 1640]. 415mm by 530mm, hand-colored.. Cut close, backed & remargined; 4 worm holes. bba June 6 (286) £200 [Winston]
SANSON D'ABBEVILLE, NICOLAS. - Les Deux Poles Arcticque ou Septentrional.... Paris, 1657. 395mm by 535mm, hand-colored in outline. Edges soiled. sg Dec 7 (160) £425

### Tasmania

WYLD, JAMES. - Tasmania, or, Van Diemen's Land. L, [1850]. 335mm by 790mmm, backed with linen, sectioned for folding, hand-colored. pba Oct 9 (191) $100

### United States

— Geological Map of a Part of the State of California Explored in 1853 by Lieut. R. S. Williamson.... [Wash., c.1855]. 560mm by 410mm, hand-colored. pba Oct 9 (63) $150
— Johnson's New Railroad & Township Copper Plate Map of Ohio, Indiana & Kentucky.... NY, 1858. 675mm by 760mm, hand-colored. Tape repairs. pba Oct 9 (107) $300
— Johnson's Texas. NY, 1866. 400mm by 558mm, hand-colored. pba Oct 9 (108) $120
— Map of Property Belonging to Nichs. Luquer in the 6th Ward of the City of Brooklyn To Be Sold At Auction by James Bleeker & Sons.... NY, [1835]. 18 by 24.75 inches. Some tears with loss; pencil marks; minor soiling. wa Feb 29 (613) $325
— Map of the United States and Their Territories.... NY, 1850. 1,100mm by 971mm, mtd on linen. Some loss of paper along margins & fold lines; some staining & soiling. cb June 25 (1755) $850
— Map Showing Portions of Adjacent Counties and Yosemite Park Reserve Including the Survey of the Merced River Railroad of the Yosemite Valley Railroad from Merced to Yosemite National Park. [N.p.]: Yosemite Valley Railroad, 1906. 29 by 70 inches, rolled, housed in tube container. pba Feb 12 (231) $600
— Military Map of the States of Kentucky and Tennessee.... Cincinnati, 1863. About 88 by 48 inches, linen-backed, folding to c.7 by 13 inches, with outline coloring. Some fold breaks & repairs. NH July 21 (212) $220
— The Northern Route to Idaho and the Pacific Ocean. Saint Paul, [1864]. With: C. A. F. Morris, Minnesota Route..., map 17-1/4 by 41-1/2 inches, cloth folder; spine ends nicked, spine of folder worn. Hand-colored. Text browned; map folds torn. Robbins copy. pba Mar 21 (227) $9,000
— Official Map of Chinatown in San Francisco. San Francisco: Board of Supervisors, July 1885. 8.5 by 21.5 inches. Repaired fold tear. pba Feb 12 (269) $225
— Plan of Central Park. NY: M. Dripps, [n.d.]. 956mm by 216mm, contemp hand-coloring, folded into orig cloth; worn, spine ends torn, pastedown split & partly peeled back. Some tears to folds & margins; 1 corner torn away affecting surface; ink stamps; some foxing & dampstaining. cb Oct 17 (167) $250
— Rand, McNally & Co's Indexed County and Township map of Arizona. Chicago, [1881]. 12mo, ptd wraps. Folding color map & 14 pp of text. Small lower are of map stained. wa Feb 29 (592) $230
— Reconnaissance of the Western Coast of the United States....From San Francisco to Umpquah River. [Wash.: U. S. Coast Survey, 1854]. 24.5 by 22 inches, mtd & shrink-wrapped. Margins chipped; some wrinkling. George Davidson's copy, sgd & annotated. pba Feb 12 (33) $160
— Die Vereinigten Staaten von Nordamerika. Nuremberg, 1799. 21 by 25.5 inches, hand-colored in outline.. Left margin cut close; dampstain to lower right. wa Feb 29 (627) $120
ANVILLE, JEAN BAPTISTE BOURGUIGNON D'. - Carte de la

Louisiane. Paris, 1752. 530mm by 920mm, hand-colored in outline. Minor soiling & marginal tears. sg Dec 7 (55) $750

ARROWSMITH, AARON. - A Map of the United States of North America. L, [1802]. 2 parts, together 48 by 54.5 inches, hand-colored, cartouche uncolored. Upper section right margin with 2 closed tears to plate mark. wa Feb 29 (624) $1,600

ARROWSMITH, AARON. - North America. From Arrowsmith's large Map. L, 1811. 185mm by 240mm, modern hand-coloring. pba Oct 9 (28) $100

ARROWSMITH, JOHN. - Map of Texas.... L, 1843. 610mm by 498mm, hand-colored in outline. Some tears; browned along edges. cb June 25 (1751) $8,000

BARBER, J. H. - Map of the State of New York. New Haven, 1852. 325mm by 370mm, hand-colored in outline, folding into orig 16mo bd case. sg Dec 7 (130) $175

BARKER, WILLIAM. - Georgia from the latest Authorities. [Phila., 1794-95]. 225mm by 405mm, backed with cloth. Fingersoiling; 3 pairs of pinholes with wrinkles along lower third of map. cb Oct 17 (211) $130

BARTHOLOMEW, JOHN. - Western States, Including California, Oregon.... Edin.: A. & C. Black, [c.1861]. 418mm by 555mm. pba Oct 9 (32) $180

BLAEU, WILLEM & BLAEU, JAN. - Nova Belgica et Anglia Nova. [Amst., 1635 or later]. 390mm by 505mm, hand-colored in outline, framed. Sold w.a.f. sg Dec 7 (60) $1,100

BLAEU, WILLEM & BLAEU, JAN. - Virginiae partis australis, et Floridae, partis orientalis.... [Amst., 1640]. 387mm by 507mm, contemp hand-coloring in outline & 2 fully colored cartouches. Dutch text on verso. Fold tear & repair; some soiling; 2 marginal tape repairs on verso; pencil notes in bottom margin. cb Oct 17 (214) $850

Anr copy. 280mm by 500mm, hand-colored in outline. Latin text on verso. Soiled; repaired. pba Oct 9 (39) $800

Anr copy. 15.25 by 20 inches, hand-colored in outline, cartouche colored in full. Dutch text on verso. wa Feb 29 (679) $700

BONNE, RIGOBERT. - Carte de la partie nord, des Etats Unis.... Paris, [c.1780]. 213mm by 320mm, hand-colored in outline, framed. CE June 15 (308) $130

Anr copy. 9 by 13.5 inches, hand-colored. F June 20 (919) $130

BOWEN, EMANUEL. - A New and Accurate Map of Louisiana, with Parts of Florida and Canada, and the Adjacent Countries.... [L, 1750 or later]. 340mm by 420mm, outline coloring, framed. CE June 15 (309) $160

BOWEN, EMANUEL. - A New and Accurate Map of New Jersey, Pensilvania.... L, [c.1760]. 360mm by 435mm, hand-colored in outline. Vertical fold partly reinforced on verso; some short creases. sg May 9 (121) $550

BUCHON, JEAN ALEXANDRE. - Carte geographique, statistique et historique de la Floride. Paris, 1825. 28.8cm by 24cm, hand-colored. Splitting at lower central crease. pba Aug 8 (111) $110

CAMPBELL, ARCHIBALD. - Sketch of the Northern Frontiers of Georgia.... L: W. Faden, 1780. 703mm by 602mm, backed with cloth. Small tears & abrasions occasionally extending into map area; fold breaks. cb Oct 17 (225) $1,100

CAREY, MATHEW. - Connecticut. Phila., 1814. 320mm by 380mm, hand-colored in outline. Browned along vertical fold. sg May 9 (138) $250

CAREY, MATHEW. - Plat of the Seven Ranges of Townships...N.W. of the River Ohio.... Phila., 1814. 14 by 13.25 inches plus margins, hand-colored in outline. Small breaks at fold ends. bbc Feb 26 (90) $270

CARRIGAIN, PHILIP. - New Hampshire. Concord NH, 1816. 60 by 46 inches plus margins, on wooden rollers. Worn, with 1 closed hole & damp spots in upper left. NH June 1 (209) $3,600

CARY, JOHN. - A New Map of Part of the United States.... L, 1811. 530mm by 595mm, hand-colored. Fold browned. sg May 9 (140) $350

CHACE, J. - Rockingham County, New Hampshire. Phila., 1857. About 48 by 60 inches, on wooden rollers. Some roughness & tender spots at top & bottom; 3 small places where the surface is gone. NH June 1 (210) $240

COLTON, JOSEPH H. - Colton's Railroad & Township Map. NY, 1871. Size not given, hand-colored, laid into cloth covers. Wrinkled; fold breaks. NH July 21 (214) $100

COLTON, JOSEPH H. - Colton's Railroad & Township Map of the State of New York. NY, 1885. 640mm by 750mm, hand-colored, folding into 12mo cloth case. sg Dec 7 (132) $300

COLTON, JOSEPH H. - Map of the United States.... NY, 1849. 21in by 19in, orig cloth; covers worn. Large folded map with text. Tears in folds. Larson copy. pba Sept 28 (583) $800

DELISLE, GUILLAUME. - Carte de la Louisiane et du Cours de Mississippi. [Amst., 1733?]. 435mm by 595mm, hand-colored in outline. Minor soiling. pba Apr 25 (28) $1,500

DERBY, GEORGE HORATIO. - The Sacramento Valley.... [Wash., 1850]. 550mm by 445mm. pba Oct 9 (91) $275

DISTURNELL, JOHN. - Mapa de los Estados Unidos de Mejico. NY, 1847. 10th Ed. 1,042mm by 745mm, attached to orig cloth folder. Hand-colored in outline. Some fold splits & tears. Streeter copy. cb June 25 (1730) $8,000

Revised Ed. 29 by 40.5 inches, cloth covers. Hand-colored Nicks at folds.. Robbins copy. pba Mar 21 (225) $10,000

DUVOTENAY, T. - Etats-Unis. [Paris, c.1840]. 178mm by 230mm, hand-colored. Left margin ragged. pba Apr 25 (35) $150

EDDY, JOHN H. - The State of New York with Part of the Adjacent States. NY, 1818. 970mm by 1,115mm, NY fully colored, adjacent states in outline, orig linen backing. sg Dec 7 (134) $900

ELWE, JAN BAREND. - Amerique spetentrionale divisee in ses principales parties. Amst., 1792. 480mm by 590mm, hand-colored. Soiling over-all. sg May 9 (153) $750

EPPINGER, J. & BAKER, F. C. - Map of Texas, Compiled from surveys recorded in the General Land Office... 1851. NY, 1851. 760mm by 590mm, hand-colored. Some tears & loss at folds. cb June 25 (1752)

# MAPS

$5,000

FADEN, WILLIAM. - A Plan of the Town...of Charlestown in South Carolina. L, 1789. 525mm by 695mm. Closed tears into image. sg Dec 7 (86) $1,300

FADEN, WILLIAM. - The United States of North America.... L, 11 Feb 1796. 531mm by 634mm, contemp hand-coloring in outline, part full coloring & full-color cartouche. Tears at ends of centerfold crossing imprint line at bottom & with tape-repair on verso; tear at upper right through border & into map area. cb Oct 17 (226) $700

GODDARD, G. H. - Britton and Rey's Reduced Map of the State of California.... San Francisco, 1858. 16 by 13 inches, cloth folder; rubbed spots. Hand-colored. Torn at folds. Robbins copy. pba Mar 21 (226) $3,000

GOODRICH, A. T. - Map of the Hudson between Sandy Hook & Sandy Hill with the Post Road between New York and Albany. NY, 1820. About 8 feet, 2 inches by 9.5 inches, backed with cloth, rolled into lea-covered tube; lacking ends to tube holder. NH July 21 (216) $1,400

GOOS, PIETER. - Paskaerte van Nova Granada en t'Eylandt California. Amst.: P. Goos, 1666. 445mm by 545mm, laid down on paper. Some browning & staining. CE June 15 (341) $4,200

GRAY, ANDREW B. - Topographical Sketch of the Southernmost Point of the Port of San Diego... Boundary Between the United States and Mexican Republic.... [Wash., 1860]. 17.5 by 22.75 inches, uncolored. Minor foxing & marginal staining. wa Feb 29 (619) $130

HACQ, J. M. - Carte de la Cote Orientale de l'Amerique Septentrionale. Paris, 1834. 660mm by 955mm. Closed tear into image; closed marginal tears. sg May 9 (160) $350

HARTMANN, CARL. - Generalkarte von Californien. Weimar, 1849. 15-1/2in by 11-1/4in, archival bd, matted shrinkwrapped. Few defs at folds. Larson copy. pba Sept 28 (585) $200

HARTMANN, CARL. - Specialkarte von Californien: Die Wichtigsten Hafen und Rheden Sowie dei Goldregion von Californien. Weimar, 1849. 14in by 9-1/2in, archival bd, matted shrinkwrapped. 2 marginal tears & 4 defs at folds. Larson copy. pba Sept 28 (586) $275

HASSLER, FERDINAND RUDOLPH. - Map of New York Bay and Harbor and the Environs. Wash., 1844. 4 (of 6) sheets, each 26.5 by 36 inches. Some marginal wear & tears. wa Feb 29 (650) $700

HILL, JOHN. - This Plan of the City of Philadelphia.... L: John & Josiah Boydell, 1 Jan, 1798. State II. 675mm by 945mm backed on linen. Dissected in 18 sections. Stained. S Oct 26 (480) £4,400 [Smith]

HOLME, THOMAS. - A Portraiture of the City of Philadelphia.... Phila., 1812. 11.75 by 17.75 inches, laid down, framed. Lower left dampstained; some browning, foxing & spotting. F Mar 28 (760) $925

HOMANN, JOHANN BAPTIST. - Amplissimae regionis Mississippi seu Provinciae Ludovicianae.... Nuremberg, [c.1720, or later]. 500mm by 590mm, hand-colored. Margins trimmed; some foxing. sg Dec 7 (93) $1,600

# AMERICAN BOOK PRICES CURRENT

Anr copy. 495mm by 590mm, Minor dampstaining along side margins, affecting image; browning along fold. sg May 9 (163) $1,600

Anr Ed. Nuremberg, [c.1687 or later]]. 19 by 22.7 inches, later hand-coloring, cartouches uncolored. Some worming at center of bottom margin. wa Feb 29 (626) $850

HOMANN, JOHANN BAPTIST. - Virginia, Marylandia et Carolina. Nuremberg, [c.1720]. 490mm by 580mm, partly colored, mtd. Cut close; tears & repairs; chipped at bottom. CE June 15 (315) $650

HOMANN'S HEIRS. - Dominia Anglorum in America Septentrionali. [Nuremberg, c.1730 or later]. 510mm by 570mm, hand-colored. Some worming on image & margins; tear at lower fold just touching image. sg Dec 7 (97) $400

Anr copy. Size not given, Repaired, top & bottom margins trimmed. sg Dec 7 (98) $425

HONDIUS, JODOCUS. - Virginiae item et Floridae...descriptio. Amst., [1606-9]. 340mm by 483mm, hand-colored. Repaired; chipped. pba Oct 9 (104) $950

HOPKINS, GRIFFITH MORGAN. - New Topographical Map of the State of Connecticut. Phila., 1859. 24 sections, 1,425mm by 1,800mm, hand-colored, linen-backed. sg May 9 (148) $1,500

JANSSONIUS, JOANNES. - Nova Belgica et Anglia Nova. Amst., [c.1647]. 390mm by 510mm, hand-colored in outline. French text on verso. Fold repaired on verso. sg May 9 (183) $1,700

JANSSONIUS, JOANNES. - Virginiae partis australis, et Floridae, partis orientalis.... [Amst., c.1640]. 385mm by 500mm, hand-colored in outline. Latin text on verso. Browning along vertical fold; repaired marginal wormholes. sg May 9 (185) $800

JEFFERSON, T. H. - Map of the Emigrant Road from Independence Mo. to San Francisco California. San Francisco, 1945. One of 300. 8-3/4 by 5-3/4 inches, orig cloth. With 4-part folding facsimile map. Robbins copy. pba Mar 21 (170) $160

JEFFERYS, THOMAS. - Plan of the Siege of Charlestown in South Carolina. L, 1787 [but 1794]. 270mm by 310mm. Minor soiling. sg May 9 (187) $425

JEFFERYS, THOMAS. - The Western Coast of Louisiana.... L, 1775. Size not given. Some soiling & spotting; tear at lower centerfold not affecting image. cb June 25 (1753) $1,500

KELLOGG, E. B. & E. C. - Map of the State of New York. Hartford, [c.1846]. 690mm by 835mm, hand-colored, folding to 8vo, in lea gilt case. Map mtd in case with cellotape, which has left marginal stain. sg Dec 7 (135) $325

LA PEROUSE, JEAN FRANCOIS GALAUP DE. - Carte Particuliere de la cote du nord-ouest de la Amerique.... Paris, [1797]. 21-1/2in by 29in Short tear at centerfold. Larson copy. pba Sept 28 (130) $120

LA PEROUSE, JEAN FRANCOIS GALAUP DE. - Plan de la baie de Monterey.... Paris, [1797]. 14-1/4in by 20-1/2in Larson copy. pba Sept 28 (133) $100

LA PEROUSE, JEAN FRANCOIS GALAUP DE. - Plan du port de St. Francois.... Paris, [1797]. 20in by 15in Marginal tears & old folds. Larson copy. pba Sept 28 (135) $200

LAURIE, ROBERT & WHITTLE, JAMES. - A New and general

Map of the Southern Dominions belonging to The United States of America.... L, 1794. 525mm by 670mm, hand-colored in outline. sg Dec 7 (115) $1,300

LAY, AMOS. - Map of the State of New York. NY, 1814. 40-section map, 1,315mmm by 1,330mm, hand-colored in outline. Browned at edges of each section; 1 worm hole; tears at intersecting sections; linen-backed. sg Dec 7 (136) $750

LOS ANGELES. - Plan of a Part of the City of Los Angeles Showing the Tract of the Aliso Homestead Association. Los Angeles, [c.1870s]. 17.25 by 21.25 inches, mtd on bd. Marginal tears tape-repaired; some wrinkling & chips. pba Feb 12 (426) $300

LOTTER, MATTHIAS ALBRECHT. - Plan of the City and Environs of Philadelphia. [Phila.], 1777. 590mm by 460mm, hand-colored. Tap remnants to margins. CE June 15 (346) $1,400

MARRIOTT, FREDERICK. - Graphic Chart of the City and County of San Francisco.... San Francisco, 1876. 51mm by 76mm, framed. Fold tears; mtd; some chips; small stamp at bottom. pba Oct 9 (151) $650

MELISH, JOHN. - United States of America. Phila., [c.1820]. 440mm by 555mm, hand-colored. sg May 9 (202) $450

MERCATOR, GERARD. - Nova Belgica et Anglia Nova. Amst.: J. Jansson, [1647]. 385mm by 497mm, hand-colored in outline. French text on verso. Repair to lower centerfold on verso; tear at upper centerfold; some soiling. pba Aug 8 (120) $600

MERCATOR, GERARD. - Nova Virginiae tabula. Amst., [1630, or later]. 370mm by 475mm, hand-colored in outline. Browned; fold chipped, framed. CE June 15 (307) $1,000

MITCHELL, SAMUEL AUGUSTUS. - County Map of Texas. Phila., 1870. 235mm by 302mm, hand-colored. pba Oct 9 (124) $140

MITCHELL, SAMUEL AUGUSTUS. - County Map of the State of California. Phila., 1874. 34cm by 27cm, hand-colored. pba Apr 25 (53) $100

MITCHELL, SAMUEL AUGUSTUS. - Mitchell's National Map of the American Republic. Phila., 1844. 1,000mm by 1,240mm, hand-colored, on wooden rollers. Yellowed from lacquer. sg Dec 7 (122) $900

MITCHELL, SAMUEL AUGUSTUS. - Mitchell's New Map of Texas, Oregon and California.... Phila., 1846. 22in by 20-1/2in, text in lea, map mounted & shrinkwrapped; covers rebacked & repaired. Folded color map. Larson copy. pba Sept 28 (588) $2,750

MITCHELL, SAMUEL AUGUSTUS. - Mitchell's Reference and Distance Map of the United States by J. H. Young. Phila., 1834. 1,255mm by 1,635mm, colored in outline, mtd on linen with rollers. Some tears & chipping. pba Oct 9 (127) $340

MOLL, HERMAN. - Virginia and Maryland. L, [1740s]. 272mm by 200mm, contemp hand-coloring in outline, framed. Some spotting & marginal worming. cb Oct 17 (239) $200

NEW YORK (COLONY & STATE). - Map of Jefferson County from Recent Surveys.... Watertown NY, 1849. 19 by 23 inches, on rollers. Some staining. NH July 21 (217) $355

ORD, EDWARD OTHO CRESAP. - Topographical Sketch of the Gold and Quicksilver District of California. Phi-

la., 1848. 21-1/4in by 15-1/4in, mounted, matted & shrinkwrapped. Larson copy. pba Sept 28 (590) $350

Anr Ed. Wash., 1848. 542mm by 390mm. Margins trimmed & chipped. pba Oct 9 (134) $300

ORD, EDWARD OTHO CRESAP. - Upper Mines and Lower Mines or Mormon Diggings. [Wash., 1848]. 8-1/4in by 6-1/4in, mounted, matted & shrinkwrapped. 2 maps on 1 plate. Larson copy. pba Sept 28 (591) $130

PREUSS, CHARLES. - Map of Oregon and Upper California from the Surveys of John Charles Fremont and Other Authorities. Wash., 1848. 16-5/8in by 19-3/4in, disbound; rebacked. Larson copy. pba Sept 28 (459) $180

ROBERT DE VAUGONDY, GILLES & DIDIER. - Partie de l'Amerique septentrionale.... Paris, 1755. 485mm by 620mm, later hand-coloring. Some soiling; horizontal crease. sg Dec 7 (152) $325

Anr Ed. [Paris, c.1863-83]. 18.8 by 24.7 inches, hand-colored in outline. Waterstain to left margin. wa Feb 29 (625) $400

RUSSELL, JOHN. - Plan of the City of Washington. L, 1800. 420mm by 540mm. Some fold breaks repaired; browning. sg May 9 (234) $400

Anr copy. 15.5 by 20.5 inches. Some fold breaks repaired; tear in upper right margin. wa Feb 29 (694) $550

Anr copy. 16 by 21 inches, cut into 6 sections, mtd on linen, framed wa Feb 29 (695) $350

SAUTHIER, CLAUDE J. - A Chorographical Map of the Province of New York.... L: Faden, 1779. 73 by 56 inches, browned, worn along creased; reinforced. NH Sept 16 (267) $2,800

SAUTHIER, CLAUDE J. - A Map of the Provinces of New-York and New-Jersey.... Augsburg, 1777. 745mm by 560mm, contemp body color. Backed. S Mar 28 (308) £700

SAYER, ROBERT & BENNETT, JOHN. - The Country Twenty-Five Miles Round New YOrk.... L, 1 Nov 1776. 612mm by 476mm overall, some outline coloring, framed. Fold repairs; some staining along vertical center fold; some soiling. CE Sept 27 (178) $5,000

SCHRAEMBL, FRANZ ANTON. - [Untitled map of the central portion of the United States] Vienna, [c.1800]. 535mm by 625mm, hand-colored. sg May 9 (246) $700

SCULL, NICHOLAS & HEAP, GEORGE. - A Map of Philadelphia, and Parts Adjacent. [Phila., 1752]. 529mm by 313mm, hand-colored in outline, mtd on linen. Some chipping. P June 5 (98) $47,500

SOLOMON, R. A. - Map of Havre de Grace, Harford Co., Md. [N.p.], 1856. 26 by 35.5 inches plus margins. Fold breaks; some soiling. bbc Feb 26 (93) $280

SPEED, JOHN. - A Map of New England and New York. L, [1676]. 385mm by 505mm, later hand-coloring in outline. Closed tears on image. sg Dec 7 (169) $1,700

Anr copy. 14.75 by 19.5 inches. English text on verso. Repair to lower right margin. wa Feb 29 (655) $1,500

STOCKDALE, JOHN. - Part of the United States of America. L, 1798. 410mm by 465mm, hand-colored in out-

line, perhaps later. pba Apr 25 (76) $225
TIDDEMAN, M. - Draught of New York from the Hook to New York Town. L: J. Mount & T. Page, [c.1758]. 450mm by 580mm, hand-colored. Trimmed; lower margin stained & repaired. CE June 15 (337) $400
TIRION, ISAAC. - Grondvlakte van Nieuw Orleans; De uitloop [De Oostelyke ingang] van de Rivier Missisippi. [Amst., c.1770, or later]. Street plan & 2 maps on 1 plate. 335mm by 450mm, hand-colored. Soiling along folds. sg May 9 (256) $450
UNION PACIFIC RAILWAY. - The Correct Map of the United States, Union Pacific Railroad, the Overland Route and Connections. [N.p.]: Rand McNally & Co., 1896. 890mm by 1,350mm, mtd on linen, overptd in red to show Union Pacific lines.; Small loss at a few folds. b June 28 (122) £500
VIELE, EGBERT L. - Sanitary & Topographical Map of the City and Island of New York. NY, 1865. 2 sheets joined, 495mm by 1,630mm, hand-colored in outline, linen-backed. sg May 9 (217) $850
VISSCHER, NICOLAUS. - Novi Belgii Novaeque Angliae nec non partis Virginiae tabula.... [Amst., c.1655 or later]. 460mm by 550mm, contemp hand-coloring, framed. Minor wear to centerfold. pn Dec 7 (195) £1,300
WALLING, HENRY F. & CHACE, J. - Map of the State of Maine. Portland, 1861. 1,570mm by 1,590mm, hand-colored, on wooden rollers. Yellowed from lacquer; some tears & chips. sg May 9 (198) $1,300
WARNER, B. - United States of America. Phila., 1820. 445mm by 650mm. Wrinkling; dampstaining to lower right corner; marginal tears extending into image. sg May 9 (264) $325
WHITNEY, JOSIAH D. - Map of a Portion of the Sierra Nevada Adjacent to the Yosemite Valley.... Sacramento: Geological Survey of California, [1868]. 20 by 29.5 inches, mtd. pba Feb 12 (200) $225
WHITNEY, JOSIAH D. - Map of California and Nevada. Berkeley: Regents of the University of California, 1874. 41.25 by 34.75 inches folded to 7 by 6, in cloth folder. Library number stamped on linen backing. pba Feb 12 (201) $325
WYLD, JAMES. - New Map of the United States.... L, [c.1880]. 335mm by 440mm, linen-backed, folding to 8vo. sg Dec 7 (179) $175

### Western Hemisphere

BELLERE, JEAN. - Brevis exactaque totius Novi Orbis.... [N.p.], 1554. 165mm by 129mm. Tear along upper fold extending into map area; some soiling. cb Oct 17 (212) $3,500
TALLIS, JOHN & CO. - Western Hemisphere. L, [c.1850]. 247mm by 335mm, hand-colored. pba Oct 9 (172) $110

### World

ARROWSMITH, AARON. - Map of the World on a Globular Projection. L, 1794. 6 sheets, 510mm by 950mm. Few tears, some repaired; wrinkles, some browning. CE Nov 8 (221) $1,900
BELLIN, JACQUES NICOLAS. - Essay d'une carte reduite, contenant les parties connuees, du globe terrestre. Paris, 1748. 495mm by 690mm. S Mar 28 (254) £200

BLAEU, WILLEM & BLAEU, JAN. - Nova et accuratissima totius Terrarum Orbis tabula. Amst., 1662. 400mm by 540mm, hand-colored. Laid down on archive tissue, repairing tears. b Jan 31 (416) £1,500
BLOME, RICHARD. - A Mapp or Generall Carte of the World.... L, [1670 or later]. 395mm by 535mm, dedication & decorative garlands hand-colored, framed. Fold creases; minor loss to armorial & dedication. b May 30 (137) £300
BOISSEAU, JEAN. - Nouvelle et exacte description de la terre universelle. Paris, 1646. 380mm by 545mm, hand-colored. b Jan 31 (417) £2,000
BONNE, RIGOBERT. - L'Ancien monde et le nouveau.... [Geneva, 1780]. 21.5cm by 41cm, hand-colored in outline. Some soiling. pba Aug 8 (110) $120
Anr Ed. [Geneva, c.1783]. 215mm by 410mm, hand-colored in outline. pba Oct 9 (42) $170
BUENTING, HEINRICH. - Die gantze Welt in ein Kleberblat. [Magdeburg, c.1581]. 258mm by 358mm, hand-colored. Margins repaired. b Sept 20 (396) £750
CHATELAIN, HENRI ABRAHAM. - Mappe-Monde. Paris, [c.1730]. 333mm by 440mm, modern hand-coloring. pba Oct 9 (67) $500
COLLIN, RICHARD. - [World Map] 190mm by 285mm.. Repair at left crease. pba Oct 9 (69) $425
COVENS, JOHANNES & MORTIER, CORNELIS. - Carte Generale de toutes les costes du monde et les pays nouvellement decouvert. Amst., [c.1730]. 2 sheets joined, 585mm by 900mm, contemp hand-coloring. b Jan 31 (418) £1,200
DANCKERTS, CORNELIS. - Nieuw Aerdsch Pleyn. [Amst., c.1696]. 600mm by 630mm. Double-page engraved circular world map surrounded by allegorical depictions. Hand-colored. Trimmed & mtd; rubbed. CE June 15 (377) $2,400
DELISLE, GUILLAUME. - Mappe monde.... Paris, 1700. 43cm by 66cm. Repairs at centerfold. pba Apr 25 (27) $1,000
DESNOS, LOUIS CHARLES. - Mappe-Monde Celeste Terrestre et Historique.... Paris, 1786. 6 sheets joined, over-all 1,040mm by 930mm, hand-colored. Remargined on 3 sides; some restoration & facsimile at lower corners & descriptive text at foot; mtd on linen. S Nov 30 (87) £4,000
DOWER, JOHN. - A New Chart of the World.... L, 1844. 127mm by 194mm, hand-colored in outline, backed with linen & sectioned for folding into lea gilt covers. Some fold breaks, covers split. pba Oct 9 (93) $150
GEELKERKEN, ARNOLDUS & GEELKERKEN, NICOLAAS. - Novae Insulae XXVI Nova Tabula. [Basel, c.1552]. 290mm by 370mm, mtd. Marginal staining. CE June 15 (374) $1,900
HALLEY, EDMOND. - Tabula Totius Orbis Terrarum Exhibens Declinationes Magneticas ad Annum 1700 composita ab Edmundo Halleyo simul cum Inclinationibus a Poundio observatis et Ventis Universalibus. [Paris, c.1700]. 195mm by 475mm, hand-colored in outline. pba Apr 25 (39) $250
HOMANN, JOHANN BAPTIST. - Planiglobi terrestris cum utroq. hemisphaerio caelesti generalis exhibitio. Nuremberg, [c.1735]. 480mm by 545mm, contemp hand-coloring, framed. Split at fold & stained at center. S Mar 28 (256) £620

HONDIUS, HENRICUS. - Nova Totius Terrarum orbis geographica.... Paris: Melchior Tavernier, 1630. 395mm by 582mm, hand-colored, mtd on linen. Side margins restored. b June 28 (127) £3,200

JAILLOT, CHARLES HUBERT ALEXIS. - Mappe-Monde geohydrographique.... Paris, 1786. 450mm by 645mm, Colored. S Oct 26 (468) £580 [Potter]

JANSSONIUS, JOANNES. - Orbis Terrarum Veteribus Cogniti Typus Geographicus. [Amst., c.1630]. 405mm by 505mm, hand-colored. Repaired on verso. sg Dec 7 (104) $750

JANVIER, JEAN. - Mappe-Monde ou Description du globe terrestre. Paris, 1775. 310mm by 460mm, hand-colored in outline. Mtd; browned & soiled. Sold w.a.f. sg Dec 7 (106) $325

KIRCHER, ATHANASIUS. - Tabula Geographico-Hydrographica motus oceani, Currentes, Abyssos, Montes Igniuomos. Amst., 1665. 345mm by 555mm. Margins trimmed. sg May 9 (191) $1,000

KITCHIN, THOMAS. - The World. L, [c.1751]. 195mm by 375mm, hand-colored. Margins trimmed. sg May 9 (193) $375

LE CLERC, JEAN. - Orbis terrae novissima descriptio. Paris, 1602. 330mm by 510mm, hand-colored. Remargined, with minor repairs. b Jan 31 (420) £1,100

LOEWITZ, G. M. - Planiglobi Terrestris. Nuremberg: Homann's heirs, 1746. 455mm by 530mm Colored. S Oct 26 (469) £600 [Wattis]

MERIAN, MATTHAEUS. - Nova totius Terrarum Orbis geographica ac hydrographica tabula. Frankfurt, 1646. 265mm by 355mm. sg May 9 (209) $1,100

MOLL, HERMAN. - A New and Corrected Map of the Whole World. L, 1719 [but c.1726]. 710mm by 1,220mm, on 2 large & 2 half-sheets joined, contemp hand-coloring. Small area of loss in sea; laid on canvas. b Jan 31 (422) £1,400

MOLL, HERMAN. - A View of ye General & Coasting Trade-Winds, Monsoons or ye Shifting Tade Winds.... L, [c.1710]. 185mm by 525mm. pba Apr 25 (57) $350

MORTIER, PIETER. - Carte generale de toutes les costes du monde.... Amst., [1693]. 582mm by 897mm, hand-colored in outline. Tape repair on reverse. pba Oct 9 (130) $1,400

MUENSTER, SEBASTIAN. - Des erst general inhaltend die beschreibung und den circkel des gantzen Erdtreighs und Moeres. [Basel, 1550, or later]. 265mm by 385mm image size. German text on verso. Some soiling & repairs. sg Dec 7 (126) $1,800

MUENSTER, SEBASTIAN. - Die erst general Tafel die beschreibung und den Circkel des gantzen Erdtrichs und Meers inhaltende. [N.p., c.1585]. 315mm by 360mm image size, later hand-coloring. German text on verso. Browned. sg Dec 7 (127) $1,700

MUENSTER, SEBASTIAN. - Die Erst General-Tafel die Beschreibung und den Cirkel des gantzen Erdtrichs und Meers innhaltende. [Basel, 1588]. 320mm by 360mm. Browned & stained; tear along fold. CE June 15 (376) $400

MUENSTER, SEBASTIAN. - Typus Orbis universalis. [Basel, c.1540s]. 253mm by 345mm. Tiny holes at centerfold; pencil notes at bottom margin. With Latin text on verso. cb June 25 (1739) $600

NOLIN, JEAN BAPTISTE. - Terrestre Plans-Hemispheres....
Paris: Crepy, [1785]. 1,180mm by 1,480mm, 4 sheets joined with attached border. Mtd on linen. S Nov 30 (86) £4,200

ORTELIUS, ABRAHAM. - Aevi veteris typus geographicus [the Ancient World]. Antwerp, [1590 or later]. 315mm by 440mm, hand-colored. Italian text on verso. Browned; creased. sg May 9 (218) $375

ORTELIUS, ABRAHAM. - Typus orbis terrarum. [Antwerp, 1570 or later]. 410mm by 565mm, hand-colored in full. Latin text on verso Central fold break; margins browned. P June 5 (307) $3,750

Anr Ed. [Antwerp, 1575]. 335mm by 490mm, hand-colored, framed. S Mar 28 (257) £2,300

Anr Ed. [Amst., c.1598]. 360mm by 490mm, hand-colored. French text on verso Minor browning. sg May 9 (223) $3,200

PHELPS, H. - World at One View. NY, 1847. 565mm by 775mm, hand-colored. Short tears closed on verso. sg May 9 (225) $475

PTOLEMAEUS, CLAUDIUS. - [Untitled map of the World.] [Rome, 1478]]. 320mm by 540mm. b Dec 5 (104) £23,000

RICCI, MATTEO. - Kunyu Wanguo Quantu [Map of the ten thousand countries of the Earth]. Vatican City, 1938. ("Il mappamondo cinese del P. Matteo Ricci....") Folio, orig half calf gilt; worn. With 30 plates. Facsimile. S Mar 28 (374) £300

SANSON D'ABBEVILLE, NICOLAS. - Mappe-Monde. Paris: P. Mariette, [1651-60]. 405mm by 520mm, with contemp outline coloring. S June 13 (583) £700

Anr Ed. Paris: Pierre Mariette, 1669. 425mm by 574mm, hand-colored in outline. Remargined at top. pba Oct 9 (152) $600

SANSON D'ABBEVILLE, NICOLAS. - Orbis vetus, et orbis veteris utraque continens. Paris, 1657. 17-3/4in by 23-1/4in Single folded sheet. Larson copy. pba Sept 28 (49) $300

Anr Ed. Paris: Pierre Mariette, 1657. 390mm by 550mm, hand-colored in outline & fully colored on field.. Marginal staining. sg May 9 (238) $1,200

SCHRAEMBL, FRANZ ANTON. - Polynesien (Inselwelt) oder Fuenfte Weltheil.... Vienna, 1789 [or later]. 470mm by 705mm, hand-colored in outline. S Mar 28 (416) £650

SPEED, JOHN. - A New and Accurat Map of the World. L: G. Humble, 1626 [or later]. 390mm by 515mm, hand-colored. Centerfold restored in Ms; remargined at top. b Jan 31 (424) £1,350

TAVERNIER, MELCHIOR. - Carte de l'Amerique.... * Carte Nouvelle de l'Europe, Asie & Afrique.... Paris, 1661. 2 sheets, each c.260mm in diameter plus border, some hand-coloring in outline. Some repairs. pba Oct 9 (173) $2,000

VALCK, GERARD. - Novus Planiglobii Terrestris per utrumque Polum Conspectus. Amst., [c.1700]. 405mm by 535mm, contemp hand-coloring. Strengthened on verso. b Jan 31 (425) £1,500

Anr copy. 420mm by 555mm, hand-colored in outline, framed. pnE Mar 20 (71) £1,400

VISSCHER, NICOLAUS. - Orbis terrarum nova et accuratissima tabula. [Amst., c.1658 or later]. 470mm by 560mm, mtd on heavy card. Some browning. CE June 15 (378) $2,200

VISSCHER, NICOLAUS. - Orbis Terrarum Tabula Recens Emendata.... [Amst., c.1657]. 308mm by 475mm, hand-colored. pba Oct 9 (183) $1,200

VISSCHER, NICOLAUS. - Orbis terrarum tabula recens emendata et in lucem edita. [Amst., c.1663). 305mm by 470mm, hand-colored. S June 13 (584) £820

WALDSEEMUELLER, MARTIN. - Diefert Situs Orgis Hydrographorum ab eo quem Ptolomeus Posuit. Strassburg, [c.1530]. Size not given early handcoloring. Latin text on verso. sg Dec 7 (175A) $3,200

WELLS, EDWARD. - A New Map of the Terraqueous Globe. Oxford, [c.1700]. 368mm by 504mm, later hand-coloring, framed. Some repairs. pba Oct 9 (185) $900

ZUERNER, ADAM FRIEDRICH. - Planisphaerium terrestre cum utroque coelesti hemisphaerio. [Amst.: P. Schenk, c.1700]. 505mm by 575mm, contemp coloring. b Jan 31 (426) £1,200

Maran, Rene, 1887-1960. See: Limited Editions Club

**Marbury, Mary Orvis**
— Favorite Flies and their Histories. Bost., 1892. 4to, orig cloth; shaken & spotted. With 32 color plates. O June 25 (193) $375

Anr copy. Orig cloth; spine ends & extremities worn. Tp & frontis lacking. pba July 11 (185) $250

**Marc, Franz, 1880-1916**
— Sechzehn Farbige Handzeichnungen aus den Skizzenbuchern. [N.p., n.d.]. One of 500. 4to, loose as issued in half-cloth portfolio. With 16 color plates. bba Oct 19 (96) £200 [Breckenridge]

**Marcati, Michele, 1541-93**
— Instruttione sopra la peste.... Rome: Vincenzo Accolto, 1576. 4to, old vellum; rebacked. With title device. Some spotting; title repaired at fore-margin. S Oct 27 (815) £360 [Zioni]

**Marcel, Jean Jacques**
— Fables de Loqman, surnomme Le Sage. Cairo, 1799. Bound with: Recueil des pieces relatives a la procedure et au jugement de Soleyman El-Hhaleby, asassin du General en Chef Kleber. Cairo, 1799-1800. 4to, contemp calf gilt; joints worn. Chatsworth copy. C June 26 (198) £3,000

**Marcellinus, Ammianus**
— Rerum gestarum.... Leiden: P. Vander Aa, 1693. Ed by Jacobo Gronovio. Folio, modern mor; joints rubbed, front hinge cracked. With 3 double-page plates & port & 14 numismatic plates. Some browning of text. sg Mar 21 (220) $200

**Marcello, Allesandro, 1684-c.1750**
— Cantate di Eterio Stinfalico Accademico Arcade. Venice: Antonio Bortoli, 1708. Oblong 4to, contemp calf gilt with arms of Casa Marcello. C June 26 (283) £380

**Marcet, Jane**
— Conversations on Political Economy.... L, 1821. 4th Ed. 12mo, later half calf; worn & scuffed. Some foxing. Signature of DeWitt Clinton on tp (slightly cropped). wa Feb 29 (154) $140

**March, J.**
— The Jolly Angler; or Water Side Companion. L: J. March, 1850. 6th Ed. 8vo, orig cloth; front joint starting. pba July 11 (186) $50

**Marchand, Prosper, d.1756**
— Histoire de l'origine et des premiers progres de l'imprimerie. The Hague, 1740. 2 parts in 1 vol. 4to, contemp half calf; rubbed, joints worn. Some foxing & browning. O Mar 26 (171) $225

**Marchand, R. F.**
— Ueber die Luftschiffahrt. Leipzig, 1850. 8vo, orig wraps; backstrip chipped. sg May 16 (60) $100

**Marchesinus, Joannes**
— Mammotrectus super Bibliam. Venice: Nicolaus Jenson, 1479. 4to, 16th-cent half mor. Some repairs & worming. 259 (of 260) leaves; lacking initial blank. Goff M-239. bba Sept 7 (173) £1,200 [Bernard]

Anr Ed. Strassburg: Johann Reinhard Grueninger, 1489. Folio, mor; extremities rubbed. 53 lines & headline; gothic letter, double column; initials in red; some letters highlighted withsiler gilt. Minor staining mainly in margins; some repairs. 160 leaves. Goff M-250. cb Feb 14 (2520) $1,500

**Marcilhac, Felix**
— Rene Lalique, 1860-1945.... Paris, [1989]. 4to, cloth, in dj. sg June 13 (228) $225

**Marck, Jan van der —&**
**Crispolti, Enrico**
— Lucio Fontana. Brussels, [1974]. 2 vols. 4to, cloth. sg Jan 11 (177) $175

**Marcus Aurelius Antoninus, 121-180**
See also: Fore-Edge Paintings
— Meditations. L: Riccardi Press, 1909. ("The Thoughts of Emperor Marcus Aurelius Antoninus.") One of 500. Trans by George Long; illus by W. Russell Flint. 4to, vellum, in dj with chip. sg Sept 14 (131) $130
— Reflexions Morales.... Paris: Didot, 1800 [An X]. 4to, orig bds; rubbed. With 2 plates. Some foxing. bba July 18 (143) £65 [Price]

**Marcy, Randolph Barnes, 1812-87**
— The Prairie Traveller: a Hand-Book for Overland Expeditions. NY, 1859. 1st Ed. 8vo, later cloth. Library markings. bbc Dec 18 (506) $460

Anr copy. Orig cloth; worn, upper joint wormed. O Mar 5 (165) $350

Anr copy. Orig cloth. Larson copy. pba Sept 28 (625) $400

**Mardersteig, Giovanni**
— The Officina Bodoni. Verona, 1980. One of 1,500. 4to, orig cloth. ds July 27 (121) $100
One of 99 with 2d vol. 2 vols. 4to, half mor. Vol II includes 10 mtd examples of leaves from books ptd at the press. bba May 9 (329) £300 [Blackwell]; cb Feb 14 (2791) $400; Ck May 31 (11) £280; P Dec 12 (120) $500
— Die Officina Bodoni. Das Werk einer Handpresse 1923-1977. Hamburg: Maximilian Gesellschaft, [1979]. One of 1,500. 4to, cloth. sg Sept 14 (259) $50
— L'Officina Bodoni; La regola e le stampe di un torchio durante i primi sei anni del suo lavoro. Verona: Officina Bodoni, 1929. One of 200. Illus by Frans Masereel. 4to, orig cloth. Some spotting. Ck May 31 (10) £180
— Pastonchi: A Specimen of a New Letter for Use on the "Monotype." Verona: Officina Bodoni, 1928. One of 200. 4to, orig half vellum. bba May 9 (609) £120 [Cox]
— Scritti...sulla Storia dei Caratteri e della Tipografia. Milan: Officina Bodoni for Edizioni Il Polifilo, 1988. One of 100, this copy for Colin Franklin. 4to, orig wraps. bba May 9 (641) £80 [Questor]

**Mardersteig, Hans.** See: Mardersteig, Giovanni

**Mardrus, Joseph Charles Victor**
— Histoire charmante de l'adolescente sucre d'amour. Paris, 1927. One of 25. Illus by F. L. Schmied. 4to, mor extra by Gruel, the upper cover with inset circular lacquer panel port of 2 lovers, by Schmied, orig wraps bound in. Inscr by Schmied to A. de Marchena. S Nov 21 (297) £33,000
— Le Marie magique. Paris, 1930. One of 125. Illus by Antoine Bourdelle. 4to, mor extra by Max Fonseque, orig wraps bound in. S Nov 21 (296) £450

**Marechal, Pierre Sylvain**
— Costumes civils actuels de tous les peuples connus. Paris, 1788. Vol IV only. Disbound. With 55 hand-colored plates. Dampstained; some tears & browning. O July 9 (131) $160
Anr copy. 4 vols. 8vo, contemp calf gilt. With hand-colored titles & 301 hand-colored plates. S Nov 30 (118) £2,200

**Marey-Monge, Edmond**
— Etudes sur l'aerostation. Paris, 1847. 8vo, orig wraps, unopened; backstrip chipped. With 9 folding plates. Foxed. sg May 16 (62) $300

**Marguerite d'Angouleme, 1492-1549**
— L'Heptameron. Berne, 1780-81. ("Les Nouvelles....") 3 vols. 8vo, 19th-cent mor gilt. Tail-piece for nouvelle X has failed to print; some spotting. Fuerstenberg - Schaefer copy. S Dec 7 (399) £1,500
— Les Nouvelles.... L, 1780-81. 3 vols. 8vo, contemp calf. With frontis by Dunker, & 73 plates. 1 plate with hole. S Oct 27 (1142) £380 [Zioni]

**Mariette, Jean**
— L'Architecture francaise. Paris & Brussels, 1927-29. Ed by Louis Hautecoeur. 3 vols. Folio, loose as issued in orig wraps. Sold w.a.f. bba Oct 19 (141) £380 [Bernett]

**Mariette Library, Pierre Jean**
— [Sale Catalogue] Catalogue raisonne des differens objets de curiosities dans les sciences et les arts, qui composaient le cabinet de feu Mr. Mariette. Paris, 1775. Compiled by Pierre Francois Basan. 8vo, contemp half vellum; cracked & rubbed. With engraved border to tp, frontis with letters plus 3 proofs later inserted in 3 states & 4 plates. Unpressed, uncut & priced. Spotting to frontis; some soiling. Fuerstenberg - Schaefer copy. S Dec 7 (401) £750

**Marinaro, Vincent**
— A Modern Dry-Fly Code. NY: Crown, [1970]. One of 350. Lea. pba July 11 (187) $200

**Marine...**
— The Marine Engineer: A Monthly Journal.... L, 1880-1921. Vols 1-43. 4to, orig cloth; worn & soiled. F June 20 (197) $475

**Marinis, Tammaro de, 1878-1969**
— Il Castello di Monselice, raccolta degli antichi libri venetiani figurati. Verona, 1941. One of 310. 4to, orig half vellum. With 2 A Ls s to Caesare Olschki loosely inserted. bba Oct 5 (46) £1,000 [Quaritch]
— La Legatura artistica in Italia nel secoli XV e XVI. Florence, 1960. One of 500. 3 vols. Folio, orig half mor. Ck Apr 12 (251) £1,100

**Marion**
— Mummy's Bedtime Story Book, by "Marion." L, [1929]. Illus by Jessie M. King. Folio, orig pictorial bds; rubbed. S Nov 2 (302) £440 [Vallejo]

**Mariotte, Edme, 1620-85**
— The Motion of Water and Other Fluids.... L, 1718. 8vo, disbound. With 7 folding plates. Inscr by the trans, J. T. Desaguliers, to Charles Labelye. b May 30 (29) £150

**Marius, Jean**
— Traite du Castor.... Paris: David fils, 1746. 12mo, contemp calf gilt. sg May 16 (446) $110

**Marius Michel**
— La Reliure francaise, depuis l'invention de l'imprimerie.... Paris, 1880. One of a few copies on bau papier du japon des fabriques du mikado. Bound with: La Reliure francaise commerciale et industrielle. Paris, 1881. 4to, citron mor a repetion by Charles Philippe de Samblanx & Jacques Weckesser, the sides a field of onlaid blue mor lozenges, each with a single gilt flower, 2 wraps bound in. With 22 plates in 1st work & 23 in 2d, plus the separate suite of 16 chromolitho plates & 3 uncolored plates to the 1st work. C May 1 (102) £7,500

## Markham, Sir Clements Robert, 1830-1916
— Antarctic Exploration: A Plea for a National Expedition.... L: Royal Geographical Society, 1898. 8vo, orig wraps; minor soiling. With folding color litho map. George Davidson's sgd copy. pba July 25 (41) $650

## Markham, Edwin, 1852-1940
— California the Wonderful. NY, [1914]. 1st Ed. Orig cloth; front cover corners bumped. Robbins copy. pba Mar 21 (228) $100
— The Man with the Hoe, and Other Poems. NY, 1899. 1st Ed, 1st Issue. 8vo, orig cloth; extremities rubbed. Inscr, explaining the issue point, fruitless on p. 35. CE Sept 27 (180) $240

## Markham, Gervase, 1568?-1637
See also: Cresset Press
— The English House-Wife. L, 1675. 8th Ed. 4to, later calf. Lacking Ppp2 and Ppp3; 1st 22 pp. dampstained, wormed in inner margin, loss at Ppp4. S Oct 12 (35) £140
— The English Hous-Wife.... L, 1656. 4to, modern half calf. Dampstained throughout; some margins shaved close affecting shoulder notes. CE June 12 (178) $700
— The English Husbandman. L, 1635. 3 parts in 1 vol. 4to, contemp sheep; rebacked, worn. Lacking blank A1; H4 lacking lower corner. S Mar 29 (766) £650
— The English Hus-wife.... L: John Beale, 1615. 1st Ed. 4to, contemp bds; worn. Inner margins ragged on title; 1st few pp. loose. S Oct 12 (107) £500
— Markhams Maister-Peece. L, 1668. ("Markham's Master-piece....") 4to, contemp calf; rebacked retaining spine, rubbed, corners repaired. Engraved title shaved, 1 of the 2 folding woodcuts with tear repaired. S Mar 29 (767) £460

**Markland, George.** See: Derrydale Press

## Marliano, Bartolomeo
— Urbis Romae topographia. Rome: Valerio & Luigi Dorico, Sept 1544. Folio, 18th-cent calf. With 23 woodcut illusts, including hand-colored double-page plan of Rome. Tp soiled & mtd on guards; upper right corner of L4 restored. P June 5 (292) $3,000

## Marlier, Georges
— Pierre Brueghel le Jeune. Brussels, 1969. Folio, cloth, in dj. sg June 13 (66) $400

## Marlowe, Christopher, 1564-93
— Doctor Faustus. L: Vale Press, 1903. One of 310. Ed by John Masefield; Illus by Charles Ricketts. Orig cloth; spine ends rubbed. pba Nov 30 (317) $170
— Works. L: William Pickering, 1850. 3 vols. 8vo, contemp calf by Bedford. pba Aug 8 (285) $225

## Marmont, Auguste Frederic Louis Viesse de, duc de Raguse
— Voyage du marechal duc de Raguse en Hongrie, en Transylvanie, dans la Russie meridionale.... Paris, 1837-39. 6 vols. 8vo & 4to, contemp half mor. With port, 12 plates & 8 folding & double-page plans & maps. S June 13 (412) £550

## Marmontel, Jean Francois, 1723-99
— Chefs-d'Oeuvre Dramatiques. Paris, 1773. 4to, modern calf gilt. With: suite of 1 plate & 17 vignettes illustrating Sophonisba. Fuerstenberg - Schaefer copy. S Dec 7 (403) £460
— Les Contes moraux. Paris, 1765. 1st Issue, with errata at foot of contents leaves. 3 vols. 12mo, contemp red mor gilt. With port, engraved titles & 23 plates. Piece torn away from foremargin of G3 in Vol III. With 6 ink drawings by Gravelot for the plates mtd within gilt frames at beginning of vols. Fuerstenberg - Schaefer copy. S Dec 7 (407) £2,400
— Les Incas, ou la destruction de l'empire. Liege, 1777. 2 vols. 8vo, contemp calf gilt; spines wormed & scratched. With frontis & 10 plates. Hole in text of A3 in Vol I. Fuerstenberg - Schaefer copy. S Dec 7 (405) £200
— Poetique francois. Paris, 1763. 3 parts in 2 vols. 8vo, contemp red mor gilt. S Dec 7 (406) £240

## Marquez, Gabriel Garcia
See also: Limited Editions Club
— El Amor en los Tiempos del Colera. Bogota: Editorial Oveja Negra, [1985]. 1st Ed, One of 1,000. In dj. pba Jan 25 (106) $300
— No One Writes to the Colonel.... NY, [1968]. 1st American Ed. In dj. pba Oct 5 (281) $275

## Marquis, Thomas B. —& Woodenlegs, Richard
— The Warrior Who Fought Custer. Minneapolis, 1931. In dj. Inscr by Marquis & by Woodenlegs's grandson, John. pba June 25 (165) $1,300

## Marra, John
— Journal of the Resolution's Voyage.... L: for F. Newbery, 1775. 8vo, contemp calf. With folding chart & 5 plates. James Bruce of Kinnaird's copy. C Nov 29 (89) £3,300
— 1st Ed. L, 1775. Ed by David Henry. 8vo, contemp calf; rehinged. With folding frontis & 5 plates. Frontis torn & repaired; 1 text leaf repaired. Robbins copy. pba Mar 21 (229) $3,000

## Marryat, Francis S., 1826-55
— Borneo and the Indian Archipelago.... L, 1848. 1st Ed. 8vo, contemp half mor gilt; extremities & joints scuffed. With engraved title, colored frontis & 20 plates. pba Apr 25 (211) $800

Anr copy. 4to, orig cloth; worn & soiled, part of spine detached, hinges cracked. With half-title 7 22 plates. 1 plate loose. S Oct 26 (590) £280 [Morrel]

Anr copy. 8vo, 19th-cent half mor gilt; rubbed. With tinted additional title & 21 tinted litho plates. S Mar 28 (398) £600

— Mountains and Molehills.... L, 1855. 1st Ed. 8vo, orig cloth; faded. With 8 color plates & 18 illus. Some stains. Larson copy. pba Sept 28 (592) $1,400

Anr copy. Later cloth; extremities worn. With 8 plates. Robbins copy. pba Mar 21 (230) $650

1st American Ed. NY, 1855. 8vo, orig cloth. With 26 illus. Larson copy. pba Sept 28 (593) $250
Anr copy. Orig cloth. Light foxing to frontis. Robbins copy. pba Mar 21 (231) $120

**Marryat, Frederick, 1792-1848**
— A Diary of America, with Remarks on its Institutions. L, 1839. 1st Ed. 3 vols. 8vo, later calf; worn & scuffed. Short tears in folding maps. wa Feb 29 (426) $85

**Marsden, Joshua, 1777-1837**
— Amusements of a Mission, or Poems.... Blackburn, 1818. 2d Ed. 8vo, contemp mor gilt prize bdg. With folding frontis & 2 woodcut plates. Frontis torn. b Dec 5 (205) £80

**Marselaer, Fridericus de**
— Legatus, libri duo. Antwerp: Plantin, 1626. 4to, orig presentation bdg of calf gilt with author's arms & motto on front cover; rubbed. C June 26 (104) £1,100

**Marsh, James B.**
— Four Years in the Rockies.... New Castle PA, 1884. 12mo, orig cloth; spine ends frayed, rubbed. bbc Dec 18 (508) $500
1st Ed. 12mo, modern half calf; rebound. With frontis port. Robbins copy. pba Mar 21 (232) $425

**Marshall, Charles H. T., 1841-1927.** See: Hume & Marshall

**Marshall, Henry Rissik**
— Coloured Worcester Porcelain of the First Period.... Newport, 1954. One of 1,200. 4to, lea gilt; front joint starting. sg Jan 11 (88) $200

**Marshall, John, Schoolmaster**
— The Village Paedagogue, a Poem.... Newcastle, 1810. 8vo, contemp mor gilt. b Dec 5 (283) £100

**Marshall, John, 1755-1835**
— The Life of George Washington. L, 1804-7. 5 vols. 4to, 19th-cent half calf; spines rubbed, joint splitting. With port & 14 plates & maps. Foxing to maps, plates & tp of Vol I. pba Nov 30 (233) $325
Anr copy. 5 vols. 8vo, half lea. With 10 maps & 6 plates. sg Oct 26 (385) $1,000
Anr Ed. Phila., 1807. Atlas vol only. 4to, half mor; needs rebdg. With 10 maps. Browned. sg Oct 26 (384) $175
— Vie de George Washington.... Paris: Dentu, 1807. 6 vols, including Atlas. 8vo & 4to, contemp calf; rubbed. With port & 16 maps & plates. O Nov 14 (118) $650

**Marsigli, Luigi Ferdinando, Count, 1658-1730**
— L'Etat militaire de l'empire ottoman.... The Hague, 1732. 2 vols in 1. Folio, contemp mor gilt; top of spine chipped. With 34 plates, 2 folding maps hand-colored in outline & 3 folding tables. Some browning, affecting plates. sg Apr 18 (81) $1,100
— La Hongrie et le Danube.... The Hague, 1741. Folio, disbound. With 28 (of 31) mostly double-page or folding mapsheets & charts. Some staining & fire damage at edges. Sold w.a.f. S Mar 28 (205) £160

**Marsilius of Inghen, d.1394**
— Questiones Marsilii super quattuor libros sententiarum. [Strassburg: Martin Flach, 1501]. Folio, contemp blindstamped calf over wooden bds; re-backed, old spine laid down. Worming; staining. Sold w.a.f. 363 (of 593) leaves; lacking dd3 & dd6 & all after zz7. S Dec 18 (60) £380 [de Palol]

**Marston, Anna Lee**
— Records of a California Family: Journals and Letters of Lewis C. Gunn and Elizabeth Le Breton Gunn. San Diego, 1928. 1st Ed, One of 300. Half bds. With 1 maps, 13 photogravures, & 3p. letter from Marston to printer. Larson copy. pba Sept 28 (505) $300

**Marston, Edward**
— Days in Clover by the Amateur Angler. L, 1892. One of 150. 8vo, ptd vellum; spine ends chipped. pba July 11 (189) $200
— Frank's Ranch or My Holiday in the Rockies.... L, 1886. 3d Ed. Calf gilt; extremities rubbed. Inscr, 1886. pba July 11 (417) $50

**Marston, John, 1575?-1634.** See: Golden Cockerel Press

**Marston, Robert Bright, 1853-1927**
— Walton and Some Earlier Writers on Fish and Fishing. L, 1894. 8vo, orig cloth; spine foot rubbed, nick to head. pba July 11 (192) $90

**Marti, Giovanni Filippo**
— Della robbia sua coltivazione e suoi usi. Florence, 1776. 1st Ed. - Engraved by Matteo Carboni. 8vo, contemp vellum. With half title, title, & 5 plates (2 folding). S Oct 26 (62) £2,400 [Quaritch]

**Marti, Giovanni Francesco**
— Viaggi per l'isola di Cipro e per la soria e Palestina fatti.... Florence, 1769-74. Vols I-VII (of 9) only. 8vo, limp bds; Vol I worn & repaired. Vol I spotted & stained. S Oct 26 (63) £400 [Zioni]

**Marti, Joaquin**
— Historia del origen, padecimientos, progresos, y porvenir de las misiones catholicas de Nueva-Holanda.... Barcelona, 1850. 8vo, contemp half mor; worn. With 2 ports. Some spotting. S Mar 28 (421) £150

**Martial Achievements...**
— The Martial Achievements of Great Britain.... L: James Jenkins, [1814-15]. 4to, contemp half mor; rubbed, spine def, lower cover detached. With 54 hand-colored plates, including titles & dedication. bba June 6 (20) £450 [Abbey Antiquarian Books]

**Martial de Paris, dit d'Auvergne**
— Aresta amorum.... Paris: Simon Colines, 1531. 8vo, 18th-cent calf gilt; rubbed. N2 corner def just touching pagination; u2 with burn-hole causing loss of text. bba July 18 (117) £420 [Maggs]

**Martialis, Marcus Valerius**
— Epigrammata. Venice: [Ptr of the 1480 Martial], 1480. Folio, contemp bds with remains of lea; stitching broken, worn. 57-line commentary surrounding text; roman letter. Some worming & staining; h3-i3 holed at inner blank margins. 216 (of 224) leaves; lacking c4-d1, E1 & final blank. Goff M-304. C June 26 (103) £550
Anr Ed. Venice: Baptista de Tortis, 1482. Folio, calf; bookplate removed from front pastedown. With hand-painted initials, 15 illuminated. Some cropping, affecting hand-painted design on a4; some staining. 198 leaves. Goff M-306. pba Nov 30 (234) $3,000
Anr Ed. Venice: Thomas de Blauis, 12 June 1482. ("Domitius Calderinus Ioanni Francisco Ludovici Principis Mantuani filio salutem.") Folio, 19th-cent mor gilt. Wormed at beginning; some dampstaining & spotting; repairs at ends; institutional release stamp at end. 216 (of 218) leaves; lacking conjugate rl.8. Goff M-305. S Nov 30 (284) £650
Anr Ed. Paris: C. Robustel & N. le Loup, 1754. ("Epigrammatum libri....") 2 vols. 12mo, mor gilt. With 2 headpieces & frontis ptd in blue. Pilkington - Fuerstenberg - Schaefer copy. S Dec 7 (408) £400

**Martin, Barthelamy**
— Traite de l'usage du lait. Paris, 1684. 1st Ed. 12mo in 8s & 4s, contemp vellum; soiled. Some gatherings pulled; N1 torn in inner margin. Ck Mar 22 (183) £360

**Martin, Benjamin, 1704-82**
— The Philosophical Grammar: Being a View of the Present State of Experimental Physiology. L, 1778. 8vo, modern cloth. Some foxing. sg May 16 (214) $100
— A Plain and Familiar Introduction to the Newtonian Philosophy.... L, 1765. 5th Ed. 8vo, contemp sheep; worn, joints cracked, 1 plate loose. With 6 folding plates. sg May 16 (212) $100

**Martin, Corneille**
— Les Genealogies, et anciennes descentes des forestiers et comtes de Flandre. Antwerp: [Robert Bruneau for] Jean Baptiste Vrints, [1608]. Folio, 19th-cent half sheep; needs rebacked. With engraved title, full-page engraving with map & arms, 41 ports & allegorical illust. Margins soiled throughout; some repairs & marginalia. sg Mar 21 (221) $175

**Martin, Don Jose.** See: Grabhorn Printing

**Martin, George R. R.**
— Songs the Dead Men Sing. Niles IL: Dark Harvest, 1983. One of 500. In dj. pba Jan 25 (251) $130
One of 500, this copy lettered P/C. Syn. O Dec 5 (227) $90

**Martin, H. B.**
— Fifty Years of American Golf. NY: Dodd, Mead, 1936. 1st Trade Ed. - Foreword by Grantland Rice. Cloth; front cover lower joint discolored. pba Nov 9 (60) $190

Anr Ed. NY, 1936. Cloth; spine dulled & rubbed. pba Apr 18 (124) $225
Anr Ed. NY: Dodd, Mead, 1936. One of 355. Cloth; spine sunned. Sgd. pba Nov 9 (61) $600
— How to Play Golf. NY, [1936]. 1st Ed. Wraps. pba Apr 18 (126) $95

**Martin, H. B. —& Halliday, A. B.**
— Saint Andrews Golf Club 1888-1938. [Hastings-on-Hudson: Rogers, Kellogg & Stillson, 1938]. One of 500. Cloth. With color frontis. Frontis dampstained. pba Apr 18 (123) $275

**Martin, J. C. —& Martin, R. S.**
— Maps of Texas and the Southwest, 1513-1900. Albuquerque, [1984]. Oblong 4to, cloth, in dj. ds July 27 (51) $225

**Martin, J. W.**
— Float Fishing & Spinning in the Nottingham Style.... L, 1885. 2d Ed. Pictorial bds; some rubbing. With 9 wood-engraved plates. pba July 11 (193) $75

**Martin, James, 1783-1860**
— Poems on Various Subjects. Cavan, 1816. 2d Ed. 8vo, orig bds; spine def. b Dec 5 (610) £70

**Martin, John, 1789-1869**
— An Account of the Natives of the Tonga Islands. L, 1817. 1st Ed. 2 vols. 8vo, contemp half calf. With frontises. b Mar 20 (122) £300
Anr Ed. Bost., 1820. 8vo, modern half mor. With folding map & 1 plate. Map backed. pba Apr 25 (213) $110

**Martin, R. S.** See: Martin & Martin

**Martin, Sarah Catherine**
— The Comic Adventures of Old Mother Hubbard and her Dog. L, 1807. 16mo, orig wraps; browned & worn. Engraved throughout. Some soiling. S May 16 (172) £160
— A Continuation of the Comic Adventures of Old Mother Hubbard and her Dog. L, 1806. 1st Ed. 16mo, orig wraps; soiled & chipped, loose. With title & 14 (of 15) leaves, each with hand-colored illust. Some crayon scribbling. S May 16 (173) £120

**Martin, Violet.** See: Derrydale Press

**Martin, W. C. L.**
— A General History of Humming-Birds. L, [c.1830]. 8vo, cloth; needs rebdg. With 16 hand-colored plates. sg May 9 (285) $200
Anr Ed. L, 1852. 8vo, cloth; needs rebdg. With 16 hand-colored plates. Some foxing & browning. sg May 9 (286) $225

**Martineau, Harriet, 1802-76**
— Society in America. L, 1837. 3 vols. 12mo, orig cloth; worn, lending-library labels on front covers & backstrips, some hinges starting. sg Oct 26 (244) $60

Ed not specified. 3 vols. 12mo, orig bds; spines chipped, joints cracked. F Mar 28 (469) $60

**Martinet, Francois Nicolas**
— Histoire des oiseaux, peints dans tous leurs aspects.... Paris, 1782-95. "An Edition unknown to the standard bibliographies". 1 (of 2) vol. Folio, later half mor. With 131 hand-colored plates on light blue paper. Bound without text; 10 plates cut down & mtd, 1 of these ptd on white paper. C May 31 (31) £10,000

Anr Ed. Paris, 1787-96. 8 vols in 9. 8vo, contemp calf; rebacked. With 423 (of 483?) hand-colored plates. Small damage by adhesion to plate facing p. 4 in Vol VII; tp to Vol V slightly defaced; some text lacking. Sold w.a.f. b June 28 (41) £5,000

Anr copy. Contemp bds; recased. With 479 (of 483?) hand-colored plates, some with orig watercolor drawing. Martin copy. C May 31 (32) £22,000

**Martini, Giambatista**
— Storia della musica. Bologna, 1757-81. 3 vols. 4to, half calf; worn & loose. Lacking 2 maps & half-titles. Vincent Novello's sgd copy. S May 15 (90) £450

**Marty, J.**
— Les quadrupedes et les insectes mis en regard ou zoologie comparee. Paris: Louis Janet, [c.1830]. 16mo, later bds. With 20 hand-colored plates, each with 2 illusts. Spotted. S Nov 2 (224) £140 [Schiller]

**Martyn, Thomas, 1735-1825**
— Flora Rustica exhibiting Accurate Figures of...Plants.... L, 1792-94. 4 vols. 8vo, contemp half calf; rubbed. With 144 hand-colored plates. S June 13 (413) £600

— Letters on the Elements of Botany.... L, 1796-99. 2 vols. 8vo, old calf; plate vol respined. With 38 hand-colored plates. Foxing at end. Met May 2 (440) $300

— Thirty-Eight Plates with Explanations: Intended to Illustrate Linnaeus's System of Vegetables. L, 1794. 8vo, old calf; broken, spine gone. With 38 hand-colored plates. Some staining & soiling. O Mar 5 (166) $225

Anr Ed. L, 1799. 8vo, orig bds; backstrip rubbed & chipped. With 38 hand-colored plates. Some spotting. b Sept 20 (479) £130

**Martyn, Thomas, fl.1760-1816**
— Aranei, or a Natural History of Spiders.... L, 1793. 4to, contemp mor by Samuel Welcher, with his ticket. With 28 hand-colored plates, including engraved title. Dampstaining in upper margin of plates; lacking the 2 numismatic plates. sg Oct 19 (169) $1,600

— The English Entomologist, Exhibiting all the Coleopterous Insects.... L, 1792. 4to, modern calf gilt. With engraved title & 42 colored plates & 2 uncolored plates of medals. French title & text bound in. Fattorini copy. C Oct 25 (76) £500

Anr copy. Contemp mor gilt by Staggemeir & Welcher. With engraved title, 2 plates of medals & 42 colored plates. S June 27 (49) £800

Anr copy. Contemp mor by Samuel Welcher, with his ticket. With 42 hand-colored plates & 2 uncolored numismatic plates. Dampstaining in upper margins. sg Oct 19 (168) $2,200

**Martyn, William, 1562-1617**
— The Historie and Lives of the Kings of England.... L, 1628. Folio, modern lea. Stain to p.129; old notes to index in rear. pba June 20 (234) $170

**Martyr, Peter, d.1525**
— De rebus oceanicis & orbe novo decades tres.... Basel: J. Bebel, 1533. Folio, contemp calf; rebacked. b May 30 (141) £2,500

— Opus epistolarum. Compluti [Alcala-en-Henares]: Miguel de Eguia, 1530. Folio, mor gilt, with Lenox arms; minor rubbing to extremities. Some staining; contemp notes throughout; lacking 4 leaves of index & final blank. cb Feb 14 (2539) $7,000

**Marulic, Marko**
— Evangelistarium. Basel: Adam Petri [for Johann Koberger, 1519]. 4to, contemp blind-tooled pigskin over wooden bds with brass catches only. Dampstained & wormed. sg Mar 21 (223) $425

**Marum, Martin van**
— Beschreibung einer Ungemein grossen Elektrifier-Maschine.... Leipzig, 1786-98. 3 vols in 1. 4to, contemp half calf; worn. With 27 plates, 9 of them colored, 21 of them folding. Some browning. Madsen copy. S Mar 14 (247) £3,200

**Marvell, Andrew, 1621-78.** See: Nonesuch Press

**Marx, Roger**
— La Loie Fuller. Evreux, 1904. One of 130, this for Paul Soufflot. 4to, mor extra by Noulhac with orchid pattern of colored mor, orig wraps bound in. With 18 colored designs ptd in relief. S Nov 21 (303) £2,500

**Mary, Princess of Liechtenstein**
— Holland House. L, 1874. 2 vols. 4to, early half mor; joints & corners worn, endpapers foxed. wa Feb 1 (20) $80

**Mary, Andre**
— Tristan. Paris, 1937. One of 150. Illus by Jean Berque. 4to, loose as issued in orig wraps. Some dampstaining. pba Aug 22 (616) $75

**Marzio, Peter C.**
— Chromolithography, 1840-1900. Bost.: Godine for Amon Carter Museum, [1979]. 4to, cloth, in dj. ds July 27 (122) $100

**Marzioli, Francesco**
— Precetti militari. Bologna, 1670. Folio, contemp vellum; spine soiled & with small tear. With engraved title, port, 27 plates & 37 illusts. Wormhole through

731

inner blank margin. Auersberg copy. C Apr 3 (146) £2,200

**Mas, Simon Alphonse**
— Le verger, ou histoire, culture et description... des varieties de fruits.... Paris, [1873]. 1st Ed. 8 vols. 8vo, orig cloth; worn & marked. With 384 color plates. Spotted. S Oct 27 (750) £2,100 [Shapero]

**Mascagni, Paolo, 1752-1815**
— Vasorum lymphaticorum corporis humani historia et ichnographia. Siena, 1787. 1st Ed. - Illus by Ciro Santi. Folio, modern half mor. With title vignette & 41 plates. Lacks dedication; 1st 12 leaves torn & repaired; last 2 plates waterstained; some foxing & soiling. CE Nov 8 (120) $1,200

**Mascardi, Vitale**
— Festa fatta in Roma, alli 25 di Febraio MDCXXXIV. Rome, [1635]. Oblong 4to, 18th-cent half vellum; head of spine with split. With engraved title & 12 plates. Traces of damp in lower margin, not affecting text or plates. C Apr 3 (147) £2,600

**Mascarenas, Jeronimo**
— Campana de Portugal por la Parte de Estremadura el Ano de 1662. Madrid: Francisco Xavier Garcia, 1762. 8vo, contemp vellum; front hinge cracked. sg Mar 21 (299) $110

**Mascha, Ottokar**
— Felicien Rops und sein Werk. Katalog.... Munich, [1910]. One of 500. Orig wraps; soiled, spine with joints tearing. bba Oct 19 (30) £160 [Ginnan]

**Masefield, John, 1878-1967**
— Salt-Water Ballads. L, 1902. 1st Ed, 1st Issue. Inscr. CE Sept 27 (182) $300; sg Sept 21 (257) $200

**Masereel, Frans, 1889-1972**
— Remember! Berne: Herbert Lang, [1945]. One of 950. Oblong folio, bds, in dj. bbc Dec 18 (309) $120

**Maskelyne, Nevil, 1732-1811**
— The British Mariner's Guide, Containing... Instructions.... L, 1763. Bound with: Murdoch, Patrick. Mercator's Sailing, Applied to the True Figure of the Earth. L, 1741 4to, contemp calf; worn. With 3 folding plates. 1 plate stained. S Oct 27 (813) £440 [Bickersteth]

**Mason, Finch.** See: Richardson & Mason

**Mason, Francis**
— Of the Consecration of the Bishops in the Church of England. L, 1613. 1st Ed. Folio, contemp vellum; worn & soiled, stained, loose. Stain to tp & prelims on to p. 14. wa Feb 29 (147) $120

**Mason, George Henry**
— The Costume of China. L, 1800. Bound with: Mason. The Punishments of China. L, 1801. Folio, contemp mor gilt; rubbed & bumped. With 60 hand-colored plates in 1st work & 22 hand-colored plates in 2d work. cb Oct 17 (105) $1,100
Anr Ed. L, 1800 [watermarked 1821]. Folio, mor gilt. With 60 hand-colored plates. pba June 20 (236) $850
1st Ed. L, 1800. Folio, mor gilt. With 60 hand-colored plates. pba Mar 7 (174) $950
Anr Ed. L, 1806 [plates watermarked 1801-11]. Folio, contemp russia gilt by Charles Hering, with his ticket; joints weak. Robyns - Fuerstenberg copy. C May 1 (103) £900
Anr Ed. L, 1806. Folio, contemp half russia gilt; spine repaired. With 60 hand-colored plates. Foxing to plates. sg May 9 (331) $850
— The Punishments of China. L, 1801 [plates watermarked 1822]. Folio, mor gilt; extremities worn & scuffed, front hinge cracked. With 22 colored plates. cb Oct 17 (106) $400
Anr Ed. L, 1801. Folio, mor gilt. With 22 colored plates. pba Mar 7 (184) $600
Anr Ed. L: W. Bulmer for Wm. Miller, 1830. 4to, contemp mor gilt; rubbed. With 22 colored plates. Titles stamped; English title torn & mtd. sg May 9 (364) $300

**Mason, James**
— The Natural Son. A Tragedy. Liverpool, 1805. 8vo, contemp calf; spine ends worn. b Dec 5 (206) £120

**Mason, John, 1600?-72?**
— A Brief History of the Pequot War.... NY: Sabin 1869. 8vo, half mor; extremities rubbed. sg Oct 26 (245) $175

**Mason, Monck, 1803-89?**
— Account of the Late Aeronautical Expedition from London to Weilburg. L, 1836. 8vo, modern syn, orig front cover label laid down. Tp spotted. sg May 16 (63) $375

**Mason, Otis Tufton**
— Indian Basketry: Studies in a Textile Art without Machinery. Wash., 1904. 8vo, orig wraps; worn. With 248 plates. sg Oct 26 (160) $60

**Mason, Timothy B.** See: Boynton & Mason

**Masons, Free and Accepted**
— A Book of the Antient Constitutions of the Free & Accepted Mason. L: B. Cole, [1729]. 1st Ed, 2d Issue. 8vo, contemp calf; rebacked. Some soiling. b Sept 20 (47) £200
— The Constitutions of the Free-Masons. L, 1723. 1st Ed of J. Anderson's version. 4to, contemp lea; worn. Frontis in facsimile; some discoloration. b Sept 20 (46) £700
Anr Ed. L, 1738. ("The New Book of Constitutions.") 4to, contemp calf; some wear. b Sept 20 (49) £400
— A Select Collection of Masonic Songs... General Charge to Masons and a List of all the Regular Lodges in England. Exeter: R. Trewman, 1767. 12mo, contemp sheep. Lacking H1. b Jan 31 (248) £60

**Maspero, Gaston**
— History of Egypt, Chaldea, Syria, Babylonia, and Assyria. L, [1903-6]. One of 1,000. 13 vols. 4to, half lea; worn & scuffed, hinges weak. sg June 13 (248) $130

**Masques II**
— Masques II: All-New Stories of Horror and the Supernatural. Balt., 1987. One of 300. Ed by J. N. Williamson. Sgd on tp by Robert Bloch, Ramsay Campbell & Joe R. Lansdale. pba Jan 25 (386) $50

**Massachusetts**
— Atlas of Essex County. Bost., 1884. Folio, disbound. With 57 hand-colored maps. Tp detached & worn. NH Sept 16 (44) $375
— Atlas of Hampden County. Springfield: Richards, 1894. Folio, cloth; broken. With 35 double-page color maps. 1 plate torn. O July 9 (13) $225
— Atlas of Springfield and longmeadow.... Springfield: Richards, 1910. Folio, cloth; broken. With 27 double-page color maps. O July 9 (14) $110
— The Charter Granted by their Majesties King William and Queen Mary, to the Inhabitants of the Province of the Massachusetts-Bay in New-England. Bost, 1759. Bound with: Acts and Laws, of His Majesty's Province of the Massachusetts-Bay in New-England. Bost., 1759. 8vo, old sheep; worn & scarred. Z June 28 (181) $450
— Debates, Resolutions and other Proceedings of the Convention...9th of January, 1788.... Bost., 1808. 2d Ed. 8vo, later half calf; scuffed. Tears to pages 7-10. pba June 13 (277) $75
— The Perpetual Laws of the Commonwealth of Massachusetts. [Bost.: Adams & Nourse, 1789]. Folio, contemp sheep; extremities worn. sg Oct 26 (248) $275

**Massachusetts Society for Promoting Agriculture.**
— Laws and Regulations of the Massachusetts Society for Promoting Agriculture. Bost.: Isaiah Thomas & Ebenezer T. Andrews, 1793. 8vo, sewn. Dogeared, minor tears. pba June 13 (299) $130

**Massialot, Francois, c.1660-1733**
— Nouvelle instruction pour les confitures, les liquers, et les fruits. Paris, 1740. 8vo, contemp calf; corners rubbed. With 4 folding plates. S Oct 12 (109) £180

**Massillon, Jean Baptiste**
— Petit Careme de Massillon suivi des Sermons. Paris, 1826. 8vo, contemp mor gilt by Vogel. sg Feb 8 (23) $90

**Masson, Andre**
— Anatomy of my Universe. NY, 1943. 1st Ed, one of 30, with orig sgd etching laid in. 4to, orig wraps; worn. cb Oct 17 (654) $500
— Bestiaire. NY, 1946. One of 135. Folio, pictorial wraps over bds; spine perished, wraps stained. With 12 litho plates. cb Oct 17 (655) $600; sg May 23 (389) $800

— Mythologies. Paris, [1946]. One of 250. 4to, orig wraps; backstrip def, some soiling. sg June 13 (249) $60

**Masson de Pezay, Alexandre Frederic Jacques, 1741-77**
— Zelis au bain. Poeme.... Geneva [but Paris], [1773]. 8vo, contemp citron mor gilt. With 4 plates & with further proof impressions of 1 headpiece & 1 tailpiece & the drawing by Eisen for the latter. Fuerstenberg - Schaefer copy. S Dec 7 (410) £360

**Masson, Frederic, 1847-1923**
— Josephine: Imperatrice et reine. Paris, 1899. One of 150. Folio, mor extra by P. Ruban, 1899. CE Sept 27 (184) $380

**Masters, Edgar Lee, 1869-1950.** See: Limited Editions Club

**Masterson, Thomas**
— Mastersons Arithmetic. L: George Miller, 1634. 8vo, 19th-cent half calf; front cover detached. Some foxing & staining; minor worming; tp browned; edges frayed & reinforced; 19th-cent owner's notes bound in. STC 17659. sg May 16 (215) $650

**Mastigouche Fish and Game Club**
— Charter and By-Laws. St. Gabriel de Brandon, 1 Jan 1922. Orig cloth; worn. With inserted list with ink corrections & with a typed addenda slip tipped in. O Feb 6 (153) $500

**Mather, Cotton, 1663-1728**
— Magnalia Christi Americana; or, the Ecclesiastical History of New England.... L, 1702. Folio, contemp calf; rebacked but hinges resplit. Lacking initial blank & map (supplied in photocopy); tp backed. pba Sept 14 (259) $1,500
Anr Ed. Hartford, 1820. 2 vols. 8vo, old sheep; rubbed. Some spotting. Z June 28 (182) $275
— A Memorial of the Present Deplorable State of New-England... by Philopolites. L, 1707. 4to, mor; spine head damaged. D4 torn & repaired, touching text. S Nov 30 (140) £2,200

**Mather, Increase, 1639-1723**
— A Brief History of the War with the Indians in New-England. L, 1676. 4to, later mor. Lacking a1; some leaves restored along fore-margin; some waterstaining. S Nov 30 (139) £2,400
— A Further Account of the Tryals of the New-England Witches.... L, 1693. 1st Ed. 4to, later calf. S Nov 30 (138) £1,800

**Mather, Samuel, 1706-85**
— The Life of the Very Reverend and Learned Cotton Mather. Bost., 1729. 8vo, later half mor; library mark on spine. Some browning & staining; library stamp on tp & B2. CE May 22 (23) $220

**Mathes, W. Michael**
— Spanish Approaches to the Island of California, 1628-1632. San Francisco: Book Club of Calif., 1975. One of 400. pba Feb 13 (136) $55

## MATHES

— Vizcaino and Spanish Expansion in the Pacific Ocean, 1580-1630. San Francisco, 1968. Orig cloth in dj. With 1 illus & 37 maps. Larson copy. pba Sept 28 (280) $55

**Matheson, Richard**
— Born of Man and Woman. Phila., 1954. In dj. Inscr. sg June 20 (262) $150
— Collected Stories. Los Angeles: Dream Press, 1989. One of 400. O Dec 5 (228) $50

**Mathews, Alfred E.**
— Gems of Rocky Mountain Scenery. NY, 1869. 1st Ed. Folio, orig cloth; faded & stained. With 20 plates. Plate stained at top margin. Robbins copy. pba Mar 21 (233) $3,000
— Pencil Sketches of Colorado. Boulder, 1961. With: Nolie Mumey. Alfred Edward Mathews. And: Interesting Narrative, Being a Journal of the Flight of Alfred E. Mathews (facsimile) One of 350. Folio, orig cloth, half cloth & wraps in box; box worn. With 23 color plates. Robbins copy. Sgd by Mumey. pba Mar 21 (234) $75

**Mathews, Anne**
— Memoirs of Charles Mathews, Comedian. L, 1838-39. 4 vols extended to 8. 8vo, mor gilt; rubbed. Extra-illus with c.210 prints & ALs. bba June 6 (27) £350 [Cherrington]

**Mathews, Eliza Kirkham**
— Poems. York, 1802. 8vo, contemp calf gilt. b Dec 5 (465) £320

**Mathews, Frederick C.** See: Howe & Mathews

**Mathias, Thomas James, 1754?-1835.** See: Fore-Edge Paintings

**Mathison, Thomas**
— The Goff. An Heroi-Comical Poem. [Far Hills, NJ]: Stinehour Press for U.S.G.A., 1981. One of 1,400. Intro by Joseph Murdoch & Stephen Ferguson. Half cloth. pba Apr 18 (127) $300

**Matisse, Henri, 1869-1954**
— Cinquante dessins. Paris, 1920. Ltd Ed. Folio, orig wraps. With orig frontis etching, sgd, & 50 plates. bba May 9 (182) £1,900 [Sims Reed]
— Dernieres oeuvres.... Paris, 1958. Folio, bds. Verve, No 35/36. wad Oct 18 (410) C$980
— Dessins: Themes et Variations. Paris: Fabiani, 1943. One of 950. 4to, loose in orig wraps. wad Oct 18 (315) C$1,450
— Gravures originales sur le theme de Chant de Minos (Les Cretois). Pour le text de H. de Montherlant. Paris, 1981. One of 25. 2 vols. 4to, loose as issued in ptd wraps & half cloth. CE Sept 27 (185) $2,400
— [-] Henri Matisse Exhibition. NY, 1915. 8vo, orig wraps. sg Sept 7 (239) $150
— [-] Homage to Henri Matisse. NY, [1970. 4to, cloth, in dj. Special No of Vingtieme Siecle. sg June 13 (306) $70

## AMERICAN BOOK PRICES CURRENT

— Jazz. Paris, 1947. One of 250 on velin d'Arches. Folio, orig wraps & bds; lower joint of wraps splitting. With 20 plates, colored by pochoir. S Nov 21 (305) £57,000

Anr Ed. NY: Braziller, [1983]. Folio, cloth. sg Sept 7 (238) $175

Anr copy. Loose as issued in cloth. sg Jan 11 (274) $120
— The Last Works of.... NY, [1958]. Folio, bds. Verve, No 35/36. pba Mar 7 (175) $750
— Portraits. Monte Carlo, 1954. Hors commerce copy. 4to, orig wraps. With litho frontis, 60 uncolored & 33 tipped-in color plates. cb Oct 17 (656) $550

Ltd Ed in French. Wraps. sg Jan 11 (275) $375

Anr copy. Wraps; prelims loose. wad Oct 18 (316) C$500

**Matrix**
— Matrix: A Review for Printers & Bibliophiles. Andoversford: Whittington Press, 1981-95. Ltd Ed. Vols 1-15 & Index for Vols 1-5. Various bdgs, in djs. bba May 9 (350) £2,500 [Ginnan]

Anr copy. Vol 8 only. Bds, in dj. bba May 9 (653) £50 [Cox]; bba May 9 (654) £65 [Ginnan]

Anr copy. Vols 1 & 3-12 in 11 plus additional folder for Vols 10 & 11. Various bdgs. sg Feb 15 (199) $1,500

Anr copy. Vol 9 only. Bds, in dj with crease. sg Feb 15 (201) $140

One of 105 specially bound in oasis mor with accompanying portfolio. sg Feb 15 (200) $250

**Mattes, Merrill J.**
— The Great Platte River Road: The Covered Wagon Mainline via Fort Kearny to Fort Laramie. [Omaha], 1969. 1st Ed. Orig cloth in dj; d/j worn. With frontis, 9 maps, & 29 illus. Some spotting. Sgd. Larson copy. pba Sept 28 (594) $90
— Platte River Road Narratives: A Descriptive Bibliography.... Urbana, 1988. 1st Ed. - Foreword by James Michener. Orig cloth. With double-page map. Robbins copy. pba Mar 21 (235) $65
— Platte River Road Narratives: A Descriptive Bibliography of Travel over the Great Central Overland Route.... Urbana, IL, 1988. 1st Ed. - Foreword by James Michener. Orig cloth. With two-page map. Larson copy. pba Sept 28 (595) $165

**Matthes, Francois E.**
— Geologic History of the Yosemite Valley. Wash., 1930. Folio, cloth. With 46 plates & 6 folding maps Adhesive marks on tp & back endpaper. U.S. Department of the Interior, Geological Survey, Professional Paper 160. pba Feb 12 (102) $60

Anr copy. Ptd wraps; rear wrap detached, along with envelope with 4 folding maps. U.S. Department of the Interior, Geological Survey, Professional Paper 160. pba Apr 25 (523) $50

**Matthews, Lieut. John, R.N.**
— A Voyage to the River Sierra-Leone.... L, 1788. 1st Ed. 8vo, later calf; rubbed. With 9 plates (1 folding)

& folding map. Title browned; few leaves stained. S Oct 26 (546) £460 [Rizzo]

**Matthews, Washington**
— The Night Chant, a Navaho Ceremony. [NY], 1902. 1st Ed. Recent calf, orig wraps bound in. With 8 plates (5 color) Some insect damage at beginning. bbc Dec 18 (493) $325

Anr copy. Orig wraps; some chipping & wear to wraps, corners bumped. Robbins copy. pba Mar 21 (236) $140

**Matthews, William, Engineer**
— Hydraulia... L, 1835. 8vo, orig cloth; spine head chipped, upper hinge split. With 5 folding maps, port & 12 plates. Piece lacking at bottom margin of tp. bbc Feb 26 (455) $200

**Matthews, William F.** See: Grolier Club

**Matthias, Eugen**
— Der Mannliche Korper. Zurich, 1931. Half cloth; worn & soiled. sg Feb 29 (228) $60

**Matthiessen, Peter**
— In the Spirit of Crazy Horse. NY: Viking, [1983]. 1st Issue. In dj. bbc Dec 18 (310) $120

**Mattioli, Pietro Andrea, 1500-77**
— Commentarii in libros sex Pedacii Dioscoridis de medica materia. Venice: Valgrisi, 1565. ("Commentarii in sex libros P. Dioscoridis de materia medica.") Folio, later calf with modern linen cover. With early hand-coloring. Lacking tp & several other leaves; last 8 leaves def; wormhole affecting last 100 leaves; some dampstaining throughout; minor tears, holes & repairs affecting portions of text. Sold w.a.f. pn Dec 7 (110) £2,800
— Commentarii in sex libros Pedacii Dioscoridis Anazarbei de medica materia. Venice: Valgrisi, 1565. 1st Enlarged Ed. Folio, later calf; some wear. Lacking Gg3 & Hh3; some dampstaining; title def & backed; extensive marginal repairs at beginning & end; last leaf backed. S Oct 27 (752) £2,600 [Bifolco]
— I Discorsi di M. Pietro Andrea Matthioli ne i sei libri di Pedacio Dioscoride...della materia medicinale. Venice: Marco Ginami, 1621. ("I Discorsi ne i sei libri di Pedacio Dioscoride....") Folio, later half calf; rubbed. Tp frayed & mtd & stamped; some browning & soiling throughout; a few leaves with small holes affecting text. Sold w.a.f. pn Dec 7 (111) £500 [Bifolco]

Anr Ed. Venice, 1645. ("I Discorsi nelli sei libri de Pedacio Dioscoride Anazarbeo della materia medicinale.") Folio, old vellum. Some tears & foxing. Met Sept 28 (379) $1,800

**Mattson, Morris**
— The American Vegetable Practice.... Bost., 1841. 2 vols in 1. 8vo, lea; broken. With 24 plates. Foxed throughout; some repairs. Met Feb 24 (317) $525

**Mauclair, Camille, 1872-1945**
— Jules Cheret. Paris, 1930. One of 730. 4to, orig wraps; tears at edges. sg June 13 (116) $120
— Louis Legrand, pientre et graveur. Paris, [1910]. 4to, half mor gilt, orig wraps bound in. sg June 13 (235) $700
— Les Poisons des pierreries. Paris, 1903. One of 312. Illus by E. Decisy after Georges Rochegrosse. 4to, mor sgd J. Weckesser, 1918, with large inset marquetry panels, the upper cover depicting a seated woman, the lower 2 entwined snakes above flames; orig wraps bound in. S Nov 21 (307) £2,000

**Maudslay, Anne C. & Alfred P.**
— A Glimpse at Guatemala.... L, 1899. 1st Ed. 4to, orig bds. Met Feb 24 (52) $900

Anr copy. Orig half cloth; soiled. S Oct 26 (518) £800 [Ortueta]

**Maugham, William Somerset, 1874-1965**
See also: Limited Editions Club
— Ashenden, or the British Agent. L, 1928. Orig cloth, in dj; extremities worn. P Dec 12 (122) $1,200
— Loaves and Fishes. L, 1924. 1st Ed. pba Aug 22 (329) $55
— The Moon and Sixpence. L, [1919]. 1st Ed, Issue not specified. Cloth; corners bumped. Browned. pba Aug 22 (331) $120
— Of Human Bondage. Garden City, 1936. One of 751. pba Jan 25 (252) $190
— Points of View. L, 1958. 1st Ed. In dj. Inscr. sg June 20 (263) $250
— Then and Now, a Novel. Garden City, 1946. Proof copy. Wraps. sg Dec 14 (212) $175
— A Writer's Notebook. Garden City, 1949. One of 1,000. pba Aug 22 (332) $170

**Maule, John.** See: Cooke & Maule

**Maund, Benjamin, 1790-1863.** See: Botanic...

**Maupassant, Guy de, 1850-93**
See also: Limited Editions Club
— Boule de Suif and Other Stories. Bost.: C. T. Brainard, [1909]. One of 1,000. 10 vols. Half calf; spine ends rubbed. pba Aug 8 (273) $120
— Contes et Nouvelles. Paris, 1885. 24mo, mor gilt by Yseux. Inscr to Alphonse Daudet. C May 1 (104) £1,600
— Deux contes: le vieux, la ficelle. Paris: la Societe Normande du Libre Illustre, 1907. One of 120. Illus by Auguste Lepere. 8vo, mor extra by Charles Meunier, orig wraps bound in. With 84 wood-engraved illusts 7 decorations colored a la poupee. S Nov 30 (348) £500
— Pierre et Jean. Paris, 1888. 1st Ed, one of 50 on japon with 3 additional suites of the illusts. Illus by Ernest Duez & Albert Lynch. 12mo, mor extra by Ch. Septier, orig wraps bound in. Watercolor drawing sgd by Ernest Duez on half-title. S Nov 21 (308) £350
— Le Vagabond. Paris, 1902. One of 115. Illus by Theophile Steinlen. 4to, mor by Marius Michel with inset panel of calf showing the Vagabond walking along a road, carved, colored & stamp-sgd by Stein-

## MAUPERTUIS

len, orig wraps preserved. Steinlin's copy, with the suite of colored lithos before text. S Nov 21 (309) £2,100

**Maupertuis, Pierre Louis Moreau de, 1698-1759**
— Oeuvres. Lyons, 1768. 4 vols. 8vo, calf; extremities rubbed. Some foxing. NH Sept 16 (376) $210

**Mauriac, Francois, 1885-1970**
— Genitrix. Paris, 1923. With: 2 autograph dedications to Adrien Lachenal; autograph note by Robert de Traz One of 20 on papier velin de cuve. 8vo, half mor by Gruel; orig wraps & d/js bound in. With port by Heudebert. S Oct 27 (1143) £150 [Viandier]

**Maurice, Frederick**
— Robert E. Lee the Soldier. Bost., 1925. 4th Impression. Orig cloth; extremities worn. Cut signature tipped to tp. cb Oct 17 (158) $500; cb Oct 17 (158) $500

**Maurice, Thomas**
— Indian Antiquities, or Dissertations Relative to the Ancient Geographical Divisions.... L, 1806. 7 vols. 8vo, contemp half mor; rubbed, extremities scuffed. With 29 folding plates. Some foxing; short tear to frontis of Vol I. pba June 20 (237) $250

**Maurois, Andre, 1885-1967**
— Le Peseur d'ames. Paris: Roche, 1931. One of 366. Illus by Francis Picabia. 4to, mor extra by R. Scheuchzer, the upper cover with 4 cutout pieces revealing crayon, watercolor & gouache drawings after Picabia, orig wraps bound in. With 9 color plates. Bound in are 15 crayon & watercolor drawings sgd by Picabia, a proof of the tp with Ms annotations & an ALs of R. Scheuchzer explaining his bdg design. S Nov 21 (310) £4,600

**Maury, Matthew Fontaine, 1806-73**
— Explanations and Sailing Directions To Accompany the Wind Current Charts.... Phila., 1854. Folio, contemp sheep; covers worn, front cover detached, lacking some lea. Dampstaining to top margins throughout; foxed. pba July 25 (185) $225
— The Physical Geography of the Sea. NY, 1855. 8vo, orig cloth. With 12 plates. NH June 1 (238) $250

**Mavor, William Fordyce, 1758-1837.** See: Fore-Edge Paintings

**Maw, George, 1832-1912**
— A Monograph of the Genus Crocus.... L, 1886. 4to, contemp mor gilt; extremities scuffed. With double-page colored map, 2 double-page distribution tables & 81 hand-colored plates. C May 31 (34) £2,400

**Mawe, John, 1764-1829**
— The Linnaean System of Conchology. L, 1823. 8vo, contemp half calf; rubbed. Ck Feb 14 (317) £200
— Travels in the Interior of Brazil.... L, 1823. 2d Ed. 8vo, disbound. With map & 5 colored plates. sg Oct 26 (252) $225

## AMERICAN BOOK PRICES CURRENT

**Mawe, Thomas —& Others**
— Every Man his Own Gardener. Dublin, 1793. 4to, contemp calf; joints cracked. Some wear to upper corners. pba Aug 22 (581) $200

**Mawson, Sir Douglas, 1882-1938**
— The Home of the Blizzard. Phila., [1915]. 1st American Ed. 2 vols. Orig cloth; rubbed, corners showing. pba July 25 (44) $375
Anr Ed. L, [1931]. Foxing to edges. pba July 25 (45) $55

**Maximilian zu Wied-Neuwied, Prince, 1782-1867**
— Reise nach Brasilien in den Jahren 1815 bis 1817. Frankfurt, 1820-21. 2 text vols only. 4to, contemp calf gilt; corner of Vol I dampstained. CE May 22 (24) $400

**Maxwell, Sir Herbert Eustace**
— Salmon and Sea Trout. L, 1898. One of 130 L.p. copies. 8vo, orig cloth; worn & shaken. Some foxing. O Feb 6 (154) $100

**Maxwell, James Clerk, 1831-79**
— A Treatise on Electricity and Magnetism. Oxford, 1873. 1st Ed. 2 vols in 1. 8vo, contemp calf prize bdg. With 20 plates. b May 30 (30) £650

**Maxwell, W. Harold & Leslie F.**
— Sweet and Maxwell's Legal Bibliography.... L, 1989. 2 vols. O May 7 (200) $60

**May, Philip William, 1864-1903**
— Phil May's ABC. L, 1897. One of 1,050. 4to, orig cloth. bba May 9 (238) £60 [Stransky]

**May, Robert, b.1588**
— The Accomplisht Cook.... L, 1678. 4th Ed. 8vo, contemp calf; worn, upper joint cracked. Short tear on gutter margin of port; some wrinkling to folding plate; a few short tears; some staining. CE June 12 (179) $1,200

**Mayakovsky, Vladimir**
— Dlya Golosa. Berlin, 1923. Illus by El Lissitsky. 8vo, orig wraps; spine discolored. Inscr to Boris Kochno. S Nov 2 (28) £1,800 [Weinbaum]
Anr copy. Orig wraps; soiled, backstrip darkened & worn, ends chipped. Some foxing; a few leaves stained; index tabs browned. sg Apr 18 (114) $850
— Ya. Moscow, [1913]. 4to, wraps; spine worn, some soiling. Browned. C June 26 (225) £280

**Maydman, Henry**
— Naval Speculations, and Maritime Politicks.... L, 1691. 1st Ed. 8vo, later half sheep; needs rebdg. sg Mar 7 (221) $800

**Mayer, Alfred Marshall, 1836-97**
— Sport with Gun and Rod...in American Woods and Waters. L, [c.1883]. 4to, pictorial cloth. sg Mar 7 (496) $130
1st Ed. NY, [1883]. 2 vols. 4to, orig cloth; worn. O Jan 9 (164) $170

Anr copy. Modern cloth. sg Mar 7 (497) $80

### Mayer, Charles Joseph
— Les Ligues Acheenne, Suisse et Hollandoise.... Geneva, 1787. 2 vols. 12mo, orig wraps. sg Oct 26 (253) $200

### Mayer, Julius Robert von, 1814-78
— Die Mechanik der Waerme in gesammelten Schriften. Stuttgart, 1867. 1st Ed. 8vo, contemp cloth. Title & some leaves spotted. Ck Mar 22 (184) £240

### Mayer, Luigi
— A Selection of the most interesting of Sir Robert Ainslie's...Collection of Views.... L, 1811-12. Part 1 only. Folio, disbound. With 24 color plates. Tp soiled & chipped; repaired tears to contents; minor soiling to plates. wa Feb 29 (128) $1,100

— Views in Egypt. L, 1804. With 48 colored plates dated 1801-4. Bound with: Mayer. Views in Palestine.... L, 1804. With 24 colored plates dated 1803-4. And: Mayer. Views in the Ottoman Empire.... L, 1803. With 24 colored plates dated 1803. And: Views in the Ottoman Dominions.... L, 1810. With 71 hand-colored plates. Bound in 2 vols. Folio, contemp half mor gilt; rubbed, 1 joint split. Charles Vignoles' copy. b June 28 (44) £4,200

Anr Ed. L, 1805. Bound with: Views in Palestine. L, 1804; Views in the Ottoman Empire. L, 1803. 3 works in 1 vol. Folio, contemp russia; rebacked, edges worn. Text in English & French. With 96 hand-colored plates. Some offsetting. S Oct 26 (169) £3,000 [Magnani]

— Views in Egypt, Palestine and other Parts of the Ottoman Empire. L, 1805-4-3. 3 vols in 1. Folio, contemp russia gilt; spine ends & corners damaged. With 92 hand-colored plates only. sg Dec 7 (280) $4,200

— Views in the Ottoman Empire. L, 1803 [c.1811]. Folio, 19th-Cent half calf. Text in English & French. With 23 (of 24) hand-colored plates. S Oct 26 (168) £950 [Chelsea Gal.]

— Vues en Egypte. L, 1802. Bound with: Views in Palestine. L, 1804; Views in the Ottoman Empire. L, 1803. Plates by Thomas Milton. 3 works in 1 vol. Folio, 20th-Cent half calf. Together, 96 hand-colored plates. Some discoloration. S Oct 26 (167) £2,900 [Harrington]

### Mayer, Wenceslaus Joseph
— Historica-philosophica descriptio picturae novae bibliothecae fornici inductae in Canonia Strahoviensi... ab Antonio Maulbertsch. Prague, 1797. 4to, contemp sheep. sg Apr 11 (228) $300

### Mayerne Turquet, Louis de
— The General Historie of Spaine. L, 1612. 1st Ed in English. Folio, contemp calf; needs rebacked. Stain in center of tp & next leaf; 3d prelim leaf frayed; may lack initial blank. sg Mar 21 (225) $300

### Mayeul Chaudon, L.
— Nouveau dictionnaire historique-portatif.... Amst.: Marc Michel Rey, 1771. 4 vols. 8vo, contemp calf; rubbed. O Mar 26 (172) $225

### Mayhew, Augustus & Henry
— The Good Genius that turned Everything into Gold.... L, 1847. 1st Ed. - Illus by George Cruikshank. 16mo, calf gilt by Root, orig cloth bound in. With frontis & 3 plates. pba Aug 22 (617) $80

### Mayhew, Edward
— The Illustrated Horse Doctor. NY, 1862. Orig cloth. pba Aug 22 (597) $70

### Mayhew, Henry, 1812-87
— 1851: or the Adventures of Mr. and Mrs. Sandboys.... L, [1851]. Illus by George Cruikshank. 8 parts. 8vo, orig wraps; Part 2 backstrip imperf. Lacking Plate 3. sg Feb 8 (268) $120

### Maynard, Charles Johnson, 1845-1929
— Eggs of North American Birds. Bost., 1890. 8vo, cloth. With 10 hand-finished litho plates. sg Dec 7 (204) $110

— A Manual of North American Butterflies. Bost., 1891. Folio, cloth; spine ends rubbed. With 10 hand-colored lithos. pba June 20 (238) $350

### Maynwaring, Everard, 1628-99?
— Tutela Sanitatis, sive Vita Protracta. The Protection of Long Life.... L, 1664. 2d Ed. 8vo, contemp calf; restored. Title & few leaves repaired; some soiling. Ck Mar 22 (186) £550

### Mayow, John, 1643-79
— Tractatus quinque medico-physici.... Oxford, 1674. 1st Ed. 8vo, contemp calf; restored. With frontis port, & 6 plates (3 folding). 2 folding plates soiled & crumpled; 3d folding plate browned & lacking segment; title thumb-soiled; later leaves dampstained. Ck Mar 22 (187) £1,000

**Mayronis, Franciscus de.** See: Franciscus de Mayronis

### Mayuyama & Co.
— Mayuyama, Seventy Years. [Tokyo, 1976]. 2 vols. Folio, cloth. sg June 13 (251) $200

### Mazal, Otto
— Europaeische Einbandkunst aus Mittelalter und Neuzeit. Graz: Akademischer Druck, 1970. 4to, orig cloth; worn. O Mar 26 (173) $140

### Mazzella, Scipio
— Descrittione del regno di Napoli. Naples: Gio. Battista Cappelli, 1601. 4to, contemp lea; most lea rubbed off. sg Mar 21 (226) $375

### Mazzocchi, Domenico, 1592-1665
— Dialoghi e sonetti posti in musica. Rome: Francesco Zannetti, 1638. Bound with: Praterent anni. elegia Urbani Papae VIII.... Rome: Ludovicus Grignanus, 1641. Oblong 4to, contemp vellum. C June 26 (273) £950

## Mazzocchius, Jacobus
— Epigrammata antiquae urbis. Rome: Jacobus Mazochius, 1521. Folio, old vellum; soiled, worn, spine deteriorating. Tp soiled; some dampstaining to top margins; some foxing; old ink notes; I3 with marginal tear; Bb1 wormed affecting a line of text; some corners chipped; lacking 1 leaf.  pba Mar 7 (176) $425

## Mead, Richard, 1673-1754
— A Treatise concerning the Influence of the Sun and Moon upon Human Bodies.... L, 1748. 1st English Ed. - Trans by Thomas Stack. 8vo, modern mor.  CE Nov 8 (121) $280

## Mead Collection, Richard
— [Sale Catalogue] Bibliotheca Meadiana. L, 1754-55. 8vo, contemp half calf; joints cracked, rubbed.  bba May 9 (46) £220 [Quaritch]

## Means, James
— Manflight. Bost., 1891. 8vo, orig ptd wraps. Aeronautic Americana 83.  b May 30 (31) £70

## Means, Sterling
— Black Devils and Other Poems. Louisville: Pentacostal Publishing Company, [1919]. Orig cloth; lettering chipped.  sg Mar 28 (201) $80

## Meares, John, 1756?-1809
— Authentic copy of the Memorial to the Right Honourable William Wyndham Grenville.... L, [1790]. 1st Ed. Modern half calf. Some foxing & darkening. Robbins-Streeter copy.  pba Mar 21 (237) $4,500
— Voyages Made in the Years 1788 and 1789.... L, 1790. 4to, orig or early cloth, purported to be by Dorothy Wordsworth; minor wear & stains, old pressmark to front pastedown. With port, 10 maps & 16 plates (has the extra plate of the Philippines facing p. 17). Minor foxing.  pba Feb 13 (137) $4,500
Anr copy. Contemp calf. With 8 folding maps & 4 plates, 2 of them folding. Tape repair to 1 leaf.  pba Apr 25 (215) $900

## Mease, James, 1771-1846
— The Picture of Philadelphia.... Phila., 1811. 1st Ed. 12mo, orig sheep; rubbed, spine gone. Folding view dampstained & lacking corner; tp & front matter dampstained.  F June 20 (375) $50

## Mecham, Clifford Henry
— Sketches & Incidents of the Siege of Lucknow.... L, 1858. Folio, loose in orig cloth; worn & stained. With litho title & 17 tinted litho plates. Dampstained & spotted affecting plates; text leaves stained & torn.  bba June 6 (48) £65 [Finney]

## Mechel, Christian von, 1737-1818
— La Passion de notre Seigneur. Basel, 1784. Illus by Hans Holbein. Folio, later bds; worn. With 12 plates. Some foxing & soiling.  sg May 9 (352) $175

## Mechnikov, Il'ia Il'ich, 1845-1916
— Lektsii o sravnetelnoipatologii vospalenija. St. Petersburg, 1892. 8vo, disbound. Tp stained.  sg May 16 (449) $1,800

## Medailles...
See: Fleurimont, G. R.; Louis XIV

## Medical Student, A.
See: Laing, Alexander

## Medina, Balthasar de, d.1697
— Vida, martyrio, y beatificacion del invicto protomartyr de el Japan San Felipe de Jesus, Patron de Mexico.... Madrid, 1751. 4to, recent vellum. With port. Some discoloration.  S Nov 30 (203) £900

## Medina, Pedro de, 1493-1567
— L'Art de naviguer. Rouen, 1633. 4to, modern vellum. Library stamp on verso of tp & final blank.  S June 13 (660) £520
— L'Arte del navegar.... Venice: G. Pedrezano, 1555 [colophon dated 1554]. 1st Ed in Italian. 4to, modern vellum bds. With woodcut map. Tp repaired & soiled.  S Nov 30 (168) £3,000
— Libro de la Verdad.... Valladolid: Francisco Fernandez de Cordova, 12 Feb 1555. 4to, contemp vellum; front cover torn. Dampstaining at ends; some worming; tp soiled; edges gnawed. Sold w.a.f.  sg Mar 21 (300) $1,200

## Mediterranean
— A collection of 12 charts [covering the Eastern Mediterranean...]. L, [1844-1862]. Engraved by J. C. Walker. Backed on linen; some soiling.  S Oct 26 (94) £400 [Martin]

## Mee, Margaret
— Flowers of the Brazilian Forest.... L, [1968]. One of 100, sgd & with orig drawing as frontis. Folio, orig vellum.  S Nov 30 (35) £1,000

## Meehan, Thomas, 1826-1901
— The Native Flowers and Ferns of the United States. Bost., 1878-80. Series I-II, in 4 vols. 4to, contemp half mor; several covers detached, spines shabby. With 193 colored plates.  wa Nov 16 (290) $400
Anr Ed. Bost., 1878-[80]. Series I, Vol 2 & Series II, Vol 1 only. 4to, orig cloth; worn, spines cropped, frayed, joints & hinges cracked, loose. With 96 chromolitho plates.  wa Feb 29 (142) $350

## Meeker, Ezra, 1830-1928
— The Busy Life of Eighty-five Years of Ezra Meeker. Seattle, 1916. Bdg not described. Library markings. Inscr to Thomas A. Edison.  pba June 13 (154) $160
— Hop Culture in the United States. Puyallup, [1883]. 8vo, orig cloth. Stamps to tp.  pba Nov 16 (171) $120

## Meggendorfer, Lothar, 1847-1925
— Always Jolly! L: H. Grevel, [1891]. 4to, orig bds; & soiled, lacking backstrip. With 8 hand-colored illusts, the moving parts operated by levers. Moving parts for 1 illust inoperative, 3 levers creased or repaired; soiled & spotted.  S Nov 2 (337) £280 [Barnsbury]
— Comic Actors. L: H. Grevel, [c.1900]. Folio, orig half cloth. With 8 full-page colored illusts, each with levers to operate moving parts. Lacking 1 lever, anr broken; head of 1 figure broken, 2 figures def; 3 mar-

gins torn; 3 leaves loose.  S Nov 2 (338) £280 [Glendale]

**Meheut, Mathurin**
— Etude de la Foret. Paris: Albert Levy, [early 20th-cent]. With Texts by Julien Noel Costantin & L, Plantefol. Vol II only. loose as issued in pictorial bd folder; joints cracked. With 60 plates, 25 of them mtd & in color.  sg Dec 7 (281) $50

**Meibom, Marcus, d.1711**
— De proportionibus dialogus. Copenhagen: Melchior Martzan, 1655. Bound with: Wilhelmi Langii epistola. Accessit Marci Meibomii responsio. Copenhagen: Petrus Morsingius, [1656]. Folio, contemp sheep.  S Mar 14 (249) £650

**Meier, Georg, Professor**
— De origine et autoritate verbi Dei.... Wittenberg: Johannes Lufft, 1550. 8vo, contemp roll-tooled calf with inner panel of acorns, with first owner's initials I.S.F. & date 1550; front cover almost detached, spine worn, corners scuffed. Bound in is a very imperf copy of Icones Mortis, Lyon, 1547. Inscr by Joannes Bugenhagen.  C Apr 3 (149) £1,300

**Meigret, Amedee**
— Questiones in libros de celo & mundi Aristotelis. Paris: Jean Petit, 14 Nov 1514. Folio, modern mor. Modern ink & color two-sided border added to margins of tp & device colored by same hand; marginal repairs at beginning; some browning; a few tears in margins.  S June 27 (343) £850

**Meigs, John**
— Peter Hurd. The Lithographs. [Lubbock, Texas], 1968. One of 300 sgd & with an orig sgd litho. 4to, mor. Inscr.  pba June 20 (203) $250

**Meikle, James.** See: Shields & Meikle

**Meinertzhagen, Richard**
— Nicoll's Birds of Egypt. L, 1930. 2 vols. 4to, cloth. With 38 color plates & 3 folding maps.  Met May 22 (389A) $350

**Meinhold, William**
— Sidonia the Sorceress. L, 1926. One of 225. 4to, vellum gilt. Library stamps.  bba Nov 16 (223) £300 [Thorp]

**Meinrad.** See: Passio...

**Meinstorff, J. F. von.** See: Fictuld, Hermann

**Meisl, Willy —& Others**
— Die Olympischen Spiele in Los Angeles 1932. Altona-Bahrenfeld, 1932. 4to, orig cloth, in worn dj; bdg extremities worn.  sg Feb 29 (291) £110

**Meisner, Leonhard Ferdinand**
— Caffe, chocolatae, herbae thee ac nicotianae.... Nuremberg, 1721. 8vo, contemp half calf; spine wormed, corners bumped. With frontis & 3 folding plates. 2 plates wormed.  Ck Mar 22 (197) £350

**Mejer, Johannes.** See: Danckwerth & Mejer

**Mejer, Johannes —&**
**Norlund, N. E.**
— Johannes Mejer's kort over det Danske Rige. Copenhagen, 1942. 3 vols. Folio, orig half cloth. With 289 color maps, some foxing. Geodaetisk Instituts Publikationer I-III. Inscr by Norlund.  S Mar 14 (96) £250

**Mejer, Wolfgang**
— Bibliographie der Buchbinderei-Literatur, 1924-1932. Leipzig, 1925-1933. 4to, modern half mor.  sg Apr 11 (55) $90

**Mela, Pomponius**
— Cosmographia. Paris: Christian Wechel, 1530. ("De orbis situ libri tres.") Bound with: Quintilianus, Marcus Fabius. institutiones oratoriae ac Declamationes. Paris, 1531. Folio, contemp blind-tooled calf over pastebd with brass catches only; joints cracked & chipped. Worming in blank margins of c.40 leaves; some dampstaining along top edges.  sg Mar 21 (227) $800
— De situ obris libri III.... Leiden, 1722. 8vo, contemp vellum. With additional title & folding map. Map browned; spotted.  S Oct 26 (456) £260 [Zioni]

**Melanchthon, Philipp, 1497-1560**
— Loci praecipui theologici. Leipzig: Valentin Papst, 1552. 8vo, contemp calf over wooden bds, elaborately blind-tooled with Bibliocal figures by an unknown atelier, with 3 raised double bands on blind-ruled spine, repoussee brass center- & cornerpieces & orig brass clasps & catches.  C May 1 (105) £2,200

**Melish, John, 1771-1822**
— A Geographical Description of the United States.... Phila., 1818. 3d Ed. 8vo, early half sheep; rebacked with cloth, endpapers renewed. Some foxing.  sg May 9 (85) $650
— Travels in the United States of America.... Phila., 1812. 1st Ed. 2 vols. 8vo, bdg not described. With 3 hand-colored & 3 uncolored maps. Foxed.  NH June 1 (218) $325

**Mellen, Peter**
— The Group of Seven. Toronto, 1970. 4to, cloth, in dj.  sg Jan 11 (277) $50

**Meller, Prosper**
— Des Aerostats. Bordeaux, 1851. Atlas vol only. Folio, 19th-cent half calf, orig front wrap bound in; extremities worn. With 5 litho plates. Inscr "Hommage a M. O. de Lalande".  sg May 16 (65) $400

**Melli, Sebastiano**
— La Comare levatrice istruita nel suo uffizio. Venice: Gio. Battista Recurti, 1738. 4to, contemp vellum bds; front free endpaper lacking. With 20 plates. Tp stained; some leaves dampstained.  sg May 16 (451) $600

## Mellick, Andrew D.
— The Story of an Old Farm. Somerville NJ: Unionist Gazette, 1889. 4to, orig cloth; worn, hinges cracked. With port & 3 A Ls s inserted. F Mar 28 (402) $145

## Melling, Antoine Ignace
— Voyage pittoresque dans les Pyrenees Francaises.... Paris, 1826-30. Oblong folio, 19th-cent half mor; worn. With port, map & 72 plates. Each plate with pbr's blindstamp at plate mark & library blindstamp; some discoloration, mainly to text. S June 27 (116) £1,000

## Mellon, James
— African Hunter. NY, [1975]. 4to, bds, in chipped & torn & repaired dj; some wear. Inscr. O Oct 10 (194) $150

Anr copy. Bds, in dj with minor wear. O Oct 10 (195) $130

## Mellon, Paul
PODESCHI, JOHN B. - Books on the Horse and Horsemanship. L, 1981. Folio, in dj. O May 7 (244) $80

Anr copy. Orig cloth in dj. sg Apr 11 (229) $120

## Mellon, Paul & Mary
— Alchemy and the Occult; a Catalogue of Books.... New Haven, 1968. One of 500. Compiled by Ian Macphail & others. Vols I & II (of 4). 2 vols. 4to, orig cloth in slipcase. sg Apr 11 (287) $300

**Mellon Collection, Paul & Mary**

Anr Ed. New Haven, 1968-77. One of 500 sets. Vols III-IV only. Orig cloth. Met Feb 24 (155) $200

## Meltzer, David
— Poems. [San Francisco: Pvtly ptd, 1957]. Bound as issued with: Schenker, Donald. Poetry. One of 25, sgd by both authors. Half cloth. pba Aug 22 (346) $55

## Melusine...
— La Melusine. Lyon: Matthias Huss, [c.1493]. Compiled by Jean d'Arras. Folio, mor gilt by Bauzonnet-Trautz. 43-44 lines; types 12:95G (text) & 10:140G (title). With 64 woodcuts. Washed; minor stains; 2 corners repaired. 128 leaves. C 3971. Essling - Yemeniz - Lignerolles - Bordes - Loncle - Schaefer copy. P Nov 1 (128) $190,000

## Melville, Henry
— Van Diemen's Land...Statistical and Other Information.... Hobart Town: Henry Melville, 1833. 8vo, orig cloth; covers spotted. Some foxing & soiling. O Nov 14 (121) $300

## Melville, Herman, 1819-91
See also: Limited Editions Club; Nonesuch Press
— Battle-Pieces and Aspects of the War. NY, 1866. 1st Ed. 12mo, orig cloth; spine ends worn, shaken. CE Feb 21 (181) $1,000

Anr copy. Orig cloth; spine ends worn, upper hinge cracked. Marginal browning. CE May 22 (331) $700

— Billy Budd, Sailor. Mt. Holly NJ: Married Mettle Press, 1987. Illus by Deborah Alterman. Orig wooden bds riveted to a patinated bronze spine with handmade hinges & the title in bronze relief, in welded bronze-framed glass folding box. P June 5 (294) $750

— Israel Potter: His Fifty Years of Exile. NY, 1855. 1st Ed, 1st ptg. 12mo, orig cloth, 1st bdg; minor rubbing. CE Feb 21 (180) $1,000

— Mardi: and a Voyage Thither. L, 1849. 1st Ed. 3 vols. 12mo, orig cloth; sides soiled, Vol I rebacked with most of orig spine laid down, some corners worn, portion of Vol II front free endpaper torn away. Small piece torn from corner of half-title. CNY Dec 15 (27) $6,500

1st American Ed. NY, 1849. 2 vols. 12mo, orig cloth. Some foxing. CE May 22 (328) $1,400

Anr copy. Orig cloth; small chips to spine tops. Cut signature laid in. K Feb 11 (274) $2,700

Anr copy. Orig cloth, variant without a blindstamped rule at top of spines. Arthur Swann copy. P Jan 30 (2149) $1,500

Anr copy. Orig cloth; library stamps to front free endpapers & titles. sg Feb 8 (321) $325

— Moby Dick. NY, 1851. ("Moby Dick; or, the Whale.") 1st American Ed. 12mo, half mor gilt. Washed. CE Sept 27 (186) $1,300

Anr copy. Orig slate brown cloth with dark orange endpapers; rebacked with orig spine laid down, rear inner hinge tender. Less foxing than usual. CNY Dec 15 (30) $5,500

Anr copy. Orig black cloth; extremities worn, abrasion from removal of plate or label from front flyleaf. Some foxing. CNY May 17 (96) $7,500

Anr copy. Orig green cloth; extremities worn, shaken. Some marginal discoloration. CNY May 17 (97) $5,000

Anr copy. Orig blue cloth with orange-coated endpapers; minor wear & dampstaining. P June 5 (293A) $10,000

Anr copy. Modern half mor gilt. Lacking ads & orig flyleaves; some dampstaining; tp with mildew marks. pba Dec 14 (106) $3,250

Anr copy. Orig cloth, 1st bdg; spine ends & joints repaired but spine splitting & creased, corners showing. Tp & some other leaves foxed. pba June 20 (242) $6,500

Anr copy. Modern half calf (amateurish bdg), part of orig covers bound in. sg Sept 21 (260) $1,700

Anr Ed. Chicago, 1930. One of 1,000. Illus by Rockwell Kent. 3 vols. 4to, orig cloth, in aluminum slipcase. cb Oct 17 (647) $800

Anr copy. Orig cloth, in aluminum slipcase. Inscr by Kent to Pat Magarick, 15 July 1965. CE Feb 21 (183) $1,800; sg Apr 18 (108) $1,400

Anr Ed. NY, 1930. Half mor gilt; spine ends scuffed. pba Aug 22 (799) $65

Anr Ed. Mt. Vernon, 1975. One of 1,500. Preface by Jacques Cousteau; illus by LeRoy Neiman. Folio, mor. With 12 double-page plates. cb Oct 17 (617) $500

Anr Ed. San Francisco: Albion Press, 1979. ("Moby-Dick, or the Whale.") One of 265. Illus by Barry Moser. Folio, orig mor. sg Oct 19 (5) $2,800
California Deluxe Ed. Berkeley, [1981]. One of 750. pba July 11 (201) $55; sg Sept 14 (35) $375
— Omoo; A Narrative of Adventures in the South Seas. NY, 1847. 1st American Ed. 12mo, orig cloth; extremities worn, ink stain on cover. Some foxing. CE May 22 (327) $1,700
Anr Ed. NY, 1924. Illus by Mead Schaffer. pba Aug 22 (809) $120
— Pierre; or, the Ambiguities. NY, 1852. 1st Ed. 12mo, orig dark brown cloth with salmon-pink endpapers; top of spine frayed, front cover soiled. Some foxing. CNY Dec 15 (31) $1,500
Anr copy. Orig cloth; wormholes at rear joint. Part of 1st blank excised; some foxing. sg Sept 21 (262) $650
— Redburn. NY, 1849. 1st American Ed, 2d ptg. 8vo, orig cloth; rubbed & stained, spine ends worn, endpapers stained. Some foxing. CE Feb 21 (177) $1,100
— Typee. L, 1846. ("Narrative of a Four Months Residence Among the Natives of the Marquesas Islands.") 1st Ed, 2d Issue, with reading "Pomare" on p. 19. 8vo, half mor. Lacking prelims to tp; trimmed at top. pba Sept 14 (268) $325
1st American Ed. NY & L, 1846. ("Typee: A Peep at Polynesian Life.") 2 vols in 1. 8vo, orig cloth, BAL B bdg; spine ends & corners worn, 1 gathering started. Foxed; possibly lacking a blank. Inscr twice to his cousin, Maria Peebles. Stockhausen copy. CNY Dec 15 (26) $24,000
Anr Ed. L, 1850. 8vo, orig cloth; spine ends frayed, joints starting. sg Feb 8 (322) $60
— White-Jacket; or the World in a Man-of-War. NY, 1850. 1st American Ed. 2 vols. 12mo, orig cloth, 1st bdg; spine ends & corners frayed. Waller Barrett copy. CE Feb 21 (178) $1,400
Anr copy. Orig cloth, 1st bdg; rebacked with orig spine laid down, splitting & chipping along edges. Some foxing & dampstaining. CE Feb 21 (179) $220
1st Ptg. Orig wraps in 1st form; splits at rear outer joints. Foxed. One of a handful of known copies in orig wraps. CNY Dec 15 (29) $24,000
Anr Ed. NY, [1892]. 8vo, half calf; extremities rubbed. F June 20 (686) $50
— Works. L, 1922-24. Standard Ed, one of 750. 16 vols. CE Feb 21 (182) $2,000

**Melville, Sir James, 1535-1617**
— The Memoires.... L, 1683. 1st Ed. Folio, calf; spine ends repaired. Tear in 1 leaf affecting 6 letters of text. pba Nov 30 (236) $350

**Melzo, Lodovico**
— Regole militari sopra il governo a servitio.... Antwerp: Gioachino Trognaesio, 1611. 1st Ed. Folio, contemp vellum gilt; soiled. With engraved title & 16 (on 15) double-page folding plates. Repair to 1 folding plate. Munby - Wright copy. C Apr 3 (150) £2,000

**Memoires...**
— Memoires pour l'histoire des sciences et de beaux arts... Mai 1743. Paris: Chaubert, 1743. 12mo, contemp red mor gilt with arms of the Marquise de Pompadour. Fuerstenberg - Schaefer copy. S Dec 7 (411) £750

**Memoirs...** See: Adams, Henry

**Men at War...**
— Men at War; The Best War Stories of All Time. NY, [1942]. Ed by Ernest Hemingway. In dj with closed tear. sg June 20 (160) $200

**Menage, Gilles, 1613-92**
— Historia mulierum philosopharum.... Lyons, 1690. 12mo, contemp vellum. Browned. sg Mar 21 (229) $110
— Les Origines de la langue francoise. Paris: Augustin Courbe, 1650. 4to, contemp calf. Tp partly detached & stamped. sg Mar 21 (228) $200

**Menagerie...**
— La Menagerie imperiale, ou collection de pres de 300 figures representant tous les quadrupedes ou les animaux les plus curieux. Paris: Saintin & Mame, 1812. 4 vols. 16mo, 19th-cent half calf gilt. With 106 plates. S Nov 2 (230) £220 [Schiller]

**Menard, Leon, 1709-67**
— Histoire des antiquites de la ville de Nismes.... Nismes, 1814. 8vo, orig wraps. With 15 plates. sg Mar 7 (159) $90

**Menasseh ben Israel**
— De la resurreccion de los muertos, libros III. Amst., 1636. 12mo, contemp calf; worn & broken. Lacking final leaf of Index; tp torn along gutter margin; a few gatherings with wormtracks affecting text; some staining & browning. Sold w.a.f. CE Dec 6 (217) $1,400

**Mencken, Henry Louis, 1880-1956**
— The American Language. NY, 1919. 1st Ed. Orig cloth, in dj; warped. bbc Dec 18 (312) $330
— A Book of Prefaces. NY, 1917. 1st Ed. Tips and corners worn. sg June 20 (265) $425
— Menckeniana: a Schimpflexikon. NY, 1928. Orig cloth; spine soiled. Sgd on tp. pba May 23 (237) $120
One of 230 L.p. copies. Half cloth. bbc June 24 (577) $300
— Newspaper Days. NY, 1941. 1st Ed. In chipped dj. Inscr to Harry Hayman. sg Dec 14 (213) $375
— Notes on Democracy. NY, [1926]. one of 200, sgd. pba May 23 (238) $160
— Ventures into Verse. NY, Balt., etc.: Marshall, Beek & Gordon, 1903. 1st Ed. 12mo, orig half cloth; spine partly split & reglued, fore-edge of front cover with fraying. Inscr to Theodore Hamberger, June 1908 & with ALs of presentation. Engelhard copy. CNY Oct 27 (108) $8,000

## Mencken, Henry Louis, 1880-1956 —& Hirshberg, Leonard Keene
— What You Ought to Know About Your Baby. NY, 1910. Inscr by Mencken to Ralph Colin, telling how the work came to be, 14 Mar 1945. CE Sept 27 (187) $1,700

## Mendeleev, Dmitri Ivanovich, 1834-1907
— Izsledovanie vodnykh rastvorov po udel'nomu vesu. St. Petersburg, 1887. 8vo, contemp half lea gilt; scuffed. sg May 16 (224) $700
— Organicheskaja khimia. St. Petersburg, 1863. 8vo, contemp half calf; spine ends & corners worn. Some browning. sg May 16 (223) $400
— Polozhenija, izbrannyja dlja zashchishchenija na stepen' magistra khimii. St. Petersburg, 1856. 8vo, modern wraps. Soiling at ends; marginal dampstaining. sg May 16 (222) $850

## Mendelsohn, Erich
— Amerika: Bilderbuch eines Architekten. Berlin, 1926. 4to, half cloth; spine rubbed. wa Dec 14 (396) $280

## Mendelssohn, Sidney
— South African Bibliography. Cambr. MA: Martino, [n.d.]. One of 175. 2 vols. O May 7 (208) $70

## Mendelssohn-Bartholdy, Felix, 1809-47
— Paulus. Oratorium... Opus 36 [full score]. Bonn; Simrock, [1837]. 4to, mor gilt; joints split. With handpainted dedication leaf to Julius Tausch [1855].. S June 13 (722) £200

## Mendes, Catulle, 1841-1909
— Le chercheur de Tares. Paris, 1898. One of 20 on papier velin de cuve. 12mo, half mor by Meunier; orig wraps & d/js bound in. With port by Laleuze. Sgd. S Oct 27 (1144) £160 [Way]
— Pour lire au Couvent. Paris, [1887]. One of 25 on chine. Illus by Lucien Metivet. 8vo, mor gilt by Emile Rousselle, orig front wrap bound in. sg Feb 15 (202) $250

## Mendes Pinto, Fernando, 1509?-83
— Les Voyages advantureux. Paris: Arnould Cotinet & Jean Roger, 1645. 4to, contemp vellum; lower hinge broken, stained & warped. Hole in Zzz1-2 affecting letters; inkstaining on RRrr4 & SSss1; some dampstaining; corners creased at ends; pencil annotations. S June 12 (77) £800
— The Voyages and Adventures.... L, 1663. 2d Ed in English. Folio, old bds; rebacked in calf. Marginal worming at end; burnhole in 2F3, affecting text. CE June 12 (227) $900

## Menestrier, Claude Francois. See: Christina, Queen of Sweden's copy

## Mengs, Antonio Raphael, 1728-79
— Oeuvres. Paris, 1787. 2 vols. 4to, contemp calf gilt; hole in joint at head of spine of Vol I. Fuerstenberg - Schaefer copy. S Dec 7 (412) £400

## Meninski, Franciscus a Mesgnien
— Linguarum orientalium turcicae, arabicae, persicae.... Vienna, 1680. Folio, contemp calf; worn. Text stained. S Oct 26 (173) £450 [Mertturkmen]

## Mennie, Donald
— The Grandeur of the Gorges. Shanghai, 1926. One of 1,000. 4to, pictorial silk over bds. With 50 photogravures. sg Feb 29 (201) $300
— The Pageant of Peking. Shanghai, 1921. 2d Ed. 4to, orig cloth; soiled. With 64 Vandyke photogravures. b Sept 20 (432) £70

## Menochius, Jacobus, d.1607
— Consilorum, sive responsorum. Venice: F. Ziletti, 1580. Folio, contemp vellum; rear cover stained. pba Mar 7 (182) $400

## Menon, ——, Sieur
— La Cuisiniere bourgeoise.... Brussels, 1761. 12mo, modern half calf. Dampstained & soiled. S Oct 12 (36) £200
Anr Ed. Paris: Guillyn, 1769. 8vo, modern half mor. S Oct 12 (38) £150
Anr copy. 2 vols. 12mo, Spotted. S Oct 12 (39) £150
Anr Ed. Brussels, 1777. 8vo, modern half mor. Lacking half-title. S Oct 12 (37) £150
— La Science du Maitre d'Hotel Confiseur. Paris, 1768. 8vo, contemp calf; spine & corners restored. With 5 folding plates. S Oct 12 (108) £180

## Menot, Michel, 1440-1518
— De federe et pace ineunda media ambassiatrice penitentia. Paris: Claude Chevallon, 3Mar 1519. 8vo, modern vellum with vellum pastedowns from Ms leaves. Early Ms annotations in margins, some shaved. S June 12 (148) £210

## Menou, Rene de. See: Pluvinel & Menou

## Menpes, Dorothy & Mortimer
— World's Children. L, [1903]. Orig cloth; worn & soiled. F June 20 (541) $50

## Merard de Saint-Just, Anne Jeanne Felicite d'Ormoy
— L'Occasion et le moment.... The Hague, 1782. 4 parts in 1 vol. 18mo, contemp calf gilt. Author's copy with holograph revisions for Anr Ed; sheet of verses inserted. Fuerstenberg - Schaefer copy. S Dec 7 (413) £560

## Meray, Antony. See: Nus & Meray

## Mercado, Tomas de
— Tratos y contratos de mercaderes y tratantes discidios y determinados. Salamanca: Mathias Gast, 1569. Modern blind-stamped mor Minor repairs at margins; underlinings & marginalia; stamp erased from tp. S Nov 30 (169) £2,600

## Mercati, Michele, 1541-93
— Metallotheca. Opus posthumum.... Rome, 1719. 2 parts in 1 vol. Folio, contemp vellum. With frontis &

5 plates, 2 of them double-page. Without port. Masden copy.   S Mar 14 (250) £2,100

**Mercator, Gerard, 1512-94 —&
Hondius, Jodocus, 1563-1611**
— Atlas Minor. [Amst., 1634]. 8vo, contemp vellum; soiled. With 146 maps. Lacking title & prelims; Moscovia map replaced by duplicate; 1 map with slight loss; water-stained throughout.   S Oct 26 (438) £3,600 [Schuster]
— L'Atlas ou Meditations cosmographiques de la fabrique du monde.... Amst., 1609. Folio, contemp calf, tooled in sepia & blind; worn. With engraved general title, 4 engraved sectional titles, & 147 maps (all but 1 double-page), hand-colored in outline. Some discoloration; a few maps misbound; some maps split at centerfold; some repairs.   S Nov 30 (78) £36,000

**Mercer, Asa Shinn**
— Big Horn Country, Wyoming. [Cheyenne, Wyoming], 1906. 12mo, orig wraps; worn & chipped, some staining. With 8 plates.   wa Feb 29 (589) $375

**Mercer, Henry Chapman, 1856-1930**
— Ancient Carpenters' Tools Illustrated.... Doylestown, Pa., 1929. Cloth; worn.   O Dec 5 (88) $130

**Mercier, Jean**
— Emblemata. [Bourges: Nicolas Levez, May 1592]. 4to, 18th-cent half calf; spine heel chipped, joints dry, corners bumped. Roman & italic types. With engraved title & 50 engravings by Queyr in text. Some discoloration; K3 with marginal paper repair. Schaefer copy.   P Nov 1 (153) $7,500

**Mercier, Louis Sebastien, 1740-1814**
— Lettres de Dulis. Londres, 1767. 8vo, mor gilt by Joly fils. Fuerstenberg - Schaefer copy.   S Dec 7 (415) £360

**Mercure...**
— Mercure de France... Paris, 1740. Vol II. 12mo, contemp red mor gilt with the arms of Queen Marie Leczinska. Fuerstenberg - Schaefer copy.   S Dec 7 (416) £320

**Mercurialis, Hieronymus, 1530-1606**
— De arte gymnastica. Paris: Jacques du Puys, 1577. 4to, 18th-cent vellum. Minor foxing; marginalia.   sg May 16 (452) $700

**Meredith, George, 1828-1909**
See also: Limited Editions Club
— Beauchamp's Career. L, 1876. 1st Ed. 3 vols. 8vo, orig cloth. Frederick Augustus Maxse's copy (model for Beauchamp) with his holograph lv on half-title of Vol I identifying characters & the election described.   S Dec 18 (198) £1,700 [Valentine]
— Farina: a Legend of Cologne. L, 1857. 8vo, orig cloth; rubbed & soiled, upper cover stained. Tear across A3 not affecting legibility of text; marginal tear on D7; some pencilled markings & a correction on p. 135. Inscr to Frederick Augustus Maxse.   S Dec 18 (199) £800 [Bertram]

— The Ordeal of Richard Feverel. L, 1859. 1st Ed. 3 vols. 8vo, orig cloth; rubbed. Some foxing.   S Apr 23 (113) £240
— Works. L, 1896-98. Ltd Ed. 32 vols. 8vo, mor extra.   cb Oct 17 (285) $1,800; Met May 22 (111) $3,100
Memorial Ed. NY, 1909-12. 37 vols.   pba June 20 (244) $225

**Meredith, Henry**
— An Account of the Gold Coast.... L, 1812. 8vo, modern bds. With folding map. Ink stamp & number on tp; browned & foxed.   bba Apr 11 (323) £650 [Waggett]

**Meredith, Louisa Anne Twamley**
— The Romance of Nature; or, the Flower-Seasons Illustrated. L, 1836. 2d Ed. 4to, contemp mor gilt; extremities rubbed, scuff mark to upper cover.   Ck Feb 14 (318) £250
— Some of my Bush Friends in Tasmania. L, 1860-[91]. 2 vols. Folio, orig cloth. With additional chromolitho title & 12 color plates in 1st series & additional chromolitho title & 13 plates in 2d series.   b Sept 20 (433) £350
Anr Ed. L, 1860. Folio, half mor; front cover detached, back cover cracked, worn. With 12 colored plates.   wd Nov 15 (95) $400

**Merian, Maria Sibylla, 1647-1717**
— Butterflies, Beetles and other Insects. The Leningrad Book.... NY, [1976]. 2 vols. 4to, text in bds, plates loose in folding case. Library markings, but plates unmarked.   sg Sept 7 (242) $100
— Dissertatio de generatione et metamorphosibus insectorum Surinamensium. Amst., 1719. ("De generatione et metamorphosibus insectorum Surinamensium.") Folio, 18th-cent calf gilt; worn, rebacked. With frontis & 72 plates, all with contemp handcoloring, letter on tp & dedication heightened in gold. Some staining & soiling, mostly to margins. Schaefer copy.   P Nov 1 (154) $47,500
Anr Ed. The Hague, 1726. Folio, later 18th-cent mor gilt. With engraved titles & 72 hand-colored plates. Lacking half-titles; small section from lower outer corner of 1st title town away; oxidation of sky in Plates 70 & 72. Fattorini copy.   C Oct 25 (78) £26,000

**Merian, Matthaeus, 1593-1650**
— Topographia Archiepiscopatum Moguntinesis, Treuirensis, et Coloniensis. Frankfurt: M. Merian, 1646. Folio, contemp calf; spine ends & corners worn, rear hinge cracked. With title, 3 double-page maps, & 40 plates & views. Some soiling & browning; map margins frayed.   CE Nov 8 (224) $4,000
— Topographia Galliae; dat ist Een Algemeene en naeukeurige Lant en Plaets-beschrijvinghe van het Machtige Koninckrijk Vranckryck. Amst.: Joost Broersz & Caspar Merian, 1660-63. Vols I-II & IV (of 4). Folio, contemp sheep gilt; needs rebacked. With 3 engraved titles, 12 double-page maps, 219 double-page city views & plans & 36 single-page plates, all hand-colored at an early date. Old stamp

on titles & on verso of most plates & recto of a few. Sold w.a.f. sg May 9 (88) $9,000
— Topographia Helvetiae. Frankfurt: Mathaeus Merian, 1642. Bound with: Topographia Alsatiae. Framkfurt: Wolfgang Hofmann for Matthaeus Merian, 1644. Folio, contemp vellum bds. 1st work with engraved title, 2 maps & 57 plates; 2d work with 2 maps & 37 plates. Zurich & Bellinzona in 1st work with short tear; tp of 2d work with library stamp; some shaving, browning & spotting. S June 27 (118) £8,500

**Merida, Carlos**
— Estampas del Popol-Vuh. Mexico City, 1943. Ltd Ed, sgd. Folio, loose as issued in bds; extremities worn, some soiling. With 10 plates. sg May 23 (391) $750
— Trajes Regionales Mexicanos. Mexico, 1945. One of 1,000. Folio, cloth portfolio; spine reinforced with tape. cb June 25 (1958) $750

**Merigot, James**
— A Select Collection of Views and Ruins in Rome.... L, 1797-99. Part 1 only. Folio, contemp half calf; spine def. With 27 (of 30) plates. b Sept 20 (252) £70

**Merimee, Prosper, 1803-70**
See also: Limited Editions Club
— Carmen. Paris: Les Cent Bibliophiles, 1901. One of 125 exemplaires nominatifs with additional suite of illusts before letters. Illus by Alexandre Lunois. Contemp mor gilt by Charles Meunier, orig wraps bound in. b Dec 5 (34) £150
One of 125 exemplaires nominatifs with additional suite of illusts before letters, this for Paul Clermont. Mor extra with a fan design by Petrus Ruban, 1903, orig wraps bound in. S Nov 21 (324) £350
Anr Ed. Paris, 1929. One of 5 on japon blanc supernacre with plates in 3 or more states. Illus by Leon Courbouleix. 4to, contemp mor gilt by A. Toumaniantz, with orig copper plate framed inside front cover. With 16 plates. Each plate preceded by orig watercolor & orig pencil drawing on half-title. b May 30 (565) £260
— Carmen, and Letters from Spain. Paris, 1931. One of 50. Illus by Maurice Barraud. Half lea. sg Sept 14 (227) $90
— Le Carrosse du St. Sacrement. Paris, [1928]. One of 20 on verge d'Arches, with 2 extra suites of plates, this copy for Pierre Legrain. Illus by Mily Possoz. 4to, mor extra with a geometric design by Pierre Legrain, orig wraps bound in. sg Apr 18 (115) $1,700

**Merivale, Charles**
— A History of the Romans under the Empire. L, 1875. 8 vols. 8vo, contemp calf gilt by Riviere. pba Sept 14 (36) $250

**Merou, Martin Garcia.** See: Fore-Edge Paintings

**Merriam, Clinton Hart, 1855-1942**
— The Dawn of the World.... Cleveland, 1910. F Mar 28 (399) $130
1st Ed. - Illus by E. W. Deming & C. J. Hittell. Orig cloth; spine ends & corners rubbed. Larson copy. pba Sept 28 (29) $130

**Merrick, George Byron**
— Old Times on the Upper Mississippi. Cleveland, 1909. Orig cloth; dampstain to spine, corners bumped, stamp to front endpaper. pba Apr 25 (530) $85

**Merrill, Catharine**
— The Soldier of Indiana in the War for the Union. Indianapolis, 1869. 8vo, orig sheep; library blinstamp on front bd, soiled. wa Feb 1 (90) $90

**Merrill, James**
— Jim's Book. NY: Pvtly ptd, 1942. Half cloth; bowed, endpapers foxed. sg Dec 14 (214) $1,100

**Merriman, Henry Seton, 1862-1903**
— The Grey Lady. L, 1897. Illus by Arthur Rackham. 8vo, orig cloth; extremities rubbed, spine soiled. Ck May 31 (109) £95

**Merriman, Henry Seton, 1862-1903 —& Tallentyre, Stephen G., Pseud.**
— The Money-Spinner, and Other Character Notes. L, 1896. Illus by Arthur Rackham. 8vo, orig cloth; extremities rubbed. With 12 plates. Ink stamps on front free endpaper & half-title; ink stains on 2 prelim leaves. Ck May 31 (107) £240

**Merritt, Abraham, 1882-1943**
— The Black Wheel. NY: New Collectors' Group, 1947. One of 1,000. Illus by Hannes Bok. pba May 4 (204) $70

**Merritt, Abraham, 1882-1943 —& Bok, Hannes**
— The Fox Woman.... NY: New Collectors' Group, 1946. One of 1,000. 4to, cloth. pba May 4 (205) $90

**Merritt, Edward Percival**
— Horace Walpole, Printer: a Paper Read at a Meeting of the Club of Odd Volumes. Bost., 1907. One of 77. Ptd by Bruce Rogers. 16mo, bds. sg Sept 14 (318) $100

**Meryman, Richard**
— Andrew Wyeth. Bost., 1968. Oblong 4to, orig cloth, in tattered dj. Foxed. O May 7 (209) $50

**Mesens, Edouard L. T.** See: Magritte & Mesens

**Mesmer, Franz Anton, 1734-1815**
— Mesmerismus. Oder System der Wechselwirkungen.... Berlin, 1814. Bound with: Wolfart, Karl Christian. Erlaeuterungen zum Mesmerismus. Berlin, 1815. 8vo, old bds. Some browning & staining. S Mar 14 (251) £460

**Metastasio, Pietro, 1698-1782**
— Opere. Paris: la veuve Herissant, 1780-82. 12 vols. 8vo, contemp mor gilt. With port & 37 plates. Ruststain on tp of Vol I; some browning. Fuerstenberg - Schaefer copy. S Dec 7 (417) £1,200

**Methodist...**
— The Methodist. A Poem. Liverpool, 1820. 8vo, modern bds. b Dec 5 (209) £50

**Methodius, Saint, Archbishop of Tyre, 827-69**
— Revelationes. Basel: Michael Furter, 14 Feb 1500. ("Revelationes divinae a sanctis angelis factae de principio mundi....") 4to, 17th-cent vellum. Types 156bG, 6:106G, 1:83G, 4:64G. With 61 woodcuts from 55 blocks colored by an early hand. Tear in b6 extending into woodcut & repaired without loss. C June 26 (105) £5,000

**Metropolitan Museum of Art**
REITZ, S. C. BOSCH. - An Exhibition of Early Chinese Pottery and Sculpture. NY, 1916. 8vo, mor gilt, orig wraps bound in, bdg sgd MK at end & with initials of George Eumorfopoulos; soiled. Inscr. bba May 30 (45) £60 [Lobo]

**Metzgar, Judson D.** See: Grabhorn Printing

**Metzinger, Jean, 1883-1956.** See: Gleizes & Metzinger

**Meung, Jean de.** See: Lorris & Meung

**Meusel, Johann G.**
— Das gelehrte Teutschland oder Lexikon.... Lemgo, 1796-1803. 10 vols. 8vo, 7 vols in contemp wraps, 3 in contemp bds; wraps frayed & soiled. O Mar 26 (174) $130

**Mexico**
— Estatutos de la real academia de San Carlos de Nueva Espana. Mexico, 1785. Folio, contemp calf. Wormhole in inner margins; some spotting. S June 27 (199) £500

**Meyer, Adolf Bernhard, 1840-1911**
— Album of Filipino - Types III. Negritos, Manguianes, Bagobos.... Dresden, 1904. 4to, loose in orig half cloth folder. With tp & 37 plates. Library stamps on titles. S June 27 (238) £1,000

**Meyer, Bernard, 1767-1856.** See: Wolf & Meyer

**Meyer, Carl**
— Bound for Sacramento: Travel-Pictures of a Returned Wanderer. Claremont, Calif., 1938. 1st English Ed, One of 450. Trans by Ruth Frey Axe. Orig cloth. With facsimile of front & rear wrap. Larson copy. pba Sept 28 (604) $80
— Nach dem Sacramento: Reisebilder eines Heimgekerten. Aarau, 1855. 1st Ed. Orig wraps; wraps frayed. Larson copy. pba Sept 28 (603) $650

**Meyer, Franz**
— Marc Chagall: Life and Works. NY: H. N. Abrams, [1964]. 4to, cloth, in pictorial dj with chip to spine. pba Aug 22 (720) $55

**Meyer, Friedrich**
— Verzeichnis einer Goethe-Bibliothek. Leipzig, 1908. 8vo, half cloth; orig wraps bound in, covers imperf. sg Apr 11 (230) $50

**Meyer, Hans Horst**
— Across East African Glaciers. L, 1891. 8vo, orig cloth. bba Nov 1 (482) £500 [Hunter]

**Meyer, Henry Leonard**
— Game Birds and their Localities.... L, [c.1848]. Oblong 4to, later half mor; spines scuffed. With 6 hand-colored plates. Small tears to initial blank, 1 repaired with adhesive tape. Fattorini copy. C Oct 25 (28) £3,600
— Illustrations of British Birds. L, [1835-41]. 4 vols. Folio, contemp cloth. With 313 hand-colored plates. Marginal spotting on c.17 plates. Fattorini copy. C Oct 25 (30) £6,500

Anr copy. Contemp mor gilt; rebacked retaining backstrips, spine heads worn, Vol II rear cover detached. With 317 hand-colored plates only. About half the plates foxed. sg May 9 (287) $1,800

Anr Ed. L, [1837-44]. 4 vols in 5. Folio, cloth. With 256 hand-colored plates only. Lacking titles & contents leaves. S June 27 (52) £2,200

Anr Ed. L, 1842-50. ("Coloured Illustrations of British Birds.") 7 vols. 8vo, contemp mor gilt. With 322 hand-colored plates of birds, 105 hand-colored plates of eggs & 8 uncolored anatomical plates. Fattorini copy. C Oct 25 (31) £2,400

**Meyer, Joachim**
— Gruendtliche Beschreibung der freyen Ritterlichen unnd Adelichen kunst des fechtens. Strassburg: Thiebolt Berger, 1570. Illus by Tobias Stimmer. 3 parts in 1 vol. Oblong 4to, contemp calf gilt; rebacked, scuffed. With woodcut arms on tp verso & 73 woodcut illusts. Some browning & staining; a4 torn without loss; lacking M4. C June 26 (106) £4,500

**Meyer's...**
— Meyers Universum. Hildburghausen, 1835-52. Vol I only. Contemp half mor. Some foxing. pba Apr 25 (217) $160

**Meyers, William H.** See: Grabhorn Printing

**Meyler, William**
— Poetical Amusement of the Journey of Life.... Bath, 1806. 8vo, contemp calf gilt; rubbed. b Dec 5 (333) £70

**Meynell, Alice, 1847-1922**
— A Father of Women and Other Poems. L, 1917. 8vo, orig wraps. Foxed. sg June 20 (266) $50

**Meynell, Francis**
— Typography; the Written Word and the Printed Word.... L: Pelican Press, 1923. bba May 9 (35) £50 [Cox]

**Meyrick, Sir Samuel Rush**
— A Critical Inquiry into Antient Armour. L, 1824. 3 vols. 4to, contemp half mor gilt with Camperdown Library crest on spines. With engraved titles, 70 hand-colored plates & 10 uncolored plates. Chapter initials hand-colored & heightened with gold. sg Apr 18 (82) $1,300

Anr Ed. L, 1842. 3 vols. 4to, later cloth. With 80 plates, 70 of them hand-colored. Lacking frontis. bba May 30 (323) £560 [R. S. Books]

Anr copy. Contemp half mor; extremities rubbed. With color frontis & 130 plates, some hand-colored. F Mar 28 (766) $1,800

2d Ed. 3 vols. Folio, contemp half mor. With 70 hand-colored plates & 10 initials. Some spotting. S Oct 26 (310) £800 [Harrington]

**Meyrick, Sir Samuel Rush —& Skelton, Joseph**
— Engraved Illustrations of Antient Arms and Armour, from the Collection...at Goodrich Court. L, 1854. 2 vols. 4to, half mor; scuffed. With port, engraved titles, frontises & 150 plates. F Mar 28 (765) $625

**Meyrick, Sir Samuel Rush —& Smith, Charles Hamilton**
— The Costume of the Original Inhabitants of the British Islands. L, 1815. Folio, contemp half calf gilt. With engraved title & 23 (of 24) colored plates. pnE Sept 20 (151) £210

**Michael de Dalen**
— Casus summarii Decretalium Sexti et Clementinarum. Basel: Michael Wenssler, 25 Aug 1479. Folio, later bds. Variable lines; double column; types 1a(Memmingen, Kunne):82G, 2(Memmingen, Kunne):134G. Dampstained & browned throughout; some worming at end. 98 (of 100) leaves; lacking initial blank. Goff M-532. S Dec 18 (61) £700 [Gabinete]

**Michael Scotus**
— Mensa philosophica. [Cologne: Cornelius de Zierikzee, c.1500]. 4to, 19th-Cent half vellum. With 52 leaves. 1st quire rehinged; some staining. Ck Mar 22 (199) £1,000
— La Physionomia natural. [N.p.], 1555. 16mo, contemp vellum. Tp clipped in lower margin & with small holes affecting printing on verso; cut close, with running head shaved on some leaves. pba June 20 (295) $130

**Michals, Duane**
— Homage to Cavafy. Danbury: Addison House, 1978. One of 1,000. 8vo, cloth, in vellum dj; dampstained. Edition page soiled. sg Feb 29 (202) $110

**Michaux, Francois Andre, 1770-1855**
— The North American Sylva.... Paris & Phila., 1817-19. Vols II-III (of 3). Early half calf; worn. With 106 colored plates finished by hand. Some foxing throughout. wa Nov 16 (170) $900

Anr Ed. Paris, 1819-18-19. 3 vols. 8vo, 19th-cent calf gilt; extremities worn. With 156 colored plates. Text foxed. sg Apr 18 (152) $1,500

**Michaux, Francois Andre, 1770-1855 —& Nuttall, Thomas, 1786-1859**
— The North American Sylva.... Phila.: Robert P. Smith, 1852. 3 vols, without Nuttall's Supplement. 8vo, orig cloth; loose. With 156 hand-colored plates. sg May 9 (310) $90

Anr copy. Mor gilt; rubbed. With 131 hand-colored plates only, in mixed issues. wa Feb 29 (144) $800

**Michel, Andre, 1853-1925**
— Histoire de l'art. Paris, 1905-08. 3 vols in 5. 4to, half mor. CE Nov 8 (225) $220

**Michelangelo Buonarotti, 1475-1564**
[-] Esequie del divino Michaelangelo Buonarotti celebrate in Firenze dall'Accademia de Pittori, Scultori, & Architetti...il di luglio MDLXIII. Florence: Giunta, 1564. Bound with: Varchi, Benedetto. Orazione funerale... fatta, e recitata... pubblicamente nell'essequie di Michelangelo Buonarotti in Firenze.... Florence: Giunta, 1564. 4to, 19th-cent half calf; rubbed, upper cover detached. C Apr 3 (151) £5,500

**Michelet, Victor Emile**
— Maufra, peintre et graveur. Paris, 1908. 4to, contemp half mor gilt, orig wraps bound in. With 8 plates. sg June 13 (250) $250

**Micheli, Pier Antonio**
— Nova Plantarum genera juxta Tournefortii methodum disposita. Florence, 1729. Folio, 19th-cent half calf. With 108 plates. Margins wormed; stain at head of last few leaves touching last 2 plates. S June 27 (54) £800

**Michener, James A.**
— Centennial. NY, [1974]. One of 500. sg June 20 (267) $275
— Chesapeake. NY, 1978. One of 500. pba May 23 (241) $55
— Facing East. NY, 1970. Illus by Jack Levine. 2 parts in 1 vol. Folio, loose in satin folding-case. With 4 orig colored lithos & 54 sheets of plates, hand-colored. bbc June 24 (578) $350; sg Sept 7 (215) $200
— The Floating World. NY, [1954]. Half cloth, in dj. pba Aug 22 (349) $325
— Hawaii. NY: Random House, [1959]. In chipped dj. pba May 23 (242) $55
One of 400. K Oct 1 (268) $325
— The Modern Japanese Print.... Rutland, [1962]. One of 510. Folio, cloth. With 10 orig sgd prints. pba June 20 (245) $2,000
— Return to Paradise. NY, [1951]. In chipped & rubbed dj with repairs. pba Aug 22 (351) $110
— Texas. NY: Random House, [1985]. One of 1,000. pba Jan 25 (257) $160
— Ventures in Editing. Huntington Beach: James Cahill, 1995. Proof copy of 26 deluxe copies. pba Aug 22 (353) $170

**Michigan**

OGLE, GEORGE. - Standard Atlas of Hillsdale County, Michigan. Chicago, 1916. Folio, half mor; extremities worn.  sg Dec 7 (27) $140

OGLE, GEORGE. - Standard Atlas of Saginaw County, Michigan. Chicago, 1916. Folio, half mor; extremities worn.  sg Dec 7 (28) $110

OGLE, GEORGE. - Standard Atlas of Van Buren County, Michigan. Chicago, 1912. Folio, half mor; needs rebdg.  sg Dec 7 (29) $110

**Middleton, Charles Theodore**

— A New and Complete System of Geography. L, 1778-79. 2 vols. Folio, contemp calf; joints & spine ends worn. Sold w.a.f.  CE May 22 (333) $220

**Middleton, Conyers, 1683-1750**

— The History of the Life of Marcus Tullius Cicero. L, 1741. 1st Ed. 2 vols. 4to, contemp calf gilt; rebacked with orig backstrips laid down, corners repaired, rubbed.  CE May 22 (334) $550

**Midwinter International Exposition.** See: California

**Mies van der Rohe, Ludwig.** See: Museum of Modern Art

**Mijatovics, Elodie Lawton**

— The History of Modern Serbia. L, 1872. 8vo, cloth.  sg Mar 7 (162) $70

**Milan**

— Statuta Mediolani. Milan: Paulus de Suardis, 20 Dec 1480. Bound after: Statuta Mediolani: Tabula. Milan: Joannes Antonius de Honate, 30 Nov 1482. Folio, 18th-cent vellum. Gothic types.. 240 leaves & 14 leaves. Goff S-716 & 717.  C Apr 3 (152) £8,500

**Miles, Eustace H.** See: Benson & Miles

**Miles, Henry Downes, 1806-89**

— The Book of Field Sports. L, [n.d.]. Vol II (of 2). 4to, calf gilt; rubbed. Some foxing & soiling.  O Jan 9 (165) $90

— British Field Sports. L: Wm. Mackenzie, [n.d.].. 4to, contemp half lea; worn, stained. Repaired tear to tp.  O Oct 10 (196) $450

**Miles, Nelson Appleton, 1839-1925**

— Personal Recollections and Observations...Civil War.... Chicago, 1896. 1st Ed, 2d Issue. 4to, orig cloth. NH July 21 (190) $100

1st Issue, with "General" at frontis port. Illus by Frederic Remington. Orig cloth; edges rubbed.  pba Apr 25 (532) $180

2d Ed. Chicago, 1897. 4to, orig cloth; dampstains to fore-edge of front cover.  pba June 25 (170) $150

**Military...**

— The Military Costume of Turkey. L, 1818. Folio, contemp mor gilt; scuffed. With hand-colored vignette on title & 30 hand-colored plates. L.p. copy.  b May 30 (285) £600

Anr copy. Mor; extremities worn & scuffed. With engraved title & 30 colored plates. cb Oct 17 (119) $800

Anr copy. Contemp mor gilt.  pba Mar 7 (177) $750

Anr Ed. L, 1818 [some plates watermarked 1830]. Folio, later half mor gilt; extremities worn. With engraved title & 29 hand-colored plates. Engraved title trimmed & inlaid.  sg Dec 7 (260) $425

**Military Order of Santiago**

— Regra: statutos e diffincoes da ordem de Sanctiaguo. Setubal: Herman de Kempis, 13 Dec 1509. Folio, 18th-cent velvet over bds; rubbed, extremities frayed. Gothic type. With 5 woodcuts ptd from 4 blocks. Some marginal defs; minor worming. Schaefer copy.  P Nov 1 (180) $32,000

**Milizia, Francesco**

— Del teatro. Rome: Arcangelo Casaletti, 1772. 8vo, modern bds.  S May 15 (416) £1,200

**Mill, Hugh Robert**

— The Siege of the South Pole. L, 1905. 8vo, orig cloth; spine rubbed, rear hinge cracked.  pba July 25 (47) $70

**Mill, John Stuart, 1806-73**

— Autobiography. L, 1873. 1st Ed. 8vo, contemp half calf.  S Apr 23 (114) £80

1st Issue. Orig cloth; corners bumped, edge wear. Some spotting.  F June 20 (455) $140

— Dissertations and Discussions Political, Philosophical, and Historical. L, 1859-75. Vols I-III (of 4). Orig cloth; tear along spines of Vols I-II. Tp & a few other leaves in Vol III trimmed at lower margins.  pba Dec 14 (109) $120

— Principles of Political Economy. L, 1848. 1st Ed. 2 vols in 4. 8vo, contemp half calf gilt; joints & corners worn. Interleaved copy. Chandos - Hefner copy.  CNY May 17 (32) $1,600

**Millais, John Guille, 1865-1931**

— British Deer and their Horns. L, 1897. Folio, orig cloth; rebacked.  b May 30 (496) £130

— Game Birds and Shooting-Sketches. L, 1892. Folio, orig half mor gilt. With 34 plates; 15 color lithos. Some foxing & edge wear.  Met Feb 24 (458) $550

— The Mammals of Great Britain and Ireland. L, 1904-6. One of 1,025. 3 vols. 4to, half cloth.  pnE Sept 20 (172) £200

Anr copy. Orig cloth.  S June 13 (448) £150

— The Natural History of the British Surface-Feeding Ducks. L, 1902. One of 600 L.p. copies. 4to, orig cloth; corners rubbed. With 41 colored plates & 25 uncolored plates & 6 photogravures.  S June 13 (444) £380

Anr copy. With 41 colored plates & 6 photogravures.  S June 13 (446) £360

— Newfoundland and its Untrodden Ways. L, 1907. Orig cloth.  sg Mar 7 (500) $100

— The Wildfowler in Scotland. L, 1901. 1st Ed. 4to, contemp half calf; joints cracked. With frontis, 8

## MILLAN

photogravure plates & 2 colored plates. b Sept 20 (482) £75

**Millan, John**
— A Succession of Colonels to All His Majesties Land Forces.... L, 1745. 8vo, contemp calf. S Oct 26 (317) £200 [Bayntun]

**Millar, George Henry**
— The New and Universal System of Geography. L, [1785]. Folio, contemp calf; rebacked preserving old spine, rubbed. With frontis, 23 maps & 84 plates. Some tears & repairs, mostly marginal; some soiling & browning. bba June 6 (49) £850 [Cox]

**Millar, John Fitzhugh**
— The Architects of the American Colonies.... Barre, 1968. Illus by Suzanne Carlson. Folio, cloth, in dj. O Dec 5 (90) $80

**Millar, Kenneth**
— The Barbarous Coast. L, [1957]. 1st English Ed. In rubbed & repaired dj; bdg skewed. sg Dec 14 (62) $50
— Black Money. NY, 1966. 1st Ed. In rubbed & discolored dj. sg Dec 14 (64) $60
— Blue City. NY, 1947. In rubbed dj. sg June 20 (273) $225
— Experience with Evil. L, 1954. In dj with wear. Inscr both as Millar & as John Ross Macdonald. sg June 20 (256) $175
— The Ferguson Affair. NY, 1960. In dj, extremities worn. sg Dec 14 (63) $140

**Millay, Edna St. Vincent, 1892-1950**
— Fatal Interview. NY, 1931. One of 525. Half cloth. pba Jan 25 (258) $120

**Miller, Alfred W.**
— Fishless Days, by Sparse Grey Hackle. NY, 1954. One of 591. O Feb 6 (156) $130
  Anr copy. Inscr as Sparse Grey Hackle to Pete Hidy. O Feb 6 (157) $350
— Sparse Grey Hackle. His Life, His Stories, and His Angling Memories. NY, 1993. One of 300. Orig cloth. O Feb 6 (158) $160

**Miller, Arthur**
  See also: Limited Editions Club
— Death of a Salesman. NY: Viking, 1949. 1st Ed. In dj with stain to spine. pba Oct 5 (285) $150
  Anr copy. In chipped dj with extremities rubbed. pba May 23 (246) $160
  Anr copy. In dj with staining. pba Aug 22 (354) $140
  Anr Ed. NY: Viking, [1981]. One of 500. sg Dec 14 (216) $130

**Miller, C. William**
— Franklin's Philadelphia Printing, 1728-1766: a Descriptive Bibliography. Phila., 1974. 4to, cloth, in dj. ds July 27 (78) $50; O May 7 (213) $70

**Miller, Charlotte**
— Fifty Drawings by Canaletto from the Royal Library, Windsor Castle. L, 1983. One of 500. Folio, text in cloth, plates unbound in half mor case. sg June 13 (71) $400

**Miller, E.** See: Fore-Edge Paintings

**Miller, Francis Trevelyan**
— Photographic History of the Civil War. NY, 1912. 10 vols. 4to, orig cloth; worn, spines def. F June 20 (334) $100

**Miller, G.** See: Gravell & Miller

**Miller, George**
— A Trip to Sea, from 1810 to 1815. Long Sutton: John Swan, 1854. 8vo, orig cloth. b Sept 20 (434) £350

**Miller, Henry, fl.1856.** See: Grabhorn Printing

**Miller, Henry, 1891-1980**
— Aller Retour New York. Paris, 1935. 1st Ed, One of 150. Orig wraps. CE May 22 (337) $1,000
— Black Spring. Paris: Obelisk Press, [1936]. 1st Ed. Orig wraps. Sgd on half-title. CE May 22 (339) $650
— Into the Night Life. [Berkeley, 1947]. One of 800. Inscr to Calvin Israel, 1975. pba Nov 30 (237) $475
— Max and the White Phagocytes. Paris, [1938]. 1st Ed. Orig wraps; spine ends worn. Inscr to George E. Howard, 10 Mar 1941. CE May 22 (342) $850
— My Life and Times. NY: Playboy Press, [1971]. Intro by Bradley Smith. In dj. Ptd insert sgd by Miller laid in; inscr by Bradley Smith to John Land. pba Aug 22 (355) $95
— Plexus. Paris: Olympia Press, [1953]. 2 vols. Orig wraps; rubbed. pba May 23 (247) $55
— Quiet Days in Clichy. Paris, 1956. 16mo, wraps; worn & chipped. sg Feb 29 (54) $350
  Anr Ed. Paris: Olympia Press, 1958. 2d Ptg. Illus by Brassai. 16mo, pictorial wraps; rubbed. sg June 20 (271) $200
— Reflections of the Death of Mishima. Santa Barbara, 1972. One of 200. Inscr. sg Dec 14 (217) $250
— The Rosy Crucifixion, Book One, Sexus. Paris: The Obelisk Press, [1949]. One of 300. 2 vols. sg June 20 (271) $225
— Scenario. Paris: Obelisk Press, 1937. One of 200. Orig wraps; spine repaired. CE May 22 (340) $300
— Tropic of Cancer. Paris: Obelisk Press, [1934]. 1st Ed. Orig wraps; edge-wear. Inscr to Jim O'Roark, 13 Feb 1977. CE May 22 (336) $8,000
  Anr Ed. NY: Grove Press, [1961]. Galley proof. Stapled at top. With pencil corrections throughout & with ink writing on front stating "Karl Shapiro - Galleys of Tropic of Cancer". Last leaf def. pba May 23 (250) $160
— Tropic of Capricorn. Paris: Obelisk Press, [1939]. 1st Ed. Orig wraps; spine ends worn. Errata slip tipped on to title. Inscr to John Martin. CE May 22 (343) $3,400
  Anr copy. Mor gilt, orig wraps bound in. pba May 23 (251) $150

Anr copy. Orig wraps; spine heel repaired with tape, rubbed. Errata slip tipped in. pba May 23 (252) $85
— What Are You Going to Do About Alf? Paris: Pvtly ptd, [1935]. Orig wraps. Inscr to Giacomo Antonini, Nov 1936. CE May 22 (338) $950
Anr Ed. Paris: Pvtly ptd, [1938]. Wraps. CE May 22 (341) $260

**Miller, Joaquin, 1839-1913**
— The Gold Seeker of the Sierra. NY, 1884. Wraps in slipcase. Larson copy [Norris copy?]. pba Sept 28 (606) $200
— Works. San Francisco, 1909-10. Author's De Luxe Ed, one of 250. 6 vols. 8vo, mor gilt. Library stamp on bottom page edges. cb Oct 17 (286) $550

**Miller, Joe.** See: Mottley, John

**Miller, John, 1715?-90?**
— Illustratio systematis sexualis Linnaei. An Illustration of the Sexual System of the genera plantarum of Linnaeus. L, 1794. 2 vols. Folio. modern half goatskin. With frontis, engraved title & 108 colored plates. Several plates torn or flawed, but the whole restored at Johns Hopkins University. wa Feb 29 (143) $6,000

**Miller, Philip, 1691-1771**
— The Gardener's Dictionary.... L, 1731. Folio, old calf; front bd detached, rear joint starting, chipped & scuffed. Lacking the 12 prelim blanks; some soiling & foxing. wa Feb 29 (178) $550

**Miller, Thomas**
— Elegy on the Death of Lord Byron's Mary. Nottingham, [c.1832]. 12mo, sewn as issued. b Dec 5 (303) £300

**Millikin, Richard Alfred**
— The River-Side, a Poem, in Three Books. Cork, 1807. 4to, contemp half calf. Last leaf laid down. b Dec 5 (611) £220

**Millin de Grandmaison Library, Aubin Louis**
— [Sale Catalogue] Catalogue des livres de la bibliotheque.... Paris, 1819. 2 vols in 1. 8vo, contemp half calf; rubbed. Bound in is Catalogue des livres rares et curieux de la bibliotheque de feu M. l'Abbe Hemey d'Auberive, 1816. O Mar 26 (175) $170

**Millot, Claude Francois Xavier**
— Tableaux de l'histoire romaine. Paris, 1796 [An IV]. Folio, contemp mor gilt. With 48 plates. Fuerstenberg - Schaefer copy. S Dec 7 (421) £180

**Mills, Anson**
— My Story. Wash., [1918]. With errata slip pasted to front pastedown. pba June 25 (173) $225

**Mills, John, d. c.1885**
— The Flyers of the Hunt. L, 1859. Illus by John Leech. 12mo, calf gilt by Zaehnsdorf, orig cover & spine bound in; rubbed. O Jan 9 (166) $170
Anr copy. Mor gilt by Root, orig cloth bound in; rubbed. With 6 colored plates. wa Nov 16 (174) $85

— Stable Secrets; Or, Puffy Doodles.... L, 1863. 8vo, half mor by Zaehnsdorf, orig covers & spine bound in; rubbed. O Jan 9 (168) $90

**Mills, Samuel J. —&**
**Smith, Daniel**
— Report of a Missionary Tour...west of the Allegany Mountains. Andover, 1815. 8vo, disbound. sg Oct 26 (260) $250

**Milman, Henry Hart, 1791-1868**
— The History of the Jews. L, 1855. 3 vols. 8vo, calf gilt prize bdgs. pba Sept 14 (226) $200

**Milmine, Georgine**
— The Life of Mary Baker G. Eddy.... L, 1909. 1st English Ed. - Ed by Willa Cather. pba Oct 5 (27) $180

**Milne, Alan Alexander, 1882-1956**
See also: Fore-Edge Paintings
— A Gallery of Children. L, 1925. One of 500. Illus by H. W. Le Mair. 4to, orig cloth. With 12 colored plates. Creases or tears to 3 plates. NH July 21 (234) $140
Anr copy. Orig cloth; stained & soiled. With 12 colored plates. S Nov 2 (306) £200 [Sotheran]
Anr copy. Orig cloth; endpapers foxed. sg Oct 19 (145) $475
— The House at Pooh Corner. L, 1928. 1st Ed. - Illus by E. H. Shepard. In dj. bba May 9 (241) £260 [Sotheran]
Anr copy. In soiled dj. cb Feb 14 (2699) $450
Anr copy. Orig lea gilt. cb June 25 (1883) $1,800
One of 350 L.p. copies, sgd by author & artist. 4to, orig half cloth, unopened, in dj. pn Dec 7 (90) £850
— Now We Are Six. L, 1927. 1st Ed. - Illus by E. H. Shepard. Mor by Bayntun Riviere with pictorial onlays after Shepard's drawing to the Morning Walk. b May 30 (566) £240
Anr copy. In dj with soiling. bba May 9 (239) £240 [Sotheran]
Anr copy. In soiled & torn dj. bba May 9 (240) £180 [Sotheran]
Anr copy. In dj. cb Feb 14 (2700) $400
Anr Ed. L, [1927]. Orig lea gilt. cb June 25 (1884) $850
Anr Ed. L, 1927. In soiled & chipped dj. pba Jan 4 (65) $190
4th Ed. L, [1928]. Calf gilt by Riviere; extremities scuffed. pba Mar 7 (185) $110
— Toad of Toad Hall.... L, [1929]. One of 200, sgd by author & Kenneth Grahame. 4to, orig half cloth, in dj with minor soil. cb Feb 14 (2701) $900
— When We Were Very Young. L, 1924. 1st Ed. - Illus by E. H. Shepard. In dj with chipped spine; bdg spine ends rubbed. Ck May 31 (68) £950
One of 100, sgd by author & artist. Orig half cloth, unopened, in dj with soiling. cb Feb 14 (2702) $2,250
— Winnie-the-Pooh. L, 1926. 1st Ed. - Illus by E. H. Shepard. Lea gilt. cb June 25 (1885) $2,000

Anr copy. In chipped dj. S May 16 (177) £380

**Milne, Christian**
— Simple Poems, on Simple Subjects. Aberdeen, 1805. 8vo, contemp half calf; rubbed. b Dec 5 (521) £120

**Milne, Colin, 1743?-1815**
— A Botanical Dictionary: Or Elements of Systematic and Physiological Botany. L, 1805. 3d Ed. 8vo, contemp calf; joints cracked, spine ends worn. With 25 plates. sg May 16 (327) $80

**Milne, John Stewart —& Burton, William Kinninmond**
— The Great Earthquake in Japan, 1891. Yokohama, [1892]. Illus by Kazumasa Ogawa. Oblong 4to, cloth; rubbed. With map & 29 plates. b Sept 20 (435) £70

**Milner, Joe E. —& Forrest, Earle Robert**
— California Joe: Noted Scout and Indian Fighter. Caldwell, Idaho, 1935. Stamp to front pastedown; some annotations; newspaper clipping affixed to front free endpaper. pba June 25 (174) $75

**Milner, John, 1752-1826**
— The History Civil and Ecclesiastical...Winchester. Winchester, [1798-1801]. 2 vols. 4to, orig half cloth; stained. Some foxing. pba June 20 (246) $55

**Milner, Joseph.** See: Fore-Edge Paintings

**Milner, Thomas**
— The Gallery of Nature. L, 1846. 4to, contemp mor gilt; joints rubbed. Some foxing. pba Aug 8 (520) $120

**Milnor, William, Jr., 1769-1848**
— An Authentic Historical Memoir of the Schuylkill Fishing Company. Phila., 1889. ("A History of the Schuylkill Fishing Company....") 8vo, half mor; rubbed. Library markings; minor stains & soiling. O Feb 6 (207) $225

Anr copy. Half calf; small crack to upper joint. Tp laid-down on archival paper. pba July 11 (273) $275

— Memoirs of the Gloucester Fox Hunting Club.... NY: Derrydale Press, 1927. One of 375. Bds; worn, spine chipped, covers spotted. With 2 mtd plates. O Jan 9 (88) $50

**Milosz, Czeslaw.** See: Limited Editions Club

**Milton, John, 1608-74**
See also: Doves Press; Fore-Edge Paintings; Golden Cockerel Press; Gregynog Press; Limited Editions Club; Nonesuch Press sg Sept 21 (35) $750L, 1835. 6 vols. 8vo, lev gilt by Bayntun
— Comus. L & NY, [1921]. Illus by Arthur Rackham. 4to, orig cloth, in frayed dj. With 24 mtd colored plates. Ck May 31 (153) $340

One of 550. Orig half vellum gilt. With 24 mtd color plates. Corner of 1 plate creased. S Nov 2 (118) £320 [Sotheran]

One of 550, sgd by artist. Orig vellum; rear joint cracked, corners worn. With 24 mtd colored plates. sg Feb 15 (255) $250
— A Defence of the People of England.... L, [Amst.?], 1692. 8vo, later half calf. Some spotting & browning. cb Feb 14 (2704) $450
— The History of Britain.... L, 1670. 1st Ed. 4to, later mor gilt by Stikeman; front cover scuffed. Marginal browning & spotting throughout; a few leaves soiled. cb Feb 14 (2705) $550
— Le Paradis perdu. Paris, 1792. 2 vols. 4to, contemp mor gilt. With 12 color plates. S Nov 30 (285) £2,300

Anr copy. Contemp mor gilt. With 12 color plates plus added port of Milton. Some spotting & browning. Fuerstenberg - Schaefer copy. S Dec 7 (422) £950
— Paradise Lost. L, 1668. 1st Ed, Amory's No 2 Issue (traditional 4th title). 4to, contemp goatskin gilt; spine ends chipped, edges rubbed, bookplate removed from front pastedown; tipped in at front is a folio leaf from an unidentified vol of Miscellanies. De Coppet copy. CNY May 17 (101) $18,000

Anr copy. Contemp calf; hinges weak, repaired. rs Nov 11 (107) $7,500

Amory's No 3 Issue. L, 1669. 4to, later calf gilt. Browned. S July 11 (122) £2,000

3d Ed. L, 1678. 8vo, later mor gilt. Some foxing, dampstaining & marginal tears & stains; some leaves cut close touching running heads; tp lacking bit of corner & with ink writing. cb Feb 14 (2706) $400

4th Ed. L, 1688. Folio, contemp calf; rubbed. With port & 12 plates. Some staining; hole on p. 7 & 41 affecting 2 letters of text. b Dec 5 (36) £650

Anr copy. Modern half calf. Soiled & frayed; 1 plate torn & repaired. CE May 22 (349) $950

Anr copy. Mor extra jewelled bdg by Sangorski & Sutcliffe. With port & 12 plates. sg Apr 18 (83) $16,000

Anr Ed. Glasgow: Foulis, 1770. Folio, contemp calf gilt; rebacked, corners repaired. Some foxing & marginal waterstaining. bba May 9 (6) £150 [Cox]

Anr copy. Later mor gilt, prize bdg. bba July 18 (195) £50 [Unsworth]

Anr copy. Contemp calf gilt; rubbed. Top margin of several leaves dampstained. F June 20 (830) $120

Anr Ed. L, 1825-27. Illus by John Martin. 2 vols in 12 parts. Imperial 4to, orig wraps; some spotting & marginal tears, 1 spine renewed. With 24 plates. Some foxing. P Nov 1 (155) $9,500

Anr Ed. L, 1827. 2 vols. Folio, 19th-cent calf gilt; rebacked, worn, endpapers & half-title of Vol I reattached with tape, dampstaining to front endpapers of Vol II. Some foxing. S July 11 (197) £360

Anr Ed. L, 1853. 4to, contemp or gilt. With 24 plates. Margins spotted or soiled. S Nov 2 (94) £200 [Bankes]

Anr Ed. L, 1882. Illus by Gustave Dore. Folio, mor gilt. pba Sept 14 (132) $225

Anr Ed. Liverpool, 1906. Illus by William Blake. 4to, half cloth; rubbed & stained, endpapers foxed. pba Aug 8 (301) $110

— Paradise Regain'd. L, 1671. 1st Ed, 1st Issue, with misprint "loah" on p. 67. Bound with Comus. L, 1670. 8vo, 18th-cent calf; rebacked, upper cover & flyleaf detached, corners repaired. A few leaves shaved; a few catchwords in Comus cropped. De Coppet copy. CNY May 17 (102) $1,900

1st Ed, Issue not indicated. 8vo, modern half mor. Stamp on p. 1; tp repaired; tp of Samson Agonistes resized; trimmed at top. pba Sept 14 (270) $1,200

2d Ed. L, 1680. 8vo, old calf. Minor dampstaining at beginning; trimmed; License leaf chipped. F June 20 (441) $370

— Poetical Works. L, 1794-97. 3 vols. Folio, half mor; 1 spine top worn, some rubbing. With 4 ports & 28 plates. Extra-illus with 9 plates. K June 23 (380) $400

Anr copy. Contemp russia gilt; rebacked, edges worn. sg Oct 19 (146) $425

Anr Ed. L, 1862. Illus by J. M. W. Turner. 8vo, contemp mor gilt; rubbed. pba Dec 14 (150) $80

— Pro populo Anglicano defensio secunda. L, 1654. 1st Ed. 8vo, contemp calf; worn, upper joint cracked. Dampstaining in lower margin throughout, affecting some text; chipped at bottom. CE May 22 (348) $450

— Samson Agonistes. Harrow Weald: Raven Press, 1931. One of 275. Illus by R. A. Maynard. 4to, orig half vellum. bba May 9 (628) £50 [Hanborough]

**Paradise Lost bound with or accompanied by Paradise Regain'd**

— 1674-80. - L. 8vo, later half lea; worn. PL tp torn & with small hole & with other tears with loss; PR with some cropping. S Mar 28 (613) £440

— 1770-66. - L. 4 vols. 4to, later calf; rebacked, hinges repaired. sg Feb 8 (84) $175

**Milton, William Wentworth Fitzwilliam, Viscount.**
See: Fitzwilliam & Cheadle

**Minadoni, Giovanni Tommaso**
— Historia della guerra fra Turchi et Persiani. Rome: G. Tornerio & B. Donangeli, 1587. 4to, contemp vellum; soiled. Lacks maps; spotted; title dust-soiled. S Oct 26 (172) £360 [Zioni]

**Miner, Harriet Stewart**
— Orchids, the Royal Family of Plants. L, 1885. 4to, orig cloth; corners bumped. With 24 colored plates. F June 20 (848) $600; sg May 9 (311) $400

**Miner's...**
— The Miner's Own Book, containing Correct Illustrations and Descriptions of the Various Modes of California Mining. San Francisco, 1858. Illus by Charles Nahl. 8vo, orig wraps. Larson copy. pba Sept 28 (528) $3,000

Anr Ed. San Francisco, 1949. One of 500. Intro by Rodman Paul. Half bds in dj. Larson copy. pba Sept 28 (529) $110

**Miniature Books**
— The Bible in Miniature. L, 1775. 44mm by 28mm, orig mor gilt with label with JHS on covers; upper joint rubbed. With engraved title & 14 plates. Tp loose; 1 leaf with loss. S Nov 2 (333) £180 [Sotheran]

— Botanical Illustrations of the Twenty-Four Classes in the Linnaen System of Vegetables. L, 1813. 75mm by 65mm, orig lea; rebacked preserving spine, new endpapers. With 48 hand-colored plates. Ink & pencil marks; some browning. S Nov 2 (160) £220 [Hirsch]

— Kern des Bybels. The Hague, 1750. 41mm by 24mm, contemp mor gilt. With 7 woodcut plates. sg Apr 18 (84) $300

— [New Testament in Greek]. Sedan: J. Jannon, 1628. 76mm by 47mm, 17th-cent silver bdg with engraved decoration including a central oval containing a mirror-monogram K.A. surmounted by an earl's coronet, with maker's mark GM on covers; contents upside down, clasp lacking. C May 1 (154) £850

— Novum Iesu Christi Domini Nostri Testamentum. Sedan: J. Jannon, 1628-29. 81mm by 47mm, 17th-cent Hungarian enamelled silver bdg set with pearls & jewels. Greek text.. D & M 4676. Abbey copy. C May 1 (16) £3,000

— A Picture Book of Birds, British and Foreign.... L: William Darton, 1822. 72mm by 56mm, orig lea gilt; rubbed, corner of lower cover & foot of spine damaged, hinges weak. With 46 (of 48) plates, a few partly colored by former owner. Lacking Plates 9 & 10; a few plates reinserted. S Nov 2 (238) £260 [Schiller]

— [Psalms] The Whole Booke of Psalmes. L, 1641. Trans by T. Sternhold & J. Hopkins. 70mm by 50mm, contemp embroidered needlework bdg; worn. b Dec 5 (185) £50

— Les Quatre Saisons. Paris: A. Pinard, [c.1820]. 4 vols. 68mm by 46mm, orig wraps. With 4 hand-colored frontises. S Nov 2 (245) £580 [Temperley]

— Queen Elizabeth's Prayer Book. [Southwood, 1893]. One of 50. 76mm by 55mm, lea. On vellum. With 2 port miniatures. S Nov 2 (336) £220 [Johnson]

— Seder Tephiloth. Amst.: Naphtali Herz Levi, 1739. 59mm by 36mm, blind-tooled dyed parchment. CE Dec 6 (132) $500

Anr copy. 58mm by 34mm, contemp calf gilt; worn, lower hinge cracked, some leaves loose. Some foremargins trimmed affecting letters; some staining & browning. CE Dec 6 (133) $600

Anr Ed. Amst.: Naphtali Herz Levi, 1761. 8vo, contemp mor gilt; textblock cracked; 1 gathering loose; stained & browned. CE Dec 6 (136) $800

BAUM, L. FRANK. - The Wonderful Wizard of Oz. Van Nuys: Collectors Editions in Miniature, 1979. One of 300. .75 by .50 inches, orig cloth. pba Jan 18 (158) $110

BOREMAN, THOMAS. - The Gigantick History of the Two Famous Giants.... L, 1740. Vol II only. 60mm by 47mm, orig Dutch floral bds; rebacked, rear endpaper torn. Small hole in final leaf of text; corners of some leaves creased. S Nov 2 (334) £1,000 [Schiller]

## MINIATURE

CLEMENS, SAMUEL LANGHORNE. - Coyote. Helmet CA: Ash Ranch Press, 1986. One of 26 lettered copies. 30mm by 25mm, Lea. pba Dec 14 (156) $110

CROSBY, HARRY. - Transit of Venus. Paris: Black Sun Press, 1929. 2d Ed, One of 200. Orig wraps. pba Nov 30 (49) $180

FORD, ALLA T. - The High-Jinks of L. Frank Baum. Hong Kong: Ford Press, 1969. One of 500. 2.5 by 2 inches, pictorial wraps with hand-painted rear cover. Inscr to George Breslin. pba Jan 18 (153) $90

FORD, ALLA T. - The Joys of Collecting Children's Books. Hong Kong: Ford Press, 1968. One of 25 with hand-painted cover. 2.25 by 1.75 inches, cloth. Inscr to George Breslin. pba Jan 18 (152) $55

HORACE. - Carmina Sapphica. Bost.: Bromer, 1983. One of 150. 35mm by 25mm, orig mor gilt. bba May 9 (587) £70 [Talerman]; bba May 9 (588) £70 [Talerman]

HORACE. - Opera. L: Wm. Pickering, 1820. 83mm by 47mm, contemp mor. With engraved title. pba June 20 (247) $300

OMAR KHAYYAM. - The Rose Garden. Worcester, Mass., 1932. 4mm by 6mm, mor. With an archive of material concerning the publication of this Ed. sg Apr 18 (85) $750

PETRARCA, FRANCESCO. - Le Rime. L, 1822. 80mm by 45mm, contemp sheep; front joint cracked. sg Sept 21 (264) $60

SHAKESPEARE, WILLIAM. - Plays. L: Pickering, 1825. 9 vols. 80mm by 44mm, later calf gilt; joints & corners rubbed, endpapers abraded. Some foxing & soiling. cb Feb 14 (2725) $850

Anr copy. 9 vols. 87mm by 50mm, orig cloth; minor wear. With port & 38 plates. S Apr 23 (129) £280

Anr Ed. NY: Knickerbocker Leather & Novelty, [1890s]. 24 vols. 3 by 2 inches mor gilt of various colors. pba Aug 8 (596) $250

Anr Ed. L, [c.1920]. 39 vols. 2 by 1.5 inches, orig cloth, in wooden bookcase. F Mar 28 (299) $230

WALCOTT, PAUL & BETTY & SOLIDAY, MARION. - Chats About Miniature Books. Bost.: Pvtly ptd, [1932]. One of 250. 38mm by 32mm, wraps. sg Apr 18 (87) $250

**Minkoff, George Robert**

— A Bibliography of the Black Sun Press. Great Neck, NY, 1970. One of 1,250. 4to, orig cloth. sg Apr 11 (233) $90

**Minnesota**

— St. Paul City Directory for 1874. St. Paul, 1874. Orig half cloth; rubbed & worn. pba Nov 16 (175) $75

**Minnigerode, Meade**

— Some Personal Letters of Herman Melville and a Bibliography. NY, 1922. One of 1,500. Half cloth, unopened, in rubbed & soiled dj. pba Aug 8 (518) $50

**Minot, Henry D.** See: Roosevelt & Minot

## AMERICAN BOOK PRICES CURRENT

**Minotaure...**

— Minotaure: Revue artistique et litteraire. Paris, 1933-39. Nos 1-13 (complete set), bound in 3 vols. Cloth, orig wraps bound in. cb Feb 14 (2768) $2,250

No 10. 4to, pictorial wraps by Matisse; soiled. sg June 13 (292) $130

No 11. Pictorial wraps by Max Ernst; repaired. Sold w.a.f. sg June 13 (293) $90

No 5. 4to, orig wraps; backstrip chipped. sg June 13 (291) $200

**Miquel, Pierre**

— Eugene Isabey, 1803-1886. Maurs-La-Jolie, 1980. 2 vols. Folio, cloth, in djs. sg Jan 11 (227) $250

**Mirabeau, Honore Gabriel Riqueti, Comte de, 1749-91**

— Considerations on the Order of Cincinnatus.... L, 1785. 8vo, contemp mor gilt. Fuerstenberg - Schaefer copy. S Dec 7 (423) £700

**Mirabeau Library, H. G. R., Comte de**

— [Sale Catalogue] Catalogue des livres.... Paris, 1791. 8vo, old calf; rebacked preserving orig spine. Library stamp. O Mar 26 (176) $500

**Miro, Joan, 1893-1974**

— Joan Miro Litografo. Barcelona: Ediciones Poligrafa, [1972-81]. Ed by Michel Leiris & Fernand Mourlot. Vols I-III (of 4). Orig cloth, in djs. sg Jan 11 (287) $400

— Lithographe. Paris, 1972-81. Ed by Michel Leiris & Fernand Mourlot. Vols I-III. In djs. CE June 12 (228) $400

— Lithographs. NY: Tudor Publishing, [1972]-81. Ed by Michel Leiris & Fernand Mourlot. Vols I-III (of 4). Folio, orig cloth, in djs. cb Feb 14 (2793) $600

Anr copy. 4 vols. Folio, cb June 25 (1960) $1,200

Anr copy. Vols I-II (of 4). Folio, cb June 25 (1961) $600

Anr copy. Vol I In dj. sg June 13 (259) $350

Vol II only. NY: Leon Amiel, [1975]. Unsewn as issued in wraps, with wrap-around band. With 2 sgd lithos. pba June 20 (248) $250

[-] Miro. Paris: Fondation Maeght, 1968. Pictorial wraps by Miro. sg June 13 (257) $200

— Peintures sur cartons. Paris: Maeght, 1965. One of 150 on velin de Rives. Text by Jacques Dupin. Folio, pictorial wraps, unbound. Sold w.a.f. Special No 151/152 of Derriere le Miroir. sg Jan 11 (289) $140

**Mirror...**

— The Mirrour of the World. Kentfield, CA: Allen Press, 1964. One of 130. 3 vols. Folio, orig wraps. From William Caxton's 1481 Ed. cb June 25 (1902) $150

**Missal**

— Missale romanum. Antwerp: Balthasar Moretus, 1631. 4to, 17th-Cent mor. With vignette title & 9 full-page illus. Rust-hole in B7 & Q5. S Oct 27 (1071) £220 [P & P Bks.]

— 1500, 16 Apr. - Missale ad usum Lugdunense. Lyon: Petrus Ungarus. Folio, 17th-cent calf gilt with supralibros of R. & H. M. Sheldon. 35 lines & headline; double column; Gothic types. With 2 full-page woodcuts, large woodcut initial T & 21 woodcut initials of 19 blocks, all illuminated in gold & colors; leaf a1r illuminated with floriated full border in penwork & colors, incorporating birds, strawberries & unidentified coat-of-arms. Worming in lower outer corner of a few leaves; some staining. 270 (of 272) leaves; lacking blanks c6 & L10. C 4156. Schaefer copy. P Nov 1 (157) $12,000

— 1520. - Missale ad usum dyocesis Monasteriensis. Paris: Wolfgang Hopyl for Franz Birckman & Gottfried Hittor. Folio, calf over wooden bds, 1 roll dated 1554, with brass clasps & plaited parchment index tabs; repaired, clasps renewed, a few tabs perished. 42 lines & headlines (variable), double column, Gothic types. With full-page Canon woodcut of the Crucifixion on v4v. Early repairs; woodcut with tear repaired; some soiling & thumbing. P June 5 (296) $2,500

— 1546. - Missale romanum. Venice: heirs of Luc Antonio Giunta. Folio, contemp blindstamped calf laid down over modern calf over wooden bds, with contemp full-page painted armorial ex-libris on verso of flyleaf. With full-page woodcut & 10 smaller woodcuts, all hand-colored. Lacking tp & final blank; some worming; 1 leaf with lower margin partly cut away & repaired; dampstaining at end. S July 11 (6) £360

— 1670. - Missale Romanum auctoritate Pauli V. pont. M. Sinice redditum a P. Ludovico Buglio Soc. Iesu Panormitano. Peking Folio, silk; spine worn. Ptd xylographically in Chinese on native paper on 1 side of folded sheets. Tp repaired with minor loss; some dampstaining. S June 27 (225) £6,800

— 1712-18-1667. - Missale Romanum.... Lyon & Paris Folio, With engraved title & 2 plates. Fuerstenberg - Schaefer copy. S Dec 7 (425) £1,200

— 1718. - Venice: Paulus Balleonius. Folio, contemp mor gilt over wooden bds with geometric strapwork border & azured strapwork center lozenge, gilt & blue edges, gauffered & painted with strapwork decoration. sg Mar 21 (50) $750

**Missolonghi**
— Ta Hellenika Khronika. Efemeris Politike ekdoseisa en Mesolongioi upo tou D. I. Mager apo A' Ianouariou 1824 - 20 Febr. 1826. Athens, 1840. Folio, contemp wraps; frayed & stained. sg Mar 7 (101) $350

**Mitchell, Edward.** See: Scarpa, Antonio

**Mitchell, Joseph.** See: Limited Editions Club

**Mitchell, Lisa.** See: Bradbury & Mitchell

**Mitchell, Margaret, 1900-49**
See also: Limited Editions Club
— Gone With the Wind. NY, 1936. 1st Ed. Mor gilt by Zaehnsdorf for Asprey. CE Sept 27 (199) $1,200

Anr copy. Inscr to Mable Search, 1 Dec 1936. CE May 22 (352) $2,500
1st Issue, with May 1936 date. In dj. A few right margins dampstained. Inscr to Carmin Jones. P Dec 12 (123) $3,000
Anr copy. In chipped & creased dj. pba May 23 (253) $1,800
Anr copy. In dj. sg Dec 14 (220) $1,900
Anr copy. In 1st dj. sg June 20 (274) $4,600
Anr copy. In 1st dj, with chips & tears. Z June 28 (195) $2,800
Anr copy. Orig cloth; rubbed, spine def. Z June 28 (196) $350
Issue not indicated. In frayed dj. Inscr. P June 5 (297) $3,500
Anr copy. In chipped later dj. Inscr. sg June 20 (275) $3,000
Anniversary Ed. NY, 1961. With booklet about the book & its author, in wraps. pba May 23 (254) $90
Anr Ed. Norwalk: Easton Press, 1968. 2 vols. 4to, lea gilt. Z June 28 (202) $60
Anr Ed. [N.p.]: Southern Classics Library, 1984. Mor gilt. Without commentary booklet. Z June 28 (203) $55
Anr copy. With commentary booklet. Z June 28 (204) $85
Anr Ed. NY: Macmillan, [1986]. In dj. Facsimile of 1st Ed. Z June 28 (205) $60

**Mitchell, Samuel Augustus, 1792-1868**
See also: Atlas
— Illinois in 1837.... Phila., 1837. 1st Ed, 2d Issue. 8vo, later half mor. With hand-colored folding map. sg Oct 26 (151) $130
— Mitchell's Ancient Atlas, Classical and Sacred. Phila., 1854. 4to, orig lea-backed bds; spine chipped. With 12 hand-colored maps on 8 sheets. sg Dec 7 (30) $225
— Mitchell's New Traveler's Guide through the United States. Phila., 1850. 16mo, orig lea gilt; extremities worn, rear hinge cracked through. With folding map, hand-colored in outline. Fold tears; some foxing. cb Feb 14 (2570) $500
— Mitchell's Traveller's Guide Through the United States. Phila., 1834. 12mo, orig lea wallet-style bdg. Map hand-colored. O July 9 (139) $300
— A New Map of Texas, Oregon and California.... Phila., 1846. Bound with: Accompaniment to Mitchell's New Map of Texas.... Phila., 1846. 16mo, orig cloth; worn. Map 23 by 21 inches, partially colored;. Some spotting & staining; ink stamps. cb June 25 (1754) $7,500
— A New Universal Atlas. Phila., 1847. Folio, disbound. With 52 hand-colored maps & 1 plate. Last few maps marginally torn; Palestine map & plate with loss. S Oct 26 (477) £1,300 [Avader]
Anr Ed. Phila., 1850. Folio, half sheep gilt; spine lacking, worn, covers detached. With engraved title & 71 (of 72) hand-colored maps. Some foxing & browning. bbc Feb 26 (20) $1,700
Anr Ed. Phila., 1858. Folio, orig half sheep; needs rebdg. sg May 9 (89) $1,900

## MITCHELL

**Mitchell, Silas Weir, 1829-1914**
— Hugh Wynne, Free Quaker. NY, 1897. 1st Ed, 1st Issue. 2 vols. 12mo, orig cloth, B bdg, in djs. K Oct 1 (272) $275

**Mitchell, Sir Thomas Livingstone, 1792-1855**
— Three Expeditions into the Interior of Eastern Australia. L, 1839. 2d Ed. 2 vols. 8vo, orig cloth; rubbed. With folding map & 51 plates, some colored Corner of Q1 in Vol II def; some foxing. bba Nov 16 (280) £450

**Mitchie, John**
— The Vices of the Tavern Dissected; or, Drunkeness Laid Open.... Rotherham, 1814. 8vo, modern bds. Some soiling. b Dec 5 (468) £100

**Mitelli, Giuseppe Maria, 1634-1718**
— Proverbi figurati consecrati al serenissimo Principe Francesco Maria di Toscana. [Bologna], 1678. Folio, old vellum; soiled. With engraved title & 47 (of 48) plates. Lacking Plate 27; tp & Plate 7 repaired; Plate 31 torn; some browning. Extra plate inserted at end. C Nov 29 (101) £3,400

**Mitford, Nancy**
— The Sun King. L, 1969. One of 265, specially bound & with added sgd title. 4to, orig mor gilt by Zaehnsdorf. sg Sept 14 (23) $375

**Mivart, St. George Jackson, 1827-1900**
— Dogs, Jackals, Wolves, and Foxes.... L, 1890. 1st Ed. 4to, modern mor gilt. With 45 hand-colored plates. Fattorini copy. C Oct 25 (79) £1,100

**Mochi, Ugo —&**
**Carter, T. Donald**
— Hoofed Mammals of the World. NY, 1953. Folio, cloth; worn. William Beach's copy. O Oct 10 (198) $190

**Model, Lisette**
— Lisette Model. NY, [1979]. Preface by Berenice Abbott. Folio, pictorial bds, in dj; bdg bumped, shaken & with tear on front pastedown. sg Feb 29 (205) $110

**Modeles...**
— Modeles d'appareils d'aviation de l'antiquite a nos jours. Paris, 1910. Oblong 4to, orig wraps; spine worn. sg May 16 (70) $60

**Modern...**
— Modern Artists in America.... NY, [1951]. Ed by Robert Motherwell & Ad Reinhardt. Pictorial bds; rubbed. sg Jan 11 (300) $110

**Moe, Jorgen I., 1813-82.** See: Asbjornsen & Moe

**Moebs, T. T.**
— Reference-iana: (1481-1899) A Concise Guide.... Williamsburg, 1989. In dj. ds July 27 (132) $70

## AMERICAN BOOK PRICES CURRENT

**Moellhausen, Balduin, 1825-1905**
— Diary of a Journey from the Mississippi to the Coasts of the Pacific. L, 1858. 2 vols. 8vo, 19th-cent half mor; extremities worn. With 11 chromolitho plates, 12 woodcut plates & 1 folding map. Dampstaining to corners of some plates, affecting small portion of images. pba Nov 16 (178) $1,400

**Moerenhout, Jacques Antoine, 1796?-1879**
— The Inside Story of the Gold Rush. San Francisco: California Historical Society, 1935. 1st Ed. - Trans & ed by Abraham P. Nasatir. Orig cloth. With frontis port, 1 map, & 7 plates. Larson copy. pba Sept 28 (608) $50

Anr copy. Trans & Ed by Abraham P. Nasatir. Orig cloth. With folding map. Robbins copy. pba Mar 21 (239) $140

**Moeurs...**
— Moeurs et coutumes des peuples. Paris: Hocquart, [1811-14]. 2 vols. 4to, contemp calf gilt; rebacked. With 143 colored plates only. sg Dec 7 (261) $1,200

**Moffett, Kenworth**
— Kenneth Noland. NY: Abrams, [1977]. Oblong folio, cloth, in plastic dj. sg Jan 11 (321) $130

**Moffett, Thomas, 1553-1604**
— Healths Improvement.... L, 1655. 4to, contemp calf; rebacked. Soiled; minor stains; corner chipped on &1 affecting a few letters of shoulder not; last leaf of text with margins frayed. CE June 12 (180) $1,300

1st Ed. 4to, late 19th-Cent half calf. With imprimatur leaf. Imprimatur torn; title & other leaves browned in margins; 2I2r soiled. Ck Mar 22 (200) £1,000

**Mohler, Olga**
— Francis Picabia. [Turin, 1975]. Folio, half cloth, in dj with piece lacking. sg June 13 (311) $140

**Moholy-Nagy, Laszlo**
— 60 Fotos. Berlin, [1930]. Essay by Franz Roh. 4to, disbound from wraps. Tp foxed & creased. sg Feb 29 (207) $375

— Bauhausbuecher No 14: Von Material zu Architektur. Munich, 1929. Orig wraps; upper cover detached, spine head chipped with loss. bba Oct 19 (145) £220 [W. English]

— L. Moholy-Nagy. Brno: Telhor, 1936. 4to, spiral-bound ptd wraps; worn & chipped. Water damage & foxing throughout. sg Feb 29 (210) $475

**Mokshin, S.** See: Frolov & Mokshin

**Moleville, Antoine Francois Bertrand de**
— The Costume of the Hereditary States of the House of Austria.... L, 1804. 4to, mor gilt. With 50 hand-colored plates. In English & French. pba Mar 7 (187) $950

Anr Ed. L, 1804 [but some plates watermarked 1819]. Folio, contemp mor gilt; endleaves creased. With 50 hand-colored plates. sg Oct 19 (147) $500

— Private Memoirs relative to the Last Year of the Reign of Lewis the Sixteenth, late King of France. L, 1797. 3 vols. Half mor; extremities rubbed. Z June 28 (25) $200

**Moliere, Jean Baptiste Poquelin de, 1622-73**
See also: Cabinet...
— Oeuvres. Paris, 1673. 8 vols. 12mo, contemp calf gilt; spines chipped. With 30 plates; Vols I-V without cancels. Some worming; plate of Psyche in Vol VI shaved at top; short tear in 2L in Vol VII affecting text. La Rochefoucauld copy. S June 27 (347) £10,000

Anr Ed. Paris, 1734. 6 vols. 4to, contemp mor gilt; ink stain on lower cover of Vol II, lower cover of Vol V repaired. With engraved titles, port & 33 plates. Some worming to inner margins of Vol I; inkstain on edge of 1st leaves of Vol II, affecting outer margins; tear in lower margin of 1st plate of Vol V. Fuerstenberg - Schaefer copy. S Dec 7 (426) £15,000

Anr Ed. Amst. & Leipzig, 1765. Illus by J. Punt. 6 vols. 12mo, contemp mor gilt. With port, frontis & 33 plates. Soiling on 1st leaves of Vol V. Fuerstenberg - Schaefer copy. S Dec 7 (427) £1,300

Anr Ed. Paris, 1773. 1st Issue. 6 vols. 8vo, contemp mor gilt. With 6 engraved titles, port & 33 plates. Fuerstenberg - Schaefer copy. S Dec 7 (428) £3,000

— Les Oeuvres. Paris, 1791. 6 vols. 4to, contemp mor gilt; covers of Vol I spotted. Didot's unillustrated Ed bound with Boucher's illusts; with port & 32 (of 33) plates & with port by Restout tipped in. Vols V & VI browned; plates browned in all vols. Fuerstenberg - Schaefer copy. S Dec 7 (429) £3,000

— Oeuvres. Paris, 1882. One of 1,000. Illus by Jacques Leman. 32 vols. 4to, mor gilt by Yseux, orig wraps bound in. With many colored illusts in 4 states. S Nov 2 (18) £450 [Frew]

— Theatre. Paris, 1878-79. One of 21 on chine. Illus by V. Foulquier. 2 vols. 8vo, mor gilt by Marius Michel. With 26 plates. b Sept 20 (630) £220

— Theatre complet. Paris, 1876-83. One of 910. Illus by Louis Leloir after Leopold Flameng. 8 vols. 8vo, half mor by Granghaud, orig wraps bound in. With port & 30 plates. cb Oct 17 (332) $500

Anr copy. Mor gilt by Pagnant. With port & 30 plates in 2 states. CE Sept 27 (206) $900

— Works. L, 1714. Trans by J. Ozell. 6 vols in 3. 12mo, contemp calf gilt; spines & edges repaired, hinges cracked. Doheny copy. C Nov 29 (131) £700

**Molina, Alonso de, d.1535**
— Vocabulario en lengua castellana y mexicana.... Mexico: Antonio de Spinoza, 1571. 2d Ed. 2 parts in 1 vol. Folio, later half sheep; extremities rubbed. Lacking tp & 1 prelim leaf (supplied in early Ms facsimile); Part 2 lacking prelim blank & last 10 leaves (similarly supplied); 1st 10 leaves with marginal repairs with minor loss; last 30 leaves with marginal repairs; some staining. cb Feb 14 (2596) $2,000

**Molina, Juan Ignacio de**
— Compendio della storia geografica, naturale, e civile, del regno del Chile. Bologna, 1776. 8vo, orig bds. With folding map & 10 plates. S June 13 (613) £500

**Molinier, Pierre.** See: Gorsen & Molinier

**Molitoris, Ulrich**
— De lamiis et phitonicis mulieribus teutonice unholden vel hexen. Reutlingen: Johann Otmar, not before 10 Jan 1489]. 4to, modern bds. 33 lines; gothic letter; with 7 full-page woodcuts. Tear in lower margin of a8 repaired, touching 1 letter of text; marginal worming & repairs; stamp on tp. 28 leaves. Goff M-795. S June 27 (349) £7,200

**Moll, Herman, d.1732**
— Atlas Geographius: or, a Compleat System of Geography. L, 1708-97. Vol I only. Contemp calf; worn, spine torn, half of each pastedown missing, 2 plates detached, 3 plates nearly detached. With 6 plates & 20 maps. cb Oct 17 (253) $700

— Atlas Minor: or a New and Curious Set of Sixty-Two Maps. L, [1732?]. Oblong folio, half calf; worn. With 62 maps, colored in outline. Marginal dampstains; some soiling; last map creased. cb Feb 14 (2558) $4,000

Anr copy. Modern half calf. With engraved title & 62 maps. World map repaired at corners; a few small repaired tears; marginal soiling. S Nov 30 (79) £3,500

— A Set of Fifty New and Correct Maps of England and Wales.... L, 1724. Oblong folio, contemp wraps; worn. With 50 maps, 2 folding. Tear to 1 map; lower outer corner gnawed throughout; tp torn with minor loss. Sold w.a.f. b Sept 20 (281) £850

Anr Ed. L, 1739. Oblong folio, modern half calf. With 2 folding maps & 48 regional & county maps. Some marginal discoloration. S Nov 30 (58) £1,600

— The World Described... L: T. Bowles, [1709-20]. Folio, contemp calf; worn, lower cover torn. With 26 (of 30) folding maps, hand-colored in outline. Lacking France, upper Italy, Rhine & Baltic. With 3 additional maps inserted. Lacking list of maps; many maps torn at margins or along centerfolds; some old repairs & browning; wormhole at head of guards just affecting maps. C Nov 29 (102) £12,500

**Molloy, Charles, 1646-90**
— De jure maritimo et navali. L, 1677. 2d Ed. 8vo, contemp sheep; front cover loose. Engraved title frayed. sg Mar 7 (222) $150

4th Ed. L, 1688. 8vo, contemp sheep. sg Mar 7 (223) $200

**Molyneux, William, 1656-98**
— Dioptrica Nova, a Treatise of Dioptricks.... L, 1709. 2d Ed. 4to, contemp calf; rebacked. With 43 folding plates. Some shaving, browning & spotting. S Mar 14 (255) £750

## MOMMSEN

**Mommsen, Theodor, 1817-1903**
— The History of Rome. L, 1868-86. 6 vols. 8vo, half mor gilt; joints & spine ends rubbed. F Mar 28 (430) $130

**Monaghan, Frank**
— French Travellers in the United States, 1765-1932. A Bibliography. NY, 1961. Library stamp on edges. ds July 27 (133) $125

**Moncrif, Francois Augustin Paradis de**
See also: Golden Cockerel Press
— Les Chats. Paris, 1727. 1st Ed. 8vo, contemp calf; rubbed, lettering-piece & endpapers renewed. With 9 plates, 2 of them double-page, & 1 genealogical folding plate. Fuerstenberg - Schaefer copy. S Dec 7 (431) £750

Anr copy. Bdg not described; spine & cover repaired, lettering-piece renewed. Inscr. Fuerstenberg - Schaefer copy. S Dec 7 (432) £650

**Mondonville, Jean Joseph**
— Les Festes de Paphos ballet heroique [full score]. Paris, [1758]. Folio, contemp calf gilt; spine ends repaired. Engraved throughout. Tp & last page stamped. S May 15 (418) £500

**Money, John**
— The History of the Campaign of 1792... L: E. Marlow, 1794. 8vo, half calf; needs rebdg. With 3 folding engraved maps, with troop positions handcolored. sg Mar 7 (176) $80

**Mongez, Antoine, 1747-1835**
— Tableaux, Statues, Bas-Reliefs et Camees, de la Galerie de Florence et du Palais Pitti. Paris, 1804. 4 vols. Folio, half mor; rubbed. K June 23 (385) £750

**Monicart, Jean Baptiste de, 1656-1722**
— Versailles immortalise. Paris, 1720. 2 vols. 4to, contemp calf; spine ends repaired, spines regilded, endpaper renewed. With 2 frontises, 1 folding map & 94 plates. Marginal tear to Vol I frontis; lower corner of Plate 53 in Vol I torn away. Fuerstenberg - Schaefer copy. S Dec 7 (434) £320

**Moniglia, Giovanni Andrea**
— Il Mondo festeggiante balletto a cavallo.... Florence, 1661. Illus by Stefano della Bella. 4to, contemp vellum gilt; lower cover def. With 3 folding plates. C June 26 (55) £2,700

**Monipennie, John**
— The Abridgement or Summarie of the Scots Chronicles.... Edin., 1650. 8vo, later lea; scuffed, extremities worn. Small hole in tp near imprint; marginal chips & tears; a few ink notes in margins. pba June 20 (249) $150

**Monk, Maria, 1817?-50**
— Awful Disclosures of Maria Monk. L, 1853. 8vo, orig cloth. sg Feb 8 (323) $100

## AMERICAN BOOK PRICES CURRENT

**Monkhouse, William Cosmo, 1840-1901**
— The Turner Gallery.... NY: Appleton, [c.1880]. 2 vols. Folio, half mor; extremities rubbed. sg June 13 (374) $550
— The Works of Sir Edwin Landseer.... L, [1879-80]. 1 vol in 2. Folio, half calf; edges rubbed. bba May 30 (12) £130 [Grey Heron Antiques]

**Monroe, James, 1758-1831**
— [Monroe Doctrine]. Wash., 1823. ("Message of the President...to Both Houses of Congress....") 8vo, contemp sheep; worn. In: A List of Reports to be Made to the House of Representatives...Dec 1, 1823. Clipped signature of President Monroe mtd to front free endpaper. sg Oct 26 (263) $850

**Monstrelet, Enguerrand de, 1390?-1453**
— Chroniques. Paris: Antoine Verard, [c.1503]. 2d Ed. 3 vols in 2. Folio, mor gilt extra fanfare bdg by Lortic. With 4 full-page miniatures in gouache & gold paint; 160 smaller column-width miniatures; 2 illuminated borders of floral & foliate ornament; many illuminated initials. Ptd chapter-headings that are obscured by miniatures copied in margins in bastarda script. Text & woodcut on x3 in Vol I in ink & painted facsimile; minor shaving & stains. Ptd on vellum. Kreisler - Kettaneh copy. C June 26 (27) £100,000

**Montagu, George, 1751-1815**
— Testacea Britannica; or, Natural History of British Shells. Romsey & L, 1803-8. 1st Ed. 3 vols, including Supplement bound in 1. 4to, old half calf; worn, joints broken, spine chipped. With engraved titles & 29 (of 30) plates. Lacking Plate 22 from Supplement. Sold w.a.f. O Mar 5 (167) $70

**Montaigne, Michel Eyquem de, 1533-92**
See also: Limited Editions Club
— Les Essais. L, 1724. 3 vols. 4to, contemp calf; worn & scuffed. b May 30 (342) £100

Anr Ed. Paris, 1725. 3 vols. 4to, half lea; some corners worn through, wormed. Met Sept 28 (115) $300

Anr Ed. Paris, 1934-36. One of 185. Illus by Louis Jou. 3 vols. 4to, orig wraps, unopened. S Nov 21 (319) £400
— The Essayes.... L, 1613. 2d Ed of Florio's trans. 8vo, contemp calf; rebacked in mor. Tp & last leaf creased & soiled in margin. CE May 22 (354) $750

Anr Ed. Bost., 1902-4. ("Essays.") One of 265. Trans by John Florio. 3 vols. Folio, half cloth, unopened. sg Oct 19 (148) $950

Anr Ed. Hillsborough, Calif.: Allen Press, 1948. One of 200. Trans by Francis Carmody; illus by Mallette Dean. pba Mar 7 (9) $190

**Montale, Eugenio**
— Poesie inedite. NY: Fondazione Schlesinger, 1986-93. One of 100. Vols I-VIII. 4to half vellum gilt. Ck May 31 (14) £480

### Montana
— Constitution of the State of Montana.... Helena, 1889. 8vo, orig wraps. pba Aug 8 (140) $50

### Montana de Monserrate, Bernardino
— Libro de la anothomia del hombre.... Valladolid: Sebastian Martinez, 1551. 1st Ed. Folio, later half mor; corners repaired, lower joint renewed. With 12 plates. Tp def; lacks D3 & R8; R7 patched in foremargin; some staining & browning. Sold w.a.f. CE Nov 8 (125) $1,200

### Montanus, Arnoldus, 1625?-83
— Atlas Japannensis.... L, 1670. 1st Ed in English. - Trans by John Ogilby. Folio, old calf; spine lacking, covers detached, worn. With engraved title, folding map & 24 double-page or folding plates. Some browing; 1 plate with long tear & old repairs with tape; some fold breaks; library stamp to tp. bbc June 24 (193) $5,000
— Gedenkwaerdige Gesantschappen der Oost-Indische Maetschappy in't Vereenigde Nederland.... Amst., 1669. Folio, early sheep gilt. With engraved title, folding map & 24 plates. sg Mar 7 (186) $4,600

### Montanus, Nicolaus
— Oratio ad Luccenses. [Rome: Johannes Bulle, c.1479]. 4to, later vellum wraps from 15th-cent Ms leaf. 35-36 lines; type 1:83G. Minor staining. 8 leaves. IGI 6708. C Apr 3 (152A) £700

### Monte, Guidobaldo del
— Planisphaeriorum universalium theorica. Pesaro: J. Concordia, 1579. Folio, contemp vellum. Some browning. Madsen copy. S Mar 14 (257) £2,800

### Monteclair, Michel Pignolet de
— Jephte. Tragedie...[full score]. Paris, 1709Paris: Boivin, [c.1737]. 3d Ed. Folio, contemp calf gilt; spine ends repaired, hinges reinforced; some browning. Engraved throughout. S Dec 1 (240) £620
— Nouvelle Methode pour apprendre la musique.... Paris, 1709. 4to, contemp calf; tears on covers. Engraved throughout. S Dec 1 (239) £500

### Monteiro, Aristides
— War Reminiscences by the Surgeon of Mosby's Comand. Richmond, 1890. 12mo, cloth; extremities worn. With port. NH July 21 (84) $275

### Monteith, William
— Kars and Erzeroum.... L, 1856. 8vo, cloth; needs rebdg. With folding map & tinted litho plate. sg Mar 7 (177) $80
— Narrative of the Conquest of Finland by the Russians in the Years 1808-9. L, 1854. 8vo, half mor. With folding map. Tears at gutter & intersecting folds; early repairs. sg Mar 7 (178) $200

### Montemayor, Jorge de, 1520?-61
— La premiere [seconde... troisieme...] partie de la Diane.... Paris, 1582. 3 parts in 2 vols. 12mo, contemp vellum; joints wormed. Some waterstaining. S Nov 30 (287) £700

### Montenay, Georgette de
— Emblematum Christianorum centuria versibus gallicis.... Zurich: C. Froschauer, 1584. 4to, 17th-cent vellum remboitage with lower cover attached along the joint, yapp edges; spotted. With hand-colored port & 100 emblems, 3 with hand-coloring. Lacking F4 blank; made-up copy, with c4, E & F quires supplied; c1 with closed tear; some soiling; tp hinges to flyleaf. This copy used as an album amicorum by an early owner. Schaefer copy. P Nov 1 (158) $3,500

### Montesquieu, Charles de Secondat, 1689-1755
— Considerations sur les causes de la grandeur des Romains et leur decadence.... Paris, 1748. 12mo, contemp red mor gilt with crowned monogram. Fuerstenberg - Schaefer copy. S Dec 7 (439) £420
— De l'esprit des loix. Geneva: Barillot, [but Paris: Prault, c.1748]. 2 vols. 4to, contemp calf. Minor foxing. bbc Feb 26 (375) $950

Anr copy. Contemp calf; rebacked. Fuerstenberg - Schaefer copy. S Dec 7 (436) £150
— Le Temple de Gnide. Paris, 1772. 8vo, mor gilt by Chambolle-Duru. With frontis & 9 plates before letters. Fuerstenberg - Schaefer copy. S Dec 7 (437) £1,050

### Montesquiou Fezensac, Jean de
— Ardance, ou la Vallee d'automne. Paris: E. Durand, 1946. Unique copy on japon for the author with extra suite of the plates in bistre with remarques, 3 preliminary drawings with notes & various additional suites all relating to the illust at p. 127, a color decomposition in 5 plates of the illust at p. 183, proof copies of 4 plates in color with remarques & 7 drawings by Gaston Hoffman. Illus by Gaston Hoffmann. 4to, mor extra in flame pattern by G. Crette, orig wraps bound in. Also bound in are a sketch by Umberto Brunelleschi & a crayon drawing by Edouard Chimot, both sgd. Laid in are A Ls s of Georges Crette & G. Gilbert. S Nov 21 (317) £3,100

Anr Ed. [Paris, 1946]. One of 2 on papier ancien du japon. Illus by Edouard Chimot. Folio, unsewn in orig wraps, the text, proofs, drawings & plates in 4 matching cloth-covered cases. With 151 proofs, some sgd, some with annotations & remarques & 73 drawings. S Nov 21 (318) £3,000

### Montesquiou Fezensac, Robert, Comte de
— Prieres de tous. Paris, 1902. Unique copy on japon for Pierre Meunier. 4to, mor extra by Charles Meunier, 1904, each cover with large inset panel of chiselled & painted calf with symbolic designs, orig wraps bound in. Bound in is a letter of praise from the author to Meunier, with related material. S Nov 21 (316) £8,000

### Montesquiou, Robert de
— Paul Helleu. Paris, 1913. 4to, half mor gilt, orig wraps bound in. With 100 plates. Some foxing. sg June 13 (182) $400

### Montessori, Maria
— Il Metodo della pedagogia scientifica applicato all' educazione infantile nell case dei bambini. Rome, 1909. 4to, disbound; Leaves at beginning chipped & with tears. bbc Dec 18 (416) $100

Anr copy. Modern half mor, orig wraps bound in. With folding plan & 15 plates. Some dampstaining. sg Oct 19 (149) $850

### Montfaucon, Bernard de, 1665-1741
— L'Antiquite expliquee et representee en figures. Paris, 1722-24. 2d Ed. 5 vols in 10 plus 5-vol Supplement. Folio, contemp calf; joints & spine ends worn. Sold w.a.f. CE May 22 (355) $2,200

### Montgomery, Charles F.
— American Furniture. The Federal Period. NY: Viking, [1966]. 4to, cloth, in dj. sg June 13 (159) $100

### Montgomery, James Eglinton
— The Cruise of Admiral D. G. Farragut. NY, 1869. 4to, orig cloth; spine chipped, hinges weak. F June 20 (280) $50

### Montgomery, Rutherford G. See: Derrydale Press

### Montgomery, Walter
— American Art and American Art Collections. Bost., [c.1889]. 2 vols. Folio, orig half mor; worn. sg Jan 11 (291) $70

### Montherlant, Henry de, 1896-1973
— La Redemption par les betes. Paris, 1959. Unique set in 2 vols, the 1st being 1 of 20 & the 2d being Montherlant's corrected proof with 20 orig designs in pencil by Bonnard. Illus by Pierre Bonnard. 4to, lev extra by Lucie Weill, orig wraps to 1st vol bound in. Inscr to Daniel Sickles by Montherlant, 30 Apr 1960. C June 26 (199) £27,000

### Montorgueil, Georges
— La Vie des boulevards Madeleine-Bastille. Paris, 1896. One of 700. Illus by Pierre Vidal. 4to, half mor, orig wraps bound in. sg June 13 (265) $250

### Montpetit, Andre Napoleon
— Les Poissons d'eau douce du Canada. Montreal, 1897. 8vo, later cloth. Frontis detached. pba July 11 (203) $60

### Montreme, —, Chevalier de
— Description abregee des principales regions de la terre. [Paris?, 1728]. 8vo, contemp calf gilt with arms of Anne Auguste de Montmorency, Prince de Robecq. Inscr to the Prince de Robecq. Fuerstenberg - Schaefer copy. S Dec 7 (441) £300

### Montule, Edouard de
— A Voyage to North America and the West Indies.... L, 1821. 8vo, modern half mor. With 6 plates (2 folding). S Oct 26 (494) £150 [Magnus]

### Moods...
— Moods and Movements in Art. NY, 1959. One of 1,000. Orig bds, in dj. Verve 27/28, with French text & accompanying booklet containing English trans. sg Sept 7 (254) $1,800

### Mooney, James E. See: Shipton & Mooney

### Moore, Adolphus Warburton
— The Alps in 1864. A Private Journal. L: [Pvtly ptd], 1867. 8vo, orig cloth; library shelf number on spine in gilt, new endpapers. With 10 maps. Stamps on tp & some map versos. bba Nov 1 (526) £950 [Hunter]

### Moore, Ann
— A Faithful Relation of Ann Moore of Tutbury, Staffordshire.... Birm., 1811. Bound with: An Account of the Extraordinary Abstinence of.... Uttoexter, 1810. A Statement of Facts Relative to.... L, 1813 4th Ed of Faithful Relation. 3 pamphlets in 1 vol. 8vo, later half calf; lower front joint split, spine & covers rubbed. Ck Mar 22 (202) £160

### Moore, Brian
— The Lonely Passion of Judith Hearne. L, [1955]. ("Judith Hearne.") In dj. pba Jan 25 (262) $250

### Moore, Charles
— The Mental Side of Golf. NY, 1929. 1st Ed. - Foreword by Gene Sarazen. Half cloth. Inscr & sgd to Rufus Steele. pba Apr 18 (128) $80

### Moore, Clement Clarke, 1779-1863
— The Night before Christmas. NY, 1837. ("A Visit from St. Nicolas.") 8vo, cloth; spine ends & corners worn. In: The New York Book of Poetry. wa Feb 29 (71) $240

— Night Before Christmas. NY, 1912. Illus by Jessie Wilcox Smith. Orig bds; bumped. Met Dec 5 (385) $425

Anr Ed. L, 1931. One of 550, sgd by artist. Illus by Arthur Rackham. Orig vellum. With 4 colored plates. S Nov 2 (113) £420 [Culpin]; sg Oct 19 (205) $1,200

### Moore, Francis
— Travels into the Inland Parts of Africa.... L, 1738. 1st Ed. 2 parts in 1 vol. 8vo, modern cloth. Map repaired on verso. sg Mar 7 (187) $275

### Moore, George, Barrister
— Grasville Abbey. L, 1797. 3 vols. 12mo, contemp half calf; spines frayed. B1 of Vol I torn at inner margin; Vol III with clean tear across F6; tear at outer margin of F11 touching text; piece torn from outer margin of F12; some spotting & soiling. Ck Sept 8 (207) £1,500

### Moore, George, 1852-1933
— A Modern Lover. L, 1883. 1st Ed. 3 vols. 8vo, orig cloth, Carter's B bdg; worn, upper hinges broken. S Apr 23 (117) £1,650

## Moore, George Henry
— Notes on the History of Slavery in Massachusetts. NY, 1866. 1st Ed. 8vo, orig cloth, unopened. Some foxing. sg Mar 28 (304) $350

## Moore, Henry Spencer
— Heads, Figures, and Ideas. L & Greenwich CT, 1958. Folio, orig half cloth, in rubbed dj. With color auto-litho loosely inserted. bba Oct 19 (66) £120 [Besley]

Anr copy. Half cloth, in dj. Inscr. wad Oct 18 (332) C$575

— Henry Moore: Catalogue of Graphic Work 1931-1979. Geneva, 1973-80. 3 vols. 4to, cloth, in djs. sg Jan 11 (293) $400

One of 100, with 3 orig sgd etchings. Cloth, in djs. wad Oct 18 (335) C$3,200

— Sketchbook 1926. L, 1976. One of 100. 2 vols. 4to, bds, with 2 sgd etchings loose in wraps. wad Oct 18 (334) C$950

## Moore, Jacob. See: Farmer & Moore

## Moore, John, 1729-1802
— A View of Society and Manners in Italy. L, 1781. 2 vols. 8vo, contemp calf; rubbed, joints split, Vol I has new endpapers. Some browning & spotting. bba May 30 (374) £70 [Tosi]

## Moore, John Hamilton
— The Practical Navigator. Newburyport: Edmund M. Blunt, 1800. ("The New Practical Navigator.") 8vo, contemp sheep. Some foxing; margins stained at end. cb Feb 14 (2540) $275

## Moore, Marianne, 1887-1972
— Collected Poems. NY, 1952. 3d Ed. Orig cloth, in dj with minor tears; frayed. Inscr to Ida Hodes. pba May 23 (255) $80

— Poems. L: Egoist Press, 1921. 1st Ed. Orig wraps; some chips, minor stains on free endpapers. CE Sept 27 (209) $200

## Moore, T. Sturge, 1870-1944. See: Eragny Press

## Moore, Thomas, 1779-1852
See also: Fore-Edge Paintings
— The Beauties of Moore, a Series of Portraits of his Principal Female Characters.... L, 1847. Illus by W. & E. Finden. Folio, contemp mor gilt; spine ends worn, extremities rubbed. With 25 plates. pba Aug 22 (765) $95

— Lalla Rookh. L, 1861. Illus by John Tenniel. 8vo, mor extra by Hayday; spine ends & extremities rubbed, front hinge weak. pba Aug 22 (861) $90

— Paradise and the Peri. L, [1860]. 4to, orig cloth; broken. pba Aug 8 (488) $360

— Poetical Works. L, 1840-41. 10 vols. 8vo, contemp half mor; scuffed, soiled. F June 20 (715) $120

Anr copy. Later mor extra. sg Feb 8 (24) $500

## Moore, Thomas, 1821-87
— The Ferns of Great Britain and Ireland. L, 1855. Folio, contemp half mor; worn. With 51 colored nature-ptd plates. Some spotting. S June 27 (55) £3,400

Anr Ed. L, 1859-60. ("The Nature-Printed British Ferns.") 2 vols. 8vo, contemp half mor; rubbed, 1 cover detached. With 122 colored nature-ptd plates. Some foxing. O Mar 5 (169) $250

## Moore, William V.
— Indian Wars of the United States. Phila., 1850. 8vo, modern cloth. Foxed. pba Aug 8 (141) $170

## Mora, Jo
— Californios: the Saga of the Hard-riding Vaqueros, America's First Cowboys. Garden City, 1949. 1st Ed. Orig cloth in dj. Larson copy. pba Sept 28 (175) $70

## Morais, Henry Samuel
— The Jews of Philadelphia. Phila., 1894. 8vo, orig cloth; worn. F June 20 (373) $170

## Morand, Paul, 1889-1977
— Noeuds coulants. Paris: Editions Lapina, 1928. One of 20 on japon. 8vo, loose in orig wraps, unopened. With frontis port by Marie Laurencin & 9 illusts by R. Grillon. Inscr to David Sickles. With 4-page autograph Ms, the orig watercolor drawings in 2 states, 5 prelim pencil drawings for the port, 3 states of the etched port & 2 suites of the wood-engraved illusts. S May 16 (24) £550

— Pascin. Paris, [1931]. One of 500. 4to, orig wraps. Some leaves loose. sg Jan 11 (333) $60

— Rues et visages de New-York. Paris, 1950. One of 10 on japon imperial, with orig drawing. Illus by Charles Laborde. Folio, unsewn in orig half vellum folder. S Nov 2 (15) £1,000 [Fluhmann]

## Morazzoni, Giuseppe
— Il Libro illustrato veneziano del settecento. Milan, 1943. 4to, bds. With 154 plates. bba Oct 5 (125) £220 [Maggs]

Anr copy. Contemp half vellum. bba May 9 (66) £140 [Brinded]

Anr copy. Orig bds, in dj. Ck Apr 12 (259) £220

## Morden, Robert
— Geography Rectified. L, 1680. 4to, contemp calf; def. With 62 miniature maps. Some text leaves stuck together; 3 maps with small losses. Sold w.a.f. b May 30 (130) £1,500

— Geography Rectified: or, a Description of the World. L, 1700. Contemp calf; worn, front hinge cracked. With 78 maps in text. Library markings; some soiling, browning & dampstaining; 1 map laid down; border of 2 maps trimmed. cb June 25 (1738) $1,300

## More, Sir Thomas, 1478-1535
See also: Ashendene Press; Limited Editions Club
— The Historie of the Pitifull Life and Unfortunate Death of Edward the Fifth.... L, 1641. 12mo, later calf;

worn & stained, front cover nearly detached. Frontises chipped at margins & 1st laid on backing leaf; some borders shaved. pba Nov 30 (243) $250

— Utopia. [Louvain]: Thierry Martin, [1516]. ("Libellus vere aureus nec minus salutaris quam festivus....") 4to, 19th-cent calf by Hering; rubbed. Inner blank margin of title abraded; some inkstains; underlined in ink throughout, with marginal annotations in a 17th-cent hand. Chatsworth - Hefner copy. CNY May 17 (33) $210,000
Anr copy. Bound with: Hugo de Sancto Victore. Allegoriarum in utrunque testamentum libri decem. Paris: Henri Estienne, 10 Oct 1517. And: Nicolaus Chappusius, De menta & memoria libellus. [Paris: Enguilbert, Jean & Geoffroy de Marnef, c.1510]. 16th-cent blind-stamped mor over bds; worn, wormed & restored, head of spine def. More with full-page woodcut view of Utopia. Worming turning into a trail through lower portion of text of Utopia; a few other wormholes affecting texts; some dampstaining throughout; fore-edge of Hugo tp trimmed away; lower corner of n5 of Chappusius torn away just touching text; More & Chappusius bound between prelims & text of the Hugo; quire a of More misgathered. Schaefer copy. P Nov 1 (159) $240,000
1st Ed of Gilbert Burnet's trans. L, 1684. 8vo, contemp calf; rebacked & recornered, worming to front cover. pba Sept 14 (277) $225

— The XII Propertees or Condicyons of a Lover. Ditchling: St. Dominic's Press, 1928. One of 250. Orig cloth. sg Sept 14 (326) $120

**Moreau de la Sarthe, Jacques Louis**
— Description des principales monstruosites dans l'homme.... Paris, 1808. Folio, contemp half calf gilt; library markings on front cover. With 42 colored plates. Last 2 plates browned; library markings on endleaves. P Dec 12 (125) $5,500

**Moreau de Saint-Mery, Mederic Louis Elie, 1750-1819**
— De la danse. Parma: Bodoni, 1803. 16mo, orig bds; rubbed with paper loss. Some foxing; library markings. sg Mar 28 (120) $225

**Moreau, Francois Joseph**
— A Practical Treatise on Midwifery. Phila., 1844. 4to, modern cloth with orig cloth laid down; hinges reinforced. With 80 uncolored plates. Marginal dampstaining; foxed, affecting plates; stamps to some plates. sg May 16 (457) $140

**Moreau, Jean Michel, 1741-1814**
— Suite d'estampes, pour servir a l'histoire des moeurs et du costume des francois dans le dix-huitieme siecle * Deuxieme Suite.... * Troisieme Suite.... Paris, 1774-77-84. 3 parts in 1 vol. Folio, contemp red mor gilt. With 36 plates. Without title & 2 leaves of text for Part 2 & title for Part 3. Fuerstenberg - Schaefer copy. S Dec 7 (238) £8,500

**Moreau-Gobard, Jean Claude.** See: Lion-Goldschmidt & Moreau-Gobard

**Moreau-Nelaton, Etienne**
— Les Clouet et leurs Emules. Paris, 1924. One of 300. 3 vols. 4to, cloth, orig wraps bound in. sg Jan 11 (298) $275

**Morejon, Pedro de, 1562-1634**
— A Briefe Relation of the Persecution lately made against the Catholike Christians, in the Kingdome of Iaponia.... St. Omer: English College Press, 1619. 8vo, 18th-cent calf; rebacked, new endpapers. Some soling & repairs to tp; P3-6 torn with loss; upper margin cut close, affecting some headings. CE June 12 (219) $7,000

**Morelli Fernandez, Maria Maddalena**
— Atti della solenne coronazione fatta in Campidoglio...della insigne poetessa.... Parma: Bodoni, 1779. 8vo, contemp sheep. bba May 9 (8) £400 [O'Keefe]

**Moreri, Louis, 1643-80**
— The Great Historical, Geographical and Poetical Dictionary. L, 1694. In 2 vols. Folio, contemp calf; spine ends worn, joints cracked, front endpaper loose. cb Feb 14 (2637) $325

**Mores, Edward Rowe, 1730-78**
See also: Grolier Club
— A Dissertation upon English Typographical Founders and Foundries. [N.p.], 1778-79. One of 100. 8vo, contemp half calf; worn & def, ink notations on front pastedown. Some foxing; tp chipped. Met May 22 (391) $2,700

**Morgagni, Giovanni Battista, 1682-1771**
— De sedibus, et causis morborum.... Venice, 1761. 1st Ed. 2 vols in 1. Folio, contemp calf; rebacked, worn. Lacking half-titles & frontis port; title laid down with repair & closed tear; P4 in vol II torn; part of 3G4 in Vol II torn away; last leaves of Vol II dampstained; beginning & end soiled; some spotting & ink stains. Ck Mar 22 (203) £800

**Morgan, Dale Lowell**
See also: Hammond & Morgan
— Jedediah Smith and the Opening of the West. Indianapolis: Bobbs-Merrill, [1953]. Inscr, 17 Oct 1953. pba Feb 13 (172) $110
1st Ed. In dj; upper edge of d/j worn, spine faded. Robbins copy. pba Mar 21 (241) $100
— Overland in 1846: The California-Oregon Trail. Georgetown CA, 1963. One of 1,000. Ed by Morgan. 2 vols. Half cloth; lower corner bumped. With facsimile map (4 parts on 2 sheets) loose in rear pocket of Vol I; folding map in Vol II. pba Nov 16 (180) $120
Anr Ed. Georgetown, Calif., 1963. One of 100. 2 vols, half mor. With 2 folded maps. Larson copy. pba Sept 28 (628) $325
— The West of William H. Ashley. Denver, 1964. 1st Trade Ed. Ed by Morgan. pba Nov 16 (14) $100
One of 250. Half calf. pba Nov 16 (13) $325; pba Feb 13 (3) $425

1st Ed. - Illus by Bodmer, Catlin, & others. Half calf; spine rubbed & faded. Robbins copy. pba Mar 21 (4) $400

**Morgan, Dale Lowell —&
Wheat, Carl I.**
— Jedediah Smith and His Maps of the American West. San Francisco, 1954. One of 530. With 7 folding maps, 3 in pocket. pba Feb 13 (139) $550
1st Ed. Orig cloth. With 7 maps (6 folding, 3 inserted loose). Robbins copy. pba Mar 21 (240) $500

**Morgan, George**
— The New Complete Sportsman; or, the Town and Country Gentleman's Recreation. L: Hogg, [c.1785]. 12mo, later half mor; rubbed. Some soiling & foxing; piece torn from margin of ad leaf & restored with minor loss. O Feb 6 (166) $400

**Morgan, John Pierpont, 1837-1913**
— Drawings by the Old Masters formed by C. Fairfax Murray. L, [1904]-1910-1912. 4 vols. 4to, contemp half mor by Leighton; slightly rubbed. With 814 collotype plates. S Oct 27 (965) £2,100 [Antiquaria]
— Porcelaines francaises. Paris, 1910. One of 150. 4to, contemp calf by Pagnant. With additional title & 50 color plates. S Oct 27 (1000) £420 [Schmidt & Grunth]

**Morgan Collection, John Pierpont**
— Collection of Watches.... L: Pvtly ptd at the Chiswick Press, 1912. One of 45 on handmade paper. Compiled by G. C. Williamson. 4to, half mor; joints rubbed. With 92 photogravure plates on chine appliqué. Frontis foxed. P Dec 12 (189) $2,500
— The Gutmann Collection of Plate now the property of J. Pierpont Morgan, Esquire. L, 1907. 4to, orig cloth. W Nov 8 (201) $300
— Porcelaines francaises. Paris, 1910. One of 150. Ed by the Comte X. de Chavagnac. Folio, calf gilt by Pagnant. sg June 13 (97) $650

**Morgan, Joseph, Miscellaneous Writer**
— A Complete History of Algiers.... L, 1731. 4to, contemp sheep; needs rebdg. Some dampstaining & browning; foxing to top edge of tp. sg Mar 7 (188) $400

**Morgan, Lewis Henry, 1818-81**
— Houses and House-Life of the American Aborigines. Wash., 1881. 1st Ed. 8vo, orig cloth; spine ends frayed, front cover stained. With color frontis. Robbins copy. pba Mar 21 (242) $120
— League of the Ho-De-No-Sau-Nee, or Iroquois. Rochester, 1851. 8vo, orig lea; spine ends worn & chipped. Repairs to folding map. NH July 21 (192) $180

**Morgan, Lady Sydney Owenson**
— The O'Briens and the O'Flahertys. L, 1827. 4 vols. 12mo, orig bds; spines chipped, lacking free endpapers. bba Oct 19 (234) £95 [Scott]
— O'Donnel. A National Tale. L, 1814. 1st Ed. 3 vols. 8vo, contemp half calf; spines rubbed & chipped. G9 of Vol I with hole touching letters; G10 of Vol III

with tear into text; no half-title in Vol I. Ck Sept 8 (208) £320

**Morgand et Fatout**
— Bulletin de la Librairie Morgand et Fatout. Paris, 1876-1904. 12 vols, including Repertoire General for 1882 & 1893. 8vo, contemp half mor, orig wraps bound in; a few covers detached, rubbed. O Mar 26 (177) $600

**Morier, Sir James Justinian, 1780?-1849**
— A Journey through Persia, Armenia, and Asia Minor.... L, 1812. 4to, contemp calf; rebacked. With 3 folding maps & 26 plates. Lacking half-title; some spotting. b May 30 (287) £600
Anr copy. 1st Journey only. 4to, contemp half calf; worn & scuffed. With 3 maps & 26 plates. Library markings; maps slightly misfolded & 1 with later paper repair on reverse. bbc June 24 (194) $350
1st Ed. 4to, contemp russia; repaired. With 3 maps & 26 plates. Q1-2 torn; some spotting. S Oct 26 (174) £200 [Finopoulos]

**Morison, Douglas, 1814-47**
— Views of the Ducal Palaces and Hunting Seats of Saxe Coburg and Gotha. L, 1846. Folio, loose as issued in half mor portfolio. With engraved title & 20 plates, all colored by hand & mtd. Some spotting. S June 27 (121) £4,000

**Morison, Samuel Eliot, 1887-1976**
See also: Limited Editions Club
— Admiral of the Ocean Sea: a Life of Christopher Columbus. Bost., 1942. 2 vols. In djs; front free endpapers with owner's stamps. pba Feb 13 (44) $160
— The European Discovery of America. NY, 1971-74-57. 2 vols. In djs. pba Feb 13 (140) $60

**Morison, Stanley**
See also: Grolier Club
— The Calligraphic Models of Ludovico degli Arrighi.... Paris, 1926. One of 300. bba May 9 (606) £300 [Cox]; Ck May 31 (1) £360; sg Oct 19 (184) £700
— The English Newspaper. Cambr., 1932. 1st Ed. Folio, orig cloth; front hinge cracked, endpapers foxed. bbc Dec 18 (134) $210

**Morison, Stanley —&
Carter, Harry**
— John Fell.... Oxford, 1967. One of 1,000. Folio, cloth, in stained dj. bba May 9 (37) £130 [Collinge & Clark]

**Morisot, Claude Barthelemy**
— Orbis maritimi sive rerum in mari et littoribus gestarum generalis historia. Dijon, 1643. Folio, contemp calf; def, covers detached. Some staining; lacking tp. Sold w.a.f. S June 13 (570) £520

**Morley, Christopher, 1890-1957**
— Kathleen. NY, 1920. Half cloth. Inscr. sg June 20 (279) $90
— Mince Pie. NY, [1919]. In repaired dj. Inscr to Percy A. Beach. sg June 20 (280) $100

## MORLEY

— Parnassus on Wheels. Garden City, 1917. 1st Ed, 1st State. Bds. Inscr. sg June 20 (281) $225
— Passport -- Hoboken Free State. Hoboken, [1929]. One of 200. 4to, orig cloth. sg June 20 (282) $130
— The Romany Stain. NY, 1926. 1st Ed. In dj. Inscr with pen drawing of a small bird. sg June 20 (285) $70
— Tales from a Rolltop Desk. NY, 1922. In dj. Inscr. sg June 20 (286) $120
— Travels in Philadelphia. Phila.: David McKay, [1920]. 1st Ed. - With intro by A. Edward Newton. In dj. Inscr. sg June 20 (288) $275
— Where the Blue Begins. L & NY, [1925]. One of 100, sgd by author & artist. Illus by Arthur Rackham. Orig half cloth; rubbed & stained. Ck May 31 (158) £220
One of 175. Orig half cloth; endpapers browned. S Nov 2 (115) £260 [Sotheran]

### Morley, Christopher, 1890-1957 —& Others
— Born in a Beer Garden. NY: Foundry Press, 1930. One of 1,000. 4to, half mor; joints tender. sg June 20 (278) $100

### Morley, Christopher, 1890-1957 —& Haley, Bart
— In the Sweet Dry and Dry. NY, 1919. Illus by Gluyas Williams. In repaired dj. Inscr by Morley & sgd by Haley & Williams. sg June 20 (289) $225

### Morley, John, Viscount, 1838-1923
— English Men of Letters. L, 1902. One of 1,000. 12mo, half mor. wa June 20 (35) $270

### Morley, Thomas, 1557-1604?
— A Plaine and Easie Introduction to Practicall Musicke. L: Humfrey Lownes, 1608. 2d Ed. Folio, later half calf. Tp laid down with some loss to outer corners; some margins shaved, affecting sidenotes; worming affecting text on O4-Q2; some stains & holes; early annotations. S May 15 (419) £2,100

### Mornay, ——
— A Picture of St. Petersburgh, represented in a Collection of Twenty Interesting Views of the City.... L, [1815]. Folio, half calf; hinges weak, spine worn. With 20 plates. Foxed. wd May 8 (74) $4,000

**Morogues, Sebastien Francois Bigot de.** See: Bicot de Morogues, Sebastien Francois

### Moroni, Gaetano, 1802-83
— Dizionario de erudizione storico-ecclesiastica. Venice, 1840-61-79. 103 vols plus 6 index vols. 8vo, orig ptd wraps; some broken. bba Oct 5 (127) £1,300 [Maggs]

### Morrell, Benjamin, 1795-1839
— A Narrative of Four Voyages.... NY, 1832. 1st Ed. 8vo, orig cloth; spine worn, front joint cracked. Browned; stamp on half-title; frontis foxed, with pencil scrawls over image. sg Mar 7 (189) $200

### Morrell, David
— First Blood. NY: Evans, [1972]. In dj. pba Aug 22 (370) $50

### Morris, Beverley Robinson
— British Game Birds and Wildfowl. L, 1855. 4to, orig half mor; extremities scuffed. With 60 hand-colored plates. Some spotting. Fattorini copy. C Oct 25 (32) £1,400
Anr copy. Orig cloth; rubbed. Some foxing. cb Feb 14 (2616) $1,600
Anr copy. Orig cloth; rebacked in mor gilt. With 60 hand-colored plates. S Mar 29 (735) £1,400
Anr copy. Contemp half mor; upper joint cracked. With 60 hand-colored plates. Some spotting. S Apr 23 (330) £1,150
Anr copy. Loose in contemp half mor. Marginal waterstaining to 2 plates. W Nov 8 (416) £1,300

### Morris, Francis Orpen, 1810-93
— A History of British Birds. L, 1851-57. 1st Ed. 6 vols. 8vo, contemp calf gilt. With 358 hand-colored plates. Sold with: Beautiful British Birds Favorite Picture Portfolio. L, [c.1853]. Containing 8 unbound hand-colored plates ptd from the blocks used for Morris's Birds. Fattorini copy. C Oct 25 (33) £750
Anr Ed. L, 1860-65. 6 vols. 8vo, contemp half calf; rubbed. With 358 colored plates. S June 13 (450) £460
Mixed Ed. L, 1860-57. 6 vols. 8vo, orig cloth; shelf numbers erased from spine. With 358 colored plates. Library markings on plates. bba Sept 7 (150) £320 [Frew]
Anr Ed. L, 1866. 6 vols. 8vo, orig cloth; extremities worn. With 358 colored plates. Some foxing. sg May 9 (288) $750
Anr Ed. L, [1888]. 8 vols. 8vo, contemp half calf gilt; rubbed. With 361 hand-colored plates. b Jan 31 (300) £340
Anr copy. Orig cloth. b Jan 31 (301) £300
Anr copy. Vols I-IV only. Orig cloth. With 160 color plates, including titles. Dampstain in blank outer margins towards end of Vol III. sg Dec 7 (282) $275
4th Ed. L, 1895. 6 vols. 8vo, orig cloth; few vols with cracked hinges. With 394 hand-colored plates. S Oct 27 (754) £500 [Hearn]
"4th" Ed. L, 1895-97. 6 vols. 8vo, lea; bumped. With 393 hand-colored plates. Some foxing. Met May 22 (442A) $475
Anr copy. Contemp mor gilt; worn, Vol V with 1st signature sprung. With 394 hand-colored plates.. wa Nov 16 (139) $650
5th Ed. L, 1903. 6 vols. 8vo, orig cloth. With 400 hand-colored plates. S Oct 27 (753) £500 [Hearn]
"5th" Ed. 6 vols. With 400 hand-colored plates. S Mar 29 (736) £600
— History of...Butterflies. L, 1864. ("A History of British Butterflies.") 4to, orig cloth. With 71 color & 2 uncolored plates. Some foxing. cb Feb 14 (2617) $400

4th Ed. L, 1872. 4to, orig cloth; extremities rubbed. With 72 colored plates. b Sept 20 (484) £80
6th Ed. L, 1891. 8vo, orig cloth. With 72 colored plates. sg May 9 (359) $90
8th Ed. L, 1895. 8vo, orig cloth; worn. With 79 colored plates. F June 20 (569) $140
Anr copy. 4to, contemp half mor gilt, orig wraps bound in. With 79 hand-colored plates. S Apr 23 (332) £180
— A Natural History of British Moths. L, 1872. 4 vols. 8vo, orig cloth. b May 30 (569) £120
— A Natural History of the Nests and Eggs of British Birds. Groombridge, 1865. 3 vols. 8vo, orig cloth. With 225 plates. b Sept 20 (485) £90
— A Series of Picturesque Views of Seats of the Noblemen and Gentlemen of Great Britain and Ireland. L, [c.1880]. Vols I-IV (of 6). Orig cloth. b Sept 20 (314) £160
Anr copy. Vols I-V only. With 199 colored plates. b Jan 31 (342) £150
Anr copy. 6 vols. 4to, orig cloth; rubbed, lower corner of 1 bd worn. bba June 6 (63) £240 [Oliver]
Anr copy. 5 vols (of 7). 4to, orig cloth; spine ends worn. With 240 color plates. Light foxing. CE Nov 8 (230) $150
Anr Ed. L: Mackenzie, [c.1880]. 6 vols. 4to, mor gilt; spines dryed & corroded. O May 7 (225) $275
Anr Ed. L, [c.1880]. 6 vols. 4to, contemp mor; joints weak. With pictorial titles & 234 chromolitho plates. S Mar 28 (58) £240

**Morris, Henry**
See also: Taylor & Morris
— Japonica: The Study and Appreciation of...Japanese Paper. North Hills, Pa.: Bird & Bull Press, 1981. One of 250. Half mor. With 44 paper specimens. sg Sept 14 (65) $275
— Omnibus: Instructions for Amateur Papermakers. [North Hills, PA], 1967. One of 500. Half lev. sg Sept 14 (66) $120
— The Paper Maker: A Survey of Lesser-Known Hand Paper Mills.... [North Hills, PA], 1974. One of 175. Half lev. sg Sept 14 (67) $600
— Roller-Printed Paste Papers for Bookbinding. North Hills, Pa.: Bird & Bull Press, 1975. Half vellum. With 25 mtd paper samples. sg Sept 14 (68) $200

**Morris's copy, Lewis**
ALEYN, JOHN. - Select Cases Reported. L, 1688. Folio, contemp calf; dried & worn, front cover detached, lacking front endpapers. Tp laid down; some browning & soiling. With Morris's bookplate. CE Sept 27 (20) $280

**Morris, William, 1834-96**
See also: Kelmscott Press
— A Book of Verse. L: Scolar Press, 1980. 4to, orig cloth. Facsimile of 1870 Ms. bba May 9 (243) £65 [Stevenson]
[-] A Brief Sketch of the Morris Movement and of the Firm founded by William Morris to carry out his Designs and the Industries revived or started by him.... L: pvtly ptd for Morris & Company, 1911. 16mo,

wraps; fragile, fore-edge of front cover chipped. sg Sept 14 (262) $100
— The Defence of Guenevere.... L, 1904. Illus by Jessie M. King. 12mo, vellum with painted cartouche, by Chivers of Bath. sg Oct 19 (151) $425
— A Tale of the House of the Wolfings.... L, 1889. Ltd Ed. 8vo, contemp half vellum. bba May 9 (465) £50 [Deighton Bell]
— Works. L, 1910-15. One of 1,050. 24 vols. Half mor by Zaehnsdorf. cb Oct 17 (287) $1,800

**Morris, Wright**
— The Inhabitants. NY, 1946. 4to, cloth, in dj with spine ends chipped. pba Jan 25 (266) $50

**Morrison, James, 1763-1807.** See: Golden Cockerel Press

**Morrison, John.** See: Fore-Edge Paintings

**Morrison, Toni**
— Jazz. NY, 1992. In dj. Inscr. pba Jan 25 (267) $120
— Sula. L, [1974]. 1st English Ed. In dj. pba Jan 25 (268) $170

**Morrow, Prince Albert**
— Atlas of Skin and Venereal Diseases. NY, 1889. 2 vols. Folio, text in orig half lea (rebacked, free endpapers renewed), plates loose in folding case. With 75 chromolitho plates & 1 photogravure plate. Tp stamped. sg May 16 (458) $275

**Morse, Edward S., 1838-1925**
See also: Hobson & Morse
— Japanese Homes and their Surroundings. L, 1886. 8vo, orig cloth; spine head torn, hinges starting. pba June 20 (250) $250

**Morse, Jedidiah, 1761-1826**
— The American Gazetteer.... Bost., 1797. 1st Ed. 8vo, contemp calf; rubbed. With 7 maps. Some fold spits or repairs. O Nov 14 (124) $275
Anr copy. Contemp sheep; worn. With 7 folding maps. Browned; tears to maps. sg Oct 26 (269) $175
— The American Geography. L, 1792. 2d Ed. 8vo, later half calf. Lacking prelims except for tp & 1 leaf of contents. sg Oct 26 (270) $120
Anr copy. Later cloth. Z Jan 30 (417) $175
3d Ed. Bost., 1796. ("The American Universal Geography.....") Part 1 only. Contemp sheep gilt; rubbed. With 17 folding maps. Some browning. S Mar 28 (313) £480

**Morse, Jedidiah, 1761-1826 —&**
**Morse, Richard C.**
— The Traveller's Guide: or, Pocket Gazetteer of the United States. New Haven, 1823. 12mo, contemp calf; some wear. With folding hand-colored map with repaired tears. pba July 25 (423) $200

**Morse, Peter**
— John Sloan's Prints: a Catalogue Raisonne.... New Haven, 1969. Folio, cloth, in dj. O May 7 (226) $125

763

Anr copy. Cloth. Bdg & contents dampstained in upper inner corner. sg Sept 7 (313) $150

Anr copy. Cloth, in dj. sg Jan 11 (401) $110

One of 150 with inserted proof of unpbd Sloan etching. Cloth. pba June 20 (305) $275; sg Jan 11 (400) $400

**Morse, Richard C.** See: Morse & Morse

**Mortensen, William**

— Monsters and Madonnas: A Book of Methods. San Francisco, [1943]. 4to, spiral-bound; some wear. sg Feb 29 (214) $225

**Morticellarium Aureum**

— Quadragesimale et adventuale de arte moriendi, quod Morticellarium aureum nuncupatur. Antwerp: Gerard Leeu, 20 Feb 1488. 4to, contemp blindstamped calf over wooden bds, with remains of brass clasps, vellum pastedowns of notarial waste; rebacked, but upper cover off. 35 lines & headline; types 4:100G (title, headlines) & 5:82G (text); rubricated. With tp woodcut. Pieces cut from upper & lower margins of tp; margin of last leaf def & poorly supplied; marginal stains at beginning. 222 leaves. Goff M-864. Schaefer copy. P Nov 1 (161) $5,500

**Mortier, Pieter**

— Atlas Royal a l'usage de Monseigneur le Duc de Bourgogne. Paris: N. de Fer, 1695 [but Amst., 1695?]. Folio, bdg not given. With engraved title & 60 (of 64) double-page maps with hand-coloring in outline (44 listed in ptd index, remainder added to index in Ms). Lacking maps 35, 60, 62 & 63; frontis cut round & remargined; some fold aprasions & repaired tears; 4 maps cropped; all maps reguarded. S June 27 (74) £7,500

**Mortimer, John, 1656?-1736**

— The Whole Art of Husbandry. L, 1707. 1st Ed. 8vo, contemp calf; worn. b Sept 20 (149) £140

**Mortimer, Ruth**

— French 16th Century Books. Cambr. MA, 1964. 2 vols. 4to, cloth. bba Oct 5 (128) £180 [Sowell]

Anr copy. Orig cloth. sg Apr 11 (234) $250

— Italian 16th Century Books. Cambr. MA, 1974. 2 vols. 4to, cloth. bba Oct 5 (129) £240 [Sowell]; bba July 18 (17) £200 [Laywood]

Anr copy. Orig cloth; spines faded. sg Apr 11 (235) $375

— Italian Sixteenth Century Books. Cambr. MA, 1974. 2 vols. 4to. bba May 9 (67) £160 [Brinded]

**Mortimer, Thomas**

— Elements of Commerce, Politics and Finances. L, 1774. 4to, contemp sheep; worn, covers detached. Some browning. sg Mar 21 (109) $110

**Morton, Samuel George, 1799-1851**

— Illustrations of Pulmonary Consumption.... Phila., 1834. 1st Ed. 8vo, contemp sheep; spine & extremities rubbed. With 12 plates, all but the last hand-colored. Lacking pages 177-83. sg May 16 (459) $60

**Morton, William Thomas Green, 1819-68**

[-] [Letters Patent granted to William T. G. Morton for the discovery of the surgical application of ether as an anesthetic] Wash, 12 Nov 1846. Single sheet, 392mm by 209mm, fold breaks. sg May 16 (362) $3,600

**Moryson, Fynes, 1566-1630**

See also: Onassis copy, Jacqueline Bouvier Kennedy

— An Itinerary.... L, 1617. 1st Ed. Folio, later calf; rebacked, rubbed. Lacking initial blank & all after Eeee6; 1st p of title cut round & mtd, 2d p with small holes, repaired & margin restored; Z4 torn; other tears & stains. bba May 30 (352) £360 [Corke]

Anr copy. Contemp calf; rebacked. Lacking 1st leaf & final blank. CE June 12 (230) $650

Anr Ed. Glasgow, 1907-8. One of 1,000. 4 vols. sg Mar 7 (191) $60

**Moscardo, Lodovico**

— Note overo Memorie del Museo di Lodovico Moscardo. Padua, 1656. 1st Ed. Folio, old vellum; soiled. Repair to margin of G2. Madsen copy. S Mar 14 (259) £4,400

**Moschetti, Alessandro**

— Principali Monumenti di Roma. Rome, [c.1846]. Oblong folio, contemp half calf. With engraved title & 53 plates. S June 13 (553) £420

— Raccolta delle principali vedute di Roma. Rome, 1843. Oblong folio, contemp half mor; stain on lower cover. With engraved title, plan & 37 plates. Some dampstaining & spotting. S June 13 (554) £220

**Moschus.** See: Bion & Moschus

**Moselly, Emile, Pseud.**

— La Charrue d'erable. [L: Eragny Press], 1912. One of 116. Illus by Esther & Lucien Pissarro after Camille Pissarro. 8vo, orig mor. b Dec 5 (18) £1,800

**Mosely, Martin Ephraim**

— The Dry-Fly Fisherman's Entomology. L, 1921. With 16 hand-colored plates of insects. O Feb 6 (167) $170

**Moses, Henry.** See: Englefield Collection, Sir Henry Charles

**Moses, Henry, 1782?-1870.** See: Fore-Edge Paintings

**Mosimann, Anton**

— Important collection of 24 working ledgers of Mosimann's menus du jour.... L, 1961-78. 25 vols. Folio, bds; some covers detached or lacking, worn. 1 vol lacks some pp.. S Oct 12 (54) £800

**Moskowitz, Ira**

— Graphics - A Catalogue Raisonne 1929-1975. Balt: Ferdinand Roten Galleries, [1975]. 4to, cloth. With color litho, numbered & sgd in pencil. wa Feb 1 (311) $85

**Mosley, Seth Lister**
— A History of British Birds. Huddersfield, 1884-87-92. 3 vols. 8vo, contemp half calf gilt. With 160 plates of birds & 116 plates of nests & eggs, all hand-colored. Fattorini copy. C Oct 25 (34) £2,000
"Superioir Ed". Huddersfield, 1884-87. 2 vols. 8vo, contemp half calf; rubbed. With 214 color plates. S Oct 27 (757) £750 [Gerrard]

**Most...** See: Reynard the Fox

**Mother...**
— Mother Goose. NY, [1944]. One of 500. Illus by Tasha Tudor. In frayed dj. O Sept 12 (185) $650

**Mother Goose**
— Mother Goose. Springfield: McLoughlin Bros., [c.1900]. Chromolitho bds. pba Aug 22 (814) $60
— Mother Goose Movies. NY, [1917]. Illus by Alice Beard. Pictorial bds; extremities rubbed. Pictures cut in half, matching the following pages by half. pba Aug 22 (812) $70

**Motherby, George, 1732-93**
— A New Medical Dictionary.... L, 1785. 2d Ed. Folio, contemp calf; front joint cracked. With 26 plates. sg May 16 (460) $175

**Motley, John Lothrop, 1814-77**
— Works. NY, [1902]. 14 vols. Half mor gilt; some wear. sg Feb 8 (85) $250

**Mott, Abigail, 1766-1851**
— Biographical Sketches and Interesting Anecdotes of Persons of Colour. NY, 1875. ("Narratives of Colored Americans.") 8vo, cloth; spine extremities worn. sg Mar 28 (209) $200

**Mott, Frank Luther**
— A History of American Magazines, 1741-1905. Cambr. MA, 1966-68. 5 vols. 4to, orig cloth; some front free endpapers gone. Library markings. F June 20 (3) $100

**Mott, Lucretia, 1798-1880**
— Discourse on Woman, delivered at the Assembly Buildings, December 17, 1849. Phila., 1869. 8vo, orig wraps; edges worn. Inscr. bbc June 24 (443) $300

**Motte, Benjamin**
— Oratio Dominica nimirum, plus centum linguis versionibus.... L, 1700. 4to, contemp calf; rubbed, rebacked. With half-title & title vignette. G1 torn & repaired; lacks final leaf. S Oct 27 (1075) £260 [Stanley]

**Motteley Library, Charles**
— [Sale Catalogue] Catalogue d'anciens livres et manuscripts.... Paris, 1841. 8vo, contemp cloth; worn & soiled, inner joints broken. Priced in margins throughout. With annotations & notes suggesting that "this might be the Silvestre house copy". O Mar 26 (180) $200
— [Sale Catalogue] Catalogue des livres de la bibliotheque.... Paris, 1824. 8vo, contemp bds; worn. Priced in margins throughout. O Mar 26 (179) $250

**Mottley, John, 1692-1750**
— Joe Miller's Jests: or, the Wits Vade-mecum. L, 1745. 8vo, 19th-cent vellum with metal catch & clasp. Last leaf soiled, creased & rehinged. sg Mar 21 (234) $600

**Moufet, Thomas.** See: Moffett, Thomas

**Mouhot, Henri**
— Travels in the Central Parts of Indo-China.... L, 1864. 1st English Ed. 2 vols. 8vo, orig cloth; shaken, hinges cracked. With folding map. Spotted. S Oct 26 (591) £320 [Remington]

**Mouillard, Louis Pierre**
— L'Empire de l'air. Paris, 1881. 8vo, later half cloth, orig front wrap bound in. Some foxing. sg May 16 (71) $375
— Le Vol sans battement. Paris, 1923. 8vo, contemp half cloth, orig front wrap bound in. With port & folding plate. sg May 16 (72) $130

**Moule, Herbert Frederick.** See: Darlow & Moule

**Moule, Horace Frederick.** See: Darlow & Moule

**Moule, Thomas**
— Bibliotheca heraldica Magnae Britanniae. L, 1822. 4to, old bds; rebacked in calf, new endpapers. Tear in blank margin of 1 leaf; minor foxing. L.p. copy. O Mar 26 (181) $140
— The English Counties Delineated.... L, 1837. 2 vols. 4to, contemp half calf; rubbed. With frontis, 1 engraved title & 61 maps, a few colored. bba Nov 1 (286) £800 [Burden]

Anr Ed. L, 1838. 2 vols. 4to, orig cloth; worn. With engraved title, frontis & 60 maps & plates. Lacking frontis in Vol II; general map of England & Wales stained & soiled; Northumberland frayed & soiled with loss; a few borders cropped. S June 13 (487) £600
— The English Counties in the Nineteenth Century. L, 1836. 4to, cloth. With frontises, 1 engraved title & 59 maps only. Sold w.a.f. b May 30 (113) £650
— Great Britain Illustrated. L, 1830. Illus by William Westall. 4to, contemp half mor; broken. With engraved title, 118 views on 59 plates, 26 early proofs before completion of sky & other parts. ALs of Westall to John Martin tipped in. Largest paper copy. Jeudwine copy. bba Nov 16 (346) £300 [Clarke]
— Winkles's Architectural and Picturesque Illustrations of the Cathedral Churches of England and Wales. L, 1851. 3 vols. 8vo, orig cloth; gutta percha of Vol III perished. With engraved titles & 181 (of 184) plates. b Jan 31 (354) £60

## Mountaine, William
— The Seaman's Vade-Mecum. L, 1783. 12mo, later half calf; needs rebdg. Library stamp on tp; without plates.   sg Mar 7 (225) $425

## Mountevans, Edward Evans, Baron, 1880-1957
— South with Scott. L, 1921. In dj. With port, folding diagram & 3 folding maps. Some leaves badly opened.  b May 30 (142) £250

## Mouradja d'Ohsson, Ignace de
— Allgemeine Schilderung des Othomanischen Reichs. Leipzig, 1788-1821. Vols I-II (of 3). 8vo, early 19th-cent bds. With 18 plates & 4 folding genealogical tables. Old stamps on titles.   sg Mar 7 (194) $225
— Tableau general de l'empire Othoman. Paris, 1787-1820. 1st Ed. 3 vols. Folio, contemp mor extra with monogram of Albrecht von Sachsen-Teschen by Georg Friedrich Krauss. With 237 illusts on 103 plates. Repair in outer margin of Vol II, 3P1r; marginal tear to 1 leaf; soiling in upper covern of plate facing p. 266 in Vol I.  Fuerstenberg - Schaefer copy.  S Dec 8 (466) £44,000

## Mourelle, Francisco Antonio
— Voyage of the Sonora in the Second Bucareli Expedition.... San Francisco, 1920. One of 230. 4to, half cloth. With port & 2 maps.  pba Feb 13 (141) $190
1st American Ed. - Trans by Daines Barrington. 4to, half cloth & bds in dj; d/j dusty. With 2 folding maps & frontis port.  Robbins copy.   pba Mar 21 (243) $275

## Mourey, Gabriel
— Albert Besnard. Paris, [1906]. 4to, half mor, orig wraps bound in. With etching by Besnard & 100 plates.  sg Sept 7 (42) $175
Anr Ed. Paris, 1906.  4to, half mor gilt, orig wraps bound in.  Some foxing, affecting plates.  sg June 13 (57) $140

## Mourlot, Fernand
See also: Buffet, Bernard; Chagall, Marc; Miro, Joan
— Art in Posters.... NY, 1959. ("The Complete Original Posters of Braque, Chagall, Dufy, Leger, Matisse, Miro, Picasso.") Folio, cloth, in dj.  pba Aug 22 (623) $95
— Lithographies de l'atelier Mourlot. L, 1965. One of 1,150. 4to, orig wraps.  sg Jan 11 (301) $275; sg Jan 11 (302) $350
— Prints from the Mourlot Press. [N.p., 1964]. 4to, orig wraps.  K Oct 1 (281) $300; sg Jan 11 (303) $275
— Souvenirs et portraits d'artistes. Paris, [1972].  One of 800 on velin d'Arches. Folio, loose in folding box. cb Feb 14 (2797) $1,000; sg Apr 18 (117) $1,000
Anr copy. Loose as issued. With 25 orig colored lithos.  sg May 23 (422) $1,000
— The Lithographs of Chagall. See: Chagall, Marc

## Mourt, George
— A Relation or Journll of the beginning and proceedings of the English Plantation setled at Plimoth in New England.... Bost., 1865. ("Mourt's Relation or Journal of the Plantation at Plymouth.") One of 4 on india. 4to, cloth.  sg Oct 26 (271) $60

## Mowry, Sylvester, 1830-71
— Arizona and Sonora: The Geography, History and Resources of the Silver Region of North America. NY, 1864. 3d Ed. 12mo, orig cloth; extremities rubbed, spine foot repaired. With frontis.  Robbins copy. pba Mar 21 (244) $275

## Moxon, James. See: Mandey & Moxon

## Moxon, Joseph, 1627-1700
— A Tutor to Astronomy and Geography. L, 1670. 4to, half syn. Frontis detached; tp & frontis soiled; marginal browning & wear.  CE May 22 (357) $300

## Mozart, Leopold, 1719-87
— Gruendliche Violinschule. Augsburg, 1769. 2d Ed. 4to, modern mor. With 3 (of 4) plates. Port & folding table at end supplied in facsimile; browned & stained; L1 misbound.  S Dec 1 (242) £400

## Mozart, Wolfgang Amadeus, 1756-91
— Adagio and Fuge in C minor, K.546. Vienna: Hoffmeister, [1788]. ("Fuga per 2 Violini, Viola, e Violoncello.") Complete parts. Folio. Engraved throughout. Some staining.  S Dec 1 (244) £3,200
— Concerto pour le Clavecin ou Piano Forte avec accompagnement de grand Orchestre [K.459]. Offenbach: Andre, [n.d.]. Size not indicated. Engraved throughout. Outer tp with dust-staining.  S May 15 (582) £1,800
— Il dissoluto punito osia Il Don Giovanni...[RISM M4502]. Leipzig: Breitkopf & Haertel, [1801]. 2 vols. Oblong 4to, early half calf; rebacked & recornered. Some foxing & staining in Vol II; a few small tears; pagination occasionally trimmed at end; a few early annotations..  S May 15 (430) £2,000
— Four Sonatas for the Harpsichord....[K.6-9]. L: for Leopold Mozart, [1765]. 4to, 19th-cent bds. Engraved throughout. Alterations in brown ink in a contemp hand; browning. Taphouse copy. S May 15 (421) £3,400
— Grande Sinfonie a plusieurs instruments... Oeuvre 34me [Linz Symphony, K.425]. Offenbach: Andre, [1793]. 1st Ed. Parts for Violin 1 & 2, violas, basso, oboes 1 & 2, bassoons 1 & 2, horns 1 & 2, clarinets 1 & 2, timpani. Folio. Engraved throughout. Lacking 1st leaf in the Violino 1 & some text near inner margin of last page.  S Dec 1 (247) £1,800
— Indomeneo, Re di Creta Seria in 3 atti.... Leipzig: bey Schmidt und Rau, [1797]. 4to, contemp half calf. With subscription list, engraved title & engraved music. Dust-marks to 1st & last pages.  S May 15 (423) £5,500
— Overtura a quatro mani per un clavicembalo del Opera La Clemenza di Tito... [Racolta di arie 159-62, 164-69 & 546]. Vienna: Artaria et Comp., 1795. 12 nos in 1 vol. Oblong 4to, contemp half calf; rebacked & restored. Engraved throughout. Also bound in are Mss of music by G. G. Ferrari & others. S May 15 (433) £1,600

— Rondeau pour le Forte-piano, ou Clavecin [K.511]. Vienna: Hoffmeister, [1787]. Oblong folio, modern bds. Engraved throughout. Lower corners thumbed. S May 15 (428) £3,600
— Six Sonates pour le clavecin... Oeuvre II [K. 376, 296, 377-80]. Vienna, [1781]. Oblong folio, parts sewn. C June 26 (272) £1,200
— Tre Quartetti per due Violini Viola e basso... Opera 18. [The King of Prussia Quartets, K.575, 589 & 590]. Vienna: Artaria, [1791]. 1st Ed. Folio, 19th-cent bds. With the memorial engraved port; engraved throughout. Some staining & browning. S Dec 1 (245) £15,500
— Trois Sonates pour le Clavecin ou Pianoforte Oeuvre. VI. [K330-332]. Vienna: Artaria, [1784]. Oblong folio, 19th-cent bds. Engraved throughout.. S May 15 (425) £5,200

**Mucha, Alphonse, 1860-1939**
— Figures decoratives. Paris: Librairie centrale des beaux arts, [n.d.]. Folio, loose as issued in orig cloth-backed pictorial portfolio; worn & lacking 2 ties, small label on lower corner of upper cover. With 40 color plates. S Nov 21 (326) £1,500

**Mudford, William, 1782-1848**
— An Historical Account of the Campaign in the Netherlands.... L, 1817. 4to, 19th-Cent half roan; rubbed. With hand-colored additional title, 2 folding maps, & 25 (of 26) plates. Plates bound in. 1 map torn, another soiled. S Oct 26 (325) £200 [Military]
Anr copy. Half mor gilt; hinges weak, rubbed. With frontis, engraved title, folding plate, folding plan of the Battle of Waterloo, folding map & 24 colored plates by George Cruikshank. Foxed; battle plan starting. wd May 8 (71) $450

**Mudie, Robert, 1777-1842**
— The Feathered Tribes of the British Islands. L, 1835. 2d Ed. 2 vols. 8vo, orig cloth; worn. With 18 hand-colored plates. F June 20 (566) $120

**Mueller, Johann Sebastian.** See: Miller, John

**Muenden, Christian**
— Danck Predigt welche am dritten Jubelfest wegen Erfindung der Loebl. Buchdrucker.... Frankfurt, 1741. 8vo, modern half lea. Some browning & soiling; library stamps. O Mar 26 (183) $150

**Muenster, Sebastian, 1489-1552**
— Canones super novum instrumentum luminarium. Basel: Andreas Cratander, 1534. 4to, half vellum bds. Madsen copy. S Mar 14 (261) £3,200
— Cosmographia. Basel: Officina Henricpetrina, 1572. ("Cosmographiae universalis libri VI.") Folio, 17th-cent calf gilt; worn. With port & 19 (of 25) double-page maps & 55 double-page woodcut town views & plans, including 3 folding panoramas. Tertia Rheni repaired; lacking prelims before a1; text censored by ink-scoring; lacking colophon leaf; GGG5 def & repaired with blank paper. S Mar 28 (182) £3,200
— La cosmographie universelle. Basel: [Heinrich Petri, 1555]. Folio, 1th-Cent calf; worn. With 900 hand-colored illus on 25 maps. Some tears, staining, soiling, & defs; some pp. loose. Sold w.a.f. S Oct 26 (440) £1,600 [Antique Bks]

**Muentz, Eugene**
— Leonardo da Vinci: Artist, Thinker, and Man of Science. L, 1898. 2 vols. contemp mor. Joints starting & slightly rubbed. CE Nov 8 (231) $500

**Muffett, Thomas.** See: Moffett, Thomas

**Mugridge, Donald H.** See: Onassis copy, Jacqueline Bouvier Kennedy

**Muhammad, Eiljah, 1897-1965**
— Message to the Black Man. Chicago: Mosque of Islam No. 2, [1965]. In chipped dj. sg Mar 28 (215) $150

**Muilman, Peter**
— A New and Complete History of Essex. Chelmsford, 1770-69-72. 1st Ed. 6 vols. 8vo, contemp calf; spines chipped, Vol VI with loss at head. With 52 plates, some folding, & 3 folding maps. Lacking engraved titles. S Apr 23 (363) £200

**Muir, John, 1838-1914**
See also: Adams, Ansel Easton; Stern, Alec
— Edward Henry Harriman. Garden City, 1911. 1st Ed. Orig cloth. Robbins copy. pba Mar 21 (245) $300
— Letters to a Friend: Written to Mrs. Ezra S. Carr, 1866-1879. Bost., 1915. 1st Ed. One of 300. Orig bds; spine ends rubbed, front joint bumped. Robbins copy. pba Mar 21 (246) $450
— The Mountains of California. NY, 1894. 1st Ed, 1st Issue. 8vo, cloth; rear cover marred, front hinge repaired. With 51 plates & 2 maps. Larson copy. pba Feb 12 (108) $650
New & Enlarged Ed. NY, 1911. Robbins copy. Sgd. pba Mar 21 (247) $550
Anr Ed. NY, [1942]. 2 vols. Orig cloth, in djs. With 51 plates & 2 maps. pba Feb 12 (110) $80
— My First Summer in the Sierra. Bost. & NY, 1911. Orig cloth; extremities worn, front hinge repaired. pba Feb 12 (111) $150
1st Ed. - Photos by Herbert W. Gleason. Half mor; rebound. Robbins copy. Sgd. pba Mar 21 (248) $600
— Our National Parks. Bost., 1909. Some pencil underlinings & marginal notations. pba Feb 12 (114) $50
Anr copy. In repaired dj. Larson copy. pba Feb 12 (120) $1,500
New & Enlarged Ed. Half mor; rebound. With 33 plates (1 double-page map). Robbins copy. Sgd. pba Mar 21 (249) $500
— Picturesque California and the Region West of the Rocky Mountains, from Alaska to Mexico. NY & San Francisco: J. Dewing, [1887-88]. Edition De Luxe, one of 750. 10 parts. Folio, orig wraps, each in pictorial silk cloth folder; folder spines perished, some wrap spines detached. pba Apr 25 (541) $1,000
India Proof Ed. 10 parts. Folio, orig wraps; soiled & loose. With 115 (of 120) plates. Additional illusts in

all vols, some on india proof paper, some on silk. Some foxing. Sold w.a.f.  cb Oct 17 (165) $650

Anr Ed. San Francisco & NY, [1888]. 2 vols. Folio, orig half mor; rebacked in calf. Lacking 5 plates. bbc June 24 (427) $350

Anr copy. Folio, orig cloth. With 60 plates. Larson copy.  pba Feb 12 (117) $500

Anr copy. 3 vols. Folio, orig mor gilt; extremities rubbed, Vol I with puncture in front cover & extending through 1st 25 leaves of text.  sg Oct 26 (272) $325

— Steep Trails. Bost.: Houghton Mifflin, 1918. One of 280. Half cloth; soiled, corners bumped.  pba Oct 5 (289) $60

1st Ed. Bost., 1918. One of 380. Ed by William F. Bade; photos by Herbert W. Gleason. Half cloth; spine label nicked, spine head bumped. With 17 plates. Robbins copy.  pba Mar 21 (250) $325

— The Story of My Boyhood and Youth. Bost., 1913. 1st Ed, 1st Issue.  pba Feb 12 (121) $75

— A Thousand-Mile Walk to the Gulf. Bost. & NY, 1916.  pba Feb 12 (123) $90

One of 550 L.p. copies. Half cloth.  pba Feb 12 (122) $190

1st Ed. - Ed by William F. Bade. Orig cloth; spine & cover rubbed. With frontis port. Robbins copy. pba Mar 21 (251) $200

— Travels in Alaska. Bost. & NY, 1915. Cloth; spine ends rubbed.  pba Feb 12 (124) $110

— Works. Bost., 1916-24. One of 750. 10 vols. 8vo, half lev gilt. Larson copy.  pba Feb 12 (126) $2,250

Anr copy. Mor; spines sunned. With 69 plates. Robbins copy.  pba Mar 21 (252) $4,250

— The Yosemite. NY, 1912. 1st Ed. Orig cloth; rubbed.  pba Feb 12 (127) $190

Anr copy. Orig cloth; spine head frayed.  pba Aug 8 (527) $70

**Muir, Percy H.** See: Carter & Muir

**Mukhopadhaya, S. C.**
— A Course in Hindoo Hypnotism and Oriental Occultism.... [N.p.]: Hindoo Occult Society, 1903. Orig ptd wraps.  pba Aug 8 (528) $80

**Mulford, Ami Frank**
— Fighting Indians in the 7th United States Cavalry.... Corning NY: Paul LIndsley Mulford, [c.1930]. Cloth, orig wraps bound in.  pba June 25 (178) $55

**Mullan, Capt. John, 1830-1909**
— Miners and Travellers' Guide to Oregon, Washington, Idaho.... NY, 1865. 1st Ed. 12mo, orig cloth. Map with tape-repaired tears.  pba Apr 25 (543) $900

— Report on the Construction of a Military Road from Fort Walla-Walla to Fort Benton. Wash., 1863. 8vo, syn. With 4 folding maps & 10 plates. 14 pp at rear bound upside down; tp stamped.  wa Dec 14 (95) $240

**Mullen, Stanley**
— Kinsmen of the Dragon. Chicago: Shasta Publishers, [1951]. In dj. Sgd.  pba May 4 (206) $110

**Muller, Frederik**
— Essai d'une Bibliographie Neerlando-Russe. Amst., 1859. 8vo, later half cloth; worn.  O Mar 26 (184) $70

**Muller, John**
See also: Revere's copy, Paul
— A Treatise containing the Elementary Part of Fortification.... L, 1756. 2d Ed. 8vo, contemp calf; rubbed. With 34 folding plates & plans. b Sept 20 (155) £100

— A Treatise Containing the Practical part of Fortification.... L, 1774. 8vo, old calf; becoming disbound, front hinge taped. With 26 folding plates & 8 tables (4 folding).  wa Feb 29 (200) $325

**Muller, Marcia —& Others**
— Criminal Intent 1. Arlington Heights: Dark Harvest, 1993. One of 250. In dj.  pba Dec 7 (141) $65

**Mulsant, Martial Etienne**
— Lettres a Julie sur l'ornithologie. Paris, [1868]. Illus by Edouard Travies. 8vo, orig half cloth; rubbed. With 16 hand-colored plates. Some text foxing.  S Oct 27 (758) £320 [St. Anns]

**Mumey, Nolie**
— The Black Ram of Dinwoody Creek. Denver: Range Press, 1951. One of 325. Half cloth; worn.  O Oct 10 (199) $90

— Bloody Trails along the Rio Grande.... Denver, 1958. Half cloth in dj. With frontis port & folding map. Robbins copy. Sgd.  pba Mar 21 (255) $50

— Calamity Jane, 1852-1903. Denver, 1950. 1st Ed, One of 200. Half cloth. With folding map. Robbins copy. Sgd.  pba Mar 21 (256) $225

— Colorado Territorial Scrip.... Boulder, 1966. One of 350, sgd.  pba Aug 8 (143) $65

— Creede: History of a Colorado Silver Mining Town. Denver, 1949. 1st Ed, One of 500. Orig cloth in dj; d/j soiled. With 3 maps (1 folding).. Robbins copy. pba Mar 21 (257) $80

— Edward Dunsha Steele, 1829-1865.... Boulder, 1960. One of 500. Half buckram. With frontis port, folding map, & 11 facsimiles. Robbins copy. Sgd.  pba Mar 21 (258) $50

— James Pierson Beckworth 1856-1866. Denver, 1957. 1st Ed, One of 500. With frontis port & folding map. Robbins copy. Sgd.  pba Mar 21 (259) $120

— John Williams Gunnison.... Denver, 1955. 1st Ed, One of 500. 4to, orig cloth; spine head rubbed. With color frontis port & folding map. Robbins copy. Sgd.  pba Mar 21 (260) $85

— Old Forts and Trading Posts of the West. Denver, 1956. 1st Ed, One of 500. Vol I only. With 37 plates & folding map. Robbins copy. Sgd.  pba Mar 21 (261) $70

— The Saga of "Auntie" Stone and her Cabin.... Boulder, Colo., 1964. Centenary Ed, one of 500, sgd. 4to, cloth, unopened.  pba Aug 22 (943) $650

— The Teton Mountains. Denver, 1947. One of 700. Half buckram. With fold-out plate. Robbins copy. Sgd. pba Mar 21 (262) $250

**Munby, Alan Noel Latimer —& Coral, Lenore**
— British Book Sale Catalogues, 1676-1800: a Union List. L, 1977. 4to, orig cloth. sg Apr 11 (23) $60

**Munckerus, Thomas, d.1652**
— Mythographi Latini. Amst., 1681. 2 vols in 1. 8vo, contemp vellum; backstrip partly detached. sg Mar 21 (235) $175

**Mundy, Francis Noel Clarke**
— Needwood Forest. Derby, 1811. Bound with: The Fall of Needwood. Derby, 1808. 4to, mor gilt. b Dec 5 (74) £100

**Mundy, Talbot**
— The Gunga Sahib. NY, 1934. In chipped & stained dj. pba May 4 (210) $60
— Hira Singh. Indianapolis: Bobbs-Merrill, [1918]. Cloth; bumped, front hinge weak. Inscr to Fletcher Ames & with photo laid on front pastedown. pba May 4 (211) $60
— Jimgrim and Allah's Peace. NY, 1936. Variant bdg of brown cloth with spine panel stained in black & gold lettering, in dj. pba May 4 (208) $50
— Om, the Secret of Arbor Valley. Indianapolis, [1924]. In dj with tears to extremities. pba May 4 (209) $50

**Munk, Joseph A.**
— Southwest Skecthes. NY, 1920. 1st Ed. Orig cloth; corners bumped. Robbins copy. pba Mar 21 (263) $65

**Munnings, Sir Alfred, 1878-1959**
See also: Onassis copy, Jacqueline Bouvier Kennedy
— Pictures of Horses and English Life. L, 1927. 4to, cloth; some wear. O Jan 9 (169) $550
Anr copy. Cloth; hinge cracked, some leaves loose. pba Nov 30 (246) $300
Anr Ed. L, 1939. 4to, orig cloth, in worn & soiled dj. With 20 colored plates. wa Nov 16 (223) $140

**Munoz, Juan Bautista**
— Historia de nuevo-mundo. Madrid, 1793. 1st Ed. Vol I (all pbd). Folio, contemp half calf; worn, covers detached. Lacking folding map; frontis & tp soiled. John Philip Kemble's copy. S Apr 23 (364) £110

**Munroe, Kirk**
— The Golden Days of '49. NY, 1889. Orig cloth. pba Nov 16 (183) $120

**Munthe, Axel**
— The Story of San Michele. NY, 1929. Sgd by George Gershwin on front free endpaper. Richard Simon's copy. CE Feb 21 (209) $280

**Murchison, Sir Roderick Impey, 1792-1871**
— The Silurian System. L, 1839. 1st Ed. 2 vols. 4to, text in contemp russia; upper cover nearly detached. With colored 3-sheet geological map in separate cloth case. S June 13 (415) £1,400

**Murchison, Sir Roderick Impey, 1792-1871 —& Others**
— The Geology of Russia in Europe and the Ural Mountains. L & Paris, 1845. 2 vols plus slipcase of folding maps. 4to, orig cloth, unopened; covers affected by damp. With 64 plates, 4 folding hand-colored maps of geological sections, 2 folding hand-colored geological maps & engraved dedication. Some spotting. C May 31 (101) £1,250

**Murdoch, Iris**
— A Year of Birds.... Compton Press, 1978. One of 50 with an extra set of proofs. Illus by Reynolds Stone. bba May 9 (429) £260 [Marks]

**Murdoch, Joseph S. F.**
See also: Johnston & Murdoch
— The Library of Golf 1743-1966. A Bibliography of Golf Books. Detroit, 1968. 1st Ed. Cloth. With Supplement 1967-1977. Inscr & sgd. pba Apr 18 (129) $850

**Murillo, Gerardo**
— Iglesias de Mexico... Texto y Dibujos del Dr. Atl. Mexico, 1924-26. Vols I-III (of 6). Folio, cloth. Library markings, but plates unmarked. sg Sept 7 (14) $225
Anr copy. 6 vols. Folio, bds; worn, some staining, some backstrips damaged. sg June 13 (23) $450

**Murphy, James Cavanah**
— The Arabian Antiquities of Spain. L, 1815. Folio, later half mor gilt; edges rubbed. With 102 plates & plans numbered 1-97. CE May 22 (358) $4,500
Anr copy. 19th-cent half mor; worn, upper joint split. With 2 engraved titles & 102 plates. Some browning. S June 27 (120) £3,500
Anr copy. Plates engraved by E. Turrell, J. Roffe, & others. 19th-Cent half mor; worn. With 2 titles, & 102 plates. S Oct 26 (176) £3,800 [Quaritch]

**Murray, Alexander Sutherland**
— Twelve Hundred Miles on the River Murray. L, 1898. Oblong 4to, orig cloth; spine weak. With 15 colored plates. Last plate repaired. S Mar 28 (422) £50

**Murray, Charles Fairfax**
— Catalogue of a Collection of Early French Books. L, 1961. Compiled by Hugh Davies. 2 vols. 4to, bds in djs. sg Apr 11 (236) $375
Anr Ed. L, 1962. 2 vols. 4to, orig cloth; spines soiled. sg Apr 11 (237) $275

**Murray Collection, Charles Fairfax**
— Catalogo dei Libri posseduti da.... L [Rome?], 1899. 2 parts in 1 vol. 4to, orig ptd bds; soiled, joints rubbed. bba Oct 5 (131) £700 [Quaritch]

**Murray, Edward Frederick Croft.** See: Croft-Murray, Edward Frederick

## MURRAY

**Murray, Florence**
— The Negro Handbook. 1944. NY, 1944. sg Mar 28 (216) $60

**Murray, Hugh, 1779-1846**
— Historical Account of Discoveries and Travels in Asia.... Edin., 1820. 1st Ed. 3 vols. 8vo, modern cloth. With 3 folding maps. Tp & maps stamped. sg Mar 7 (197) $70

**Murray, Johann Anders**
— Apparatus medicaminum tam simplicium quam praeparatorum et compositorum in praxeos adjumentum consideratus. Goettingen, 1776-90. 6 vols. 8vo, contemp bds; minor defs. Titles stamped; some stains. sg May 16 (461) $225

**Murray, Keith**
— The Modocs and Their War. Norman, [1959]. 1st Ed, 2d Printing. Orig cloth in dj. With 2 illus by Joe Beeler. Larson copy. pba Sept 28 (32) $50

**Murray, Robert A.**
— Fort Laramie: "Visions of a Grand Old Post." Fort Collins CO: Old Army Press, [1974]. One of 250. pba June 25 (179) $60

**Murray, Thomas Boyles**
— Pitcairn: the Island, the People and the Pastor. L, 1853. 8vo, orig cloth; extremities rubbed, endpapers lacking. Some dampstaining. sg Mar 7 (198) $90

**Murray-Oliver, Anthony**
— Captain Cook's Artists in the Pacific.... Christchurch, 1969. One of 2,000. Oblong folio, orig half mor. pba Nov 16 (349) $130

**Murray's...**
— Murray's Adventures in the Adirondacks. Bost., [1869]. Orig cloth; soiled. Each cover with folding map in pocket. pba July 11 (362) $120

**Murrell, John**
— Murrels Two Bookes of Cookerie and Carving. L, 1631. 8vo, contemp vellum; soiled, hinges cracked, loose. CE May 22 (359) $1,300

**Musaeus**
See also: Golden Cockerel Press
— Ero e Leandro, una leggenda greca. Verona: Officina Bodoni, 1977. One of 100. 4to, orig half mor. S July 27 (349) £280 [Quaritch]

**Muscatine, Charles**
— The Book of Geoffrey Chaucer.... [San Francisco], 1963. One of 450. Folio, cloth. With orig leaf from c.1551 Ed of Chaucer. pba June 20 (252) $110
Anr copy. Cloth. With orig leaf from c.1551 Ed of Chaucer. pba Aug 22 (624) $90

**Muse...**
— La Muse lyrique dediee a la Reine.... Paris: Baillon, 1779. 8vo, contemp bds; worn. Engraved through-

## AMERICAN BOOK PRICES CURRENT

out. Some staining & tears; old ownership stamps on tp. S June 13 (665) £260

**Musee...**
— Musee des dames et des demoiselles. Paris: Marcilly Aine, [c.1830]. 6 vols: papillons, insectes, oiseaux, fleurs, mineraux, coquillages. 12mo, orig bds & orig box with gilded sides. With 6 hand-colored frontises. S Nov 2 (227) £420 [Temperley]

**Musee du Louvre**
GRANDJEAN, SERGE. - Catalogue des tabatieres, boites et etuis dex XVIIIe et XIXe siecles du Louvre. Paris, 1981. 4to, cloth, in dj. sg June 13 (345) $150

**Museum...**
— Museum van Naturlyke Historie voor Kinderen. Amst.: E. Maaskamp, [c.1820]. With: Warande van Vreemde Dieren ten vevolge van het Museum van Natuurlyke Historie voor Kinderen. Amst.: E. Maaskamp, [c.1820]. 6 vols. 8vo, orig bds; worn, joints cracked, backstrips chipped. With 64 hand-colored plates. Van Veen set. S Nov 2 (226) £320 [Schiller]

**Museum of Modern Art**
— Ludwig Mies van der Rohe. Drawings in the Collection of.... NY, 1969. Notes by Ludwig Glaeser. Oblong folio, bds; scratched. With 31 plates. CE Sept 27 (207) $100

**Musper, H. T.**
— Die Urausgaben der hollaendischen Apokalypse und Biblia pauperum. Munich, [1961]. 3 vols. 4to, bds in slipcase. sg Apr 11 (156) $80

**Musschenbroek, Peter van, 1692-1761**
— Inledning til Naturkunnigheten.... Stockholm, 1747. 1st Ed in Swedish. 8vo, contemp vellum; soiled. With 26 folding plates; with errata leaf. S Mar 14 (263) £700

**Musset, Alfred de, 1810-57**
— Les Nuits. Montagnola di Lugano: Officina Bodoni, 1924. One of 225. Folio, orig vellum gilt, unopened. Ck May 31 (15) £180
— Works. NY: Pvtly ptd, 1908. One of 1,000. 10 vols. Half mor; spine ends rubbed. pba Dec 14 (36) $130

**Mustafa Ibn 'Abd Allah.** See: Katib Chelebi

**Mutis, Jose Celestino —& Others**
— Flora de la real expedicion botanica del Nuevo Reino de Granada. Madrid, 1954-69. Vol 7 only. Orig lea. With 53 plates, 49 of them in color. K Feb 11 (303) $350

**Myers, Thomas**
— A New Comprehensive System of Modern Geography. L, 1822. 2 vols. 4to, contemp half calf; joints cracked, 1 vol disbound. With 50 hand-colored plates & 62 uncolored plates. Some tears & staining, 1 double-page plate torn with loss. b Jan 31 (458) £250

## Mylius, Gottlieb Friedrich
— Memorabilium Saxoniae subterraneae. Leipzig, 1709-18. 2 parts in 1 vol. 4to, later cloth-backed wraps. With frontis & 28 plates. Some leaves cut down at head; some dampstaining & browning. S Mar 14 (264) £800

## Myres, Sandra L.
— Ho fo California! Women's Overland Diaries from the Huntington Library. San Marino, 1980. Linen. With 13 illus by J. Goldsborough Bruff, William Hays Hilton, Charles Nahl, & others. Larson copy. pba Sept 28 (614) $65

## Myrick, Thomas S.
— The Gold Rush: Letters of.... Mount Pleasant: Cumming Press, [1971]. One of 487. Orig cloth. Larson copy. pba Sept 28 (615) $50

Myrrour... See: Baldwin, William

# N

N., G. See: Nichol, George

## Nabokov, Vladimir, 1899-1977
— Despair. NY, [1966]. In repaired dj. sg June 20 (292) $130
— Lolita. NY, [1955]. 1st American Ed. In chipped & soiled dj. pba May 23 (256) $120
1st Ed. Paris, 1955. 2 vols. Wraps; spine repaired. With price of 900 Francs. b May 30 (409) £900
Anr copy. Orig wraps; joints chipped. CE May 22 (362) $2,200
Anr copy. Wraps; abrasion to rear joint of Vol II. sg Dec 14 (221) $700

## Naef, Hans
— Die Bildniszeichnungen von J. A. D. Ingres. Bern, [1977]. 5 vols. 4to, syn, in djs. sg Jan 11 (225) $550

Naef, Weston. See: Grolier Club

## Nagler, Georg Kaspar, 1801-66
— Die Monogrammisten und diejenigen bekannten und unbekannten Kuenstler aller Schulen. Munich, 1879-1920. 6 vols, including Index. Half cloth; rebound & shaken. sg June 13 (270) $150
— Neues allgemeines Kuenstler-Lexikon. Vienna, 1924. 22 vols only. sg June 13 (271) $400
Anr Ed. Leipzig, [n.d.]. 25 vols. Orig cloth. bba Oct 5 (135) £340 [Halwas]

## Naipaul, V. S.
— Miguel Street. L, 1959. In dj. S Dec 18 (410) £130 [Williams]

## Nanino, Giovanni Bernardino
— Madrigali a cinque... libro terzo. Rome: Zanetti, 1612. Complete parts. 4to, modern mor by Missol. Minor worming; some spotting & staining; minor paper loss on upper margin of Canto. S Dec 1 (253) £2,000

## Nansen, Fridtjof, 1861-1930
— Farthest North. L, 1897. 2 vols. 8vo, orig cloth. b Sept 20 (437) £60
— Hunting & Adventure in the Arctic. L, 1925. Orig cloth; rubbed. Some foxing. O June 4 (201) $50

Nanteuil, Robert. See: Petitjean & Wickert

## Napier, Sir Charles James, 1782-1853
— The War in Syria. L, 1842. 1st Ed. 2 vols. 8vo, recent half calf. S Oct 26 (177) £150 [Folios]

## Napier, Mark
— A Letter to Sir William Stirling Maxwell.... [N.p.: Pvtly ptd, 1872]. Ltd Ed. 4to, orig cloth; worn. Maxwell's copy with 3 A Ls s from Napier to Maxwell. O Mar 26 (186) $170

## Napier, Sir William Francis Patrick, 1785-1860
— The History of the War in the Peninsula.... L, 1832. 6 vols. 8vo, half calf. pba Sept 14 (279) $300

## Naples
— Aviso de la sollennita e festa fatta in la citta di Napoli in lo giuramento & hommagio dato al... Filippo de Austria Re d'Inghilterra e, de Napoli. [Naples: Mattia Cancer, 1554]. 4to, early 19th-cent calf gilt; rubbed. Waterstain in upper margin. C Apr 3 (158) £1,100

## Napoleon I, 1769-1821
— Correspondance publiee par ordre de l'Empereur Napoleon III. Paris, 1858-69. 32 vols. 4to, contemp half lea; rubbed. S Mar 28 (538) £2,000
[-] L'Hymen et la naissance, ou poesies en l'honneur de leurs majestes imperiales et royales. Paris: Firmin Didot, 1812. 8vo, green mor gilt by Bozerian jeune. With frontis & engraved dedication leaf. Fuerstenberg - Schaefer copy. S Dec 7 (307) £450
— Le Sacre de S. M. L'Empereur Napoleon.... Paris, [1806]. Folio, orig bds; soiled, upper joint split. With title, & 38 plates. Some spotting & offsetting. S Oct 27 (1145) £1,700 [Chelsea Gal.]

## Nardi, Giovanni
— Noctes geniales. Bologna: Giovanni Baptista Ferroni, 1656. 4to, modern half vellum. Some dampstaining, mostly marginal. S Mar 29 (705) £180

## Narinsky, S.
— The Holy Land. Jerusalem, 1921. 4to, loose in folding case. With 102 sgd plates. sg Mar 7 (200) $300

## Narkiss, Bezalel
— Hebrew Illuminated Manuscripts in the British Isles. Jerusalem, [1969]. Folio, orig cloth in dj; worn. With 61 tipped-in color plates. Inscr & sgd. sg Apr 11 (182) $90

## Nash, Joseph, 1809-78
— The Mansions of England in the Olden Time. L, 1839-49. Series 1-4. 4 vols in 8. Folio, half mor; rubbed & soiled. With 104 colored plates, mtd on card. CE Feb 21 (195) $4,700

Anr copy. Series 1-4. 4 vols. Folio, loose in half mor folding cases; some rubbing & defs. With 106 colored plates, mtd on card. CE June 12 (231) $3,800

5 vols including text vols. Folio & 8vo. Plates loose in half mor folding cases, text in orig cloth with upper cover nearly detached. With 4 hand-colored litho titles & 100 hand-colored plates mtd on heavy card within gilt-ruled borders. Tp mount in Vol III stained. CE Sept 27 (212) $7,500

### Nash, Paul, 1889-1946
— Places. L, 1922. One of 210. 4to, orig half cloth; corners rubbed. Inscr by Bernard Berenson to Richard Smart. S May 16 (121) £260

### Nash, Treadway Russell
— Collections for the History of Worcestershire. L, 1799. 2 vols. Folio, modern half mor; joints cracked. With 2 engraved dedication leaves, port, 88 plates & 2 maps. Port with marginal waterstaining. bba Nov 1 (253) £600 [Freddie]

### Nast, Thomas, 1840-1902
— Christmas Drawings for the Human Race. NY, 1890 [1889]. 1st Ed. 4to, orig cloth; worn & soiled. With 60 plates. Dampstained at margins. wa Feb 29 (117) $160

### Natalis, Hieronymus
— Evangelicae historiae imagines. Antwerp: [Martinus Nutius?], 1593. Folio, contemp calf; extremities rubbed, joints cracked. With engraved title & 153 plates. Some foxing. cb Feb 14 (2521) $1,200

Anr copy. 19th-cent calf gilt; spine ends & edges rubbed. With engraved title & 152 (of 153) plates. Engraved title laid down; tp & endpapers wormed. CE June 12 (232) $400

### Nathan, Fernand
— Pour la Beaute Physique de ton Enfant! Gymnastique Figurative. Paris, 1927. 4to, ptd wraps; creased. Some foxing & soiling. sg Feb 29 (230) $225

### National...
— National Antarctic Expedition, 1901-1904. L, 1908. Album of Photographs and Sketches & Portfolio of Panoramic Views. 2 vols. 4to, cloth & portfolio. With 165 plates, 24 panoramas & 2 maps. pba July 25 (48) $1,300

— The National Era. Wash., 1847-59. Ed by G. Bailey & John G. Whittier. 300 weekly issues. K Feb 11 (22) $1,550

— The National Portrait Gallery of Distinguished Americans. Phila., 1836 [i.e., 1834]-1839.. 4 vols. 4to, bdg not described but def. Some foxing. F June 20 (625) $100

Anr copy. Mor gilt. sg Feb 8 (73) $600

Anr copy. Orig mor gilt; spines worn, Vol IV scuffed. With engraved titles & 147 plates. wa Feb 29 (240) $180

### National Maritime Museum
— Catalogue of the Library. L, 1968-76. Vols I-III (of 5) in 5 vols. ds July 27 (136) $325

Anr Ed. L, 1968. Vol I only. 4to, orig cloth in dj; worn. sg Apr 11 (238A) $100

Anr Ed. L, 1968-76. Vol III, Parts 1-2, in 2 vols. In djs. sg May 9 (24) $475

### Natrus, Leendert van —& Others
— Groot volkomen moolenboek; of naauwkeurig Ontwerp, van allerhande tot nog toe bekende soorten van moolens. Amst., 1734-36. Bound with: Lindberg, Pehr. Architectura mechanica, of moole boek. Amst., 1727. Folio, late 18th-cent half calf with gilt C.T. stamped into upper cover; extremities worn, old spine laid down. P June 5 (305) $3,250

### Natura...
— Natura Exenterata or Nature Unbowelled. L, 1655. 8vo, 19th-Cent mor. With frontis. Title repaired at margin. S Oct 12 (80) £360

### Natural...
— The Natural History of Birds. L, 1791. 6 parts in 3 vols. 12mo, modern half calf. With 116 hand-colored plates. Tear in 1 plate. S Nov 2 (194) £900 [Temperley]

Anr copy. Disbound. With 114 hand-colored plates only. Some foxing & browning. sg May 9 (289) $200

— Natural History of Birds. Their Architecture, Habits, and Faculties. NY, 1840. 12mo, orig cloth; soiled & stained. Some spotting & staining. Audubon family copy, with pencil initials of John James Audubon on tp & with bookplate of Maria R. Audubon. sg Apr 18 (142) $600

— Natural History of the World. L: J. Bysh, 1818. 24mo, orig wraps with engraved pictorial label; soiled. With frontis, pictorial title & 10 leaves, each with hand-colored illust. Engraved throughout. S Nov 2 (232) £550 [Schiller]

### Naturalist...
— The notebook of an English naturalist. N.p., early 19th-Cent. 8vo, half roan. With 32 watercolor illus leaves. 1st leaf stained. S Oct 27 (725) £300 [Astor]

### Naturalist's...
— The Naturalist's Pocket Book. L, 1797. Illus by barlow. 12mo, mor; rubbed & soiled, stitching broken. With title, color vignette, calendar, & 13 hand-color plates. S Oct 27 (759) £1,100 [Antiquariat]

### Nature...
— Nature. L, 7 Jan - 24 June 1939. Vol 143. With Index. 3 vols. Cloth, Index in wraps. sg May 16 (221A) $800

### Naturforschende...
— Naturforschende Gesellschaft Versuche und Abbhandlungen. Danzig, 1747-56. 3 vols. 4to, contemp calf. With 14 folding plates. Some soiling. S Mar 14 (94) £1,600

**Naumann, Johann Andreas, 1747-1826**
— Naturgeschichte der Voegel Mitteleuropas. Gera-Untermhaus: Koehler, [1895]-97-1905. 12 vols. Folio, half mor. With 439 chromolitho plates & 10 uncolored plates. Some spotting. S June 27 (56) £2,000

**Naumann, Johann Andreas, 1747-1826 —& Bouvier, A.**
— Iconographie des oiseaux d'Europe et de leurs oeufs. Paris, 1910. Folio, modern half mor, orig wraps bound in. With 409 chromolitho plates & 5 uncolored plates. Some spotting; some plates with section tissue adhering to image surface. Fattorini copy. C Oct 25 (80) £1,500

**Naval Achievements...**
— The Naval Achievements of Great Britain.... L: James Jenkins, 1817. 4to, half mor; joints rubbed & weak. With engraved title, 1 plain & 55 hand-colored plates. Lacking the 2 ports. P Dec 12 (131) $4,250

Anr Ed. L: James Jenkins, [c.1825]. 4to, 19th-cent half mor gilt; rubbed. With engraved title, 1 plain & 55 hand-colored plates. Lacking the 2 ports & list of subscribers. S Nov 30 (228) £3,200

**Navalon, Sebastian C.**
— El grabado en Mexico.... Mexico, 1933. 4to, orig ptd wraps. ds July 27 (139) $150

**Navone, Giandomenico —& Cipriani, Giovanni Battista, 1727-85**
— Nuovo Metodo per apprendere insieme le Teorie, e le pratiche della scelta architettura civile.... Rome: Luigi Perego Salvioni, 1794. Folio, early 19th-cent half sheep gilt; spine worn. With 55 plates. Dampstaining in upper outer corners; foxed, affecting some plates. sg Sept 7 (16) $750

**Naya, C.**
— Catalogue general des photographies editees par Mr. C. Naya, photographe de S.M. le roi Victor Emanuel II.... Venice, 1872. 8vo, ptd wraps; worn & soiled, corners repaired with tape. NH June 1 (303) $275

**Naylor, Gloria**
— The Women of Brewster Place. NY, [1982]. In dj with short tears; ink mark on top of fornt free endpaper. pba Aug 22 (376) $90

Anr copy. In dj. Dampstaining in lower margins; edges foxed. sg Mar 28 (217) $70

**Neal, Arthur**
— Edward Thomas: A Centenary Celebration with Etchings.... Cambr.: Rampant Lions Press, 1978. One of 25 with additional suite of 4 sgd etchings. 4to, orig cloth, plates loose as issued in orig cloth portfolio. bba May 9 (333) £90 [Deighton Bell]

**Neal, Daniel**
— The History of New England.... L, 1720. 2 vols. 8vo, modern lea gilt. Short tear on map extending into image. Z June 28 (218) $375

**Neale, Adam, d.1832**
— Travels through some Parts of Germany, Poland, Moldavia, and Turkey. L, 1818. 4to, half calf. With 11 plates. A few plate imprints cropped. b Sept 20 (351) £260

1st Ed. 4to, modern half mor. With 11 hand-colored plates. Some offsetting & discoloration. S Oct 26 (178) £200 [Lach]

**Neale, John Preston**
— Views of the Seats of Noblemen and Gentlemen.... L, 1818-29. 1st Series: 6 vols. 2d Series: 5 vols. Together, 11 vols. 8vo, later half calf; rubbed, a few covers detached. C Oct 25 (137) £700

Anr copy. Contemp calf; rebacked. With engraved titles & 722 plates. Some spotting. S Mar 28 (56) £1,800

Anr copy. Later half calf gilt. sg Mar 7 (242) $400

1st Series only. 6 vols. 4to, contemp half mor; rubbed. With engraved titles & 426 plates. S Mar 28 (57) £400

**Neander, Joannes, b.1596**
— Tabacologia. Leiden: Elzevier, 1626. 4to, contemp calf; rebacked, worn. Dampstained throughout. Sold w.a.f. CE May 22 (364) $300

**Nebenzahl, Kenneth**
— A Bibliography of the Printed Battle Plans of the American Revolution, 1775-1795. Chicago, [1975]. In dj. pba Apr 25 (222) $65

**Necker, Jacques, 1732-1804**
— De l'administration des finances de la France. [Paris], 1784. 1st Ed. 3 vols. 8vo, contemp red mor gilt with arms of Antoine Jean Amelot de Chaillou; repaired tear to lower cover of Vol I, upper hinge of Vol III split. Some browning & spotting. Fuerstenberg - Schaefer copy. S Dec 7 (447) £3,200

**Nederlandsch Historisch Scheepvaart Museum**
— Catalogus der Bibliotheek. Amst., 1960. 2 vols. pba July 25 (445) $160

**Needham, John Tuberville, 1713-81**
— An Account of Some New Microscopical Discoveries. L, 1745. 8vo, modern half cloth. With 1st title & 6 folding plates. Tp & dedication spotted; marginal stains. S June 12 (273) £320

**Negri, Cesare**
— Nuove invenzioni di balli.... Milan: Girolamo Bordone, 1604. Folio, 18th-cent vellum. With port. Some browning. C Apr 3 (159) £9,000

**Negro...**
— The Negro in New York. NY: Urban League, [1931]. Wraps. sg Mar 28 (221) $60

— The Negro Pew; Being an Inquiry Concerning the Propriety of Distinctions in the House of God, on Account of Color. Bost.: Isaac Knapp, 1837. 12mo, half cloth; rubbed, piece of front free endpaper torn away. Some foxing. sg Mar 28 (218) $150

## NEGRO...

— Negro U. S. A. NY: Graphics Workshop, 1942. Intro by Herbert Aptheker. Folio, loose as issued in wraps. With 25 lithos. sg Mar 28 (188) $300

**Nehru, Jawaharlal, 1889-1964**
— Jawaharlal Nehru: An Autobiography.... L, [1955]. New Ed. In dj. Inscr to Marion Anderson. sg Mar 28 (219) $375

**Neihardt, John G.**
— The Lonesome Trail. NY, 1907. 8vo, pictorial cloth; rippling to rear cover. sg Feb 8 (326) $100

**Neihardt, John G. —& Black Elk**
— Black Elk Speaks: Being the Life Story of A Holy Man of the Ogalala Sioux. NY, 1932. Illus by Standing Bear. Bdg not described but spine ends frayed, soiled, corners rubbed. Inscr by Neihardt to John Popovich. pba June 25 (180) $130

**Neill, John R.**
— Lucky Bucky in Oz. Chicago: Reilly & Lee, [1942]. 1st Ed, 1st State. Later hand-coloring to design on front free endpaper. pba Jan 18 (162) $140
— The Scalawagons of Oz. Chicago: Reilly & Lee, [1941]. In 1st dj. K Feb 11 (83) $400; pba Jan 18 (163) $190
— The Wonder City of Oz. Chicago: Reilly & Lee, [1940]. Orig cloth; spine ends rubbed, rear hinge cracked. pba Jan 18 (164) $225

**Neill, Patrick, 1776-1851**
— Journal of a Horticultural Tour...Flanders, Holland, and the North of France.... Edin., 1823. 8vo, orig bds; backstrip chipped, covers detached. With 7 plates. Foxed. sg May 16 (328) $50

**Nelson, Battling**
— Life, Battles and Career of Battling Nelson.... Hegewisch, 1909. Pictorial cloth. Inscr to Dr. Frederick Kroll, 1923. pba Apr 4 (78) $250

**Nelson, Byron**
— The Byron Nelson Story. [Cincinnati, 1980]. One of 600. Calf. pba Apr 18 (132) $120
— How I Played the Game. Dallas, [1993]. One of 500. Foreword by Arnold Palmer. Cloth. pba Apr 18 (131) $140
   1st Ed. Dallas: Taylor Publishing, [1993]. Cloth. Sgd. pba Nov 9 (62) $130
— Shape Your Swing the Modern Way. [NY, 1976]. 1st Ed. - Intro by Tom Watson. In dj. Inscr & with sgd photo. pba Nov 9 (63) $90
— Winning Golf. NY, [1946]. 1st Ed. In dj. Sgd. pba Apr 18 (133) $80

**Nelson, Henry Loomis, 1846-1908**
— The Army of the United States. NY, [1889]. Ltd Ed. Illus by H. A. Ogden. Folio, library cloth. With 47 colored plates. Text to Plates XLIV-XLVII lacking; library markings. NH Sept 16 (111) $375

**Nelson, Horatio Nelson, Viscount, 1758-1805**
— Letters to Lady Hamilton. L, 1814. 2 vols. 8vo, later half mor. b May 30 (410) £140
   Anr copy. Later bds; 1 joint splitting. Some spotting & soiling; ephemera mtd inside. bba Oct 19 (260) £150 [Scott]
[-] Ode on the Death of Vice-Admiral Lord Viscount Nelson...Spoken at the Christmas Exhibition, Stonyhurst, December 19th, 1805. Preston, [1805]. 4to. Fold creases. b Dec 5 (211) £100
[-] A Pindaric Ode to the Immortal Memory of the Late Lord Nelson. Warrington, 1807. 4to, modern bds. Some staining. b Dec 5 (212) £160

**Nelson, Robert.** See: Fore-Edge Paintings

**Nemerov, Howard**
— The Image and the Law. NY, 1947. In dj; Editorial copy handstamp on rear endpaper. Inscr to Miriam. Z June 28 (220) $170

**Nemes, Sylvester**
— The Soft-Hackled Fly Addict. Chicago, [1981]. One of 276 with fly attached to limitation page. Syn gilt. O Feb 6 (168) $110

**Nenna, Pomponio**
— L'Ottavo libro de madrigali a cinque voci. Rome: G. B. Robletti, 1618. 1st Ed. Complete parts for Canto, Quinto, Alto, Tenore & Basso. 4to, 17th-cent wraps, alto & basso parts rebound. SMall tear in E5. S Dec 1 (255) £2,400
— Il sesto libro di madrigali a cinque voci. Venice: Angelo Gardano & fratelli, 1609. 2d Ed. Complete parts for Canto, Quinto, Alto, Tenore & Basso. 4to, 17th-cent wraps. S Dec 1 (254) £2,000

**Neptune...**
— Le Neptune francois, ou atlas marine nouveau. Paris, [c.1750s-1820s]. Vol I only [Western coasts of France]. Folio, later half calf. With engraved title & 53 mostly double-page charts, 1 colored. Some repairs with loss; a few maps backed. S Mar 28 (176) £2,500

**Neralco, Pastore Arcade, Pseud.**
— I Tre Ordini d'Architettura dorico, ionico e corintio.... Rome, 1744. Folio, contemp vellum; edges worn, some peeling to lower cover. With 76 plates. Lacking half-title; front blank loose; dampstain at top margin of 1st few leaves. bbc Dec 18 (161) $850

**Nerciat, Andrea de**
— Le Diable au corps, oeuvre posthume de tres-recommandable Dr. Cazzone.... [Brussels: Poulet-Malassis, c.1865]. Illus by Felicien Rops. 3 vols. 12mo, contemp half mor gilt, orig wraps bound in. With 12 plates. L.p. copy on holland, with plates in 3 or 4 states. S May 16 (48) £1,700

**Nericault-Destouches, Philippe, 1680-1754**
— Oeuvres. Paris, 1811. 6 vols. 8vo, contemp mor gilt. With port before letters & 10 plates before letters. Fuerstenberg - Schaefer copy. S Dec 7 (165) £850

**Nerucci, Gherardo**
— Sette Novelle Montalesi. Verona: Officina Bondoni for Cento Amici del Libro, 1960. One of 116, this copy for Aldo Borletti dell'Acqua d'Arosio. Illus by Dario Cecchi. Folio, contemp mor over bds. Ck May 31 (16) £400

**Neruda, Pablo**
— L'Espagne au Coeur. Paris: Edition Denoel, [1938]. One of 6 hors commerce. Ptd wraps. Inscr to Jorge Caceres, 1938. sg June 20 (296) $325
— Hacia la Ciudad Esplendida. [Stockholm, 1972]. 1st Ptg. Ptd wraps, stapled; rubbed. Inscr. sg June 20 (295) $350
— Oda a la Tipografia. Isla Negra: Editorial Nacimento, 1956. One of 150. Ptd wraps. pba May 23 (257) $170

**Nescher Library, Daniel Georg**
— Forteckning uppa framl. Olver-Inspectoren Daniel Georg Neschers esterlemnade Samling at Manuscripter, Boecker, Chartor och Estamper.... Stockholm: Nestius, 1828. 8vo, later half calf; rubbed. Some browning & foxing. O Mar 26 (187) $190

**Neue...**
— Neue Deutsche Biographie. Berlin, 1971-94. 15 vols. 8vo, orig cloth. sg Apr 11 (240) $900

**Neumann, Arthur H.**
— Elephant Hunting in East Equatorial Africa. L, 1898. 8vo, orig cloth; worn, hinges starting. NH June 1 (167) $270

**Nevada**
— Manhattan Silver Mining Company of Nevada. Report of Adelberg & Raymond. NY, 1865. 8vo, orig ptd wraps stabled into modern stiff wraps. pba Apr 25 (553) $800
KELLY, J. H. WELLS. - First Directory of Nevada Territory.... San Francisco: Valentine & Co., 1862. 8vo, orig half lea; spine perished, covers nearly detached, loose. Some staining. pba Nov 16 (151) $3,500

**Nevill, Ralph**
— Old English Sporting Books. L, 1924. One of 1,500. 4to, orig cloth; soiled, spine-tips frayed. O June 25 (195) $50
Anr copy. Some foxing. sg Mar 7 (502) $50
— Old English Sporting Prints and their History. L, 1923. One of 1,500. 4to, orig cloth; worn. O Jan 9 (170) $110; sg Jan 11 (314) $50

**Nevins, Iris**
— Varieties of Spanish Marbling. Newtown: Bird & Bull Press, 1991. One of 250. Half cloth. With 12 marbled samples. sg Feb 15 (49) $225

**New...**
— New Coterie: A Quarterly. L, 1925-27. Nos 1-6. Orig wraps; some spines chipped. cb Oct 17 (493) $450

— The New Gallery of British Art.... NY: Appleton, [c.1880]. Folio, mor gilt; worn. With 121 plates, including engraved title. Dampstain to top fore-edge margin of last 10 plates in Vol I. wa Feb 1 (336) $170
— A New Geographical Dictionary. L, 1759-60. 2 vols. Folio, contemp calf; worn. With frontis, 97 plates & 45 maps. Vol II tp creased. S June 13 (382) £650
— The New Naturalist: A Survey of British Natural History. L, 1945-94. 1st Eds. Vols I-LXXXI (all published). 8vo, orig cloth in djs; some minor tears. S Oct 27 (654) £1,800 [Old Hall]
— The New Naturalist Monographs: A Survey of British Natural History (Special Volume). L, 1948-71. 1st Eds. Vols I-XXII. 8vo, orig cloth in djs. S Oct 27 (655) £550 [Old Hall]
— The New Negro Forget-Me-Not Songster. Cincinnati: Stratton & Barbard, 1848. 18mo, half mor; worn. Some foxing & staining. sg Mar 28 (220) $200

**New England...**
— The New England Primer, Enlarged and Improved.... Bost.: J. W. Folsom, [c.1785]. 32mo, wooden bds. Some browning. rs Nov 11 (141) $950
Anr Ed. Bost.: Samuel Hall, [n.d.]. 16mo, paper-covered wooden bds. Met Dec 5 (339) $750

**New Guide...**
— New Guide for Travellers Through the United States of America.... Bost.: J. Haven, 1851. 12mo, cloth; worn & loose. With folding hand-colored map. NH Sept 16 (264) $325

**New Hampshire**
— Acts and Laws of His Majesty's Province of New-Hampshire. Portsmouth: Daniel & Robert Fowle, 1771. Folio, contemp calf; dampstained. Dampstaining at beginning; tp damaged with loss. cb Feb 14 (2598) $200

**New York...**
— The New York Herald. NY, 1 May-30 June 1863. Nos 9725-85, lacking 9756. Bound in 1 vol in recent lea. bbc Apr 22 (20) $525

**New York (City)**
— Atlas of New York and Vicinity.... NY, 1867. Folio, half sheep; nearly detached, worn. With full-page table, 9 plates & 51 hand-colored maps. Folding maps torn. Sold w.a.f. bbc Feb 26 (10) $600
Anr copy. Disbound. With 50 maps, table of distances, & 9 views. Large folding map backed with linen & with tears. Met May 22 (280) $450
Anr copy. Orig half mor; very worn. Lacking 1 map; edge tears; minor dampstaining in margins; 1 map def. Sold w.a.f. sg Dec 7 (35) $500
Anr Ed. NY, 1868. Folio, orig half lea; def. Lacking 1 map; prelims def. Sold w.a.f. sg Dec 7 (36) $325
— New York, New York. NY Graphic Society, 1983. One of 35. Folio, loose as issued. With 8 prints by Indiana, Rivers, Rauschenberg, Kitaj, Rosenquist, Katz, Motherwell & Grooms. sg May 23 (532) $4,000

### New York (Colony & State)

— Annual Report of the Forest Commission of the State of New York for... 1891. Albany, 1892. Orig bdg NH July 21 (1) $120

— Atlas of Clinton Co.... NY, 1869. Folio, half mor; extremities rubbed. Marginal dampstaining; lacking 4 maps. Sold w.a.f. sg Dec 7 (37) $150

— Geology of New-York. Albany, 1842-43. 4 vols. 4to, orig cloth; worn & frayed, spine ends chipped. With 4 engraved titles & 122 plates. Large folding map torn & separated. Part of Natural History of New-York series. wa Feb 29 (213) $250

— New Topographical Atlas of Jefferson Co., New York. Phila., 1864. Folio, orig bds; rebacked, new endpapers. With 36 hand-colored mapsheets. Laid in is repaired, folded, hand-colored county map. Some repairs. NH July 21 (24) $550

— Robinson's Atlas of Jefferson County New York. NY, 1888. Folio, orig half lea; spine & corners worn. With 33 colored plates. NH July 21 (26) $625

NEW-YORK STATE LIBRARY. - Catalogue of the Books on Bibliography, Typography and Engraving. Albany, 1858. 8vo, orig half lea; rubbed. O Mar 26 (189) $50

### New York Public Library

— Descriptive Catalogue of the Work of John Taylor Arms. NY, 1962. 2 vols. 4to, cloth. Photocopy of a typescript catalogue. sg Jan 11 (25) $200

### Newcastle, William Cavendish, Duke of, 1592-1676

— A General System of Horsemanship. L, 1743. 2 vols in 1. Folio, contemp calf gilt; joints broken, worn. With double-page engraved title dated 1658 & 62 plates, most of them double-page. Some browning & spotting; 2 plates torn. Ck Feb 14 (326) £4,200

— Methode et invention nouvelle de dresser les chevaux.... Antwerp, 1658. Folio, contemp calf; upper hinge split, extremities worn. With double-page engraved title & 42 double-page plates. Browned; 1 plate trimmed into left border; a few tears repaired. C May 31 (35) £3,200

— Methode nouvelle et invention extraordinaire de dresser les chevaux.... "Jouxte la Copie a Londres", 1674. 8vo, contemp vellum; loose, some wear & soiling. O Jan 9 (67) $170

### Newcomb, Franc Johnson

— Navajo Omens and Taboos. Santa Fe: Rydal Press, [1940]. Inscr. pba Apr 25 (557) $150

— Sandpaintings of the Navajo Shooting Chant. NY, [1937]. Folio, cloth; soiled, hinge starting. With 35 color plates. Met May 22 (78) $200

### Newcomb, Rexford

— The Old Mission Churches and Historic Houses of California. Phila., 1925. 1st Ed. Orig cloth in dj. Larson copy. pba Sept 28 (177) $140

Anr Ed. Phila. & L, 1925. pba Apr 25 (558) $65; pba Aug 8 (145) $130

### Newell, Peter, 1862-1924

— The Hole Book. NY, 1908. 4to, cloth; upper corner of front cover chewed. pba Aug 22 (818) $60; sg Sept 21 (267) $150

— Jungle-Jangle. NY, 1909. 4to, unbound. The 1st 3 leaves with cut-outs in illusts of pair of eyes & grin. Stain at left portion of 1st leaf. bbc Dec 18 (321) $450

### Newgate Calendar

— The Newgate Calendar.... L: J. Cooke, [1773?]. 5 vols. 8vo, recent half calf; new endpapers. 3 plates & 1 text leaf in facsimile; 1 title lacking corner; 1 plate margin def, anr repaired with 1 word in caption supplied. bbc Feb 26 (122) $550

### Newhall, Beaumont

See also: Kirstein & Newhall

— Photography 1839-1937 [Catalogue of exhibition at Museum of Modern Art]. NY, [1937]. 4to, cloth; minor wear. sg Feb 29 (223) $140

### Newhall, Beaumont —& Edkins, Diana E.

— William H. Jackson. Dobbs Ferry, [1974]. 4to, cloth, in rubbed dj. sg Feb 29 (165) $100

### Newhall, Nancy

See also: Strand, Paul

— Ansel Adams. The Eloquent Light. San Francisco, [1963]. Folio, cloth, in rubbed & chipped dj. sg Feb 29 (11) $50

— Time in New England. NY, 1950. 1st Ed. - Illus by Paul Strand. 4to, cloth, in rubbed & chipped dj. sg Feb 29 (308) $100

### Newland, Henry

— Forest Scenes in Norway and Sweden. L, 1858. 12mo, contemp half calf; rubbed. Some foxing & soiling. O Feb 6 (169) $60

### Newman, John B.

— The Illustrated Botany. NY, 1846. Vol I (all pbd). 8vo, cloth; worn & repaired. Some foxing. pba Aug 8 (340) $160

### Newman, W.

— Moveable Shadows. L: Dean, [1857]. 8vo, orig pictorial bds; worn & broken. With pictorial tp & 8 colored plates, each with a figure moved sideways by a lever to reveal the shadow behind. O Sept 12 (123) $850

— Moveable Shadows for the People. Second Series. L: Dean, [1858]. 8vo, orig pictorial bds; scuffed, spine chipped. With pictorial tp & 8 colored plates, each with a figure moved sideways by a lever to reveal the shadow behind. Some foxing & soiling. O Sept 12 (124) $900

### Newmark, Harris

— Sixty Years in Southern California. NY, 1916. 1st Ed. pba Feb 12 (429) $90

**Newton, Alfred Edward, 1863-1940**
See also: Bible in Latin
— The Greatest Book in the World.  Bost., [1925].  One of 470.  pba Aug 22 (561) $50
— Thomas Hardy, Novelist or Poet?  [Oak Knoll: Pvtly Ptd, 1929].  4to, half cloth.  Inscr.  pba Aug 8 (533) $60

**Newton, Sir Charles Thomas, 1816-94**
— Travels and Discoveries in the Levant.  L, 1865.  2 vols. 8vo, later half calf.  With 41 plates & maps.  b May 30 (288) £240
Anr copy.  Orig cloth; spotted, extemities worn, some signatures loose.  bbc June 24 (196) $350

**Newton, Sir Charles Thomas, 1816-94 —& Pullan, Richard Popplewell, 1825-88**
— A History of Discoveries at Halicarnassus....  L, 1862.  3 vols, including Atlas. 8vo & folio, orig cloth.  With folding map & 14 plates in text vols; Atlas with litho title & 97 plates & plans.  b Sept 20 (352) £1,600

**Newton, Huey P. —& Erikson, Erik H.**
— In Search of Common Ground.  NY, [1973].  In d/j  Inscr by Newton.  sg Mar 28 (222) $300

**Newton, Sir Isaac, 1642-1727**
— The Mathematical Principles of Natural Philosophy.  L, 1729.  1st Ed in English. - Trans by Andrew Motte.  2 vols. 8vo, needs rebdg.  With 2 frontises, 2 folding tables & 47 folding plates.  Last several leaves in Vol II gnawed in outer margins.  Sold w.a.f.  sg May 16 (229) $1,400
Anr Ed. L, 1803.  Trans by Motte.  3 vols. 8vo, contemp calf; rubbed.  Some folding plates repaired.  CE May 22 (365) $650
— The Method of Fluxions and Infinite Series....  L, 1737. ("A Treatise of the Method of Fluxions and Infinite Series....") 8vo, cloth; dampstained.  Some foxing.  Met Feb 24 (319) $325
Anr copy.  Modern cloth.  Some dampstaining.  sg Feb 8 (327) $70
— Observations upon the Prophecies of Daniel....  L, 1733. 1st Ed. 2 parts in 1 vol. 4to, contemp calf.  pba Sept 14 (280) $375
Anr copy.  Remains of old calf.  Prelims with minor staining & foxing.  wa Dec 14 (180) $350
— Opticks....  L, 1718. 2d Ed, 2d Issue. 8vo, contemp calf; worn & broken.  With 12 folding plates.  Rust-hole in S1 affecting text; some diagrams trimmed at foot.  S Mar 14 (267) £400
— Philosophiae naturalis principia mathematica.  L, 1726.  "3d" Ed. 4to, contemp calf; worn, small loss to spine head.  b Sept 20 (157) £950
Anr copy.  Contemp calf; rebacked, 3 corners rubbed.  S Mar 29 (670) £1,700
Anr copy.  Contemp calf; worn.  Lacking ad leaf at end.  S Mar 29 (672) £1,300
Anr Ed. Glasgow, 1871. ("Principia.") 4to, mor gilt by Spottiswode.  Reprint of the 1726 Ed.  pba Mar 7 (192) $170

— A Treatise of the System of the World....  L, 1728.  1st Ed in English. 8vo, contemp calf; rebacked. Tp soiled & repaired; some foxing.  sg May 16 (227) $1,700

**New-York State Library.**  See: New York (Colony & State)

**Nials-Saga**
— Nials-Saga: Historia Niali et filiorum....  Copenhagen: Johannis Rudolphi Thiele, 1809.  4to, 19th-cent half calf; extremities worn, joints tender.  Foxed.  pba Aug 22 (599) $140

**Nibby, Antonio, 1792-1839**
— Itinerarie de Rome et de ses environs.  Rome, 1829.  4to, orig wraps; soiled.  sg Mar 7 (244) $225

**Niblick, Pseud**
— Hints to Golfers.  Boston: O. K. Niblick, [1913].  15th Ed, One of 1,000.  Cloth.  pba Nov 9 (64) $85

**Niccolini, A.**
— Fouilles de Pompei: Monuments choisis.  Naples, [c.1900].  Folio, orig bds; chipped, spine worn, piece of upper corner of rear cover gone.  With 36 colored or tinted plates.  Some foxing.  K Feb 11 (293) $500

**Nichol, George**
— The Story of the Three Bears.  L, 1837.  1st Ed. Oblong 8vo, half calf.  In The Doctor, Vol IV. Sold as part of a set of Vols I-VII.  pba Sept 14 (133) $250

**Nichols, Jeannette Paddock**
— Alaska. A History of its Administration, Exploitation, and Industrial Development....  Cleveland, 1924 [1923]. 1st Ed. Buckram; spine sunned.  With 2 ports & 1 (of 2) maps.  Robbins copy.  pba Mar 21 (265) $160

**Nichols, John, 1745-1826**
— The History and Antiquities of the County of Leicester.  L, 1795-1815.  4 vols in 8. Folio, modern cloth.  With 462 plates & maps.  bba Nov 1 (153) £1,200 [Maynard & Bradley]
— Literary Anecdotes of the Eighteenth Century.  L, 1812-16.  Vols I-IX in 10 vols. 8vo, later half mor gilt by Birdsall.  S Apr 23 (123) £1,100

**Nicholson, Ben.**  See: Russell, John

**Nicholson, George**
— The Illustrated Dictionary of Gardening.  L, 1887.  7 vols. 4to, orig cloth; some wear.  With 22 chromolitho plates.  F June 20 (628) $120

**Nicholson, Peter, 1765-1844**
— The Carpenter's New Guide....  Phila., 1818.  4to, contemp sheep; worn & chipped, text separated at center.  With 84 plates.  Some foxing & staining; 2 plates with small holes; 1 text leaf with marginal hole.  bbc June 24 (146) $375
— The New Practical Builder and Workman's Companion.  L, 1823-25.  In 2 vols. 4to, contemp calf gilt;

## NICHOLSON

spine ends & edges rubbed, contents leaf misbound. With frontis & 183 plates; 1 engraved title only. bba Oct 19 (146) £70 [Sotheran]

**Nicholson, William, 1785-1845**
— The History of the Wars Occasioned by the French Revolution L, 1817. Folio, half calf; worn. With hand-colored frontis, & 20 (of 21) hand-colored plates. Some discoloration. S Oct 26 (312) £260 [Barker]

**Nicholson, William, 1872-1949**
— An Alphabet. NY, 1898. 2d impression. 4to, pictorial bds; soiled, frayed, free flyleaves detached. With 26 colored plates. wa Feb 29 (118) $260
— The Book of Blokes. L, [1929]. One of 50 with orig sketch. Orig bds. S Nov 2 (104) £280 [Newman]
— Characters of Romance. NY, 1900. Orig cloth portfolio; worn. With 16 color plates. bba June 6 (31) £450 [Frew]
— London Types, Quatorzains by W. E. Henley. L, 1898. 4to, orig vellum; rebacked, some stains. With 12 colored plates. bba May 9 (245) £200 [Sotheran]

**Nicolai, Heinrich**
— De pane. Danzig, 1651. 2d Ed. 4to, modern bds; old calf relaid. Some marginal repairs to title; some browning. Ck Mar 22 (204) £380

**Nicolaus de Ausmo**
— Supplementum summae pisanellae.... Milan: Leonardus Pachel & Uldericus Scinzenzeler, 22-30 Apr 1479. Folio, contemp goatskin over wooden bds elaborately blindstamped & with small punched roundels colored in glue & yellow gesso, with 4 brass catches on lower cover; rubbed, spine worn, lacking some lea on lower cover. 50 lines; double column; type 4:145G, 2:79G. Worming, affecting some letters. 350 leaves. Goff N-369. C Apr 3 (160) £4,000

**Nicolaus de Blony**
— Tractatus de sacramentis. Strassburg: Martin Flach, 1492. 4to in 8's, old vellum. With 125 (of 126) leaves, 35 lines & headline, double column. Soiled & stained; lacking m7; contemp annotations. S Oct 27 (1076) £400 [Gabinete]

**Nicolaus de Lyra, 1270?-1340?**
— Moralia super totam Bibliam. [Strasbourg: Georg Husner, c.1479]. Folio, contemp blind-tooled pigskin over wooden bds; lacking metal fittings. 57 lines; double column; goth letter; rubricated. Dampstaining in lower margins throughout; some marginal worming; repair in upper margin of Fol. 2. 225 (of 226) leaves; lacking final blank. Goff N-112. S June 27 (350) £1,500

**Nicolaus Pergamenus**
— Dialogus creaturarum moralisatus. Gouda: Gerard Leeu, 3 June 1480. Folio, 19th-cent half russia. 34 lines; type 2:108G; rubricated. With 122 woodcuts. Small hole in cut on a6v; top of borderpiece on a2r shaved. 102 (of 104) leaves; lacking the 2 blanks.

## AMERICAN BOOK PRICES CURRENT

Goff N-151. Liechtenstein - Loncle - Schaefer. P Nov 1 (76) $475,000

Anr Ed. Antwerp: Gerard Leeu, 4 Apr 1481. ("Twijspraeck der creaturen.") Folio, modern vellum. 34 lines; gothic type 2:108. With 122 woodcut illusts. Tear in 31 repaired; wormhole through final quire affecting letters; tear in penultimate leaf; marginal staining towards end. 126 leaves. HC 6135. C June 26 (161) £150,000

**Nicolay, John George, 1832-1901 —& Hay, John Milton, 1838-1905**
— Abraham Lincoln: a History. NY, 1890. 10 vols. 8vo, later cloth. wa Dec 14 (82) $95

**Nicolay, Nicolas de, 1517-83**
— Les quatre premiers livres des navigations et peregrinations orientales. Lyon, 1568. 2d Issue. Folio, later calf; worn, rebacked. With 58 (of 61) plates colored by a contemp hand, including 2d version of plate facing p. 144. Tp & 1 plate cut down & mtd; 12 plates repaired; lacking 1 blank; 1 leaf torn with loss, anr torn & repaired. C Nov 29 (103) £1,000
— Vier Bucher von der Raisz und Schiffart in die Turckey... Antwerp: Guillaume Silvius, 1576. 2d German Ed. 4to, 18th-Cent vellum; rubbed. With title & 61 illus, all hand-colored, some heightened in gold. Title discolored; water-stain affecting leaves after 2C; rustmark on 2L3. S Oct 26 (193) £11,000 [Chelsea Rare]

**Nicole, Pierre, 1625-95.** See: Arnauld & Nicole

**Nicols, Thomas**
— A Lapidary: or, the History of Pretious Stones.... L, 1653. ("Arcula Gemmea: or, a Cabinet of Jewels.") 1st Ed, 2d Issue. 4to, early 19th-cent half calf gilt; spine rubbed. Lacking initial blank; folding table bound upside down & with short tear; marginal dampstain. sg Oct 19 (235) $3,200

**Nicolson, Benedict**
— Joseph Wright of Derby. L & NY, 1968. 2 vols. 4to, orig cloth, in djs. sg Jan 11 (471) $100

**Nicolson, William, 1655-1727**
— The English Historical Library. L, 1736. ("The English, Scotch and Irish Historical Libraries.") Folio, contemp calf; worn. b Sept 20 (158) £90

**Nidever, George**
— The Life and Adventures of George Nidever.... Berkeley, 1937. In dj. pba July 25 (190) $65

**Niebuhr, Carsten, 1733-1815**
— Description de l'Arabie. Amst. & Utrecht, 1774. Trans by F. L. Mourier. 4to, orig bds; rebacked, worn. With half-title, title vignette, folding map, folding table, & 24 plates (7 folding, 2 hand-colored). S Oct 26 (179) £680 [Chelsea Gal.]

**Nieder, Mattheus Broverius van**
— Kabinet van Nederlandsche en Kleefsche Outheden.... Amst., 1727-33. Illus by Abraham Rademaker. 6

vols. 4to, early 19th-cent vellum gilt; warped. Some foxing. sg Apr 18 (176) $1,200
Anr Ed. Amst., 1792-95. Vols I-VII (of 8). 8vo, orig wraps; spine ends chipped. With 129 plates. sg May 9 (374) $800

**Niedieck, Paul**
— Cruises in the Bering Sea. L, 1909. Orig cloth; worn & discolored. O Oct 10 (201) $170

**Nielsen, Carl P. —&**
**Berg, R.**
— Danmarks Bogbindere Gennem 400 Aar. Copenhagen, 1926. 4to, wraps; worn. O Mar 26 (190) $60

**Nielsen, Lauritz Martin**
— Dansk typografisk atlas, 1482-1600. Copenhagen, 1934. Folio, orig half vellum bds; some wear. O Mar 26 (191) $60

**Nierdorf, Karl.** See: Blossfeldt, Karl

**Nieremberg, Joannes Eusebius, 1595?-1658**
— Historia naturae maxime peregrinae libris XVI distincta.... Antwerp: Plantin, 1635. Folio, 19th-cent half calf; scuffed. Minor browning. F June 20 (856) $1,400

**Nietzsche, Friedrich Wilhelm, 1844-1900**
See also: Limited Editions Club
— Also sprach Zarathustra. Leipzig, 1908. One of 530. Folio, vellum; some soil. S Mar 14 (270) £700

**Nieuhoff, Jan**
— L'Ambassade de la Compagnie Orientale des Provinces Unies vers l'empereur de la Chine.... Leiden, 1665. 1st Ed in French. 2 parts in 1 vol. Folio, contemp calf; rebacked, edges repaired. With engraved title, port, folding map & 34 double-page plates. Some spotting; waterstained at end; edges repaired. S June 27 (251) £1,300
— Ambassades memorables de la Compagnie des Indes Orientales des Provinces Unies vers les Empereurs du Japon. Amst., 1680. 2 parts in 1 vol. Folio, contemp calf; very worn, spine def at head. With engraved title, folding map & 25 plates. Some soiling; library stamps on tp. Madsen copy. S Mar 14 (256) £2,400
Anr copy. Contemp calf; corners & joints repaired, upper hinge repaired. With frontis & 24 (of 25) double-page or folding plates & folding map. S June 27 (236) £2,400
— An Embassy from the East-India Company of the United Provinces, to the Grand Tartar Cham, Emperor of China.... L, 1673. 2d Ed in English. - Trans by John Ogilby. Folio, later calf; worn, cover detached. With 20 plates, including engraved title, folding map & folding plan. Corner torn from 1 plate; split in surface of 1 port plate. bba Nov 30 (104) £700 [Shapiro]
— Gedenkweerdige Brasiliaense Zee-en Lant-Reise door de voornaemste Landschappen van West en Oostindien. Amst., 1682. Folio, contemp vellum; recased. Lacking 6 plates & 1 map. Stamp on tp;

worming & foxing. Sold w.a.f. sg Dec 7 (286) $2,200
Anr copy. Contemp vellum; front joint cracked. With 4 folding maps & 46 plates. Some foxing. sg Apr 18 (164) $4,800
— Legatio Batavaica ad Magnum Tartarie.... Amst., 1668. Folio, later cloth. With engraved title, folding map & 35 double-page plates. Tp & engraved title cropped & stamped; browned & stained throughout; plate margins repaired. CE June 12 (233) $320

**Niger, Stephanus**
— Dialogus, quo quicquid in graecarum literarum penetralibus reconditum./ Milan: Officina Minutiana, 1517. Folio, later half sheep; worn. Prelims stained; lacking 2 blanks at end; contemp annotations; library markings. cb June 25 (1769) $300

**Night and Day**
— Night and Day. L, 1 July to 23 Dec 1937. Ed by Graham Greene & John Marks. 26 issues (all pbd). 4to, cloth, orig pictorial wraps bound in. Hobson set. S June 28 (179) £750

**Night Visions**
— Night Visions 1. Niles IL: Dark Harvest, 1984. Printer's copy, sgd by all contribs. Ed by Alan Ryan. In dj. pba Dec 7 (166) $100
— Night Visions 2. Arlington Heights: Dark Harvest, 1987. One of 300, sgd by all contribs. In dj. pba Dec 7 (52) $70
— Night Visions 2-9 Arlington Heights: Dark Harvest, 1987-91. Ltd Ed, sgd by all contribs. 8 vols plus uncorrected proofs for Night Visions 4, 7 & 8, spiral-bound ptd wraps. O Dec 5 (231) $300
— Night Visions 3. Arlington Heights: Dark Harvest, 1987. One of 400, sgd by all contribs. In dj. pba Dec 7 (125) $80
— Night Visions 4. Arlington Heights: Dark Harvest, 1987. One of 500, sgd by all contribs. In dj. pba Dec 7 (126) $80

**Nightingale, Florence, 1820-1910**
— Notes on Nursing.... L, 1860. New Ed. 8vo, later half vellum by Birdsall. Inscr to Douglas Galton, 26 Aug 1860. S Apr 23 (293) £850
1st American Ed. NY, 1860. 8vo, orig cloth; covers rubbed, extremities worn. Foxed. CE Nov 8 (125A) $100

**Nightingale, Joseph**
— English Topography. L, 1816. 4to, disbound. With 59 hand-colored maps. Some pp. of text missing; some discoloration. S Oct 26 (374) £480 [Franks]
Anr copy. Folio, contemp half calf; rubbed, hinges weak. With 58 maps with contemp hand-coloring. Some spotting & discoloration. S Mar 28 (88) £380

**Nignon, Edouard**
— Les plaisirs de la table. Paris, [1926]. 4to, modern half calf. S Oct 12 (58) £150
Anr copy. Illus by P. F. Grignon. S Oct 12 (112) £130

**Niles, John M., 1787-1856**
— History of South America and Mexico.... Hartford, 1839. 2 vols in 1. 8vo, lea; worn. With 2 hand-colored folding maps & 3 plates. Some foxing. NH July 21 (380) $400

**Nimrod.** See: Apperley, Charles J.

**Nin, Anais, 1903-77**
— The House of Incest. Paris, 1936. 1st Ed, One of 249. Folio, orig wraps. b Jan 31 (194) £100

**Niphus, Augustinus, 1473?-1538?**
— De falsa diluvii prognosticatione. Bologna, 1520. 8vo, 19th-cent vellum bds, with arms of the Prince d'Essling; soiled. C Apr 3 (161) £1,000

**Nisbet, Alexander, 1657-1725**
— An Essay on the Ancient and Modern Use of Armories. Edin., 1718. 4to, old calf; worn, covers detached. wa Feb 1 (160) $85

**Nissen, Claus**
— Die botanische Buchillustration. Stuttgart, 1951. Folio, orig cloth. sg Apr 11 (289) $250
— Die Botanische Buchillustration. Stuttgart, 1966. 2nd Ed. 3 parts in 1 vol. 4to, orig cloth. bba Oct 5 (385) £220 [Maggs]
— Die botanische Buchillustration. Mansfield CT: Martino, [n.d.]. One of 225. 2 vols in 1. 4to, cloth; worn. O May 7 (231) $80
— Die illustrierten Vogelbuecher, ihre Geschichte und Bibliographie. Stuttgart, [1976]. Folio, orig cloth. sg Apr 11 (291) $225
— Die Zoologische Buchillustration. Stuttgart, 1969-78. 2 vols, with Vol II in 8 orig parts. Folio, orig cloth or wraps. bba Oct 5 (387) £280 [Cody]
— Die zoologische Buchillustration. Stuttgart, 1969-78. 2 vols. Folio, orig cloth. sg Apr 11 (290) $425
— Die Zoologische Buchillustration. Stuttgart, 1969-78. 1st Ed. 2 vols. 4to, half mor; orig wraps preserved. With port. S Oct 27 (692) £520 [Sawyer]

**Nissen, Georg Nikolaus von**
— Biographie W. A. Mozarts.... Leipzig: G. Senf, 1828. 2 parts in 1 vol. 8vo, contemp half mor. With port & 17 plates. Some spotting throughout. S May 15 (420) £520

**Nivedita, Sister —&**
**Coomaraswamy, Ananda Kentish, 1877-1947**
— Myths of the Hindus & Buddhists. L, 1913. Calf; extremities rubbed. With 23 color plates. pba Aug 8 (394) $90

**Nivelle de la Chausee, Pierre Claude, 1692-1754**
— Oeuvres. Paris: Prault, 1762. 5 vols. 12mo, contemp mor gilt. With the Supplement bound at the end of Vol V. Fuerstenberg - Schaefer copy. S Dec 7 (448) £180

**Nixon, Howard M.**
— Broxbourne Library: Styles and Designs of Bookbindings from the Twelfth to the Twentieth Century. L, 1956. One of 300. 4to, orig half vellum; rubbed & marked. bba May 9 (143) £500 [Ogino]

**Nixon, Richard M., 1913-94**
— Real Peace. NY, 1983. Ltd Ed for Medal of Honor winners & Vietnam POWs. In dj. Sgd. pba June 13 (77) $300
— The Real War. [NY, 1980]. In dj. Sgd on laid-in bookplate. pba June 13 (79) $85
— RN: The Memoirs of Richard Nixon. NY, 1978. Ltd Ed, sgd. pba June 13 (78) $275
— Seize the Moment. NY, 1992. One of 250. Syn. pba Oct 26 (295) $325
— Six Crises. NY, 1962. Bookclub Ed. Orig cloth; soiled, spine ends worn. Inscr to Ann & Walter Smith (2 water smears blurring 4 words in inscr). wa Feb 29 (248) $150

**Noailles, Anna Elisabeth, Comtesse de, 1876-1933**
— Ame des paysages. Paris: Cent Femmes Amies des Livres, 1928. One of 130, this for Mme la Marechale Petain. Illus by Pierre Bouchet after the author. 4to, pink calf extra with art deco flowers in gilt & gold by the Vicomtesse G. de Mentque. Inscr to Mme Petain & with poem written out & sgd opposite. ALs tipped in & postcard loosely inserted. S Nov 21 (331) £1,700
— Les Climats. Paris, 1924. One of 125. Illus by F. L. Schmied. 4to, mor extra by Esther Founes, orig wraps bound in. b Sept 20 (639) £2,600
— L'Ombre des jours. Paris, 1938. One of 110, this for Max Girard. Illus by J. E. Laboureur. 4to, mor extra by Georges Levitzky, orig wraps bound in; spine rubbed. S Nov 21 (332) £1,900

**Noble...**
— The Noble Knight Paris & the Fair Fienne. Kentfield, Calif.: Allen Press, 1956. One of 130. Half vellum. sg Sept 14 (14) $325

**Noble, Mark, 1754-1827**
— An Historical Genealogy of the Royal House of Stuart. L, 1795. 4to, later half calf. CG June 12 (15) £160

**Nocq, Henry**
— Le Poincon de Paris, repertoire des maitres orfevres de la jurisdiction de Paris.... Paris, 1926-31. One of 600. 5 vols. 4to, orig wraps. W Nov 8 (131) £900

**Noctes Binanianae...**
— Noctes Binanianae: Certain Voluntary and Satyrical Verses and Compliments.... L: Pvtly ptd, 1939. One of 25. Orig wraps. Verses by John Hayward, Geoffrey Faber, T. S. Eliot & Frank Morley. Laid in is typed reminiscence sgd by Morley, Oct 1967. Hobson copy. S June 28 (55) £2,800

**Nodder, Frederick P.** See: Shaw & Nodder

**Nodier, Charles, 1780-1844**
— Bibliotheque Sacree Grecque-Latine.... Paris, 1826. 8vo, contemp blindstamped calf; spine head chipped, joints worn. Some foxing. O Mar 26 (193) $70

**Noe, Amedee Charles Henri, Comte de, 1819-79**
— L'Art d'engraisser et de maigrir a volonte par cham. Paris, [c.1860]. Folio, contemp cloth; corners restored; covers stained. Some spotting. Ck Mar 22 (206) £120

**Noe, Bianchi**
— Viaggio da Venetia al Santo Sepolcro.... Venice, 1658. 8vo, contemp wraps; worn, 3 leaves loose. Some browning; paper loss to B2 & 15. b May 30 (289) £350

Anr Ed. Bassano: Giovanni Antonio Remondini, 1734. 8vo, 19th-cent lea gilt by Pratt. With 157 large & small woodcuts, including 4 double-page views. Tp & following leaf damaged & repaired with a few letters supplied by hand; last leaf repaired; some top margins cut close. C June 26 (107) £650

**Noe, Marc Antoine de, 1724-1802**
— Discours prononce dans l'eglise metropolitaine d'Auch, pour la benediction des guidons du Regiment du Roi, Dragons, le 28 September 1781. Pau: P. Daumon, 1781. 4to, contemp mor French military bdg bound for Louis PIerre Charles de la Baig, Comte de Viella, with his arms on lower cover. C May 1 (112) £8,000

**Noguchi, Isamu**
— Isamu Noguchi: A Sculptor's World. NY, [1968]. Intro by R. Buckminster Fuller. 4to, cloth, in dj. sg Jan 11 (318) $150

**Noguchi, Yone, 1875-1947**
— Emperor Shomu and the Shosoin. Tokyo, 1941. 2 vols. Pictorial wraps. wa Dec 14 (524) $100
— Hiroshige. NY, 1921. One of 750. String-bound wraps. F June 20 (315) $60

Anr copy. String-bound wraps; spotted. With color frontis & 19 collotype plates. sg Jan 11 (319) $60
Anr Ed. L & Tokyo, 1940. 2 vols. 4to, pictorial wraps bound in the Japanese manner. wa Dec 14 (533) $130
— Korin. L, 1922. One of 450. 4to, orig wraps in cloth sleve with ivory clasps. sg Jan 11 (320) $150
— Lafcadio Hearn in Japan.... NY, [1911]. Pictorial bds with silk string ties. Inscr by Hearn's great-grandson, Bon Koizumi. sg Dec 14 (146) $225

**Nogues, Marie Germain**
— La Coutume de Barege.... Toulouse, [1760]. 8vo, contemp mor gilt. Fuerstenberg - Schaefer copy. S Dec 7 (449) £550

**Nolan, Edward Henry**
— The Illustrated History of the British Empire in India and the East. L, [1855-57]. 2 vols in 8. 8vo, orig cloth; spine ends frayed. In orig parts, with titles & prelims bound at rear of last part. sg Mar 7 (247) $400

**Nolhac, Pierre de, 1859-1936**
— Francois Boucher. Paris, 1907. One of 500. 4to, early half lev, orig wraps bound in; scuffed & soiled. wa Nov 16 (273) $150

**Nollet, Jean Antoine, 1700-70**
— Lecons de physique experimentale. Paris, 1749-64. 6 vols. 12mo, contemp calf; worn. S Mar 14 (273) £450.

**Nonesuch Press—London**
— Bible, The Holy. 1924-27. One of 1,000 & 1,250. 5 vols, including Apocrypha S Nov 2 (41) £360 [Chong Yap Seng]
One of 1,000, Apocrypha out-if-series for review. 5 vols, including Apocrypha. wa Nov 16 (25) $300
One of 75 on Arnold rag paper. 5 vols, including Apocrypha sg Sept 14 (274) $200
— The Book of Ruth. 1923. One of 250. bba May 9 (592) £85 [Dowdall]; wa Nov 16 (23) $200
— Genesis: The First Chapter. 1924. One of 375. S May 16 (59) £450
— The Greek Portrait. 1934. One of 425. Mor gilt by Zaehnsdorf, orig cloth bound in. sg Sept 14 (272) $325; sg Sept 14 (273) $140
— The Nonesuch Century. 1936. One of 750. bba May 9 (326) £180 [Maggs]; sg Sept 14 (286) $250
BLAKE, WILLIAM. - The Writings. 1925. One of 1,500. 3 vols. pba Sept 14 (58) $225; pba Nov 30 (56) $275
BURTON, ROBERT. - The Anatomy of Melancholy. 1925. One of 750. 2 vols. S Nov 2 (39) £260 [Dowdall]; sg Feb 15 (213) $325; wa Nov 16 (26) $120
Anr copy. Bdg soiled. wa Nov 16 (27) $80
CERVANTES SAAVEDRA, MIGUEL DE. - Don Quixote. 1930. One of 1,475. 2 vols. b Jan 31 (195) £180; wa Nov 16 (28) $170
COLERIDGE, SAMUEL TAYLOR. - Selected Poems. 1935. One of 500. sg Sept 14 (268) $200; sg Feb 15 (214) $130
COLLIER, JOHN. - The Devil and All. 1934. One of 1,000. pba May 23 (77) $65
CONGREVE, WILLIAM. - The Complete Works. 1923. One of 900. 4 vols. wa Nov 16 (29) $100
DANTE ALIGHIERI. - La Divina Commedia. 1928. One of 1,475. bba Nov 16 (226) £260 [Sotheran]; sg Sept 14 (270) $400; sg Oct 19 (182) $325; sg Feb 15 (215) $325
DICKENS, CHARLES. - Works. 1937-38. One of 877. 25 vols including Dickensiana & steel plate. Jan Masaryk's copy, sgd on front free endpapers & with Ls by Arthur Waugh. bba Sept 7 (377) £2,800 [Sims Reed]
Anr copy. 23 vols, including 1 orig metal plate. CE Sept 27 (101) $2,300
Anr copy. 25 vols, including steel-faced plate. CE Feb 21 (87) $4,000
DREYFUS, JOHN. - A History of the Nonesuch Press. 1981. One of 950. bba May 9 (328) £130 [Cox]; sg Sept 14 (108) $150
FARQUHAR, GEORGE. - Works. 1930. One of 100 on handmade paper. 2 vols. bba May 9 (602) £110 [Dowdall]; bba May 9 (603) £100 [Deighton Bell]
HERODOTUS. - The History. 1935. One of 675. bba May 9 (325) £170 [Heritage]; sg Feb 15 (216) $225
HOMER. - The Iliad. 1931. One of 1,450. Ed by Alexander Pope. sg Sept 14 (275) $140
HOMER. - The Iliad & The Odyssey. 1931. One of 1,450 & 1,400. Ed by Alexander Pope. 2 vols. sg Sept

14 (276) $275
HOPKINS, GERARD MANLEY. - Selected Poems. 1954. One of 1,100. sg Sept 14 (277) $400
LAWRENCE, DAVID HERBERT. - Love Among the Haystacks, and Other Pieces. 1930. One of 1,600. sg June 20 (208) $140
MARVELL, ANDREW. - Miscellaneous Poems. 1923. One of 20 specially bound in vellum. sg Oct 19 (181) $500
MELVILLE, HERMAN. - Benito Cereno. 1926. One of 1,650. bba May 9 (18) £55 [Cox]; bba May 9 (322) £50 [Wall]
MILTON, JOHN. - The Mask of Comus. 1937. One of 950. sg Sept 14 (279) $90
MILTON, JOHN. - Poems in English. 1926. One of 1,450. 2 vols. NH July 21 (283) $240; sg Sept 14 (280) $120; wa Nov 16 (30) $200
OTWAY, THOMAS. - Works. 1926. One of 90. 3 vols. bba May 9 (595) £60 [Dowdall]; bba May 9 (596) £60 [Deighton Bell]
PLUTARCH. - The Lives of the Noble Grecians and Romans. 1929-30. One of 1,550. 5 vols. sg Sept 14 (283) $120; wa Nov 16 (31) $75
RICKETTS, CHARLES DE SOUSY. - Some Recollections of Oscar Wilde. 1932. One of 800. cb Oct 17 (683) $160
ROCHESTER, JOHN WILMOT. - Works. 1926. One of 975. wa Nov 16 (22) $170
ROUSSEAU, JEAN JACQUES. - The Confessions. 1938. One of 800. 2 vols. bba May 9 (423) £180 [Baring]; pba Aug 8 (581) $65; sg Feb 15 (217) $150
SHAKESPEARE, WILLIAM. - Works. 1929-33. One of 1,600. 7 vols. K June 23 (399) $600; S Nov 2 (45) £440; S Nov 2 (46) £550 [Frew]
VANBRUGH, SIR JOHN. - Works. 1927. One of 110 on hand-made paper. 4 vols. bba May 9 (600) £160 [Baring]
Out-of-series copy. wa Nov 16 (24) $65
WALTON, IZAAK. - Works. 1929. One of 1,600. pba July 11 (321) $130; sg Feb 15 (218) $120
WALTON, IZAAK & COTTON, CHARLES. - The Compleat Angler. 1929. One of 1,600. bba May 9 (323) £160 [Blackwell]; sg Sept 14 (288) $200
WHITE, GILBERT. - The Writings. 1938. One of 850. 2 vols. sg Sept 14 (289) $700
WILSON, MONA. - The Life of William Blake. 1927. One of 1,480. Rex Harrison's copy. pba June 20 (69) $110; sg Feb 15 (220) $60

**Nonne, Max**
— Syphilis und Nervensystem. Berlin, 1902. 8vo, half mor; rubbed. O Mar 5 (172) $90

**Nonnius, Ludovicus**
— Diaeteticon, sive de re cibaria, libri IV. Antwerp, 1627. 1st Ed. 8vo, contemp vellum. With title device. Small hole in title inner margin; Pp7 & Pp8 marginally repaired; upper margin of some leaves stained. Ck Mar 22 (208) £160

**Noorden, Carl Harko von, 1858-1944**
— Die Zuckerkrankheit und ihre Behandlung. Berlin, 1895. 1st Ed. 8vo, modern cloth. Outer margins affected by damp. Ck Mar 22 (210) £80

**Nordenskiold Collection, A. E.**
— The A. E. Nordenskiold Collection in the Helsinki University Library: Annotated Catalogue of Maps made up to 1800. Stockholm, 1979-89. 4 vols. 4to, cloth. sg May 9 (27) $400

**Nordenskjold, Nils Adolf Erik, 1832-1901**
— Periplus. An Essay on the Early History of Charts.... NY, [1964]. Folio, orig cloth. bba Oct 5 (358) £280 [Franks]

**Nordenskjold, Nils Otto Gustav, 1869-1928 —& Andersson, Johan Gunnar**
— Antarctica; or, Two Years amongst the Ice.... NY, 1905. 1st American Ed. Orig cloth; rebacked with orig spine laid on, new endpapers. Library markings; eradicated stamp from frontis verso causing holes; lacking half-title. pba July 25 (49) $170

Anr copy. Orig cloth; spine ends split. wa Dec 14 (118) $120

**Nordheimer, Isaac**
— A Critical Grammar of the Hebrew Language.... NY, 1838-41. 2 vols in 1. 8vo, contemp sheep; covers loose. With folding chart. sg Oct 26 (179) $80
— A Grammatical Analysis of Selections from the Hebrew Scriptures. NY, 1842. 2 vols in 1. 8vo, orig half cloth; extremities worn. sg Oct 26 (181) $80

**Nordhoff, Charles Bernard, 1887-1947.** See: Limited Editions Club

**Norie, John William, 1772-1843**
— The New Seaman's Guide and Coaster's Companion. L, 1821. Oblong 8vo, later cloth; front cover loose. sg Mar 7 (228) $90

**Norie, W. Drummond**
— The Life and Adventures of Prince Charles Edward Stuart. L & Edin., [n.d.]. One of 850. 4 vols. 4to, orig cloth. CG June 12 (11) £110; CG June 12 (35) £130

**Norlund, N. E.** See: Mejer & Norlund

**Norlund, Poul**
— Golden Altars: Danish Metal Work from the Romanesque Period. Copenhagen, 1926. Folio, bds; worn, hinge cracked. sg June 13 (253) $50

**Norman, Benjamin Moore, 1809-60**
— Rambles in Yucatan, or Notes of Travel.... NY, 1843. 2d Ed. 8vo, contemp lea; extremities worn, residue of library jacket on pastedown, interior hinge weak. Met Feb 24 (354) $225

**Norman, Dorothy**
— Dualities. NY, 1933. Half vellum. Inscr by the dedicatee, Alfred Stieglitz, to Joan Baker, 2 Oct 1937. pba June 20 (312) $325

**Norman, Jeremy —& Hook, Diana H.**

— The Haskell F. Norman Library of Science & Medicine. San Francisco, 1991. 2 vols. Ck Apr 12 (242) £450

**Norris, Thaddeus**
— The American Angler's Book.... Phila., 1864. 1st Ed. 8vo, cloth; rebacked preserving spine. O June 25 (199) $160
Anr copy. Cloth; spine ends frayed, hinges cracked. pba July 11 (210) $375
Memorial Ed. Phila., 1865. 8vo, orig cloth; hinges weak. pba July 11 (211) $120

**Norris Collection, Thomas Wayne**
— A Descriptive & Priced Catalogue...Collection of Thomas Wayne Norris, Livermore, Calif. Oakland: Holmes Book Co., 1948. One of 500. Folio, half cloth. With frontis. pba July 25 (329) $80

**Norroena...**
— Norroena: Anglo-Saxon Classics, Embracing the History and Romance of Northern Europe. L, [1905]-11. One of 500. 15 vols. Calf gilt; rubbed & scuffed. pba Sept 14 (282) $300

**North American...**
— North American Big Game Hunters. L & Munich, 1963-64. One of 250. Ed by Alphonse Stock. Folio, orig mor gilt; rubbed. O Jan 9 (219) $1,000; wd Nov 15 (71) $450

**North, Andrew.** See: Norton, Alice Mary

**North, Arthur Walbridge**
— Camp and Camino in Lower California. NY, 1910. In chipped dj. pba Aug 8 (146) $90

**North, Roger, 1653-1743**
— The Life of...Francis North, Baron of Guildford.... L, 1742. 4to, contemp calf gilt; joints split. bba July 18 (185) £90 [C. L. Edwards]

**Northumberland County History Committee**
— A History of Northumberland. Newcastle-upon-Tyne, 1893-1940. 15 vols. 4to, modern cloth. bba Nov 1 (167) £400 [Turton]
Anr copy. Orig cloth; spines rubbed & torn. Library bookplates. bba Nov 16 (347) £380 [Turton]

**Norton, Alice Mary**
— Android at Arms. NY, [1971]. In dj. Sgd bookplate laid in loose. pba May 23 (259) $70
— At Swords' Point. NY: Harcourt, [1954]. In dj. pba May 23 (260) $90
— The Beast Master. NY: Harcourt, [1959]. In dj. ANs laid in loose; sgd on tp by jacket illustrator Richard M. Powers. pba May 23 (261) $110
— Breed to Come. NY: Viking, [1972]. In dj. Sgd bookplate laid in. pba May 23 (262) $140
— Dark Piper. NY, [1968]. In dj. Sgd on tp. pba May 23 (264) $70
— The Day of the ness. NY: Walker [1975]. Illus by Michael Gilbert. In dj. Sgd by Norton & Gilbert & with ink drawing by Gilbert on front free endpaper. pba May 23 (265) $120

— Galactic Derelict. Cleveland: World, [1959]. In rubbed dj. Sgd bookplate laid in. pba May 23 (269) $80
— Grand Master's Choice. Cambr.: NESFA, 1989. One of 275. In dj. pba May 23 (271) $70
— Ice Crown. NY: Viking, [1970]4]. Bdg A, in dj. Inscr. pba May 23 (272) $70
— Lord of Thunder. NY: Harcourt, [1962]. In dj. Inscr. pba May 23 (276) $75
— Night of Masks. NY: Harcourt, 1964. In dj. Inscr. pba May 23 (277) $100
— Octagon Magic. Cleveland: World, [1967]. In dj. Inscr to her grand-niece, Debbie. pba May 23 (278) $65
— Ordeal in Otherwhere. Cleveland, 1964. In dj. Sgd on tp. pba May 23 (279) $50
— Plague Ship. NY: Gnome Press, [1956]. 1st bdg of tan bds lettered in black, in dj. pba May 23 (280) $100
— Postmarked the Stars. NY, [1969]. In dj. Sgd bookplate laid in. pba May 23 (281) $70
— Rebel Spurs. Cleveland, [1962]. In dj. pba May 23 (283) $225
— Ride, Proud Rebel! Cleveland: World, [1961]. In rubbed dj. pba May 23 (284) $300
— Sargasso of Space. NY: Gnome Press, [1955]. In dj. Inscr as North & as Norton. pba May 23 (285) $85
— Sea Siege. NY: Harcourt, [1957]. In dj. Sgd bookplate laid in loose. pba May 23 (287) $110
— Space Pioneers. Cleveland: World, [1954]. Ed by Norton. In chipped & creased dj. pba May 23 (319) $80
— Space Service. Cleveland: World, [1953]. In dj. pba May 23 (317) $90
— Stand to Horse. NY: Harcourt, [1956]. In dj. Inscr. pba May 23 (290) $250
— Star Born. Cleveland: World, [1957]. In dj. Inscr, May 1957. pba May 23 (291) $425
— Star Gate. NY: Harcourt Brace, [1958]. In 2 djs. pba May 4 (219) $75
— Star Guard. NY: Harcourt Brace, [1955]. In dj. pba May 23 (292) $85
— Star Man's Son, 2250 A.D. L: Staples Press, [1953]. In rubbed dj. pba May 23 (294) $140
— The Stars are Ours! Cleveland, [1954]. In dj with rubbing & tears. pba May 4 (222) $95
— The Time Traders. Cleveland: World, [1958]. In dj. Cut signature at bottom of typed letter mtd to front free endpaper. pba May 23 (297) $95
— Uncharted Stars. NY: Viking, [1969]. In dj. Sgd on tp. pba May 23 (298) $60
— Victory on Janus. NY: Harcourt, [1966]. In dj. Sgd on tp. pba May 23 (299) $55
— Were-Wrath. New Castle VA: Cheap Street, [1984]. One of 123. Illus by Judy King-Rieniets. In wood veneer dj. pba May 23 (300) $110
— The X Factor. NY: Harcourt, [1965]. In dj. Inscr. pba May 23 (301) $65
— Yankee Privateers. Cleveland: World, [1955]. In dj with tear & crease to spine foot. Inscr, 1959. pba May 23 (302) $600

**Norton, Andre, Pseud.** See: Norton, Alice Mary

**Norton, C. Goodwin**
— The Lantern and How to Use It. L, 1901. Some soiling. pba Mar 7 (159) $50

**Norton, E. F.**
— The Fight for Everest: 1924. L, 1925. 1st Ed. Cloth; stains to front cover. sg Mar 7 (193) $80

**Norton, Oliver Willcox**
— The Attack and Defense of Little Round Top, Gettysburg July 2, 1863. NY, 1913. 8vo, orig cloth; worn & soiled. Inscr to Gen. Ellis Spear. wa Feb 29 (345) $260

**Norton, Thomas, 1532-84**
— A Bull graunted by the Pope to Doctor Harding.... L: John Daye, [1570]. 8vo, later calf gilt; front free endpaper detached. Verso of tp blank. Huth copy. CE June 12 (234) $450

**Norway, Nevil Shute, 1899-1960.** See: Shute, Nevil

**Norwich.** See: England

**Norwich, Oscar**
— Maps of Africa. Johannesburg, 1983. 4to, cloth, in dj. sg May 9 (28) $225

**Nostitz, Countess Paulene Mathilde**
— Travels of Doctor and Madame Helfer in Syria, Mesopotamia, Burmah and other lands. L, 1878. 1st English Ed. - Trans by Mrs. George Sturge. 2 vols in 1. 8vo, cloth; spine faded. With frontis. S Oct 26 (144) £300 [Brunt]

**Nostradamus, Michel de, 1503-66**
— The True Prophecies or Prognostications. L, 1672. Folio, contemp calf; rubbed, front bd detached. cb Oct 17 (446) $1,500

Anr copy. Contemp calf; rebacked but detached. Lacking frontis; tp browned; wormed, browned & stained. Sold w.a.f. CE May 22 (366) $550

Anr copy. Old calf; worn & rubbed, covers detached, spine splitting. Tear in tp; lacking port. K Feb 11 (294) $800

Anr copy. Old calf; rubbed. pba Nov 30 (254) $1,800

**Notitia...**
— Notitia utraque cum orientis tum occidentis, ultra Arcadii Honoriique Caesarum tempora.... Basel: Froben, 1552. 1st Complete Ed. Folio, disbound in contemp vellum; vellum worn. 1st & last leaf soiled; last leaf torn. S Oct 26 (180) £900 [Zioni]

**Nott, Stanley Charles**
— A Catalogue of Rare Chinese Jade Carvings. St. Augustine, 1940. 4to, cloth; shelf number on spine, which is chipped. Inscr. sg June 13 (203) $90

— Chinese Jade Throughout the Ages. L, 1936. 4to, orig cloth. With 148 plates, 39 in color. sg June 13 (202) $90

— Chinese Jades in the Stanley Charles Nott Collection. West Palm Beach, 1942. Ltd Ed. 4to, cloth; front joint cracked. With port & 118 plates. sg June 13 (204) $175

**Nouvelle...**
— La Nouvelle Omphale, comedie representee par les comediens italiens ordinaires du Roi, devand leur Majestes le 22 November 1782.... [Paris: Valleyre, 1785]. 12mo, orig wraps. With engraved hand-colored title & 4 folding plates, each in the nature of an overslip disclosing anr scene below on unfolding. Fuerstenberg - Schaefer copy. S Dec 7 (14) £3,500

**Nouvelles Devantres...**
— Nouvelles Devantres et Agencements d Magasins Parisiens. Paris: Rene-Herbst, [n.d.]. 3d Series. Folio, cloth, scuffed, spine ends worn. Owner's handstamp throughout. sg Feb 29 (16) $150

**Novella...**
— Novella del grasso legnaiuolo. Florence: sotto il Corridore di Sua Altezza, 1576. 6 leaves. 4to, mor gilt by Lloyd, Wallis & Lloyd. Repaired tear in A4 touching 3 lines; top margins restored, affecting 1st word of tp & a few words of text. C Apr 3 (162) £1,700

**Novelli, Gastone**
— Scritto sul Muro. Rome, 1938. One of 200. 4to, white lea heightened with glitter. sg Sept 7 (260) $130

**Novotny, Fritz —&**
**Dobai, Johannes**
— Gustav Klimt.... L, 1967. One of 1,250. 4to, cloth, in dj. Library markings. sg Sept 7 (206) $250

**Nuew Modelbuch...**
— Nuew Modelbuch allerley gattungen Daentelschnuer so diser zyt in hoch Tuetschlanden gong und bruechig sind...erstmals in truck verfergket durch R. M. [Zurich: Christoph Froschauer, c.1561]. 4to, mor gilt by Asper, sgd, floral wraps bound in. Gothic letter; large woodcut on tp & 164 woodcuts of lace patterns on 39 pages. Some thumbing; tp with dampstain at upper right. C June 26 (93) £13,000

**Nugae...**
— Nugae venales, sive Thesaurus ridendi & iocandi. Londini, 1741. 12mo, contemp mor gilt; spine browned. Fuerstenberg - Schaefer copy. S Dec 7 (452) £110

**Nunez Cabeca de Vaca, Alvar, 1490?-1557?.** See: Grabhorn Printing

**Nunis, Doyce B., Jr.**
— Los Angeles and Its Environs in the Twentieth Century.... Los Angeles: Ward Ritchie Press, 1973. In dj. pba Feb 12 (402) $55

— The Hudson's Bay Company's First Fur Brigade to the Sacramento Valley.... Sacramento: Sacramento Book Collector's Club, 1968. 1st Ed. Orig cloth. With 1 map. Larson copy. pba Sept 28 (141) $65

**Nunn, John.** See: Clarke, William Barnard

**Nuova...**
— Nuova Raccolta di 25 vedute antiche e moderne di Roma.... [Rome, c.1780]. Bound with: Acquaroni, Antonio. Nuova raccolta di vedute antiche della citta de Roma. Rome, [c.1780] Oblong folio, contemp wraps. With engraved title & 23 plates in 1st work & engraved title & 24 plates in 2d work. Dampstaining in upper margins, affecting a few images; some foxing. sg May 9 (378) $600

**Nuremberg Chronicle**
SCHEDEL, HARTMANN. - Das Buch der Croniken.. Augsburg: Johann Schoensperger, 18 Sept 1496. Folio. bdg not described. Some staining & browning. Lacking c.12 leaves; some leaves torn & repaired; other repairs. bba Sept 7 (195) £3,400

SCHEDEL, HARTMANN. - Liber chronicarum. Nuremberg: Anton Koberger, 12 July, 1493. 13 leaves. 385mm by 230mm, 4 sheets hand-colored 1 sheet with hole; 1 repaired. S Oct 26 (463) $320 [Zioni]

Anr Ed. Nuremberg: Anton Koberger, 12 July 1493. Folio, modern half calf. Stained; some tears with repairs; some views with names penned in ink within the images. 313 (of 326) leaves; lacking tp, 1st text leaf, 2 blanks, colophon leaf & blanks at rear. Goff S-307. bbc June 24 (268) $12,000

Anr copy. 19th-cent calf antique; broken, worn. Types 16:110GB (text), 9:165G (headings), 2 columns, 64 lines. Europe bound at end as folding sheet; tear into 1 leaf repaired; worming at ends touching some lettters, cuts & final map; dampstain along edge at end. 324 (of 328) leaves; lacking blanks & fo. 53/6, which is blank but for ptd headline (supplied in facsimile). Goff S-307. C Oct 25 (146) £14,500

Anr copy. 19th-cent mor gilt; free endpaper detached. Some repaired tears; 2 leaves with large repairs affecting woodcuts; some soiling & dampstaining. 306 (of 326) leaves; lacking tp, 15 leaves of index, 3 text leaves & 3 blanks. cb Feb 14 (2524) $20,000

Anr copy. 92 leaves only. Folio. cb Feb 14 (2525) $2,500

Anr copy. 26 leaves only. Folio. pn Dec 7 (34) £460 [Bifolco]

Anr copy. 31 leaves only. Folio. rs Nov 11 (117) $1,200

2d Latin Ed. Augsburg: Johann Schoensperger, 1 Feb 1497. Issue with the double-page map of Northern & Central Europe at end. Folio, 18th-cent sheep; extremities worn, head of spine chipped. 51 lines & headline; gothic letter; 2 xylographic titles, c.1809 woodcuts & double-page map. Tp with overslip on lower portion; some repairs; some shaving, affecting headlines; map of Germany with 2 repaired tears, 1 with small image loss; early annotations; tp with 2 deleted ownership inscriptions. 368 (of 366) leaves. Goff S-308. Wessel copy. P June 5 (330) $5,000

**Nus...**
— Nus: La Beaute de la Femme. Paris: Daniel Masclet, [1933]. 4to, wraps; backstrip cracked. With 96 plates. sg Feb 29 (229) $400

**Nus, Eugene, 1816-94 —&**
**Meray, Antony**
— Les Papillons metamorphoses terrestres des peuples de l'air. Paris: Gabriel de Gonet, [1852]. Illus by Amedee Varin. 2 vols. 8vo, contemp half mor; rubbed. With hand-colored frontises & 33 hand-colored plates. Some spotting. b Sept 20 (632) £550

**Nuttall, Thomas, 1786-1859.** See: Michaux & Nuttall

**Nuttall, William**
— Rochdale; A Fragment.... Rochdale, 1810. 8vo, modern bds. Tp with tape marks; 1 leaf with tear affecting a few letters. b Dec 5 (210) £120

**Nutting, Judge**
— The History of One Day Out of Seventeen Thousand. Oswego, 1889. 12mo, pictorial bds; worn. O June 25 (200) $250

**Nye, Russell Scudder**
— Scientific Duck Shooting in Eastern Waters. Falmouth, 1895. Cloth; worn. O June 25 (201) $275

# O

**O Cathasaigh, P.** See: O'Casey, Sean

**Oakes, Alma**
— The National Costumes of Holland. L, 1932. One of 550. Illus by Gratiane de Gardilanne & Elizabeth Whitney Moffat. Folio, half mor; worn & tape-repaired, some plates detached, 1 plate misbound. With 50 colored plates. wa Feb 29 (101) $140

**Oates, Joyce Carol**
— Miracle Play. Santa Barbara: Black Sparrow Press, 1974. One of 350. Half cloth. pba Aug 22 (382) $60

— Night-Side. NY, [1977]. In rubbed dj. Inscr. sg Dec 14 (222) $70

— Will You Always Love Me? Huntington Beach: James Cahill, 1994. One of 26. wa Feb 29 (72) $65

Proof copy of 26 specially bound copies. pba Aug 22 (383) $70

**Oberhummer, Eugen**
— Die Insel Cypern. Munich, 1903. 8vo, half calf. With half title, color folding map, & 4 plates. Map repaired. S Oct 26 (68) £2,200 [Cyprus Pop. BK]

**Oberleitner, Andreas.** See: Jahn & Oberleitner

**O'Brien, Francis M.**
— A Backward Look: 50 Years of Maine Books and Bookmen. Portland, 1986. One of 50. Frontis by Leonard Baskin. O Dec 5 (104) $50; O Dec 5 (105) $60

## O'Brien, John
— Leaving Las Vegas. Wichita: Watermark Press, [1990]. In dj. Sgd on tp, 15 June 1991. pba Aug 22 (379) $250

## O'Brien, Robert
— California Called Them: A Saga of Golden Days and Roaring Camps. NY, [1951]. Illus by Antonio Sotomayor. Orig cloth. With original drawing. Sgd. Larson copy. pba Sept 28 (617) $50

## Obsequens, Julius
— Des Prodiges.... Lyons: de Tournes, 1555. 8vo, later vellum. S June 12 (84) £850

## Observateur...
— L'Observateur, journal periodique, par Herald-Dumesle. No XI Cayes, 1819. 8vo, wraps. Marginal dampstaining. sg Mar 28 (123) $300

## Observations...
— Observations sur la physique, sur l'histoire naturelle, et sur les arts. Paris, 1774-1800. Vols 1-50, in 26 vols. Contemp sheep; needs rebdg. Browned; marginal dampstains. Sold w.a.f. sg May 16 (230) $275

## Obsessions...
— Obsessions: Chilling New Tales.... Arlington Heights: Dark Harvest, 1991. One of 500. In dj. pba Dec 7 (161) $65

## O'Casey, Sean, 1880-1964
— The Silver Tassie. L, 1928. Half cloth; rubbed. Inscr to Maggie, 1928 & with 4-line poem. sg Dec 14 (223) $120
— The Story of the Irish Citizen Army. Dublin, 1919. 1st Issue. Ptd wraps. Met Feb 24 (207) $200
Anr copy. Small paper remnant on half-title. sg June 20 (298) $200

## Ockley, Simon, 1678-1720
— The History of the Saracens. L, 1718. 2d Ed. 2 vols. 8vo, modern cloth. Browned throughout; library stamps on titles. sg Mar 7 (248) $120
Anr copy. Early half sheep; needs rebdg. sg Mar 7 (249) $60

## O'Connor, Flannery
— A Good Man Is Hard To Find. NY, 1955. 1st Ed. In dj with minor soiling. CE May 22 (367) $320
Anr copy. In chipped & creased dj. pba May 23 (327) $250

## O'Connor, Jack
See also: Derrydale Press
— The Best of Jack O'Connor. Clinton NJ: Amwell Press, [1977]. One of 1,000. sg Mar 7 (505) $200
— The Big Game Animals of North America. NY, [1961]. Folio, cloth. sg Mar 7 (506) $50
— Hunting in the Rockies. NY, 1947. In frayed & chipped dj; some wear. Some dampstaining in upper blank margin. O Oct 10 (207) $130
— The Hunting Rifle. NY: Winchester Press, [1970]. One of 100. Half lea; some wear. O Oct 10 (208) $130

## O'Connor, John
— The Wood-engravings of John O'Connor. Andoversford: Whittington Press, 1989. One of 350. Ed by Jeannie O'Connor. Folio, orig half cloth. bba May 9 (398) £130 [Bankes Books]

## Oddi, Oddus de
— De coenae et prandii portione libri II. Venice: Gulielmo de Fontaneto, January, 1532. 8vo, in 4s, 18th-Cent bds; extrems rubbed. Ck Mar 22 (212) £800

**Odo de Meung.** See: Gueroult, Guillaume

**Odo Magdunensis.** See: Gueroult, Guillaume

## O'Donnell, T. C.
— The Ladder of Rickety Rungs. Chicago: P. F. Volland, [1923]. Pictorial bds. pba June 20 (92) $65

**O'Donoghue, Freeman.** See: British Museum

## O'Dwyer, E. J.
— Thomas Frognall Dibdin.... Pinner: Private Libraries Association, [1967]. One of 1,400. In dj. pba Dec 14 (38) $85

## Oecolampadius, Johannes
— In epistolam... demegoriae, hoc est homiliae una & XX enuo per authorem recognitae. Basel: Cratander, 1525. 8vo, old sheep with later patterned paper on covers; worn, covers detached. Lacking colophon leaf. sg Mar 21 (237) $300

## Oeconomy...
— The Oeconomy of Human Life. L, 1795. Illus by Sylvester Harding. 8vo, calf gilt; hinges weak. L.p. copy. wd May 8 (72) $150

## Oeder, Georg Christian von
— Flora Danica. Copenhagen, 1761-1883. ("Icones plantarum sponte nascentium in Regnis Daniae et Norvegiae....") Vols I-VII, fascicle 20 only, bound in 8 vols. Folio, modern half mor. With 1,200 hand-colored plates. Vol VII lacking tp; tp & last plate in each vol backed; plates stamped. Sold w.a.f. S Nov 30 (39) £5,500
Anr Ed. Copenhagen, 1761-83. 17 vols plus 3 supplementary parts bound in 2 vols. Together 19 vols. Folio, early 20th-cent calf gilt. With 3,240 hand-colored or colored plates. Minor dampstaining in Vols 1-13; Part 39 in Vol 13 stained & discolored; small hole in Plate 72 of Vol IV; a few plates trimmed; tp to Vol 12 slightly def & repaired; lacking fascicle titles to parts 24-26. This copy with German titles to Vols I-IV with Latin title-pages thereafter. Madsen copy. S Mar 14 (131) £64,000

**Oehler, Richard.** See: Lanckoronska & Oehler

**Oeuvre...**
— L'Oeuvre et l'Image. Paris, 1900-2. Vols I-II in 3. 4to, half cloth. sg Sept 7 (262) $325

**Official...**
— Official Records of the Union and Confederate Armies in the War of the Rebellion. Wash., 1880-1901. 127 (of 128) vols; lacking Series 2, Vol IV Orig half mor; some spines def or repaired. bbc Apr 22 (154) $775
— Official Records of the Union and Confederate Navies in the War of the Rebellion. Wash., 1894-1922. Series I, Vols 1-27 & Series II, Vols 1-3. bbc Apr 22 (155) $375

Anr copy. Series I, in 30 vols, plus 1961 Index. cb Oct 17 (150) $400
— Official Report of the Battle of Chickamauga. Richmond, 1864. 8vo, disbound. Some chipping. sg Oct 26 (64) $250
— Official Reports of Battles.... NY, 1863. 8vo, orig cloth; worn & soiled. F Mar 28 (179) $110

**Officina Bodoni**
— The Officina Bodoni: The Operation of a Hand-Press during the First Six Years of its Work. Paris & NY, 1929. One of 500. Folio, cloth, in soiled & frayed dj. bba May 9 (22) £480 [Mandle]

Anr copy. Cloth; front hinge cracked. cb Oct 17 (675) $225

**Officium**
— 1501, 26 Aug. - Officium Beate Marie Virginis ad usum Romane ecclesie. Lyons: [Jacobinus Suigus & Nicolaus de Benedictis] for Boninus de Boninis. 8vo, 16th-cent sheepskin over wooden bds. Type 80G. With 17 metalcuts; all pages surrounded with 6-part metalcut borderpieces. Ptd on vellum. Schaefer copy. P Nov 1 (119) $16,000
— 1662. - L'Office de la semaine sainte.... Paris 8vo, contemp red mor gilt with arms of Marie Therese d'Autriche, queen of Louis XIV, possibly by Pierre Rocolet. With 3 engravings & with 7 plates by Jacques Callot inserted. Some spotting. C May 1 (116) £1,400
— 1703. - Office de la Semaine sainte...a l'usage de Rome et de Paris. Paris 8vo, contemp red mor gilt with monogram of the Duc D'Orleans surmounted by a crown; corners & edges rubbed & bumped. Staining to very edge of 1st few leaves; rust-hole in N2. Fuerstenberg - Schaefer copy. S Dec 8 (454) £480
— 1723. - Office de la Semaine sainte.... Paris 8vo, contemp olive mor gilt with royal arms of France. With engraved title & 4 plates. Fuerstenberg - Schaefer copy. S Dec 8 (455) £750
— 1726. - Office de la Semaine Sainte. Paris 8vo, 18th-cent mor gilt with arms of Marie Francoise de Bourbon; scuffed, stain in upper inner corner of front cover, lacking front free endpaper. sg Sept 21 (269) $175
— 1728. - Office de la Semaine sainte.... Paris: J. Collombat. 8vo, contemp red mor gilt with arms of Cardinal de Rohan. Fuerstenberg - Schaefer copy. S Dec 8 (456) £1,100

— 1728. - Paris: la veuve Mazieres et Garnier. 8vo, contemp red mor gilt a la fanfare with arms of Maria Leczinska; endpaper & half-title loose. A few words inked out. Fuerstenberg - Schaefer copy. S Dec 8 (457) £500
— 1743. - Paris: J. Collombat. 8vo, contemp red mor gilt. Fuerstenberg - Schaefer copy. S Dec 8 (458) £600
— 1746. - Office de la Semaine sainte... a l'usage de la maison de madame la Dauphine. Paris: la veuve Mazieres et Garnier. 8vo, contemp red mor gilt to a pointille style, with arms of Marie Joseph [Olivier 2526.2]. A few leaves browned. Fuerstenberg - Schaefer copy. S Dec 8 (460) £450
— 1748. - Office de la Semaine Sainte. Paris 8vo, contemp red mor gilt with arms of Marie Leczinska. Fuerstenberg - Schaefer copy. S Dec 8 (461) £3,100
— 1755. - Uffizio della B. Vergine Maria. Rome: Fratelli Pagliarini. 5 parts in 1 vol. 8vo, contemp red mor gilt from the Vatical Bindery, with large central aureole enclosing profile head of the Virgin on upper cover 7 emblem of the Passion on lower cover. C Apr 3 (45) £1,100
— 1765. - Officia propria sanctorum ad usum capituli.... Rome: Typographia Vaticana. 8vo, contemp red mor gilt with a cardinal's arms incorporating the Rezzonico arms, by the Salvioni atelier. C Apr 3 (44) £380
— 1774. - Office de la nuit, de laudes et de prime.... Paris: au depens des libraires associes. 12mo, contemp velvet over wooden bds, each cover with silver embossed covering. Fuerstenberg - Schaefer copy. S Dec 8 (465) £480

**Offray de la Mettrie, Julien, 1709-51**
— Oeuvres philosophiques. Amst., 1764. 3 vols in 2. 12mo, contemp calf; worn. Fuerstenberg - Schaefer copy. S Dec 7 (346) £360

**O'Flaherty, Liam, 1896-1984**
— I Went to Russia. L, [1931]. In chipped dj. Sgd on front free endpaper. pba Jan 25 (276) $70
— The Wild Swan and Other Stories. L, 1932. One of 550. pba May 23 (328) $55

**Ogawa, Kazumasa**
— Famous Castles and Temples of Japan. Tokyo, [c.1890s]f. 4to, bds; dampstained. Some soiling. pba Aug 8 (147) $425
— Sights and Scenes in Fair Japan. Tokyo: Imperial Government Railways, [c.1910]. Oblong folio, orig cloth; rubbed. With 2 maps & 48 tinted photographic plates. b May 30 (156) £190

**Ogilby, John, 1600-76**
— Africa, being an Accurate Description.... L, 1670. Folio, contemp calf gilt; worn, lower cover detached. With frontis, 33 plates & 14 maps. Browned. bba Nov 30 (106) £1,900 [Graves-Johnston]
— America, being the Latest and most Accurate Description.... L, 1671. Folio, half calf; rubbed, bottom of spine worn, hinges reinforced. With engraved title, 6 ports, 30 folded views & 10 (of 19) maps. Some soiling, foxing & staining; some fold tears. cb Feb 14 (2599) $3,250

## OGILBY

— Britannia.... L, 1698. 2d Ed. Folio, contemp calf; worn. With 100 double-page road maps. Old dampstaining; 7 maps shaved into image area; marginal tears; 13 maps & To the Reader with ink ownership stamp on verso; tp & 4 maps creased. C May 31 (62) £4,000

Anr copy. Later half calf; worn, upper cover becoming detached. With 99 (of 100) double-page road maps. General map of England & Wales inserted & wormed with loss; lacking Plate 100; tp torn with loss; some plates shaved; Plates 1 & 19 with margins torn; hole in Plate 39; Plate 99 torn with loss; some rustholes; marginal fraying. S Nov 30 (59) £3,800

### Ogilby, John, 1600-76 —& Senex, John, d.1740
— The Roads through England Delineated. L, 1762. Oblong 4to, recent half mor. With engraved title, full-page general map & 101 (on 51) road maps. Hole in last 2 pages. S June 13 (488) £360

### Ogilvie, John, 1733-1813
— Britannia: a National Epic Poem.... Aberdeen, 1801. 4to, contemp bds; worn. b Dec 5 (522) £120

### Ogilvie, William Henry
— Scattered Scarlet. L, 1923. 4to, cloth. Corners of most plates chipped or torn. Harry Worcester Sith's copy, with 2 A Ls s from Ogilvie to Smith tipped in. O Jan 9 (173) $110

### Ogilvie-Grant, William Robert —& Others
— The Gun at Home and Abroad. British Game Birds and Wildfowl. L, 1912. One of 950. 4to, orig mor gilt; scuffed. With frontis & 30 color plates. bba May 30 (459) £80 [Classic Bindings]

Anr copy. Orig mor gilt; rubbed. O Feb 6 (155) $400

**Ogle, George.** See: Michigan

**O'Hara, Frank.** See: Limited Editions Club

### O'Hara, John, 1905-70
— Appointment in Samarra. NY, [1934]. 1st Ed, 1st Issue. In dj with wear; date stamped on front free endpaper. sg June 20 (300) $375
— Pal Joey. NY, [1940]. 1st Ed, Review copy. In dj. sg June 20 (302) $200
— Sermons and Soda-Water. NY, [1960]. 1st Ed. 3 vols. Cloth. Vol I sgd by O'Hara on tipped-in leaf. pba Aug 22 (380) $80

### O'Henry Memorial Award...
— O'Henry Memorial Award Prize Stories. NY, 1933-40. Ed by Harry Hansen. 8 vols, for 1933-40 In djs. Each vol inscr by Hansen. sg June 20 (6) $200

### Ohm, Georg Simon, 1789-1854
— Die galvanische Kette, mathematisch Bearbeitet. Berlin, 1827. 1st Ed. 8vo, contemp calf; rubbed. Library stamp on tp; some pencil annotations. Madsen copy. S Mar 14 (275) £4,200

### Ohnefalsch-Richter, Max
— The Owl Science Literature and Art. [Nicosia, 1888]. Nos. 1-9. 4to, Sold w.a.f. S Oct 26 (69) £320 [Bank of Cyprus]

### O'Keeffe, Georgia, 1887-1986
— Georgia O'Keeffe. NY, 1976. Out-of-series copy. Folio, cloth. With 108 color plates & extra suite of 16 color plates. sg June 13 (275) $850
— Georgia O'Keeffe: One Hundred Flowers. NY, 1987. Folio, cloth, in dj. With 100 plates. sg Sept 7 (263) $60

### Olbrich, Joseph Maria
— Architektur. Berlin: Ernst Wasmuth, [1904]. 4 vols. Folio, later half sheep; worn & abraded, some joints cracked, spine ends torn. With 300 photolitho plates. Library markings; soiling affecting images; marginal dampstaining; perforated stamp on titles. cb Oct 17 (92) $3,750

### Old...
— The Old Water-Colour Society.... L, 1924-46. Vols I-XXIV. 4to, orig cloth & half bds. S Oct 27 (1002) £300 [Frazer]

**Old Etonian.** See: Terry, George W.

### Old Pretender...
— Old Pretender Scotch-Loyalty Exemplify'd, in the Behavior of the Dean of the Faculty...in relation to the Reception of a Medal of the Pretender.... L: for S. Popping, [1717]. Single sheet, 13.2 by 7.75 inches, soiled & laid down. Bound with: The Scotch Medal Decipher'd and The New Hereditary-Right Men Display'd. L, 1711. 8vo, 19th-cent calf; hinges weak. CG June 12 (1) £200

### Old, Robert O.
— Colorado... Including a Comprehensive Catalogue of Nearly Six Hundred Samples of Ores. L: British & Colorado Mining Bureau, [1869]. 8vo, modern half cloth, orig wraps bound in. Chip to corner of tp. pba Apr 25 (565) $1,000

### Old Settler
— The Garden of the World, or the Great West.... Bost., 1856. 12mo, later cloth. sg Oct 26 (86) $80

Anr copy. Orig cloth. Some foxing. sg Oct 26 (118) $80

**Oldfield, Otis.** See: Grabhorn Printing

### Oldham, James Basil
— Blind Panels of English Binders. Cambr., 1958. 1st Ed. Folio, orig cloth; some wear. O Mar 26 (195) $90
— English Blind-Stamped Bindings. Cambr., 1952. 1st Ed, one of 750. Folio, orig cloth; lower cover stained. bba May 9 (146) £55 [Besley]
— Shrewsbury School Library Bindings. Catalogue Raisonne. Oxford, 1941. ("Shrewsbury School Bindings: Catalogue Raisonne.") Proof copy. Bound in 2 vols. Folio, cloth; rubbed. Some text

creased or with minor tears. Annotated. bba May 9 (145) £1,100 [Hunt]
1st Ed. Oxford, 1943. one of 200. 4to, orig cloth; rubbed & marked, spine head damaged. ALs tipped in. bba May 9 (144) £140 [Maggs]

**Olearius, Adam**
— Des Welt-beruehmten Adami Olearii colligirte und viel vermehrte Reise-Beschreibungen.... Hamburg: Zacharias Hertel & Thomas von Wiering, 1696. 5 parts in 1 vol. Folio, contemp calf; worn. With 4 engraved titles, 5 ports & 21 double-page maps & plans & 2 full-page plates. Large folding map strengthened at folds without loss. Madsen copy. S Mar 14 (276) £1,400

**Olearius, Johannes**
— Christliche Bet-Schule auff Unterschiedliche Zeit, Personen, Verrichtungen. Nuremberg: W. E. Felssecker for G. H. Fromman, 1667. 12mo, contemp velvet, the covers with gold enamelled mounts with naturalistic flowers, the upper cover with central ornament of crowned pierced monogram IMHSZ within wreath with enamelled date 1658. C May 1 (118) £5,000

**Oleson, W. B.** See: Stevens & Oleson

**Olin, Stephen, 1797-1851**
— Travels in Egypt, Arabia Petraea, and the Holy Land. NY, 1843. 2 vols in 1. 8vo, 19th-cent half calf. With 3 maps & 12 plates. S Mar 28 (297) £240

**Olina, Giovanni Pietro**
— Uccelliera. Rome, 1684. 4to, old vellum; soiled. Lacking 26 leaves (facsimiles of text supplied). Sold w.a.f. S Mar 29 (738) £440

**Oliphant, Laurence, 1829-88**
— A Journey to Katmandu.... L, 1852. 8vo, orig bds; lacking backstrip. bba May 30 (368) £160 [Fabricant]
— Narrative of the Earl of Elgin's Mission to China and Japan.... L, 1859. 1st Ed. 2 vols. 8vo, contemp calf; rubbed. With 5 folding maps & 20 plates, some in color. b May 30 (173) £160
— The Russian Shores of the Black Sea in the Autumn of 1852.... NY, 1854. 1st American Ed. 8vo, cloth. pba July 25 (425) $50

**Oliphant, Margaret, 1828-97**
— Jerusalem. L, 1893. 8vo, calf extra by Riviere. sg Feb 8 (25) $130
— The Makers of Florence. L, 1903. 8vo, vellum gilt with 4 hand-painted miniature ports, by Giulio Giannini. sg Sept 21 (85) $700

**Oliver, Stephen, the Younger.** See: Chatto, William Andrew

**Olivier, Eugene —& Others**
— Manuel de l'amateur de reliures armoriees francaises. Paris, 1924-38. One of 1,000 on velin. 30 vols, including Index. 4to, loose in orig wraps; some torn. bba Oct 5 (139) £600 [Lamstead]

— Manuel de reliures armoriees francaises. Paris, 1924-35. Vols I-XXIX (of 30). 4to, wrapper portfolios; loose as issued. lacks index. sg Apr 11 (56) $700

**Olmstead, Frederick Law, 1822-1903**
— Yosemite and the Mariposa Grove: A Preliminary Report, 1865 Yosemite National Park: Yosemite Association, [1993]. One of 100. Intro by Victoria Post Ranney. pba Feb 12 (139) $110

**Olney, J.**
— New and Improved School Atlas to Accompany the Practical System of Modern Geography. NY, 1837. 4to, orig wraps; stained. With 13 hand-colored plates, some of them double-page. No text. sg Dec 7 (39) $150

**Olschki, Leo Samuel**
— Choix de livres anciens rares et curieux.... Florence, 1907-36 & Rome, 1940. 13 vols, including supplement. Ck Apr 12 (263) £700
— Le Livre en Italie a travers les siecles. Florence, 1914. 4to, orig wraps, in dj. Z Jan 30 (126) $100

**Olsen, Tillie**
— Tell Me a Riddle. [NY, 1978]. One of 100. pba Jan 25 (277) $60

**Olson, Charles —& Creeley, Robert**
— Charles Olson & Robert Creeley: The Complete Correspondence. Santa Barbara: Black Sparrow Press, 1980-82. One of 250. 4 vols. Half cloth. pba Jan 25 (278) $130

**Olympic Games**
— Die Olympischen Spiele 1936 in Berlin und Garmisch-Partenkirchen. Berlin, 1936. 2 vols. 4to, orig cloth with orig viewer. cb Feb 14 (2798) $325

Anr copy. Vol II only. Orig cloth; edges worn. wa Feb 1 (278) $55
— Report of the American Olympic Committee: Games of the XIth Olympiad, Berlin Germany August 1 to 16, 1936.... NY, 1936. Ed by Frederick W. Rubien. pba Aug 8 (535) $120

**Omar Khayyam, d. c.1123.** See: Golden Cockerel Press; Gregynog Press; Limited Editions Club

### The Rubaiyat
— 1872. - L. 4to, in Doves bdg designed by T. J. Cobden-Sanderson, bound by Charles Wilkinson & finished by Charles McLeish, 1903. Lacking 1st & last blanks. C May 1 (117) £1,600
— 1899. - L. 8vo, ornate calf gilt bdg by Cedric Chivers. b May 30 (571) £500
— 1900. - Bost. One of 300. Half cloth. sg Sept 14 (319) $140
— 1903 [1904]. - L: De la More Press Trans by Edward Fitzgerald; illus by Blanche McManus. 4to, contemp mor by Ramage, elaborately tooled & gilt. With 12 hand-colored illusts. Reprint of the 1st Ed of 1859. sg Apr 18 (165) $500

— [1909]. - L: Hodder & Stoughton Illus by Edmund Dulac. 4to, orig cloth. With 20 colored plates. b Sept 20 (615) £120; b May 30 (430) £120
Copy numbered 0000 & sgd by Dulac. Orig vellum gilt. sg Oct 19 (77) $650
One of 750. Orig vellum gilt. bba Sept 7 (382) £500 [M. Edwards]
Anr copy. With 20 colored plates. S Nov 2 (82) £440 [Hirsch]; S May 16 (108) £440
— [1909]. - L. Illus by Willy Pogany. Folio, mor extra by Riviere, with onlaid design of Eve in the Garden of Eden. CE Sept 27 (226) $1,400
— [1909]. - NY: Crowell Illus by Willy Pogany. sg Feb 15 (238) $80
— 1913. - L. One of 250. Illus by Rene Bull. 4to, mor gilt by Zaehnsdorf for Asprey. CE Sept 27 (66) $650
— [c.1915]. - L. Illus by Edmund Dulac. 4to, cloth, in repaired dj. sg Feb 15 (98) $225
— 1916. - L: Leonard Jay One of 100. 8vo, mor extra by G. Hedberg of Stockholm, 1925. b May 30 (572) £400
— 1920. - L: Constable & Co. One of 50. Illus by Ronald Balfour. 4to, orig cloth. b Jan 31 (197) £750
— 1930. - L. One of 750. Illus by Willy Pogany. 4to, mor gilt. With 12 colored plates. b May 30 (576) £180
— 1973. - L. One of 75. Illus by Susan Allix. 4to, mor by Sangorski & Sutcliffe. sg Sept 14 (20) $1,000
— 1980. - L. One of 200. 2 vols. 4to, mor gilt by Sangorski & Sutcliffe. b Sept 20 (633) £170

**O'Meara, Barry Edward, 1786-1836**
— Napoleon in Exile; or, a Voice from St. Helena. L, 1888. ("Napoleon at St. Helena.") 2 vols. 8vo, half calf by MacDonald. With 1 plain & 5 colored plates. pba Mar 7 (194) $110

**Omont, Henri.** See: Carey & Omont

**Omwake, John**
— Conestoga Six-Horse Bell Teams of Eastern Pennsylvania. Cincinnati, 1930. 4to, cloth; bumped. Ls laid in & with related material. pba Aug 8 (536) $100

**On the Ambitious Projects**
— On the Ambitious Projects in regard to North West America... by an Englishman. San Francisco: Book Club of California, 1955. One of 400. Bds. With frontis map after Robert Greenhow's 1840 map. Larson copy. pba Sept 28 (116) $120

**Onassis copy, Jacqueline Bouvier Kennedy**
— East Side House Winter Antiques Show... Seventh Regiment Armory... January 19th through January 25th, 1962. NY, [1962]. Cloth with supralibros of Mrs. John F. Kennedy; bumped. P Apr 23 (172) $7,000
— In the Russian Style. NY, [1976]. Half calf gilt. With 2 other copies of the work, in d/j & in wraps. P Apr 23 (211) $3,000
— Inaugural Addresses of the Presidents of the United States from George Washington 1789 to John F.
Kennedy 1961. Wash., 1961. Orig wraps; residue from removed bookplate. John F. Kennedy's copy, with his own address marked & corrected in his own hand & with his wife's note that this was done at Hyannis in July 1963. P Apr 23 (51) $120,000
— Inauguration of the British Memorial to John F. Kennedy by Her Majesty Queen Elizabeth II at Runnymede on the 14th May 1965. L, [1965]. Mor gilt by Tollit & Harvey with supralibros of Jacqueline Bouvier Kennedy. Extra-illus with 8 tipped-in silverprint photographs. P Apr 23 (50) $3,000
— Memorial Addresses in the Congress of the United States and Tributes in Eulogy of John Fitzgerald Kennedy, Late a President of the United States. Wash., 1964. Mor gilt with title, federal eagle & supralibros of Mrs. John F. Kennedy. P Apr 23 (189) $30,000
— Oratio Dominica. Parma: Franco Maria Ricci, 1967. Copy for Mrs. John F. Kennedy, dated 30 Jan 1967 & bearing signatures of Pope Paul VI & U Thant. 2 vols. Folio, mor gilt with papal arms. P Apr 23 (195) $4,000
— The White House: An Historic Guide. Wash., 1962. Mor gilt with initials J.B.K., orig paper covers bound in. P Apr 23 (201) $11,000
ACHESON, DEAN. - Power and Diplomacy. Cambr. MA, 1958. In chipped dj. Annotated throughout by John F. Kennedy. P Apr 23 (50L) $21,000
BABB, JAMES TINKHAM. - The White House Library: A Short-Title List. Wash., 1967. One of 300. Sgd by Onassis on front free endpaper. P Apr 23 (47) $8,000
BEMELMANS, LUDWIG. - On Board Noah's Ark. NY, [1962]. 4to, half cloth in dj. Inscr "To Jackie with love, Love Ludwig". P Apr 23 (180) $4,500
BEN-GURION, DAVID. - Israel: Years of Challenge. NY, 1963. In dj. Inscr "To Mrs. Jacqueline B. Kennedy with deep admiration. D. Ben-Gurion, Sdeh-Boker, 18.12.63". P Apr 23 (193) $54,000
BETJEMAN, SIR JOHN. - Summoned by Bells. L, 1960. 1st Ed. Orig cloth, in dj. Inscr "Christmas 1960. For Jackie, with love on a memorable Xmas. John". P Apr 23 (205) $5,000
BILLINGS, LEMOYNE. - Creative America. NY: Ridge Press, 1962. Inscr to her by Billings & sgd by her "Jacqueline Kennedy, March 28, 1963". P Apr 23 (191) $4,000
CAPOTE, TRUMAN. - Selected Writings. NY, [1963]. Orig cloth, in repaired dj. Inscr "for Jackie with Truman's admiration and affection, 5 June 1963". P Apr 23 (207) $6,000
CASTAREDE, J. - A Complete Treatise on the Conjugation of French Verbs. Phila.: David McKay, [n.d.]. Orig cloth wraps; frayed. Sgd "Jacqueline Bouvier, Form 2, Tel - Woodley 4020" on front cover, & with fashion sketches. P Apr 23 (166) $37,000
CERVANTES SAAVEDRA, MIGUEL DE. - The History and Adventures of the Renowned Don Quixote.... L, 1755. Trans by Tobias Smollett. 2 vols. 4to, contemp calf; rebacked. Inscr "To Jacqueline From her Man of La Mancha in the winter of our Quest. D.". P Apr 23 (208) $5,000
CHURCHILL, RANDOLPH SPENCER. - Lord Derby. L, 1959. In worn dj. Inscr "Jacqueline, with love from Ran-

dolph. Washington, June 1960". P Apr 23 (188) $5,500

DE ANDREA, MIGUEL. - Pensamiento Cristiano y Democratico de Monsenor de Andrea. Buenos Aires: Imprenta del Congreso de la Nacion, 1965. Mor gilt. Inscr to her by the Vice President of Argentina, Carlos Perette, 5 Apr 1966. P Apr 23 (199) $2,000

EBAN, ABBA. - Heritage: Civilization and the Jews. NY: Summit, [1984]. In dj. Inscr to her by Eban, 17 Jan 1990. P Apr 23 (192) $6,000

HAMMER, ARMAND. - The Quest of the Romanoff Treasure. NY: Paisley Press, 1936. In dj. Inscr to President & Mrs. Kennedy, 15 Sept 1961. P Apr 23 (679) $11,000

HOLT, J. C. - Magna Carta. Cambr., 1965. One of 3 specially bound by the pbr for presentation. Mor gilt. Presentation slip from Cambridge University Press laid in. P Apr 23 (190) $5,000

JACKSON, ABRAHAM VALENTINE WILLIAMS. - History of India. L, [1906-7]. Baroda Ed. 9 vols. 8vo, orig cloth; bumped. P Apr 23 (661) $2,500

KENNEDY, JOHN F. - The John F. Kennedy Memorial at Runnymede: Dedicatory Remarks May Fourteenth, Nineteen Hundred Sixty-Five. Pvtly ptd & bound for Mrs. John F. Kennedy, Dec 1965. One of 100. Calf gilt with presidential seal. P Apr 23 (186) $4,000

KENNEDY, JOHN F. - Profiles in Courage. NY, 1964. Memorial Ed, One of 2 specially bound, this for Mrs. John F. Kennedy. Mor extra. P Apr 23 (48) $60,000

KENNEDY, JOHN F. - Why England Slept. NY, 1940. 1st Ed. Dedication copy with Rose Kennedy's bookplate & presidential bookplate of John F. Kennedy. P Apr 23 (49) $40,000

KUNHARDT, PHILIP B. - Lincoln. NY, 1992. In dj. Inscr to Mrs. Onassis, Christmas 1992; also sgd by collaborators Philip B. Kunhardt III & Peter W. Kunhardt. With picture of group of Union officers including Capt. John Vernon Bouvier, sent to Mrs. Onassis by Kunhardt. P Apr 23 (196) $4,000

LAYARD, SIR AUSTEN HENRY. - The Monuments of Nineveh. Series I & II. L, 1849-53. Vol I only. Contemp half mor; worn. With litho title & 99 plates, 4 hand-colored & mtd on heavier stock. Some dampstaining. P Apr 23 (668) $2,250

LIBERMAN, ALEXANDER. - Greece: Gods and Art. NY, 1968. In dj. Inscr "To Jacqueline Onassis, with profound admiration" by Liberman. P Apr 23 (177) $3,500

MACKENZIE, SIR EDWARD MONTAGUE COMPTON. - On Moral Courage. L: Collins, 1962. In stained dj. On front free endpaper are the then Mrs. Kennedy's holograph notes about her meeting with Charles De Gaulle. P Apr 23 (50N) $9,500

MAILER, NORMAN. - Harlot's Ghost. NY, 1991. In dj. Inscr to her by Mailer, Sept 1991. P Apr 23 (176) $10,000

MANCHESTER, WILLIAM. - Portrait of a President. Bost., 1962. In dj. Inscr to Mrs. Kennedy, 11 Nov 1962. P Apr 23 (194) $9,850

MCCARTHY, JOE. - The Remarkable Kennedys. NY: Dial Press, 1960. In dj. Inscr to Jack & Jackie Kennedy. P Apr 23 (187) $5,500

MORYSON, FYNES. - An Itinerary.... L, 1617. 1st Ed. Folio, contemp mor gilt; extremities worn. Inscr to her by John Fleming, June 1984. Formerly the Boies Penrose copy. P Apr 23 (181) $4,000

MUGRIDGE, DONALD H. - The Presidents of the United States 1789-1962: A Selected List of References. Wash.: Library of Congress, 1963. Mor gilt with emblem of the Library of Congress & supralibros Jacqueline Bouvier Kennedy. P Apr 23 (204) $12,000

MUNNINGS, SIR ALFRED. - Pictures of Horses and English Life. L, 1927. 4to, orig cloth; rubbed & shaken. With her note saying that Hugh Auchincloss gave the book to her because she loved it when growing up at Merrywood. P Apr 23 (218) $15,000

PARKER, FRED G. - Forty-Minute Plays from Shakespeare. NY, 1939. Orig cloth; endpapers with erasures & annotations. Sgd "J. Bouvier" in pencil & with passages marked & notes of her grades on rear free endpaper. P Apr 23 (210) $10,000

PARKS, FANNY. - Wanderings of a Pilgrim in Search of the Picturesque. L, 1850. 2 vols. 8vo, contemp mor gilt. With 49 (of 50) plates, some hand-colored. P Apr 23 (675) $2,750

RAJAH RAM CHUTTRAPUTTEE. - Diary of the late Rajah of Kolhapoor, during his Visit to Europe in 1870. L, 1872. Ed by Edward W. West. Contemp mor gilt; extremities rubbed. With accomplished presentation leaf forwarding the book to Mrs. Borthwick from the family of the late Rajah of Kolhapur. P Apr 23 (663) $3,250

ROWSE, A. L. - Homosexuals in History. NY: Macmillan, [1977]. In dj. With holograph notes by Mrs. Onassis on rear flyleaves & free endpaper. P Apr 23 (182) $4,500

SLOANE, ERIC. - Remember America. NY, 1975. Inscr, 1984, "To the J. K. O. Library, with infinite admiration" & with large drawing of covered bridge on front free endpaper. P Apr 23 (168) $3,000

SOONG, MEI-LING (MME. CHIANG KAI-SHEK). - Selected Speeches, 1958-1959. Taipei, 1959. With: The Sure Victory. Westwood NJ, 1965. Both in dj. Inscr to Mrs Kennedy, Dec 1964. P Apr 23 (197) $10,000

STEVENSON, ADLAI E. - What I. Think. NY, [1956]. Inscr to John F. Kennedy, 26 Feb 1956. P Apr 23 (50M) $27,000

TATUM, GEORGE B. - Penn's Great Town: 250 Years of Philadelphia Architecture Illustrated.... Phila., [1961]. One of 200, this copy 2. Orig cloth with seal of City of Philadelphia, in cloth folding case with supralibros Mrs. John F. Kennedy. With ptd & calligraphic inscr to her, sgd by Mayor Richardson Dilworth & City Representative F. R. Mann. P Apr 23 (175) $28,000

UNITED STATES CAPITOL HISTORICAL SOCIETY. - We, the People: The Story of the United States Capitol. Wash., 1963. Mor gilt with Mrs. Kennedy stamped in gilt on upper cover, orig wraps bound in. P Apr 23 (184) $2,500

**Onassis, Jacqueline Bouvier Kennedy, 1929-94 — & Radziwill, Lee Bouvier**

— One Special Summer. NY, 1974. Out-of-series copy belonging to Mrs. Onassis. P Apr 23 (167) $8,000

## Ondaatje, Michael
— The Collected Works of Billy the Kid. Toronto: Anasi Press, 1970. Wraps. pba Jan 25 (282) $90
— The Dainty Monsters. Toronto: Coach House Press, [1967]. 2d Ed. Wraps. Sgd on tp. pba Jan 25 (283) $110
— The English Patient. L, 1992. Uncorrected Proof copy. Wraps. pba Jan 25 (284) $90

## O'Neal, Hank
— Berenice Abbott, American Photographer. NY, [1982]. In dj. pba Aug 8 (560) $55
Anr copy. In worn dj. Sgd by Abbott. sg Feb 29 (1) $250

## O'Neill, Eugene, 1888-1953
See also: Limited Editions Club
— Ah, Wilderness! NY, [1933]. One of 325. Calf; spine ends rubbed. sg Dec 14 (234) $175
— Anna Christie. NY, 1930. One of 775. Illus by Alexander King. 4to, orig bds, in soiled & wrinkled dj. F Mar 28 (319) $110
Anr copy. Half cloth; def. sg Dec 14 (232) $250
— Dynamo. NY, 1929. One of 775. Vellum; bowed. pba May 23 (329) $60; sg Dec 14 (229) $50
— The Emperor Jones. NY, 1928. One of 775 L.p. copies. Illus by Alexander King. 4to, half cloth. With 8 colored plates. sg Dec 14 (228) $200
— The Emperor Jones. Diff'rent. The Straw. NY, [1921]. 1st Ed. In soiled dj. sg June 20 (303) $150
— The Great God Brown. The Fountain. The Moon of the Caribbees and other Plays. NY, 1926. 1st Ed. Cloth; rubbed & askew, rear hinge cracked. Inscr. sg Dec 14 (224) $250
— The Hairy Ape. NY, 1929. One of 775 L.p. copies. Illus by Alexander King. 4to, half cloth, in dj. rms Nov 30 (259) $300
Anr copy. Half cloth. sg Dec 14 (231) $200
— Lazarus Laughed. NY, 1927. One of 775. Half vellum; def. sg Dec 14 (225) $90
— Marco Millions. NY, 1927. 1st Ed, One of 450. Half vellum; def. sg Dec 14 (226) $150
— Mourning Becomes Electra. NY, [1931]. One of 550. Vellum. sg Dec 14 (233) $250
Anr copy. Vellum gilt, unopened. Bookplate of Detroit Public Library on front pastedown. Sgd by O'Neill & by 20 cast members, including Nazimova. sg June 20 (304) $950
— Strange Interlude. NY, 1928. Cloth, in repaired dj. sg June 20 (305) $140
One of 775. Orig vellum over bds; soiled. pba Oct 5 (290) $130; sg Dec 14 (227) $180

## O'Neill, Rose
— The Loves of Edwy. Bost., [1904]. Orig cloth; worn & dusty. Inscr. O July 9 (149) $90

## Ongania, Ferdinando, 1842-1911
— L'Arte della Stampa nel Rinascimento Italiano Venezia. Venice, 1894. 4to, contemp half vellum. sg Apr 11 (157) $50
— Calli e canali in Venezia. [Venice], 1891-96. Bound in 1 vol. Folio, later half mor; extremities worn, spine ends worn away & def, joints cracked. With photolitho title & 110 photogravure plates. Marginal notes in pencil; marginal soiling. cb Oct 17 (53) $450

## Onis, Luis de, 1769-1830
— Memoria sobre las Negociaciones entre Espana y los Estados-Unidos de America. Madrid, 1820. Part 1. Sq 8vo, later half calf. With folding map. sg Oct 26 (282) $375
Anr Ed. Madrid, 1826. Part 1. Sq 8vo, old calf; hinges starting. With 15 folding charts in rear. Met May 22 (361) $600

## Open...
— The Open Window. L, 1910-11. Nos 1-12 Ptd wraps. Ck Nov 17 (131) £240
Anr copy. Nos 1-12, bound in 2 vols. Orig cloth, 1 vol in dj. Ck Nov 17 (132) £240
Anr copy. Nos 1-12 Ptd wraps; spines browned & chipped. Ck Apr 12 (163) £150

## Opera moralissima...
— Opera moralissima de diversi auctori.... Venice: Georgio di Ruschoni ad instantia di Nicolo Zopino & Vincenzo compagni, 28 Nov 1516. 8vo, 19th-cent mor gilt. Large woodcut on tp. Lacking final blank. C June 26 (108) £1,100

## Operation...
— Operation Deep Freeze, 1957-1958: The Story of Task Force 43 and its Service to Science...IGY Antarctic Program. Paoli PA: Dorville, [1958]. pba July 25 (376) $80

## Opie, Amelia Alderson, 1769-1853
— The Negro Boy's Tale.... Norwich, 1824. 8vo, orig wraps. Tp browned. b Dec 5 (252) £200

## Oppenort, Gille Marie
— Livres de fragments d'architecture recueillis et dessines a Rome d'apres les plus beaux Monuments. Paris: Huquier, [c.1725]. 8vo, contemp calf; spine heel repaired, lettering-piece renewed. With 14 suites of 168 plates, each composed of 3 leaves with 6 2-part plates. Fuerstenberg - Schaefer copy. S Dec 8 (467) £3,000

## Oppianus
— De piscibus libri V. Eiusdem de venatione libri IIII. Venice: Aldus, 1517. 8vo, 18th-cent calf gilt with arms of the Foscarini family; joints & corners rubbed. Jeanson 1392. C Apr 3 (164) £4,000

## Oratio...
— Oratio Dominica CL Linguis Versa. Paris, 1805. 4to, contemp calf. sg Oct 19 (142) $2,000; sg Oct 19 (142) $2,000
— Oratio Dominica Polyglottos.... L: Dan. Brown et al., 1713. 4to, modern cloth. sg Mar 21 (208) $325

## Orcutt, William Dana
— The Kingdom of Books. Bost., 1927. One of 475. pba Aug 8 (330) $70

**Orczy, Emmuska, Baroness, 1865-1947**
— The Elusive Pimpernel. L, 1908. Cloth; skewed, ink signature on front cover. sg Dec 14 (235) $50

**Ordem de Sanctiaguo.** See: Military Order of Santiago

**Ordeman, John T.**
— To Keep a Tryst with the Dawn: An Appreciation of Roland Clark. Henderson NC, [1989]. One of 100. 4to, half lea; some wear. O Oct 10 (209) $70

**Orden...**
— Orden de las oraciones cotidianas. Amst., 1733. Bound with: Cinco libros de la Ley Divina. Amst., 1733. 8vo, later mor gilt over wooden bds; bowed. Upper margins cut close, affecting running heads. CE Dec 6 (129) $1,700
Anr Ed. Amst., 1734. 32mo, mor gilt. CE Dec 6 (130) $4,800
Anr Ed. Amst., 1772. 12mo, modern lea. Lacking ginal leaf; R1, R8 & R9 with horizontal tears crossing text; some tears tape-repaired; browning & staining. CE Dec 6 (213) $600
— Orden de los cinco Tahaniot. Amst., 1648. 8vo, modern lea. Tp chipped in upper margin & repaired with cellotape; some staining & browning; early marginalia. CE Dec 6 (210) $1,600
— Orden de Ros Asanah y Kypur. Amst.: Joria Trigg for Yona Abravanel & Efraim Bueno, 1652. 8vo, modern lea. Worming in 1st 4 gatherings affecting letters; A8 with gutter margin renewed & tape-repaired; browned & stained. CE Dec 6 (211) $380

**Ordre...**
— The Ordre or Trayne of War. L: R. Wyer for J. Gough, [c.1540]. 8vo, 18th-cent mor gilt. 24 lines; catchwords; no headlines or foliation; 2 woodcut initials & 5 woodcut illusts. Minor damage with loss of margin at top right corners of ff. g1-4. "Only known copy" of STC 18841.7. S Dec 18 (116) £11,000 [Quaritch]

**Ordre de St. Michel**
— Statuts de l'Ordre de St. Michel. Paris, 1725. 4to, contemp mor gilt with arms of France. Some browning. Fuerstenberg - Schaefer copy. S Dec 8 (582) £1,600

**Oregon**
— The Resources of Southern Oregon: Statistical Information.... Salem, 1890. Orig wraps; stamp at bottom of front wrap & tp, front wrap foxed. pba Nov 16 (204) $75

**Oregon Pioneer Association**
— Constitution and Quotations from the Register.... Salem OR, 1875. Bound with: Transactions of the Third [-Fourteenth] Annual Re-Union, 1876-87. And: indexes. Contemp half sheep; worn & rubbed. pba Nov 16 (203) $300

**Oribasius Sardianus**
— Collectorum medicinalium libri XVII.... Paris: Bernard Turrisan, 1555. 8vo, lea; rebound. Dampstained. CE Nov 8 (126) $130

**Oriental Ceramics...**
— Oriental Ceramics: The World's Great Collections. Tokyo, [1980-82]. 10 (of 11) vols. 4to, orig cloth. S Mar 28 (430) £500

**Original...**
— Original Etchings by American Artists. NY: Cassell, [1883]. Folio, orig cloth; worn & soiled. With 20 plates. Marginal soiling; dampstain to bottom margins of 2 plates. wa Nov 16 (579) $700

**Orland, Ted**
— Man & Yosemite. A Photographer's View of the Early Years. Santa Cruz: The Image Continuum Press, [1986]. One of 250 with tipped-in photo & sgd. In dj. pba Feb 12 (140) $170

**Orlando, Matteo**
— Directorium chori. Rome: Jacomo Fei, 1668. 4to, contemp blindstamped calf with central feature of Virgin & child; rebacked, torn on lower cover. Foot of tp cut away & repaired; some browning; small tear on O4. S Dec 1 (265) £500

**Orleans, Anne d', Duchesse de Montpensier**
— Memoires. Londres [but Paris], 1746. 7 vols. 12mo, contemp calf; worn. Joseph "Consul" Smith's copy. bba May 9 (51) £65 [O'Keefe]

**Orleans, Charles, Duc d', 1394-1465**
— Poemes. Paris, 1950. One of 1,230. Illus by Henri Matisse. Folio, mor, orig wraps bound in. S Nov 21 (75) £1,200

**Orleans, Jean**
— La Genealogie des illustres Comtes de Nassau. Leiden, 1615. Folio, contemp sewn bds without covering; worn. With 40 double-page plates & 1 double-page map; title within engraved historiated architectural border, with Nassau arms on verso. sg Mar 7 (181) $600

**Orleans Collection, Louis, Duc d'**
— Description des principales pierres gravees du cabinet de.... Paris, 1780-84. 2 vols. Folio, contemp red mor gilt with added arms of Louise Marie Adelaide de Bourbon Penthievre, duchesse d'Orleans; joints weak, spine of Vol II chipped at head. With frontis & 179 plates. Without the 7 medal plates. Fuerstenberg - Schaefer copy. S Dec 7 (324) £500

**Orlers, Jan —&**
**Haestens, Henrik van**
— The Triumphs of Nassau. L, 1613. Folio, contemp calf gilt with initials I & S; covers detached, endpapers renewed. Blank corner off 2N3. sg Mar 7 (180) $325

**Orme, Edward**
— Collection of British Field Sports.... [Guildford: Chas. W. Traylen, 1955]. Ltd Ed. Oblong folio, orig half mor. Facsimile of the 1807 Ed. b Sept 20 (486) £220
— Historic, Military, and Naval Anecdotes.... L, [1819]. 4to, contemp half mor; worn. With 40 colored

plates. 1 plate watermarked 1831 & torn in margin; 1 plate detached along lower plate mark. b June 28 (49) £1,300

Anr copy. Half mor gilt; hinges cracked, worn. With 40 plates. Foxed & browned; tear to last leaf. wd May 8 (73) $2,800

**Ormerod, George, 1785-1873**
— The History of the County Palatine and City of Chester. L, 1819. 3 vols. Folio, contemp calf gilt; worn, Vol III covers detached. With hand-colored double-page map & 48 plates, 3 of them hand-colored, 1 heightened with gold. Some spotting & browning. bba Nov 1 (29) £320 [Charwick]

2d Ed. L, 1882. 3 vols. Folio, modern cloth; later endpapers. With double-page hand-colored map & 58 plates, 2 of them hand-colored. bba Nov 1 (30) £400 [Spread Eagle]

**Ornithologia...**
— Ornithologia Nova, or a New General History of Birds. Salop & Birm., 1744. 2 vols. 12mo, 19th-cent half calf; rubbed. Tp worn & laid down; some tears & repairs; ink marks. S Nov 2 (233) £950 [Schiller]

Anr Ed. L: J. Osborn, 1745. ("New General History of Birds.") 2 vols. 12mo, modern calf. S Nov 2 (234) £400 [Temperley]

**Orosius, Paulus**
— Historiae adversus paganos. Venice: Bernardinus Venetus de Vitalibus, 1500. Folio, modern half calf. 44 lines & headline; roman letter. Some dampstaining; a1 def at head. 80 leaves. Goff O-101. S Dec 18 (63) £500 [Frew]

**O'Rourke, John, Count**
— A Treatise on the Art of War.... L, 1778. 4to, contemp calf; lower cover repaired, edge-wear. With 14 plates. bbc Feb 26 (374) $475

**Orphen, R.**
— The Comic Irish Alphabet for the Present Time. "Porkopolis" OH: Young Ireland & Co, [c.1893]. Folio, pictorial wraps. Lithographed throughout. pba Aug 22 (824) $170

**Orr, Eric**
— Zero Mass: The Art of Eric Orr. Lund, 1990. Steel, with ceramic sphere in 2-piece styrofoam box; wear to spine. Tear in 1 leaf. sg Jan 11 (329) $90

**Orsino, Cesare**
— Magistri Stopini... capriccia macaronica. Venice: Jacobus Sarzina, 1636. 12mo, old vellum. sg Mar 21 (238) $200

**Orta, Garcia da —&**
**Acosta, Cristoval de, 1597-1676?**
— Tractado de las drogas y medicinas de las Indias orientales. Burgos, 1578. 1st Ed. 4to, contemp vellum; endleaves renewed. With 46 woodcut plates & port. P Dec 12 (37) $3,750

**Ortelius, Abraham, 1527-98**
— Epitome. Antwerp: P. Galle for Christopher Plantin, 1585. ("Theatri Orbis Terrarum Enchiridion, minor tabulis.") 4to, contemp calf. With engraved allegorical illust, 5 (of 6) double-page maps & 76 miniature maps (of 77). Lacking World & America maps; some fold breaks; tp soiled & stained. C May 31 (65) £2,200

— Theatrum orbis terrarum. Antwerp, 1573. Folio, later calf; worn. With 70 double-page maps. Many maps reguarded; some browning; Map 1 repaired at left with loss; Map 3 with rusthole below title; Map 18 with repaired marginal tears, affecting surface; some worming, affecting Maps 38-40. S June 27 (81) £13,000

Anr Ed. Antwerp: Christopher Plantin, 1584. Folio, late 18th-cent russia gilt with contemp mor panels mtd on covers, armorial bdg; rubbed & scuffed, small tear to lower cover. With engraved title, port & 112 maps with contemp hand-coloring. Tp & dedication leaf repaired at outer margin; tp soiled; Ireland from a smaller copy; some rust holes; 4 maps torn at centerfold; marginal annotations in a 17th-cent hand. C May 31 (64) £30,000

Anr Ed. Antwerp: Plantin, 1595. Bound with: Ortelius. Parergon.... Antwerp: Plantin, 1595. And: Nomenclator ptolemaicus. Folio, 17th-cent mor gilt to a cottage-roof pattern, by Roger Bartlett. Theatrum with port, hand-colored engraved title & 115 hand-colored maps; Parergon with woodcut title & 31 (of 32) double-page mapsheets; lacking Aevi veteris. All 146 mapsheets hand-colored in full throughout in a contemp hand, the titles, port & 1st 5 mapsheets heightened with gold. Some centerfolds repaired, occasionally touching surface; a few tiny rustholes to surface. S June 27 (80) £109,000

Anr Ed. Antwerp: Officina Plantiniana for Jan Baptist Vrients, 1602. ("Theatro d'el orbe de la tierra.") Folio, contemp vellum over bds with covers gilt-panelled; soiled, spine damaged by damp & repaired. With engraved allegorical title, engraved arms of Philip III of spain, 120 10-line woodcut historiated initials, 33 smaller woodcut initials, woodcut historiated tailpiece, port of Ortelius & 149 maps on 120 copperplates & ptd on 117 mapsheets. Tp, arms, port, maps, all large & most small woodcut initials all colorec by a contemp hand & title heightened with gold. Rusthole to world map touching platemark; some fold breaks; a few maps with short marginal tears; some soiling. Schaefer copy. P Nov 1 (162) $130,000

Anr Ed. Antwerp, 1612. Folio, 19th-cent vellum gilt. With hand-colored title with hand-colored arms on verso, port & 127 double-page maps only, colored throughout in a contemp hand. Lacking all after the map of Morocco; some shaving; a few small holes & wear to corners of sheets & at centerfolds; some discoloration; first few quires affected by damp & with margins repaired; a section of the table of maps supplied in Ms. C May 31 (63) £42,000

Anr Ed. Florence: Giunti, 1991. One of 998. Folio, orig bds, in dj. Facsimile of 1595 Ed. Ck Apr 12 (264) £140

**Orvis, Charles F. —& Cheney, A. Nelson**
— Fishing with the Fly.... Manchester VT: Orvis, 1883. 8vo, cloth; worn, remnant of library pocket. O June 25 (203) $225

Anr copy. Orig cloth; hinges cracked, becoming disbound. pba July 11 (217) $275

**Orwell, George, 1903-50**
— Animal Farm. L, 1945. 1st Ed. In dj. With facsimiles of letters of rejection from Jonathan Cape & T. S. Eliot to Orwell's agent, Leonard P. Moore. Hobson copy. S June 28 (185) £850

1st American Ed. NY: Harcourt, Brace, [1946]. In def dj. pba Aug 22 (385) $80

Advance proof copy. Wraps; spine tanned. sg June 20 (306) $150

Anr Ed. [Munich, 1947]. ("Colgost Tvaryn.") Orig wraps; spine worn, chipped, contemp Russian newspaper review sewn to inner cover with signs of thread showing through. sg June 20 (307) $1,000

— The Collected Essays, Journalism and Letters.... L, [1968]. 1st Ed. - Ed by Sonia Orwell & Ian Angus. 4 vols. In djs. Hobson copy. pba Aug 22 (386) $130

— Coming Up for Air. L, 1939. 1st Ed. In dj with minor defs. Hobson copy. S June 28 (183) £5,500

— Critical Essays. L, 1946. Orig cloth, in chipped dj. sg June 20 (308) $90

— Dickens, Dali and Others. NY: Reynal and Hitchcock, 1946. 1st Ed. In dj. Author's copy, with 4 holograph corrections. Hobson copy. S June 28 (186) £850

— Down and Out in Paris and London. L, 1933. Hobson copy. S June 28 (180) £380

Anr Ed. NY, 1933. Orig cloth, in chipped & soiled dj. F Mar 28 (531) $140

Anr copy. Orig cloth. sg Dec 14 (236) $90

— The English People. L, 1947. Orig bds, in dj. With 8 colored plates. sg June 20 (309) $90

— Keep the Aspidistra Flying. L, 1936. 1st Ed. In dj with minor defs. Hobson copy. S June 28 (182) £600

— Nineteen Eighty-Four. L, 1949. 1st Ed. Orig cloth, in red dj with short tears. Hobson copy. S June 28 (188) £650

1st American Ed. NY, 1949. In chipped dj. pba Jan 25 (288) $85

Advance Reading Copy. Orig wraps; repaired. sg June 20 (310) $225

**Osborn, Sherard, 1822-75**
— A Cruise in Japanese Waters. L, 1859. 8vo, orig cloth. b May 30 (174) £280

**Osborne, Edgar**
— The Osborne Collection of Early Children's Books. Toronto, 1958-75. Compiled by Judith St. John. 2 vols. 8vo, orig cloth. sg Apr 11 (76) $175

**Osborne, Thomas, d.1767**
— A Collection of Voyages and Travels.... L, 1765. Vol II only. Folio, contemp calf; worn. Sold w.a.f. b May 30 (126) £680

**O'Shaughnessy, M. M.**
— Hetch Hetchy: Its Origin and History. San Francisco, 1934. One of 1,000. Folio, cloth. pba Apr 25 (563) $85

**Osler, Sir William, 1849-1919**
— Aequanimitas. Phila., 1904. 1st Ed. Orig cloth; backstrip torn, corner of front free endpaper chipped. sg May 16 (463) $110

— Bibliotheca Osleriana: a Catalogue of Books.... Montreal & L, 1969. 4to, orig cloth. bbc Feb 26 (188) $275

— Lectures on Angina Pectoris and Allied States. NY, 1901. 8vo, orig cloth; worn, rear hinge cracked. sg May 16 (462) $175

— Lectures on the Diagnosis of Abdominal Tumors. L, 1896. 8vo, cloth; spine ends chipped. pba June 20 (241) $110

— The Principles and Practice of Medicine. NY, 1893. later Issue. 8vo, orig half sheep; worn & scraped, spine top chipped, endpapers foxed. Some foxing. bbc Feb 26 (447) $250

**Osley, A. S.**
— Mercator. A Monograph on the lettering of Maps.... L, 1969. Foreward by R. A. Skelton. 4to, cloth, in soiled & torn dj. Contents & d/j rippled from dampness. pba Apr 25 (156) $120

**Osorio da Fonseca, Jeronimo, 1506-80**
— De rebus Emmanuelis regis Lusitaniae.... Cologne: heirs of Arnold Birckmann, 1574. 8vo, contemp calf; worn. Marginal tears; some staining. b Sept 20 (439) £170

**O'Sullivan, Vincent**
— The Houses of Sin. L, 1897. Ltd Ed. Illus by Aubrey Beardsley. 8vo, orig vellum gilt. S Nov 2 (75) £120 [Schonthal]

**Osumi, Tamezo**
— Printed Cottons of Asia. Tokyo & Rutland, [1963]. Folio, half cloth, in dj. With 103 mtd color plates. sg Jan 11 (417) $175

Anr copy. Half cloth, in worn dj. With 88 tipped-on color plates. wa Nov 16 (376) $120

**Oswald de Lasko**
— Sermones dominicales.... Hagenau: Heinrich Gran for J. Rymman, 17 Feb 1502. 4to, old vellum; spine repaired. Dampstaining throughout. S Mar 14 (278) £140

**Others.** See: Anthoine-Legrain & Others; Kosch & Others; Olivier & Others; Singer & Others; Totok & Others

**Otis, George A.**
— A Report on Amputations at the Hip-Joint. Wash., 1867. 4to, orig wraps; foxed & chipped, needs rebacking. With 9 litho plates, 5 of them in color. Maringal foxing. War Department, Surgeon General's Office, Circular No 7. sg May 16 (465) $60

**Ottino, Giuseppe —& Fumagall, Giuseppe**
— Bibliotheca Bibliographica Italica. Graz, 1957. 8vo, orig cloth. sg Apr 11 (243) $150

**Ottley, William Young, 1771-1836**
— The Italian School of Design. L, 1823. Folio, orig half cloth; front hinge broken & repaired. 2 text leaves & 1 plate bound upside down. wad Oct 18 (342) C$650

**Ottley, William Young, 1771-1836 —& Tomkins, Peltro William**
— Engravings of the most Noble Marquis of Stafford's Collection of Pictures. L, 1818. 4 vols in 2. Folio, contemp mor gilt. pba Sept 14 (284) $350
Anr copy. Contemp calf gilt; rubbed, bds detached. With 13 plans & 126 plates on india paper. S Apr 23 (248) £340

**Ottolander, K. J. W. —& Others**
— Nederlandsche Flora en Pomona.... Groningen, 1876-79. 2 vols. 4to, orig cloth; worn. With 81 chromoliths. Minor foxing. O Mar 5 (175) $1,800

**Ottonelli, Gian Domenico —& Berretini da Cortona, Pietro**
— Trattato della pittura, e scultura, uso, et abuso loro. Florence: Giovanni Antonio Bonardi, 1652. 4to, contemp vellum; soiled. C Apr 3 (165) £1,800

**Otway, Thomas, 1652-85.** See: Nonesuch Press

**Oudaan, Joachim**
— Roomse Moogentheid, bevat in een naauwkeurige Beschrijving van de Magt en Heerschappy der Oude Roomse Keizeren.... Leiden: Hendrik van Damme, 1723. 4to, contemp vellum; corners worn. Dampstaining in outer margins towards end, with some traces of mold. sg Mar 21 (239) $200

**Oudry, Jean Baptiste, 1686-1755**
— Collection de vingt-six Estampes, representant les scenes...du Roman Comique de Scarron. Paris: Desnos, [c.1735]. Folio, modern half mor. With 26 plates, all double-page. Fuerstenberg - Schaefer copy. S Dec 8 (574) £2,000

**Ouimet, Francis Desales, 1893-1967**
— A Game of Golf.... Bost.: Houghton Mifflin, 1932. One of 550. Intro by Bernard Darwin. Cloth in glassine. pba Apr 18 (138) $1,400
1st Ed. Cloth & glassine; spine & extrems sunned. Sgd. pba Nov 9 (65) $1,100

**Our Daily Fare**
— Our Daily Fare. Phila., 1864. Nos 1-12 (8-21 June). Folio, unbound & uncut. pba Aug 22 (594) $140

**Our Lady's Choir**
— Our Lady's Choir. A Contemporary Anthology of Verse by Catholic Sisters. Bost., 1931. One of 50 on Kelmscott handmade paper, this copy unnumbered. Ed by W. S. Brathwaite; foreword by Hugh Francis Blunt; intro by Ralph Adams Cram. 8vo, silk, unopened. O Dec 5 (21) $100

**Ouseley, Thomas John**
— A Vision of Death's Destruction. Leicester, 1837. 8vo, contemp mor gilt. Inscr. b Dec 5 (231) £100

**Outerbridge, Paul**
— Photographing in Color. [NY, 1940]. 1st Ed. 4to, cloth, in chipped dj. pba Aug 8 (561) $100
Anr copy. Cloth; worn & soiled. Some foxing. sg Feb 29 (233) $80
— A Singular Aesthetic, Photographs & Drawings 1921-1941. Santa Barbara, 1981. One of 1,500. Folio, cloth, in dj. sg Feb 29 (234) $350

**Overbeke, Bonaventura ab**
— Reliquiae antiquae urbis Romae.... Amst., 1708. 3 vols in 1. Folio, 19th-cent half mor; edges rubbed. With frontis, double-page map & 146 plates, 1 double-page. Library stamp on each plate. S Nov 30 (06) £1,600

**Overland...**
— The Overland Monthly, Devoted to the Development of the Country. San Francisco, 1868. Vol 1, Nos 1-6. 8vo, orig cloth; hinges cracked, lacking free endpapers, rear leaf (flyleaf or final text page) & general title. Last 100 pages stained. pba Dec 14 (182) $325
Anr Ed. San Francisco, 1868-75. Ed by Bret Harte. Vols I-XV (complete run). 15 vols. 8vo, orig wraps in half mor slipcases; wraps darkened & worn, some spines worn. Robbins copy. pba Mar 21 (268) $3,500

**Ovid, 43 B.C.-17? A.D.**
See also: Limited Editions Club
— L'Art d'aimer. Paris, 1923. One of 22 on japon with 2 additional suites & an orig watercolor. Illus by Andre Lambert. 4to, mor extra with onlays in fruit design by Creuzevault. S Nov 21 (336) £750
Anr Ed. [Lausanne: Philippe Gonin, 1935]. One of 225, this copy with additional suite of the lithos in sanguine & impressions of 3 of the woodcuts avant champlevure. Illus by Aristide Maillol. Folio, mor extra with geometric patterns, by Pierre Legrain. With 12 lithos & 15 woodcuts (including initials & cover design). Bound in are 4 drawings by Maillol on 2 sheets. S Nov 21 (337) £7,000
— Elegies. L, 1925. One of 625. Trans by Christopher Marlowe, together with the Epigrams of Sir John Davies; illus by John Nash. Half calf by Bayntun. bba May 9 (590) £80 [Deighton Bell]
— Epistolae heroidum. Toscolano: Alexandrus Paganinus, 1533. 4to, 19th-cent half calf gilt; backstrip partly detached. sg Mar 21 (243) $500
— Fastorum libri.... Toscolano: Alexandrus Paganinus, 1527. 4to, 19th-cent half calf gilt; joints starting. Repaired wormholes in lower margins, occasionally entering text. sg Mar 21 (242) $450
— Heroidum epistolae. Verona: Bodoni, 1953. ("Heroides.") One of 166. Illus by Francesco Messina. Folio, orig half vellum. Ck May 31 (17) £300

— Opera. Venice: Aldus, 1516. ("Annotationes in omnia Ouidij opera.") 8vo, early vellum; soiled. Wormhole affecting final 50 leaves. Francis Throckmorton's copy. b June 28 (69) £450

Anr Ed. Leiden: Officina Hackiana, 1670. 3 vols. 8vo, vellum gilt sgd by Bozerian jeune. With 3 engraved titles, port & 15 full-page illusts in text. Fuerstenberg - Schaefer copy. S Dec 8 (468) £1,800

— Tristium libri.... Toscolano: Alexandrus Paganinus, 1526. 4to, 19th-cent half calf gilt; joints cracked. sg Mar 21 (241) $300

### English Versions of Metamorphoses

— Metamorphoses. L, 1717. Folio, contemp sheep; extremities worn, needs rebacked. Browned. sg Mar 21 (245) $475

— Shakespeare's Ovid, being Arthur Golding's translation of the Metamorphoses edited by W. H. D. Rouse. L: De La More Press, 1904. King's Library Ed, One of 350. Folio, orig half cloth. bba May 9 (483) £75 [Collinge & Clark]

— 1732. - Amst. 2 vols in 1. Folio, later calf; rebacked, joints weak. sg Mar 21 (247) $800

### French Versions of Metamorphoses

— Les Metamorphoses. Bruges: Colard Mansion, May 1484. Bound in 2 vols. Folio, calf over wooden bds, covered with red velvet. 33 lines; double column; type 1:162B; rubricated. With 16 (of 17) page-width woodcuts & 12 (of 17) column-width woodcuts. Leaf 31/5 supplied from a shorter copy, but rubricated by same hand; some worming & waterstaining. 368 (of 389) leaves; lacking quires 1-2. Goff O-184. Schaefer copy. P Nov 1 (164) $55,000

Anr copy. 1 leaf only: D7. Folio. Piece torn from inner margin. Schaefer collection. P Nov 1 (165) $700

— Les metamorphoses. Paris, 1738. 2 vols. 4to, contemp calf; rubbed. With 133 illus. S Oct 27 (1150) £430 [Zioni]

— Traduction des fastes...avec des notes...par M. Bayeux. Rouen, 1783-88. 4 vols. 4to, 19th-cent calf gilt. With frontis & 6 plates. Marginal worming in Vol I; marginal dampstains in Vol II. L.p. copy. Fuerstenberg - Schaefer copy. S Dec 8 (478) £320

### Italian Versions of Metamorphoses

— Le Trasformationi. Venice: G. Giolito, 1553. Trans by Lodovico Dolce. 4to, vellum; rebacked with cloth. Tp soiled. CE May 22 (369) $320

— La Vita et metamorfoseo.... Lyons: G. de Tournes, 1559. 8vo, 18th-cent calf with peacock-feather decoration painted on edges. Some inkstains & annotations. S June 12 (85) £800

### Latin & French Versions of Metamorphoses

— Les Metamorphoses. Amst., 1732. 2 vols in 1. Folio, lea gilt; worn & broken. Foxed. NH Sept 16 (157) $475

Anr copy. Contemp red mor gilt; rubbed. With frontis & 124 illusts in text plus 6 inserted plates. Some leaves browned & spotted. Fuerstenberg - Schaefer copy. S Dec 8 (469) £1,000

Anr Ed. Paris, 1767-71. 4 vols. 4to, 18th-cent mor gilt; some wear & scratching, upper hinge of Vol I split. With frontis & 139 plates. Marginal tears repaired. S June 27 (355) £1,500

Anr Ed. Paris, 1771. 4 vols. 4to, contemp mor gilt by Bradel-Derome. With 141 plates & the "fin des estampes". Fuerstenberg - Schaefer copy. S Dec 8 (472) £5,500

Anr Ed. Paris, 1806. One of 2 ptd on vellum, with plates before letters on chine. 4 vols. 4to, contemp mor gilt by Bradel; Vol I stitching weak. With frontis & 3 plates in prelims of Vol I & 135 numbered plates ptd on chine & pasted to vellum leaves. Minor discoloration. Fuerstenberg - Schaefer copy. S Dec 8 (475) £9,500

### Latin Versions of Metamorphoses

— Metamorphoses. Toscolano: A. Paganini, 1526. 4to, 19th-cent half calf gilt; backstrip detached. Some soiling & staining; lacking final blank. sg Mar 21 (240) $700

Anr Ed. Antwerp: Plantin, 1591. 8vo, modern mor gilt. With engraved title, port & 178 plates. Minor staining; repaired tear in a2. Schaefer copy. P Nov 1 (166) $3,000

— 1583. - Metamorphoses Ovidii. Paris 16mo, old vellum; backstrip cracked. With 172 (of 178) woodcut illusts in text. Tp soiled, torn & partly repaired; erotic woodcuts on H1r & H2r inked over; lacking I2-7. Sold w.a.f. sg Mar 21 (244) $60

**Oviedo y Valdes, Gonzalo Fernandez de.** See: Limited Editions Club

**Ovington, John**
— An Essay upon the Nature and Qualities of Tea. L, 1699. 1st Ed. 8vo, later half calf; rubbed. With frontis. Frontis & title browned; lacking blank A1. Ck Mar 22 (214) £550

**Ovington, Mary White**
— The Shadow. NY, 1920. sg Mar 28 (226) $90

**Owen, John, of the Middle Temple —& Bowen, Emanuel, d.1767**
— Britannia Depicta or Ogilby Improv'd. L, 1730. 8vo, contemp sheep; needs rebdg. With engraved title, 2 leaves of engraved contents & 136 engraved leaves of road maps. sg May 9 (92) $850

Anr Ed. L, 1764. 8vo, contemp half calf; worn, rebacked. With 273 road maps on 137 sheets. Maps 174 & 175 duplicated in place of maps 178 & 179; tp & 1st leaf loose. pn Dec 7 (180) £540

**Owen, Major John, 1818-89**
— The Journals and Letters of.... NY, 1927. One of 50 L.p. copies. 2 vols. Half vellum, unopened. O Dec 5 (106) $500

1st Ed, One of 50 L.p. sets. Ed by Seymour Dunbar. 2 vols. Half vellum. With 30 plates & 2 folding maps. Robbins copy. Inscr from Edward Eberstadt to Frederick Beinecke. pba Mar 21 (269) $650

### Owen, Wilfred, 1893-1918
— Thirteen Poems, with Drawings by Ben Shahn. Northampton, Mass: Gehenna Press, 1956. One of 35 specially bound & with proof port sgd by Shahn & Baskin. Folio, orig half mor. CE Feb 21 (106) $420

One of 400, sgd by Leonard Baskin. Half mor; joints rubbed. sg Feb 15 (125) $225

### Owl...
— The Owl: A Miscellany L, 1919. Ed by Robert Graves. Nos 1 & 2. 4to, orig wraps. S Nov 2 (103) £180 [Wendler]

### Oxford...
— The Oxford Book of English Verse. Oxford, 1907. Mor gilt by Sangorski & Sutcliffe; joints scuffed. Cs & inscr by Stanley Bray inserted. F June 20 (723) $80

Anr Ed. Oxford, 1910. Ed by Sir Arthur Quiller-Couch. Lev gilt by Bayntun. sg Sept 21 (86) $200

— The Oxford Broom. Oxford, 1923. Ed by Harold Acton & Alfred Nicholson. Vol I, Nos 1-3 (all pbd). Orig wraps, those for Nos 2-3 ptd from linocuts by Evelyn Waugh. No 3 contains Waugh's short story, "Antony, who sought things that were lost". Short tear in margin of No 2 tp. Harold Acton's copy, with holograph revisions. Hobson copy. S June 28 (233) £1,800

— The Oxford Gazette [later London Gazette]. L, 1665-1979. In c.1,450 vols. Folio, various bdgs. Some library stamps. bba Sept 7 (255) £32,000 [Hughes]

### Oxford English Dictionary
— A New English Dictionary on Historical Principles. Oxford, 1888-1933. 11 vols in 21, including Supplement. Folio, contemp half mor. b May 30 (411) £170

Anr Ed. Oxford, 1970-75. 13 vols. 4to, orig cloth in djs. S Oct 27 (1022) £180 [Baring]

Compact Microprint Ed. Oxford, 1971. 2 vols. Folio, cloth. Lacking magnifying glass. F Mar 28 (113) $50

Compact Ed. NY, [1987]. 3 vols. Folio, cloth, in orig case with magnifying glass. O May 7 (236) $150

### Oxley, T. Louis
— Jacques Balmat, or the First Ascent of Mont Blanc. L, 1881. 8vo, orig cloth. bba Nov 1 (335) £400 [Atlas]

### Ozanne, Nicholas Pierre
— Recueil de combats et d'expeditions maritimes. Paris, 1797-[1803]. 5 parts in 1 vol. Folio, orig bds; worn. Tp torn at fore-edge & becoming loose; stain at upper inner margin not touching images. S Mar 28 (423) £800

— Recueil de vues et perspectives des ports de France. [Paris: the author, c.1790]. 4to, contemp red mor gilt. Engraved throughout. Fuerstenberg - Schaefer copy. S Dec 8 (479) £4,600

## P

P., T. See: Palfreyman, Thomas

Pacheco, Jose Ramon. See: Iturbide, Agustin de

### Pachymeres, Georgius
— Andronicus Palaeologus sive Historia rerum ab Andronico seniore in imperio gestarum.... Venice: Bartholomaeus Javarina, 1729. Folio, contemp calf; worn, needs rebacked. Old stamp on tp. sg Mar 21 (249) $225

### Paciaudi, Paolo Maria, 1710-85
— Memoira ed orazione intorno del P. Paolo M. Paciaudi intorno la Biblioteca Parmense. Parma: Bodoni, 1815. 8vo, contemp bds; soiled. O Mar 26 (196) $200

### Packard, Ralph C.
— Rifles That I Have Used and Designed. [N.p.]: Pvtly ptd, 1939. Ltd Ed. Cloth; worn. O Oct 10 (210) $70

### Packman, Ana Begue
— Early California Hospitality.... Gendale, 1938. 1st Ed. pba Apr 4 (130) $120

### Paddock, Judah
— A Narrative of the Shipwreck of the Ship Oswego.... L, 1818. 4to, mor. Foxed & browned. sg Oct 26 (283) $80

### Paden, Irene Dakin
— The Wake of the Prairie Schooner. NY, 1943. With: Paden, Prairie Schooner Detours, 1949 1st Ed. Orig cloth in dj; 1st d/j chipped, 2d worn. With 11 maps. Sgd. Larson copy. pba Sept 28 (630) $85

### Paden, Irene Dakin —& Schlichtmann, Margaret E.
— The Big Oak Flat Road. San Francisco, 1955. 1st Ed, one of 1,000. pba Nov 16 (207) $55

Anr copy. With modern sepia-tone print from 1903 Boysen negative of horses & a wagon on the road, framed. Larson copy. pba Feb 12 (141) $65

Anr copy. Robbins copy. Inscr & sgd. pba Mar 21 (270) $100

Page, Harry S. See: Derrydale Press

### Page, Margaret
— In Childhood Land. Akron: Saalfield Publishing, 1907. Illus by Katharine H. Greenland. Folio, pictorial bds; corners rubbed, creases to front free endpaper & half-title. pba Aug 22 (825) $50

### Pageant...
— The Pageant. L, 1896-97. Ed by C. H. Shannon & J. W. Gleeson White. Vols I & II (all pbd). 4to, orig cloth. bba July 18 (272) £75 [Cox]

— A Pageant of Youth. Moscow: State Art Publishers, 1939. 4to, cloth; hinges starting & dampstained. sg Feb 29 (276) $475

## Pages...

— Pages from the Past: A Collection of Original Leaves from Rare Books and Manuscripts. NY: Foliophiles, [c.1967]. One of 20. 4 portfolios. Folio, in folding lea drop-front boxes. With c.158 ptd leaves, Ms leaves, papyri, clay tablets, etc. pba June 20 (260) $3,500

## Pagninus, Santes, 1470-1541

— Thesaurus linguae sanctae.... [Paris]: R. Estienne, 21 Jan 1548. 4to, contemp gold-tooled bdg of flexible vellum. C June 26 (113) £6,000

## Paijkull, Carl Wilhelm

— A Summer in Iceland. L, 1868. 8vo, cloth; spine ends frayed, hinges cracked, library numbers on backstrip. sg Mar 7 (290) $140

## Pain, William, 1730?-90?

— The Builder's Golden Rule, or the Youth's Sure Guide.... L, 1782. 2d Ed. 2 parts in 1 vol. 8vo, contemp calf; worn, spine def, front cover & 1st 3 leaves detached. With 106 plates. Some foxing; text leaf with old tear closed up. cb Oct 17 (37) $200

## Paine, Thomas, 1737-1809

See also: Limited Editions Club

— Common Sense. Newburyport: John Mycall, [1776]. 8vo, limp calf; worn. CE May 22 (26) $2,800

1st Ed. Phila.: R. Bell, 1776. 1st Issue. 12mo, contemp sheep. Some foxing; tear to 1 leaf; stain in lower inner margin of quires D through K; some stains to gutter. Bound after, Rights of Man, 1791, & Thomas Clarkson's Essay on the Slavery and Commerce of the Human Species, 1786. Engelhard copy. CNY Jan 26 (153) $110,000

10th Ed. Providence, 1776. 4to, unbound; spine reinforced with sewn cloth tape. Some tears & creases. sg Oct 26 (284) $3,600

— Droits de l'homme.... Paris, 1791. 8vo, contemp sheep gilt; extremities worn. Marginal dampstaining. sg Oct 26 (285) $800

— The Genuine Trial of Thomas Paine, for a Libel contained in the Second Part of Rights of Man. L, 1792. 8vo, modern calf. sg Oct 26 (286) $400

[-] The Whole Proceedings of the Trial... Against Thomas Paine... before... Lord Kenyon. L, 1793. 2d Ed. 8vo, modern bds. Owner's stamp. F Mar 28 (448) $325

— Works. NY, [1908]. One of 500. Ed by D. E. Wheeler. 10 vols. wa Feb 1 (114) $170

## Palafox y Mendoza, Juan de, 1600-59

— Vida interior. Seville: Lucas Margin 1691. 4to, contemp vellum. With port. CE Sept 27 (218) $240

## Palatino, Giovanni Battista

— Libro...nel qual s'insegna a scrivere ogni sorte lettera. Rome: Antonio Blado, [1553]. 4to, old bds. Some soiling. sg Apr 18 (166) $1,900

## Palau y Dulcet, Antonio

— Manual del librero Hispano-Americano. Barcelona, 1948-1977. 28 vols. Modern half cloth. bba Oct 5 (142) £850 [Baker]

## Palazzi, Giovanni

— Fasti Cardinalium omnium Sanctae Romanae Ecclesiae.... Venice, 1703. 5 vols in 4. Folio, contemp vellum. bba Oct 5 (143) £320 [Maggs]

## Palemonio, Giovanni Giacomo

— L'Ornamento della oratione. Venice: Giovanni Pietro Brigonci, 1663. Bound with: Panegirici in prosa, et in versi. Venice, 1663. 32mo, contemp mor gilt by Gregorio Andreoli for Camillo Robpigliosi, with coronetted arms of Rospigliosi impaled with those of his wife, Lucrezia Cellesi. C Apr 3 (166) £1,700

## Palestrina, Giovanni Pierluigi da

— Il Primo Libro de Madrigali a quattro voci.... Rome: Gardano, 1605. Complete parts. Oblong 8vo, contemp wraps. Some browning. S Dec 1 (266) £2,000

— Il Secondo Libro de Madrigali a quattro voci.... Venice: heirs of Girolamo Scotto, 1586. Complete parts. 8vo, contemp wraps. Title of Alto creased. S Dec 1 (267) £5,000

## Palfreyman, Thomas

— The Treatise of Heavenly Philosophie. L, 1578. 4to, contemp calf; rebacked, lacking endpapers. Lacking 1 leaf. CE June 15 (235) £450

## Palgrave, William Gifford, 1826-88

— Narrative of a Year's Journey Through Central and Eastern Arabia. L, 1865. 1st Ed. 2 vols. 8vo, orig cloth; rubbed, shaken. Folding map with tear. With ALs to Capt. William Beaumont Selby inserted. b May 30 (290) £400

3d Ed. L, 1866. 2 vols. 8vo, orig cloth; hinges repaired or cracked. With frontis & 5 maps. Tape repair to 1 map. sg Mar 7 (253) $350

## Palha, Fernando

— Catalogue de la Bibliotheque. Lisbon, 1896. 4 vols. 4to, orig wraps; worn, spines crudely repaired. sg Apr 11 (244) $130

## Palissot de Montenoy, Charles, 1730-1814

— Oeuvres. Paris, 1788. 4 vols. 8vo, mor gilt. With port & 18 plates. Fuerstenberg - Schaefer copy. S Dec 8 (480) £550

## Palladino, Lawrence Benjamin

— Indian and White in the Northwest.... Balt., 1894. 8vo, orig cloth; worn & shaken. With folding color map, 90 plates, 55 ports. wa Feb 29 (458) $130

## Palladio, Andrea, 1518-80

— The Architecture. L, 1676. ("The First Book of Architecture....") 3d Ed. 4to, contemp calf; def. Lacking 1 plate (of 70); 3 plates torn with loss; some waterstaining & spotting. b Sept 20 (160) £130

Anr Ed. The Hague, 1726. ("Architecture de Palladio....") 4 parts in 1 vol. Folio, contemp calf; worn.

# PALLADIO

With frontis, port, & 172 plates. CE Nov 8 (232) $1,500

Anr Ed. L, 1738. ("The Four Books of....") Folio, buckram; rebound. With title, & 203 plates. Browned. Sold w.a.f. CE Nov 8 (233) $1,000

Anr Ed. L, 1742. 2 vols. 4to, later sheep; lea peeled in several places, spine ends frayed, joints tender. With 232 plates. Some foxing & dampstaining; dampstain to upper margins throughout Vol II, sometimes affecting text; marginal tears or holes. cb Feb 14 (2639) $1,700

— Architettura.... Venice: Bartolomeo Carampello, 1581. ("I Quattro Libri dell architettura.") Folio, 17th-cent vellum; soiled, edges rubbed. Some spotting; wormhole affecting lower margin of 1st 5 gatherings. C June 26 (111) £1,700

**Pallas, Peter Simon, 1741-1811**

— Travels through the Southern Provinces of the Russian Empire.... L, 1802-3. 2 vols. 4to, mor gilt by Bayntun-Riviere. With 4 folding maps & 51 hand-colored plates, many folding. b May 30 (175) £950

Anr copy. Modern cloth; rubbed. Lacking 2 plates; some foxing; 1 plate loose. Met Sept 28 (358) $300

2d Ed. L, 1812. 2 vols. 4to, contemp calf; worn, 1 cover detached. With 55 plates, maps & plans (44 handcolored), & 28 handcolored illus. Plate 22 in vol I torn. S Oct 26 (290) £360 [Harrington]

**Pallavicino, Ortensio**

— D.O.M. Austriaci Casesres Mariae Annae... Reginae in dotale auspicium... exhibiti. Milan: Lodovico Monti, 1649. Illus by Federigo Agnelli. 4to, contemp vellum; tears to spine. With etched title & 13 oval ports. C Apr 3 (168) £2,200

**Pallegoix, Jean Baptiste**

— Dictionarium linguae Thai sive Siamensis interpretatione Latina, Gallica, et Anglica illustratum. Paris, 1854. 1st Paris Ed. 4to, 19th-Cent half mor. With half-title. Text in Thai, romanized Thai, Latin, French, and English. Title creased; some spotting.. S Oct 26 (599) £360 [Antiquariat]

**Palliser, Fanny Bury**

— History of Lace. L, 1902. In chipped dj. sg Sept 7 (265) $50

**Palliser, John, 1807-87**

— Solitary Rambles and Adventures of a Hunter in the Prairies. L, 1853. 1st Ed. 8vo, orig cloth; bumped, frayed, hinges weak. With frontis, engraved title & 6 plates. Met Feb 24 (408) $650

**Pallucchini, Rodolfo —& Guarnati, G. F.**

— Les Eaux-Fortes de Canaletto. Venice, [1945]. One of 1,000. Oblong folio, half cloth; soiled, lower corner of front cover gouged, affecting prelims. With 18 plates. sg June 13 (72) $60

# AMERICAN BOOK PRICES CURRENT

**Palma di Cesnola, Luigi**

— Cyprus.... NY, 1878. 8vo, pictorial cloth; spine ends & corners worn. With 2 maps & port. Inscr & with ALs to the widow of Senator Ira Harris, who would have been the dedicatee if he had been alive. bbc Feb 26 (462) $150

Anr copy. Pictorial cloth; spine ends & corners worn. Inscr & with ALs to the widow of Senator Ira Harris, who would have been the dedicatee if he had been alive. S June 27 (137) £1,500

Anr copy. Pictorial cloth; spine ends frayed, shelf numbers on backstrip. sg Mar 7 (254) $60

2d Ed. 8vo, pictorial cloth; edge wear. With 2 maps & 59 plates. S Mar 28 (298) £190

**Palmer, Bradley Webster**

— Moisie River. [N.p., 1995]. One of 50. 4to, cloth. Facsimile of 1938 Ed. O June 25 (204) $90

**Palmer, C. H.**

— The Salmon Rivers of Newfoundland. Bost., 1928. 8vo, ptd wraps; worn, library stamp on inside of rear wrap & on tp. O June 25 (205) $120

**Palmer, Harry Clay**

— Athletic Sports in America, England and Australia.... Phila.: Hubbard Brothers, [1889]. 4to, half cloth; new endpapers. Ink stamp on verso of some plates & text leaves. bbc June 24 (340) $290

**Palmer, James Croxall**

— Thulia: A Tale of the Antarctic. NY: Samuel Colman, 1843. 8vo, orig cloth; front flyleaf excised. Foxing & soiling. pba July 25 (53) $500

**Palmer, John Williamson**

— The New and the Old; or, California and India in Romantic Aspects. NY, 1859. Orig cloth; spine ends & corners rubbed. pba Aug 8 (148) $55

**Palmer, Shirley**

— The Swiss Exile, a Poem. Lichfield, 1804. 4to, orig wraps. With frontis. Small paper repair. b Dec 5 (347) £120

**Palmer, Thomas Fyshe**

— A Narrative of the Sufferings of.... Cambr., 1797. 2d Ed. 8vo, later half lea. Dampstaining on margins not affecting text. Met May 22 (313) $1,100

**Palmerin**

— Historia del valoroissimo cavalliere Palmerino d'Oliva.... Venice: Michele Tramezino, 1547. 8vo, contemp vellum. Wormhole in text of a few leaves towards end. S June 27 (356) £1,100

**Palmquist, Peter**

— Redwood and Lumbering in California Forests. San Francisco: Book Club of California, [1983]. One of 600. 4to, orig cloth. pba Feb 12 (164) $50

**Palou, Francisco, 1722?-89?**

— The Expedition into California of the Venerable Padre Fray Junipero Serra.... San Francisco, 1934. One of 400. Trans by Thomas W. Temple II. Half vellum

800

in dj; d/j stained & spine chipped. With frontis port, 1 map, & 4 facsimiles. Larson copy. pba Sept 28 (239) $60

— Historical Memoirs of New California. Berkeley, 1926. 4 vols. pba Feb 13 (145) $275

1st Ed. - Ed by Herbert E. Bolton. 4 vols, orig cloth. Larson copy. pba Sept 28 (179) $250

1st English Ed. - Ed by Herbert Eugene Bolton. 4 vols. Robbins copy. pba Mar 21 (273) $275

— Life and Apostolic Labors of the Venerable Father Junipero Serra.... Pasadena, 1913. 1st Complete English Ed. - Trans by C. Scott Williams. Intro by George Wharton James. Orig cloth. With facsimiles of tp, frontis & map from 1787 Ed. Larson copy. pba Sept 28 (242) $70

— Life of Fray Junipero Serra. Wash., 1955. pba Feb 13 (147) $75

— Life of Ven. Padre Junipero Serra. San Francisco, 1884. Trans by J. Adam. 8vo, orig cloth. With frontis port. 1 page corner chipped. Larson copy. pba Sept 28 (241) $50

— Noticias de la Nueva California. San Francisco: Edouardo Bosqui, 1874. 1st Separate Ed, One of 100. Intro by John T. Doyle. 4 vols. 8vo, orig half mor; scuffed. With 18 albumen photos. Robbins copy. pba Mar 21 (271) $3,500

— Relacion historica de la vida y apostolicas tareas del venerable Padre Fray Junipero Serra.... Mexico, 1787. 4to, orig vellum; discolored & scorched. With frontis port & folded map. Map repaired. Larson copy. pba Sept 28 (240) $2,500

Anr copy. Orig vellum; discolored, minor wear, hinges weak. With port & folding map. Eames - Crane copy. pba Feb 13 (146) $2,500

1st Ed. 4to, orig vellum in mor slipcase. With port plate & folding map. Robbins copy. pba Mar 21 (272) $3,250

**Pancoast, Charlie Edward, 1818-1906**

— A Quaker Forty-Niner: The Adventures of Charles Edward Pancoast on the American Frontier. Phila., 1930. 1st Ed. Orig cloth; spine rubbed. Larson copy. pba Sept 28 (631) $95

**Pancoast, Joseph**

— A Treatise on Operative Surgery. Phila., 1844. 1st Ed. 4to, cloth; rebound. With 80 plates. Text & plates foxed; some dampstaining. CE Nov 8 (127) $450

3d Ed. Phila., 1852. 4to, modern cloth with orig cloth covers laid down. With 79 (of 80) plates. Last 2 leaves laminated; some plates with owner's stamp on image; tp repaired; some foxing. sg May 16 (467) $140

**Pann, Abel**

— Genesis: from the Creation until the Deluge. Jerusalem, [c.1926-30]. One of 100. Folio, cloth; extremities worn. With 25 color lithos, sgd in pencil. cb Oct 17 (662) $650

**Panofsky, Erwin, 1892-1968**

— Early Netherlandish Painting. Cambr. MA, 1953. 2 vols. Folio, cloth. sg Jan 11 (332) $120

**Panormitanus de Tedeschis, Nicolaus**

— Lectura super V libris decretalium. Venice: Johannes de Colonia & Johannnes Manthen, 1476. Vol II (of 6) only. Folio, 18th-cent mor gilt. Michael Wodhull's copy. 291 leaves. Goff P-44. C Apr 3 (168) £2,200

Anr Ed. Venice: Andreas Torresanus de Asula, 13 May 1483. Vol V only. Folio, half calf; spine ends repaired. 69 lines & headline; double column; gothic letter. Some staining in margins; early Ms annotations. 208 leaves. Goff P-49. S Dec 18 (65) £550 [Sokol]

Anr Ed. Basel: Johann Amerbach, 1487-88. Parts 1 & 3 (of 6) in 2 vols. Folio, contemp Nuremberg bdg by Kyriss workshop 113 of wooden bds rebacked with calf. 60 lines & headline; types 4*:165G (headings, headlines) & 11:82G (text); double column Piece torn from lower margin of a2; minor worming; some leaves dampstained in margins; A3 with upper third cut away with loss; hand-painted initial partially restored; some worming & staining. 353 (of 354, lacking a1) leaves & 268 leaves. Goff P-51. S Dec 18 (66) £1,200 [Zioni]

**Panvinio, Onofrio, 1529-68**

— Fasti et triumphi...a Romulo...ad Carolum V. Venice, 1557. Folio, later vellum; extremities worn, soiled, new endpapers, text block cracked. Tp soiled & dampstained; some soiling & browning; wormhole at inner margins of last few leaves; last leaf torn. cb Feb 14 (2526) $300

**Paoli, Paolo Antonio**

— Antichita di Pozzuoli.... [Naples], 1768. Folio, contemp half vellum; spine torn. With 38 engraved leaves of text & 69 plates. Some browning; 1 fold torn; owner's stamp on frontis. C Apr 3 (169) £1,800

**Papacino d'Antoni, Alessandro Vittorio.** See: Antoni, Alessandro Vittorio Papacino d'

**Papa's...**

— Papa's Present, or Pictures of Animals with Descriptions in Verse. L, 1818. 16mo, orig wraps; rebased with backstrip strengthened, soiled & worn. With 11 (of 12 hand-colored plates. Lacking The Horse; browned & soiled. S Nov 2 (235) £140 [Schiller]

**Papi, Lorenzo**

— Marino Marini: Paintings. Turin, [1989]. In dj. sg June 13 (247) $200

**Papin, Denys, 1647-1712?**

— La Maniere d'amolir les os.... Paris, 1682. 1st French Ed. 12mo in 4s & 2s, contemp calf; restored. With 2 folding plates. 1 plate soiled & with closed internal tear; ink stain at foot of R3r. Ck Mar 22 (215) £280

## PAPWORTH

**Papworth, John Buonarotti**
— Select Views of London. L: Ackerman, 1816. 1st Ed in Book form. 8vo, contemp russia gilt to a cathedral window design; rebacked, extremities worn. With 76 hand-colored plates, 5 folding. P Dec 12 (134) $2,000

**Paracelsus, 1493?-1541**
— Labrinthus medicorum errantium. Nuremberg: Valentinus Neuberus for B. Vischer, 1553. 8vo, 18th-cent calf; worn, spine chipped. With port on title. Some browning. P Dec 12 (135) $2,000

**Paradin, Claude**
— Devises heroiques. Lyons: Jean de Tournes & Guilliame Gazeau, 1551. 16mo, 18th-cent bds; worn, tears to joints. Roman & italic types; page number shaved on e8r; duplicate stamp of the Herzog August Bibliothek, Wolfenbuettel. Schaefer copy. P Nov 1 (167) $2,500

**Parangon...**
— Le Parangon de Nouvelles, honetes & delectables.... Lyon: Denis de Hansy for Romain Morin, 1532. 2 parts in 1 vol. 8vo, mor gilt by Bauzonnet-Trautz; joints starting, corners bumped. Gothic types. Minor soiling; A3 with repair & pen facsimile in upper corner; Jesuit stamp on tp; washed. P June 5 (310) $6,500

**Parboni, Achille**
— Nuova raccolta delle principali vedute antiche, e moderne dell'alma citta di Roma e sue vicinanze. Rome: Giacomo Antonelli, 1829. Oblong 8vo, orig wraps; worn. With 50 plates, 1 folding & with additional tinted litho view bound in at end. Some spotting & dampstaining, plates at beginning with caption affected. S Nov 30 (07) £800

**Pardoe, Julia, 1806-62**
— The Beauties of the Bosphorus. L, 1838. Illus by W. H. Bartlett. 4to, contemp calf; worn, lacking part of spine, covers detached. With port, map & 78 plates. Foxed. bba June 6 (50) £320 [Eurobooks]

Anr Ed. L, [c.1840]. Bound with: Beattie, William. The Danube.... [L, c.1840]. 4to, later syn. Some spotting & soiling. wad Oct 18 (456) C$1,150

**Pare, Ambroise, 1510?-90**
— Oeuvres. Paris, 1585. 4th Ed. Folio, 17th-cent calf gilt; joints restored but cracked, corners worn. Some foxing; marginal worming; stain through M1-6; lacking port. sg May 16 (468) $3,000

Anr Ed. Paris, 1614. Folio, old calf; scratched, bumped & chipped. Engraved title creased & chipped, repaired & mtd; port loose; dampstained; edges worn. Met May 22 (396) $850

10th Ed. Lyons, 1641. Folio, modern mor. Tp & prelims repaired, affecting text; tp mtd; some browning; lacking a2, a6 & last leaf. Sold w.a.f. sg May 16 (469) $750

— Works. L, 1649. Folio, modern half vellum retaining old bds. With 4 woodcut plates on 3 leaves. Tp def & mtd; c.30 leaves repaired, sometimes affecting sidenotes or text; 4F1 with full-page cut trimmed & inverted; 4G5 with 2 full-page cuts def. S June 12 (275) £1,000

Anr Ed. Pound Ridge, 1968. Folio, orig bdg. Facsimile of the 1634 Ed. sg May 16 (470) $400

**Parenti, Marino**
— Prime Edizioni Italiane. Manuale di Bibliografia Pratica.... Florence, 1951. 8vo, cloth in dj; spine panel darkened. sg Apr 11 (245) $70

**Paris**
— Atlas administratif des egouts de Paris 1889. Paris, 1889. Illus by L. Wuher. Folio, contemp bds; rubbed. With 16 double-page plans. S Oct 26 (257) £360 [Quaritch]

— Paris 1937-57. Paris: Centre Georges Pompidou, 1981. 4to, pictorial wraps. sg Jan 11 (330) $50

— Paris dans sa splendeur: monuments, vues, scenes.... Paris, 1861-63. 3 vols. Folio, later half mor; minor wear, lea peeled in several places, joints tender. With 100 plates. Some foxing; library markings & card pockets. cb Oct 17 (200) $450

— Plans des hopitaux et hospices civils de la ville de Paris. Leves par ordre du Conseil general d'Administration de ces Etablissemens. Paris, 1820. Illus by J. E. Thierry after H. Bessat & E. Poulet Galimard. Folio, contemp calf gilt; rebacked. With 29 hand-colored double-page plates, including 1 large folding plate (small tear). b June 28 (36) £4,000

**Park, Lawrence, 1873-1924**
— Gilbert Stuart, an Illustrated Descriptive List of his Works. NY, 1926. 4 vols. 4to, cloth. bbc Feb 26 (244) $425

Anr copy. Cloth; rubbed, shaken. sg Jan 11 (409) $325

**Park, Mungo, 1771-1806**
— Travels in the Interior Districts of Africa. Phila., 1800. 1st American Ed. 4to, contemp calf; rubbed. With folding frontis map. Closed tears to lower creases of map. pba July 25 (427) $325

**Park, Willie, Jr.**
— The Art of Putting. Edin.: J. & J. Gray, 1920. 1st Ed. Cloth; spine head bumped, lower spine faded, cover spotted. pba Apr 18 (140) $1,200

— The Game of Golf. L: Longmans, Green, 1896. 1st Ed. Cloth; spine ends & joints rubbed. Foxed; some pencil notations. pba Nov 9 (66) $550

2d Ed. Cloth; joints & spine ends rubbed. pba Apr 18 (139) $425

**Parker, Amos Andrew**
— Trip to the West and Texas, comprising a Journey of Eight Thousand Miles.... Concord, NH, 1835. 1st Ed. 12mo, orig cloth; rebacked with orig spine strip laid on. Soiled & stained. pba Aug 8 (149) $475

## Parker, B.
— Arctic Orphans. L, [c.1910]. Oblong 4to, chromolitho bds. O Sept 12 (130) $550
— Lays of the Grays. L, [1909]. Oblong 4to, chromolitho bds. With chromolithos of elephants at home & at play. pba Jan 4 (74) $225

## Parker, Emma —&
## Cowen, Nell Barrow
— Fugitives: The Story of Cyde Barrow and Bonnie Parker. Dallas: The Ranger Press, [1934]. In dj. CE May 22 (61) $650

## Parker, Fred G. See: Onassis copy, Jacqueline Bouvier Kennedy

## Parker, Henry Walter
— The Rise, Progress, and Present State of Van Diemen's Land.... L, 1834. ("Van Diemen's Land; its Rise, Progress and Present State....") 2d Ed. 12mo, calf; rebacked. With hand-colored folding map. b Sept 20 (440) £160

## Parker, John Henry
— A Glossary of Terms Used in Grecian, Roman, Italian and Gothic Architecture. Oxford, 1850. 3 vols. 8vo, half mor; edges worn. wa Nov 16 (256) $110

## Parker, Sir Karl Theodore
— Antoine Watteau: Catalogue complet de son oeuvre dessine. Paris, [1957-58]. 2 vols. 4to, cloth, in djs. sg Jan 11 (461) $650

## Parker, Nathan Howe
— Iowa As It Is in 1855. Chicago, 1855. 12mo, orig cloth. Lacking the map but with 9 rather than 2 plates. sg Oct 26 (163) $60

## Parker, Robert B.
— The Godwulf Manuscript. Bost., 1974. In dj. pba Oct 5 (292) $190; pba May 23 (332) $55

## Parker, Samuel, 1779-1866
— Journal of an Exploring Tour Beyond the Rocky Mountains. Ithaca, NY, 1842. 12mo, orig cloth; rebacked with mor but with orig cloth back retained. Foxed. sg Oct 26 (288) $80

## Parkinson, James, d.1824
— Organic Remains of a Former World.... L, 1833. 3 vols. 4to, orig cloth; chipped. With 2 frontises & 51 partly colored plates. S Mar 29 (739) £450

## Parkinson, John, 1567-1650
— Paradisi in sole paradisus terrestris.... L, 1629. 1st Ed. Folio, bdg not described but rebacked & repaired. Lacking last 2 leaves & Rr4; 1 leaf with ink blot; waterstained. K June 23 (312) $1,700
   Anr Ed. L, 1656. Folio, old calf; rebacked, rubbed. Foxed, soiled 7 stained. O Mar 5 (176) $1,700
— Theatrum botanicum.... L, 1640. Folio, old calf; rebacked. 2 leaves supplied in facsimile. W Mar 6 (208) £620

## Parkinson, Richard
— A Treatise on the Breeding and Management of Livestock. L, 1810. 2 vols. 8vo, orig bds; broken. Titles stamped & with upper margins excised; some foxing. sg May 16 (331) $300

## Parkinson, Sydney. See: Cook, Capt. James

## Parkman, Francis, 1823-93
   See also: Dickens's copy, Charles; Limited Editions Club
— The California and Oregon Trail. NY, 1849. 1st Ed, 1st Ptg. 12mo, orig cloth; rubbed & frayed. With ads 1-8 [7] at end. Some foxing; Hasty Pudding Club Library bookplate. bbc June 24 (437) $1,500
   2d Ptg. Orig cloth; spine sunned, covers rubbed. With frontis & added title. Faint marginal darkening; mild foxing. Robbins copy. pba Mar 21 (274) $1,900
   Anr Ed. Bost., 1892. ("The Oregon Trail.") Illus by Frederic Remington. 8vo, orig sheep; rebacked with orig spine strip laid on, rubbed. pba Aug 8 (166) $130
— Count Frontenac and New France under Louis XIV. Bost., 1877. One of 75 L.p. copies. 8vo, orig cloth; spine ends frayed. sg Oct 26 (289) $110
— A Half-Century of Conflict. Bost., 1892. One of 75 L.p. copies. 2 vols. 8vo, orig cloth. sg Oct 26 (291) $110
— History of the Conspiracy of Pontiac, and the War of the North American Tribes.... Bost., 1851. 1st Ed. 8vo, orig cloth. sg Oct 26 (292) $50
— The Oregon Trail. Bost., 1892. 1st Remington Ed. - Illus by Frederic Remington. 8vo, orig sheep; spine ends rubbed, head torn, corners & edges rubbed. With 10 plates. Robbins copy. pba Mar 21 (296) $190
   Anr Ed. Bost., 1925. One of 975. Illus by N. C. Wyeth & Frederic Remington. With 5 color & 5 monochrome plates. Pages edges darkened. Robbins copy. pba Mar 21 (275) $225
— Works. Bost., 1892-93. 12 vols. 8vo, contemp half mor; spines discolored, worn. F Mar 28 (617) $110
   Champlain Ed. Bost., 1897-98. 20 vols. 8vo, half mor gilt by James MacDonald; spine ends scuffed. pba June 20 (262) $750
   Frontenac Ed. Bost., 1902. 12 vols only. Half mor. cb Oct 17 (289) $700
   LaSalle Ed, one of 500. Vols 1-10 (of 20). Contemp mor gilt. sg Sept 21 (36) $600

## Parks, Fanny. See: Onassis copy, Jacqueline Bouvier Kennedy

## Parmachenee Club
— Constitution, By-Laws, Rules and List of Officers and Members 1916. NY, [1916]. Bds. Sidney A. Kirkman's copy. O Feb 6 (177) $375

## Parmentier, Antoine Augustin, 1737-1813
— L'Art de faire les eaux-de-vie, d'apres la doctrine de Chaptal. Paris, 1805. 8vo, modern vellum bds. With half-title, 1 folding table, & 5 plates (2 folding).

Half-title creased & with small repair; some spotting. Ck Mar 22 (216) £50
— Dissertation sur la nature des eaux de la Seine. Paris, 1787. 1st Ed. 8vo, later half calf; lightly rubbed. Some spotting. Ck Mar 22 (217) £50
— Experiences et reflexions relatives a l'analyse du bled et des farines. Paris, 1776. Bound with: Parmentier & Vauz, A. A. Cadet de. Discours prononces a l'overture de l'ecole gratuite de boulangerie. Paris, 1780. maniere de faire le pain de pommes de terre.... Paris, 1779. Instruction sur la conservation et les usages des pommes-de-terre.... Paris, [n.d.]. Avis aux bonnes menageres des villes et campagnes.... [Paris, 1777]. Silvestre, A. F. Essai sur les moyens de perfectionner les arts economiques en France. Paris, [1801]. Fourcroy, A. F. Discours sur l'etat actuel des sciences et des arts dans la Republique Francaise. [Paris, c.1793] 1st Eds, except Fourcroy. 7 works in 1 vol. 8vo, contemp half calf; spine head chipped; rubbed. Some spotting & dampstaining; lacking 1 half-title. Ck Mar 22 (218) £700
— Traite de la chataigne. Paris, 1780. 1st Ed. 8vo, contemp half calf; spine rubbed. Outer corner of B3 torn away. Ck Mar 22 (224) £280

**Parmentier, Antoine Augustin, 1737-1813 —& Delalause, L'Abbe**
— Traite theorique et pratique sur la culture des grains.... Paris, 1802 [An X]. 1st Ed. 2 vols. 8vo, contemp calf; Vol II joints cracked; Vol II spine almost detached, head & tails chipped. With 15 folding plates & 1 folding map. X3 in vol I torn; map margin browned & brittle; corner of Y7 & margin of R2 in vol II torn away. Ck Mar 22 (228) £200

**Parmentier, Antoine Augustin, 1737-1813 —& Deyeux, Nicolas**
— Precis d'experiences et observations sur les differentes especes de lait. Strassburg, 1799 [An VII]. 1st Ed. 8vo, contemp wraps. With half-title. Part of title torn away; Q3 with marginal hole; lower corner of Cc1 torn away. Ck Mar 22 (227) £60

**Parnasse...**
— Le Parnasse libertin, ou recueil de poesies libres. Paillardisoropolis [Paris]: Le dru, 1772. 8vo, contemp half calf. With plate. b Sept 20 (36) £90

**Parnell, Thomas, 1679-1718.** See: Goldsmith & Parnell

**Parnell, W. G.**
— The Kaleidoscope; or, a Poem, Descriptive of the Exhibition at the Sheffield Music Hall.... Sheffield, 1839. 2 vols. 16mo, early wraps; def. b Dec 5 (474) £90

**Parrish, Morris L.**
— Victorian Lady Novelists.... L, 1933. One of 150. 4to, orig cloth; stain at foot of spine. Inscr to Carroll A. Wilson. O Mar 26 (197) $325

**Parrot, Jules**
— Clinique des nouveau-nes.... Paris, 1877. 1st Ed. - Illus by F. Renadout. 8vo, contemp half roan;

rubbed. With 4 hand-colored plates. Spotted. Ck Mar 22 (229) £130

**Parry, Caleb Hillier, 1755-1822**
— An Inquiry into... the Syncope Anginosa, commonly called Angina Pectoris. Bath & L., 1799. 1st Ed. 8vo, contemp tree calf; rebacked, corners worn. With half-title. D4r soiled at margin. Ck Mar 22 (230) £90

**Parry, William**
— The Last Days of Lord Byron.... L, 1825. 8vo, contemp half vellum; worn. With frontis & 3 hand-colored plates. Lacking half-title. b May 30 (291) £180
Anr copy. Calf gilt by Root. With frontis & 3 hand-colored plates. sg Oct 19 (53) $350

**Parry, Sir William Edward, 1790-1855**
— A Supplement to the Appendix of Captain Parry's Voyage.... L, 1824. 4to, disbound. Some soiling, foxing & fraying. O Nov 14 (137) $270

**Parseval, August von, 1861-1942**
— Motorballon und Flugmaschine. Weisbaden, 1908]. 8vo, orig wraps; spine rubbed. sg May 16 (74) $150

**Parseval-Grandmaison, Francois Auguste, 1759-1834**
— Les Amours epiques. Paris, 1804 [An XII]. 12mo, contemp citron mor gilt by Bozerian, with initials of the Empress Josephine. Inscr to the Empress Josephine with verses. Fuerstenberg - Schaefer copy. S Dec 8 (481) £1,000

**Parsons, George F.**
See also: Grabhorn Printing
— The Life and Adventures of James W. Marshall. Sacramento, 1870. 12mo, orig cloth. pba Feb 12 (527) $85

**Parsons, James, 1705-70**
— Remains of Japhet.... L, 1767. 4to, contemp calf; worn, covers detached. With map, 2 plates & 2 tables. Tp stamped & loose; map loose; some worming in upper inner corners. sg Mar 21 (250) $175

**Parsons, Joseph**
— Religion recommended to the Soldier. Bost., 1744. 8vo, disbound. Lacking half-title. sg Oct 26 (101) $130

**Paruta, Paolo, 1540-98**
— Discorsi politici. Venice, 1629. 2 parts in 1 vol. 4to, contemp vellum; marked. bba July 18 (124) £80 [Robertshaw]
— The History of Venice.... L, 1696. Folio, contemp calf; covers detached, backstrip damaged. Some browning & staining. sg Mar 21 (251) $300

**Pascal, Blaise, 1623-62**
See also: Bremer Press; Limited Editions Club
— Pensees. Paris, 1812. 2 vols. 8vo, contemp calf. Inscr by W. E. Gladstone to his brother, 28 June 1831. S Apr 23 (58) £140

**Pascale, Giovanni**
— Liber de morbo composito vulgo Gallico appellato authore Suessano. Naples: Giovanni Antonio de Caneto, 9 Dec 1534. 4to, 18th-cent bds. Worming at bottom of final leaf. C Apr 3 (170) £450

**Pascin, Jules**
— Erotikon. Brussels, 1933. One of 40 on chine. Folio, each separately mtd in orig wraps. With 9 plates. S Nov 21 (339) £2,500

**Pashino, Petr Ivanovich**
— Turkestanskij Kraj b 1866 Godu. St. Petersburg, 1868. 4to, contemp half sheep; extremities worn. With 20 tinted litho plates. Old stamp on tp. sg Mar 7 (365) $400

**Pasquali, Giovanni Battista.** See: Smith Library, Joseph

**Passeri, Giovanni Battista, 1610?-79**
— Picturae Etruscorum in vasculis. Rome, 1767-75. 3 vols. Folio, contemp russia gilt; rebacked. With 3 frontises, 2 engraved dedications & 301 plates; hand-colored throughout & all but 2 initials hand-colored; 1 uncolored plate & 4 tables in Vol III Vol I frontis shaved & repaired, minor damage to margins of tp & following 4 leaves; repaired tears to D1-E4, tear in Plate CII; Vol II with k3 lacking lower corner; tear to Plate CXLIII; Vol III with repaired tear to blank margin of K3. C Apr 3 (172) £6,500

**Passero, Felice**
— La Vita di San Placido.... Venice: Giolito, 1589. 4to, contemp vellum; spine wormed. Waterstain in lower margin; library stamp on tp. S Mar 28 (491) £150

**Passio...**
— Passio S. Meynradi. Basel: Michael Furter, 20 Sept 1496. 4to, modern mor gilt by Trautz-Bauzonnet. 38 lines; gothic types. With 21 woodcuts from 19 blocks. 14 leaves. Goff P-142. C June 26 (171) £11,000

**Pasternak, Boris, 1890-1960**
See also: Limited Editions Club
— Doctor Zhivago. L, 1958. 1st Ed in English. In repaired dj. sg Dec 14 (239) $175

**Pataroli, Laurenzo**
— Series Augustorum, Augustarum, Caesarum, et tyrannorum omnium. Venice: Jo. Baptista Pasquali, 1743. 8vo, contemp sheep gilt; worn, joints chipped & cracked. With 15 folding plates. sg Mar 21 (253) $70

**Patchen, Kenneth**
— The Famous Boating Party. [NY, 1954]. 4to, bds, in dj with tear to front flap crease. pba May 23 (333) $50
— Hurrah for Anything. Highlands, N.C.: Jonathan Williams, 1957. One of 100 "prepared & painted by Kenneth Patchen". 8vo, pictorial bds, painted by Patchen. cb Oct 17 (461) $500
— The Love Poems.... San Francisco: City Lights, [1960]. One of 300. 12mo, orig cloth; dampstaining to upper edges. pba May 23 (334) $50
— When We Were Here Together. NY: New Directions, [1957]. One of 75, sgd. 4to, bds, spine & covers painted by author. cb Oct 17 (463) $275

**Patents...**
— Patents for Inventions. Abridgements of Specifications. Class 119: Small-Arms, 1855-1929. L, 1903-22. 4 vols. 8vo, cloth; some wear. O June 4 (211) $160

**Pater, Walter, 1839-94**
See also: Limited Editions Club
— An Imaginary Portrait. Oxford: Daniel Press, 1894. One of 250. Half calf, orig wraps bound in. sg Sept 21 (270) $175
— Sebastian Van Storck. L & NY, 1927. One of 1,050, with 1 plate sgd. Illus by Alastair. 4to, orig cloth; soiled. With 8 colored illusts. Soiling to margin of 1 plate. cb June 25 (1896) $225
— Works. L, 1895-1900. 9 vols. Half mor gilt by Hatchards. pba Mar 7 (198) $250

**Paterculus, Marcus Velleius.** See: Tacitus & Paterculus

**Paterson, George**
— The History of New South Wales. Newcastle, 1811. 8vo, contemp calf; rubbed. With folding map, plan & 2 (of 3) plates. Some spotting. b Mar 20 (151) £200

**Paterson, William, 1658-1719**
— An Enquiry into the State of the Union of Great Britain.... L, 1717. 8vo, contemp calf; rubbed. b Sept 20 (162) £300

**Patin, Charles**
— Imperatorum romanorum numismata. Strasbourg, 1671. Folio, lea gilt; wormed, hinges starting. Met Sept 28 (150) $300

**Paton, Lucy Allen**
— Selected Bindings from the Gennadius Library. Bost., 1924. Ltd Ed. 4to, orig cloth; rubbed. bba May 9 (147) £220 [Brindel]

**Patri, Giacomo**
— White Collar: Novel in Linocuts. [N.p., c.1940]. 2d Ed. Spiral-bound wraps. sg Feb 15 (225) $175

**Patrick, Mrs. F. C.**
— Poems Founded on the Events of War in the Peninsula. Hythe, 1819. 8vo, modern bds. b Dec 5 (152) £70

**Patte, Pierre, 1723-1814**
— Memoires sur les objets les plus importans de l'architecture. Paris, 1769. 4to, contemp calf gilt; rebacked retaining orig backstrip. With 27 plates, all but 1 folding. sg June 13 (24) $650

**Patten, B. A.** See: Barry & Patten

**Patten, Edmund**
— A Glimpse at the United States.... L, 1853. 8vo, orig cloth; worn & soiled, spine end frayed. Foxed. wa Feb 29 (486) $130

**Patten, Robert**
— The History of the Late Rebellion.... L, 1745. ("The History of the Rebellion.") 4th Ed. 8vo, contemp calf; worn. Marginal worming; anr 18th-cent work bound at end. bba May 30 (101) £75 [Young]

**Patten, William**
— The Book of Sport. NY, 1901. One of 450. 4to, half lev; scuffed. Dampstain to edges. bbc June 24 (366) $210
Autograph Ed, One of 50. 4to, mor gilt by Blackwell; rubbed, corners worn. Frontis is orig sgd watercolor drawing by J. Burton Smith after a painting by Henry Hutt. O Jan 9 (175) $475

**Patterson, Lawson B.**
— Twelve Years in the Mines of California.... Cambr. MA, 1862. 1st Ed. 12mo, modern half mor. Some soiling. Robbins copy. pba Mar 21 (276) $180
Anr Ed. Cambr., MA, 1862. 12mo, orig cloth. Light foxing, lacking 1 endpaper. Larson copy. pba Sept 28 (633) $130

**Patteson, Edward**
— A General and Classical Atlas. L, 1825. 4to, modern bds. With 66 mapsheets. Minor browning. sg May 9 (93) $375

**Pattie, James O.**
— The Personal Narrative of James O. Pattie of Kentucky.... Cincinnati, 1833. Orig or contemp tree sheep; calf scuffed. With 5 plates. Several pp. darkened; front free endpaper missing. Larson copy. pba Sept 28 (180) $2,250

**Pattison, Mark, 1813-84.** See: Grabhorn Printing

**Paul, Elliot.** See: Quintanilla, Luis

**Paul, Rodman W.**
— The California Gold Discovery: Sources, Documents.... Georgetown CA, 1966. One of 100. Half mor. pba Apr 25 (585) $85
1st Ed. Georgetown, Calif., 1966. Half bds in dj. Larson copy. pba Sept 28 (635) $55

**Paul Wilhelm, Duke of Wuerttemberg**
— Early Sacramento. San Francisco, 1973. One of 400. 4to, half cloth. pba Feb 12 (564) $55

**Paulding, James Kirke, 1778-1860**
— The Merry Tales of the Three Wise Men of Gotham. NY, 1826. 1st Ed. 12mo, orig half cloth; worn. Browned throughout. Sold w.a.f. sg Sept 21 (271) $150

**Paulhan, Jean, 1884-1968**
— Fautrier l'enrage. Paris, 1949. One of 29 with an additional suite of the engravings on Tonkins. Illus by Jean Fautrier. Folio, mor janseniste by J. P. Miguet, orig wraps bound in. S Nov 21 (340) £2,200

**Paulli, Simon, 1603-80**
— A Treatise on Tobacco, Tea, Coffee, and Chocoloate.... L, 1746. 1st Ed in English. - Trans by Dr. R. james. 8vo, old vellum; soiled. With 2 folding plates & half-title. Upper margin of half-title torn; title torn with loss, & repaired; C1 torn & repaired; F1 holed with loss; plate II with piece torn away. Ck Mar 22 (231) £400

**Paulsen, Martha**
— "Follow Me" Animal Book. Akron: Saalfield Publishing, 1945. Illus by Vivienne Blake. In dj with tear along joint. pba Aug 22 (826) $50

**,Paulson, Ronald**
— Hogarth's Graphic Works. L, 1989. 4to, cloth, in dj. bba Oct 19 (69) £50 [Sims Reed]

**Paulus Aegineta**
— Opus de re medica.... Paris: S. Colin, 1532. 7 parts in 1 vol. Folio, old vellum. Tp def; leaves at beginning & end dampstained; lacks KKK8; some margins damaged & repaired. Sold w.a.f. CE Nov 8 (129) $160
— The Seven Books. L: Sydenham Society, 1844-47. Trans & Ed by Francis Adams. 3 vols. 8vo, cloth; Vol II needs rebacking. sg May 16 (473) $140

**Pauly, Theodore de**
— Description Ethnographique des peuples de la Russie. St. Petersburg, 1862. Folio, contemp mor; rubbed, spine head worn. With 60 (of 63) chromolitho plates only & double-page colored map. Browned; some leaves spotted. C May 31 (107) £800
Anr copy. Orig mor. With 62 chromolitho plates, chromolitho map & double-page table. Some discoloration in text towards end; a few plate margins marked. S Nov 30 (08) £6,500

**Pausanias**
— Pausaniae veteris Graeciae descriptio. Florence: Lorenzo Torrentino, 1551. Folio, 17th-cent calf; spine ends chipped. S June 12 (89) £340

**Pavlov, Ivan Petrovich, 1849-1936**
— Dvadtsatiletniy Opyt Ob'yektivnogo Izucheniya Vysshey Nervnoy Deyatelnosti (Povedeniya) Zhivotnykh. Uslovnye Refleksy. Moskow & Leningrad, 1923. 8vo, orig wraps; spine ends & bottom edges chipped. sg May 16 (474) $300
— Lektsii o Rabote Bol'shikh Polusharii Golovnogo Mozga. Moscow, 1927. 8vo, orig wraps; worn & shaken, top half of backstrip missing. sg May 16 (475) $250
— Lektsii o rabotie glavnykh pishchevaritelnykh zhelyoz. St. Petersburg, 1897. 8vo, contemp half cloth. Some discoloration at beginning. C June 26 (228) £4,500

## Paxton, John Adams

— An Alphabetical List of All the Wards, Streets... Philadelphia. Phila., [1811]. For 1813. 12mo, orig bds backed in mor; extremities worn. With folding map. F June 20 (376) $230

## Paxton, Sir Joseph, 1801-65

See also: Lindley & Paxton

— The Magazine of Botany, and Register of Flowering Plants. L, 1834-49. Vols 1-10. Contemp half mor gilt. With 452 hand-colored & 3 uncolored plates. Some plates shaved. C May 31 (37) £2,800

Anr copy. Vol 2 only. 8vo, contemp half lea gilt; scuffed. With 41 (of 43) hand-colored plates. sg Dec 7 (229) $600

Anr copy. Vols I-XV (of 16). Half mor; extremities rubbed, backstrips dried. With 698 hand-colored plates. Some foxing. sg May 9 (313) $6,500

**Payne, John R.** See: Goldstone & Payne

## Payne-Gallwey, Sir Ralph

— Letters to Young Shooters. L, 1894-99. Mixed Ed. 3 vols. 8vo, orig cloth. Foxed. O June 4 (212) $100

## Payson, George

— Golden Dreams and Leaden Realities. NY, 1853. 1st Ed. Orig cloth; worn & fading. Light foxing. Larson copy. pba Sept 28 (636) $120

**Paz, Octavio.** See: Limited Editions Club

## Pazdirek, Franz

— Universal-Handbuch der Musik-Literatur aller Zeiten und Voelker. Vienna, [1904-10]. 14 vols. Contemp bds. S May 15 (126) £500

**Peabody, George Augustus.** See: Peabody Museum

## Peabody Museum—Salem MA

BREWINGTON, MARION VERNON. - The Peabody Museum Collection of Navigating Instruments. 1963. One of 1,000. rce July 25 (65) $200

BREWINGTON, MARION VERNON & BREWINGTON, DOROTHY. - Marine Paintings and Drawings in the Peabody Museum. 1981. 4to, cloth. O Dec 5 (112) $80

Anr copy. Cloth, in dj. O May 7 (69) $90

PEABODY, GEORGE AUGUSTUS. - South American Journals, 1858-59. 1937. One of 100. 4to, half cloth, unopened. O Dec 5 (113) $110

## Peachie, John

— Some Observations made upon the Russia Seed.... L, 1694. 1st Ed. 4to, recent wraps. Title restored. Ck Mar 22 (235) £550

## Peacock, Lucy

— The Adventures of the Six Princesses of Babylon.... L, 1785. 1st Ed. 4to, modern wraps. Half-title stained & with small loss to outer margin. b May 30 (412) £450

## Peake, Mervyn, 1911-68

— Captain Slaughterboard Drops Anchor. L: Country Life, 1939. 4to, orig pictorial bds, in soiled, def & torn dj. S Nov 2 (309) £1,350 [Blackwell]

## Pearce, Helen

— The Enchanted Barn. NY: Watch Hill Press, 1929. One of 100. Illus by Asa Chaffetz. 4to, bds. sg Feb 15 (69) $80

## Pearce, Thomas, fl.1722-56

— The Laws and Customs of the Stannaries in...Cornwall and Devon. L, 1725. Folio, later calf; rebacked. Some foxing & soiling at ends. bba Nov 1 (37) £420 [Brewer]

## Pearson, Edwin

— Banbury Chap Books and Nursery Toy Book Literature.... L, 1890. 1st Ed, One of 500. 4to, orig cloth; spine faded. sg Apr 11 (77) $150

## Pearson, John, 1613-86

— An Exposition of the Creed. L, 1701. 7th Ed. Folio, contemp calf. Some worming. pba Nov 30 (255) $170

## Pearson, Susanna

— Poems, Dedicated...to The Right Honourable the Countess Fitzwilliam. Sheffield, 1790. 4to, modern bds. b Dec 5 (475) £340

## Peary, Robert Edwin, 1856-1920

— Northward over the "Great Ice." L, 1898. 2 vols. 8vo, orig cloth; extremities worn. NH July 21 (326) $120

— Secrets of Polar Travel. NY, 1917. In dj with edgewear. sg Mar 7 (293) $200

## Peasants...

— The Peasants of Chamouni, Containing an Attempt to reach the Summit of Mont Blanc.... L, 1823. 12mo, contemp half lea; upper cover detached. bba Nov 1 (514) £700 [Hunter]

Anr copy. Contemp half lea, prize bdg. bba Nov 1 (578) £700 [Hunter]

## Pease, Z. W.

— The Catalpa Expedition. New Bedford, 1897. 12mo, orig cloth. Inscr by Capt. Anthony of the expedition, 1909. pba July 25 (429) $130

## Peaton, Arthur

— Pictures of East Coast Health Resorts. L, [1894]. 4to, orig cloth; stained. With 14 illusts after Arthur Rackham. Ck May 31 (102) £650

## Peck, Charles Horton, 1833-1917

— Annual Report of the State Botanist of the State of New York. Albany, 1897. 4to, orig cloth; extremities worn. With 40 color plates only. Library markings; perforated stamp on tp; plates unstamped. sg Dec 7 (230) $110

Anr copy. With 43 color plates. sg May 9 (320) $150

### Peck, Francis, 1692-1743
— Desiderata Curiosa; or, a Collection...Relating to...English History. L, 1779. 2 vols in 1. 4to, calf gilt by James Toovey; joint worn. pba Mar 7 (199) $275

### Peck, John M., 1789-1858
— A Gazetteer of Illinois.... Jacksonville, 1834. 1st Ed. 16mo, contemp sheep. sg Oct 26 (152) $800

### Pedersen, Carl Henning
— Himlens Trompeter. [Paris, 1982]. One of 500. 4to, cloth, in dj. sg Sept 7 (104) $140
— Solens Latter. Copenhagen, 1968. One of 600. 4to, pictorial bds. sg Sept 7 (105) $140

### Peer, Frank Sherman
— Cross Country with Horse and Hound. NY, 1902. 4to, half mor; rubbed. O Jan 9 (176) $70
— The Hunting Field with Horse and Hound.... NY, 1910. 4to, cloth; worn. O Jan 9 (177) $60; O June 4 (213) $50

### Peignot, Gabriel, 1767-1849
— Dictionnaire critique, litteraire et bibliographique des principaux livres condamnes au feu, suprimes ou censures. Paris, 1806. 1st Ed. 2 vols in 1. 8vo, contemp half calf; rubbed. O Mar 26 (198) $250
— Manuel du bibliophile, ou traite du choix des livres. Paris: Renouard, 1823. 2 vols. 8vo, contemp half mor; extremities worn. O Mar 26 (200) $50
— Opuscules... extraits de divers journeaux.... Paris, 1863. One of 200. 8vo, half mor by Belz-Niedree; rubbed. O Mar 26 (201) $225
— Opuscules philosophiques et poetiques de Frere Jerome. Paris, 1796. 1st Ed. 12mo, contemp calf; rubbed. O Mar 26 (202) $200
— Repertoire Bibliographique Universel. Paris, 1812. 1st Ed. 8vo, contemp half mor; extremities worn. Some foxing. sg Apr 11 (246) $250
  1st Eds. Bound with: Bibliotheque Choise de Classiques Latins, Paris, 1813 2 vols in 1. 8vo, contemp half roan; spine ends worn, joints cracked at bottom. sg Apr 11 (247) $130

### Pelham, Camden, Pseud.
— Chronicles of Crime, or the New Newgate Calendar. L, 1886. Illus by Hablot K. Browne. 2 vols. 8vo, half calf by Whitman Bennett. pba June 20 (77) $120

### Pellico, Silvio, 1789-1854
— Tratado de los deberes del hombre.... Puerto Rico, 1840. 4to, contemp wraps; spine broken. b Sept 20 (441) £160

### Pemberton, Thomas
— Historical Journal of the American War. Bost.: Belknap, 1795. 8vo, contemp calf; rubbed, bookplate removed. Some soiling, foxing, staining & browning. O Nov 14 (138) $225

### Pembroke, Henry Herbert, 10th Earl of, 1734-94
— Military Equitation; or a Method of Breaking Horses. L, 1778. 8vo, orig bds; worn & soiled, lacking backstrip. With 17 plates. Stain to tp. wa Feb 29 (167) $270

### Pena, Petrus. See: L'Obel & Pena

### Penalosa y Zuniga Fernandez de Velasco, Clemente
— Oratio habita in regio ac Pontificio Angelorum-Populi Palafoxiano Seminario in laudem Angelici Doctoris D. Thomae Aquinatis.... Puebla de Los Angeles, 1771. 4to, recent vellum. With frontis (shaved at foot). Lacking final blank. S Nov 30 (176) £400

### Penhallow, Samuel, 1665-1726
— The History of the Wars of New-England, with the Eastern Indians. Cincinnati, 1859. 4to, orig bds; extremities worn. sg Oct 26 (294) $325

### Penick, Harvey — & Shrake, Bud
— Harvey Penick's Little Red Book. NY: Simon & Schuster, [1992]. 1st Ed. In dj. Inscr & sgd. pba Nov 9 (67) $160

### Penkethyman, John
— Artachthos or a New Booke Declaring the Assise or Weight of Bread.... L, 1638. 4to modern half calf. Dampstained throughout. CE June 15 (236) $650
— Authentic Accounts of the History and Price of Wheat.... L, 1765. 8vo in 4s, modern wraps. With folding frontis, folding tables, & 11 folding leaves. Ck Mar 22 (236) £550

### Penn, Irving
— Momenti, otto saggi in immagini e parole. Milan, [1960]. Folio, cloth, in dj. sg Feb 29 (235) $350
— Moments Preserved. [NY, 1960]. 4to, cloth, in rubbed dj. sg Oct 7 (281) $325
  Anr copy. Orig cloth, in dj with small tear. Sgd. sg Feb 29 (236) $900
— Worlds in a Small Room. [NY, 1974]. In stained & rubbed dj; pencil notation on rear free endpaper. sg Feb 29 (237) $70

### Penn, Richard, 1735-1811
— Maxims and Hints for an Angler.... Phila., 1855. 1st American Ed. 12mo, orig cloth. With 12 plates. Some foxing & soiling. O Feb 6 (179) $60
  Anr copy. Some foxing. O Feb 6 (180) $90

### Penn, William, 1644-1718
— The Christian Quaker and his Divine Testimony Vindicated by Scripture.... L: T. Sowle, 1699. ("The Christian Quaker and his Divine Testimony Stated and Vindicated....") 8vo, calf; worn, front cover detached, spine def. K Oct 1 (296) $700
— Primitive Christianity Revived in the Faith and Practice of the People called Quakers. Phila., 1783. 2 vols in 1. 8vo, contemp half calf; worn with paper peeled off, joints repaired. Tp with tear repaired through imprint; stains to prelims & rear flyleaves. pba June 13 (279) $400

— Some Fruits of Solitude. L: Essex House Press, 1901. One of 250. 4to, orig vellum; soiled. pba Mar 7 (101) $160; sg Sept 14 (122) $275

**Pennant, Thomas, 1726-98**
— Arctic Zoology. L, 1784-85. 1st Ed. 2 vols. 4to, contemp calf; some wear. With frontis & 23 plates. Some discoloration. b May 30 (178) £400
Anr Ed. L, 1784-87. 3 vols, including Supplement. 4to, 18th-cent calf gilt. With 2 folding maps & 24 hand-colored plates. pnE Sept 20 (140) £1,300
— British Zoology. L: J. & J. March, [1761]-66. Folio, 18th-cent mor gilt with Spencer arms, by Kalthoeber, with his ticket. With 132 hand-colored plates. A few plates slightly discolored; neat repair to outer margins of ff.6 & 7. Spencer - Rylands - Fattorini copy. C Oct 25 (35) £26,000
Anr Ed. L, 1776-77. 4 vols. 8vo, old calf; worn & broken, spines gone. Staining & soiling. Sold w.a.f. O Mar 5 (177) $250
— Indian Zoology. L, 1790 [1791]. 2d Ed. 4to, old half calf; rebacked, worn. With engraved title & 16 plates. Some soiling & foxing. O Mar 5 (178) $225
— Of London. L, 1793. ("Some Account of London.") "3d" Ed. 4to, contemp calf; rubbed, upper cover detached. Margins browned. bba May 30 (388) £70 [Price]
Anr Ed. L: printed for the Illustrator, [1814]. In 4 vols. Folio, mor gilt; minor wear, joints tender. Extra-illus with over 300 plates. cb Oct 17 (201) $400
— A Tour in Scotland and Voyage to the Hebrides. L, 1776. Vol I only. Later half calf. pba Sept 14 (288) $225

**Pennell, Elizabeth Robins, 1855-1936**
— My Cookery Books. Bost. & NY, 1903. 1st Ed, One of 330. 4to, orig half cloth; chipped, worn. With 28 tipped-in reproductions of tps, frontises, etc.. S Oct 12 (113) £200

**Pennell, Elizabeth Robins, 1855-1936 —& Pennell, Joseph, 1857-1926**
— The Glory of New York. NY, 1926. One of 355. Folio, orig half cloth. sg Sept 14 (295) $275
Anr copy. Cloth; spotted & discolored. With 24 colored plates. Inscr by Elizabeth Pennell to Justice & Mrs. Harlan Fiske Stone. sg Jan 11 (336) $200

**Pennell, Joseph, 1857-1926**
See also: Pennell & Pennell
— The Adventures of an Illustrator.... Bost., 1925. Ltd Ed. 4to, half calf. sg Jan 11 (335) $90
— The Graphic Arts: Modern Men and Modern Methods. Chicago, 1920. One of 150 on Japan vellum, sgd & with additional frontis. 4to, half cloth; rubbed & soiled. wa Nov 16 (351) $110

**Pennell, Joseph, 1857-1926 —& Dillaye, Blanche**
— Views on the Old Germantown Road. [N.p., not before 1883]. One of 20. Folio, loose as issued in cloth portfolio. With 16 mtd proof plates & additional unidentified proof etching by Pennell. K June 23 (414) $700

**Penney, James Cash ("J. C."), 1875-1971**
BEASLEY, NORMAN. - Main Street Merchant - The Story of the J. C. Penney Company. NY, 1948. In dj. Inscr by Penney to Wm. F. Edwards, 1951. pba June 13 (164) $130

**Pennsylvania**
— Combination Atlas Map of Lancaster County Pennsylvania. Phila., 1875. Folio, half lea; worn. K Feb 11 (31) $275
— Proceedings and Debates of the General Assembly of Pennsylvania. Taken in Short-hand by Thomas Lloyd. Phila. 1787-88. 2 vols. 8vo, contemp calf. Trimmed; minor browning. rs Nov 11 (111) $3,300

**Pennsylvania Gazette**
— Pennsylvania Gazette. Phila.: Franklin & Hall, 1762. No 1737, for 8 Apr 1762. pba Oct 26 (137) $950

**Pennsylvania Magazine...**
— Pennsylvania Magazine: Or American Monthly Museum. Phila., 1805. For Oct 1775. Disbound from larger vol. pba Nov 16 (361) $100

**Pepler, Hilary Douglas Clerk**
— Plays for Puppets. Ditchling: St. Dominic's Press, 1929. One of 450. Orig half cloth; rubbed. bba May 9 (341) £50 [Otten]

**Pepusch, Johann Christoph**
— The Additional Songs in the Operas of Thomyris and Camilla. [L: Walsh & Hare, 1719]. Folio, modern bds. Some staining. S May 15 (443) £780

**Pepys, Samuel, 1633-1703**
See also: Limited Editions Club
— Memoires relating to the State of the Royal Navy of England.... [L], 1690. 1st Ed, 2d Issue. 8vo, modern mor. Corrections to text in contemp hand on 4 leaves; minor loss to margin on lower forecorner of C2; some browning. S Dec 18 (109) £300 [Way]
Anr copy. 19th-cent cloth. Lacking port; tp soiled & dampstained. Adm. Benjamin William Page's copy, with sgd leaf of notes. sg Mar 7 (230) $350
— Memoirs.... L, 1825. 1st Ed. 2 vols. 4to, contemp calf gilt; rebacked, corners worn. Some foxing. CE Feb 21 (198) $550
Anr copy. 2 vols extended to 7. 4to, calf gilt; rebacked, extremities worn. Extra-illus with 2 orig watercolor drawings & several hundred prints. P June 5 (312) $5,500
2d Ed. L, 1828. 5 vols. 8vo, cloth; leaning. Z June 28 (224) $280
3d Ed. L, 1848. ("Diary and Correspondence.") Ed by Richard Lord Braybrook. 5 vols. 8vo, contemp calf. b Jan 31 (100) £220
Anr Ed. L, 1924. ("Diary....") Ed by Henry B. Wheatley. 8 vols in 3. 8vo, half mor. wa Feb 29 (16) $180

# PEPYS

Anr Ed. L, 1928. ("The Diary....") 8 (of 10) vols in 3. Contemp half mor gilt by Hatchards. C July 1 (325) £280
Anr copy. 10 vols. calf gilt by Riviere. sg Sept 21 (37) $700
Anr Ed. NY, 1928. ("Everybody's Pepys.") Ed by O. F. Morshead; illus by E. H. Shepard. Later half mor, orig map endpapers bound in. Frontis stained. wa Dec 14 (25) $70
Anr Ed. L, 1935. Illus by E. H. Shepard. 8vo, mor gilt by Riviere, with onlaid design of a yawning Pepys holding a candlestick. CE Sept 27 (256) $450

**Peralta Grant.** See: Trials

**Perau, Gabriel Louis Calabre**
— Description historique de l'Hotel Royal des Invalides. Paris: G. Desprez, 1756. Folio, contemp calf gilt; spine ends repaired. With 108 plates, 31 of them double-page. Fuerstenberg - Schaefer copy. S Dec 8 (485) £1,400

**Percier, Charles, 1764-1838 —&**
**Fontaine, Pierre Francois Leonard, 1762-1853**
— Choix des plus celebres maisons de plaisance de Rome.... Paris, [n.d.]. New Ed. Folio, later half mor gilt; spine ends worn, joints cracked, endpapers brittle. With 97 engravings on 83 plates, 2 of them double-page. cb Oct 17 (38) $275

**Percival, MacIver**
— The Chintz Book. L, 1923. Met Dec 14 (238) $275

**Percy, Thomas, 1729-1811**
— Percy Folio of Old English Ballads and Romances. L: De La More Press, 1905-10. One of 320 on handmade paper. 4 vols. Folio, half cloth. wa Nov 16 (3) $80
— Reliques of Ancient English Poetry. L, 1765. 1st Ed. 3 vols. 8vo, calf; rubbed. Z June 28 (227) $300
New Ed. L, 1844. 3 vols. 8vo, contemp mor gilt. sg Sept 21 (38) $275

**Percy, Walker**
— The Last Gentleman. NY, 1966. 1st Ed. In dj with chip to spine head. pba Dec 7 (154) $50
— The Second Coming. NY, [1980]. One of 450. sg Dec 14 (240) $150

**Percyvall, Richard**
— A Dictionarie in Spanish and English. L: Edm. Bollifant, 1599. Bound with: Percyvall. A Spanish Grammar. L: Edm. Bollifant, 1599. Folio, 18th-cent calf; rebacked preserving orig spine, corners bumped. Hole in last leaf repaired with a few words in facsimile; soiled. Masterman Sykes copy. S June 27 (357) £300

**Perelle, Gabriel**
— Veues des belles maisons de France. Paris: Chez N. Langlois, [n.d.]. 7 parts in 1 vol. Oblong 4to, early calf; worn. With engraved titles & 283 plates on 252 leaves. Some browning; 1 folding plate with small tear. b June 28 (52) £3,800

**Perelman, Sidney Joseph, 1904-79**
— The Most of S. J. Perelman. NY, 1958. In worn dj. Inscr to Earl Wilson. sg June 20 (312) $110

**Peret, Benjamin**
— La Brebis galante. [Paris, 1949]. One of 300. Illus by Max Ernst. 8vo, orig wraps; soiled. With 21 plates & 3 etchings. Met Feb 24 (24) $900
Anr copy. Orig bds, in dj. With 3 plates & with an extra suite of the etchings & pochoirs. sg Apr 18 (121) $2,400
— Dormir, dormir dans les pierres. Paris, 1927. One of 205. Illus by Yves Tanguy. 4to, orig wraps; soiled. sg Apr 18 (119) $1,600
— Feu Central. Paris, 1947. One of 200. Illus by Yves Tanguy. 4to, orig double wraps designed by Tanguy. sg Apr 18 (120) $175

**Perez de Allecio, Matteo**
— Iveri Ritratti della guerra & dell'assedio & assalti dati al la isola di Malta dall'armata turchesca l'anno 1565.... Rome, 1582. Oblong folio, 19th-cent bds, edge-bound. With engraved title & 14 double-page plates. Worming at extreme edges, not affecting surface. S June 27 (154) £28,000

**Perez de Guzman, Fernan, 1377?-1460?**
— Cronica del Senor Don Juan, Segundo de este Nombre en Castilla y en Leon.... Valencia: Benito Monfort, 1779. Folio, 19th-cent sheep gilt; spine & extremities worn. sg Mar 21 (301) $550

**Perez de Valencia, Jaime**
— Centum ac quinquaginta psalmi Davidici cum expositione.... Lyons: Bernardus Rosier & Johannes Thomas for Stephanus Gueynardus, 1512. 3 parts in 1 vol. Folio, 16th-cent blind-tooled pigskin over wooden bds, with 2 brass clasps. With 6 woodcuts of 4 blocks. Gothic type, 1 word in Greek. Minor worming at end with minimal loss; some marginalia & underlinings; waterstaining at front. Mantz - Morris - Schaefer copy. P Nov 1 (170) $1,900

**Perez, Judah Leon de Joseph**
— Fundamento solido, baza y typo de la sacra, sancta y divina Ley. Amst., 1729. 8vo, modern lea. Wormholes penetrating text block affecting a few letters; browned & stained throughout. CE Dec 6 (223) $750

**Perez Quintana, Josef**
— Explicacion de las maquinas e instrumentos de que se compone una fabrica para telillas angostas de lana. Seville, 1785. 4to, contemp pigskin gilt. With 10 folding plates. Waterstaining throughout. S Nov 30 (330) £580

**Pergolesi, Michele Angelo**
— [Designs for various ornaments]. L, [plates dated 1777-92]. Folio, modern cloth with calf corners. With engraved dedication & 66 plates. Sold w.a.f. Ck Sept 8 (46) £820

**Perkins, Charles Elliott**
— The Pinto Horse. Santa Barbara, 1927. 1st Ed. - Illus by Edward Borein. Foreword by Owen Wister. 4to, orig cloth; front cover edge faded. With color frontis. Robbins copy. pba Mar 21 (29) $1,400

**Perkins, Elisha Douglass**
— Gold Rush Diary: Being the Journal of Elisha Douglass Perkins on the Overland Trail in the Spring and Summer of 1849. L, 1967. 1st Ed. - Ed by Thomas D. Clark. Orig cloth in dj. With 6 maps. Larson copy. pba Sept 28 (638) $60

**Perkins, John, d.1545**
— A Profitable Booke...Treating of the Lawes of England.... L, 1597. 12mo, contemp calf; front cover detached. Black letter. Some worming in outer margins, which are trimmed. sg Mar 21 (189) $850

**Perkins, Justin**
— A Residence of Eight Years in Persia. Andover & NY, 1843. 8vo, cloth; extremities worn. With folding map, 4 plain & 23 hand-colored plates. sg Mar 7 (259) $150

**Perkins, William, of Canada**
— Three years in California: William Perkin's Journal of Life at Sonora, 1849-1852. Berkeley, 1964. 1st English Ed. - Ed by Dale Morgan and James Scobie. Buckram. With frontis port, 2 maps & 8 illus. Larson copy. pba Sept 28 (639) $55

**Perlot, Jean-Nicolas**
— Gold Seeker: Adventures of a Belgian Argonaut during the Gold Rush Years. New Haven, [1985]. 1st English Ed. - Trans by Helen Harding Bretnor. Ed by Howard R. Lamar. Orig cloth in dj. With 23 illus on 8 pages. pba Sept 28 (640) $75

**Peron, Francois —& Others**
— Voyage de decouvertes aux Terres Australes. Paris, 1807-16. Historique, 2 vols; Atlas, 2 parts in 1 vol. With Freycinet's Voyage: Navigation et Geographie, plus Atlas. Folio & 4to, contemp half mor gilt, Atlas bound recently to match. Historique with 3 folding tables; Peron Atlas with 54 plates; Freycinet Atlas with engraved title & 32 maps & charts. S Nov 30 (222) £8,000

**Perottus, Nicolaus, 1430-80**
— Cornucopiae linguae latinae. Venice: Paganinus de Paganinis, 14 May 1489. Folio, contemp blind-stamped goatskin over wooden bds; repaired, some lea renewed. 374 leaves. Goff P-288. C Apr 3 (174) £3,600

Anr Ed. Venice: Bernardinus de Cremona & Simone de Luero, 1490. Folio, 18th-cent calf; rubbed. Some stains. Sold w.a.f. 301 (of 320) leaves; lacking Sigs. a & b, 2 leaves from Sig. P & final blank. Goff P-289. O Mar 5 (179) $450

**Perrault, Charles, 1628-1703**
See also: Eragny Press
— La Belle au bois dormant.... Paris, 1910. Illus by Edmund Dulac. 4to, orig wraps; 2 closed tears on rear wrap. With 28 mtd color plates. Met Dec 5 (154) $250

— Le cabinet des beaux arts.... Paris, 1690. Folio, contemp calf; worn, joints cracked & chipped. With additional title & 12 plates. Lacks last text leaf; spotted & stained. S Oct 27 (848) £360 [Shapero]

— Le Cabinet des beaux arts.... Paris, 1690. Oblong folio, half calf; worn & chipped. With 12 plates. Some soiling & dampstaining; worming to c.5 leaves at gutter margin; tape-repair to folding plate. wa Dec 14 (441) $220

— Cendrillon et les fees. Asnieres-sur-Seine: Boussod-Valadon, 1886. Bound with: La Barbe bleue et la belle au bois dormant. Asnieres-sur-Seine, 1887. Both are one of 200. Illus by Edouard de Beaumont. 4to, mor extra by Marius Michel; endpapers discolored at inner margin. S Nov 21 (342) £1,600

— Contes. Paris: Au Sans Pareil, 1928. One of 17 on velin de cuve for the Amis du Sans Pareil. 4to, mor extra with concentric circles & cones with titles of the 10 Contes, art deco bdg by Paul Bonet [Carnets 100], bound by Ferdinand Giraldon & finished by Andre Jeanne, 1929-30. With 11 engraved plates, 11 lithos & 11 colored wood-engravings, each by a different artist. Orig recipient's name erased from colophon leaf. Extra-illus with 12 proofs (1 sgd), 6 planches refusees & prospectus. C May 1 (124) £20,000

— Contes des fees. Paris: Lamy, 1781. 2 parts in 1 vol. 12mo, contemp calf. With frontis & 12 headpieces. Marginal repair to p.416. Fuerstenberg - Schaefer copy. S Dec 8 (486) £700

— Histoires ou contes du temps passe.... Paris, 1843. ("Contes du temps passe de ma mere l'oye.") 8vo, mor gilt by Cuzin, orig wraps bound in. Engraved throughout, each leaf interleaved with a blank. S Nov 21 (343) £2,500

Anr Ed. Paris, 1854. 8vo, orig half mor. Library markings. sg Sept 21 (273) $200

— Les Hommes illustres qui ont paru en France pendant ce siecle.... Paris, 1696-1700. 2 vols. Folio, contemp calf; rebacked retaining orig spine, rubbed. With engraved title & 102 ports. Some browning. S June 12 (91) £450

— Perrault's Popular Tales. Oxford, 1888. Ed by Andrew Lang. 8vo, half vellum. pba June 20 (263) $90

**Perrault, Claude, 1613-88**
— Description anatomique de divers animaux dissequez dans l'Academie Royale des Sciences. Paris, 1682. Part 1 only. 4to, contemp blind-stamped vellum; upper edges of covers worn. With 5 folding plates. 1 short tear repaired. J. F. Blumenbach's copy, sgd on verso of tp. S Mar 29 (708) £150

— Memoires pour servir a l'histoire naturelle des animaux. Paris, 1671-76. 3 vols in 1. Folio, contemp calf gilt; extremities worn, most of backstrip missing. Dampstaining & traces of mold; some foxing at end. Sold w.a.f. sg May 16 (332) $750

— Ordonnance de cinq especes de colonnes selon la methode des anciens. Paris, 1683. Folio, contemp calf;

joints & corners repaired. With 6 plates. Some browning. C Apr 3 (173) £700

— A Treatise of the Five Orders of Columns in Architecture.... L, 1722. Folio, modern half mor; spine head chipped, rubbed. With engraved title, dedication leaf & 6 full-page plates. cb Oct 17 (39) $425

**Perrinchief, Richard, 1623?-73**
— The Royal Martyr. L, 1676. 8vo, old calf; worn. wa Feb 29 (164) $180

**Perrinet D'Orval, Jean Charles**
— Essay sur les feux d'artifice pour le spectacle et pour la guerre. Paris, 1745. 1st Ed. 8vo, contemp calf; joints cacking. With 13 plates. bba Sept 7 (209) £350 [Sotheran]

**Perrissin, Jean, c.1536-c.1611.** See: Tortorel & Perrissin

**Perrot, Ferdinand**
— Marines dessinees d'apres nature et lithographiees. Paris, [c.1840]. Bound with: Cuvillier, Ad. Marines pittoresques lithographiees. Oblong folio, 19th-cent half calf, orig front wrap bound in. With 24 lithos in 1st work, 12 lithos in 2d work & 3 litho plates by others bound in. pba July 25 (431) $800

**Perrot, Georges, 1832-1914 — & Chipiez, Charles**
— A History of Art in Chaldaea & Assyria. L, 1884. 2 vols. 8vo, old half mor. pba Aug 8 (544) $120

— A History of Art in Primitive Greece: Mycenian Art. L, 1894. 2 vols. 8vo, old half mor; extremities rubbed, front joint of Vol II starting. pba Aug 8 (543) $120

**Perrott, Charlotte Louisa Elizabeth**
— A Selection of British Birds.... L, 1835. Part I (all pbd). Folio, sewn as issued in orig wraps; frayed, some soiling. With 5 hand-colored plates. Fattorini copy. C Oct 25 (37) £12,000

Anr copy. Sewn in orig wraps; upper cover repaired. C May 31 (38) £5,500

**Perry, George, Conchologist**
— Conchology, or the Natural History of Shells. L, [1810]-1811. Folio, contemp half mor; rebacked, 2 corners replaced. With 61 hand-colored plates. C May 31 (39) £2,000

Anr Ed. L, 1811. Folio, contemp mor gilt; worn, covers detached, spine lacking. With 61 hand-colored plates. Lacking half-title. S Nov 30 (40) £1,800

Anr Ed. L, [plates dated 1810, text watermarked 1823]. Folio, half mor. With 61 hand-colored plates. Some foxing. P Dec 12 (220) $3,000

**Perry, John, 1670-1732**
— The State of Russia, under the Present Czar.... L, 1716. 1st Ed. 8vo, modern calf; new endpapers. pba Nov 16 (358) $275

**Perry Library, Marsden J.**
— A Preliminary List of Books and Manuscripts Relating to the Life and Writings of William Shakespeare Forming the Collection of.... Providence: Pvtly ptd, 1891. Out-of-series copy in 4to. Later wraps with most of orig front cover laid on; worn & soiled. O Mar 26 (203) $325

**Perry, Matthew Calbraith, 1794-1858**
— Narrative of the Expedition of an American Squadron to the China Seas and Japan. Wash., 1856. 3 vols. 4to later cloth. With 140 litho plates (17 hand-colored) 3 lithos of colored woodblock prints & 7 charts (4 folding). Brittle; some browning, foxing & chipping; 2 folding charts torn in half along folds. Sold with material relating to the expedition. cb Feb 14 (2541) $1,200

Anr copy. 3 vols. 4to, orig cloth; Vol I in green, II-III in brown. Sold w.a.f. CE May 22 (370) $750

Anr copy. Lea presentation bdg; extremities rubbed. With 76 plates & 11 folding maps. NH June 1 (183) $775

Anr copy. Orig cloth; worn & soiled, loose, some gatherings detached. With 133 plates (18 hand-colored) & 18 folding maps. Some soiling. S June 27 (252) £1,100

Anr copy. Orig cloth; Vol I rebacked with orig cloth retained & some gatherings loose. Inscr to the New York Natural History Lyceum. sg Oct 26 (296) $1,700

Anr copy. Vol I only. Orig cloth. With 88 (of 89) tinted litho plates. sg Oct 26 (297) $350

Anr copy. 3 vols. 4to, later half lea. With 167 plates & 2 maps. Plate 144 trimmed & detached; notations on front free endpaper & table of contents. sg Apr 24 (599) $2,400

Anr Ed. NY, 1857. 4to, orig lea; extremities rubbed. With the nude bathing plate & the photography plate. sg Oct 26 (298) $600

**Perse, St. John**
— Winds / Vents. NY: Pantheon Books, [1953]. 1st American Ed. Folio, in chipped dj. pba Aug 8 (545) $75

**Pershing, John J., 1860-1948**
— My Experiences in the World War. NY, 1931. Ltd Ed, sgd. 2 vols. Orig cloth; rubbed & scratched. CE Sept 27 (221) $120

**Persius Flaccus, Aulus, 34-62.** See: Juvenalis & Persius Flaccus

**Person, David**
— Varieties, or a Surveigh of Rare and Excellent Matters.... L, 1635. 5 parts in 1 vol. 4to, contemp vellum; hole in backstrip, free endpapers renewed. sg May 16 (232) $550

**Person of Honour, A.** See: Ancillon, Charles

## 1995 - 1996 · BOOKS

**Persoz, Jean Francois**
— Traite theorique et pratique de l'impression des tissus. Paris, 1846. Vol IV only. Modern cloth. With 207 specimens of textiles mtd in text. Met Dec 14 (222) $250

**Perthuis, Leon**
— Traite d'architecture rurale. Paris, 1810. Contemp sheep gilt; rebacked retaining orig backstrip. With 26 folding plates. Some foxing. sg June 13 (25) $550

**Perucci, Francesco**
— Pompe funebri di tutte le nationi del mondo.... Verona, 1639. 1st Ed. 4to, 19th-cent bds. Marginal dampstaining. sg Mar 21 (255) $300

**Peter...** See: Goodrich, Samuel Griswold

**Peter, Armistead, 3d**
— Tudor Place. Designed by Dr. William Thornton and Built Between 1805 and 1816 for Thomas and Martha Peter. Georgetown, 1969. Printer's copy. Folio, half lea; minor wear. O Dec 5 (114) $475

**Peterkin, Julia**
— Roll, Jordan, Roll. NY, 1933. 1st Ed. - Illus by Doris Ulmann. sg Feb 29 (329) $175

**Peters, Charles**
— Autobiography.... Sacramento, [c.1915]. 1st Ed. - Illus by Lesley Jones. Orig wraps; spine fades. With frontis port & 14 illus. Larson copy. pba Sept 28 (641) $55

**Peters, DeWitt Clinton**
— Kit Carson's Life and Adventures. Hartford, 1873. 8vo, orig cloth; spine head & foot frayed. With double-frontis. Frontis foxed. Robbins copy. pba Mar 21 (277) $60
— The Life and Adventures of Kit Carson. Hartford, 1873. ("Kit Carson's Life and Adventures.") 8vo, later half calf; joints rubbed. sg Oct 26 (299) $60

**Peters, Harry Twyford**
— America on Stone.... Garden City, 1931. One of 751. 4to, orig cloth. b Sept 20 (532) £90
Anr Ed. Garden City, 1976. One of—751. 4to, cloth; soiled. Reprint of 1931 Ed. O May 7 (239) $130
— California on Stone. Garden City, 1935. 1st Ed, One of 501. 4to, buckram in dj; d/j sunned & torn. Robbins copy. pba Mar 21 (278) $325
Anr copy. Folio, orig cloth in dj & slipcase; torn, spine ends cracked. sg Apr 11 (248) $225
— Currier & Ives.... Garden City, 1929-31. One of 501. 2 vols. 4to, orig cloth; spine ends chewed, inner joint broken. O Mar 5 (180) $120
Anr copy. Cloth. sg Sept 7 (271) $400

**Petis de la Croix, Francois, the Elder**
— Histoire du Grand Genghizcan... Paris: widow Jombert, 1710. 12mo, later calf gilt; spine ends chipped, upper hinge weak. bba July 18 (132) £180 [Seydi]

## PETRARCA

**Petit...**
— Le Petit Neptune francais; or French Coasting Pilot. L, 1793. 1st Ed. 4to, contemp calf; rebacked. With 40 maps, charts & plans. 1 map in facsimile. S Mar 28 (181) £340
3d Ed. L, 1805. 4to, contemp half sheep; needs rebacked. With frontis & 41 folding maps. Frontis dampstained in margins. sg May 9 (94) $300

**Petit, Jean Louis, 1674-1750**
— Traite des maladies des os.... Paris, 1758. 2 vols. 12mo, modern bds. With 2 folding plates & folding table. sg May 16 (476) $225

**Petitjean, Charles —&**
**Wickert, Charles**
— Catalogue de l'oeuvre grave de Robert Nanteuil. Paris, 1925. One of 750. 4to, orig cloth, unopened. bba Oct 5 (291) £120 [Quaritch]
Anr copy. 2 vols. 4to, orig wraps & unsewn as issued. With 231 (of 234) plates. sg Jan 11 (307) $50

**Petity, Jean Raymond, Abbe de**
— Etrennes francoises, dediees a la ville de Paris.... Paris, 1766. 4to, 19th-cent half calf. With 8 plates & inserted port. Fuerstenberg - Schaefer copy. S Dec 8 (487) £480
Anr copy. Wraps. Fuerstenberg - Schaefer copy. S Dec 8 (488) £160

**Petrarca, Francesco, 1304-74**
See also: Limited Editions Club
— De remediis fortunae. Cremona: Bernardinus de Misintis & Caesar Parmensis, 17 Nov 1492. Folio, modern mor. 44 lines; tye 1:102R. Wormed at beginning & end; u6 lacking small section of outer blank margin. 166 leaves. Goff P-409. C Nov 29 (67) £1,700
— De remediis utriusque fortunae. Cremona: Bernardinus de Misintis & Caesar Parmensis, 17 Nov 1492. Folio, 19th-cent half mor; extremities rubbed, hinges reinforced. Some soiling & dampstaining. 165 (of 166) leaves; lacking final blank. Goff P-409. cb Feb 14 (2527) $1,200

### Canzonieri

— Petrarca don doi commenti sopra Sonetti & Canzoni. Venice: Albertinus Vercellensis, 26 Sept 1503. Folio, 19th-cent calf gilt; rubbed, upper cover detached, spine loose. With port of Petrarch on tp & 6 full-page woodcuts. Repairs to fore-margin of 1st 11 leaves; some staining; library stamp on tp. C Apr 3 (176) £2,200
— 1513. - Li Sonetti, canzone e triumphi.... Venice: Bernardino Stagnino. Bound in 2 vols. 4to, later half sheep; joints cracked, rubbed. Some staining & repairs. bba Sept 7 (197) £520
— 1514. - Il Petrarca.... Venice: Aldus. 8vo, 19th-cent mother-of-pearl overlaid with cut-out wooden frame, the whole decorated in gold, blue & red, central panel on upper cover with Aldine device. Some staining; 1st leaf wormed & remargined & supplied from anr copy. S June 12 (150) £310

## PETRARCA

— 1532. - Il Petrarca con l'espositione d'Alessandro Vellutello. Venice: Bernardino dei Vitali. 8vo, mor elaborately gilt with ivy-leaf design, lettered at center non a caso e virtute on upper cover & quest opere son frali on lower cover; joints rubbed, partly cracked at bottom. Lacking 2 leaves in quire A; name cut from blank upper margin of tp; some staining. Brunet - Gruel - d'Annunzio - Montesquiou copy, inscr by d'Annunzio to Robert de Montesquiou, 13 Dec 1910.   C Apr 3 (177) £8,000

— 1533. - Il Petrarca. Venice: heirs of Aldus Manutius & Andreas Torresanus. 8vo, mor gilt by Cape, with strapwork design in inlaid mor & gilt. Minor repairs to blank section of tp; soiled at beginning & end. Holden - Kalbfleisch - Doheny copy.   C May 1 (125) £4,000

— 1546. - Venice: Aldus. 8vo, 19th-cent half calf; worn. Oily stains to tp & last leaf.   pba Nov 30 (259) $200

— 1547. - Venice: Gabriel Giolito de Ferrari. 12mo, contemp citron mor gilt with enamelling in red & green by the Pecking Crow Binder; endleaves & silk ties renewed, portion of enamelling renewed. Dampstaining in upper margin of 1st few leaves. Ashburnham - Holford copy.   C May 1 (127) £12,000

— 1548. - Sonetti, canzoni, et capitoli. Venice: al segno de la Speranza. 8vo, 16th-cent goatskin gilt with paid of clasps hands at center. Hole at top of 1st few leaves touching 2 letters.   C May 1 (126) £2,200

— 1560. - Il Petrarca.... Venice: Gabriel Giolito. 8vo, old calf; rebacked. Tp rubbed.   sg Mar 21 (256) $325

— 1819-20. - Le Rime. Padua 2 vols. 4to, contemp bds. With frontis, port & 6 plates. Some spotting.   S Mar 28 (528) £240

**Petronio, Alexander Trajanus**

— De victu romanorum et de santitate tuenda libri quinque.... Rome, 1581-82. 1st Ed. 8vo, 17th-Cent vellum; soiled & wormed, spine torn. With title vignette. Title spotted; outer margins wormed; some soiling.   Ck Mar 22 (238) £800

**Petronius Arbiter.** See: Limited Editions Club

**Petrus de Abano, 1250?-1316?**

— Conciliator differentiatum philosophorum et medicorum. Venice: Giunta, 1565. ("Conciliator controversiarum, quae inter philosophos et medicos versantur.") Folio, old vellum; spine & fore-edges damaged. Lacking final blank.   sg May 16 (477) $600

**Petrus de Alliaco.** See: Alliaco, Petrus de

**Petrus de Harentals**

— Collectarius super libros Psalmorum. Reutlingen: Johann Otmar, 1488. Folio, contemp blind-stamped pigskin over wooden bds; worn. 50 lines & headline; double column; types 6:81G, 7:170G. Lower outer corners of 1st & last few leaves frayed & def through damp; some dampstaining. 208 (of 210) leaves; lacking C2 & C7. Goff P-474.   S Dec 18 (67) £650 [de Palol]

**Petrus de Palude**

— In Quartum Sententiarum. Venice: Bonetus Locatellus for Octavianus Scotus, 20 Sept 1493. Folio, modern vellum. 66 lines & headline; double column; gothic letter. Wormed; b1r soiled; marginal stains. 232 (of 248) leaves only. Goff P-502.   S Dec 18 (68) £260 [Aspin]

**Petrus Lombardus, 1100?-c.1160**

— Glossa magistralis Psalterii. [Nuremberg: Johann Sensenschmidt & Andreas Frisner, 1475-76]. Folio, contemp pigskin over wooden bds; lacking clasps. 45 lines; gothic letter. Marginal repairs; dampstaining; worming at end. 412 (of 415) leaves; lacking 1st blank & 2 text leaves. Goff P-476.   S Nov 30 (289) £750

— Sententiarum. Venice: Vindelinus de Spira, 10 Mar 1477. Folio, calf antique. 43 lines & headline; double column; gothic letter. Outer margins at end damaged & repaired; a few leaves dampstained; tear in 1 leaf. 241 (of 246) leaves; lacking a1 blank, a10, b1, penultimate leaf & final blank. Goff P-480.   S Dec 18 (69) £380 [de Palol]

Anr Ed. Basel: Nicolaus Kesler, 1486. ("Sententiarum libri IV.") Folio, 16th-cent blind-stamped pigskin; lacking clasps. 54 lines & headline; double column; gothic letter. Some worming, mostly margin. 232 leaves. Goff P-484.   S Dec 18 (70) £1,900 [Maggs]

Anr Ed. [Nuremberg]: Anton Koberger, [after 2 Mar 1491]. ("Quaestiones super IV libros Sentientiarum Petri Lombardi cum textu eiusdam.") Parts 3 & 4 only in 1 vol. Folio, contemp blind-stamped calf over wooden bds with metal fittings; rebacked. 64 lines of commentary & headline; double column; gothic letter. Dampstaining at fore-edge throughout; foremargin of last leaf of Part 4 repaired. 217 (of 218, lacking 1st blank) & 271 (of 272, lacking K1) leaves. Goff P-486.   S Dec 18 (72) £900 [Aspin]

Anr Ed. [Basel], 1516. ("Sententiarum textus....") Folio, 18th-cent calf; spine chipped, joints rubbed. Lacking 1 text leaf; wormed at ends; last leaf torn with minor loss; some dampstains & repairs.   S Mar 28 (492) £180

**Petry, Ann**

— The Street. Bost., 1946. Proof copy. Orig wraps.   sg Mar 28 (231) $275

**Pettenkofer, Max von**

— Ueber einen neuen Respirations-Aparat. Munich, 1861. 4to, modern half cloth; orig wraps bound in, wraps detached & brittle. With 3 folding plates. Plates browned & torn. Inscr to Prof. Ernst Bucher.   Ck Mar 22 (239) £550

**Pettigrew, James Bell**

— Animal Locomotion.... L, 1873. 8vo, orig cloth; spine ends & corners frayed.   sg May 16 (75) $150

**Pettigrew, Thomas Joseph**

— A History of Egyptian Mummies. L, 1834. 4to, orig half cloth; corners retouched, new endpapers. Some foxing.   pba June 20 (264) $325

— On Superstitions Connected with the History and Practice of Medicine and Surgery. L, 1844. 8vo, orig cloth; spine foot rubbed. Foxed. pba Jan 4 (333) $130

**Pettingal, John**
— An Enquiry into the Use and Practice of Juries among the Greeks and Romans. L, 1769. 4to, disbound. Tp & last leaf soiled. sg Mar 21 (191) $250

**Pettingill, Olin Sewall, Jr.**
— The American Woodcock. Bost., 1936. 4to, cloth; worn. O June 25 (207) $70

**Pettus, Sir John, 1613-90**
— Fleta Minor. The Laws of Art and Nature, in...Metals. L, 1686. 2 parts in 1 vol. Folio, old calf; recased & restored. With engraved port. Browned; tear to lower margin of port. Madsen copy. S Mar 14 (281) £1,000
— Fodinae regales.... L, 1670. Folio, later calf gilt; rubbed, upper bd detached. With frontis, 2 engraved plates & 2 letterpress plates. O2 torn at lower edge; some foxing. bba Nov 1 (291) £550 [P & P Books]

**Petty, Sir William, 1623-87**
— The Political Anatomy of Ireland. L, 1691. 1st Ed. 8vo, contemp calf; rubbed. Tear affecting text of G3; some spotting. b Sept 20 (163) £1,300
  2d Ed. L, 1719. ("Political Survey of Ireland....") 8vo, contemp calf; rubbed. b Sept 20 (164) £250

**Petzendorfer, Ludwig**
— Schriftenatlas.... Stuttgart, [early 1900s]. Folio, cloth; worn. sg Apr 11 (322) $150

**Petzholdt, Julius**
— Bibliotheca Bibliographica. Leipzig, 1866. 8vo, contemp half calf; rubbed, upper joint repaired, lower joint broken, spine dried & corroded. O Mar 26 (204) $80
  Anr Ed. Nieuwkoop, 1972. 8vo, orig cloth; rubbed & shaken. sg Apr 11 (249) $50

**Peyrey, Francois**
— Les Premiers Hommes-Oiseaux: Wilbur et Orville Wright. Paris, 1908. Contemp half cloth, orig wraps bound in. Inscr to Marcel Lheureux, 8 Sept 1908. sg May 16 (76) $300
  One of 10 on japon. Contemp bds, orig wraps bound in. sg May 16 (77) $375

**Peyrot, Jean Claude, 1709-95**
— Poesies patoises et francoises. En Rouergue [Villefranche de Rouergue: Vedelhie], 1774. 8vo, 19th-cent mor gilt by A. Motte with monograms of the Baron de Ruble. Fuerstenberg - Schaefer copy. S Dec 8 (489) £400

**Pfaeffle, Suse**
— Otto Dix: Werkverzeichnis der Aquarelle und Gouachen. Stuttgart, 1991. 4to, cloth, in dj. sg Jan 11 (143) $110

**Pfeffel, Theophile Conrad**
— Fables et poesies choises. Strassburg, 1840. 8vo, contemp mor by Simier. With frontis port, 5 color lithos, & 4 other lithos. Some foxing. Inscr by Paul Lehr to Louis-Philippe. S Oct 27 (1153) £260 [Robertshaw]

**Pfefferkorn, Ignaz**
— Sonora. Albuquerque, 1949. In dj with minor wear. With facsimile frontis, 5 photographic plates & folding map. pba Nov 16 (212) $55
  Anr copy. In chipped dj. pba Aug 8 (151) $65

**Pfennig, Johann Christoph**
— Historische Nachricht von der Nicolai Kirchen Bibliothek zu Alten Stettin. Stettin, 1791. 8vo, orig wraps; worn & soiled. Minor foxing & soiling. O Mar 26 (205) $190

**Pfnor, Rudolph**
— Architecture, decoration et ameublement Epoque Louis XVI. Paris, 1865. Folio, later half mor; worn & soiled, joints rubbed, spine ends worn & torn, front hinge cracked through, endpapers brittle. With 50 plates on india paper. cb Oct 17 (40) $475

**Pfyffer von Altishofen, Carl**
— Relazione della condotta del reggimento delle Guardie Svizzere nella giornata del 10 agosto 1792. Naples, 1826. 4to, orig wraps. With litho title, engraved dedication & additional title with port, 2 folding litho plates & 5 full-page plates. Some spotting. S Mar 28 (162) £200

**Phair, Charles.** See: Derrydale Press

**Phelps, William D.**
— Fremont's Private Navy: The 1846 Journal of Captain William Dane Phelps. Glendale, Calif., 1987. One of 500. Ed by Briton Cooper Busch. Orig cloth in dj. Larson copy. pba Sept 28 (642) $65

**Philadelphia**
— Desilver's Philadelphia Directory and Stranger's Guide for 1828. Phila., 1835. 8vo, orig half sheep; worn. Without the United States Register. sg Oct 26 (301) $225

**Philatelist...**
— Philatelist: an Illustrated Magazine for Stamp Collectors. L, 1867-76. 10 vols (all pbd). 8vo, orig cloth. bba May 30 (66) £340 [Fabricant]

**Philby, Harry St. John Bridger, 1885-1960.** See: Golden Cockerel Press

**Phileleutherus Dubliniensis.** See: Delany, Patrick

**Philelphus, Franciscus, 1398-1481**
— Epistolae. Venice: Joannes Rubeus Vercellensis, 28 Jan 1487. Folio, modern vellum. 54 lines; roman letter. Dampstaining, especially at end. 123 (of 126) leaves; lacking a1 blank & n3-4. Goff P-585. S Dec 18 (73) £400 [Carter]

— Odae. [Brescia]: Angelus Britannicus, 4 July 1497. 4to, 18th-cent sheep, with gilt arms at foot of spine. 29 lines; type 11:110R. Some staining; 1st 2 leaves guarded. 94 leaves. Goff P-606. C Apr 3 (175) £1,300

**Philip, Duke of Edinburgh —&**
**Fisher, James**
— Wildlife Crisis. L, 1971. One of 265, specially bound & with an added title, sgd by Prince Philip. 4to, mor by Zaehnsdorf. sg Sept 14 (55) $325

**Philipot, Thomas, d.1682**
— Villare Cantianum, or Kent Surveyed.... L, 1659. 1st Ed. Folio, 19th-cent half mor; rubbed, new endpapers. Map torn & repaired. bba Nov 1 (132) £600 [Marrin]
Anr copy. Contemp calf gilt; rebacked, new endpapers. With folding map. Map laid down & worn at folds; corrections & an index in a contemp hand. S Apr 23 (370) £600

**Philippe de Pretot, Etienne Andre**
— Recueil de Cartes pour l'Etude de L'Histoire Sainte. Paris, 1787. 4to, contemp half sheep; worn. With 13 folding maps Some dampstaining to about half the maps. sg May 9 (95) $400

**Phillipps Library, Sir Thomas**
— [Sale Catalogue] Bibliotheca Phillippica. Medieval Manuscripts. L, 1965-76. New Series: Parts 1-11. 4to, bds. ds July 27 (143) $225

**Phillips, Catherine Coffin**
See also: Grabhorn Printing
— Cornelius Cole: California Pioneer and United States Senator. San Francisco: John Henry Nash, 1929. 1st Ed. Orig cloth in slipcase. With frontis port & 27 plates. Inscr & sgd to Frederick Webb Hodge. With ALs of Cornelius Cole to W. P. Fessenden. Larson copy. pba Sept 28 (382) $120
One of 250. Illus by Will Wilke. Orig cloth; spine faded, corners bumped. Robbins copy. Sgd. pba Mar 21 (279) $50; pba Apr 25 (589) $55
— Portsmouth Plaza.... San Francisco: John Henry Nash, 1932. 4to, half vellum; 1 flyleaf missing, 1 corner of vellum darkened. Inscr. pba Feb 12 (370) $95
Anr copy. Half vellum. Inscr. pba July 25 (333) $120

**Phillips, Christopher**
— Steichen at War. NY, [1981]. 4to, cloth, in rubbed & soiled dj; shaken. sg Feb 29 (293) $70

**Phillips, Duncan**
— Alfred Hutty. NY, [1929]. One of 75. 4to, cloth. American Etchers, Vol II. sg Sept 7 (190) $150

**Phillips, Henry, 1801-76**
— The True Enjoyment of Angling. L, 1843. One of 100. 8vo, orig cloth; front hinge cracked, with frontis & next pages detached. pba July 11 (223) $50

**Phillips, Jayne Anne**
— Sweethearts. Carrboro: Truck Press, 1976. One of 400. Pictorial wraps; spine repaired. Cs to John & Elaine Gill laid in. pba Jan 25 (290) $100

**Phillips, John Charles**
— Wenham Great Pond. Salem: Peabody Museum, 1938. One of 100. Unopened. O Dec 5 (115) $130
One of 400. O Dec 5 (116) $80

**Phillips, John Charles —&**
**Hill, Lewis Webb**
— Classics of the American Shooting Field. Bost. & NY, 1930. With Complimentary Copy bookplate. O June 25 (210) $100; sg Mar 7 (511) $250
One of 150. O June 25 (209) $160

**Phillips, Paul C.**
— The Fur Trade. Norman OK, 1961. With concluding chapters by J. W. Smurr. 2 vols. pba Nov 16 (213) $110
Anr copy. Library markings. pba Apr 25 (593) $75

**Phillips, Philip, Engineer**
— The Forth Bridge in its Various Stages of Construction. Edin.: R. Grant & Son, [1889]. Oblong folio, orig cloth; rubbed. bbc Dec 18 (155) $425

**Phillips, Philip A. S.**
— Paul de Lamerie, Citizen and Goldsmith of London. L, 1935. One of 250. Folio, orig cloth. bba Apr 11 (24) £520 [Sims Reed]; W Nov 8 (82) £500
Anr Ed. L, 1968. Folio, cloth, in dj. W Nov 8 (83) £240

**Phillips, Philip Lee**
— A List of Geographical Atlases in the Library of Congress.... Amst., 1971. 2 vols. Reprint of 1909-20 Ed. sg Dec 7 (41) $425
— Lowery Collection: a Descriptive List.... Wash., 1912. Inscr. sg May 9 (30) $325

**Phillips, Philip Lee —&**
**LeGear, Clara E.**
— A List of Geographical Atlases in the Library of Congress.... Wash., 1909-20 & 1958-74. Vols V-VIII only. Cloth; worn, erasures on front free endpapers. bbc Dec 18 (116) $300
Anr Ed. Wash., 1909-20, 1958-74. 8 vols. 4to, orig cloth; rubbed. bba Oct 5 (363) £750 [Sims Reed]

**Phillips, Sarah**
— Physiologie du vie de champagne, par deux buveurs d'eau. Paris, 1841. Illus by Mm. Elmerich & Rouget. 12mo, orig wraps; backstrip torn. S Oct 12 (114) £150

**Phillips, W. S.**
— Indian Tales for Little Folks. NY, [1928]. In chipped dj. With 11 color plates. pba Aug 22 (827) $50

**Phillips, Wendell, 1811-84**
— Discours sur Toussaint l'Ouverture. Paris, Dec 1879. 12mo, cloth-backed ptd wraps; reinforced with cardbd. sg Mar 28 (126) $70

## 1995 - 1996 · BOOKS

**Phillpotts, Eden, 1862-1960**
— The Dartmoor Novels. L, 1927-28. One of 1,500, sgd. 20 vols. Half vellum; spines & flyleaves foxed. ACs laid in. pba Aug 22 (628) $70
— A Dish of Apples. L & NY, [1921]. Illus by Arthur Rackham. 4to, contemp mor gilt by Rennerds; scuffed. With 3 colored plates. F June 20 (530) $110
One of 500. Orig cloth; soiled. With 3 colored plates. pba June 20 (277) $650

**Philogenes Pandonius.** See: Brathwaite, Richard

**Philomela.** See: Rowe, Elizabeth

**Philomneste Junior.** See: Brunet, Gustave

**Phinney, Mary Allen**
— Allen-Isham Genealogy. Rutland VT: Tuttle, [1946]. One of 200. Inscr. pba June 25 (192) $375

**Phoenix, John.** See: Derby, George Horatio

**Photographic...**
— The Photographic History of the Civil War. NY, 1911-12. Ed by Francis Trevelyan Miller. 10 vols. 4to, orig cloth; worn, hinge cracked. Some staining & soiling, lower edges of Vol IV waterstained. wa Dec 14 (74) $210
— Photographic Times. NY, 1899-1912. Vols XXXI-XLVII in 18 vols. Half cloth; worn. Library markings. O July 9 (157) $550

**Photographie**
— Photographie. Paris: Art et Metiers Graphiques, 1930-47. 11 vols (all pbd). 4to, wraps, spiral bound. P Oct 5 (329) $4,000

**Physician...**
— Physician's Anatomical Aid. Chicago: Western Publishing House, [c.1890]. Folio, cloth; library code on spine. With 10 color plates only, backed with linen, several with overlaid sections.. Met May 22 (397) $300

**Piale, S.**
— Raccolta di 50 vedute antiche e moderne della citta di Roma. Rome, [c.1840]. Oblong 4to, modern half vellum. With engraved title & 50 plates. S June 27 (125) £400

**Piatigorsky, Gregor, 1903-76**
— Cellist. NY, 1976. One of 1,000. pba June 13 (220) $50

**Piazzetta, Giovanni Battista, 1682-1754**
— Studi di pittura. Venice, 1760. Oblong folio, later bds; lower joint split, extremities rubbed. With port & 48 plates of 24 subjects plus additional engraved title from anr Ed. Repair to margin. C Apr 3 (178) £5,200

**Picabia, Francis, 1879-1953**
— Chois de poemes. Paris, 1947. One of 749. Orig wraps. sg June 20 (368) $90

## PICASSO

— La Lois d'accomodation chez les Borgnes: "Sursum Corda." Paris, 1928. One of 365. 4to, orig wraps. sg Feb 15 (229) $225
— Poemes et dessins de la fille nee sans mere. Lausanne, 1918. 8vo, orig wraps. With 18 plates. sg Apr 18 (122) $450
— Rateliers platoniques. Lausanne, 1918. 8vo, orig wraps; some wear. Inscr incorporating 9-line poem & drawing to Pierre de Massot. sg Apr 18 (123) $3,400
— Unique Eunuque.... Paris, 1920. One of 1,025. Preface by Tristan Tzara. 12mo, orig wraps. sg Apr 18 (125) $200

**Picard, Edmond**
— Le jure. Brussels, 1887. One of 100. Illus by Odilon Redon. 4to, mor gilt by Sangorski & Sutcliffe. S Nov 21 (347) £4,000

**Picart, Bernard**
— The Ceremonies and Religious Customs of the...World.... L, 1733-39. 7 vols in 6. Folio, contemp calf; worn. With 215 (of 223) plates. Some worm-holes. S Oct 26 (191) £650 [Pollack]
— Ceremonies et coutumes religieuses de tous les peuples du monde. Amst., 1723-43. 9 vols in 8. Folio, contemp calf; worn, some hinges cracked. Sold w.a.f. pba Apr 25 (225) $2,250
Anr Ed. Amst., 1723-37. Vols I-VII only. Folio, contemp calf gilt; spines chipped. With 223 plates, some double-page. S Apr 23 (372) £900
— Impostures innocentes.... Amst., 1734. Folio, contemp calf; upper joint split, spine chipped. With port & 78 plates. S Mar 28 (527) £600
— The Religious Ceremonies and Customs of the...World. L, 1733-39. ("The Ceremonies and Religious Customs of the...World....") Vol III only. Contemp calf; scuffed & worn, joints tender. Some soiling. pba June 20 (266) $350
2d Issue. 5 (of 7) vols. Folio, contemp calf; rebacked. Sold w.a.f. CE Sept 27 (224) $900
Anr copy. Vol I only. Folio, contemp calf; scuffed. F June 20 (850) $600
— Le Temple des muses.... Amst., 1733. Folio, 18th-cent mor gilt; scraped. With engraved title & 59 (of 60) plates. Lacking Plate XXV; tear at head of Plate IX; tear in G1 repaired without loss; some spotting. Fuerstenberg - Schaefer copy. S Dec 7 (320) £650
— The Temple of the Muses. Amst., 1733. Folio, disbound with old calf bds. With 60 plates. Damage to endpapers, tp & 1st few leaves of text; some damp-staining. Sold w.a.f. Met May 22 (418) $1,050
Anr copy. Contemp sheep; badly worn, covers detached. Opening leaves dampstained in outer margin with traces of mold & corrosion along fore-edges; lacking engraved title. Sold w.a.f. sg Dec 7 (290) $850

**Picasso, Pablo, 1881-1973**
[-] Photographs of Picasso by Gjon Mili and Robert Capa. NY, 1950. Folio, acetate covers with plastic multi-ring binder, the front cover ptd with Alexander Liberman's name. With 20 silver-print photographs,

## PICASSO

mtd on bds, the 1st inscr & dated by Mili. Inscr by Mili to Alexander Liberman. sg Feb 29 (203) $1,800
— Picasso a Vallauris. Paris, 1951. Folio, orig wraps. Verve Nos 25/26. sg Jan 11 (357) $50
— Picasso lithographe. Monte Carlo, 1949-50-56-64. Text by Fernand Mourlot. 4 vols. Folio, orig wraps; stains on top edges. sg Jan 11 (354) $1,300
Vol I. Orig wraps; spine ends chipped. Some foxing to front & end matter. F Mar 28 (776) $450
Vol I. Orig wraps; spine ends worn. sg June 13 (313) $300
Vols I-II. Orig wraps. Ck May 31 (74) £200
— Quarante dessins en marge du Buffon. Paris, 1957. Folio, unsewn as issued in orig wraps. S May 16 (26) £900
— Sueno y mentira de Franco. [Paris, 1939]. One of 850 on verge. Folio, orig wraps, unsewn. With 2 etchings with aquatint, each with 9 illusts. First plate creased at lower corner; some spotting. S Nov 21 (348) £2,000
— Suite de 180 dessins.... Paris, 1954. Folio, bds. Verve No 29/30. b May 30 (476) £140
Anr copy. Bds; covers scratched. Verve No 29/30. sg June 13 (314) $400
Anr copy. Bds; front hinge weak, lacking front free endpaper. Verve No 29/30. wa Dec 14 (567) $220
— A Suite of 180 Drawings, 1953-54. NY, [1954]. Folio, orig bds, in chipped & torn dj. Verve Nos 29/30. sg Jan 11 (356) $300
Anr copy. Orig bds, in worn dj; bdg edges worn, front hinge weak. Verve Nos 29/30. wa Feb 1 (373) $160
ZERVOS, CHRISTIAN. - Picasso: Oeuvres de 1895-1972. Paris, 1942-78. Parts 1-33 in 34 vols. 4to, half mor, orig wraps bound in. P Dec 12 (136) $20,000
Anr copy. Parts 1-19 in 20 vols. 4to, orig wraps. P June 5 (314) $6,500

### Piccolpasso, Cipriano
— The Three Books of the Potter's Art. L, 1934. Ltd Ed. Folio, orig cloth, in chipped dj. sg June 13 (99) $300

### Picerli, Silverio
— Specchio secondo di musica.... Naples: Matteo Nucci, 1631. 4to, contemp vellum; new liners. Tear in A2; some staining. S Dec 1 (271) £1,100

### Pichl, Wenzel, 1741-1804
— Tre Quartetti per il clarinetto violino, viola e violoncello... Opera XVI. Amst, [c.1795]. Folo, unbound. Complete parts. C June 26 (277) £650

### Pichon, Jerome, Baron
— Vie de Charles Henry Comte de Hoym.... Paris, 1880. 2 vols. 8vo, half vellum, orig wraps bound in; worn. Minor marginal dampstains. O Mar 26 (206) $130

### Pickering, Harold G. See: Derrydale Press

### Pictorial...
— Pictorial Photography in America. NY, 1920. Vol I. Folio, half cloth; worn & soiled. sg Feb 29 (265) $120

### Picturesque...
— Picturesque America.... NY, [1872-74]. Ed by William Cullen Bryant. 2 vols. 4to, orig mor gilt; scuffed. With 49 plates, including engraved titles. Some foxing; minor marginal dampstaining. F June 20 (72) $150
Anr copy. Half lea gilt; extremities rubbed. With 49 plates. LIbrary markings; some foxing. NH June 1 (118) $200
Anr copy. Lea gilt; extremities worn. With 2 engraved titles & 45 (of 47) plates. NH June 1 (119) $240
Anr copy. Orig half lea. Minor dampstaining to bottom edge of plates. NH July 21 (121) $200
Anr copy. Lea; rubbed. Some foxing. O July 9 (159) $200
Anr copy. Mor gilt. pba Sept 14 (83) $325
Anr copy. Orig half lea gilt; scuffed. Stamps on tp versos. sg Oct 26 (302) $225
Anr copy. Vol II only. Pictorial cloth; needs rebdg. sg May 9 (322) $175
Anr copy. 2 vols. 4to, orig mor gilt. Plates in Vol II dampstained at top margin. wa Nov 16 (380) $260
Anr copy. Mor gilt; scuffed. With 49 plates. wa Feb 29 (126) $375
Anr copy. Orig mor gilt; worn & scuffed. With 49 plates. Foxed. wa Feb 29 (127) $260
— A Picturesque Description of North Wales. L, 1823. Oblong 4to, 19th-cent half calf. With 20 colored plates. Some discoloration. S Mar 28 (59) £460
— Picturesque Representations of the Dress and Manners of the English. L, 1814. 8vo, half calf; def. With 50 hand-colored plates. A few plates with foxing or soiling. sg May 9 (332) $500
— The Picturesque World: or, Scenes in Many Lands. Bost., 1882. 2 vols. Folio, orig half lea. With 88 plates. sg Dec 7 (291) $175

### Piedagnel, Alexandre
— Jules Janin. Paris, 1876. One of 10 on chine. 8vo, mor by David, orig wraps bound in. ANs of Janin tipped in. O Mar 26 (207) $130

### Pierce, Franklin, 1804-69
— Message from the President...at the Commencement of the 1st Session of the 34th Congress. Wash, 1856. Part IV: Illustrations Belonging to Reports Accompanying the Message. 4to, orig cloth. Inscr, 22 Nov 1856. K June 23 (424) $325

### Pierce's copy, Franklin
ANDREWS, C. C. - Minnesota & Dacotah in Letters Descriptive of a Tour through the North-West. Wash., 1857. Calf gilt; rubbed. Inscr by Andrews to Pierce. K June 23 (423) $600

## 1995 - 1996 · BOOKS

**Pierotti, Ermete**
— Jerusalem Explored. L, 1864. 1st Ed. 2 vols. Folio, half mor; vol II resewn. With 63 plates, maps & plans. S Oct 26 (192) £420 [Pollack]

**Pierres, Philippe Denis, 1741-1808**
— Description d'une nouvelle presse d'imprimerie. Paris, 1786. 4to, orig wraps. With 2 folding plates. Fuerstenberg - Schaefer copy. S Dec 8 (491) £1,400

**Pigafetta, Antonio, 1491-1534?**
— Magellan's Voyage... New Haven & L, 1969. 2 vols. Folio, cloth. pba Feb 13 (150) $180
  Anr copy. Cloth; soiled. pba Apr 25 (226) $120
— Primo viaggio intorno al globo terracqueo.... Milan, 1800. Trans by Carlo Amoretti. 4to, contemp calf gilt. With 2 folding maps & 4 hand-colored plans. C Apr 3 (179) £1,800

**Pigafetta, Filippo, 1553-1603.** See: Lopes & Pigafetta

**Pigage, Nicolas de**
— La Galerie electorale de Dusseldorff.... Basel, 1778. Oblong 4to, old mor gilt by Kalthoeber. With engraved title & 30 plates. Fuerstenberg - Schaefer copy. S Dec 8 (492) £4,000
  Anr copy. 19th-cent half lea gilt; rear joint cracked. With engraved title & 30 plates. Plate versos stamped. sg Sept 7 (279) $225

**Pignoria, Lorenzo, 1571-1631**
— Mensa isiaca, qua, sacrorum apud aegyptios ratio & simulacra subjectis tabulis aeneis simul exhibentur & explicantur. Amst: Andreas Fries, 1669. Bound with: Magnae deum matris ideae & attidis initia. Amst.: Andreas Fries, 1669. 4to, contemp vellum. With 12 plates, all but 1 folding, & 7 full-page illusts. Stamp on tp & at end. sg Mar 21 (262) $325

**Pigot & Co., James**
— A Pocket Topography and Gazetteer of England. L, [1842?]. Vol I only. 12mo, contemp calf gilt; rubbed & stained. With 21 maps & 21 plates, with contemp outline color. Some browning & marginal staining. S Mar 28 (89) £260

**Pigott, Charles**
— The Female Jockey Club, or, a Sketch of the Manners of the Age. NY, 1794. 1st American Ed. 12mo, contemp sheep; spine ends lacking. Browned. sg Feb 8 (329) $180

**Pigott, Grenville**
— A Manual of Scandanavian Mythology.... L, 1839. Half mor by J. Larkins; spine ends & joints worn. pba Nov 30 (249) $95

**Pike, Albert**
— State or Province? Bond or Free? Addressed Particularly to the People of Arkansas. Little Rock, 1861. 8vo, ptd wraps; chipped & frayed. Some soiling. O Nov 14 (143) $250

## PINART

**Pike, Gustavus D.**
— The Singing Campaign for Ten Thousand Pounds of the Jubilee Singers in Great Britain. NY: American Missionary Association, 1875. Ed by Theodore F. Seward. 8vo, cloth; worn. sg Mar 28 (238) $80

**Pike, Nicholas, U.S. Consul, Mauritius**
— Sub-Tropical Rambles in the Land of the Aphanapteryx.... NY, 1873. 8vo, cloth. sg Mar 7 (261) $175

**Pike, Nicolas**
— A New and Complete System of Arithmetic.... Newburyport, 1788. 8vo, contemp calf; worn. Some leaves loose & frayed; browned. O Mar 5 (182) $70

**Pike, Zebulon Montgomery, 1779-1813**
— An Account of Expeditions to the Soures of the Mississippi.... Phila., 1810. 1st Ed. 2 vols including Atlas. 8vo & 4to, contemp calf & contemp bds; both rebacked. With frontis port, 6 maps (5 folding), & 3 folding tables. Maps foxed & some crease tears. Robbins copy. pba Mar 21 (280) $7,500
— The Expeditions to Headwaters of the Mississippi River.... NY, 1895. One of 150 on handmade paper. Ed by Elliot Coues. 3 vols. 8vo, orig half cloth in djs; d/js soiled & worn. Robbins copy. pba Mar 21 (281) $650
— Reize Naar Nieuw-Mexico.... Amst.: C. Timmer, 1812-13. 2 vols. 8vo, orig bds; joints weak. With 3 folding maps. Ink stamps on titles; occasional browning. cb Feb 14 (2601) $750

**Piles, Roger de**
— Conversations sur la connoissance de la peinture.... Paris, 1677. 1st Ed. 12mo, contemp calf gilt; spine ends chipped, front joint cracked, later paper label on front cover. sg Sept 7 (279A) $400

**Pilkington, Matthew**
— The Gentleman's and Connoisseur's Dictionary of Painters. L, 1798. 4to, contemp calf gilt; joints & spine ends worn. Extra-illus with c.30 ports, most trimmed. bba July 18 (336) £60 [Basso]

**Pillement, Jean —& Others**
— The Ladies Amusement; or, Whole Art of Japanning Made Easy. L: for Robert Sayer, [c.1762]. Oblong half-sheets, 198mm by 322mm, wraps; worn. With 200 hand-colored plates. Corners thumped; worn & soiled; marginal repairs; 1 plate with tear along right plate mark. Schaefer copy. P Nov 1 (173) $40,000

**Pillsbury, Aetheline B.**
— The Real Yosemite. Oakland: Pillsbury Picture Company, 1908. Pictorial wraps bound with lea thongs. With 20 mtd photos. pba Feb 12 (220) $375

**Pinart, Alphonso L.**
— Journey to Arizona in 1876. Los Angeles: Zamorano Club, 1962. One of 500. Half cloth. pba July 25 (197) $55
— Voyages a la cote nord-ouest de l'Amerique.... Paris, 1875. Vol I, Part 1 (all pbd). 4to, orig wraps; spine split. pba July 25 (339) $50

## Pinch...

— A Pinch—of Snuff...by Dean Snift of Brazen-Nose. L, 1840. 8vo, mor gilt with mor onlays depicting hands taking a pinch of snuff, by Kelliegram, orig front wrap bound in. CE Sept 27 (54) $480

## Pinckney, Pauline A.

— American Figureheads and their Carvers. NY,[1940]. In chipped dj. sg Mar 7 (231) $50

— Painting in Texas. Austin, 1967. In dj. ds July 27 (145) $175; ds July 27 (146) $150

## Pindar, 522?-443 B.C.

### Odes

— 1928. - Stratford: Shakespeare Head Press One of 250. 4to, half cloth, unopened. wa Nov 16 (37) $170

## Pindar, Peter. See: Wolcot, John

## Pinder, Ulrich

— Speculum passionis domini nostri Jesu christi. Nuremberg, 30 Aug 1507. Illus by Hans Schaeufelein. Folio, contemp orange-painted vellum over pastebd, with remnants of lea ties; extremities rubbed, occasionally to pastebd, spine ends with tears, small sections lacking from lower outer corners. Roman type. With 39 full-page woodcuts. Minor repairs; wormhole at foot of last 2 leaves; some soiling; marginal notes in an early hand. C June 26 (114) £7,000

## Pine, John

— The Tapestry Hangings of the House of Lords. L, 1739. Folio, contemp calf; worn, upper cover detached. With engraved title, 10 double-page plates of sea battle; 1 double-page map & 5 double-page plates each with 2 maps. Wormed at inner margin affecting surface of 6 plates; most others with 1 small wormhole; lacking the 2 maps of Cornwall & Devon and the Thames. S June 27 (272) £3,000

## Pinelli Library, Maffei

— Bibliotheca Maphaei Pinellii Veneti magno jam studio collecta.... Venice, 1787. 6 vols. 8vo, orig bds; rubbed. Margin of Y2 in Vol VI repaired. bba May 9 (47) £600 [O'Keefe]

## Pinet, D. See: Gosse & Pinet

## Pinkerton, Allan, 1819-84

— The Detective and the Somnambulist. Chicago, 1875. Orig cloth. pba Dec 14 (116) $50

## Pinkerton, John, 1758-1826

— A General Collection of the Best and Most Interesting Voyages.... L, 1808-14. 17 vols. 4to, contemp calf; spines def. Sold w.a.f. CE June 15 (238) $950

Anr copy. 15 (of 17) vols. Contemp half lea; spines def. CE June 15 (239) $1,600

Anr copy. 17 vols. 4to, later cloth; extremities rubbed. Marginal dampstaining; some foxing. pba July 25 (443) $1,800

— Modern Geography. L, 1802. 2 vols. 4to, contemp calf; worn & broken. Some foxing. Sold w.a.f. O Mar 5 (183) $200

## Pinkerton, Robert

— Russia: or, Miscellaneous Observations on the Past.... L, 1833. 8vo, contemp mor gilt. With 8 hand-colored plates. Inscr to Dr. Bonnet. b Sept 20 (353) £100

Anr copy. Contemp calf; rebacked. With 8 hand-colored plates. Some foxing. sg Mar 7 (262) $150

## Pinter, Harold. See: Fowles & Pinter

## Pioneer...

— The Pioneer; or, California Monthly Magazine. San Francisco, 1854-55. Ed by F. C. Ewer. Vols I-IV in 24 nos. 8vo, contemp half mor & cloth; orig wraps not present; light stains, some shelf wear. Robbins copy. pba Mar 21 (59) $2,500

## Pious...

— The Pious Christian Instructed in the Nature... of the... Exercises... Used in the Catholic Church. Dublin: P. Wogan, 1823. 8vo, contemp calf; worn & warped, joints cracked. Dampstaining. F June 20 (117) $60

## Piozzi, Hester Lynch Thrale, 1741-1821

— Letters to and from the late Samuel Johnson. L, 1788. 1st Ed. 2 vols. 8vo, orig bds. sg Oct 19 (191) $1,600

## Piranesi, Francesco, 1748-1810. See: Piranesi & Piranesi

## Piranesi, Giovanni Battista, 1720-78

— Alcune vedute di archi trionfali. Rome, [after 1778]. 2 parts in 1 vol. Folio, bds; lea covering worn away, spine gone. With 2 engraved titles, 3 engraved leaves of text & 32 plates. Old stain along top edge throughout. K June 23 (425) $2,500

— Le Antichita Romane. Rome, 1756. 4 vols. Folio, 19th-cent half russia; spines def, joints broken. With port & 218 plates (with 2 anonymous plates at end of Vol IV of the Circus of Caracalla). S June 27 (285) £18,000

— Della magnificenza ed architetture de' Romani. Paris, 1836. Bound with: Piranesi. Osservazioni...sopra la lettere de M. Mariette. Folio, contemp half mor; worn. With 2 engraved titles, port & 41 plates. Plate guards browned. S Nov 30 (239) £1,800

— Vasi, candelabri, cippi.... [Paris, c.1836]. 3 vols. Folio, half mor gilt by Sangorski & Sutcliffe.. With engraved title & 111 plates. Some plates with blindstamps; a few plates discolored in margin. S Nov 30 (240) £5,000

## Piranesi, Giovanni Battista, 1720-78 —& Piranesi, Francesco, 1748-1810

[A collection of works bound in 25 vols, in half mor gilt by Tessier, sold at Sotheby's on 30 Nov 1995, lot 238, for £120,000]

## Pirsson, Louis Valentine, 1860-1919

— Fly-Fishing Days or the Reminiscences of an Angler. Wash.: Pvtly ptd, 1946. Half cloth; spine ends & corners worn. pba July 11 (225) $180

**Pirstinger, Bertholdus**

— Theologia Germanica. Augsburg, 1531. Bound with: Onus ecclesiae temporibus hisce deplorandis apocalypseos suis aeque conveniens. Folio, contemp blind-stamped calf over wooden bds; lacking clasps & catches. S Nov 30 (290) £600

**Pisanelli, Baldassare**

— Doctoris medici bononiensis de alimentorum facultatibus libellus aureus. Brussels, 1662. 12mo, modern half bds. With vignette title. Title soiled. S Oct 12 (63) £200

— Trattato della natura de'cibi et del bere. Venice: J. B. Porta, 1584. 4to, later 18th-Cent half vellum; spine wormed. With title vignette & blank A4. Some dampstains. Ck Mar 22 (243) £700

Anr Ed. Turin, 1612. 16mo in 8s, contemp vellum; soiled & wormed, upper hinge split. With vignette title. Soiled. S Oct 12 (62) £260

Anr Ed. Venice, 1666. 12mo, orig half bds. With vignette title. S Oct 12 (61) £200

**Piscatorial Society**

— The Book of the Piscatorial Society, 1836-1936. L, [c.1936]. 4to, orig cloth. pba July 11 (226) $120

**Pita Andrade, Jose Manuel**

— Les Tresors de L'Espagne d'Altamira aux rois catholiques. [Geneva, 1967]. 2 vols. 4to, cloth, in djs. sg June 13 (348) $175

**Pitcairn, Robert**

— Ancient Criminal Trials in Scotland. Edin., 1833. 3 vols. 8vo, later half mor gilt. pnE Sept 20 (157) £330

**Pitiscus, Bartholomew**

— Trigonometry, or the Doctrine of Triangles. L, 1630. Bound with: A Canon of Triangles. L, 1630. 4to, old half calf. 1st work lacking M8; A4 def; tp pasted to inside of front cover; 1st 4 leaves frayed & loose; some browning, staining & marginal worming. 2d work lacking all after K3; last few leaves frayed & loose. Sold w.a.f. STC 19967 & 19966. bba May 30 (418) £130 [Denniss]

**Pitt, Moses**

— The English Atlas. Oxford, 1680-81-83-82. 4 vols in 2. Folio, contemp half calf; spines chipped, corners bumped, much of marbled paper off bds. With engraved title, frontis, double-page plate & 174 maps, 169 of them double-page. Minor tears to folds, occasionally affecting surface; 1 map with tear in margin; engraved title & frontis bound as titles. C May 31 (67) £15,200

**Pla, Joseph**

— Obres de museu. Barcelona, 1980. One of 150 with bronze medallion inset into pocket inside upper cover. Illus by Salvador Dali. Folio, contemp mor over shaped wooden bds, with inset port of Gala Dali, by Jordi de la Rica. S Nov 2 (8) £500 [SMR Associates]

**Plaisted, Bartholomew**

— A Journal from Calcutta in Bengal.... L, 1757. 2 parts in 1 vol. 8vo, contemp calf; rebacked. With cancel-title (K4). S Oct 26 (73) £420 [Bank of Cyprus]

Anr copy. Recent half calf. With cancel-title (K4). Some marginalia & spotting. S Oct 26 (74) £700 [Christodoulou]

**Plakat...**

— Das Plakat: Mitteilungen des Vereins der Plakatfreunde. Berlin, 1910-21. Vols 1-12. 4to, cloth, orig wraps bound in. With inserted specimens including cards, notepaper, menus, etc.. P June 5 (237) $11,000

**Plath, Sylvia**

— The Bell Jar. L, [1963]. Bds, in rubbed dj. b Sept 20 (552) £280

— Three Women. L: Turret, 1968. One of 180. pba Jan 25 (293) $95

**Platina, Bartholomaeus Sacchi de, 1421-81**

— De honesta voluptate et valetudine. Venice: Laurentius de Aquila & Sibylinus Umber, 13 June, 1475. Folio, 17th-Cent vellum wraps; rebacked. With 93 (of 94) leaves. Spotting & dampstaining; last leaf mended; worming at extreme margin of a few leaves. Ck Mar 22 (244) £3,500

Anr Ed. Venice: Laurentius de Aquila & Sibylinus Umber, 13 June 1475. Folio, mor janseniste by Riviere. 32 lines; type 1:117R, 117Gk. Worming occasionally touching text. 93 leaves. Goff P-762. C Apr 3 (181) £21,000

Anr Ed. Venice: Tacuinus, 28 July, 1503. 4to, late 19th-Cent vellum. Some soiling & browning; t4 waterstained. Ck Mar 22 (245) £1,600

— Vitae pontificum. [Venice]: Johannes de Colonia Agripiensi & Johannes Manthen de Gheretzem, 11 June 1479. 1st Ed. Folio, 18th-cent calf gilt; rebacked, some tears on both covers. 40 lines; roman letter. Dampstaining at top of a few leaves; 1st & last leaf rebacked; tear in last leaf with loss to colophon; worming to some inner margins. 240 leaves. Goff P-768. S Nov 30 (291) £900

— Le vite di tutti i pontefici da S. Piero.... Venice: Bernardo Basa & Barezzo Barezzi, 1598. 8vo, old vellum; stained, upper hinge split. V2 torn & repaired with loss. S Oct 27 (1082) £210 [Zioni]

**Plato, 427?-347 B.C.**

See also: Limited Editions Club

— Le Banquet. Paris, 1928. One of 60, with a decomposition of the frontis, a suite of illus in blue & a decomposition of 1 illust. Illus by Sebastien Laurent. 4to, mor extra with geometric pattern by G. Crette, orig wraps bound in. With 25 colored plates, including frontis wood-engraved by Camille Beltrand. S Nov 21 (349) £2,200

— The Cratylus, Phaedo, Parmenides, and Timaeus. L, 1793. 8vo, modern half calf. Tp foxed. pba June 20 (325) $850

## PLATO

— Crito: A Socratic Dialogue.... Paris: The Pleiad, 1926. One of 475. Orig bds. bba May 9 (21) £190 [Heritage]
— Opera. Venice: Aldus, 1513. 1st Ed in Greek. 2 parts in 1 vol. Folio, 17th-cent sheep gilt, with arms of Armand de Monchy D'Hoquincour, Bishop of Verdun [Olivier 2042]; minor damage to surface. C Apr 3 (182) £30,000

Anr Ed. Basel, 1534. Folio, old vellum; needs rebdg. Stamp on tp verso; inkstain to lower margins throughout. Sold w.a.f. sg Mar 21 (263) $2,000

Anr Ed. Basel: Henricus Petri, Mar 1556. Folio, late 18th-cent sheep; front cover surface def. Early marginalia in Greek & Latin throughout; marginal dampstaining on last several index leaves. In Greek. sg Apr 18 (168) $1,300

Anr Ed. [Geneva]: Henr. Stephanus, 1578. 3 vols. Folio, 17th-cent mor; extremities rubbed. Occasional marginal soiling; some corners jammed; occasional worming in Vol II; Vol III with closed marginal tears in tp & following 2 leaves. The Garden - Hefner copy. CNY May 17 (34) $15,000

Anr Ed. Lyon: Guillelmus Laemarius, 1590. Folio, contemp vellum over bds; torn & cracked at spine, front hinge split. Lacking front blanks; tp wrinkled. In Greek & Latin. bbc Dec 18 (420) $450

— Opere. Lyons: J. Tornaesius, 1550. 5 vols. 12mo, 18th-cent calf; worn. Contemp annotations, possibly by l'Abbe Andre Morellet. S June 12 (96) £420
— Works. L, 1720. 2 vols. Calf; spine ends rubbed & repaired. pba Nov 30 (266) $200

**Platt, Sir Hugh**
— The Jewel House of Art and Nature.... L, 1594. 1st Ed. 4to, 19th-cent half calf; worn, upper hinge starting. Marginal tears to 2 leaves; marginal dampstaining & worming & repairs; last leaf with repaired tears & partly inlaid. S Dec 18 (113) £850 [Seeber]
— Sundrie New and Artificiall Remedies against Famine. L: P. Short, 1596. 4to, mor by Sangorski & Sutcliffe. Title affected by damp, with repair to margin; A2 also repaired; C3r soiled; E1 torn & repaired. Ck Mar 22 (247) £1,700

**Platt, P. L. —& Slater, N.**
— Traveler's Guide Across the Plains.... San Francisco: John Howell Books, 1963. One of 475. Intro by Dale L. Morgan. Half bds. With facsimiles of orig tp & map. Larson copy. pba Sept 28 (626) $50; pba Apr 25 (600) $55

**Plattes, Gabriel**
— A Discovery of Infinite Treasure, hidden since the World's Beginning.... L: for George Hutton, 1639. 4to, modern half mor; spine head rubbed. S Mar 29 (772) £460

**Plautus, Titus Maccius, 254?-184 B.C.**
— Comedies. L, 1769-74. 5 vols. 8vo, contemp calf; joints cracked or starting. sg Mar 21 (265) $225

## AMERICAN BOOK PRICES CURRENT

— Comoediae. Venice: Aldus, July 1522. 8vo, 19th-cent mor, with unidentified arms. Soiling & staining to tp; marginal foxing. sg Mar 21 (264) $1,200

**Playford, John**
— A Brief Introduction to the Skill of Musick. L, 1660. 8vo, old sheep; rebacked, new endpapers. Plate of a viol player loosely inserted; lacking port; D5-8 repaired in fore-margins with slight loss of text; marginal repairs; wormed at end. S May 15 (444) £850
— An Introduction to the Skill of Musick. L, 1694. 12th Ed. 8vo, 19th-Cent half roan; rubbed. With 2 illus. Lacking frontis & some music; p.1 torn; H3 with printing fault; browned. S Oct 27 (945) £200 [Schneider]

**Plea...**
— A Plea for Polygamy. NY: Panurge Press, [1929]. One of 1,010. Orig cloth. With frontis. pba June 20 (273) $150

**Pleasants, William J.**
— Twice Across the Plains.... San Francisco, 1906. pba Apr 25 (601) $950

**Plesch, Arpad**
— [Sale Catalogue] The Magnificent Botanical Library.... L, 1975-76. 3 vols. 4to, bds; vol 2 joints cracked. Includes price lists. sg Apr 11 (24) $130

**Plesch Library, Arpad**
Anr copy. Parts 1-3 (complete set) in 3 vols. 4to, With price lists. sg May 9 (308) $120; sg May 16 (334) $140

**Pletsch, Oscar**
— Was willst du werden? Berlin, [1862]. 4to, pictorial bds; worn & soiled. With pictorial title & 22 wood-engraved plates. O Mar 5 (24) $275

**Plinius Secundus, Gaius, 23-79**
— Buecher und schrifften von der Natur.... Frankfurt: Peter Schmidt for S. Feyerabend & S. Hueter, 1565. Folio, old half calf; corners worn. Browned & dampstained; A6 & B1 def. Sold w.a.f. sg May 16 (337) $1,100
— Historia naturalis. Basel, 1539. ("Historia mundi, libri XXXVII....") With dedicatory epistle by Desiderius Erasmus. Folio, 18th-cent calf; extremities worn, joints cracked. Dampstaining; cropped marginalia; old stamp on tp & next leaf. sg May 16 (335) $325

Anr Ed. Basel: Froben, 1545. ("Historiae mundi libri XXXVII...."). Folio, old calf; becoming disbound, most of spine gone. Outer leaves frayed; tp with Ms notes & hole below ptr's device; some foxing & soiling. Sold w.a.f. O Mar 5 (185) $450

Anr Ed. Lyons: Godefridus & Marcellus Beringus, 1548. ("Historia mundi, libri triginta septem.") Folio, old half sheep; rebacked. Tp creased & spotted; early marginalia; marginal dampstaining towards end; hole in gutter of last index leaf affecting a few words. sg May 16 (336) $350

Anr Ed. Paris, 1685. ("Naturalis historiae....") 5 vols. 4to, later calf; worn, some bds detached. Some spotting.  bba July 18 (130) £125 [Therese]
— The Historie of the World.... L, 1601. 1st Ed in English. - Trans by Philemon Holland. 2 vols in 1. Folio, contemp calf; worn, joints cracked. Lacking 4 leaves in vol I & final blank; tp repaired; some tears & holes. Sold w.a.f.  CE Nov 8 (133) $300
Anr Ed. L: Adam Islip, 1601. 2 vols in 1. Folio, calf; rebacked, old spine laid down, corners worn. Marginal tears to tp & prelims of Vol I; lacking b5 & 2 blanks; a few small holes in text.  S Mar 14 (285) £550
Anr Ed. L, 1634. 2 vols in 1. Folio, contemp calf; hinges cracked, spine heal repaired, fragment of Ms antiphonal on vellum bound in at beginning, rear free endpaper torn. Some shaving affecting sidenotes; dampstained at ends; ad leaf torn.  S June 12 (98) £360
Anr Ed. L, 1635. 2 vols in 1. Folio, contemp sheep; rebacked, worn. Tp reinforced at gutter; some foxing & browning.  cb June 25 (1789) $450
Anr copy. Contemp calf; joints worn. Marginal dampstaining.  CE June 15 (241) $650

**Plinius Secundus, Gaius Caecilius, 62-113**
— Epistolae. Paris: Jodocus Badius & Jean Roigny, 1533. ("Epistolarum, libri X.") Folio, 18th-cent calf with onlaid arms of Lee impaling those of Egerton. S June 12 (97) £250
Anr Ed. L, 1790. 8vo, mor extra by Henry Walther for Antoine Auguste Renouard. Renouard - Holford copy.  C Nov 29 (116) £550

**Plomer, Henry Robert**
— English Printers' Ornaments. L, 1924. One of 75, sgd & with 4 additional plates. 4to, orig half vellum; worn, corners bumped. Crosby Gaige's copy.  O Mar 26 (208) £120

**Plomer, William, 1903-73 —& Britten, Benjamin, 1913-76**
— Gloriana: An Opera in Three Acts. L, 1953. Out-of-series copy. Folio, orig vellum gilt.  bba May 9 (330) £280 [Williams]

**Plon, Eugene**
— Benvenuto Cellini. Paris, 1883-84. One of 30 L.p. copies on japon, with plates in 3 states. 2 vols in 1. Folio, lev extra by Chambolle-Duru.  sg Oct 19 (58) $1,000

**Ploos van Amstel, Cornelis**
— Collection d'imitations de dessins d'apres les principaux maitres hollandais et flamands. L, 1821-28. One of 100. 2 vols. Folio, contemp mor gilt by Charles Murton; scuffed, corners bumped, nick to spine of Vol II. With engraved title, port & 105 plates on 103 mounts, some in color or with color highlights added. Many plate versos stamped; some spotting & discoloration to margins & mounts. Schaefer copy.  P Nov 1 (174) $32,000

**Plot, Robert**
— The Natural History of Oxfordshire. Oxford, 1677. Folio, later half calf. With folding map & 16 plates. Tear to map fold.  bba Nov 1 (180) £550 [Old Hall]
— The Natural History of Staffordshire. Oxford, 1686. Folio, modern half calf. With folding map & 37 plates. Lacking leaf "Armes omitted"; folding map & some plates repaired.  bba Nov 1 (205) £700 [Baldwin]
Anr copy. Contemp calf gilt; 1 scratch on lower cover, crack to upper joint. With folding map dated 1682, port of Charles II (cut round & mtd opposite tp) & 38 plates, 26 of them double or folding. Some browning & staining; map folds strengthened; marginal repairs to plates; lacking subscribers' list. Schaefer copy.  P Nov 1 (175) $1,600

**Plowden, Francis, LL.D.**
— Jura Anglorum: The Rights of Englishmen. Dublin, 1792. 8vo, calf; broken, library bookplates.  pba Nov 30 (267) $120

**Pluche, Noel Antoine**
— Schau-Platz der Natur. Vienna, 1746-53. 8 vols. 8vo, contemp calf; rubbed.  S Mar 14 (288) £750

**Plumbe, John, Jr.**
— A Faithful Translation of the Papers Respecting the Grant made by Governor Alvarado to John A. Sutter. Sacramento: Sacramento Book Collectors Club, 1942. One of 80. Intro by Neal Harlow. Half bds. With frontis illus. Larson copy.  pba Sept 28 (693) $300

**Plutarch, 46?-120?**
See also: Limited Editions Club; Nonesuch Press
— Lives. Venice: Nicolaus Jenson, 2 Jan 1478. ("Virorum illustrium vitae...in latinum versa.") 2 vols. Folio, contemp blind-tooled Italian goatskin over wooden bds, the center decorated in Islamic style with 8-pointed star & knotwork; spine repaired. Type 1:115(111)R, 50 lines. Unrubricated. Stained. 234 & 228 leaves. Goff P-832. Abrams copy.  C Apr 3 (183) £24,000
Anr Ed. Venice: Ioannem Rigatium de Monteferato, 7 Dec 1491. ("Vitae illustrium virorum.") Folio, early vellum; worn & soiled. Some staining; wormed; last leaf detached; contemp marginal notes. Goff P-833.  cb Feb 14 (2528) $2,500
Anr Ed. Venice: Giolito, 1569-68. ("Vite de gli huomini illustri Greci et Romani.") 2 parts in 2 vols. 4to,, 18th-cent calf. Hole with loss on X5 in Vol I; washed annotations; 2 holes & repair in margin on H6; small repair affecting sidenote on R1.  S June 12 (103) £520
Anr Ed. Venice: Felice Valgrisi, 1582. ("Vite de Plutarco....") 3 vols. 4to, red mor gilt with arms of Mme de Pompadour.  C May 1 (129) £3,200
Anr Ed. L, 1612-10. ("The Lives of the Noble Grecians and Romanes....") 2 parts in 1 vol. Folio, later calf; upper cover detached. Lacking a prelim leaf; tp stained, repaired & laid down; some corners restored;

minor worming at beginning. bba May 30 (76) £160 [Rix]

Anr Ed. L, 1657. ("The Lives of the Noble Grecians and Romains....") Folio, contemp calf; worn & def. S June 12 (102) £220

Anr Ed. L, 1727. 8 vols. 8vo, contemp calf; glue to joints. pba Nov 30 (268) $425

Anr Ed. Phila., 1825. 4 vols. Calf gilt. pba June 20 (268) $85

Anr Ed. L, 1826. 6 vols. 12mo, later half calf gilt. sg Feb 8 (87) $275

Anr Ed. Bost., 1872. Dryden's trans revised by A. H. Clough. 5 vols. 8vo, contemp half calf gilt. sg Sept 21 (39) $275

— Moralia. L, 1704. ("Plutarch's Morals....") 5 vols. Contemp calf. pba Sept 14 (293) $225

— Les Vies des hommes illustres, grecs et romains. Paris: M. Vascosanus, 1559. 2 vols. Folio, 18th-cent calf with arms of the Duke of Sutherland; rebacked, rubbed. S June 12 (101) £250

— Works. NY: Colonial, 1906. One of 1,000. 10 vols. 8vo, pigskin. cb Oct 17 (290) $800

Anr copy. Half mor gilt; spine ends worn. pba Dec 14 (117) $140

**Pluvinel, Antoine de, 1555-1620 —& Menou, Rene de**

— L'Exercice de monter a cheval. Ensemble le maneige royal. Paris: Etienne Loyson, 1660. 2 parts in 1 vol. 8vo, contemp sheep gilt; rubbed, joints starting spine head chipped. With 6 folding plates. sg Mar 7 (512) $325

**Podarok...**

— Podarok detyam v' pamyat 1812 goda. [N.p., c.1814]. 34 hand-colored cards each with letter of the alphabet in top right corner, in orig pictorial box. S Nov 2 (330) £2,300 [Schiller]

**Podeschi, John B.** See: Mellon, Paul

**Poe, Edgar Allan, 1809-49**

See also: American...; Graham's...; Limited Editions Club; Sartain's...

— The Bells, and other Poems. L, [1912]. Illus by Edmund Dulac. 4to, orig cloth. With 28 colored plates. b Jan 31 (155) £130

One of 750, sgd by the artist. Orig lea; rubbed. With 28 colored plates. O Sept 12 (133) $650

— The Black Cat. [N.p.]: Cheloniidae Press, 1984. One of 60 in quarter lea with drypoint & extra suite of the wood engravings. Illus by Alan James Robinson. sg Feb 15 (70) $375

— La Chute de la Maison Usher. Paris: Editions Orion, 1929. One of 336. Illus by Alexandre Alexeieff. 4to, ptd wraps; backstrip chipped & splitting. With frontis & 8 illusts. sg Feb 15 (2) $150

— Eureka. Paris, 1864. 1st French Ed. - Trans by Charles Baudelaire. 12mo, contemp mor. S Oct 27 (1154) £50 [Robertshaw]

— Eureka: a Prose Poem. NY, 1848. 1st Ed. 8vo, orig cloth, in later cloth dj; spine ends reinforced, staining to front pastedown. pba Dec 14 (121) $1,000

— The Masque of the Red Death. Balt.: Aquarius Press, 1969. ("The Mask of the Red Death.") One of 25. Illus by Federico Castellon. 2 vols. Folio, half calf. With 16 lithos & with a separate folio containing 28 sgd lithos. sg May 23 (279) $800

— The Murders in the Rue Morgue. Antibes, France: Allen Press, 1958. One of 150. pba Nov 30 (11) $140; pba June 20 (25) $140

— The Narrative of Arthur Gordon Pym.... L, 1838. 12mo, orig cloth; stained, spine ends repaired, 1st signature sprung. Thomas Woomer's copy. K June 23 (427) $700

Anr copy. Orig cloth; spine ends frayed, front joint torn. Some foxing & browning; owner's stamp on tp verso. sg Sept 21 (276) $100

— Poetical Works. L: Addey & Co., 1853. Orig cloth; upper hinge cracked. CE May 22 (380) $200

— The Poetical Works. L, 1858. 8vo, mor extra jeweled bdg by Sangorski & Sutcliffe; upper hinge repaired. P June 5 (315) $6,500

— The Purloined Letter. Phila., 1845 [1844]. 1st Issue. 8vo, orig mor gilt; scuffed, a few signatures sprung, piece lacking from front free endpaper. With 7 (of 8) plates. Plates foxed. In: The Gift: A Christmas, New Year, and Birthday Present. bbc Feb 26 (333) $400

— Quinze histoires.... Paris: Les Amis des Livres, 1897. One of 13 for presentation, this for Mme Terah-Haggin, with additional suite of the etchings. Trans by Charles Baudelaire; illus by Louis Legrand. 4to, mor extra by Chambolle-Duru, orig wraps bound in. Rahir copy. S Nov 21 (350) £700

— The Raven. NY, 1884. Illus by Gustave Dore. Folio, orig cloth; worn & soiled. With 26 plates. Some fingersoiling; 1 plate loose. wad Oct 18 (74) C$320

Anr Ed. Berlin: Rogall Hand-Press-Laboratory, [1924]. One of 50. Illus & with calligraphy by Rafaello Busoni. Folio,; half vellum. Lithographed throughout. sg Feb 15 (235) $225

Anr Ed. Brooklyn: F. K. Lane, [1962]. Ltd Ed. Illus by Augustine Mantia. 4to, orig cloth; loose. Ptd from wood blocks. sg Feb 15 (236) $140

— The Raven, and Other Poems. L, 1846. 1st English Ed. 8vo, orig cloth; rebacked with orig backstrip laid down, endpapers renewed. Some staining. CE May 22 (378) $900

— Tales. NY, 1845. 1st Ed, 1st Issue. 8vo, contemp half lea; rubbed, spine heel with small split. Lacking ads; dampstain to foremargin. CNY May 17 (103) $4,500

— Tales of Mystery and Imagination. L, 1919. Illus by Harry Clarke. 4to, cloth; some wear, endpapers browned. With 24 plates. sg Feb 15 (74) $150

Anr Ed. L & NY, [1923]. 4to, mor gilt by Whitman Bennett; joints & spine head worn. Ls from Bennett about the bdg inserted. sg Sept 14 (91) $100

Anr Ed. L, 1935. Illus by Arthur Rackham. 4to, orig cloth; warped & rubbed. bba May 30 (314) £60 [Clancey]

Anr copy. Syn gilt, in dj. Ck May 31 (170) £280

Anr copy. Orig cloth, in repaired dj. sg Oct 19 (212) $425

One of 460. Vellum gilt. CE Sept 27 (239) $1,600; pn Dec 7 (98) £580; sg Feb 15 (257) $1,600

Anr copy. Vellum gilt; spine browned. wd Nov 15 (103) $1,100

Out-of-series Presentation copy. Orig vellum gilt. With 12 colored plates. sg Oct 19 (211) $1,200

— Tales of the Grotesque and Arabesque.... Phila., 1840. 1st Ed. 2 vols. 12mo, orig cloth; stained, free endpapers lacking in Vol I; split at outer joint & front hinge broken on Vol I. Stain at gutter of tp. Hogan - Hersholt copy. CE Feb 21 (199) $2,800

— Works. NY, 1850-56. Vols I-III (of 4). 12mo, orig cloth; joints repaired, some wear. Minor staining & foxing. CE May 22 (379) $850

Anr Ed. NY, 1850. 1st Ptg. 2 vols. Orig cloth, A bdg but with tan endpapers. Z June 28 (228) $300

Anr Ed. Chicago, 1894-95. 10 vols. 8vo, half mor. pba Dec 14 (125) $1,900

Anr Ed. L, 1895. One of 100. 8 vols. 8vo, half mor; extremities worn, 1 hinge cracked. sg Feb 8 (88) $225

Arnheim Ed. NY, [1902]. one of 500. 10 vols. Mor gilt. cb Oct 17 (291) $3,250

Tamerlane Ed. NY, 1902. one of 300. 10 vols. Half vellum gilt; soiled. F June 20 (501) $100

Centenary Ed. Akron, [1908]. One of 1,000. 10 vols. Half lea gilt; some nicks & edge-wear. CE Sept 27 (227) $700

**Poellnitz, Carl Ludwig, Baron von**

— La Saxe galante. Amst., 1734. 8vo, contemp calf with Bedford arms. Bedford - Astor copy. b May 30 (331) £150

Anr copy. 19th-cent mor gilt by Hardy-Mennil, armorial bdg. Fuerstenberg - Schaefer copy. S Dec 8 (497) £450

**Poem...**

— A Poem upon the Undertaking of the Royal Company of Scotland trading to Africa and the Indies. Edin.: James Wardlaw, 1697. 8vo, early 19th-cent half calf gilt; extremities worn. Soiled & dampstained. sg Mar 21 (98) $1,500

**Poetas...**

— Los Poetas del Mundo defienden al Pueblo Espanol. Chapelle-Reanville, 1937. 6 nos. Folio, unsewn as issued. Each annotated by Nancy Cunard in pencil. Hobson set. S June 28 (154) £3,800

**Poetic...**

— A Poetic Epistolary Description of the City of York.... York, 1811. 8vo, orig wraps. Some discoloring & paper repairs. Sometimes attributed to N. Knelland. b Dec 5 (476) £80

**Poetical...**

— The Poetical Magazine. L: R. Ackermann, 1809-11. Vols I-IV. 8vo, contemp half mor by Tout. With 52 hand-colored plates. Lacking 2 engraved titles & To Readers leaves. S Apr 23 (279) £520

**Poetry...**

— Poetry of the College Magazine. Windsor, 1819. Disbound. b Dec 5 (2) £200

— The Poetry Quartos. NY, 1929. One of 475. 12 parts. Orig wraps. pba May 23 (344) $60

**Poets...**

— The Poets of the Nineteenth Century. L, 1857. 4to, mor gilt. pba Dec 14 (8) $55

**Pogany, Willy, 1882-1956**

— Willy Pogany's Mother Goose. NY, [1929]. 4to, pictorial cloth, in frayed & repaired dj. O Sept 12 (134) $425

**Poggendorf, Johann Christian, 1796-1877**

— Biographisch-literarisches Handwoerterbuch zur Geschichte der exacten Wissenschaften.... Amst., 1965. Reprint of 1863 Ed. Vols I-V in 6. 8vo, orig cloth; spines faded & rubbed. sg Apr 11 (293) $600

**Poggiali, Gaetano**

— Serie de' Testi di Lingua Stampati... Accademici della Crusca. Livorno: Masi, 1813. 2 vols. 8vo, contemp bds. Some foxing. O Mar 26 (209) $100

**Poingdestre, John Edmund**

— Nevada County Mining and Business Directory, 1895.... Oakland: Pacific Press, [1895]. Half lea; missing piece of cloth, joints cracked. Tape-repaired tear to map. pba Aug 22 (950) $170

**Poisson, Simeon Denis, 1781-1840**

— Traite de mechanique. Paris, 1833. 2 vols. 8vo, contemp half calf gilt; extremities worn, front joint starting & spine worn on Vol II. Some foxing. sg May 16 (235) $225

**Poissonnier Desperrieres, Antoine, 1722-93**

— Memoire sur les avantages qu'il auroit a changer absolument la nourriture des gens de mer. Paris, 1771. 1st Ed. 4to, disbound. Ck Mar 22 (248) £160

**Poldo d'Albenas, Jean**

— Discours historial de l'antique et illustre cite de Nismes. Lyons, 1560. Folio, vellum with yapp edges; 15th-cent liturgical Ms used as spine reinforcement, extremities worn, some staining, cockling & creasing. With 17 double-page woodcuts & 16 woodcuts in text. Dampstain to lower right of gatherings a-e; city view shaved at fore-edge. Schaefer copy. P Nov 1 (176) $4,000

**Poleni, Giovanni**

— Miscellanea.... Venice, 1709. 1st Ed. 4to, contemp half sheep; rubbed, spine foot & corners chipped. With engraved title & 9 folding plates. Inkstamp removed from tp; small stain to half-title; Plates 1-3 with short tears along platemarks. CNY May 17 (35) $6,500

**Polidori, John William**

— The Vampyre. L, 1819. 2d Issue. 8vo, modern lea gilt by Geoffrey Moore. Z June 28 (230) $600

### Polignac, Melchior de
— L'Anti-Lucrece. Paris, 1749. 2 vols in 1. 8vo, contemp mor gilt with added arms of the marquis de Trans-Flayosc. Fuerstenberg - Schaefer copy. S Dec 8 (495) £400

### Politi, Leo
— Pedro, Angel of Olvera Street. NY, [1946]. In dj. Inscr. pba Aug 22 (828) $60

### Politianus, Angelus, 1454-94
— Illustrium virorum epistole. Paris: Jodocus Badius, 1526. 4to, old sheep gilt; extermities worn, covers detached, spine ends chipped. Browned; some marginalia. sg Mar 21 (267) $350
— Opera. Venice: Aldus, July 1498. Folio, modern pigskin with rebus of Wilfred Merton stamped in gilt, by Katherine Adams, sgd. 38 lines & headline; types 2:114R, 7:114Gk. 452 leaves. Goff P-886. Domenico Lazzarini's annotated copy. C June 26 (116) £12,000

### Poliziano, Angelo. See: Politianus, Angelus

### Polk, Dora Beale
— The Island of California. Spokane, 1991. pba Feb 13 (152) $75
Anr copy. In dj. pba July 25 (199) $60

### Polk, James K., 1795-1849
— Message from the President of the United States to the Two Houses of Congress at the Commencement of the Second Session of the Thirtieth Congress. Wash., 1848. 8vo, later wraps. With 6 folding & 1 hand-colored map. Some darkening & aging. Robbins copy. pba Mar 21 (49) $1,200
**Polk's copy, James K.**
RUSH, RICHARD. - Letter from the Secretary of the Treasury...in Relation to the Growth and Manufacture of Silk.... Wash., 1828. 8vo, orig bds; rebacked, rubbed. Some foxing. Sgd by Polk on front cover & on tp. sg Sept 28 (218) $1,500

### Pollard, Alfred William
See also: Bartlett & Pollard; Short-Title Catalogue
— Cobden-Sanderson and the Doves Press. San Francisco: John Henry Nash, 1929. One of 27 with inserted vellum leaf. Folio, orig vellum gilt. sg Sept 14 (107) $550
One of 339. Vellum. sg Sept 14 (298) $325
— Early Illustrated Books. L, 1893. pba Aug 8 (333) $95
— Shakespeare Folios and Quartos. L, 1909. Folio, half cloth. With taped catalog cuttings. Endpapers browned. sg Apr 11 (252) $300

### Pollard, Edward Albert, 1831-72
— Southern History of the War. NY, 1863-66. ("The First [-Second -Third - Last] Year of the War....") 8vo, orig cloth; some wear & fraying. Lacking map in 1st vol; some foxing. F Mar 28 (178) $120

### Pollard, Graham. See: Carter & Pollard

### Pollard, Hugh Bertie Campbell
— The Gun Room Guide. L, 1930. One of 225. 4to, orig half vellum; minor wear. O June 25 (215) $275

### Polley, Jacobus. See: Horst & Polley

### Polo, Marco, 1254?-1324?
See also: Limited Editions Club
— Il Milione. Milan: Lucini, 1982. One of 125. Folio, contents loose in wraps as issued. With 8 orig lithos, each sgd by the artist. Ck Apr 12 (266) £350
— The Travels.... L, 1818. 4to, modern half calf. Upper corner of tp replaced. pba Sept 14 (295) $275

### Polwhele, Richard
— The History of Cornwall. L, 1816. 7 vols in 2, including Whitaker's Supplement. 4to, library cloth. Mount's Bay plates torn at folds. bba Nov 1 (39) £300 [Phelps]

### Polyaenus
— Stratagems of War. L, 1796. 4to, later half mor; broken. wa Feb 29 (201) $120

### Polybius, 205?-125? B.C.
— Histoire.... Paris, 1753. 7 vols. 4to, contemp calf gilt; worn, joints weak. With 3 folding maps & 123 plates, some folding. Some foxing. bbc Feb 26 (132) $600

### Pomet, Pierre
— A Compleat History of Druggs.... L, 1712. 2 vols in 1. 4to, contemp calf; rebacked retaining orig backstrip. With 86 plates. Browning to 3 plates. sg Oct 19 (172) $850
Anr Ed. L, 1725. 4to, 19th-cent half russia; spine & upper bd torn. With 86 plates. Many plates shaved; last 2 leaves soiled. S June 12 (307) £420
— Histoire generale des drogues.... Paris, 1694. 1st Ed. 3 (of 4) parts in 1 vol. Folio, contemp sheep; worn, front cover & half-title loose. Some worming, occasionally entering text. sg Dec 7 (231) $225

### Pomier, Louis
— L'Art de Cultiver les Muriers-Blancs.... Orleans, 1763. ("Traite sur la culture des muriers blancs....") 8vo, contemp red mor gilt with arms of Louis Joseph de Bourbon-Conde. Fuerstenberg - Schaefer copy. S Dec 8 (498) £950

### Pompadour, Jeanne Antoinette, Marquise de, 1721-64
— Suite d'estampes gravees par Madame la marquise de Pompadour d'apres les pierres gravees de Guay graveur du Roy. Paris, [1782]. 4to, contemp calf; joints repaired, spine chipped at head. With frontis & 70 plates plus port of Mme de Pompadour inserted. Browned. Fuerstenberg - Schaefer copy. S Dec 8 (499) £1,150

### Pompei, P. P.
— Etat actuel de la Corse.... Paris, 1821. 8vo, contemp half mor; extremities rubbed. sg Mar 7 (305) $130

## Pomposo Fernandez de San Salvador, Agustin

— El Modelo de los cristianos presentado a los insurgentes de America. Mexico, 1814. One of 12 bound in lea. Contemp calf gilt. S Nov 30 (170) £600

## Poncelet, Polycarpe

— Chimie du gout et de l'odorat. Paris, 1755. 1st Ed. 8vo, modern calf; spine faded. With frontis by B. Audran, & 6 plates. Frontis torn; title soiled; marginal soiling & dampstaining. Ck Mar 22 (249) £220

## Pontanus, Johannes Isaac, 1571-1640

— Historiae Gelricae libri XIV. Harderwijk, 1639. Folio, contemp blind-stamped vellum. With engraved title, 4 ports, 4 double-page plans & 5 double-page maps. Ink notes on front blank. sg Apr 18 (170) $1,400

— Rerum et urbis Amstelodamensium historia.... Amst., 1611. Folio, contemp vellum. Browned; marginal dampstains; tp frayed & rehinged. sg Mar 7 (306) $1,100

Anr copy. Some browning. sg Apr 18 (169) $4,000

## Pontanus, Johannes Jovianus, 1426-1503

— Opera. Venice: Aldus 1518-19. 3 vols. 4to, later vellum. Repairs to 1st few leaves of Vol I; colophon of Vol I stained; staining to Vols I & III; a few leaves discolored; some old notes in margins. cb Feb 14 (2529) $1,200

## Pontifical

— Pontificales Romanum Clementis VIII primum. Rome: ex typographia Medicea, 1611. Folio, contemp calf gilt over wooden bds with Jesuit monogram; worn, lacking 2 clasps. S Mar 14 (290) £600

## Ponting, Herbert George

— The Great White South. Being an Account.... L, 1921. 8vo, orig cloth; spine repaired, 1 plate detached but present. pba July 25 (57) $140

## Pontoppidan, Erik, 1698-1764

— Den Danske Atlas eller konge-riget Dannemark. Copenhagen, 1763-81. 7 vols. 4to, contemp calf; repaired. With 95 folding maps & plans & 201 folding plates. A few fold tears; some discoloration. Madsen copy. S Mar 14 (292) £1,300

Anr copy. Contemp calf gilt; rubbed. With 94 (of 95) folding maps & town plans & 201 folding plates. Some tears without loss. S June 13 (556) £1,300

— The Natural History of Norway. L, 1755. 1st English Ed. Folio, contemp half calf; rebacked. With folding map & 28 plates. Some spotting. S Oct 26 (291) £360 [Sutton]

— Theatrum Daniae veteris et modernae. Bremen: Hermann Jaeger, 1730. 2 parts in 1 vol. 4to, contemp calf; rubbed. With folding general map & 34 plates. Map repaired at fold without loss; some spotting. S Mar 14 (291) £550

## Poole, George Ayliffe —& Hugall, J. W.

— An Historical & Descriptive Guide to York Cathedral and its Antiquities. York, 1850. 4to, orig bds; worn, joints cracked. With 38 plates. sg Sept 7 (18) $130

## Poor, Charles Lane. See: Derrydale Press

## Poor's...

— Poor's Manual of the Railroads of the United States. [N.p.], 1888-1915. 28 vols. 8vo, orig cloth, 1888 vol in later cloth; varying wear. Library markings. K Feb 11 (328) $2,700

## Poortenaar, Jan

— The Technique of Prints and Art Reproduction Processes. L, [1933]. 4to, half cloth; smoke damage to covers. pba Aug 8 (570) $130

## Pope, Alexander, 1688-1744

— Works. L, 1751. 9 vols. 8vo, contemp calf; rebacked. With 24 plates. b Jan 31 (103) £80

Anr Ed. L, 1753. 9 vols. 8vo, contemp calf gilt; some wear. b May 30 (413) £140

Anr Ed. L, 1776. 6 vols. 12mo, contemp sheep; some joints weak. sg Feb 8 (89) $175

## Pope, Richard, 1799-1859

— An University Prize Poem.... Cork, 1817. 8vo, orig ptd bds; soiled. b Dec 5 (612) £80

## Pope, Walter, c.1629-1714

— The Memoires of Monsieur Du-Vall.... L, 1670. 1st Ed. 4to, modern calf. Last leaf with repaired chip. CE May 22 (384) $130

## Popham, Arthur Ewart

— Catalogue of the Drawings of Parmigianino. New Haven, 1971. 3 vols. 4to, orig cloth. CE Feb 21 (196) $600; sg June 13 (277) $650

## Porcacchi, Thomaso

— L'Isole piu famose del mondo. Venice, 1604. 4to, later sheep; def. Tp def, affecting imprint; last leaf of preface lacking; 1st leaf of text obscured with paper; dampstained throughout. Sold w.a.f. sg May 9 (96) $2,400

Anr Ed. Venice, 1605. Folio, disbound. With engraved title & 23 maps only (of 48). Sold w.a.f. S Mar 28 (183) £460

## Porfiry, Konstantin Aleksandrovich Uspensky, Bishop of Chigirin

— Vostok Khristianskij, Egipet i Sinaj. Moscow, 1857. Oblong folio, contemp half sheep; needs rebacked. With 83 litho plates, including title. Lower margin of tp repaired; some foxing; old stamp in blank gutter of several plates. Sold w.a.f. sg Dec 7 (292) $800

## Porny, Marc Antoine, Pseud.

— The Elements of Heraldry. L, 1787. 4th Ed. 8vo, calf. With 24 plates. pba Nov 30 (176) $200

**Porta, Giovanni Battista della, 1538-1615**
— De humana physiognomonia.... Vico Equense: J. Cacchium, 1586. Folio, old vellum; lower corners gnawed. Tp & 1st few leaves with ink notations in old hand; marginal browning & staining. CE May 22 (385) $1,000
— Magia naturalis, oder Haus-Kunst-und Wunder-Buch. Nuremberg, 1680. 2 vols. 8vo, contemp vellum. With frontis & 20 plates. Madsen copy. S Mar 14 (293) £1,700

**Portalis, Roger**
— Honore Fragonard: sa vie et sone oeuvre. Paris, 1889. One of 1,100. 4to, half mor gilt, wraps bound in. sg June 13 (149) $140

**Portalis, Roger —&**
**Beraldi, Henri**
— Les Graveurs du dixhuitieme siecle. Paris, 1880-82. One of 50 on papier Whatman. 3 vols in 6. Contemp half mor by Rousselle; rubbed. Some foxing. O Mar 26 (210) $375

**Porter, Anna Maria**
— Walsh Colville: or, a Young Man's First Entrance into Life. L, 1797. 1st Ed. 8vo, contemp calf. Heavily annotated for a new Ed. Inscr by Jane Porter. b May 30 (414) £3,600

**Porter, David, 1780-1843**
— Journal of a Cruise made to the Pacific Ocean... in the United States Frigate Essex.... NY, 1822. 2d Ed. 2 vols in 1. 8vo, contemp half calf; worn. With 2 ports, folding table, folding chart of the Galapagos islands & 7 plates (browned). Repaired tear to blank margin of 2d title. ANs presenting the book tipped in; extra-illus with port of Ingraham & 2 of Porter. Edge-Partington copy. b Mar 20 (173) £520
— A Voyage in the South Seas.... L: R. Phillips, 1823. 8vo, half calf; rebacked. With folding map & 2 plates. Some discoloration. b Mar 20 (174) £120
Anr copy. Cloth. With folding map & 2 plates. sg Mar 7 (307) $140

**Porter, Eliot**
— All Under Heaven: The Chinese World. NY, 1983. One of 250. Text by Jonathan Porter. 4to, cloth. Frontis thumbed. sg Feb 29 (266) $600

**Porter, George Richardson**
— The Nature and Properties of the Sugar Cane. L, 1830. 8vo, orig cloth; worn, spine foot chipped. With 5 plates (4 folding) & folding chart. Some foxing. F Mar 28 (476) $160

**Porter, James A.**
— Modern Negro Art. NY: Dryden Press, 1943. Orig cloth; spine ends worn. sg Mar 28 (239) $175

**Porter, Jane, 1776-1850**
— The Scottish Chiefs, a Romance. NY, 1921. Illus by N. C. Wyeth. In dj with extremitiy tears. With pictorial title & 14 plates. pba Apr 4 (548) $500

**Porter, John W. H.**
— A Record of Events in Norfolk County, Virginia, From April 19th, 1861 to May 10th, 1862. Portsmouth VA, 1892. 8vo, orig cloth; worn, insect damage. wa Feb 29 (346) $130

**Porter, Katherine Anne, 1890-1980**
— A Christmas Story. NY, [1967]. One of 500 with an additional frontis. Illus by Ben Shahn. Sgd twice by author. pba May 23 (348) $65
— French Song-Book. [Paris]: Harrison of Paris, 1933. Ltd Ed, sgd. Half cloth, in stained & chipped dj. Inscr by Glenway Wescott. sg Feb 15 (160) $90
— Hacienda. [NY]: Harrison of Paris, [1934]. One of 895. pba Aug 22 (394) $50

**Porter, Sir Robert Ker, 1772-1842**
— Travels in Georgia, Persia, Armenia, Ancient Babylonia. L, 1821-22. 1st Ed. 2 vols. 4to, 19th-Cent calf; rubbed. With 2 folding maps, & 87 plates (4 color). Some spotting, discoloration, & marginalia. S Oct 26 (195) £480 [Waggett]

**Porter, Rufus**
— Aerial Navigation: the Practicability of Traveling Pleasantly and Safely from New York to California.... San Francisco, 1935. One of 200. Half cloth. Marginal crease to frontis. pba Apr 25 (603) $50

**Porter, Whitworth, 1827-92 —&**
**Watson, Charles M.**
— History of the Corps of Royal Engineers. L, 1889-1915. Vols I-II (of 3). Orig cloth; worn & soiled, hinges cracked. With frontises, 4 color lithos & 7 folding maps. wa Feb 29 (192) $95

**Porter, William Sydney ("O. Henry"), 1862-1910**
See also: Limited Editions Club
— The Gift of the Magi. L, 1939. One of 105. Illus by Stephen Gooden. Orig half mor. sg Sept 14 (176) $300
— Works. Garden City, 1917. One of 1,075. Illus by Gordon Grant. 14 vols. Half mor. b Sept 20 (573) £950

**Portfolio...**
— The Portfolio. L, 1894-95. Ed by Philip Gilbert Hamerton. Nos 1-24. 4to, contemp half vellum by Birdsall, orig wraps bound in. S Apr 23 (239) £360

**Portlock, Nathaniel**
— A Voyage Round the World. L, 1789. 1st Ed. 4to, contemp russia gilt; rebacked with calf, corners repaired. With port, 5 hand-colored & 8 plain plates & with 6 folding maps. Washed; some foxing to frontis & soiling to tp. pba Feb 13 (153) $3,000
Anr copy. Contemp calf. With 19 (of 20) plates. Earlier leaves with dampstain to lower gutter corner; large chart creased with tears. pba July 25 (444) $750
Anr copy. Contemp calf gilt; joints cracked, edges rubbed. With port & 19 charts & plates, the bird plates hand-colored. Some spotting & staining. wa Feb 29 (478) $2,500

**Portlock, William Henry**
— A New Complete and Universal Collection of...Voyages and Travels.... L, [1794]. Folio, contemp calf; worn. Lacking initial gathering. Sold w.a.f.  sg Mar 7 (308) $130

**Portoghesi, Paolo.** See: Bonelli & Portoghesi

**Portoghesi, Paulo**
— Roma Barocca: The History of an Architectonic Culture. Cambr. MA, [1970]. 4to, cloth, in dj. wa Dec 14 (397) $95

**Portulano...**
— Portulano de la America Setentrional. Madrid, 1818. 4 parts in 1 vol. Oblong folio, disbound. With engraved title & 107 charts only. Tp & last chart detached, worn & soiled; some foxing & dampstaining. cb Oct 17 (254) $3,750

**Posner, David**
— A Rake's Progress. L: Lion and Unicorn Press, 1967. 4to, orig cloth; loss to lower backstrip. b Jan 31 (175) £90

**Posten, Charles D.**
— Apache-Land. San Francisco, 1878. 1st Ed. Orig cloth; extremities rubbed. With 13 plates. Robbins copy.  pba Mar 21 (283) $170

**Poster...**
— The Poster: An Illustrated Monthly Chronicle. L, 1898-1901. Vols I-VI in 4 vols (complete set). 4to, contemp cloth, orig pictorial wraps. S Nov 2 (97) £1,300 [Sims Reed]

**Posthius, Joannes**
— Tetrasticha in Ovidii metamor. lib XV. Frankfurt: G. Corvinum, 1563. 8vo, modern calf. Marginal soiling & staining. sg Apr 18 (172) $1,100

**Potier Library, L.**
— [Sale Catalogues] Catalogue des livres rares et precieux manuscripts.... Paris, 1870-82. 3 vols in 2. 8vo, half mor, orig wraps bound in; worn. Part 1 with ptd prices realized bound in; Parts 2 & 3 priced by hand. O Mar 26 (211) $170

**Potter, Beatrix, 1866-1943**
— The Fairy Caravan. Phila.: David McKay, [1929]. 8vo, cloth, in frayed dj. O Sept 12 (137) $400
— The Roly-Poly Pudding. L, [c.1927]. ("The Tale of Samuel Whiskers or the Roly-Poly Pudding.") 12mo, orig bds; front hinge reinforced. Some leaves creased. Sgd on half-title. cb Feb 14 (2717) $1,500
— The Story of a Fierce Bad Rabbit. L, 1906. 1st Ed. 16mo, orig cloth wallet-type bdg; lacking flap to tab-slot, slot frayed.  S Nov 2 (315) £280 [Thurnham]
— The Story of Miss Moppet. L, 1906. 1st Ed. 16mo, orig cloth wallet-type bdg; tab-slot & joint frayed.  S Nov 2 (314) £400 [Sotheran]
  Anr copy. Orig cloth wallet-type bdg; soiled, lacking tab. S May 16 (183) £150; S May 16 (184) £180

— The Tailor of Gloucester. L, 1902. 1st Ed, One of 500. 16mo, orig bds; minor spotting. Ck May 31 (77) £2,000
  Anr copy. Orig bds; soiled, corners rubbed, backstrip worn at ends, endpapers browned. With 16 colored plates. S Nov 2 (311) £1,000 [Schuster]
  Anr copy. Orig bds; soiled, backstrip browned & chipped. Inscr to Cicely Roscoe, 16 Jan 1903. S May 16 (180) £1,950
  1st Pbd Ed. L & NY, 1903. 16mo, orig bds; small spot to front cover. pba Aug 22 (831) $95
— The Tale of Jemima Puddle-Duck. L, 1908. 1st Ed. 16mo, orig bds; lower joint cracked, backstrip chipped. Inscr to Nellie Wilkinson Meadhurst. S May 16 (185) £500
— The Tale of Mr. Jeremy Fisher. L, 1906. 1st Ed. 16mo, orig bds. Ck May 31 (81) £480
  Anr copy. Orig cloth; rubbed & soiled. S May 16 (182) £260
— The Tale of Mrs. Tiggy-Winkle. L, 1905. 1st Ed. 16mo, orig bds. b Jan 31 (201) £140
— The Tale of Mrs. Tittlemouse. L & NY, 1910. 1st Ed. 16mo, orig bds; outer margin of front cover dampstained, small stain to rear cover. With colored frontis & 26 plates. Ck May 31 (82) £260
  Anr Ed. L, 1911. 16mo, orig bds; spine def. Inscr, Christmas 1911. b Jan 31 (202) £240
  Anr Ed. L, 1979. One of 500. 16mo, orig mor. Facsimile of the Ms. b May 30 (578) £80
— The Tale of Peter Rabbit. L, [Dec 1901]. 1st Pvtly Ptd Ed, 1st Issue. One of 250. 16mo, orig bds; lower cover slightly marked, backstrip creased, spotting to endpapers. Minor spotting to lower edge of tp & to a few other leaves. In Potter's hand on tp is "F. Warne & Co. 15 Bedford St. Strand to be published in the autumn 1902". S Nov 2 (310) £18,000 [James]
  1st Commercial Ed. L, Oct 1902. 16mo, variant bdg or brown cloth with red lettering with mtd pictorial label on upper cover; rubbed, upper joint broken, blue pencil doodles on back endpapers. Ck May 31 (85) £600
  2d Pvtly Ptd Ed. [L], Feb 1902. 16mo, orig bds; front cover spotted. Lacking prelim blank; upper stitching of gathering B loosened; minnor spotting at beginning. Ck May 31 (84) £2,800
  Anr Ed. Phila: Henry Altemus, 1904. Pictorial cloth. pba Apr 4 (535) $275
— The Tale of Pigling Bland. L, [1913]. 1st Ed. 16mo, orig bds; rubbed, spine heel rubbed, half-title & frontis detached. bba May 9 (256) £50 [Benster]
— The Tale of Squirrel Nutkin. L, 1903. 1st Ed. 16mo, orig bds; backstrip chipped, hinge cracked. With 27 colored illusts. Frontis reinserted; some soiling. S May 16 (181) £550
— The Tale of the Faithful Dove. L, 1955. 1st Ed, one of 100. 4to, orig cloth, in dj. Ck Apr 12 (172) £1,500
— The Tale of Timmy Tiptoes. L, 1911. 1st Ed. 16mo, orig bds. Inscr to Nellie Wilkinson. S May 16 (187) £750

## POTTER

1st American Ed. NY, 1911. 16mo, orig bds; worn with some staining on back bd, hinge weak. Met Dec 5 (336) $250
— The Tale of Tom Kitten. L, 1907. 1st Ed. 16mo, orig bds. b Jan 31 (204) £140; b Jan 31 (205) £100
— The Tale of Two Bad Mice. L, [c.1935]. 16mo, pictorial bds; rebacked with new spine, rubbed. Sgd, Feb 1942. cb Feb 14 (2719) $850
— Wag-by-Wall. L & NY, [1944]. 1st Ed. 16mo, cloth, in dj with pieces lacking. pba Aug 22 (832) $95

**Potthast, August, 1824-98**
— Bibliotheca historica medii aevi.... Berlin, 1896. 2 vols. 8vo, buckram; rebound, spines worn. sg Apr 11 (254) $60

**Pottinger, George**
— Muirfield and the Honourable Company. Edin., 1972. 1st Ed. Cloth in dj. With color frontis. pba Apr 18 (143) $75

**Pouchet, Felix Archimede**
See also: Fore-Edge Paintings
— Theorie positive de l'ovulation spontanee.... Paris, 1847. 2 vols, including Atlas. 8vo & 4to, contemp half calf & orig bds; soiled. With folding table & 20 colored plates. Some dampstaining & foxing to text in both vols. S June 12 (276) £360

**Pouchot, Francois**
— Memoires sur la derniere guerre de l'Amerique septentrionale.... Yverdon, 1781. 3 vols. 12mo, contemp sheep; rubbed. With 3 folding maps. Tp & half-title to Vol III detached; tear to margin of general map; contemp annotations on the general map in red ink. C June 26 (201) £2,400

**Poulain, Roger**
— Ecoles. Paris, [1923]. 4to, loose in half cloth folder; joints cracked. With 104 plates. sg Jan 11 (14) $60

**Pound, Ezra, 1885-1972**
See also: Limited Editions Club
— Canto CX. Paris: Herne, 1967. One of 224. Wraps. pba Jan 25 (308) $55
— Cantos LII-LXXI. L, [1940]. 1st Ed. Orig cloth, unopened; endpapers foxed. Inscr to Pearl Buck. Engelhard copy. CNY Oct 27 (116) $1,800
— Cantos XXVIII, XXIX and XXX. [N.p.]: Hound & Horn, Apr-June 1930. 8vo, orig bdg; creased. Some dust-staining. Sold w.a.f. In: Hound & Horn, Spring, 1930. Pound's own copy, so inscr on front cover. S Dec 18 (414) £320 [Mandl]
— Cathay. L, 1915. 1st Ed. Ptd wraps; some soiling. pba Jan 25 (310) $180
— Cavalcanti Poems. New Directions [Ptd at Verona, Officina Bodoni], 1966. One of 200. 4to, orig half vellum. bba May 9 (616) £520 [Heritage]; sg Oct 19 (186) $1,100
— A Draft of XVI Cantos. Paris: Three Mountains Press, 1925. One of 70. Folio, orig half vellum; some wear & soiling. Engelhard copy. CNY Oct 27 (113) $6,500

## AMERICAN BOOK PRICES CURRENT

— A Draft of XXX Cantos. Paris: Hours Press, 1930. 1st Ed, one of 200. Orig cloth; backstrip with discoloration. Waterstained in lower margin. bba May 30 (295) £375 [Finch]

Anr copy. Orig cloth, unopened. Engelhard copy. CNY Oct 27 (115) $2,900

Out-of-series copy. Orig bds; spine browned. Hobson copy. S June 28 (148) £400
— Drafts & Fragments of Cantos CX-CXVII. NY: New Directions, [1968]. 1st Ed, one of 310. Folio, cloth. sg June 20 (315) $375
— Gaudier-Brzeska, a Memoir. L, 1916. 1st Ed. bba Oct 19 (376) £95 [Poetry Bookshop]
— A Lume spento. In the City of Aldus. [Venice], 1908. 1st Ed, one of 100. Contemp cloth; spine with wear. Derby - Engelhard copy. CNY Oct 27 (109) $12,000
— Lustra. [L, 1916). 1st Ed, 2d Impression. sg June 20 (316) $90

One of 200. Inscr to Lord Carlow. Gilvarry - Engelhard copy. CNY Oct 27 (112) $9,500
— Part of Canto XX. [N.p.], 1927. Broadside, 4to. Engelhard copy. CNY Oct 27 (114) $500
— Personae. L, 1909. 1st Ed. Orig bds; spine chipped. Inscr to Sir Francis Meynell. Goodwin - Engelhard copy. CNY Oct 27 (110) $950
— The Pisan Cantos. [NY]: New Directions, [1948]. 1st Ed, Issue not specified. Bd in chipped dj. pba Jan 25 (309) $55
— Quia pauper amavi. L: The Egoist, [1919]. 1st Ed, one of 500. Orig half cloth; spine ends chipped, corners rubbed. pba Jan 25 (315) $95
— Redondillas, or Something of that Sort. [NY]: New Directions, [1967]. 1st Ed, one of 110. 4to, orig cloth. b Jan 31 (207) £160
— Ripostes. L, 1912. 1st Ed, 1st Issue. Orig cloth. Inscr to May Sinclair, 30 Nov 1912. Engelhard copy. CNY Oct 27 (111) $1,000

**Pouqueville, Francois Charles Hugues Laurent**
— Voyage dans la Grece. Paris, 1826-27. 2d Ed. 6 vols. 8vo, contemp calf; rebacked. With 7 folding maps & 30 plates. b Sept 20 (354) £420

**Pourtraits...**
— Pourtraits divers. Lyons: Jean de Tournes, 1556. 8vo, 18th-cent bds. With 62 woodcuts. Minor dampstaining; many leaves with blind impress. Harth - Schaefer copy. P Nov 1 (177) $4,250

Anr Ed. Lyons: Jean de Tournes, 1557. 8vo, modern calf; joints worn, inner hinge split, spine ends worn. With 60 woodcuts only. Tp soiled & repaired; marginal repairs. Schaefer copy. P Nov 1 (178) $1,800

**Powell, Adam Clayton**
— Against the Tide. An Autobiography. NY, 1938. Cloth; rubbed. Sgd. sg Mar 28 (244) $200

**Powell, H. M. T.** See: Grabhorn Printing

**Powell, John Wesley, 1834-1902**
— Exploration of the Colorado River of the West and its Tributaries.... Wash., 1875. 1st Ed. 8vo, orig cloth; spine chipped & worn. With folding map & folding profile. Robbins copy.  pba Mar 21 (284) $375
— Report on the Lands of the Arid Region of the United States.... Cambr. MA, 1962. Ed by Wallace Stegner. In dj with dampstain to corners.  pba Jan 25 (345) $75

**Powell, Lawrence Clark**
— Robinson Jeffers: the Man & His Work. Los Angeles: The Primavera Press, 1934. One of 750. In dj. Inscr by Jeffers to Charles Erskine Scott Wood & Sara Bard.  pba Oct 5 (197) $650

**Powell, William H. —&**
**Shippen, Edward**
— Officers of the Army and Navy...in the Civil War. Phila., 1892. 4to, orig half lea; shaken, spine taped. NH July 21 (88) $130

**Powers, Stephen**
— Afoot and Alone: a Walk from Sea to Sea by the Southern Route. Hartford, 1872. 1st Ed. 8vo, orig cloth; spine ends & corners frayed. With 12 plates. Robbins copy.  pba Mar 21 (285) $160

**Powers, Tim**
— The Drawing of the Dark. Eugene OR: Hypatia Press, 1991. One of 30 lettered copies. Lea. O Dec 5 (234) $60
— An Epitaph in Rust. Cambr. MA: NESFA Press, 1989. One of 225. In dj by Jim Gurney. O Dec 5 (237) $50
— On Stranger Tides. NY: Ace Books, [1987]. One of 150 from the Ultramarine Publishing Co., specially bound by Denis Gouey. Half mor. O Dec 5 (238) $50
— The Skies Discrowned. Huntington Beach: James Cahill, [1993]. One of 300. In dj. pba Oct 5 (295) $80
Anr copy. Syn, in 2 djs. wa Feb 29 (75) $60

**Pownall, Thomas, 1722-1805**
— Principles of Polity, being the Grounds and Reasons of Civil Empire. L, 1752. 4to, 18th-cent calf; hinges & covers repaired. C Nov 29 (132) £240
— A Treatise on the Study of Antiquities as the Commentary to Historical Learning. L, 1783. 8vo, early 19th-cent half cloth. With 5 folding plates. Fraying & fold breaks to 1st plate.  sg Mar 21 (269) $200

**Powys, Llewelyn, 1884-1939**
See also: Golden Cockerel Press
— The Twelve Months. L, 1936. Ltd Ed, sgd by author & artist. Illus by Robert Gibbings. bba May 9 (375) £170 [Brook]

**Pozzo, Andrea, 1642-1709**
— Perspectiva pictorum et architectorum. Augsburg, 1708-9. 2 vols in 1. Folio, contemp vellum over bds; soiled, rear turn-ins lifting. With 2 frontises & 222 plates. Lacking Vol I tp.  pn Dec 7 (36) £800

— Rules and Examples of Perspective Proper for Painters and Architects. L, [1707]. Folio, contemp calf; worn, joints cracked. With frontis, titles, & 103 plates. Text in Latin & English. Dampstained; 1st few leaves wrinkled. CE Nov 8 (235) $1,100
Anr Ed. L, 1707. Folio, early 19th-cent half russia; covers detached. With frontis & 101 plates. Minor marginal soiling.  sg June 13 (26) $950

**Prain, Eric**
— The Oxford and Cambridge Golfing Society, 1898-1948. L, [1949]. 1st Ed. Cloth in dj; d/j torn & chipped.  pba Apr 18 (144) $170

**Prangey, Joseph Philibert Girault de**
— Choix d'ornements Moresques de l'Alhambra. See: Girault de Prangey, Joseph Philibert

**Prasse, Leona**
— Lyonel Feininger: a Definitive Catalogue.... Cleveland, [1972]. 4to, cloth, in dj.  sg Jan 11 (170) $275

**Prateius, Pardulphus**
— Lexicon juris civilis, et canonici.... Venice: Hieronymus Scotus, 1572. Folio, early 19th-cent half sheep; extremities rubbed. Old stamps on tp; some words scored & oxidized with resulting hole; minor marginal dampstain at end.  sg Mar 21 (192) $400

**Pratt, Anne, 1806-93**
— The Flowering Plants, Grasses, Sedges, and Ferns of Great Britain. L, [c.1860]. 6 vols. 8vo, orig cloth. With 319 color plates. b Sept 20 (488) £240
Anr Ed. L, [c.1873]. Vol I only. 19th-cent half calf. With 80 hand-colored plates. sg May 9 (314) $175
Anr Ed. L, [c.1880]. 6 vols. 8vo, contemp half mor; worn. Lacking 1 plate. b May 30 (497) £220
Anr Ed. L, 1899-1900. 4 vols. 8vo, orig cloth. With 1 uncolored & 317 chromolitho plates. pnE Mar 20 (128) £220
Anr Ed. L & NY, 1899-1900. 4 vols. 8vo, orig cloth; spines stained. S Oct 27 (767) £260 [Bifolco]

**Pratt, F. M.**
— California Gold Regions, with a Full Account of Their Mineral Resources. NY, [1849]. 1st Ed. Later mor. Larson copy.  pba Sept 28 (646) $6,500

**Pratt, Fletcher.** See: De Camp & Pratt

**Pratt, Parley Peter**
— The Millennium. A Poem. Bost., 1835. 12mo, old plain wraps. K Oct 1 (279) $5,600
— A Voice of Warning.... Plano IL, 1863. Revised Ed. 12mo, contemp half cloth; rubbed, edges worn. First 8 pages, including tp, dampstained. pba Apr 25 (607) $85

**Pratt, Samuel Jackson**
— An Apology for the Life and Writings of David Hume.... L, 1777. 1st Ed. 8vo, contemp wraps; broken, edge wear.  CE May 22 (389) $700

## PRATT

— Gleanings through Wales, Holland and Westphalia.... L, 1795. 3 vols. 8vo, orig bds. Minor foxing. bba May 30 (355) £70 [Price]
— The Pupil of Pleasure. L, 1776. 3 vols. 12mo, contemp half calf; spines worn. Ck Sept 8 (209) £550

**Prayer Books**
— [Prayers in Hebrew & Yiddish] Amst.: Shlomo Proops, 1714. 2 parts in 1 vol. 8vo, 16th-cent silver-gilt bdg with central rectangular panel, filled with cast & pierced repeating scrollwork against a gilt foil ground & 4 surrounding panels engraved with C-scrolls & husks, with 2 clasps. Abbey copy. C May 1 (158) £24,000

**Praz, Mario**
— Studies in Seventeenth Century Imagery. Rome, 1964. 2d Ed. 8vo, orig cloth in dj. sg Apr 11 (255) $120; sg Apr 11 (256) $150

**Preece, Louisa.** See: Symonds & Preece

**Preissler, Johann Daniel**
— Theoretisch-Praktischer Unterricht im Zeichnen. Nuremberg, 1798-1807. 7 parts in 1 vol. Folio, 19th-cent half sheep; spine worn, front hinge split. Prelims of 1st part foxed. Sold w.a.f. sg Jan 11 (144) $350

**Prelleur, Peter**
— Instructions upon the Hautboy.... L: Printing-Office in Bow Church-Yard, [c.1738]. 8vo, wraps. Engraved throughout; with 1 folding plate. Some staining; marginal gnawing with some loss. S May 15 (438) £450

**Presas, Jose**
— Memorias secretas de la princesa del Brasil.... Bordeaux: Carlos Lawalle Sobrino, 1830. 8vo, calf. b Dec 5 (136) £180

**Prescott, William Hickling, 1796-1859**
See also: Limited Editions Club
— History of the Conquest of Mexico. NY, 1843. 1st American Ed. 3 vols. 8vo, orig cloth; endpapers browned. With 4 plates & 2 double-page maps. sg Oct 26 (304) $225
— Works. L, 1850-64. 13 vols, including Ticknor's Life. 8vo, half mor by Zaehnsdorf; spines browned. pba Aug 22 (556) $400
Anr Ed. L, 1867-70. 14 vols. 8vo, half mor gilt; worn. b Jan 31 (105) £110
Aztec Ed. Phila., [1904]. one of 250. Ed by Wilfred Harold Munro. 22 vols. Half mor. cb Oct 17 (292) $750

**Present...**
— Present Day Impressions of the Far East and Prominent Progressive Chinese at Home and Abroad. [N.p.]: Globe Encyclopaedia, 1917. Ed by W. Feldwick. 4to, orig cloth; rubbed. b May 30 (202) £750

**Present State...**
— The Present State of Liberty in Great Britain and Her Colonies. By An Englishman. L, 1769. 12mo, contemp wraps; splitting, chipped. Sometimes attributed to Joseph Priestley. pba June 13 (289) $200

**Presidents of the United States**
— A Compilation of the Messages and Papers of the Presidents. Wash., 1897. Ed by James D. Richardson. 11 vols. 8vo, orig mor; spine ends chipped. CE Nov 8 (238) $100

**Prestwich, John**
— Prestwich's Dissertation on Mineral, Animal & Vegetable Poisons.... L, 1775. Bdg not described. With 8 hand-colored plates only. sg May 16 (480) $200

**Prevost d'Exiles, Antoine Francois, 1697-1763**
— Manon Lescaut. Amst., 1753. ("Histoire du Chevalier des Grieux, et de Manon Lescaut.") 1st Ed. 2 vols. 12mo, 19th-cent mor by Trautz-Bauzonnet. With 8 plates plus an eau-forte of the plate at p.96. Fuerstenberg - Schaefer copy. S Dec 8 (501) £2,200
Anr Ed. Paris: Didot l'aine, 1797. ("Histoire du chevalier Des Grieux, et de Manon Lescaut.") 2 vols. 8vo, contemp mor gilt by Bozerian. With 8 plates, all in 2 states, on slightly smaller leaves. Fuerstenberg - Schaefer copy. S Dec 8 (502) £2,100
Anr Ed. Stamford: Overbrook Press, 1958. One of 200. Illus by T. M. Cleland. sg Feb 15 (75) $175

**Prevost, Florent —&**
**Lemaire, C. L.**
— Histoire naturelle des oiseaux exotiques. Paris, [c.1845]. 8vo, early sheep; extremities worn. With 80 hand-colored plates & 2 uncolored plates. Foxing & browning. sg Dec 7 (205) $2,800

**Preziosi, Amadeo**
— Stamboul. Paris, 1865. Folio, orig cloth; worn. With litho title & 28 color plates mtd on card. Tp & mounts spotted. b May 30 (292) £4,000

**Price, Charles Matlack**
— Posters: a Critical Study of the Development of Poster Design.... NY, 1913. One of 250. 4to, cloth. sg Sept 7 (284) $325
Out-of-series copy. Cloth. Inscr. sg June 13 (321) $375

**Price, Edmund E.**
— Science of Self Defence. NY, [1867]. Half cloth. pba Apr 4 (105) $170

**Price, Francis, d.1753**
— The British Carpenter: or, A Treatise on Carpentry.... L, 1735. 2d Ed. 2 vols, including Supplement, in 1. 4to, old calf; worn, front bd detached. Some stains & soiling. wa Feb 29 (88) $210

**Price, Frederick**
— Ootacamund. A History. Compiled for the Government of Madras. Madras, 1908. 4to, contemp half mor gilt. With folding map & 24 plates & plans. b May 30 (181) £80

## 1995 - 1996 · BOOKS

**Price, J. —& Haley, C. S.**
— The Buyer's Manual and Business Guide.... San Francisco, 1872. pba Aug 8 (159) $130

**Price, Lake**
— Tauromachia, or the Bull-Fights of Spain.... L, 1852. Folio, contemp half mor with edges restored in mor. With 26 hand-colored plates, including extra title. Some spotting. S June 27 (124) £10,000

**Price, Richard, 1723-91**
— Observations on Reversionary Payments; on Schemes for providing Annuities.... L, 1783. 2 vols. 8vo, contemp sheep; spines worn, covers detached. Some foxing. sg Mar 21 (112) $110

**Price-Mars, Jean**
— La Vocation de l'Elite. Port-au-Prince, 1919. Ptd wraps; spine chipped. Owner's blindstamp on front cover. sg Mar 28 (128) $140

**Prideaux, Humphrey, 1648-1724**
— The Old and New Testament Connected in the History of the Jews. L, 1718. 2 vols. 4to, contemp calf; worn & rubbed, front free endpapers loose. With 5 maps (4 double-page) & double-page plan of a temple. K Feb 11 (234) $325

**Prideaux, Sara T.**
— A Catalogue of Books Bound by S. T. Prideaux.... L, [1900]. Ltd Ed. 8vo, orig half cloth. sg Sept 14 (299) $90

**Pridgen, Tim**
— The Story of Modern Cockfighting. Bost., 1938. pba Jan 4 (184) $65

**Priestley, Joseph, 1733-1804**
— Directions for Impregnating Water with Fixed Air. L, 1772. 1st Ed. 8vo, modern cloth. With folding plate. Ck Mar 22 (252) £320
— Geschichte und Gegenwaertiger Zustand der Optik. Berlin, 1772. Bound with: Schmidt, Georg Christoph. Beschreibung einer Elektrisir-Maschine.... Jena, 1773. 4to, contemp half calf; rubbed, spine chipped at head. With 8 folding plates in 1st work & 2 folding plates in 2d. Tp of 1st work stamped. ALs of Priestley, 12 Aug 1788, inserted. S Mar 14 (296) £850
 Anr Ed. Leipzig, 1775-76. 2 parts in 1 vol. 4to, contemp half calf; rubbed. With 16 folding plates. Some browning & spotting. S Mar 14 (295) £400
— Histoire de l'electricite. Paris, 1771. 3 vols. 12mo, contemp calf. With 9 folding plates. Short tear in 1 plate. S Mar 14 (297) £260
— The History and Present State of Discoveries Relating to Vision, Light and Colours. L, 1772. 1st Ed. 2 vols in 1. 4to, early calf gilt, with arms of the 3d Earl of Bute; rebacked. With 25 folding plates. Lacking Vol II tp. sg Apr 18 (173) $1,100
 Anr copy. 2 vols. 4to, contemp calf; broken, worn, endpapers stamped. Vol I tp with tear repaired; Vol II tp stamped. sg May 16 (238) $700

## PRINT...

**Priestley, Sir Raymond E.**
— Antarctic Adventure: Scott's Northern Party. L, 1914. 1st Ed. Orig cloth; rubbed & soiled, a few signatures sprung. Some foxing; marginal dampstaining at rear. pba July 25 (58) $170
 Anr copy. Orig cloth; worn, inner hinges cracked. Some foxing. wa Feb 29 (134) $280

**Priestly, Herbert Ingraham**
— Franciscan Explorations in California. Glendale, 1946. 1st Ed. With 2 maps (1 folding). Robbins copy. pba Mar 21 (286) $180

**Prime, Samuel Irenaeus, 1812-85**
— Under the Trees. NY, 1874. 8vo, orig cloth. pba July 11 (363) $75

**Prime, William Cowper, 1825-1905**
— I Go A-Fishing. NY, 1873. 8vo, half mor; joints & extremities rubbed. Inscr. pba July 11 (229) $110

**Primum...**
— Primum pactum confoederationis Helveticae MCCXCI. Montagnola: Bodoni, June 1925. One of 275. Folio, orig half vellum. Ck May 31 (19) £280

**Prince, L. Bradford**
— Spanish Mission Presses of New Mexico. Cedar Rapids: Torch Press, 1915. Orig cloth; spine ends rubbed, front hinge tender, circular stain to front cover. pba Aug 8 (160) $60

**Prince, Nancy**
— The Narrative of the Life and Travels of.... Bost., 1853. 12mo, orig cloth; lacking front free endpaper. Waterstain through lower corner of text. sg Mar 28 (334) $150; sg Mar 28 (335) $200

**Prince, Thomas, 1687-1758**
— The Salvations of God in 1746. Bost., 1746. 8vo, disbound. Library stamp on tp. sg Oct 26 (102) $80
— A Sermon Delivered at the South Church in Boston, N.E., August 14, 1746...for the great Deliverance of the British Nations.... Bost., 1746. 1st Ed. 4to, disbound. Library stamp on tp. sg Oct 26 (103) $275

**Pringle, Sir John, 1707-82**
— A Discourse upon Some Late Improvements... for... Preserving the Health of Mariners. L, 1776. 1st Ed. 4to, contemp half calf; spine chipped at head, extrems rubbed. With half-title, & title device. Title soiled. Ck Mar 22 (253) £4,200

**Prinsep, Henry Thoby, the Elder**
— History of the Political and Military Transactions in India.... L, 1825. 2 vols. 8vo, contemp half sheep; extremities worn, hinges reinforced. Some maps with tears into image. sg Mar 7 (310) $225

**Print...**
— Print Collector's Quarterly. NY, 1911-42. Vol I, No 1 through Vol XXVI, No 4 in 68, & Index for Vols I-XXIII. Orig cloth or wraps; rubbed. bba Oct 5 (295) £550 [Sime Reed]

833

## PRINT...

— Print Collector's Quarterly: An Anthology of Essays on Eminent Printmakers of the World. Millwood, 1977. 10 vols. sg June 13 (323) $500

**Prior, George**
— United States Commercial Register.... NY, 1852. 12mo, orig cloth. Tp browned; frontis or several flyleaves lacking before title. sg Oct 26 (306) $60

**Prior, Matthew, 1664-1721**
— Poems on Several Occasions. L, 1718. Folio, contemp mor gilt. Subscriber's copy, inscr by Edward Harley, 2d Earl of Oxford. sg Oct 19 (193) $1,400
Anr Ed. L, 1754. 2 vols. 12mo, later half mor gilt. sg Feb 8 (90) $100

**Prior, Thomas**
— An Authentic Narrative of the Success of Tar-Water in Curing.... Dublin, 1746. 8vo, contemp calf; spine chipped, front joint cracked. sg May 16 (481) $300

**Prip-Moller, Johannes**
— Chinese Buddhist Monasteries. Hong Kong, [1967]. Folio, later cloth. Library markings. sg June 13 (27) $70

**Prisse D'Avennes, Achille Constant T. Emile**
— L'Art Arabe, d'apres les monuments du Kaire.... Paris, 1877. 3 plate vols, folio & text vol, 4to, later half sheep; scuffed, extremities worn, corners showing, spine ends lacking & spines def. With 199 (of 200) plates in plate vols & 34 plates in text vol. Library stamps on plates; some soiling & foxing. cb Oct 17 (202) $4,000

**Pritchard, James Avery, 1816-62**
— The Overland Diary.... [Denver], 1959. In soiled d/j, unopened. pba Apr 25 (608) $55
Anr copy. Ed by Dale Morgan. Orig cloth in dj; d/j worn. With frontis port, 3 maps(2 folded), & 1 folded chartt. Also, with T.L.s of Morgan to Francis Farquhar. Sgd by Morgan & Hugh Williamson. Larson copy. pba Sept 28 (647) $100

**Pritt, Thomas Evan**
— An Angler's Basket.... Manchester, 1896. Orig cloth. A. Nelson Cheney's copy. pba July 11 (239) $80
— North-Country Flies. L, 1886. 8vo, orig cloth; worn. With 11 hand-colored & 1 plain plate. O Feb 6 (183) $275
— Yorkshire Trout Flies. Leeds, 1885. One of 200. 8vo, half mor; rebacked preserving orig spine. With 11 hand-colored plates & 1 plain plate. O Feb 6 (184) $600

**Pritzel, Georg August**
— Thesaurus literaturae botanicae, omnium gentium. Leipzig, 1851. 4to, contemp half mor; rubbed, joints worn. Interleaved with blanks. O Mar 26 (212) $140
Anr Ed. Koenigstein, 1972. Folio, orig cloth. sg Apr 11 (294) $110

## AMERICAN BOOK PRICES CURRENT

Anr Ed. Mansfield CT: Martino, [n.d.]. One of 150. 4to, orig cloth; some wear. O May 7 (254) $90

**Procaccino, Calisto**
— Libellus de nutritione humani corporis in re medica. Rome, 1650. 8vo, contemp calf in impresa binding; rebacked, extrems worn. With title vignette. Title browned; margins dampstained; spotted. Ck Mar 22 (254) £900

**Processo...**
— Processo formado de Orden del Rey N. Senor por la Junta de Generales... sobre la conducta, que tuvieron en la Defensa... de la Habana.... Madrid, 1763-64. Folio, sheep; rubbed, hinges cracked. With 12 folding tables. CE Nov 8 (181) $1,800

**Processus...**
— Processus judiciarius Mascaron contra genus humanum. [Augsburg: Guenther Zainer, before 5 June 1473]. 1st Ed. Folio, 19th-cent half vellum; soiled. 35 lines; type 2:118G; 4-line initial in red. 10 leaves. Goff P-1001. C Nov 29 (68) £900

**Procopius of Caesarea**
— De Rebus Gothorum, Persarum ac Vandalorum Libri VII.... Basel, 1531. 1st Ed. Folio, contemp calf by John Reynes, with lettered fore-edge; repaired where clasps missing; both covers wormed & rebacked. Small hole on tp; some worming, dampstaining & early annotations. S June 12 (105) £420

**Proctor, Robert George Collier, 1868-1903**
— The Printing of Greek in the Fifteenth Century. Oxford, 1900. 1st Ed. 4to, half cloth; rear joint cracked. sg Apr 11 (158) $200

**Proksch, Johann Karl**
— Die Litteratur ueber die venerischen Krankheiten. Nieuwkoop, 1966. 5 vols in 3. 8vo, orig cloth. sg Apr 11 (295) $150

**Promptuaire...**
— La Premiere Partie du promptuaire des Medalles.... Lyon: Guillaume Rouille, 1553. 2 parts in 1 vol. 4to, 16th-cent calf gilt; rebacked, new endpapers. Lacking final blank; some staining throughout. S June 12 (66) £550

**Pronostico...**
— Pronostico e profecia delle cose debbeno succere giiralmente maxime delle guere comentiate per magni potentati contra Venetiani adi. xx. di zenaro. M.v.x. Ferrara, [1510]. 4to, mor janseniste by Trautz-Bauzonnet. Maglione - Essling copy. C Apr 3 (185) £3,200

**Prontuario...**
— Prontuario de le medaglie de piu illustri, & fulgenti huomini & donne.... Lyons: G. Rouille, 1553. 4to, old half calf; spine ends worn. Small repair to tp; some browning & staining. CE June 12 (142) $200

## Prony, Gaspard, Baron de
— Nouvelle architecture hydraulique.... Paris, 1790-96. 2 vols. 4to, 19th-cent half calf. With 53 folding plates & 11 tables. S Mar 14 (298) £600

## Propertius, Sextus
— Elegies.... Paris, 1802. 2 vols. 8vo, contemp red mor gilt by Bozerian jeune. With 5 plates before letters. Fuerstenberg - Schaefer copy. S Dec 8 (503) £800

## Proud, Robert, 1728-1813
— The History of Pennsylvania in North America.... Phila., 1797-98. 2 vols. 8vo, 19th-cent cloth; worn. With port & folding map. Some spotting; map torn; tp of Vol I loose. F June 20 (352) $60

Anr copy. Later half calf. With port & folding map. wa Feb 29 (491) $240

## Proudhon, Pierre Joseph, 1809-65
— Systeme des contradictions economiques, ou philosophie de la misere. Paris, 1846. 2 vols. 8vo, contemp half calf. b May 30 (5) £600

## Proulx, E. Annie
— The Shipping News. NY, [1993]. 1st Ed. In dj. pba Dec 7 (159) $160

## Proust, Marcel, 1871-1922
See also: Atget, Eugene

— 47 lettres inedites a Walter Berry. Paris: Black Sun Press, 1930. One of 200. 4to, wraps; spine soiled. pba Nov 30 (43) $100

One of 50. Wraps. pba Nov 30 (42) $200

— Du cote de chez Swann. Paris, 1914 [wraps dated 1913]. 1st Ed, 1st Issue. Orig wraps; minor tears. Inscr to Princess Marthe Bibesco. C June 26 (333) £7,000

— Les Plaisirs et les jours. Paris, 1896. Illus by Madeleine Lemaire. 4to, orig wraps. b Jan 31 (208) £150

## Prout, Samuel, 1783-1852
— Facsimiles of Sketches Made in Flanders and Germany. L, [1833?]. Folio, modern half mor. With litho title, dedication & 50 plates. Lacking subscribers' list. P Nov 1 (179) $2,750

## Proverbe
— Proverbe. Paris, Feb-Apr 1920. Ed by Paul Eluard. Nos 1-3. Wraps. sg June 13 (286) $325

## Pryce, William, 1725?-90
— Mineralogia Cornubiensis; a Treatise on...Mining. L, 1778. 1st Ed. Folio, contemp mor gilt; rubbed, rebacked, later endpapers. Dedication torn & repaired. bba Nov 1 (40) £450 [Henly]

## Pryce-Tannatt, T. E. See: Tannatt, Thomas Edwin Pryce

## Pryer, Ada
— A Decade in Borneo. Hong Kong, 1893. 8vo, orig cloth. S Mar 28 (402) £340

## Prynne, William, 1600-69
— The History of King John, King Henry III.... L, 1670. Folio, modern cloth. Old library stamps on tp; some browning & soiling. sg Mar 21 (270) $275

## Psalmanar, George, 1679-1763
— Description de l'ile Formosa.... Amst., 1705. 12mo, later half calf; rubbed. With title, folding map, & 17 plates (2 folding). S Oct 26 (592) £520 [Baynton-William]

## Psalms & Psalters

### English Versions
— The Whole Books of Psalmes.... L: J. L. for the Company of Stationers, 1640. Bound with: [The New Testament.] L, 1640 24mo, contemp satin; worn, some loss. N.T. lacks title & final leaf. S Oct 27 (860) £200 [Clark]

— 1641. - The Whole Book of Psalms. L. 8vo, contemp needlework bdg in silver thread; worn. rs Nov 11 (68) $400

— 1977. - The Psalms of David and Others, as rendered into English by Arthur Golding. San Francisco: Arion Press One of 200. Folio, half vellum. With the Companion vol in wraps. bba May 9 (298) £120 [Blackwell]; sg Sept 14 (29) $450

### French Versions
— 1694. - Pseaumes de David et cantiques.... Paris 8vo, lev gilt by Chambolle-Duru. With port & 24 plates. Washed. sg Apr 18 (24) $400

### Greek Versions
— 1685. - Psalterion David. Rome: Giovanni Battista Bussotti. 4to, contemp sheep gilt; spine ends damaged. Old stamp on tp; minor stains; interlinear Latin trans in early hand through most of vol. sg Mar 21 (43) $175

### Hebrew & Latin Versions
— 1662. - Basel: Johannes koenig. 12mo, contemp vellum; soiled. Some staining & browning. St. 535. CE Dec 6 (36) $220

### Hebrew & Spanish Versions
— [1671]. - Las Albancas de Santidad. Kodesh Hilulim. Amst. 8vo, modern lea gilt. Some worming, staining & browning. CE Dec 6 (209) $420

— 1671. - Amst. 8vo, contemp calf gilt; rebacked retaining backstrip, hinges reinforced. Marginal dampstaining; worming to opening leaves, affecting text. sg Mar 21 (44) $750

### Hebrew Versions
— 1576. - Sefer Tehillim. Wittenberg: Johannis Cratonis. 8vo, contemp pigskin over wooden bds with port stamps, with engraver's monogram H. W.; extremities worn. Early marginalia on tp; some foxing & browning. Roest 199. CE Dec 6 (18) $1,000

— 1634. - Amst. 16mo, contemp calf; spine ends & corners worn, broken, loose. Tp shaved. St. 463. CE Dec 6 (28) $850

## PSALMS

— 1637. - Leiden: Johannes Le Maire. 12mo, contemp vellum. Some soiling. D & M 5125. CE Dec 6 (29) $420

— 1644. - Amst.: Immanoel Benveniste. Bound with: Seder tefillot ke-minhag Ashkenaz. Amst.: Immanoel Benveniste, 1644. 16mo, contemp vellum stained brown; broken. Staining & browning. CE Dec 6 (105) $1,200

— 1650. - Leiden: Johannes Le Maire. 12mo, contemp vellum with edges stained black. Tp soiled; some browning & foxing. CE Dec 6 (32) $350

— 1717. - Likkutei Tehillim. Welhermsdorf; Hirsch ben Chaim of Fuerth 12mo, 18th-cent mor gilt; corners worn. A few leaves with margins trimmed or worn. CE Dec 6 (51) $420

— 1833. - Safed: Israel ben Abraham Bak. 8vo, contemp half calf. Zedner 132. CE Dec 6 (62) $1,000

### Latin Versions

— 1509, 31 July. - Quincuplex psalterium. Paris: Henri Estienne. Folio, 18th-cent calf; rebacked & repaired, retaining orig spine, new endpapers. Tp cut down & md; some worming & staining; tears in text of last few leaves with loss; marginal repairs in last 2 gatherings with minor loss. S July 11 (20) £2,800

— 1545, Sept. - Psalterium Davidis Carmine Redditum. Strassburg: Crato Mylius. 8vo, contemp sheep over wooden bds; spine ends & corners worn through, lacking metalwork. Wormhole through blank outer margin towards end. sg Mar 21 (45) $500

— 1587. - Psalmi Davidis vulgata editione.... Paris: l'Huillier. Folio, contemp mor gilt for J. A. de Thou with his arms as a bachelor. Jeudwine copy. C Nov 29 (31) £2,400

— 1955. - Novum Psalterium PII XII: An Unfinished Folio Edition of Brother Antoninus.... Los Angeles One of 20 containing 6 leaves from Everson's abandoned Psalter. Folio, cloth. sg Sept 14 (124) $800

### Micmac Versions

— 1859. - [Psalms] Bath 8vo, contemp sheep; covers detached. With frontis. Some browning. D & M 6785. sg Oct 26 (17) $300

### Polyglot Versions

— 1516. - Psalterium Hebraeum, Graecum, Arabicum & Chaldaeum.... Genoa: Petrus Paulus Porrus. 4to, late 16th-cent calf gilt; rebacked in 18th-cent mor with Lamoignon shelfmark, spine chipped at top. C June 26 (119) £6,500

### Swedish Versions

— 1697. - Then Swenska Psalm-Boken.... Stockholm: Burchard for J. J. Genath. 9 parts in 1 vol. 12mo, contemp silver filigree bdg over silver-gilt ground; minor damage to filigree caps. Minor marginal spotting; 1st frontis def; 1 text leaf torn. Abbey - Schaefer copy. P Nov 1 (27) $2,500

### Syriac & Latin Versions

— 1625. - Psalmi Davidis. Paris Ed by Gabriel Sionita. 4to, contemp bdg for presentation to the dedicatee, Dominique de Vic, in red mor gilt with arms [Olivier 472, fer 2]; minor rubbing. D & M 8961. C June 26 (44) £2,600

### Yiddish Versions

— [1661-68]. - Sefer Tehillim. Gar wol far taysht gemakht. Prague: Judah ben Jacob Bak. 4to, vellum from Ms missal; endleaves renewed. Browning & marginal staining; a few marginal tears. St. 1272. CE Dec 6 (35) $6,000

## Ptolemaeus, Claudius

— Almagestum.... Venice: L. A. Giunta, 1528. Folio, old half vellum; worn. Some marginal woodcut diagrams cropped; worming to margins at ends; some worming to text; lacking final blank. CE May 22 (393) $4,800

— Composition mathematique. Paris, 1813-16. 2 vols. 4to, calf gilt; worn & scuffed, joints starting. Some foxing. wa Feb 29 (187) $230

### Geographia

— Geographia. Venice: Vincenzo Valgrisi, 1562. 3 parts in 1 vol. 4to, 19th-Cent half vellum; covers detached. With title device & 64 double-page maps. Lower part of title missing; wormed, with severe loss at map cenetrfolds; pp. loose. S Oct 26 (441) £380 [Ostby]

— 1542. - Geographia universalis.... Basel: Henricus Petrus. Folio, 17th-cent calf; rubbed, split at head of upper hinge, chip at foot of spine. With 48 double-page maps. Some fold tears; tears at foot of Map 37 affecting image; upper right corner of tp torn away; a few leaves with marginal stains; marginalia & ink scoring in various hands. C May 31 (68) £7,500

— 1552, 1 Mar. - Basel: Henricus Petrus. Folio, contemp blind-tooled calf over pastebds; repaired, worn. With 54 double-page maps. Tp soiled. S Nov 30 (81) £8,000

— 1562. - Geographia. Venice: Vincenzo Valgrisi. 2 parts in 1 vol. 4to, contemp blind-stamped pigskin over pastebds with gilt ornaments added. With 64 double-page maps. Tp repaired at foot & laid down. S Nov 30 (80) £3,400

— 1584. - Geographiae libri octo.... Cologne: G. von Kempen. Folio, old vellum; cockled. With engraved title, 27 double-page engraved maps & 1 small folding map. Some staining & discoloring. S June 27 (82) £4,000

— 1597-98. - Geografia, cioe descrittione universale della terra. Venice: Galignani. 4to, later half vellum. With 63 maps, mostly inset in the text. Lacking double-hemisphere map; tp margin repaired; marginal stains & soiling. cb June 25 (1746) $2,000

— 1597. - Geographiae universiae. Cologne: Petrus Keschedt. 2 parts in 1 vol. 4to, half sheep with gilt stamp of an eagle on front cover; rubbed, bds pockmarked. With 2 pictorial titles & 64 maps, all hand-colored, including a double-page map of the world. Minor marginal dampstaining; tp repaired & inserted on linen stub; marginal repairs. pba Nov 30 (269) $5,600

— 1730. - Orbis antiqui tabulae geographicae secundum. Amst. Folio, later half mor; corners bumped, endpa-

pers reattached. With hand-colored engraved title & 28 double-page maps, hand-colored in outline. Some dampstaining & soiling. cb Oct 17 (255) $5,500
— 1974. - Geographia. Plymouth One of 250. Folio, orig lea. Facsimile of the Strassburg 1520 Ed. CE June 15 (299) $300

**Puaux, Rene.** See: Aspiotis & Puaux

**Puccini, Giacomo, 1858-1924**
— Turandot, dramma lirico. Milan: Ricordi, 16 Apr 1926. One of 100. 4to, orig calf gilt & silver with hand-painted central feature of Princess Turandot by Leopoldo Metlicovitz. S May 15 (585) £1,000

**Puch...**
— Das Puch von dem Entkrist. [Leipzig, 1925]. One of 500. 4to, half vellum. Color facsimile of block book. sg Apr 11 (159) $130

**Pueckler-Muskau, Hermann Ludwig Heinrich von, Prince**
— Andeutungen ueber Landschaftsgaertnerei, verbunden mit der Beschreibung ihrer praktischen Anwendung in Muskau. Stuttgart, 1834. 2 vols. 8vo, contemp half calf & modern half cloth portfolio; scuffed. With 4 double-page or folding plans & 45 litho plates, 1 double-page. C Apr 3 (187) £4,500

**Pufendorf, Samuel, Baron von, 1632-94**
— The Compleat History of Sweden. L, 1702. 8vo, contemp half sheep; needs rebdg. Final text leaf lacking a corner & c.10 words of text. sg Mar 7 (311) $140
— Introduction a l'histoire generale et politique de l'univers.... Amst., 1743-45. 8 vols. 12mo, calf; extremities rubbed. With 51 maps & plates. Some dampstaining. sg May 9 (98) $325
— An Introduction to the History of the Kingdoms and States of Asia, Africa and America.... L, 1705. Contemp calf; joints & spine head rubbed. pba Apr 25 (227) $180

**Puget de la Serre, Jean**
— Histoire de l'entree de la Reyne Mere du Roy Tres-Chrestien, dans la Grande-Bretagne. L, 1639. Folio, 18th-cent bds; shaken, backstrip chipped. With engraved title & 7 plates, 1 double-page, & 7 full-page illusts. Engraved title soiled; spotted; lacking last leaf. sg Apr 18 (175) $1,400

**Pugh, Edward, d.1813**
— Cambria Depicta: a Tour through North Wales. L, 1816. 1st Ed. 4to, old half calf; rebacked preserving spine, worn, chipped. With 70 (of 71) plates. Lacking Plate 41; foxed & soiled. Sold w.a.f. O Mar 5 (186) $150

**Pugin, Augustus Charles, 1762-1832**
— Gothic Furniture. L, [c.1828]. 4to, orig cloth-backed wraps; rubbed. With 27 uncolored plates. Tp spotted. Ck Jan 24 (664) £260

**Pugin, Augustus Charles, 1762-1832 —& Others**
— Examples of Gothic Architecture. L, 1831-38. 5 parts in 3 vols. 4to, cloth; worn, spines def. Foxed, affecting plates; library markings. Sold w.a.f. sg June 13 (28) $140

**Pugin, Augustus Charles, 1762-1832 —& Heath, Charles, 1785-1848**
— Paris and its Environs. L, 1829-31. 2 vols. 4to, contemp calf; worn. b Jan 31 (464) £100
  Anr copy. 2 vols in 3. 4to, mor gilt; worn. With 200 mtd plates. pba Mar 7 (215) $70
  Anr copy. 2 vols. 4to, contemp calf. With 2 engraved titles & 351 views on 175 leaves. S June 13 (557) £160
  Anr Ed. L, 1831. 2 vols. 4to, cloth; needs rebdg. Some foxing. sg Mar 7 (312) $200

**Pugin, Augustus Welby Northmore, 1812-52**
— A Treatise on Chancel Screens and Rood Lofts. L, 1851. 4to, half mor; spine ends damaged. With frontis & 13 plates. bba Oct 19 (150) £60 [Pagan]
— The True Principles of Pointed or Christian Architecture. L, 1841. 4to, half mor gilt; rubbed, backstrip def. With frontis & 9 plates. bba Oct 19 (149) £70 [Fetzer]

**Pulci, Luigi, 1432-84**
— Morgante maggiore. Florence: Bartolomeo Sermartelli, 1574. ("Il Morgante.") 4to, 18th-cent vellum, with Bagot arms. H8 torn at margin; small hole on Aa4, affecting text; some staining, mostly confined to upper margin. S June 12 (107) £260
  Anr Ed. Londra, 1768. 3 vols. 12mo, contemp mor gilt, with arms of the king of Sweden. With port & 3 titles. Fuerstenberg - Schaefer copy. S Dec 8 (504) £500

**Pullan, Matilda Marian**
— The Lady's Manual of Fancy-Work.... NY, 1859. 8vo, orig cloth; hinges cracked. Marginal dampstain. pba Jan 4 (378) $60

**Pullan, Richard Popplewell, 1825-88**
See also: Newton & Pullan
— The Designs of William Burges. L, [1885]. Illus by F. Bedford. Folio, loose in cloth-covered case with reproduction of tp on upper cover. With 23 photographs. Photographs removed from their orig mounts & placed within acetate inside new mounts, with some annotations from the original mounts preserved. S Nov 21 (352) £2,000

**Pullen, Henry William**
— The Fight at Dame Europa's School.... L, [1871]. 8vo, contemp mor gilt. With 10 orig ink illusts. Text & illusts mtd; browned. bba May 30 (337) £140 [Ferret Fantasy]

**Pullen-Burry, Bessie**
— Ethiopia in Exile. L, 1905. sg Mar 28 (252) $120

## Pulman, George Philip Rigney
— The Vade-Mecum of Fly-Fishing for Trout. L, 1851. 3d Ed. 16mo, orig cloth. O Feb 6 (185) $100

## Pulphouse...
— Pulphouse: The Hardback Magazine. Eugene: Pulp House Publishing, 1988-91. One of 1,000. Ed by Kristine Kathryn Rusch. Nos 1-11. pba Dec 7 (165) $80

## Pulton, Ferdinand
— De pace regis et regni. L, 1609. Folio, contemp calf; spine dry, sprung. Wrinkling to margins. CE June 15 (246) $220

**Punshon, Morley.** See: McFee, William

## Purchas, Samuel, 1575?-1626
— Purchas his Pilgrimage.... L, 1626. 4th Ed. Vol V only. Folio, contemp calf; worn. With 23 maps & 1 plate. Lacking folding map; pp.769-772 inserted from another copy; some pp. torn & frayed. S Oct 26 (457) £850 [Remington]
— Purchas his Pilgrimes. L, 1625. ("Hakluytus Posthumus or Purchas His Pilgrimes.") 1st Ed. With: Purchas his Pilgrimage. L, 1626. 4th Ed. 5 vols. Folio, disbound. Lacking all inserted engraved matter, including the folding maps; stamp excised from titles. Sold w.a.f. sg May 9 (99) $1,900

Anr Ed. Glasgow, 1905-7. One of 1,000. 20 vols. Library markings. pn Dec 7 (166) £300; sg Mar 7 (313) $800

## Pushkin, Aleksandr Sergyeevich, 1799-1837
See also: Limited Editions Club
— Bakhchisaraisky Fontan. Moscow, 1824. 1st Ed. 12mo, contemp half mor. A few leaves soiled. C June 26 (229) £1,100
— Boris Godunov. St. Petersburg, 1831. 1st Ed. 8vo, contemp half calf; spine ends worn. Spotted. C June 26 (232) £2,400
— Gabriel: a Poem in One Song. NY, 1929. One of 750. Trans by Max Eastman; illus by Rockwell Kent. Vellum, unopened. pba Aug 22 (606) $130
— Povesti Pokoinago Ivana Petrovicha Byelkinka. St. Petersburg, 1831. 1st Ed. 12mo, contemp half calf; spine worn. Dampstaining throughout; tear in margin of last leaf repaired; short tear in margin of contents leaf. S June 27 (362) £500
— [The Gypsies]. Moscow, 1827. With: A.L.s in French, Moscow, 1 Jan 1945 1st Ed. 8vo, later bds; orig wraps bound in, soiled. Browned & stained; margins torn. S Oct 27 (1156) £160 [Stavrovski]
— Tsygany. Moscow, 1827. Bound with: Poltava, poema. St. Petersburg, 1829. 12mo, contemp mor gilt; spine scuffed, recased. Marginal worming in last 3 leaves of 2d work; 1st work with some soiling. C June 26 (230) £2,400

1st Ed. 12mo, contemp calf gilt; new endpapers. Lacking final blank. C June 26 (231) £750

## Puss...
— Puss In Boots. NY: Blue Ribbon Books, [1934]. Illus by C. Carey Cloud & Harold B. Lentz. Pictorial bds; scratched & pieces lacking. With 3 colorful pop-up illusts. pba June 20 (274) $130

## Puteanus, Ericius
— Pompa funebris...Alberti...Archiducis Austriae. Brussels, 1729. ("Pompe funebre du...Albert Archiduc d'Autriche.") Folio, 18th-cent calf; needs rebacked. With double-page engraved title & 65 plates; Old stamp on tp. sg Apr 18 (52) $1,000

## Putnam's...
— Putnam's Monthly Magazine. NY, 1853-87. Jan 1853 to Jan 1857 in 8 vols. 8vo, orig cloth; repair to 1 spine. CE May 22 (330) $320

## Puydt, Paul Emile de
— Les Orchidees. Paris, 1880. 8vo, later cloth. With 50 hand-finished colored plates. Piece cut from tp & final leaf & repaired, with loss; some soiling. O Mar 5 (187) $700

## Puzo, Mario
— The Godfather. NY, [1969]. 1st Ed, Advance copy. Wraps, in trial dj. sg June 20 (320) $425

## Pyaduishev, —
— Geograficheskiy Atlas' Rossiyskoiy Imperii, Tsarstva Pol'skago i Velikago Knyazhestva Finlyandskago. St. Petersburg, 1834. Oblong folio, contemp half lea; worn & repaired. With engraved title, engraved index sheet & 60 maps on 81 sheets, some folding or double-page, the maps hand-colored in outline. Some leaves soiled, mostly in outer margin. C May 31 (66) £1,700

## Pyle, Howard, 1853-1911
— Howard Pyle's Book of the American Spirit. NY, 1923. 1st Ed. - Compiled by Merle Johnson. 4to, half cloth, in dj with edge tears; bdg bumped. pba Aug 22 (834) $130
— Stolen Treasure. NY, 1907. 4to, cloth, in def dj with insect damage. pba Jan 4 (81) $130
— The Story of the Grail and the Passing of Arthur. NY, 1910. 4to, cloth. sg Sept 14 (300) $150

## Pynchon, Thomas
— The Crying of Lot 49. Phila., [1966]. 1st Ed. Orig cloth, in chipped & creased dj; bdg bumped, edges worn. F June 20 (49) $90
— Gravity's Rainbow. NY, [1973]. In dj; tape residue on covers. pba Dec 7 (160) $120
— V. Phila: Lippincott, [1963]. 1st Ed, Advance copy. Orig wraps; joint split. Leaves curling at ends. wa Feb 29 (76) $210

## Pyne, William Henry
— The Costume of Great Britain. L, 1804 [plates watermarked 1819-20]. Folio, contemp mor gilt; scuffed. With 60 colored plates. Some soiling & foxing; lacking half-title. F June 20 (837) $625

Anr Ed. L, 1804. Folio, mor gilt. With hand-colored engraved title & 60 hand-colored plates. pba Mar 7 (216) $800

Anr copy. Early mor gilt; def, most leaves loose. With 52 (of 60) hand-colored plates. Minor soiling to plates. sg Dec 7 (262) $250

Anr Ed. L, 1808 [some plates watermarked 1819]. Folio, mor gilt. With 60 hand-colored plates. pba June 20 (275) $800

— The History of the Royal Residences.... L, 1819. 3 vols. 4to, contemp mor gilt. With 100 hand-colored plates.. b Sept 20 (317) £4,500

Anr copy. Contemp half mor; vol I & III joints repaired. With 100 color plates. Soiled; some plates stained. CE Nov 8 (237) $4,800

Anr copy. Mor gilt by Bayntun; joints of Vols I & II broken. With 100 hand-colored plates. Leaf Bb2 torn in Vol II; cleaned & pressed; 2 plates sprung. CNY May 17 (104) $4,000

Anr copy. Modern mor gilt by Sangorski & Sutcliffe. With 100 hand-colored plates, some heightened with gum arabic. Lacking half-titles; 1 plate marked. S Nov 30 (61) £3,000

— Microcosm, or a Picturesque Delineation.... L, 1808. 2 vols in 1. Oblong folio, contemp half calf; rubbed, joints splitting, partly misbound. With frontis & 115 (of 120) plates. Duplicate of Miscellaneous I bound in Vol II; 1 leaf of text torn; 1 leaf shaved at head. bba June 6 (33) £480 [Ingol Maps & Prints]

— Wine and Walnuts; or, After Dinner Chit-Chat. By Ephraim Hardcastle.... L, 1824. 2 vols. 8vo, contemp calf gilt; spine ends & joints worn. pba Mar 7 (217) $60

**Pyritz, Hans**
— Goethe-Bibliographie. Heidelberg, 1965-68. 2 vols. 8vo, cloth & half imitation lea. Volume I with corrigenda booklet laid in. sg Apr 11 (260) $110

**Pyron du Martre, Antoine.** See: Porny, Marc Antoine

# Q

**Quackenbos, John Duncan, 1848-1926**
— Geological Ancestors of the Brook Trout.... NY, 1916. One of 300. Lea gilt; rubbed, joints & spine-tips rubbed. Inscr. O Feb 6 (186) $200

**Quartermain, L. B.**
— South to the Pole. L, 1967. In creased & rubbed dj. pba July 25 (59) $65

**Queen, Ellery, Pseud.**
— Ellery Queen's The Tragedy of X. NY, 1940. In chipped dj. Sgd "Ellery Queen" on tp. pba Aug 22 (398) $55

**Queen's...**
— The Queen's Majesty's Entertainment at Woodstock 1575. Oxford: Daniel Press, 1903 & 1910. One of 115. 4to, orig half cloth. Attributed to George Gascoigne. bba May 9 (481) £120 [Collinge & Clark]

**Queen's Coronation Procession...**
— The Queen's Coronation Procession From the Palace to the Abbey. L: Joseph Robins, 1838. 4.25 by 6.75 inches, Cloth. With hand-colored litho 20 panel fold-out. Minor edge-wear; 1 panel tape repaired. rs Nov 11 (142) $425

**Queeny, Edgar M.**
— Cheechako: the Story of an Alaskan Bear Hunt. NY, 1941. One of 1,200. Inscr. O Oct 10 (219) $140

Anr copy. Inscr. O Oct 10 (220) $100; O Oct 10 (221) $110

— Prairie Wings: Pen and Camera Flight Studies. NY, 1947. Illus by Richard E. Bishop. 4to, cloth. pba July 11 (428) $110

**Quenot, J. P.** See: Vatout & Quenot

**Querard, Joseph Marie, 1797-1865**
— Les Supercheries litteraries devoilees. Paris, 1872-89. 8 vols, including Brunet's Supplement. 8vo, half mor by Stroobants; rubbed. O Mar 26 (216) $900

**Querelles, Emmanuel Michel, Chevalier de**
— Hero et Leandre, poeme nouveau.... Paris: Didot l'aine, 1801. 4to, modern half mor. With frontis & 8 hand-finished color plates. Fuerstenberg - Schaefer copy. S Dec 8 (505) £550

Anr copy. Illus by Louis Philibert Debucourt. 19th-cent mor gilt by Chambolle-Duru. With plain frontis & 8 plates ptd in color & hand-finished. L.p. copy on papier velin. C May 1 (133) £1,500

**Quevedo y Hoyos, Antonio de**
— Libro de indicios y tormentos.... Madrid: Francisco Martinez, 1632. 4to, contemp vellum; cockled. Some marginalia; light discoloration & waterstains. S Nov 30 (181) £950

**Quevedo y Villegas, Francisco de**
— Ensenanza entretenida i donairosa moralidad.... Madrid, 1648. 1st Collected Ed. 4to, loose in old limp vellum. Lacking pp.287/288, 331-350, & 391-396; 1st & last leaves frayed & torn with loss; holes & tears in text; stained & browned. S Oct 27 (1157) £500 [Calero]

— The Visions.... L, 1667. 8vo, contemp calf; backstrip def at ends. Worming in lower inner corners; upper outer corner of last leaf torn with loss; lacking license leaf. sg Mar 21 (302) $150

**Queverdo, Francois Isidore, 1748-97**
— Premier cayer des panneaux, frises et sujets arabesques.... Paris, [c.1788). 3 parts in 1 vol. Bdg not described. With 12 lettered & numbered plates & 14 other plates. Fuerstenberg - Schaefer copy. S Dec 8 (506) £850

**Quiller-Couch, Sir Arthur, 1863-1944**
— In Powder and Crinoline: Old Fairy Tales.... L, [1913]. Illus by Kay Nielsen. 4to, orig half cloth; worn & shaken. With 24 colored plates. cb Oct 17 (658) $400

## QUILLER-COUCH

Anr copy. Cloth; spine ends worn. sg Feb 15 (212) $275

One of 500, sgd by Nielsen. Orig vellum gilt; extremities rubbed. With 26 colored plates. pba Nov 30 (253) $3,750

— The Sleeping Beauty and Other Fairy Tales.... L, [1910]. Illus by Edmund Dulac. 4to, orig cloth. b May 30 (431) £140

One of 1,000. Mor gilt. With 30 colored plates. cb Oct 17 (629) $850

One of 150. Mor extra with onlaid design of a cavalier with sword, by Bayntun-Riviere. CE Sept 27 (109) $3,000

### Quillinan, Edward

— Stanzas, by the Author of "Dunluce Castle". Lee Priory, Kent, 1814. 4to, orig wraps; rebacked & soiled. b Dec 5 (154) £120

### Quin, Edward

— An Historical Atlas. L, 1836. 4to, contemp half calf. With 20 folding maps. Tp foxed. b Sept 20 (384) £70

### Quin, Edwin Richard Windham, 3d Earl of Dunraven

— Notes on Irish Architecture. L, 1875-77. 2 vols. Folio, orig cloth; spines & extremities worn, repaired. With 125 mtd autotype plates (5 double-page), 13 litho plans & 161 wood-engraved text illusts. Plate mounts warped; some foxing. sg June 13 (29) $3,000

### Quincy, Josiah, 1744-75

— Observations on the Act of Parliament commonly called the Boston Port-Bill.... L, 1774. 8vo, later wraps. Foxed; old ink blot on 1 leaf. John Dickinson's copy. K Oct 1 (138) $2,200

### Quinn, David Beers. See: Hulton & Quinn

### Quintanilla, Luis

— All the Brave. NY, [1939]. One of 440. Text by Elliot Paul & Jay Allen; preface by Ernest Hemingway. 4to, orig half mor; spine scuffed. pba Aug 22 (236) $110

### Quintilianus, Marcus Fabius

— Institutiones oratoriae. Venice: Aldus, 1521. ("Institutionum oratorarium libri XII.") 8vo, blind-tooled mor. Small hole on F6 affecting 1 letter; some dampstaining. S June 12 (108) £420

### Quintos Horatius Flaccus, 65-8 B.C

— Carmina Alcaica. See: Ashendene Press

### Quinze Joyes...

— Les Quinze Joyes de Mariage. Paris: Rene Kieffer, 1930. One of 50 on japon, with watercolor drawing, additional suite in orange & a suite of 56 additional illusts. Illus by J. Touchet. Mor extra by G. Levitzky showing a frantic man caught in a lobster trap. S Nov 21 (353) £600

## AMERICAN BOOK PRICES CURRENT

### Quirini, Angelo Maria, Bishop of Brescia

— Liber singularis de optimorum scriptorum editionibus.... Lindau, 1761. 4to, modern half calf. Some dampstains & foxing. O Mar 26 (217) $250

### Quirola, Antonio

— Nuova smorfia del giuco del lotto disposta per ordine alfabeatico.... Naples, 1846. 12mo, modern half lea. Some soiling & staining. O Sept 12 (146) $350

### Quiz, Peter. See: Egerton, Daniel Thomas

# R

### R., F.

— The Year of Jubilee. A Poem, Commemorative of the Centenary of Wesleyan Methodism, 1839. Beverley, [1839]. 8vo, modern bds. b Dec 5 (477) £50

### Rabaut Saint-Etienne, Jean Paul, 1743-93

— Almanach historique de la revolution francoise pour l'annee 1792.... Paris, [1792]. 2 parts in 1 vol. 18mo, contemp mor gilt. Plates before letters. Marginal dampstains. Fuerstenberg - Schaefer copy. S Dec 8 (507) £240

### Rabelais, Francois, 1494?-1553

See also: Limited Editions Club

— Les Cinq Livres de Rabelais. Paris, 1876. One of 25 on chine with the plates before letters. Illus by E. Boilvin. 4 vols. 16mo, mor gilt by Zaehnsdorf. With an extra suite of port & 15 plates by anr artist. b Dec 5 (44) £160

— Oeuvres. Amst., 1711. 3 vols. 8vo, 18th-cent mor gilt. With port, map & 3 folding plates. Fuerstenberg - Schaefer copy. S Dec 8 (508) £800

Anr Ed. Amst., 1741. Ed by Le Duchat. 3 vols. 4to, contemp calf. With 2 engraved titles, frontis, port, 12 plates, 3 topographical plates & 1 folding map. A few biographical notes in French. Fuerstenberg - Schaefer copy. S Dec 8 (509) £1,700

Anr Ed. Paris, 1798 [An VI]. 3 vols. 4to, calf gilt by Bozerian. With port & 75 plates, proofs before letters. L.p. copy. Fuerstenberg - Schaefer copy. S Dec 8 (510) £1,150

Anr copy. Later mor gilt by Birdsall. With port & 75 plates. S Apr 23 (132) £500

### Rabinowitz, Shalom, 1859-1916. See: Sholem Aleichem

### Racine, Jean Baptiste, 1639-99

— Oeuvres. Paris, 1783. One of 200. 3 vols. 4to, 19th-cent mor gilt by Chilliat. Fuerstenberg - Schaefer copy. S Dec 8 (513) £1,300

Anr Ed. Paris: Didot jeune for Deterville, 1796. 4 vols. 8vo, contemp calf gilt; spine of Vol I damaged at head. With port & 12 plates, all but 1 in 2 states. Fuerstenberg - Schaefer copy. S Dec 8 (514) £400

Anr Ed. Paris, 1807. Copy on papier velin. 5 vols. 8vo, contemp red mor gilt by Bozerian jeune. With port & 12 plates before letters. Plates foxed. Fuerstenberg - Schaefer copy. S Dec 8 (515) £1,100

**Racinet, Auguste**
— Le Costume historique. Paris, [1876-88]. 5 vols only; lacking Vol I with into text & 12 plates of diagrams. Folio, mor extra. With 473 plates only, 277 in color. S June 13 (732) £1,000
Anr Ed. Paris, 1888. 5 (of 6) vols; lacking Vol IV. Half mor; rubbed. cb Oct 17 (115) $800
Anr copy. 6 vols. 4to, lea; spine & hinges weak, endpapers split. Met Dec 14 (254) $1,050
— L'Ornement polychrome. Paris, [c.1870]. Folio, later cloth, orig cover laid down. With 100 plates. Plates browned, with short tears reinforced on verso; some soiling. cb June 25 (1967) $800
— L'Ornement polychrome. 1st Series. Paris, [c.1870]. Folio, later half mor; worn. With 100 color plates. Some foxing & soiling; marginal dampstains. cb Oct 17 (43) $700
— L'Ornement polychrome. 2d Series. Paris, 1885-86. Folio, later half mor; some wear. With 120 plates. Some soiling & foxing; marginal dampstains. cb Oct 17 (44) $700
— Polychromatic Ornament. L, 1873. Folio, contemp half mor, orig cover bound in. With 100 color plates. Prelims & text foxed. cb June 25 (1966) $1,000

**Rackham, Arthur, 1867-1939**
— The Arthur Rackham Fairy Book. L, 1933. One of 460. 4to, orig vellum gilt. With 8 colored plates. bba May 9 (412) £800 [Baring]; CE Sept 27 (240) $1,000; pn Dec 7 (95) £650 [Shapero]; S Nov 2 (127) £440 [Hirsch]; sg Oct 19 (209) $900; wd Nov 15 (101) $850
— Arthur Rackham's Book of Pictures. L, 1913. 4to, orig cloth; covers spotted. With 44 colored plates. sg Feb 15 (245) $550
One of 1,030. Later lev gilt by Bayntun-Riviere. With 44 colored plates. sg Oct 19 (198) £425
Anr copy. Mor gilt by Zaehnsdorf for E. Joseph. W Mar 6 (34) £700
— Mother Goose: The Old Nursery Rhymes. L, [1913]. One of 1,130. 4to, cloth; stained, rubbed. Half-title spotted. Ck May 31 (142) £320
Anr copy. Orig cloth; soiled. Half-title browned; some spotting to text. Ck May 31 (179) £400
Anr copy. Orig cloth; stained. S Nov 2 (110) £260 [McCulloch]
Anr Ed. NY: Century, [1913]. One of 150. 4to, cloth; spine with stains, some soiling. pba June 20 (276) $1,200
Anr copy. Cloth; soiled. sg Sept 21 (279) $550
— Some British Ballads. L, [1919]. 4to, orig cloth. bba May 9 (261) £70 [Clancey]
Anr copy. Orig half vellum. S Nov 2 (123) £440 [Toledano]
Anr copy. Lev gilt by Bayntun-Riviere. With 16 mtd color plates. sg Feb 15 (260) $175
One of 575. Orig half vellum; stained. Ck May 31 (149) £140
Anr copy. Orig half vellum; endpapers browned. S Nov 2 (112) £260 [Sotheran]
Anr copy. Later mor gilt by Zaehnsdorf. sg Oct 19 (199) $700

Anr copy. Orig half vellum. W Mar 6 (35) £300

**Rackham, Bernard**
— Catalogue of the Glaisher Collection of Pottery and Porcelain. Cambr., 1935. 2 vols. 4to, half lea gilt. With 302 plates, 36 of them in color. Library markings. sg June 13 (100) $400
— Early Netherlands Maiolica. L, 1926. 4to, orig cloth, in torn & chipped dj. sg June 13 (101) $100

**Radcliffe, Ann, 1764-1823**
— The Mysteries of Udolpho. Dublin, 1795. 3 vols. 12mo, contemp calf; spine ends repaired. sg Feb 8 (331) $140

**Radcliffe, Frederick Peter Delme**
— The Noble Science: a Few General Ideas on Fox-Hunting.... L, 1839. 1st Ed. 8vo, orig cloth. O Jan 9 (183) $80
Anr copy. Pictorial cloth; soiled. Some foxing. O Jan 9 (184) $90

**Radcliffe, John, of the Chetham Library, Manchester**
— Bibliotheca Chethamensis. Manchester, 1791-1826. Vols I-III (of 6). 8vo, old bds or old cloth; rebacked. Some stains & soiling. O Mar 26 (219) $100
Anr copy. Vols I-III (of 6) bound in 5 vols. 8vo, half calf; worn. Interleaved with blanks. Some foxing. O Mar 26 (220) $100

**Radcliffe, William**
— Fishing from the Earliest Times. L, 1921. Half cloth. pba July 11 (242) $180

**Rademaker, Abraham**
— Kabinet van Nederlandsche Outheden en Gezichten. Hamburg & Amst., 1730. 4to, contemp calf; worn. With 300 illus, & text in Dutch, French, & English. S Oct 26 (292) £750 [Lemmers]

**Rademaker, Abraham —& Others**
— Arcadie Hollandaise; ou, Collection Choisie de Six-Cent Vues Pittoresques. Amst., 1807. 2 vols. Folio, contemp bds; worn, Vol II needs rebacked. With 519 plates only. sg May 9 (373) $2,600

**Radiguet, Raymond, 1903-23**
— Le Diable au corps. Paris, 1957. One of 30 for collaborators, this with 2 additional suites of the uncolored lithos, 2 sgd pencil drawings for the plate facing p. 80. Preface by John Cocteau; illus by Paul Emile Becat. Mor mosaic bdg with onlaid sterling silver by Jack Craib, 1987. With litho frontis & 15 hand-colored plates. S Nov 21 (357) £900

**Radziwill, Lee Bouvier.** See: Onassis & Radziwill

**Rae, W. F.**
— Westward by Rail: The New Route to the East. L, 1870. Orig cloth; worn, front joint cracked, free endpaper detached. With frontis map having water portions hand-colored. Pencil marks to tp, which has pbr's presentation blindstamp. pba Nov 16 (218) $120

# RAEMAEKERS

**Raemaekers, Louis, 1869-1956**
— Raemaekers' War Cartoons.... NY, 1917. One of 1,050. 2 vols. Folio, orig cloth, in cloth djs. Marginal dampstaining. O July 9 (178) $110

**Raffald, Elizabeth**
— The Experienced English Housekeeper.... L, 1788. 8vo, modern half bds. With port frontis, & 3 folding plates. 1 plate torn & repaired; p.343 torn with loss; spotted. S Oct 12 (65) £200

Anr Ed. L, 1795. 8vo, contemp calf; rubbed & rebacked. With port & 3 folding plates. Small tears in lower margin of 2 plates; frontis & 1st few pages dampstained at upper margin & wormed. S Mar 28 (563) £150

Anr Ed. L, 1808. 8vo, contemp calf; rubbed. With frontis & folding plate. Browned. bba May 30 (124) £120 [Hawley]

**Raffles, Sir Thomas Stamford, 1781-1826**
— The History of Java. L, 1817. 1st Ed. 2 vols. 4to, mor gilt by Cassidy, 1899. On papier velin. With large folding map hand-colored in outline at end of Vol II, 2 folding tables & 65 plates, 10 of them hand-colored. Some margins shaved. S June 27 (241) £220

**Rafinesque-Schmaltz, Constantine Samuel, 1783-1840**
— Caratteri di alcuni nuovi generi e nuove specie di animali e piante della Sicilia. Palermo, 1810. 4to, 19th-cent half cloth, unopened, orig wraps bound in. sg May 16 (338) $1,300
— Florula Ludoviciana; or, a Flora of the State of Louisiana. NY, 1817. 8vo, half lea. Tp repaired; other repairs; foxed. Met Feb 24 (321) $1,700

**Rahir, Edouard**
— [Sale Catalogue] La Bibliotheque de feu Edouard Rahir.... Paris, 1930-37. 5 parts (of 6) in 5 vols. 4to, orig wraps; worn, first 2 parts shaken, part 2 spine ends repaired. Part 1 priced throughout in pencil. sg Apr 11 (25) $275

**Rahir Collection, Edouard**
— Livres dans de riches reliures des seizieme, dix-septieme, dix-huitieme et dix-neuvieme siecles. Paris, 1910. Folio, modern half mor, orig wraps bound in; soiled. bba May 9 (142A) £100 [Maggs]

Anr copy. Ptd wraps; soiled & chipped. With 50 plates. O Mar 26 (221) $130
— [Sale Catalogue] La Bibliotheque de feu Edouard Rahir.... Paris, 1930-31. 2 vols. 4to, recent cloth, wraps bound in. Partially priced in pencil. bba May 9 (120) £170 [Maggs]

**Raht, Carlysle Graham**
— The Romance of Davis Mountain and Big Bend Country. El Paso, [1919]. Orig cloth; hinge cracked before tp, extremities worn. With port & 13 plates with images on both sides & double-page map. pba Apr 25 (609) $130

# AMERICAN BOOK PRICES CURRENT

**Rail-Roads...**
— The Rail-Roads, History and Commerce of Chicago. Chicago, 1854. 8vo, orig wraps. sg Oct 26 (153) $550

**Rainwater, Robert.** See: Arntzen & Rainwater

**Raisor, Gary**
— Less Than Human. Woodstock: Overlook Connection Press, [1993]. One of 300. Cloth, in wooden velvet-lined coffin-shaped case. O Dec 5 (240) $150

**Rajah Ram Chuttraputtee, Maharajah of Kolhapur.** See: Onassis copy, Jacqueline Bouvier Kennedy

**Raleigh, Sir Walter, 1552?-1618**
— The History of the World. L, 1666. Folio, contemp calf; rebacked & recornered. With port, engraved title & 8 double-page maps. b Jan 31 (107) £320

Anr Ed. L, 1677. Folio, contemp calf; very worn. With frontis, port & 8 double-page maps & plates. b Sept 20 (167) £320

Anr Ed. L, 1687. Folio, contemp calf; joints cracked, worn. With engraved title, port & 8 double-page maps & plates. CE June 15 (247) $700
— Judicious and Select Essayes and Observations upon the First Invention of Shipping.... L, 1650. 8vo, old calf; discount. Some dampstaining & foxing on tp & frontis & along margins. Met May 22 (316) $275; Met May 22 (317) $225
— Remains. L, 1702. 12mo, contemp sheep; spine ends chipped, joints cracked. With port. sg Mar 21 (271) $150
— Works. L: R. Dodsley, 1751. 2 vols. 8vo, contemp calf; worn & rubbed, front cover of Vol I detached. K Feb 11 (202) $275

**Raleigh, Sir Walter A., 1861-1922 —& Jones, Henry Albert**
— The War in the Air. Oxford, 1922-37. 9 vols, including Appendix vol & 2 portfolios of maps. pn Dec 7 (131) £400

**Ralfe, James**
— The Naval Chronology of Great Britain. L, 1820. 3 vols. 8vo, early calf with orig cloth spines laid down inside lower cover. With 60 hand-colored plates. Some spotting. b June 28 (57) £1,000

Anr copy. Mor gilt by Riviere. With 60 hand-colored plates. S Nov 30 (230) £2,100

**Ralph, James.** See: Sidney & Ralph

**Ralph, Julian, 1853-1903**
— On Canada's Frontier. NY, 1892. Illus by Frederic Remington. 8vo, orig cloth; spine ends & corners rubbed. pba Apr 25 (621) $120

**Ramade, Louis**
— Nouveau recueil pratique d'enseignes decoratives a l'usage des peintres. Paris: Monrocq Freres, [c.1900]. Half cloth, plates loose as issued; spine cracked & frayed, portfolio bds rubbed & mildewed. With 19 (of 20) chromolitho plates. Plate edges spotted. cb Oct 17 (93) $800

**Ramal, Walter.** See: De la Mare, Walter

**Ramazzini, Bernardino**
— L'Art de conserver la sante des princes et des personnes du premier rang.... Leiden, 1724. 1st Ed in French. - Trans by Etienne Coulet. 8vo, contemp calf; upper joints cracked, spine repaired. Some soiling.   Ck Mar 22 (255) £200

**Rameau, Jean Philippe, 1683-1764**
— Les Surprises de l'amour, ballet.... Paris, 1757. 4 parts in 1 vol. 4to, contemp vellum bds. Some browning.   S Dec 1 (288) £1,200

**Ramelli, Agostino**
— Le Diverse et artificiose machine.... Paris, 1588. Folio, contemp vellum; rubbed. With engraved title, port & 194 plates numbered to 195 (Nos 148-149 a single double-page plate). Perforation to tp affecting background of port on verso; tp soiled; some creasing to lower forecorners at beginning; some double-page engravings regarded; a few engravings rubbed; quire Ii misbound after I; P1 with tear entering image; marginal tears & dampstaining; Hh1 stained. Hefner copy.   CNY May 17 (36) $14,000
Anr copy. Modern half vellum. With engraved title, port & 194 plates. Washed; fore-margin of H1 torn out & repaired at edge of plate; repairs in text of Gg5 with loss; other marginal repairs; gathering F misbound.   S Nov 30 (331) £5,000

**Ramey, Earl**
— The Beginnings of Marysville. San Francisco: California Historical Society, 1936. 1st Ed. Bds; corners bumped, some sunning. With folding map. Robbins copy.   pba Mar 21 (288) $120

**Ramiro, Erastene, Pseud.**
— Catalogue descriptif et analytique de l'oeuvre grave de Felicien Rops. Paris, 1893. Bound with: Supplement. Paris, 1895. One of 200 & 750. 4to, half mor by Charles Meunier, orig wraps bound in; joints & edges rubbed.   S Nov 21 (358) £2,100
— Cours de danse fin de siecle. Paris, 1892. One of 49 on japon with 3 additional suites of the etchings & an additional suite of all the decorations. Illus by Louis Legrand. 8vo, contemp vellum, upper cover painted by Louis Legrand, orig wraps bound in. With frontis & 11 color plates. Bound in are a chalk drawing & a crayon & watercolor drawing, both by Louis Legrand.   S Nov 21 (359) £4,500
— Faune Parisienne. Paris: Gustave Pellet, 1901. One of 140. Illus by Louis Legrand. 4to, mor extra with floral onlays by Rene Kieffer, orig wraps bound in. With additional suite of plates in black only, prelim ink & watercolor drawing (sgd by Legrand) for the vitnette on p. 38 & unsgd watercolor drawing.   S Nov 21 (361) £1,600
— Louis Legrand: Peintre Graveur, catalogue de son oeuvre grave et lithographie. Paris, 1896. One of 250. 4to, wraps; loose. With etched cover & 6 etched plates. Inscr.   sg June 13 (236) $800
One of 50 on japon. Half mor, orig wraps bound in. With additional state of cover design & frontis, 43 extra etchings, a crayon & pencil drawing sgd by Legrand, 5 contemp exhibition invitations & ALs to Marc Peter presenting the book.   S Nov 21 (360) £2,700

**Ramsay, A. Maitland**
— Atlas of External Diseases of the Eye. Glasgow, 1898. 4to, contemp half lea; rebacked. With 30 chromolitho & 18 photogravure plates.   sg May 16 (483) $175

**Ramsay, Andrew Michael, 1686-1743**
— The Travels of Cyrus. L, 1730. 4th Ed. 4to, contemp calf; rebacked in calf. Stamp to bottom of tp & dedication leaf; ink note to tp verso.   pba Mar 7 (219) $100

**Ramusio, Giovanni Battista, 1485-1557**
— Delle navigationi et viaggi. Venice, 1563-64-65. 3 vols. Folio, old mor; 2 spine heads chipped. Vol I lacking 3 double-page maps; tp laid down; upper margins cut close, occasionally touching headlines; tear at inner margins of ccc8-10 with loss of letters on ccc8. Vol II with tear in 335; bifolium h3.6 duplicated. Vol III with fold of 1 plan repaired; double-page map of New World shaved at foot with minor loss to caption; marginal worming.   C Apr 3 (186) £4,500

**Ranby, John, 1703-73**
— The Method of Treating Gunshot Wounds. L, 1744. 1st Ed. 8vo, modern half mor. Title soiled & repaired; K1 torn; K4 chipped.   CE Nov 8 (138) $480

**Rand, Ayn**
— Atlas Shrugged. NY: Random House, [1957]. In rubbed dj.   pba May 23 (353) $160
Anr copy. In backed & restored 1st dj.   sg June 20 (321) $700
— The Fountainhead. Indianapolis, [c.1948]. In worn dj; bdg stained. Inscr.   sg Dec 14 (245) $550

**Randall, David A.** See: Van Winkle & Randall

**Randolph, Bernard, 1643-90?**
— The Present State of the Morea.... L, 1689. 3d Ed. With folding map & 2 double-page plates. Bound with: Randolph. The Present State of the Islands in the Archipelago.... Oxford, 1687. 1st Ed. With folding map & 4 plates. 4to. Contemp calf, needs rebdg. Some fold breaks to maps; some repairs to plates. Sold w.a.f.   sg Mar 7 (314) $375

**Randolph, Mary**
— The Virginia Housewife: or, Methodical Cook. Balt., 1828 [preface dated 1831]. Stereotype Ed. 12mo, calf; front cover detached.   pba Nov 30 (100) $160
4th Ed. Wash., 1830. 12mo, calf; spine worn, corners rounded, hinges cracked. Foxed.   pba June 20 (101) $110

**Ransome, Arthur.** See: Arabian Nights

**Ransome, John Crowe**
— Grace after Meat. L: Hogarth Press, 1924. One of 400. Intro by Robert Graves. Orig bds. sg Dec 14 (168) $200

**Ransonnette, Nicolas, 1745-1810.** See: Krafft & Ransonnette

**Raphael Sanzio d'Urbino, 1483-1520**
— La Favola di Psiche disegnata.... Rome, [c.1840]. Oblong 4to, half mor; worn. With 30 plates. sg May 9 (376) $90
— I Freschi delle Loggie Vaticane... illustratai per cura di Agostino Valentini. Rome, [c.1840]. Folio, orig pictorial bds. With 41 plates. sg Sept 7 (288) $600
— Les Loges de Raphael... [Rome, 1772-77?]. Folio, unbound in portfolio. With 86 engraved sheets. Some dampstaining, soiling & marginal tears. C Nov 29 (105) £6,500
— La Sacra Genesi. Rome, 1773. 4th state. Oblong 4to, early wraps. With engraved title & 17 plates. Some foxing. sg Dec 7 (294) $375

**Raphall, Morris Jacob, 1798-1868**
— Bible View of Slavery. NY, 1861. 8vo, ptd wraps; repaired, joint splitting. sg Mar 28 (309) $550

**Rapicius, Jovita**
— De numero oratorio libri quinque.... Venice: Aldus, 1554. Folio, old carta rustica. Tear in margin of final leaf repaired; some foxing at beginning. S Nov 30 (293) £950

**Rapin de Thoyras, Paul, 1661-1725**
— The History of England.... L, 1728-31. Trans by N. Tindal. 15 vols. 8vo, half mor. With 29 plates & 6 folding tables & 4 folding maps. NH Sept 16 (164) $325
Anr Ed. L, 1763. 2 vols. Folio, contemp calf; rubbed, hinges weak. Worming at beginning of Vol II; small loss at p. 331 of Vol I & minor tear at p. 543. S June 12 (192) £200

**Rapin, Rene, 1621-87**
— The Modest Critick.... L: William Witwood & Mrs. Feltham, 1691. 8vo, contemp sheep; worn, needs rebacked. Tp stamped. sg Mar 21 (272) $150

**Raponi, Ignazio Maria**
— Recueil de pierres antiques gravees concernant l'historie... des anciens peuple.... Rome, 1786. Port by Angelo Campanella. Illus by Giovanni Bruno. Folio, 18th-Cent half calf; spine worn. With title vignette, port, & 88 plates. S Oct 26 (338) £1,100 [Lyon]

**Rapport...**
— Rapport officiel sur la deuxieme exposition internationale de locomotion aerienne organisee par l'Association des Industriels de la Locomotion Aerienne au Grand-Palais (15 Octobre - 2 Novembre 1910). Paris, 1911. Folio, orig wraps; shaken, backstrip & glassine outer wrap chipped. sg May 16 (83) $175
— Rapport officiel sur la premiere exposition internationale de locomotion aerienne organisee par l'Association des Industriels de la Locomotion Aerienne au Grand-Palais (Octobre 1909). Paris, 1910. Folio, orig wraps; shaken, backstrip & glassine outer wrap chipped. sg May 16 (82) $175
— Rapport sur le premier salon d'aeronautique, Grand Palais, Decembre 1908. Paris, 1908. 4to, orig wraps; spine ends chipped. Tp stamped. sg May 16 (80) $175
Anr copy. Syn, orig front wrap laid down. Henri Hegener's annotated copy. sg May 16 (81) $225

**Rashleigh, Philip**
— Specimens of British Minerals. L, 1797-1802. 2 parts in 1 vol. 4to, later half mor & contemp bds; rebacked. With 54 plates, most hand-colored. bba Nov 1 (41) £3,500 [Phelps]

**Raspe, Rudolph Erich, 1737-94**
See also: Limited Editions Club
— The Adventures of Baron Munchausen. L: Frederick Warne, [1878]. Illus by A. Bichard. 4to, orig cloth-backed pictorial bds. With 18 chromolitho plates. With 12 of Bichard's watercolor designs, each sgd, mtd in card folders. S Nov 21 (365) £8,000

**Rastell, William**
— A Table Collected of the Yeres of Our Lorde God, and of the Yeres of the Kinges of England.... L: J. Waley, 1567. 8vo, later calf. Sold w.a.f. CE June 12 (143) $160

**Rathbone, Hannah Mary Reynolds**
— The Poetry of Birds Selected from various Authors.... Liverpool, 1833. 4to, contemp mor; rubbed, rebacked, recornered. With 21 hand-colored plates. Slight soiling & spotting. S Oct 27 (769) £280 [Gerrard]
— The Poetry of Birds Selected from Various Authors.... Liverpool & L, 1833. One of c.25. 4to, contemp mor calf; minor rubbing to joints. With 21 hand-colored plates. Inscr to her brother, Richard Rathbone, 1833. Fattorini copy. C Oct 25 (38) £1,900

**Rathborne, Aaron**
— The Surveyor in Foure Bookes. L, 1616. 1st Ed. Folio, contemp calf; rubbed. With engraved title & 2 ports. Lacking initial blank. S Mar 29 (773) £1,700

**Rattray, Harriet**
— Country Life in Syria. L, 1876. 1st Ed. 8vo, cloth; rubbed. Lacks front fly-leaf. S Oct 26 (147) £180 [Brunt]

**Rau, Bernd**
— Hans Arp. Die Reliefs. Oeuvre-Katalog. Stuttgart, 1981. 4to, cloth. sg Jan 11 (26) $130

**Raumer, Frederick von**
— America, and the American People. NY, 1846. Orig cloth; stained & worn. Some foxing & marginal dampstains. pba Aug 8 (161) $200

**Rauschenberg, Robert**
— XXXIV Drawings for Dante's Inferno. NY, 1964. One of 300. 4to, orig cloth portfolio; broken & stained, text bound in pictorial wraps. Met May 22 (89) $500

Anr copy. Orig cloth portfolio; soiled. sg May 23 (533) $1,400

**Ravier, Emile**
— Bibliographie des oeuvres de Leibniz. Hildesheim, 1966. 8vo, orig cloth. sg Apr 11 (261) $120

**Ravilious, Eric William, 1903-42**
— The Complete Wedgwood Designs of Eric Ravilious. Dalrymple Press, 1986. One of 750. In dj. bba May 9 (417) £130 [Goddard]
— The Wood Engravings of Eric Ravilious. L: Lion and Unicorn Press, 1972. Ltd Ed. bba May 9 (416) £380 [Thomsen]

Anr copy. With 113 plates, 3 folding. S May 16 (140) £360

**Rawling, Cecil Godfrey**
— The Great Plateau being an Account of Exploration in Central Tibet, 1903, and of the Gartok Expedition, 1904-1905. L, 1905. 1st Ed. With 2 folding maps. bba Nov 1 (456) £300 [Chessler]

**Rawlings, Marjorie Kinnan**
— The Sojourner. L, [1953]. Inscr & with sgd Christmas Card laid in. wa Feb 1 (66) $100

**Rawlinson, George**
— The Five Great Monarchies of the Ancient Eastern World. L, 1879. 3 vols. 8vo, contemp vellum gilt. pba Oct 9 (14) $65

**Rawls, James J.**
— Dan De Quille of the Big Bonanza. San Francisco: Book Club of California, 1980. One of 650. Half cloth, in dj. pba Feb 12 (499) $55

**Rawstorne, Lawrence**
— Gamonia: or, the Art of Preserving Game. L: Ackermann, 1837. 8vo, orig mor gilt. With 15 handcolored plates. sg Mar 7 (516) $400

**Ray, Edward**
— Golf Clubs and How to Use Them. NY: Robert McBride, 1922. 1st Ed. Bds; soiled, lacking piece at spine foot. pba Apr 18 (146) $85

**Ray, Gordon N.**
— The Art of the French Illustrated Book.... NY, 1982. 2 vols. Folio, orig cloth in djs. sg Apr 11 (263) $200
— The Illustrator and the Book in England from 1790 to 1914. NY, 1976. 4to, cloth. sg Sept 14 (313) $80

Anr copy. Folio, orig cloth. sg Apr 11 (262) $120

**Ray, Man**
— Alphabets for Adults. Beverley Hills, 1948. One of 500. 4to, half cloth. sg Jan 11 (371) $350

Anr Ed. Beverly Hills, 1948. One of—500. 4to, orig bds. Inscr to Max Edel, 13 Dec 1948. sg Apr 18 (129) $650

— Electricite. Paris: La Compagnie Parisienne de Distribution d'Electricite, 1931. One of 500. Intro by Pierre Bost. Folio, orig wraps, in transparent dj. With 10 mtd photogravures from rayographs. P Oct 5 (333) $20,000
— La Photographie n'est pas l'art. [Paris], 1937. Foreword by Andre Breton. Unsewn in orig wraps; corners creased. sg Apr 18 (128) $950
— Photographs by Man Ray, Paris 1920-1934. Hartford, [1934]. 4to, plastic multi-ring binder; extremities worn. sg Feb 29 (193) $1,500
— Self-Portrait. L: Andre Deutsch, [1963]. Tattered dj laid in. Inscr, with ink sketch of an open eye. With autograph postcard, sgd by Julie Ray. pba June 20 (279) $375

**Ray, Patrick Henry**
— Report of the International Polar Expedition to Point Barrow, Alaska. Wash., 1885. 4to, cloth. George Davidson's sgd copy. Larson copy. pba Feb 12 (39) $350

**Raymond, Alex**
— Flash Gordon: The Tournament of Death. Chicago: Pleasure Books, [1935]. Pictorial bds; soiled, rubbed, spine chipped. With 3 color pop-ups. pba May 4 (244) $275

**Raymond, Henry Jarvis, 1820-69**
— History of the Administration of President Lincoln. NY, 1864. 8vo, orig cloth; spine ends worn, corners showing. pba June 13 (291) $55

**Raymond, Oliver**
— The Art of Fishing on the Principle of Avoiding Cruelty. L, 1866. 8vo, half mor by Larkins; rubbed. O June 25 (217) $160

Anr copy. 4to, orig cloth, unopened. pba July 11 (243) $100

**Raynal, Guillaume Thomas Francois, 1713-96**
See also: Floyd's copy, William
— Atlas de toutes les parties connues du globe terrestre.... [Geneva, 1780]. 4to, orig bds; def. With 50 double-page maps. S June 13 (509) £700

Anr Ed. [Geneva: Pellet, 1780]. Maps by Rigobert Bonne. 4to, contemp half calf; spine chipped with loss; worn. With 50 double-page maps. World map repaired, slight loss. S Oct 26 (443) £700 [Zioni]

Anr copy. Contemp tree calf; rubbed. With 50 double-page maps & 23 tables. S Oct 26 (444) £850 [Zioni]

— Histoire philosophique et politique des establissemens et du commerce des Europeens dans les deux Indes. Geneva, 1780. 5 vols. 4to, contemp calf; rebacked. Mildewed. Sold w.a.f. CE June 15 (248) $300

Anr copy. Contemp mor gilt. With 23 tables, port, 4 plates & 50 double-page maps hand-colored in outline. Fuerstenberg - Schaefer copy. S Dec 8 (517) £5,000

— The Revolution of America. Dublin, 1781. 12mo, orig bds; worn & rebacked with lea. Foxed; 1 leaf torn. pba June 13 (292) $60

**Rayner, Simeon**
— The History and Antiquities of Haddon Hall. Derby & L, 1836. Folio, contemp calf; rebacked, rubbed. With hand-colored frontis & 32 plates (23 are proofs on india paper mtd), 6 supplementary plates. Some spotting. Ck Feb 14 (310) £130

**Reach, Angus B.**
— Clement Lorimer, or the Book with the Iron Clasps. L, [c.1849]. Illus by George Cruikshank. 8vo, calf gilt by Riviere; rubbed. pba June 20 (280) $180

**Read, Alexander**
— Somatographia Anthropine, or a Description of the Body of Man by Artificial Figures Representing the Members.... [L]: T. Cotes, 1634. 2 parts in 1 vol. 8vo, modern cloth. Lacking M5 & initial leaf; rustholes to E5 & Z1 with small loss. Sold w.a.f. pn Dec 7 (46) £340

**Read, George Willis**
— A Pioneer of 1850.... Bost., 1927. 1st Ed. - Ed by Georgia Willis Read. Orig cloth in dj; d/j spine faded. With frontis port & 1 folded map. Larson copy. pba Sept 28 (648) $50

**Read, J. A. & D. F.**
— Journey to the Gold Diggins by Jeremiah Saddlebags. Cincinnati, 1849. 1st Ed, 1st Issue. 12mo, orig wraps; spine ends worn, front wrap corner reinforced. With 112 illusts. Robbins copy. pba Mar 21 (289) $5,000
Anr Ed. NY, [1849]. 2d Issue. Oblong 12mo, orig wraps; broken, piece lacking from upper cover. Foxed; some corners lacking. bbc Dec 18 (549) $400

**Reade, Charles, 1814-84**
See also: Limited Editions Club
— Works. L, 1896-98. Library Ed. 17 vols. 8vo, half calf; some chipping. b Sept 20 (574) £420

**Reagan, Ronald**
— An American Life. NY, 1990. In dj. Sgd bookplate mtd to front blank. pba Oct 26 (305) $250

**Real...**
— Real cedula de ereccion de la Compania de Filipinas de 10 de marzo de 1785. Madrid: Joaquin Ibarra, [1785]. Folio, modern mor gilt. With frontis with Spanish royal arms. Small wormhole running through text, anr through margin; some marginal staining. S June 27 (240) £750
— Real Museo Bobonico. Naples, 1824-57. 16 vols. 8vo, 19th-cent half vellum. With 977 plates, 32 of them folding, 8 in color, 1 double-page. K June 23 (45) $475

**Real, Daniel**
— Les Batiks de Java.... Paris: A. Calavas, [c.1924]. 4to, Loose as issued in bd folder; extremities worn, front joint partly cracked. With 47 plates on 46 leaves. sg June 13 (357) $120

**Reales...**
— Reales Ordenanzas para la direccion.... Madrid, 1783. Folio, contemp half calf. S Nov 30 (171) £400

**Reau, Louis**
— Houdon, sa vie et son oeuvre. Paris, 1964. 2 vols. Folio, cloth, in djs. sg Jan 11 (221) $175

**Reaumur, Rene Antoine Ferchault de, 1683-1757**
— L'Art de faire eclore et d'elever en toute saison des oiseaux domestiques. Paris, 1749. 2 vols in 1. 12mo, contemp calf; worn. With 15 folding plates. Some leaves stained at beginning of Vol ii. S June 12 (280) £200

**Rechberg, Charles de —&**
**Depping, George Bernhard**
— Les Peuples de la Russie.... Paris, 1812-13. 2 vols. Folio, contemp half calf; corners worn, spines lacking. With 96 hand-finished colored plates. Lacking Cosaques du Don in Vol I; here replaced by Agoun Tartare. S Nov 30 (11) £2,400

**Recollections...** See: Beckford, William Thomas

**Recueil...**
— Recueil de diverses pieces, sur la philosophie, la religion naturelle, l'histoire, les mathematiques, &c. Amst., 1720. Ed by Pierre Des Maizeaux. 2 vols. 12mo, contemp mor gilt; joints weak. Fuerstenberg - Schaefer copy. S Dec 7 (372) £320
— Recueil de la diversite des habits qui sont de present en usaige tant es pays d'Europe, Asie.... Paris: Richard Breton, 1567. 8vo, modern mor gilt. With 121 woodcuts of figures in costume. Tp repaired; other repairs; 1st 2 leaves of costumes each with tiny wormhole; minor creasing & soiling. pba Sept 14 (126) $6,500
— Recueil des festes, feux d'artifices et pompes funebres ordonnees pour le Roi. Paris, 1756. Folio, contemp mor gilt, with arms of France; covers scratched, corners bumped, spine ends repaired. With 14 plates, most double-page. Fuerstenberg - Schaefer copy. S Dec 8 (519A) £2,400
— Recueil des loix constitutives des colonies angloises, confederees sous la demoniation d'Etats-Unis. Phila. & Paris, 1778. 12mo, orig wraps; spine & corners worn. Some dampstaining. CE May 22 (13) $550
— Recueil des portraits de quelques deputes celebres, a l'Assemblee nationale de France, en 1789. Paris, [n.d.]. Illus by J. Guerin. 4to, contemp bds. With 12 mezzotint ports on papier velin. Fuerstenberg - Schaefer copy. S Dec 7 (281) £180
— Recueil d'estampes representant les differents evenemens de la guerre qui a procure l'independence aux Etats de l'Amerique. Paris, [1784?]. 4to, contemp paste-paper covered bds; rubbed, rebacked. Engraved throughout, with 16 plates & maps (including title). bba June 6 (32) £350 [Robertshaw]
Anr copy. Wraps. With engraved title, 2 maps & 13 plates. S Nov 30 (144) £500
— Recueil d'estampes representant les differents evenemens de la guerre qui a procure l'independance aux Etats Unis.... Paris, [1784?]. 4to, modern bds. En-

graved throughout, with title, 2 maps & 13 plates. Marginal spotting. Fuerstenberg - Schaefer copy. S Dec 7 (15) £1,100

**Redgrave, Gilbert Richard.** See: Short-Title Catalogue

**Redi, Francesco, 1626?-98**
— Esperienze intorno alla generazione degl'insetti. Florence, 1668. 4to, contemp vellum. With 28 plates, 2 of them double-page & 10 full-page engravings in text. Some browning. S June 12 (277) £1,100

**Redoute, Pierre Joseph, 1759-1840**
— Album de Redoute. L, 1954. Folio, pictorial wraps. With 24 plates. sg Jan 11 (373) $120
— Choix des plus belles fleurs. Paris, 1827-[33]. Bound in 2 vols. Folio, contemp half calf; joints worn. With 144 hand-finished colored plates. The paper of a few plates discolored or with faint spotting. L.p. copy. Vilmorin—de Belder copy. P June 5 (324) $120,000
— Les Liliacees. Paris, 1802-[16]. 8 vols. Folio, near-contemp half mor gilt; edge of lower bd knocked. With 1 plain & 484 hand-finished color plates & with additional suite of the plates ptd in black on ochre paper bound in. Lacking port of Redoute & dedication to Chaptal. P June 5 (322) $325,000

**Redoute, Pierre Joseph, 1759-1840 —&**
**Thory, Claude Antoine**
— Les Roses. Paris: Didot, 1817-21-24. 1st Ed. 3 vols. Folio, mor gilt by Bayntun. With port, frontis & 169 plates, all ptd in color & finished by hand. Some spotting & discoloration. L.p. copy. P June 5 (323) $140,000
3d 8vo Ed. Paris, 1828-30. Issue not indicated. Half mor; extremities worn, cloth soiled. With 184 hand-colored plates & 2 ports. Some soiling & foxing. cb Oct 17 (138) $9,000

**Redpath, James**
— Echoes of Harper's Ferry. Bost., 1860. 1st Ed. 16mo, orig cloth; extremities worn, tear to spine cloth. pba Apr 25 (170) $90

**Reed, Henry M.**
— The A. B. Frost Book. Rutland VT, [1967]. 4to, cloth; worn. O June 25 (218) $90
Anr copy. Cloth, in dj with minor wear. Sgd by Reed. pba July 11 (452) $130

**Reed, Ronald**
— The Nature and Making of Parchment. [Leeds, 1975]. Ltd Ed. 4to, half vellum. sg Sept 14 (116) $110

**Rees, Abraham**
— The Cyclopaedia.... Phila., [c.1806]. ("The New Encyclopedia or, Universal Dictionary of Arts and Sciences.") Vol I, Part 1 to Vol XXVI, part 1 & 2 vols of plates. Together, 53 vols. 4to, orig ptd bds; worn, a few covers missing. Some stains & foxing. Sold w.a.f. O Mar 5 (190) $650
Anr Ed. L, 1819-20. ("The Cyclopaedia; or Universal Dictionary of Arts, Sciences, and Literature.") 45 vols, including 6 vols of plates. 4to, contemp calf gilt; rubbed & scratched, lower bd of 1 vol detached, some staining, crude ink illust on 1 bdg. bba Oct 19 (263) £600 [Lynn]

**Reeve, J. Stanley.** See: Derrydale Press

**Reeve, Lovell Augustus, 1814-65**
— Reeve's Popular Natural History Series. L, 1849-58. 19 9of 24) vols. 8vo, orig cloth; faded & chipped, 1 vol lacks spine. Some staining & spotting. Sold w.a.f. S Oct 27 (663) £300 [Egglishaw]

**Reeve, Sophia**
— The Flowers at Court. L, 1809. 1st Ed. 12mo, orig lea gilt; spine rubbed. With 10 watercolor illusts. Inscr to Mary Worth. S Nov 2 (246) £550 [Schiller]

**Reeves, James**
— Arcadian Ballads. Andoversford: Whittington Press, [1977]. One of 200. bba May 9 (356) £100 [Ginnan]; bba May 9 (651) £220 [Ginnan]

**Reeves, Richard Stone —&**
**Robinson, Patrick**
— Classic Lines. Birm., [1975]. Oblong folio, half lea, in dj. Sgd by both. sg Mar 7 (517) $50
— The Golden Post. NY, [1985]. Oblong folio, lea gilt. Sgd by both. sg Mar 7 (518) $50

**Reff, Theodore**
— The Notebooks of Edgar Degas. Oxford, 1976. 2 vols. 4to, cloth, in dj. bba Oct 19 (13) £65 [Maclashlan]

**Regenfuss, Franz Michael**
— Auserlesne Schnecken, Muscheln und andere Schaalthiere. Copenhagen, 1758. Vol I (all pbd). Folio, 19th-cent half mor gilt; extremities scuffed. With 12 hand-colored plates. Text in German & French. Lacking port; old dampstain to lower blank margins. C May 31 (40) £9,000

**Regenvolscius, Adrianus**
— Systema Historico-Chronologicum, ecclesiarum Slavonicarum.... Utrecht, 1652. 4to, contemp vellum; worn. Some stains & browning. O Mar 26 (222) $100

**Regimen...**
— Regimen sanitatis.... L: Thomas Berthelet, 1541. ("Regimen Sanitatis Salerni. This Boke Teachinge all People to Governe Them in Helthe....") 4to, contemp blind-tooled calf; rebacked. Lacking 5 prelims; frayed; repaired tears & restoration to penultimate leaf; some edge-softening. CE June 15 (249) $700
Anr Ed. Frankfurt: C. Egenolph, [1553]. ("De conservanda bona valetudine, opusculum Scholae Salernitanae....") 8vo, 19th-cent mor gilt. Tp, B2, C4 & T3 washed, leaving stains. C June 26 (122) £1,600
Anr Ed. Frankfurt: C. Egenolph, 1559. ("De conservanda bona valetudine liber scholae salernitanae....") 8vo, 19th-cent half mor; spine faded, rubbed. Lacks tp; A-C dampstained; 1st & last pp repaired. Sold w.a.f. CE Nov 8 (140) $110

**REGIMEN...**

— Regimen Sanitatis Salerni; or, The Schoole of Salernes Regiment of Health.... L, 1649. 4to, 18th-Cent calf; rebacked. Browned; some soiling & staining; some corners torn away. Ck Mar 22 (267) £220
— Regimen Sanitatis Salerni. This Boke Teachinge all People to Governe Them in Helth.... L, 1541. 4th Ed. - Trans by Thomas Paynel. 4to, modern calf. Text in Latin & English. Title marginally damaged & laid down; prelims soil-marked; some pen trials & ink stains; B4v with crayon-mark; S2 soiled; b4 with outer margin part town away; f1 to end dampstained; quires h & i wormed; lacking i4. Ck Mar 22 (266) £420

**Reglamento...**

— Reglamento y Aranceles Reales para el Comercio Libre de Espana a Indias de 12. de Octubre de 1778. Madrid: Pedro Marin, [1779]. Folio, contemp calf gilt. S Nov 30 (184) £900

**Regnard, Jean Francois, 1655-1709**

— Oeuvres. Paris, 1789-90. 6 vols. 8vo, contemp mor gilt with crowned monogram of Prince Eugene de Beauharnais (later Herzog von Leuchtenberg); shelfmarks removed from spines. S Dec 8 (520) £3,000

**Regnery, Dorothy F.**

— The Battle of Santa Clara, January 2, 1847. San Jose, 1978. One of 100. Illus by William H. Meyers & William H. Dougal. Linen in slipcase. With 17in by 11in color sketch. Larson copy. pba Sept 28 (650) $50

**Regnier, Henri Francois Joseph, 1864-1936**

— La Double Maitresse. Paris, 1928. One of 1,075. Illus by Georges Barbier. 4to, half mor gilt, orig wraps bound in. S Nov 21 (363) £225

**Regny, Jane**

— Le Zodiaque. Paris, 1928. One of 50 on japon with plates in 2 states. Half lea by Canape & Corriez. cb Feb 14 (2767) $300

**Reichard, Gladys A.**

— Navajo Shepherd and Weaver. NY: J. J. Augustin, [1936]. Orig burlap over bds. pba Apr 25 (614) $130
— Sandpaintings of the Navajo Shooting Chant. NY, [1937]. Ltd Ed. Folio, burlap over bds. With 35 color plates. Robbins copy. Sgd by Reichard & Franc Newcomb. pba Mar 21 (290) $375

**Reid, James D.**

— The Telegraph in America.... NY, 1879. 4to, orig cloth; front hinge reinforced, prelims & 1 port rehinged. Library markings. Inscr. sg Oct 26 (309) $50

**Reid, William**

— Golfing Reminiscences: The Growth of the Game, 1887-1925. Edin.: J. & J. Gray, [1925]. 1st Ed. Cloth. pba Apr 18 (148) $475

**AMERICAN BOOK PRICES CURRENT**

**Reiderer, Johann Bartholomaeus**

— Nachrichten zur Kirchen- Gelehrten- und Buecher-Geschichte. Altdorf, 1764-68. 4 vols. 8vo, old bds; soiled. Some foxing & browning. Kraus copy. O Mar 26 (231) $275

**Reigart, J. Franklin**

— The Life of Robert Fulton. Phila., 1856. 8vo, orig cloth; worn. With 26 plates. F Mar 28 (395) $90
— The United States Album. Phila., 1844. 4to, calf gilt; worn & broken. Helen M. Chapman copy, with additional actual signatures of many notables of the 1840s, including J. Q. Adams, Daniel Webster, John C. Calhoun & others. P June 5 (6) $1,500

**Reiger, George**

— The Bonefish. Stone Harbor: Meadow Run Press, [1994]. One of 100. Illus by Peter Corbin. O Feb 6 (187) $140

**Reimar, Johann Albert Heinrich**

— Vom Blitze. Hamburg, 1778. 3 parts in 1 vol. 8vo, contemp half vellum. S Mar 14 (300) £400

**Rein, J. J.**

— The Industries of Japan, with an Account of its Agriculture.... NY, 1889. 8vo, pictorial cloth. With 3 maps, 44 illusts & 4 lithos of fabrics & lacquers. sg June 13 (330) $375

**Reinagle, George Philip**

— Particolari della Battaglia di Navarino.... Naples, 1828. Folio, contemp bds; rebacked. With litho map & 12 litho views. Tp lacking; text leaf & map spotted. C Oct 25 (140) £3,000

**Reinhardt, Johann Christian**

— Collection de costumes suisses des XXII Cantons. Basel, 1819 [some plates watermarked to 1823]. 4to, recent mor gilt by J. Kulbsho. With 46 plates in color & gouache. Minor restoration to Plate 46 just touching image. S Nov 30 (112) £7,500

**Reinhardt, Robert —& Others**

— Palast-Architektur von Ober-Italien und Toscana.... Berlin, 1886-1911. 5 vols. Folio, later half sheep; worn, spines perished, 3 covers detached. With 501 photolitho plates, some in color, 32 double-page. Library markings; some foxing & soiling affecting some images; ink stamp to each plate; some perforated stamps. cb Oct 17 (85) $300

**Reinhold, Erasmus**

— Prutenicae tabulae coelestium motuum. Tubingen: U. Morhardus, 1551. 4to, contemp blind-stamped pigskin over wooden bds, by Michael Fadner of Nuremberg, initialled & dated 1553. Lacking 3 folding tables; repair to upper margin of Ss1. Madsen copy. S Mar 14 (301) £1,800

**Reisch, Gregorius, d.1525**

— Margarita philosophica. [Freiburg im Breisgau: Johann Schott, 16 Mar 1504]. ("Aepitoma omnis phylosophiae. alias Margarita phylosophica tractans....") 4to, contemp blind-stamped calf-backed

848

bds; lacking 2 clasps & catches, spine ends torn. With 22 full-page hand-colored woodcuts & 2 folding woodcut diagrams. World map from anr copy & repaired; worming at ends; some staining; tear in text of ss4. Madsen copy. S Mar 14 (302) £3,400

**Reiss, Lionel S.**
— My Models were Jews. NY: Gordon Press, 1938. One of 1,200. With 178 illusts. pba June 20 (281) $130

**Reiss-Befert...**
— Reiss-Befert durch Ober- und Nieder-Teutschland. Augsburg: Andreas Knortzen Seel. for Christoph Riegel, 1686. 12mo, contemp vellum; spine def. With engraved double-page title & 18 (of 120) town views & plans. Engraved title bound upside down; A1 torn away at lower corner with loss; Leiden at P.413 torn & repaired; some staining. Madsen copy. S Mar 14 (307) £2,200

**Reissner, Adam**
— Ierusalem, die alte Haubstat der Iuden. Frankfurt, 1565. 2d Ed. 2 vols in 1. Folio, contemp blind-tooled pigskin over wooden bds, with brass clasps. C May 1 (138) £1,400

**Reitz, S. C. Bosch.** See: Metropolitan Museum of Art

**Relacion...**
— Relacion de todo lo sucedido en estas provincias de la Nueva Espana, desde la formacion de la Armada Real de Barlovento.... [Mexico, 1642]. 4 pp. Folio. b June 28 (4) £600

**Reland, Adrian**
— Palaestina ex monumentis veteribus illustrata. Nuremberg, 1716. 4to, contemp vellum; soiled. With frontis port, & 13 maps & plates (7 double-page or folding). Some tears. S Oct 26 (197) £200 [Mayersdorf]

**Relation...**
— Relation des fetes donnees par la ville de Strasbourg a leurs Majestes Imperiales et Royales, les 22 et 23 janvier 1806.... Strassburg, 1806. Folio, contemp red mor gilt with imperial eagle, crowned & at center a gilt N, crowned; bdg bumped & with small repair to upper cover. With 5 plates. Napoleon's copy, ptd on vellum. Fuerstenberg - Schaefer copy. S Dec 8 (523) £4,000

**Rellstab, Ludwig**
— Berlin und seine naechsten Umgebungen in malerischen Originalansichten. Darmstadt, [c.1850]. 8vo, orig mor gilt; upper joint weak. With engraved title, frontis & 54 plates. Some spotting. Madsen copy. S Mar 14 (304) £1,200

**Remarque, Erich Maria, 1898-1970.** See: Limited Editions Club

**Remington, Frederic, 1861-1909**
— Crooked Trails. NY, 1898. 1st Ed. 8vo, orig cloth; spine & cover sunned. With 49 plates. Robbins copy. Inscr Xmas 1898. pba Mar 21 (291) $300; pba Apr 25 (615) $170
— Done in the Open. NY, 1902. Intro & verses by Owen Wister. Folio, half cloth; worn, soiled. Some foxing. O Mar 5 (192) $375
— Frederic Remington: Paintings and Drawings of the Old West. Alhambra CA: C. F. Braun, 1963. Intro by John G. Braun. Half mor. pba Aug 8 (165) $50
— Frontier Sketches. Chicago, [1898]. 1st Ed. Oblong 4to, orig bds; soiled, sunned & rubbed. With 15 plates. Robbins copy. pba Mar 21 (292) $550
— Men with the Bark On. NY & L, 1900. 1st Ed, 1st Issue. Orig cloth; covers foxed & rubbed. With 32 plates. Robbins copy. pba Mar 21 (293) $100
1st Issue. Orig cloth; insect damage to spine. pba Apr 25 (617) $55
— Pony Tracks. NY, 1895. 1st Ed. 8vo, orig cloth; card pocket removed. NH July 21 (394) $200
Anr copy. Orig cloth; edges & extremities worn. Robbins copy. pba Mar 21 (294) $300
Anr copy. Cloth; extremities rubbed. pba July 25 (341) $250
Anr copy. Cloth. With holograph signature on small piece of paper. pba Aug 8 (163) $325

**Remmelin, Johann**
— Catoptrum microcosmicum, suis aere incisis visionibus splendens.... Augsburg: D. Franck, 1619. Folio, disbound with old bds present. With engraved title with port on verso & 3 plates of anatomical figures, each with numerous superimposed flaps revealing details of the make-up of the body. Lacking some flaps; chipped; some dampstaining. Met May 22 (400) $1,500

**Remondino, P. C.**
— The Mediterranean Shores of America. Phila., 1892. 1st Ed. Orig cloth; extremities worn. Illusts include 2 folding color charts on tissue. pba July 25 (204) $50

**Remsburg, John E. & George J.**
— Charley Reynolds, Soldier, Hunter, Scout and Guide. Kansas City, 1931. One of 175. pba June 25 (198) $140

**Remy.** See: Renault, Gilbert

**Renaudot, Eusebius, the Elder**
— Another Collection of Philosophical Conferences of the French Virtuosi.... L, 1665. Folio, disbound. Tp stamped. sg May 16 (241) $225

**Renault, Gilbert**
— Memoires d'un agent secret de la France Libre. Cannes, 1946. Ltd Ed, this copy for Col. & Mrs. Guy Westmacott. Illus by Empile Compard. 2 vols. 4to, loose as issued in wraps. Inscr. bba May 9 (185) £70 [Clancey]

### Rench, W. Steuart
— Realities of Irish Life. L, 1869. Orig cloth; front hinge cracking, spine head chipped. pba Aug 8 (482) $65

### Reneaulme, Paul
— Specimen historiae plantarum. Paris, 1611. 2 parts in 1 vol. 4to, contemp vellum; worn. With 22 (of 25) plates. Lacking pp 95-104. Sold w.a.f. O Mar 5 (193) $200

**Rennell, James Rodd, Baron.** See: Rodd, James Rennell

**Renner, Frederic G.** See: Carter Collection, Amon G.

**Rennie, George, 1791-1866.** See: Cooke & Rennie

### Rennie, James
— Alphabet of Scientific Angling.... L, 1833. 12mo, later wraps. Name stamped on tp. pba July 11 (246) $50

### Rennie, Sir John, 1794-1874
— An Historical, Practical and theoretical Account of the Breakwater in Plymouth Sound. L, 1848. Folio, late half mor. With frontis port & 25 plates (3 color). Title & dedication creased; 1 plate torn; spotted. S Oct 26 (339) £460 [Elliott]

### Rennolds, Edwin H.
— A History of the Henry County Commands which Served in the Confederate State Army. Jacksonville, 1904. 8vo, cloth; soiled. Some soiling & foxing. K Feb 11 (123) $450

**Reno, Marcus A.** See: Graham, William A.

### Renouard, Antoine Augustin
— Annales de l'Imprimerie des Alde.... Paris, 1803-12. 1st Ed. 3 vols. 8vo, contemp wraps; worn, spines rubbed at extremities. Ck Apr 12 (268) £550
— Annales de l'Imprimiere des Alde.... Paris, 1834. 3d Ed. 8vo, 19th-cent half mor; extremities scuffed. With 2 ports & 10 facsimile plates. sg Apr 11 (265) $225

#### Renouard Library, Antoine Augustin
— [Sale Catalogue] Catalogue d'une precieuse collection de livres, manuscrits, autographes, dessins et gravures... Paris, 1854. 8vo, later half cloth, orig front wrap bound in; worn. Some soiling. O Mar 26 (224) $100

### Renouard, Paul
— La Danse. Vingt dessins.... Paris, 1892. One of 275. Folio, mtd on thin bds individually, in portfolio. cb Feb 14 (2800) $400

### Renouard, Philippe
— Bibliographie des impressions et des oeuvres de Josse Badius Ascensius.... NY, [1967]. 3 vols. 4to, cloth. Reprint of 1908 Ed. bba May 9 (132) £70 [Librairie Farfouille]

### Renouvier, Jules
— Des gravures sur bois dans les livres de Simon Vostre.... Paris, 1859. One of 200. 8vo, mor by Hardy; rubbed. O Mar 26 (225) $100

### Renversement...
— Renversement de la morale chretienne par les desordres du monachisme. Holland, [c.1690]. 2 parts in 1 vol. 4to, mor gilt by Bozerian jeune; minor rubbing. With frontis & 50 grotesque plates of degenerate clerics. pn Dec 7 (37) £920

### Report...
See also: Chadwick, Sir Edwin
— Report of the Committee of the Board of Agriculture concerning the Culture and Use of Potatoes. L, 1795. 4to, contemp tree calf; rebacked, rubbed. With 7 plates. Ck Mar 22 (44) £70

Anr copy. With 7 plates. Lacking half-title; 3 holes in leave margins. Ck Mar 22 (45) £70

### Reports...
— Reports of Explorations and Surveys...for a Railroad from the Mississippi River to the Pacific Ocean.... Wash., 1855-61. Vol I. Orig half calf; spine stained, front joint cracked. Inscr by the Hon. G. W. Morrison. pba July 25 (330) $85

Vol VI only. Orig bds. Lacking 2 maps. F Mar 28 (159) $80

Vol VIII. Orig half calf; worn, spine ends chipped. Foxing & staining to plates. pba July 25 (331) $70

Anr Ed. Wash., 1856. Vol V only. 4to, half calf; worn. With 23 color lithos, 39 (of 40) uncolored plates, 4 color maps & 7 folding sectional drawings (2 in color). Some foxing; lacking 1 plate; all folding charts poorly refolded with tears. Sold w.a.f. wa Feb 1 (117) $55

### Reps, John W.
— Cities on Stone. Fort Worth: Amon Carter Museum, [1976]. In dj. ds July 27 (167) $50

### Repton, Humphrey
— Observations on the Theory and Practice of Landscape Gardening. L, 1805. 2d Ed. 4to, contemp half calf; worn & def, covers detached. With port, 5 steel-engraved plates & 27 aquatint plates (10 hand-colored, 10 with hinged flaps); 2 hand-colored aquatint vignettes with hinged overlays. Frontis detached. cb Oct 17 (95) $2,000
— Sketches and Hints on Landscape Gardening. L, 1794. Oblong folio, contemp russia gilt; laid down, rubbed. With 10 hand-colored plates with overlays & 6 uncolored plates (3 with overlays). Tears to 2 double-page plates, 1 just touching surface; some soiling. C Oct 25 (142) £3,000

### Reresby, Sir John
— The Travels and Memoirs of.... L, 1813. 8vo, contemp calf gilt; rebacked preserving most of orig spine. With 40 plates, some hand-colored. pba Nov 30 (274) $190

**Resen, Peder Hansen, 1625-88**
— Inscriptiones Haffnienses Latinae, Danicae et Germanicae.... Hanau, 1668. 4to, contemp vellum; front endpapers renewed. With 3 folding woodcut plates & 2 folding engraved plates. sg May 16 (136) $850

**Resenius, P. J.** See: Resen, Peder Hansen

**Reste, Bernard de**
— Histoire des peches, des decouvertes et des etablissemens des Hollandois dans les mers du nord.... Paris, 1801. 3 vols. 8vo, contemp tree-calf; worn. With frontis & 27 plates. Spotted; few pages marginally torn with loss. S Oct 12 (66) £400

**Restif de la Bretonne, Nicolas Edme, 1734-1806**
[A set of the so-called Serie des Graphes (Le Pornographe, La Mimographe, Les Gynographes & L'Andrographe), 1770-82, the former Fuerstenberg - Schaefer set sold at S on 8 Dec 1995, lot 524, for £14,000]
— La derniere avanture d'un homme de quarante-cinq ans. Geneva, 1783. 1st Ed. 2 vols. 12mo, contemp calf; spines wormed. Without the Catalogue des Livres qui se trouvent chez Regnault; soiling to margin of last plate affecting surface; spot on F12. Fuerstenberg - Schaefer copy. S Dec 8 (527) £1,200
— L'Ecole des peres. Paris, 1776. 3 vols. 8vo, contemp calf gilt. Fuerstenberg - Schaefer copy. S Dec 8 (525) £3,000
— Monument du costume physique et moral de la fin du dix-septieme siecle.... Neuwied, 1789. Folio, orig bds; scuffed, inner hinges repaired. With 26 plates by (24) Moreau le Jeune & (2) Freudeberg. Some spotting & old dampstaining. C Apr 3 (188) £1,800
— Le Paysan et la paysane pervertis.... The Hague, 1784. 4 vols. 12mo, modern mor gilt by Fikencher, 1922. Made-up copy. Lacking 2 plates; 1 plate misbound; 2 plates repaired. Fuerstenberg - Schaefer copy. S Dec 8 (528) £240

**Restout, Jean, 1692-1768**
— Galerie francoise, ou portraits des hommes et des femmes celebres.... Paris, 1771-72. 2 vols. Folio, contemp half calf. With 40 plates. Fuerstenberg - Schaefer copy. S Dec 8 (530) £320

**Retzius, Magnus Gustaf**
— Das Affenhirn in bildicher Darstellung. Stockholm & Jena, 1906. Folio, contemp half cloth; light rubbing. Browned. Presentation copy, sgd. CE Nov 8 (141) $100

**Reuchlin, Johannes, 1455-1522**
— De arte cabalistica, libri tres. Hagenau: T. Anshelmum, 1517. Folio, contemp calf gilt, the upper cover with owner's stamp on top of central ornament; worn, joints cracked, lacking front flyleaf. Marginal worming & staining; extensive marginalia & Latin poetry. Jacobus Conrad Praetorius's copy. CE Sept 27 (243) $8,500
Anr copy. Modern vellum. Tp soiled, softened & with adhesive stain affecting woodcut; wormtrack to fore-margins of 1st 3 leaves; worming throughout; dampstaining to most lower fore-corners; marginal tear to N6. CE Dec 6 (176) $5,000

**Reume, August Joseph de**
— Genealogie de la noble famille Elsevier. Brussels, 1850. One of 200. 8vo, half calf, orig wraps bound in; worn. O Mar 26 (226) $70
— Varietes bibliographiques et litteraires. I. Imprimeurs Belges. Brussels, 1848. One of 100. 8vo, mor, orig wraps bound in; worn. O Mar 26 (227) $110

**Reusner, Nicolaus**
— Icones sive imagines virorum literis illustrium.... Strassburg, 1584. Bound with: Ianuarius, siue fastorium sacrorum et histoiricorum liber Primus. Strassburg: B. Jobin, 1584. 2 vols in 1. 8vo, mor gilt by Lloyd, Wallis & Lloyd. With 100 port woodcuts in 1st work; large folding tble for 2d work misbound in 1st work. Fairfax Murray copy. P June 5 (326) $2,750

**Reuss, Jeremias David**
— Das Gelehrte England, oder Lexikon der Jeztlebenden Schriftsteller.... Berlin & Stettin, 1791. 8vo, contemp calf; rubbed, extremities worn. Foxing & soiling. O Mar 26 (228) $80

**Revere, Joseph Warren**
— Naval Duty in California. Oakland, 1947. One of 1,000. Orig cloth. With 6 plates & map. Sgd by Joseph Sullivan to Joseph Seeger. Larson copy. pba Sept 28 (653) $65
— A Tour of Duty in California.... NY, 1849. 1st Ed. 12mo, cloth; staining & wear, stabhole to spine. With folding map & 6 plates. Marginal dampstains; short stub tear to map. pba Apr 25 (622) $200
Anr copy. Ed by Joseph N. Balestier. Orig cloth; spine faded, extremities worn. With folded map & 6 plates. Inscr by ed. Larson copy. pba Sept 28 (652) $400
Anr copy. Orig cloth; covers stained, spine faded & rubbed. With 6 plates & folding map. Some foxing. Robbins copy. pba Mar 21 (297) $750

**Revere's copy, Paul**
MULLER, JOHN. - A Treatise of Artillery. L, 1757. 8vo, orig calf; worn. Lacking frontis & portions of tp & some plates. Sgd by Revere 4 times. Phila., 1779 Ed of this work included in the lot. CNY May 17 (295) $23,000

**Revett, Nicholas, 1720-1804.** See: Stuart & Revett

**Revilla Gigedo, Conde de**
— Instruccion reservada que el conde de Revilla Gigedo.... Mexico: Imprenta de la Calle de las Escalerillas, a Cargo del C. Agustin Guiol, 1831. 1st Ed. 8vo, contemp sheep; covers & spine scuffed. With port. Lower corner of contents page missing. Robbins copy. pba Mar 21 (298) $400

**Revue...**
— La Revue indigene. Port-au-Prince, 1927-28. Nos 4-6 in 2 vols. 8vo, ptd wraps; worn & chipped, 2d vol lacking rear wrap. sg Mar 28 (133) $50

**Rey, Agapito.** See: Hammond & Rey

**Reynard the Fox**
— Reynaert den Vos ofte het oordeel der dieren.... Antwerp: J. H. Heyliger, [1670?]. 4to, later ptd bds with vellum spine strip. With partly-colored woodcut on title. Tp & last leaf soiled; some browning; library bookplate. cb June 25 (1771) $425
— Reynard the Fox. L, 1681. ("The Most Pleasing and Delightful History of....") 2 parts in 1 vol. 12mo, half calf. Portion only, beginning in middle of Chapter V of Part 1 & going to Chapter XXXII of Part 2 & these sections possibly incomplete. pba Mar 7 (220) $85

**Reynardson, Charles Thomas Samuel Birch**
— "Down the Road." Or Reminiscences of a Gentleman Coachman. L, 1875. 2d Ed. 8vo, half mor by Larkins; rubbed. Some foxing. O Jan 9 (188) $180

**Reynolds, John, of King's Norton**
— A Discourse upon Prodigious Abstinence Occasioned by the Twelve Months Fasting of Martha Taylor. L, 1669. 4to, modern half calf. Ck Mar 22 (256) £350

**Reynolds, John, 1788-1865**
— The Pioneer History of Illinois. Belleville IL, 1852. 1st Ed. 12mo, orig cloth; def. sg Oct 26 (154) $300
— Sketches of the Country on the Northern Route from Belleville, Illinois to the City of New York.... Belleville, Illinois, 1854. 1st Ed. 12mo, orig cloth. sg Oct 26 (315) $1,100

**Reynolds, John N.**
— Pacific and Indian Oceans; or, the South Sea Surveying and Exploring Expedition. NY, 1841. 8vo, orig cloth. Foxed. sg Mar 7 (317) $325

**Reynolds, Sir Joshua, 1723-92**
— A Discourse, Delivered... the Royal Academy.... L, 1769-90. 1st Eds. 6 discourses. 4to, modern mor by Zaehnsdorf. 4 are presentation copies with inscr. S Oct 27 (1001) £420 [Spelman]

**Reyrac, François Philippe de Laurens de**
— Hymne au soleil. Paris: Imprimerie Royale, 1783. 8vo, contemp red mor gilt with arms of France. Fuerstenberg - Schaefer copy. S Dec 8 (531) £1,950

**Rezanov, Nikolai Petrovich**
— Rezanov Reconnoiters California, 1806.... San Francisco: Book Club of Calif., 1972. One of 450. pba Feb 13 (156) $60
— The Rezanov Voyage to Nueva California.... San Francisco, 1926. One of 260. Half cloth, in rubbed dj. pba Feb 13 (155) $170

Anr copy. Trans by Thomas C. Russell. Half bds. Larson copy. pba Sept 28 (207) $140

**Rhazes, 850-923**
— Ob usum experimentiamque multiplicem.... Basel: Henrichi Petri, [1544]. 1st Ed of this Latin version. - Ed by Alban Thorer; trans by Vesalius & others. Folio, modern half vellum. Some marginalia on title, underlinings on leaves; some marginal wear, browning & foxing. CE Nov 8 (142) $3,800

**Rhead, George Woolliscroft**
— History of the Fan. L, 1910. One of 450. Folio, orig cloth; worn, bumped, label on lower spine, hinges reinforced. With 26 color & 100 uncolored plates. cb Oct 17 (116) $350

Anr copy. Orig cloth; upper hinge split. S June 12 (332) £150

**Rheede tot Draakestein, Henrik Adrian van**
— Hortus Indicus Malabaricus, continens regni malabarici apud Indos celeberrimi omnis generis plantas rariores.... L, 1774. Ed by Sir John Hill. Part 1 only. 4to, cloth. With 57 plates, some folding. Met Sept 28 (376) $2,300

**Rhine...**
— The Rhine, its Scenery and Monuments.... L, 1862. Folio, half mor; worn & stained. With 50 colored plates. pnE Mar 20 (215) £2,400

**Rhoads, Asa**
— An American Spelling-Book.... NY: for Daniel S. Dean & Joseph Talcott, 1798. Part 1 (of 2). 12mo, contemp calf; minor stains, pp. 89-92 bound upside down. Piece torn from blank margin of last leaf. Evans 24443. O Sept 12 (151) $425

**Rhode Island**
— "At the General Assembly of the Governor and Company of the English Colony of Rhode Island..." [1st official & pbd declaration of independence by a colony]. Providence: J. Carter, [1803]. 8vo, sewn. sg Oct 26 (316) $300

**Rhode Island Historical Society**
— The John Brown House Loan Exhibition of Rhode Island Furniture.... Providence, 1965. rce Nov 18 (748B) $90

**Rhodes, Eugene Manlove**
— Bransford in Arcadia.... NY, 1914. Orig cloth; spine ends & corners rubbed. Foxing to prelim list of books. pba Apr 25 (625) $50
— The Little World Waddies. Chico, [1946]. One of 1,000. Intro by J. Frank Dobie; illus by Harold Bugbee. Cloth, in torn & chipped dj. pba Apr 25 (627) $140
— Once in the Saddle and Paso Por Aqui. Bost. & NY, 1927. Orig cloth, in dj with spine stained, front panel rubbed. pba Apr 25 (628) $60
— Penalosa. Santa Fe: Writers' Editions, [1934]. One of 500. Orig wraps; some creasing & wear. Inscr. pba Apr 25 (629) $100

## Rhune, Michel
— L'Ile enchantee. Paris, [1908]. Illus by Edmund Dulac. 4to, half mor gilt, orig wraps bound in. sg Sept 14 (112) $200

## Rhyme...
— The Rhyme and Reason of Country Life. NY, 1855. 8vo, mor gilt. Inscr to Laurentine by 4 people, including William H. Brewer. pba June 20 (63) $200

## Ribadeneyra y Barrientos, Antonio Joaquin de
— Manual compendio de el Regio Patronato Indiano.... Madrid, 1755. 1st Ed. 4to, later calf; some wear & peeling, 2 wormholes in front cover extending into text block. Some dampstains; soiling & foxing; tp holed & repaired; marginal tears & worming; annotated in ink. cb Oct 17 (204) $300

Anr copy. Contemp calf. With port. Minor discoloration. S Mar 28 (338) £400

Anr copy. Contemp calf gilt, with Spanish royal arms; lower cover & spine wormed. Tp & A1 browned. S June 27 (211) £900

## Ribera, Franciscus
— In Sanctum Iesu Christi Evangelium secundum Johannem Commentarius. Lyons: Jean Cardon & Pierre Cavellat, 1623. 8vo, contemp red mor extra profusely decorated. Dedication copy, given to the library of the Jesuit General. Fuerstenberg copy. C May 1 (139) £1,800

## Ribot, Theodule Armand
— Psychologie de l'attention. Paris, 1889. 12mo, orig wraps. Inscr to Herbert Spencer & with Spencer's stamp on front cover & title. sg May 16 (487) $100

## Ricard, Samuel
— Traite general du commerce. Amst., 1781. 2 vols. 4to, contemp sheep; needs rebacked. sg Mar 21 (113) $225

## Ricardo, David, 1772-1823
— On the Principles of Political Economy and Taxation. L, 1817. 1st Ed. 8vo, later 19th-cent half calf; spine rubbed. Some foxing & pencil markings. bbc June 24 (328) $6,200

Anr copy. Contemp cloth with later label. Lacking final ad leaf; some foxing. sg Oct 19 (216) $11,000

2d Ed. L, 1819. 8vo, contemp calf. Some discoloration to tp. S June 12 (112) £800

3d Ed. L, 1821. 8vo, 19th-cent calf; spine broken & def. Minor foxing. C Nov 29 (134) £600

## Riccardi, Pietro
— Biblioteca Matematica Italiana. Milan, [1952]. 2 vols. Folio, orig cloth. sg Apr 11 (296) $200

## Ricci, Elisa
— Antiche trine italiane. Bergamo, 1908. 2 vols. Folio, bds. wad Oct 18 (35) C$580

## Ricci, Marco
— Viro clarissimo Josepho Smith... primas has decem et octo Tabulas.... Venice, [c.1740]. Bound with: Fossati, Davide. Francisco Comiti Algarotto... Hasce XXIV Tabulas... quae extant in aedibus Joseph Smith, e Antonii Mariae Zanetti.... Venice, 1743. Oblong folio, contemp half calf; repaired. With 2 frontises & 36 plates. C Apr 3 (189) £28,000

## Rice, Anne
— Beauty's Punishment. NY, [1984]. In dj with crease to front flap. pba May 23 (357) $120
— Beauty's Release. NY, [1985]. In dj. pba May 23 (358) $100
— The Claiming of Sleeping Beauty. NY, [1989]. In dj. Sgd by Rice as Rice & as Roquelaure. pba May 23 (355) $250
— Cry to Heaven. NY, 1982. In dj. pba Dec 7 (162) $65

Anr copy. In dj. Inscr. pba May 23 (359) $85
— The Feast of All Saints. NY, [1979]. In dj. pba May 23 (362) $70

Uncorrected proof copy. Orig wraps; spine soiled. pba May 23 (361) $50
— Interview with the Vampire. NY, 1976. In dj with spine ends rubbed. CE Feb 21 (203) $160

Anr copy. In dj. CE May 22 (404) $380; O Dec 5 (241) $170

Anr copy. In chipped & rubbed dj. pba May 23 (365) $275

Anr copy. In dj with crease. Inscr. sg June 20 (323) $400

Special Preview Ed. Wraps; soiled, corners roughened. pba Aug 22 (405) $225

Uncorrected proof. Wraps; soiled, staple to front cover. pba May 23 (363) $700
— The Queen of the Damned. NY, 1988. One of 124. Half lea. O Dec 5 (242) $80
— The Vampire Lestat. NY, 1985. In dj. O Dec 5 (244) $50; pba Dec 7 (164) $90

Anr copy. In dj. Sgd on tp. pba May 23 (370) $140

Uncorrected proof. Ptd wraps. pba May 23 (369) $200

## Rice, Grantland
See also: Travers & Rice
— The Bobby Jones Story, from the writings of O. B. Keeler. Atlanta, [1953]. 1st Ed. In dj; d/j spine darkened & rubbed. pba Apr 18 (149) $110
— The Duffer's Handbook of Golf. NY: Macmillan, 1926. 1st Trade Ed. - Illus by Clare Briggs. Cloth; spine ends rubbed, lower front corner rubbed. pba Nov 9 (69) $100

## Rice Library, John A.
— [Sale Catalogue] Catalogue... to be Sold...on March 21st 1870.... NY, 1870. 8vo, half mor; rubbed. O Mar 26 (229) $60

## Rice, Maj. Gen. William
— "Indian Game" (from Quail to Tiger). L, 1884. 8vo, cloth; worn. Minor foxing. O June 25 (219) $225

## Rich, Claudius James
— Narrative of a Residence in Koordistan. L, 1836. 2 vols. 8vo, contemp half calf; def. With folding dia-

gram, 2 folding maps & 10 plates. Some discoloration. Freya Stark's copy. b May 30 (293) £270

**Rich, Obadiah**
— Bibliotheca Americana Nova; or, A Catalogue of Books...relating to America. L, 1835-46. One of 250. Vol I only. Modern cloth. Some foxing & library stamps. O Mar 26 (230) $60

**Richards, Addison**
— American Scenery. NY, [1854]. 4to, bind-stamped mor with inlaid mor gilt pictorial center cartouche. With 32 plates after Bartlett. sg Feb 8 (29) $400

**Richards, J. M.**
— High Street. L, 1938. Illus by Eric Ravilious. Orig bds; spine ends lacking. With 24 colored lithos. S June 12 (351) £250

**Richards, Walter**
— Her Majesty's Army.... NY: John Beacham, [c. 1890]. 4 vols. 4to, orig cloth; soiled. With 2 chromolitho titles & 29 chromolitho plates. b Jan 31 (276) £110

**Richardson, Albert Edward —&**
**Eberlein, Harold Donaldson**
— The Smaller English House of the Later Renaissance, 1660-1830. NY, [1925]. 4to, cloth; spine ends repaired, bumped. Inscr by Eberlein. sg June 13 (30) $120

**Richardson, Charles, Sportsman**
— Cassell's New Book of the Horse. L, 1911. 4 vols. 4to, cloth. With 29 color plates, including 3 anatomical frontises with multiple superimposed flaps. sg Mar 7 (519) $110

**Richardson, Charles, Sportsman —& Others**
— Racing at Home and Abroad. L, 1923-31. One of 475. Vol I only. Mor gilt; spine rubbed. bba May 30 (460) £70 [Allen]

**Richardson, Dorothy M., 1870-1957**
— John Austen and the Inseparables. L, 1930. One of 125. With woodcut, sgd by Austen, laid in. sg Feb 15 (15) $100

**Richardson, John, F.S.A.**
— A Grammar of the Arabick Language. L, 1776. 4to, orig bds; backstrip missing. b May 30 (294) £220

**Richardson, John, 1787-1865**
— Arctic Searching Expedition: A Journal of a Boat Voyage...in Search of...Sir John Franklin. NY, 1852. 8vo, orig cloth. Foxed. pba July 25 (446) $80

**Richardson, John, 1787-1865 —&**
**Gray, John Edward, 1800-75**
— The Zoology of the H. M. S. Erebus and Terror under the Command of Captain Sir James Clark Ross, during the Years 1839-1843. L, 1844-75. 7 parts in 3 vols. 4to, orig wraps. With color chart frontis, & 197 (of 198) plates (49 hand-colored, 10 supplied in photocopy). Some spotting. S Oct 27 (772) £950 [Maggs]

**Richardson, John Munsell —&**
**Mason, Finch**
— Gentleman Riders Past and Present. L: Vinton, 1909. 4to, half vellum. Some foxing & soiling. O Jan 9 (189) $100

**Richardson, Lee**
— Lee Richardson's B.C.: Tales of Fishing.... Forest Grove OR: Champoeg Press, [1978]. With 16 plates, 8 colored & in rear cover envelope. ALs to Vernon Hidy laid in. O Feb 6 (189) $140

Anr copy. Unopened. O June 25 (220) $90; O June 25 (221) $80

— You Should Have Been Here Yesterday. Beaverton OR: Touchstone Press, 1974. One of 1,200. 4to, half syn. ANs to Vernon Hidy laid in. O Feb 6 (190) $190

**Richardson, Mary E.**
— The Life of a Great Sportsman (John Maunsell Richardson). L, 1919. 4to, pictorial cloth; worn. Some foxing & dampstaining. O Jan 9 (190) $70

**Richardson, Samuel, 1689-1761**
— Clarisse Harlowe. Traduction nouvelle.... Geneva, 1785-86. 10 vols. 8vo, contemp half sheep. With port & 21 plates, proofs before letters. Fuerstenberg - Schaefer copy. S Dec 8 (533) £800

— Works. Oxford: Shakespeare Head Press, 1929-31. ("Novels.") 18 vols. Half cloth, unopened; soiled & bumped. wa Nov 16 (38) $300

**Richie, Donald —&**
**Weatherby, Meredith**
— The Masters' Book of Ikebana. Tokyo, [1966]. Folio, silk with wooden cover label & wrap-around title band. pba Aug 8 (481) $65

**Richman, Irving Berdine**
— California under Spain and New Mexico, 1535-1847. Bost., 1911. 1st Ed. Orig cloth. With folded chart, folded map, & 20 other maps, charts & plans. Larson copy. pba Sept 28 (209) $55

— San Francisco Bay and California in 1776: Three Maps with Outline Sketches.... Providence, 1911. One of 125. Drawn by Father Pedro Font. 16in by 11-3/4in, bds in org box; box slightly damaged. Larson copy. pba Sept 28 (102) $325

**Richmond, Leonard**
— The Technique of the Poster. L, 1933. 4to, cloth; worn. Half-title torn & repaired with tape. sg Sept 7 (285) $225

**Richter, Hans**
— Filmgegner von Heute -- Filmfreunde von Morgen. Berlin, 1929. 4to, cloth; dampstained & bowed, hinges starting. Foxed. sg Feb 29 (268) $175

**Rickett, Harold William**
— Wild Flowers of the United States. NY, 1966-73. Vols I-VI in 14 vols. wa Dec 14 (444) $600
Vol IV in 2 vols. NY, 1966-71. cb Oct 17 (139) $110

**Ricketts, Charles de Sousy.** See: Nonesuch Press

**Ricketts, Edward F.** See: Steinbeck & Ricketts

**Rickey, Don, Jr.**
— $10 Horse, $40 Saddle: Cowboy Clothing, Arms, Tools and Horse Gear of the 1880s. Fort Collins CO: Old Army Press, [1976]. Illus by Dale Crawford. In dj. With orig pencil sketch by Crawford, sgd to John Popovich. pba June 25 (201) $190
— History of Custer Battlefield. Billings MT, [1967]. Wraps; title inked on spine. pba June 25 (202) $55

**Rickman, John.** See: Cook, Capt. James

**Rickmers, Willy Rickmer**
— The Duab of Turkestan. L, 1913. 4to, orig cloth. b Jan 31 (468) £160

**Ricord, Philippe, 1800-89**
— Traite complet des maladies veneriennes. Paris, 1851. 4to, modern half mor. With port & 66 colored plates. Text spotted & marginally stained; port & tp laminated with Japanese tissue; some corners repaired. bba July 18 (89) £150 [Westwood]

**Riding, Laura**
See also: Graves & Riding
— Love as Love, Death as Death. L, 1928. One of 175. Hobson copy. S June 28 (191) £140
— Though Gently. Majorca: Seizin Press, 1930. One of 200. Hobson copy. S June 28 (195) £120

**Ridinger, Johann Elias, 1698-1767**
— [Vorstellung der Pferde nach ihren Hauptfarben....]. [Augsburg, c.1770]. 2 parts in 1 vol. Folio, contemp half calf. With colored engraved title & 47 (of 50) colored plates. Some foxing, staining & hand-soling. O Jan 9 (193) $7,200

**Riefenstahl, Leni**
— Kampf in Schnee und Eis. Leipzig, [1933]. Pictorial cloth. sg Feb 29 (269) $150
— Schoenheit im Olympischen Kampf. Berlin, 1936. 4to, cloth, in chipped dj. sg Feb 29 (270) $500

**Riemer, Jacob de, 1678?-1762**
— Beschryving van 's Graven-Hage. Delft, 1730-39. 2 vols in 3. Folio, old half calf; needs rebacked. Lacking 1 plate; some dampstaining with traces of mold on some plates; tear in Plate 15. sg May 9 (377) $1,600

**Rieter, Jacob**
— Danske Nationale Klaededragter. Copenhagen: Rothes Boghandling, [1805-6]. 12 parts in 1 vol. Folio, recent mor by Anker Kyster, orig wraps preserved. With 72 hand-colored plates. Some spotting. S Mar 28 (235) £2,900

**Riggs, Lynn.** See: Limited Editions Club

**Righi, Francois**
— Fleche-en-Ciel. [N.p., 1975]. One of 9 on velin d'Arches. Loose as issued in wraps. sg Sept 7 (297) $100

**Rigoley de Juvigny, Jean Antoine**
— De la decadence des lettres et des moeurs depuis les Grecs et les Romains jusqu'a nos jours. Paris, 1787. 4to, 18th-cent mor gilt; spine wormed. With inserted port. Fuerstenberg - Schaefer copy. S Dec 8 (535) £260

**Riis, Jacob August, 1849-1914**
— The Children of the Poor. NY, 1892. 1st Ed. 8vo, cloth; spine ends chipped. pba Aug 8 (580) $100

**Rikhoff, Jim**
— Hunting the World's Mountains: An Anthology. Clinton: Amwell Press, [1984]. One of 1,000. 2 vols. lea; worn. O Oct 10 (175) $100
Anr copy. Lea; worn. O Oct 10 (228) $100

**Riland, John**
— Memoirs of a West-India Planter. Hamilton, 1827. 1st Ed. 12mo, half calf; rubbed. S Oct 26 (522) £140 [Druett]

**Riley, James, 1777-1840**
— Loss of the American Brig Commerce.... Chillicothe, 1820. ("An Authentic Narrative of the Loss of the American Brig Commerce....") 12mo, contemp calf. Leaf Dd2 with loss to c.20 words along margin; 1 other leaf with paper loss, affecting several words. sg Oct 26 (318) $80

**Riley, James Whitcomb, 1849-1916**
— All the Year Round. Indianapolis: Bobbs Merrill, [1912]. Illus by Gustave Baumann. pba June 20 (50) $150
Anr copy. Orig cloth; soiling & orners bumped. With 12 woodcuts ptd in colors. Tear to margin of 1 leaf. pba Aug 22 (690) $160
Anr copy. Orig cloth; some soiling. With 12 woodcuts ptd in colors. sg Sept 21 (281) $225
— Armazindy. Indianapolis, 1894. 1st Ed. 12mo, cloth, in chipped dj; spine ends rubbed. pba Dec 14 (127) $300
Anr copy. Cloth. Inscr. pba May 23 (374) $85
— A Child-World. Indianapolis, 1897. 1st Ed, 2d Issue. 12mo, orig cloth; some wear & soiling. Inscr. F June 20 (480) $80
— The Flying Islands of the Night. Indianapolis, [1913]. Illus by Franklin Booth. In chipped dj. pba Dec 14 (128) $190
— "The Old Swimmin'-Hole" and 'Leven More Poems. Indianapolis, 1883. 1st Ed. 12mo, orig wraps; soiled & stained. ALs tipped in. rs Nov 11 (114) $375
Anr copy. Orig wraps; repair to corner of front cover. Sgd & with 8-line holograph poem sgd as Johnson. sg Sept 21 (282) $600

### Rilke, Rainer Maria, 1875-1926
See also: Limited Editions Club
— Duineser Elegien. L: Hogarth Press, 1931. One of 8 on vellum with initials heightened in gold. Trans by V. & E. Sackville-West. Orig mor gilt. C Nov 29 (122) £8,500
— The Lay of the Love and Death of Cornet Christoph Rilke. San Francisco: Arion Press, 1983. One of 300. 4to, cloth. sg Sept 14 (36) $90; sg Feb 15 (9) $100

### Rimbaud, Arthur, 1854-91
See also: Limited Editions Club
— Deux Poemes. Maastricht: Stols for Baron van der Borch van Verwolde, 1932. One of 30. Illus by John Buckland Wright. 4to, orig wraps. Inscr. S Nov 2 (79) £650 [Collinge & Clark]
— Une Saison en enfer. Brussels, 1873. 1st Ed. 12mo, orig wraps, with tissue outer wrap; small tear at bottom of front cover & small fox mark at top. Engelhard copy. CNY Oct 27 (118) $6,000

Anr Ed. [Paris, 1951]. One of 100. Illus by Lucien Coutaud. 8vo, unsewn in orig wraps. sg Feb 15 (268) $300

### Rimmel, Eugene
— The Book of Perfumes. L, 1867. 5th Ed. 4to, orig cloth; rubbed. O July 9 (181) $80

### Rinder, Frank
— D. Y. Cameron: An Illustrated Catalogue.... Glasgow, 1932. One of 600. 4to, cloth; joints cracked. sg Sept 7 (66) $150

### Rinehart, Frank
— The Face of Courage. Ft. Collins, CO: Old Army Press, [1972]. One of 100. Intro by Royal Sutton. 4to, pictorial lea gilt; rubbed. With over 100 sepiatoned, full page repro of his Native-American ports & views of the Trans-Mississippi Exposition in Omaha. Sgd. With 3 copy print ports by Rinehart laid in. pba June 25 (203) $170
— Rinehart's Indians. Omaha, 1899. 8vo, orig cloth. With 46 halftone & 4 color reproductions of photos. bbc Apr 22 (249) $475

### Ring...
— The Ring Record Book and Boxing Encyclopaedia. NY, 1954-87. 16 vols. Cloth, last 3 in djs. pba Apr 4 (89) $250

### Ringgold, Cadwalader, 1802-67
— A Series of Charts, with Sailing Directions, Embracing Surveys of the... Bay of San Francisco.... Wash., 1851. 1st Ed. - Illus by W. H. Dougal. 4to, orig cloth; covers spotted, corners bumped, spine repaired. With 12 illusts on 8 plates, & 6 folding charts. 1 chart with stub tear. Robbins copy. Inscr to Hon. E. B. Hall. pba Mar 21 (299) $1,500

Anr Ed. Wash., 1852. 8vo, orig cloth; covers spotted. With 12 views on 8 plates & 6 folding maps. Foxed; maps with stub tears & chipping; 1 map creased. pba July 25 (205) $800

4th Ed. - Engraved by William H. Dougal. 8vo, orig cloth. With 8 plates of 12 illus, & 6 folded charts. Larson copy. pba Sept 28 (655) $900

### Rinhart, Floyd & Marion
— American Daguerreian Art. NY, 1967. 4to, cloth; worn. sg Feb 29 (110) $60

### Rink, Evald
— Technical Americana: A Checklist of Technical Publications Printed before 1831. Millwood, [1981]. 4to, cloth; some wear. O May 7 (261) $70

### Rinman, Sven
— Anleitung zur Kentniss...Eisen und Stahlveredlung und deren Verbesserung. Vienna, 1790. 8vo, contemp bds; worn. Dampstain in upper outer corner throughout. sg May 16 (243) $110
— Foersoek till Jaernets Historia.... Stockholm, 1782. 2 vols. 4to, contemp calf; rubbed. With engraved titles & 2 folding plates. Owner's stamp on titles; minor staining. S Mar 14 (308) £280

### Riolan, Jean, 1577-1657
— A Sure Guide, or the Best and Nearest Way to Physick and Chyrurgery.... L, 1671. 3d Ed. Folio, contemp sheep; recased, front joint cracked, endpapers renewed. With 24 plates. Dampstained in upper margin. sg May 16 (488) $700

### Riopelle, Jean Paul
— Ficelles et autres jeux. Paris, 1972. 4to, pictorial wraps. sg Sept 7 (106) $130

### Rios, Francois de los
— Bibliographie instructive, ou notice de quelques livres rares. Avignon & Lyons, 1777. 8vo, contemp calf; rubbed. Lacking port. O Mar 26 (162) $175

### Riou, Stephen
— The Grecian Orders of Architecture. L, 1768. Folio, contemp half calf; rubbed. With engraved titles & 28 plates. Blackmer copy. S Nov 30 (130) £2,600

### Ripley, Roswell S.
— The War with Mexico. L, 1850. 1st English Ed. 2 vols. 8vo, later half mor; worn & scuffed, some scrapes. Foxed. wa Feb 29 (503) $260

### Ripley, S. Dillon
— Rails of the World. Toronto, [1977]. Folio, cloth, in dj. With 41 color plates. sg May 16 (339) $70

### Rire...
— Le Rire: journal humoristique. Paris, 5 Sept 1908. New Series, No 292. 4to, orig pictorial wraps; fragile & loose. Front cover has chromolitho image of Wilbur Wright Sold w.a.f. sg May 16 (98) $150

### Ristow, Walter W.
— American Maps and Mapmakers.... Detroit, 1985. Oblong 4to, cloth, in dj. sg May 9 (34) $175

### Ritchie, Anne Thackeray. See: Thackeray, Anne Isabella

**Ritchie, Robert Welles**
— The Hell-Roarin' Forty-niners. NY, [1928]. 1st Ed. Orig cloth in dj. With 13 illus on 8 plates. Larson copy. pba Sept 28 (656) $85

**Ritchie, Ward**
— Merle Armitage: His Loves and his Many Lives. Laguna Verde, [1982]. One of 60. Wraps. Inscr to Mel Smith. pba May 23 (375) $90

**Ritson, Joseph, 1752-1803**
— An Essay on Abstinence from Animal Food, as a Moral Duty. L, 1802. 1st Ed. 8vo, contemp half calf; lower joints split, extrems rubbed. Title margin adhering to blank; B1r soiled; browned. Ck Mar 22 (257) £110
— Robin Hood: a Collection of All the Ancient Poems, Songs, and Ballads.... L, 1887. 2 vols. 8vo, half vellum. With the Bewick engravings on chine, mtd. NH July 21 (359) $155

**Rittenhouse, Jack D.**
— Carriage Hundred: A Bibliography on Horse-Drawn Transportation. Houston: Stagecoach Press, 1961. One of 450. In dj. ds July 27 (168) $100

**Ritter, Abraham**
— Philadelphia and Her Merchants.... Phila., 1860. 8vo, orig cloth; spine head repaired. With 20 plates. F June 20 (372) $80

**Ritter, Wilhelm Leonard, 1799-1862.** See: Hardouin & Ritter

**Rituals**
— Liber Sacerdotalis nuperrime ex libris Sanctae Romanae ecclesiae.... Venice: Vittor de Ravanni, 1537. Ed by Alberto da Castello. 4to, old vellum; soiled & creased, new liners. Some creasing & minor paper loss to outer leaves; small hole in 1st 2 gatherings & cover; lacking final blank. S Dec 1 (296) £520

**Ritz, Charles**
— A Fly Fisher's Life. NY, [1960]. One of 250. Mor. pba Jan 4 (231) $170

**Rivaz, C. A. G.**
— Indian Small-Game Shooting for Novices. L, 1912. In chipped dj. sg Mar 7 (522) $60

**Rive, John Joseph**
— La Chasse aux bibliographes et antiquaires mal'avises.... Londres [Aix], 1789. 2 vols. 8vo, contemp wraps; shaken, spine split. O Mar 26 (232) $180

**Rives, Reginald W.** See: Derrydale Press

**Riviere, Lazare, 1589-1665**
— Methodus Curandarum Febrium. Gouda, 1649. 8vo, modern half lea; rebacked retaining orig backstrip. sg May 16 (489) $130
— The Practice of Physick.... L, 1678. Folio, later half calf; spine ends worn. Tp browned & repaired in margin; other marginal repairs, browning & staining. CE Nov 8 (143) $300

**Rizzi, Aldo**
— The Etchings of the Tiepolos. NY, [1979?]. 4to, cloth. sg Jan 11 (420) $110

**Robaut, Alfred**
— L'Oeuvre complet de Eugene Delacroix. Paris, 1885. 4to, later half cloth, orig wraps bound in; spine def. sg Jan 11 (138) $250

**Robbe-Grillet, Alain**
— Jealousy. Kentfield, CA: Allen Press, 1971. One of 140. Illus by Michele Forgeois. 4to, orig pictorial bds. CE Feb 21 (4) $140

**Robert de Vaugondy, Gilles & Didier**
— Atlas o compendio geographico del Glovo terestre. Madric, 1756. Oblong 8vo, contemp mor gilt, armorial bdg. With 14 maps, hand-colored in outline. sg Dec 7 (43) $1,900
— Atlas universel. Paris, 1757-[58]. Folio, contemp calf; worn, jonits cracked, upper cover partly detached. With engraved title & 108 maps, hand-colored in outline. Marginal spotting; a few maps browned. C Oct 25 (143) £4,800
— Nouvel atlas portatif. Paris, 1795. 4to, contemp bds; def. With title & 54 maps. Some small stains; 1 map torn; some creasing & marginal soiling. S Oct 26 (446) £600 [Yingst]

**Roberts, David, 1796-1864**
— Picturesque Sketches in Spain. L, 1837. Folio, contemp calf gilt. With 26 mtd hand-colored plates before letters, mtd on stiff paper. Lacking litho title & plate list; 1st plate creased at lower margin; foxed. Schaefer copy. P Nov 1 (181) $16,000

### Egypt and Nubia
— Egypt and Nubia, from Drawings Made on the Spot.... L, 1846-49-49. 3 vols in orig 20 parts in 10. Folio, orig half cloth wraps; disbound, most backstrips def, some wraps creased. With 3 tinted litho titles & 121 plates (61 full-page, 60 half-page). Some fraying & marginal soiling. C May 31 (106) £16,000
Anr copy. 3 vols. Folio, 19th-cent half mor; extremities rubbed. With 3 pictorial titles, 61 tinted litho plates, 60 tinted litho text illusts & map. Some foxing. Schaefer copy. P Nov 1 (183) $22,000
— Egypt and Nubia, from Drawings made on the Spot.... L, 1846-49. 3 vols in 2. Folio, 19th-Cent half mor; rubbed. With 3 titles, full-page map, & 121 plates. Some spotting & light water-staining. S Oct 26 (204) £13,000 [Map House]
— Roberts' Sketches in Egypt and Nubia. Part XII. L, [1840s]. Folio, lea-backed pictorial cloth; def. With 14 hand-colored lithos only on 4to sheets, each mtd to folio sheets. Lacking the text leaves; some foxing. Sold w.a.f. sg Dec 7 (295) $2,200

### Sets of Holy Land and Egypt
— The Holy Land, Syria, Idumea, Arabia, Egypt and Nubia. With: Egypt and Nubia. L, 1842-49. 6 vols.

Folio, mor gilt. With 247 plates, including titles, 2 maps & port. C Oct 25 (144) £19,000

Anr copy. Contemp half mor gilt; scuffed. With 247 plates, including titles, 2 maps & port. Lacking subscribers list. P June 5 (327) $30,000

Anr copy. Half mor gilt by Hayday. With 6 litho titles, 241 plates, port (uncolored) on india paper & 2 maps, the titles & plates hand-colored & mtd on card. Guarded throughout. A few plates just slightly cockled. Colored copy. S Nov 30 (131) £80,000

Anr Ed. L, 1855-56. 6 vols in 3. 4to, contemp half mor; rubbed. With 248 tinted litho plates & 2 maps. b Sept 20 (371) £1,900

Anr copy. Contemp half mor; edges rubbed, joints of Vol I weak. With 250 plates. Mostly marginal foxing. K June 23 (441) $3,500

Anr copy. 6 vols in 5. 4to, cloth; worn, vol I-II spine repaired. With 6 titles, 2 maps, & 242 plates. Some plates working loose; no port. S Oct 26 (203) £1,850 [Frew]

Anr copy. 6 vols in 3. 4to, contemp half mor gilt. With 6 tinted titles & 240 plates, port & 3 maps. S June 13 (595) £2,800

### The Holy Land

— The Holy Land, Syria, Idumea, Arabia, Egypt and Nubia. L, 1842-49. 20 orig parts in 10. Folio, orig cloth-backed wraps; disbound, most backstrips def, some covers torn. With port on india paper mtd, 1 litho map, 3 tinted litho titles & 120 plates. Some spotting; margins of c.6 leaves torn; some fraying. C May 31 (105) $8,000

Anr Ed. L, 1842-43-49. 3 vols in 2. Folio, 19th-cent half mor. With 124 lithos, including port & 3 titles. Foxed; stain at lower margin of Port of Tyre leaf. P Nov 1 (182) $10,000

Anr Ed. L, 1842-49. 3 vols. Folio, contemp mor gilt. With uncolored port, 6 litho titles with hand-colored vignette views & 121 plates, hand-colored & mtd on card & 2 maps. Some spotting; some plates cockled; 1 prelim leaf from Vol I of Holy Land bound in Vol II; 2 plate captions shaved. Colored copy. S June 27 (157) £72,000

**Roberts, E. L.**
— Test Cricket Cavalcade 1877-1946. L, 1947. Sgd by 60 national team members, 1948-49. pn Oct 12 (324) £70

**Roberts, Elizabeth Maddox**
— The Time of Man. NY, 1926. In chipped dj. sg June 20 (324) $140

**Roberts, Emma**
— Hindostan. L, 1845-47. 2 vols. 4to, orig cloth; rebacked with sheep, endpapers renewed. With engraved titles & 99 plates. sg Dec 7 (296) $400

**Roberts, Henry**
— The Green Book of Golf.... San Francisco: Ellis & Roberts, 1925-26. 3d Ed. Cloth; extrems chipped & torn. Dampstained. pba Apr 18 (150) $200

**Roberts, Kenneth, 1885-1957**
— Trending Into Maine. Bost., 1938. One of 1,075. Illus by N. C. Wyeth. sg Sept 14 (346) $250

**Roberts, Mary**
— The Royal Exile; or, Poetical Epistles of Mary, Queen of Scots.... Sheffield, 1822. 2 vols. 8vo, orig bds; rubbed. With frontis. b Dec 5 (480) £70

**Roberts, Robert**
— The House Servant's Directory.... Bost. & NY, 1827. 1st Ed. 12mo, orig half cloth; spine cracked, front cover loose, newspaper cutting mtd on rear endpaper. Some foxing. Inscr by William E. Payne to Mrs. S. F. Lyman. sg Mar 28 (256) $3,200

**Roberts, Samuel, 1763-1848**
— Tales of the Poor, or Infant Sufferings.... Sheffield, 1813. 12mo, orig bds; spine def. b Dec 5 (481) £220

**Roberts, William.** See: Ward & Roberts

**Robertson, Bryan**
— Jackson Pollock. NY, [1960]. In dj. sg Jan 11 (361) $250

**Robertson, David, fl.1794**
— A Tour through the Isle of Man. L, 1794. 8vo, orig bds; rebacked. S Mar 28 (61) £160

**Robertson, George, 1750?-1832**
See also: Crawfurd & Robertson
— A Genealogical Account of the Principal Families in Aurshire.... Edin. & Irvine, 1823-27. 4 vols, including Supplement. 8vo, mor gilt by Riviere. Inscr to J. Fullarton & with his annotations. pnE May 15 (85) £500

**Robertson, John, 1712-76**
— The Elements of Navigation. L, 1764. 2d Ed. 2 vols. 8vo, contemp sheep; needs rebdg. With 16 folding maps & charts. sg Mar 7 (232) $175

5th Ed. L, 1786. 2 vols. 8vo, contemp sheep; joints cracked. With 16 folding maps & charts. Stamps on front endpapers & half-titles; foxed. sg Mar 7 (233) $90

**Robertson, John Wooster.** See: Grabhorn Printing

**Robertson, Merle Greene**
— The Sculpture of Palenque. Princeton, [1983-85]. Vols I-III. 4to, cloth, in djs; some wear. O May 7 (262) $250

**Robertson, W. Graham**
— Gold, Frankincense, and Myrrh. L, 1906. Orig cloth; worn & soiled. Some spotting. F June 20 (677) $70

Anr Ed. L, 1907. Orig cloth, in soiled dj; bdg edges worn. wa June 20 (292) $140

**Robertson, William, 1721-93**
— The History of America. L, 1788. 3 vols. 4to, half calf; spine ends of Vol I worn. pba June 20 (284) $275

7th Ed of Vols I-III, 1st Ed of Vol IV. L, 1796. 4 vols. 4to, contemp calf; Vol I spine head chipped, cover nearly detached. With 4 folding maps & folding plate. pba Nov 30 (276) $110
— The History of the Reign of the Emperor Charles V.... L, 1769. 1st Ed. 3 vols. 4to, 19th-cent calf; some glue at spine heads. pba Nov 30 (277) $140

Anr copy. Contemp calf gilt; rebacked. Lacking frontis in Vol I. sg Feb 8 (26) $140

**Robertus Monachus, Abbot of St. Remigius**
— Bellum Christianorum principum, praecipue Callorum, contra Saracenos. Basel, [1533]. Folio, mor gilt with Lenox arms; extremities rubbed. Some soiling & spotting; 1 leaf with minor repair; lacking a blank; library stamp on tp. cb Feb 14 (2581) $1,500

**Robeson, Kenneth**
— The Land of Terror. NY, [1933]. Pictorial bds; spine ends rubbed. pba May 4 (246) $55
— The Man of Bronze. NY, [1933]. Pictorial bds; spine ends rubbed, front hinge starting, stains to front endpapers & tp. pba May 4 (247) $50
— Quest of the Spider. NY, [1933]. Pictorial bds; corners bumped. pba May 4 (245) $50

**Robida, Albert, 1848-1926**
— La Vieille France. Paris, [c.1885]. 4to, half cloth, orig wraps bound in; rubbed. sg Mar 7 (319) $90

**Robinson, Alan James**
— Songbirds. Easthampton MA: Cheloniidae Press, 1983-84. One of 50. 2 vols. Folio, unbound as issued in half mor folding case. With 30 hand-colored etchings. P June 5 (193) $800

**Robinson, Alfred, 1806-95**
— Life in California before the Conquest. San Francisco, 1925. One of 250. Half cloth, in stained dj. With 7 colored plates. Inscr. pba Apr 25 (634) $50

Anr Ed. Oakland, 1947. One of 750. Buckram; spine faded. With 8 plates. Larson copy. pba Sept 28 (214) $60
— Life in California during a Residence of Several Years.... NY, 1846. Bound with: Doyce Nunis. A Commentary on Alfred Robinson... half mor. With 9 plates. Frontis marginally chipped; other marginal tears repaired. Larson copy. pba Sept 28 (212) $375

1st Ed. 2 vols in 1. 12mo, orig cloth; extremities worn. With 9 plates. Foxed & soiled. Robbins copy. pba Mar 21 (300) $350

1st London Ed. L, 1851. Orig cloth; worn & damaged, front hinge cracked. Foxed & lightly stained. Larson copy. pba Sept 28 (213) $50

**Robinson, Charles N.**
— Old Naval Prints, their Artists and Engravers. L: The Studio, 1924. One of 1,500. 4to, orig cloth. sg Jan 11 (369) $150

**Robinson, Doane**
— A History of the Dakota or Sioux Indians. Aberdeen SD, 1904. 8vo, cloth; worn. Pp. 63-78 bound upside down & backwards. South Dakota Historical Collections, 1904, Part 2. pba June 25 (204) $250

**Robinson, Edwin Arlington, 1869-1935**
— The Children of the Night.... Bost., 1897. 1st Ed, one of 450. 12mo, orig cloth; tear in front flyleaf. Inscr to Richard Henry Stoddard & with ALs to Stoddard laid in. Engelhard copy. CNY Oct 27 (120) $750

Anr copy. Orig cloth; rubbed, mull exposed at rear inner hinge. K June 23 (442) $225

Anr copy. Orig cloth; rubbed. Waterstain at bottom margin at beginning. Inscr, 22 Sept 1899. Z June 28 (237) $200
— The Torrent and the Night Before. Gardiner, Maine: Ptd for the Author, 1896. 1st Ed. 12mo, orig ptd wraps; recased with front cvoer rehinged & repair to front cover. Inscr to H. E. Scudder. With 2 A Ls s from Robinson to Paul Lemperly. Engelhard copy. CNY Oct 27 (119) $1,900

**Robinson, Ellen**
— A Tribute of Sorrow and Affection to the Memory of a Beloved Son.... Liverpool, [c.1821]. 8vo, contemp wraps; worn. Some browning. b Dec 5 (213) £75

**Robinson, Henry Crabb, 1775-1867**
— Diary, Reminiscences, and Correspondence. L, 1869. 3 vols. 8vo, contemp calf gilt. Extra-illus with plates & ports. S Apr 23 (134) £250

**Robinson, Henry Peach**
— Pictorial Effect in Photography. L, 1869. 8vo, orig cloth; stained & worn. With 3 mtd Woodburytype illusts & 3 photo-etchings. b May 30 (63) £110

**Robinson, Patrick.** See: Reeves & Robinson

**Robinson, William, 1838-1935**
— Flora and Sylva. L, 1903-5. 3 vols. 4to, contemp half vellum gilt; soiled. Ck Feb 14 (321) £350

Anr copy. Orig cloth; some wear. Library markings. pba Sept 14 (304) $325

Anr copy. 3 vols (all pbd). S Apr 23 (316) £360

Anr copy. 3 vols. 4to, orig half vellum. With 66 chromolitho plates. S June 13 (417) £420

Anr copy. Half mor; spines dried & cracked, ends frayed. Not collated. Sold w.a.f. sg Dec 7 (233) $425

**Robinson, William Heath, 1872-1944**
— Railway Ribaldry. L, 1935. 4to, orig wraps; spotted. bba May 30 (317) £90 [Mandl]
— Some "Frightful" War Pictures. L, 1915. 4to, orig half cloth. bba May 9 (264) £100 [Trevett]

**Robinson, William Wilcox**
— Maps of Los Angeles. Los Angeles, 1966. One of 380. Inscr. pba Feb 12 (446) $275

### Robley, Augusta J.
— A Selection of Madeira Flowers. L, 1845. Folio, orig cloth; marked. With 8 hand-colored plates. Tipped in at beginning are 6 watercolors, 5 by Mrs. Robley. S June 27 (60) £1,500

### Robley, Horatio Gordon
— Moko; or Maori Tattooing. L, 1896. 4to, orig cloth; worn & bumped. Met May 22 (92) $210

### Robson, George Fennell
— Scenery of the Grampian Mountains. L, 1819. Oblong folio, 19th-cent half mor; worn. With map & 41 hand-colored plates. Library stamps, sometimes touching images. S Nov 30 (62) £500

### Robson, Joseph
— The British Mars. L, 1763. 1st Ed. 8vo, orig bds. Some foxing. sg Mar 21 (274) $1,200

### Robson, Joseph Philip
— Poetic Gatherings; or, Stray Leaves from my Portfolio. Gateshead, 1839. 12mo, orig wraps; spine def. b Dec 5 (110) £70

### Roby, John
— Lorenzo, or the Tale of Redemption! Rochdale, 1820. 2d Ed. 8vo, orig bds; worn. b Dec 5 (214) £60

### Rocca, ——, Abbe della
— Traite complet sur les Abeilles. Paris, 1790. 3 vols. 8vo, early 19th-cent half calf gilt; joints rubbed & starting, spine heads worn, 2 prelims bound out of order in Vol II. With 5 folding plates. sg Apr 18 (153) $375

### Rocca, Angelo, Bishop of Tagasti. See: Roccha, Angelo

### Roccha, Angelo, Bishop of Tagasti
— De campanis commentarius. Rome: Facciottus, 1612. 4to, later bds. With 4 plates. Trimmed with some loss to engraved surfaces on folding plates A & B & folds reinforced on verso; some worming repaired on tp & later leaves; some worming to plates; 1 leaf with marginal hole; Plates C & D misbound; some browning. S Dec 1 (297) £500

### Rocha Pitta, Sebastiao da
— Historia da America Portugueza.... Lisbon, 1730. Folio, 18th-cent calf gilt; later endpapers. Old writing removed from foot of tp. S Nov 30 (183) £11,500

### Rochefort, Charles de, b.1605
— The History of the Caribby-Islands, viz., Barbados, St. Christophers.... L, 1666. 1st English Ed. - Map by T. Kitchen. 2 parts in 1 vol. Folio, contemp calf; rebacked, rubbed. With 9 plates, additional folding plate, & map. Some browning; table with fore-edge repaire. S Oct 26 (524) £460 [Remington]

### Roches, Michael de la
— Memoirs of Literature.... L, 1722. 8 vols. 8vo, contemp calf; rubbed, spines worn & dried. Some foxing & browning. O Mar 26 (234) $110

### Rochester, John Wilmot, Earl of, 1647-80. See: Nonesuch Press

### Rochon de Chabannes, Marc Antoine Jacques
— Le Jaloux, comedie en cinq actes.... Paris: la veuve Duchesne, 1785. 8vo, contemp red mor gilt with arms of Rochon de Chabannes. Owner's stamp on tp. Author's copy. Fuerstenberg - Schaefer copy. S Dec 8 (538) £1,100

### Rockwell, Norman
— My Adventures as an Illustrator. Garden City, 1960. Sgd. pba Aug 22 (639) $65

Anr copy. In dj. Inscr by both Norman & Thomas Rockwell. pba Aug 22 (844) $85

Anr copy. In dj. Sgd. wa Feb 29 (257) $140

### Rocky Mountain...
— The Rocky Mountain Directory and Colorado Gazetteer for 1871.... Denver: S. S. Wallihan, [1870]. 8vo, orig cloth; covers stained, extremities worn, front hinge cracked, a few signatures sprung. pba Nov 16 (59) $600

### Rocque, John
— A New and Accurate Survey of the Cities of London and Westminster.... L, 1748. Folio, 19th-Cent half calf; rubbed. With title vignette & 16 double-page sheets. Title stained; sheet VI torn in 2 with some fraying; sheet XI with repaired tear; sheet XII with small stains; some marginal tears & staining. S Oct 26 (401) £950 [Bankes]

### Rocques de Montgaillard, Jean Gabriel Maurice, Comte
— L'An Mille Sept-Cent Quatre-Vingt-Quinze.... Hamburg, 1795. 8vo, contemp wraps, unopened; spine ends chipped, front cover starting. sg Mar 21 (275) $250

### Rodd, James Rennell, Baron Rennell
— Rose Leaf and Apple Leaf. Phila., 1882. Intro by Oscar Wilde. 8vo, orig vellum. S Dec 18 (239) £300 [Sumner & Stillman]

1st Ed. 8vo, orig vellum. S Oct 27 (1206) £350 [Swales]

### Roddenberry, Gene
— The Star Trek Guide. [N.p.]: Norway Productions, 1967. 3d Revision. Ptd wraps, bound with brass tacks. pba May 23 (389) $275

### Rodenberg, Julius, 1831-1914
See also: Simon & Rodenberg
— Deutsche Pressen: Eine Bibliographie. Vienna, [n.d.]. 8vo, orig cloth in dj. With supplement for 1925-30. sg Apr 11 (266) $400

### Rodman, Selden
— Horace Pippin. NY, 1947. 4to, cloth. Inscr to Phil Petrie. sg Mar 28 (258) $200

Anr copy. Cloth, in chipped & repaired dj. sg Mar 28 (259) $200

**Rodney, George Brudges**
— As a Cavalryman Remembers. Caldwell: Caxton Printers, 1944. 1st Ed. Orig cloth in torn & chipped dj. Robbins copy.   pba Mar 21 (301) $70

**Rodrigues, Eugene.** See: Ramiro, Erastene

**Rodriguez, A., Dramatist**
— Coleccion general de los trages que en la actualidad se usan en Espana. Madrid, 1801. 8vo, contemp wraps; backstrip def. With 112 hand-colored plates. Lacking the 4 supplementary plates.  sg Apr 18 (177) $1,700

**Roe, Charles Francis**
— Custer's Last Battle. [NY: Robert Bruce, 1927]. 2 parts in 1 vol. Folio, pictorial wraps.  pba June 25 (205) $90

**Roe, Frances**
— Army Letters from an Officer's Wife, 1871-1888. NY, 1909. Orig cloth; rubbed, hinges repaired.  pba June 25 (206) $80

**Roediger, Virginia More**
— Ceremonial Costumes of the Pueblo Indians. Berkeley, 1941. 4to, orig cloth, in dj.  pba Nov 16 (196) $140

**Roesel von Rosenhof, August Johann**
— De Natuurlyke Historie der Insecten. Haarlem & Amst., 1764-68.  5 vols in 8, including Supplement. 4to, contemp half lea; rubbed. With 3 hand-colored frontises, port & 381 plates on 310 leaves only. Marginal tears repaired in Plate XIV in Vol II & Plate XI in Vol IV; 4 plates bound upside down.  S June 27 (62) £2,800

**Roesslin, Eucharius**
— Der swangern Frauwen und Hebammen Rosegarten. Strassburg: Martinus Flach, 1513. 4to, contemp vellum with overflap, unpressed.  C June 26 (120) £35,000

**Roest, M.**
— Catalog der Hebraica und Judaica aus der L. Rosenthal'schen Bibliothek. Amst., 1966. 2 vols. 4to, cloth. Reprint of 1875 Ed.  F Mar 28 (244) $80
   Anr copy. 2 vols. 8vo, orig cloth.  sg Apr 11 (183) $175

**Roger-Marx, Claude**
— Bonnard: Lithographe. Monte Carlo, 1952. 4to, orig wraps; spine head torn.  Ck May 31 (88) £90
— L'Oeuvre grave de Vuillard. Monte Carlo, [1948]. 4to, orig wraps.  sg Jan 11 (453) $325; sg Jan 11 (454) $325
   Anr copy. Orig wraps; soiled.  sg June 13 (379) $300

**Rogers, Bruce, 1870-1957**
— Paragraphs on Printing Elicited from Bruce Rogers in Talks with James Hendrickson.... NY, 1943. 4to, cloth. Inscr.  sg Sept 14 (316) $150

— The Work of Bruce Rogers: Catalogue of an Exhibition Arranged by the A.I.G.A. NY, 1939. In chipped & frayed dj. Laid in is ptd Christmas greeting, initialled by Rogers.  O Mar 26 (235) $70

**Rogers, David Banks**
— Prehistoric Man of the Santa Barbara Coast. Santa Barbara: Museum of Natural History, [1929].  pba July 25 (207) $85

**Rogers, Edward H.**
— Reminiscences of Military Service in the Forty-Third Regiment, Massachusetts Infantry.... Bost., 1883. 8vo, orig cloth; spine ends worn. With 4 plates. frontis loose.  NH July 21 (90) $135

**Rogers, Fairman**
— A Manual of Coaching. L, 1900. 8vo, orig cloth; worn & rubbed, puncture to spine, front hinge cracked.  wa Feb 29 (148) $140

**Rogers, Fred B.**
See also: Grabhorn Printing
— Bear Flag Lieutenant: The Life Story of Henry L. Ford.... San Francisco: California Historical Society, 1951. One of 250. Illus by Alexander Eduoart. Orig cloth. With frontis port & 5 full-page plates. Larson copy.  pba Sept 28 (657) $75
— Montgomery and the Portsmouth. San Francisco: John Howell Books, 1958. 1st Ed, One of 750. Orig cloth. With frontis port, 4 facsimiles, & 3 illus; 2 carte-de-vistes, 2 prospectuses, & 2 book reviews laid in. Larson copy.  pba Sept 28 (658) $75

**Rogers, Robert, 1731-95**
— Journals of Major Robert Rogers.... L, 1765. 1st Ed. 8vo, half mor gilt.  sg Oct 26 (321) $1,900

**Rogers, Samuel, 1763-1855**
See also: Byron & Rogers; Fore-Edge Paintings
— The Pleasures of Memory. L, [1865]. 8vo, orig cloth. Some discoloration throughout.  b May 30 (64) £80
— Poems. L, 1834. 8vo, mor gilt by Hayday; rubbed. sg Feb 8 (27) $110
   Anr Ed. L, 1839. 8vo, orig cloth; worn, hinges repaired. Inscr to Mary Shelley.  S Dec 18 (201) £400 [Spademan]

**Rogers, Will, 1879-1935**
— The Illiterate Digest. NY, 1924. One of 250. Inscr. pba Nov 30 (279) $250

**Rogerson, Ian**
— Agnes Miller Parker. Wakefield: Fleece Press, 1991. One of 300. Folio, orig half cloth.  bba May 9 (487) £120 [Dowdall]

**Rohan, Henri, Duc de, 1579-1638**
— The Memoires.... L, 1660. Trans by George Bridges. 2 parts in 1 vol. 8vo, calf; glue to spine ends & rear joint.  pba Nov 30 (280) $160
— Les Memoires du Duc de Rohan. [N.p.], 1644. 2 parts in 1 vol. 16mo, vellum with yapp edges.  pba Mar 7 (223) $150

## Rohault, Jacques
— Traite de physique. Paris, 1671. 1st Ed. 2 vols in 1. 4to, contemp calf; upper joint wormed. With 2 (of 3) folding plates. Tear in inner margin of folding plate; some dampstaining. S Mar 14 (309) £260

## Rohrbach, Carl
— Die Trachten der Voelker vom Beginn der Geschichte.... Leipzig, 1886. 2d Ed. - Illus by J. G. Bach. 4to, orig cloth; rubbed, bumped, shaken. With extra colored title & 104 plates. Met May 22 (437) $350

## Rojas, Fernando de
— La Celestine. Paris, 1971. One of 18 exemplaires nominatifs, this copy for Docteur Jean Stehlin. Illus by Pablo Picasso. 4to, orig vellum. Inscr & with large ink drawing by Picasso on first flyleaf. S Nov 30 (351) £17,000

## Rolewinck, Werner, 1425-1502
— Fasciculus temporum. Utrecht: Johann Veldener, 14 Feb 1480. ("Dat Boeck dat men hiet Fasciculus Temporum....") Folio, early 16th-cent calf over wooden bds; spine repaired, endleaves & 2 fore-edge clasps renewed. 38 lines & 3 columns in table; types 5:114G, 4:89B. With 35 woodcuts form 20 blocks. The 2 woodcut borders trimmed; some staining; corner of 33/2 mended; tears in 29/7,8 affecting 1 letter. 339 (of 340) leaaves only; lacking final blank. C June 26 (172) £9,000

Anr Ed. Venice: Erhard Ratdolt, 28 May 1484. Folio, 19th-cent half vellum, armorial bdg. 57 lines; types 4:76G, 6:56(75)G, 9:130G. With 55 woodcuts. 74 leaves. Goff R-270. C June 26 (123) £1,500

Anr Ed. [Strassburg: Johann Pruess, not before 1490]. Folio, modern blind-stamped calf; edges rubbed. 50 lines; gothic letter; full-page woodcut on tp verso. Some dampstaining; early Ms annotations. 94 (of 96) leaves; lacking 2 blanks. Goff R-276. S Dec 18 (77) £1,150 [Zioni]

## Rolfe, Ann
— Miscellaneous Poems for a Winter's Evening. Colchester, [c.1840]. 8vo, contemp half calf gilt. b Dec 5 (115) £85

## Rolli, Paolo
— Di canzonette e di cantate libri due. L: Thomas Edlin, 1727. 8vo, 18th-cent calf. With frontis & 24 pages of engraved music. S May 15 (476) £460

**Romance...** See: Malory, Sir Thomas

## Romanian Liturgy
— [Handbook to Church Festivals] Snagov: the monk Anthimos, June 1701. 4to, contemp calf gilt tooled to a post-fanfare pattern, with the initials I.K.B. & the date in the center. S Nov 30 (294) £3,200

## Romanov, Nikolai Mikhailovich, Grand Duke, 1859-1919
— Memoires sur les Lepidopteres. St. Petersburg, 1884-93. Vols I-VII (of 10). 4to, contemp half mor or cloth (Vol VII); joints weak, spines rubbed. With 112 colored & 3 uncolored plates & 1 folding colored map. Some browning; stamps removed from titles; tear to fold of map; 1st 4 plates mtd to size. Fattorini copy. C Oct 25 (82) £2,000

## Rome
— Statuti del secro monte della pieta di Roma, rinovati nell'anno MDCCLXVII. Rome: Alla Stamperia Ermateniana, [1767]. Bound with: Bolle e privilegi del sacro monte della pieta di Roma. 4to, contemp mor gilt by the Vatican Bindery for Cardinal Giovanni Anglo Braschi, with the Cardinal's arms. C Apr 3 (228) £1,600

— Vedute antiche e moderne le piu interessanti della citta di Roma. Rome: Veneziano Monaldi, [c.1820]. 4to, contemp half mor; rubbed. With frontis & 100 views on 50 plates. b June 28 (58) £200

## Ronalds, Alfred
— The Fly-Fisher's Entomology. L, 1836. 1st Ed. 8vo, modern half mor. W Nov 8 (390) £440

Anr Ed. L, 1856. 8vo, orig cloth; inner joint cracked. With 20 hand-colored plates. Some foxing & soiling. O Feb 6 (194) $160

7th Ed. L, 1868. 8vo, contemp cloth; spine torn. With frontis & 19 hand-colored plates & with canvas wallet with orig flies inserted into pockets (some lacking). S June 13 (459) £150

Anr Ed. L, 1901. pba July 11 (256) $160

Anr Ed. Liverpool, 1913. Ltd Ed. 2 vols. 4to, orig cloth; worn. With 7 plain & 14 hand-colored plates, plus 48 specimen flies on sunken mounts. b Sept 20 (489) £600

Anr copy. Orig half mor gilt. W Nov 8 (392) £900

One of 250. Orig half mor gilt; worn. With 7 plain & 14 hand-colored plates, plus 48 specimen flies on sunken mounts. O Feb 6 (82) $1,900

Anr copy. Half mor; rubbed. With 48 flies mtd in thick recessed card. Minor foxing. O Feb 6 (195) $2,500

Anr copy. Mor gilt by Birdsall for Scribner's. With 7 plates of rivers & 13 hand-colored plates; 48 flies on 9 leaves of sunken mounts. P June 5 (328) $2,250

## Ronsard, Pierre de, 1524-85
— Florilege des amours. Paris, 1948. One of 20 with a suite of 8 extra lithos & the 12 planches refusees ptd on Japanese vellum & sgd with initials by Matisse. Illus by Henri Matisse. Folio, mor extra irradiant bdg by Paul Bonet, 1966 [Carnets 1538], orig wraps bound in. S Nov 21 (377) £26,000

Anr copy. Loose as issued in orig wraps. wd Nov 15 (93) $7,500

— Songs & Sonnets. NY, 1903. One of 425. Designed by Bruce Rogers. Mor gilt. b Dec 5 (48) £140

## Roo, Gerard von
— Annales rerum belli domique ab Austriacis Habspurgicae gentis principibus a Rudolpho primo, usque ad Carolum V. Gestarum.... Innsbruck: Joannes Agricola, 1592. 1st Ed. Folio, contemp half bdg with blind-tooled pigskin spine & corners with vellum sides; corners worn. With port, full-page genealogi-

cal tree & engraved & woodcut coats-of-arms. Minor staining. C June 26 (125) £450

**Roop, Guy**
— Villas & Palaces of Andrea Palladio.... Milan, 1968. Folio, calf gilt. pba Aug 8 (232) $85

Anr copy. Syn. sg Jan 11 (15) $100

Anr copy. Pictorial bds. wa Feb 1 (301) $65

**Roosen, Gerhard**
— Christliches Gemuths-Gesprach von dem Geistlichen und Seligmachenden Glauben.... Ephrata: Ephratae Typis Societatis, 1769. 8vo, contemp sheep; rubbed. Some dampstaining; ink annotations at foot of tp. F Mar 28 (445) $160

**Rooses, Max, 1839-1914**
— Christophe Plantin, imprimeur anversois. Antwerp, 1890. 4to, half mor, orig front wrap bound in; rubbed, joints worn. O Mar 26 (236) $60
— Dutch Painters of the Nineteenth Century. L, 1898-1901. 4 vols. 4to, orig cloth; some hinges cracked, 1 bdg soiled. sg June 13 (142) $225

**Roosevelt, Franklin D., 1882-1945**
— Addresses of Franklin D. Roosevelt and Winston Churchill. Wash., 1942. One of 21 lettered copies for presentation. 4to, mor gilt. pba Mar 7 (224) $2,500
[-] The Democratic Book. [Phila.], 1936. One of 898. 4to, orig syn CE June 12 (106) $700

Anr copy. 4to, mor gilt. sg June 6 (158) $550
— F.D.R.: His Personal Letters. NY, [1947-50]. Foreword by Eleanor Roosevelt. Inscr by Eleanor Roosevelt in last vol, 7 Mar 1951, to Mary Norton. pba Oct 26 (306) $250
— Looking Forward. NY, 1933. 1st Ed. Library markings. Inscr to Charles Edison. sg Sept 28 (232) $350
— Records of the Town of Hyde Park. Hyde Park, 1928. One of 100. 4to, orig cloth; shaken. O Nov 14 (153) $250

**Roosevelt, Robert B.**
— Game Fish of the Northern States of America.... NY, 1862. 8vo, orig cloth; spine ends frayed. pba July 11 (259) $50

**Roosevelt, Robert B. —&**
**Green, Seth, 1817-88**
— Fish Hatching, and Fish Catching. Rochester: Union & Advertiser, 1879. 8vo, cloth. pba July 11 (257) $70

**Roosevelt, Theodore, 1858-1919**
— African Game Trails. L, 1910. Orig cloth. pba July 25 (208) $70

Anr copy. Half mor; extremities rubbed. sg Mar 7 (523) $175
— Applied Ethics. Cambr., 1911. Inscr by Martha Bulloch Roosevelt & with her inscr calling card. sg Oct 26 (322) $110

— Fear God and Take Your Own Part. NY, [1916]. Inscr to Russell Bowen, 3 Apr 1916. sg Sept 28 (240) $1,100
— Outdoor Pastimes of an American Hunter. NY, 1905. pba Apr 25 (229) $65

One of 260 L.p. copies. 4to, half pigskin; extremities rubbed. sg Mar 7 (524) $1,800
— Ranch Life and the Hunting-Trail. L, [1888]. Illus by Frederick Remington. Folio, cloth; worn, hinges cracked. sg Mar 7 (525) $60

1st Ed. - Illus by Frederic Remington. Folio, orig buckram. Half-title detaching. Robbins copy. pba Mar 21 (304) $850

Anr Ed. NY, [1888]. Illus by Frederick Remington. Folio, cloth; some soiling. pba Aug 8 (168) $75

Anr Ed. NY, 1902. Illus by Frederic Remington. Cloth; extremities rubbed. sg Oct 26 (323) $50
— The Wilderness Hunter: An Account of the Big Game of the United States.... NY, [1888]. 1st Ed, One of 200. 8vo, orig cloth. Robbins copy. pba Mar 21 (305) $275
— The Winning of the West. NY, 1900. One of 200 L.p. sets. 4 vols. 4to, half mor. sg Oct 26 (324) $1,300
— Works. NY, 1923-26. Memorial Ed, one of 1,050. 24 vols. Unopened copy. K Oct 1 (331) $500; pba Mar 7 (225) $800

**Roosevelt, Theodore, 1858-1919 —&**
**Grinnell, George Bird, 1849-1938**
— American Big-Game Hunting. NY, 1893. 8vo, cloth; some wear. O Oct 10 (231) $110

Anr Ed. NY, 1901. 8vo, cloth; worn. O Oct 10 (232) $80
— Hunting in Many Lands. NY, 1895. Cloth; worn. O Oct 10 (233) $180

Anr copy. Pictorial cloth; some wear, rear inner joint broken. O Jan 9 (194) $100
— Trail and Camp Fire. The Book of the Boone and Crockett Club. NY, 1897. Orig cloth; worn, inner joint broken. O Oct 10 (149) $50

**Roosevelt, Theodore, 1858-1919 —&**
**Minot, Henry D.**
— The Summer Birds of the Adirondacks in Franklin County, NY. [Salem, 1877]. 4 pp, 8vo, unbound. Stain in blank corner of p.3. sg Oct 26 (325) $1,100

**Root, Edward Wales**
— Philip Hooker: a Contribution to the Study of the Renaissance in America. NY, 1929. One of 750. 4to, cloth, in repaired dj. sg Jan 11 (16) $70

**Root, Frank A. —&**
**Connelley, William Elsey, 1855-1930**
— The Overland Stage to California. Topeka, 1901. Orig cloth; 1 corner showing, inner hinges weak. Extra folds to map at rear. wa Feb 29 (484) $190

1st Ed. Robbins copy. pba Mar 21 (306) $325

**Root, Marcus A.**
— The Camera and the Pencil.... Phila., 1864. 1st Ed. 8vo, orig mor gilt; joints & edges rubbed. Inscr to James Russell Lowell. CE May 22 (408) $380

**Root, Riley**
— Journal of the Travels... St. Josephs to Oregon.... Galesburg, 1850. 1st Ed. 8vo, facsimile wraps. Light wear; 1st 16pp chipped in corner. Robbins copy. pba Mar 21 (307) $7,000

**Roper, J.** See: Cole & Roper

**Roper, Moses**
— Hanes Bywyd A Ffoedigaeth... O Gaethiwed Americanaidd. Aberysthwyth, 1842. 24mo, orig bds. F June 20 (412B) $350
— A Narrative of the Adventures and Escape of Moses Roper from American Slavery. Phila., 1838. 8vo, wraps; spine def. Some foxing. Met Feb 24 (411) $200
Anr Ed. L, 1839. 12mo, cloth. sg Mar 28 (336) $175

**Roquefeuil, Camille de**
— A Voyage Round the World.... L, 1823. 1st Ed in English. 8vo, modern half calf. Some soiling & marginal tears. pba Feb 13 (159) $450

**Roquelaure, A. N.** See: Rice, Anne

**Rosa, Salvator, 1615-73**
— Has ludentis otii Carolo Rubeo singularis pignus D.D.D. Nuremberg: J. J. de Sandrart, [c.1670?]. Folio, later mor gilt; extremities worn, joints cracked, spine perished. With 33 plates only. Lacking tp; 5 plates detached but present. cb Oct 17 (685) $1,000

**Rosborough, E. H. ("Polly")**
— Tying and Fishing the Fuzzy Nymphs. Manchester, [1969]. One of 50. In frayed dj. O Feb 6 (196) $70

**Roscoe, Thomas, 1791-1871**
— Wanderings and Excursions in South Wales. L, [1837]. 8vo, mor extra; extemities worn. With 48 plates. sg Mar 7 (322) $225

**Roscoe Library, William**
— [Sale Catalogue] Catalogue of the...Library. Liverpool, 1816. 8vo, half lea; backstrip def, front bd & 1st gathering detached. Lacking port. Priced; interleaved.. bba Sept 7 (27) £620 [Bowers]

**Rose, Barbara**
— Alexander Liberman. NY, [1981]. 4to, cloth, in dj. sg Sept 7 (218) $80
— Frankenthaler. NY, [1970]. Oblong folio, cloth, in soiled plastic dj. Designed by Robert Motherwell. sg Jan 11 (181) $120

**Rose, George**
— The Great Country; or, Impressions of America. L, 1868. 8vo, early calf; rebacked. sg Oct 26 (326) $60

**Rosenbach, A. S. W., 1876-1952**
See also: Widener Library, Harry Elkins
— The All-Embracing Doctor Franklin. Phila., 1932. Out-of-series copy. Half mor. O Dec 5 (126) $80
— Books and Bidders: the Adventures of a Bibliophile. Bost., 1927. One of 785 L.p. copies. Half cloth. pba Aug 22 (563) $65
— The Collected Catalogues.... NY, [1967]. 10 vols. 8vo, orig cloth. sg Apr 11 (266A) $375
— Early American Children's Books. Portland, 1933. Out-of-series exhibition copy on Zerkall Halle. 4to, pigskin. With the Cock Robin chapbook in mor case, as issued. O Dec 5 (127) $1,100

**Rosenberg, Harold**
— De Kooning. NY, [1974]. Oblong 4to, cloth, in dj. sg Sept 7 (123) $600; sg Jan 11 (137) $375

**Rosenberg, Isaac**
— Poems.... L, 1922. 1st Ed. Orig cloth; creased. Inscr by T. S. Eliot to Lady Ottoline Morrell, 1923. Hobson copy. S June 28 (189) £850

**Rosenberg, Marc**
— Der Goldschmiede Merkzeichen. Frankfurt, 1890. 4to, bds with earlier contemp calf backstrip. Dampstain to fore-edge of tp & contentes leaves. wa Dec 14 (544) $130

**Rosenthal, Leonard**
— Au royaume de la perle. Paris, [1920]. Ltd Ed. Illus by Edmund Dulac. 4to, orig bds; hinges weak. With 10 colored plates. Met Dec 5 (155) $225

**Rosinus, Joannes**
— Antiquitatum Romanarum corpus absolutissimum. Geneva, 1620. 4to, contemp citron mor gilt, with arms of the Comte de Richelieu; small piece torn from front free endpaper. With 2 folding plates. Some foxing; tp stamped. sg Mar 21 (276) $300
— Romanarum antiquitatum libri decem. Lyons, 1609. 4to, contemp calf gilt; rebacked, spotted. pba Mar 7 (226) $110

**Ross, Alexander, 1591-1654**
— Arcana Microcosmi: or, the Hid Secrets of Man's Body Discovered.... L, 1652. 2d Ed. 8vo, half vellum; rubbed & soiled. Some worming affecting text; lower fore-margin torn from F2. S June 12 (278) £450

**Ross, Alexander, 1783-1856**
— The Fur Hunters of the Far West. L, 1855. 1st Ed. 2 vols. 8vo, orig cloth; recased, spine head repaired, hinges cracking or repaired, spines sunned. With 2 frontises & 1 folding map. Foxed. Robbins copy. pba Mar 21 (308) $700

**Ross, Sir James Clark, 1800-62**
— A Voyage of Discovery and Research in the Southern and Antarctic Regions... L, 1847. 1st Ed. 2 vols. 8vo, orig cloth; stained, hinges weak. With frontises & 14 plates & maps. Inscr to Admiral Sir William Parker. pba Oct 9 (16) $700

### Ross, Janet Ann
— Florentine Villas. L, 1901. One of 200. Folio, orig cloth. Spotting at beginning. Ck Feb 14 (313) £140
Anr copy. Cloth; soiled, scratched, some wear, endpapers foxed. With 24 plates. Tp & endpaper stamped. wa Dec 14 (398) $300

### Ross, Sir John, 1777-1856
— Narrative of a Second Voyage in Search of a North-West Passage.... L, 1835. 2 vols (including Appendix). 8vo, orig cloth. With frontises, 43 plates (21 of them colored), 5 charts & a folding map. Tear at map fold; minor spotting. b May 30 (183) £380
Anr copy. Half lea. With 50 plates & maps. Folding chart lacking. Met Sept 28 (361) $300
Vol I only. Orig bds; worn & rubbed, prelims loose, split in half at middle of book but spine intact. With 31 maps & plates. Foxed. K Feb 11 (27) $250
1st American Ed. Phila., 1835. 8vo, contemp half cloth; front endpaper lacking. With folding map (wrinkled, repaired in gutter). O Nov 14 (154) $275
— A Voyage of Discovery, Made under the Orders of the Admiralty...for the Purpose of Exploring Baffin's Bay.... L, 1819. 1st Ed. 4to, contemp calf; extremities worn. With 32 plates, maps & charts. With the errata slip. sg Oct 26 (327) $1,100

### Rossberg, Christian Gottlieb
— Systematische Anweisung zum Schoenschreiben. [Dresden, 1817]. 2 vols in 1 (lacking the 3 text vols). Oblong folio, modern bds. Engraved throughout, with 2 titles & 139 plates of lettering, numbering & calligraphy. bba Oct 5 (215) £600 [Frognal]

### Rosselli, Cosma
— Thesaurus artificiosae memoriae. Venice: A. Padovani, 1579. 4to, old half vellum; upper bd dampstained. With folding woodcut plate & 27 woodcuts in text; worming in text of 1st 3 leaves; gathering F browned; a few leaves towards end wormed in inner margins; tear in Ee4; Ms notes. S Nov 30 (332) £650

### Rosselmini, Niccolo
— Dell' obbedienza del cavallo. Livorno, [1764]. 4to, contemp half mor. With half-title, pictorial title by G. Lapi, & 2 folding plates. Some discoloration. S Oct 27 (773) £280 [Zioni]

### Rosset, Pierre Fulcrand de
— L'Agriculture, poeme. Paris, 1774-82. 1st Ed. Part 1 only. 4to, contemp mor gilt. With port & 8 plates. Fuerstenberg - Schaefer copy. S Dec 8 (539) £550

### Rossetti, Christina Georgina, 1830-94
See also: Eragny Press
— Goblin Market. L, 1933. One of 10 with orig drawing on free endpaper. Illus by Arthur Rackham. Orig vellum; some discoloration. With 4 colored plates. P Dec 12 (156) $6,500
One of 410. Orig vellum. CE Sept 27 (241) $650; Ck May 31 (169) £380
Anr copy. Orig vellum; joints cracked. sg Sept 14 (306) $425

— Poems. L, 1891. 8vo, mor gilt by Worsfold. b May 30 (580) £340
— Verses. L, 1847. 1st Ed. 8vo, orig wraps, sewn. Minor marginal dampstaining. CE Sept 27 (245) $4,000

### Rossetti, Dante Gabriel, 1828-82
See also: Kelmscott Press
— Ballads and Sonnets. Leipzig, 1882. 8vo, vellum painted with rampant lion holding an escutcheon, by Giulio Giuliani, in cloth dj. sg Feb 8 (28) $300

### Rossi, Domenico
— Raccolta di statue antiche e moderne. Rome, 1704. Folio, 19th-cent calf; scuffed, covers detached. With engraved title & 163 plates. Tp soiled; some spotting; some text leaves browned. C May 31 (108) £1,700
— Romanae magnitudinis monumenta quae urbum illam orbis dominam velut redivivam exhibent posteritati.... Rome, 1699. Oblong folio, contemp vellum; minor wear, a few plates loose. With engraved title & 137 plates. Some dampstaining. cb Feb 14 (2801) $850
— Studio d'architettura civile sopra gli ornamenti di porte e finestre tratti da alcune fabbriche insigni de Roma. Rome, 1702-[21]. 3 vols in 2. Folio, contemp vellum; rebacked, old spines laid down, resewn. With 3 engraved titles, engraved dedication & 281 plates.. C Apr 3 (192) £2,200

### Rossi, Giovanni Giacomo de
— Insignium Romae templorum prospectus.... Rome, [1684]. Folio, contemp vellum; affected by damp. Engraved throughout, with 88 plates, 2 folding. Tear to lower blank; margin of Plate 4; some spotting. C Apr 3 (193) £900
— Mercurio geografico overo guida geografica in tutte le parti del mondo. Rome, 1692-94. 2 parts in 1 vol. Folio, 19th-cent half calf; worn, wormed. With engraved title & 91 double-page maps. Lacking Malta but including a twin-hemispherical world map & 2 of Americas; wormed & waterstained throughout with loss. S Mar 28 (184) £720

### Rossi, Giovanni Giacomo de —& Falda, Giovanni Battista
— Il Nuovo Teatro delle fabriche et edificii, in prospettiva di Roma moderna. Rome, 1665. Parts 1-3 (of 4) in 1 vol. 4to, old vellum. Engraved throughout, with 3 titles, 3 dedication leaves & 82 unnumbered plates. C Apr 3 (93) £2,000
Anr Ed. Rome, 1665-99. 4 parts in 1 vol. Oblong folio, contemp vellum. With 142 plates, including titles & dedication leaves. Spotting to Part 1. S Nov 30 (99) £3,000
Anr Ed. [Rome, 1739]. 5 parts in 1 vol. Folio, buckram; rebound. With 174 plates. 1st few leaves soiled. CE Nov 8 (239) $2,600
— Vedute delle fabriche, piazze et strade fatte fare nuovamente in Roma dalla...Alessandro VII. Rome, 1665. Oblong folio, contemp vellum; soiled. With engraved title & 33 plates. Repair to 1 plate in margin. b Sept 20 (253) £550

**Rossignol, Louis**
— Nouveau livre d'ecriture d'apres les meilleures exemples.... Paris: Daumont, [c.1760]. Folio, later half mor. With title by Babel & 17 plates by Le Parementier & Lattre. S Oct 27 (1159) £200 [Fonseca]

**Rossini, Gioachino, 1792-1868**
— [Sale Catalogue] Catalogue of the Unpublished Compositions of Gioachino Rossini... which will be sold by Auction... on Thursday, May 30, 1878. L, 1878. Bound with: a catalogue for the sale of MMe Rossini's jewelry, Paris, 1878. Half lea, orig wraps bound in. S May 15 (132) £600

**Rossit, Claudio.** See: Lago & Rossit

**Rostand, Edmond, 1868-1918**
See also: Limited Editions Club
— L'Aiglon. Paris, 1900. 8vo, mor gilt by Zaehnsdorf. b Dec 5 (5) £200
— Cyrano de Bergerac. L: Corvinus Press, 1937. One of 30. bba May 9 (472A) £170 [Collinge & Clark]

**Rostand, Maurice**
— La Vie amoureuse de Casanova. Paris: E. Flammarion, [1930]. One of 20 on hollande with additional suite with remarques & 2 unused etchings with remarkes, all on japon imperial. Illus by Charles Martin. 4to, calf extra pictorial bdg by Louis Pinard, orig wraps bound in. Plesch copy. S Nov 21 (385) £500

**Rota, Bernardino**
— Delle rime del S. B. Rota. Naples, 1572. 4to, later vellum. Library markings; some staining, soiling & worming. Sold w.a.f. O Feb 6 (198) $350

**Rotario, Sebastiano**
— Ragioni... contra l'Uso del Salasso. Verona, 1699. 4to, orig bds. Single wormhole through last c.40 pages. bba July 18 (89A) £80 [Weiner]

**Roth, Henry**
— Call It Sleep. NY, [1934]. 1st Ed, Advance copy. Orig wraps. K June 23 (446) $3,200

**Roth, Henry Ling**
— The Natives of Sarawak.... L, 1896. One of 700. 2 vols. 8vo, orig cloth; rubbed. S Mar 28 (404) £550

**Rothschild Library, Nathan James Edouard**
— Catalogue des livres composant la bibliotheque.... Paris, 1884-1920. Ed by Emile Picot. 5 vols. Ck Sept 8 (49) £400

**Rothschild, Baron Nathan James Edouard, 1844-81**
— Catalogue des livres composant la bibliotheque.... NY, [1965]. 5 vols. 4to, orig cloth. sg Apr 11 (267) $175

**Roth-Scholtz, Friedrich**
— Bibliotheca Chemica, oder Catalogus von Chymischen-Buechern.... Nuremberg & Altdorff, 1727. Parts 1 & 2 (of 5) in 1 vol. 16mo, 19th-cent half cloth; worn. Some cropping & dampstaining. S Mar 14 (310) £150

**Rotz, John.** See: Roxburghe Club

**Rouard Library, Etienne Antoine Benoit**
— [Sale Catalogue] Catalogue des livres, manuscrits.... Paris: Morgand & Fatout, 1879. 8vo, later half mor, orig wraps bound in; worn. O Mar 26 (238) $100

**Rouart, Denis —& Wildenstein, Daniel**
— Edouard Manet: Catalogue raisonne. Paris, [1975]. Vol I only. In dj. sg June 13 (242) $350

**Rouault, Georges, 1871-1958**
— Cirque de l'etoile filante. Paris: Vollard, 1938. One of 280. Folio, orig wraps; spine lacking. With 5 aquatints only (of 17) & 72 woodcuts only (of 82). Some soiling; loose. Ck May 31 (89) £3,600
— Stella Vespertina. Paris, 1947. Folio, loose signatures in cloth-backed bds; extremities worn, spine ends & joints frayed. With 12 mtd colored plates. Adhesion residue to 1 plate. pba Aug 22 (641) $50

**Roubo, Andre Jacob**
— L'Art du menuisier. Paris, 1769-75. 4 parts in 3 vols. Folio, later half sheep; spine ends frayed. With 364 plates only. Mainly marginal foxing. cb Feb 14 (2641) $1,200

**Rouille, Guillaume**
— Promptuarii Iconum insigniorum a seculo hominum.... Lyons, 1553. Bound with: Strada, Jacobus de. Epitome thesauri antiquitatum.... Lyon: (Jean de Tournes for) Jacobus de Strada & Thomas Guerin, 1553 1st Ed. 4to, contemp mor gilt by Christoph Heusler of Nuremberg for the Roemer family. Hoe - Coolidge - Schaefer copy. P Nov 1 (186) $9,500
Anr copy. 2 parts in 1 vol. 4to, contemp vellum; some discoloration. Tp foxed & soiled. pba Sept 14 (306) $475

**Rouquet, J. A.**
— The Present State of the Arts in England. L, 1755. 8vo, half lea; joints & spine ends rubbed. pba Aug 22 (763) $130

**Rouquette, Louis Frederic**
— Le Grand Silence blanc. [Paris], 1928. One of 725. Illus by Clarence A. Gagnon. 4to, orig wraps; backstrip split. wad Oct 18 (219) C$1,200

**Rousseau, Jean Jacques, 1712-78**
See also: Nonesuch Press
— Les Confessions.... Geneva, 1782. 1st Ed. 2 vols. 8vo, contemp calf; corners rubbed, wormhole in spine of Vol II. Fuerstenberg - Schaefer copy. S Dec 8 (547) £550
— Discours sur l'origine et les fondemens de l'inegalite parmi les hommes. Amst., 1755. 1st Ed. 8vo, contemp calf; bds showing at edges, spine head chipped, pastedown with partially removed label. Minor foxing & soiling. pba June 20 (287) $1,700

— Emile, ou de l'education. "A La Haye: Chez Jean Neaulme," 1762. 4 vols. 8vo, contemp mor gilt. With 5 plates. Some leaves spotted. Fuerstenberg - Schaefer copy. S Dec 8 (544) £7,800
— Lettres de deux amants, habitants d'une petite ville.... Amst., 1761. 6 vols. 12mo, contemp calf; stamp on flyleaves. With 12 plates. Fuerstenberg - Schaefer copy. S Dec 8 (546) £1,700
— Oeuvres. Londres [but Brussels], 1774-83. 12 vols. 4to, contemp calf gilt; spines scuffed, some chipping to spines. With port & 37 plates by Moreau le Jeune & Le Barbier. Some browning, ocasionally heavy. C Nov 29 (135) £950

Anr copy. Plate vol only. Mor gilt by Smeers; scuffed, upper hinge with small split. With port & 37 plates by Moreau le Jeune & Le Barbier. Bound in are 3 additional ports & 11 ptd titles from the works. C June 26 (205) £1,300

Anr Ed. Geneva, 1782. 15 vols, including 3 vol Supplement. 4to, early 19th-cent mor gilt. Some browning. Extra-illus with plates. ALs to the marquise de Crequi inserted. Fuerstenberg - Schaefer copy. S Dec 8 (542) £6,500

Anr Ed. Geneva, 1782-89. 17 vols. 4to, contemp calf; spines chipped, rubbed, pieces of lea lacking. S June 12 (114) £950

**Rousselet, Louis**
— India and its Native Princes.... NY, 1876. 4to, modern half cloth, with orig elephant gilt from orig front cover retained. sg Mar 7 (323) $200

**Rousset de Missy, Jean.** See: Dumont & Rousset de Missy

**Rouveyre, Andre**
— Repli. Paris, 1947. One of 370. Illus by Henri Matisse. 4to, unsewn in orig wraps. wad Oct 18 (323) C$2,200

**Roux de Rochelle, Jean Baptiste Gaspard**
— Estados-Unidos de America. Mexico, 1841. ("Estados Unidos de Norte America.") 8vo, half sheep. With folding map & 96 plates. Some foxing. bbc Dec 18 (552) $210

**Rouyer, Eugene**
— L'Art architectural en France.... Paris, 1867-66. 2 vols. Contemp half mor; rubbed, Vol II spine reinforced with tape, hinges reinforced. With 195 (of 200) plates. cb Oct 17 (47) $180

**Rowan, John J.**
— The Emigrant and Sportsman in Canada. L, 1876. 8vo, cloth; worn. O Oct 10 (234) $350

**Rowe, Elizabeth, 1674-1737**
— Poems on Several Occasions. L, 1696. 8vo, later mor gilt; extremities worn, spine ends def, hinges cracked. Some foxing. cb Feb 14 (2745) $225

**Rowe, George**
— Forty-Eight Views of Cottages and Scenery at Sidmouth, Devon. Sidmouth: John Wallis [1826]. Oblong 4to, contemp half mor gilt. With 48 plates on india paper mtd. Some spotting. S Mar 28 (62) £550
— Linton & Lynmouth. Cheltenham: G. Rowe, [1825]]. Oblong 4to, contemp half mor; worn. With 25 plates. All plates loose, some frayed, 2 torn; some soiling. S Mar 28 (63) £360
— Picturesque Scenery of Hastings.... Hastings: P. M. Powell, [c.1820]. Oblong 4to, 19th-cent half mor. With 24 plates, 6 of them colored. S Mar 28 (64) £280

**Rowell, Galen A.**
— The Vertical World of Yosemite. Berkeley: Wilderness Press, [1974]. In dj. pba Feb 12 (144) $50

**Rowell, George S.**
— The Great Raid. Presque Isle, 1874. 12mo, later mor. With 3 woodcut plates. Frontis backed & restored; some soiling. O Feb 6 (199) $2,200

**Rowland, Daniel**
— An Historical and Genealogical Account of the Noble Family of Nevill. L, 1830. Folio, contemp half mor; joints rubbed. Inscr to G. N. Nevill, 1831. Ck Apr 12 (2) £480

**Rowland, Kate Mason**
— The Life of Charles Carroll of Carrollton, 1737-1832. NY & L, 1898. One of 750. 2 vols. 8vo, orig cloth. wa Feb 29 (433) $130

**Rowlands, Henry**
— Mona Antiqua Restaurata, an Archaeological Discourse...of the Isle of Anglesey. L, 1766. 2d Ed. 4to, contemp calf; corners bumped, rebacked. With map & 12 plates. Browned. bba May 30 (404) £70 [Classic Bindings]

Anr copy. Half calf; needs rebdg. Dampstained at beginning. sg Mar 7 (324) $100

**Rowlandson, Thomas, 1756-1827**
— Loyal Volunteers of London & Environs.... L: Ackermann, 1798-99. 4to, lev gilt by Morrell. With engraved hand-colored title & 86 hand-colored plates, some heightened with silver & gold. sg Apr 18 (178) $6,500

**Rowley, William, 1742?-1806**
— The Translation into English of the Principal References to the Sixty-Six Anatomical Plates of the Latin Edition of Schola Medicinae Universalis Nova.... L, 1796. 4to, contemp wraps; needs rebacking. Stain in lower inner corner of front cover & title. sg May 16 (491) $110

**Rowse, A. L.** See: Onassis copy, Jacqueline Bouvier Kennedy

**Rowson, Susanna Haswell**
— Charlotte. A Tale of Truth. Harrisburg, 1801. 2 vols in 1. Contemp calf; lacking front free endpaper. pba June 20 (288) $100

## ROXBURGHE

**Roxburghe Club—London**
— Elton Manorial Records 1279-1351. 1946. bba May 9 (101) £160 [Lam]
BARKER, NICOLAS. - Bibliotheca Lindesiana. L, 1977. 4to, orig cloth; worn. sg Apr 11 (31) $50
ROTZ, JOHN. - The Maps and Text of the Boke of Idrography.... 1981. CE June 15 (300) $300
SCOTTOWE, JOHN. - Alphabet Books. 1974. O Mar 26 (12) $100
SKELTON, RALEIGH ASHLIN & SUMMERSON, JOHN. - A Description of Maps and Architectural Drawings. 1971. CE June 15 (302) $150
WORMALD, FRANCIS. - An Early Breton Gospel Book. 1977. bba May 9 (110) £100 [Lam]

**Roxby, Robert**
— The Lay of the Reedwater Minstrel... By a Son of Reed. Newcastle, 1809. 4to, bdg not described. Bound at end is a single sheet, Hotspur: a Ballad...By Mr. William Richardson. Sgd. b Dec 5 (289) £85

**Roy, Claude**
— La France de profil. Lausanne, 1952. Illus by Paul Strand. 4to, wraps, in dj. sg Feb 29 (312) $250

**Roy, William, 1726-90**
— The Military Antiquities of the Romans in Britain. L, 1793. 1st Ed. Folio, half russia; rebacked. With 51 plates. b Sept 20 (319) £140

**Royal...**
See also: Stevens, Capt. John
— The Royal Navy; in a Series of Illustrations.... Portsmouth, 1881. Intro by Francis Elgar. 2 vols in 1. 4to, orig pictorial cloth. With 49 color plates. pn Dec 7 (125) £680

**Royal Artillery...**
— The Royal Artillery War Commemoration Book. L, 1920. Folio, lev gilt by Zaehnsdorf. pba Nov 30 (333) $140

**Royal Society of London**
— Philosophical Transactions....Abridged. L, 1738-41. ("Memoirs... being a New Abridgment....") 10 vols. 8vo, contemp sheep gilt; worn, covers detached or starting. Sold w.a.f. sg May 16 (245) $250

**Royal Swedish Academy of Sciences**
— Abhandlungen, aus der Naturlehre, Hausaltungskunst und Mechanik.... Hamburg & Leipzig, 1749-72. Vols 1-31. 8vo, contemp calf; rubbed. Sold w.a.f. Christian Horrebow's set. Madsen set. S Mar 14 (311) £720

**Royall, Anne**
— Sketches of History, Life, and Manners in the United States. By a Traveller. New Haven, 1826. 12mo, 19th-cent half sheep; worn. sg Oct 26 (328) $200

**Royce, C. C.**
— John Bidwell, Pioneer, Statesman, Philanthropist.... Chico, 1906-07. One of 100. 2 vols in 1. 8vo, half mor. With frontis port. Larson copy. pba Sept 28 (318) $650

## AMERICAN BOOK PRICES CURRENT

**Royce, Sarah**
— A Frontier Lady: Recollections of the Gold Rush and Early California. New Haven, 1932. 1st Ed. - Ed by Ralph Henry Gabriel. Orig cloth. With 1 map. Larson copy. pba Sept 28 (660) $95

**Royer, Louis Charles**
— Vaudou Roman de Moeurs Martiniquaises. Paris, 1944. Ltd Ed. 4to, orig wraps. With title vignette & 8 plates colored through stencil. ALs loosely inserted. bba May 9 (186) £75 [Collins]

**Ruano Llopis, Carlos**
— Mi Tauromaquia. Mexico City, 1943. One of 1,000. 4to, calf. pba June 20 (226) $100

**Rubens, Peter Paul, 1577-1640**
— La Gallerie du Palais de Luxembourg. Paris, 1710. Folio, calf. With port, engraved title & 24 plates. 2 plates browned. Fuerstenberg - Schaefer copy. S Dec 8 (550) £1,150
Anr copy. Contemp calf; worn. Lacking 4 plates. Fuerstenberg - Schaefer copy. S Dec 8 (551) £380
Anr copy. With engraved title, port & 24 plates, 3 of them double-page. S Apr 23 (250) £1,300

**Rubin, William S.**
— Dada, Surrealism, and their Heritage. NY: Museum of Modern Art, [1968]. 4to, cloth, in dj. wa Dec 14 (550) $80

**Rubner, Max**
— Die Gesetze des Energieverbrauchs bei der Ernaehrung. Leipzig & Vienna, 1902. 1st Ed. 8vo, contemp cloth. Inscr. Ck Mar 22 (259) £100

**Rucellai, Giovanni, 1475-1525**
— Le Api. [Florence], 1539. 8vo, 19th-cent half lea. C Apr 3 (196) £1,900

**Ruda, Jeffrey**
— Fra Filippo Lippi. NY, 1993. 4to, cloth, in dj. sg Jan 11 (258) $60

**Rudbeck, Olof, the Younger**
— Book of Birds. A Facsimile of the Original Watercolors...in the Leufsta Collection in Uppsala University Library. Stockholm, 1986. One of 500. Folio, orig cloth. With 165 color plates. b Sept 20 (490) £140

**Rudder, Samuel, d.1801**
— A New History of Gloucestershire. Cirencester, 1779. Folio, modern cloth. With 18 plates. Lacking map; tp reinforced with tape. bba Nov 1 (87) £380 [Spake]

**Ruding, Walt**
— An Evil Motherhood: An Impressionist Novel. L, 1896. 1st Ed, 1st State, with suppressed frontis by Aubrey Beardsley. 8vo, pictorial cloth. S Nov 2 (69) £240 [Zioni]

## Ruemann, Arthur
See also: Lanckoronska & Ruemann
— Alte Deutsche Kinderbuecher. Vienna, 1937. 8vo, orig cloth. sg Apr 11 (78) $90
— Das illustrierte Buch des XIX. Jahrhunderts in England, Frankreich, und Deutschland, 1790-1860. Leipzig, 1930. 4to, orig cloth; spine rubbed. sg Apr 11 (268) $150

## Rueppell, Eduard, 1794-1884
— Neue Wirbelthiere, zu der Fauna von Abyssinien gehoerig.... Frankfurt, 1835-40. 4 parts in 1 vol. Folio, contemp half mor, orig wraps bound in; worn & soiled. With 95 plates, 80 of them hand-colored. All plates with library blindstamps; some plates spotted; tp soiled & backed. S Nov 30 (43) £3,000

## Ruettimann, Johann
— Das Nordamericanische Bundesstaatsrecht.... Zurich, 1867-76. 2 vols in 3. 8vo, contemp half cloth. pba Apr 25 (232) $160

## Ruggieri, Ferdinando
— Scelta di architetture antiche e moderne della citta di Firenze. Florence, 1755. 4 vols in 2. Folio, 18th-cent half russia gilt. With 4 engraved titles, double-page map of Florence, 3 ports & 279 plates. Minor dust-soiling. S June 27 (287) £5,000
— Sudio d'architettura civile sopra gli ornamenti di porte, e finestre colle misure.... L, 1722-24-28. 3 vols. Folio, contemp sheep gilt; extremities scuffed. With 3 engraved titles, 3 frontises & 237 plates. C Apr 3 (197) £3,000

## Rumford, Benjamin Thompson, Count, 1753-1814
— Essais politiques, economiques et philosophiques.... Geneva, 1799. 8vo, contemp sheep; scuffed. With 6 folding plates. F Mar 28 (470) $100
— Essays, Political, Economical, and Philosophical. L, 1796. 1st Separate Issue. Essay III, Of Food and Drink, only. 8vo, modern vellum; orig wraps bound in. Ck Mar 22 (260) £350

## Runyon, Damon, 1880-1946
— Guys and Dolls. NY, 1931. In repaired dj. Inscr to Doc Morris, Sept 1931. sg June 20 (325) $10,000
— Take It Easy. NY, 1938. In dj rubbed at head of spine. sg June 20 (326) $300

**Rural...** See: Johnson, Richard

## Ruscha, Edward
[-] Edward Ruscha (ed-werd rew-shay) Young Artist. Minneapolis, 1972. 4to, pictorial bds; rubbed, joints starting, front free endpaper & following page detached but present. sg Feb 29 (275) $250
— Every Building on the Sunset Strip. Los Angeles: Pvtly ptd, 1966. 12mo, wraps; spine creased. With folding panorama. wa Feb 1 (283) $130
— Nine Swimming Pools and a Broken Glass. [N.p.]: Pvtly ptd, 1968. 12mo, wraps. wa Feb 1 (284) $65

## Rush's copy, Benjamin
— The Holy Bible. Oxford, 1772. 8vo, contemp mor gilt; rubbed, prelims loose & secured with cellotape. Inscr to his daughter, Ann Emelia, & with AL of presentation. sg Feb 1 (210) $8,000

**Rush, Richard, 1780-1859.** See: Polk's copy, James K.

## Rushdie, Salman
— East, West. L, [1994]. In dj. Sgd on tp. pba Jan 25 (325) $75
— Midnight's Children. L, 1981. In dj. S Dec 18 (418) £130 [Macnamara]
— The Moor's Last Sigh. L, [1995]. One of 200. pba Jan 25 (326) $110
— The Satanic Verses. NY: Viking, [1988]. In dj. pba May 23 (376) $90
— Two Stories. L: Rampant Lions Press, 1989. One of 60. S Dec 18 (346) £400 [Gekoski]

## Rushworth, John, 1612?-90
— Historical Collections. L, 1680-1701. Mixed Ed. 8 vols. Folio, calf; rebacked, library numbers on spine. With 6 ports & 2 folding plates. Vol III lacking prelims including tp & pp. 1333-34. wa Feb 29 (161) $180
— The Tryal of Thomas, Earl of Strafford.... L, 1680. Folio, contemp calf; worn. Lacking last leaf. bba May 30 (86) £130 [Unsworth]

## Ruskin, John, 1819-1900
See also: Fore-Edge Paintings; Stone's copy, Marcus
— The Ethics of the Dust. L, 1866. 8vo, orig cloth. Inscr to Amy Yule. b Jan 31 (219) £90
— The King of the Golden River. L, 1851. 1st Ed. - Illus by Richard Doyle. 4to, mor gilt by the Doves Bindery, 1904, orig wraps bound in. sg Oct 19 (218) $2,200

Anr Ed. L, 1932. One of 570. Illus by Arthur Rackham. Orig vellum gilt. With 4 colored plates. CE May 22 (397) $400

Anr copy. Orig vellum; stained. Some staining. Ck May 31 (165) £90; sg Oct 19 (207) $250

Anr Ed. L: Smith Elder, [n.d.]. Illus by Richard Doyle. 8vo, mor extra by Kelliegram, orig wraps bound in. b May 30 (581) £360
— Modern Painters. L, 1846-60. Vol I only. 4to, seal-skin gilt by the Doves Bindery, 1902. CE Sept 27 (107) $850

Anr Ed. L, 1873. One of 1,000. 5 vols. 4to, orig cloth; backstrips chipped. b Jan 31 (218) £160

Anr copy. Orig cloth; nicked. bba Oct 19 (33) £130 [Astill]

Anr Ed. Orpington, 1888. 6 vols, including Index. 4to, contemp cloth; bumped. L.p. copy. S Apr 23 (141) £180

2d Ed in small form. Orpington & L, 1898. 6 vols. 8vo, half calf; extremities worn & scuffed. Some foxing. cb Oct 17 (687) $550

Anr Ed. L, [c.1900]. 5 vols. 8vo, half calf gilt; rubbed. sg Sept 21 (40) $200
— Notes on Some of the Principal Pictures of Sir John Everett Millais, exhibited at the Grosvenor Gallery,

## RUSKIN

1886. L, [1886]. 8vo, lev gilt by Charles McLeish, 1914. L.p. copy. C May 1 (142) £300
— Notes on the Construction of Sheepfolds. L, 1851. 8vo, contemp calf gilt by Mansell. Tp soiled & torn. S Apr 23 (144) £220
— Sesame and Lilies. East Aurora: Roycroft Shop, 1897. One of 40 hand-illuminated & sgd by Elbert Hubbard. 8vo, mor extra by L. Broca. wd May 8 (39) $550
— The Stones of Venice. L, 1873-74. New Ed, one of 1,500. 3 vols. 8vo, orig cloth. bba Oct 19 (34) £150 [Ulysses]
— Works. L, [various pbrs], 1886-85. 36 works in 41 vols. 8vo & 4to, white mor gilt by William Mansell, specially bound by Ruskin for Kate Greenaway. Inscr in 5 vols to Kate Greenaway. S Dec 18 (203) £5,800 [Cann]
Illustrated Sterling Ed. Bost., [c.1890]. 13 vols. 8vo, contemp half calf gilt. sg Sept 21 (41) $650
Library Ed. L, 1903-12. Ed by E. T. Cook & A. Wedderburn. 39 vols. Half mor. cb Oct 17 (295) $4,500

**Russell, Alexander, 1715?-68**
— The Natural History of Aleppo.... L, 1794. 2d Ed. 2 vols. 4to, contemp calf gilt; worn, 1 cover detached. With map & 19 plates, 6 of them folding. Minor soiling; 1st gathering of Vol II loose. pn Dec 7 (168) £750
1st Ed. L, 1856 [but 1756]. 4to, contemp calf; covers detached. With 13 (of 17) plates. Tp stamped. sg Mar 7 (325) $375

**Russell, Bertrand, 3rd Earl, 1872-1970.** See: Whitehead & Russell

**Russell, C. E. M.**
— Bullet and Shot in Indian Forest.... L, 1900. 2d Ed. 8vo, orig cloth; worn. Some foxing. O Oct 10 (237) $225

**Russell, Charles Marion, 1864-1926**
— Back-Trailing on the Old Frontiers. Great Falls, MT, 1922. 1st Ed. Orig wraps; extremities worn. Robbins copy. pba Mar 21 (309) $500
— Forty Pen and Ink Drawings. Pasadena, [1947]. One of 1,000. Cloth, in dj. pba July 25 (345) $110
— Good Medicine. Garden City, 1930. 1st Trade Ed. - Intro by Will Rogers. In soiled dj. Robbins copy. pba Mar 21 (310) $325
— More Rawhides. Great Falls, 1925. 1st Ed. 4to, orig wraps; chipped & torn. Inscr & with a sketch by Russell. pba July 25 (346) $950
— Paper Talk: Illustrated Letters.... Fort Worth: Amon Carter Museum, [1962]. Folio, pictorial bds, in mylar dj. Sgd by the Ed, Frederic G. Renner. ds July 27 (171) $100
— Rawhide Rawlins Rides Again.... Pasadena: Trail's End, [1948]. One of 300. Calf. Robbins copy. pba Mar 21 (311) $850
— Rawhide Rawlins Stories. Pasadena: Trail's End, 1946. 4to, pictorial cloth, in dj. pba Apr 25 (637) $50

— Trails Plowed Under. Garden City, 1927. pba Apr 25 (638) $75

**Russell, Frank**
— Explorations in the Far North.... Iowa: Published by the University, 1898. 4to, orig ptd wraps; chipped, spine repaired with tape. With 21 photographic plates & folding map. pba Apr 25 (644) $110

**Russell, John, Writer on Art**
— Ben Nicholson: Drawings, Paintings and Reliefs, 1911-1968. L, 1969. One of 60 with orig sgd etching. 4to, orig cloth, in dj. pn Dec 7 (75) £600

**Russell, John Scott, 1808-82**
— The Modern System of Naval Architecture. L, 1865. 3 vols. Folio, orig half mor; sides spotted, upper hinge of Vol I partly split. With frontis & 167 plates. S June 27 (273) £1,900

**Russell, Osborne**
— Journal of a Trapper, or Nine Years in the Rocky Mountains.... Portland, 1955. 3d Ed, One of 750. Ed by Aubrey L. Haines. Robbins copy. pba Mar 21 (314) $90

**Russell, Sir William Howard, 1820-1907**
— My Diary, North and South. NY, 1863. 8vo, orig cloth; worn & soiled. wa Dec 14 (75) $170

**Russia**
— Oude en Nieuwe Staat van 't Russiche of Moskovische Keizerryk.... Utrecht, 1744. 2 vols. 4to, orig bds; rubbed & soiled. With half-title, 4 titles, 4 folding maps, & 5 plates. Some browning. S Oct 26 (296) £250 [Anderson]

**Russians...**
— The Russians in California. San Francisco: California Historical Society, 1933. 1st Ed. With 2 plates (1 color), 1 sketch, 1 view, & folding facsimile map. pba Feb 21 (161) $50
Anr copy. Robbins copy. pba Mar 21 (315) $160

**Russoli, Franco**
— Marino Marini: Paintings and Drawings. NY, 1963. 4to, cloth, in dj. wa Feb 1 (358) $50

**Rutherforth, Thomas, 1712-71**
— A System of Natural Philosophy.... Cambr., 1748. 2 vols. 4to, contemp calf; worn, front covers detached. pba Oct 9 (17) $160
Anr copy. Contemp calf gilt; worn. With folding map & 31 folding plates. Some browning & staining; some corners wormed towards end of Vol II; half-title creased in Vol I. S Mar 14 (313) £160

**Rutherston, Albert.** See: Drinkwater & Rutherston

**Ruttenber, Edward M.**
— History of the County of Orange.... Phila., 1821. ("History of Orange County, New York....") 4to, orig half lea. Tp repaired. NH July 21 (273) $110

**Rutter, Owen, 1889-1944.** See: Golden Cockerel Press

**Rutty, John.** See: Wight & Rutty

**Ruxton, George Frederick**
— Adventures in Mexico and the Rocky Mountains. L, 1847. 1st Ed. 16mo, Orig cloth; rear joint split, hinges cracked. Robbins copy. pba Mar 21 (316) $450

1st American Ed. NY, 1848. Orig cloth; some wear & staining. Contents dampstained. pba Apr 25 (645) $75

— Life in the Far West. NY, 1849. 1st American Ed. 8vo, orig cloth; shelf wear. Foxed. Robbins copy. pba Mar 21 (317) $325

**Ruzicka, Rudolph.** See: Grolier Club

**Ryan, William Redmond**
— Personal Adventures in Upper and Lower California in 1848-9.... L, 1850. 1st Ed. 2 vols. 12mo, orig cloth; rebacked. With 23 plates. Larson copy. pba Sept 28 (662) $2,250

Anr copy. Modern cloth. With 23 plates. Some foxing & marginal staining; pp. 309-10 with top corner torn off. pba Nov 16 (235) $275

Anr copy. Orig cloth; recased. With 23 plates (3 color). Robbins copy. pba Mar 21 (318) $3,250

**Rycaut, Sir Paul**
— Die Neu-eroeffnete Ottomannische Pforte.... Augsburg, 1694. 1st German Ed. Folio, contemp calf; worn. With frontis. D1 torn; small hole in i2i4. S Oct 26 (199) £400 [Finopoulos]

**Rychkov, Nikolai Petrovich, 1746-84**
— Dnevnyia zapiski puteshestviia v Kirgis-kaisatskoi stepe. St. Petersburg, 1772. Bound with: Prodolzhenie zhurnala ili dnevnykh zapisok. St. Petersburg, 1772. 4to, later half calf gilt; rubbed, lower hinge split. L.p. copy. C May 31 (109) £950

**Ryder, Hugh**
— New Practical Observations in Surgery.... L, 1685. 8vo, contemp calf; worn & loose. Some soiling & marginal tears; hole in C7 affecting letters. C June 26 (207) £1,000

**Ryff, Walther Hermann**
— New Kochbuech fuer die Kranken. Frankfurt: Christian Egenolff, 1545. 1st Ed. 4to, early 20th-Cent half calf. With hand-colored title vignette. 1st 8 leaves dampstained; some thumb soiling. Ck Mar 22 (262) £4,000

— Spiegel und Regiment der Gesundheit. Frankfurt: Christian Egenolff, 1544. 1st Ed. 4to, early 20th-Cent half calf; extrems rubbed. With hand-colored title vignette. Title soiled; outer margins frayed & limp; laminated paper repair to margin of f1; k1v with ink stain. Ck Mar 22 (263) £1,600

**Rymill, John**
— Southern Lights. NY & L, 1939. 1st American Ed. 4to, orig cloth, in worn dj; lower corner of front cover bumped. pba July 25 (60) $130

**Rymsdyk, John & Andrew van**
— Museum Britannicum. L, 1778. Folio, contemp half sheep; extremities worn, needs rebacked. Tp & some plates stamped. sg May 16 (342) $225

# S

**Sa, Jose Antonio de**
— Dissertacoes Philosophico-Politicas sobre o Trato das Sedas na Comarca de Moncorvo. Lisbon: Academia Real das Ciencias, 1787. 4to, contemp sheep; wear along front joint & top of front cover. sg May 16 (346) $80

**Saavedra Fajardo, Diego de, 1584-1648**
— Idea principis christiano-politici.... Pest: J. G. Mauss, 1748. Folio, contemp mor gilt with arms of Emperor Francis I. Some foxing & staining. Schaefer copy. P Nov 1 (187) $2,600

**Sabartes, Jaime**
— Les Menines et la Vie. Paris, [1958]. Illus by Pablo Picasso. 4to, pictorial bds; joints starting. One plate wrinkled. sg Jan 11 (355) $50

— Picasso: Toreros. L & Monte Carlo, 1961. Oblong 4to, orig cloth, in dj. With 4 lithos, 1 colored. CE Sept 27 (225) $500; sg Sept 7 (276) $425; sg Sept 7 (277) $475; sg Sept 7 (278) $425

**Sabbatini, Luigi Antonio**
— Elementi teorici della musica. Rome, 1798-90. 3 vols in 1. Oblong 4to, contemp half vellum. Old stamp on tp; some worming in table 2; some staining & browning. S Dec 1 (303) £520

**Sabin, Arthur K.** See: Hardie & Sabin

**Sabin, Edward Legrand**
— Kit Carson Days.... Chicago, 1914. 1st Ed. 8vo, orig cloth; extremities worn, front hinge cracked. With frontis port. Larson copy. pba Sept 28 (351) $160

Anr Ed. NY, 1935. Illus by Howard Simon. 2 vols. Robbins copy. pba Mar 21 (319) $100

**Sabin, Joseph, 1821-81**
— A Dictionary of Books Relating to America. Amst., 1961-62. ("Bibliotheca Americana: A Dictionary of Books....") 29 vols in 15. bba Oct 5 (397) £440 [Israel]; bba May 9 (102) £320 [Maggs]

Min-Print Ed. NY, [1967]. 29 vols in 2. 4to, orig cloth. sg Apr 11 (269) $450

Mini-Print Ed. 29 vols in 2. Oblong 4to, orig cloth. bbc Feb 26 (204) $325

Anr copy. Tp wrinkled. ds July 27 (175) $275; sg Oct 26 (329) $425

**Sabine, Lorenzo, 1803-77**
— Notes on Duels and Duelling.... Bost., 1856. 8vo, modern mor gilt. sg Mar 7 (526) $150

**Sack, Albert von, Baron**
— A Narrative of a Voyage to Surinam.... L, 1810. 4to, cloth. Met Sept 28 (366) $225

## Sackville-West, Victoria, 1892-1962
— Nursery Rhymes. L: Dropmore Press, 1947. 1st Ed, one of 550. 4to, orig cloth, in rubbed dj. sg Dec 14 (251) $100

## Sacramento...
— Sacramento Illustrated: A Reprint of the Original Edition Issued by Barber & Baker in 1855. Sacramento: Sacramento Book Collectors Club, 1950. One of 300. pba Apr 25 (647) $150

## Sacranus, Johannes
— Elucidarius errorum ritus Ruthenici. [Cracow: Johannes Haller, c.1506]. 4to, mor gilt; scratched, joints worn, vaulted. 36 leaves; Gothic types; full-page woodcut on A1r.. Dyson Perrins - Broxbourne - Schaefer copy. P Nov 1 (188) $3,250

## Sacrobosco, Johannes
— Annotationi sopra la lettione della Spera del Sacro Bosto.... Florence, 1550. 4to, 19th-cent half calf. Some browning. b June 28 (59) £900
— Sphaera mundi. Venice: Johannes Lucilius Santritter & Hieronymus de Sanctis, 31 Mar 1488. 4to, modern mor by Leighton; joints & extremities scuffed. 35 lines; roman letter; 1st paragraph on A2r ptd in red; woodcut of an armillary sphere on A4v; woodcut diagrams, including several partly ptd in colors. 69 leaves. Goff J-407. C Nov 29 (70) £2,400

Anr copy. Contemp calf over wooden bds; 1 clasp renewed, some wear to spine. 35 lines; types 5:82R, 10:65G & 24bis:55G. With 2 full-page woodcuts & many diagrams, 8 of them ptd in colors. A1 & A8 supplied from shorter copy; some leaves loose; some staining. 69 leaves. Goff J-407. C Apr 3 (199) £1,600

Anr Ed. Venice: [Bonetus Locatellus] for Octavianus Scotus, 4 Oct 1490. 4to, recent vellum bds. 41 lines; types 6:105R & 5:80R. Ms notes, thos on tp washed; some marginal stains. 48 leaves. Goff J-409. S June 27 (335) £3,800

Anr Ed. Antwerp, 1543. ("Libellus de sphaera.") 8vo, contemp calf with large panel stamp; rebacked, worn & loose. Lacking volvelles & prefaces by Melanchthon, whose name is obliterated from titles. Sold w.a.f. sg May 16 (247) $300
— Sphera volgare novamente tradotta.... Venice: B. Zanetti, 1537. Trans by Marco Mauro. 4to, modern vellum. Without errata leaf; 1 letter trimmed from illust heading on last leaf. b June 28 (43) £1,500

Anr copy. Mor gilt by Lortic. Lacking the errata & a volvelle part. Church copy. C Nov 29 (69) £1,000

## Sade, Donatien Alphonse Francois, Marquis de, 1740-1814
— Justine.... Hollande: chez les libraires associes, 1791. 2 vols in 1. 8vo, contemp calf gilt; upper joints cracked & repaired, corners rubbed, spine head chipped. Fuerstenberg - Schaefer copy. S Dec 8 (553) £10,500
— La Philosophie dans le boudoir.... Londres: aux depens de la Compagnie, 1795. 2 vols. 18mo, early bds. With frontis & 4 plates. b May 30 (535) £2,900

## Sadeler, Marco
— Vestigi delle antichita di Roma... Rome, 1660. Oblong folio, contemp half calf; spine def. With engraved title & dedication & 49 plates. Stain to 1 plate; some spotting. b Sept 20 (170) £650

## Sadie, Stanley
— The New Grove Dictionary of the Opera. L: Macmillan, 1994. 4 vols. pba Mar 7 (227) $425

## Sadleir, Michael, 1888-1957
— Daumier, the Man and the Artist. L, 1924. One of 100. 4to, cloth; worn, cracked, discolored. O May 7 (267) $70
— XIX Century Fiction. A Bibliographical Record. L, 1951. One of 1,025. 2 vols. 4to, orig cloth, Vol II in dj. Inscr to Cecil & Woodham, Feb 1951. b Jan 31 (40) £150

Anr copy. Orig cloth, in frayed djs. O Mar 26 (240) $150

Anr Ed. Cambr. MA: Martino, [n.d.]. One of 350. 2 vols. 4to, orig cloth; some wear. O May 7 (268) $50

## Sagan, Francoise
— Toxique. Paris, 1964. Illus by Bernard Buffet. 4to, orig wraps; soiled, tear at bottom joint of front cover. sg June 13 (67) $250

## Sage, Dean
— The Ristigouche and its Salmon Fishing.... Goshen: Angler's & Shooter's Press, 1973. One of 250. 4to, mor gilt. O June 25 (224) $650

## Sage, Rufus B.
— Scenes in the Rocky Mountains.... Phila., 1846. 1st Ed. 12mo, orig cloth; extremities worn, recased. With folding frontis map Map torn & repaired. Robbins copy. pba Mar 21 (320) $5,500

## Saggi...
— Saggi di naturali esperienze.... Florence, 1667. Bound with: Riccioli, Giambattista. Geographicae crucis fabrica et usus. Bologna: G. B. Ferroni, 1643. Folio, 18th-cent calf gilt with arms of Calori-Stremiti of Modena; repaired. S Mar 14 (7) £2,500

2d Ed. Florence, 1691. Folio, later vellum; lower cover marked. With port & 74 plates. Hole in lower margin of V3. S Mar 14 (8) £700

## Sagra, Ramon de la
— Album d'oiseaux de l'Ile de Cuba. Paris, 1842-43. Folio, modern half mor. With 33 hand-colored plates. Blindstamp on plates; Spanish title backed; lacking Spanish half-title; some foxing, mainly to text. S Nov 30 (15) £1,600
— Histoire physique, politique et naturelle de l'Ile de Cuba. Paris: A. Bertrand, [1839]. 2 vols in 1. Folio, crude bd bdg. With 40 hand-colored plates. Some dampstaining & foxing. Met May 22 (450) $1,200

## Sahagon, Bernardino de, 1499?-1590
— Historia general de las cosas de Nueva Espana.... Mexico, 1829-30. 3 vols. 4to, contemp half roan; vols I & II spines def; vol III rebacked, old spine laid down. With 1 folding plate. Bibliotheca Lindesiana copy. S Oct 26 (525) £480 [Dalleggio]

## Saincts Devoirs...
— Les Saincts Devoirs de l'ame devote. Paris: Coulon, 1645. 8vo, contemp mor gilt attributed to Le Gascon. O Mar 5 (96) $600

## Sainsbury, John
— Catalogue of the Napoleon Museum. [N.p., 1843]. 16 pp, ptd on pink paper, 8vo, creased, in lea case. With note by W. N. Sainsbury stating that this copy was used by the Duke of Wellington on 25 May 1843. S May 15 (249) £150

## Saint...
— Saint Chaterine - 25 Novembre 1946. Paris, 1946. 4to, pictorial wraps by Matisse; joints & spine ends def. With color plates by Matisse, Laurencin, Picasso & Berard. sg Sept 7 (240) $150

## Saint German, Christopher
— The Dialogue in English, betweene a Doctor of Divinitie, and a Student in the Lawes of England. L: R. Tottel, 1569. Later calf; worn. Worming with loss; early Ms annotations throughout. S June 12 (151) £240

## Saint-Amand, Marc Antoine Gerard, Sieur de, 1594-1661?
— Le Oeuvres. Paris, 1635. 8vo, later vellum. With title vignette. Dampstained. S Oct 12 (68) £300

## Sainte-Marthe, Scevole de
— La Maniere de nourrir les enfans a la mammelle. Paris, 1698. 8vo, contemp red mor gilt with arms of Paulin Prondre de Guermantes et de Bussy; spine repaired. Some leaves browned. Fuerstenberg - Schaefer copy. S Dec 8 (568) £400

— Paedotrophia; or the Art of Nursing and Rearing Children.... L, 1797. 8vo, modern calf gilt. sg May 16 (492) $225

## Saint-Exupery, Antoine de, 1900-44
— Le Petit Prince. NY: Reynal & Hitchcock, [1943]. One of 260. In soiled dj. pba June 20 (290) $1,800

— Terre des hommes. Paris: Gallimard, [1939]. 1st Ed, One of 36 with double suite of plates. Loose as issued in orig wraps, prints in separate ptd folder. bbc Dec 18 (342) $200

— Wind, Sand and Stars. NY, [1939]. Half cloth. Inscr to Julie Aulick. CE May 22 (413) $1,400

## Saint-Foix, Germain Francois Poullain de
— Oeuvres. Paris: veuve Duchesne, 1778. 6 vols. 8vo, red mor gilt by Bozerian. Some spotting. Fuerstenberg - Schaefer copy. S Dec 8 (554) £1,900

## Saint-Gelais, Mellin de, 1491-1558
— Ouevres poetiques. Paris, 1719. 18mo, contemp mor gilt. Fuerstenberg - Schaefer copy. S Dec 8 (555) £80

## Saint-Lambert, Jean Francois de
— Les Saisons, poeme. Amst., 1769. 8vo, contemp calf gilt. With 5 plates. Fuerstenberg - Schaefer copy. S Dec 8 (556) £160

Anr Ed. Paris, 1796. 4to, contemp mor gilt. With 4 plates. Stamp of Russian Imperial Library on tp. Fuerstenberg - Schaefer copy. S Dec 8 (559) £650

## Saint-Martin, Michel de
— Moiens faciles et eprouves, dont Monsieur de l'Orme.... Caen, 1682. 1st Ed. Part I (of 2) only. 12mo in half sheets, contemp vellum; soiled, recased. Title frail; ownership inscr cut away; early leaves margins affected by damp; dampstain from 3Z to end; A3 & 2K2 torn. Ck Mar 22 (264) £65

## Saint-Non, Jean Claude Richard de
— Recueil de griffonis, de vues, paysages, fragments antiques.... [Paris, c.1791?]. Folio, contemp half mor; partly misbound. With title & 156 leaves of plates. Fuerstenberg - Schaefer copy. S Dec 8 (563) £6,000

— Voyage pittoresque ou description des royaumes de Naples et de Sicile. Paris, 1781-86. 4 vols in 5. Folio, disbound. With all plates, including the priapic plate & the 14 plates of doubles medailles; the illusts of vases are in color. Foxing to 1 plate; 1 plate bound upside down. C Oct 25 (145) £7,500

Anr copy. Contemp red mor gilt by Derome le jeune, with his ticket. With 306 plates before letters, maps & plans. Some spotting. Fuerstenberg - Schaefer copy. S Dec 8 (561) £21,000

## Saint-Real, Cesar Vichard, Abbe de
— Histoire de la conjuration des espagnols contre la republique de Venise.... Paris, 1795. One of 5 on vellum. Folio, contemp half lea. Fuerstenberg - Schaefer copy. S Dec 8 (567) £1,600

## Saint-Sauveur, Hector
— Les Beaux Jardins de France. Paris, [1926]. Folio, loose as issued in half cloth folder. With 44 photographic plates. sg Sept 7 (211A) $250

## Saintsbury, George
— Specimens of English Prose Style from Malory to Macaulay. L, 1885. One of 50 L.p. copies. 8vo, lev extra exhibition bdg by Zaehnsdorf. sg Oct 19 (219) $550

## Saint-Victor, Jacques M. B. Bins de
— Tableau historique et pittoresque de Paris.... Paris, 1808-11. 1st Ed. Vol I (of 3). Contemp sheep; needs rebdg. With 59 plates. Some foxing & browning. sg May 9 (369) $200

## Sala, Angelo
— Saccarologia darinnen erstlich von der Natur Qualiteten.... Rostock, 1637. 1st Ed. 8vo, later bds. 3 leaves dampstained. Ck Mar 22 (265) £900

## SALA

**Sala, George Augustus, 1828-95**
— William Hogarth, Painter, Engraver, Philosopher. L, 1866. 1 vol in 2. Folio, contemp mor gilt by Mansell. Extra-illus with 191 ports & views selected by Horace Pym & with A Ls s & 3 etchings by Sala. S Apr 23 (251) £800

**Salaman, Malcolm Charles**
— The Etchings of Sir Francis Seymour Haden. L, 1923. One of 200. Folio, half lea gilt. With envelope containing 16 duplicate plates. sg Jan 11 (207) $225

**Sale, William Meritt**
— Samuel Richardson: A Bibliographical Record. New Haven, 1936. O Mar 26 (242) $60

**Salignac de la Mothe, Francois Fenelon de.** See: Fenelon, Francois de Salignac de la Mothe

**Salinas, Francisco**
— De musica libri septem.... Salamanca: Mathias Gast, 1577. Folio, contemp vellum; rebacked retaining part of old spine. Woodcart arms on title (inserted). Some browning & staining; tear in E5. S Dec 1 (306) £4,000

**Salinger, J. D.**
— The Catcher in the Rye. Bost., 1951. 1st Ed. In repaired dj. sg June 20 (328) $950
— Nine Stories. Bost., [1953]. In dj with minor wear & chipping. bbc Dec 18 (343) $275
Anr copy. In chipped dj. CE May 22 (414) $420

**Salk, Jonas**
— Vaccination Against Paralytic Poliomyelitis: Performance and Prospects. [N.p.], 1955. Orig wraps. Inscr to Marshall Bean. rms Nov 30 (293) $400

**Sallengre, Albert Henri de**
— Memoires de literature. The Hague, 1715-17. 2 vols in 4. 8vo, contemp half calf; spines chipped & corroded, joints broken. O Mar 26 (243) $80

**Sallustius Crispus, Caius, 86-34 B.C.**
— Opera. Venice: Joannes Tacuinus de Tridino, 20 July 1500. Folio, 19th-cent calf. 61 lines of commentary & headline; roman letter. Woodcut on tp; a few initials colored. Inner margins of 1st few leaves repaired with edge loss; tear in margin repaired with minor loss; dampstained throughout; some worming at beginning. 113 (of 114) leaves; lacking final blank. Goff S-85. S Dec 18 (80) £550 [Quaritch]
Anr Ed. Paris: Vivant, 1539. ("De la guerre que les romains feirent a lencontre de Iugurtha....") 8vo, 19th-cent mor gilt. S June 12 (116) £280
Anr Ed. Madrid: Ibarra, 1772. ("La Conjuracion de Catalina y la guerra de Jugurta.") Folio, contemp mor extra by P. Carsi y Vidal; spine ends repaired. Fuerstenberg - Schaefer copy. S Dec 8 (569) £8,500
Anr copy. Contemp mor gilt with onlays; rubbed & stained. Fuerstenberg - Schaefer copy. S Dec 8 (570) £2,600

## AMERICAN BOOK PRICES CURRENT

**Salmon, Andre**
— Le Manuscrit trouve dans un chapeau. Paris, 1919. One of 750. Illus by Pablo Picasso. 4to, orig wraps. sg Sept 14 (296) $650
Anr copy. Later half sheep, orig front wrap bound in. sg Feb 15 (231) $200

**Salmon, Joseph Whittingham**
— Moral Reflections in Verse.... Nantwich, 1796. 8vo, orig bds; worn. Inscr to Mrs. Cooper. b Dec 5 (52) £100

**Salmon, Richard**
— Trout Flies. NY, 1975. One of 589. 4to, lea gilt. With mtd samples of fly-tying materials. O June 25 (233) $190

**Salmon, Thomas, 1679-1767**
— Modern History. L, 1739. 3 vols. 4to, contemp calf; joints cracked, worn. End of Vol III dampstained. CE June 15 (295) $1,100
— A New Geographical and Historical Grammar.... L, 1749. 8vo, contemp calf; worn. With 21 folding maps & 1 plate. b Sept 20 (171) £160
Anr Ed. L, 1762. 8vo, contemp sheep; needs rebdg. With 23 folding maps. sg Dec 7 (44) $225
Anr Ed. Edin., 1771. 8vo, calf; worn. With 21 (of 222) folding maps & 2 plates. Lacking frontis map; worming in bottom margin; last few leaves dampstained. NH Sept 16 (210) $270
Anr Ed. L, 1772. 8vo, modern sheep. sg May 9 (100) $550

**Salmon, William, 1644-1713**
— Botanologia. The English Herbal. L, 1710-11. Vol I only. Contemp calf; def, covers & prelims detached. Sold w.a.f. CE May 22 (268) $120
Anr copy. 2 vols in 1. Folio, contemp calf gilt; worn, joints cracked. Lacking the 3-leaf "Index Morborum"; stamp on tp & next leaf. sg Apr 18 (154) $700
— Pharmacopoeia Londinensis, or the New London Dispensatory.... L, 1685. 8vo, contemp calf; spine ends chipped, joints cracked. sg May 16 (493) $350
— Polygraphice; or the Art of Drawing, Engraving.... L, 1675. 3d Ed. 8vo, later half calf; spine partly detached. With port, engraved title & 17 plates. 2 plates repaired. S June 12 (335) £280
"5th" Ed. L, 1685. 8vo, contemp sheep; rebacked retaining orig backstrip. With 16 plates only. Tear to p. 49; last leaf mtd inside rear cover; some soiling & dampstaining. Sold w.a.f. sg Sept 7 (304) $120

**Salmond, J. B.**
— The Story of the R. A..... L, 1956. 1st Ed. - Foreword by Bernard Darwin. In dj; d/j rubbed & torn. pba Apr 18 (152) $130

**Salmony, Alfred, 1890-1958**
— Carved Jade of Ancient China. Berkeley, 1938. 4to, orig cloth; worn. sg June 13 (205) $150

**Salomon, Jacques**
— Vuillard. Paris, 1961. One of 25 with pencil drawing by Vuillard. 4to, unsewn as issued in orig cloth box. Inscr by Salomon. S Nov 21 (391) £800

**Salt, Sir Henry**
— A Voyage to Abyssinia. L, 1814. 4to, contemp calf gilt; rebacked. With 34 plates & charts, 5 of them folding. b May 30 (184) £450

**Salter, Thomas Frederick**
— The Angler's Guide, or Complete London Angler.... L, 1815. ("The Angler's Guide, Being a Complete Practical Treatise....") 2d Ed. 8vo, modern half lea. O Feb 6 (202) $225

3d Ed. 8vo, bds; joints cracking, spine soiling & chipped. Some staining, browning & soiling. O Feb 6 (203) $50

Anr Ed. L, 1833. ("The Angler's Guide, Being a Plain and Complete Practical Treatise....") 8vo, 19th-cent half mor; front joint cracked, library bookplate to front pastedown. Some leaves trimmed. pba July 11 (267) $140

— The Troller's Guide. L, 1820. 12mo, contemp half calf; spine perished. pba July 11 (268) $150

**Salusbury, Thomas**
— Mathematical Collections and Translations in Two Parts. L, 1967. One of 200. Folio, orig calf. sg May 16 (248) $450

**Saluste du Bartas, Guillaume de.** See: Du Bartas, Guillaume de Saluste
— His Devine Weekes and Workes. See: Du Bartas, Guillaume de Saluste

**Salvado, Rudesindo, Bishop**
— Memorias historicas sobre la Australia.... Barcelona, 1853. 8vo, contemp calf; rubbed. With folding map, 2 ports & 12 plates. Some spotting. S Mar 28 (425) £150

**Salvandi, N. A. de**
— De l'Emancipation de Sant Domingue dans ses rapports avec la politique interieure et exterieure de la France. Paris: Chez Ponthieu, 1825. 8vo, modern half lea. Repair to half-title & last leaf. sg Mar 28 (134) $60

**Salverte, Eusebe**
— The Occult Sciences: the Philosophy of Magic.... NY, 1847. 2 vols. 12mo, orig cloth; spine ends chipped. Some foxing. sg May 16 (249) $50

**Saly, Jacques Francois**
— Vasa. A. Se. Inventa Atq. sudii. causa. delin. et incisa D. U. C. Iacobus Saly. Paris, 1746. Folio, contemp calf gilt; corners rubbed, some repairs, lower cover cracked near spine heel. With allegorical tp & 30 plates. Tp with spotting. Fuerstenberg - Schaefer copy. S Dec 8 (571) £8,500

**Salzmann, Christian Gotthilf, 1744-1811**
— Gymnastics for Youth. Phila., 1803. 8vo, contemp sheep; worn, shaken. With 10 plates. Foxed. F June 20 (114) $150

**Sambucus, Joannes, 1531-84**
— Emblemata, cum aliquot nummis antiqui operis. Antwerp: Plantin, 1564. 8vo, 19th-cent mor gilt by Bedford; front cover detached. With port & 166 emblems in text. Schaefer copy. P Nov 1 (189) $2,750

**Samples...**
— Samples. A Collection of Stories.... NY: Boni & Liveright, [1927]. In dj with spine wear. sg Dec 14 (103) $225

**Sampson, John.** See: Gregynog Press

**Sams, William**
— A Tour through Paris. L, [plates watermarked 1827-28]. Folio, contemp half mor gilt; spine def. With 21 hand-colored plates. Soiling at plate margins & on interleaves. S Nov 30 (114) £1,000

Anr copy. 19th-cent half mor; spine ends worn, joints starting. With 21 hand-colored plates. sg Apr 18 (179) $1,500

**Samson, Jack**
— The Grizzly Book. Clinton: Amwell, [1981]. One of 1,000. Illus by Al Barker. sg Mar 7 (527) $80

**Samuels, Edward Augustus, 1836-1908**
— With Fly-Rod and Camera. NY, 1890. 8vo, orig cloth. pba July 11 (269) $140
— With Rod and Gun in New England and the Maritime Provinces. Bost., 1897. pba July 11 (432) $90

**Samwell, David**
— A Narrative of the Death of Captain James Cook. San Francisco: David Magee, 1957. ("Captain Cook and Hawaii.") One of 750. Unopened copy. pba Feb 13 (164) $85

**San Francisco**
— Annual Report of the Board of Health of the City and County of San Francisco. San Francisco, 1898. Orig cloth; spine ends rubbed. pba Nov 16 (28) $160
— Guide Book and Street Manual of San Francisco, California. San Francisco: F. W. Warner, 1882. 12mo, cloth; hinges cracked, worn. Owner's stamp on 1st page. pba Feb 12 (323) $60
— Proceedings of the Friends of a Rail-Road to San Francisco, at the Public Meeting, Held at the U.S. Hotel, in Boston, April 19, 1849.... Bost., 1849. 3d Ed. Orig wraps; worn, soiled & with tear. pba Nov 16 (219) $110
— San Francisco Municipal Reports, 1859-60. San Francisco, 1860. Calf; worn. Some foxing. pba Feb 12 (362) $130
— San Francisco Municipal Reports for the Fiscal Year 1867-8. San Francisco, 1868. Mor gilt presentation bdg to Henry H. Haight; rebacked, with orig spine strip laid on, extremities scuffed. pba Nov 16 (240) $55

— San Francisco Municipal Reports for the Fiscal Year 1871-72. San Francisco, 1872. Cloth. pba Feb 12 (363) $85
— San Francisco Municipal Reports for the Fiscal Year 1886-87. San Francisco, 1887. Orig cloth. With folding map outlined in color. Map repaired. pba Feb 12 (364) $85
GOLDEN GATE PARK. - Second Biennial Report of the San Francisco Park Commissioners, 1872-73. San Francisco, 1874. 8vo, orig wraps; soiled. With 1 plate & 2 folding maps. pba Feb 12 (318) $75
SAN FRANCISCO EARTHQUAKE. - The California Earthquake of April 18, 1906: Report of the State Earthquake Investigation Commission. Wash., 1908. 2 vols in 3 plus Atlas. Orig wraps, Atlas in cloth; Atlas bdg soiled & spine deteriorating. With 145 plates & 3 maps in text vols & 25 maps & 15 seismographs in Atlas. Piece cut from top blank margin of several leaves. pba Feb 12 (286) $1,300
SAN FRANCISCO PRESIDIO. - [Sealed-paper petition of Francisco Rochin, soldier of the Presidio, for discharge because of physical disability. San Francisco, 3 Aug 1831. Single sheet, 12.5 by 8.5 inches. "Earliest sealed-paper to be printed". Larson copy. pba Sept 24 (219) $1,000

**San Francisco Earthquake.** See: San Francisco

**San Francisco Presidio.** See: San Francisco

**San Lazzaro, Giovanni di**
[-] San Lazzaro et ses amis. Hommage au fondateur de la revue XXe siecle. Paris, 1975. One of 500. Folio, loose in orig wraps. With 15 colored plates. cb Feb 14 (2795) $700

**Sanchez, Nellie van de Grift**
— Spanish and Indian Place Names of California.... San Francisco, 1922. 2d Ed. Orig cloth. With news clipping laid in. Inscr by Luisa Vallejo Emparan to Lachryma Montis. Larson copy. pba Sept 28 (216) $50

**Sanctorius, Sanctorius, 1561-1636**
— Medicina Statica. L, 1676. 2d Ed in English. 12mo, old calf; spine worn, joints cracked, covers chipped. With frontis. Ck Mar 22 (269) £350

**Sand, George, 1804-76**
— La Mare au diable. Paris, 1846. 2 vols. 8vo, later mor, 1 set of orig wraps bound in; joints worn. CE May 22 (418) $250
— Works. Phila.: Geo. Barrie, [1910]. ("The Masterpieces of George Sand.") Japan Vellum Ed, one of 1,000. 20 vols. 8vo, mor gilt. cb Oct 17 (296) $2,750

**Sandburg, Carl, 1878-1967**
— Abraham Lincoln: The War Years. NY, [1939]. One of 525. 4 vols. pba Oct 5 (297) $350; sg Oct 26 (221) $185
— Always the Young Strangers. NY, [1953]. One of 600 L.p. copies. pba Oct 5 (298) $60

Anr copy. In mylar dj. sg Dec 14 (253) $140
— Chicago Poems. NY, 1916. 1st Ed. Orig cloth; some soiling. Inscr to Anna Proctor & with holograph fair copy of his poem Fog. Engelhard copy. CNY Oct 27 (121) $1,700
— Good Morning America. NY, 1928. Sgd. pba Oct 5 (299) $50
— A Lincoln and Whitman Miscellany. Chicago: Holiday Press, 1938. One of 250. 4to, half cloth. sg Dec 14 (252) $140
— Remembrance Rock. NY, [1948]. One of 1,000. 2 vols. pba Oct 5 (300) $75
— Steichen the Photographer. NY, [1929]. One of 925. 4to, cloth. P June 5 (335) $600
Anr copy. Cloth; worn. sg Feb 29 (294) $1,200

**Sandby, Paul, 1725-1809**
— A Collection of One Hundred and Fifty Select Views in England, Scotland, and Ireland. L, 1781. 2 vols in 1. Oblong 4to, contemp half mor; worn. With 150 plates. Some browning & dampstaining. bba June 6 (64) £600 [Ingol Maps & Prints]

**Sandels, G. M.** See: Grabhorn Printing

**Sandeman, Fraser**
— Angling Travels in Norway. L, 1895. 4to, orig half cloth; cloth on covers lacking, rubbed, hinges cracked. L.p. copy. pba July 11 (271) $200

**Sander, August**
— Men Without Masks, Faces of Germany 1910-1938. Greenwich, 1973. 4to, cloth, in creased & torn dj; handstamp to front & rear free endpapers. sg Feb 29 (281) $175

**Sander, Max**
— Le Livre a figures italien depuis 1467 jusque a 1530. Mailan, 1942-69. 7 vols in 5 plus Supplement. 4to, cloth. bba Oct 5 (166) £650 [Maggs]
Anr copy. 7 vols, including Supplement. 4to, orig cloth; spines browned. Ck Apr 12 (272) £450
Anr Ed. Milan, 1969. 7 vols, including Supplement, in 6. 4to, orig cloth; spines browned. Ck Apr 12 (273) £360

**Sanders, Daniel C.**
— A History of the Indian Wars.... Montpelier, 1812. 1st Ed. 16mo, mor gilt by Pratt. sg Oct 26 (331) $750

**Sanders, Robert, 1727-83.** See: Spencer, Nathaniel

**Sanderson, George P.**
— Thirteen Years among the Wild Beasts of India.... L, 1882. 3d Ed. O Oct 10 (241) $150

**Sanderson, Thomas, 1759-1829**
— Original Poems. Carlisle, 1800. 12mo, orig wraps; spine def. b Dec 5 (171) £80

**Sanderus, Antonius, 1586-1664**
— Bibliotheca Belgica Manuscripta.... Insulis, 1641-44. Vol I. 4to, contemp vellum; worn. O Mar 26 (244) $70

**Sandford, Christopher & Lettice**
— Clervis & Belamie. Heathercomb: Boars Press, 1932. One of 100.  bba May 9 (458) £75 [Rush]

**Sandford, Francis, 1630-94**
— The History of the Coronation of James II and Queen Mary. L, 1687. Folio, contemp calf; rubbed, rebacked & repaired. With 31 plates.  S June 12 (152) £750

**Sandford, John F. A., Report of the Decision of the Supreme Court of the United States...**
— Report of the Decision of the Supreme Court of the United States...in the Case of Dred Scott versus John F. A. Sandford. See: Howard, Benjamin C.

**Sandoz, Mari**
— The Battle of Little Big Horn. NY, 1966. 1st Ed, One of 249. Half mor; corner bumped. With double-page map, folding plate, & orig Ms page sgd. Robbins copy.  pba Mar 21 (321) $300
— The Beaver Men: Spearheads of Empire. NY, [1964]. 1st Ed, One of 185 sgd & with two sgd pp of orig typescript bound in. 2 vols. Half lev. With large folding color map in vol II. Robbins copy.  pba Mar 21 (322) $450
— The Cattlemen, from the Rio Grande Across the Far Marias. NY, [1958]. 1st Ed, One of 199. With folding color frontis by Neil Egenhoffer. Robbins copy. Sgd.  pba Mar 21 (323) $150
— Crazy Horse, the Strange Man of the Oglalas.... NY, 1942. In dj.  pba Apr 25 (653) $250
— Old Jules. Bost., 1935. 1st Ed. In dj with tear. Robbins copy.  pba Mar 21 (324) $50
— Old Jules Country. NY, 1965. One of 250. Illus by Bryan Forsyth. Half lev. With folding map. Robbins copy. Sgd.  pba Mar 21 (325) $50

**Sandoz, Maurice**
— La Maison sans fenetres. Paris, [1949]. Illus by Salvador Dali. 4to, wraps; unopened. With 7 colored plates.  sg Feb 15 (84) $150

**Sandwith, Humphry**
— A Narrative of the Siege of Kars. L, 1856. 12mo, contemp calf gilt. With frontis & 2 maps.  sg Mar 7 (182) $90

**Sandys, George, 1578-1644**
— Anglorum Speculum, or the Worthies of England.... L, 1684. 8vo, old calf; worn & chipped. Trimmed; some browning & staining; early pen annotations.  wa Feb 29 (165) $140
— A Relation of a Journey.... L, 1627. 3d Ed. Folio, 19th-cent calf; rebacked, spine laid down. Engraved title trimmed; folding map & folding plate laid down.  CE June 15 (255) $320
4th Ed. L, 1637. Folio, contemp calf; rebacked, worn, joints starting. Piece missing along top of map; tp margins foxed; early marginalia & underlining.  CE May 22 (419) $300
— A Relation of Journey begun An. Dom 1610... Description of the Turkish Empire. L, [1670]. 5th Ed. - Illus by Natale Bonifacio. Folio, recent vellum;

soiled. With title by Francis Delaram, & 47 illus. Lacking map & 1 plate; title & 1st pp torn & frayed; some soiling, discoloration, & few tears.  S Oct 26 (200) £180 [Mertturkmen]
— Sandys Travailes.... L, 1658. 6th Ed. Folio, contemp calf; rebacked, worn. With title from 5th Ed, double-page map, folding map, & 47 illus. Some soiling; some tears affecting letters.  S Oct 26 (77) £280 [Zioni]
— Travells.... L, 1670. 6th Ed. Folio, contemp calf; rubbed & marked. With folding map, folding plate, & 47 illus. Map & plate torn; F6 verso poorly printed; K5 repaired; o6 with hole.  S Oct 26 (202) £260 [Gray]

**Sanger, Margaret**
— An Autobiography. NY, [1938]. Library markings. Inscr to Mrs. Charles Edison.  sg Sept 28 (246) $175

**Sannazaro, Jacopo, 1458-1530**
— Arcadia. Venice: Bernardino da Vercelli, 1502. ("Libro pastorale nominato arcadio.") 4to, 19th-cent half calf. Marginal repairs; soiled & waterstained.  C Apr 3 (201) £2,000

**Sanson d'Abbeville, Nicolas**
— L'Asie en plusieurs cartes.... Paris, [1652-53]. 4to, contemp calf. With 17 colored double-page maps., but with a map of Hungary substituted for Japan. Marginal dampstains.  sg Dec 7 (45) $900
— L'Asie en plusieurs cartes nouvelles, et exacte. Paris, [1670]. 4to, contemp calf; spine worn. With 19 double-page maps. Lacking title.  S Oct 26 (565) £820 [Adams]
— Atlas nouveau. Paris, [1648-1710]. Folio, contemp vellum; spine label torn, extremities rubbed. With 139 double-page maps, hand-colored in outline; double-page view of Orleans by Inselin. Some maps creased, a few shaved to image; view of Orleans & map of Italy torn.  C May 31 (69) £13,000
— Cartes generales de toutes les parties du monde.... Paris, 1658. Folio, contemp calf; rubbed. With 85 double-page maps, hand-colored in outline. Ms contents list; a few maps shaved or frayed; some staining at ends; last map stained & laid down.  S Nov 30 (82) £5,600

**Sansovino, Francesco**
— Gl'Annali Turcheschi overo vite de principi della casa Othomana. Venice: Enea de Alaris, 1573. 4to, contemp limp vellum decorated by Cesare Vecellio & with fore-edge painting (of a Turk in red robes) for the Pillone library, with orig drawings in ink of a sultan on the front cover & a Turkish swordsman on rear cover. Pillone - Bazolle - Brooke - Beres copy.  C May 1 (144) £36,000
— Cronologia del mondo.... Venice, 1580. 4to, contemp vellum; worn & soiled. Dampstaining.  F June 20 (189) $120

**Santa Maria, Vincente**
— The First Spanish Entry into San Francisco Bay, 1775. San Francisco: John Howell Books, 1971. One of 5,000. Ed by John Galvin. Orig cloth in dj; d/j

spine sunned. With 4 maps & 6 color illus. Larson copy. pba Sept 28 (220) $80

**Santa Teresa, Giovanni Giuseppe di**
— Istoria delle guerre del regno del Brasile.... Rome, 1698. 1st Ed. 2 parts in 1 vol. Folio, contemp vellum; worming on spine ends. With frontis, 2 ports & 23 maps & plans. Some browning on upper margin of 3 plates. b June 28 (60) £11,000

**Santangelo, Antonio**
— The Development of Italian Textile Design from the 12th to the 18th Century. L, 1964. 4to, cloth, in dj. sg June 13 (358) $120

**Santarem, Manuel Francisco de Barros, 2d Visconde de, 1791-1856**
— Atlas compose de Mappemondes et de cartes hydrographiques et historiques.... Paris, 1842-49. 2 vols in 1. Folio, later half mor gilt; endpapers renewed. With 82 plates. sg May 9 (35) $4,600

**Santayana, George, 1863-1952**
— Works. NY, 1936-40. Triton Ed, one of 940. 15 vols. Orig half cloth. Met Feb 24 (209) $300
Anr copy. Vols 1-14 (of 15). pba June 20 (291) $375

**Santee, Ross**
— Cowboy. NY, 1928. Orig cloth; rubbed & soiled. Front free endpaper has orig ink sketch & inscr to Uncle Bill, 24 Aug 1938. pba Aug 8 (176) $600
— Dog Days. NY, 1955. 1st Ed. In dj with edge-wear. Robbins copy. Sgd & with orig watercolor on front free endpaper. pba Mar 21 (326) $425
— Men and Horses. NY & L: Century, [1926]. Inscr, including 3 orig drawings, 1926. pba Mar 7 (228) $300
Anr copy. With 2 orig ink sketches on front free endpaper & inscr to Emily Young, 1926. pba Aug 8 (177) $900

**Santini, Francois**
— Atlas universel dresse sur les meilleures cartes modernes. Venice, 1776-[84]. 2 vols. Folio, contemp calf; worn, joints cracked, upper spine compartment of Vol II lacking. With engraved title & 135 double-page maps, hand-colored in outline. Minor staining to 1st few leaves in Vol I. C May 31 (70) £9,000

**Santini, Piero.** See: Derrydale Press

**Santo Tomas de Aquino, Manuel de**
— Verdadero caracter de Mahometa y de su religion. Velancia, 1793-95. 4 parts in 1 vol. 4to, contemp tree calf; worn. 1st few leaves with worm-holes. S Oct 26 (205) £360 [Folios]

**Santorini, Giovanni Domenico, 1681-1737**
— Anatomici summi septemdecim tabulae.... Parma, 1775. 1st Ed. 4to, modern half mor. With port & 42 plates. Title soiled & stained; some foxing. CE Nov 8 (145) $2,400

**Sanz, Gaspar**
— Instruccion de musica sobre la guitarra espanola.... Saragossa: heirs of Diego Dormer, 1697. 3 vols in 1. Oblong folio, later wraps. With 17 (of 18) plates in Vol I; 12 plates in Vol II; 8 (of 10) plates in Vol III. Tape-repaired at beginning & end; some paper loss on last leaf; tp to Vol I holed; some browning & staining. S Dec 1 (307) £2,200

**Sappho**
— [Fragments] Paris, 1933. One of 40 with a suite of the etchings on chine. Illus by Mariette Lydis. 4to, mor extra by H. Lappersonne & G. H. Lillaz. S Nov 21 (394) £800

**Sarayna, Torellus**
— De origine et amplitudine civitatis Veronae. Verona, 1540. 1st Ed. Folio, 17th-cent calf gilt with arms of Henri Feydau, seigneur de Brou. With woodcut title, port & 29 woodcuts, plans & views. Repaired tear in top margin of M1; partly repaired tear in K1 with minor damage to illust. C July 21 (55) £65 [Bury]

**Sarazen, Gene —& Others**
— From Tee to Cup by the Four Masters. N.p.: Wilson Sporting Goods, 1937. 1st Ed. Cloth. Sgd by Ralph Guldahl. pba Nov 9 (70) $90

**Sardou, Victorien**
— Rabagas. Paris, 1872. 12mo, mor gilt by Lortic, orig wraps bound in. With 81 orig watercolor vignettes in the margins, the final one sgd "Henriot" [Henri Maigrot]. Extra-illus with c.7 full-page watercolors, Ms fragment of Sardou & other materials. S Nov 21 (393) £300

**Sargent, Charles Lennox**
— The Life of Alexander Smith, Captain of the Island of Pitcairn.... Bost., 1819. 8vo, half calf. Some foxing. b Mar 20 (184) £1,300

**Sargent, Shirley**
— Pioneers in Petticoats. Yosemite's Early Women. Los Angeles, [1966]. In dj. Inscr & with related material. pba Feb 12 (151) $110
— Solomons of the Sierra. Yosemite: Flying Spur Press, 1989. Pictorial bds. Inscr. pba Feb 12 (153) $120
— Theodore Parker Lukens, Father of Forestry. Los Angeles: Dawson's Book Shop, 1969. Inscr. pba Feb 12 (154) $70
— Yosemite's Rustic Outpost: Foresta, Big Meadow. Yosemite: Flying Spur Press, 1983. Inscr. pba Feb 12 (158) $65

**Sargent, Winthrop, 1825-70**
— The History of an Expedition against Fort Du Quesne, in 1755.... Phila., 1856. 8vo, later cloth. sg Oct 26 (332) $100
— The Life and Career of Major John Andre. Bost., 1861. One vol in 3. 8vo, mor; spines rubbed. Extra-illus with 291 ports & views. wd Nov 15 (104) $200

**Sarmiento de Gamboa, Pedro**
— Viage al Estrecho de Magallanes.... Madrid, 1768. 4to, modern calf. With 3 folding plates. Tp foxed; some marginal stains. cb Feb 14 (2542) $1,200

**Saroyan, William, 1908-81**
— Harlem as Seen by Hirschfeld. NY, [1941]. One of 1,000. Illus by Al Hirschfeld. Folio, orig cloth; lower joint split. CE May 22 (420) $550

Anr copy. Cloth; spine off. Met Sept 28 (11) $1,400

Anr copy. Pictorial cloth; front cover detached, spine def. Lacking last plate. Sold w.a.f. sg Mar 28 (145) $750

— Peace, It's Wonderful. NY, 1939. Ptd wraps; extremities rubbed. Inscr to Paul Bowles, 15 Apr 1939. sg Dec 14 (254) $325

**Sarpi, Paolo, 1552-1623**
— The Historie of the Councel of Trent. L, 1629. 2d Ed in English. - Trans by N. Brent. Folio, contemp calf; rebacked, corners restored, joints starting. Marginal dampstaining at ends. sg Mar 21 (280) $150

— The History of the Quarrels of Pope Paul V. with the State of Venice. L, 1626. 1st Ed in English. 4to, contemp calf; spine ends chipped, covers detached. Library stamp on tp & colophon leaf. sg Mar 21 (279) $150

**Sarre, Friedrich, 1865-1945**
— Islamic Bookbindings. L, [1923]. One of 550. Folio, contemp half mor; extremities worn, corners worn or bumped. With 36 color plates. Some soiling. cb Oct 17 (607) $700

**Sarre, Friedrich, 1865-1945 — & Trenkwald, Hermann**
— Old Oriental Carpets.... Vienna & Leipzig, 1926-29. 2 vols. Folio, orig cloth. With 120 plates, 68 of them in color. cb Oct 17 (98) $1,800

Anr copy. Vol I only. Some soiling. Met Feb 24 (152) $600

**Sartain's...**
— Sartain's Union Magazine. Phila., 1849. July-Dec 1849 bound in 1 vol. 4to, contemp half mor; spine worn, joints cracked. Nov issue contains The Bells. pba Oct 5 (293) $160

**Sarti, Giuseppe, 1729-1802**
— Giulio Sabino. Vienna, [1781 or later]. Full score, oblong folio, contemp mor gilt. Engraved throughout. Minor marginal tears. S May 15 (135) £620

**Sarton, George, 1884-1956**
— An Introduction to the History of Science. Baltimore, 1927-48. 3 vols in 5. 4to, orig cloth; vols 2/1 & 2/2 spines faded & hinges cracked. sg Apr 11 (297) $300

— Introduction to the History of Science. Wash., [1953]. 3 vols in 5. 4to, cloth. sg May 16 (250) $225

**Sartre, Jean Paul, 1905-80**
— The Wall and Other Stories. NY: New Directions, [1948]. Ltd Ed. Half cloth. pba Jan 25 (330) $110

Out-of-series copy on specially made paper, sgd. Half cloth. CNY May 17 (105) $1,600

**Sarychev, Gavrila Andreevich**
— Account of a Voyage of Discovery to the North-East of Siberia.... L, 1806-7. 2 vols in 1. 8vo, 19th-cent half calf; spine ends frayed. With 5 plates, 2 of them hand-colored. sg Mar 7 (297) $450

**Sassoon, Siegfried, 1886-1967**
— Memoirs of an Infantry Officer. L, 1931. One of 320. Unopened. sg June 20 (329) $250

— Sherston's Progress. L, 1936. 1st Ed, One of 300 on homemade paper. sg June 20 (330) $200

— To My Mother. L, [1928]. One of 500 L.p. copies, sgd. Illus by Stephen Tennant. sg June 20 (331) $175

— Vigils. [Bristol], 1934. One of 272, sgd. Illus by Stephen Gooden. Pigskin; bowed. sg Sept 14 (177) $300

**Satchell, Thomas.** See: Westwood & Satchell

**Satie, Erik, 1866-1925**
— 3 Moreaux en forme de poire.... Paris, [1911]. 1st Ed. 4to, ptd wraps; repaired. Inscr to Marcelle Meyer. S Dec 1 (308) £750

**Saude, Jean**
— Traite d'enluminure d'art au pochoir. Paris, 1925. One of 500. 4to, contemp half mor with orig cloth-backed bd sleeve with color pochoir front cover label by Benedictus. With 30 color pochoir plates. sg Apr 18 (130A) $3,400

Anr copy. Loose as issued in half-cloth portfolio. wa Feb 1 (374) $2,700

**Sauer, Martin**
— An Account of a Geographical and Astronomical Expedition to the Northern Parts of Russia.... L, 1802. 1st Ed. 2 parts in 1 vol. 4to, contemp calf gilt with Signet stamp; rebacked, some discoloration. With folding map & 15 plates. Foxed. pba Feb 13 (167) $1,400

Anr copy. Modern half calf. Plates & chart bound in after errata sheet at beginning & in reverse order; some foxing. pba Feb 13 (168) $1,100

**Sauerlandt, Max**
— Emil Nolde. Munich, 1921. Folio, cloth. Some foxing. O May 7 (269) $90

**Saulo Phantino, Pietro**
— Trastullo delle donne da far ridere la brigata. Florence: Francesco di Iacopo della Spera, [before 1519]. 4to, mor gilt by Lortic with Essling arms. With full-page woodcut. C Apr 3 (202) £15,000

**Saunders, Charles Francis**
— The Southern Sierras of California. Bost., 1923. With 32 plates. pba Feb 12 (159) $60

# SAUNDERS

— Under the Sky in California. NY, 1913. With 51 illusts on 48 plates. pba Feb 12 (160) $70

**Saunders, Louise**
— The Knave of Hearts. NY, 1925. Illus by Maxfield Parrish. Folio, orig cloth; rubbed & shaken. cb Oct 17 (665) $800
Anr copy. Pictorial cloth; upper corners bumped. Some creasing. Inscr to Walter Oakman. sg Sept 14 (294) $700
Anr copy. Orig cloth. sg Oct 19 (190) $1,900
Anr Ed. Racine, [1925]. Folio, orig pictorial wraps; worn & soiled. O Sept 12 (158) $270

**Saunderson, Nicholas, 1682-1737**
— The Method of Fluxions applied to a Select Number of Useful Problems.... L, 1756. 1st Ed. 8vo, needs rebdg. With 12 folding plates. Lacking half-title or initial blank; plates partly dampstained; old stamp on tp. sg May 16 (251) $100

**Savage, George, Writer on Ceramics**
— English Pottery and Porcelain. NY, [1961]. 1st American Ed. 4to, cloth, in worn & repaired dj. wa Dec 14 (420) $70

**Savary, Claude Etienne**
— Letters on Egypt.... L, 1787. 2 vols. 8vo, contemp calf. With 3 folding maps & 1 folding plate. Tear to 1 map. b Sept 20 (372) £170

**Savigny, Marie Jules Cesar Lelorgne de**
— Histoire naturelle de L'Egypte. Zoologie. Oiseaux. Paris: Imprimerie Imperiale, 1808. Folio, contemp French red mor gilt by Tessier, elaborate bdg with arms of Napoleon at center of both covers. Engraved throughout. With 10 plates showing 31 birds from drawings by Barraband engraved & ptd in colors by Bouquet, all without name of artist & without Savigny's name; all plates interleaved with blanks. Most plates with light staining surrounding the figures of the birds; Plate 3 slightly cockled; library stamp of Hermitage on tp; Hermitage cancellation stamp on tp & on verso of each plate. S June 27 (21) £22,000

**Savile, Sir Henry, 1549-1622**
— Rerum Anglicarum scriptores post Bedam praecipui.... Frankfurt am Main: Wechelianis, 1601. Folio, contemp calf; repaired. Light discoloration; imprint defaced affecting letters. S Oct 26 (78) £280 [Quaritch]

**Saville, Albany**
— Thirty-Six Hints to Sportsmen. Okehampton: Simmons, [n.d.]. 16mo, calf by Sangorski & Sutcliffe; rubbed. O Jan 9 (195) $150

**Savonarola, Girolamo, 1452-98**
— Compendio di revelatione. Florence: Francesco Bonaccorsi, 18 Aug 1495. 8vo, modern calf. 54 leaves. Goff S-179. C Apr 3 (203) £1,100
— Del sacramento della messa e regola utile. [Florence: Bartolommeo di Libri, c.1495]. 4to, 19th-cent half calf. 33 lines; type 97R1. With title woodcut & 2 lombard initials. Minor staining. 4 leaves. Goff S-241. C Apr 3 (210) £1,700
— Dell' umilta. Florence: Gian Stephano di Carlo da Pavia, [c.1505]. 4to, modern vellum, stamped with Essling supralibros. 38 lines; type 87R; 2 woodcuts. C Nov 29 (71) £1,100
Anr copy. 19th-cent half mor. 10 leaves. Goff S-281. C Apr 3 (204) £900
— Esposizione sopra l'Ave Maria. [Florence: Bartolommeo di Libri, c.1495]. 4to, 19th-cent vellum. 28 lines; type 2:114R2. 12 leaves. Goff S-197. C Apr 3 (206) £1,300
— La Expositione del Pater Noster Composta per frayre Girolomo de Ferrara. [Florence: Bartolommeo de Libri, c.1495]. 4to, vellum wrap. 34 lines; type 1:97R1, 3:114G. Some spotting. 24 leaves. Goff S-199. C Apr 3 (205) £1,600
Anr Ed. [Florence: Antonio Tubini et al., after 1500]. 4to, modern mor. 38 lines; type 1:86R. 20 leaves. Goff S-202. C Apr 3 (212) £1,200
— Expositione del psalmo lxxviiii tradocto in lingua fiorentina. Florence: [Lorenzo Morgiani & Johannes Petri], 8 June 1496. 4to, modern half mor. 35 lines; type 4:85R. 16 leaves. Goff S-222. C Nov 29 (73) £950
— Predica fatta ad di 25 di Febbraio, 1497. [Florence: Bartolommeo di Libri, after 25 Feb 1497/98]. 4to, modern vellum. 20 leaves. Goff S-256. C Nov 29 (73) £950
— Prediche nuovamente venute in luce.... Venice: Agostino de Zanni, 1528. 1st Italian Ed. - Trans by Girolamo Gianoti da Pistoia. 8vo, later limp vellum. With woodcut title. Final blank & few leaves discolored. S Oct 27 (1084) £600 [Zioni]
— Regola del ben vivere. [Florence: Bartolommeo di Libri], 1498. 4to, mor by Sangorski & Sutcliffe. 28 lines; gothic letter; woodcut of Crucifixion on tp & of the wayfarer praying on f4 verso. 4 leaves. Goff S-237. C Apr 3 (207) £1,600
— Sermone dell'orazione. [Florence: Bartolommeo di Libri, c.1495]. 4to, modern mor by Sangorski & Sutcliffe. 34 lines; types 1:97R, 3:114G. With 2 woodcuts. 14 leaves. Goff S-266. C Apr 3 (208) £1,400
— Tractato contra li Astrologi. [Florence: Bartolommeo di Libri, c.1497]. 4to, modern half mor by Lortic. 33 lines; types 1:97R2, 2:114R. 34 (of 36) leaves; lacking final 2 leaves of errata. Goff S-175. Landau copy. C June 26 (131) £2,000
— Triumphis crucis. [Florence: Bartolommeo di Libri, 1497?]. Folio, modern bds. 34 lines & headline; types 2:114R2, 3:114G. Erasure on tp repaired on verso. 98 leaves. Goff S-274. C Apr 3 (211) £1,100
— Vita viduale. [Florence: Bartolommeo di Libri, c.1495]. 4to, modern mor. 33 lines; types 1:97R1, 3:114G. With woodcut. 19 (of 20) leaves; lacking final blank. Goff S-287. C Apr 3 (209) £1,800

**Savoy...**
— The Savoy: an Illustrated Quarterly. L, 1896. Ed by Arthur Symons; illus by Aubrey Beardsley. Nos 1-

2. 4to, orig bds; spines & corners worn, 1 bdg stained. pba June 20 (52) $110

Anr copy. Nos 3-5. Orig cloth; spine ends chipped, extremities rubbed. pba Aug 22 (534) $100

Anr copy. Nos 1-8 (complete set) in 3 vols. 4to, orig cloth. With the Beardsley Christmas card inserted in No 1. S Nov 2 (71) £800 [Sims Reed]

Anr copy. Nos 1-2. 4to, orig bds; chipped. Some foxing to prelims. sg Feb 15 (40) $650

**Sawyer, Anna**
— Poems on Various Subjects. Birm., 1801. 8vo, contemp mor-backed bds. b Dec 5 (24) £190

**Sawyer, Charles J. —& Darton, Frederick Joseph Harvey**
— English Books, 1475-1900. L, 1927. 2 vols. Half mor by Sangorski & Sutcliffe. sg Sept 21 (287) $130

**Sawyer, Charles Winthrop**
— Firearms in American History. Bost., 1910-20. 3 vols. Cloth; worn. O June 4 (231) $50

**Sawyer, Eugene T.**
See also: Grabhorn Printing
— History of Santa Clara County.... Los Angeles, 1922. Folio, half mor; joints cracked, spine strip split through at front joint. pba Aug 22 (957) $95
— The Life and Career of Tiburcio Vasquez.... [San Jose, 1875]. 8vo, orig wraps; soiled, spine ends worn. With 2 port plates. Robbins copy. pba Mar 21 (328) $2,500

**Sawyer, Lorenzo**
— Way Sketches containing Incidents of Travel Across the Plains. NY, 1926. One of 35. Half vellum; some soiling. pba Nov 16 (243) $250

Anr copy. Half parchment. With frontis port. Robbins-Streeter copy. Inscr to Streeter from Edward Eberstadt. pba Mar 21 (330) $450

**Saxby, Henry L.**
— The Birds of Shetland.... Edin., 1874. 1st Ed. 8vo, orig half mor. With 8 tinted lithos. Browned. bba July 18 (98) £95 [Sotheran]

**Saxe, John Godfrey.** See: Fore-Edge Paintings

**Saxe, Maurice, Comte de, 1696-1750**
— Reveries, or Memoires upon the Art of War. L, 1757. 4to, old calf; broken, worn. With 40 plates on 34 leaves. Tp clipped at top margin; some foxing. wa Feb 29 (202) $475
— Les Reveries ou memoires sur l'art de guerre.... The Hague, 1756. Folio, modern half calf; worn. Some foxing, staining & soiled; library markings; early annotations. O Mar 5 (199) $325

**Saxo Grammaticus, 1150?-1220?**
— Danorum regum heroumque historie.... Frankfurt: Andreas Weschel, 1576. ("Danorum historiae libri XVI.") Bound with: Hopper, Joachim. De juris arte. Louvain: Stephanus Gualtherus, 1553. Folio, old vellum; bumped, front hinge cracked, 1st signature detached. Hopper lacking prelims & is soiled & waterstained. wd May 8 (79) $225

**Saxton, Christopher**
— An Atlas of England and Wales. L, 1979. One of 500. Folio, half calf gilt. Facsimile of 1579 Ed. CE June 15 (301) $150

**Say, Thomas, 1787-1834**
— American Entomology. Phila., 1824-28. 3 vols. 8vo, half lea; rubbed & bumped, hinges repaired. With 53 (of 54) hand-colored plates & engraved title. Met Sept 28 (417) $650

**Sayers, Dorothy L., 1893-1957**
— Hangman's Holiday. NY, [1933]. 1st Ed. In rubbed dj. sg Dec 14 (67) $90
— Papers relating to the Family of Wimsey. [N.p.: Pvtly ptd, 1936]. 1st Ed, one of 500. Orig wraps. Inscr to Nancy Pearn. Ck Nov 17 (158) £480

**Sayers, Frank, 1763-1817**
— Poems. Norwich, 1792. 8vo, modern bds. b Dec 5 (254) £200

**Sayger, C. —& Desarnod, A.**
— Album d'un Voyage en Turquie fait par Ordre de sa Majeste Empereur Nicolas 1 en 1829 et 1830. Paris: Engelmann, [c.1830]. Folio, contemp half mor, spine with crowned monogram. With litho tp & 51 plates, 4 hand-colored. Spotting affecting some plates; stamp on each plates. S June 27 (160) £2,200

**Sayre, Eleanor**
— Late Caprichos of Goya: Fragments from a Series. NY, 1971. One of 25. 4to, mor gilt by Arno Werner, with extra suite of plates in cloth portfolio. pba June 20 (178) $550

**Scaliger, Julius Caesar, 1484-1558**
— Exotericarum exercitationum liber xv de subtilitate ad Hieronymum Cardanum. Paris: Michael Vascosan, 1557. 4to, contemp vellum. Wormhole in upper margin of 1st few leaves; dampstained at head of last few leaves; margins spotted. S Mar 14 (314) £800

**Scammon, Charles M.**
— The Marine Mammals of the North-Western Coast of North America.... Riverside: Manessier Publishing, [1969]. 4to, cloth. With 27 plates. Facsimile of the 1874 Ed. pba Apr 25 (234) $50

Anr copy. Cloth. Facsimile of the 1874 Ed. pba July 25 (215) $110

**Scammon, L. N.** See: Grabhorn Printing

**Scamozzi, Vincenzo, 1552-1616**
— Dell' idea della architettura universale. Piazzola, 1687. 2 parts in 2 vols. Folio, contemp vellum. With 86 engraved illusts, 8 of them double-page. Hole in F3 of Vol I with loss of a few characters; some shaving at top into headlines. C Apr 3 (220) £1,300

## SCANLAND

**Scanland, John Milton**
— The Life of Pat F. Garrett and the Taming of the Border Outlaw. El Paso, [1908]. 1st Ed. Orig wraps; lower edge torn. With 5 illusts. Robbins-Streeter copy.   pba Mar 21 (331) $6,500

**Scantrel, Felix Andre Yves.** See: Suares, Andre

**Scapula, Johann**
— Lexicon Graeco-Latinum.... L, 1652. Folio, contemp calf; rubbed & broken. Library markings.   F June 20 (193B) $60

**Scarlatti, Domenico**
— Pieces pour le Clavecin. Lyon: Brotonne, [c.1738]. 2 vols. Folio, calf; upper cover detached.   S May 15 (484) £800

**Scarpa, Antonio, 1747-1832**
— Engravings of the Cardiac Nerves, the Nerves of the Ninth Pair.... Edin., 1829. 2d Ed. 4to, modern cloth. With 25 plates. Stained. Sold w.a.f.   sg May 16 (494) $140

**Scarron, Paul, 1610-60**
— Oeuvres. Paris, 1715-20. 10 vols. 12mo, contemp calf gilt; spine worn.   sg Sept 21 (42) $300
— Le Roman comique. Paris, 1796 [An IV]. 3 vols. 8vo, contemp mor gilt by Tessier. With port & 15 plates before letters. Tear in fore-margin of D1 in Vol III. Hoe - Fuerstenberg - Schaefer copy.   S Dec 8 (572) £2,600

**Scenen...**
— Scenen aus der Wiener Revolution, 1848. Vienna, [n.d.]. Oblong folio, contemp half mor; scuffed. With 10 litho plates..   bbc Feb 26 (1) $400

**Sceve, Maurice**
— La Magnifica et Triumphale Entrata del Christianissimo Re di Francia Henrico Secondo...alli 21 di Septembre 1548. Lyons: Guillaume Rouille, 1549. 4to, contemp vellum; front pastedown torn at top & bottom. With 14 full-page woodcuts. Spotting & browning. Hoe - Rahir - Schaefer copy.   P Nov 1 (190) $4,000

**Schachtzabel, E.**
— Illustriertes Prachtwerk saemtlicher Tauben-Rassen. Halle, [1925]. Orig cloth; spine frayed, 1 plate loose. With 104 color plates.   sg Dec 7 (206) $325

**Schaefer, Heinrich, Professor**
— Ethnographische Denkmale von Catalonien. Darmstadt: J. W. Heyer, 1828. Folio, contemp half calf. With engraved title & 30 plates. Lower right corner affected by damp.   C May 31 (110) £600

**Schaefer, Otto**
— Katalog der Bibliothek... Teil I: Drucke, Manuskripte, und Einbaende des 15. Jahrhunderts. Stuttgart, [1984]. One of 800. 2 vols. Folio, orig cloth.   sg Apr 11 (160) $200

## AMERICAN BOOK PRICES CURRENT

**Schaeffer, D. F.**
— Der Weltumsegler. Oder Reise durch alle fuenf Theile der Erde. Berlin, 1801-20. Vols I-VI (of 7). 4to, 19th-cent half calf. With 2 colored maps & 48 colored plates, plus map of Ruegen not called for in Vol VI. Text spotted.   S Mar 14 (318) £700

**Schaeffer, Jacob Christian**
— Abbildung und Beschreibung des Bestaendigen Electricitaettraegers. Regensberg, 1776. Bound with: Kraefte, Wirkungen und Bewegungsgesetze des bestaendigen Electricitaettragers. Regensburg, 1776. And: Fernere Versuche mit dem bestaendigen Elictricitaettraeger. Regensburg, 1777. 4to, contemp half calf.   S Mar 14 (316) £900

**Schaeffer, Luther M.**
— Sketches of Travels in South America, Mexico and California. NY, 1860. 1st Ed. 12mo, orig cloth. Robbins copy.   pba Mar 21 (332) $85

**Schaldach, William J.**
— Carl Rungius, Big Game Painter. West Hartford VT, [1945]. One of 1,250. 4to, cloth; worn.   O June 25 (235) $475; O June 25 (236) $500
Anr copy. Orig cloth.   sg Apr 18 (155) $650
One of 160 with orig sgd etching as frontis. Cloth. Inscr by Rungius to Sam Webb & with 8-line inscr by Webb.   O Oct 10 (242) $4,000
— Fish by Schaldach. L, 1937. One of 1,560. Folio, cloth; worn.   O June 25 (238) $130
Anr Ed. Phila., 1937. One of 1,500. Folio, cloth; minor stains & soiling along edges.   sg Mar 7 (528) $120
— The Wind on Your Cheek. Rockville Centre: Freshet Press, [1973]. One of 200. 4to, half lea. With mtd sgd etching.   O Feb 6 (206) $160; O June 25 (240) $200

**Schammade...**
— Die Schammade (dilettanten erhebt euch). Cologne: Schloemilch Verlag, 1920. Ed by Max Ernst & J. T. Baargeld. 4to, orig wraps with woodcut by Arex & Ernst's Dadameter; soiled, loss to lower corners at fold, stamp on lower cover. With tp design by Ernst & 8 mtd preproductions by Ernst, Arang & Hoerle; 2 large illusts by Picabia & Baargeld. Some browning at extremities.   P June 5 (222) $10,000

**Schedel, Hartmann.** See: Nuremberg Chronicle

**Scheele, Carl Wilhelm, 1742-86**
— The Chemical Essays.... L, 1786. 1st Ed. 8vo, bds.   b May 30 (38) £900
— Chemical Observations and Experiments on Air and Fire.... L, 1780. 8vo, contemp calf; repaired.   b May 30 (37) £1,300
— Chemische Abhandlung von der Luft und dem Feuer. Upsala & Leipzig, 1777. 8vo, contemp half calf; rubbed. Lacking initial blank & with 2-leaf Foreword misbound in its orig position. Honeyman - Hefner copy.   CNY May 17 (37) $16,000

## Schefferus, Joannes, 1624-77
— The History of Lapland.... Oxford, 1674. Folio, contemp calf; rebacked, rubbed. Owner's stamp on tp. CE June 15 (256) $750

## Scheidt, Caspar
— Wol gerissnen und geschnidten Figuren ausz der Neuwen Testament. Lyons: J. de Tournes, 1564. 8vo, 19th-cent mor janseniste by Chambolle-Duru. Italic types. With 96 woodcuts in text. Some soiling. P Nov 1 (32) $1,800

## Scheler, Lucien
— Sillage intangible. Paris: Iliazd, 1958. On of 50. Illus by Pablo Picasso. 4to, unsewn as issued in wraps covered with vellum. With 1 drypoint etching. S Nov 30 (352) £900

## Schenk, Peter
— Atlas contractus sive mapparum geographicarum Sansoniarum.... Amst., [c.1705]. Folio, later half calf; rubbed. With engraved title, engraved contents & 26 double-page or folding maps in contemp body color. All maps backed; abrasion at fold of 4 maps with minor loss; most maps split at lower fold; reguarded throughout; some creasing & soiling. S June 27 (83) £3,600
— Schouwtoneel van den Oorlog beginnende met Koning Karel den Tweeden... afgebeeld in twe-hondert, en agt-en-dertig Historische Figuren. Amst., [c.1727]. Folio, 18th-cent half vellum; worn. With double-page engraved general fortification plate & 32 double-page plates. Worming with minor loss. S Nov 30 (83) £850
— Theatrum Belgicum.... Amst., 1712. Folio, contemp sheep; worn. With 153 maps & views on 17 double-page sheets & 1 double-page plate. Some fold tears. C Oct 25 (147) £900

## Schenker, Donald. See: Meltzer, David

## Scherzer, Karl von
— Narrative of the Circumnavigation of the Globe by the Austrian Frigate Novara.... L, 1861-63. 3 vols. 8vo, orig cloth. b Mar 20 (185) £130

## Scheuchzer, Johann Jacob, 1672-1733
— Kupfer-Bibel. Augsburg & Ulm, 1731-35. 1st Ed. 4 vols. Folio, 19th-cent half calf; joints weak, 1 cover detached. Rusthole & stain in Plate 340b; some browning & tears to margins. S Mar 14 (320) £3,600
— Natur-Geschichte des Schweitzerlandes samt seinen Reisen ueber die Schweitzerische Gebuerge. Zurich: David Gessner, 1746. 2 vols in 1. 4to, 19th-cent half mor; spines worn. With 31 plates, 48 of them bound at end of Vol I is J. G. Sulzer's Untersuchung von dem Ursprung der Berge, 1746. Some worming in lower margins of Vol II repaired; inner margin of 1st tp repaired. S June 12 (308) £650

## Schiff, Gert
— Johann Heinrich Fuessli. Zurich & Munich, 1973. 2 vols. 4to, orig cloth, in djs. sg Jan 11 (189) $475

## Schiller, Friedrich von, 1759-1805
— Das Lied von der Glocke. Offenbach: Rudolf Koch & Rudolf Gerstung, 1919. One of 100. Vellum with hand-painted vignettes of flowers surrounded by rule-border in gilt; discoloration along outer edges. cb Oct 17 (648) $850
— Werke. Stuttgart & Tuebingen, 1830. 8vo, contemp purple mor extra by Brand. Fuerstenberg copy. C May 1 (147) £1,300

Anr copy. Contemp green mor extra by A. Schillings. C May 1 (148) £1,200
— William Tell, a Drama....... L, 1829. 8vo, mor extra presentation bdg by Hering. Queen Adelaide's copy, sgd on tp. CE May 22 (421) $550
— Works. Phila., [1883]. Ed by J. G. Fischer. 4 vols. 4to, half mor. pba Dec 14 (129) $70

## Schiotz, Eiler H.
— Itineraria Norvegica. A Bibliography.... Oslo, [1970-86]. 2 vols. In djs. Inscr. wa Dec 14 (10) $90

## Schlegel, Hermann, 1804-84
— De Vogels van Nederland. Leiden, [1859-61]. 3 vols. 8vo, modern half mor by Sangorski & Sutcliffe. With 362 hand-colored plates. Some discoloration of plate paper. S Oct 27 (775) £750 [Grahame]
— De Vogels van Nederlandsch Indie. Leiden & Amst., 1863-66. 1st Ed. 3 parts in 1 vol. 4to, half mor by Sangorski & Sutcliffe, orig wraps bound in; rubbed, joints worn. With 50 plates, 48 of them hand-colored. Some plates chipped; minor soiling & foxing. O Mar 5 (200) $1,200
— Natuurlijke Historie van Nederland. De Dieren van Nederland. Harrlem, 1860-61. 2 vols. 8vo, contemp half mor; orig wraps bound in. With 53 plates (51 hand-colored). Slight offsetting to text. S Oct 27 (776) £260 [Grahame]

## Schlichtmann, Margaret E. See: Paden & Schlichtmann

## Schmalenbach, Werner
— Kurt Schwitters. NY, [1967]. 4to, cloth, in dj. sg Jan 11 (387) $300

## Schmidt, Adolf, of Darmstadt
— Bucheinbaende aus dem XIV.-XIX. Jahrhundert in der Landesbibliothek zu Darmstadt. Leipzig, 1921. Folio, orig cloth; front cover blistered. With 10 plates. Some plates dampwrinkled. sg Apr 11 (56A) $325

## Schmidt, F. A.
— Mineralienbuch, oder Allgemeine und Besondere Beschreibung der Mineralien. Stuttgart, 1850. 4to, orig cloth; hinges cracked. With 44 hand-colored plates, some heightened with glitter. Some foxing to text. sg Apr 18 (180) $1,000

## Schmidt, Max
— Kunst und Kultur von Peru. Berlin, [n.d.]. Met Feb 24 (63) $300

## Schmidt, P.
— Die Illustration der Lutherbibel. Basel, [1962]. Folio, orig cloth in dj. sg Apr 11 (272) $110

## Schmidt, Robert
— Chinesische Keramik von der Han-Zeit bis zum XIX Jahrhundert. Frankfurt, 1924. 4to, cloth, in dj cracked across spine panel. With 132 plates. sg June 13 (102) $100
— Eugene Boudin, 1824-1898. Paris, 1973. One of 1,200. 3 vols. 4to, orig cloth. sg Jan 11 (58) $1,800

## Schmied, Wieland
— Alfred Kubin. NY, 1969. 4to, cloth, in dj. sg Jan 11 (250) $120

## Schmitt, Joseph
— L'Ile d'Anticosti, whose Wild and Barbaris Charm.... Hartford: Pvtly ptd, 1940. One of 50 on Rives Liampre. Calf; rubbed. With 9 mtd photographs & folding map in rear cover pocket. O June 25 (242) $375

## Schmitt, Martin F. —& Brown, Dee
— Fighting Indians of the West. NY, 1948. In worn & repaired dj; bdg corners bumped & showing. pba June 25 (210) $50

## Schmitz, Hermann
— For Hundert Jahren Festraume und Wehnzimmer des Deutscher Klassizismus und Biedermeier. Berlin, 1920. Oblong folio, bds; worn & chipped. With 28 color plates, loose as issued. wd Nov 15 (61) $500

## Schmoller, Hans
— Mr. Gladstone's Washi: A Survey of Reports.... Newtown PA: Bird & Bull Press, 1984. One of 500. 4to, half mor. With extra set of prints in portfolio. bba May 9 (455) £95 [Cox]
Anr copy. Orig half mor. sg Sept 14 (69) $175
Anr copy. Half mor. With extra set of prints in portfolio. sg Feb 15 (51) $175

## Schmoller, Hans —& Others
— Chinese Decorated Papers Newtown PA, 1987. One of 325. 4to, half mor. sg Sept 14 (70) $150; sg Feb 15 (50) $150

## Schmookler, Paul
— The Salmon Flies of Major John Popkin Traherne. Millis MA: The Complete Sportsman, [1993]. One of 300. Half lea; minor wear. O June 25 (243) $125

## Schneider, Antoine. See: Bory de Saint-Vincent & Schneider

## Schoberl, Frederick
— Austria. L: Ackermann, [1823]. ("The World in Miniature: Austria.") 2 vols. 12mo, later half mor. With 32 hand-colored plates. sg Mar 7 (330) $275
— Picturesque Tour from Geneva to Milan.... L: Ackermann, 1820. 8vo, contemp half mor; rubbed. With plan & 36 colored plates. Lacking last 4 leaves of ads; some browning & spotting. C Oct 25 (98) £1,200
— The World in Miniature. L: Ackermann, 1821-27. Ed by Schoberl. 43 vols. 12mo, mor gilt by Birdsall; 1 bdg scuffed. P June 5 (149) $8,000
— The World in Miniature: South Sea Islands. L: Ackermann, [1824]. 2 vols in 1. 12mo, orig bds; worn, loose. With facsimile & 25 colored plates. b Mar 20 (191) £140

## Schoelcher, Victor
— Conference sur Toussaint l'Ouverture.... Paris, 1879. 12mo, ptd wraps. sg Mar 28 (135) $50

## Schoene, Albrecht. See: Henkel & Schoene

## Schoepflin, Johann Daniel, 1694-1771
— Vindiciae Typographicae. Strassburg, 1760. 1st Ed. 4to, contemp wraps. With 7 folding facsimiles. Some soiling & foxing. O Mar 26 (245) $225
Anr copy. Calf; hinges cracked. Marginalia in pencil. Z June 28 (246) $275

## Schoonebeek, Adriaan
— Kurtze und grundliche Histori von dem Ursprung der heistlichen Orde...Ordens-Kleider.... Augsburg, 1695. 8vo, 19th-cent cloth. With 73 plates. Tear across Plate 9 repaired; marginal tear to plates 20 & 24 slightly affecting image. sg Mar 21 (281) $300

## Schopenhauer, Arthur, 1788-1860
— The Basis of Morality. L, 1903. sg Sept 21 (288) $60

## Schott, Albert —& Hagen, Karl
— Die Deutschen Kaiser, nach den Bildern des Kaiser-Saales im Roemer zu Frankfurt.... Frankfurt, 1847. Folio, 19th-cent cloth. With engraved title with hand-colored vignette, uncolored india-proof plates & 49 hand-colroed ports. Sir Henry Irving's copy. sg Feb 8 (334) $250

## Schott, Gaspar
— Mechanica hydraulico-pneumatica. Wuerzburg, 1657-[58]. 4to, contemp vellum over wooden bds with arms of Peucher of Bavaria & initials I.G.B.D.P. in gilt on upper cover. With engraved title, leaf of instruction to the binder & 46 plates. Engraved title shaved. S Mar 14 (321) £2,000
— Physica curiosa, sive mirabilia naturae et artis, libris XII. Wuerzburg, 1662. 2 vols. 4to, contemp calf; worn, spine of Vol I cracked & upper cover renewed. With 57 (of 60) plates. Marginal staining at beginning of Vol I. S June 12 (281) £580
— Technica curiosa, sive mirabilia artis. Nuremberg, 1664. 4to, contemp calf gilt with arms of August, Herzog von Schleswig-Holstein-Sondenburg in Beck; worn, spine torn. With frontis, port, full-page coat-of-arms & 63 plates on 62 sheets. Most of Plate 28 torn away; hole in center of 1st few leaves; tear in headline of K1; tear in Plates 17 & 20 repaired; a few other tears & marginal repairs; some browning. Madsen copy. S Mar 14 (322) £1,400

Anr Ed. Wuerzburg, 1664. 2 parts in 1 vol. 4to, contemp calf gilt with arms of August, Herzog von Schleswig-Holstein; worn & rubbed, spine torn. With frontis, engraved coat-of-arms & 63 plates on 62 sheets. Lacking 4F4; most of Plate 28 torn away; hole in center of 1st few leaves; tear in headline of K1; tear in Plates 17 & 20 repaired. S June 12 (309) £480

**Schouten, Willem Corneliszoon**
— Iournael ofte Beschryvinghe van de Wonderlijke Reyse.... Amst.: Blaeu, 1618. Contemp vellum gilt; some wear, pastedowns splitting along vellum turn-ins, notes on endpapers. With engraved title vignette & 8 folding maps & plates, all hand-colored. Some soiling; lacking 1 map. cb Oct 17 (205) $6,000

**Schouten, Wouter**
— Ost-Indische Reyse: worin erzehlt wird viel gedenckwuerdiges und ungemeine seltsame Sachen.... Amst., 1676. 2 parts in 1 vol. Folio, contemp vellum; spine split, front cover nearly detached & dampstained. With engraved title, port & 20 plates. Some dampstain at beginning; some browning. cb Feb 14 (2543) $450

**Schrdt, Hermann**
— Paris 1900: Masterworks of French Poster Art. NY, [1970]. Folio, cloth, in dj with wear. With 72 tipped-in color plates. Library markings. sg Sept 7 (286) $70

**Schreber, Johann Christian Daniel**
— Beschreibung der Graeser. Leipzig, 1769-1810. 2 vols. Folio, later half cloth; worn. With 54 plates. Some browning; library markings to tp & last text leaves & bottom margin of dedication leaf. bbc June 24 (301) $360

**Schreiber, Alois**
— Ouvrage representant en 70 a 80 feuilles les vues les plus pittoresques des bords du Rhin.... Schaffhausen: Louis Bleuler, [c.1839]. Oblong folio, contemp half mor gilt with ticket of William Muir of Hamilton; rubbed. With engraved title & 80 hand-colored plates, many heightened with gum-arabic. Tp spotted; 1st plate with soft crease; final plate with oxidation in sky-area. S June 27 (127) £60,000

**Schreiber, Lady Charlotte, 1812-95**
— Fans and Fan Leaves. L, 1888. Folio, contemp vellum gilt; scuffed & soiled. With 161 plates. Some fingersoiling. Ck Sept 8 (50) £600

**Schreiber, Fred**
— The Estiennes: An Annotated Catalogue of 300 Highlights of Their Various Presses. NY, [1982]. One of 600. bba May 9 (39) £95 [Maggs]
Anr copy. 8vo, orig cloth. sg Apr 11 (275) $225

**Schreiber, Wilhelm Ludwig**
— Der Buchholzschnitt im 15. Jahrhundert. Munich, 1929. One of—100. Folio, orig cloth box. With 43 (of 55) mounted leaves, & text brochure. S Oct 27 (1086) £450 [Pirages]

**Schretlen, Martinus Joseph**
— Dutch and Flemish Woodcuts of the Fifteenth Century. Bost., 1925. 4to, cloth. sg June 13 (333) $70
One of 20 on cheval chinois & bound in mor, with an extra suite of the plates in a folding case. Mor; rubbed. bba May 30 (25) £100 [Bifolco]

**Schrevelius, Theodorus**
— Harlemias of Eerste Stichting der Stad Haarlem. Haarlem, 1754. 2d Ed. 2 vols. 4to, contemp red mor gilt, with arms of the De Pinto family; rubbed, spines rubbed with loss. With engraved title, plan & 47 folding plates. Tear along mounts of 2 plates; paperclip mark on Vol I title; some cropping to dedication engraving. Dedication copy bound for Aron de Pinto & including orig drawings for the engraved title & armorial engraving. CE Dec 6 (193) $3,800

**Schreyvogel, Charles**
— My Bunkie and Others. NY, 1909. Oblong folio, disbound. With 36 plates. Some soiling & spotting. O July 9 (186) $90

**Schroder, Timothy B.**
— The Gilbert Collection of Gold and Silver. [Los Angeles, 1988]. 4to, cloth, in dj. sg June 13 (171) $80

**Schroeder, John F.**
— The Life and Times of Washington. NY: Johnson, Fry & Co., [1857-61]. 2 vols. 4to, lea. Some foxing. O July 9 (187) $100

**Schubert, Franz, 1797-1828**
— Am Erlafsee [D.586]. [N.p.], 1818. 1st Ed. 4to, in modern case. In: Mahlerisches Taschenbuch fuer Freunde interessanter Gegenden Natur-und Kunst Merkwuerdigkeiten der Oesterreichischen Monarchie... sechster Jahrgang. S May 15 (486) £3,000
— Symphonie C Dur fuer grosses Orchester, D.944. Leipzig; Breitkopf & Haertel, [1849]. 1st Ed. 4to, contemp half calf by Reichert of New Orleans. Engraved throughout. S June 13 (738) £240

**Schubert, Gotthilf Heinrich von, 1780-1860 —& Bernatz, Johann Martin**
— Bilder aus dem heiligen Lande. Stuttgart, [c.1842]. 2d Ed. 8vo, contemp half mor. Text in German & French. With 37 (of 38) plates (1 folding). Some spotting. S Oct 26 (207) £200 [Kosa]

**Schulberg, Budd**
— Waterfront. NY, [1955]. In laminated dj with discoloration. Inscr. sg June 20 (332) $100
— What Makes Sammy Run? NY: Random House, [1941]. In dj. sg June 20 (333) $375

**Schulte-Strathaus, E.**
See also: Bremer Press
— Bibliographie der Originalausgaben deutscher Dichtungen im Zeitalter Goethes.... Munich & Leipzig, 1913. 8vo, orig bds; crudely rebacked, edges chipped. sg Apr 11 (276) $90

## Schultz, James Willard
— Blackfeet Tales of Glacier National Park. Bost., 1916. 1st Ed. - Illus by R. W. Reed. Orig cloth; spine sunned, spine ends rubbed. With 24 plates. Robbins copy. pba Mar 21 (333) $170
— Questers of the Desert. Bost., 1925. pba Apr 25 (659) $70
— William Jackson, Indian Scout. Bost., 1926. Illus by Frank E. Schoonover. pba Feb 24 (277) $225

## Schultze, Eberhard
— Geographisches handbuechlein. Tuebingen, 1655. 2d Ed. 12mo, contemp vellum; soiled. With additional title, 3 tables, & 7 folding maps & plates. Title & 1st pp repaired; some small tears. S Oct 26 (206) £850 [Antiquariat]

## Schultze, Walter. See: Schouten, Wouter

## Schumann, Robert, 1810-56
— Der Rose Pilgerfahrt, Op. 112. Leipzig: Kistner, [1852]. Early Issue. Folio, orig wraps. Piano score; engraved music with litho title on wraps & pictorial frontis. Some spotting, staining & repairs. Inscr to Jenny Lind (as Goldschmidt). S Dec 1 (311) £2,500

## Schurman, Anna Maria van
— Opuscula Hebraea, Graeca, Latina, Gallica: Prosaica & metrica. Leiden: Elzevir, 1648. 1st Ed. 8vo, old vellum. Port loose, with later pencil notes on verso. sg Mar 21 (282) $750

## Schwartz, Aubrey
— Mothers and Children. [Brooklyn, 1958]. One of 60. 32mo, mor gilt by the Harcourt Bindery. With 18 plates. Inscr. sg Sept 7 (309) $375

## Schwartz, Seymour I. —& Ehrenberg, Ralph E.
— The Mapping of America. NY, [1980]. 4to, cloth, in dj. sg Dec 7 (46) $200; sg May 9 (36) $130; sg May 9 (37) $130

## Schwartze, Moritz Gotthilf
— Das alte Aegypten.... Leipzig, 1843. 4to, half calf; worn. Some discoloration. S Oct 26 (208) £450 [Lewis]

## Schwarz, Arturo
— Man Ray: the Rigour of Imagination. NY, 1977. One of 500. 4to, half cloth. sg Jan 11 (371) $350; sg Jan 11 (372) $110

## Schwarz, Ignaz
— Wiener Strassenbilder im zeitalter des Rokoko. Vienna, 1914. One of 30. 4to, mor gilt by Ferdinand Bakala. With 59 color plates & 57 uncolored plates. b June 28 (74) £400

## Schwarz, Karl
— Das Graphische Werk von Lovis Corinth. Berlin, 1917. One of 60. Folio, orig cloth. sg Jan 11 (115) $650

## Schwatka, Frederick, 1849-92
— Along Alaska's Great River. NY, [1885]. 8vo, orig cloth; extremities rubbed, front hinge cracked. pba Nov 16 (246) $120
— A Summer in Alaska. St. Louis, 1893. 8vo, orig cloth; worn & soiled. wa Feb 29 (270) $65

## Schwenter, Daniel
— Deliciae Physico-Mathematicae. Oder Mathemat. und Philosophische Erquickstunden. Nuremberg, 1636. 4to, contemp vellum; soiled, lower outer corner of upper cover torn. Some browning & staining. S Mar 14 (330) £480

## Schwerdt, C. F. G. R.
— Hunting, Hawking, Shooting.... L, 1928-37. One of 300. 4 vols. 4to, orig half mor gilt; several covers detached. CE Sept 27 (249) $500

## Schwiebert, Ernest George
— Matching the Hatch. NY, 1955. In dj with tears to extremities. Inscr to William Kaufmann. pba July 11 (274) $140
— Salmon of the World. NY: Winchester Press, [1970]. One of 750. Folio, half cloth. With 30 color plates loose in portfolio. O June 25 (245) $375
— Trout. NY, [1978]. 2 vols. 4to, cloth. Sgd. O Feb 6 (209) $130

Anr copy. Cloth. Inscr. O June 25 (246) $130

One of 750, with an artificial fly in sunken mount. Cloth; scuffed. O Feb 6 (208) $275

## Schwing, Ned
— The Winchester Model 42. Iola, 1990. 4to, syn gilt; some wear. O Oct 10 (246) $60

One of 42. Half syn; worn. O Oct 10 (245) $120
— Winchester Slide-Action Rifles. Iola, 1992. One of 22. 2 vols. 4to, half syn; some wear. O Oct 10 (244) $140
— Winchester's Finest. The Model 21. Iola, 1990. One of 50. 4to, syn gilt; some wear. Affixed to front pastedown are 5 snapshots of Winchester engravers. O Oct 10 (247) $250

Anr Ed. Fredericksburg TX, 1991. One of 100. 4to, syn gilt; some wear. O Oct 10 (248) $140

## Schwob, Marcel, 1867-1905
— Vies imaginaires. Paris, 1929. One of 120. Illus by Georges Barbier. 4to, mor extra by Rene Aussourd reproducing the orig upper wrap design, orig wraps bound in. S Nov 21 (396) £5,000

## Scidmore, Eliza Ruhamah, 1856-1928
— Appleton's Guide-Book to Alaska and the Northwest Coast. NY, 1897. 8vo, pictorial cloth. sg Oct 26 (2) $50

## Science...
— La Science Curieuse, ou traite de la Chyromance. Paris, 1667. 2d Ed. 4to, contemp calf; spine repaired. With 90 plates. Some worming to lower margin; a few leaves dampstained. S July 11 (273) £250

**Scientific...**
— Scientific American. A Journal of Practical Information in Art, Sciences, Mechanics.... NY, 1874-1923. 54 vols. Folio. Lacking some leaves & plates. Sold w.a.f.  NH July 21 (288) $930

**Sclater, Philip Lutley**
— A Monograph of the Jacamars and Puff-Birds. L, [1879-82]. 4to, contemp half mor; extremities rubbed. With 55 hand-colored plates. Mtd on guards throughout; some spotting; c.6 plates with marginal browning. Fattorini copy.  C Oct 25 (85) £2,500
— Nitzch's Pterylography. L, 1867. 4to, half mor; front cover almost detached.  pba June 20 (66) $160

**Sclater, Philip Lutley —&
Hudson, William Henry, 1841-1922**
— Argentine Ornithology. L, 1888-89. 2 vols. 8vo, orig bds; soiled, discolored, bumped, hinges starting, stamp on pastedown. With 20 colored plates. Met May 22 (451) $1,200

**Sclater, Philip Lutley —&
Thomas, Michael R. Oldfield**
— The Book of Antelopes. L, 1894-1900. 4 vols. 4to, later cloth. With 100 colored plates. Fattorini copy. C Oct 25 (84) £3,200

Anr copy. Orig cloth, 12 orig wraps bound in. With 100 colored plates. Vol II with both the cancellans & candellanda versions of C2; bound with the temporary titles & provisional contents lists in Vols I-III, with sheets for final titles & prelim leaves for Vols I-III loosely inserted. C May 31 (41) £4,000

**Sclater, William Lutley.** See: Shelley & Sclater

**Scollard, Clinton**
— The Epic of Golf. Bost.: Houghton Mifflin, 1923. 1st Ed. Half cloth in dj; d/j spine chipped.  pba Nov 9 (72) $160

**Scores...**
— Scores & Biographies of Celebrated Cricketers. L, 1862-1925. Vols 1-15, lacking Vol 14. 8vo, various bdgs; some covers detached, spines cracked, soiled. G. B. Buckley's annotated set.  pn Oct 12 (209) £1,200

**Scoresby, William, 1789-1857**
— An Account of the Arctic Regions.... Edin., 1820. 1st Ed. 2 vols. 8vo, contemp half calf. With 2 folding frontises, 4 tables, 4 maps & 18 plates. pnE Sept 20 (120) £580

**Scot, Reginald, 1538-99**
— The Discoverie of Witchcraft.... L, 1665. 3d Ed. Folio, later calf; rebacked preserving orig spine. Some spotting & staining; lacking half-title & X5-X6; some rustholes affecting text; some staining & soiling; a few leaves with marginal tears. S July 11 (274) £480

**Scotland...**
— Scotland: Her Songs and Scenery. L, 1868. 4to, orig cloth. With 14 mtd albumen prints. Some spotting. b May 30 (65) £150

**Scotland's...**
— Scotland's Industrial Souvenir. A Pictorial Description.... [Derby & L, c.1904]. Folio, orig cloth; spotted. With 32 litho plates in gold & colors. O Mar 5 (201) $350

**Scots...**
— Scots Magazine [continued from 1817 as the Edinburgh Magazine]. Edin., 1739-1817. Vols 1-79. 8vo, contemp calf gilt. pnE May 15 (39) £10,800

**Scott, Dred.** See: Howard, Benjamin C.

**Scott, E. B.**
— The Saga of Lake Tahoe. Lake Tahoe: Sierra-Tahoe Publishing, 1957. Folio, in dj. Sgd on half-title. pba Aug 8 (179) $55

**Scott, Genio C.**
— Fishing in American Waters. NY, 1869. 8vo, cloth; worn. O June 25 (247) $90

Anr copy. Cloth; worn, spine ends frayed. sg Mar 7 (529) $60

Anr Ed. NY: Orange Judd, [1875]. 8vo, orig cloth. Library markings; lower corner of tp lacking. pba July 11 (276) $50

**Scott, George Cole**
— Sixty Packs 1921-1956. Richmond VA, 1957. Ltd Ed, this being copy 10. 4to, looseleaf binder; some cover wear & stains. Mimeographed typescript, with photographs tipped in. Inscr to J. Watson Webb. O Jan 9 (196) $170

**Scott, George Gilbert**
— Gleanings from Westminster Abbey. Oxford, 1861. Half mor; rubbed. Extra-illus with plates. pba Mar 7 (229) $75

**Scott, Harvey W.**
— History of the Oregon Country. Cambr. MA, 1924. One of 500. 6 vols. In chipped djs. pba Nov 16 (247) $200

**Scott, Job**
— Journal of the Life, Travels and Gospel Labours.... NY, 1797. 12mo, old calf; front joint cracked. Lacking prelims before tp.  pba Aug 8 (586) $85

**Scott, John**
— British Field Sports. See: Lawrence, John

**Scott, John, 1730-83**
— The Poetical Works. L, 1782. 8vo, contemp bds; def. With port & 11 plates, 4 engraved by William Blake. b Jan 31 (141) £110

## Scott, John, 1783-1821
— A Visit to Paris in 1814. L, 1816. 5th Ed. 8vo, early calf; loose. sg Mar 7 (332) $50

## Scott, Sir Michael. See: Michael Scotus

## Scott, Peter
— Morning Flight. L, 1935. One of 750. 4to, orig cloth; stain to spine. O June 25 (248) $150
— Wild Chorus. L, 1938. One of 1,250, sgd. 4to, cloth, in chipped dj. sg Mar 7 (530) $140

## Scott, Capt. Robert Falcon, 1868-1912
— Scott's Last Expedition. L, 1913. 2 vols. Orig cloth; worn & soiled. wa Dec 14 (119) $70
   Anr copy. Half mor by Brian Frost. wa Feb 29 (226) $375
   Anr Ed. Toronto, [1913?]. pba July 25 (65) $225
— The Voyage of the "Discovery." L, 1905. 2d Impression. 2 vols. Orig cloth; extremities rubbed, spine heads bumped. pba July 25 (64) $350

## Scott, Sir Walter, 1771-1832
See also: Fore-Edge Paintings; Limited Editions Club
— The Abbot. Edin., 1820. 1st Ed. 3 vols. 12mo, contemp half calf. pba Mar 7 (232) $160
— The Antiquary. Edin., 1816. 1st Ed. 3 vols. 12mo, contemp calf; spines, joints & edges rubbed. pba Aug 22 (643) $130
— The Border Antiquities.... L, 1814-17. 1st Ed. 2 vols. 4to, mor gilt. pba Sept 14 (313) $275
   Anr copy. 2 vols in 1. 4to, 19th-cent lea gilt. With engraved titles & 93 plates, all mtd india-proofs. Some plate mounts foxed. sg Dec 7 (297) $375
— Catalogue of the Library at Abbotsford. Edin., 1838. 1st Ed. 4to, contemp half mor; rubbed. bba July 18 (3) £260 [Laywood]
— Ivanhoe. Edin., 1820. 1st Ed, State not given. 3 vols. 12mo, later half calf. bba May 28 (151) £110 [N. Williams]
— The Journal.... Edin., 1890. 1st Ed, One of 6 on japon for presentation by the pbr, this copy for Dean Sage. 2 vols. 8vo, cloth. Inscr by & with ALs from the pbr, David Douglas, to Dean Sage. Z June 28 (247) $400
— The Lady of the Lake. Edin., 1819. 4to, contemp mor gilt; spine ends & extremities worn. Inscr by Lord Sandwich, 1826. pba Aug 8 (264) $110
— Letters on Demonology and Witchcraft.... L, 1830. 1st Ed. 12mo, lev gilt by Wood. Extra-illus with 12 plates by George Cruikshank separately issued, all in 3 states. sg Oct 19 (239) $950
— The Life of Napoleon. Phila., 1827. 3 vols. 8vo, orig bds; some wear & dampstaining. Dampstained & spotted. F June 20 (447) $100
— The Pirate. Edin., 1822. 1st Ed. 3 vols. 8vo, contemp half calf gilt. sg Sept 21 (290) $350
— Quentin Durward. Edin., 1823. 1st Ed. 3 vols. 8vo, contemp half calf. pba Mar 7 (230) $140
— Redgauntlet.... Edin., 1824. 1st Ed. 3 vols. 8vo, contemp half calf. pba Mar 7 (231) $140
— Rob Roy. Edin., 1818. 1st Ed. 3 vols. 12mo, contemp half calf; scuffed. F June 20 (443) $70

— Tales of a Grandfather. Bost., 1870. 3 vols. Half calf. pba Dec 14 (130) $90
— Tales of My Landlord. Edin., 1817-18. 2d Ed of 1st Series, 1st Ed of 2d Series. 8 vols. 12mo, contemp half mor; rubbed. bba May 30 (272) £110 [Scott]
— Waverley.... Edin., 1814. 1st Ed. 3 vols. 8vo, contemp half calf & bds; extremities worn, bindings tightened. Leaf O5 chipped. CE Nov 8 (240) $600
— Woodstock; or, the Cavalier. Edin., 1826. 1st Ed. 3 vols. 8vo, contemp half mor gilt; soiled. Some foxing. pba Mar 7 (233) $120
   Anr copy. Contemp half calf; rubbed. pba Aug 8 (589) $50
— Works. L, 1842-47. ("Waverley Novels.") Abbotsford Ed. 12 vols. 8vo, orig half mor; rubbed. ALs tipped in. S Apr 23 (150) £360
   Victoria Ed. L, 1897. 25 vols. 8vo, contemp calf gilt. sg Sept 21 (43) $650
   "New Abbotsford" Ed. Boston, 1900. ("Waverley Novels.") One of 1,000. 54 vols. Contemp half mor; spines faded, spine ends worn. CE Nov 8 (241) $150
   Edition de Grande Luxe. L: Merrill & Baker, [c.1900]. one of 500. 33 vols. Half mor. cb Oct 17 (297) $2,500
   Edition des Amateurs. L, [c.1900]. one of 250. 33 vols. Half mor gilt. pba Nov 30 (286) $800
   Anr Ed. NY, 1900. ("Waverley Novels.") 24 (of 25) vols; lacking Vol 13. 8vo, half calf. pba Aug 8 (287) $450
   Anr Ed. NY, [c.1900]. 12 vols. 8vo, half calf gilt. sg Feb 8 (91) $650

## Scott, William Henry. See: Lawrence, John

## Scott, Zachary
— John Emery. NY: Pvtly ptd, 1964. One of 200. Half mor. Contains 2-page essay by John Steinbeck about Emery. This copy with typed correction of pbr mtd to tp. pba Aug 22 (425) $1,100

## Scottowe, John. See: Roxburghe Club

## Scribner, Romeyn B.
— Senior Golf: Golf is More Fun After Fifty-Five. Golf, IL: Evans Scholars Foundation, [1960]. 1st Ed, One of 1,000. Ed by Frank Matey. Cloth. Inscr & sgd by Chick Evans to Frederick B. Alexander & Alfred V. Ednie. pba Nov 9 (73) $190

## Scrope, William
— Days and Nights of Salmon Fishing in the Tweed. L, 1843. 1st Ed. 8vo, modern half lea, preserving orig cloth sides. With 13 tinted lithos, including hand-colored plate of artificial fles. Some foxing, staining & soiling. O Feb 6 (210) $450
   Anr copy. Early half mor; backstrip held on with tape. sg Mar 7 (531) $475
   Anr copy. Contemp calf; rebacked. W Nov 8 (398) £350

## Scrutator. See: Horlock, H. W.

### Scudder, Samuel Hubbard, 1837-1911
— Every-Day Butterflies: A Group of Biographies. Bost., 1899. Cloth; spine spotted. pba Aug 8 (351) $55

### Scudery, George de
— Curia Politae: or the Apologies of Several Princes.... L, 1673. 2d Ed in English. Folio, contemp sheep; worn, covers detached, endpapers renewed. Tp stamped. sg Mar 21 (283) $100

### Seabury, George J.
— An Ode to the Lake Bass. NY, 1890. 8vo, cloth; spine ends & corners rubbed. pba July 11 (278) $110

### Seaver, James E.
— A Narrative of the Life of Mrs. Mary Jemison.... Buffalo, 1877. ("Life of Mary Jemison.") 12mo, orig cloth; joints splitting. sg Oct 26 (157) $120

### Seavey, Charles A.
— Mapping the Transmississippi West, 1540-1861: An Index to the Cartobibliography. Winnetka IL: Speculum Orbis Press, 1992. Map & Geography Round Table of the American Library Association, Occasional Paper No 3. pba Feb 13 (199) $85

### Sechenov, Ivan Mikhailovich
— Fiziologiia nervnoi sistemy. St. Petersburg, 1866. 8vo, contemp half lea; chipped at top. Some foxing. sg May 16 (495) $425
— Psikhologicheskie Etiudy. St. Petersburg, 1873. 8vo, contemp half sheep; scuffed. sg May 16 (496) $225

### Sedaine, Michel Jean, 1719-97
— La reine de Golconde, opera.... Versailles, 1782. 8vo, contemp red mor gilt, with arms of Louis XVI. Fuerstenberg - Schaefer copy. S Dec 8 (575) £900

### Seder, Anton
— Das Thier in der decorativen Kunst. Vienna: Gerlach & Wiedling, [c.1896-1903]. Folio, loose in orig bds as issued; rubbed. With litho title & 29 plates, all but 3 in color. Soiling, browning, marginal wear. CE June 15 (258) $1,600

Anr copy. Loose in orig bds as issued; edges soiled & worn. With 29 lithos, all but 3 in color. S Nov 21 (397) £1,100

### Sed-Rajna, Gabrielle
— L'Art Juif. [Paris, 1975]. Folio, cloth. sg Sept 7 (198) $70

### Seebohm, Henry, 1832-95
— A History of British Birds. L, 1883-85. 1st Ed. 4 vols. 8vo, contemp half mor gilt; rubbed. With 68 colored plates. Browned. bba July 18 (99) £65 [Pendlebury]

### Seelen, Johann Heinrich von
— Selecta Litteraria.... Luebeck, 1726. 8vo, contemp bds. Library stamp on both sides of tp; some browning & foxing. O Mar 26 (248) $90

### Segard, W. —& Testard, Francois Martin
— Picturesque Views of Public Edifices in Paris. L, 1814. 4to, contemp half sheep; needs rebdg. With 20 plates. Some plates with inked notes beneath caption; library stamps. sg Mar 7 (333) $250

### Seguin, Lisbeth Gooch
— Rural England. L, [1881]. One of 600. Folio, orig vellum; soiled. sg Mar 7 (334) $200

### Seguy, E. A.
— Les Fleurs et leurs applications decoratives. [Paris, c.1925]. Folio, loose in half-cloth portfolio. With 30 chromolitho plates numbered 31-60. Marginal chipping & soiling. sg May 9 (337) $650
— Insectes. Paris: Editions Duchartre et Van Buggenhoudt, [1926]. Folio, unbound as issued in orig half cloth portfolio; covers soiled. With 20 colored plates. pba Nov 30 (287) $1,500; sg Apr 18 (157) $3,200
— Papillons. Paris, [1925]. Folio, loose as issued in half cloth portfolio. With 10 (of 20) colored plates. Sold w.a.f. cb Oct 17 (100) $850

Anr copy. Pictorial bd portfolio; soiled. With 20 colored plates. pba Nov 30 (288) $1,900

Anr copy. Loose in later half cloth folder. sg Apr 18 (156) $3,400
— Samarkande. Paris, [c.1925]. Folio, loose, lacking bdg. With 20 color pochoir plates plus 14 duplicate plates. Marginal soiling & browning. sg May 9 (338) $400

### Selby, Prideaux John
— Illustrations of British Ornithology. Edin., 1841. 4 vols. 8vo & folio, contemp half mor gilt. With 2 engraved titles with hand-colored vignettes, 4 plain & 218 hand-finished colored plates. Creases to 2 titles & 2 plates; captions shaved with loss on 2 plates; outermargin shaved into image on 1 plate; 1 repaired tear. Fattorini copy. C Oct 25 (40) £16,000
— Parrots. Edin., 1836. 8vo, orig cloth; needs rebdg. With engraved title & 30 hand-colored plates. The Naturalist's Library, Vol XV (Ornithology Vol VI). sg May 9 (290) $300

### Selden, John, 1584-1654
— Mare clausum seu de dominio maris libri duo. L, 1635. 1st Ed. Folio, old calf; rebacked, upper cover & front blanks detached, spine scuffed. Text rippled. bbc June 24 (189) $500
— Of the Dominion, or Ownership of the Sea. L, 1663. ("Mare Clausum: the Right and Dominion of the Sea....") 2d Ed in English. 2 parts in 1 vol. Folio, contemp calf; worn & loose. Frontis def; library stamp on tp. sg Mar 7 (234) $300
— Of the Judicature in Parliaments.... L, 1681. 1st Ed. 8vo, old calf; becoming disbound. Some dampstaining to lower edges. wa Feb 29 (163) $160
— Titles of Honour. L, 1614. 1st Ed. 4to, contemp calf; rebacked. Ms notes on front endpapers. b Jan 31 (113) £95

2d Ed. L, 1631. 4to, later calf gilt; worn, lower cover detached. Some foxing & browning. bba May 30 (79) £100 [Wall]

Select... See: Smith, John

**Seligman, Germain**
— Roger de la Fresnaye. L, 1969. One of 900. 4to, cloth, in dj. sg Jan 11 (251) $150

**Seligmann, Charles Gabriel**
— The Melanesians of British New Guinea. Cambr., 1910. Orig cloth; stained. With folding map. S Mar 28 (406) £100

Sellar, W. Y. See: Fore-Edge Paintings

**Selous, Frederick Courteney, 1851-1917**
— Recent Hunting Trips in British North America. L, 1907. Orig cloth; recased with new endpapers. Some foxing. O Oct 10 (249) $170
Anr copy. Cloth; worn. O Oct 10 (250) $160
Anr copy. Some foxing. sg Mar 7 (533) $130

**Selz, Peter**
— Sam Francis. NY, [1975]. Oblong 4to, cloth, in dj. sg Jan 11 (182) $110
Revised Ed. NY, [1982]. Oblong 4to, cloth, in dj. Sgd by Francis. cb Oct 17 (688) $350

**Semivskii, Nikolai Vasil'evich**
— Noveishiia... povestvovaniia o vostochnoi Sibiri.... St. Petersburg, 1817. 2 parts in 1 vol. 8vo, orig wraps, unopened; torn. With engraved title (loose), engraved dedication, 10 plates & 2 folding maps, 1 hand-colored in outline. Some leaves towards end waterstained. C May 31 (111) £750

**Semmes, Raphael, 1809-77**
— Captains and Mariners of Early Maryland. Balt., 1937. 1st Ed. Sgd. wa Dec 14 (86) $80

**Semple, Miss ——**
— The Costume of the Netherlands.... L: Ackermann, 1817 [label dated 1819]. 4to, orig bds; worn. With engraved title & 30 hand-colored plates. Some soiling. S Mar 28 (153) £200

**Semple, Robert, 1766-1816**
— Walks and Sketches at the Cape of Good Hope. L, 1803. 8vo, old calf; spine & hinges repaired. Met May 22 (317) $225

**Senault, Louis**
— Petit Office de la Ste. Vierge.... Paris: chez l'auteur, [c.1680]. 8vo, 19th-cent mor extra by Thouvenin. Engraved throughout. Fuerstenberg - Schaefer copy. S Dec 8 (576) £1,290

**Sendak, Maurice**
— Where the Wild Things Are. NY, 1963. In dj. Sgd & with 2 orig sgd ink sketches laid in. O Sept 12 (159) $650

Anr Ed. NY, [c.1964]. In later dj. With gift record. Inscr & with sketch of Max dated May 1965. Met Dec 5 (379) $225
Anr Ed. NY, 1988. One of 220 with orig sgd ink sketch. Met Dec 5 (381) $900

**Seneca, Lucius Annaeus, 54? B.C.-39 A.D.**
— Opera philosophicae. Antwerp: Plantin, 1652. Folio, contemp vellum gilt; soiled. With engraved title & frontis. Some browning & foxing. cb June 25 (1772) $425
— Proverbia. Deventer: Richard Pafraet, 13 Feb 1490. 4to, unbound. 38 lines.. 6 leaves. HC 14646. C Nov 29 (74) £850

**Senex, John, d.1740**
See also: Ogilby & Senex
— A New General Atlas. L, 1721. Folio, early half mor. With 12 (of 34) double-page maps only. Lacking 1st gathering & plates of subscribers arms; 2 maps with fold breaks. sg Dec 7 (47) $1,400

**Senior, William**
— Travel and Trout in the Antipodes. Melbourne, etc., 1880. 8vo, calf gilt; rubbed, rear cover detached. ALs with initials to R. B. Marston laid in. O Feb 6 (211) $375

Sept... See: Giraudoux & Others

**Septem sapientes Romae**
— Historia septem sapientum Rome. Delft: Christian Snellaert, 1495. 4to, modern vellum using old material. 36 lines; gothic types. With 15 woodcuts. Minor marginal repairs. 46 leaves. HC 8726. Schaefer copy. P Nov 1 (192) $22,000
— Les sept saiges de Romme. Lyons: Olivier Arnoullet, [c.1520]. 4to, mor janseniste by Chambolle-Duru. Bastarda type. With 24 woodcuts. Washed & pressed. Schaefer copy. P Nov 1 (193) $17,000

**Sergent-Marceau, Antoine Francois, 1751-1847**
— Portraits des grands hommes, femmes illustres.... Paris, [1787-88]. Folio, 19th-Cent half calf. With title, & 80 color ports. Some marginal thumbing, & discoloration. Sold w.a.f. S Oct 27 (1105) £780 [Galleria San.]
Anr Ed. Paris: Pierre Blin, [c.1792]. 4to, 19th-cent russia gilt; rebacked, orig backstrip laid down, extremities rubbed. With colored title, engraved dedication & 192 color plates. Small tear along platemark of Plate 78; some foxing. CNY May 17 (106) $1,900
Anr copy. Contemp calf gilt; recased, spine head repaired. With colored title, engraved dedication & 192 hand-finished colored plates. Fuerstenberg - Schaefer copy. S Dec 8 (577) £1,200

**Serlio, Sebastiano, 1475-1554**
— Il Settimo Libro d'Architettura. Venice: Francesco de' Franceschi, 1584. 4to, old vellum; spine damaged. With 120 full-page woodcuts. sg June 13 (33) $750

### Sermon, William
— A Friend to the Sick; or, The Honest English Mans Preservation.... L, 1673. 1st Ed. 8vo, contemp calf; rebacked. With port frontis & title. Page edges browned; C5 torn; M1 with paper fault. Ck Mar 22 (272) £950

### Serna Santander, Carlos Antonio de la
— Memoire historique sur la Bibliotheque dite De Bourgogne, presentement Bibliotheque Publique de Bruxelles. Brussels, 1809. 8vo, orig wraps; spine ends chipped. Some foxing. Inscr to the Institute Royal de Hollande. O Mar 26 (249) $275
— Memoire sur l'origine et le premier usage des signatures et des chiffres, dans l'art typographique. Brussels, 1796 [An IV]. 8vo, half calf; worn. With 6 folding plates. Bound in is the 6-page Supplement, 1803 & the Prefatio Historico, 1800. O Mar 26 (250) $70

### Serpilius, Georg, Pseud.
— S. S. Verzeichnuess einiger Rarer Buecher. Frankfurt, 1723. 3 parts in 1 vol. 12mo, old bds with vellum tips. O Mar 26 (251) $400

### Serra, Junipero
See also: Grabhorn Printing
— [Confirmation record of the Missions of Santa Barbara, San Antonio de Padua, San Buenaventura, and San Luis Obispo....] [California, c.1783]. 11-3/4 in by 8 inches, mor slipcase. 1 leaf, 80 lines. Robbins copy. pba Mar 21 (334) $17,000
— Writings. Wash., 1955-66. 1st Eds. - Ed by Antonine Tibesar. 4 vols, orig cloth. Larson copy. pba Sept 28 (225) $325

### Serrano, Carmen Sotos
— Los Pintores de la Expedicion de Alejandro Malaspina. Madrid: Real Academia de la Historia, 1982. 2 vols. Folio, pictorial wraps; corner of Vol II plates. pba Apr 25 (207) $90

### Servaes, Franz
— Giovanni Segantini, sein Leben und sein Werk. Vienna, 1902. Oblong folio, bds; rebacked, rehinged. With 63 plates. sg June 13 (334) $200

### Serven, James E.
— Colt Firearms, 1836-1954. Santa Ana, 1954. Folio, orig bdg, in dj with light wear. pba Apr 25 (661) $50

### Servetus, Michael, 1511-53
— Dialogorum de trinitate libri duo. [Regensburg, 1721?]. 8vo, later mor; corners worn, rebacked. CE Nov 8 (146) $380

### Service, Douglas. See: Taverner & Service

### Serviss, Garrett Putnam, 1851-1929
— Edison's Conquest of Mars. Los Angeles: Carcosa House, 1947. One of 1,500. In repaired dj with piece lacking. pba May 4 (248) $60

### Sesti, Giovanni Battista
— Piante delle citta, piazze e castelli fortificati in questo stato di Milano. Milan, [1718]. 4to, contemp calf; spine ends chipped. With folding map, folding plan & 22 full-page plans, some hand-colored with green wash. b June 28 (64) £1,900

### Seton, Ernest Thompson, 1860-1946
— The Arctic Prairies. A Canoe-Journey.... NY, 1917. Inscr. sg Mar 7 (534) $225
— Lives of Game Animals. Garden City, 1925-28. One of 177. 4 vols. 4to, orig bdgs. This copy not sgd but with sgd presentation of seated bear mtd on larger sheet & taped to front pastedown. sg May 16 (344) $1,500
— Monarch, the Big Bear of Tallac. NY, 1904. Orig cloth; spine rubbed. pba Aug 22 (849) $50
— Studies in the Art Anatomy of Animals. L, 1896. 4to, orig cloth; 1 corner bumped. Some foxing & soiling, mainly to prelims. cb Feb 14 (2724) $225

### Seton-Thompson, Ernest. See: Seton, Ernest Thompson

### Setoun, Gabriel
— The Child World. L, 1896. 8vo, mor extra by Kelly, orig wraps bound in. b Sept 20 (640) £220

### Seuphor, Michel
— La Peinture abstraite en Flandre. Brussels, 1963. 4to, cloth. sg Jan 11 (390) $60

### Seuss, Dr.
— The 500 Hats of Bartholomew Cubbins. NY, [1938]. 1st Ed. 4to, pictorial bds; wraped at bottom left corner. pba June 20 (297) $120
— Horton Hears a Who! NY: Random House, [1954]. 4to, pictorial bds, in dj with rubbing to extremities. pba Mar 7 (234) $750
— If I Ran the Circus. NY: Random House, [1956]. 4to, pictorial bds, in repaired dj. pba Mar 7 (235) $900
— Yertle the Turtle and Other Stories. NY, [1958]. 1st Ed. 4to, pictorial bds; extremities rubbed. pba Mar 7 (236) $55

Anr copy. Cloth, in dj. pba June 20 (298) $250
— You're Only Old Once! NY, [1986]. One of 500. sg Dec 14 (258) $200

### Seutter, Matthaeus
— Atlas Minor.... Augsburg, [1744?]. Oblong 8vo, orig calf; rubbed. With engraved title & 63 maps, all hand-colored. Some marginal spotting. C May 31 (72) £2,300
— Atlas Novus. Augsburg, [1740?]. Folio, contemp calf; hinges weak. With colored allegorical title & 49 double-page maps with contemp body color. Lacking tp & text; 3 maps repaired at margins; some fold breaks & repairs. S June 27 (84) £4,200
— Atlas novus indicibus instructus oder neur mit Wort-Registern versehener Atlas. Augsburg & Vienna, 1730-[38]. Folio, contemp calf; upper cover detached. With hand-colored frontis & 52 double-page hand-colored maps. Several maps split at fold without loss; worming at guards occasionally affecting

image, with slight loss; some soiling. S Nov 30 (84) £5,500

**Severi, Francesco**
— Salmi passaggiati per tutte le voci nella maniera che si cantano in Roma.... Rome: Nicola Borboni, 1615. Oblong 12mo, contemp vellum. Some plates trimmed at top; tp & top margins with staining. Thurston Dart's sgd copy. S May 15 (491) £3,000

**Severini, Gino, 1883-1966**
— Fleurs et masques. L, 1930. One of 125. Folio, orig vellum; browned at joints, spine ends chipped. With 16 plates colored through stencils & heightened with gold. S May 16 (127) £9,000

**Sevigne, Marie de Rabutin-Chantal, Marquise de, 1626-96**
— Letters. Phila., 1927. Intro by A. E. Newton. 7 vols. Half calf gilt by Sangorski & Sutcliffe. pba Aug 22 (644) $80

**Sewall, Samuel, 1652-1730**
— The Selling of Joseph: a Memorial. [Northampton, Mass.: Gehenna Press, 1968]. One of 100. Half mor. With port by Leonard Baskin. Inscr by Baskin; with additional port laid in. sg Feb 15 (29) $175

**Sewall, Stephen**
— An Hebrew Grammar.... Cambr., 1806. 8vo, orig half sheep. sg Oct 26 (182) $40

**Seward, George H.**
— Chinese Immigration, in its Social and Economical Aspects. NY, 1881. Orig cloth; spine spotted & frayed. pba Aug 8 (180) $65

**Seward, William Henry, 1801-72**
— Argument of William H. Seward, in defence of William Freeman, on his Trial for Murder, at Auburn, July 21st & 22d, 1846. Auburn, 1846. 8vo, orig wraps; backstrip reinforced, some chipped, inked note on front cover. sg Mar 28 (312) $250
— Russian America. Message from the President of the United States.... [Wash., 1868]. Loose in cloth slipcase. Top edges scorched. Robbins copy. pba Mar 21 (337) $130

**Seward, William Wenman**
— The Hibernian Gazetteer.... Dublin, 1789. 12mo, sheep; worn. With folding map. sg Mar 7 (336) $90

**Sewel, William, 1653-1720**
— The History of the Rise, Increase, and Progress of the Christian People Called Quakers. L, 1725. Folio, mor gilt; extremities scuffed. pba Nov 30 (290) $160
— A Large Dictionary English and Dutch. Amst., 1754. 2 parts in 1 vol. 4to, contemp calf; rubbed, lower free endpaper def. bba July 18 (137) £140 [Maggs]

**Sewell, Anna, 1820-78**
— Black Beauty. Bost.: American Humane Education Society, [1890]. 1st American Ed. 12mo, orig bds;

spine ends chipped. Chipped at top. bbc June 24 (606) $260

**Sewell, Mary Young, fl.1777-1809**
— Poems. Egham & Chertsey, 1803. Bound with: Costello, Louisa Stuart. Redwald; a Tale of Mona.... Brentford, 1819. 8vo, contemp half calf; worn. b Dec 5 (373) £70
— Trafalgar: a Poem, to the Memory of Lord Nelson.... Egham & Chertsey, 1806. 4to, orig wraps; creased. b Dec 5 (374) £320

**Seyd, Ernest**
— California and its Resources.... L, 1858. 1st Ed. 8vo, orig cloth. With 2 folding maps & 18 plates. Larson copy. pba Feb 12 (172) $1,300

**Seymour, Robert, 1800-36**
— Seymour's Humorous Sketches. L, 1872. 8vo, half mor gilt, orig cover & spine bound in. sg Feb 8 (92) $80
— Sketches. L, [c.1840]. 5 vols in 1. 8vo, half mor gilt by Bayntun. With 5 etched titles & 180 plates. Some plates browned along edges. sg Apr 18 (181) $300

**Shackleton, Sir Ernest Henry, 1874-1922**
— The Heart of the Antarctic. L, 1909. 1st Ed. 2 vols. 4to, orig cloth; 1 backstrip off, some wear. wa Feb 29 (135) $730

Anr Ed. Phila., 1909. 2 vols. Orig cloth; corners showing, rear joint of Vol I split, lacking free endpapers. pba July 25 (69) $325
— South.... NY, 1920. 1st American Ed. pba July 25 (70) $100
— Aurora Australis. See: Aurora...

**Shadwell, Thomas, 1642?-92**
— Works. L: Fortune Press, 1927. One of 90. 5 vols. 4to, orig half mor. bba May 9 (492) £220 [Marks]

**Shafer, L. A.**
— The Cup Races. Being a History in Pictures of the Winning and Defense of the America's Cup. NY, [1899?]. Folio, orig bds. S Oct 27 (835) £220 [Dennistoun]

**Shaffer, Ellen Kate**
— The Garden of Health. An Account of Two Herbals. [San Francisco]: Ptd for the Book Club of California, 1957. Folio, orig bds. With an orig leaf from the 1499 Hortus Sanitatis bound in. pba June 20 (299) $180

Anr copy. Orig bds. With an orig leaf from the 1499 Hortus Sanitatis bound in. pba Aug 8 (595) $170

**Shaftesbury, Anthony Ashley Cooper, 3d Earl, 1671-1713**
— Characteristicks of Men, Manners, Opinions, Times. Birm.: Baskerville, 1773. 5th Ed. - Illus by S. Gribelin. 3 vols. 4to, contemp calf. With frontis Offset. S Oct 27 (1176) £200 [Sotheran]

892

## Shahn, Ben
— An Alphabet of Creation.... NY, [1954]. One of 50 on Umbria. Orig drawing on leaf facing tp. K June 23 (456) $650

One of 50, with a sgd ink drawing. 4to, cloth. Inscr. sg Feb 15 (271) $850

— Love and Joy about Letters. NY, 1963. 4to, cloth. Sgd. F Mar 28 (557) $160

## Shakers
— A Brief Exposition of the Established Principles and Regulations of the United Society of Believers Called Shakers. NY, 1879. 8vo, orig ptd wraps; minor soiling & wear. pba Aug 8 (181) $60
— Shaker Music, Original Inspirational Hymns and Songs. NY: Pond for the North Family, 1884. 8vo, orig cloth; worn, hinges cracked. sg Oct 26 (335) $60

## Shakespear, Henry
— The Wild Sports of India.... L, 1862. 2d Ed. 8vo, orig cloth; worn, inner joint broken. Some foxing & soiling. O Jan 9 (197) $80

## Shakespeare...
— Shakespeare's Seven Ages of Man. Hammersmith, 1799. Illus by Thomas Stothard. Folio, half cloth. With tp & 7 plates, all hand-colored. S July 11 (131) £400

## Shakespeare, William, 1564-1616
See also: Cranach Press; Doves Press; Fore-Edge Paintings; Golden Cockerel Press; Grabhorn Printing; Kelmscott Press; Limited Editions Club; Nonesuch Press
— Antony and Cleopatra. Guildford: Circle Press, 1979. One of 40 with artist's proof frontis. Illus by Ronald King. Folio, unsewn as issued in white ptd wraps. bba May 9 (467) £120 [Hanborough]
— As You Like It. L: Hodder & Stoughton 1909]. Illus by Hugh Thomson. With 40 colored plates. b May 30 (458) £60
— Hamlet. L: Selwyn & Blount, [1922]. ("Hamlet, Prince of Denmark.") Illus by John Austen. 4to, orig bds; spine & corners worn, spine def at head. Sgd by John Austen. cb Oct 17 (596) $170
— King Lear. San Francisco, [1930]. One of 200. Cloth; faded. sg Feb 15 (190) $90

Anr Ed. Bangor ME: Theodore Press, 1986. ("The Tragedie of King Lear.") One of 160. Illus by Claire Van Vliet. Folio, half pigskin. Schaefer copy. P Nov 1 (194) $1,000

— The Merchant of Venice. L, [c.1909]. Illus by James D. Linton. 4to, orig cloth; bowed, worn. With 36 color plates. F June 20 (533) $70

One of 500. Mor gilt with onlaid design depicting Shylock, by Bayntun-Riviere. With 36 color plates. CE Feb 21 (16) $2,000

Anr copy. Orig vellum gilt. S May 16 (128) £190
— The Merry Wives of Windsor. L, 1910. One of 350, sgd by the artist. Illus by Hugh Thomson. 4to, vellum gilt; endpapers foxed. sg Sept 14 (332) $300

Anr Ed. NY, 1910. 4to, orig cloth. With 40 colored plates. pba Apr 4 (222) $170
— A Midsummer-Night's Dream. L, 1908. Illus by Arthur Rackham. 4to, orig cloth. bba May 9 (403) £260 [Wai Chen]

Anr copy. Cloth; endpapers foxed. sg Feb 15 (258) $150

One of 1,000. Orig vellum gilt. S Nov 2 (117) £370 [Bayntuns]

One of 1,000, sgd by Rackham. Vellum gilt; light staining. Ck May 31 (133) £420

Anr copy. Mor gilt by Riviere. sg Oct 19 (196) $800

1st American Ed. NY, 1908. 4to, half cloth; covers foxed, edges worn, 1 plate detached & creased, shaken. With frontis & 39 colored plates. pba Aug 22 (838) $75
— The Tempest. L: Hodder & Stoughton, [1908]. One of 500, sgd by Dulac. Illus by Edmund Dulac. 4to, orig vellum. K Oct 1 (142) $1,000

Anr copy. Prelims foxed. sg Oct 19 (76) $900; W Mar 6 (104) £520

Anr Ed. Montagnola di Lugano: Officina Bodoni, 1924. One of 10 specially bound in mor. sg Oct 19 (183) $1,200

Anr Ed. L, 1926. Illus by Arthur Rackham. 4to, orig cloth, in dj with short tear. Ck May 31 (159) £220

Anr Ed. L, [1926]. One of 520. 4to, orig vellum gilt, in soiled & chipped dj. P Dec 12 (154) $1,000

Anr copy. Orig vellum gilt; discolored. With 21 color plates. S Nov 2 (107) £420 [Fox]

Anr copy. Orig vellum gilt; spine ends worn. sg Oct 19 (202) $1,200

Anr copy. Orig vellum gilt; spine soiled. With 21 color plates. sg Feb 15 (259) $950
— Titus Andronicus. L, 1687. 4to, half calf; hinges rubbed. Marginal dampstains; trimmed; browned & soiled. Sold w.a.f. CE June 15 (259) $300
— Twelfth Night. L, [1908]. One of 350, sgd by artist. Illus by W. Heath Robinson. 4to, orig vellum gilt. With 40 colored plates. sg Sept 14 (315) $600
— Venus and Adonis. Paris, 1930. One of 440. Half vellum. sg Sept 14 (228) $100

### 2d Folio
— Comedies, Histories, and Tragedies. L, 1632. Mor gilt by Riviere; inner hinges split, chip to tail of spine, lower flyleaf creased. Leaf "To the Reader" lacking & supplied in facsimile; tp heavily restored & resized; port with disfiguring ink facsimile work; last leaf remargined catching rule border; repaired tears, that to oo2v with loss to 4 or 5 words; small holes to D4, I6, S5 & x1, each catching 1 or 2 letters; filled holes to dd5 & hh1; marginal repairs, a few entering rule borders; a few borders shaved; 1st few leaves foxed; some soiling & staining. CNY May 17 (107) $12,000
— The Life of King Henry the Fift; The Second Part; The Third Part. L, 1632. Modern calf. Trimmed at beginning; some repairs, staining & browning. CE May 22 (425) $650

# SHAKESPEARE

— A Midsommer Nights Dreame. L, 1632. Modern half calf. Cropped, browned & stained. S Mar 28 (494) £150

— Richard the Second * Henry IV, Part 2 L, 1632. Disbound. Headlines cropped, affecting top line of text; 1st leaf frayed along edges with loss; minor stains. sg Mar 21 (287) $150

— Romeo and Juliet * Timon of Athens. L, 1632. Disbound. Puncture through outer margin of 1st several leaves; minor stains. sg Mar 21 (288) $300

### 3d Folio

— Comedies, Histories, and Tragedies. L, 1664. 2d Issue. Later sheep; worn, front cover detached, spine ends perished. First 11 & last 6 leaves supplied in facsimile & some out of order; marginal dampstaining touching text; some tears into text; some soiling. cb Oct 17 (342) $4,000

### 4th Folio

Anr Ed. L, 1685. Contemp calf; worn, rebacked, new endpapers. Tear in tp repaired; lacking port; tear in Gg2 & Eee4; crude repairs to Ii2-4, Mm3, Nn1 & Qq5-6; small burn-hole in Qq6 & Aaa5; corner of Ll6 burnt; some worming; partly erased stamp on blank leaf preceding title. S Dec 18 (117) £2,500 [Heritage]

Anr copy. Calf. Rubbed Port from anr copy, washed & sized, with residual soiling; tp & last leaf rehinged & remargined; c.35 leaves supplied; minor foxing, staining & repairs. sg Apr 18 (182) $15,000

1st state of imprint without Chiswell's name. Mor gilt by Riviere. Small restoration to port margin; corner of final leaf restored affecting line border. b Dec 5 (187) £16,000

Anr copy. 19th-cent mor gilt by Pratt; rebacked with orig backstrip laid down, front free endpaper detached. Frontis repaired & with margins extended; tp restored & with repaired tear at foot; dedication leaf bound after List of Actors & Catalogue leaf; c.120 leaves with at least 1 margin extended, occasionally affecting border rules or a few letters; many marginal repaired tears; I6, L12 & c.10 other leaves with longer repaired tears affecting text, with letters & rules supplied in Ms facsimile; some 18th-cent annotations. CNY May 17 (108) $14,000

— King Lear * Othello * Anthony and Cleopatra. L, 1685. Disbound, pp. 87-164. Some browning & chipping. bbc Feb 26 (345) $600

— Pericles * The London Prodigal. L, 1685. Pp. 193-226, modern cloth. Stain to top half inch of pages. pba Sept 14 (315) $300

— Timon of Athens * Julius Caesar * Macbeth. L, 1685. Disbound, pp. 1-58. Some chipping & browning. bbc Feb 26 (344) $525

— Troilus and Cressida * Coriolanus. L, 1685. Disbound, pp. 258-84. Burnhole to pp, 259-60. pba Sept 14 (316) $250

### Collected Works

— 1709-10. - L: Jacob Tonson Ed by N. Rowe. 7 vols. 8vo, contemp calf; Vol I rebacked, joints starting, endpaper in Vol VII repaired. cb Oct 17 (339) $1,900

— 1723-25. - Works. L: Jacob Tonson Ed by Alexander Pope. 6 vols. 4to, contemp calf; rebacked. pba Nov 30 (292) $2,000

— 1725-23. - L. Vols I-VI (of 7). 4to, contemp calf; joints weak. pba June 20 (303) $700

— 1768. - L. Ed by Samuel Johnson. 8 vols. 8vo, contemp calf; spines rubbed. b Sept 20 (173) £300

— 1788. - L. 20 vols. 12mo, old calf; rubbed, rebacked. K Oct 1 (340) $600

— 1802. - L.Boydell Ed. - Ed by George Steevens. 9 vols. Folio, mor gilt; rubbed & scraped. With 96 plates (additional plate bound at p. 62 of Richard the Third). Minor repairs; some spotting; some plates misbound. cb Oct 17 (341) $3,250

— 1802. - The Dramatic Works.... L.Boydell Ed. - Ed by George Steevens. 9 vols. Folio, contemp mor gilt. With 96 (of 100) plates. Foxing to plates. sg Oct 19 (241) $1,700

— 1813. - L. Ed by I. Reed. 21 vols. 8vo, contemp calf gilt; joints & spines rubbed. Ck Sept 8 (124) £750

— 1821. - L.Malone's Variorum Ed. 21 vols. 8vo, contemp calf gilt; joints rubbed. F Sept 21 (417) $675

— 1823. - Chiswick: C. Whittingham for Thomas Tegg et al.. 12mo, mor lavishly gilt in the style of books bound for Pietro Duodo. sg Apr 18 (183) $800

— 1832-34. - L: A. J. Valpy. 15 vols. 12mo, contemp calf. b Jan 31 (115) £140

— 1840. - The Pictorial Edition of the Works.... L. 7 vols. 8vo, contemp half calf; rubbed. b May 30 (417) £110

— 1847. - NY 3 vols. 4to, orig gilt-pictorial mor gilt. sg Feb 8 (93) $300

— 1857. - L. 15 vols. 12mo, half calf; rubbed. sg Sept 21 (44) $325

— c.1865. - L.Imperial Ed. - Ed by Charles Knight. 2 vols. Folio, orig half mor; spine ends chipped. CE Nov 8 (242) $400

— 1875-76. - L & NY: Virtue. Imperial Ed. 2 vols. Folio, gilt-pictorial mor. sg Feb 8 (94) $600

Anr copy. Mor gilt. sg Feb 8 (95) $325

— 1881. - NY Ed by Charles Knight. 6 vols. 8vo, half calf; spine ends worn. pba June 20 (302) $170

— 1887. - Bost. 12 vols. 8vo, contemp lea, in contemp lea travelling library case; dried, 1 hinge cracked. CE Sept 27 (252) $400

— 1891-93. - L.Cambr. Ed. 9 vols. 8vo, contemp calf; rebacked. sg Sept 21 (45) $600

— 1899-1900. - L.Larger Temple Ed, one of 175. Ed by Israel Gollancz. 12 vols. 8vo, contemp calf gilt; joints & edges rubbed. CE Feb 21 (204) $550

— 1900-3. - L: Vale Press Ed by T. Sturge Moore. 36 (of 39) vols in 18. 8vo, orig cloth. S May 16 (56) £260

— [c.1900]. - Phila.: J. P. Lippincott. 20 vols. 8vo, half mor gilt; rubbed. sg Sept 21 (46) $425

— 1901-4. - Edin.Remarque Ed, One of 15. Ed by W. E. Henley. 20 vols. Folio, mor extra with port of Shakespeare in gilt & blue more onlays, comedy & tragedy masks in gilt & white mor onlays. P Dec 12 (164) $12,000

— 1904. - L: Grant Richards. Extended to 20 vols. Mor gilt. According to tp, a "unique, extra illustrated set, extended to twenty volumes by the insertion of numerous engravings and other fine illustrations, many of which are colored by hand". cb Oct 17 (340) $8,500

— 1904-7. - Stratford: Shakespeare Head Press One of 1,000. 10 vols. 4to, orig cloth. bba May 9 (635) £430 [Heritage]

— 1926. - Phila.: J. B. Lippincott Ed by Horace Howard Furness. 27 vols. pba Mar 7 (239) $225

### Facsimile Editions

— The National Shakespeare. L: W. Mackenzie, [n.d.]. Illus by J. Noel Paton. 3 vols. Folio, orig pictorial mor; shelf label on spines. Facsimile of 1st Folio. b May 30 (416) £320

— 1807-8. - L. Folio, contemp calf; rebacked. First Folio facsimile. cb Oct 17 (337) $500

— [1867]. - The National Shakespeare. L. Folio, mor gilt. pba June 20 (301) $350

— 1968. - The Norton Facsimile. NY Folio, half mor. The First Folio. pba Aug 22 (647) $75

### Poems, Sonnets, etc.

— A Collection of Poems.... L: Bernard Lintot, [c.1709-10]. 2 vols in 1. 8vo, contemp calf; rebacked. S July 11 (130) £1,290

— A Collection of Poems, viz. I. Venus and Adonis. II. The Rape of Lucrece.... L: Bernard Lintott, [c.1709-10]. 2 parts in 1 vol. 8vo, contemp calf; rebacked. Some repaired tears. pba Nov 30 (291) $2,000

— Poems. L: Essex House Press, 1899 [1900]. One of 450. 4to, vellum; minor discoloration. S Nov 2 (53) £320 [Chong Yap Seng]

Anr copy. Contemp mor gilt; extremities rubbed. Tipped in on blank is inscr to Lady Glenconner from F. W. Bain. S May 16 (54) £700

— Songs and Sonnets. L, [c.1930]. Illus by Charles Robinson. 4to, contemp calf by Bayntun Riviere, with central panel with embossed & painted image of a young man in a landscape. b Sept 20 (642) £190

— Songs from Shakespeare's Plays. Verona: Officina Bodoni, 1974. One of 300. 4to, orig half mor. bba May 9 (618) £260 [Blackwell]

— The Sonnets. L, 1881. One of 50 L.p. copies. 8vo, lev extra by Zaehnsdorf. sg Feb 8 (335) $550

— Sonnets. New Rochelle: George D. Sproul, 1901-2. Ltd Ed, ptd on vellum. Illuminated titles & 154 initials in colors & gilt by Ross Turner. 2 vols. 4to, mor gilt with onlays by Trautz-Bauzonnet. Initials rubbed on tp of Vol I. P Dec 12 (165) $4,000

### Shaler, William

— Journal of a Voyage between China and the North-Western Coast of America. Claremont, Calif., 1935. One of 700. Half cloth. pba Apr 25 (235) $130

Anr copy. Half cloth, in dj with minor tears. pba July 25 (216) $110

### Shapiro, Karl

— Poems. Balt.: Waverly Press, 1935. One of 200. bbc June 24 (609) $350

### Sharp, Granville, 1735-1813

— A Declaration of the People's Natural Right to a Share in the Legislatures.... L, 1774. 8vo, contemp calf; rubbed. b Sept 20 (174) £170

— A Representation of the Injustice and Dangerous Tendency of Tolerating Slavery. L, 1769. 8vo, disbound. sg Mar 28 (313) $600

### Sharp, Samuel, 1700?-78

— Letters from Italy Describing the Customs and Manners.... L, 1766. 8vo, old calf gilt; worn, front cover detached. wa Dec 14 (162) $70

### Sharpe, Richard Bowdler, 1847-1909

— An Analytical Index to the Works of the Late John Gould. L, 1893. 4to, cloth. Lacking port. b Sept 20 (466) £200

### Sharshun, Sergei

— Dadaizm (Kompiljatsija). Berlin: European Homeopath, [c.1922]. 8vo, orig wraps; fragile, spine def, stains on rear cover. sg Apr 18 (133) $500

### Shaw, D. A.

— El Dorado or California as Seen by a Pioneer, 1850-1900. Los Angeles, 1900. Orig cloth. With frontis port & 7 illus. Larson copy. pba Sept 28 (664) $85

### Shaw, Frederick George

— The Science of Fly Fishing for Trout. NY, 1925. sg Mar 7 (536) $130

### Shaw, George, 1751-1813

— General Zoology. L, 1800-15. 20 vols. 8vo, contemp calf; dried, some covers & spines detached. Some plates browned & spotted. Sold w.a.f. CE Nov 8 (243) $650

— General Zoology, or Systematic Natural History. L, 1800-26. 13 vols.. 8vo, calf or disbound; some bds detached. Some foxing. Met Feb 24 (465) $450

— Zoological Lectures. L, 1809. 2 vols. 8vo, contemp russia; worn, rebacked. With 167 plates. Some spottng. S Oct 27 (779) £200 [Egglishaw]

### Shaw, George, 1751-1813 —& Nodder, Frederick P.

— The Naturalist's Miscellany. L, [1789]-1790-1813. 18 (of 24) vols in 9. Lea gilt. With 631 (of 772) hand-colored plates. Some foxing. Sold w.a.f. Met Sept 28 (413) $2,900

### Shaw, George Bernard, 1856-1950

See also: Gregynog Press

— The Apple Cart. L, 1930. 1st Ed. In dj & protective cloth dj. Inscr to Harold Downs, 19 Dec 1930. sg June 20 (334) $400

— Man and Superman. L, 1903. 1st Ed. Orig cloth; worn, rear hinge cracked. With ALs & ACs to Philip H. Lee Warner & with related material by Warner. sg Sept 21 (292) $650

## SHAW

Anr Ed. NY, 1905. Inscr. sg June 20 (336) $225
— Selected Plays. NY, [1948]. 8vo, mor gilt by Maurin. wa Feb 29 (17) $350
— Three Plays for Puritans. L, 1901. 1st Ed. Orig cloth; front hinge cracked, spine ends worn. Inscr to Frank Harris. sg Feb 8 (336) $325
— Works. NY, 1930-32. Ayot St. Lawrence Ed, one of 1,790. Vols 1-30 (of 33). pba Mar 7 (240) $425

**Shaw, Henry, 1800-73**
— Alphabets, Numerals, and Devices of the Middle Ages. L, 1845. 4to, orig cloth. With 48 plates, many color. Preliminaries & last few plates foxed. sg Apr 11 (305) $300
— The Decorative Arts, Ecclesiastical and Civil, of the Middle Ages. L, 1851. Folio, contemp half mor; rubbed. With 41 plates. b May 30 (479) £80
— Dresses and Decorations of the Middle Ages. L, 1843. 2 vols. 4to, later half cloth; earlier spine laid down, rubbed. cb Feb 14 (2805) £325

Anr Ed. L, 1858. 2 vols. 4to, contemp half mor; rubbed & marked. With engraved title & 93 plates, some colored. bba May 30 (324) £170 [Disa]
— The Encyclopedia of Ornament. L, 1842. Folio, half calf; corners worn, extremities scuffed. With 60 color plates. pba Sept 14 (319) $550

**Shaw, John, of Throstle Nest**
— Woolton Green: a Domestic Tale.... Liverpool, [1825]. Bound with: Don Juan. Canto XVII, 1824. And: Don Juan, Canto XVIII, 1825. 8vo, contemp mor gilt. Inscr, 1826. b Dec 5 (216) £520

**Shaw, Ralph R. —& Shoemaker, Richard H.**
— American Bibliography; a Preliminary Checklist for 1801-1819.... [Methuen, N.J.], 1958-66. 22 vols. Ck Apr 12 (274) £100
— American Bibliography; a Preliminary Checklist for 1801-37. [Metuchen NJ], 1958-86. 37 vols; lacking vol for 1806 but with index vols for 1801-19 & 1820-29. ds July 27 (160) $425

**Shaw, Stebbing**
— The History and Antiquities of Staffordshire. L, 1798-1801. Vols I & II, Part 1 (all pbd). Folio, later half mor; rubbed, spine of Vol I worn, lower cover detached. bba Nov 1 (207) £550 [Sparkes]

**Shaw, Thomas, 1694-1757**
— Travels or Observations relating to Several Parts of Barbary and the Levant. Oxford, 1738. 1st Ed. Folio, contemp vellum; soiled. With half title, title, & 32 plates & maps. S Oct 26 (79) £850 [Chelsea Rare]

Anr Ed. L, 1757. 4to, later mor. With 38 plates, some of them folding. Tear at fold of 1 plate. bba May 30 (325) £220 [Harrison's]

2d Ed. 4to, contemp sheep. With 34 (of 36) maps & plates. Marginal worming. sg Mar 7 (338) $200

## AMERICAN BOOK PRICES CURRENT

**Shaw, William, 1749-1831**
— Memoirs of the Life and Writings of the late Dr. Samuel Johnson. L, 1785. Bound with: Selden, John. Table-Talk. L, 1777. 8vo, old bds; rebacked in calf, edges worn, some discoloration. Half-title discolored. pba June 20 (304) $350

**Shcheglov, Nikolai**
— Khozjzjstvennaja Botanika. St. Petersburg, 1828. Parts 1-3 in 1 vol. 4to, contemp half calf gilt; front joint cracked. With 52 hand-colored plates. Old stamp on general title. sg Dec 7 (234) $700

**Shea, John Gilmary, 1824-92**
— Early Voyages Up and Down the Mississippi.... Albany, [1902]. One of 500. 8vo, cloth. Facsimile of the 1861 Ed. sg Oct 26 (336) $140

**Shearer, Thomas**
— The Cabinet-Makers London Book of Prices. L, 1793. 4to, half calf; rubbed. With engraved title & 20 plates. bba June 6 (36) £160 [Kennedy]

**Sheldon, Charles**
— The Wilderness of Denali. Explorations...in Northern Alaska. NY & L, 1930. Orig cloth; worn. O Oct 10 (252) $190
— The Wilderness of the North Pacific Coast Islands. NY, 1910. Orig cloth; worn. Frontis foxed. pba July 25 (449) $160

Anr Ed. NY, 1912. O Oct 10 (255) $130
— The Wilderness of the Upper Yukon.... NY, 1911. Orig cloth; some wear. O Oct 10 (254) $250

**Shelley, George Ernest**
— A Monograph of the Nectariniidae, or Family of Sun-Birds. L, 1876-80. 4to, contemp mor gilt by R. H. Porter. With 121 hand-colored plates. Author's copy. Fattorini copy. C Oct 25 (86) £6,800

**Shelley, George Ernest —& Sclater, William Lutley**
— The Birds of Africa, Comprising all the Species... in the Ethiopian Region. L, 1896-1906. Vols I-IV, and V part 1 (of 2) in 6 vols. 4to, orig cloth; spines rubbed 7 faded. With 49 hand-colored plates. S Oct 27 (780) £1,300 [Maggs]

**Shelley, Mary Wollstonecraft, 1797-1851**
See also: Limited Editions Club
— Frankenstein.... L, 1818. 1st Ed. 3 vols. 12mo, contemp calf gilt; corners worn, covers abraded. Some staining throughout; D12 in Vol I with marginal tear; Vols II & III lacking ads. Hefner copy. CNY May 17 (38) $38,000

Anr copy. 19th-cent calf; worn, spines lacking, lacking upper cover of Vol II, upper cover of Vol III detached. S Dec 18 (204) £1,000 [Heritage]
— Frankenstein; or, the Modern Prometheus. L, 1831. 3d Ed. 2 vols. 8vo, orig cloth. Vols 9 & 10 in Bentley's Standard Novels series, with other works. S Dec 18 (205) £1,200 [Buddenbrooks]

Anr Ed. NY, 1845. 8vo, orig wraps; def, edges curled. Some dampstaining. Met Feb 24 (211) $450

Anr Ed. NY: Grosset & Dunlap, [1931]. In dj with front panel repro of illust by Mach Tey from the motion-picture posters; some chips, creases & soiling. With 7 plates from stills from the motion picture starring Boris Karloff. Met Sept 28 (36) $350; pba May 4 (249) $750

**Shelley, Percy Bysshe, 1792-1822**
See also: Golden Cockerel Press; Kelmscott Press; Limited Editions Club
— Adonais. Pisa, 1821. 1st Ed. 4to, modern wraps. Foxed throughout. sg Apr 18 (184) $2,800
— Epipsychidion. Montagnola: Officina Bodoni, 1923. One of 222. 4to, orig vellum gilt. Ck May 31 (21) £350
— History of a Six Weeks' Tour through a Part of France, Switzerland, Germany, and Holland. L, 1817. 1st Ed. 8vo, modern lev extra, stamp-sgd C. L.. sg Oct 19 (242) $1,900
— Laon and Cythna. L, 1818. ("The Revolt of Islam.") 2d Ed, 2d Issue, with 1818 date on title. 8vo, mor extra by Zaehnsdorf. Shorter blank inserted following tp. CE Sept 27 (254) $1,200
— Ode to the West Wind. Florence: Allen Press, 1951. One of 100. pba June 20 (27) $65
— The Poetical Works. L, 1839. 1st Collected Ed. - Ed by Mary Shalley. 4 vols. 8vo, contemp calf; joints & spine ends worn & repaired, few hinges cracked. With frontis port by Finden. CE Nov 8 (245) $130
Anr copy. Ed by May Shelley. 4 vols. 12mo, half mor by Root. wd May 8 (80) $400
Anr Ed. Cambr. MA, 1892. One of 250 L.p. copies. 4 vols in 8. 8vo, half mor gilt; wormed, 1 spine end rubbed. cb Feb 14 (2807) $700
— Rosalind and Helen. L, 1819. 1st Ed. 8vo, mor extra exhibition bdg by Zaehnsdorf. Terry copy. b May 30 (584) £800
Anr copy. Contemp calf; upper cover detached, spine ends chipped. Lacking ads at rear. H. W. Poor - C. B. Tinker copy. CE Sept 27 (255) $600
— The Sensitive Plant. L & Phila., [c.1911]. Illus by Charles Robinson. Orig vellum gilt. With 18 colored plates. S Nov 2 (142) £280 [Sotheran]

**Shelvocke, Capt. George**
— A Voyage Round the World.... L, 1726. 1st Ed. 8vo, period calf; joints cracking, light cover wear. With folding frontis map, & 4 plates (2 folding). Robbins copy. pba Mar 21 (338) $3,000

**Shepherd, Thomas Hosmer**
— Bath and Bristol, with the Counties of Somerset and Gloucester.... L, 1829. 4to, contemp mor gilt. Some spotting. Ck Feb 14 (325) £180

**Shepherd, Thomas Hosmer —&**
**Elmes, James, 1782-1862**
— London and its Environs in the Nineteenth Century. L, 1829. Bound with: Metropolitan Improvements. L, 1830. 4to, contemp calf; rubbed, joints broken. Together, with 2 titles, 1 map, & 353 views on 161 leaves. Spotted & browned. S Oct 26 (404) £320 [Storey]

Anr copy. Bound with: Metropolitan Improvements. L, 1830. contemp half calf; rubbed. Spotted. S Oct 26 (405) £290 [Squire]
— Metropolitan Improvements; or London in the Nineteenth Century. L, 1827. 4to, contemp half mor gilt; rejointed. With engraved title & 82 plates & plan of Regent's Park. Foxed. sg Sept 7 (19) $175

**Shepperd, Tad.** See: Derrydale Press

**Sherer, John**
— The Classic Lands of Europe. L, [n.d.]. 2 vols. 4to, contemp half calf. With engraved titles & 118 plates. b May 30 (296) £750
Anr copy. Lea gilt; extremities rubbed. With 151 plates. NH Sept 16 (182) $300

**Sheridan, Philip Henry, 1831-88 —&**
**Sherman, William Tecumseh, 1820-91**
— Reports of Inspection Made in the Summer of 1877... of Country North of the Union Pacific Railroad. Wash., 1878. 1st Ed. 8vo, orig cloth. With 10 folding maps & 5 plates. Robbins copy. pba Mar 21 (339) $550

**Sheridan, Richard Brinsley, 1751-1816**
— The School for Scandal. L, [1911]. One of 350. Illus by Hugh Thomson. 4to, vellum. sg Sept 14 (333) $275
Anr Ed. Oxford: Shakespeare Head Press, 1930. One of 475. 4to, half vellum. sg Sept 14 (323) $110
— Works. L, 1821. 2 vols. 8vo, contemp calf gilt by Worefols; minor rubbing. pba Aug 8 (289) $80
Anr Ed. L, 1884. 2 vols. 8vo, contemp calf gilt, armorial bdgs. pba Aug 8 (288) $130

**Sheridan, Thomas, 1646-88**
— A Discourse of...Parliaments. L, 1677. 8vo, contemp calf; rubbed. Stain in outer margins. b Sept 20 (175) £170

**Sherman, Edwin A.**
— The Life of the Late Rear-Admiral John Drake Sloat.... Oakland, 1902. Enlarged Monumental Ed. Orig cloth. Sgd. Larson copy. pba Sept 28 (672) $100

**Sherman, Frederic Fairchild**
— Early American Portraiture. NY, 1930. One of 250. Half cloth; some wear. O Dec 5 (130) $90

**Sherman, William Tecumseh, 1820-91**
See also: Sheridan & Sherman
— Memoirs of General William T. Sherman. By Himself. NY, 1875. 1st Ed. 2 vols, orig cloth; Some wear, soiling & abrasion of covers. Vol I page tops spotted. Larson copy. pba Sept 28 (666) $500

**Shewell, John Talwin**
— A Tribute to the Memory of William Cowper.... Ipswich, 1808. 4to, modern wraps. Half-title repaired. b Dec 5 (366) £80

**Shibley, Fred Warner**
— Aspinwall Island. NY: Pvtly ptd, 1916. O Feb 6 (212) $130

**Shields, George Oliver**
— American Game Fishes: Their Habits, Habitat, and Peculiarities. Chicago & NY, 1892. Ed by Shields. 8vo, orig cloth. pba July 11 (222) $180

Anr copy. Half mor; extremities rubbed. sg Mar 7 (539) $50

**Shields, Henry —& Meikle, James**
— Famous Clyde Yachts 1880-87. Glasgow, 1888. Folio, orig cloth; worn. With frontis & 31 mtd chromolitho plates. Marginal spotting to top margins; 2 small stamps. W Nov 8 (420) £1,300

**Shiels, Archie W.**
— Little Journeys into the History of Russian America and the PUrchase of Alaska. Bellingham WA, 1949. One of 125. Typescript on rectos only. pba Apr 25 (265) $190
— San Juan Islands: The Cronstadt of the Pacific. Juneau, 1938. 1st Ed, One of 500. Lea. With frontis map. Robbins copy. Inscr & sgd. pba Mar 21 (340) $150

**Shillibeer, Lieut. John**
— A Narrative of the Briton's Voyage to Pitcairn's Island.... L, 1817. 2d Ed. 8vo, contemp bds; rebacked. With frontis & 16 (on 12) plates. b Mar 20 (187) £260

3d Ed. L, 1818. 4to, contemp calf-backed mor. b Mar 20 (188) £220

**Shimada, Shujiro**
— Japanese Paintings in Western Collections. Tokyo, 1969. 3 vols in 6. Folio, orig bdgs. sg June 13 (206) $500

**Shinn, Charles Howard**
— Mining Camps. NY, 1885. 1st Ed. 8vo, orig cloth. Larson copy. pba Sept 28 (670) $300

Anr copy. Orig cloth. Robbins copy. pba Mar 21 (341) $850
— The Story of the Mine as Illustrated by the Great Comstock Lode of Nevada. NY, 1896. 8vo, orig cloth. Inscr to Dan De Quille. pba Feb 12 (555) $160

**Shinn, Earl, 1837-86**
— Mr. Vanderbilt's House and Collection. Bost., [1883-84]. One of 500 on japan vellum. 4 vols. Folio, orig mor; extremities worn, joints cracked, some covers loose. cb June 25 (1975) $1,800

**Shipley, Conway**
— Sketches in the Pacific: The South Sea Islands. L, 1851. Folio, orig cloth; rebacked. With litho title & 25 plates. Marginal spotting. b Mar 20 (190) £7,200

**Shipley, William**
— A True Treatise on the Art of Fly-Fishing.... L, 1838. 12mo, orig cloth; worn, spine torn along rear joint. Frontis & text vignettes are mtd india proofs Some foxing. L.p. copy. O Feb 6 (213) $120

**Shippen, Edward.** See: Powell & Shippen

**Shipton, Clifford Kenyon —& Mooney, James E.**
— National Index of American Imprints through 1800. [Worcester, Mass.], 1969. 1st Ed. 2 vols. 4to, cloth; worn. O May 7 (274) $90

**Shirley, Rodney W.**
— The Mapping of the World.... L, [1983]. Folio, cloth, in dj; rear joint starting. sg May 9 (39) $275

**Shirley, Thomas, Angler**
— The Angler's Museum.... L, 1784. 12mo, contemp calf; rebacked. W Nov 8 (399) £300
— The Angler's Museum. Or, the Whole Art of Float and Fly Fishing. L, 1784. 1st Ed. 12mo, recent lea gilt. John Gerard Heckscher's copy. O Feb 6 (214) $225

**Shirley, William, 1694-1771**
— A Letter from William Shirley, Esq; Governor of Massachuset's Bay.... L, 1748. 8vo, half lea gilt; spine worn, endpaper & flyleaf detached. Met Sept 28 (163) $300

**Shoberl, Frederick.** See: Schoberl, Frederick

**Shoel, Thomas**
— Glastonbury Tor. A Poem. Sherborne, 1818. 8vo, contemp wraps. b Dec 5 (98) £110
— Miscellaneous Pieces, in Verse. Yeovil, 1819. 8vo, sewn as issued. b Dec 5 (337) £90

**Shoemaker, Richard H.** See: Shaw & Shoemaker

**Sholem Aleichem, 1859-1916**
— Zakoldovannii portnoi. Moscow, 1957. Illus by Anatoli Kaplan. Loose in folder with orig litho cover design. S Nov 2 (25) £400 [Trotter]

**Short...** See: Frere, George

**Short, Richard, of Bury**
— Peri Psychroposias, of Drinking Water.... L, 1656. 8vo, 19th-cent half calf. Some discoloration throughout. b Sept 20 (224) £190

**Short, Thomas, 1690?-1772**
— A Dissertation upon Tea.... L, 1730. 1st Ed. 4to, modern half calf. Margins spotted; F4r ink stained; final leaves dampstained. Ck Mar 22 (273) £400

**Short-Title Catalogue**
— A Short-Title Catalogue of Books Printed in England, Scotland & Ireland...1475-1640. L, 1950. Ed by A. W. Pollard & G. R. Redgrave. 4to, cloth; worn. Reprint of 1926 Ed. O May 7 (245) $50
2d Ed. L, 1976-1991. Ed by A. W. Pollard and G. R. Redgrave. 3 vols. Folio, orig cloth in djs. sg Apr 11 (253) $375

**Shostakovich, Dmitri, 1906-75**
— Shestaya Simfoniya, Sechste Symphonie... Op.53. Leningrad, 1941. 4to, orig bds. Inscr to Ilya Osipovich Brik. S Dec 1 (320) £1,200

**Shrake, Bud.** See: Penick & Shrake

**Shurtleff, Nathaniel B.**
— Records of the Colony of New Plymouth in New England. Bost., 1855-61. 12 vols in 10. 4to, cloth; worn. NH July 21 (102) $425
— Records of the Governor and Company of the Massachusetts Bay.... Bost., 1853-54. In 6 vols. 4to, cloth; worn, library markings. NH July 21 (103) $300

**Shute, E. L.** See: Dodgson presentation copy, Charles Lutwidge

**Shute, Nevil**
— On the Beach. L, 1957. In dj. sg June 20 (337) $250

**Sibyllinorum...**
— Sibyllinorum Oraculorum Libri VIII. Basel: Joannes Oporinus, [1555]. 8vo, half calf. Side-notes cropped; x1 torn with small loss. b May 30 (527) £160

**Sichel, Jules**
— Spectacles: their Uses and Abuses. Bost., 1850. 1st Ed in English. - Trans by H. W. Williams. 8vo, orig cloth; spine ends chipped. sg May 16 (499) $60

**Siddons, Anne Rivers**
— The House Next Door. Atlanta, 1993. One of 26 lettered copies. Lea. O Dec 5 (247) $60

**Sidney, Algernon, 1622-83**
— Discourses Concerning Government.... L, 1763. 4to, contemp sheep gilt designed by & bound for Thomas Hollis; some wear, a few dents, corners bumped. P Dec 12 (91) $2,500

**Sidney, Algernon, 1622-83 —& Ralph, James**
— Of the Use and Abuse of Parliament.... L, 1744. 2 vols. 8vo, orig bds covered in later paper. pba Mar 7 (218) $65

**Sidney, Sir Philip, 1554-86**
— The Countesse of Pembrokes Arcadia. L: H. L. for Matthew Lownes, 1623. Folio, contemp calf; worn. Margins browned & frayed at ends. CE May 22 (428) $200

Anr Ed. L, 1627-[28]. Folio, contemp calf gilt, with arms of Henry Fiennes, 7th Earl of Lincoln; rebacked preserving most of orig spine. Marginal dampstaining. S July 11 (123) £220

— The Sonnets. L: Vale Press, 1898. One of 210. Illus by Charles Ricketts. 8vo, mor gilt, orig wraps bound in. sg Feb 15 (305) $150

**Sidney, Samuel**
— The Book of the Horse. L, [1879-81]. 4to, contemp half mor; worn. With 25 colored plates. Tear in 1 text leaf. b May 30 (498) £310

3d Ed. L, [1884-86]. Bound in 2 vols. 4to, contemp cloth; 1 spine def, some leaves loose. With 25 chromolitho plates. b Jan 31 (277) £260

**Sidney-Smythe, George Autustus Frederick Percy, Viscount Strangford**
— Angela Pisani. L, 1875. 3 vols. 8vo, orig cloth; rubbed & marked, hinges cracked. bba May 30 (219) £130 [Ferret Fantasy]

**Sidonius, Caius Sollius Apollinaris, 430-c.483**
— Epistolae et poemata. Milan: Uldericus Scinzenzeler for Hieronymus de Asula & Johannes de Abbatibus, 4 May 1498. Folio, modern calf gilt. 57 lines of commentary; roman letter. Lower blank half of tp annotated by a former owner; stamp removed from upper half of tp leaving holes affecting text on verso; minor worming partly repaired. 144 leaves. Goff S-494. S Dec 18 (78) £800 [Zioni]

**Siebeck, Rudolph**
— Guide pratique du jardienier paysagiste.... Paris, 1867. Folio, orig bds; rubbed. With half-title, 24 double-page hand-colored plates. S Oct 26 (340) £800 [Arader]

**Siegel, Henry A. —& Others**
— The Derrydale Press: A Bibliography. Goshen, Conn.: The Angler's & Shooter's Press, 1981. One of 1,250. O June 25 (48) $70; O June 25 (252) $100; sg Mar 7 (541) $150

**Siemienowicz, Casimir**
— The Great Art of Artillery.... L, 1729. 1st Ed in English. Folio, contemp calf; front joint cracked. With frontis & 22 folding plates. Outer margin of frontis cropped. sg Oct 19 (236) $300

**Siena**
— La Biblioteca Pubblica di Siena disposta secondo le materie da Loranzo Ilari. Catalogo.... Siena, 1844-48. 7 vols in 3. 4to, 19th-cent half lea; rubbed. Library markings. O Mar 26 (253) $60

**Sienkiewicz, Henryk, 1846-1916.** See: Limited Editions Club

**Sierra Club**
— Base Camp '52. San Francisco, [1952]. Pictorial wraps. Mimeographed text with ptd photographs. pba Feb 12 (174) $80

**Sigaud de la Fond, Joseph Aignan**
— Essai sur differentes especes d'air qu'on signe le nom d'air fixe.... Paris, 1779. 1st Ed. 8vo, contemp half calf; lower front joint split, joints rubbed. With half-title & 5 folding plates. Half-title corner torn away; a5 inner margin holed; 1st 12 leaves browned; some spotting. Ck Mar 22 (274) £150

Anr copy. Contemp calf; joints rubbed. Some spotting. Ck Mar 22 (275) £170

## SIGEL

**Sigel, Gustav A.**
— Deutschlands Heer und Flotte in Wort und Bild. Akron OH, 1900. Folio, half cloth; spine ends & corners worn & frayed, front hinge repaired. With 41 colored plates. Text in German & English. bbc June 24 (245) $250

Anr copy. Orig cloth; worn. Text in German & English. F June 20 (839) $350

**Signature...**
— The Signature. L, 1915. Nos 1-3 (all pbd). Orig wraps. With contribs by Katherine Mansfield, D. H. Lawrence & J. Middleton Murry. Ck Nov 17 (149) £1,000

— Signature: A Quadrimestrial of Typography and Graphic Arts. L, 1935-54. First Series, Nos 1-15; New Series, Nos 1-18 (complete set). Together, 33 nos. 4to, orig wraps. bba May 9 (40) £480 [Morris]

Anr Ed. L, 1935-40. First Series, Nos 1-15. 4to, wraps. sg Sept 14 (82) $325

Anr Ed. L, 1946-54. New Series, Nos 1-18. 4to, orig wraps. bba May 9 (133) £120 [Boutle & King]

**Sigorgne, Pierre, Abbe, 1719-1809**
— Institutions leibnitiennes, ou precis de la monadologie. Lyon: freres Perisse, 1767. 8vo, contemp calf gilt with crowned monogram of Maire Amelie de Bourbon, Queen of France; upper joint cracked, repair at upper corner of lower cover, possibly a remboitage. Fuerstenberg - Schaefer copy. S Dec 8 (578) £650

**Silius Italicus, Caius, 25-101 A.D.**
— De bello Punica. Venice: Baptista de Tortis, 6 May 1483. ("Punica.") Folio, 18th-cent mor gilt; hinges repaired. 64 lines of commentary; types 1:114R, 2:78R. Worming at beginning touching letters. 178 leaves. Goff S-507. C Nov 29 (75) £1,500

— De Bello Punico. Venice: Bonetus Locatellus for Octavianus Scotus, 18 May 1492. ("Punica cum Commentariis Petri Marsi.") Folio, modern calf. 62 lines of commentary & headline; double column; roman letter. Washed copy; each leaf mtd on a guard; device from final leaf cut out & pasted down. 152 (of 156) leaves; lacking a1, g2 & 7, u6. Goff S-508. S Dec 18 (79) £300 [Zioni]

**Silko, Leslie Marmon**
— Laguna Woman. Greenfield Center: Greenfield Review Press, [1974]. Wraps; some soiling. pba Jan 25 (337) $1,100

**Sillar, David**
— Poems. Kilmarnock, 1789. 1st Ed. 8vo, orig bds; upper cover detached. Spotting & discoloring. b Dec 5 (527) £140

**Silliman, Benjamin, 1779-1864**
— Elements of Chemistry. New Haven, 1830-31. 2 vols. 8vo, contemp sheep; rubbed. sg May 16 (256) $250

## AMERICAN BOOK PRICES CURRENT

**Silliman, Benjamin, 1816-85 —& Others**
— The World of Science, Art and Industry, illustrated from Examples in the New-York Exhibition, 1853-54. NY, 1854. 2 parts in 1 vol. Folio, orig cloth; soiled, spine ends worn. With 5 plates. Some foxing. wa Feb 1 (355) $60

**Sillitoe, Alan**
— The Loneliness of the Long-Distance Runner. L, 1959. In dj with spine ends rubbed & some soiling. pba Jan 25 (338) $85

**Siltzer, Frank**
— The Story of British Sporting Prints. NY, [1925]. Cloth; worn. Some foxing. O Jan 9 (199) $50

Anr copy. With 20 plates. O June 25 (253) $70

**Silva...** See: Evelyn, John

**Silva y Figueroa, Garcia**
— L'Ambassade... en Perse, contenant la politique de ce grand empire.... Paris: Jean du Puis, 1667. 4to, modern half calf. Some waterstaining. b Jan 31 (473) £500

**Silver...**
— Silver Scream. Arlington Heights: Dark Harvest, 1988. One of 500, sgd by the 20 contributors. Ed by David J. Schow. In dj. pba Dec 7 (168) $60

**Silverberg, Robert**
— Lord Valentine's Castle. NY: Harper & Row, [1980]. One of 250. sg Dec 14 (263) $50

**Silverer, Victor**
— Im Ballon! Eine Schilderung der Fahrten des Wiener Luftballons "Vindobona" im Jahre 1882.... Vienna, 1883. 8vo, orig cloth. With 14 wood-engraved plates. sg May 16 (86) $130

**Simak, Clifford D.**
— Cosmic Engineers. NY: Gnome Press, [1950]. In dj with edge wear & chipping, Currey's A bdg. pba May 4 (250) $110

**Simcoe, John Graves, 1752-1806**
— Simcoe's Military Journal.... NY, 1844. 12mo, contemp bds; rebacked in cloth, worn. With 10 folding maps. Library stamp to copyright page; some foxing. wa Feb 29 (301) $475

**Simeon Simonovich, Archimandrite, of Jerusalem**
— Opisanie svjatago bozhija grada Ierusalima.... [Moscow], 1771. 4to, half mor; extremities worn. Engraved throughout, with 70 views of churches & holy places all ptd on rectos only. Marginal soiling & staining. P June 5 (333) $3,750

**Simeoni, Gabriele**
— Dialogo pio et speculativo. Lyons, 1560. 4to, later wraps. Lacking several leaves, including folding map. Stains to upper gutters. pba Mar 7 (241) $140

**Simmons, Albert Dixon.** See: Derrydale Press

## Simmons, Amelia
— American Cookery... Salem, Mass, 1804. 5th Ed. Orig wraps in cloth case; wraps laid down, rubbed, resewn. Spotted & dampstained. S Oct 12 (119) £1,550

## Simmons, Dan
— Carrion Comfort. Arlington Heights: Dark Harvest, 1989. Copy lettered P/C. In dj. O Dec 5 (250) $60
— Entropy's Bed at Midnight. Northridge: Lord John Press, 1990. One of 300. O Dec 5 (252) $120
— Hyperion. NY: Doubleday, [1989]. Uncorrected proof copy. In dj. pba Jan 25 (339) $110
— Phases of Gravity. L: Headline, [1989]. One of 250. Syn. O Dec 5 (254) $50
— Prayers to Broken Stones. Arlington Heights: Dark Harvest, 1990. One of 52 lettered copies. Syn in dj. O Dec 5 (255) $60
— Song of Kali. NY: Bluejay Books, [1985]. 1st Ed. In dj. Inscr. O Dec 5 (257) $130

## Simon, Andre Louis
— Bibliotheca Bacchia.... L, [1978]. 2 vols in 1. Folio, orig cloth in dj. sg Apr 11 (306) $80
— The Noble Grapes and the Great Wines of France. NY: McGraw-Hill, [n.d.]. 4to, mor gilt by Zaehnsdorf. pba Nov 30 (294) $75

## Simon, Barbara Anne
— The Hope of Israel. L, 1829. 8vo, orig bds; front cover loose, backstrip cracked. sg Mar 7 (339) $80

## Simon, Oliver —&
## Rodenberg, Julius, 1831-1914
— Printing of To-day.... L & NY, 1928. 4to, half cloth, in dj with small piece lacking & small stain. pba Mar 7 (243) $75
Anr copy. Cloth. pba Aug 22 (648) $120

## Simoneta, Joannes
— La Sforziada. Milan: Antonius Zarotus, 1490. 1st Ed in Italian. Folio, 17th-cent vellum. 44 lines; type 5:111Rb4. Stained; wormhole touching a few letters in final 3 quires. 199 (of 202) leaves; lacking 1st leaf & 2 blanks. Goff S-534. C Apr 3 (224) £900

## Simonini, Francesco Antonio
— Scielta di Battaglie. Bologna: Luigi Guidotti, 1760. Oblong 4to, later bds. With port, title, dedication & 33 plates. Some marginal soiling & staining; tp & dedication loose. sg Apr 18 (185) $450

## Simons, Mathew
— A Direction for the English Traveller. L, 1643. 8vo, contemp half vellum; repaired. Lacking 1 map; some spotting & soiling. S June 13 (489) £550
Anr Ed. L, [1250]. 8vo, contemp calf; spine ends & 1 corner repaired. Engraved throughout, with 40 maps. Cambridgeshire with small rust-hole. bba June 6 (369) £700 [Sharpe]

## Simpkinson, Francis Guillemard —&
## Belcher, Edward
— H.M.S. Sulphur at California, 1837 and 1839: Being the Accounts of.... San Francisco: Book Club of California, 1969. One of 450. Half bds. With 1 facsimile & 1 port. Larson copy. pba Sept 28 (251) $80

## Simplex...
— Simplex Buyers Guide of Standard Merchandise. [N.p.], 1923-24. Met June 6 (468) $200

## Simpson, Charles
— Leicestershire & its Hunts. L, 1926. One of 75. Half cloth. C July 1 (339) £110

## Simpson, Christopher
— The Division-Violist... L, 1659. Folio, contemp sheep gilt; rebacked, knife cuts on upper cover, new endpapers. Lacking blank P1; tear in port repaired; minor staining. S May 15 (498) £4,000

## Simpson, G. Wharton
— On the Production of Photographs in Pigments.... L, 1867. 8vo, cloth; recased with new endpapers. With port by R. Faulkner. Prelims & fore-edge foxed. sg Apr 24 (601) $250

## Simpson, Sir George, 1792-1860
— Narrative of a Voyage to California Ports. San Francisco, 1930. One of 250. 4to, half bds in dj. With 2 ports. Larson copy. pba Sept 28 (252) $170
Anr copy. Orig cloth in dj. With 2 ports, folding map, & holograph report. Robbins copy. pba Mar 21 (342) $170

## Simpson, James H., 1813-83
— Journal of a Military Reconnaissance, from Santa Fe.... Phila., 1852. 8vo, orig cloth; extremities worn, rear bd discolored. Some dampstaining & foxing. Met Feb 24 (414) $375

## Simpson, Sir Walter Grindlay
— The Art of Golf. Edin., 1887. 1st Ed. 8vo, half calf; rebacked, residue of tape in spine, soiled, hinges reinforced. pba Nov 9 (74) $650
Anr copy. Half calf; spine head & joints scuffed, corners bumped. pba Apr 18 (154) $1,000

## Simpson, William, 1823-99
— The Seat of the War in the East. First and Second Series. L, 1855-56. 2 vols in 1. Folio, half mor; worn, covers detached, spine def. With litho titles & 79 plates. Plates with old waterstain at bottom of image. Sold w.a.f. K Oct 1 (355) $950

## Sinclair, Sir John, 1754-1835
— The History of the Public Revenue of the British Empire. L, 1785-90. 3 parts in 2 vols. 4to, contemp half russia gilt; worn, needs rebacked. Library stamps. sg Mar 21 (115) $350
— Specimen of Statistical Reports. L, 1793. 8vo, old wraps; backstrip def, front cover loose. Library stamps. sg Mar 21 (116) $400

**Sinclair, Upton, 1878-1968.** See: Limited Editions Club

**Singer, Charles —&**
**Others**
— A History of Technology Oxford, 1954-58. Vols I-V. 5 vols. 4to, orig cloth; shaken, vol I hinges cracked. sg Apr 11 (298) $250

**Singer, Isaac Bashevis, 1904-91**
See also: Limited Editions Club
— The Family Moskat. NY, 1950. In dj. wa Dec 14 (58) $140
— A Little Boy in Search of God. NY, 1976. 1st Ed, One of 150. sg Dec 14 (264) $110
— Lost in America. Garden City, 1981. One of 500. Illus by Raphael Soyer. With sgd plate by Soyer laid in. sg Dec 14 (266) $110
— Satan in Goray. NY, [1981]. One of 350. Illus by Ira Moskowitz. 4to, half mor. sg Feb 15 (275) $350
— Yentl the Yeshiva Boy. NY, [1983]. One of 450. Illus by Antonio Frasconi. sg Dec 14 (268) $120
— A Young Man in Search of Love. Garden City, 1978. One of 300. Illus by Raphael Soyer. With numbered color print sgd by Soyer laid in loose. sg Dec 14 (265) $110

**Sinibaldus, Johannes Benedictus**
— Geneanthropeiae sive de hominis generatione decateuchon.... Frankfurt, 1669. 4to, contemp blind-tooled pigskin with gilt armorial bookstamp of Abbot Gottfried of the Benedictine monastery of Gottweig in Austria, with brass clasps; lacking catches. Some browning. sg May 16 (499A) $225

**Sinibuldi, Guittone, 1270-1337**
— Rime. Rome, [1559]. 1st Ed. 2 parts in 1 vol. 8vo, 19th-cent gilt bdg; parts bound in reverse order. Lacking final blank; minor spotting. C June 26 (132) £800

**Sinistrari d'Ameno, Louis Marie**
— Demoniality, or Incubi and Succubi. L, [1927]. One of 1,290. Trans by Montague Summers. pba Aug 8 (598) $50

**Siodmak, Curt**
— Donovan's Brain. NY, 1943. In dj. sg June 20 (339) $110

**Siqueiros, David Alfaro**
— Mountain Suite. NY, [1969]. One of 250. Folio, loose as issued in orig cloth portfolio. With 10 color lithos. Marginal foxing. sg May 23 (446) $1,900

**Sirelius, Uuno Taavi**
— The Ryijy-Rugs of Finland. Helsinki, 1926. 4to, half mor, in dj. With 93 color plates. sg June 13 (80) $140

**Siren, Osvald, 1879-1966**
— Chinese Painting: Leading Masters and Principles. L, [1956-58]. 7 vols. 4to, orig cloth. CE Sept 27 (257) $300

— Chinese Paintings in American Collections. Paris & Brussels, 1927-28. 3 vols. 4to, loose in wraps as issued; def. sg Jan 11 (394) $120
— Gardens of China. NY, [1949]. 4to, cloth. With 11 color plates. sg June 13 (232) $350
— Histoire des arts anciens de la Chine. Paris, 1929-30. 4 vols. Folio, wraps. With 476 photographic plates. sg Jan 11 (395) $375
— A History of Early Chinese Painting. L, 1933. One of 525. 2 vols. Folio, cloth. Library markings. sg Sept 7 (313) $150

**Siringo, Charles A., 1855-1928**
— Riata and Spurs: The Story of a Lifetime Spent in the Saddle.... Bost., 1927. Orig cloth; extremities worn. pba Nov 16 (250) $75

**Siskind, Aaron**
— Aaron Siskind, Photographer. Rochester, 1965. 4to, cloth, in soiled dj. sg Feb 29 (286) $110

**Sitgreaves, Lorenzo, 1811-88**
— Report of an Expedition Down the Zuni and Colorado Rivers. Wash., 1853. 1st Ed. 8vo, orig half mor; cover fore-edges worn. With 79 plates (1 fold-out) & 1 folding map. Map torn & repaired; some foxing. Robbins-Merriam copy. pba Mar 21 (344) $500
Anr copy. Early half mor. Tp fore-edge margin excised; lacking map. 32d Congress, 2d session, Senate Exec. Doc. 59. sg Oct 26 (337) $130
Anr Ed. Wash., 1854. 2d Issue. 8vo, orig cloth. pba Apr 25 (667) $425

**Sitgreaves, Lorenzo, 1811-88 —&**
**Woodruff, Israel Carle**
— Northern and Western Boundary Line of the Creek Country.... Wash., 1858. 1st Ed. Disbound from larger work, with remains of stitching. With folding map. Adhesion damage along gutter of 1st page. pba Aug 8 (187) $100

**Sitwell, Sacheverell —& Others**
— Fine Bird Books.... L, 1953. Folio, orig half cloth, in dj. b Sept 20 (494) £120
Anr copy. Orig half cloth. Met Sept 28 (24) $250
Anr copy. Library bookplate & release stamp. sg Oct 19 (173) $550
Anr copy. Orig half cloth, in dj. sg Apr 18 (158) $250

**Sitwell, Sacheverell —&**
**Blunt, Wilfrid Jasper Walter**
— Great Flower Books. L, 1956. One of 1,750. Folio, orig half cloth, in dj. sg Apr 18 (159) $250
One of 295. Half cloth; worn. O Mar 5 (202) $200
1st Ed. Folio, orig half mor. Sgd. S Oct 27 (696) £340 [Sawyer]

**Sitwell, Sacheverell —&**
**Madol, Roger**
— Album de Redoute. L, 1954. One of 25 with an orig Redoute plate. Folio, half vellum bds gilt. S Nov 30 (42) £1,000

**Six...**
— Les Six Ages de Leontine. Paris: Marcilly aine, [c.1825]. 6 vols. 12mo, orig bds with hand-colored label, in orig box. S Nov 2 (255) £650 [Hirsch]

**Sixteen...**
— Sixteen Beasts for the Amusement of Children. L: William Darton, [plates dated 1824]. 16mo, orig ptd wraps; soiled. With 16 hand-colored plates. S Nov 2 (256) £260 [Schiller]

**Skelton, Joseph**
See also: Meyrick & Skelton
— Engraved Illustrations of the Principal Antiquities of Oxfordshire.... Oxford, 1823. 4to, contemp half russia; worn, upper cover detached. With frontis, title, map, & 49 plates on india paper. Plates in 2 states; some plates spotted. S Oct 26 (407) £440 [Levy]
— Oxonia antiqua restaurata. Oxford, 1823. 2 vols. 4to, contemp half russia; rubbed, 1 joint split. With folding frontis, & 134 plates on india paper. Spotted. S Oct 26 (406) £380 [Kentish]

Anr copy. Contemp russia; upper hinge weak, spine chipped. With 134 plates & plans & folding map. Tear to 1 plate not affecting image; undescribed drawing loosely inserted. S June 13 (465) £280

**Skelton, Raleigh Ashlin.** See: Roxburghe Club

**Skene, James Henry**
— The Danubian Principalities, the Frontier Lands of the Christian and the Turk. L, 1854. 3d Ed. 2 vols. 8vo, cloth. With half-title, plate, & folding map. S Oct 26 (209) £140 [Scott]

**Sketches...**
See also: Home, Henry; Royall, Anne
— Sketches of Mission Life Among the Indians of Oregon. NY, 1854. Orig cloth; worn & stained. Lacking 1 plate; some soiling & staining. pba Nov 16 (211) $140

**Skinner, Andrew.** See: Taylor & Skinner

**Skipp, John —&**
**Spector, Craig**
— Book of the Dead. Williamantic: Zeising, 1989. One of 500, sgd by the contributors. In dj. O Dec 5 (258) $60

**Skrebneski, Victor**
— Portraits, a Matter of Record. NY, [1978]. 4to, cloth, in torn & chipped dj; bdg soiled, front cover damp-wrinkled. Sgd. sg Feb 29 (289) $130

**Skues, George Edward MacKenzie**
— Minor Tactics of the Chalk Stream. L, 1910. 8vo, cloth; some wear. Minor foxing. O Feb 6 (216) $250; pba July 11 (285) $110
— Nymph Fishing for Chalk Stream Trout. L, 1939. Lev gilt by Bayntun. sg Mar 7 (543) $300
— Side-Lines, Side-Lights & Reflections. Phila., [c.1932]. Orig cloth; tear to cloth at front joint head. pba July 11 (286) $95

— The Way of a Trout with a Fly.... L, 1921. pba July 11 (287) $90

**Sladek, John.** See: Disch & Sladek

**Slare, Frederic**
— Experiments and Observations upon Oriental and Other Bezoar-Stones.... L, 1715. 1st Ed. 8vo, contemp calf; rebacked, corners worn. With woodcut diagram on F7r. H1 torn in margin; some spotting & browning. Ck Mar 22 (276) £200

**Slater, N.** See: Platt & Slater

**Slavery**
— The Fugitive Slave Bill: its History and Unconstitutionality; with an Account of the Seizure and Enslavement of James Hamlet.... NY: American & Foreign Anti-Slavery Society, 1850. 12mo, disbound. Dampstain to tp & 1st leaf. sg Mar 28 (331) $400

**Sleeman, Sir William Henry**
— Rambles and Recollections of an Indian Official. L, 1844. 1st Ed. 2 vols. 8vo, contemp cloth; rebacked. With 2 color frontises, & 30 plates. Plates spotted & margins browned. Ck Mar 22 (277) £220

**Sleidanus, Johannes, 1506?-56**
— De quatuor monarchiis.... Canterbury, 1686. 12mo, contemp calf; rubbed, lower hinge cracked. Tp with corner torn away with loss & laid down; lacking 1 prelim leaf; 1st 2 gatherings wormed in upper margin; a few leaves dust-soiled. S June 12 (155) £200

**Sloan, Samuel, 1817-1907**
— The Model Architect: a Series of Original Designs for Cottages, Vollas, Suburban Residences.... Phila., [1852]. 1st Ed. 21 (of 24) parts. Folio, orig wraps; some soiled or detached. Marginal tears & wrinkling to some plates. Sold w.a.f. K Oct 1 (16) $450

Anr copy. 2 vols. Folio, half mor; dampstained. Foxed throughout; repairs to tp of Vol II. wad Oct 18 (10) C$580

**Sloane, Eric.** See: Onassis copy, Jacqueline Bouvier Kennedy

**Sloane, William Milligan, 1850-1928**
— Life of Napoleon Bonaparte. NY, 1906. 4 vols. 4to, contemp half mor. CE Feb 21 (211) $850

**Slocum, Joshua**
— Sailing Alone around the World. NY, 1900. 1st Ed. 8vo, cloth; rubbed & shaken, hinges cracked. pba July 25 (217) $100

Anr Ed. NY, 1906. Inscr to Ira E Lute, 23 May 1906. pba July 25 (218) $80

**Slop-Basin...**
— The Slop-Basin; or, Two or Three LInes WIthout a Preface. Stockton: William Robinson, [c.1838]. 12mo, orig cloth. Minor spotting. Inscr to Richard Knight Ord, 1838. b Dec 5 (111) £50

**Small, Henry Beaumont**
— The Canadian Handbook and Tourist's Guide. Montreal, 1867. 8vo, orig cloth; spine frayed. With 10 mtd albumen prints by Notman. O Feb 6 (218) $250

Anr copy. Orig cloth; worn, rebacked, endpapers renewed. With 8 mtd albumen prints by Notman. Soiled throughout. sg Feb 29 (225) $90

**Smalridge, George, Bishop of Oxford**
— Sixty Sermons Preached on Several occasions. Oxford, 1724. Folio, contemp calf elaborately gilt with gauffered edges to design of floral volutes with stags & birds, accented with paint. sg Mar 21 (51) $700

**Smart, Christopher, 1722-71**
— Poems on Several Occasions. L, 1752. 4to, contemp half calf; rubbed, upper joint cracked. Spotting to 1st 4 leaves. William Mason's copy. S Dec 18 (138) £320 [Quaritch]

**Smart, James Francis**
— The Steam Packet.... Bristol, 1823. 8vo, orig bds. With folding litho frontis. b Dec 5 (37) £150

**Smeaton, John, 1724-92**
— A Narrative of the Building... of the Edystone Lighthouse. L, 1813. 2d Ed. Folio, cloth; worn. With title & 23 maps & plates. Title & 4 plates torn; 1 plate loose; some plates marked. S Oct 26 (342) £250 [Jeffery]

**Smellie, William, 1697-1763**
— An Abridgement of the Practice of Midwifery.... Bost.: J. Norman, [1786]. 8vo, contemp sheep; rubbed. With 38 (of 39) plates. Lacking Plate 4; some staining & foxing. sg May 16 (500) $500

**Smiles, Samuel, 1812-1904**
— Lives of the Engineers. L, 1862. 3 vols. 8vo, contemp calf; spines rubbed & faded. With frontis port. Some foxing. Inscr to Joseph Whitaker. S Oct 26 (344) £170 [Sotheran]

**Smith, Aaron, fl.1823-52.** See: Golden Cockerel Press

**Smith, Abram P.**
— History of the Seventy-Sixth Regiment New York Volunteers.... Cortland NY, 1867. 8vo, orig cloth; spine worn. NH July 21 (95) $120

**Smith, Adam, 1723-90**
— An Inquiry into the Nature and Causes of the Wealth of Nations. L, 1776. 1st Ed. 2 vols. 4to, contemp calf; joints weak or split, spines scuffed & chipped at ends. Tear to margin of 3B2; corner of 3G4 lacking. C June 26 (209) £17,000

Anr copy. Bds, uncut. Vol I tp & Vol II half-title cut away; Vol I tp foxed; 2 catchwords punched out; some marginal tears & foxing. Chichester Cathedral copy. CNY Dec 15 (37) $19,000

Anr copy. Contemp calf; corners worn, rebacked. Foxed; Vol I with L4 torn, lacking final blank & with marginal worming at end; Vol II with tear at gutter margin of half-title. CNY May 17 (110) $16,000

Anr copy. Contemp calf; spines repaired, hinges weak, rubbed, bumped. Lacking half-title in Vol I; minor foxing; Vol II with some corners creased. rs Nov 11 (118) $21,000

Anr Ed. L, 1784. 3 vols. 8vo, contemp calf gilt; spines worn & scuffed, joints cracked, upper cover of Vol II detached. Some foxing & browning. bbc Dec 18 (394) $950

Anr Ed. L, 1789. 3 vols. 8vo, half calf by Bayntun. Z June 28 (254) $425

Anr Ed. L, 1793. 3 vols. 8vo, contemp bds; def. Lacking half-titles. b Sept 20 (213) £160

Anr Ed. L, 1796. 3 vols. 8vo, contemp calf; rubbed. bba Nov 16 (152) £350 [Axe]

Anr Ed. Phila.: Dobson, 1796. 3 vols. 12mo, early calf gilt, stamped Academia Jacobi VI Scotorum Regis Edinensis; joints & edges rubbed, front joints split. wa Nov 16 (218) $240

9th Ed. L, 1799. 3 vols. 8vo, contemp calf. pba Sept 14 (323) $375

Anr Ed. Edin., 1806. 3 vols. 8vo, contemp calf; joints cracked, front cover detached from Vol III. pba Jan 4 (398) $160

New Ed. L, 1822. 3 vols. 8vo, half calf; 1 spine marred. pba Aug 8 (601) $130

Anr copy. Later calf; scuffed, Vol III joints weak. wa Feb 29 (227) $270

— The Theory of Moral Sentiments. L, 1761. 2d Ed. 8vo, modern half calf; some page edges stained. S June 12 (122) £1,150

Anr Ed. Phila., 1817. 2 vols. 8vo, contemp calf; extremities worn, joints cracked. pba Nov 30 (296) $170

**Smith, Albert Richard, 1816-60**
— The Adventures of Mr. Ledbury and his Friend Jack Johnson. L, 1886. Illus by John Leech. 4to, half mor gilt. With hand-colored frontis & 21 uncolored plates. sg Feb 8 (96) $110

— The Struggles and Adventures of Christopher Tadpole. L, 1848. Illus by John Leech. 8vo, calf gilt by Hatchards. pba June 20 (306) $75

**Smith, Amanda**
— Autobiography. The Story of the Lord's Dealings with Mrs. Amanda Smith, the Colored Evangelist. Chicago, 1893. 8vo, cloth; corner of front cover worn. With port. sg Mar 28 (351) $350

**Smith, Sir Andrew, 1797-1872**
— Illustrations of the Zoology of South Africa.... L, [1838]-49-[50]. 5 vols in 3. 4to, contemp half mor gilt; worn & stained, 1 bd def at upper outer corner. With 11 plain & 268 hand-colored plates. Margins at beginning of Mammalia brittle, chipped & torn, affecting a few plates & text leaves; Plate 32 of Aves with crude modern coloring; title to Reptilia torn in inner margin. S June 27 (65) £2,000

**Smith, Bernard.** See: Joppien & Smith

**Smith, Bertha H.**
— Yosemite Legends. San Francisco, [1904]. With 13 plates. pba Feb 12 (179) $80; pba Apr 25 (669) $65; pba July 25 (351) $55

**Smith, Charles**
— The Aberdeen Golfers: Records and Reminiscences. [L]: Ellesborough Press, [1982]. One of 200. Mor; spine sunned. Sgd by J. S. R. Cruickshank, Capt. Royal & Ancient Golf Club St. Andrews. pba Apr 18 (46) $250

**Smith, Charles, Bookseller**
— General Atlas.... L, 1808. Folio, contemp half calf; rubbed & worn. With engraved title & 42 maps on 46 double-page mapsheets, with contemp hand-coloring. S Nov 30 (63) £950

**Smith, Charles Hamilton**
See also: Meyrick & Smith
— Selections of the Ancient Costume of Great Britain and Ireland. L, [c.1821]. ("The Ancient Costume of Great Britain and Ireland.") Folio, half mor; spine ends perished, front cover partly detached, some plates & leaves detached. With 61 colored plates. cb Oct 17 (117) $400

**Smith, Charlotte, 1749-1806**
— Elegiac Sonnets and Other Poems. Worcester MA: Isaiah Thomas, 1795. 12mo, contemp calf gilt; front joint cracked. With 5 plates. Some spotting. 1st American book ptd on wove paper. Dard Hunter's copy. sg Apr 18 (186) $330

**Smith, Clark Ashton, 1893-1961**
— The Double Shadow and Other Fantasies. Auburn CA: Auburn Journal Print, 1933. Folio, half mor, orig wraps bound in; spine browned. Pencil corrections in Smith's hand to 4 pages. pba May 4 (252) $350
— The Star Treader and Other Poems. San Francisco, 1912. In dj. Inscr, 1937 & with orig address label from Smith laid in. pba May 4 (253) $300

**Smith, Daniel.** See: Mills & Smith

**Smith, Edmund Ware**
See also: Derrydale Press
— The Further Adventures of the One-Eyed Poacher. NY: Crown, [1947]. One of 750. pba July 11 (435) $65; sg Mar 7 (544) $130

**Smith, Edward E., 1890-1965**
— Gray Lensman. Reading: Fantasy Press, 1951. One of 500. In rubbed dj. cb Oct 17 (567) $140

**Smith, Edwin, The Edwin Smith Surgical Papyrus, Published in Facsimile...**
— The Edwin Smith Surgical Papyrus.... See: Breasted, James Henry

**Smith, Elizabeth**
— Poems on Malvern and Other Subjects. Worcester, 1829. 8vo, orig cloth; stained. b Dec 5 (418) £70

**Smith, Ernest Bramah, 1868-1942.** See: Bramah, Ernest

**Smith, Francis Hopkinson, 1838-1915**
— American Illustrators. NY, 1892. 5 parts. Folio, loose as issued in wraps. sg May 9 (381) $60

**Smith, Garden G.**
See also: Hilton & Smith
— Side Lights on Golf. L: Sisley's, [c.1907]. 1st Ed. Cloth; soiled & spotted. pba Apr 18 (155) $250
— The World of Golf: The Isthmian Library. L: A. D. Innes, 1898. 1st Ed. - Preface by Temple Chambers. Cloth. With frontis illus. Frontis stained. pba Apr 18 (156) $325

**Smith, Capt. George, of the Royal Artillery**
— An Universal Military Dictionary. L, 1779. 4to, contemp calf; worn, front cover detached, rear joint split. With 16 plates (14 folding). Some cropping. wa Feb 29 (203) $475

**Smith, Sir Grafton Elliot —& Dawson, Warren Royal**
— Egyptian Mummies. L, 1924. 4to, orig cloth; worn & soiled, notes on endpapers & half-title. wa Feb 1 (149) $100

**Smith, Harold Clifford**
— Buckingham Palace. L, 1931. Folio, orig cloth, in dj. b Sept 20 (536) £55

**Smith, Harry B., 1860-1936**
— A Sentimental Library.... [N.p.]: Pvtly ptd, 1914. Half vellum, in frayed dj. Inscr. O Mar 5 (205) $130
  Anr copy. Half vellum, in chipped dj; worn. O Mar 26 (255) $130

**Smith, Harry Worcester**
— A Sporting Family of the Old South. Albany: J. B. Lyon, 1936. 4to, cloth; rubbed, shaken. Some foxing. O June 4 (250) $50
— A Sporting Tour through Ireland, England, Wales and France.... Columbia, SC, 1925. Bookplate Ed, with tipped-in bookplate & slip sgd by Smith. 2 vols. Inscr & with 8-line holograph poem. O Jan 9 (201) $110

**Smith, Hendrik, 1495-1563**
— Henrik Smids Laegebog.... Copenhagen: Andreas Gutterwitz for Balter Kaus, 1577. 4to in 8s,. 17th-cent calf rubbed. A few leaves repaired in margins, affecting catchwords; loss at edges of text in index to Part 6; some dampstaining. Madsen copy. S Mar 14 (336) £420

**Smith, Miss J.**
— Studies of Flowers from Nature. Adwick Hall, near Doncaster, 1818. Folio, contemp half mor; worn. With engraved title within hand-colored border of a wreath of flowers & 20 plates in uncolored & hand-colored states. With 2 leaves of subscribers. b June 28 (66) £5,000

# SMITH

**Smith, J. B.**
— Seaton Beach; a Poem.... Exeter, 1835. 8vo, orig bds; spine def.  b Dec 5 (91) £75

**Smith, Col. James**
— An Account of the Remarkable Occurrences in the Life and Travels of.... Phila., 1831. 18mo, orig half lea; rubbed.  sg Oct 26 (345) $900

**Smith, Sir James Edward, 1759-1828**
See also: Sowerby & Smith
— Plantarum icones hactenus ineditae.... L, 1789-1801. 3 parts in 1 vol. Folio, cloth. With 75 uncolored plates. Some foxing & dampstaining. Met Feb 24 (328) $1,000

**Smith, Jedediah**
— The Southwest Expedition of Jedediah S. Smith.... Glendale, 1977. 2d Ptg. Ed by George R. Brooks. With 3 maps.  pba Feb 13 (171) $55

**Smith, Jerome V. C.**
— Natural History of the Fishes of Massachusetts. Bost., 1833. 8vo, orig cloth; spine tips frayed. Some foxing & soiling. Gee - Van Winkle copy. O June 25 (254) $225

**Smith, John, Picture Dealer**
— A Catalogue Raisonne of the Works of the Most Eminent Dutch, Flemish and French Painters. L, 1908. One of 1,250. 9 vols, including Supplement. Facsimile reprint of the 1829-42 Ed. sg June 13 (344) $60

**Smith, John, Professor of Dartmouth College**
— A Hebrew Grammar. Bost., 1803. 8vo, early half sheep; worn. Portion of upper margin of tp excised, affecting 1 word of title. sg Oct 26 (184) $60

**Smith, John, 1747-1807**
— Galic Antiquities, consisting of a History of the Druids.... Edin., 1780. 1st Ed. 4to, modern half calf with incorrect date on spine. pba Nov 30 (297) $225

**Smith, John, 1749-1831**
— Select Views in Italy.... L, 1792-96. 2 vols. Folio, early 19th-Cent half roan; rubbed. With map frontis, & 72 plates. Vol I plate 21 creased; vol II plate 37 frayed; plates 40-42 misbound; 2 leaves torn & repaired; some spotting. S Oct 26 (299) £1,100 [Zioni]
Anr Ed. L, 1796 [engraved title dated 1830]. 2 vols in 1. 4to, contemp mor gilt; extremities rubbed. Ck Feb 14 (319) £700

**Smith, Capt. John, 1580-1631**
— A Description of New England.... Bost., 1865. One of 250. 4to, half mor. Some dampstaining. pba July 25 (451) $80
— The Generall Historie of Virginia, New-England, and the Summer Isles.... L, 1632. Bound with: Smith. The True Travels, Adventures, and Observations.... L, 1630. Folio, later mor gilt. Engraved title laid down; some soiling; chipped; 2d work lacking plate, Contents & B1. cb Feb 14 (2603) $36,000

Anr Ed. [Cleveland, 1966]. Folio, vellum gilt with arms of King James I. Facsimile of the 1624 Ed. pba Aug 8 (188) $70
— The True Travels, Adventures and Observations.... L, 1630. Folio, crudely recased into contemp calf. With folding plate in 2d state. Extra-illus with c.54 ports of Smith & his contemporaries. pba Oct 9 (19) $2,750

**Smith, John Calvin**
— The Illustrated Hand-Book.... NY, 1848. 16mo, orig cloth; rubbed. With folding map hand-colored in outline. Dampstain in lower corners of 1st few leaves; fold breaks in map. NH Sept 16 (15) $300

**Smith, John Chaloner**
— British Mezzotinto Portraits. L, 1883-78-83. 4 vols. 8vo, contemp half mor. S June 12 (336) £300

**Smith, John Thomas, 1766-1833**
— Antiquities of London and its Environs. L, 1791-[1800]. 4to, later half mor; extremities rubbed. Small tear at p. 75. S Apr 23 (373) £130
— A Book for a Rainy Day: or, Recollections of the Events of the Last Sixty-Six Years. L, 1845. 8vo, contemp calf gilt by Root. Extra-illus with c.100 plates. pba Aug 22 (764) $85
— The Cries of London. L, 1842. 4to, calf gilt by Root; rebacked retaining backstrip. With engraved title & 30 hand-colored plates. Bishop copy. sg Sept 21 (295) $475

**Smith, Joseph, 1682-1770**
— Bibliotheca Smithiana, seu catalogus librorum D. Josephi Smithii Angli. Venice, 1755. Compiled by Giovanni Battista Pasquali. 2 parts in 1 vol. 4to, contemp calf gilt; upper joint cracked, extremities worn. Some waterstaining. Sir Thomas Phillipps' annotated copy. bba May 9 (49) £700 [Marlborough]
— Catalogus librorum rarissimorum, ab artis typographicae inventoribus aliisque artis principibus.... [Venice: Pasquali, 1737]. 8vo, contemp vellum. bba May 9 (48) £1,000 [Brindel]

**Smith Library, Joseph**
— Bibliotheca Smithiana, seu catalogus librorum D. Josephi Smithii Angli. Venice, 1755. Compiled by Giovanni Battista Pasquali. 4to, contemp vellum. Some soiling. O Mar 26 (257) $300

**Smith, Joseph, 1805-44**
— The Book of Mormon. Palmyra, NY, 1830. 1st Ed. 8vo, orig sheep; hinges cracked, joints splitting, spine worn. With 2-page preface & testimonial leaf at end & without index. Page iv numbered vi. Library stamp on tp verso; minor stains. cb Oct 17 (171) $7,500
Anr copy. Orig lea; rubbed. Tp stamped; lacking preface. NH July 21 (245) $8,200
Anr Ed. Liverpool, 1854. Flake 603. 12mo, lea. Z June 28 (31) $250
Anr Ed. Salt Lake City, 1877. 16mo, contemp mor; recased, with repairs to spine. pba Aug 22 (942) $200

Anr Ed. Salt Lake City: Deseret News, 1888. 16mo, contemp mor gilt. pba Aug 22 (941) $110
— The Holy Scriptures, Translated and Corrected by the Spirit of Revelation.... Plano IL, 1867. 12mo, contemp mor gilt; scuffed, stain to rear cover. pba Apr 25 (538) $450

**Smith, Michael A.**
— Landscapes 1975-1979. Revere PA: Lodima Press, [1981]. One of 1,000. 4to, cloth with mtd photographic reproduction & orig plastic outer wrap; spine ends rubbed. With 42 tipped-in duotones. sg Feb 29 (290) $150

**Smith, Nathan Ryno, 1797-1877**
— Surgical Anatomy of the Arteries. Balt., 1835. 4to, modern cloth. With 20 hand-colored plates. Foxing; marginal dampstaining throughout. sg May 16 (502) $90

**Smith, Nora Archibald**
— Boys and Girls of Bookland. NY, 1923. Illus by Jessie Willcox Smith. In dj; bdg spine ends rubbed. pba Aug 22 (855) $110

**Smith, Patti**
— Robert Mapplethorpe. [N.p.]: Bellport Press, 1987. 4to, cloth, in rubbed & soiled dj. sg Feb 29 (200) $110

**Smith, Robert, 1689-1768**
— A Compleat System of Opticks. Cambr., 1738. 2 vols. 4to, contemp calf; joints split, sides rubbed. With 83 folding plates, 1 ad leaf & binder's instructions. Plates browned. Madsen copy. S Mar 14 (338) £1,200
— Vollstaendiger Lehrbegriff der Optik. Altenburg, 1755. 4to, contemp half vellum; rubbed & soiled. With 22 folding plates. S Mar 14 (339) £360

**Smith, Samuel, 1720-76**
— The History of the Colony of Nova-Caesaria, or New-Jersey... Burlington, 1765. 1st Ed. 8vo, contemp calf; scuffed. Foxed; prelims with worming to bottom left corner. wd Nov 15 (105) $500

**Smith, Stevie, Pseud.**
— A Good Time Was Had by All. NY, 1937. In chipped & soiled dj. pba Jan 25 (344) $75

**Smith, Thomas, 1638-1710**
— Remarks upon the Manners, Religion and Government of the Turks. L, 1678. 1st Ed. Bound with: Georgirenes, Joseph. A Description of the Present State of Samos, Nicaria, Patmos and Mount Athos. L, 1678. 1st Ed. Lacking the 2 prelim leaves. Text in Greek. 8vo, contemp calf; worn, cover detached. S Mar 28 (299) £900

Anr copy. 1st Ed. Bound with: Georgirenes, Joseph. A Description of the Present State of Samos, Nicaria, Patmos and Mount Athos. L, 1678. 8vo, contemp sheep; rubbed. S June 27 (161) £900

**Smith, Sir Thomas, 1513-77**
— De Republica Anglorum. The Maner of Governement of England. L: Henry Midleton for Gregory Seton, 1584. 4to, mor by Morrell preserving 18th-cent bookplate of Sir Francis Palgrave. Some headlines shaved. b May 30 (419) £700

**Smith, Thomas W.**
— A Narrative of the Life, Travels and Sufferings.... Bost., 1844. 12mo, contemp sheep; worn, 1st signature sprung, stained. Some foxing. wa Feb 29 (584) $240

**Smith, Thorne**
— Topper. NY, 1926. In dj with insect damage & chipping. pba May 4 (254) $750

**Smith, W. Eugene**
— Eugene Smith Photography. Minneapolis: University of Minnesota, 1954. Ptd wraps; rust stains on fold. Soft creases on a few plates. sg Oct 7 (335) $130

**Smith, William, LL.D.**
— A Dictionary of the Bible. L, 1860-63. 3 vols. 8vo, contemp mor gilt; joints rubbed. pba Sept 14 (22) $130

**Smith, William, 1728-93**
— The History of the Province of New-York.... L, 1757. 1st Ed. 4to, contemp calf; rebacked, corners repaired. Folding view split along fold; some browning & soiling. CE May 22 (29) $1,600

**Smith, William, 1769-1839**
— [A Geological Survey Atlas of England]. L, 1819-24. 24 maps with platemark measurement of 600mm by 520mm, in cloth portfolio. Maps hand-colored. Cumberland soiled; Surrey with tear along platemark; Kent with repaired tear touching platemark. Hefner copy. CNY May 17 (40) $10,000
— A Delineation of the Strata of England and Wales.... L, 1815-[17]. With: A Memoir to Smith's Map and Delineation.... L, 1815. Folio, contemp half calf, memoir in orig wraps lacking backstrip; rubbed. With engraved title & 15 hand-colored double-page mapsheets, divided into 32 sections & laid down on orig linen backed in marbled paper. Memoir with 2 folding tables, the 2d engraved & partly hand-colored. Some staining; ink stain in blank area below title; some fold breaks. Honeyman - Hefner copy. CNY May 17 (39) $19,000

**Smith, William A.**
— Lectures on the Philosophy and Practice of Slavery.... Nashville: Stevenson & Evans, 1856. 8vo, cloth; extremities worn. sg Mar 28 (340) $120

**Smith, William Rudolph, 1787-1868**
— Observations on the Wisconsin Territory.... Phila., 1838. 1st Ed. 12mo, modern half cloth. With colored folding map. Library stamp on p. 81; map backed. Met May 22 (374) $450

Anr copy. Orig cloth; worn, ring stain to back cover. 2 of 3 tears to map repaired. wa Feb 29 (587) $475

**Smith, Yvonne**
— John Haley Bellamy: Carver of Eagles. Portsmouth NH, 1982. 4to, cloth, in dj. NH July 21 (20) $110

**Smithwick, Noah**
— The Evolution of a State or Recollections of Old Texas Days. Austin, [1900]. 12mo, orig cloth; rubbed. With 5 plates. Tp with small erasure smudge. wa Feb 29 (523) $280

**Smollett, Tobias, 1721-71**
See also: Limited Editions Club
— The History of England. L, 1758-65. ("A Complete History of England.") 3d Ed of Vols 4-16, 2d Ed of Vols 1-3. 16 vols. 8vo, contemp calf; rubbed. S Mar 28 (580) £440

Anr Ed. L, 1788. 5 vols. 8vo, contemp calf. pba Sept 14 (325) $275
— Works. L, 1797. 8 vols. 8vo, calf gilt; extremities scuffed. F Sept 21 (423) $350

Anr Ed. Oxford: Shakespeare Head Press, 1925-26. One of 780. 11 vols. Unopened, in djs. wd Nov 15 (106) $150

Anr Ed. Bost., 1926. One of 500. 11 vols. Half mor. cb Oct 17 (299) $600

**Smyth, Charles Piazzi**
— Teneriffe, an Astronomer's Experiment.... L, 1858. 8vo, orig cloth. With 20 stereographs & 1 map. Margins of 1 stereograph cut away; library stamps. b May 30 (66) £160

**Smyth, Garden G.** See: Hilton & Smyth

**Smyth, Henry DeWolf**
— A General Account of the Development of Methods of Using Atomic Energy for Military Purposes.... [Wash.: Adjutant General's Office, Aug 1945]. Lithoprint version. 4to, orig wraps; soiled. Leaf I-9/I-10 in duplicate, but text on p. IX-2 dropped. wa Feb 29 (137) $450

**Smyth, William**
— English Lyricks. Liverpool, 1797. 8vo, uncut sheets. Minor spotting. b Dec 5 (219) £80

**Smyth, William Henry, 1788-1865**
— Memoir Descriptive of the Resources, Inhabitants, and Hydrography of Sicily.... L, 1824. 1st Ed. 4to, contemp half calf; rubbed. With folding map, & 14 views on 13 leaves. Some spotting. Sir Thomas Phillipps copy. S Oct 26 (300) £280 [Tosi]

**Smythies, Miss —**
— The Stage-Coach, containing the Character of Mr. Manly.... L, 1753. 2 vols. 12mo, contemp calf; rubbed, joints cracked. Ink stain on tp of Vol I. bba Oct 19 (230) £260 [Axe]

**Snape, Andrew, Farrier**
— The Anatomy of an Horse.... L, 1683. 1st Ed. 2 parts in 1 vol. Folio, contemp mor gilt; rubbed. With 49 plates. Lacking port. some stains & foxing. O Jan 9 (203) $1,400

**Snelgrave, William**
— A New Account of Some Parts of Guinea, and the Slave Trade. L, 1734. 1st Ed. 8vo, calf. With folding map. b May 30 (186) £180

**Snell, Roy J.**
— The Strangeland Bird Life. Chicago: Just Right Books, [1924]. Illus by Cobb X. Shinn. pba Aug 22 (857) $70

**Snelling, William Joseph, 1804-48**
— Indian Nullification of the Unconstitutional Laws of Massachusetts Relative to the Mashpee Tribe.... Bost., 1835. 12mo, cloth; hinges cracked. Some foxing. Met May 22 (328) $200

**Snift, Dean, of Brazen-Nose.** See: Pinch...

**Snodgrass, John James**
— Narrative of the Burmese War. L, 1827. 8vo, orig bds; backstrip def. With folding map & 2 plates. Map torn. sg Mar 7 (183) $90

**Snow, Jack**
— The Magical Mimics in Oz. Chicago, [1946]. 1st Ed, 1st State. Orig cloth; repaired tear along upper front joint. pba Jan 18 (165) $120
— The Shaggy Man of Oz. Chicago: Reilly & Lee, [1949]. In chipped dj; short tear to bdg cloth at spine head. pba Jan 18 (166) $225
— Who's Who in Oz. Chicago: Reilly & Lee, [1954]. In dj. pba Jan 18 (167) $275

**Snow, William Parker**
— A Paper on the Lost Polar Expedition.... L, 1860. 8vo, orig wraps. Inscr. sg Mar 7 (298) $1,200

**Snow, William R.**
— Sketches of Chinese Life and Character. L: Dickinson Bros, [1860]. 3 parts in 1 vol. Folio, contemp half mor gilt. With 18 hand-colored plates. Lacking title & text. S Nov 30 (213) £4,600

**Snowden, Eleanor**
— The Maid of Scio. Dover, 1829. 16mo, contemp calf. Inscr. b Dec 5 (156) £150

**Snowman, Abraham Kenneth**
— Eighteenth Century Gold Boxes of Europe. Bost., 1966. In dj. sg June 13 (346) $60

**Snyder, John P.**
— The Mapping of New Jersey. New Brunswick, [1973]. In dj. sg May 9 (40) $350

**Soane, Sir John, 1753-1837**
— Description of the House and Museum on the North Side of Lincoln's Inn Fields. L, 1830. 4to, orig bds; spine & corners worn, upper hinge weak. With 17 plates. Some plates foxed or dampstained. Inscr to Sir Charles Flint. S June 27 (289) £700

Anr Ed. L, 1835. One of 150. 4to, orig half mor gilt; worn. Inscr to Miss Paterson. b Sept 20 (79) £900

— Sketches in Architecture. L, 1793. Bound with: Parkyns, George Isham. Six Designs for Improving and Embellishing Grounds. L, 1793. Folio. 1st Ed. Contemp half calf; worn. 1st work, 43 plates & plans; 2d work, 11 plates & plans. S Apr 23 (252) £820

2d Ed. L, 1798. Bound with: Parkyns, George Isham. Six Designs for Improving and Embellishing Grounds. L, 1798. 2 parts in 1 vol. Folio, contemp half calf; rebacked, worn. With half-title, divisional title, & 54 plates. Some discoloration & spotting in margins. S Oct 26 (345) £850 [Sotheran]

**Soby, James Thrall**
— The Early Chirico. NY, 1941. 4to, cloth, in dj with spine ends rubbed. sg Jan 11 (111) $225
— The Prints of Paul Klee. NY, 1947. 4to, loose as issued in pbr's case. With 40 plates. sg Jan 11 (245) $130

**Socard, Emile**
— Catalogue de la Bibliotheque de la Ville de Troyes. Troyes, 1875-80. 7 vols. 8vo, contemp half mor; rubbed. O Mar 26 (258) $120

**Societe Anonyme**
— Modern Art at the Sesqui-Centennial Exhibition. NY, 1926. Text by Christian Brinton. 4to, orig wraps. sg Sept 7 (314) $300

**Society for the Diffusion of Useful Knowledge**
— Maps. L, 1844. 2 vols in 1. 4to, contemp half calf; def. With 206 maps only, hand-colored in outline. Some marginal tears; lacking some text. Sold w.a.f. b May 30 (131) £1,100

Anr copy. Vol I (of 2) only. Folio, contemp half calf; worn, upper cover detached. With 112 maps. Some discoloration & fraying; few pp. becoming loose. S Oct 26 (447) £280 [Verdi]

Anr copy. 2 vols in 1. 4to, contemp half mor gilt; rubbed. With 218 mapsheets, most hand-colored in outline. Folding maps strengthened; some discoloration or spotting. S Nov 30 (85) £1,700

Anr copy. 3 vols. 4to, contemp half russia; worn. With 195 (of 218) maps & plans, hand-colored in outline. S June 13 (418) £1,400

Anr copy. 2 vols. 4to, contemp half calf; worn. With 212 maps hand-colored in outline. Lacking star charts; marginal annotations; some staining & soiling. S June 13 (510) £1,600

Anr copy. Contemp half mor; rubbed & soiled. With 218 maps, hand-colored in outline. S June 13 (511) £1,700

— The Penny Cyclopaedia.... L, 1833-44. 27 vols, plus 2-vol Supplement. 4to, contemp half calf gilt; rubbed. S June 12 (208) £300

**Society of Antiquaries of Scotland**
— Proceedings. Edin., 1851-1969. Vols 1-101 in 102; lacking Vol 10, Part 2. 4to, various bdgs. Library markings. pnE Mar 20 (142) £400

**Society of California Pioneers**
— Quarterly of.... San Francisco, 1924-1933. 1st Ed. 37 issues, unbroken run, Orig wraps. Robbins copy. pba Mar 21 (345) $275

**Soeiro, Joao, 1566-1607**
— Abkai ejen-i enduringge tachiya i oyonggo gisun. [Peking, c.1670]. Folio, modern fabric bdg. 10 leaves, ptd xylographically on native paper; in Manchu. S June 27 (230) £6,000

**Solano Ortiz de Rozas, Josef**
— Idea del imperio otomano. Madrid, 1793. 8vo, contemp calf. With folding map & 3 folding plates. Some tears to map; fold breaks to table; last leaf partly detached; some staining. S June 13 (597) £300

**Solinus, Caius Julius**
See also: Camers, Giovanni
— De situ orbis. Venice: Jenson, 1473. 4to, 18th-cent calf; rebacked. Type 1:114R, 33 lines. Unrubricated. Occasional staining. Ms notes in a humanistic hand. 68 leaves. Goff S-615. Jeudwine-Abrams copy. C Apr 3 (225) £10,000

**Solis y Ribadeneyra, Antonio de, 1610-86**
— Historia de la conquista de Mexico.... Mexico: Ignacio Cumplido, 1844-46. 3 vols, including Supplement. 4to, calf gilt; rubbed. With chromolitho titles & 1 plate plus 70 plates & folding map in Supplement. Some foxing; library stamps on titles. sg Oct 26 (303) $140
— The History of the Conquest of Mexico.... L, 1724. 1st Ed in English. Folio, contemp calf; rebacked, rubbed. With engraved port & 2 maps & 6 plates. Blindstamp on tp. cb Oct 17 (206) $1,000

**Solis-Cohen, Emily**
— David the Giant Killer and Other Tales of Grandma Lopez. Phila., 1908. Illus by Alfred Feinberg. Color pictorial title label applied to cloth,; soiled, hinges starting. pba Jan 4 (56) $170

**Solleysell, Jacques, Sieur de**
— Le Parfait Mareschal.... The Hague, 1691. 2 parts in 1 vol. 4to, contemp calf; rubbed. With port, extra pictorial title & 2 plates. Some browning, minor stains & foxing. O Jan 9 (204) $120

**Solvyns, Frans Baltasar**
— The Costume of Hindostan. L, 1804. 4to, contemp mor gilt with floral & greek-key pattern border. With 60 hand-colored plates. Marginal soiling; some spotting. C May 1 (164) £900

Anr Ed. L, 1807. Folio, contemp mor gilt; rebacked retaining orig spine. With 60 colored plates. S June 13 (641) £700

Anr Ed. L, 1807 [plates watermarked 1815-16]. Folio, mor gilt; broken, taped, library markings. With 60 colored plates. Lacking English text leaf for Plate 39; Plate 46 stained; Plate 52 taped in margin; some marginal foxing. wa Feb 29 (102) $375

— Les Hindous. Paris, 1808-12. 4 vols. Folio, contemp bds; rebacked with mor, worn. With 288 hand-

# SOLZHENITSYN

colored plates. Some discoloration & spotting. In French & English. S Nov 30 (214) £6,500

**Solzhenitsyn, Alexander**
— One Day in the Life of Ivan Denisovich. L, 1963. 1st English Ed. In dj. sg Dec 14 (270) $150

**Some...**
— Some Observations on the Assiento Trade. L, 1728. 8vo, disbound. sg Mar 28 (341) $700

**Some Recollections...**
— Some Recollections of the Upper Ammonoosuc Valley. [N.p.]: R. M. Kauffmann, 1948. Cloth; endpapers possibly supplied. pba July 11 (19) $325

**Somerville, Edith**
See also: Derrydale Press
— Slipper's A.B.C. of Fox Hunting. L, 1903. Folio, orig cloth; corners bumped. bba May 30 (462) £180 [Cathach]

**Somerville, William, 1675-1742**
— The Chase. L, 1735. 1st Ed. 4to, old calf; rubbed. Minor foxing & soiling. O Jan 9 (205) $80
Anr copy. Contemp calf; rubbed. Inscr, 12 Aug 1735. S June 13 (419) £160
Anr Ed. L, 1796. Illus by Thomas Bewick. 8vo, contemp bds; spine chipped. O Jan 9 (206) $130
Anr Ed. L: Albion Press, 1804. ("The Chase; to which is annexed Field Sports.") 12mo, modern calf gilt; front joint weak. With 9 hand-colored plates. sg Mar 7 (545) $250
Anr Ed. L, 1817. 12mo, mor gilt by Thomas Gosden; some rubbing. O Jan 9 (207) $275

**Somm, Henry**
— La Berline de l'emigre. Paris, 1885. Ltd Ed. 12mo, mor extra with design of a hanging sign, orig wraps bound in. WIth 6 orig drawings, including the tp. S Nov 21 (406) £300

**Sommier, Francois Clement.** See: Somm, Henry

**Songs...**
— Songs and Spirituals of Negro Composition. Chicago: Progressive Book Company, 1928. Orig wraps. sg Mar 28 (224) $150
— Songs of the Chace. L, 1811. 2d Ed. 8vo, mor by Taffin. Some foxing & soiling. O Jan 9 (208) $100
Anr copy. Gilt-pictorial calf by Thomas Gosden; worn. Some soiling & foxing. O Jan 9 (209) $60
Anr copy. Half mor; front cover nearly detached, extremities rubbed. pba July 11 (436) $55

**Songster's...**
— The Songster's Favourite Companion; A Collection of New and Musch-Esteemed Songs... Flute, Voice, and Violin. Glasgow, [c.1810]. 8vo, later half mor by Tout. S Apr 23 (295) £70

**Sonneck, Oscar George, 1873-1928**
— Bibliography of Early Secular American Music. [Wash.], 1945. Revised by W. T. Upton. Cloth; worn. O Mar 26 (260) $50

# AMERICAN BOOK PRICES CURRENT

**Sonnets...**
— Sonnets et eaux-fortes. Paris, 1869. One of 350. 4to, mor gilt by Sangorski & Sutcliffe. With 42 plates. S Nov 21 (407) £3,200

**Sonoma County.** See: California

**Soong, Mei-ling (Mme. Chiang Kai-shek).** See: Onassis copy, Jacqueline Bouvier Kennedy

**Sophocles, 496?-406 B.C.**
See also: Limited Editions Club
— Antigone. Bost., 1930. One of 550. Half vellum; spine soiled. pba Aug 8 (603) $55
Anr Ed. Greenbrae: Allen Press, 1978. One of 130. bba May 9 (441) £75 [Collinge & Clark]; pba June 20 (28) $110; sg Sept 14 (16) $150
— Ediop Re. Verona: Officina Bodoni, 1968. One of 105. Illus by Giacomo Manzo. 4to, unsewn in vellum bds. With 7 etchings. Ck May 31 (22) £1,000
— Tragoediae septem. Venice: Aldus, 1502. 1st Ed. 8vo, 19th-cent calf gilt, with arms of the 1st Duke of Sutherland. Fingersoiling to 1st quire; tp spotted. C Apr 3 (226) £5,200
Anr Ed. Strasbourg, 1786. 5 parts in 1 vol. 4to, 19th-cent half calf; spines rubbed & dry, corners scuffed. Some foxing. pba Aug 22 (650) $110

**Sorbait, Paul de**
— Praxios medicae, auctae, et a plurimis typi mendis.... Vienna, 1701. Folio, old bds; rebacked in calf. Marginal dampstaining with traces of mold. sg May 16 (503) $120

**Sorel, Charles, Sieur de Souvigny**
— La Bibliotheque Francoise. Paris, 1664. 12mo, old calf; rebacked, rubbed. Sussex copy. O Mar 26 (261) $180

**Sorgeloos, Claude**
— Labore et Constantia: a Collection of 510 Editions issued by Christopher Plantin from 1555 til 1589. Brussels, 1990. One of 800. 8vo, orig cloth. sg Apr 11 (250) $140

**Soria, Abraham**
— Oracion panejirico doctrinal sobre la mala tentacion. Livorno: Juan Pablo Fantechi, 1751. 8vo, modern lea. Worming at beginning. CE Dec 6 (225) $420

**Sorlier, Charles**
— The Ceramics and Sculptures of Chagall. Monaco, 1972. 4to, orig cloth, in dj. sg Jan 19 (107) $200

**Sotheby, William, 1757-1838**
— A Tour through Parts of Wales.... L, 1794. 4to, contemp half calf; rubbed. With 12 plates. b Jan 31 (346) £110

**Sotheran, Henry**
— Bibliotheca Chemico-Mathematica.... L, 1921-52. Compiled by Heinrich Zeitlinger. 2 vols, with 3 supplements in 4 vols. Together, 6 vols. 8vo, orig cloth; 1st 3 vols worn, spines faded, front hinge split on 1st supplement. sg Apr 11 (299) $425

**Soucek, Ludvik**
— Brassai. Prague: SNKLU, 1962. 4to, pictorial wraps; rubbed. sg Feb 29 (52) $70
— Laszlo Moholy-Nagy. Prague: SNKLU, 1965. 12mo, pictorial wraps; minor wear. sg Feb 29 (209) $325

**Soule, Frank —& Others**
— The Annals of San Francisco. NY, 1855. 1st Ed. 8vo, modern mor gilt. With 6 plates & folding map. Marginal dampstaining. pba Nov 16 (253) $200

Anr copy. With Griffin's 1935 Index. 2 vols. 8vo, orig cloth; Index with library markings & removed pocket. With 2 maps (1 folding & by John Bartlett) & 6 plates. Larson copy. pba Feb 12 (378) $325

Anr copy. 8vo, orig mor. With 6 plates & 2 maps. Title & frontis foxed. Robbins copy. pba Mar 21 (347) $375

Anr copy. Orig mor; rebacked with modern mor. With 2 maps.. pba Apr 25 (672) $160

Anr copy. Modern cloth. Some foxing. pba Apr 25 (673) $110

Anr copy. Orig half calf; worn & scuffed, joints cracked. With 6 plates & 2 maps, 1 folding. pba July 25 (352) $130

Anr copy. Orig mor gilt; worn, front joint starting. With 6 plates & 2 maps. Short fold break to 1 map. wa Feb 29 (329) $500

**South Carolina**
— Charleston South Carolina in 1883: With Heliotypes.... Bost., 1883. Folio, orig cloth; extremities worn, stain to front cover, hinges cracked. With 39 plates. pba Apr 25 (238) $225

**South Sea Company**
— The Particulars and Inventories of the Estates of the Late Sub-Governor, Deputy-Governor, and Directors.... L, 1721. 33 parts in 2 vols. Folio, contemp sheep; worn, joints cracked. Some browning; Vol I wormed in blank corner at beginning. sg Mar 21 (118) $1,200

**Southard, Charles Z.**
— Trout Fly-Fishing in America. NY, 1914. 4to, cloth; soiled, spine ends rubbed. pba July 11 (289) $120

**Southern, Terry**
— Candy. Paris: Olympia Press, [1958]. Orig wraps; creased. Thumbed. bbc Feb 26 (347) $125

**Southey, Robert, 1774-1843**
See also: Fore-Edge Paintings
— Poetical Works. Paris, 1829. Mor gilt by J. Clarke. pba Aug 8 (265) $55

**Southey's copy, Robert**
HOMER. - [Odyssey in Greek] Oxford, 1782. Vol I only (of 4). Contemp half calf. Interleaved & with Ms notes in Southey's hand. S Dec 18 (265) £400 [Spedding]

**Souvenir...**
— A Souvenir of the Trans-Continental Excursion of Railroad Agents, 1870. By One of the Party. Albany, 1871. Orig cloth. With color litho. cb Feb 14 (2604) $1,100

**Sou'Wester...**
— The Sou'Wester: Published Quarterly by the Pacific County Historical Society. Raymond WA, 1966-74. Vol I, No 1 to Vol IX, No 4. 36 issues. Wraps. pba Aug 8 (208) $60

**Sovetska Filmova...**
— Sovetska Filmova Fotografie Dvacatych Let. Prague: Odeon, [1979]. 4to, pictorial wraps; minor wear. sg Feb 29 (94) $175

**Soviet...**
— [Soviet Cosmonautics, in Russian]. Moscow, 1981. In dj. Inscr by Gherman Titov to Vladimir A. Khokhlov & sgd by c.100 other early Soviet cosmonauts, designers, flight engineers, commanders of the Biakunur Cosmodrome, defense department officials, leaders of the rocket & space industries & space journalists. P Mar 18 (363) $1,000

**Sowerby, James, 1757-1822**
— British Mineralogy. L, 1804-17. 1st Ed. Vols I-II. Later calf; scuffed, hinges rubbed. With 200 colored plates. wd Nov 15 (107) $325

**Sowerby, James, 1757-1822 —&**
**Smith, Sir James Edward, 1759-1828**
— English Botany. L, 1790-1814. Vols 1-15 only. Contemp half calf; rubbed, spines cracked. With 1,283 hand-colored plates only. S Mar 29 (746) £800

Anr copy. 36 vols in 18 plus vol of Indexes. 8vo, contemp half calf; spines worn & def. With 2,592 colored plates. Some browning; 6 plates repaired in margins; some shaving. Sold w.a.f. S Mar 29 (748) £1,900

Anr copy. 36 vols in 18 & General Index. 8vo, 19th-cent half calf; rubbed. With 2,592 color plates (some with hand-coloring). Some browning & spotting; a few plates trimmed within plate-mark at lower edge. Sold w.a.f. S June 27 (66) £2,000

Anr copy. Vols I-XXXI (of 36). 19th-cent half lea gilt; worn. sg May 9 (316) $3,200

2d Ed. L, [1832]-46. Vols I-VII only. Contemp cloth; 4 vols rebacked retaining backstrips. Sold w.a.f. S Mar 29 (747) £340

3d Ed. L, 1877. 12 vols. 8vo, contemp half mor, vol XII in orig cloth; worn. Some plates loose. Sold w.a.f. S Oct 27 (671) £450 [Bifolco]

Anr Ed. L, 1913. 13 vols. Later mor gilt; hinges cracked. S Mar 29 (749) £520

**Sowerby, John E., 1825-70.** See: Johnson & Sowerby

**Soyer, Alexis, 1809-58**
— The Pantropheon, or History of Food.... L, 1853. With: The Gatronomic Regenerator, L, 1861, 9th Ed. 1st Ed. 2 vols. 8vo, modern half mor & half calf. With 2 frontises. Spotted. S Oct 12 (70) £320

## SOYER

— Soyer's Culinary Campaign.... L, 1857. 1st Ed. 8vo, orig cloth; worn, rear hinge broken. Browned. wa Dec 14 (137) $65

### Spackman, W. H.
— Trout in New Zealand. Wellington, 1892. 8vo, cloth; worn. Stamp on tp. pba July 11 (208) $250

### Spafar'ev, Leonti Vasilevich, 1765-1845
— Atlas Finskago Zaliva.... St. Petersburg: Naval Printing Office, 1823. Folio, contemp half russia; rubbed. With engraved title in Russian, French & English; 12 charts, most double-page or folding, with lighthouses colored in red; 1 plate of a lighthouse tower & lamp. Guarded throughout; litho privilege leaf dated 1813 laid down on rear pastedown. C Nov 29 (106) £2,800

### Spalding, Albert Goodwill, 1850-1915
— Spalding's Official Baseball Guide, 1889. Chicago, 1889. Orig wraps; upper corner of front wrap lacking. Some corners worn. pba Sept 14 (12) $275

### Spallanzani, Lazzaro, 1729-99
— Dissertazioni di fisica animale, e vegetabile. Modena, 1780. 1st Ed. 2 vols. 8vo, contemp wraps; spines repaired. With 3 folding plates. Title & 1st few leaves with wormhole; lower margin of other leaves torn away. Ck Mar 22 (278) £900
— Experiences pour servir a l'histoire de la generation des animaux et des plantes. Geneva, 1785. 8vo, contemp half calf. With 3 folding plates. A few pencil marks in margins. S June 12 (283) £150
— Memoirs on Respiration. L, 1804. 1st Ed. - Ed by John Senebier. 8vo, contemp bds; rebacked, spine faded, corners bumped, covers rubbed. Half-title & title soiled; some spotting. Ck Mar 22 (280) £80
— Nouvelles recherches sur les decouvertes microscopiques.... Paris, 1769. 2 vols. 8vo, contemp calf; worn. With 8 plates, 5 folding. Some foxing. S June 12 (282) £160

### Spanish Inquisition
— Apologia por los curas del Sagrario de la Santa Patriarcal Iglesia de esta ciudad de Sevilla... los Ingleses, prisoneros de guerra, que abjuraron sus errores.... Madrid: Manuel de Sancha, 1783. 8vo, contemp calf. b Dec 5 (171) £150

### Spare, Austin Osman
— Earth Inferno. L, 1905. One of 265. Folio, orig vellum with watercolor drawing by Spare, 1906; new endpapers, slight staining to vellum. S Nov 21 (409) £1,400

### Sparfvenfeldt, Johann Gabriel
— Catalogus centuriae librorum rarissimorum.... Uppsala, 1706. 1st Ed. 4to, disbound. sg Apr 11 (308) $350

### Sparke, Edward
— Scintilla-Altaris, Being a Pious Reflection on Primative Devotion in the Feasts and Fasts of the Church of England. L, 1660. 2d Ed. 8vo, contemp mor gilt; joints reinforced. With 39 plates. Some soiling. pba Nov 30 (298) $190

### Sparks, William
— The Apache Kid, and Other True Stories of the Old West. Los Angeles, 1926. Orig wraps; vertical creases to spine. pba Apr 25 (681) $160

**Sparrman, Anders.** See: Golden Cockerel Press

### Sparrow, Walter Shaw
— Angling in British Art. L, 1923. 4to, orig cloth. pba July 11 (290) $80; sg Mar 7 (546) $130; sg Mar 7 (547) $70
— Ben Alken. L & NY, 1927. One of 250. 4to, orig cloth; covers spotted & soiled. O Jan 9 (214) $180
— A Book of Sporting Painters. L, 1931. 4to, cloth; some wear. O Jan 9 (210) $120

Anr copy. Orig cloth; worn. O Jan 9 (211) $110
— British Sporting Artists from Barlow to Herring. L & NY, 1922. 4to, cloth; some wear. O Jan 9 (212) $110; sg Mar 7 (548) $60
— George Stubbs and Ben Marshall. L & NY, 1929. 4to, cloth; some wear. O Jan 9 (213) $170

### Spaulding Edward S.
— Adobe Days along the Channel. Santa Barbara: Schauer Printing Studio, 1957. Grizzly Ed, one of 1,015. 4to, cloth. pba July 25 (223) $55

### Spaulding, Thomas M. —& Karpinski, Louis C.
— Early Military Books in the University of Michigan Libraries. Ann Arbor, 1941. 1st Ed. 4to, orig cloth in dj; chipped. sg Apr 11 (300) $300

### Spears, John R., 1850-1936
— Captain Nathaniel Brown Palmer.... NY, 1922. 12mo, orig cloth, in worn dj. pba July 25 (72) $50
— Illustrated Sketches of Death Valley.... Chicago, 1892. 1st Ed. 12mo, orig cloth. With map & 57 illus. Robbins copy. pba Mar 21 (349) $400

### Specimens...
— Specimens of German Romance. L, 1826. Frontises by George Cruikshank. 3 vols. 8vo, lev. pba June 20 (111) $140

Anr copy. Later half calf gilt; rubbed. sg Feb 8 (270) $175

### Spectator
— The Spectator [By Addison, Steele & others]. L, [1750]. 8 vols. 8vo, contemp calf; rubbed. Some spotting. bba May 30 (273) £160 [Frew]

Anr Ed. L, 1775. 8 vols. 8vo, contemp calf; joints starting. Some foxing. wa Nov 16 (159) $130

Anr Ed. L, 1789. 8 vols. 8vo, contemp calf; gouges & rubbing. pba Aug 22 (535) $85

Anr Ed. L, 1819. 8 vols. 8vo, half calf; rubbed. pba Sept 14 (12pUS225)

**Spector, Craig.** See: Skipp & Spector

**Speculum...**

— Speculum animae peccatricis. Paris: for Denis Roce, [after 1495].. 8vo, mor gilt by Chambolle-Duru. 27 lines; gothic letter. 36 leaves. Goff S-648. S Nov 30 (270) £750

— Speculum exemplorum omnibus christicolis.... Strassburg: [Printer of the 1483 Jordanus de Quedlinburg], 4 Dec 1495. Folio, 19th-cent calf, with stamp of Signet Library; covers detached. Wormed, affecting some letters; 1 leaf holed. 259 (of 286) leaves; lacking the 27 leaves following the title. Goff S-655. S Nov 30 (297) £520

— Speculum Humanae Salvationis. Munich, 1925. One of 550. 2 vols. 8vo, facsimile in vellum, text in wraps, in chipped djs. sg Feb 15 (277) $140

Anr copy. Facsimile in vellum, text in wraps, in djs; worn. sg Apr 11 (161) $100

**Speechly, William**

— A Treatise on the Culture of the Pine Apple.... York, 1779. 8vo, contemp calf; joints cracked, spine ends worn. With 2 plates, 1 folding. Wormed at end, affecting folding plate. CE June 15 (263) £320

— A Treatise on the Culture of the Vine. L, 1790. 1st Ed. 4to, contemp half calf; worn. With half-title, list of subscribers, & 5 plates (3 folding). Plate 1 leaf torn, no loss; spotted. S Oct 12 (120) £300

**Speed, John, 1552-1629**

### Abridgement of Theatre

— England, Wales, Scotland and Ireland Described.... L, 1627. Part 1 (of 2) only; lacking "A Prospect of the World". Oblong 8vo, contemp calf; def & loose. With engraved title & 61 (of 63) maps. Some maps cropped; 1 with large tear. b Sept 20 (179) £950

Anr Ed. L, [1662]. 2 parts in 1 vol. Oblong 8vo, modern half calf. With 61 (of 63) hand-colored maps & 20 uncolored maps. Lacking British Isles & Yorkshire. S June 27 (91) £1,900

### Theatre

— The Theatre of the Empire of Great Britaine. L, 1616. ("Theatrum imperii magnae Britanniae....") 4 parts in 1 vol. Folio, contemp calf; contents on later guardes & recased. With 67 double-page maps. Tp with repaired tears & some restoration to surface in lower right corner; Berkshire with small hole; tears without loss to Berkshire, Middlesex; some discoloration. b Dec 5 (60) £24,000

Anr copy. 4 parts in 1 vol (without A Prospect...). Bound with: Speed. The Historie of Great Britain. L, 1611. Folio, contemp calf; covers laid down preserving gilt-panelled calf. Theatre with tp & 1st leaf strengthened at margin; Kingdome of England worn & abraded at fold; Hereford with repaired split; Derbyshire split at fold; Yorkshire with repaired tear; maps repaired at fold. Historie lacking last 484 pp; some repairs. S Nov 30 (64) £24,000

Anr Ed. L, 1676. ("The Theatre of the Empire of Great Britain.") Issue with A Prospect..... 4 (of 5) parts in 1 vol; lacking Ireland. Folio, old half calf; worn, covers detached. With 64 double-page maps & 3 distance tables & 27 double-page maps in Prospect. Lacking map of East India in Prospect; lacking leaves D1, D2 & 2 tables & half of the map of Great Britain & several leaves of index; marginal repairs with loss; some soiling & staining; map of Canaan with severe loss; many lower margins strengthened. C Nov 29 (107) £33,000

**Speigelius, Adrianus, 1578-1625**

— Opera. Amst., 1645. 1st Ed. 2 vols. Folio, modern mor; rebound, orig calf covers laid down. With tp, port, & 117 plates. Dampstained throughout; some marginal repairs. CE Nov 8 (147) $3,200

**Spelman, Sir Henry, 1564?-1641**

— Reliquiae Spelmannianae. Oxford, 1698. Folio, contemp sheep; worn, joints cracked, spine ends def. Some browning & dampstaining; old stamps on tp. sg Mar 21 (306) $100

**Spelman, Sir John, 1594-1643**

— The Life of Alfred the Great. Oxford, 1709. 8vo, contemp calf; rubbed, cover loose. Some browning. bba July 18 (174) £100 [Stanley]

**Spence, Joseph, 1699-1768**

— An Essay on Pope's Odyssey. Oxford, 1726-27. 2 parts in 1 vol. 12mo, contemp mor gilt by Thomas Sedgley of Oxford; upper joint partially cracked. S Dec 18 (135) £520 [Edwards]

— A Parallel in the Manner of Plutarch.... Strawberry Hill, 1758. 1st Ed. 8vo, contemp half calf; top of spine chipped, front joint cracked. Some foxing. sg Sept 21 (298) $200

— Polymetis.... L, 1747. 1st Ed. Folio, contemp sheep gilt; joints cracked. With port & 41 plates. sg Mar 21 (307) $325

**Spence, Sydney Alfred**

— Captain Wm. Bligh, R.N. (1754-1817) & Where to Find Him. Sydney, 1970. One of 5 specially bound. 4to, orig half mor gilt. Inscr & with holograph additions & corrections. b Mar 20 (194) $240

**Spencer, Capt. Edmund**

— Travels in Circassia, Krim Tartary.... L, 1837. 2 vols. 8vo, orig cloth. With 2 hand-colored frontises & 2 folding maps. S June 13 (421) £340

**Spencer, H. McDonald**

— Pacific Coast Golf & Outdoor Sports. San Francisco: Pacific Golf Publishing, 1913. 1st Ed. Wraps; front wrap creased, extrems soiled. pba Nov 9 (76) $275

**Spencer, J. W.**

— Reminiscences of Pioneer Life in the Mississippi Valley. Davenport, 1872. 8vo, orig cloth; staining & water damage to covers. Page edges scorched. pba Apr 25 (497) $75

**Spencer, John, 1630-93**

— A Discourse concerning Prodigies.... L, 1665. 2 parts in 1 vol. 8vo, later half lea; new endpapers, rubbed & cracked. F7 & F8 lacking corner. Z June 28 (256) $350

## SPENCER

**Spencer, Nathaniel**
— The Complete English Traveller. L, 1773. Folio, contemp calf; rebacked, worn, loose. With frontis, 57 plates & 3 maps. S June 13 (506) £650

**Spencer, Oliver M.**
— Narrative... of his Captivity among the Mohawk Indians. L, 1854. 12mo, orig cloth; cloth at joints splitting. sg Oct 26 (158) $100

**Spender, Stephen**
— At Night. [Cambr.]: ptd for Frederic Prokosch, Christmas 1935. Special copy on Leipzig. Orig wraps. Hobson copy. S June 28 (207) £150
— Fraternity. [Paris], 1939. One of 113. Trans by Louis Aragon. 4to, loose in portfolio. With 9 orig etchings by Kandinsky, Miro, Wright, each sgd. Hobson copy. S June 28 (206) £6,900
— Perhaps. [Bryn Mawr]: ptd for Frederic Prokosch, 1933. One of 2 on Deane. Orig wraps. Hobson copy. S June 28 (202) £120
— Poem. [Bryn Mawr]: ptd for Frederic Prokosch, 1934. One of 5 on japan vellum. Orig wraps. Hobson copy. S June 28 (204) £260
— Twenty Poems. Oxford, [1930]. 1st Ed, One of 75. Orig wraps; soiled. Inscr to Anthony Hobson. S June 28 (201) £230

**Spender, Stephen —& Hockney, David**
— China Diary. L, 1982. One of 1,000. With orig litho, Red Square and the Forbidden City, sgd, loosely inserted. Ck May 31 (91) £200

**Spengler, Joseph**
— Optick, Catoptrick und Dioptrick. Augsburg: M. Rieger, 1775. 8vo, orig bds; spine worn. With 14 folding plates. Library stamp on tp; some spotting. S Mar 14 (342) £500

**Spenser, Edmund, 1552?-99**
See also: Ashendene Press; Cresset Press; Kelmscott Press; Limited Editions Club
— The Faerie Queene. L: William Ponsonby, 1590-96. 1st Ed. 2 vols. 4to, mor gilt by Zaehnsdorf, 1910. Tp in facsimile; Kk6 torn across & repaired, affecting text; repairs to margins affecting catchword & 1 letter of text on K1; X7 with spaces left for the Welsh words, but with extra leaf loosely inserted showing variant with Welsh ptd. S July 11 (125) £1,700
Anr Ed. L, 1751. 3 vols. 4to, later half calf. With 32 plates. bba July 18 (186) £150 [Price]
Anr Ed. Cambr., 1909. One of 350. 2 vols. 4to, orig vellum bds gilt; front hinge cracked. pba June 20 (309) $100
— Works. L, 1611-13. ("The Faerie Queene: The Shepheards Calendar: Together with Other Works of England's Arch-Poet.") 1st Collected Ed, STC 23084. Folio, contemp calf gilt; rebacked. Some leaves stained; top margin of 2 leaves restored; contemp notes on flyleaves. cb Oct 17 (474) $1,200
Anr copy. Contemp calf gilt; joints & corners worn. Marginal dampstaining & soiling. CE June 15 (264) $1,700

## AMERICAN BOOK PRICES CURRENT

Anr Ed. L, 1617. NSTC 23085. Folio, contemp calf; worn, rebacked. General title trimmed & mtd; browning & staining throughout; a few tears in text; partly misbound. Sold w.a.f. CE May 22 (432) $420
STC 23085. 17th-cent calf; rubbed, rebacked, new endpapers. Lacking A1; first 3 leaves present dampstained & shaved at fore-edge, affecting woodcuts; also lacking Q5-6. S June 12 (123) £380

Anr Ed. L, 1679. Folio, contemp calf gilt; front joint cracked. pba Sept 14 (331) $225

Anr Ed. Oxford: Shakespeare Head Press, 1930-32. One of 375. 8 vols. 4to, orig half calf. bba May 9 (344) £420 [Baring]

Anr copy. Orig half calf; minor wear. S Nov 2 (57) £400 [Dowdall]

**Spielmann, Marion Harry**
— The History of "Punch". L, 1895. One of 250 L.p. copies. 4to, orig cloth, unopened. Sgd on endleaf by John Tenniel, George Du Maurier, Phil May, Bernard Partridge, Linley Sambourne, T. E. Reed, T. Anstey Guthrie, R. C. Lehmann, H. W. Lucy, Arthur W. a Beckett, F. C. Burnand & E. J. Milliken. S Apr 23 (216) £220

**Spielmann, Marion Harry —& Layard, George Somes, 1857-1925**
— Kate Greenaway. NY & L, 1905. O Mar 5 (208) $110

One of 500, sgd by John Greenaway & with pencil sketch by Kate laid in. 4to, orig cloth. b May 30 (547) £520

Anr copy. Orig cloth. Austin Dobson's copy, with holograph correction to his verse appreciation in the intro. Inscr by Christopher Dobson to his daughter. With ALs of Greenaway to Austin Dobson, 1881.. S Nov 2 (297) £1,000 [Hirsch]

**Spiera, Ambrosius de**
— Quadragesimale de floribus sapientiae. [Venice: Vindelinus de Spira, 18 Dec 1476]. Folio, 18th-cent calf; rebacked. 46 lines; double column; gothic letter. Tears in lower margin y4 repaired with adhesive tape; some contemp Ms annotations; 1 gathering misbound. 507 (of 512) leaves; lacking 1 leaf of register & 4 blanks. Goff S-678. S Dec 18 (81) £920 [Zioni]

Anr Ed. Venice: Bonetus Locatellus for Octavianus Scotus, 20 Feb 1488/9. 4to, contemp Aubsburg bdg by Kyriss workshop 81 of blind-stamped calf over wooden bds; lacking 2 clasps; some stains. 60 lines & headlines; double column; types 3:62G & 2:130G. Annotations in margins; some marginal worming. 312 (of 314) leaves; lacking 2 blanks. Goff S-681. Madsen copy. S Mar 14 (343) £800

**Spies, Werner**
— Max Ernst Oeuvre-Katalog. Houston & Cologne, 1975-79. One of 1,500. Vols I-II (of 4). 4to, cloth, in djs. sg Jan 11 (167) $800

**Spignesi, Stephen J.**
— The Shape Under the Sheet. Woodstock: Overlook Press, 1991. One of 350. 4to, pictorial bds. O Dec 5 (197) $80

**Spillane, Mickey**
— The Deep. NY: Dutton, [1961]. In dj. Inscr. pba Aug 22 (417) $100
— I, the Jury. NY, 1947. In rubbed dj with chip to top of spine. cb Oct 17 (475) $325

**Spiller, Burton L.** See: Derrydale Press

**Spiller, Robert E. —& Blackburn, Philip C.**
— A Descriptive Bibliography of James Fenimore Cooper. NY, 1934. One of 25. Calf gilt; spine ends rubbed. pba Nov 30 (78) $150

**Spilsbury, Francis B.**
— Picturesque Scenery in the Holy Land and Syria. L, 1801. 1st Ed. - Port by Bell after Chandler. Folio, rcent half mor. With port, & 19 hand-colored plates. S Oct 26 (215) £1,900 [Magnani]

Anr Ed. L, 1823. 4to, bds. With 19 hand-colored plates. S Oct 26 (214) £370 [Hollin]

**Spink, Alfred H.**
— The National Game. A History of Baseball.... St. Louis, 1910. Orig bdg; hinges weak. Z June 14 (314) $275

**Spon, Jacob, 1647-85**
— The History of the City and State of Geneva. L, 1687. 1st Ed in English. Folio, contemp calf; worn, needs rebacking. With engraved title, 2 folding views, woodcut numismatic plate & map. Bottom edge of titles trimmed. sg Mar 7 (344) $150
— Traitez nouveaux et curieux du cafe, du the et du chocolate. Lyons: J. Girin & B. Riviere, 1685. 12mo, contemp calf; spine chipped, head repaired, corners bumped. With title, title device, & 3 full-page illus. Some browning & dampstaining. Ck Mar 22 (282) £420

**Sporting...**
— Sporting Magazine: Or, Monthly Calendar.... L, 1792-1815. Vols 1-46. 8vo, contemp half calf; rubbed. Lacking 58 plates; 1 plate with loss; some dampstaining. Sold w.a.f. S June 13 (460) £850

**Sportsman**
— The Sportsman. Concord, 1927-37. Vols 1-21, lacking Vol 11. Half lea; rebacked in cloth. Z Jan 30 (450) $1,800

**Sportsman's...**
— The Sportsman's Dictionary. L, 1778. ("The Sportsman's Dictonary, or the Gentleman's Companion for Town and Country....") 4to, contemp calf; rubbed, spine ends worn. With 16 plates. Some foxing & soiling. O Jan 9 (218) $250

**Sportsmen's Association of Cheat Mountain**
— Sportsmen's Association of Cheat Mountain, 1889. Cheat Mountain WV, 1889. Cloth; insect damage to covers. With orig albumen photo & 2 folding maps. pba July 11 (412) $180

**Spotts, David L.**
— Campaigning with Custer and the Nineteenth Kansas Volunteer Cavalry.... Los Angeles, 1928. One of 800. In repaired dj. pba June 25 (219) $200

**Sprague, Isaac, 1811-95**
— Beautiful Wild Flowers of America. Bost., 1882. Ed by A. B. Hervey. 4to, orig pictorial cloth; worn, spine ends torn. With 14 color plates. Margin of 1 plate chipped. wa Feb 29 (106) $210

**Sprague, John T.**
— The Origin, Progress, and Conclusion of the Florida War. NY, 1848. Issue with 10 plates. 8vo, orig cloth; worn. Some foxing to folding map. wa Feb 29 (371) $475

**Sprat, Thomas, 1635-1713**
— The History of the Royal Society of London. L, 1734. 4th Ed. 4to, contemp sheep; worn, covers detached. With 2 folding plates. Old stamp on tp. sg May 16 (258) $80

**Spratt, Thomas Abel Bremage, 1811-88**
— Travels and Researches in Crete. L, 1865. 2 vols. 8vo, orig cloth; rebacked preserving orig spines. With 2 folding colored maps. War Office stamps on titles. b Sept 20 (357) £500

Anr copy. Orig cloth; rubbed. With 12 tinted litho plates & 2 hand-colored folding maps. Library markings. pn Dec 7 (171) £300

1st Ed. 2 vols. 8vo, orig cloth; soiled, spines chipped, hinges weak. With 17 plates & 2 hand-colored folding maps. 1 plate loose. S Oct 26 (216) £600 [Basil]

**Spratt, Thomas Abel Bremage, 1811-88 —& Forbes, Edward, 1815-54**
— Travels in Lycia, Milyas and the Cibyratis. L, 1847. 2 vols. 8vo, calf. With 2 frontises, folding map & 25 maps & plates. Some maps cut close. b Sept 20 (356) £320

**Sprengel, Kurt, 1766-1833**
— An Introduction to the Study of Cryptogamous Plants. L, 1807. 8vo, contemp half calf; scuffed. With 10 folding plates. Owner's name clipped from top margin of tp; some bad folding to plates. bbc Feb 26 (453) $210

**Sprunt, Alexander**
— Florida Bird Life. NY, [1954]. 4to, cloth, in creased & soiled dj; bdg corners bumped. F June 20 (703) $80

**Squatter, A.** See: Lloyd, E.

**Squier, Ephraim George, 1821-88**
— Travels in Central America.... NY, 1853. 1st Ed. 2 vols. 8vo, orig cloth; shaken, spines chipped. S Oct 26 (529) £260 [Ortueta]

**St. Albans Chronicle**
— Chronicles of England [St. Alban's Chronicle]. See: Chronicles

**St. Andrews**
— The Book of St. Andrews Links.... [L]: Ellesborough Press, [1984]. One of 200. Mor; spine sunned. Sgd by J. Stewart Larson, Capt. Royal & Ancient Golf Club St. Andrews. pba Apr 18 (45) $200

**St. Bernard Fish and Game Club**
— Club Book. NY: Press of T. A. Wright, 1901. Ed by William W. Henry. Orig wraps; worn & frayed. Sgd by Henry on front endpaper. O Feb 6 (124) $325

**St. Clair, Philip R.**
— Frederic Remington: The American West. Kent, 1978. Oblong 4to, cloth. pba Aug 8 (164) $55

**St. John, James Augustus, 1801-75**
— Oriental Album. L, 1848. Illus by A. C. T. E. Prisse d'Avennes. Folio, contemp half mor gilt; worn. With colored title & 31 mtd plates, partly colored by hand. A few tears repaired. S Nov 30 (133) £4,200

**St. John, Spenser, 1825-1910**
— Life in the Forests of the Far East. L, 1863. 2 vols. 8vo, orig cloth; some wear. With 2 folding maps, 12 tinted lithos & 4 hand-colored lithos. S Mar 28 (408) £350

**St. Quentin, Dominique de**
— A Poetical Chronology of the Kings of England.... Reading, 1795. 12mo, contemp half calf; joints cracked. b Dec 5 (8) £240

**Stace, Machell**
— John Bon and Mast Person. [L, 1808]. One of 25 on vellum. 4to, 19th-cent cloth; spine head & foot chipped. With proof illust laid down. Inscr to Richard Heber. b May 30 (406) £160

**Stackhouse, Thomas**
— A New Universal Atlas.... L, 1786. 2d Ed. Folio, later half mor; some wear, especially to spine & corners, hinges cracked. With 43 maps with contemp hand-coloring (39 in full, 4 in outline). Some leaves cut close; 1 corner off; marginal tears; library markings. cb Oct 17 (257) $1,100

**Stael-Holstein, Anne Louise Germaine, Baronne de, 1766-1817**
— Considerations sur les principaux evenemens de la Revolution Francaise. Paris, 1818. 3 vols. 8vo, contemp calf gilt by Meslant; 2 spines chipped, short tear at head of upper joint of Vol II. La Rochefoucauld copy. S June 27 (370) £2,900
— Germany. L, 1813. 3 vols. 8vo, contemp half calf; worn. Minor foxing. sg Apr 18 (188) $325

**Stagg, John**
— Miscellaneous Poems. Carlisle, 1790. 12mo, later half calf. b Dec 5 (174) £340

**Stagi, Andrea**
— Amazonida. Venice, 18 Jan 1503. 8vo, mor gilt by Trautz-Bauzonnet; scuffed. Repair to lower corner of D1; some repairs to wormtracks in margins. C Apr 3 (227) £4,200

**Stalker, John**
— A Treatise of Japaning and Varnishing.... Oxford, 1688. Folio, disbound. Stained throughout. H Oct 29 (248) £650 [Weinreb]
Anr copy. Contemp calf gilt; rubbed, rebacked. With 24 plates. Schaefer copy. P Nov 1 (196) $11,000

**Stammhammer, Josef**
— Bibliographie der Social-Politik. Jena, 1896. 2 vols. 4to, buckram; rebound. sg Apr 11 (310) $100
— Bibliographie des Socialismus und Communismus.... Aalen, 1963-64. 3 vols. 8vo, orig cloth. sg Apr 11 (311) $100

**Standing Bear, Chief Luther**
— My People the Sioux. Bost., 1928. In chipped dj. Inscr. pba Nov 16 (254) $200

**Standish, Arthur**
— The Commons Complaint. L, 1611. 4to, modern half calf. Lacking folding woodcut; 17th-cent annotations shaved. S Mar 29 (776) £200

**Stanfield, Clarkson, 1793-1867**
— Stanfield's Coast Scenery: a Series of Views in the British Channel. L, 1836. 4to, mor gilt; scuffed, lower front corner bumped. wa Dec 14 (588) $120

**Stanger, Frank M. —& Brown, Alan K.**
— Who Discovered the Golden Gate? The Explorers Own Accounts.... San Mateo County, 1969. One of 1,500. Buckram. Larson copy. pba Sept 28 (255) $95

**Stanhope, Leicester Fitzgerald Charles, 5th Earl of Harrington**
— Greece in 1823 and 1824.... L, 1825. Bound with: Sketch of the History and Influence of the Press in British INdia. L, 1823. 8vo, contemp mor gilt. Inscr to Laetitia Bonaparte Wyse. b May 30 (297) £550

**Staniforth Collection, Thomas**
— A Collection of Early English Spoons.... L, 1898. 4to, mor gilt by C. Fox; scuffed. W Nov 8 (59) £460

**Stanislas Leczinski, King of Poland**
— Oeuvres du philosophe bienfaisant. Paris, 1763. 4 vols. 8vo, contemp red mor gilt. With port. Fuerstenberg - Schaefer copy. S Dec 8 (581) £1,200

**Stanley, Arthur Penrhyn.** See: Fore-Edge Paintings

### Stanley, Sir Henry Morton, 1841-1904

— In Darkest Africa. L, 1890. 1st Ed. 2 vols. 8vo, orig cloth; extremities worn, shaken. Tear to 1 folding map. CE June 15 (270) $220

Anr copy. Orig cloth; corners bumped. With 4 maps, 3 of them folding. Some foxing. F June 20 (562) $100

Anr copy. Cloth; edges rubbed. With 2 folding maps. Maps torn. S Oct 26 (549) £170 [Bordiu]

Anr copy. Folding map with small fold breaks. sg Mar 7 (345) $80

One of 250 L.p. copies, sgd. 2 vols. 4to, orig half mor gilt; soiled. P Dec 12 (168) $1,700

1st American Ed. NY, 1890. ("In Darkest Africa, or the Quest, Rescue, and Retreat of Emin, Governor of Equatoria.") 2 vols. 4to, contemp half mor; spines scuffed & chipped. The 3 folding maps with small nicks at folds & rear pockets splitting. pba Apr 25 (240) $65

Anr Ed. NY, 1891. 2 vols. 8vo, orig cloth; rubbed, dampstaining to front joint of Vol I. With 3 folding maps in back pockets. Tears to map creases. pba Aug 8 (190) $75

— Through the Dark Continent. L, 1878. 2 vols. 8vo, half mor; extremities worn. sg Mar 7 (346) $120

Anr Ed. NY, 1878. 2 vols. 8vo, orig cloth; extremities rubbed. With 9 (of 10) maps, including 1 folding in rear pocket of Vol I. Lacking folding map of western half of Equatorial Africa. pba Nov 16 (359) $225

Anr copy. Orig half mor; rubbed, joints tender. With 10 maps, 3 folding in endpaper pockets. Some tearing to map creases. pba July 25 (453) $150

Anr Ed. NY, 1879. 2 vols. 8vo, orig cloth; worn & rubbed, front joint of Vol II splitting, endpapers of Vol II damaged & reglued. Lacking 1 (of 10) folding map. pba Oct 9 (20) $100

### Stanley, Thomas, 1625-78

— The History of Philosphy. L, 1656. 8 parts in 1 vol. 4to, later half calf. With port & 15 plates. Port def; stains & tears. Sold w.a.f. b Sept 20 (214) £50

### Stansbury, Howard

— An Expedition to the Valley of the Great Salt Lake.... Phila, 1852. 1st Ed. The 2 folding maps in folder only. Folder split at spine. pba Oct 9 (30) $300

Anr copy. 8vo, orig cloth; rubbed. With 57 litho plates, a few folding & with folding map. Lacking the portfolio of 2 aps; foxed; 1 plate torn & lacking half. pba Apr 25 (685) $160

### Stanwood, Avis A.

— Fostina Woodman, the Wonderful Adventurer. By Miss. A. A. Burnham. Bost., 1850. 8vo, orig wraps; foxed & stained, corners chipped. With 8 woodcuts, including frontis, illust on tp & front wrap. Some foxing. pba Aug 8 (191) $225

### Stapley, Mildred. See: Byne & Stapley

### Starbuck, Alexander

— History of the American Whale Fishery. NY: Argosy, 1964. One of 750. 2 vols. Facsimile reprint. pba July 25 (224) $80

### Stark, Freya

— Space, Time & Movement in Landscape. L, [n.d.]. One of 500. Oblong 4to, orig half lea; corners rubbed. bba May 9 (268) £100 [Hamilton]

### Stark, William

— Works. L, 1788. 1st Ed. 4to, modern calf; joints rubbed. With 3 folding plates. Lacking half-title & final leaf; title soiled in margins; some ink stains; plates spotted & marginally torn; last plate almost detached; some soiling. Ck Mar 22 (283) £350

### Starr, Walter A., Jr.

— Guide to the John Muir Trail and the High Sierra Region. San Francisco: The Sierra Club, 1934. In dj. With port & folding map. pba Feb 12 (180) $225

Anr copy. Inscr to Emma McLaughlin from Walter & Carmen Starr. pba Apr 25 (686) $50

### Stassen, Franz. See: Wagner, Richard

### Statius, Publius Papinius, 45?-96?

— Opera. Venice: Aldus, Aug-Nov 1502. ("Sylvarum, libri quinque; Thebaidos libri duodecim; Achilleidos duo.") 8vo, 18th-cent vellum. Worming in lower margin; dampstaining to lower outer corners of 1st 10 quires; a1 & a4-5 of Orthographia soiled. C Apr 3 (229) £450

### Statuts...

— Les Statuts de l'ordre du St. Esprit estably par Henri III. Paris, 1703. 4to, contemp mor gilt, with arms of Louis X; repaired, stained. S Mar 28 (521) £300

### Stauffer, David McNeely, 1845-1913. See: Grolier Club

### Staunton, Sir George Leonard, 1737-1801

— An Authentic Account of an Embassy from the King of Great Britain to the Emperor of China. L, 1797. Text only: 2 vols. Contemp half calf; joints cracked, spine ends rubbed. S Mar 29 (676) £250

— Voyage dans l'interieur de la Chine.... Paris, 1804. 5 vols plus Atlas. 4to, contemp calf gilt. With port, 40 maps & plates, including 3 large folding maps. C May 31 (113) £600

### Staunton, Schuyler. See: Baum, L. Frank

### Stavorinus, Jan Splinter, 1739-88

— Voyages to the East Indies. L, 1798. 3 vols. 8vo, contemp half calf; worn, scuffed & stained, 2 covers detached, library shelfmarks on spines. With 4 folding maps. Library stamps; Vol III soiled & stained. cb Oct 17 (207) $250

### Stealingworth, Slim

— Tom Wesselmann. NY, [1980]. Oblong 4to, cloth, in acetate dj. sg Jan 11 (463) $60

### Steaman, Ralph
— Cherrywood Cannon, Based on a Story Told to him by Dimitri Sidjanski. NY: Paddinton Press, [1978]. In dj. Sgd on half-title. pba May 23 (391) $50

### Stearn, William T.
— The Australian Flower Paintings of Ferdinand Bauer. L: Basilisk Press, 1976. One of 550. Folio, half mor. sg Oct 19 (174) $325

### Stebbing, Henry, 1799-1883
— The Christian in Palestine. L, [1847]. 4to, contemp half calf. With title, map, & 78 plates (1 double-page). Spotted. S Oct 26 (217) £240 [Brunt]

### Stebbins, T.
— The Life and Work of Martin Johnson Heade. New Haven, 1975. 4to, cloth. wa June 20 (344) $190

### Stebbins, Theodore E., Jr. —& Keyes, Norman, Jr.
— Charles Sheeler: The Photographs. Bost., [1987]. 4to, cloth, in dj. With 90 plates. sg Feb 29 (284) $90

### Steck, Amos, 1822-1908
— Amos Steck... Forty-niner.... Denver, 1981. One of 200. Ed by Nolie Mumey. Orig cloth in dj. With 10 photos. Larson copy. pba Sept 28 (675) $50

### Stedman, Charles, 1753-1812
— The History of the Origin, Progress, and Termination of the American War. L, 1794. 1st Ed. 2 vols. 4to, contemp calf. sg Oct 26 (350) $3,200

Anr copy. Early half calf; worn, front bd of Vol II detached. With 15 maps, 11 of them folding. Vol I dampstained; 2-inch tape residue stain to verso of Bunker Hill, which has its overslip. wa Feb 29 (302) $2,100

### Stedman, John Gabriel
— Narrative of a Five Years' Expedition against the Revolted Negroes of Surinam.... L, 1813. 2 vols. 4to, contemp calf; vol I spine worn, vol II rebacked with old spine laid down. With 78 plates & 3 folding maps. Some soiling & offsetting. S Oct 26 (530) £480 [Franklin]

Anr Ed. Barre: Iprint Society, 1971. 2 vols. 4to, half cloth. pba Apr 25 (242) $50

### Steel, Flora Annie, 1847-1929
— English Fairy Tales. NY, 1918. One of 250 L.p. copies. Illus by Arthur Rackham. 4to, orig white calf. wa Feb 29 (119) $1,000

### Steele, John. See: Caxton Club

### Steele, Oliver G.
— The Western Guide Book, and Emigrant Directory. Buffalo, 1836. 12mo, orig half lea; worn & soiled. With folding color map. Foxed. wa Feb 29 (390) $375

### Steele, Sir Richard, 1672-1729. See: Spectator

### Steele, Sir Richard, 1672-1729 —& Gillmore, Joseph
— An Account of the Fish-Pool.... L, 1718. 1st Ed. 8vo, modern bds. Title browned. Ck Mar 22 (284) £220

### Steele, Thomas Sedgwick
— Canoe and Camera: a Two Hundred Mile Tour through the Maine Forests. NY, 1880. Orig cloth; spine ends & corners rubbed. pba July 11 (439) $80
— Paddle and Portage, from Moosehead Lake to the Aroostook River.... Bost., 1882. 8vo, orig cloth; some wear. With map. NH June 1 (204) $220

### Steevens Library, George
— [Sale Catalogue] Bibliotheca Steevensiana: a Catalogue.... [L, 1800]. 8vo, later wraps. Priced in several different hands Library stamp on both sides of title leaf. O Mar 26 (264) $80

Anr copy. Contemp bds; rebacked, library bookplate. L.p. copy. O Mar 26 (265) $200

Anr copy. Contemp half calf; rubbed. Priced in ink. pba Aug 22 (559) $50

### Stefansson, Vilhjalmur, 1879-1962
— Ultima Thule. NY, 1940. One of 100. Z Oct 27 (289) $110

### Steffen, Randy
— United States Military Saddles, 1812-1943. Norman, [1973]. In dj. Inscr to John Popovich, with sketch of Custer's head. pba June 25 (222) $90

### Steffens, Henrik, 1773-1845
— Indledning til philosophiske Forelaesninger. Copenhagen: Andreas Seidelin, 1803. 8vo, contemp half calf. S Mar 14 (344) £180

### Stegmann, Carl Martin von —& Geymuller, Heinrich von
— The Architecture of the Renaissance in Tuscany. NY, [1924?]. 2 vols. Folio, orig cloth; spine ends worn, lettering on lower spines. Library markings; foxing & marginal dampstaining to Vol II. cb Oct 17 (94) $160

Anr copy. Orig cloth, in worn djs. wa Nov 16 (258) $140

### Stegner, Wallace
— 20-20 Vision: In Celebration of the Peninsula Hills. Palo Alto: Green Foothills Assoc., [1982]. Pictorial wraps. pba May 23 (395) $70
— All the Little Live Things. NY: Viking, 1967. In dj with minor rubbing. Inscr. pba May 23 (392) $140
— Angle of Repose. Garden City, 1971. In dj with tear at spine head. pba Oct 5 (306) $160
— Beyond the Hundredth Meridian. Bost., 1954. In dj with tears to lower corners. Sgd on half-title. pba Oct 5 (308) $375

One of 250. pba Oct 5 (307) $425
— The Big Rock Candy Mountain. NY, [1943]. In dj. bbc June 24 (614) $240

Anr copy. In dj with tears & creases to extremities. pba Oct 5 (313) $650

Anr copy. Orig wraps; spine rubbed & creased, adhesion residue from tape along front joint. pba Nov 30 (300) $250

Anr copy. In dj with minor defs. Inscr. pba May 23 (393) $1,100
— Mormon Country. NY, [1942]. In torn & chipped dj. pba Oct 5 (310) $60
— On the Writing of History. [N.p.], 1989. One of 100 to benefit the Duveneck Family History Room. Ptd wraps. pba May 23 (394) $170
— The Potter's House. Muscatine IA: Prairie Press, 1938. One of 490. pba Oct 5 (315) $1,100
— Remembering Laughter. NY, 1937. In dj. pba Oct 5 (311) $150
— Wolf Willow. NY, [1962]. In dj with spine ends rubbed. pba Oct 5 (318) $100

Anr copy. In dj with tear to front panel & chips to spine ends. pba Jan 25 (347) $100

Anr copy. In dj. pba Aug 22 (420) $130
— The Women on the Wall. Bost., 1950. In dj with chipping to spine head. pba Oct 5 (316) $170

## Steichen, Edward, 1879-1972
— Rodin's Balzac and Ten Drawings by Rodin. NY: Brentano's, [n.d.]. 4to, half mor; spine ends worn. With 4 plates after Steichen & 3 (of 6) reproductions of Rodin's drawings. sg Apr 24 (602) $1,400

## Stein, Gertrude, 1874-1946
— An Acquaintance with Description. L, 1929. 1st Ed, One of 225. Hobson copy. S June 28 (192) £280

Out-of-series copy without the limitation slip. Inscr to Bob Brown. Engelhard copy. CNY Oct 27 (125) $900
— The Autobiography of Alice B. Toklas. NY, [1933]. 1st Ed. In chipped dj. sg Dec 14 (272) $200

3d Issue. In dj. wa Feb 1 (70) $80
— A Book Concluding with As a Wife Has a Cow. Paris, [1926]. 1st Ed, one of 90. Illus by Juan Gris. 4to, orig wraps; minor chips. C June 26 (211) £2,400
— Dix portraits. Paris, [1930]. 1st Ed, one of 65 on velin d'Arches. Trans by Georges Hugnet & Virgil Thomson. Orig wraps, in glassine dj with wear to spine ends. Waller Barrett - Engelhard copy. CNY Oct 27 (127) $1,600
— Four Saints in Three Acts. NY, 1934. 1st Ed. In chipped dj. Inscr to Charles H. Tenney. Also sgd by Alice B. Toklas. CE Sept 27 (261) $420

Anr copy. In dj with tears & edge-wear. Inscr. sg June 20 (345) $290
— Geography and Plays. Bost., [1922]. 1st Ed. 1st bdg, in dj with nicks at spine head. sg June 20 (346) $200
— Morceaux choisis de la fabrication des americains. Paris, [1929]. One of 5 on japan vellum with page of autograph Ms. Orig wraps, in glassine dj; corners bumped. With additional page of autograph Ms, sgd. Engelhard copy. CNY Oct 27 (126) $2,500
— Portrait of Mabel Dodge at the Villa Curonia. [Florence, 1912]. 1st Ed, one of 300. 4to, orig wraps; some wear to spine. CNY Oct 27 (124) $1,000

— Portraits and Prayers. NY, [1934]. 1st Ed. Orig cloth; soiled. F June 20 (620) $80

## Stein, Sir Marc Aurel, 1862-1943
— Ancient Khotan: Detailed Report of Archaeological Explorations in Chinese Turkestan. NY: Hacker Art Books, 1975. 2 vols in 1. Folio, cloth. Reprint of 1907 Ed. pba Nov 16 (360) $120
— Ruins of Desert Cathay. L, 1912. 2 vols. Library markings; 1 map reinforced at fold with tears. pn Dec 7 (174) £200 [R. S. Books]

## Steinbeck, John, 1902-68
See also: Limited Editions Club
— Bombs Away: The Story of a Bomber Team. NY, 1942. In dj with minor defs. pba Oct 5 (319) $75

Anr copy. Cloth, in worn dj. sg Dec 14 (274) $50

Anr copy. Cloth, in rubbed dj with tear along front joint. sg June 20 (347) $50
— Burning Bright. NY, 1950. In dj. pba Oct 5 (320) $65; pba May 23 (399) $80; pba Aug 22 (422) $70
— Cannery Row. NY, 1945. 1st Ed. Orig cloth. Inscr to Major Bob. CE Feb 21 (230) $1,500

Anr copy. In chipped & repaired dj. CE Feb 21 (232) $800

Anr copy. Orig cloth, 2d bdg, in dj. Dedication copy, inscr to Ed Ricketts (with bird & fish drawings) & sgd by Ricketts on front flyleaf 20 Dec 1944. CE Feb 21 (233) $32,000

Anr copy. 2d state bdg, in dj. pba Oct 5 (321) $140

Anr copy. 2d bdg, in dj. pba Jan 25 (349) $120

Anr copy. 2d State bdg in dj. pba May 23 (401) $95

Advance copy. Orig wraps. CE Feb 21 (231) $220
— The Collected Poems of Amnesia Glasscock. South San Francisco: Manroot, 1976. One of 250. Wraps. pba May 23 (402) $65
— Cup of Gold: a Life of Henry Morgan.... NY, 1929. 1st Ed, 1st Issue. In chipped & repaired dj. CE Feb 21 (213) $3,000

Anr copy. In repaired dj with some areas recolored, laid down on paper. CE Feb 21 (214) $480

Anr copy. In dj. pba Oct 5 (323) $13,000

Anr copy. In chipped dj; crease to spine. pba Jan 25 (350) $3,750

Anr Ed. NY, [1936]. In dj with piece lacking from upper front joint. pba Aug 22 (423) $80
— Cup of Gold: A Life of Sir Henry Morgan.... NY, [1936]. 2d Ed. In dj; minor insect damage to bdg spine. pba May 23 (403) $70
— De Souris de des Hommes. Paris, [1939]. pba Oct 5 (324) $50

Anr Ed. Paris: Arts et Metiers Graphiques, [1948]. One of 390. Illus by Reynold Arnould. Orig wraps. pba Oct 5 (325) $80
— East of Eden. NY, 1952. 1st Ed. Orig cloth, in repaired dj. CE Feb 21 (237) $180

Anr copy. In trimmed dj. pba Jan 25 (351) $250

Anr copy. In chipped dj. pba May 23 (404) $130; pba Aug 22 (424) $70

Anr copy. In dj. sg June 20 (348) $350

One of 1,500.  cb Oct 17 (478) $700; pba Oct 5 (326) $1,000

Anr Ed. [Bronxville]: Pvtly ptd, 1952. ("Chapter Thirty-Four from the Novel East of Eden.") One of 125.  pba Oct 5 (322) $750

— The First Watch. [Los Angeles: Ward Ritchie Press], 1947. 1st Ed, one of 60. 16mo, orig wraps, without mailing envelope. CE Feb 21 (236) $2,400

Anr copy. Orig wraps, with a mailing envelope. pba Oct 5 (327) $3,250

[-] El Gabilan. 1919.  Salinas, Cal, 1919.  [High School Yearbook] 4to, orig cloth, ends of spine frayed.  With 3 contribs by Steinbeck. Goodwin - Engelhard copy. CNY Oct 27 (129) $1,200

— The Grapes of Wrath.  L, [1939].  1st English Ed.  In dj with extremities rubbed.  pba Oct 5 (330) $325

1st Ed.  NY, [1939].  In dj.  cb Oct 17 (479) $1,900; CE May 22 (436) $1,900

Anr copy.  In dj with extremities rubbed.  pba Oct 5 (328) $800

Anr copy.  In browned, rubbed, chipped & repaired dj; cloth covers & spine foxed.  pba Mar 7 (245) $350

Anr copy.  In dj with crease to spine.  pba May 23 (405) $800

Anr copy.  In dj.  sg June 20 (349) $1,000; sg June 20 (350) $1,300

Anr copy.  In rubbed & worn dj.  sg June 20 (351) $350

Advance salesman's dummy copy of the 1st Ed, consisting of the prelims & 1st 10 pp of text. Orig cloth; small stain to spine. CE Feb 21 (222) $1,300

— How Edith McGillcuddy Met RLS.  Cleveland: Rowfant Club, 1943. 1st Ed, one of 152, ptd at the Grabhorn Press. 4to, orig half cloth, in dj (faded). CE Feb 21 (229) $900

— In Dubious Battle.  NY, [1936]. 1st Ed.  In dj with minor stains & tears; rear bd warped.  cb June 25 (1887) $500

Anr copy.  In dj with minor wear.  Inscr to Mrs. Tim Lowry.  CE Feb 21 (220) $1,600

Anr copy.  In dj with short tear.  Inscr to Harold Baily on tp.  pba Oct 5 (332) $3,250

Anr copy.  In repaired dj.  sg June 20 (352) $225

— John Steinbeck Replies.  [N.p., 1940].  Single sheet, folded to 8vo.  CE Feb 21 (225) $450

Anr copy.  Orig wraps; tear to rear wrap.  pba Oct 5 (333) $600

— Letters to Elizabeth: A Selection.... San Francisco: Book Club of California, 1978. One of 500. Half cloth, in dj. Book Club of California No 157.  pba Oct 5 (334) $95

Anr copy. Half cloth, in dj.  Book Club of California No 157.  pba Aug 22 (426) $80

— The Log from the Sea of Cortez. NY, 1951. 2d Ed. Cloth, in chipped dj.  pba Oct 5 (335) $130

— The Long Valley.  NY, 1938. 1st Ed.  In dj.  pba Oct 5 (336) $225

— The Moon is Down.  NY, 1942. 1st Ed. In worn & badly repaired dj. Inscr to Alice Sheridan, 1942.  sg Sept 28 (256) $325

1st Issue. In rubbed dj with rear panel soiled.  Inscr to Elizabeth & Larry Otis & with ALs to Elizabeth Otis. Engelhard copy.  CNY Oct 27 (132) $2,300

Anr copy. In dj.  pba Oct 5 (337) $100

2d Issue. In chipped dj.  pba Oct 5 (338) $550

— "Nothing So Monstrous": a Story. [NY], 1936. 1st Separate Ed, one of—50 for Elmer Adler. Orig half cloth.  Inscr to Jean Hersholt by Elmer Adler & with related Ls from Adler.  pba Oct 5 (339) $1,100

— Of Mice and Men.  L, [1937]. 1st English Ed.  b May 30 (457) £140

1st Ed.  NY, [1937].  1st Issue. In slightly shorter dj.  pba Jan 25 (353) $550

Anr copy.  In dj with 3 small holes.  sg June 20 (353) $325

— Once There Was a War.  NY, 1958. Half cloth, in glassine wrap.  pba May 23 (407) $80

— The Pastures of Heaven.  NY, 1932. 1st Ed, 1st Issue. In dj with light wear, minor chipping to spine & edges strengthened; leaning.  CE Feb 21 (216) $950

Anr copy.  In chipped dj, with piece lacking from spine.  pba Jan 25 (354) $850

— The Pearl.  NY, 1947. In dj, with Steinbeck looking to his left in photo; bdg spine ends rubbed.  Inscr to Dorothy, sgd & with pigasus logo.  CE Feb 21 (234) $3,000

Anr copy.  In frayed dj, with Steinbeck looking to his right in photo; bdg spine worn, front hinge weak. Frontis repaired.  Inscr to Peter Kriendler.  CE Feb 21 (235) $1,400

Anr copy.  In repaired 2d dj.  sg June 20 (354) $200

— The Red Pony.  NY, 1937. 1st Ed, one of 699.  Inscr to Harold Baily on tp.  pba Oct 5 (340) $1,000

Anr Ed. NY, 1945.  one of—699.  Illus by Wesley Dennis.  Half mor by Bennett Book Co..  Inscr to Paulette Greene.  pba May 23 (409) $1,500

— Saint Katy the Virgin.  [NY: Covici-Friede, 1936]. 1st Ed, one of 199. Orig bds; spine ends & corners rubbed.  With the "Merry Christmas" slip laid in. pba Oct 5 (341) $1,400

— Steinbeck. A Life in Letters.  NY: Viking Press, 1975. Ed by Elaine Steinbeck & Robert Wallsten, One of 1,000.  pba Aug 22 (435) $50

— Sweet Thursday.  NY, 1954. In chipped, rubbed & repaired dj.  Inscr to Paulette Greene.  pba May 23 (411) $2,680

Anr copy.  In rubbed & creased dj.  pba May 23 (412) $65

Anr copy.  In dj with wear to spine.  sg June 20 (355) $50

— To a God Unknown.  NY: Robert O. Ballou, [1933]. 1st Ed, 1st Issue. Orig cloth, in chipped dj.  CE Feb 21 (217) $700

Anr Ed. NY, [1933].  1st Issue. In dj & cloth case. Inscr to Robert Rau. Goodwin - Engelhard copy. CNY Oct 27 (130) $3,500

Anr Ed. NY: Robert O. Ballou, [1933].  1st Issue. In dj with minor chipping.  pba Oct 5 (343) $4,250

Anr Ed. NY: Covici-Friede, [1933].  2d Issue.  In dj. CE Feb 21 (218) $240

Anr copy. In soiled & chipped dj. sg June 20 (356) $250
— Tortilla Flat. NY, [1935]. 1st Ed. Orig cloth, in dj; spine darkened. With rubber stamp on front endpaper stating "Covici Friede Inc./ Sample Copy/ Not for Sale." Inscr to Robert Rau. Goodwin - Engelhard copy. CNY Oct 27 (131) $2,300
Anr copy. Orig cloth, in dj. Inscr to Harold Baily. pba Oct 5 (344) $11,000
One of 500 advance copies in wraps. Orig wraps. pba Oct 5 (345) $700; pba Aug 22 (430) $800
Trial Ed with Viking Press on tp & d/j & with ptd dedication leaf to Susan Gregory of Monterey. Orig cloth, in repaired dj. CE Feb 21 (219) $700
— Travels with Charley in Search of America. NY, 1962. Advance galley proofs. Unbound. CE Feb 21 (241) $1,400
— Las Uvas de la Ira. Santiago de Chile: Zig-Zag, 1940. Pictorial wraps. Inscr in Spanish to Natalya Lovejoy. CE Feb 21 (224) $650
— The Wayward Bus. NY, 1947. 1st Ed. In scraped & rubbed dj. Sgd twice & inscr to Selma & Jack, 1948. pba Nov 30 (304) $1,700
— The Winter of our Discontent. NY, 1961. Advance galley proofs. Unbound. CE Feb 21 (239) $1,200
— Zapata. Covelo CA: Yolla Bolly Press, 1991. One of 257. Illus by Karin Wikstrom. Orig half cloth & mailing box. CE Feb 21 (243) $300

**Steinbeck, John, 1902-68 —& Ricketts, Edward F.**
— Sea of Cortez. NY, 1941. 1st Ed. Inscr to Dr. Hoyt by Ricketts. CE Feb 21 (226) $750
Anr copy. Cloth, in chipped dj. CE Feb 21 (226A) $220
Anr copy. Cloth, in dj. pba Oct 5 (348) $425
Anr copy. Cloth; spine ends rubbed. pba Oct 5 (349) $95
Anr copy. In rubbed & chipped dj. Inscr by Steinbeck to Gene Fowler, with drawing. pba Nov 30 (303) $2,750

**Steinberg, Saul**
[-] Steinberg. Paris, 1966. Hors commerce copy. Folio, unsewn in orig wraps. With 1 colored & 2 plain lithos. Derriere le miroir No 157. Inscr by Steinberg on front cover. sg Sept 7 (316) $225
One of 150. Unsewn in orig wraps. With 1 colored & 2 plain lithos. Derriere le miroir No 157. bba May 9 (178) £95 [Gidal]
Anr copy. Unsewn in orig wraps. Derriere le miroir No 157. pba Mar 7 (246) $180

**Steinberger, Irene.** See: Carroll & Steinberger

**Steiner, Ralph**
— Ten Photographs from the Twenties and Thirties & One From the Seventies. NY: Pvtly ptd, [n.d.]. One of 25. Intro by Willard Van Dyke. Folio, loose in linen clamshell box. With 10 sgd & mtd photographs. P Oct 5 (164) $3,750

**Steinert, Otto**
— Akt International. Munich: Bruder Auer, [1954]. 4to, orig cloth, in chipped & soiled dj; bdg front cover dampstained. sg Feb 29 (227) $200

**Steingass, F.** See: Lawrence's copy, T. E.

**Stennett, R.**
— Aldiborontiphoskyphorniostikos, a Round Game for Merry Parties.. L, 1823. 8vo, ptd wraps; worn & marked. With hand-colored frontis & 15 hand-colored plates. Minor tears; some browning. bba May 30 (342) £120 [Ginnan]

**Step, Edward**
— Favourite Flowers of Garden and Greenhouse. L, [1896-97]. 4 vols. 8vo, contemp half mor; rubbed. With 316 chromolitho plates. b Jan 31 (303) £750
— Favourite Flowers of the Garden and Greenhouse. L, 1896-97. 1st Ed. 4 vols. 8vo, contemp half mor. With 316 color plates. Some spotting; few plates loose. S Oct 27 (676) £740 [MacDonnell]

**Stephanopoli, Dimo & Nicolo**
— Voyage... en Grece. Paris, [1800]. 2 vols. 8vo, later half calf. With 8 plates (2 folding). Text discolored. S Oct 26 (218) £400 [Theotoky]

**Stephen, Thomas**
— Stephen's Philadelphia Directory. Phila., [1796]. For 1796. 12mo, contemp half mor; rubbed, front cover detached. Lacking map & end matter; 1 leaf torn. F June 20 (377) $140

**Stephens, James, 1882-1950**
— The Crock of Gold. L, 1926. One of 525. Illus by Thomas Mackenzie. 4to, half vellum, in dj; spine rubbed. With 12 mtd colored plates. bba May 9 (421) £95 [Marks]
— Irish Fairy Tales. L, 1920. Illus by Arthur Rackham. 4to, orig cloth, in rubbed & soiled dj. With 16 colored plates. bba May 9 (407) £180 [Heritage]
One of 520, sgd by Rackham. Orig half vellum; slightly discolored, endpapers spotted. S Nov 2 (137) £700 [Hirsch]

**Stephens, John, Writer on Australia**
— The Land of Promise: being an Authentic...History of South Australia.... L, 1839. 8vo, orig cloth; hinges weak, spine worn. With folding map, folding plan, folding table & 4 litho plates. Dampstained & spotted. S June 13 (663) £180

**Stephens, John Lloyd, 1805-52**
— Incidents of Travel in Central America, Chiapas, and Yucatan. L, 1843. 2 vols. 8vo, orig cloth; bumped. With 2 folding frontises, folding map & 74 plates. Met Feb 24 (362) $200
Anr Ed. L, 1854. 8vo, orig cloth; spine ends rubbed. pba July 25 (454) $110
— Yucatan. NY, 1843. ("Incidents of Travel in Yucatan.") Illus by F. Catherwood. 2 vols. 8vo, modern half calf. Foxed & browned throughout; frontis backed. sg Oct 26 (257) $90

## Stephens, Lorenzo Dow
— Life Sketches of a Jayhawker.... [San Jose], 1916. One of 300. Orig wraps; spine chipped, minor tears. pba Feb 12 (51) $110
  Anr copy. Orig wraps; edges worn, spine head chipped. pba Apr 25 (689) $50

## Stephenson, George
— A Description of the Safety Lamp.... L, 1817. 2d Ed. 8vo, wraps; split on backstrip. With 4 plates. CE Nov 8 (149) $100

## Stephenson, Russell M.
— Eighty Sketches in Water Colour from Nature. L: St. Catherine Press, 1926. Ltd Ed. 4to, mor gilt. Corner crease to frontis. pba Nov 30 (305) $550

## Sterling, George, 1869-1926
— Beyond the Breakers. San Francisco, 1914. 1st Ed. John Myers O'Hara's copy with 5 letters or poems & 1 postcard from Sterling to O'Hara mtd to prelims. pba Oct 5 (355) $800
— The Caged Eagle and Other Poems. San Francisco, 1916. 1st Ed. Mor gilt; rubbed. Inscr. pba May 23 (415) $50
  1st Issue. In chipped dj. Inscr. pba Oct 5 (356) $95
— Yosemite: An Ode. San Francisco: A. M. Robinson, 1916. Wraps over bds. pba Feb 12 (181) $60

## Stern, Alec
— Etchings of Yosemite by Alec Stern. Worlds of John Muir. San Mateo: Studio of Alec Stern, 1979. One of 1,000. With port & 40 illusts. pba Feb 12 (182) $70

## Stern, Frederic Claude
— A Study of the Genus Paeonia. L, 1946. Folio, orig bds. With 15 colored plates. Met Feb 24 (467) $350

## Sterne, Laurence, 1713-68
  See also: Limited Editions Club
— Letters...to his Most Intimate Friends. L, 1775. 1st Ed. 3 vols. 8vo, contemp calf; scuffed. F June 20 (442) $60
  Anr copy. Contemp calf; spine heads rubbed. S June 13 (423) £200
— Lettres d'Yorick a Eliza et d'Eliza a Yorick. Lausanne: Chez Mourer Cadet, 1786. 12mo, contemp sheep; stained, splits in spine ends. Frontis stained along bottom margin. P Nov 1 (198) $50
— The Life and Opinions of Tristram Shandy. [York] & L, 1760-67. 3d Ed of Vols I-II, 2d Ed of Vol III, 1st Ed of Vols IV-VI & IX. 9 vols in 6. 8vo, contemp calf; rebacked, joints of Vol VI starting. Sold w.a.f. Vols V, VII & IX sgd. CE May 22 (438) $380
  Anr Ed. San Francisco: Arion Press, 1988. One of 400. Illus by John Baldessari. 4to, half calf. With book of photo-collages by John Baldessari & a booklet containing Melvyn New's commentary. sg Sept 14 (38) $550
  Anr copy. Orig half calf. With book of photo-collages by John Baldessari & a booklet containing Melvyn New's commentary. sg Oct 19 (6) $300

— A Sentimental Journey.... L, 1809. 12mo, later calf gilt; rebacked with orig spine laid down. With 2 hand-colored plates by Thomas Rowlandson. sg Sept 21 (285) $110
  Anr Ed. NY: J. W. Bouton, 1884. Illus by Maurice Leloir. 4to, mor, orig wraps bound in. sg Sept 21 (250) $200
  Anr Ed. L, 1897. 8vo, mor gilt by Sangorski & Sutcliffe. sg Sept 14 (56) $175
  Anr Ed. L: Fraser Press, 1971. Lev gilt by A. W. Lumsden. sg Sept 14 (57) $175
— Voyage sentimental, suivi des letters d'Yorick a Eliza.... Paris, 1799. 2 vols. 4to, 19th-cent calf gilt. With 6 plates before letters; English text & French translation on facing pages.. L.p. copy. Fuerstenberg - Schaefer copy. S Dec 8 (583) £480
— Works. L, 1783. 7 vols. 12mo, early 19th-cent half calf gilt; edges worn. CE Sept 27 (265) $480
— Yoricks empfindsame Reise durch Frankreich und Italien. Bremen: J. H. Cramer, 1776-73. Mixed Ed. 4 vols in 2. 8vo, contemp half calf; worn. S Mar 14 (346) £50

**Steuart, Sir James.** See: Denham, Sir James Steuart

## Stevens, Charles W.
— Fly-Fishing in Maine Lakes.... Bost., 1881. 8vo, cloth. pba July 11 (291) $120

## Stevens, Henry, 1819-86
— Bibliotheca Geographica & Historica, or a Catalogue of a Nine Days' Sale.... L, 1872. Part l (all pbd). 8vo, ptd wraps with lea spine; worn, chipped. First few leaves with tide mark in lower margin. Inscr to Joseph Sabin. O Mar 26 (266) $160

## Stevens, Capt. John, d.1726
— A New Collection of Voyages and Travels.... L, 1711. Vol II only. 4to, recent half calf. Slight discoloration. S Oct 26 (81) £450 [Cyprus Pop. BK]
— The Royal Treasury.... L, 1725. 8vo, contemp calf; broken, spine ends chipped. Library stamp on tp. sg Mar 21 (119) $90

## Stevens, John L. —& Oleson, W. B.
— Picturesque Hawaii. Phila: Edgewood Publishing, [c.1894]. 4to, orig cloth; circular stain to front cover, shaken. pba Apr 25 (189) $100

## Stevens, Wallace, 1879-1955
— Esthetique de Mal. Cummington: Cummington Press, 1945. One of 300. Half calf; spine scuffed & nicked. bbc Dec 18 (350) $300
— Harmonium. NY, 1923. Orig cloth, remains of dj laid-in. pba May 23 (417) $120
— Poems. San Francisco: Arion Press, 1985. One of 300. Frontis by Jasper Johns. Half mor. sg Sept 14 (39) $1,900

## Stevens-Nelson Paper Corp.
— Specimens: a Stevens-Nelson Paper Catalogue. [NY, 1953]. Text designed or ptd by Bruce Rogers, Mardersteig, Dropmore, Golden Cockerel, etc.. 4to, half

lev. With over 100 specimen sheets of handmade & mouldmade paper. pba Mar 7 (197) $75; pba June 20 (261) $100; sg Feb 15 (276) $225

**Stevenson, Adlai E., 1900-65.** See: Onassis copy, Jacqueline Bouvier Kennedy

**Stevenson, Edward Luther, 1858-1944**
— Terrestrial and Celestial Globes: Their History and Construction.... New Haven, 1921. 2 vols. bba Oct 5 (172) £200 [Phillips]

**Stevenson, Robert Louis, 1850-94**
See also: Grabhorn Printing; Limited Editions Club
— Acoss the Plains. L, 1892. One of 100 L.p. copies. 4to, half calf; rubbed & scuffed, recased with later endpapers. pba Mar 7 (247) $65
— Across the Plains. Hillsborough: Allen, 1950. One of 200. Illus by Mallette Dean. pba June 20 (8) $110; sg Sept 14 (17) $225
— Catriona. A Sequel to "Kidnapped...." L, 1893. 1st English Ed in Book form. 8vo, orig cloth; upper corner of front free endpaper clipped. pba Dec 14 (134) $80
— The Charity Bazaar: an Allegorical Dialogue. [Edin., 1868]. 4to, mor gilt. Sgd at end. cb Feb 14 (2727) $1,100
— A Child's Garden of Verses. L, 1885. 1st Ed. 8vo, orig cloth; soiled. cb Oct 17 (481) $1,200
Anr copy. Orig cloth; extremities rubbed, endpapers browned. CE Sept 27 (268) $1,300; S Apr 23 (157) £170
Anr copy. Orig cloth; spine bumped. S July 11 (203) £460
Anr copy. Orig cloth; spine ends & corners rubbed, endpapers browned. sg Oct 19 (243) $800
— Island Nights' Entertainments. L, 1893. 8vo, orig cloth; spine ends rubbed, tear to gutter of front free endpaper. pba May 23 (418) $75
— Kidnapped. Being Memoirs of the Adventures of David Balfour.... L, 1866. 1st Ed. 8vo, orig wraps. CE May 22 (439) $1,800
Anr Ed. L, 1886. 1st Issue. 8vo, orig cloth; leaning, corners rubbed, spine ends with small splits. CE Feb 21 (257) $300
2d Issue. Later half calf. CG June 12 (19) £260
— The Pentland Rising. A Page of History. Edin., 1866. 8vo, orig wraps; worn & soiled. cb Feb 14 (2728) $1,700
— La Porte de maletroit. Cagnes-sur-Mer, 1952. One of 300. Wraps. sg Sept 14 (18) $70
— Some Letters. NY: Cheltenham Press for Ingalls Kimball, 1902. One of 50 on japan vellum. 8vo, mor extra with onlays by Sangorski & Sutcliffe, 1903; joints & corners scuffed. bbc June 24 (109) $225
— The Strange Case of Dr. Jekyll and Mr. Hyde. L, 1886. 1st English Ed. 8vo, contemp half mor, orig wraps with date altered bound in; rubbed. b Jan 31 (117) £220
Anr copy. Orig cloth; worn & cockled. Lacking ad leaf at end; some soiling. bba May 30 (232) £380 [Williams]

Anr copy. Orig wraps with dates altered in ink from 1885 to 1886; backstrip def, repaired. CE Feb 21 (256) $1,400
Anr copy. Orig cloth; small mark on upper cover, spine soiled. S Apr 23 (156) £850
Anr copy. Orig cloth; upper cover rubbed, spine bumped. S July 11 (204) £620
Anr copy. Orig wraps; upper wrap with minor soiling & chipped. Prelims slightly dog-eared. S July 11 (205) £1,050
Anr copy. Orig wraps; repaired, date altered by hand. sg Feb 8 (337) $900
Anr copy. Half calf. sg Feb 8 (338) $475
— The Suicide Club. NY, [1941]. One of 100. Illus by Karl Schrag. 4to, wraps. With 18 orig aquatint etchings. sg Sept 14 (258) $425; sg Oct 19 (244) $325
— Treasure Island. L, 1883. 1st Ed. 8vo, mor gilt by Bayntun-Riviere with onlaid design of Capt. Silver, orig cloth bound in; extremities worn. Lacking rear ads. CE Sept 27 (267) $1,600
1st Issue. Orig cloth; spines bumped. Minor foxing; small tear in lower margin of 1 leaf. S July 11 (206) £2,600
Anr Ed. NY, 1932. Illus by N. C. Wyeth. Orig cloth; front cover smudged. pba Aug 22 (880) $100
— Virginibus Puerisque and other Papers. L, 1881. 1st Ed. 8vo, orig cloth; rubbed & soiled, rear inner hinge tightened. Thomas Stevenson's copy (RLS's father). At end of dedication & of each essay RLS has written in indelible purple pencil the name of the place where the piece was composed. McCutcheon - Mills - Benz copy. CE Sept 27 (266) $1,900
Anr copy. Half mor; spine ends & corners rubbed, spine discolored. pba Dec 14 (135) $60
Anr Ed. L, 1910. One of 250. Illus by Norman Wilkinson. 4to, mor extra by Denise Lubett. sg Sept 14 (58) $800
— When the Devil was Well. Bost., 1921. 1st Ed. Bds. sg Sept 21 (300) $130
— Works. L, 1894-1901. Edinburgh Ed, one of 1,035. 32 vols, including Balfour's life orig cloth. With corrected leaf for Macaire loosely inserted at end of Vol 23. bba May 30 (268) £420 [Classic Bindings]
Anr Ed. NY, 1898-99. 24 vols. 8vo, half mor gilt. CE Sept 27 (269) $1,900
Anr Ed. NY, 1899-1901. ("The Novels and Tales....") 26 vols. 8vo, half mor. CE Nov 8 (246) $1,400
Anr Ed. NY, 1900. 26 vols. pba Aug 8 (605) $170
Pentland Ed. L, 1906-7. one of 1,550. 20 vols. Contemp calf. sg Sept 21 (47) $1,700
Swanston Ed. L, 1911-12. 25 vols. Contemp half calf. b Jan 31 (118) £650; bba May 30 (269) £260 [Classic Bindings]
Anr Ed. NY, 1911-17. 27 vols. Cloth; extremities dampstained. pba June 20 (310) $140

**Stevenson, Roger**
— Military Instructions for Officers Detached in the Field. Phila., 1775. 12mo, contemp sheep; worn, joints split, covers held on with tape. With 12 plates,

7 folding. Names clipped from top edge of tp & dedication; browned. wa Feb 29 (438) $1,300

**Stevin, Simon, 1548-1620**
— Les Oeuvres mathematiques.... Leiden: Elzevir, 1634. Folio, contemp sheep; worn, needs rebacked. Lacking final leaf of instructions to the binder; browned. sg May 16 (260) $275

**Stewart, Basil**
— Subjects Portrayed in Japanese Colour-Prints. L, 1922. Folio, half cloth; rear cover abraded. Foxed at ends. sg Sept 7 (321) $175

Anr copy. Orig bds; endpapers renewed, later cloth back. Library markings. sg Jan 11 (405) $130

**Stewart, C. G.** See: Browne & Stewart

**Stewart, Charles Samuel**
— A Visit to the South Seas, in the U.S. Ship Vincennes.... NY, 1833. 2 vols. 8vo, orig cloth; spine ends frayed. sg Mar 7 (349) $100

**Stewart, George R.**
— The Opening of the California Trail.... Berkeley, 1953. With: Stewart, The California Trail: An Epic with Many Heroes, 1962, 1st Ed 1st Ed, One of 350. 2 vols, orig cloth. With 2 ports, 2 maps, & 14 illus. Larson copy. pba Sept 28 (684) $55
— Ordeal by Hunger. NY, [1936]. 1st Ed. Orig cloth. With 5 maps & 12 illus. Sgd. Larson copy. pba Sept 28 (426) $70

**Stewart, James Lindsay**
— Golfiana Miscellanea.... L, 1887. 1st Ed. Cloth; spine chipped, rubbed, & dulled. pba Apr 18 (159) $800

**Stewart-Murphy, Charlotte A.**
— A History of British Circulating Libraries.... Newton: Bird & Bull Press, 1992. One of 185. Half lea. sg Feb 15 (52) $225

**Stickney, Sarah.** See: Ellis, Sarah Stickney

**Stieglitz, Alfred, 1864-1946**
— Alfred Stieglitz, Photographs and Writings. Wash., [1983]. Compiled by Sarah Greenough & Juan Hamilton. Folio, cloth, in soiled & repaired dj. Soiling to prelims & fore-edge. sg Feb 29 (300) $110
— America and Alfred Stieglitz. Garden City, 1934. Ed by Waldo Frank & others. Half cloth. Inscr, 22 Jan 1935. CE May 22 (372) $550

**Stieler, Adolph, 1775-1836**
— Hand Atlas ueber alle Theile deer Erde. Gotha: Justus Perthes, [c.1837]. Folio, contemp half sheep; worn, spine def. With 52 full-page mapsheets, hand-colored in outline. Stained & spotted. S Mar 28 (185) £170

**Stiff, Edward**
— Cincinnati: George Conclin, 1840 8vo, contemp sheep; rebacked with modern calf, corners worn. Lower half of map lacking & remainder split into 3 pieces; foxing & soiling. pba Aug 8 (193) $350

**Stigand, Chauncey Hugh**
— Hunting the Elephant in Africa.... NY, 1913. Cloth; worn & stained. O Oct 10 (259) $180

**Stille, Charles J.**
— Major-General Anthony Wayne and the Pennsylvania Line in the Continental Army. Phila., 1893. 8vo, orig cloth; worn. wa Feb 29 (303) $110

**Stillingfleet, Benjamin**
— Miscellaneous Tracts Relating to Natural History. L, 1759. 8vo, contemp half calf; worn. Some worming. Ck Feb 14 (308) £50

Anr Ed. L, 1775. 8vo, contemp calf; rubbed. b Sept 20 (182) £110

**Stillman, Jacob D. B., 1819-88**
— The Horse in Motion.... Bost., 1882. Illus by Eadweard Muybridge. 4to, orig cloth; rubbed, ring on front cover, hinges cracked. pba Jan 4 (374) $325

**Stillman, William James**
— Poetic Localities of Cambridge. Bost., 1876. 4to, cloth; extremities worn, spine cracked, 1st plate detached. With 12 plates. Some foxing. sg Feb 29 (303) $130

**Stirling-Maxwell, Sir William, 1818-78**
— Annals of the Artists of Spain. L, 1848. 1st Ed. 3 vols. 8vo, later calf gilt. sg Jan 11 (407) $475

**Stith, William**
— The History of the First Discovery and Settlement of Virginia. NY, 1865. One of 250. 8vo, orig cloth; bumped. Minor staining. Reprint of the Williamsburg 1747 Ed. wa Feb 29 (539) $160

**Stobaeus, Johannes**
— The Sayings of the Seven Sages of Greece.... Verona: Officina Bodoni, 1976. One of 160. 8vo, orig half vellum. sg Sept 14 (293) $350

**Stockton, Frank R., 1834-1902**
— The Lady, or the Tiger?... NY, 1885. 8vo, pictorial cloth; rubbed. sg Sept 21 (301) $110

**Stoddard, W. L.**
— The New Golfer's Almanac...for the year 1910. Bost., 1909. Illus by A. W. Bartlett. 8vo, cloth-backed pictorial bds; extremities worn. sg Mar 7 (454) $60

**Stoddart, Thomas T., 1810-80**
— An Angler's Rambles and Angling Songs. Edin., 1866. 1st Ed. 12mo, orig cloth; front hinge starting. pba July 11 (294) $50
— The Art of Angling as Practised in Scotland. Edin., 1835. 12mo, cloth; shaken, inner joint broken, 1st few leaves detached. O Feb 6 (221) $70

**Stoecklein, Joseph**
— Allerhand so lehr-als geisteiche Brief-Schrifften und Reis Beschreibungen.... Augsburg, 1726-28. 8 parts (of 38) in 1 vol. Folio, later half vellum. Some foxing & marginal dampstaining; marginal tears & repairs; 2 maps with repairs on verso. cb Oct 17 (208) $800

**Stoker, Bram, 1847-1912**
See also: Limited Editions Club
— Dracula. L, 1897. 1st Ed. 8vo, orig cloth; rubbed, minor stain on lower cover. Without ads. b Jan 31 (119) £550

Anr copy. Orig cloth; soiled. S July 11 (210) £2,300

Anr Ed. NY, 1899. 8vo, orig cloth; rubbed & with chip beneath title. sg June 20 (357) $750

Photoplay Ed. NY: Grosset & Dunlap, [1931]. In dj. pba May 4 (257) $700

**Stokes, Isaac Newton Phelps**
— The Iconography of Manhattan Island.... NY, 1915-28. One of 360. 6 vols. 4to, orig half vellum gilt, in frayed & soiled djs. Abbey copy. S Nov 30 (142) £2,200

One of 42 on japan vellum. Orig half vellum. P June 5 (336) $4,750

Anr Ed. NY, 1967. 6 vols. 4to, cloth. Facsimile of 1915-28 Ed. O May 7 (281) $700

**Stokes, Isaac Newton Phelps —& Haskell, Daniel Carl**
— American Historical Prints.... NY, 1933. 4to, cloth. sg Oct 26 (352) $110; sg June 13 (350) $90

**Stokes, John Lort**
— Discoveries in Australia. L, 1846. 2 vols. 8vo, recent mor gilt. With 8 folding maps in pockets & 25 plates. Some faint marks in text. S June 27 (270) £700

**Stolle, Gottlieb, 1673-1744**
— Kurtze Nachricht von den Buechern und deren Urhebern in der Stollischen Bibliothec. Jena, 1733-43. 18 parts in 3 vols. 4to, contemp half vellum & contemp bds; some wear & soiling. Browning & foxing. Kraus copy. O Mar 26 (269) $1,200

**Stone, George Cameron**
— A Glossary of the Construction, Decoration, and Uses of Arms and Armor.... Portland ME, 1934. 4to, cloth; worn. O Dec 5 (136) $90

**Stone, Irving**
— Men to Match My Mountains. Garden City, 1956. Ltd Ed. Syn. Sgd. pba Apr 25 (691) $60; pba Aug 8 (194) $65; pba Aug 22 (440) $85

— Sailor on Horseback: The Biography of Jack London. Cambr. MA, 1938. Review copy. In chipped & rubbed dj. Inscr to Clive Saig, 1 Oct 1938. pba Oct 5 (278) $90

**Stone, John A.**
— Put's Golden Songster Containing the Largest and Most Popular Collection of California Songs Ever Published. San Francisco: D. Appleton & Co., [1858]. Orig pictorial wraps. pba Feb 12 (510) $85

**Stone, Livingston, 1836-1912**
— Domesticated Trout. Charlestown NH: Cold Spring Trout Ponds, 1877. 3d Ed. 8vo, orig cloth. Inscr to J. D. Young. pba July 11 (296) $110

4th Ed. Charlestown NH: Cold Spring Trout Ponds, 1896. 8vo, orig cloth. Inscr to John Simpson, 1897. pba July 11 (297) $75

**Stone's copy, Marcus**
RUSKIN, JOHN. - Notes on Some of the Principal Pictures Exhibited in the Rooms of the Royal Academy...No III - 1857. L, 1857. Bound with: Thornbury, Walter. The May Exhibition. A Guide to the Pictures in the Royal Academy. L, 1860. 8vo, contemp cloth. Decorated by Stone with penwork marginal drolleries. S Nov 21 (389) £300

**Stone, Reynolds**
— Engravings. L, 1977. Ltd Ed. 4to, mor, with portion of copper plate inset in cover, by Audrey P. Tomlinson. Sgd wood-engraving loosely inserted. bba May 9 (152) £150 [Lam]

Anr copy. Orig cloth. Sgd wood-engraving loosely inserted. bba May 9 (428) £220 [Bankes Books]

**Stone, Wilbur Macey**
— The Gigantick Histories of Thomas Boreman. Portland, ME: Southworth Press, 1933. One of 250. 4to, half cloth, unopened. O Dec 5 (137) $120

— The Triptych's Penny Toys. NY: Pvtly ptd for the Triptych, 1924. One of 99. Pictorial bds; worn. O Sept 12 (173) $225

**Stoneback, H. R.**
— Cartographers of the Deus Loci: The Mill House. North Hills PA: Bird & Bull Press, 1982. One of 240. Half vellum. sg Feb 15 (53) $90

**Stoneman, Vernon C.**
— John and Thomas Seymour: Cabinetmakers in Boston, 1794-1816. Bost., 1959. 4to, cloth; spine spotted. Inscr. sg June 13 (160) $80

**Stoner, Frank**
— Chelsea, Bow, and Derby Porcelain Figures. Newport, [1955]. Folio, cloth. sg Jan 11 (89) $80

**Stonham, Charles**
— The Birds of the British Islands. L, 1906-11. 5 vols. 4to, orig cloth. S June 13 (424) £320

**Storck, Anthony**
— An Essay on the Medicinal Nature of Hemlock. Edin., 1762. 12mo, modern mor. With 1 folding plate. Margin edges browned & worn; text obscure on gutter of Aa2v. CE Nov 8 (151) $100

**Storer, James S.**
— The Antiquarian Itinerary.... L, 1815-18. 7 vols. 8vo, contemp mor gilt; worn, spines soiled. Some foxing.  wa Nov 16 (249) $160
— History and Antiquities of the Cathedral Churches of Great Britain. L, 1814-19. 4 vols. 4to, contemp half calf; joints worn. Some foxing, staining & soiling.  O Mar 5 (209) $100

**Storer, James S. —& Greig, John**
— Antiquarian and Topographical Cabinet. L, 1807-11. 10 vols. 8vo, half mor. With 480 plates. Some foxing.  pba Nov 30 (308) $350

**Storer, Tracey.** See: Grinnell & Storer

**Storer, Tracy.** See: Grinnell & Storer

**Stork, William**
— A Description of East-Florida, with a Journal kept by John Bartram of Philadelphia.... L, [1766]. ("An Account of East-Florida, with a Journal, Kept by John Bartram of Philadelphia....") 2 parts in 1 vol. 8vo, later 19th-cent half mor; extremities rubbed. Stamp on leaf after title. Benjamin Matlack Everhart's copy.  sg Oct 26 (353) $1,600

**Storm...**
— The Storm. A Poem.... Bridlington: George Furby, [c.1812]. 12mo, modern bds.  b Dec 5 (489) £140

**Storr, Gottlieb Conrad Christian**
— Museum physiognosticum.... Stuttgart, 1807. 4to, bdg not described.  b May 30 (41) £60

**Storrs, Augustus**
— Answers... to Certain Queries upon the... Trade and Intercourse, between Missouri and the Internal Provinces of Mexico.... Wash., 1825. 1st Ed. 8vo, modern half mor. With 6pp. from Niles Register laid in. Stained & foxed. Robbins-Streeter copy.  pba Mar 21 (350) $150

**Story...**
— The Story of Mary and her Little Lamb as told by Mary and her Neighbors and Friends. Dearborn; Mr. & Mrs. Henry Ford, 1928. Pictorial bds.  pba Aug 22 (731) $60

**Story, Joseph, 1779-1845**
— Commentaries on the Constitution of the United States. Bost., 1833. 1st Ed. 3 vols. 8vo, contemp calf; scuffed, worn & refurbished. Foxed.  pba June 13 (297) $130

**Stott, Raymond Toole**
— Circus and Allied Arts, a World Bibliography.... Derby, 1958-71. One of 1,200. Vols I-II. Orig cloth.  Z June 14 (8) $225
— Maughamiana: the Writings of W. Somerset Maugham. L, [1950]. In dj with discoloration to spine foot.  pba Aug 22 (330) $55

**Stoupi, Edmund S. J. de**
STOUPI LIBRARY, EDMUND S. J. DE. - [Sale Catalogue] Catalogue des livres de la bibliotheque.... Liege: J. J. Tutot, 1786. 8vo, contemp wraps; worn & soiled.  O Mar 26 (270) $275

**Stoupi Library, Edmund S. J. de.** See: Stoupi, Edmund S. J. de

**Stout, Rex, 1886-1975**
— Murder by the Book. NY, 1951. In dj with some wear.  sg June 20 (358) $175
— Silent Speaker. NY, 1946. In creased & repaired dj.  sg Dec 14 (68) $90
— Too Many Cooks. NY, [1938]. In dj with minor defs.  sg June 20 (359) $900

**Stowe...**
— Stowe: A Description of the Magnificent House and Gardens of the Right Honourable Richard Grenville Temple.... Buckingham, 1777. 8vo, contemp sheep; worn & soiled, rebacked with much of orig spine laid down. With folding frontis & 20 plates. Tear to frontis repaired; 1 other folding plate with tears repaired.  wa Nov 16 (251) $100

**Stowe, Harriet Beecher, 1811-96**
See also: Limited Editions Club
— Dred. Bost., 1856. 1st Ed. 2 vols. 12mo, orig cloth; corners worn, spine ends chipped.  wa Dec 14 (59) $95
   Fiftieth Thousand. NY, 1856. 2 vols. 12mo, cloth; rubbed, extremities worn, leaning. Some foxing & soiling.  pba June 13 (298) $95
— A Key to Uncle Tom's Cabin. Bost., 1853. 1st Ed. 8vo, contemp half mor; rubbed. Dampstained & foxed.  sg Mar 28 (360) $50
— Uncle Tom's Cabin.... Bost., 1852. 1st Ed, 1st Ptg. 2 vols. 8vo, orig cloth; joints & spine ends repaired, rubbed, some gatherings sprung. Minor foxing.  CE Feb 21 (259) $600
   Anr copy. Orig cloth, BAL B bdg; frayed. Engelhard copy.  CNY Oct 27 (134) $8,500
   Anr copy. Half mor; rubbed.  O Mar 5 (210) $400
   Anr copy. Lev gilt, Blanck's C bdg bound in.  sg Mar 28 (356) $2,600
   Anr Ed. L: Clarke & Co., 1852. 8vo, later half mor gilt; spine head chipped, front joint cracked.  sg Mar 28 (359) $130
   Anr Ed. L, 1852. Illus by George Cruikshank. 8vo, orig cloth; rubbed, a few gatherings sprung.  CE Feb 21 (260) $350
   Anr copy. Orig 13 parts. Orig ptd wraps. With port & 27 plates. Lacking ad at end of Part 6.  CE May 22 (442) $1,200
   Anr copy. Illus by the Dalziel brothers. 8vo, pictorial cloth.  sg Mar 28 (358) $250
   Anr Ed. Bost., 1892. 8vo, orig cloth; extremiteis worn. Inscr, 6 July 1893, to Elizabeth Alden Curtis.  P June 5 (338) $2,250
— Works. Cambr., Mass., 1896-97. 17 vols. 8vo, half mor. L.p. copy.  cb Oct 17 (300) $2,500

**Strabo, 63 B.C.-24 A.D.**
— Geographia. Basel: Valentinus Curio, 1523. Folio, old half vellum; worn. Some leaves at beginning stained & frayed; some tears. O Mar 5 (211) $500

Anr Ed. [Geneva], 1587. ("Rerum geographicarum.") Folio, later sheep; worn, covers detached. In Greek & Latin. With folding world map laid in (dampstained, cropped, partly separated at folds). Heavily dampstained. Sold w.a.f. sg May 9 (101) $550

Anr Ed. Paris, 1620. Folio, 17th-cent calf; worn, covers detached. Tp stamped. sg Mar 7 (351) $275
— Geographie. Paris, 1805-19. 5 vols. 4to, early 19th-cent bds; Vol I front joint cracked, Vol IV backstrip partly detached. Foxed; ink notes on some endleaves. sg Mar 7 (350) $175
— Geographikon bibloi. rerum geographicarum libri xvii. Amst., 1707. 2 vols in 1. Folio, contemp Dutch vellum; upper joint split. S Oct 27 (1089) £550 [Theotoky]

**Straccha, Benvenuto**
— Tractatus de mercatura seu mercatore. Venice: Michael Bonelli, 1575 [1576]. 8vo, later bds. Tears from paper faults in B1, Q7 & Pp7 just affecting text. C Apr 3 (230) £450

**Strada, Famiano, 1572-1649**
— De Bello Belgico. L, 1650. 1st Ed in English. Folio, 18th-cent half calf; joints cracked, spine chipped at foot. With 14 ports. sg Mar 21 (308) $350

**Strada, Jacobus de, d.1588**
— Epitome du thresor des antiquitez. Lyons: J. de Tournes for the author & Thomas Guerin, 1553. 4to, 18th-cent calf; worn. Marginal dampstaining; bb3 repaired at fore-edge. S June 12 (125) £280

**Strahan, Edward.** See: Shinn, Earl

**Strahorn, Carrie A.**
— Fifteen Thousand Miles by Stage.... NY, 1911. wa Feb 29 (485) $325

2d Ed. NY, 1915. Orig cloth; shaken. pba Apr 25 (692) $120

**Strambotti...**
— Strambotti d'ogni sorte. Sonetti alla bergamasca. [Rome: Eucharius Silber, c.1500]. 4to, modern vellum with Essling supralibros; lettering strip partly detached from spine. Early writing washed from foot of last leaf. C Apr 3 (231) £4,500

**Strand, Paul**
— The Mexican Portfolio. NY: Da Capo Press, [1967]. One of 1,000. Folio, loose as issued in portfolio. sg Feb 29 (305) $2,500
— Paul Strand: A Retrospective Monograph.... Phila.: Phila. Museum of Art, [1971]. 2 vols in 1. 4to, pictorial bds. sg Feb 29 (307) $100
— Photographs 1915-1945. NY: Museum of Modern Art, [1945]. Text by Nancy Newhall. sg Feb 29 (306) $150

— Photographs of Mexico. NY, 1940. One of 250. Folio, loose as issued in soiled portfolio. With 20 plates. sg Feb 29 (304) $6,500
— Tir a'Mhurain: Outer Hebrides. L, [1962]. 4to, cloth; worn. Some foxing. sg Feb 29 (311) $175

**Strang, William, 1859-1921**
— The Earth Fiend. A Ballad.... L, 1892. Ltd Ed. 4to, orig cloth; rubbed & marked. bba July 18 (336) £65 [Cox]

Anr copy. Cloth; rubbed & rebacked. With 11 plates. sg Sept 21 (302) $150

**Strange, Edward F.**
— Chinese Lacquer. L, 1926. One of 500. With 55 plates. sg June 13 (225) $130

**Strange, John**
— Lettera sopra l'origine della carta naturale di Cortona. Pisa, 1764. 4to, 18th-Cent calf; rubbed. S Oct 27 (1167) £150 [Zioni]

**Strassoldo-Grafenberg, Michael, Count —& Cesaris, Angelo**
— Atti della Distribuzione dei Premii d'Industria. Milan: Imperiale Regia Stamperia, 1822. 8vo, contemp mor gilt bound for presentation to Emperor Francis I of Austria. C Apr 3 (233) £950

**Strater, Henry**
— Twenty-four Drawings. With Foreword by the Artist. Ogunquit, 1958. One of 50. Folio, half cloth, in dj; minor stain on upper cover. O Dec 5 (138) $140

**Stratton, Royal B.**
— Captivity of the Oatman Girls.... San Francisco, 1857. 2d Ed. 12mo, orig wraps; stained, front wrap torn. Tp & last leaves with fox spots. Robbins-Cowan copy. pba Mar 21 (351) $2,750

Anr Ed. Salem OR: Oregon Teachers Monthly, 1909. Revised & abridged by Charles H. Jones. 12mo, orig wraps. pba Apr 25 (693) $55

**Straub, Peter.** See: King & Straub

**Strauss, Johann, 1825-99**
— Die Fledermaus. Leipzig: Cranz, [c.1897]. Folio, half calf. Full score. With performance markings, later annotations & mtd annotations. C Nov 29 (254) £400

**Strauss, Joseph B.**
— The Golden Gate Bridge: Report of the Chief Engineer.... [San Francisco: Golden Gate Bridge & Highway District], 1937. Folio, cloth, in dj. Inscr by the general manager of the district. With related material. pba Feb 12 (316) $180

**Street, Alfred Billings**
— Woods and Waters, or the Saranacs and Racket. NY, 1860. 12mo, cloth; spine ends chipped, tear to cloth along rear joint. pba July 11 (364) $120

**Streeter, Edwin William**
— Catalogue, with Designs and Prices, of Diamond Ornaments, and Machine-Made Jewellery.... L, [1872]. 8vo, half cloth; shaken. sg Sept 7 (194) $140

**Streeter, Thomas Winthrop**
— [Sale Catalogue] The Celebrated Collection of Americana. NY, 1966-70. 8 vols. 8vo, bds, index in cloth; backstrips faded or discolored, vol I rear joint cracked. Rear endpaper torn out. sg Apr 11 (27) $325

**Streeter Library, Thomas Winthrop**
— Bibliography of Texas. Cambr., Mass, 1955-60. One of 600. Parts 1-3, Vol I; lacking Part 3, Vol II. O Dec 5 (139) $250
— [Sale Catalogue] The Celebrated Collection of Americana. NY, 1966-70. 8 vols, including Index. 4to, bds. bba Oct 5 (399) £240 [Forbes Smiley]; cb Feb 14 (2575) $650
Anr copy. Orig bds. Ck Apr 12 (277) £220
Anr copy. Bds. Vols I, IV & Index "well used". ds July 27 (180) $425
Anr copy. Bds. Warren Howell's annotated copy. Sold with a copy of Streeter's Americana - Beginnings. Robbins copy. pba Mar 21 (352) $2,500; sg Oct 26 (354) $500; sg Oct 26 (355) $225

**Strickland, Agnes, 1796-1874**
— Lives of the Queens of England. L, 1854. 8 vols. 12mo, contemp calf gilt. pba June 20 (314) $120
Anr Ed. L, 1869. 6 vols. 8vo, calf gilt. pba Sept 14 (332) $225
Anr Ed. L, 1885. 8 vols. Half calf gilt. sg Sept 21 (48) $475
Imperial Ed. Phila., [1902-3]. one of 1,000. 16 vols. Mor gilt; spines rubbed. cb Feb 14 (2746) $800
Victoria Ed. 16 vols. Half mor gilt; joints worn, spine foot worn. pba Dec 14 (138) $375
— Seven Ages of Women.... Bungay, 1827. 8vo, orig bds; backstrip renewed. Library stamp on tp & at end. b Dec 5 (369) £150

**Strickland, William, 1787?-1854**
— Reports on Canals, Railways, Roads, and Other Subjects.... Phila., 1826. 1st Ed. Oblong folio, orig half lea; worn & stained. With 73 views on 62 plates. Some browning, including plates; old dampstain at top edge. bbc Feb 26 (408) $850

**Stringa, Giovanni**
— Vita di S. Marco Evangelista.... Venice: Francesco Rampazetto, 1610. 8vo, contemp vellum, with traces of painted enamel arms. sg Mar 21 (309) $175

**Strong, James C.**
— Wah-Kee-Nah and her People.... NY, 1893. 12mo, orig cloth; extremities rubbed. pba Apr 25 (694) $55

**Strong, Leonard Alfred George, 1896-1958.** See: Golden Cockerel Press

**Strong, Roy**
— The English Icon: Elizabethan and Jacobean Portraiture. L, 1969. 4to, cloth, in dj. bba Oct 19 (77) £70 [Sims Reed]
— Tudor & Jacobean Portraits.... L: National Portrait Gallery, 1969. 2 vols. 4to, cloth; shelf label removed from spines. sg Jan 11 (310) $200

**Strother, David Hunter, 1816-88**
— The Blackwater Chronicle. A Narrative of an Expedition....By "The Clerke of Oxenforde." NY, 1853. 8vo, orig cloth; spine worn & chipped. Some foxing & soiling. O Feb 6 (222) $250

**Strouse, Norman H.**
— The Passionate Pirate. North Hills PA: Bird & Bull Press, 1964. One of 200. Half mor. sg Sept 14 (71) $325

**Strubberg, Friedrich Armand**
— The Backwoodsman, or Life on the Indian Frontier. Bost., 1866. 12mo, cloth; spine ends & corners worn with glue repairs. With 8 plates. pba Aug 8 (195) $550

**Struck, Hermann**
— Die Kunst des Radierens. Berlin, 1919. 4to, orig bds; spine lacking. With 5 plates. Some foxing. wd May 8 (733) $400
5th Ed. Berlin, 1923. 4to, orig cloth; extremities worn, stain to top of back cover, hinges cracked, front free endpaper lacking. With 5 plates. sg June 13 (351) $100

**Strunsky, Anna.** See: London & Strunsky

**Strutt, Jacob George**
— Sylva Britannica. L, 1822-26. Folio, half mor; loose. With 50 mtd India-proofs. Some foxing & browning. sg Dec 7 (235) $425

**Strutt, Joseph, 1749-1802**
— A Complete View of the Dress and Habits of the People of England.... L, 1842. 2 vols. 4to, half mor gilt; joints scuffed. With 153 hand-colored plates. F Sept 21 (241) $580
— Glig-Gamena Angel-Deod.... L, 1810. ("The Sports and Pastimes of the People of England.") 2d Ed. 4to, contemp half sheep; needs rebdg. With hand-colored frontis & 39 plates. Library markings. sg Mar 7 (549) $175
Anr Ed. L, 1831. 8vo, early half mor gilt. sg Mar 7 (550) $120
Anr Ed. L, 1845. 4to, half mor; rubbed. O Jan 9 (221) $200

**Struve, Burcard Gotthelf**
— Bibliotheca Philosophic a in suas Classes Distributa. Jena, 1707. 8vo, modern bds; worn. O Mar 26 (271) $130
— Neuester Gelehrter Staat von Paris.... Jena, 1724. 8vo, contemp bds. Some foxing. O Mar 26 (272) $475

**Stryker, Roy Emerson —& Wood, Nancy**
— In This Proud Land. Greenwich, [1973]. 4to, cloth, in worn dj. sg Feb 29 (131) $90

**Stryker, William S.**
— The Battles of Trenton and Princeton. Bost., 1898. 8vo, orig cloth. NH July 21 (358) $100

**Stuart, Charles Edward.** See: Stuart & Stuart

**Stuart, Granville**
— Forty Years on the Frontier.... Cleveland, 1925. 2 vols. Orig cloth; worn & soiled. wa Feb 29 (583) $230

1st Ed. - Ed by Paul C. Phillips. 2 vols. Orig cloth; corners bumped. With 10 plates. Robbins copy. pba Mar 21 (353) $600

— Montana As It Is. NY, 1865. 1st Ed. 19th-cent half mor; joints repaired; extremities scuffed. Tp dampstained. Robbins copy. pba Mar 21 (354) $19,000

**Stuart, James, 1713-88 —& Revett, Nicholas, 1720-1804**
— The Antiquities of Athens. L, 1762-1830. 4 vols, plus Supplement. Folio, modern half calf. With 2 ports & 368 plates, folding map of Greece in Vol III hand-colored in outline. Some foxing. S June 27 (163) £19,000

**Stuart, James, 1775-1849**
— Three Years in North America. NY, 1833. 1st American Ed. 2 vols. 12mo, orig half cloth; joints weak. Browned. sg Oct 26 (356) $110

**Stuart, John, LL.D.**
— Sculptured Stones of Scotland. Edin.: Spalding Club, 1856-67. 2 vols. Folio, half mor; scuffed. Some foxing. sg June 13 (352) $175

**Stuart, John Sobieski Stolberg —& Stuart, Charles Edward**
— The Costume of the Clans. Edin., 1892. One of 500. Folio, half mor; worn & stained. With engraved title & 36 plates. CG June 12 (25) £400

**Stuart, Moses**
— A Grammar of the Hebrew Language. Andover, 1831. 8vo, orig half cloth; extremities worn. sg Oct 26 (185) $70

Anr Ed. Andover, 1838. 8vo, orig half cloth; needs rebdg, front free endpaper & flyleaf lacking. sg Oct 26 (186) $70

— A Hebrew Chrestomathy. Andover, 1829. 8vo, early half sheep; needs rebdg. sg Oct 26 (187) $60

— A Hebrew Grammar with a Praxis on Select Portions of Genesis and the Psalms. Andover: Codman Press, 1823. 8vo, early half sheep; loose. Library markings. sg Oct 26 (188) $50

— A Hebrew Grammar without the Points. Andover, 1813. 8vo, early half calf. sg Oct 26 (189) $110

**Stuart, Robert, 1785-1848**
— The Discovery of the Oregon Trail. NY, 1935. Ed by P. A. Rollins. 8vo, cloth. pba Nov 16 (259) $110; pba July 25 (356) $110

1st English Ed. 8vo, buckram in dj; d/j soiled & darkened, spine head chipped, cover stained. Robbins copy. Inscr to Graff from E. Eberstadt. pba Mar 21 (355) $170

Anr Ed. NY, [1936]. pba Feb 13 (179) $150

**Stubbe, Henry, 1632-76**
— The Indian Nectar... Chocolata. L, 1662. 1st Ed. 8vo, late 19th-Cent mor. Title with repaired hole & marginal tear; G3 torn; H2 with burn mark; I2v with ink stain; some browning & spotting. Ck Mar 22 (285) £1,400

**Stuck, Hudson, 1863-1920**
— Voyages on the Yukon and its Tributaries.... NY, 1917. Orig cloth; corners bumped, worn. F June 20 (62) $90

**Studer, Jacob Henry**
— The Birds of North America. NY, 1888. Folio, orig half calf; broken, worn. With 119 colored plates. Old dampstain to a few margins; minor smudging & marking to text. bbc June 24 (286) $290

Anr copy. Half mor; spine head bumped, corners worn. With port & 120 chromolitho plates, including 2 copies of Plate 36. Some soiling. cb Oct 17 (140) $250

Anr Ed. NY, 1897. 4to, orig lea gilt; spine ends chipped, joints cracked. sg Dec 7 (209) $350

Anr copy. Half sheep; front cover & first few leaves loose. With 119 colored plates. sg May 9 (291) $300

Anr Ed. NY, 1903. Folio, cloth; joints & hinges cracked, insect damage to cloth. With 119 colored plates. pba June 20 (315) $190

— Studer's Popular Ornithology: The Birds of North America. Columbus, Ohio, [1874]-78. Illus by Theodore Jasper. Together, 2 vols in 1. 4to, mor gilt; hinges reinforced. Some rubbing to plates. rs Nov 11 (120) $250

Anr Ed. Columbus, Ohio, & NY, 1881. Folio, mor gilt; becoming disbound, stained. With litho title & 119 colored plates. rs Nov 11 (121) $300

Anr copy. Later half mor; extremities worn. With litho title & 119 colored plates. Marginal repairs to prelims. sg Dec 7 (207) $550

Anr copy. Modern cloth; index bound before title. With litho title & 119 colored plates. sg Dec 7 (208) $400

**Studies...**
— Studies from Leading Photographers. Chicago: C. Hetherington, [c.1880]. 4to, cloth; worn & soiled, both inner hinges cracked. NH June 1 (304) $200

**Studio...**
— The Studio: An Illustrated Magazine of Fine and Applied Art. L, 1893-1903. Vols 1-27. Later cloth. S May 16 (148) £640

## STUDIO...

Vols 1-48. L, 1893-1910. Orig cloth; some spines chipped. S May 16 (147) £1,500
Yearbooks, 69 vols. L, 1906-78. Cloth or wraps, all but 4 in orig bdgs. S May 16 (149) £2,300

**Stuermer, H.**
— Sammlung von National-Trachten und andern zu Charakter-Masken passenden Kostuemen. Berlin: L. W. Wittich, 1826. 8vo, later half calf. With 26 hand-colored plates. Tp in Ms. S Mar 28 (154) £300

**Sturgis, William B.** See: Derrydale Press

**Sturt, Capt. Charles, 1795-1869**
— Narrative of an Expedition into Central Australia. L, 1849. 1st Ed. 2 vols. 8vo, mor by Baynutn-Riviere. With 1 folding map, 2 uncolored & 4 hand-colored lithos, 10 engraved plates. Without the large folding map. S June 27 (253) £750
— Two Expeditions into the Interior of Southern Australia.... L, 1833. 1st Ed. 2 vols. 8vo, orig cloth, unopened; rebacked in calf, 1 gathering loose. With 15 plates & maps, 4 hand-colored. Foxing to uncolored plates & 2 of them chipped; library stamps on titles. S June 27 (254) £460

**Styron, William**
— Lie Down in Darkness. Indianapolis & NY, [1951]. 1st Ed. In dj. sg Dec 14 (275) $175; sg June 20 (363) $250
— Sophie's Choice. NY, [1979]. 1st Ed, One of 500. pba Aug 22 (445) $75; sg Dec 14 (276) $175; sg June 20 (365) $110
— This Quiet Dust. NY, 1982. 1st Ed, One of 250. sg June 20 (366) $80

**Suares, Andre, Pseud.**
— Voyage du condottiere. Paris, 1930. One of 30 on japon with additional suite of the illusts, 4 unused illusts & a watercolor sketch sgd by the artist. Illus by Louis Jou. Folio, mor extra by Gruel, orig wraps bound in. S Nov 21 (417) £500

**Suckling, Sir John, 1609-42.** See: Golden Cockerel Press

**Sudek, Josef**
— Janacek-Hukvaldy. Prague, 1971. 4to, cloth, in dj. sg Feb 29 (314) $225
— Praha. Prague, 1948. 4to, cloth, in worn dj with tears; bdg with split on spine. sg Feb 29 (315) $110
— Praha panoramatika. Prague, 1959. Oblong 4to, cloth, in dj. sg Apr 24 (605) $600
— Pro Fily 1: Josef Sudek. Prague, 1980. Folio, loose with pamphlet in portfolio with pictorial folding jacket. With 18 photographs. sg Feb 29 (319) $200

**Sudhoff, Karl**
— Erstlinge der paediatrischen Literatur. Munich, 1925. 4to, orig vellum. sg May 16 (506) $80

**Sue, Eugene, 1804-57**
— The Wandering Jew. L, 1844-45. 1st Ed in English. 3 vols. 8vo, calf gilt by Zaehnsdorf. cb Oct 17 (301) $325

## AMERICAN BOOK PRICES CURRENT

**Suess, Eduard**
— The Face of the Earth. Oxford, 1904-8. 3 vols. bba May 30 (414) £75 [Henly]

**Suetonius Tranquillus, Caius**
See also: Limited Editions Club
— De vitae XII Caesarum. [Venice: Printer of the 1480 Valla], 1480. Folio, 18th-cent vellum over paper bds; tear in rear cover & stain on front. 38 lines; types 112R, 112Gk. With 12 initials in gold opening each book with white-vine decoration on red, green & blue background with white dots; 1st initial with 3-sided border & armorial in lower border. Wormhole in final quires touching letters. 108 (of 110) leaves; with b7,8 cancelled. Goff S-820. C Apr 3 (232) £5,500

Anr Ed. Venice, 1506. ("Vitae duodecim Caesarum.") Folio, contemp half pigskin over wooden bds; lacking catches & clasps, lower outer corner of front cover chipped, crack in rear cover. Marginal dampstaining at ends; some underscoring & marginalia; k3.6 browned. sg Apr 18 (189) $1,000

Anr Ed. Lyons: Joannem Frellonium, 1548. ("Duodecim Caesares.") Folio, 17th-cent mor with gilt arms of Paul Petau; tooled inscr erased from lower edge of upper cover, rubbed. S June 12 (127) £2,100

— The Historie of Twelve Caesars, Emperors of Rome. L, 1606. Bound with: Justinus, Marcus Junianus. The History of Justine. L, 1606. Folio, calf; worn & stained, lacking free endpaper. 1st tp soiled; 1 leaf at rear with split up gutter; marginal ink marks & a few notes to 1st work. STC 23423 & 24923. pba June 20 (317) $1,500

Anr Ed. L, 1677. Calf; front cover detached, rear joint rubbed, last page adhered to rear pastedown. pba Aug 22 (654) $150

Anr Ed. L, 1931. Ltd Ed. Trans by Philemon Holland. Unopened. wa Nov 16 (34) $80

**Sueyro, Emanuel**
— Anales de Flandes. Antwerp, 1624. 1st Ed. 2 vols in 1. Folio, old calf gilt; spine ends chipped, covers detached. Browned. sg Mar 21 (305) $750

**Suffolk...**
— The Suffolk Garland: or, A Collection of Poems, Songs.... L, 1818. 8vo, later mor gilt by Birdsall. S Apr 23 (296) £80

**Sullivan, Sir Arthur, 1842-1900.** See: Gilbert & Sullivan; Limited Editions Club

**Sullivan, Eleanor**
— Whodunit: A Biblio-Bio-Anecdotal Memoir of Frederic Dannay. NY, 1984. 1st Ed, One of 150. O Dec 5 (122) $50

**Sullivan, Francis Stoughton**
— An Historical Treatise on the Feudal Law.... Dublin, 1772. 8vo, disbound. Marginal dampstaining throughout. sg Mar 21 (193) $175

## Sullivan, Mark, 1874-1952
— Our Times, 1900-1925. NY, 1926-35. Avondale Ed, One of 20 presentation sets. 6 vols. Half mor. Vol V with creasing & some pencil marks to prelims. Inscr. pba Aug 8 (608) $225

## Sullivan, Maurice S.
— The Travels of Jedidiah Smith.... Santa Ana CA, 1934. With frontis & 11 plates & folding facsimile map. pba Feb 13 (173) $200

## Sully, Maximilien de Bethune, Duc de
— Memoires des sages et royales oeconomies d'estat, domestiques, politiques...de Henry le Grand. Londres [Paris], 1745. 3 vols. 4to, contemp calf gilt, armorial bdg; scuffed, hinges weak. wd May 8 (81) $150

Anr Ed. Londres [Paris], 1747. 3 vols. 4to, contemp calf; worn. With 66 ports within ornamental borders. S Apr 23 (165) £180

Memoirs. L, 1810. 5 vols. 8vo, contemp russia gilt. pba Sept 14 (338) $225

## Summerhayes, Martha
— Vanished Arizona. Salem, [1911]. 2d Ed. Orig cloth; covers rubbed. Robbins copy. pba Mar 21 (356) $55

## Summerson, John. See: Roxburghe Club

## Sumner, Charles, 1811-74
— Speech of Hon. Charles Sumner on the Cession of Russian America to the United States. Wash., 1867. 8vo, orig wraps; spine lacking, wraps detached & worn & stamped Library of Congress Duplicate. With folding colored map. Map detached & with closed tears. wa Feb 29 (271) $325
— Works. Bost., 1870. 15 vols. 8vo, contemp half calf gilt; Vol I front cover detached. Sgd in Vol I. sg Sept 21 (49) $300

## Sun Artists
— Sun Artists. L, 1889-91. Nos 1-8. Folio, Disbound. With 32 plates. sg Apr 24 (606) $2,000

## Sunderland Library, Charles Spencer, 3d Earl of
— [Sale Catalogue] Bibliotheca Sunderlandiana. Catalogue of the Sunderland or Blenheim Library. L, 1881-83. 6 vols in 1 (including Returned Imperfects). 8vo, contemp cloth. Price lists bound in for Parts 1-5. Adrian McLaughlin's annotated copy. bba May 9 (122) £85 [Maggs]

## Sunshine...
— Sunshine in the Country. A Book of Rural Poetry. L, 1861. Illus by J. Grundy. 4to, orig cloth; spine ends worn, joints cracked, hinge repaired, prelims detached. With 20 albumen photos. sg Feb 29 (124) $325

## Surrealism...
— Le Surrealisme, meme. [Paris, 1956-59]. Ed by Andre Breton. Nos 1-5 (all pbd). 8vo, pictorial wraps; creased. Lacking the 2 separate booklets. bba July 18 (25) £120 [Breckenridge]

## Surtees, Robert Smith, 1803-64
— The Analysis of the Hunting Field. L: Ackermann, 1846. 1st Ed, Issue not stated. 8vo, mor by Riviere, orig bdg bound in; rubbed. With 7 hand-colored plates, including engraved title. Some foxing & soiling. O Jan 9 (5) $325

Anr Ed. L, 1903. One of 50 with plates in 2 states. Orig vellum. With engraved title & 12 plates in 2 states. sg Mar 7 (551) $100

— "Ask Mama...." L, 1858. 1st Ed in Book form. - Illus by John Leech. 8vo, 19th-cent half mor; joints & extremities rubbed. F Mar 28 (297) $90

— Handley Cross, or the Spa Hunt. L, 1854. 2d Issue. 8vo, orig cloth; some wear. O Jan 9 (224) $160

Anr Ed. L: Edward Arnold, [c.1910]. ("Handley Cross or Mr. Jorrocks's Hunt.") One of 250. Illus by Cecil Aldin. 2 vols. Half cloth; endpapers foxed. With 24 color plates. K June 23 (478) $325

— Hawbuck Grange. L, 1847. 8vo, orig cloth. Minor soiling & foxing. O Jan 9 (226) $80

— Hillingdon Hall, or the Cockney Squire.... L, 1845. 3 vols. 12mo, contemp mor-backed calf. Some foxing & soiling. O Jan 9 (227) $140

— Jorrocks's Jaunts and Jollities. L: Ackermann, 1843. 2d Ed. - Illus by Henry Alken. 8vo, mor gilt by Riviere. With 15 hand-colored plates. O Jan 9 (228) $1,400

Anr copy. Mor gilt by Riviere, orig wraps bound in; spine rubbed. With 14 hand-colored plates. rs Nov 11 (122) $200

3d Ed. L, 1869. 8vo, orig cloth; rubbed. With 16 hand-colored plates, including tp & frontis. b Sept 20 (496) £70

Anr copy. Lea; extremities worn. NH July 21 (374) $150

Anr copy. Modern half lev gilt; bookplate removed. With 16 color plates, including tp & frontis. sg Mar 7 (554) $90

Anr Ed. L: Kegan Paul, [1901]. 4to, half mor gilt. sg Mar 7 (555) $100

— Mr. Facey Romford's Hounds. L, 1865. 1st Ed in Book form. 8vo, mor by Tout, orig wraps & ads bound in. With 24 hand-colored plates. Upper corner chewed; some foxing & soiling. O Jan 9 (229) $200

— Mr. Sponge's Sporting Tour. L, 1853. 1st Ed in Book form. 8vo, orig cloth; rebacked retaining orig backstrip, spine & front cover blistered. sg Mar 7 (556) $90

— [Sporting Novels]. L, 1853-88. Mixed Ed (1 vol not a 1st Ed). 6 vols. 8vo, calf gilt. b Sept 20 (575) £380

Anr Ed. L: Bradbury, Agnew & Co., [1890s]. 6 vols. 8vo, half mor gilt; extremities rubbed. sg Mar 7 (558) $200

## Sutherland Collection, Alexander Hendras
— Catalogue of the Sutherland Collection. L, 1837. 2 vols. Folio, orig half mor. bba May 30 (17) £65 [Baker]

## SUTHERLAND

**Sutherland, James**
— A Narrative of the Loss of his Majesty's Ship the Litchfield.... L, 1761. 8vo, mor. b May 30 (188) £220

**Sutherland, R. Q. —& Wilson, R. L.**
— The Book of Colt Firearms. Kansas City, [1971]. 4to, cloth, in frayed dj; some wear. O Oct 10 (262) $160
One of 500. Lea gilt; some wear. Inscr by both. O Oct 10 (260) $275
Anr Ed. Minneapolis, [1993]. One of 150. 4to, syn gilt; minor wear. O Oct 10 (272) $150

**Sutphen, W. G. van T.**
— The Golfer's Alphabet. NY, 1898. 1st Ed. - Illus by A. B. Frost. 4to, half cloth; extrems rubbed. pba Nov 9 (77) $400

**Sutter, John A., 1803-80**
See also: Grabhorn Printing
— Statement Concerning Early California Experiences. Sacramento: Sacramento Book Collectors Club, 1943. One of 160. Ed by Allan R. Ottley. Orig cloth. With frontis port. Larson copy. pba Sept 28 (702) $160

**Sutton, Martin H. F. —& Others**
— Golf Courses: Design, Construction and Upkeep. L: Simpkin Marshall, 1933. 1st Ed. - Intro by Bernard Darwin. Cloth; extrems & spine ends rubbed. Endpapers foxed. pba Nov 9 (78) $550

**Svoboda, Alexander**
— The Seven Churches of Asia. L, 1869. 4to, orig cloth. With 20 mtd photographs. b May 30 (69) £400

**Swainson, Isaac**
— An Account of Cures by Velnos' Vegetable Syrup. L, 1790. 12mo, modern half calf. Ck Mar 22 (293) £120

**Swainson, William, 1789-1855.** See: Bligh Collection, William

**Swallow, George Clinton**
— Geological Report of the Country along the Line of the South-Western Branch of the Pacific Railroad, State of Missouri. St. Louis, 1859. 8vo, cloth; worn, spine frayed. With folding color map & 2 plates. wa Feb 24 (457) $220

**Swammerdam, Jan, 1637-80**
— The Book of Nature; or, the History of Insects.... L, 1758. Folio, modern half calf. With 53 plates. Library stamp on tp & each plate; some foxing; marginal stains. S Mar 29 (713) £340
Anr copy. Contemp russia gilt; rubbed. Foxed. S June 12 (286) £460
— Bybel der natuure, of historie der insecten.... Leiden, 1737-38. 2 vols. Folio, contemp half calf gilt; worn. With 53 plates. Marginal tear repaired in Plate 31; some browning. S Nov 30 (333) £1,000

## AMERICAN BOOK PRICES CURRENT

— Historia insectorum generalis.... Utrecht, 1693. 4to, contemp vellum; worn & soiled. With folding table & 13 plates. marginal repair to last leaf; some browning. S June 12 (285) £250

**Swan, Abraham**
— The British Architect: or, The Builder's Treasury of Stair-Cases. L, 1745. 1st Ed. Folio, recent half calf; new endpapers. With 60 plates. Tp margin repaired. bba Sept 7 (41) £450 [Ash]
— The British Architect: or, the Builder's Treasury of Stair-Cases. L, 1750. 2d Ed. Folio, 19th-cent half sheep; spine & corners worn. With 59 (of 60) plates; lacking Plate 40. Browned. sg Jan 11 (17) $325
— The Carpenters Complete Instructor.... L, 1768. Folio, contemp half calf; worn & scuffed, cracks at joint ends. With 55 plates. Some browning, foxing & finger-soiling; tp nearly detached; tp stained at bottom; lacking all blanks & free endpapers; old dampstain at bottom of last 10 plates. bbc Feb 26 (253) $650

**Swan, James**
— The Northwest Coast; or, Three Years' Residence in Washington Territory. NY, 1857. 8vo, bds; joint split, minor worming to rear joint & hinge. A few stains; folding map frayed at edge. wa Feb 29 (479) $160

**Swarbreck, Samuel D.**
— Sketches in Scotland. L, 1839. Folio, contemp half mor; spine def. With litho title & 24 plates. Marginal dampstaining; some spotting; a few plates loose. bba June 6 (68) £450 [Grant & Shaw]
Anr copy. Half roan; covers loose. With title, dedication, & 23 (of 24) plates. Spotting & some fraying at edges. S Oct 26 (409) £400 [Map House]

**Swasey, W. F.**
— The Early Days and Men of California. Oakland, 1891. 1st Ed. 8vo, orig mor; front & rear joints cracked. With 4 plates. Larson copy. pba Sept 28 (704) $375

**Swaysland, Walter**
— Familiar Wild Birds. L, 1883-[88?]. Series 1-2 (of 4) in 2 vols. Pictorial cloth. With 80 color plates. sg May 9 (292) $110

**Swedenborg, Emanuel, 1688-1772**
— Opera philosophica et mineralia. Dresden & Leipzig, 1734. 3 vols. Folio, contemp calf; worn. With port (cut close) & 156 on 125 plates, some folding. Some plates trimmed at outer edge; folding plate at P.412 of Vol III torn & repaired; some staining & browning. Sold w.a.f. Madsen copy. S Mar 14 (349) £3,200

**Sweet, Robert, 1783-1835**
— The British Warblers. L, 1823-[29]. 8vo, orig bds; backstrip torn, small tears in endpapers. With 16 hand-colored plates. Fattorini copy. C Oct 25 (47) £500

— Flora Australasica.... L, 1827-28. 8vo, orig cloth; spine splitting & def at top, endleaves fragile. With 56 hand-colored plates. Met May 22 (453) $2,700

## Swift, Jonathan, 1667-1745

See also: Golden Cockerel Press; Limited Editions Club

— The Drapier's Letters. L, 1730. ("The Hibernian Patriot: being a Collection of the Drapier's Letters.") 8vo, contemp sheep; worn, joints cracked. sg Mar 21 (120) $275

— Gulliver's Travels. L, 1726. ("Travels into Several Remote Nations of the World.") Teerink's "AA" Ed (2d 8vo Ed). 2 vols. Modern calf gilt; Vol I front cover detached. sg Mar 21 (312) $1,300

Anr Ed. Dublin, 1792. 8vo, contemp calf; loss to upper cover. With 4 maps. N2 with tear. b May 30 (421) £55

Anr Ed. L & NY, 1909. Illus by Arthur Rackham. 4to, orig cloth. With 12 colored plates. pba Aug 22 (839) $95

Anr copy. Half calf gilt; extremities worn. With 12 color plates. sg Sept 14 (307) $90

One of 750. Orig cloth; soiled. With 13 colored plates. Some discoloration. S Nov 2 (136) £420 [Sotheran]

Anr copy. With 13 colored plates. sg Sept 14 (308) $550

Anr copy. Orig cloth; spine ends frayed, soiled. sg Feb 15 (261) $300

— A Tale of a Tub. L, 1710. 5th Ed. 8vo, calf gilt; some wear & soiling. With 8 plates. NH Sept 16 (394) $210

— Voyages de Gulliver. Paris, 1797 [An V]. 2 vols in 4. 12mo, contemp mor gilt. With 10 plates. Fuerstenberg - Schaefer copy. S Dec 8 (584) £900

— Works. L, 1766. 27 vols. 8vo, contemp calf; vol I cover detached & repaired, spines worn. CE Nov 8 (247) $150

Anr Ed. Dublin, 1774. Ed by John Hawkesworth. 8vo, contemp calf gilt; spine ends chipped, Vol IV with front cover detached. pba Apr 4 (413) $200

Anr Ed. L, 1784. 17 vols. 8vo, contemp calf; scraped. Some discoloration & spotting. S June 13 (426) £200

## Swinburne, Algernon Charles, 1837-1909

See also: Golden Cockerel Press; Kelmscott Press

— Ode on the Proclamation of the French Republic.... L, 1870. 8vo, orig wraps; front hinge reglued, corners soiled & worn. pba June 20 (321) $50

— Songs Before Sunrise. L: Florence Press, 1909. One of 12 on vellum. 4to, orig vellum gilt. bba May 9 (490) £600 [Sotheran]

Anr copy. Mor extra mosaic bdg by Riviere. sg Oct 19 (245) $3,800

— The Springtide of Life. L, 1918. Illus by Arthur Rackham. 4to, orig cloth, in dj with spine wear. With 8 colored plates. sg Feb 15 (262) $225

One of 765. Half vellum; rubbed. With 9 colored plates. Some foxing. bba May 9 (260) £100 [Bankes Books]

Anr copy. Half vellum; discolored. With 9 colored plates. S Nov 2 (133) £200 [Sotheran]

— William Blake: A Critical Essay. L, 1868. 2d Ed. 8vo, later wraps. With 9 hand-colored plates. pba Dec 14 (11) $50

— Works. L, 1927. Bonchurch Ed, One of 780. 20 vols, including Wise's Bibliography Half mor. cb Oct 17 (302) $1,500

## Swinburne, Henry, 1743-1803

— Picturesque Tour through Spain. L, 1810. Oblong folio, modern half calf. With frontis & 20 plates. Waterstaining at outer edges affecting surface of 10 plates.. S Nov 30 (116) £1,200

Anr Ed. L, 1823. Folio, contemp half calf; covers detached. With frontis & 20 plates. b May 30 (189) £420

Swire, Herbert, d.1934. See: Golden Cockerel Press

## Sydenham, Thomas, 1624-89

— Works. L, 1705. 4th Ed. 8vo, contemp half calf; worn. Some dampstaining. CE Nov 8 (152) £110

## Sykes Library, Sir Mark Masterman

— [Sale Catalogue] Catalogue of the Splendid, Curious, and Extensive Library.... L, 1824. 3 parts in 1 vol. 8vo, contemp mor; rebacked. With frontis port. S Oct 27 (1035) £420 [Heuer]

Anr copy. 20th-Cent half calf. Lacks frontis port; title creased & soiled. S Oct 27 (1036) £240 [Maggs]

## Sykes, Sir Percy Molesworth, 1867-1945

— A History of Persia. L, 1930. 2 vols. Orig cloth; rubbed. Tear to folding map. bba July 18 (372) £100 [Lester]

Sylva... See: Evelyn, John

## Sylvester, Joshua, 1563-1618

— The Parliament of Vertues Royal.... [L: for H. Lownes], 1614-15-[17]. 8vo, contemp calf; soiled. Marginal inkstain on A1-2. b Sept 20 (184) £140

## Sylvius, Jacobus, 1478-1555

— De medicamentorum simplicum delectu, praeparationibus, mistionis modo, libri tres. Leiden: Jean de Tournes & Gulielmus Gazieus, 1548. Bound with: Galen, Claudius. De alimentorum facultatibus libri tres. Lyons: Guillaume Rouille, 1547. 2 works in1 vol. 16mo, contemp calf; extremis & covers repaired. With 2 title devices. Silvius: title & a2 soiled; G1 stained. Galen: lacking R4 & R5; R6 upper corner torn away; 3 leaves dampstained. Ck Mar 22 (294) £300

## Sylwan, Vivi

— Svenska Ryor. Stockholm, [1934]. 4to, half calf; hinges cracked. With 98 color plates. sg June 13 (81) $225

## Symbolum...

— Symbolum Apostolicum. A Facsimile... Paris, 1927. One of 150. 2 vols. 8vo, facsimile in vellum, text in wraps; edges cracked. sg Apr 11 (162) $110

### Syme, Patrick

— A Treatise on British Song-Birds. Edin., 1823. 8vo, contemp half calf; joints split. With 15 hand-colored plates. Fattorini copy. C Oct 25 (49) £380

Anr copy. Illus by R. Scott. Orig cloth; discolored, rebacked, old spine laid down. With 15 hand-colored plates. Some offsetting. S Oct 27 (786) £200 [Grahame]

### Symes, Michael

— Relation de l'Ambassade Anglaise.... Paris, 1800. 1st Ed in French. 3 vols; without Atlas. 8vo, contemp half mor gilt; minor wear. sg Mar 7 (352) $500

### Symonds, Mary —&
### Preece, Louisa

— Needlework through the Ages. L, 1928. 4to, half vellum; some soiling. sg June 13 (273) $225

### Symonds, Robert Wemyss

— Furniture Making in Seventeenth and Eighteenth Century England. L, 1955. Folio, orig cloth, in soiled dj. bba Apr 11 (137) £320 [Sims Reed]
— Thomas Tompion. L, 1951. One of 350. 4to, orig half mor gilt. pba Nov 30 (310) $300; sg May 16 (261) $140

### Symons, Arthur, 1865-1945

— Notes on Joseph Conrad. L, 1926. One of 250, sgd. In dj. sg Sept 21 (136) $130

### Symons, George James

— The Eruption of Krakatoa.... L, 1888. Ed by Symons. 4to, orig cloth; rubbed, rebacked retaining backstrip. With double-page chromolitho frontis & 45 plates, maps & charts, some folding. sg May 16 (262) $550

### Synge, John Millington, 1871-1909

— The Playboy of the Western World. Dublin, 1907. 1st Ed, one of 25 on handmade paper. Orig cloth. Engelhard copy. CNY Oct 27 (135) $2,600
— The Shadow of the Glen and Riders to the Sea. L, 1905. Orig wraps. Rupert Brooke's copy, sgd on verso of half-title, 1906. CE Sept 27 (270) $850

### Szarkowski, John

— The Photographer's Eye. NY, [1966]. In dj. sg Feb 29 (238) $200

### Szyk, Arthur, 1894-1951

— Ink & Blood: a Book of Drawings. NY, 1946. One of 1,000. Folio, mor. pba Mar 7 (411) $460

Anr copy. Mor gilt; spine scuffed. wa Dec 14 (582) $450

One of 1,000, sgd. Mor; spine worn & chipped. sg Feb 15 (289) $300
— The New Order. NY, [1941]. 4to, cloth, in dj with edge-tears. sg Feb 15 (291) $70

## AMERICAN BOOK PRICES CURRENT

— Washington and his Times. Vienna, 1932. With 30 (of 38) colored miniatures, matted to 4to & enclosed in a folding case Lacking tp & prelims. sg Feb 15 (292) $750

# T

### Tabard, Maurice

— Maurice Tabard. Paris, [1987]. Folio, cloth, in worn dj; bdg extremities soiled. With 103 plates. sg Feb 29 (322) $100

### Tableaux...

— Tableaux historiques de la Revolution Francaise. Paris, 1802. 3 vols. Folio, contemp calf gilt; spines rubbed, chip to spine of Vol III. With frontises & 153 plates. Fuerstenberg - Schaefer copy. S Dec 8 (585) £750

Anr Ed. Paris, 1804. 3 vols. 4to, contemp half calf; worn. With frontises & 153 plates & 66 ports. Library stamps on titles. S June 12 (178) £750

### Tachard, Gui

— Voyage de Siam de Peres Jesuites. Paris, 1686. Bound with: Choisy, Francois Timoleon de. Journal du voyage de Siam.... Paris, 1687. 4to, contemp vellum; soiled, worn. With 20 plates. Some discoloration. S Nov 30 (206) £600

Anr Ed. Paris, 1688. 12mo, contemp calf; rebacked, corners worn, some crackling, hinges repaired but cracked. With frontis & 30 plates, most folding. Brown stain affecting several leaves at top inner margin. cb Oct 17 (209) $650

### Tacitus, Publius Cornelius

— Oeuvres. Paris, 1582. Folio, contemp red mor gilt a la fanfare, with feuillage decoration, attributed to Nicolas or Clovis Eve. C May 1 (168) £4,000
— Opera. Antwerp: Plantin, 1588. 8vo, contemp calf; rubbed, joints broken. Some soiling & foxing. O Mar 5 (214) $120

Anr Ed. Antwerp, 1607. Folio, contemp vellum; soiled & worn, front free endpaper affixed to pastedown. pba June 20 (322) $55
— Tibere, ou les six premiers livres des Annales.... Paris, 1768. 3 vols. 12mo, contemp calf gilt. Fuerstenberg - Schaefer copy. S Dec 8 (587) £240
— Works. L, 1728-31. 1st Ed of Thomas Gordon's trans 2 vols. Folio, contemp calf; covers detached. sg Mar 21 (314) $150

### Tacitus, Publius Cornelius —&
### Paterculus, Marcus Velleius

— Scripta quae exstant. Paris, 1608. 3 parts in 1 vol. Folio, contemp mor gilt for J. A. de Thou, with his arms & those of his 2d wife, Gasparde de la Chastre. Jeudwine copy. C Apr 3 (234) £1,300

### Tacquet, Andreas

— Opera mathematica. Antwerp, 1707. Folio, contemp blind-stamped pigskin, with clasps; rubbed & soiled. With engraved title, port & 87 folding plates. Marginal worming. S Mar 14 (353) £900

**Tagaultius, Joannes**
— La chirurgie. Paris: Augustin Courbe, 1629. 8vo, old vellum; lacking free endpapers. Some browning & spotting. S Mar 29 (716) £150

**Taglang, Jacques.** See: Chevalier & Taglang

**Tagore, Rabindranath, 1861-1941**
— L'Offrande lyrique. Paris: F. L. Schmied, 1925. Out-of-series copy. Illus by F. L. Schmied after Jean Berque. Folio, loose as issued in wraps. pba Sept 14 (342) $2,500

**Taillandier, Yvon**
— The Indelible Miro.... NY, 1972. Folio, cloth, in dj. pba Aug 22 (620) $100

**Taine, John, 1883-1960**
— The Forbidden Garden. Reading: Fantasy Press, 1947. One of 500. In chipped dj. Stain to half-title. pba May 4 (260) $50
— The Purple Sapphire. NY, [1924]. In dj with pieces lacking from spine ends & short tears. pba May 4 (261) $50

**Taisnier, Joannes, b.1509**
— Opusculum Perpetua Memoria Dignissimum.... Cologne, 1562. 4to, modern wraps. With port of author. D3 stained. Madsen copy. S Mar 14 (354) £3,200
Anr copy. Modern vellum; warped. Lacking plate with duplicate port & final blank. sg May 16 (263) $650

**Talbot, Marion & Edith.** See: Aldrich, Thomas Bailey

**Talbot, Theodore**
— The Journals...with the Fremond Expedition of 1843.... Portland OR, 1931. Cloth. pba Apr 25 (697) $80

**Talbot, William Henry Fox, 1800-77**
— Sun Pictures in Scotland. L, 1845. 4to, contemp calf gilt. With 23 mtd calotype plates. Notice to the Reader mtd on 2d page of the plate list. P Oct 5 (8) $18,000

**Tallack, William**
— The California Overland Express. Los Angeles: Historical Society of Southern California, 1935. One of 150. Half cloth; lower corners bumped. pba Apr 25 (698) $170

**Tallentyre, Stephen G., Pseud.** See: Merriman & Tallentyre

**Tallis, John & Co.**
See also: Gaspey, William
— History and Description of the Crystal Palace. L, [1851]. 3 vols. 4to, contemp lea gilt; covers detached or starting. Library markings, plates unmarked. sg Sept 7 (165) $350

**Tamayo, Rufino**
— Tamayo. [Mexico City: Galeria de Arte Misrichi, 1967]. One of 100 specially bound, but lacking the additional sgd drawing. Folio, hand-painted calf. sg Feb 15 (297) $150

**Tan, Amy**
— The Hundred Secret Senses. NY, [1995]. 1st Ed, one of 175. pba Jan 25 (359) $60
— The Joy Luck Club. NY, [1989]. 1st Ed, Advance Reading copy. Orig wraps. pba Jan 25 (360) $250

**Tanaka, Ichimatsu**
— Wall Paintings in the Kondo Horyuji Monastery. Tokyo, 1951. Folio, loose as issued in portfolio; worn. With 36 plates, 26 of them in color. wa Dec 14 (521) $50

**Tangye, Sir Richard**
— Reminiscences of Travel in Australia, America, and Egypt. Birm., 1883. 1st Ed. 8vo, orig cloth. pba Aug 8 (198) $50

**Tannatt, Thomas Edwin Pryce**
— How to Dress Salmon Flies. L, 1914. Orig cloth; spine torn & repaired. With 12 color plates. pba July 11 (241) $100

**Tanning, Dorothea**
[-] Dorothea Tanning. Paris, [1977]. 4to, cloth. Special No of Vingtieme Siecle. sg June 13 (307) $200

**Tanselle, G. Thomas**
— Guide to the Study of United States Imprints. Cambr. MA, 1971. 2 vols. sg Oct 26 (359) $60

**Taplin, William**
— The Sporting Dictionary. L, 1803. 2 vols. 8vo, contemp calf; worn, joints broken. Some foxing. O Jan 9 (234) $140
— The Sportsman's Cabinet.... L, 1803-4. 2 vols. 4to, contemp calf; def. With engraved titles & 26 plates. b Sept 20 (497) £400

**Targ, William**
— Bibliophile in the Nursery. Cleveland, [1957]. pba Aug 22 (860) $55

**Tarkington, Booth, 1869-1946**
— The Fascinating Stranger, and other Stories. Garden City, 1923. One of 377 L.p. copies. Half cloth; some wear. F June 20 (319) $60

**Tarleton, Sir Banastre, 1754-1833**
— A History of the Campaigns of 1780 and 1781 in the Southern Provinces of North America. L, 1787. 4to, contemp sheep; worn, joints split. With folding map & 4 folding plans, all with routes colored. Repaired tear to folding map. wa Feb 29 (518) $1,700

**Taschenbuch...**
— Taschenbuch der Luftflotten... 1. Jahrgang. Munich, 1914. Orig cloth; soiled, rear joint worn. sg May 16 (87) $120

**Tassin, Christophe**
— Description de tous les cantons des Suisses. Paris: Michel Vanlochom, 1635. Oblong 8vo, contemp

## TASSIN

vellum; soiled. With engraved title & 35 views & folding map. Some soiling. S Nov 30 (92) £1,600

**Tassin, Nicolas**
— Les Plans et profils de toutes les principales villes et lieux considerables de France. [Paris: Tavernier, 1636]. 2 vols. Oblong 4to, contemp vellum. Worming to c.20 leaves in 1 vol & 60 in the other, not affecting images; library markings. sg May 9 (102) $2,800

**Tasso, Torquato, 1544-95**
— Aminta.... Paris, 1745. 12mo, contemp citron mor gilt with arms of La Live de Jully; lower joint cracked, 1 corner of lower cover rubbed. Fuerstenberg - Schaefer copy. S Dec 8 (588) £1,200

Anr Ed. Parma, 1789. 4to, contemp half mor gilt; minor worming to upper cover. Tp duplicated; some browning. bba May 9 (9) £190 [R. Franklin]

Anr copy. Later lev gilt. pba Nov 30 (58) $400

Anr Ed. Paris: Renouard, 1800. 12mo, citron mor gilt by Bozerian. Fuerstenberg - Schaefer copy. S Dec 8 (590) £360

— Discorsi...dell'Arte Poetica. Venice: G. Vassalini, 1587. 4to, old vellum. Some staining. pba Nov 30 (311) $500

— Il Forno.... Vicenza, 1581. 4to, old bds. sg Mar 21 (315) $300

— La Gerusalemme liberata. Genoa, 1617. Folio, late 17th-cent calf gilt, with arms of Archbishop Jacques-Nicolas Colbert. With frontis, title with port of Tasso & 20 plates. Frontis partly detached. C Apr 3 (235) £650

Anr Ed. Paris: Prault, 1744. ("La Gierusalemme liberata....") 2 vols. 12mo, 18th-cent mor gilt. With frontis & engraved titles. Fuerstenberg - Schaefer copy. S Dec 8 (591) £200

Anr Ed. Venice, 1745. Illus by G. B. Piazzetta. Folio, contemp calf; rebacked preserving orig spine, corners repaired. With frontis, port & 20 plates & double-port. Old marginal staining. C Apr 3 (236) £3,200

Anr Ed. Venice: A. Groppo, 1760-61. ("Il Goffredo....") 2 vols. 4to, later vellum; spines rubbed, that of Vol II wormed. cb Feb 14 (2808) $750

Anr copy. Contemp calf gilt; spine ends & corners worn, scuffed. Minor marginal repairs. CE Sept 27 (273) $750

Anr Ed. Paris, 1771. ("La Gierusalemme liberata.") 2 vols. 4to, contemp mor gilt. Tear in lower margin of Pp3 in Vol I; some browning. L. p. copy on papier de Hollande. Fuerstenberg - Schaefer copy. S Dec 8 (592) £9,500

Anr copy. 2 vols. 8vo, contemp red mor gilt to a design by Gravelot, probably by Derome le jeune. On papier de Hollande. Fuerstenberg - Schaefer copy. S Dec 8 (593) £1,500

Anr copy. Tirages-a-part & prospectus. 8vo, orig wraps. Fuerstenberg - Schaefer copy. S Dec 8 (594) £250

Anr Ed. Florence: Marenigh, 1820. 2 vols. Folio, later half mor; joints cracked, lea peeled, spine strip of Vol I detached along 1 edge. Some foxing & browning, affecting some images; marginal dampstains. cb Feb 14 (2729) $300

— Godfrey of Bulloigne.... L, 1624. ("Godfrey of Boulogne....") Folio, old calf; rebacked, worn & detached. Engraved title soiled & worn. wa Feb 1 (186) $150

Anr Ed. L, 1687. 8vo, modern half lev; new endpapers & binder's blanks. A8 recorneed. Z June 28 (266) $275

**Tassoni, Alessandro, 1565-1635**
— La Secchia rapita.... Oxford, 1737. 2 vols in 1. 8vo, 18th-cent mor gilt, with arms of Simon-Pierre Merard de Saint-Just. Fuerstenberg - Schaefer copy. S Dec 8 (597) £250

**Tate, Allen, 1899-1979**
— The Vigil of Venus. Cummington MA: Cummington Press, [1943]. Review copy. pba June 20 (114) $90

**Tate, Nahum, 1652-1715**
— The Kentish Worthies, a Poem. L, 1701. Folio, unbound. Marginal tears & annotations. bba May 30 (91) £400 [C. L. Edwards]

**Tatler...**
— The Tatler of California. Los Angeles, 1912. Vol V, no. 23 only, Wraps. pba Apr 18 (64) $80

**Tattersall, George**
— The Pictorial Gallery of English Race Horses. L, 1844. 8vo, half mor by Bayntun; rubbed. Some marginal restoration; some foxing & soiling. O Jan 9 (235) $475

— Sporting Architecture. L, 1841. 4to, orig cloth; spine chipped. Some foxing, soiling & staining. O Jan 9 (236) $150

Anr copy. Half mor; rubbed. Minor soiling, foxing & staining. O Jan 9 (237) $275

**Tatum, George B.** See: Onassis copy, Jacqueline Bouvier Kennedy

**Taubert, Sigfried**
— Bibliopola. Hamburg, L & NY, 1966. 2 vols. Folio, cloth. bba May 9 (108) £60 [Laywood]

**Taullard, Alfredo**
— Tejidos y ponchos indigenas de Sudamerica. Buenos Aires, 1964. 4to, cloth. Met Feb 24 (154) $250

**Tausk, Petr**
— Josef Sudek. Prague: Mezinarodni Fotografie/Pressfoto, 1977. Illus with photos by Sudek. 4to, silver-pictorial folding jacket. With an essay booklet laid-in & 13 photos on 12 sheets. sg Feb 29 (316) $350

Anr copy. Silver-pictorial folding jacket; worn, front cover creased. sg Feb 29 (317) $375

**Taverner, Eric —& Others**
— Trout Fishing from all Angles. L, 1933. In dj with sine ends rubbed. pba July 11 (181) $50

**Taverner, Eric —& Service, Douglas**
— The Flyfishers' Club: Library Catalogue, 1935. L, [1935]. Orig cloth. pba July 11 (299) $140

**Tayler, A. Chevallier**
— The Empire's Cricketers. L, 1905. Folio, orig cloth. With 48 chromolitho plates. A few imprints shaved. pn Oct 12 (216) £1,500

**Taylor, Arthur V.**
— Origines Golfianae: The Birth of Golf.... Woodstock, VT: Elm Tree Press, 1912. One of 500. Half cloth; spine rubbed. pba Apr 18 (160) $800

**Taylor, Bayard, 1825-78**
— Eldorado, or Adventures in the Path of Empire. NY, 1850. With: A.L.S. of Taylor, 1849; carte-de-viste with port of Taylor 1st Ed. 2 vols. 12mo, orig cloth; covers rubbed. With 8 color plates. Larson copy. pba Sept 28 (706) $1,100

Anr copy. Orig cloth; rubbed, spine ends worn, corners showing. With 8 plates. Some foxing & soiling. pba Nov 16 (260) $950

Anr copy. Orig cloth; spines & covers faded. With plates. Robbins copy. pba Mar 21 (357) $1,500

— Life and Letters of Bayard Taylor. Bost., 1884. 1st Ed. - Ed by Marie Hansen-Taylor & Horace E. Scudder. 2 vols, orig cloth; spine faded, light wear on covers at extremities. With 8 illus & 1 facsimile. Larson copy. pba Sept 28 (708) $80

— Picturesque Europe: A Delineation by Pen and Pencil.... NY, [1875-79]. Ed by Bayard Taylor. 3 vols. Folio, lea; front bds detached. Foxed. O July 9 (160) $190

Anr copy. Orig mor gilt. pba June 20 (323) $275; sg Feb 8 (339) $275

Anr copy. Vols I & II (of 3) only. Folio, half mor gilt; extremities worn. sg Mar 7 (355) $225

Anr Ed. L, [1876-79]. 5 vols. 4to, half mor; rubbed. Some staining & foxing; half-title detached in Vol V. rs Nov 11 (109) $225

Anr copy. Contemp half mor. With engraved titles & 60 plates. S Apr 23 (371) £380

— Works. NY, 1865-70. 13 vols. 8vo, contemp half calf; rubbed. bba May 30 (275) £160 [Heritage]

**Taylor, Benjamin F.**
— Short Ravelings from a Long Yarn.... Santa Ana, 1936. 2d Ed. - Foreword by Henry Raup Wagner. Half mor; spine head chipped, cover margins sunned. With 3 facsimiles. Robbins copy. pba Mar 21 (390) $180

**Taylor, Clyde Romer Hughes**
— A Pacific Bibliography. Wellington, 1951. pba Feb 13 (181) $100

Anr Ed. Oxford, 1965. In dj. pba Oct 9 (21) $70

**Taylor, Frederick**
— Recollections of a Horse Dealer. 1, 1861. 1st Ed. 12mo, orig bds; spine frayed. Some foxing & soiling. O Jan 9 (238) $60

Anr copy. Half lea, orig wraps bound in; rubbed. O Jan 9 (239) $70

**Taylor, George —& Skinner, Andrew**
— Maps of the Roads of Ireland. Dublin, 1778. 8vo, contemp calf; loose. Frontis map backed. sg May 9 (103) $1,100

Anr Ed. L, 1778. 8vo, modern half mor. With engraved title, folding map & 288 strip maps on 144 leaves. S Mar 28 (14) £240

— Survey and Map of the Roads of Scotland. Edin., [1800-38]. 8vo, contemp half calf; worn. With title, general map, & 178 pp. of strip maps. General map loose; some browning & soiling. S Oct 26 (375) £200 [Tooley]

**Taylor, Mrs. H. J.**
— Yosemite Indians and Other Sketches. San Francisco, 1936. One of 400. In dj. Inscr. pba Feb 12 (183) $60; pba Apr 25 (700) $65

**Taylor, James, 1813-92**
— The Pictorial History of Scotland. L: Virtue, [c.1870]. 2 vols in 4. 4to, contemp half mor; worn & soiled. F June 20 (82) $130

**Taylor, Jeremy, 1613-67**
— The Rule and Exercises of Holy Living. L, 1674. 10th Ed. 12mo, contemp calf. pba June 20 (324) $110

— Theologia eklektike. A Discourse of the Liberty of Prophesying. L, 1647. 1st Ed. 4to, contemp sheep; spine chipped. Marginal pencil markings throughout. sg Mar 21 (316) $300

**Taylor, John H.**
See also: Beldam & Taylor

— Taylor on Golf: Impressions, Comments and Hints. L: Hutchinson, 1902. 1st Ed. Cloth. With 48 illus. 1 plate detached. pba Nov 9 (79) $650

Anr Ed. L, 1902. Cloth; front cover tarnished. With 48 illus. Sgd on frontis verso, 28 June 1902. pba Apr 18 (161) $900

**Taylor, Joshua**
— The Art of Golf. L: T. Werner Laurie, [c.1912]. 1st Ed. Cloth; spine ends shelf worn. Sgd. pba Nov 9 (80) $275

**Taylor, L.**
— Hunting Big Game in North Western North America. Portsmouth OH, 1915. Orig cloth; some wear. O Oct 10 (265) $475

**Taylor, Paul Schuster**
— An American Exodus: A Record of Human Erosion. NY, [1939]. Illus by Dorothea Lange. In chipped & worn dj. sg Feb 29 (177) $150; wa Feb 1 (250) $55

**Taylor, Capt. Philip Meadows, 1808-76**
— Confessions of a Thug. L, 1839. 1st Ed. 3 vols. 12mo, orig half cloth; rubbed & spotted, 1 joint split. bba Nov 1 (462) £350 [Bolton]

**Taylor, Ray**
— Hetch Hetchy. The Story of San Francisco's Struggle to Provide a Water Supply.... San Francisco, 1926. One of 650. With 23 plates. Inscr & with Ls. pba Feb 12 (381) $170

**Taylor, Samuel.** See: Lang & Taylor

**Taylor, Samuel, Angler**
— Angler in all its Branches.... L, 1800. 1st Ed. 8vo, modern half mor. Some soiling. O Feb 6 (223) $100

**Taylor, Silas, 1624-78 —& Dale, Samuel, 1659?-1739**
— The History and Antiquities of Harwich and Dovercourt. L, 1730. 1st Ed. - Ed by Samuel Dale. 4to, contemp calf; rebacked, rubbed. With 11 plates. Bookseller's description stuck on tp. bba Nov 1 (78) £320 [Baldwin]

**Taylor, T. Griffith**
— With Scott: The Silver Lining.... L, 1916. pba July 25 (74) $350

**Taylor, Thomas, 1758-1835**
— A Dissertation on the Eleusinian and Bacchic Mysteries. L, [1790]. 8vo, modern half calf gilt. pba June 20 (326) $600

**Taylor Library, Thomas**
— [Sale Catalogue[ Catalogue of the Singularly Curious Library.... L: Sotheby, 1836. Bound after a biographical essay on Taylor extracted from a larger work. And: A Brief Notice of Mr. Thomas Taylor.... L, 1831. 8vo, old cloth; worn. Some stains & soiling. O Mar 26 (274) $1,100

**Taylor, W. Thomas —& Morris, Henry**
— Twenty-One Years of Bird & Bull. [North Hills, Pa.]: Bird & Bull Press, 1980. One of 350. Half lev. NH July 21 (44) $110

Anr Ed. [North Hills PA]: Bird & Bull Press, 1980. One of—350. Half mor. sg Sept 14 (73) $300

Anr Ed. [North Hills, Pa.]: Bird & Bull Press, 1980. One of—350. Half mor. With a portfolio containing Bird & Bull specimens and ephemera. sg Feb 15 (54) $300

**Taylor, William**
— Seven Years Street Preaching in San Francisco.... NY: Pvtly ptd, [n.d.]. 22d Thousand. 8vo, orig cloth. With sgd holograph note. pba Feb 12 (382) $50

**Taylor, Zachary, 1784-1850**
— Message from the President...in relation to California and New Mexico. Wash., 1850. 8vo, sheep; rear cover detached. With 7 maps. 31st Congress, 1st Session, Senate Rep. Com. No. 18. K Feb 11 (113) $300

**Tchaikovsky, Peter Ilyich, 1840-93**
— Suite No. 3 pour Orchestre Op. 55. Berlin, [1885]. Folio, contemp bds; worn & stained. Lithographed throughout. Inscr to the conductor Gustav Kogel, 8 Feb 1888 & with annotations, probably by Kogel. S Dec 1 (364) £2,600

**Tchemerzine, Stephane & Avenir**
— Bibliographie d'editions originales et rares d'auteurs francois des XVe, XVIe, XVIIe et XVIIIe siecles. Paris, 1927-33. 10 vols in 30. 8vo, orig wraps, unopened; 1 lower cover detached. bba Oct 5 (175) £520 [Franks]

**Teasdale, Sara, 1884-1933**
— Dark of the Moon. NY, 1926. One of 250. pba May 23 (425) $110

**Teasdale-Buckell, George Teasdale**
— Experts on Guns and Shooting. L, 1900. 8vo, cloth; worn. Some stains & soiling. Sold w.a.f. O June 4 (265) $110

**Techener, Jacques Joseph**
— Description bibliographique des livres choisis en tous genres.... Paris, 1855-58. 2 vols. 8vo, contemp half calf. Minor foxing. Inscr to Charles Pieters in Vol II. O Mar 26 (275) $50

**Tedeschi, Niccolo.** See: Panormitanus de Tedeschis, Nicolaus

**Teesdale, Henry**
— New British Atlas. L, 1831. Folio, contemp half mor; rubbed. With engraved title, 3 folding maps & 45 double-page county maps, all hand-colored. Small holes in title & in lower margin of N. Wales. bba June 6 (371) £900 [Baskes]

— A New General Atlas of the World. L, 1841. Folio, contemp mor; def, covers detached. With engraved title & 46 maps, hand-colored in outline. Folding map torn; tp loose. pn Dec 7 (182) £320

**Teixeira da Mota, Avelino.** See: Cortesao & Teixeira da Mota

**Teixidor, Joan.** See: Jouffroy & Teixidor

**Telehor...**
— Telehor 1-2. Brno, 1936. 4to, wire-bound pictorial wraps. Issue devoted to Laszlo Moholy-Nagy. sg Sept 7 (250) $275

**Telephone...**
— Telephone Directory. New Haven, Conn., Nov 1878. Vol I, No. 1. 8vo, orig wraps. Honeyman-Hefner copy. CNY May 17 (42) $18,000

**Telford, Thomas, 1757-1834**
— A Survey and Report...Highlands of Scotland. L, 1803-17. 8 parts in 2 vols. 4to, contemp half mor; rubbed. With 6 folding maps, hand-colored in out-

line, & 1 plate. Library stamp on tp.  b Jan 31 (349) £200

**Temoinages...**
— Temoinages pour L'Art Abstrait 1952. Paris: Editions "Art D'Aujourd'Hui", 1952. One of 1,500 with 30 pochoir plates. Ed by Julien Alvard & R. V. Gindertael. Orig printed wraps; chipped.  sg Sept 7 (325) $500

**Temple, Sir Richard Carnac**
— The Thirty-Seven Nats, a Phase of Spirit Worship Prevailing in Burma.... L, 1906. Folio, orig bds; chipped. With color title. Some spotting.  S Oct 26 (597) £360 [Randall]

**Temple, Samuel**
— Works. L, 1731. 2 vols. Folio, half mor gilt. Titles with owner's stamp & with upper extremities replaced.  pba Sept 14 (343) $300

**Temple, Sir William, 1555-1627**
— Memoirs of What Past in Christendom, from...1672 to...1679. L, 1700. 8vo, contemp calf; rebacked.  pba Aug 8 (614) $65

**Templeman, Daniel**
— The Secret History of the Late Directors of the South-Sea Company. L, 1735. 8vo, disbound.  sg Mar 21 (121) $350

**Templo, Jacob Jehuday Leon**
— Retrato del tabernaculo de Moseh. Amst.: Gillis Joosten, 1654. 4to, contemp vellum; remnants of early calf rebacking. Browned & stained throughout; early marginalia on tp.  CE Dec 6 (181) $1,900

**Tencin, Claudine Alexandrine Guerin de, 1685-1749**
— Le Siege de Calais, nouvelle historique. Paris: Didot l'aine, 1781. 2 vols. 18mo, contemp mor gilt. Fuerstenberg - Schaefer copy.  S Dec 8 (599) £360

**Tenesles, Nicola**
— The Indians of New England and the North-Eastern Provinces.... Middletown CT, 1851. 1st Ed - Ed by Joseph Barratt. 12mo, wraps preserving part of orig wrap. Phillipps copy.  S Nov 30 (143) £300

**Teniers, David, 1610-92**
— Theatrum pictorium.... Brussels, 1660. Folio, 17th-cent sheep; worn. With 120 plates only. Margins restored throughout affecting text or images; some dampstaining & worming. Sold w.a.f.  sg Dec 7 (299A) $550

**Tennent, Sir James Emerson, 1804-69**
— Ceylon. L, 1860. 2 vols. 8vo, contemp half mor gilt.  b Sept 20 (448) £90

**Tennessee**
— Nashville Business Directory. Nashville, 1857. Vol III - 1857. 12mo, orig cloth; worn, rebacked with plastic tape. Dampstained throughout.  sg Oct 26 (274) $225

**Tennyson, Alfred, Lord, 1809-92**
See also: Fore-Edge Paintings; Kelmscott Press; Limited Editions Club
— The Holy Grail. L, 1870. 8vo, mor gilt by Zaehnsdorf, 1911.  b Dec 5 (50) £190
— Idylls of the King. L, 1859. 1st Ed, 1st Issue. 8vo, mor gilt by Bayntun.  pba Mar 7 (250) $90
— In Memoriam. L, 1883. 8vo, mor gilt by the Doves Bindery, 1898, designed by T. J. Cobden-Sanderson, bound by Charles Wilkinson & finished by Charles McLeish.  C May 1 (170) £1,900
Anr Ed. L, 1900. One of 320. Illus by Charles Ricketts. 8vo, mor gilt by Putnam's.  pba June 20 (345) $550
— The Lady of Shalott. [NY, 1881]. Illus by Howard Pyle. 4to, orig gray-green pictorial cloth; free endpaper creased.  bbc Feb 26 (334) $300
— Poems, Chiefly Lyrical. L, 1830. 1st Ed. 12mo, mor gilt by Alfred Mathews.  b Dec 5 (49) £260
Anr copy. Mor extra by Cobden-Sanderson, 1890. Schimmel - Schaefer copy.  P Nov 1 (200) $19,000
— Works. Bost., 1871. 10 vols. 32mo, half lea, in orig box; rubbed.  NH June 1 (59) $410
Anr Ed. L, 1872-73. 6 vols. 8vo, contemp calf gilt.  sg Sept 21 (50) $400
Anr Ed. L, 1877. 7 vols. 8vo, mor gilt by Ramage; joints rubbed. Inscr to Richmond Thackeray-Ritchie & Annie Thackeray, July 1877, & to William Thackeray Ritchie in Vol III; with slip in Vol III with inscr to W. M. D. Thackeray, 1886 pasted on flyleaf.  bba May 30 (191) £2,400 [Mandl]
Anr Ed. Bost.: Estes & Lauriat, 1895-98. One of 1,000. 12 vols. 8vo, mor gilt.  cb Oct 17 (303) $1,800

**Tentzel, Wilhelm Ernst**
— Saxonia numismatica.... Dresden, 1705. 2 vols. 4to, contemp half vellum; Vol I with outer corners off front cover. Lower outer corner of opening leaves dog-eared; browned throughout.  sg Mar 21 (318) $375

**Terentius Afer, Publius, 185-159 B.C.**
— Andria. Verona: Bodoni, 1971. One of 160. 4to, orig half vellum gilt.  Ck May 31 (24) £260
— Les Comedies.... Rotterdam, 1717. 3 vols. 12mo, 18th-cent mor gilt. Fuerstenberg - Schaefer copy.  S Dec 8 (602) £1,100
Anr Ed. Paris, 1771. 3 vols. 8vo, mor gilt. Fuerstenberg - Schaefer copy.  S Dec 8 (604) £750
— Comoediae. Strassburg: Johann (Reinhard) Gruninger, 11 Feb 1499. ("Terenti' cum directorio vocabulorum....") Folio, modern bds. Some browning, soiling & staining; many initials in brown ink by a later hand; crude coloring or inking to woodcuts; some tears or holes. 174 (of 178) leaves; lacking prelim blank, tp, bi & cviii. Goff T-101.  cb June 25 (1774) $1,200
Anr Ed. Venice, 1558. 8vo, contemp calf gilt with forged Apollo & Pegasus plaquette on both covers. Tp soiled & nicked; some soiling & spotting throughout; t8 lacking.  P June 5 (340) $700

## TERENTIUS

Anr Ed. Amst., 1727. 2 parts in 1 vol. 4to, contemp calf; rebacked, scuffed. pba Nov 30 (312) $350

**Ternois, Daniel**
— Jacques Callot: Catalogue complet de son oeuvre dessine. Paris, [1962]. Folio, cloth, in dj. sg Jan 11 (74) $225

**Terracina, Laura**
— Discorso sopra tutti li primi canti d'Orlando Furioso. Venice: Gabriel Giolito, 1550. Landi, Ortensio. Lettere di molte valorose donne.... Venice: Giolito, 1548. 8vo, contemp calf; worn, rebacked, upper cover loose. C Apr 3 (237) £1,100

**Terry, Alfred H.**
— The Field Diary of General Alfred H. Terry. Bellevue NE: Old Army Press, [n.d.]. One of 50 bound in lea. Ed by Michael J. Koury. Inscr by Koury to John Popovich. pba June 25 (227) $225

**Terry, Daniel**
— British Theatrical Gallery.... L, 1825. Folio, contemp half mor; worn. With 20 plates. guards removed; a few leaves loose; minor spotting. Extra-illus with 18 plates, a watercolor, a drawing & a sheet of facsimile signatures. S Apr 23 (228) £400

**Terry, Ellen, 1847-1928**
— Ellen Terry and Bernard Shaw: A Correspondence. NY & L, 1931. 1st Ed. Inscr to Hugh Beaumont ("Binkie") by John Gielgud, June 1939. sg June 20 (335) $200

**Terry, George W.**
— The Alphabet Annotated for Youth and Adults in Doggerel Verse, by an Old Etonian. L, [c.1885]. 4to, orig cloth. Margin of 2 leaves frayed, affecting text. bba May 30 (343) £90 [Blankevoort]

**Tesnohlidek, Rudolf**
— The Cunning Little Vixen. NY, 1985. One of 250. Illus by Maurice Sendak. sg Dec 14 (257) $130

**Tessarini, Carlo**
— Concerti a Cinque... Opera Prima, Libro Primo... Secondo.... Amst.: Le Cene, [n.d.]. Folio, contemp bds. Complete parts. S May 15 (518) £550

**Testard, Francois Martin.** See: Segard & Testard

**Tevjashov, E. N.**
— Opisanie neskol'kikh gravjur i litografij. St. Petersburg, 1903. 4to, floral brocade cloth; extremities frayed. With 132 mtd plates. sg Sept 7 (327) $60

**Texte...**
— Texte des coustumes de la prevoste & Vicomte de Paris. Paris: Denis Thierry, 1668. Bound with: Ordonnance de Louis XIV, roy de France et de Navarre. Donnee a S. Germain en Laye au mois d'Avril 1667. Paris, 1730. 8vo, 18th-cent red mor gilt, with arms of the comte de Courbert. Fuerstenberg - Schaefer copy. S Dec 8 (606) £160

## AMERICAN BOOK PRICES CURRENT

**Thackeray, Anne Isabella**
— Alfred, Lord Tennyson and his Friends. L, 1893. One of 400. Folio, orig cloth; worn, hinges cracked. With 20 plates. bbc June 24 (592) $900

Anr copy. Orig cloth; bumped, extremities rubbed, soiled. With 25 plates. Prelims spotted. S Nov 21 (423) £200

Anr copy. Orig cloth; soiled, endpapers foxed. With frontis & 25 plates. sg Feb 29 (80) $1,500

**Thackeray, William Makepeace, 1811-63**
See also: Fore-Edge Paintings; Limited Editions Club

— An Essay on the Genius of George Cruikshank. [L], 1840. 1st Ed in Book form. Bound in 2 vols. 8vo, contemp half calf; rebacked preserving orig spines, rubbed. With 17 plates. Extra-illus with c.150 illusts by Cruikshank, all inlaid or mtd on folio leaves. Inscr by Cruikshank to Samuel Gurney & an unsgd plate bound in; some other annotations in Cruikshank's hand. bba May 30 (178A) £1,000 [Mandl]

Anr copy. 8vo, calf gilt by Worsfold; front joint starting. Tape remains to verso of frontis & extremities of a few leaves. pba Mar 7 (251) $80

Anr Ed. L, 1884. 4to, later half mor by Tout. With all of the woodcuts from the 1st Ed & a new port. L.p. copy. Extra-illus with 67 plates. S Apr 23 (218) £240

— Etchings...while at Cambridge.... L, 1878. 8vo, orig half cloth; soiled. With 11 illusts on 8 plates. S Apr 23 (217) £100

— The Four Georges.... L, 1861. 1st English Ed in Book form, 1st Issue. 8vo, orig cloth. Half-title & tp foxed. sg Sept 21 (303) $90

— The Loving Ballad of Lord Bateman. L, 1839. 1st Ed, 1st Issue. Preface & notes by Charles Dickens; illus by George Cruikshank. 16mo, orig cloth; a few leaves loose. sg Feb 8 (340) $650

— Mrs. Perkins's Ball. [L, 1847]. 1st Ed. 4to, 19th-cent half mor gilt, orig wraps bound in; rubbed. With 22 colored plates. Folding frontis backed with linen. sg Feb 8 (341) $70

— The Newcomes. L, 1853-55. 1st Ed. Orig 24/23 parts. 8vo, orig wraps; corner restored to 1st part. Some wear & foxing. cb Oct 17 (483) $600

— Notes of a Journey from Cornhill to Grand Cairo. L, 1846. 1st Ed. 12mo, contemp half mor. With hand-colored frontis. b May 30 (298) £100

— The Paris Sketch Book. L, 1840. 1st Ed. 2 vols. 12mo, later half mor. With 12 plates. B2 in Vol II torn & repaired; 1 plate repaired; some staining & spotting. bba May 30 (178) £85 [Walpole]

— Pendennis. L, 1848-50. ("The History of Pendennis.") 1st Ed in 24/23 parts, Issue not indicated. 8vo, orig wraps; some detached. pba Mar 7 (252) $140

— Roundabout Papers.... L, 1863. 1st Ed. 8vo, orig cloth; corners bumped. Inscr to Lady Martin, Christmas 1862. S Dec 18 (212) £800 [Mandl]

— The Students' Quarter or Paris Five-and-thirty Years Since. L: John Camden Hotten, [c.1874]. 1st Ed, 1st

Issue. 3 vols. 8vo, contemp half calf. With 5 colored plates. S Apr 23 (170) £130
— Vanity Fair. L, 1848. 1st Ed in Book form. 8vo, orig cloth; spine ends & joints worn, hinges cracked. CE May 22 (446) $600
1st Issue. Lev gilt; front joint rubbed. sg Sept 21 (304) $350
Issue not stated. Mor gilt by Zaehnsdorf. Edward FitzGerald's copy, with 2 notes on the flyleaves. cb Feb 14 (2730) $600
— The Virginians. L, 1857-59. 1st Ed. Orig 24 parts. 8vo, orig wraps; minor wear. Lacking some ads. bbc Feb 26 (348) $925
— Works. L, 1869. 24 vols. 8vo, half lea by Wood; some staining. Met Feb 24 (229) $400
Anr Ed. L, 1879-86. 24 vols. 12mo, contemp half calf gilt; rubbed. C July 1 (326) £250
Anr Ed. NY, 1884. 11 vols. 8vo, contemp half calf gilt. sg Sept 21 (51) $375
Anr Ed. L, 1898-99. 26 vols. 8vo, half calf gilt. b Jan 31 (122) £320
Biographical Ed. 13 vols. 8vo, orig cloth; soiled. bba May 30 (270) £130 [Classic Bindings]
Anr Ed. L, 1902. 26 vols. 8vo, half calf gilt by Ramage. pnE Sept 20 (56) £360
Anr Ed. NY, 1903-4. 32 vols. pba June 20 (333) $180

**Tharaud, Jerome & Jean**
— Un Royaume de Dieu. Paris, 1925. One of 20 lettered copies but this copy lacking extra plates & watercolor. Illus by Lucien Madrassi. 4to, mor extra with geometric onlay, by Pierre Legrain. Sold as a bdg. C June 26 (195) £3,800

**Thayer, Emma Homan**
— Wild Flowers of the Pacific Coast.... NY, [1887]. Folio, cloth; spine worn, joints split, adhesion damage to front pastedown. Library markings. pba Apr 25 (702) $80
Anr copy. Cloth; soiled & rubbed. With 24 chromolitho plates. pba July 25 (358) $110

**Thayer, James Bradley**
— A Western Journey with Mr. Emerson. Bost., 1884. In dj. Larson copy. pba Feb 12 (59) $325
1st Ed. Wraps in dj; d/j chipped & torn, darkened extremities are detaching. Robbins copy. pba Mar 21 (358) $100
Anr Ed. San Francisco: Book Club of California, 1980. One of 600. In dj. Larson copy. pba Feb 12 (60) $80

**Theakston, Michael**
— A List of Natural Flies that are Taken by Trout.... Ripon, 1853. 12mo, half mor; rebacked preserving most of older spine gilt, rubbed. Dean Sage's copy. O Feb 6 (224) £350

**Theatre...**
— The Theatre: A Monthly Review of the Drama.... L, 1878-82. 9 vols. 8vo, orig half mor; not uniform, rubbed, some covers detached, Vol I lacking spine. Some spotting. bba May 30 (221) £120 [Maggs]

**Theatrum...**
— Theatrum chemicum. Strassburg: Lazarus Zetzner, 1613. Vols I-IV (of 5). 8vo, contemp blind-stamped vellum; minor stains, Vol IV front joint partly cracked & reinforced, hinges wormed. With 6 folding tables. Browned; early underscoring; titles stamped. sg Oct 19 (238) $2,000

**Thegliatus, Stephanus**
— Oratio in die Omnium Sanctorum. [Rome: Andreas Freitag, after 1 Nov 1492]. 4to, 19th-cent bds. 34 lines; roman letter. 8 leaves. Goff T-124. S Dec 18 (82) £300 [Tenschert]

**Theilhaber, Felix A.**
— Juedischer Flieger im Weltkreig. Berlin, 1924. Bds; bumped. Met Sept 28 (222) $150

**Thelwall, John, 1764-1834**
— Poems Chiefly Written in Retirement. Hereford, 1801. 8vo, contemp half calf; rebacked using orig spine. b Dec 5 (133) £240
2d Ed. 8vo, half calf. b Dec 5 (134) £140

**Theobaldus Episcopus**
— Physiologus Theobaldi Episcopi. Bloomington: Indiana University Press, [1964]. One of 325. Illus by Rudy Bozzatti. Folio, unbound as issued. sg Feb 15 (241) $200

**Theocritus, Bion & Moschus**

### Idylls

— 1495, Feb. - Eidyllia.... Venice: Aldus 1st Issue. Folio, 18th-cent vellum. 30 lines; types 1:146Gk, 2:114R & 6:83R. Stamps & writing washed from 1st & last leaves. 140 leaves. Goff T-144. C Apr 3 (239) £7,000
— 1516, 15 Jan. - [Rome]: Zacharias Callierges. 2 parts in 1 vol. 8vo, modern mor. Some foxing; early marginalia in Greek throughout. sg Mar 21 (319) $1,200
— 1767. - L: Dryden Leach. 8vo, calf; spine head & front joint glued. pba Nov 30 (313) $110
— 1922. - The Idyls. L: Riccardi Press One of 500. Trans by Andrew Lang; illus by W. Russell Flint. 2 vols. 4to, orig half cloth, in djs. b Sept 20 (619) £60
Anr copy. Half cloth; 1 hinge repaired. sg Sept 14 (132) £120
— 1971. - Sixe Idyllia. NY One of 417. Illus by Anthony Gross. Folio, orig half cloth. bba May 9 (626) £95 [Besley]

**Therese...**
— Therese philosophe, ou memoires pour servir a l'histoire de D. Dirrag & de Mademoiselle Eradice. Londres, 1785. 2 vols in 1. 12mo, contemp mor gilt. With 20 plates. 2 leaves torn affecting text. b May 30 (536) £320

## THEROUX

**Theroux, Paul**
— Fong and the Indians. Bost., 1968. In dj. Sgd on half-title. pba Aug 22 (449) $95
— The Mosquito Coast. Bost., 1982. 1st American Ed, One of 350. pba Aug 22 (450) $60

**Thesaurus...**
— Thesaurus Geographicus. A New Body of Geography.... L: for Abel Swall & Tim Child, 1695. Folio, later calf; worn, joints starting, front pastedown torn at 1 corner, rear pastedown pulling loose. Stain at lower part of tp; some browning, soiling & marginal dampstaining; some soiling. cb Feb 14 (2559) $900
Anr Ed. L, 1695. Folio, contemp calf; rebacked & repaired, many leaves loose. With 58 maps & plans, most within text. Frayed. S Mar 28 (186) £240

**Thesiger, Wilfred Patrick**
— The Marsh Arabs. L, 1964. 1st Ed. 8vo, cloth; worn. Some discoloration. Inscr. S Oct 26 (222) £450 [Al-Ankauy]

**Thevenot, Jean de**
— The Travels.... L, 1687. 1st English Ed. Folio, contemp calf; rubbed. With frontis port, & 3 full-page plate. Some rust-holes, affecting text; 2 pp torn. S Oct 26 (223) £1,000 [Christodoulou]

**Thielmann, Max von**
— Journey in the Caucasus, Persia and Turkey.... L, 1875. 2 vols 12mo, contemp half calf gilt; extremities worn. With folding map & 14 plates. Library markings, but plates unmarked. sg Mar 7 (357) $225

**Thieme, Ulrich —&**
**Becker, Felix**
— Allgemeines Lexikon der Bildenden Kuenstler von der Antike bis zur Gegenwart. Leipzig, 1907-50. 37 vols. 4to, contemp half lea. bba Oct 5 (311) £1,200 [Maggs]
Anr Ed. Leipzig, [n.d.]. 37 vols. 4to, half syn. sg June 13 (363) $1,000

**Thiers, Louis Adolphe, 1797-1877**
— The History of the French Revolution. L, 1828. 2 vols. 4to, contemp calf; worn, spines shabby. Foxed. wa Feb 1 (158) $75

**Thissell, G. W.**
— Crossing the Plains in '49. Oakland, 1903. 12mo, orig cloth; minor wear. With 11 plates. pba Apr 25 (703) $250

**Thomas a Kempis, Saint, 1380-1471**
See also: Fore-Edge Paintings
— De imitatione Christi. Augsburg: Erhard Ratdolt, 1488. 2 parts in 1 vol. 4to, 19th-cent vellum gilt. 40 lines & headline; double column. Some headlines trimmed. 46 leaves. Goff I-16. C June 26 (138) £1,200
Anr Ed. L: R. Daniell for John Clarke, 1654. ("The Christians Pattern, or Imitation of Christ.") 24mo, modern half vellum with covers from 17th-cent em-

## AMERICAN BOOK PRICES CURRENT

broidered bdg laid down, gilt edges, with painted floral decoration. sg Mar 21 (52) $500

Anr Ed. L, 1908. ("Of the Imitation of Christ.") Illus by W. Russell Flint. Lev gilt by Bayntun-Riviere. With 12 mtd color plates. Last 10 leaves stained in right margin. sg Sept 14 (133) $325

— Opera. Nuremberg: Caspar Hochfeder, 29 Nov 1494. Folio, 19th-cent bds; some wear. 53 lines & headline; double column; types 2:168aG (title, headlines) & 1:83G (text). Last 18 leaves from anr copy & mtd on guards; outer margin of 12 repaired. 183 (of 184) leaves; lacking [*3]. Goff T-352. S Dec 18 (83) £500 [Aspin]

**Thomas, Alfred Barnaby**
— The Plains Indians and New Mexico 1751-1778. Albuquerque, 1940. In rubbed & torn dj. pba Nov 16 (198) $80

**Thomas Aquinas, Saint, 1225?-74**
See also: Limited Editions Club
— Enerrationes. Paris, 1546. Folio, modern half calf. Inkstains to y5-6; tear on Aa1-2; last 5 leaves frayed. S June 12 (129) £250
— Prima pars secunde partis summe theologie. Paris: Pierre Olivier for Francois Regnault, 19 Mar 1521. 8vo, elaborate red mor gilt of c.1575 with plaque of strapwork & azured leaves. Lower blank margin of tp & a1 cut away & tp repaired; some sidenotes at end trimmed. S Nov 30 (300) £1,600
— Summa theologicae. [Cologne: Ulrich Zel, c.1468?]. ("Summa theologicae prima pars.") Folio, contemp South German blindstamped calf over wooden bds with brass bosses, with chain & hasp; rebacked preserving part of orig spine, lacking clasps. 47-50 lines, double column, gothic letter; promptmarks for rubricator supplied in lower margins by printer or binder. Waterstaining affecting lower margins of 1st few leaves; marginal tear to f.49. 254 leaves. Hain 1439. Unpressed copy. William Morris's copy. b June 28 (68) £26,000

Anr Ed. Venice: Joannes Rubeus Vercellensis, 1497-96. ("Summa theologiae, secunda pars, pars prima [pars secunda].") 2 parts in 2 vols. Folio, contemp calf over wooden bds (wormed, rebacked) & 19th-cent half calf. Worming & staining. 131 (of 132, lacking tp) leaves & 179 (of 180, lacking last blank) leaves. Goff T-207 & T-218. S Dec 18 (85) £700 [Zioni]

Anr Ed. Venice: Andreas Torresanus de Asula et Socii, 5 Dec 1502. ("Tertia parts Sancti Thome.") Folio, modern mor. Tp & index leaves browned, with clean tears repaired; foxing & marginalia. sg Mar 21 (321) $300

— Super tertium sententiarum. Venice: Hermannus Liechtenstein, 26 Apr 1490. Folio, half sheep; bds wormed, lacking 2 clasps & catches, upper hinge split. 68 lines & headline; gothic letter. Worming at beginning & endf. 150 leaves. Goff T-167. S Dec 18 (84) £600 [Zioni]

**Thomas, Arthur Hermann**
— Formes et Couleurs. [Paris: Librairie Centrale des Beaux-Arts], 1921]. Folio, loose as issued in bd folder. With 20 pochoir-colored plates. Met Dec 14 (246) $400

**Thomas Cantipratensis**
— Der byen boeck. Leiden: I. Severz, 16 Nov 1515. Folio, contemp vellum wraps, with endpapers from a vellum Ms passionary from the 1st half of the 12th cent. Tp & last leaf torn & rebacked with loss; hole in text of I2. S Mar 28 (496) £1,400

**Thomas, Dylan, 1914-53**
— 18 Poems. L: Fortune Press, 1934. 1st Ed, 1st Issue. In dj with tear. bba Oct 19 (391) £420 [Thornton]
Anr copy. In dj. cb Feb 14 (2731) $800
Anr copy. In def dj. Inscr "Caitlin's copy lent to Emma Swan. 1938". Engelhard copy. CNY Oct 27 (137) $3,000
Anr copy. In foxed dj with chip at head of spine. Hobson copy. S June 28 (215) £800
Anr copy. Orig cloth, in torn & foxed dj. S July 11 (349) £700
— A Child's Christmas in Wales. Norfolk, [1954]. In dj. sg June 20 (369) $300
— Quite Early One Morning. L: Dent, [1954]. 1st English Ed. In repaired dj. sg June 20 (373) £70
— Twelve More Letters. N.p.: Turret Books, 1969. One of 175. 4to, cloth. pba Jan 25 (362) $50
— Twenty-Six Poems. L [ptd Verona, 1949]. One of 140. Folio, half cloth. Hobson copy. S June 28 (221) £950
Anr Ed. NY: New Directions, [1950]. One of—140. Folio, orig half cloth. Engelhard copy. CNY Oct 27 (138) $2,000
— Under Milk Wood. L, 1954. In dj. Ck Apr 12 (175) £240
Advance proof copy of the 1st Ed. Orig wraps with proof stamp; stain to lower cover, lower extremities bumped. Ck Apr 12 (174) £320
— The World I Breathe. Norfolk CT, [1939]. Orig cloth; stained & bubbled. Inscr, May 1940. Hobson copy. S June 28 (217) £1,400

**Thomas, George C., Jr.**
— Golf Architecture in America.... Los Angeles: Times-Mirror Press, 1927. 1st Ed. Cloth in dj; d/j chipped, torn, pieces missing. With color frontis. Half-title foxed. Inscr & sgd. pba Apr 18 (162) $3,250
Anr copy. Cloth. With color frontis. pba Apr 18 (163) $425

**Thomas, H. P.**
— Old English Cricket. L, 1923-29. 6 vols in 1. Inscr by A. W. Shelton to E. V. Lucas. pn Oct 12 (330) £180

**Thomas, Isaiah, 1750-1831**
— The History of Printing in America.... Albany, 1874. 2d Ed. 2 vols. 8vo, later cloth; worn. O Mar 26 (277) $100

**Thomas, Joseph B.** See: Derrydale Press

**Thomas, Lewis**
— Could I Ask You Something? NY: Library Fellows of the Whitney Museum, 1984. One of 120. Illus by Alfonso Ossorio. Folio, orig foiled bds. CE Sept 27 (217) $500

**Thomas, Michael R. Oldfield.** See: Sclater & Thomas

**Thomas, Patrick J.**
— Our Centennial Memoirs.... San Francisco, 1877. 1st Ed. 8vo, orig cloth; covers soiled, worn, front hinge cracked. Larson copy. pba Sept 28 (163) $95

**Thomas, Ralph**
— Sketches of Turkey in 1831 and 1832. By an American. NY, 1833. 8vo, modern cloth. Some spotting. b May 30 (270) £50

**Thomas, Robert, 1753-1835**
— The Modern Practice of Physic. NY, 1811. 8vo, contemp sheep; worn, joints cracked. Minor stains. sg May 16 (514) $50

**Thomas, Ronald Stuart**
See also: Gregynog Press
— The Minister. Newtown, 1953. Orig wraps. Hobson copy. S June 28 (225) £190
— The Mountains. NY: Chilmark Press, [1968]. One of 110 with an extra set of the 10 engravings. Illus by John Piper. Folio, orig half mor. Hobson copy. S June 28 (227) £260

**Thomassy, Raymond**
— Geologie pratique de la Louisiane. New Orleans, 1860. 4to, modern half mor. With 1 plate & 6 folding maps. Some foxing & browning; minor stains & soiling. O Nov 14 (176) $375

**Thome de Gamond, Aime, 1807-75**
— Carte d'etude pour le trace et le profil du canal de Nicaragua.... Paris, 1858. 4to, orig half cloth. With colored folding map. b Sept 20 (420) £150

**Thome, James A. —& Kimball, J. Horace**
— Emancipation in the West Indies. NY: American Anti-Savery Society, 1838. 8vo, wraps. sg Mar 28 (342) $90

**Thomes, William H.**
— On Land and Sea, or California in the Years 1843, '44 and '45. Bost., 1884. 1st Ed. - Illus by Childe Hassam. Cloth; worn. Larson copy. pba Sept 28 (257) $475

**Thompson & West**
— Reproduction of Thompson & West's History of Nevada, 1881. Berkeley, 1958. Ed by Myron Angel. With H. J. Poulton's Index, 1881. pba Apr 25 (554) $50
— Reproduction of Thompson & West's History of Sacramento County.... Berkeley, 1960. Intro by Allan

## THOMPSON

R. Ottley. Folio, cloth, in torn & def dj. pba Apr 25 (646) $80
— Reproduction of Thompson & West's History of Santa Barbara & Ventura Counties.... Berkeley, 1961. pba Apr 25 (655) $55

**Thompson, Charles John Samuel, 1862-1943**
— The History and Evolution of Surgical Instruments. NY, 1942. Ltd Ed. sg May 16 (512) $200

Thompson, David, 1770-1857. See: Henry & Thompson

**Thompson, Francis, 1859-1907**
— Poemes. Paris, 1939 [1942]. One of 205. Illus by Maurice Denis. Loose as issued in wraps. With 13 chromolitho plates. Small ink line on tp. cb Oct 17 (620) $1,300

**Thompson, Hunter S.**
— Hell's Angels. NY, [1967]. 8vo, orig cloth, in dj. CE May 22 (447) $350

**Thompson, Robert A.**
— Conquest of California.... Santa Rosa, Calif., 1896. 8vo, wraps; spine & edges worn, chip to front wrap. pba Apr 25 (704) $75
1st Ed. 8vo, orig wraps; front wrap detached, edges worn. With 4 plates. Robbins copy. pba Mar 21 (359) $250

**Thompson, Ruth Plumly**
— Captain Salt in Oz. Chicago, [1936]. 1st Ed. 4to, orig cloth, in 1st dj with minor chipping; minor discoloration to lower outer corner of covers. sg Oct 19 (37) $225
Anr Ed. Chicago: Reilly & Lee, [1936]. Illus by John R. Neill. Orig cloth; spine head bumped. pba Jan 18 (168) $160
— The Cowardly Lion of Oz. Chicago, [1923]. 1st Ed, 1st State. In secondary bdg. F Mar 28 (74) $140
Anr copy. Orig cloth, 1st bdg; spine ends rubbed. pba Jan 18 (170) $200
1st Canadian Ed. [Toronto, 1923]. 4to, orig cloth; spine warped, spine ends rubbed, hinges cracked, most of rear free endpaper lacking. pba Jan 18 (171) $95
Anr copy. Orig cloth, in dj with wear & crack at fold of rear flap. sg Feb 8 (177) $1,600
Anr copy. Orig cloth; tips rubbed. sg Feb 8 (178) $110
— The Curious Cruise of Captain Santa. Chicago, [1926]. 1st Ed. Orig cloth; tears along spine & extremities, hinges cracked. pba Jan 18 (169) $110
— The Giant Horse of Oz. Chicago, [1928]. 1st Ed 1st State. F Mar 28 (71) $130
Anr copy. Orig cloth; spine ends rubbed, hinges cracked. pba Jan 18 (172) $150
— The Gnome King of Oz. Chicago, [1927]. 1st Ed. Emerald green cloth; front hinge starting. pba Jan 18 (173) $140
1st Canadian Edition. Toronto: Copp Clarke, [1927]. Emerald green cloth; spine ends frayed, rear cover discolored. Lacking 1 plate. pba Jan 18 (174) $50

— Grampa in Oz. Chicago, [1924 but c.1930]. 1st Ed, 2d Issue. In def dj. With 12 color plates. pba Jan 18 (176) $130
Anr Ed. Chicago, [1924]. Early state. Orig cloth; corners bumped, worn & soiled. F Mar 28 (73A) $130
Anr copy. Orig cloth; corners bumped, soiled. F June 20 (660A) $130
Anr copy. Orig cloth; joints spotted, hinge cracked. Crease to dedication page. pba Jan 18 (175) $200
Anr copy. Orig cloth; extremities rubbed. pba Aug 22 (686) $100
— Handy Mandy in Oz. Chicago, [1937]. 1st Ed, 1st State. 4to, orig cloth. pba Jan 18 (177) $190
— The Hungry Tiger of Oz. Chicago, [1926]. 1st Ed, 1st State, with plate stock coated only on ptd side. pba Jan 18 (178) $190
Earliest state. Orig cloth; worn & soiled. F June 20 (659) $130
— Jack Pumpkinhead of Oz. Chicago, [1929]. 1st Ed. Orig cloth; edge-wear. F Mar 28 (70) $110
Anr copy. Orig cloth, in chipped dj with def spine. F June 20 (657) $140
Anr copy. Orig cloth; tear at spine head. pba Jan 18 (179) $200
— Kabumpo in Oz. Chicago, [1922]. 1st Ed, 1st State. F Mar 28 (75) $140
Anr copy. Orig cloth; hinges starting, spine ends rubbed. pba Jan 18 (180) $140
Early State. Orig cloth, in chipped & repaired dj. With sgd 8-line holograph verse about Dick Martin on verso of front free endpaper, 17 July 1970. Dick Martin copy. sg Oct 19 (35) $3,200
— The Lost King of Oz. Chicago, [1925]. 1st Ed, 1st Issue. Orig cloth; worn & soiled. F June 20 (660) $130
1st State, with plate stock coated only on ptd side. In dj with pieces lacking & short tears. pba Jan 18 (181) $700
Anr copy. Orig cloth. pba Jan 18 (182) $225
Anr copy. Orig cloth; rubbed, front hinge cracked, tape stains to front free endpaper. pba Aug 22 (689) $65
— Ojo in Oz. Chicago, [1933]. 1st Ed, 1st State. 4to, orig cloth. With 12 color plates. pba Jan 18 (183) $225
2d Ed. 4to, orig cloth. With 12 color plates. K Feb 11 (73) $200
— Ozoplaning with the Wizard of Oz. Chicago: Reilly & Lee, [1938]. 1st Ed. - Illus by John R. Neill. In dj with tears & chipping & with piece lacking from spine. pba Jan 18 (184) $300
— Pirates in Oz. Chicago, [1931]. 1st Ed. bbc Dec 18 (203) $180; K Feb 11 (74) $160
1st State. Orig cloth; bumped. With 12 color plates. pba Jan 18 (185) $140
Anr copy. 4to, orig cloth; front hinge cracked. With 12 colored plates. pba Jan 18 (186) $110
Anr Ed. Toronto, [1931]. Canadian Issue. Orig cloth; glue wear to spine, front hinge starting. Lacking plate facing p.272. pba Jan 18 (187) $60

— The Princess of Cozytown. Chicago, [1922]. 1st Ed. Orig bds; joints & extremities rubbed. pba Jan 18 (188) $170
— The Purple Prince of Oz. Chicago, [1932]. 1st Ed. Orig cloth, 1st bdg. pba Jan 18 (189) $180
— The Royal Book of Oz. Chicago, [1912]. 1st Ed, 1st State. Orig cloth; spine heel rubbed, lower edges of covers flattened. pba Jan 18 (190) $190

Anr copy. Orig cloth; front hinge repaired, small hand-coloring to front free endpaper. pba Jan 18 (191) $150

Anr copy. Orig cloth; soiled, front hinge weak. Marginal tears repaired. pba Jan 18 (192) $250

Anr copy. Orig cloth, in dj with edge wear & 2 minor repairs. Dick Martin copy. sg Oct 19 (34) $1,900

Anr Ed. Chicago, [1921]. F Mar 28 (76) $170

Anr copy. 4to, orig cloth; worn & scuffed. With 12 colored plates. F June 20 (662) $110

1st Canadian Ed, from 1st issue American sheets. Toronto: Copp Clark, [1921]. 4to, orig cloth; lacking front endpaper, rear hinge repaired. sg Feb 8 (176) $200

— The Silver Princess in Oz. Chicago: Reilly & Lee, [1938]. 1st Ed, 1st Issue. Illus by John R. Neill. pba Jan 18 (194) $275

— The Wishing Horse of Oz. Chicago, [1935]. 1st Ed. In dj with closed tears. sg Feb 8 (182) $400

Anr Ed. Chicago: Reilly & Lee, [1935]. Illus by John R. Neill. Orig cloth. With 12 colored plates. pba Jan 18 (195) $180

— Yankee in Oz. [Kinderhook, Ill.]: The International Wizard of Oz Club, [1972]. 1st Ed. - Illus by Dick Martin. 2d bdg of light blue cloth; spine ends bumped. Inscr to Justin Schiller & with Ls to Shiller laid in. pba Jan 18 (196) $425

Anr copy. 1st bdg of colored wraps. pba Jan 18 (197) $120

— The Yellow Knight of Oz. Chicago, [1930]. 1st Ed, 1st State. 4to, orig cloth; scuffed. F June 20 (656) $80

Anr Ed. Chicago: Reilly & Lee, [1930]. Illus by John R. Neill. Orig cloth; bumped, front hinge cracking. With 12 colored plates. pba Jan 18 (198) $180

**Thompson, Vincent**
— St. Helier, the Hermit.... St. Helier, 1834. 8vo, contemp half mor. b Dec 5 (143) £800

**Thompson, Winfield M. —& Lawson, Thomas W.**
— The Lawson History of the America's Cup. Bost., 1902. 4to, cloth; soiled. pba Jan 4 (393) $140

**Thomson, J., Curate of Netherwitton**
— Poems, Moral, Descriptive, and Elegaic. Newcastle, 1806. 12mo, contemp half mor; rubbed. b Dec 5 (292) £70

**Thomson, James, 1700-48**
See also: Fore-Edge Paintings
— The Poetical Works. Glasgow: Andrew Foulis, 1784. 2 vols. Folio, contemp calf. S June 12 (130) £440

— Les Saisons. Paris: Chambert & Herissant, 1759. 8vo, 18th-cent mor gilt, armorial bdg. With 4 plates. Lacking the ptd not about the trans; some browning. Fuerstenberg - Schaefer copy. S Dec 8 (609) £240

Anr copy. 18th-cent red mor gilt. With 4 plates. Fuerstenberg - Schaefer copy. S Dec 8 (610) £650

— The Seasons. Glasgow: Andrew Foulis, 1776. 12mo, contemp vellum gilt in the style of Edwards of Halifax, with painted Farrer/Armytage arms. sg Oct 19 (246) $750

Anr Ed. L, 1797. Illus by F. W. Bartolozzi & P. W. Tomkins after W. Hamilton. Folio, contemp mor gilt by Kalthoeber, inside front cover are large gilt letters FD below a coronet; minor rubbing. With frontis, 5 plates & 15 vignettes. b Sept 20 (215) £320

Anr copy. Contemp russia gilt; extremities worn, joints broken. With frontis, dedication, 6 plates & 14 illusts. Spotting, affecting 2 plates. pn Dec 7 (41) £240

**Thomson, James, 1800-83**
— Retreats: a Series of Designs.... L, 1827. 4to, orig bds. With 10 plans & 31 hand-colored plates. From the library of Louis-Philippe. S Nov 30 (241) £1,000

**Thomson, James, 1834-82**
— The City of Dreadful Night. L, 1880. 1st Ed. 8vo, orig cloth; spine ends frayed, wear at front outer joint. With 18 revisions by Thomson in ink on 17 pp. CE May 22 (448) $350

**Thomson, John.** See: Clark Library, Clarence H.

**Thomson, John, Cartographer**
— The Atlas of Scotland.... Edin., 1832. Folio, half mor gilt; broken. With 2 double-page hand-colored plates, 1 index map & 29 (on 58) maps hand-colored in outline. pnE May 15 (262) £1,300

— A New General Atlas. Edin., 1817. Folio, contemp half cloth; worn. With 70 hand-colored maps only. Lacking tp & prelims; minor defs to several maps. P Dec 12 (169) $3,250

Anr copy. Contemp calf-edged bds; def, upper cover detached. With dedication, 74 hand-colored mostly double-page map sheets & 1 double-page engraved diagram. Dedication & some prelims dampstained; many maps loose; some browning. pn Dec 7 (183) £1,200 [R. S. Books]

Anr copy. 19th-cent half mor; worn. With 46 (of 74) double-page maps only. Lacking tp & prelims; some tears & repairs. S June 13 (512) £1,200

**Thomson, Thomas, 1773-1852**
— Travels in Sweden during the Autumn of 1812. L, 1813. 1st Ed. 4to, contemp half mor; rebacked. With 8 plates & 5 maps. sg Mar 7 (358) $250

**Thomson-Seton, Ernest.** See: Seton, Ernest Thompson

**Thor, George**
— Cheiragogica Heliana. A Manuduction to the Philosophers Magical Gold.... L, 1659. 8vo, later calf gilt. Met May 22 (115) $550

**Thorburn, Archibald**
— Birds of Prey. Lamarsh, 1985. One of 145. Folio, half mor. Facsimile of the 1919 Ed. sg May 16 (348) $140

**Thoreau, Henry David, 1817-62**
See also: Limited Editions Club
— Cape Cod. Bost., 1865. 1st Ed. 12mo, orig cloth; spine ends worn. CE May 22 (454) $600
Anr Ed. Bost., 1865 [1864]. 12mo, orig cloth, B bdg; spine head chipped, front hinge cracked. pba Aug 22 (656) $325
Anr Ed. Bost., 1865. 12mo, orig cloth, D bdg; spine frayed. Z June 28 (271) $160
— Excursions. Bost., 1863. 8vo, orig cloth; spine rubbed. CE Feb 21 (262) $320
Anr copy. Some foxing to prelims. K Feb 11 (362) $350
Anr copy. Orig cloth; spine frayed, rubbed. Z June 28 (272) $290
— In the Maine Woods. Bost., 1864. 8vo, orig purple cloth. CE May 22 (452) $700
Anr copy. Orig blue-gray cloth. CE May 22 (453) $700
Anr copy. Orig cloth; rubbed, spine ends def. Z June 28 (273) $190
— On the Duty of Civil Disobedience. New Havin: At the Sign of the Chorobates, 1928. One of 300. Tp decoration by Rockwell Kent. Orig cloth; discolored. Z June 28 (274) $100
— Walden. Bost., 1854. 1st Ed. 8vo, orig cloth; worn, corners bumped, spine ends frayed. Spotted; 1 leaf roughly opened. F Mar 28 (623) $4,500
Anr copy. Half mor. Tp mtd at gutter; lacking map & ads. sg Sept 21 (306) $250
— A Week on the Concord and Merrimack Rivers. Bost. & Cambr., 1849. 1st Ed. 8vo, orig cloth; spine ends worn, minor staining. With ad leaf for Walden at rear. CE Feb 21 (261) $3,500
1st Issue. Orig cloth, BAL A bdg. Parsons - Engelhard copy. CNY Oct 27 (141) $10,000
Anr copy. Orig cloth; rear inner hinge & spine ends repaired, forecorners with wear. Inscr to Thomas Wentworth Higginson. Engelhard copy. CNY Oct 27 (142) $23,000
Anr Ed. Bost., 1862. 2d Issue, comprising sheets from the 1849 ptg with a new tp. 8vo, orig cloth, C bdg; spine head frayed. NH July 21 (383) $875
— Works. Bost., [1893-94]. Riverside Ed. 11 vols. 8vo, cloth. pba Aug 8 (627) $180
Manuscript Ed. Bost., 1906. one of 600, with leaf of autograph Ms in Vol I. 20 vols. Half mor. cb Oct 17 (305) $7,000
Anr copy. Half mor gilt. pba Dec 14 (146) $11,000
— A Yankee in Canada.... Bost., 1866. 1st Ed. 8vo, orig cloth. CE Feb 21 (264) $750

Anr copy. Orig cloth; front cover with minor wear, some soiling at ends, upper joint starting. CE May 22 (455) $380
Anr copy. Orig cloth, A bdg; worn, loose. NH July 21 (384) $340

**Thorer, Alban**
— De re medica.... Basel: Andreas Cratander, 1528. Folio, bds; rebound. Colophon wormed & repaired; browned. CE Nov 8 (154) $260

**Thorley, John**
— Melissologia, or the Female Monarchy...of Bees. L, 1744. 1st Ed. 8vo, half calf. With frontis & 4 plates. Folding plate torn without loss; frontis frayed def. bba July 18 (100) £120 [Price]

**Thornborough, John**
— A Discourse Plainely Proving the Evident Utilitie and Urgent Necessitie of the Desired Happie Union of the Two Famous Kingdomes of England and Scotland.... L, 1604. 4to, old half calf; rebacked. Lacking A1; library markings. STC 24035. CE June 15 (271) $180

**Thorndike, Lynn, 1882-1965**
— A History of Magic and Experimental Science. NY, [1923-58]. 8 vols. 8vo, orig cloth. sg Apr 11 (301) $325
Anr Ed. NY, 1947-58. 8 vols. bba Oct 5 (178) £320 [Kitazawa]
Anr Ed. NY, 1958-60. 8 vols. ds July 27 (187) $200; sg May 16 (265) $225

**Thorndyke, Helen Louise.** See: Garland's copy, Judy

**Thornton, Jessy Quinn**
— Oregon and California in 1848.... NY, 1849. 1st Ed. 2 vols. 12mo, orig cloth; spines repaired, soiled. With folding map & 12 plates. Dampstained & browned throughout; folding map wrinkled at margins. CE May 22 (30) $140
Anr copy. Period tree calf; lea worn, front joints beginning to crack. With 12 illus & 1 folded map. Larson copy. pba Sept 28 (713) $850
Anr copy. 12mo, orig cloth; spine ends chipped & frayed. With 12 plates & folding map. Robbins copy. pba Mar 21 (360) $1,400
2d Ed. NY, 1855. Vol II only. orig cloth; rubbed & stained. Inscr, 9 Jan 1873, to a clergyman. pba Aug 22 (967) $60

**Thornton, Robert John**
— New Illustration of the Sexual System of...Linnaeus. Comprehending...The Temple of Flora.... L, [1799]-1807-[10].. 3 parts in 1 vol. Folio, modern mor gilt by Hedberg of Stockholm. With engraved title on 2 leaves, engraved dedication to Queen Charlotte, engraved half-title, engraved contents leaf, port of Linnaeus wearing Lapland dress in hand-colored & plain states, 30 plates ptd in colors & finished by hand. Night-Blowing Cereus in Buchanan's B state; Superb Lily engraved by Ward. Asculapius, etc honoring the Bust of Linnaeus short in margin & probably from

anr copy; some plates reinforced along plate line; lacking Flora dispensing her Favours on the Earth. S June 27 (68) £32,000

**Thornton, Col. Thomas, 1757-1823**
— Sporting Tour through the Northern Parts of England.... L, 1804. 4to, half mor gilt by Bayntun. With 16 plates.  pba July 11 (441) $180

**Thornton, William**
— Cadmus; or, A Treatise on the Elements of Written Language.... Phila., 1796. Later half cloth. Waterstaining to margins. Phillipps copy. Z Oct 27 (84) $180

**Thoroughbred...**
— Thoroughbred Types, 1900-1925. NY: Pvtly ptd, 1926. One of 250. 4to, half cloth; some wear. O Jan 9 (248) $130

**Thory, Claude Antoine.** See: Redoute & Thory

**Thrale, Hester Lynch Salusbury**
— Letters to and from the late Samuel Johnson. See: Piozzi, Hester Lynch Thrale

**Thrapp, Dan L.**
— Encyclopedia of Frontier Biography. Spokane: Arthur H. Clark, 1990. 2d Ptg. pba Apr 25 (706) $85

**Thrasher, Max**
— Tuskegee. Bost., 1900. 8vo, pictorial cloth; spine rubbed. Cut signature of Booker T. Washington mtd on front free endpaper. sg Mar 28 (363) $130

**Three Lions...**
— Three Lions and the Cross of Lorraine.... Newtown, 1992. One of 138. Folio, half mor. With woodcut facsimiles & orig leaf from Winken de Worde's Ed of De Proprietatibus Rerum. sg Feb 15 (55) $425

**Thucydides, 471?-400? B.C.**
See also: Ashendene Press; Limited Editions Club
— De bello Peloponnesiaco, libri octo. Venice: Aldus, May 1502. Folio, mor gilt by Bedford; rebacked, extremities rubbed. 55 lines & headline; Greek types. Washed & pressed; lacking final blank; last 2 leaves foxed. Flaxley Abbey - Aldenham - Hefner copy. CNY May 17 (43) $6,500

Anr copy. 19th-cent mor gilt; new endpapers. Washed & resized; AA7 stained in margins; lacking 2 blanks. S June 27 (376) £4,600

Anr Ed. [Geneva]: H. Stephanus, 1564. Folio, old calf; rebacked, worn scuffed. Text browned; old stamp on tp.  wd May 8 (82) $250
— The History of the Peloponnesian War. L, 1634. ("Eight Bookes of the Peloponnesian Warre....") Folio, later calf; extremities worn, front joint & bottom of spine cracked, endpapers renewed. With 3 plates & 2 maps. First plate cropped in outer margin affecting image; engraved title trimmed & mtd. sg Mar 21 (322) $700

Anr Ed. L, 1676. ("The History of the Grecian War....") Trans by Thomas Hobbes. Folio, contemp calf; rubbed. With engraved title, 2 plates & 3 folding maps. 1 map cropped with paper repair. b Jan 31 (278) £150

**Thumb, Tom**
[-] Biography of the Only and Original P. T. Barnum's General Tom Thumb.... NY: Popular Publishing, [n.d.]. Orig hand-colored pictorial wraps. pba Aug 8 (629) $75

**Thurah, Lauritz de**
— Den Danske Vitruvius.... Copenhagen, 1746-49. 1st Ed. 2 vols in 1. Folio, early 19th-cent mor extra from the workshop of Niels Anthon; scuffed, joints rubbed. With 281 plates. Small repair to tp verso & to fold of 1st plate.  C Apr 3 (240) £8,500

Anr copy. 2 vols. Folio, contemp calf; rubbed. With engraved title & 281 plates. Engraved title repaired in lower margin, as are 4 other plates; 1 text leaf repaired in margin. S June 27 (290) £3,600
— Hafnia hodierna.... Copenhagen, 1748. 4to, contemp calf gilt; repaired, later endpapers. With engraved frontis & 110 plates. Some staining throughout; some leaves repaired at fore-margins. S June 13 (560) £480

**Thurber, James, 1894-1961**
— The Last Flower: a Parable in Pictures. NY & L, 1939. Oblong 4to, pictorial bds, in dj. sg June 20 (375) $60
— My World and Welcome to It. NY, [1942]. Inscr "Jim & Helen". K Feb 11 (363) $140

**Thwaites, Reuben Gold.** See: Early...

**Thwrocz, Johannes de**
— Chronica Hungariae. Augsburg: Erhard Ratdolt for Theobaldus Feger in Buda, 3 June 1488. 2d Ed. 4to, contemp blindstamped calf with brass fittings; rebacked & restored. 38 lines; type 7:92G. With 62 woodcuts from 32 blocks, all colored by the contemp hands of the Master of the Hungarian Chronical and anr artist. Small hole in a1 affecting a few letters; stains at inner margin of c8-d4. 172 (of 174) leaves; lacking blank v3-4. Goff T-361. C June 26 (176) £12,000

**Tibbitts, John**
— Poems. Stourport, 1811. 8vo, contemp bds; rebacked. b Dec 5 (420) £70

**Tielenburg, Gerrit**
— Gezichten der Steeden Londen, Canterbury en Colchester.... Amst., [c.1740]. 2 vols in 1. 8vo, modern half calf. With 82 plates & maps, 1 folding. Tp repaired; waterstaining affecting a few plates; some spotting. S Mar 28 (66) £550

**Tiger's...**
— The Tiger's Eye. Westport, 1947-49. Nos 1-9. 4to, pictorial wraps; worn. sg Jan 11 (421) $140

**Tighe, Mary, 1772-1810.** See: Fore-Edge Paintings

## Tight...

— Tight Lines and a Happy Landing. Anticosti, 1937. One of 300. Half cloth; worn. O June 25 (14) $200

## Tilden, Freeman

— Following the Frontier with F. Jay Haynes, Pioneer Photographer.... NY, 1964. In dj with soiling. pba Apr 25 (449) $50

## Tillotson, John, 1630-94

— Sermons. L, 1694-1704. 20 vols. 8vo, contemp mor; spine ends worn. CE Nov 8 (170) $550

## Tilton, Cecil G.

— William Chapman Ralston, Courageous Builder. Bost., [1935]. In chipped dj. pba Apr 25 (707) $50

## Timlin, William M.

— The Ship that Sailed to Mars. L, [1923]. 4to, half mor gilt. With calligraphic text & 48 colored plates mtd on gray sheets. b May 30 (587) £500

Anr copy. Mor gilt by Zaehnsdorf. With calligraphic text & 48 colored plates. Tears along edges crudely repaired. S Nov 2 (146) £440 [Hirsch]

Anr copy. Orig half vellum; shelf label on spine. Library markings on tp verso. sg Sept 14 (334) $850

**Tindale, Harriet Ramsay.** See: Tindale & Tindale

## Tindale, Thomas Keith —& Tindale, Harriet Ramsay

— The Handmade Papers of Japan. Rutland, Vt., 1952. 4 vols, including Atlas of samples. 4to, orig wraps, envelope & card portfolio. F June 20 (832) $3,600

## Ting, Wallasse

— Hot and Sour Soup. [N.p.: Sam Francis Foundation, 1969]. One of 1,050. Folio, unbound as issued in wraps. With 22 color lithos. Inscr. sg June 13 (364) $120

Anr Ed. [Copenhagen, 1970]. One of 800. Folio, loose as issued in wraps. sg Sept 7 (330) $175

— My Shit and My love: 10 Poems. Paris, 1961. One of 1,099. Folio, orig wraps. sg Sept 7 (331) $130

— One-Cent Life. Berne, 1964. Folio, unsewn in orig cloth folder. Inscr & with ink drawing. sg Sept 7 (328) $1,600

## Tinkham, George H.

— A History of Stockton.... San Francisco, 1880. 8vo, orig cloth; rebacked with orig spine strip laid on, worn, endpaper hinges repaired. pba Nov 16 (262) $250

## Tippett, Sir Michael

— String Quartet III. L: Schott, [n.d.]. 4to, orig wraps. Miniature score. Inscr to Mary Behrens, the dedicatee. Ck Nov 17 (165) £50

## Tipping, Henry Avray

— English Gardens. L, 1925. Folio, cloth. Ck Jan 24 (667) £110

— English Homes. L, 1920-29. Vols I-VI in 8 vols. Folio, cloth, some in djs. W Mar 6 (18) £410

Anr Ed. L, 1927-37. 6 (of 9) vols. Folio, orig cloth. S Oct 27 (1003) £380 [Sotheran]; S Oct 27 (1004) £380 [Sims Reed]

## Tiraboschi, Girolamo, 1731-94

— Biblioteca Modenese.... Modena, 1781-86. 6 vols. 4to, contemp vellum-backed bds; worn & soiled, minor spine tears. Institutional stamp on titles. O Mar 26 (279) $425

— Bibliotheca Modenese. Modena, 1781-86. 6 vols plus 1833-37 continuation in 5 vols. Together, 11 vols. 4to, later half calf; some spines wormed, rubbed. bba Oct 5 (179) £620 [Maggs]

## Tissandier, Gaston, 1843-99

— Bibliographie aeronautique: catalogue de livres d'histoire.... Paris, 1887. 4to, modern half cloth. Minor foxing to a few leaves. sg May 16 (92) $375

— En Ballon! pendant le Siege de Paris. Paris, 1871. 18mo, modern half cloth, orig front wraps bound in. Some foxing. sg May 16 (89) $150

— Observations meteorologiques en Ballon. Paris, 1879. 12mo, lev gilt by A. Knecht, orig wraps bound in. sg May 16 (91) $90

## Tizac, H. d'Ardenne de

— Animals in Chinese Art. L, 1923. One of 250. Folio, contemp calf with design of dragon in colored lea inlaid on upper cover; rebacked preserving spine. bba May 30 (50B) £150 [Harrison's Books]

## Tobacco...

— Tobacco: Its History and Associations, Use and Abuse.... L: Pvtly ptd by W. Davy of Long Acre for his friend J. Gibbs, Sept 1836. 3 vols. Folio, 19th-cent half mor gilt; edges rubbed. Each vol with specially ptd title, several hundred mtd items & engravings & ephemera. bba June 6 (280) £1,600 [C. L. Edwards]

## Tocqueville, Alexis de, 1805-59

— Democracy in America. L, 1835-40. 1st Ed in English. - Trans by Henry Reeve. 4 vols. 8vo, half mor gilt; extremities rubbed. Lacking the map. sg Oct 26 (367) $3,800

1st Eds of both parts. Paris, 1835-40. ("De la democratie en Amerique.") 4 vols. 8vo, contemp half calf gilt by Le Brun, with his stamp. With hand-colored folding map. Lacking blank at end of Vols I & IV; some foxing & browning. Hefner copy. CNY May 17 (44) $15,000

2d American Ed. NY, 1838. 8vo, orig cloth; re-cased with covers refurbished. Foxed. pba Aug 22 (969) $150

**Todd, John.** See: Fore-Edge Paintings

## Toderini, Giovanni Battista, 1728-99

— Letteratura turchesca. Venice, 1787. 1st Ed. 3 vols. 8vo, contemp half calf; spines wormed & rubbed. With 2 folding sheets of music. 1 music sheet detached; vol III dampstained. S Oct 26 (224) £850 [Dessy]

**Todhunter, John.** See: Ashendene Press

## Toepffer, Rodolphe, 1799-1846
— Histoire de Mr. Jabot. Geneva: Freydig, [1833]. 8vo, contemp half lea; head of spine torn, corners bumped. With 52 litho plates. Graphite affecting image on tp; marginal soiling. Schaefer copy. P Nov 1 (202) $300

## Toesca, Maurice
— Six contes fantastiques. Paris, 1953. One of 225. Illus by Pablo Picasso. Folio, half mor, orig wraps bound in. With 6 plates. S Nov 21 (426) £1,100

## Toesca, Pietro
— L'Ufiziolo Visconeo Landau-Finaly donato alla Citta di Firenze. Florence, 1951. One of 215. Folio, orig half cloth. bba May 9 (614) £240 [Van Eyk]

## Toke, Monroe Tsa. See: Grabhorn Printing

## Token...
— The Token and Atlantic Souvenir. A Christmas and New Year's Present. Bost., 1837. 8vo, orig calf; worn, spine ends def. Contains first appearances of 8 works by Nathaniel Hawthorne. Inscr by the Pbr to Mrs. Alexander. wa Feb 29 (39) $80

## Toland, Mary B. M.
— Tisayac of the Yosemite. Phila., [1890]. Orig cloth; front hinge cracked. pba Feb 12 (184) $50

## Toledo Osorio y Mendoza, Fadrique de
— Relacion embiada por Don Fadrique de Toledo.... Seville: Francisco de Lira, 1630. Folio, unbound. Palau 333046. S Nov 30 (186) £1,300

## Toletus, Franciscus, Cardinal
— Commentaria una cum quaestionibus in tres libros Aristotelis. Cologne: Geoffroy Kempens pour Birckmann, 1583. 4to, modern half mor. G3 torn with loss; ink annotations on tp & front free endpaper; some waterstaining. bba July 18 (118) £275 [Poole]

## Tolkien, John Ronald Reuel, 1892-1973
— The Hobbit. L, 1937. 1st Ed. Sgd; holograph annotations on 24 pp. Ck Nov 17 (166) £420
— The Lord of the Rings. L, 1954-55. 1st Ed. 3 vols. In djs. pba Oct 5 (359) $7,500
 Anr Ed. Bost., 1967. 3 vols. In rubbed djs. pba May 4 (262) $110
— A Middle English Vocabulary. Oxford, 1922. Orig wraps; spot to front wrap, spine wrap mostly lacking. pba Jan 25 (363) $170
— The Return of the King. L, 1956. 1st American Ed. In chipped dj. pba May 4 (263) $160
— Smith of Wotton Major. Bost., 1967. 1st American Ed. In soiled dj. pba May 4 (264) $55
 **Tolkien's copy, John Ronald Reuel**
 COWLING, GEORGE H. - A Preface to Shakespeare. L, 1925. Sgd, 1925 in pencil on flyleaf. cb Feb 14 (2732) $400

## Tollens, Hendrik
— L'Hivernage des Hollandais a la Nouvelle-Zemble.... Maestricht, 1839. Trans by August Claverau. 4to, orig bds; worn, needs rebacking. With port & 8 litho plates, all mtd India-proofs. Foxed. sg Mar 7 (299) $130

## Tolley, Cyril J. H.
— The Modern Golfer. NY, 1924. 1st American Ed. Cloth; spine sunned. With frontis port. pba Apr 18 (164) $85

## Tolnay, Charles de. See: De Tolnay, Charles

## Tolstoy, Leo, 1828-1910
 See also: Ashendene Press; Limited Editions Club
— Anna Karenina. Moscow, 1878. 1st Ed. 3 vols. 8vo, contemp half calf. Minor stains to some leaves in Vol II. C June 26 (233) £2,400
 Anr copy. Modern half calf. Lacking final blank in Vol III; a few leaves in Vol II with tears affecting words; spotted. C June 26 (234) £1,350
— War and Peace. Moscow, 1868-69. ("Voina i Mir.") 1st Ed. 6 vols. 8vo, contemp half calf. Vol II lacking final blank. C June 26 (235) £5,800

## Tombleson, William —& Fearnside, William Gray
— Eighty Picturesque Views on the Thames and Medway. L, [1834]. 4to, orig cloth; bumped. With engraved title & 79 plates. S Mar 28 (67) £550
 Anr Ed. L, [c.1845]. 4to, contemp cloth; rubbed, backstrip split. With 80 plates. bba June 6 (69) £380 [Sharpe]
— Views of the Rhine. L, 1832-[34]. 2 vols, including The Upper Rhine. 8vo, later half calf gilt. With 2 engraved titles, folding ap, 67 plates in 1st Rhine & 69 plates in Upper Rhine. pnE Mar 20 (144) £380
 Anr Ed. L, [c.1840]. 2 vols. 8vo, orig cloth; broken, spine perished. wd May 8 (83) $200

## Tome, Philip
— Pioneer Life; or, Thirty Years a Hunter. Buffalo, 1854. Orig cloth; rebacked, new endpapers. Foxed; dampstains at inner margins at begining & along bottom margins throughout. K June 23 (488) $600

## Tomkins, Peltro William. See: Ottley & Tomkins

## Tomkinson, Geoffrey Stewart
— A Select Bibliography of the Principal Modern Presses.... L, 1928. One of 1,000. 4to, orig half cloth, in chipped dj. pba Nov 30 (315) $100

## Tomlinson, Charles F. R. S.
— Winter in the Arctic Regions and Summer in the Antarctic Regions. L, [1872]. 1st Ed. 8vo, orig cloth; spine darkened. With 2 folding maps. Some foxing. pba July 25 (75) $120

## Toms, William Henry. See: Badeslade & Toms

## Tooke, John Horne, 1736-1812
— Epea Ptereonta. Or, the Diversions of Purley. L, 1829. ("The Diversions of Purley.") 2 vols. 8vo, half mor. pba Mar 7 (257) $275

**Toole, John Kennedy**
— A Confederacy of Dunces. Baton Rouge, 1980. In dj. pba Aug 22 (452) $475

**Tooley, Ronald Vere**
— California as an Island.... L, [1964]. Orig wraps. Map Collectors' Series No 8. pba Feb 13 (183) $55
— Collectors' Guide to Maps of the African Continent.... L, 1969. 4to, cloth, in dj. sg May 9 (41) $200
— The Mapping of America. L: Holland Press, 1980. In dj. sg Dec 7 (49) $200; sg May 9 (42) $225; sg May 9 (43) $300
— The Mapping of Australia. L, 1979. 4to, cloth, in dj. sg May 9 (44) $120
— Tooley's Dictionary of Mapmakers. Tring, 1979. 1st Ed in Book form. In dj. sg May 9 (45) $325

**Toomer, Jean**
— Essentials. Chicago: Pvtly ptd, 1931. 1st Ed, out-of-series copy. In dj. sg Mar 28 (364) $500

**Toor, Frances**
— Diego Rivera. Mexico: Fischgrund Publishing Co., [late 1930s]. Folio, wraps. With 12 mtd color plates. Sgd by Rivera. sg Apr 18 (130) $650

**Torneri, Arnaldo**
— La corsa delle slitte in Vicenza nel Carnovale MCDDLXXXIV. Vicenza: Giovanni Battista Vendramini Mosca for Giacomo Leoni, 1784. 8vo, contemp bds. With 16 folding plates with contemp hand-coloring, heightened with gold & silver. C Apr 3 (241) £11,000

**Tornero, Recaredo S.**
— Chile ilustrado.... Valparaiso, 1872. 4to, orig cloth; worn, front hinge cracked. With litho port & 9 litho plates. b Jan 31 (475) £120

**Torniello, Augustine**
— Annales sacri et profani. Frankfurt: Heirs of Jacob Fischer, [1616?]. Folio, contemp vellum. With 23 maps & plates. Some discoloration to text. b June 28 (88) £1,500

**Torquemada, Juan de**
— Primara parte de los veinte i un libros rituales i monarchia Indiana. Madrid, 1723. 2d Ed. 3 vols. Folio, half mor; spines faded, 1 cover detached. With color folding map, & 3 titles by Irala. Titles washed & reinforced; few tears. Sold w.a.f. CE Nov 8 (248) $1,000

**Torre, Alfonso de la, c.1410-60**
— Vision delectable. Toulouse: Johannes Parix & Stephan Cleblat, 1489. Folio, 17th-cent vellum; later endpapers. 36 lines & headline; types 4:111G, 5:98G, 76?G. With 22 woodcuts from 16 blocks. Some staining; some corners at end repaired; 1st leaf rehinged. 102 leaves. Goff T-389. C May 1 (172) £20,000

**Torre Farfan, Fernando de la**
— Fiestas de la S. Iglesia Metropolitana y Piarcal de Sevilla.... Seville, 1671. Folio, 19th-cent sheep gilt; joints worn, corners bumped. With etched title, 2 ports, 9 folding plates & 9 plates of emblems & devices. Small rusthole on etched title; some folding plates with repaired tears. Freidus - Schaefer copy. P Nov 1 (138) $9,000

**Torre y Sevil, Francisco de la.** See: Jesuits

**Torres Martinez Bravo, Joseph de**
— Reglas generales de acompanar, en organo, clavicordio, y harpa.... Madrid, 1702. 4to, old vellum. R2 cropped at foot. S Dec 1 (369) £1,200

**Torrey, John, 1796-1873**
— A Flora of the Northern and Middle Sections of the United States. NY, 1824. Vol I. 8vo, cloth; dampstaining. Foxed; pencil notations. Met Feb 24 (330) $325
— A Flora of the State of New York. Albany, 1843. 2 vols. 4to, 19th-cent lea; needs rebacked. With 162 colored plates. Some plates foxed. sg Dec 7 (236) $425

Anr copy. Orig cloth; worn. Browning & foxing to plates. sg May 9 (318) $375

Anr copy. Orig cloth; frayed & chipped. With 2 engraved titles & 161 plates, 57 of them hand-colored. 2 plates foxed. Part of Natural History of New-York series. wa Feb 29 (216) $170

**Torricelli, Evangelista, 1608-47**
— Lezioni accademiche.... Florence, 1715. 4to, 19th-cent half calf gilt; wormed. Minor marginal tear to half-title. Honeyman - Hefner copy. CNY May 17 (45) $1,600

**Torsellini, Horatio.** See: Jesuits

**Tortorel, Jacques —&**
**Perrissin, Jean, c.1536-c.1611**
— Premier Volume, contenant quarante tableaux ou histoires diverses qui sont memorables touchant les guerres, massacres & troubles advenus en France.... [Geneva, after 1570]. Folio, 19th-cent half sheep; worn, needs rebacked. With 32 double-page plates only. Trimmed with occasional loss to headlines; mtd; marginal soiling; some dampstains; Plate 24 creased & torn with loss, with duplicate impression of Plate 5 on verso; some plates are faint impressions; lacking Avis au Lecteur. Sold w.a.f. sg Mar 21 (254) $4,700

**Tory, Geofroy, 1480?-1533?**
See also: Grolier Club
— Champ fleury auquel est contenu lart & science de la...proportio[n] des lettres attiques. Paris: Geofroy Tory & Giles Gourmont, 1529. 1st Ed. Folio, mor gilt by Godillot. 50 lines & headline; roman & greek types. With 116 woodcut designs, 13 woodcuts of alphabets & 10 ciphers. Library stamp on a1v. C Apr 3 (242) £32,000

## Totok, Wilhelm —& Others
— Handbuch der bibliographischen Nachschlagewerke.... Frankfurt am Main, [1984]. 2 vols. 8vo, orig cloth in djs. sg Apr 11 (317) $150

## Touchstone, S. F., Pseud.
— History of Celebrated English and French Thorough-Bred Stallions. L, 1890. One of 520. Oblong folio, half lea; shaken, some tears & chips to endpapers. O Jan 9 (241) $1,000

## Toulouse-Lautrec, Henri de, 1864-1901
— Affiches. Basel, [1946]. Folio, loose as issued in bds; tape remnants on front cover. With 10 color plates. sg Jan 11 (427) $110

— Les Affiches de Toulouse-Lautrec. Monte Carlo, [1950]. Intro by Edouard Julien. 4to, pictorial wraps; some wear. With 32 color plates. O May 7 (285) $140; sg Jan 11 (431) $225; sg Jan 11 (432) $200

Anr copy. Pictorial wraps; spine ends worn, front joint split. With 32 lithos. sg June 13 (368) $150

Anr copy. Pictorial wraps; spine creased. With frontis, 31 poster designs & a decomposition of 1 poster in 6 progressive states. Several little stains to fore-edge. wa Nov 16 (378) $100

— Au Cirque. Monte Carlo, [1952]. One of 1,500. 4to, wraps. sg Jan 11 (428) $250

— The Circus. NY, 1952. One of 1,500. Wraps. With 39 color plates. sg Jan 11 (429) $225

— Submersion: Album de quarante-neuf dessins inedits a la plume. Paris, [1938]. One of 200. 4to, loose as issued in orig wraps; def. sg Sept 7 (332) $200

## Tournefort, Joseph Pitton de
— A Voyage into the Levant. L, 1718. 2 vols. 4to, contemp calf gilt; rebacked. With 153 plates & maps. Foxed. b Sept 20 (359) £700

1st English Ed. 2 vols. 4to, contemp calf; rebacked. With 152 plates, maps & plans. Some spotting. S Oct 26 (228) £1,400 [Squire]

## Tousard, Anne Louis de
— American Artillerist's Companion, or Elements of Artillery. Phila., 1809. Vol III only. 4to, old half calf; front bd detached, worn. With 65 double-page plates. Marginal worming to 10 plates; other plates foxed or browned. wa Feb 29 (443) $425

## Toussaint, Franz
— Le Jardin des caresses. Paris, 1914. One of 100 on japon with 2 additional suites. ILlus by Leon Carre. 4to, mor extra by Cl. Lande, orig wraps bound in. Watercolor drawing sgd by Leon Carre bound in. S Nov 21 (429) £1,700

## Toussaint, Manuel
— Arte Colonial en Mexico. Mexico, 1948. Oblong 4to, cloth, in dj. sg June 13 (369) $60

## Towler, John
— The Silver Sunbeam.... Hastings-on-Hudson, [1969]. 8vo, cloth, in dj. Stain on prelim page. Reprint of 1864 Ed. sg Feb 29 (323) $110

## Town, Laurence
— Bookbinding by Hand. L, [1951]. 8vo, orig cloth, in chipped dj; bdg worn. F June 20 (516) $50

## Towne, Charles Hanson
— An April Song. NY, [1937]. 8vo, orig cloth; backstrip frayed at head. Inscr to "Jerome Salinger, for his unfailing attention in the Spring Course, 1939, at Columbia University". CE May 22 (415) $170

## Townsend, John Kirk, 1809-51
— Narrative of a Journey Across the Rocky Mountains to the Columbia River.... Phila., 1839. 1st Ed. 8vo, orig cloth; spine ends chipped. Some foxing. bbc Dec 18 (561) $325

Anr copy. Orig cloth; edges worn. Dampstaining & foxing. Met Sept 28 (365) $200

Anr copy. Orig cloth; loss to spine. Library stamp on 1 leaf. Met May 22 (369) $200

Anr copy. Orig cloth; covers worn & stained, possibly recased. Some foxing. Robbins copy. pba Mar 21 (362) $300

## Townshend Library, George, 2d Marquis
— [Sale Catalogue] A Catalogue of the Magnificent Library.... L: Leigh & Sotheby, 1912. 8vo, old half calf. Priced in margins throughout. Some foxing & soiling. O Mar 26 (281) $300

## Townshend, James
— The Royal Farrier; or the Art of Farriery Display'd. L: Isaac Fell, [c.1750]. 12mo, contemp calf; worn. Some foxing & soiling; minor tears. O Jan 9 (242) $325

## Toye, Nina —& Adair, Arthur H.
— Petits & grands verres. Paris, [1927]. Copy for the artist, with additional suite of plates & watercolor for 1 of the plates, all sgd. Illus by J. E. Laboureur. 4to, mor gilt, orig wraps bound in. S Nov 21 (430) £800

## Traffichetti, Bartolomeo
— L'Arte di conservare la sanita. Pesaro, 1565. 1st Ed. 4to, contemp vellum; lower extrems chipped. Wormholes in title, 1st gathering, & last 3 leaves; Q8 torn; lower margins creased; light marginal spotting. Ck Mar 22 (300) £480

## Tragi-Comic...
— The Tragi-Comic History of the Burial of Cock Robin. Phila.: J. Bouvier for Johnson & Warner, 1811. 8vo, orig wraps; split to spine. With 8 plates. Browned. sg Feb 8 (255) $100

Traits... See: Grabhorn Printing

### Transformateurs...
— Les Transformateurs d'Energie: Generateurs, Accumulateurs, Moteurs. Paris, 1910. 2 vols. Folio, orig cloth; loose in bdg, with backstrip partly detached, Atlas shaken. With 22 chromolitho plates with multiple die-cut overlays on 13 mounts. Sold w.a.f. sg May 16 (220) $400

### Trapier, Paul
— The Gospel to be Given to Our Servants. Charleston, 1847. 8vo, ptd wraps; loose, spine def, repaired. sg Mar 28 (344) $200

### Trask, John B.
— Report of the Geology of Northern and Southern California.... Sacramento: B. Redding State Printer, 1855. 8vo, removed from larger vol with remains of stitching. California Assembly Doc. No 14, Session of 1855. pba Aug 8 (201) $80
  Anr Ed. Sacramento: California Senate, 1856. 8vo, later cloth. California Senate Doc. No 14, Session of 1856. pba Feb 12 (186) $75
— Report of the Geology of the Coast Mountains and Part of the Sierra Nevada.... Sacramento: California Assembly, 1854. 8vo, later cloth. Some creasing, small tears & foxing. California Assembly Doc. No 9, Session of 1854. pba Feb 12 (185) $100

### Trautman, Milton B.
— The Fishes of Ohio. [N.p.], 1957. 4to, cloth, in dj; rear hinge starting. sg Mar 7 (562) $140

### Trautwine, John C.
— Rough Notes of an Exploration for an Inter-Oceanic Canal Route.... Phila., 1854. 8vo, orig cloth; spine ends & corners frayed. With 14 color litho plates. bbc June 24 (197) $325

### Traven, B., 1890?-1969
— Die Brueck im Dschungel. Berlin: Buechergilde Gutenberg, 1930. Orig cloth; spine frayed, tear along rear joint. pba May 23 (430) $130
— Der Busch. Berlin: Buechergilde Gutenberg, 1930. Orig cloth. Stamp to lower tp. pba May 23 (431) $130
— Death Ship. NY, 1934. In soiled & chipped dj. wa Dec 14 (60) $170
— The Treasure of the Sierra Madre. NY, 1935. 1st American Ed. In chipped dj. CE May 22 (458) $500

### Travers, Jerome D.
— Travers' Golf Book. NY: Macmillan, 1913. 1st Ed. Cloth. With frontis. Lacking front free endpaper. pba Apr 18 (165) $110

### Travers, Jerome D. —& Rice, Grantland
— The Winning Shot. Garden City, 1915. 1st Ed. Cloth; spine head chipped, spine smudged. pba Apr 18 (166) $100

### Travers, Pamela Lyndon
— Mary Poppins. NY, [1934]. Illus by Mary Shepard. Cloth, in chipped dj. bbc June 24 (559) $230
— Mary Poppins Comes Back. L, 1935. Illus by Mary Shepard. In rubbed dj. Inscr. bbc Dec 18 (360) $250

### Travies, Edouard, 1809-65
— Types du regne animal; Buffon en estampes.... Paris, [1860]. 1st Ed. Folio, mor; rubbed & soiled. With frontis & 24 hand-colored plates. S Oct 27 (787) £520 [Grahame]

### Travis, Walter J.
— Practical Golf. NY: Harper, 1902. 2d Ed. Cloth; spine ends rubbed. pba Apr 18 (167) $140
  Anr Ed. NY: Harper, 1903. Cloth; spine ends rubbed. Endpapers foxed. pba Nov 9 (82) $130

### Treaties
— Convention Between His Britannick Majesty and the King of Spain... the 28th Day of October, 1790. L, 1790. 4to, modern wraps. Robbins copy. pba Mar 21 (267) $2,750
— Declaration and Counter-Declaration... at Madrid, the 24th of July, 1790.... L, 1790. 4to, modern wraps. Text in Spanish & English. Robbins-Streeter copy. pba Mar 21 (266) $4,000
— Tratado de Paz, Amistad... entre la Republica Mexicana y los Estados-Unidos de America.... Queretaro, 1848. Bound with: Esposicion Dirigida al Supremo Gobierno por los Comisionadosque Firmaron el Tratado... 1st Eds. 4to, late tree sheep with orig wraps; front cover creased. Text in Spanish & English. Marginal soiling in rear. Robbins copy. pba Mar 21 (363) $1,100
— Tratado de paz, Armistad... Entre la Republica Mexicana y los Estados-Unidos de America.... Mexico, 1848. 2d Ed. Wraps; lacking orig printed wraps. Text in Spanish & English. Larson copy. pba Sept 28 (717) $250
  1st Ed. Queretaro, 1848. 4to, wraps; lacking orig printed wraps. Text in Spanish & English. Larson copy. pba Sept 28 (716) $1,300
— Tratado de paz y amistad concluido entre Espana y la Republica del Ecuador en 16 de Febrero de 1840. Madrid, 1841. 4to, recent vellum bds; upper cover gnawed. S Mar 28 (326) £160
— Tratado definitivo de paz concluido entre SS. MM. Christianissima, y Britanica, y los Estados Generales de la Provincias Unidas, en Aix la Chapelle a 18 de Octubre de 1748. Madrid, 1749. 4to, recent calf. Waterstains at beginning. S Mar 28 (343) £300
— The Treaty Between the United States and Mexico.... Wash., 1848. With: Richard Griswold del Castillo, The Treaty of Guadalupe Hidalgo, Norman, 1990 1st American Ed. Together, 2 vols, modern cloth. Larson copy. pba Sept 28 (718) $150
— Treaty of Amity, Commerce, and Navigation, between His Britannic Majesty, and the United States.... Phila, 2 Nov 1795. 8vo, half calf; def. Bottom margin excised on last leaf. sg Oct 26 (373) $300
— Treaty of Versailles. L, 1920. ("The Treaty of Peace Between the Allied and Associated Powers and Germany....") Orig ptd wraps; spine worn & chipped. Paperclip stain to first few leaves. David Lloyd

# 1995 - 1996 · BOOKS

George's copy. Forbes copy. CNY Dec 15 (259) $4,000

Anr Ed. L, [n.d.]. 4to, half mor; spine head torn. Some spotting. wa Feb 1 (193) $110

**Tredgold, Thomas**
— Elementary Principles of Carpentry. L, 1820. 1st Ed. 4to, disbound. With 22 plates. Minor foxing; 2 pieces excised from blank portions of tp. sg June 13 (371) $60

3d Ed. L, 1840. 4to, later cloth. With 47 plates. Inked ownership stamp on tp & 1 index page. sg June 13 (372) $50

**Trembecki, Stanislas**
— Sophiowka, Poeme Polonais. Vienna, 1815. 4to, contemp half calf; loose in bdg. With port & 6 plates ptd in sanguine. Foxing & minor stains; old stamps on tp. sg Sept 21 (308) $150

**Trembley, Abraham, 1700-84**
— Memoires pour servir a l'histoire d'un genre de polypes d'eau douce.... Leiden, 1744. 8vo, contemp half calf; rubbed & soiled. With 13 folding plates. S June 12 (287) £600

Anr copy. Contemp calf; worn. With 13 folding plates. Marginal worming at end. Sgd by William Bateson on front endpaper. Andrade copy. S June 12 (288) £700

Anr Ed. Paris, 1744. 2 vols. 8vo, contemp calf; 1 spine damaged. S June 12 (289) £320

**Trench, Richard Chenevix.** See: Fore-Edge Paintings

**Trenkwald, Hermann.** See: Sarre & Trenkwald

**Tresham, Henry —& Others**
— The British Gallery of Pictures.... L, 1818. Folio, contemp half mor; rubbed, joints worn. With 25 plates. Some foxing & soiling. O Mar 5 (227) $550

Anr copy. Contemp calf gilt; loose, head of spine def. With 25 plates. S Apr 23 (257) £360

**Treussart, Gen. —**
— Memoires sur les mortiers hydrauliques et sur les mortiers ordinaires. Paris, 1829. 4to, contemp half russia. With folding plate. Foxed. sg May 16 (266) $50

**Trew, Abdias.** See: Cantzler & Trew

**Trials**
— The Case of Impotency Debated, in the late Famous Trial at Paris; between the Marquis de Gesures and his Lady, Mademoiselle de Mascranny; who, after three years of marriage, commences a suite against him for Impotency. L, 1715. 2d Ed. 2 vols. Contemp calf; rebacked, front joint of Vol I cracked. pba Mar 7 (178) $70

— Trial of John Y. Beall, as a Spy.... NY, 1865. 8vo, wraps. sg Oct 26 (57) $90

PERALTA GRANT. - In the United States Court of Private Land Claims, Santa Fe District: James Addison Peraltareavis and Dona Sofia Loreto Micaela de Peraltareavis... vs. the United States.... Santa Fe,

1895. 8vo, contemp half sheep; rubbed & scuffed. Some soiling. pba Apr 25 (588) $1,000

**Tricot, Xavier**
— James Ensor. L, [1992]. 2 vols. 4to, coth, in djs. sg Sept 7 (142) $110

**Trifles...**
— Trifles from Harrogate. Harrogate, 1797. 8vo, orig wraps. Minor spotting. b Dec 5 (494) £260

**Triggs, Henry Inigo**
— The Art of Garden Design in Italy. L, 1906. Folio, later cloth; extremities worn, soiled. With 73 collotype, 28 halftone & 27 photolitho plates. Marginal tape repairs to 1 plate; some soiling. cb Oct 17 (51) $160

— Formal Gardens in England and Scotland. L, 1902. 2 vols. Folio contemp half mor. With 122 plates. Subscriber's copy. b Jan 31 (305) £220

Anr copy. Half lea; worn, spine bumped. Met Sept 28 (26) $275

**Trimble, Isaac P.**
— A Treatise on the Insect Enemies of Fruit and Fruit Trees. NY, 1865. 4to, orig cloth; rebacked in mor, some wear. With 2 plain & 9 hand-colored plates. Some smudging. wa Feb 29 (181) $210

**Triompho...**
— Triompho di Reggio alle donne reggiane dedicato. Parma: Seth Viotto, 1551. 4to, 19th-cent russia gilt. Stains to tp. C June 26 (141) £1,400

**Trissino, Giovanni Giorgio, 1478-1550**
— Epistola del Trissino de le lettere nuovamente aggiunte ne la lingua Italiana. Rome: Ludovico Arringhi da Vicenza & Lautizio Perugino, [1524]. 1st Issue. 4to, 19th-cent half cloth. Some spotting. C Apr 3 (244) £1,500

2d Issue. 19th-cent half mor; upper joint cracking, spine chipped. Some foxing; wormhole to last 3 leaves. bba May 9 (1) £550 [Breman]

— La Italia liberata da Gotthi. Venice, 1548. 1st Ed. 3 vols in 2. 8vo, 18th-cent vellum. With folding plan & folding map. Device at end of Vol III shaved; tear in fold of folding plan; lower margins at beginning of Vol I repaired with occasional loss of signature. S Nov 30 (302) £450

Anr Ed. Paris, 1729. ("L'Italia liberata da' Goti....") 3 vols. 8vo, mor gilt by Riviere. Lacking privilege leaf at end of Vol I. Ptd on vellum. Fuerstenberg - Schaefer copy. S Dec 8 (613) £1,500

**Tristan de Leonnoys**
— Histoire de Tristan de Leonois et de la Reine Yseult. Paris: Deterville, [1799]. 2 vols. 12mo, Mor. With 5 plates. b Dec 5 (51) £130

**Tristram, W. Outram**
— Coaching Days and Coaching Ways. L, 1888. Illus by Herbert Railton & Hugh Thomson. 4to, mor gilt by Riviere, with scene of horses on upper cover in mor. b May 30 (588) £280

## TRITHEMIUS

**Tritheim, Johann.** See: Trithemius, Joannes

**Trithemius, Joannes, 1462-1516**
— Polygraphiae libri sex. [Oppenheim: J. Koebel], 1518. 2 parts in 1 vol. Folio, 19th-cent calf gilt; rubbed. Lacking b6; q3 torn & repaired; prelims wormed; some marginal staining. Honeyman - Hefner copy. CNY May 17 (46) $4,500

**Triumphe...**
— Le Triumphe des neuf preux.... Abbeville: Pierre Gerard, 30 May 1487. Folio, 18th-cent calf gilt with added arms of the Mareste family; rebacked, orig strip laid down. 34 lines & headline, double column, batarde type Gerard 1:109. With full-page woodcut & 10 half-page woodcuts; contemp rubrications. Some worming at ends touching text; minor stains. 288 leaves. Goff T-458. C June 26 (177) £62,000

**Trogus Pompeius.** See: Justinus, Marcus Junianus

**Troil, Uno von, 1746-1803**
— Letters on Iceland. L, 1780. 8vo, contemp sheep; needs rebdg. With frontis & folding map. Library stamps on tp. sg Mar 7 (301) $275

**Troisieme...**
— Troisieme Congres International d'Art et d'Archeologie Iraniens; Memoirs, Leningrad, Septembre 1935. Leningrad, 1939. Folio, cloth, in dj. With 123 plates. sg June 13 (195) $130

**Trollope, Anthony, 1815-82**
See also: Limited Editions Club
— The Belton Estate. L, 1866. 1st Ed. 8vo, half mor by Sangorski & Sutcliffe. Ink stamps to a few upper corners; lacking pbr's cat at end of Vol III but with Jones' Circulating Library ad, laid down. pn Dec 7 (49) £380 [Shapero]
— Can You Forgive Her? L, 1864-65. 1st Ed in Book form. 2 vols. 8vo, half mor by Sangorski & Sutcliffe. Some foxing. pn Dec 7 (48) £200 [Sotheran]
— The Chronicles of Barsetshire. L, 1889. 8 vols. 8vo, half calf by Zaehnsdorf. pba Sept 14 (352) $375
— The Duke's Children. L, 1880. 1st Ed. 3 vols. 8vo, orig cloth; rubbed & soiled, remains of library stickers on upper covers. S July 11 (222) £320
— Framley Parsonage. L, 1861. 1st Ed in Book form. 3 vols. 8vo, orig cloth; spines repaired & partially rebacked. Some foxing. S July 11 (217) £420
— The Golden Lion of Granpere. L, 1872. 1st Ed in Book form. 8vo, orig cloth; rubbed. S July 11 (229) £420
— He Knew He Was Right. L, 1869. 1st English Ed in Book form. 3 vols. 8vo, orig cloth; rubbed, new endpapers. Lacking plate opposite p.25; half-title of Vol II torn & remtld. S July 11 (232) £200
— How the "Mastiffs" Went to Iceland. l, 1878. 1st Ed. 4to, orig cloth gilt; spine ends & corners worn, endpapers cracked at inner hinges. Inscr to Mrs Carnegie. CE Sept 27 (278) $1,200
— Is he Popenjoy? L, 1878. 1st Ed in Book form. 3 vols. 8vo, orig cloth; rubbed. S July 11 (225) £550

## AMERICAN BOOK PRICES CURRENT

— Lady Anna. L, 1874. 1st English Ed in Book form. 2 vols. 8vo, half mor by Sangorski & Sutcliffe. Some spotting. pn Dec 7 (51) £220 [Sotheran]
— The Landleaguers. L, 1883. 1st Ed. 3 vols. 8vo, orig cloth; endpapers slightly foxed. S July 11 (228) £950
— The Last Chronicle of Barset. L, [1866-67]. 1st Ed, in orig 32 parts. 8vo, orig wraps; minor repairs to 3 spines. Most slips & ads present. sg Sept 21 (309) $1,900

1st English Ed in Book form. L, 1867. 2 vols. 8vo, half lev gilt. pba Dec 14 (148) $275
— Marion Fay. L, 1882. 1st Ed in Book form. 3 vols. 8vo, half mor by Sangorski & Sutcliffe. Some foxing at beginning. pn Dec 7 (54) £270 [Sotheran]
— The Noble Jilt. A Comedy.... L, 1923. One of 500. Ed by Michael Sadleir. sg Feb 8 (342) $60
— North America. NY, 1862. 2 vols. 8vo, cloth; extremities rubbed & frayed, tear on front free endpaper. Z June 28 (276) $225
— The Prime Minister. L, 1876. 1st English Ed in Book form. 4 vols. 8vo, orig cloth; rubbed. S July 11 (234) £380
— Ralph the Heir. L, 1871. 1st Ed in Book form. 3 vols. 8vo, orig cloth; worn, rebacked, preserving spines. S July 11 (219) £380
— The Small House at Allington. L, 1864. 1st Ed in Book form. 2 vols. 8vo, half mor. Some foxing. pba Dec 14 (149) $225

Anr copy. Orig cloth; rubbed & stained, rebacked, preserving most of orig spines. Some foxing & soiling. S July 11 (224) £220
— The Warden. L, 1855. 1st Ed. 8vo, orig cloth; recased with spine repair. Some browning. Pbr's presentation copy with blindstamp on tp. S July 11 (233) £380

Anr copy. Orig cloth, 2d bdg; rubbed, some loss of cloth to spine extremities. sg Feb 8 (343) $225
— Works. L, 1906-13. ("Barsetshire Novels.") 8 vols. Contemp half mor gilt. b May 30 (422) $300

Anr Ed. Stratford: Shakespeare Head Press, 1929. One of 525. Ed by Michael Sadleir. 14 vols, orig cloth. S Oct 27 (1228) £260 [Harrington]

**Trollope, Frances, 1780-1863**
— Belgium and Western Germany in 1833. L, 1834. 2 vols. 12mo, orig bds; joints rubbed. sg Mar 7 (362) $110
— Domestic Manners of the Americans. L, 1832. 1st Ed. 8vo, early half calf. With 24 plates. sg Oct 26 (368) $275

**Trollope, Thomas Adolphus, 1774-1835**
— Beppo the Conscript. L, 1864. 1st Ed. 2 vols in 1. 8vo, contemp half calf; rubbed. Lacking half-titles; some spotting. bba May 30 (214) £100 [Finch]
— A Summer in Western France. L, 1841. Ed by Frances Trollope. 2 vols. 8vo, orig cloth. sg Mar 7 (363) $80

**Troncon, Jean**
— L'Entree triomphante de leurs maiestez Louis XIV... et Marie Therese d'Austriche... dans la ville de Paris. Paris, 1662. Folio, contemp calf; extremities rubbed. With frontis, port, engraved dedication & 21 plates, 14 of them double-page. Tear to lower margin of frontis.   C May 31 (115) £850

**Tropfke, Johannes**
— Geschichte der Elementar-Mathematik in systematischer Darstellung. Leipzig, 1902-3. 2 vols.   sg May 16 (267) $60

**Trotsky, Leon, 1879-1940**
— The History of the Russian Revolution. NY, 1932. 3 parts in 1 vol. Inscr to Richard Simon, 3 Mar 1932.   CE Feb 21 (210) $2,600

**Trotta, Giovanni Battista**
— Praxis horologiorum expeditissima per quam varia horologiorum genera. Naples, 1631. 1st Ed. 2 parts in 1 vol. 4to, contemp vellum; wormed, spine worn. Some browning.   S Oct 27 (820) £580 [Antiquarian]

**Trotter, Thomas, 1760-1832**
— An Essay, Medical, Philosophical and Chemical on Drunkenness.... Phila., 1813. 12mo, orig sheep; worn, spine def, front cover detached.   F June 20 (115) $200

**Troublesome...**
— The Troublesome and Hard Adventures in Love... Written in Spanish, by... Michael Cervantes.... L, 1652. 4to, modern mor janseniste; front joint rubbed. Wormholes in lower outer corners, occasionally affecting text. Palau 53554.   sg Apr 18 (35) $1,400

**Trower, H. F.** See: Longman & Trower

**True...**
— The True History of a Little Boy who Cheated Himself.... L, 1809. 16mo, orig wraps; soiled, backstrip split at foot. With 12 full-page hand-colored illusts. Browned.   S May 16 (195) £400

**Trueheart, James L.**
— The Perote Prisoners, being the Diary. San Antonio, 1934. Ed by Frederick Chabot.   pba Apr 25 (335) $65

**Truman, Harry S., 1884-1972**
— Memoirs. Garden City, NY, [1955-56]. 2 vols. Cloth, in dj. Inscr.   pba Oct 26 (327) $450
   Anr Ed. Garden City, 1955-56. Vol I only. Library markings. Sgd on half-title.   sg Sept 28 (268) $225
— Mr. Citizen. NY, 1960. Sgd.   Met May 22 (167) $210
— Mr. President. NY, 1952. Interviews by William Hillman. Inscr to Phil Regan, 13 Sept 1952. Also inscr by Cabinet members & others in the Truman White House.   CE June 12 (120) $600
— Truman Speaks. NY, 1960. In dj. Inscr to Milton Maidenberg.   pba Oct 26 (328) $250

**Trusler, John, 1735-1820**
— The Honours of the Table.... L, 1788. 8vo, half calf.   b May 30 (311) £320

**Truth, Sojourner, 1797?-1883**
— Narrative of Sojourner Truth, a Northern Slave.... Bost., 1853. 12mo, orig front wrap only.   sg Mar 28 (338) $2,400

**Tryon, Thomas, 1634-1703**
— The Way to Health, Long Life and Happiness.... L, 1691. 2d Ed. 8vo, contemp calf; corners repaired, spine rebacked. Soiled; inner margins of 1st 2 leaves repaired.   S Oct 12 (121) £320

**Tseng Hien-ch'i.** See: Hoyt Collection, Charles B.

**Tsiolkovsky, Konstantin Eduardovich, 1857-1935**
— [Dreams of the Earth and the Sky, in Russian]. Moscow, 1935. Orig wraps. Alexei A. Leonov's copy.   P Mar 16 (5) $500
— [Nirvana]. Kaluga, 1914. Orig ptd wraps; detached. Inscr to Nikolay Polikarpovich Glukharyov, 1919. Yuri Baginsky's copy.   P Mar 16 (1) $2,700
— [The Goal of Space Flight, in Russian]. Kaluga, 1929. Orig ptd wraps. Carried aboard Soyuz 4 & so inscr on front cover by cosmonaut Vladimir A. Shatalov.   P Mar 16 (153) $800

**Tsuji, S.**
— Etude historique de la cuisine Francaise. Tokyo, 1977. One of 1,250. Folio, cloth. Text in English, French and Japanese, & 3 photo plates. Sgd by Monsieurs Lenotre, uthier, L'Oasis, & Paul Bocuse.   S Oct 12 (17) £320
   Anr copy. Cloth in dj. Text in English, French and Japanese.   S Oct 12 (18) £280

**Tuchman, Maurice —& Barron, Stephanie**
— David Hockney: A Retrospective. Los Angeles, [1988]. 4to, cloth, in dj.   sg Jan 11 (217) $50

**Tucker, Ephraim W.**
— Five Months in Labrador and Newfoundland, during the Summer of 1838. Concord NH, 1839. 16mo, orig cloth; worn. Foxed.   NH Sept 16 (33) $350

**Tucker, St. George, 1752-1827**
— The Probationary Odes of Jonathan Pindar.... Phila., 1796. 8vo, modern half mor; new endpapers. Stained throughout; 1 leaf repaired.   Z June 28 (277) $200

**Tuckey, James Kingston, 1776-1816**
— Relation d'une expedition entreprise en 1816... pour reconnoitre le Zaire.... Paris, 1818. 3 vols, including Atlas. 8vo & 4to, contemp calf gilt by Meslant; upper joint of Atlas wormed, small scratch on spine of Vol I. With folding map & 15 plates in Atlas. Small hole in 1 text leaf.   S June 27 (217) £1,300

**Tuer, Andrew White, 1838-1900**
— 1,000 Quaint Cuts. L: Leadenhall Press, [1896]. 4to, half cloth; worn. O July 9 (210) $50
— Bartolozzi and his Works.... L, 1881. 2 vols. 4to, orig bds; shaken. Library markings. sg Sept 7 (35) $70
 One of 100 L.p. copies. 2 vols. Folio, orig vellum gilt. Extra-illus with port & 36 plates, ALs from the pbr & a prospectus. S Apr 23 (256) £820
— History of the Horn-Book. L, 1896. 2 vols. 4to, orig vellum gilt. With 7 facsimile horn books in end pocket. Related material, including ALs & the auction catalogue for the sale of Tuer's collection. S May 16 (201) £600
 2d Ed. Edin., 1897. 4to, orig cloth; worn & soiled. F June 20 (520) $210

**Tufts, Richard S.**
— The Principles Behind the Rules of Golf. Pinehurst, NC, [1960]. 1st Ed. In dj; d/j chipped & rubbed. pba Apr 18 (168) $150

**Tull, Jethro, 1671-1741**
— The New Horse-Houghing Husbandry.... L, 1731. 1st Ed. 4to, contemp calf; worn. Some waterstaining. b Sept 20 (189) £4,500
 Anr Ed. L, 1733. ("The Horse-Hoing Husbandry....") Folio, contemp half calf; rubbed, upper joint split. With 6 folding plates. S Mar 29 (777) £800

**Tulloch, W. W.**
— The Life of Tom Morris..... L: T. Werner Laurie, [c.1908]. 1st Ed. 8vo, cloth; spine ends & joints rubbed, cover label scratched, some insect damage. With 27 photos. pba Nov 9 (83) $1,400
 Anr copy. Cloth; shelf worn. Wit 27 photos. pba Apr 18 (169) $1,300
 Anr Ed. [L]: Ellesborough Press, [1982]. One of 200. Mor; spine sunned. With frontis photo. Sgd by J. H. Neill, Capt. Royal & Ancient Golf Club St. Andrews. pba Apr 18 (47) $180

**Tulpius, Nicolaus**
— Observationes medicae. Amst., 1652. 8vo, later calf; lower rear joints cracked, joints rubbed, corners bumped. With title, & 18 full-page illus. Lacking final blank; spotted & dampstained; modern illus laid down at end. Ck Mar 22 (303) £280

**Tunney, Gene**
— A Man Must Fight. Bost.: Houghton Mifflin, 1932. One of 550. Half cloth; front hinge starting. pba Apr 4 (110) $200

**Tunon de Lara, Manuel**
— From Incas to Indios. Paris: Robert Delpire, [1956]. 4to, cloth, in worn dj. With photographic plates by Robert Frank, Werner Bischof & Pierre Verger. sg Feb 29 (138) $100

**Tupper, Martin Farquhar.** See: Fore-Edge Paintings

**Turchi, Nicolo**
— La Tavola rotonda. Botogna: Nicolo Tebaldini, 1639. 4to, 18th-cent floral wraps. With 3 folding plates. Some spotting. C Apr 3 (247) £2,600

**Turf...**
— The Turf. A Satirical Novel. L, 1831. 2 vols in 1. 8vo, contemp half cloth. Foxed. O Jan 9 (243) $110

**Turgan, L.**
— Histoire de l'aviation. Paris, 1909. Later half cloth. sg May 16 (93) $90

**Turgenev, Ivan, 1818-83**
 See also: Limited Editions Club
— Russian Life in the Interior, or the Experiences of a Sportsman. Edin., 1855. 8vo, cloth; bumped. Pbr's presentation copy. sg Sept 21 (311) $425
— Works. NY, 1903-4. ("The Novels and Stories.") Trans by Isabel F. Hapgood. 16 vols. 8vo, half mor; rubbed. Some dampstaining. O Mar 5 (228) $850

**Turgot, Michel Etienne**
— Plan de Paris. Paris, 1739. Folio, contemp mor gilt with arms of Paris; rebacked, rubbed. Double-page key map & perspective plan on 20 double-page sheets (sheets 18 & 19 joined). Some browing; a few inner folds; light dampstain at top edge of a few sheets. C May 31 (73) £2,200

**Turkish...**
— Turkish Tales... with the History of the Sultaness of Persia... Written... by Chec Zade.... L: for J. Tonson, 1708. 12mo, contemp calf; rebacked. With frontis. Piece torn from 1 leaf with loss. bba Oct 19 (222) £100 [Attias]

**Turnebus, Adrianus.** See: Gallandius & Turnebus

**Turner, Daniel, 1667-1741**
— The Art of Surgery.... L, 1722. 2 vols. 8vo, contemp calf; extremities worn, covers detached or starting. sg May 18 (518) $425

**Turner, Joseph Mallord William, 1775-1851**
— Liber studiorum. L, 1899. One of 150. 2 vols. Oblong folio, orig cloth; rebacked retaining orig backstrips. With frontis & 70 plates. sg June 13 (373) $400
— Picturesque Views on the Southern Coast of England. L, 1826. 2 vols. Folio, contemp half mor; rubbed. With 80 plates on india paper. Spotted; 1 plate dampstained. S Oct 26 (410) £1,000 [Muller]
 Anr copy. Contemp half mor gilt; rubbed. With 80 plates on india paper, 48 of them full-page. Some spotting. S Mar 28 (69) £1,000
— The Rivers of France. L, 1837. 4to, lea gilt; spine loose. With 95 plates. Met May 22 (456) $250
— The Turner Gallery: a Series of Sixty Engravings.... L, 1875. Folio, contemp half mor gilt; rubbed. With port & 60 plates. Some spotting; a few leaves loose. S Apr 23 (258) £460

Anr Ed. L: Virtue, [n.d.]. Folio, contemp half mor gilt; rubbed. With port & 60 plates. S June 12 (340) £330

**Turner, Laurence Arthur**
— Decorative Plasterwork in Great Britain. L, 1927. Folio, orig cloth; stained. Dampstaining on prelims & several leaves; preface leaf detached. sg June 13 (375) $80

**Turner, Samuel, 1749?-1802**
— An Account of an Embassy to the Court of the Teshoo Lama, in Tibet. L, 1806. 2d Ed. 4to, contemp half calf; joints cracked, edges rubbed. With 13 plates & folding map. Map with marginal wear; some browning & staining. CE June 15 (273) $700

**Turpin, Francois Rene, 1709-99**
— La France illustre, ou le Plutarque francais.... Paris, 1780-86. 4 vols. 4to, contemp mor gilt; Vol IV with small tear & rubbing on upper cover. With 48 plates. Half-titles in Vols II & III only; near-contemp Ms list of plates pasted onto tp verso. Fuerstenberg - Schaefer copy. S Dec 8 (615) £800

**Turrecremata, Johannes de, 1388-1468**
— Expositio psalterii. [Basel: Johann Amerbach, not after 1482]. ("Expositio super toto psalterio.") Folio, contemp half pigskin over wooden bds, bound in Landshut, Kyriss 165; crack to front corner repaired, lacking 1 clasp. 41 lines & headline; double column; types 1:185G, 5:106(92)G, 3:92a. Wormholes touching some letters. 124 leaves. Goff T-530. C Nov 17 (223) £200
— Quaestiones evangeliorum de tempore et de sanctis.... Basel: Johann Amerbach, [not after 1484]. Folio, 19th-cent mor; rebacked. 47 lines; gothic type. Wormholes at end; 1 leaf with tear. 193 (of 194) leaves (without the Flos theologiae). Goff T-553. S Dec 18 (89) £1,000 [Zioni]
— Summa de ecclesia. Venice: Michele Tramezini, 1561. 2 parts in 1 vol. 4to, early blind-stamped pigskin over pastebds; soiled. Hole in 2A at foremargin. S June 12 (158) £130
— Summa de Ecclesia.i. Lyon: Johannes Treschel, 20 Sept 1496. Folio, 16th-cent blind-stamped calf; rubbed & worn, repaired, rebacked. Some worming at beginning; 1 leaf lacking corner. 270 leaves. Goff T-556. bba Sept 7 (175) £900 [R. Clark]

**Turrell, W. J.**
— Ancient Angling Authors. L, 1910. 1st Ed. Cloth. pba July 11 (306) $80

**Turton, William, M.D.**
— Manual of the Land and Fresh-Water Shells of the British Islands. L, 1840. 2d Ed. 12mo, orig cloth; def. With 12 hand-colored plates. sg Dec 7 (252) $110

**Tuscarora Club**
— Tuscarora Club's Forty-Year History 1901-1941. [N.p.: Pvtly ptd], 1941. One of 100. O Feb 6 (236) $400

**Tusser, Thomas, 1524?-80**
— Five Hundreth Pointes of good Husbandrie.... L: Henrie Denham, 1585. 4to, 19th-cent mor gilt; spine rubbed. Black letter. Tp discolored & with minor repairs to margins. S Mar 29 (780) £850

**Tute, George**
— Leon Underwood: His Wood Engravings. Woolley: Fleece Press, [1986]. One of 200. Folio, half mor. sg Jan 11 (439) $100

**Twain, Mark.** See: Clemens, Samuel Langhorne

**Twamley, Louisa Anne.** See: Meredith, Louisa Anne Twamley

**Tweedie, Major-Gen. William**
— The Arabian Horse: his Country and People. Edin., 1894. 4to, cloth; shaken, spine tips frayed. Drawing on frontis verso. O Jan 9 (244) $800
One of 100 L.p. copies. Orig half mor gilt. S Mar 29 (797) £1,700

**Twice a Year...**
— Twice a Year: A Semi-Annual Journal of Literature, the Arts, and Civil Liberties. NY, 1938-47. Nos 1-15 in 9 vols as issued. Orig wraps & ptd bds; rubbed & chipped. bbc Apr 22 (236) $300

**Twining, Edward Francis, Baron Twining**
— A History of the Crown Jewels of Europe. L, [1961]. 4to, cloth; library markings to covers & text. bbc June 24 (270) $200

**Twining, William J.** See: Campbell & Twining

**Twiss, Richard**
— Voyage en Portugal et en Espagne fait en 1772 & 1773. Berne, 1776. 8vo, contemp calf gilt with monogram (PB) on spine of the Empress Josephine & a later library stamp of Malmaison on tp. Fuerstenberg - Schaefer copy. S Dec 8 (616) £420

**Twitchell, Ralph Emerson**
— The Leading facts of New Mexican History. Cedar Rapids: Torch Press, 1911-12. 1st Ed. 2 vols. Robbins copy. pba Mar 21 (364) $350
— The Spanish Archives of New Mexico. Cedar Rapids: Torch Press, 1914. 1st Ed. 2 vols. Orig cloth in djs; d/js chipped & torn, hinges cracked. Robbins copy. pba Mar 21 (365) $300

**Twyne, Brian**
— Antiquitatis academiae Oxoniensis apologia. Oxford: J. Barnes, 1608. 4to, later half calf. Tp worn & repaired; some annotations. bba May 30 (75) £220 [R. Clark]

**Twysden, Sir Roger, 1597-1672**
— Historiae Anglicanae scriptores X.... L, 1652. 1st Ed. 2 vols. Folio, later sheep; repaired. With half title, title, & errata leaf 2N4. Lacks 4F3; errors in pagination; some discoloration; some worming touching letters. S Oct 26 (84) £400 [Cyprus Pop. BK]

**Tyler, Anne**
— Breathing Lessons. NY, 1988. Inscr. pba May 23 (436) $55
— If Morning Ever Comes. NY, 1964. In repaired but def dj. sg Dec 14 (283) $650
— A Slipping-Down Life. NY, 1970. In chipped dj. bbc June 24 (626) $290

**Tyler, Daniel, b.1816**
— A Concise History of the Mormon Battalion in the Mexican War, 1846-1847. Salt Lake City, 1881. 1st Ed. 8vo, orig cloth; covers stained, corners & spine ends rubbed. Robbins copy. pba Mar 21 (366) $1,300

Anr Ed. [Salt Lake City, 1882]. Orig cloth; cover extremities worn. Larson copy. pba Sept 28 (610) $300

**Tyler, Rev. Josiah**
— Livingstone Lost and Found.... Hartford, 1873. Orig cloth; rear hinge & joint weak. pba Aug 22 (933) $80

Anr copy. Orig cloth; rubbed. Short tear in prelims. sg Mar 7 (367) $50

**Tyler, Ron**
— Posada's Mexico. Wash., 1979. 4to, pictorial wraps. ds July 27 (148) $150

**Tymms, William Robert —&**
**Wyatt, Sir Matthew Digby, 1820-77**
— The Art of Illuminating as Practised in Europe.... L, [1859] 1860. Folio, contemp mor gilt; rubbed, joints & tips worn. With chromolitho title & 99 chromolitho plates. O Mar 5 (231) $200

Anr Ed. L, [1859]-60. 4to, orig cloth; rebacked retaining orig backstrip. With chromo title & 101 plates. sg Apr 11 (319) $80

Anr copy. Contemp half lea; rebacked. sg Apr 11 (320) $80

**Tyrrell, Frederick, 1793-1843**
— A Practical Work on the Diseases of the Eye.... L, 1840. 1st Ed. 2 vols. 8vo, contemp half lea; With 1 plain & 8 colored plates.. Stain in gutter of Vol I. O Mar 5 (232) $160

**Tyrrell, Henry**
— The History of the War with Russia.... L, [c.1856]. Vols I-II (of 3) bound in 1 vol. Contemp half mor. pba Apr 25 (249) $50

**Tyson, George E.**
— Arctic Experiences. NY, 1874. Ed by E. Vale Blake. Later cloth; hinges cracked. sg Mar 7 (273) $60

**Tyson, Henry**
— The Plan for the Improvement of the Channel of Jones' Falls.... Balt., 1871. 4to, cloth; spine lacking, worn, library stamp to front free endpaper. bbc June 24 (372) $300

**Tyson, James L.**
— Diary of a Physician in California.... NY, 1850. Contemp half lea; front hinge & joint cracked, worn & scuffed. Some foxing. Larson copy. pba Sept 28 (721) $800

**Tyson, Philip T.**
— Report of the Secretary of War Communicating Information in Relation to the Geology and Topography of California. Wash., 1850. 8vo, modern half mor. With 13 folding maps. Waterdamage to bottom of leaves; some foxing to maps. 31st Congress, 1st Session, Sen. Exec. Doc. 47. Larson copy. pba Feb 12 (187) $600

**Tyssot de Patot, Simon**
— Voyages et avantures de Jaques Masse. Bordeaux [i.e., The Hague], 1710. 12mo, contemp vellum. With port. sg Mar 21 (323) $300

**Tytler, Alexander Fraser, Lord Woodhouselee.** See: Fore-Edge Paintings

**Tzara, Tristan, 1896-1963**
— L'Antitete. Paris, 1949. One of 23 on Hollande. 3 vols. 4to, unsewn in orig wraps; stained. With 23 plates, plus an extra suite, hand-colored, of the plates in Vols I & II, & a different set of 8 plates in Vol III. sg Apr 18 (136) $15,000
— La Main Passe. Paris, 1935. One of 30 on vellum sgd by author & with etched frontis in 2 states, 1 sgd by the artist. Illus By Wassily Kandinsky. 4to, mor extra with abstract design, by Pierre Lucien Martin, 1959. b May 30 (557) £10,000
— Midis gagnes. Paris, [1939]. One of 1,000. Illus by Henri Matisse. 4to, orig wraps, unopened. sg Feb 15 (196) $200
— La Premiere aventure celest de Mr. Antipyrine. Zurich: J. Heuberger, 1916. Illus by Marcel Janco. Orig ptd wraps; partly separated at top of spine, tape stains on inside covers. With 6 colored illusts & 1 uncolored illust. Sgd by Tzara & Janco. sg Apr 18 (135) $2,400

# U

**Uchard, Mario**
— Mon Oncle Barbassou. Paris: J. Lemonnyer, 1884. One of 50 on chine. Illus by Paul Avril. 8vo, olive lev extra by Petrus Ruban, 1898, bound for the Vicomte Lacroix-Laval, to over-all oriental design of stylized lotus flowers surmounted by small star & crescent moon, alternating with stylized pistil & stamen, within rhomboid compartments. C May 1 (174) £9,500

**Udell, John**
— Incidents of Travel to California.... Jefferson, OH, 1856. 1st Ed. 12mo, orig cloth; spine cloth frayed at top & bottom, rear cover & pastedown marred. With errata slip & frontis port Foxed & dampstained; pp.245-303 torn at bottom. Sgd & inscr on port. Larson copy. pba Sept 28 (723) $600

# 1995 - 1996 · BOOKS

Anr Ed. Jefferson OH, 1856. 12mo, orig cloth; recased, spine rubbed, spine ends & corners worn. With frontis port. Foxed & soiled. Robbins copy. Inscr & sgd. pba Mar 21 (368) $2,250
— Journal Kept During a Trip Across the Plains.... Los Angeles, 1946. With: facsimile reprint of 1859 Ed by Yale U. Library Intro by Lyle H. Wright. 2 items, orig cloth. With facsimile of 1868 Ed tp. Larson copy. pba Sept 28 (724) $50

**Uemura, Rokuro**
— Old Art Treasures from Japan's Needles and Looms. Kyoto, 1949. Folio, Plates loose in folio orig wooden folding case; text in wraps laid in.. With 50 colored plates, mtd. sg June 13 (360) $175

**Ullrich, Hermann**
— Robinson und Robinsonaden. Teil I. Bibliographie. Weimar, 1898. 8vo, half vellum. sg Apr 11 (323) $110

**Ulmann, Doris**
— The Darkness and the Light. NY, [1974]. Text by Robert Coles. 4to, cloth, in soiled dj; notations on front free endpaper. sg Feb 29 (328) $130

**Ultonius, Virgilius, Pseud.**
— The Civic Wreath, an Anniversary Poem.... Belfast, 1818. 8vo, modern half cloth. b Dec 5 (597) £50

**Umbstaetter, H. D.**
— The Red-Hot Dollar and Other Stories from the Black Cat. Bost., 1911. 1st Ed. - Intro by Jack London. Orig cloth; covers spotted. pba Aug 22 (311) $65

**Umfreville, Edward**
— The Present State of Hudson's Bay.... L, 1790. 1st Ed. 8vo, disbound. Folding chart repaired. Met Feb 24 (365) $525
Anr copy. Contemp bds; shelf-number at foot of spine, bookplate removed from rear pastedown. With 1 plate & 2 folding tables. O Nov 14 (179) $2,050

**Underhill, Francis T.**
— Driving for Pleasure; or, the Harness Stable.... NY, 1896. 1st Ed. 4to, calf & gilt-pictorial suede; rubbed. O Jan 9 (245) $325

**Underwood, Lamar**
— The Bobwhite Quail Book. Clinton: Amwell, 1980. One of 1,000. Illus by Donald Shoffstall. Syn gilt; worn. O Oct 10 (267) $30

**Unger, Franz, 1800-70**
— Wissenschaftliche Ergebnisse einer Reise in Griechenland und in den jonischen Inseln. Vienna, 1862. 1st Ed. 8vo, half mor. With half-title, folding map, 3 plates, & 27 illus. S Oct 26 (229) £140 [Theotoky]

**Union Pacific Railway**
— The Union Pacific Railroad: A Trip Across the North American Continent.... NY: T. Nelson, [1874].

# UNITED

12mo,. cloth worn & rubbed, hinges repaired, new free endpapers. pba July 25 (327) $110
— The Union Pacific Railroad Company...Progress of their Road West.... NY, Apr 1868. Pamphlet Ed. Orig wraps; chipped. With frontis map. Library stamps. pba Aug 8 (202) $50

**United States Capitol Historical Society.** See: Onassis copy, Jacqueline Bouvier Kennedy

**United States of America**
See also: Morton, William Thomas Green; Official...
— Abstract of Infantry Tactics; Including Exercises and Manoeuvres.... Phila., 1853. Orig cloth; stained & worn. pba June 25 (125) $80
— Acts Passed at a Congress of the United States of America...Wednesday the Fourth of March.... NY, 1789. 8vo, contemp sheep; rebacked with lea. Some foxing. pba June 13 (300) $3,250
Anr Ed. Richmond: Augustine Davis for the Gneneral [sic] Assembly of Virginia, [1789]. 8vo, later half cloth. Tp soiled & reinforced with minor loss; library markings. cb Oct 17 (172) $8,000
— Annual Report of the Superintendent of the Coast Survey.... Wash., 1851. 4to, orig cloth; spine taped. With 58 charts & plans. Some charts split at folds. NH July 21 (211) $200
— A Bill to Provide for Organizing, Arming and Disciplining the Militia of the United States. Phila., 18 Feb 1795. 8vo, disbound. P June 5 (106) $2,500
— Complete Regular Army Register of the United States for One Hundred Years (1779 to 1879). Wash., 1880. 8vo, orig cloth; worn & soiled. wa Feb 29 (311) $160
— The Infantry Exercise of the United States Army, Abridged.... Montpellier VT, 1820. 12mo, contemp calf; rubbed. With 9 plates. Some foxing & browning. O Jan 9 (158) $100
— Journal of the First Session of the Senate...March 4th, 1789.... NY, 1789. 1st Ed. Folio, orig wraps; becoming detached. Tp soiled; corner of last few leaves worn; library bookplate. cb Oct 17 (173) $8,500
— Journal of the Proceedings...at Philadelphia, May 10, 1775. L, 1776. 8vo, disbound. sg Oct 26 (372) $600
— The Laws of the United States of America. Phila.: R. Folwell, 1796-[97]. 3 vols. With: Acts Passed at the First Session of the Fifth Congress. Phila., [1799]. Together, 4 vols. 8vo, contemp sheep; worn, library labels to rear covers. Some browning. wa Feb 29 (416) $290
— Progress-Report upon Geographical & Geological Explorations and Surveys West of the One Hundredth Meridian.... Wash., 1874. Folio, orig wraps; spine splitting. George Davidson's copy, sgd at top of front wrap. pba July 25 (246) $110
— Report of Professor Alexander D. Bache, Superintendent of the Coast Survey, showing the Progress of that work for the year ending October 1850. Wash., 1850. 8vo, orig wraps; worn, backstrip split, repaired. With 27 folding maps & charts. Some soiling & foxing. wa Feb 29 (621) $200

## UNITED

— Report of the Superintendent of the Coast Survey, showing the Progress of the Survey during the Year 1850. Wash., 1851. 8vo, wraps. With 27 maps & plates. Minor fold tears & foxing. wa Feb 29 (616) $170
— Report of the Superintendent of the Coast Survey, showing the Progress of the Survey during the Year 1852. Wash., 1853. 4to, orig cloth; worn & chipped. With 37 charts & diagrams. pba July 25 (230) $350
— Report of the Superintendent of the Coast Survey, showing the Progress of the Survey during the Year 1853. Wash., 1854. 4to, orig cloth; some wear. With 54 folding charts, tables & diagrams. Minor tears to plates. pba July 25 (231) $350
— Report of the Superintendent of the Coast Survey, showing the Progress of the Survey during the Year 1854. Wash., 1855. 4to, orig cloth; worn & chipped, adhesion damage to front pastedown. pba July 25 (232) $350
  Anr copy. Orig cloth; rebacked, endpapers renewed. Tp & last leaf foxed; tears in several plates. sg May 9 (387) $300
— Report of the Superintendent of the Coast Survey, showing the Progress of the Survey during the Year 1855. Wash., 1856. 4to, orig sheep; worn, glue-repairs. With 60 charts & diagrams. pba July 25 (233) $325
— Report of the Superintendent of the Coast Survey, showing the Progress of the Survey during the Year 1856. Wash., 1856. 4to, cloth; worn & cracked, front cover detached. With 67 plates & diagrams. Buzzards Bay chart torn. NH Sept 16 (266) $275
— Reports upon Geographical & Geological Explorations and Surveys West of the One Hundredth Meridian. Wash., 1875. Vol V (of 7). 4to, orig cloth; shabby. Dampstained at all edges. wa Feb 29 (236) $190
— Sketches Accompanying the Annual Report of the Superintendent of the United States Coast Survey, 1851. Wash., 1851. 8vo, cloth; spine torn, corners showing. With 58 charts 7Z diagrams, most folding. Tears to a few plates. 32d Congress, 1st Session, Senate Ex. Doc 3. pba July 25 (229) $450
  Anr copy. Orig cloth. With 58 folding maps & sketches. 32d Congress, 1st Session, H of R Ex. Doc 26. Z Jan 30 (415) $200
DEPARTMENT OF AGRICULTURE. - Report on the Big Trees of California. Prepared in the Division of Forestry.... Wash., 1900. 3d Issue. Orig cloth; insect damage to covers. pba Aug 8 (17) $75
HOUSE OF REPRESENTATIVES. - Journal of the House of Representatives of the United States. NY, 1790. Folio, contemp half calf; worn, joints split. wa Feb 29 (400) $210

### Universal Exhibition—Paris, 1878
— The Chefs-d'Oeuvre d'Art of the International Exhibition, 1878. Phila., 1878. Folio, mor gilt; corners & extremities rubbed. Some foxing. pba June 20 (313) $100

**University Excursion Party.** See: Le Conte, Joseph

### University of Edinburgh
— Catalogue of the Printed Books in the Library.... Edin., 1918-23. 3 vols. 4to, cloth; worn. O Mar 26 (86) $80

**Untermeyer, Louis.** See: Limited Editions Club

### Updike, Daniel Berkeley
— Printing Types. Cambr. MA, 1937. 2d Ed. 2 vols. In djs with tears. bba May 9 (41) £55 [Morris]

### Updike, John
— Baby's First Step. Huntington Beach: James Cahill, [1993]. Artist's copy. pba Dec 7 (186) $65
  Author's copy. pba Jan 25 (365) $60
  One of 100. pba Oct 5 (360) $80; wa Feb 29 (79) $50
— Marry Me. NY, 1976. 1st Ed, One of 300. sg Dec 14 (286) $70
— Picked-Up Pieces. NY, 1975. One of 250. In dj. sg Dec 14 (285) $50
— The Poorhouse Fair. NY, 1959. In dj with minor crease to spine & small scrape to rear flap. pba Aug 22 (465) $95
— Rabbit Is Rich. NY, 1981. In dj. Sgd. pba Aug 22 (467) $55
  Anr copy. In dj. Inscr. sg June 20 (379) $120
— Rabbit Redux. NY, 1971. In dj. Inscr. sg Dec 14 (284) $110
— Rabbit, Run. Franklin Center: Franklin Mint, [1977]. Ltd Ed. Lea. sg Dec 14 (287) $50
— Roger's Version. NY, 1986. One of 350. sg Dec 14 (289) $70
— Talk from the Fifties. Northridge CA: Lord John Press, 1979. 1st Ed, One of 300. sg June 20 (380) $80
— The Twelve Terrors of Christmas. NY: Gotham Book Mart, [1994]. Illus by Edward Gorey. pba Jan 25 (366) $65
— The Witches of Eastwick. Franklin Center, 1984. Ltd Ed. Mor gilt. Dampstaining to extremities of sgd leaf. pba Jan 25 (367) $55

### Upham, Charles Wentworth
— Life, Explorations and Public Services of John Charles Fremont. Bost., 1856. Variant Issue. 8vo, orig cloth; spine ends frayed. With frontis port & 13 plates. Robbins copy. pba Mar 21 (369) $50

### Upham, Samuel Curtis
— Notes of a Voyage to California via Cape Horn.... Phila., 1878. 1st Ed. 8vo, orig mor; light wear & scuffing. With 45 plates. Inscr to John Sickels. Larson copy. pba Sept 28 (726) $1,700
  Anr copy. Orig cloth; spine faded, front hinge cracking. With double-frontis ports. Robbins copy. pba Mar 21 (370) $700

### Upton, Bertha & Florence K.
— The Golliwogg in Holland. L, 1904. Oblong 4to, pictorial bds; worn & soiled, corner bent, 1 leaf detached. wa Feb 29 (94) $190

— The Golliwogg in War. L, 1903. Oblong 4to, orig pictorial bds; worn & soiled, shaken. Child's scrawls on tp & text. F Mar 28 (570) $100
— The Golliwogg's Air-Ship. L & NY: Longmans, [1902]. Oblong 4to, pictorial bds; chipped. Some corners chipped. F Mar 28 (572) $140
— The Golliwogg's Auto-Go-Cart. L, 1901. Oblong 4to, pictorial bds; chipped. Some tears & scrawls. F Mar 28 (571) $130

### Urban, Martin
— Emil Nolde: Catalogue Raisonne of the Oil Paintings. L & NY, 1987. 2 vols. 4to, cloth, in djs. sg Jan 11 (324) $200

### Urfe, Honore d', 1568-1625
— L'Astree. Paris: P. Witte & Didot, 1733. 5 vols in 10. 8vo, contemp calf. With 60 plates. Fuerstenberg - Schaefer copy. S Dec 8 (617) £320

### Urquinaona y Pardo, Pedro de
— Relacion documentada del origen y progresos del trastorno de las provincias de Venezuela hasta la exoneracion del Capitan General Don Domingo Monteverde.... Madrid, 1820. 4to, modern half calf. Tp & a few leaves browned. S Nov 30 (189) £650

### Ursula, Saint
— The Legend of Saint Ursula and Her Companions. L, 1869. 4to, mor extra by Mansell. With 22 chromolitho plates. b May 30 (522) £200

### Usage...
— De l'usage du caphe, du the, et du chocolate. Lyons: J. Girin & B. Riviere, 1671. 1st Ed. 12mo, contemp calf; spine rubbed, covers scuff marked. With woodcut illus on *8. Library perforation to title, A8, & E1; G4 with burn mark. Ck Mar 22 (281) £420

### Usher, James
— A Body of Divinity, or the Summe and Substance of Christian Religion. L, 1645. 1st Ed. Folio, contemp calf; rubbed, covers detached. Tp & last leaf loose; browned. bba May 30 (81) £75 [Cathach]

### U.S.S.R....
— U.S.S.R., The Soviet Worker. Moscow: State Art Publishers, 1939. Designed by El Lissitzky. Oblong 4to, lea; soiled. sg Feb 29 (278) $600

### Utilite...
— Utilite de la Flagellation dans les plaisirs de l'amour et du Mariage.... L, 1885. 8vo, half mor; front cover detached. With 2 albumen photographs. Sold w.a.f. sg Feb 29 (133) $300

### Utley, Robert M.
— Custer's Last Stand.... Dayton IN, [1949]. Orig ptd wraps. Tp & front wrap stamped. Sgd. pba June 25 (233) $50
— Frontier Regulars. NY, [1973]. In dj. Inscr to John Popovich. pba June 25 (234) $70

### Uttenhofer, Caspar
— Circinus geometricus, zu teutsch Mess-Circkel.... Nuremberg, 1626. Bound with: Albrecht, Andreas. Instrument zur Architectur damit die fuenff Seuelen.... Nuremberg, 1622. And: Eigentlicher Abriss und Beschreibung. Eines sonderbaren nutzlich und notwendigen mechanischen Instruments.... Nuremberg: J. Duemmler, [n.d.]. 4to, contemp vellum. Madsen copy. S Mar 14 (359) £4,000

### Uzanne, Octave, 1852-1931
— Dictionnaire bibliophilosophique, typologique, iconophilesque, bibliopegique et bibliotechnique. Paris, 1896. One of 176, this copy for Ernest Chaze. 8vo, mor extra by Canape et Corriez, orig wraps bound in. With 32 full-page plates, 2 colored, & decorated borders throughout. S Nov 21 (436) £650
— The Fan. L, 1884 [1883]. Illus by Paul Avril. 8vo, mor extra by Riviere, upper cover with 5 watercolor port miniatures inset behind glass; upper joint weak, upper hinge repaired. S Nov 21 (434) £3,500
— Fashion in Paris: the Various Phases of Feminine Taste. L, 1898. Illus by Francois Courboin. 8vo, orig cloth; worn & shaken. With 100 hand-colored plates. sg Jan 11 (126) $175
— The Sunshade, the Muff, the Glove. L, 1883. Illus by Paul Avril. 4to, mor extra by Riviere from designs by J. J. Stonehouse, a Cosway bdg with upper cover inset with 5 watercolor miniatures on ivory by C. B. Currie. S Nov 21 (433) £4,600

### Uztariz, Geronimo de
— Theorica y practica de comercio y de marina.... Madrid: Antonio Sanz, 1757. Folio, contemp mor gilt with name of Don Josef Benito Cistue stamped in guilt on upper cover, presentation copy of the Real Sociedad Economica de Amigos del Pais de Zaragoza; repair to head of spine. S June 27 (378) £950

# V

### Vade, Jean Joseph, 1720-57
— Oeuvres poissardes.... Paris, 1796. One of 300. 4to, contemp mor gilt. Library stamp washed form half-title; paper cockled; some spotting. S Nov 30 (304) £600
Anr copy. Contemp calf gilt; lower joint repaired. Paper browned & cockled. Fuerstenberg - Schaefer copy. S Dec 8 (620) £500

### Vaenius, Otto
— Amoris divini emblemata. Antwerp: Plantin, 1660. 4to, later sheep; some lea peeled away, joints rubbed, spine ends def. With 61 plates. Some soiling, staining & browning; marginal worming. cb Feb 14 (2809) $500
— Amorum emblemata. Antwerp, 1608. 1st Ed. Oblong 4to, contemp vellum; soiled, later lettering-piece on spine. With 1 full-page enblematic illust & 124 engraved emblems within frames. Rustmark on Q4. STC 24627a.8. C June 26 (142) £3,200
Anr copy. 17th-cent vellum over thin bds, with yapp edges; stains to bds. With 124 (of 125) engravings

## VAENIUS

in text. Lacking B1; partly misbound; tp with erasures; some soiling. Schaefer copy. P Nov 1 (203) $2,000
— Emblesmes de l'amour divin. Paris, [c.1690]. Bound with: Herman Weyen. [Scenes from the Passion.] N.p., n.d. 2 vols in 1. 4to, contemp calf; worn. Together, 40 plates. Stained; 1 plate repaired. S Oct 27 (1172) £240 [D'Arte]
— Le Theatre morale de la vie humaine.... Brussels: F. Foppens, 1678. Folio, 18th-cent calf. With port & 102 (of 103) plates. Lacking Dd2; a few small wormholes; Tableau de Cebes torn along 1 fold & repaired. S Mar 14 (146) £360

### Vaile, P. A.

— Golf on the Green. NY, 1915. 1st Ed. Cloth; spine ends rubbed. pba Apr 18 (170) $110
— The Soul of Golf. L, 1912. 1st Ed. Cloth; upper corners bumped. Clapcott copy. pba Apr 18 (172) $250

### Valades, Didaco

— Rhetorica christiana ad concionandi, et orandi usum accommodata. Perugia: P. Petrutium, 1579. 4to, 17th-cent vellum; wormed. With engraved title & 12 plates on 9 leaves & 14 illusts, 5 of them full-page. some staining; tp shaved at margins with restorations. C June 26 (143) £5,500

### Valens, E. G.

— Magnet. Cleveland, [1964]. Illus by Berenice Abbott. In chipped & worn dj. sg Feb 29 (3) $90

### Valentijn, Frans, 1656-1727

— Verhandeling der Zee-Horenkens en Zee-Gewassen in en omtrent Amboina en de Nabygelegene Eilanden... Dordrecht: Joannes van Braam, 1726. Folio, contemp half calf; repaired. With folding table & 40 maps & plates. With additional material bound in. b Sept 20 (447) £1,500

### Valentine and Orson

— Cy commence l'hystoire des deux vaillans chevaliers valentin et orson filz de lempereur de grece et nepueux du tresvaillant et debouvte roy pepin iadis roy de france. Paris: Jean Trepperel or his widow with Jean Heannot, [c.1512-21]. 4to, contemp doeskin; worn. Lacking Sig A & leaves B2-4, O1 & P8; tear with loss in B5. C Apr 3 (249) £1,900

### Valentiner, Wilhelm Reinhold

— Rembrandt Paintings in America. NY, 1931. One of 200. Folio, lea gilt, in plain dj; rubbed. With port & 175 plates. Inscr. O May 7 (287) $100

### Valentini, Michael Bernard

— Museum museorum, oder Vollstaendige Schau-Buehne aller Materialien und Specereyen. Frankfurt, 1714. 2d Ed. Vol I only. Folio, contemp calf; both covers detached. A few leaves with later illusts pasted over text. Sold w.a.f. S Mar 14 (360) £220

## AMERICAN BOOK PRICES CURRENT

### Valerius Flaccus, Caius

— Argonauticon, libri octo. Bologna: Hieronymus Plato de Benedictus, 1519. ("Argonautica....") Folio, 18th-cent bds; later endpapers, joints splitting. Some soiling & staining. bba Sept 7 (181) £500 [Hubert]

### Valerius Maximus, Gaius

— Dictorum et factorum memorabilium.... Venice: Joannes & Gregorius de Gregoriis, de Forlivio, 8 Mar 1487. ("Facta et dicta memorabilia.") Folio, contemp calf over wooden bds; rebacked in sheep with fragments of orig calf, clasps lacking, hinges starting. 59 lines commentary & headline; types 10:109R (text), 11:82R & occasional 80 Greek. Rubricated. 247 (of 248) leaves; lacking initial blank. Goff V-36. P June 5 (343) $1,400

Anr Ed. Venice: Bartholomaeus de Zanis, 22 Mar 1497. Folio, modern half calf. 62 lines & headline; roman letter. Tear in text of e3 repaired without loss; ink stains on f3; some other staining; library stamp on tp. S Nov 30 (305) £850

Anr Ed. Paris: Ascensi, 1513. ("Valerius Maximus cum duplici comentario....") Folio, 17th-cent sheep gilt. Marginal dampstaining at ends; outer margin of tp cropped; clean tear in gutter of last leaf. sg Mar 21 (324) $400

### Valery, Paul, 1871-1945

— Degas, danse, dessin. Paris, 1936. One of 305. 4to, half mor, orig wraps bound in. S Nov 21 (444) £1,500
— Eupalinos or the Architect. L, 1932. One of 250. sg Dec 14 (290) $200; sg June 20 (383) $120
— Odes. Paris, 1920. One of 25. Illus by Paul Vera. 4to, mor extra by Marot-Rodde, orig wraps bound in. Inscr to Louis Barthou, with a stanza from Palme, & with 2 A Ls s, 1 to Barthou & 1 to an unidentified recipient & with an AL in pencil by Pierre Louys to Valery. S Nov 21 (440) £1,500
— Pieces dur l'art. [Paris: Darantiere, 1931]. One of 26 hors commerce. 4to, ptd wraps, unopened. sg June 20 (384) $175

### Valery, Paul, 1871-1945 —& Others

— Paul Bonet. Paris, 1945. One of 50 with 6 additional plates. 4to, mor extra irradiant bdg by Paul Bonet for Jacques Millot, executed 1945-46 by Rene Desmules & Collet. Extra-illus with 5 orig designs by Bonet. C May 1 (175) £10,000

### Vallance, Aylmer

— The Art of William Morris. L, 1897. One of 220. Folio, orig half cloth; shaken, lower hinge cracked. S Nov 21 (438) £950

Anr copy. Orig half cloth; lower cover marked, hinges cracked. Benz copy. S Nov 21 (439) £1,000
— William Morris: His Art, his Writings, and his Public Life. L, 1897. 4to, mor gilt; spine ends & corners scuffed. Tp stamped & bookplate of Brooklyn Public Library. pba Nov 30 (244) $275

## Valle, Guglielmo della
— Storia del duomo di Orvieto. Rome, 1791. 4to, contemp half russia by C. Lewis; joints rubbed. Some spotting. Beckford - Rosebery copy. S Mar 28 (508) £200

## Vallee, Leon
— Bibliographie des Bibliographies. Paris, 1883. 1st Ed. 8vo, later half cloth; orig wrappers bound in. sg Apr 11 (325) $140
— Courtiers and Favourites of Royalty. L: Merrill & Banker, [n.d.]. 20 vols. 8vo, mor gilt; joints & extremities rubbed. F Mar 28 (622) $220

## Vallejo, Mariano Guadalupe
— Ecsposicion Que hace el Comdanante General Interino de la Alta California al Gobernador de la Misma. Sonoma, Aug 17 1837. 5-3/4in by 3-3/4in, wraps. Larson copy. pba Sept 28 (262) $5,500
— Informe de la Comsion Especial Sobre la Derivacion y Definicion de los Nombres de los Diferentes Condados del Estado de California. [San Jose, 1850]. Wraps; spotted. Larson copy. pba Sept 28 (266) $2,000
— Proclama el C. Mariano G. Vallejo en el acto de prestar el juramento de las baces adoptadad por la ecselentisima diputacion de la Alta California. Monterey, Nov 29 1836. 12in by 8.5in, Some chipping & foxing & creases where folded. Larson copy. pba Sept 28 (261) $4,750

## Vallier, Dora
— Henri Rousseau. NY: Abrams, [c.1962]. 4to, cloth, in dj. sg Jan 11 (383) $50
— Ten Works...with a Discussion by the Artist. NY, [1963]. One of 35 with a sgd litho. Illus by Georges Braque. Folio, loose with text booklet in half-cloth folder. With 10 matted reproductions. wad Oct 18 (174) C$1,800

## Valpy, Richard
— Poetical Chronology of Ancient and English Poetry.... Reading, 1795. 12mo, contemp calf. b Dec 5 (9) £70

## Valtellina Massacre
— Piadoso memorial del Clero y Catholicos de la Valtelina, presentado al Rey Nuestro Senor por el Orador particular que embio para este efeto a la Corte por el mes de Otubre del ano de 1621... con el traslado de una determinacion heche por los predicantes hereges Grisones. Barcelona: Estevan Liberos, 1622. 4to, vellum gilt. S Nov 30 (306) £420

## Valton, Emilio
— Impresos mexicanos del siglo XVI.... Mexico, 1935. One of 50. Folio, contemp lea, orig wraps bound in; spine head loose, joints rubbed. Inscr. ds July 27 (190) $80

## Valverde de Hamusco, Juan
— Anatomia del corpo humano.... Rome, 1560. 1st Ed, 2d Issue of the Italian trans. Folio, contemp vellum; spine renewed. With engraved title & 42 plates. Tp stained, with small hole in right margin & contemp writing in lower margin; blank portion of B6 renewed; plate on f.95 torn & repaired; some staining throughout. P Dec 12 (171) $2,250

1st Italian Ed. Rome: Salamanca & Lafrerj, 1560. Folio, modern half mor. With 41 (of 42) illus. Lacks S1; stained at ends; marginal staining & defs. CE Nov 8 (155) $500
— La Anatomia del corpo umano. Venice: Giunta, 1586. Folio, contemp vellum. With engraved title with port on verso & 46 plates. Lacking P1-P6 & A1-A5; S1 torn; soiling & dampstaining throughout. Sold w.a.f. CE Feb 21 (266) $400

## Van de Water, Frederic
— Glory-Hunter: A Life of General Custer. Indianapolis: Bobbs-Merrill, [1934]. pba June 25 (237) $150

## Van Dine, S. S.
— The Greene Murder Case. NY, 1928. In chipped dj. pba Aug 22 (480) $50
— The Kennel Murder Case. NY, 1933. In chipped dj; bdg spine leaning. pba Aug 22 (481) $65
— The Scarab Murder Case: A Philo Vance Story. NY, 1930. In chipped dj; bdg spine leaning. pba Aug 22 (482) $60

**Van Dyke, Henry, 1852-1933.** See: Derrydale Press

## Van Dyke, John C.
— The Desert. NY, 1901. pba Feb 12 (188) $85

## Van Dyke, Theodore Strong
— The City and County of San Diego Illustrated.... San Diego, 1888. 8vo, cloth wraps; dog-eared. pba Apr 25 (710) $80

**Van Dyne, Edith.** See: Baum, L. Frank

## Van Gogh, Vincent, 1853-90
— The Complete Letters.... Greenwich CT: New York Graphic Society, [1958]. 3 vols. 4to, cloth; minor wear. sg Sept 7 (336) $175

## Van Gulik, Robert, 1910-67
— The Chinese Maze Murders. The Hague, 1956. 1st Ed. In dj, with wrap-around band having Agatha Christie's endorsement,; minor discoloration to white portions of d/j. sg Dec 14 (74) $300
— The Given Day: An Amsterdam Mystery. San Antonio: Dennis McMillan, 1984. One of 300. Postscript by Janwillem Van de Wetering. In dj. pba Aug 22 (485) $130

## Van Hengel, Steven J. H.
— Early Golf. N.p., [1982]. 1st Ed. In dj. pba Apr 18 (173) $65

## Van Laun, Henri
— History of French Literature. L, 1882. 3 vols. Half mor. pba Aug 8 (291) $130

### Van Lennep, Henry John, 1815-89
— Travels in Little-Known Parts of Asia Minor. L, 1870. 2 vols. 8vo, orig cloth; some wear. b Sept 20 (360) £260

### Van, Melvin
— The Big Heart. San Francisco, [1957]. Illus by Ruth Bernhard. 4to, bdg not described, in rubbed dj. sg Feb 29 (33) $90

### Van Nieder, Mattheus Broverius. See: Nieder, Mattheus Broverius van

### Van Nostrand, Jeanne
See also: Coulter & Van Nostrand
— Edward Vischer's Drawings of the California Missions, 1861-1878. San Francisco: Book Club of California, 1982. One of 600. In dj. pba Apr 25 (711) $75
— A Pictorial and Narrative History of Monterey, Adobe Capital of California, 1770-1847. San Francisco, 1968. 1st Ed. Mor by Edna Peter Fahey. Larson copy. pba Sept 28 (274) $100

Anr copy. Orig cloth in dj. Larson copy. pba Sept 28 (275) $50

Anr copy. Orig cloth in dj. pba Feb 13 (184) $65
— San Francisco, 1806-1906 in Contemporary Paintings, Drawings.... San Francisco: Book Club of California, 1975. One of 500. Book Club of California No 150. pba Feb 12 (384) $85

Anr copy. Book Club of California No 150. pba Feb 13 (185) $85

### Van Tramp, John C.
— Prairie and Rocky Mountain Adventures. Columbus, 1858. 8vo, orig lea; front joint cracked. pba Apr 25 (712) $65

### Van Urk, John Blan. See: Derrydale Press

### Van Vechten, Carl, 1880-1964
— Fragments from an Unwritten Autobiography. New Haven, 1955. 2 vols. Ls laid in. pba Aug 22 (486) $65

### Van Vogt, Alfred Elton
— Slan. Sauk City, 1946. 1st Ed. In chipped & rubbed dj. pba May 23 (440) $110
— The Voyage of the Space Beagle. NY, 1950. Advance copy. In chipped dj. pba May 4 (268) $60
— The Weapon Makers. Providence: Hadley, [1947]. In dj. sg Dec 14 (291) $250
— The World of A. NY, 1948. In dj with extremity wear. pba May 4 (270) $30

### Van Winkle, William Mitchell —& Randall, David A.
— Henry W. Herbert: a Bibliography.... Portland ME, 1936. One of 250. Unopened. O Dec 5 (146) $120

### Vanbrugh, Sir John, 1664-1726. See: Nonesuch Press

### Vance, Jack
— To Live Forever. NY: Ballantine Books, 1956. Currey's A bdg, in dj. pba May 4 (272) $300
— Vandals of the Void. Phila.: Winston, [1953]. In dj with short tear. pba May 23 (439) $110

### Vancouver, George, 1757-98
— Vancouver in California, 1792-1794. Los Angeles, 1954. Ed by Marguerite E. Wilbur. Orig cloth. With 4 illus by John Sykes. Larson copy. pba Sept 28 (273) $50
— Voyage de decouvertes, a l'Ocean Pacifique du Nord, et autor du monde.... Paris, [1800]. 1st French Ed. 3 vols plus atlas. 4to, orig bds; scuffed & worn, spines faded; atlas worn with crude repairs to covers. With 16 maps & charts, & 18 plates. Some stains. Larson copy. pba Sept 28 (272) $3,000
— A Voyage of Discovery to the North Pacific Ocean and Round the World. L, 1798. 1st Ed. 3 vols (lacks atlas). 4to, later half calf; light scuffing, extremities worn. With 18 plates. Larson copy. pba Sept 28 (271) $1,700

Anr copy. 4 vols, including Atlas. 4to & folio, contemp calf, Atlas in bds; all rebacked in calf. With 17 plates & 1 chart in text vols; Atlas with 10 folding charts & 6 plates. Foxing to plates in text vols; marginal worming at beginning of Vol I; foxing to Atlas profile views only. pba Feb 13 (186) $15,000

Anr copy. 20th-cent half mor; Atlas cover worn. With 23 plates & 11 charts. Foxed; some maps with minor crease tears, several verso repairs. Robbins copy. pba Mar 21 (371) $11,000

Anr Ed. L, 1801. 6 vols. 8vo, calf; rebacked, joints worn. With 2 folding maps & 17 folding plates. Repairs to both maps; some foxing. wa Feb 29 (531) $1,400

1st Ed. Amst.: N. Israel, [1967]. 4 vols, including Atlas. 4to & folio, syn gilt. Facsimile reprint of 1798 Ed. pba July 25 (235) $300

### Vanderbilt, William K., 1878-1944
— Taking One's Own Ship Around the World. NY: Pvtly ptd, 1929. Out-of-series copy. 4to, half mor; soiled. sg Mar 7 (240) $100
— West Made East, with the Loss of a Day.... NY: Pvtly ptd, 1933. One of 200. 4to, half mor; some discoloration to rear cover. pba Apr 25 (237) $170

### Vanderpoel, Emily Noyes
— American Lace & Lace-Makers. New Haven, 1924. Folio, pictorial cloth; extremities rubbed. With 111 plates. Some foxing. sg June 13 (223) $60

### Vandiveer, Clarence A.
— The Fur-Trade and Early Western Exploration. Cleveland, 1929. 1st Ed. Robbins copy. pba Mar 21 (372) $190

### Vane, Sir Henry, 1613-62
[-] The Tryal of Sir Henry Vane.... [L], 1662. 4to, calf; rebacked, worn, lea pulling away. Port rehinged; some foxing; underlining & marginal notations. NH July 21 (119) $270

**Vanel, ——**
— The Royal Mistresses of France.... L, 1695. 2 parts in 1 vol. 8vo, contemp calf; front cover detached, lacking front free endpaper. Browned; tp creased & chipped. sg Mar 21 (326) $120

**Vanity...**
— The Vanity Fair Album. L, 1869-83. Vols 1-18. Orig cloth; spine head rubbed. Sold w.a.f. S June 13 (428) £4,200

Vols 1-38 & 40 only & Index in 2 vols. Folio. L, 1869-1908. Folio, orig cloth; rubbed & loose. With 2,020 colored plates plus 2 vols of Vanity Fair for 1876 with 29 plates. Sold w.a.f. C Oct 25 (153) £7,000

Vols 26-29. L, 1894-97. One of 10 proof sets before letters. Orig lea gilt; recased. Vol 29 half-title & tp foxed. sg Oct 19 (250) $2,200

**Vankuli, Mehmed ben Mustafa**
— Kitab-i Lugat-i Vankuli. Constantinople: press of Ibrahim Mueteferika, 1141 H [1729]. One of 1,000. 2 vols. Folio, contemp Turkish sheep; restored. Lacking pp.483-4 & 497-8 in vol. II; some waterstains; some tears. S Oct 26 (225) £1,500 [Heald]

**Vansittart, Robert.** See: Gregynog Press

**Vardon, Harry**
— The Complete Golfer. NY: McClure Phillips, 1907. 1st Ed. Cloth; insect damage to spine & front cover. With frontis port. pba Nov 9 (85) $85

10th American Ed. NY: McClure Philips, 1908. Cloth. With 65 illus. pba Apr 18 (174) $65

— The Gist of Golf. NY: George H. Doran, [1922]. 1st American Ed. Cloth; spine ends rubbed. pba Apr 18 (175) $60

— How to Play Golf. NY: George W. Jacobs, [1912]. 1st American Ed. Cloth. pba Apr 18 (176) $85

— My Golfing Life. L: Hutchinson, [1933]. 1st Ed. Cloth in dj; d/j chipped & lacking pieces, cloth torn at spine head. pba Apr 18 (177) $300

— Progressive Golf. L: Hutchinson, [1920]. 1st Ed. Cloth in dj; d/j in pieces. Endpapers browned; marginal pencil notes. pba Apr 18 (178) $85

**Vardon, Harry —& Others**
— Success at Golf. Bost., 1914. 2d American Ed. - Intro by John Anderson. Cloth; front cover offset. With frontis. pba Apr 18 (179) $140

**Varignon, Pierre**
— Nouvelle Mecanique ou statique. Paris, 1725. 2 vols. 4to, contemp calf; spine ends restored, corners worn, Vol II front joint cracked. With 64 folding plates. Dampstaining to upper inner corners in Vol I. sg May 16 (269) $600

**Varlo, Charles**
— The Essence of Agriculture.... L, 1786. 8vo, contemp calf; top of spine chipped, joints cracked. Wormhole through opening leaves minimally affecting text. sg May 16 (352) $300

**Varro, Marcus Terentius, 116-27 B.C.**
— Opera. Dordrecht: Joannes Berewout, 1619. 2 vols. 8vo, late 18th-Cent mor. Some spotting. S Oct 27 (1090) £260 [Zioni]

**Vasari, Giorgio, 1511-74**
See also: Limited Editions Club
— Stories of the Italian Artists. L, 1906. 4to, early vellucent bdg by Cedric Chivers with painted panel of Virgin & Child enthroned & mother-of-pearl inlays. b Sept 20 (609) £420
— Vite de piu eccellenti pittori scultori e architetti. Milan, 1807-11. 16 vols in 8. 8vo, contemp vellum. Some vols dampstained. CE Nov 8 (250) $320

**Vasi, Giuseppe Agostino**
— Delle magnificenze di Roma antica e moderna. Rome, 1786. ("Raccolta delle piu belle vedute antiche e moderne di Roma.") Vol I (of 2) only. Remnants of calf-backed bds; separated & worn. Some soiling & foxing. wa Dec 14 (513) $1,700

**Vastey, Pompee Valentine de**
— De Negerstaat van Hayti.... Amst., 1821. 8vo, orig wraps; spine def. With folding map. sg Mar 28 (139) $300
— Reflexions politiques sur quelques ouvrages et journaux francais, concernant Hayti. Sans-Soucci [i.e., Port au Prince], 1817. 8vo, later half calf; joints worn. Some worming in gutter of pp. 201-6. sg Mar 28 (141) $800

**Vatout, Jean**
— Histoire lithographique du Palais-Roayl.... Paris, [1834]. Bound with: Histoire de Palais-Royal. Paris, 1830. Folio & 8vo, Mor gilt by Simier, with the arms of Marie-Amelie. With engraved title & 39 mtd plates. Pbr's blindstamp on each plate. Minor discoloration. S Nov 30 (242) £4,000

**Vatout, Jean —& Quenot, J. P.**
— Histoire lithographique de son Altesse Royale Monseigneur de Duc d'Orleans. Paris, [c.1820]. Vol II only. Folio, contemp mor gilt. With 76 india-proof plates. b Sept 20 (517) £650

**Vaughan, William, 1577-1641**
— Directions for Health, Natural and Artifical.... L, 1626. 2 parts in 1 vol. 4to, early 20th-Cent mor; joints rubbed & split at head. Several margins torn & frayed; some oxydisation spots. Ck Mar 22 (304) £380

**Veen, Otto van.** See: Vaenius, Otto

**Vega Carpio, Lope Felix de, 1562-1635.** See: Gregynog Press

**Vegetius Renatus, Flavius**
— De re militari. Paris: C. Wechel, 1532. Folio, modern half mor. Minor staining. S June 27 (379) £1,800

Anr Ed. Venice, 1540. ("Vegetio de l'arte militare ne la commune lingua....") 8vo, contemp vellum;

worn & wormed. Worming to 1st 3 leaves affecting woodcut illust on tp & letters on following leaf. pba June 20 (347) $250

Anr Ed. Antwerp, 1607. 5 parts in 1 vol. 4to, limp vellum. Some browning, spotting; few water-stains; title repaired. S Oct 27 (1091) £220 [Zioni]

— Du Fait de guerre, et fleur de chevalerie.... Paris, 1536. 1st Ed of Nicole Volkyr de Serouville's trans. Folio, modern vellum. With 121 hand-colored woodcuts. Upper corners repaired, def or wormed, affecting some text. S June 12 (132) £600

**Veilroc, Francois.** See: Corlieu, Francois de

**Veitch, James Herbert**
— Hortus Veitchii. L, 1906. 4to, orig cloth; extremities worn. Met Feb 24 (332) $260

**Veitia Linage, Jose**
— Norte de la contratacion de las Indias Occidentales. Sevile, 1672. 2 parts in 1 vol. Folio, contemp vellum; cockled, lacking front free endpaper. Some waterstains at fore-margins; some worming; engraved title frayed. S Nov 30 (187) £3,500

**Velazquez y Sanchez, Jose**
— Anales del Toreo. Madrid, [c.1868]. Folio, contemp calf gilt; extremities worn. With litho title & 29 tinted litho plates, many double-page. Some foxing. sg Dec 7 (241) $1,500

**Velpeau, Alfred Armand Louis Marie**
— Nouveaux elements de medecine operatoire. Paris, 1839. 5 vols. 8vo & 4to, orig wraps, Atlas in bds with ptd wraps laid down on sides; spines of text vols worn. With 22 plates. Some spotting & dampstaining. S Mar 29 (718) £170

**Venegas, Miguel**
— El Apostel Mariano Representado en la vida del V.P. Juan Maria de Salvatierra. Mexico: Don Maria de Ribera, 1754. 1st Ed. 4to, contemp vellum; wrinkled & worn, front joint darkened, possibly recased. Marginal worming with repairs; endpapers crudely attached. Robbins copy. pba Mar 21 (373) $3,250
— Juan Maria de Salvatierra of the Company of Jesus.... Cleveland, 1929. 1st English Ed. - Trans & Ed by Marguerite Eyer Wilbur. With double-page map. Robbins copy. pba Mar 21 (374) $250
— A Natural and Civil History of California.... L, 1759. 1st Ed in English. 2 vols. 8vo, modern calf; rebacked. With folding map & 4 plates. Repaired tear to map. pba Feb 13 (188) $750

Anr copy. Half calf; worn, lacking 2 covers. With 3 plates only. Lacking map; waterstained. S Mar 28 (315) £50

1st English Ed. 2 vols. 8vo, orig lea; hinges cracked, rear covers almost separated. With 8 illus & 1 folded map. Map torn & repaired with stain. Larson copy. pba Sept 28 (277) $600

— Noticia de la California, y de su conquista....hasta el tiempo presente.... Madrid, 1757. 3 vols. 4to, contemp calf; extremities rubbed. With 4 folding maps. Marginal dampstaining to a number of leaves in Vol I; marginal tear in Vol II repaired; marginal worming in Vol III. Doheny copy. pba Feb 13 (187) $2,500

Anr copy. 19th-Cent half mor; rubbed. 1st map torn in folds; tears & holes in text. S Oct 26 (498) £3,400 [Antiquariat]

1st Ed. 3 vols. 4to, modern vellum. With 4 folding maps. Some foxing. Robbins copy. pba Mar 21 (375) $2,500

**Venezuela**
— Acte d'independance, manifeste, constitution de la Republique Federale de Venezuela.... Paris, 1817. 8vo, orig wraps. S Nov 30 (190) £1,500
— Exposicion que ha dirigado al augusto Congreso Nacional el Ayuntamieno de la Cuidad de Santigao de Leon de Caracas. Cadiz, 1813. 4to, contemp wraps. S Nov 30 (191) £1,400

**Venice**
— Il modo de la elettione del Serenissimo Principe de Venetia.... Venice, [c.1546]. 8vo, calf gilt by Bedford. Gothic letter, with 2 sonnets at end in roman. Woodcut on tp. Huth copy. C June 26 (147) £1,600

**Venne, Adriaen van de**
— Tafereel van de belacchende werelt en des self geluckige Eeuwe. The Hague, 1635. 4to, vellum. With engraved title & 12 half-page plates. 2 leaves dampstained. Schaefer copy. P Nov 1 (204) $1,200

**Venner, Tobias**
— A Briefe and Accurate Treatise of Tobacco. San Francisco: Book Club of Calif., 1931. One of 200. 4to, cloth. pba June 20 (370) $60

**Venture...**
— Venture: an Annual of Art and Literature. L, 1905. 4to, orig cloth; bumped. Some browning. CE May 22 (290) $700

**Ver Mehr, J. L.**
— Checkered Life in the Old and New World. San Francisco, 1877. 1st Ed. Orig cloth; front & rear hinge cracking. Sgd by grandson of au. Larson copy. pba Sept 28 (732) $50

**Verbiest, Ferdinand, 1623-88**
— Compendium latinum proponens xii posteriores figuras Libri Observationum nec non priores vii figuras libri organici. [Peking, not before 1674]. 2 parts. Folio, text sewn into a wrap, plates loose in anr wrap. With xylographic text & 20 double-page astronomical plates. b Dec 5 (141) £41,000
— Epistola... die 15 Augusti ex curia Pekinensi in Europam ad socios missa. [Peking, 1678]. 10 leaves, folio, modern cloth. Repairs at ends in inner margins. S June 27 (227) £9,800

**Verdet, Andre**
— Georges Braque le solitaire. Paris, [1959]. Ltd Ed. 4to, cloth. With 8 plates. sg Sept 7 (59) $110

**Verdi, Giuseppe, 1813-1901**
— Rigoletto. Milan: Ricordi, [1895]. 3 vols. Folio, half cloth. Some conductor's markings in pencil & crayon. S May 15 (587) £1,600
— Simon Boccanegra. Venice: Teresa Gattei, 1857. 8vo, later bds. Libretto for the premiere. S Dec 1 (373) £450

**Vere, Sir Francis, 1560-1609**
— The Commentaries.... Cambr., 1657. 1st Ed. Folio, contemp calf; rebacked. With 6 plates & 4 folding maps. Minor marginal staining. b Dec 5 (188) £200
Anr copy. Contemp sheep; worn, needs rebacking. With 7 folding plates 7 maps & 1 (of 3) port. sg Mar 21 (327) $275

**Vergil, Polydore, 1470?-1555**
— Anglicae historiae libri XXVI..... Basel: Jo. Bebelius, 1534. Folio, disbound. Marginal dampstaining; cropped marginalia; wormholes through opening leaves; tp soiled & mtd, with old signatures; next leaf remargined. sg Mar 21 (328) $250

**Vergilius Maro, Publius, 70-19 B.C.**
See also: Cranach Press; Limited Editions Club
— Les Oeuvres. Paris, 1743. 2 vols. 8vo, contemp olive mor gilt. With 2 ports & 18 plates. Henault - Fuerstenberg - Schaefer copy. S Dec 8 (621) £950
— Opera. Venice: Jacob Rubeus, 1475. Folio, mor gilt by H. Zucker. 65 lines of commentary; types 1:113R (text), 2:80R. Some initials roughly supplied in later pencil or ink; some marginalia; soiled; some margins tape-repaired. 233 (of 284) leaves; lacking initial blank & last 5 quires. P June 5 (344) $1,800
Anr Ed. Paris: Jean Barbier for Francois Regnault, [1515]. 2 parts in 1 vol. Folio, contemp half pigskin over wooden bds, with brass catches; lacking clasps, wormed. Early marginalia throughout; tear across tp repaired with cellotape; wormed at end. sg Mar 21 (330) $800
Anr Ed. Venice: Giunta, 1552. Folio, old vellum; worn, split between 2 gatherings in middle of vol. Marginal dampstaining at ends; some leaves dogeared at end. Sold w.a.f. sg Mar 21 (331) $550
Anr Ed. Amst., 1746. 4 vols. 4to, contemp mor gilt; marked. A few leaves browned. Fuerstenberg - Schaefer copy. S Dec 8 (622) £1,800
Anr Ed. L, 1750. ("Bucolica, Georgica, et Aeneis.") 2 vols. 8vo, contemp mor; rubbed. F Mar 28 (415A) £90
Anr Ed. Birm: Baskerville, 1766. ("Bucolica, Georgica, et Aeneis....") 8vo, contemp mor gilt; scuffed. Cut close. F June 20 (165I) £90
Anr Ed. L, 1796. 2 vols. 8vo, old half calf. wd May 8 (84) $175
Anr copy. Illus by Gilbert Wakefield. Contemp mor. S Oct 27 (884) £480 [King]
Anr Ed. Paris: Didot l'aine, 1798. ("Bucolica, Georgica, et Aeneis.") One of 250. Folio, contemp mor gilt. With frontis & 23 plates plus 2 inserted plates. Vernon - Holford - Fuerstenberg - Schaefer copy. S Dec 8 (622A) £1,200

— Bucolica, Georgica, et Aeneis.... One of 250 L.p. copies numbered & sgd by Pierre Didot l'aine & 1 of 100 with plates before letters. Contemp red mor extra by Bozerian, sgd; some scuffing. With frontis & 22 plates. C June 26 (212) £2,500
Anr Ed. Brussels: J. L. de Loubers, [c.1800]. 5 vols in 2. 8vo, contemp goatskin gilt; stained, spines rubbed. Engraved throughout by Marcus Pitteri. bba May 30 (111) £400 [Unsworth]
Anr Ed. L, 1800. ("Bucolica, Georgica, et Aeneis.") 2 vols. 8vo, contemp mor by Hering. With 15 plates. Some waterstaining; 1 plate loose. S Apr 23 (175) £120
— Works. L, 1697. 1st Ed of Dryden's trans. Folio, half mor gilt by Bayntun. With frontis & 101 plates. Some text leaves browned. sg Oct 19 (251) $700
Anr copy. Contemp calf; needs rebdg. With 102 plates. Tear across frontis & tp repaired; some prelims torn in lower margins; some browning to text & c.20 plates; hole through plate facing p. 31 affecting image. L.p. copy. sg Mar 21 (332) $850
Anr Ed. Birm.: Baskerville, 1766. 8vo, later mor gilt; lacking clasp & catch. sg Mar 21 (333) $300

**Aeneid in English**
— The Aeneid of Virgil. Bost., 1906. One of 650. 2 vols. 4to, mor extra; joints worn. CE Sept 27 (281) $300

**Aeneid in French**
— L'Eneide. Paris: Estienne Loyson, 1658. 2 vols. 4to, modern calf. Tp & engraved title of Vol I ink-stained at upper cover; tp & A3 of Vol II with tears; illusts shaved; some browning in Vol II. S June 12 (134) £480
Anr copy. Illus by Abraham Bosse. 2 vols in 1. 4to, With engraved titles & 10 half-page illusts. Some browning in Vol II. sg Apr 18 (193) $800
Anr Ed. Paris, 1804. 4 vols. 4to, contemp mor gilt by Prunet. With 4 frontises & 9 plates plus a proof before letters of 1 frontis loosely inserted. Some browning. Fuerstenberg - Schaefer copy. S Dec 8 (624) £1,300

**Bucolica & Georgica in Latin**
— Bucolica et georgica.... L: Pine, 1774. 2 vols in 1. 8vo, early calf; rebacked. sg Mar 21 (334) £150

**Bucolica in English**
— An English Version of the Eclogues. L, 1883. Illus by Samuel Palmer. Folio, mor gilt by Sangorski & Sutcliffe. Half-title spotted. S Nov 21 (458) £350
Anr Ed. L, 1884. Folio, orig vellum gilt. b May 30 (443) £350

**Georgica in French**
— Les Georgiques. Paris: C. Bleuet, 1783. 4to, contemp mor gilt. With port & 4 plates. Fuerstenberg - Schaefer copy. S Dec 8 (626) £700
Anr Ed. Paris, 1937-43-[50]. One of 750. Illus by Aristide Maillol. 2 vols. 4to, loose as issued in orig wraps. Ck Sept 8 (22) £450

Anr copy. Half mor, orig wraps bound in. With 2 extra suites of the 104 illusts, 1 black & 1 sanguine. S Nov 21 (461) £1,300

Anr copy. Loose in orig wraps as issued. sg Oct 19 (143) $1,700

Anr Ed. Paris, 1944 [1947]. One of 175. Trans by Michel de Marolles; illus by Andre Dunoyer de Segonzac. 2 vols. Folio, wraps. bba May 9 (190) £1,700 [Sims Reed]

Anr copy. With 99 plates. S Nov 21 (460) £1,500

**Verhaeren, Emile, 1855-1916**
— Belle chair. Paris, 1931. One of 5 on japon Pelletan, with additional suite of the lithos, 2 additional unused lithos, all on chine, & with a suite of the wood-engravings on japon. Illus by Aristide Maillol. 4to, mor extra by Semet & Plumelle, orig wraps bound in. S Nov 21 (445) £3,250
— Les Villes tentaculaires. Paris, 1919. With: Les Campagnes hallucinees. Paris, 1927. Hors commerce copies. Illus by Frank Brangwyn. 4to, in matching mor extra bdgs, 1 green & the other gold, with designs of factories and gears, by Paul Bonet [Carnets 94 & 95], commissioned by Carlos Scherer. S Nov 21 (446) £20,000

**Verheiden, Jacobus**
— The History of the Moderne Protestant Divines. L, 1637. 8vo, 19th-Cent mor. With additional title & 45 port illus. Lacking 1st & last blank leaves. S Oct 27 (1092) £700 [Pardue]

**Verheyen, Philip**
— Corporis humani anatomia. Leipzig, 1705. 4to, contemp calf; rebacked. With port & 31 plates. pba Sept 14 (266) $225

**Verino, Ugolino.** See: Ashendene Press

**Verkler, Linda A.** See: Zempel & Verkler

**Verlaine, Paul, 1844-96**
— Les Amies. Paris, 1921. One of 437. Illus by Gustave Buchet. Half mor, orig wraps bound in. S Nov 21 (449) £200
— Femmes. Paris, 1917. one of 11 on japon, with additional suite of illusts. Illus by J. G. Daragnes. 8vo, calf extra by L. Houades, orig wraps bound in & calf-backed & edged folder. S Nov 21 (448) £1,000
— Hashish and Incense. [N.p.]: Paul Verlaine Society, 1929. One of 50. Illus by Mahlon Blaine. Sgd by Blaine on illust tipped-in before tp. pba Aug 22 (866) $95
— Les Poetes maudits.... Paris, 1937. One of 200. Illus by Luc Albert Moreau. 4to, mor extra by A. Cerutti. b Sept 20 (646) £450

**Verne, Jules, 1828-1905**
See also: Limited Editions Club
— The Baltimore Gun Club. Phila: King & Bard, [1874]. Cloth; extermities rubbed, spine ends rubbed. pba May 4 (273) $120
— In Search of the Castaways. Phila., [1873]. 8vo, orig cloth; spine ends rubbed. pba Dec 14 (201) $180

— Mistress Branican. NY: Cassell, [1891]. 1st American Ed. Orig cloth; spine ends rubbed & bumped, lower front joint scuffed. pba Dec 14 (202) $110
— The Tour of the World in Eighty Days. Bost., 1874. 12mo, orig cloth; spine ends rubbed. pba May 4 (274) $375

**Verner, Collie**
— The Printed Maps of Virtinia 1590 to 1800. [N.p., c.1963]. 4to, wraps. Photocopy of typescript. bba Oct 5 (375) £1,000 [Forbes Smiley III]

**Vernet, Carle, 1758-1835**
— Tableaux historiques de campagnes d'Italie depuis L'An IV jusqu'a la bataille de Marengo. Paris, 1806. Folio, later half calf. With half-title, additional title, 2 divisional title ports, 1 double-page map, & 26 plates. Some discoloration or water-staining. S Oct 26 (302) £950 [Mariotti]

**Verney, Lady Frances**
— Florence Nightingale's Pet Owl, Athena.... San Francisco: Grabhorn-Hoyem, 1970. One of 300. 4to, orig cloth. sg Sept 14 (187) $80

**Verniquet, Edme**
— Atlas de plan general de la ville de Paris. Paris, [1791]. Folio, recent half calf. With 72 double-page mapsheets. Tp spotted & soiled; a few edges softening. S June 27 (129) £2,000

**Verrue Library, Comtess Jeanne d'Albert de Luynes de**
— [Sale Catalogue] Catalogue des livres.... Paris: Gabriel Martin, 1737. 8vo, contemp calf; rubbed. Priced in margins in a contemp hand. Some staining & foxing. O Mar 26 (284) $350

**Vertes, Marcel**
— The Stronger Sex. NY, [1941]. Text by Janet Flanner. Folio, pictorial cloth; soiled. sg Jan 11 (446) $50

Anr copy. Cloth. With 24 mtd plates. sg June 13 (377) $200

**Verve...**
— Verve: An Artistic and Literary Quarterly. Chicago, 1937. No 1. 4to, orig wraps. wa Nov 16 (349) $190
— Verve: Revue artistique et litteraire. Paris, 1937-58. Nos 1-36 in 25 vols. 4to, orig wraps or bds. S Nov 21 (453) £5,000

No 1. Paris, 1937. Wraps. In English. sg Jan 11 (447) $175

Anr copy. Orig wraps; soiled, loose. sg June 13 (297) $80

Anr copy. Wraps. sg June 13 (298) $90

Nos 2-4 in 1 vol. Paris, 1938-39. sg Jan 11 (448) $250

Nos 3-4 in 1 vol. pba Aug 22 (867) $225

No 4. Paris, 1939. Wraps. pba Aug 22 (868) $65; sg Feb 15 (198) $110

No 5/6. Wraps; rubbed. pba Mar 7 (259) $400

Anr copy. Wraps; spine chipped. pba June 20 (350) $325

Anr copy. Wraps; spine head chipped. pba Aug 8 (642) $80

Anr copy. Wraps; very worn. French text. Sold w.a.f. sg June 13 (300) $110

Nos 5-8 in 3 vols. Paris, 1939-40. Wraps. sg Jan 11 (449) $120

Nos 5/6. Paris, 1939. Wraps. English text. sg June 13 (301) $200

No 7. Paris, 1940. Wraps. sg June 13 (299) $50

No 13. Paris, 1943. Bds, in dj. sg June 13 (302) $425

Nos 27/28. Paris, 1952. Bds; backstrip def. sg Jan 11 (450) $1,200; wa June 20 (372) $900

**Verwey, Albert, 1865-1937**

— Het Eigen Rijk. The Hague: De Zilverdistel, 1912. One of 100. Contemp snakeskin(?) gilt, with floral-patterned silk doublures & endleaves designed by Josef Hoffmann. sg Apr 18 (192) $950

**Vesalius, Andreas, 1514-64**

See also: Bremer Press

— De humani corporis fabrica. Basel: Johannes Oporinus, June 1543. 1st Ed. Folio, contemp blind-stamped calf over wooden bds. Tp repaired at bottom & with small hole; wormed at end; colophon holed at bottom; H2 & I 4 repaired; some stains. Honeyman - Hefner copy. CNY May 17 (47) $155,000

2d Folio Ed. Basel: Joannes Oporinus, [1555]. Folio, contemp pigskin over bds; upper cover bowed, worn, & revarnished; bottom half of upper joint cracked. With pictorial title, port, 2 folding diagrams, & 200 illus (21 full-page & 2 double-page). Tp & endpaper edges soiled & frayed, marginal tear repaired; foxing & dampstaining throughout; some marginal staining & worming. CE Nov 8 (156) $19,000

Anr Ed. Nieuwendijk: de Forel, 1975. Folio, half mor, separate booklet by Lindeboom in wraps. pba Mar 7 (260) $250

Anr Ed. [Kodansha, 1976]. Folio, orig mor. Facsimile of the Basel 1543 Ed. S June 12 (310) £190

— Opera. Leiden, 1725. Illus by Jan Wandelaar. 2 vols, contemp calf; spine ends & edges chipped & rubbed. With title, port & 83 plates. Some plates marginally dampstained; some folding plates wrinkled & torn; foxed & browned throughout; 1st few pages of Vol I wormed. CE Nov 8 (157) $4,500

**Vesling, Johann, 1598-1649**

— Syntagma anatomicum.... Padua, 1647. 2d Ed. - Illus by Giovanni Georgi. 4to, contemp vellum over pastebd. With frontis & 24 full-page plates. C June 26 (148) £1,400

**Vespucci, Amerigo, 1454-1512.** See: Grabhorn Printing

**Vestal, Stanley**

— Fandango: Ballads of the Old West. Bost., 1927. In dj with spine ends worn. pba Nov 16 (269) $60

**Veyssiere de la Croze, Mathurin**

— Histoire du christianisme des Indes. The Hague, 1724. Bound with: Remarques...sur son Histoire du christianisme. Amst., 1737. 8vo, 18th-cent bds; rebacked in vellum. S Mar 28 (380) £160

**Vialart, Charles, Bishop of Avranches**

— Geographia sacra. Amst: Franciscus Halma, 1703. Folio, contemp vellum; some wear & soiling, piece replaced in rear cover. With engraved title, dedication & memorial leaf & 10 double-page folding maps, hand-colored in outline, with cartouches colored in full. Marginal dampstaining to several leaves. cb Oct 17 (258) $1,500

**Vianoli, Alessandro Maria**

— Historia Veneta. Venice: G. G. Hertz, 1680. 2 vols. 4to, contemp calf; rubbed. With full-page ports & 105 oval ports in text. b June 28 (73) £450

**Viborg, Erik —&**
**Young, —**

— Memoires sur l'Education...du Porc. Paris, 1823. 8vo, contemp half calf gilt. With 3 plates. sg May 16 (353) $175

**Vicentio, Ludovico degli Arrighi**

— Calligraphic Models.... Paris, 1926. One of 300. Orig half vellum. bba May 9 (15) £400 [Quaritch]

**Victoria, Queen of England, 1819-1901**

— Leaves from the Journal of Our Life in the Highlands. L, 1868. 1st Pbd Ed. - Ed by Arthur Helps. 8vo, orig cloth; worn, inner hinges split. Inscr to Lord Sheffield, 22 Sept 1891. Ck Nov 17 (172) £70

— More Leaves from the Journal of a Life in the Highlands. L, 1884. 1st Ed. 8vo, orig cloth. Inscr to Lord Henry, 26 Feb 1884. b May 30 (378) £85

Anr copy. Pictorial mor gilt by Mansell. Inscr to the Marquis of Breadalbane, 14 June 1895 & with ALs laid in. pnE May 15 (93) £800

**Victoria's copy, Queen**

— Scripture Reading Lessons for Little Children. [N.p., n.d.]. 8vo, wraps backed with calf. Sgd & dated Nov 1844 & with dates she began the work with each of her children. pn June 13 (216) £500 [Maggs]

**Vida, Marcus Hieronymus, 1480?-1566**

— Poetica... d'heroici latini, in versi toschi sciolti trapportata.... Venice, [c.1550]. 8vo, half vellum. Tp margin repaired on verso. b Dec 5 (179) £100

**Vidal, Gore**

— The Judgment of Paris. NY, 1952. In rubbed & worn dj. Sgd on half-title. wa Feb 1 (75) $85

**Vidius, Vidus, c.1500-69.** See: Guidi, Guido

**Vieillard, Roger**

— Elements. Paris, 1957. One of 60. Folio, loose in orig wraps. bba May 9 (189) £220 [Andrews]

## Vien, Joseph Marie
— Caravanne du Sultan a la Mecque.... [Paris: Fessard, 1748]. Folio, mor gilt by Lortique, with arms of Prince Victor Massena. Engraved throughout; with title & 31 plates. Fuerstenberg - Schaefer copy. S Dec 8 (628) £13,000

Anr Ed. Paris: Fessard, [1768]. 8vo, loose sheets, tied at a later date through top margin. Engraved throughout, with title & 24 (of 30) plates. Top frayed; some marginal dampstaining. S June 27 (164) £1,900

## Viereck, George Sylvester —& Eldridge, Paul
— The Invincible Adam. NY: Liveright, [1932]. One of 100. In dj with chips & tears. pba May 4 (275) $65

## Vierte Wand...
— Die Vierte Wand. Magdeburg, 1926-27. Vols 1-22 (all pbd), in 21 parts. 4to, orig wraps; No 1 lacking top fore-corner of upper wrap. bba May 30 (224) £180 [Mytze]

## Views...
— Views of Preventing and Curing Blindness; Realised by the Institution of the London Ophthalmic Infirmary.... L, 1828. 12mo, contemp mor gilt by T. Armstrong, with upper cover lettered History of the British Opthalmic Institutions originating with Saunders. b Sept 20 (221) £160

## Vignier, Nicolas
— Sommaire de l'histoire des Francois. Paris: Sebastien Nivelle, 1579. Folio, 18th-cent half sheep gilt; spine ends chipped, joints cracked. sg Mar 21 (329) $200

## Vigny, Alfred de, 1797-1863
— Daphne. Paris: F. L. Schmied, 1924. One of 140 on velin d'Arches. Illus by F. L. Schmied. 4to, red lacquer sgd Dunand after Schmied, the upper cover with abstract design, orig wraps bound in. Schmied's own copy, bound to his design, with additional impression of 1 of the illusts & full-page watercolor, heightened with silver, sgd. S Nov 21 (457) £10,000

## Vigo, Johannes de
— Works. L: T. East, 1571. 3 parts in 1 vol. 4to, contemp calf over wooden bds; rebacked, endpapers renewed, wormholes through front cover & opening leaves. Tear in S5. sg May 16 (521) $5,400

## Villena, Enrique de Aragon
— Los trabajos de Hercules. Zamora: Antonio de Centenera, 15 Jan 1483. Folio, 19th-cent calf gilt with supralibros of the Biblioteca Vicente & Pedro de Salva. 40 lines; double column; type 1:93G; rubricated. With 11 woodcuts. Washed & pressed; minor worming affecting letters. 30 leaves. Goff V-275. Schaefer copy. P Nov 1 (205) $80,000

## Villenfagne d'Ingihoul, Hilarion Noel, Baron de
— Recherches historiques sur l'ordre-equestre de la principaute de Liege.... Liege, 1792. Bound with: Eclaircissemens sur Raes de Dammartin.... Liege, 1793. 8vo, contemp bds. S Nov 30 (308) £300

## Villere, Charles J.
— Review of Certain Remarks Made by the President When Requested to Restoe General Beauregard to the Command of Dapartment No 2. Charleston, 1863. 8vo, wraps. Upper margin of tp excised. Inscr & sgd twice by Beauregard to Alexander Hamilton Stephens. sg Oct 26 (65) $1,700

## Villon, Francois, b.1431
See also: Eragny Press
— The Ballads and Poems.... San Francisco: Windsor Press, 1927. One of 200 hand-illuminated by Julian A. Links. 4to, vellum gilt; bowed. sg Sept 14 (343) $90
— Oeuvres. Paris, 1723. 3 parts in 1 vol. 8vo, 19th-cent mor gilt. A few leaves browned. Fuerstenberg - Schaefer copy. S Dec 8 (630) £400

## Vincent, Augustine, 1584?-1626
— A Discoverie of Errours in the First Edition of the Catalogue of Nobility.... L, 1622. Folio, contemp calf; worn. Tp cropped; marginal dampstaining. Ck Feb 14 (332) £300

## Vincent, William, 1739-1815
— The Voyage of Nearchus from the Indus to the Euphrates. L, 1797. 4to, contemp calf; lower cover detached. With frontis & 6 maps. b May 30 (301) £160

## Vineis, Raimundus de
— La vida dela seraphica sancta Catherina de Sena.... Valencia: Johan Joffre, 17 Sept 1511. Bound with: Obras fets en lahor dela seraphica senta Catherina.... [Valencia: Johan Joffre, after 29 Sept 1511] 4to, modern vellum wallet-style bdg. Gothic types. 1st work with 36 mostly full-page woodcuts surrounded by borderpieces. 1st work with strengthening to tp & inner margin of a1 & a8; some soiling at beginning. Last leaf of 2d work with hole costing 2 letters & lower corner torn off without loss; some leaves strengthened in inner margins; lacking bifolium 1.10. Schaefer copy. P Nov 1 (206) $5,500

## Vingtieme Siecle
— Le Surrealisme: Edition speciale des etudes parues dans les numeros 42 et 43.... Paris, 1975. In dj with chip to spine head. pba Mar 7 (249) $200
— XXe Siecle: Cahiers d'art. Paris, 1939. No 5/6. Wraps; spine ends frayed. sg Jan 11 (441) $475
New Series, No 10. Paris, 1958. Pictorial wraps. sg Jan 11 (442) $450
New Series, No 24. Paris, 1964. Bds. sg June 13 (303) $50
New Series, No 26. Paris, 1966. Bds. sg Jan 11 (443) $90
New Series, No 29. Paris, 1967. Bds. sg June 13 (114) $90

New Series, No 28. Bds. sg June 13 (304) $80
Chagall Monumental. Paris, 1973. 4to, cloth, in dj. sg Jan 11 (108) $80

**Viola Zanini, Giuseppe**
— Della architettura...libri due. Padua: Francesco Bolzetta, 1629. 4to, 17th-cent calf; rebacked retaining orig backstrip. sg June 13 (35) $1,100

**Viollet-le-Duc, Eugene Emmanuel, 1814-79**
— Dictionnaire raisonne du mobilier francais.... Paris, 1858-75. 6 vols. 8vo, contemp half mor; rubbed, 1 hinge cracked. CE Feb 21 (267) $650

**Virchow, Rudolf, 1821-1902**
— Der Cellularpathologie.... Berlin, 1858. 1st Ed. 8vo, contemp bds; rebacked in mor. S June 12 (290) £1,900
Anr copy. Modern lea. Foxed; library stamps on tp & in text. sg May 16 (522) $3,000

**Virely, Andre**
— Rene Charles Guibert de Pixerecourt.... Paris, 1909. One of 74 on papier velin. Mor by Riviere, orig wraps & spine bound in at the end; rubbed. O Mar 26 (285) $90

**Virgil.** See: Vergilius Maro, Publius

**Virgin, P. S.**
— Chloride Mining District, Mohave County, Arizona. Chloride AZ, [1916]. Orig wraps; worn & stained. Repair to panoramic frontis. pba July 25 (250) $250

**Virginia**
— A Collection of all Such Acts of the General Assembly of Virginia...as are now in Force. Richmond: Thomas Nicolson & William Prentis, 1785. Folio, modern half calf. Tp stamped; foxed; some lower corners lacking. pba Nov 30 (318) $425

**Vischer, Edward**
— Drawings of the California Missions, 1861-1878. San Francisco: Book Club of California, 1982. One of 600. Oblong 4to, orig cloth, in dj. With colored frontis & 43 colored plates. pba Apr 25 (714) $70
— Missions of Upper California 1872. Notes on the California Missions, a Supplement to Vischer's Pictorial of California, Dedicated to its Patrons. San Francisco, 1872. 4to, orig white wraps laid in stiff tan wraps; outer wraps soiled. pba Feb 12 (191) $75
— Vischer's Pictorial of California. San Francisco, 1870. 2 vols. 4to, text in cloth, drawings in portfolio.. With 110 (of 114) mtd albumen photographs & 1 index card. Larson copy. pba Feb 12 (189) $7,500
— Vischer's Views of California. The Mammoth Tree Grove, Calaveras County, California, and its Avenues. San Francisco, [1862]. 1st Ed, 3d Issue, B variant. 13 cards including tp & 12 plates containing 25 litho illusts with 4 (facsimile) sheets of explanatory text, 11 by 13.5 inches, in orig envelope with reproduction of tp on front. Marginal dampstain to 1 plate. Larson copy. pba Feb 12 (190) $4,000

**Visconti, Ennio Quirino, 1751-1818.** See: Canova & Visconti

**Visconti, Zacharias**
— Complementum artis exorcisticae. Milan, 1637. 8vo, contemp vellum. Marginal traces of mold. sg Mar 21 (335) $325

**Vision...**
— The Vision for Coquettes. An Arabian Tale. Liverpool, 1804. 4to, modern bds. Some browning. b Dec 5 (225) £260

**Visscher, Nicolaus**
— Afbeeldingen der Voornaamste Historien.... Amst., [1700?]. 4to, contemp vellum; front cover detached. With engraved title & 280 half-page illusts. sg Mar 21 (36) $325
— Atlas minor sive totius orbis terrarum contracta delineata. Amst., [c.1717]. Folio, old half mor covered in paper in 19th-cent; scuffed & bumped. Engraved throughout, with hand-colored title & 46 double-page or folding maps. 10 maps with fold tears, 7 shaved, 2 with marginal tears affecting surface, last 5 maps with old dampstaining. C May 31 (75) £6,500

**Vitruvius Pollio, Marcus**
— De architectura libri decem. Strassburg: Officina Knoblochiana for Georgius Machaeropoeus, August, 1550. 4to, contemp vellum. With title & final blank. Inner upper margin wormed throughout; wormhole in last 20 leaves; some dampstaining, underlining & annotations. Ck Mar 22 (307) £800

*Architecture in English*
— The Architecture. L, 1812. ("The Civil Architecture.") 4to, half calf. With 42 plates. Library markings; stamps on plate versos. bba Oct 19 (164) £50 [Owens]

*Architecture in Latin*
— De Architectura. Florence: Giunta, 1522. 8vo, 19th-cent half vellum; joints broken. Underlining in red ink; Ms marginalia; later leaves waterstained. S Mar 28 (497) £600
Anr Ed. Lyons: Jean de Tournes, 1552. 4to, contemp vellum; spine holed. Wormhole in outer blank margin of tp; old repair to outer margin of z1. C Nov 29 (112) £900
Anr Ed. Lyons: J. Tornaesium, 8 Feb 1552. 4to, 19th-cent half calf; rubbed. With folding plate. Some staining & rust-marks. S June 12 (136) £650
— De architectura, libri decem. Strassburg: In Officina Knoblochiana per Georgium Machaeropioeum, 1543. 3 parts in 1 vol. 4to, contemp vellum; soiled. Marginal worming; paper repairs; 2 leaves with marginal ink smudges; some browning. b Sept 20 (190) £480

*Architecture in Italian*
— I Dieci libri dell'architettura. Como: Gottardo da Ponte, 15 July 1521. ("De architectura....") Folio, old vellum painted yellow; small splits in spine. Stained throughout, mainly in margins; some worm-

ing, mainly in margins, but with occasional loss of characters. C Apr 3 (258) £4,000
— I Dieci Libri dell'architettura. Venice, 1524. ("De architectura....") Folio, later half vellum; rubbed. Lacking last leaf; some soiling; marginal worming. Ck Sept 8 (59) £420
Anr Ed. Venice: Turrini, 1641. ("L'Architettura.") 4to, later half sheep gilt; scuffed. With frontis & 25 plates. Some dampstaining. bbc Dec 18 (196) $300

### Architecture in French
— Les Dix Livres d'architecture. Paris, 1674. 2d Ed of Perrault's trans. Folio, contemp calf gilt; joints & corners repaired. With frontis tipped-in & 68 plates, some double-page. Final leaf of title made up in near-contemp Ms; lacking colophon after the index; marginal staining; 1 plate tape-repaired in margins. bba Oct 19 (163) £650 [Pagan]
Anr Ed. Paris, 1684. Folio, contemp calf; rebacked, worn. With frontis & 68 plates. Stain at upper inner margin throughout. S Mar 28 (165) £460
2d French Ed. Folio, later calf; worn. Few gatherings browned. CE Nov 8 (251) $1,000

**Vivarium...** See: Shaw & Nodder

**Vivero, Matias.** See: Jesuits

### Vivian, Sir Arthur Pendarves
— Wanderings in the Western Land. L, 1879. 8vo, cloth; crease to front cover. With 2 folding maps. Library markings; frontis detached. pba Apr 25 (715) $50

### Viviani, Niccolo
— Ero e Leandro. Parma: Bodoni, 1794. 8vo, contemp vellum gilt. Fuerstenberg - Schaefer copy. S Dec 8 (631) £240

### Viviani, Viviano
— Trattato di custodire la sanita. Venice, 1626. 1st Ed. 8vo, contemp vellum; spine worn. With title vignette. Marginal dampstaining & spotting. Ck Mar 22 (308) £550

**Vivielle, J.** See: La Roerie & Vivielle

**Vizcaino, Sebastian.** See: Grabhorn Printing

### Vizetelly, Henry, 1820-94
— A History of Champagne.... L, 1882. 4to, orig cloth; worn. F June 20 (611A) $100
— The Story of the Diamond Necklace. L, 1881. 3d Ed. Cloth; spine ends chipped. Owner's stamp to tp. pba Aug 8 (435) $70

### Voch, Lukas
— Abhandlung von Feuerspruetzen. Augsburg: M. Rieger, 1781. 8vo, contemp wraps. With 8 plates. S Mar 14 (362) £290

### Voet, J.
— De jure militari. Utrecht, 1670. Bound with: G. Feltman. Artikel-Brief ofte ordonnatie op de discipline militaire. Groningen, 1676 2 work in 1 vol. 8vo, contemp vellum; stained, upper hinge broken. Paper browned. S Oct 27 (1094) £190 [Zioni]

### Voet, Johann Eusebius, d.1778
— Catalogus systematicus coleopterorum. The Hague, 1806. 2 vols. 4to, contemp calf; needs rebacking. With 105 hand-colored plates. Vol I stamped in blank upper corners; owner's typed description mtd on half-titles. sg Dec 7 (273) $900

### Voet, Leon —&
### Voet-Grisolle, Jenny
— The Plantin Press (1555-1589): A Bibliography.... Amst., [1980-83). 6 vols. 8vo, cloth. ds July 27 (191) $900
1st Ed. 6 vols. 8vo, orig cloth. sg Apr 11 (251) $950

**Voet-Grisolle, Jenny.** See: Voet & Voet-Grisolle

### Vogt, Johann, 1695-1764
— Catalogus historico-criticus librorum rariorum. Hamburg, 1738. 8vo, contemp vellum; worn. O Mar 26 (286) $180
Anr Ed. Frankfurt, etc., 1793. 8vo, contemp half vellum; soiled. O Mar 26 (287) $120

### Vogue, Marie Eugenee Melchior de, Vicomte
— Le Temple de Jerusalem. Paris, 1864. Illus by E. Duthoit. Folio, contemp half mor. With half-title, 37 plates (12 color). S Oct 26 (231) £1,700 [Pollack]

### Voight, Hans Henning
— Forty-Three Drawings. L, 1914. One of 500. 4to, orig cloth. S May 16 (95) £260

### Voisenon, Claude Henri de Fusee de, 1708-75
— Romans et contes.... Paris: Bleuet jeune, [1798]. 18mo, contemp mor gilt. Bishop - Fuerstenberg - Schaefer copy. S Dec 8 (632) £320

### Volboudt, Pierre
— Les Assemblages de Jean Dubuffet: signes, sols, sorts. Paris, 1958. One of 650. Illus by Jean Dubuffet. 4to, unsewn in orig wraps. sg Jan 11 (146) $225

### Volkmann, Daniel G.
— Fifty Years of the McCloud River Club. San Francisco: Pvtly ptd, 1951. One of 150. 4to, half cloth. pba July 11 (307) $200
— Memories of a Fishing Journey to New Zealand Made in 1950 by Dean and Helen Witter.... San Francisco, 1950. One of 100. Bds. pba July 11 (308) $275

### Vollard, Ambroise
— La Vie et l'oeuvre de Pierre-Auguste Renoir. Paris, 1919. One of 525. Folio, contemp half mor; spine worn. Library markings, but plates clean. sg Sept 7 (294) $2,200

### Vollmer, Carl G. W.
— Kalifornien och Guldfebern. Stockholm, [1862]. 1st Ed. Orig half calf; worn. With 8 color plates. Pages darkened. Larson copy. pba Sept 28 (756) $200

## Vollmer, Hans
— Allgemeines Lexikon der Bildenden Kunstler des XX. Jahrhunderts. Leipzig, 1953-62. 6 vols, including supplement. 4to, half syn. sg June 13 (378) $300

## Vollstaendiges...
— Vollstaendiges Voelkergallerie in getreuen Abbildungen aller Nationen. Meissen, c.1835-40. 3 parts in 2 vols. 4to, half mor; rubbed. With 141 hand-colored plates. Some foxing & browning. cb Feb 14 (2752) $600

## Volney, Constantin Francois, Comte de
— A View of the Soil and Climate of the United States.... Phila., 1804. 8vo, contemp calf; worn & soiled. With 2 maps & 2 plates, all folding. Some foxing; contents page torn at fore-edge with loss of page numbering. wa Feb 29 (540) $100

## Volpi Library, Gaetano
— La Libreria de' Volpi, e la stamperia cominiana. Padua, 1756. 8vo, contemp vellum. bba May 9 (52) £380 [Maggs]

**Volt.** See: Ciotti, Vittorio Fani

## Volta, Alessandro, 1745-1827
— Lettere... Sull' Aria infiammabile native delle Paludi al Padre Carlo Giuseppe Campi. Milan: Giuseppe Marelli, [c.1776]. 8vo, single folded sheet, unbound, unopened & uncut, as issued. Minor fold breaks & dust-soiling. Hefner copy. CNY May 17 (48) $7,500
— Lettres...sur l'air inflammable des Marais. Strassburg, 1778. 8vo, contemp wraps; backstrip def. sg May 16 (272) $175

## Voltaire, Francois Marie Arouet de, 1694-1778
See also: Limited Editions Club
— Candide. NY, 1927. One of 1,000. Illus by Clara Tice. Half cloth; ink stamps on endpapers. With 10 colored plates. sg Feb 15 (300) $110

Anr Ed. NY, 1928. One of 1,470. Illus by Rockwell Kent. 4to, cloth; rubbed. sg Sept 14 (248) $70

Anr Ed. NY: Pantheon, [1944]. One of 50 hand bound by Gerlach & with 2 extra suites of the illusts, on white & yellow paper. Illus by Paul Klee. 4to, half lev. sg Feb 15 (179) $500
— Candide, ou l'optimisme. L [Geneva: Cramer], 1759. 1st Ed. 12mo, contemp half vellum; extremities worn & rubbed, spine soiled, front hinge cracked. cb Oct 17 (492) $4,250

Anr Ed. Paris, 1893. One of 75 on chine with plates in 3 states. Illus by Adrien Moreau. 8vo, mor extra by Rapalier. b Sept 20 (647) £120
— Elemens de la philosophie de Neuton. Amst., 1738. 8vo, later calf; rubbed. With frontis & port. S Mar 14 (363) $300
— La Henriade. L, 1728. 4to, contemp mor gilt. Lacking subscribers' list. Fuerstenberg - Schaefer copy. S Dec 8 (634) £800

Anr Ed. Paris, 1770. 2 vols. 8vo, contemp mor gilt. With 10 engraved headpieces, all with extra proofs inserted & with frontis & 10 plates before letters. S Dec 8 (636) £550

Anr Ed. Kehl, 1789. 4to, contemp mor gilt; spine repaired. Fuerstenberg - Schaefer copy. S Dec 8 (638) £360
— The History of the Russian Empire Under Peter the Great. L: J. Nourse et al, [1763]. 1st Ed in English. 2 vols. 8vo, calf; needs rebdg. pba Nov 30 (321) $150
— Nanine, comedie en vers dissillabes. Paris: la compagnie des libraires associes, 1749. 12mo, contemp red mor gilt with arms of the comte de Pont de Veyle. Fuerstenberg - Schaefer copy. S Dec 8 (645) £320
— Oeuvres. Kehl, 1785-89. 70 vols. 8vo, contemp red mor gilt by Derome le jeune, with his ticket. With port, engraved dedication with port & 93 plates. Fuerstenberg - Schaefer copy. S Dec 8 (633) £3,400

Anr copy. 70 vols, plus 2 vols Index, 1801. Together, 72 vols. 8vo, contemp calf gilt, Vols 37 & 38 bound in 19th-cent sheep gilt; minor wear. Some foxing. sg Oct 19 (252) $2,000

Anr Ed. Paris, 1817-21. 55 (of 56) vols; lacking Vol IX but with Pieces inedites, 1920. 8vo, 19th-cent half mor; scuffed, some spine ends chipped. Minor foxing & soiling. bbc June 24 (111) $450

Anr Ed. Paris, 1883-85. 52 vols. 8vo, contemp half calf; spines discolored. With 199 plates. Some spotting. S Mar 29 (677) £520
— La Princesse de Babylone. Paris, 1948. One of 12 on Japon ancien, with 3 suites of the plates; in black, in colors & in black on Chine. Illus by Kees Van Dongen. 4to, mor extra with swirling onlaid design by Paul Bonet [Carnets, 1007], this being 1 of 6 bdgs commissioned by members of the Societe Scripta et Picta, this the example for Dr. Roudinesco. S Nov 21 (465) £23,000
— La Pucelle d'Orleans. Paris: Didot le Jeune, 1795 [An III]. 2 vols. Folio, contemp half mor; rubbed, tear in upper cover of Vol I. With port before letters & 21 plates in 2 states. Spotted. Fuerstenberg - Schaefer copy. S Dec 8 (641) £1,200
— Romans et contes. Bouillon, 1778. 3 vols. 8vo, contemp mor. S Dec 8 (643) £1,200
— Zadig, ou la destine. Paris, 1893. One of 115, this for M. Lagorce, with additional suite of plates in 3 or 4 states of color decomposition. 4to, mor extra by Marius Michel with art-nouveau-style orchid motifs, orig wraps bound in. With 8 color-ptd etchings. S Nov 21 (464) £20,000

## Von Hagen, Victor Wolfgang
— La Fabricacion del papel entre los Aztecas y los Mayas. Mexico: Editorial Nuevo Mundo, [1945]. One of 750. 4to, bdg not described. ds July 27 (192) $100

## Vonnegut, Kurt, Jr.
— Galapagos. Franklin Center, 1985. Ltd Ed. Lea gilt. Sgd on front flyleaf. sg Dec 14 (296) $120
— Jailbird. NY, 1979. One of 500. sg Dec 14 (294) $120

## VONNEGUT

— Palm Sunday. NY, [1981]. One of 500. sg Dec 14 (295) $120
— Slapstick: Or Lonesome No More! NY: Delacorte, [1976]. One of 250. sg Dec 14 (293) $120
— Slaughterhouse-Five or the Children's Crusade. NY, 1969. In soiled dj. sg June 20 (387) $90

### Voorn, Hendrick
— Old Ream Wrappers. [North Hills, Pa.]: Bird & Bull Press, 1969. One of 375. Half mor. Lacking the portfolio with 2 extra copper-engraved plates. pba June 20 (65) $55

### Voragine, Jacobus de, 1230?-98?
See also: Kelmscott Press
— Legenda aurea. Venice: Christophorus Arnoldus, not after 6 May 1478. Folio, old vellum. 49 lines; double column; gothic letter; initials in red. Margins of a1 & c4 repaired & c4 from shorter copy; last leaf cut round & mtd; tear in lower margin of L7 & m2; tears in last few leaves with loss. 265 (of 266) leaves; lacking initial blank. Goff J-89. S Dec 18 (44) £1,600 [Tenschert]

Anr Ed. Ulm: Johann Zainer, [c.1481]. Folio, 18th-cent calf; rubbed & wormed. 40 lines; gothic letter. Some worming & stains; marginal repairs. 314 (of 398) leaves only. Goff J-100. S Dec 18 (45) £420 [de Palol]

Anr Ed. Lyon: Nicolaus Philippi & Marcus Reinhard, [c.1482]. ("La legende doree.") Folio, mor by Chambolle-Duru. 48 lines, double column, type 98G. With 2 full-page woodcuts & 176 column-width woodcuts.. 291 (of 294) leaves; lacking 1st 2 leaves & final blank. Fairfax Murray, French, 589. Seilliere - Fairfax Murray - Gillet - Schaefer copy. P Nov 1 (125) $55,000

Anr Ed. Strassburg: Printer of the 1481 Legenda Aurea, 1482. Folio, 16th-cent blind-stamped pigskin over bevelled bds; repaired, clasps renewed. 43 lines; double column; types 1:180G, 2:97bG. Some worming at beginning; marginal repairs. 361 (of 362) leaves; lacking initial blank. Goff J-104. S Dec 18 (47) £1,400 [Buchel]

Anr Ed. Nuremberg: Anton Koberger, 1 Oct 1482. Folio, contemp blind-stamped calf over wooden bds; spine ends def, 1 clasp remaining. 54 lines & headline; gothic letter; large initial in red & blue on fol. 2r. Some worming, affecting text; browning & staining. 184 leaves. Goff J-103. S Dec 18 (46) £2,200 [Zioni]

Anr Ed. [Reutlingen: Michael Greyff], 1483. Folio, contemp blind-stamped calf over wooden bds; rebacked, new endpapers, corners worn. 46 lines; gothic letter. Some dampstaining & worming. 326 leaves. Goff J-109. S Dec 18 (49) £2,200 [Tenschert]

Anr Ed. Cologne: Ludwig van Renchen, 1485. Folio, 18th-cent calf; rebacked with old spine laid down. 46 lines; gothic letter. Tp repaired in upper margin; some worming; tear in B7; last 3 leaves hole in outer margin. Goff J-112. S Dec 18 (50) £1,400 [Frew]

Anr Ed. Strassburg: Printer of the 1483 Jordanus de Quedlinburg, May 1496. ("Lombardica historia que a plerisque aurea legenda sanctorum appelatur.") Folio, contemp wooden bds; rebacked with calf. 46 lines; double column; gothic letter. Tp stained & creased; marginal stains; a few leaves damaged in extreme upper margins; some worming in margins at ends. 263 (of 264) leaves; lacking last blank. Goff J-133. S Dec 18 (52) £900 [Tenschert]

Anr Ed. Antwerp: Henrick Eckert van Homberch, 20 May 1505. ("Passionael, of die Gulden Legende.") 2 parts in 1 vol. Folio, calf over wooden bds; rubbed, repaired, new endpapers. Some staining; soiling to last leaf; worming touching text; tear in b1v repaired with a few letters in pen facsimile. C June 26 (168) £7,000

### Vorreiter, Ansbert
— Kritik der Drachenflieger. Berlin, 1909. sg May 16 (94) $90

### Vosburgh, Walter S.
See also: Derrydale Press; Hervey & Vosburgh
— "Cherry and Black." The Career of Mr. Pierre Lorillard on the Turf. [NY], 1916. Orig cloth; worn. O Jan 9 (247) $50

### Vosmaer, Arnout
— Natuurkundige Beschrijving van zeldsaame gedierten.... Amst., [1766]-1804. 4to, modern wraps. With hand-colored engraved title & 35 hand-colored plates. Sold w.a.f. pba June 20 (352) $700

### Vosmeer, Michael
— Principes Hollandiae et Zelandiae.... Antwerp, 1578. Folio, contemp vellum gilt. With 36 ports. Lower margin of 1 plate repaired; other marginal repairs. CE June 15 (279) $350

### Voyage...
— The Voyage of the Racoon: A "Secret" Journal of a Visit to Oregon, California and Hawaii, 1813-1814. San Francisco: Book Club of California, 1958. One of 400. Ed by John A. Hussey. Tp & decorations by Henry Rusk. Bds. With 1 map. Larson copy. pba Sept 28 (140) $85

**Voyages...** See: Tyssot de Patot, Simon

### Voynich, W. M.
— A First-[Ninth] List of Books offered for Sale at the Net Prices affixed. L, [1898]-1902. 11 parts in 1 vol, including supplement and index. 8vo, contemp cloth; worn, rebacked in buckram. sg Apr 11 (327) $120

### Vrba, Frantisek
— Paul Strand. Prague: SNKLU, 1961. 12mo, pictorial wraps; minor wear. sg Feb 29 (309) $200

**Vredius, Olivier de.** See: Wree, Olivier de

**Vries, Hugo de.** See: De Vries, Hugo

## VVV
— VVV. Poetry, Plastic Arts, Anthropology, Sociology, Psychology. NY, 1942-44. No 1. Orig wraps by Max Ernst; waterstained. Last 5 leaves waterstained. sg June 13 (296) $475

## Vyner, Robert Thomas
— Notitia Venatica: a Treatise on Fox-Hunting. L, 1892 [1891]. 8vo, mor gilt with hunting tools, by Zaehnsdorf; rubbed. With 12 hand-colored plates. b May 30 (589) £80

Anr copy. 4to, half lea; some wear. O June 4 (270) $130

Anr copy. 2 vols. 4to, orig cloth; front bd of Vol I soiled. wa Feb 29 (230) $160

# W

## W., S.
— Human Nature, Poems, Dedicated by (Permission,) to Otho Manners.... [Stamford: Markham], 1828. 8vo, orig bds; worn & stained. Tp stained. b Dec 5 (235) £75

## Waddington, George
— A History of the Church.... L, 1833. 8vo, half calf. pba Aug 8 (267) $90

## Waddy, Ruth G. See: Lewis & Waddy

## Wadsworth, Edward
— The Black Country. L, 1920. Intro by Arnold Bennett. 4to, orig cloth, with front panel of dj loosely inserted. b Jan 31 (224) £180

## Wadsworth, Edward —& Windeler, Bernard
— Sailing Ships and Barges of the Western Mediterranean and Adriatic Seas. L, 1926. One of 450. Folio, orig half canvas. bba May 9 (578) £170 [Rush]

## Wafer, Lionel, 1660?-1705?
— A New Voyage and Description of the Isthmus of America.... L, 1699. 1st Ed. 8vo, half lea; worn & chipped, interior hinge starting, front endpaper & tp disbound. With map & 3 folding plates. Repair to 1 plate. Met May 22 (323) $425

## Wagenaar, Jan
— Amsterdam, in zyne opkomst, aanwas, geschiednissen.... Amst., 1760-88. Vols I-III. Old half calf. Lacking some plates. Sold w.a.f. pba Apr 25 (252) $850

## Waghenaer, Lucas Jansz
— The Mariners Mirrour.... L: [J. Charlewood, 1588?]. Folio, disbound. With 45 double-page charts. Lacking 1st 6 prelims before A1, including tp, dedication & arms; also lacking B3 & B4; frontis to Part 2 replaced by a blank; small section of Map 16 in Part 1 excised; general chart of Europe detached with lower margin browned. Sold w.a.f. C Nov 29 (114) £16,000

— Speculum nauticum super navigatione maris occidentalis confectum.... Antwerp & Amst., 1591. 2 parts in 1 vol. Folio, contemp vellum over pastebd tooled in dutch-metal (oxidised to black); tears & worming to extremities, lower outer corner of upper cover reinforced. With engraved title, 2 engraved illusts (1 with overslips), 1 woodcut & 47 coastal charts (1 folding, 46 double-page). Title to 1st part & 2 following leaves supplied in photofacsimile; 5 charts browned. C May 31 (76) £13,000

## Wagner, Arthur L. —& Kelley, James Douglas Jerrold, 1847-1922
— The United States Army and Navy. Akron, 1899. Folio, pictorial cloth; extremities worn. With 43 colored plates. Tear in title of Navy section; small tears in margins of several leaves. NH Sept 16 (113) $325

## Wagner, Henry Raup
See also: Garcia Icazbalceta & Wagner; Grabhorn Printing

— Bullion to Books: Fifty Years of Business and Pleasure. Los Angeles, 1942. 1st Ed. 8vo, orig cloth in dj; spine panel bottom stained. sg Apr 11 (328) $60

— California Voyages, 1539-1541. San Francisco, 1925. Orig cloth. With 8 plates of maps. Inscr to Charles L. Camp. Larson copy. pba Sept 28 (282) $475

— The Cartography of the Northwest Coast of America.... Amst., 1968. 2 vols in 1. 4to, cloth. pba Oct 9 (24) $190; pba Apr 25 (162) $200; sg May 9 (48) $425

— The Cartography of the Northwest Coast of America to the Year 1800. Berkeley, 1937. 2 vols. 4to, orig cloth, in djs. Crease & edge tear to 2 leaves in Vol II. pba Feb 13 (193) $375

1st Ed. 2 vols. 4to, orig cloth in soiled djs. Robbins copy. pba Mar 21 (376) $425

— Juan Rodriguez Cabrillo: Discoverer of the Coast of California. San Francisco, 1941. One of 750. Half bds. With color frontis. Larson copy. pba Sept 28 (281) $100; pba Feb 13 (190) $80; pba Apr 25 (717) $85

— The Plains and the Rockies.... Columbus, 1953. Revised by Charles L. Camp. pba Feb 13 (194) $90

4th Ed. San Francisco, 1982. Revised by Charles L. Camp & then by Robert H. Becker. Cloth; worn. O May 7 (291) $100; pba Feb 13 (195) $85; sg Oct 26 (379) $90

— Published Writings. Santa Ana, 1934. One of 125. Orig wraps; chipped & with edge-tears. sg Oct 26 (377) $70

— The Rise of Fernando Cortes. [Los Angeles], 1944. 1st Ed, One of 300. Robbins copy. Inscr. pba Mar 21 (377) $180

— Sir Francis Drake's Voyage around the World.... San Francisco, 1926. 1st Ed. Buckram; spine faded, rear cover bumped. Robbins copy. pba Mar 21 (378) $160

One of 100. Half mor; spine faded & spotted. Larson copy. Inscr to Charles L. Camp. pba Sept 28 (91) $350

— Spanish Explorations in the Strait of Juan de Fuca. Santa Ana, 1933. One of 425. 4to, cloth. pba Apr 25 (718) $225

1st Ed. With 13 maps. 1 map cut at fold during binding & repaired. pba Feb 13 (191) $350

Anr copy. With 13 maps. Robbins copy. pba Mar 21 (379) $375

— The Spanish Southwest, 1542-1794. An Annotated Bibliography. Berkeley, 1924. 1st Ed, One of 20. Orig vellum; discolored. With 15 specially inserted facsimiles. Some darkening. Robbins copy. Sgd. pba Mar 21 (381) $1,600

— Spanish Voyages to the Northwest Coast of America in the Sixteenth Century. San Francisco, 1929. Inscr to Willard S. Morse. pba Feb 13 (192) $325

1st Ed. Robbins copy. pba Mar 21 (380) $325

Anr Ed. Amst., 1966. Reprint of 1929 Ed. pba Oct 9 (23) $120

Anr copy. Reprint of 1929 Ed. pba July 25 (239) $75

**Wagner, Lauren McGraw.** See: McGraw & Wagner

**Wagner, Richard, 1813-83**
— The Flying Dutchman. L: Corvinus Press, 1938. Out-of-series copy. 4to, orig vellum gilt; bowed. Inscr by Carlow. bba May 9 (472B) £80 [Cox]
— Das Nibelungen Lied. Berlin: Askanischen Verlag, 1933. Memorial Ed, ptd for the Deutsch-Nordischen Richard Wagner Gesellschaft, this copy for Augusta Taissle. 4to, vellum gilt. wa Nov 16 (74) $130
— Ouverture zu der Oper der Fliegende Hollaender.... Dresden: Meser, [1861]. Folio, orig wraps; spotted. Tp spotted; contemp annotations. Inscr. S Dec 1 (383) £1,000
— Parsifal. L, 1912. One of 525. Illus by Willy Pogany. Folio, mor extra with a central panel of mor decorated with a banner of silk inlay raised form a design of flowering lilies & thorns worked with chalice of mirrored glass in center. b Dec 5 (42) £650
— Das Rheingold und die Walkyre. Berlin, 1922. ("Der Ring des Nibelungen I: Das Rheingold.") Illus by Franz Stassen. Folio, orig upper cover only. With 24 lithos, most in 2 or mor colors, some heightened with gold, each sgd in pencil, 1 dated in 1922, all in separate card mounts. With letterpress tp, dedication & contents on 3 leaves. S Nov 21 (466) £2,000
— The Rhinegold & the Valkyrie. L, 1910. Illus by Arthur Rackham. 4to, later cloth. Some spotting. F June 20 (531) $70

Anr copy. Orig cloth; corner bumped. pba Aug 22 (840) $200

One of 1,150. Mor gilt by Bayntun-Riviere. b Dec 5 (47) £260

Anr copy. Orig vellum gilt; stained. Some spotting & browning. Ck May 31 (138) £240; sg Feb 15 (263) $350

Anr copy. Later calf gilt. sg Feb 15 (264) $400

Anr copy. Orig vellum gilt; soiled. wd May 8 (78) $400

Anr Ed. L, [1920]. Mor; rubbed. CE Feb 21 (202) $160

— Siegfried & the Twilight of the Gods. L, 1911. One of 1,150. Illus by Arthur Rackham. 4to, vellum gilt; lower joint cracked. With 30 color plates. b May 30 (579) £190

Anr copy. Vellum gilt; stained. Some spotting & browning. Ck May 31 (140) £280

Anr copy. Later calf gilt. Small def on plate facing p.10. sg Feb 15 (265) $800

Anr Ed. NY, 1911. Illus by Arthur Rackham. 4to, pictorial bds; corners showing. With 30 mtd plates. pba Aug 22 (841) $75

— The Tale of Lohengrin. L, [1913]. Illus by Willy Pogany. b Dec 5 (43) £75

One of 525. 4to, orig vellum; bowed, minor soiling, front hinge cracked. cb June 25 (1965) $600

— Tannhauser. L, 1911. Illus by Willy Pogany. 4to, orig cloth; soiled & rubbed. sg Feb 15 (237) $140

One of 525. Mor with onlaid mor design of Wolfram von Eschenbach holding a lute, by Bayntun-Riviere. CE Feb 21 (11) $800

**Wagstaff, Alexander E.**
— Life of David S. Terry.... San Francisco: Continental Publishing, 1892. Orig cloth; extremities worn. With frontis & 5 wood-engraved plates. pba Aug 8 (206) $160

**Wagstroem, C. B.**
— Observations of the Slave Trade.... L, 1789. 1st Ed. 8vo, modern bds. S Oct 26 (550) £320 [Rizzo]

**Wahl, Gustave.** See: Liebmann & Wahl

**Wahl, Ralph**
— Come Wade the River. Seattle: Salisbury Press, [1971]. One of 250. Folio, cloth; worn. ANs from Ralph Wahl to Pete Hidy laid in. O Feb 6 (50) $250

**Wahlstedt, Jacob J.**
— Iter in Americam. Uppsala, [1725]. 8vo, disbound. Some foxing. Met Feb 24 (422) $375

**Wain, Louis.** See: Burnaby & Wain

**Waitz, Jacob Sigismund von**
— Abhandlung von der Electricitaet. Berlin, 1745. 4 parts in 1 vol. 4to, contemp half calf. Minor worming in lower margins. S Mar 14 (365) £300

**Wakefield, Edward**
— An Account of Ireland, Statistical and Political. L, 1812. 2 vols. 4to, half calf; Vol II rebacked preserving backstrip. Lacking the frontises; some holes in text. bba Nov 1 (114) £450 [Emerald Isle]

**Wakefield, Priscilla**
— Excursions in North America. L, 1810. 12mo, contemp sheep; worn. With folding map. sg Oct 26 (380) $80
— An Introduction to Botany.... L, 1818. 8vo, contemp half mor; spine def. With 9 hand-colored plates. Contemp ink annotations. b May 30 (501) £50

**Wakeman, Bryarly.** See: Geiger & Wakeman

## Wakeman, Capt. Edgar
— The Log of an Ancient Mariner. San Francisco, 1878. 1st Ed. 8vo, orig cloth; spine faded, extremities rubbed. With frontis port. Robbins copy. pba Mar 21 (382) $120

Anr copy. Ed by his daughter. Orig cloth; spine faded. With frontis port & 1 plate. Larson copy. pba Sept 28 (734) $75

## Wakeman, Geoffrey
— Graphic Methods in Book Illustration. Loughborough: Plough Press, 1981. One of 120. Folio, laid in cloth folding case with 18 paper folders containing explanatory text & loose specimen leaves, as issued. sg Sept 14 (338) $200

## Walcott, Derek. See: Limited Editions Club

## Walcott, John
— Synopsis of British Birds. L, 1789. 2 vols in 1. 4to, contemp half calf; rebacked, old spine laid down. With 255 hand-colored half-page plates. Author's copy. Fattorini copy. C Oct 25 (50) £2,600

## Walcott, Mackenzie E. C.
— Battle Abbey; with notices of the Parish Church and Town. Battle, 1866. 8vo, orig cloth. With 9 mtd photographic plates & folding plan. b May 30 (72) £70

## Walcott, Mary Vaux, 1860-1940
— North American Wild Flowers. Wash., 1925-29. 5 vols. In portfolios. With 400 plates. pba Sept 14 (358) $550; wa Nov 16 (171) $850

## Waldberg, Patrick
— Rene Magritte. Brussels, 1965. 4to, cloth, in dj. sg Jan 11 (261) $50
— Un Reve a commettre. Paris, 1973. One of 180. Folio, unsewn in wraps. With 11 color etchings. sg Feb 15 (308) $225

## Walden, Arthur
— List of Birds Known to Inhabit the Philippine Archipelago. L, 1875. 4to, half lea. Extracted from: Zoological Society of London, Vol IX, Part 2, Apr 1875. Met Sept 28 (419) $350

## Walden, Howard T. See: Derrydale Press

## Wales, George Canning
— Etchings and Lithographs of American Ships.... Bost., 1927. One of 500. Folio, cloth, in dj; some wear. O May 7 (292) $130

Anr copy. Half cloth, in chipped dj. sg Sept 7 (342) $200

## Waley, Arthur, 1889-1966
— The Lady Who Loved Insects. L, 1929. One of 550. sg Sept 14 (80) $110

Out-of-series presentation copy for Humbert Wolfe. bba May 9 (457) £55 [Hanborough]

## Walker, Adam, 1730-1821
— A Journal of Two Campaigns of the Fourth Regiment of U.S. Infantry. Keene, NH, 1816. 12mo, orig half lea; front bd lacking part of covering. NH June 1 (24) $1,100

## Walker, Aldace
— The Vermont Brigade in the Shenandoah Valley, 1864. Burlington VT: Free Press Association, 1869. 8vo, orig cloth; some wear. wa Feb 29 (347) $180

## Walker, Alexander
— Intermarriage. L, 1838. 8vo, contemp half calf; rubbed. F June 20 (101A) $70

## Walker, Mrs. Alexander
— Female Beauty, as Preserved and Improved by Regimen, Cleanliness and Dress. L, 1837. 8vo, orig mor gilt. With hand-colored frontis & 11 plates, 10 hand-colored, each with hand-colored overlay. b Jan 31 (284) £320

Anr copy. Early half mor; worn, 1 plate loose. With hand-colored plates, 10 with overlays. Minor foxing. sg Dec 7 (263) $175

## Walker, Francis A., 1840-97
— Statistical Atlas of the United States.... Wash., 1874. Folio, half sheep; extremities worn, covers spotted. sg Dec 7 (51) $375

Anr Ed. [New Haven], 1874. Folio, orig half sheep; worn. With 60 litho maps, some in color. Text browned & repaired; tear & repair to 1 plate. bbc Feb 26 (25) $200

## Walker, James, 1748-1808. See: Atkinson & Walker

## Walker, James, 1781-1861
— Liverpool and Manchester Railroad: Report to the Directors...on the Comparative Merits of Locomotive and Fixed Engines.... Phila.: Carey & Lea, 1831. 8vo, orig half cloth; extremities worn. sg May 9 (375) $120

Anr copy. With frontis, map & 2 folding charts. Bound with: Stephenson, Robert, & Locke, Joseph. Observations on the Comparative Merits.... Phila., 1831. And: Booth, Henry. An Account of the Liverpool and Manchester Railway. Phila., 1831. orig half cloth; spine rubbed. Foxed; stamps on tp & endleaves. sg May 16 (274) $60

## Walker, James P.
— Book of Raphael's Madonnas. NY, 1860. Illus by E. Hufnagel. 4to, mor gilt. With 11 orig mtd albumen photographs, 1 hand-colored. pba Aug 22 (870) $80

## Walker, John & Charles
— The British Atlas. L, 1851. Folio, contemp half russia; rubbed, upper cover detached. With 49 maps. Lacking tp. S June 13 (429) £480

## Walker, Joseph Cooper
— An Historical Essay on the Dress of the Ancient and Modern Irish. Dublin, 1788. 4to, contemp half calf; needs rebdg. With frontis & 13 plates. Some dampstaining. sg Mar 7 (372) $250

**Walker, Judson Elliott**
— Campaigns of General Custer.... NY, 1881. 8vo, orig wraps; backstrip frayed & def, worn. wa Feb 29 (358) $180

**Walker, Margaret**
See also: Limited Editions Club
— Jubilee. Bost., 1966. In dj with wear. sg Mar 28 (367) $50

**Walker, Mary Adelaide**
— Through Macedonia to the Albanian Lakes. L, 1864. 8vo, orig cloth; rebacked using orig backstrip. With 4 color & 8 tinted lithos. One leaf loose. b May 30 (302) £350

**Walker, Mary Willis**
— The Red Scream. NY, [1994]. In dj. Sgd on tp. pba May 23 (447) $75

**Wall, Bernhardt, 1872-1953**
— The Etched Monthly. Lime Rock CT, 1928-31. Vol I, Nos 1-12, Oct 1928 to Sept 1929.. Orig wraps; frayed, creases, 2 free endpapers stuck together. cb Feb 14 (2810) $1,000
— Following Abraham Lincoln. Lime Rock CT, 1931-[39]. One of 100. Vols 1-54 (of 85). 4to, orig half cloth, plain djs on all but vols II & IV. sg Oct 19 (254) $3,200
— Lincoln's New-Salem: A Pilgrimage. New Preston, 1926. One of 103. 4to, orig half cloth. Etched throughout. Inscr. sg Oct 26 (381) $150

**Wall, John F.**
— Thoroughbred Bloodlines: an Elementary Study. Columbia SC: Pvtly ptd, [1946]. One of 1,000. Folio, cloth; worn. O Jan 9 (249) $90

**Wallace, Alfred Russel, 1823-1913**
— The Malay Archipelago. L, 1869. 2 vols. 8vo, orig cloth; library label removed from upper covers, hinges weak, rubbed. S June 13 (430) £360

**Wallace, Edward S.** See: Herr & Wallace

**Wallace, Lew, 1827-1905**
See also: Limited Editions Club
— Ben-Hur. NY, 1892. 2 vols. 8vo, orig cloth; minor soiling. pba Nov 30 (323) $50

**Waller, Edmund, 1606-87**
— Poems, &c. Written upon Several Occasions.... L, 1664. 2d Ed. 8vo, 18th-cent calf gilt; joints & extremities rubbed. Cut close with minor loss to some running heads. F June 20 (119) $120
5th Ed. L, 1686. 8vo, contemp mor gilt. Endleaves with 2 poems in Ms. Astor - Bagot copy. b May 30 (423) £900

**Wallhausen, Johann Jacobi von**
— Art militaire a cheval. Frankfurt, 1616. Folio, contemp vellum. With engraved title, dedication with engraved arms & 43 (of 44) plates, most double-page. Lacking Plate 11 but with an unnumbered plate bound in at end; 5 plates cropped; dampstaining in upper margin. S Mar 28 (164) £420

**Wallihan, Allen Grant & Mary A.**
— Hoofs, Claws and Antlers of the Rocky Mountains by the Camera. Denver, 1894. 4to, pictorial cloth; extremities worn, covers soiled, hinges cracked. sg Mar 7 (463) $50

**Wallis, John, 1616-1703**
— Operum mathematicorum. Oxford, 1657-56. 2 vols in 1. 4to, contemp calf; upper cover detached. Tp & prelims soiled; minor worming to upper margin of c.100 leaves. b Sept 20 (192) £3,000

**Wallraf-Richartz Museum**
— Kunst der sechziger Jahre im Wallraf-Richartz Museum. Cologne, 1970. 4th Revised Ed. 4to, in clear plastic binder, as issued. sg June 13 (319) $250

**Walmsley, Hugh Mulleneux**
— Stories of the Battle Field; and Sketches in Algeria. L, [c.1860]. 8vo, cloth; hinges cracked. sg Mar 7 (184) $175

**Walpole, Horace, 4th Earl of Orford, 1717-97**
— Anecdotes of Painting in England. L, 1828. 5 vols. 8vo, half lea; worn & chipped. O May 7 (293) $160
— The Castle of Otranto. Edin., 1811. 4to, contemp half mor gilt; front joint tender. With added frontis; bookplates, including that of Walpole, tipped in before engraved title. sg Sept 21 (319) $275
— A Catalogue of the Royal and Noble Authors of England.... Strawberry Hill, 1758. 1st Ed, 1st state with "to be partial," vol I, A2v, line 3. 2 vols. 8vo, contemp mor; rubbed. David Garrick's copy. S Mar 28 (616) £620
Anr Ed. L, 1806. 5 vols. 8vo, later 19th-cent calf gilt; rubbed. With 150 ports. O Mar 26 (288) $160
Anr copy. Contemp mor gilt; hinges rubbed. wd Nov 15 (113) $100
— Essay on Modern Gardening. Strawberry Hill, 1785. 4to, 19th-cent half mor. Plate trimmed to edge with slight loss. Fuersterberg - Schaefer copy. S Dec 8 (653) £700
Anr copy. Contemp sheep with 19th-cent arms of Baron Stuart de Rothesay; front joint cracked. Later pencil marginalia on 1 leaf. sg Oct 19 (176) $325
— Letters Addressed to the Countess of Ossory. L, 1903. 3 vols. Half mor by William Winter; marginalia & pencil notes on rear endpapers. sg Sept 21 (322) $120
— The Mysterious Mother, a Tragedy. Strawberry Hill, 1768. One of 50. 8vo, 18th-cent mor gilt by Kalthoeber; joints rubbed. Lacking final blank. C Nov 29 (141) £2,700
— Works. L, 1798. 5 vols. 4to, contemp calf; rubbed, some joints starting. wa Dec 14 (196) $600

**Walpole Library, Horace**
— [Sale Catalogue] A Catalogue of the Classic Contents of Strawberry Hill.... L: Geo. Robins, [1842]. 4to, later half mor. Some prices in ink; frontis browned at margins. Ck Apr 12 (4) £110

Anr copy. Later half lea. Library markings. O Mar 26 (289) $160

**Walpole, Robert, 1781-1856**
— Travels in Various Countries of the East. L, 1820. 4to, contemp calf; rebacked. With 2 maps & 11 plates. Plates & maps foxed. b Sept 20 (361) £160

**Walsh, James E.** See: Harvard University

**Walsh, Robert, 1772-1852**
— Constantinople and the Scenery of the Seven Churches of Asia Minor. L, [c.1839]. Illus by Thomas Allom. 2d Series only. Contemp calf gilt; rebacked. b May 30 (303) £250

Anr Ed. L: Fisher, Son & Co., [1839?]. 1st & 2d Series. 2 vols in 1. 4to, contemp half calf; spine rubbed. With 2 maps & 96 plates, including additional titles. Some spotting. S June 13 (599) £550

— Notices of Brazil in 1828 and 1829. L, 1830. 2 vols. 8vo, modern half calf. With 2 folding maps & 19 plates. Some foxing. bba Nov 16 (303) £350 [Waggett]

**Walsh, Robert, 1784-1859**
— An Appeal from the Judgments of Great Britain respecting the United States of America. Phila., 1819. 2d Ed. 8vo, contemp sheep; worn. sg Oct 26 (382) $175

**Walsh, Capt. Thomas**
— Journal of the late Campaign in Egypt.... L, 1803. 2d Ed. 4to, bds. With 42 plates (6 hand-colored). Discolored. S Oct 26 (233) £200 [Fsadni]

**Walsingham, Thomas, d.1422?**
— Historia brevis.... L: H. Binneman, 1574. Folio, contemp calf, remboitage; spine head torn, upper cover almost off. CE June 15 (280) £230

**Walter, John, 1738-1812**
— Miscellanies in Prose and Verse intended as a Specimen of the Types at the Logographic Printing Office. L, 1785. 1st Ed. 8vo, modern mor by Riviere. Spotted & stained. S Oct 27 (1202) £550 [Marlborough]

**Walter, Richard**
— Anson's Voyage Round the World. L, 1928. One of 1,500 of the American issue, with Lauriat imprint on spine. 8vo, half cloth; corner bumped. pba Feb 13 (2) $150

Anr copy. Half cloth; corners bumped. pba July 25 (89) $90

**Walters Library, Henry**
— Incunabula Typographica: a Descriptive Catalogue to the Books...in the Library.... Balt., 1906. 4to, calf; worn. O Mar 26 (290) $130

**Walters, Lettice d'Oyley**
— The Year's at the Spring. L, 1920. Illus by Harry Clarke. 4to, mor gilt by Bayntun-Riviere. bba May 9 (275) £130 [Page]

**Walters, Lorenzo D.**
— Tombstone's Yesterday. Tucson AZ: Acme Printing Co., 1928. Orig cloth, in chipped & repaired dj; spine head frayed. Inscr to Eugene Manlove Rhodes. wa Feb 29 (516) $230

**Walters, Minette**
— The Sculptress. L, [1993]. Uncorrected Proof copy. Wraps. Sgd on tp. pba Jan 25 (374) $85

**Walterstorff, Emelie von**
— Textilt Bildverk Stockholm, 1925. One of 700. 4to, sheep gilt. sg June 13 (361) $90

**Walther, Rudolph**
— An Hundred, Threescore and Fiftene Homelyes or Sermons, uppon the Actes of the Apostles.... L, 1572. Folio, contemp calf; upper cover detached, corners worn. Black letter. Tp supplied; marginal staining & soiling. STC 25013. CE June 15 (281) $480

**Walton, Izaak, 1593-1683**
See also: Limited Editions Club; Nonesuch Press
— The Life of Dr. Sanderson.... L, 1678. 2 parts in 1 vol. 8vo, contemp calf; rebacked with orig spine laid down. Marginal staining & fraying. bba Oct 19 (220) £60 [Clark]
— The Life of John Donne. L, 1658. 12mo, contemp calf; worn. Lacking initial blank. b Sept 20 (116) £130
— The Lives of Dr. John Donne, Sir Henry Wotton.... L, 1670. 1st Collected Ed. 8vo, calf by Riviere; rebacked preserving most of spine. With 4 ports. O Feb 6 (246) $275

**Walton, Izaak, 1593-1683 —&**
**Cotton, Charles, 1630-87**

### Compleat Angler

— 1655. - L.2d Ed. 12mo, contemp calf; extremities worn. Some leaves cropped, affecting headlines. cb Oct 17 (495) $5,500
— 1750. - L.1st Moses Brown Ed. 16mo, calf gilt by Riviere. pba July 11 (310) $375
— 1759. - L. 16mo, contemp calf; rubbed. C July 1 (336) £190
— 1760. - L.1st Hawkins Ed. 2 parts in 1 vol. 8vo, modern calf gilt. pba July 11 (311) $375
— 1784. - L.4th Hawkins Ed. 8vo, modern half lea; most of early calf spine laid on, worn. Some staining, foxing & soiling. O Feb 6 (238) $120
— 1808. - L. 8vo, contemp calf; rebacked in mor, rubbed. O Feb 6 (239) $130
Anr copy. Calf. pnE Mar 20 (173) £240
— 1815. - L: Samuel Bagster. 2 parts in 1 vol. 8vo, later half mor; rubbed. Some browning & soiling. O Feb 6 (240) $60
Anr copy. Modern half mor. pba July 11 (312) $110
— 1823. - L. Intro by John Major. 16mo, mor gilt by Gosden; covers detached. With 14 mtd india-proof plates. L.p. copy. O Feb 6 (241) $325
Anr copy. Lev gilt to a cottage-roof design by Birdsal; spine browned. With 13 mtd india-proof plates

& engraved leaf of music. L.p. copy. sg Mar 7 (565) $500
— 1824. - L. 8vo, contemp calf gilt. Edward Fitzgerald's copy with his note "Given to me by William Thackeray December 1829". bba May 30 (197) £460 [Devitt]
Anr copy. Bds. pba July 11 (313) $130
— 1836. - L. Ed by Sir Harris Nicolas. 2 vols. 4to, mor gilt. rce Nov 16 (47) $400
Anr copy. Mor gilt by Hayday. L.p. copy. sg Mar 7 (566) $800
— 1847. - NY1st American Ed. 2 vols in 1. 12mo, orig cloth; spine ends chipped. Tp stamped; tear across 1 leaf. sg Mar 7 (567) $175
— 1856. - L. 12mo, half mor gilt. Dampstaining in margins. sg Mar 7 (568) $100
— 1860. - L. 2 vols. 8vo, lev gilt by Wright. sg Mar 7 (569) $325
— 1880. - NY 2 vols. 8vo, cloth; worn, library bookplates. Some foxing & soiling. O Feb 6 (243) $160
One of 100. 2 vols. 4to, contemp half mor; rubbed, joints worn. Some foxing. O Feb 6 (242) $300
— 1883. - L.12th Major Ed. 8vo, cloth. With 8 plates in 2 states & 74 text wood-illusts, each a mtd India proof. pba July 11 (314) $225
— 1887. - L.4th Nicolas Ed. 8vo, cloth. pba July 11 (315) $110
— 1888. - L. One of 500. 2 vols. 4to, half mor, Coigney's 2d bdg. pba July 11 (316) $550
— 1889. - L. 8vo, modern half mor gilt. sg Mar 7 (570) $110
2d Nimmo Ed. 2 parts in 1 vol. 8vo, orig cloth; spine ends & joints rubbed, rear hinge cracked. pba July 11 (318) $85
— 1893. - L.Tercentenary Ed, one of 350. 2 vols. 4to, half vellum, in frayed cloth djs. O Feb 6 (244) $130
Anr copy. Half vellum. R. B. Marston's copy. pba July 11 (319) $400
— 1905. - Chiswick: Caradoc Press One of 350. Calf; rubbed & dried. O Feb 6 (245) $80
— 1925. - L: Navarre SocietyMor by Bayntun-Riviere, the upper cover with central inset colored miniature port of Walton. S Mar 29 (798) £380
— 1930. - L. One of 450. Illus by Frank Adams. 4to, half vellum; spine yellowed. bba May 9 (276) £50 [Katrina]
— 1931. - L. Illus by Arthur Rackham. 4to, cloth, in dj. With 12 colored plates. sg Sept 14 (309) $150
One of 775. Orig vellum gilt; spine stained. CE May 22 (398) $450
Anr copy. Orig vellum gilt; minor staining. With 12 colored plates. Ck May 31 (164) £220
Anr copy. Orig vellum gilt, unopened. sg Oct 19 (206) $600
Anr copy. Orig vellum gilt. sg Feb 15 (266) $450

Walton, J. See: Fielding & Walton

**Walton, William, 1843-1915**
— World's Columbian Exposition...Official Illustrated Publication: Art and Architecture. Phila., [1893]. 2 vols. Folio, orig lea gilt; joints rubbed. sg Sept 7 (109A) $100

**Wandrei, Donald**
— Dark Odyssey. St. Paul: Webb Publishing, 1931. One of 400. Illus by Howard Wandrei. Orig cloth; spine ends rubbed. Inscr. sg June 20 (388) $90
— The Web of Easter Island. Sauk City: Arkham House, 1948. In dj. pba May 23 (448) $55

**Waningen, Hendrick**
— Thresoor van't Italiaens Boeck-Houden. Rotterdam: Pieter van Waesberge, 1652. Folio, old vellum; worn & shaken. sg Mar 21 (122) $700

**Wanostrocht, Nicholas**
— Felix on the Bat. L, 1845. 4to, orig cloth; stained. With 10 litho plates & 7 color plates. Some foxing. pn Oct 12 (333) £450

**Wansey, Henry**
— The Journal of an Excursion to the United States of North America.... Salisbury & L, 1796. 8vo, contemp half calf; rubbed. With frontis & folding plate. Foxed. pba Apr 25 (253) $160

**War...**
— The War; Being a Faithful Record of the Transactions of the War...declared on the 18th June 1812. NY, 1812-14. Vols I-II. 104 issues in 1 vol. 4to, early half mor; broken, worn. Some browning & staining; cropped, affecting page numerals. wa Feb 29 (544) $100
— The War of the Rebellion: a Compilation of the Official Records of the Union and Confederate Armies. Wash., 1880-1902. 128 vols. 8vo, orig cloth; various defs, some covers detached, call numbers on spines. Lacking Atlas. Library markings; several pages torn & def in Vol XXXII, Part 2. cb Oct 17 (149) $850

**Warburton, John, of Dublin —& Others**
— History of the City of Dublin. L, 1818. 2 vols. 4to, contemp calf; needs rebdg. sg Mar 7 (374) $350

**Warburton, Roland E. Egerton**
— Hunting Songs, Ballads, &c. Chester, 1834. 8vo, calf by Riviere; rubbed. O Jan 9 (250) $100

**Ward, Sir Adolphus William**
— Dickens. L, 1882. 8vo, half calf gilt by Bayntun. Extra-illus with materials including photos of Dickens & Wilkie Collins. wa Dec 14 (35) $110

**Ward, Humphry —& Roberts, William**
— Romney: a Biographical and Critical Essay. L, 1904. One of 350. 2 vols. 4to, orig half lea gilt; spine ends worn. sg Sept 7 (300A) $150

**Ward, Mrs Humphry.** See: Ward, Mary Augusta

## Ward, Lynd
— Gods' Man, a Novel in Woodcuts. NY, [1929]. One of 405. Owner's stamp to front free endpaper & top edges. pba Apr 4 (431) $325
— Madman's Drum. NY, [1930]. Orig bds; edges worn. F June 20 (687) $50

Anr copy. In soiled dj. pba May 23 (449) $140
— Song Without Words. NY, 1936. One of 1,250. Orig bds; extremities & spine ends rubbed, front hinge starting. pba June 20 (354) $170
— Vertigo, a Novel in Woodcuts. NY, 1937. In dj. pba Apr 4 (433) $160

## Ward, Mary Augusta, 1851-1920
— Works. Bost. & NY, 1909-12. ("The Writings of Mrs. Humphry Ward.") Autograph Ed. 16 vols. Half mor. cb Oct 17 (308) $475

## Ward, Rowland
— Records of Big Game. L, 1962. ("Rowland Ward's Records of Big Game.") XIth Ed (Africa). - Ed by G. Dollman & J. B. Burlace. 4to, orig cloth; worn. O June 4 (273) $60
— Rowland Ward's Records of Big Game. L, 1910. 6th Ed. Some soiling. O June 4 (271) $110

8th Ed. L, 1922. Ed by G. Dollman & J. B. Burlace. 4to, orig cloth; worn, front hinge starting. Inscr by Burlace to Gerald Burrard. O June 4 (272) $70

## Warden, David Baillie, 1778-1845
— A Chorographical and Statistical Description of the District of Columbia. Paris, 1816. 12mo, modern cloth; soiled & rubbed. Library markings; map foxed & with tear. wa Feb 1 (97) $210

## Warden, William, 1777-1849
— Letters Written on Board His Majesty's Ship the Northumberland.... L, 1817. 8vo, contemp half calf. With folding frontis & 1 plate. b May 30 (193) £60

## Ware, Isaac, d.1766
— A Complete Body of Architecture.... L, 1756. 2 vols. Folio, contemp half calf; worn. With frontis, title, & 114 plates. Sold w.a.f. CE Nov 8 (252) $900
— The Plans, Elevations, and Sections; Chimney-Pieces, and Ceilings of Houghton in Norfolk.... L, 1760. Folio, later bds. With engraved title & 35 plates. Some staining. b Sept 20 (80) £300

## Ware, Sir James, 1594-1666
— The Antiquities and History of Ireland. Dublin, 1705. 8vo, contemp calf; bumped. pba Sept 14 (362) $375

## Ware, Joseph
— The Emigrant's Guide to California. Princeton, 1932. Reprint of 1849 Ed. - Intro by John Caughey. Orig cloth. With facsimile of orig tp, 1 plate & 1 folded map. Larson copy. pba Sept 28 (627) $110

## Ware, William Rotch
— The Georgian Period: A Collection of Papers.... NY, 1908. 12 parts in 4 vols. Half mor; worn. With 451 plates. Some plates soiled. cb Oct 17 (55) $200

## Warhol, Andy, d.1987
[-] Andy Warhol. Bost.: Boston Book & Art, [1968]. 4to, stiff pictorial wraps. sg Jan 11 (455) $120
— Andy Warhol's Index Book. NY, 1967. 4to, pictorial foil wraps. Some soiling. pba June 20 (355) $275

Anr copy. The various pop-ups & devices loose or otherwise def. Sold w.a.f. sg Sept 7 (344) $200; sg Jan 11 (456) $90

Anr copy. Half cloth; worn, mark to front cover. Tomato can need repair; lacking balloon, Velvet Underground record & For a Big Surprise. wa June 20 (401) $150
— A is an Alphabet by Corky and Andy. NY, 1953. One of c.100. 4to, orig wraps. With 26 illusts. Discoloration to right edge of 1st 3 prints. sg May 23 (546) $850
— The Philosophy of Andy Warhol (from A to B & Back Again). NY: Harcourt Brace Jovanovich, [1975]. Half cloth, in dj. Inscr to Alan Weiner with sketch. CE May 22 (463) $140

Anr copy. Half cloth, in dj. Sgd with initials. pba Mar 7 (264) $55

Anr copy. Half cloth, in dj. Initialled on half-title. pba May 23 (450) $80

Anr copy. Half cloth, in dj. Initialed by Warhol. pba Aug 22 (491) $85

Anr copy. Half cloth, in dj. Sgd on half-title & with soup-can sketch & initials on tp. sg June 6 (187) $550
— Portraits of the 70's. NY: Random House, [1979]. One of 200. Essay by Robert Rosenblum; Ed by David Whitney. 4to, cloth. sg June 13 (380) $425

## Warhol, Andy, d.1987 —& Colacello, Bob
— Andy Warhol's Exposures. NY, [1979]. 4to, orig cloth, in dj. Sgd on half-title & upper cover. S May 16 (150) £150

## Waring, John Burnley
— Art Treasures of the United Kingdom. L, 1858. Folio, orig calf gilt with royal arms; broken, worn. Small piece cut from top of title. K Feb 11 (30) $375
— Masterpieces of Industrial Art and Sculpture.... L, 1863. 3 vols. Folio, orig lea gilt; spines rubbed, rear joints restored, hinges renewed. Some tears; minor foxing affecting a few plates. sg June 13 (381) $1,300

## Waring, John Burnley —& Macquoid, T. R.
— Examples of Architectural Art in Italy and Spain.... L, 1850. Folio, loose in cloth portfolio; back repaired. With litho title & 63 plates. Some soiling, edge tears; stain through lower outside margin, touching some images. wad Oct 18 (11) C$400

**Waring, S.**
— The Minstrelsy of the Woods. L, 1832. 12mo, orig cloth; corners bumped, 1 plate loose. With 18 hand-colored plates. F June 20 (565) $180

**Warner, Charles Dudley, 1829-1900**
— My Winter on the Nile, Among the Mummies and Moslems. Hartford, 1876. 1st Ed. Orig cloth. pba Aug 8 (207) $70

**Warner, Sir George Frederic**
— The Library of James VI. Edin., 1893. One of 40. 8vo, orig cloth; worn & shaken. Inscr to J. A. Herbert. O Mar 26 (292) $70

**Warner, Juan J. —& Others**
— An Historical Sketch of Los Angeles County, California.... [Los Angeles]: Louis Lewin, 1876. 8vo, orig wraps; partial splitting of joint. Larson copy. pba Feb 12 (452) $800

**Warner, Sir Pelham Francis**
— Imperial Cricket. L, 1912. Ltd Ed. 4to, orig cloth; stained. pn Oct 12 (335) £85

**Warner, Richard, 1763-1857**
— Antiquitates Culinariae, or Curious Tracts Relating to the Culinary Affairs of the Old English. L, 1791. 1st Ed. 4to, later half calf; worn, upper hinge cracked. With title, & 2 aquatint plates (1 folding). Some spotting; upper margins stained. S Oct 12 (123) £450
— The History of Bath. L, 1801. 2 parts in 1 vol. 4to, 19th-cent mor gilt; joints & edges worn. Extra-illus with plates, an orig drawing & a watercolor view. CE May 22 (464) $700

**Warner, Sylvia Townsend.** See: Cresset Press

**Warren, Benjamin Harry**
— Report on the Birds of Pennsylvania. Harrisburg, 1890. 2d Ed. 8vo, later cloth. With 100 plates, 99 colored. wa Dec 14 (125) $85

**Warren, Edward**
— The Life of John Collins Warren, M.D. Bost., 1860. 2 vols. 8vo, orig cloth. sg May 16 (524) $110

**Warren, John Collins, 1778-1856**
— A Letter Addressed to a Republican Member of the House of Representatives of ... Massachusetts...New Incorporation, to be entitled "A College of Physicians." Bost., 1812. 12mo, wraps; soiled, edges worn. sg May 16 (525) $225
— Surgical Observations on Tumours, with Cases and Operations. Bost. & L, 1839. 1st English Ed. 8vo, orig cloth; spine ends worn. With 16 hand-colored plates, & blank C2. Yale Medical Library bookplate & stamp. Inscr "Gift of Dr. Harvey Cushing". S Mar 29 (719) £300

**Warren, Robert Penn**
See also: Limited Editions Club
— Audubon: A Vision. NY, 1969. 1st Ed, One of 300. In dj. bbc Dec 18 (368) $100

— Chief Joseph of the Nez Perce. NY, [1983]. One of 250. sg Dec 14 (299) $140
— Rumor Verified. Poems 1979-1980. NY, 1981. 1st Ed, One of 250. sg Dec 14 (298) $60
— Selected Poems: New and Old, 1923-1966. NY, [1966]. Ltd Ed. sg Dec 14 (297) $70

**Wars...** See: Combe, William

**Warton, Thomas, 1728-90**
— The History of English Poetry. L, 1774-1806. 1st Ed. 3 vols. 4to, contemp calf; rubbed. Without the unfinished Vol IV & index. bba May 30 (118) £220 [Besley]

**Waseurtz, G. M.** See: Grabhorn Printing

**Washington, Booker T., 1856-1915**
— The Negro in Business. [Bost.: Hertel Jenkins, 1907]. Probable pbr's dummy or advance copy, lacking imprint. 8vo, lea gilt; spine def. sg Mar 28 (374) $150
— The Story of Slavery. Dansville NY: F. A. Owen Publishing Company, [1913]. 8vo, pictorial wraps; stapled, spine soiled. sg Mar 28 (375) $175
— Up from Slavery: An Autobiography. Garden City, [1937]. In dj. Inscr by Washington's son. sg Mar 28 (376) $100

**Washington, George, 1732-99**
See also: Grabhorn Printing
— Official Letters to the Honourable American Congress.... L, 1795. 1st English Ed. 2 vols. 12mo, old calf; worn, becoming disbound. Fore-edge of Vol II stained. wa Feb 29 (566) $180
[-] The Washingtoniana: Containing a Sketch of the Life and Death.... Lancaster, 1802. Ed by F. Johnston & W. Hamilton. 8vo, contemp sheep; rubbed, joints splitting, frontis detached & def. pba Apr 25 (254) $110
— Writings.... NY, 1847-48. 12 vols. 8vo, half pigskin; some spine heads chipped, a few corners bumped. cb Oct 17 (309) $850

**Washington's copy, George**
JEFFRIES, JOHN. - A Narrative of the Two Aerial Voyages of Doctor Jeffries with Mons. Blanchard...from London into Kent...from England into France. L, 1786. 4to, contemp calf; rebacked, most of orig spine laid down; corners restored. Sgd by Washington on tp. Schiff - Forbes copy. CNY Dec 15 (254) $46,000

**Washington, M. Bunch**
— The Art of Romare Bearden. NY, [1972]. 4to, cloth; shaken. Library markings. sg Sept 7 (37) $130
Anr copy. Cloth, in dj. sg Mar 28 (21) $450; sg June 13 (53) $225

**Wasson, Robert Gordon**
— Soma: Divine Mushroom of Immortality. NY: Harcourt, Brace & World [ptd at Officina Bodoni, Verona], 1968. One of 680. 3 parts in 1 vol. Orig half mor. sg Oct 19 (187) $350

**Wasson, Valentina P. & Robert G.**
— Mushrooms, Russia and History. NY, 1957. One of 510. 2 vols. 4to, orig cloth. pba Nov 30 (325) $850; sg Oct 19 (185) $950

**Watelet, Claude Henri, 1718-76**
— L'Art de peindre: poeme. Paris, 1760. 4to, contemp mor gilt; rebacked, recornered, rubbed. With engraved title, 2 plates & with inserted port of Watelet. Fuerstenberg - Schaefer copy. S Dec 8 (655) £320
Anr copy. Contemp mor gilt. Hamilton - Fuerstenberg - Schaefer copy. S Dec 8 (656) £800
— Essai sur les jardins. Paris, 1774. 8vo, contemp calf. Marginal markings on pp. 16-17; hole in D4. Fuerstenberg - Schaefer copy. S Dec 8 (658) £440

**Waterhous, Edward**
— The Gentlemans Monitor; or a Sober Inspection.... L, 1665. 1st Ed. 8vo, old calf; rebacked preserving most of orig spine, rubbed & dried. Some soiling; lacking A1. O Mar 5 (236) $225

**Waters, Frank**
— The Man Who Killed the Deer. Flagstaff: Northland Press, [1965]. One of 1,250. Half cloth. pba Oct 5 (362) $100

**Wathen, James**
— Journal of a Voyage, in 1811 and 1812, to Madras and China.... L, 1814. 1st Ed. 4to, contemp mor gilt; scuffed, extremities rubbed. With 24 hand-colored plates. Some foxing. F June 20 (844) $1,300

**Watson, Alfred E. T.**
— Fur, Feather, and Fin. L, 1890-98. 12 vols. 8vo, orig cloth. S Apr 23 (317) £350

**Watson, Charles M.** See: Porter & Watson

**Watson, Douglas S.**
See also: Grabhorn Printing
— California in the Fifties. San Francisco, 1936. One of 50 on Alexandra japan. Oblong 4to, half mor, in worn & torn dj; extremities scuffed. With the portfolio & orig document. pba Apr 25 (723) $500
One of 850. Cloth. pba Nov 16 (273) $200
One of 100. Lithos by Kuchel & Dresel. 4to, half mor in dj; edges worn, d/j torn & repaired. With 50 plates, & portfolio of duplicate prints. Larson copy. pba Sept 28 (561) $900
— West Wind, the Life Story of Joseph Reddeford Walker.... Los Angeles, 1934. 1st Ed, One of 100. 4to, half mor; spine rubbed. With frontis port, 5 plates, & folding map. Robbins copy. pba Mar 21 (384) $325

**Watson, Frank John Bagolt**
— The Wrightson Collection. NY, 1966-73. 5 vols. 4to, orig cloth. wa Feb 1 (335) $700

**Watson, John, 1725-83**
— Memoirs of the Ancient Earls of Warren and Surrey. Warrington, 1782. 1st Ed. 2 vols. 4to, contemp calf gilt; rebacked, rubbed. Ck Feb 14 (320) £450

**Watson, John Fanning, 1779-1860**
— Annals of Philadelphia; Being a Collection of Memoirs.... [Phila.] & NY, 1830. 8vo, half lea; worn. Some spotting. O July 9 (223) $50

**Watson, William.** See: Jenyns & Watson

**Watson, Sir William, 1715-87**
[A collection of Watson's works on electricity, bound in 1 volume, sold in the Madsen sale at Sotheby's on 14 Mar 1996, lot 105, for £1,250]

**Watt, James Cromar**
— Examples of Greek and Pompeian Decorative Work. L, 1897. Folio, orig cloth; rubbed & marked. With 60 plates. bba Oct 19 (210) £55 [Graves-Johnston]

**Watts, Alaric A.**
— Lyrics of the Heart. L, 1851. 2 vols in 1. 8vo, lev gilt by Bickers. With 41 plates. ALs tipped in. pba Sept 14 (29) $200

**Watts, William, 1752-1851**
— The Seats of the Nobility and Gentry.... L, 1799. Oblong 4to, contemp half mor; cover detached. With engraved title & 84 plates. Some waterstaining. b Jan 31 (353) £520

**Watts, William Lord**
— Across the Vatna Jokull.... L, 1876. 8vo, cloth. With 2 maps & 2 plates. sg Mar 7 (302) $150

**Waugh, Evelyn, 1903-66**
— Basil Seal Rides Again. L, [1963]. 1st Ed, one of 750. Ck Apr 12 (176) £140; pba Aug 22 (492) $160
Anr copy. Hobson copy. S June 28 (267) £130
— Black Mischief. L, 1932. 1st Ed. In dj. "Fine copy in d/j". sg June 20 (389) $950
One of 250. In dj with 1 short tear. Hobson copy. S June 28 (244) £650
— Brideshead Revisited. L, 1945. 1st Ed. Mor gilt by Sangorski & Sutcliffe. Inscr to Daniel Bolton, July 1950. b Jan 31 (225) £520
One of 50 specially issued. Orig wraps. Inscr to Christopher Sykes. Hobson copy. S June 28 (259) £4,200
Anr Ed. L: Chapman & Hall [ptd in Melbourne], [1946]. In rubbed & repaired dj. Browned. sg Dec 14 (300) $100
— Decline and Fall. L, 1928. 1st Ed. In dj. With review slip. Hobson copy. S June 28 (239) £1,800
Anr copy. Orig cloth, in dj with slight tears; upper hinge fragile, covers & spine worn. S July 11 (351) £800
— Edmund Campion. L, [1935]. One of 50. Hobson copy. S June 28 (247) £500
— A Handful of Dust. L, 1934. In dj with Book Society wrap-around band inserted. Sgd, Nov 1934. Hobson copy. S June 28 (246) £2,000
— Helena. L, 1950. 1st Ed. Orig cloth; some soiling & discoloration. Inscr to Ronald Knox, 1 Oct 1950. S Dec 18 (360) £1,650 [Blackwell]
Anr copy. L.p. copy. Inscr to Christopher Sykes, 1 Oct 1950. Hobson copy. S June 28 (258) £650

## WAUGH

— The Holy Places. L, 1952. 1st Ed, One of 50. Illus by Reynolds Stone. Orig mor, in dj with minor soiling & tear on spine. Hobson copy. S June 28 (260) £320

One of 950. In soiled dj. bba May 9 (425) £75 [Virgo]

— Labels, a Mediterranean Journal. L, 1930. 1st Ed, One of 110, with a leaf of Ms bound in. Hobson copy. S June 28 (241) £900

— The Life of the Right Reverend Ronald Knox.... L, 1959. In dj with small tears; some scratches to bdg. Inscr to Christopher Sykes & with misprint on tp corrected by Waugh; annotated by Sykes. Hobson copy. S June 28 (265) £280

— A Little Learning. L, 1964. 1st Ed. In dj; small def to upper cover of bdg. Inscr to Christopher Sykes. Hobson copy. S June 28 (269) £420

— Love Among the Ruins. L, 1953. 1st Ed, one of 250. Illus by Stuart Boyle. pba Aug 22 (493) £170

Anr copy. Hobson copy. S June 28 (262) £240

— The Loved One. L, [1948]. 1st Ed, one of 250. Illus by Stuart Boyle. Inscr "Mr. E. F. Morice's copy". S June 28 (256) £400

Anr copy. Inscr to Hedingren's Bokhandel. wa Feb 29 (82) $425

— Mr Loveday's Little Outing.... L, 1936. In dj with corner defs & small slits on spine. Hobson copy. S June 28 (249) £500

— Ninety-Two Days: The Account of a Tropical Journey.... L, 1934. 1st Ed, 1st Issue. In repaired dj. S June 28 (245) £1,200

— The Ordeal of Gilbert Pinfold. L, 1957. L.p. issue. Inscr to Christopher Sykes. Hobson copy. S June 28 (264) £1,300

— P. R. B, An Essay on the Pre-Raphaelite Brotherhood.... L, 1926. 1st Ed, One of 50. Orig half cloth. Inscr to Elspeth Waugh by Arthur Waugh, father of Evelyn & brother of Elspeth, & by Evelyn Waugh. Hobson copy. S June 28 (231) £3,200

— Pansy Pakenham. The Old Expedient. L, 1928. In dj with small tears on lower cover. S June 28 (240) £240

— Put Out More Flags. L, 1942. In dj; bookplate removed from endleaf. Hobson copy. S June 28 (253) £340

— Remote People. L, 1931. 1st Ed. In dj with chipped spine. bba Oct 19 (396) £650 [Thornton]

Anr copy. In repaired dj. Inscr to Thomas Balston. Hobson copy. S June 28 (243) £1,000

— Robbery under Law. L, 1939. 1st Ed. In d/j. S June 28 (252) £400

— Rossetti: His Life and Works. L, 1928. 1st Ed. Inscr to Thomas Balston & with Ls from Arthur Waugh to Balston inserted. Hobson copy. S June 28 (237) £780

— Scoop. L, 1938. 1st Ed. In worn dj. Ck Nov 17 (173) £240

Anr copy. In def 2d dj with Daily Beast logo. Hobson copy. S June 28 (251) £200

— Tactical Exercise. Bost., 1954. In dj with minor wear. Inscr. Hobson copy. S June 28 (263) £380

— Tourist in Africa. Bost., 1960. Half mor. Inscr to Christopher Sykes & with the words "A Potboiler by" inserted in Waugh's hand on tp. Hobson copy. S June 28 (266) £380

— Vile Bodies. L, 1930. 1st Ed. In repaired dj. Hobson copy. S June 28 (242) £2,200

— Waugh in Abyssinia. L, 1936. 1st Ed. In 1st dj. Inscr. Hobson copy. S June 28 (250) £900

— Work Suspended. L, 1942. One of 500. In dj; corner of bdg bumped. Dedication copy, inscr to Alexander Woollcott, Christmas 1942. Hobson copy. S June 28 (254) £1,900

**Weale, John**
— Quarterly Papers on Architecture. L, 1844-45. 2 vols. 4to, half lea. Plate count not given. NH June 1 (36) £280

**Weatherby, Meredith.** See: Richie & Weatherby

**Weaver, Sir Lawrence.** See: Jekyll & Weaver

**Webb, Edith Buckland**
— Indian Life at the Old Missions. Los Angeles, [1952]. 1st Ed. Orig cloth in dj. Larson copy. pba Sept 28 (169) $90

**Webb, F. R.**
— Manual of the Canvas Canoe. NY, 1898. Orig cloth; soiled, spine head rubbed. Tp with short tears. pba July 11 (445) $140

**Webb, Francis**
— Poems. Salisbury, 1790. 4to, disbound. b Dec 5 (411) £90

**Webb, Laura S.**
— Custer's Immortality: A Poem.... NY: Evening Post, [n.d.]. Orig cloth; hinges repaired. With map. pba June 25 (241) $130

**Webb, Walter Prescott**
— The Texas Rangers.... Bost., 1935. In chipped dj. pba Nov 16 (274) $140

Anr copy. In tattered & def dj. pba Apr 25 (724) $50

**Webb, William Seward, 1851-1926**
— California and Alaska, and over the Canadian Pacific Railway. NY, 1890. One of 500. 4to, orig mor gilt; rubbed. O Jan 9 (251) $325

**Webber, Charles Wilkins**
— The Hunter-Naturalist.... Phila., 1852. 8vo, orig cloth; worn, chipped. With 10 chromolitho plates. Most plates dampstained. wa Feb 29 (231) $90

— Old Hicks the Guide; or, Adventures in the Camanche Country in Search of a Gold Mine. NY, 1848. 12mo, orig cloth; rebacked with orig spine cloth laid on. pba Aug 8 (209) $100

**Weber, Bruce**
— Bear Pond. NY, 1990. 4to, cloth, in dj; corners bumped. sg Feb 29 (334) $350

— Bruce Weber. NY, [1989]. Folio, cloth, in dj with minor wear. sg Feb 29 (335) $200

— O Rio de Janeiro, A Photographic Journal.... NY, [1986]. Folio, cloth, in dj. sg Feb 29 (336) $550

**Weber, Carl Jefferson**
— A Bibliography of Jacob Abbott. Waterville ME, 1948. 8vo, cloth, in frayed dj with edge stains. O Dec 5 (147) $160

**Weber, Msgr. Francis J.**
— Following Bernhardt Wall, 1872-1956: Bio-Bibliographical Sketch. Austin: Castle Press & Patrick Reagh for Book Club of Texas, 1994. One of 195. 4to, orig bds. ds July 27 (194) $300

**Weber, Johann Carl**
— Die Alpen-Pflanzen Deutschlands und der Schweitz. Munich, n.d.-1879. 4 vols. 12mo, vols I-II orig cloth, II-IV later half cloth. With 400 hand-colored plates. Some spotting. S Oct 27 (683) £500 [Galerie aux Tro]

**Weber, Max, 1881-1961**
— Primitives: Poems and Woodcuts. NY, 1926. One of 350. Intro by Benjamin de Casseres. Orig bds; spine ends chipped, front joint cracked. Inscr, 11 Mar 1934. sg Oct 19 (256) $650

**Webster, Daniel, 1782-1852**
— Works. Bost., 1851. 6 vols. 8vo, later half calf; rubbed. Sgd. F June 20 (409) $180

Anr copy. Cloth; edges & spine ends chipped & worn, spine of Vol VI torn. Sgd. wa Feb 29 (570) $110

Anr Ed. Bost., 1857-60. 6 vols. 8vo, 19th-cent calf gilt. sg Sept 21 (53) $600

**Webster, George G.**
— Around the Horn in '49.... Wethersfield CT: L. J. Hall, 1898. 2d Ed. 8vo, orig cloth; spine ends & corners rubbed. pba Aug 8 (210) $120

**Webster, Harold M.** See: Beebe & Webster

**Webster, Kimball**
— The Gold Seekers of '49. Manchester, 1917. 1st Ed. - Intro by George Waldo Browne. Orig cloth; spine & cover partly faded. With 2 ports & 3 plates. Larson copy. pba Sept 28 (737) $50

**Webster, Noah, 1758-1843**
— An American Dictionary of the English Language. L, 1832. 2 vols. 4to, contemp half calf; rubbed. b Jan 31 (126) £150
— A Compendious Dictionary of the English Language. Hartford & New Haven, 1806. 12mo, contemp sheep; backstrip reinforced with tape. sg Oct 26 (388) $150

**Wecker, Johann Jakob, 1528-86**
— De Secretis Libri XVII. Basel, 1642. 8vo, calf; rubbed, rebacked. Marginal tears & repairs; c5 torn with loss of letters. Sold w.a.f. bba July 18 (126) £55 [Robertshaw]

**Weegee**
— Naked City. NY, [1945]. 1st Ed. Cloth; damp-stained, fore-edge soiled. Half-title creased. sg Feb 29 (338) $175
— Weegee by Weegee: An Autobiography. NY, 1961. In torn & soiled dj. With 116 plates. Prelims foxed. sg Feb 29 (337) $110

**Weeks, Edward**
— The Moisie Salmon Club. Barre, 1971. 4to, cloth. Inscr. O June 25 (280) $120
One of 1,500. Cloth. O June 25 (281) $95; pba July 11 (326) $80

**Weelkes, Thomas, 1576-1623**
— Madrigals to 3.4.5.&6 voyces. L: Thomas East, 1597. Cantus primus part only (of 6). 4to, modern half calf. S May 15 (537) £500

**Wegner, Robert**
— Wegner's Bibliography on Deer and Deer Hunting. Deforest, 1992. One of 100. Syn gilt; minor wear. O Oct 10 (270) $160

**Weichenham, Erasmus**
— Christiche Betrachtungen. Germantown: Billmyer, 1791. 4to, orig calf; extremities rubbed, clasps def. Some spotting; minor dampstaining to end matter. F June 20 (109) $100

**Weidenmann, Jacob**
— Beautifying Country Homes: A Handbook.... NY: O. Judd, [1870]. Folio, orig cloth; worn & spotted, inner joints broken, shaken. With 24 color plates. Some foxing & soiling. O Mar 5 (237) $750

**Weigel, Christoph, 1654-1725**
— Abbildung der Gemein-Nuetzlichen Haupstaende von denen Regenten.... Regensburg, 1698. 4to, contemp vellum; soiled. With 211 (of 212) plates. Marginal repairs. S Mar 14 (367) £5,800
— Biblia ectypa. Bildnussen aus Heilige Schrift.... Augsburg, 1695. 2 parts in 1 vol. Folio, modern half lea. With 2 frontises, 2 (of 8) engraved titles & 210 plates. Some plates repaired with loss; some spotting & soiling. Sold w.a.f. S July 11 (7) £250
— Passio Domini nostri Jesu Christi. Augsburg, 1693. 4to, contemp vellum; soiled. With engraved title, frontis & 100 plates. b Sept 20 (42) £220

**Weigel, Rudolph.** See: Andresen & Weigel

**Weigel Library, T. O.**
— [Sale Catalogue] Katalogue fruehester Erzeugnisse der Druckerkunst.... Leipzig, 1872. 8vo, half calf; rubbed. ALs from William Brenchley Rye tipped in. O Mar 26 (293) $300

**Weik, Jesse W.** See: Herndon & Weik

**Weiler, Milton C.**
— The Classic Decoy Series. NY, 1969. Ltd Ed, sgd. Folio, wraps. With 24 colored plates. rce Nov 16 (44) $290

**Weinberger, Bernhard Wolf**
— An Introduction to the History of Dentistry. St. Louis, 1948. 1st Ed. 2 vols. In djs with soiling & edge wear. Some foxing. O Mar 5 (238) $250

**Weindel, Henri de**
— Histoire des Soviets. Paris, 1922. Parts I-VI (complete). Folio, orig wraps, in portfolio. bbc Dec 18 (422) $200

**Weirotte, Franz Edmund**
— Oeuvre...contenant pres de deux cent paysages & ruines, dessines d'apres nature.... Paris: chez Bassan & Poignant, [1775]. Folio, contemp half mor gilt. With port & 19 series of views on 92 leaves including 6 folding plates. Fuerstenberg - Schaefer copy. S Dec 8 (661) £4,400

**Weiss, Margaret R.**
— Ben Shahn, Photographer, an Album from the Thirties. NY, 1973. Oblong 4to, cloth, in soiled dj. sg Feb 29 (283) $60

**Weisse, Franz**
— The Art of Marbling. [North Hills PA]: Bird & Bull Press, 1980. One of 300. Half lev. sg Sept 14 (75) $250

**Weitenkampf, Frank**
— The Eno Collection of New York City Views. NY, 1925. Wraps. sg May 9 (26) $200

**Weizsaecker, Heinrich, 1862-1945**
— Adam Elsheimer der maler von Frankfurt. Berlin, 1936-52. Vols 1-2 in 3. 4to, orig cloth. S Oct 27 (987) £400 [Schmidt & Grunth]

**Weld, Charles Richard**
— A History of the Royal Society.... L, 1848. 2 vols. 8vo, later half calf; spines scuffed, joints worn. sg May 16 (275) $400

**Weld, Isaac, 1774-1856**
— Travels through the States of North America.... L, 1799. 1st Ed. 4to, later half calf; upper cover detached, worn & scuffed. With 16 plates, plans & maps. Some browning & foxing. bbc Dec 18 (566) $375

Anr copy. Contemp half calf; broken, spine worn. With 16 plates, including colored folding map & frontis. CE May 22 (31) $900

2d Ed. 2 vols. 8vo, modern half mor gilt by Bennett. With 16 maps & plates. Lacking ad leaves. sg Oct 26 (389) $225

**Weld, Theodore**
— American Slavery As It Is.... NY: American Anti-Slavery Society, 1839. 8vo, later half mor. Browned. sg Mar 28 (346) $600

**Wellcome Historical Medical Library**
— Catalogue of Printed Books.... L, 1962-76. 3 vols. 4to, cloth. bba Oct 5 (187) £310 [Malavasi]
Anr copy. 3 vols. bbc Feb 26 (187) $210

**Weller, Emil**
— Die falschen und fingierten Druckorte. Hildesheim, 1970. 3 vols. 8vo, orig cloth. sg Apr 11 (330) $100

**Welles, Gideon, 1802-78**
— Lincoln and Seward. NY, 1874. 12mo, orig cloth. sg Oct 26 (222) $80

**Wellington, Arthur Wellesley, 1st Duke, 1769-1852**
— The Dispatches of Field Marshal the Duke of Wellington.... L, 1837-39. 13 vols. 8vo, contemp calf gilt by Burn & Son; extremities worn. Some spotting. S Mar 28 (546) £600

**Wellman, Manly Wade**
— Worse Things Waiting. Chapel Hill: Carcosa, 1973. Illus by Lee Brown Coye. In dj. pba May 4 (278) $55

**Wells, Edward, 1667-1727**
See also: Dionysius Periegetes
— A New Sett of Maps both of Ancient and Present Geography. L: T. W. for J. Walthoe & Others, [c.1700]. Folio, later half cloth; worn. With 41 double-page maps, all on stubs. Lacking final 2 text leaves; some soiling & marginal tears. C Oct 25 (154) £4,400
Anr Ed. L: T. W. for R. Bonwicke, J. Walthoe, etc. [1722]. Folio, contemp half sheep; worn. With 41 folding maps. Browned; most maps with small tears at folds; some larger tears repaired; 2 maps town with loss to surface. C May 31 (74) £2,000

**Wells, H. G., 1866-1946**
See also: Limited Editions Club
— The Door in the Wall and Other Stories. NY & L, 1911. One of 600. Folio, half cloth; notations on front free endpaper. With frontis & 9 plates after A. L. Coburn. sg Feb 29 (99) $600
— The First Men in the Moon. Indianapolis, [1901]. Orig cloth; insect damage. pba Aug 22 (498) $130
1st Ed. L, 1901. Orig cloth, Currey's bdg C. sg Feb 8 (354) $225
— The Food of the Gods. L, 1904. Colonial Issue. Cloth; front cover discolored. sg Dec 14 (305) $140
— In the Days of the Comet. L, 1906. 1st Ed in Book form, Colonial Issue. Cloth; endpapers foxed. sg Dec 14 (306) $130
— The Invisible Man: A Grotesque Romance. L, 1897. 1st Ed in Book form. 8vo, orig cloth; rubbed. pn Dec 7 (55) £240
Anr copy. Orig cloth; soiled, front hinge cracked. Browned. sg Feb 8 (355) $425
— Little Wars. L: Frank Palmer, [1913]. 1st Ed. Orig cloth; piece lacking from spine head, spine lettering worn off. pba May 23 (452) $160
— Love and Mr. Lewisham. L & NY, 1900. 8vo, orig cloth; soiled. Inscr, July 1902. cb June 25 (1889) $300
— The Passionate Friends, a Novel. L, 1913. Inscr to Henry James. Gilvarry - Engelhard copy. CNY Oct 27 (89) $3,800
— Star-Begotten: A Biological Fantasia. NY, 1937. 1st American Ed. In dj. pba May 4 (279) $85

— The Time Machine. An Invention. L, 1895. 1st Ed. 8vo, orig cloth; rubbed & soiled. pn Dec 7 (56) £240

Anr copy. Orig cloth, Currey's A bdg. sg Feb 8 (356) $1,200

Anr copy. Orig cloth, Currey's B bdg. sg Feb 8 (357) $650

— The War in the Air. And Particularly How Mr. Bert Smallways Fared.... L, 1908. 1st Ed in Book form. Orig cloth; hinges cracked. With 16 plates. sg May 16 (95) $175

Colonial Issue. Some foxing. sg Dec 14 (307) $175

— The War of the Worlds. L, 1898. 1st Ed. 8vo, orig cloth with monogram on lower cover; rubbed & soiled, upper hinge pulled. Minor foxing. bba May 30 (300) £320 [Mead]

Anr copy. Orig cloth, later state of bdg; extremities rubbed, staining to spine & rear cover, front free endpaper lacking. pba May 23 (453) $130

Anr copy. Orig cloth; upper hinge broken. Browned. S July 11 (355) £3,200; sg Feb 8 (358) $650

— The Wife of Sir Isaac Harman. L, 1914. 1st Ed. Inscr to Sir Thomas of Sandhurst. cb June 25 (1890) $300

— Works. L, 1924-27. Atlantic Ed, One of 620. 28 vols. Half calf by Bayntun. b Sept 20 (576) £2,000; cb Oct 17 (334) $850; cb June 25 (1976) $800

**Wells, Harry Laurenz**

— History of Nevada County, California.... Oakland, 1880. Oblong folio, orig half lea; worn, possibly recased. Tp torn & repaired, reinserted on stub. pba Oct 9 (12) $800

Anr copy. Later cloth; new endpapers. Library markings. pba Apr 25 (552) $350

— History of Siskiyou County, California.... Oakland, 1881. 1st Ed. Orig half lea; spine ends & joints scuffed, hinge cracked. Robbins copy. pba Mar 21 (343) $900

**Wells, Henry P.**

— The American Salmon Fisherman. NY, 1886. 8vo, orig cloth; worn, tips showing. Wells's sgd copy. O June 25 (282) $120

Anr copy. Orig cloth; worn. O June 25 (283) $80

Anr copy. Orig cloth; spine head rubbed. pba July 11 (328) $120

— Fly-Rods and Fly-Tackle: Suggestions as to their Manufacture.... NY, 1885. 8vo, cloth. O Feb 6 (249) $70

Anr copy. Cloth; worn. O June 25 (284) $130

Anr copy. Orig cloth. pba July 11 (327) $300

Anr copy. Cloth. sg Mar 7 (572) $175

**Wells, Nathaniel Armstrong**

— The Picturesque Antiquities of Spain. L, 1846. 8vo, orig cloth; worn, frontis & front free endpaper loose. With 10 plates. bba July 18 (375) £75 [Shand]

**Wells, Richard**

— The Remains of Richard Wells.... Boston, 1827. 8vo, orig wraps; worn. b Dec 5 (236) £70

**Wells, William Charles, 1757-1817**

— Two Essays: One upon Single Vision with Two Eyes; the Other on Dew.... L, 1818. 8vo, modern half calf. S June 12 (293) £250

**Welsch, Hieronymous**

— Warhafftige Reiss-Beschreibung... von Deutschland.... Stuttgart, 1658. 4to, contemp bds. sg Mar 7 (375) $500

**Welty, Eudora**

— Acrobats in a Park. Northridge CA: Lord John Press, 1980. One of 300. Half cloth. sg Dec 14 (311) $80

— Delta Wedding. NY, [1946]. In dj with edge-wear. sg June 20 (393) $175

— The Eye of the Story. NY, 1977. 1st Ed, One of 300. sg Dec 14 (310) $90

— In Black and White. Northridge: Lord John Press, 1985. One of 100. 4to, half cloth. sg Dec 14 (312) $130

— The Ponder Heart. NY, [1954]. In dj with rubbing & creasing. Inscr. pba May 23 (454) $90

— Women!! Make Turban in Own Home! [N.p.]: Palaemon Press, [1979]. 1st Ed, one of 200. Bds. sg Dec 14 (309) $70

**Wendler, Pietro Giovanni**

— Istruzione per la coltivazione del tabacco nello Stato Pontifico. Rome, 1780. 8vo, contemp wraps. With title vignette. S Oct 27 (819) £200 [Antiquarian]

**Wengenroth, Stow**

— The Lithographs of Stow Wengenroth. Bost. & Huntington NY, [1974-82]. One of 100. Ed by Ronald & Joan Stuckey. Without Supplement. 4to, half calf. pba June 20 (358) $375

— Stow Wengenroth's New England. Barre, 1969. One of 350 with orig litho. Oblong 4to, half cloth. pba June 20 (357) $325

**Wenger-Ruutz, Lisa**

— Von Sonne, Mond und Sternen in Bildern und Versen. Stuttgart: Gustav Weise, [n.d.]. Oblong 4to, pictorial bds; spine tips frayed, shaken. O Sept 12 (197) $300

**Wenley, A. G.** See: Freer Gallery of Art

**Wentz, Roby**

— The Grabhorn Press: A Biography. San Francisco: Book Club of California, 1981. One of 750. Half cloth, in dj. Book Club of California No 168. pba Aug 8 (455) $120

**Wertheim, Maurice, 1886-1950**

— Salmon on the Dry-Fly. NY, 1948. One of 500. Half cloth. O June 25 (285) $100

## WESCOTT

**Wescott, Glenway**
— A Calendar of Saints for Unbelievers. Paris: Harrison, 1932. One of 695. Illus by Pavel Tchelitchev. 8vo, cloth, in dj. sg Sept 14 (229) $150

**Wesley, Charles H.**
— The History of Alpha Phi Alpha. A Development in Negro College Life. Wash., 1950. 6th ptg. Orig cloth; discolored. sg Mar 28 (377) $80

**Wesley, John, 1703-91**
— Primitive Physick. L, 1747. 1st Ed. 12mo in 6s, contemp calf; rubbed, spine head frayed. B6 repaired & torn; corners creased. Ck Mar 22 (311) £1,300

**Wesson, Douglas B.**
— I'll Never Be Cured & I Don't Much Care. NY: J. H. Sears, [1928]. 1st Ed. - Illus by Wyncie Green. Cloth; spine & cover spotted, spine head rubbed. With frontis. pba Apr 18 (181) $55

**West, James E. —&**
**Lamb, Peter O.**
— He Who Sees in the Dark: The Boys' Story of Frederick Burhham, the American Scout. NY, 1932. Sgd by West on pbr's tipped-in leaf. pba Aug 22 (703) $160

**West, Jane**
— The Infidel Father. L, 1802. 1st Ed. 3 vols. 12mo, contemp half calf. Scorch mark to prelims of Vol II; 2 leaves with marginal defs. Ck Sept 8 (214) £550

**West, Nathanael**
— A Cool Million. NY, [1934]. 1st Ed. Orig cloth; sides foxed. Inscr to Robert M. Coates. Engelhard copy. CNY Oct 27 (144) $2,800
— The Dream Life of Balso Snell. Paris & NY: Contact Editions, [1931]. 1st Ed, one of 500. Orig wraps; spine ends chipped, stains to front cover. Inscr to Robert M. Coates. Engelhard copy. CNY Oct 27 (143) $1,200
— Miss Lonelyhearts. NY, [1933]. 1st Ed. sg June 20 (395) $800

**West, Paul Clarendon —&**
**Denslow, William Wallace**
— The Pearl and The Pumpkin. NY, [1904]. 1st Ed. Spine rubbed. pba Jan 18 (151) $140

**Westall, Richard**
— Victories of the Duke of Wellington. L, 1819. Folio, half mor; hinges weak, spine head repaired. With 12 hand-colored plates. wd May 8 (85) $600

**Westcott, Thompson, 1820-88**
— Centennial Portfolio: A Souvenir of the International Exhibition at Philadelphia. Phila., 1876. Oblong folio, orig cloth; extremities rubbed, loose. With map & 52 colored plates. bba July 18 (361) £100 [Sims Reed]
Anr copy. Orig cloth; worn & soiled, lacking front free endpaper. With 52 tinted lithos. Tp stained & repaired. wa Feb 29 (85) $270

## AMERICAN BOOK PRICES CURRENT

**Western...**
— Western Photography, May 1946. Los Angeles, 1946. Ed by Cyril Mipaas & Harold Dreyfus. Orig maquette with 21 leaves of paste-up, photo-pictorial wraps; chipped, some leaves detached. Comprising 5 photographs by Man Ray, 8 photographs by George Barrows & Fred Ragsdale & orig layout & typography, including an open letter, sgd by Man Ray. Chipped throughout. sg Feb 29 (195) $8,000

**Westminster...**
— The Westminster Review. NY, 1840. American Ed. Vol VIII, No 2. 8vo, ptd front wrap only. Some corners creased. sg Feb 29 (340) $175

**Westminster, Archibald Constable.** See: Stoker, Bram

**Weston, Brett.** See: Grabhorn Printing

**Weston, Charis W.** See: Weston & Weston

**Weston, Edward**
— My Camera on Point Lobos. Yosemite National Park & Bost., 1950. Folio, spiral bdg, in worn dj. sg Feb 29 (344) $140

**Weston, Edward —&**
**Weston, Charis W.**
— Edward Weston: Nudes. [NY]: Aperture, 1977. In dj. pba Aug 22 (660) $95

**Westphal, Karl Georg Heinrich**
— Diaetetik fuer solche Personen.... Quedlinburg & Leipzig, 1824. 8vo, contemp bds; spine partly torn, rubbed & scuffed. Some spotting. Ck Mar 22 (312) £130

**Westropp, Michael Seymour Dudley**
— Irish Glass. L, [1920]. 4to, orig cloth. sg June 13 (169) $200

**Westwood, John Obadiah, 1805-93.** See: Humphreys & Westwood

**Westwood, Thomas**
— In Memoriam Izaak Walton. L: Wm. Satchell, [c.1880]. 4to, half calf; rebacked, orig spine strip laid on. Newberry Library stamps. pba July 11 (332) $110

**Westwood, Thomas —&**
**Satchell, Thomas**
— Bibliotheca Piscatoria: a Catalogue of Books on Angling.... L, 1883. 8vo, cloth; spine ends chipped, front hinge cracking, library bookplate. pba July 11 (330) $400
Anr Ed. L: Dawsons, 1966. Reprint of 1883 Ed. sg Mar 7 (573) $80
— A New Bibliotheca Piscatoria; or General Catalogue of Angling and Fishing Literature.... L, 1861. 8vo, orig cloth; front cover spotted. pba July 11 (331) $120

## Wethered, Joyce
— Golfing Memories and Methods. L: Hutchinson, [1933]. 3d Ed. Cloth. pba Apr 18 (182) $100

## Wethered, Joyce & Reginald
— Golf from Two Sides. L, 1925. 3d Ed. Cloth; shelf worn. pba Apr 18 (183) $65

## Wethered, Joyce & Reginald —& Others
— The Game of Golf.... L: Seeley Service, 1931. 1st Trade Ed. Cloth; front hinge starting. With 100 photos. Lonsdale copy. pba Apr 18 (113) $150
2d Ed. L: Seeley Service, [c.1931]. Cloth in dj; d/j chipped. With 100 photos. Lonsdale copy. pba Apr 18 (114) $100
1st American Ed. Phila.: J. B. Lippincott, 1931. Cloth; spine ends rubbed. With 100 photos. Lonsdale copy. pba Apr 18 (115) $110

## Wetzel, Charles M.
— American Fishing Books: A Bibliography.... Newark DE, 1950. One of 200. 4to, half lea; extremities worn. Met Feb 24 (156) $600
Anr copy. Half lea; some wear. O June 25 (286) $1,000
Anr Ed. Newark, Del., 1950. One of—200. 4to, half lea; rubbed. O Feb 6 (252) $1,300
— Practical Fly Fishing. Bost.: Christopher, [1943]. In tattered dj. O June 25 (288) $120
Anr copy. Orig cloth; spine head rubbed. pba July 11 (333) $180
— Trout Flies: Naturals and Imitations. Harrisburg, [1955]. 4to, cloth, in dj with piece lacking from lower rear cover. pba July 11 (334) $90

## Whaling...
— The Whaling Directory of the United States in 1869.... New Bedford, 1869. 8vo, orig cloth. With 14 pp of hand-colored litho representations of signal flags. sg Mar 7 (376A) $900

## Wharton, Charles H.
— A Poetical Epistle to His Excellency George Washington.... L, 1780. 12mo, half mor by Sangorski & Sutcliffe. With port. cb Feb 14 (2607) $300

## Wharton, Edith, 1862-1937
See also: Limited Editions Club
— The Age of Innocence. NY, 1920. Orig bdg; rehinged. pba May 23 (455) $55
Anr copy. Orig cloth; offset from laid-in newspaper clipping to front endpapers. pba Aug 22 (500) $170
— A Backward Glance. NY, 1934. 1st Ed. pba May 23 (456) $75
— The Children. NY, 1928. pba May 23 (457) $65
— Ethan Frome. NY, 1911. 1st Ed, 1st Issue. Orig cloth; worn. F June 20 (473) $80
Issue not indicated. sg Feb 8 (360) $225
— French Ways and their Meaning. NY, 1919. pba May 23 (458) $85
— The Glimpses of the Moon. NY, 1922. 1st Ed. Orig cloth; spine creased. pba Aug 22 (504) $60

— The Greater Inclination. NY, 1899. 8vo, gilt-pictorial bds; spine chipped, tips rubbed. sg Feb 8 (361) $120
— Italian Backgrounds. NY, 1905. Illus by Ernest Peixotto. pba May 23 (459) $180
— Italian Villas and their Gardens. NY, 1904. 1st Ed. - Illus by Maxfield Parrish. 4to, orig cloth; some wear & fraying. Minor staining. bbc Feb 26 (331) $250; pba June 20 (361) $650
— Quartet: Four Stories. Kentfield, CA: Allen Press, 1975. One of 140. 4to, cloth. pba June 20 (29) $190; sg Sept 14 (19) $375
— A Son at the Front. NY, 1923. 1st Ed. pba May 23 (462) $85

## Wheat, Carl I.
See also: Grabhorn Printing; Morgan & Wheat
— Mapping the Transmississippi West. Mansfield CT: Martino, [n.d.]. One of 350. 5 vols in 6. 4to, cloth. bba July 18 (24) £130 [Hay Cinema]
Anr copy. Cloth; some wear. O May 7 (297) $275
— Mapping the Transmississippi West. 1540-1857: A Preliminary Survey. Worcester MA: American Antiquarian Society, 1954. One of 350. Later cloth. pba Feb 13 (196) $130
— The Maps of the California Gold Region. Storrs: Martino, [1995]. pba Aug 22 (974) $170

## Wheat, Ellen Harkins
— Jacob Lawrence. American Painter. Seattle, [1986]. 4to, cloth, in dj. Inscr. sg Mar 28 (187) $100

## Wheatley, Henry Benjamin, 1838-1917
— Les Reliures remarquables du Musee Britannique.... Paris, 1889. One of 200. 4to, later half mor, front wrap bound in. bba May 9 (149) £120 [Laywood]

## Wheatley, Phillis, 1753?-84
— Memoir and Poems of.... Bost., 1835. 2d Ed. 8vo, half cloth; spine def. Library markings; some foxing. Met May 22 (372) $400
— Poems on Various Subjects.... L, 1773. 8vo, contemp sheep; rebacked, corners recapped or worn. Engelhard copy. CNY Oct 27 (145) $5,000
Anr copy. Later mor by Riviere. sg Mar 28 (378) $5,400

## Wheeler, Daniel
— Extracts from the Letters and Journal.... L, 1839. 8vo, orig cloth; spine ends & corners worn. pba Apr 25 (255) $110

## Wheeler, Ella
— Poems of Passion. Chicago, 1883. 8vo, mor extra by Bumpus. b May 30 (590) £130

## Wheeler, George M. See: United States of America

## Wheeler, Gervase
— Rural Homes; or, Sketches of Houses Suited to American Country Life. NY, 1851. 8vo, half calf; chipped, front hinge weak. With frontis & 8 plates. Some foxing. Inscr to his mother. wa Nov 16 (260) $150

**Wheeler, Olin D.**
— The Trail of Lewis and Clark, 1804-1904. NY, 1904. 1st Ed. 2 vols. Orig cloth; front hinges cracked. pba Aug 22 (975) $225

**Wheelman...**
— The Wheelman: An Illustrated Magazine of Cycling Literature and News. Bost., 1883. Vols I-II (all pbd). 8vo, half mor; edges worn. Tape repair to 1 leaf. wa Feb 29 (140) $160

**Wheelock, Eleazar, 1711-79**
[A collection of materials relating to the Indian Charity-School & Dartmouth, bound in 1 vol, sold at Met on 22 May 1996, lot 336, for $8,500]

**Wheelock, John Hall.** See: Brooks & Wheelock

**Whigham, H. J.**
— How to Play Golf. Chicago: Herbert S. Stone, 1897. 1st Ed. Cloth. Prelim flyleaf clipped; half-title torn. pba Nov 9 (86) $225

Anr copy. Photos by E. Burton Holmes. Cloth; spine head chipped, upper cover bumped. pba Apr 18 (184) $225

**Whipple, Amiel W.**
— Report of Lieutenant Whipple's Expedition from San Diego to the Colorado. [Wash.], 1851. Senate Issue. 8vo, modern cloth. pba July 25 (365) $160
— Report upon the Indian Tribes. Wash., 1855. 4to, later cloth. Spotted. sg Oct 26 (390) $80

**Whistler, James Abbott McNeill, 1834-1903**
— The Gentle Art of Making Enemies. L, 1890. 4to, orig half cloth; front joint repaired. Inscr with butterfly signature on front free endpaper. sg Sept 7 (348) $200

One of 250. Mor extra Peacock bdg by Sangorski & Sutcliffe, orig cloth backstrip & paper from front cover bound in. sg Oct 19 (258) $5,200

Anr Ed. NY, 1890. Ed by Sheridan Ford. 12mo, jeweled peacock bdg by Sangorski & Sutcliffe, with port miniature of Whistler contained in upper doublure. Sold as a bdg. P June 5 (348) $11,000

Anr copy. Orig half cloth; spine rubbed & bumped, extremities rubbed. With 19 orig drawings by various artists. S Nov 2 (147) $800 [Hirsch]

Anr copy. Orig stiff wraps; joints cracked. sg Sept 21 (323) $325

— Mr. Whistler's "Ten o'Clock". L: T. Way, 1885. Trial Issue. 8vo, loose in contemp wraps. Spotting at beginning & end. sg Oct 19 (257) $850

Anr Ed. L, 1888. Bound with: Notes - Harmonies - Nocturnes. L, 1884. 8vo, cloth, orig wraps bound in. Walter Hamilton's copy, with related material. pba June 20 (362) $325

**Whistler, Laurence**
— The Imagination of Vanbrugh and his Fellow Artists. L, 1954. In chipped dj. bba Oct 19 (166) £260 [Pagan]

**Whistler, Rex, 1905-44**
— The Koenigsmark Drawings. L, 1952. One of 1,000. Intro by Laurence Whistler. 4to, orig cloth; rubbed. bba May 9 (284) £55 [Bankes Books]

**Whitaker, Charles H.**
— Bertram Grosvenor Goodhue: Architect and Master of Many Arts. NY, 1925. Folio, cloth; backstrip spotted, some leaves loose. sg Jan 11 (19) $80

**Whitaker, Frederick**
— A Complete Life of Gen. George A. Custer. NY: Sheldon, [1876]. Orig cloth; frayed, rear hinge repaired. pba June 25 (244) $150

**Whitaker, Thomas Dunham**
— The History and Antiquities of the Deanery of Craven. L, 1812. 2d Ed. 4to, modern cloth. Lacking 2 plates but with 18 plates inserted. Sold w.a.f. bba Nov 1 (274A) £340 [Woodcock]
— An History of Richmondshire.... L, 1823. 2 vols. Folio, contemp half mor; rubbed, upper bd of Vol I detached. 6E of Vol II torn & tape-repaired. bba Nov 1 (275) £300 [Turton]

Anr copy. Contemp calf; rebacked. With 45 plates & maps. Some spotting. S Mar 28 (71) £360

**White...**
— The White House Gallery of Official Portraits of the Presidents. NY, 1901. Folio, remains of orig mor gilt bdg. Some leaves worn. wa Feb 29 (387) $100

Anr Ed. NY, 1907. Folio, sheep gilt; spine lacking covers worn & detached. With 24 plates. A few leaves at front partly torn. bbc Feb 26 (404) $230

Anr copy. Orig mor gilt; worn, joints starting. wa Feb 29 (250) $150

**White, Alain Campbell —& Others**
— The Stapelieae. Pasadena, 1933. 4to, orig cloth, in dj. With tipped-in color frontis. sg May 16 (355) $60

Anr Ed. Pasadena, 1937. 3 vols. 4to, orig cloth. sg May 16 (356) $110

— The Succulent Euphorbieae. Pasadena, 1941. 2 vols. 4to, orig cloth. sg May 16 (354) $275

**White, Rev. C. C.**
— No Quittin' Sense. Austin, 1969. In dj. sg Mar 28 (379) $90

**White, Charles, 1728-1813**
— A Treatise on the Management of Pregnant and Lying-in Women. Worcester, MA, 1793. 1st American Ed. 8vo, contemp sheep; extremities rubbed. With 2 plates. Some browning. F June 20 (101) $425

**White, Christopher —&**
**Boon, Karel G.**
— Rembrandt's Etchings: An Illustrated Critical Catalogue. Amst., [1969]. 2 vols. 4to, cloth, in djs. bba Oct 5 (300) £300 [Rozza]

## White, Elwyn Brooks
— Charlotte's Web. NY, [1952]. 1st Ed. In dj. cb Feb 14 (2736) $800
— Stuart Little. NY, 1945]. Illus by Garth Williams. In dj. cb Feb 14 (2737) $550
Anr copy. In repaired dj. pba May 23 (465) $140
Anr copy. In dj with small chips. sg June 20 (401) $80

## White, George, 1802-87
— Statistics of the State of Georgia.... Savannah, 1849. 1st Ed. 8vo, orig cloth. With folding colored map. Tear to map; some foxing. NH Sept 16 (201) $270

## White, Gilbert, 1720-93
See also: Limited Editions Club; Nonesuch Press
— The Natural History and Antiquities of Selborne. L, 1789. 1st Ed. 4to, contemp mor gilt; rebacked. With 2 engraved titles & 7 plates. Inscr on slip bound before title, to the Rev T. Arnold. sg Oct 19 (177) $1,500
Anr Ed. L, 1813. 2 parts in 1 vol. 4to, later half mor; scuffed, joints cracking. With 10 mostly full-page hand-colored plates. bbc June 24 (200) $275
Anr Ed. L, 1833. 8vo, mor gilt by Kelly, with vari-colored mor doublures showing views of Selborn Street & Rogate. sg Sept 21 (324) $450
Anr Ed. L, 1851. 8vo, contemp mor gilt. CE May 22 (466) $150

## White, Henry Kirke, 1785-1806. See: Fore-Edge Paintings

## White, Jack
— Easier Golf. L: Methuen, [1924]. 1st Ed. Cloth. With 51 illus. Some soiling. pba Nov 9 (87) $55

## White, John, fl.1788-96
— Journal of a Voyage to New South Wales. L, 1790. 1st Ed. 4to, later calf. Some foxing. Met Sept 28 (367) $2,300

## White, John Blake, 1781-1859
— Foscari, or the Venetian Exile.... Charleston, 1806. 12mo, later half mor. K June 23 (466) $225

## White, Minor
— Mirrors Messages Manifestations. NY, 1969. 4to, cloth, in rubbed & chipped dj. sg Feb 29 (349) $110

## White, Terence Hanbury, 1906-64
— The Ill-Made Knight. NY, 1940. In chipped & rubbed dj. pba May 23 (468) $200
— The Witch in the Wood. NY, 1939. In chipped dj. pba May 23 (467) $120

## White, Walter
— A Rising Wind. NY, 1945. In dj. sg Mar 28 (380) $50

## White, William F.
— A Picture of Pioneer Times. San Francisco, 1881. 1st Ed. 8vo, orig cloth; spine faded. 1 page torn & repaired. Larson copy. pba Sept 28 (499) $75

## Whitehead, Alfred North —& Russell, Bertrand, 3rd Earl, 1872-1970
— Principia mathematica. Cambr., 1910-13. Vol I only. Orig cloth; rippling of cloth, shaken. pba June 20 (363) $1,100

## Whitehead, Charles Edward, 1829-1903
— The Camp-Fires of the Everglades. Edin., 1897. 8vo, orig cloth; shaken, frayed, lower spine edge torn, back cover & spine detached. O June 4 (284) $70

## Whitehead, Henry S.
— Jumbee and Other Uncanny Tales. Sauk City, 1944. In dj with small piece lacking. pba Aug 22 (505) $85

## Whitehead, John, 1860-99
— Exploration of Mount Kina Balu. L, 1893. Folio, recent cloth; stained. With 1 uncolored & 11 hand-colored natural history plates & 20 tinted litho plates of views. Some spotting. S Mar 28 (412) £600

## Whitehouse, Francis C.
— Sport Fishing in Canada. Vancouver, 1948. One of 1,200. With remnant of dj. O June 25 (289) $100

## Whitehouse, W. F.
— Agricola's Letters and Essays on Sugar Farming in Jamaica. L [Jamaica ptd], 1845. 8vo, half calf. b Sept 20 (451) £250

## Whitely, Henry, 1817-98
— British Birds. Woolwich, 1847-48. Parts 2 & 3 only (of 3). 12mo, orig cloth; backstrips split. With 16 hand-colored plates. With a duplicate of Part 2. Wilson - Fattorini copy. C Oct 25 (51) £500

## Whiting, William
— Military Arrests in Time of War. Wash., 1863. 8vo, orig wraps. Inscr to Brig. Gen. Graham. sg Oct 26 (58) $90

## Whitman, Malcolm D.
— Fly Fishing Up to Date.... N.p.: Pvtly ptd, 1924. Half cloth; worn. Some foxing. Inscr. O Feb 6 (253) $80

## Whitman, Walt, 1819-92
See also: Grabhorn Printing; Limited Editions Club
— Drum Taps. NY, 1865. 1st Ed, 2d Issue, with the "Sequel". 12mo, orig cloth; some wear to extremities. CE May 22 (467) $850
— Grashalme. Berlin, [1920]. One of 200. Illus by Willi Jaeckel. 4to, half lea; worn, spine def. With 13 plates. sg Feb 15 (167) $120
— Leaves of Grass. Brooklyn, 1855. 1st Ed, 1st State. 4to, orig cloth; spine ends rubbed, corners bumped, traces of removals from pastedown. Frontis foxed. P Dec 12 (174) $27,000
Anr copy. Orig cloth; spine ends frayed. Tipped to endpaper is broadside letter from Ralph Waldo Emerson to Walt Whitman, 21 July 1855. With ANs, 1856 about revising the work & ALs to W. S. Kennedy, 28 Jan 1889. Bucke copy. rs Nov 11 (127) $43,000

2d State. Orig cloth; bumped, spine def & chipped, some foxing on pastedown. Some spotting; review quire loose. P June 5 (120) $16,000
State not indicated. Late 19th-cent half mor; scuffed. Frontis foxed; some browning. P Dec 12 (175) $9,500
Anr Ed. Phila.: David McKay, 1883. 8vo, orig cloth; worn, spine chipped, front hinge cracked. Library stamp on tp. Check, sgd, 2 Aug 1889, tipped to front free endpaper. cb Oct 17 (498) $900
Anr Ed. Phila., 1888. 8vo, cloth; some discoloration, front hinge started. sg Feb 8 (362) $400
Anr Ed. Mount Vernon, N.Y.: Peter Pauper Press, [1943]. One of 1,100. Folio, half mor. sg Feb 15 (228) $200
— November Boughs. Phila., 1888. 1st Ed. 8vo, limp maroon cloth. L.p. copy. Inscr to Richard J. Hinton, 6 Jan 1889. rs Nov 11 (128) $2,700
Anr copy. Orig cloth, D bdg; rubbed, spine frayed, front hinge broken. Z June 28 (286) $100
— Out of the Cradle Endlessly Rocking. Santa Cruz & San Francisco: Labyrinth Editions, 1976-78. One of 65. 10 loose leaves, each in its own japanese tissue envelope, the whole in linen bds. bba May 9 (470) £60 [Hanborough]
— Specimen Days. Bost., 1971. 4to, cloth, in worn dj. sg Feb 29 (350) $70
— Specimen Days & Collect. Phila.: David McKay, 1882-83. 1st Ed. 12mo, cloth; rubbed & soiled, spine head chipped. Ink stamp on tp. Inscr to Dr. William A. Hawley, 17 June 1884. cb Oct 17 (499) $1,100
— Two Rivulets. Camden, 1876. Author's Ed. 8vo, orig half calf gilt; some rubbing & soiling. With photo frontis. Inscr on frontis & on front free endpaper to Alfred Webb. CE Feb 21 (268) $5,000
— Works. NY, [1902]. Camden Ed, One of 500. 10 vols. Half vellum, in orig linen djs; soiling to d/js, some bdg corners bumped. cb Oct 17 (335) $700

**Whitney, Harry**
— Hunting with the Eskimos. NY, 1910. One of 150. Half mor. sg Mar 7 (574) $350

**Whitney, Henry C.**
— The Life and Art of Dwight William Tryon. Bost., 1930. 8vo, half cloth; hinges starting. sg Jan 11 (435) $140
— Life on the Circuit with Lincoln. Bost: Estes & Lauriat, [1892]. 8vo, cloth. sg Oct 26 (223) $450

**Whitney, Joel P.**
— Silver Mining Regions of Colorado. NY, 1865. 16mo, modern half cloth, orig front wrap bound in. Adhesion spots to blank portion of preface page. pba Apr 25 (732) $1,100

**Whitney, Josiah D., 1819-96**
— Contributions to American Geology, Volume I: The Auriferous Gravels of the Sierra Nevada of California. Cambr. MA, 1880. 4to, cloth; flap detached from rear map pocket. With 3 heliotype plates after Carleton Watkins, 1 double-page plates & 20 maps & plans. Larson copy. pba Feb 12 (194) $200
— Geological Survey of California, J. D. Whitney, State Geologist. Geology. Volume I. Report of Progress and Synopsis of the Field-Work from 1860 to 1864. Sacramento: Legislature of California, 1865. 4to, cloth; hinges cracked. Larson copy. pba Feb 12 (193) $1,600
— The Yosemite Book.... NY, 1868. One of 250. 4to, orig half mor; scuffed, endpapers foxed, front hinge cracked. With 28 mtd photos (24 of them by Carleton Watkins, 4 by W. Harris) & 2 folded maps. Spot of glue residue to 1 image. Larson copy. pba Feb 12 (195) $8,500
1st Ed. [Sacramento], 1868. Illus by Carleton Watkins. 4to, orig half mor; rebacked, spine scuffed. With 28 albumen photos & 2 folding maps. Marginal stains to early leaves; photos faded. Robbins copy. pba Mar 21 (385) $4,250
— The Yosemite Guide-Book. NY, 1869. 8vo, orig cloth; extremities rubbed. Lacking the map of the Yosemite Valley; map of area adjacent with tears at folds. pba July 25 (367) $130
Anr Ed. Sacramento: California State Legislature, 1869. 8vo, cloth; spine worn at top. With 8 plates & 2 folding maps. pba Feb 12 (196) $1,100
Anr Ed. Sacramento: California State Legislature, 1871. 12mo, cloth; spine worn at top. With 2 folding map. pba Feb 12 (197) $200
Anr Ed. Sacramento: California Legislature, 1874. 16mo, orig cloth; ink stain on rear cover. With 2 folding maps & 1 single map; lacking that of Yosemite Valley. pba Feb 12 (198) $180

**Whitted, J. A.**
— A History of the Negro Baptists of North Carolina. Raleigh, 1908. Orig cloth; spotted & stained. Foxed; marginal dampstaining. sg Mar 28 (381) $225

**Whittier, John Greenleaf, 1807-92**
See also: Limited Editions Club
— Anti-Slavery Reporter, a Periodical Containing Justice and Expediency.... NY, Sept 1833. Vol I, No 4. 4to, sewn. Dampstained. sg Mar 28 (350) $200
— Works. Cambr., 1888-94. L.p. Ed, One of 400. 9 vols. 8vo, mor gilt. ALs bound in. cb Oct 17 (310) $500
Riverside Ed. Bost. & NY: Houghton, Mifflin, 1892. 7 vols. 8vo, contemp half calf gilt. ANs, 1883, laid in. sg Sept 21 (54) $425

**Whittington Press**
— A Miscellany of Type. Andoversford, 1990. One of 530. Folio, half cloth. sg Feb 15 (312) $200

**Whittle, James.** See: Laurie & Whittle

**Whitwell, Catherine Vale**
— An Astronomical Catechism; or, Dialogues between a Mother and her Daughter. L, 1823. 8vo, contemp half calf; rubbed, upper cover detached. With hand-colored frontis & 24 plates, 3 of them hand-

colored, 7 folding. Browned. bba May 30 (344) £170 [Devitt]

**Whymper, Edward, 1840-1911**
— Chamonix and the Range of Mont Blanc. L, 1899. Bound with: The Valley of Zermatt and the Matterhorn. L, 1899. 8vo, orig cloth; stained. Both inscr to Louis Sers. bba Nov 1 (549) £400 [Mandl]

**Whyte-Melville, George John, 1821-78**
— Works. L, 1898-1902. Ed by Sir Herbert Maxwell. 24 vols. 8vo, calf gilt by Riviere. sg Sept 21 (55) $1,300

**Wiater, Stanley**
— Dark Dreamers: Conversations with the Masters of Horror. Novato: Underwood-Miller, 1990. One of 297. Half mor. O Dec 5 (264) $50

**Wickert, Charles.** See: Petitjean & Wickert

**Widekind, Melchior Ludwig**
— Ausfuehrliches Verzeichnis von Raren Buechern.... Berlin, 1753-55. 4 parts in 1 vol. 8vo, old cloth; some wear. Foxed; early owner's stamp on tp. Kraus copy. O Mar 26 (294) $450

**Widener Library, Harry Elkins**
— A Catalogue of the Books and Manuscripts of Robert Louis Stevenson in the Library.... Phila.: Pvtly ptd, 1913. One of 150. With a Memoir by A. S. W. Rosenbach. 4to, mor by Zucker; rubbed. O Mar 26 (295) $160

**Widener Collection, Peter Arrell Brown**
— Pictures in the Collection at Lynnewood Hall, Elkins Park. Phila., 1913-15-16. One of 200. 3 vols. Folio, mor gilt by Riviere; some scratches, several endleaves & doublures def. sg June 13 (385) $425

**Wiegel, Christoph, 1624-1725**
— Biblia Ectypa. Augsburg, 1695. Folio, old calf; worn, repaired. With 211 plates & 1 mezzotint. Some soiling & some repairs. Sold w.a.f. S Oct 27 (1047) £420 [Beccarini]

**Wierzbicki, Felix Paul, 1815-60**
See also: Grabhorn Printing
— California as it is.... San Francisco, 1849. 1st Ed. Orig wraps; restored. Some foxing. Robbins copy. pba Mar 21 (386) $55,000

**Wiesel, Elie**
— The Golem. NY, [1983]. One of 250. Illus by Mark Podwal. sg Dec 14 (317) $110

**Wiggin, Kate Douglas, 1856-1923**
— Rebecca of Sunnybrook Farm. Bost., 1903. 2d or 3d ptg. Orig cloth, 2d bdg. ACs mtd to front pastedown. wa Feb 1 (327) $50
— Works. Bost., [1917]. One of 500. 10 vols. Half mor; 2 spines chipped. Sgd on the extra frontis. cb Oct 17 (311) $180

**Wight, John**
— More Mornings at Bow Street. L, 1827. 8vo, later calf gilt by Morrell. Lacking ads. pba June 20 (365) $100
— Mornings at Bow Street. L, 1824. 1st Ed, Later Issue. Illus by George Cruikshank. 8vo, later calf gilt by Morrell. With 11 plates plus engravings in the text. Lacking ad. pba June 20 (366) $100
3d Ed. L, 1925. 8vo, later half mor gilt; some rubbing. With 12 plates. wa Nov 16 (291) $75

**Wight, Thomas —&**
**Rutty, John**
— A History of the Rise and Progress of the...Quakers in Ireland. Dublin, 1751. 4to, later cloth. Last index leaf worn & with margin trimmed; some tears & holes; blanks with later ink family notations. bbc June 24 (264) $230

**Wightwick, George**
— The Palace of Architecture. L, 1840. 4to, half mor gilt; joints weak, library bookplate & pocket, endpaper stuck to pastedown. With 41 plates. Some spotting. wa Feb 29 (89) $70

**Wikgren, Allen P.**
— The Coverdale Bible. San Francisco: Book Club of California, 1974. One of 425. With facsimile reproductions & an orig leaf. bba May 9 (134) £80 [Heritage]
Anr copy. With facsimile reproductions & an orig leaf. pba June 20 (59) $375

**Wilberforce, William, 1759-1833**
— An Appeal to the Religion, Justice and Humanity of the Inhabitants of the British Empire.... L, 1823. 1st Ed. 8vo, disbound. Library stamp on 1 text leaf. Sgd "From the Author" on half-title. sg Mar 28 (349) $275
— A Letter on the Abolition of the Slave Trade. L, 1807. 1st Ed. 8vo, contemp wraps. b May 30 (6) £550

**Wilbrand, Johann Bernhard, 1779-1846**
— Handbuch der Botanik. Darmstadt, 1837. Orig bds. Interleaved throughout with holograph notes & pencil & ink drawings. pba Aug 8 (341) $100

**Wilbur, Homer.** See: Lowell, James Russell

**Wilcox, Michael**
— Twelve Bindings. Austin: W. Thomas Taylor, 1985. One of 10 in Wilcox bdg. Folio, mor gilt inlaid with mor rectangles & a butterfly & bird. sg Sept 14 (339) $500
One of 225. Cloth. bba May 9 (154) £65 [Deighton Bell]; bba May 9 (155) £70 [Maggs]
Anr copy. Cloth, in dj. Stamp of Stella Patri to front free endpaper. pba Nov 30 (63) $120

**Wild, Frank**
— Shackleton's Last Voyage. The Story of the Quest. NY, [1923]. 1st American Ed. 8vo, orig cloth; spine ends worn. With color frontis & 100 b&w plates. pba July 25 (79) $250

**Wilde, Oscar, 1854-1900**
See also: Grabhorn Printing; Limited Editions Club
— The Ballad of Reading Gaol. L, 1898. 3d Ed, one of 99. 8vo, contemp mor gilt by The Hampstead Bindery; minor rubbing. S Dec 18 (230) £1,400 [Rieden]

Anr Ed. L, 1924. One of 450. Illus by Frans Masereel. Orig half cloth, in chipped dj. b Jan 31 (229) £110

Anr copy. Orig half cloth, in dj. b Jan 31 (230) £100

Anr Ed. NY, 1928. Ltd Ed. Illus by John Vassos. Half cloth. pba May 23 (469) $60

Anr Ed. NY, 1930. 4to, half cloth, in dj. sg Feb 15 (306) $130

— De Profundis. L, [1905]. One of 200. S Dec 18 (222) £420 [Cathach]

One of 50 on Japanese vellum. Orig vellum gilt; bowed. CE May 22 (471) $750; S Dec 18 (223) £1,200 [Cathach]

— The Happy Prince and Other Tales. L, 1888. 1st Ed. - Illus by Walter Crane & Jacomb Hood. 4to, mor gilt by Sangorski & Sutcliffe. Inscr to Joseph Skipsey, Apr 1889. b Jan 31 (231) £1,400

Anr Ed. L, 1889. 4to, orig bds; bumped. sg June 20 (397) $150

— A House of Pomegranates. L, 1891. 1st Ed. 4to, orig cloth; hinges repaired with tape. CE May 22 (470) $420

Anr copy. Orig cloth; discoloured. With 4 plates. S Nov 2 (141) £200 [Sotheran]

Anr copy. Orig cloth; soiled. Inscr to Byron Webber, 1892. S Dec 18 (240) £6,800 [Edwards]

— An Ideal Husband. L, 1899. 1st Ed, One of 1,000. 4to, orig cloth; spine faded. S Oct 27 (1203) £300 [Cathach]

Anr copy. Orig cloth; slightly skewed, minor discoloration to upper cover. sg June 20 (398) $550

One of 100 L.p. copies. Orig cloth bds. Sgd. S Dec 18 (216) £1,800 [Levin]

— The Importance of Being Earnest. L, 1899. 1st Ed, one of 100 L.p. copies on Van Gelder Zonen. 4to, orig cloth; spine soiled. ALs to Leonard Smithers tipped in. P Dec 12 (179) $3,500; S Dec 18 (242) £2,800 [Hawthorn Bks]

— Intentions. L, 1891. 1st Ed. 8vo, cloth; slightly skewed. sg June 20 (399) $130

— Lady Windermere's Fan. L, 1893. 1st Ed. 4to, orig half cloth. S Dec 18 (224) £1,100 [Levin]

One of 500. Orig cloth; faded & soiled. S Oct 27 (1204) £400 [Cathach]

Pirated Ed. Paris [Ptd in England], 1903. Orig cloth; pin-pricks to small portion of front cover. sg June 20 (400) $70

— Lord Arthur Savile's Crime and other Stories. L, 1891. 1st Ed. 8vo, orig bds; rubbed, skewed. sg Feb 8 (370) $250

— Phrases and Philosophies for the Use of the Young. L: Privately ptd, 1894 [but c.1902]. Pirated Ed, one of 75. 8vo, wraps; spine splitting. pba Oct 5 (363) $65

— The Picture of Dorian Gray. L, [1891]. 1st Ed, one of 250 L.p. copies, sgd. 4to, mor gilt. P June 5 (349) $2,500

Anr copy. Orig half vellum gilt; spine worn. S Dec 18 (229) £1,600 [Rieden]

Anr copy. Orig half vellum gilt; worn. S Dec 18 (243) £4,500 [Symonds]

1st Ed in Book form, 1st Issue. 8vo, orig bds; front hinge starting. CE Sept 27 (284) $1,300

Anr copy. Orig bds; discoloration, possibly recased. CE Sept 27 (285) $1,300

Anr copy. Orig bds with vellum spine. S Dec 18 (228) £1,100 [Sumner & Stillman]

— Poems. L, 1881. 1st Ed, one of 250. 8vo, orig vellum gilt; free endpapers browned. CE Sept 27 (283) $700

Anr copy. Orig vellum; rubbed & discolored, lacking front free endpaper. Wear to edges. pba Nov 30 (327) $500

Anr copy. Orig vellum; lightly soiled. S Dec 18 (225) £1,400 [Buddenbrooks]

Anr copy. Orig vellum; soiled. S July 11 (239) £400

Anr Ed. L, 1892. One of 220. 8vo, orig cloth; rubbed. b Sept 20 (555) £1,000

Anr copy. Orig cloth; spine lacking, endpapers repaired, lacking flyleaf. Met May 22 (159) $2,100

Anr copy. Orig cloth; spine def, front free endpaper loose. S Dec 18 (226) £1,200 [Rieden]

Anr copy. Orig cloth; water damage to bds, small tears to cloth on spine. Dampstaining to outer margins of prelims. S July 11 (238) £1,200

— Ravenna. Oxford, 1878. 1st Ed. 8vo, orig wraps; tear to lower wrap. CE May 22 (469) $900

Anr copy. Cloth, orig wraps bound in. S Dec 18 (213) £260 [Cathach]

— Salome. A Tragedy in One Act. L & Bost., 1894. One of 100 L.p. copies on Japanese vellum. Trans by Lord Alfred Douglas; illus by Aubrey Beardsley. 4to, half mor gilt; rubbed. With 10 plates. ALs to Stuart laid in. P Dec 12 (178) $2,250

Anr copy. Orig silk bds gilt; covers with minor browning, spotting & soiling. S July 11 (240) £750

Anr Ed. Bost., 1907. Illus by Aubrey Beardsley. 4to, orig cloth; worn. sg Feb 15 (314) $90

Anr Ed. L, 1907. 4to, cloth; free endpapers browned. With 16 plates, including title & plate list. sg Apr 18 (197) $250

— The Sphinx. L, 1894. 1st Ed, one of 200. Illus by Charles Ricketts. 4to, orig vellum gilt. S Dec 18 (232) £1,700 [Copus]

Anr copy. Orig vellum gilt; slightly warped. sg Oct 19 (259) $3,400

Anr Ed. L, 1920. One of 1,000. Illus by Alastair. 4to, orig cloth. b May 30 (460) £210; sg Sept 14 (1) $400

— A Woman of No Importance. L, 1894. 1st Ed, one of 50. 4to, orig cloth; slightly discolored. Michael Sadleir's copy. S Dec 18 (215) £1,100 [Levin]

One of 500. Orig bds gilt. Inscr to Arthur Clifton. S Dec 18 (214) £2,600 [Edwards]

— Works. L, [1907]. Uniform Ed, one of 1,000. 15 vols. Contemp mor; 3 covers detached. b Jan 31 (232) £320
Edition de Grande Luxe. L & NY, 1907. one of 100. 15 vols. Mor gilt with floral onlay in mor, by Tapley. cb Oct 17 (312) $1,700
Anr Ed. L, 1908. One of 1,000. 14 vols. Half mor by Bayntun Riviere. b Sept 20 (577) £1,400; S Dec 18 (235) £680 [Harrington]

**Wildenstein, Daniel**
See also: Rouart & Wildenstein
— Claude Monet: Biographie et catalogue raisonne. Paris, [1974-85]. Vol IV only. In dj. sg June 13 (262) $250

**Wildenstein, Georges.** See: Jamot & Wildenstein

**Wilder, Mitchell A.**
— Georgia O'Keeffe: An Exhibition.... Fort Worth: Amon Carter Museum, 1966. 4to, pictorial wraps. Sgd by O'Keeffe, 17 Mar 1966. ds July 27 (141) $200
— Santos: The Religious Folk Art of New Mexico. Colorado Springs, [1943]. 4to, cloth. pba Apr 25 (734) $70

**Wilder, Thornton, 1897-1975**
See also: Limited Editions Club
— The Angel that Troubled the Waters.... L, 1928. One of 260 L.p. copies. pba Oct 5 (364) $110
Anr Ed. NY, 1928. One of 775 L.p. copies. In chipped dj. sg Dec 14 (318) $275
— The Bridge of San Luis Rey. L, 1927. In chipped dj. Inscr. Met May 22 (160) $225
Anr Ed. NY, 1927. One of 21. In repaired dj. pba Oct 5 (366) $1,300
Anr Ed. NY, 1929. One of 1,100. Illus by Rockwell Kent. 4to, cloth; some soiling. pba Oct 5 (367) $170
Anr copy. Cloth; covers foxed, bumped. pba May 23 (472) $80
Anr copy. Cloth; spine soiled. pba Aug 22 (507) $150
— The Cabala. NY, 1926. 1st Ed, 1st Issue. In chipped & repaired dj. CE May 22 (473) $240
— Heaven's My Destination. NY, 1938. Review copy. In dj. With ALs to reviewer Kenneth A. Fowler, Jan 1935, mtd to front free endpaper. pba Oct 5 (370) $175

**Wildman, Thomas**
— A Treatise on the Management of Bees.... L, 1778. 3d Ed. 2 parts in 1 vol. 8vo, contemp calf. With 3 folding plates. b Sept 20 (500) £80

**Wiley, Hugh**
— The Prowler. NY, 1924. In dj. sg Mar 28 (383) $80

**Wiley, William H. & Sara King**
— The Yosemite, Alaska, and the Yellowstone. L: Offices of Engineering, [1893]. Folio, later cloth. Library markings; some staining. pba Apr 25 (735) $50

**Wilkes, Charles, 1798-1877**
— Exploring Expedition.... Maderia, Brazil, Southern Cruise.... NY, 1858. 4to, orig cloth; extremiteis worn, front joint nicked, hinge cracked. With 8 plates & folding map. Some foxing. pba Apr 25 (736) $55
— Narrative of the United States Exploring Expedition, during the Years 1838-42. Phila., 1845. 5 vols, including Atlas. 4to, half mor, orig cloth upper covers bound in. With 64 plates & 14 maps (with tears repaired). Lacking 2 titles; some foxing. b Sept 20 (452) £1,300
Anr copy. 6 vols, including Atlas. 4to, orig cloth; backstrip of Vol IV gone, some wear. With 64 plates & 9 maps plus 6 additional maps in Atlas. Minor dampstaining. F Mar 28 (49) $1,700
Anr copy. 5 vols (lacks atlas). 8vo, orig cloth. Larson copy. pba Sept 28 (288) $550
Anr copy. 6 vols, including Atlas. 4to, orig cloth; Vol I lacking front free endpaper, Vol IV with gouge to spine, spine ends frayed. With 64 plates & 9 double-page maps in text vols; Atlas with 5 large folding maps, 1 hand-colored. pba July 25 (80) $1,700
3d Ed. 6 vols, including Atlas. 4to, orig cloth; spine ends worn, vol I rear joint split along top. With 64 plates, 13 double-page maps (1 folding, 1 hand-colored). Maps in Atlas torn at stub. Robbins copy. pba Mar 21 (387) $4,000
Anr Ed. Phila., 1849. 5 vols. 4to, orig calf; spines chipped & dried, & def, some wear 7 scuffing. Some foxing. bbc June 24 (201) $475
Anr copy. Orig sheep gilt; dry, extremities rubbed. cb June 25 (1720) $500
Anr Ed. Phila., 1850. 5 vols. 4to, half lea. With 64 plates & 11 (of 13) maps. Some foxing. NH June 1 (124) $550
Anr Ed. NY, 1856. Vols I-IV (of 5); lacking Vol II. 4to, half calf; 2 vols with bds separated, other scuffed. With 52 plates & 12 maps, 11 of them folding. wa Dec 14 (108) $180
— Western America, including California and Oregon.... Phila., 1849. 1st Ed. 8vo, later wraps; worn. With 3 folding maps. 2d map with 2 crease tears. Robbins copy. pba Mar 21 (388) $850

**Wilkie, Sir David, 1785-1841**
— Sketches Spanish and Oriental.... L, 1846. 4to, loose in orig cloth portfolio; worn, rebacked in mor. With 25 plates, hand-colored & mtd on card. Text leaf frayed & torn. S June 27 (130) £3,000

**Wilkins, H. St. Clair**
— Reconnoitring in Abyssinia. L, 1870. 8vo, cloth; front joint split, head of spine frayed. With 10 color litho plates. sg Mar 7 (377) $300

**Wilkins, John, 1614-72**
— A Discovery of a New World.... L, 1684. 2 parts in 1 vol. 8vo, contemp sheep; worn, covers detached. Browned; stamp on tp. sg May 16 (96) $350
— Mathematicall Magick.... L, 1691. 4th Ed. 8vo, contemp calf; rebacked. With port. L4 shaved at head. b June 28 (75) £350

**Wilkinson, Henry**
— Engines of War.... L, 1841. 8vo, orig cloth; backstrip repaired, front joint chipped. Ads dated Feb 1841. sg May 16 (276) $225
Later Issue. Orig cloth; spine ends chipped. Ads dated Mar 1856. Inscr & with 2 A Ls s. sg May 16 (277) $150

**Wilkinson, James, East India Merchant**
— Hau Kiou Choaan, or the Pleasing History.... L: R. & J. Dodsley, 1761. 4 vols. 8vo, contemp calf; rebacked. With 4 frontists; half-title in Vol I only. Margins "slightly blackened". bba Oct 19 (228) £100 [Scott]

**Wilkinson, Sir John Gardner, 1797-1875**
— The Manners and Customs of the Ancient Egyptians. L, 1841. 2d Series only. 3 vols. 8vo, orig cloth; rubbed, 1 front hinge repaired. Plate vol with 67 lithos, including 2 in color. pba June 20 (368) $225
2d Ed of Vols I-III, 1st Ed of 2d Series & Supplement vols. L, 1841-42. 6 vols. 8vo, calf gilt; rebacked. pba Nov 30 (328) $600
Anr Ed. L, 1878. Ed by Samuel Birch. 3 vols. 8vo, orig cloth; worn & soiled, Vol I front hinge broken. Pencil annotations. wa Feb 1 (150) $75

**Wilkinson, Robert, Publisher**
— A General Atlas. L, [1809-16]. 4to, modern half calf. With engraved title, plate-list & 48 maps with contemp hand-coloring. S Mar 28 (187) £460
Anr Ed. L, 1809. 4to, disbound. With engraved title, plate-list & 48 colored maps. Tp repaired; stained throughout. S June 13 (514) $340
— Londina Illustrata. L, 1819. Vol I only. 4to, later half mor; rubbed. With title & 107 plates. Some spotting. S Oct 26 (414) £200 [Storey]

**Wilks, Lieut. Col. Mark**
— Historical Sketches of the South of India.... L, 1810-17. 3 vols. 4to, contemp calf; rebacked, Vol I front joint starting. With 2 folding hand-colored maps. Half-title lacking in Vol II. sg Mar 7 (378) $400

**Will & Finck, Cutlers**
— Boller's Pantomime Book. San Francisco, [c.1900]. 8.25 by 5.5 inches, self-wraps; hole in spine. With 3 internal pages on which are pictures of 12 figures, with strips of central page folding to alter pictures. pba Nov 16 (280) $120

**Willeford, Charles**
— The Burnt Orange Heresy. NY, [1971]. 1st Ed. In dj. pba Aug 22 (509) $75
— Cockfighter Journal. Santa Barbara: Neville, 1989. One of 300. pba Aug 22 (510) $70
— Proletarian Laughter. Yonkers: Alicat Bookshop Press, 1948. Pictorial wraps. pba Aug 22 (511) $65

**Willement, Emily Elizabeth**
— A Bouquet from Flora's Garden, Botanically described for Lovers of Flowers among Little Folks. Norwich, 1841. 12mo, orig cloth. With 19 hand-colored plates. Short tear at foot of tp. S Nov 2 (270) £220 [Elizabeth Grant]

**Willems Library, Alphonse**
— [Sale Catalogue] Catalogue de livres anciens rares et pricieux.... Paris, 4-7 May 1914. 8vo, bds with hand-painted vellum spine depicting a skeleton carrying a stack of books; worn. O Mar 26 (296) $120

**Williams, Arthur Bryan**
— Game Trails in British Columbia. L, 1925. O June 25 (291) $130
Anr Ed. NY, 1925. Orig cloth; shaken, some wear. O Oct 10 (271) $70

**Williams, Ben Ames.** See: Derrydale Press

**Williams, Benjamin Samuels**
— The Orchid-Grower's Manual.... L: Victoria & Paradise Nurseries, 1894. Orig cloth; spine ends rubbed, hinges starting. pba June 20 (259) $95

**Williams, David, 1738-1816**
— The History of Monmouthshire. L, 1796. 4to, later half mor; rubbed, later endpapers. With map & 36 plates. Some browning. bba Nov 1 (238) £320 [Hughes]

**Williams, Edward, of Glamorgan**
— Vox populi vox dei! or, Edwards for Ever! Swansea, [1818]. 12mo, modern wraps. b Dec 5 (509) £90

**Williams, Henry Smith**
— The History of the Art of Writing.... L, [1902]. 4 vols. Folio, loose as issued in 4 cloth portfolios; spines worn. With 225 plates, some in color. O Mar 5 (239) $110

**Williams, Henry T.**
— The Pacific Tourist: Williams' Illustrated Transcontinental Guide of Travel. NY, 1878. 8vo, orig cloth; hinges cracked, rubbed. Frontis & front ad leaf detached; lacking 1 rear ad leaf. pba Aug 8 (213) $75

**Williams, Hugh W., 1773-1829**
— Select Views in Greece. L, 1829. 2 vols. 4to, contemp mor gilt. With 64 plates. b May 30 (305) £500
Anr copy. Mor gilt; scuffed. bbc June 24 (202) $525
Anr copy. Contemp half mor; corners rubbed. Some spotting. Ck Feb 14 (328) £450
1st Ed. 2 vols. in 1. 4to, later half mor. With 64 plates. Some discoloration; lacking list of plates. S Oct 26 (234) £380 [Map House]
Anr copy. 2 vols. 4to, contemp half mor. Some spotting; lacking list of plates. S Oct 26 (236) £340 [Frew]

**Williams, Iolo A.**
— Early English Watercolours. L, 1952. 4to, cloth, in chipped & frayed dj. O May 7 (299) $50

**Williams, John, 1664-1729**
— The Redeemed Captive, Returning to Zion.... Bost.: John Boyle, 1774. 5th Ed. 8vo, orig front wrap. Last leaf detached. NH June 1 (25) $210

**Williams, John H.**
— Yosemite and its High Sierra. Tacoma, 1914. Orig cloth with color illust tipped to front cover. Folding map inside rear cover. pba Feb 12 (202) $120

Anr copy. Orig cloth with color illust tipped to front cover; lacking front free endpaper. With 8 color plates. pba Apr 25 (737) $55

**Williams, John Jay**
— The Isthmus of Tehuantepec. NY, 1852. 1st Ed. Atlas vol only. 8vo, cloth binder; worn, all maps detached. With 8 folding litho maps. Some browning & foxing, small fold breaks. bbc Feb 26 (411) $160

**Williams, Juanita H.** See: Hallenbeck & Williams

**Williams, Margery.** See: Bianco, Margery Williams

**Williams, Mary Floyd**
— History of the San Francisco Committee of Vigilance of 1851. Berkeley, 1921. pba Feb 12 (580) $60

**Williams, Samuel, 1743-1817**
— The Natural and Civil History of Vermont. Walpole, N.H., 1794. 8vo, contemp sheep; worn, covers detached. With folding map by J. Whitelaw.. F June 20 (394) $300

Anr copy. Small portion of upper margin excised & restored, with loss of 1 letter. sg Oct 26 (392) $120

2d Ed. Burlington, 1809. 2 vols. 8vo, early calf; rebacked with orig backs retained. Lacking the map; some foxing. sg Oct 26 (393) $50

**Williams, Sidney Herbert**
— Some Rare Carrolliana. L: Pvtly ptd, 1924. One of 79. Inscr to Falconer Maden. sg Feb 8 (245) $475

**Williams, Tennessee, 1911-83**
See also: Limited Editions Club
— Androgyne, Mon Amour. NY, 1977. One of 200. sg Dec 14 (322) $200
— Battle of Angels. Murray, Utah: Pharos No 1/2, 1945. Wraps; spine with pieces lacking. pba Aug 22 (513) $100
— Cat on a Hot Tin Roof. NY, 1955. In dj with rubbing. pba May 23 (474) $110
— The Glass Menagerie. NY, [1945]. pba May 23 (475) $170
— Memoirs. NY, 1975. Ltd Ed, sgd. sg Dec 14 (321) $200
— One Arm and other Stories. New Directions, [1948]. One of 1,500. Half cloth. pba Oct 5 (373) $80
— I Rise in Flame, Cried the Phoenix. [Norfolk, Conn.]: New Direction, [1951]. 1st Ed, one of 300. 4to, orig half cloth. sg June 20 (403) $425
— A Streetcar Named Desire. New Directions, [1947]. In chipped dj. Sgd. CE Sept 27 (287) $900; pba Oct 5 (372) $250

— Suddenly Last Summer. NY, 1958. In dj. sg June 20 (404) $200
— Summer and Smoke. NY, 1948. In dj with spine ends chipped. pba May 23 (479) $65

**Williams, Thomas Lanier, 1911-83.** See: Williams, Tennessee

**Williams, William Carlos, 1883-1963**
— The Clouds, Aigeltinger, Russia, &c. Wells College & the Cummington Press, 1968. One of 310. pba Jan 25 (380) $180
— An Early Martyr. NY: Alcestis Press, 1935. One of 165. Orig wraps; discolored at edges. sg June 20 (405) $300
— Four Poems. Chicago, 1913. Wraps. In: Poetry: A Magazine of Verse, Vol II, No 3. pba Jan 25 (381) $130
— Paterson. NY, 1946-59. 1st Ed. 5 vols. Orig cloth, in djs. CE May 22 (475) $950
— Paterson (Book Two). [Norfolk: New Directions, 1948]. 1st Ed. Cloth, in dj. pba May 23 (483) $60
— Poems. [Rutherford, N. J.: Pvtly ptd by Reid Howell], 1909. 1st Ed, 2d State, with the ptg errors corrected. one of 100. 16mo, orig wraps, in half mor case; front wrap & front flyleaf detached, a few stains on cover. Inscr dated 1910. With postcard sgd by Williams discussing the scarcity of the work laid in. Goodwin - Engelhard copy. CNY Oct 27 (146) $28,000

**Williamson, George Charles, 1858-1942.** See: Manners & Williamson

**Williamson, Robert Stockton**
— Report upon the Removal of Blossom Rock, San Francisco Harbor, California. Wash., 1871. Folio, cloth. pba Feb 12 (356) $130

Anr copy. Orig cloth; spine torn & tape-repaired, library bookplate. pba July 25 (248) $110

**Williamson, Capt. Thomas**
— The Complete Angler's Vade-Mecum.... L, 1808. 8vo, half calf; rubbed, joints worn. With 10 plates. Some foxing. O Feb 6 (254) $200

**Williamson, Capt. Thomas —& Howitt, Samuel, 1765?-1822**
— Oriental Field Sports. L, 1807. Oblong folio, contemp half lea gilt, orig wraps cut round & mtd on upper cover of each vol; spines worn. With colored engraved title & 40 colored plates. Engraved title torn in margin & creased; Plate 2 stained; 3 plates creased; Plate 36 chipped in lower margins; 2 leaves of index creased at end of Vol IV. S June 27 (243) £8,500

Anr Ed. L, 1819. Oblong folio, contemp mor; broken, worn. With 40 hand-colored plates. Some text leaves with pencil markings. bbc June 24 (367) $850

Anr copy. In 2 vols. Oblong folio, contemp mor; rebacked preserving spine. With 40 hand-colored plates. O June 25 (292) $4,100

Anr Ed. L, 1819 [plates watermarked 1820s]. Oblong folio, contemp mor gilt. With 41 hand-colored plates. Lacking half-title. S June 13 (642) £800

**Willichius, Jodocus**
— Ars magirica hoc est, coquinaria, de cibariis, ferculis opsoniis.... Zurich: Jacob Gesner, [1563]. Bound with: Gesner, Jacob. Sanitatis tuendae praecepta. 1st Ed. - Ed by Konrad Gesner. 8vo, 18th-Cent calf; rebacked, extrems worn. Title browned. Ck Mar 22 (313) £1,400

**Willis, Nathaniel Parker, 1806-67**
— American Scenery. L, 1840. Illus by W. H. Bartlett. 2 vols. 4to, contemp mor; rebacked, corners repaired. With 2 engraved titles, hand-colored port, map & 117 hand-colored plates. CE May 22 (32) $2,200

Anr copy. Half calf; spines & corners rubbed. With 2 engraved titles, map & 117 plates. Lacking port. CE May 22 (33) $600

Anr copy. Contemp blind-stamped mor. With 2 engraved titles, port, map & 117 plates. S June 13 (615) £580

Anr copy. Contemp half calf; rubbed & stained. With 2 engraved titles, port, map & 116 plates. Lacking Plate 22 in Vol I; some spotting & staining; engraved title in Vol I is same as that in Vol II. S June 13 (616) £300

Anr copy. Illus W. H. Bartlett. Contemp calf; cover detached. Marginal age-darkening. CE Nov 8 (253) $130

— Canadian Scenery. L, 1842. Illus by W. H. Bartlett. 2 vols. 4to, contemp calf gilt; rubbed. With engraved frontises, additional vignette titles, map & 115 plates. Lacking port; foxed. bba June 6 (51) £280 [Ribbons]

Anr copy. Contemp mor gilt; rubbed. With engraved titles, port & 117 plates. wad Oct 18 (466) C$1,150

— Pencillings by the Way. L, 1835. 3 vols. 8vo, bds; worn. S Oct 26 (238) £140 [Scott]

**Willis, Nathaniel Parker, 1806-67 —&**
**Coyne, Joseph Stirling, 1803-68**
— The Scenery and Antiquities of Ireland. L: Virtue, [1841]. 2 vols in 5. 4to, orig cloth. With engraved titles, map & 118 plates. S Apr 23 (375) £220

Anr copy. 2 vols. 4to, mor gilt; worn & soiled. With engraved titles, map & 114 (of 118) plates. Lacking port. wa Nov 16 (387) $110

**Willis, Thomas, 1621-75**
— Opera. Amst., 1682. 2 vols. 4to, half lea; rebound. With port frontis, title, & 36 plates. Port & title repaired; plates stained. CE Nov 8 (159) $500

— Pathologiae cerebri et nervosi generis specimen.... Amst., 1668. 12mo, contemp calf; rubbed. Browned. bba July 18 (91) £360 [Perkin]

**Willkie, Wendell, 1892-1944.** See: Limited Editions Club

**Willmott, Ellen Ann**
— The Genus Rosa. L, 1910-14. 2 vols. Folio, contemp half mor, orig wraps bound in; corners bumped. With 132 chromolitho plates, 15 uncolored plates & 68 full-page illusts. C May 31 (46) £1,600

Anr copy. 2 vols in orig 25 parts. Folio, orig wraps in 2 portfolios. With 132 chromolitho plates. O Mar 5 (240) $2,500

**Willughby, Francis**
— Ornithologiae libri tres. L, 1676. Folio, contemp calf; worn, rebacked. With 2 tables & 77 plates. Upper fore-corner of tp damaged; some marginal tears repaired; a few small holes in text; some browning. Samuel Pepys's copy. S June 27 (69) £1,700

— The Ornithology.... L, 1678. 1st Ed in English. 3 parts in 1 vol. Folio, modern half calf. With 2 tables & 78 (of 80) plates & 2 ptd tables. Several plates with portions of image torn away; others with marginal repairs. S Mar 29 (678) £320

**Willyams, Cooper, 1762-1816**
— A Selection of Views in Egypt, Palestine, Rhodes.... L, 1822. Folio, contemp half mor; worn. With 36 colored plates. bba June 6 (54) £420 [Eurobooks]

— A Voyage Up the Mediterranean. L, 1802. 1st Ed. 4to, orig bds; covers detached, stitching broken. With engraved dedication 2 double-page maps, 1 double-page & 40 full-page plates.. L.p. copy. Lady Hamilton's copy. C May 31 (117) £1,900

Anr copy. Contemp calf gilt; rebacked, rubbed, corners repaired. With engraved dedication with hand-colored arms, 2 hand-colored maps & 40 hand-colored plates. Spotted & dust-soiled. L.p. copy. C May 31 (118) £1,100

**Wilmerding, John**
— A History of American Marine Painting. Bost., [1968]. In dj with light wear. O Dec 5 (150) $80

**Wilson, Adrian**
— The Work and Play.... Austin: W. Thomas Taylor, 1983. One of 325. Folio, half lev. pba Nov 30 (329) $150

Anr copy. Half mor. sg Sept 14 (340) $175

**Wilson, Alexander, 1766-1813**
— Poems. Paisley, 1790. 8vo, orig bds; upper cover & spine detached. b Dec 5 (585) £100

**Wilson, Alexander, 1766-1813 —&**
**Bonaparte, Charles Lucien, 1803-57**
— The American Ornithology. L, 1832. 3 vols. 8vo, contemp half mor; extremities rubbed. With 97 hand-colored plates. Some foxing to plates. cb Feb 14 (2622) $1,100

**Wilson, Alexander, 1766-1813 —&**
**Bonaparte, Charles Lucian, 1803-57**
— The American Ornithology. L, 1832. 3 vols. 8vo, contemp half mor; vol I upper hinge broken, rubbed & chipped. With frontis port & 97 hand-colored

plates. Some offsetting, few leaves loose. S Oct 27 (789) £320 [Egglishaw]

**Wilson, Alexander, 1766-1813 —& Bonaparte, Charles Lucien, 1803-57**
— The American Ornithology. L, 1832. 3 vols. 8vo, contemp half mor; rubbed. With port & 97 hand-colored plates. Vols I-II lacking half-titles. S June 27 (70) £800

Anr Ed. Phila., [1871]. 4 vols, including 3 text vols & 1 (of 2) Atlas vols. 8vo & folio, later cloth; worn. With 103 hand-colored plates. Some marginal tears & chipping; 1 plate repaired on verso. cb June 25 (1721) $5,000

**Wilson, Andrew, Traveler**
— Photographic Album Accompanying the Ever Victorious Army. Edin., 1868. Folio, orig cloth; spine torn with loss. With 22 photographs. Some leaves loose; some spotting. bba July 18 (339) £650 [Fine Books Oriental]

**Wilson, Angus**
— The World of Charles Dickens. L: Arcadia Press, 1971. One of 265. 4to, mor extra by Zaehnsdorf. b Sept 20 (648) £100

**Wilson, Benjamin, 1721-88**
— A Series of Experiments Relating to Phosphori.... L, 1776. ("A Series of Experiments on the Subject of Phospori....") 2d Ed. 4to, modern cloth. Library stamp on tp. sg May 16 (278) $225

**Wilson, Charles Henry**
— The Polyanthea: or, a Collection of Interesting Fragments in Prose amd Verse. L, 1804. 2 vols. Half mor. Vol I prelims chipped at top. pba June 20 (369) $50

— The Wanderer in America, or Truth at Home.... Thirsk, 1822. 2d Ed. 12mo, bds; rebacked with cloth. sg Oct 26 (394) $50

**Wilson, Sir Charles William**
— Picturesque Palestine.... L, [1880-84]. Vols II-III only. Orig cloth. With 21 plates & 1 map. b Sept 20 (374) £50

Anr copy. 5 vols, including Supplement (Social Life in Egypt, by Stanley Lane-Poole). 4to, orig cloth; worn & rubbed, some leaves loose in Supplement. S Mar 28 (300) £260

Anr Ed. L, [1881-84]. 5 vols. 4to, mor; worn. S Oct 26 (239) £280 [Sevens]

Anr Ed. NY, [1881]-84. 2 vols. Folio, half mor. pba Mar 7 (204) $325

Anr copy. Minor dampstaining in 1 vol. sg Mar 7 (382) $150

Anr copy. Orig mor gilt; scuffed. wa Nov 16 (382) $350

**Wilson, Edmund, 1895-1972**
— The Boys in the Back Room. San Francisco: Colt Press, 1941. Ltd Ed, sgd. In chipped dj. sg June 20 (406) $90

— To the Finland Station. NY, [1940]. 1st Ed, Review copy. In chipped & soiled dj. sg Dec 14 (324) $70

**Wilson, Edward**
— Diary of the Discovery Expedition to the Antarctic Regions 1901-1904. NY, [1967]. 1st American Ed. 4to, orig cloth, in laminated dj. pba July 25 (81) $60

**Wilson, Elijah Nicholas**
— Among the Shoshones. Salt Lake City, [1910]. 1st Ed. With 8 plates. Robbins copy. pba Mar 21 (389) $650

1st Issue. With 8 plates. K Feb 11 (376) $275

**Wilson, Eugene E.**
— A Pilgrimage of Anglers. [Hartford, 1952]. One of 450. 8vo, half lea. Inscr. O June 25 (293) $80

**Wilson, F. Paul**
— Nightworld. Arlington Heights: Dark Harvest, 1992. One of 26 lettered copies. Syn, in dj. O Dec 5 (267) $60

— Reborn. Arlington Heights: Dark Harvest, 1990. One of 52 lettered copies. Syn, in dj. O Dec 5 (268) $60

— Reprisal. Arlington Heights: Dark Harvest, 1991. One of 26 lettered copies. Syn, in dj. O Dec 5 (269) $60

— Sibs. Arlington Heights: Dark Harvest, 1991. One of 26 lettered copies. Syn, in dj with edge tears. O Dec 5 (270) $60

**Wilson, Harrison Corbett**
— The Artillery Officer's Bride. Southam, 1838. 8vo, orig ptd wraps. b Dec 5 (403) £50

**Wilson, Henry —& Caulfield, James, 1754-1826**
— Wonderful Characters L, 1821. 3 vols. Calf gilt, armorial bdg; extremities rubbed, joints cracked. pba Aug 8 (293) $140

**Wilson, Job**
— An Inquiry into the Nature and Treatment of...Spotted Fever.... Bost., 1815. 8vo, contemp calf; rubbed. With 5 plates. Some foxing & browning. O Nov 14 (195) $250

**Wilson, John Albert**
— History of Los Angeles County.... Berkeley: Howell-North, 1959. Folio, cloth, in dj. With 111 plates & 1 color map. Facsimile of the 1880 Ed. pba Feb 12 (450) $70

**Wilson, Mona.** See: Nonesuch Press

**Wilson, Obed G.**
— My Adventures in the Sierras. Franklin, 1902. 1st Ed. Orig cloth. With frontis port. Larson copy. pba Sept 28 (741) $60

**Wilson, R. L.**
See also: Sutherland & Wilson
— Colt. An American Legend. NY: Abbeville, [1985]. Sesquicentennial Ed. - Photography by Sid Latham.

# WILSON

Oblong 4to, lea gilt with colt coin inset onto front cover. O Oct 10 (273) $140
— Colt Pistols 1836-1976. Dallas: Jackson Arms, [1976]. Oblong 4to, syn gilt, upper cover with large metallic medallion inset of a colt. O Oct 10 (274) $130
— L. D. Nimschke. Firearms Engraver. Teaneck: John J. Malloy, [1965]. One of 200. 4to, cloth, in frayed dj; some wear. Inscr by the pbr. O Oct 10 (277) $140
— Winchester Engraving. Palm Springs CA: Beinfeld, [1989]. 2d Ed, One of 50. 4to, mor; some wear. O Oct 10 (278) $375

**Wilson, Sir Robert Thomas, 1777-1849**
— History of the British Expedition to Egypt. L, 1802. 1st Ed. 4to, contemp half calf. Lacking half-title. b May 30 (304) £220

**Wilson, Sir Samuel, 1832-95**
— Salmon at the Antipodes. L, 1879. 8vo, pictorial cloth; worn. Some foxing. Inscr "With the Author's Compliments" on half-title. O Feb 6 (257) $190

**Wilson, Scott B. —& Evans, Arthur Humble**
— Aves Hawaiienses: The Birds of the Sandwich Islands. Hawaii, 1989. One of 250. 4to, in cloth & wood box. With 60 color plates. Met Sept 28 (420) $325

**Wilson, T., Rev.** See: Clark, Samuel

**Wilson, William, Chief Mate of the Ship Duff**
— A Missionary Voyage to the Southern Pacific Ocean. L, 1799. 1st Ed. 4to, contemp bds; rebacked. Some spotting. b Mar 20 (97) £380

Anr copy. Contemp tree calf; rebacked. With 7 maps (6 folding) & 6 plates. 1st map torn & repaired; some spotting & offsetting. S Oct 26 (614) £280 [Harrington]

**Wilson, William, Topographer**
— The Post-Chaise Companion or Traveller's Directory through Ireland. Dublin, 1786. 8vo, contemp calf; worn, covers detached, opening leaves loose. With engraved title & 4 plates. Frontis mtd. sg Mar 7 (383) $90

Anr Ed. Dublin, 1803. 8vo, later cloth; needs rebdg. Browned throughout. sg Mar 7 (384) $60

Anr Ed. Dublin, 1805. 8vo, later half mor; extremities worn. sg Mar 7 (385) $175

**Wilson, William Rae**
— Travels in Egypt and the Holy Land. L, 1824. 8vo, contemp half calf; extremities worn, spine ends chipped. With 6 (of 12) plates. sg Mar 7 (386) $150

**Wiltsee, Ernest A.**
See also: Grabhorn Printing
— The Pioneer Miner and the Pack Mule Express. San Francisco: California Historical Society, 1931. 1st Ed. Orig cloth. With 8 plates, & 1 facsimile of 1849 restaurant menu. Larson copy. pba Sept 28 (743) $80

**Wimer, James**
— Events in Indian History, Beginning with an Account of the Origin of.... Lancaster, Pa., 1841. 1st Ed. 8vo, modern half mor. With 8 plates, most with some coloring. Some plates with short tears or repaired tears; dampstaining to text. sg Oct 26 (395) $120

**Winans, Walter**
— The Sporting Rifle. NY, 1908. 4to, cloth; some wear & spotting. O Oct 10 (279) $200

**Winckelmann, Johann Joachim, 1717-68**
— Critical Account of the Situation and Destruction by the First Eruptions of Mount Vesuvius, of Herculaneum, Pompeii, and Stabia. L, 1771. 8vo, contemp calf; needs rebacking. sg May 16 (279) $130
— Lettre... a Monsieur le comte de Bruehl.... Dresden, 1764. 4to, contemp red mor gilt, with arms of Henri, comte de Calenberg. Fuerstenberg - Schaefer copy. S Dec 8 (664) £1,000
— Monumens inedits de l'antiquite.... Paris, 1808-9. 3 vols in 2. 4to, contemp calf gilt; rebacked retaining orig backstrips. With 225 color or tinted plates. sg Apr 18 (198) $600

**Wind, Herbert Warren.** See: Hogan & Wind

**Windeler, Adolphus**
— The California Gold Rush Diary of a German Sailor. San Francisco, [1969]. 1st Ed. - Ed by W. Turrentine Jackson. Orig cloth in dj. With 2 plates. Larson copy. pba Sept 28 (744) $60

**Windeler, Bernard.** See: Wadsworth & Windeler

**Windsor, Edward, Duke of, 1894-1972**
— A King's Story. L, 1951. 1st Ed, one of 250. 8vo, orig mor gilt, with royal arms. With 22 plates. bbc Dec 18 (77) $260

**Wing, Donald**
— Short-Title Catalogue of Books Printed in England...1641-1700. NY, 1945-51. 3 vols. 4to, cloth. ds July 27 (199) $400

1st Ed. 3 vols. 4to, orig cloth. sg Apr 11 (332) $375

2d Ed. NY, 1972. Vol I (of 3). 4to, orig cloth. sg Apr 11 (333) $60

Anr Ed. NY, 1994-82-88. 3 vols. 4to, orig cloth. S June 12 (369) £320

**Wingate, George W.**
— Through the Yellowstone Park on Horseback. NY, 1886. Orig cloth; spine ends frayed. With folding map loose in rear endpaper pocket. pba Apr 25 (738) $85

**Wingate's copy, Orde**
— Bible. Oxford, [c.1911]. Bdg not described; worn & detached. Inscr inside front cover & annotated. Used by Wingate from the age of 12 throughout his life.. S July 11 (374) £2,100

## Wingert, Paul S.
— The Sculpture of William Zorach. NY, 1938. In chipped dj. Sgd twice & inscr.  sg Jan 11 (474) $80

## Wingler, Hans Maria
— The Bauhaus. Cambr. MA, 1969. Folio, cloth.  wa June 20 (322) $100

Anr Ed. Cambr., Mass., 1969. Folio, cloth.  sg June 13 (386) $140

## Winkler, Rolf Arnim
— Die Fruehzeit der deutschen Lithographie. Katalog der Bilddruck von 1796-1821. Munich, [1975]. 1st Ed. 4to, orig cloth in dj.  sg Apr 11 (334) $120

## Winkles, B.
— French Cathedrals. L, 1837. 4to, orig cloth; rebacked, front hinge cracked. Foxing affecting plates.  sg Sept 7 (21) $60

## Winship, George Parker
— The Merrymount Press of Boston. An Account.... Vienna, 1929. One of 350. Folio, orig bds; worn, spine head torn. Inscr to Alfred Reginald Allen & with ALs to Allen laid in, along with Merrymount ephemera.  O Mar 26 (297) $140
— William Caxton and the First English Press. NY, 1928. 4to, orig mor in dj. With orig leaf of the Polycronicon mtd at end.  sg Oct 19 (56) $900

## Winslow, Henry
— The Etching of Landscapes. Chicago: Chicago Society of Etchers, [1914]. One of 250 with 2 loose pencil-sgd etchings. 4to, orig bds; soiled, marked, spine bumped.  wa Nov 16 (301) $120

## Winsor, Justin, 1831-97
— Narrative and Critical History of America. Bost., [1884-89]. 8 vols. 4to, orig cloth; extremities worn, 1 front hinge cracked.  ds July 27 (200) $100

Anr copy. Orig cloth; worn, front hinges weak.  wa Feb 29 (585) $350

1st Ed. Bost., 1889. One of 550. 8 vols. 4to, later cloth.  sg Oct 26 (398) $200

## Winter...
— A Winter in Paris; or, Memoirs of Madame de C**** written by herself. L, 1811. 3 vols. 12mo, contemp half calf; spines worn. Minor defs; lacking ad leaf at end of Vol III.  Ck Sept 8 (194) $750
— Winter Sports. NY: McLoughlin Brothers, [n.d.]. Foldout book, 12 feet long.  Met Dec 5 (280) $375

## Winter, Douglas E.
— Prime Evil. West Kingston RI: Donald M. Grant, [1988]. One of 1,000. Ed by Winter. Syn gilt. Sgd by all the contributors.  pba May 4 (283) $150

## Winter, George, 1809-76
— The Journals and Indian Paintings of George Winter, 1837-1839. Indianapolis, 1948. 4to, cloth.  sg Sept 7 (350) $50

## Winter, George Simon
— Wolberittener Cavallier.... Nuremberg, 1678. Folio, contemp blindstamped pigskin over bds. With frontises & 171 plates, 66 of them double-page. Small wormhole in 1st 3 plates & last 4 leaves. Fugger copy.  b June 28 (78) £4,200

## Winter, William H. See: Johnson & Winter

## Winther, Oscar Osburn
— The Story of San Jose, 1777-1869.... San Francisco: California Historical Society, 1935. 1st Ed, One of 150. Illus by William Smyth & J. W. Revere. With color frontis, 1 illus, & 1 plate. Robbins copy.  pba Mar 21 (391) $130

## Winthrop, John, 1588-1649
— A Journal of the Transactions and Occurences in the Settlement of Massachusetts.... Hartford, 1790. 1st Ed, 1st Ptg. Ed by Noah Webster. 8vo, old calf; front bd bowed, joints starting. Some foxing.  wa Feb 29 (586) $280

## Winthrop, Theodore, 1828-61
— The Canoe and the Saddle, Adventures Among the Northwestern Rivers and Forests.... Bost., 1863. 8vo, orig cloth; extremities rubbed, stained.  pba July 25 (369) $100

## Wisconsin
— Information for Emigrants. The City of Superior and the Lake Superior Region. Superior, 1858. 8vo, orig ptd wraps; lower cover stained. Some foxing & creasing.  bbc Dec 18 (587) $400

## Wisden, John
— Cricketers' Almanack. L, 1868. Modern cloth.  pn Oct 12 (247) £1,000

Anr Ed. L, 1888. Orig wraps; broken.  pn Oct 12 (253) £150

Anr Ed. L, 1889-90. 2 vols. Orig wraps; spines cracked.  pn Oct 12 (254) £400

Anr Ed. L, 1891-92. Orig wraps; soiled.  pn Oct 12 (255) £380

Anr Ed. L, 1893-94. 2 vols. Orig wraps; spines cracked.  pn Oct 12 (256) £270

Anr Ed. L, 1895-97. 3 vols. Orig wraps (1897) & later cloth.  pn Oct 12 (257) £240

Anr Ed. L, 1896-1900. 5 vols. Later cloth. Lacking 1 plate.  pn Oct 12 (226) £320

Anr Ed. L, 1898. Orig hard bdg.  pn Oct 12 (258) £500

Anr Ed. L, 1899. Orig hard bdg.  pn Oct 12 (259) £720

Anr Ed. L, 1900. Orig cloth. Inscr to R. M. Poore by Henry Luff of Wisden & Co.  pn Oct 12 (248) £720

Anr Ed. L, 1900-7. 8 vols.  pn Oct 12 (260) £460

Anr Ed. L, 1901-9. 9 vols. Various cloth bdgs. Lacking 1 plate.  pn Oct 12 (227) £300

Anr Ed. L, 1902-7. 6 vols. Orig wraps; spines def.  b May 30 (505) £240

## WISDEN

Anr Ed. L, 1908-15. 8 vols. Orig wraps; some spines cracked or creased. b May 30 (506) £260

Anr copy. Orig wraps; spines cracked. Some soiling. pn Oct 12 (261) £420

Anr Ed. L, 1910-15. 6 vols. Later cloth. pn Oct 12 (228) £220

Anr Ed. L, 1916. Orig wraps. b May 30 (507) £320

Anr copy. Later cloth. pn Oct 12 (262) £260

Anr Ed. L, 1917-19. 3 vols. Orig wraps; spines creased. b May 30 (508) £320

Anr copy. Orig wraps; spines cracked. Some staining. pn Oct 12 (263) £340

Anr Ed. L, 1920-29. 10 vols. Orig wraps; spines creased, 4 reinforced with tape. b May 30 (509) £320

Anr copy. Various cloth, 1924 in orig wraps. 1929 lacking pp 1-20. pn Oct 12 (229) £300

Anr copy. Orig wraps; spines cracked, some repairs. pn Oct 12 (264) £380

Anr Ed. L, 1922-29. 8 vols. Orig wraps; spines cracked. pn Oct 12 (249) £320

Anr Ed. L, 1930-39. 10 vols. Orig wraps or cloth; 1 spine tape-repaired. b May 30 (510) £450

Anr copy. Orig bdgs. pn Oct 12 (230) £480

Anr Ed. L, 1930-37. 8 vols. Orig bdgs. pn Oct 12 (250) £520

Anr Ed. L, 1930-39. 10 vols. Various orig bdgs; some spines cracked, repairs. pn Oct 12 (265) £700

Anr Ed. L, 1936. Orig cloth; rubbed. Tape repair to plate & facing page. pn Oct 12 (237) £160

Anr Ed. L, 1937. Orig bds. pn Oct 12 (238) £190

Anr Ed. L, 1940-49. 10 vols. Orig cloth. b May 30 (503) £580

Anr Ed. L, 1940-41. 2 vols. pn Oct 12 (266) £340

Anr Ed. L, 1942. Orig cloth; rubbed. Ink stamp. pn Oct 12 (239) £440

Anr Ed. L, 1942-43. 2 vols. pn Oct 12 (267) £280

Anr Ed. L, 1943. Orig cloth; rubbed. pn Oct 12 (240) £180

Anr Ed. L, 1944. Orig cloth. pn Oct 12 (241) £200

Anr copy. Orig bdg. pn Oct 12 (252) £85

Anr Ed. L, 1944-45. 2 vols. pn Oct 12 (268) £220

Anr Ed. L, 1945. Orig cloth. pn Oct 12 (242) £200

Anr Ed. L, 1946. Orig cloth. pn Oct 12 (243) £65

Anr Ed. L, 1946-49. 4 vols. pn Oct 12 (269) £130

Anr Ed. L, 1947-50. 4 vols. Orig cloth; rubbed. pn Oct 12 (244) £220

Anr Ed. L, 1950-66. 17 vols. b May 30 (504) £200

Anr Ed. L, 1950-69. 20 vols. Orig bdgs. pn Oct 12 (232) £340

Anr Ed. L, 1950-92. 43 vols. pn Oct 12 (270) £480

Anr Ed. L, 1951-64. 14 vols. pn Oct 12 (245) £360

Anr Ed. L, 1965-92. 28 vols plus Index for 1864-1984. In djs. pn Oct 12 (246) £400

Anr Ed. L, 1970-94. 25 vols. Orig bdgs. pn Oct 12 (233) £160

## AMERICAN BOOK PRICES CURRENT

**Wise, Henry Augustus, 1819-69**

— Los Gringos or an Inside View of Mexico and California. NY, 1849. 1st Ed. Contemp half mor; worn. Larson copy. pba Sept 28 (745) $110

**Wise, Thomas James, 1859-1937**

— A Bibliography of the Writings... of George Gordon Noel, Baron Byron. L: Privately ptd, 1932. 1st Ed, One of 180. 2 vols. 4to, orig cloth; spines faded. sg Apr 11 (335) $400

— A Byron Library. L: Privately ptd, 1928. One of 200. 4to, orig cloth. bba May 9 (73) £95 [Ogino]

— A Complete Bibliography of the Writings in Prose and Verse of John Ruskin. L, 1893. One of 250. 2 vols. 4to, half mor, orig upper wraps bound in; rubbed, corners worn. Some foxing; pencilled marginalia by a former owner. O Mar 26 (299) $90

— A Conrad Library. L: Pvtly ptd, 1928. One of 180. 4to, orig cloth. pba June 20 (372) $180

— A Swinburne Library. L, 1925. One of 170. Inscr. O Mar 26 (298) $100

**Wistar, Isaac Jones, 1827-1905**

— Autobiography, 1827-1905. Phila., 1914. 1st Ed, One of 250. 2 vols. 4to, orig half bds; light shelf wear. With 4 ports & 1 folded map. Larson copy. pba Sept 28 (746) $300

2d Ed. Phila., 1937. Orig cloth in dj; d/j spine faded. With 4 ports & 1 folded map. Larson copy. pba Sept 28 (747) $50

**Wister, Owen, 1860-1938**

See also: Limited Editions Club

— A Journey in Search of Christmas. NY, 1904. 1st Ed. - Illus by Frederic Remington. Orig cloth; extremities rubbed, some staining. pba July 25 (370) $90

**Withering, William, 1741-99**

— A Systematic Arrangement of British Plants. Birm., 1796. ("An Arrangement of British Plants.") 3d Ed. 4 vols. 8vo, contemp bds; 1 backstrip def, rubbed. With 31 plates, 1 of them colored, 1 folding. bba May 30 (451) £80 [Price]

**Withers, Alexander S.**

— Chronicles of Border Warfare, or a History.... Clarksburg VA, 1831. 12mo, contemp calf. Some foxing & staining. pba Apr 25 (257) $200

**Witherspoon, John, 1723-94**

— The Dominion of Providence over the Passions of Men.... Phila.: R. Aitken, 1776. 8vo, sewn. Some foxing; large piece torn from bottom corner of last leaf. NH Sept 16 (21) $775

— Works. Phila., 1802. 4 vols. 8vo, contemp sheep; worn. sg Oct 26 (399) $450

**Witsen, Nicolaas**

— Aeloude en Hedendaegsche Scheeps-Bouw en Bestier. Amst., 1671. 1st Ed. Folio, 18th-cent half calf; joints cracked, rubbed. With etched title, port & 113 plates, 1 double-page. Lacking text leaf Ooo2 & Plate B of Appendix. C Oct 25 (156) £1,800

## Witteman, A.
— Mit dem Luftschiff ueber den atlantischen Ozean. Die Amerika fahrt des Z.R. III. Weisbaden, 1925. Orig bds; spine chipped at top.  sg May 16 (97) $150

## Wodehouse, Pelham Grenville, 1881-1975
— Bill the Conqueror.... NY, [1924]. Cloth; edges foxed.  sg Dec 14 (327) $70
— The Code of the Woosters. NY, 1938. In dj; some soiling to d/j & bdg.  F Mar 28 (66) $100
— The Crime Wave at Blandings. Garden City, 1937. In dj with minor tear to front panel. F Mar 28 (67) $100
— Eggs, Beans and Crumpets. L, 1940. In dj with tears. sg Dec 14 (335) $200
— Full Moon. L, [1947]. In dj.  sg Dec 14 (337) $120
— Gaa, Baa, Black Sheep. L, 1930. Wraps; some discoloration.  sg Dec 14 (331) $100
— Golf Without Tears. NY: George H. Doran, [1924]. 1st American Ed. Cloth; soiled, spine ends rubbed. pba Apr 18 (187) $55
— Laughing Gas. Garden City, 1936. Cloth; spine discolored.  sg Dec 14 (333) $50
— Leave it to Psmith. L, 1924. Some foxing.  sg Dec 14 (326) $60
— Love Among the Chickens. NY, 1909. 1st American Ed, Advance copy. With 6 plates. Ck Nov 17 (180) £320
— The Luck of the Bodkins. Bost., 1936. Orig cloth, in chipped dj.  F Mar 28 (68) $80
— Money in the Bank. L, [1946]. In dj.  sg Dec 14 (336) $60
— A Prefect's Uncle. L, 1903. Orig cloth; spine ends def, joints split. Some foxing at ends.  cb June 25 (1892) $400
   Anr copy. Orig cloth; inner hinges weak, bumped. Spotted throughout.  Ck Nov 17 (178) £380
— Quick Service. NY, 1940. Colonial Issue. In repaired dj.  sg Dec 14 (334) $175
— The Small Bachelor. L, 1928. Some foxing.  sg Dec 14 (328) $60
   Anr Ed. NY, [1928]. In dj with edges rubbed.  sg Dec 14 (330) $275
— Ukridge. L, 1924. 1st Ed. Orig cloth. Some foxing. sg Dec 14 (325) $70
— Uncle Dynamite. L, [1948]. In dj.  sg Dec 14 (338) $120
— Uncle Fred in the Springtime. NY, 1939. In chipped dj.  F Mar 28 (65) $110
— Young Man in Spats. L, [1936]. 2d Ptg. In rubbed dj with tear. Sgd on tp.  bba Oct 19 (402A) £160 [Mandl]

## Wofford, J. D.
— Sunalei Akvlvgi No'gwisi Alikalvvsga Zvivgi Gesvi.... NY, 1824. 12mo, orig half sheep; def.  sg Oct 26 (159) $225

## Wolcot, John, 1738-1819
— The Works of Peter Pindar, Esq. L, 1794-1801. 5 vols. 8vo, early half calf. Minor foxing.  bbc Feb 26 (137) $240

## Wolf, Eclan Isaac
— Von den Krankheiten der Juden. Mannheim, 1777. 1st Ed. 8vo, contemp bds; rubbed. Dampstained. Ck Mar 22 (314) £600

## Wolf, Edwin, 2d —& Fleming, John F.
— Rosenbach: a Biography. Cleveland, [1960]. 1st Ed. In worn dj. Graham Greene's sgd copy.  bba May 9 (109) £110 [Mandl]

## Wolf, Johann, 1765-1824 —& Meyer, Bernard, 1767-1856
— Naturgeschichte der Voegel Deutschlands in getreuen Abbildungen und Beschreibungen. Nuremberg: J. F. Frauenholz, 1805-[21]. One of 16. 2 vols. Folio, calf gilt by C. Smith. With 176 (of 180) hand-colored plates. Botfield copy.  C May 31 (45) £30,000

## Wolf, Johann Christian
— Monumenta typographica, quae artis hujus...originem.... Hamburg, 1740. 2 vols. 8vo, later cloth; worn. Browned throughout.  O Mar 26 (300) $800

## Wolf, Johannes, Jurisconsult
— Lectionum memorabilium et reconditarum centenarii XVI. Lauingen: L. Rheinmichel, 1600. Bound with: Linsius, Johannes Jacobus. Lectionum memorabilium et reconditarum... index absolutiss. methodice. Lauingen: Jacob Winter, 1608. 2 vols. Folio, 17th-cent mor gilt; corners worn, rubbed.  S Mar 14 (371) £300

## Wolf, Joseph, 1820-99
— Pheasant Drawings by Joseph Wolf.... Kingston upon Hull, Allen Publishing Co., 1988. One of 250. Folio, orig half mor gilt.  sg Oct 19 (179) $1,500

## Wolf, Joseph, 1820-99 —& Elliot, Daniel Giraud, 1835-1915
— The Life and Habits of Wild Animals. L, 1874. Folio, contemp mor gilt.  S Apr 23 (338) £240

## Wolfart, Peter
— Historia naturalis Hassiae inferioris pars prima.... Cassel, 1719. 4to, bds; spine worn. With 25 plates, 2 of them folding. Some staining; 1 plate with tear repaired, anr with neatline cropped; no frontis or port.  b May 30 (42) £70

## Wolfe, Richard J.
— Jacob Bigelow's American Medical Botany..... [North Hills, Pa.]: Bird & Bull Press, 1979. Half lev. With 1 colored & 1 plain plate.  bba May 9 (451) £50 [Deighton Bell]
   Anr copy. Half mor.  sg Sept 14 (76) $250
— Three Early French Essays on Paper Marbling 1642-1765. Newtown: Bird & Bull Press, [1986]. One of 310. Ed by Wolfe. Half mor.  sg Sept 14 (77) $90

**Wolfe, Richard J. —& McKenna, Paul**
— Louis Herman Kinder and Fine Bookbinding in America. Newtown: Bird & Bull Press, 1985. One of 325. Half mor. sg Sept 14 (78) $225

**Wolfe, Thomas, 1900-38**
— Look Homeward, Angel. NY, 1929. 1st Ed. Orig cloth, with remains of dj; spine ends frayed, browned at front free endpaper & half-title from mtd newspaper reviews. Inscr in pencil, 1 Nov 1929. bbc Feb 26 (355) $400
  Anr copy. Later wraps. Inscr to Charles Tenney, 24 Dec 1935; additionally sgd & dated 9 July 1935. CE Sept 27 (288) $2,200
  Anr copy. Orig cloth, in 1st state of dj (frayed). Engelhard copy. CNY Oct 27 (149) $2,300
— Of Time and the River. NY, 1935. 1st Ed. In dj. Inscr to Helen Trafford Moore, 31 Aug 1937. Goodwin - Engelhard copy. CNY Oct 27 (150) $1,800

**Wolferstan, Elizabeth Pipe**
— Fairy Tales, in Verse. Lichfield, 1830. 8vo, wraps. b Dec 5 (350) £90

**Wolff, Joseph, 1795-1862**
— A Narrative of a Mission to Bokhara. L, 1845. 2d Ed. 2 vols. 8vo, orig cloth. With 9 plates. S June 13 (431) £620
  1st American Ed. NY, 1845. 2 vols. 8vo, orig cloth; soiled. With 9 plates. b Sept 20 (362) £200

**Wolff, Paul, Photographer**
— Meine Erfahrungen mit der Leica. Frankfurt, [1934]. 4to, cloth, in def dj; bdg worn & soiled. wa Feb 1 (290) $65

**Wolffenstein, Richard.** See: Cremer & Wolffenstein

**Wolffheim, Werner —& Wollfheim Collection, Werner**
— Versteigerung der Musikbibliothek des Herrn Dr. Werner Wolffheim. Berlin, 1928-29. 2 parts in 4 vols. 4to, orig wraps. sg Apr 11 (28) $475

**Wolhuter, Harry**
— Memories of a Game Ranger. Johannesburg, [1948]. Illus by C. T. Astley-Maberly. 4to, cloth. sg Mar 7 (575) $150

**Wollaston, Thomas Vernon, 1822-78**
— Insecta Maderensia. L, 1854. 4to, cloth; needs rebdg. With 13 colored plates. Some foxing; plates browned at edges. sg May 9 (360) $175

**Wollfheim Collection, Werner.** See: Wolffheim & Wollfheim Collection

**Wollick, Nicolaus**
— Enchiridion musices.... Paris: for Jehan Petit & Francois Regnault, 1512. 4to, old vellum. Some foxing. S May 15 (559) £2,800
— Opus Aureum. Musice castigatissimum de Gregoriana et Figurativa.... Cologne: Heinrich Quentell, 1504. 4to, modern calf bds. Lacking final blank; some staining, affecing tp. S May 15 (560) £2,500

**Wollstonecraft, Mary, 1759-97**
— Letters Written during a Short Residence in Sweden, Norway and Denmark. L, 1796. 1st Ed. 8vo, contemp calf. Some foxing. S Apr 23 (181) £520
  Anr copy. Contemp half calf; rubbed. Some spotting. S June 12 (196) £500
— Original Stories from Real Life. L, 1791. Illus by William Blake. 12mo, contemp lea; rebacked in later lea, corners restored. With frontis & 5 plates. K Oct 1 (71) $1,500
— Posthumous Works of the Author of a Vindication of the Rights of Woman. L, 1798. 8vo, contemp calf; joints cracked. Lacking half-titles. S Apr 23 (180) £1,150
— A Vindication of the Rights of Woman.... L, 1792. 8vo, calf; worn, hinges cracked. Some foxing. NH Sept 16 (411) $300
  Anr copy. Calf; rebacked. pba Nov 30 (332) $800

**Woloshuk, Nicholas**
— E. Irving Couse, 1866-1936. Santa Fe, 1976. Sgd. sg Jan 11 (127) $80

**Wolters, Friedrich**
— Herrschaft und Dienst. Berlin: Einhorn Presse, 1909. One of 500. Folio, half vellum gilt; minor rubbing. bbc Dec 18 (362) $325

**Woman...**
— Woman: In All Ages and in All Countries. Phila.: George Barrie, [1907-8]. One of 1,000 on japan vellum. 10 vols. Half vellum. wa Feb 1 (192) $65

**Wonders...**
— Wonders of the Circus: Men, Monkeys, and Dogs. NY: McLoughlin Bros., [1905]. Pictorial bds. pba June 20 (93) $120

**Wood, Anthony a, 1632-95**
— Historia et antiquitates Universitatis Oxoniensis.... Oxford, 1674. 1st Ed. 2 parts in 1 vol. Folio, 19th-cent half sheep; worn, needs rebacking. With engraved title & folding plate. Tear to corner of folding plan; minor worming in outer margins. sg Mar 21 (339) $225

**Wood, Casey Albert**
— The Fundus Oculi of Birds.... Chicago, 1917. 4to, orig cloth; label removed from front free endpaper. With 61 color plates on 31 leaves. sg May 16 (357) $200
— An Introduction to the Literature of Vertebrate Zoology. L, 1931. 4to, orig cloth; white ink shelf number on spine. McGill University Publications. Series XI (Zoology). No 24. sg May 16 (358) $300

**Wood, Charles Erskine Scott**
— Maia: A Sonnet Sequence. [N.p., 1918]. One of 186. Folio, half cloth. pba Aug 8 (648) $90

**Wood, Ellen Lamont.** See: Grabhorn Printing

## Wood, Erskine
— Fishing. [N.p.]: Christmas, 1968. One of 150. Inscr to Pete Hidy on tp. O Feb 6 (258) $70

## Wood, Harry B.
— Golfing Curios and the Like. L, 1910. 1st Trade Ed. Cloth; spine & extrems sunned, spine ends rubbed. pba Nov 9 (88) $1,400

Reprint Ed. Manchester, [1980]. Calf in dj; corners bumped. pba Apr 18 (188) $90

## Wood, John
— [Town Atlas of Scotland.] Edin., 1818-27. Folio, orig half cloth. With 47 double-page plans on 48 leaves, the streets on most with pale yellow wash. pnE May 15 (256) £4,000

## Wood, John George, F.S.A.
— The Principles and Practice of Sketching Landscape Scenery from Nature. L, 1813-15. 1st Ed. Oblong 4to, contemp calf gilt over thin bds; rebacked. With 64 soft ground etchings with engraving, including plate with overslips. Some soiling & discoloration; pencil annotations; a few plates cropped, affecting captions. P Nov 1 (208) $1,400

2d Ed. L, 1816. 4 parts in 1 vol. Oblong folio, half calf; worn & broken. With 64 plates, 1 with overlay, 1 in a series of 6 overlays. wa Feb 29 (130) $140

## Wood, John George, 1827-89
— The ABC of Swimming.... L: Frederick Warne, [c.1870]. 16mo, orig cloth; rear cover warped. pba Aug 8 (611) $100
— Animate Creation. NY, [1885]. Ed by Joseph B. Holder. 3 vols. Folio, cloth. pba Jan 4 (440) $250

Anr Ed. NY, [1898]. 6 vols. Orig half mor; worn & scuffed. With 34 mtd chromolitho plates. bbc Dec 18 (99) $375

## Wood, Mark
— Remarks during a Journey to the East Indies. Lichfield, 1875. 4to, orig mor gilt. With frontis map & 2 folding pedigrees. bba July 18 (376) £80 [Sotheran]

## Wood, Nancy. See: Stryker & Wood

## Wood, R. E.
— The Life and Confessions of James Gilbert Jenkins: The Murderer of Eighteen Men. Napa City, 1864. 1st Ed. 8vo, orig wraps; lower wrap fore-edge torn. With frontis port & 1 plate. Robbins copy. pba Mar 21 (393) $350

## Wood, Silas
— Speech of Mr. Wood, of New-York, on the Missouri Question. Wash., 1820. 8vo, disbound. sg Mar 28 (303) $110

## Wood, Stanley
— An Unattended Journey or Then Thousand Miles by Rail.... Chicago, 1895. Orig pictorial wraps; front wrap nearly detached, worn. pba Aug 8 (215) $60

## Wood, William
— A Survey of Trade. L, 1718. 8vo, contemp calf; spine ends chipped, covers detached. sg Mar 21 (123) $300

Anr Ed. L, 1722. 8vo, contemp calf; spine ends chipped, covers detached. Tp stamped. sg Mar 21 (124) $175

## Wood, William, 1774-1857
— General Conchology, or a Description of Shell.... L, 1835. 8vo, contemp half mor; rubbed. With 60 hand-colored plates. Some spotting & offsetting. S Oct 27 (684) £420 [Galleria San Gi]
— Index Testaceologicus, or a Catalogue of Shells, British and Foreign.... L, 1828. 2d Ed of Vol I, 1st Ed of Supplement. 2 vols. 8vo, contemp lea gilt; extremities rubbed. With 46 hand-colored plates. sg Dec 7 (253) $425

## Woodall, John
— The Surgeon's Mate, or Military & Domestique Surgery L, 1639. 2d Ed. 4 parts in 1 vol. Folio, contemp calf; rebacked, corners restored. With frontis port, title, folding table, & 4 plates (1 folding). Title soiled with laminated repair; N3 holed with loss; some leaves soiled; some dampstaining. Ck Mar 22 (310) £6,000

## Woodard, Capt. David
— The Narrative of Captain Woodard and four Seamen who Lost their Ship.... L, 1805. 2d Ed. 8vo, contemp calf; joints weak. With port & 4 plates, 2 of them folding. b Mar 20 (201) £200

## Woodbridge, Hensley C. —& Others
— Jack London: A Bibliography. Georgetown CA: Talisman Press, 1966. In dj. pba Oct 5 (280) $110

## Woodbridge, William Channing, 1794-1845
— He Hoikehonua, he mea ia e hoakaka' i ke ano o ka honua nei. Oahu, 1845. 12mo, modern half lea. sg Oct 26 (133) $950

## Woodcut...
— The Woodcut, an Annual. L: The Fleuron, 1928-30. Ltd Ed. Vols I-IV (all pbd) 4to, orig half cloth, 2 vols in djs. One plate worn. bba May 9 (295) £300 [Sims Reed]

## Woodenlegs, Richard. See: Marquis & Woodenlegs

## Woodley, George
— Cornubia: a Poem.... Truro, 1819. 8vo, contemp calf; spine rubbed. b Dec 5 (65) £140

## Woodruff, Israel Carle. See: Sitgreaves & Woodruff

## Woods, Daniel B.
— Sixteen Months at the Gold Diggings. NY, 1851. 12mo, orig cloth; worn. Some foxing. wa Feb 29 (384) $300

1st Ed. 12mo, orig cloth; spine top cloth chipped, corners worn. Last 80pp. waterstained in upper corner; some foxing. Larson copy. pba Sept 28 (750) $190

**Woods, Isaiah Churchill**
— Report to Hon. A. V. Brown, Postmaster General, on the Opening and Present Condition of the United States Overland Mail Route Between San Antonio, Texas, and San Diego, California. Wash., [1858]. 8vo, disbound. wa Feb 29 (483) $210

**Woods, Shirley E.**
— Angling for Atlantic Salmon. Goshen CT, [1976]. One of 990. O June 25 (9) $90; O June 25 (298) $80

**Woodville, William, 1752-1805**
— Medical Botany. L, 1790-94. 4 vols, including Supplement. 4to, contemp half mor; joints repaired but covers detached. With 274 hand-colored plates. Marginal tears to a few plates. pba Mar 7 (267) $1,700

Anr copy. Vol III only. Contemp half calf. With 75 hand-colored plates. Minor stains to 1 plate; a few plates with coloring smudged. pn Dec 7 (118) £280

**Woodward, David**
See also: Harley & Woodward
— Five Centuries of Map Printing. Chicago, [1975]. In dj. pba Apr 25 (163) $65

**Woodward, John, 1665-1728**
— An Essay toward a Natural History of the Earth.... L, 1695. Bound with: Whiston, William. A New Theory of the Earth. L, 1696. 8vo, contemp calf with initials CC in gilt on sides; worn, upper cover detached. S Mar 14 (374) £580

**Wooldridge, H. Ellis, 1845-1917.** See: Bridges & Wooldridge

**Wooldridge, Jessie Walton**
— History of the Sacramento Valley, California. Chicago, 1931. 3 vols. Library markings to bdg & text. cb Oct 17 (176) $180

**Woolf, Virginia, 1882-1941**
— Beau Brummell. NY, 1930. 1st Ed, one of 550. Folio, orig half cloth; extremities worn. sg Dec 14 (342) $375
— Jacob's Room. Richmond: Hogarth Press, 1922. 1st Ed. With subscriber's slip, sgd & issued to Pernel Strachey. Hobson copy. S June 28 (276) £3,000
— Kew Gardens. Richmond: Hogarth Press, 1919. 1st Ed, 2d State of woodcut. Variant bdg of pink wallpaper with flowers in colors by Omega Workshops. Cancel slip over imprint. Clive Bell's copy. Hobson copy. S June 28 (272) £3,800
— Monday or Tuesday. L: Hogarth Press, 1921. 1st Ed. Orig half cloth; scuffed, bumped. bbc June 24 (647) $350

Anr Ed. L, 1921. Orig bds. Hobson copy. S June 28 (275) £550
— Night and Day. L, 1919. 1st Ed. Hobson copy. S June 28 (274) £320

1st American Ed. NY, 1920. Orig cloth; spine ends rubbed. pba Jan 25 (387) $95

— On Being Ill. L: Hogarth Press, 1930. 1st Ed, one of 250. In dj with minor defs. Hobson copy. S June 28 (279) £620
— Orlando. NY: Crosby Gaige, 1928. ("Orlando, a Biography.") 1st American Ed, One of 861. Hobson copy. S June 28 (277) £440
— A Room of One's Own. L: Hogarth Press, 1929. 1st English Ed, One of 492. sg Dec 14 (341) $800

Anr Ed. NY, 1929. One of—492. Orig cloth. Sgd on half-title. P Dec 12 (190) $1,000

1st Ed. Hobson copy. S June 28 (278) £850
— Street Haunting. San Francisco, 1930. one of 500. Mor gilt by Drury; spine head chipped. cb June 25 (1893) $325
— The Voyage Out. L, 1915. 1st Ed. Orig cloth; upper joint repaired. b Jan 31 (234) £180

Anr copy. Duff Cooper copy. Hobson copy. S June 28 (273) £440
— The Waves. L, 1931. 1st Ed. In chipped dj. sg June 20 (407) $150

**Woolf, Virginia & Leonard**
— Two Stories. Richmond, 1917. 1st Ed, one of 150. Orig thin yellow wraps. Issue lacking initial & final leaves. Hobson copy. S June 28 (271) £5,200

Anr copy. Orig wraps; outer edges smudged. S July 11 (358) £3,800

**Woollen, William Watson**
— The Inside Passage to Alaska, 1792-1920. Cleveland, 1924. 1st Ed, One of 1,000. 2 vols. Robbins copy. pba Mar 21 (394) $375

**Woolley, Sir Charles Leonard, 1880-1960 —& Lawrence, Thomas Edward, 1888-1935**
— The Wilderness of Zin. L, [1915]. 4to, orig half cloth, in glassine dj. Sold with the other 5 vols in the Palestine Exploration Fund set. S July 11 (315) £500

1st Ed. L, 1915. 4to, orig bds. With 37 plates. S Oct 26 (240) £180 [Watkins]

**Woolman, John, 1720-72**
— A Journal of the Life and Travels of John Woolman.... L: Essex House Press, 1901. One of 250. 16mo, orig vellum. sg Sept 14 (123) $100

**Wooster, David**
— Alpine Plants. L, 1872-74. 1st & 2d Series. 2 vols. 8vo, orig cloth; worn & soiled, a few signatures in Vol I sprung. With 108 color woodcuts. wa Nov 16 (172) $400

1st Series. L, 1872. 8vo, orig cloth; broken & loose, spine worn & partly detached. With 54 colored plates. Some spotting. bba June 6 (38) £50 [Eurobooks]

Anr copy. Orig cloth; extremities rubbed. Some plates spotted. Ck Feb 14 (301) £50

**Worcester...**
— The Worcester Collection of Sacred Harmony. Worcester MA: Isaiah Thomas, 1786. Oblong 8vo, bdg not described. Some repairs at beginning. Met Sept 28 (171) $300

**Wordsworth, William, 1770-1850**
See also: Fore-Edge Paintings
— A Guide through the District of the Lakes in the North of England.... Kendal, 1835. 8vo, orig cloth; spine ends worn. K June 23 (508) $225
— Intimations of Immortality from Recollections of Early Childhood. L: Simon King Press, 1991. One of 15. Folio, half mor by Angela Thompson. pba Mar 7 (242) $130
— Poems. L, 1807. 1st Ed. 2 vols. 12mo, orig bds; corners worn, spines def. With errata slip in Vol I. Some leaves roughly opened; foxing & dampstaining. S Dec 18 (268) £850 [Finch]
Anr Ed. L, 1815. 2 vols. 12mo, half mor gilt by Bayntun. Some foxing. S Dec 18 (276) £240 [Franklin]
— Poetical Works. L, 1864. 6 vols. 8vo, calf gilt by Bickers. pba Sept 14 (366) $350
— Selections from the Poems.... L, 1834. 8vo, orig cloth; repaired on spine. S July 11 (246) £1,050
— The Sonnets. L, 1838. 1st Ed. 12mo, orig cloth. S June 13 (432) £240
— Works. Bost., 1910. One of 500 L.p. copies. 10 vols. Half mor. cb Oct 17 (313) $800
Anr copy. Half mor gilt; scuffed. wad Oct 18 (469) C$180
**Wordsworth presentation copy**
HUDSON, JOHN. - A Complete Guide to the Lakes.... Kendal & L, 1842. 8vo, orig cloth; rubbed. Inscr to his son William Wordsworth, Jr. S Dec 18 (275) £1,300 [Finch]

**Wordsworth, William, 1770-1850 —&**
**Coleridge, Samuel Taylor, 1772-1834**
— Lyrical Ballads. L, 1800. 2d Ed of Vol I, 1st Ed, 1st Issue of Vol II. 2 vols. 8vo, contemp calf gilt; rebacked preserving orig spines. Some foxing & browning. S Dec 18 (273) £1,800 [Finch]

**Workman, Fanny Bullock —&**
**Workman, William Hunter**
— Ice-Bound Heights of the Mustagh. NY, 1908. Tape repair to 1 map. bba Nov 1 (397) £400 [Old Hall Bookshop]
— Peaks and Glaciers of Nun Kun. NY, 1909. Orig cloth; rubbed. With frontis & 91 plates, some colored. Folding map with tear; some foxing & browning. bba Nov 1 (491) £420 [Mountaineering Books]

**Workman, William Hunter.** See: Workman & Workman

**World...**
— The World Displayed; or, a Curious Collection of Voyages and Travels. L, 1760-61. Vol I 2d Ed; other vols 1st Ed. 20 vols in 10. 16mo, contemp calf; worn. Sold w.a.f. b Sept 20 (193) £110

**World War I.** See: England

**World's...**
— The World's Worst Marbled Papers; being a Collection of Ten Contemporary San Serriffean Marbled Papers Showing the Lowest Level of Technique, the Worst Combination of Colors, the most Inferior Execution Known since the Dawn of the Art of Marbling. [N.p.]: San Serriffe Publishing Co [but ptd at the Bird & Bull Press], 1978. One of 400, all numbered 1. 4to, wraps. pba Aug 8 (539) $50; Z Jan 30 (164) $150

**World's Columbian Exposition**
— The Columbian Gallery: A Portfolio of Photographs.... Chicago: Werner, [1894]. 4to, half mor; spine ends def. pba Apr 25 (258) $85
— The World's Columbian Exposition Reproduced. Chicago, 1894. 4to, cloth. With photographic illusts. pba Apr 25 (165) $55

**Worlidge, John, fl.1669-98**
— Systema Agriculturae; The Mystery of Husbandry Discovered.... L, 1675. 2d Ed. 3 parts in 1 vol. Folio, contemp calf; joints cracked, spine & corners rubbed. Explanation leaf & engraved title with wormhole in lower margin. S Mar 29 (781) £300
— Vinetum Britannicum: or, a Treatise of Cider. L, 1676. 1st Ed. 8vo, 18th-cent half sheep; worn, upper cover detached. With 3 plates. Frontis cropped; some headlines shaved. S June 12 (161) £260

**Wormald, Francis.** See: Roxburghe Club

**Wornum, Ralph Nicolson.** See: Turner, Joseph Mallord William

**Worrall, John, d.1771**
— Bibliotheca Legum: or, a Catalogue of the Common and Statute Law Books.... L, 1782. 12mo, contemp calf; rebacked in calf, rubbed. Some browning & fraying. O Mar 26 (301) $120

**Worsley, Sir Richard**
— The History of the Isle of Wight. L, 1781. 4to, contemp calf; rebacked. With 31 plates & 1 folding map hand-colored in outline. Map repaired at fold map. Inscr. b Jan 31 (355) £90
Anr copy. Modern half mor. With folding map hand-colored in outline, 12 double-page & 19 single-page plates. Short tear in map. Related ephemera inserted in an envelope. S Mar 28 (72) £180

**Wotton, Sir Henry, 1568-1639**
— The Elements of Architecture. L, 1624. 1st Ed. 4to, old sheep; rebacked. Lacking 1st blank; minor soiling & dampstaining at beginning. C Apr 3 (260) £950
— Reliquiae Wottonianae.... L: for B. Tooke & T. Sawbridge, 1685. 8vo, contemp calf; glue to joints. Marginal piece lacking to lower frontis. pba Nov 30 (334) $150

**Wraxall, Sir Nathaniel William**
— Memoirs of the King of France.... L, 1777. 2 vols. 8vo, half calf; front joints starting. pba June 20 (373) $50
— Posthumous Memoirs of his own Time. L, 1836. 2d Ed. 3 vols. 8vo, half calf. pba Aug 8 (294) $55

**Wreden, Otto Just**
— Deutlicher und gruendlicher Unterricht von der Nutrition.... Hanover, 1731. 1st Ed. 8vo, modern vellum. With woodcut vignette. 1st gathering ink-stained; browned throughout. Ck Mar 22 (315) £100

**Wree, Olivier de**
— Sigilla comitum Flandriae et inscriptiones diplomatum. Bruges, 1639. 2 parts in 1 vol. Folio, contemp vellum. sg Mar 21 (341) $750

**Wren Society**
— The First [-Twentieth] Volume of the Wren Society. L, 1924-43. 20 vols. 4to, orig bds; soiled. bba Oct 19 (168) £400 [Bernett]

**Wright, Arnold**
— Twentieth Century Impressions of British Malaya. L, 1908. 4to, orig mor. b May 30 (231) £1,600

**Wright, Blanche Fisher**
— Our Child's Favorites. Chicago, [1913]. Folio, cloth; soiled. pba Aug 22 (876) $50

**Wright, Cedric**
— Words of the Earth. San Francisco: Sierra Club, [1960]. Ed by Nancy Newhall; foreword by Ansel Adams. Folio, cloth. Sgd by Adams. pba Feb 12 (206) $60

**Wright, Edgar W.**
— Lewis & Dryden's Marine History of the Pacific Northwest.... NY: Antiquarian Press, 1961. One of 750. pba Nov 16 (285) $95; pba July 25 (371) $85
Anr copy. Unopened. Smudge to tp. pba July 25 (459) $110

**Wright, Edward**
— Certain Errors in Navigation Detected and Corrected.... L, 1610. 3 parts in 1 vol. 4to, old calf; rubbed & chipped. Hole in C4 affecting a few letters; tear to margin of P1; Z5 shaved with minor loss to illust on verso. C June 26 (214) £3,800
— Some Observations Made in Travelling through France.... L, 1764. 2 vols. 4to, contemp vellum gilt in the manner of Edwards of Halifax. With 40 engraved plates & woodcut plate & folding plan. sg Apr 18 (199) $650

**Wright, Frank Lloyd, 1869-1959**
— Ausgefuerhte Bauten und Entwuerfe. Berlin, 1910. In 2 portfolios. Folio. With 72 plates & 32 tissue overlays. cb Oct 17 (60) $18,000
— The Disappearing City. NY: William Farquar Payson, 1932. Orig cloth; discolored. sg June 13 (39) $80
— Drawings for a Living Architecture. NY, 1959. 1st Ed. In chipped dj. sg Jan 11 (20) $475
[-] Frank Lloyd Wright. NY, Jan 1938. Spiral bdg. Offprint from Architectural Forum LXVIII. sg June 13 (41) $130
— The Future of Architecture. NY, 1953. 4to, cloth, in dj with wear to top edge. sg Sept 7 (23) $225
— Genius and the Mobocracy. NY, [1949]. 1st Ed. 4to, cloth, in chipped dj; bdg soiled. Inscr. sg Jan 11 (21) $650
[-] The Life-Work.... Santpoort (Holland), 1925-[26]. 1st Ed. 7 parts in 1 vol. 4to, orig cloth. cb Oct 17 (56) $650
Anr copy. Later cloth. sg June 13 (40) $650
— Modern Architecture. Princeton, 1931. cb Oct 17 (57) $1,200
Anr copy. Library markings. cb Feb 14 (2644) $1,400
— The Natural House. NY: Horizon Press, 1954. In chipped dj. sg Sept 7 (24) $80
— Selected Drawings. NY, 1977-82. Portfolios I-III. 3 vols. Folio, loose in glassine wraps. With 150 mtd color plates. cb Oct 17 (63) $3,250
One of 500. Loose in wraps in 3 cloth folding cases with ivory clasps. With 150 mtd color plates. sg Jan 11 (23) $6,500
— A Testament. NY, [1957]. 1st Ed. 4to, cloth, in dj with extremities rubbed. pba Aug 8 (656) $85

**Wright, George Newenham**
— China in a Series of Views.... L, [1843]. Illus by Thomas Allom. Vols I-II (of 4). Orig cloth; spine ends worn, Vol II front joint cracked. With 64 plates, including additional titles. sg Dec 7 (301) $300
— Landscape-Historical Illustrations of Scotland and the Waverley Novels.... L, [c.1850]. 2 vols. 4to, contemp half mor; rubbed. With port & 103 plates. F June 20 (647) £130
— The Rhine, Italy and Greece. L, [1841]. 2 vols in 1. 4to, contemp half mor; upper hinge cracked. With engraved titles, frontises & 69 plates. Some foxing. b May 30 (306) £380
— The Shores and Islands of the Mediterranean. L, [1840]. 4to, orig half mor; rubbed. With engraved title, folding map & 63 plates. Some spotting. b Sept 20 (256) £350
Anr copy. Contemp half calf. b May 30 (307) £380

**Wright, Harry**
— A Short History of Golf in Mexico and the Mexico City Country Club. NY, 1938. Ltd Ed. - Illus by R. Winslow Myers & Andres Audiffred. Cloth; covers bowing. Half-title foxed. Sgd to Bartlett Cocke. pba Nov 9 (89) $275
Anr copy. Cloth. With supplement laid in. Sgd to Bartlett Cocke. pba Apr 18 (189) $200

**Wright, James, 1643-1713**
— The History and Antiquities of the County of Rutland. L, 1684. Folio, contemp calf; rebacked & repaired. C July 1 (333) £420

**Wright, John, Horticulturist**
— The Fruit Grower's Guide. L: Virtue, [1891-94]. Vols I & III only. 4to, orig cloth; loose & shaken. With 27 (of 28) color plates. 1 leaf torn. S Oct 27 (794) £400 [Whiteson]
— The Vegetable Grower's Guide. L: Virtue, [c.1895]. 4 vols. 4to, cloth; some wear. O July 9 (231) $150

**Wright, John Michael**
— Ragguaglio della solenne comparsa, fatta in Rome.... Rome: Ercole, [1687]. Folio, 19th-cent calf by Guillemy. With frontis & 14 (of 15) plates. S June 12 (162) £320

**Wright, Lewis**
— The Illustrated Book of Poultry. L, 1885. 4to, orig cloth; shaken. With 50 color plates. 1 plate loose & soiled; some spotting. S Oct 27 (795) £550 [Whiteson]

Anr Ed. L, [1886]. 4to, contemp half mor; partly misbound. With 50 colored plates. pba Mar 7 (118) $250

Anr Ed. L, 1890. 4to, orig cloth; spine detached, scuffed. S June 13 (453) £720

**Wright, Lyle Henry**
— American Fiction, 1774-1850...1851-1875...1876-1900. San Marino: Huntington Library, 1965-78. 3 vols. In djs. ds July 27 (201) $50

**Wright, Magnus von —& Others**
— Svenska faglar efter naturen och pa sten ritade. Stockholm, 1917-29. Text by Einar Lonnberg. 3 vols. 4to, orig lea gilt. With 364 colored lithos. C Oct 25 (93) £1,000

**Wright, Robert M.**
— Dodge City. The Cowboy Capital.... [Wichita: Wichita Eagle Press, 1913]. 1st Ed. Orig cloth; worn. wa Feb 29 (411) $210

**Wright, Thomas, 1810-77**
— The History and Topography of the County of Essex. L, [1831]-36. 2 vols. 4to, orig cloth. With engraved titles, folding map & 97 plates. Minor staining. b Jan 31 (356) £170

Anr copy. Orig cloth; def. With 1 engraved title & 96 plates only. Sold w.a.f. b May 30 (121) £120

Anr copy. Orig cloth; worn & loose. Lacking 2 plates; some spotting. Sold w.a.f. bba June 6 (71) £200 [Cox]

Anr copy. Orig cloth; spine ends worn, some splitting, front hinges broken. Some foxing; some plates & letterpress detached; plates in Vol II dampstained in bottom margin. wa Feb 1 (389) £120

— A History of Domestic Manners and Sentiments in England During the Middle Ages. L, 1862. Half calf by Zaehnsdorf for John Wanamaker; front joint starting. pba Aug 8 (252) $160

**Wright, Willard Huntington, 1888-1939.** See: Van Dine, S. S.

**Wright, William, of Nevada**
— History of the Big Bonanza.... Hartford, 1876. 8vo, orig cloth. With ALs of Mark Twain to Wright as De Quille laid in. Larson copy. pba Feb 12 (496) $3,500

1st Ed. - Intro by Mark Twain. 8vo, orig cloth. With double frontis & 90 plates. Robbins copy. pba Mar 21 (395) $800

— A History of the Comstock Silver Lode.... Virginia [City, Nev., 1889]. 12mo, orig wraps; ptd label affixed to top of spine, lower inch of spine paper lacking. Snapshot, c.1905, of Mark Twain laid in. pba Nov 16 (286) $110

Anr copy. Orig wraps; chipped. pba Apr 25 (739) $150

1st Ed. Virginia [City NV, 1889]. 12mo, period mor. Robbins copy. pba Mar 21 (396) $225

— Washoe Rambles. Los Angeles: Dawson's Book Shop, 1963. One of 50. 12mo, mor gilt. pba Feb 12 (498) $55

**Wroth, Lawrence C.**
See also: Grolier Club
— The Colonial Printer. Portland ME, 1938. One of 1,500. O Dec 5 (152) $80

Anr Ed. Portland, Me., 1938. One of—1,500. O Dec 5 (31) $90

— A History of Printing in Colonial Maryland.... Balt., 1922. One of 125. Contemp mor gilt by Bayntun. bbc Dec 18 (150) $220

**Wuerth, Louis A.**
— Catalogue of the Etchings of Joseph Pennell. Bost., 1928. One of 465. Cloth, in dj. With an orig etching by Pennell. NH Sept 16 (323) $310

Anr Ed. San Francisco, 1988. In dj. sg Sept 7 (270) $100

— Catalogue of the Lithographs of Joseph Pennell. Bost., 1931. One of 425. 4to, orig half calf. sg Jan 11 (337) $250

**Wulff, Lee**
— The Atlantic Salmon. NY, 1958. One of 200. 4to, half lea; worn, spine soiled. O Feb 6 (259) $325

Anr copy. Half mor; spine stained. O June 25 (300) $160

Anr copy. Half goatskin. pba July 11 (337) $600

— Leaping Silver: Words and Pictures on the Atlantic Salmon. NY, [1940]. One of 540. 4to, half mor; rubbed. O Feb 6 (260) $450

**Wundt, Theodor**
— Wanderbilder aus den Dolomiten. Stuttgart, [n.d.]. Folio, loose as issued in pictorial bd portfolio; rubbed & soiled, some wear to flaps. With 16 plates, 8 in color. bba Nov 1 (561) £680 [Highton]

**Wurzbach, Alfred Wolfgang von, 1846-1915**
— Niederlaendisches Kuenstler-Lexicon. Vienna & Leipzig, 1906-11. One of 100. 3 vols in 5. Contemp half mor; joints rubbed, top of spines worn. sg Sept 7 (352) $400

**Wyatt, Claude W.**
— British Birds. L, 1894-99. 2 vols. 4to, contemp half mor gilt; extremities scuffed. With 67 hand-colored lithos. Fattorini copy. C Oct 25 (52) £2,000

**Wyatt, Sir Matthew Digby, 1820-77**
See also: Tymms & Wyatt
— The Industrial Arts of the Nineteenth Century. L, 1851-53. 40 parts. Folio, orig wraps; several covers

loose or starting, parts & unbound plates in 2 contemp half lea portfolios. With 159 (of 160) chromolitho plates. Lacking Plate 47; Plate 21 supplied. sg June 13 (175) $1,400

**Wyeth, Andrew**
— The Four Seasons. NY: Art in America, [1963]. One of 500. Folio, loose as issued. sg Jan 11 (472) $350

**Wyeth, Betsy James**
— Wyeth at Kuerners * Christina's World. Bost., 1976. One of 200. Illus by Andrew Wyeth. 2 vols. Oblong 4to, half lea, boxed together. O May 7 (300) $275

**Wyeth, Jamie**
— Jamie Wyeth. Bost., 1980. One of 500. Oblong 4to, half mor. sg June 13 (388) $90

**Wyld, James, 1812-87**
— An Atlas of the World. L, 1838. 4to, contemp half mor; rubbed, hinges weak. With engraved title, 4 comparative tables & 43 hand-colored maps. Folding map torn & strengthened; some spotting. S Mar 28 (188) £320
— A General Atlas. Edin., [c.1825]. Folio, half calf; worn, spine heel chipped. With engraved title & 43 maps, hand-colored in outline & 2 tables. Some soiling; lacking world map. wa Feb 29 (610) $800

**Wyndham, John, Pseud.**
— The Midwich Cuckoos. NY: Ballantine, [1957]. In dj with wear at extremities. pba May 4 (286) $350

**Wyse, Sir Thomas, 1791-1862**
— An Excursion in the Peloponnesus.... L, 1865. 2 vols. 8vo, orig cloth; shelf label on upper covers. Titles stamped. b May 30 (308) £410

**Wytfliet, Cornelius —&**
**Magini, Giovanni Antonio**
— Histoire universelle des indes occidentales et orientales. Douai: Francois Fabri, 1607. Bound with: Herrera, Antonio de. Description des Indes Occidentales... le Nouveau Monde. Amst., 1622. Folio, contemp calf; worn & rubbed, hinges weak in Wytfliet. In Herrera: 1 illus. Lacking all maps in both works; Wytfliet browned. S Oct 26 (460) £170 [Rix]

# X

**Xantus, Janos**
— Utazas Kalifornia deli Reszeiben. Pesten, 1860. With: Ann Zwinger, John Xantus: The Fort Tejon Letters, 1857-59. Together, 2 items, modern half mor; rebound. With 8 plates. Larson copy. pba Sept 28 (754) $950

**Xenophon, c.430-c.355 B.C.**
See also: Gregynog Press; Limited Editions Club
— Le Guerre de Greci.... Venice, 1550. 4to, contemp calf gilt with gilt motto of Thomas Mahieu; upper hinge cracked, corners rubbed, spine heel damaged with small loss. Sunderland - Spencer-Churchill - Bordes - Loncle - Schaefer. P Nov 1 (210) $80,000
— History of the Affairs of Greece.... L, 1770. 8vo, calf; joints cracked, front cover nearly detached. pba June 20 (374) $95
— Opera. [Geneva: H. Estienne], 1581. 3 parts in 2 vols. Folio, old half sheep; worn, needs rebacked. Worming in lower margins of Vol II affecting text. sg Mar 21 (342) $425

**XXe Siecle.** See: Vingtieme Siecle

# Y

**Yarrell, William, 1784-1856**
— A History of British Birds. L, 1845. 2d Ed. 4 vols, including Supplement. 8vo, orig cloth. b Jan 31 (306) £50
Anr Ed. L, 1871-85. 4 vols. 8vo, calf. b Sept 20 (502) £130
— A History of British Fishes. L, 1836. 2 vols plus Supplements to 1860. 4 vols in 3. 8vo, contemp half mor gilt; minor rubbing. b May 30 (591) £90

**Yarrow, William —&**
**Bouche, Louis**
— Robert Henri: his Life and Works. NY, 1921. One of 900. Folio, bds; rebacked retaining most of discolored backstrip. sg June 13 (183) $120

**Yashiro, Yukio**
— Sandro Botticelli. L: Medici Society, 1925. One of 630. 3 vols. Folio, orig cloth; soiled, spine age-darkened, spine ends worn. CE Nov 8 (254) $80
Anr copy. Cloth; soiled & stained. sg Jan 11 (57) $450

**Yato, Tamotsu**
— Naked Festival. NY, [1969]. Intro by Yukio Mishima. 4to, cloth, in repaired dj. wa Feb 1 (291) $65
— Young Samurai. NY, [1967]. Intro by Yukio Mishima. 4to, cloth, in dj. sg Feb 29 (42) $325
Anr copy. Cloth, in worn dj. wa Feb 1 (292) $65

**Yciar, Juan de.** See: Iciar, Juan de

**Yeats, William Butler, 1865-1939**
See also: Beltaine; Cuala Press; Limited Editions Club
— Cathleen ni Hoolihan. L: Caradoc Press, 1902. Orig half mor; spine rubbed, soiled. Met Feb 24 (216) $250
Anr copy. Orig half mor; spine head worn. Hobson copy. S June 28 (293) £220
— The Celtic Twilight. L, 1893. 1st Ed. 8vo, orig cloth with pbr's name at spine foot entirely in capitals; bumped. Sgd on tp. Hobson copy. S June 28 (287) £700
— Deirdre. L & Dublin, 1907. 1st Ed. Half cloth; insect damage & soiling to cloth. With the 4-page Alterations in Deidre tipped in. pba Aug 22 (529) $85

Anr copy. Orig half cloth. Author's copy, sgd on tp & with 7 revised lines in his hand. Hobson copy. S June 28 (300) £7,200
— Easter, 1916. [L: Pvtly ptd by Clement Shorter, 1916]. One of 25. 4to, orig ptd wraps. S June 28 (306) £7,800
— Essays. NY, 1924. One of 250. pba Oct 5 (375) $250
— The Green Helmet. Stratford-upon-Avon: Shakespeare Head Press, 1911. Orig wraps. Sgd on tp. Hobson copy. S June 28 (301) £260
— The Hour-Glass, Cathleen ni Houlihan, The Pot of Broth.... L, 1904. 1st English Ed. Orig half cloth; soiled. pba Aug 22 (530) $65
— Ideas of Good and Evil. NY, 1903. 1st American Ed form the English sheets. Orig cloth; rubbed & bumped. sg June 20 (410) $100
— Is the Order of R. R. & A. C. to remain a Magical Order? L, 1901. 1st Ed. Orig wraps, unopened. Tp spotted. Quinn - Hobson copy. S June 28 (291) £2,800
— The King's Threshold. NY, 1904. One of—100. Orig bds. Hobson copy. S June 28 (298) £750
— The Land of Heart's Desire. L, 1894. 4to, orig wraps. Minor foxing. Hobson copy. S June 28 (284) £580
— Leda and the Swan. [Florence: ptd for Frederic Prokosch, 1935 or 1936]. One of 5 bound in Sardinia paper. Orig wraps. Inscr by Prokosch "in Florence 1936" & inscr by him to Rupert Hart-Davis in 1949 & with Prokosch ALs to Wade. Hobson copy. S June 28 (320) £380
— Mosada. A Dramatic Poem. Dublin, 1886. 1st Ed. 8vo, orig unlined wraps; some spotting. Nelson - Hobson copy. S June 28 (283) £42,000
— Nine Poems. L: Pvtly Ptd by Clement Shorter, Oct 1918. One of 25. 4to, orig wraps, unopened. Hobson copy. S June 28 (307) £4,000
— Nine Poems Chosen from the Works of.... NY: Pvtly Ptd for John Quinn & his Friends by Mitchell Kennerley, 1 Apr 1914. One of 25. Orig wraps; edges with wear & staining. Inscr to Mrs Jefferson. Gielgud - Hobson copy. S June 28 (305) £4,200
— On Baile's Strand. Dublin, 1905. Orig wraps. Abbey Theatre series, Vol VI. pba Aug 22 (531) $100
— Plays for an Irish Theatre. L, 1911. 1st Ed. pba Jan 25 (394) $225
— Poems. L, 1895. 1st Ed, one of 25 on japan vellum. 8vo, orig vellum gilt. Hobson copy. S June 28 (288) £2,600
— The Poems of W. B. Yeats. L, 1949. One of 375. 2 vols. 4to, orig cloth. S Dec 18 (358) £780 [Cathach]
Anr copy. Orig cloth. Hobson copy. S June 28 (323) £1,500
— A Postscript to Essay called "Is the Order of R. R. & A. C. to remain a Magical Order?" L, 1901. Orig wraps. Hobson copy. S June 28 (292) £4,600
— Reveries over Childhood and Youth. L, 1916. Advance review copy. Half cloth. With colored frontis & 2 plates. K June 23 (512) $375
— The Singing Head and the Lady. Italy: ptd for Frederic Prokosch, 1934 [but 1951]. One of "4 preliminary trial copies in Elzevir". Orig wraps. With marked proof of all but tp laid in. Hobson copy. S June 28 (319) £440
Anr Ed. [Bryn Mawr: Ptd by Frederic Prokosch, Christmas 1934]. One of 6 on Oland. Orig wraps. Hobson copy. S June 28 (318) £280
— A Speech and Two Poems. Dublin, 1937. One of 70. Orig wraps. Inscr by George Yeats, 1945. Hobson copy. S June 28 (321) £1,600
— The Tables of the Law. The Adoration of the Magi. L, 1897. 1st Ed, one of 110. 8vo, orig cloth. Some foxing. Inscr to his uncle, George Pollexfen. S June 28 (295) £2,000
— The Tower. L, 1928. 1st Ed. In dj with minor fraying. Hobson copy. S June 28 (315) £750
— The Wanderings of Oisin.... L, 1889. 1st Ed, One of 500. 8vo, orig cloth; some scratching to upper cover. Hobson copy. S June 28 (285) £850
— Where There is Nothing. NY, 1902. One of 10. Orig wraps. Esher - Hobson copy. S June 28 (294) £1,700
Anr copy. Vellum, orig wraps preserved. Inscr to Lady Gregory with note that only 10 ptd (pace Wade). S July 24 (410) £1,900 [Taylor]
— The Winding Stair. L, 1933. ("The Winding Stair and Other Poems.") pba Aug 22 (533) $65
— The Winding Stair and Other Poems. NY: Fountain Press, 1929. ("The Winding Stair.") One of 642. bbc June 24 (649) $325

**Yellow...**
— The Yellow Book: an Illustrated Quarterly. L, 1894-97. Vols 1-13 (all pbd). 8vo, orig cloth; soiled, rubbed, darkened. CE May 22 (485) $180
Anr copy. Orig cloth; soiled. sg Sept 21 (326) $700
Anr copy. Orig cloth; rubbed, spines darkened. sg Apr 18 (200) $600
Vols 1-13 (all pbd). 8vo, orig cloth; soiled. sg Feb 8 (373) $650

**Yelverton, Therese, Pseud.** See: Longworth, Maria Theresa

**Yemeniz Library, M. N.**
— [Sale Catalogue] Catalogue de la Bibliotheque de M. N. Yemeniz. Paris, 1867. 8vo, contemp half cloth; some wear. O Mar 26 (303) $50

**Yerushalmi, Yosef Hayim**
— Haggadah and History. Phila., 1975. 4to, orig cloth in dj; worn. Inscr & sgd. sg Apr 11 (184) $100

**Yon, L. Gabriel**
— Note sur la direction des Aerostats. Paris, 1880. 4to, orig wraps; chipped. With frontis & 15 plates. Inscr to the balloonist Brissonet. sg May 16 (100) $200

**Yorke, Henry Vincent.** See: Freen, Henry

**Yorke, James, fl.1640**
— The Union of Honour. L, 1640. 1st Ed. 3 parts in 1 vol. Folio, contemp calf; spine ends & corners worn, joints cracked, lacking endpapers, upper hinge rein-

forced. Lacking frontis; marginal browning & staining.  CE June 15 (283) $250

**Yorke, Philip, 1743-1804**
— The Royal Tribes of Wales. Wrexham, 1799. 8vo, contemp russia gilt; rebacked in calf, adhesion residue to covers, new cloth-backed endpapers.  pba Nov 30 (335) $120

**Yosemite**
— Yosemite Illustrated in Color. San Francisco: Crocker, 1890. Folio, half lea; worn & soiled. With 13 colored plates. Larson copy.  pba Feb 12 (28) $550
— The Yosemite Valley and the Mammoth Trees and Geysers of California. NY: T. Nelson & Sons, [c.1871]. 8vo, orig cloth; front hinge cracked. With map & 12 chromolitho plates. One of Nelson's Pictorial Guide-Books.  pba Feb 12 (138) $50

**Young, —.** See: Viborg & Young

**Young, Andrew M. —& Others**
— The Paintings of James McNeill Whistler. New Haven, 1980. 2 vols. 4to, cloth in djs.  sg Jan 11 (466) $100; sg Jan 11 (467) $120

**Young, Arthur, 1741-1820**
— Travels during the Years 1787, 1788, and 1789...Kingdom of France. Bury St. Edmunds, 1792. 1st Ed. 4to, bdg not described. With 2 folding maps, 1 colored.  b Sept 20 (363) £120

Anr copy. Contemp half calf gilt; worn. With 3 folding maps, including hand-colored map of France.  pba Sept 14 (368) $425

2d Ed. L & Bury St. Edmunds, 1794. 2 vols. 4to, contemp half calf; rebacked retaining orig spines, corners repaired.  S June 13 (434) £180

**Young, E.**
— Elementar-Gymnastik...nach den Werken... Clias und Guts-Muths bearbeitet.... Milan, 1827. 8vo, contemp red mor gilt with arms of the Duchess of Parma, Placenza & Guastalla, being the Empress Marie Louise.  C May 1 (179) £3,200

**Young, Edward, 1683-1765**
See also: Fore-Edge Paintings
— The Complaint: or, Night Thoughts.... L, 1797. ("The Complaint, and the Consolation; or Night Thoughts.") Illus by William Blake. Folio, 19th-cent half mor gilt; some rubbing. A few leaves trimmed to edge of illusts.  pba Nov 30 (57) $4,000

Anr copy. Half mor, uncut. Lacking explanation leaf; some spotting; tears in lower edge of a few leaves; edges soiled or browned.  S Apr 23 (260) £2,600

**Young, Francis Marion.** See: Hafen & Young

**Young, George Orville**
— Alaskan Trophies Won and Lost. Bost., [1928]. O Oct 10 (6) $190

Anr copy. Orig cloth; some wear, spine ends frayed.  O Oct 10 (289) $190

**Young, John, 1755-1825**
— A Catalogue of the Collection of Pictures of the Marquess of Stafford at Cleveland House.... L, 1825. 2 vols. Folio, contemp half mor; rubbed.  bba Oct 19 (82) £90 [Walpole]
— A Catalogue of the Pictures at Grosvenor House. L, 1820. Folio, half lea; worn & loose, spine chipped & torn. With 46 plates. Some foxing.  O Mar 5 (251) $120
— A Series of Portraits of the Emperors of Turkey from the Foundation of the Monarchy to the Year 1815. L, [1815]. Folio, contemp half mor; worn. With letter-press subtitles in English & French, color title, & 31 hand-colored plates. Final plate creased; some rubbing & spotting; without dated general title.  S Oct 26 (241) £25,000 [Champbell]

**Young, John Philip**
— San Francisco.... San Francisco & Chicago, [1912]. Ltd Ed, sgd. 2 vols. Folio, later half sheep; worn, call numbers on spine. With port & 145 photographic plates (1 folding) & 4 maps (3 folding). Perforated stamps; a few leaves detached & tipped in; some fraying; holes at folds of folding plates.  cb Oct 17 (177) $170

Anr copy. Half mor gilt; scuffed.  pba Feb 12 (388) $90

Anr copy. Half mor gilt; joints rubbed, 1 bdg with corners showing.  pba Aug 8 (220) $140

**Young, Thomas, 1773-1829**
— An Account of Some Recent Discoveries in Hieroglyphical Literature.... L, 1823. 8vo, orig bds; rebacked in later cloth.  pba Aug 8 (221) $80

**Young, Sir William, 1749-1815**
— An Account of the Black Charaibs in the Island of St. Vincent's. L, 1795. 1st Ed. 8vo, contemp half calf; rebacked.  S Oct 26 (534) £500 [Keynes]

**Young, William Weston**
— Proposals for Publishing...British Ornithology, or history of Birds. L, [c.1800-10]. 8vo, modern mor gilt by Zaehnsdorf. Hand-colored specimen plate & leaf of text, with leaf giving details. "Unrecorded and perhaps unique". Fattorini copy.  C Oct 25 (53) £650

**Youngblood, Charles L.**
— Adventures of Chas. L. Youngblood during Ten Years on the Plains. Chicago, 1890. ("A Mighty Hunter. The Adventures of....") 8vo, orig cloth; worn.  pba Aug 8 (222) $250

**Younghusband, Sir Francis Edward**
— The Wonders of the Himalaya. NY, [1924]. 1st American Ed.  pba July 25 (460) $120

**Yount, George C.**
— George C. Yount and his Chronicles of the West.... Denver, 1966. One of 1,250. Ed by Charles L. Camp. Unopened.  pba July 25 (100) $50

# Z

**Zacconi, Lodovico**
— Prattica di musica.... Venice: Girolamo Polo, 1592. Folio, modern vellum bds. Some staining. S Dec 1 (393) £2,000

**Zachariae, Just Friedrich Wilhelm, 1726-77**
— Les Quatre Parties du jour.... Paris, 1769. Illus by Baquoy after Eisen. 8vo, orig wraps. With frontis & 4 plates. Fuerstenberg - Schaefer copy. S Dec 8 (665) £300

**Zaehnsdorf, Joseph, 1816-86**
— The Art of Bookbinding. ·L, 1903. Mor gilt by Zaehnsdorf; joints & spine ends rubbed. Inscr, 1904 & with related material. pba June 20 (375) $450

**Zaharias, Babe Didrickson**
— This Life I've Led: My Autobiography. NY: A. S. Barnes, [1955]. 1st Ed. In dj; d/j chipped. Sgd. pba Apr 18 (190) $900

**Zahn, Joannes**
— Oculus artificialis teledioptricus sive telescopium.... Nuremberg, 1702. 1st Ed. Folio, vellum; stained, new endpapers. Madsen copy. S Mar 14 (378) £1,700
— Specula physico-mathematico-historica. Nuremberg, 1696. 1st Ed. 3 vols in 1. Folio, contemp blind-stamped pigskin over wooden bds, 2 clasps & catches. With 3 frontises, 3 ports & 55 plates & maps. Tear along fold of 1 plate; tears in a few other plates. Madsen copy. S Mar 14 (377) £3,200

**Zamorano, Rodrigo**
— Compendo de la Arte de Navegar. Seville: Andrea Pescioni, 1582. 2d Ed (with tp date of 1581 altered by hand to 1582 & colophon reading 1582). 4to, contemp calf with trace of clasps; spine repaired, extremities worn, tail of spine loose. Library stamps on tp; some spotting; E gathering on heavy paper, folding volvelle plate at end in modern facsimile. P Dec 12 (191) $2,500

**Zanetti, Antonio Maria, the Elder & the Younger**
— Delle antiche statue greche e romane che nell'antisala della libreria di San Marco.... Venice, 1740-43. 2 parts in 2 vols. Folio, contemp sheep; rebacked, Vol I front cover detached, worn. With frontis, port & 100 plates. Some plates in Vol I dampstained in lower inner corner; a few plates in Vol II spotted. sg June 13 (389) $2,200

**Zanotto, Francesco**
— Storia Veneta. Venice, 1863. 2d Ed. - Plates by A. Viviani after G. Gatteri. 2 vols. Folio, cloth. With frontis & 150 plates. Plates 44-45 misbound; some discoloration. S Oct 26 (86) £1,050 [Severis]

**Zapf, Georg Wilhelm**
— Merkwuerdigkeiten der Zapfischen Bibliothek. Augsburg, 1778. 1st Ed. 2 parts in 1 vol. 8vo, 19th-cent bds; worn, spine chipped. O Mar 26 (304) $500

**Zapf, Hermann**
— Manuale Typographicum. Frankfurt, 1968. Folio, half syn. Library markings. sg Sept 14 (348) $150
— Typographische Variationen. Frankfurt, [1963]. Folio, bds. sg Sept 14 (349) $200

**Zarlino, Gioseffo**
— Le Istitutioni harmoniche. Venice, 1558. Folio, contemp vellum Ms over bds; repaired. Wormhole in inner margin of 1st 18 leaves & in lower margin of last 4 leaves; ownership inscr on tp deleted; bookseller's stamp. S May 15 (561) £4,800
— Le Istitutioni harmonische. Venice: F. Senese, 1562. 2d Ed. Folio, modern vellum. Italic type with roman, letterpress music. Foremargins of tp & 9 following leaves repaired & strengthened; some dampstaining. C Apr 3 (157) £700
— Opere. Venice: Francesco Franceschi, 1588-89. 4 vols in 2. Folio, contemp vellum; soiled. Lacking 2 leaves at end of Vol IV; stamps removed from titles of 3 vols; folding woodcut diagram in Vol III torn at fold; bottom parts of C6 & G2 in Vol IV cut away with loss to catchwords; G7 trimmed; some worming in Vols I & II, touching 1 woodcut; lacking 3 blanks in Vol III. S Dec 1 (394) £1,200

**Zavattini, Cesare**
— Un Paese. [Turin, 1955]. Illus by Paul Strand. 4to, cloth, in rubbed dj. sg Feb 29 (313) $425

**Zeis, Eduard**
— Die Literatur und Geschichte der plastischen Chirurgie. Leipzig, 1863. 1st Ed. 8vo, modern cloth; rebound. CE Nov 8 (161) $1,000

**Zeisberger, David, 1721-1808**
— Essay of a Delaware-Indian and English Spelling-Book.... Phila., 1776. 8vo, old half calf; dried. Jasper Yeates's copy. CE May 22 (34) $6,000

**Zeise, H.**
— Die Aeronautik einst und jetzt, nebst theoretischen und praktischen Vorschlaegen.... Altona, 1850. 8vo, later half cloth. Some browning towards end. sg May 16 (101) $250

**Zeising, Heinrich**
— Theatrum machinarum. Altenburg: Johann Meuschken, 1612-14. Part 2 only (of 6). Oblong 4to, contemp vellum. Lacking title; A2 7 anr leaf repaired; some browning. S June 12 (311) £160

**Zelazny, Roger**
— The Changing Land. San Francisco: Underwood-Miller, 1981. One of 200. In dj. pba May 23 (488) $50
— Dilvish, the Damned. San Francisco: Underwood-Miller, 1983. 1st Ed, one of 333. In dj. pba May 23 (490) $50
— The Guns of Avalon. L, [1974]. In dj. Sgd on tp. pba May 23 (493) $50
— Nine Princes in Amber. Garden City, 1970. In dj. pba May 4 (287) $1,000

## ZELAZNY

Anr copy. In dj. Sgd on tp & with autograph postcard, sgd, laid in. pba May 23 (491) $1,400

Anr Ed. L, [1972]. In dj. Sgd on tp. pba May 23 (492) $110

**Zeller, Ludwig**
— Alphacollage. Erin, 1979. One of 200. 4to, cloth. sg Sept 7 (356) $200

**Zempel, Edward N. —&
Verkler, Linda A.**
— Book Prices: Used and Rare. Peoria: Spoon River Press, 1993-96. 4 vols. 4to, cloth. wa June 20 (19) $230

**Zentner, L.**
— A Select Collection of Landscapes from the Best of Old Masters. L, 1791. Oblong 4to, half calf; worn, spine repaired. With 56 plates. bba Nov 30 (109) £330 [Finney]

**Zern, Ed**
— To Hell with Fishing.... NY, [1945]. Illus by H. T. Webster. In chipped & torn dj. Inscr. Also inscr by Pete Hidy to Jim Leisenring & other members of the Leisenring family. O Feb 6 (261) $100

**Zervos, Christian**
See also: Picasso, Pablo
— Pablo Picasso. Paris, [1949]. Vol 3 only. 4to, orig cloth; worn & soiled. With 41 mtd plates. Some dampstaining. F Mar 28 (775) $125

**Zibrt, Cenek**
— Bibliografie Ceske Historie. Prague, 1900-12. 5 vols in 11. 4to, orig cloth. sg Apr 11 (338) $140; sg Apr 11 (339) $150

**Zichy, Michael, 1827-1906**
— Liebe. Leipzig, 1911. Ltd Ed. Oblong folio, half mor gilt, orig vellum gilt spines bound in; With 40 plates. Milford Haven copy. pnE Mar 20 (265) £500

Anr copy. Half mor; spine & corners worn. With 40 plates. S May 16 (53) £360

**Ziegenfuss, Werner —&
Jung, Gertrud**
— Philosophen-Lexikon. Berlin, 1949-50. 2 vols. 8vo, orig cloth. sg Apr 11 (340) $130

**Zimmer, Heinrich Robert, 1890-1943**
— The Art of Indian Asia. NY, [1955]. Ed by Joseph Campbell. 2 vols. Folio, cloth, in worn djs. wa Nov 16 (321) $85

**Zimmerman, E. A. W. von**
— Taschenbuch der Reisen oder unterhaltende Darstellung der Entdeckungen des 18 Jahrhunderts.... Lepizig, 1805. 1st Ed. Orig bds; covers scuffed. With frontis port, 2 folding maps, & 7 plates (6 folding). Larson copy. pba Sept 28 (289) $3,000

**Zimmerman, William**
— Waterfowl of North America. Louisville, [1974]. One of 1,000. Oblong folio, half mor with metal seal to front cover; stain to front cover. With 42 color plates & with 2 extra sgd plates laid-in loose. pba July 11 (451) $275

**Zimmermann, Johann Georg, 1728-95.** See: Fore-Edge Paintings

**Zinner, Ernst**
— Geschichte und Bibliographie der astronomischen Literatur in Deutschland zur Zeit der Renaissance. Stuttgart, 1964. 8vo, orig cloth in dj. sg Apr 11 (304) $175

**Zischka, Gert A.**
— Index Lexicorum. Bibliographie der lexikalischen Nachschlagewerke. Vienna, [1959]. 1st Ed. 8vo, wrappers. sg Apr 11 (341) $100

**Zoar Community**
— Sammlung auserlesener Geistlicher Lieder.... Zoar OH, 1867. 8vo, orig sheep; rubbed. sg Oct 26 (402) $175

**Zobel, Christoff**
— Sachsenspiegel auffs newe ubersehen.... Leipzig: E. Voeglin, 1563 [1561]. Folio, contemp vellum with arms of Bodenhausen, initials HVB & date 1597 in gilt; some worming to both covers. Some worming at ends; browned throughout. S June 27 (366) £1,400

**Zocchi, Giuseppe**
— Scelta di XXIV vedute delle principali contrade, piazze, chiese, e palazzi della citta di Firenze. Florence, 1754 [plan dated 1755]. Folio, contemp vellum gilt; scuffed, joints split. Engraved & double-page throughout, with title, map & 24 views Some fold tears; 1 plate browned; 1 marginal tear. C Apr 3 (261) £9,500

— Vedute delle ville, e d'altri luoghi della Toscana. Florence, 1757. Oblong folio, contemp half sheep; spine wormed. With engraved title, dedication & 50 plates. C Apr 3 (262) £7,000

**Zocchi, Giuseppe —& Others**
— Serie di ritratti d'uomini illustri Toscani. Florence: Giuseppe Allegrini, 1766-73. Vols I-II (of 4). Contemp vellum; soiled, stitching weak. With engraved titles, frontises & 101 ports. Some soiling, mainly marginal. C Nov 29 (113) £950

**Zoega, Georg**
— De origine et usu obeliscorum. Rome, 1797. Folio, contemp calf gilt by the Vatican Bindery, presentation bdg. With engraved title vignette & 8 folding plates. C Apr 3 (263) £1,400

**Zogbaum, Rufus F., 1849-1925**
— Horse, Foot, and Dragoons: Sketches of Army Life.... NY, 1888. 8vo, orig cloth; extremities rubbed, hinges cracking. pba June 25 (248) $170

## Zola, Emile, 1840-1902

— J'Accuse...! Lettre au President de la Republique. Paris, 13 Jan 1898. Folio. 4 pp, folded. A few fold breaks & small holes, affecting a few letters. In: L'Aurore, deuxieme annee, No 87. With related newspaper material on the Dreyfus affair. CE Feb 21 (270) $5,000

Anr copy. 1st leaf only (of 4). Folio. Framed. Browned; repaired. Sold w.a.f. In: L'Aurore, deuxieme annee, No 87. S Nov 30 (310) £600

— Travail. Paris, 1901. 1st Ed, One of 200 on hollande. 2 vols. 8vo, half mor; spines faded, orig wraps bound in. S Oct 27 (1174) £70

— Works. Phila.: George Barrie, [n.d.]. One of 1000. 12 vols. Half mor. With plates in 2 states.. cb Oct 17 (314) $1,100

## Zompini, Gaetano

— Le Arti che vanno per via nella Citta di Venezia. [N.p., 1753]. Folio, orig bds; worn. With engraved title, engraved plate list & 60 plates. Minor worming through lower margin of msot plates; minor staining. bba Sept 7 (210) £4,200 [Chelsea Gallery]

## Zonaras, Johannes

— Historia Imperatorum Romanorum a Constantino Magno. Frankfurt am Main, 1578. 3 parts in 1 vol. Folio, 18th-Cent calf; worn. With title port. Lacking blank at part II; few leaves loose. S Oct 27 (1096) £170 [Anastassakis]

## Zonca, Vittorio

— Nova teatro di machine et edificii. Padua, 1607. 4to, old vellum; rebacked, recased, resewn. With engraved title & 42 plates. Inner margins strengthened. C Apr 3 (264) £2,200

## Zoological Society of London

— Proceedings. L, 1831-1950. Vols 1-119 bound in 128 plus 8 index vols. Together, 136 vols. 8vo, half mor or contemp cloth, orig wraps bound in. C Oct 25 (94) £5,800

## Zorgdrager, Cornelius Gijsbertsz

— Bloeijende opkomst der aloude en hedendaagische Groenlandsche Visschery.... Amst., 1728. Ed by Abraham Moubach. 4to, contemp blindstamped vellum; recased, vellum partly cracked. sg Mar 7 (241) $600

## Zouch, Thomas, 1737-1815

— The Life of Isaac Walton; including Notices of his Contemporaries. L, 1823. 4to, contemp half calf; rebacked, rubbed. Some foxing. O Feb 6 (262) $180

**Zuallardo, Giovanni.** See: Zuallart, Jean

## Zuallart, Jean

— Il Devotissimo viaggio di Gerusalemme. Rome, 1595. 4to, modern mor gilt. With 2 folding plates. b May 30 (309) £1,300

## Zuniga y Ontiveros, Mariano

— Calendario manual y guia de forasteros en Mexico.... [Mexico, 1803]. 8vo, contemp calf gilt. With frontis, folding plan & folding map. S Nov 30 (172) £460

## Zurla, Placido

— Di Marco Polo e degli altri Viaggiatori Veneziani piu illustri Dissertazioni.... Venice, 1818. 2 vols in 1. 4to, early half vellum. With 4 folding maps. Library stamps. sg Mar 7 (304) $600

**Zurlauben, Beat Fidel Antoine, Baron de.** See: Laborde & Zurlauben

## Zwicker, C.

— Compendium horologico-sciotericum et geometricum oder kurtzer aber doch gruendlicher unterricht.... Nuremberg, 1675. 4to, bds; worn. With 32 plates & engraved title. Some foxing & dampstaining. NH Sept 16 (224) $375

## Zyll, Gisbertus a

— Monumenta illustrium virorum, et elogia.... Utrecht, 1671. Folio, contemp leaf; surface pitted, lacking backstrip, corner gone from front free endpaper. With engraved title & 127 plates. Sold w.a.f. sg Mar 21 (343) $300

A book auction at Sotheby's, circa 1800,